DATE DUE

DEMCO 38-296

Contemporary Authors

Contemporary Authors

**A Bio-Bibliographical Guide to
Current Writers in Fiction, General Nonfiction,
Poetry, Journalism, Drama, Motion Pictures,
Television, and Other Fields**

FRANCES CAROL LOCHER
Editor

volumes 85-88

GALE RESEARCH COMPANY • THE BOOK TOWER • DETROIT, MICHIGAN 48226

CONTEMPORARY AUTHORS

Published by
Gale Research Company, Book Tower, Detroit, Michigan 48226
Each Year's Volumes Are Revised About Five Years Later

Frederick G. Ruffner, *Publisher*   James M. Ethridge, *Editorial Director*

Christine Nasso, *General Editor, Contemporary Authors*

Frances Carol Locher, *Editor, Original Volumes*

Ann Factor Ponikvar, *Associate Editor*

Victoria France Hutchinson, B. Hal May, Nancy M. Rusin,
Leslie D. Stone, David Versical, Barbara A. Welch,
and Martha G. Winkel, *Assistant Editors*
Juanita M. Krygier, Susan L. Rose, Norma Sawaya,
Shirley Seip, and Laurie M. Serwatowski, *Editorial Assistants*

Alan E. Abrams, Jane A. Bowden,
Otto Penzler, and Adele Sarkissian, *Contributing Editors*
Andrea Geffner, Martha J. Abele, Arlene True,
and Benjamin True, *Sketchwriters*

Eunice Bergin, *Copy Editor*
Michaeline Nowinski, *Production Director*

Special recognition is given to the staffs of
Journalist Biographies Master Index
and
Yesterday's Authors of Books for Children

Questions and Answers About
Contemporary Authors

What types of authors are included in *Contemporary Authors?* More than 57,000 living authors of nontechnical works (and such authors who have died since 1960) are represented in the series. *CA* includes writers in all genres—fiction, nonfiction, poetry, drama, etc.—whose books are issued by commercial, risk publishers or by university presses. Authors of books published only by known vanity or author-subsidized firms are not generally included. Since native language and nationality have no bearing on inclusion in *CA,* authors who write in languages other than English are also included in *CA* if their works have been published in the United States or translated into English.

Although *CA* focuses primarily on persons whose work appears in book form, the series now also encompasses prominent writers of interest to the public whose work appears in other media: newspaper and television reporters and correspondents, columnists, newspaper and periodical editors, syndicated cartoonists, screenwriters, television scriptwriters, and other media people.

Among the authors of particular interest included in this volume are Richard Aldington, Yves Bonnefoy, Willy Brandt, Italo Calvino, John Leonard Clive, Marc Connelly, Louis Ferdinand Destouches (best known for writings under the pseudonym Louis-Ferdinand Celine), W. E. B. Du Bois, Lyle Kenyon Engel, Antonia Fraser, Max Frisch, Athol Fugard, Richard Howard, Aldous Huxley, Robinson Jeffers, Thomas Keneally, Sidney Kingsley, Paer Lagerkvist, Marcel Marceau, Jacques Maritain, John P. Marquand, Henry de Montherlant, Jawaharlal Nehru, Robert Pinget, John Cowper Powys, David Rabe, Jules Romains, Ntozake Shange, Georges Simenon, Jean Toomer, and Evelyn Waugh.

Prominent media writers represented in this volume include Milton Caniff, John Cassavetes, Ivan Greenberg, Ben Hecht, James Kenneth McManus, Nicolas Nabokov, N. Richard Nash, Tim O'Brien, Clifford Odets, Laurence Stern, Robert Stone, and Melvin Van Peebles.

How is *Contemporary Authors* compiled? Most of the material in *CA* is furnished by the authors themselves. Questionnaires are sent regularly to authors as their new books appear and are reviewed as well as to prominent media personalities. Information provided by the authors in their questionnaires is then written in the distinctive *CA* format, and the proposed entries are sent to the authors for review and approval prior to publication.

How are entries prepared if authors do not furnish information? If authors of special interest to *CA* users fail to reply to requests for information, material is gathered from various other reliable sources. Biographical dictionaries are checked (a task made easier through the use of Gale's *Biographical Dictionaries Master Index* and *Author Biographies Master Index*), as are bibliographical sources, such as *Cumulative Book Index, The National Union Catalog,* etc. Published interviews, feature stories, and book reviews are examined, and often material is supplied by the author's publishers.

As with entries prepared from questionnaires, sketches prepared through extensive research are also sent to the authors for approval prior to publication. If the authors do not respond, the listings are published with an asterisk (*) following them to indicate that the material has not been personally verified by the authors.

Why are obituary notices included in *Contemporary Authors,* and how can they be distinguished from full-length sketches? To be as timely and comprehensive as possible, *CA* publishes obituary notices on recently deceased authors. These notices provide date and place of birth and death, highlight the author's career and writings, and list other sources where additional biographical information and obituaries may be found. To distinguish them from full-length sketches, obituaries are identified with the heading *Obituary Notice.*

CA includes obituary notices both for authors who already have full-length sketches in earlier *CA* volumes, thus effectively completing the sketches, and for authors not yet sketched in the series. Deceased authors of special interest presently represented in the series only by obituary notices are scheduled for full-length sketch treatment in forthcoming *CA* volumes.

Will you please explain the unusual numbering system used for *Contemporary Authors* volumes? The unusual four-volume numbering system used today reflects *CA*'s publication history. To meet the urgent need for information about authors as quickly as possible, *CA* began as a quarterly publication, with each book carrying a single volume number. The numbering system was changed to double-volume numbers when Volumes 5-6 was published with twice as many entries as a quarterly volume. With the appearance of Volumes 25-28, the numbering system was altered once more to indicate that each physical volume of *CA* represents four of the original quarterly volumes.

Now, all *CA* volumes are available as four-volume units, including the revised volumes. As early volumes of *CA* were revised, they were combined into the four-volume units presently being issued. For example, when Volumes 1, 2, 3, and 4 were revised, the material was updated, merged into a single alphabet, and is available today as Volumes 1-4, First Revision.

An unusual number of biographical publications have been appearing recently, and the question is now often asked whether a charge is made for listings in such publications. Do authors listed in *Contemporary Authors* make any payment or incur any other obligation for their listings? Some publishers charge for listings or require purchase of a book by biographees. There is, however, absolutely no charge or obligation of any kind attached to being included in *CA*.

Cumulative Index Should Always Be Consulted

Since *CA* is a multi-volume series which does not repeat author entries from volume to volume, the cumulative index published in alternate new volumes of *CA* should always be consulted to locate an individual author's listing. Each new volume contains authors not previously included in the series and is revised approximately five years after its original publication. The cumulative index indicates the original or revised volume in which an author appears. Authors removed from the revision cycle and placed in the *CA Permanent Series* are listed in the index as having appeared in specific original volumes of *CA* (for the benefit of those who do not hold *Permanent Series* volumes), *and* as having their finally revised sketches in a specific *Permanent Series* volume.

For the convenience of *CA* users, the *CA* cumulative index also includes references to all entries in three related Gale series—*Contemporary Literary Criticism,* which is devoted entirely to current criticism of major authors, poets, and playwrights, *Something About the Author,* a series of heavily illustrated sketches on juvenile authors and illustrators, and *Authors in the News,* a compilation of news stories and feature articles from American newspapers and magazines covering writers and other members of the communications media.

As always, suggestions from users about any aspect of *CA* will be welcomed.

CONTEMPORARY AUTHORS

Indicates that a listing has been compiled from secondary sources believed to be reliable, but has not been personally verified for this edition by the author sketched.

A

ACOMB-WALKER, Evelyn 1910-
(Evelyn Martha Acomb)

PERSONAL: Born September 25, 1910, in Donora, Pa.; daughter of William Edward (a mechanical engineer) and Dorothea (Gray) Acomb; married Herman Walker (a college professor and foreign service officer), January 26, 1969. *Education:* Wellesley College, A.B., 1931; Columbia University, A.M., 1932, Ph.D., 1941. *Home:* 231 Old Ford Rd., New Paltz, N.Y. 12561. *Office:* Department of History, State University of New York College, New Paltz, N.Y. 12561.

CAREER: Rutgers University, Douglass College, New Brunswick, N.J., instructor in history, 1941-42; U.S. Department of State, Washington, D.C., research assistant in political studies, 1942-43; College of William and Mary, Williamsburg, Va., acting assistant professor of history, 1943-46; Hunter College (now of the City University of New York), New York, N.Y., acting assistant professor of history, 1946-49; State University of New York College at New Paltz, associate professor, 1949-60, professor of history, 1960-77, professor emeritus, 1977—. *Member:* American Historical Association, American Association of University Professors, American Association of University Women, Society for French Historical Studies (co-founder; president, 1959-60), Berkshire Conference of Women Historians, New York State Association of European Historians (president, 1954-55), Phi Beta Kappa, Mid-Hudson Wellesley Club.

WRITINGS—All under name Evelyn Martha Acomb: *The French Laic Laws, 1879-1889,* Columbia University Press, 1941, 2nd edition, Octagon, 1967; (editor and translator) *The Revolutionary Journal of Baron Ludwig von Closen, 1780-1783,* University of North Carolina Press, 1958; (editor with Marvin Brown, Jr.) *French Society and Culture Since the Old Regime,* Holt, 1966. Contributor to French studies journals.

WORK IN PROGRESS: Research on French feminism under the Second Empire and Third Republic.

SIDELIGHTS: Evelyn Acomb-Walker comments: "I believe a knowledge of history is essential for an educated person."

AVOCATIONAL INTERESTS: Travel in France.

ADAMS, J(ames) Mack 1933-

PERSONAL: Born August 14, 1933, in Marfa, Tex.; son of Glen Wayne (a surveyor) and Albene (Hughes) Adams; married Joe Ann Davis (a secretary), March 30, 1952; children: Mack Lane, Mark Wayne. *Education:* Texas Western College (now University of Texas at El Paso), B.S., 1954; attended University of Pittsburgh, 1955-56; New Mexico State University, M.S., 1960, Ph.D., 1963. *Residence:* Las Cruces, N.M. *Office:* Department of Computer Science, New Mexico State University, Las Cruces, N.M. 88003.

CAREER: Westinghouse Electric Corp., Pittsburgh, Pa., associate scientist, 1954-56; Flight Simulation Laboratory, White Sands Missile Range, N.M., mathematician, 1956-58, supervisory mathematician, 1958-60, mathematician, 1961-62, research mathematician, electronics research and development activity, 1963, supervisory mathematician, 1963-64; University of Texas at El Paso, associate professor of mathematics, 1964-65; New Mexico State University, Las Cruces, professor of computer science and department head, 1965—. Fulbright-Hayes lecturer at La Universidad Catolica, Santiago, Chile, 1972. *Member:* Mathematical Association of America, Association for Computing Machinery (national lecturer, 1972), Sigma Xi, Phi Kappa Phi. *Awards, honors:* Special Act Service award, White Sands Missile Range, 1964.

WRITINGS: (With Robert Moon) *Introduction to Computer Science,* Scott, Foresman, 1970; (with Douglas Haden) *Computers: Appreciation, Applications, Implications; An Introduction,* Wiley, 1973; (with Haden) *Social Effects of Computer Use and Misuse,* Wiley, 1976.

WORK IN PROGRESS: Research in software engineering and programming language design.

SIDELIGHTS: Adams told *CA:* "Although my current activities are of a technical nature, I have an abiding interest in the social and philosophical implications of science in general and computer science in particular. My current sabbatical leave at the Programming Research Group of Oxford University contributes to both my technical and non-technical interests, and during my previous sabbatical leave at La Universidad Catolica in Santiago, Chile, I studied and lectured on the social implications of computer usage in developing countries."

ADAMS, Philip R. 1908-

PERSONAL: Born November 19, 1908, in Fargo, N.D.; son of Charles Ryan (a Presbyterian minister) and Myra (Old-father) Adams; married Marie Constance LeMercier du-Quesnay (deceased); married Mary Rosan Krippendorf, September 17, 1947; children: Jeremy duQuesnay, Philip LeMercier. *Education:* Ohio State University, B.A., 1929; graduate study at Princeton University, 1930-31; New York University, M.A., 1931. *Religion:* Presbyterian. *Home:* 3003 Observatory Ave., Cincinnati, Ohio 45208.

CAREER: Tulane University, New Orleans, La., instructor in art and lecturer in fine arts, 1931-34; Columbus Gallery of Fine Arts, Columbus, Ohio, assistant director, 1934-36, director, 1936-45; Cincinnati Art Museum, Cincinnati, Ohio, director, 1945-74, director emeritus, 1974—; writer, 1974—. *Member:* Association of Art Museum Directors (vice-president, 1969; honorary vice-president, 1975). *Awards, honors:* Litt.D. from Miami University, Oxford, Ohio, and Cincinnati College; D.F.A. from Wittenberg College; L.H.D. from University of Cincinnati, Hebrew Union College, and Jewish Institute of Religion.

WRITINGS: Rodin, Hyperion Press, 1945; *Mary Callery Sculpture,* Wittenborn, 1961; *Walt Kuhn, Painter: His Life and Work,* Ohio State University Press, 1978. Contributor to professional and literary journals and popular magazines, including *Harper's Bazaar, Commonweal,* and *Kenyon Review.*

* * *

AGINSKY, Bernard W(illard) 1905-
(Burt W. Aginsky)

PERSONAL: Born February 10, 1905, in New York, N.Y.; son of Samuel (in real estate and building) and Bessie (Shenkin) Aginsky; married Ethel Goldberg (an anthropologist), April 7, 1929. *Education:* New York University, B.S., 1931, M.A., 1932; Columbia University, Ph.D., 1934. *Home:* 939 Coast Blvd., 19-DE, La Jolla, Calif. 92037. *Agent:* Julian Bach Literary Agency, Inc., 249 East 48th St., New York, N.Y. 10017. *Office:* Institute for World Understanding, 939 Coast Blvd., La Jolla, Calif. 92037.

CAREER: Columbia University, New York City, research associate, 1934-36; University of California, Berkeley, research associate, 1936; Yenching University, Yenching, China, visiting professor of anthropology and language, 1936-37; Columbia University, research associate, 1937-38; New York University, New York City, instructor in anthropology and sociology, 1938-41, director of Social Science Field Laboratory, 1939-41; Hunter College (now of the City University of New York), New York City, lecturer in sociology and anthropology, 1946; City College of the City University of New York, New York City, professor of anthropology and sociology, 1946-65, head of department, 1947-52; Syracuse University, Syracuse, N.Y., director of Social Science Field Laboratory Institute, 1947-48; Institute for World Understanding, La Jolla, Calif., director, 1965—. Member of faculty at New York Psychoanalytic Institute, 1939; visiting professor at University of Buenos Aires, 1958; Sperry-Hutchinson Lecturer at University of Miami, Coral Gables, Fla., 1965. Member of board of directors of Museum of Man, 1973, Senior Adult Services, 1973—, School of Medicine Associates (head of board of directors), 1974, Children's Center, 1974—, and La Jolla Cancer Institute; member of board of visitors at University of San Diego, 1974—. Representative to White House Conference on Youth Problems, 1961. *Military service:* U.S. Army, Infan-

try, 1942, professor of military science and tactics at University of Iowa, 1943-46.

MEMBER: International Congress of Americanists, American Academy of Political and Social Sciences, American Anthropological Association (fellow; member of council, 1935—), American Association for the Advancement of Science (fellow), American Association of University Professors, American Ethnological Society, American Folklore Society (member of council, 1953—), American Sociological Association, Society for Applied Anthropology, United Nations Association (member of San Francisco board of directors, 1973; local vice-president, 1974), Eastern Sociological Society, Southwestern Anthropological Association, New York Academy of Science (fellow). *Awards, honors:* Social Science Research Council grants, 1934, 1935-36, 1939; Rockefeller Foundation grant, 1939; Wenner-Gren Foundation grant, 1947-50; Research Institute for the Study of Man grants, 1964, 1965.

WRITINGS: Kinship Systems and the Forms of Marriage, American Anthropological Association, 1935; *Culture Element Distribution: Central Sierra,* University of California Press, 1943; (under name Burt. W. Aginsky) *This Man-Made World,* Rinehart, 1949; (with wife, Ethel G. Aginsky) *Selected Papers of B. W. and E. G. Aginsky,* Printing Unlimited, 1955; (under name Burt W. Aginsky, with E. G. Aginsky) *Deep Valley: A Presentation of the Pomo Indians,* Stein & Day, 1967; (under name Burt W. Aginsky, with E. G. Aginsky) *Anthropotentialism and Language,* Brigham Young University Press, 1978. Contributor to *Encyclopaedia Britannica.* Contributor to anthropology and sociology journals, including *Annals of the American Academy of Political and Social Science.*

WORK IN PROGRESS: Research on anthropotentialism and holistic presentation, based on the development of methodology resulting from the study of the modern world, containing a presentation of "how the potential culture of Mankind can be ascertained and then how Man can select from that potential the culture in which he desires to live," with a book expected to result.

SIDELIGHTS: Aginsky writes: "To me, the world of Man and the natural universe in which we live has always constituted the greatest mystery which Man has been in the process of solving bit by bit, but which still constitutes the most exciting challenge. One of the most intriguing items is the inability of Man to solve his problems without aggression and warfare.

"As an anthropologist I am interested in the whole of Man and his accomplishments and have concentrated on what could be called civilizational anthropology. I am also involved in establishing a 'system of universal transmitting and receiving' through computers, whereby every person will speak and hear his own language. The computer will do the translating. Research and travel has been with a number of American Indian tribes and more than fifty nations. This includes visits and research in almost every great civilizational center of the past."

AVOCATIONAL INTERESTS: Painting, sculpture, playing the harp.

* * *

AI 1947-

PERSONAL: Birth-given name, Florence Anthony; known professionally as Ai; born October 21, 1947, in Albany,

Tex.; *Education:* University of Arizona, B.A.; University of California, Irvine, M.A., 1971. *Home:* 69 Cedar Dr., Miller Place, N.Y. 11764.

CAREER: Poet. *Awards, honors:* Guggenheim fellow, 1975; Radcliffe fellow, 1975; Massachusetts Arts and Humanities fellowship, 1976.

WRITINGS: Cruelty (poems), Houghton, 1973; *Killing Floor* (Lamont poetry selection), Houghton, 1979. Contributor of articles and poems to magazines, including *Ms.*

SIDELIGHTS: Ai has been called "All woman—all human" by Anne Sexton, while the subjects of her first book were labeled by the *Times Literary Supplement* as "the cruelty of intimate relationships and the delights of perverse spontaneity—e.g. the joy a mother gets from beating her child." Alicia Ostriker saw no parallel between such assessments when she wrote: "'All woman—all human'; she is hardly that. She is more like a bad dream of Woody Allen's, or the inside story of some Swinburnean Dolorosa, or the *vagina-dentata* itself starting to talk. Woman, in Ai's embodiment, wants sex. She knows about death and can kill animals and people. She is hard as dirt. Her realities—very small ones—are so intolerable that we fashion female myths to express our fear of her. She, however, lives the hard life below our myths."

Whether Ai is "all woman" or not, she undoubtedly puts to shame "everyone who has ever thought, secretly or otherwise, that a woman, writing naturally, about things that concern her, would have to come up with a string of cliches and roses." The speakers in her poems are not the poet but individuals (sometimes men) "playing out the drama of their lives in isolated small-town and small-farm settings." Simply, and with "no begging, no pleading, and no self-pity," they can say "I see your stomach is flat as an iron. / You've done it, as you warned me you would" ("Abortion"), or "The street coughs blood / in a linen handkerchief, / as I strut down to the river" ("The Suicide").

Ostriker explained that the lives behind these voices "count for nothing more than that of a slaughtered goat, where desire is like the smell of fresh meat. Each is savage, each is victim.... Their cruelty is theirs because it is nature's." And in portraying these lives, "Ai has not spared herself or mistrusted the reality of her own perception of experience," reasoned Alice Walker. "She has chosen honesty over politics. Expressions of personal knowledge are always arguable; if you want nice poems to 'like' this is not your book."

Ai herself has not been sheltered from struggles of her own, particularly in regards to her heritage. In her article "On Being 1/2 Japanese, 1/8 Choctaw, 1/4 Black, and 1/16 Irish," she revealed her own mother's traumatic pregnancy; her difficulty in keeping a racial identity as she grew older; her problem of deciding whether to be "loyal to myself as a multiracial person or be immersed in the black struggle for identity with which I had little in common"; and eventually her success in finding identity through the "aesthetic atmosphere fostered by the [University of Arizona] Oriental Studies faculty, by books, records, and my own fantasies."

Ai detailed her feelings on race when she wrote: "People whose concept of themselves is largely dependent on their racial identity and superiority feel threatened by a multiracial person. The insistence that one must align oneself with this or that race is basically racist. And the notion that without a racial identity a person can't have any identity perpetuates racism.... Since I believe that clinging to one's race tears one apart, and that letting go makes one whole, I wish I could say that race isn't important. But it is. More than ever, it is a medium of exchange, the coin of the realm with which one buys one's share of jobs and social position. This is a fact which I have faced and must ultimately transcend. If this transcendence were less complex, less individual, it would lose its holiness."

It is apparent that as Ai has wrestled with the problem of her racial identity she has never affirmed any definition of her self other than her own. Similarly, Ostriker felt that Ai as a poet, "though she is just beginning, ... has set herself in a league with Faulkner's novels, or with Ted Hughes's 'Crow'; with those who will not take yes for an answer."

BIOGRAPHICAL/CRITICAL SOURCES: Kirkus Reviews, August 15, 1973; *New York Times Book Review,* February 17, 1974; *Times Literary Supplement,* March 29, 1974; *Ms.,* June, 1974, June, 1978; *Contemporary Literary Criticism,* Gale, Volume 4, 1975.*

* * *

AICHINGER, Ilse 1921-

PERSONAL: Born November 1, 1921, in Vienna, Austria; married Guenter Eich (a poet and radio dramatist), 1953 (died, 1972); children: three. *Education:* University of Vienna, 1946-48. *Home:* 8232 Bayerisch Gmain, Postfach 27, West Germany.

CAREER: Novelist, short story writer, radio dramatist, poet. S. Fischer (publisher), publisher's reader in Frankfurt, East Germany, and Vienna, Austria, 1949-50; Hochschule fuer Gestaltung (Academy of Design), Ulm, West Germany, assistant to the founder, Inge Scholl. *Member:* German P.E.N. Center, Bavarian Academy of Fine Arts, Berlin Academy of Arts. *Awards, honors:* Group 47 Prize, 1952; Austrian State Prize for the Encouragement of Literature, 1952; Literary Prize of the City of Bremen, 1955; Immermann Prize of the City of Duesseldorf, 1955; Bavarian Literature Prize, 1961; Nelly Sachs Prize, Dortmund, 1971.

*WRITINGS—*In English: *Die groessere Hoffnung: Roman* (novel), Bermann-Fischer (Amsterdam), 1948, translation by Cornelia Schaeffer published as *Herod's Children,* Atheneum, 1963; *Rede unter dem Galgen* (title means "Speech Under the Gallows"), Jungbrunnenverlag (Vienna), 1951, published as *Der Gefesselte,* Fischer (Frankfurt), 1953, translation by Eric Mosbacher published as *The Bound Man and Other Stories,* Secker & Warburg, 1955; (contributor) Anna Otten, *Mensch und Zeit: An Anthology of German Radio Plays,* Irvington Books, 1966; *Ilse Aichinger: Selected Short Stories and Dialogue,* edited and translated by James C. Alldridge, Pergamon, 1966; *Ilse Aichinger,* edited and translated by Alldridge, Wolff, 1969.

Other works: *Zu keiner Stunde* (dialogues; title means "Never at Any Time"), Fischer, 1957; *Besuch im Pfarrhaus: Ein Hoerspiel, Drei Dialoge* (title means "A Visit to the Vicarage: A Radio Play, Three Dialogues"), Fischer, 1961; *Wo ich wohne: Erzaehlungen, Gedichte, Dialoge* (title means "Where I Live: Short Stories, Poems, Dialogues"), Fischer, 1963; *Eliza, Eliza* (short stories), Fischer, 1965; *Auckland: Four Hoerspiele* (title means "Auckland: Four Radio Plays"), Fischer, 1969; *Nachricht vom Tag: Erzaehlungen* (title means "News of the Day: Short Stories"), Fischer, 1970; *Dialoge, Erzaehlungen, Gedichte* (title means "Dialogues, Short Stories, Poems"), Reclam, 1971; *Schlechte Woerter* (title means "Bad Words"), Fischer, 1976.

Also author of radio plays, "Knoepfe" (title means "Buttons"), first broadcast in 1953, and "Belvedere."

SIDELIGHTS: Ilse Aichinger grew up in Vienna and in

Linz, enjoying an unremarkable childhood until 1938, when Hitler annexed Austria. Being of partly Jewish blood, she was forced to work in an Austrian factory and suffered in other ways, not least in her education. Unable to matriculate until after World War II, she then entered the University of Vienna, intending to become a doctor. It was during her two years at the university that she wrote her novel *Die groessere Hoffnung*. When it was published in 1948, Aichinger abandoned her medical studies.

Die groessere Hoffnung introduced many of the themes that have preoccupied Aichinger in all her work. Set in a country dominated by the Nazis, it centers on Ellen, a precociously perceptive child who is half Jewish. We see through her eyes how a group of children devise an "emigration" game which is a rehearsal for a real escape attempt. Although Ellen is eventually killed, the novel offers the "greater hope" of its title—the hope that, even in the midst of chaos and suffering, "all things work together for good in them that love God." James C. Alldridge in his monograph on Aichinger wrote that the children's escape plan is obviously impracticable, but that "the tension and the possibility are kept alive by the 'double' life the children lead; the half-preposterous hope of an exit visa is fanned and kept alive by the imaginative and 'parabolic' scenes of the children's games, re-enacting as they frequently do events from the New Testament. . . . The juxtaposition throughout the work of a pitiless world writhing in the horrors of war and death, and a serener world of a soaring spirit, is most skilfully contrived." When the novel was published in English as *Herod's Children*, reviewers were reminded variously of Kafka and of *The Diary of Anne Frank*. Some were confused, unable to distinguish easily between what was happening in the streets and what occurred only in the imagination of the children. Other critics were moved, however: one in the *Times Literary Supplement* called it "a first work of astonishing maturity" and Kay Boyle praised "the beauty of the author's remarkable prose" as well as her "poetic fury and spirited tenderness."

Thereafter Ilse Aichinger wrote no more novels, concentrating her attention on shorter literary forms which, it has been suggested, may seem to her more expressive of the fragmented and impermanent spirit of the age. Many of her short stories and radio plays are parables, like the well-known story "The Bound Man," which gave its title to her first collection. Her debt to Kafka is nowhere more evident than in this piece, whose central character wakes up one morning and finds that he has been bound with cords that allow him only slight freedom of movement. Paradoxically, it is in this condition that he achieves most; when he is freed, his personality disintegrates. The point of this parable for some readers was that perfect freedom lies in bondage to God. For James C. Alldridge, however, it bears upon what he regards as Aichinger's central theme, "mankind in the bondage caused and nourished by his lack of concern for the spiritual life of his fellows." "From this position," Alldridge writes, "She moves on in her stories through a mythical, almost grotesque dreamland, but she maintains an extreme logical sequence and avoids getting lost in surrealist phantasmagoria. None of her settings is tied to a particular time, though her inspiration has arisen out of her experience in her own time, and the remarkable variety of scene in her work would be bewildering, were it not for the sympathy and understanding we feel at once for every one of her characters, in spite of the apparent unreality of the actual setting. . . . The wisdom and understanding in her work are given to the world in a concentrated, abbreviated, almost codified form." Rolf Schroers has spoken of her "unreal tales of overwhelming

reality," while an English reviewer of *The Bound Man*, who found the endings of some of her stories unsuitably contrived, concluded that "there is no denying the irrational power and deep feeling of almost every story in the book."

There has been a similar reception for Aichinger's radio plays. "Buttons," the first of her plays to be broadcast, evokes with great economy the loss of individuality of several characters who devote their working lives to the mindlessly repetitive routines of a button factory, and whose fate it is to become buttons themselves. A much more ancient literary form, the dialogue, has in Aichinger's hands been given a new lease of life. She uses it as Plato did, to show how one person may gain information or guidance from another, or how two people might debate together to solve a problem of mutual concern. In "Belvedere" the same technique is used to illustrate a failure of communication that is at first funny and then increasingly menacing, in a way reminiscent of Ionesco. Aichinger has also published a number of poems, distinguished by the same economy and ambiguity, the same lyrical strangeness, as her prose.

Alldridge, discussing the themes and images that pervade Ilse Aichinger's work, has referred to the preponderance of dream imagery, her frequent use of characters from folklore, and her profound religious sense: "Night, thought of as an approach to the shades of death, the transitoriness of all individual life, the tolling of bells and concern for a state beyond the immediate, the present, and the obvious"—all these preoccupations are an extension of her religious concerns. The consistency with which she uses her recurrent symbols, Alldridge points out, suggests a familiarity with the pattern of archetypal dream symbols posited by Jung. Speaking of the modest, low-keyed, and scrupulous nature of her work, he says that "one has often had the impression, when reading one of her works for the first time, of a silent figure, by whom one has been observed and of whose existence one had been unaware."

BIOGRAPHICAL/CRITICAL SOURCES: Times Literary Supplement, January 4, 1952, September 16, 1955; *Time,* October 25, 1963; *New York Times Book Review,* November 24, 1963; James C. Alldridge, editor and translator, *Ilse Aichinger: Selected Short Stories and Dialogue,* Pergamon, 1966; Alldridge, editor and translator, *Ilse Aichinger,* Wolff, 1969; Siegfried Mandel, *Group 47,* Southern Illinois University Press, 1973; Frederick Ungar, editor, *Handbook of Austrian Literature,* Ungar, 1973.*

* * *

ALBERTI, Rafael 1902-

PERSONAL: Born in Puerto de Santa Maria, Cadiz, Spain; immigrated to Rome, Italy; married Maria Tersa Leon; children: Aitana (a daughter). *Education:* Attended a Jesuit academy in Spain. *Residence:* Rome, Italy.

CAREER: Poet, dramatist, and painter. *Awards, honors:* National Prize for Literature (Spain), 1924, for *Marinero en tierra.*

WRITINGS—All poetry, except as noted; in English: *Sobre los angeles (1927-1928)* (also see below), Editorial Plutarco, 1924, reprinted, 1959, translation by Geoffrey Connell published as *Concerning the Angels,* University of California Press, 1966; *A Spectre Is Haunting Europe: Poems of Revolutionary Spain,* translation from the original Spanish manuscript by Ira Jan Wallach and Angel Flores, Critics Group (New York, N.Y.), 1936; *La arboleda perdida y otras prosas* (also see below), Editorial Seneca, 1942, translation by Gabriel Berns published as *The Lost Grove: Autobiography of a Spanish Poet in Exile,* University of California Press,

1976; *Rafael Alberti: Selected Poems*, edited by Ben Belitt, translation by Lloyd Mallan, New Directions, 1944; *Poesias completas*, Losada, 1961, translation by Mark Strand published as *The Owl's Insomnia* (text in English and Spanish), Atheneum, 1973; *A Year of Picasso's Paintings*, translation by Anthony Kerrigan, Abrams, 1971.

In Spanish: *Marinero en tierra*, Losada, 1924, 4th edition, 1970; *La amante canciones* (also see below), Editorial Plutarco, 1925; *El alba del alheli* (also see below), Buenos Aires, 1927; *Cal y canto*, Revista de Occidente, 1929; *El hombre deshabitado*, Gama (Madrid), 1930; *La poesia popular en la lirica espanola contemporanea*, W. Gronan, 1933; *Poesia, 1924-1930* (title means "Poetry, 1924-1930"), Ediciones del arbol, 1934; *Verte y no verte: A Ignacio Sanchez Mejias*, Fabula (Mexico), 1935; *Nuestra diaria palabra*, [Madrid], 1936; *Trece bandas cuarenta y ocho estrellas*, [Madrid], 1936; *Entre el clavel y la espada (1939-1940)*, illustrations by Maria Carmen, Losada, 1941; *El poeta en la Espana de 1931*, [Buenos Aires], 1942; *Eh, los toros!*, illustrations by Luis Seoane, Emece, 1942; (editor) Federico Garcia Lorca, *Antologia poetica*, Losada, 1942, revised edition, 1972; (compiler and author of introduction) *Eglogas y fabulas castellanas*, two volumes, Pleamar, 1944; (compiler and author of introduction) *Romancero general de la guerra espanola*, illustrations by Gori Munoz, Patronato Hispano Argentino de Cultura, 1944; *Pleamar (1942-1944)*, Losado, 1944; *A la pintura; cantata de la linea y del color*, Imprenta Lopez, 1945.

Buenos Aires en tinta china, edited by Attilio Rossi, Losada, 1951; *Retornos de lo vivo lejano (1948-1952)*, Losada, 1952; *Ora maritima, seguido de Baladas y canciones del Parana* (also see below), illustrations by Juan Batte Planas, Losada, 1953; *Maria Carmen Portela*, Losada, 1956; (editor with Guillermo de Torre) Garcia Lorca, *Antologia poetica (1918-1936)*, Losada, 1957; (with Maria Teresa Leon; self-illustrated) *Sonrie China*, J. Muchnik, 1958; *Cal y canto, Sobre los angeles, Sermones moradas*, Losada, 1959; *El otono, otra vez*, [Lima], 1960; *Los viejos olivos*, Direccion de Cultura y Bellas Artes, Departmento de Publicationes, 1960; *Poemas escenicos*, Losada, 1962—; (self-illustrated) *Suma taurina: Verso, prosa, teatro*, edited by Rafael Montesinos, Editorial R. M., 1963; *Diez sonetos romanos*, Ediciones Galeria Bonino, 1964; *Rafael Alberti* (anthology), edited by Eduardo Gonzales Lanuza, Ediciones Culturales Argentines, 1965; (editor and compiler) Lope Felix de Vega Carpio, *Poesias* (title means "Poetry"), Losada, 1965; *El Poeta en la calle, poesia civil, 1931-1965*, compiled by Pablo Neruda, Editions de la Librairie du Globe, 1966; (contributor) Angel Caffarena Such, *Homenaje que ofrecen Picasso*, El Guadalhorce, 1966; *Poemas de amor* (title means "Poems of Love"), Alfaguara, 1967; *Roma, peligra para caminantes, 1964-1967*, J. Mortiz, 1968; *Libro del mar*, compiled by Aitana Alberti, illustrations by F. Catal Roca, Lumen, 1968; *Poesias anteriores a marinero en tierra, 1920-1923*, Editiones V.A., 1969.

Los ocho nombres de Picasso, y No digo mas que lo que no digo (1966-1970), inscribed by Pablo Picasso, Editorial Kairos, 1970; *Prosas encontradas (1924-1942)*, compiled by Robert Marrast, Ayuso, 1970; (compiler and author of introduction) *Antologia poetica: Antonio Machado, Juan Ramon Jimenez, Federico Garcia Lorca*, illustrations by Jaume Pla, Nauta, 1970; *Canciones del alto valle del Aniene y otros versos y prosas, 1967-1972*, Losada, 1972; *Retornos de lo vivo lejano 1948-1956*, Libres de Sinera (Barcelona), 1972; *Obras completas* (title means "Complete Works"), Aguilar, 1972—; *La arboleda perdida: Libros I y II de memorias*,

Seix Barral, 1975; *Picasso, el rayo que no cesa*, Poligrafa, 1975; *Poemas del destierro y de la espera* (anthology), compiled by J. Corredor-Matheos, Espasa-Calpe (Madrid), 1976; *Alberti* (anthology), Ediciones Litoral, 1976; *Coplas de Juan Panadero (1949-1977) seguida de Vida bilingue de un refugiado espanol en Francia (1939-1940)*, Editorial Mayoria, 1977. Also author of *Costa sur de la muerte* (title means "The South Coast of Death"), 1936, *Cantata de los heroes y la fraternidad de los pueblos* (title means "Cantato of Heroes and the Fraternity of Peoples"), and *El burro explosivo*.

Other works: *Imagen primera de Federico Garcia (1940-1944)*, Losada, 1945; (editor) *El gran amor de Gustavo Becquert*, Losada, 1946; *Raul Soldi*, Losada, 1963; *Lope de Vega y la poesia contemporanea seguita de la pajara pinta* (also see below), introduction by Marrast, Centre de recherches de l'Institut d'etudes hispaniques, 1964; *Picasso en Avignon, commentaires a une peinture en mouvement*, translation from original Spanish manuscript by Georges Franck, Editions Cercle d'art, 1971. Also contributor to *Martin Fierro*, by Jose Hernandez Pueyrnedon, 1968.

Translator: Gloria Alcorta, *Visages (rostros)*, Botella al mar, 1951; (and editor with Leon) *Doinas y baladas populares rumanas*, Losado, 1963; *Abierto a todas horas (1960-1963)*, A. Aguado, 1964.

Plays: *La pajara pinta* (title means "The Game of Forfeits"), Argentina, 1925; *De un momento a otro* (title means "From One Moment to the Next"), Editorial Bajel (Buenos Aires), 1942; *El adefesio* (three-act; title means "The Folly"; also see below), Losada, 1944, reprinted, 1976; *Teatro: El hombre des habitado, El trebol florido, La gallarda* (also see below), Losada, 1950; *Noche de guerra en el Museo del Prado* (one-act), Ediciones Losange, 1956; *Teatro: El hombre des habitado, El trebol florido, El adefesio, La Gallarda*, Losada, 1959; *Teatro: La lozana andaluza, De un momento a otro, Noche de guerra en el Museo del Prado*, Losado, 1964. Also author of "Fermin Gala."

Works included in numerous anthologies in Spanish and English.

SIDELIGHTS: Rafael Alberti and Garcia Lorca are considered the most prominent contemporary Spanish surrealist poets. Alberti is not well known on an international level. Only a few of his books have been translated into English. Comparing Alberti to Garcia Lorca, editor Ben Belitt called Alberti "more intellectual." In *Rafael Alberti: Selected Poems*, Belitt wrote: "Alberti found his subjects more and more in himself, in his own contradictions and problems. . . . He lacked Lorca's instinctive joy and instinctive melancholy: his gifts were more varied and more conflicting." Making the same comparison, Ruth Stephan commented in *Poetry*, "Those who know Spain say these two poets, one impulsive and sensuous, the other subjectively wise, are complementary components of the Spanish character."

Both Alberti and Garcia Lorca belonged to an avant garde group, "The Generation of 1929," which also included Spanish surrealist painter Salvador Dali. In his autobiographical collection, *The Lost Grove*, Alberti relates anecdotes concerning this coterie of writers and artists. *Best Sellers* called the work "a truly lovely book," in which Alberti "evokes all the joys, the sorrows, the embarrassments, and the longings of a boy growing up, and unashamedly presents all the pleasant and all the bitter reflections of the man looking back on himself as a youth."

"Alberti is so accomplished a craftsman of verse and so well trained in its different forms that he has no difficulty in finding the right measures for his different moods," said Luis

Monguio in *The Poetry of Rafael Alberti: An Introduction.* In his early period of writing, Alberti wrote popular poetry such as that in *Marinero en tierra,* for which he won the National Prize for Literature. *Cal y canto* has been classified as "Gongoristic," after sixteenth-century poet Gongora, while *Sobre los angeles* is a surrealistic work. It is in this collection that "Alberti approaches nearest to pure poetry," critic Erik Proll once wrote. Alberti's later works are more spiritual in mood.

During the Spanish Civil War Alberti sympathized with the Popular Front and eventually became a self-imposed political exile in Paris, in Buenos Aires, and in Italy, where he now lives. Much of his poetry is still banned in Spain for being of a revolutionary nature. *Sobre los angeles* reflects Alberti's strong political views. It deals with a "terrible crisis in which Alberti finds that for no explicable reason he has lost his trust in himself and his hold on existence, that things which have hitherto meant much to him and guided and sustained him have suddenly left him," and he has lost all that "gives savour and significance to life," wrote Monguio. Alberti speaks not only for himself, "who has lost a most precious possession but of a generation which fears that it has lost its way in the world," Monguio continued. Because of his ability to identify with the working class, Alberti has been called "a poet of the proletariat."

The Owl's Insomnia contains fifty selected poems from Alberti's *Poesias completas,* a work over one thousand pages in length. Reviewing the poetry in *Prairie Schooner,* Hilda Gregory remarked, "They are beautiful and strange, more moving when read in the company of their fellows than as single pieces."

Alberti has traveled and studied in France, Germany, and Russia, and has toured both North and South America.

BIOGRAPHICAL/CRITICAL SOURCES: Luis Monguio, *The Poetry of Raphael Alberti: An Introduction,* University of California Press, 1966; C. B. Morris, *Rafael Alberti's "Sobre los angeles": Four Major Themes,* University of Hull, 1966; Morris, *A Generation of Spanish Poets 1920-1936,* Cambridge University Press, 1969; *Times Literary Supplement,* October 15, 1971; *Publishers Weekly,* June 26, 1972, November 22, 1976; *Newsweek,* December 11, 1972; *Nation,* May 28, 1973, January 11, 1975, April 16, 1977; *Choice,* April, 1974, July/August, 1977; *Village Voice,* June 20, 1974; *Poetry,* August, 1974; *Poet,* August, 1974; *Prairie Schooner,* fall, 1974; *Parnassus: Poetry in Review,* fall/winter, 1974; *American Poetry Review,* November, 1976; *Best Sellers,* May, 1977; Jose Miguel Velloso, *Conversaciones con Rafael Alberti,* Sedmay Ediciones (Madrid), 1977; *Contempory Literary Criticism,* Gale, Volume 7, 1977.*

*   *   *

ALBIN, Peter S(teigman) 1934-

PERSONAL: Born December 20, 1934, in New York, N.Y.; son of Joseph (an engineer) and Minna (a teacher; maiden name, Steigman) Albin; married Patricia Elson (a political scientist), July 13, 1958; children: Nancy, John. *Education:* Yale University, B.A., 1956; Princeton University, M.A., 1959, Ph.D., 1964. *Politics:* Social Democrat. *Home:* 505 Laguardia Pl., New York, N.Y. 10012. *Agent:* Hy Cohen Literary Agency Ltd., 111 West 57th St., New York, N.Y. 10019. *Office:* 445 West 54th St., New York, N.Y. 10019.

CAREER: New York University, New York City, assistant professor, 1964-67, associate professor, 1967-72, professor of economics, 1972-74; City University of New York, John

Jay College of Criminal Justice, New York City, professor of economics and head of department, 1974- . Faculty visitor at Cambridge University, 1968-69; visiting professor at University of California, Berkeley, 1973-74, and at Vienna's Institute for Advanced Studies, 1978; professor at City University of New York Graduate Center, 1974—; Lindner Lecturer at New School for Social Research, 1978. Partner and chief economist of Unicorn Group (assets management firm); consultant to World Bank, U.S. Congress, and National Organization for Women. *Member:* American Economic Association. *Awards, honors:* National Science Foundation grant, 1978.

WRITINGS: Analysis of Complex Socioeconomic Systems, Lexington Books, 1975; *Progress Without Poverty,* Basic Books, 1978. Contributor to economic, business, and finance journals.

WORK IN PROGRESS: Workplace (tentative title), an analysis of the complexity of technical and industrial systems and an assessment of the human impact of that complexity; *Structure and Complexity* (tentative title), a more abstract analysis of the structural characteristics of economic and social systems, using the algebraic theory of automata.

SIDELIGHTS: Albin writes: "My interest over the past decade has been in finding better ways to describe the structural forms which characterize continuously-adapting socioeconomic systems. This has led me toward methods which derive from linguistics, mathematical logic, and computer science. Although the approach is not yet well-established, it is beginning to produce practical results pertaining to system properties and the planning and control of real-world economics.

"I am naive enough to believe that this is a humanistic endeavor—that the way to check 'technologically inevitable' ecological and social disasters is to understand the development of industrial systems and the implications of technique better than the technicians who rely on mystification to cover up their conceits. The spirit of my research can be read from the subtitle of *Progress Without Poverty:* 'socially responsible economic growth.'

"I have also been writing some fiction. I have completed one children's fantasy, and I am well into a novel (which I take seriously)."

AVOCATIONAL INTERESTS: Tennis, music, playing *Go.*

*   *   *

ALDINGTON, Richard 1892-1962

PERSONAL: Born in 1892, in Hampshire, England; came to United States during World War II; died July 28, 1962, in Lere, France; married Hilda Doolittle (a poet), 1913 (divorced, 1937); married Netta McCulloch, 1937. *Education:* Attended Dover College and University of London.

CAREER: Writer. *Military service:* Served in infantry during World War I; became officer. *Awards, honors:* James Tait Black Memorial Prize, 1947, for *Wellington.*

WRITINGS—Poetry: Images, 1910-1915, Poetry Bookshop, 1915, revised edition published as *Images, Old and New,* Four Seas, 1916; *Images,* Egoist Ltd., 1919; *Images of War,* Allen & Unwin, 1919; *Images of Desire,* Elkin Mathews, 1919; *War and Love,* Four Seas, 1919; *Exile and Other Poems,* Allen & Unwin, 1923; *A Fool i' the Forest, a Phantasmagoria,* Allen & Unwin, 1925; *The Love of Myrrhine and Konallis, and Other Prose Poems,* P. Covici, 1926; *Hark the Herald,* Hours Press, 1928; *Collected Poems,* Friede, 1928; *The Eaten Heart,* Hours Press, 1929; *A Dream in the Luxembourg,* Chatto & Windus, 1930; *Love and the Luxembourg,* Friede, 1930; *Collected Poems, 1914-1923,* Allen & Unwin, 1933; *The Poems of Richard Aldington,* Doubleday, 1934; *Life Quest,* Doubleday, 1935; *The Crystal World,* Heinemann, 1937, Doubleday, 1938; *The Complete Poems of Richard Aldington,* Wingate, 1948; Norman Timmins Gates, editor, *The Poetry of Richard Aldington: A Critical Evaluation and an Anthology of Uncollected Poems,* Pennsylvania State University Press, 1975.

Novels: *Death of a Hero,* Friede, 1929, reprinted, Scholarly Press, 1972; *The Colonel's Daughter,* Doubleday, 1931; *Stepping Heavenward, a Record,* Chatto & Windus, 1931, Doubleday, 1932; *All Men Are Enemies, a Romance,* Doubleday, 1933, reprinted, Cedric Chivers, 1968; *Women Must Work,* Doubleday, 1934; *Seven Against Reeves, a Comedy-Farce,* Doubleday, 1938; *Rejected Guests,* Heinemann, 1939; *Romance of Casanova,* Duell, Sloan & Pearce, 1946.

Other: *Medallions in Clay,* Knopf, 1921; *Literary Studies and Reviews,* Dial, 1924, reprinted, Books for Libraries Press, 1968; *Voltaire,* Dutton, 1925, reprinted, Folcroft Library Editions, 1977; *French Studies and Reviews,* Allen & Unwin, 1926, reprinted, Books for Libraries Press, 1967; *At All Costs* (short stories), Heinemann, 1930; *Roads to Glory* (short stories), Chatto & Windus, 1930, Doubleday, 1931, reprinted, Books for Libraries Press, 1970; *Two Stories,* E. Mathews, 1930; *Last Straws* (short story), Hours Press, 1930, reprinted, Folcroft Library Editions, 1976; *Balls: And Another Book for Suppression,* privately printed, 1932, reprinted, Norwood, 1977; *Soft Answers* (short stories), Doubleday, 1932, reprinted, Southern Illinois University Press, 1967; *Artifex: Sketches and Ideas,* Chatto & Windus, 1935, Doubleday, 1936; (with Derek Patmore) *Life of a Lady: A Play in Three Acts,* Doubleday, 1936; *Very Heaven,* Heinemann, 1937; *Rejected Guest,* Viking, 1939; *W. Somerset Maugham: An Appreciation,* Doubleday, 1939, reprinted, Norwood, 1977.

Life for Life's Sake; A Book of Reminiscences, Viking, 1941, Cassell, 1968; *The Duke; Being an Account of the life and Achievements of Arthur Wellesley, 1st Duke of Wellington,* Viking, 1943 (published in England as *Wellington: Being an Account of the Life and Achievements of Arthur Wellesley, 1st Duke of Wellington,* Heinemann, 1946); *Four English Portraits, 1801-1851,* Evans Brothers, 1948; *The Strange Life of Charles Waterton,* Duell, Sloan & Pearce, 1949.

D. H. Lawrence: Portrait of a Genius But . . . , Duell, Sloan & Pearce, 1950 (published in England as *Portrait of a Genius But . . . , The Life of D. H. Lawrence, 1885-1930,* Heinemann, 1950); *Pinorman; Personal Recollections of Norman Douglas,* Heinemann, 1954; *Lawrence of Arabia: A Biographical Inquiry,* Regnery, 1955, new edition, Collins, 1969; *Introduction to Mistral,* Heinemann, 1956, reprinted, Southern Illinois University Press, 1960; *Frauds,* Heinemann, 1957; *Portrait of a Rebel; The Life and Work of Robert Louis Stevenson,* Evans Brothers, 1957; Alister Kershaw, editor, *Richard Aldington: Selected Critical Writings,* Southern Illinois University Press, 1970; Miriam Benkovitz, editor, *A Passionate Prodigality: Letters to Alan Bird From Richard Aldington,* New York Publishing Library, 1976.

Editor: (And translator) *A Book of 'Characters' From Theophrastus; Joseph Hall, Sir Thomas Overbury, Nicolas Breton, John Earle, Thomas Fuller, and Other English Authors; Jean de La Bruyere, Vauvenargues, and Other French Authors,* Dutton, 1924; (and translator) Voltaire, *Letters of Voltaire and Frederick the Great,* [England], 1927; (and author of introductory essay) Marchioness Sevigne, *Letters of Madame de Sevigne,* [England], 1927; (and translator) *Fifty Romance Lyric Poems,* C. Gaige, 1928; (with G. Orioli and others) D. H. Lawrence, *Last Poems,* [England], 1932, new edition edited by Aldington with introduction, [England], 1933; Lawrence, *Selected Poems,* Secker & Warburg, 1934; (and author of introduction) Lawrence, *The Spirit of Place: An Anthology,* [England], 1935.

The Viking Book of Poetry of the English-Speaking World, Viking, 1941, revised edition, Viking, 1958; (and author of introduction) *Oscar Wilde: Selected Works,* [England], 1946; (and author of introduction) *Great French Romances,* Pilot Press, 1946; Walter Horatio Pater, *Selected Works,* Duell, Sloan & Pearce, 1948; Oscar Wilde, *The Portable Oscar Wilde,* Viking, 1963.

Also author of *Reverie, a Little Book of Poems for H. D.,* 1917, and *The Poet and His Age,* 1922. Translator and author of introduction to numerous works. Literary editor of *Egoist.* Critic of French literature for *Times Literary Supplement.* Contributor to periodicals.

SIDELIGHTS: Aldington began his career as a poet of the same Imagist school that included his wife Hilda Doolittle. In contrasting Aldington with Doolittle, Douglas Bush wrote, "In intention and technique his early Hellenic-Imagist poems were much the same as H. D.'s, but with a more diffuse softness, a more openly Victorian weariness and nostalgia." Aldington had achieved some recognition for his poetry when he enlisted during World War I. Many critics have noted how Aldington's attitudes as a writer changed after that war.

When he was discharged, Aldington suffered severely from shell shock. Upon recovery eight years later, he began writing novels. Considered by critics as extremely bitter accounts of war, Aldington's novels have been praised for their poetic power. "When he is willing to be serious," noted Frank Swinnerton, "as he is in the scenes of *Death of a Hero* which picture War experience, this author fully demonstrates his quality, which is considerable." Swinnerton added that Aldington possessed "great capacity for emotion." However, Swinnerton implied that Aldington's bitter feelings towards his countrymen hampered his writing. He wrote that as "indignation dies in him, and elderly age steals forward, if he continues to write novels he will find that his native kindness and gentleness will recover their sway over mind and pen, and a gentler view of his fellow-countrymen will supervene."

But many critics observed that Aldington's bitterness failed to diminish in its intensity. In a review of *Very Heaven,* Louis Macneice wrote, "Mr. Aldington is essentially a bitter writer and perhaps, therefore, ill-adapted to gestures of acceptance, but it is the aggressive parts of this book which strike me as so bad." Aldington's bitter style was also evident in his biography of T. E. Lawrence. In a review of *Lawrence of Arabia,* Robert Graves Wrote, "Personally I cannot read this book without revulsion. Instead of a carefully considered portrait of Lawrence, I find the self-portrait of a bitter, bedridden, leering, asthmatic, elderly hangman-of-letters—the live man who thinks himself better than the dead lion because he can at least scratch himself and snarl." Concerning the same biography, Graves also claimed that "Mr. Aldington was . . . not a proper person to write it, because he did not know Lawrence at all and has made little attempt to understand him, or even to consult those who did. . . ."

Not all critics denounced Aldington for the absence of "hero-worship" in his biographies. In a review of *D. H. Lawrence: Portrait of a Genius But . . . ,* James Stern wrote,

"Just because it lacks this quality, disclaims literary criticism, is not a personal memoir or even a biography, but an objective portrait . . . , Aldington's volume on D. H. Lawrence will undoubtedly stand the test of time better than anything else so far in print." Richard Mayne called Aldington "the reverse of a hostile critic." Summing up Aldington's book, *Mistral,* Mayne wrote, "He quotes and translates admirably, and writes with great fondness of Mistral and the life he stood for."

Assessing Aldington's work in retrospect, Bush wrote that "the mold of Mr. Aldington's Imagism was, along with other things, broken by the war." Bush commented that after the war "Mr. Aldington turned from Imagism to verse of the Pound-Eliot kind, and then to the novel, and has made a career of disillusioned bitterness." Richard McLaughlin, in a review of Aldington's autobiography, *Life for Life's Sake,* found justification for Aldington's apparent bitterness. "Never judge a man by his novels," cautioned McLaughlin. "Those who know Richard Aldington through his fiction will be agreeably surprised by his memoirs. Having thought of him as one of the embittered post-War generation, they will find his cynicism lies deeper than the smart nay-saying of his day. It is born of a striving for perfection, a distaste for the sham and second-rate in the literary and social worlds. It lifts him above the iconoclasts and gives him a detachedness which sets his reminiscences apart from the cant and bleatings of little men."

BIOGRAPHICAL/CRITICAL SOURCES: Saturday Review of Literature, April 28, 1934; *Nation,* May 30, 1934; *Poetry,* October, 1934, June, 1938; Frank Swinnerton, *The Georgian Scene,* Farrar & Rhinehart, 1934; *Spectator,* March 19, 1937, April 30, 1954; *South Atlantic Quarterly Review,* April 28, 1934; *Commonweal,* March 7, 1941; Robert Aldington, *Life for Life's Sake,* Viking, 1941; *New York Herald Tribune,* May 21, 1950; *New Republic,* May 21, 1955; *Time and Tide,* December 22, 1956; Douglas Bush, *Mythology and the Romantic Tradition in English Poetry,* Harvard University Press, 1957.*

*   *   *

ALEIXANDRE, Vicente 1898-

PERSONAL: Born April 26, 1898, in Seville, Spain; son of Cirilo (an engineer) and Elvira (Merlo). *Education:* Attended University of Seville; University of Madrid, licence in law and diploma in business, both in 1919. *Home and office:* Velintonia 3, Parque Metropolitano, Madrid 3, Spain.

CAREER: Worked as journalist for *La Semana Financiera* (financial magazine); lectured in commercial law at School of Business Studies in Madrid and worked for railroad company; full-time writer and poet, 1925—. Lecturer. Member of Spanish Academy, 1949—. *Member:* Puerto Rico Academy of Science and Arts, Hispanic Society of America, Professors of Spanish (U.S.; honorary fellow), Malaga Academy, Hispano-American Bogota Academy, Monde Latin Paris Academy. *Awards, honors:* National Prize, Spain, 1933, for *La destruccion o el amore;* Spanish Critics Prize, 1969 and 1970; Nobel Prize for Literature, Swedish Academy, 1977; awarded Grand Cross of the Order of Carlos III, 1977.

WRITINGS—All poetry, except as noted; in English: *Poems* (text in Spanish and English), translation from the Spanish by Ben Belitt, Alan Brilliant, and others, Ohio University Department of English, 1969; *Vicente Aleixandre and Luis Cernuda: Selected Poems* (text in Spanish and English), translation from the Spanish by Linda Lehrer and others,

Copper Beech Press, 1974; *The Cave of Night,* translation by Jeoffrey Bartman, Solo Press, 1976; Lewis Hyde, editor, *Twenty Poems,* translation from the Spanish by Hyde and Robert Bly, Seventies Press, 1977; *Poems-Poemas,* Unicorn Press, 1978.

In Spanish: *Espadas como labios* (title means "Swords Like Lips"; also see below), Espasa-Calpe, 1932; *La destruccion o el amor* (title means "Destruction or Love"), Signo, 1935, 2nd edition, 1967; *Quando comeco a cantar,* Faro, 1943; *Sombra del Paraiso* (title means "Shadow of Paradise"), Adan, 1944, reprinted, Castalia, 1976; *Intencionais,* Faro, 1945; *Pasion de la tierra: poemas 1928-1929* (title means "Passion of the Earth"; also see below), [Madrid], 1946; *Mundo a solas, 1934-36,* illustrations by Gregorio Prieto, Clan, 1950; *Nacimiento ultimo* (title means "Final Birth"), Insula, 1953; *Historia del corazon* (title means "Story of the Heart"), Espasa-Calpe, 1954; *Ochos poemas: seleccionados por su autor* (title means "Eight Poems: Selected by the Author"), Montivideo, 1955; *Mis poemas mejores,* Gredos, 1956; *Espadas como labios, 1930-1931. Pasion de la tierra, 1928-1929,* Losada, 1957; *Ambito, 1924-1927* (title means "Ambit, 1924-1927"), [Madrid], 1959, reprinted, Corazon, 1976.

Poesias completas, introduction by Carlos Bousono, Aguilar, 1960; *Poemas amorosos* (anthology), Losada, 1960; (contributor) Francisco Sabadell Lopez, *Desnudos,* Vallodolid, 1961; *Antiqua casa madrilena,* Hnos. Bedia, 1961; (contributor) Angel Caffarena Such, editor, *Picasso,* El Guadalhorce, 1961; *En un vasto dominio* (title means "In a Vast Dominion"), Revista de Occidente, 1962; *Presencias,* Editorial Seix Barral, 1965; *Retratos con nombres* (title means "Portraits With Names"), El Barda, 1965; *Dos vidas,* Liberia Anticuaria El Guadalhorce, 1967; *Sombra del paraiso,* Losada, 1967; *Poemas de la consumacion* (title means "Poems of Consummation"), Plaza & Janes, 1968; *Obras completas* (title means "Complete Works"), introduction by Carlos Bousono, Aguilar, 1968.

Mundo a solas (1934-1936), Ediciones Javalambre, 1970; *Poesia superrealista* (anthology), Barral Editores, 1971; Javier Lostale, editor, *Antologia del mar y la noche,* Al-Borak, 1971; *Sonido de la guerra,* Fomento de Cultura Ediciones, 1972; *Dialogos conocimiento* (title means "Dialogues of Insight"), Plaza & Janes, 1974; Pere Gimferrer, editor, *Antologia total,* Seix Barral, 1975; *Pasion de la tiera,* notes and commentaries by Luis Antonio de Villena, Narceu, 1976; Leopoldo de Luis, editor, *Antologia poetica,* Castalia, 1976.

Other works: *El nino ciego de Vasquez Diaz,* Ateneo, 1954; *Algunos caracteres de la nueva poesia espanola,* Imprunta Gongora, 1955; *Papeles de son Armadans,* Palma, 1956; *Los encuentros* (title means "The Meetings"), Editorial Guadarrama, 1958; (with others) *Homenaje a Luis Cernuda,* La Cana gris, 1962; (author of epilogue) Federico Garcia Lorca, *Obras completas* (title means "Complete Works"), Aguilar, 1963; *Estudios sobre Antonio Machado,* Ariel, 1977.

Also author of introduction of *Poesia en linea,* by G. Preto, 1950, and of *Antologia,* by J. Maruri Alvarez, 1957. Works represented in other anthologies, including *Contemporary Spanish Poetry,* edited by E. C. Turnbill, 1945, *Penguin Book of Spanish Verse,* 1956, *Modern European Poetry,* edited by W. Barnstone, 1966, and *Cuatro poetas espanoles contemporaneos,* compiled by Pablo Luis Avila, La goliardica, 1968. Contributor of poetry to Spanish journals.

SIDELIGHTS: Surrealist poet Vincente Aleixandre is the first Spaniard not in exile to receive the Nobel Prize for Literature since the 1930's. Aleixandre won the award, a spokesman for the Swedish Academy told the *New York Times,* because his poetry "with roots in the traditions of Spanish lyric verse and in modern currents illuminates man's condition in the cosmos and in present-day society."

When Aleixandre received the award reviewers and poets alike responded with praise for him. In *New Republic,* Allen Josephs hailed Aleixandre as "the mentor and foreground godfather to all post war Spanish poets as well as many outside of Spain." Poet and translator Lewis Hyde described him as follows: "He is a poet of intellectual vigor, spiritual vigor, spiritual depth and tenacity.... He went far down into the soul and brought back pieces of life as a gift for the rest of us."

In his youth, Aleixandre was a member of Spain's "Generation of 1927," an avant garde group that included, among others, Federico Garcia Lorca, Rafael Alberti, Damaso Alonso, and Alberti Jorge Guillen. Suffering from ill health most of his life, Aleixandre remained in Spain during the Franco regime (1939-1975) while most of the poets fled to other countries. Many of his works were banned in Spain, however, for being revolutionary, and are still banned there today.

Although Aleixandre has been involved in writing poetry since the age of eighteen, he did not let it be known until he was twenty-seven, thinking there was nothing remarkable about his work. Whether it was remarkable or not evidently did not matter to him: he merely wanted to write. As Aleixandre told *New York Times* reviewer Eric Pace: "Since my youth, I have had a defined and definite vocation.... I have always wanted to work." This devotion to writing poetry was again illustrated in Aleixandre's response to winning the Nobel Prize for Literature, as quoted in *Time:* "My life won't change with this prize. It was a very pleasant surprise, but I'll go on working with my regular application until the end."

Many of Aleixandre's works have also been translated into French and German.

AVOCATIONAL INTERESTS: Foreign languages.

BIOGRAPHICAL/CRITICAL SOURCES: La poesia de Vicente Aleixandre, [Madrid], 1950, 2nd edition, 1968; *Times Literary Supplement,* May 17, 1957, July 10, 1969, May 23, 1975; Kessel Schwartz, *Vicente Aleixandre,* Twayne, 1970; *Time,* October 17, 1977; *Newsweek,* October 17, 1977; *New York Times Book Review,* October 30, 1977; *New Republic,* December 24, 1977; *World Literature Today,* winter, 1977; *Nation,* March 4, 1978.

*   *   *

ALEXANDER, Martha 1920-

PERSONAL: Born May 25, 1920, in Augusta, Georgia; divorced; children: a son and a daughter. *Education:* Graduate of Cincinnati Academy of Fine Arts. *Residence:* Sag Harbor, N.Y.

CAREER: Writer; illustrator. *Awards, honors: Nobody Asked Me if I Wanted a Baby Sister* was chosen as Children's Book Showcase title, 1972; Christopher Award, 1973, for *I'll Protect You From the Jungle Beasts.*

WRITINGS—All self-illustrated; published by Dial: *Maybe a Monster,* 1968; *Out! Out! Out!,* 1968; *Blackboard Bear,* 1969; *The Story Grandmother Told,* 1969; *We Never Get to do Anything,* 1970; *Bobo's Dream,* 1970; *Sabrina,* 1971; *Nobody Asked Me if I Wanted a Baby Sister,* 1971; *And My Mean Old Mother Will Be Sorry, Blackboard Bear,* 1972; *No*

Ducks in Our Bathtub, 1973; *I'll Protect You From the Jungle Beasts,* 1973; *I'll Be the Horse if You'll Play With Me,* 1975; *I Sure Am Glad to See You, Blackboard Bear,* 1976.

Illustrator only: Charlotte Zolotow, *Big Sister and Little Sister,* Harper, 1966; Janice Udry, *Mary Ann's Mud Day,* Harper, 1967; Lois Wyse, *Grandmothers Are to Love,* Parents' Magazine Press, 1967; Wyse, *Grandfathers Are to Love,* Parents' Magazine Press, 1967; La Verne Johnson, *Night Noises,* Parents' Magazine Press, 1968; Lois Hobart, *What Is a Whispery Secret?,* Parents' Magazine Press, 1968; Doris Orgel, *Whose Turtle?,* World Publishing, 1968; Lillie D. Chaffin, *I Have a Tree,* David White, 1969; Liesel Moak Skorpen, *Charles,* Harper, 1971; Corothea Frances Fisher, *Understood Betsy,* Holt, 1972; Joan M. Lexau, *Emily and the Klunky Baby and the Next-Door Dog,* Dial, 1972; Carol K. Scism, *The Wizard of Walnut Street,* Dial, 1973; *Poems and Prayers for the Very Young,* Random House, 1973; Jean Van Leeuwen, *Too Hot for Ice Cream,* Dial, 1974; Liesel M. Skorpen, *Mandy's Grandmother,* Dial, 1975. Also illustrator of *You,* by Louis Untermeyer, 1970.

BIOGRAPHICAL/CRITICAL SOURCES: Washington Post Book World, July 28, 1968, June 21, 1978; *Top of the News,* April, 1973.*

*   *   *

ALEXANDER, (Eben) Roy 1899(?)-1978

PERSONAL: Born c.1899, in Omaha, Neb.; died October 30, 1978, in Roslyn, N.Y.; married Mary Louise Webb; children: Patricia Alexander LaMothe, Rosemary, Harriet Alexander Garzero, Hollis Alexander Nichols, Roy, Charles C., Stephen W. *Education:* Received degree from St. Louis University. Attended Massachusetts Institute of Technology, c.1920.

CAREER/WRITINGS: St. Louis Star, 1921-25; *St. Louis Post-Dispatch,* 1925-39, became assistant city editor; *Time* magazine, New York, N.Y., writer, 1939-46, assistant managing editor, 1946-49, managing editor, 1949-60, executive assistant, 1960-66. Part-time test pilot at Grumman aircraft plant, Long Island, N.Y., during World War II. *Military service:* U.S. Marine Corps, c.1918-19; Missouri Air National Guard, 1920-39.

SIDELIGHTS: During his career at *Time* magazine, Roy Alexander attained the publication's highest editorial position, that of managing editor. He held the post for eleven years, longer than anyone has since 1923, when the magazine was founded by Henry R. Luce. Alexander also worked as executive assistant to Luce from 1960 until his retirement in 1966. He was described in *Time* as "equally at home in subjects as diverse as politics, religion, music, foreign affairs and the classics."

Alexander was also a pilot, having learned to fly at Massachusetts Institute of Technology following his service in the Marine Corps.

OBITUARIES: Washington Post, November 1, 1978; *Chicago Tribune,* November 2, 1978; *Time,* November 13, 1978.*

*   *   *

ALLEN, John Logan 1941-

PERSONAL: Born December 27, 1941, in Laramie, Wyo.; son of John Milton (in business) and Nancy (Logan) Allen; married Anne Gilroy (an elementary school teacher), August 9, 1964; children: Traci Kathleen, Jennifer Lynne. *Education:* University of Wyoming, B.A. (honors), 1963, M.A.

(distinction), 1964; Clark University, Worcester, Mass., Ph.D., 1969. *Politics:* Democrat. *Religion:* Congregationalist. *Home:* 21 Thomas Dr., Storrs, Conn. 06268. *Office:* Department of Geography, University of Connecticut, Storrs, Conn. 06268.

CAREER: University of Connecticut, Storrs, instructor, 1967-69, assistant professor, 1969-73, associate professor of geography, 1973—, head of department, 1976—. Member of Lewis and Clark Trail Heritage Foundation. Environmental sciences consultant. *Member:* Association of American Geographers, American Geographical Society, Society for Historians of the Early American Republic, Western History Association, Royal Geographical Society (fellow), Eastern Historical Geographers Association. *Awards, honors:* Meritorious achievement award from Lewis and Clark Trail Heritage Foundation, 1976, for *Passage through the Garden.*

WRITINGS: Passage Through the Garden, (nonfiction), University of Illinois Press, 1975.

Contributor: D. Lowenthal and M. Bowden, editors, *Geographies of the Mind,* Oxford University Press, 1975; R. E. Ehrenberg, editor, *Pattern and Process: Research in Historical Geography,* Howard University Press, 1975; B. Blouet and M. Lawson, editors, *Images of the Plains,* University of Nebraska Press, 1975; D. Ward, editor, *Geographic Perspectives on America's Past,* Oxford University Press, 1978.

Contributor of articles and reviews to geography and history journals.

WORK IN PROGRESS: The Eagle Screams: John Charles Fremont and the Image of the American West (tentative title), publication expected in 1981.

SIDELIGHTS: Allen wrote: "Born and raised a Westerner, I have always had a deep interest in the idea of (and ideas about) the American West, particularly in the initial evaluations of land quality and in myths of a geographical nature. These interests developed early and were encouraged by an amateur historian father and a librarian mother. I have traveled extensively throughout the American West, including wilderness travel."

Allen continued: "My first book, *Passage Through the Garden,* is an outgrowth of my interests and deals with the Lewis and Clark expedition and its role as a shaper of American images of the West. My current work deals with the same area and ideas in the 1840's and basically is a study of the impact of Fremont's expeditions on American attitudes at midcentury. A projected third volume on the impact of the great surveys of the 1870's will complete a trilogy of works dealing with nineteenth-century attitudes toward the West."

*   *   *

ALLEN, Ruth Finney   1898(?)-1979

OBITUARY NOTICE: Born c. 1898 in Chicago, Ill.; died March 20, 1979, in Washington, D.C. Journalist. Described in the 1930's as "the only woman to write lead political stories for a national string of newspapers," Allen covered President Harding's death, the Teapot Dome oil scandals, and Sacco and Vanzetti's executions, as well as national conventions for forty years or more. She earned the name "Poison Ivy Finney" for her coverage of a government investigation of utility holding company procedures. Allen was one of the first women to become a city editor, a position she reached at the *Sacramento Star.* Obituaries and other sources: *New York Times,* March 21, 1979; *Washington Post,* March 21, 1979.

ALLINSMITH, Wesley   1923-

PERSONAL: Born May 21, 1923; U.S. citizen born abroad; son of Harry Bryan (a business executive) and Corinne (Allin) Allinsmith; married Beverly Balch, June 30, 1947 (divorced, 1975); married Anne Gallitte, June 13, 1975; children: Bryan Balch, Wendy, Craig Lewis. *Education:* Princeton University, A.B., 1947, graduate study, 1947-48; University of Michigan, M.A., 1949, Ph.D., 1954. *Home:* 8995 Cherryblossom Lane, Cincinnati, Ohio 45231. *Office:* Department of Psychology, University of Cincinnati, Ohio 45221.

CAREER: University of Michigan, Ann Arbor, staff psychologist, 1952-53, instructor and research associate in psychology, 1953-55; Harvard University, Cambridge, Mass., assistant professor, 1955-57, lecturer in human development, 1957-60, assistant professor of psychology, 1960-61, research associate of Laboratory of Human Development, 1955-56, assistant director, 1956-57, associate director, 1957-60; University of Cincinnati, Cincinnati, Ohio, professor of psychology, 1961—, head of department, 1961-68, fellow of Graduate School, 1966—. *Military service:* U.S. Army Air Forces, 1943-46.

MEMBER: American Association for the Advancement of Science (fellow), American Psychological Association (fellow), American Sociological Association, American Association of Sex Educators, Counselors, and Therapists, Society for the Psychological Study of Social Issues (fellow), National Council on Family Relations, American Association of University Professors, Sigma Xi.

WRITINGS: (With D. R. Miller, G. E. Swanson, and others) *Inner Conflict and Defense,* Holt, 1960; (contributor) P. H. Odegard, editor, *Religion and Politics,* Oceana, 1960; (with G. W. Goethals) *The Role of Schools in Mental Health,* Basic Books, 1962; (editor with Judy F. Rosenblith, and contributor) *The Causes of Behavior: Readings in Child Development and Educational Psychology,* Allyn & Bacon, 1962, 3rd edition (with Rosenblith and Joanna P. Williams), 1972; (contributor) R. G. Kuhlen, editor, *Studies in Educational Psychology,* Blaisdell, 1968; (editor with Rosenblith and Williams, and contributor) *Readings in Educational Psychology,* Allyn & Bacon, 1973; (editor with Rosenblith and Williams) *Readings in Child Development,* Allyn & Bacon, 1973. Contributor to psychology and education journals. Consulting editor of *Merrill-Palmer Quarterly of Behavior and Development,* 1960-79.

WORK IN PROGRESS: Research for a book based on four thousand anonymous university students' sex lives and sexual value systems.

SIDELIGHTS: Allinsmith writes: "Looking back over my thirty-five years of adulthood, I see my energies as having focused on a few topics. The preoccupations of my personal life have been mirrored in my research, writing, and teaching—a parallelism between inner struggles and career that authors, preachers, shrinks, and behavioral scientists get to indulge in. In my case, the themes have been superego, sexuality, childrearing practices, and the effects of devoutness and fundamentalism.

"Concretely, I have been interested in prohibitions and ideals; resistance to temptation and yielding; remorse and restitution; types of self-deception (in defense against guilt feelings, shame, or anxiety); belief and blasphemy; compulsive over-compliance and conscientiousness coupled with rebellions—covert and overt; and the determinants of all these in childhood experiences (those of self, parents, grandparents) having to do with social class; social mobility, upward and downward; the influences of denomination crossed with irreligion; school teachings and identifications with school teachers; self-teachings; home teachings intended and unintended, especially moral exhortations leading to emotional survival by subterfuge.

"Having for many years taught personality development in childhood and adolescence, I now conduct a course in human sexuality that enrolls eleven hundred students annually. For recreation, I climb low mountains in Maine, ride a trail motorcycle, and sail, while pondering the irrational in behavior."

Allinsmith gave some examples of the irrational behavior with which he is most concerned: "The sharing of guilt and the insufficient or unilateral communication in organizational groups, which allow individuals to participate actively or passively in unethical decisions such as one that permitted the continuing production of an auto gas tank too capable of exploding, and others that have stifled warnings of dams in peril of collapse; the slowness of women and men, collectively through their leaders and representatives, to act decisively to forestall foreseen disasters whether they consist of an excess of births over deaths, the accumulation of radioactive wastes and other pollutants, or the disappearance of public transportation which could alleviate a looming shortfall in available fuels; and the fettering of some human beings by moral inhibitions, self-reproaches, and inner conflicts acquired from partly-troubled forebears (who also had strengths), together with the liberation of the same beings by similarly-acquired perspectives, aspirations, and long-range goals that have kept them from entirely frittering life away in mundane absorptions and neurotic symptomatology."

Allinsmith continued: "I have taught that adults are children with a veneer. In fact, I have usually felt that I am a child, a grey-haired bearded boy venturing daily into a fearsome world. (Why then do I court danger by mounting motorcycle or helming sloop far from shore? I take pride in surmounting risks by knowing every safety measure and employing it.) It's apt to label me as truly a 'child psychologist.'"

*   *   *

ALLMAN, John 1935-

PERSONAL: Born July 27, 1935, in New York, N.Y.; son of John King (a truck driver) and Helen (in sales; maiden name, Burghard) Allman; married Eileen Jorge (a professor), August 18, 1962; children: Jennifer. Education: Hunter College of the City University of New York, B.A., 1963; Syracuse University, M.A., 1967. Politics: "I am too cynical to have any 'politics.'" Religion: None. Home address: R.D. 4, Frances Dr., Katonah, N.Y. 10536. Office: Department of English, Rockland Community College, 145 College Rd., Suffern, N.Y. 10901.

CAREER: Greystone Press, New York, N.Y., editorial coordinator, 1963; Syracuse University, Syracuse, N.Y., part-time instructor in English, 1964-67; Cazenovia College, Cazenovia, N.Y., assistant professor of English, 1967-71; Rockland Community College, Suffern, N.Y., associate professor of English, 1971—. Awards, honors: State University of New York faculty fellowship in fine arts, 1973, 1979; Bullis Prize from Poetry Northwest, 1976, for "The Weeper," "The Soul Grown Lazy," and "The Knuckler".

WRITINGS: Walking Four Ways in the Wind (poems), Princeton University Press, 1979. Contributor to literary journals, including Paris Review, Poetry Now, and American Poetry Review.

WORK IN PROGRESS: Dostoevsky at Semyonov Square, a book of poems on historical subjects, 1849-1948.

SIDELIGHTS: Allman writes: "I am moving away from the lyric poem toward longer, more narrative forms. My previous work with and in fiction is now serving me well in the long poems. I live for my family and my work."

*   *   *

ALMY, Millie 1915-

PERSONAL: Born June 19, 1915, in Clymer, N.Y.; daughter of Joseph Egbert (a farmer) and Edna (Wood) Almy. Education: Vassar College, A.B., 1936; Columbia University, A.M., 1945, Ph.D., 1948. Office: School of Education, University of California, Berkeley, Calif. 94720.

CAREER: Columbia University, Teachers College, New York, N.Y., instructor in curriculum and teaching, 1944-48; University of Cincinnati, Cincinnati, Ohio, associate professor of child development and director of nursery school, 1948-52; Columbia University, Teachers College, began as associate professor, professor of psychology and education, 1952-71; University of California, Berkeley, professor of education, 1971—, coordinator of interdisciplinary program for the preparation of personnel for key positions in day care and related child development services, 1974-78. Member: Association for Childhood Education International, American Educational Research Association, American Association for the Advancement of Science (fellow), American Psychological Association (fellow), National Association for the Education of Young Children, Society for Research in Child Development.

WRITINGS: Children's Experiences Prior to First Grade and Success in Beginning Reading, Bureau of Publications, Teachers College, Columbia University, 1949; (with R. Gans and C. Stendler) Teaching Young Children in Nursery School, Kindergarten, and the Primary Grades, World Book Co., 1952; Ways of Studying Children, Bureau of Publications, Teachers College, Columbia University, 1959; Young Children's Thinking About Natural Phenomena: A Follow-Up Study, Horace Mann-Lincoln Institute for School Experimentation, Teachers College, Columbia University, 1961; (with Edward Chittenden and P. Miller) Young Children's Thinking: Studies of Some Aspects of Piaget's Theory, foreword by Jean Piaget, Teachers College Press, 1966; (with Joel Davitz and Mary Alice White) Ugandan Children in School, Teachers College Press, 1970; (with Chittenden, Lilly Dimitrovsky, and others) Logical Thinking in Second Grade, Teachers College Press, 1970; The Early Childhood Educator at Work, McGraw, 1975; (with Celia Genishi) Ways of Studying Children: An Observation Manual for Early Childhood Teachers, Teachers College Press, 1978. Also author of Psychological Foundations of the Science Curriculum Improvement Study, 1967.

Contributor: Integration of Mental Health Concepts With the Human Relations Professions, Bank Street College of Education, 1962; A. H. Passow and R. R. Leeper, editors, Intellectual Development: Another Look, Association for Supervision and Curriculum Development, 1964; D. E. Huebner, editor, A Re-Assessment of the Curriculum, Bureau of Publications, Teachers College, Columbia University, 1964; Joe L. Frost, editor, Issues and Innovations in the Teaching of Reading, Scott, Foresman, 1967; (author of introduction) Susan Isaacs, The Nursery Years: The Mind of the Child From Birth to Six Years, Schocken, 1968; Frost, editor, Early Childhood Education Rediscovered, Holt, 1968; W. Jacobson and A. Kondo, editors, SCIC Elementary

Science Sourcebook, University of California Press, 1968; H. F. Clarizio, editor, *Mental Health and the Educative Process*, Rand McNally, 1969; C. P. Torrance and W. F. White, editors, *Issues and Advances in Educational Psychology: A Book of Readings*, University of Georgia Press, 1969.

A. R. Binter, editor, *The Psychology of the Elementary School Child*, Rand McNally, 1970; J. M. Hall and other editors, *Readings in Social Science Education: A Geographic Perspective*, Wiley, 1971; Myron F. Rosskopf, Leslie P. Steffe, and Stanley Taback, editors, *Piagetian Cognitive-Development Research and Mathematical Education*, National Council of Teachers of Mathematics, 1971; Robert H. Andersen, editor, *Education in Anticipation of Tomorrow*, Charles A. Jones Publishing, 1973. Contributor of about thirty-five articles and reviews to academic journals and popular magazines, including *Saturday Review* and *Woman's Home Companion*.

* * *

ALPERS, Paul (Joel) 1932-

PERSONAL: Born October 16, 1932, in Philadelphia, Pa.; son of Bernard J. (a physician) and Lillian (Sher) Alpers; married Svetlana Leontief (a professor of art history), January 31, 1958; children: Benjamin, Nicholas. *Education:* Harvard University, A.B., 1953, A.M., 1955, Ph.D., 1959. *Home:* 1411 Hawthorne Ter., Berkeley, Calif. 94708. *Office:* Department of English, University of California, Berkeley, Calif. 94720.

CAREER: Harvard University, Cambridge, Mass., instructor in English, 1959-61; University of California, Berkeley, began as assistant professor, professor of English, 1962—. Fellow of Center for Advanced Study in the Behavioral Sciences (Stanford, Calif.), 1976. *Member:* Modern Language Association of America, Renaissance Society of America, English Institute (head of supervising committee, 1977-78). *Awards, honors:* American Council of Learned Societies fellowships, 1966-67, 1972-73; award from *Explicator*, 1968, for *The Poetry of "The Faerie Queene"*.

WRITINGS: *The Poetry of "The Faerie Queene"*, Princeton University Press, 1967; (editor) *Elizabethan Poetry: Modern Essays in Criticism*, Oxford University Press, 1967; (editor) *Edmund Spenser* (critical anthology), Penguin, 1969; *The Singer of the "Eclogues": A Study of Virgilian Pastoral* (includes a new translation of the *Eclogues*), University of California Press, 1979.

WORK IN PROGRESS: Pastoral Poetics.

* * *

AMENT, Pat 1946-

PERSONAL: Born September 3, 1946, in Denver, Colo.; married wife, Paula (a rock climber).

CAREER: Professional rock climber; teacher; writer.

WRITINGS: (With Cleveland McCarty) *High Over Boulder: A Climber's and Hiker's Guide to Boulder*, High Over Publications, 1967, 3rd edition, March Press, 1976; *Master of Rock: The Biography of John Gill*, Westview Press, 1977. Contributor to climbing magazines.

* * *

AMICHAI, Yehuda 1924-

PERSONAL: Born in 1924, in Germany; immigrated to Palestine in 1936; naturalized Israeli citizen.

CAREER: Poet and writer. *Military service:* Served in Israeli Army during 1948 war.

*WRITINGS—*In English: *Lo me-'akhshav, lo mi kan* (novel), [Tel-Aviv], 1963, translation by Shlomo Katz published as *Not of This Time, Not of This Place*, Harper, 1968; *Selected Poems*, translation from the original Hebrew by Assia Gutmann, Cape Goliard Press, 1968, published as *Poems*, introduction by Michael Hamburger, Harper, 1969; *Selected Poems of Yehuda Amichai*, translation from the original Hebrew by Gutmann, Harold Schimmel, and Ted Hughes, Penguin, 1971; *Songs of Jerusalem and Myself* (poetry), translation from the original Hebrew by Schimmel, Harper, 1973; *Amen* (poetry), translation from the original Hebrew by the author and Hughes, Harper, 1977.

In Hebrew: *Akhshav uba-yamim na-aherim* (poetry; title means "Now and in the Other Days"), [Tel-Aviv], 1955; *Ba-ginah ha-tsiburit* (poetry; title means "In the Park"), [Jerusalem], 1958-59; *Be-merhak shete tikrot* (poetry), [Tel-Aviv], 1958; *Be-ruah ha-nora'ah ha-zot* (stories), Merhavya, 1961; *Masa' le-Ninveh* (play), 1962; *Shirim, 1948-1962* (title means "Poetry, 1948-1962"), [Jerusalem], 1962-63. Also author of *'Akshav ba-ra'nsh*, 1968, *Mah she-karah le-Roni bi-Nyu-York*, 1968, *Pa 'amonim ve-rakavot*, 1968, *Mi yitneni malon* (title means "Hotel in the Wilderness"), 1972, *Ve-lo 'al menat lizkor* (poetry), 1971, and *Me-ahore kol zeh mistater osher gadol* (poetry), 1974. Translator of German works into Hebrew.

SIDELIGHTS: According to M. L. Rosenthal, Yehuda Amichai "is Israel's best-known living poet." Born in Germany, Amichai left that country in 1936 with his family and journeyed to Palestine. During the 1948 war, he fought with the Palmach or the Israeli defense forces prior to the creation of the state and the Israeli Army. In his novel, *Not of This Time, Not of This Place*, Amichai struggles with "the torment of being buried alive in the irrelevant past." The novel's hero is torn between returning to the German town where he grew up and staying in Jerusalem and "immersing himself in a love affair with an outsider who has had no part in it." Anthony West in his review of the novel in *New Yorker* explained: "The alternatives are both impossibilities. The past is still going on back in Germany, and it is inescapable in Israel: the knowledge of what men are and what they can do that was acquired in the years of Hitler's "final solution" cannot be discarded or ignored, and it is no easier to live with when one is in the country of the ex-butchers than it is in that of the ex-victims."

In his review, Amos Elon highlighted the theme of struggle for identity in *Not of This Time, Not of This Place:* "Amichai has been brought up in Israel, but the question of his identity sits heavily on his mind as much as with his Jewish-American fellow writers. He attempts a synoptic view of modern Jewish existence; its keys are ambivalence and disintegration, rather than clarity, unity or nationalistic simplicities." The treatment of this identity struggle is different, however, from other novels dealing with Holocaust themes. Robert Alter observed: "The fact of his German childhood, his awareness of kin and earliest friends murdered by the Nazis, clearly determines the broad direction of the sections of his novel set in Germany, and yet the general attempt of the book to make moral contact with the destruction and its perpetrators is eminently that of an Israeli beyond the experience, not of a European Jew actually torn by it. Indeed, the peculiar structure of the novel—a brilliant but not fully worked out invention of Amichai's—provides a kind of diagrammatic illustration of the difficulties Israeli writers have in trying to imagine this ultimate catastrophe and how one can live with the knowledge of it.''

Leon Wieseltier commented that "Amichai's poems must compel the attention not only of devotees of modern Hebrew literature, but of anyone concerned with the state of contemporary poetry in general.'' In a review of *Poems,* Aaron Kramer wrote: ''[Amichai] makes us leap from association to association, metaphor to metaphor—arriving finally at the hush of understanding. His sense of disorientation, noncommunication, and despair at times seems too pervasive—perilously close to self-pity. But the volcanic lyricism of this German-born Israeli poet bursts through again and again.... There are many superlative songs of love, war, and loss.''

Chad Walsh of *Book World* commented: ''A Jewish poet, like a Greek, has the enormous advantage of an immense history and tradition which he can handle with an easy familiarity, and play with as a foil to the homogenized culture that is spreading over the globe like a universal parking lot. This combination of the old and the new speaks very powerfully in Amichai's poetry and makes him, as it were, a contemporary simultaneously of King David the psalmist and Eric Sevareid.''

Amen is Amichai's latest collection of poems in English. ''The most important thing,'' wrote Rochelle Ratner, ''that Amichai teaches us is that the universal can only be approached through one's most personal experience. There is no anger and little guilt in these poems, only a quiet acceptance and a depression which strives to fill itself with love and caring. In many poems, the poet is alone, remembering and regretting, but silence doesn't have to be empty—Amichai knows that.''

BIOGRAPHICAL/CRITICAL SOURCES: New York Times Book Review, August 4, 1965, July 3, 1977; Robert Alter, *After the Tradition: Essays on Modern Jewish Writing,* Dutton, 1969; *New Yorker,* May 3, 1969; *Library Journal,* July, 1969, July, 1977; *Book World,* February 15, 1970; *Commentary,* May, 1974; *Contemporary Literary Criticism,* Volume 9, Gale, 1978.*

*   *   *

ANDERSEN, Jefferson 1955(?)-1979

OBITUARY NOTICE: Born c. 1955; died February 19, 1979, in San Francisco, Calif. Author of *Sun Signs: Moon Signs.* At the time of his death, Andersen was writing a novel, *On the Edge.* Obituaries and other sources: *Publishers Weekly,* March 26, 1979.

*   *   *

ANDERSON, Arthur J(ames) O(utram) 1907-

PERSONAL: Born November 26, 1907, in Phoenix, Ariz.; son of Arthur Cyril Edwin James (in business) and Grace Elizabeth (an educator; maiden name, Greaves) Anderson; married Christine Vivian Hayler (a musician), March 30, 1937. *Education:* San Diego State College (now University), B.A., 1930; Claremont Colleges, M.A., 1931; University of Southern California, Ph.D., 1940. *Residence:* San Diego, Calif.

CAREER: San Diego State College (now University), San Diego, Calif., assistant instructor in English, 1933-37; Riverside Junior College, Riverside, Calif., instructor in English, 1938; Eastern New Mexico College (now University), Portales, associate professor, 1939-40, professor of anthropology and geography, 1940-45, head of Social Science Division, 1942-45; Museum of New Mexico, Santa Fe, curator of history and editor of publications, 1945-57; El Camino College, Torrance, Calif., instructor in anthropology and sociology, 1957-61; San Diego State University, assistant professor, 1961-63, associate professor, 1963-67, professor of anthropology, 1967-75; writer and researcher, 1975—. Visiting professor at San Diego State College, summer, 1950, visiting lecturer, 1953-54; visiting professor at Occidental College, summer, 1952, special lecturer, 1957-58; visiting professor at Universidad de Madrid, 1968-69. Director of Roosevelt County Museum of Art, History, and Archaeology, 1939-45; associate in charge of departments of history and publications at School of American Research, Santa Fe, N.M., 1945-57. *Awards, honors:* Guggenheim fellow in Europe, 1955, 1957; honorary fellow of School of American Research; honorary curator of Latin American ethnography at San Diego Museum of Man; grant from Del Amo Foundation, summer, 1964.

WRITINGS: (Translator from Nahuatl, editor, and annotater, with Charles E. Dibble) Fray Bernardino de Sahagun, *Florentine Codex: Historia general de las cosas de Nueva Espana* (title means ''General History of the Things of New Spain''), University of Utah Press, Part 2, Book I: *The Gods,* 1950, revised edition, 1970, Part 3, Book II: *The Ceremonies,* 1951, revised edition, 1979, Part 4, Book III: *The Origin of the Gods,* 1952, 2nd edition, 1978, Part 8, Book VII: *The Sun, Moon, and Stars, and the Binding of the Years,* 1953, Part 9, Book VIII: *Kings and Lords,* 1954, Part 13, Book XII: *The Conquest of Mexico,* 1955, revised edition, 1975, Part 5, Book IV: *The Soothsayers,* 1957, Part 6, Book V: *The Omens,* 1957, Part 10, Book IX: *The Merchants,* 1959, Part 11, Book X: *The People,* 1961, Part 12, Book XI: *Earthly Things,* 1965, Part 7, Book VI: *Rhetoric and Philosophy,* 1969, Part 1 (including introduction and indices), 1979.

Rules of the Aztec Language: Classical Nahuatl Grammar–A Translation With Modifications of Francisco Xavier Clavijero's ''Reglas de la lengua mexicana,'' with exercise book, University of Utah Press, 1973; (editor, annotator, and author of introduction) Francisco Xavier Clavijero, *Reglas de la lengua mexicana, con un vocabulario* (monograph; title means ''Rules of the Mexican Language, With a Vocabulary''), Instituto de Investigaciones Historicas, Universidad Nacional Autonoma de Mexico, 1974; (contributor) Munro S. Edmonson, editor, *Sixteenth-Century Mexico: The Work of Sahagun,* University of New Mexico Press, 1974; (translator and editor, with Frances Berdan and James Lockhart), *Beyond the Codices: The Nahua View of Colonial Mexico,* University of California Press, 1976; (with Dibble) *War of Conquest: How It Was Waged Here in Mexico–The Aztecs' Own Story as Given to Fray Bernardino de Sahagun, Rendered Into Modern English,* University of Utah Press, 1978.

Contributor of more than twenty-five articles and reviews to scholarly journals. Editor of *El Palacio,* 1947-57; associate editor of *New Mexico Historical Review,* 1946-57; member of editorial advisory board of *New Scholar.*

WORK IN PROGRESS: Translating from Nahuatl, editing, and annotating proceedings of the city council of Tlaxcala, New Spain, with James Lockhart and Frances Berdan.

SIDELIGHTS: Anderson's research has taken him to Mexico, Spain, England, France, Italy, Greece, and Peru. He feels his translations in progress are important, not only for their wealth of historical information, but for their contributions to philosophy and linguistics. Other current work includes popularizing more of the *Florentine Codex.*

BIOGRAPHICAL/CRITICAL SOURCES: Natural History, December, 1970.

*   *   *

ANDERSON, Ian Gibson 1933-

PERSONAL: Born June 7, 1933, in Dumfries, Scotland; son of Daniel Gibson (a lawyer) and Margaret (a teacher; maiden name, Stothart) Anderson. *Education:* University of Edinburgh, M.A., 1953. *Home:* 10 Gaynesford Rd., London SE23 2UQ, England.

CAREER: Associated with Dumfriesshire Libraries, Dumfries, Scotland, 1956-57, Signet Library, Edinburgh, Scotland, 1957-58, and Guildhall Library, London, England, 1958-68; CBD Research Ltd., Beckenham, Kent, England, editor, 1968—. *Military service:* British Army, 1953-55. *Awards, honors:* McColvin Medal from Library Association, 1970, for *Councils, Committees, and Boards.*

WRITINGS: (Editor) *Current British Directories,* CBD Research, 5th edition (Anderson was not associated with earlier editions), 1966, 9th edition, 1979; (editor) *Marketing and Management: A World Register of Organisations,* CBD Research, 1969; (editor) *Councils, Committees, and Boards: A Handbook of Advisory, Consultative, Executive, and Similar Bodies in British Public Life,* CBD Research, 1970, 3rd edition, 1977; (editor) *Directory of European Associations,* CBD Research, Part I, 1971, 2nd edition, 1976, Part II, 1975, 2nd edition, 1979; (editor) *Current African Directories, Incorporating "African Companies: A Guide to Sources of Information": A Guide to Directories Published in or Relating to Africa,* and to *Sources of Information on Business Enterprises in Africa,* CBD Research, 1972. Also editor of *Current Asian and Australasian Directories,* 1978.

*   *   *

ANDERSON, Jeanne 1934(?)-1979

OBITUARY NOTICE: Born c. 1934 in Little Falls, Minn.; died May 5, 1979, in Washington, D.C. Editor and author. Anderson was a senior analyst with the Government Research Corp. She edited the *Washington Drug and Device Letter* and *Textile Week,* and was Washington correspondent for *Medical World News.* Earlier, Anderson had been Minnesota Governor Orville L. Freeman's press aide and speech writer. She also wrote food articles for the *Washington Post* and co-authored *Two in the Kitchen.* Obituaries and other sources: *Washington Post,* May 6, 1979.

*   *   *

ANDERSON, Patrick (John MacAllister) 1915-1979

OBITUARY NOTICE: Born August 4, 1915, in Ashtead, Surrey, England; died in 1979. Educator, poet, and travel writer. In 1946 Anderson was awarded the Harriet Monroe Memorial Prize. His collections of poetry include *A Tent for April, The White Centre,* and *The Colour is Naked.* In addition, he wrote *Snake Wine, Dolphin Days, The Smile of Apollo, A Visiting Distance,* and other travel books. Anderson also co-founded the magazine *Preview.* Obituaries and other sources: *Contemporary Poets,* 2nd edition, St. Martin's, 1975; *AB Bookman's Weekly,* April 16, 1979.

*   *   *

ANDERSON, Robert C(harles) 1930-
(Charles Cottle)

PERSONAL: Born May 22, 1930, in Sault Ste. Marie, Mich.; son of James O. (a lockmaster) and Nesta Grace (Cottle) Anderson; married Frances Theresa Merimee, July 25, 1952; children: James R., Helen C. Anderson Doepel. *Education:* University of Michigan, B.A., 1957. *Home:* 904 Elm, Winnetka, Ill. 60093. *Office: Success Unlimited,* 401 North Wabash Ave., Suite 530, Chicago, Ill. 60611.

CAREER: Chicago Tribune, Chicago, Ill., reporter, 1957-64, assistant magazine editor, 1964-69, feature editor, 1969-72; *Oui,* Chicago, managing editor, 1972-75; *Professional Photographer,* Des Plaines, Ill., editor, 1975-78; *Success Unlimited,* Chicago, editor, 1978—. *Military service:* U.S. Army, Infantry, 1948-52; served in Korea; became first sergeant. *Member:* American Society of Journalists and Authors, Midwest Writers, Chicago Press Club.

WRITINGS: (With Ray Kroc) *Grinding It Out: The Making of McDonald's,* Contemporary Books, 1977. Contributor to magazines and newspapers, including *Discovery, Woman, Saturday Evening Post, Chicago Tribune Magazine,* and BBC's *Radio Times.* Also contributor of articles to magazines under pseudonym Charles Cottle.

WORK IN PROGRESS: Little Giant, a biography of W. Clement Stone.

SIDELIGHTS: Anderson told *CA:* "My interest in writing personality profiles brought me into contact with Ray Kroc, who wanted to write his autobiography and asked me to help him after interviewing several writers. My aim in writing the book was to capture the ideas, life, and times of this colorful entrepreneur so future generations would have a perspective on his contribution to business."

About the story of Kroc's life, Michael Gartner wrote: "It took hard work, vision and guts, and [Kroc] demonstrates that he has all three plus a certain amount of ruthlessness. Although his book is filled with Kroc homilies ('if you think small, you'll stay small') and an occasional 'cripes almighty!,' it tells a fascinating story that would make Horatio Alger jealous."

BIOGRAPHICAL/CRITICAL SOURCES: Wall Street Journal, July 7, 1977; *St. Louis Post Dispatch,* August 16, 1977.

*   *   *

ANDERSON, Teresa 1944-
(Teresa McCarthy)

PERSONAL: Born April 14, 1944, in Hays, Kan.; daughter of Clair Morton (a pilot) and Marguerite (a teacher and secretary; maiden name, Fesler) Anderson; married John McCarthy, September 3, 1966 (divorced August, 1976); children: Denis B. *Education:* Attended University of Grenoble, 1965; University of Oklahoma, B.A., 1966, M.A., 1976. *Politics:* "Radical Feminist-Socialist." *Home:* 2144 Mason, Houston, Tex. 77006. *Agent:* Tom James, 1145 Jackson, Wichita, Kan. 67502. *Office:* Texas Commission on the Arts and Humanities, Austin, Tex. 78711.

CAREER: University of Chicago, Chicago, Ill., instructor at laboratory school, 1967-69; teacher at private school in Chicago, 1972-73; Texas Commission on the Arts and Humanities, Austin, poet-in-residence, 1978—. Director of writing workshop. *Member:* Phi Beta Kappa.

WRITINGS: (Contributor, under name Teresa McCarthy) *New Poets: Women,* Les Femmes, 1976; *Speaking in Sign* (poetry), West End, 1979. Also author of "The Way Back," a three-act play.

WORK IN PROGRESS: The Endless Request, love poems; translating *Soleil et Tristesse,* by Philippe Canaletti, from the French; with Fred Whitehead, translating *Incitacion al Nixoncidio,* by Pablo Neruda, for West End Press.

SIDELIGHTS: Anderson comments: "My first and last mother is the Midwest, with her endless dry seas and harsh winds and her small fragile towns that somehow manage to cling to life after every emergence from her howling winters. I have been saved from the narrow smothering confinement of these places by the rising of women all over the land. Our growing strength and collective voice have been my refuge and my reason to continue fighting for an end to the oppression of all people everywhere."

*　　*　　*

ANGOFF, Charles 1902-1979
(Richard W. Hinton)

OBITUARY NOTICE—See index for *CA* sketch: Born April 22, 1902, in Minsk, Russia (now U.S.S.R.); died May 3, 1979, in New York, N.Y. Editor, educator, and author of some thirty books, including *H. L. Mencken: A Portrait From Memory.* Angoff was associated with H. L. Mencken's literary review, *American Mercury,* for twenty-five years, first as a member of the editorial staff and later as managing editor. Although he and Mencken had their differences and often disagreed about whose work to include in the publication, Mencken once called Angoff "the best managing editor in America." Angoff also did editorial work for both *American Spectator* and *North American Review* and was co-editor of *Literary Review.* He was a professor of English at Fairleigh Dickinson University from 1954 until his retirement in 1976. Best known for his series of eleven autobiographical novels on Jewish-American life, Angoff was also a poet and served two terms as president of the Poetry Society of America. Obituaries and other sources: *Current Biography,* Wilson, 1955; *Who's Who in World Jewry,* Pitman, 1972; *Who's Who in America,* 40th edition, Marquis, 1978; *New York Times,* May 4, 1979; *Time,* May 14, 1979; *AB Bookman's Weekly,* May 21, 1979.

*　　*　　*

ANHALT, Edward
(Andrew Holt)

PERSONAL: Born in New York, N.Y.; married wife, Edna (a writer).

CAREER: Writer. Member of faculty of Loyola University. *Awards, honors:* Co-winner of Academy Award for best original story from Academy of Motion Picture Arts and Sciences, nomination from Writer's Guild, both 1950, both for "Panic in the Streets"; co-nominee for Academy Award for best screen story, 1952, for "The Sniper"; Academy Award for best screenplay and award from Writer's Guild, both 1964, both for "Becket"; Edgar Allen Poe award from Mystery Writers of America, 1968, for "The Boston Strangler."

WRITINGS—Screenplays: (Under pseudonym Andrew Holt) "Avalanche," Producers Releasing Corp., 1946; (under Holt pseudonym) "Strange Voyage," Monogram, 1946; (with wife, Edna Anhalt) "Bulldog Drummond Strikes Back" (adapted from the novel by H. C. McNeile), Columbia, 1947; "The Gentleman From Nowhere," Columbia, 1948; "The Crime Doctor's Diary," Columbia, 1949.

(Screen story; with Edna Anhalt) "Panic in the Streets," Twentieth Century-Fox, 1950; (contributor with Edna Anhalt) John Lucas Meredyth, George F. Slavin, and George W. George, "Red Mountain," Paramount, 1952; (screen story; with Edna Anhalt) "The Sniper," Columbia, 1952; (with Edna Anhalt) "The Member of the Wedding" (a-dapted from the play by Carson McCullers), Columbia, 1952; (with Edna Anhalt) "Not as a Stranger" (adapted from the novel by Morton Thompson), United Artists, 1955; (with Edna Anhalt) "The Pride and the Passion" (adapted from the novel by C. S. Forester, *The Gun*), United Artists, 1957; "The Young Lions" (adapted from the novel by Irwin Shaw), Twentieth Century-Fox, 1957; "In Love and War" (adapted from the novel by Anton Myrer), Twentieth Century-Fox, 1958; "The Restless Years" (adapted from the play by Patricia Joudry, "Teach Me How to Cry"), Universal, 1959.

"The Sins of Rachel Cade" (adapted from the novel by Charles Mercer, *Rachel Cade*), Warner Bros., 1961; (with J. P. Miller) "The Young Savages" (adapted from the novel by Evan Hunter, *A Matter of Conviction*), United Artists, 1961; (with Allan Weiss) "Girls! Girls! Girls!," Paramount, 1962; "A Girl Named Tamiko" (adapted from the novel by Ronald Kirkbride), Paramount, 1962; "Wives and Lovers" (adapted from the play by Jay Presson Allen), Paramount, 1963; "Becket" (adapted from the play by Jean Anouilh), Paramount, 1964; (with James Clavell) "The Satan Bug" (adapted from the novel by Ian Stuart), United Artists, 1965; "Boeing, Boeing" (adapted from the play by Marc Camoletti), Paramount, 1965; "Hour of the Gun," United Artists, 1967; "The Boston Strangler" (adapted from the book by Gerold Frank), Twentieth Century-Fox, 1968; (with Alfred Hayes) "In Enemy Country" (adapted from the story by Sy Bartlett), Universal, 1969; "The Madwoman of Chaillot" (adapted from the play by Jean Giraudoux), Warner Bros., 1969.

(With John Milius) "Jeremiah Johnson" (adapted from the novel by Vardis Fisher, *Mountain Man,* and the story by Raymond W. Thorp and Robert Bunker, *Crow Killer*), Warner Bros., 1972; "The Man in the Glass Booth" (adapted from the play by Robert Shaw), American Film Theatre, 1975. Also author of "Luther," 1974.

Also wrote educational screenplays, including "Thunder of the Sea" for World Lutheran Congress, and "Problem Child" for Columbia University. Author of teleplays, including "Three Lives," "A Time for Killing," and "QB VII."

Contributor to magazines with wife, Edna Anhalt, under joint pseudonym Andrew Holt.*

*　　*　　*

ANNIS, Linda Ferrill 1943-

PERSONAL: Born September 10, 1943, in South Bend, Ind.; daughter of Everett William (a professor) and Mary (Chapman) Ferrill; married David Boyden Annis (a professor), August 22, 1964. *Education:* Ball State University, B.S., 1964; University of Illinois, M.Ed., 1967; Purdue University, Ph.D., 1976. *Home:* 39 Bayberry Lane, R.R. 12, Muncie, Ind. 47302. *Office:* Department of Educational Psychology, Ball State University, Muncie, Ind. 47306.

CAREER: Junior high school teacher of English and social studies in Champaign, Ill., 1964-69; Ball State University, Muncie, Ind., assistant professor, 1969-78, associate professor of educational psychology, 1978—. Visiting research psychologist at Educational Testing Service, Princeton, N.J., 1976-77. *Member:* American Psychological Association, American Educational Research Association, American Federation of Teachers, Indiana Psychological Association, Indiana Educational Research Association, Pi Lambda Theta, Alpha Chi Omega (president of alumnae, Muncie, 1971-73). *Awards, honors:* National Science Foundation grant, 1977-78; named Outstanding Young Woman of America, 1978; Lilly Open Faculty fellowship, 1979-80.

WRITINGS: The Child Before Birth (Macmillan Book Club selection), Cornell University Press, 1978. Contributor to education and philosophy journals, including *Journal of Experimental Education* and *Journal of Educational Research,* and to *Expecting.*

WORK IN PROGRESS: Research on study technique effectiveness, cognitive styles, prenatal development, and sex role development.

SIDELIGHTS: Linda Annis writes: ''I think of myself primarily as a teacher. Through my teaching and my daily interactions with students I get many ideas for my research and writing. I teach many courses in human growth and development. My book, *The Child Before Birth,* evolved out of great student interest in prenatal development. In my courses we would spend so much of the term on the topic that I would finally say we had to continue and at least get the child born. Then my students would ask what they could read for more information on prenatal development. When I realized there was no appropriate current book I decided to write one myself and that is how *The Child Before Birth* was born.''

AVOCATIONAL INTERESTS: Reading, travel, long walks.

*   *   *

ANTSCHEL, Paul   1920-1970
(Paul Celan)

PERSONAL: Born November 23, 1920, in Cernowitz, Rumania; died May 1, 1970, in Paris, France; married Gisele Lestrange (an artist), 1950. *Education:* Earned *licence es lettres* in Paris, 1950.

CAREER: Poet and translator. Lecturer at Ecole Superieure of University of Paris during 1950's. *Awards, honors:* Literature Prize of City of Bremen, 1958; Georg Buechner Prize, 1960.

WRITINGS—All under pseudonym Paul Celan; poetry in English: *Speech-Grille and Selected Poems* (contains *Sprachgitter;* also see below), translation from the German by Joachim Neugroschel, Dutton, 1971; *Nineteen Poems,* translation by Michael Hamburger, Carcanet Press, 1972; *Selected Poems,* translation by Hamburger and Christopher Middleton, Penguin, 1972. Also author of *Breath Crystal: Translations of Paul Celan,* translation by Walter Billeter, Ragman Productions (Australia).

Poetry in German: *Der Sand aus den Urnen,* [Germany], 1948; *Mohn und Gedaechtnis* (title means ''Poppy and Memory''), Germany, 1952; *Von Schwelle zu Schwelle* (title means ''From Threshold to Threshold''), Deutsche Verlags-Anstalt, 1955; *Sprachgitter* (title means ''Speech-Grille''; also see above), S. Fischer, 1959; *Der Meridian,* S. Fischer, 1960; *Die Niemandsrose* (title means ''The No Man's Rose''), S. Fischer, 1963; *Atemkristall,* Brunidor, 1965; *Gedichte* (title means ''Poetry''), Moderner Buchclub, 1966; *Atemwende,* Suhrkamp, 1967; *Ausgewaehlte Gedichte,* Suhrkamp, 1968; *Lichtwzang,* Suhrkamp, 1970; *Schneepart,* Suhrkamp, 1971; *Gedichte: In 2 Bd.,* Suhrkamp, 1975; *Zeitgehoeft: Spaete Gedichte aus d. Nachlass,* Suhrkamp, 1976.

Other poetry: *Strette. Suivis du Meridien et d'Entretien dans la montagne,* Mercure de France, 1971; *Poesie/Paul Celan; a cura di Moshe Kahne e Marcella Bagnasco,* A. Mondadori [Italy], 1976.

Also author of *Conversation in the Mountains,* translation by Rosmarie Waldrop. Translator of numerous works into German. Also author of works represented in anthologies, including *Modern German Poetry, 1910-1960,* edited by Hamburger and C. Middleton, 1962, *Twentieth Century German Verse,* edited by P. Bridgewater, 1963, and *Modern European Poetry,* edited by W. Barnstone, 1966.

SIDELIGHTS: Celan is regarded as one of the most important poets to emerge from post-World War II Europe. According to one critic, he ''made a more original and substantial contribution to modern poetry than any other German-language poet of his generation.'' His work bears the influence of both the French surrealists and Rilke in terms of poetic devices and linguistic stylization. His thematic obsession, however, is the extermination of the Jews during World War II. A writer for *Times Literary Supplement* wrote that Celan ''makes us aware of the horror of our age in a way that is the more powerful for being oblique. The humble and familiar images . . . combine with others that suggest blinding, mutilation and empaling, burning, whipping and shooting, hunting down and shutting in with walls and barbed wire—festering memories of Auschwitz which are relevant not only to Germany and not only to an era that ended in 1945.''

Celan began writing poetry shortly after the war. His first book in 1947 caused little stir in the German literary community. His second collection, ''Poppy and Memory,'' received much more critical attention and Celan quickly became a reputable poet. Among his most popular poems is ''Death Fugue,'' a stark recreation of activities at Auschwitz which was featured in both of the early collections. Paul Auster called it ''literally a fugue composed of words, and the incessant, rhythmical repetitions and variations of phrases evoke a nightmare more devastating than any forthright description could.'' This description is exemplified in the stanza which includes the lines ''death is a master from Germany / his eye is blue / he shoots you with bullets of lead / his aim is true / a man lives in the house your / golden hair Margarete / he sets his hounds on us he gives / us a grave in the air / he plays with the serpent and / dreams death is a master from / Germany.'' Despite its high regard, ''Death Fugue'' was later refuted by Celan as, according to Auster, ''too obvious and superficially realistic,'' and he disallowed its inclusion in collections.

As Celan progressed, his poetry became increasingly inaccessible. ''The poems grow shorter,'' observed John Hollander, ''denser and less easily rewarding toward the end of the poet's career, and more starkly impressive.'' His poetry also became less depressing. One critic wrote, ''The worst, we are made to feel, has been faced, and out of despair has come a new beauty which *is* truth. . . .'' The same reviewer added that the collection *Atemwende* ''shows a poet projecting his breath into emptiness and feeling it return . . . charged with a numinous power.'' Aside from its rather positive stance, *Atemwende* was also noted for its attention to the language itself. ''The author of *Atemwende* is obsessed by words and obsessed by forms,'' contended a writer for *Times Literary Supplement.* The critic attributed Celan's brighter outlook to his new interest in words. ''And this new reality has been uniquely embodied in language,'' the critic claimed: ''language, in fact, has helped not just to shape it, but to bring it life.''

Celan pursued his interest in economy of form in *Lichtzwang,* a collection published the same year as his death. A reviewer for *Times Literary Supplement* wrote that ''his poems are very much word-sculptures.'' Jerry Glenn believed that Celan was moving towards a union of his early realist style with his later structure-conscious poems. He also noted in a review of *Lichtzwang*, "There are some fine poems here, poems which will justly become a part of the permanent legacy of Germany literature...."

Celan's drowning suicide in 1970 was lamented by many writers. Auster called him "one of the truly great poets of our time." In the same article, he observed that by reading the collected works, one could perceive a developing sense of despair within Celan. Referring to the poems, Auster wrote, "One feels both a shrinking and an expansion in them, as if, by traveling to the inmost recesses of himself, Celan had somehow vanished, joining with the greater forces beyond him, and at the same time sinking more deeply into his terrifying sense of isolation...." Celan once revealed, "I have tried to write poetry in order to acquire a perspective of reality for myself." Perhaps he forecast his own fate when he wrote, "You were my death: / you I could hold / when all fell away from me."

BIOGRAPHICAL/CRITICAL SOURCES: Times Literary Supplement, December 7, 1967, September 18, 1970; *Books Abroad*, spring, 1971; *New York Times Book Review*, July 18, 1971; Paul Celan, *Speech-Grille and Selected Poems*, Dutton, 1971; Celan, *Selected Poems*, Penguin, 1972; Jerry Glenn, *Paul Celan*, Twayne, 1973; *Commentary*, February, 1976; *Contemporary Literary Criticism*, Volume 10, Gale, 1979.*

* * *

APITZ, Bruno 1900-1979

OBITUARY NOTICE: Born April 28, 1900, in Leipzig, East Germany; died in 1979. Journalist and novelist recognized as the originator of proletarian literature. A member of the Communist Party, Apitz was imprisoned for eight years by the Nazis. Five of those years were spent in Buchenwald prison camp, an experience Apitz depicted in his highly acclaimed novel, *Naked Among Wolves*. Obituaries and other sources: *Cassell's Encyclopaedia of World Literature*, revised edition, Morrow, 1973; *AB Bookman's Weekly*, May 21, 1979.

* * *

APPEL, Martin E(liot) 1948-
(Marty Appel)

PERSONAL: Surname is pronounced A-*pell;* born August 7, 1948, in Brooklyn, N.Y.; son of Irving (an insurance broker) and Celia (a secretary; maiden name, Mann) Appel; married Patricia Alkins (a social worker), October 26, 1975. *Education:* State University of New York College at Oneonta, B.A., 1970. *Home:* 95 Wellford Rd., White Plains, N.Y. 10607. *Office:* Office of the Baseball Commissioner, 75 Rockefeller Plaza, New York, N.Y. 10019.

CAREER: New York Yankees, Bronx, N.Y., director of public relations, 1968-77; Garagiola/Appel Enterprises, Tarrytown, N.Y., president, 1977-78; New York Apples (tennis team), New York City, director of public relations, 1978; presently associated with the Office of the Baseball Commissioner, New York City. *Member:* Society of American Baseball Research. *Awards, honors: Baseball's Best* was named outstanding sports reference book by American Library Association, 1977.

WRITINGS: (With Matt Winick) *Illustrated Digest of Baseball*, five volumes, Stadia Sports Publishing, 1971-75; (with Burt Goldblatt) *Baseball's Best: The Hall of Fame Gallery*, McGraw, 1977; (with Thurman Munson) *Thurman Munson:*

An Autobiography (Sports Illustrated Book Club selection), Coward, 1978; (under name Marty Appel, with Fred Stolle) *Tennis Tips for Youngsters*, Wanderer Books, in press; (editor, under name Marty Appel) *Batting Tips for Youngsters*, Wanderer Books, in press. Contributor to *Baseball Digest* and *Baseball Quarterly*. Senior editor of *Baseball Quarterly*.

SIDELIGHTS: Appel was raised in New York as a Yankee fan, went from college to work in the team's front office, and later, to the league commissioner's office. He feels "few have managed to be this fortunate—crossing over from fan to the 'inside' and gaining the opportunity to write about it."

* * *

APPLEBAUM, Stan 1929-
(Robert Keith)

PERSONAL: Born March 1, 1929, in Newark, N.J.; son of William and Julia (Knoll) Applebaum; married second wife, Cecelia Notov (an educator and television personality), March 3, 1971; children: (first marriage) Jody Karin, Jonathan Todd; (second marriage) Edward Norman. *Home and office:* 330 West 58th St., New York, N.Y. 10019.

CAREER: Musical arranger, composer, conductor, and writer. Arranger for big band directors, including Harry James and Benny Goodman; musical arranger and orchestrator for "The Goldbergs," 1950-51, "Jimmy Durante," 1951-52, "Eddie Cantor" and "Martin and Lewis," 1953, "The Hit Parade," 1956-57, and Studio One," 1960; eastern artists and repertory director for Warner Brothers Records, 1961-63.

MEMBER: National Academy of Recording Arts and Sciences (member of board of governors), American Society of Composers, Authors, and Publishers, Society of Advertising Music Producers, Arrangers, Composers (head of technical and information committee). *Awards, honors:* Awards of merit from Communication Arts Society, 1967, for music campaigns for Bristol Myers Co. and Eastern Airlines; international broadcasting awards from Hollywood Radio and Television Society, 1967, for music in Pan American World Airlines advertisement, and 1969, for music in Sears, Roebuck & Co. advertisement; award from American Television and Radio Commercials Festival, 1968, for music in Pan American World Airlines advertisement; award from Cannes International Festival of Film Publicity, 1969, for music in WTS Pharmacraft Products advertisement.

WRITINGS—Children's nature books: A Not So Ugly Friend, Holt, 1973; *The Flying Janitor*, Golden Press, 1973; *Nature's Carpet Sweeper*, Golden Press, 1973; *The Knight in Crusty Armor*, Golden Press, 1973; *Nature's Smallest Gravedigger*, Golden Press, 1973; *The Laughing Garbage Disposal*, Golden Press, 1973; *Nature's Assistant*, Golden Press, 1973; *Going My Way?*, Harcourt, 1975; *Nature's Doubles*, Golden Press, 1975.

Music books: *How to Improvise*, C. Colin, 1954; *Advanced Trumpet Duets*, two volumes, C. Colin, 1955; *Folk Music: Bach Style*, Schroeder & Gunther, 1972; *Creative Rhythmic Reading at the Piano*, Schroeder & Gunther, 1972; *Sound/World*, Schroeder & Gunther, 1974; *Bach Music: Simple Style*, Schroeder & Gunther, 1975; *Double Play*, Schroeder & Gunther, 1975.

Also author of plays with Gerald Dietz, including "Heavenly Chase," "Hogan's Utopia," "Pithead," "Bride of the Bayou," "Mr. Nathan and the Nafke," and "Catherine's Daughter."

Composer of music for television and radio commercials,

records for leading performers, motion pictures, pieces for band and orchestra, jazz instrumentals, chamber and choral music, choral arrangements, dance band music, piano music, and children's songs, some under pseudonym Robert Keith, many published by Chappell, Inc., E. Shuberth & Co., E. H. Morris, and other leading music publishers.

WORK IN PROGRESS—All children's books: *The Words We Live By; I See With My Ears; Three Different Places; I Can Be Positive; I've a Friendship With the Lord; The Apple, the Bee, the Bird, and Me; The Five of Us; Music Primer.*

SIDELIGHTS: Applebaum's prolific career in music has spanned several generations and covered nearly all aspects of composition and arrangement. Beginning with the big-band era, he later moved into television and radio work. Subsequently, he arranged the music for hit records by such popular recording artists as Joanie Sommers, Bobby Vinton, Brook Benton, and Connie Francis. He has also composed dozens of pieces for beginning and advanced music students.

AVOCATIONAL INTERESTS: Archaeology, travel in Mexico, ham radio, carpentry, botany, painting, jogging, swimming, baseball.

* * *

APPLEGATE, Richard 1913(?)-1979

OBITUARY NOTICE: Born c. 1913; died February 13, 1979, in Boston, Mass. Journalist and free-lance writer. Applegate was a correspondent and Chicago bureau chief for the National Broadcasting Corp. (NBC). During the Korean War he served as a war correspondent for United Press International. In 1950, while sailing on a yacht in the South Pacific, Applegate and some friends were captured by a Chinese gunboat near Lantao Island and held captive for several weeks for invading Chinese territory. In 1954 Applegate wrote of this experience in a series published in the *New York World Telegram* and the *Baltimore Sun.* Obituaries and other sources: *New York Times,* February 14, 1979.

* * *

APPLEWHITE, James W(illiam) 1935-

PERSONAL: Born August 8, 1935, in Stantonsburg, N.C.; son of James W. (a farmer) and Jane Elizabeth (Mercer) Applewhite; married Janis Forrest (an executive secretary), January 28, 1956; children: Lisa, Jamey, Jeff. *Education:* Duke University, A.B., 1958, M.A., 1960, Ph.D., 1969. *Home:* 606 November Dr., Durham, N.C. 27712. *Office:* Department of English, 336 Carr Building, Duke University, Durham, N.C. 27706.

CAREER: Poet. Associate professor of English at Duke University, Durham, N.C. *Member:* Poetry Society of America. *Awards, honors:* Emily Clark Balch Prize from *Virginia Quarterly Review,* 1966, for "The Journey"; National Endowment for the Arts grant, 1974; Borestone Mountain Poetry Awards, 1975, for "Roadside Notes" and 1977, for "William Blackburn, Riding Westward"; Guggenheim fellowship, 1976.

WRITINGS: Statues of the Grass (poems), University of Georgia Press, 1975.

Work represented in anthologies, including *American Poetry Anthology,* 1970.

WORK IN PROGRESS: Iron Age Flying, a long poem.

SIDELIGHTS: "Applewhite's first volume of poems establishes him as an enormously gifted writer. He can make the English language float or sing. I have not been so enthralled by the magic wedding of imagery and music in many recent years of reading contemporary poetry," Clair Hahn wrote in a review of *Statues of Grass.* Other critics also marveled over Applewhite's talent. Fred Chappel called *Statues of Grass* a "first work which is also the work of a master," while Henry Taylor termed the book "a splendid achievement."

A native of the South, Applewhite's poems are concerned with that area and with the relationship between the past and the present. "Applewhite is very much aware that the southern popular world from which he writes is disappearing, and there is an elegiac tone to many of the poems in *Statues of Grass,*" D. E. Richardson noted. A reviewer for *Choice* pointed out that "these poems sift the memories of a childhood and a region (the South) for their resonances of thought and feeling in the present. Typical lyrics assay the possible meanings for a modern sensibility of the Civil War as well as World War II, the racial taboos of very few decades ago, a grandfather's funeral, the testaments of gravestones, the 'wisdom' assumed at adulthood, and the inevitable change of the South by bulldozer and concrete."

Applewhite told *CA:* "I am working to re-introduce the narrative element into poetry. *Iron Age Flying* begins from a child's point of view. Style evolves as the chronology progresses. The guiding myth is that of the fall from innocence into knowledge."

BIOGRAPHICAL/CRITICAL SOURCES: Appalachian Journal, spring, 1976; *Southern Poetry Review,* spring, 1976; *Southern Review,* autumn, 1976; *Choice,* July/August, 1976; *Commonweal,* October 22, 1976.

* * *

ARAFAT, Ibtihaj Said 1934-

PERSONAL: Born January 24, 1934, in Nablus, Palestine; came to the United States in 1964, naturalized citizen, 1977; daughter of Said Omar (a lawyer) and Khadija Arafat. *Education:* Arab States Fundamental Education Center, diploma, 1957; Oklahoma State University, B.S., 1967, M.S., 1968, Ph.D., 1970. *Religion:* Moslem. *Home:* 115 East 87th St., Apt. 10-B, New York, N.Y. 10028.

CAREER: United Nations Relief and Works Agency, headmistress of girls' secondary school in Jordan, 1951-55; UNESCO, expert on women's education in Libya, 1957-60, Yemen, 1960-63, and Paris, France, 1963-64; City College of the City University of New York, N.Y., assistant professor of demography and social research, 1970-78; University of Aleppo, Aleppo, Syria, member of economics faculty and senior United Nations international demography expert, 1978—. Participant in professional conventions.

MEMBER: American Sociological Association, American Statistical Association, Population Association of America, American Society of Criminology, Southern Sociological Society, Midwest Sociological Association, Mid-Southern Sociological Association, Oklahoma Academy of Science. *Awards, honors:* UNESCO fellowship, 1955-57, for study in Egypt; Institute for International Education fellowship, 1965-67.

WRITINGS: The New Woman: Attitude, Behavior, and Self Image, C. E. Merrill, 1976. Contributor of about forty articles to social science journals.

WORK IN PROGRESS: The Middle East in Progress: Politically, Economically, and Socially; Urban Identity and Ethnicity in New York City.

SIDELIGHTS: Ibtihaj Arafat writes: "I am engaged in a housing survey in Aleppo as part of my job with the United Nations. I am training four local professors to work in the survey so that they can take over when I leave. My major area of interest in demography is fertility."

* * *

ARDIZZONE, Tony 1949-

PERSONAL: Born August 18, 1949, in Chicago, Ill.; son of Anthony and Mary (Biederman) Ardizzone; married Diane Kondrat (an actress), August, 1975. *Education:* University of Illinois, B.A. (honors), 1971; Bowling Green State University, M.F.A., 1975. *Religion:* Roman Catholic. *Home:* 1406 Melrose Parkway, Norfolk, Va. 23508. *Agent:* Ray Lincoln Literary Agency, P.O. Box 2907, Philadelphia, Pa. 19141. *Office:* Department of English, Old Dominion University, Norfolk, Va. 23508.

CAREER: St. Mary Center for Learning, Chicago, Ill., instructor in English, 1971-73; Bowling Green State University, Bowling Green, Ohio, instructor in English, 1975-78; Old Dominion University, Norfolk, Va., assistant professor of English, 1978—. Director of seminars and workshops; gives readings at schools and on television and radio. *Member:* Poets and Writers. *Awards, honors:* First prize from *Black Warrior Review* literary contest, 1977, for story "But You Can Call Me Thaddeus."

WRITINGS: (Editor) *Saint Mary's Anthology of Women Writers,* St. Mary Center for Learning, Volume I, 1972, Volume II, 1973; *In the Name of the Father* (novel), Doubleday, 1978.

Work represented in anthologies, including *Itinerary I,* Bowling Green State University Press, 1974, and *Itinerary IV,* Bowling Green State University Press, 1977. Contributor of stories, poems, and articles to literary magazines, including *Quarterly West, Texas Quarterly, Seattle Review,* and *Epoch.* Fiction editor of *Penny Dreadful,* 1974-75; managing editor of *Intro 10,* 1978-79.

WORK IN PROGRESS: The People and the Stones, a short story collection.

* * *

ARKUSH, Arthur Spencer 1925-1979

OBITUARY NOTICE: Born June 22, 1925, in Chicago, Ill.; died March 22, 1979, in Chicago, Ill. Publisher. Arkush was publisher and president of *Pro Football Weekly* from 1967 until his death. Obituaries and other sources: *Who's Who in America,* 40th edition, Marquis, 1978; *Chicago Tribune,* March 24, 1979.

* * *

ARMERDING, George D. 1899-

PERSONAL: Born October 17, 1899, in New Jersey; son of Ernst (in construction) and Gebke (Kretzmer) Armerding; married Helen L. Warren, August 22, 1925; children: Mary Jane Armerding Searle, George W., Robert L. *Education:* Attended New Jersey State Agricultural College, 1917-18. *Politics:* Democrat. *Religion:* Protestant. *Home:* 3805 Maybelle Ave., Apt. 2, Oakland, Calif. 94619.

CAREER: Mojonnier Brothers, Chicago, Ill., food process engineer, 1930-65; writer, 1965—. Lecturer at land grant colleges. Christian Business Committee International, head, 1963, and past member of board of directors; honorary member of board of directors of Christian Business Men's Committee, Chattanooga. *Member:* California Diary Industries Association (life member).

WRITINGS: (With Paul Hubert Tracy and Harold W. Hannah) *Dairy Plant Management,* McGraw, 1958; *Evaporation Methods as Applied to the Food Industry,* Academic Press, 1966; *Fragrance Ascending,* Western Book Co., 1975; *The Dollars and Sense of Honesty,* Harper, 1979; *Fragrance of the Lord,* Harper, 1979. Contributor to trade journals.

WORK IN PROGRESS: Chino, the Adventurous Salmon, a novel.

* * *

ARNY, Thomas Travis 1940-

PERSONAL: Born June 2, 1940, in Montclair, N.J.; son of Robert Allan and Mary (Travis) Arny; married Linda Ray Cowan (a librarian), March 31, 1968. *Education:* Haverford College, B.A., 1961; University of Arizona, Ph.D., 1965. *Office:* Department of Astronomy, University of Massachusetts, Amherst, Mass. 01003.

CAREER: Amherst College, Amherst, Mass., research associate, 1965-66, assistant professor of astronomy, 1966-69; University of Massachusetts, Amherst, associate professor, 1969—. *Member:* International Astronomical Union, American Astronomical Society, Royal Astronomical Society. *Awards, honors:* National Science Foundation grant, 1967-71.

WRITINGS: (Author of revision) Nicholas Pananides, *Introductory Astronomy,* Addison-Wesley, 1979. Contributor to scientific journals.

WORK IN PROGRESS: Research on meteorological optics and on stars and interstellar dust.

SIDELIGHTS: Arny told *CA:* "My formal research interests concern the formation of stars and the curiously shaped gas clouds often found near them. My informal interests cover most areas of natural history, especially birds. I can't decide which I find more miraculous—that stars form to light our sky, or that a bird weighing a few ounces can fly nonstop over two thousand miles of ocean to a place it has never seen using those same stars as guide posts. I'd like to follow those birds sometime."

* * *

ARONSON, Harvey 1929-

PERSONAL: Born May 17, 1929, in Jamaica, N.Y.; son of Isadore (an auto wrecker) and Anna (Schoenberg) Aronson; married Phyllis Ziman, June 13, 1953; children: Beth, Linda, Bruce. *Education:* Syracuse University, B.A., 1950. *Politics:* Independent. *Religion:* Jewish. *Residence:* East Northport, N.Y. *Agent:* Sterling Lord Agency, Inc., 660 Madison Ave., New York, N.Y. 10021.

CAREER: Newsday, Garden City, N.Y., 1953-70, variously worked as editor, copy editor, reporter, feature writer, and columnist; free-lance writer. Member of board of directors, East Northport Youth Development Association. *Military service:* U.S. Army, Signal Corps, 1950-52. *Awards, honors:* New York Society of Silvrians award for reporting and feature writing.

WRITINGS: (Editor with Mike McGrady) Penelope Ashe (a group pseudonym), *Naked Came the Stranger,* Lyle Stuart, 1969; (with F. Lee Bailey) *The Defense Never Rests,* Stein & Day, 1972; (with McGrady) *Establishment of Innocence,* Ballantine, 1978. Also author of *The Killing of Joey Gallo,* Putnam. Contributor of articles to periodicals, including

New York, Cosmopolitan, Sports Illustrated, Good House-keeping, Seventeen, True, and *Newsweek.*

WORK IN PROGRESS: Whistler's Landing, a novel, for publication by Ballantine; some work on nonfiction book ideas.

SIDELIGHTS: Aronson told *CA* that his occupation is writing. He gives credit to his agent for supporting him in his free-lance work: "Sterling Lord has a great deal to do with my being able to survive as a freelancer." Aronson also wrote: "I work out of an office on Main Street, Northport, and I can see the harbor from my window. I spend a great deal of time in the sweet-shop across the street, where most of the resident philosophers come in for coffee."

* * *

ARTHUR, Ruth M(abel)   1905-1979

OBITUARY NOTICE—See index for *CA* sketch: Born May 26, 1905, in Glasgow, Scotland; died March 6, 1979, in Oxford, England. Educator and author of over fifteen books for children and young adults. Arthur was a kindergarten teacher in both Scotland and England before retiring to raise six children and write such books as *A Candle in Her Room, Requiem for a Princess, My Daughter, Nicola,* and *The Whistling Boy.* All of her books have been published in the United States and several have appeared in foreign translations. Obituaries and other sources: *The Author's and Writer's Who's Who,* 6th edition, Burke's Peerage, 1971; *Publishers Weekly,* March 19, 1979.

* * *

ASHLEY, Paul P(ritchard)   1896-1979

OBITUARY NOTICE—See index for *CA* sketch: Born July 2, 1896, in Fostoria, Ohio; died February 5, 1979, in Maui, Hawaii. Attorney, educator, and author of five books on law. Ashley was admitted to the State Bar of Washington in 1926 and practiced law in Seattle for over fifty years. An expert on libel, Ashley was best known for his book, *Say It Safely,* currently in its fifth edition. He was the first editor of the *Washington Law Review* and the author of *You and Your Will, Essentials of Libel, Cases on Business Law,* and *Oh Promise Me, But Put It in Writing.* Obituaries and other sources: *Who's Who in America,* 40th edition, Marquis, 1978; *New York Times,* February 7, 1979.

* * *

ASPRIN, Robert Lynn   1946-

PERSONAL: Born June 28, 1946, in St. John's, Mich.; son of Daniel D. (a machinist) and Lorraine (an elementary school teacher; maiden name, Coon) Asprin; married Anne Brett (a bookkeeper), December 28, 1968; children: Annette Maria, Daniel Mather. *Education:* Attended University of Michigan, 1964-65. *Home:* 1214 Westport, Ann Arbor, Mich. 48103. *Agent:* Kirby McCauley Ltd., 60 East 42nd St., New York, N.Y. 10017. *Office:* 204 South Fourth Ave., Ann Arbor, Mich. 48104.

CAREER: University Microfilm, Ann Arbor, Mich., accounts payable clerk, 1966-69, accounts receivable correspondent, 1969-70, payroll-labor analyst, 1970-74, junior cost accountant, 1974-76, cost accountant, 1976-78; writer, 1978—. *Military service:* U.S. Army, 1965-66. *Member:* Science Fiction Writers of America. *Awards, honors:* Hugo nomination from World Science Fiction Convention, 1976, for "The Capture."

WRITINGS: The Cold Cash War (science fiction novel), St. Martin's, 1977; *Another Fine Myth* (fantasy novel), Donning, 1978; *The Bug Wars* (science fiction novel), St. Martin's, 1979; *Myth Conception* (fantasy novel), Donning, 1979; *The Star Stulkers* (science fiction novel), Playboy Press, 1979; *Thieves World* (fantasy anthology), Ace Books, 1979; *The Demon Blade* (occult fiction), St. Martin's, 1980; *Tambu* (science fiction novel), Ace Books, 1980; *Tambu Anthology* (science fiction stories), Ace Books, 1980; *Myth Direction* (fantasy novel), Donning, 1980; (with Lynn Abbey) *Act of God* (science fiction novel), Ace Books, 1980.

Author of "The Capture," a script for a comedy slide show, produced by Boojums Press, 1975.

SIDELIGHTS: Asprin writes: "Philippine-Irish in ancestry, I look like a stereotyped revolutionary (which I'm not). This image has been aided by my hobbies, which are primarily martial in nature. I fenced and coached all three weapons, foil, saber, and epee, and served a term as vice-chairman of the Michigan Division of the Amateur Fencing League of America. Furthermore, I have studied the Japanese, Okinawan, and Chinese forms of armed and unarmed combat, and am passable with firearms and archery. To round out the picture, I was active for several years in the Society for Creative Anachronism, which practices full-force combat with mock-ups of swords, spears, axes, and maces. As Yang the Nauseating, I organized and ran a 'household' patterned after a Mongol horde.

"There is, of course, a gentler side to my nature. I raise and breed tropical fish, and have long been involved with music and theater. I have acted in several amateur productions, and occasionally supplemented my income playing folk guitar in coffee houses and bars.

"As for my writing, I am first and foremost a storyteller. Most of my current work falls into the category of science fiction or fantasy, the fields giving the widest range to a writer's imagination and inventiveness. My primary reading for years has been action-adventure novels, and that style of writing has influenced my own work heavily. I find long drawn-out descriptions of explanations of mathematical theorems to be extremely boring, and therefore exclude them from my own stories. You do not have to know how to build a clock to tell time or understand a jet engine to ride in a plane.

"I have long been afraid of being 'typed,' and have made a concentrated effort to avoid letting my work fall into a rut, particularly in subject matter. As an example, my first three books are intentionally dissimilar. *The Cold Cash War* is speculative near-future fiction involving corporate takeover of world government. *Another Fine Myth* is a sword and sorcery farce full of dragons, stranded demons, and very bad puns. *The Bug Wars* does not have a human in the entire book. It was written 'first-person alien, reptile to be specific' and has been one of my greatest writing challenges to date.

"If there is an overall message in my work, it would have to be stated as the case for Everyman. Like all science fiction writers, I promote space travel and development. I feel, however, that we will never see it until the average guy on the street can see a place for himself in space. We will have to have the support of the common man, not just the scientists and test pilots. *Tambu* contains what I feel is a realistic crew for a spaceship. It is not only co-educational, there are several racial types, ages ranging from teens to old-timers, and a wide cross-section of educational backgrounds. That is what life on Earth is all about, and that is what it is going to be like in space. We are going to need grease monkeys as well as computer programmers. Few people see themselves as Superman, and as long as science fiction writers portray space travelers in that light, the taxpayers and voters could not care less about getting off the planet."

* * *

AUERBACH, Nina 1943-

PERSONAL: Born May 24, 1943, in New York, N.Y.; daughter of Arnold Malcolm (a writer) and Justine (Rubin) Auerbach. *Education:* University of Wisconsin—Madison, B.A., 1964; Columbia University, M.A. (high honors), 1967, Ph.D. (distinction), 1970. *Politics:* "Feminist." *Religion:* Jewish. *Home:* 135 South 18th St., Philadelphia, Pa. 19103. *Office:* Department of English—D1, University of Pennsylvania, Philadelphia, Pa. 19104.

CAREER: Cleveland State University, Cleveland, Ohio, instructor in English, summer, 1968; Hunter College of the City University of New York, New York, N.Y., adjunct professor of general studies, 1969-70; California State University, Los Angeles, assistant professor of English, 1970-72; University of Pennsylvania, Philadelphia, assistant professor, 1972-77, associate professor of English, 1977—. *Member:* Modern Language Association of America, Victorian Society of America, Northeast Victorian Association, Phi Beta Kappa, Phi Kappa Phi. *Awards, honors:* Ford Foundation fellow, 1975-76; fellow of Radcliffe Institute, 1975-76.

WRITINGS: (Contributor) Mark Spilka, editor, *Toward a Poetics of Fiction,* Indiana University Press, 1977; *Communities of Women: An Idea in Fiction,* Harvard University Press, 1978; (contributor) Sandra Gilbert and Susan Gubar, editors, *Shakespeare's Sisters: Women Poets, Feminist Critics,* Indiana University Press, 1979. Contributor of about twenty articles and reviews to literature journals.

WORK IN PROGRESS: Victorian Womanhood and Literary Character (tentative title); "Jane Austen and Romantic Imprisonment," to be included in *Jane Austen and Society,* edited by David Monaghan, Macmillan, 1980.

SIDELIGHTS: Nina Auerbach comments: "My first book, *Communities of Women,* has a personal origin, translated into academic criticism—the understanding and support I received from women (not necessarily feminists) during my painful probation in the male-dominated academic world. I think all good criticism has an autobiographical origin, disguised but intense, though we claim we are being objective and disinterested. As a critic, I find it more interesting to write about my own experience as I perceive it outside myself, having lived it once already."

* * *

AUSTIN, M(ichel) M(ervyn) 1943-

PERSONAL: Born July 2, 1943, in Brisbane, Queensland, Australia; son of Lloyd James (a university professor) and Jeanne F. (Guerin) Austin. *Education:* Jesus College, Cambridge, M.A., 1965, Ph.D., 1968. *Religion:* None. *Home:* 4 Radernie Pl., St. Andrews, Fife KY16 8QR, Scotland. *Office:* Department of Ancient History, University of St. Andrews, St. Andrews, Fife, Scotland.

CAREER: University of St. Andrews, St. Andrews, Scotland, lecturer in ancient history, 1968—. *Member:* Hellenic Society (member of council, 1973-75), Association des Etudes Grecques, Cambridge Philological Society.

WRITINGS: Greece and Egypt in the Archaic Age, Cambridge Philological Society, 1970; (with Pierre Vidal-Naquet) *Economies et societes en Grece ancienne,* Armand

Colin, 1972, 2nd edition, 1973, translation published as *Economic and Social History of Ancient Greece: An Introduction,* University of California Press, 1977.

WORK IN PROGRESS: A sourcebook in translation, covering the Hellenistic world from Alexander to the second century B.C., publication by Cambridge University Press expected in 1980.

SIDELIGHTS: Austin told *CA:* "My main interest in ancient history is in Greek history from the eighth to second centuries B.C., with special reference to social, economic, and institutional history. This is the connecting element in my published work so far and will also be represented in the sourcebook on the Hellenistic world." *Avocational interests:* Classical music, playing the violin, current affairs, travel.

* * *

AVAKIAN, Arra S(teve) 1912-

PERSONAL: Born February 27, 1912, in Boston, Mass.; son of Setrak S. and Takoohi (Kazarossian) Avakian; married Georgia Keosaian (a clerk), July 1, 1939; children: Arsine Avakian Peterson, Armine Avakian Kotin, Arra E., Armen, Arten. *Education:* Massachusetts Institute of Technology, S.B., 1933, Sc.D., 1935. *Home and office:* 6149 North Ninth St., Fresno, Calif. 93710.

CAREER: Metropolitan Life Insurance Co., New York, N.Y., actuary, 1935-40; researcher in science and technology at York Industries, York, Pa., at Vectron, Inc., at Waltham, Mass., at research and development division, Avco, Wilmington, Mass., and at advanced development laboratory, Raytheon Co., Bedford, Mass., 1946-63; Aerospace Corp., Washington, D.C., director of eastern operations, 1963-68; Cybernetics Research Institute, Washington, D.C., chief scientist, 1968-70; California State University, Fresno, professor of Armenian studies, 1970-74; independent research and study, 1974-76; American Armenian International College, La Verne, Calif., professor of Armenian studies, 1976—. *Military service:* U.S. Army, Ordnance Corps, 1940-46; became colonel.

WRITINGS: The Armenians in America, Lerner, 1977. Contributor of numerous articles to periodicals.

WORK IN PROGRESS: The Armenians of Fresno, publication expected in 1981.

SIDELIGHTS: Avakian told *CA* he is active "in the Armenian community, particularly in the Armenian Church where I am an ordained senior deacon, a choirmaster, and at times a member of the governing council of the Armenian Church in America. I am also active in Armenian educational and charitable organizations."

AVOCATIONAL INTERESTS: Travel.

* * *

AXELROD, Herbert Richard 1927-

PERSONAL: Born in 1927, in Bayonne, N.J.; married Evelyn Miller. *Education:* City College (now of City University of New York), B.S.; New York University, M.S., Ph.D. *Home:* 245 Cornelison Ave., Jersey City, N.J. 07302. *Office:* T.F.H. Publications, Inc., 211 West Sylvania Ave., Neptune, N.J. 07753.

CAREER: Instructor at New York University; publisher of *Tropical Fish Hobbyist;* president and chief executive officer of Miracle Pet Products, Inc.; president of T.F.H. Publications, Inc. *Member:* American Association of Herpetologists and Ichthyologists.

WRITINGS: (With William Vorderwinkler) *Color Guide to Tropical Fish*, 1955; *Axelrod's Tropical Fish Book*, Arco, 1964; *Breeding Aquarium Fishes*, T.F.H. Publications, Book I (with Susan Shaw), 1968, Book II, 1971, Book III (with Lourdes Burgess), 1973, Book IV, 1976; *Tropical Fish as a Hobby*, McGraw, revised edition, 1969; *Photography for Aquarists*, T.F.H. Publications, 1970; (with Leonard P. Schultz) *Handbook of Tropical Aquarium Fishes*, T.F.H. Publications, 1970; (with Warren Burgess) *Pacific Marine Fishes*, T.F.H. Publications, Books I-VII, 1972-76; *Tropical Fish for Beginners*, T.F.H. Publications, 1972; (co-author) *Exotic Marine Fishes*, T.F.H. Publications, 1973; *African Cichlids of Lakes Malawi and Tanganyika*, T.F.H. Publications, 1973; *Koi of the World*, T.F.H. Publications, 1973; (with William Vorderwinkler) *Tropical Fish in Your Home*, Barnes & Noble, 1973; (with Edwin C. Welty, Jr.) *Pigeon Racing*, Sterling, 1973; *Freshwater Fishes*, Book I, T.F.H. Publications, 1974; (with Vorderwinkler) *Encyclopedia of Tropical Fishes*, T.F.H. Publications, revised edition, 1975; *Sand Painting for Aquariums and Terrariums*, T.F.H. Publications, 1975; (editor) *Heifetz*, Paganiniana Publications, 1976. Also author of *Guppies, Saltwater Aquarium Fishes, The Educational Aquarium, Catfishes for the Advanced Hobbyist*, and *Exotic Tropical Fishes*. Contributor to *Tropical Fish Hobbyist*.*

*   *   *

AYALA, Francisco 1934-

PERSONAL: Born March 12, 1934, in Madrid, Spain; came to United States in 1961, naturalized citizen, 1971; son of Francisco (in business) and Soledad (Pereda) Ayala; married Mary Henderson, May 27, 1968; children: Francisco Jose, Carlos Alberto. *Education:* University of Madrid, B.S., 1955; Columbia University, M.A., 1963, Ph.D., 1964. *Home:* 747 Plum Lane, Davis, Calif. 95616. *Office:* Department of Genetics, University of California, Davis, Calif. 95616.

CAREER: Providence College, Providence, R.I., assistant professor of biology, 1965-67; Rockefeller University, New York, N.Y., assistant professor of biology, 1967-71; University of California, Davis, associate professor, 1971-74, professor of genetics, 1974—, director of Institute of Ecology and associate dean of environmental studies, both 1977—. Member of national advisory council of Institute of General Medical Sciences. *Member:* Society for the Study of Evolution (vice-president, 1973), American Society of Naturalists (secretary, 1973-76), Genetics Society of America, Ecological Society of America, American Genetics Association, Society for the Study of Evolution (president, 1979-80). *Awards, honors:* Johns Hopkins University centennial scholar, 1975; Guggenheim fellow, 1977; American Academy of Arts and Sciences fellow, 1977.

WRITINGS: (Editor) *Studies in the Philosophy of Biology*, Macmillan, 1974; (editor) *Molecular Evolution*, Sinauer, 1976; (with Theodosius Dobzhansky, G. L. Stebbins, and J. W. Valentine) *Evolution*, W. H. Freeman, 1977; (with Valentine) *Evolving*, W. A. Benjamin, 1979. Contributor of more than two hundred articles to scientific journals.

WORK IN PROGRESS: A book on the philosophy of science, publication by Harvard University Press expected in 1981; a book on general genetics, for W. A. Benjamin.

SIDELIGHTS: Ayala told *CA:* "*Evolution* is an authoritative statement of the current theory of evolution that integrates modern biochemical as well as ecological studies of evolution, besides the more traditional approaches to the subject. It also contains a long chapter on philosophical issues related to biological evolution. My interest on the philosophical, ethical, and humanistic components of science are also reflected in the book I edited in 1974 and the book to be published by Harvard University Press."

B

BACH, Kent 1943-

PERSONAL: Born July 10, 1943, in San Francisco, Calif.; son of Karl (in insurance) and Meryl (a musician; maiden name, Coleman) Bach. *Education:* Harvard University, A.B., 1964; University of California, Berkeley, Ph.D., 1968. *Home:* 3767 Army St., San Francisco, Calif. 94110. *Office:* Department of Philosophy, San Francisco State University, San Francisco, Calif. 94132.

CAREER: University of Nebraska, Lincoln, assistant professor of philosophy, 1968-69; San Francisco State University, San Francisco, Calif., assistant professor, 1969-72, associate professor, 1972-78, professor of philosophy, 1978—. *Member:* American Philosophical Association, American Association of University Professors, Society for Philosophy and Psychology.

WRITINGS: Exit—Existentialism, Wadsworth, 1973; (with Robert M. Harnish) *Linguistic Communication and Speech Acts,* M.I.T. Press, 1979. Contributor to philosophy journals, including *Philosophical Studies, Mind,* and *Journal for the Theory of Social Behavior.*

WORK IN PROGRESS: Action and the Mind; various papers on the theory of knowledge and the philosophy of mind.

SIDELIGHTS: Bach told *CA:* "My philosophizing is a quest for contemporary answers to the central question of philosophy: what are the conceptual relationships between the world and how we view it and between ourselves and our self-conceptions?" *Avocational interests:* Music, basketball, tennis, chess, backgammon.

* * *

BACKER, Dorothy 1925-

PERSONAL: Born January 16, 1925, in West New York, N.J.; daughter of William T. (a manufacturer) and Anna (Schwarz) McShea; married Eric F.L. Backer (a finance director), October 17, 1953; children: Anna Mary Liot. *Education:* University of London, B.A. (honors), 1960, M.A., 1962, Ph.D., 1968. *Politics:* "Liberal, but not dogmatic." *Religion:* None. *Home:* 10 Waterside Plaza, New York, N.Y. 10010. *Agent:* Roslyn Targ Literary Agency, Inc., 250 West 57th St., Suite 1932, New York, N.Y. 10019.

CAREER: University of London, London, England, lecturer in French at St. Mary's College, Twickenham, 1964-66, and Birkbeck College, 1966-69; St. John's University, Jamaica,

N.Y., assistant professor of French, 1969-73; Dickinson College, Carlisle, Pa., assistant professor of French, 1973-75, head of department, 1974-75; writer, 1975—. *Member:* Modern Language Association of America, Society for French Studies.

WRITINGS: Precious Women (nonfiction), Basic Books, 1974; *The Parma Legacy* (novel), Norton, 1978. Contributing editor of *Practical Psychology.*

WORK IN PROGRESS: A suspense novel, set in Greece; a sequel to *The Parma Legacy,* set in France, completion expected in 1980.

SIDELIGHTS: Dorothy Backer writes: "My life began in disaster, tuberculosis, which claimed eight years of my youth. It wasn't all wasted: I learned languages, read everything, and waited. When the end came, my travels began. I have lived all over the world and used all my ten languages (including Persian, Swahili, and modern Greek). And I was an academic for eleven years.

"In middle age I threw over the academic career to write; it was like coming home after a long exile. But my writing is closely influenced by the academic training, so I guess that wasn't wasted either. I'm a meticulous, fussy writer. I work long hours and throw most of it away."

* * *

BACON, Martha Sherman 1917-

PERSONAL: Born in 1917, in California; married Philip Oliver-Smith (marriage ended); married Ronald Ballinger (a history professor). *Education:* Educated in Massachusetts and Italy; also attended the American Academy of Dramatic Arts. *Residence:* Rhode Island.

CAREER: Member of the staff for the *Atlantic Monthly;* lecturer in English at Rhode Island College, Providence; novelist and poet.

WRITINGS: Lament for the Chieftains, and Other Poems, Coward, 1942; *Things Visible and Invisible* (poems), Coward, 1947; *A Star Called Wormwood* (novel), Random House, 1948; *A Masque of Exile,* C. N. Potter, 1962; *Puritan Promenade,* Houghton, 1964; *Sophia Scrooby Preserved,* illustrations by David Omar White, Little, Brown, 1968; *The Third Road,* illustrations by Robin Jacques, Little, Brown, 1971; *In the Company of Clowns: A Commedia,* Little, Brown, 1973; *Moth Manor,* Little, Brown, 1978.

SIDELIGHTS: In reviewing Bacon's *Things Visible and Invisible,* a critic for *Saturday Review* wrote, "Miss Bacon's poetic gift is deepening and maturing. . . . Her poetry is subjective, disciplined; the emotion tempered and restrained." A reviewer for the *Christian Science Monitor* noted its "skillfully turned lyrics, showing depth and delicacy of feeling, but not sufficiently original in statement or diction to be distinguished."

A Star Called Wormwood was Bacon's first novel. "The real and rather astonishing merits of *A Star Called Wormwood* lie in the writing and in the characterizations of the Meredith children. . . . [This book] clearly adds a new name to the short list of first-rate novelists who still care for style and form in their craft," commented a critic for the *New York Herald Tribune.* A *Kirkus* reviewer called it "a rather brilliant, if not always focussed, novel whose sight, sound and feel has its own power."

Bacon has traveled extensively, especially in Africa. The author used her knowledge of the country as a backdrop for *Sophia Scrooby Preserved.* In reviewing the book, a *New York Times* critic noted, "Martha Bacon has a lively style and when she is sure of her scene, writes with wit and perception. Her story opens promisingly and is most appealing when it pictures life in an African village. . . ."

AVOCATIONAL INTERESTS: Traveling.

BIOGRAPHICAL/CRITICAL SOURCES: Christian Science Monitor, April 26, 1947; *Saturday Review of Literature,* May 31, 1947; *Kirkus,* September 15, 1948; *New York Herald Tribune Weekly Book Review,* November 14, 1948; *New York Times Book Review,* October 20, 1968.*

*　　*　　*

BADILLO, Herman 1929-

PERSONAL: Surname is pronounced Ba-*dee*-yo; born August 21, 1929, in Caguas, Puerto Rico; came to United States in 1940; son of Francisco and Carmen (Rivera) Badillo; married Norma Lit, 1948 (divorced, 1960); married Irma Deutsch Liebling (a governor's assistant), May 7, 1961; children: David Alan; stepchildren: Loren, Mark. *Education:* City College (now of the City University of New York), B.B.A. (magna cum laude), 1951; Brooklyn Law School, LL.B. (cum laude, valedictorian), 1954, J.D. (cum laude), 1967. *Politics:* Democrat. *Home:* 405 West 259th St., Bronx, N.Y. 10471. *Office:* City Hall, New York, N.Y. 10007.

CAREER: Ferro, Berdon & Co. (certified public accountants), New York City, accountant, 1951-55; admitted to the Bar of New York State, 1955; Permut & Badillo (law firm), New York City, partner of firm, 1955-61; became certified public accountant, 1956; New York City Department of Real Estate, New York City, deputy commissioner, 1962; New York City Department of Relocation, New York City, commissioner, 1962-65; Borough of Bronx, Bronx, N.Y., president, 1966-69; Stroock & Stroock & Lavan (Wall Street law firm), partner of firm, 1970-73; U.S. House of Representatives, congressman from 21st New York district, 1970-78, serving on the Education and Labor Committee, also member of several subcommittees; appointed deputy mayor for management, New York City, 1978—. Delegate to New York State Constitutional Convention, 1966. Adjunct professor at the Graduate School of Urban Education, Fordham University, 1970—. Member of board of directors of Mount Sinai Hospital, New York City. *Member:* Alpha Beta Psi, Beta Gamma Sigma, Sigma Alpha. *Awards, honors:* LL.D., City College of the City University of New York, 1972.

WRITINGS: (With Milton Haynes) *A Bill of No Rights: Attica and the American Prison System,* Outerbridge & Lazard, 1972.

SIDELIGHTS: Herman Badillo is one of the most prominent Puerto Rican-born politicians in the United States. Orphaned at the age of five, Badillo was sent to the United States to live with relatives. He spent most of his childhood in the East Harlem section of New York City.

Badillo's political career began in 1960 when he was chairman of the East Harlem Kennedy for President committee. The next year he challenged Alfred E. Santangelo, the regular Democratic candidate, for the post of district leader of the sixteenth assembly district. He lost by only seventy-five votes and demanded a recount, but before a decision was made he was appointed deputy of the New York City Real Estate Commission.

In 1965 Badillo won the November election for Bronx borough president. Two weeks after the election the Federal Court invalidated a literacy provision of the Voting Rights Act which had been passed that year. This act had allowed over four thousand Puerto Ricans to vote in November who had not previously been allowed to cast ballots. Since Badillo had won by only 2,086 votes, his incumbent Republican opponent demanded a new election. The court, however, upheld Badillo's victory.

While serving as Bronx president, Badillo announced his intention to run for mayor of New York. Although he placed third in the 1969 primary election, this was considered a good showing since it was his first citywide campaign. Badillo was more successful in 1970 when he was elected congressman from New York's twenty-first district. The Democratic primary race was close, with the district divided between Puerto Rican, black, Irish, Italian, and Jewish voters, but Badillo defeated a large number of candidates and went on to win the November election by a wide margin. He became the first Puerto Rican to hold a voting membership in Congress.

BIOGRAPHICAL/CRITICAL SOURCES: New York Post, September 1, 1965, June 5, 1969; *New York Times,* November 4, 1965; *New York,* February 10, 1969; *New Yorker,* June 2, 1973.

*　　*　　*

BAHLMAN, Dudley Ward Rhodes 1923-

PERSONAL: Born March 19, 1923, in Cincinnati, Ohio; son of William T. and Janet (Rhodes) Bahlman; married Jean Mitchell, December 29, 1951; children: Dudley R., Anne M. *Education:* Yale University, B.A., 1946, M.A., 1947, Ph.D., 1951. *Home address:* Sabin Dr., Williamstown, Mass. 01267.

CAREER: Yale University, New Haven, Conn., instructor, 1951-54, assistant professor of history, 1954-59; Williams College, Williamstown, Mass., associate professor, 1962-67, professor of history, 1967—, dean of faculty, 1968-75, head of department, 1978—. *Military service:* U.S. Army Medical Corps, 1943-46. *Member:* American Historical Association, Royal Historical Society (fellow), Elizabethan Club. *Awards, honors:* Morse fellowship from Yale University, 1957-58; Guggenheim fellow, 1965-66.

WRITINGS: The Moral Revolution of 1688, Yale University Press, 1957; *The Diary of Sir Edward Hamilton,* Oxford University Press, 1972. Contributor to *Victorian Studies.*

WORK IN PROGRESS: Deceased Wife's Sister, a historical study of a Victorian legislative folly; an article on politics and church patronage in the Victorian age.

BAILEY, Lloyd Richard 1936-

PERSONAL: Born October 29, 1936, in Burnsville, N.C. *Education:* Attended Mars Hill Junior College, 1954-56; Duke University, B.A., 1958, B.D., 1961; Hebrew Union College—Jewish Institute of Religion, New York, N.Y., Ph.D., 1967. *Office:* Divinity School, Duke University, Durham, N.C. 27706.

CAREER: Union Theological Seminary, New York, N.Y., assistant professor of Old Testament, 1967-71; Duke University, Durham, N.C., associate professor of Old Testament, 1971—.

WRITINGS: Where Is Noah's Ark?, Abingdon, 1978; *Biblical Perspectives on Death,* Fortress, 1979. Editor of supplement to *Interpreter's Dictionary of the Bible.*

*   *   *

BAIN, Carl E. 1930-

PERSONAL: Born February 9, 1930, in Jackson, Miss.; married Billye Joan Brothers, June 17, 1969; children: John Roderick. *Education:* Baylor University, B.A., 1952, M.A., 1953; Johns Hopkins University, Ph.D., 1961. *Home:* 1248 Lively Ridge Rd. N.E., Atlanta, Ga. 30329. *Office:* Department of English, Emory University, Atlanta, Ga. 30322.

CAREER: Teacher of English and mathematics at military school in Bainbridge, Md., 1953-56, head of department of mathematics, 1955-56; Johns Hopkins University, Baltimore, Md., junior instructor in English, 1956-60; Emory University, Atlanta, Ga., instructor, 1960-62, assistant professor, 1962-65, associate professor of English, 1966—, acting dean of Graduate School, 1969-70. Part-time instructor at Maryland Institute, 1958-60. Executive secretary of South Atlantic Graduate English Cooperative Agreement, 1967—. *Member:* Modern Language Association of America.

WRITINGS: The Norton Introduction to Literature: Drama, Norton, 1973, abridge edition (with Jerome Beaty and J. Paul Hunter), 1973, 2nd abridged edition, 1977; *The Norton Introduction to Literature: Drama—Questions and Suggestions,* Norton, 1973, abridged edition (with Beaty and Hunter), 1973, 2nd abridged edition, 1977. Contributor of articles and reviews to literature journals. Head of editorial board of *Emory University Quarterly,* 1966-68.

WORK IN PROGRESS: An Experience of Demons, on trends in drama, 1945-65.

*   *   *

BAIN, Chester Ward 1919-

PERSONAL: Born August 11, 1919, in Bradshaw, Va.; son of Hubert Ward and Nellie May (Gwynne) Bain; married Sylvia Rubinowitz, August 6, 1944; children: Eugene Ward, Charles Lynwood, Douglas Gwynne. *Education:* Attended Roanoke College, 1937-38; University of Virginia, B.A., 1948, M.A., 1950, Ph.D., 1955. *Religion:* Methodist. *Home:* 1634 Green St., #3, Columbia, S.C. 29201. *Office:* Department of Political Science, University of South Carolina, Columbia, S.C. 29208.

CAREER: University of Virginia, Charlottesville, member of faculty, 1951-57, associate professor of political science, 1957-60; University of South Carolina, Columbia, professor of political science and head of department, 1960-63; Emory University, Atlanta, Ga., professor of political science, 1963-66, head of department, 1964-66; University of South Carolina, Olin D. Johnson Professor of Political Science, 1966—, dean of College of Humanities and Social Sciences,

1976—. Visiting professor at West Virginia University, 1957-58, and Case Western Reserve University, 1974-75. Volunteer for International Executive Service Corps. *Military service:* U.S. Army, 1941-45; received Legion of Merit. *Member:* American Political Science Association, Southern Political Science Association (president, 1979-80), Phi Sigma Alpha.

WRITINGS: Annexation in Virginia: The Use of the Judicial Process for Readjusting City-County Boundaries, University Press of Virginia, 1966; *A Body Incorporate: The Evolution of City-County Separation in Virginia,* University Press of Virginia, 1967; (contributor) William C. Havard, editor, *The Changing Politics of the South,* Louisiana State University Press, 1972. Contributor to political science journals.

*   *   *

BAIRD, J(oseph) L. 1933-

PERSONAL: Born April 15, 1933, in Gastonia, N.C.; son of David H. and Bertis L. (Barrett) Baird; married Lorrayne Yates (a professor), May 13, 1961; children: Bertis Eve. *Education:* Appalachian State University, B.S., 1957, M.A., 1959; University of Kentucky, Ph.D., 1966. *Home:* 336 Park Ave., Kent, Ohio 44240. *Office:* Department of English, Kent State University, Kent, Ohio 44242.

CAREER: Kent State University, Kent, Ohio, staff member in department of English, 1964—. *Member:* Mediaeval Academy of America.

WRITINGS: Rossignol, Kent State University Press, 1978; *La Querelle de la rose,* University of North Carolina Press, 1978. Contributor to literature journals.

WORK IN PROGRESS: Translating the Latin chronicle of Salimbene de Adam, three volumes.

SIDELIGHTS: Baird's main academic interests are medieval literature, from *Beowulf* to Chaucer, including old French, medieval Latin, and Italian literature.

*   *   *

BAKALIS, Michael J. 1938-

PERSONAL: Born March 23, 1938, in Berwyn, Ill.; son of John Bakalis; married January 21, 1961; wife's name Desi; children: Patti, Erin. *Education:* Northwestern University, B.A., 1959, M.A., 1962, Ph.D., 1966. *Politics:* Democrat. *Religion:* Greek Orthodox. *Home:* 1460 Coral Berry, Downers Grove, Ill. 60515. *Agent:* Sam Freifeld, 33 North La Salle St., Chicago, Ill. 60602. *Office:* Office of the State Comptroller, 160 North La Salle St., Chicago, Ill. 60601.

CAREER: Former high school social studies teacher in Evanston, Ill., former junior high school teacher of language arts in Illinois; state superintendent of public instruction for State of Illinois, 1971-75; Northwestern University, Evanston, visiting professor of education, 1975-76; State of Illinois, Chicago, state comptroller, 1976—. Held positions at Rosary College (River Forest, Ill.) and at Sangamon State University; guest lecturer at Harvard University, 1973. Member of National Institute of Education task force on ethnic education; member of National Science Foundation advisory committee, 1973.

AWARDS, HONORS: Awards from Hellenic Professional Society and Chicago Kent College of Law, both in 1971, from State Minority Caucus, Michael Reese Medical Center, Illinois Association of Student Governments, Illinois Association of School Administrators, and Baptist General State Conference, all in 1973, from Chicago Manpower Area

Planning Council, Operation PUSH, and Illinois Television Commission, all in 1974, and from Puerto Rican Educators and Illinois Association of School Boards, both in 1975.

WRITINGS: A Strategy for Excellence: Reaching for New Standards in Education, Archon Press, 1974; *A Sense of Purpose,* Nelson-Hall, 1978. Contributor to professional journals.

* * *

BAKER, James T. 1940-

PERSONAL: Born February 5, 1940, in Clarksville, Tex.; son of Marvin P. (a teacher) and Gladys (a teacher; maiden name, Wood) Baker; married Jill Withrow (an artist), August 25, 1963; children: Virginia Wood, Elizabeth Ann. *Education:* Baylor University, B.A., 1962; Southern Baptist Seminary, B.D., 1965; Florida State University, M.A., 1966, Ph.D., 1968. *Home:* 335 Sumpter, Bowling Green, Ky. 42101. *Office:* Western Kentucky University, Bowling Green, Ky. 42101.

CAREER: Ordained Baptist minister; pastor of Baptist churches; Florida State University, Tallahassee, chaplain, 1964-68; Western Kentucky University, Bowling Green, professor, 1968—. Fulbright professor, 1977. *Member:* Society of American Church Historians. *Awards, honors:* Robert Connor Award for writing, 1978.

WRITINGS: Thomas Merton, Social Critic, University Press of Kentucky, 1971; *Faith for a Dark Saturday,* Judson, 1973; *Under the Sign of the Waterbearer,* Love Street Books, 1976; *A Southern Baptist in the White House,* Westminster, 1977; (with Mary Ann Kearny) *Life, Liberty, and the Pursuit of Happiness,* Newbury House, 1978.

WORK IN PROGRESS: Eric Hoffer: The Passionate Mind.

* * *

BAKER, John F. 1931-

PERSONAL: Born December 21, 1931, in Lincoln, England; son of Louis A. (a bank official) and Gladys (Firth) Baker; married wife, Lila, November 8, 1958 (separated). *Education:* Received M.A. from Oxford University. *Home:* 7 East 14th St., New York, N.Y. 10011.

CAREER/WRITINGS: Yorkshire Post, Leeds, England, editorial writer, 1954-57; Reuters News Agency, New York City and London, England, desk editor, 1957-64; *Venture* (magazine), New York City, articles editor, 1964-71; Readers Digest Books, New York City, senior editor, 1971-73; *Publishers Weekly,* New York City, managing editor and contributor of regular interviews, 1973-77; *Bookviews,* New York City, editor-in-chief and contributor of regular interviews, 1977-79. Contributor to *Pages,* Gale, *Conversations With Writers,* Gale, *The Author Speaks,* Bowker, and *PW Interviews,* Bowker. Contributor of articles and reviews to *Venture, Holiday, Diversion, Better Homes and Gardens,* and *Family Circle. Military service:* British Army, Education Corps, 1950-52.

* * *

BAKER, Robert G. 1928-
(Bobby Baker)

PERSONAL: Born November 12, 1928, in Easley, S.C.; son of Ernest R. (a postman) and Mary E. (Norman) Baker; married wife, Dorothy, November 24, 1949 (divorced February 16, 1976); children: Robert, Jr., James P., Cissy, Lynda, Lyndon (deceased). *Education:* Received degree from

George Washington University; American University, L.L.B. *Politics:* "Democrat—Independent." *Religion:* Baptist. *Home and office:* 2000 M St. NW, Washington, D.C. 20036. *Agent:* Sterling Lord Agency, 660 Madison Ave., New York, N.Y. 10021.

CAREER: Attorney; builder and developer, 1953—; writer and movie producer, 1976—. Secretary to the Democratic majority of the U.S. Senate, 1955-63. Chairman of the board and chief executive officer of Mecklenburg Enterprises. *Member:* American Bar Association, Delta Theta Phi, University Club.

*WRITINGS—*Under name Bobby Baker: (With Larry L. King) *Wheeling and Dealing: Confessions of a Capitol Hill Operator,* Norton, 1978.

WORK IN PROGRESS: A book about the twenty-five best and twenty-five worst U.S. senators, 1933-1980.

SIDELIGHTS: Baker told *CA:* "My single greatest motivation is to tell a truthful story about a tragedy that never happened."

Baker began his career in government at the age of fourteen as a Senate page boy and quickly garnered a reputation for knowing which members of the Senate had fondnesses for women, drink, or bribes. Lyndon Johnson, then the Senate majority leader, took the young Baker under his wing, and, as Baker reported, said to him: "Mr. Baker, I understand you know where the bodies are buried in the Senate. I'd appreciate it if you'd come to my office and talk with me." Baker was subsequently hired as the secretary to the Democratic majority, a position he used to great advantage. Regarded by many to be the second most powerful man in the Senate, Baker was called "the 101st Senator" by John Kennedy. His mentor Johnson said of Baker, "He is the first person I talk to in the morning and the last one at night."

"I was industrious, hard-working, ambitious, and I cared about my job," Baker said in explanation of his rapid success. "I very early grew to love the Senate: its air of excitement and sense of making history, its aura of power." Baker was also successful in transforming his $19,600 salary to a $2 million fortune in cattle, insurance, vending machines, and gambling concessions in the Caribbean. He wrote in *Wheeling and Dealing:* "Like my bosses and sponsors in the Senate, I was ambitious and eager to feather my personal nest.... As they presumed their high stations to entitle them to accept gratuities or hospitalities from patrons who had special axes to grind, so did I. As they took advantage of privileged information to get in on the ground floor of attractive investments, so did I. As they used their powerful positions to gain loans or credit that otherwise might not have been granted, so did I."

Baker's empire began to crumble when in 1963 he was accused of delivering bribery money to Senator Robert Kerr of Oklahoma. Kerr, a powerful senator known for his greed, had accepted a $400,000 bribe from savings and loan associations in exchange for voting as they wished him to. ("Money was Senator Kerr's God," wrote Baker.) "It was over this money that I went to jail," said Baker, who delivered part of the bribe to Kerr but was later accused of keeping $50,000 of the money. In 1967, Baker was indicted by a grand jury on nine criminal counts of tax evasion, theft, and fraud. He began serving his sixteen-month jail sentence in January, 1971.

Baker still denies his guilt of the charges on which he was convicted. He recently told Larry Swindell: "It was a time when just about everybody in the Senate was on the take, without having to feel good about it. It's just the way things were done then. I wouldn't deny being involved in little cover-ups here and there, but nothing that had to do with the charges that were brought against me—the charges on which I was convicted, the crimes of which I was innocent.''

Refusing to implicate any other party members or to plea bargain, Baker explained, ''The Democratic Party was damn good to me and I'd have destroyed a lot of people if I'd testified.'' After his conviction, however, party members were no longer so helpful. Despite the fact that Baker was almost a surrogate son to Johnson, he dropped Baker almost immediately when his troubles began. ''Friendship with Lyndon Johnson was a one-way street,'' Baker wrote. He believed Johnson to be ''a coward for letting me down. I certainly understood why, under the circumstances, I had to be sacrificed. The presidency was at stake. But he could have talked to me . . . he could have telephoned. Well, he didn't.''

When ex-President Johnson finally asked to see Baker after he had served his prison term, Johnson told his protege: ''If there was any way in the world I could have turned off the investigation when I became President I'd have gladly done it. But I knew it would be politically disastrous.'' When Baker left the ranch, he noticed that Johnson did not ask him to sign the guest book.

BIOGRAPHICAL/CRITICAL SOURCES: People, January 23, 1978; *New York Times Book Review*, May 28, 1978; *New Times*, June 12, 1978; *New York Review of Books*, July 20, 1978; *Philadelphia Inquirer*, September 7, 1978; Bobby Baker and Larry L. King, *Wheeling and Dealing: Confessions of a Capitol Hill Operator*, Norton, 1978.

* * *

BALAKIAN, Nona 1919-

PERSONAL: Born September 4, 1919, in Constantinople (now Istanbul), Turkey; came to United States, 1925; daughter of Diran (a physician) and Koharig (Panosyan) Balakian. *Education:* Barnard College, B.A., 1942; Columbia University, M.S., 1943. *Home:* 600 West 116th St., New York, N.Y. 10027. *Agent:* John Schaffner, 425 East 51st St., New York, N.Y. 10022. *Office:* New York Times, 229 West 43rd St., New York, N.Y. 10036.

CAREER: New York Times, New York, N.Y., assistant to book review editor, 1943—, associate editor of *New York Times Book Review*, 1963—, book reviewer, essayist. Consultant to BOA Editions (poetry publisher). *Member:* Author's Guild, P.E.N. American Center (member of executive board, 1972—), National Book Critics Circle (member of executive board, 1974—; secretary 1974-76).

WRITINGS: (Editor, with Charles Simmons) *The Creative Present: Notes on Contemporary American Fiction*, Doubleday, 1963; *Critical Encounters: Literary Views and Reviews, 1953-1977*, Bobbs-Merrill, 1978. Contributor to periodicals, including *New Leader, New Republic, Kenyon Review, New York Times, Columbia Journalism Review*, and *Christian Science Monitor*. Member of editorial staff of *Ararat Quarterly*.

WORK IN PROGRESS: A critical work on William Saroyan.

SIDELIGHTS: Balakian told *CA:* ''I am eager to promote and encourage literary journalism in America—it is vital to our culture to expand book reviewing on a higher level throughout the country. I feel fortunate in having been connected with the best journal of book reviewing in the United States, but would like to see its example spread. (I have writ-

ten on the subject and talked about it over the air as well as on panel discussions.) The future of our literature depends on it.''

Critical Encounters has been highly praised for pushing for an expansion and refinement in book reviewing. In a review in *New York Times Book Review*, William H. Pritchard acknowledged Balakian as an expert reviewer of book reviewing. He noted that ''Balakian is in a position to speak with insight and authority about the state of American literary journalism, and the moments in which she occupies herself with the subject are the best ones in the book.''

Joyce Carol Oates called Balakian's *Critical Encounters* ''superb.'' ''The individual essays are, almost without exception, extremely well done,'' declared Oates, who found the book extraordinary in a number of ways. ''*Critical Encounters* is, then, something of an anomaly,'' wrote Oates, ''a highly literate, informative, sensitive, and perhaps even prophetic book by a professional journalist who has been, since 1943, at the very center of the most dizzying literary activity imaginable.''

BIOGRAPHICAL/CRITICAL SOURCES: Publishers Weekly, May 8, 1978; *New Republic*, May 20, 1978; *Los Angeles Times*, June 16, 1978; *New York Times Book Review*, June 25, 1978; *Saturday Review*, September 30, 1978; *Washington Post Book World*, October 22, 1978; *New York Times*, November 16, 1978.

* * *

BALET, Jan (Bernard) 1913-

PERSONAL: Born July 20, 1913, in Bremen, Germany; came to United States in 1938, naturalized citizen; children: Peter. *Education:* Attended Arts and Crafts School and Academy of Fine Arts, both in Munich, Germany. *Residence:* New York, N.Y., and Long Island, N.Y.

CAREER: Writer; illustrator; painter. Former art director of *Mademoiselle* and *Seventeen* magazines, both in New York City. Former illustrator for New York City department stores and for many national advertising firms. Participant in Art Directors Club exhibitions. *Awards, honors:* Received two gold medals and fifteen awards of merit from Art Directors Club.

WRITINGS—All self-illustrated: *Amos and the Moon*, Oxford University Press, 1948, Walck, 1959; *Ned and Ed and the Lion*, Oxford University Press, 1949; *What Makes an Orchestra*, Walck, 1951; *The Five Rollatinis*, Lippincott, 1959; *Joanjo: Eine Geschichte aus Portugal*, Betz (Munich), 1965, translation published as *Joanjo: A Portuguese Tale*, Delacorte, 1967; *The Gift: A Portuguese Christmas Tale*, Delacorte, 1967; *Der Koenig und der Besenbinder*, Betz, 1967, translation published as *The King and the Broom Maker*, Delacorte, 1968; *Ladismus, oder, Die Vorteile einer hoeheren Schulbildung*, Betz, 1969, translation published as *Ladismouse; or, The Advantages of Higher Education*, Walck, 1971; *Jan Balet: Bamaelde* (paintings), H. Holzinger, 1969.

Illustrator: Dorothea Zack Hanle, *The Golden Ladle*, Ziff-Davis, 1945; Pedro Antonio de Alarcon, *Tales From the Spanish*, Story Classics, 1948; Helen Wing, *Rosalinde*, Container Corp., 1952; Patricia Jones, *Rumpelstiltskin* (adapted from *Grimms' Fairy Tales*), Container Corp., 1955; Jones, *Fair, Brown and Trembling: An Irish Fairy Tale* (adaptation), Container Corp., 1957; Martha Bennett King, *Birthday Angel*, Container Corp., 1959; King, *The Snow Queen* (adaptation of the story by Hans Christian Anderson), Container Corp., 1961; *The Princess and the Pea*, Parents' Magazine Press, 1962; *The Magic Fishbone*, Parents' Magazine Press, 1963; George Selden, *The Mice, the Monks and the Christmas Tree*, Macmillan, 1963; Aileen Brothers and Cora Holsclaw, *Just One Me*, Follett, 1967; James Kruess, *Ein-, Eich- & Mondhorn*, Betz, 1968. Contributor of illustrations to various magazines, including *Glamour, Good Housekeeping, Vogue,* and *House and Gardens*.

SIDELIGHTS: Balet's painting has been influenced by Egyptian, Greek, and Roman primitive art, as well as by Lautrec, Picasso, Miro, and other modern French artists. He has traveled through Yugoslavia, Italy, France, Spain, Rumania, Switzerland, and Austria. *Avocational Interests:* Flying his own plane.

BIOGRAPHICAL/CRITICAL SOURCES: American Artist, November, 1946, January, 1951; *Graphis,* No. 51, 1954.*

* * *

BALL, Edith L. 1905-

PERSONAL: Born September 4, 1905, in New York, N.Y. *Education:* Columbia University, B.S., 1926, M.A., 1927; New York University, Ed.D., 1953. *Religion:* Episcopalian. *Home:* 6110 East Fifth St., Apt. 223, Tucson, Ariz. 85711.

CAREER: Worked as girls' club leader at York Settlement House, 1925, and as elementary school physical education teacher, 1926-27; Kent State College (now University), Kent, Ohio, assistant professor of health and physical education, 1927-29; Columbia University, Teachers College, New York City, technical assistant in health education, 1929-30; University of Maryland, College Park, director of physical education for women, 1930-31; Western Reserve University (now Case Western Reserve University), Cleveland, Ohio, director of physical education and recreation for School of Nursing, 1931-37; supervisor of recreation, district director of communities, and director of war service activities for Works Progress Administration in Maryland, Delaware, and District of Columbia, 1937-43; War Department, Washington, D.C., employee counselor on housing, finances, and organization, 1943; Office of Residence Halls, Washington, D.C., 1943-47, began as assistant director, became director of recreation and education; Stuyvesant Neighborhood House, New York City, executive director, 1947-50; New York University, New York City, 1950—, began as instructor, became professor emeritus, 1973—; writer, 1973—. Dance teacher, 1926-27. Head of Maryland State Division of Girls' and Women's Sports, 1937-42; committee member of National Social Welfare Assembly; member of board of directors of New York City's Neighborhood House, 1963-72, and American Youth Hostels; member of Youth Division of Federation of Protestant Welfare Agencies. Speaker at national and international meetings; adviser and consultant.

MEMBER: American Recreation Society (head of hospital section, 1956-57, vice-president of section, 1954; president, 1962), American Association for Health, Physical Education and Recreation, National Association of Social Work, American Association of University Professors, American Camping Association, National Recreation Association, American Association of University Women, National Recreation and Park Association (member of board of trustees, 1965—), Adult Education Association, District of Columbia Association for Health, Physical Education and Recreation (vice-president, 1946-47), Pi Lambda Theta (president of Rho chapter, 1955; national vice-president, 1957-61), Kappa Delta Pi, Alpha Kappa Delta, College Women's Club of Jackson Heights.

WRITINGS: Developing Volunteers for Service in Recreation Programs (monograph), National Recreation Association, 1958; *Hosteling* (monograph), American Youth Hostels, 1971; (with Robert Cipreone) *Leisure Services Preparation*, Prentice-Hall, 1978. Also editor of *Creative Activites for Older People.* Contributor to physical education, recreation, and education journals.

WORK IN PROGRESS: A study of recreation functions and personnel in private agencies; research on the contribution of recreation to the hospitalized chronically ill.

* * *

BANDI, Hans-Georg 1920-

PERSONAL: Born September 3, 1920, in Thun, Switzerland; son of J. H. and V. (Thomas) Bandi; married Regula Klipstein, October 1, 1945. *Education:* University of Fribourg, Ph.D., 1945. *Home:* Scharnachtalstrasse 12, Berne, Switzerland. *Office:* Seminar fuer Urgeschichte, University of Berne, 7P, Berne, Switzerland.

CAREER: Voelkerkundemuseum, Basel, Switzerland, assistant curator, 1945-50; University of Berne, Berne, Switzerland, professor of prehistoric archaeology, 1950—. Visiting professor at Brown University, 1959 and 1962-63, and University of Alaska, 1962-63. Curator of Berne Historical Museum, 1950—. *Military service:* Swiss Air Force; became colonel. *Member:* Swiss Academy of Humanities (honorary member), German Archaeological Institute.

WRITINGS—In English: (With Joergen Meldgaard) *Archaeological Investigations on Clavering Island, Northeast Greenland,* C. A. Reitzel, 1952; (with Johannes Maringer) *Art in the Ice Age, Spanish Levant Art, Arctic Art,* translated by Robert Allen, Praeger, 1953; *Urgeschichte der Eskimo,* Gustav Fischer Verlag, 1964, translation by Ann E. Keep published as *Eskimo Prehistory,* University of Washington Press, 1969; (with others) *The Art of the Stone Age,* translated by Keep, Crown, 1961, 2nd edition, Methuen, 1970.

Other: *Das Magdalenien der Schweiz,* Chur, 1947; *Die Schweiz zur Rentierzeit, Kulturgeschichte der Rentierjaeger am Ende der Eiszeit,* Huber, 1947; (with Maringer) *Kunst der Eiszeit,* Holbein-Verlag, 1952; (with Roland Bay and others) *Birsmatten-Basisgrotte; Eine mittelsteinzeitliche Fundstelle im unteren Birstal,* Staempfli, 1964; *Alaska. Urgeschichte Geschichte, Gegenwart,* Kohlhammer, 1967.

WORK IN PROGRESS: "Evaluation of archaeological field work on St. Lawrence Island, Alaska; interpretation of the art of hunter populations, through collaboration of prehistory, zoology, and ethnology."

* * *

BARAM, Phillip J(ason) 1938-

PERSONAL: Surname is pronounced Ba-*ram;* born July 29, 1938, in Woonsocket, R.I.; son of Max (in textiles) and Eva (Gertz) Baram; married Eleanor Chalet, August 29, 1965; children: Yoav, Yaakov. *Education:* Brown University, B.A. (cum laude), 1959; Hebrew University of Jerusalem, certificate, 1960; Harvard University, M.A., 1961; Boston University, Ph.D., 1976. *Religion:* Jewish. *Home:* 110 Warren St., #11, Brighton, Mass. 02135. *Office:* Employment and Economic Policy Administration, City of Boston, 15 Beacon St., Boston, Mass. 02108.

CAREER: Abelard-Schuman Ltd., New York City, book editor, 1961-62; *New York Jewish Post and Opinion,* New York City, reporter, 1961; high school teacher of history and geography at schools in Southbridge, Braintree, and Reading, Mass., 1963-67; Boston University, Boston, Mass., teaching fellow and lecturer in history, 1967-70; Worcester State College, Worcester, Mass., assistant professor of history, 1970-73; Roxbury Community College, Roxbury, Mass., associate professor of history, 1973-75; Massachusetts Rehabilitation Commission, Brookline, Mass., occupational research specialist, 1976-77; City of Boston, program manager in Youth Division of Employment and Economic Policy Administration, 1978—. Adjunct professor at Boston State College, 1976—. Lecturer in Middle Eastern issues. Has made television appearances. *Member:* American Historical Association, Society of Historians of American Foreign Relations, National Education Association, Association of American Professors for Peace in the Middle East, Sierra Club. *Awards, honors:* Truman Library grant, summer, 1977.

WRITINGS: The Department of State in the Middle East, 1919-1945, University of Pennsylvania Press, 1978. Contributor to history and Middle East studies journals, including *Historian* and *Jerusalem Journal of International Relations.*

WORK IN PROGRESS: Research on U.S.-Saudi Arabian relations since 1945, on the U.S. Department of State since Acheson, and on an employment program in the energy conservation field in the Boston area.

SIDELIGHTS: Baram told *CA:* "Israel, the Arab Middle East, and U.S. foreign policy have been longtime interests that I sought to synthesize when I wrote my book. While literature on the Middle East is enormous, much is polemical and/or based on secondary sources. In my work I have dealt chiefly with hitherto untapped primary sources. That fact, plus the fact that my book tries to present a comprehensive perspective of the period and the areas under review—a sculpture-in-the-round effect, as it were—has given me the satisfaction of knowing that I have spaded new ground on topics of much interest to different publics. I might add that the research and writing represented a long, laborious solo effort."

AVOCATIONAL INTERESTS: Hiking, backpacking, gardening, jogging, meditation, playing the piano, ecology, *gestalt,* the Bible.

* * *

BARBER, Jesse 1893-1979

OBITUARY NOTICE: Born in 1893 in Charlotte, N.C.; died January 27, 1979. Clergyman, university official, and author. A Presbyterian minister, from 1941 to 1950 Barber was dean of Lincoln University's theological seminary in Pennsylvania. He was also active in several civil rights organizations, including the National Association for the Advancement of Colored People (NAACP); his goal was a "nonsegregated church in a nonsegregated society." He was editor of *New Advance* magazine and author of *Climbing Jacob's Ladder.* Obituaries and other sources: *Washington Post,* January 29, 1979.

* * *

BARCLAY, Hartley Wade 1903-1978

PERSONAL: Born December 3, 1903, in Gladbrook, Iowa; died November 13, 1978, in Rye, N.Y.; son of Wade Crawford and May (Hartley) Barclay; married Marjorie Kathleen Whitley, February 16, 1924 (died, 1967); married Lois Beveridge Wilson, October 28, 1967; children: (first marriage) Jean Marjorie (deceased), Hartley Wade, James Crawford.

Education: Ohio Wesleyan University, A.B., 1924. *Home:* King St., Port Chester, N.Y. 10573. *Office address:* P.O. Box 811, Port Chester, N.Y. 10573.

CAREER: Machine shop worker at Lukenheimer Company; McGraw-Hill Publishing Company, New York City, research director of electrical trades division, 1930-31; editorial director and secretary of Conover-Mast Corporation, 1931-42; *New York Times,* New York City, business writer, 1947-52, industrial advertisement manager, 1952-56; publisher of *Tide* magazine, 1956-59; *Automotive Industries,* Radnor, Penn., editor and publisher, 1959-70; Chilton Company (trade publishing house), Radnor, vice president and director, 1962-70; editor and publisher of *Foundation Survey of Corporate and Industrial Systems Communications,* 1970. Founder of Management Research Institute, 1942; eastern vice president and engineer at Nova-Chrome, Inc. Lecturer on industrial production management at U.S. Army Industrial College; instructor in aeronavigation, meteorology, and regulations for the Federal Aviation Administration; lecturer to educational, government, engineering, and business groups. Head of Hartley W. Barclay and Associates (aeronautical consulting firm); consultant to Taft-Pierce Manufacturing Company, Marine Products Company, Henry G. Thompson & Son Company, General Motors Corporation, Copper & Brass Research Association, and Rye, N.Y.; special adviser to New York State Legislature Select Joint Committee on Economic Affairs. Editor of *Mill and Factory.*

MEMBER: American Ordnance Association, American Society for Testing and Materials, American Society for Metals, American Institute of Industrial Engineers, National Press Club, Civil Air Patrol, Institute of Management Sciences, Society of Manufacturing Engineers (founder; chairman of Westchester chapter), Protestant Episcopal Church (perpetual deacon), Edison Pioneers, Tri-State Yacht Club, Bahamas Automobile Club, Engineers Society of Detroit, Sigma Delta Chi, Phi Gamma Delta, Pi Delta Epsilon. *Awards, honors:* Distinguished service award, New York State Society of Professional Engineers, 1952; named honorary member of 25th Infantry Division and 101st Airborne Division of U.S. Army, 1965.

WRITINGS: Ford Production Methods, Harper & Brothers, 1936; *Labor's Stake in the American Way,* Atlantic, 1938; *Red Labor Marches in Mexico,* Conover-Mast, 1938; (editor) *How Your Business Can Help Win the War,* Simon & Schuster, 1942; *The Postwar Strategy of Peace,* [Port Chester, N.Y.], 1943; *MRI Standard Industrial News Subjects,* Management Research Institute, 1970. Also author of *Survey of Industrial Distribution,* 1931, and *The Timetable of Dictatorship,* 1940, and editor of *The Foundation Survey of Production and Sales Planning, The First Standard Manual of Public Information Procedures, Making Money in New York,* 1976, and *Preacher's Kid,* 1977. Contributor to *Atlantic, New York Times,* and other publications.

OBITUARIES: New York Times, November 14, 1978.*

* * *

BARDI, Pietro Maria 1900-

PERSONAL: Born February 21, 1900, in La Spezia, Italy; son of Pasquale (a merchant) and Elisa (Viggiani) Bardi; married Lina Bo (an architect). *Religion:* Roman Catholic. *Home:* Rua General Moura 200, Morumby, Sao Paulo, Brazil. *Office:* Museu de Arte, Caixa Postal 6789, Sao Paulo, Brazil.

CAREER: Museu de Arte, Sao Paulo, Brazil, director, 1974—.

WRITINGS—In English: *Art Treasures of the Sao Paulo Museum and the Development of Art in Brazil,* translated by John Drummond, Abrams, 1956; *The Arts in Brazil: A New Museum at Sao Paulo,* translated by Drummond, Edizioni del Milione, 1956; *Lasar Segall, 1891-1957,* [published], 1957, translation by Drummond published as *Lasar Segall,* Edizioni del Milione, 1959; (editor) *Sixteen Paintings of Giorgio Morandi,* Edizioni del Milione, 1957; (editor) Marino Marini, *Graphic Work and Paintings,* Abrams, 1960; *I giardini tropicali di Burle Marx,* G. G. Goerlich, 1964, translation published as *The Tropical Gardens of Burle Marx,* Reinhold, 1964; *New Brazilian Art,* translated by Drummond, Praeger, 1970, published in Holland as *Profile of the New Brazilian Art,* Kosmos, 1970; *Architecture: The World We Build,* F. Watts, 1972.

Other: *Emilio Gola,* Istituto Nazionale l'Unione Cinematografica Educativa, 1930; *Federico Faruffini,* Istituto Nazionale l'Unione Cinematografica Educativa, 1934; (editor) *Ernesto de Fiori,* Hoepli, 1950; *Museu de Arte de Sao Paulo* (title means "Museum of Art of Sao Paulo"), Editora Codex, 1968; *Berco Udler: Meninos, namorados, morte* (title means "Berco Udler: Boys, Lovers, Death"), Kosmos, 1969; *L'opera completa di Velazquez* (title means "Velazquez's Complete Works"), Rizzoli, 1969; *Viaggio nell' architettura* (title means "Travel Into Architecture"), Rizzoli, 1972, translation published as *Architecture: The World We Build; Museu de Arte de Sao Paulo "Assis Chateaubriand"* (title means "Sao Paulo Museum of Art 'Assis Chateaubriand'"), Graficos Brunner, 1973; *Historia da arte brasileira: Pintura escultura, arquitetura, outras artes* (title means "History of Brazilian Art: Painting, Sculpture, Architecture and Other Types of Art"), Edicoes Melhoramentos, 1975.

Author of exhibition catalogs. Editor of *Belvedere,* 1928-30, *Quadrante,* 1931-33, *Habitat,* 1950-53, and *Mirante das Artes,* 1967-68.

WORK IN PROGRESS: Historia da Arte da Prata no Brasil (title means "History of the Art of Silver in Brazil").

*   *   *

BARNARD, Howard Clive   1884-

PERSONAL: Born June 7, 1884, in London, England; son of Howard Barnard (a journalist); married Edith Gwendolen Wish (died August 20, 1956); children: Edward John, Edith Mary Joan Clifford. *Education:* Brasenose College, Oxford, M.A., 1910, B.Litt., 1911; London School of Economics and Political Science, M.A., 1912, D.Litt., 1926; also studied in France and Germany. *Home:* 54 Grosvenor Rd., Caversham, Reading, Berkshire, England.

CAREER: Headmaster of grammar school, Gillingham, Kent, England, 1925-37; University of Reading, Reading, England, professor of education, 1937-51, professor emeritus, 1951—. Also external examiner at various times for University of London, Cambridge University, Oxford University, University of Wales, Civil Service Commission, College of Preceptors, and other organizations and universities. Fellow of Trinity College of Music, London, 1930—. *Member:* College of Preceptors (fellow). *Awards, honors:* D.Litt. from University of Reading, 1974.

WRITINGS: The Little Schools of Port-Royal, Cambridge University Press, 1913; (translator and editor) *The Port-Royalists on Education,* Cambridge University Press, 1918; (editor) *The Expansion of the Anglo-Saxon Nations,* A. & C. Black, 1920; (general editor) *The Making of the British Empire,* two volumes, A. & C. Black, 1922; *The French Tradi-*

tion in Education: Ramus to Mme. Necker de Saussure, Cambridge University Press, 1922, reprinted 1970; *Principles and Practice of Geography Teaching,* University Tutorial Press, 1933; *Madame de Maintenon and Saint-Cyr,* A. & C. Black, 1934, reprinted, S. R. Publishers, 1971; *A History of English Education: From 1760 to 1944,* University of London Press, 1947, revised edition published as *A History of English Education from 1760,* 1961, published with amendments, 1970; *An Introduction to Teaching,* University of London Press, 1952, 2nd edition, 1966; *Girls at School Under the Ancien Regime* (collection of lectures), Burns & Oates, 1954; (with Joseph Albert Lauwwreys) *A Handbook of British Educational Terms, including an Outline of the British Educational System,* Harrap, 1961; (editor) Francois de Salignac de la Mothe Fenelon, *Fenelon on Education,* Cambridge University Press, 1966; *Education and the French Revolution,* Cambridge University Press, 1969; *Were Those the Days?,* Pergamon Press, 1970; *A Clowder of Cats,* Cats' Production League, 1978. Also author of geography and history text books, 1910-25.

AVOCATIONAL INTERESTS: Music, playing the organ and the piano.

*   *   *

BARNES, J.   1944-

PERSONAL: Born November 28, 1944, in Bridlington, England; son of Thomas Charles (a physician) and Joyce Margaret Barnes; married Polly Ann Rector, June 1, 1968; children: Jane Mary Barnes McDowell, Brendan Paul. *Education:* University of London, B.Sc., 1966; University of New Mexico, M.A., 1967; University of Birmingham, diploma in planning, 1969; further graduate study at University of Madrid, 1969-70. *Politics:* "Jaded." *Religion:* "Hopeful." *Home:* 10 Queen Elizabeth's Walk, London N16 OMX, England. *Office:* Bexley London Borough, Broadway, Bexley, Kent, England.

CAREER: University of Liverpool, Liverpool, England, tutor in economics, 1970-71; University of Illinois at Chicago Circle, Chicago, visiting instructor in systems engineering, 1972-73; currently chief housing officer of Bexley London Borough, Bexley, England.

WRITINGS: (With George Bugliarello and others) *The Impact of Noise Pollution: A Socio-Technological Introduction,* Pergamon, 1976.

WORK IN PROGRESS: Revising *The Impact of Noise Pollution.*

*   *   *

BARNES, Mary   1923-

PERSONAL: Born February 9, 1923, in Portsmouth, Hampshire, England. *Educaton:* Educated in England. *Home:* St. Dympna's Harepath Hill, Seaton, Devonshire, England. *Religion:* Christian.

CAREER: Writer; artist. Former nurse and teacher of nursing. Paintings shown at exhibitions entitled "Painting of the Last Hundred Years," and "Search for Identity," Milan, Italy, both in 1974. Has also held one-woman exhibits. Member of Hampstead Arts Council. *Military service:* Served as nurse in British Army, 1945-49.

WRITINGS: (With Joseph Berke) *Two Accounts of a Journey Through Madness,* MacGibbon & Kee, 1971, published as *Mary Barnes: Two Accounts of a Journey Through Madness,* Harcourt, 1972. Author of script for Swedish made-for-television screenplay based on her book.

WORK IN PROGRESS: Breath of Life for Ronnie, a collection of essays and stories.

SIDELIGHTS: In Mary Barnes's first book, *Two Accounts of a Journey Through Madness,* she relates the story of her long battle with mental illness. She tells how she was raised in a family situation where angry feelings were never allowed to surface. Suppression of negative emotions was so extreme that her younger brother Peter, unable to find an acceptable outlet for the stress he felt within himself, suffered a mental breakdown. Just in his early teens, Peter was diagnosed as schizophrenic and was institutionalized. Later, when Barnes was working as a nurse, she found herself frequently suffering from anxiety attacks; she often felt dead. Eventually she too broke down and was hospitalized until, ostensibly, she recovered. At the age of forty-two, Barnes again found herself on the verge of collapse and had herself admitted to the therapeutic community of controversial psychiatrist R. D. Laing in London. At Kingsley Hall Barnes did break down completely. Schizophrenic like her brother, she reverted to infancy, and, under the guidance of American-born psychotherapist Joseph Berke, fought her way back to sanity.

To give the story perspective, two versions of Mary Barnes's experiences at Kingsley Hall are described in *Two Accounts of a Journey Through Madness.* Barnes records events as she saw them; Berke, who coauthored the book, tells what happened from his point of view. "This is a book that must be fully experienced as painful, disgusting and frightening, or else pushed out of the mind altogether." wrote a *Times Literary Supplement* critic. "The reader who perseveres will be forced to feel something of what Mary Barnes and her therapists went through for years." Christopher Lehmann-Haupt noted that what he "found particularly moving is the faith the book expresses in the resiliency of the human spirit: that no matter how damaged the soul, there remains a part of it that always grows toward wholeness. . . .''

David Edgar wrote a play based on Barnes's ordeal entitled "Mary Barnes." It was first produced in Birmingham, England, at Birmingham Repertory Theatre, August, 1978.

Barnes has often been interviewed on radio and television programs.

BIOGRAPHICAL/CRITICAL SOURCES: Times Literary Supplement, October 29, 1971; *Kirkus Reviews,* February 1, 1972; *Publishers Weekly,* February 14, 1972; *New York Times,* April 3, 1972; *New Leader,* May 15, 1972; *New York Times Book Review,* July 2, 1972; *Choice,* December, 1972.

* * *

BARNHOUSE, Ruth Tiffany 1923-

PERSONAL: Born October 23, 1923, in LaMur, Isere, France; came to united States in 1925; daughter of Donald Grey (a minister) and Ruth (Tiffany) Barnhouse; married Francis C. Edmonds, Jr. (a physician), August 11, 1941 (divorced, July, 1947); married William F. Beuscher (a physician), April 4, 1950 (divorced, 1968); children: (first marriage) Francis C. III, Ruth T.; (second marriage) Robert Conrad, William David, Christopher Grey, Thomas Frederick, John Franklin. *Education:* Attended Vassar College, 1940-41; Barnard College, B.A., 1945; Columbia University, M.D., 1950; Weston College of Theology, Th.M., 1974. *Politics:* Independent. *Religion:* Episcopalian. *Home and office:* 2311 Connecticut Ave. N.W., Apt. 402, Washington, D.C. 20008.

CAREER: Monmouth Memorial Hospital, Long Branch,

N.J., intern, 1950-51; McLean Hospital, Waverly, Mass., resident in psychiatry, 1953-55; Massachusetts General Hospital, Boston, fellow in psychiatry, 1955-56; private practice of psychiatry in Boston, Mass., 1955-78, and Washington, D.C., 1978—. Diplomate of American Board of Psychiatry and Neurology; director of clinical psychiatry at children's unit of Metropolitan State Hospital, Waltham, Mass., 1956-57; staff psychiatrist at Massachusetts Mental Health Center, 1958-59; staff physician at McLean Hospital, 1958-78; clinical assistant in psychiatry at Harvard University, 1959-78; associated with Sibley Hospital courtesy staff, 1979—. Lecturer at Weston College of Theology, 1971-76; adjunct professor at Virginia Theological Seminary and Loyola College, Columbia, Md., 1978—. Member of C. G. Jung Center of New England; member of board of advisers of Foundation for Education in Human Relations, 1976—. Lecturer and workshop leader on psychiatry and religion; member of state and national commissions of the Episcopal Church.

MEMBER: American Academy of Psychoanalysis (Scientific associate), American Psychiatric Association (fellow), American Medical Womens Association, American Association for the Advancement of Science, Washington Psychiatric Society, Boston Vassar Club (president, 1973-75), Anchor Society (member of board of directors, 1975—). *Awards, honors:* Fellow of U.S. Public Health Service at Harvard University, 1955-56; fellow of College of Preachers, Washington, D.C., 1976.

WRITINGS: (Contributor) Robert J. Heyer, editor, *Women and Orders,* Paulist/Newman, 1974; (editor with Urban T. Holmes III) *Male and Female: Christian Approaches to Sexuality,* Seabury, 1976; *Homosexuality: A Symbolic Confusion,* Seabury, 1977. Contributor to theology and psychiatric journals. Assistant science and religion editor for *Anglican Theological Review,* 1977—.

WORK IN PROGRESS: Ethics for the Person-in-the-Street; research for a book on the relationship between psychotherapy and religious development.

AVOCATIONAL INTERESTS: Playing the piano, writing poetry, painting, sewing and needlework, travel (especially Europe), reading (especially mystery novels).

* * *

BARNOUW, Victor 1915-

PERSONAL: Born May 25, 1915, in The Hague, Netherlands; came to United States in 1919, naturalized citizen, 1924; son of Adriaan Jacob and Anne E. (Midgley) Barnouw; married Sachiko Miyagawa, January 7, 1964. *Education:* Attended Princeton University, 1933-35; Columbia University, A.B., 1940, Ph.D., 1948. *Home:* 2518 North Terrace Ave., Milwaukee, Wis. 53211. *Office:* Department of Anthropology, University of Wisconsin—Milwaukee, Milwaukee, Wis. 53201.

CAREER: Brooklyn College (now of the City University of New York), Brooklyn, N.Y., instructor in anthropology, 1945-48; University of Buffalo (now State University of New York at Buffalo), visiting assistant professor of anthropology, 1948-51; University of Pennsylvania, South Asia Regional Studies Department, researcher in South Asia, 1951-52, and in India, 1952-53; teacher at private school in Verde Valley, Ariz., 1953-54; University of Illinois at Urbana-Champaign, research associate, 1955-56, visiting assistant professor of anthropology, 1956-57; University of Wisconsin—Milwaukee, assistant professor, 1957-61, associate professor, 1961-65, professor of anthropology, 1965—, head of department, 1976-79. *Member:* American Anthropological Association (fellow). *Awards, honors:* Stirling Award from American Anthropological Association, 1968, for "Cross-Cultural Research With the House-Tree-Person Test."

WRITINGS: Acculturation and Personality Among the Wisconsin Chippewa, American Anthropological Association, 1950, reprinted, AMS Press, 1977; *Culture and Personality,* Dorsey, 1963, 3rd edition, 1979; *Dream of the Blue Heron* (juvenile novel), Delacorte, 1966; *An Introduction to Anthropology,* Volume I: *Physical Anthropology and Archaeology,* Volume II: *Ethnology,* Dorsey, 1971, 3rd edition, 1978; *Programmed Learning Aid for Cultural Anthropology,* Learning Systems Co., 1972; *Plaid for Physical Anthropology and Archaeology,* Learning Systems Co., 1972; *Programmed Learning Aid for Physical Anthropology and Archaeology,* Learning Systems Co., 1973; (editor with Joseph B. Casagrande, Ernestine Friedl, and Robert E. Ritzenthaler) *Wisconsin Chippewa Myths and Tales and Their Relation to Chippewa Life,* University of Wisconsin Press, 1977; *Anthropology: A General Introduction,* Dorsey, 1979. Contributor of stories to popular magazines, including *Vogue* and *New Yorker.* Member of advisory board of *Journal of Psychological Anthropology.*

SIDELIGHTS: Barnouw writes: "Although my main profession has been teaching anthropology, I have also written fiction. My novel, *Dream of the Blue Heron,* was my major effort in this field. My fiction is 'anthropological,' usually being related to my field work. The novel, for instance, is about a Chippewa Indian boy."

*   *   *

BAROODY, Jamil Murad   1905-1979

OBITUARY NOTICE: Born August 8, 1905, in Souk el-Gharb, Lebanon; died March 4, 1979, in New York. Diplomat, writer, and poet. Baroody was ambassador of Saudia Arabia, dean of United Nations (U.N.) delegates, U.N. spokesman for Saudi Arabia, and an avid opponent of Zionism. His reputation for delivering candid oratory was highlighted during the Middle East debates that took place in the Security Council and the General Assembly. Baroody was an adviser for the Arabic edition of *Reader's Digest,* contributed to magazines, and for three years wrote free-lance articles on international affairs. A book of his poetry was published in 1936. Obituaries and other sources: *Esquire,* September, 1974; *Who's Who in the World,* 4th edition, Marquis, 1978; *New York Times,* March 5, 1979.

*   *   *

BAROOSHIAN, (Dickran) Vahan   1932-

PERSONAL: Born January 21, 1932, in Chelsea, Mass.; son of Vahan (in business) and Charlotte (Basmajian) Barooshian; married Barbara Ann Kalman, September 7, 1957; children: Daniel, Sarah. *Education:* University of Massachusetts, B.A., 1960; Brown University, earned M.A. and Ph.D. *Home address:* Wells Rd., Aurora, N.Y. 13026. *Office:* Department of Russian, Wells College, Aurora, N.Y. 13026.

CAREER: Wells College, Aurora, N.Y., professor of Russian, 1963—. Consultant to National Endowment for the Humanities, 1975—. *Military service:* U.S. Coast Guard, 1952-56. *Member:* American Association of University Professors. *Awards, honors:* International Research & Exchanges Board senior scholar, 1971-72, 1974-75; fellow of Harvard University, 1971-72, 1976-77.

WRITINGS: Russian Cubo-Futurism, 1910-1930, Mouton, 1974; *Brik and Mayakovsky,* Mouton, 1978. Contributor to Russian studies journals.

WORK IN PROGRESS: A biography of Anastas Mikoyan, *The Crisis of Detente in East-West Relations.*

AVOCATIONAL INTERESTS: Cooking, auto mechanics, thoroughbred racing and breeding.

*   *   *

BARRETT, Harry B(emister)   1922-
(Henry Bemister)

PERSONAL: Born May 29, 1922, in Port Dover, Ontario, Canada; son of Theobald B. (a farmer and federal member of parliament) and Marjorie (Clarke) Barrett; married Hellen M. Browne, October 9, 1943; children: Toby, Jennifer, Barbara Barrett Hourigan, Elizabeth, Hugh Massey. *Education:* University of Toronto, B.S.A. (with honors), 1949. *Politics:* Conservative. *Religion:* Anglican. *Home:* 11 Bridge, Port Dover, Ontario, Canada N0A 1N0. *Office:* Department of Norfolk School of Agriculture, Fanshawe College, Box 10, Simcoe, Ontario, Canada.

CAREER: Farmer in Norfolk County, Ontario, 1945-59; high school teacher of agriculture and science in Hagersville, Ontario, 1959-61; teacher of agricultural science and head of department in Simcoe, Ontario, 1961-69; Fanshawe College, Simcoe, teacher of animal science and soil and crop science, principal of Norfolk School of Agriculture, and coordinator of farm business management, 1969—. Executive and provincial appointee to Long Point Region Conservation Authority; member of Nanticoke architectural conservation advisory committee; secretary of Long Point Bird Observatory. *Military service:* Canadian Militia, 1939-41. Royal Canadian Navy Volunteer Reserve, 1941-45; became lieutenant; received combat medals.

MEMBER: Agricultural Institute of Canada, Soil Conservation Society of America, Ontario Institute of Agrologists (past local president), Federation of Ontario Naturalists (past member of board of directors), Norfolk Historical Society (past president), Norfolk Field Naturalists (past founding president), Dover Mills Heritage Association (founding president), Simcoe Rotary Club, Port Dover Erie Lodge.

WRITINGS: Nineteenth-Century Journals and Paintings of William Pope, M. F. Feheley, 1976; *Burning of Dover, 1814* (booklet), Cline Press, 1976; *Lore and Legend of Long Point,* Burns & MacEachern, 1978.

Author of "Norfolklore," a weekly nature column in *Haldimand-Norfolk News,* under pseudonym Henry Bemister, 1975-76. Contributor to *Treasures of Canada, Nature Canada* and *Ontario Naturalist.* Past editor of *Ontario Science, Agriculture Teachers Bulletin, Norfolk Historical Society Bulletin,* and *Norfolk Naturalists Bulletin.*

WORK IN PROGRESS: Writer for "Treasures of Canada," about museums and art galleries across Canada; research on Great Lakes schooner captains.

SIDELIGHTS: Barrett wrote: "Although I have always enjoyed writing and researching local history (the Long Point country is alive with it), my activities were limited to local nature and history organization bulletins until 1967 when an article on W. M. Pope for Canada's centennial was published in the *Ontario Naturalist* in 1967: the first issue to use colour with several of Pope's paintings. This led to 'Budd' (M. F.) Feheley asking me to produce a text to go with a coffee-table-type book of Pope's paintings, 36 of which were chosen.

''Speaking engagements with historical and naturalist societies (I do quite a bit of this using slides of historical or floral and faunal interest) led to my next book. Barney Sandwell, a hunting club member on Long Point, saw my presentation on that area and asked that I write what became much more than he originally planned: *Lore and Legend of Long Point* is already into its second printing in less than a year from publication. Lee d'Anjou, the chief editor of *Treasures of Canada,* who also edited my book, asked me to be a writer for her on this rather ambitious and expensive guide book.

''I am concerned about the effects our modern technology is having on the environment and I am increasingly convinced that we could wipe out one animal species—Homo Sapiens—perhaps quite inadvertently in the same way D.D.T. put so many animals and birds on the list of endangered or even extinct species. Our love of the quick buck and lack of concern for long range benefits or concern for our fellow man may well be our undoing. Are we going to *die* to see the cockroach inherit the earth?

''Hopefully my books sound an alarm of this nature while preserving a small part of our local heritage. If they stimulate some interest in our youth along these lines, I will be well satisfied.''

AVOCATIONAL INTERESTS: Local history, local flora and fauna, the outdoors, photography, boating in Long Point Bay and Haliburton district of Ontario.

*   *   *

BARRETT, Michael Dennis 1947-

PERSONAL: Born October 24, 1947, in Washington, D.C.; son of Francis A. (a surgeon) and Harriett (Holland) Barrett; married Paula Anne Follings (an airline agent); children: Eryn Alia. *Education:* Attended American College of Switzerland, 1966-67, Seattle University, 1969-70, Seattle Central Community College, 1970-71, and University of Wyoming, 1972-74. *Home address:* P.O. Box 325, Cheyenne, Wyo. 82001. *Agent:* Susan Ann Protter, 156 East 52nd St., New York, N.Y. 10022.

CAREER: Writer. Copy writer for Amazing Advertising, 1976. Also worked as cab driver, interviewer, landscaper, garbage collector, railroad worker, and rock music promoter. *Military service:* U.S. Army, 1967-69.

WRITINGS: Asylum and Circus, Manor, 1978.

WORK IN PROGRESS: An Ordinary, Unfinished Journey; Mover of Winds Toward Sails; John William Ash: The Memoirs of Gunther Palido.

SIDELIGHTS: Barrett comments: ''As you can see, I have performed in a variety of ways to gain the money necessary to ward off starvation and arrest. This is a losing battle. As for 'being a writer,' this is only a technicality brought about by my being published. I have always written and shall continue to do so; however, I am a bit upset at the publishing business because I have seen how a simple book has been exploited and cheapened so much that it is akin to the transformation that takes place from a virginal Wisconsin teenager to a nickel-and-dime whore in Times Square. It seems to me that in order to support yourself as a writer in these fine times it is necessary to write a book about a love affair on the rim of a black hole in space or else hold a few dozen people hostage in a bank, have an affair with a politician, assemble a great body of cliches in the form of self-help, or, in desperation, get yourself caught violating some part of the Constitution.''

BARRY, Anne 1940-

PERSONAL: Born April 18, 1940, in Boston, Mass.; daughter of Theodore and Helen (Coleman) Barry. *Education:* Radcliffe College, B.A., 1962. *Agent:* Helen Brann, The Helen Brann Agency, 14 Sutton Place S., New York, N.Y. 10022.

CAREER: Dial Press, New York City, managing editor, 1965-66; free-lance writer, 1966—. Writing instructor at New School for Social Research, New York City, 1978—. Adjunct assistant professor at Fordham University, 1979—. *Member:* American Society of Journalists and Authors.

WRITINGS: Bellevue Is a State of Mind (nonfiction), Harcourt, 1970. Contributor to popular magazines, including *Esquire, McCall's, Cosmopolitan, Glamour,* and *Self,* and to newspapers.

*   *   *

BARSON, John 1936-

PERSONAL: Born April 26, 1936. *Education:* Amherst College, B.A., 1957; Princeton University, A.B.D., 1961. *Office:* Department of French and Italian, Stanford University, Stanford, Calif. 94305.

CAREER: Stanford University, Stanford, Calif., faculty member in department of French and Italian. *Member:* American Association of Teachers of French, American Association of University Professors.

WRITINGS: La Grammaire a l'oeuvre, Holt, 1970; *Textuellement,* Holt, 1974; *Espanol esencial,* Holt, 1974; *Intrigues* (intermediate reader), Holt, 1978.

*   *   *

BARUK, Henri Marc 1897-

PERSONAL: Born August 8, 1897, in Saint-Ave, France; son of Jacques (a psychiatrist) and Marie (Brechon) Baruk; married Suzanne Sorano, December 29, 1947. *Education:* Faculte de medecine, Paris, M.D. *Home:* 5 quai de la Republique, 94410 Saint Maurice (Seine), Paris 368, France.

CAREER: Psychiatrist; specialist in neuropsychiatry. Intern in hospitals in Paris, France, 1921-26; Faculte de medecine, Paris, professor, 1926-30; House of Charenton, Charenton-le-Pont, France, chief physician, 1932-68; director at L'Ecole Pratique des Hautes Etudes, Sorbonne, University of Paris; currently consulting physician at St. Antoine Hospital, Paris. Member of Committee of Public Health. *Member:* National Academy of Medicine (Paris), American International Academy (honorary member).

WRITINGS—In English: *Civilisation hebraique et science de l'homme,* Editions Zikarone, translation by Philip Polak published as *Hebraic Civilization and the Science of Man,* World Federation for Mental Health, 1961, published as *Tsedik: Where Modern Science is Examined and Where it is Attempted to Save Man From Physical and Spiritual Enslavement* (includes three chapters translated from *Tsedek, droit hebraique et science du paix;* also see below), Swan House, 1972; Jean Laborde, compiler, *Des hommes comme nous: memoires d'un neuropsychiatre* (autobiography), Laffont, 1976, translation by Eileen Finletter and Jean Ayer published as *Patients Are People Like Us: The Experiences of Half a Century of Neuropsychiatry,* Morrow, 1977.

Other—All published by Presses universitaires de France, except as noted: *Les Troubles mentaux dans les humeurs cerebrales,* (Paris), 1926; *Psychiatrie medicale physiologique et experimentale,* Masson, 1938; *Psychiatrie morale experimentale, individuelle et sociale: haines et reactions de culpabilite*, 1945; *Psychoses et nevroses*, 1946; (with Maurice Buchet) *Le Test "tsedek": le jugement moral et la delinquance*, 1950; *La Psychiatrie sociale*, 1955; *Psychiatrie, dermatologie, notions d'electroradiologie et de physiotherapie*, Masson, 1959; *Traite de psychiatrie*, Masson, 1959; *Precis de psychiatrie*, Masson, 1959.

Les Therapeutiques psychiatriques, 1960; *Titres et travaux scientifiques*, Masson, 1963; *La Psychopathologie experimentale*, 1964; *La Psychiatrie et la science de l'homme*, Editions du Levain, 1965; *L'Ethique juive face a l'assimilation*, Trait-d' Union, 1965; *La Psychiatrie francaise de Pinel a nos jours*, 1967; *Colloque international sur l'histoire de la psychiatrie francaise par rapport aux autres psychiatries, Paris, 1967*, 1969; *Savoir interpreter les examens complementaires neuropsychiatriques*, De Visscher (Brussels), 1969; *Les Examens complementaires neuropsychiatriques*, De Visscher, 1969.

Tsedek: droit hebraique et science de la paix, Edition Zikarone, 1970; *Psychiatrie* (title means "Psychiatry"), Foucher, 1970; *L'Hypnose et les methodes derivees*, 1972; *Essais sur la medecine hebraique dans le cadre de l'histoire juive*, Editions Zikarone, 1973.

WORK IN PROGRESS: Two Books.

SIDELIGHTS: An eminent French neurologist and psychologist, Baruk believes in what he calls "moral psychiatry." For this reason he has studied both the Talmud and the Bible in addition to medicine, he told *CA*.

It is Baruk's philosophy that charity and justice, as well as science, must prevail if man is to grow and even survive. The Hebrew term for this concept is *Tsedek*, which is also the title of Baruk's book on the subject.

Baruk is responsible for the creation of a neural laboratory for the study of catatonia at the Sorbonne.

BIOGRAPHICAL/CRITICAL SOURCES: Best Sellers, November 15, 1972; Henri Marc Baruk, *Patients Are People Like Us: The Experiences of Half a Century of Neuropsychiatry*, Morrow, 1977; *New York Times Book Review*, February 12, 1978.

*   *   *

BASICHIS, Gordon (Allen) 1947-

PERSONAL: Surname is pronounced Ba-*seek*-as; born August 23, 1947, in Philadelphia, Pa.; son of Martin (a furniture refinisher) and Ruth (an antique shop owner; maiden name, Gordon) Basichis; married Marcia Hammond (a media program executive), September 10, 1974. *Education:* Temple University, B.S., 1969. *Agent:* Mike Marcus, Paul Kohner, Michael Levy Agency, 9169 Sunset Blvd., Los Angeles, Calif. 90069. *Office address:* P.O. Box 3264, Beverly Hills, Calif. 90212.

CAREER: News reporter in Philadelphia, Pa., 1967-69, and Santa Fe, N.M., 1969-71; publicity and advertising writer and account executive in Los Angeles, Calif., 1971-74; filmmaker and scriptwriter in Los Angeles, 1974—. Operator of boutique shops in Santa Fe, N.M., and New York, N.Y. *Member:* Writers Guild of America.

WRITINGS: The Constant Travellers, Putnam, 1978; *Fataxe!*, Pocket Books, in press. Script writer of feature film "Blizzard" for National Broadcasting Co. (NBC-TV).

Author of three television screenplay scripts.

WORK IN PROGRESS: A novel; writing script for screenplay adaptation of "The Constant Travellers."

SIDELIGHTS: Basichis writes: "I intend to create new mythologies, combine elements of cultures and histories for appropriate mythologies for the coming era, for what I believe amounts to new evolutionary eras. I learned much of writing drama from early 'street' and travel experience. I try to combine passions of life and colors of the sensual with the volatile mystical experience."

*   *   *

BATTEN, Charles Linwood, Jr. 1942-

PERSONAL: Born December 31, 1942, in Norfolk, Va.; son of Charles Linwood and Daisy (Graham) Batten; married Anne Cummings, June 14, 1972; children: Katharine Margaret, Caroline Elizabeth. *Education:* University of Virginia, B.A., 1965; University of Chicago, M.A., 1966, Ph.D., 1971. *Religion:* Episcopalian. *Home:* 4647 Cerrillos Dr., Woodland Hills, Calif. 91364. *Office:* Department of English, University of California, Los Angeles, Calif. 90024.

CAREER: University of California, Los Angeles, assistant professor, 1969-77, associate professor of English, 1977—, vice-chairman of department, 1977-78. Editor for Augustan Reprint Society.

WRITINGS: Pleasurable Instruction, University of California Press, 1978.

*   *   *

BAUER, Harry C(harles) 1902-1979

OBITUARY NOTICE—See index for *CA* sketch: Born July 22, 1902, in St. Louis, Mo.; died in 1979 in Washington, D.C. Librarian, educator, and author of a book of essays. Bauer was librarian at the University of Washington, Seattle, and professor of library science until his retirement in 1967. An expert in bibliographic dowsing, he was founder and president of the Bibliographic Dowsers of America. Bauer was best known for his witty and informative journal articles. Obituaries and other sources: *A Biographical Directory of Librarians in the United States and Canada*, 5th edition, American Library Association, 1970; *Who's Who in America*, 40th edition, Marquis, 1978; *AB Bookman's Weekly*, February 5, 1979.

*   *   *

BAUM, Robert J(ames) 1941-

PERSONAL: Born October 19, 1941, in Chicago, Ill.; son of Adam (a clergyman) and Jean (TerMeer) Baum; married Gail May Ingrish (a teacher); children: Aimee Joy. *Education:* Northwestern University, B.A. (with honors), 1963; Ohio State University, Ph.D., 1969. *Office:* Department of Philosophy, Rensselaer Polytechnic Institute, Troy, N.Y. 12181.

CAREER: U.S. Peace Corps, Washington, D.C., visiting lecturer in mathematics at Middle East Technical University, Ankara, Turkey, 1965-67; Rensselaer Polytechnic Institute, Troy, N.Y., assistant professor, 1969-73, associate professor, 1973-79, professor of philosophy, 1979—, director of Center for the Study of the Human Dimensions of Science and Technology, 1976—. Program director for National Science Foundation, 1974-76. *Member:* American Philosophical Association, American Association for the Advancement of Science, Philosophy of Science Association, American Society for Engineering Education, American Association of University Professors, American Civil Liberties Union.

WRITINGS: (Editor with James Randell) *Ethical Arguments*

for Analysis, Holt, 1973, 2nd edition, 1977; *Philosophy and Mathematics,* Freeman, Cooper, 1974; *Logic,* with workbook, Holt, 1975, revised edition, 1980; (editor with Albert Flores) *Ethical Problems in Engineering,* Rensselaer Polytechnic Institute, 1978. Contributor to philosophy and scientific journals. Editor of *Business and Professional Ethics.*

* * *

BAXTER, Douglas Clark 1942-

PERSONAL: Born September 20, 1942, in Flint, Mich.; son of Clark J. and Rose K. (Bosch) Baxter; married Phyllis F. Field (a professor), January 1, 1977. *Education:* Wayne State University, A.B., 1964; University of Wisconsin, Madison, M.A., 1966; University of Minnesota, Ph.D., 1971. *Home:* 127 Franklin Ave., Athens, Ohio 45701. *Office:* Department of History, Ohio University, 58-E Bentley Hall, Athens, Ohio 45701.

CAREER: Ohio University, Athens, instructor, 1969-71, assistant professor, 1971-76, associate professor of history, 1976—. *Member:* American Historical Association, Society for French Historical Studies (life member), Phi Beta Kappa.

WRITINGS: Servants of the Sword: French Intendants of the Army, 1630-70, University of Illinois Press, 1976.

WORK IN PROGRESS: Research on French military administration in the Ancien Regime and on the *commis* in the Bureau de Guerre.

* * *

BAYH, Marvella (Hern) 1933-1979

OBITUARY NOTICE: Born February 14, 1933, in Enid, Okla.; died of cancer, April 24, 1979, in Maryland. Civic worker and author. First stricken with cancer in 1971, Bayh zealously devoted the rest of her life to combating the disease. She spoke on numerous television programs and lectured around the United States as a special representative of the American Cancer Society. She also was a proponent of women's rights. In 1951, Bayh was the first woman to win the American Farm Bureau national speaking contest, prevailing over her future husband, Senator Birch Bayh. She was the author of *Marvella: A Personal Journey,* and contributed to magazines, including *McCall's, Ladies' Home Journal,* and *Today's Health.* Obituaries and other sources: Myra MacPherson, *Power Lovers,* Putnam, 1975; *Ladies' Home Journal,* January, 1975; *Newsweek,* December 29, 1975; *New York Times,* April 25, 1979; *Washington Post,* April 25, 1979; *Chicago Tribune,* April 26, 1979.

* * *

BAYLESS, Raymond 1920-

PERSONAL: Born January 30, 1920, in Los Angeles, Calif.; married Marjorie Ann Brinkman (a dress designer), December, 1957. *Education:* Attended public schools in Los Angeles, Calif. *Home and office:* 11348 Cashmere St., Los Angeles, Calif. 90049.

CAREER: Parapsychologist in Los Angeles, Calif., 1948—; realistic and romantic landscape artist. *Member:* American Society for Psychical Research, English Society for Psychical Research, Toronto Society for Psychical Research, New Horizons Research Foundation.

WRITINGS: The Enigma of the Poltergeist, Parker Press, 1967; *Animal Ghosts,* University Books, 1970; *Experiences of a Psychical Researcher,* University Books, 1972; *The*

Other Side of Death, University Books, 1972; *Apparitions and Survival of Death,* University Books, 1973; *Voices From Beyond,* University Books, 1976; (with D. Scott Roco) *Telephone Calls From the Dead?,* Prentice-Hall, 1978.

Also author of technical papers on parapsychology. Contributor of articles to various magazines.

WORK IN PROGRESS: An autobiography; a novel; short stories; fantasy-horror stories.

* * *

BAYLEY, John (Oliver) 1925-

PERSONAL: Born March 27, 1925, in Lahore, India; son of Frederick (an army officer) and Olivia (Heenan) Bayley; married Iris Murdoch (a novelist), 1956; *Education:* Attended Eton College, 1938-43; New College, Oxford, B.A., 1950. *Home:* Cedar Lodge, Steeple Aston, Oxford, England.

CAREER: University of Oxford, Oxford, England, St. Anthony's College and Magdalen College, staff member, 1951-55, New College, lecturer, 1955-74, St. Catherine's College, Warton professor of English, 1974—. *Military service:* British Army, served in Grenadier Guards and Special Intelligence, 1943-47. *Awards, honors:* Heinemann Literary Award, 1971, for *Tolstoy and the Novel.*

WRITINGS: El Dorado: The Newdigate Prize Poem, (poetry), Blackwell, 1951; *In Another Country,* (novel), Coward, 1955; *The Romantic Survival: A Study in Poetic Evolution,* Constable, 1957, Basic Books, 1961; (contributor) *Proceedings of the British Academy 48,* Oxford University Press, 1963; *Tolstoy and the Novel,* Chatto and Windus, 1966, Viking, 1967; (author of introduction) Thomas Hardy, *Jude the Obscure,* Heritage Press, 1969; (contributor) Barbara Hardy, editor, *Critical Essays on George Eliot,* Routledge, 1970; *Pushkin: A Comparative Commentary,* Cambridge University Press, 1971; (contributor) *New Literary History,* [Charlottesville, Va.], 1974; (author of introduction) Thomas Hardy, *Far From the Madding Crowd,* Macmillan, 1974; (contributor) *Essays in Criticism,* [Oxford], 1975; *The Uses of Division: Unity and Disharmony in Literature,* Viking, 1976; *An Essay on Hardy,* Cambridge University Press, 1978; (editor) *The Portable Tolstoy,* Viking, 1978.

WORK IN PROGRESS: Research on Shakespearean tragedy.

SIDELIGHTS: Although an author in his own right, Bayley is primarily noted for his literary criticisms of such writers as Leo Tolstoy, Aleksander Pushkin, Thomas Hardy, and George Eliot. Bayley has been praised for providing new insights into writings that have already been extensively studied. Herbert Leibowitz explained that "even when one disagrees with them Bayley's readings of poems, plays and novels force one to rethink long-held assumptions and judgments."

Tolstoy and the Novel studies Tolstoy specifically as a novelist, and includes a detailed analysis of *War and Peace* as well as comparisons with Western literature. Bayley provides many extremely acute observations, noted W. M. Frohock, but he "refuses so resolutely to impose his conclusions on his reader that the latter occasionally loses the thread of the development." Kathryn Feuer declared that Bayley's book achieved "a wonderful freshness and insight, a striking depth and variety, an affectionate and creative renewal of Tolstoy's great art."

Times Literary Supplement called *Pushkin: A Comparative*

Commentary "the first detailed critical study in English of Pushkin's writings." Describing the book as "brilliant [and] provocative," Helen Muchnic stated, "Bayley's own understanding of Pushkin is indisputable, and his admiration is ardent enough to satisfy even a Russian."

In *The Uses of Division: Unity and Disharmony in Literature* Bayley suggests that division and disunity give vitality to writing and thus should not be considered a flaw. Under this assumption he studies Dickens, Kipling, Shakespeare, and other authors. In a *Times Literary Supplement* review, W. C. Booth implied that Bayley's theories were insufficient to support his judgments, causing the book to be unclear, although Booth also commented that Bayley's interpretations of the authors and their works were "often sensitive, persuasive, and original." Herbert Leibowitz declared that Bayley's "mind is commodious, nimble, exacting, skeptical" and that in *The Uses of Division* "he speaks in a voice of humane reason and passionate sense . . . [which] should lure readers back to the vanishing pleasures of literary controversy."

Bayley told *CA:* "The background of my novel was my experience in the army in Germany at the end of the war. It is not a bad novel. Then I wrote the others, but they did not seem to me good enough. By that time I had married a really good novelist and I cooperated a certain amount on her earlier novels, particularly *The Bell,* published in 1958. I am now called in as an adviser on technical matters: cars, food, geography, and history.

"As a critic, I don't use any special approach. I brood over an author a long time and say whatever seems to me worth saying."

BIOGRAPHICAL/CRITICAL SOURCES: New York Times Book Review, April 23, 1967, May 1, 1977; *Virginia Quarterly Review,* summer, 1967, winter, 1972; *Yale Review,* autumn, 1967; *New York Review of Books,* September 14, 1967, October 7, 1971, April 14, 1977, June 15, 1978; *Times Literary Supplement,* July 30, 1971, July 23, 1976, July 28, 1978; *New Statesman,* August 6, 1971, May 11, 1976; *Choice,* November, 1971, January, 1977, September, 1978; *Encounter,* July, 1978.

*   *   *

BEACH, Stewart   1899-1979

OBITUARY NOTICE: Born December 17, 1899, in Pontiac, Mich.; died February 21, 1979, in New York. Magazine editor and author. Beach was a former editor of *House Beautiful* and executive editor of *This Week* magazine from 1947 to 1966. He was the author of several books, including *Samuel Adams, Lexington and Concord,* and *The Short-Short Story,* and co-authored a Broadway play. Beach contributed short stories to the *Saturday Evening Post, Cosmpolitan,* and other leading magazines. Obituaries and other sources: *New York Times,* February 23, 1979.

*   *   *

BEASER, Herbert W.   1913(?)-1979

OBITUARY NOTICE: Born c. 1913 in Boston, Mass.; died May 11, 1979, in Silver Spring, Md. Lawyer, legislative adviser, and author. Beaser was former chief counsel of the Federal Security Agency and consultant to the Department of Health, Education, and Welfare (HEW). When Eleanor Roosevelt represented the United States in the United Nations, he served as her adviser. Beaser wrote about various government concerns and was co-author of *Vietnam Folly,*

published in 1968. Obituaries and other sources: *Washington Post,* May 16, 1979.

*   *   *

BEATY, Jerome   1924-

PERSONAL: Surname is pronounced *Beet*-y; born October 12, 1924, in Baltimore, Md.; son of Harry C. (a printer) and Rose (Savage) Beaty; married Laurel Abrams, September 7, 1947 (divorced, June, 1970); married V. Elaine Brown (a teacher), October 9, 1970; children: (first marriage) Shawn, Andrew; (second marriage) Meaghan, Caelin. *Education:* Johns Hopkins University, B.A., 1947, M.A., 1948; University of Illinois, Ph.D., 1956. *Home:* 893 Vistavia Circle, Decatur, Ga. 30033. *Office:* Department of English, Emory University, Atlanta, Ga. 30322.

CAREER: Virginia Military Institute, Lexington, assistant professor of English, 1953-56; University of Washington, Seattle, instructor, 1956-58, assistant professor of English, 1958-60; Emory University, Atlanta, Ga., associate professor, 1960-64, professor of English, 1964—. Visiting assistant professor at New York University, summer, 1959; visiting associate professor at University of Illinois, summer, 1961; visiting professor at University of Wisconsin, Madison, 1965-66. Head of screening committee for Fulbright senior awards, 1978-79. Speaker at universities in the United States, Canada, England, and Scotland; consultant to publishers. *Military service:* U.S. Marine Corps Reserve, active duty, 1943-44. U.S. Naval Reserve, active duty, 1944-46; served in Atlantic theater; became lieutenant junior grade. *Member:* Modern Language Association of America, English Institute, Dickens Society, South Atlantic Modern Language Association. *Awards, honors:* Guggenheim fellow, 1962-63.

WRITINGS: "*Middlemarch*" *From Notebook to Novel,* University of Illinois Press, 1960; (with William Matchett) *Poetry: From Statement to Meaning,* Oxford University Press, 1965; *Norton Introduction to Fiction,* Norton, 1973; (with C. E. Bain and J. Paul Hunter) *Norton Introduction to Literature,* Norton, 1973, 2nd edition, 1977, classroom guide for fiction, 1977; *Norton Introduction to Fiction: Questions and Suggestions* (pamphlet), Norton, 1973.

Contributor: Gordon S. Haight, editor, *A Century of George Eliot Criticism,* Houghton, 1965; Barbara Hardy, editor, "*Middlemarch*": *Critical Approaches to the Novel,* Athlone Press, 1967; Clyde de L. Ryals, editor, *Nineteenth-Century Literary Perspectives: Essays in Honor of Lionel Stevenson,* Duke University Press, 1974; A. E. Dyson, editor, *The English Novel: Select Bibliographical Guides,* Oxford University Press, 1974; Richard Levine, editor, *The Victorian Experience,* Ohio University Press, 1976. Contributor of more than fifteen articles and reviews to literature journals. Member of editorial board of *Victorian Poetry.*

WORK IN PROGRESS: Charlotte Bronte's Hippograph: "*Jane Eyre*" *in the Context of the Contemporary Novel; Charles Dickens and the Victorian World Order.*

*   *   *

BECK, James (H.)   1930-

PERSONAL: Born May 14, 1930, in New York, N.Y.; son of Samuel (in business) and Margaret (Weisz) Beck; married Darma Tercinod (a secretary), April 9, 1956; children: Eleonora, Lawrence. *Education:* Oberlin College, B.A., 1952; New York University, M.A., 1954; Columbia University, Ph.D., 1963. *Home:* 54 Carthage Rd., Scarsdale, N.Y.

10583. *Office:* Department of Art History, Columbia University, 815 Schermerhorn Hall, New York, N.Y. 10027.

CAREER: Rotron Manufacturing Co., Woodstock, N.Y., factory worker, 1956-58; University of Alabama, Tuscaloosa, assistant professor of art, 1958-59; Arizona State University, Tempe, assistant professor of art, 1958-60; Columbia University, New York, N.Y., instructor, 1961-64, assistant professor, 1964-68, associate professor, 1969-72, professor of art history and archaeology, 1972—, director of graduate studies. *Awards, honors:* Institute for Advanced Study fellow, 1968; Villa I Tatti fellow, 1968-69; Guggenheim fellow, 1973-74.

WRITINGS: Taccola: Liber Tertius de Inceneis (title means "Taccola's Third Book of Inventions"), Edizioni il Polifilo, 1969; *Jacopo della Quercia e il portale di San Petronio a Bologna* (title means "Jacopo della Quercia's Portal Sculpture on the Church of San Petronio in Bologna"), Edizioni Alfa, 1970; *Michelangelo: A Lesson in Anatomy,* Viking, 1975; *Raphael,* Abrams, 1976; *Masaccio: The Documents,* J. J. Augustin, 1978; *Leonardo and Modern Art,* Viking, 1979. Contributor to art journals.

WORK IN PROGRESS: A History of Italian Renaissance Painting, for Harper; also, "a work of fiction that deals with the external and to a greater extent the inner life of a very old man (age eighty-six), what goes on in his mind and in his thoughts."

SIDELIGHTS: Beck told *CA:* "The impetus for writing the book on the old man comes from a series of diaries I have from my maternal grandfather who loyally made entries from the age of sixteen until the last day of his life (age ninety-two). So far, what has become clear to me is that even in extreme old age, one does not really undergo any emotional change from other periods in a life. The needs (for affection and stimulation) are identical. What is perhaps most troubling is that it seems that radical alteration of character is unusual, even rare, after childhood.

"I find that this also is true concerning the development of artists as manifested in their 'styles': once they have trained and achieved a truly personal style, change in basic language and sets of choices is never fundamental."

*   *   *

BECKER, Jurek   1937-

RESIDENCE: Germany.

CAREER: Playwright and novelist. *Awards, honors:* Silver Bear for East Germany at Berlin Film Festival, 1974, for a screenplay.

WRITINGS: Jakob der Luegner, Aufbau-Verlag, 1969, translation with introduction by Melvin Kornfeld published as *Jacob the Liar,* Harcourt, 1975; *Irrefuehrung der Behoerden* (novel), Suhrkamp, 1973; *Der Boxer,* Hinstorff (Rostock, Germany), 1976. Also author of plays and screenplays.

SIDELIGHTS: Jurek Becker's style of writing was described by a *Times Literary Supplement* critic as having "a sense of proportion, humour, lightness of touch." His first novel, *Jacob the Liar,* is set in a Nazi-run concentration camp, a place Becker knows about from first-hand experience. In the book, he "achieved the exact balance of detached involvement necessary to create a work of art," the critic observed. The novel was written from Becker's less successful screenplay version of the story.

Irrefuehrung der Behoerden was not as widely acclaimed as *Jacob the Liar.* According to reviewers, its main weakness is that the story is about the author as he currently is and, as a result, there are few surprises contained in the narrative. The *Times Literary Supplement* writer added that the parts of the story which Becker calls "incidental," such as "the intending thieves who set about building a new road to facilitate their robbery," are the highlights of this book.

BIOGRAPHICAL/CRITICAL SOURCES: Times Literary Supplement, December 21, 1973, February 6, 1976; *Booklist,* February 1, 1974, December 15, 1975; *New Statesman,* January 20, 1976; *Encounter,* May, 1976; *National Observer,* May 15, 1976; *Contemporary Literary Criticism,* Gale, Volume 7, 1977.*

*   *   *

BECKER, Lawrence C(arlyle)   1939-

PERSONAL: Born April 26, 1939, in Lincoln, Neb.; son of Albert Carlyle (a clergyman) and Harriette (Toren) Becker; married Charlotte Burner, June 10, 1967. *Education:* Midland College, B.A., 1961; University of Chicago, M.A., 1963, Ph.D., 1965; postdoctoral study at Oxford University, 1971-72. *Home address:* P.O. Box 9641, Hollins College, Roanoke, Va. 24020. *Office:* Department of Philosophy and Religion, Hollins College, Hollins College, Va. 24020.

CAREER: Hollins College, Hollins College, Va., instructor, 1965-67, assistant professor, 1967-71, associate professor, 1971-78, professor of philosophy, 1978—, head of department of philosophy and religion, 1972-75. *Awards, honors:* Woodrow Wilson fellowships, 1961-62, 1964-65; National Endowment for the Humanities junior fellowship, 1971-72; American Council of Learned Societies fellowship, 1975-76; visiting fellow at Harvard University, 1975-76.

WRITINGS: On Justifying Moral Judgments, Humanities, 1973; *Property Rights: Philosophic Foundations,* Routledge & Kegan Paul, 1977. Contributor of about twenty articles to philosophy journals.

SIDELIGHTS: Becker describes his first book as "an attempt to lay out a comprehensive set of procedures for the reasoned justification of moral judgments. It is argued that axiological, deontological, and agent morality approaches should be given coordinate status. A scheme for grounding moral judgments is proposed in which the existence of certain human species characteristics shifts the burden of proof to the sceptic. Solutions are proffered for problems of the meaning of value judgments, the logic of the move from is to ought, the dilemma raised by the notion of determinism, and others. It is acknowledged that the procedures proposed in the book are not decision procedures in the technical sense, but it is argued that they are occasionally adequate to yield decisions, and that that is enough to defeat moral scepticism.

"*Property Rights* gives a detailed analysis of the nature of rights *per se* and property rights in particular; gives equally detailed analyses of the major forms of argument for and against private property (first occupancy, the labor theory, utility, liberty, and property-worthiness); and sketches the results of the analysis for questions of specific justification (e.g., whether full ownership of land is justifiable). In sum, the book offers the rationale for rejecting both thoroughgoing libertarianism and thoroughgoing socialism, and lays the philosophic foundations for a new theory of property rights which lies between those two extremes.

"I don't write 'wisdom literature'—for the very good reason that, while I am fairly knowledgeable (and perhaps reasonable), I am not very wise. I also don't pay much attention to matters of style—being preoccupied instead with matters of validity and truth. My method is reasoned argument; my subject matter is substantive moral philosophy; my hope is to make a significant contribution directly to other professionals in the field, and through the profession as a whole, to others.''

*   *   *

BEDRIJ, Orest (John) 1933-

PERSONAL: Born May 24, 1933, in the Ukraine; came to the United States in 1949, naturalized citizen, 1955; son of Eustachy and Olga (Banach) Bedrij; married Oksana Cymbalista, 1956; children: Orest, Roksana, Chrystyna. *Education:* Rochester Institute of Technology, B.S.E.E., 1956. *Office:* Securities Council, Inc., 11 Lincoln Dr., Poughkeepsie, N.Y. 12601.

CAREER: International Business Machines Corp. (IBM), Poughkeepsie, N.Y., and Los Angeles, Calif., manager, 1956-68; Securities Council, Inc., Poughkeepsie, president and member of board of directors, 1965—. Technical director of Jet Propulsion Laboratory Space Flight Facility at California Institute of Technology, 1961-62. Founder of Intersil, Inc., Iomec, Inc., and Xytex, Inc. Member of executive committee and board of directors of Harvard University's Ukrainian Studies Fund, 1959—. *Military service:* Honorable discharge, 1963. *Awards, honors:* Outstanding contribution award from International Business Machines Corp.

WRITINGS: Yes, It's Love: Your Life Can Be a Miracle, Pyramid Publications, 1974; *ONE by Orest,* Strawberry Hill Press, 1977, 2nd edition, 1978.

SIDELIGHTS: Bendrij reflected: "The key to the understanding of truth is the mind. It is the mind that perceives mathematical laws. It is the mind that verifies these laws by experimentation. It is the mind that thinks; it is the mind that knows and decides. Simply, the mind is our new frontier! The mind can be improved! The mind is the key to our peace, freedom, and understanding of the innermost secret of who we are."

*   *   *

BEESLY, Patrick 1913-

PERSONAL: Born June 27, 1913, in Barnt Green, Worcestershire, England; son of Gerald (an engineer) and Helen (Chamberlain) Beesly; married Pamela Mary Wildman, September 1, 1939; children: Carolina Elizabeth Beesly Gay, Judith Mary Beesly Evans. *Education:* Trinity College, Cambridge, B.A. (with honors), 1934; private study in France, Belgium, and Germany, 1934-36. *Politics:* Conservative. *Home:* 8 Nelson Place, Lymington, Hampshire SO4 9RT, England. *Agent:* Campbell, Thomson & McLaughlin Ltd., 31 Newington Green, London N16 9PU, England.

CAREER: Keith Shupton & Co. Ltd., London, England, insurance broker, 1936-39; British European Airways, London, head of passenger relations, 1946-48; Henry Hope & Sons Ltd. (window manufacturers), Smethwick and Birmingham, England, 1949-64, director, 1954-64, managing director, 1964, Crittal-Hope Ltd. (amalgamation of Henry Hope & Sons; became Crittal-Hope Engineering Ltd.), Smethwick and Braintree, England, director, 1964-74; writer, 1974—. *Military service:* Royal Naval Volunteer Reserve, Naval Intelligence, 1939-58; became lieutenant commander; received American Legion of Merit.

WRITINGS: Very Special Intelligence: The Story of the Admiralty's Operational Intelligence Centre, 1939-1945, Hamish Hamilton, 1977, Doubleday, 1978. Contributor to naval journals.

WORK IN PROGRESS: Research on the life of Admiral John Godfrey (1888-1971) and on naval intelligence in general.

SIDELIGHTS: Beesly reports: "*Very Special Intelligence* was extremely highly praised by all the British national papers and by British and American naval and military journals. Unfortunately, it appeared in the United States during the New York newspaper strike and received less press coverage there than in England. It was the first book based on a study of the recently released secret naval intelligence records and, of course, on my own intimate knowledge of them and of events resulting from my service in the submarine tracking room. It shows not only what information was available but how it was put to practical use and the contribution which it made to the Allied victory in the Battle of the Atlantic. It is, I believe, easy and exciting reading for the lay reader as well as essential for the professional.

"The role of intelligence in wartime decision making is usually ignored by historians and by the great commanders in their autobiographies. In fact, it is crucial. I was concerned to draw attention to it not only for a proper understanding of past history but as an essential ingredient in the future defense of the Western World.

"Having failed to realize an ambition to join the Royal Navy at the age of thirteen, I have always been deeply interested in naval history and consider it quite an achievement to have had such success with a first book written at the age of sixty-four. It has brought me much correspondence with such famous historians as Professor Marder of the United States, Captain Roskill of Great Britain, and Professor Rohwer of Germany, and with hundreds of individuals from all over the world. I have been invited to lecture in Canada, Germany, Norway, and the United States, as well as in England. I have also appeared on British and German television. In fact, you might say that I have started, rather late in life, on a new career—exhausting and only moderately rewarding financially (due to British taxation), but of absorbing interest."

AVOCATIONAL INTERESTS; Yachting, military history ("particulary that of the American Civil War—the first 'modern' war").

*   *   *

BEILENSON, Edna 1909-
(Elisabeth Deane)

PERSONAL: Surname is pronounced *Bee*-lenson; born June 16, 1909, in New York, N.Y.; daughter of John (an artist) and Anna (Beilenson) Rudolph; married Peter Beilenson, July 20, 1930 (died January 20, 1962); married Joseph E. Barmack, June 19, 1966 (divorced, 1975); children: Anthony C., Roger N., Elizabeth R. Beilenson Schildkraut. *Education:* Hunter College (now the City University of New York), A.B. (cum laude), 1928. *Home and office:* 1035 Fifth Ave., New York, N.Y. 10028.

CAREER: Peter Pauper Press, Inc., Mt. Vernon, N.Y., 1932—, worked as bookkeeper, typesetter, cover designer, and other jobs, became president; free-lance designer of children's books, 1935; Walpole Printing Office, Inc., Mt. Vernon, president, 1962-78. American Institute of Graphic Arts, vice-president, 1956, president, 1958-60; Goudy Society, director, 1965, chairman of board, 1968-74 and 1978, honorary chairman of board, 1974-78, president, 1975-78;

president of Distaff Side; trustee of American Printing History Association. *Member:* Royal Society of Arts (fellow), Grolier Club (New York City). *Awards, honors:* Woman of the Year in Business, Marquis's *Who's Who,* 1968.

WRITINGS—All published by Peter Pauper Press: *Holiday Cook Book,* 1950; (compiler) *Festive Cookery,* 1951; *Cooking to Kill! The Poison Cook-book: Comic Recipes for the Ghoul, Cannibal, Witch, and Murderer,* 1951; (compiler) *Recipes Mother Used to Make,* 1952; (compiler) *Holiday Goodies and How to Make Them,* 1952; *Holiday Punches, Party Bowls, and Soft Drinks,* 1953; (compiler) *Holiday Candies,* 1954; (compiler) *Holiday Cookies,* 1954; *The Merrie Christmas Cook Book,* 1955; *Queen of Hearts Cook Book,* 1955; *The Little Quiz Book,* 1956; (compiler) *Holiday Party Casseroles,* 1956; (compiler) *Holiday Party Desserts,* 1956; *Cupid's Almanack: A Collection of Epigrams Witty and Wise About Love and Marriage, Arranged for Your Delight According to the Seasons of the Year,* 1956; *Abalone to Zabaglione: Unusual and Exotic Recipes,* 1957; *The Christmas Stocking Book,* 1957; *The Melting Pot: A Cookbook of All Nations,* 1958; (compiler) *Festive Seafood Cookery,* 1969; *The Zodiac Cook Book,* 1969; (editor) *Friendship Is Forever,* 1979.

"ABC of Cookery" series; published by Peter Pauper Press: *The ABC of Canapes,* 1953; . . . *Chafing Dish Cookery,* 1956; . . . *Gourmet Cookery,* 1956; . . . *Herb and Spice Cookery,* 1957; . . . *Wine Cookery,* 1957.

"Simple Cookery" series; compiler; published by Peter Pauper Press: *Simple French Cookery,* 1958; . . . *Italian Cookery,* 1959; . . . *Oriental Cookery,* 1960; . . . *Viennese Cookery,* 1960; . . . *Jewish Cookery,* 1962; . . . *New England Cookery,* 1962; . . . *Continental Cookery,* 1963; . . . *Hawaiian Cookery,* 1964; . . . *German Cookery,* 1965.

"Gifts of Gold" series; compiler under pseudonym Elisabeth Deane; published by Peter Pauper Press: *Gentle Thoughts: A Collection of Tender and Wise Sayings From Sundry Authors of Wisdom and Renown,* 1969; *Gift of Friendship: A Collection of Warm, Beautiful Thoughts About the Love of One Heart for Another,* 1969; *Words of Love: A Collection of Love Poems, Love Letters, and Meaningful Sayings Pertaining to Love and Loving,* 1969; *Wisdom of the East: Precious Jewels of Great Wisdom Garnered From the Sages of India and the Far Orient,* 1970; *A Gift of Mistletoe: Thoughts for a Merrie Christmas,* 1971; *Gift of Prayer: A Selection of Prayers Designed to Make the Burdens Lighter and the Hours Less Lonely,* 1971; *The Listening Heart: A Collection of Warm, Discerning Sayings for the Heart That Listens With Sympathy and Understanding,* 1971.

Under pseudonym Elisabeth Deane; published by Peter Pauper Press: (Compiler) *Smiles, Chuckles, and Chortles,* 1971; *The Heart of a Friend,* 1973; (compiler) *A Gift of Tenderness,* 1979.

WORK IN PROGRESS: A history of the Peter Pauper Press.

SIDELIGHTS: Peter Pauper Press was formed in 1928 by Edna Beilenson's cousin, Peter Beilenson, whom she later married. His goal was to publish fine books at a low price. Most of the books were small in size, 64 pages long, made of high quality paper, and sold for one dollar. Today the price of these books is still only $2.95. A year later Beilenson also opened the Walpole Printing Office, which printed quality books, including over a dozen for George Macy's Limited Edition Club.

Edna Beilenson joined her husband as a business partner at Peter Pauper and Walpole Printing in 1932. Over the years she worked in bookkeeping, typesetting, promotion and general sales, and general operations, but her largest contribution was in cover designing. She felt that the style and color of the cover were important selling points, and she had a flair for choosing the right design. Her husband once wrote: "She looks at a book as would a dress designer or an interior decorator. Our output soon showed the feminine influence in the use of delightful patterned bindings. She also taught me how much better a book can be when it has color inside, too; when the printed pages, the binding and even the slipcase are in harmony."

After her husband's death in 1962 Edna Beilenson took over the business, which has continued to prosper. She told Chandler B. Grannis her secret of success: "I love people and I love the books I make—which is a good combination when it comes to selling."

Before she became involved in publishing, Beilenson had planned to be a journalist and novelist.

Beilenson told *CA:* "My career at the Peter Pauper Press has been a lifelong romance. Although I was taught to set the early books by hand, we now use machine-set type, but the accent is still on the craft of the book, and it is that aspect of publishing to which I have devoted my life."

BIOGRAPHICAL/CRITICAL SOURCES: Publishers Weekly, November 27, 1978.

*   *   *

BEIM, Norman 1923-

PERSONAL: Surname is pronounced "Bime"; born October 2, 1923, in Newark, N.J.; son of Herman (a tavern owner) and Frieda (Tall) Beim; divorced. *Education:* Attended Ohio State University, 1941-42, Hedgerow Theatre School, 1946-47, and Institute of Contemporary Art, Washington, D.C., 1949. *Home:* 425 West 57th St., New York, N.Y. 10019.

CAREER: Playwright, 1946—; actor in productions for stage, film, television, and radio, and on tour, 1948—; director, 1949—. *Military service:* U.S. Army, Field Artillery, 1942-45. *Member:* Actors Equity Association, Screen Actors Guild, American Federation of Television and Radio Artists, Dramatists Guild. *Awards, honors:* Second prize from National Theatre Conference, 1944, for "Inside"; first prize from Samuel French competition, 1978, for "The Deserter."

WRITINGS: The Deserter (one-act play; first produced Off-Off Broadway at Troupe Theatre, April 17, 1978), Samuel French, 1979.

Unpublished plays: "Inside" (one-act), first produced in New York City at Provincetown Playhouse, 1951; "The Battle of Valor" (two-act), first produced in New York City at Ansonia Hotel, 1967; "David and Jonathan" (two-act), first produced in New York City at Assembly Theatre, 1967; "Guess Who's Not Coming to Dinner" (three-act), first produced in New York City, 1968; "The World of Dracula" (two-act), first produced Off-Off Broadway at Troupe Theatre, February 3, 1978; "The Failure" (one-act), first produced Off-Off Broadway at Troupe Theatre, April 17, 1978; "A Queen's Revenge" (one-act), first produced Off-Off Broadway at Troupe Theatre, April 17, 1978; "Marvelous Party" (two-act comedy), first produced Off-Off Broadway at Troupe Theatre, July 31, 1978; "A Marriage of Convenience" (two-act comedy), first produced Off-Off

Broadway at Troupe Theatre, October 23, 1978; "The Professor Graduates" (two-act), first produced Off-Off Broadway at Troupe Theatre, February 11, 1979. Also author of "The Lively Art" (three-act Comedy), first produced in New York City at Studio Theatre.

Unproduced plays: "Echo and Narcissus" (two-act), 1949; "Springtime in New York" (two-act), 1961; "The Haircut" (two-act), 1968; "The Establishment" (two-act), 1969; "Success" (two-act), 1969; "The Disintegration of Della Longstreet" (two-act), 1970; "Ida the Indomitable" (two-act), 1970; "Food Stamps" (two-act), 1971; "The Dark Corner of an Empty Room" (two-act), 1972; "The Liberation of Linda Dwarkin" (two-act), 1972; "Pygmalion and Galatea" (two-act), 1973; "Kingdom by the Sea" (two-act), 1973; "Pickled Peppers" (two-act), 1976; "The First Mistake" (two-act), 1976; "The Tyranny of Love" (two-act), 1977; "Dancing in the Dark" (two-act), 1977; "The Jealous Critic" (two-act), 1978; "Archies Comeback" (two-act), 1978.

WORK IN PROGRESS: A play about David and Bathsheba, a dramatic study of the corruption of power.

SIDELIGHTS: Beim told *CA:* "I intended first to be a novelist, but after taking acting classes at Ohio State I became involved in theatre and began writing plays. My first one-act effort, "Inside," won second prize in a nationwide contest (I received the award while I was fighting in Germany during World War II) and I was hooked. I have been writing almost continually for these many years. Despite very meagre rewards, I have persisted because playwriting is really compulsive with me.

"I earn my living as an actor. Writing, my first love, is really an avocation. The closest I have come to Broadway has been an option ("Success"), but the production failed to materialize. There is still production interest in that play and it may be done Off Broadway next season. I consider myself a fool to have persisted for so long at my writing with nothing to show for it. I have learned my craft, but knowledge, unfortunately, does not pay the rent. Perhaps all true artists are fools at heart, or maybe I must cling to that belief as a crutch.

"I try to write almost every morning (early) for two to three hours. It is a relief, it is therapy, and it is a necessity." Beim added that his "favorite playwright is Moliere. Of course Shakespeare's poetry is imperishable. I admire Ibsen, Chekov, Strindberg, and Tennessee Williams."

BIOGRAPHICAL CRITICAL SOURCES: New York Times, March 20, 1979.

* * *

BELFER, Nancy 1930-

PERSONAL: Born July 30, 1930, in Buffalo, N.Y.; daughter of Albert and Helen Barback; married Bernard Belfer (a teacher), September 2, 1951; children: Lauren. *Education:* State University of New York College at Buffalo, B.S., 1951; Rochester Institute of Technology, M.F.A., 1962. *Residence:* Buffalo, N.Y. *Office:* Department of Design, State University of New York College at Buffalo, 1300 Elmwood Ave., Buffalo, N.Y. 14222.

CAREER: State University of New York College at Buffalo, assistant professor, 1960-67, associate professor, 1967-72, professor of textile design (weaving), 1972—. Work exhibited in group and solo shows, in national tours sponsored by Smithsonian Institution, and in OBJECTS: USA. Lecturer and workshop leader. *Member:* Handweavers Guild of

America (state representative), American Crafts Council, Surface Design Association, New York State Craftsmen, Buffalo Craftsmen. *Awards, honors:* Golden Eagle Awards from Council on International Nontheatrical Events, for each of her films.

WRITINGS: Designing in Batik and Tie Dye, Davis Publications (Worcester, Mass.), 1971, revised edition, Prentice-Hall, 1977; *Designing in Stitchery and Applique,* Davis Publications, 1972, revised edition, Prentice-Hall, 1977; *Weaving: Design and Expression,* Davis Publications, 1975. Contributor to magazines, including *Everyday Art* and *School Arts.*

Films; all for ACI: "Batik"; "Weaving on Looms You Can Make"; "With Fabric and Thread"; "Tie-Dye: Designing with Color."

WORK IN PROGRESS: A series of wall hangings for a textile exhibition.

SIDELIGHTS: Nancy Belfer writes: "My three books all deal with various aspects of textile design. My writing activities stem from two important and related facets of my life: my creative work as an exhibiting fiber artist and my teaching. Thus the books are technical on the one hand, but also, I would like to think, something more in that the focus is not primarily on the 'how-to-do-it' directions. They are books for those who wish to learn skills, which are certainly necessary in fiber arts. However, the books are also for those who wish to develop their ability to see beyond the obvious and the commonplace in visual design. I have tried to show that working in the various techniques of the textile arts can offer a fascinating challenge, a creative experience of deep pleasure and accomplishment."

* * *

BELIN, David W. 1928-

PERSONAL: Born June 20, 1928, in Washington, D.C.; son of Louis I. and Esther (Klass) Belin; married Constance Newman (a university regent), September 14, 1952; children: Jonathan L., James M., Joy E., Thomas R., Laura R. *Education:* University of Michigan, A.B., 1951, M.B.A., 1953, J.D., 1954. *Residence:* Des Moines, Iowa. *Office:* Belin, Harris, Helmick & Lovrien, 2000 Financial Center, Des Moines, Iowa 50309.

CAREER: Belin, Harris, Helmick & Lovrien, Des Moines, Iowa, partner, 1954—. Counsel to President's Commission on the Assassination of President Kennedy (Warren Commission), 1964; executive director of Commission on C.I.A. Activities Within the United States (Rockefeller Commission), 1975. Member of corporate boards of directors. *Military service:* U.S. Army, 1946-47. *Member:* Phi Beta Kappa, Phi Kappa Phi, Coif.

WRITINGS: November 22, 1963: You Are the Jury, Quadrangle, 1973. Contributor to popular magazines, including *National Review,* and newspapers.

BIOGRAPHICAL/CRITICAL SOURCES: New York Times Book Review, November 18, 1973; *Best Sellers,* January 1, 1974.

* * *

BELL, Arthur 1939-

PERSONAL: Born November 14, 1939, in Brooklyn, N.Y.; son of Samuel (a manufacturer of children's clothing) and Claire (a designer; maiden name, Bodan) Bell. *Education:* Attended commercial high school in Montreal, Ontario,

Canada. *Politics:* Democrat. *Religion:* Jewish. *Home:* 1446 First Ave., New York, N.Y. 10021. *Agent:* Betty Anne Clarke, International Creative Management, 40 West 57th St., New York, N.Y. 10019. *Office: Village Voice,* 80 University Place, New York, N.Y. 10003.

CAREER: Viking Press, Inc., New York City, publicity director for children's books, 1960-68; Random House, Inc., New York City, publicity director for children's books, 1968-70; *Village Voice,* New York City, feature writer and author of column "Bell Tells," 1970—. *Awards, honors:* Runner-up award in nonfiction from *Playboy* for adaptation of *Kings Don't Mean a Thing* and best nonfiction award from *Where It's At* for *King Don't Mean a Thing,* both 1978.

WRITINGS: Dancing the Gay Lib Blues: A Year in the Gay Liberation Movement, Simon & Schuster, 1971; *Kings Don't Mean a Thing: The John Knight Murder Case,* Morrow, 1978. Contributor to magazines and newspapers, including *Esquire, Playboy, Cosmopolitan,* and *New York Times.*

WORK IN PROGRESS: Another nonfiction book.

SIDELIGHTS: Bell writes: "I've probably had more articles on the gay lifestyle published in non-gay media than anyone else in America. Additionally, I cover crime stories and write a good deal about the entertainment world. I'm published weekly in the *Weekly Voice,* and the subjects and personalities in my column really run the gamut. When time permits, I write features for other magazines."

BIOGRAPHICAL/CRITICAL SOURCES: Christopher Street, January, 1979.

* * *

BELLAK, Leopold 1916-

PERSONAL: Born June 22, 1916, in Vienna, Austria; came to United States in 1938, naturalized in 1942; son of Siegfried and Marie (Weiler) Bellak; married Sonya Sorel (a sculptor), December 20, 1950; children: Karola, Katrina. *Education:* Attended University of Vienna, 1935-38; Boston University, M.A., 1939; Harvard University, M.A., 1942; New York University, M.D., 1944. *Residence:* Larchmont, N.Y. *Agent:* James Brown Associates, Inc., 22 East 60th St., New York, N.Y. 10022. *Office:* 22 Rockwood Dr., Larchmont, N.Y. 10538.

CAREER: St. Elizabeth's Hospital, Washington, D.C., 1944-46, began as intern, became resident; private practice in psychiatry, Larchmont, N.Y., 1946—; City Hospital, New York City, director and psychiatrist, 1958-64; New York University, New York City, clinical professor of psychology, 1965—; Albert Einstein College of Medicine, New York City, clinical professor of psychiatry, 1971—. Visiting professor or lecturer at New School for Social Research, 1947-55, City College of New York (now of the City University of New York), 1948-54, Columbia University, 1956-69, and George Washington University, 1970-76. Principal investigator and project director for the National Institute of Mental Health grants, 1951—. Established Trouble Shooting Clinic in New York City, 1958. Consultant to Jewish Board of Guardians, 1947-48, Altro Health and Rehabilitation Service, 1947-57, U.S. Military Academy, 1966—, and RAND Corp., 1969—. Member of board of advisers of New Rochelle Guidance Center, 1960—. *Military service:* U.S. Army Medical Corps, 1942-46.

MEMBER: American Psychoanalytic Association (life fellow), American Psychological Association (life fellow), American Psychiatric Association (life fellow), American Orthopsychiatric Association (fellow), Royal Society of Medicine (fellow), Society for Projective Techniques and Rorschach Institute (fellow; president, 1952-56, 1957-58), Westchester Psychoanalytic Society (president, 1962-63), Sigma Xi. *Awards, honors:* Annual merit award from New York Society of Clinical Psychologists, 1964; award for contribution to the theory and practice of community psychiatry from Psychiatric Outpatient Centers of America, 1976.

WRITINGS: Dementia Praecox: The Past Decade's Work and Present Status; A Review and Evaluation (Basic Book Club selection), Grune, 1948; (editor with Lawrence E. Abt, and contributor) *Projective Psychology: Clinical Approaches to the Total Personality* (Basic Book Club selection), Knopf, 1950; *Manic-Depressive Psychosis and Allied Disorders* (Basic Book Club selection), Grune, 1952; (editor and contributor) *The Psychology of Physical Illness: Psychiatry Applied to Medicine, Surgery and the Specialties,* Grune, 1952; *The Thematic Apperception Test and the Children's Apperception Test in Clinical Use,* Grune, 1954, 2nd edition, 1971; (editor with P. K. Benedict, and contributor) *Schizophrenia: A Review of the Syndrome* (Basic Book Club selection), Logos Press, 1958; (editor, conference chairman, and contributor) *Conceptual and Methodological Problems in Psychoanalysis,* New York Academy of Sciences, 1959.

(Co-editor) Emilio Mira y Lopez, *Myokinetic Psychodiagnosis,* Logos Press, 1960; (editor) *Contemporary European Psychiatry,* Grove, 1961; (editor and contributor) *A Handbook of Community Psychiatry and Community Mental Health,* Grune, 1964; (with Leonard Small) *Emergency Psychotherapy and Brief Psychotherapy,* Grune, 1965, 2nd edition, 1978; *The Broad Scope of Psychoanalysis: Selected Papers of Leopold Bellak,* edited by Donald P. Spence, Grune, 1967; (editor with Laurence Loeb) *The Schizophrenic Syndrome,* Grune, 1969; (editor with Harvey H. Barten, and contributor) *Progress in Community Mental Health,* Grune, Volume I, 1969, Volume II, 1972, Volume III, Brunner, 1975.

The Porcupine Dilemma, Citadel, 1970; (with Marvin Hurvich and Helen Gediman) *Ego Functions in Schizophrenics, Neurotics, and Normals* (selection of Behavioral Science Book Service, Macmillan Book Clubs), Wiley, 1973; (editor and contributor) *A Concise Handbook of Community Psychiatry and Community Mental Health,* Grune, 1974; *The Best Years of Your Life: A Guide to the Art and Science of Aging,* Atheneum, 1975; *Overload: The New Human Condition,* Behavioral Publications, 1975; *The Thematic Apperception, Test, Children's Apperception Test, and Senior Apperception Technique in Clinical Use,* Grune, 3rd edition, 1975; (editor with Toksoz B. Karasu, and contributor) *Geriatric Psychiatry: A Handbook for Psychiatrists and Primary Care Physicians,* Grune, 1976; (editor and contributor) *Disorders of the Schizophrenic Syndrome,* Basic Books, 1979.

Contributor: E. A. Spiegel, editor, *Progress in Neurology and Psychiatry,* Volumes IV-X, Grune, 1949-55; L. W. Crafts, T. C. Schneirla, and others, editors, *Recent Experiments in Psychology,* revised edition, McGraw, 1950; E. Shneidman and others, editors, *Thematic Analysis,* Grune, 1951; G. Bychowski and J. L. Despert, editors, *Specialized Techniques in Psychotherapy,* Basic Books, 1952; Daniel Brower and L. E. Abt, editors, *Progress in Clinical Psychology,* Grune, 1952; A. A. Roback, editor, *Present-Day Psychology,* Philosophical Library, 1955; J. M. McCary, editor, *Psychology of Personality,* Logos Press, 1956; Albert I. Rabin and Mary R. Haworth, editors, *Projective Techniques with Children,* Gruen, 1960; W. Klopfer, *The Psychological Test Report,* Grune, 1961; J. Massermann, editor, *Current Psychiatric Therapy,* Grune, 1962, Robert W. White, editor,

The Study of Lives, Atherton Press, 1963; Morton Hunt, *The Talking Cure,* Harper, 1963; A. Abrams, editor, *Unfinished Tasks in the Behavioral Sciences,* Williams & Wilkins, 1964; Abt and S. Weissman, editors, *Acting Out: Theoretical and Clinical Aspects,* Grune, 1965; Haworth, *The C.A.T.: Facts About Fantasy,* Grune, 1965; Louis A. Gottschalk and Arthur H. Auerbach, editors, *Methods of Research in Psychotherapy,* Appleton-Century-Crofts, 1966; Jacob B. Chassan, *Research Design in Clinical Psychology and Psychiatry,* Appleton-Century-Crofts, 1966; *Viewpoint on Mental Health* (transcript of an interview on WNYC-TV with Marvin Perkins), New York City Community Mental Health Board, 1967; S. Lesse, editor, *An Evaluation of the Results of the Psychotherapies,* C. C Thomas, 1968; P. Davidson and C. Costello, editors, *N=1: Experimental Studies of Single Cases,* Van Nostrand, 1969; R. Cancro, editor, *The Schizophrenic Reactions,* Brunner, 1970; C. Chiland and P. Bequart, editors, *Traitements au long cours des etats psychotiques,* Editions Privat, 1974; Benjamin B. Wolman, editor, *Clinical Diagnosis of Mental Disorders: A Handbook,* Plenum, 1978.

Contributor to *International Encyclopedia of Social Sciences,* 1968. Contributor of many articles and occasional book reviews to professional journals, magazines, and newspapers.

WORK IN PROGRESS: A book with Toksoz B. Karasu, *Specialized Techniques in Psychotherapy,* for Brunner; a book, *Adult Psychiatric States With Minimal Brain Dysfunction,* for Grune; articles about psychiatry to be published in professional journals.

AVOCATIONAL INTERESTS: Writing detective stories, karate and aikido (black belt), judo (brown belt).

BIOGRAPHICAL/CRITICAL SOURCES: New York Times Book Review, September 14, 1975; *Contemporary Psychology,* December, 1975, July, 1977.

*   *   *

BELTRAN, Pedro (Gerardo) 1897-1979

OBITUARY NOTICE: Born February 17, 1897, in Lima, Peru; died of a heart attack, February 16, 1979, in Lima. Politician, economist, diplomat, farmer, entrepreneur, and publisher. As publisher of the internationally recognized *La Prensa,* one of Peru's most highly esteemed newspapers, Beltran fought for freedom of the press. He was hailed as a national hero in the 1950's when President Manuel Odria halted the printing of *La Prensa* several times and had Beltran imprisoned for advocating free elections. When President Prado was voted in a free election to replace Odria, Beltran was appointed prime minister of Peru and minister of finance. A proponent of democracy and free enterprise, Beltran implemented a free-exchange policy that helped stabilize Peru's shaky economy. While he was in office, Beltran obtained financial assistance from the United States and fostered the development of much-needed housing facilities. Following an unsuccessful campaign for the presidency of Peru, he relinquished his political posts in 1961, returning to the publication of *La Prensa.* When the paper was shut down for the last time in 1975 by a new military regime, Beltran went into exile. He received the Maria Moors Cabot Prize for inter-American journalism from Columbia University and the Hero of the Press gold medal from the Inter-American Press Association. Obituaries and other sources: *Current Biography,* Wilson, 1967; *Biography News,* Volume II, Gale, 1975; *New York Times,* February 18, 1979.

BENET, Laura 1884-1979

OBITUARY NOTICE—See index for *CA* sketch: Born June 13, 1884, in Brooklyn, N.Y.; died February 17, 1979, in New York, N.Y. Social worker, newspaper editor, poet and author. After her retirement from social work, Benet worked for several New York newspapers, including the *New York Evening Post.* In addition to writing children's books, novels, and literary biographies, Benet was also the author of two books on her brothers, Stephen Vincent and William Rose Benet. She wrote numerous volumes of poetry, including *Bridge of a Single Hair,* published in 1974. Obituaries and other sources: *Authors of Books for Young People,* 2nd edition, Scarecrow, 1971; *Who's Who in America,* 38th edition, Marquis, 1974; *New York Times,* February 19, 1979.

*   *   *

BENNETT, Judith   ?-1979

OBITUARY NOTICE: Died May 25, 1979, in an airplane crash in Chicago, Ill. Psychologist and senior editor of *Forum* magazine. Obituaries and other sources: *New York Times,* May 31, 1979.

*   *   *

BENNETT, Thomas L(eroy) 1942-

PERSONAL: Born September 25, 1942, in Norwalk, Conn.; son of Thomas L. and Gertrude (employed by National Park Service; maiden name, Richardson) Bennett; married Jacqueline Beekman, August 5, 1972; children: Dean, Shannon, Brian, Laurie. *Education:* University of New Mexico, B.A., 1964, M.S., 1966, Ph.D., 1968. *Religion:* Presbyterian. *Home:* 213 Camino Real, Fort Collins, Colo. 80524. *Office:* Department of Psychology, Colorado State University, Fort Collins, Colo. 80523.

CAREER: California State University, Sacramento, assistant professor of psychology, 1968-70; Colorado State University, Fort Collins, assistant professor of psychology, 1970-73, associate professor, 1973-77, professor of psychology, physiology, and biophysics, 1977—. *Member:* American Psychological Association, Society for Neuroscience, Rocky Mountain Psychological Association, Sigma Xi.

WRITINGS: (Editor) *Readings in the Psychology of Perception,* MSS, 1971; (editor) *Perception: An Adaptive Process,* MSS, 1973; *Brains and Behavior,* Brooks/Cole, 1977; *The Sensory World,* Brooks/Cole, 1978; (with H. C. Ellis, T. C. Daniel, and E. J. Rickert) *The Psychology of Learning and Memory,* Brooks/Cole, 1979; (with D. P. Cantrell) *Exploring the Sensory World,* Brooks/Cole, 1979. Contributor of about forty articles to academic journals.

WORK IN PROGRESS: Revising *Brains and Behavior,* publication by Brooks/Cole expected in 1981; *The Psychological World,* publication by Brooks/Cole expected in late 1981 or early 1982.

SIDELIGHTS: Bennett comments: "I love writing, and a major goal has been to write technical, yet readable and stimulating books. Textbook writing has vastly changed in the last ten years. Authors must write in a personal style to capture the students' interest, and short, illustrative, personalized examples drive a point home. In addition, I find it helpful to read novels on the side: it loosens up my own writing. Technical writing need not be boring!

"I am also an active researcher. Most of work is in the area of physiological psychology. Our goal is to gain a better understanding of how the brain regulates behavior. A major area of research has examined changes in the brain waves that occur as an animal or human performs different behaviors. The Electroencephalagram (EEG) method allows us to 'listen in on' the brain as it is doing its job. We use sophisticated computer analysis to look at the fine features of the brain waves.''

AVOCATIONAL INTERESTS: Camping, fishing, cooking, square dancing, racquetball, weight lifting, gardening.

* * *

BENSON, Herbert 1935-

PERSONAL: Born April 14, 1935, in Yonkers, N.Y.; son of Charles (a merchant) and Hannah (Schiller) Benson; married Marilyn Joan Wilcher; children: Jennifer Caron, Gregory Charles. *Education:* Wesleyan University, Middletown, Conn., B.A., 1957; Harvard University, M.D., 1961. *Office:* Beth Israel Hospital, 330 Brookline Ave., Boston, Mass. 02215.

CAREER: King County Hospital, Seattle, Wash., intern, 1961-62; University of Washington, Seattle, assistant resident in medicine at University Hospital, 1962-63; Harvard University, Cambridge, Mass., research fellow in medicine, 1965-67, and physiology, 1967-68, instructor, 1969, assistant professor, 1970-72, associate professor of medicine, 1972—. Research and clinical fellow in medicine at Boston City Hospital's Thorndike Memorial Laboratory, 1965-67, research associate, 1969-74, assistant visiting physician, 1967-71, associate visiting physician, 1971-74, assistant program director at General Clinical Research Center, 1970-72, program director, 1972-78; associate physician at Beth Israel Hospital, 1974—, director of hypertension section, 1974—, behavioral medicine section, 1977-78, and Division of Behavioral Medicine, 1978—. Research assistant in medicine at University of Puerto Rico, 1964-65. Head of steering committee of Boston Health Promotion Council, 1977-78; member of executive committee and board of directors of Medical Foundation (and head of committee on community health and education), 1978—; consultant to President's Special Action Office for Drug Abuse Prevention and National Institute of Mental Health. *Military service:* U.S. Public Health Service, surgeon at National Heart Institute, 1963-65; became lieutenant commander.

MEMBER: American Medical Association, American Heart Association, American College of Cardiology (fellow), American Physiological Society, American Psychosomatic Society, American Association for the Advancement of Science, American Federation for Clinical Research, Academy of Behavioral Medicine Research, Society for Behavioral Medicine, Massachusetts Medical Society, Massachusetts Heart Association (member of local board of directors, 1972-75), Sigma Xi. *Awards, honors:* Medical Foundation fellow, 1967-69.

WRITINGS: (Contributor) G. Onesti, K. E. Kim, and J. H. Moyer, editors, *Hypertension: Mechanisms and Management,* Grune, 1973; (contributor) R. S. Eliot, editor, *Contemporary Problems in Cardiology,* Volume I: *Stress and the Heart,* Futura Publishing, 1974; *The Relaxation Response,* Morrow, 1975; (contributor) Onesti and A. M. Brest, editors, *Hypertension: Mechanisms, Diagnosis, and Treatment,* F. A. Davis, 1978; *The Mind/Body Effect,* Simon & Schuster, 1979.

Contributor of about sixty-five articles to medical and business journals and popular magazines, including *Science* and *Scientific American.* Associate editor of *Journal of Behavioral Medicine,* 1977—; member of editorial board of *Psychotherapy and Psychosomatics, Journal of Biofeedback*

and Self Regulation, and *Journal of Human Stress,* all 1974—.

SIDELIGHTS: Benson's first book has been published in Finland, France, Italy, Japan, Spain, the Netherlands, Germany, Denmark, and Brazil.

* * *

BENSON, Kathleen 1947-

PERSONAL: Born February 10, 1947, in Keene, N.H.; daughter of Roland F. (a technical representative) and Margaret (a bookkeeper; maiden name, Bliss) Benson. *Education:* University of Connecticut, B.A., 1969. *Residence:* New York, N.Y. *Office:* Museum of the City of New York, Fifth Ave. at 103rd St., New York, N.Y. 10029.

CAREER: Museum of the City of New York, New York, N.Y., assistant dean of education, 1969—. Member of board of directors of Children's Book Review Service. *Member:* Phi Beta Kappa, Phi Kappa Phi, Mortar Board.

WRITINGS: (With Jim Haskins and Ellen Inkelis) *The Great American Crazies,* Condor, 1977; (with Haskins) *Scott Joplin: The Man Who Made Ragtime,* Doubleday, 1978; (with Haskins) *The Stevie Wonder Scrapbook,* Grosset, 1978; *A Man Called Martin Luther,* Concordia, 1980. Contributor of articles to *Now* and of crossword puzzles to newspapers.

WORK IN PROGRESS: Methodists, publication by Concordia expected in 1981.

SIDELIGHTS: Benson comments: ''Research fascinates me. Nothing is more exciting than making a discovery about which no one else knows; e.g., identifying Scott Joplin's German music professor or mentor.'' Her advice to aspiring writers is ''to read as much really good writing as possible and always to keep trying.''

BIOGRAPHICAL/CRITICAL SOURCES: Washington Post, July 24, 1978.

* * *

BENTOV, Itzhak 1923(?)-1979

OBITUARY NOTICE: Born c. 1923 in Czechoslovakia; died May 25, 1979, in an airplane crash in Chicago, Ill. Business consultant and author. Bentov wrote *Stalking the Wild Pendulum,* published in 1977. Obituaries and other sources: *Publishers Weekly,* June 11, 1979.

* * *

BERENDZEN, Richard (Earl) 1938-

PERSONAL: Born September 6, 1938, in Walters, Okla.; son of Earl Emmanuel (a retail merchant) and Florine (Harrison) Berendzen; married Gail Edgar (an educator), November 26, 1964; children: Deborah, Natasha. *Education:* Massachusetts Institute of Technology, B.S., 1961; Harvard University, M.A., 1967, Ph.D., 1968. *Home:* 5301 Westbard Circle, Bethesda, Md. 20016. *Office:* American University, Washington, D.C. 20016.

CAREER: Geophysics Corporation of America, Bedford, Mass., resident scientist, 1959-64; Ling-Temes-Vought Corp., astronautics division, Dallas, Tex., resident scientist, 1962-63; Boston University, Boston, Mass., lecturer, 1965-67, assistant professor, 1967-71, associate professor of astronomy, 1971-74, acting department chairman, 1971-72; American University, Washington, D.C., associate professor of physics and dean of College of Arts and Sciences, 1974-76, professor of physics and university provost, 1976—. Visiting lecturer in astronomy at Harvard University, summer, 1964 and 1966; has lectured frequently for professional and popular organizations. Consultant or adviser to Harvard Project Physics, American Institute of Physics, American Council on Education, Association of American Colleges, National Academy of Sciences, National Aeronautics and Space Administration (NASA), Smithsonian Institution, and numerous other organizations.

MEMBER: International Association of University Presidents (associate member), International Astronomical Union, American Association for the Advancement of Science (fellow), American Association for Higher Education, American Association of Physics Teachers, American Association of University Administrators (chairman of task force on international development, 1978—), American Association of University Professors, American Astronomical Society, American Conference of Academic Deans, National Science Teachers Association, Astronomical Society of the Pacific, History of Science Society, New York Academy of Sciences, Washington Institute of Foreign Affairs, Kappa Mu Epsilon, Phi Eta Sigma, Phi Kappa Phi, Sigma Xi, Cosmos Club (Washington, D.C.). *Awards, honors:* Mortar board distinguished faculty award from American University, 1977; selected as one of the "100 top young leaders in the American academy" by *Change* magazine, 1978.

WRITINGS: Structure of the Universe in the Development of Modern Astronomy, Boston University, 1969; (editor) *Education in and History of Modern Astronomy,* New York Academy of Sciences, 1972; (contributor) Stephen George Brush and John Gordon King, editors, *History in the Teaching of Physics,* University Press of New England, 1972; (contributor) *Astronomy and Astrophysics for the 1970's,* National Academy of Sciences, Volume I, 1972, Volume II, 1973; (editor) *Life Beyond Earth and the Mind of Man,* U.S. Government Printing Office, 1973; (with Garritt Vershuur and H. M. Gurin) *Careers in Astronomy* (booklet), American Astronomical Society, 1973; (contributor) Arthur Beer and K. A. Strand, editors, *Copernicus Yesterday and Today,* Pergamon, 1975; (with Richard Hart and Daniel Seeley) *Man Discovers the Galaxies,* Science History Publications, 1976. Contributor to *Dictionary of Scientific Biography,* and contributor of more than one hundred articles and reviews to magazines and professional journals. Founding editor of *Journal of College Science Teaching;* member of founding editorial board of *Search: The First Magazine About the Search for Extra-Terrestrial Life,* 1978. Guest editor of *Journal of College Science Teaching,* December, 1973.

SIDELIGHTS: Berendzen was featured in two educational films, "Life Beyond Earth and the Mind of Man," 1974, and "Who's Out There?," 1975, both produced by the National Aeronautics and Space Administration. He has also hosted or participated in several dozen radio and television programs in the U.S. and abroad, including the "Scientific Search for Life Beyond Earth," shown by NBC-TV throughout 1975, "The David Susskind Show," televised nationally in October, 1975, and "Two Hundred Years of American Astronomy," an NBC-TV special related to the Bicentennial.

BIOGRAPHICAL/CRITICAL SOURCES: Sky and Telescope, February, 1973, December, 1973, April, 1977; *Washington Post Book World,* October 28, 1973; *Science,* May 10, 1974; *Psychology Today,* June, 1974; *Scientific American,* April, 1977; *American Scholar,* autumn, 1977.

* * *

BERENY, Gail Rubin 1942-

PERSONAL: Original name, Gail Rubin; name legally changed in 1965; born June 24, 1942, in Davenport, Iowa; daughter of David and Ruth (Wiseman) Rubin. *Education:* University of Michigan, B.A., 1963; also attended San Francisco State University and University of California, San Francisco. *Politics:* "Changes daily." *Religion:* Jewish. *Home and office:* 200 Southeast 15th Rd., Miami, Fla. 33129.

CAREER: KPIX-TV, San Francisco, Calif., associate director and producer, 1974-75; WTVJ-TV, Miami, Fla., press information manager, 1976—. Producer and narrator for documentary program on KPFA-Radio, 1973. Director of research for "Persons" project, WPBT-TV, Miami, 1975. *Member:* Common Cause.

WRITINGS: MsAdventures: World Travelguide for Independent Women, Chronicle Books, 1978. Author of "Heroin in the Bay Area," a documentary, KPFA-Radio, 1973. Author of television documentaries for private production companies. Associate editor of "Focus" for KQED-TV, 1974-75.

WORK IN PROGRESS: A novel.

* * *

BERGER, Yves 1934-

PERSONAL: Surname is pronounced Bur-*zhay*; born January 14, 1934, in Avignon, France; son of Leon (in transportation) and Marie (Coutelin) Berger. *Education:* University of Montpellier, License es lettres, 1955; Sorbonne, University of Paris, diplome d'etudes superieures, 1956. *Home:* Villa des Ternes, 12 Avenue de Verzy, Paris 75017, France. *Office:* Editions Bernard Grasset, 61 rue des Saints-Peres, Paris 75006, France.

CAREER: Editions Bernard Grasset, Paris, France, editor-in-chief, 1960—. Consultant to French television, 1970-74.

WRITINGS: Boris Pasternak, Seghers, 1958; *Le Sud* (novel), Grasset, 1962, translation by Robert Baldick published as *The Garden,* Braziller, 1963 (translation published in England as *The South,* Weidenfeld & Nicholson, 1963); *America: cinquante annees de l'histoire des Etats-Unis* (title means "America: Fifty Years of United States History"), A. Barret (Paris), 1975; *Le Fou d'Amerique,* Grasset, 1976, translation by Patrick O'Brian published as *Obsession: An American Love Story,* Putnam, 1978; *Les Luberons* (essay; title means "The Luberons"), Chene, 1977; *Les Indiens des plaines* (title means "The Indians of the Plains"), Dargaud, 1978.

SIDELIGHTS: Berger's first novel, *The Garden,* is the story of a Frenchman's fantasy about the state of Virginia. In his mind, it is a place of pastoral beauty reminiscent of a less complicated era. The man's daughter, Virginnie, tries unsuccessfully to dissuade her brother, who is also the narrator, from being caught up in the same dream. Reviewing the book in *Book Week,* Susan Sontag noted that *The Garden* "is not too long; it is beautifully written without being overwritten, and it is full of intelligences. . . . M. Berger has spun a really gothic tale of psychological horror, swathing the gothic elements—emotional thralldom, the transformation of a person into an automaton, lively incest between brother and sister—in his finely wrought, no-comment, thoroughly inward prose." Critic L. S. Roudiez commented in the *Saturday Review* that "M. Berger has talent: if he were willing to join the rest of us who have accepted the fact that we live in the twentieth century, he might give us a thing of value—a work that would not only involve Berger the literary craftsman but his total being as well."

"The Garden", Berger told *CA*, "is the story of a youth whose father tries to raise him in the south of France in 1962 as if they were living in Virginia in 1842. This novel explores the fear of death and the passing of time; it evokes Rimbaud's famous verse "True life is elsewhere" ("La vraie vie est ailleurs"). For my hero, true life is in North America, the more so as he spent his childhood in France during the German occupation and his father and mother endlessly spoke of the day when the Americans would arrive to liberate France."

Berger added a word about two of his other books: "*Les Luberons* is an essay about a very beautiful part of southern France, le Luberon, about fifty miles north of Marseilles. I researched *Les Indiens* through reading lots of books, traveling a great deal throughout the United States, and visiting more than thirty Indian reservations."

AVOCATIONAL INTERESTS: Collecting North American Indian artifacts ("My collection includes three katchina dolls from the Hopi Indians, a Blackfeet war bonnet, a very large Haida cup, a Northern Cheyenne pair of pearled mocassins, and many other items, all made in North America before 1880").

BIOGRAPHICAL/CRITICAL SOURCES: New York Times Book Review, September 8, 1963; *Saturday Review*, September 14, 1963; *Book Week*, September 15, 1963; *Commonweal*, October 18, 1963; *Times Literary Supplement*, October 18, 1963, September 17, 1976.

* * *

BERGIER, Jacques 1912-1978

PERSONAL: Born in 1912; died November 24, 1978, in Paris, France, of cerebral hemorrhage; married Jacqueline Bernardeau. *Education:* Educated in France.

CAREER: Writer and scientist. Co-founder of *Planete*. *Military service:* Served in French Underground during World War II; captured by German Gestapo and sent to concentration camp, 1943, released in 1945. *Awards, honors:* Legion of Honor; Croix de Guerre; Rosette de la Resistance.

WRITINGS—In English: *The Secrets of Living Matter*, translation by L. R. Celestin, Barrie & Rockliff, 1959; *The Dawn of Magic*, translation by Rollo Meyers, A. Gibbs & Phillips, 1964; (with Louis Pauwels) *Le Matin des magiciens*, Gallimard, c. 1960, translation published as *The Morning of the Magicians*, Stein & Day, 1964; *Admirations* (history and criticism of fantasy-fiction), C. Bourgois, 1970; (with Pauwels) *Impossible Possibilities*, Stein & Day, 1971; (with Pauwels) *L'Homme eternal*, Gallimard, 1970, translation published as *The Eternal Man*, Souvenir Press, 1972, Mayflower, 1973; *Extraterrestrial Visitations From Prehistoric Times to the Present*, Regnery, 1973; (compiler and contributor) *Extraterrestrial Intervention: The Evidence*, Regnery, 1974; *Visa pour une autre terre*, A. Michel, 1974, translation by Nicole Teghert published as *Secret Doors of the Earth*, Regnery, 1975; *Secret Armies: The Growth of Corporate and Industrial Espionage* (contains *L'Espionnage industriel*, *L'Espionnage scientifique*, and *L'Espionnage strategique*; also see below), Bobbs-Merrill, 1975.

Other: *Agents secrets contre armes secretes*, Arthaud, 1955; *Mysteres de la vie*, Le Centurion, 1957; *L'Energie H.*, Editions du Cap, 1958; *Les Murailles invisibles*, Del Duca, 1960; (editor) *Encyclopedie des sciences et des techniques*, Editions de l'Encyclopedie des sciences, 1961; (editor) *Les Meilleures histoires de science-fiction sovietique*, Robert Laffont, 1963; *A l'ecoute des planetes*, Fayard, 1963; *Rire*

Avec les savants, Fayard, 1964; (co-editor with Jacques Sternberg) *Les Chefs-d'oeuvre de l'epouvante*, Editions Planete, 1965; (co-editor with Sternberg) *Les Chefs d'oeuver du rire*, Editions Planete, 1966; (with Pierre Nord) *L'Actuelle guerre secrete*, Editions Planete, 1967; (co-editor with Sternberg) *Les Chefs d'oeuvre du fantastique*, Editions Planete, 1967; *La Guerre secrete du petrole*, Denoeel, 1968; (translator) Howard Phillips Lovecraft, *Epouvante et surnaturel en litterature*, Christian Bourgois, 1969; *L'Espionnage industriel* (also see above), Hachette, 1969.

(With Victor Alexandrov) *Guerre secrete sous les oceans*, Editions maritimes et et d'outremer, 1970; *Aux limites du connu*, Casterman, 1971; *Les Frontieres du possible*, Casterman, 1971; *L'Espionnage scientifique* (also see above), Hachette, 1971; *Vous etes paranormal*, Hachette, 1972; (compiler and contributor) *Le Livre de l'inexplicable*, A. Michel, 1972; *Les Empires de la chimie moderne*, A. Michel, 1972; *L'Espionnage politique*, A. Michel, 1973; (with John Philippe Delaban) *L'espionnage strategique*, Hachette, 1973; (editor) Bernard le Bovier de Fontenelle, *Entretiens sur la pluralite des mondes*, Editions Gerard, 1973.

SIDELIGHTS: Bergier is best known for his activities during World War II. Working with the French Underground, Bergier was instrumental in devising a radio network as well as numerous devices used in sabotage. He also organized the group of scientists responsible for discovering where the German Army was constructing their V-2 rockets. The cite was later bombed by Allied forces. In 1943 Bergier was captured by Gestapo agents and placed in a concentration camp. The effects of interrogation remained with Bergier all his life. However, he refused to cooperate with the Germans. He later received recognition for his activities during the war.

Bergier devoted most of his writing to science books. Later he also embraced science fiction. The *New York Times* reported that Bergier was interested in "the borderland between science and speculation. . . ."

OBITUARIES: New York Times, November 25, 1978.*

* * *

BERLIN, Isaiah 1909-

PERSONAL: Born June 6, 1909, in Riga, Latvia (now U.S.S.R.); son of Mendel (a timber merchant) and Marie (Volshonock) Berlin; married Aline Elizabeth Yvonne de Gunzburg, 1956. *Education:* Corpus Christi College, Oxford, B.A., 1932, M.A., 1935. *Agent:* Curtis Brown Ltd., 1 Craven Hill, London W2 3EW, England. *Office:* All Souls College, Oxford University, Oxford, England.

CAREER: Oxford University, Oxford, England, lecturer in philosophy at New College, 1932-50, fellow of All Souls College, 1932-38, 1950-67, 1975—, Chichele Professor of Social and Political Theory, 1957-67, president of Wolfson College, 1966-75. Visiting professor at Harvard University, 1949, 1951, 1953, 1962, Bryn Mawr College, 1952, Princeton University, 1965, City University of New York, 1966-71, Australian National University, Canberra, 1975; Northcliffe Lecturer at University College, London, 1953; Alexander White Professor at University of Chicago, 1955; Mellon Lecturer at National Gallery of Art, Washington, D.C., 1965; Danz Lecturer at Washington University, 1971. Member of award committee, Commonwealth Fellowships, 1960-64, Kennedy Scholarships, 1967—; member of academic advisory committee, University of Sussex, 1963-66. Member of board of governors, Hebrew University of Jerusalem, 1955—; member of board of directors, Royal Opera House,

Covent Garden, 1954-65, 1974—; trustee, National Gallery, 1975—. *Wartime service:* Staff member with Ministry of Information, New York, N.Y., 1941-42, and British Embassy, Washington, D.C., 1942-46, Moscow, 1945-46.

MEMBER: British Academy (vice-president, 1959-61; president, 1974-78), Aristotelian Society (president, 1963-64), American Academy of Arts and Sciences, American Academy and Institute of Arts and Letters, American Philosophical Society, British Friends of the University of Jerusalem (president), Athenaeum, Brooks's Club, Century Club (New York). *Awards, honors:* Commander, Order of the British Empire, 1946; knighted, 1957; Order of Merit, 1971. Numerous honorary degrees, including: LL.D. from Hall University, 1965; D.Litt. from University of Glasgow, 1967, Columbia University, 1968, Cambridge University, 1970, and University of London, 1971; D.Phil. from Tel-Aviv University, 1973, and University of Sussex, 1979.

WRITINGS: (Editor) *Karl Marx: His Life and Environment,* Thorton Butterworth, 1939, 4th edition, Oxford University Press, 1978; (translator) Ivan Turgenev, *First Love,* Hamish Hamilton, 1950; *The Hedgehog and the Fox: An Essay on Tolstoy's View of History,* Simon & Schuster, 1953; (editor, and author of introduction and interpretive commentary) *The Age of Enlightenment: The Eighteenth Century Philosophers,* Houghton, 1956; *Historical Inevitability* (lecture; also see below), Oxford University Press, 1957; *Chaim Weizmann* (lecture), Farrar, Straus, 1958; *Two Concepts of Liberty* (lecture; also see below), Clarendon Press, 1958; *The Life and Opinions of Moses Hess* (lecture), Heffer, 1959; *History and Theory: The Concept of Scientific History* (essay), Mouton, 1960; *John Stuart Mill and the Ends of Life* (lecture; also see below), Council of Christians and Jews (London), 1962; *Does Political Theory Still Exist?* (essay), Basil Blackwell, 1962; *Mr. Churchill in 1940* (pamphlet), Houghton, 1964; *Four Essays on Liberty* (contains "Political Ideas in the Twentieth Century," "Two Concepts of Liberty," "Historical Inevitability," and "John Stuart Mill and the Ends of Life"), Oxford University Press, 1969; *Fathers and Children* (Romanes lecture), Clarendon Press, 1972; *Essays on J. L. Austin,* Clarendon Press, 1973; *Vico and Herder: Two Studies in the History of Ideas,* Viking, 1976; *Russian Thinkers* (collection of essays and lectures), edited by Henry Hardy and Aileen Kelly, Viking, 1978; *Concepts and Categories,* edited by Hardy, Viking, 1979. Contributor of articles to journals, including *Spectator, Twentieth Century,* and *Foreign Affairs.*

WORK IN PROGRESS: A study of some intellectual sources of European Romanticism.

SIDELIGHTS: Irving Howe found *Four Essays on Liberty* "peculiarly relevant to our time" even though the book "lacks just about everthing that now brings intellectual acclaim: the apocalyptic turgidity of a Marcuse, the fixed moralism of a Noam Chomsky, to say nothing of the antics of the small fry who follow these thinkers." Howe praised Berlin for his "capacity . . . in making refined and significant distinctions" and noted that he read the book with "that pleasure one gains from an encounter with a strong, disciplined mind." Norman S. Care in *New Republic* called *Four Essays* a collection of "brilliant lectures in the history of ideas."

In a review of *Concepts and Categories,* John Leonard wrote: "History is what informs these difficult essays. Sir Isaiah would just as soon be talking to Spinoza as to A. J. Ayer, because the problems are the same, and the individuals might have been interesting back then. He is the skeptic

who aspires to faith and complains all the way along the rode [sic] to Oz. Thought, for him, requires embodiment, a person with whom to argue. It needs the angle of the ages. Any single notion of value presides, if at all, with spurs."

Avocational interests: Music and travel.

BIOGRAPHICAL/CRITICAL SOURCES: New York Times, February 9, 1966, August 13, 1969, April 20, 1979; *New Republic,* November 1, 1969; *Commonweal,* January 30, 1970; *Harper's,* August, 1970.

*   *   *

BERLIN, Sven 1911-

PERSONAL: Born September 14, 1911, in Sydenham, London, England; son of Karl Gustav (a merchant) and Mary Louise (Hughes) Berlin; married Helga Groom, 1938 (deceased); married Juanita Fisher Barlow, 1953 (divorced, 1963); married Julia Pamela Lenthall, September 6, 1963; children: (first marriage) Paul, Janet, Jasper. *Education:* Attended Redruth College of Art and University of Exeter, both 1934, 1939-40. *Politics:* "Humanity." *Religion:* "Unorthodox." *Home and office:* Higher Gaunts, Stanbridge, Wimborne, Dorsetshire BH21 4JD, England.

CAREER: Sculptor, painter, and writer, 1945—. Has had more than twenty-four solo exhibitions in England and the United States. Lectured in poetry and the visual arts at Poole College of Further Education. Also worked as dancer, engineer, and teacher. *Military service:* British Army, Royal Artillery, 1942; served in France, Belgium, the Netherlands. *Member:* New Forest Association, Bladon Art Society, Chelsea Arts Club, Penwith Society of Arts (founding member), Crypt Group (founding member).

WRITINGS: Alfred Wallis (Primitive), Nicholson & Watson, 1948; *I Am Lazarus* (war story), Norton, 1961; *Dark Monarch* (novel), Dent, 1962; *Jonah's Dream* (meditation on fishing), Dent, 1964, William Kaufmann, 1975; *Dromengro: Man of the Road,* Collins, 1971; *Pride of the Peacock: Evolution of an Artist,* Collins, 1972; *Amergin: Enigma of the Forest* (novel), David & Charles, 1978.

Documentary television films: "Casting a Bronze," BBC-TV, 1958; "Portrait in Time," BBC-TV, 1960; "New Forest: Summer '67," BBC-TV, 1967; "Shapes in the Wilderness," ITV-TV, 1970; "Augustus John," BBC-TV, 1978.

WORK IN PROGRESS: Violet Man: A Personal Testament on Creation; Circe Under a Clock, a novel; *Ben Blossom: A Secret Childhood; Sacred River: A Spring Sacrifice,* a novel; poems; sculpture; painting.

SIDELIGHTS: Berlin writes: "I have always had to contend with the problems of painting, sculpture, and writing as three aspects of one personal expression in an attempt to reach full realization and understanding of the world in which I find myself, which is the purpose of my life—and to invest material experience with spirit by imagination. Beauty of form with poetic insight is the unattainable target."

BIOGRAPHICAL/CRITICAL SOURCES: "Casting a Bronze" (television documentary), BBC-TV, 1958; "Portrait in Time" (television documentary), BBC-TV, 1960; Denys Val Baker, *The Timeless Land: The Creative Spirit in Cornwall,* Adams, 1973.

*   *   *

BERMAN, Eleanor 1934-

PERSONAL: Born May 7, 1934, in Birmingham, Ala.; daughter of Abraham and Bertha (Sirote) Greenwald; children: Thomas, Eric, Terry Ellen. *Education:* Smith College, B.A., 1955. *Home:* 1791 Long Ridge Rd., Stamford, Conn. 06903.

CAREER: City of Stamford, Conn., director of Commission on Aging, 1968-71; Stamford Museum, Stamford, director of public information, 1971-74; Macmillan Publishing Co., Inc., New York City, publicist in General Books Division, 1974-75, publicity manager, 1975-76; Robert Marston & Associates (public relations firm), New York City, account executive, 1977—. *Member:* American Society of Journalists and Authors, Women in Communications.

WRITINGS: The Cooperating Family, Prentice-Hall, 1977; *The Best of Families,* Prentice-Hall, 1980; *Re-Entering,* Prentice-Hall, 1980. Special travel correspondent for *Newsday.* Contributor to popular magazines, including *Harpers' Bazaar, Family Circle, Parade, Parents' Magazine,* and *Family Health.*

SIDELIGHTS: Eleanor Berman comments: "Most of my writing has followed my own interests and life phases. I began writing magazine articles as a stay-at-home mother, and continued to write as a single working mother. My first book was a description of the beneficial changes in our household when I took a full-time job and the children began to share responsibility. My subsequent books are concerned with changing family roles and with providing guidance to mature women who are re-entering the job market. I also write about my own state, Connecticut, and historic towns, a special interest."

AVOCATIONAL INTERESTS: Travel.

* * *

BERNHARD, Thomas 1931-

PERSONAL: Born September 11, 1931, in Heerland, Holland; emigrated to Austria. *Education:* Studied music in Vienna and Salzburg. *Office:* c/o Alfred A. Knopf, Inc., 201 East 50th St., New York, N.Y. 10022.

CAREER: Novelist, dramatist, poet, and journalist. Has worked as a reporter, critic, and librarian. *Awards, honors:* Austrian State Prize for Literature, 1967; George Buechner Prize from German Academy of Language and Literature, 1970.

WRITINGS—In English: Vestoerung (novel), Insel, 1967, translation by Richard Wilson and Clara Wilson published as *Gargoyles,* Knopf, 1970; *Das Kalkwerk* (novel), Suhrkamp, 1970, translation by Sophie Wilkins published as *The Lime Works,* Random House, 1973; *Die Macht der Gewohnheit: Komoedie* (play, also see below), Suhrkamp, 1974, translation by Neville Plaice and Stephen Plaice published as *The Force of Habit: A Comedy,* Heinemann Educational, 1976, text edition published as *National Theatre Plays: The Force of Habit, a Comedy.*

Other works: *Auf der Erde und in der Hoelle* (poetry), Mueller (Salzburg), 1957; *Unter dem Eisen des Mondes* (poetry), Kipenheuer & Witsch, 1958; *In hora mortis* (poetry), Mueller, 1958; *Die Rosen der Einoede: fuenf Saetze fuer Ballett, Stimmen und Orchester,* S. Fischer, 1959; *Frost* (novel), Insel, 1963; *Amras* (prose), Suhrkamp, 1967; *Ungenach* (prose), Suhrkamp, 1968; *Watten: ein Nachlass* (prose), 1969; *Ereignisse,* Literarisches Colloquium, 1969; *An der Baumgrenze* (novel), illustrations by Anton Lehmden, Residenz, 1969.

Ein Fest fuer Boris (play; title means "A Party for Boris"), Suhrkamp, 1970; *Gehen,* Suhrkamp, 1970; *Midland in Stilfs,* Suhrkamp, 1970; *Der Italiener* (screenplay; title means "The

Italian"), Residenz, 1971; *Der Ignorant und der Wahnsinnige* (play; first produced in Salzburg, Austria, at Salzburg Festival; title means "The Ignoramus and the Maniac"), Suhrkamp, 1972; *Der Kulterer* (screenplay), Residenz, 1974; *Die Jagdgesellschaft,* Suhrkamp, 1974; *Die Salzburger Stuecke* (also includes *Die Macht der Geowohnheit*), Suhrkamp, 1975; *Der Praesident* (title means "The President"), Suhrkamp, 1975; *Die Ursache: eine Andeutung* (also see below), Residenz, 1975; *Korrektur* (novel), Suhrkamp, 1975; *Der Wetterfleck,* illustrations by Otto F. Best, Reclam, 1976; *Die Beruehmtem,* Suhrkamp, 1976; *Der Keller* (sequel to *Die Ursache*), Residenz, 1976; *Minetti: ein Portrait des Kuenstlers als alter Mann,* photographs by Digne Meller Marcovicz, Suhrkamp, 1977.

SIDELIGHTS: Bernhard's pessimistic view of life is everpresent in his controversial plays and novels. Critic Stella Rosenfeld commented on his writing, "Thomas Bernhard has reached the point where the near obsessional fidelity to himself and his work must be given new artistic form, lest his powerfully disturbing theme lose in impact and conviction."

Although not widely read in the United States, Bernhard's first novel, *Vestoerung,* translated as *Gargoyles,* was very popular in Europe. Called "Kafkaesque" by reviewers, *Gargoyles* reveals Bernhard's belief in the hopelessness of the human condition. In the story, "the patients are the gargoyles of the title and their peculiar arrangements could be well skipped were it not for the brilliance, erudition, and suggestiveness with which Bernhard writes about them," commented a critic in *Antioch Review.*

In *Ein Fest fuer Boris,* thirteen legless guests attend a party hosted by a wealthy woman who also has no legs. The woman, misnamed the "Gute" or "Good," is married to Boris, also legless, who dies while pounding on a drum; because the guests are absorbed in sharing their morbid experiences and dreams with one another, they don't notice until the end of the party. "Taken as a whole, the meaning of the play is opaque," wrote a *Books Abroad* reviewer. "Still it communicates messages typical of Thomas Bernhard: life is insufferable, a stifling routine in which human relations are based on mutual hatred and intimidation; social injustice prevails." The play version of the story proved more successful than the book, which Rosenfeld described as "unpalatable, frustratingly cryptic, and generally unrewarding."

Das Kalkwerk, The Lime Works in English, is narrated by a life-insurance salesman who weaves the story from rumors about a frustrated Austrian writer who has blasted his crippled wife in the head with a shot from her own rifle. A *New Republic* reviewer wrote: "The book is a jungle of meaning, the opposite of simplistic allegory, and a major achievement because of this. . . . *The Lime Works* invites comparison with the run-on novels of Beckett." Ronald De Feo concluded in *National Review* that in this book Bernhard again "proves himself to be one of the most substantive and intense of today's young, experimental German writers."

BIOGRAPHICAL/CRITICAL SOURCES: Saturday Review, October 31, 1970; *Antioch Review,* fall, 1970; *Book World,* January 3, 1971; *Times Literary Supplement,* February 12, 1971, September 29, 1972, February 13, 1976, June 11, 1976; *Booklist,* February 15, 1971, July 15, 1975; *New Republic,* December 15, 1973; *National Review,* February 1, 1974; *Contemporary Literary Criticism,* Volume 3, Gale, 1975; *World Literature Today,* summer, 1977, winter, 1978.*

* * *

BERQUE, Jacques Augustin 1910-

PERSONAL: Born June 4, 1910, in Moliere, Algeria; son of

Augustin and Florentine (Migon) Berque; divorced; children: Augustin, Marie-Salsa Berque Brossollet, Valerie, Isabelle Berque Jeannot, Maximillen, Emmanuel, Julien. *Education:* University of Algiers, licence et lettres, 1929, M.A., 1930; Sorbonne, University of Paris, Ph.D., 1955. *Home:* 11 place Marcelin Berthelot, Paris V 75005, France. *Office:* Department of Social History of Contemporary Islam, College de France, Paris 75005, France.

CAREER: Administrative officer in Morocco, 1934-53; United Nations Educational, Scientific, and Cultural Organization, Egypt, international expert in education, 1953-56; College de France, Paris, France, professor of social history of contemporary Islam, 1956—. *Military service:* French Army, 1932-33, 1939-40. *Member:* Academy of Cairo (corresponding member. *Awards, honors:* Chevalier of Legion of Honor, 1960.

WRITINGS—In English: *Les Arabes d'hier a demain,* Seuil, 1960, revised and enlarged edition, Seuil, 1969, translation by Jean Stewart published as *The Arabs, Their History and Future,* Praeger, 1964; *Le Maghreb entre deux guerres,* Seuil, 1962, revised and enlarged edition, Seuil, 1970, translation by Stewart published as *French North Africa: The Maghrib Between Two World Wars,* Praeger, 1967; *Egypt: Imperialism and Revolution,* translated from the French by Stewart, Praeger, 1972; *Languages arabes du present,* Gallimard, 1974, translation by Basima Bezirgan and Elizabeth Fernea published as *Cultural Expression in Arab Society Today,* University of Texas Press, 1978.

Other: *Contribution a l'etude des contrats nord-africains (les pactes pastoraux Beni Meskine),* Imprimerie la typolitho et J. Carbonel reunies, 1936; *Structures sociales du haut atlas,* Presses universitaires de France, 1955; *Histoire sociale d'un village egyptien au XXeme siecle,* Mouton, 1957; *Al-Yousi: problemes de la culture marocaine au XVIIeme siecle,* Mouton, 1958; *Les Arabes* (title means "The Arabs"), Delpire, 1959, revised and enlarged edition, Sinbad, 1973.

Depossession du monde, Seuil, 1964; *Problemes de la culture arabe contemporaine,* [Beyrouth], 1965; *Groupe de recherche et d'action pour le reglement du probleme palestinien: pour un juste reglement du probleme palestinien,* Temoignage chretien, 1967(?); (with Jean Paul Charnay), *L'Ambivalence dans la culture arabe,* Anthropos, 1967; *L'Egypte, imperialisme et revolution,* Gallimard, 1967.

L'Orient second Gallimard, 1970; *Languages arabes du present,* Gallimard, 1974; *Maghreb, histoire et societes,* Duculot, 1974; *Aujourd'hui l'histoire,* Editions Sociales, 1974; *Les Palestiniens et la crise israelo-arabe,* Editions Sociales, 1974; *Nomades et vagabonds,* Union generale d'editions, 1975; *Les Arabes par leurs archives,* Centre nationale de la Recherche, 1976; (with Julien Couleau) *Le Marc,* P.U.F., 1977; *L'Interieur de Maghreb,* Gallimard, 1978; *De l'Euphrate a l'Atlas,* two volumes, Sinbad, 1978.

WORK IN PROGRESS: Classical Arab Poetry: Dynamics of Present Islam.

SIDELIGHTS: Berque told *CA* that, since childhood, he has been devoted to studying and synthesizing the cultures of the northern shore of the Mediterranean with those of the southern shore. "I have followed by analysis and, at times, by action, the evolution of the Arabs," he wrote. "I am now turning toward larger perspectives: those of the role of the Islam in becoming a world in itself."

BERRY, Burton Yost   1901-

PERSONAL: Born August 31, 1901, in Fowler, Ind.; son of Burton Bowers (a lawyer and judge) and Jessie (Yost) Berry. *Education:* Indiana University, earned A.B. and A.M. *Politics:* Republican. *Religion:* Presbyterian. *Home:* 4172 Combe Way, San Diego, Calif. 92122. *Agent:* Kenan Ball, 299 Madison Ave., New York, N.Y. 10017.

CAREER: U.S. Department of State, Washington, D.C., foreign service officer until 1954; writer and researcher, 1954—. *Awards, honors:* LL.D. from Indiana University.

WRITINGS: Turkish and Greek Island Embroideries From the Burton Yost Berry Collection in the Art Institute of Chicago, Art Institute of Chicago, 1964; *A Selection of Ancient Gems,* Museum of Art, Indiana University, 1965; *Ancient Gems From the Collection of Burton Y. Berry,* Museum of Art, Indiana University, 1968; *A Numismatic Biography,* privately printed, 1971; *Teenage Styles and Trends, 1967-71: A Retrospect* (photographs; with text), privately printed, 1972; *Out of the Past: The Istanbul Grand Bazaar* (memoirs), Arco, 1977. Contributor to magazines.

WORK IN PROGRESS: A book about life in the Middle East in the late 1920's.

SIDELIGHTS: Berry writes: "After my retirement from the foreign service I continued to live in the Near East, spending my time studying the artifacts of the area, collecting them, and eventually giving them to American institutions that could make use of them: for example, coins to the American Numismatic Society of New York, textiles to the Art Institute of Chicago, and archaeological artifacts to the Metropolitan Museum in New York, the Museum of Fine Arts in Boston, and the Museum of Art at Indiana University."

* * *

BERRY, Henry   1926-

PERSONAL: Born June 30, 1926, in Hartford, Conn.; son of Harold James (a merchant) and Jane (Tracy) Berry; married Diana Weeks (a fund raiser and school director), February 12, 1955; children: Jane, Harold, Diana. *Education:* Kenyon College, B.A., 1951. *Religion:* Christian. *Home:* 74 Christie Hill Rd., Darien, Conn. 06820. *Office: Business Week,* 300 Broad St., Stamford, Conn.

CAREER: Business Week, Stamford, Conn., in advertising sales, 1960—. Lecturer on baseball humor and on World War I. *Military service:* U.S. Marine Corps Reserve, 1943-46.

WRITINGS: The Boston Red Sox, Macmillan, 1975; (coauthor) *A Baseball Century,* Macmillan, 1976; *Poosh 'em Up Struck Out* (booklet), Xerox, 1976; *Make the Kaiser Dance,* Doubleday, 1978. Editor-in-chief of *DKE Quarterly,* 1976—.

WORK IN PROGRESS: The autobiography of General James Van Fleet, with Van Fleet; a book on American prisoners of war.

* * *

BERRY, Jane Cobb   1915(?)-1979
(Jane Cobb)

OBITUARY NOTICE: Born c. 1915; died March 31, 1979, in Norwalk, Conn. Columnist, critic, and author of children's books. Berry co-authored the "Sue Barton" and "Carol Page" series of novels with Helen Dore Boylston as a "silent collaborator." A columnist in the *New York Times* during the 1940's, Berry also reviewed numerous books for the same publication. In addition, she contributed stories under her maiden name to a variety of magazines. Obituaries and other sources: *New York Times*, April 2, 1979; *AB Bookman's Weekly*, April 16, 1979; *Publishers Weekly*, April 16, 1979.

* * *

BERTCHER, Harvey (Joseph) 1929-

PERSONAL: Born January 9, 1929, in New York, N.Y.; son of Samuel (a credit manager) and Anna (Mendes) Bertcher; married Gloria Kline, June 17, 1951; children: Quincey (daughter), Corey (son). *Education:* Olivet College, B.A., 1949; Columbia University, M.A., 1951; University of Denver, M.S.W., 1955; University of Southern California, D.S.W., 1966. *Residence:* Ann Arbor, Mich. *Office:* School of Social Work, University of Michigan, Ann Arbor, Mich. 48109.

CAREER: Troy Jewish Community Center, Troy, N.Y., director of youth activities, 1951-53; Hathaway Home for Children, Los Angeles, Calif., director of group work and recreation, 1955-58; Special Service for Groups, Los Angeles, Calif., group work specialist, 1958-59; Adolescent Treatment Center, Salt Lake City, Utah, director of social group work, 1959-61; University of Southern California, Los Angeles, lecturer in social work, 1963-64; University of Michigan, Ann Arbor, assistant professor, 1964-67, associate professor, 1967-72, professor of social work, 1972—. Clinical assistant at University of Utah, 1959-61, field work instructor, 1960-61. Member of board of directors of Washtenaw County Office of Economic Opportunities, 1967, and Jewish Cultural School, 1971-73; vice-president of Manpower Science Services, 1968-76; chairman of citizens' advisory action council at Maxey Boys Training School, 1974-77. National consultant in social work to U.S. Air Force, 1973-77. Has worked as social caseworker, music and folk dance specialist, recreation worker, and camp counselor. Participates in and organizes professional institutes and meetings. *Member:* National Conference on Social Welfare, Council on Social Work Education, National Association of Social Workers (charter member; local vice-president, 1957-58, 1969-70), Academy of Certified Social Workers. *Awards, honors:* National Institute of Mental Health career teacher training grant, 1963-64; grants from U.S. Department of Labor, 1967-68, 1968-70, 1970-72, 1972-75.

WRITINGS: (With Charles Garvin) *Staff Development in Social Welfare Agencies*, Campus Publishers, 1969; (with Jesse E. Gordon, Michael E. Hayes, and Harry Mial) *Role Modeling, Role Playing: A Manual for Employability Development Agencies*, Manpower Science Services, 1969; (with Frank Maple) *Group Composition: An Instructional Program*, Campus Publishers, 1972; (with Gordon) *Techniques of Group Leadership*, Manpower Science Services, 1973; (with John Milnes) *Verbal Empathic Responding*, Campus Publishers, 1975; (with Robert Kozma and Rand Anderson) *Local Office* (with Gordon, Mel Lawson, and Jerome Muncey) *Simulation Imitation* (guidebook and audio-cassette tapes), Manpower Science Services, 1970, revised edition, 1979; *Decision-Making and Implementation: A Self-Managed Workshop*, Manpower Science Services, 1975; (with Lynn Nybell, Tom Morton, Pat Ruby, and Roy Grant) *Staff Development for Supervisors*, University of Michigan, School of Social Work, 1977; (with Maple) *Creating Groups*, Sage Publications, 1977; *Group Participation: Techniques for Leaders and Members*, Sage Publications, 1979. Contributor to social work and child care journals.

WORK IN PROGRESS: Staff Development: A Guidebook;

revising *Verbal Empathic Responding* for a more generic audience.

SIDELIGHTS: Bertcher comments: "My primary interest in writing is to provide practical guidelines for human service organization professionals and students, to help them help people in need. We do need theoretical conceptualizations to guide our thinking and shape our perceptions, but we also need research based, easily used practitioner-oriented instructional packages that avoid abstract esoteric language. In my teaching and development of instructional materials I've tried to simplify without being simplistic so that learners can gain confidence in their ability to be helpful.

"Currently, I've become interested in the problems associated with stress on the job—a condition labeled 'burnout.' I am convinced that human services workers burnout because they feel ineffective in their ability to help people, their ability to maintain their integrity, and their ability to focus in bureaucratic organizations. I hope that my work can help to overcome the burnout problem."

* * *

BETHGE, Eberhard 1909-

PERSONAL: Born August 28, 1909, in Warchau, Germany; son of Wilhelm (a pastor) and Elisabeth (Nietzschmann) Bethge; married Renate Schleicher, May 15, 1943; children: Dietrich, Gabriele Bethge Bode, Sabine Bethge Moffett. *Education:* Attended University of Berlin, University of Tuebingen, and University of Halle, 1929-33. *Home:* Flachsgraben 9, D 5307, Wachtberg-Villip, West Germany.

CAREER: Expelled from official church seminary, Wittenberg, Germany, when he, along with friends, refused obedience to the Nazi-Reichsbishop, 1934; joined the anti-Nazi Confessing Church Seminary, Finkenwalde, Germany, assistant to director Dietrich Bonhoeffer, 1935-40; arrested and imprisoned by the Nazis, 1944-45; after the war, he served in Berlin, Germany, as assistant to Bishop Dibelius and as student chaplain; pastor for a German congregation in London, England, 1953-61; Institute for Continuing Education for Clergy of the Evangelical Church in the Rhineland, Rengsdorf, West Germany, director, 1961-75; Union Theological Seminary, New York City, visiting professor, 1976-77. Visiting lecturer at Harvard University, 1957-58; visiting professor at Chicago Theological Seminary, 1966-67, Union Theological Seminary, New York City, 1966-67, and Bryn Mawr College, 1978; visiting scholar at Broadway Presbyterian Church, 1976-77. *Member:* P.E.N. International. *Awards, honors:* Honorary doctoral degrees from University of Glasgow, 1962, University of Berlin, East Berlin, 1967, and University of Bern, 1975; honorary professorship from University of Bonn, 1969.

WRITINGS: The Editing and Publishing of the Bonhoeffer Papers, Andover Newton Theological School, 1959; *The Challenge of Dietrich Bonhoeffer's Life and Theology*, Chicago Theological Seminary, 1961; *Dietrich Bonhoeffer: Theologe, Christ, Zeitgenosse* (biography), Kaiser, 1967, translation by Eric Mosbacher published as *Dietrich Bonhoeffer: Man of Vision, Man of Courage*, Harper, 1970 (published in England as *Dietrich Bonhoeffer: Theologian, Christian, Contemporary*, Collins, 1970); *Ohnmacht und Muedigkeit* (title means "Powerlessness and Maturity"), Kaiser, 1969; *Bonhoeffer: Exile and Martyr* (collection of essays and lectures), Seabury, 1975; *Dietrich Bonhoeffer in Selbstzeugnissen und Bilddokumenten/dargest* (title means "Dietrich Bonhoeffer Presented in Quotations, Documents, and Pictures"), Rowohlt, 1976.

Editor: Dietrich Bonhoeffer, *Ethik*, Kaiser, 1949, translation by Neville Horton Smith published as *Ethics*, Macmillan, 1955; Bonhoeffer, *Widerstand und Ergebung*, Kaiser, 1951, translation by Reginald H. Fuller published as *Letters and Papers From Prison*, S.C.M. Press, 1953, Macmillan, 1954, revised and enlarged edition, S.C.M. Press, 1971; Bonhoeffer, *Dein Reich komme*, Furche, 1957, translation by John D. Godsey published as *Preface to Bonhoeffer: The Man and Two of His Shorter Writings*, Fortress, 1965; Bonhoeffer, *Gesamelte Schriften* (title means "Collected Writings"), six volumes, Kaiser, 1958-74, three volume English edition: translation by Edwin H. Robertson and John Bowden of Volume I published as *No Rusty Swords: Letters, Lectures, and Notes, 1928-36*, Harper, 1965, translation by Robertson and Bowden of Volume II published as *The Way to Freedom: Letters, Lectures, and Notes, 1935-39*, Harper, 1966, translation by Bowden of abridged edition of Volume III published as *Christ the Center*, Harper, 1966 (published in England as *Christology*, Collins, 1966), translation by Richarson and Bowden published as *True Patriotism: Letters, Lectures, and Notes, 1939-45*, Harper, 1973; Bonhoeffer, *Das Gebetbuch der Bibel*, M.B.K., 1958, translation by James H. Burtness published as *Psalms: The Prayer Book of the Bible*, Augsburg, 1970.

WORK IN PROGRESS: Studies in Christian-Jewish relations; autobiographical reflections.

SIDELIGHTS: "Early in 1933," Bethge told *CA*, "I was drawn into the ecclesiastical opposition to the Third Reich's attempts to nazify the church. Slowly, I learned that this meant political opposition as well and, therefore, resistance with its consequences." As a consequence of his opposition to the Nazis, Bethge was imprisoned in October, 1944, until April, 1945, when he was freed by the Russians.

Before his arrest, however, Bethge had served from 1935 to 1940 as an assistant to Dietrich Bonhoeffer, the theologian and director of the Confessing Church Seminary who was executed as a co-conspirator in the plot to overthrow Hitler. He and Bonhoeffer became close friends during those years, and, as a result of their friendship, Bethge became the editor of Bonhoeffer's writings. "By having had the experience of being a political prisoner of the Nazis myself," Bethge explained, "and by noticing the astonishing response to the figure of Bonhoeffer and to his thoughts all over the world, I sank more and more into research of the whole period and let flow my resources into files, articles, and books." Bethge's research produced *Dietrich Bonhoeffer: Man of Vision, Man of Courage*, which some reviewers regard as the definitive biography of Bonhoeffer. In his review of the book, Clifford Greene said: "It is one of the major biographies of this century.... We owe an immense debt of gratitude to Bethge.... Modesty, avoidance of the faddish, and freedom from adulation mark his writing." Bethge told *CA:* "I tried to catch the history of those years in Germany in their manifold aspects of the church, of the open or hidden Christian anti-Semitism, and of culture and family life. I was greatly helped in this endeavor by periods of living in Britain and the United States that offered me the opportunity to view the experiences of my own country more detachedly and to learn from those countries with their great tradition of writing biographies."

Another and more recent examination of Bonhoeffer's thought is made in *Bonhoeffer: Exile and Martyr*. This collection of essays and lectures, which were delivered in South Africa by the author, traces the chronological development of Bonhoeffer's theology and attempts to relate some of his major ideas to issues that have arisen since the theologian's death in 1945. John Begley wrote: "Bethge's

own reflections on what he terms Bonhoeffer's inner exile' and modern martyrdom . . . are valuable for their originality and depth. Other readers may well find Bethge's observations on the similarities (the differences are also recognized) between the situation of Christians in South Africa today and the situation of Christians in Germany in the 1930s more timely and thought-provoking."

BIOGRAPHICAL/CRITICAL SOURCES: New Statesman, April 17, 1970; *Times Literary Supplement*, May 21, 1970; *Saturday Review*, May 30, 1970; *New York Times Book Review*, June 21, 1970, October 24, 1976; *Christian Century*, July 1, 1970; *Critic*, July, 1970; *New Republic*, September 19, 1970; *Commonweal*, October 2, 1970; *Best Sellers*, July, 1976; *America*, August 7, 1976.

* * *

BETTS, Richard K(evin) 1947-

PERSONAL: Born August 15, 1947, in Easton, Pa.; son of John Rickards (a professor of history) and Cecelia (Fitzpatrick) Betts. *Education:* Harvard University, B.A. (magna cum laude), 1969, M.A., 1971, Ph.D., 1975. *Politics:* Democrat. *Home:* 4740 Connecticut Ave. N.W., Apt. 303, Washington, D.C. 20008. *Office:* Brookings Institution, 1775 Massachusetts Ave. N.W., Washington, D.C. 20036.

CAREER: Harvard University, Cambridge, Mass., lecturer in government, 1975-76; Brookings Institution, Washington, D.C., research associate in foreign policy, 1976—. Visiting professor at Johns Hopkins University, 1978, and Columbia University, 1979. Staff member of U.S. Senate Select Committee on Intelligence (Church Committee), 1975-76; consultant to National Security Council. *Military service:* U.S. Army Reserve, Military Intelligence, 1969-71; became second lieutenant. *Member:* International Studies Association, American Political Science Association, Academy of Political Science, Arms Control Association, Council on Foreign Relations, Inter-University Seminar on Armed Forces and Society.

WRITINGS: Soldiers, Statesmen, and Cold War Crises, Harvard University Press, 1977; (with Leslie H. Gelb) *The Irony of Vietnam: The System Worked*, Brookings Institution, 1979. Contributor to political science journals.

WORK IN PROGRESS: A book on regional security problems and nuclear proliferation, with Joseph Yager, publication by Brookings Institution expected in 1980; a monograph on surprise attacks, their history, and the implications for defense planning, publication by Brookings Institution expected in 1980.

SIDELIGHTS: Betts comments: "I rationalize frying my brain by spending most of my time thinking about war and nuclear weapons, by figuring that if a lot of bright people don't do so, more than my brain will wind up fried. If the Soviets—and the Chinese, Vietnamese, Cubans, Israelis, Arabs, Iranians, Yemenis, and almost everybody else—would just behave and put military policy analysts like me out of business, I'd be happy to return to my avocation of American cinema history. Barring such a Utopian evolution, I plan to keep writing about how and why nations kill and prepare to kill large numbers of people in other nations."

* * *

BEUF, Ann H(ill) 1939-

PERSONAL: Surname is pronounced "buff"; born October 1, 1939, in Philadelphia, Pa.; daughter of Erle G. (a metallurgist) and Helen (a social worker; maiden name, Harper)

Hill; married Francesco Gallatin Beuf (a physician), March 21, 1959; children: Helen, Carlo, Peter. *Education:* Bryn Mawr College, A.B., 1969, M.A., 1970, Ph.D., 1972. *Home:* 800 North Valley Rd., Paoli, Pa. 19301. *Office:* Women's Studies Program, University of Pennsylvania, Philadelphia, Pa. 19104.

CAREER: University of Pennsylvania, Philadelphia, assistant professor of sociology, 1972-77, director of women's studies, 1977—. Visiting professor at Villanova University, autumn, 1979. Member of United Nations Committee on Stigmatized Children. Member of board of directors of Little People's Nursery School of Paoli. *Member:* American Sociological Association, National Women's Studies Association, Society for the Study of Social Problems, Sociologists for Women in Society, Indian Rights Association, Delaware Valley Women's Studies Consortium.

WRITINGS: Red Children in White America, University of Pennsylvania Press, 1977; *Biting Off the Bracelet: A Study of Children in Hospitals,* University of Pennsylvania Press, 1979. Also editor with Dorothy Kurz of "Childhood: A Social Construct," 1977. Contributor to medical and education journals. Editor of newsletter of Delaware Valley Women's Studies Consortium; member of editorial board of *American Medical Women's Association Journal.*

WORK IN PROGRESS: Editing *Encyclopedia of American Women,* publication by McGraw expected in 1981; continuing research on women as patients.

SIDELIGHTS: Beuf writes: "I am interested in the status of women and children in societies—especially the manner in which bureaucratization limits and controls their opportunities for controlling their own destinies.

"Biting Off the Bracelet came out of my increasing concern about the bifurcation of the physician's role into two separate roles. The role of impartial, scientific, dispassionate medicator is filled by those we call doctors. The other role, that of carer, is increasingly delegated to someone other than the physician, such as a social worker, psychologist, or volunteer. We will not have decent health care in this society until both of these roles are played by the physician."

*   *   *

BEYERS, Charlotte K(empner) 1931-

PERSONAL: Born December 8, 1931, in New York, N.Y.; daughter of Sigmund Marshall (a banker) and Charlotte Kempner; married Gerald Davis (divorced, 1965); married Robert West Beyers (a university public relations director), June 14, 1971; children: (first marriage) Pam, Nancy, Alan, Cynthia. *Education:* Stanford University, B.A., 1952, M.A., 1970. *Politics:* Democrat. *Religion:* Jewish. *Home and office:* 330 Santa Rita Ave., Palo Alto, Calif. 94301. *Agent:* Julian Bach Literary Agency, Inc., 3 East 48th St., New York, N.Y. 10017.

CAREER/WRITINGS: Correspondent for *New York Times,* and *London Times Higher Educational Supplement,* 1978—. Free-lance writer on science and medicine, 1967—. Notable assignments include an article on Jane Goodall for *Saturday Review* in 1974. Research associate in department of psychiatry at Stanford University Medical School, 1971-73. Past member of board of directors of Nairobi School. Public relations consultant. *Member:* American Society of Journalists and Authors, American Medical Writers Association, National Press Club.

WORK IN PROGRESS: Medical writing

SIDELIGHTS: Charlotte Beyers comments: "I became a

medical writer as a result of the journal I kept when my seven-year-old son had open heart surgery. My first article in 1965 was about congenital disease, and it appeared in a magazine for physicians." *Avocational interests:* Travel (including Nepal).

*   *   *

BIAGI, Shirley 1944-

PERSONAL: Born June 21, 1944, in San Francisco, Calif.; daughter of Herbert H. and Gerbina Mary (Biagi) Rickey; married Victor J. Biondi (a state government executive), 1964; children: Paul and Tom (twins), David. *Education:* California State University, Sacramento, B.A., 1967, M.A., 1975. *Office:* California State University, 6000 J St., SSC-302, Sacramento, Calif. 95819.

CAREER/WRITINGS: California Journal, Sacramento, assistant editor, 1970-72; California State University, Sacramento, lecturer, 1972-75, assistant professor of journalism, 1975—. Contributor of articles to *Parade, Writer's Digest, Family Circle, Christian Science Monitor,* and *Antioch Review. Member:* American Society of Journalists and Authors, American Association of University Women, Sigma Delta Chi. *Awards, honors:* Literary merit award from Sacramento Regional Arts Council, 1974.

WORK IN PROGRESS: Research on Hollywood labor activity in the 1930's.

SIDELIGHTS: Biagi comments: "I have become particularly interested in Hollywood unionism because I have done extensive interviews over the last two years with screenwriters, union activists, and reporters who believe this is an overlooked topic in California history. So for now this seems a valuable way to spend my time."

*   *   *

BIANCO, Andre 1930-

PERSONAL: Born April 19, 1930, in Ugine, France; son of Jules Ambroise (a businessman) and Lucie Anna (Poensin) Bianco; married Marie-Louise Mazagol, August 6, 1955; children: Sylvie, Jean-Francois. *Education:* Attended Ecole normale superieure, 1952-57; Sorbonne, University of Paris, agregation d'histoire, 1957; Institut national des langues orientales, diploma in Chinese, 1962. *Home:* 54 rue de Docteur-Babin, Forges-les-Bains, 91470 Limours, France. *Office:* 54 faubourg Raspail, Paris 75270, France.

CAREER: Teacher in Beauvais, France, 1959-60, and in Paris, France, 1960-61; director of L'Ecole pratique des hautes etudes, 1961-69; Ecole des hautes etudes en sciences sociales, Paris, director of studies, 1969—, director of Center of Research and Documentation Contemporary China (CRDCC), 1977—. Professor at Institut d'Etudes Politiques. Visiting professor at Princeton University, 1971. *Military service:* Served in French Army, 1957-59. *Member:* Association of Asian Studies (Ann Arbor, Mich.), Association Europeene d'Etudes Chinoises (Paris), Societe d'-Histoire Moderne (Paris).

WRITINGS: Les Origines de la revolution chinoise 1915-1949, Gallimard, 1967, translation by Muriel Bell published as *Origins of the Chinese Revolution, 1915-1949,* Stanford University Press, 1971; (editor) *Das modern Asien,* Fischer Buecherei, 1969; *Les Paysans et la revolution en Chine de 1919 a 1949,* Centre d'etude du Sud-Est asiatique et de l'Extreme-Orient, 1969; *Mouvements populaires et societes secretes en Chine aux XIXe et XXe siecles,* F. Maspero, 1970, translation published as *Popular Movements and Se-*

cret Societies in China, 1840-1950, Stanford University Press, 1972; (with others) Inde et Extreme-Orient contemporains, Bordas, 1971; (with others) Regards froids sur la Chine, Seuil, 1976. Contributor to Le Monde.

WORK IN PROGRESS: Peasant Movement in Republican China.

* * *

BIANCO, Pamela 1906-

PERSONAL: Born December 31, 1906, in London, England; came to the United States in 1921, naturalized citizen, 1930; daughter of Francesco Guiseppe (a bibliographer and poet) and Margery (a writer; maiden name, Williams) Bianco; married Robert Schlick, 1930 (divorced, 1955); married Georg Theodor Hartmann (an artist), July 25, 1955 (died August 7, 1976); children: (first marriage) Lorenzo Bianco. Education: Educated privately. Home: 428 Lafayette St., New York, N.Y. 10003.

CAREER: Artist and writer for children, 1917—. Worked for Italian Division of U.S. Office of Censorship, 1943-45. Work is represented in more than a dozen solo exhibitions since 1919, as well as group shows in Europe and the United States, and public and private collections, including Museum of Modern Art and Hirshhorn Museum. Awards, honors: Natives of Rock was listed among fifty best books of the year by American Institute of Graphic Arts, 1956.

WRITINGS: Sing a Song of Journeys (poems), Grosset, 1937; (contributor) Anne Carroll Moore and Bertha Mahoney Miller, editors, Writing and Criticism: A Book for Margery Bianco, Horn Book, 1951; (contributor) Eleanor Whitney Field, editor, Horn Book Reflections, Horn Book, 1969.

Self-illustrated children's books: The Starlit Journey, Macmillan, 1933; Beginning With A, Oxford University Press, 1947; Playtime in Cherry Street, Oxford University Press, 1948; Joy and the Christmas Angel, Oxford University Press, 1949; Paradise Square, Oxford University Press, 1950; Little Houses Far Away, Oxford University Press, 1951; The Look-Inside Easter Egg, Oxford University Press, 1952; The Doll in the Window, Oxford University Press, 1953; The Valentine Party, Lippincott, 1954; Toy Rose, Lippincott, 1957.

Illustrator: Flora: A Book of Drawings by Pamela Bianco With Illustrative Poems by Walter de la Mare, Heinemann, 1920; Margery Williams Bianco, The Little Wooden Doll, Macmillan, 1925; Glenway Wescott, Natives of Rock (poems), privately printed, 1925; M. W. Bianco, The Skin Horse, Doran, 1927; William Blake, The Land of Dreams (poems), Macmillan, 1928; Oscar Wilde, The Birthday of the Infanta, Macmillan, 1929; Juliana Horatia Ewing, Three Christmas Trees, Macmillan, 1930; Hans Christian Andersen, The Little Mermaid, Holiday House, 1935; Alice Isabel Hazeltine and Elva Sophronia Smith, selectors, The Easter Book of Legends and Stories, Lothrop, 1947; John Symonds, Away to the Moon, Lippincott, 1956.

Contributor to The Illustrator's Notebook. Contributor of illustrations to national magazines, including Theatre Arts and Harper's Bazaar.

WORK IN PROGRESS: A volume of early memoirs.

SIDELIGHTS: Bianco writes: "My approach to the writing of a book for children is very much like my approach to the painting of a canvas. First comes the idea. This is carried around in my mind for a very long time, usually for weeks or months (sometimes even for years) until finally it crystallizes and evolves into a plot. The plot is then worked out in its en-

tirety, and all the problems therein solved. Only then does the actual writing take place. When writing for children I try to keep the words and sentences as simple as possible, while at the same time striving to give a particular rhythm to the paragraphs.

"With the exception of Paradise Square, which is about my brother Cecce and me when we were small children living in Gelder's Green, London; and of Little Houses Far Away, which was inspired by a happening in my early childhood, all my books for children have thus far been written entirely from the imagination. The idea for Little Houses Far Away is based upon a strange experience I went through as a very small child, while travelling by train through the Alps from France to Italy. Quite suddenly, as seen by me through the train window, all the houses and the people on the mountainsides looked so very tiny I could not believe that they were proper-sized real houses and people, and not doll houses and dolls—even though my parents and Cecce tried their very best to convince me that they were.

"When writing about children I try to place them in a world in which only children dwell; a world wherein grown-ups are permitted to appear only when strictly necessary, although dolls and stuffed animals are forever welcome there. Especially dolls. For ever since I can remember I have been fascinated by them (as recreation I sometimes design and sew dresses for my two old-fashioned dolls Maribel and Chrystabel). Also, ever since I can remember I have loved to observe children at play. Thus, some of the little girls in my illustrations were seen by me as they played in the Valentine Gardens at Turin, Italy, when I too was a little girl."

* * *

BICANIC, Rudolf 1905-1968

PERSONAL: Born in 1905, in Bjelovar, Croatia; died, 1968; married wife, Sonia (a university teacher of philosophy). Education: Studied law in Zagreb, Yugoslavia, and Paris, France.

CAREER: Political activist and journalist, 1935-39; Yugoslav Board for Foreign Trade, director, c.1939; National Bank of Yugoslavia, deputy governor in exile in London, England, c.1942; employed by Government of Yugoslavia in Belgrade, 1942-46; University of Zagreb, Zagreb, Yugoslavia, head of economic policy in Faculty of Law, 1946-68. Visitor at University of Texas and Center for Advanced Studies in the Behavioral Sciences; lecturer at colleges and universities all over the world.

WRITINGS: Problems of Planning: East and West, Mouton, 1967; Turning Points in Economic Development, Mouton, 1972; Economic Policy in Socialist Yugoslavia, Cambridge University Press, 1973.

Not in English: Kako zivi narod: Zivot u pasivnim krajevima (title means "How the People Live"), Tisak Tipografija, 1936; Ekonomsky podloga Hrvatskog pitanja (title means "The Economic Foundation of the Croatian Question"), V. Macek, 1938; Pogled iz svetske perspektive i nasa ekonomsky orientacija, [Zagreb, Yugoslavia], 1939; Doba manufakture u Hrvatskoj (title means "The Early Factory Period in Croatia"), 1951; Problemi vanjske trogovine, Izd. Instituta za medunarodno pravoi medunarodne odnose, 1954; Ekonomsky politika FNRJ (title means "Economic Policy of the Yugoslav Federation"), [Zagreb, Yugoslavia], 1962. Contributor to professional journals in the United States and Europe.

SIDELIGHTS: In the foreword to Economic Policy in So-

cialist Yugoslavia, Michael Kaser wrote: "Rudolf Bicanic was to the study of Yugoslav economic conditions and policy as Pigou was to Marshallian economics: he infused it with a social consciousness generated by his innate humanitarianism, and fostered by his early experiences."*

* * *

BIERMAN, Arthur K(almer) 1923-

PERSONAL: Born November 15, 1923, in Madison, Neb.; son of Arthur G. (a farmer) and Elsie C. (Kalmer) Bierman; married, 1945; children: Megan, Benjamin. *Education:* University of Michigan, B.A., 1947, M.A., 1948, Ph.D., 1955; graduate study at University of California, Berkeley, 1948-49. *Agent:* Gerard McCauley Agency, Inc., P.O. Box AE, Katonah, N.Y. 10536. *Office:* Department of Philosophy, San Francisco State University, San Francisco, Calif. 94132.

CAREER: San Francisco State University, San Francisco, Calif., began as instructor, 1952, became professor of philosophy, 1965—. Co-founder of San Francisco Neighborhood Arts Program, 1967. *Military service:* U.S. Navy, 1943-45. *Member:* American Philosophical Association, United Professors of California (president, 1971-72, 1975-76).

WRITINGS: Logic: A Dialogue, Holden-Day, 1964; (editor with James Gould) *Philosophy for a New Generation,* Macmillan, 1970, 3rd edition, 1977; (editor with Gould and Jacob Needleman) *Religion for a New Generation,* Macmillan, 1973, 2nd edition, 1977; *The Philosophy of Urban Existence,* Ohio University Press, 1973; *Life and Morals,* Harcourt, 1980. Contributor to philosophy journals.

* * *

BIGGS, John, Jr. 1895-1979

OBITUARY NOTICE: Born October 6, 1895, in Wilmington, Del.; died of a heart attack, April 15, 1979, in Wilmington, Del. Judge and author. Appointed by President Franklin D. Roosevelt, Biggs was one of the youngest men inexperienced in judicial matters to become senior judge of the United States Court of Appeals Third Circuit. He was responsible for banning Bible reading in Delaware's public schools and ordered the desegregation of the school system. A former roommate of F. Scott Fitzgerald, Biggs wrote three novels and other books, as well as short stories and articles. He won the Benjamin N. Cardoso Award from the American Psychiatric Association for *The Guilty Mind.* Obituaries and other sources: *Who's Who in America,* 40th edition, Marquis, 1978; *New York Times,* April 17, 1979.

* * *

BIKLEN, Douglas Paul 1945-

PERSONAL: Born September 8, 1945, in Washington, D.C.; son of Paul Frederick (an advertising executive) and Anne (a teacher; maiden name, Chenoweth) Biklen; married Sari Knopp (a writer), November 28, 1970; children: Noah, Molly. *Education:* Bowdoin College, B.A., 1967; Syracuse University, M.R.P. and Ph.D., both 1973. *Home:* 314 Stratford St., Syracuse, N.Y. 13210. *Office:* Center on Human Policy, Syracuse University, 216 Ostrom Ave., Syracuse, N.Y. 13210.

CAREER: U.S. Peace Corps, Washington, D.C., volunteer community development worker in Sierra Leone, 1967-69; Syracuse University, Syracuse, N.Y., coordinator for legal advocacy at Center on Human Policy, 1971-72, advocacy director, 1973-74, associate director of center, 1975, direc-

tor, 1976—, assistant professor, 1973-75, associate professor of special education and rehabilitation, 1976—, coordinator of summer workshops on human abuse, protection, and public policy, 1972-73, also director of Publications in Education, director of print media for television series, "Feeling Free," and co-director of Developmental Disabilities Rights Center. Member of board of directors of Mohican Children's Foundation, 1974—, Onondaga Neighborhood Legal Services, and Protection and Advocacy System for Developmental Disabilities, Inc.; participant in national professional meetings.

MEMBER: Society for the Study of Social Problems, Council for Exceptional Children, American Association on Mental Deficiency, National Committee for Citizens in Education, American Association of University Professors, National Association for Retarded Citizens. *Awards, honors:* Grant from U.S. Office of Education, 1976—.

WRITINGS: Let Our Children Go: An Organizing Manual for Advocates and Parents, Human Policy Press, 1974; (editor with Bogdan and Burton Blatt) *An Alternative Textbook in Special Education: People, Schools, and Other Agencies,* Love Publishing, 1977; *The Elementary School Administrator's Practical Guide to Mainstreaming,* Scholastic, 1978; (with Ellen Barnes and Carol Berrigan) *What's the Difference: Teaching Positive Attitudes Toward People with Disabilities,* Human Policy Press, 1978; (with Barnes) *You Don't Have to Hear to Cook Pancakes: A Workbook in Understanding People,* Human Policy Press, 1978; (with Michele Sokoloff) *What Do You Do When Your Wheelchair Gets a Flat Tire?,* Scholastic, 1978; (editor with Bogdan) *Unconditional Care,* Canadian Educational Programmes, 1978.

Contributor: Burton Blatt, editor, *Souls in Extremis,* Allyn & Bacon, 1973; Sol Gordon, editor, *Living Fully: A Guide for People Who Have Handicaps, Their Parents, and Professionals,* Crowell, 1975; E. Sontag, J. Smith, and N. Certo, editors, *Educational Programming for the Severely/Profoundly Retarded,* Council for Exceptional Children, 1977; Miles Santamour, editor, *The Mentally Retarded Citizens and the Criminal Justice System,* James L. Maher Center, 1977; Stanley Brodsky and Constance Fischer, editors, *The Prometheus Principle,* Transaction Books, 1978; Judith S. Mearig, editor, *Working for Children,* Jossey-Bass, 1978; H. Carl Haywood, editor, *Designing Environments for the Developmentally Disabled,* American Association on Mental Deficiency, 1979.

Co-editor of monograph series, "Segregated Settings and the Problem of Change," Syracuse University Press, 1976—; editor of "Notes from the Center," Center on Human Policy, Syracuse University, 1971-74. Contributor to *Consent Handbook* and *Resource Handbook on TV Programming and Children With Special Needs.* Contributor of about thirty articles and reviews to education and social science journals. Editor of Human Policy Press, 1976—; associate editor of *Exceptional Children.*

WORK IN PROGRESS: From Charity to Rights: The Politics of Mental Retardation.

* * *

BILLMEYER, Fred Wallace, Jr. 1919-

PERSONAL: Born August 24, 1919, in Chattanooga, Tenn.; son of Fred W. (an automobile dealer) and Eleanor (Salmon) Billmeyer; married Annette Trzcinski, August 4, 1952; children: Fred S., Eleanor (Mrs. Paul Puffe), Dean W., David M. *Education:* California Institute of Technology, B.S., 1941; Cornell University, Ph.D., 1945. *Home:* 2121 Union

St., Schenectady, N.Y. 12309. *Office:* Department of Chemistry, Rensselaer Polytechnic Institute, Troy, N.Y. 12181.

CAREER: E. I. du Pont de Nemours & Co., Wilmington, Del., chemist, 1945-64; Rensselaer Polytechnic Institute, Troy, N.Y., professor of analytical chemistry, 1964—. Member of International Commission on Illumination. *Member:* American Association of Textile Chemists and Colorists, American Chemical Society, Optical Society of America (fellow), American Physical Society (fellow), American Association for the Advancement of Science, American Society for Testing and Materials, Canadian Society for Color, The Color Group (Great Britain), Society of Dyers and Colourists (Great Britain), Council for Optical Radiation Measurements, Inter-Society Color Council, Munsell Color Foundation, Society of Plastics Engineers, New York Society for Coatings Technology. *Awards, honors:* Browning Award from Federation of Societies for Coatings Technology, 1977; Macbeth Award from Inter-Society Color Council, 1978.

WRITINGS: Textbook of Polymer Chemistry, Wiley, 1957; *Textbook of Polymer Science,* Wiley, 1961, 2nd edition, 1971; (with Max Saltzman) *Principles of Color Technology,* Wiley, 1966; *Synthetic Polymers,* Doubleday, 1972; (with Edward A. Collins and Jan Bares) *Experiments in Polymer Science,* Wiley, 1973; (with Richard N. Kelley) *Entering Industry,* Wiley, 1975. Contributor of about two hundred articles to scientific journals. Editor-in-chief of *Color Research and Application.*

WORK IN PROGRESS: A revision of *Principles of Color Technology,* with Max Saltzman, publication by Wiley expected in 1980; a revision of *Textbook of Polymer Science,* publication by Wiley expected in 1981.

SIDELIGHTS: Billmeyer told CA: "Much of my writing is purely scientific, and must conform to the rather artificial style of the technical journal or book: concise, precise, impersonal. When I have the luxury of departing from this style, I prefer to write in the first person and to involve the reader as much as possible in the narrative, even though the content is still basically the exposition of science.

"My greatest challenge and greatest enjoyment is to attempt to make a scientific topic as simple as possible for the reader. My co-author Max Saltzman and I took this as our objective in writing *Principles of Color Technology;* we have never quite decided whether it is an indication of success or failure that no one ever complained that the book was too simple. Twelve years later, we are finding it a major task to incorporate the many new developments in the field into a book of about the same length without losing that simplicity.

"In a sense the scientific writer is like a part-time hired copywriter. When he is called upon to write a technical article—and this may occupy only a very small fraction of his time—it is usually to address a specific, delineated, set of objectives, dictated usually by the results of his scientific research. Seldom if ever does he have the freedom to create in the same sense as the novelist or poet.

"Yet, as I continually remind my students, communication through the written word is of vital importance throughout any scientific career. To do it well requires, I believe, more practice than talent. Again, this is not the same situation faced by the writer of fiction."

* * *

BILLOUT, Guy Rene 1941-

PERSONAL: Surname sounds like "be-you"; born July 7,

1941, in Decize, France; son of Rene George (a journalist) and Christiane (Vichard) Billout. *Education:* Attended Ecole Des Arts Appliques De Beaune, France, 1956-60. *Home and office:* 222 West 15th St., New York, N.Y. 10011.

CAREER: Free-lance illustrator; writer. Worked six years as designer in Paris, France. *Awards, honors: Number 24* listed among ten best books by *New York Times,* 1973; two gold medals from Society of Illustrators, 1974.

WRITINGS—Self-illustrated: *Number 24,* Quist, 1973; *By Camel and by Car,* Prentice-Hall, 1979.

BIOGRAPHICAL/CRITICAL SOURCES: New York Times Book Review, November 4, 1973; *New York,* December 17, 1973.

* * *

BINGER, Walter 1888(?)-1979

OBITUARY NOTICE: Born c. 1888; died March 17, 1979, in New York, N.Y. Civil engineer, executive, and author. Binger was a New York City official under Mayor La Guardia. Later, he became president of the Jacob Valeria Langelogh Foundation. He also acted as engineering consultant to the governments of Britain and Iran, and from 1952 to 1954 was national director of the Society of Civil Engineers. Binger is author of several publications on engineering and other topics. Obituaries and other sources: *New York Times,* March 19, 1979.

* * *

BIRCH, Alison Wyrley 1922-

PERSONAL: Born March 11, 1922, in New York, N.Y.; daughter of Sydney (a writer) and Marjorie (a writer; maiden name, Barstow) Greenbie; married Richard Wyrley Birch (an engineer), August 5, 1942; children: Wendy Wyrley Birch Martinez, Laurie Wyrley Birch Kendall. *Education:* Attended Western Connecticut State College, 1962-63. *Politics:* Republican. *Religion:* Congregationalist. *Home Address:* Macedonia Rd., Kent, Conn. 06757. *Agent:* Paul Reynolds, Inc., 12 East 41st St., New York, N.Y. 10017.

CAREER: Feature writer for *New Castle News,* Chappaqua, N.Y., and for *Bedford Villager,* Bedford, N.Y., 1945-56; *Reader's Digest,* Pleasantville, N.Y., member of editorial staff, 1956-66; free-lance writer, 1966—; poet. Gives poetry readings and public lectures; has appeared on national television and radio programs. *Member:* Authors League of America, Society for the Prevention of Drug Addiction (member of board of directors, 1970—), Poetry Society of New Hampshire. *Awards, honors:* Two prizes, *Writer's Digest* short story contest, 1945; Bag Press poetry contest, first prize for "Conversation Stillborn," 1967, third prize for "The Old Mill," 1968.

WRITINGS: Say Ah-h (poetry) Traversity Press, 1959; *A Little of This and That* (poetry), Mitre Press, 1965; *East of Manhattan* (poetry), Traversity Press, 1965; *Poetry for Peace of Mind* (poetry), Doubleday, 1978; *History of Dover Township* (prose and poetry), [Dover, N.Y.], 1979.

Work represented in fourteen anthologies, including: *Poetry on the Air,* Poetry House, 1947; *The Spring Anthology,* Mitre Press, 1964, 1965, 1966, 1967, 1968; *Golden Quill Anthology,* edited by Paul Scott Mowrer and Clarence E. Farrar, 1968, 1969.

Author of "Classroom Candids," column in *Lakeville Journal,* 1967-73, and "All Things Considered," column in *Con-*

necticut Republican and *Lakeville Journal*, 1974—. Contributor of articles and poems to national magazines and newspapers, including *Reader's Digest* and *Christian Science Monitor.*

WORK IN PROGRESS: Rhymes for a Reason, poetry and prose; *Make Mine Maine; How to Be Very Kind to Yourself.*

SIDELIGHTS: Birch told *CA:* "I am a traditional poet using mostly the classical forms and—yes—even rhyming. I believe that the poet's job is to express the most intense feelings that reside in all of us with rhythm and beat, and to evoke by his music and unique expression a universal response. The classical, traditional forms are to me what makes the difference between prose and poetry although good prose has a rhythm too. I use the reading and writing of poetry in workshops in hospitals for the mentally ill, with the mentally retarded, alcoholics, drug addicts, and elderly people in nursing homes. Poetry therapy is a modality used by hundreds of psychiatrists across the country and its remarkable success supports my belief that a true poem is one that creates a universal response.

"While the bulk of my writing is prose, for economical reasons I like to get a poetic sense and rhythm and flow into it, particularly in essays that are, in a sense, a form of poetry. In magazine pieces I concentrate on upbeat material that will be helpful to the reader. I've written on health problems, education, government and private programs as well as personalities and their accomplishments. Writing either prose or poetry is only useful when it serves others.

"My book *Poetry for Peace of Mind* is both prose and poetry and explains how to use poetry as therapy for anxiety, grief, loneliness, etc. A *Book Views* critic wrote: '*Poetry for Peace of Mind* by Alison Wyrley Birch is a significant book in that it explores how poetry can be used to break through moments of depression, anxiety or boredom. Ms. Birch has plowed some new land in this excellent book which social workers, psychologists, physicians and others should read along with the rest of us.'

"Much modern poetry disturbs me because it seems to be esoteric prose. The universality of emotion is missing; the inevitability of word following word that makes the reader of a good poem feel that it couldn't have been said otherwise. Robert Frost was a genius at this. I believe in simplicity and intensity and rhythm and use of the best, most poignant language and unforced rhyming. Unrhymed poetry should have, as Dylan Thomas's poetry did, a majestic rhythm and unique always beautiful choice and positioning of words that instantly emotionally affects the reader."

Birch's free-lance assignments have taken her all over the United States and Canada, and to Europe, Mexico, and the Caribbean. Her book *East of Manhattan* has become recommended reading in New York secondary schools.

BIOGRAPHICAL/CRITICAL SOURCES: New Milford Times, July, 1978; *Book Views*, September 10, 1978; *Ellsworth American*, October, 1978; *Waterbury Republican*, October 8, 1978.

*   *   *

BIRCH, Cyril   1925-

PERSONAL: Born March 16, 1925, in Bolton, Lancastershire, England; son of Archie and Annie (Worsley) Birch; married Dorothy Nuttall, July 31, 1946; children: David Geoffrey, Catherine Anne Birch Epstein. *Education:* School of Oriental and African Studies, London, B.A. (first class honors), 1948, Ph.D., 1954. *Religion:* Protestant. *Home:* 635

Santa Barbara Rd., Berkeley, Calif. 94707. *Office:* Department of Oriental Languages, University of California, Berkeley, Calif. 94720.

CAREER: University of London, School of Oriental and African Studies, London, England, lecturer in Chinese, 1948-50; University of California, Berkeley, associate professor, 1960-65, professor of Oriental languages, 1965—, head of department, 1964-66, associate dean of College of Letters and Science, 1966-69. *Military service:* British Army, Intelligence Corps, 1944-47; became lieutenant. *Member:* Association for Asian Studies. *Awards, honors:* Rockefeller Foundation fellow, 1958; Guggenheim fellow, 1964.

WRITINGS: Stories From a Ming Collection, Bodley Head, 1958; *Chinese Myths and Fantasies*, Oxford University Press, 1960; (editor) *Chinese Communist Literature*, Praeger, 1963; (editor) *Anthology of Chinese Literature*, Grove, 1965, Volume II, 1972; *Studies in Chinese Literary Genres*, University of California Press, 1974; (with S. H. Chen and Harold Acton) *Peach Blossom Fan*, University of California Press, 1976; (contributor) Merle Goldman, editor, *Modern Chinese Literature of the May Fourth Era*, Harvard University Press, 1977. Translator of Tang Xianzu's play, *The Peony Pavilion*. Contributor to Chinese studies and language journals.

WORK IN PROGRESS: A critical study of Ming drama.

SIDELIGHTS: Birch writes: "I count myself very fortunate to have been trained in two of the world's richest languages, Chinese and English. I don't know whether I translate for the vicarious satisfaction of my urge to create stories and plays, or to share and tell the delights of Chinese literature, or just to show off. It's a worrisome, agonizing, but in the end marvelously fortifying, occupation. It's also a form of criticism. For the rest of my writing, I try to practice the sort of criticism that will reveal the original author's skillful exploitation of form and thereby clarify total meaning. Chinese experience of life and love, suffering and peril, has been so rich—by passing some of it on to my students and to a broader public of readers, perhaps I can express something of my own eclectic philosophy."

AVOCATIONAL INTERESTS: Travel (Hong Kong, Japan, Taiwan, China, Australia).

*   *   *

BIRD, Harrison K.   1910-

PERSONAL: Born September 1, 1910, in New York; son of Harrison K., Sr. (in finance) and Grace (Gillette) Bird; married Harriette Jansen, January 7, 1957. *Education:* Attended Williams College, 1930-32. *Politics:* Independent. *Religion:* Christian. *Home and office:* Bluff Head, Huletts Landing, N.Y. 12841.

CAREER: Estate manager in New York, 1947—. Vice-president of Lake George Park Commission, 1961-76. *Military service:* Canadian Army, 1940-46; served in Europe; became captain; received Military Cross. *Member:* Company of Military Historians (past president; past member of board of governors). *Awards, honors:* Bronze medal from Society of Colonial Wars; Order of St. Barbara.

WRITINGS: Navies in the Mountains, Oxford University Press, 1961; *March to Saratoga*, Oxford University Press, 1962; *Battle for a Continent*, Oxford University Press, 1964; *Attack on Quebec*, Oxford University Press, 1966; *War for the West*, Oxford University Press, 1969. Contributor to military journals.

SIDELIGHTS: Bird writes that his general interests are soldiers, sailors, and airmen in wars and in training, with emphasis on the eighteenth century in America and World Wars I and II. He is also interested in archaeology and expeditions dealing with North American Indians.

* * *

BIVINS, John 1940-

PERSONAL: Born October 10, 1940, in High Point, N.C.; son of John Franklin and Louise (McNabb) Bivins; married Lucy Hudgens (a fraktur artist), June 1, 1968; children: Matthew Evan. *Education:* Attended Duke University, 1959-63; Guilford College, B.A., 1964. *Politics:* "Bipartisan." *Religion:* "Deist." *Home:* 200 Wicklow Rd., Winston-Salem, N.C. 27106. *Office:* Museum of Early Southern Decorative Arts, Winston-Salem, N.C. 27108.

CAREER: Hall Printing Co., High Point, N.C., in printing production, 1964-66; North Carolina Department of Archives and History, Raleigh, curator of furnishings, 1966-68; Old Salem, Inc., Winston-Salem, N.C., curator of collections, 1968-75; writer and custom gunmaker, 1975—; Museum of Early Southern Decorative Arts, Winston-Salem, director of publications, 1979—. Member of Winston-Salem Historic Properties Commission; member of board of directors of North Carolina League of Creative Arts; member of publications committee of Old Salem, Inc. *Member:* North Carolina Rifle and Pistol Association (member of board of directors), Pennsylvania German Society, North Carolina Historical Society, Kentucky Rifle Association. *Awards, honors:* North Carolina Mayflower Award and award of merit from American Association for State and Local History, both 1972, both for *Moravian Potters in North Carolina.*

WRITINGS: Longrifles of North Carolina, Shumway, 1968; *Moravian Potters in North Carolina,* University of North Carolina Press, 1972; *The Compleat Firelock,* Brownell's, 1979. Contributor to exhibit catalogs, antiques magazines, and gunmaking journals.

WORK IN PROGRESS: Furniture of the North Carolina Tidewater, completion expected in 1981; *American Gunmakers,* completion expected in 1982; *North Carolina Piedmont Furniture,* completion expected in 1983.

SIDELIGHTS: Bivins writes: "My chief interest lies in the applied arts, both work of the Baroque and Rococo periods and work done today. My intention is to spend my career trying to understand and interpret the decorative arts, not only through cataloging studies and monographs, but with my own hands as well, particularly in the areas of relief-carving and engraving."

* * *

BLACK, Ivan 1904(?)-1979

OBITUARY NOTICE: Born c. 1904 in Trenton, N.J.; died of emphysema, March 25, 1979, in New York, N.Y. Publicity agent and poet. Black designed houses until the stock market crashed in 1929. Afterward he became an enthusiastic publicity agent, representing Lena Horne, Patti Page, Imogene Coca, and other now-famous performers. Black worked largely with night club acts and Broadway and Off-Broadway shows. He promoted the popular musical production, "Jacques Brel is Alive and Well and Living in Paris." It was Black who suggested that the then-aspiring comedian Sam Mostel change his given name to the more singular "Zero" because he was beginning from nothing. Black wrote a collection of surrealistic poems, some of which he read in Greenwich Village cafes. Obituaries and other sources: *New York Times,* March 27, 1979.

* * *

BLACK, Malcolm Charles Lamont 1928-

PERSONAL: Born May 13, 1928, in Liverpool, England; son of Kenneth (an oil company sales representative) and Althea Black; married Charla Doherty (a publicist), June 9, 1967; children: two sons. *Education:* Attended Old Vic School, 1948-50. *Office:* Theatre New Brunswick, P.O. Box 566, Fredericton, New Brunswick, Canada.

CAREER: Stage and television actor and director, 1950-56; currently managing director of Theatre New Brunswick. Professor at University of Washington, Seattle, 1968-70, at Queens College of the City University of New York, 1970-74, and at York University, 1974-78. Actor and stage manager for drama department of Arts Council of Great Britain, 1950, 1952; performer for BBC-TV, 1950-53, studio manager, 1954-56; stage director and production manager for Toronto's Crest Theatre, 1957-59; administrator and instructor at American Shakespeare Festival Theater and Academy, 1959-61; artistic director for Playhouse Theater Company, Vancouver, British Columbia, 1964-67; director and choreographer of Society of Stage; producer and director for regional theatre. Member of Canada Council Advisory Arts Panel. *Military service:* British Army, 1946-48; became second lieutenant. *Member:* Canadian Actors Equity Association.

WRITINGS: From First Reading to First Night, University of Washington Press, 1975. Comedy writer for CBC-TV. Contributor to magazines and newspapers.

SIDELIGHTS: Black told *CA:* "My written work is currently restricted by my commitment to my theatre, but I intend to write more books after I leave here."

* * *

BLACKWELL, Lois S. 1943-

PERSONAL: Born January 6, 1943, in North Carolina; daughter of William Glen (a manager of a textile company) and Gladys (a bookkeeper; maiden name, Thompson) Schuler; married C. Kenneth Blackwell (a television news reporter), April 17, 1962; children: Jonathan Eric, Christian Alexander. *Education:* Attended University of North Carolina at Chapel Hill and University of North Carolina at Asheville. *Politics:* Democrat. *Religion:* Lutheran. *Home and office:* 7730 Enfield Ave., Apt. 203, Norfolk, Va. 23505.

CAREER: Board of Elections, Hendersonville, N.C., secretary, 1968-70; Metrogas, Inc., Hendersonville, bookkeeper, 1972-74; Hendersonville Junior High School, Hendersonville, teacher of English, 1975-76; writer, 1976—. Part-time hostess of a television talk show. Lecturer at schools and colleges, including Old Dominion University. Orientation director for Women's Job Corps; has taught illiterate adults and mentally retarded children.

WRITINGS: The Wings of the Dove: The Story of Gospel Music in America, Donning Co., 1978. Contributor to magazines, including *Western North Carolina TV Guide* and *Christian Herald.*

WORK IN PROGRESS: A pictorial history of the Christian Broadcasting Network; a book on the humor and psychological nuances of baseball; a nationally syndicated radio series on gospel music.

SIDELIGHTS: Lois Blackwell writes: "I have done a great

deal of public speaking at high schools, libraries, and clubs. I enjoy television and would like to have my own local program. American and English history have been my major areas of study, and I prefer to write history with comments emphasizing the social scene. I plan to go to England soon and would at some time like to write a book on some aspect of English history.''

*   *   *

BLACKWOOD, Caroline 1931-

PERSONAL: Born July, 1931, in Ireland; married Robert Lowell (a poet), 1972 (died, September 12, 1977); children: Robert Sheridan. Home: 15 West 67th St., New York, N.Y. 10023.

CAREER: Essayist, short story writer, and novelist.

WRITINGS: For All That I Found There (short stories and nonfiction), Duckworth, 1973, Braziller, 1974; The Stepdaughter (novel), Duckworth, 1976, Scribner, 1977; Great Granny Webster (novel), Duckworth, 1977, Scribner, 1978.

SIDELIGHTS: For All That I Found There is divided into three sections—Fiction, Fact, and Ulster—and according to Carole Horn, it is an unusual collection in that "the witty sardonic fiction frequently seems to embrace as much of truth as her journalistic accounts do unreality." Francis Wynham commented: "If Caroline Blackwood is intensely amused by human silliness, she is also fascinated by human extremity—by horror, ugliness and pain. Instead of sensitively shrinking from such subjects she nervously dwells on them, as though perversely fingering a wound. Her approach is bold—perhaps almost morbidly obsessed—but never callous." Horn further remarked: "Most of Blackwood's characters are 'poor trapped prisoners of the temporal,' though only some recognize it. Those who appear most intense, most lovely, are as likely as any to be rotted within, to suffer the psychological equivalent of that macabre form of leprosy in which a person, though riddled with the disease, appears perfectly normal until he suddenly, horribly disintegrates."

Blackwood's first novel is set in New York City and is written in the form of letters from a woman, K, to an imaginary friend. "Anxiously assuming an interested audience, the writer of letters is free to practise unburdening and evasiveness in equally large quantities," Susannah Clapp wrote. "Much of Caroline Blackwood's success in her good first novel comes from the witty recognition of this. The undispatched letters which make up the narrative of The Stepdaughter are, bleakly, addressed to an infinitely patient and cherishable nobody and tell a story which could only have been less self-aware presented as straight dramatic monologue, and more cumbersome as full dialogue."

K relates the bitter account of her life in a high-rise apartment with a four-year-old daughter, an adolescent stepdaughter, and an au pair girl, after her husband has left her for a younger woman. Jane Larkin Crain was bothered by what she considered Blackwood's "venomously controlled attack" on the Manhattan archetype K represents. "However much one might relish a clear-eyed view of those 'victimized' matrons with too much time and money on their hands, there is about The Stepdaughter a facile, monochromatic nastiness that robs it of resonance," Crain wrote. "True, the novel does a handy stiletto job on its few characters, but what, finally, is the point?. . . The book manifests a disdain for the way we live now that seems too easily won, and that defuses its rather brilliant bitchiness."

Crain's negative view was overshadowed by more positive comments. John Mellors, for example, praised Blackwood for her "unblinking, observant eye, and a penetrating, acid wit. . . . The Stepdaughter is like an etching sharp, precise and sensitive." And James Price remarked: "With its unblinking view of man's selfishness and woman's dependence The Stepdaughter is a notable contribution to the women's movement, though it contains a scene with a woman friend which serves to protect it from too facile a categorisation. It is also, I should hazard, a philosophical and religious novel. It begins with a cry of pain, which can be seen to be a philosophical position. It ends with a sense of loss, which can be seen to be a religious one. It is an unusual and affecting experience."

BIOGRAPHICAL/CRITICAL SOURCES: New Statesman, November 30, 1973, June 4, 1976, August 26, 1977; Times Literary Supplement, April 5, 1974, May 21, 1976, September 2, 1977; Washington Post Book World, June 2, 1974; London Magazine, October/November, 1974; Contemporary Literary Criticism, Gale, Volume 6, 1976, Volume 9, 1978; Listener, May 20, 1976; Encounter, September, 1976, January, 1978; New York Review of Books, September 15, 1977; New York Times Book Review, September 18, 1977; New Yorker, October 17, 1977; Observer, December 18, 1977, August 28, 1977.*

*   *   *

BLAKE, Gary 1944-

PERSONAL: Born July 25, 1944, in New York, N.Y.; son of George (a producer and director) and Jean (a travel agent; maiden name Ullman) Blake; married Eve Butterman (a journalist), May 16, 1971. Education: University of Wisconsin—Madison, B.S. (cum laude), 1966, M.S., 1967; City University of New York, Ph.D., 1973. Home: 510 East 85th St., New York, N.Y. 10028.

CAREER: City University of New York, New York City, lecturer at City College and Hunter College, 1968-73, assistant professor of speech at Bernard M. Baruch College, 1973-78; writer, 1978—. Lecturer at New School for Social Research, 1968-70; speech consultant. Member: American Theatre Association, Speech Communication Association of America, National Book Critics Circle, American Society for Theatre Research, Dramatists Guild (associate member), Drama Desk, American Society of Journalists and Authors.

WRITINGS: The Status Book, Doubleday, 1978. Author of "Punch Line" (one-act play), first produced in New York City at Hunter College, April, 1974. Contributor of articles and reviews to magazines and newspapers, including Playbill, Family Circle, Travel and Leisure, and American Home. Book review editor of Performing Arts Review.

WORK IN PROGRESS: Expertease: How to Sound Like an Expert on Almost Everything.

SIDELIGHTS: Blake commented: "Although I write about a wide variety of subjects—travel, theatre, food, health, collectibles, and ideas—I consider myself a satirist, a philosopher.

"I have haggled for years over the meaning of 'good,' 'right,' 'duty,' 'morality,' 'responsibility,' and whether or not draperies should match the couch. I've tossed around a number of philosophical positions in an attempt to find one that sounded right for me. When you find a philosophical stance which sounds right, the philosophy behind it will be right. For example, take 'hedonist.' You don't even have to know what a hedonist is, to know that being one sounds like a lot of fun.

"I never stop experimenting with alternative philosophical positions. Positivist. Empiricist. Pragmatist. Cockeyed Optimist.

"I've read all the great philosophers in an attempt to make up my mind: Kant, Nietzsche (who believed in the *ubermensch*, a person who was not bound by conventional morality; in short, a person who never clips his fingernails or sends Mother's Day cards), Mill, Aquinas, Bacon, Wayne Dyer. I've read the works of a Rationalist, a Diest, a Podiatrist. Diests, in effect, compare God to a clockmaker and the world to a giant clockradio, but forgot to allow for daylight savings time. Of course, I've gone through periods of being a skeptic, a cynic, an agnostic (an agnostic is someone who addresses his prayers 'to whom it may concern'). I've pondered the age-old debate between the Naturalists and the Utilitarians over the statement: 'Your car is double-parked.' And I've read Socrates who said, 'Because I doubt, I know I exist.' And Descarte who said, 'I think, therefore I am.'

"Which calls to mind the story of the philosophy teacher who began his academic career in the red light district, but soon grew weary of putting Descartes before the whores.

"I've even thought of joining Philosopher's Anonymous, made up of people who once had a thinking problem.

"I've learned that if you want to astound your friends with your knowledge of philosophy, you can't rush into the big problems of mankind. You have to start small. At the end of this paragraph is an ageless question which philosophers have debated for many thousands of years. What are your thoughts on this ancient subject?: Where does you lap go when you stand up?''

* * *

BLAKE, James 1922-1979

OBITUARY NOTICE: Born in 1922 in Edinburgh, Scotland; died of cancer, February 19, 1979, in Arlington, Va. Musician and author. As a jazz pianist, Blake accompanied singer Anita O'Day, comedian Lord Buckley, and other notable performers. He spent a total of thirteen years in the Florida State Penitentiary, usually for petty larceny. Viewing himself as "the world's most inept burglar," Blake relished imprisonment. *The Joint,* published by Doubleday in 1971, is a collection of letters he wrote to Simone de Beauvoir, Jean Paul Sartre, and other friends while he was behind bars. Blake also contributed to *Paris Review, American Scholar, Washingtonian, Esquire,* and other periodicals. Obituaries and other sources: *New York Times,* February 20, 1979; *Washington Post,* February 21, 1979.

* * *

BLAKEMORE, Colin (Brian) 1944-

PERSONAL: Born June 1, 1944, in Stratford-on-Avon, England; son of Cedric Norman and Beryl (Smith) Blakemore; married Andree Elizabeth Washbourne, August 28, 1965; children: Sarah Jayne, Sophie Ann. *Education:* Corpus Christi College, Cambridge, B.A., 1965, M.A., 1969; University of California, Berkeley, Ph.D., 1968. *Office:* Physiological Laboratory, Cambridge University, Cambridge CB2 3EG, England.

CAREER: Cambridge University, Cambridge, England, demonstrator at Physiological Laboratory, 1968-72, lecturer, 1972—, fellow and director of medical studies at Downing College, 1971—. Visiting professor at New York University, 1970, and Massachusetts Institute of Technology, 1971; Reith Lecturer for British Broadcasting Corp., 1976; Lethaby Professor at Royal College of Art, 1978.

MEMBER: International Brain Research Organization (member of central council, 1973—), European Brain and Behaviour Society (member of committee, 1974-76), Physiological Society, Experimental Psychology Society, Brain Research Association (member of national committee, 1973-77), Cambridge Philosophical Society (member of council, 1975—), Sigma Xi. *Awards, honors:* Robert Bing Prize for Research in Neurology from Swiss Academy of Medical Sciences, Locke research fellowship from Royal Society, 1976—; Copeman Medal for Medical Research from Corpus Christi College, Cambridge, 1977; Richardson Cross Medal from Southwestern Ophthalmological Society, 1978; named man of the year by Royal Association for Disability and Rehabilitation, 1978.

WRITINGS: (Editor with M. S. Gazzaniga) *Handbook of Psychobiology,* Academic Press, 1975; *Mechanics of the Mind,* Cambridge University Press, 1977. Writer (and broadcaster) for British Broadcasting Corp. Contributor to learned journals and popular magazines, including *Sciences* and *Nature.* Member of editorial board of *Perception, Trends in Neurosciences, Behavioural and Brain Sciences,* and *Journal of Developmental Physiology.*

WORK IN PROGRESS: A book on perception and art.

* * *

BLAKEY, Scott 1936-

PERSONAL: Born November 19, 1936, in Nashua, N.H.; son of Elmer F. and Mildred (Chaloner) Blakey; married Jacquelyn Ann Jacobs, November 30, 1963 (divorced, 1969); married Lone Erting (a textile company president), July 18, 1970; children: Laura Mayer (stepdaughter), Nicholas. *Education:* Attended University of New Hampshire, 1955-59, and University of California, Berkeley, 1969. *Home and office:* 35 Douglass St., San Francisco, Calif. 94114. *Agent:* Phyllis Seidel Literary Agency, 164 East 93rd St., New York, N.Y. 10028.

CAREER: Nashua Telegraph, Nashua, N.H., reporter and photographer, 1960-63; U.S. House of Representatives, Washington, D.C., legislative assistant for press affairs, 1963-64; *Concord Daily Monitor,* Concord, N.H., managing editor, 1964-68; *San Francisco Chronicle,* San Francisco, Calif., urban affairs writer, 1968-70; KQED-TV, San Francisco, urban affairs correspondent for "Newsroom," 1970-71, associate news editor and writer/producer, 1971-74; freelance writer, 1974—. *Member:* American Air Mail Society, California Academy of Science, Smithsonian Associates. *Awards, honors:* First prize from New England News Executives Association, 1965, for political reporting, three achievement awards for newspaper design and graphics, 1965-68; Emmy Awards in news and documentary film from Academy of Television Arts and Sciences, 1974, for "2251 Days"; DuPont-Columbia citation from Columbia University, 1975, for "2251 Days."

WRITINGS: San Francisco, Les Editions du Pacifique, 1975; *Prisoner at War: The Survival of Commander Richard A. Stratton* (selection of Reader's Digest Book Club and American Heritage Book Club), Doubleday, 1978.

Author of "Delicate Strategem" (one-act play), first produced in Durham, N.H., May, 1959.

Documentary films: "Death of Cannery Row," released by KQED-TV, 1972; "2251 Days," KQED-TV, 1973; "The Edifice Complex," U.S. Information Agency, 1974. Contributor to *Schoener Wohnen.*

WORK IN PROGRESS: Canary, a book on the escape of

Danish Jews in 1943, publication by Random House expected in 1981.

* * *

BLANCK, Gertrude 1914-

PERSONAL: Born January 8, 1914, in New York, N.Y.; daughter of Irving and Elizabeth (Green) Sacks; married Rubin Blanck (a psychoanalyst), June 21, 1940; children: Susan A. Blanck Franzen. *Education:* Hunter College (now of the City University of New York), B.A., 1936; Columbia University, M.A., 1944; New York University, Ph.D., 1963. *Home and office:* 30 West 60th St., New York, N.Y. 10023.

CAREER: Private practice of psychoanalysis and psychotherapy in New York, N.Y., 1949—. Supervisor at Theodor Reik Clinic, 1955-59, and Community Guidance Service, 1960-69. Instructor at Institute for Psychoanalytic Training and Research, 1966-68; director of training at Washington Square Institute for the Study of Psychotherapy and Mental Health, 1966-70; faculty member and curriculum director at Institute for the Study of Psychotherapy, 1970—. *Member:* American Psychological Association.

WRITINGS: Education for Psychotherapy (monograph), Institute for Psychoanalytic Training and Research, 1962; (with husband, Rubin Blanck) *Marriage and Personal Development,* Columbia University Press, 1968; (with R. Blanck) *Ego Psychology: Theory and Practice,* Columbia University Press, 1972; (contributor) B. Wolman, editor, *The Therapist's Handbook,* Van Nostrand, 1976; (with R. Blanck) *Audiotapes on Ego Psychology,* Jason Aronson, 1976; (with R. Blanck) *Ego Psychology II: Psychoanalytic Developmental Psychology,* Columbia University Press, 1979. Contributor to psychology and social work journals.

* * *

BLAU, Abram 1907-1979

OBITUARY NOTICE: Born January 19, 1907, in Montreal, Quebec, Canada; died May 14, 1979, in New York, N.Y. Psychiatrist, psychoanalyst, and author. Blau held the post of chief psychiatrist of child-adolescent psychiatry at Mount Sinai Hospital for twenty-four years, and was a psychoanalyst in private practice. He helped found the New York Council on Child Psychiatry and the American Academy of Child Psychiatry. He wrote *The Master Hand* and contributed a number of articles to medical journals. Obituaries and other sources: *Who's Who in World Jewry,* Pitman, 1972; *Who's Who in America,* 40th edition, Marquis, 1978; *New York Times,* May 16, 1979.

* * *

BLAU, Eric 1921-
(Milton Blau)

PERSONAL: Born June 1, 1921, in Bridgeport, Conn.; son of Alexander and Julia Blau; married Eleanor Stone (a singer), September, 1962; children: John Paul, Peter, Matthew. *Education:* Attended City College (now of the City University of New York). *Residence:* New York, N.Y. *Agent:* Joan Meyer, 141 East 55th St., New York, N.Y. 10022.

CAREER: Writer, theatre and film producer, and lyricist. President of a public relations firm in New York City, 1950-60. *Military service:* U.S. Army, 1942-45.

WRITINGS: (Under name Milton Blau) *Brief Journey* (poems), International Publishers, 1950; *Jacques Brel Is Alive and Well and Living in Paris* (autobiography), Dutton,

1971; *Let Me Tell You About Moses: An Experience of Israel* (poetry), Bobbs-Merrill, 1972; (contributor) *Great Songs of the Sixties,* Quadrangle, 1972.

Also author of plays, "Jacques Brel Is Alive and Well and Living In Paris" (and producer), "O Oysters," "How To Get Rid of It," "The Cockeyed Tiger," and "Dori." Ghost writer for professional athletes.

WORK IN PROGRESS: Key to Billy Tillio, a suspense novel; *Julia of the Harp,* a drama.

AVOCATIONAL INTERESTS: Cooking and gardening.

BIOGRAPHICAL/CRITICAL SOURCES: Eric Blau, *Jacques Brel Is Alive and Well and Living in Paris,* Dutton, 1971.

* * *

BLAUFARB, Douglas S(amuel) 1918-

PERSONAL: Born May 12, 1918, in Brooklyn, N.Y.; son of Jacob (a furrier) and Bessye (Klein) Blaufarb; married Celia Marjorie Warrilow (an editor), November 15, 1944; children: Ingrid (Mrs. Arthur Hughes), Nora, David, William. *Education:* Harvard University, A.B., 1939; Columbia University, M.S., 1941. *Home:* 1661 Crescent Pl., N.W., Washington, D.C. 20009.

CAREER: WQWR-Radio, New York City, news editor, 1941-44; Office of War Information, London, England, news editor and commentator, 1944-45; U.S. Information Service, New York City, news editor and commentator; 1945-50; Central Intelligence Agency (C.I.A.), Washington, D.C., operations officer in Athens and Saigon, operations officer and station chief in Singapore, and station chief in Vientiane, 1950-70. Vice-president of residential cooperative in Washington, D.C. Consultant to RAND Corp., 1970-72, and to National Security Council staff, 1972; consultant to various research organizations. *Member:* Association of Former Intelligence Officers. *Awards, honors:* Medal of Merit, Central Intelligence Agency, 1966; grant from Earhart Foundation, 1973-74.

WRITINGS: The Counterinsurgency Era, Free Press, 1977. Assistant editor of bulletin of Association of Former Intelligence Officers.

WORK IN PROGRESS: Research on the Meo guerrilla movement against Pathet Lav and the North Vietnamese, 1960-74.

SIDELIGHTS: Blaufarb comments: "I am a liberal of the Roosevelt-Truman stripe and am opposed to all forms of totalitarianism. When I joined the C.I.A. it did not seem to me that my decision represented a departure from that principle, and it still doesn't. While the C.I.A. made some serious mistakes, the nature of the world requires that the United States maintain both an effective intelligence service and a capability to intervene covertly in vital areas to protect major U.S. interests. I am afraid that at the moment the furor over the C.I.A. has undermined both capabilities. They will probably not be restored until some future crisis demonstrates unmistakably that a critical gap exists in our arsenal.

"As for my book, I wrote it because I seemed to be the best qualified person to attempt the subject who also had the requisite background, skills and interest. I am not really drawn to writing for its own sake. I can only willingly become involved in the laborious work called for if I see some broader purpose."

BLEDSOE, Jerry 1941-

PERSONAL: Born July 15, 1941, in Danville, Va.; son of Gurney F. (a builder) and Jean (Atkins) Bledsoe; married Linda Boyd, July 11, 1964; children: Erik. *Home address:* Route 6, Box 634, Asheboro, N.C. 27203. *Agent:* Sterling Lord Agency, Inc., 660 Madison Ave., New York, N.Y. 10021. *Office: Charlotte Observer,* P.O. Box 32188, Charlotte, N.C. 28232.

CAREER: Greensboro Daily News, Greensboro, N.C., columnist, 1966-71; *Louisville Times,* Louisville, Ky., feature writer, 1971; *Greensboro Daily News,* columnist, 1972-77; *Charlotte Observer,* Charlotte, N.C., columnist, 1977—. *Military service:* U.S. Army, 1960-63. *Awards, honors:* Ernie Pyle Memorial Award from Scripps-Howard Foundation, 1968-70; National Headliners Award, 1969; young newspaperman award from International Newspaper Promotion Association, 1971.

WRITINGS: The World's Number One, Flat-Out, All Time Great Stock Car Racing Book, Doubleday, 1975; *You Can't Live on Radishes,* Grape Hill Press, 1976. Contributing editor of *Esquire,* 1972-75.

WORK IN PROGRESS: Winecoff, on the Atlanta hotel fire in 1946; *Tank, the Last Revenooer,* tales of mountain moonshiners.

* * *

BLEIER, Robert Patrick 1946-
(Rockey Bleier)

PERSONAL: Born March 5, 1946, in Appleton, Wis.; son of Robert Thomas and Ellen Joan (McGu) Bleier; married Aleta Lynn Giacobine, September 7, 1975; children: Samantha Aspen Giacobine-Bleier, Adri-James Giacobine-Bleier. *Education:* University of Notre Dame, B.B.A., 1968. *Religion:* Catholic. *Home:* 580 Squaw Rd. E., Pittsburgh, Pa. 15238. *Office:* Russell, Rea, Bleier & Zappalla, Roosevelt Bldg., Pittsburgh, Pa. 15219.

CAREER: Pittsburgh Steelers (professional football team), Pittsburgh, Pa., runningback, 1968—; Hinsdale Associates, Hinsdale, Ill., insurance agent, 1971-74; Russell, Rea, Bleier & Zappalla, Pittsburgh, investment banker, 1976—. Instructor at Joe Namath Football Camp. Member of board of directors of National Society for Multiple Sclerosis, Council for the Mentally Retarded, and the President's Board for War Veterans; member of national board of directors, U.S.O. (United Service Organization). *Military service:* U.S. Army, 1968-70; received Purple Heart and Bronze Star, both 1969. *Member:* Council for Sports Vision. *Awards, honors:* Byron "Wizard" White Award, 1975; Vince Lombardi Award, 1975; named Brookland Player of the Year, 1975; named most courageous player of the year by N.F.L. Sports Writers of America, 1975; University of Nortre Dame award; General Mathew Ridgeway Award, 1977; Kennedy Foundation Award, 1979, for contributions to the Special Olympics.

WRITINGS: (With Terry O'Neil; under name Rocky Bleier) *Fighting Back,* Stein & Day, 1976.

WORK IN PROGRESS: Screenplay based on *Fighting Back.*

SIDELIGHTS: Among the numerous hard-playing pro football players stands Rocky Bleier, a Pittsburgh Steelers halfback, who has overcome serious physical obstacles in his desire to play the game. Early in his football career Bleier played for the University of Notre Dame and waited with anticipation for the possibility of joining a professional team.

In 1968, Bleier was drafted twice: first by the Pittsburgh Steelers, then by the U.S. Army. Bleier was sent to Vietnam where he was later shot in the left leg while on patrol. He was injured again when a grenade exploded at his feet while he crawled to safety.

During his rehabilitation Bleier was told by doctors that football was out of the question—that even walking would be difficult at first. The grenade had destroyed part of his right foot, and now he wears two shoe sizes: 10 and 10½. Despite a painful rehabilitation and against medical opinions, Bleier was determined to return to pro football and the Pittsburgh Steelers. *Fighting Back* is the story of his personal courage and strength in overcoming physical disabilities and the odds against him in order to build the pro career that he now enjoys.

In *Fighting Back* Bleier revealed a strenuous regimen that eventually led him to play in Super Bowl IX. After the victory over the Minnesota Vikings, Bleier recalled "the memory of those first, horrifying weeks, when nothing seemed to work . . . and the memory of an alarm clock stirring me up at 5:30 a.m. . . . . My body still sore from yesterday, and the day before, and the day before that." Finally the training paid off, but only after he resisted the temptations to sleep in or quit on "a thousand painful mornings."

Why did he do it? Bleier wrote: "Ultimately, I did it all for myself. I did it so I couldn't ask myself, ten years later, 'What if I'd rehabilitated? What if I'd gotten into super condition: could I have made the team?'"

BIOGRAPHICAL/CRITICAL SOURCES: Rocky Bleier and Terry O'Neil, *Fighting Back,* Stein & Day, 1976.

* * *

BLISS, George William 1918-1978

PERSONAL: Born July 21, 1918, in Denver Colo.; died by his own hand September 11, 1978, in Oak Lawn, Ill.; son of William and Marie (Bresnan) Bliss; married Helen Jeanne Groble, June 29, 1940 (died June, 1959); married Therese O'Keefe, August 11, 1960 (died September 14, 1978); children: (first marriage) William R., George L., Dennis M., Marianne, Carol, Helen Jeanne; (second marriage) Terrence. *Education:* Attended Northwestern University, 1938. *Home:* 9605 S. Lawndale Ave., Evergreen Park, Ill. 60642. *Office:* 435 North Michigan Ave., Chicago, Ill. 60611.

CAREER/WRITINGS: Journalist. *Chicago Evening American,* Chicago, Ill., 1937-42; *Chicago Tribune,* Chicago, 1942-53, labor editor, 1953-68; Better Government Association, chief investigator, 1968-71; *Chicago Tribune,* director of investigative task force, 1971-78. *Military service:* U.S. Naval Reserves, World War II. *Member:* Chicago Newspaper Reporters Association, Press Club, Illinois Athletic Association. *Awards, honors:* Edward Scott Beck Award, *Chicago Tribune,* 1954, 1958, 1973; spot news reporting award, Chicago Newspaper Guild, 1957; spot news reporting award, Associated Press, 1958, 1959; Pulitzer Prize for local reporting, 1962, 1973, 1976; news writing award, Associated Press of Illinois, 1972, 1974; Jacob Scher Award, 1973; news writing award, Associated Press Editors Association, 1974; Inland Daily Press Association Award, 1974; news award, United Press International, 1974.

SIDELIGHTS: George Bliss won numerous awards for his investigative reporting for the *Chicago Tribune.* In 1962 he earned his first Pulitzer Prize for a series on scandal in the city's municipal sanitary district. Bliss later exposed election fraud in Chicago and waste in federal housing programs, thus earning two more Pulitzer Prizes for the *Tribune* in 1973 and 1976.

Time reported that Clayton Kirkpatrick, the editor of the *Chicago Tribune,* described Bliss as a "perfectionist who agonized over details and in effect became a victim of his own intense devotion to journalism." On September 11, 1978, Bliss apparently committed suicide after shooting his wife. She died three days later. Bliss had been "suffering from severe depression for several months" before his death, according to *Newsweek.*

OBITUARIES: New York Times, November 6, 1978; *Newsweek,* September 25, 1978; *Time,* September 25, 1978.*

*　　*　　*

BLOCK, Stanley Byron 1939-

PERSONAL: Born October 4, 1939, in Corpus Christi, Tex.; son of Abe Bernard and Mary Helen (Orshanski) Block; married Mary Ann Ritzwoller, March 30, 1969; children: Michelle, Randy. *Education:* University of Texas, B.B.A., 1961; Cornell University, M.A., 1964; Louisiana State University, Ph.D., 1967. *Religion:* Jewish. *Home:* 3716 Lands End, Fort Worth, Tex. *Office:* Department of Decision Science and Finance, Texas Christian University, 2800 South University Dr., Fort Worth, Tex. 76129.

CAREER: Texas Instruments, Dallas, Tex., financial analyst, 1965; Louisiana State University, Baton Rouge, staff assistant, 1965-67; Texas Christian University, Fort Worth, assistant professor, 1967-70, associate professor, 1971-73, professor of finance, 1974—, head of department of decision science and finance, 1967—. Member of board of Block Realty Co., 1974-75, and of directors of Pressure Vessels, Inc., 1977—. Chairholder of Fort Worth National Bank, 1974—. Active member of Fort Worth Jewish Community Center, 1975-76. *Member:* Mortgage Bankers Association of America (fellow), Financial Management Association, Financial Executives Institute (member of board of directors), Financial Analysts Federation, Southern Casewriters Association, Jewish Club, B'nai B'rith.

WRITINGS: Problems in Basic Business Finance, Harper, 1973; *Foundations of Foundation Management,* Irwin, 1978. Contributor to business and finance journals.

*　　*　　*

BLOEM, Diane Brummel 1935-

PERSONAL: Born October 10, 1935, in Grand Rapids, Mich.; daughter of William (in sales) and Mary (Voss) Brummel; married Robert C. Bloem (an electronic field engineer), September 15, 1955; children: William Dirk, Bethel Joy, Mary Dee. *Education:* Attended Calvin College, 1953-55. *Religion:* Christian Reformed. *Home:* 1110 Burgis Court S.E., Kentwood, Mich. 49508.

CAREER: Bank teller, 1954-55; writer and editor, 1955—.

WRITINGS—All published by Zondervan: *Bible Word Search Puzzles,* 1974; *Favorite Hymns Word Search,* 1976; *Challenging Bible Crossword Puzzles,* 1977; *A Woman's Workshop on Proverbs,* with Student Manual and Leader's Guide, 1978; *Challenging Bible Crossword Puzzles 2,* 1979; (with husband, Robert C. Bloem) *Messages From Bible Marriages,* with student manual and leader's guide, 1980.

SIDELIGHTS: Diane Bloem has been a Bible leader for women's groups throughout Michigan since 1957, and a volunteer worker for Friends in Service Here (FISH). She organized and now directs a local high school career opportun-

ities program. She writes: "I vigorously encourage women to use their talents in the Lord's service, but have published my opposition to women's ordination to the priesthood or ministry because I believe the Bible teaches the headship of males in home and church. I am thankful for recognition of women's rights and abilities. I am also alarmed at contemporary emphasis on individual achievement when this conflicts with or overshadows Christ's call to His followers to serve one another."

*　　*　　*

BLOOME, Enid P. 1925-

PERSONAL: Born July 29, 1925, in New York, N.Y.; daughter of Paskes F. (a lawyer) and Marion (Gans) Marks; married Selwyn Bloome (a consulting engineer), May 30, 1948; children: David Michael, Robert Steven. *Education:* Adelphi College (now Adelphi University), B.A.; University of Hartford, M.Ed.; further graduate study at Fairfield University. *Home:* 5 Wake Robin Rd., Norwalk, Conn. 06851. *Agent:* Ruth Aley, Maxwell Aley Associates, 145 East 35th St., New York, N.Y. 10016. *Office:* Norwalk Public Schools, Norwalk, Conn.

CAREER: Elementary school teacher, 1949—; currently in Norwalk Public Schools, Norwalk, Conn. *Member:* Authors Guild.

WRITINGS—All juveniles: *Dogs Don't Belong on Beds!,* Doubleday, 1971; *The Air We Breathe,* Doubleday, 1971; *The Water We Drink,* Doubleday, 1971. Contributor to education journals and *Highlights for Children.*

WORK IN PROGRESS—All juveniles: *Economics for Children; More Dogs Don't Belong on Beds!; The Land We Use;* the story of Lady, a show dog.

SIDELIGHTS: Enid Bloome writes: "Most of my motivation comes from the children I teach: the needs in the classroom and the interests of these children. My first three books grew out of kindergarten activities and the need for pollution material for the very young. My fourth-graders are currently interested in my hobby of raising and showing our champion yellow Labrador retrievers."

*　　*　　*

BLY, Thomas J. 1918(?)-1979

OBITUARY NOTICE: Born c. 1918 in Shrewsbury, N.Y.; died March 15, 1979, in Red Bank, N.J. Journalist. Bly was executive editor of the *Register* in Shrewsbury, N.J., since 1962. Earlier in his career, he had written for the *New York Herald Tribune* and worked as a sports reporter for the *New York Times.* Bly received a Bronze Star for his service in Europe during World War II. Obituaries and other sources: *New York Times,* March 17, 1979.

*　　*　　*

BODO, Peter T. 1949-

PERSONAL: Born June 19, 1949, in Klagenfurt, Austria; son of Frank Alexander (a commercial artist) and Elizabeth (Kalotay) Bodo. *Education:* Attended Seton Hall University, 1967-71. *Home:* 151 East 81st St., New York, N.Y. 10028.

CAREER: Passaic Herald-News, Passaic, N.J., staff writer, 1972-74; *Star,* New York, N.Y., sportswriter, 1974-76; *Tennis,* Norwalk, Conn., contributing editor, 1976-78; freelance writer, 1978—.

WRITINGS: (With David Hirshey) *Pele's New World,* Norton, 1976; *Soccer: America's New Sport,* Walker & Co., 1978. Contributor to magazines, including *New York,* and newspapers.

WORK IN PROGRESS: A book about the professional tennis tour, for Delacorte.

SIDELIGHTS: Bodo remarks: "I like to write because it can never be done well enough, and it's not as exhausting as loading trucks."

* * *

BOKENKOTTER, Thomas 1924-

PERSONAL: Born August 19, 1924, in Cincinnati, Ohio; son of Anthony J. and Gertrude P. (Wessel) Bokenkotter. *Education:* St. Gregory Seminary, A.B., 1947; graduate study at Mount St. Mary Seminary, 1947-50; Angelicum, Rome, Italy, lic.theol., 1951; University of Louvain, Ph.D., 1954. *Home and office:* 6616 Beechmont Ave., Cincinnati, Ohio 45230.

CAREER: Ordained Roman Catholic priest; currently professor of history at St. Gregory Seminary. Director of Over the Rhine Kitchen; member of United Farm Workers' Support Committee. *Member:* American Historical Association, American Association of University Professors, Catholic Historical Association.

WRITINGS: Cardinal Newman as an Historian, Duculot, 1959; *A Concise History of the Catholic Church,* Doubleday, 1977. Contributor to *New Catholic Encyclopedia.* Contributor of articles and reviews to history and theology journals.

WORK IN PROGRESS: Research on social history.

SIDELIGHTS: Bokenkotter writes: "I have a strong interest in prison reform and serve on a number of church commissions dedicated to reform of prisons. Major influences on my concept of history have been Cardinal Newman and Lord Acton." *Avocational interests:* European travel.

* * *

BOLLOTEN, Burnett 1909-

PERSONAL: Born June 24, 1909, in Bangor, Wales; came to United States, 1949; naturalized U.S. citizen, 1955; son of Joseph (a businessman) and Betty (Cohen) Bolloten; married Gladys Evie (an actress), August 27, 1938 (divorced, 1955); married Betty Bieders, May 30, 1955; children: Gregory Max. *Education:* Educated in England and Switzerland. *Home and office:* 491 Raquel Ct., Los Altos, Calif. 94022.

CAREER: Author and journalist. Worked in father's business in London, England, until 1930; worked as English teacher, bookkeeper and hotel receptionist in Bastia, Corsica, as secretary in Tunis, North Africa, for British consulate in Lebanon, and for Royal Air Force station in Ismailia, Egypt, 1929-32; financial writer for stockbroker in London, 1934; journalist with United Press of America and British United Press (now combined as United Press International) in London, 1936-38. Lecturer at Stanford University, 1962-65. Notable assignments include coverage of Spanish civil war.

WRITINGS: The Grand Camouflage: The Communist Conspiracy in the Spanish Civil War, Praeger, 1961, revised and expanded edition with introduction by Hugh Trevor-Roper, Praeger, 1968; *La Revolucion Espanola,* California Institute of International Studies, 1964, translation published as *The Spanish Revolution,* University of North Carolina Press, 1979; (contributor) Raymond Carr, editor, *The Republic and the Civil War in Spain,* Macmillan, 1971.

WORK IN PROGRESS: "I am presently working on the third (and final) volume of the Spanish Revolution, which I hope to complete by 1986 (the 50th anniversary of the outbreak of the Spanish civil war) or at the latest by 1989 (the 50th anniversary of the end of the civil war)."

SIDELIGHTS: Bolloten told *CA:* "On July 18, 1936, I arrived in Spain for my summer vacation only to find myself a few hours later in the midst of the civil war and revolution. Little did I imagine that for the next forty years or more I would be gathering, organizing, digesting, and assimilating the largest collection of materials on the subject ever assembled by a single person. The United Press at first assigned me to the Aragon front, then to Madrid, Valencia, and Barcelona, the main centers of political activity, where I began collecting all available material.

"In 1938, I left Spain, married, and sailed for Mexico, where I planned to write a brief account of some of the political events of the civil war, but a few months later the war ended and thousands of refugees arrived. I then decided to widen my aim and write a comprehensive history, taking advantage of the new materials and information fortuitously made available to me. Aided by my wife, and financed by my small savings, by a modest legacy, and by the sale of some of my materials to U.S. libraries, I undertook the work of research and investigation on a scale commensurate with the need. From that time on, I consulted and reconsulted more than one hundred thousand issues of newspapers and periodicals published during the civil war and the years of exile, over three thousand books and pamphlets, and a large number of published and unpublished documents. This massive documentation was not available in any one institution or in any one country, but had to be obtained from Spain, Great Britain, France, Germany, Italy, and the U.S., as well as from Mexico and other Latin American republics, where thousands of Spaniards took refuge after the civil war. In the course of forty years of research and inquiry, I corresponded with or interviewed a large number of refugees, and combed and recombed essential institutions and libraries for fresh material. From these sources alone I obtained 125,000 microfilm frames, and years went by in an effort to bring order and meaning into this chaotic welter of material, much of which had to be consulted several times.

"In 1949, I immigrated to the United States.... By then, my financial resources were nearing exhaustion, forcing me to lower my sights and settle for a smaller book than the one projected. In 1953, without abandoning my search for new material, I joined Sears, Roebuck & Co. and for five years sold their encyclopedia from door to door. In 1959 I went into real estate business to make myself financially independent, so that I could eventually resume full-time work on my project."

* * *

BONANNO, Margaret Wander 1950-

PERSONAL: Born February 7, 1950, in Brooklyn, N.Y.; daughter of William H. (an accountant) and Patricia M. (Gosse) Wander; married Russell E. Bonanno (a teacher and actor), April 3, 1971; children: Danielle, Michaelangelo. *Education:* St. Joseph's College, Brooklyn, N.Y., B.A., 1971. *Politics:* "Independent, with a slight tilt to the left." *Religion:* "Ex-Catholic." *Residence:* Staten Island, N.Y. *Agent:* Scott Meredith Literary Agency, Inc., 845 Third Ave., New York, N.Y. 10022.

CAREER: New York City Board of Education, New York, N.Y., teacher of English and remedial reading, 1971-72;

free-lance writer for a local newspaper, 1972—. Acting member of Adelphian Players, 1969—.

WRITINGS: A Certain Slant of Light (novel), Seaview Books, 1979.

WORK IN PROGRESS: A novel based on her Irish-Newfoundland origins, publication by Seaview Books.

SIDELIGHTS: A Certain Slant of Light is the story of a friendship between two women. Sarah Morrow is an elderly professor trying to combat recent disabilities incurred by a stroke. She is looked up by Joan who once studied under Sarah and is now faced with several problems: her eight-year marriage has collapsed, she has custody of her three-year-old son, and she has no job.

At Sarah's request, Joan reads to her on weekends. At first Joan is uncomfortable with the situation but eventually takes note of her own intellectual and spiritual revitalization as a result of the visits. Eventually Sarah is rehabilitated to the extent that the two women unite in an effort to have Sarah granted her former academic position. With Sarah's help, Joan also takes steps necessary for her well-being: she decides to enroll in law school (with Sarah's financial assistance) and by novel's end, has moved in with Sarah.

In a review of the novel, Elizabeth Forsythe Hailey noted that "Bonanno has created a strong and vivid character [Sarah] who will evoke memories of real-life counterparts for many readers." She called the book "a compelling first novel." Hailey also quoted Bonanno as stating that her goal with the novel was to say that "a strong person can hold her own against all possible adversity." According to Hailey, "It is a message that needs stating in today's world . . . and *A Certain Slant of Light* proclaims it with originality and eloquence."

BIOGRAPHICAL/CRITICAL SOURCES: Washington Post, April 19, 1979.

* * *

BONE, Quentin 1918-

PERSONAL: Born September 3, 1918, in Bond County, Ill.; son of Herbert E. and Cordia (Kimbro) Bone; married wife, Elizabeth, June 20, 1958; children: Polly Jane. *Education:* University of Illinois, A.B., 1940, M.A., 1941, Ph.D., 1954. *Home:* 2332 North Seventh St., Terre Haute, Ind. 47804. *Office:* Department of History, Indiana State University, Terre Haute, Ind. 47809.

CAREER: High school social studies teacher, 1941-42; master of private school, 1946-48; high school teacher in East Peoria, Ill., 1948-52; Fairmont State College, Fairmont, W.Va., assistant professor of history, 1954-55; Indiana State University, Terre Haute, professor of history, 1955—. *Military service:* U.S. Army Air Forces, 1942-46. *Member:* American Historical Association, Phi Beta Kappa, Phi Alpha Theta.

WRITINGS: Henrietta Maria: Queen of the Cavaliers, University of Illinois Press, 1972.

* * *

BONNEFOY, Yves 1923-

PERSONAL: Born July 24, 1923, in Tours, France; son of Elie and Helene (Maury) Bonnefoy; married Lucille Vine, 1968; children: one daughter. *Education:* University of Paris, degree in philosophy. *Home:* 63 rue Lepic, Paris 18e, France.

CAREER: Writer. Has taught literature at various universi-

ties, including Brandeis, 1962-64, Johns Hopkins, Princeton, Yale, and Geneva. Co-founder of *L'ephemere* (art and literature journal), 1967. *Awards, honors:* Prix de l'Express, for *Hier regnant desert,* and *L'Improbable,* 1958; Cecil Hemly Award, 1967, for *On the Motion and Immobility of Douve;* Prix des Critiques, 1971; Prix Montaigne, 1978.

WRITINGS—Poetry: Du mouvement et de l'immobilite de Douve, Mercure de France (Paris), 1953, translation by Galway Kinnell published as *On the Motion and Immobility of Douve,* Ohio University Press, 1968; *Hier regnant desert* (title means "In Yesterday's Desert Realm") Mercure de France, 1958; *Anti-Platon* (title means "Against Plato"), Maeght (Paris), 1962; *Pierre ecrite,* Mercure de France, 1965, bilingual edition with translation by Susanna Lang published as *Pierre ecrite-Words in Stone,* University of Massachusetts Press, 1976; *Selected Poems,* translation by Anthony Rudolf, J. Cape, 1968; *Dans le leurre du seuil* (title means "In the Lure of the Threshold"), Mercure de France, 1975; *Poemes,* Mercure de France, 1978.

Criticism: Peintures murales de la France gothique (title means "Mural Paintings of Gothic France"), P. Hartmann (Paris), 1954; *L'Improbable* (title means "The Improbable"), Mercure de France, 1959; *La Seconde Simplicite* (title means "The Second Simplicity"), Mercure de France, 1961; *Rimbaud par lui-meme,* Seuil, 1961, translation by Paul Schmidt published as *Rimbaud,* Harper, 1973; *Miro,* La Bibliotheque des arts (Paris), 1964, translation by Judith Landry published as *Miro,* Viking, 1967; *Un reve fait a Mantoue* (title means "A Dream Dreamt in Mantoue"), Mercure de France, 1967; *La Poesie francaise et le principe d'identite* (title means "French Poetry and the Principle of Identity"), Maeght, 1967; *Rome 1630: l'horizon du premier baroque* (title means "Rome 1630: Early Baroque and Its Context"). Flammarion, 1970; *L'arriere-pays* (title means "The Hinterland"), Editions d'Art Albert Skira (Geneva), 1972; (with Jacques Thuillier) *Garache,* Maeght, 1975; *L'Ordalie* (title means "The Ordeal"), Maeght, 1975; *Terre seconde* (title means "The Second World"), Association des Amis de Ratilly, 1976; *Rue traversiere* (title means "The Cross Street"), Mercure de France, 1977; *Le Nuage rouge* (title means "The Red Cloud"), Mercure de France, 1977.

Translator: Leonora Carrington, *Une chemise de nuit de flanelle,* Les Pas perdus, 1951; William Shakespeare, *Henri IV, Jules Cesar, Hamlet, Le Conte d'hiver, Venus et Adonis,* [and] *Le Viol de Lucrece* (also see below), Club Francais du Livre, 1957-60; Shakespeare, *Jules Cesar,* Mercure de France, 1960; Shakespeare, *Hamlet* (also see below), Mercure de France, 1962; Shakespeare, *Le Roi Lear* (also see below), Mercure de France, 1965; Shakespeare, *Romeo et Juliette,* Mercure de France, 1968; Shakespeare, *Hamlet* [and] *Le Roi Lear, Gallimard, 1978.*

English translations of poetry collected in numerous anthologies, including: C. A. Hackett, *An Anthology of Modern French Poetry,* Basil Blackwell, 1964; W. Barnstone, *Modern European Poetry,* Bantam, 1966; S. W. Taylor, *French Writing Today,* Penguin, 1968; Serge Gavronsky, *Poems and Texts,* October House, 1969; Graham Dunstan Martin, *Anthology of Contemporary French Poetry,* Edinburgh University Press, 1972; Stanley Appelbaum, *French Poetry: A Selection From Charles D'Orleans to Yves Bonnefoy,* Peter Smith, c. 1978.

WORK IN PROGRESS: Collected essays.

SIDELIGHTS: In a review of Galway Kinnell's translation of *Du mouvement et de l'immobilite de Douve* in *Poetry,* Ralph J. Mills, Jr. pointed out that "by general critical consensus Yves Bonnefoy is one of the finest poets to emerge in France since World War II.'' He has been placed in the tradition of Baudelaire, Rimbaud, and Jouve, and has been associated as well with the post-war surrealists. A metaphysical poet, he is distinguished, according to critic Michael Hamburger, by the conviction that ''poetry has to do with truth and with salvation.''

Bonnefoy's first volume of poetry established his reputation. A sequence of short poems separated into several sections, *Douve* is a difficult work, described by Mills as ''reminiscent in part of the hermetic qualities of Mallarme and Valery and others whose technique involves obliquity, spiritual plenitude and vacancy.'' The title entity, ''Douve,'' is a female principle, which Bonnefoy himself defined as the relationship between consciousness and nothingness, and she variously represents earth, woman, love, and poetry. The progress of the poem portrays changing moods and metaphysical transformations and sets up dialectics such as mind/spirit, hope/despair, and life/death.

The difficulty of Bonnefoy's poetry arises in part from its remoteness from modern English and American poetry. Hamburger explained: ''Its language functions in a radically different way, its movement proceeds in a radically different direction; and above all ... it assumes an order of pure ideas, or of pure subjectivity, that can be evoked poetically with a minimum of sensuous substantiation.'' These distinctions are reinforced by what Bonnefoy calls the ''semi-transparency'' of French words, as contrasted with the earthy opaqueness of English. It is his view that the very language in which he writes is fraught with dangers and deficiencies for the poet, against which he must constantly struggle to sustain a ''passionate intensity.''

Bonnefoy is a respected critic and scholar, as well as a poet, and has written essays on literature, art, and architecture. His translations of Shakespeare are considered among the best in French.

BIOGRAPHICAL/CRITICAL SOURCES: Richard Kostelanetz, editor, *Yale French Studies 21*, 1958; *On Contemporary Literature*, Avon, 1964; *Poetry*, January, 1969; Serge Gavronsky, *Poems and Texts*, October House, 1969; Michael Hamburger, *The Truth of Poetry*, Harcourt, 1970; *Poetry*, June 1976; *Contemporary Literary Criticism*, Volume 9, Gale, 1978; *World Literature Today*, summer, 1979.

* * *

BONOMA, T(homas) V(incent) 1946-

PERSONAL: Born September 18, 1946, in Cleveland, Ohio; son of Emil and Marie Bonoma; married; children: one. *Education:* Ohio University, B.A. (cum laude), 1968; University of Miami, Coral Gables, Fla., M.S., 1969; State University of New York at Albany, Ph.D., 1972. *Office:* Graduate School of Business, University of Pittsburgh, Pittsburgh, Pa. 15260.

CAREER: State University of New York at Albany, instructor in psychology, 1971-72; Institute for Juvenile Research, Chicago, Ill., senior research fellow, 1972-74, senior research scientist, 1974-75; University of Pittsburgh, Pittsburgh, Pa., associate professor of business administration and psychology, 1975—, research associate of Center for International Studies and research fellow at Center for Arms Control and International Security Studies, 1975—, director of Bureau of Business Research, 1978—. Lecturer at Roosevelt University, 1973-74, and Loyola University, Chicago, Ill., 1974-75; visiting assistant professor at Northwestern University, 1974-75. Speaker at professional gatherings;

marketing and management consultant to major American businesses.

MEMBER: International Peace Research Society, International Studies Association, American Institute for Decision Sciences, American Marketing Association (member of local board of directors), American Psychological Association, American Association for the Advancement of Science, Association for Consumer Research, Society for the Psychological Study of Social Issues, Conflict Research Group, Eastern Psychological Association, Blue Key. *Awards, honors:* Grants from Marketing Science Institute, 1975, 1977-78; senior Fulbright-Hays grant, 1978.

WRITINGS: (With J. T. Tedeschi and B. R. Schlenker) *Conflict, Power, and Games: The Experimental Study of Interpersonal Relations*, Aldine, 1973; *Escalation and De-Escalation: A Social Psychological Perspective*, Sage Publications, 1975; (with Gerald Zaltman and W. J. Johnston) *Industrial Buying Behavior* (monograph), Marketing Science Institute, 1977; (editor with Zaltman) *The 1978 Review of Marketing*, American Marketing Association, 1978; (with D. P. Slevin) *Executive Survival Manual*, Wadsworth, 1978; (editor with Zaltman) *Organizational Buying* (monograph), American Marketing Association, 1978; (with Zaltman) *Psychology for Managers*, Wadsworth, 1979.

Contributor: Zaltman, Philip Kotler, and Ira Kaufman, editors, *Creating Social Change*, Holt, 1972; Tedeschi, editor, *The Social Influence Processes*, Aldine, 1972; Dennis Krebs, editor, *Readings in Social Psychology: Contemporary Perspectives*, Harper, 1976; M. Kaplan and S. Schwartz, editors, *Human Judgment and Decision Processes in Applied Settings*, Academic Press, 1977; Daniel Druckman, editor, *Negotiation: A Social Psychological Perspective*, Sage Publications, 1978; Zaltman, editor, *Handbook of Nonprofit Management*, American Management Association, 1979; Zaltman, editor, *Consumer Behavior*, Wiley, 1979; R. Bagozzi, editor, *Sales Management*, Marketing Science Institute, 1979; *Marketing Survival Manual*, CBI Publishing, 1980; *Industrial Marketing*, Business Publications, 1980.

Contributor of more than fifty articles and reviews to journals in the behavioral sciences, marketing, and management. Co-editor of *Journal of Social Issues*, 1977, *American Behavioral Scientist*, 1978, and of *Annual Review of Marketing;* member of editorial review board of *Behavioral Science*.

WORK IN PROGRESS: Social Conflict, with T. W. Milburn.

SIDELIGHTS: Bonoma's professional interests include behavioral and industrial marketing, consumer influence processes, social power, social conflict and resolution, group dynamics, individual and social decision-making, social evaluation, and application of scientific findings to practical and managerial concerns.

* * *

BONOMI, Patricia U(pdegraff) 1928-

PERSONAL: Born January 16, 1928, in Longview, Wash.; daughter of Winston R. (a publisher) and Kathryn (Mathews) Updegraff; married John G. Bonomi (an attorney), August 22, 1953; children: Kathryn, John. *Education:* University of California, Los Angeles, B.A., 1948; New York University, M.A., 1963; Columbia University, Ph.D., 1970. *Office:* Department of History, New York University, New York, N.Y. 10003.

CAREER: Herbert H. Lehman College of the City University of New York, Bronx, N.Y., part-time lecturer, 1967-70, visiting assistant professor of history, 1970; New York University, New York, N.Y., assistant professor, 1970-72, associate professor, 1972-78, professor of history, 1978—. Visiting lecturer at colleges and universities. *Member:* American Historical Association, Society of American Historians (fellow), Institute for Early American History and Culture. *Awards, honors:* Book prize from Berkshire Conference of Women Historians, 1973, for *A Factious People;* American Council of Learned Societies fellowship, 1973-74; Guggenheim fellowship, 1976-77; fellow at Davis Center for Historical Studies, Princeton University, 1979-80.

WRITINGS: A Factious People: Politics and Society in Colonial New York, Columbia University Press, 1971; (contributor) Alden T. Vaughan and George A. Billias, editors, *Perspectives on Early American History: Essays in Honor of Richard B. Morris,* Harper, 1974; (contributor) Jacob Judd and Irwin Polishook, editors, *Aspects of Early New York Society and Politics,* Sleepy Hollow Restorations, 1974; (contributor) *The Genesis of the Empire State,* New York State Bicentennial Commission, 1977; (editor) *Party and Political Opposition in Revolutionary America,* Sleepy Hollow Restorations, 1979. Contributor of articles and reviews to history and political science journals. Member of editorial board of *New York History,* 1973—.

WORK IN PROGRESS: The Formation of an American Religious Culture (tentative title).

* * *

BONSAL, Philip Wilson 1903-

PERSONAL: Born May 22, 1903, in New York, N.Y.; son of Stephen, Sr. (a correspondent and diplomat) and Henrietta (Morris) Bonsal; married Margaret Lockett, April 10, 1929. *Education:* Yale University, A.B., 1924. *Home:* 3142 P St. N.W., Washington, D.C. 20007.

CAREER: Employed by American Telephone & Telegraph in Cuba, Spain, and Chile, 1926-35; Federal Communications Commission, Washington, D.C., telephone expert, 1935-37; U.S. Department of State, Washington, D.C., vice-consul in Havana, Cuba, 1938, third secretary at embassy in Havana, 1938-39, division assistant in Washington, 1939, assistant chief of Division of American Republics, 1940, acting chief, 1940-42, chief, 1942-44, deputy director of Office of American Republic Affairs, 1944, first secretary at embassy in Madrid, Spain, 1944-46, *charge d'affaires,* 1946-47, first secretary of embassy in The Hague, Netherlands, 1947-48, political adviser in Paris, France, 1948-50, minister of embassy in Paris, 1950-52, director of Office of Philippine and Southeast Asian Affairs in Washington, 1952-54, Far Eastern adviser to U.S. delegation to the United Nations, 1954, ambassador to Colombia in Bogota, 1955-57, ambassador to Bolivia, 1957-59, ambassador to Cuba in Havana, 1959-61, ambassador to Morocco, 1961-62, in Washington, 1962-65; writer, 1965—. *Military service:* U.S. Army Reserve, Field Artillery, 1924-29; became second lieutenant. *Member:* Colombian Academy (Bogota; corresponding member), Metropolitan Club, Century Club.

WRITINGS: Cuba, Castro, and the United States, University of Pittsburgh Press, 1971. Contributor of foreign affairs articles and reviews to magazines.

SIDELIGHTS: Bonsal spent much of his boyhood abroad, attending schools in the Philippines and Switzerland. While some of his diplomatic assignments took him to Europe and Morocco, he spent most of his working years in Latin America, where he made clear his preference for democracy over dictatorship.

* * *

BOOTY, John Everitt 1925-

PERSONAL: Born May 2, 1925, in Detroit, Mich.; son of George Thomas and Alma (Gamauf) Booty; married Catherine Louise Smith, June 10, 1950; children: Carol Holland, Geoffrey Rollen, Peter Thomas, Catherine Jane. *Education:* Wayne State University, B.A., 1952; Virginia Theological Seminary, B.D., 1953; Princeton University, M.A., 1957, Ph.D., 1960. *Politics:* Democrat. *Home:* 165 Cambridge Turnpike, Concord, Mass. 01742. *Office:* 99 Brattle St., Cambridge, Mass. 02138.

CAREER: Ordained Episocopal minister, 1953; curate of Christ Episcopal church in Dearborn, Mich., 1953-55; Virginia Theological Seminary, Alexandria, Va., assistant professor, 1958-64, associate professor of church history, 1964-67; Episcopal Divinity School, Cambridge, Mass., professor of church history, 1967—. Acting director of Institute for Theological Research, 1974-76. *Member:* American Historical Association, American Society of Church History, Renaissance Society of America, Modern Language Association of America. *Awards, honors:* Fulbright scholar at University of London, 1957-58; award from American Philosophical Society, 1964; fellow of Folger Shakespeare Library, 1964, and National Endowment for the Humanities, 1978-79.

WRITINGS: John Jewel as Apologist of the Church of England, S.P.C.K., 1963; (editor) Jewel, *An Apology of the Church of England,* Cornell University Press, 1963; *Yearning to Be Free,* Greeno, Hadden, 1974; (editor) *The Book of Common Prayer, 1559: The Elizabethan Prayer Book,* University Press of Virginia, 1976; *Three Anglican Divines on Prayer: Jewel, Andrewes, and Hooker,* Cowley Fathers, 1978; *The Church in History,* Seabury, 1979; (editor) Richard Hooker, *Works,* Volume IV, Harvard University Press, 1980. Contributor to *Encyclopaedia Britannica, World Book Encyclopedia,* and *Westminster Dictionary of Church History.* Contributor to theology and history journals, and newspapers. Member of editorial committee of Richard Hooker's *Works,* Harvard University Press, 1977—.

WORK IN PROGRESS: Studying *The Book of Common Prayer.*

SIDELIGHTS: Booty comments: "My scholarly efforts (and writing) seem to be concentrated on sixteenth-century Anglican liturgy and piety. But my interests are broader, encompassing work on the seventeenth-century metaphysical poets and the Christian understanding of history. To further that understanding, I have recently written five short stories in sixteenth century settings."

* * *

BORDOW, Joan (Wiener) 1944-
(Joan Wiener)

PERSONAL: Born April 21, 1944, in Brooklyn, N.Y.; daughter of Merf (owner of an oil drum company) and Mildred (Males) Kernis; married Richard Wiener, October 1, 1966 (marriage ended, 1975); married Robert Bordow (an engineer and drummer), March 16, 1975; children: Daisy, Dandelion. *Education:* Attended Emerson College, 1961. *Politics:* "Buddhist." *Home:* 5915 Faught Rd., Santa Rosa, Calif. 95401. *Agent:* Collier Associates, 280 Madison Ave., New York, N.Y. 10016.

CAREER: Writer, 1969—. *Awards, honors:* Tastemakers Award from R. T. French Co., 1973, for best natural foods cookbook.

*WRITINGS—*Under name Joan Wiener: *Victory Through Vegetables,* Holt, 1970; *Swami Satchidananda: His Biography,* Straight Arrow Books, 1970; (editor) *Integral Yoga: Hatha,* Holt, 1970; *Get Your Health Together,* Lancer Books, 1971; (with Sharon Rosenberg) *The Illustrated, Hassle-Free Make Your Own Clothes Book,* Straight Arrow Books, 1971; (with Rosenberg) *Son of Hassle-Free Sewing,* Straight Arrow Books, 1972; (with Diana Collier) *Bread: Making It the Natural Way,* Lippincott, 1973; (with Pat Hills) *The Leathercraft Book,* Random House, 1973; (with Joyce Glick) *A Motherhood Book: Adventures in Pregnancy, Childbirth, and Being a Mother,* Macmillan, 1974; *The Denim Book,* Spectrum, 1978; *Child Death* (nonfiction), Grove, 1980.

WORK IN PROGRESS: Soap Opera, a novel; a book on money, with Paul Rest; a children's cookbook, with Claire Rosenthal; film and television scripts.

SIDELIGHTS: Joan Bordow writes: "I always wrote. I was always a writer. My credentials, however, didn't arrive until the publication of my first book, which had very little to do with writing, and which served as a springboard so that I could present other work with professional credibility. My life has come to be about experiencing life—and that experience isn't conscious a hell of a lot. When it is, then I see myself in everything—in the writing, in relating with people, in people relating with other people, in washing the dishes, in being with my husband and children, in everything. More and more I am approaching writing as a service to others and a way to share myself, rather than as a way for me to prove my existence and to dominate others with my credentials."

*   *   *

BOROWITZ, Albert (Ira)   1930-

PERSONAL: Born June 27, 1930, in Chicago, Ill.; son of David (a business executive) and Anne (Wolkenstein) Borowitz; married Helen Osterman (an art museum curator), July 29, 1950; children: Peter Leonard, Joan, Andrew Seth. *Education:* Harvard University, B.A., 1951, M.A., 1953, J.D., 1956. *Home:* 2561 Coventry Rd., Shaker Heights, Ohio 44120. *Agent:* Vivienne Schuster, John Farquharson Ltd., Bell House, Bell Yard, London WC2A 2JU, England. *Office:* Hahn, Loeser, Freedheim, Dean & Wellman, 800 National City-East 6th Building, Cleveland, Ohio 44114.

CAREER: Hahn, Loeser, Freedheim, Dean & Wellman, Cleveland, Ohio, associate, 1956-62, partner, 1956—. Member of board of directors of Bobbie Brooks, Inc. *Member:* American Bar Association, American Law Institute, Great Lakes Shakespeare Association (member of board of trustees; past vice-president), Ohio State Bar Association, Bar Association of Greater Cleveland (member of board of directors, 1976-79), Friends of the Cleveland Public Library (member of board of trustees), Union Club, Rowfant Club.

WRITINGS: Fiction in Communist China, M.I.T. Press, 1955; *Innocence and Arsenic: Studies in Crime and Literature* (essays), Harper, 1977. Contributor of articles to journals, including *Opera News, American Scholar, Nineteenth-Century French Studies,* and *American Bar Association Journal.*

WORK IN PROGRESS: The Woman Who Murdered Black Satin: The Bermondsey Horror.

SIDELIGHTS: Borowitz told *CA:* "My special interest is the study of criminal cases that have directly involved writers and artists, either as murderers, victims, witnesses, or spectators, or that have inspired significant works of art or literature."

In the preface to his collection of essays on crime, *Innocence and Arsenic,* Borowitz wrote: "I am drawn to works based on actual criminal experience because of the intriguing ambiguity of real crimes. There is uncertainty often as to guilt or innocence, and uncertainty oftener as to the motivations of the criminal and other participants in the drama. The appeal of such literature seems to me to be just the opposite of that of the classic detective story, where all doubts and suspense are finally resolved by the ingenious detective and the evil are firmly separated from the innocent. The ambiguity of historical crime is closer to the state of constant suspense in which we live. In the detective novel the puzzle is solved at the end, but in the study of crime, as in life, the puzzle goes on forever. In the title of my collection, I adopt a famous phrase from the work of the great nineteenth-century Swedish novelist C.J.L. Almqvist. The full quotation is: 'Two things are white: innocence and arsenic.' There can be no better statement of the ambiguity of criminal conduct, or any other human conduct, for that matter.

"As I planned the essays, I decided to stake out a special area of the crime field for my writing. Having great interest in literature and music, I decided to concentrate on cases in which writers or musicians are brought into direct confrontation with crime (as participants in criminal cases or trials, as spectators of crime or punishment, or as the subjects of murder legends), and on crimes that provide the basis for significant literary works. In addition, because I like to study foreign languages and cultures, I chose material from many countries and periods rather than limiting myself to Britain and America, as many of my predecessors have done. I hoped to communicate my enthusiasm for the varied social settings of crimes, for nothing can show better how people live than the strange circumstances under which they are sometimes done to death."

BIOGRAPHICAL/CRITICAL SOURCES: Albert Borowitz, *Innocence and Arsenic: Studies in Crime and Literature,* Harper, 1977.

*   *   *

BORSTEN, Orin   1912-

PERSONAL: Born February 19, 1912, in Lithonia, Ga.; son of Joseph (a merchant) and Minnie (Zilberstein) Borsten; married Laura G. Rapaport, November 2, 1946; children: Joan Paula, Joseph Samson. *Education:* Attended high school in Thomaston, Ga. *Politics:* Democrat. *Religion:* Jewish. *Home:* 10736 Wrightwood Lane, Studio City, Calif. 91604. *Agent:* Francis Greenburger, Sanford J. Greenburger Associates, Inc., 825 Third Ave., New York, N.Y. 10022.

CAREER: Stage actor in Atlanta, Ga., in the 1920's and 1930's; Southern Newspaper Enterprises, Atlanta, editor, 1932-38; actor, appearing in "The American Way" in New York City, 1938-39; Hollywood Beach Hotel, Hollywood, Fla., publicity director, 1939-42; Hy Gardner Office, New York City, entertainment publicist, 1942; Russell Birdwell Office, Beverly Hills, Calif., publicist, 1944-47; independent publicist in Los Angeles, Calif., 1947-57; playwright and television writer in New York City, Los Angeles, and Westport, Conn., 1957-65; publicist in Los Angeles, 1965-77; free-lance writer, 1977—. Press editor at Universal Pictures and publicist for films, including "Topaz," "Hellfighters," "The War Wagon," "Texas Across the River," and "The

Great Waldo Pepper.'' *Military service:* U.S. Army, 1942-44; became technical sergeant. *Member:* Publicists Guild of America (past vice-president), Academy of Motion Picture Arts and Sciences, Writers Guild of America (West), Dramatists Guild.

WRITINGS: (With Meta Carpenter Wilde) *A Loving Gentleman: The Love Story of William Faulkner and Meta Carpenter,* Simon & Schuster, 1976. Also author of screenplay (with Paul Mason and Samuel Roeca) ''Angel Baby,'' Allied Artists, 1960.

Plays: ''Fever for Life'' (three-act), first produced in New York at Hyde Park Playhouse, August 5, 1957.

Television scripts include ''The Case of the Missing Wife'' on ''U.S. Steel Hour,'' 1960, and scripts for series ''Naked City,'' ''The Outer Limits,'' and ''The Eleventh Hour.''

Author of ''Spotlight: Hollywood,'' an interview column self-syndicated to about one hundred fifty outlets, 1969-73. Associate editor of syndicated column, ''Erskine Johnson's Hollywood,'' 1950-55.

WORK IN PROGRESS: Going Under for the Third Time, a contemporary novel set in Atlanta, Ga.

SIDELIGHTS: Borsten writes: ''For many years I considered myself primarily as a playwright, and I continue to feel that it is the form in which I am most comfortable and which brings me the greatest fulfillment. With the lack of financing for American plays on Broadway, the meager gains to be made off-Broadway, except in special cases, I turned to television and motion pictures in 1960, the year in which 'Angel Baby,' starring George Hamilton and Salome Jens, was released as my first motion picture credit.

''My friendship with Meta Wilde began in 1944; more than thirty years later I was to begin writing her story in *A Loving Gentleman.*

''I devote myself wholly to creative writing today. All my plays have been set in the South. On completion of my novel, I will concentrate on productions of three full-length plays which I withdrew from the marketplace a decade or so ago, and a stage production of 'The Innocents of Summer,' screen rights to which are owned by Metro-Goldwyn-Mayer.

''Screenwriters rarely see all their work translated into film. I have written many screenplays and television plays that—for one reason or another, never because of lack of quality—have never seen the light of day. Producers fail to raise financing. Programs go off the air. Studio executives leave and others replace them, sweeping the boards clean of properties identified with their predecessors.

''I am a plodding writer, seemingly taking forever to finish a work, when I am engaged in developing a play or book.

''Although I am drawn obsessively to the South in my work, I have no special affection for the South. It is simply that I find its darker side rich in conflict, its people vivid, its speech patterns poetic and colorful. My earliest imagery is tied up with the South; I draw from it as from a bottomless well.

''I have never written about myself.

''Although I have lived in Los Angeles for more than thirty years and have been associated with the film industry, I have never attempted to write a Hollywood novel. But in *Going Under for the Third Time* my narrator is a Hollywood assistant director on vacation in Atlanta, and that is the closest I have come to juxtaposing my two worlds.''

AVOCATIONAL INTERESTS: Collecting signed, limited, numbered graphics and collecting contemporary British and American first edition novels, plays, and books of poems.

*　　　*　　　*

BOURDON, Sylvia Diane Eve 1949-

PERSONAL: Born January 29, 1949, in Kirchen, Germany. *Education:* Attended London School of Economics and Political Science, London. *Home and office:* 16 Rue des Grands Augustins, 75006 Paris, France.

CAREER: Writer; interpreter for films (in four languages). Employed by an art gallery specializing in erotic art.

WRITINGS: L'Amour est une fete, Belfond, 1976, translation by Sam Flores published as *Love Is a Ball,* J. Calder, 1977, Grove, in press.

*　　　*　　　*

BOURET, Jean 1914-

PERSONAL: Born August 8, 1914, in Paris, France; son of Georges (a horticultural engineer) and Elisabeth (Protat) Bouret; married Mauricette Chaineux, August 19, 1935; children: Alain. *Education:* Sorbonne, University of Paris, Licence es lettres, Diplome des Hautes Etudes, Certificat d'Ethnologie, Faculte des Lettres. *Home:* 86 rue du Bac, Paris 7, France. *Office:* 104 faubourg Saint Honore, Paris 8, France.

CAREER: Writer; art critic. Teacher of French literature at College de Gisors, Eure, France, 1936-40; Musee de l'homme, Paris, France, attache in department of the ocean, 1941; editor of *Arts,* 1948-52; art historian for *France-Tireur,* 1952-56, and for *Lettres francaises,* 1958-72; writer for *Nouvelles litteraires,* 1973—. Director of *Regards,* 1946-47, and of *Marco-Polo,* 1952-60; vice-president of French section of A.I.C.A. United Nations Educational, Scientific and Cultural Organization (UNESCO). Organized contemporary art exhibitions. *Member:* Association Internationale des Critiques d'Art.

WRITINGS—In English: Leo Michelson (text in English, French, and German), translation from the French by Rainer Esslen, Arts, 1963; *Henri Rousseau,* Ides et calendes, 1961, translation by Martin Leake published as *Henri Rousseau,* New York Graphic Society, 1961; *Henri Rousseau* (booklet), Beaverbrook Newspapers (London), 1962; *Douanier Rousseau,* Fawcett, 1963; *Andre Derain,* Hirschl & Adler Galleries (New York, N.Y.), 1964; *Degas,* Somogy, 1965, translation by Daphne Woodward published as *Degas,* Tudor, 1965; *Deux cents recettes secretes de la cuisine francaise,* Stock, 1966; *Bifron's Secret Recipes From the French Cuisine,* Award Books, 1966; *Bonnard: Seductions,* International Art Book, 1967, translation published as *Bernard: The Magic Ring,* French & European Publications, 1967; (with Arbit Blatas) *Resnik: Ten Original Lithographs,* Editeur Archee, 1969; *Pulga* (text in English, French, and Italian), Le Musee de poche, 1970; *L'Ecole de Barbizon et le paysage francais au XIXe siecle,* Ides et calendes, 1972, translation published as *The Barbizon School and 19th Century French Landscape Painting,* New York Graphic Society, 1973.

Other: *Simon Segal,* PLF (Paris), 1950; (author of preface) Pablo Picasso, *Dessins,* Editions des deux mondes, 1950; (with others) *Bernard Lorjou: l'age atomique,* PLF, 1950; *Joseph Pressmane,* PLF, 1952; *Helman,* Editions les Gemeaux, 1951; *A. Hambourg,* PLF, 1952; *Vinay,* PLF, 1952; *Fra Angelico,* Amiot-Dumont, 1953; *Giotto: gli affreschi nella chiesa superiore d'Assisi* (text in Italian), Sidera,

1953; (editor) Bernard Buffet, *Le Cirque*, [Paris], 1956; *L'Art abstrait, ses origines, ses luttes, sa presence*, Club francais du livre, 1957; *Eloge de Francois Desnoyer*, M. Bruker, 1958; *Bernard Ruffet*, [Paris], 1958; *Robert Wehrlin: Ausstellung* (text in German), Museum of Allerheiligen [Schaffhausen, Germany], 1958; *Despierre, oeuvres recentes*, [Paris], 1961; *Eloge de Louis Neillot*, M. Bruker, 1962; *Michelson, le peintre entre le reel et le reve*, Somogy, 1963; *Toulouse-Lautrec*, Somogy, 1964; *Galerie Marcel Guiot: Marzelle 1962-1965*, P. Gaudin, 1965; *Peske*, [Paris], 1967; *Desnoyer: peintures a l'huile et aquarelles, 1930-1972*, [Saint-Denis, France], 1972; *Un peintre de l'Ecole de Paris: Emile Lahner*, Biblioteque des arts, 1974; *Genis*, Ides et calendes, 1976.

WORK IN PROGRESS: A dictionary of French landscape paintings from 1800-1900; an essay on contemporary art; an essay on Valery Larbaud.

SIDELIGHTS: Bouret told *CA:* "I don't think there could be a better career than that of a writer whose greatest joys are to read, fish for trout, and collect rare books and paintings." *Avocational interests:* Hunting, fishing.

* * *

BOURGUIGNON, Erika (Eichhorn) 1924-

PERSONAL: Born February 18, 1924, in Vienna, Austria; came to United States in 1939, naturalized citizen, 1945; daughter of Leopold H. (a businessman) and Charlotte (a physician; maiden name, Rosenbaum) Eichhorn; married Paul-Henri Bourguignon (an artist), September, 1950. *Education:* Attended New School for Social Research, 1944, and University of Connecticut, 1945; Queens College (now of the City University of New York), B.A., 1945; Northwestern University, Ph.D., 1951. *Office:* Department of Anthropology, Ohio State University, 208 Lord Hall, 124 West 17th Ave., Columbus, Ohio 43210.

CAREER: Yale University, New Haven, Conn., research assistant at Laboratory of Applied Psychology, summer, 1945; Northwestern University, Evanston, Ill., research fellow in Haiti, 1947-48; University of Chicago, Chicago, Ill., research assistant, 1948-51; Ohio State University, Columbus, instructor, 1949-56, assistant professor, 1956-60, associate professor, 1960-66, professor of anthropology, 1966—, co-director of African summer program, 1957-58, head of anthropology department, 1972-76. Instructor at Washington University, St. Louis, Mo., 1952; lecturer at Columbus State Hospital, 1962, 1965. Member of board of directors of Human Relations Area Files, Inc., 1976—. Conducted field work with Ojibwa Indians. Broadcaster on radio.

MEMBER: American Anthropological Association (fellow), American Ethnological Society (fellow), Current Anthropology (associate member), Society for Psychological Anthropology, Ethnologia Europaea (founding associate member), R. M. Bucke Memorial Society for the Study of Religious Experience, Central States Anthropological Society, Sigma Xi (fellow). *Awards, honors:* Grant from National Institute of Mental Health, 1963-68.

WRITINGS: (With Lenora Greenbaum) *Diversity and Homogeneity: A Comparative Analysis of Societal Characteristics Based on the Data of the Ethnographic Atlas*, Department of Anthropology, Ohio State University, 1968; *Trance Dance* (monograph), Dance Perspectives Foundation, 1968; (editor and contributor) *Religion, Altered States of Consciousness, and Social Change*, Ohio State University Press, 1973; (with Greenbaum) *Diversity and Homogeneity in World Societies*, Human Relations Area File Press, 1973; *Possession*, Chandler & Sharp, 1976; *Psychological Anthropology: An Introduction to Human Nature and Cultural Differences*, Holt, 1979; (editor and contributor) *A World of Women*, J. F. Bergin, 1979.

Contributor: M. E. Spiro, editor, *Context and Meaning in Cultural Anthropology*, Free Press, 1965; Andre Caquot and Marcel Leibovici, editors, *La Divination*, Presses Universitaires de France, 1968; Raymond Prince, editor, *Trance and Possession States*, R. M. Bucke Memorial Society for the Study of Religious Experience, 1968; N. E. Whitten, Jr. and J. F. Szwed, editors, *Afro-American Anthropology: Contemporary Perspectives*, Free Press, 1970; Szwed, editor, *Black America*, Basic Books, 1970; Wolfram Keup, editor, *Origin and Mechanisms of Hallucination*, Plenum, 1970; F.L.K. Hsu, editor, *Psychological Anthropology*, new edition, Schenkman, 1972; (author of foreword) F. D. Goodman, J. H. Henney, and Esther Pressel, *Trance, Healing, and Hallucination: Three Studies in Religious Behavior*, Wiley, 1974; I. I. Zaretsky and M. P. Leone, editors, *Religious Movements in Contemporary America*, Princeton University Press, 1974; Agehananda Bharati, editor, *World Anthropology, the Realm of the Extra-Human: Ideas and Actions*, Mouton, 1976; William Lebra, editor, *Culture-Bound Syndromes, Ethno-Psychiatry, and Alternative Therapies*, University Press of Hawaii, 1976; Simon Ottenberg, editor, *Festschrift for W. R. Bascom*, University of Washington Press, 1979; Brian M. duToit, editor, *Drugs, Ritual, and Altered States of Consciousness*, Balkema, 1977; G. D. Spindler, editor, *The Making of Psychological Anthropology*, University of California Press, 1978; E. Norbeck, editor, *Symposium on Forms of Play Among North American Indians*, West Publishers, 1979; W. Schoene and W. M. Pfieffer, editors, *Psychopathologie in transkultureller Sicht*, Thieme, 1979; Jean Rouch, editor, *Cultes de possession*, Editions du Centre National de la Recherch Scientifique, 1979; Robert Baron, editor, *The Haitian Cultural Impact Upon the Caribbean World*, Brooklyn Museum, 1979. Also author of *The Status of Women: A Cross-Cultural Bibliography*, in press.

Contributor to *Proceedings*, U.S. Society for Education Through Art, 1978. Contributor to *Handbook of Social and Cultural Anthropology, Collier's Encyclopedia, Encyclopedia Americana, Encyclopedia International, American Oxford Encyclopedia*, and *World Book Encyclopedia*, and of more than sixty articles and reviews to scientific journals. Member of editorial board of Ohio State University Press, 1971—; advisory editor of *Behavior Science Research*, 1975—; associate editor of *Journal of Psychological Anthropology*, 1977—.

SIDELIGHTS: Bourguignon told *CA:* "To say that writing is part of my work as an anthropologist and as a teacher would be only part of the truth. No, writing, for me, is more than that. I write because I like to put on paper what I see and hear. And I hear a lot because I like to listen to what people around me have to say: the mailman, the grocer, the neighbor, and the cabdriver. It is of what they say that the stuff of anthropology is made. I like to write in order not to forget what I hear and see, and with the hope that someone, somewhere, may be interested in my observations. In fact, nothing pleases me more than to get a letter from someone I never met, whose first sentence is: 'I heard you were interested in . . .' and then goes on to tell me about the missionary nurse who went to a Pentecostal church in the Middle West and then claimed that someone there who was speaking in tongues actually spoke in a New Guinea language only she, among all those present, was able to recognize. The letter writer was right: I was interested in this tale, and in a hundred and one other things. And that is why I had decided, one day a long time ago, to become an anthropologist.

"That, too, is why I enjoy reading widely, not only in my own field, but also in history, biography, and autobiography, diaries and letters of people in other times and places, and I like to read them in the original languages. Art and music are also rich sources of personal satisfaction. Together with my readings, they often shed startling light on the riches of the human heritage that are so often neglected.

"I have been interested in altered states of consciousness ever since I conducted field work in Haiti. Developments in this country in the 1960's made this research timely. Yet here too, only a broad appreciation of cultural varieties has allowed me to arrive at some understanding of the phenomena involved. This is also the reason for my interest in societies of the past, such as that of France in the seventeenth and eighteenth centuries, and not only in a handful of contemporary societies."

* * *

BOURJAILY, Monte Ferris 1894-1979

OBITUARY NOTICE: Born February 28, 1894, in Lebanon; died May 6, 1979, in South Pasadena, Fla. Journalist and author. Bourjaily was founder, president, and editor of the Globe Syndicate for forty years. He also served as general manager and editor of the United Features Syndicate. Bourjaily wrote a daily column entitled "Everyday Editorials," and was the author of *People's Business in the Fifth City.* Obituaries and other sources: *Who's Who in America,* 40th edition, Marquis, 1978. *Washington Post,* May 11, 1979.

* * *

BOWEN, Ezra 1927-

PERSONAL: Born April 2, 1927, in Easton, Pa.; son of Ezra (a professor) and Catherine (a writer; maiden name, Drinker) Bowen; married Joan Williams (divorced, 1970); married Keren Widmann (divorced, 1974); children: Ezra D., Matthew W. *Education:* Amherst College, A.B., 1949. *Politics:* Liberal Democrat. *Religion:* Episcopalian. *Home:* 5 Stony Brook Rd., Westport, Conn. 06880. *Agent:* Julian Bach Literary Agency, Inc., 3 East 48th St., New York, N.Y. 10017.

CAREER: Newsweek, New York City, reporter, 1950-54; *Sports Illustrated,* New York City, senior editor, 1954-64; Time-Life Books, New York City, senior editor, 1964-76, assistant managing editor, 1973-76; *American Heritage,* New York City, editor-in-chief of books, 1976-78; writer, 1978—. *Military service:* U.S. Navy, 1945-46. *Awards, honors:* Service medal from government of Austria, 1964.

WRITINGS: The Book of American Skiing, Lippincott, 1963; (with Wilfred Owen) *Wheels,* Time-Life, 1967; *The Mid-Atlantic States,* Time-Life, 1968; (with Willy Schaeffler) *Le Ski,* Editions de l'homme, 1968; *High Sierra,* Time-Life, 1972; *Henry and Other Heroes: An Informal Memoir of High Dreams and Vanished Seasons,* Little, Brown, 1974. Editor of Time-Life series "The Old West" and "This Fabulous Century."

SIDELIGHTS: Bowen writes: "My special interest areas are America's westward expansion, 1840-1890, wild land and animal conservation, the coal-steel-rail empire in America, 1890-1940, and the Constitutional period of American history." *Avocational interests:* Classical music from baroque to Tchaikovsky, tennis, skiing, sailing, boxing, baseball.

BOWMER, Angus L(ivingston) 1904-1979

OBITUARY NOTICE: Born September 25, 1904, in Bellingham, Wash.; died May 26, 1979, in Ashland, Ore. Educator and author who founded the Ashland Elizabethan Theatre and Oregon Shakespeare Festival. A professor of drama for thirty-nine years, Bowmer produced all plays at the Shakespeare Festival from 1935 until 1971, when he became developing consultant. In 1974 Bowmer was made presidential appointee to the National Council of the Arts. Bowmer is the author of an autobiography, *As I Remember Adam.* Obituaries and other sources: *The Biographical Encyclopaedia and Who's Who of the American Theatre,* James Heineman, 1966; *Who's Who in America,* 40th edition, Marquis, 1978; *New York Times,* May 29, 1979.

* * *

BOYLE, J(ohn) A(ndrew) 1916-1979

OBITUARY NOTICE—See index for CA sketch: Born March 10, 1916, in Worcester Park, Surrey, England; died in 1979 in England. Educator, diplomat, linguist, translator, and author of books on Persian history and language. Boyle was affiliated with the British Foreign Office from 1942-50 before he began an academic career. He was professor of Persian studies at the University of Manchester. In addition to his books on Persian history and culture and Mongolian history, Boyle translated several books of Persian writers, including some works by a Sufi poet. Obituaries and other sources: *The Author's and Writer's Who's Who,* 6th edition, Burke's Peerage, 1971; *The Writers Directory, 1976-78,* St. Martin's, 1976; *Who's Who,* 131st edition, St. Martin's, 1979; *AB Bookman's Weekly,* February 5, 1979.

* * *

BOZEMAN, Theodore Dwight 1942-

PERSONAL: Born January 27, 1942, in Gainesville, Fla.; son of Simuel (in sales) and Kathleen F. (a teacher; maiden name, Jacobus) Bozeman; married Hannelore Wagner, July 29, 1973. *Education:* Eckerd College, B.A., 1964; Union Theological Seminary, New York, N.Y., B.D., 1968; Union Theological Seminary, Richmond, Va., Th.M., 1970; Duke University, Ph.D., 1974. *Office:* School of Religion, University of Iowa, Iowa City, Iowa 52242.

CAREER: Ordained Presbyterian minister, 1974; University of Iowa, Iowa City, instructor, 1974, assistant professor, 1974-78, associate professor of religion, 1978—. *Member:* American Society of Church History, American Association of University Professors, American Academy of Religion, Southern Historical Association.

WRITINGS: Protestants in an Age of Science: The Baconian Ideal and Antebellum American Religious Thought, University of North Carolina Press, 1977.

WORK IN PROGRESS: A book on Puritanism, completion expected in 1981.

SIDELIGHTS: Bozeman explained that *Protestants in an Age of Science* "examines the relationship between science and religion in nineteenth-century America before Darwin."

* * *

BRADFORD, Benjamin 1925-

PERSONAL: Born October 28, 1925, in Alexandria, La.; son of Robert Lee (in railroad work) and Edith (Turner) Bradford; married Elizabeth Wheeler (a merchant), April 2, 1946; children: Alison Bradford Harrington, Megan Bradford Hughes, Benjamin Todd. *Education:* Attended Louisiana State Northwestern University, 1942, and Mississippi College, 1943-44; Louisiana State University, M.D., 1948; postdoctoral study at Tulane University. *Politics:* Democrat. *Religion:* Episcopalian. *Home:* 122 Hilldale Lane, Paducah, Ky. 42001. *Agent:* Earl Graham, Graham Agency, 451 West 44th St., New York, N.Y. 10019. *Office:* 2320 Broadway, Paducah, Ky. 42001.

CAREER: United States Public Health Service, New York, N.Y., and New Orleans, La., internship and residence, 1948-54; private practice of medicine in Paducah, Ky., 1954—. Visiting playwright, Clarion State University, 1972; playwright-in-residence, University of Kentucky, 1973-75. Founding member and former president of Markethouse Theatre. Member of executive committee and regional arts panel. Member of Kentucky Arts Commission. *Military service:* U.S. Navy, 1943-46. U.S. Public Health Service, 1948-54. U.S. Naval Reserve, 1954—; now commander.

MEMBER: American Medical Association, American Society of Authors, Dramatists Guild, American Guild of Authors and Composers, American Society of Composers, Authors, and Publishers, Southeastern Theatre Conference, Kentucky Medical Society, Kentucky Theatre Association, McCracken County Medical Society. *Awards, honors:* Golden Windmill Award from Radio Nederland, 1971, for "Post Mortem"; John Gassner Memorial Award from New England Theatre Conference, 1968, for "Concentric Circles," 1969, for "You Don't See Many Red Cars From Montana," and 1970, for "Look Away, Look Away"; Kent Messenger Drama Award, 1969, for *Where Are You Going, Hollis Jay?;* award from Theatre Guild of Webster Grove, 1972, for "Concentric Circles"; best play award from *Variety,* 1974, for "Lunch" and "You Don't See Many Red Cars From Montana."

WRITINGS—Plays: *Segments of a Contemporary Morning* (five-act; first produced in New York City at Old Reliable Theatre, 1972), Holiday House, 1971; *Princess* (one-act; first produced in Los Angeles at Staircase Theatre, 1974), Performance Publishing, 1976; *Loving Kindness* (one-act), Performance Publishing, 1976; *The Goats* (one-act; first produced in Los Angeles at Melrose Theatre, 1973), Performance Publishing, 1977; *Where Are You Going, Hollis Jay?* (two-act; first produced in Canterbury, Kent, England, at University of Kent, 1969), Samuel French, 1979.

Plays produced only: "A High Structure Falls Farther" (three-act), first produced in New York City at Old Reliable Theatre, 1970; "Losing Things" (one-act), first produced at University of Wisconsin at Earplay Theatre, 1973; "Code Ninety-Nine" (five-act), first produced at University of Wisconsin, 1973; "Good Days, Bad Days" (one-act), first produced at University of Wisconsin at Earplay Theatre, 1973; "Lunch" (one-act), first produced in Los Angeles at Garden Theatre Festival, 1974; (with Blatz Harrington) "To Make a Man" (two-act musical), first produced in Lexington, Ky., at University of Kentucky, 1974; "Look Away, Look Away" (one-act), first produced in New York City at Three Muses Theatre, 1977.

Unpublished and unproduced plays: "Game" (one-act), 1967; "Megalith" (one-act), 1967; "Circumstance" (one-act), 1967; "A Matter of Time" (three-act), 1967; "Geometric Progression" (one-act), 1968; "A Double Fraktur L" (one act), 1968; "Parabus Objective" (one-act), 1968; "A Game of Kings and Queens" (three-act), 1968; "Instructions for a Sand Castle" (three-act), 1969; "Fancy" (one-act), 1970; "Spartans" (three-act), 1971; "The Anthropolo-

gists" (one-act), 1970; "The Ideal State" (one-act), 1970; "The Purgation List" (one-act), 1971; "Rendezvous" (one-act), 1971; (with others) "Bugs" (two-act musical), 1971; "Touch and Go" (one-act), 1971; "The Three Fence War" (one-act), 1971; "Conversation Piece" (one-act), 1971; "The Sack of Oak Pack" (one-act), 1971; "Rainbow" (one-act), 1971; "The Boa Constrictor" (one-act), 1971; "The Middle Ground" (two-act), 1972; "Life and Death in a Public Place" (four-act), 1972; "Sing Your Song America" (musical), 1974; "Birds of Passage" (one-act), 1974; "The New Woman" (three-act), 1974; "The Moon Bridge" (three-act), 1974; "Love" (two-act), 1976; "Bingo" (two-act), 1977; "Cowboy" (two-act musical), 1978; "The Rabbit" (one-act), 1978; "Doillies" (one-act), 1978.

Also author of "Quatre Jours," an episode, 1973, with Dexter Freeman, of "Favorite Son," a television series, 1974, and of *Princess Reluctant,* a music book, 1975. Contributor to theater journals, including *DeKalb Literary Journal* and *Geometric Progression,* 1979.

WORK IN PROGRESS: A Christmas Pageant; A Jigsaw Puzzle Look at American Life With Several Pieces Missing, a musical in 34 scenes; The Adorable Dodo, "a new American musical" in two acts; Sons, a novel.

SIDELIGHTS: Bradford comments. "Why do I write? A compulsion, I think, to overachieve, to compete, to create. What else is there?"

*   *   *

BRAND, Sandra   1918-

PERSONAL: Name originally Roma Brand; born August 26, 1918, in Vienna, Austria; came to United States in 1947, naturalized citizen, 1953; daughter of Leyzor (in business) and Pepa (Rumelt) Brand; married Mark Rathauser (an attorney), 1936 (died, 1942); married Arik Weintraub (a businessman); children: (first marriage) Bruno (deceased). *Politics:* Democrat. *Religion:* Jewish. *Home:* 305 West 28th St., Apt. 6-J, New York, N.Y. 10001. *Agent:* Rita Marcus, 21 Marlin Lane, Port Washington, N.Y. 11050.

CAREER: Worked as Polish-German interpreter, 1942-45; partner and treasurer, Globe Optical Imports, 1970—. *Member:* Organization for Rehabilitation Through Training, Warsaw Ghetto Resistance Organization, B'nai B'rith, Hadassah.

WRITINGS: I Dared to Live (autobiography), Shengold, 1978.

WORK IN PROGRESS: Between Two Forces, nonfiction; *Russian Occupation; And the Wind Blowed Away,* a nonfiction "Chassidic" story.

SIDELIGHTS: Sandra Brand lost both her first husband and her son in the Holocaust. She escaped almost certain extermination by assuming the identity of a Polish Catholic; her blonde, "Aryan" appearance made the masquerade easier. While working as a factory administrator in Warsaw under her new identity, Brand helped other Jews to escape from their impending doom. *I Dared to Live* is the story of her struggle.

Brand writes: "I hope to make people aware that another Holocaust is possible if we don't stop the 'small' fascistic excesses. Also I try to underline that throughout that period of time when debasement reigned, some decent individuals of every faith, every nationality extended help to victims of the Nazi regime by putting their own lives in jeopardy."

BRANDT, Willy 1913-

PERSONAL: Birth-given name, Herbert Ernst Karl Frahm; name legally changed; born December 18, 1913, in Lubeck, Germany (now West Germany); naturalized Norwegian citizen, 1940; renewed German citizenship, 1947; son of Martha Frahm; married Carlota Thorkildsen, 1940 (divorced); married Rut Hansen (a journalist), 1948; children: (first marriage) Ninja; (second marriage) Peter, Lars, Matthias. *Education:* Attended University of Oslo, 1934-35. *Office:* German Social Democratic Party, Erich-Ollenhauer-Haus, 53 Bonn, Federal Republic of Germany.

CAREER: Apprentice ship broker in Lubeck, Germany, 1932; fled from Lubeck to Norway to escape Hitler's Gestapo, 1933; journalist in Norway and Sweden, 1933-45; Norwegian press attache in Berlin, Germany, 1945-48; German Federal Parliament (Bundestag), member, 1949-57, 1969—, member of European Parliament; chief editor of Berlin Stadtblatt, 1950-51; German Federal Council (Bundesrat), president, 1957-58, vice-president, 1958-59; governing mayor of city of West Berlin, 1957-66; German Federal Republic, minister of foreign affairs and vice-chancellor, 1966-69, chancellor, 1969-74. Became member of German Social Democratic party (SPD), 1930, broke with party and joined Socialist Workers party, 1931, rejoined SPD, 1945, party worker, 1945-48, executive secretary of SPD in Berlin, 1948-49, deputy chairman, 1954-58, chairman, 1958-63, deputy chairman, 1962-64, chairman, 1964—. Secretary of Norwegian charity, 1933-40; involved in German and Norwegian resistance movements, 1940-45. Writer. Berlin Chamber of Deputies, member, 1950-69, president, 1955-57; president of German Conference of Mayors, 1958-63; president of Socialist International, 1976—; founder and head of Independent Commission on International Development, 1977—.

MEMBER: Society Germany Indivisible (member of executive committee), German Society of Foreign Politics, German Horticultural Society, German Society of the United Nations, Society for Christian-Jewish Cooperative, Max Planck Society (senator), Ernest Reuter Society. *Awards, honors:* Dr. h.c., University of Pennsylvania, 1958, University of Maryland, 1960, Harvard University, 1963, and Weizmann Institute of Israel, 1973; Freedom Award from Freedom House, 1961, for contribution to strengthening cause of world freedom; D.C.L., Oxford University, 1969; decorated Grosses Verdienstkreuz (Germany), 1959; 1st Class Star of Uprising (Jordan), 1959; Order of St. Olaf grand cross (Norway), 1960; Order of King of Greece grand cross, 1961; made honorary citizen of Berlin, 1970, and Lubeck, 1972; Nobel Peace Prize, 1971; Reinhold Niebuhr Award, 1972; Aspen Institute for Humanistic Studies prize, 1973.

WRITINGS—In English: (With Leo Lania) *Mein Weg nach Berlin,* Kindler, 1960, translation published as *My Road to Berlin,* Doubleday, 1960; *Koexistenz, Zwang zum Wagnis,* Verlags-Anstalt, 1963, translation published as *The Ordeal of Coexistence,* Harvard University Press, 1963; (with Gunter Struve) *Draussen, Schriften wahrend der Emigration,* Kindler, 1966, translation by R. W. Last published as *In Exile: Essays, Reflections and Letters, 1933-47,* University of Pennsylvania Press, 1971; *Friedenspolitik in Europa,* S. Fischer, 1968, translation by Joel Carmichael published as *A Peace Policy for Europe,* Holt, 1969; *Frieden: Reden und Schriften des Friedensnobelpreistragers,* Verlag Neue Gesellschaft, 1971, translation published as *Peace: Writings and Speeches of the Nobel Peace Prize Winner,* Verlag Neue Gesellaschaft, 1971; *Begegnungen und Einsichten: Die Jahre 1960-1975,* Hoffmann & Campe, 1976, translation

by J. Maxwell Brownjohn published as *People and Politics: The Years 1960-75,* Little, Brown, 1978.

Other: *Norge fortsatter kampen,* Bonnier (Stockholm) 1941; *Krieg in Norwegen,* Europa Verlag, 1942; *Efter segern,* Bonnier, 1944; *Nurnberg-Norge-dommen,* Aschehoug (Oslo), 1946; *Forbrytere og andre tyskere,* Aschehoug, 1946; *Tyskland under Adenauer: Den Tyske forbundsrepublikken,* Aschehoug, 1954; (with Richard Lowenthal) *Ernst Reuter, ein Leben fur die Freiheit: Ein Politische* (biography), Kindler, 1957; (with Otto Uhlitz and Horst Korber) *Von Bonn nach Berlin: Eine Dokumentation zur Hauptstadtfrage,* Arani, 1957; *Pladoyer fur die Zukunft: Zwolf Beitrage zu deutschen Fragen,* Europaische Verlagsanstalt, 1961; *Mit Herz und Hand: Ein Mann in der Bewahrung,* Verlag fur Literature und Zeiteschehen, 1962; *Begegnungen mit Kennedy,* Kindler, 1964; *Reden, 1961-65,* Verlag Wissenschaft und Politik, 1965; *Friedenssicherung in Europa,* Berlin-Verlag, 1968; *Aussenpolitik, Deutschlandpolitik, Europapolitik,* Berlin-Verlag, 1968; *Friedrich Engels und die soziale Demokratie,* Verlag Neue Gesellschaft, 1970, published as *Die Partei der Freiheit: Reden uber August Bebel, Karl Marx, Friedrich Engels und Otto Wels,* 1974; (with Otto Wolff von Amerongen and Albrecht Duren) *Kurs Marktwirtschaft,* Handelstag, 1971; *Der Wille zum Frieden: Perspektiven der Politik,* Hoffmann & Campe, 1971; *Reden und Interviews,* Hoffmann & Campe, 1971; *Bundestagsreden* (speeches), Verlag AZ-Studio, 1972; *Nicht auf halbem Wege stehenbleiben,* German Social Democratic Party, 1972; *Das Grundgesetz verwirklichen: Parteitag Hannover, 1973,* German Social Democratic Party, 1973; *Uber den Tag Hinaus: Eine Zwischenbilanz,* Hoffmann & Campe, 1974; (with Bruno Kreisky and Olaf Palme) *Briefe und Gesprache, 1972-75,* Europaische Verlagsanstalt, 1975; (with Helmut Schmidt and Jurgen Kellermeier) *Deutschland 1976: 2 Sozialdemokraten im Gesprach,* Rowohlt, 1975; *Frauen heute,* Europaische Verlagsanstalt, 1978.

SIDELIGHTS: Willy Brandt and politics have been synonymous for nearly fifty years. Alongside his work for the German Social Democratic party (SPD), Brandt has served West Germany in positions ranging from house representative to chancellor. Known early for his anti-Nazism, his major accomplishment in later years, as chancellor, was his *Ostpolitik*—the pursuit of peaceful relations with the Soviet Union, its allies, and East Germany. Though domestic problems and an internal scandal resulted in Chancellor Brandt's resignation in 1974, he still remains active in politics, continually working for a unified Europe and world peace.

Brandt's political persuasions developed early when his maternal grandfather introduced him to Germany's SPD youth movement. By the age of fourteen he was writing articles for a Social Democratic newspaper, and by seventeen he had gained full membership in the party. This association with the party broke in 1931 when the "uncompromised enemy of Nazism" decided he could fight Hitler more effectively as a member of the Socialist Workers party. In 1933, fear of arrest by the Gestapo forced the young Herbert Frahm to leave Germany for Norway, where he organized an exile office and adopted his pseudonym, Willy Brandt, as his own name.

In Norway, Brandt continued his work in politics and journalism. He wrote for the Norwegian Labor party's newspaper and covered the Spanish Civil War as a Scandinavian correspondent. Brandt chaired the Refugee Federation in Oslo and traveled to several European countries championing the anti-fascist cause. He even posed as a Norwegian student in Berlin while helping organize underground activities. The 1940 German invasion of Norway left Brandt imprisoned in a Norwegian camp for a month, from where he picked up and headed for Sweden to continue his work. After post-war assignments as a Nuremberg trial reporter and as a Norwegian press attache, Brandt decided to return permanently to his native country. He renewed his citizenship in 1947.

Upon his return, Brandt began service in a series of influential political positions. Beginning as director of the SPD's Berlin liason office, he eventually became a house representative, a parliament representative, and then mayor of West Berlin. One key event in establishing his popularity occurred in 1956, when Brandt quelled a riotous mob about to raid the gates to East Berlin in protest of the Soviet invasion of Hungary. As mayor, Brandt strongly resisted Soviet and East German claims that West Berlin belonged to Soviet influenced East Germany. He also countered Soviet Premier Nikita Khrushchev's demands by insisting West Berlin would not become an entity independent of West Germany.

Brandt's prominence in the SPD led him through two chancellorship campaigns, in 1961 and 1965, before he was finally elected West Germany's highest officer in 1969. Spurred by West German foreign policy accomplishments during his vice-chancellorship, which most notably reestablished diplomatic ties with Romania and Yugoslavia, Brandt continued to emphasize a neighborly coexistence among European nations during his early years in office. As a result of his *Ostpolitik* he signed an anti-force agreement with the Soviets, signed the Treaty of Warsaw with Poland, and urged Great Britain's admittance into the European Common Market. Brandt even sought peace with East Germany, hoping for "two German states within one German nation." The success of *Ostpolitik* was recognized in 1971 when a forty-member committee voted unanimously to award him the Nobel Peace Prize. "Brandt is the first German since Ossietzky to receive the peace prize," wrote *Nation*, "and the first to deserve it."

The rationale behind many of Brandt's foreign policy decisions had been outlined previously in his book, *A Peace Policy for Europe*. "His argument," summarized a *Times Literary Supplement* reviewer, "is that the solution of Germany's problem and the solution of Europe's problems are inseparable." Brandt emphasized that Germany's prominence in the future depended on its ability to acknowledge its past. "Even twenty-five years after the end of the war we still have to beat the consequences of Hitlerism," he declared. "No one who fails to realize this can forge a wise policy for Germany, and anyone who believes himself capable of managing without an emphatic break with that past will founder. Neo-Nazism is treason to fatherland and nation." Brandt offered his "creative" foreign policy proposals while exemplifying the attitude necessary for their success. Inis L. Claude appraised Brandt's dignified approach to his subject: "One might have expected so important a German official to be highly intelligent, but neither the history of international relations in general nor of Germany in particular would permit us to take it for granted that that country . . . would exhibit the patience and moderation, the reasoned restraint, and the constructive urge for reconciliation that the author, speaking for the government, displays in this volume."

While Brandt's successes were not limited to the foreign front, his domestic policy was never considered quite as strong. A self-proclaimed "chancellor of domestic reform," he initiated, for example, an insurance program for schoolchildren and laborers and fought for a restructuring of the tax system to reduce the poor's disproportionate burden. Yet

Brandt's chancellorship still fell victim to pressing domestic and internal issues. A rising inflation rate, defecting party members, and the resignation of his economics and finance minister all tempered the gains made abroad; but not enough to earn him less than a convincing 1972 reelection victory. A London *Times* assessment indicated Brandt's political strength at the start of his second term: "It is almost inconceivable that he would not be elected President of Europe against any competition."

Within only a year, however, confidence in Brandt's office had been visibly shaken. His *Ostpolitik* was being criticized as ineffective, and East Germany had begun to reduce contacts with the West. His own party bickered over domestic reform proposals while critics called his reaction to the energy crisis lackadaisical. To intensify Brandt's problems, his own personality fell under attack for being elusive and aloof. As *Time* reported, "to those around him, he increasingly gives the impression of a man who is tired and bored, as if the frustrations of domestic politics are too much to bear after the heady sweep of his foreign policy successes." Nonetheless, the West German public held Brandt the man, if not his policies, in high esteem. "He is a bit weak," admitted one citizen, "but you can trust him. He is a decent man."

Beneath all these troubles, a much more damaging one was about to surface. In the spring of 1974, West German officials arrested one of Brandt's closest aides, Gunter Guillaume, on charges that he, his wife, and four others were East German spies. What at first seemed to be another blemish on Brandt's chancellorship became its demise; Brandt soon resigned, saying "I accept the political responsibility for negligence in connection with the Guillaume espionage affair."

The resignation spurred contentions that Brandt had played more than an incidental role in the affair. *Newsweek* revealed the Chancellor "had been recruited by his own security service to set a trap" for Guillaume. "The tactic worked, the traitor was caught—but so, as it turned out, was Brandt. . . . For knowingly or not, Brandt had been deceived by the Communists, with whom he tried to make peace, by colleagues in whom he placed his highest trust and, perhaps, even by the women he loved." Brandt's relationship with Guillaume had been close—the two had recently vacationed together in Norway—and some claimed the aide had access to important West German documents. Allegations continued that Guillaume had threatened to reveal damaging information about Brandt unless he could be guaranteed a safe return to East Germany.

Despite the flourish of rumors, many observers believed the incident an ostensible, rather than actual, cause for resignation. His campaign promise of more tax and education reform had fallen against conservative Free Democrat resistance. The winter's oil crisis, an incessantly rising inflation rate, and public service strikes further increased his political vulnerability. Brandt's foreign policy, his forte, had also suffered disturbing setbacks. Britain's new labor government threatened Brandt's dream for an economically integrated Europe by demanding a renegotiation of the terms on which it had entered the European Common Market. His *Ostpolitik* process, too, had slowed, as critics accused him of giving more to the Communists than he had received in return. And, on a personal level, Brandt's own melancholy led him to speak secretly of resignation among his closest friends. The Guillaume incident and his ensuing resignation, then, apparently culminated a string of political problems.

Even after leaving office, Brandt's political and personal image remained highly favorable. Continued popular support was obvious as tens of thousands of West Germans marched through their streets pleading for his return. In *Newsweek's* assessment, though, Brandt had "displayed some very human frailties . . . , he nevertheless will go down as one of the towering figures in modern German history." As mayor, "he had courageously defied the Communists and guarded his city's ties to the Western world," and "as foreign minister and then Chancellor, Brandt was one of the first leaders to come out of the cold war." Altogether, "he was *unser Willy* ('our Willie'), the man who had made them proud to be Germans again." Whatever humiliation Brandt felt throughout his last months in office, his resignation did not mean an end to his ever-expanding political legacy. "One period of my life ended this week," he said after leaving. "But for me there is no flight from duty."

Part of Brandt's duty was to continue his focus on peaceful coexistence between countries. In his recent book, *People and Politics,* he shifted his foreign policy emphasis from Europe to the North-South conflict. Amid reflections on *Ostpolitik,* sketches of major personalities, and summaries of meetings with world leaders, *People and Politics* demonstrated Brandt's concern for the Third World. "Our species of democracy and liberal society is increasingly threatened," he wrote, "by the growing gulf between affluence and poverty. . . . There is a new and no longer silent majority in the world—a majority of undernourished nations. . . . The world's leaders will be those who respond to the global needs of humanity with relevant and realistic ideas and can put those ideas into practice."

Brandt transformed his theories into a course of action by forming the Independent Commission on International Development. The ex-chancellor acknowledged the difficulty of improving relations between the economically depressed Third World and the wealthy industrial countries and warned of the need for a tactful resolution. "If we treat the people of the Third World the way the narrowminded old capitalists treated workers," he said, "then we will have a clash between the starving and the well-fed nations that could go as far as war." Yet, Brandt still offered reasons for hope: "Because we're under no pressure to succeed and are free from outside instructions, we can perhaps work toward mutually acceptable solutions in at least some areas."

BIOGRAPHICAL/CRITICAL SOURCES: Times Literary Supplement, October 18, 1963, July 31, 1969; *Time,* June 17, 1966, June 28, 1968, October 3, 1969, October 31, 1969, November 14, 1969, January 26, 1970, March 16, 1970, March 23, 1970, April 20, 1970, August 30, 1970, December 21, 1970, January 4, 1971, November 1, 1971, January 10, 1972, May 15, 1972, July 10, 1972, July 17, 1972, October 9, 1972, October 16, 1972, November 27, 1972, December 4, 1972, April 2, 1973, May 14, 1973, May 28, 1973, June 4, 1973, June 18, 1973, January 21, 1974, May 6, 1974, May 20, 1974, November 24, 1975.

Business Week, December 3, 1966, December 12, 1977; *Newsweek,* April 1, 1968, November 3, 1969, November 10, 1969, January 5, 1970, January 26, 1970, March 2, 1970, March 30, 1970, May 11, 1970, July 27, 1970, August 10, 1970, November 23, 1970, June 21, 1971, November 1, 1971, March 27, 1972, May 8, 1972, October 2, 1972, November 20, 1972, November 27, 1972, January 29, 1973, April 23, 1973, May 21, 1973, February 4, 1974, May 6, 1974, May 20, 1974, May 27, 1974, June 2, 1975, December 12, 1977.

Washington Post Book World, February 23, 1969, October 22, 1978; *Life,* March 7, 1969; *Saturday Review,* March 29,

1969, December 9, 1972, May 8, 1973; *Christian Science Monitor,* May 14, 1969; *Spectator,* June 21, 1969; *Commentary,* June, 1969, *Virginia Quarterly Review,* summer, 1969, summer, 1972; *Nation,* October 13, 1969, November 8, 1971, April 10, 1972, June 8, 1974; *U.S. News and World Report,* October 13, 1969, November 3, 1969, March 30, 1970, April 20, 1970, February 8, 1971, June 14, 1971, May 8, 1972, October 2, 1972, December 4, 1972, April 30, 1973; *National Review,* October 21, 1969, June 30, 1970, September 8, 1970, April 12, 1974, June 21, 1974; *New Republic,* November 8, 1969, January 23, 1971, October 6, 1973; *New York Times Magazine,* November 30, 1969.

Look, April 21, 1970; *New Statesman,* November 27, 1970, April 9, 1971, May 10, 1974; Hermann Otto Bolesch and Hans Dieter Leicht, *Willy Brandt: A Portrait of the German Chancellor,* translated by Alice Denes, Erdmann, 1971; Klaus Harpprecht, *Willy Brandt: Portrait and Self-Portrait,* translated by Hank Keller, Nash Publishing, 1971; *Economist,* April 3, 1971; *New York Times Biographical Edition,* October 21, 1971; *Christian Century,* November 3, 1971, May 29, 1974; *Foreign Affairs,* April, 1972; *America,* December 9, 1972; David Binder, *The Other German: Willy Brandt's Life and Times,* New Republic, 1973; Alma Homze and Edward Homze, *Willy Brandt: A Biography,* Thomas Nelson, 1974; Terence Cornelius Farmer Prittie, *Willy Brandt: Portrait of a Statesman,* Schocken, 1974; *New Yorker,* January 14, 1974; Viola Herms Drath, *Willy Brandt: Prisoner of His Past,* Chilton, 1975; *Macleans,* November 6, 1978.

*   *   *

BRANIN, M(anlif) Lelyn   1901-

PERSONAL: Born January 27, 1901, in Camden, N.J.; son of Manlif L. and Sarah E. (Patterson) Branin; married Edith M. Dowling, October 22, 1926 (divorced); married Helen Hass Ream, December, 1965; children: Edith Branin Herrick. *Education:* Purdue University, B.S., 1923; graduate study at Yale University, 1926-27; Columbia University, A.M., 1930; University of Michigan, M.S., 1933, Ph.D., 1934. *Religion:* Protestant. *Home and office:* 239 Hamilton Ave., Princeton, N.J. 08540.

CAREER: Columbia University, Bard College, Annandale-on-Hudson, N.Y., assistant professor of biology, 1937-40; University of Delaware, Newark, instructor in chemistry, 1940-41; Pennsylvania Military College, Chester, associate professor, 1941-42, professor of chemistry and head of department, 1942-46; Newark College of Engineering, Newark, N.J., professor of chemistry and head of department, 1946-66; writer and researcher, 1966—. Assistant division chief for Bituminous Coal Consumers Counsel, 1942-43; vice-president in research for Asphaltic Specialties Co., 1951-54; consultant to Bituminous Coal Institute, 1943-46. *Member:* American Chemical Society, Society for the Preservation of New England Antiquities, New Jersey Academy of Science (fellow); vice-president, 1954-65; president, 1965-66; executive secretary, 1968-78), Maine Historical Society, Sigma Xi. *Awards, honors:* Past president award, 1968, and award for outstanding contribution and service, 1972, both from New Jersey Academy of Science; New Jersey Authors Citation, 1979, for *The Early Potters and Potteries of Maine.*

WRITINGS: The Early Potters and Potteries of Maine, Wesleyan University Press, 1978. Contributor of articles and reviews to technical journals. Editor of *Bulletin* of New Jersey Academy of Science, 1954-66; associate editor of *MECHannual, Mechanization,* and *Coal Utilization,* 1943-57.

WORK IN PROGRESS: The Early Potters and Potteries of New Jersey (tentative title), publication expected in 1981; another book on New England.

SIDELIGHTS: Branin told *CA:* "My interest in ceramics goes back to the time when I accompanied my grandfather to occasional county sales. He was interested in stoneware for storage purposes. . . . The book on early Maine potteries is an in-depth study of the early redware and stoneware potteries. . . . It was stimulated initially by my realization of how little of this information had previously been published and thus made available. *Avocational interests:* Pre-industrial cultural history (especially in New England), travel.

* * *

BRAUER, Carl M(alcolm) 1946-

PERSONAL: Born September 13, 1946, in Jersey City, N.J.; son of Julius L. (in business) and Beatrice (Kleimer) Brauer; married Nancy J. Schieffelin (a psychiatric social worker), August 23, 1975; children: Jacob. *Education:* Rutgers University, B.A., 1968; Harvard University, M.A., 1969, Ph.D., 1973. *Home:* 1807 Rugby Place, Charlottesville, Va. 22903. *Office:* Department of History, Randall Hall, University of Virginia, Charlottesville, Va. 22903.

CAREER: University of Missouri, Columbia, visiting assistant professor of history, 1973-74; Brown University, Providence, R.I., visiting assistant professor of history, 1974-75; University of Virginia, Charlottesville, assistant professor of history, 1975—. *Member:* American Historical Association, Organization of American Historians, Social Welfare History Group, Southern Historical Association, Phi Beta Kappa. *Awards, honors:* Woodrow Wilson fellow, 1968; National Endowment for the Humanities fellow, 1978-79; Charles Warren fellow at Harvard University, 1978-79.

WRITINGS: John F. Kennedy and the Second Reconstruction, Columbia University Press, 1977.

WORK IN PROGRESS: A History of the War on Poverty, publication expected in 1982; research on the Vietnam war in American politics and society.

SIDELIGHTS: Brauer wrote: "As a political historian, I am interested in the distribution and exercise of power through government, but I believe in viewing politics broadly and so I am concerned with the cultural and economic forces that shape politics. Writing about recent public policy is particularly exciting to me because of the opportunities it provides to use new sources, to interview actors in my story, and to pioneer in the historical interpretation of a subject. However, it also requires an unusual degree of detachment and the sheer volume of pertinent sources can be staggering, though vital information may, at the same time, be inaccessible. It is very challenging work."

* * *

BRAVMANN, Rene A. 1939-

PERSONAL: Born December 10, 1939, in Marseilles, France; son of Max Moses (a baker) and Isabelle (Edelstein) Bravmann; married Stephanie Gail Luster, September 15, 1963; children: Paul H., Rachel L. *Education:* Case Western Reserve University, B.A., 1961; graduate study at University of Wisconsin, Madison, 1961-63; Indiana University, M.A., 1965, Ph.D., 1971. *Home:* 16280 Agate Point Rd., Bainbridge Island, Wash. 98110. *Office:* School of Art, University of Washington, Seattle, Wash. 98195.

CAREER: University of Washington, Seattle, assistant professor, 1968-72, associate professor, 1972-77, professor of art

history, 1977—. Consultant to Social Science Research Council and National Endowment for the Humanities. *Member:* College Art Association of America, African Studies Association. *Awards, honors:* Grants from Social Science Research Council, 1971-72, American Council of Learned Societies, 1972, and American Philosophical Society, 1974; Guggenheim fellow, 1974.

WRITINGS: West African Sculpture, University of Washington Press, 1970; *Open Frontiers: The Dynamics of Art in Black Africa,* University of Washington Press, 1973; *Islam and Tribal Art in West Africa,* Cambridge Univeristy Press, 1974.

WORK IN PROGRESS: Art and Urbanization in Africa.

SIDELIGHTS: Bravmann has traveled extensively in Europe and Africa since 1966. In addition to French and German, he speaks the Twi language of Ghana and Bobo, of Upper Volta.

* * *

BREWSTER, Dorothy 1883-1979

OBITUARY NOTICE—See index for *CA* sketch: Born in 1883 in St. Louis, Mo.; died April 17, 1979, in Lancaster, Pa. Educator and author. A specialist in modern fiction and short story writing, Brewster was a member of the English faculty at Columbia University until her retirement in 1950. She was the author of numerous books on American literature and literary biographies. Obituaries and other sources: *The Author's and Writer's Who's Who,* 6th edition, Burke's Peerage, 1971; *Who's Who in America,* 39th edition, Marquis, 1976; *Directory of American Scholars,* Volume II: *English, Speech, and Drama,* 7th edition, Bowker, 1978; *New York Times,* April 28, 1979.

* * *

BRIDGEMAN, Harriet 1942-

PERSONAL: Born March 30, 1942, in Durham, England; daughter of Ralph Meredith (a solicitor) and Mary Blanche (Chetwynd-Stapleton) Turton; married Robin John Orlando Bridgeman (a stockbroker), December 10, 1968; children: Will Orlando Caspa, Luke Orlando Robinson, Esmond Frances Ralph Orlando. *Education:* Trinity College, Dublin, Ireland, M.A., 1964. *Politics:* Conservative. *Religion:* Protestant. *Home:* Watley House, Sparsholt, Winchester, Hampshire, England. *Agent:* Abnerstein, 43 Albany Mansions, Albert Bridge Rd., SW11, England. *Office:* 19 Chepstow Rd., London W.2, England.

CAREER: Lady, London, England, editor, 1964-65; executive editor of *The Masters,* 1965-68; worked as editor for various organizations, 1968-73; company director of Cooper-Bridgeman Library. *Member:* British Association of Picture Libraries and Agencies.

WRITINGS: (Editor and compiler) *Erotic Antiques; or, Love Is an Antic Thing,* Lyle Publications, 1974; *The British Eccentric,* M. Joseph, 1975; (editor with Elizabeth Drury) *The Encyclopedia of Victoriana,* Country Life, 1975; *Society Scandals,* David & Charles, 1977; (compiler with Drury) *Beside the Seaside: A Picture Postcard Album,* Elm Tree Books, 1977; *An Illustrated History of Needlework,* Paddington, 1978.

WORK IN PROGRESS: Guide to Gardens of Europe; The History of Lights and Lighting; The History of Knives, Forks, and Spoons; An Antique Browser's Handbook; Guide to Houses and Castles of Europe; a children's anthology.

BRILL, Steven

PERSONAL—Education: Yale University, earned bachelor degree, LL.M., 1975. *Agent:* c/o Simon & Schuster, Inc., 630 Fifth Ave., New York, N.Y. 10020.

CAREER: Assistant to Mayor John Lindsay, New York, N.Y., 1971-73; currently founder and editor-in-chief of *The American Lawyer.* Contributing editor to *New York* and *Harper's* magazines; law columnist and contributing editor to *Esquire* magazine. Consultant to the Police Foundation, Washington, D.C., 1975-77. *Awards, honors:* John Hancock Award, 1977, for excellence in business reporting.

WRITINGS: Firearm Abuse: A Research and Policy Report, Police Foundation, 1977; *The Teamsters,* Simon & Schuster, 1978.

SIDELIGHTS: Before Steven Brill's *The Teamsters* appeared in print, there was speculation that it provided the solution to Jimmy Hoffa's murder. Rumors circulated that Brill had a taped confession about the Hoffa murder—a charge that Brill flatly denied. Actually, Brill's reconstruction of the crime is similar to the one previously made by the FBI. Brill theorizes that the Mafia, alarmed by Hoffa's determination to resume leadership of the Teamsters, decided to end the labor leader's life. He asserts that Anthony Provenzano (Tony Pro) was involved in the killing, and charges that Provenzano received orders from Russell Bufalino, a New York mobster. One new piece of information in *The Teamsters* is its claim that Hoffa's body was destroyed at a refuse-disposal plant owned by two Detroit crime figures. Thus far, no witnesses have come forth to confirm Brill's suspicions.

It should not be assumed, however, that *The Teamsters* is merely a muckraking book about Hoffa. As the title indicates, the book is primarily a history of the Teamsters Union. "My book is less than 10 percent about Hoffa," Brill explained to an interviewer. "In some respects, it's a very positive story about the teamsters. In fact, I've had an offer to go to work for the teamsters as a public-relations consultant—which I turned down." Walter Clemons agreed with Brill's assessment of the book. He called *The Teamsters* "an ambitious effort to clarify the operations of the union to which 2.3 million Americans belong," and praised Brill's portrayals of Teamster officials.

BIOGRAPHICAL/CRITICAL SOURCES: New York Times, June 29, 1978; *Newsweek,* October 2, 1978.*

*   *   *

BRINK, Wellington 1895-1979

OBITUARY NOTICE: Born in 1895 in Kalamazoo, Mich.; died of a stroke, March 22, 1979, in Easton, Md. Journalist and author. Brink edited agriculture journals and contributed to trade publications before joining the American Red Cross as assistant national director of information. He later took a position with the Soil Conservation Service, where he remained for twenty-one years. Brink wrote a biography in 1951 on Hugh Bennett, a prominent figure in the field of agriculture. Obituaries and other sources: *Washington Post,* March 24, 1979.

*   *   *

BRINKERHOFF, Dericksen Morgan 1921-

PERSONAL: Born October 4, 1921, in Philadelphia, Pa.; son of Robert Joris and Marion (Butler) Brinkerhoff; married Mary Dean Weston, December 20, 1946; children: Derick W., Elizabeth (Mrs. John Clarke), Jonathan D., Carolyn

(Mrs. David Peterson). *Education:* Williams College, B.A., 1943; Yale University, M.A., 1947; further graduate study at University of Zurich, 1948-49; Harvard University, Ph.D., 1958. *Home:* 4985 Chicago Ave., Riverside, Calif. 92507. *Office:* Department of the History of Art, University of California, Riverside, Calif. 92521.

CAREER: Rhode Island School of Design, Providence, associate professor of history, 1952-59, head of department, 1955-56, head of Division of Liberal Arts, 1956-59; Pennsylvania State University, University Park, associate professor of art history, 1961-62; Temple University, Philadelphia, Pa., associate professor of art history, 1962-65; University of California, Riverside, associate professor, 1965-67, professor of art history, 1967—, head of department, 1965-71. Instructor at Brown University, 1952-55; and at University of California, Berkeley, 1968-69. Member of American Research Center of Egypt and of Los Angeles County Museum of Art. *Military service:* U.S. Army Air Forces, 1943-46; served in Burma; became sergeant.

MEMBER: Associazione internazionale di Archeologia classica, American Numismatic Society, American Association of University Professors, Archaeological Institute of America, College Art Association of America, Society for the Promotion of Roman Studies, Classical Society (of American Academy in Rome), Art Historians of Southern California, Riverside Art Association (member of board of trustees, 1968-72). *Awards, honors:* Prize from American Numismatic Society, 1952; Belgian-American Educational Foundation fellow, summer, 1959; senior fellow of American Academy in Rome, 1959-61; American Philosophical Society grant, 1960-61; award from California Humanities Institute, 1971-72.

WRITINGS: A Collection of Sculpture in Classical and Early Christian Antioch (monograph), edited by Anne C. Hanson, New York University Press, 1970; *Hellenistic Statues of Aphrodite: Studies in the History of Their Stylistic Development,* Garland Publishing, 1978. Contributor to art and archaeology journals.

WORK IN PROGRESS: Roman Sarcophagi at the Hearst Monument, San Simeon, California; The Attalid War Memorial on the Athenian Acropolis; The Arch of Titus in the Roman Forum.

SIDELIGHTS: Brinkerhoff writes: "I find the history of art endlessly fascinating as an index to the way we were and how we arrived where we are. My motivations are intellectual curiosity and a desire to explain how it was and how it all fits together." *Avocational interests:* Wine, finance, touring.

*   *   *

BRITT, Steuart Henderson 1907-1979

OBITUARY NOTICE—See index for *CA* sketch: Born June 16, 1907, in Callaway County, Mo.; died March 15, 1979, in Evanston, Ill. Marketing consultant, educator, attorney, editor, and author. Britt practiced law for two years and taught psychology before he entered the fields of marketing and advertising. He was professor of marketing at the Graduate School of Management of Northwestern University for eighteen years and professor of advertising at the university's Medill School of Journalism. Britt was also president of his own marketing firm, and was the author and editor of more than fifteen books and two-hundred articles. Obituaries and other sources: *American Men and Women of Science: The Social and Behavioral Sciences,* 12th edition, Bowker, 1973; *Who's Who in America,* 40th edition, Marquis, 1978; *Chicago Tribune,* March 17, 1979.

BROBECK, Florence 1895-1979

OBITUARY NOTICE: Born in 1895 in Ashville, Ohio; died in Manhattan, N.Y., March 10, 1979. Magazine editor, columnist, and author of cookbooks. Brobeck was associate editor of *McCall's* magazine for seven years and wrote a weekly food column for the *New York Times* magazine. Many of her cookbooks, which include *Scandinavian Cookery for Americans* and *The Best of All Cookbook,* were best sellers. Brobeck also wrote *New York's Restaurants Reflower* and *The Cat on the Mat.* She contributed articles to *Good Housekeeping, American, New Yorker, Town and Country,* and other periodicals. Obituaries and other sources: *New York Times,* March 11, 1979.

*   *   *

BRODIN, Pierre Eugene 1909-

PERSONAL: Born September 19, 1909, in Paris, France; son of Theophile E. and Madeleine Brodin; married Dorothy R. (a professor), 1948; children: Alain S. *Education:* Sorbonne, University of Paris, bachelier-es-lettres in Latin, Greek, and philosophy, 1926, licence-es-lettres in history and geography, 1930, agrege, 1931, docteur-es-lettres, 1935. *Home:* 825 West End Ave., New York, N.Y. 10025. *Office:* Lycee Francais de New-York, 3 East 95th Ave., New York, N.Y. 10028.

CAREER: Instructor in history at Lycee Clemenceau, Nantes, France, 1931-33; Lycee Francais de New-York, New York City, professor of French and director of studies, both 1935-76; Ecole libre des Hautes Etudes, New York City, a professor of French literature and civilization, 1941—, director of Faculte des Lettres, 1945—. Professor at Brooklyn College of the City University of New York, 1935-37, at Hunter College of the City University of New York, 1935-37, at Adelphi University, 1942-60, at Columbia University, 1943-45, and at the United Nations, 1948-56. Summer professor at Middlebury College, 1933-40, at Pennsylvania State College (now University), 1936-37, at Mills College, California, 1938, at Columbia University, 1939, at Oklahoma State University, 1941, and at McGill University, 1949, 1958. Literary critic for *France-Amerique* (newspaper), 1958-76.

MEMBER: Societes des Professeurs Francais en Amerique (president, 1938-52), American Association of Teachers of French (honorary member). *Awards, honors:* Harvard University Chapman fellow, 1932; Rockefeller fellow for social studies, 1933; chevalier of the Legion d'Honneur, 1953; chevalier of the Ordre National de la Republique de Madagascar, 1964; officier of the Order de Leopold, 1966; officier of the Palmes Academiques, 1967.

WRITINGS: Les Quakers en Amerique au dix-septieme siecle et au debut du dixhuitieme (title means "Quakers in America in the Seventeenth Century and Beginning of the Eighteenth Century"), Librairie des Amis, 1935; *Le Roman regionaliste americain: esquisse d'une geographie morale et pittoresque des Etats-Unis* (title means "The Regionalist Novel in America"), Maisonneuve, 1937; *Les Idees politiques des Etats-Unis d'aujourd'hui* (title means "Political Ideas in America Today"), Maisonneuve, 1940; *Les Ecrivains francais de l'entre-duex-guerres* (title means "French Writers Between the Two Wars"), Valiquette, 1942, revised edition, Editions Brentano (New York, N.Y.), 1943; *Loti,* Parizeau (Montreal), 1945; *Esquisse de la France* (title means "A Sketch of France"), Parizeau, 1946; *Les Ecrivains americains de l'entre-deux-guerres* (title means "American Writers Between the Two Wars"), Horizons de

France, 1946; *Les Maitres de la litterature americaine* (title means "Master of American Literature"), Horizons de France, 1948; *Thomas Wolfe,* translated by Imogene Riddick, Stephens Press, 1949.

Presences contemporaines: Litterature (title means "Contemporary Writers"), three volumes, Debresse, 1954-57, revised and enlarged edition published in one volume as *Presences contemporaines: Auteurs francais du XXe siecle,* French and European Publications, 1972; *Julien Green,* Editions universitaires, 1957; *Ecrivains americains d'aujourd'hui* (title means "American Writers Today"), Debresse, 1964; *Vingt Cinq Americains* (title means "Twenty-Five Americans"), Debresse, 1969; *France* (juvenile), Doubleday, 1973; *Continuateurs et novateurs: Ecrivains americains d'aujourd'hui,* Debresse, 1973.

Textbooks: (With J. Boorsch and L. Chapard) *La Revolution francaise* (title means "The French Revolution"), Cordon Co. (New York), 1937; (with Boorsch and Chapard) *Madame de Sevigne,* Cordon Co., 1937; (with Jacob Greenberg) *Le Francais et la France* (title means "The French and France"), two volumes, Merrill, 1938; (with Frederic Ernst) *La France et les francais* (title means "France and the French")' Holt, 1960, revised and enlarged edition, 1965; (with Ernst) *Gens de France dans l'histoire et la litterature* (title means "French Men and Women in History and Literature"), Holt, 1968.

Translator: A. A. Vasiliev, *Histoire de l'empire byzantin* (title means "A History of the Byzantine Empire"), Picard, 1932; C. Van Doren, *Benjamin Franklin,* Aubier-Montaigne, 1963. Also translator of L. Steffens, *L'Enfant a cheval* (title means "Boy on Horseback"), 1966; F. R. Dulles, *Le Chemin de Teheran* (title means "The Road to Teheran"), 1963; and Ernie Pyle, *G.I. Joe,* 1966.

Contributor to *Encyclopedia Americana, Encyclopaedia Britannica,* and *Americana Annual.* Contributor of articles to many periodicals, including *Figaro, France-Etats-Unis, Revue de Paris, French Review, Gants du Ciel* (Montreal), *Flambeau* (Brussels), *France-Amerique* (New York), and *Nouveau Monde* (Haiti).

SIDELIGHTS: Brodin explained that graduates of the Lycee Francais de New York either enter American colleges or universities in advanced placement, or are admitted to schools of higher learning abroad. He further noted that the Ecole Libre des Hautes Etudes, also located in New York City, "was founded in 1941 as a University of the French in exile."

BIOGRAPHICAL/CRITICAL SOURCES: Modern Language Journal, February, 1969, March, 1971.

*   *   *

BROOKE, Brian 1911-

PERSONAL: Born September 27, 1911, in Sabie, South Africa; son of Thomas (an army officer) and Kate (Shires) Brooke; married Petrina Fry, July 28, 1939; children: Michael, Jacqueline Stephens, Clive, Alan. *Education:* Attended Graham College. *Religion:* Church of England. *Home:* 9 Houghton Mansions, Louis Botha Ave., Leoville, Johannesburg 2000, South Africa. *Office:* Brooke Theatre, 7 de Villiers St., Johannesburg 2000, South Africa.

CAREER: Writer, actor, and producer of motion pictures. Worked as electrical engineer, 1929-34; actor in productions, including "The Odd Couple," "Harvey," "Mary, Mary," "The Teahouse of the August Moon," and "Champagne Complex"; producer of productions, including "The Boy

Friend," "Irma La Douce," "Oliver," "The Sound of Music," and "How to Succeed in Business Without Really Trying"; currently managing director of Brian Brooke Co., in London, England, and Rhodesia. Chairman of Brian Brooke Bowling Centres. *Military service:* British Army, 1939-46; became captain. *Member:* South African Association of Theatrical Managements, Bryanston Country Club.

WRITINGS: Art in London, D. White, 1966; (with John Russell Taylor) *The Art Dealers,* Scribner, 1969; *My Own Personal Star,* Limelight Press, 1978. Also author of plays, including "The Crescent Moon," "The Platonic Nymph," and "The Aging Adolescent."

WORK IN PROGRESS: History of Theatre in South Africa From 1954 to 1979.

* * *

BROUMAS, Olga 1949-

PERSONAL: Born May 6, 1949; daughter of Nicholas Constantine (in Greek Army) and Claire Antonia (Pendeli) Broumas. *Education:* University of Pennsylvania, B.A., 1970; University of Oregon, M.F.A., 1973. *Residence:* Pullman, Wash.

CAREER: University of Oregon, Eugene, instructor in English and women's studies, 1972-76; conducted lecture tour around the United States, 1977-78; University of Idaho, Moscow, visiting associate professor of English, autumn, 1978; poet and writer.

WRITINGS: Caritas, Jackrabbit Press, 1976; *Beginning With O* (poems), Yale University Press, 1977; *Namaste* (poetry chapbook), Copper Canyon Press, 1978. Contributor to literary journals, including *Heresies, Chrysalis,* and *Northeast Review.*

SIDELIGHTS: Olga Broumas writes: "I am interested in linguistics and linguistic theory. I speak French and modern Greek, and can read Italian, Spanish, Old English, Latin, and ancient Greek. I am interested (and still sometimes active) in visual arts, architecture, and spatial design. I enjoy traveling and overdo it. I also enjoy any strenuous physical activity, including straining the mind and the imagination: I am currently studying physics. 'The imagination wants to dance, not march, to her destination.'"

* * *

BROWN, Sterling Allen 1901-

PERSONAL: Born May 1, 1901, in Washington, D.C.; married Daisy Turnbull. *Education:* Williams College, A.B., 1925; Harvard University, A.M., 1930. *Office:* Department of English, Howard University, Washington, D.C. 20001.

CAREER: Worked as teacher at Fisk University, Nashville, Tenn., Virginia Seminary and College, Lynchburg, Va., and Lincoln University, Jefferson City, Mo.; Howard University, Washington, D.C., professor of English, 1929—. Visiting professor at New York University, New School for Social Research, Sarah Lawrence College, and Vassar College. Worked on the Federal Writer's Project and the Carnegie-Myrdal Study of the Negro. *Member:* Phi Beta Kappa. *Awards, honors:* Guggenheim fellowship for creative writing.

WRITINGS: Southern Road (poetry), Harcourt, 1932, revised edition, Beacon Press, 1974; *The Negro in American Fiction,* Associates in Negro Folk Education, 1937, Argosy-Antiquarian, 1969, also published with *Negro Poetry and Drama* (also see below); *Negro Poetry and Drama,* Associates in Negro Folk Education, 1937, revised edition, Atheneum, 1969, also published with *The Negro in American Fiction* (also see below); (editor with Arthur P. Davis and Ulysses Lee) *The Negro Caravan,* Dryden, 1941, revised edition, Arno, 1970; *Negro Poetry and Drama and the Negro in American Fiction,* Atheneum, 1969; (with George E. Haynes) *The Negro Newcomers in Detroit* [and] *The Negro in Washington,* Arno, 1970; *The Last Ride of Wild Bill, and Eleven Narrative Poems,* Broadside Press, 1975. Also author of *A Negro Looks at the South,* 1943, and *What the Negro Wants,* 1948. Contributor of poetry and articles to many anthologies and journals.

SIDELIGHTS: Sterling Brown is a teacher, folklorist, storyteller, and poet of the Black Renaissance. He grew up at Howard University, an important center of the black intellectual world, where his father taught at the School of Religion. Here he was exposed to such great men as his neighbor Paul Laurence Dunbar, Frederick Douglas, whom his father had known, Kelly Miller, Alain Locke, and W. E. B. Dubois.

As a teacher, Brown became known as a "red ink man" because he covered his students' papers with so many red corrections. But he learned from his students as well, collecting many of the black folk songs and sayings of their local lore. From these and "out of his fascinating past," said Hoyt W. Fuller, "he serves up a living history of the past forty years."

Although Brown has published many of his poems and stories, "he regrets having written no shelf of books, but his books are everywhere that men and women go away from his Howard University classes and his bull sessions and his rollicking, instructive speeches." His vivid storytelling has been captured for the reader in a phonodisc, "Sixteen Poems by Sterling Brown," Folkways Records, 1973.

BIOGRAPHICAL/CRITICAL SOURCES: Rosey E. Pool, editor, *Beyond the Blues,* Hand and Flower Press, 1962; *Negro Digest,* April, 1967; *Contemporary Literary Criticism,* Volume 1, Gale, 1973; Arthur P. Davis, *From the Dark Tower,* Howard University Press, 1974; *Choice,* January, 1976; *Ebony,* October, 1976; *Black Scholar,* March, 1977; *New Republic,* February 11, 1977.

* * *

BROWN, Susan Jenkins 1896-

PERSONAL: Born August 10, 1896, in Pittsburgh, Pa.; daughter of Reuben John (a steel maker) and Jane (Evans) Jenkins; married James Light (deceased); married William Slater Brown (divorced); children: (second marriage) Gwilym S. *Education:* Pittsburgh Normal College, certificate, 1916. *Politics:* Democrat. *Religion:* Protestant. *Home address:* Route 37, Box 135, Sherman, Conn. 06784.

CAREER: United Neighbors Houses, New York City, chief aide to executive director during the 1930's; Henry Street Settlement, New York City, head of consumer education during the 1940's. Writer. Book editor for Macauley Publishing. *Member:* Sherman Historical Society.

WRITINGS: (Translator from German) *Fever House,* Macauley, 1929; (editor) *Robber Rocks: Letters and Memories of Hart Crane, 1923-1932,* Wesleyan University Press, 1968. Also translator from French, Philippe Soupault, *The Last Nights of Paris,* 1930. Contributor to local newspapers. Editor of *Telling Tales,* and *Ranch Romances.*

WORK IN PROGRESS: Assisting biographers of Katherine Anne Porter, Edna St. Vincent Millay, and Allen Tate.

AVOCATIONAL INTERESTS: Travel (Wales, Denmark, England).

BIOGRAPHICAL/CRITICAL SOURCES: Publishers Weekly, October 13, 1969; *New York Times,* December 5, 1969; *Commonweal,* February 6, 1970; *Times Literary Supplement,* March 19, 1970.

* * *

BROWN, Warren (William) 1894-1978

PERSONAL: Born in 1894; died November 19, 1978, in Forest Park, Ill.; married; children: Bill, Roger, Mary Elizabeth Brown Rempe. *Education:* Received degree from University of San Francisco. *Residence:* Forest Park, Ill.

CAREER: Played minor league baseball with San Francisco team in Pacific Coast League, c.1914; worked as sportswriter for the *San Francisco Call-Post,* beginning c.1915; later became sports editor of the *New York Evening Mail* and then the *Chicago Herald Examiner;* finished career in Chicago as columnist for the *Chicago Herald-American,* the *Chicago Sun,* and finally, *Chicago's American.*

WRITINGS: Rockne, Reilly & Lee, 1931; *The Chicago Cubs,* Putnam, 1946; *Win, Lose, or Draw,* Putnam, 1947; *The Chicago White Sox,* Putnam, 1952.

SIDELIGHTS: "I've written about every damn thing under the sun," Warren Brown once said, "I even did theatrical and vaudeville reviews." Though the veteran journalist reported some politics and general news stories, he was most widely known for his sportswriting. He covered nearly every major sporting event in his career, including forty-five World Series and forty Kentucky Derbies. Brown was also a friend of two other famed sportswriters, Damon Runyon and Grantland Rice.

As might be expected in a journalist's books, Brown relied on anecdotes to convey his impressions of the sporting world. In reviewing Brown's first book, *Rockne,* Caswell Adams reported that Brown probably knew the legendary Notre Dame football coach "more intimately than any other newspaper man. . . . He writes of Rockne the man, and from him we learn of the humor, the genius, the generosity, the sincerity of the stocky, baldheaded coach. He, in a terse, not unpleasant style, hurriedly sketches the coach by telling us wisecracks, his satirical shafts." Similarly, in his books on Chicago's baseball teams Brown added an entertaining style to a foundation of facts. "Brown has done an exhaustive job of research and brightened the resulting text with a leavening of anecdotes," wrote Robert Cromie in his review of *White Sox.*

Win, Lose, or Draw included Brown's reflections on his sportswriting career and his association with many great sporting personalities. Harold Kaese took a tongue-in-cheek look at the book: "By being so witty, entertaining and informative, Warren Brown probably has done the sportswriting industry irreparable harm in writing his memoirs. . . . There will be no salary increases in the near future for sports writers whose publishers read Brown's expose of our charming circle and find it a strong argument for less money and longer hours."

BIOGRAPHICAL/CRITICAL SOURCES: New York Herald-Tribune Books, June 21, 1931; *New York Times,* September 22, 1946, February 8, 1948, April 20, 1952; *Chicago Tribune,* March 30, 1952, November 22, 1978.*

* * *

BROWNING, Robert L(ynn) 1924-

PERSONAL: Born June 19, 1924, in Gallatin, Mo.; son of Robert Watson (a physician) and Nell (Trotter) Browning; married Jean Beatty (died, July, 1977); children: Robert Gregory, David James, Peter Douglas, Lisa Anne. *Education:* Missouri Valley College, B.A., 1945; Union Theological Seminary, New York, N.Y., M.Div., 1948; further graduate study at Columbia University, 1951-53; Ohio State University, Ph.D., 1960, postdoctoral study, 1967-68, 1972-73; further study at Oxford University, 1978-79. *Home:* 120 Longfellow Ave., Worthington, Ohio 43085. *Office:* Department of Christian Education, Methodist Theological School, Delaware, Ohio 43015.

CAREER: Ordained Methodist minister, 1949; pastor and minister of education at Methodist churches in Meadville, Pa., and Mt. Vernon, N.Y., 1946-59; Methodist Theological School, Delaware, Ohio, assistant professor, 1959-63, associate professor, 1964-67, professor of Christian education, 1967-72, William A. Chryst Professor of Pastoral Theology, 1972—. Vice-president of Methodist Conference on Christian Education, 1965-67, president, 1967-69; executive director of Commission on the Role of the Professions in Society, 1974-76. Past member of board of directors of Southside Settlement, Tracy-Lee Center, Neighborhood House, Wesley Foundation, and Ohio State University. Public speaker. *Military service:* U.S. Navy, 1942-45.

MEMBER: Association of Professors and Researchers in Religious Education, Association for Professional Education for the Ministry (member of executive committee), Christian Educators Fellowship, United Methodist Professors of Christian Education, Pi Gamma Mu. *Awards, honors:* Paul M. Hinkhouse Award from Religious Public Relations Council of America, 1972, for audio-tape series, "Communicating the Faith With Children"; fellow of Academy for Contemporary Problems, 1974-76.

WRITINGS: (Contributor) Herman Peters, editor, *Counseling: Selected Readings,* Charles E. Merrill, 1962; *What on Earth Are You Doing?* (juvenile), with teacher's book, Methodist Publishing House, 1966, 3rd edition, 1972; (contributor) Carlton E. Beck, editor, *Guidelines for Guidance,* W. C. Brown, 1966, revised edition published as *Philosophical Guidelines for Counseling,* 1971; (contributor) Marvin Taylor, editor, *Introduction to Christian Education,* Abingdon, 1966; *Communicating With Junior Highs,* Graded Press, 1968, revised edition, Abingdon, 1972.

Guidelines for Youth Ministry, Program Council, United Methodist Church, 1970; (contributor) Ben Ard, Jr., editor, *Counseling and Psychotherapy: Classics on Theories and Issues,* Science & Behavior Books, 1975; (contributor) Marion Brown, editor, *Church School: Decision Point,* St. Paul's School of Theology, 1976; (contributor) Marvin Taylor, editor, *Christian Education in an Era of Change,* Abingdon, 1976.

Audio-tape series, with self-instruction guides: "Communicating the Faith With Children," Board of Christian Education, United Methodist Church, 1971; "Ways the Bible Comes Alive," Abingdon, 1975; "Ways Persons Become Christians," Abingdon, 1976; (with Charles R. Foster and Everett Tilson) *Looking at Leadership Through the Eyes of Biblical Faith,* Discipleship Resources, United Methodist Church, 1978. Also author of church school curriculum material. Contributor to religious journals for clergy, educators, and laymen, including *Christian Home, Christian Advocate, Religious Education,* and *Church School.*

WORK IN PROGRESS: Teaching and Learning in the United Methodist Church; research on sacramental theology and the stages of life, and its relation to education and liturgy.

SIDELIGHTS: Browning comments: "I have been a generalist in Christian education, writing in several sub-fields related to leadership, philosophy of education, theological assumptions, youth and children's ministry, group work, administration, adult education, and family life. I have also worked in the area of interdisciplinary and interprofessional education—between Christian education and other fields, and between theology, medicine, law, social work, education, and nursing; I was responsible for designing interprofessional courses at Ohio State University that deal with ethics, values, and clinical cooperation.

"I have sought to integrate theory and practice not only in my teaching and writing but also by relating to local churches, boards and agencies as a resource person, consultant, and, in the process, a learner and interpreter. This involvement in the field has informed my writing and has meant that much of my writing and speaking are in response to concrete problems and the educational and theological issues implied."

*   *   *

BRUGGER, Robert J. 1943-

PERSONAL: Surname is pronounced *Broo*-ger; born February 8, 1943, in New Haven, Conn.; son of John R. (an educational broadcasting consultant) and Angeline M. (a Montessori teacher) Brugger. *Education:* University of Notre Dame, A.B., 1965; University of Maryland, M.A., 1967; Johns Hopkins University, Ph.D., 1974. *Home address:* Route 2, Box 254, Charlottesville, Va. 22901. *Office:* Corcoran Department of History, University of Virginia, Randall Hall, Charlottesville, Va. 22903.

CAREER: University of Virginia, Charlottesville, assistant professor of history, 1974—. Mellon faculty fellow at Harvard University, 1978-79. *Military service:* U.S. Marine Corps, 1967-70; became captain. *Member:* American Historical Association, Organization of American Historians, Southern Historical Association. *Awards, honors:* Woodrow Wilson fellowship, Ford Foundation fellowship, Daniel Coit Gilman fellowship, essay award from Phi Alpha Theta, 1972.

WRITINGS: Beverley Tucker: Heart Over Head in the Old South, Johns Hopkins Press, 1978.

WORK IN PROGRESS: An anthology of essays and excerpts on American history, drawing on psychological theory; a comparative study of intellectual life in antebellum America, both north and south.

*   *   *

BRUNS, Frederick R., Jr. 1913(?)-1979

OBITUARY NOTICE: Born c. 1913, in New York, N.Y.; died of cancer, March 24, 1979, in Washington, D.C. Curator, philatelist, columnist, and writer. Bruns served as curator of the division of postal history in the Smithsonian Institution. In addition, he wrote a syndicated column on stamp and coin collecting for more than forty years, and edited and contributed to over twenty philately publications. Bruns was a co-founder and former president of the American Philatelic Congress. Obituaries and other sources: *New York Times,* March 27, 1979; *Chicago Tribune,* April 1, 1979.

*   *   *

BRUNSKILL, Ronald (William) 1929-

PERSONAL: Born January 3, 1929, in Lowton, England; son of William and Elizabeth (Hannah) Brunskill; married

Miriam Allsopp, June 20, 1960; children: Lesley, Robin (daughters). *Education:* Victoria University of Manchester, B.A. (honors), 1951, M.A., 1952, Ph.D., 1963. *Home:* Three Trees, Overhill Rd., Wilmslow, Cheshire, England. *Office:* Department of Architecture, Victoria University of Manchester, Manchester 13, England.

CAREER: Massachusetts Institute of Technology, Cambridge, visiting fellow, 1956-57; William Deacon's Bank Ltd., Manchester, England, architect, 1957-60; Victoria University of Manchester, Manchester, England, lecturer, 1960-73, senior lecturer in architecture, 1973—. Visiting professor at University of Florida, 1969-70. Partner of Carter, Brunskill & Associates, 1965-73. Member of Historic Buildings Council and Wilmslow Trust (chairman, 1974-76, vice-president, 1978—). *Military service:* British Army, Royal Engineers, 1953-55; became lieutenant. *Member:* Royal Institute of British Architects, Royal Architectural Institute, Society of Antiquaries, Vernacular Architecture Group (president, 1974-77), Association for the Preservation of Technology, Society for Folk Life Studies, Society of Architectural Historians, Cumberland and Westmorland Antiquarian and Architectural Society (vice-president, 1975—), Lancashire and Cheshire Antiquarian Societies. *Awards, honors:* Awards from Royal Institute of British Architects, 1952, 1962, and Manchester Society of Architects, 1977.

WRITINGS: Illustrated Handbook of Vernacular Architecture, Faber, 1971, revised edition, 1978; *Vernacular Architecture of the Lake Counties,* Faber, 1974; (with Alec Clifton-Taylor) *English Brickwork,* Ward, Lock, 1977. Contributor to architecture, archaeology, and history journals.

WORK IN PROGRESS: Research on vernacular architecture, including the planning of domestic and farm buildings, and the use of building materials and education in such subjects, with publication expected to result.

SIDELIGHTS: Brunskill comments: "The study and publication of information on vernacular architecture has risen from a background and education which included both urban and rural context, from an awareness through architectural practice of the problems of building conservation, and from an understanding through many years of teaching of the ways in which students and the public can be made aware of their architectural heritage. I have made contact with, and have attempted to encourage, the developing 'American movement toward the study of vernacular architecture over many years."

*   *   *

BUCHHEIM, Lothar-Guenther 1918-

PERSONAL: Born February 6, 1918, in Germany. *Office:* c/o Alfred A. Knopf, Inc., 201 East 50th St., New York, N.Y. 10022.

CAREER: Writer.

*WRITINGS—*In English: *Picasso: eine Bildbiographie,* Kindler, 1958, translation by Michael Heron published as *Picasso: A Pictorial Biography,* Viking, 1959; *Graphik des deutschen Expressionismus,* Buchheim Verlag, 1958, published as *The Graphic Art of German Expressionism,* Universe Books, 1960; *Das Boot,* R. Piper, 1973, translation by J. Maxwell Brownjohn published as *U-Boat,* Collins, 1974, translation by Helen Lindley and Denver Lindley published as *The Boat,* Knopf, 1975; *U-Boot-Krieg,* R. Piper, 1976, published as *U-Boat War,* Knopf, 1978.

In German: *Tage und Naechte steigen aus dem Strom,* S. Fischer, 1941; (author of introduction) Marc Chagall,

Swischen Tag und Traum, Buchheim, 1955; (author of foreword) Raoul Dufy, *Festliche Welt: Zeichnungen und Radierungen,* Buchheim, 1955; (editor) *Knaurs Lexikon moderner Kunst,* T. Knaur Nachf, 1955; (author of introduction) Fernand Leger, *Menschen und Objekte: Zeichnungen,* Buchheim, 1955; *Deutsche Graphik des XX,* Buchheim, 1956; *Die Kuenstlergemeinschaft Bruecke: Erich Heckel, Ernst Ludwig Kirchner, Otto Mueller, Emil Nolde, Max Pechstein, Karl Schmidt-Rottluff,* Buchheim, 1956; (author of foreword) Erich Heckel, *Holzschnitte aus den Jahren, 1905-1956,* Buchheim, 1957; *Der Blaue Reiter un die "Neue Kuenstlervereingung Muenchen,"* Buchheim, 1959.

(Editor) *Abstrakt und zugenaeht! Eine ganz und gar echte Sensation: Enthuellungen Dokumente. Die moderne Kunst—ein Schwindel?,* Feldafing, 1962; *Otto Meuller: Leben und Werk,* Buchheim, 1963; (author of foreword), *Max Kaus: Fruehe Lithographien,* Buchheim, 1964; *Jugendstilplakate,* Buchheim, 1969.

Also author of texts on art.

SIDELIGHTS: Although the majority of Buchhcim's writings are devoted to art, he is best known in the United States for his novel, *The Boat.* The book was praised for its humanizing of the Germany Army of World War II. Buchheim filled his tale of submarine warfare with "real people," wrote Robert J. Myers, "people who complained about their leaders, drank, whored, loved and died...."

The Boat was subject to a variety of critical interpretations. R. Z. Sheppard called it "an exciting adventure yarn, full of battle tensions and long bouts of boredom on long patrols." Peter Prescott wrote that *The Boat* was "more an act of journalism than a work of art...." Edward Weeks summed up the book as "surely the most vivid and human picture of the underseas war ever written...."

BIOGRAPHICAL/CRITICAL SOURCES: New Republic, May 24, 1975; *Newsweek,* May 26, 1975; *Time,* June 2, 1975; *Saturday Review,* June 28, 1975; *Atlantic,* July, 1975; *Contemporary Literary Criticism,* Volume 6, Gale, 1976.*

* * *

BUNDY, Clarence E(verett) 1906-

PERSONAL: Born April 12, 1906, in Bondurant, Iowa; son of Hubert J. (a farmer) and Cary (a teacher; maiden name, Armbruster) Bundy; married Mildred Loraine Larson, June 7, 1933; children: D. James, Robert C. *Education:* Iowa State College (now University), B.S., 1929, M.S., 1934; attended University of Iowa, 1931, and Ohio State University, summers, 1938-40. *Politics:* Republican. *Religion:* Lutheran. *Home:* 1607 Bel Air Dr., Ames, Iowa 50010.

CAREER: Teacher of vocational agriculture in public schools in Iowa Falls, Iowa, 1929-47, principal of junior high school, 1931-37, and senior high school, 1942-44; Iowa State University, Ames, assistant professor, 1947-56, associate professor, 1956-59, professor of agricultural education, 1959-73, professor emeritus, 1973—, head of department, 1968-71; writer and researcher, 1971—. Member of part-time faculty at Iowa State College (now University), 1938-47; visiting professor at University of Nebraska, summers, 1953, 1960, University of Illinois, summer, 1955, and University of Missouri, summer, 1957. Past member of general educational advisory committee for Iowa Training School for Boys; member of board of trustees of National Future Farmers of America Foundation. Judge at state fairs and congresses; speaker at state conferences.

MEMBER: National Education Association (life member),

American Vocational Association (past chairman of teacher education council), National Vocational Agriculture Teachers Association (life member), American Vocational Education Research Association (charter member), American Association of Teacher Educators in Agriculture (life member; past president), Iowa State Education Association (life member), Iowa Vocational Agriculture Teachers Association (past president; member of board of directors), Iowa Association of Future Farmers of America (member of board of directors), Alpha Zeta, Gamma Sigma Delta, Phi Kappa Phi, Phi Delta Kappa (life member), Alpha Tau Alpha. *Awards, honors:* Honorary American farmer degree from National Association of Future Farmers of America, 1936, V.I.P. Award, 1977; outstanding educator award from Phi Delta Kappa, 1964; citation from National Vocational Agriculture Teachers Association, 1969; centennial achievement award from Ohio State University, 1970.

WRITINGS: (With Ronald V. Diggins) *Livestock and Poultry Production,* Prentice-Hall, 1954, 4th edition (with Diggins and Virgil W. Christensen), 1975; (with Diggins) *Dairy Production,* Prentice-Hall, 1950, 4th edition (with Diggins and Christensen), 1979; (with Diggins) *Beef Production,* Prentice-Hall, 1956, 3rd edition, 1971; (with Diggins) *Swine Production,* Prentice-Hall, 1956, 4th edition (with Diggins and Christensen), 1976; (with Diggins) *Sheep Production,* Prentice-Hall, 1958; (with Diggins) *Poultry Production,* Prentice-Hall, 1960; (with Barton Morgan and Glenn E. Holmes) *Methods in Adult Education,* Interstate, 1960, 3rd edition, 1976. History editor for *Agricultural Education,* 1975-79.

WORK IN PROGRESS: Research for 5th editions of *Livestock and Poultry Production,* with Diggins and Christensen, publication by Prentice-Hall expected in 1982, and *Swine Production,* with Diggens and Christensen, for Prentice-Hall, 1983.

SIDELIGHTS: Bundy told *CA:* "I discovered, as a teacher of agriculture at the secondary level and as an educator at the university level, a serious lack of reference material suitable for student use. Some writers beamed their material toward those with low reading levels. Others used terminology understandable only by those with university backgrounds. Our objective as a team of authors was to prepare reference materials for use by secondary and postsecondary students, and by livestock farmers, that would provide technical information concerning livestock production in an understandable manner in as few words as possible."

Bundy concluded that he and his coauthors write with the realization that their readers will retain information about only those subjects that interest them, in language they understand. For added interest, the authors "use large numbers of very carefully selected pictures, graphs and charts."

* * *

BURCHFIELD, Joe D(onald) 1937-

PERSONAL: Born September 14, 1937, in Gastonia, N.C.; son of Wade Donald (a clerk and truck driver) and Faye (Price) Burchfield; married Martha Geiger (a nurse), June 29, 1963; children: Aline, Daniel. *Education:* Furman University, B.S. (cum laude), 1959; University of North Carolina, M.S., 1963; Johns Hopkins University, Ph.D., 1969. *Home:* 157 Terrace Dr., DeKalb, Ill. 60115. *Office:* Department of History, Northern Illinois University, DeKalb, Ill. 60115.

CAREER: North Carolina Wesleyan College, Rocky Mount, instructor in physics, 1961-62; Vassar College,

Poughkeepsie, N.Y., instructor in physics, 1962-64; Northern Illinois University, DeKalb, assistant professor, 1968-74, associate professor of history, 1974—. Consultant to National Science Foundation. *Member:* History of Science Society (member of council, 1978-80), Society for the History of Technology, British Society for the History of Science, Royal Institution of Great Britain, Midwest Victorian Studies Association (member of executive committee, 1977-80), Sigma Xi. *Awards, honors:* American Philosophical Society grant, 1972; National Science Foundation grant, 1975-79; National Endowment for the Humanities grant, 1979-80.

WRITINGS: Lord Kelvin and the Age of the Earth, Science History Publications, 1975. Contributor of articles and reviews to historical and scientific journals.

WORK IN PROGRESS: John Tyndall and the London Scientific Community, 1850-1890, completion expected in 1981.

SIDELIGHTS: Burchfield writes: "My interest in the history of science grew naturally out of my interests and experience as a neophyte scientist; my interest in the Victorians, perhaps, from a kind of premature nostalgia. I am most interested in the human dimensions of science: scientists as individual social beings, and scientific ideas as cultural artifacts. Such a perspective can, I believe, help to make the history of science accessible to scientists and non-scientists alike and thus (if it still remains an issue) can contribute to bridging the gap between 'the two cultures.'"

*   *   *

BURGER, Robert E(ugene) 1931-

PERSONAL: Born June 21, 1931, in Yerington, Nev.; son of Edmund Ganes (in business) and Rose Catherine (Kobe) Burger; married Mary Theresa Dunne, June 26, 1954; children: Eileen, Marlene, Robert, Diane, Elisabeth, Joseph, Daniel, John, Clare, Christopher. *Education:* University of California, Berkeley, A.B., 1954, M.A., 1955. *Religion:* Roman Catholic. *Home:* 1 El Camino Real, Berkeley, Calif. 94705. *Agent:* Sheri Safron Associates, 866 United Nations Plaza, New York, N.Y. 10017.

CAREER: Electronic Navigation Co., San Francisco, Calif., founder and president, 1958-60; Burger, Felix & Wood (advertising agency), San Francisco, founder and president, 1960—. Lecturer at Stanford University, 1964, and University of California, Hayward, 1972. *Member:* U.S. Chess Federation (member of board of directors), Authors Guild, British Chess Problem Society (fellow), California Chess Federation (vice-president).

WRITINGS: (With Richard M. Garvin) *Where They Go to Die: The Tragedy of America's Aged*, Delacorte, 1968; (editor with Jan T. Slavicek) *How to Get Out From Under by Using Your Financial Bill of Rights*, Sherbourne, 1969; (with Garvin) *The World of the Twilight Believers*, Sherbourne, 1970; (with Pietro Pinoni) *Pietro on Wine*, Delphic Press, 1971; *The Love Contract: Handbook for a Liberated Marriage*, Van Nostrand, 1973; (with Edmond G. Addeo) *Ego-Speak*, Chilton, 1973; (with Karl Bach) *How I Sell Twenty-Five Million Dollars of Life Insurance Year After Year*, Chilton, 1973; (with Slavicek) *The Layman's Guide to Bankruptcy*, Van Nostrand, 1974, reprinted as *The Simplified Guide to Personal Bankruptcy*, Crown, 1975; (with Addeo) *Inside Divorce*, Chilton, 1975; (with Donald A. Moses) *Are You Driving Your Children to Drink?*, Van Nostrand, 1975; *The Chess of Bobby Fischer*, Chilton, 1975; (with Steven Fredman) *Forbidden Cures: How the FDA Suppresses Drugs that Could Help Save Your Life*, Stein & Day, 1976; *Jog-*

ger's Catalog, M. Evans, 1977; (with Bobby Vinton) *The Polish Prince*, M. Evans, 1978; *Shubert: An Historical Fiction*, Crowell, 1980. Also author of *McCarthy: Words to Remember*, 1969.

SIDELIGHTS: Burger was U.S. chess master from 1965 to 1979, and is an international problem judge. He comments: "Any book or any piece of writing requires the full output of the writer. He should not feel he can hold anything back on any assignment. When 'later' comes, so will inspiration."

BIOGRAPHICAL/CRITICAL SOURCES: Best Sellers, November 1, 1968; *New York Times Book Review*, November 10, 1968; *Nation*, November 18, 1968.

*   *   *

BURICK, Si(mon) 1909-

PERSONAL: Surname is pronounced *Byoo*-rick; born June 14, 1909, in Dayton, Ohio; son of Samuel F. (a rabbi) and Lillian (Solnitzky) Burick; married Rachel Siegel (a teacher), June 28, 1935; children: Lenore Burick Goldman, Marcia Burick Goldstein. *Education:* Attended University of Dayton, 1926-27. *Politics:* Democrat. *Religion:* Jewish. *Home:* 563 Heather Dr., Dayton, Ohio 45405. *Office: Dayton Daily News*, Dayton, Ohio 45401.

CAREER: Dayton Daily News, Dayton, Ohio, sports editor, 1928—. Notable assignments include every World Series but one since 1934, all thirteen Super Bowl games to date, the Kentucky Derby each year since 1933, the Olympics four times, numerous college football bowl games, golf championships, and numerous heavyweight title boxing matches since 1931. Member of board of directors of Dayton Newspapers, Inc.; Commissioner of Dayton—Montgomery County Park District; former charter member of local Human Relations Council and Jewish Community Council; former chairman of United Jewish Campaign and of National Foundation for Infantile Paralysis, Montgomery County chapter; board member of Dayton Boys' Club.

MEMBER: National Sportswriters and Sportscasters Association (president, 1974), Football Writers Association of America (president, 1973), Basketball Writers Association, Baseball Writers Association, Turf Writers Association, U.S. Golf Writers Association, Dayton Bicycle Club, Dayton Agonis Club, B'nai B'rith. *Awards, honors:* D.H.L. from University of Dayton, 1977; named Ohio sportswriter of the year by Ohio writers and broadcasters, 1964-75, 1977, 1978; honorary doctorate from University of Dayton, 1977.

WRITINGS: Alston and the Dodgers, Doubleday, 1966; *The Main Spark*, Doubleday, 1978. Contributor to sports magazines and local periodicals.

WORK IN PROGRESS: Memoirs.

SIDELIGHTS: Burick writes: "Several careers have been offered to me (I left pre-medical courses at University of Dayton for the opportunity to work for *Dayton Daily News*), but printer's ink has gotten under my nails and I've stuck to my typewriter. I enjoy the travel accompanying sports events and feel very fortunate to have done fifty years of sports writing."

*   *   *

BURN, Barbara 1940-

PERSONAL: Born January 24, 1940, in Boston, Mass.; daughter of Henry J. and Louise Marie (Buff) Burn; married John C. Kohr, July 11, 1964 (divorced January 31, 1967); married Emil P. Dolensek (a veterinarian), May 15, 1976.

Education: Smith College, B.A., 1961; graduate study at New York University, 1961-65. *Home:* 21 Tier St., City Island, N.Y. 10464. *Office:* Viking Press, Inc., 625 Madison Ave., New York, N.Y. 10022.

CAREER: Solomon R. Guggenheim Museum, New York City, administrative assistant, 1961-65; Viking Press, New York City, editor, 1965—, editorial director of studio books, 1978—. *Member:* New York Zoological Society.

WRITINGS: (With husband, Emil P. Dolensek) *A Practical Guide to Impractical Pets,* Viking, 1976, reprinted as *The Penguin Book of Pets,* Penguin, 1978; (with Steven Price, Gail Rentsch, and David Spector) *Whole Horse Catalog,* Simon & Schuster, 1977; (with Nancy Dolensek) *Mutt,* C. N. Potter, 1978; *The Horseless Rider,* St. Martin's, 1979; *The Morris Method* (on cat care), Morrow, 1979. Contributor to *Better Homes and Gardens* and *American Home.*

SIDELIGHTS: Barbara Burn writes: "My experience as an editor of other writers' books, combined with my marriage to a veterinarian and renewed interest in owning pets and horseback riding, managed to result in a group of books in which I could focus on my favorite subjects, popularize serious information, and share some of my personal experiences."

* * *

BURNS, Vincent Godfrey 1893-1979
(Bobby Burns)

OBITUARY NOTICE—See index for *CA* sketch: Born October 17, 1893, in Brooklyn, N.Y.; died February 3, 1979, in Epping Forest, Md. Minister, educator, poet, and author. Burns was ordained a Congregational minister in 1920 and was pastor of Congregational and Episcopal churches until 1958. In 1962, he was named poet laureate of the state of Maryland, a position which he tenaciously held on to all of his life. Burns, who once described himself as a "dedicated patriot," was conservative in both political and religious thought and often expressed his convictions in poetry. In the poem "Down at the Old Watergate," he declared that Richard M. Nixon was slandered and victimized by that political scandal. Burns gained notoriety during the trial of Bruno Richard Hauptmann for the kidnapping of the Lindbergh baby when he shouted in the courtroom, "this man is innocent." He later wrote his account of the kidnapping and murder and stated that a strange man had come to him and confessed to the crime. In the late 1960's attempts were made to oust Burns from his appointed position as poet laureate, but all efforts failed. He was the author of *I Am a Fugitive From a Chain Gang,* based on the experiences of his older brother, and *Female Convict.* Obituaries and other sources: *The Author's and Writer's Who's Who,* 6th edition, Burke's Peerage, 1971; *Authors in the News,* Volume II, Gale, 1976; *Who's Who in America,* 40th edition, Marquis, 1978; *Washington Post,* February 7, 1979.

* * *

BURSK, Christopher 1943-

PERSONAL: Born April 23, 1943, in Cambridge, Mass.; son of Edward C. (a professor and editor) and Catherine (Irwin) Bursk; married Mary Ann Adzanto, June 19, 1967; children: Christian, Norabeth, Justin. *Education:* Tufts University, B.A., 1965; Boston University, Ph.D., 1975. *Politics:* Democrat. *Religion:* Episcopalian. *Home:* 704 Hulmeville Ave., Langhorne Manor, Pa. 19047. *Office:* Department of Language and Literature, Bucks County Community College, Swamp Rd., Newtown, Pa. 18940.

CAREER: Shaw University, Raleigh, N.C., assistant professor of English, 1968-69; Bucks County Community College, Newtown, Pa., associate professor of language and literature, 1970—. Volunteer counselor for local prison-probation program. *Member:* Amnesty International.

WRITINGS: (With Paul Hannigan and William Corbett) *Three New Poets* (poems), Pym-Randall Press, 1968; *Standing Watch* (poems), Houghton, 1978. Contributor to literary magazines, including *Sun, Xanadu, Images,* and *Poetry Now.*

* * *

BURSTEIN, Alvin G(eorge) 1931-

PERSONAL: Born March 31, 1931, in Omaha, Neb.; son of Harry and Jennie (Gersteen) Burstein; married Helen O'-Grady, April, 1951 (divorced, 1976); married Sandra Loucks (a clinical psychologist), April 15, 1978; children: Gregory (deceased), Jessica Lee, Daniel James. *Education:* University of Chicago, B.A., 1950, M.A., 1958, Ph.D., 1959; also attended George Washington University, 1956. *Residence:* San Antonio, Tex. *Office:* Department of Psychiatry, Health Science Center, University of Texas, 7703 Floyd Curl, San Antonio, Tex. 78284.

CAREER: Institute for Nuclear Studies, Chicago, Ill., junior chemist, 1953-54; Billings Hospital, Chicago, intern in psychiatry, 1959-60; University of Chicago, Chicago, lecturer in history of psychology, 1960; University of Michigan, Ann Arbor, assistant professor of psychology, 1960-63; University of Illinois, Neuropsychiatric Institute, Chicago, associate professor of psychology and assistant director of Inpatient Service, 1963-69, professorial lecturer, 1964-69, director of psychology training program, 1963-69; University of Texas, Health Science Center, San Antonio, professor of psychiatry and chief of Division of Psychology, 1970—. Diplomate of American Board of Professional Psychology. Lecturer at Northwestern University, Chicago, 1958-59. Consultant. *Military service:* U.S. Army, in chemical research, 1954-56.

MEMBER: American Psychological Association (fellow), Association of Psychology Internship Centers (head of executive committee, 1978-79), Midwest Psychological Association, Southwestern Psychological Association (president, 1978-79), Texas Psychological Association (president, 1975), Sigma Xi. *Awards, honors:* Citation from Texas Psychological Association, 1975.

WRITINGS: (Contributor) Oscar K. Buros, editor, *Sixth Mental Measurements Yearbook,* Gryphon, 1965; (contributor) Buros, editor, *Seventh Mental Measurements Yearbook,* Gryphon, 1972; (with Charles Bowden) *The Psychosocial Basis of Medical Practice: Introductory Text,* Williams & Wilkins, 1974; (contributor) J. Claghorn, editor, *Successful Psychotherapy,* Brunner, 1976; (contributor) Sally Andrade, editor, *Chicano Mental Health: The Case of Cristal,* Hogg Foundation for Mental Health, University of Texas, 1978. Contributor of more than thirty-five articles to journals in the behavioral sciences. Advisory editor of *Contemporary Psychology;* past member of editorial board of *International Journal of Psychiatry in Medicine.*

WORK IN PROGRESS: Research on psychotherapy, personality theory, psychodiagnostics, and social systems.

SIDELIGHTS: Burstein told CA: "My theoretical orientation is psychoanalytic. I am particularly interested in the recent contributions to psychoanalytic technique and theory of Heinze Kohut. My wife, Dr. Louks, and I are currently involved in developing an improved Rorschach scoring manual.''

*   *   *

BURYN, Ed(ward Casimir)   1934-

PERSONAL: Born May 29, 1934, in Union City, N.J.; son of Kazimierz (a baker) and Josephine (in business; maiden name, Solecka) Buryn; married Jo-Ann Hughes (an artist), November 10, 1956 (divorced, 1966); lived with Stephanie Mines (a poet) 1969-73; children: Jan, Sierra. *Education:* Attended University of Miami, Coral Gables, Fla., 1955-56; Pasadena City College, A.A., 1958. *Politics:* "No preference." *Religion:* "No preference." *Home:* 601 Diamond St., San Francisco, Calif. 94114. *Office address:* P.O. Box 31123, San Francisco, Calif. 94131.

CAREER: Electronics technical writer for Radiation, Inc., Melbourne, Fla., Honeywell, Duarte, Calif., Philco, Palo Alto, Calif., and Lynch Communications, San Francisco, Calif., 1957-67; free-lance writer and photographer, 1968—. *Military service:* U.S. Navy, 1951-55. *Member:* Authors Guild of Authors League of America.

WRITINGS: Hitch-Hiking in Europe (with own photographs), Hannah Associates, 1969; *Vagabonding in Europe and North Africa* (with own photographs), Random House, 1971, revised edition, 1973; (photographer), Janet Brown, Eugene Lesser, and Stephanie Mines, *Two Births,* Random House, 1972; *Vagabonding in America* (with own photogtaphs), Random House, 1973, revised edition, privately printed, 1976; (chief photographer) Andrew Fluegelman, *New Games Book,* Headlands Press, 1976; *Floating Island II* (portfolio of photographs), Floating Island Publications, 1977; *Vagabonding in the U.S.A.* (with own phtographs), And/Or Press, 1979.

SIDELIGHTS: Buryn commented: "Although I had always wanted to write because of a certain interest and aptitude for it, early circumstances led me into an electronics career—courtesy of the Navy, where I received my first vocational training. Afterwards, I became an electronics writer for various corporations, fully intending to live out a normal middle-class existence as corporate slave. However, as time went by I became increasingly dissatisfied with that role, and I finally 'dropped out' to go traveling in Europe as a foot-loose vagabond for almost a year (1964-1965). That experience changed my head around, and also became the focus of my subsequent work as free-lance photographer, nonfiction writer, and popularizer of a 'vagabonding' approach to life.

"Writing is difficult work for me, very time-consuming in its demands for rationalistic clarity. My photography, on the other hand, comes intuitively and easily, and I enjoy it more than writing. As a photographer, I would call myself a humanistic photo-journalist. Although I consider myself more of a photographer than a writer, I don't take either of these labels too seriously. I became a writer and photographer in response to my opportunities and situations; future situations may elicit new responses."

BIOGRAPHICAL/CRITICAL SOURCES: Berkeley Barb, May 13, 1977.

*   *   *

BUSE, Renee   1914(?)-1979
(R. F. Buse; Robert Benton, Michael King, pseudonyms)

OBITUARY NOTICE: Born c. 1914 in Trieste, Italy; died of emphysema, March 15, 1979, in New York, N.Y. Editor, executive, and author. Buse was editor-in-chief of two fact-oriented crime magazines, *True Detective* and *Master Detective,* from 1951 until 1960. In addition to writing crime articles, she worked on the editorial staffs of *Parents' Magazine* and Platt & Munk Publishers. In 1973 she took a position with World Health Information Services and in 1976 was named vice-president of Health Projects International. Buse is the author of *The Deadly Silence.* Obituaries and other sources: *New York Times,* March 16, 1979.

C

CABLE, James Eric 1920-

PERSONAL: Born November 15, 1920, in London, England; son of Eric Grant (a consul-general) and Margaret (Skelton) Cable; married Viveca Hollmerus, 1954; children: Charles. *Education:* Corpus Christi College, Cambridge, Ph.D., 1973. *Office:* British Embassy, Helsinki, Finland.

CAREER: Diplomatic Service, London, England, served in H. M. Forces, 1941-46, joined H. M. Foreign Service, 1947, vice-consul in Batavia (now Djakarta), 1949, second secretary in Djakarta, 1950, *charge d'affaires,* 1951-52, second secretary in Helsinki, Finland, 1952, and in Foreign Office in London, 1953, became first secretary, 1953, member of British delegation to Geneva Conference on Indo-China, 1954, first secretary in Budapest, Hungary, 1956, head of chancery and consul in Quito, Ecuador, 1959, *charge d'affaires,* 1959-60, in Foreign Office, 1961-63, head of Southeast Asia department, 1963-66, counselor in Beirut, Lebanon, 1966, *charge d'affaires,* 1967-69, head of western organizations department at Foreign and Commonwealth Office, 1970-71, counselor in contingency studies, 1971, head of planning staff, 1971-75, assistant under-secretary of state, 1972-75, ambassador to Finland in Helsinki, 1975—. Research associate at Institute for Strategic Studies, 1969-70. *Member:* International Institute for Strategic Studies, Royal Automobile Club, Athenaeum Club. *Awards, honors:* Companion of Order of St. Michael and St. George, 1967; knight commander of Royal Victorian Order, 1976.

WRITINGS: Gunboat Diplomacy, Praeger, 1971; *The Royal Navy and the Siege of Bilbao,* Cambridge University Press, 1979.

WORK IN PROGRESS: Books on international relations, Scottish social history, and naval theory.

SIDELIGHTS: Sir James says he writes "because I enjoy it."

*   *   *

CABRERA INFANTE, G(uillermo) 1929-
(Guillermo Cain)

PERSONAL: Born April 22, 1929, in Gibara, Cuba; immigrated to London, England, 1966; naturalized British citizen; son of Guillermo Cabrera Lopez (a journalist) and Zoila Infante; married second wife, Miriam Gomez, in 1961; children: (first marriage) Ana, Carola. *Education:* Received baccalaureate in 1948; additional study at Havana University, 1949, 1950-54. *Home:* 53 Gloucester Rd., London SW7, England. *Agent:* Brandt & Brandt, 101 Park Ave., New York, N.Y. 10017.

CAREER: Film critic; journalist; translator; writer. *Awards, honors:* Biblioteca Breve prize for novels, 1964, and Prix du Meilleur Livre Etranger, Paris, 1971, both for *Tres tristes tigres;* Guggenheim fellowship for creative writing, 1970.

WRITINGS—In English: (And translator, with Donald Gardner and Suzanne Jill Levine) *Tres tristes tigres,* published, 1965, translation published as *Three Trapped Tigers,* Harper, 1971; *Exorcismos de estilo* (text in English, French, and Spanish; title means "Exorcising Style"), Editorial Seix Barral, 1976; *A View of Dawn in the Tropics,* translated by Levine, Harper, 1978.

Other works: *Asi en la paz como en la guerra: cuentos* (title means "In Peace as in War"), Revolucion (Havanna, Cuba), 1960; (with G. Cain) *Un oficio del siglo veinte* (title means "A Twentieth-Century Job"), illustrations by Sergio Haban and R. M. Haban, Revolucion, 1963; *Vista del amancecer en el tropico,* Editorial Seix Barral, 1974; *O/G. Cabrera Infante* (autobiography), Editorial Seix Barral, 1975; *O* (collection of articles and essays), Editorial Seix Barral, 1975. Also author of *Arcadia todas las noches* (title means "Arcadia Every Night"), 1978.

Screenplays; under pseudonym Guillermo Cain: "Wonderwall," released in England, 1968; "Vanishing Point," Twentieth Century-Fox Film Corp., 1970. Author of a series of lectures on American screenplays.

Translator into Spanish of stories by Mark Twain, Ambrose Bierce, Sherwood Anderson, Ernest Hemingway, William Faulkner, Dashiell Hammett, J. D. Salinger, Vladimir Nabokov, and other major authors, and of the *Dubliners,* by James Joyce.

Contributor to *New Yorker, New Republic,* and to Latin-American and Spanish periodicals. Editor of *Lunes de Revolucion,* 1959-61.

WORK IN PROGRESS: La Habana Para un Infante Difunto and *Cuerpos Divinos* ("Divine Novels"), both novels to be published by Harper; "Under the Volcano," a screenplay based on the novel by Malcolm Lowry.

SIDELIGHTS: Although Cabrera Infante is currently in disfavor in his native Cuba, he is said to have much influence on modern Cuban writers. One of his most noted works is

Asi en la paz como en la guerra, a collection of short stories about Cuba in the 1950's during the dictatorship of Batista.

Cabrera Infante is probably best known, however, for his award-winning *Three Trapped Tigers,* the title of which was taken from a Spanish tongue-twister. The novel takes place before the revolution that ousted Batista. In the heart of Havanna, the characters, including a photographer, a drummer, a writer, and an actor, each tell their story. "It is a political novel," Cabrera Infante told *CA,* "because it is apolitical."

In *Three Trapped Tigers,* Cabrera Infante uses a language that is like actual speech, Cuban colloquialisms included, according to David Gallagher in the *New York Times Book Review.* The language is also humorous, a quality not often found in Hispanic literature. "I doubt a funnier book has been written since Don Quixote," wrote Gallagher. It has "savagely refreshed an often portentously solemn heritage. It is also one of the most inventive novels that has come out of Latin America, and that is saying a great deal." Its "comedy is a strategy against sadness, against mediocrity, against the limitations of an underdeveloped land."

Much of the humor is revealed through puns that are liberally scattered throughout the book. *Newsweek* reviewer Walter Clemons wrote that while Cabrera Infante displays "ferocious verbal energy," he is a "terrible pedant. The second half of 'Three Trapped Tigers' dries up into a sandy waste of Joycean punning (what we need least is a Cuban Joyce), heavy literary parodies and assorted monkey tricks of an avant-garde 50 years to the rear." But in *Modern Latin-American Literature,* Gallagher expressed his view that "like everything else in the novel, the puns are often just funny, gratuitously, defiantly stupid, part of the book's frequent enterprise to be plain ridiculous for the sake of it."

Gallagher called *Three Trapped Tigers* a local novel. He also pointed out that it is universal in the sense that it is a "celebration of the small things that oblivion or time demolishes."

Cabrera Infante told *CA:* "It all began with a parody. If it were not for a parody I wrote on a Latin American writer who was later to win the Nobel Prize, I wouldn't have become a professional writer and I wouldn't qualify to be here at all. My parents wanted me to go to University and I would have liked to become a doctor. But somehow that dreadful novel crossed my path. After reading a few pages (I just couldn't stomach it all, of course) and being only seventeen at the time, I said to myself, 'Why, if that's what writing is all about—*anch'io sono scrittore* [I'm also a writer]!' To prove I too was a writer I wrote a parody of the pages I had read. It was a dreadfully serious parody and unfortunately the short story I wrote was taken by what was then the most widely-read publication in Latin America, the Cuban magazine *Bohemia.* They paid me what at the time I considered a fortune and I was hooked: probably hooked by fortune, probably hooked by fame but certainly hooked by writing.

"I wrote many short stories, parodies all, in the coming years. Then I tried writing on films, movies being central to my life, which was not the case with books. Later the crooked arm of the law intruded in my plans and I was accused of publishing a short story with four-letter words in English (which was true) and of corrupting Cuban morals (which was false: they were already corrupt) and I was put in jail, tried, and fined for what the judge called 'writing English profanities.' Harder than the sentence was the professional penalty: I couldn't write with my own name in the best Cuban publications—but there was a kind loophole: I could use a pseudonym. As I didn't want to lose my name,

which is my face, for a mask I chose to shorten my two last names and minimize my first name to its initial. The result was G. Cain, a name that was synonymous with jealousy, fraternal envy, and murder. To avoid such fate I became my alter ego's keeper. The movie column I wrote weekly grew overpoweringly and it was only in 1960 that I was able to publish my first book, a collection of short stories, under my too full name. But I had to kill Cain first to attain this. In 1963 I managed to bury him in a book, with samples of his film criticism and my euphoric eulogy. I have published other books in other voices but I've succeeded in signing them with my own name.

"But I still do the writing in different voices. American readers can verify this by reading my *Three Trapped Tigers,* a gallery of voices. The same parodic element is present in the book I've just finished. It is called *La Habana Para un Infante Difunto.* The title is of course a send-up of Ravel's *Pavane pour une Infante Defunte.* Parody starts with the title and it should be so, for parody is what writing is all about. Literature is a parody of life. But then, what is life a parody of? I have an answer for that too. When Einstein said that God does not play dice with the Universe, he certainly didn't have the courage of his equation at the time. I have no doubt that God is a colossal parodist. Otherwise, why did He create man?"

BIOGRAPHICAL/CRITICAL SOURCES: Book World, October 3, 1971; *New York Times Book Review,* October 17, 1971, December 5, 1971; *Newsweek,* October 25, 1971; *New Leader,* November 1, 1971; *Commonweal,* November 12, 1971; *Best Sellers,* December 1, 1971; *New York Review of Books,* December 16, 1971; *Time,* January 10, 1972; *New Yorker,* January 19, 1972, September 19, 1977; Rita Guibert, *Seven Voices,* Knopf, 1973; *Modern Latin-American Literature,* Oxford University Press, 1973; *National Observer,* March 24, 1973; Raymond D. Souza, *Major Cuban Novelists,* University of Missouri Press, 1976; *Contemporary Literary Criticism,* Volume 5, Gale, 1976; *World Literature Today,* spring, 1977; *Nation,* November 4, 1978.

* * *

CAHN, Sammy 1913-

PERSONAL: Born June 18, 1913, in Manhattan, N.Y.; son of Abraham (a restaurateur) and Elka (a restaurateur; maiden name, Reiss) Cahn; married Gloria Delson, September 5, 1945 (divorced May, 1964); married Tita Curtis; children: Steve, Laurie. *Education: Politics:* "Liberal Democrat." *Religion:* "Jewish-American." *Residence:* New York, N.Y.; and Beverly Hills, Calif. *Office:* Traubner/Flynn, 2049 Century Park E., Los Angeles, Calif. 90067.

CAREER: Lyricist and performer. Formed band with Saul Chaplin; appeared in one-man show on Broadway, "Words & Music." *Member:* National Academy of Popular Music (president), American Society of Composers, Authors, and Publishers (member of board), Christian Scientists, Sigma Delta Chi. *Awards, honors:* Thirty nominations for best song from Academy of Motion Picture Arts and Sciences; Academy Award for best song, 1954, for "Three Coins in the Fountain," 1957, for "All the Way," 1959, for "High Hopes," and 1963, for "Call Me Irresponsible"; Emmy Award from Television Academy of Arts and Sciences for music for "Our Town"; inducted into Songwriters' Hall of Fame.

WRITINGS: I Should Care: The Sammy Cahn Story, Arbor House, 1974. Lyricist for stage productions, including "High Button Shoes," "Skyskraper," and "Walking Happy,'' and for motion pictures, including "Anchors Aweigh," 1945, "Romance on High Seas," 1948, "Three Coins in the Fountain," 1954, "Some Came Running," 1958, "Robin and the Seven Hoods," 1964, and "Thoroughly Modern Millie," 1967. Also author of countless songs, including "The Tender Trap," "Teach Me Tonight," "I'll Walk Tonight," "Call Me Irresponsible," "Let It Snow, Let It Snow, Let It Snow," "Please Be Kind," "Until the Real Thing Comes Along," "Shoe Shine Boy," and "Victory Polka." Work featured in numerous songbooks.

SIDELIGHTS: Cahn told *CA:* "I would rather write lyrics than do anything else. My vocation is my marriage, 'The Second Time Around.' My avocation is writing lyrics. A day doesn't go by that I don't write a special lyric for someone. Writing is the easiest thing I do and I never let anyone watch me write because if they saw how easy it is they wouldn't pay me! There is no greater career than a SUCCESSFUL, underline and repeat *SUCCESSFUL,* songwriting career. The rewards are incredible financially but, more important, aesthetically. One college student asked me, 'What is wrong with a successful architectural career?' 'Nothing,' I said, 'but who walks down the street humming a building?'"

*   *   *

CAILLOIS, Roger   1913-1978

OBITUARY NOTICE—See index for *CA* sketch: Born March 3, 1913, in Reims, Marne, France; died December 21, 1978, in Paris, France. Critic, sociologist, editor, and author. Caillois founded the French Institute of Buenos Aires in 1941. He served as the editor of the literary journals *Lettres francaises* and *La France libre.* Before he became chief editor of *Diogenes* in 1953, Caillois was affiliated with the United Nations Educational, Scientific and Cultural Organization (UNESCO) as director of the divisions of cultural activities and letters. The author of over thirty books, Caillois was best known for *Man and the Sacred,* a study of the sociological and mythological aspects of religion. Obituaries and other sources: *Encyclopedia of World Literature in the Twentieth Century,* updated edition, Ungar, 1967; *The International Who's Who,* Europa, 1978; *Who's Who in the World,* 4th edition, Marquis, 1978; *World Literature Today,* spring, 1979.

*   *   *

CAINE, Jeffrey (Andrew)   1944-

PERSONAL: Born December 16, 1944, in London, England; son of Henry (a store manager) and Fay (Rosenberg) Caine; married Lorna Williams (a secretary and personal assistant), July 7, 1969; children: Helena, Lisa. *Education:* University of Sussex, B.A., 1967; University of Leeds, M.A., 1968. *Politics:* "Liberal-democratic." *Religion:* None. *Residence:* St. Martins, Shropshire, England. *Agent:* Erica Spellman, International Creative Management, 40 West 57th St., New York, N.Y. 10017.

CAREER: Taught English at all levels from junior high school to college, with posts in London and Shrewsbury, England, and Cardiff, Wales, 1968-73; writer, 1973—. *Member:* British Society of Authors, Authors' Guild.

WRITINGS—Novels: *Hamlet, My Boy,* Deutsch, 1972; *The Cold Room,* W. H. Allen, 1976, Knopf, 1977; *Heathcliff,* W. H. Allen, 1977, Knopf, 1978.

SIDELIGHTS: Caine writes: "I seem to be fascinated by the bizarre, by obsession and the workings of obsessed minds. Don't ask my why, or why I have a black imagination and

sense of humor. I think I must work from the unconscious. My conscious, social self is apparently healthy and safely balanced. One personal preoccupation that governs my work is a longing to be versatile, never to repeat myself. When people ask me, 'What kind of novels do you write?' I answer, 'Different kinds.' I have, therefore, the ambitions of a junk collector. And like junk collectors everywhere, I dream of finding an original, a one-of-its-kind idea for a unique book. Now that I think of it, that does sound obsessive, doesn't it?"

Reviewing *The Cold Room,* Newgate Callendar wrote: "It's altogether a virtuoso job with a Grand Guignol ending. In addition Caine captures the drabness, meanness, and danger of East Berlin, as seen through the eyes of a bright, rebellious adolescent."

About *Heathcliff,* Katha Pollit remarked: "This is a witty, elegant, fast-paced story.... Caine is a clever narrator and an artful stylist, and he goes about his task with a dash and good humor...." Jerome Charyn said in his review: "Heathcliff's story is told with gusto and imagination..., a very energetic book."

The Cold Room and *Heathcliff* are being adapted as films.

BIOGRAPHICAL/CRITICAL SOURCES: New York Times Book Review, March 6, 1977, March 5, 1978; *Time,* February 13, 1978; *Saturday Review,* March 18, 1978.

*   *   *

CALHOUN, Don Gilmore   1914-

PERSONAL: Born February 8, 1914, in New York, N.Y.; son of Harold Gilmore (a lawyer) and Dorothy (a writer and editor; maiden name, Donnell) Calhoun; married Esther Ball, April 2, 1937 (died February 1, 1974); married Susana Watts (an artist), June 5, 1974; children: Michael, John, Stephen, Faith Calhoun Gordon. *Education:* University of California, Los Angeles, B.A.; attended Academie Julien and Oxford University. *Politics:* "Republican (sometimes)." *Religion:* None. *Home and office:* 320 Ponus Ridge, New Canaan, Conn. 06840. *Agent:* Mrs. Carlton Cole, Waldorf Towers Apartments, New York, N.Y.

CAREER: McMann Erickson Advertising Agency, New York City, vice-president and creative director, 1953-60; Jack Tinker & Partners, New York City, partner and creative director, 1960-63; Interpublic, Inc., New York City, consultant to chairman of board of directors, 1963-69; writer, 1969—. Art work exhibited in Paris, France. *Military service:* U.S. Navy, 1944-46; served in Pacific theater; received two Bronze Stars. *Awards, honors:* Art Directors Award for Distinctive Merit, 1947.

WRITINGS: Dear Kids (self-illustrated), Ziff-Davis, 1946; *The Little President* (self-illustrated), Crowell, 1946; *Dando Shaft* (novel), Stein & Day, 1966; *Is There Life After Advertising?,* Stein & Day, 1974. Contributor of stories, articles, and illustrations to magazines, including *Esquire, Look,* and *Motion Picture.*

WORK IN PROGRESS: Four novels, *The Taming of Hannible Boone, Young Dando, The Island Game,* and *Crazy World;* two books for children, *The Horse in the House* and *The Wonderful Thunderful Storm.*

AVOCATIONAL INTERESTS: Travel, painting.

*   *   *

CALVINO, Italo   1923-

PERSONAL: Born October 15, 1923, in Santiago de Las

Vegas, Cuba; son of Mario (a botanist) and Eva (a botanist; maiden name, Mameli) Calvino; married Chichita Singer (a translator), February 19, 1964; children: one daughter. *Education:* University of Turin, graduated, 1947. *Office:* Giulio Einaudi Editore, Via Umberto Biancamano 1, Turin, Italy.

CAREER: Writer. Member of editorial staff of Giulio Einaudi Editore, 1947—; lecturer. *Military service:* Italian Resistance, 1943-45. *Awards, honors:* Premio Feltrinelli per la Narrativa, 1972; honorary member of the American Academy and Institute of Arts and Letters, 1975; Oesterreischiches Staatspreis fuer Europeische Litteratur, 1976.

WRITINGS—In English; all originally published by Einaudi, unless otherwise indicated: *Il sentiero dei nidi di ragno* (novel), 1947, translation from the Italian by Archibald Colquhoun published as *The Path to the Nest of Spiders*, Collins, 1956, Beacon Press, 1957; *La formica argentina* (novella), 1952, translation by Colquhoun and Peggy White published as *Adam, One Afternoon and Other Stories* (also contains selections from *Ultimo viene il corvo* and *L'entrata in guerra;* also see below), Collins, 1957; *Il visconte dimezzato* (novel), 1952, translation by Colquhoun published as *The Non-Existent Knight and The Cloven Viscount* (also contains translation of *Il cavaliere inesistente;* also see below), Random House, 1962; (editor) *Fiabe italiane; raccolte della tradizione popolare durante gli ultimi cento anni e transcritte in lingua dai vari dialetti,* 1956, translation by Louis Brigante published as *Italian Fables,* Orion Press, 1959; *Il barone rampante* (novel), 1957, translation by Colquhoun published as *The Baron in the Trees,* Random House, 1959; *Il cavaliere inesistente* (novel), 1959, translation by Colquhoun published as *The Non-Existent Knight and The Cloven Viscount* (also contains translation of *Il visconte dimezzato*), Random House, 1959.

La giornata d'uno scrutatore (stories), 1963, translation published as *The Watcher and Other Stories,* Harcourt, 1971; *Le cosmicomiche* (stories), 1965, translation by William Weaver published as *Cosmicomics,* Harcourt, 1968; *Ti con zero* (stories), 1967, translation by Weaver published as *T Zero,* Harcourt, 1969, published in England as *Time and the Hunter,* J. Cape, 1970; *Tarocchi,* F. M. Ricci, 1969, translation by Weaver published as *Tarot; The Visconti Pack in Bergamo and New York,* F. M. Ricci, 1975; *Le citta invisibili,* 1972, translation by Weaver published as *Invisible Cities,* Harcourt, 1974; *Il castello dei destini incrociati,* 1973, translation by Weaver published as *The Castle of Crossed Destinies,* Harcourt, 1977.

Other; all published by Einaudi: *L'entrata in guerra* (short stories; title means "Entry Into War"; also see above), 1954; *I racconti* (short stories), 1958; *Ultimo viene il corvo* (short stories; title means "Last Comes the Crow"; also see above), 1959; *I nostri antenati: Il cavaliere inesistente, Il visconte dimezzato, Il barone rampante,* 1960; (editor) Cesare Pavese, *Poesie edite e inedite,* 1962; (editor) Pavese, *La letterature americana e altri saggi,* 4th edition, 1962; *La speculazione edilizia* (novel; title means "A Plunge in Real Estate"), 1963; *Marcovaldo; ovvero, Le stagioni in citta* (title means "M.; or, The Seasons in the City"), 1963; *La nuvola di smog, e La formica argentina* (novellas), 1965; (editor) Pavese, *Lettere, 1945-50,* 1966; (editor) Pavese, *Lettere, 1926-1950,* 1968; *Gli amori difficili,* 1970.

Work anthologized in *Italian Short Stories,* 1965, and *Italian Writing Today,* 1967.

SIDELIGHTS: Calvino is best known in the U.S. for his collection of short stories, *Cosmicomics,* in which the characters resemble mathematical formulas. The main character is Qfwfq, whose specific origin is ignored. As Donald Heiney noted, Qfwfq "has recapitulated the whole history of evolution in his personal experience, and thus remembers being a number of higher and lower animals at various epochs in his past." Qfwfq's recall encompasses the age of dinosaurs, a period when the moon and earth were extremely close, and "a time," according to Heiney, "when the entire substance of the universe was contracted into a single point." Michael Feingold wrote, "If Calvino's tales are good jokes on the cosmos, it is because of the terrifying emptiness sandwiched between the first splutter of amusement and the gigantic, warming irony that is our victory over existence."

Attempting to define Calvino as a writer, Anatole Broyard found him unique from others in the science-fiction genre. "Calvino brings a number of people to mind," declared Broyard, specifically mentioning Borges, Kafka, and the later Becket. "He differs from science-fiction writers in focusing on the poignant possibilities, the ambiguities and inevitable maladjustments of scientific progress, rather than on its glamorous gadgetry and cocky perspectives." In reviewing *T Zero,* Heiney noted a similar uniqueness. "Rather than projections into the future with more or less human characters, like the fiction of Wells or Asimov, they [the stories] are, so to speak, fairy tales constructed around scientific premises."

T Zero contains more stories with Qfwfq of *Cosmicomics.* Included in the collection are such tales as "Soft Moon," in which the moon actually begins to drip onto the earth, and another in which a divided cell undergoes an identity crisis. John Ashbery found *T Zero* "more interesting" than *Cosmicomics* but also found it to be "more uneven." He wrote that, with *T Zero,* Calvino had "a horror of vacuums: he has trimmed these stories to the bone, using long run-on sentences that keep skidding out from under one as idea engenders idea."

But if Calvino is attempting stylistic changes, he is at least continuing to deal with off-beat and unique ideas. Aside from his first novel, *The Path to the Nest of Spiders,* a realistic account of the Italian Resistance, most of Calvino's writings have embraced the unusual. *The Non-Existent Knight* concerns the daily goings of a knight who's been severed completely in half; "The Argentine Ant," one of the tales in *The Watcher and Other Stories,* is about a couple who become, as H. T. Anderson noted, "totally demoralized, absolutely demoralized," by their inability to combat ants inhabiting the couple's new home. As Anderson noted, "Mr. Calvino is a genius. He knows his craft, he knows reader needs, he is boldly imaginative: an important writer."

In 1974 the appearance of the English translation of *Le citta invisibili,* entitled *Invisible Cities,* spurred a new interest in Calvino's work. American critics raved about *Invisible Cities.* Joseph McElroy lauded the originality of the book and declared that "Calvino's book is like no other I know." John Updike was also lavish with his praise; he wrote that Calvino "has produced a consummate book, both crystalline and limpid, adamant and airy, intricate and ingenuous, playful yet 'worked' with a monkish care upon materials of great imaginative density and resonance."

BIOGRAPHICAL/CRITICAL SOURCES: New York Times Book Review, August 25, 1968, October 12, 1969, November 17, 1974, April 10, 1977; *Christian Science Monitor,* August 29, 1968, October 16, 1969; *New Republic,* November 2, 1968; *Book World,* September 7, 1969; *Best Sellers,* February 1, 1971; *Time,* February 22, 1971; *New York Review of*

Books, May 30, 1974; *New Yorker*, February 24, 1975; *Contemporary Literary Criticism*, Gale, Volume 5, 1976, Volume 8, 1978.

*　　*　　*

CAMPBELL, Kenneth　1901(?)-1979

OBITUARY NOTICE: Born c. 1901, in Pittsburgh, Pa.; died February 27, 1979, in New York. Journalist. As a *New York Times* foreign correspondent and reporter for twenty-five years, Campbell occasionally wrote for the editorial page and critiqued plays and books as well. Part of his job was preparing advance articles on noteworthy people to be printed in the newspaper after they died. A U.S. patriot and francophile, he was named chevalier of the Legion of Honor and won the French Croix de Guerre for military valor. Some of his writing is anthologized in *America at Random*. Obituaries and other sources: *New York Times*, February 28, 1979.

*　　*　　*

CANIFF, Milton (Arthur)　1907-

PERSONAL: Surname is pronounced Can*iff*; born February 28, 1907, in Hillsboro, Ohio; son of John William (a printer) and Elizabeth (Burton) Caniff; married Esther Parsons, August 23, 1930. *Education:* Ohio State University, B.A. 1930. *Home:* 375 West Vista Chino, Palm Springs, Calif. 92262. *Agent:* Toni Mendez, 140 East 56th St., New York, N.Y. 10022. *Office:* King Features, 235 East 45th St., New York, N.Y. 10017.

CAREER: Journal Herald, Dayton, Ohio, staff artist, 1922-25; *Miami News*, Miami, Fla., staff artist, summer, 1925; *Columbus Dispatch*, Columbus, Ohio, staff artist, 1925-32; Associated Press Feature Service, New York, N.Y., staff artist, 1932-34, creator of "Dickie Dare" and "The Gay Thirties" cartoon strips; creator of "Terry and the Pirates" cartoon strip, *Chicago Tribune*, and *New York News* Syndicate, 1934-46; staff artist, and creator of "Steve Canyon" cartoon strip, Field Newspaper Syndicate, and King Features, 1947—. Artwork exhibited at institutions in the United States and abroad, including the Metropolitan Museum of Art, the Louvre Museum, and the Renoir Museum. *Member:* National Cartoonists Society (president, 1948-49; honorary chairman), National Press Club, National Aviation Club, Society of Illustrators, Playors Club, Overseas Press Club (Palm Springs), Palm Springs Racquet Club, Dutch Treat Club. *Awards, honors:* Reuben award, National Cartoonists Society, 1946, 1972; Doctor of Laws, Atlanta Law School, 1948; Doctor of Fine Arts, Rollins College (Florida), 1956; Freedoms Foundation National Service medal, 1967, for "creative editorials and cartoons which brilliantly espouse the precepts of human freedom'; Distinguished Eagle award, Boy Scouts of America (Columbus, Ohio), 1969; first Segar award, San Francisco Press Club, 1971; Doctor of Humane Letters, Ohio State University, 1974; Doctor of Fine Arts, University of Dayton, 1979; recipient of numerous other awards from U.S. Air Force and other organizations, for distinguished service.

WRITINGS: Terry and the Pirates, Adapted From the Famous Comic Strip by Milton Caniff, Random House, 1946; *Male Call: The First Complete Collection of the Uninhibited Adventures of Every GI's Dream Girl—Miss Lace*, new edition, Grosset, 1959.

Collections of previously published cartoons: *Terry and the Pirates*, Nostalgia Press, 1970; *Enter the Dragon Lady: From the 1936 Classic Newspaper Strip*, Nostalgia Press,

1975; *Meet Burma*, Nostalgia Press, 1975; *Let's See if Anyone Salutes: A Cartoon Story for New Children*, Sheed & Ward, 1976; (with others) G. B. Trudeau, editor, *Cartoon Stories for New Children*, Sheed, Andrews & McMeel, 1976; Bill Chadbourne, editor, *Terry and the Pirates: The Normandie Affair*, Nostalgia Press, 1977; William Chadbourne, editor, *Terry and the Pirates: China Journey*, Nostalgia Press, 1977.

"Steve Canyon" series; all published by Grosset, 1959: *Steve Canyon; . . . Operation Convoy; . . . Operation Eel Island; . . . Operation Foo Ling; . . . Operation Snowflower*.

WORK IN PROGRESS: Research and travel that "may serve as background for a topical cartoon story sequence."

SIDELIGHTS: A *Newsweek* reviewer once described Milton Caniff as "the most widely aped artisan" today in his field. It was Caniff who invented the popular comic strip, "Terry and the Pirates" when *New York News* publisher Colonel Joseph M. Patterson suggested he create an adventure sequence "so powerful that nobody could eat his breakfast without reading it." John Steinbeck once wrote of the series: "When my grandchildren speak of their sugarplum eroticisms, I can say 'You see? This is how it was in my day. This Dragon Lady (from 'Terry') with the figure of a debutante . . . was one of your old man's girlfriends."

Success came quickly to another Caniff brainchild, the comic strip "Steve Canyon," featuring the adventures of a U.S. Air Force colonel. The strip is currently circulated in six hundred newspapers throughout the country with an estimated readership of thirty million. Caniff has received many awards from the U.S. Air Force for "Steve Canyon," and the cartoon colonel himself was honored with a special "Steve Canyon Day" at the 1964 World's Fair.

More than once, ideas used by Caniff in "Steve Canyon" have become a reality. In one instance, Canyon discovered that Captain Shark, a woman submarine expert from a formidable foreign country, was moving prefabricated submarines to warm-water ports over land. A year and a half later, it became known that the U.S.S.R. was actually transporting prefabricated submarines in much the same way. Then Canyon captured Shark in her snorkel submarine, an innovation that was in fact later developed. A reconnaissance plane used for guiding naval vessels was another idea preconceived by Caniff.

"Terry and the Pirates," "Steve Canyon," and the other Caniff creations might never have appeared in print if Caniff had pursued a career in acting, something he once seriously considered. But he changed his mind when *Columbus Dispatch* cartoonist Billy Ireland advised him, "Stick to your inkpots, kid. Actors don't eat regularly."

A self-professed "working stiff," Caniff spends from fourteen to sixteen hours every day at the drawing board. Expressing his philosophy in creating each comic strip, Caniff wrote: "I have always admonished myself to write for the man on the bus or the woman who is having her second cup of coffee after her husband and children have been sent off for the day. At these moments we are alone together, and I bring to them an uninterrupted display of my wares. The playwright can have the advantage of chain reaction emotion stemming from mutual appreciation by many people crowded together. I am happy to have my reader alone for the few minutes each day during which we rendezvous."

In addition to being a cartoonist, Caniff is also a painter in oils. After viewing some of Caniff's paintings exhibited at the Julian Levy Gallery in New York, an art critic described him as a "genuine creative talent in the field of modern Americana."

BIOGRAPHICAL/CRITICAL SOURCES: New Yorker, January 8, 1944; J. P. Adams, *Rembrandt of the Comic Strips,* McKay, 1946; *Time,* January 13, 1947; *Newsweek,* April 24, 1950; *Life,* December 7, 1959; *Los Angeles Times,* April 21, 1974; *Authors in the News,* Volume I, Gale, 1976.

*   *   *

CARETTE, Louis 1913-
(Felicien Marceau)

PERSONAL: Born September 16, 1913, in Cortenberg, Belgium; naturalized French citizen, 1959; son of Louis (a civil servant) and Marie (Lefevre) Carette; married Bianca Licenziati, December 30, 1953. *Education:* University of Louvain Law School, licence en philosophie et lettres, 1936. *Agent:* Societe des Auteurs 9, rue Ballu, Paris 75442, CEDEX 09.

CAREER: Full-time writer. Writer for Institut National Belge de Radiodiffusion, Belgium, 1936-42. *Member:* L'Academie francaise. *Awards, honors:* Prix Pelman du Theatre, 1954, for *Caterina;* Prix Interallie, 1955, for *Les Elans de coeur;* Prix Goncourt, 1969, for *Creezy;* Prix Litteraire de la Fondation Prince Pierre de Monaco, 1974; Grand Prix de la Societe de Auteurs et Compositeurs Dramatiques, 1975.

WRITINGS—All under pseudonym Felicien Marceau, except as noted; plays: *L'Ecole des moroses* (title means "School for the Morose"; one-act play; first produced in Paris at Theatre Hebertot, October 10, 1952), published in *Les Oeuvres Libres,* [Paris], 1953; *Caterina* (three-act; first produced in Paris at Theatre de l'Atelier, October 20, 1954), published in *Les Oeuvres Libres,* [Paris], 1954; *L'Oeuf* (two-act; first produced in Paris at Theatre de l'Atelier, December 18, 1956), translation by Robert Schlitt produced as "The Egg" on Broadway at the Cort Theatre, January 8, 1962), Gallimard, 1957, translation by Charles Frank published as *The Egg,* Faber, 1958; *La Bonne Soupe* (three-act; first produced in Paris at Theatre du Gymnase, October 1, 1958, adaptation by Garson Kanin produced as "The Good Soup" on Broadway at the Plymouth Theatre, March 2, 1960; also see below), Gallimard, 1958.

L'Etouffe-Chretien (title means "The Smothered Christian"; two-act; first produced in Paris at Theatre de la Renaissance, October 31, 1960), [Paris], 1961; "Tibere" (title means "Tiberius"; one-act radio play), published in *New French Writing,* edited by Georges Borchardt, Grove Press, 1961; *Les Cailloux* (title means "The Pebbles"; two-act play; first produced in Paris at Theatre de L'Atelier, January 27, 1962), Gallimard, 1962; "La Preuve par quatre" (title means "The Proof by Four"; two-act; first produced in Paris at Theatre de la Michodiere, February 3, 1964), published in *Theatre I,* Gallimard, 1964; "La Mort de Neron" (one-act radio play), and "Madame Princesse" (two-act; first produced in Paris at Theatre du Gymnase, 1965), both published in *Theatre II,* Gallimard, 1965; *Un Jour j'ai rencontre la verite* (two-act; first produced in Paris at Theatre de la Comedie des Champs Elysees, 1967), Gallimard, 1968; *Le Babour* (two-act play), Gallimard, 1969; *L'Ouvre-Boite* (title means "The Can Opener"; five-act play), Gallimard, 1972; *L'Homme en question* (title means "The Man in Question"; two-act play), Gallimard, 1974; (translator with Giorgio Strehler) de Goldoni, *La Trilogie de la Villegiature* (first produced in Paris at Theatre de l'Odeon, 1978), Editions de la Comedie Francaise, 1978.

Screenplays: "La Bonne Soupe" (adapted from play; also

see above), Twentieth Century-Fox, 1960; "Les Sept Peches capitaux" (title means "The Seven Capital Sins"), Films Gibe, 1962; "Trois de perdues," Nordisk Films, 1963; "L'Oeuf," Columbia, 1973; "La Race des seigneurs," Films La Boetie, 1973; "Les Corps de mon ennemi" (title means "The Body of My Enemy"; adapted from the novel; also see below), Films Cerito, 1976.

Novels: (Under name Louis Carette) *Le Peche de Complication* (title means "The Complicated Sin"), Editions de la Toison d'or, 1942; (under name Louis Carette) *Le Cadavre exquis* (title means "The Exquisite Corpse"), Editions du Houblon, 1943; *Chasseneuil: ou la nouvelle melusine,* Gallimard, 1948, translation by Arthur Rhodes published as *By Invitation Only,* 1955; *Chair et cuir* (title means "Chair and Leather"), Gallimard, 1951, translation by Margaret Crosland published as *The Flesh in the Mirror,* 1953; *Capri petite ile* (title means "Capri Little Island"), Gallimard, 1951; *L'Homme du roi,* Gallimard, 1952, translation by David Hughes and M. J. Mason published as *The King's Man,* 1954; *Bergere legere,* Gallimard, 1953, translation by Hughes and Mason published as *The China Shepherdess,* Abelard, 1957; *En de secretes noces* (title means "In the Secret Nuptial"), Calmann-Levy, 1953; *Les Elans du coeur,* Gallimard, 1955, translation by Hughes and Mason published as *The Flutterings of the Heart,* A. Barker, 1957, published as *Heart Flights,* Abelard, 1958; *Les Belles Natures* (title means "The Good Kind"), Gallimard, 1957; *Les Diamants de Mademoiselle Antoinette* (title means "Miss Antoinette's Diamonds"), P. Noordhoff, 1960; *Creezy* (also see above), Gallimard, 1969, translation by J. A. Underwood published as *Creezy,* Orion Press, 1970; *Le Corps de mon ennemi* (title means "The Body of My Enemy"), Gallimard, 1975.

Essays: *Naissance de Minerve* (under name Louis Carette; title means "The Birth of Minerva"), Houblon, 1943; *Casanova ou l'anti-Don Juan* (title means "Casanova or the Anti-Don Juan"), Presses de la Cite, 1948; *Balzac et son monde,* Gallimard, 1955, translation by Derek Coltman published as *Balzac and His World,* Orion Press, 1966; (with Jean Giono and Georges Pillement) *Rome I Love You,* Editions Sun, 1958; *Les Personnages de la "Comedie humaine"* (title means "The Characters of the 'Human Comedy'"), Gallimard, 1977; *Le Roman en liberte* (title means "The Novel Set Free"), Gallimard, 1977.

Other: (Contributor) Georges Borchardt, *New French Writing,* Criterion, 1961; *Les Annees Courtes* (memoirs; title means "The Fleeting Years"), Gallimard, 1968.

Also author of prefaces to works by Balzac, Anouilh, and Flaubert.

SIDELIGHTS: Critics generally classify Marceau as a satirist, elaborating on the term with such adjectives as "brutal," "corrosive," and "derisive." This satire is also distinctly "social" in that he deals in both his plays and fiction with such themes as alienation and conformity. Marceau's name is often linked with Samuel Beckett and Jean Anouilh, for like these authors he confronts in his work the individual's struggle against absurdity and despair. He examines the human condition and faces its meaninglessness and anguish with cynicism.

Outside of the United States, particularly in France, Marceau has met with great popular success. But when *The Egg,* for example, opened in New York, it closed within a week. Reviewers rejected the play's cynical view of the world as a rotten egg and its lack of poetic justice for the rotten hero (who moves successfully through seduction, adultery, and theft to murder in order to "make it" in society). Yet Robert Brustein saw the play as "a work of unexampled moral idealism." For though it "celebrated the progress of the hipster," it was not to be taken seriously. It was, Brustein said, "the most consistently amusing light entertainment of the year."

American critics more frequently had good things to say about Marceau's novel *Creezy*. The story is familiar: a tragic love affair between a young, successful fashion model, Creezy, and Jacques, a middle-aged politician with a wife and children. But Marceau extends the form. First of all, he tells the story through Jacques, whose "confessional urgency," Naomi Bliven maintained, "creates the fluency of good story-telling." She also liked the fact that "the book's solid structure is unobtrusive" and that the minor characters are drawn "concisely, vividly, and realistically." Other critics praised different aspects of *Creezy*'s style. Martin Levin pointed out Marceau's ability "to accelerate his story with bursts of wonderfully lean dialogue." Laurent LeSage wrote, "In the narrative parts Marceau's sentences rush about like the characters in their world of steel and cement"; and he said, "Character portrayal is as brutal and bold as a camera flashbulb."

Bliven further noted Marceau's extensive use of the element of decor and the importance of Creezy's apartment as a symbol of the modern world, "a symptom of impersonality, alienation, and dehumanization." But while Bliven found this symbolism of set and props distracting, LeSage felt the book successfully produces "the impression of a frightening mechanical universe in which mankind itself has become a sort of souped-up machine."

"The Egg" was produced as a film in 1972.

BIOGRAPHICAL/CRITICAL SOURCES: Georges Borchardt, *New French Writing*, Criterion, 1961; Robert Brustein, *Seasons of Discontent*, Simon & Schuster, 1967; *The New York Times Book Review*, January 25, 1970; *The Saturday Review*, February 21, 1970; *The New Yorker*, August 1, 1970.

* * *

CARGO, Robert T. 1933-

PERSONAL: Born November 20, 1933, in Hanceville, Ala.; married Helen McCain; children: Rose Caroline, Robert T., Jr. *Education:* Birmingham-Southern College, B.A., 1955; University of Alabama, M.A., 1956; further graduate study at Sorbonne, University of Paris, 1959-60; University of North Carolina, Ph.D., 1965. *Home:* 405 Caplewood Dr., Tuscaloosa, Ala. *Office:* Department of Romance Languages, University of Alabama, University, Ala. 35486.

CAREER: Snead Junior College, Boaz, Ala., instructor in French, 1956-59; University of Caen, Caen, France, lecturer in English, 1960-61; University of North Carolina, Chapel Hill, instructor in French, 1963-65; University of Alabama, University, assistant professor, 1965-68, associate professor, 1968-72, professor of French, 1972—. Consultant to Canada Council. *Member:* Modern Language Association of America, American Association of Teachers of French, Alabama Association of Foreign Language Teachers (vice-president, 1969-70). *Awards, honors:* Fulbright scholar in France, 1959-61; National Endowment for the Humanities grant, summer, 1971.

WRITINGS: A Concordance to Baudelaire's "Les Fleurs du Mal", University of North Carolina Press, 1965; *Baudelaire Criticism, 1950-1967; A Bibliography With Critical Commentary*, University of Alabama Press, 1968; (translator) Pierre

Emmanuel, *Baudelaire: The Paradox of Redemptive Satanism*, University of Alabama Press, 1970; *A Concordance to Baudelaire's "Petits Poèmes en Prose"*, University of Alabama Press, 1971; (editor with Emanuel Micke, and contributor) *Studies in Honor of Alfred G. Engstrom*, University of North Carolina Press, 1972. Contributor of about a dozen articles and reviews to language and literature journals. Associate editor of *South Atlantic Bulletin* and *Oeuvres et Critiques* (member of advisory board, 1976—).

BIOGRAPHICAL/CRITICAL SOURCES: French Review, Volume XXXIX, number 5, 1966, Volume XLV, number 3, 1972, Volume XLVII, number 2, 1973; *Modern Language Notes*, Volume LXXXI, number 3, 1966; *Romance Philology*, Volume XXI, number 3, 1968; *French Studies*, April, 1970.

* * *

CARNES, Conrad D(ew) 1936-

PERSONAL: Born January 14, 1936, in New York, N.Y.; son of Sidney Cecil (a writer) and Elizabeth (Dew) Carnes; married Marilyn Brown, August 16, 1958; children: Walter B., Lincoln Cecil, Matthew G. *Education:* Ohio State University, B.A., 1958, J.D., 1965; graduate study at Indiana University, 1961-63. *Politics:* Independent Republican. *Religion:* Christian. *Home and office:* 3506 Stratton Dr., Fort Collins, Colo. 80525. *Agent:* Francis Greenburger, Sanford J. Greenburger Associates, Inc., 825 Third Ave., New York, N.Y. 10022.

CAREER: Attorney in private practice in Cincinnati, Ohio, 1965-67, and in Columbus, Ohio, 1967-73; Ohio State University, Mansfield, Ohio, instructor in real estate law, 1973-77; Westland Group, Fort Collins, Colo., attorney, 1978—. *Military service:* U.S. Naval Reserve, 1958—; present rank, commander. *Member:* American Bar Association, Ohio Bar Association, Columbus Bar Association.

WRITINGS: (With Gene Church) *The Pit* (nonfiction), Dutton, 1972.

WORK IN PROGRESS: Planning Your Personal Finance, with John Sestina; *The Community*, a novel.

SIDELIGHTS: Carnes writes: "My novel in progress deals with the formation of a religious separatist/agrarian community. As in all novels, the characters will live out the author's fantasy. I have traveled nearly everywhere, and speak Greek, Hebrew, Spanish, French, with some German, Russian, and Hindustani."

* * *

CARNES, Paul N(athaniel) 1921-1979

OBITUARY NOTICE: Born February 1, 1921, in Jeffersonville, Ind.; died of cancer, March 17, 1979, in Boston, Mass. Minister and author of books on religion, known primarily as president of the Unitarian Universalist Association of North America. Described as an "intellectual with charisma," Carnes received numerous awards for his efforts in promoting civil rights. He was captured by the Germans while serving in the U.S. Army in World War II, and acted as the prison camp's chaplain during his three-year incarceration. Books by Carnes include *For Freedom and Belief, Longing of the Heart*, and *Introduction to Unitarianism*. Obituaries and other sources: *New York Times*, March 19, 1979.

* * *

CARR, Robert K(enneth) 1908-1979

OBITUARY NOTICE: Born February 15, 1908, in Cleveland, Ohio; died February 21, 1979, in Elyria, Ohio. Educator, author, and authority on constitutional law and civil liberties. In 1947, Carr served as director of President Truman's Commission on Civil Rights and was the principal author of the federal report *To Secure These Rights*. A former president of Oberlin College (1960-70), Carr wrote *The Supreme Court and Judicial Review, Federal Protection of Civil Rights*, and *The House Committee on Un-American Activities*. Obituaries and other sources: *Current Biography*, Wilson, 1961; *American Men and Women of Science: The Social and Behavioral Sciences*, 12th edition, Bowker, 1973; *Leaders in Education*, 5th edition, Bowker, 1974; *Who's Who in America*, 40th edition, Marquis, 1978; *Washington Post*, February 23, 1979; *New York Times*, February 23, 1979.

* * *

CARRAS, Mary C(alliope)

PERSONAL: Born in New York, N.Y.; daughter of Louis and Urania (Georgiou) Carras. *Education:* Hunter College of the City University of New York, B.A. (cum laude), 1962; University of Pennsylvania, Ph.D., 1969. *Home:* 11 MacArthur Blvd., Westmont, N.J. 08108. *Office:* Department of Political Science, Rutgers University, Camden, N.J. 08102.

CAREER: Cedar Crest College, Allentown, Pa., assistant professor of political science, 1968-70; Rockford College, Rockford, Ill., assistant professor of political science and head of department, 1970-73; Rutgers University, Camden, N.J., associate professor of political science, 1973—. *Member:* American Political Science Association, Association for Asian Studies, American Academy of Political and Social Science, American Association of University Women, Phi Beta Kappa, Pi Sigma Alpha. *Awards, honors:* National Defense Education Act foreign language fellow, 1962-64; Fulbright-Hays fellow in India, 1964-66; American Association of University Women founders' fellow in India, 1974-75; American Philosophical Society grant, 1974-75.

WRITINGS: The Dynamics of Indian Political Factions, Cambridge University Press, 1972; *Indira Gandhi in the Crucible of Leadership*, Beacon Press, 1979. Contributor of articles and reviews to economic, political science, and Asian studies journals.

WORK IN PROGRESS: Research on social and occupational problems of women in South Asian cultures.

SIDELIGHTS: Mary Carras writes: "I consider India one of the most important Third-World countries because of its potential for economic and political power, its strategic location, its vast population, and its possible impact on international and Asian stability. Once developed, India could radically change international political and economic alignments.

"I was in India for nearly two years, between 1964 and 1966, conducting research for my first book. In 1975 I researched my book on Indira Gandhi, and returned to New Delhi for a month in 1978. I have studied Hindi and Marathi."

* * *

CARRERA ANDRADE, Jorge 1903-1978

OBITUARY NOTICE: Born September 18, 1903, in Quito, Ecuador; died December, 1978, in Quito, Ecuador. Poet, essayist, and diplomat in Ecuador's foreign service. As a diplomat, Carrera Andrade traveled extensively throughout the world, and in Spain he took an active part in the procla-

mation of the Republic. At fifteen he edited a literary review and was later regarded as Ecuador's leading poet, as well as one of the most important of contemporary Latin-American poets. His works of poetry, noted for a brief, terse, and strongly imagistic style, include *Estanque inefable, La guirnalda del silencio, Antologia poetica, 1922-1939, Canto al puente del Oakland–To the Bay Bridge*, and *Secret Country*. Obituaries and other sources: *Books Abroad*, autumn, 1941, April, 1943; *Poetry*, February, 1942; *Encyclopedia of World Literature in the Twentieth Century*, updated edition, Ungar, 1967; *The Penguin Companion to American Literature*, McGraw, 1971; *Cassell's Encyclopaedia of World Literature*, revised edition, Morrow, 1973; *Who's Who in the World*, 2nd edition, Marquis, 1973; *World Literature Today*, spring, 1979.

* * *

CARROLL, Jackson W(alker) 1932-

PERSONAL: Born January 29, 1932, in Chester, S.C.; son of Jackson W. (a grocer) and Eileen (a teacher; maiden name, Little) Carroll; married Anne Ewing (in real estate sales), August 25, 1954; children: Susan Ewing, Frances Ewing. *Education:* Wofford College, A.B. (magna cum laude), 1953; Duke University, B.D., 1956; further graduate study at Princeton University, 1965-68, and New School for Social Research, 1966; Princeton Theological Seminary, Ph.D. (with honors), 1970. *Politics:* Democrat. *Home:* 7 Bear Ridge Dr., Bloomfield, Conn. 06002. *Office:* Hartford Seminary Foundation, 111 Sherman St., Hartford, Conn. 06105.

CAREER: Ordained United Methodist minister, 1956; assistant pastor of Church of Scotland in Dumfries, Scotland, 1956-57; pastor of Methodist church in Rock Hill, S.C., 1957-61; Duke University, Durham, N.C., Methodist chaplain, 1961-65; Princeton University, Princeton, N.J., lecturer in sociology, 1968; Emory University, Atlanta, Ga., assistant professor, 1968-73, associate professor of sociology and religion, 1973-74, also director of Religious Research Center at Candler School of Theology; Hartford Seminary Foundation, Hartford, Conn., coordinator of research for church and ministry program, 1974—, director of program, 1978—. Member of Bloomfield Human Relations Commission; member of board of directors of Capitol Region Conference of Churches.

MEMBER: American Sociological Association, American Association of University Professors, Society for the Scientific Study of Religion, Religious Research Association (member of board of directors, 1974—), Southern Sociological Society, Phi Beta Kappa. *Awards, honors:* Research grants from United Methodist Church, 1970, 1971, Social Science Research Council, 1971, and Lilly Endowment, 1976, 1976-77.

WRITINGS: (Contributor) Earl D. C. Brewer, editor, *Transcendence and Mystery*, IDOC International Documentation, 1976; (editor and contributor) *Small Churches Can Be Beautiful*, Harper, 1977; (with Douglas W. Johnson and Martin E. Marty) *Religion in America: 1950 to the Present*, Harper, 1978. Contributor of about twenty-five articles and reviews to theology and sociology journals. Member of editorial board of *Review of Religious Research*.

WORK IN PROGRESS: With Robert L. Wilson, *Too Many Shepherds: The Employment Situation of the Clergy;* a book on women clergy in Protestant churches, completion expected in 1982.

SIDELIGHTS: Carroll comments: "During the years that I

was a parish and campus minister, I regularly discovered the importance of sociological perspectives on the church and its functioning. Often I discovered this in retrospect, sometimes painfully. The more I read the more I realized that I wanted to become a sociologist and to function primarily at the intersection of theory and practice. In my teaching and writing I have attempted to draw on sociological perspectives to illuminate aspects of contemporary religious life."

AVOCATIONAL INTERESTS: Breeding Shetland sheepdogs, tennis, cross-country skiing.

* * *

CARROLL, Jeffrey 1950-

PERSONAL: Born April 26, 1950, in Buffalo, N.Y.; son of Glenn Arthur (in sales) and Doris (Kirkgasser) Carroll; married Tamara Lynn Zielinski (a graphic artist), November 24, 1971. *Education:* Reed College, B.A., 1972. *Residence:* Honolulu, Hawaii.

CAREER: Writer.

WRITINGS: Climbing to the Sun, Seabury, 1977.

WORK IN PROGRESS: Three novels, *Safe Joins, The Palm Tree Hanging,* and *White Luck;* a poem cycle, *The Condition of Her.*

* * *

CARROLL, Loren 1904-1978

PERSONAL: Born March 5, 1904, in Scanlon, Minn.; died October 21, 1978, in Chevy Chase, Md.; married Sheila Baker; children: Alexander, Nicholas. *Education:* Attended University of Chicago and Sorbonne, University of Paris. *Residence:* Chevy Chase, Md.

CAREER: International News Service correspondent in Paris, France, 1933-34; *New York Herald Tribune,* Paris, city editor of European edition, 1934-37; *Newsweek,* New York, N.Y., staff member, 1937-40, foreign editor, 1940, chief of Paris bureau, 1945-c.51; public affairs officer for U.S. mission to North Atlantic Treaty Organization (NATO), in London and in Paris; U.S. Government, state department, consul general in Quebec, 1956-60, consul general in Palermo, Italy, 1960-64. Notable assignments include coverage of murder trial of defendants Nathan Leopold and Richard Loeb, 1924. *Military service:* Chief of psychological warfare operations of office of war information in London, and press attache for American diplomatic mission in Algiers and for American Embassy in Paris, all during World War II.

WRITINGS: Wild Onion, Dodd, 1930; *Conversation, Please: A Clinic for Talkers,* Bobbs-Merrill, 1939.

SIDELIGHTS: As a reporter covering the trial of Nathan Leopold and Richard Loeb (the "thrill killers"), the men accused of murdering Bobby Franks, Carroll became friends with defense counselor Clarence Darrow.

Wild Onion reflects the life of Chicago gangster and bootlegger Joe Dulac.

OBITUARIES: Washington Post, October 27, 1978.*

* * *

CARROTT, Richard G. 1924-

PERSONAL: Born July 3, 1924, in Greenwich, Conn.; son of O. Browning (in business) and Jane (Green) Carrott. *Education:* Wesleyan University, B.A. (with distinction), 1950; New York University, M.A., 1955; Yale University, Ph.D.,

1961. *Politics:* "Whig." *Religion:* Roman Catholic. *Home:* La Tourelle, 78730 Rochefort-en-Yvelines, France. *Office:* Department of Art History, University of California, Riverside, Calif. 92506.

CAREER: Sweet Briar College, Sweet Briar, Va., instructor in art history, 1955-58; University of California, Riverside, assistant professor, 1961-67, associate professor, 1967-76, professor of art history, 1976—, head of department, 1962-65, 1971-73, 1977—. Visiting associate professor at University of California, Berkeley, 1969, 1976. National coordinator of Committee to Rescue Indian Art, 1966-67; Riverside Cultural Heritage Board, member, 1971-74, head of board, 1973-74. *Military service:* U.S. Army, Combat Infantry, 1943-45. *Member:* College Art Association of America, Society of Architectural Historians (member of board of directors, 1964-66), Art Historians of Southern California. *Awards, honors:* Comite d'honneur from Societe Augusta, 1965; committee of honor from Metropolitan Museum of Art, 1968, for exhibit "Age of Fresco."

WRITINGS: (Editor) *Thomas Moran, 1837-1926,* University of California, Riverside, 1963; *The Egyptian Revival: Its Monuments, Sources, and Meaning,* University of California Press, 1978. Contributor to *New Catholic Encyclopedia.* Contributor to *Antiques* and architectural history journals.

WORK IN PROGRESS: Marie Antoinette's Hameau at Versailles; The Gothic Revival in France; a monograph on the Church of Rochefort-en-Yvelines.

SIDELIGHTS: Carrott told *CA* that "when not teaching or doing research my life seems mostly to be spent battling with the twentieth century. I find that all change is for the worse."

* * *

CASSAVETES, John 1929-

PERSONAL: Born December 9, 1929, in New York, N.Y.; married Gena Rowlands (an actress), March 19, 1954; children: Nicholas, Alexander, Xan. *Education:* Attended Mohawk College, Colgate University, and New York Academy of Dramatic Art. *Residence:* New York, N.Y.; and Los Angeles, Calif. *Office:* c/o Public Relations, United Artists, 729 Seventh Ave., New York, N.Y. 10017.

CAREER: Actor, screenwriter, and director of motion pictures. Actor in motion pictures, including "Taxi," 1952, "Crime in the Streets," 1957, "The Killers," 1964, "The Dirty Dozen," 1967, "Rosemary's Baby," 1967, "Husbands," 1970, "Mikey and Nicky," 1974, "The Fury," 1978; actor in teleplays, including "The Expendable House," "There Are the Hip and There Are the Square," 1963, and "Murder Case," 1964; also appeared in numerous television programs, including "Philco Goodyear Television Playhouse," "Channing," "Bob Hope Theatre," and "Kraft Mystery Theatre"; starred in television series, "Johnny Staccato," 1959-60; director of motion pictures, including "Shadows," 1960, and "A Child Is Waiting," 1963. *Awards, honors:* Nomination for Academy Award for best supporting actor from Academy of Motion Picture Arts and Sciences, 1967, for "The Dirty Dozen"; five awards from Venice Film Festival, 1968, for "Faces."

WRITINGS—Screenplays; and director: *Faces* (released by Walter Reade Organization, 1968), compiled by Al Ruban, New American Library, 1970; *Minnie and Moskowitz* (released by Universal, 1971), Black Sparrow Press, 1973. Also author of *Husbands* (released in 1970), Scripts Limited.

Unpublished screenplays; all as director: "Shadows," Lion,

1961; (with Richard Carr) "Too Late Blues," Paramount, 1962; "A Woman Under the Influence," 1974; "The Killing of a Chinese Bookie," Faces Distribution Corp., 1976.

SIDELIGHTS: Cassavetes broke into films as an actor specializing in psychopathic young hoodlums. In performances in films such as "The Night Holds Terror" and "Crime in the Streets," he played basically the same character. When he obtained a role outside the "street-crime" genre, as with the western film, "Saddle the Wind," it was also as a psychopathic character. Television offered more of the same for Cassavetes. However, here he also developed a second stereotype: that of the virtuoso composer, intense but sensitive.

While Cassavetes was acting in what Jack Edmund Nolan called "various shoddy productions," he also found time to teach method acting in New York City. The classes were going so well that his students suggested they employ their improvisational exercises in a film. Cassavetes agreed and after obtaining financial support from friends, he filmed "Shadows": the story of a black nightclub singer living with his brother and sister and how they are victimized by racism. With its stark realism and improvisational atmosphere, "Shadows" proved quite successful in Europe, where Cassavetes was hailed as the American new wave equivalent of Jean-Luc Godard. But Cassavetes has insisted that his role was secondary to the actors. "The director is the most expendable person in the film," he claimed. "If you have a good script and good actors, all the director has to do is aim the camera and keep things going. Act as a go between, because what the people really look at on the screen is the people, not what the director did to them."

Following its success in Europe, "Shadows" was released in the United States where it attracted sizeable crowds at art-house theatres. Moguls at Paramount were impressed with the fact that "Shadows" had cost only $40,000 to film and so hired Cassavetes to direct a quality low-budget film for them. He made "Too Late Blues," the story of a struggling jazz pianist. Although Nolan deemed it "perhaps his very best feature," Cassavetes's other critics were ambivalent. His next work, "A Child Is Waiting," was a documentary on retarded children which also featured actors. This film, too, failed to impress critics although Cassavetes was not entirely to blame. Noted for his slow-paced editing, Cassavetes was given only a few weeks to cut the film; studio executives then decided to edit Cassavetes's version still further. The result was a less than successful film.

After "A Child Is Waiting," Cassavetes waited four years, until 1968, to direct another film. Meanwhile, he was repeating his patented psycho-hoodlum roles in various teleplays and films. Finally, in 1965, he even played a role which combined his stereotyped acting talents. According to Nolan, when Cassavetes played in "Free of Charge," he "combined his two personae, the genius composer who was *also* a full-time psychotic." But if Cassavetes was unable to obtain roles aside from composers and psychotics, he at least began to gain recognition for his ability within his confining stereotype. In 1967, he was nominated for an Academy Award for his portrayal of a psychopathic convict-soldier in "The Dirty Dozen." He followed that performance with another one of note in Roman Polanski's "Rosemary's Baby," in which he played an actor who furthers his career by cooperating with a Satanic cult.

When Cassavetes finally returned to directing, it was with the much heralded "Faces." The story of emotional crises in a middle-class couple's marriage received several awards when it was shown at the Venice Film Festival. It also dupli-

cated the atmosphere of "Shadows" as it too was filmed in what would become known as the Cassavetes style: highly improvised acting in a realist manner, filmed on a low-budget, with extensive use of a hand-held camera.

After "Faces," Cassavetes made "Husbands," the story of three men who learn of the death of a close friend and react by going on a drunk-binge. Like the previous films, "Husbands" was also praised for its unique style. But beyond that, it also received attention as a film of social comment. Writing in the *New York Times,* Betty Friedan declared: "'Husbands' zeroes in on the real state of love and sex in our time. It shows the actual crisis between men and women in America today, that is sickly reflected in the elimination of women from the boys-together films and the dehumanized death-of-sex skin flicks." Friedan also observed that the film "confronts the reality of the alienation, loneliness, un-met need for human love and intimacy—the frustrations, hostilities and resentments which pose almost impossible barriers to love between men and women today."

"Husbands" also marked Cassavetes's only major role in one of his own films. Although the role of Gus, one of the three lamenting friends, offered a departure for him from his usual psychopaths and composers, Cassavetes expressed doubts as to whether he'd create another large role for himself. "No, I don't think I'll direct myself again," he remarked. "It doesn't work. When others in the film have a good role you tend to slough off your own. And in a scene, it's very difficult. They will say, 'Are you going to be in this scene too?' . . . So, well, no, I don't think I'll do it again."

Cassavetes's sixth film, "Minnie and Moscowitz," is a comedy about a relationship between two middle-class people: the woman is confused but beautiful, the man is a Jewish "hippie" parking-lot attendant. Vincent Canby called it Cassavetes's most "ambitious film" but expressed disappointment with it as a comedy. "Mr. Cassavetes's use of exaggerated slapstick gestures," observed Canby, "to underscore the loneliness and fears of his characters is more interesting in theory than funny or moving in actual fact."

Canby did applaud Cassavetes's choice of actors though. "As an actor," declared Canby, "he appreciates actors and their mysterious art, as well as their awful dependency on the work of others. This explains why he casts his films so abundantly." Cassavetes revealed his attitude toward actors in an interview with Corinne F. Hammett. "I think it's important that all actors keep open a feeling of innocence," he commented, "a feeling that they don't know everything yet. I don't like professional groups that take this away from an actor, preventing him from being responsive, fresh."

Following the release of "Minnie and Moscowitz," Cassavetes divided his time between two projects: writing a play that would feature his wife, actress Gena Rowlands; and acting, notably in Elaine May's "Mikey and Nicky." Unfortunately for him, neither project was going smoothly. After completing the play, he was informed by his wife that although it was well written, her part was far too demanding to be done on a daily basis. And funds for May's film had run out before she'd completed it. Finally Cassavetes completed a second draft of his play but that too was rejected by his wife. Similarly, "Mikey and Nicky" was rejected by critics after its release in 1974. The story of two old friends involved in the underworld was considered an odd mix of realism and implausibility. May gave the film its realism by shooting it in a style similar to Cassavetes's. However, the film relies on a plot device which features one friend financing a murder-contract on the other, then staying with him to guarantee his death. Considered pretentious and overdone, "Mikey and Nicky" was withdrawn from circulation soon after it had been released.

Meanwhile Cassavetes had completed a third revision for his wife and, like the previous two, it was rejected. "I read it and didn't think I could survive it, mentally," claimed Rowlands in reference to the first version. "It was a demanding role, and to do that every night and then matinees too. I didn't think I could physically handle it." This decision forced Cassavetes to compromise. "So I wrote another play," he recalled, "brought the husband in more, and the family and the children. Then that didn't work out so I wrote a third version. By then we decided to do a movie script instead so I took all three scripts and wrote the fourth."

Cassevetes's perseverence resulted in "A Woman Under the Influence," a film described by Paul Zimmerman as one "flailing away at us with its heavy-breathing hysteria, boring us with its repetitiousness, wounding us to the heart with the tender combat of its loving, hating characters, making us confront our own deepest feelings even as we cry, 'Stop, enough!'" The film is a chronicle of the mental breakdown of Mabel Longhetti, played by Rowlands. The film ends on an ironic note when Mabel returns home after being institutionalized by both her mother-in-law and husband; she is greeted by them upon her return, as Pauline Kael noted, "prepared to do her in all over again."

Kael called the film "a tribute to the depth of feelings that people can't express" and compared Cassavetes's perception of human emotion as akin to Harold Pinter's. "His special talent," wrote Kael, "is for showing intense suffering from nameless causes; Cassavetes and Pinter both give us an actor's view of human misery. It comes out as metaphysical realism: we see the tensions and the power plays but never know the why of anything." Kael's main objection with "A Woman Under the Influence" is the aforementioned obliqueness of motivation. She described Cassavetes's direction as possessing "a muffled quality: his scenes are often unshaped and so rudderless that the meanings don't emerge."

"In a way we took a chance with this movie," said Cassavetes of "A Woman Under the Influence." "It's naive in that sense, because we weren't sure that people would want to see family life, family life with problems, not hyped up. . . ." For most of his filmmaking career, Cassavetes has been taking chances: he risks his reputation by refusing to make cliche-ridden films. "He's always on the verge of hitting the big time," observed Kael, "but his writing and directing are grueling. . . ." Zimmerman agreed. "Every film is a risk," he noted, "but Cassavetes is the biggest gambler around, betting that he can make enough magic out of inspiration and improvisation to keep his characters from boring us to death. For two and a half hours, he wins and loses from scene to scene until, battered, exasperated but close to tears, we surrender."

Cassavetes's most recent film, "The Killing of a Chinese Bookie," did not fare well with many critics. Charles Champlin wrote, "Watching this stumbling story of a strip-joint owner forced into murder to square a gambling debt, you get the impression the film maker could not decide whether to make a 'popular' picture in something close to the gangster tradition, or another of his studies of contemporary American society. . . ." Judith Crist was more direct. She called the film "a mess, as sloppy in concept as it is in execution, as pointless in thesis as it is in concept." Similarly, Frank Rich complained that "the style intentionally obscures what pal-

try drama there is. . . ." However, Jack Kroll found some redeeming things in the film. He called it "a rewarding film that asks only that you stay alert and use your senses." He was also impressed with Cassavetes's growth as a filmmaker. "Visually stunning," he wrote, "stylistically extravagant, this film converts Cassavetes' excesses to a prodigal poetry."

BIOGRAPHICAL/CRITICAL SOURCES: New York Times, January 31, 1971, December 23, 1971; *Playboy,* July, 1971; *Baltimore News-American,* October 27, 1974; *Newsweek,* December 9, 1974, March 15, 1976; *New Yorker,* December 9, 1974; *Films in Review,* December, 1974; *Biography News,* January/February, 1975; *New York Post,* February 16, 1976; *Los Angeles Times,* February 17, 1976; *Saturday Review,* April 3, 1976.*

*   *   *

CATLIN, George E(dward) G(ordon)   1896-1979

OBITUARY NOTICE—See index for *CA* sketch: Born July 29, 1896, in Liverpool, England; died in 1979 in England. Educator, political scientist, editor, and author of about twenty books on political theory and philosophy. Catlin was a drafter of the International Declaration in Support of the Independence of India in 1943, and was adviser to such British political leaders as Arthur Greenwood and Harold Wilson. An expert on Atlantic Community affairs, Catlin was joint founder of the British Commonwealth Association, now the English-Speaking Union. Catlin was co-founder with H. G. Wells of *Realist,* and was co-editor of the magazine from 1929-30. His autobiography was entitled *For God's Sake, Go!* Obituaries and other sources: *The Writers Directory, 1976-78,* St. Martin's, 1976; *Who's Who in the World,* 3rd edition, Marquis, 1976; *The International Who's Who,* Europa, 1978; *Who's Who,* 131st edition, St. Martin's, 1979; *AB Bookman's Weekly,* April 16, 1979.

*   *   *

CHAFFEE, John   1946-

PERSONAL: Born October 24, 1946, in New York, N.Y.; son of Hubert Roe (an engineer and U.S. Coast Guard captain) and Charlotte (Hess) Chaffee; married Heide Lange (a literary agent), May 27, 1974. *Education:* Johns Hopkins University, B.A., 1967; New York University, Ph.D., 1972. *Home:* 102 Christopher St., New York, N.Y. 10014. *Agent:* Heide Lange, Sanford J. Greenburger Associates, Inc., 825 Third Ave., New York, N.Y. 10022.

CAREER: Johns Hopkins Hospital, Baltimore, Md., research assistant at Phipps Psychiatric Clinic, 1966; DuPont Co., London, England, personnel trainee, 1967; New York State Division for Youth, New York City, researcher, 1967-68; Human Resources Administration, New York City, social worker, 1968-78; writer, 1978—. Furniture designer and cabinetmaker, 1972—. Assistant professor at LaGuardia Community College of the City University of New York, 1976—. *Member:* Phi Beta Kappa.

WRITINGS: (Contributor) *Juvenile Delinquency in New York State,* New York State Division for Youth, 1968; *Designing and Making Fine Furniture* (selection of Better Homes and Gardens Book Club, Playboy Book Club, and Macmillan Book Club), A & W Publishers, 1978; (with sister, Judi Culbertson) *Games America Played: An Informal History of Board Games in America,* Scribner, 1979.

WORK IN PROGRESS: Unconscious: Search for Your Inner Self.

SIDELIGHTS: Chaffee writes: "Completing my doctorate in philosophy in 1972, I found that full-time teaching positions were hard to come by. Casting around for a means to supplement my income, I decided on woodworking. Five years later, at the suggestion of my agent, who also doubles as my wife, I wrote a book on woodworking which emphasizes functional elegant designs and simple straightforward techniques. I enjoyed the experience of writing so much that I decided to continue.

"I presently divide my time between writing, teaching philosophy and communication arts, designing and making furniture, restoring early American houses (including my own), collecting antique toys and woodworking tools, and participating actively in a number of sports.

"I believe very strongly that it is important for human beings to develop as many of their potentials as possible. Experiencing the many diverse dimensions of yourself is synergistically productive, avoids the staleness that often accompanies narrow interests, and enhances your vitality and aliveness as a person."

* * *

CHAMBERLIN, J. E(ward) 1943-

PERSONAL: Born June 29, 1943; married Jane Clement; children: two. Education: University of British Columbia, B.A., 1964; Oxford University, B.A., 1966; University of Toronto, Ph.D., 1969. Office: University College, University of Toronto, Toronto, Ontario, Canada M5S 1A1.

CAREER: Writer. Associated with University of Toronto, Toronto, Ontario. Consultant to pipeline agencies.

WRITINGS: The Harrowing of Eden: White Attitudes Toward Native Americans, Seabury, 1975; Ripe Was the Drowsy Hour: The Age of Oscar Wilde, Seabury, 1977.

WORK IN PROGRESS: A book on Arthur Cravan; a book of essays on decadence in the late nineteenth century.

* * *

CHAMBERS, Jane 1937-

PERSONAL: Born March 27, 1937, in Columbia, S.C.; daughter of Carroll J. (an engineer) and Clarice (a bookkeeper; maiden name, Summerour) Chambers. Education: Attended Rollins College, 1953-54, and Pasadena Playhouse, 1955-56; Goddard College, B.A., 1971. Residence: Greenport, N.Y. Agent: Gloria Safier, Inc., 667 Madison Ave., New York, N.Y. 10021.

CAREER: Stage actress, 1956-61; free-lance journalist, 1962-64; WMTW-TV, Poland Spring, Maine, writer and broadcaster, 1964-66; Poland Spring Job Corps Center, Poland Spring, director of avocation, 1967-69; Jersey City Job Corps Center, Jersey City, N.J., director of avocation, 1969-71; television writer and playwright, 1971-77; full-time writer, 1977—.

AWARDS, HONORS: Rosenthal Award from Religious Arts Guild, 1971, for poem, "Ejected"; Connecticut Educational Television Award, 1971, for play, "Christ in a Treehouse"; Eugene O'Neill fellowship, 1972; award from Writers Guild of America, 1973, for "Search for Tomorrow"; award from Office of Advanced Drama Research, 1976, for "The Common Garden Variety"; grant from Creative Artists Public Service Program, 1977.

WRITINGS: Burning (novel), Jove Press, 1978.

Work represented in anthologies, including Along With All the Once Beloved Things (poetry anthology), edited by Jeanne Foster Hill, Worship Arts Clearing House, Unitarian Universalist Association, 1972, and Gay Plays: The First Anthology, edited by William Hoffman, Avon, 1979.

Stage plays: "Tales of the Revolution and Other American Fables" (three-act), first produced in Waterford, Conn., at Eugene O'Neill Memorial Theatre, August, 1972; "Random Violence" (two-act), first produced in New York City at Interart Theatre, March, 1973; "Mine!" (one-act), first produced in New York City at Interart Theatre, May, 1974; "The Wife" (one-act), first produced in New York City at Interart Theatre, May, 1974; "Jamboree" (one-act), first produced in New York City at Town Hall, January, 1974; "A Late Snow" (two-act), first produced in New York City at Clark Center for the Performing Arts, May-June, 1974; "The Common Garden Variety" (two-act), first produced in Los Angeles, Calif., at Mark Taper Laboratory, February, 1976.

Film scripts and television plays include: "Christ in a Treehouse," produced by Connecticut Educational Television, August, 1971; "Curfew," WNYC-TV, January, 1972; "Here Comes the Iceman," 1972; "Grass Roots," 1973; "Gotcha," 1975. Writer for "Search for Tomorrow," serial broadcast on CBS-TV, 1973-74. Contributor to magazines and newspapers.

WORK IN PROGRESS: "The Bluff," a three-act play set in the lesbian subculture; a novel set in the contemporary South.

SIDELIGHTS: Chambers comments: "I write from my experience and interests. I have always felt a strong identification with the underdog and much of my work is set in minority or ethnic subcultures. I am not writing about social injustice—I am writing about specific people who happen to be victims of that injustice. I do not consciously create my characters—I just look up one day and notice that they are standing in front of my typewriter. They are a determined lot who will not budge until I write a story or a play for them to live in. Sometimes I love the process of writing, other times I despise it, but always I must do it. I have never felt I have a choice. To survive, I must eat, sleep, love, and write—though not necessarily in that order."

* * *

CHANCE, Michael R(obin) A(lexander) 1915-

PERSONAL: Born January 19, 1915, in Birmingham, England; son of Clinton Frederick (a farmer and stockbroker) and Janet (an author and social reformer; maiden name, Whyte) Chance; married Marie Eleanor Kohn, November 7, 1942; children: Neil Peter, Clive (deceased), Annette. Education: University of London, B.Sc., 1936; University of Birmingham, Ph.D., 1948, D.Sc., 1957. Religion: Agnostic. Home: Rocks Cottage, Kemerton, Tewkesbury, Gloucestershire, England. Office: School of Medicine, University of Birmingham, Birmingham, England.

CAREER: National Institute for Medical Research, London, England, researcher in endocrinology, 1937-38; Glaxo Laboratories, Greenford, Middlesex, England, pharmacologist, 1938-46; Pioneer Health Centre, Peckham, England, director of laboratory, 1946; University of Birmingham, Birmingham, England, lecturer in experimental pharmacology, 1946-66, reader in ethology, 1966—. Member of University of Sussex Centre for Research in Collective Psychopathology, 1966; research adviser in anthropology at University of California, Berkeley, 1966, 1969; visiting professor at Rutgers University, 1969. Director of ethology laboratories at Uffculme Clinic and All Saints' Hospital, 1958;

honorary adviser in ethology for Birmingham Regional Hospital Board, 1958; honorary research associate of University of London, 1965.

MEMBER: British Pharmacological Society, Society of Experimental Biology, Institute for the Study of Animal Behaviour, Institute of Biology (fellow), Royal Anthropological Institute, British Association for the Advancement of Science (president of anthropology section, 1977), Current Anthropology (associate), Savile Club.

WRITINGS: (With Clifford Jolly) *Social Groups of Monkeys, Apes, and Men,* Dutton, 1970; (editor with R. R. Larsen) *The Social Structure of Attention,* Wiley, 1976.

Contributor: S. L. Washburn, editor, *Social Life of Early Man,* Viking Fund, 1961; Ashley Montagu, editor, *Culture and the Evolution of Man,* Oxford University Press, 1962; C.R.B. Joyce, editor, *Psychopharmacology: Dimensions and Perspectives,* Tavistock Publications, 1968; F. J. Ebling, editor, *Biology and Ethics,* Academic Press, 1969; S. H. Foulkes and G. S. Prince, editors, *Psychiatry in a Changing Society,* Tavistock Publications, 1969; J. Benthall, editor, *The Limits of Human Nature,* Dutton, 1973; Robin Fox, editor, *Biosocial Anthropology,* Malaby Press, 1975; Mario Von Cranach, editor, *Methods of Inference From Animal to Human Behavior,* Aldine, 1977; M. T. McGuire and L. A. Fairbanks, editors, *Ethological Psychiatry: Psychopathology in the Context of Evolutionary Biology,* Grune, 1977; Lionel Tiger and Joan Fowler, editors, *Female Hierarchies,* Aldine, 1978.

Author of "Social Life of a Macaque Colony," a film released by British Film Institute and London Zoo, 1954. Contributor to *Handbook of Psychopharmacology.* Contributor of nearly seventy articles and reviews to scientific, medical, and social science journals, and to popular magazines, including *Man* and *Nature.*

WORK IN PROGRESS: Continuing research on the social structure of attention, modes of operation of intelligence, and ethology of cognition.

SIDELIGHTS: Chance writes: "As a biologist I have more and more realized the imbalance of information which the pattern of current research supplies to us on the subject as a whole. A particular deficit lies in the field of the organism's powers and ways of adaptation to its environment which, in the higher primates and man in particular, becomes converted into powers of creation, based on intelligence or the ability to base behaviour on *awareness* of reality. This power originally deployed on the external environment is now being redeployed on awareness of self and the social relations and enhances the individual's powers of personality growth. Insight into the way this takes place is assisted by the recognition of two modes of mental operation, the agonic and hedonic (subject of my later publications), originally discovered through the study of the social structure of attention. Human rights supporting the freedom of thought by individuals are the preconditions for the growth of intelligence which itself is made possible by the worldwide dissemination of information and the freedom of individuals to have access to it."

* * *

CHARBONNEAU, Louis (Henry) 1924-
(Carter Travis Young)

PERSONAL: Born January 20, 1924, in Detroit, Mich.; son of Louis Henry (a lawyer) and Mary Ellen (Young) Charbonneau; married Hilda Sweeney, December 15, 1945. *Edu-*

cation: University of Detroit, A.B., 1948, M.A., 1950. *Politics:* Democrat. *Home:* 1015 Cynthia Ave., Pasadena, Calif. 91107. *Agent:* Scott Meredith Literary Agency, Inc., 845 Third Ave., New York, N.Y. 10022. *Office:* Security World Publishing Co., 2639 South La Cienega Blvd., Los Angeles, Calif. 90034.

CAREER: University of Detroit, Detroit, Mich., instructor in English, 1948-52; Mercury Advertising Agency, Los Angeles, Calif., copywriter, 1952-56; *Los Angeles Times,* Los Angeles, staff writer, 1956-71; free-lance writer, 1971-74; Security World Publishing Co., Los Angeles, book editor, 1974—. *Military service:* U.S. Army Air Forces, 1943-46; became staff sergeant. *Member:* Western Writers of America.

WRITINGS—Novels; under name Louis Charbonneau: *No Place on Earth,* Doubleday, 1958; *Night of Violence,* Dodd, 1959; *Nor All Your Tears,* Dodd, 1959; *Corpus Earthling,* Zenith, 1960; *The Sentinel Stars,* Bantam, 1963; *Psychedelic-40,* Avon, 1965; *Way Out,* Avon, 1966; *Down to Earth,* Bantam, 1967; *The Sensitives* (novelization), Bantam, 1968; *Down From the Mountain,* Doubleday, 1969; *And Hope to Die,* Ace Books, 1970; *Barrier World,* Lancer Books, 1970; *From a Dark Place,* Dell, 1974; *Embryo* (novelization), Warner Paperback, 1976; *Intruder* (Reader's Digest Condensed Book Club selection), Doubleday, 1979; *The Lair,* Fawcett, 1979; *The Macimer File,* Doubleday, 1980.

Western novels; under pseudonym Carter Travis Young: *The Wild Breed,* Doubleday, 1960; *Shadow of a Gun,* Fawcett, 1961; *The Savage Plain,* Doubleday, 1962; *The Bitter Iron,* Doubleday, 1964; *Long Boots, Hard Boots,* Doubleday, 1965; *Why Did They Kill Charlie?,* Doubleday, 1967; *Winchester Quarantine,* Doubleday, 1970; *The Pocket Hunters,* Doubleday, 1972; *Winter of the Coup,* Doubleday, 1972; *The Captive,* Doubleday, 1973; *Blaine's Law,* Doubleday, 1974; *Guns of Darkness,* Doubleday, 1975; *Red Grass,* Doubleday, 1976; *Winter Drift,* Doubleday, 1980.

Author of radio and television plays, including scripts for "Outer Limits."

SIDELIGHTS: Charbonneau told *CA:* "I think of myself as a professional writer and a storyteller rather than as a carrier of messages. At the same time I find that many of my novels turn upon what Joseph Conrad once called the 'moral pivot.' My first novel, *No Place on Earth,* dealt with questions raised by a situation in which the world's overpopulation had led inevitably to population control. (Perhaps understandably, that book has remained continuously in print in Japan for twenty years.) My first western, *The Wild Breed,* dealt with a middle-aged man who came to a violent Western town simply to claim the body of his son, a gunfighter, but who, against his nature, was forced into violent action himself. One of my most recent novels, *Intruder,* is a contemporary story which dramatizes the potential for mischief in a computerized society which as yet lacks adequate security for the technology it has created. Moral pivots these stories may have, but in my own mind they are primarily 'entertainments,' to borrow Graham Greene's felicitous word.

"I like to write of the West because it is a marvelously enduring myth, and because there are such limitless possibilities for strong drama in a fictional world where right and wrong, honor and dishonor, are so clearly perceived. My early speculative fiction tended to be projections of contemporary problems into a possible future time, social rather than scientific explorations.

"My characters, whether of the past, present, or future, are usually average people rather than giants, caught up (often reluctantly) in crises not of their own choosing. *The Macimer File* is a story about a career FBI man who is forced to reexamine what has happened to himself, to the Bureau and to the public's perception of it over the past twenty years or so. Having said that, I must add that the story is a novel of suspense, not a tract. When they work, such stories may help us to understand who and what we are, but they do so by engaging the emotions on behalf of imaginary lives."

One of Charbonneau's novels, *Corpus Earthling*, was adapted for the television series "Outer Limits."

BIOGRAPHICAL/CRITICAL SOURCES: *Roundup*, February, 1977; *New York Times Book Review*, April 22, 1979.

* * *

CHARLES-ROUX, Edmonde 1920-

PERSONAL: Born April 17, 1920, in Neuilly-sur-Seine, France; daughter of Francois (an ambassador) and Gounelle (Sabine) Charles-Roux; married Gaston Defferre (mayor of Marseille, France). *Education:* Marseille Hospital, diploma in nursing, 1940. *Politics:* Socialist Party. *Religion:* Catholic. *Home:* 7 rue des St. Peres, Paris 64, France. *Agent:* Georges Borchardt, 145 East 52nd St., New York, N.Y. 10022.

CAREER: *Elle*, Paris, France, columnist, 1946-48; *French Vogue*, Paris, columnist, 1948-52, editor-in-chief, 1952-66; writer. *Wartime service:* Served as nurse in French Army, 1940. *Awards, honors:* Croix de guerre, 1940, 1945: Prix Goncourt, 1966, for *Oublier Palerme*.

WRITINGS—In English: *Oublier Palerme* (novel), Grasset, 1966, translation by Helen Eustis published as *To Forget Palermo*, Delacorte, 1968; *L'Irreguliere: ou mon itineraire Chanel*, Grasset, 1974, translation by Nancy Amphoux published as *Chanel: Her Life, Her World, and the Woman Behind the Legend She Herself Created*, Knopf, 1975.

Other: *Don Juan d'Autriche, 1547-1578*, Del Duca, 1959; *Guide du savoir vivre*, Grasset, 1965; *Elle, Adrienne*, Grasset, 1971; *Les Femmes et le travail du moyen-age a nos jours*, Editions de la Courtille, 1975.

WORK IN PROGRESS: A photo album of the life of Gabrielle Chanel, for Chene.

SIDELIGHTS: Charles-Roux's first novel, *To Forget Palermo*, winner of the Prix Goncourt, "is not only a work of great literary beauty, but an eminently readable novel as well—two qualities that do not often concur in French prize novels," noted a *Publishers Weekly* reviewer. It is a saga beginning with two Sicilian families, one of noble heritage, the other of tougher stock, who eventually settle in the Italian section of New York City. The "young Italian-American politician's rise," wrote the reviewer, "is as pithy and pungent as the late Edwin O'Connor's delineation of the Boston Irish political scene. This is a novel that goes right to the heart of the conflict between the old and the new, the folk yearnings of an ancient ancestry and the pragmatism of 20th century America."

Chanel: Her Life, Her World, Charles-Roux's latest book to be translated into English, was met with conflicting reviews. A critic for *Publishers Weekly* said, "The book, a top bestseller in France, has intelligence and width of cultural reference that would make it absorbing even if its subject were unworthy of them which is not the case." *New York Times* reviewer Rachael Billington instead found the author's style of writing "irritating." She further commented: "A certain kind of high-flown French does not come out well in English.

The verbosity and an awful tone of self-congratulation often blurs any real sense of what was going on. This would, no doubt, have pleased Chanel, who apparently took endless pains, including straightforward lying, to hide her background and real self.... All is circumlocution, padding, 19th-century pomposity," which, Billington added, is "in depressing contradiction to everything Chanel herself stood for." Charles-Roux told *CA* that because of the popularity of the book in Europe, she has been in great demand as a speaker at cultural centers and universities there.

Charles-Roux was wounded twice while in nurse's training during World War II and twice was awarded the Croix de Guerre. Besides *Chanel*, editions of *To Forget Palermo* and *Elle Adrienne* have also appeared in other European countries.

BIOGRAPHICAL/CRITICAL SOURCES: *Times Literary Supplement*, March 2, 1967; *Publishers Weekly*, April 1, 1968, September 8, 1975; *Kirkus Reviews*, April 1, 1968, August 15, 1975; *Book World (Washington Post)*, May 26, 1968, August 31, 1975; *Harper's*, June 1, 1968; *Saturday Review*, June 8, 1968; *Best Sellers*, July 1, 1968; *New York Times Book Review*, July 14, 1968, November 2, 1975; *Listener*, September 26, 1968; *Booklist*, July 15, 1975, November 1, 1975; *Books and Bookmen*, December, 1976; *West Coast Review of Books*, March, 1977.

* * *

CHARVET, John 1938-

PERSONAL: Born June 21, 1938, in Cairo, Egypt; son of Guy (a banker) and Nadege (Off) Charvet; married Barbara Keeling (a teacher), August 7, 1964; children: Guy, Emma. *Education:* Cambridge University, B.A., 1960; Oxford University, B.Phil., 1962. *Politics:* Conservative. *Home:* 6 Croftdown Rd., London NW5 1EH, England. *Office:* Department of Government, London School of Economics and Political Science, University of London, London WC2A 2AE, England.

CAREER: London School of Economics and Political Science, London, England, assistant lecturer, 1965-67, lecturer in political philosophy and history of political philosophy, 1967—.

WRITINGS: *The Social Problem in the Philosophy of Rousseau*, Cambridge University Press, 1974. Contributor to philosophy and political science journals.

WORK IN PROGRESS: A book on freedom and equality; research for a book on feminism.

BIOGRAPHICAL/CRITICAL SOURCES: *Times Literary Supplement*, July 26, 1974.

* * *

CHASE, James S(taton) 1932-

PERSONAL: Born July 2, 1932, in Richmond, Va.; son of Francis Seabury (an educator) and Sue (Elder) Chase. *Education:* College of William and Mary, B.A., 1953; University of Chicago, M.A., 1957, Ph.D., 1962. *Politics:* Democrat. *Religion:* Episcopalian. *Home:* 1606 West Center St., Fayetteville, Ark. 72701. *Office:* Department of History, University of Arkansas, Fayetteville, Ark. 72701.

CAREER: University of Texas, Austin, assistant professor of history, 1961-68; University of Arkansas, Fayetteville, associate professor, 1968-73, professor of history, 1973—, chairman of department, 1970-76. Member of Arkansas Bicentennial Commission, 1973-76; member of state board of directors of Arkansas Humanities Program, 1974-76. *Military service:* U.S. Army, 1954-55. *Member:* American Historical Association, Organization of American Historians, Southern Historical Association, Southwestern Social Science Association, Arkansas Historical Association, Arkansas Association of College History Teachers (president, 1974-76).

WRITINGS: The Emergence of the Presidential Nominating Convention, 1789-1832, University of Illinois Press, 1973. Contributor to history and social science journals.

WORK IN PROGRESS: A biography of William Wirt.

* * *

CHATWIN, (Charles) Bruce 1940-

PERSONAL: Born May 13, 1940, in Great Britain; son of Charles Leslie (a lawyer) and Margarita (Turnell) Chatwin; married Elizabeth Chanler, 1965. *Education:* Attended private secondary school in Marlborough, England. *Home:* Holwell Farm, Ozleworth, Wotton-under-Edge, Gloucestershire, England.

CAREER: Sotheby & Co. (art auctioneers), Great Britain, picture expert, 1958-66, director, beginning 1965. Writer. *Awards, honors:* Hawthornden Prize, 1978, for *In Patagonia.*

WRITINGS: In Patagonia (travel adventure), J. Cape, 1977, Summit Books, 1978. Contributor to London newspapers.

WORK IN PROGRESS: Slave Trade to Brazil.

SIDELIGHTS: Chatwin's South American quest story, *In Patagonia,* evolves around the search for a piece of giant sloth skin. Tom Zito praised "the scope of Chatwin's vision" as it provided readers with "a veritable liberal arts education." Zito called the book "a good text in what's best about travel writing."

BIOGRAPHICAL/CRITICAL SOURCES: Washington Post Book World, July 26, 1978.

* * *

CHESS, Stella 1914-

PERSONAL: Born March 1, 1914, in New York, N.Y.; daughter of Benjamin and Clara (Schwartzman) Chess; married Alexander Thomas, June 28, 1938; children: Joan, Richard, Leonard, Kenneth. *Education:* Smith College, B.A., 1935; New York University, M.D., 1939; postdoctoral study at New York Medical College, 1946-49. *Home:* 10 Mitchell Pl., New York, N.Y. 10017. *Office:* 333 East 49th St., New York, N.Y. 10017.

CAREER: Bellevue Hospital, New York City, extern in pediatric psychiatry, 1939-40; Montefiore Hospital, New York City, intern, 1940-41; Grasslands Hospital, Valhalla, N.Y., resident in psychiatry, 1941; private practice of pediatric psychiatry in New York City, 1942—. Resident in psychiatry at Pleasantville Cottage School, 1941-45, and Riverdale Children's Association, 1942-54; psychiatrist at Northside Center for Child Development, 1946-47, chief coordinating psychiatrist, 1947-58; attending psychiatrist at Metropolitan Hospital, 1958-60, director of child psychiatry clinic, 1960-66; associate attending psychiatrist at New York University Medical Center; visiting psychiatrist at Bird S. Coler Hospital, 1958-66, and Bellevue Hospital, 1966—. Associated with New York Medical College, 1949-54, professor, 1954-66, director of child psychiatry, 1960-66; professor at New York University. *Member:* American Psychiatric Association (fellow), American Orthopsychiatric

Association (fellow), American Academy of Child Psychiatry (fellow; charter member), American Women's Medical Association, Society for Research in Child Development, New York Society for Clinical Psychiatry.

WRITINGS: An Introduction to Child Psychiatry, Grune, 1959, 2nd edition, 1969; (with Herbert G. Birch and husband, Alexander Thomas) *Your Child Is a Person: A Psychological Approach to Parenthood Without Guilt,* Viking, 1965; (with Birch and Thomas) *Temperament and Behavior Disorders in Children,* New York University Press, 1968; (editor) *Annual Progress in Child Psychiatry and Child Development,* nine volumes, Brunner, 1968-76; (with Thomas) *The Origin of Personality,* W. H. Freeman, 1970; (with Sam J. Korn and Paulina B. Fernandez) *Psychiatric Disorders of Children With Congenital Rubella,* Brunner, 1971; (with Jane Whitbread) *How to Help Your Child Get the Most Out of School,* Doubleday, 1974; (with Thomas) *Temperament and Development,* Brunner, 1977; (with Whitbread) *Daughters: From Infancy to Independence,* Doubleday, 1978. Also author of *Behavior Individuality in Early Childhood,* 1963. Contributor to medical journals. Editor of *Journal of Autism and Childhood Schizophrenia,* 1972-73; associate editor of *Journal of the American Academy of Child Psychiatry,* 1975—.

WORK IN PROGRESS: Continuing research on individual behavioral characteristics of children, mentally retarded children, and children with congenital rubella.

* * *

CHEVALIER, Louis 1911-

PERSONAL: Born May 29, 1911, in Vendee, France; son of Jules (a merchant) and Leontine (Maillard) Chevalier. *Education:* Attended Ecole Normale Superieure, 1932. *Home:* 71 Rue du Cardinal Lemoine, 75005 Paris, France. *Office:* Department of History, College de France, Place Marcelin Berthelot, 75005 Paris, France.

CAREER: Professor at Institut d'Etudes Politiques of University of Paris; College of France, Paris, professor of history, 1958—. Technical adviser to Seine Prefecture. President of scientific council of International Center for the Study of Human Problems (Monaco); member of Economic and Social Council of District of Paris. *Member:* Institut National d'Etudes Demographiques. *Awards, honors:* Honorary degree from Columbia University.

WRITINGS—In English: *Classes laborieuses et classes dangereuses a Paris pendant la premiere moitie du dix-neuvieme siecle,* Plon, 1958, translation by Frenk Jellinek published as *Laboring Classes and Dangerous Classes in Paris During the First Half of the Nineteenth Century,* Fertig, 1973.

Other works: *Documents sur l'immigration,* Presses universitaires de France, 1947; *Les Paysans: Etude d'histoire et d'economie rurales,* Societe des editions Denoel, 1947; *Le Probleme demographique nord-africain,* Presses universitaires de France, 1947; *Histoire del vingtieme siecle* (title means "History of the Twentieth Century"), three volumes, Cours de droit, 1949; *Problemes de la population,* three volumes, Cours de droit, 1950; *La Formation de la population parisienne au dix-neuvieme siecle,* Presses universitaires de France, 1950; *Demographie generale,* Dalloz, 1951; *Madagascar: Populations et ressources,* Presses universitaires de France, 1952; (editor) *Le Cholera: La Premiere Epidemie du dix-neuvieme siecle–Etude collective,* Impr. centrale de l'Ouest, 1958; *Les Parisiens* (title means "The Parisians"), Hachette, 1967; (with Pierre Billard) *Cinema et civilisation,* three volumes, Cours de droit, 1968; *Histoire anachronique des francais,* Plon, 1973; *L'Assassinat de Paris,* Calmann Levy, 1977.

WORK IN PROGRESS: A study of pleasure and crime in Montmartre.

SIDELIGHTS: Two traits remain constant among the many subjects Chevalier treats in his studies of Paris. First of all, he prefers the qualitative fact over the quantitative; the image and the anecdote over statistics and surveys. Secondly, to strengthen his perspective of history, Chevalier reads historical documents in the light of great literary works, and vice versa.

*　　*　　*

CHICAGO, Judy 1939-

PERSONAL: Original name, Judy Cohen; name legally changed; born July 20, 1939, in Chicago, Ill.; daughter of Arthur M. (a union organizer) and May (a medical secretary; maiden name, Levenson) Cohen; married Jerry Gerowitz, 1961 (died, 1965); married Lloyd Hamrol, 1970 (divorced, 1979). *Education:* University of California, Los Angeles, B.A., 1962, M.A., 1964. *Residence:* Santa Monica, Calif. *Agent:* Peri Winkler, 535 Evelyn, Beverly Hills, Calif.

CAREER: Artist and writer. California State University, Fresno, assistant professor and founder of women's art program, 1969-71; California Institute of the Arts, Valencia, member of faculty and co-founder of feminist art program, 1971-73; Feminist Studio Workshop, Los Angeles, Calif., founder and instructor, 1973-74. Work featured in exhibitions, including Pasadena Museum of Art, 1969, Kenmore Galleries, 1974, JPL Fine Arts, 1975, Quay Ceramics, 1976, Ruth S. Schaffner Gallery, 1977. Organizer and co-curator of "Visible/Invisible" exhibit, Long Beach Museum of Art, 1972; co-director of "Womanhouse," 1972; co-founder of Womanspace, an alternative women's art gallery, 1972, and Woman's Building, an alternative arts institution, 1974. *Member:* Phi Beta Kappa. *Awards, honors:* Tamarind fellowship, 1972; Named Outstanding Woman of the Year in Art by *Mademoiselle,* 1973; grants from National Endowment for the Arts, 1976, 1977.

WRITINGS: Through the Flower: My Struggle as a Woman Artist, Doubleday, 1975; (and artist) *The Dinner Party: A Symbol of Our Heritage,* Anchor, 1979.

WORK IN PROGRESS: The Dinner Party Needlework, for Anchor.

SIDELIGHTS: Chicago is highly regarded in the art community, both as a feminist and as an artist. "Chicago was the first all-out feminist artist of the new movement," declared Lucy R. Lippard, "the first to get it together as a painter, a woman, and a political force; and the first with enough vision, energy, intelligence, and emotion to build a community of female peers, independent of the established art world that has heartily rejected women's art for so long." However, Chicago told Jan Butterfield that she is not a separatist-feminist. "Look, I think that there are some separatist feminists," she acknowledged, "but I don't think that there are a whole lot of them. I think that most feminists are interested in remaking the world, in new terms. It is not that we don't want to work with men: we just won't let men work with us in the old way. If they work with us, they cannot bring authoritarianism and dominance into the group. I think that women need to gain full control until men make changes."

Chicago's first book, *Through the Flower: My Struggle as a Woman Artist,* was cited by Adrienne Rich as "important

... for the future of education; it examines the woman teacher/woman student relationship, the imagery and skills and self-knowledge that can develop in a women's studio...." Lippard wrote, "Actually it is two books: an event-filled autobiography, which oozes with the juices of real life; and a concise summary of the development and sources of recent women's art—probably the best summary published so far...."

Chicago told *CA:* "*The Dinner Party* is a tribute to women in Western civilization. A monumental sculpture, *The Dinner Party* is a symbolic history of women's achievements and struggles told through thirty-nine china-painted plates and elaborately embroidered runners which cover a triangular table. The table rests on a porcelain tile floor which has inscribed the names of 999 historically important women. I worked on this traveling museum exhibition for five years and it was executed in cooperation with a working community of 400 women and men." "The studio and the project are *not collaborative,*" she asserted in an interview. "They are cooperative." She also added, "Everybody has an equal voice in this project, but *I retain aesthetic control.* In other words, if I don't like something, that is the bottom line." But she also insisted that she was not an authoritarian. "I try and give people a tremendous amount of space to make their own decisions and to take their own responsibilities. I want them to extend themselves, to bring their own ideas into it."

BIOGRAPHICAL/CRITICAL SOURCES: Partisan Review, Volume XLII, number 1, 1975; *Village Voice,* March 24, 1975; *Ms.,* August, 1975; *New West,* August 1, 1977; *Los Angeles Times,* April 6, 1978; *The Spokeswoman,* June 15, 1978; *ARTnews,* January, 1979; *Mother Jones,* January, 1979; *Newsweek,* April 2, 1979.

*　　*　　*

CHICOREL, Marietta

PERSONAL: Born in Vienna, Austria; came to United States in 1939, naturalized citizen, 1945; daughter of Paul (a manufacturer) and Margaret (Gross) Selby; married Albert Chicorel, April 26, 1942 (divorced, 1961). *Education:* Wayne State University, B.A., 1952; University of Michigan, M.A.L.S., 1960. *Home:* 275 Central Park W., #14-D, New York, N.Y. 10024. *Office:* Chicorel Library Publishing Corp., 275 Central Park W., New York, N.Y. 10024.

CAREER: University of Washington, Seattle, assistant chief acquisitions librarian, 1962-66; R. R. Bowker Co., New York City, chief editor of *Ulrich's International Periodicals Directory,* 1966-68; Crowell Collier Macmillan Information Sciences, Inc., New York City, project director, 1968-69; Queens College of the City University of New York, Flushing, N.Y., assistant professor of library science, 1971-73; Chicorel Library Publishing Corp., New York City, president, 1969— . Head of Library Material Price Index Commission, 1965-68; member of board of governors of Book League of New York, 1975— . Member of Washington Committee on the Status of Women, 1963-65. *Member:* American Library Association (member of Technical Services Division executive board, 1965-68; member of council, 1969-73), American Society for Information Sciences, Pacific Northwest Library Association, New York Library Club, New York Technical Services Librarians.

*WRITINGS—*Editor; all published by Chicorel Library Publishing: *Chicorel Theater Index to Plays in Anthologies, Periodicals, Discs, and Tapes,* two volumes, 1970-71; *Chicorel Theater Index to Plays in Collections, Anthologies, Periodicals, and Discs in England: Plays in Print and on Records*

Published in England, 1972; *Chicorel Bibliography to the Performing Arts*, 1972; *Chicorel Index to Poetry in Collections in Print, on Discs and Tapes: Poetry on Discs, Tapes, and Cassettes*, 1972; *Chicorel Theater Index to Plays in Anthologies, Periodicals, Discs, and Tapes*, 1973.

Chicorel Index to Poetry in Anthologies and Collections in Print, four volumes, 1974; *Chicorel Theater Index to Plays for Young People in Periodicals, Anthologies, and Collections*, 1974; *Chicorel Bibliography to Books on Music and Musicians*, 1974; *Chicorel Index to Abstracting and Indexing Services: Periodicals in Humanities and the Social Sciences*, two volumes, 1974, 2nd edition, 1978; *Chicorel Index to Short Stories in Anthologies and Collections*, four volumes, 1974, revised edition, two volumes, 1977; *Chicorel Index to the Crafts: Needlework, Crochet to Tie-Dyeing*, 1974; *Chicorel Index to Reading Disabilities: An Annotated Guide*, 1974; *Chicorel Index to Biographies*, two volumes, 1974.

Chicorel Index to Poetry in Anthologies and Collections: Retrospective, four volumes, 1975; *Chicorel Index to the Spoken Arts on Discs, Tapes, and Cassettes*, four volumes, 1975, new edition, 1977; *Chicorel Index to the Crafts: Glass, Enamel, Metal*, 1975; *Chicorel Index to the Crafts: Education, Recreation, and Therapy*, 1975; *Chicorel Index to Environment and Ecology*, two volumes, 1975; *Chicorel Index to Urban Planning and Environmental Design*, two volumes, 1975; *Chicorel Index to Learning Disorders: Books*, two volumes, 1975, 1977 annual, 1977; *Chicorel Index to Poetry and Poets: Literature*, two volumes, 1975; *Chicorel Theater Index to Drama: Literature*, 1975; *Chicorel Theater Index to Drama: Books and Periodicals*, 1975; *Chicorel Index to Film Literature*, two volumes, 1975.

Chicorel Abstracts to Reading and Learning Disabilities: Periodicals, 1976, 1976 annual, 1976, 1977 annual, 1977; *Chicorel Index to Mental Health Book Reviews*, 1976, 1977 annual, 1977; *Chicorel Index to the Crafts: Ceramics, Leather, Wood*, 1977; *Chicorel Index to Parapsychology and the Occult: Books*, 1977; *Chicorel Theater Index to Plays in Anthologies, 1970-1976*, 1976, 1976 annual, 1976, 1977 annual, 1977; *Chicorel Index to Video: Tapes and Cassettes*, 1977; *Chicorel Index to Literary Criticism: Prose*, three volumes, 1978; *Chicorel Index to Poetry, 1974-1977*, two volumes, 1979.

Contributor to library journals.

WORK IN PROGRESS: Additional volumes in the "Chicorel Index" series.

SIDELIGHTS: Chicorel writes: "As a publisher to librarians, I feel a great deal of satisfaction in furthering the aims of the profession to which I also belong. I work out the titles to be published with the advice of librarians in the field and my former colleagues. At their request we are providing bibliographic coverage where it did not adequately exist before; and new fields are added to our indexing services as the literature, and demand for access to it, grows. Also, the system of indexing is flexible enough to give support in the best manner possible in each area."

AVOCATIONAL INTERESTS: Hiking, bicycling, jogging, attending theater and musical events.

*   *   *

CINBERG, Bernard L.   1905-1979

OBITUARY NOTICE: Born in 1905; died May 13, 1979, in New York, N.Y. Obstetrician, gynecologist, conservationist, educator, and author. Cinberg was a staff physician at Roosevelt Hospital and the New York Infirmary, as well as professor emeritus at French and Polyclinic Hospital. His conservation work included efforts to save the Neversink River, a popular trout stream in the Catskills, from the pollution caused by the construction of Neversink Reservoir. He was named New York State's Conservationist of the Year in 1975. Cinberg wrote twenty novels under various pseudonyms, three medical textbooks under his own name, and a popular book on obstetrics and gynecology called *For Women Only.* Obituaries and other sources: *New York Times*, May 16, 1979.

*   *   *

CLARK, George Norman   1890-1979

OBITUARY NOTICE—See index for *CA* sketch: Born February 27, 1890, in Halifax, England; died in 1979. Historian, educator, editor, and author of over twenty books on British and European history. Clark was a professor of history at both Oxford University and Cambridge University and, in 1943, became Regius Professor of Modern History at Cambridge. Knighted in 1953, Clark was the editor of the fifteen volume series, *The Oxford History of England.* Obituaries and other sources: *The Author's and Writer's Who's Who*, 6th edition, Burke's Peerage, 1971; *The International Who's Who*, Europa, 1978; *Who's Who*, 131st edition, St. Martin's, 1979; *AB Bookman's Weekly*, April 16, 1979.

*   *   *

CLAVEL, Maurice   1920-1979

OBITUARY NOTICE: Born in 1920; died of a heart attack, April 23, 1979, in Vezelay, France. Writer, political activist, and the Resistance commander who liberated Chartres and greeted Charles de Gaulle on the cathedral steps. Clavel also took a leading role in the French student revolt of 1968, and was the author of a weekly column in *Le Nouvel Observateur.* His other writings include the novels *Le Jardin de Djemila* and *Saint Euloge de Cardoue*, and numerous critical and political essays. Obituaries and other sources: *Chicago Tribune*, April 29, 1979; *Newsweek*, May 7, 1979.

*   *   *

CLEGG, Alexander Bradshaw   1909-
(Alec Clegg)

PERSONAL: Born June 13, 1909, in Sawley, Derbyshire, England; son of Samuel (a school principal) and Mary (Bradshaw) Clegg; married Jessie Coverdale Phillips, September 14, 1940; children: Andrew Samuel, John, Peter Alexander. *Education:* Clare College, Cambridge, B.A., 1931; Institute of Education, London, M.A., 1936. *Politics:* "I have voted in rotation for all three major parties." *Home address:* Dam Lane, Saxton, Tadcaster, Yorkshire LS24 9QF, England.

CAREER: Assistant schoolmaster in London, England, 1932-36; Birmingham Education Authority, Birmingham, England, administrative assistant, 1936-39; Cheshire Education Authority, Chester, England, assistant education officer, 1939-42; Worcestershire Education Authority, Worcester, England, deputy education officer, 1942-45; West Riding Education Authority, Wakefield, England, deputy education officer, 1945, chief education officer, 1945-74; writer and researcher, 1974—. Past member of Furniture Development Council and Council for Industrial Design; past member of council of Open University; member of board of trustees of Darlington Hall Trust; chairman of board of governors of Centre for Education and Advice on Educational Disadvantage. *Member:* Chief Education Officers Association (president, 1965). *Awards, honors:* Smith-Mundt scholarship, 1954; Etoile noire, French Legion d'Honneur, 1960; named Knight Bachelor, 1965; LL.D., University of Leeds, and DL.H., Loughborough University of Technology, both, 1972; LL.D., University of Bradford, 1979.

WRITINGS: (Editor) *The Excitement of Writing,* Chatto & Windus, 1964, Schocken, 1972; *The Middle School: A Symposium,* Schoolmaster Publishing, 1967; (with Barbara Megson; under name Alec Clegg) *Children in Distress,* Penguin, 1968, 2nd edition, 1973; *Recipe for Failure,* National Children's Home, 1972; (editor) *The Changing Primary School: Teachers Speak on Adapting to New Ways,* Schocken, 1972 (published in England as *The Changing Primary School: Its Problems and Priorities–A Statement by Teachers,* Chatto & Windus, 1972); (editor) *Enjoying Writing,* Chatto & Windus, 1973. Contributor to education journals.

WORK IN PROGRESS: Studying the problems of the disadvantaged child.

SIDELIGHTS: Clegg writes: "I believe that Western civilization is too concerned with the bright child and insufficiently concerned with the child of below-average ability, and if no change occurs in this attitude it will lead to social disaster. One of the absurdities of Western education is that we teach what can be marked and measured. We attach importance to this kind of grading and overlook the more important aspects of a child's education—his loves and his hates, his sympathies and his antipathies, his imagination, his compassion, his sensitivity. We put our emphasis on what the child knows rather than on the sort of person he is growing into. Yet in every group of children anywhere on earth there will be one who is least liked, one who is the most timid, one who is least articulate, one who likes his teacher least, and so on. It is these and points like them which matter far more than the information which can be pushed into him."

AVOCATIONAL INTERESTS: Travel.

* * *

CLEMENS, Virginia Phelps 1941-

PERSONAL: Born April 7, 1941, in Bronxville, N.Y.; daughter of James F. (in real estate) and Florence (Bassford) Phelps; married Douglas Clemens (in sales), June 22, 1961; children: Ted, Greg, Shari. *Education:* Attended Syracuse University, 1959-61, and Trenton State College, 1968. *Home:* 218 Green Dr., Churchville, Pa. 18966.

CAREER: Council Rock School District, Bucks County, Pa., in public relations, 1971-76; writer, 1977—.

WRITINGS: A Horse in Your Backyard (juvenile), Westminster, 1977; *Super Animals and Their Unusual Careers* (juvenile), Westminster, 1979.

WORK IN PROGRESS: A book for teenage girls.

SIDELIGHTS: Clemens commented: "I strongly object to writers who do not write for readers. Whether it is to entertain or to inform, I feel that a writer's main concern should be to be read. To be read and to be accurate (not to impress with big words and difficult phrases) are my primary objectives whether I am writing a book, an article, or a press release."

* * *

CLEVELAND, Carles 1952-

PERSONAL: Born March 8, 1952, in Miami, Fla.; son of Jonas and Zephanorah (Williams) Cleveland; children: La-

Shone E. *Education:* Attended Bernard M. Baruch College of the City University of New York, 1970-72. *Home:* 400 West 43rd St., #41P, New York, N.Y. 10036. *Agent:* Curtis Brown, Ltd., 575 Madison Ave., New York, N.Y. 10022. *Office:* 523 West 121st St., #41, New York, N.Y. 10027.

CAREER: Al Fann Theatrical Ensemble, New York, N.Y., stage manager, 1972-74. Actor in motion pictures, including "The Wiz," 1978, and "Slow Dancing in the Big City," 1978, and stage productions, including "Hail Hail the Gangs!" "Anna Lucasta," "A Raisin in the Sun," and "In Splendid Error." Also actor in television commercials. Vice-president and secretary of Cleveland-de Jongh Associates, Inc. Writer. *Member:* American Federation of Television and Radio Artists (AFTRA), Screen Actors Guild, Writers Guild of America, East, Harlem Writers' Guild, Frederick Douglass Creative Arts Center. *Awards, honors:* Nomination for Audelco Recognition Award for best black theatre play, 1976, for "Hail Hail the Gangs!"; fiction award from Creative Artists Projects Service, 1977-78.

WRITINGS—All with James de Jongh: "Hail Hail the Gangs!: A Theatre Piece" (play), first produced in New York City at New York Theatre Ensemble, April, 1976; *City Cool: A Ritual of Belonging* (novel), Random House, 1978; "City Cool: A First Draft Screenplay," Warner Bros., 1978; *Till Victory* (historical novel), Random House, in press. Contributor to periodicals, including *BOPP* and *Penthouse.*

SIDELIGHTS: Cleveland told *CA* that he and de Jongh "write novels, dramas, and screenplays dealing with universal themes drawn from our experiences as black men living in America." Their latest novel, *Till Victory,* traces "the rise and fall of black Harlem in the fictional character of Alexander Hamilton Shakespeare (1880-1942), lover, philanthropist, sportsman, and number banker."

* * *

CLIFFORD, John McLean 1904-1979

OBITUARY NOTICE: Born December 9, 1904, in Salt Lake City, Utah; died March 10, 1979, in Santa Barbara, Calif. Lawyer and businessman. Clifford was a divisional head of the Federal Securities and Exchange Commission, a State Lands Commissioner in California, and an administrative executive with NBC and the RCA Corporation. From 1962 until 1968, he was a vice-president and president of the Curtis Publishing Company during a period of severe financial crisis. His efforts to rescue the company that published *Saturday Evening Post, Ladies' Home Journal,* and *Holiday* failed, and he was eventually forced to resign. Obituaries and other sources: *The International Who's Who,* Europa, 1978; *Who's Who in America,* 38th edition, Marquis, 1974; *New York Times,* March 11, 1979.

* * *

CLIVE, John Leonard 1924-

PERSONAL: Born September 25, 1924, in Berlin, Germany; came to United States in 1940, naturalized citizen, 1943; son of Bruno and Rose (Rosenfeld) Clive. *Education:* University of North Carolina, A.B., 1943; Harvard University, M.A., 1947, Ph.D., 1952. *Home:* 38 Fernald Dr., Cambridge, Mass. 02138. *Office:* 247 Widener Library, Harvard University, Cambridge, Mass. 02138.

CAREER: Harvard University, Cambridge, Mass., instructor, then assistant professor of history and literature, 1952-60; University of Chicago, Chicago, Ill., assistant professor,

1960-61, associate professor of history, 1961-65; Harvard University, professor of history and literature, 1965—. Fellow of Center for Advanced Study in the Behavioral Sciences, 1964-65. *Military service.* U.S. Army, 1943-46; became second lieutenant. *Member:* American Historical Association, Mid-West Conference of British Historical Studies (secretary, 1961-64), Massachusetts Historical Society, Phi Beta Kappa. *Awards, honors:* Guggenheim fellowship, 1957-58; American Council of Learned Societies grant, 1962-63; National Book Award in history, 1974, for *Macaulay: The Shaping of the Historian.*

WRITINGS: *Scotch Reviewers: The Edinburgh Review, 1802-1815,* Harvard University Press, 1957; (editor) Thomas Carlyle, *History of Friedrich II of Prussia, Called Frederick the Great,* University of Chicago Press, 1969; (editor with H. J. Hanham) Henry T. Buckle, *On Scotland–the Scottish Intellect,* University of Chicago Press, 1970; (editor with Geoffrey Best) R. W. Church, *Oxford Movement: Twelve Years, 1833-1845,* University of Chicago Press, 1970; (editor with Thomas Pinney) Thomas Babington Macaulay, *Selected Writings,* University of Chicago Press, 1972; *Macaulay: The Shaping of the Historian,* Knopf, 1973 (published in England as *Thomas Babington Macaulay–the Shaping of the Historian,* Secker & Warburg, 1973); (editor with Isaac Kramnick) *Lord Bolingbroke: Historical Writings,* University of Chicago Press, 1974; *Edward Gibbon and "The Decline and Fall of the Roman Empire,"* Harvard University Press, 1977. Also editor and translator, with O. Handlin, of *Journey to Pennsylvania* by Gottlieb Mittelberger.

SIDELIGHTS: Nominated for the 1974 National Book Award in both history and biography, and winner of the award in the former category, Clive's biography of the Victorian historian Macaulay has drawn praise from numerous critics. Lionel Stevenson of *South Atlantic Quarterly* observed that Clive "combines expertise in history and literature" in this "major work" on Thomas Babington Macaulay. Stevenson praised Clive's scholarly efforts and cited the "large archives of unpublished letters and diaries" that were consulted for the book.

Critics from *Time* magazine and *Virginia Quarterly Review* both noted the difficulty of writing about Macaulay. As William H. Nelson of the *Quarterly* explained: "The adjectives 'common' and 'vulgar' so often used to describe his [Macaulay's] appearance also regularly found their way into comments on his mind and work.... John Stuart Mill thought him 'an intellectual dwarf—rounded off and stunted, full grown broad and short, without a germ of principle of further growth in his whole being.'" Indeed, Queen Victoria once commented to Lord Melbourne that Macaulay was "'uncouth, and not a man of the world.'" But Clive, according to Nelson, found "the real Macaulay under this forbidding surface.... [and] sensibly enough, in his own early family life, from whose oppressions and joys, in Clive's view, Macaulay never escaped.... Cold and striving to the wider world, he was tender, solicitous, playful, charming, and flirtatious towards his adoring sisters."

Although Melvin Maddocks praised the "respectable case for a respectable Macaulay" that Clive was able to build, he was surprised at the popularity of the book: "Why is this potential doorstop winning such acclaim? Are readers ... really that willing to plow through 25 pages of hearsay evidence on Macaulay's eloquence as a parliamentary orator from 1832 to 1834?" Perhaps it is because, as Maddocks proposed, "Clive ... livens his exposition by suggesting the obligatory sinister Victorian flaw. Macaulay, a lifelong bachelor, loved his younger sisters ... more than a brother

should." He continued: "Working from this clue of psychological incest, Clive submits that Macaulay was a suppressed romantic, smoldering behind a mask of rationality.... A historian [however] can no more make this preacher of 'middlingness' very heroic than he can make him very wicked.... [Macaulay] was every inch a Victorian, and that fact finally provides the best explanation of the book's success."

Stevenson also noticed that Clive drew "a sympathetic picture of Macaulay in his social and political context, displaying him as more complex in his personality and more discriminating in his attitudes than is assumed by those who have not read his essays and speeches." But for Stevenson, Clive's style tended "to be wooden and repetitive, though perhaps this impression results from contrast with his subject's floridity." On the other hand, Victor Howes of *Christian Science Monitor,* stated, "It is to Clive's praise that his work reads like a great Victorian novel.... Macaulay looms forward from the pages of his biography like a firedrake, glittering, capacious, burning, dangerous."

Finally, almost all critics have agreed that Clive's book has simply whet their appetite for learning more about Macaulay. As Howes observed, "He leaves Macaulay at 40, on the threshold of writing his 'History of England,' the book on which his modern fame most securely rests." Nelson, however, considered this one of the book's drawbacks: "If Clive is persuasive and sure in explaining Macaulay's personal life and its relationship to his career, he is less satisfying when it comes to Macaulay's importance. Partly, no doubt, this is because this volume ends when Macaulay is thirty-eight and about to begin his "History," and Clive consequently deals with him as a historian only *en passant....* Perhaps if Clive had probed and delved more, had speculated more vigorously on the relationship between Macaulay and those to and for whom he spoke, this book might have been revelational, instead of merely informative, humane, and suggestive."

To many critics, Clive's book was more than simply a biography of an important historian. For R. Rea of *Library Journal* it was "also a marvelous survey of the evangelical, utilitarian, middle-class milieu of pre-Victorian Britain." For Maddocks it was a book in which "we find between all those lines an obituary on that soul of respectability that is fast fading but still not quite dead within ourselves."

BIOGRAPHICAL/CRITICAL SOURCES: *Library Journal,* January 15, 1973; *Atlantic,* April, 1973; *New York Times Book Review,* April 1, 1973, June 10, 1973, June 2, 1974, October 23, 1977; *Christian Science Monitor,* April 4, 1973; *New Yorker,* April 14, 1973; *New Leader,* April 16, 1973; *New Republic,* May 5, 1973; *Observer,* June 24, 1973; *Listener,* June 28, 1973; *Times Literary Supplement,* June 29, 1973; *New Statesman,* June 29, 1973; *Newsweek,* August 6, 1973; *Time,* December 31, 1973, April 22, 1974; *Virginia Quarterly Review,* winter, 1974; *Washington Post Book World,* April 20, 1975; *South Atlantic Quarterly,* spring, 1975.*

* * *

COE, Fred(erick) 1914-1979

OBITUARY NOTICE: Born December 23, 1914, in Alligator, Miss.; died April 29, 1979, in Los Angeles, Calif. Producer, director, and television writer. Coe was a major pioneer in translating theatre to the medium of television. During the golden age of live television drama, Coe produced more than 500 hour-long teleplays, including "Peter

Pan," "Marty," "The Last Tycoon," and "What Makes Sammy Run?" At NBC-TV he was in charge of the "Philco-Goodyear Theatre" and the "Mr. Peepers" programs. He later headed "Playhouse 90" at CBS-TV. His Broadway productions included "Two for the Seesaw" and "The Miracle Worker." He also produced the motion picture "The Left-Handed Gun" and was filming "The Miracle Worker" for NBC at the time of his death. *Obituaries and other sources: Current Biography,* Wilson, 1959; *The Biographical Encyclopaedia and Who's Who of the American Theatre,* James Heineman, 1966; *Who's Who in the Theatre,* 15th edition, Pitman, 1972; *Who's Who in America,* 38th edition, Marquis, 1974; *International Motion Picture Almanac,* Quigley, 1975; *Esquire,* May, 1973; *New York Times,* May 1, 1979.

*   *   *

COHEN, Amnon 1936-

PERSONAL: Born August 1, 1936, in Tel Aviv, Israel; son of Yoel (an accountant) and Sara Cohen; married Amalia Teper (a teacher), November 28, 1961; children: Noam, Tal, Inbal. *Education:* Hebrew University of Jerusalem, B.A., 1958, M.A., 1966, Ph.D., 1971. *Religion:* Jewish. *Home:* 33 Harav Berlin, Jerusalem, Israel. *Office:* Institute of Asian and African Studies, Hebrew University of Jerusalem, Jerusalem, Israel.

CAREER: School of Political Sciences, Jerusalem, Israel, instructor in Arabic and chief instructor of Middle Eastern history, 1957-58; Hebrew University of Jerusalem, Jerusalem, lecturer, 1971-73, senior lecturer, 1973-78, associate professor in history of Muslim countries, 1978—, head of department, 1974-76. Visiting history professor at York University, Toronto, Canada, 1978-79. *Military service:* Israeli Army, 1958-61, 1969-71, 1973-75; became colonel. *Member:* Middle East Studies Association; Israeli Oriental Society.

WRITINGS: Palestine in the Eighteenth Century: Patterns of Government and Administration, Magnes University Press, 1973; *Yehude Yerushalayim ba-mea ha-shesh 'esre* (title means "The Jewish Community of Jerusalem in the Sixteenth Century"; text in Hebrew and summary in English, with original documents in Turkish) Yad Ben Zvi, 1975; (with Bernard Lewis) *Population and Revenue in the Cities of Palestine in the Sixteenth Century,* Princeton University Press, 1978; *Ha-Tequfa Ha-'Othmanit,* editor, *Yerushalayim be-reshit* (title means "Jerusalem in the Early Ottoman Period"), Yad Ben Zvi, 1979.

WORK IN PROGRESS: The Jewish Community in Sixteenth-Century Jerusalem; research on political parties of Israel's West Bank under Hashemite rule, 1950-1967.

*   *   *

COLLIER, Kenneth Gerald 1910-

PERSONAL: Born March 24, 1910, in East Sheen, Surrey, England; son of Frank (a civil engineer) and Mary (Humphreys) Collier; married Gwendoline Halford, December 28, 1938; children: Peter, Anthony. *Education:* St. John's College, Cambridge, M.A., 1935; Oxford University, diploma in education, 1945. *Religion:* Church of England. *Home:* 4 Branksome Rd., Norwich, Norfolk NR4 6SN, England. *Office:* Centre for Applied Research in Education, University of East Anglia, Norwich NR4 7TJ, England.

CAREER: Worked as technical translator in Stockholm, Sweden, 1931-32; teacher of science and mathematics at var-

ious schools in Sussex, Norfolk, and Yorkshire, England, 1933-41; Royal Ordnance Factories, Cumberland, England, chemist and safety officer, 1941-44; senior physics master at private school in Sussex, 1944-49; St. Luke's College of Education, Exeter, England, head of education department, 1949-59; College of the Venerable Bede, Durham, England, principal, 1959-75; consultant on teacher education overseas, 1975—. Visiting professor at Temple University, 1965, 1968; research fellow at University of East Anglia, 1978—. Consultant to National Council for Educational Technology, 1971. *Member:* National Association of Teachers in Further and Higher Education, Society for Research into Higher Education (member of governing council), Royal Over-Seas League.

WRITINGS: The Science of Humanity, Thomas Nelson, 1949; (contributor) *Sixth Form Citizens,* Oxford University Press, 1950; (contributor) *Religious Faith and World Culture,* Wiley, 1951; *The Social Purposes of Education,* Routledge & Kegan Paul, 1959.

New Dimensions in Higher Education, Longmans, Green, 1968; (editor and contributor) *Innovation in Higher Education,* National Foundation for Educational Research, 1974; (editor with John Wilson and Peter Tomlinson, and contributor) *Values and Moral Development in Higher Education,* Croom Helm, 1974; (editor and contributor) *Evaluating the New B.Ed.,* Society for Research into Higher Education, 1978. Contributor to education journals. Editor of *Education for Teaching,* 1953-58.

WORK IN PROGRESS: Research on small-group teaching techniques in higher education; evaluation of an in-service M.A. course for teachers; analysis of job responsibilities of junior management in educational technology.

SIDELIGHTS: "My principal concern has been the quality of education received by pupils at all ages," Collier told *CA.* "This quality largely depends on the personal quality of the teachers; hence my concern with teacher education and with the influence of staff relationships on teacher performance. In my opinion, education—whether one is educating teachers or five-year-old children—is a matter of creating situations in which the learner becomes mentally engaged, whether in intellect or in imagination or in both. This is an art of great subtlety that requires imaginative sympathy with individuals and understanding of their backgrounds. Much education places too great an emphasis on instruction and factual information; much of it gives too little attention to the value-implications of pupils' life and works; much of it gives too little attention to what the pupils should be getting from work or to assessing how effective the teacher has been."

AVOCATIONAL INTERESTS: Local history, music, film, gardening.

*   *   *

COLMER, John (Anthony) 1921-

PERSONAL: Born October 2, 1921, in Plymouth, England; son of Vyvyan (a physician) and Jessie (Paton) Colmer; married Dorothy Mildred Penson (a university tutor), March 2, 1951; children: Rosemary Colmer Pearson, Vivienne. *Education:* Keble College, Oxford, B.A., 1949; University of London, Ph.D., 1955. *Home:* 4 Everard St., Glen Osmond, Adelaide, South Australia 5064. *Office:* Department of English Language and Literature, University of Adelaide, G.P.O. Box 498, Adelaide, South Australia 5001.

CAREER: University of Khartoum, Khartoum, Sudan, lecturer, 1949-53, senior lecturer in English, 1953-60; University of Birmingham, Birmingham, England, senior research fellow, 1960-61; University of Adelaide, Adelaide, Australia, senior lecturer, 1961-64, reader, 1964, professor of English, 1964—, head of department of English language and literature, 1968-70. *Military service:* British Army, Royal Armoured Corps, 1941-46; became sergeant. *Member:* Australasian Universities Language and Literature Association, Australian Academy of the Humanities (fellow), Association for the Study of Australian Literature, Commonwealth Language and Literature Association, Centre for Research into the New Languages in English, Modern Humanities Research Association, English Association.

WRITINGS: Coleridge: Critic of Society, Clarendon Press, 1959; (editor) *Coleridge: Selected Poems,* Oxford University Press, 1965; (editor) William Shakespeare, *Henry IV, Part I,* Longman, 1965; (editor) *Approaches to the Novel,* Rigby, 1966; *E. M. Forster: "A Passage to India",* Edward Arnold, 1967; (editor) *New Choice,* F. W. Cheshire, 1967; (editor with wife, Dorothy Colmer) *Mainly Modern,* Rigby, 1969; (contributor) R. L. Brett, editor, *S. T. Coleridge,* G. Bell, 1971; *E. M. Forster: The Personal Voice,* Routledge & Kegan Paul, 1975; (editor) *Coleridge: On the Constitution of the Church and State,* Princeton University Press, 1976; *Patrick White's Riders in the Chariot,* Edward Arnold, 1978; *Coleridge to Catch-22: Images of Society,* Macmillan, 1978.

General editor of "Studies in Australian Culture," a book series, Edward Arnold, 1977—. Contributor to language and literature journals. Past editor of *Southern Review.*

WORK IN PROGRESS: A critical study of Edward Carpenter, publication expected in 1981.

SIDELIGHTS: Colmer writes: "What I think gives unity to my critical writings is a central preoccupation with the relationship between literature and politics. This emerges clearly in my books on the poet Coleridge, the liberal humanist E. M. Forster, and my general study of nineteenth and twentieth century society, *Coleridge to Catch-22: Images of Society.* My future plans include writing about the two most momentous periods of my own life (experience of tank warfare in the Western Desert and the independence movement in Sudan between 1950 and 1959), and developing new theories about Australian cultural history.

"As an Englishman I choose to live and work in Australia because of the fine wines, the beautiful climate, and the chance to swim, fish, and play tennis all through the year."

* * *

CONNELLY, Marc(us Cook) 1890-

PERSONAL: Born December 13, 1890, in McKeesport, Pa.; son of Patrick Joseph (an actor and hotel owner) and Mabel Louise (an actress; maiden name, Cook) Connelly; married Madeline Hurlock, 1930 (divorced, 1935). *Education:* Attended Trinity Hall, Washington, Pa., 1902-07. *Home:* 25 Central Park West, New York, N.Y. 10023.

CAREER: Pittsburgh Press and *Gazette Times,* Pittsburgh, Pa., reporter, 1908-16; *New York Morning Telegraph,* New York, N.Y., reporter, 1916-21; Yale University, Graduate School of Drama, New Haven, Conn., professor of playwriting, 1946-50. Lecturer and teacher at several colleges and universities throughout the United States. Actor in plays, including "Our Town," New York City Center, January 10, 1944, in films "The Spirit of St. Louis," Warner Bros., 1957, and "Tall Story," Warner Bros., 1959, and in the television series "The Defenders," 1963. Director of Broadway plays, including many of his own, beginning with

"The Wisdom Tooth," 1926. *Member:* American Federation of TV & Radio Artists, Authors' League of America (past president), National Institute of Arts and Letters (president, 1953-56), Actors Equity Association, Dramatists' Guild (founding member), Screen Actors Guild, Players Club (New York), Dutch Treat Club (New York), Savage Club (London). *Awards, honors:* O. Henry Short Story Prize, 1930, for "Coroner's Inquest"; Pulitzer Prize for Drama, 1930, for *The Green Pastures;* honorary degrees from Bowdoin College, 1952, and Baldwin-Wallace College, 1962.

WRITINGS: A Souvenir From Qam (novel), Holt, 1965; *Voices Off-Stage: A Book of Memoirs,* Holt, 1968. Also author with others of *Webster's Poker Book,* 1925.

Plays: "2.50" (one-act), first produced in Pittsburgh, 1914; (author of lyrics) "The Amber Express," produced in New York at the Globe Theatre, September 19, 1916; "Erminie" (a revision of the operetta by Henry Paulton), first produced in New York at the Park Theatre, January 3, 1921; (with George S. Kaufman) *Dulcy* (three-act; first produced in New York at the Frazee Theatre, August 13, 1921), Putnam, 1921; (with Kaufman) *To the Ladies!* (three-act; first produced in New York at the Liberty Theatre, February 20, 1922), Samuel French, 1923; (with Kaufman) "The '49ers" (a review), first produced in New York at the Punch and Judy Theatre, November 7, 1922; (with Kaufman) *Merton of the Movies* (four-act; an adaptation of the story by Harry Leon Wilson; first produced on Broadway at the Cort Theatre, November 13, 1922), Samuel French, 1925.

(With Kaufman) "Helen of Troy, New York" (musical comedy), first produced in New York at the Selwyn Theatre, June 19, 1923; (with Kaufman) "The Deep Tangled Wildwood" (comedy), first produced in New York at the Frazee Theatre, November 5, 1923; (with Kaufman) *Beggar on Horseback* (comedy; first produced on Broadway at the Broadhurst Theatre, February 12, 1924), Liveright, 1925, also contained in *Three Plays About Business in America,* edited by Joseph E. Mersand, Washington Square Press; (with Kaufman) "Be Yourself" (musical comedy), first produced in New York at the Harris Theatre, September 3, 1924; *The Wisdom Tooth: A Fantastic Comedy* (three-act; first produced on Broadway at the Little Theatre, February 15, 1926), Samuel French, 1927; (with Herman J. Mankiewicz) "The Wild Man of Borneo" (comedy), first produced in New York at the Bijou Theatre, September 13, 1927; "How's the King?" (musical comedy), first produced in New York, 1927.

The Green Pastures: A Fable Suggested by Roark Bradford's Southern Sketches "Ol' Man Adam an' His Chillun" (first produced in New York at the Mansfield Theatre, February 26, 1930), Farrar & Rinehart, 1929, reprinted, Holt, 1959, also contained in *Contemporary Drama, Eleven Plays,* edited by E. Watson and Benfield Pressy, Scribner, 1956, film version co-directed by Connelly for Warner Bros., 1936, adapted for television for "The Hallmark Hall of Fame," National Broadcasting Company, 1957; "The Survey" (a skit), published in *New Yorker,* 1934; (with Frank B. Elser) "The Farmer Takes a Wife" (comedy; an adaptation of the novel *Rome Haul* by Walter Edmonds), first produced on Broadway at the Forty-Sixth Street Theatre, October 30, 1934, abridged edition contained in *Best Plays of 1934-35,* edited by Burns Mantle, Dodd, 1935; *Little David: An Unproduced Scene From "The Green Pastures"* (one-act), Dramatists Play Service, 1937, also contained in *The Best One-Act Plays of 1937,* edited by J. W. Marriott, Harrap, 1938; (with Arnold Sundgaard) "Everywhere I Roam," first produced in New York at the National Theatre, December 29, 1938; *The Traveler* (one-act), Dramatists Play Service, 1939.

"The Flowers of Virtue" (comedy), first produced on Broadway at the Royale Theatre, February 5, 1942; "Story for Strangers" (comedy), first produced on Broadway at the Royale Theatre, September 21, 1948; "Hunter's Moon," first produced in London at the Winter Garden Theatre, February 26, 1958.

Screenplays: "Whispers," 1920; "Exit Smiling," Metro-Goldwyn-Mayer, 1926; "The Bridegroom," "The Suitor," and "The Uncle" (film shorts), 1929; "The Unemployed Ghost" (film short), 1931; "The Cradle Song," Paramount, 1933; "The Little Duchess" (film short), 1934; (with others) "Captains Courageous," Metro-Goldwyn-Mayer, 1934; "I Married a Witch," Paramount, 1936; "Crowded Paradise," Tudor, 1956.

Radio Plays: "The Mole on Lincoln's Cheek," first broadcast by Canadian Broadcasting Corp., March 2, 1941, published in *The Free Company Presents,* edited by James Boyd, Dodd, 1941.

Author of lyrics for "The Lady of Luzon," 1914, and "Follow the Girl," 1915. Contributor of articles and stories to magazines, including *New Yorker, Collier's, Life, Saturday Review, Reader's Digest,* and others.

SIDELIGHTS: Joseph Wood Krutch once distinguished Marc Connelly from other Broadway playwrights "by the fact that he is not in the least 'hard-boiled.' Somehow or other he has managed to escape from the tough tradition which rules our stage.... His plays are never vulgar and never, like the typical product, somehow unpleasantly brassy. Below the surface of his sophistication is a delicate fancy, an essentially gentle spirit." The writer of romantic and charming plays, Connelly is primarily noted by critics in three capacities: as George S. Kaufman's collaborator, as a member of the Algonquin literary circle, and, especially, as the author of the Pulitzer Prize winning *Green Pastures.*

Connelly's friendship with George S. Kaufman and their subsequent collaboration on a number of Broadway plays solidified his career in the theatre and established his reputation as a writer of light satire. Their first joint effort, "Dulcy," was a box office success, popularizing the title characterization of a scatter-brained yet well-intentioned young woman. But the Connelly/Kaufman team achieved more than financial success by contributing to the development of American theatre. For example, "Merton of the Movies" brought to the stage the cinematic technique of rapid scene shifts and "Beggar on Horseback" employed the methods of expressionism already being experimented with in America by such playwrights as Elmer Rice.

In 1919 a group called the Round Table began to gather at the Algonquin Hotel in New York City. The group included such writers as Robert Benchley, the drama critic for the *New Yorker,* Dorothy Parker, a columnist for *Vanity Fair,* and Alexander Woollcott, the drama critic for the *New York Times,* as well as Heywood Broun, Edna Ferber, George S. Kaufman, and Marc Connelly. Another writer, Franklin P. Adams (F.P.A.) made the group famous by reporting their witticisms in his renowned *New York World* column, "The Conning Tower." Edna Ferber wrote of the group: "Their standards were high, their vocabulary fluent, fresh, astringent and very, very tough. Theirs was a tonic influence, one on the other, and all on the world of American letters." In fact, the founding of the *New Yorker* is sometimes attributed to Harold Ross's association with the members of the Round Table, most of whom, Connelly among them, at some time wrote for the magazine.

But beyond his associations with Kaufman and the rest of the Algonquin wits, Connelly's contribution to American drama rests on "The Green Pastures." Its genesis was *Ol' Man Adam an' His Chillun* by Roark Bradford, the son of a Tennessee plantation owner, who based his collection of black folk versions of Bible stories on the religious beliefs of black field hands he had observed. In adapting the tales for the stage, Connelly made the central figure a black Jehovah and interposed Negro spirituals during scene changes. Others of the play's features considered radical at the time were its use of contemporary black idiom and an all black cast.

A film version of "The Farmer Takes a Wife" was produced by Warner Brothers in 1935.

Connelly's manuscript collection is housed at the University of Wisconsin—Madison.

BIOGRAPHICAL/CRITICAL SOURCES: Nation, November 14, 1934; *Saturday Review,* April 7, 1951; *Phylon,* spring, 1959; Marc Connelly, *Voices Off-Stage: A Book of Memoirs,* Holt, 1968; *New York Times,* October 3, 1968; Paul T. Nolan, *Marc Connelly,* Twayne, 1969; *American Heritage,* February, 1970; Susan Edmiston and Linda Cirine, *Literary New York,* Houghton, 1976; *Contemporary Literary Criticism,* Volume 7, Gale, 1977.*

*   *   *

CONRAN, Terence Orby 1931-

PERSONAL: Born October 4, 1931; married first wife, Shirley (divorced); married Caroline Herbert (a writer), 1963; children: (first marriage) Sebastian, Jasper; (second marriage) Tom, Sophie, Edmund. *Education:* Attended Central School of Art, 1948-49. *Home:* Barton Court, Kintbury, Newbury, Berkshire, England. *Office:* The Studio, Barton Court, Kintbury, Newbury, Berkshire, England.

CAREER: Chairman of Conran Holdings Ltd., 1965-68; co-chairman of Ryman Conran Ltd., 1968-71; chairman of Habitat Design Holdings Ltd., 1971—. Chairman of Habitat America Holdings, Inc. and Habitat Europe Ltd.; director of Neal Street Restaurant, Conran Ink, Creative Business, and Conran Associates. Member of Royal Commission on Environmental Pollution, 1973-76. Member of council of Royal College of Art, 1978—, and advisory council of Victoria and Albert Museum, 1979-81. *Member:* Society of Industrial Artists and Designers. *Awards, honors:* Presidential medals for design management from Royal Society of Arts, 1968, 1975.

WRITINGS: The House Book, Mitchell Beazley, 1974; (with Maria Kroll) *The Vegetable Book,* Collins, 1976; *The Kitchen Book,* Mitchell Beazley, 1977; *The Bed and Bath Book,* Mitchell Beazley, 1978.

WORK IN PROGRESS: The Cook's Book; The Furniture Book.

AVOCATIONAL INTERESTS: Gardening, cooking.

*   *   *

CONROY, Pat 1945-

PERSONAL: Born October 26, 1945, in Atlanta, Ga.; son of Don (a military officer) and Peg (Peek) Conroy; married wife, Barbara; children: Jessica, Melissa, Megan. *Education:* The Citadel, B.A., 1967. *Home:* 71 Maddox Dr. N.E., Atlanta, Ga. 30309. *Agent:* Julian Bach Literary Agency, 3 East 52nd St., New York, N.Y. 10017. *Office:* 1069 Juniper St. N.E., Atlanta, Ga. 30309.

CAREER: Writer. Worked as schoolteacher in Daupauski, S.C., 1969.

WRITINGS: The Boo, McClure, 1970; *The Water Is Wide,* Houghton, 1972; *The Great Santini,* Houghton, 1976.

WORK IN PROGRESS: A novel, *Lords of Discipline.*

SIDELIGHTS: Conroy's experiences as a schoolteacher were the subject matter for his second book, *The Water Is Wide.* In it, he tells of his graduation from college, when he was filled with liberalism and the desire to erase the racism which was so prevalent in the South. Unfortunately, after Conroy got his job he succeeded in turning numerous school officials against him and he was removed within a year.

At first he saw *The Water Is Wide* as a means by which he could criticize his opponents in the school system, but the time spent writing opened his mind. "When I began to write the first chapters I was blazing," he told an interviewer. "What concerned me most was denouncing the people who had brought me down. But when I began to cool off (and rewrite) I realized I had played a major part in my own downfall."

After his dismissal from teaching, Conroy was drafted. There seemed to be no end to his hardships. However, he was able to receive a deferment. He returned to writing *The Water Is Wide* and finished it with the help of several friends who acted as typists. Although the publication of the book practically guaranteed some animosity from the community, Conroy insisted that he would remain there. "I don't want to be accused of nailing people to the wall in the book and then fleeing."

Conroy's *The Water Is Wide* was adapted as the motion picture "Conrack" in 1974.

BIOGRAPHICAL/CRITICAL SOURCES: Publishers Weekly, May 15, 1972; *Authors in the News,* Volume 1, Gale, 1976.

* * *

COOPER, Matthew (Heald) 1952-

PERSONAL: Born July 6, 1952, in London, England; son of William Heald (a banker) and Beryl (Davies) Cooper. *Education:* King's College, London, B.A. (honors), 1973. *Home:* 69 Cornwall Gardens, London S.W. 7, England. *Agent:* Bolt & Watson Ltd., 8/12 Old Queen St., London S.W.1, England. *Office:* House of Commons, London S.W.1, England.

CAREER: Imperial War Museum, London, England, library assistant, 1970; House of Commons, London, England, officer dealing with parliamentary procedure, 1974—. Member of board of directors of Cooper & Lucas Ltd. *Member:* Royal United Services Institution.

WRITINGS: (With James Lucas) *Hitler's Elite,* Macdonald & Jane's, 1974; (with Lucas) *Panzer: The Armoured Force of the Third Reich,* Macdonald & Jane's, 1976; (with Lucas) *Panzer Grenadiers,* Macdonald & Jane's, 1977; *The German Army, 1933-1945: The Political and Military Failure,* Stein & Day, 1978; *The Phantom War,* Stein & Day, 1979.

WORK IN PROGRESS: Research on the development of Parliament since 1066.

SIDELIGHTS: Cooper writes: "I am especially interested in the relationship of the individual to government, above all in totalitarian societies. Apart from writing, my great interest is travel; at the moment I am fortunate enough to spend roughly four months a year in other countries."

COOPER, Michele F(reda) 1941-

PERSONAL: Born March 16, 1941, in New York, N.Y.; daughter of Philip I. (a lawyer) and Helen (a secretary; maiden name, Davis) Delfin; married Marve H. Cooper (an artist and gallery owner), September 4, 1960; children: Petrina Lee, Jesse David Cutt. *Education:* Queens College of the City University of New York, B.A., 1962; New York University, M.A., 1964, doctoral study, 1964-71. *Politics:* "International." *Religion:* Jewish. *Home:* 46 Second St., Newport, R.I. 02840. *Office:* Department of English, Queens College of the City University of New York, 65-30 Kissena, Flushing, N.Y. 11367.

CAREER: Queens College of the City University of New York, Flushing, N.Y., lecturer in English, 1964—. Instructor in English, Rhode Island School of Design, 1976—; instructor, Art Association of Newport, 1976—; lecturer at New England Art Teachers Conference, 1977—. Member of American Friends Service Committee and Jung Center.

WRITINGS: (Contributor) Mario Pei, editor, *Language of the Specialists,* Funk, 1966; *The Freshman Writer,* Harper, 1971; (editor with Susan Cahill) *The Urban Reader,* Prentice-Hall, 1971; *The Freshman Reader,* Harper, in press. Contributor of more than forty-five essays, articles, and reviews to arts journals and local periodicals. Editor of *Newport Review: A Journal of Art, Literature, and Ideas.*

WORK IN PROGRESS: Symbolism From the Natural World; Isis and the Magic Tree, based on an Egyptian myth; *Dragon From Arcadium,* a fantasy; "Izabella and the Hand of God," a two-act play; "Young Goodman Brown," a one-act play.

SIDELIGHTS: Michele Cooper writes: "The creative impulse is uroboric, like Demeter and Charybdis in harmony. I nurse on her energy and believe in her, also in myself, my husband and children, good teaching, home cooking, antifascism, intuition, potent literature, Jewish culture, Quaker activism, love, maturation, and writing time. Nurturing these, and now a garden, is the essential dynamic, a personal metaphor for the process of individuation. It is a difficult and stimulating path with all those dark nights of the soul and extra-ordinary dawns and green things. One needs, as always, both love and good work to know and feed the Self."

* * *

COPELAND, Thomas Wellsted 1907-1979

OBITUARY NOTICE—See index for *CA* sketch: Born July 10, 1907, in East Cleveland, Ohio; died January 31, 1979, in Northampton, Mass. Educator, editor, and author. Copeland was emeritus Commonwealth Professor of English at the University of Massachusetts, Amherst, and was considered an authority on Edmund Burke. In addition to his biography of the author, Copeland directed a team of American, English, and Irish scholars in editing the complete writings of Edmund Burke. Obituaries and other sources: *The Author's and Writer's Who's Who,* 6th edition, Burke's Peerage, 1971; *Directory of American Scholars,* Volume II: *English, Speech, and Drama,* 7th edition, Bowker, 1978; *New York Times,* February 3, 1979.

* * *

CORMAN, Avery 1935-

PERSONAL: Born November 28, 1935, in New York, N.Y.; married; wife's name, Judy (an interior decorator), November 5, 1967; children: Matthew, Nicholas. *Education:* Attended New York University. *Agent:* International

Creative Management, 40 West 57th St., New York, N.Y. 10019.

CAREER: Playwright, educational film writer, book collaborator, and novelist.

WRITINGS: (With Marcia Seligson and Mort Gerberg) *What Ever Happened to . . . ?,* Price, 1965; (with Seligson and Gerberg) *You Have a Hang-up If . . . ,* Essandess, 1967; (with Seligson and Gerberg) *The Everything in the World That's the Same as Something Else Book,* Simon & Schuster, 1969; (with Seligson and Gerberg) *More What Ever Happened to . . . ?,* Price, 1971; *Oh, God!: A Novel,* Simon & Schuster, 1971; *Kramer Versus Kramer: A Novel* (Book-of-the-Month Club alternate selection), Random House, 1977; *The Bust-Out King* (novel), Bantam, 1977. Also author of plays.

Contributor of articles to magazines, including *Esquire, Cosmopolitan, McCall's,* and *New York.*

SIDELIGHTS: For years Corman struggled through the anonymous apprenticeship served by most aspiring writers. He wrote plays at first, then educational films and collaborative works with friends, and supplemented it all with magazine articles. Corman once said: "I really thought that if you work hard enough and learn enough, eventually you get rewarded with fame and money and interviews . . . , and just as I realized the danger and folly of such an attitude, it happened." His first novel, *Oh, God!,* was purchased by Warner Brothers, produced as a major motion picture with George Burns and John Denver, and re-released as a paperback by Bantam in 1977. His next effort, *Kramer Versus Kramer,* enjoyed the same success.

In the main, *Oh, God!* won appreciative reviews. The book is a comic, often satiric treatment of God's return to earth and a free-lance writer's unsuccessful efforts to inform the world. The writer is rejected, acclaimed, arrested, detained in Bellevue, and dismissed by a world ecumenical board of miracle examiners. Martin Levin found the book "highly instructive and very funny" with a satire that is "all the more effective because it is so airily presented." While Corman admitted that he wanted just to write a novel and prove his talent for comedy, he applied a more serious approach to his next book.

With *Kramer Versus Kramer,* Corman hoped to capture a feeling, to "isolate a man's emotions in as accurate a way as possible, [and] portray what it means to be a father and to love a small child." The story follows the growing relationship between Ted Kramer and his son Billy, after Joanna Kramer leaves the family and pursues her own career. Years later, Joanna launches a custody fight for Billy and wins, despite Ted's demonstrated competence as a father, deciding finally to return him to Ted's custody. "It takes a couple of topics that are both universal and timely," remarked Christopher Lehmann-Haupt, "and works them into a story told with maximum emotional effect." David Finkle added: "The style of *Kramer Versus Kramer* is spare but the sentiment is not. Good writers have many talents, but stacking a wealth of love between the lines is not a commonplace one; Corman has that enviable facility." Asserting that his novel is not political, Corman noted that a new fatherhood has arisen as a result of the women's liberation movement. "Do you remember 'henpecked?'" he asked. "Now you never hear that word anymore. . . . Men no longer feel they're not masculine if they show they love their children."

Kramer Versus Kramer has been adapted by Robert Benton into a motion picture for Columbia Pictures, starring Meryl Streep and Dustin Hoffman.

BIOGRAPHICAL/CRITICAL SOURCES: New York Times Book Review, October 24, 1971, October 23, 1977; *Best Sellers,* November 15, 1971; *Critic,* March, 1972; *Village Voice,* September 5, 1977; *New York Times,* October 7, 1977, October 21, 1977; *Publishers Weekly,* October 10, 1977.

*   *   *

CORMAN, Sidney 1924-
(Cid Corman)

PERSONAL: Born June 29, 1924, in Boston, Mass. *Education:* Tufts College (now University), B.A., 1945; graduate study at University of Michigan, 1946-47, University of North Carolina, 1947, and Sorbonne, University of Paris, 1954-55. *Home:* Fukuoji-cho 82, Utano-Ku, Kyoto 616, Japan.

CAREER: WMEX Radio, Boston, Mass., poetry broadcaster, 1949-51; *Origin* magazine and Origin Press, Ashland, Mass., and Kyoto, Japan, editor, 1951—. Teacher in Europe and Japan. *Awards, honors:* Chapelbrook Foundation grant, 1967-69; National Endowment for the Arts grant, 1974; Lenore Marshall Memorial Poetry Award for outstanding new book of poems from Book-of-the-Month Club, 1974, for *O/I.*

WRITINGS—All under name Cid Corman; poems: *subluna,* privately printed, 1944; *Thanksgiving Eclogue,* Sparrow Press, 1954; (with others) *Ferrini and Others,* Berlin Gerhardt, 1955; *The Responses,* Origin Press, 1956; *The Marches and Other Poems,* Origin Press, 1967; *Stance and Distances,* Origin Press, 1957; *A Table in Province,* Origin Press, 1959; *Clocked Stone,* Origin Press, 1959; *Cool Gong,* (adaptations of well-known Japanese poems), Origin Press, 1959; *The Descent From Daimonji,* Origin Press, 1959.

For Sure, Origin Press, 1960; *January,* [Kyoto], 1960; *For Instance,* Origin Press, 1962; *Sun Rock Man,* Origin Press, 1962; *In No Time,* [Kyoto], 1963; *In Good Time,* Origin Press, 1964; *All in All,* Origin Press, 1964; *For Good,* Origin Press, 1964; *Nonce,* Elizabeth Press, 1965; *Stead,* Elizabeth Press, 1966; *For You,* Origin Press, 1966; *Words for Each Other,* Rapp & Carroll, 1967; *For Granted,* Elizabeth Press, 1967; *No Less,* Elizabeth Press, 1968; *Hearth,* Origin Press, 1968; *& Without End,* Elizabeth Press, 1968; *No More,* Elizabeth Press, 1969; *Plight,* Elizabeth Press, 1969.

For Keeps, Origin Press, 1970; *Livingdying,* New Directions, 1970; *Nigh,* Elizabeth Press, 1970; *Of The Breath Of,* Maya, 1970; *For Now,* Origin Press, 1971; *Out and Out,* Elizabeth Press, 1972; *Be Quest,* Elizabeth Press, 1972; *A Language Without Words,* Byways 6, 1972; *Poems—Thanks to Zuckerkandl,* Sceptre Press, 1973; *Three Poems,* Sceptre Press, 1973; *So Far,* Elizabeth Press, 1973; *O/I,* Elizabeth Press, 1974; *Yet,* Elizabeth Press, 1974; *RSVP,* Sceptre Press, 1974; *For Dear Life,* Black Sparrow Press, 1975; *Un Less,* Serendipity, 1975; *Once and for All: Poems for William Bronk,* Elizabeth Press, 1975; *'S,* Elizabeth Press, 1976; *Auspices,* Pentagram, 1978. Also author of *Not Now.*

Other works: *At: Bottom,* Caterpillar, 1966; (editor) Franco Beltrametti, *Face to Face,* GR/EW Books, 1973; (editor and author of introduction) *The Gist of Origin 1951-71: An Anthology,* Grossman, 1975; *William Bronk: An Essay,* Truck Press, 1976; *Word for Word: Essays on the Art of Language,* Black Sparrow Press, 1977.

Translator: Matsuo Basho, *Cool Melon,* Origin Press, 1959; Corman, *Cool Gong,* Origin Press, 1959; (with Kamaike Susumu) Shimpei Kusano, *Selected Frogs,* Origin Press, 1963; Basho, *Back Roads to Far Towns,* Mushinsha (Tokyo), 1967; (with Susumu) Kusano, *Frogs and Others:*

Poems, Mushinsha, 1968, Grossman, 1969; Francis Ponge, *Things*, Grossman, 1971; Rene Char, *Leaves of Hypnos*, Grossman, 1973; Philippe Jaccottet, *Breathings*, Grossman, 1974.

SIDELIGHTS: Alicia Ostriker viewed Cid Corman as "a poet's poet: a writer neither very profuse—all his books are 'slender' ones—nor very aggressive, but central. To read Corman is to become conscious of one's breathing, how slightly it separates us from things like stones. The pure language, in minimal lines like those of Williams or Creeley, makes one think of other arts in their purity: a clean tone of harpsichord music, or flute, or lute, or Matisse colors, or *sumi* painting or the Zen archer, shooting well." Ian Hamilton furthered the comparison to Creeley in his comments on *Words for Each Other:* "He has much of Robert Creeley's wistful, abstract, openheartedness, but is less mannered than Creeley, less anxiously naive."

Corman's characteristic poem, said Hayden Carruth, "has a somewhat Oriental look about it: brief lines, measured by syllabic count, with much interplay of tones and accents, usually turning on a point of acute perception." Not only is this poem "devilishly hard to write," continued Carruth, "I detect in his work a Yankee toughness and existential lucidity that raise it far above trivia." Similarly, Robert J. Griffin tasted "an Oriental flavor" in Corman's *Livingdying*, a flavor "so strong in some poems that they seem not original works but carefully literal translations. At its worst this flavor may smack of cross-cultural belch, like pseudo-Zen gnomics or Pound pretentiously wagging his pigtail.... But that isn't typical. Corman lives in Japan, really *lives* there, and in most of his short pieces the Eastern note is earned and genuinely resonant."

In his overview of Corman's work, Michael Heller compared the poems of the six or seven years before 1976 to *Sun Rock Man:* "These poems, no longer quests, are certainly different in tone from the anguished work of *Sun Rock Man* with its ache of excess being.... That the meanings adhere to the language at depth and complexity testifies to the visionary nature of Corman's craft."

Corman extracted highlights from two decades of his magazine to produce *The Gist of Origin.* Included in this chronological collection of poetry, short prose, and reviews are some early works of Creeley, Charles Olson, and Denise Levertov alongside later efforts by William Carlos Williams and Wallace Stevens. Corman provided his own introduction, which *Choice* termed "thoughtful, specific, candid, and invaluable as social history." The magazine itself earned praise from Heller: "What I have said of Corman's poetry strikes me as no less true of his editorship of *Origin;* like the poems, it is an enterprise, a meditation of exile. Its pages testify anew to what makes the American literary scene such a curiosity, such a contradictory set of patterns and influences."

BIOGRAPHICAL/CRITICAL SOURCES: Observer, February 11, 1968; *Books and Bookmen,* May, 1968; *Nation,* July 20, 1970; *Partisan Review,* spring, 1972; *Choice,* November, 1975; *New York Times Book Review,* May 16, 1976; *Parnassus: Poetry in Review,* spring-summer, 1976; *Contemporary Literary Criticism,* Volume 9, Gale, 1978.*

*   *   *

CORN, Ira George, Jr. 1921-

PERSONAL: Born August 22, 1921, in Little Rock, Ark.; son of Ira George and Martha (Vickers) Corn; married Louise Touchstone, February 8, 1947 (divorced, March,

1961); children: Jay, John, Laura. *Education:* Attended Little Rock Junior College, 1939-41; University of Chicago, A.B., 1947, M.B.A., 1948. *Politics:* "Advocate of free market system and enlightened capitalism." *Religion:* Presbyterian. *Home:* 4829 Forest Lane, Dallas, Tex. 75234. *Office:* Dallas Federal Tower, 8333 Douglas St., Dallas, Tex. 75225.

CAREER: General Electric Co., New York, N.Y., marketing trainee, 1947-48; Southern Methodist University, Dallas, Tex., assistant professor of marketing, 1948-54; corporate financial consultant in Dallas, 1954-66; C & H Transportation Co., Dallas, chairman, 1966-68; Michigan General Corp., Dallas, co-founder and head of board of directors, 1968—. Co-founder and member of board of directors of Tyler Corp., 1966—; president of Dallas Community Water Service, 1960—. Captain of world champion Aces' Bridge Team. Member of executive committee of Committee of Publicly Owned Companies. Member of board of directors of Aberrant Behavior Center and Dallas Academy. *Military service:* U.S. Army, 1942-46; became sergeant. *Member:* American Management Association, National Association of Business Economists, American Contract Bridge League (life master; member of board of directors), Sons of the American Revolution, University of Chicago Alumni Association (head of local chapter, 1955—), Sigma Chi.

WRITINGS: Aces on Bridge, Fawcett, 1972; *The Story of the Declaration of Independence,* Corwin, 1977. Author of radio scripts. Author of "Aces on Bridge," a column distributed by United Features Syndicate to nearly one hundred-fifty outlets, 1978—. Contributor to finance and marketing journals, *Vital Speeches, Southwestern Home Furnishings,* and newspapers.

WORK IN PROGRESS: A question-and-answer manual on an independent economic system; a political novel, completion expected in 1981; revising *The Story of the Declaration of Independence,* 1981.

SIDELIGHTS: Corn writes that he is well-known for his speeches and articles on the U.S. independent economic system; he has held more than thirty seminars on the subject at colleges. But he adds that he is best known for founding and co-founding business ventures, more than twenty-four since 1950. He has twenty years of experience as a marketing, general management, and financial consultant for more than seventy-five companies. His background includes "twenty-one years as a lecturer and scholar, and a lifetime as an analytical observer of the human condition," including work as a freight handler, orchestra leader, film extra, camp counselor, life insurance agent, grocer, loan broker, art collector, securities analyst, public underwriting manager, export sales manager, cost analyst, and market researcher.

BIOGRAPHICAL/CRITICAL SOURCES: Dallas, December, 1972; *Christian Science Monitor,* July 14, 1976; *Dallas Times Herald,* October 17, 1976, November 11, 1977.

*   *   *

CORSARO, Francesco Andrea 1924-
(Frank Corsaro)

PERSONAL: Born December 22, 1924, in New York, N.Y.; son of Joseph (a tailor) and Marie (Guarino) Corsaro; married Mary Cross Lueders (an actress), May 30, 1971; children: Andrew. *Education:* Attended Yale School of Drama, 1945-48, City College (now of the City University of New York), and Actor's Studio. *Home:* 33 Riverside Dr., New York, N.Y. 10023.

CAREER: Director of plays and operas; actor. Director of plays, including "No Exit," 1947, "The Scarecrow," 1953, "A Hatful of Rain," 1955-56, "The Night of the Iguana," 1959, 1961, "Oh Dad, Poor Dad, Mama's Hung You in the Closet and I'm So Sad," 1961, "The Sweet Enemy," 1965, "Cold Storage," 1978, and "Whoopee!" (musical), 1979, and operas, including "Madame Butterfly," 1967, "Faust," 1968, "Prince Igor," 1969, "Don Giovanni," 1972-73, "The Makropulos Case," 1972, "A Village Romeo and Juliet," 1973; "Die Tete Stadt," 1975, and "Treemonisha," 1975; actor in plays, including "The Would-Be Gentleman," 1949, "The Taming of the Shrew," 1951, "Mrs. McThing," 1952, and "The Merchant of Venice," 1953. Resident stage director of New York City Opera Co., 1966—; artistic adviser and principal stage director of Houston Grand Opera, 1977—; teacher of acting at University of Houston, 1977—. *Member:* National Endowment for the Arts, National Opera Institute, Actors Equity Association, American Guild of Musical Artists, Screen Directors Guild, Society of Stage Directors-Choreographers.

WRITINGS—Under name Frank Corsaro: (And director) "A Piece of Blue Sky" (three-act play), first performed in Fort Lee, N.J., at Fort Lee Playhouse, in 1958; *L'Histoire du soldat* (adapted from original Ramuz text), Belwin-Mills, 1975; *Maverick: A Director's Personal Experience in Opera and Theater,* Vanguard, 1978. Also author of libretto, *Before Breakfast* (adapted from the play by Eugene O'Neill), Belwin-Mills.

WORK IN PROGRESS: Two film scripts; a novel; a reincarnation thriller; a memoir.

SIDELIGHTS: Corsaro has been involved in theater as a writer, director, and actor. He also appeared in the film "Rachel, Rachel," and directed his play "A Piece of Blue Sky" when it was performed on television. But he is best known for his original and sometimes outrageous directorial methods with plays and operas.

In opera, Corsaro has left quite an impression. His highly innovative stagings inevitably become involved in controversy. He is often known to tamper with *fermate,* the pauses in a score for which no action has been written. In a production of Stravinsky's "Histoire du soldat," Corsaro had characters on stage consuming hamburgers and milk shakes. Of course, this approach was none too popular with critics and traditionalist opera buffs. In a more popular alteration, Corsaro removed candles in a scene in Verdi's "La Traviata," thus creating an environment of dark shadows. Corsaro has also been known to employ multi-media effects in some shows, notably for "Die Tote Stadt," and his displays of sexuality are considered much more pronounced than is usually associated with opera. As Peter Andrew noted, Corsaro's "heritage is theater and not opera, and he seeks new theatrical solutions to old operatic problems." Corsaro himself claimed, "Opera *is* theater, and you create theater on a live stage, not in a museum." This approach has sometimes led to new characters being created and, in the case of "Doktor Faust," having the doctor enter as a composer at his own birthday party, during which he endures a heart attack and finds himself as Faust, the subject of one of his own unfinished compositions! However, for all his innovations, Corsaro insists that the music remain constant. "The music is sacred," he revealed, "as the essence of the musical drama."

Maverick offers an explanation of Corsaro's unique approach to opera and even Donal Henahan, though he apparently disagreed with Corsaro's style, felt that the book was valuable as a "discussion of stylization and the delicate relationship between singing and acting." And R. F. Young wrote that Corsaro displays "insight into his theories on dramatic, particularly operatic productions ... the man makes his point strongly and deserves a hearing." Defending his style, Corsaro declared: "I approach each new work, old or new, as if regarding a clear, clean space. The most thumbnailed musical chestnut becomes virgin territory; no matter how rouged or battered by time, each time is the first time...."

AVOCATIONAL INTERESTS: Painting, tennis, piano, ice skating.

BIOGRAPHICAL/CRITICAL SOURCES: Dance magazine, March, 1969; *Music Journal,* May, 1971; *Opera News,* August, 1972; *New York Times Magazine,* November 12, 1972; *Horizon,* October, 1977; *People,* April 3, 1978; *Best Sellers,* April, 1978; *New York Times,* June 24, 1978; *Esquire,* September 26, 1978.

* * *

COSGROVE, Mark P. 1947-

PERSONAL: Born January 16, 1947, in Kansas City, Mo.; son of William A. (in business) and Yolanda (Auteri) Cosgrove; married Jo Ann Walker, April 2, 1977; children: Walker. *Education:* Creighton University, B.A., 1969; Purdue University, M.S., 1971, Ph.D., 1973. *Office:* Taylor University, Upland, Ind. 46989.

CAREER: Probe Ministries, Dallas, Tex., research associate, 1974-76; Taylor University, Upland, Ind., assistant professor, 1976—. *Military service:* U.S. Army Reserve, 1971-79. *Member:* American Scientific Affiliation, Midwestern Psychological Association, Sigma Xi.

WRITINGS: The Essence of Human Nature, Zondervan, 1977; (with James Mallory) *Mental Health: A Christian Approach,* Zondervan, 1977; *Psychology Gone Awry,* Zondervan, 1979.

WORK IN PROGRESS: Studying Christian psychology.

* * *

COSTELLO, John E(dward) 1943-

PERSONAL: Born May 3, 1943, in Greenock, Scotland; son of John E. (an engineer) and Patricia S. Costello. *Education:* Cambridge University, M.A., 1965. *Politics:* "Radical liberal." *Religion:* "Thought." *Home:* 2 Lincoln Sq., New York, N.Y. 10023. *Agent:* Paul R. Reynolds, Inc., 12 East 41st St., New York, N.Y. 10017. *Office:* 29 Smith St., London S.W.3, England.

CAREER: McCann Erickson, London, England, advertising copywriter, 1965; Haymarket Press, London, magazine editor, 1965-67; London Weekend Television, London, television director, 1967-69; British Broadcasting Corp. (BBC), London, writer of documentary film scripts, 1969-71; Atlantic Communications Ltd., producer of documentary films and audio visual presentations, 1971—.

WRITINGS: D-Day, Macmillan, 1974; *The Concorde Conspiracy,* Scribner, 1976; *Jutland, 1916,* Holt, 1976; *Battle of the Atlantic,* Dial, 1977; *A History of Pan-American and U.S. Aviation,* Holt, 1979; *Battle for the Pacific,* Dial, in press.

Author of filmscripts, including "H.M.S. *Belfast:* The Ship That Survived," "Operation Neptune: Prelude to D Day," and "Concorde: The Twenty-Four Hour World."

WORK IN PROGRESS: Hitler's Germany, publication by Putnam expected in 1981.

SIDELIGHTS: Costello told *CA* his "objective in writing books is to present a total history for the general audience through the drama, the visual immediacy, and the relevance of the television documentary."

AVOCATIONAL INTERESTS: Aviation, politics, skiing, food and wine, music, painting, travel, archives, military history, New York City.

BIOGRAPHICAL/CRITICAL SOURCES: Washington Post, November 24, 1977.

* * *

COUTURE, Andrea 1943-

PERSONAL: Born May 26, 1943, in Methuen, Mass.; daughter of Sylvio H. (a businessman) and Cecile B. (Gagnon) Couture; *Education:* Emmanuel College, B.A., 1965. *Politics:* "Non-doctrinaire left." *Religion:* "Non-institutional humanist." *Home and office:* 279 Beacon St., Boston, Mass. 02116.

CAREER: Lawrence Eagle Tribune, Lawrence, Mass., cub reporter, summers, 1963-64; Nowels Publications, Menlo Park, Calif., editor, 1967-69; North Shore Weeklies, Inc., Ipswich, Mass., reporter and news editor, 1969-71; Unitarian-Universalist Service Committee, Boston, Mass., communications director, 1972-76; free-lance writer and communications consultant, 1976—. Has held photography exhibits in Boston, including "The Aymara Indians of Peru," and "Four Studies."

MEMBER: Women in Communications, National Academy of Television Arts and Sciences, Word Guild, New England Woman's Press Association. *Awards, honors:* Journalism awards include first prize for news story from New England Press Association, for "Quinlan Sweats Out First Big Defeat," special award for series, "Leather: Local Industry Threatened," and second prize for feature story, "No Need to Chime the Hour," all 1970. Silver medals from Boston Art Directors Club, 1974 and 1975, for annual report writing; certificate of distinction from *Creativity,* 1975, for annual report writing.

WRITINGS: For the People, for a Change (nonfiction), Beacon Press, 1978.

SIDELIGHTS: Andrea Couture began her career in journalism as a college student, working in the city room of the local daily newspaper. Then she edited a weekly newspaper in a California black community during the height of the "war on poverty," and after that, she traveled throughout the "third world."

Couture returned to Massachusetts to report on mental health, retardation, the elderly, and other social issues of growing public concern. Her work for the Unitarian-Universalist Service Committee included travel in Latin America and the Caribbean, and reports on such subjects as public health, irrigation, and political prisoners.

She writes: "I am interested in the fate of the oppressed and in articulating their struggle, and in the confluence of forces that keep people down. Perhaps in the description can come more understanding as the first step toward compassion and the beginnings of true change in the individual destinies that collectively form an oppressed group.

"Also, I am preoccupied with the impact of the emotional rationale on human behavior and how it is present and frequently intrusive in the most intellectual of situations regardless of culture. In my opinion, the telling of any story is incomplete without giving this human factor its due. This governs my work into the personal profile as my best means of expressing what I see, hear, smell.

"And someday I hope to push it all the way and write a novel, the ultimate relief from the storing up of impression, anecdote, grievance. For I write because I observe compulsively and words become my kind of collage-making where I can select, juxtapose and sometimes even order my experience in a fashion that has meaning. What I have written about frequently has not been pretty to see, but it is my way of edging along toward something better."

* * *

COUZYN, Jeni 1942-

PERSONAL: Born July 26, 1942, South Africa; *Education:* University of Natal, B.A., 1962, B.A. (with honors), 1963. *Home:* 17 Willow Rd., London NW3, England.

CAREER: Worked as a drama teacher in Rhodesia, 1964; African Music and Drama Association, Johannesburg, South Africa, producer, 1965; Special School, London, England, teacher, 1966; Camden Arts Centre, London, poetry organizer and gallery attendant, 1967; free-lance poet, 1968—. Teacher of creative writing at Lynden Centre and Loughton College of Further Education. Has been commissioned to write poems for several organizations and individuals, including the Globe Playhouse Trust and Whitechapel Gallery; director of poetry workshops for the Arvon Foundation in Devon, England; organizer of poetry readings at the Camden Festival, 1969, 1970; founder and director of Poetry Round. *Member:* The Poetry Society (executive member), National Poetry Secretariat (chairman). *Awards, honors:* Art Council of Great Britian grant, 1971, 1974; Canada Council Arts grant, 1977.

*WRITINGS—*Poems: *Flying,* Workshop Press, 1970; (editor) *Twelve to Twelve: Poems Commissioned for Poetry D-Day, Camden Arts Festival 1970,* London Poets' Trust, 1970; *Monkey's Wedding,* J. Cape, 1972; *Christmas in Africa,* Heinemann, 1975; *House of Changes,* Heinemann, 1978; *The Happiness Bird,* Sono Nis, 1978. Poems represented in many anthologies, including *The Puffin Book of Magic Verse, Poetry Dimension 4,* and Borestone Mountain Poetry Awards' *Best Poems of 1969* and *Best Poems of 1972.* Contributor to numerous magazines,, including *Vogue, Harper's,* and *Transatlantic Review.* Author of several radio broadcasts for British Broadcasting Corporation (BBC).

* * *

COWDEN, Jeanne 1918-

PERSONAL: Born December 5, 1918, near Durban, South Africa; daughter of John and Ida Mary (Williams) Cowden. *Education:* Attended secretarial college. *Home:* 62 Lagoon Drive, Umhlanga Rocks, 4320, South Africa. *Office address:* P.O. Box 1755, Durban, 4000, South Africa.

CAREER: Writer. Currently in advertising.

WRITINGS: For the Love of an Eagle, McKay, 1973; *Chameleons: The Little Lions of the Reptile World,* McKay, 1977. Also co-author of screenplay with Arthur Bowland, "For the Love of an Eagle."

WORK IN PROGRESS: Preliminary research for a first novel.

SIDELIGHTS: Cowden told *CA:* "My father was a Scot who came to South Africa at an early age. He was a man of imagination and love of freedom who found a Scottish village a little irksome to his independent spirit. My mother came of a well-known pioneer family whose ancestors came from Wales and Yorkshire in England. All of their children seem to have inherited these traits of not wanting to be confined!

"In my early days I wanted to be a veterinary surgeon, but this would have meant study in Edinburgh at great cost. I recognized that my scholastic shortcomings did not warrant this. Secretarial college and a job as survey draughtswoman held my attention before I embarked on *Barcarolle,* a small steam yacht bound for Britain. The journey, during which the passengers helped run the little craft, took about six weeks, traveling up the west coast of Africa.

"I now live in one of the few old homes right on the sea front at Umhlanga Rocks, once a small village twelve miles north of metropolitan Durban, but fast becoming a sophisticated resort." It was in her own garden that Cowden studied and photographed chameleon activity, which was the subject of her book, *Chameleons: The Little Lions of the Reptile World.* Her research uncovered some little known facts about mating rituals and other aspects of chameleon life.

"I spend all my spare time," Cowden continued, "in the indigenous forest, river, and lagoons that are nearby and still untouched by 'progress.' There I keep an eye on the wild and look out for poacher snares that strangle small buck in the bush. When not there I am in the lovely mountain range 140 miles inland, called the Drakensberg (mountains of the dragon), a home to eagles and lammergeyer. *For the Love of an Eagle* was drawn from my experiences in these mountains."

Cowden's books were acclaimed by critics for their well-written texts and beautiful photography. An American Humane Society reviewer described Cowden as "a keen, caring observer and writer of emotional power and grace . . . who fills her pages with brilliantly recorded insights and vivid images of untamed beauty." A *Natal Mercury* critic commented, "Her love of all things wild shows through very clearly and makes the book *Chameleons* a pleasure to read."

BIOGRAPHICAL/CRITICAL SOURCES: American Humane Society Book Review, February, 1977; *Libri Natales,* March, 1978; *AAAS Science Books and Films,* May, 1978; *Natal Mercury,* October 8, 1978.

*   *   *

COWEN, Ron(ald) 1944-

PERSONAL: Born September 15, 1944, in Cincinnati, Ohio. *Education:* University of California, Los Angeles, B.A., 1966; attended University of Pennsylvania, 1967-68. *Home:* 147 West 79th St., New York, N.Y. 10024. *Agent:* Audrey Wood, International Creative Management, 40 West 57th St., New York, N.Y. 10019.

CAREER: Dramatist. Taught at New York University, 1969. Associate trustee of University of Pennsylvania. *Awards, honors:* Wesleyan University fellowship, 1968; Vernon Rice Drama Desk Award, 1968, for *Summertree;* Pulitzer Prize nomination, 1968, for *Summertree.*

*WRITINGS—*Plays: *Summertree* (three-act; first produced in Waterford, Conn., at the Eugene O'Neill Memorial Theatre Foundation, 1967; produced off-Broadway at the Players Theatre, December, 1969), Dramatists Play Service, 1968; "Valentine's Day," first produced in Waterford at the Eugene O'Neill Memorial Theatre Foundation, 1968, revised version with music by Saul Naishtat produced in New York at Manhattan Theatre Club, 1975; (with Stephen Glasse) *Billy* (musical; based on Herman Melville's *Billy Budd*), first produced on Broadway at the Billy Rose

Theatre, March, 1969; *Saturday Adoption* (also see below), Dramatists Play Service, 1969; "Porcelain Time," first produced in Waterbury, Conn., 1972; *The Book of Murder* (also see below), Dramatists Play Service, 1974; "Lulu" (based on plays by Frank Wedekind), first produced in New York, 1974, produced in New York as "Inside Lulu," 1975. Also author of play, "Gene and Jean," as yet neither published nor produced.

Teleplays: "Saturday Adoption" (also see above), Columbia Broadcasting System (CBS-TV), 1968; "The Book of Murder" (also see above), American Broadcasting Companies (ABC-TV), 1974; "I Am a Fool," Public Broadcasting Service (PBS-TV).

Also author of screenplay, "45 Day Excursion."

SIDELIGHTS: Ron Cowen was only twenty-two when he wrote *Summertree,* one of the first plays to deal with American involvement in the Vietnamese War. Many viewers were deeply touched by the play, which through a series of flashbacks examines the life of a young man killed in Vietnam. Edith Oliver commented: "Mr. Cowen has been able to catch the elusive feelings of a particular young man—and, by extension, of many young men—trapped in the tragic, bewildering nineteen-sixties. . . . by making his hero human and specific, he has given him a universality that many more experienced (and inferior) writers try for and miss." Clive Barnes was also generous with his praise: "The play has a quality of compassion that will always be rare in the theater. The sparse writing, uninflected prose, is beautifully telling. I wonder when young lovers were depicted on stage with such simple honesty? Perhaps not since John Osborne wrote 'Look Back in Anger.' I wonder when a father-son relationship was so carefully, almost unemotionally depicted? Would you have to go back to Arthur Miller?"

Other reviewers, however, were not so enthusiastic about *Summertree.* "The play is full of emotion, which is not necessarily the same as sensitivity," a critic for *Variety* pointed out. Dick Brukenfeld complained about the "skim surface ability that doesn't stick" and the "slickly drawn, typical characters who do their endearingly familiar thing, constantly." A *Nation* reviewer gave a lukewarm assessment of *Summertree,* calling it "a nice boy's play—a first step. . . . The domestic scenes (with father, mother, junior brother, girl friend) are all as simple as can be, not at all maudlin, and in their primal candor they appeal to folk for whom such attributes are sufficient. No errors, no hits, no runs—a neat bunt."

The stage is not Ron Cowen's only medium; he has also written for television. The efforts of a white college student and a black seventh grader to bridge the gaps between their vastly different worlds are portrayed in "Saturday Adoption," which was aired on CBS-TV in 1968. Doyle Dane Bernbach derided the teleplay, calling it "a strikeout in every department and a 90-minute exercise in tedium." In contrast, Jack Gould considered "Saturday Adoption" to be "a delicately poignant, if frequently uneven, drama on the multiple agonies and occasional rewards of trying to establish communication between human beings."

Summertree was produced as a motion picture by Columbia in 1971.

BIOGRAPHICAL/CRITICAL SOURCES: New Yorker, March 16, 1968; *New York Times,* March 17, 1968, December 5, 1968, December 10, 1969; *Partisan Review,* summer, 1968; *Variety,* December 11, 1968, December 24, 1969; *Village Voice,* December 18, 1969; *Nation,* February 2, 1970.*

CRADDOCK, William J(ames) 1946-
(William James)

PERSONAL: Born July 16, 1946, in San Jose, Calif.; son of William O. (an executive) and Camille J. (Hatch) Craddock; married Carole Anne Bronzich, November 27, 1967 (divorced); married Teresa Lynn Thorne (a fashions buyer), July 27, 1975. *Education:* Attended San Jose State College (now University), 1964-67. *Politics:* None. *Religion:* None. *Agent:* Joan Stewart, William Morris Agency, 1350 Avenue of the Americas, New York, N.Y. 10019. *Office:* 2872 Chesterfield Dr., Santa Cruz, Calif. 95062.

CAREER: Writer. Worked as ditch digger, 1962. *Member:* National Rifle Association, National Muzzle Loading Rifle Association, Lompico Volunteers, Night Riders Motorcycle Club (secretary-treasurer, 1966-67; vice-president, 1967—).

WRITINGS: Be Not Content, Doubleday, 1970; *Twilight Candelabra,* Doubleday, 1972. Author of unpublished novels, including "Backtrack," 1970, "The Fall of Because," 1973, "The Fading Grass," 1975, and "A Passage of Shadows," 1976. Columnist for *Los Gatos-Saratoga Times Observer,* 1963-67. Contributor of articles to periodicals, including *Easyriders,* and to other publications, sometimes under pseudonym William James. Editor and publisher of *Mobius Strip,* 1966-67.

SIDELIGHTS: Craddock told *CA:* "Doubleday tentatively accepted *Be Not Content* in 1968. They asked me to omit certain chapters detailing the effects of LSD-25 and revise various 'too esoteric' passages they felt would be 'incomprehensible to the reading public . . . which is'—they reminded me—'largely unfamiliar with drugs or the underground drug culture.' (Even in 1968 I thought they were being just a bit conservative—but didn't wanna argue the point.)

"While waiting for the anticipated wild joy of actual publication I wrote a second and much longer novel (intended as a sequel and wrap-up of *Be Not Content*) entitled 'Backtrack,' which followed the first book's main characters through the disillusioning reentry years immediately after the winter of 1967 and the death of hippie-hope. This grand opus was rejected after due consideration."

After Craddock received an advance for his novel *Twilight Candelabra,* he "moved back into the mountains where, for the next three years, I did any number of things besides write. I managed to do a short and admittedly unmarketable book called 'The Fall of Because,' a satire overlaying a serious allegorical treatment of 'modern magick,' which was submitted to and rejected by Doubleday, thereby meeting and completing my second contract with them.

"I remarried and was moved (not to say enticed) to a lovely old house above Los Gatos, Calif., where I wrote a novel about the transitional early 1970's entitled 'The Fading Grass.' From the 'quaint village of my birth,' my wife and I then moved to the Santa Cruz mountains and, once settled, I did an occult novel called 'A Passage of Shadows.'"

Craddock has attempted to resolve the dilemma of his unpublished manuscripts by acquiring an agent. "In the meanwhile—having stumbled past my thirtieth birthday, somewhat less enthusiastic than I was ten years ago about the idea of filling pages with cloudy reflections of personal visions, suddenly able to report 'nostalgic Americana' firsthand in the wake of a motorcycle accident that put me in the hospital for the first time in a decade-and-a-half of constant riding, still unable to adjust my waking hours with the sun—I have begun a book on certain selected people throughout history who fall (usually inadvertently) into a particular category."

AVOCATIONAL INTERESTS: Motorcycles, collecting antique firearms, writers (including Peter S. Beagle, Philip K. Dick, and Anne Steinhardt), paintings of Richard Dadd, drawings of Martin Van Maele and George Metzger, and miniature replicas of human skulls.

* * *

CRAIG, H(enry) A(rmitage) L(lewellyn) 1921-1978

PERSONAL: Born in 1921, in West Cork, Ireland; died October 24, 1978, in Rome, Italy, of lung cancer; married wife, Peggy; children: Tom, Sean, Siobhan. *Education:* Attended Kilkenny College. *Residence:* Rome, Italy.

CAREER: Writer.

WRITINGS: Bilal (fiction), Quartet Books, 1977.

Screenplays: "Anzio," Columbia, 1968; (with Sergei Bondarchuk) "Waterloo," Paramount, 1971.

Author of ballad-operas with Dominic Behan, including "Come All You Gallant Poachers," and "A Grand Year for Mushrooms." Also writer for British Broadcasting Corporation's Third Programme.

SIDELIGHTS: Bilal is a fictionalized account of the first convert of Mohammed told in autobiographical style.

OBITUARIES: New York Times, November 17, 1978.*

* * *

CRANE, R(onald) S(almon) 1886-1967

PERSONAL: Born January 5, 1886, in Tecumseh, Mich.; died July 12, 1967; married Julia L. Fuller, 1917; children: two. *Education:* University of Michigan, B.A., 1908; University of Pennsylvania, Ph.D., 1911.

CAREER: Literary critic. Northwestern University, Evanston, Ill., instructor, 1911-15, assistant professor, 1915-20, associate professor of English, 1920-24; University of Chicago, Chicago, Ill., associate professor, 1924-25, professor of English, 1925-50, chairman of department, 1935-47, distinguished service professor, 1950-51, professor emeritus, 1951-67. Visiting professor and Alexander lecturer, University of Toronto, 1952; visiting professor at Cornell University, 1952-53, Carleton College, 1953, University of Oregon, 1954, Stanford University, 1954-55, Indiana University, 1955-56, and Cornell University, 1957. *Awards, honors:* L.H.D. from University of Michigan, 1941.

WRITINGS: The Vogue of Guy Warwick From the Close of the Middle Ages to the Romantic Revival, Modern Language Association, 1915; *The Vogue of Medieval Chivalric Romance During the English Renaissance,* George Banta, 1916, reprinted, Folcroft Library Editions, 1971; (contributor and co-editor) *Critics and Criticism: Ancient and Modern,* University of Chicago Press, 1952, abridged edition, 1957; *The Languages of Criticism and the Structure of Poetry,* University of Toronto Press, 1953, revised edition, 1953; *The Idea of the Humanities and Other Essays Critical and Historical,* two volumes, University of Chicago Press, 1967; *Critical and Historical Principles of Literary History,* University of Chicago Press, 1971.

Editor: (With William Frank Bryan) *The English Familiar Essay: Representative Texts,* Ginn, 1916; Oliver Goldsmith, *New Essays,* University of Chicago Press, 1927, reprinted, Greenwood Press, 1968; (with F. B. Kaye and Moody Prior) *A Census of British Newspapers and Periodicals, 1620-1800,* University of North Carolina Press, 1927, reprinted, Johnson Reprint Corp., 1963; *A Collection of English Poems, 1660-1800,* two volumes, Harper, 1932, reprinted, Granger

Books, 1978; (with Arthur O. Lovejoy and others) *A Documentary History of Primitivism and Related Ideas*, Johns Hopkins Press, 1935; *English Literature, 1660-1800: A Bibliography of Modern Studies*, Princeton University Press, 1950.

Contributor to periodicals, including *University Review*. Editor of *Modern Philology*, 1930-52.

SIDELIGHTS: Crane is recognized in the literary world as a major exponent of "pluralism," a mode of criticism which embraces a variety of possible interpretive devices. Crane's method of determining which particular mode of reference is used is based on practicality. He proposed that different critical devices could be chosen depending on what in particular was being criticized. Working from Richard McKeon's division of criticism into two modes, the literal and the didactic, Crane suggested that a multiplicity of derivative critical modes, each one capable of addressing a particular aspect of literature, could be used.

Crane also devoted much of his critical attention to what he believed to be the most effective mode within the division of literal criticism: the Aristotelian method. It was Crane's belief that the Aristotelian method alone was useful in dealing with certain basic critical inquiries.

BIOGRAPHICAL/CRITICAL SOURCES: The Verbal Icon: Studies in the Meaning of Poetry, University of Kentucky Press, 1954; *The Charted Mirror: Literary and Critical Essays*, Routledge & Kegan Paul, 1960.*

*   *   *

CRAVENS, Gwyneth

PERSONAL—Home: 327 Central Park West, Apt. 17A, New York, N.Y. 10025.

CAREER: Writer; contributing editor to *Harper's* magazine.

WRITINGS: (Editor with Tony Jones and Judith Appelbaum) *The Big Picture: A Wraparound Book*, Harper's Magazine Co., 1976; (with John S. Marr) *The Black Death*, Dutton, 1976. Contributor to *New Yorker*, *Harper's*, and *Transatlantic Review*.

SIDELIGHTS: Reviewing *The Black Death*, a *Newsweek* critic commented: "Admirers of Albert Camus's moral parable about an outbreak of pestilence may want to leave this novel alone. It's subliterary stuff, overlong and burdened with an outrageous love story, but for what it is, it's first rate: on par with *Seven Days in May*, for instance, or *The Andromeda Strain*. The authors are knowledgeable about the plague; and their grim insistence that it's only a matter of time before their story comes true may make some of us regret having passed up our swine-flu shots." A *Times Literary Supplement* critic pointed out that "the authors' anger is one of the book's strengths: another is that the medical data are fascinating, authoritative, and clear. The local colour/human interest is only occasionally obtrusive . . . and there is an amazing climax."

A *New York Times Book Review* critic also observed, that in addition to the authenticity of the epidemiology, "the crowded, festering New York scene, which the authors depict with ripe imagery, . . . could be a superb host for any pandemic. The corpse-by-corpse timing of the book is good too, as the death multiplies in geometric progression. When they come to causality, however, the authors project a touch of Dr. Strangelove paranoia that is a bit much."

BIOGRAPHICAL/CRITICAL SOURCES: Publishers Weekly, November 1, 1976; *Newsweek*, January 10, 1977; *New York Times Book Review*, January 30, 1977; *Times Literary Supplement*, May 6, 1977.*

*   *   *

CRAWFORD, Christina 1939-

PERSONAL: Born June 11, 1939, in Hollywood, Calif.; adopted daughter of actress Joan Crawford; married second husband C. David Koontz (a writer and producer), February 14, 1976; stepchildren: David. *Education:* Attended Carnegie Mellon University and Neighborhood Playhouse Professional School; University of California, Los Angeles, B.A. (magna cum laude), 1974; University of Southern California, M.A., 1975. *Home:* 21395 Castillo St., Woodland Hills, Calif.

CAREER: Writer. Worked as actress in films, television, and stock productions, 1959-72; handled corporate communications in a public relations department. Representative of Annenberg School of Communications, University of Southern California Alumni Board of Governors.

WRITINGS: Mommie Dearest, Morrow, 1978.

WORK IN PROGRESS: Screenplay based on *Mommie Dearest;* a novel.

SIDELIGHTS: Adopted by movie queen Joan Crawford in 1940, Christina Crawford was a "Hollywood child" whose life was unstable and double edged. As a little girl Christina would often pose for photographs with lovely unwrapped Christmas presents, only to see them later taken away and rewrapped as future birthday gifts for the children of other Hollywood stars. The beautiful matching mother and daughter outfits were to be worn only for photographers—the public; in private Joan had ripped to shreds Christina's favorite dress during one "night raid" and made her wear it that way for one week.

Mommie Dearest is the story of Christina's life as the often abused daughter of Joan Crawford. Molly Haskell in the *New York Times Book Review* called it "a horror story that goes beyond showbiz scandal-mongering to become a morbidly disturbing saga of inverted mother-love and emotional bondage." Among the horrors related in this saga are the "night raids" by a drunken mother who ransacked her children's bedroom and later demanded that they clean up their "own" mess, and the outbursts of Joan's rage at minor "childhood transgressions" which preceded excessively strict disciplinary action. Although Christina provided lurid details of the abuse by her mother, Haskell observed that she wrote about the incidents in "a remarkably contained, even placid, tone of voice."

Still the book has rocked the memory of one of Hollywood's most glamorous movie stars. Termed an "expose" and an "indictment," *Mommie Dearest* has evoked unfavorable reactions from some critics. Christopher Lehmann-Haupt of the *New York Times* conceded that "perhaps Christina Crawford is justified in committing 'Mommie Dearest' against her late adoptive mother," however he called the book "Gretel's revenge on the ugly old witch." Lehmann-Haupt also doubted Christina's "blather about forgiving Joan and loving her despite all." "To forgive requires understanding," he wrote, "and understanding Joan Crawford requires considerably more than perceiving that she wanted children merely for the sake of show." James McCourt in his *Washington Post Book World* review agreed and called the book "an unremittingly acrimonious account which amazingly asks its readers to believe that the septic bondage between a harridan lush and a hapless child somehow evolved into an authentic relationship."

Joan Crawford's final act of "abuse" toward her daughter and son was to make no provisions for them in her will. However, Joan went beyond merely leaving them out of her will; she specifically mentioned that both children were disinherited "for reasons which are well known to them." Christina considered the act an insult.

Joan Crawford died in May, 1977, and Christina recently stated: "In the summer of 1977 I reached a point in my life where it was time to write the truth. I was 37 then and had been a public figure since I was a baby. I wanted to tell what it was like growing up as a Hollywood child—including the child abuse."

In a *Washington Post* article Christina Crawford discussed child abuse and the role of her book as a testimony to this crime: "For many, many years, society has held the view that the child is the property of the parent. That the child has no rights as a human being. I survived because I came to the decision at some early age that I wanted to live more than I wanted to die. It was a terrifying journey because I was so alone. But many people, whether from wealthy Hollywood, or more ordinary circumstances, have not survived. My hope is that the revelations in my book will give other people hope."

To her critics and to her mother's fans Christina Crawford offered this insight: "Before reading it, some people mixed up the dream of Joan Crawford with the reality. But I didn't write her biography, I wrote my autobiography."

BIOGRAPHICAL/CRITICAL SOURCES: Christina Crawford, *Mommie Dearest,* Morrow, 1978; *Washington Post,* November 1, 1978; *Washington Post Book World,* November 26, 1978; *New York Times,* December 6, 1978; *New York Times Book Review,* December 24, 1978, January 14, 1979.*

* * *

CRAWFORD, Oliver 1917-

PERSONAL: Birth given name, Oliver Kaufman; professional name, Oliver Crawford; born August 12, 1917, in Chicago, Ill.; son of Alex (a milkman) and Bertha Pearl (Farkas) Kaufman; married Bertha Ethel Pikus, March 31, 1941; children: Jo Ann, Kenneth, Vicki Sue. *Education:* Attended Kenneth Sawyer Goodman School of Drama, 1937-38, and Actors Laboratory, 1946-48. *Politics:* "Well intentioned." *Religion:* None. *Home:* 6553 Colgate Ave., Los Angeles, Calif. 90048. *Agent:* International Creative Management, 8899 Beverly Blvd., Los Angeles, Calif. 90048.

CAREER: Screenwriter and author. Loyola University of Los Angeles, Los Angeles, Calif., part-time instructor in writing, 1979—. Has also worked as salesman, welder, clerk, freight handler, cartoonist, actor, and postman. Story consultant for television series, including "Iron Horse," "Medical Center," and "Madigan." *Military service:* U.S. Army, 1943-46; served in Pacific Theatre. *Member:* Writers Guild of America (member of board of directors, 1964-72, 1974—; chairman of history committee), Authors Guild, Dramatists Guild. *Awards, honors:* Nomination for Emmy Award from Academy of Television Arts and Sciences, 1959, for script for television series "Climax!," and 1960, for script for television series "Lineup"; Brotherhood Award ~~m~~ National Conference of Christians and Jews, 1963, for ~~t~~ for television program "Death Valley Days"; nomi- ~~from Writers Guild of America, 1965, for script for~~ ~~n series "Outer Limits."~~

~~S: *Blood on the Branches* (novel), Ace Publish-~~ ~~e Execution* (novel), St. Martin's, 1978.~~

Screenplays: (With Maurice Klauber) "Girl in the Woods" (adapted from own novel, *Blood on the Branches*), Republic, 1958; (author of screen story, with Niven Busch) "The Man From the Alamo," Universal, 1953. Contributor of "The Hostages" sequence in "The Steel Cage," United Artists, 1954.

Recordings: (With Sid Kuller) Bob Hope, "This Country Is Two Hundred Years Old and There Is Still Hope," Capitol Records, 1976.

Contributor of scripts to numerous television series, including "Kraft Theatre," "Lux Video Theatre," "Theatre Guild of the Air," "Climax," "Lineup," "Rawhide," "Ben Casey," "The Fugitive," "Four Star Theatre," "Quincy," "Big Valley," "Bonanza," "Telephone Time," "Schlitz Playhouse of Stars," "The Jazz Singer," "Rifleman," "Wagon Train," "I Spy," "Perry Mason," "Ironside," "Star Trek," "Love—American Style," "Wild, Wild West," "Kojak," "Gilligan's Island," "The Bold Ones," "Six Million Dollar Man," "Kaz," and "Movie of the Week."

WORK IN PROGRESS: A "whodunit" novel about life in the year 2030, *Laugh, Clone, Laugh;* a screenplay of own novel, *The Execution;* a pilot script, "California Beat," for Lorimar Productions and National Broadcasting Co. (NBC).

SIDELIGHTS: Crawford told *CA:* "I am indebted to many people who have been supportive.... I may have ego, but not conceit, for the world is not waiting for my next line.... If I did not write I would be ill-qualified to do much else of anything.... I believe the world is on a doomsday course. God (if there is one) screwed up when he/she/it created man. I understand man's need for God but why God's need for man?"

Crawford continued: "Early in my career I was predominantly an actor, doing poorly, and thought a similar sounding name, and Anglicized, might change my luck. As I acted less and wrote more, the name stuck. Legally, I am still Oliver Kaufman, also known as Oliver Crawford.

"Incidentally, I still act, occasionally performing in a one-act play for 'Plays for the Living,' a division of Family Service of Association of America. We play in churches, synagogues, summer camps, at seminars, and even in living rooms. It's nice to be able to put something back into the pot."

AVOCATIONAL INTERESTS: Acting, baseball, gardening.

* * *

CREEL, Herrlee G(lessner) 1905-

PERSONAL: Born January 19, 1905, in Chicago, Ill.; son of HerrLee Glessner (a writer) and Lena (Peterson) Creel; married Lorraine Johnson, August 28, 1937. *Education:* Attended University of Oklahoma, 1923-24, and Creighton University, 1924; University of Chicago, Ph.B., 1926, A.M., 1927, Ph.D., 1929. *Residence:* Palos Park, Ill. 60464. *Agent:* Curtis Brown Ltd., 575 Madison Ave., New York, N.Y. 10022.

CAREER: Newspaper reporter and editor, 1922-24; Lombard College, Galesburg, Ill., assistant professor of psychology, 1929-30; University of Chicago, Chicago, Ill., instructor, 1936-37, assistant professor, 1937-40, associate professor, 1940-49, professor, 1949-64, Martin A. Ryerson Distinguished Service Professor of Chinese History, 1964-73, professor emeritus, 1974—. *Military service:* U.S. Army, research analyst in Military Intelligence, 1943-45; became lieutenant colonel. *Member:* American Oriental Society (president, 1955-56), Association for Asian Studies, Authors Guild of Authors League of America. *Awards, honors:* Fellowships from American Council of Learned Societies, 1930-31, 1932-33, and Harvard-Yenching Institute, 1931-32, 1933-35; Gordon J. Laing Prize from University of Chicago Press, 1971, for *The Origins of Statecraft in China,* Volume I.

WRITINGS: Sinism: A Study of the Evolution of the Chinese World-View, Open Court, 1929; *The Birth of China: A Survey of the Formative Period of Chinese Civilization,* J. Cape, 1936, John Day, 1937, reprinted, Ungar, 1963; *Studies in Early Chinese Culture,* First Series, Waverly, 1937; (with Chang Tsung-ch'ien and Richard C. Rudolph) *Literary Chinese by the Inductive Method,* University of Chicago Press, Volume I: *The Hsiao Ching,* 1938, revised edition, 1948, Volume II: *Selections from the Lun Yu,* 1939, Volume III: *The Mencius, Books I-III,* 1952; (with Teng Ssu-yu and others) *Newspaper Chinese by the Inductive Method,* University of Chicago Press, 1943; *Chinese Writing* (pamphlet), American Council on Education, 1943; *Confucius: The Man and the Myth,* John Day, 1949, reprinted as *Confucius and the Chinese Way,* Harper, 1963.

Chinese Thought: From Confucius to Mao Tse-Tung, University of Chicago Press, 1953, reprinted, 1977; *The Origins of Statecraft in China,* Volume I: *The Western Chou Empire,* University of Chicago Press, 1970; *What Is Taoism? and Other Studies in Chinese Cultural History,* University of Chicago Press, 1970; *Shen Pu-hai: A Chinese Political Philosopher of the Fourth Century B.C.,* University of Chicago Press, 1974.

WORK IN PROGRESS: Additional volumes of *The Origins of Statecraft in China;* research on Chinese philosophy.

SIDELIGHTS: Creel's books have been published in England, France, Japan, Italy, and Spain. He writes: "My principal concern is to understand the origins and the early history of humanity's most continuously enduring civilization, that of China."

* * *

CRITCHLEY, Julian (Michael Gordon) 1930- (William Beaufitz)

PERSONAL: Born December 8, 1930, in Chelsea, England; married Paula Joan Baron, 1955 (divorced, 1965); married Heather Goodrick, 1965; children: (first marriage) Neil Clercley, Susannah; (second marriage) Melissa, Joshua. *Education:* Attended Sorbonne, University of Paris, 1950; Pembroke College, Oxford, M.A., 1954. *Religion:* Church of England. *Home:* Brewer's House, 18 Bridge Sq., Farnham, Surrey, England.

CAREER: Conservative member of Parliament from Rochester, Chatham, England, 1959-64; Conservative member of Parliament from North Hampshire, England, 1970-74, and Aldershot, England, 1970—. Head of Bow Group, 1966-67; head of Conservative party's media committee, 1976—, vice-chairman of defense committee, 1976-78, also former vice-chairman of broadcasting committee; delegate to Council of Europe and Western European Union (head of defense committee). Public affairs consultant. *Member:* Atlantic Association of Young Political Leaders (president, 1968-70), Coningsby Club, Oxford Union Society.

WRITINGS: (With Otto Pick) *Collective Security,* Macmillan, 1976; *Warning and Response: A History of Surprise Attack in the Twentieth Century,* Leo Cooper, 1978. Also

author of *Great Expectations: A History of Detente,* with Pick, 1979. Author of pamphlets for Bow Group. Restaurant correspondent under pseudonym William Beaufitz.

SIDELIGHTS: Critchley writes: "I am a moderately rightwing, cynical, and disenchanted English Conservative. I am interested in Europe, nineteenth-century England, nineteenth-century poetry, and nineteenth-century music." *Avocational interests:* Watching boxing, the country, reading military history, "making love and ends meet."

* * *

CROCETTI, Guido M. 1920-1979

PERSONAL: Born January 2, 1920, in New York, N.Y.; died May 28, 1979; married, 1941; children: two. *Education:* Rutgers University, B.Sc., 1941; attended Johns Hopkins University, 1959-61; Columbia University, Ph.D., 1973. *Office:* Institute of Mental Health Sciences, College of Medicine and Dentistry, Rutgers University, Piscataway, N.J. 08854.

CAREER: Dickinson College, Carlisle, Pa., instructor in sociology, 1948-50; Columbia University, New York City, research associate for Bureau of Applied Social Research, 1951; City College (now of the City University of New York), New York City, lecturer in sociology, 1952-55; New York Community Mental Health Board, director of research, 1955-58; Johns Hopkins University, Baltimore, Md., assistant professor of mental hygiene, 1959-69; Rutgers University, Medical School, Camden, N.J., associate professor of psychiatry, 1973—. Labor organizer for Textile Workers of America and United Retail Distribution and Warehouse Workers; member of New Jersey Collective Bargaining Agents Committee. Research associate of Hospital Council of Greater New York, 1952-55, and Richard Manville Research Institute, 1953-54. Participant in seminars; consultant to Iran's Ministry of Health and Scientific Management Corp. *Military service:* U.S. Coast Guard Reserve, active duty, 1942-45.

MEMBER: American Public Health Association, American Sociological Association, American Association of Public Opinion Research, American Association of University Professors (local president, 1974-75; chief negotiator, 1972-73, 1974-75, 1975-76), National Association for Prevention of Addiction, New Jersey Association for Mental Health. *Awards, honors:* Award of merit from Public Health Association of New York City, 1957.

WRITINGS: (With Peter Rogatz) *Organized Home Medical Care in New York City: A Study of Nineteen Programs,* Harvard University Press, 1956; (contributor) Leopold Bellack, editor, *Schizophrenia: A Review of the Syndrome,* Logos International, 1958; (contributor) Lewis E. Weeks and John R. Griffith, editors, *Progressive Patient Care: An Anthology,* University of Michigan Press, 1962; (contributor) Alfred M. Freeman and Harold I. Kaplan, editors, *Comprehensive Textbook of Psychiatry,* Williams & Wilkins, 1967; (with Herzl R. Spiro and Iradj Siassi) *Contemporary Attitudes Toward Mental Illness,* University of Pittsburgh Press, 1973. Also editor of *Mental Health Resources in New York City.* Contributor of more than thirty articles to public and mental health journals.

WORK IN PROGRESS: Psychiatric Care Through Collective Bargaining, with Herzl R. Spiro and Iradj Siassi.

* * *

CRONIN, Thomas E(dward) 1940-

PERSONAL: Born March 18, 1940, in Milton, Mass.; son of

Joseph M. (in business; a lawyer) and Mary M. Cronin; married Taniaz Zaroudny, 1966; children: Alexander. *Education:* Holy Cross College, A.B., 1961; Stanford University, M.A., 1962, Ph.D., 1968. *Politics:* Democrat. *Religion:* Roman Catholic. *Home:* 30 Thompson Lane, Milton, Mass. 02186. *Office:* Department of Political Science, University of Delaware, Newark, Del. 19711.

CAREER: White House aide in Washington, D.C., 1966-67; University of North Carolina, Chapel Hill, assistant professor of political science, 1967-70; Brookings Institution, Washington, D.C., research political scientist, 1970-73; Center for the Study of Democratic Institutions, Washington, D.C., research political scientist, 1972-74; University of Delaware, Newark, professor of political science, 1976—. Visiting professor at Brandeis University, 1975-77, and Colorado College, 1979. Lecturer at more than a hundred U.S. colleges and universities. Member of board of directors of Center for the Study of the Presidency; consultant to Congressional committees.

MEMBER: American Political Science Association, American Society of Public Administration, Common Cause (member of board of directors; head of Massachusetts board of directors, 1976-78).

WRITINGS: (Editor and contributor) *The Presidential Advisory System,* Harper, 1969; *The State of the Presidency,* Little, Brown, 1975; *The Presidency Reappraised,* Praeger, 1977; *Government by the People,* Prentice-Hall, 1978; *America in the Seventies,* Little, Brown, 1977; *State and Local Politics,* Prentice Hall, 1978. Contributor to newspapers, journals and magazines, including *Saturday Review, Politics Today, Commonweal, Science, Society, Public Administration Review, Skeptic,* and *Washington Monthly.* Consulting editor of *National Journal* and *Presidential Studies Quarterly.*

WORK IN PROGRESS: A study of direct democracy in America.

SIDELIGHTS: Cronin comments: "My major interest is helping to clarify and explain American politics, our policy-making processes, and our leadership institutions. Experience in the White House, in Congress, in state and national politics has shaped and informed much of my research and writing."

*   *   *

CROW, Duncan 1920-

PERSONAL: Born September 14, 1920, in Aberdeen, Scotland; son of Henry (a barrister and civil servant) and Margaret (Ballantyne) Crow; married August 30, 1945. *Education:* University College, London, B.A. (honors), 1940. *Home address:* c/o Midgeley & Co., 315 Regent St., London W1R 7YB, England. *Office:* 36 Golden Sq., London W1R 4AH, England.

CAREER: Food and Agricultural Organization of the United Nations, London, England, information officer in the United Kingdom, 1946-48; Central Office of Information, London, production controlling officer in Films Division and scriptwriter for Crown Film Unit, Beaconsfield, England, 1948-50; Political and Economic Planning, London, senior researcher, 1950-52; free-lance writer, 1952-58; Granada Television, Manchester and London, researcher, writer, producer, and executive, 1958—. Member of board of directors of Intermediate Technology Publications; past member of history selection committee of National Film Archive. *Military service:* British Army, Royal Armoured Corps, Royal Innis-

killing Dragoon Guards, 1940-46; served in France and Germany; became captain. *Member:* Society of Authors, British Academy of Film and Television Arts.

WRITINGS: The British Film Industry: Its History and Organisation, Political and Economic Planning, 1952; *Commonwealth Education: Britain's Contribution,* Central Office of Information, 1959, revised edition, 1961; *Henry Wikoff: The American Chevalier,* MacGibbon & Kee, 1963; *World in Action '63,* Consul Books, 1963; *World in Action: Second Series,* Mayflower, 1965; *A Man of Push and Go: The Life of George Macauley Booth,* Hart-Davis, 1965; *Theresa: The Story of the Yelverton Case,* Hart-Davis, 1966; *The First Summer* (novel), Hart-Davis, 1967; *Clem Atlee: The Granada Historical Records Interview,* Panther, 1967; *The Crimson Petal* (novel), Hart-Davis, 1969; *From the North* (history of Granada Television), privately printed, 1970; *The Victorian Woman,* Allen & Unwin, 1971, Stein & Day, 1972; *U.S. Armor-Cavalry 1917-1967: A Short History,* Doubleday, 1973; *British and Commonwealth Armoured Formations 1916-1946,* Profile Publications, 1973; (with H.B.C. Watkins) *Panzer Divisions of World War II,* Profile Publications, 1974; (with Robert J. Icks) *Encyclopedia of Tanks,* Chartwell Books, 1975; (with Icks) *Encyclopedia of Armoured Cars,* Chartwell Books, 1976; *The Edwardian Woman,* St. Martin's, 1978; *A Grave Danger of Invasion,* Profile Publications, 1980.

Editor: (And contributor) *Armored Fighting Vehicles in Profile,* Volume I: *AFVs of World War I,* Doubleday, 1970, Volume II: *British AFVs, 1919-1940,* Doubleday, 1970, Volume III: *British and Commonwealth AFVs, 1940-1946,* Doubleday, 1971, Volume IV: *American AFVs of World War II,* Doubleday, 1972, Volume V: *Armored Fighting Vehicles of Germany, World War II,* Arco, 1978, published in Canada as *Armoured Fighting Vehicles of the World,* Profile Publications, Volumes I and II, 1970, Volume III, 1971, Volume IV, 1972, Volume V: *German AFVs of World War II,* 1973, reprinted as *Armoured Fighting Vehicles of Germany, World War II,* Arco, 1978; Icks, *Modern U.S. Armored Support Vehicles,* Profile Publications, 1971; Nigel Duncan, *79th Armoured Division: Hobo's Funnies,* Profile Publications, 1971; Peter Chamberlain and Chris Ellis, *Making Tracks: The British Carrier Story, 1914-1972,* Profile Publications, 1973; *The State of the Nation: Parliament,* Granada Television, 1973; *Disappearing World,* Granada Television, 1973; Chamberlain and Terry Gander, *88 Flak and Pak,* Profile Publications, 1976; (and contributor) *Modern Battle Tanks,* Arco, 1978.

Contributor: Herbert Van Thal, editor, *The Prime Ministers,* Allen & Unwin, 1975.

Author of documentary film scripts, including "British Housing," released by Crown Film Unit, 1950; "In the Know," Ministry of Labor, 1951; "Introducing: United Kingdom," NATO, 1954; "The Grenadier Guards," Anvil Films, 1956; "Isotopes," United Kingdom Atomic Energy Authority, 1959; "The Engineer and the Atom," United Kingdom Atomic Energy Authority, 1959; "Shift-Working," British Productivity Council, 1960; "All Change for Tomorrow," British Productivity Council, 1961; "The Road to Hiroshima," Granada Television, 1961; "The Great Exhibition of 1851," Granada Television, 1962; "Sir Thomas Beecham," Granada Television, 1979.

Author of booklets and pamphlets. Editor of "AFV/Weapons Profiles," a monograph series, Profile Publications, 1969—. Contributor to *Encyclopaedia Britannica* and *Academic American Encyclopedia.* Contributor to magazines, including *Sight and Sound, Economist,* and *Independent Broadcasting.*

WORK IN PROGRESS: A trilogy, consisting of *Dragons Come Later, Upon a Frieze,* and *Court of Owls;* a book of photographs on Edwardian landed gentry.

SIDELIGHTS: Duncan Crow's *The Victorian Woman* shattered some misconceptions about the Victorian era. "This rich, learned and readable study makes it plain that the present image of the Victorian woman is precisely that with which generations of lively, intelligent Victorian women refused to conform and struggled to destroy," a *Times Literary Supplement* reviewer wrote. He went on: "In all but one dimension the Victorian age appears as it was: a period not of prunes and prisms but of rough, vivid, violent development in which rigid codes of behaviour served to control the pressures which might otherwise have exploded. That dimension is the religious one. Although Mr. Crow stresses 'the predominance of religion' he does not seem to be aware of its meaning." W. H. Archer also admired *The Victorian Woman,* calling it "vivid" and "illuminating." "To use 'Victorian' as a term of denigration becomes impossible after pondering Mr. Crow's study of the complex forces at work during the nineteenth century in the United States and Great Britain," Archer commented.

Crow told *CA:* "*A Grave Danger of Invasion* and the book of photographs of Edwardian landed gentry that I'm writing are both spin-offs from *The Edwardian Woman.* One of the worries in Edwardian England was the growth of German sea power and the conviction that Germany would invade England. There were many fictional invasions; e.g., William Le Queux's *The Invasion of 1910. A Grave Danger* describes the projected invasions during the past two hundred years and looks at the auxiliary forces which were set up to defend the country and how technological advances such as steam navigation and airborne troops affected the situation. *Dragons Come Later* is set in England in 1939 and 1940, and covers the period of Dunkirk and the threat of invasion immediately after it. I seem to be in an invasion syndrome at the moment!

"The book of Edwardian pictures arises from a cache of several thousand photographs that came into my possession a year or two ago, a few of which I used in *The Edwardian Woman.* I hope to be able to show, by using two well-known Yorkshire families, how the county families of the turn of the century lived: their holidays in the highlands of Scotland, Switzerland, and Algeria, their motor cars, as they called them, their amateur dramatics, and so on. My writing interests are basically concerned with social and military history."

BIOGRAPHICAL/CRITICAL SOURCES: Times Literary Supplement, September 17, 1971, May 5, 1978; *New Statesman,* December 24, 1971; *Best Sellers,* April 15, 1972.

*   *   *

CROW, Jeffrey J(ay) 1947-

PERSONAL: Born May 29, 1947, in Akron, Ohio; son of David O. (a personnel manager) and Gwendolyn (McClellan) Crow. *Education:* Ohio State University, B.A., 1969; University of Akron, M.A., 1972; Duke University, Ph.D., 1974. *Politics:* Independent Democrat. *Home:* 1803 Arlington St., Raleigh, N.C. 27608. *Office:* North Carolina Division of Archives and History, 109 East Jones St., Raleigh, N.C. 27611.

CAREER: Duke University, Durham, N.C., instructor in

history, 1973-74; North Carolina Bicentennial Committee, Raleigh, N.C., historian, 1974-76; North Carolina Division of Archives and History, Raleigh, editor of historical publications, 1976—. *Member:* Southern Historical Association, Historical Society of North Carolina, Phi Beta Kappa. *Awards, honors:* William R. Davie Award from state chapter of Sons of the American Revolution, 1977, for pamphlet series, "North Carolina in the American Revolution."

WRITINGS: A Chronicle of North Carolina During the American Revolution, 1763-1789 (pamphlet), North Carolina Division of Archives and History, 1975; (with Robert F. Durden) *Maverick Republican in the Old North State: A Political Biography of Daniel L. Russell,* Louisiana State University Press, 1977; *The Black Experience in Revolutionary North Carolina* (pamphlet), North Carolina Division of Archives and History, 1977; (editor with Larry E. Tise) *The Southern Experience in the American Revolution,* University of North Carolina Press, 1978.

Co-author of film script, "Majority of One," released by North Carolina Department of Cultural Resources in 1976. Editor of pamphlet series, "North Carolina in the American Revolution," fourteen volumes, North Carolina Bicentennial Committee, 1974-78. Contributor of articles and reviews to history journals. Editor of *Carolina Comments,* 1977—.

WORK IN PROGRESS: Populism and Fusion in North Carolina, publication by University of North Carolina Press expected in 1981; research on conflict and slave rebellion in Revolutionary North Carolina, 1775-1802.

SIDELIGHTS: Crow comments: "History must be rewritten by each new generation. Although the past does not change, the present does, and thus succeeding generations of historians bring new questions, different assumptions, and more finely honed methodological tools to the examination of historical evidence. The uncritical celebration of 'progress' in American history is giving way to more tough-minded analysis as the historical scene shifts away from the halls of Congress, White House, and plantation to the farm, factory, and ethnic ghetto. Although historians can recover only a tiny fragment of the past, they have yet to recover a 'usable' past—rich in textures, complexity, and meaning for contemporary America. The decline of the study of history in our schools attests to this failure, but it is not too late to reverse the trend."

AVOCATIONAL INTERESTS: Sports, film, music, golf, tennis, basketball, fishing.

*   *   *

CUDDIHY, John Murray 1922-

PERSONAL: Born January 22, 1922, in New York, N.Y.; son of H. Lester (a publisher) and Julia (Murray) Cuddihy; married Harriet Pray Dettaven (in flower business); children: Heidi, Johnny, Julia. *Office:* Department of Sociology, Hunter College of the City University of New York, 695 Park Ave., New York, N.Y. 10021.

CAREER: Presently associate professor of sociology at Hunter College of the City University of New York, New York City. Previously a faculty member at Columbia University, New York City, Vassar College, Poughkeepsie, N.Y., William Alanson White Institute of Psychiatry, New School for Social Research, New York City, and Rutgers University, New Brunswick, N.J. *Awards, honors:* National Book Award nomination, for *The Ordeal of Civility.*

WRITINGS: The Ordeal of Civility: Freud, Marx, Levi-

Strauss, and the Jewish Struggle With Modernity, Basic Books, 1974; *No Offense: Civil Religion and Protestant Taste,* Seabury, 1978.

BIOGRAPHICAL/CRITICAL SOURCES: Stephen Birmingham, *Real Lace: America's Irish Rich,* Harper, 1975; *New York Times Book Review,* July 9, 1978.

* * *

CULBERTSON, Judi 1941-

PERSONAL: Born March 1, 1941, in Norfolk, Va.; daughter of Hubert Roe (an engineer and U.S. Coast Guard captain) and Charlotte (Hess) Chaffee; married Paul Culbertson, June 21, 1962 (marriage ended, 1970); married Thomas Randall (a social worker), June 22, 1974; children: (first marriage) Andrew William. *Education:* Wheaton College, Wheaton, Ill., B.A., 1962. *Home:* 211 Hawthorne St., Port Jefferson, N.Y. 11777. *Agent:* Hiede Lange, Sanford J. Greenburger Associates, Inc., 825 Third Ave., New York, N.Y. 10022. *Office:* Suffolk County Department of Social Services, Patchogue, N.Y. 11772.

CAREER: Eternity (magazine), Philadelphia, Pa., editorial assistant, 1962-64; Middle Country School District II, Centereach, N.Y., substitute teacher, 1966-70; Suffolk County Department of Social Services, Patchogue, N.Y., social worker, 1970—.

WRITINGS: (With Patti Bard) *Games Christians Play,* Harper, 1967; (with Bard) *The Little White Book on Race,* Lippincott, 1970; (with brother, John Chaffee) *Games America Played: An Informal History of Board Games in America,* Scribner, 1980. Contributor to *Glamour, Christian Herald,* and *Writer's Digest.*

WORK IN PROGRESS: Teddy Bear, Teddy Bear, a mystery novel set in the postwar era of 1949, evoking the atmosphere of that time as well as murder, infant stealing, and suspense; *Lost Parents, Lost Children,* a critical look at foster care based, in part, on interviews with former foster children.

SIDELIGHTS: Judi Culbertson writes: "I am particularly interested in mysteries, and would love to be the American Agatha Christie, but my books, serious or satirical, all center around a fascination with human behavior and are written with the hope of further identifying or illuminating it." *Avocational interests:* Running, travel, reading, antiques.

* * *

CUNNINGHAM, Laura 1947-

PERSONAL: Born January 25, 1947, in New York, N.Y.; daughter of Laurence Moore (an aviator) and Rose Weiss; married Barry Cunningham (a journalist), December 4, 1966. *Education:* New York University, B.A., 1966. *Residence:* Tuxedo Park, N.Y.; and New York, N.Y. *Agent:* Owen Laster, William Morris Agency, 1350 Avenue of the Americas, New York, N.Y. 10019.

CAREER: Author. *Member:* Writers Guild of America, Girl Scouts of America, Authors Guild, Poets and Writers, Writer's Community.

WRITINGS: Sweet Nothings (novel), Doubleday, 1977. Contributor of articles and reviews to magazines and newspapers, including *Atlantic Monthly* and *Village Voice.*

WORK IN PROGRESS: A novel, tentatively titled *Third Parties,* examining the relationship between inflation and sex ("it isn't good").

SIDELIGHTS: Laura Cunningham writes: "I have a typical writer's personal history, that is: atypical. I am of Jewish-Southern Baptist descent, was orphaned at age eight, and raised by two unmarried uncles (both writers). I'm a third generation author: my grandparents also wrote stories and books. Motivation? I didn't know there was anything else to be. Had I known, I would have been a ballerina."

* * *

CUNNINGHAM, Lawrence 1935-

PERSONAL: Born September 23, 1935, in Pittsburgh, Pa.; son of Lawrence (a teacher) and Helen (Shimkus) Cunningham; married Cecilia Davis (a potter), October 13, 1972. *Education:* St. Bernard's Seminary and College, A.B., 1957; Pontifical Gregorian University, S.T.L., 1961; Florida State University, M.A., 1963, Ph.D., 1969. *Politics:* Democrat. *Religion:* Roman Catholic. *Home address:* P.O. Box 607, Crawfordville, Fla. 32327. *Office:* Department of Religion, Florida State University, Tallahassee, Fla. 32306.

CAREER: Florida State University, Tallahassee, instructor, 1966-69, assistant professor, 1969-73, associate professor of religion, 1973—, assistant director of university center in Florence, Italy, 1970-72. *Member:* American Academy of Religion, College Theology Society.

WRITINGS: (Editor) *Brother Francis,* Harper, 1972; *Saint Francis of Assisi,* Twayne, 1976; (translator) Saint Bonaventure, *Mind's Journey to God,* Franciscan Herald, 1979. Contributor to magazines, including *Commonweal, America,* and *Christian Century.*

WORK IN PROGRESS: A revisionist book on Roman Catholic saints, publication expected in 1981.

SIDELIGHTS: Cunningham comments: "I am interested in Catholicism and its cultural matrix." *Avocational interests:* Gardening, beekeeping, Italian opera, collecting art.

* * *

CURLER, (Mary) Bernice 1915-
(Mary Bernice Davis)

PERSONAL: Born December 4, 1915, in Los Angeles, Calif.; daughter of Charles E. and Josephine Babette (Meier) Davis; married Albert Elmer Curler, April 10, 1938; children: Daniel Jay, Dawna Dee. *Education:* Attended Woodbury College, 1934, 1935. *Home and office:* 8156 Waikiki Dr., Fair Oaks, Calif. 95628.

CAREER: U.S. Navy Ship Yards, Bremerton, Wash., in personnel, 1944-45; WSAP-Radio, Portsmouth, Va., copy writer, 1945; associated with Hillman, Shane & Bryon Advertising Agency, Los Angeles, Calif., 1945-46; free-lance writer, 1957—. Instructor at Cosumnes River College, 1970-77; assistant director and instructor at Sierra Writing Camp, 1975-77; conducts writing seminars. *Member:* American Society of Journalists and Authors, California Writers' Club (past president; past member of board of directors). *Awards, honors:* Literary achievement award from Sacramento Regional Arts Council, 1974.

WRITINGS: (Contributor) Lyle E. Schaller and Edgar R. Trexler, editors, *Creative Congregations,* Abingdon, 1972; *Story of a Medal: A Family Heritage* (nonfiction), Jay-Dee Press, 1976.

Author of "Mazie's Red Garter" (one-act play), first produced in Carmichael, Calif., 1962.

Contributor of articles and stories (sometimes under name Mary Bernice Davis) to a wide variety of trade journals and popular magazines, including *House Beautiful, Young Miss, McCall's, Parents' Magazine,* and *Modern Maturity,* and newspapers.

WORK IN PROGRESS: In Search of Calafia (tentative title), a historical novel; research on early California.

SIDELIGHTS: Curler comments: "Writing has always been a way of life for me—first only a dream, then at last fulfillment when my thoughts and emotions appeared in print—and others read them. Short fiction was the first vehicle, followed by a number of years of writing nonfiction: articles about far-away places, social issues, craft projects, and fascinating people. But now I'm back to fiction in novel form—releasing the true creative impulses. I feel I have finally come home."

*   *   *

CURRIER, Frederick P(lumer) 1923-

PERSONAL: Born December 6, 1923, in Grand Rapids, Mich.; married Caroline Elizabeth Musselman, July 14, 1951; children: Nancy, Amelia, Rebecca. *Education:* Attended Grinnell College, 1942-43, and University of Chicago, 1943-44, 1949-51; University of Illinois, A.B., 1948, M.A., 1949. *Politics:* Independent. *Religion:* Congregationalist. *Residence:* Birmingham, Mich. *Office:* 28 West Adams, Detroit, Mich. 48226; and Suite 2055, Commerce Court W., Toronto, Ontario, Canada M5L 1E7.

CAREER: Morristown Sun, Morristown, Tenn., vice-president and co-publisher, 1952-54; bank loan analyst in Detroit, Mich., 1954-55; *Detroit Free Press,* Detroit, research manager, 1955-62; Market Opinion Research, Detroit, and Canadian Opinion Research, Toronto, Ontario, vice-president, 1962-68, president, 1968—. Adjunct professor at University of Michigan; instructor in marketing and economics at University of Illinois, Detroit Institute of Technology, Wayne State University, and University of Michigan. Member of the American Marketing Association National Census Advisory Committee for the Bureau of the Census and American Newspaper Publishers Association Newspaper Advertising Bureau; co-founder of American Newspaper Publishers Association Research Advisory Council; secretary-treasurer of National Council on Public Polls. *Military service:* U.S. Air Force, 1943-46. *Member:* American Economic Association, American Marketing Association (president of Detroit chapter, 1961), American Newspaper Publishers Association, United Community Service Assembly, Economic Club of Detroit, University of Chicago National Alumni Board, Detroit Alumni of University of Chicago (past chairman).

WRITINGS: (Contributor) R. E. Heibert, editor, *The Political Image Merchants,* Acropolis Books, 1971. Also author of "The *Detroit News* Poll of Election Trends," 1968—. Contributor to *Journalism Quarterly.*

SIDELIGHTS: Currier's Market Opinion Research, one of the twenty-five largest survey research firms in the United States, has handled the survey research for the last two incumbent U.S. presidents. His Canadian Opinion Research has been involved in national surveys for the past two federal elections in Canada. Currier has spent nearly a quarter century in consumer research and attitude measurement and has pioneered the ticket-splitter concept of political behavior and various aspects of media measurement.

AVOCATIONAL INTERESTS: Photography, writing.

D

DAHL, Georg 1905-

PERSONAL: Born November 23, 1905, in Sunnemo, Sweden; son of Anders Wilhelm (a forest officer) and Emmy (Carlsson) Dahl; married Marta Althen, February 12, 1937 (divorced February 12, 1974); married Naemi Gustafsson, March 15, 1974; children: (first marriage) Leif Georg, Sven Ottar Wilhelm. *Education:* Attended secondary school in Karlstads, Sweden. *Home address:* Posseberg, Kristinehamn, Sweden S-681 00.

CAREER: High school teacher in Colombia, 1949-58; Universidad Nacional de Colombia, Bogota, professor of ichthyology, 1958-61; Department of Fisheries Research, Cartagena, Colombia, director, 1961-67; writer, 1967—. *Member:* Traveller's Club.

WRITINGS: The Metamorphosis From Leptocephalus to Postlarval Stage in the Common Tarpon (pamphlet; Spanish-English bilingual edition), Corporacion Autonoma Regional de los Valles del Magdalena y del Sinu, 1965; *Two Children's Stories for Physicians and Other Wise Men,* Bell Museum of Pathobiology, School of Medicine, University of Minnesota, 1973.

Other: *Aeventyrens maen: Beraettelser om Latin amerikas eroevring* (historical essays), Fahlcrantz & Gumaelius, 1946; *Jakt paa aender och vadare* (nonfiction), Fahlcrantz & Gumaelius, 1948; *Oernoega och aaskgudinnans tempel* (juvenile nonfiction), Bonnier, 1959; *Mangroveland: Syner och minnen* (essays and stories), Bonnier, 1963; (with Federico Medem and Alonso Ramos Henao) *El "Bocachico": Contribution al estudio de su biologia y de su ambiente,* Corporacion Autonoma Regional de los Valles del Magdalena y del Sinu, 1963; (with Medem) *Informe sobre la fauna acuatica del Rio Sinu,* Corporacion Autonoma Regional de los Valles del Magdalena y del Sinu, 1965; *Den sista floden: Tjugo aar i Colombias urskogar* (memoirs), Bonnier, 1967; *Min vaen Jose Dolores: En bok om Colombia* (nonfiction), Bonnier, 1968; *De vilda vaegarna: En faerdkroenika fraan Orinocos bifloder* (nonfiction), Bonnier, 1969; *Under min grannes traed* (essays), Bonnier, 1970; *Los peces del norte de Colombia* (nonfiction), Instituto de Desarrollo de los Recursos Naturales Renovables, 1971; *Fraan mitt afrikanska vattenhaal* (nonfiction), Bonnier, 1973.

Also author of *Snoepaels,* 1926, *De graa fraan grottan,* 1928, *De snabba vingarna,* 1929, *Sommarliv i Lappmarken,* 1931, *Djuren i vaara skogar,* 1932, *Sjoearnas och aelvarnas djur,* 1933, *Djuren i vaar fjaellvaerld,* 1936, *Guld och vilt,* 1938, *Jaguar,* 1939, *Tvaa aar som indian,* 1940, *Djungelfeber,* 1943, *Sedan kommo spanjorerna,* 1945, *De odoedlige conquistadoren,* 1947, *Oernoega och krigsgudens baage,* 1958, *Oernoega och folket ovan molnen,* 1961, *Vaermlandsminnen,* 1970, *En vaermlaendsk loeskerkarl,* 1971; *Den laanga rodden,* three volumes, 1973-75, *En jaegare minns.*

SIDELIGHTS: Dahl's deepest interest since childhood has been the natural world, especially the areas of zoology and protection of the environment and wildlife. He writes that he has spent twenty-five years in Latin America, especially Colombia, Venezuela, and Panama. But he has also traveled in Turkey, North Africa, West Africa, Portugal, Spain, and the United States. He speaks and writes in English, Spanish, and German, as well as the Scandinavian languages, and his books have also been translated for publication in the Soviet Union.

AVOCATIONAL INTERESTS: Fishing, hunting.

* * *

DAKERS, Elaine Kidner 1905-1978
(Jane Lane)

PERSONAL: Born in 1905, in Rorslip, England; died January 6, 1978; daughter of Mason and Enid Kidner; married Andrew Dakers, 1937; children: Stewart. *Education:* Attended schools in Middlesex, England. *Residence:* Sussex, England.

CAREER: Writer, 1933-78.

WRITINGS—Novels; under pseudonym Jane Lane: *King's Critic,* Rich & Cowan, 1935; *Prelude to Kingship,* Rich & Cowan, 1936, reprinted, International Publications Service, 1969; *Sir Devil-May-Care,* Methuen, 1937, reprinted, Muller, 1971; *He Stooped to Conquer,* Dakers, 1943, reprinted, International Publications Service, 1968; *England for Sale,* Dakers, 1943; *Gin and Bitters,* Dakers, 1945, reprinted, Muller, 1966, published as *Madame Geneva,* Rinehart, 1946; *His Fight Is Ours,* Dakers, 1946, *London Goes to Heaven,* Dakers, 1947; *Parcel of Rogues,* Rinehart, 1948.

Fortress in the Forth, Dakers, 1950; *Dark Conspiracy,* R. Hale, 1952; *Thunder on St. Paul's Day,* Newman Press, 1954; *Conies in the Hay,* R. Hale, 1957, published as *Rabbits in the Hay,* Newman Press, 1958; *Command Performance,* R. Hale, 1957; *Sow the Tempest,* Muller, 1960; *Ember in the Ashes,* Muller, 1960; *A Wind Through the Heather: A Novel of the Highland Clearances,* International Publications Service, 1965; *From the Snare of the Hunters*, International Publications Service, 1968; *The Young and Lonely King*, Muller, 1969.

The Questing Beast, International Publications Service, 1970; *A Call of Trumpets*, International Publications Service, 1971; *The Severed Crown*, P. Davies, 1972, Simon & Schuster, 1973; *Bridge of Sighs*, P. Davies, 1973, John Day, 1975; *Heirs of Squire Harry*, P. Davies, 1974; *A Summer Storm*, P. Davies, 1976; *A Secret Chronicle*, P. Davies, 1977. Also author of *Undaunted*, 1934, *Be Valiant Still*, 1935, *Come to the March*, 1937, *You Can't Run Away*, 1940, *The Sealed Knot*, 1952, *The Lady of the House*, 1953, *The Phoenix and the Laurel*, 1954, *Queen of the Castle*, 1958, Sphere Books, 1971, *Cat Among the Pigeons*, 1959, *Farewell to the White Cockade*, 1961, *The Crown for a Lie*, 1962, and *A State of Mind*, 1964.

Nonfiction; all under pseudonym Jane Lane: *King James the Last*, Dakers, 1942; *Titus Oates*, Dakers, 1949; *Puritan, Rake, and Squire*, Richard West, 1950; *The Reign of King Covenant*, R. Hale, 1956.

For children; all under pseudonym Jane Lane: *Escape of the King*, illustrations by Jack Mathews, Evans, 1950; *The Escape of the Prince*, Evans, 1951. Also author of *Desperate Battle*, 1953, *The Escape of the Queen*, 1957, *The Escape of the Duke*, 1960, *The Escape of the Princess*, 1962, *The Trial of the King*, 1963, *The Return of the King*, 1964, *The March of the Prince*, 1965, *The Champion of the King*, 1966.

SIDELIGHTS: Stewart Dakers writes: "Jane Lane believed strongly that a writer was no different from any other worker; that in effect, background, personal status, and any other sociological data were irrelevant and intrusive. As a person she was a private individual, known to her friends; as a writer she was known to her readers. To confuse the two was, to her, anathema."

[Sketch verified by son, Stewart Dakers]

* * *

DALTON, Elizabeth 1936-

PERSONAL: Born December 25, 1936, in New York, N.Y.; daughter of James Leo and Alice (Carville) Dalton. *Education:* University of California, Berkeley, B.A., 1957; Columbia University, Ph.D., 1975. *Residence:* New York, N.Y. *Office:* Department of English, Barnard College, New York, N.Y. 10014.

CAREER: American Consulate, Paris, France, translator and clerk, 1958-59; administrative assistant for an international cultural foundation, 1959-62; administrative assistant in New York City, 1962-65; Barnard College, New York City, instructor, 1965-75, assistant professor of English, 1975—. *Member:* International P.E.N., Phi Beta Kappa. *Awards, honors:* Fulbright scholar in France, 1957-58; Rockefeller Foundation humanities fellow, 1977-78.

WRITINGS: Unconscious Structure in "The Idiot": A Study in Literature and Psychoanalysis, Princeton University Press, 1979. Contributor of stories, articles, and reviews to magazines, including *New Yorker* and *Commentary*. Assistant editor of *Partisan Review*.

* * *

DALTON, Stephen 1937-

PERSONAL: Born October 2, 1937, in Kingswood, Surrey, England; son of Douglas and Stephanie (Olver) Dalton; married Elizabeth Mac Andrew, June 24, 1977; children:

Joanna, Philip, Lee. *Education:* Regent Street Polytechnic, diploma in photography, 1964. *Religion:* Christian. *Home:* Holly Farmhouse, Cob Lane, Ardingly, Sussex, England.

CAREER: Wildlife photographer and author. Work exhibited at Kodak Galleries, Photographers Gallery, and Pentax Gallery, all London, England. *Military service:* Royal Air Force, 1956. *Member:* Royal Photographic Society (honorary fellow), Institute of Incorporated Photographers (fellow). *Awards, honors:* Kodak scholarship in advance photography, 1962; Kodak Award, 1970, for development of specialized high speed flash equipment; Hood Medal, 1971, and Silver Progress Medal, 1978, both from Royal Photographic Society; named animal photographer of the year by Rothmans, 1972; Nikon Award, 1977.

WRITINGS: Borne on the Wind, Reader's Digest Press, 1975; *The Miracle of Flight*, Samson Low, 1977, McGraw, 1978. Also author of *Ants From Close-up*, Crowell, *Bees From Close-up*, Crowell, and *Looking at Nature*, Jarrolds. Contributor of articles on photography and wildlife subjects to professional journals and magazines.

WORK IN PROGRESS: Photographing bats.

SIDELIGHTS: Stephen Dalton began photographing wildlife when he was a young boy after receiving from his photographer father a box Brownie. Fascinated by insects, Dalton began work on the development of high speed flash equipment, lens, and camera shutter that would enable him to photograph insects during free flight, a feat no photographer had yet accomplished. He enlisted the aid of Ron Perkins, an electronics scientist with the Central Unit of Scientific Photography and together they worked for more than two years. The result of their endeavors was a sensor-trigger system that would react to a human hair passing through its beam. Dalton then photographed over two-hundred different species of insects during free flight in the Florida Everglades and the Upper Amazon. Dalton noted that he's taken "as many as 900 exposures of a single insect."

Prior to the development of this new system insects were never photographed during free flight; they were tethered or suspended in harnesses. The reason being, of course, that they fly too fast and as Dalton stated that they "zigzag indiscriminately." The beat of the wings of even the slowest insect is a problem for most photographers as the wings themselves often appear blurred to the human eye. Some insects register up to 1,000 wing beats per second.

Dalton considers photographing birds "relatively easy. They fly in straight lines, and they have to come back to the nest. You could wait 500 years for a specific species of insect to arrive, though, and still not get your picture."

Much as he enjoys flying, Dalton sometimes finds it disappointing after studying the flying abilities of the insect. "Perhaps if I went up in a Tiger Moth," he told *Radio Times* reporter Gordon Burns, "and did acrobatics, then I might get more satisfaction out of it; perhaps then I might feel free of the earthly constraints. Because, ordinarily, you're just flying on a set course, sitting there twiddling, watching dials."

Dalton and his work were the subject of a documentary special, entitled "Secrets on the Wing," for the British Broadcasting Corp. (BBC) program "The World Around Us," 1978.

AVOCATIONAL INTERESTS: Flying, hang-gliding, playing the harpsichord.

BIOGRAPHICAL/CRITICAL SOURCES: Practical Photography, May, 1978; *Radio Times*, May 20-26, 1978.

DALY, Mary Tinley   1904(?)-1979

OBITUARY NOTICE: Born c. 1904 in Council Bluffs, Iowa; died March 13, 1979, in Washington, D.C. Former director of public relations at Catholic University and syndicated columnist. Daly wrote a weekly newspaper column about family life called "At Our House," which was an account of the doings in the Daly household. The column was syndicated by the National Catholic News Service (now NC News Service) and appeared in Catholic newspapers throughout the United States and Canada for twenty-one years. She also wrote articles for *Parents', Coronet,* and *Baby Talk.* Obituaries and other sources: *Washington Post,* March 14, 1979; *Chicago Tribune,* March 18, 1979.

*   *   *

DANA, Richard H(enry)   1927-

PERSONAL: Born June 14, 1927, in Bronxville, N.Y.; son of Richard Henry and Hilda (Jackson) Dana. *Education:* Princeton University, B.A. (honors), 1949; University of Illinois, M.S., 1951, Ph.D., 1953. *Office:* Department of Psychology, University of Arkansas, Fayetteville, Ark. 72701.

CAREER: Veterans Administration Hospital, Danville, Ill., clinical psychology trainee, 1950-52; Veterans Administration Hospital, Fresno, Calif., clinical psychology trainee, 1952-53; Veterans Administration Hospital, Denver, Colo., clinical psychologist, 1953—. Clinical psychologist, Winona County Dependency Project, 1953-54; research associate and clinical psychologist, St. Louis State Hospital, 1954-56; assistant professor of psychology, University of Wisconsin—Milwaukee, 1956-57; assistant professor of psychology, University of Nevada, 1957-61; West Virginia University, Morgantown, associate professor, 1961-63, professor of psychology, 1963-64; visiting professor of psychology, University of South Florida, 1964-65; professor of psychology, University of Wyoming, 1965-67; Marquette University, Milwaukee, Wis., professor of psychology and psychiatry, 1967-69, head of department of psychology, 1968-69; University of Arkansas, Fayetteville, professor of psychology, 1969—, director of clinical training program, 1971-74. Visiting professor at New Mexico Highlands University, summer, 1955; distinguished visiting professor at University of Montana, summer, 1972. Diplomate of American Board of Professional Psychology; private practice of clinical psychology, 1957-61. *Military service:* U.S. Army, 1945-46.

MEMBER: American Psychological Association (fellow), Society for Personality Assessment (fellow; president-elect, 1978), Sigma Xi. *Awards, honors:* James McKeen Cattell Fund grant, 1956-57; grants from U.S. Department of Health, Education and Welfare, 1963-66, 1966-69, 1972-75; Cancer Research Foundation grant, 1964-65.

WRITINGS: Foundations of Clinical Psychology: Problems in Personality and Adjustment, Van Nostrand, 1966; (contributor) Lewis Bernstein and B. Burris, editors, *The Contribution of the Social Sciences to Psychotherapy,* C. C Thomas, 1967; (editor and contributor) *Readings in Personality Assessment,* MSS Educational Publishing, 1969.

(Editor) *Readings in Abnormal Behavior: Toward a Sociopsychological Model,* MSS Educational Publishing, 1970; (with Lewis Bernstein) *Interviewing and the Health Professions,* Appleton, 1970, revised edition, with Bernstein and R. S. Bernstein, published as *Interviewing: A Guide for Health Professionals,* 1974; (with James Turner) *Coupling: An Exploration in Living and Loving,* Printing Services, University of Arkansas, 1975; (with Marian Gilliam) *Self-Exploration and Self-Appraisal: A Course-in-Oneself,* Print-

ing Services, University of Arkansas, 1975; *Manual for a Course-in-Oneself,* Printing Services, University of Arkansas, 1975; *Self-Assessment for Paraprofessional Trainees,* Printing Office, University of Arkansas, 1977, revised edition, 1978; (with Jeff Brookings) *A Self-Assessment Manual for Human Service Paraprofessionals,* Printing Office, University of Arkansas, 1978; (with C. E. Brian) *Some Paraprofessional Resources and Activities in Northwest Arkansas,* Printing Office, University of Arkansas, 1978; (with Brian and G. L. Tabor) *A Training Manual for Paraprofessional Helping Skills,* Printing Office, University of Arkansas, 1978. Also author of *So You Want to Be a Clinical Psychologist?: Graduate Training and Informed Choice–A Student's Guide to Decision-Making,* 1977.

Contributor to *International Encyclopedia of Neurology, Psychiatry, Psychoanalysis, and Psychology* and *Encyclopedia of Clinical Assessment.* Contributor of about a hundred articles and reviews to psychology journals. Consulting editor of *Journal of Personality Assessment.*

WORK IN PROGRESS: Psychological Assessment; A Human Science Model for Psychological Research and Practice.

SIDELIGHTS: Dana told *CA:* "Since 1969 I have been concerned that my research and practice expressed a value system that speaks to quality of life and humanization. My work has been accordingly focused on giving away what we know as psychologists: training, growth, and self-development.

AVOCATIONAL INTERESTS: Poetry, travel (Europe and South America), backpacking, rural lifestyle.

*   *   *

DANGAARD, Colin (Edward)   1942-

PERSONAL: Born May 1, 1942, in Monto, Australia; immigrated to United States in 1969; son of Alan (a businessman) and Millie (Thompson) Dangaard; married Kay Hooper (a publicist and writer), March 27, 1963 (divorced, March, 1978); children: Christian. *Education:* Educated in North Queensland, Australia. *Office:* International Features, Inc., P.O. Box 987, Malibu, Calif. 90265.

CAREER: Cairns Post, Cairns, North Queensland, Australia, cadet, 1961; *Rotorua Post,* Lake Taupo, New Zealand, staff member, 1962; *Fiji Times,* Fiji, staff member, 1963; *Sydney Sun,* Sydney, Australia, staff member, 1964; *Hongkong Star,* Hong Kong, China, reporter, 1966-67, editor, 1967-68; *Sunday Times,* Johannesburg, South Africa, feature writer, 1968; *Miami Herald,* Miami, Fla., staff member, 1970; free-lance writer, 1972—; owner of International Features, Inc. Has also lived and worked in Greece, the Caribbean, and Europe.

WRITINGS: English Comprehension (short stories), Longmans, Green, 1978. Contributor of numerous articles to newspapers and magazines. Contributing editor, *Us* magazine.

SIDELIGHTS: Dangaard has realized his dream of being an internationally syndicated writer. Circulation of periodicals containing articles by him exceed forty million issues weekly. Recalling his upbringing in Australia's outback, Dangaard wrote: "Where I come from, you either went south to a big city and worked in a bank, or north to a cattle property, to move the big herds, break horses, or build fences. The first choice seemed dull, and, having cattle property in the family, I knew I wasn't tough enough for the second." Instead, Dangaard chose the field of journalism. He began his career as a cadet reporter for the *Cairns Post* in

Australia, moved on to New Zealand, and subsequently worked in "15 other countries, changing jobs about every six months, all the while assembling an international network of contacts to be used later in building International Features, Inc."

In 1969, Dangaard sailed to the United States from Cape Town, South Africa, on a thirty-four foot wooden boat. Eventually, he ended up in Hollywood where he focused his writing on show business, "figuring that was what most of the people in most of the countries wanted to read."

Dangaard told *CA:* "At the *Cairns Post* I was the world's poorest journalist; so poor I could not afford to obey the order when they first fired me. Since then I decided I would become the world's richest print journalist. This is still my aim. I want to show that journalism can be big dollars, and that we are actually worth a lot of money. I am also motivated to entertain rather than inform. I write for a living because any other occupation is dull by comparison."

AVOCATIONAL INTERESTS: Raising quarter horses, surfing, jogging, entertaining.

* * *

DANILOFF, Nicholas 1934-

PERSONAL: Born December 30, 1934, in Paris, France; married in 1961; children: two. *Education:* Harvard University, A.B. (cum laude), 1956; Magdalen College, Oxford, B.A., 1960, M.A., 1965. *Home:* 3713 Warren St. N.W., Washington, D.C. 20016. *Office:* United Press International, 315 National Press Bldg., Washington, D.C. 20045.

CAREER: United Press International, staff member in London, England, 1959, bureau manager in Geneva, Switzerland, 1960-61, correspondent in Moscow, Russia, congressional and diplomatic correspondent in Washington, D.C., 1966—. Adjunct professor at American University, 1975—. *Member:* Overseas Writers (president, 1976-77), State Department Correspondents Association (president, 1969-70). *Awards, honors:* Nieman fellow at Harvard University, 1973-74.

WRITINGS: The Kremlin and the Cosmos, Knopf, 1972.

WORK IN PROGRESS: Foreign Affairs Reporting, a textbook describing the problems of a diplomatic correspondent in Washington, Moscow, and Peking; *Soviet-American Relations Since 1962: The Struggle to Live Together.*

SIDELIGHTS: Daniloff told *CA:* "*The Kremlin and the Cosmos* is a book for the general reader describing the interest in space flight in Russia in the nineteenth century, and tracing developments to the early 1970's. The book focuses on the pioneers of the 1920's, the forward leap brought on by World War II, and the efforts at U.S.-Soviet cooperation in space. *Soviet American Relations Since 1962* grows out of my experience as a U.S. correspondent in Moscow during the Cuban missiles crisis, and later in Washington during the end of the Vietnam war, and of the long struggle to achieve a SALT treaty with Moscow."

* * *

DANSON, Lawrence Neil 1942-

PERSONAL: Born November 10, 1942, in New York, N.Y.; married, 1967; two children. *Education:* Dartmouth College, B.A., 1964; Oxford University, M.A., 1966; Yale University, Ph.D., 1969. *Office:* Department of English, Princeton University, Princeton, N.J. 08540.

CAREER: Princeton University, Princeton, N.J., instruc-

tor, 1968-70, assistant professor, 1970-76, associate professor of English, 1976—. *Member:* Modern Language Association of America, Shakespeare Association of America.

WRITINGS: Tragic Alphabet: Shakespeare's Drama of Language, Yale University Press, 1974; *The Harmonies of "The Merchant of Venice",* Yale University Press, 1978. Contributor to language and literature journals.

* * *

DASHTI, Ali 1894-

PERSONAL: Born March 31, 1894, in Karbala, Iraq; son of Abdol Hossine and Mariam Dashti. *Education:* Attended Darol Elm Islami Ghavam. *Religion:* Moslem. *Home:* 10 Ave., Gholhak, Tehran, Iran. *Office:* Majles, Sena Sepah St., Tehran, Iran.

CAREER: Writer. Member of department of parliament of Iran, 1926-46; ambassador of Iran to Egypt, 1948-50, and Lebanon, 1963-64; senator of government of Iran, 1954—.

WRITINGS—In English: Dami Ba Khayyam, 1965, translation from the Persian by L. P. Elwell-Sutton published as *In Search of Omar Khayyam,* Columbia University Press, 1971.

Also author of *Ayyam-E-Mahbass,* 1922; *Fetnah,* 1943; *Saieh* (title means "Shadow"), 1947; *Jadou* (title means "Magic"), 1954; *Hendou,* 1954; *Nagh shi Az Hafiz,* 1957; *Seiri Dar Divan Shams,* 1958; *Ghalamoro Sa'adi,* 1959; *Shaeri Dir Ashna,* 1967; *Naghshi From Hafez* (title means "Part of Hafez"), 1970.

WORK IN PROGRESS: Naser Khosro; "some writings about society's problems."

AVOCATIONAL INTERESTS: "Walking is my best sport."

* * *

DAVID, Alfred 1929-

PERSONAL: Born March 31, 1929, in Hamburg, Germany; came to United States in 1938, naturalized citizen, 1944; son of Albert S. (an accountant) and Edith (Moses) David; married Mary Elizabeth Meek, June 12, 1957 (marriage ended, 1968); married Linda Utz, June 15, 1968; children: Benjamin. *Education:* Harvard University, A.B., 1951, A.M., 1954, Ph.D., 1957. *Home:* 422 South Hawthorne, Bloomington, Ind. 47401. *Office:* Department of English, Indiana University, Bloomington, Ind. 47401.

CAREER: Indiana University, Bloomington, instructor, 1958-61, assistant professor, 1961-65, associate professor, 1965-68, professor of English, 1968—. *Military service:* U.S. Army, 1951-53. *Member:* Modern Language Association of America, Mediaeval Academy of America. *Awards, honors:* Guggenheim fellowship and Fulbright fellowship, both 1966-67.

WRITINGS: (Editor and translator with Mary Elizabeth David) *The Frog King and Other Tales of the Brothers Grimm,* New American Library, 1964; (editor and translator with M. E. David) *The Twelve Dancing Princesses and Other Fairy Tales,* New American Library, 1964, revised edition, Indiana University Press, 1974; *The Strumpet Muse: Art and Morals in Chaucer's Poetry,* Indiana University Press, 1976; (editor with George B. Pace) *The Chaucer Varorium,* Part I: *The Minor Poems,* University of Oklahoma Press, 1980.

* * *

DAVIDSON, James West 1946-

PERSONAL: Born December 21, 1946; *Education:* Haverford College, B.A., 1968; Yale University, M.Phil., 1971, Ph.D., 1973. *Office:* c/o Yale University Press, 92A Yale Station, New Haven, Conn. 06520.

CAREER: Writer.

WRITINGS: (With John Rugge) *The Complete Wilderness Paddler,* Knopf, 1976; *The Logic of Millennial Thought: Eighteenth Century New England,* Yale University Press, 1977. Contributor to magazines, including *Canoe* and *New England Quarterly.*

* * *

DAVIDSON, Morris 1898-1979

OBITUARY NOTICE: Born December 16, 1898, in Rochester, N.Y.; died April 13, 1979, in Piermont, N.Y. Painter and teacher of art. Davidson exhibited his paintings in thirty one-man shows throughout the United States. Many of his works are in private collections and museums, including the Jerusalem Museum, the Baltimore Museum, and the Schenectady Museum of Art. He directed the Morris Davidson School of Art in New York for many years, ran his own art school in Provincetown, and was a founder of the American Federation of Modern Painters and Sculptors. His books include *Understanding Modern Art* and *An Approach to Modern Painting.* Obituaries and other sources: *Who's Who in World Jewry,* Pitman, 1972; *Who's Who in American Art,* Bowker, 1978; *New York Times,* April 16, 1979.

* * *

DAVIES, Merton E(dward) 1917-

PERSONAL: Born March 13, 1917, in St. Paul, Minn.; son of Albert Daniel (in insurance) and Lucile (McCabe) Davies; married Margaret Louise Darling, February 6, 1946; children: Deidra Louise Davies Stauff, Albert Karl, Merton Randel. *Education:* Stanford University, A.B., 1938, graduate study, 1938-39. *Home:* 1414 San Remo Dr., Pacific Palisades, Calif. 90272. *Office:* RAND Corp., 1700 Main St., Santa Monica, Calif. 90406.

CAREER: University of Nevada, Reno, instructor in mathematics, 1938-40; Douglas Aircraft Co., El Segundo, Calif., mathematics group leader, 1940-48; RAND Corp., Santa Monica, Calif., senior staff member, 1948—, liaison with U.S. Air Force in Washington, D.C., 1959-62. Inventor with patents in the field of planetary space science; consultant to National Science Foundation.

MEMBER: International Astronomical Union, American Astronomical Society, American Geophysical Union, American Society of Photogrammetry, American Association for the Advancement of Science, American Institute of Aeronautics and Astronautics (associate fellow). *Awards, honors:* George W. Goddard Award from Society of Photo-Optical Instrumentation Engineers, 1966; Talbert Abrams Award from American Society of Photogrammetry, 1974, for patented spin-pan space camera.

WRITINGS: (With Bruce C. Murray) *The View From Space: Photographic Exploration of the Planets,* Columbia University Press, 1971; (with Stephen E. Dwornick, Donald E. Gault, and Robert G. Strom) *Atlas of Mercury,* U.S. Government Printing Office, 1978.

SIDELIGHTS: Davies writes: "I believe that we are in the midst of man's most exciting period of exploration—that of examining the major planets of the solar system at close range by means of robot spacecraft. This ancient dream began to be realized early in the space age and now initial contacts have been made with the moon, Venus, Mars, Jupiter,

and Mercury; Saturn will soon be added to this list, and will be followed later by Uranus, Neptune, and Pluto. The sophisticated instruments carried on these deep-space missions yield large amounts of data about the planets' surfaces, lower and upper atmospheres, magnetospheres, and trapped radiation. As a member of the television science experimenter team on a number of these flight missions, I have participated firsthand in the adventure.

"Most of my writing is found in scientific journals. My two books reflect my interest in the exploration of the planets and the continuing program to map the surfaces of the major bodies of the solar system."

* * *

DAVIS, Frank G(reene) 1915-

PERSONAL: Born October 13, 1915; son of Greene (a farmer) and Eliza Davis; married Joy Powell; children: Frank G., Jr., Matel, Dwight. *Education:* Howard University, B.A., 1935; Ohio State University, M.A.; Iowa State University, Ph.D., 1939. *Home:* 901 Sixth St. S.W., #614, Washington, D.C. 20024. *Office:* Department of Economics, Howard University, Washington, D.C. 20059.

CAREER: Professor of economics, Prairie View State College, 1939-42; economist for Social Security Board and U.S. Department of Defense, 1942-51; Foreign Aid Program, Liberia, U.S. economic adviser, 1951-54; Internal Revenue Service, Washington, D.C., statistician, 1954-57; *Ebony,* Chicago, Ill., research director for Negro market, 1957-60; City University of New York, New York, N.Y., lecturer in statistics, 1957-60; Fairleigh Dickinson University, Rutherford, N.J., associate professor of economics, 1960-68; Lincoln University, Lincoln, Pa., professor of economics and head of department, 1968-71; Howard University, Washington, D.C., professor, 1971-73, research professor of economics, 1973—, head of department, 1971-73. Member of District of Columbia Citizens Commission on Pension Policy, 1978. Guest speaker on television programs and at public meetings. Consultant to National Science Foundation and Ford Foundation. *Member:* American Economic Association, Caucus of Black Economists (head of education committee). *Awards, honors:* Ford Foundation grant, 1963; award from New Jersey governor's economic policy council, 1967.

WRITINGS: The Economics of Black Community Development, Rand McNally, 1972; *Cost-Benefit Under Social Security: The Case of Poor Blacks,* Institute of Urban Affairs and Research, Howard University, 1976; *The Black Community's Social Security,* University Press of America, 1977. Also contributor to *Black Economic Development,* 1975. Contributor to economic journals.

WORK IN PROGRESS: Research on black and white *per-capita* income, black and white life expectancies, the relation of personal and social security taxes to welfare reform, the future of black labor, and inequality between black and white workers in American industry.

* * *

DAVIS, Grania 1943-
(Mama G.)

PERSONAL: Born July 17, 1943, in Milwaukee, Wis.; married Avram Davidson (a writer), February, 1961 (marriage ended, 1963); married Stephen Davis (a physician), June 2, 1968; children: (first marriage) Ethan; (second marriage) Seth. *Education:* University of Hawaii, B.A. (Buddhist studies), 1976; Sonoma State University, B.A. (literature), 1976. *Politics:* "Hopeless." *Religion:* "Jewish/Buddhist." *Agent:* Richard Curtis Literary Agency, 156 East 52nd St., New York, N.Y. 10022.

CAREER: Writer; also worked as travel agent.

WRITINGS: (Editor) *The Proud Peacock and The Mallard* (Buddhist tales for children), Dharma, 1976; *Dr. Grass,* Avon, 1978; *The Great Perpendicular Path,* Avon, 1978. Author of "Mama G.," a column in *Marin Scope.* Contributor to science fiction and fantasy magazines and to *Tibetan Review.*

WORK IN PROGRESS: The Rainbow Annals, a novel set in Tibet; research for a novel set in the Caribbean.

SIDELIGHTS: Grania Davis writes: "I seem to have a special talent for anticipating trends. My books are generally considered 'far out,' but eventually everyone else catches up with them. *Dr. Grass* is a perfect example.

"My main preoccupation is travel. I've lived in Mexico, the jungles of Central America, Europe, and Tibetan refugee camps in India. Right now, I'm busy packing to move to Japan!"

* * *

DAVIS, James Robert 1945-
(Jim Davis)

PERSONAL: Born July 28, 1945, in Marion, Ind.; son of James William (a farmer) and Anna C. (Carter) Davis; married Carolyn Altekruse (in public relations), July 26, 1969. *Education:* Attended Ball State University, 1963-67. *Politics:* Republican. *Religion:* Protestant. *Office:* 413 Wayne St., Muncie, Ind. 47303.

CAREER/WRITINGS: Free-lance advertising artist, 1969-78; assistant to author of "Tumbleweeds" cartoon strip, 1969-78; writer and cartoonist, under name Jim Davis, of "Garfield" cartoon strip, syndicated internationally by United Feature Syndicate, 1978—. Muncie Civic Theatre (member, 1970—; board member, 1974-76). *Member:* National Cartoonists Society. *Awards, honors:* Outstanding Young Men of America Award, 1972.

SIDELIGHTS: Davis told *CA:* "My philosophy for my work is to entertain. While humor and editorial comment are obviously not mutually exclusive, I write strictly for humorous content. Any editorial comment in 'Garfield' is there to serve a humorous end." When asked how he gets ideas for his cartoon strips, Davis replied," When writing a gag for a humor strip, I simply imagine my character in a funny situation; then I back up three frames and cut it off."

He added: "My wife and I are family people, so we'll probably continue to live in the Midwest near our families. I like tennis, chess, and hamburgers. My favorite humor strip is 'B.C.'"

BIOGRAPHICAL/CRITICAL SOURCES: Chicago Sun-Times, November 2, 1978; *Fort Wayne Journal Gazette,* November 2, 1978; *Editor and Publisher,* November 18, 1978; *Cartoonist Profiles,* December, 1978.

* * *

DAVIS, Tom Edward 1929-

PERSONAL: Born June 11, 1929, in Akron, Ohio; son of David Edward (a lawyer) and Edith (Larson) Davis; married Patricia Ann Elwin, June 13, 1953; children: Derek, Heather. *Education:* Tufts College (now University), A.B. (magna cum laude), 1950; Johns Hopkins University, M.A.,

1952, Ph.D., 1956. *Home:* 2211 North Triphammer Rd., Ithaca, N.Y. 14850. *Office:* Department of Economics, Cornell University, Ithaca, N.Y. 14853.

CAREER: University of Chicago, Chicago, Ill., assistant professor, 1956-58, associate professor of economics, 1958-62; Cornell University, Ithaca, N.Y., associate professor, 1962-67, professor of economics, 1967—, head of department, 1967-70, director of Latin American studies program, 1965-67, 1971-76, director of National Bureau of Economic Research, 1969-71. Head of Latin American Research Review Board, 1965-67. Consultant to U.S. Department of State. *Member:* American Economic Association, Latin American Studies Association. *Awards, honors:* Fulbright fellow at London School of Economics and Political Science, 1953-55, 1970-71; Social Science Research Council fellow at London School of Economics and Political Science, 1953-55; Ford Foundation fellow, 1965-66.

WRITINGS: (Contributor) Baer and Kerstenetsky, editors, *Inflation and Growth in Latin America,* Yale University Press, 1964. Also editor and contributor of *Mexico's Recent Economic Growth,* University of Texas Press. Contributor to economic journals.

WORK IN PROGRESS: Economic History of Latin America (tentative title).

* * *

DAVIS-GOFF, Annabel 1942-

PERSONAL: Born February 19, 1942, in Ireland; daughter of Ernest and Cynthia (an art dealer; maiden name, Woodhouse) Davis-Goff; married Mike Nichols (a film and stage director); children: Max, Jenny. *Religion:* Church of Ireland. *Agent:* Joan Stewart, William Morris Agency, 1350 Ave. of the Americas, New York, N.Y. 10019.

CAREER: Free-lance film technician in England and Hollywood, Calif., 1963-73; writer.

WRITINGS: Night Tennis, Coward, 1978. Author of screen adaptation of *Life Signs,* by Johanna Davis.

WORK IN PROGRESS: A screen adaptation of *Night Tennis;* a novel, *Tail Spin,* for Coward.

* * *

DAWSON, Fielding 1930-

PERSONAL: Born August 2, 1930, in New York, N.Y. *Education:* Attended Black Mountain College. *Address:* 49 East 19th St., New York, N.Y. 10003.

CAREER: Painter, illustrator, writer, and essayist.

WRITINGS: An Emotional Memoir of Franz Kline, Pantheon, 1967; *Krazy Kat, The Unveiling, and Other Stories,* Black Sparrow Press, 1969; *Open Road* (novel), Black Sparrow Press, 1970; *The Black Mountain Book,* Croton Press, 1970; *The Mandalay Dream,* Bobbs-Merrill, 1971; *The Dream/Thunder Road: Stories and Dreams, 1955-1965,* Black Sparrow Press, 1972; *A Great Day for a Ballgame: A Conscious Love Story,* Bobbs-Merrill, 1973; *The Greatest Story Ever Told: A Transformation,* Black Sparrow Press, 1973; *The Sun Rises Into the Sky, and Other Stories, 1952-1966,* Black Sparrow Press, 1974; *The Man Who Changed Overnight, and Other Stories and Dreams,* Black Sparrow Press, 1976; *Penny Lane* (novel), Black Sparrow Press, 1977; *Two Penny Lane* (novel), Black Sparrow Press, 1977; *The Second Diplomat,* Ferry Press, 1977; *Delayed: Not Postponed,* edited by Maureen Owen, Telephone Books, 1978.

SIDELIGHTS: "Fielding Dawson is a journalist in that word's constantly essential, all-but-forgotten meaning: He is both a seer and a messenger, a bringer of news: not impaled by the present, but sped by the energies which converge in the present—Fielding Dawson with the news," wrote Donald Phelps in *Caterpillar.* Phelps noted that Dawson's short stories have a number of distinguishing characteristics. They are written in a heroic mode and in a style similar to that of an artist, for Dawson "enlists the process-rhythms of painting and choreography in the rippling, guileless complexity of his typical prose." When Dawson is at his best, Phelps observed, his stories "have the sharp linear focus, the crystalline acuteness, the expressive grace which only mobility, governed by awareness can bring," but when he fails it is the result of "an over-determined consciousness" which causes him to lose "the larger human reverberations, the reality, for the narrower actuality." Eric Mottram elucidated Dawson's themes: "A main horror is to feel nothing is happening as time draws a man on in boredom, mechanism and waste. Intimations of mortality urge throughout Dawson's work: it must be now or never that we love, paint, write, taste, drink, field that ball, strike."

Dawson's archives are at the University of Connecticut.

BIOGRAPHICAL/CRITICAL SOURCES: Caterpillar, fall, 1970; *Vort,* Number 4, fall, 1973; *Contemporary Literary Criticism,* Volume 6, Gale, 1976.

*   *   *

DAWSON, Minnie E.   1906-1978

OBITUARY NOTICE: Born in 1906 in Baltimore, Md.; died of Parkinson's Disease, December 30, 1978, in Washington, D.C. Government worker and poet. Dawson was an administrative assistant at the Federal Housing Administration and at the Department of Housing and Urban Development. Her humorous verses on the medical profession appeared in the *American Medical Journal,* and she wrote a book of poems, *Love and Laugh: A Refresher Course in Living, Loving, and Laughing.* She was also a recipient of the Peabody Award for literature. Obituaries and other sources: *Washington Post,* January 12, 1979.

*   *   *

DAY, Albert M.   1897-1979

OBITUARY NOTICE: Born April 2, 1897, in Humboldt, Neb.; died January 21, 1979, in Harrisburg, Pa. Biologist and environmentalist. Day was a former director of the U.S. Fish and Wildlife Service and of wildlife research for the Arctic Institute of North America. He also served as an environmental consultant for several government agencies. He was the author of a number of publications in his field, including *Making a Living in Conservation: A Guide to Outdoor Careers* and *Hunters Handbook.* Obituaries and other sources: *Current Biography,* Wilson, 1948; *American Men and Women of Science: The Physical and Biological Sciences,* 12th edition, Bowker, 1971-73; *Washington Post,* January 24, 1979.

*   *   *

DAY, Price   1907-1978

PERSONAL: Born November 4, 1907, in Plainview, Tex.; died December 9, 1978, in Baltimore, Md.; son of John Walter and Zillah (Price) Day; married Alice Alexander, December 28, 1931; children: Anthony, Joseph, Thomas, James. *Education:* Princeton University, A.B., 1929. *Home:*

West Lake Ave., Baltimore, Md. 21210. *Office:* Baltimore *Sun,* 501 North Calvert St., Baltimore, Md. 21203.

CAREER/WRITINGS: Journalist. Worked as cartoonist and free-lance writer in New York and Florida, 1929-35; *Fort Lauderdale Daily News,* Fort Lauderdale, Fla., reporter, 1930; ticket seller at Hialeah Park, Hialeah, Fla.; free-lance writer, 1935-41; *Fort Lauderdale Times,* city editor, 1942; *Baltimore Sun,* Baltimore, Md., war correspondent in Mediterranean and European Theatre, 1943-45, field correspondent, 1945-60, editor-in-chief, 1960-75. Notable assignments include coverage of surrender of German Army at Rheims, France, Nuremberg trials, interviewing Mahatma Gandhi, and independence of India. *Awards, honors:* Pulitzer Prize for international reporting, 1949, for coverage of independence of India.

OBITUARIES: Washington Post, December 11, 1978.*

*   *   *

DAYTON, Edward R(isedorph)   1924-

PERSONAL: Born April 21, 1924, in Brooklyn, N.Y.; son of Charles R. (a dentist) and Florence (Risedorph) Dayton; married Marjorie Buermann (a marriage and family counselor), October 11, 1944; children: Jill Dayton Davis, Patricia Dayton Van Dalfsen, Leigh Dayton Fitz, Robert J. *Education:* New York University, B.S.A.E., 1948; Fuller Theological Seminary, M.Div., 1967. *Politics:* None. *Religion:* Evangelical Protestant. *Home:* 8544 Larkdale Rd., San Gabriel, Calif. 91775. *Office:* World Vision International, 919 West Huntington Dr., Monrovia, Calif. 91016.

CAREER: Sperry Gyroscope Co., Great Neck, N.Y., section head in system engineering, 1948-59; Lear Siegler, Instrument Division, Grand Rapids, Mich., division manager, 1959-64; Lear Siegler, Heater Division, Los Angeles, Calif., assistant to president, 1964-66; World Vision International, Monrovia, Calif., director of Missions Advanced Research and Communication Center, 1966—. *Military service:* U.S. Army, 1941-46. *Member:* American Scientific Association, American Society of Missiology, Psi Epsilon. *Awards, honors:* Ford Foundation fellow, 1964-65.

WRITINGS: (With Paul Friesen Barkman and Edward L. Gruman) *Christian Collegians and Foreign Missions,* Missions Advanced Research and Communications Center, World Vision International, 1969; (editor) *Medicine and Missions,* Medical Assistance Programs, 1969; *Tools for Time Management: Christian Perspectives on Managing Priorities,* Zondervan, 1974; *God's Purpose/Man's Plans,* Missions Advanced Research and Communication Center, World Vision International, 1975; (with Theodore Wilhelm Engstrom) *The Art of Management for Christian Leaders,* Word, Inc., 1976; (with Engstrom) *Strategy for Living: How to Make the Best Use of Your Time and Abilities,* Regal Books, 1976; (editor) *Mission Handbook: North American Protestant Ministries Overseas,* Missions Advanced Research and Communication Center, World Vision International, 1977; (with Engstrom) *The Christian Executive,* Word, Inc., 1979; (with Engstrom) *Strategy for Leadership,* Revell, 1979. Author of monographs on management and cross-cultural missions. Co-editor of *Christian Leadership Letter,* 1973—.

WORK IN PROGRESS: Editing a book of essays, publication expected in 1980; research on strategy for Christian missions; devotional study of the Bible's Book of James.

SIDELIGHTS: Edward Dayton writes: "I have always been an avid writer, but the only things I wrote for publication were in my role as an engineering manager. The turning point in my career was at Fuller Theological Seminary, at age forty. This led to my work with World Vision International, a large Christian service organization, where I was able to combine my technical and theological skills to found a division known as Missions Advanced Research and Communication Center (MARC).

"Teaching management naturally led to a number of books on management and leadership. These in turn led to the institution of the *Christian Leadership Letter.*

"A major interest is the integration of theology and management within various Christian enterprises. This has been enhanced by travel to a large number of foreign countries and has brought my interest into the cross-cultural communication of management theory."

*   *   *

DEARSTYNE, Howard B(est) 1903-1979

OBITUARY NOTICE: Born August 2, 1903, in Albany, N.Y.; died March 7, 1979, in Alexandria, Va. Photographer, architectural historian, and educator. Dearstyne was assistant architectural records editor for Colonial Williamsburg and lectured on architecture at the College of William and Mary. His photographs were featured in a number of one-man shows and appeared in exhibitions at Chicago's Art Institute, Howard University, and the Photokina in Cologne, Germany. He held teaching positions at several colleges, contributed articles to magazines, and was the co-author of two books, *Colonial Williamsburg: Its Buildings and Gardens* and *Shadows in Silver: A Record of Virginia, 1850-1900.* Obituaries and other sources: *Who's Who in America,* 40th edition, Marquis, 1978; *Washington Post,* March 10, 1979.

*   *   *

DeBEAUBIEN, Philip Francis 1913-1979
(Homer Holiday)

OBITUARY NOTICE: Born February 9, 1913, in Conneaut, Ohio; died April 28, 1979, in Ormond Beach, Fla. Banker, publisher, and newspaper columnist. DeBeaubien was associated with *Good Housekeeping* and *Look* magazines before becoming the publisher of the *Detroit Times.* He was also a vice-president of Commonwealth Bank in Daytona Beach, Fla. He wrote a nationally syndicated column, "Ticker Tempo," under the pseudonym Homer Holiday. Another column, "You Name It," appeared in the *Daytona Beach News-Journal.* Obituaries and other sources: *Who's Who in the South and Southwest,* 15th edition, Marquis, 1976; *New York Times,* April 30, 1979.

*   *   *

DECKER, Hannah S(hulman) 1937-

PERSONAL: Born March 19, 1937, in New York, N.Y.; daughter of Samuel (a carpenter) and Eugenia (Foss) Shulman; married Norman Decker (a psychiatrist), August 11, 1957; children: Ruth Leonora, William Karl. *Education:* Barnard College, A.B., 1957; Columbia University, M.A., 1958, Ph.D., 1971. *Home:* 5026 Glenmeadow, Houston, Tex. 77096. *Office:* Department of History, University of Houston, Houston, Tex. 77004.

CAREER: Albert Einstein College of Medicine, Bronx, N.Y., clinical instructor in psychiatry, 1972-74; University of Houston, Houston, Tex., assistant professor, 1974-78, associate professor of history, 1978—. Fellow of Cornell

University, 1967-73, clinical instructor in psychiatry, 1973-74; adjunct assistant professor at University of Texas, Medical Branch, Galveston, 1974-77, and Baylor University, 1979—. Member of board of directors of Houston Friends of Music. *Member:* Cheiron: International Society for the History of the Behavioral and Social Sciences, American Historical Association, Conference Group on Central European History, Group for the Use of Psychology in History.

WRITINGS: Freud in Germany: Revolution and Reaction in Science, International Universities Press, 1977; (contributor) Jacques M. Quen and Eric T. Carlson, editors, *American Psychoanalysis: Origins and Development,* Brunner/ Mazel, 1978; (contributor) William E. Fann, Ismet Karacan, Alec D. Pokorny, and Robert L. Williams, editors, *Phenomenology and Treatment of Schizophrenia,* Spectrum, 1978. Contributor to journals in medicine and the behavioral sciences.

WORK IN PROGRESS: A history of the physician-patient relationship since 1800; studying the reception of Freud's concept of sublimation in the United States and Germany (a comparative study in national character).

SIDELIGHTS: Reviewers of *Freud in Germany* were impressed with Decker's scholarship. "Decker has carried out an exhaustive examination of the medical, psychological, and general literature of Wilhelmine Germany," noted Louise E. Hoffman, "including periodicals, conference proceedings, monographs, textbooks, and semipopular works."

Critics also praised Decker for refuting the long-held belief that Freud's theories were unpopular in his lifetime. "One of Prof. Decker's major accomplishments in this book," wrote Elizabeth Long, "is the destruction of the notion, perpetuated by Freud and his followers, that initially Freud stood in 'splendid isolation,' his ideas either ignored or greeted with total hostility." Similarly, Hoffman declared, "Decker convincingly demonstrates several important points. First: Freud's early work did receive considerable attention, particularly from physicians and the lay public. Second, much of this attention was favorable or neutral, and even critical notices were usually polite and accepted Freud as a serious worker."

Decker told *CA:* "My interest in German history began in childhood as I watched my mother cry when she received letters from friends and relatives in the Cracow ghetto.

"*Freud in Germany* was written to show that the reactions to psychoanalysis are diverse and should not be reduced to generalizations about Victorian prudery, the critics neurotic resistances, and Freud's Jewishness.

"At present, as for the past twenty years, I share my psychiatric and psychoanalytic interests with my husband. In my teaching, I preach the inherent complexity of all matters."

AVOCATIONAL INTERESTS: Music.

BIOGRAPHICAL/CRITICAL SOURCES: American Historical Review, February, 1979; *Houston Chronicle,* April 29, 1979.

*   *   *

DEGH, Linda 1920-

PERSONAL: Born in 1920, in Budapest, Hungary; came to the United States in 1964, naturalized citizen, 1977; daughter of Karoly and Jolan (Engl) Degh; married Andrew Vazsonyi (a doctor and researcher). *Education:* Pazmany Peter Tudomanyegyetem, Ph.D., 1943. *Office:* Department of Folklore, Indiana University, 506-8 North Fess St., Bloomington, Ind. 47405.

CAREER: Szabo Ervin Municipal Library, Budapest, Hungary, research assistant, 1946-47; East European Research Institute, Budapest, research associate, 1948-51; Eotvos University, Budapest, adjunct professor of folklore, 1951-58, docens, 1958-64; Indiana University, Bloomington, visiting professor, 1964-65, associate professor, 1965-68, professor of folklore, 1968—. Visiting professor at Wayne State University, 1976, and University of California, Berkeley, 1978; lecturer at Nordic Institute of Folklore, 1977. *Member:* American Folklore Society (first vice-president, 1971-73; president of fellows, 1977—), American Hungarian Educator's Association (member of executive board, 1975—), Hoosier Folklore Society (president, 1966-69). *Awards, honors:* International Pitre Prize from Palermo, Italy, 1963; Guggenheim fellow, 1970-71.

WRITINGS: *Folktales of Hungary,* University of Chicago Press, 1965; *Folktales and Society: Story-Telling in a Hungarian Peasant Community,* Indiana University Press, 1969; *People in the Tobacco Belt: Four Lives,* National Museums of Man, 1975; (editor with Felix Oinas and Henry Glassie, and contributor) *Folklore Today: A Festschrift for Richard M. Dorson,* Research Center for Language and Semiotic Studies, Indiana University, 1976; (editor) *East European Folk Narrative Studies,* American Folklore Society, 1978; *Folklore of Indiana,* Indiana University Press, 1980.

Not in English: *Pandur Peter het bagi meseje* (title means "Seven Tales by Peter Pandur From Bag"), Officina, 1940; *Pannandur Peter mesei* (title means "Tales of Peter Pandur"), two volumes, Franklin (Budapest, Hungary), 1942; *Bodrog-kozi mesek* (title means "Tales from Bodrogkoz"), privately printed, 1945; *Utmutato 48-asnep hagyomany gyujtesehez* (title means "Fieldworker's Guide for Researching Historical Traditions of 1948-49"), [Budapest], 1947; *A magyar nepi szinjatek kutatasa* (title means "Hungarian Folk Drama Research"), Teleki Pal Tudomanyos Intezet, 1947; (with Inre Katona and Laszlo Peter) *Torteneti enekek es katona-dalock* (title means "Historical Songs and Soldier's Songs"), Tankonyvkiado, 1952; *A szabadsagharc nepkolteszete* (title means "Folklore of the War of Independence"), Akademiai Kiado, 1952; *Szepen szol a Kossuth muzsikaja* (contains selected songs from the Revolution of 1848), Mora, 1953; *Nepkolteszet* (title means "Folk Literature"), Eotvos University Publications, 1953; (with Katona and Tekia Domotor) *Magyarorszagi munkasdalok* (title means "Worker's Songs From Hungary"), Muvelt nep, 1955; *Kakasdi nepmesek* (title means "Folktales From Kakasd"), Akademiai Kiado, Volume I, 1955, Volume II, 1960; (with Agnes Kovacs) *Magyar nepmesek* (title means "Hungarian Folktales"), three volumes, Szepirodalmi Kiado, 1960; *Gonaquadate a viziszorny* (North American Indian tales), Europa, 1960; *A vilagjaro kiralyfi* (North European folktales), Mora, 1961; *Marchen, Erzahler und Erzahlge-meinschaft dargestellt an der ungarischen Volksueber-lieferung* (title means "Tale, Storyteller, and Folk Tradition as Represented by Hungarian Folklore"), Akademie-Verlag, 1962; *Tolna megyei szekely nepmesek* (title means "Szekely Folktales From Tolna County"), Megyei Tanacs, 1965.

Contributor: Wayland Hand, editor, *American Folk Legend: A Symposium,* Univeristy of California Press, 1971; Richard M. Dorson, editor, *Folklore and Folklife: An Introduction,* University of Chicago Press, 1972; Dan Ben-Amos and Kenneth S. Goldstein, editors, *Folklore, Performance, and Communication,* Mouton, 1975; Ben-Amos, editor, *Folklore Genres,* University of Texas Press, 1976; *Folk Narrative Research,* Studia Fennica XX, 1976; Dorson, editor, *Folk-*

lore in the Modern World, The Hague, Mouton, 1978; Juha Pentikainen and Tuula Juutikka, editors, *Studies in Turkish Folklore,* Turkis Studies Association, 1978; Ilhan Basgoz and Mark Glazer, editors, *East European Folk Narrative,* American Folklore Society, 1978.

Associate editor of "Uralic and Altaic Series," published by Research Center for Language and Semiotic Studies, Indiana University, 1965-76. Contributor of about seventy articles to ethnography, anthropology, and folklore journals in the United States and Europe. Editor of *Indiana Folklore,* 1968—; associate editor of *Journal of American Folklore,* 1973—; member of editorial board of *Journal of the Folklore Institute,* 1965—.

WORK IN PROGRESS: *Irrationality Explosion: The Folk Legend of Our Time,* in press.

SIDELIGHTS: Degh writes: "Since early childhood I was always interested in the life of little people and their creativity. I observed the simple folk—peasants, illiterates in the rural countryside, mountaineers, fishermen, shepherds, craftsmen, peddlers, and the urban poor—and tried to communicate their feelings by publishing and interpreting their spontaneous expression as represented in folktales, legends, life histories, and manifestations of their fantasies."

* * *

de JONGH, James 1942-

PERSONAL: Surname is pronounced de-*Young;* born September 23, 1942, in St. Thomas, Virgin Islands; came to United States in 1960; son of Percy Leo and Mavis (in business; maiden name, Bentlage) de Jongh. *Education:* Williams College, B.A. (honors), 1964; Yale University, M.A., 1967; further graduate study at New York University, 1967-70. *Home:* 523 West 121st St., New York, N.Y. 10027. *Agent:* Curtis Brown Ltd., 575 Madison Ave., New York, N.Y. 10022. *Office:* Department of English, City College of the City University of New York, New York, N.Y. 10031.

CAREER: E. L. Reilly Opinion Research Corp., New York City, writer and researcher, 1966-67; Baldridge Reading and Study Skills, Inc., Greenwich, Conn., assistant to president, 1967-69; Rutgers University, Newark, N.J., instructor in English, 1969-70; City College of the City University of New York, New York City, lecturer in English, 1970—, president of Black Action Council, 1971-73. *Member:* Screen Actors Guild, Actors' Equity Association, American Federation of Television and Radio Artists (AFTRA), Writers Guild of America, East, Harlem Writers' Guild (vice-president, 1976—), Frederick Douglass Creative Arts Centers. *Awards, honors:* Fiction award from creative Artists Projects Service, 1977, for *City Cool: A Ritual of Belonging;* National Endowment for the Arts fellow, 1978.

WRITINGS: (With Carles Cleveland) "Hail Hail the Gangs!: A Theatre Piece" (play), first produced in New York City at New York Theatre Ensemble, April, 1976; (with Cleveland) *City Cool: A Ritual of Belonging* (novel), Random House, 1978; (co-author) "Do Lord Remember Me: A Theatre Piece" (play), first produced in New York City at Woodie King, Jr.'s New Federal Theatre, April, 1978; (with Cleveland) "City Cool: A First Draft Screenplay," Warner Bros., 1978; (with Cleveland) *Till Victory* (historical novel), Random House, in press. Contributor to *BOPP* and *Penthouse.*

SIDELIGHTS: De Jongh comments: "I collaborate with Carles Cleveland, with whom I worked at the Al Fann Theatrical Ensemble in Harlem. We write novels, dramas, and screenplays dealing with universal themes drawn from our experiences as black men living in America.'' Their latest novel, *Till Victory,* traces ''the rise and fall of black Harlem in the fictional career of Alexander Hamilton Shakespeare (1880-1942), lover, philanthropist, sportsman, and number banker.''

*   *   *

DE KOVEN, Bernard 1941-
(Bernie De Koven)

PERSONAL: Born October 15, 1941, in Appleton, Wis.; son of Ralph (a rabbi) and Esther (Shatzky) De Koven; married Rosanne Friedlander, June 27, 1965; children: Shael, Elyon. *Education:* Temple University, B.A., 1964; Villanova University, M.A., 1967. *Politics:* ''Global.'' *Religion:* Jewish. *Home and office address:* R.D. 1355, Fleetwood, Pa. 19522.

CAREER: Curriculum development specialist in public schools in Philadelphia, Pa., 1968-72; writer, designer of educational games, and consultant, 1972—. Founder and developer of Games Preserve and Games Board; past director of New Games Foundation. *Member:* International Playground Association, Anthropological Association for the Study of Play.

WRITINGS: (Contributor, under name Bernie De Koven), Andrew Fluegelman, editor, *The New Games Book,* Dolphin, 1976; *The Well-Played Game,* Doubleday, 1978; (contributor, under name Bernie De Koven) James McCullagh, editor, *Ways to Play,* Rodale Press, 1978.

Plays: ''The Manner of Prayer of Daniel the Blessed'' (three-act), first produced in Villanova, Pa., 1967; ''I You and Sometimes Why'' (two-act), first produced in Philadelphia, Pa., 1970; ''The Fabled Lot of Elmwood Tree'' (seven scenes), first produced in Philadelphia, 1971; ''Planetaria'' (choral reading), first produced in Philadelphia at Fels Planetarium, 1971; ''The Painted Dessert,'' first produced in Philadelphia at the Philadelphia Museum of Art, 1975.

Author of curriculum materials. Contributor to education and games journals. Contributing editor of *Simulation/Gaming/News,* and of *Games,* 1977—.

WORK IN PROGRESS: A book on the relationship between games and social/psychological interaction structures, publication expected in 1980; a book on facilitating play from early childhood through late adulthood, with Brian Sutton-Smith, completion expected in 1980.

SIDELIGHTS: De Koven writes: ''My major interest is in understanding the nature and function of play and its relation to structure—it's a quest for understanding the relationship between the spirit and community. Before I found play, I was writing poetry. That led me to searching for some other medium in which I could share the poetic experience more directly, which was theater. After I worked with children, I realized that there is something earlier and more powerful and easier to use than theater, and that is play. Since then, my whole life has become centered around the exploration of play.

''My work centers around a very familiar theme. All that I describe are merely elaborations on the understanding that, 'it's not whether you win or lose, it's how you play the game that counts.' The ramifications of that old saw have enabled me to find ways to create healthy, growth producing experiences for any population, in any setting. I am continually amazed at the power of this knowledge. *The Well-Played Game* is a record of the insights I have found through exploring 'the way you play the game.' Everybody knows the value of a good game. Everybody knows that there are games that are so good that it really doesn't matter who wins or loses. Everybody has experienced, through play, a heightening of power of consciousness. The book is a study of the politics of arranging for such experiences, of providing for access to the well-played game. As such, it enlarges the concept of what a game is or can be, and though I try to avoid it, the implications of such a study on understanding how to make the game of life well-played are unavoidable. I've been exploring variations of the theme in all my works, showing people how games can be changed, the relationship between play and games, the freedom to change rules, to quit, to be angry, whatever. It's the freedom of play, the spontaneity and creativity that results from playing even the most traditional and restrictive of games, the heightened awareness, the universality of the experience.

''I found the same thing in theatre when a group of actors played well together. In my plays, I provided for more and more spontaneity, beginning with scripts, and ending with bare outlines, scores. I found in games a form of theatre that was more universal, easier to understand, as formal or as informal as anyone wished to be, as secular or religious as what people want to play with. I consider myself a fool, a player who, at times, arrives at a remarkable clarity, and at other times, revels in nonsense. ''The Manner of Prayer of Daniel the Blessed'' was about a boy who talked to a tree. When the children made fun of his insanity, he tried to chop the tree down. He wasn't strong enough, but he interpreted that as a message. The tree didn't want to be chopped down. It wanted to talk to him. So, he continued talking to the tree, and eventually, the children saw the sense of it, and listened, with him, to what the tree had to say. See? The power of nonsense. The tree speaks.

''I founded the Games Preserve in 1971. It's a non-profit corporation, educational. We produce what we are calling The Play Curriculum. This program enables us to recommend games to any individual or group. We have a library of cards describing commercial, non-commercial, traditional, and educational games. Subscribers send us a list of the games that are currently enjoyed by themselves, family, or group, and we select games that are similar and send them back descriptions of ten such games. I'm very excited about this service because it allows people I work with to have access to an on-going support system.''

*   *   *

De La ROCHE, Mazo 1885-1961

PERSONAL: Surname is pronounced De La *Roshe;* born in Toronto, Ontario, Canada; died July 12, 1961; daughter of a farmer; children: (adopted) Renee, Esme. *Education:* Attended University of Toronto and School of Art, Toronto. *Residence:* Windrush Hill, York Mills, Ontario, Canada.

CAREER: Writer. *Awards, honors:* Two Daughters of the British Empire prizes, 1925, for plays; *Atlantic Monthly* prize, 1927, for *Jalna;* awarded Lorne Pierce Medal, Royal Society of Canada.

*WRITINGS—*All novels, except as noted: *Explorers of the Dawn* (collection of previously published sketches), foreword by Christopher Morley, Knopf, 1922; *Possession,* Macmillan, 1923, reprinted, C. Chivers, 1973; *Delight,* Macmillan, 1926; *Come True* (play; first produced in Toronto at Hart House Theatre; also see below), Macmillan, 1927; *Low Life and Other Plays* (plays; contains ''Low Life,'' ''Come True,'' and ''The Return of the Emigrant'' [also see below]; all first produced in Toronto at Hart House

Theatre), Little, Brown, 1929; *The Return of the Emigrant* (play), Little, Brown, 1929; *Lark Ascending*, Little, Brown, 1932; *Beside a Norman Tower*, illustrations by A. H. Watson, Little, Brown, 1934; *Whiteoaks* (play adapted from the author's novel entitled *Whiteoaks of Jalna*; first produced in Toronto at Hart House Theatre), Macmillan (Toronto), 1936; *The Very House*, Little, Brown, 1937; *Growth of a Man*, Little, Brown, 1938; *The Sacred Bullock and Other Stories*, illustrations by Stuart Tresilian, Little, Brown, 1939, reprinted, Books for Libraries Press, 1969; *The Two Saplings*, Macmillan, 1942; *Quebec: Historic Seaport* (nonfiction), Doubleday, 1944; *A Boy in the House, and Other Stories*, Little, Brown, 1952; *The Song of Lambert* (for children), illustrations by Eileen A. Soper, Little, Brown, c.1955; *Ringing the Changes* (autobiography), Little, Brown, 1957; *Bill and Coo* (for children), illustrations by Soper, Little, Brown, c. 1958; *Delight*, introduction by Desmond Pacey, McClelland, & Stewart, 1961.

"Jalna" series—all published by Little, Brown, except as noted: *Jalna*, 1927; *Whiteoaks of Jalna*, 1929, reprinted, Fawcett, 1977; *Finch's Fortune*, 1931; *The Master of Jalna*, 1933, reprinted, Fawcett, 1975; *Young Renny*, 1935; *Whiteoak Harvest*, 1936; *Whiteoak Heritage*, 1940, reprinted, Fawcett, 1974; *Wakefield's Course*, 1941; *The Building of Jalna*, 1944; *Return to Jalna*, 1946, reprinted, Fawcett, 1977; *Mary Wakefield*, 1949, reprinted, 1977; *Renny's Daughter*, 1951, reprinted, Fawcett, 1975; *Variable Winds at Jalna*, 1954, reprinted, Fawcett, 1975; *Centenary at Jalna*, 1958; *Morning at Jalna*, 1960. Contributor of short stories to magazines in the United States.

SIDELIGHTS: Mazo De La Roche wrote a variety of novels and some plays, but her masterwork is the "Jalna" series, a saga in the tradition of the *Matriarch* novels of G. B. Stern. The chronicle encompasses several generations of the Whiteoak family, beginning in the 1850's. It evolves around a lakeside Ontario estate named Jalna, ruled by the indomitable Adeline. The household is also comprised of Adeline's son, the pragmatic children from his first marriage who manage Jalna, and the artistic and temperamental children from his second marriage. Adeline's husband, an officer in the English-Indian Army, rarely appears in the narrative. The matriarch lives to celebrate her centennial birthday, and, following her death, is succeeded by her equally spirited grandson Renny. De La Roche's own belief in independence, the family unit, and decorum pervade the story.

The "Jalna" series has been praised for its exceptional characterization and concise construction. While some critics considered De La Roche's characters more British than Canadian, others noted their universality. The saga won the author the distinction of being the most popular Canadian novelist of her time in Europe: editions of the books have been published in France, Germany, Portugal, Poland, and Czechoslovakia. The dramatized version of the story, "Whiteoaks," was well-received in New York and in England. Ethel Barrymore was one of the actresses who played Adeline.

AVOCATIONAL INTERESTS: Dogs, horses.

BIOGRAPHICAL/CRITICAL SOURCES: George Hendrick, *Mazo de la Roche*, Twayne, 1970; Ronald Hambleton, *Secret of Jalna*, Paper-Jacks, 1972; Mazo De La Roche, *Ringing the Changes*, Chivers, 1973.*

* * *

DELGADO, Ramon (Louis) 1937-

PERSONAL: Born December 16, 1937, in Tampa, Fla.; son of Eloy Vincent (a grocer) and Hildegard (Chapman) Delgado. *Education:* Stetson University, B.A. (cum laude), 1959; Baylor University, M.A., 1960; Yale University, M.F.A., 1967; Southern Illinois at Carbondale, Ph.D., 1976. *Home:* 16 Forest, Apt. 107, Montclair, N.J. 07042. *Office:* Department of Speech and Theater, Montclair State College, Upper Montclair, N.J. 07043.

CAREER: Chipola Junior College, Marianna, Fla., instructor in speech and theater, 1962-64; Kentucky Wesleyan College, Owensboro, assistant professor, 1967-69, associate professor of speech and theater, 1969-72; Hardin-Simmons University, Abilene, Tex., associate professor of speech and theater, 1972-74; St. Cloud State College (now University), St. Cloud, Minn., assistant professor of theater, 1976-78; Montclair State College, Upper Montclair, N.J., associate professor of speech and theater, 1978—. Play director for Act Two, 1971-72, and Stearns County Theatrical Company, 1978.

MEMBER: Speech Communication Association of America, American Theatre Association, Dramatists Guild (associate member). *Awards, honors:* First place awards from Theta Alpha Phi, 1959, for "Waiting for the Bus," Baylor University, 1966, for "Nest Among the Stars," and University of Missouri, 1971, for "The Knight-Mare's Nest"; award from *Earplay*, 1973, for "The Longest Day of the Year"; first place award from Southern Illinois University, 1975, for "The Fabulous Jeromes," and 1976, for "A Little Holy Water"; fellow of Dale Wasserman's Midwest Professional Playwrights Workshop, 1978.

WRITINGS: Waiting for the Bus (one-act play; first produced in DeLand, Fla., at Stetson University, November, 1958), Baker's Plays, 1972; *The Little Toy Dog* (one-act play; first produced in Longwood, Fla., at Lyman High School, March, 1960), Baker's Plays, 1972; *Sparrows of the Field* (one-act play; first produced in Carbondale, Ill. at Lutheran Center, May 7, 1975), Baker's Plays, 1973; *Omega's Ninth* (one-act play; first produced in New Haven, Conn., at Playwright's Lab Theatre, Yale School of Drama, March, 1967), Stage Magic, 1975.

Produced plays: "Time Out for Love" (three-act musical), first produced in Longwood, Fla., at Lyman High School, April, 1961; "Nest Among the Stars" (three-act), first produced in Marianna, Fla., at Chipola Junior College, June 11, 1964; "Hedge of Serpents" (three-act), first produced in Owensboro, Ky., at Kentucky Wesleyan College, November 19, 1969; "Brambles on the Sheepskin" (three-act), first produced in Owensboro, Ky., at Kentucky Wesleyan College, November 18, 1970; "Brothers of Dragons" (three-act), first produced in Abilene, Tex., at Hardin-Simmons University, October 23, 1973; "Snowbird" (one-act), first produced in Washington, D.C., at American Theatre Association, August 11, 1975; "Bug on a Sweet Potato Vine" (one-act), first aired in Carbondale, Ill., on WSIU-TV, August, 1975; "Song of the Goose" (one-act), first aired in Carbondale, Ill., on WSIU-TV, August, 1975; "Lady Crickets Don't Sing" (one-act), first aired in Carbondale, Ill., on WSIU-TV, April, 1976; "A Little Holy Water" (three-act), first produced in St. Cloud, Minn., at St. Cloud State University, October 20, 1976; "Once Below a Lighthouse" (one-act), first produced in New York City, at Glines, February 2, 1977; "Waiting for the Bus" (one-act), first produced in New York City, at No Smoking Playhouse, June 8, 1977; "The Fabulous Jeromes" (two-act), first produced in St. Cloud, Minn., at St. Cloud State University, November 12, 1978.

Unproduced plays: "The Youngest Child of Pablo Peco"

(one-act), 1960; "Fear of Angels" (three-act), 1966; "The Jerusalem Thorn" (one-act), 1974; "Farewell to the Curlew" (three-act), 1975; "The Great American (Southern-Fried) Ice Cream Party" (two-act musical), 1978.

Work represented in anthologies, including: *Ten Great One-Act Plays*, Bantam, 1968; *Best Short Plays, 1972*, Chilton, 1972; *A Pocket Full of Wry*, Stage Magic, 1974.

Contributor of articles, plays, and poems to theater and speech journals and to *Stetson Review*.

WORK IN PROGRESS: Expanding "The Jerusalem Thorn" into a two-act play.

SIDELIGHTS: Delgado told *CA:* "It is not the business of the writer to indulge in non-productive speculation concerning his own motives and meanings in his work. That is a function best left to the critics, who generally have nothing better to do anyway. If a work communicates to its auditors, the impact defies explanation and is greater than the sum of its parts; if it fails, no amount of explanation from author or critic will salvage the effect.

"Subject matter for my plays has run the gambit from historical drama to contemporary social and psychological material; style ranges from the ironic tragedy in "Brother of Dragons" to the black farce of "The Knight-Mare's Nest." As a theatre director and occasional actor I have developed an appreciation for the concept of the playscript as the score for a theatrical event. The playwright, then, must use words economically, revealing only the tip of the dramatic iceburg while the unspoken inner actions of the characters are brought to the surface through performance."

I. E. Clark, editor of *Stage Magic*, once wrote, "Delgado has a keen perception which enables him to look at the tragedy of modern life with a sense of humor—the kind of humor we desperately need to shake us back onto the road to the American dream."

* * *

De LOACH, Allen (Wayne) 1939-

PERSONAL: Born August 21, 1939, in Jacksonville, Fla.; son of Robert Earl, Sr. (an engineer) and Wyolin Lavina (Sweat) De Loach; married Barbara Agler, May 27, 1960 (divorced, October, 1970); married Joan Ford, July 5, 1971; children: (first marriage) Allen Wayne, Jr., Karsten Devin Agler. *Education:* Attended University of Florida, 1958-61; State University of New York at Buffalo, B.A. (honors), 1967, Ph.D., 1979. *Politics:* Liberal Democrat. *Religion:* "Unlabeled." *Home:* 106 Gillette Ave., Buffalo, N.Y. 14214. *Office address:* P.O. Box 1423, Buffalo, N.Y. 14214.

CAREER: State University of New York Empire State College, State Springs, assistant professor of English, 1971-78. Surveyor; creator and producer of more than a dozen multimedia presentations for galleries, museums, Indian reservations, and other institutions in the state of New York; has had group exhibitions of photographs. Member of board of directors of Artists Committee of Western New York, 1975, and Ashford Hollow Foundation for the Visual and Performing Arts, 1978. *Member:* Committee of Small Magazine Editors and Publishers, Niagara-Erie-Writers (publications director, 1978).

WRITINGS: Elegy: For Walt Whitman (poems), Anonym Press, 1967; *From Maine* (poems), University Press at Buffalo, 1970; *Third Part Unordered* (poems), Unicorn Press, 1970; *Buffalo Cold Spring Precinct 23 Bulletin*, 23 Club Series, 1971.

Editor: Walter Lowenfels, *We Are All Poets, Really*, Intrepid Press, 1968; *The East Side Scene*, Doubleday, 1972; *Intrepid Anthology: A Decade and Then Some*, Intrepid Press, 1977.

Editor and publisher of "Beau Fleuve Series," chapbooks, 1970—. Contributor to literary magazines, including *River Styx, Poetry Review of England*, and *Daedalus*. Editor and publisher of *Intrepid*, 1964—.

WORK IN PROGRESS: Mudhead Kachina: Poems and Photographs of Hopiland; Hopi-Tu Shin-U-Mu (title means "Poems and Photographs of the Little People of Peace"); *The Jig-Saw of Association: Methods and Materials in the Writings of William Burroughs*.

SIDELIGHTS: In 1967 De Loach made "New Jazz Poets," an album for Folkways Records. He has also conducted video-taped interviews with poets Allen Ginsberg and Lawrence Ferlinghetti.

De Loach writes: "Strong influences and spiritual practices are Hindu/Buddhist and Hopi. As an artist I focus on the intersection/interaction of visual and verbal images. My primary interest is social history ('who does what to whom?') and other interest include the poetics of 'beats,' 'Black Mountain,' and 'ethnoPoetics,' Whitman, Pound, and Williams."

* * *

DEMING, Barbara 1917-

PERSONAL: Born July 23, 1917, in New York, N.Y.; daughter of Harold S. (a lawyer) and Katherine (a singer; maiden name, Burritt) Deming. *Education:* Bennington College, B.A., 1938; Western Reserve University (now Case Western Reserve University), M.A., 1941. *Politics:* "Radical pacifist lesbian feminist." *Religion:* "Yes, but no longer believe in God as 'Father.'" *Home:* Rt. 2, Box 36D, Sugarloaf Key, Fla. 33042. *Agent:* Elaine Markson, 44 Greenwich Ave., New York, N.Y. 10011.

CAREER: Writer and political activist. Co-director of Bennington Stock Theatre, summers, 1938 and 1939; teaching fellow at Bennington School of the Arts, summers, 1940 and 1941; film analyst for Library of Congress film project, 1942-44. *Member:* P.E.N., American Society of Journalists & Authors, Women's Institute for Freedom of Press, Feminist Writers Guild. *Awards, honors:* Peace award from War Resisters League, 1967.

*WRITINGS—*All published by Grossman: *Prison Notes*, 1966; *Running Away From Myself: A Dream Portrait of America Drawn From the Films of the 40's*, 1969; *Revolution and Equilibrium*, 1971; *Wash Us and Comb Us* (stories), 1972; *We Cannot Live Without Our Lives*, 1974.

Contributor of poems, stories, and essays on politics, movies and theatre to magazines, including *New Yorker, Partisan Review, Paris Review, Nation*, and *Hudson Review*. Editor of *Liberation* magazine, 1962-69.

WORK IN PROGRESS: Remembering Who We Are, a book of dialogues; *A Book of Travail*, a novel.

SIDELIGHTS: Deming was apolitical until 1960 when she was forty-three. At that time she began reading Gandhi and identified with his activist pacifism. In the 1960's she was very active with the Committee for Nonviolent Action (a Gandhian group) in the civil rights and anti-war movements.

In retrospect, Deming told Leah Fritz: "Those struggles in which I took part—the struggle against my countrymen's abuse of blacks, the Cuban people, the Vietnamese—each of these struggles reverberated deeply a so-called apolitical struggle I'd been waging on my own, in a lonely way up until then, as a woman and a lesbian: the struggle to claim my life as my own, to affirm that it didn't belong to the patriarchs, it belonged to *me.* . . . Now I can see that the reason I gave my support with such passion was that I was waging my own fight by analogy. What an amazing feeling it was to be struggling at last not just by myself but in community.''

Deming told *CA:* ''I now believe that the earlier struggle I'd made but not presumed to name political is really the *fundamental* political struggle. For sexism is the *root* of imperialism—the root, I believe of all violence. The struggle against it, however, has to be waged consciously and collectively. I now place all my hopes in this struggle. At this point of history patriarchal rule threatens the very continuance of life on this planet. I think an awakening into feminist consciousness is an absolute necessity.''

BIOGRAPHICAL/CRITICAL SOURCES: Ms., November, 1978.

* * *

DENMARK, Florence L. 1932-

PERSONAL: Born January 28, 1932, in Philadelphia, Pa.; daughter of Morris and Minna (Sharkis) Levin; married Stanley J. Denmark, June 7, 1953 (divorced); married Robert W. Wesner (a publisher), September 5, 1973; children: Valerie, Richard and Pamela (twins). *Education:* University of Pennsylvania, A.B. (honors), 1952, A.M., 1954, Ph.D., 1958. *Home:* 17-85 215th St., Bayside, N.Y. 11360. *Office:* Ph.D. Programs in Psychology, City College of the City University of New York, 33 West 42nd St., New York, N.Y. 10036.

CAREER: City University of New York, Queens College, Flushing, N.Y., instructor, 1959-66, Hunter College, New York City, instructor, then assistant professor, 1964-70, associate professor, 1970-74, professor of psychology, 1974—, head of department of academic skills, 1968-70, City College, New York City, executive officer of Ph.D. programs in psychology, 1972—. Member of board of trustees of Puerto Rican Family Institute. *Member:* American Psychological Association (fellow; president-elect), Eastern Psychological Association (member of board of governors), New York State Psychological Association (vice-president), Psi Chi. *Awards, honors:* George N. Shuster fellowships, 1968, 1970; Mellon scholar at St. Olaf's College, 1977; Kurt Lewin Award from New York State Psychological Association, 1978.

WRITINGS: Probe: A Program for Planning Ahead Educationally, Transnat Programs Corp., 1972; (co-editor) *Woman: Dependent or Independent Variable?,* Psychological Dimension, 1975; (editor with Kurt Salzinger) *Psychology: The State of the Art,* Volume 309, New York Academy of Sciences, 1978; (editor with others) *Women,* Volume I, Psychological Dimensions, in press; (editor with J. A. Sherman) *The Psychology of Women: Future Directions in Research,* Psychological Dimensions, in press. Contributor to *International Encyclopedia of Neurology, Psychiatry, Psychoanalysis, and Psychology* and *Dictionary of the Behavioral Sciences.* Associate editor of *International Journal of Group Tensions;* member of editorial board of *Sex Roles: A Journal of Research* and *Psychology of Women Quarterly.*

WORK IN PROGRESS: The Psychology of Mothering, Status, and Leadership: A Non-Verbal Analysis; studying androgyny and somatic complaints.

SIDELIGHTS: Florence Denmark writes: ''My areas of vocational interest include social psychology (including urban conflicts), minority group achievement, status and leadership, and the psychology of women.''

* * *

DENNYS, Rodney Onslow 1911-

PERSONAL: Born July 16, 1911; married Elisabeth Katharine Greene, 1944; children: one son, two daughters. *Education:* Attended London School of Economics and Political Science. *Home:* Heaslands, Steep, near Crowborough, Sussex, England. *Office:* College of Arms, Queen Victoria St., London EC4V 4BT, England.

CAREER: Foreign Office, London, England, member of legation in The Hague, Netherlands, 1937-40, member of staff at Foreign Office, 1940-41, first secretary at British Middle East Office in Egypt, 1948-50, embassy in Turkey, 1950-53, and Paris, France, 1955-57; College of Arms, London, England, assistant to Garter King of Arms, 1958-61, Rouge Croix Pursuivant of Arms, 1961-67, Somerest Herald of Arms, 1967—. Member of staff at Sir Winston Churchill's funeral and the Prince of Wales's investiture. Freeman of the City of London. Head of Sussex branch of Council for the Preservation of Rural England, 1972—, member of national executive committee, 1973—. Member of court of University of Sussex. *Military service:* British Army, Intelligence Corps, 1941-44; became lieutenant colonel. Regular Army Reserve of Officers, 1946.

MEMBER: Academie Internationale d'Heraldique (associate member), Society of Antiquaries (fellow), Royal Society of Arts (fellow), Harleian Society (member of council), Society of Genealogists (member of executive committee), Devon Association, Garrick Club. *Awards, honors:* Member of Order of the British Empire, 1943; member of Royal Victorian Order, 1969.

WRITINGS: The Heraldic Imagination, Barrie & Jenkins, 1975, C. N. Potter, 1976. Also author of *Flags and Emblems of the World* and *Royal Princely Heraldry of Wales.* Contributor to magazines.

AVOCATIONAL INTERESTS: Sailing, ornithology.

* * *

DESTOUCHES, Louis Ferdinand 1894-1961
(Louis-Ferdinand Celine)

PERSONAL: Born May 27, 1894, in Courbevoie, France; died July 4, 1961, in Paris, France; son of Ferdinand-Auguste Destouches, (an insurance executive) and Marguerite-Louise-Celine Guilloux, (a businesswoman); married Edith Follett, 1919 (divorced, 1928); married Lucette Almanzor (a dancer), 1943; children: Colette. *Education:* Rennes Medical School, 1924.

CAREER: Medical doctor, 1924-1961; Rockefeller Foundation, New York, N.Y., 1925-28. *Military service:* French Army, 1912-15.

WRITINGS—All under pseudonym Louis-Ferdinand Celine; in English: *Voyage au bout de la nuit,* Denoel, 1932, reprinted, Gallimard, 1972, translation by J. P. Marks published as *Journey to the End of Night,* Little, Brown, 1934; *Mort a credit,* Denoel, 1936, reprinted, Gallimard, 1969, translation by Marks published as *Death on the Installment Plan,* Little, Brown, 1938, new translation by Ralph Manheim, New Directions, 1966; *Mea culpa, suivi de la vie et l'oeuvre de Semmelweis,* Denoel, 1937, translation by Robert A. Parker published as *Mea Culpa and the Life and Work of Semmelweis,* Little, Brown, 1937; *Guignol's Band,* Denoel, 1941, Gallimard, 1967, translation by B. Frechtman and J. T. Nile published as *Guignol's Band,* New Directions, 1954; *D'un chateau a l'autre,* Gallimard, 1957, translation by Manheim published as *Castle to Castle,* Delacorte, 1968; *Nord,* Gallimard, 1960, tranlation by Manheim published as *North,* Delacorte, 1972; *Rigodon,* Gallimard, 1969, translation by Manheim published as *Rigadoon,* Delacorte, 1974.

Other: *La Quinine en therapeutique* (title means "Quinine as Therapeutic"), Doin (Paris), 1925; *L'Eglise* (five-act play; title means "The Church"), Denoel, 1933; *Secrets dans l'ile* (title means "Secrets of the Island"), Gallimard, 1936; *Hommage a Zola* (title means "Hommage to Zola"), Denoel, 1936; *Bagatelles pour un massacre* (title means "Trifles for a Massacre"), Denoel, 1937; *Van Bagaden,* Denoel, 1937; *L'Ecole des cadavres* (title means "The School of Corpses"), Denoel, 1938; *Les Beaux Draps* (title means "Grave Situations"), Nouvelles editions francaises, 1941; *Preface pour Bezons a travers les ages* (title means "Preface for Bezons Across the Ages"), Denoel, 1944; *A l'agite du bocal* (title means "Agitating the Bowl"), P. L. de Tartas, 1948; *Foudres et fleches* (title means "Thunderbolts and Shafts"), C. de Jonquieres, 1949; *Casse-pipe* (title means "Shooting-gallery"), F. Chambriand, 1949.

Scandale aux abysses (title means "Scandal in the Abysses"), F. Chambriand, 1950; *Feerie pour un autre fois* (title means "Enchantment for Another Time"), Gallimard, 1952; *Normance,* Gallimard, 1954; *Entretiens avec le professor Y* (title means "Conversations with Professor Y"), Gallimard, 1955; *Ballet sans personne, sans musique, sans rien* (title means "A Ballet Without Anyone, Without Music, Without Anything"), Gallimard, 1959; *La Naissance d'une fee* (ballet; title means "The Birth of a Fairy"), Gallimard, 1959; *Voyou Paul. Pauvre Virginie* (title means "Guttersnipe Paul. Poor Virginie"), Gallimard, 1959; *Vive l'amnistie Monsieur* (title means "Long Live the Amnestied Man"), Editions Dynamo, 1963; *Le Pont de Londres* (title means "London Bridge"), Gallimard, 1964; *Oeuvres de Louis-Ferdinand Céline* (title means "The Works of Louis-Ferdinand Celine"), Balland, Volume I, 1966, Volumes II-IV, 1967, Volume V, 1969.

SIDELIGHTS: The misanthropy of Celine's first and best-known novels, coupled with his later fascistic and anti-Semitic outpourings, has obstructed general appreciation of his work. However, as a critic for *Choice* pointed out, "Celine, for all his garrulous ranting, was one of the most important voices in modern French fiction, and his influence on American as well as French novelists cannot be underestimated."

Allen Thiher, author of *Celine: the Novel as Delirium,* noted that Celine's work grew out of "the recognition of man's horrible necessity to grow sick and die and of the anguish that accompanies that recognition." His novels are expressions of this "intolerable awareness of human misery." Thus what has been interpreted as misanthropy and hate is actually a nightmarish representation of what Celine saw as the absurdity and despair of man's existence.

To portray this vision in language, Celine relied on the metaphors of madness and hallucination. Bettina Knapp in *Celine: Man of Hate,* described his linguistic landscape: "Huge verbal frescoes loom forth, horrendous-looking giants trample about, paraplegics, paralytics, gnomes, bloodied remnants hover over the narrations: scenes of dismemberment, insanity, murder, disease parade before the readers' eyes in all of their sublime and hideous grandeur." Consequently, Celine's fiction has been compared to the paintings of Breughel, Duerer and Goya, artists who glimpsed a primal world of decay and death.

Stylistically, Celine has been associated with James Joyce and Marcel Proust. Like theirs, his novels are psychological, subjective, and semi-autobiographical. Knapp praised especially the virility of Celine's word power, "the ambiguous and complex cacaphonies, the strident, jarring, even deafening sounds, the tremulous notes, the juxtaposition of rhythms." In *Book World,* Paul West noted the "dense inconsecutiveness" of his prose, which vaults the reader "from one salient image to another"; and several critics have made much of the use of his favorite device, the "three dots," which contribute to the discontinuous, antirational tenor of his work.

BIOGRAPHICAL/CRITICAL SOURCES: Milton Hindus, *The Crippled Giant: A Bizarre Adventure in Contemporary Letters,* Bear's Head Books, 1950; *Cahiers de L'Herne,* Numbers 3 and 5, [Paris], 1963; David Hayman, *Louis-Ferdinand Celine,* Columbia University Press, 1965; Erika Ostrovsky, *Celine and His Vision,* New York University Press, 1967; Allen Thiher, *Celine: the Novel as Delirium,* Rutgers University Press, 1972; *Book World,* January 30, 1972; *Choice,* May, 1972; *Contemporary Literary Criticism,* Gale, Volume 1, 1973, Volume 3, 1975, Volume 4, 1975, Volume 7, 1977, Volume 9, 1978; Bettina Liebowitz Knapp, *Celine, Man of Hate,* University of Alabama Press, 1974.*

* * *

DIAMOND, Graham   1945-
(Rochelle Leslie)

PERSONAL: Born August 18, 1945, in Manchester, England; came to United States in 1948, naturalized citizen, 1953; son of Louis (a furniture designer and refinisher) and Marsha (Tresman) Diamond; married Miriam Disman, March 25, 1967; children: Rochelle, Leslie. *Education:* Attended State University of New York, 1964-65. *Residence:* Rego Park, N.Y. *Agent:* Nat Sobel, 128 East 56th St., New York, N.Y. 10017. *Office: New York Times,* 229 West 43rd St., New York, N.Y. 10036.

CAREER: Macmillan Publishing Co., Inc., New York City, designer, 1968-69; *New York Times,* New York City, editorial artist, 1969—. *Member:* Poets and Writers, Science Fiction Writers of America.

WRITINGS—All fantasy, except as noted: *The Haven,* Playboy Press, 1977; *Lady of the Haven,* Playboy Press, 1978; *Dungeons of Kuba,* Playboy Press, 1979; *The Thief of Kalimar,* Fawcett, 1979; (under pseudonym Rochelle Leslie) *Riverwild* (historical novel), Berkley, 1979; *Captain From Bagdad,* Fawcett, 1980; *Samarkand,* Playboy Press, 1980; *Samarkand Dawn,* Playboy Press, 1980; *The Falcon of Eden,* Playboy Press, in press.

WORK IN PROGRESS: Yellow Sky, Yellow Sky, a historical novel set in the Argentine pampas in the nineteenth century.

SIDELIGHTS: Diamond writes: "I hope to create a whole new *Arabian Nights* in my fantasy stories: tales that will never go stale and will be enjoyed by the young of all ages. Just as other authors inspired me, my greatest wish is for my own work to inspire other young people to do creative writing of their own.

"I enjoy creating new worlds and in-depth characters (never superheroes) who are thrown against elements beyond their control and somehow must prevail, even when they don't believe they can. I live with my characters, laugh with them, cry with them. Only in this way can they be real to me and, thus, real to my readers."

DIAMOND, John 1934-

PERSONAL: Born August 9, 1934, in Australia; married Betty Peele (an administrator). *Education:* University of Sydney, M.D. (cum laude), 1957. *Office:* Institute of Behavioral Kinesiology, P.O. Drawer 37, Valley Cottage, N.Y. 10989.

CAREER: Private practice of psychiatry in United States and Australia; attending psychiatrist at Beth Israel Medical Center, New York City; professor of psychiatry at Mount Sinai Medical School, New York City; founder and director of Institute of Behavioral Kinesiology, Valley Cottage, N.Y. Charter diplomate of International College of Applied Kinesiology. Founder and director of Archaeus Research Foundation. Participant in professional seminars in the United States and abroad. *Member:* International Academy of Preventive Medicine (fellow; president; member of board of trustees), Royal Australian and New Zealand College of Psychiatrists, Royal College of Psychiatry. *Awards, honors:* Naughton-Manning Prize for Psychiatry.

WRITINGS: Collected Papers of John Diamond, M.D., Archaeus Press, 1977; *Behavioral Kinesiology and the Autonomic Nervous System,* Archaeus Press, 1978; *Behavioral Kinesiology for Dentists: An Introduction,* Archaeus Press, 1978; *Lectures on a Spiritual Basis of Medical Practice,* Archaeus Press, 1979; *Speech, Language, and the Power of the Breath,* Archaeus Press, 1979; *BK: Behavioral Kinesiology,* Harper, 1979; *Some Contributions of Behavioral Kinesiology to Art,* Archaeus Press, 1979. Contributor to medical journals, popular magazines, and newspapers. Co-editor of *Behavioral Kinesiology Report;* associate editor of journal of International Academy of Preventive Medicine and *Homeopathic Digest.*

WORK IN PROGRESS: Continuing research on behavioral kinesiology, bioharmonics, and psychoaesthetics.

SIDELIGHTS: After moving to the United States, Diamond gradually changed his professional focus from psychiatry to preventive medicine. Since that time he has integrated and synthesized developments in a wide variety of fields, including nutrition, music, speech, lifestyle retraining, and stress reduction, to create a new medical/scientific speciality which he has named "behavioral kinesiology."

Much of Diamond's research and writing has been concentrated on the thymus gland. He has also created musical and sound tapes designed to "balance the cerebral hemispheres and reduce stress," one of the tangible results of his research on the therapeutic qualities of sounds, music, and performance. Another of his developments is a field of research he calls "psychoaesthetics," which involves "the study of music, art, literature, drama, poetry and prose, architecture, body movement and dance, and gesture and posture as they relate to human functioning and stress reduction via the aesthetic experience."

Other research work contributing to the development of his theories includes studies of psychosomatic medicine, psychiatry and psychoanalysis, neurophysiology, pharmacology, medical climatology, immunology, myofunctional therapy, acupuncture, meditative techniques, cultural anthropology, ethology, comparative religion, philosophy, political science, folklore, mythology, motivational research, and bioharmonics.

AVOCATIONAL INTERESTS: Organic gardening, music.

* * *

DIAMONSTEIN, Barbaralee D.

PERSONAL: Born in New York, N.Y.; daughter of Rubin Robert and Sally Harriet (Simmons) Dworkin; married Alan A. Diamonstein (divorced). *Education:* New York University, received doctorate, 1963. *Home:* 4 East 70th St., New York, N.Y. 10021. *Agent:* Julian Bach Literary Agency, Inc., 6 East 48th St., New York, N.Y. 10017.

CAREER: White House, Washington, D.C., assistant, 1963-66; City of New York, N.Y., director of cultural affairs, 1966-67; writer and editor, 1967—; television broadcaster and interviewer, 1969—. Interviewer and producer for "Barbaralee Diamonstein and . . . ," a series on WNYC-TV, 1975—. Adjunct associate professor at Hunter College of the City University of New York, 1974-77; lecturer at New School for Social Research, 1976—; guest lecturer at Duke University, spring, 1978. J. Clawson-Mills fellow and project director of Architectural League centennial, 1979; director of international museum exhibition for Eastern Europe, sponsored by International Communications Agency, 1979. Member of New York City Landmarks Preservation Commission, 1972—, New York City Cultural Commission, 1974—, and Committee in the Public Interest, 1975—. Member of governor's Commission on the Arts and Cultural Life of New York State, 1974—. Member of board of advisers of Museum of African Art, 1976—, board of overseers of Emerson College, 1976—, and board of directors of Film Anthology Archives, 1970—, New York Landmarks Conservancy, 1973—, and Interface, 1974—. *Awards, honors:* Winifred Fisher Award, 1976; Rockefeller Foundation Fellow at Aspen Institute, 1979.

WRITINGS: Open Secrets: Ninety-Four Women in Touch With Our Time, Viking, 1972; *Our Two Hundred Years: Tradition and Renewal,* National Endowment for the Humanities, 1975; (editor) *The Art World: Seventy-Five Years of ARTnews* (Book-of-the-Month Club alternate selection), Rizzoli International, 1977; *Buildings Reborn: New Uses, Old Places,* Harper, 1978.

Documentary films—All for CBS-TV: "But Not on My Block," aired January 28, 1976; "Rubenism," October 21, 1976; "Light on the Dark Continent," February 20, 1977.

Author of "Whatever Happened to Men?", a series distributed by Field Newspaper Syndicate, 1975, and "Culture and the Cities," Field Newspaper Syndicate, 1976. Author of "Emphasis," a monthly column in *Harper's Bazaar,* 1969-71. Contributor of articles and reviews to popular magazines, including *Vogue, Partisan Review, Saturday Review, Ladies Home Journal, Ms.,* and *Good Housekeeping.* Editor of special supplements for popular magazines, including *Harper's Bazaar* and *McCall's.* Editor and publisher of "Calendar of the American Issues Forum," American Revolution Bicentennial Administration, 1976. Special projects editor of *ARTnews* and *Antiques World,* 1974—.

WORK IN PROGRESS: Inside New York's Art World, a collection of interviews with artists, architects, photographers, critics, and music directors.

SIDELIGHTS: Barbaralee Diamonstein's career has encompassed numerous aspects of the field of communications, including television and teaching. She has conducted forums on such topics as "Womanpower in Action" and "Black Awareness," and traveling museum exhibitions, including one in 1978 under the auspices of Smithsonian Institution Traveling Exhibition Service and another in 1979 to commemorate the one hundredth anniversary of the Architectural League.

Her television interviews have brought her into contact with nationally-known entertainers, politicians, writers, and publishers, and the subjects under discussion have reflected her own interests in politics, the arts, education, and social reform.

*   *   *

DICKINSON, William Boyd   1908-1978

PERSONAL: Born May 18, 1908, in Kansas City, Mo.; died September 12, 1978, in Philadelphia, Pa., of cancer; son of William Boyd and Alice G. (Hillman) Dickinson; married Aileen Robinson (died); married Joan S. Younger; children: William Boyd III, Beverly Dickinson Albertson, Theresa Joan, Rosalind Alice Dickinson Babcock, Diana Mary Dickinson Weyman. *Education:* Kansas City Junior College, A.A., 1927; University of Kansas, A.B., 1929. *Home and office:* 2020 Delancey Pl., Philadelphia, Pa. 19103.

CAREER/WRITINGS: Kansas City Star, Kansas City, Mo., reporter, 1929-30; United Press International, New York City, manager of business in Denver, Colo., Minneapolis, Minn., and New York City, business representative in Chicago, Ill., news editor in London, England, Southwest Pacific manager and war correspondent, 1930-47, foreign news editor in New York City, 1947-49; *Philadelphia Evening Bulletin,* Philadelphia, Pa., news editor, Washington bureau chief, and associate city editor, 1949-56, assistant managing editor, 1956-59, managing editor, 1959-69, executive editor, 1969-73. Notable assignments include coverage of Japanese surrender of World War II. Member of United States Privacy Protection Study Commission, 1975-77. *Member:* American Society of Newspaper Editors, Associated Press Managing Editors Association, National Press Club, Philadelphia Press Association, Sigma Delta Chi, Delta Tau Delta.

OBITUARIES: Washington Post, September 13, 1978.*

*   *   *

DICKSTEIN, Morris   1940-

PERSONAL: Born February 23, 1940, in New York, N.Y.; son of Abraham and Anne (Reitman) Dickstein; married Lore Willner (a writer), January 3, 1965; children: Jeremy, Rachel. *Education:* Columbia University, B.A., 1961; Yale University, M.A., 1963, Ph.D., 1967; attended Clare College, Cambridge, 1963-64. *Home:* 230 West 105th St., New York, N.Y. 10025. *Agent:* Georges Borchardt, Inc., 136 East 57th St., New York, N.Y. 10022. *Office:* Department of English, Queens College of the City University of New York, Flushing, N.Y. 11367.

CAREER: Columbia University, New York, N.Y., instructor, 1966-67, assistant professor of English, 1967-71; Queens College of the City University of New York, Flushing, N.Y., associate professor, 1971-75, professor of English, 1976—. *Member:* International P.E.N., Modern Language Association of America, National Book Critics Circle. *Awards, honors:* Woodrow Wilson fellowship, 1961; Guggenheim fellowship, 1973; American Council of Learned Societies fellowship, 1977; National Book Critics Circle nomination in criticism, 1977, for *Gates of Eden.*

WRITINGS: Keats and His Poetry, University of Chicago Press, 1971; *Gates of Eden: American Culture in the Sixties,* Basic Books, 1977; (editor with Leo Braudy) *Great Film Directors,* Oxford University Press, 1978. Contributing editor, *Partisan Review,* 1972—; consultant, Basic Books, 1972—.

WORK IN PROGRESS: Research on the aesthetics of popular culture and on America in the 1930's.

SIDELIGHTS: Dickstein writes: "I started out as a student of the English Romantic poets, which is still my most solid academic field. I've written a book on Keats and hope to write another on Wordsworth some day. I have a special interest in a number of other English writers such as Blake, Carlyle, Matthew Arnold, and D. H. Lawrence. I've often reviewed current writers, and this eventually led to my book on the sixties and to an expanding interest in American cultural history.

"I've always been fascinated by politics, usually from a distance. While still an undergraduate at Columbia I developed a strong attraction to the ways literature and society, culture and politics, intersect. That's the basic approach of *Gates of Eden* and I'd like to apply it to earlier phases of American culture, such as the 1930's.

"Because my teaching and writing have a ravenous appetite for new material, these vocations tend to swallow up my avocations. This happened recently when I began teaching film courses."

In *Gates of Eden* Dickstein offered a "combination of literary criticism, cultural history, politics, and personal reminiscence" of the 1960's. Dickstein characterized the decade as a time when the "search for personal authenticity" was combined with "the quest for social justice." The decade's cultural life was a reflection of this, Dickstein contended, as politics and culture were entwined. Most reviewers found the book to contain valuable insights into the culture of the 1960's although several disagreed with either Dickstein's choice of format or with some of his conclusions. Perry Meisel was perhaps voicing the critical consensus when he commented that while Dickstein made few brilliant or novel observations, *"Gates of Eden* is likely to become the official history of the 1960's because it organized what is already familiar into a sustained critical vision that finds recurrent designs in everything it engages."

"Dickstein makes two arresting general claims for the culture of the '60s," Walter Clemons declared. "The first is that the "sexual revolution' is the most misleading of the simplistic labels attached to it; the deeper insurgency, he agrees with [Paul] Goodman, was spiritual and religious. The second is that the radical activism of the period did not entirely disintegrate it its violent final phase but 'made available to us not only critical habits of mind but strategies of direct action that continue to be used on particular issues and local encounters.' His book, with its combination of fresh cultural commentary and personal testimony, justifies Dickstein's hope that 'criticism, which is often tempted to be hermetic, can tell us something about the real world.'"

As a trained literary critic, Dickstein concentrated on the major literary figures of the decade, and included discussions of Allen Ginsberg, Norman Mailer, Philip Roth, Joseph Heller, and Kurt Vonnegut, as well as of such influential cultural critics as Herbert Marcuse, Norman O. Brown, and Paul Goodman. The 1960's was a decidedly anti-intellectual era and Dickstein proclaimed that "the line between high culture and popular culture gave way in the 60's and on some fronts was erased entirely." Nonetheless Dickstein chose to analyze the few writers who did contribute to the intellectual framework of the decade. Meisel was heartened by Dickstein's "emphasis on the literary and philosophical" and called it "a welcome relief."

Other critics thought that Dickstein had missed the central cultural achievement of the decade—the disavowal of traditional artistic means of expression. Dickstein admitted that he "slighted cultural phenomena for which I felt little affinity," and emphasized verbal, written forms of expression (literature and a smattering of rock music). He neglected art, dance, film, theatre, and other less easily categorized forms of expression. "Dickstein's sense of the Important Subject is completely predictable," Robert Christgau complained, "there's no art for art's sake here, no indigestible wierdness. . . . For finally this is a timid book. By sticking close to fiction, Dickstein neatly avoids all of the decade's more recondite avant-gardisms, and, fiction maven though he may be, he also fails to mention two quintessentially '60s genres, science fiction and pornography, which is perhaps a clue to one totally incomprehensible omission: William S. Burroughs."

Reviewer Geoffrey Wolff wrote: "If *Gates of Eden* spends excessive energy on what it will do, what it has not been about, what it meant to do—if it signals its punches always—let it also be recorded that there are some extraordinary wing shots taken, some brilliant observations brought down." He cited the book's discussions of Heller, Thomas Pynchon, Vonnegut, Donald Barthelme, and Mailer as being particularly praiseworthy: "It sounds these writers deeply and resourcefully."

Dickstein's chapter on black authors was judged "fairly perfunctory" by Christopher Lehmann-Haupt. But C. Michael Curtis found it "interesting" and noted: "He weaves carefully through the complicated clashes between an old guard (Baldwin and Ellison) and aggressive newcomers such as Eldridge Cleaver and Ishmael Reed. The bottom line, however, is that a black novelist is a good novelist when his (her) fiction meets 'conventional standards,' which means an organized plot, believable characters, and a controlling sensibility we're willing to listen to."

"Whose reading list does Dickstein think he has assembled?" Miller exclaimed. "Those 'whose culture enshrined music and films and drugs' were more interested in assuaging their discontent than rationalizing it, and were not likely to get much of a kick out of Marcusean dialectics or neo-Freudian polemics." Miller thought that *I Ching* or *Stranger in a Strange Land* would have been more appropriate choices as representative books of the 1960's. He continued: "*Gates of Eden* obscures the fact that the Sixties' upheavals began with the young, not with the New York intelligentsia; and since those young people were not great readers, Dickstein's notion of a basic countercultural bibliography is highly improbable."

Although several critics quibbled with Dickstein's choice to allow his own experiences in the decade to intrude in the narrative, Christgau was more appreciative. He wrote: "Dickstein's need to bring his own experiences to bear on his analysis is a significantly '60s-ish impulse. Its effect is to bring what he has to say down to human scale; almost by definition, he does not pontificate or claim absolute validity, and that's gratifying." Christgau conceded, however, that this method had mixed results. On the one hand, it lead to "relatively brave and—in terms of Dickstein's milieu—idiosyncratic judgments." Finally, though, Dickstein's "critical self-indulgence" distorted his subject, according to Christgau.

Dickstein's discussion of the relationship between the culture of the 1950's and the 1960's was also controversial among critics. Dickstein explained in the book's epilogue that the disjunction between the two decades was personally important to him. "What probably has marked me more than anything," he wrote, "was that I came to consciousness between the generations; my formative experiences bridged both the fifties and the sixties, and I never felt wholly comfortable in either world, though both were passionately important to me in their turn." In an interview with Philip French, Dickstein remarked: "Without being fully conscious of it, I was trying to maintain a dialogue with the conservative literary sensibility that I had grown up with and that had been dominant in the '50s. And I was trying to show that a good deal of the culture of the '60s not only would last but made it even by the standards of the literary culture of the '50s, though the critics of the '50s, or a good number of them, were simple unable to recognise the complexity that existed in the arts of the '60s."

Paul Starr explained his conception of the disjunction in Dickstein's book. "A radical contrast between the 1950s and '60s—a shift from political caution to political enthusiasm, from constriction to release of vitality, from inwardness and self-absorption to engagement and self-display—functions as the ruling dialectic of Dickstein's book," Starr wrote. "While in the '50s politics were characterized by the 'narrow range of permissible debate,' in the '60s they opened up and became a matter of intense moral concern. By the end of *Gates of Eden,* the two decades seem to symbolize for Dickstein two sides of his own personality—the '50s more reticent and restrained, the '60s more fervent and uninhibited."

Lehmann-Haupt decided that Dickstein was "at his best when identifying the 'new shoots' among the 'old roots' of the 50's, and merely very good when it comes to explaining the breakthrough of new forms in the 60's." However, he realized that "it's simply too soon to tell what was of lasting importance about the 60's." Lehmann-Haupt concluded: "But even his [Dickstein's] intelligence can't describe what hasn't yet come into perspective. Even he can't see what isn't yet there." Wolff remarked: "It requires courage and security to offer as accurate representations of cultural topography such grossly distinct and superficial contours. But not only is the judgment brave, it is accurate, and displays Dickstein's principal ambition: to codify the conceptual nature of polar eras."

Other critics found fault with Dickstein's assessment of the 1950's. While citing Dickstein's "excellent literary judgment," Lasch remarked that Dickstein's "picture of the fifties, however, is a caricature that does not do credit to a cultural historian of Dickstein's intelligence." Miller found Dickstein's depiction to be "too rigid" and also complained that it "prevents a fair appraisal of the liberal and radical positions of the period."

Lasch concluded that the book was a worthwhile portrait of the 1960's despite its several flaws. He wrote: "I still find excessive Dickstein's estimate of the period's cultural achievements, but I can see that his book makes the unqualified opposition of such critics as Philip Rahv, Saul Bellow, and Daniel Bell seem flat and uninformative by comparison. Those writers, notwithstanding the validity of many of their judgments, simply refused to take the period seriously. Dickstein has shown, conclusively, the inadequacy of this position. He makes it clear that we learn more about the period by taking it seriously than by writing it off as the triumph of the 'trendy.'"

BIOGRAPHICAL/CRITICAL SOURCES: Morris Dickstein, *Gates of Eden: American Culture in the Sixties,* Basic Books, 1977; *New York Times,* March 9, 1977; *New York Times Book Review,* March 13, 1977; *Newsweek,* March 28, 1977; *Nation,* April 23, 1977; *Village Voice,* April 25, 1977; *Washington Post Book World,* May 1, 1977; *New Times,* May 13, 1977; *New Republic,* May 21, 1977; *Atlantic,* June,

1977; *Commentary,* July, 1977; *New York Review of Books,* August 4, 1977; *Encounter,* June, 1978.

* * *

DIEHL, James M(ichael) 1938-

PERSONAL: Born December 4, 1938, in Los Angeles, Calif.; son of James Raymond (a tool planner) and Mary Catherine (in sales; maiden name, Stroud) Diehl; married Roberta Lloyd (an editor), July, 1962. *Education:* University of California, Berkeley, B.A., 1963, M.A., 1965, Ph.D., 1972. *Residence:* Bloomington, Ind. *Office:* Department of History, Indiana University, Bloomington, Ind. 47401.

CAREER: Northwestern University, Evanston, Ill., assistant professor of history, 1972-73; Indiana University, Bloomington, assistant professor, 1973-77, associate professor of history, 1978—. *Member:* American Historical Association, Conference Group for Central European History, Phi Beta Kappa.

WRITINGS: Paramilitary Politics in Weimar Germany, Indiana University Press, 1977.

WORK IN PROGRESS: Research on war veterans and right-wing radicalism in post-World War II Germany.

* * *

DILLER, Edward 1925-

PERSONAL: Born December 15, 1925, in Cleveland, Ohio; son of Isaac (a hat manufacturer) and Frieda (Kuflick) Diller; married Lois Kater (a dance therapist), December 18, 1954; children: Amie, Kevin, Steven. *Education:* Attended Los Angeles City College, 1946-48, University of Basel, 1949-50, University of Innsbruck, 1950-51, and University of California, Los Angeles, 1951-52, 1955-56; Mexico City College, B.A., 1952; Los Angeles State College, M.A., 1955; additional study at University of Zurich, 1957; Middlebury College, D.M.L., 1961. *Home:* 2089 Potter St., Eugene, Ore. 97405. *Office:* Department of German, University of Oregon, Eugene, Ore. 97403.

CAREER: Teacher of German at public schools in Beverly Hills, Calif., 1958-62; Colorado College, Colorado Springs, assistant professor of German and co-director of German summer school, 1962-65; University of Oregon, Eugene, assistant professor, 1965-66, associate professor, 1967-71, professor of German, 1972—. Fulbright professor at Carolo-Wilhemina Technische Hochschule, autumn, 1967, University of Regensburg, spring, 1968, and University of Freiburg, 1977-78; visiting professor at University of Dortmund, autumn, 1969. President of Northwest Regional Honors Council, 1976-77; participant in conferences in the United States and Germany; director of language workshops. *Member:* American Association of Teachers of German (member of executive council, 1972-75; president, 1977-80), American Council on German Studies (member of board of directors, 1977), Modern Language Association of Southern California (member of executive council, 1961).

WRITINGS: (Contributor) Samuel Levenson and Robert Kendrick, editors, *Readings of Foreign Languages for the Elementary School,* Blaisdell, 1967; (with James R. McWilliams) *Unterwegs* (title means "Along the Way"), Random House, 1969; (with McWilliams and Roger Nicholls) *Meisterwerke der deutschen Sprache* (title means "Masterpieces of the German Language"), Random House, 1970; (editor with Eberhardt Reichmann, Klaus Mueller, and others) *The Teaching of German: Problems and Methods,* Carl Schurz Association, 1970; (contributor) Horst S. Daemm-

rich and Diether Haenicke, editors, *The Challenge of German Literature,* Wayne State University Press, 1970; (with Armin Wishard) *Spiel und Sprache* (title means "Play and Language"), Norton, 1972; (with Wishard) *Noch einmal Spiel und Sprache* (title means "Play and Language, Once Again"), Norton, 1974; *Guenter Grass: Mythic Journey on a Tim Drum,* University Press of Kentucky, 1974; (with Wishard and Ellen Lavroff) *Cuentos y Juegos* (title means "Stories and Games"), Norton, 1975; (with Wishard and Ronnie Morrison) *Tout a fait francais* (title means "Entirely in French"), Norton, 1979.

Contributor of about twenty articles to language and education journals. Editor of *PEALS* (of Colorado Congress of Foreign Language Teachers and State Department of Education), 1963-65; associate editor of *Unterrichtspraxis,* 1972-77, special edition editor, spring, 1973.

WORK IN PROGRESS: Franz Kafka: Author of Ambiguity; articles on Franz Kafka.

SIDELIGHTS: Diller told *CA:* "After thirty years of research and writing I am firmly convinced that scholarly writing is as personal and subjective in most respects as is the writing of fiction itself. Whereas fiction writers take their cues from life and experience, scholars share in the process in a similar fashion but choose to explore the consciousness of the best of artistic minds as well as the world and language which the author expresses. Here the scholar must pick and choose aspects of another reality that resonates most accurately with his own but stands in need of greater clarification, of greater discovery. And how much more challenging and adventurous the process if the consciousness to be explored has been placed in another language and an alien culture! Writing comes after the fact; first discovery of self and others, then thinking and reason, then writing to capture the ideas with the right words and phrases, then finally, and most important, editing—the final line between substance and trivia."

* * *

DIMOND, E(dmunds) Grey 1918-

PERSONAL: Born December 8, 1918, in St. Louis, Mo.; son of Edmunds Grey and Gertrude Ruth (Schmidt) Dimond; married Mary Dwight Clark (a writer), 1944; children: Sherri, Lark, Leagrey. *Education:* Attended Purdue University, 1938-40; Indiana University, B.S., 1942, M.D., 1944. *Politics:* Democrat. *Religion:* None. *Home:* 2501 Holmes St., Kansas City, Mo. 64108. *Agent:* John Cushman Associates, Inc., 25 West 43rd St., New York, N.Y. 10036. *Office:* 2220 Holmes St., Kansas City, Mo. 64108.

CAREER: Indiana University Medical Center, Department of Medicine, resident physician, 1945-46, 1947-48; Massachusetts General Hospital, Clinical Fellow in Medicine and Cardiology, 1949-50; University of Kansas, Medical Center, Kansas City, assistant professor, 1950-51, associate professor, 1951-53, professor of medicine, 1953-60, chairman of department, 1953-60; Scripps Clinic and Research Foundation, LaJolla, Calif., director of Institute for Cardiopulmonary Disease, 1960-68; University of Missouri, Kansas City, distinguished professor of medicine, 1968—, provost for health sciences, 1970—. Fulbright professor in the Netherlands, 1956; visiting professor at England's National Heart Institute, 1959. University of California, San Diego, research associate, 1964-67, professor-of-medicine-in-residence, 1967-68. Member of U.S. State Department specialists abroad programs in the Philippines, Taiwan, Colombia, Chile, Czechoslovakia, Ceylon, Indonesia, and Vietnam;

consultant to U.S. Bureau of Labor. *Military service:* U.S. Army, Medical Corps, 1946-48; became captain. *Member:* American College of Physicians, American College of Cardiologists (president, 1961).

WRITINGS: Electrocardiography and Vectorcardiography, Little, Brown, 1952, 4th edition, 1967; (editor) *Digitalis,* C. C Thomas, 1957; *The Exercise Electrocardiogram,* C. C Thomas, 1961; *More Than Herbs and Acupuncture,* Norton, 1975. Editor-in-chief of *ACCEL* (journal of American College of Cardiology), 1969—.

WORK IN PROGRESS: Research on cardiovascular physiology.

SIDELIGHTS: Referring to his book *More Than Herbs and Acupuncture,* Dimond wrote: "It describes my experiences as the first clinician to be invited to the People's Republic of China in September of 1971, immediately following the ping-pong diplomacy. It further describes my personal friendship with Edgar Snow, and the role I played in developing the first medical exchanges between the People's Republic of China and the United States in 1971 and 1972. The book is essentially devoted to the political history of that time and is not a medical book, nor is it related to herbs and acupuncture as the title clearly expresses."

*   *   *

DiPEGO, Gerald F(rancis) 1941-

PERSONAL: Born August 3, 1941, in Chicago, Ill.; son of George (a cook) and Margaret (Carli) DiPego; married Pauline Samargis, October 4, 1963 (divorced); children: Justin, Zachary. *Education:* Northern Illinois University, B.S., 1963; graduate study at University of Missouri, 1967-68. *Politics:* Liberal. *Religion:* None. *Residence:* Santa Monica, Calif. *Agent:* Ziegler-Diskant, 9255 Sunset Blvd., Los Angeles, Calif.

CAREER: Joliet Spectator, Joliet, Ill., reporter, 1963-64; Department of Mental Health, Elgin, Ill., in public relations, 1964-65; *Menominee Herald Leader,* Menominee, Mich., reporter, summer, 1965; high school teacher of English and journalism in Menominee, 1965-66; free-lance writer, 1968—. *Awards, honors:* Christophers Award, 1974, for film "I Heard the Owl Call My Name."

WRITINGS: With a Vengeance (novel), McGraw, 1977; *Forest Things* (novel), Delacorte, 1979.

Author of about fifteen filmscripts and adaptations for television, including "Born Innocent," for National Broadcasting Co. (NBC-TV), "The Stranger Who Looks Like Me," American Broadcasting Co. (ABC-TV), 1974, "I Heard the Owl Call My Name," Columbia Broadcasting System (CBS-TV), 1974, "A Family Upside-Down," NBC-TV, 1978, and "Four Feathers," NBC-TV, 1978.

Work anthologized in *Great Television Plays,* Volume II, Dell, 1975.

WORK IN PROGRESS: Scripts for feature films.

SIDELIGHTS: DiPego writes: "I prefer to write from an emotional base. I must feel deeply about a character, event, or scene before I start to write. People are more interesting to me than facts or processes. I see a crowd of strangers, and I watch the faces, and I ask 'what does he want, what are her dreams, what is this one afraid of, what makes that one laugh or cry?' I ask the same questions of each of my characters and try to create full human beings on the page.

"I love the peace and strength of the mountains. My new novel, *Forest Things,* deals on a real level—three weeks at a

resort in the Adirondacks of New York—but on another level it creates a new mountain myth, a legend."

AVOCATIONAL INTERESTS: Hiking, camping, riding in the mountains.

BIOGRAPHICAL/CRITICAL SOURCES: New York Times, April 24, 1977.

*   *   *

DODDS, Tracy 1952-

PERSONAL: Born March 11, 1952, in Lafayette, Ind.; daughter of William F. and Joann (Thoma) Dodds. *Education:* Indiana University, B.A. *Office: Milwaukee Journal,* Milwaukee, Wis.

CAREER: Milwaukee Journal, Milwaukee, Wis., sports writer, 1974—. *Awards, honors:* National second place award in investigative sports reporting from Associated Press, 1976, first place award, 1977.

WRITINGS: (With Marvin Fishman) *Bucking the Odds,* Raintree, 1978; (contributor) *Best Sports Stories 1978,* Dutton, 1978.

*   *   *

DOHAN, Mary Helen 1914-

PERSONAL: Born February 15, 1914, in Cincinnati, Ohio; daughter of Joseph Francis (a representative for machine tool companies) and Anastasia (Enneking) Dohan; married Robert D. Samsot (an attorney), 1938; children: Kathleen Samsot Hawk, Robert Louis. *Education:* Tulane University, B.A., 1934, M.A., 1938. *Home:* 321 Audubon Blvd., New Orleans, La. 70125.

CAREER: Tulane University, Newcomb College, New Orleans, La., assistant professor of English, 1934-38; Dominican College, New Orleans, assistant professor of English, 1962-64; writer, 1938—.

WRITINGS: Our Own Words (nonfiction), Knopf, 1974. Work represented in *Best American Short Stories,* 1966. Contributor of stories, poems, and articles to periodicals, including *Atlantic, Redbook,* and *Smithsonian.*

WORK IN PROGRESS: Another book on language and a biographical novel.

SIDELIGHTS: Dohan writes: "In keeping with the mores of time, place, and conservative upbringing, I gave up my career upon my marriage, and became a full-time wife and mother, a demanding and (yes!) rewarding role. My first love, writing, wandered the edges of my world, though, never letting me forget. Some day there would be time! And there was—is. If I had done more writing earlier, as I should have, I'd have written differently, I am sure, of different things. What cries out to be said changes with the years—or perhaps it is our voice that changes. I regret what is lost but cherish what is not: life, the opportunity to write, a wonderful family."

AVOCATIONAL INTERESTS: Jogging, tennis, gourmet cooking.

*   *   *

DONALDSON, John W. 1893(?)-1979

OBITUARY NOTICE: Born c. 1893; died February 23, 1979, in Tucson, Ariz. Financier. A New York financial executive in the 1930's, Donaldson subsequently served as special assistant to the president of the Export-Import Bank of the United States during the John Kennedy and Lyndon Johnson Administrations. In 1943, Putnam published his edited version of Thomas Malory's *Morte d'Arthur* under the title *Arthur Pendragon of Britain.* The book featured illustrations by Andrew Wyeth, and critics remarked that for the first time the English classic had continuity, coherence, and animation. Obituaries and other sources: *New York Times,* February 28, 1979.

* * *

DONALDSON, Robert Herschel 1943-

PERSONAL: Born June 14, 1943, in Houston, Tex.; son of Herschel Arthur (in sales) and Vera (True) Donaldson; married Judy Johnston (a computer programmer), June 27, 1964; children: Jennifer Gwynne, John Andrew. *Education:* Harvard University, A.B., 1964, A.M., 1966, Ph.D., 1969. *Politics:* Republican. *Religion:* Methodist. *Home:* 2810 White Oak Dr., Nashville, Tenn. 37215. *Office:* Office of the Dean, College of Arts and Sciences, Vanderbilt University, 232 Kirkland Hall, Nashville, Tenn. 37240.

CAREER: Vanderbilt University, Nashville, Tenn., assistant professor, 1968-73, associate professor of political science, 1974—, associate dean of arts and sciences, 1975—. Visiting research professor at U.S. Army War College, 1978-79. *Member:* International Studies Association, American Association for the Advancement of Slavic Studies, Ripon Society (vice-president for research, 1973-74), United Nations Association (local vice-president, 1976-78), Phi Beta Kappa. *Awards, honors:* Fellowship from Council on Foreign Relations, 1973-74.

WRITINGS: (With Derek J. Waller) *Stasis and Change in Revolutionary Elites: A Comparative Analysis of the 1956 Party Central Committees in China and the U.S.S.R.,* Sage Publications, 1972; *Soviet Policy Toward India: Ideology and Strategy,* Harvard University Press, 1974. Contributor to political science journals.

WORK IN PROGRESS: Soviet Foreign Policy Since World War II, with Joseph L. Nogee; *The U.S.S.R. and the North-South Dialogue.*

SIDELIGHTS: Donaldson writes: "I have traveled to the U.S.S.R. and Eastern Europe, and to South Asia (India, Pakistan, Nepal, and Bangladesh). My writing on international politics and my teaching to undergraduates is primarily motivated by a desire to contribute to a shaping of 'global citizens' in this country. America in an interdependent world cannot afford a parochial outlook."

* * *

DONDIS, Donis A(snin) 1924-

PERSONAL: Born May 10, 1924; married Harold Dondis (a lawyer). *Education:* Massachusetts College of Art, B.F.A., 1948; Boston University, M.S., 1965. *Office:* School of Public Communication, Boston University, 640 Commonwealth Ave., Boston, Mass. 02215.

CAREER: William Filene's Co., Boston, Mass., graphic designer and media specialist in advertising department, 1949-52; R. H. White Co., Boston, graphic designer and media specialist in advertising department, 1952-54; John C. Dowd Co., Boston, graphic designer and media specialist in art department, 1954-55; Harvard University, Graduate School of Business Administration, Boston, staff consultant on publications, 1955-63; Boston University, Boston, lecturer, 1963-68, assistant professor, 1968-73, associate professor, 1973-78, professor of public communication, 1978—, *ad interim* dean of School of Public Communication, 1978—,

founder and director of Public Communication Institute, summers, 1973—. Research associate at Massachusetts Institute of Technology; member of advisory board of Radcliffe College Forum. Film producer; photographer and painter, with exhibitions in New England galleries. Public speaker. Vice-president of Newport International Television Festival; member of board of directors of Millay Colony for the Arts; patron of Alice James Press.

MEMBER: International Visual Literacy Association (founding member; member of board of directors), American Association of University Professors, Women in Communications, National Multiple Sclerosis Society (member of state board of directors), New England Screen Educators Association, Edna St. Vincent Millay Literary Society (member of board of directors), Newport Cultural Society (member of board of directors). *Awards, honors:* Jury's choice award for painting from Boston Arts Festival, 1965; Litt.D., Emerson College, 1978.

WRITINGS: A Primer of Visual Literacy, M.I.T. Press, 1973; *Print Media: A Handbook,* Eikon Press, 1975; *Educational Television and the Arts,* National Endowment for the Arts, 1978. Contributor to media journals.

WORK IN PROGRESS: Visualistics: A New View of Television, and *Source and Resource: The Art in Film,* both for M.I.T. Press.

SIDELIGHTS: Dondis's *A Primer of Visual Literacy* has been translated into Spanish and Japanese.

* * *

DORNAN, James E., Jr. 1938(?)-1979

OBITUARY NOTICE: Born c. 1938 in Brooklyn, N.Y.; died in an automobile crash, January 25, 1979, in Arlington, Va. Educator. Dornan was an associate professor and chairman of the political science department at Catholic University. A nationally known authority on U.S. foreign relations and military strategy, Dornan was the author of national security studies, including *U.S. Strategy in Northeast Asia* and *Soviet Perceptions of the United States.* He had also edited *U.S. National Security Policy in the Decade Ahead* and *The U.S. War Machine.* Obituaries and other sources: *Washington Post,* January 26, 1979.

* * *

DOTHARD, Robert Loos 1909(?)-1979

OBITUARY NOTICE: Born c. 1909; died in 1979 in Brattleboro, Vt. Printer, editor, and book designer. Dothard was associated with Stephen Greene Press and designed books for several publishers, including the Limited Editions Club, David R. Godine, and the Imprint Society. He also headed R. L. Dothard Associates and owned E. L. Hildreth & Co. Obituaries and other sources: *AB Bookman's Weekly,* April 16, 1979.

* * *

DOUGHTY, Paul L(arrabee) 1930-

PERSONAL: Born February 27, 1930, in Beacon, N.Y.; son of Thomas J. (an attorney) and Hazel (Larrabee) Doughty; married Mary French, 1952; children: Carol F., Thomas H. *Education:* Ursinus College, B.A., 1952; graduate study at University of Pennsylvania, 1955-57; Cornell University, Ph.D., 1962. *Politics:* Democrat. *Religion:* Society of Friends (Quakers). *Home:* 2155 Northwest Third Pl., Gainesville, Fla. 32603. *Office:* Department of Anthropology, University of Florida, Gainesville, Fla. 32611.

CAREER: Cornell University, Ithaca, N.Y., project research coordinator in Peru, 1962-64; Indiana University, Bloomington, assistant professor, 1964-68, associate professor of anthropology, 1969-71, director of Latin-American studies, 1968-71; University of Florida, Gainesville, professor of anthropology and Latin American studies, 1971—, chairman of anthropology department, 1971-76. Member and field director of rural village service units in community development in Mexico and El Salvador with American Friends Service Committee, 1953-55. Member of Bloomington Human Relations Advisory Board, 1968-70. Consultant to U.S. Agency for International Development, National Science Foundation, and Brookings Institution.

MEMBER: American Anthropological Association (fellow), Society for Applied Anthropology (fellow), American Ethnological Society, American Association for the Advancement of Science, American Academy of Political and Social Science, Latin American Studies Association (vice-president, 1973; president, 1974), Council on Anthropology and Education.

WRITINGS: (With wife, Mary French Doughty) *Huaylas: An Andean District in Search of Progress,* Cornell University Press, 1968; (editor with H. F. Dobyns and Harold Lasswell, and contributor) *Peasants, Progress, and Applied Social Change,* Sage Publications, Inc., 1971; (with Dobyns) *Peru: A Cultural History,* Oxford University Press, 1976. Contributor of more than thirty articles, reviews, and photographs to professional and popular journals, including *Life.*

WORK IN PROGRESS: Research and writing on the social and cultural impact of earthquakes in Peru since 1970 and Guatemala in 1976; a study of land reform projects in Peru since 1950; research on the socio-cultural effects of modernization and development projects in Latin America and the United States.

SIDELIGHTS: Doughty writes: "Much of my career interest derives from work in community development in the 1950's with the American Friends Service Committee in Mexico, and subsequent involvement with disaster relief, land reform, and development programs in Peru. I also have special interests in archaeology, ethnohistory, urbanization and planning, and the use of photography in research."

* * *

DOUTY, Esther M(orris) 1911-1978

OBITUARY NOTICE—See index for *CA* sketch: Born March 24, 1911, in Mount Vernon, N.Y.; died of cancer, December 13, 1978, in Washington, D.C. Educator, social worker, and author. Best known for her biographies for children, Douty was director of the workshop in junior biography of the Writers' Conference at Georgetown University. Obituaries and other sources: *Washington Post,* December 16, 1978.

* * *

DOWD, Merle E(dward) 1918-

PERSONAL: Born May 27, 1918, in Wellington, Kan.; son of John Edward (a station agent) and Nellie Anna (Brown) Dowd; married Nora Viola Gensen, April 2, 1942 (died October 30, 1943); married Anne Hemenway (a secretary), June 17, 1949; children: Jerry Edward, Stephen Christopher, Richard Owen, Timothy Francis. *Education:* Attended Kansas State University, 1936-38, and University of Washington, Seattle, 1942-43; Northwestern University, B.S.,

1947, M.B.A., 1954. *Politics:* Republican. *Religion:* Presbyterian. *Home and office:* 7438 Southeast 40th St., Mercer Island, Wash. 98040. *Agent:* Barthold Fles Literary Agency, 507 Fifth Ave., New York, N.Y. 10017.

CAREER: Boeing Co., Seattle, Wash., field service engineer, 1941-45; Northwestern University, Evanston, Ill., assistant professor, 1948-52; *Science and Mechanics,* Chicago, Ill., associate editor, 1952-54; Dowd-Swartwout Associates, Evanston, Ill., partner in graphics, 1954-56; Ford Motor Co., Dearborn, Mich., financial analyst, 1956-57; Boeing Co., engineer and manager, 1957-70; founder and owner of Writing Works, Inc. *Member:* American Society of Journalists and Authors, Pacific Northwest Writers Conference (member of board of trustees, 1970-74; president, 1972), Seattle Free Lancers, Pi Kappa Pi, Sigma Delta Chi, Tau Beta Pi, Pi Tau Sigma, Mercer Island Rotary Club.

WRITINGS: How to Live Better and Spend Twenty Percent Less, Parker & Son, 1966, 3rd edition, 1979; *How to Save Money When You Buy and Drive Your Car,* Parker & Son, 1967; *How to Get More Money in Running Your Home,* Parker & Son, 1968; *How to Earn a Fortune and Become Independent in Your Own Business,* Parker & Son, 1971; *How to Get Out of Debt and Stay Out,* Regnery, 1971; *Estate Planning for Wives: A Family's Financial Guide,* Regnery, 1971; (with William E. Garrison) *Handcrafting Jewelry: Designs and Techniques,* Regnery, 1972; (with Frances Call) *The Practical Book of Bicycling,* Dutton, 1974; *How to Earn More Money From Your Crafts,* Doubleday, 1976; (with Archie Satterfield) *The Seattle Guidebook,* Writing Works, 1976, new edition, 1977.

Author of columns, including "Money Talk," and "Managing Your Family's Money." Contributor of about four hundred articles to magazines.

WORK IN PROGRESS: Superincome: One Way to Beat Inflation; Layoff: When the Lights Dimmed at Boeing.

SIDELIGHTS: Dowd writes: "Striking out in business by organizing Dowd-Swartwout Associates was a major step up. Now my wife and I own and operate Writing Works, Inc., a publisher of regional books.

"I am aghast at the domineering role of the federal government in our lives and am considering writing a book about the inefficiencies and out-of-line costs of bureaucracies."

AVOCATIONAL INTERESTS: Tennis, skiing, hiking in the Pacific Northwest.

* * *

DOWIE, Mark 1939-

PERSONAL: Born May 20, 1939, in Toronto, Ontario, Canada; came to the United States in 1949; son of Ian R. and Shan (Campbell) Dowie; married Eve Pell (a writer), April 22, 1971; children: Daniel, Mark, Peter, John. *Education:* Denison University, B.A., 1962. *Politics:* Democratic socialist. *Religion:* Taoist. *Home:* 221 Hillside, Mill Valley, Calif. 94941. *Office:* 625 Third St., San Francisco, Calif. 94107.

CAREER: Former staff economist for Bank of America, San Francisco, Calif.; Industrial Indemnity, San Francisco, member of long range economic planning staff, 1966-69; Transitions, Inc., San Francisco, executive director, 1969-74; Phoenix Corp., San Francisco, president, 1974-76; writer, 1976—. Member of board of directors of New School for Democratic Management and Center for Investigative Reporting. *Member:* Investigative Reporters and Editors. *Awards, honors:* National Magazine Award from Columbia

University School of Journalism, 1978, for article "Pinto Madness"; public service award from Sigma Delta Chi; Penney-Missouri Award from University of Missouri School of Journalism, for consumer reporting; award from National Press Club.

WRITINGS: Transitions to Freedom, Edwards, 1973. Contributor to magazines.

WORK IN PROGRESS: A long-term investigation of the export of banned and hazardous products.

SIDELIGHTS: Dowie comments: "I believe that well-researched and documented investigative reporting is a tremendously powerful force. Though I doubted it for years, I have come to believe that the pen *is* mightier than the sword. I am particularly interested in investigating and exposing business and government practices that are *legal* but nonetheless reprehensible—like dumping chemicals and consumer goods on the Third World. My 1973 book *Transitions to Freedom* was written with the belief that greater community understanding of ex-prisoners' re-entry problems would result in lower recidivist rates."

*   *   *

DOWLING, Thomas, Jr. 1921-
(Tom Dowling)

PERSONAL: Born February 7, 1921, in Springfield, Mass.; son of Thomas (a postman) and Nell (Ferris) Dowling; married Barbara Bolce, October 18, 1941 (died September 17, 1960); married Virginia Corey, March 17, 1961; children: Thomas III, Maureen, Sandra, Michael. *Education:* Attended high school. *Religion:* Roman Catholic. *Home:* 247 West 41st Ave., San Mateo, Calif. 94403.

CAREER: Editor and publisher of a weekly newspaper, 1947-48; Naval Facilities Engineering Command, San Bruno, Calif., writer and analyst, 1956-72; free-lance writer, 1972—. Past president of Peninsula Baseball League. *Military service:* U.S. Army, 1943-46; received Purple Heart and Bronze Star. *Member:* National Writers Club (professional member).

WRITINGS—Under name Tom Dowling: *Coach: A Season With Lombardi,* Norton, 1970. Contributor of several hundred articles to magazines, including *Family Weekly, Modern Maturity, Scholastic, America,* and *Sunday Digest.*

WORK IN PROGRESS: Land as Dark as Midnight, a novel.

SIDELIGHTS: Dowling writes: "My main interest in writing is to bring the best human qualities into focus, to throw the light of hope and faith into dark corners of the mind, to attempt to prove the existence of God through the inspired action of His creatures, and to learn from these actions just what it is that should be written."

BIOGRAPHICAL/CRITICAL SOURCES: Best Sellers, October 15, 1970; Catherine Marshall, *Something More,* McGraw, 1974.

*   *   *

DOYLE, Richard 1948-

PERSONAL: Born in January, 1948, in Guernsey, Channel Islands. *Education:* Attended Oxford University. *Residence:* Dublin, Ireland. *Agent:* Desmond Elliott, Arlington Books, Ltd., 3 Clifford St., Mayfair, London W1X 1RA, England.

CAREER: Worked for accounting firm in England; investment analyst with London Stock Exchange, London, England; free-lance writer, 1974—.

WRITINGS: Deluge (novel), Arlington Books, 1976, Bantam, 1978; *Imperial 109* (novel), Arlington Books, 1977, Bantam, 1978.

WORK IN PROGRESS: A novel about an American shipbuilding family in England.

SIDELIGHTS: Richard Doyle, a descendant of Sir Arthur Conan Doyle and the *Punch* illustrator "Dickie" Doyle, balks at the idea that perhaps heredity influenced his decision to write. He states that in 1974 he made a "very conscious decision" to write and his recent best-sellers are a good example of his talent.

Doyle cites his early life experiences as the factors which provided him with the background for his novels. When he was three, doyle's family relocated first to Kuwait, then to Libya, and finally to Ethiopia. Educated in England, Doyle would often travel between England and his parents' homes. He states that many of the airfields were primitive and, after frequent visits, became fascinating to the young boy. *Imperial 109* is a product of Doyle's fascination with old airplanes. It is the story of a pre-World War II craft described as a "flying boat," and its flight from South Africa to New York. Doyle believes it to be the predecessor of the jumbo jets of today.

*   *   *

DRAKE, Donald C(harles) 1935-

PERSONAL: Born January 12, 1935, in New York, N.Y.; son of Albert (an artist) and Gloria (a photographer; maiden name, Walters) Drake; married Anne Bunting, February 18, 1955 (divorced); children: Valerie. *Education:* Attended New York University, 1953-56. *Politics:* None. *Religion:* None. *Home:* 220 Locust St. Apt. 21A, Philadelphia, Pa. 19106. *Agent:* Jay Acton, Edward J. Acton, Inc., 17 Grove St., New York, N.Y. 10014. *Office: Philadelphia Inquirer,* 400 North Broad St., Philadelphia, Pa. 19101.

CAREER: Patent Trader, Westchester, N.Y., reporter, 1956-57; *New Haven Register,* New Haven, Conn., reporter, 1957-58; *Newsday.* Long Island, N.Y., science writer, 1958-66; *Philadelphia Inquirer,* Philadelphia, Pa., medical writer, 1966—. *Member:* National Association of Science Writers (past president), Council for the Advancement of Science Writing. *Awards, honors:* About twenty-five journalism awards, including Golden Typewriter Award from Philadelphia Press Association, 1967, for a series on hospital costs; Russell L. Cecil Writing Award from Arthritis Foundation, 1968, for a column on gout; John S. Packard Award from Pennsylvania Tuberculosis and Health Society, 1968, for a series or respiratory disease; Howard W. Blakeslee Award from American Heart Association, 1969, for a series on heart research, and 1976, for a story on coronary resuscitation; Walter J. Donaldson Award from Pennsylvania Medical Society, 1970, for a series on city hospital, and 1971, for a series on medical costs; Keystone Press Award from Pennsylvania Newspaper Publishers Association and Pennsylvania Society of Newspaper Editors, 1974, for a series on dying city hospital, 1975, for a series on medical students, 1976, for a series on coronary care ambulance, 1977, for a story on Legionnaire's Disease, 1978, for a story on separating Siamese twins, and 1979, for a story on the ethics of neonatal care. Claude Bernard Award from National Society for Medical Research, 1978, for experimental evaluation of artificial lung; awards from Associated Press Managing Editors, National Conference of Christians and Jews, and American Academy of Pediatrics, all 1978, all for a story on separating Siamese twins.

WRITINGS: Medical School, Rawson, Wade, 1978.

Unpublished, unproduced plays: (With Joseph Gelmis) "The Best Tailor in Brooklyn" (three-act), 1965; (with Gelmis) "A Living Doll" (one-act), 1966; (with Gelmis) "House for Sale" (three-act), 1966; "Okay for You, Honey" (one-act), 1966.

WORK IN PROGRESS: Writing on the singles life in the American city.

SIDELIGHTS: Drake writes: "My work as a medical writer on a newspaper has been influenced greatly by my hobby as a playwright. I have tried, with some success, to use playwriting techniques in reporting on medical advances. Using dramatic techniques of suspense and anticipation enhances medical reports, making them as interesting and dramatic as television documentaries, if not dramas.

"I feel that newspaper stories and series in the nation's great newspapers are becoming increasingly more literate and authoritative as the audience of the daily press dwindles, leaving a distillate of the better educated and more serious readers.

"Increasing numbers of newspaper series are being turned into books. Only salaried writers can afford to spend years researching one book, as I spent four years gathering material for *Medical School.* Gone are the Ben Hecht days of semi-literate journalists bumming from city to city, getting jobs for only a few months at a time on this newspaper or that. Today's newsmen are much better educated, more serious in their approach to writing and, on the average, more responsible authors."

Reviewing *Medical School,* Lawrence K. Altman commented that Drake "offers valuable insights into the process of medical education.... For all the warts he reveals, he says he 'cannot help but think that medicine in this country will be improved because these people [medical students] are becoming a part of it.'"

BIOGRAPHICAL/CRITICAL SOURCES: New York Times, June 5, 1979.

* * *

DRAWSON, Blair 1943-

PERSONAL: Born October 16, 1943, in Winnipeg, Manitoba, Canada; son of Richard Robert and Florence (Carter) Drawson; married Noel Saville (divorced, 1973); married Bibi Caspari (a mime and dancer), October 19, 1974. *Education:* Attended Ontario College of Art, 1963-66. *Politics:* "Anti-political." *Religion:* "Religious, but no church affiliation." *Home and office:* 69 Westmoreland Ave., Toronto, Ontario, Canada M6H 2Z8. *Agent:* John Locke, 15 East 76th St., New York, N.Y. 10021.

CAREER: Illustrator in Toronto, Ontario, 1966-70, 1975—, in St. Helena, Calif., 1970-73, and in Norwalk, Conn., 1974-75. Illustrator for various magazines throughout the United States and Canada. Held exhibition at "Vintage 1864" in Yountville, Calif. in 1972.

WRITINGS—Author and illustrator: *The Bug and Her Friends,* Harcourt, 1976; *I Like Hats!,* Gage, 1977; *Do Something Special on Your Birthday,* Gage, 1977; *Arthur, Their Very Own Child,* Gage, 1978; *Flying Dimitri,* Groundwood Books, 1978.

Illustrator: Barbara Brenner, *Mystery of the Plumed Serpent,* Houghton, 1972; Eleanor Kay, *Read About the School Nurse,* F. Watts, 1972; Addie, *The Silly Book of Animals,* Golden Press, 1973; Jerry Lane, *In the Zoo,* Ginn, 1974; Patty Wolcott, *I'm Going to New York to Visit the Queen,*

Addison-Wesley, 1974; Wolcott, *Pickle Pickle Pickle Juice,* Addison-Wesley, 1975; *Mary Margaret's Tree,* Groundwood Books, 1979.

SIDELIGHTS: Drawson told *CA:* "It seems that the work of the artist is to provide a gentle reminder of what we may have lost in 'growing up.' When we were children, the world looked, felt, smelled, and tasted in ways that are more or less only faintly recalled in adult life. The impressions we received then—terrifying as they were at times—were fueled and made exquisite by our great innocent sense of possibility. This was the possibility of finding things and finding things out.

"Until I was about nine, I thought myself to be the only person in the world named Blair. It seemed to me that there was perhaps a magical property to my name. On several occasions a curious thing happened to demonstrate this. While washing my face or brushing my teeth at the bathroom sink, I would find myself staring at my reflection in the mirror. I would then begin to whisper, over and over, the incantation, "Blair, Blair, your name is *Blair.*" These words released a mechanism whereby I would seem to float up in the air and sort of hover there in the vicinity of the light fixture. From there I could look down at the back of my head and see my own face gazing at its image in the glass. It was altogether an awesome sensation, and one which I came to write about in a book entitled *Flying Dimitri.*"

Explaining how his career as an illustrator began, Drawson continued: "My earliest awareness of pictures was in the realm of cartoons and movie posters. Whenever I drew a picture, I put in a special effort to make it funny. I enjoyed the reactions of my classmates when they perceived some *bon mot* of mine depicted on school drawing paper, or in the margins of texts and notebooks. Indeed, some drawings were done on the blackboard itself, encouraged by the teacher.

"Years later, upon leaving art school in my third year, I found myself living hand-to-mouth in an abandoned mansion. It occurred to me that it might be fun to do some water color paintings of comical animals. I showed the results to a publisher in Toronto and was asked to illustrate a story for their school series. I knew absolutely nothing about illustration then, having devoted my time at school to fine art drawing and painting only. Therefore, it soon became plain that learning the technical side of illustration was going to be a process of painful trial and error. Eventually I decided to try my hand at writing manuscripts. That too was a matter of trial and error. Lately I have begun to do easel paintings again, to supplement my illustration in water color."

When asked about his traveling experiences, Drawson commented, "I spent several months in Mexico and Central America, poking about in ruins, and bumbling along in Spanish. (I also bumble along in French.)"

Drawson's influences are "widespread and never-ending; they come from all of history and the entire world of phenomena. In terms of writers of children's books, I have the deepest respect for William Steig, and in a broader context, for C. G. Jung."

AVOCATIONAL INTERESTS: Jazz (he is an amateur jazz musician).

* * *

DRESCHER, Sandra 1957-

PERSONAL: Born October 12, 1957, in Orrville, Ohio; daughter of John M. (a clergyman and writer) and Betty

(Keener) Drescher. *Education:* Eastern Mennonite College, B.S., 1979. *Religion:* Mennonite. *Home address:* Route 1, Box 157, Scottdale, Pa. 15683.

CAREER: Philhaven Hospital, Lebanon, Pa., creative therapist, summer, 1977; Virginia Correctional Center for Women, Goochland, assistant chaplain, summer, 1978.

WRITINGS: Just Between God and Me (meditations), Zondervan, 1977.

SIDELIGHTS: "As the daughter of a writer whom I admired greatly, I grew up wondering what my first book would be—not if I'd write one," Sandra Drescher told *CA.* "As a teenager, I felt like I didn't have any particularly superior knowledge I could share, so I began writing meditations about things God had been teaching me. Beyond the satisfaction I found in writing, I wrote mainly to aid other teenagers, showing how my faith in God had helped me in the typical teenage struggles of life. I wanted to share both the joys and hard times of my relationship with Christ. I began writing *Just Between God and Me* the summer following my graduation from high school. Throughout my first year in college, I gathered ideas and stories and finished writing my book the following summer."

Drescher's college degree is in social work. She commented that "I don't know yet what special field I'll enter. I enjoy working with elderly people and with the mentally disturbed, and in corrections."

Just Between God and Me has been translated into Spanish.

AVOCATIONAL INTERESTS: Creating things, outdoor activities, music.

* * *

DRISCOLL, R(obert) E(ugene) 1949-

PERSONAL: Born March 10, 1949, in Billings, Mont.; son of James T. (a farmer) and Inez (Loendorf) Driscoll; married Margaret L. Cooper. *Education:* Carroll College, Helena, Mont., B.A., 1971; University of Texas, M.A., 1973. *Residence:* Montrose, N.Y. *Office:* Fund for Multinational Management Education, 684 Park Ave., New York, N.Y. 10021.

CAREER: Fund for Multinational Management Education, New York, N.Y., executive director, 1973—. Member of board of directors of Public Affairs Systems, Inc. *Member:* Academy of International Business.

WRITINGS: (Editor with H. W. Wallender) *Technology Transfer and Development: An Historic and Geographic Perspective,* Fund for Multinational Management Education, 1974; *The Social and Economic Impacts of Multinational Corporations: Case Studies of the U.S. Paper Industry in Brazil,* Fund for Multinational Management Education, 1977.

WORK IN PROGRESS: Short articles on technology transfer, control of multinational corporations and codes of conduct for journals such as *PLUS,* and for edited compendia.

SIDELIGHTS: Driscoll told *CA:* "My writings are designed to elucidate the role of private enterprise and the multinational corporation in economic development and in relations between developed and developing countries. I attempt to deal with current issues of major importance to governmental bodies, and which affect the lives of the world's people. As executive director of the Fund for Multinational Management Education, I work with a variety of authors seeking to resolve key policy problems in economic development. These issues will become even more important as the world becomes more interdependent, and as the benefits of economic progress are distributed for a wider population."

Driscoll's books have been published in Spanish.

* * *

DRUTMAN, Irving 1910-1978

PERSONAL: Born July 28, 1910, in New York, N.Y.; died September 20, 1978, in New York, N.Y., of cancer.

CAREER: Writer. Worked as free-lance publicist of motion pictures.

WRITINGS: (Editor) Janet Flanner, *Paris Was Yesterday, 1925-1939,* Viking, 1972; (editor) Flanner, *London Was Yesterday, 1934-1939,* Viking, 1975; *Good Company: A Memoir, Mostly Theatrical,* Little, Brown, 1976. Also songwriter for motion pictures, including songs "Mama Never Told Me," "Bel Ami," and "My Imaginary Love." Contributor to newspapers and periodicals, including *New York Herald-Tribune,* 1939-1966, and *New York Times.*

WORK IN PROGRESS: Editing another collection of Janet Flanner's writings, tentatively titled *Dateline Europe, 1932-1975,* for Harcourt.

OBITUARIES: Publishers Weekly, October 9, 1978.*

* * *

Du BOIS, W(illiam) E(dward) B(urghardt) 1868-1963

PERSONAL: Born February 23, 1868, in Great Barrington, Mass.; immigrated to Ghana, 1960; became Ghanian citizen, 1963; died August 27, 1963, in Accra, Ghana; buried in Accra; son of Alfred and Mary (Burghardt) Du Bois; married Nina Gomer, 1896 (died, 1950); married Shirley Graham (an author), 1951 (died, 1977). children: Burghardt (deceased), Yolande Du Bois Williams (deceased). *Education:* Fisk University, B.A., 1888; Harvard University, B.A. (cum laude) 1890, M.A., 1891, Ph.D., 1896; graduate study at University of Berlin, 1892-1894. *Politics:* Joined Communist Party, 1961.

CAREER: Wilberforce University, Wilberforce, Ohio, professor of Greek and Latin, 1894-96; University of Pennsylvania, Philadelphia, assistant instructor in sociology, 1896-97; Atlanta University, Atlanta, Ga., professor of history and economics, 1897-1910; National Association for the Advancement of Colored People (NAACP), New York City, director of publicity and research and editor of *Crisis,* 1910-1934; Atlanta University, professor and chairman of department of sociology, 1934-1944; NAACP, director of special research, 1944-48; Peace Information Center, New York City, director, 1950. Co-founder and general secretary of Niagra Movement, 1905-09. Organizer of the Pan-African Congress, 1919. Vice-chairman of the Council of African Affairs, 1949. American Labor Party candidate for U.S. Senator from New York, 1950. *Awards, honors:* Spingarn Medal from NAACP, 1932; elected to the National Institute of Arts and Letters, 1943; Lenin International Peace Prize, 1958; Knight Commander of the Liberian Humane Order of African Redemption conferred by the Liberian Government; Minister Plenipotentiary and Envoy Extraordinary conferred by President Calvin Coolidge; LL.D. from Howard University, 1930, and Atlanta University, 1938; Litt.D., Fisk University, 1938; L.H.D., Wilberforce University, 1940; honorary degrees from Morgan State College, University of Berlin, and Charles University (Prague).

WRITINGS—Novels: The Quest of the Silver Fleece, A. C.

McClurg, 1911, reprinted, Kraus Reprint, 1974; *Dark Princess: A Romance*, Harcourt, 1928, reprinted, Kraus Reprint, 1974; *The Ordeal of Mansart* (first novel in trilogy; also see below), Mainstream Publishers, 1957; *Mansart Builds a School* (second novel in trilogy; also see below), Mainstream Publishers, 1959; *Worlds of Color* (third novel in trilogy; also see below), Mainstream Publishers, 1961; *The Black Flame* (trilogy; includes *The Ordeal of Mansart, Mansart Builds a School, Worlds of Color*), Kraus Reprint, 1976.

Poetry: *Selected Poems*, Ghana University Press, c. 1964, reprinted, Panther House, 1971.

Plays: "Haiti," included in *Federal Theatre Plays*, edited by Pierre De Rohan, Works Progress Administration, 1938. Also author of pageants, "The Christ of the Andes," "George Washington and Black Folk: A Pageant for the Centenary, 1732-1932," and "The Star of Ethiopia."

Works edited in conjunction with the annual Conference for the Study of Negro Problems; all originally published by Atlanta University Press: *Mortality Among Negroes in Cities*, 1896, reprinted, Octagon, 1968; *Social and Physical Condition of Negroes in Cities*, 1897, reprinted, Octagon, 1968; *Some Efforts of American Negroes for Their Own Social Benefit*, 1898, reprinted, Octagon, 1968; *The Negro in Business*, 1899, reprinted, AMS Press, 1971; *The College-Bred Negro*, 1900, reprinted, Octagon, 1968; *A Select Bibliography of the American Negro: For General Readers*, 1901; *The Negro Common School*, 1901, reprinted, Octagon, 1968; *The Negro Artisan*, 1902, reprinted, Octagon, 1968; *The Negro Church*, 1903, reprinted, Arno Press, 1968; *Some Notes on Negro Crime, Particularly in Georgia*, 1904, reprinted, Octagon, 1968; *A Select Bibliography of the Negro American*, 1905, reprinted, Octagon Books, 1968; *The Health and Physique of the Negro American*, 1906, reprinted, Octagon, 1968; *Economic Co-operation Among Negro Americans*, 1907, reprinted, Russell & Russell, 1969; *The Negro American Family*, 1908, reprinted, M.I.T. Press, 1970; *Efforts for Social Betterment Among Negro Americans*, 1909, reprinted, Russell & Russell, 1969; (with Augustus Grandville Dill) *The College-Bred Negro American*, 1901, reprinted, Russell & Russell, 1969; (with Dill) *The Common School and the Negro American*, 1911, reprinted, Russell & Russell, 1969; (with Dill) *The Negro American Artisan*, 1912, reprinted, Russell & Russell, 1969; (with Dill) *Morals and Manners Among Negro Americans*, 1914, reprinted, Russell & Russell, 1969.

Other: *The Suppression of the African Slave-Trade to the United States of America, 1638-1870*, Longmans, Green, 1896, reprinted, Kraus Reprint, 1973; *The Conservation of Races*, American Negro Academy, 1897, reprinted, Arno Press, 1969; *The Philadelphia Negro*, University of Pennsylvania, 1899, reprinted, Kraus Reprint, 1973; *The Souls of Black Folk: Essays and Sketches*, A. C. McClurg, 1903, reprinted, Kraus Reprint, 1973; (with Booker Taliaferro Washington) *The Negro in the South: His Economic Progress in Relation to His Moral and Religious Development* (lectures), G. W. Jacobs, 1907, reprinted, Metro Books, 1972; *John Brown* (biography), G. W. Jacobs, 1909, reprinted, Kraus Reprint, 1973; *The Negro*, Holt, 1915, reprinted, Kraus Reprint, 1975.

Darkwater: Voices From Within the Veil (semi-autobiographical), Harcourt, 1920, reprinted, Kraus Reprint, 1975; *The Gift of Black Folk: The Negroes in the Making of America*, Stratford Co., 1924, reprinted, Kraus Reprint, 1975; *Africa: Its Geography, People and Products* (also see below), Haldeman-Julius Publications, 1930; *Africa: Its Place in*

Modern History, Haldeman-Julius Publications, 1930, reprinted in a single volume with *Africa: Its Geography, People and Products*, KTO Press, 1977; *Black Reconstruction: An Essay Toward a History of the Part Which Black Folk Played in the Attempt to Reconstruct Democracy in America, 1860-1880*, Harcourt, 1935, reprinted, Kraus Reprint, 1976; *Black Folk, Then and Now*, Holt, 1939, reprinted, Kraus Reprint, 1975; *Dusk of Dawn: An Essay Toward an Autobiography of a Race Concept*, Harcourt, 1940, reprinted, Kraus Reprint, 1975; *Color and Democracy: Colonies and Peace*, Harcourt, 1945, reprinted, Kraus Reprint, 1975; *The World and Africa: An Inquiry Into the Part Which Africa Has Played in World History*, Viking, 1947, reprinted, Kraus Reprint, 1976; (editor) *An Appeal to the World: A Statement on the Denial of Human Rights to Minorities in the Case of Citizens of Negro Descent in the United States of America and an Appeal to the United Nations for Redress*, [New York], 1947; *In Battle for Peace: The Story of My 83rd Birthday* (autobiography), Masses and Mainstream, 1952, reprinted, Kraus Reprint, 1976.

An ABC of Color: Selections From Over a Half Century of the Writings of W.E.B. Du Bois, Seven Seas Publishers (Berlin), 1963; *The Autobiography of W.E.B. Du Bois: A Soliloquy on Viewing My Life From the Last Decade of Its First Century*, International Publishers, 1968; Philip S. Foner, editor, *W.E.B. Du Bois Speaks: Speeches and Addresses*, Pathfinder Press, 1970; Walter Wilson, editor, *The Selected Writings of W.E.B. Du Bois*, New American Library, 1970; Meyer Weinberg, editor, *W.E.B. Du Bois: A Reader*, Harper, 1970; Julius Lester, editor, *The Seventh Son: The Thought and Writings of W.E.B. Du Bois*, Random House, 1971; Andrew G. Paschal, editor, *A W.E.B. Du Bois Reader*, Macmillan, 1971; Daniel Walden, editor, *W.E.B. Du Bois: The Crisis Writings*, Fawcett Publications, 1972; Henry Lee Moon, editor, *The Emerging Thought of W.E.B. Du Bois: Essays and Editorials From "The Crisis,"* Simon & Schuster, 1972; Herbert Aptheker, editor, *The Correspondence of W.E.B. Du Bois*, University of Massachusetts Press, Volume I, 1973, Volume II, 1976; Herbert Aptheker, editor, *The Education of Black People: Ten Critiques, 1906-1960*, University of Massachusetts Press, 1973; Virginia Hamilton, editor, *The Writings of W.E.B. Du Bois*, Crowell, 1975; Herbert Aptheker, editor, *Book Reviews*, KTO Press, 1977.

Columnist for newspapers, including *Chicago Defender, Pittsburgh Courier, New York Amsterdam News*, and *San Francisco Chronicle*. Contributor to numerous periodicals, including *Atlantic Monthly* and *World's Work*. Founder and editor of numerous periodicals, including *Moon*, 1905-06, *Horizon*, 1908-10, *Brownies' Book*, 1920-21, and *Phylon Quarterly*, 1940. Editor in chief of *Encyclopedia of the Negro*, 1933-46. Director of *Encyclopaedia Africana*.

SIDELIGHTS: W.E.B. Du Bois was at the vanguard of the civil rights movement in America. Of French and African descent, Du Bois grew up in Massachusetts and did not begin to comprehend the problems of racial prejudice until he attended Fisk University in Tennessee. Later he was accepted at Harvard, but while he was at that institution he voluntarily segregated himself from white students. Trained as a sociologist, Du Bois began to document the oppression of black people and their strivings for equality in the 1890's. By 1903 he had learned enough to state in *The Souls of Black Folk* that "the problem of the twentieth century is the problem of the color line," and he spent the remainder of his long life trying to break down racial barriers.

The Souls of Black Folk was not well received when it first came out. Houston A. Baker, Jr. explained that white Americans were not "ready to respond favorably to Du Bois's scrupulously accurate portrayal of the hypocrisy, hostility, and brutality of white America toward black America." Many blacks were also shocked by the book, for in it Du Bois announced his opposition to the conciliatory policy of Booker T. Washington and his followers, who argued for the gradual development of the Negro race through vocational training. Du Bois declared: "So far as Mr. Washington apologizes for injustice, North or South, does not rightly value the privilege and duty of voting, belittles the emasculating effects of caste distinctions, and opposes the higher training and ambition of our brighter minds—so far as he, the South, or the Nation, does this—we must unceasingly and firmly oppose him. By every civilized and peaceful method we must strive for the rights which the world accords to men." In retrospect, many scholars have pointed to *The Souls of Black Folk* as a prophetic work. Harold W. Cruse and Carolyn Gipson noted that "nowhere else was DuBois's description of the Negro's experience in American Society to be given more succinct expression. . . . *Souls* is probably his greatest achievement as a writer. Indeed, his reputation may largely rest on this remarkable document, which had a profound effect on the minds of black people."

A few years after *The Souls of Black Folk* was published, Du Bois banded with other black leaders and began the Niagra Movement, which sought to abolish all distinctions based on race. Although this movement disintegrated, it served as the forerunner of the National Association for the Advancement of Colored People (NAACP). Du Bois helped to establish the NAACP and worked as its director of publicity and research for many years. As the editor of *Crisis,* a journal put out by the NAACP, he became a well-known spokesman for the black cause. In 1973 Henry Lee Moon gathered a number of essays and articles written by Du Bois for *Crisis* and published them in a book, *The Emerging Thought of W.E.B. Du Bois.*

In addition to the articles and editorials he wrote for *Crisis,* Du Bois produced a number of books on the history of the Negro race and on the problems of racial prejudice. In *Black Reconstruction,* Du Bois wrote about the role that blacks played in the Reconstruction, a role that had been hitherto ignored by white historians. The history of the black race in Africa and America was outlined in *Black Folk: Then and Now.* H. J. Seligmann found the book impressive: "No one can leave it without a deepened sense of the part the Negro peoples have played and must play in world history." An even higher compliment was paid by Barrett Williams: "Professor Du Bois has overlooked one of the strongest arguments against racial inferiority, namely, this book itself. In it, a man of color has proved himself, in the complex and exacting field of scholarship, the full equal of his white colleagues."

Although Du Bois's novels did not attract as much notice as his scholarly works, they also were concerned with the plight of the black race. His first novel, *The Quest of The Silver Fleece,* dramatized the difficulties created by the low economic status of the Southern Negro. *Dark Princess* dealt with miscegenation. After reading *Dark Princess,* a reviewer for the *Springfield Republican* observed: "The truth is, of course, that DuBois is not a novelist at all, and that the book judged as a novel has only the slightest merit. As a document, as a program, as an exhortation, it has its interest and value."

Du Bois gradually grew disillusioned with the moderate policies of the NAACP and with the capitalistic system in the United States. When he advocated black autonomy and "non-discriminatory segregation" in 1934, he was forced to resign from his job at the NAACP. Later he returned to the NAACP and worked there until another rift developed between him and that organization's leaders in 1944. More serious conflicts arose between Du Bois and the U.S. government. Du Bois had become disenchanted with capitalism relatively early. In *Darkwater: Voices From Within the Veil,* he had depicted the majority of mankind as being subjugated by an imperialistic white race. In the 1940's he returned to this subject and examined it in more detail. *Color and Democracy: Colonies and Peace* presented a case against imperialism. "This book by Dr. Du Bois is a small volume of 143 pages," H. A. Overstreet observed, "but it contains enough dynamite to blow up the whole vicious system whereby we have comforted our white souls and lined the pockets of generations of free-booting capitalists." *The World and Africa* contained a further indictment of the treatment of colonials. Du Bois "does not seek exaggeration of Africa's role, but he insists the the role must not be forgotten," Saul Carson remarked. "And his insistence is firm. It is persuasive, eloquent, moving. Considering the magnitude of the provocation, it is well-tempered, even gentle."

Du Bois not only wrote about his political beliefs; he acted upon them. He belonged to the Socialist party for a brief time in the early 1900's. Later he conceived a program of Pan-Africanism, a movement that he called "an organized protection of the Negro world led by American Negroes." In 1948 he campaigned for the Progressive Party in national elections, and in 1950 he ran for senator from New York on the American Labor Party ticket. Du Bois's radical political stance provoked some run-ins with the U.S. government, the first of which occurred in 1949, when he accepted an honorary position as vice-chairman of the Council on African affairs. This organization was labelled as "subversive" by the Attorney General. His work with the Peace Information Center, a society devoted to banning nuclear weapons, also embroiled him in controversy. Along with four other officers from the Peace Information Center, Du Bois was indicted for "failure to register as an agent of a foreign principal." The case was brought to trial in 1951 and the defendants were acquitted.

After the trial was over, Du Bois wanted to travel outside the United States, but he was denied a passport on the grounds that it was not in "the best interests of the United States" for him to journey abroad. Later the State Department refused to issue a passport to him unless he stated in writing that he was not a member of the Communist Party, a condition that Du Bois rejected. In 1958 the Supreme Court handed down a decision which declared that "Congress had never given the Department of State any authority to demand a political affidavit as prerequisite to issuing a passport." This decision enabled Du Bois and his wife to leave the country in that same year. For several months they traveled in Europe, the U.S.S.R., and China.

Du Bois's travels abroad had a profound influence on his thinking. In 1961 he joined the Communist Party. He explained in his autobiography how he reached this decision: "I have studied socialism and communism long and carefully in lands where they are practiced and in coversation with their adherents, and with wide reading. I now state my conclusion frankly and clearly: I believe in communism. . . . I believe that all men should be employed according to their ability and that wealth and services should be distributed according to need. Once I thought that these ends could be attained under capitalism, means of production privately owned, and used in accord with free individual initiative. After earnest observation I now believe that private ownership of capital and free enterprise are leading the world to disaster."

After joining the Communist party, Du Bois moved to Ghana at the invitation of President Nkrumah. While there he served as the director of the *Encyclopaedia Africana* project. In August, 1963, the ninety-five-year-old leader inspired a protest march on the U.S. Embassy in Accra to show support for the historic "March for Jobs and Freedom" taking place in Washington, D.C. that same month. Shortly afterward, Du Bois died. Although Du Bois was a controversial figure in his lifetime, his reputation has grown in the past decade. A large number of books and scholarly studies have recently appeared about him. In a discussion of the revival of interest in Du Bois, Crus and Gipson wrote: "It is important to remember that he continued to plead for a truly pluralistic culture in a world where the superiority of whites is still an *a priori* assumption. In so far as he grasped the basic dilemma of Western blacks as being a people with 'two souls, two thoughts, two unreconciled strivings,' DuBois's attitudes have been vindicated. He was, as we can now see, one of those unique men whoses ideas are destined to be reviled and then revived, and then, no doubt, reviled again, haunting the popular mind long after his death."

Some of Du Bois's books have been published in French and Russian.

BIOGRAPHICAL/CRITICAL SOURCES: W.E.B. Du Bois, *Darkwater: Voices From Within the Veil,* Harcourt, 1920, reprinted, Kraus Reprint, 1975; *Springfield Republican,* May 28, 1928; *Boston Transcript,* June 24, 1939; *Saturday Review of Literature,* July 29, 1939, June 23, 1945; Du Bois, *Dusk of Dawn: An Essay Toward an Autobiography of Race Concept,* Harcourt, 1940, reprinted, Kraus Reprint, 1975; *New York Times,* March 9, 1947; Du Bois, *In Battle for Peace: The Story of My 83rd Birthday,* Masses and Mainstream, 1952, reprinted, Kraus Reprint, 1976; Robert A. Bone, *The Negro Novel in America,* Yale University Press, revised edition, 1965; Elliott M. Rudwick, *W.E.B. Du Bois: Propagandist of the Negro Protest,* Atheneum, 1968; Du Bois, *Autobiography of W.E.B. Du Bois: A Soliloquy on Viewing My Life From the Last Decade of Its First Century,* International Publications, 1968; Rayford W. Logan, editor, *W.E.B. Du Bois: A Profile,* Hill & Wang, 1971; Emma Gelders Sterne, *His Was the Voice: The Life of W.E.B. Du Bois,* Crowell-Collier, 1971; Shirley Graham Du Bois, *His Day Is Marching On: A Memoir of W.E.B. Du Bois,* Lippincott, 1971; Houston A. Baker, Jr., *Black Literature in America,* McGraw, 1971; *Newsweek,* August 23, 1971; *Contemporary Literary Criticism,* Gale, Volume 1, 1972, Volume 2, 1974; *New Republic,* February 26, 1972; *New York Review of Books,* November 30, 1972; *Ebony,* August, 1972, August, 1975; Hugh Hawkins, editor, *Booker T. Washington and His Critics: Black Leadership in Crisis,* Heath, 1974; Arnold Rampersad, *Art and Imagination of W.E.B. Du Bois,* Harvard University Press, 1976.*

*   *   *

DUGARD, C. J(ohn) R.   1936-

PERSONAL: Born August 23, 1936, in Fort Beaufort, South Africa; son of Jack (an educator) and Rita (an educator; maiden name, Worthington) Dugard; married Jennifer Jane Irwin (a teacher), July 20, 1963; children: Jacqueline, Justin. *Education:* University of Stellenbosch, B.A., 1956, LL.B., 1958; University of Cambridge, LL.B., 1965. *Home:* 45 Rut-

land Ave., Craighall Park, Johannesburg, South Africa. *Office:* School of Law, University of Witwatersrand, Johannesburg, South Africa.

CAREER: University of Witwatersrand, Johannesburg, South Africa, professor of law, 1969—. Visiting professor at Princeton University, 1969, and Duke University, 1974-75. *Member:* South Africa Institute of Race Relations (president, 1978-79).

WRITINGS: (Editor) *The South West Africa/Namibia Dispute: Documents and Scholarly Writings on the Controversy Between South Africa and the United Nations.* University of California Press, 1973; (with J. D. van der Vyver and J.H.P. Serfontein) *South West Africa/Namibia: A Symposium,* South African Institute of International Affairs, 1976; *Introduction to Criminal Procedure,* Juta, 1977; *Human Rights and the South African Legal Order,* Princeton University Press, 1978.

WORK IN PROGRESS: Study of international law aspects of South Africa's race policies, with special reference to denationalization.

SIDELIGHTS: Dugard told *CA:* "I believe that lawyers have a special responsibility for promoting human rights in South Africa. At present human rights are undermined in South Africa by racially discriminatory and politically repressive laws. While the South African Government is sensitive to the unacceptability of discriminatory laws and claims to be moving away from discrimination under pressure from home and abroad, there is little sign of awareness of the extent to which repressive laws depart from civilized norms. South African courts do not have the power of judicial review, but judges and practicing lawyers can still exercise influence by pressing for the abolition or modification of such laws."

BIOGRAPHICAL/CRITICAL SOURCES: Journal of Politics, August, 1975; *American Political Science Review,* September, 1975.

*   *   *

DUIKER, William J.   1932-

PERSONAL: Born August 28, 1932, in Evanston, Ill.; married; two children. *Education:* Dickinson College, B.A., 1954; Georgetown University, B.S.F.S., 1955, M.A., 1961, Ph.D., 1968. *Home:* 430 Sylvan Circle, State College, Pa. 16801. *Office:* College of Liberal Arts, Pennsylvania State University, 514 Liberal Arts Tower, University Park, Pa. 16802.

CAREER: U.S. Department of the Army, Geographic Analysis Branch, civilian foreign affairs analyst, 1959-61; U.S. Department of State, Washington, D.C., member of Soviet and East European exchanges staff in Washington, D.C., 1961-62, studied Mandarin Chinese in Washington, D.C., and Taichung, Taiwan, 1962-64, economic reporting officer at U.S. embassy in Saigon, South Vietnam, 1964-65; Pennsylvania State University, University Park, 1967—, began as assistant professor, currently professor of history, director of international program development, 1974-78. *Military service:* U.S. Army, 1955-58; served in Austria. *Member:* Association of Asian Studies (member of Mid-Atlantic Regional Conference and Vietnam Studies Group), Phi Alpha Theta. *Awards, honors:* National Endowment for the Humanities grant, summer, 1968.

WRITINGS: (Contributor) Zasloff and Brown, editors, *Communism in Indochina: New Perspectives,* Heath, 1975; *The Rise of Nationalism in Vietnam, 1900-1914* (monograph), Cornell University Press, 1976; *Ts'ai Yuan p'ei:*

Educator of Modern China (monograph), Pennsylvania State University Press, 1977; *Cultures in Collision: The Boxer Rebellion* (monograph), Presidio Press, 1978. Contributor to Asian studies journals.

WORK IN PROGRESS: Continuing research on Chinese intellectual history, Chinese education, nationalism and communism in East and Southeast Asia, and contemporary Vietnam and Southeast Asia.

* * *

DUMAS, Henry L. 1934-1968

PERSONAL: Born July 20, 1934, in Sweet Home, Ark.; died May 23, 1968, in New York, N.Y. *Education:* Attended City College (now of the City University of New York), and Rutgers University, 1958-61; studied in residence with the musician-philosopher Sun Ra.

CAREER: International Business Machines (IBM), New York City, operator of printing machines, 1963-64; social worker for the State of New York, New York City, 1965-66; Hiram College, Hiram, Ohio, assistant director of Upward Bound, 1967; Southern Illinois University, Carbondale, teacher-counselor and director of language workshops for the University's Experiment in Higher Education, 1967-68. Editor, publisher and distributor of little magazines, including *Anthologist, Untitled, Camel, Hiram Poetry Review,* and *Collection,* 1953-68. *Military service:* U.S. Air Force, 1953-57. *Awards, honors:* Several awards for creative writing published in Air Force newspapers and magazines, 1953-57; Editors Award for Creative Writing, *Untitled* magazine, 1963; creative writing award from *Anthologist.*

WRITINGS: Poetry for My People, edited by Hale Chatfield and Eugene Redmond, Southern Illinois University Press, 1970; *Ark of Bones, and Other Stories,* edited by Chatfield and Redmond, Southern Illinois University Press, 1970; *Play Ebony, Play Ivory* (poetry), edited by Redmond, Random House, 1974; *Jonoah and the Green Stone* (novel), arranged by Redmond, Random House, 1976.

Work represented in many anthologies, including: *Black Fire,* edited by Imamu Amiri Baraka and Roy Neal, Morrow, 1968; *Black Out Loud,* edited by Arnold Adoff, Macmillan, 1970; *Brothers and Sisters,* edited by Adoff, Macmillan, 1970; *The Poetry of Black America,* edited by Adoff, Harper, 1973; *Open Poetry,* edited by Ronald Gross, Simon & Schuster, 1972; *Understanding the New Black Poetry,* edited by Stephen Henderson, Morrow, 1973; *Cutting Edges,* compiled by Jack Hicks, Holt, 1973.

Contributor to periodicals, including *Negro Digest, Freedom Ways, Umbra, Trace, Anthologist, Hiram Poetry Review,* and *American Weave.*

SIDELIGHTS: Henry Dumas did not live to see his poetry and fiction published in book form. On May 23, 1968, he was shot and killed by a policeman on the Harlem Station platform of the New York Central Railroad. The reasons and circumstances behind his death are uncertain, but critics agree that the bullet cut down a promising young writer. When *Poetry for My People* appeared in 1970, Jascha Kessler observed, "His work indicates that Dumas was an ambitious writer aware of the current obsessions of black poets. He seems to have been working his way through styles, dictions, and forms—trying to assemble the black heritage through its history and memories . . . and music, while maintaining a powerful ideological sweep." Julius Lester found *Play Ebony, Play Ivory* to be evidence that "Henry Dumas was the most original Afro-American poet of the sixties."

One quality of Dumas's work consistently praised by critics is the authenticity of his poetic voice. About *Play Ebony, Play Ivory,* a reviewer for *Choice* said, "His ear captures the language of black America of the fifties and sixties and in the best of these verses that language achieves considerable strength and grace." Lester pointed out that "Dumas's authentic voice is heard most clearly when he writes from within what seems to have been his subject: Africa and Nature. He is the first Afro-American poet to speak convincingly in the voice of an African."

Dumas's fiction has also attracted favorable notices. His collection of short stories, *Ark of Bones,* inspired John Deck to write, "Dumas had a rich and varied talent, and he was foremost an original." Angela Jackson lauded the characterizations in *Ark of Bones* and noted that "these stories are close to Biblical in their shape, though these myths are less leaden in tone and embrace. They sing with a humor that moves the way we normally do, not overdone. There is, too, a moral exactness that our tradition has cherished. There is spine and point." Describing *Ark of Bones* as "a collection of extraordinary short stories," a reviewer for *New Yorker* lamented: "Mr. Dumas was thirty-four when he died. One of the saddest things about his book is that it leaves no doubt in the reader's mind that there were even better books to come."

The *Hiram Poetry Review* sponsors an Annual Henry Dumas Memorial Poetry Contest, and Southern Illinois University's Experiment in Higher Education has a Henry Dumas Memorial Library.

BIOGRAPHICAL/CRITICAL SOURCES: Saturday Review, October 2, 1971; *New York Times Book Review,* October 20, 1974, January 19, 1975; *New Yorker,* January 6, 1975, May 10, 1976; *Black World,* January, 1975; *Choice,* March, 1975; *Contemporary Literary Criticism,* Volume 6, Gale, 1976; *Commonweal,* April 29, 1977.*

* * *

DUNBAR, Robert E(verett) 1926-

PERSONAL: Born November 24, 1926, in Quincy, Mass.; son of Charles Wheeler and Eva Emma (Duquette) Dunbar; married Sally Arseneault (a teacher and artist), June 26, 1954; children: Yvette Maria, Jesse Robert. *Education:* Marietta College, B.A., 1951; Northwestern University, M.S., 1954. *Religion:* Roman Catholic. *Home and office address:* Dunbairn, East Neck Rd., Nobleboro, Maine 04555. *Agent:* Janet A. Loranger, P.O. Box 113, West Redding, Conn. 06896.

CAREER: Continental Assurance Co., Chicago, Ill., assistant editor of publications, 1954-57; Junior Achievement, Chicago, director of public relations, 1957-58; *Selling Sporting Goods,* Chicago, editor, 1958-67; American Society of Anesthesiologists, Park Ridge, Ill., director of communications, 1967-70; American Fund for Dental Education and Health, Chicago, director of Public Information Division, 1970-74; free-lance writer, 1975—. Partner of Dunbairn Gallery. Adjunct assistant professor at University of Health Sciences, Chicago Medical School, 1973-75. *Military service:* U.S. Naval Reserve, active duty, 1944-45.

MEMBER: American Medical Writers Association (fellow; co-chairman of national education committee, 1970-74), Authors Guild, Authors League of America, Nobleboro Historical Society (member of board of trustees), Sigma Delta Chi. *Awards, honors:* Beth Fonda Award for excellence in medical feature writing from American Medical Writers Association, 1974, for *Learning to Cope With Arthritis, Rheumatism, and Gout.*

WRITINGS: Learning to Cope With Arthritis, Rheumatism, and Gout, Budlong, 1973; *A Man's Sexual Health,* Budlong, 1976; *Zoology Careers* (juvenile), F. Watts, 1977; *Heredity* (juvenile), F. Watts, 1978; *Mental Retardation* (juvenile), F. Watts, 1978; *The Planets* (juvenile), Pantheon, 1979; *Destination Jupiter* (young adult science fiction novel), F. Watts, 1979; *How Doctors Solve Mysteries* (juvenile), Garrard, 1980. Contributor to magazines and newspapers, including *Down East.* Former contributing editor of *Dental Economics.*

SIDELIGHTS: Dunbar writes: "I have wanted to be a writer from early childhood, with the desire mounting through my college years. I have written poetry, short stories, and essays, and now I am strongly into nonfiction as well as fiction in the juvenile and young adult fields. I have a universal interest in all subjects and feel I could write about almost any subject for general readership."

*   *   *

DUNCAN, (Reid) Bingham   1911-

PERSONAL: Born December 2, 1911, in Athens, Ala.; divorced; children: Susan Duncan McDougald. *Education:* University of Mississippi, B.A., 1932, M.A., 1933; Cornell University, Ph.D., 1938. *Home:* 1475 Clairmont Rd., Decatur, Ga. 30033. *Office:* Department of History, Emory University, Atlanta, Ga. 30322.

CAREER: Westminster College, New Wilmington, Pa., 1939-41, began as instructor, became assistant professor; Emory University, Atlanta, Ga., assistant professor, 1941-46; associate professor of history, 1946—. Fulbright lecturer in Taiwan, 1959-60. *Military service:* U.S. Army, 1943-46, 1951-52; became first lieutenant; received Bronze Star. *Member:* Society for Historians of American Foreign Relations, Southern Historical Association, Southern Center for International Studies. *Awards, honors:* Frank Luther Mott Award from Kappa Tau Alpha, 1975-76, for *Whitelaw Reid.*

WRITINGS: Whitelaw Reid: Journalist, Politician, Diplomat, University of Georgia Press, 1975. Contributor to history journals.

WORK IN PROGRESS: A series on U.S. foreign relations, especially correspondence with the legation in China.

*   *   *

DUNLAP, Joseph R(iggs)   1913-

PERSONAL: Born February 8, 1913, in Weihsien, Shantung, China; came to the United States in 1927; son of Robert Weyer (a physician) and Alice Lyon (Logan) Dunlap; married Leonie Coan, August 9, 1940 (divorced, 1970); married Barbara Jane Wood (a librarian), September 3, 1970; children: (first marriage) Bryan R., Arthur M.; (second marriage) Andrew R., Anthony L. *Education:* College of Wooster, A.B., 1936; Columbia University, B.S., 1937, A.M., 1942, D.L.S., 1972. *Politics:* Democrat. *Religion:* Presbyterian. *Home:* 420 Riverside Dr., New York, N.Y. 10025.

CAREER: City College of the City University of New York, New York, N.Y., library fellow, 1937-38, library assistant, 1938-51; assistant librarian, 1951-61; associate librarian, 1961-65; associate professor in library department, 1965-73. Participant in civic activities. *Military service:* U.S. Army, served as medic in infantry, 1943-46. *Member:* William Morris Society (North American secretary, 1957—), Kipling Society (North American secretary, 1971—), American Printing History Society, Modern Language Association of America, Victorian Society of America, Research Society

for Victorian Periodicals, Browning Institute, Housman Society, D. L. Sayers Society, Northeast Victorian Study Association, New York Shavians, Typophiles, Andiron Club.

WRITINGS: William Caxton and William Morris (pamphlet), William Morris Society, 1964, abridged edition, Cambridge University Press, 1976; (with Martin Kuhn) *Debate Index: Second Supplement,* H. W. Wilson, 1964; *The Book That Never Was,* Oriole, 1971; *On the Heritage of William Morris,* Typophiles, 1976; (with Paul Needham and John Dreyfus) *William Morris and the Art of the Book,* Pierpont Morgan Library, 1976.

Contributor to scholarly journals. Editor of *News From Anywhere* (of William Morris Society).

WORK IN PROGRESS: Continuing research on William Morris and on printing history in general.

SIDELIGHTS: Dunlap writes: "My early interest in the Middle Ages, which culminated in a master's degree, turned into curiosity about how the people of the nineteenth century viewed that period.

"William Morris combined both medievalism and a secure place in the history of the book arts, and when I came to know the extent of his work in literature, art, and other fields, he became my chief enthusiasm. I have done research on Morris's decorated manuscripts and early attempts at book design, some years before he founded the Kelmscott Press for which he is famous. This aspect of his art is less known, but is intrinsically interesting. Morris's passion for social justice, his pioneering in architectural preservation and the protection of the environment, as well as his emphasis on the vital importance of beauty in all useful things, have appealed to me for many years. When I lecture on Morris, I usually draw on my large collection of slides, since he was a very visual Victorian.

"Morris is by no means my only serious interest, but he has evoked most of such writing as I have done."

*   *   *

DUNSTER, Mark   1927-

PERSONAL: Born May 15, 1927. *Education:* Harvard University, B.A., 1950; Columbia University, M.A., 1963. *Home:* 27 West 11th St., New York, N.Y. 10011.

CAREER: Editor with Oxford University Press, Abingdon Press, *Colliers Encyclopedia,* and Columbia Pictures. Playwright. *Awards, honors:* Second prize, University of Chicago Sergel Award, 1962, for play, "Bianca"; Bellamann Foundation special award for exceptional promise in the field of playwriting, 1967; California Olympiad of the Arts, third prize for "C and P," and commendation for "Skelton," both 1968; first prize for poetic comedy, Quadrennial Contests in the Arts, Saratoga, Calif., 1972, for "Mermaid."

WRITINGS—Plays; produced only: "Mermaid," first produced at New York University, 1966; "Sojourner Truth" (one-act), first produced at University of Delaware, 1969; "Dialog" (one-act), produced by Teaneck Theatre Guild in Teaneck, N.J., 1970; "Ry," first produced in New York City, at Clark Center, 1971; "Storkwood," first produced at Clark Center, 1973.

Published only: *Jinny,* Linden Publishers, 1972; *Playboy,* Linden Publishers, 1974; *Portraits,* 2nd edition, Linden Publishers, 1976; *Druce,* Linden Publishers, 1976. Also author of "Bianca," "C and P," and "Skelton."

Contributor of plays to *New York Times Book of Verse,*

Macmillan, 1970, *Drama and Theatre,* and *Dramatika.* Contributor of poetry to journals, newspapers, and periodicals, including *Esquire, After Dark,* and *New York Times.*

* * *

DUPEE, F(rederick) W(ilcox) 1904-1979

OBITUARY NOTICE—See index for *CA* sketch: Born June 25, 1904, in Chicago, Ill; died of a drug overdose, January 19, 1979, in Carmel, Calif. Educator, editor, and author. Dupee was professor of English at Columbia University from 1948 to 1971, where he often took part in student demonstrations. An active Marxist, he once had a new set of porcelain teeth made before he joined the picket lines at Columbia knowing full well that they would probably be knocked out—and they were. In addition to writing two biographies of Henry James, Dupee also edited a collection of stories by Marcel Proust and some correspondence by Charles Dickens. He was a founding editor of *Partisan Review.* Obituaries and other sources: *Directory of American Scholars, Volume II: English, Speech, and Drama,* 6th edition, Bowker, 1974; *Who's Who in America,* 40th edition, Marquis, 1978; *New York Times,* January 22, 1979; *AB Bookman's Weekly,* February 5, 1979; *Time,* February 5, 1979

* * *

DUSKY, Lorraine 1942-

PERSONAL: Born June 13, 1942, in Detroit, Mich.; daughter of Harry (a numismatist) and Victoria (Wrozek) Dusky; married William A. Nixon III, 1968 (divorced, 1973). *Education:* Wayne State University, B.A., 1964. *Residence:* Hartsdale, N.Y. *Agent:* Rhoda A. Weyr, William Morris Agency, 1350 Avenue of the Americas, New York, N.Y. 10019.

CAREER: Saginaw News, Saginaw, Mich., reporter, 1964-65; *Rochester Democrat and Chronicle,* Rochester, N.Y., reporter, 1965; *Knickerbocker News,* Albany, N.Y., science and medical writer, 1966-68; *New York Times,* New York City, staff member, 1968-69; worked in public relations, 1969-72; free-lance writer, 1972-75; *Town and Country,* New York City, senior editor, 1975-76; free-lance writer, 1976—. Founding director of Adoptees Liberty Movement Association.

MEMBER: American Society of Journalists and Authors, National Press Club. *Awards, honors:* Journalism awards include award from New York State Health Department and New York chapter of American Medical Association, 1966, for excellence in medical reporting; public service award from American Optometric Association, 1974, for an article on vision therapy published in *Town and Country.*

WRITINGS: (With Richard Kavner) *Total Vision,* A & W Publishers, 1979; *Birthmark* (on adoption), M. Evans, 1979. Contributor to *Town and Country.*

WORK IN PROGRESS: A novel; a short story.

SIDELIGHTS: Lorraine Dusky writes: "I decided to become a writer when I was ten. I have had many rejections, but apparently enough successes to keep me going. Talent is important, but without endurance, the talent remains a babble in the wind, potential unfulfilled."

* * *

DYER, George Bell 1903-1978

PERSONAL: Born April 12, 1903, in Washington, D.C.,

died November 8, 1978, of a heart attack, in New Hope, Pa.; son of George Palmer and Dorothy (Bell) Dyer; married Charlotte Levitt (an editor). *Education:* Yale University, Ph.B., 1925; University of Pennsylvania, M.A., 1948, Ph.D., 1950. *Addresses:* Diabase Farm, Box 109, Route 2, New Hope, Pa. 18938; and Silverado, Calistoga, Calif.

CAREER: Worked as insurance salesman, 1926; *San Francisco Examiner,* San Francisco, Calif., reporter, 1929-30; free-lance writer, 1930—. Instructor in political science at Army General School, Fort Raleigh, Kan., 1950-52, at University of Pennsylvania, 1955-67, and at Yale University, 1957-58. Co-founder of Dyer Institute of Interdisciplinary Studies, 1951. *Military service:* U.S. Army, 1940-53; became lieutenant colonel; received Bronze Star. *Member:* American Military Institute (life member; trustee), Society of American Military Engineers, Authors League of America, National Rifle Association (life member), Company of Military Historians, Zeta Psi, Players Club (New York, N.Y.), Cosmos Club (Washington, D.C.).

WRITINGS—Mystery novels: *The Three-Cornered Wound,* Houghton, 1931; *The Five Fragments,* Houghton, 1932; *A Storm Is Rising,* Houghton, 1934; *The Catalyst Club,* Scribner, 1936; *The Long Death,* Scribner, 1937; *Adriana,* Scribner, 1939; *The People Ask Death,* Scribner, 1940.

Nonfiction—All with wife, Charlotte Leavitt Dyer; all published by Dyer Institute of Disciplinary Studies: *An Introduction to Strategic Intelligence,* 4th edition, 1957; *The World Analyst,* 1958; *Exercises on an Assumption of Violence: A Sensible and Active American Family Approach to the Peculiar Problems of Our Times,* 1962.

Also author of *The History of the Twelfth Corps,* 1947, *The Beginning of a U.S. Strategic Intelligence System in Latin America,* 1950, *A Century of Strategic Intelligence Reporting,* 1954, *A Strategic Intelligence Lesson,* 1955, *Estimating National Power and Intentions,* 1960, and *On Ritualization of War,* 1975.

AVOCATIONAL INTERESTS: Horseback riding.

OBITUARIES: New York Times, November 11, 1978.*

* * *

DYGARD, Thomas J. 1931-

PERSONAL: Born August 10, 1931, in Little Rock, Ark.; son of Thomas J. (a tailor) and Nannie (Smith) Dygard; married Patricia Redditt, November 23, 1951; children: Thomas J., Nancy Adams. *Education:* University of Arkansas, B.A., 1953. *Home:* 626 Lynden Lane, Arlington Heights, Ill. 60005.

CAREER: Arkansas Gazette, Little Rock, sportswriter and reporter, 1949-53; Associated Press, reporter in Little Rock, 1954-56, Detroit, Mich., 1956-58, Birmingham, Ala., 1958-62, and New Orleans, La., 1962-64, head of bureau in Little Rock, 1964-66, Indianapolis, Ind., 1966-71, and Chicago, Ill., 1971—. *Member:* Chicago Headline Club (president, 1974), Chicago Press Club (president, 1978).

WRITINGS—All novels for young adults: *Running Scared,* Morrow, 1977; *Winning Kicker,* Morrow, 1978; *Outside Shooter,* Morrow, 1979.

WORK IN PROGRESS: Sports novels for young adults, on soccer, football, and basketball.

SIDELIGHTS: Dygard comments: "I started writing young-adult fiction about four years ago for the fun and satisfaction of it, and it's still fun and satisfying, and I think it always will be." *Avocational interests:* Canoe camping, travel (Mexico,

Haiti, Scandinavia, Great Britain, Spain, France, Morocco).

BIOGRAPHICAL/CRITICAL SOURCES: New York Times Book Review, April 23, 1978.

E

EARLE, William Alexander 1919-

PERSONAL: Born February 18, 1919, in Saginaw, Mich.; son of James H. and Elsie G. Earle. *Education:* University of Chicago, A.B., 1941, Ph.D., 1951; University of Aix-Marseille, D.U., 1948. *Politics:* Independent. *Home:* 1237 Jarvis Ave., Chicago, Ill. 60626. *Office:* Department of Philosophy, Northwestern University, Evanston, Ill. 60201.

CAREER: Northwestern University, Evanston, Ill., associate professor, 1948-60, professor of philosophy, 1960—. Visiting lecturer at Yale University, 1955-56, and Harvard University, 1958. *Military service:* U.S. Army, 1941-46; became first lieutenant. *Member:* American Philosophical Association, American Society for Aesthetics, Society for Phenomenology and Existential Philosophy, Metaphysical Society of America, Hegel Society. *Awards, honors:* Rockefeller Foundation fellowship for University of Aix-Marseille, 1947-48; American Council of Learned Societies fellowship, 1959-60; Carnegie Foundation fellowship, 1965-66.

WRITINGS: Objectivity, Noonday, 1956, revised edition, Quadrangle, 1968; *Christianity and Existentialism,* Northwestern University Press, 1963; *Autobiographical Consciousness,* Quadrangle, 1972; *Public Sorrows and Private Pleasures,* Indiana University Press, 1976.

WORK IN PROGRESS: Mystical Reason.

* * *

EASTMAN, Addison J. 1918-

PERSONAL: Born October 6, 1918, in Flint, Mich.; son of Orville Peter (a clergyman) and Margaret (Watson) Eastman; married Thetis Deemer (a clerk), July 18, 1941; children: James A., Sheila J. Eastman Moran. *Education:* Taylor University, B.A., 1942; New York Theological Seminary, M.Div., 1946; Hartford Theological Seminary, M.A., 1951. *Politics:* "Mid-Liberal." *Home and Office:* 4514 Declaration Lane, Madison, Wis. 53704.

CAREER: Ordained Baptist minister; missionary in Rangoon, Burma, 1946-58; executive director of South Asia department of National Council of Churches, 1958-70; senior minister of Baptist church in Lakewood, Ohio, 1970-77; Green Lake Center, Green Lake, Wis., director of special services, 1977-78; Kodaikanal-Woodstock Foundation, Madison, Wis., executive director, 1978—.

WRITINGS: (Editor) *Branches of the Banyan,* Friendship, 1966; *This Is Southeast Asia Today,* Friendship, 1968; *A Handful of Pearls: The Epistle of James,* Westminster, 1978.

WORK IN PROGRESS: A book contrasting present-day Burma with the period leading to independence in 1948.

AVOCATIONAL INTERESTS: International travel.

* * *

EBERLE, Irmengarde 1898-1979
(Allyn Allen, Phyllis Ann Carter)

OBITUARY NOTICE—See index for *CA* sketch: Born November 11, 1898, in·San Antonio, Tex; died February 27, 1979. Editor and author of children's books. Eberle was a fabric designer and magazine editor before she became a full-time writer in 1937. She was the author of sixty-three children's and young adult books, including nature stories, biography, and fiction. Obituaries and other sources: *Current Biography,* Wilson, 1946; *Authors of Books for Young People,* 2nd edition, Scarecrow, 1971; *Who's Who in America,* 40th edition, Marquis, 1978; *Publishers Weekly,* April 2, 1979.

* * *

EBERT, Alan 1935-

PERSONAL: Born September 14, 1935, in New York, N.Y.; son of Philip Don (a plumber) and Mollie (Grosswirth) Ebert. *Education:* Brooklyn College (now of the City University of New York), B.A., 1957; Fordham University, M.A., 1975. *Home:* 353 West 56th St., New York, N.Y. 10019. *Agent:* Jane Rotrosen Agency, 318 East 51st St., New York, N.Y. 10022.

CAREER: NBC-TV, New York City, public relations coordinator, 1963-67; MSI (public relations firm), New York City, executive vice-president, 1967-71; free-lance writer, 1971—. *Member:* American Society of Journalists and Authors.

WRITINGS: The Homosexuals (nonfiction), Macmillan, 1977; *Every Body Is Beautiful* (nonfiction), Lippincott, 1978; *Feelings* (nonfiction), Dell, 1980. Contributor to periodicals, including *Family Circle, Essence, Look, Us,* and *Good Housekeeping.*

SIDELIGHTS: Ebert writes: "My work is primarily about people—what they *feel* as well as what they think. It is about that so-called 'human condition.' In magazines, the focus of my work is on celebrities—to find their inner workings and to show readers how, on a feeling level, celebrities are no different from 'civilians.' My books take me all over the country to the *people* to learn about *them*—their wants, needs, fears, hopes, and dreams."

* * *

ECKHARDT, Robert Christian 1913-
(Bob Eckhardt)

PERSONAL: Born July 16, 1913, in Austin, Tex.; son of Josephus Carl Augustus (a physician) and Norma (Wurzbach) Eckhardt; married Orissa Stephenson, 1940 (died, 1962); married Celia Buchan Morris (a writer), September 6, 1977; children: (first marriage) Orissa Eckhardt Arend, Rosalind, Sarah. *Education:* University of Texas, B.A., 1935, LL.B., 1939. *Religion:* Presbyterian. *Home:* 122 Third St. S.E., Washington, D.C. 20003. *Office:* U.S. House of Representatives, 1741 Longworth House Office Building, Washington, D.C. 20515.

CAREER: Practicing attorney in Austin, Tex., 1939-42; Office of the Coordinator of Inter-American Affairs, Austin, southwest regional director, 1946-48; practicing attorney in Dallas, Tex., 1948-50, and in Houston, 1950-66; member of Texas House of Representatives, Austin, 1958-60; U.S. House of Representatives, Washington, D.C., Democratic representative from Texas, 1967—, member of standing committees on interstate and foreign commerce, interior and insular affairs, and energy, member of House and Senate joint committee on the national energy act, 1977—. Adams House Lecturer at Harvard University, 1970; George Sherman Union Lecturer at Boston University, 1976; faculty member of Haverford College, 1977. Lecturer at more than twenty-five U.S. colleges and universities. Participant in symposia. Guest on television programs, including "Face the Nation" and "Sixty Minutes." *Military service:* U.S. Army Air Forces, flying instructor, 1942-44.

MEMBER: Americans for Democratic Action, Lamar Society, Members of Congress for Peace through Law, Texas Bar Association, Harrison County Democrats. *Awards, honors:* Congressional Award from National Parks and Recreation Association, 1974; Presidential Award from Immigration and Nationality Lawyers Association, 1976; Philip Hart Public Service Award from Consumer Federation of America, 1978.

WRITINGS—All under name Bob Eckhardt: (Editor) *Death of Galveston Bay,* Wildlife Management Institute, 1968; (with Charles L. Black, Jr.) *Tides of Power: Conversations on the American Constitution,* Yale University Press, 1975. Contributor to law journals and *Nation.*

WORK IN PROGRESS: The Legislative Process.

SIDELIGHTS: Eckhardt writes that his legislative interests include consumer protection, an equitable tax system, energy, a competitive economy, urban improvement, and environmental protection. He wrote the Toxic Substances Control Act to govern uses of new chemical substances, and has also worked toward a more open government and more representative rule within the Congress. *Avocational interests:* Cartooning, horses.

BIOGRAPHICAL/CRITICAL SOURCES: Washington Post Book World, August 15, 1976.

* * *

EDER, George Jackson 1900-

PERSONAL: Born September 5, 1900, in New York, N.Y.; married Marceline Gray, June 18, 1927 (died January 25, 1971); children: Donald Gray, Richard Gray, Luisa Eder Gray, Elizabeth Eder McCulloch. *Education:* Attended Columbia University, 1918; National University, Washington, D.C., B.Sc., 1928, LL.B., 1928; George Washington University, J.D., 1968. *Politics:* Independent Republican. *Home and Office:* 4545 Connecticut Ave., Washington, D.C. 20008. *Agent:* Collier Associates, 280 Madison Ave., New York, N.Y. 10016.

CAREER: Standard Statistics Corp. (now Standard & Poor's), New York City, manager of International Securities Division, 1932-37; Pan American Management Corp., Buenos Aires, Argentina, general manager, 1937-38; International Telephone & Telegraph Corp., New York City, South American attorney, 1938-46, assistant general attorney, 1938-61; Harvard University, Cambridge, Mass., research associate, 1961-63; University of Michigan, Ann Arbor, associated with graduate school of business administration, 1963-67; private practice of law in Washington, D.C., 1968-76. Founder and executive director of Bolivian National Monetary Stabilization Council; economic adviser to president of Bolivia, 1956-57. Past member of advisory board of California Institute of International Studies. Sponsor of Arena Stage. *Military service:* U.S. Army, 3rd Cavalry, 1917-19; became sergeant; received three battle stars. U.S. Army Reserve, 1925-37; became first lieutenant. *Member:* American Bar Association, American Economic Association, Bar Association of the District of Columbia, President's Club (University of Michigan).

WRITINGS: American Legislation on Bills and Notes (bilingual Spanish-English edition), Inter-American High Commission, 1925; *International Competition in Argentine Trade,* Carnegie Endowment for International Peace, 1930; *Taxation in Colombia,* School of Law, Harvard University, 1964; *Inflation and Development in Latin America,* University of Michigan, 1968; *What's Behind Inflation and How to Beat It,* Prentice-Hall, 1979. Contributor to economic and law journals.

WORK IN PROGRESS: A book for the traveler in Spain.

SIDELIGHTS: Eder comments: "I would be labeled a conservative by those who would call themselves 'liberals,' but in truth I am a Jeffersonian Republican, believing that the best government 'is that which governs least,' and that all that 'is necessary to make us a happy and prosperous people [is] a wise and frugal government which shall restrain men from injuring one another, which shall leave them otherwise free to regulate their own pursuits of industry and improvement, and shall not take from the mouth of labor the bread it has earned.' "

AVOCATIONAL INTERESTS: Travel (including Europe and Japan).

* * *

EDWARDS, Anne-Marie 1932-

PERSONAL: Born October 29, 1932, in York, England; daughter of Wilfrid (an engineer) and Margaret (an artist; maiden name, Jackson) Calvert; married Michael Edwards (a pilot and writer), January 8, 1955; children: Julie, Christopher. *Education:* Victoria University of Manchester, B.A. (honors), 1954; University of Southampton, M.A., 1967. *Home:* 2 Woodlands Rd., Ashurst, Southampton SO4 2AD, England.

CAREER: High school English teacher and department head in Romford, England, 1959-62; Northeast Essex Technical

College, Colchester, England, lecturer in English, 1965-66; University of Southampton, School of Navigation, Southampton, England, lecturer in English, 1969; Workers Educational Association, Southampton and Kendal, England, lecturer in English, 1969—. Radio broadcaster for British Broadcasting Corp. *Member:* Society of Authors, Thomas Hardy Society, Jane Austen Society, Southampton Poets.

WRITINGS—All published by British Broadcasting Corp.: *New Forest Walks,* 1975; *Discovering Hardy's Wessex,* 1978; *In the Steps of Jane Austen,* 1979; *New Forest Walks 2,* 1979. Contributor to magazines and newspapers, including *She, Country Life,* and *This England.* Co-editor of *Mayflower.*

WORK IN PROGRESS: With husband, Michael Edwards, a broadcast series based on her books, for British Broadcasting Corp.

SIDELIGHTS: Anne-Marie Edwards writes: "My husband and I both feel it is important that people should have vision as a saving factor in ordinary life. By relating authors to their worlds and involving the reader personally as a visitor to these worlds we hope to help people realize their own potential abilities and derive more pleasure and fulfillment from their own surroundings. My husband's book involves his readers in the world of flying. I hope that mine involve the reader in a deeper appreciation of man and nature."

*   *   *

EDWARDS, Corwin D. 1901-1979

OBITUARY NOTICE—See index for *CA* sketch: Born November 1, 1901, in Nevada, Mo.; died April 20, 1979, in Dallas, Tex. Economist, educator, and author of books on domestic economic policy and international trade. A specialist in anti-trust economics, Edwards was economic adviser and assistant chief economist to the Federal Trade Commission and the Antitrust Division of the Department of Justice. He retired from his professorship at the University of Oregon in 1971. In addition to the seven books he wrote, Edwards also contributed to some fourteen other books on economics. Obituaries and other sources: *American Men and Women of Science: The Social and Behavioral Sciences,* 12th edition, Bowker, 1973; *The Writers Directory, 1976-78,* St. Martin's, 1976; *The International Who's Who,* Europa, 1978; *Who's Who,* 131st edition, St. Martin's, 1979; *New York Times,* April 25, 1979.

*   *   *

EDWARDS, Michael 1932-

PERSONAL: Born May 22, 1932, in Birmingham, England; son of Tom (an engineer) and Mabel (Horton) Edwards; married Anne-Marie Calvert (a broadcaster, teacher, and writer), January 8, 1955; children: Julie, Christopher. *Education:* Attended University of Melbourne, 1948-49, and Royal Air Force College, Cranwell, 1950-53. *Home:* 2 Woodlands Rd., Ashurst, Southampton SO4 2AD, England.

CAREER: Royal Air Force, pilot, 1950-65, flying officer, 1953-55, flight lieutenant, 1956-64, left service as squadron leader, 1965; College of Air Training, Southampton, England, flying instructor, 1966-72; Civil Aviation Authority, Stansted, England, captain and senior flight examiner, 1972—. *Member:* British Air Line Pilots Association, Society of Authors, Aircraft Owners and Pilots Association (member of executive committee).

WRITINGS: The Aviator's World, David & Charles, 1974.

WORK IN PROGRESS: With wife, Anne-Marie Edwards, a

series of books and radio broadcasts, based on the "works and wanderings" of well-known British authors, for British Broadcasting Corp.

SIDELIGHTS: Michael Edwards told *CA:* "As a child in Hitler's Blitz of Coventry I was brought up in a community where all sections had a warm regard and understanding of each other. Military men, professional and commercial people, artists and writers simply had to pull together—or perish! During my own career as a military (and later civil) flier I have watched groups grow steadily further apart; individuals are engrossed more and more in their own activities, taking less interest in what the fellow next door is doing. In my first book I have tried to open up the world of the professional aviator to the layman, and I hope to go on opening doors and building bridges in an effort to counter the increasing divisive forces in our modern society."

BIOGRAPHICAL/CRITICAL SOURCES: Books and Bookmen, December, 1974.

*   *   *

EDWARDS, Paul 1923-

PERSONAL: Born September 2, 1923, in Vienna, Austria; naturalized U.S. citizen; son of Ignace (a lawyer) and Lotte (Hubel) Edwards. *Education:* University of Melbourne, B.A. (first class honors), 1944, M.A. (first class honors), 1947; Columbia University, Ph.D., 1951. *Religion:* Atheist. *Home:* 390 West End Ave., New York, N.Y. 10024. *Office:* Department of Philosophy, Brooklyn College of the City University of New York, Brooklyn, N.Y. 11210.

CAREER: University of Melbourne, Parkville, Victoria, Australia, faculty member, 1945-47; New York University, New York, N.Y., 1949-66, began as instructor, became associate professor of philosophy; Brooklyn College of the City University of New York, Brooklyn, N.Y., associate professor, 1966-68, professor of philosophy, 1968—. Has also held teaching positions at City College of the City University of New York, Columbia University, University of California, Berkeley, and New School for Social Research. *Awards, honors:* Guggenheim fellow, 1964-65.

WRITINGS: The Logic of Moral Discourse, Free Press, 1955; (editor with Arthur Pap) *A Modern Introduction to Philosophy,* Free Press, 1957, 3rd edition, 1973; *Buber and Buberism: A Critical Evaluation,* University Press of Kansas, 1969; *Heidegger and Death: A Deflationary Critique,* Open Court, 1979; *The Philosophy and Psychology of Death,* Free Press, in press. Editor-in-chief of *The Encyclopedia of Philosophy* (Book-of-the-Month Club selection), eight volumes, Macmillan, 1967. Contributor to philosophy journals.

*   *   *

EGERTON, George W(illiam) 1942-

PERSONAL: Born May 6, 1942, in Winnipeg, Manitoba, Canada; son of Wilfred and Elizabeth (Edmonds) Egerton; married Manya Samarin, May 10, 1971; children: Graham. *Education:* University of Manitoba, B.A., 1963; University of Minnesota, M.A., 1964; University of Toronto, Ph.D., 1970. *Religion:* Anglican. *Home:* 2080 West 36th Ave., Vancouver, British Columbia, Canada V6M 1K9. *Office:* Department of History, University of British Columbia, Vancouver, British Columbia, Canada V6T 1W5.

CAREER: Memorial University of Newfoundland, St. John's, assistant professor of history, 1970-72; University of British Columbia, Vancouver, assistant professor, 1972-76, associate professor of history, 1976—. *Member:* Canadian Institute of International Affairs, American Historical Association.

WRITINGS: Great Britain and the Creation of the League of Nations, University of North Carolina Press, 1978. Contributor to history journals.

WORK IN PROGRESS: Research on the nature and function of political memoirs; on the political writings of Lloyd George; on Woodrow Wilson and the creation of the League of Nations; on aspects of modernization and secularization in Canadian society; and on British foreign policy and the League of Nations.

AVOCATIONAL INTERESTS: History of the piano, restoring old pianos.

* * *

EGERTON, John (Walden) 1935-

PERSONAL: Surname is pronounced *Edge*-er-ton; born June 14, 1935, in Atlanta, Ga.; son of William Graham (in sales) and Rebecca (White) Egerton; married Ann Bleidt, June 6, 1957; children: Brooks B., March W. *Education:* Attended Western Kentucky State College, 1953-54; University of Kentucky, A.B., 1958, M.A., 1960. *Politics:* Independent. *Religion:* Unaffiliated. *Home and office:* 4014 Copeland Dr., Nashville, Tenn. 37215.

CAREER: University of Kentucky, Lexington, member of public relations staff, 1958-60; University of South Florida, Tampa, member of public relations staff, 1960-65; *Southern Education Report,* Nashville, Tenn., staff writer, 1965-69; *Race Relations Reporter,* Nashville, staff writer, 1969-71; free-lance writer, 1971—. Writer for Atlanta's Southern Regional Council, 1973-75. Journalist-in-residence at Virginia Polytechnic Institute and State University, 1977-78. Member of board of directors of Nashville's Family and Children's Services, 1975-77. *Military service:* U.S. Army, 1954-56.

WRITINGS: A Mind to Stay Here, Macmillan, 1970; *The Americanization of Dixie,* Harper Magazine Press, 1974; *Visions of Utopia,* University of Tennessee Press, 1977; *Nashville: The Faces of Two Centuries,* Nashville Magazine, 1979. Contributor of more than two hundred articles to magazines. Contributing editor of *Saturday Review of Education,* 1972-73, *Race Relations Reporter,* 1973-74, and *Southern Voices,* 1974-75.

WORK IN PROGRESS: A book of American social and cultural history, based on the lives of more than a hundred people who comprise four generations of a middle-class American family.

SIDELIGHTS: Egerton told *CA:* "I have been writing since I was twelve. I never really had a choice, though I was thirty years old before I understood and accepted that. It has not been easy to make a living doing what I want to do and I couldn't in good conscience recommend it as a livelihood to beginners. It may be that survival for writers is becoming less and less possible with each passing year, and writers at the *end* of the twentieth century may be like blacksmiths at the *beginning,* or calligraphers in the age of Gutenberg. Nevertheless, people will keep on doing it because they have the urge, or holds their interest and stirs in them vague dreams of immortality. It's a crazy pursuit in a crazy world. God help me, I love it, as George Patton supposedly said about war."

EGUCHI, Shinichi 1914-1979

OBITUARY NOTICE: Born in 1914; died April 22, 1979, near Tokyo, Japan. Poet and editor. Eguchi was a prize-winning editor and a Christian poet who founded the "Salt of the Earth" movement in 1956 to help poor laborers in need of money to travel home. He was found hanged in his home, an apparent suicide. Obituaries and other sources: *Chicago Tribune,* April 29, 1979.

* * *

EHRLICH, Otto Hild 1892-1979

OBITUARY NOTICE: Born in 1892 in Vienna, Austria; died May 26, 1979, in East Orange, N.J. Ehrlich was emeritus professor of economics at the New York University Graduate School of Arts and Science. He wrote several economic studies, including *Inflation in the United States* and *The Utility of Time.* Ehrlich also founded and edited *Economics Abstracts.* Obituaries and other sources: *New York Times,* May 27, 1979.

* * *

EILAND, Murray L(ee) 1936-

PERSONAL: Born September 9, 1936, in Taft, Calif.; son of Murray Lee, Sr. (a judge) and Frances (a teacher; maiden name, Perrigo) Eiland; married Astrid Hilweg (a nurse), November 19, 1967; children: Murray Lee III. *Education:* Attended University of California, Los Angeles, 1954-57; University of California, Berkeley, B.A., 1958; University of California, San Francisco, M.D., 1961. *Residence:* Berkeley, Calif. *Office:* Napa State Hospital, Imola, Calif. 94558.

CAREER: U.S. Public Health Service Hospital, Staten Island, N.Y., intern, 1961-62; Langley Porter Neuropsychiatric Institute, San Francisco, Calif., resident, 1962-65; Napa State Hospital, Imola, Calif., psychiatrist, 1965—. President of Oriental Rug Co., Inc., 1974—. *Member:* American Psychiatric Association, California Medical Association, Northern California Psychiatric Association, Phi Beta Kappa.

WRITINGS: Oriental Rugs: A Comprehensive Guide, New York Graphic Society, 1973, expanded edition, 1976; *Chinese and Other Exotic Oriental Rugs,* New York Graphic Society, 1979.

WORK IN PROGRESS: A critical study of the radical psychotherapy and human potential movements.

* * *

EISENSTEIN, Phyllis 1946-

PERSONAL: Born February 26, 1946, in Chicago, Ill.; daughter of Irving (a grocer) and Sylvia (Davidson) Kleinstein; married Alex Eisenstein (an artist and writer), September 8, 1966. *Education:* Attended University of Chicago, 1963-66, and University of Illinois at Chicago Circle, 1978—. *Residence:* Chicago, Ill. *Agent:* Kirby McCauley Ltd., 310 East 46th St., New York, N.Y. 10017.

CAREER: Writer. Grocery stock clerk and butcher, 1963-65. *Member:* Science Fiction Writers of America (Nebula trustee, 1976—).

*WRITINGS—*All science fiction novels: *Born to Exile,* Arkham, 1978; *Sorcerer's Son,* Del Rey Books, 1979; *Shadow of Earth,* Dell, 1979. Contributor to science fiction magazines, including *Analog, Galaxy, New Dimensions,* and *Isaac Asimov's Science Fiction Magazine.*

SIDELIGHTS: Phyllis Eisenstein comments: "I am interested in crackpot science and science fiction. My parents tried to discourage me from writing science fiction and fantasy, but I ignored them. This is the only field in which true creativity is possible." *Avocational interests:* Anthropology, archaeology, mythology, astronomy, old movies.

* * *

EISLER, Colin (Tobias) 1931-

PERSONAL: Born March 17, 1931, in Hamburg, Germany; naturalized U.S. citizen; son of George B. (a publisher) and Kate (Basseches) Eisler; married Benita Blitzer, June 23, 1960; children: Rachel. *Education:* Yale University, B.A., 1952; graduate study at Oxford University, 1952-53; Harvard University, M.A., 1954, Ph.D., 1957. *Office:* Institute of Fine Arts, New York University, 1 East 78th St., New York, N.Y. 10021.

CAREER: Yale University, New Haven, Conn., instructor in art history and curator in art gallery's department of prints and drawings, 1955-57; New York University, New York, N.Y., assistant professor, 1958-60, associate professor, 1960-61, professor of art history, 1968—, currently Robert Lehman Professor of the History of Art. Fellow of Princeton University's Institute for Advanced Study, 1957-58. Member of Fulbright Board, 1967; participant in international congresses; consultant to museums.

MEMBER: College Art Association of America, Renaissance Society of America, National Committee on the History of the Arts, Drawing Society. *Awards, honors:* Guggenheim fellow, 1966-67; National Endowment for the Humanities senior fellow, 1972-73.

WRITINGS: Primitifs flamands: New England Museums, Centre national de recherches primitifs flamands (Brussels), 1961; *Flemish and Dutch Drawings from the Fifteenth to the Eighteenth Centuries,* Shorewood, 1963; *German Drawings,* Shorewood, 1963; *Early Netherlandish Paintings in New England,* de Sikkel, 1963; *The Seeing Hand,* Harper, 1975; *The Master of the Unicorn,* Abaris, 1978; *Durer's Animals,* Viking, 1979. Also editor of *The Athlete of Virtue and the Iconography of Asceticism: Essays in Honor of Erwin Panofsky,* 1961. Contributor to art journals. Member of editorial board of College Art Association of America.

WORK IN PROGRESS: Luke and Pygmalion: The Allegory of Art; The Jewish Way of Death.

SIDELIGHTS: Eisler comments: "I hope to write in an interesting and responsible fashion. Art history is meaningless unless the writer can express the quality and character of his subject. I do my best."

* * *

ELLIOTT, Malissa Childs 1929(?)-1979
(Malissa Redfield)

OBITUARY NOTICE: Born c. 1929 in St. Louis, Mo.; died of a brain tumor, March 20, 1979, in Hanover, N.H. Government worker, writer, and editor. Elliott was a specialist in Soviet affairs at the Intelligence Division of the U.S. State Department and the U.S. Information Agency. She had previously been on the editorial staffs of *Fortune* magazine and the *New York Times Sunday Magazine.* At the U. S. Information Agency she edited an Arab language magazine and *Amerika,* a magazine distributed in the Soviet Union. Elliott also wrote two novels, *The Country of Love,* and *Game of Chance With Strangers,* and a book about her impressions of Vermont, *Scenes From Country Life.* She pub-

lished under the name of Malissa Redfield. Obituaries and other sources: *Washington Post,* March 21, 1979; *New York Times,* March 21, 1979; *Publishers Weekly,* April 2, 1979.

* * *

ELLIOTT, Ward E(dward) Y(andell) 1937-

PERSONAL: Born August 6, 1937, in Cambridge, Mass.; son of William Yandell (a professor) and Louise (Ward) Elliott; married Myrna Krahn (a career planning counselor), June 7, 1969; children: William Yandell, Christopher David. *Education:* Harvard University, A.B., 1959, A.M., 1968, Ph.D., 1968; University of Virginia, LL.B., 1964. *Politics:* "Teddy Roosevelt Republican." *Religion:* Christian. *Home:* 875 North College Ave., Claremont, Calif. 91711. *Office:* Department of Political Science, Pitzer Hall, Claremont Men's College, Claremont, Calif. 91711.

CAREER: Covington & Burling, Washington, D.C., law associate, 1964; Claremont Men's College, Claremont, Calif., assistant professor, 1968-73, associate professor of political science, 1973—. President of Group Against Smog and Pollution (GASP); vice-president of California Coalition for Clean Air; member of district advisory council of South Coast Air Quality Management District; member of board of directors of Planning and Conservation League. *Military service:* U.S. Army, 1959-61; became first lieutenant. *Member:* American Association for the Advancement of Science, Sierra Club. *Awards, honors:* Henry Salvatori fellowship from Claremont Men's College, 1968-73; Earhart fellowship from Earhart Foundation, 1974-75; National Institutes of Health fellowship, 1976; National Endowment for the Humanities fellowship, 1979; distinguished civilian service medal, 1973.

WRITINGS: (Contributor) Erica Dolgin and Richard Sims, editors, *Federal Environmental Law,* West Publishing, 1974; *The Rise of Guardian Democracy: The Supreme Court's Role in Voting Rights Disputes,* Harvard University Press, 1975.

WORK IN PROGRESS: Federal Law and Population Control.

SIDELIGHTS: Elliott writes: "I am interested in the interactions between public law and public policy; between short-run and long-run objectives; and between the perspectives of various academic disciplines. Each of these tells us very different things, and few of us have the breadth or the patience to try to reconcile them."

* * *

ELLIOTT, William Yandell 1896-1979

OBITUARY NOTICE: Born May 12, 1896, in Murfreesboro, Tenn.; died January 9, 1979, in Haywood, Va. Government official and educator. Elliott was a professor of history and political science at Harvard University and an adviser to numerous government agencies. He directed the preparation of more than one hundred doctoral dissertations, including those of former Secretary of State Henry A. Kissinger, former Prime Minister Pierre Elliott Trudeau, and McGeorge Bundy, an adviser to Presidents Kennedy and Johnson. "Whatever I have achieved," Kissinger once wrote, "I owe importantly to his [Elliott's] inspiration." The charismatic teacher was regarded as a legend by many of his students, while others knew him as the conscience of political study at Harvard. In the lecture hall, he was known to argue so vehemently against Communism and Marxist theory that he would draw hisses from his students. He would often hiss back. As a government official, Elliott had served as vice-chairman of the War Production Board, staff director of the House Committee on Foreign Affairs and the House Select Committee on Foreign Aid, and as an adviser to Vice-President Nixon. His writings include *The Pragmatic Revolt in Politics, The Need for Constitutional Reform, Western Political Heritage,* and *Industrial Mobilization and the National Security.* Obituaries and other sources: *American Men and Women of Science: The Social and Behavioral Sciences,* 12th edition, Bowker, 1973; *New York Times,* January 11, 1979; *Washington Post,* January 12, 1979.

*   *   *

ELLIS, J(ohn) R(ichard) 1938-

PERSONAL: Born December 16, 1938, in Melbourne, Australia; son of Edward Lawrence (an accountant) and Gladys Mary (Womersley) Ellis; married Dallas Elizabeth Symes (a teacher), May 7, 1960; children: Michael, Jennifer, Miranda. *Education:* Graylands Teachers College, teaching certificate, 1957; University of Western Australia, B.A. (honors), 1964; Monash University, Ph.D., 1970. *Politics:* Liberal. *Religion:* None. *Home address:* Dunstan St., Frankston, Victoria, Australia 3199.

CAREER: Elementary school teacher in Tammin, Western Australia, 1958-60, and Claremont, Western Australia, 1961-64; faculty member at Monash University, Clayton, Victoria, Australia. Head of Victoria Greek and Roman Histories Committee and Panels of Examiners, 1971-77. *Member:* Australian Society for Classical Studies, British School of Archaeology at Athens.

WRITINGS: (Editor) *AULLA Thirteenth Congress: Proceedings,* Monash University, 1970; (with R. D. Milns) *The Spectre of Philip,* Sydney University Press, 1970; *Philip II and Macedonian Imperialism,* Thames & Hudson, 1976. Contributor to history and classical studies journals.

WORK IN PROGRESS: Characters in the Sicilian Expedition; a monograph on Thucydidean historiography; research on Macedonian history.

SIDELIGHTS: Ellis writes: "My main motivations are the importance of the past to the present and the need to be critical."

AVOCATIONAL INTERESTS: Classical music, classical and contemporary art, literature, travel (especially to centers of European civilization).

*   *   *

ELLIS, John O(liver) 1917-

PERSONAL: Born November 30, 1917, in Atlanta, Ga.; son of Frampton Erroll (an attorney) and Eloise (an artist; maiden name, Oliver) Ellis; married Gene Palfrey, May 21, 1946; children: John O., Jr., Gene (Mrs. Hugh McCutcheon). *Education:* Emory University, A.B., 1941; Medical College of Georgia, M.D., 1944. *Religion:* Presbyterian. *Home:* 3531 Paces Valley Rd., Atlanta, Ga. 30327. *Office:* 384 Peachtree St., Atlanta, Ga. 30308.

CAREER: Charlotte Memorial Hospital, Charlotte, N.C., intern, 1944-45; Charity Hospital, New Orleans, La., resident and radiology trainee, 1945-48; private practice as a radiologist in Atlanta, Ga., 1948—. Member of Colony Medical Group, 1949—. Institutional representative of Boy Scouts of America. Photographer for *Atlanta Medical Bulletin. Military service:* U.S. Army, 1940-44.

WRITINGS: (photographer) Alex W. Bealer, *The Tools That*

Built America, Crown, 1976; (with Bealer) *The Log Cabin: Homes in the American Wilderness,* Crown, 1978. Contributor to local medical journals.

WORK IN PROGRESS: Historical studies; research on the American Indian; studies on World War II uniforms, historical buildings of Georgia, and geneology of Georgia and South Carolina.

SIDELIGHTS: Ellis told *CA:* "My writing and photography usually revolves around my collecting hobbies. My American Indian artifacts collection is the largest in the Southeast."

*   *   *

EMERSON, Rupert 1899-1979

OBITUARY NOTICE—See index for *CA* sketch: Born August 20, 1899, in Rye, N.Y.; died February 9, 1979, in Cambridge, Mass. Educator and author of eight books on Asia and Africa. Emerson was on the faculty of Harvard University for forty-three years before his retirement in 1970. A specialist on nationalism in Asia and Africa, he often guest lectured at universities in East Africa. Obituaries and other sources: *American Men and Women of Science: The Social and Behavioral Sciences,* 12th edition, Bowker, 1973; *Who's Who in America,* 40th edition, Marquis, 1978; *New York Times,* February 11, 1979.

*   *   *

ENGEL, Lyle Kenyon 1915-

PERSONAL: Born May 12, 1915, in New York, N.Y.; son of George Stevens (an inventor and publisher) and Beatrice (Michaels) Engel; married Marla Helen Ray (an editor), June, 1975; children: (previous marriage) George. *Education:* Attended New York University, 1930-32, and New York College of Music, 1933-34. *Residence:* Canaan, N.Y. *Office:* Book Creations, Inc., Schillings Crossing Rd., Canaan, N.Y. 12029.

CAREER: Book producer and creator of such paperback series as "Nick Carter—Killmaster," "The Kent Family Chronicles," and "Wagon West." Song Lyrics, Inc., New York, N.Y., editor of *Song Hits Magazine,* 1935-41, head of company, 1941-49; producer of low-priced paperback books, beginning, 1950; independent public relations executive with such accounts as Universal Pictures, United Artists Pictures, and American Broadcasting Co. (ABC), 1950-52; producer of record albums for RCA Victor, Decca, Grand Award, and other companies, 1955-61; Book Creations, Inc., Canaan, N.Y., president and producer of books, 1973—. Creator and promotion consultant of songs for motion pictures, including "The Moon Is Blue," and "Moulin Rouge," 1950-52. *Awards, honors:* Cash Box Award for Best Song from a Motion Picture from Music Industry of America, 1953, for "The Song From Moulin Rouge"; Direct Mail Advertising Association Award, 1953.

WRITINGS: (Compiler) *"500" Songs That Made the All-Time Hit Parade,* Bantam, 1964; *The Complete Book of Auto Racing,* Bantam, 1970; *Mario Andretti: The Man Who Can Win Any Kind of Race,* Arco, 1970; *The Incredible A. J. Foyt,* Arco, 1970, 2nd edition, 1977. Columnist for TV and film industry magazines and for *Seventeen* magazine. Author of recording, "Candyland Express," Hallmark, 1967.

SIDELIGHTS: Lyle Kenyon Engel estimates that he has produced more than one thousand paperback titles in his career as a book producer. In a local newspaper article he described his concept of the book producer: "I think I'm the only producer of books in the industry. Whatever has to be done to get that book out, that's what I do. I'm an expeditor. I'm basically an idea man. I create the whole thing." One of his creations is the popular "American Bicentennial—The Kent Family Chronicles" series. As with other books, Engel sold his original idea or concept of this best-selling series to a publisher, wrote the outline, and then found an author (John Jakes) to write the books. This is standard operating procedure for Engel. His authors are both famous and unknown. Some write under pseudonyms. All, according to Engel, make top money writing for him.

Engel's success as a book producer may be due largely to his ability to discern what the public will want to read and his own voracious appetite for books. Engel suffered from osteomyelitis for twelve years as a teenager and was hospitalized for treatment. It was during these years that he began to read everything from Dickens and Dumas to the *Encyclopaedia Britannica*. He still keeps up with new publications: "I read everything I can get my hands on, any new series, any new idea, anything new that comes out on the market. I have a tremendous library that I go through constantly, all current things. I read anything that will teach me something, as well as the current fiction. . . . You have to get tuned in to what you're doing. I'm interested in producing books, so I'm tuned in mentally to what would make a good book, whether it's fiction or nonfiction, whether it's a series or whatever."

About the type of fiction he produces, Engel stated: "What we're selling in these books is entertainment, not undying literature. We offer an outlet for life's cares and problems by presenting heroes whose adventures can be vicariously enjoyed and identified with. However, among our books are a number which will eventually become classics in their fields."

BIOGRAPHICAL/CRITICAL SOURCES: Publishers Weekly, January 13, 1975, August 14, 1978; *Catham Courier–Rough Notes*, May 13, 1976; *Berkshire Sampler*, May 16, 1976; *New York Times Book Review*, June 20, 1976, July 25, 1976; *Writer's Digest*, October, 1977.

* * *

ENGEL, Madeline H(elena) 1941-

PERSONAL: Born February 11, 1941, in Bronx, N.Y.; daughter of William Francis (in telephone repair work) and Adelaide (Boitano) Engel; married Thomas P. Moran (a teacher of mathematics), April 18, 1970; children: Magdalene. *Education:* Barnard College, B.A., 1961; Fordham University, M.A., 1963, Ph.D., 1966. *Politics:* Democrat. *Religion:* Roman Catholic. *Residence:* Bronx, N.Y. *Office:* Department of Sociology, Herbert H. Lehman College of the City University of New York, Bedford Park Blvd. W., Bronx, N.Y. 10468.

CAREER: Columbia University, New York City, research assistant in sociology, summers, 1959-61; Fordham University, Bronx, N.Y., instructor in sociology, summers, 1963-64; Hunter College of the City University of New York, New York City, lecturer in sociology, 1964-66; Herbert H. Lehman College of the City University of New York, Bronx, instructor, 1966-69, assistant professor, 1969-72, associate professor of sociology, 1972—. Research associate at Fordham University's Institute for Social Research, 1966—. *Member:* American Sociological Association, American Criminological Society, Eastern Sociological Society, Amigos (member of board of directors).

WRITINGS: (Editor with S. M. Tomasi) *The Italian Experi-*

ence in the United States, Center for Migration Studies, 1970; *Inequality in America,* Crowell, 1971; *The Drug Scene,* Hayden, 1974. Member of editorial board of *International Migration Review,* 1966-71.

WORK IN PROGRESS: A study of women working as lawyers and college teachers.

SIDELIGHTS: Madeline Engel writes: "My particular interests within sociology are minorities and criminology. In part this stems from the fact that I am myself a member of a minority. Within the criminology field, my work focused on training schools, community-based programs for juveniles, political delinquency, the juvenile justice system, heroin addiction and its treatment in therapeutic communities as well as by means of methadone maintenance, and illicit trafficking in methadone.

"After studying delinquents and drug addicts for thirteen years, I have now decided to turn my attention toward another group of 'deviants'—professional women. Recently I have joined with a colleague at Lehman College to study women in law and college teaching in an effort to better understand their backgrounds and experiences. I am particularly interested in the effects of ethnicity and race on their career choices and progress. Regardless of the topic I happen to be studying at a given time, my basic concern is always the same, to use a sociological perspective to make people more understanding of others, especially of those labeled 'deviants' in our society."

* * *

ENGLAND, Anthony Bertram 1939-

PERSONAL: Born July 29, 1939, in Grimsby, England; son of Bertram (a grocer) and Nellie (Bodfield) England; married Elizabeth Helen Halley (a gardener), August 8, 1964; children: Jacyntha, Matthew. *Education:* University of Manchester, B.A., 1961, M.A., 1963; Yale University, Ph.D., 1969. *Home:* 567 Monterey Ave., Victoria, British Columbia, Canada V8S 4T8. *Office:* Department of English, University of Victoria, Victoria, British Columbia, Canada.

CAREER: University of Manchester, Manchester, England, assistant lecturer in English, 1963-64; University of British Columbia, Vancouver, instructor in English, 1964-66; University of Victoria, Victoria, British Columbia, assistant professor, 1969-75, associate professor of English, 1975—.

WRITINGS: Byron's "Don Juan" and Eighteenth-Century Literature, Bucknell University Press, 1974; *Energy and Order in the Poetry of Swift,* Bucknell University Press, 1980. Contributor to literature journals.

WORK IN PROGRESS: Research on Restoration and eighteenth-century burlesque poetry and on Byron and the will.

* * *

ENGLISH, Deirdre (Elena) 1948-

PERSONAL: Born May 4, 1948, in Washington, D.C.; daughter of Maurice (a poet and publisher) and Fanita (a psychotherapist; maiden name, Blumberg) English. *Education:* Graduated from Sarah Lawrence College, 1970; State University of New York at Stony Brook, M.S.W., 1975. *Home:* 445 Noe St., San Francisco, Calif. 94114.

CAREER: State University of New York, College at Old Westbury, Old Westbury, lecturer in American studies and women's studies, 1971-75; free-lance writer and lecturer, 1976—. Instructor in women's studies and psychology at

National Congress of Neighborhood Women College, Brooklyn, N.Y., 1976. Producer and director of films, "D.C. III," 1971, and "The Year of the Tiger," 1974. *Awards, honors:* First prize at the Film Festival for Peace in Vietnam, 1972, for "D.C. III."

WRITINGS—All with Barbara Ehrenreich: *Witches, Midwives and Nurses: A History of Women Healers* (booklet), Feminist Press, 1973; *Complaints and Disorders: The Sexual Politics of Sickness* (booklet), Feminist Press, 1974; *For Her Own Good: 150 Years of the Experts' Advice to Women*, Anchor, 1978. Work represented in anthologies, including *Seizing Our Bodies: The Politics of Women's Health*, edited by Claudia Dreifus, Vintage, 1977. Contributor of articles to *Socialist Revolution* magazine.

SIDELIGHTS: English wrote to *CA:* "Barbara Ehrenreich and I probably first became interested in witches because we thought that if any group of women had been so much maligned, there must be something good about them. When we found out that witches had been midwives, herbalists, and all-around healers, it led us on to study how women got to be excluded from medicine when it was professionalized in America and how, in turn, medicine has treated and mistreated women ever since. With our first two short books we became part of the Feminist Press, a small collectively run women's publishing house that produces an exceptionally fine list. Although the books were never advertised and rarely reviewed, the sales ran to 150,000 copies in the 'invisible market' of women's studies courses, feminist bookstores, and mail-order purchases. The little books became surprisingly well-known (among women) and five foreign editions were published.

"In the meantime we went to work on a major exploration—and expose—of sexual bias in particularly every profession which has specialized in doling out 'scientific advice' to women. We studied gynecologists and child psychologists, sociologists and psychoanalysts (including Freud), home economists and pediatricians (including Spock), and again and again we uncovered a scientific literature filled with arrogant and unscientific judgments about women's body, mind, and nature. In *For Her Own Good* we present our thoroughly documented findings.

"All this goes to show that we don't think of ourselves only as writers, but as women who want to help bring about change—in the medical professions, and in the publishing industry, too—that might help to do women in general some *real* good."

* * *

EPAND, Len 1950-

PERSONAL: Born August 19, 1950, in New York, N.Y.; son of Harold (in business) and Jacqueline (Rosenberg) Epand; married Joan Gilbertson (a teacher of mathematics), September 5, 1971; children: Daniel. *Education:* University of Wisconsin, Madison, B.A., 1972. *Home:* 6511 Quartz Ave., Woodland Hills, Calif. 91367. *Agent:* Peter Skolnik, Sanford J. Greenburger Associates, Inc., 825 Third Ave., New York, N.Y. 10022. *Office:* Polydor Records, 6255 Sunset Blvd., #1126, Hollywood, Calif. 90028.

CAREER: Free-lance journalist, 1972-74; *Zoo World* (pop music magazine), Hollywood, Calif., West Coast editor, 1974; free-lance journalist, 1975-76; Polydor Records, Hollywood, Calif., West Coast publicity director, 1976—.

WRITINGS: (With Kenny Rogers) *Making It With Music*, Harper, 1978. Investigative reporter for *Eco* (of Friends of

the Earth). Contributor to magazines and newspapers. West Coast editor of *Circus;* music critic for *Rolling Stone.*

WORK IN PROGRESS: A biography of a leading female rock singer of the 1960's.

SIDELIGHTS: Epand writes: "Kenny Rogers and I wrote our book to help musicians achieve their goals with less difficulty and confusion, and to explain the business to those interested in pop music generally. As a former rock musician and music critic, I could relate to the biographical material offered by Rogers and the material I gathered from top professionals in the field.

"My general goals in writing are to weave the human story of music with a cultural and social perspective, and to keep the music scene of today alive for posterity. I'm fascinated by greatness, its qualities, components, effect, value, meaning, and price."

* * *

ERICKSON, Stephen A(nthony) 1940-

PERSONAL: Born September 1, 1940, in Fairmont, Minn.; son of Chris L. (a lawyer) and Venus (Walters) Erickson; married Martha Wiggert, June 9, 1961 (divorced, September, 1971); married Edith Roloff Howe (a professor), June 28, 1975; children: (first marriage) Christopher Lon, Ericka Liv. *Education:* St. Olaf College, B.A. (summa cum laude), 1961; Yale University, M.A., 1963, Ph.D., 1964. *Home:* 640 Occidental Dr., Claremont, Calif. 91711. *Office:* Department of Philosophy, Pomona College, Claremont, Calif. 91711.

CAREER: Claremont Colleges, Pomona College, Claremont, Calif., instructor, 1964-66, assistant professor, 1966-68, Wig Distinguished Assistant Professor, 1968, associate professor, 1968-73, professor of philosophy and religion, 1973—, head of department of philosophy, 1971-74, Claremont Graduate School, instructor, 1964-66, assistant professor, 1966-68, associate professor, 1968-73, professor, 1973—. Visiting lecturer at Max Planck Institut fuer Verhaltensphysiologie, 1970.

MEMBER: Society for Phenomenology and Existential Philosophy, Metaphysical Society of America, Phi Beta Kappa. *Awards, honors:* Fellowship from Student Project for Amity Among Nations, 1960, for travel in Poland and the Soviet Union; Danforth fellow, 1961-64; Woodrow Wilson fellowship, 1961-62; National Endowment for the Humanities grant, 1968; Wenner-Gren Foundation grant, 1969; Graves Award from American Council of Learned Societies, 1969.

WRITINGS: (Contributor) James Edie, editor, *New Essays in Phenomenology: Studies in the Philosophy of Experience*, Quadrangle, 1969; *Language and Being: An Analytic Phenomenology*, Yale University Press, 1970. Contributor to *Philosophical Aspects of Thanatology*, 1976. Contributor to *World Book Encyclopedia*. Contributor of about fifty articles and reviews to philosophy journals.

WORK IN PROGRESS: Human Presence: At the Boundaries of Meaning.

SIDELIGHTS: Erickson writes: "I am concerned with the intersection of psychiatry and religion in their attempt to understand human nature."

* * *

ERLANGER, Ellen (Louise) 1950-

PERSONAL: Born November 14, 1950, in Canton, Ohio; daughter of Robert H. (a retailer) and Rose (a volunteer worker; maiden name, Marx) Erlanger. *Education:* University of Michigan, B.A. (highest honors), 1972, M.A. (highest honors), 1976; further graduate study at Ohio State University, Indiana University, and University of Akron. *Home:* 4547 Kenny Rd., #D, Columbus, Ohio 43220. *Office:* Jones Junior High School, 2100 Arlington Ave., Columbus, Ohio 43221.

CAREER: High school history teacher in Ann Arbor, Mich., 1972, and Canton, Ohio, 1972-75; director of education at synagogue in Canton, 1976-77; Jones Junior High School, Columbus, Ohio, history teacher and head of social studies department, 1977—. Also worked as camp director. Member of Columbus Center of Science and Industry; member of advisory board of Canton Cultural Center. *Member:* National Council for the Social Studies, National Education Association, National Association of Temple Educators, Social Studies Supervisors Association, Association for Supervision and Curriculum Development, Society for Nutrition Education, Ohio Tennis Coaches Association, Ohio Council for the Social Studies, Phi Beta Kappa, Alpha Epsilon Phi (past vice-president).

WRITINGS: Senator Hubert Humphrey: The Happy Warrior (juvenile), Lerner, 1979; *America Is* (juvenile), C. E. Merrill, 1979. Contributor to education, juvenile, and general interest magazines, including *Seventeen* and *Senior Scholastic.*

WORK IN PROGRESS: A collection of essays; short stories; light verse on jogging; research on anorexia nervosa; further juvenile biography works, including possible weekly newspaper column in this field.

SIDELIGHTS: Ellen Erlanger comments: "I have enjoyed writing since my adolescent years, but began taking freelancing quite seriously about a year ago. When I began teaching junior high school American history, I recognized a need for more lively resource books about prominent Americans. As the career of Senator Humphrey drew to a close, I was inspired to make this leader my first subject in the field of juvenile biography. My success in completing and marketing my first book has given me great encouragement and satisfaction. Now I can feel a whole array of ideas clicking, and I'm determined to give them a whirl. My typewriter tags along now wherever I go.

"In coming summers I plan to visit China and travel to new (for me, at least) areas of the United States. It's important to me to keep widening my exposures and experiences. Physical well-being is a major concern as well as intellectual expansion, so I also take an interest in new, well-validated findings in the field of nutrition and health.

"Why do I write? Because I feel that thoughtful, creative communication shows the beauty of human capability—and because it's fun! I also have a deep interest in dispelling myths when I can, and in applying touches of humor and 'the critical eye' to my work. Soon I hope to expand my writing efforts into educational television and film as well as print media."

AVOCATIONAL INTERESTS: Reading, tennis, golf, jogging, water sports, politics, art, music, film, theater, astronomy.

*   *   *

ERNST, Eldon G(ilbert) 1939-

PERSONAL: Born January 27, 1939, in Seattle, Wash.; son of Kenneth G. (a teacher) and Bydell (a teacher; maiden name, Painter) Ernst; married Joy Skogland (in toy-recycling business), June 12, 1959; children: Michael, David,

Peter, Samuel. *Education:* Linfield College, B.A., 1961; Colgate Rochester Divinity School, B.D., 1964; Yale University, M.A., 1965, Ph.D., 1968. *Politics:* Democrat. *Religion:* Christian. *Home:* 1855 San Antonio Ave., Berkeley, Calif. 94707. *Office:* 2515 Hillegass Ave., Berkeley, Calif. 94704.

CAREER: Ordained American Baptist minister, 1964; pastor of Baptist church in Mt. Carmel, Conn., 1965-66; American Baptist Seminary of the West, Berkeley, Calif., instructor, 1967-68, assistant professor, 1968-69, associate professor, 1969-73, professor of American religious history, 1973—; Graduate Theological Union, Berkeley, associate professor, 1969-73, professor of American religious history, 1973—. *Member:* American Academy of Religion, American Society of Church History, American Baptist Historical Society (vice-president), American Association of University Professors.

WRITINGS: Moment of Truth for Protestant America: Interchurch Campaigns Following World War I, Scholars' Press, 1974; *The American Bicentennial and the Church,* Glide Urban Center Publications, 1975; *Without Help or Hindrance: Religious Identity in American Culture,* Westminster, 1977; (contributor) J. Needham and G. Baker, editors, *Understanding the New Religions,* Seabury, 1978. Contributor of articles and reviews to theology and history journals. Editor of *Foundations,* 1975-77.

WORK IN PROGRESS: Religion in America During the Progressive Era; research on American religious historiography.

SIDELIGHTS: Ernst writes: "In my writing I try to convey the results of highly specialized studies to non-specialist readers. My particular concern is to broaden people's tolerance of other people's religious experiences and to seek historical understanding of religious persons and groups and their reasons for thinking and acting as they do. American religious freedom and pluralism provide my raw historical data."

AVOCATIONAL INTERESTS: "Born into a family of musicians, I am a pianist with a life-long interest in music. I am also becoming increasingly caught up in Toyground, my wife's creative toy-recycling business. We may write about this experience, which has had national publicity. I have traveled in northern Europe, and plan eventually to see most of the world."

*   *   *

ESSLIN, Martin (Julius) 1918-

PERSONAL: Born June 8, 1918, in Budapest, Hungary; came to Great Britain, 1939; naturalized British citizen, 1947; son of Paul (a journalist) and Charlotte (Schiffer) Pereszlenyi; married Renate Gerstenberg, 1947; children: one daughter. *Education:* Attended University of Vienna, 1936-38; received degree from Reinhardt Seminar of Dramatic Art, Vienna, 1938. *Home:* 64 Loudon Rd., London N.W.8, England; and Ballader's Plat, Winchelsea, Sussex, England. *Agent:* Curtis Brown Ltd., 1 Craven Hill, London W2 3EW, England. *Office:* Department of Drama, Stanford University, Stanford, Calif. 94305.

CAREER: Director and writer on theatre. British Broadcasting Corp. (BBC), London, England, 1940-77, producer and scriptwriter for European services, 1941-55, became assistant head of European productions, 1955, became assistant head of drama (sound), 1961, head of drama (radio), 1963-77; Stanford University, Stanford, Calif., professor of drama,

1977—. Visiting professor of theatre at Florida State University, 1969-76. *Member:* Arts Council of Great Britain (member of drama panel), Garrick Club. *Awards, honors:* Title of Professor by president of Austria, 1967; member of the Order of the British Empire, 1972; D. Litt., Kenyon College, 1978.

WRITINGS: Brecht: A Choice of Evils; A Critical Study of the Man, His Work, and His Opinions, Eyre & Spottiswoode, 1959, published as *Brecht: The Man and His Work,* Doubleday, 1960, revised edition, Norton, 1974; *The Theatre of the Absurd,* Doubleday, 1961, third edition, Overlook Press, 1973; (editor with others) *Sinn oder Unsinn? Das Groteske im Modernen Drama,* Basilius, 1962; (editor) *Samuel Beckett: A Collection of Critical Essays,* Prentice-Hall, 1965; (editor) *Absurd Drama,* Penguin (London), 1965; *Harold Pinter,* Friedrich Verlag, 1967; (editor and author of introduction) *The Genius of the German Theater,* New American Library, 1968; *Bertolt Brecht,* Columbia University Press, 1969; *Reflections: Essays on Modern Theatre,* Doubleday, 1969 (published in England as *Brief Chronicles: Essays on Modern Theatre,* Maurice Temple Smith, 1970).

(Editor) *The New Theatre of Europe,* Volume IV, Dell, 1970; *The Peopled Wound: The Work of Harold Pinter,* Doubleday, 1970, revised edition published as *Pinter: A Study of His Plays,* Methuen, 1973, Norton, 1976; *An Anatomy of Drama,* T. Smith, 1976, Hill & Wang, 1977; *Artaud,* J. Calder, 1976, Penguin, 1977; (editor and author of introduction) *The Encyclopedia of World Theater,* Scribner, 1977 (published in England as *The Illustrated Encyclopaedia of World Theatre,* Thames & Hudson, 1977).

Contributor of essays on theatre and reviews to numerous periodicals. Advisory editor of *Drama Review;* drama editor of *Kenyon Review.*

SIDELIGHTS: Martin Esslin has been a prominent, and sometimes controversial, critic of contemporary theatre. Besides volumes on individual playwrights such as Bertolt Brecht, Antonin Artaud, and Harold Pinter, he has authored and edited numerous other books on theatre, most notably, *The Theatre of the Absurd.*

Esslin's *The Theatre of the Absurd* is considered a major study of the school of avant-garde dramatists who emerged in the late 1950's and early 1960's. Such playwrights as Samuel Beckett, Jean Genet, and Eugene Ionesco had bewildered many critics and audiences who found no recognizable plot, theme, characterization, or any other "typical" elements of drama in their work. Instead, in Esslin's words, viewers saw an expression "of the senselessness of the human condition and the inadequacy of the rational approach by the open abandonment of rational devices and discursive thought." To better comprehend these works, then, a new set of judgments had to be used, those which Esslin sought to define and clarify in his book.

One of Esslin's major theses held that these plays, often dismissed as "nonsense or mystification, *have* something to say and *can* be understood." Essentially, he said, the "theatre of the absurd reflected the absurdity of human life not by argument or theory, but by actually presenting the experience; it strove for "an integration between the subject matter and the form." Esslin cited changing critical response to *Waiting for Godot* as evidence that audiences have come to look past their preconceived notions of what a play should be: While the 1955 premier of Beckett's play met "a wide measure of incomprehension," its 1964 London revival was criticized for having "one great fault: its meaning and symbolism were a little too obvious."

Though Esslin is most widely known for coining the term "the theatre of the absurd," he has expressed concern over misuse of the phrase. In the preface of the book's second edition he wrote: "Indeed, in some respects the book's success . . . has given the author some cause for misgivings. 'The Theatre of the Absurd' has become a catch-phrase in its own right which is often thoughtlessly used." Instead, he emphasized, it is a "working hypothesis, a device to make certain fundamental traits which seem to be present in the works of a number of dramatists accessible to discussion by tracing the features they have in common."

Critics have shared diverse opinions towards Esslin and his other critical works. John Mortimer reacted positively to Esslin's 1970 book on Harold Pinter, *The Peopled Wound:* "[Esslin's] is not only by far the best critical appraisal of Harold Pinter's plays, it contains many pages I read with real excitement for their discoveries about modern dramatic writing." Meanwhile, *Reflections: Essays on Modern Theatre* prompted Marilyn Stasio to say "the man is one of the most important critics of the drama writing today." *Variety,* on the other hand, called the same book an example of "the afterthoughts and second-guesses of minor stage commentators." Another Esslin detractor, Irving Waddle, felt him to be anathema to the critical world: "To the rest of the reviewing fraternity he is a source of fear and exasperation. He knows more than we do; and he is not prepared to do the gentlemanly thing and let us get away with it."

BIOGRAPHICAL/CRITICAL SOURCES: Martin Esslin, *The Theatre of the Absurd,* revised edition, Anchor Books, 1969; *Variety,* August 20, 1969; *Christian Science Monitor,* September 30, 1969; *Cue,* October 25, 1969; *Drama Review,* winter, 1970, spring, 1974; *Guardian Weekly,* July 11, 1970, July 7, 1973; *Times Literary Supplement,* July 23, 1970, July 6, 1973, December 17, 1976; *Plays and Players,* August, 1970; *Listener,* August 20, 1970; *Observer,* August 23, 1970; *New York Times Book Review,* September 13, 1970, July 17, 1977; *Time,* October 12, 1970; *New Statesman,* November 27, 1970, October 22, 1976; *New York Review of Books,* December 17, 1970, June 3, 1971; *Economist,* October 23, 1976; *Books and Bookmen,* January, 1977, March, 1978; *Theatre Crafts,* May, 1978; *World Literature Today,* summer, 1978.

*   *   *

ESTLEMAN, Loren D. 1952-

PERSONAL: Born September 15, 1952, in Ann Arbor, Mich.; son of Leauvett Charles (a trucker) and Louise (a postal clerk; maiden name, Milankovich) Estleman. *Education:* Eastern Michigan University, B.A., 1974. *Residence:* Whitmore Lake, Mich. *Agent:* Ray Puechner, 2625 North 36th St., Milwaukee, Wis. 53210. *Office: Dexter Leader,* 8071 Main St., Dexter, Mich. 48130.

CAREER: Michigan Fed, Ann Arbor, Mich. cartoonist, 1967-70; *Community Foto-News,* Pinckney, Mich., editor-in-chief, 1975-76; *Ann Arbor News,* Ann Arbor, reporter, 1976-77; *Dexter Leader,* Dexter, Mich., staff writer, 1977—. Instructor for Friends of the Dexter Library; speaker at colleges.

WRITINGS—Novels: The Oklahoma Punk, Major Books, 1976; *The Hider,* Doubleday, 1978; *Sherlock Holmes Versus Dracula,* Doubleday, 1978; *Dr. Jekyll and Mr. Holmes,* Doubleday, 1979; *Stamping Ground,* Doubleday, 1979. Contributor to *Alfred Hitchcock's Mystery Magazine.*

WORK IN PROGRESS: "A hard-boiled private eye novel set in contemporary Detroit, research for which has taken me back three hundred years to the beginning of the settlement, and has included walking trips, at the risk of my life, down some of the meanest streets in this raw, violent city.''

SIDELIGHTS: Estleman writes: "The three writers whose works have had the most profound influence on my writing are all dead, which should prove some indication of my opinion of most writers who have since arisen. Edgar Allan Poe, Jack London, and Raymond Chandler have impressed me since childhood with their lyrical, poetical approach to action and adventure. The literature of violence is purely an American development and only the English language, that most elusive, infinitely fascinating of tongues, fulfills all the requirements for its proper expression. The icy deliberation of the murderer in Poe's 'A Cask of Amontillado,' the tortured psyche of the brutal Wolf Larsen in London's *The Sea Wolf,* and the parade of grotesques that march through all of Chandler's best works are products of the American experience beside which the elements of the great fiction of Europe seem tame as a houseplant. That there is a prejudice in literary circles against these three masters is evidence of how far we still have to go to cast off the shackles forged by those potentially great writers who accepted the restrictions of Victorian society during literature's so-called Golden Age. Shakespeare was aware of the importance of violence in human nature, as were Homer and Dostoevski, but today's civilization prefers to forget that it even exists.

"All of this may sound strange coming from the author of *Sherlock Holmes Versus Dracula.* Indeed, one or two reviewers commented upon a rather bloody scene in that book and said that Conan Doyle would have been repelled by it. If they'd taken the trouble to read one or two of the original Holmes adventures, they'd have recognized his debt to Poe and his own 'morbid' fascination with brutality and the grotesque.

"I've never killed anyone off the written page. I am, however, a hunter, and I doubt that I'm being original in saying that people and animals die similarly. I'm a good boxer, a fair wrestler, and with a name like Loren I saw my share of schoolyard fights. Although I hardly appreciated it then, those tussles have come in handy every time I've sat down to write a fight scene. Since we have no memory of pain, though, I've occasionally had to remind myself of certain sensations, which has entailed slugging myself in the jaw while seated at the typewriter. Writing was never more painful than this.''

BIOGRAPHICAL/CRITICAL SOURCES: Ann Arbor Observer, July, 1978; *Time,* July 31, 1978; *Eastern Echo,* September 8, 1978; *Ann Arbor News,* September 24, 1978; *Detroit News,* May 18, 1979.

*   *   *

ETTINGHAUSEN, Richard   1906-1979

OBITUARY NOTICE—See index for *CA* sketch: Born February 5, 1906, in Frankfurt-on-Main, Germany; died of cancer, April 2, 1979, in Princeton, N.J. Museum curator, educator, editor, and author of sixteen books on Islamic art. An authority on Islamic art, Ettinghausen supervised the installation of the Islamic art galleries at the Metropolitan Museum of Art in New York City, where he was consultative chairman of the Islamic Department. He was also head curator of the Department of Near Eastern Art of the Freer Gallery of Art of the Smithsonian Institution from 1961, and was adjunct curator of the Los Angeles County Museum of Art. Ettinghausen co-organized the tour of the exhibition "Art Treasures of Turkey" and helped to establish the permanent

exhibit of Islamic art in the Mayer Memorial Museum of Islamic Art in Jerusalem. His book, *Islamic Art,* is considered a definitive study of the subject. Obituaries and other sources: *Who's Who in American Art,* Bowker, 1978; *Directory of American Scholars,* Volume I: *History,* 7th edition, Bowker, 1978; *The International Who's Who,* Europa, 1978; *Who's Who in America,* 40th edition, Marquis, 1978; *New York Times,* April 3, 1979; *Washington Post,* April 4, 1979.

*   *   *

EVANS, Albert   1917-

PERSONAL: Born December 11, 1917, in New York, N.Y.; son of Jack and Claire (Munchberg) Evans; married Charlotte Goldstein (in accounting); children: Linda Lipitz-Mayer, Marc Lipitz. *Education:* City College of the City University of New York, B.B.A., 1940, additional study, 1946-48; also attended Institute for Advanced Study Theatre Arts, 1962-65. *Home and office:* 3800 Independence Ave., Bronx, N.Y. 10463. *Agent:* Elly Burke, Independent Artists, 200 West 108 St., New York, N.Y.

CAREER: Williams Advertising Agency, New York City, copywriter, 1958-61; Playgirl Hats (wholesaler), New York City, sales representative, 1961-71; Riverdale Showcase, Bronx, N.Y., resident playwright, 1971-75; Lab Theatre, New York City, artistic director, 1975-78; playwright. Dramaturge at Peace Theatre, New York City, 1969-71. Member of Washington Heights Arts Interaction Committee. *Military service:* U.S. Army Air Forces, 1941-45; medic. *Member:* Dramatist Guild, Broadway Drama Guild. *Awards, honors:* Bronx Council of Arts award, 1970, for "The Big Gate," and 1977, for "Visitation"; New York State Council on Arts award, 1971, for "The Big Gate," and 1974, for "Self Destruct"; Boro Park Jewish Community award, 1972, for "I Never Saw Another Butterfly."

WRITINGS—Plays: "I Never Saw Another Butterfly" (one-act), first produced in Brooklyn at Reformed Temple of Israel, 1963; "The Big Gate" (one-act), first produced in New York City at Sheridan Square Playhouse, May 2, 1964; "Ghost Town" (three-act), first produced in Riverdale, N.Y., at Peace Theatre, 1968; "The Medal of Honor Winner" (one-act), first produced in Riverdale at Peace Theatre, 1969; "Antigone Baby" (two-act; adapted from the play by Richard Allen Shur), first produced in Riverdale at Riverdale Showcase, January, 1970; "Self Destruct" (one-act), first produced in New York City at Lab Theatre, 1973; "Visitation," first produced at Lab Theatre, 1975; "The Reconciliation" (three-act), first produced in Washington Heights, N.Y., at Lab Theatre, 1976; "American Iceberg," first produced in New York City at Lab Theatre, 1978. Also author of "Summer Camp" (three-act), first produced in Riverdale at Riverdale Showcase.

WORK IN PROGRESS: The Fractured Man, "a metaphysical novel dealing with a love relationship if the same event were to happen at different times in the lives of each party"; "Summer Camp," a three-act play about "the holocaust in metaphoric terms."

SIDELIGHTS: As each person is ushered into the theatre he or she is handed a fight program and a scorecard. The customary boxing match refreshments are being peddled while an announcer asks the audience to rise, face the flag, and sing the national anthem. Before they know it, the spectators are swept into Evans's play, "The Big Gate." "The Big Gate" is actually a reference to declining middleweight boxing champion Matt Davidson's last fight: should he go through with it or not? He is not physically fit enough to triumph in the boxing ring, but decides to face his contender nonetheless. "The action is so fast moving, so engaging, so brilliantly articulated that it isn't until the final moment of this American folk tale that we become fully conscious of its tragic impact," Dick Brukenfeld observed. A critic for *Show Business* called "The Big Gate" a "technical knockout," but commented that "it was a bit unfortunate that the least involving and least new aspect of the production was the script. In fact it seems to be a live recreation of any fight movie."

Evans told *CA* that his primary motivation in becoming a writer was "to create a body of work that would perhaps shed a new light on the human condition and to sound the alarm to the individual dangers that surround all who are born human. I was turned on to the stage as my major effort after having read in one week, *Strange Interlude* by O'Neill, *Waiting for Lefty* by Odets, and *The Male Animal* by Nugent-Thurber. I was also profoundly moved by Elmer Rice's *Street Scene.*

"I was motivated to write the novel, *The Fractured Man,* when my wife and I were faced with a personal problem and I wondered how we would handle it if not only were our ages reversed (I becoming younger than she), but if it had occurred during a different time span of our lives; say if she were thirty-five instead of forty-five, and I was twenty-five instead of fifty.

"I started writing the drama, "Summer Camp," when I came to the conclusion that the story and horror of the death camps needed to be told over and over to each succeeding generation, but realized that a realistic telling of it would only have a deadening effect, and might even trivialize the brutality itself. And so I chose the metaphorical method being employed in the script."

BIOGRAPHICAL/CRITICAL SOURCES: Village Voice, July 3, 1969; *Show Business,* July 5, 1969, January 31, 1970.

*   *   *

EVANS, Glen 1921-
(Glenn Eirelin)

PERSONAL: Born April 29, 1921, in Dallas, Tex.; son of P. F. and Elga (Hacker) Evans; married Margaret Wanex (a sales and service manager), January 15, 1961; children: Lisa Glyn. *Education:* Attended Carson-Newman College, 1943-44; University of Missouri, B.J., 1949. *Politics:* Independent Liberal. *Home and office:* 7 Mead Ave., Cos Cob, Conn. 06807. *Agent:* Connie Clausen Associates, 250 East 87th St., New York, N.Y. 10028.

CAREER: Maytag Co., Newton, Iowa, editor of *Maytag News,* 1949-54; Maytag Southeastern Co., Atlanta, Ga., advertising and sales promotion manager, 1954-60; free-lance writer, 1960—. *Military service:* U.S. Navy, 1940-46; served in Europe, Asia, and the Philippines; became chief yeoman. *Member:* American Society of Journalists and Authors, National Press Club. *Awards, honors:* Scholarship from Sigma Delta Chi, 1949; magazine editing awards from Iowa Industrial Editors, 1951, and International Council of Industrial Editors, both 1951, both for *Maytag News.*

WRITINGS: Family Circle Guide to Self-Help, Ballantine, 1979.

Work represented in anthologies, including *Milestones to Excellence,* edited by Ira E. Aaron and others, Scott, Foresman, 1975. Contributor to popular magazines (sometimes under pseudonym Glenn Eirelin), including *True, Parade, Boy's Life, Easy Living,* and *Catholic Digest.*

WORK IN PROGRESS: Hair Transplantation: Winning the Battle Against Baldness, with L. Lee Bosley.

SIDELIGHTS: Evans writes: "If you would be a writer, especially a free-lance writer, success for you can be summed up in three words—work, work, and work! Learn to listen for a few years, then listen to learn. Listen to all the conversations of our world between nations, between interest groups, and between individuals. They are, of course, the stuff about which you will write. My most valuable allies as a writer have been Niebuhr's 'Serenity Prayer'—and a working wife."

*   *   *

EVANS, J. Martin 1935-

PERSONAL: Born February 2, 1935, in Cardiff, Wales; son of Evan A. E. (an architect), and Edith (Loveluck) Evans; married Mariella Lafranchi, August 5, 1963; children: Jessica Rachel, Joanna Rebecca. *Education:* Jesus College, Oxford, B.A., 1958; Merton College, Oxford, M.A. and D.Phil., both 1963. *Office:* Department of English, Stanford University, Stanford, Calif. 94305.

CAREER: Stanford University, Stanford, Calif., assistant professor, 1963-68, associate professor, 1968-75, professor of English, 1975—, associate dean of humanities and sciences, 1977—. *Military service:* Royal Air Force, 1953-55; became pilot officer.

WRITINGS: Paradise Lost and the Genesis Tradition, Oxford University Press, 1968; *Paradise Lost,* Volumes IX-X, Cambridge University Press, 1973; *America: The View From Europe,* Stanford University Press, 1976. Also author of a monograph, *The Road From Horton: Looking Backwards in "Lycidas,"* 1979.

WORK IN PROGRESS: Knowledge and Virtue: A History of the Analysis and Representation of Moral Choice.

SIDELIGHTS: Evans writes: "I am chiefly interested in the history of ideas in both the philosophy and the literature of the Middle Ages and the Renaissance. As an immigrant to the United States, I have also developed an interest, reflected in my third book, in the history of European ideas about the New World. I have taught at the Stanford overseas campuses in the United Kingdom and Italy."

*   *   *

EVANS, John Lewis 1930-

PERSONAL: Born May 6, 1930, in Villanova, Pa.; son of Rowland and Elizabeth (Wharton) Evans; married Banning Grange, March 21, 1958; children: Banning, Catharine, Annabelle, John, Atlee, Anne. *Education:* Yale University, B.A., 1955; Georgetown University, M.A., 1966; University of North Carolina, Ph.D., 1968. *Religion:* Episcopalian. *Home:* 1530 Via Tuscany, Winter Park, Fla. 32789. *Office:* Department of History, Florida Technological University, Orlando, Fla. 32816.

CAREER: Teacher at private school in Washington, D.C., 1961-65; Stetson University, DeLand, Fla., assistant professor of history, 1967-72; Florida Technological University, Orlando, assistant professor of history, 1972—. *Military service:* U.S. Army, 1951-53. *Member:* American Historical Association.

WRITINGS: The Communist International, 1919-1943, Pageant-Poseidon, 1973; *The Petrashevskij Circle, 1845-1849,* Mouton, 1974.

WORK IN PROGRESS: Continuing research on Russian history.

SIDELIGHTS: Evans comments: "I have visited the U.S.S.R. ten times since 1960. On six of these occasions I have led tours there."

*   *   *

EVANS, Joseph 1909(?)-1978

PERSONAL: Born in 1909(?); died September 12, 1978. *Education:* Received degree from Yale University, 1931.

CAREER/WRITINGS: New York Herald-Tribune, New York City, worked as reporter and editor during 1930's; *Newsweek,* New York City, member of European staff during 1940's; spokesman for Marshall Plan in London during 1940's and early 1950's; director of information and cultural affairs activities for U.S. Embassy in London; inspector general of United States Information Agency (USIA), 1958-62; director of public affairs for United States civil administration of Ryukyu Islands until retirement in 1971. Notable assignments include coverage of battle of Britain. *Awards, honors:* Medal of Freedom, 1945; Outstanding Civilian Service Medal from U.S. Army.

OBITUARIES: Washington Post, October 6, 1978.*

*   *   *

EVELY, Louis 1910-

PERSONAL: Born November 5, 1910, in Brussels, Belgium; son of Fernand (a physician) and Emilie Evely; married Marie Vandermeersch (an artist), December 4, 1971. *Education:* College Sainte Marie, Brussels, Belgium, diploma in humanities, 1924; University of Louvain, Louvain, Belgium, doctor of law, 1932, doctor of Thomistic philosophy, 1933. *Home:* Piegros La Clastre, 26400 Crest, France.

CAREER: Ordained Roman Catholic priest, 1937; priest in diocese of Malines, 1937-68; writer. *Wartime service:* Chaplain in Belgian Army, 1938-39.

WRITINGS: Notre Pere, aux sources de notre fraternite, Fleurus, 1956, translation by James Langdale published as *We Dare to Say Our Father,* Herder, 1965; *L'Eglise et les sacrements,* Editions de pensee catholique, 1956, translation by Imelda L'Italien published as *Love Your Neighbor,* Herder, 1969, translation by Salvator Attanasio published as *The Church and the Sacraments,* Dimension Books, 1971; *C'est toi, cet homme,* introduction by Yves Congar, Editions universitaires, 1957, translation by Edmond Bonin published as *That Man Is You,* Newman Press, 1964; *Souffrance,* [France], 1957, translation by Marie-Claude Thompson published as *Suffering,* Herder, 1967; *Une religion pour notre temps,* [France], 1964, translation by B. Thompson and M.-C. Thompson published as *A Religion for Our Time,* Herder, 1968; *Fraternite et evangile,* [France], 1963, translation by Sister Mary Agnes published as *We Are All Brothers,* Image Books, 1967; *Spiritualite des laics* [France], 1964, translation by B. Thompson and M.-C. Thompson published as *In the Christian Spirit,* Herder, 1969; *Credo: causeries de l'abbe Louis Evely aux fraternites seculieres Charles de Foucald,* [France], 1966, translation by Rosemary Sheed published as *Credo,* Fides (Notre Dame, Ind.), 1967; *Teach Us How to Pray,* translation of *Apprennez-nous a prier* and *Sur la priere,* by Edmond Bonin, Newman Press, 1967, new edition, 1974; *Dieu et le prochain* (title means "In His Presence"), Diffedit, 1967; *Eduquer en s'eduquant,* [France], 1967, translation by Bonin published as *Training Children for Maturity* (also contains essays), Newman Press, 1967; *Dieu et le prochain,* Diffedit, 1967, translation by J. F. Stevenson published as *In His Presence,* Image Books, 1970;

Amour et mariage, [France], 1967, translation by John Drury published as *Lovers in Marriage,* Herder, 1968; (contributor) Donald Brophy, compiler, *Does God Punish?,* Paulist Press, 1968; *La Priere d'un homme moderne,* Seuil, 1969, translation by Paul Burns published as *Our Prayer,* Image Books, 1969; *The Faith of a Modern Man,* Dimension Books, 1969.

L'Evangile sans mythes, Editions universitaires, 1970, translation by J. F. Bernard published as *The Gospels Without Myth,* Doubleday, 1971; *Si l'Eglise ne meurt,* Editions universitaires, 1971, translation by Bernard published as *If the Church Is to Survive . . . ,* Doubleday, 1972; *Meditations d'Evangiles (St. Matthieu, St. Marc, St. Luc) suivant le nouveau cycle liturgique,* Editions universitaires, 1973, translation by Bernard published as *Rejoice! Gospel Meditations,* Doubleday, 1974; *Questions de vie et de mort,* [France], 1979, translation published as *Facing Death,* Seabury Press, 1979.

SIDELIGHTS: French priest Louis Evely's writings, most of which have been translated into English, are considered classics in the field of religion. He "has influenced many Catholic seminarians in a day when few spiritual writers reach them," wrote a reviewer in *Christian Century.* Although Evely's religious view is traditional, critics said he is singular in that his books are clearly and warmly written.

Evely's first book, a collection of daily meditations entitled *We Dare To Say Our Father,* was especially popular in Europe. A *Critic* reviewer noted that with this book he "does the Christian community a real service," in his "sharp way of contrasting habitual acceptance of religious doctrine and practices with what would actually be the case were their full implication realized."

In another book, *Lovers in Marriage,* Evely writes of "the much deeper relationship of love and faith between men and women that precedes sexual harmony, and he writes with such persuasive enthusiasm about the limitless possibilities of growth in marriage that he seems capable of inspiring even the most jaded of couples to make a fresh start," Myrtle Passantino wrote in *America.* She added that the book deserves to be "read and reread." But a reviewer in *Critic* commented that the last chapter, on procreation and birth control, was already out of date by the time the English edition was published.

The Gospels Without Myth, written for "the marginal Catholic layman who is so fed up with 'the stubborn resistance of the Church to the truth,'" J. P. Crossley noted in *Christian Century,* "is living proof that one can be harshly critical of traditional Catholic doctrine and practice yet be a buoyant man of faith." To S. E. Smith, who reviewed the book in *America,* it is "frankly an embarrassment." The reviewer reasoned, "No responsible exegete today approaches the mythology of the New Testament with the simplistic fundamentalism and anti-intellectualism which characterizes Evely's angry book."

"Evely is shooting at the bishop again," observed *Commonweal* reviewer Elliott Wright, referring to *If the Church Is to Survive. . . .* "He uses good ammunition (the 'people of God' vs. church imperialism); aims carefully (the hierarchy is responsible for a crisis in Catholic confidence), and fires with resolve (a united church, led by Christ, must serve the world)." H. A. Kennedy commented that "Catholic readers will find the book stimulating" and "will be challenged to reassess many a long-held conviction."

Evely told *CA* that, having written just for himself for a long while, he was finally encouraged by friends to publish his first two books. He had believed that no one else would be interested in his thoughts, and was amazed to find that his books were being widely read. "Others had taken the same route as I, where I had thought myself alone," Evely wrote. He noted that he is now one of the eighteen most translated French authors, "after Camus and Teilhard, and before Maurois."

BIOGRAPHICAL/CRITICAL SOURCES: America, November 28, 1964, March 6, 1965, February 11, 1967, February 18, 1967, March 1, 1969, June 12, 1971; *Critic,* April, 1965, April, 1967, April, 1969; *Times Literary Supplement,* July 29, 1965; *Christian Century,* January 18, 1967, December 22, 1971; *Commonweal,* May 28, 1971, May 25, 1973; *Best Sellers,* December 1, 1972.

F

FALK, Louis A. 1896(?)-1979

OBITUARY NOTICE: Born c. 1896; died March 10, 1979, in Paramus, N.J. Businessman. In the 1930's, Falk joined the efforts of Jewish war veterans to call attention to the growth of the Nazis. He was long active in Jewish affairs and had been a vice-president of the Zionist Organization of America, as well as a founder of the American Jewish League for Israel. Falk was editor-in-chief of *The Jewish Veteran,* a monthly publication, and the co-author of the book *Jews in American Wars.* Obituaries and other sources: *New York Times,* March 12, 1979.

* * *

FARNHAM, Marynia F. 1900(?)-1979

OBITUARY NOTICE: Born c. 1900 in Red Wing, Minn.; died May 29, 1979, in Brattleboro, Vt. Psychiatrist and author. Farnham was in general psychiatric practice at New York State Psychiatric Institute and at Presbyterian Hospital, specializing in the treatment of children and adolescents. She was also an assistant professor of psychiatry at the College of Physicians and Surgeons. In 1947, she created a stir with her book *Modern Woman: The Lost Sex,* which held that women who abandoned their traditional roles as wives and mothers made themselves and society unhappy. Farnham also wrote *The Adolescent* and contributed many articles to various magazines and journals. Obituaries and other sources: *New York Times,* May 30, 1979.

* * *

FAULKNER, (Herbert Winthrop) Waldron 1898-1979

OBITUARY NOTICE: Born January 21, 1898, in Paris, France; died May 11, 1979, in Washington, D.C. Architect. Faulkner worked for several years as an architect in New York City before establishing his Washington, D.C., firm of Faulkner, Stenhouse, Fryer & Faulkner. His architectural works include the headquarters of the Brookings Institution, the museums of the National Collection of Fine Arts and the National Portrait Gallery, and George Washington University. He wrote several books on the use of color in architecture, including *Architecture and Color.* Obituaries and other sources: *Washington Post,* May 14, 1979.

FAUROT, Ruth Marie 1916-

PERSONAL: Born March 28, 1916, in Amsterdam, Mo.; daughter of Ira N. (a clergyman) and Grace (Hiatt) Faurot. *Education:* Park College, A.B., 1938; University of Kansas, M.A., 1940; University of North Carolina, Ph.D., 1953. *Office:* Department of English, Elbert Covell College, University of the Pacific, Stockton, Calif. 95204.

CAREER: Scottsbluff Junior College, Scottsbluff, Neb., instructor in English, 1940-46; Inter-American University of Puerto Rico, San Juan, instructor, 1946-52, associate professor, 1952-56, professor, 1956-62; University of the Pacific, Stockton, Calif., professor of English and English as a second language, 1962—. *Member:* Modern Language Association of America, Teachers of English to Speakers of Other Languages, Phi Kappa Phi.

WRITINGS: Jerome K. Jerome, Twayne, 1974. Contributor to language and literature journals.

WORK IN PROGRESS: Research on new humorists, W. W. Jacobs, and Dickens and semantics; an anthology of the new humorists.

* * *

FAUTSKO, Timothy F(rank) 1945-
(Employee X)

PERSONAL: Born December 27, 1945, in Canton, Ohio; son of Frank F. (a territory sales manager) and Helen E. (a personnel assistant; maiden name, Gozdan) Fautsko; married Carol Jean Kraig, November 9, 1974; children: Timothy Matthew, David Franklin. *Education:* Walsh College, Canton, Ohio, B.A., 1967; University of Colorado, M.H.S., 1972. *Politics:* Democrat. *Religion:* Roman Catholic. *Home address:* Flagstaff Mountain, Kossler Rd., Boulder, Colo. 80302. *Office:* Training/Systems Design, Inc., P.O. Box 2024, Boulder, Colo. 80306.

CAREER: University of Colorado, Boulder, field instructor in social sciences, 1967-72; National Information Center on Volunteerism, Boulder, Colo., director of training, 1972-76; State of Colorado, Boulder, court administrator, 1976—. Part-time instructor at University of Colorado. Consultant to Law Enforcement Assistance Administration and National Center on Voluntary Action. *Member:* American Society for Training and Development, Association of Trial Court Administrators.

WRITINGS: *Volunteers in Prevention/Diversion Programs,* U.S. Department of Health, Education & Welfare, 1973; *QUID: How You Can Make the Best Decisions of Your Life,* Walker & Co., 1978; (with James D. Jorgensen) *Solving Problems in Meetings,* Nelson-Hall, 1980. Contributor of more than thirty articles to professional journals and to *New Woman* and *Alternative.*

WORK IN PROGRESS: *How to Survive From 9:00 to 5:00,* with Jorgensen, under pseudonym Employee X; *Planning for the Death of Your Life,* with Jorgensen, completion expected in 1980; *Affadavit,* with Jorgensen, completion expected in 1981.

SIDELIGHTS: Fautsko told *CA:* "As a professional in human services, I have trained more than ten thousand people in forty states, and have developed and copywritten many training techniques that are used nationally by professional trainers. My books are an extension of this work; they not only instruct the reader, but give him/her 'life survivor skills' as well."

* * *

FEININGER, Andreas (Bernhard Lyonel) 1906-

PERSONAL: Born December 27, 1906, in Paris, France; son of Lyonel (a painter) and Julia (Lilienfeld) Feininger; married (Gertrud) Wysse Haegg, August 30, 1933; children: Tomas. *Education:* Bauhaus, Weimar, Germany, earned degree, 1925; Staatliche Bauschule, Weimar and Dessau, Germany, earned degree, 1928. *Home:* 18 Elizabeth Lane, New Milford, Conn. 06776.

CAREER: Kurt Elster, Dessau, Germany, architect, 1929; Karstadt, Hamburg, Germany, architect, 1930-31; Le Corbusier, Paris, France, architect, 1932-33; professional photographer specializing in architectural and industrial photography, Stockholm, Sweden, 1933-39; free-lance photographer in New York City, 1940-43; Time, Inc., New York City, staff photographer for *Life* magazine, 1943-62. One-man exhibition of photographs held at Smithsonian Institution, 1963, and at International Center of Photography, 1976. *Member:* American Society of Photographers in Publication (ASMP). *Awards, honors:* Robert Levitt Award from American Society of Magazine Photographers (now American Society of Photographers in Publication), 1966.

WRITINGS: *New Paths in Photography,* American Photographic Book Publishing, 1939; (photographer) John Erskine and Jacqueline Judge, *New York,* Ziff-Davis, 1945; *Feininger on Photography,* Ziff-Davis, 1949; *Advanced Photography,* Prentice-Hall, 1952; (photographer) Susan E. Lyman, *The Face of New York,* Crown, 1954; *Successful Photography,* Prentice-Hall, 1954, revised edition, 1975; *Successful Color Photography,* Prentice-Hall, 1954; *The Creative Photographer,* Prentice-Hall, 1955, revised edition, 1975; (photographer) Patricia Dyett, *Changing America,* Crown, 1955; *The Anatomy of Nature,* Crown, 1956.

Man and Stone, Crown, 1961; (photographer) Henry Miller and J. Bon, *Maids, Madonnas, and Witches,* Abrams, 1961; *Total Picture Control,* Crown, 1961; *The World Through My Eyes,* Crown, 1963; (photographer) Kate Simon, *New York,* Viking, 1964; *The Complete Photographer,* Prentice-Hall, 1965, revised edition, 1978; (photographer) T. Lux Feininger, *Lyonel Feininger: City at the Edge of the World,* Praeger, 1965; *Forms of Nature and Life,* Viking, 1966; *Trees,* Viking, 1968; *The Color Photo Book,* Prentice-Hall, 1969.

Basic Color Photography, American Photographic Book Publishing, 1972; W. Emerson, *Shells,* Viking, 1972; *Photographic Seeing,* Prentice-Hall, 1973; *Principles of Composition in Photography,* American Photographic Book Publishing, 1973; *Darkroom Techniques,* American Photographic Book Publishing, 1974; *The Perfect Photograph,* American Photographic Book Publishing, 1974; *Roots of Art,* Viking, 1975; *Light and Lighting in Photography,* American Photographic Book Publishing, 1976; *The Mountains of the Mind,* Viking, 1977; *New York in the Forties,* Dover, 1978; *Experimental Work,* American Photographic Book Publishing, 1978.

SIDELIGHTS: Feininger writes that he has traveled extensively in the United States and Europe, and speaks English, German, and Swedish fluently.

BIOGRAPHICAL/CRITICAL SOURCES: Peter Pollack, *The Picture History of Photography,* Abrams, 1969; Liliane De Cock, editor, *Andreas Feininger* (monograph), Morgan & Morgan, 1973; *Andreas Feininger: Experimental Work,* Amphoto, 1978.

* * *

FERGUSON, Rowena 1904-

PERSONAL: Born December 24, 1904, in Little Rock, Ark.; daughter of William Benson and Mary (Proudfoot) Ferguson. *Education:* Randolph-Macon Woman's College, A.B., 1925; graduate study at Vanderbilt University and Columbia University. *Home:* 3525 West End Ave., Nashville, Tenn. 37205.

CAREER: Methodist Publishing House, Nashville, Tenn., editor, 1930—, director of department of youth publications, 1958-71. Delegate to religious conferences in Norway, India, England, and Canada. Member of White House Conference on Children and Youth, 1960. Member of Tennessee Council on Human Relations. *Member:* Women's National Book Association (local president, 1956-57), Phi Beta Kappa. *Awards, honors:* D.D. from Iowa Wesleyan College, 1967.

WRITINGS: *Youth and the Christian Community,* Abingdon, 1954; *Hunger and Hope,* Friendship, 1955; *Editing the Small Magazine,* Columbia University Press, 1958, 2nd edition, 1976; *Everywhere: A Look at the World-Wide Church,* Friendship, 1959; *The Church's Ministry With Senior Highs: A Guide for Adult Workers,* Graded Press, 1963; *My Life: What Will I Make of It?,* Rand McNally, 1966. Also author of *Teenagers: Their Days and Ways,* 1950.

* * *

FERNANDEZ, Benedict J. (III) 1936-

PERSONAL: Born April 5, 1936, in New York, N.Y.; son of Benedict J. and Palma (Perella) Fernandez; married Siiri Aarismaa (a fashion designer), October 27, 1957; children: Benedict J. IV, Tiina. *Education:* Attended Columbia University, 1954-56; private studies in photography. *Residence:* North Bergen, N.J. *Office:* Department of Photography, New School for Social Research, 66 West 12th St., New York, N.Y. 10011.

CAREER: Parsons School of Design, New York City, instructor in photography, 1965-70; New School for Social Research, New York City, staff member in department of photography, 1970—, head of department. Resident photographer for Joseph Papp's Public Theater, 1966-72. Instructor at Rutgers University, 1973-74. Member of steering committee of Alexy Brodovich's Design Laboratory, 1968—; member of New York State Council on the Arts, 1970-73, and Massachusetts Council on the Arts, 1975—. Work represented in about fifteen group and solo exhibitions throughout the United States and in Puerto Rico, and in permanent collections, including Boston Museum of Fine Arts, Smithsonian Institution, and Museum of the City of New York. *Awards, honors:* Guggenheim fellowship, 1970-71; National Endowment for the Arts fellowship, 1973.

WRITINGS: In Opposition: The Right to Dissent, Da Capo Press, 1968; *Four Generations,* Museum of the City of New York, 1977. Contributor to *Avant-Garde, Culture Hero, Civil Libertarian,* and *Folio.*

WORK IN PROGRESS: Photographic projects on Ellis Island, Hoboken, N.J., Puerto Rico, Speaker's Corner in England, and on "mental poverty."

SIDELIGHTS: Fernandez writes: "After photographing 'Protest,' I began 'Mental Poverty.' The antidote to mental poverty is an affluent mind. My quest is to fulfill whatever my fertile imagination can develop."

*   *   *

FERRANTE, Joan M(arguerite Aida) 1936-

PERSONAL: Born November 11, 1936, in Jersey City, N.J.; daughter of Nicholas H. (a pharmacist and social worker) and Josephine (an administrator; maiden name, Pisacane) Ferrante. *Education:* Attended Radcliffe College, 1954-55; Barnard College, B.A. (magna cum laude), 1958; Columbia University, M.A., 1959, Ph.D., 1963. *Residence:* New York, N.Y. *Office:* Department of English and Comparative Literature, Columbia University, New York, N.Y. 10027.

CAREER: Hunter College of the City University of New York, New York City, lecturer in English, 1961; Barnard College, New York City, lecturer in English and Italian, 1962-63; Columbia University, New York City, instructor, 1963-66, assistant professor, 1966-70, associate professor, 1970-74, professor of comparative literature, 1974—, director of Casa Italiana, 1977—. Visiting lecturer at Swarthmore College, 1968, and Fordham University, 1976. Organizes and participates in professional conferences.

MEMBER: International Arthurian Society, Modern Language Association of America, Mediaeval Academy of America (member of council, 1977-80), Dante Society of America (member of council, 1977-80; vice-president, 1978-79), Renaissance Society of America, Phi Beta Kappa. *Awards, honors:* Woodrow Wilson fellowship, 1958; summer grant from Council for Research in the Humanities, 1965; American Council of Learned Societies fellowship, 1969.

WRITINGS: The Conflict of Love and Honor: The Medieval Tristan Legend in France, Germany, and Italy, Mouton, 1973; (translator and author of commentary) *Guillaume d'Orange: Four Epics,* Columbia University Press, 1974; (editor with George D. Economov, and contributor) *In Pursuit of Perfection: Courtly Love in Medieval Literature,* Kennikat, 1975; *Woman as Image in Medieval Literature: From the Twelfth Century to Dante,* Columbia University Press, 1975; (translator and author of commentary, with Robert Hanning) *The Lais of Marie de France,* Dutton, 1978; (contributor) W.T.H. Jackson, editor, *The Interpretation of the Medieval Lyric,* Macmillan, 1979.

Contributor of about thirty-five articles and reviews to literature journals. Member of advisory board of *Speculum,* 1975-78; member of editorial advisory board of Columbia University Press, 1971-73, consulting editor, 1975—.

WORK IN PROGRESS: The Political Vision of the Divine Comedy; "Learned Women of the Middle Ages: Fact and Fancy," to be included in *Reyond Their Sex,* edited by Patricia Labalme.

AVOCATIONAL INTERESTS: Travel (Europe and Latin America), chamber music (plays piano and viola), architecture (Romanesque, classical ruins, Indian pyramids), cooking.

*   *   *

FIFE, Dale (Odile) 1910-

PERSONAL: Born August 24, 1910, in Toledo, Ohio; daughter of Herman and Mary (Ehret) Hollerbach; married Frank Fife, June 10, 1929 (deceased); children: Duncan. *Education:* Attended San Francisco State University. *Religion:* Catholic. *Home:* 764 Edgewood Rd., San Mateo, Calif. 94402. *Agent:* Curtis Brown, 575 Madison Ave., New York, N.Y. 10022.

CAREER: Author of children's books. Also worked as registrar for a military academy, secretary, columnist, and as editor of San Mateo (Calif.) Chamber of Commerce *Bulletin.*

WRITINGS—All juvenile, except as noted; all published by Coward, except as noted: *Weddings in the Family* (adult fiction), Farrar, Straus, 1956; *The Unmarried Sister* (adult fiction), Farrar, Straus, 1958; *A Stork for the Belltower,* 1964; *Who's in Charge of Lincoln?,* 1965; *The Fish in the Castle,* 1965; *Cross A Narrow Bridge,* 1966; *A Dog Called Dunkel,* 1966; *The Boy Who Lived in the Railroad Depot,* 1968; *Joe and the Talking Thristmas Tree,* 1968; *Bluefoot,* Lothrop, Lee & Shepord, 1967; *What's New, Lincoln?,* 1970; *ABC,* 1971; *What's the Prize, Lincoln?,* 1971; *Ride the Crooked Wind,* 1972; *Who Goes There, Lincoln?,* 1973; *The Little Park,* Whitman, 1973; *Imagine That?,* Ginn & Co., 1974; *Who'll Vote for Lincoln?,* 1976; *North of Danger,* Dutton, 1978. Contributor to periodicals.

SIDELIGHTS: Dale Fife commented that she always does research in the area that she's writing about. Her latest book, *North of Danger,* took her to Norway and to Spitsbergen, a group of islands north of Norway in the Arctic Ocean. She also told *CA* that she has traveled extensively in Alsace, France, Germany, other areas of Europe, South America, and Mexico for research for her books.

Fife also draws upon her experiences at various Paiute reservations in Nevada. There she observed Indian students in reservation classrooms and visited the boarding school where fifty Indian tribes were represented. Her research on Indians for the book, *Ride the Crooked Wind,* was extensive and the book itself was, according to Fife, the most difficult work that she ever wrote.

AVOCATIONAL INTERESTS: Gardening, cooking, bridge.

*   *   *

FINK, Eli E. 1908(?)-1979

OBITUARY NOTICE: Born c. 1908; died May 2, 1979, in Highland Park, Ill. Attorney. Fink began his law career at the Chicago firm of Hall, Spitz, & Rooks and later worked for Paramount and R.K.O. Pictures. At one time he represented stage comedienne Fanny Brice in her $750,000 suit against Twentieth Century-Fox Film Corp. Brice, who won her case in 1940, had alleged that her life story was dramatized without her consent in the film "Rose of Washington Square." Fink also founded "Poet's Corner" in the American Bar Association's journal and published a book of poetry. Obituaries and other sources: *Chicago Tribune,* May 4, 1979.

FINKELSTEIN, Bonnie B(lumenthal) 1946-

PERSONAL: Born July 17, 1946, in Philadelphia, Pa.; daughter of Herman B. II (a certified public accountant) and Elaine (Belsinger) Blumenthal; married Richard M. Finkelstein (a physician), June 23, 1968; children: Joel Blumenthal. *Education:* University of Pennsylvania, A.B. (magna cum laude), 1968; Columbia University, M.A. (with honors), 1969, Ph.D. (with distinction), 1972. *Home:* 1021 Melrose Ave., Melrose Park, Pa. 19126. *Office:* Department of English, Montgomery County Community College, Blue Bell, Pa. 19422.

CAREER: McGraw-Hill Book Co., New York City, editor, writer, and researcher, summer, 1969; New York University, Medical Center, New York City, tutor in premedical research and education program, 1970-71; Montgomery County Community College, Blue Bell, Pa., assistant professor, 1972-76, associate professor of English, 1976—. *Member:* Modern Language Association of America, National Organization for Women, Phi Beta Kappa.

WRITINGS: Forster's Women: Eternal Differences, Columbia University Press, 1975. Contributor to *English Literature in Transition.*

WORK IN PROGRESS: A mystery novel.

SIDELIGHTS: Finkelstein writes: "My current research and teaching interest is women in literature, and I am looking for a contemporary feminist novel that acknowledges the difficulties of marriage but still presents a successful egalitarian attempt at a happy one; I may have to write it.

"I have received enormous support from my parents and my husband, who has never felt 'that he must lead women, though he knew not whither, and protect them, though he knew not against what.'"

AVOCATIONAL INTERESTS: Reading detective novels.

* * *

FIORE, Edith 1930-

PERSONAL: Born September 13, 1930, in Scarsdale, N.Y.; daughter of Frank (a portrait and landscape artist) and Edith (a hotel owner; maiden name, Gobel) Fiore; married Greg LeMons (a filmmaker), June 5, 1976; children: Gail de Nava, Dana Plays, Leslie Luxenberg. *Education:* Attended Mount Holyoke College, 1948-50; Goucher College, B.A., 1960; University of Maryland, M.A., 1964; University of Miami, Coral Gables, Fla., Ph.D., 1969. *Agent:* Helen McGrath, 1406 Idaho Court, Concord, Calif. 94521. *Office:* 20688 Fourth St., Saratoga, Calif. 95070.

CAREER: Children's Psychiatric Center, Miami, Fla., staff psychologist, 1969-70; private practice of clinical psychology in Miami, Fla., 1970-73, and in Saratoga, Calif., 1973—. *Member:* International Society of Clinical Hypnosis, American Psychological Association, American Society of Clinical Hypnosis, California Psychological Association, San Francisco Academy of Hypnosis, San Jose Society of Clinical Hypnosis. *Awards, honors:* Honored by Santa Clara County branch of National League of American Pen Women, 1978, for *You Have Been Here Before.*

WRITINGS: You Have Been Here Before: A Psychologist Looks at Past Lives, Ballantine, 1979. Also author of *Grandma: A Child's Book of Death and Rebirth.* Contributor to *Saga.*

WORK IN PROGRESS: The Interim: Between Life and Rebirth.

SIDELIGHTS: Edith Fiore comments: "As a result of doing past-life therapy for four years I have felt my findings *must* be shared, both with my colleagues and the general public. My interest in metaphysics has grown tremendously and I am taking a cruise to the healing centers with a group of other people in the healing arts. I also feel that Yoga is extremely important to self-unfoldment. I have been studying Yoga for five years and will be studying at the Yoga-Schule in the Swiss Alps. I am a member of the Solar Cross, an educational organization aimed at understanding our universe via the telepathic information received from our space brothers and sisters."

* * *

FIORINA, Morris Paul, Jr. 1946-

PERSONAL: Born May 16, 1946, in Greensburg, Pa.; son of Morris Paul and Helen (Plachta) Fiorina; married Mary Elizabeth Ritschard, 1968; children: Michael. *Education:* Allegheny College, B.A., 1968; University of Rochester, M.A., 1971, Ph.D., 1972. *Home:* 1286 Avocado Ter., Pasadena, Calif. 91104. *Office:* Division of Humanities and Social Studies, California Institute of Technology, Pasadena, Calif. 91125.

CAREER: California Institute of Technology, Pasadena, assistant professor, 1972-74, associate professor, 1974-77, professor of political science, 1977—. Head of workshops; participant in professional meetings. *Member:* Phi Beta Kappa. *Awards, honors:* National Science Foundation grants, 1974, 1976; political book award from *Washington Monthly,* 1977, for *Congress: Keystone of the Washington Establishment.*

WRITINGS: Representatives, Roll Calls, and Constituencies, Heath, 1974; (contributor) Norman Ornstein, editor, *Change in Congress,* Praeger, 1975; *Congress: Keystone of the Washington Establishment,* Yale University Press, 1977; (contributor) Peter C. Ordeshook and Richard D. McKelvey, editors, *Game Theory and Political Science,* New York University Press, 1978. Contributor of about fifteen articles to academic journals. Member of editorial board of *Public Choice* and *American Journal of Political Science,* both 1975—.

WORK IN PROGRESS: Research on retrospective voting in American national elections, congressional elections, congressional policymaking, and executive-legislative relations.

* * *

FISHER, Esther Oshiver 1910-

PERSONAL: Born April 5, 1910, in Philadelphia, Pa.; daughter of Harry James (an artist) and Rebecca (Saidikoff) Oshiver; married Mitchell Salem Fisher (an attorney), June 25, 1933; children: Franklin, Joanne Fisher Wang, Wesley. *Education:* University of Pennsylvania, B.S.Ed., 1929, J.D., 1932; Columbia University, Ed.D., 1962. *Politics:* Liberal. *Religion:* Jewish (conservative). *Home and office:* 1050 Park Ave., New York, N.Y. 10028.

CAREER: Institutes of Religion and Health, New York, N.Y., teacher and head of training in marriage and divorce counseling, 1958-75, consultant, 1975—. Private practice in clinical marriage and divorce counseling, 1958—. *Member:* American Association of Marriage and Family Counselors (past national chairman of legislation and public policy; national vice-president, 1972-73), American Psychological Association, American Orthopsychiatric Association (fellow), American Association of Sex Educators and Counselors (fellow), Society for the Scientific Study of Sex, American Association of Marital Therapists, National Council on Family Relations, University of Pennsylvania Law Alumni Association, Kappa Delta Pi, Pi Delta Theta.

WRITINGS: Help for Today's Troubled Marriages, Hawthorn, 1968; (contributor) *Marriage: For and Against,* introduction by Harold H. Hart, Hart Publishing, 1972; *Divorce: The New Freedom,* Harper, 1974. Author of script for "Divorce Counseling," Psychotherapy Tape Library, 1976. Contributor to *Family Coordinator.* Editor of *Journal of Divorce,* 1976—; member of editorial board of *Journal of Marriage and Family Counseling,* 1974—.

*   *   *

FISHER, Sterling Wesley 1899(?)-1978

PERSONAL: Born May 24, 1899, in San Antonio, Tex.; died December 1, 1978, of complications following a stroke, in Tarrytown, N.Y.; son of Sterling and Sue (Harper) Fisher; married Jean Alice Callahan, November 28, 1923; children: Sterling, William Murray. *Education:* Attended Southern Methodist University, 1916-18; University of Texas, A.B., 1919; attended Columbia University, 1921-22; University of California, A.M., 1924. *Religion:* Methodist. *Home:* 181 Wilson Park Dr., Tarrytown, N.Y. 10591. *Office: Reader's Digest,* Pleasantville, N.Y. 10570.

CAREER/WRITINGS: Journalist. Himeji Middle School, Himeji, Japan, instructor in English, 1919-21; Georgia Institute of Technology, Atlanta, Ga., 1922-23; University of Western Japan, Kobe, Japan, professor of English, 1924-29; *Springfield Republican,* Springfield, Mass., member of editorial staff, 1929; Associated Press, New York, N.Y., member of editorial staff, 1930; Far East expert and correspondent in China, Japan, and Manchuria, for *New York Times,* 1930-37; Columbia Broadcasting System, Inc. (CBS Radio), director of education, 1937-42; National Broadcasting Co., Inc. (NBC Radio), assistant public service counselor, 1942-48; manager of public affairs and education department, 1948-50; *Reader's Digest,* general manager in the Far East, 1950-56, director of public affairs, 1956-67. Executive director of Reader's Digest Foundation; chairman of the board of World Press Institute, Macalester College of Advanced Broadcasting, U.S. Department of State, 1942-47; served as mayor of Tarrytown, N.Y., 1947-49. Member of U.S. Committee on International Intellectual Cooperation, and Federal Radio Education Commission, 1940-42, and 1948-56; member of advisory committee of Chicago Radio Council. Director of Joseph C. Brew Foundation, 1952-56; director of International House (Tokyo); founder of School of the Air of the Americas. Notable assignments include securing a map of the concealed U.S.S.R. Baikal-Amur Mainline (B.A.M.) strategic railroad in Siberia, for the *New York Times. Military service:* U.S. Marine Corps, 1918.

MEMBER: American Museum of Natural History, Philosophical Society of History, American-Japan Society (Tokyo; vice-president, 1951-56); American Chamber of Commerce (Tokyo division; president, 1951-52), Philosophical Society of Texas, Sigma Delta Chi, Pi Kappa Alpha. *Awards, honors:* National School of Broadcasting Conference award, 1941, for promoting better relations between North and South America by radio; Magazine Digest award, 1946, for outstanding public service.

Editor of *Talks, CBS Student Guide, Americans at Work,* and many other radio booklets. Contributor to periodicals, including *New York Times* and *Current History.*

SIDELIGHTS: As a reporter, Fisher was able to talk himself out of at least one predicament, thanks to a proficiency in the Japanese language. As a correspondent in China for the *New York Times* in the 1930's, Fisher was required to fly from Shanghai to Tientsin on an assignment calling for photographs. Preparing to land in Tientsin, he was surprised to notice that aircraft on the field below belonged to the Japanese. After Fisher landed, Japanese officers announced that they had orders to check all incoming planes for cameras and confiscate those found. While Fisher did in fact have a camera with him, the officers abandoned the search in their delight to discover that he could converse in their native tongue.

AVOCATIONAL INTERESTS: Tennis, reading.*

*   *   *

FISKE, Edward B. 1937-

PERSONAL: Born June 4, 1937, in Philadelphia, Pa.; son of Edward R., Jr. and Jean (Bogardus) Fiske; married Dale Alden Woodruff, July 12, 1963; children: Julia Woodruff, Suzanna Rawson. *Education:* Wesleyan University, Middletown, Conn., B.A. (summa cum laude), 1959; Princeton Theological Seminary, M.A., 1963; Columbia University, M.A., 1965; also attended Graduate School of International Relations, Geneva, Switzerland, 1961-62. *Office: New York Times,* 229 West 43rd St., New York, N.Y. 10036.

CAREER: John Knox House, Geneva, Switzerland, member of staff, 1961-62; *Trentonian,* Trenton, N.J., journalist, 1962-63; *Packet,* Princeton, N.J., journalist, 1962-63; *New York Times,* New York City, news clerk, 1964-65, religion reporter, 1965-68, acting chief of Rome bureau, 1967, religion editor, 1968-74, education news editor and editor of quarterly education supplement, 1974—. Contributor of articles and reviews to popular magazines, including *Redbook, Saturday Review,* and *Reader's Digest,* and to newspapers. Member of editorial board of *Theology Today. Member:* Phi Beta Kappa.

SIDELIGHTS: Fiske writes: "I have traveled throughout Europe, the middle East, Africa, and the Far East on assignment. As education editor, I have written on topics ranging from early childhood education and school finance to curriculum reform, continuing education, and testing and education of the handicapped."

*   *   *

FITCH, George Ashmore 1883-1979

OBITUARY NOTICE: Born January 23, 1883, in Soochow, China; died January 21, 1979, in Pomona, Calif. Pastor and Y.M.C.A. worker. Fitch was secretary to the International Committee of the Y.M.C.A. for forty years and a resident of China from 1909 to 1946. During World War II, he worked in Nanking to provide minimal comforts and necessities to Chinese soldiers. When the Chinese government fled the invading Japanese army, he was left as acting mayor of the city and head of the International Safety Zone. He photographed many of the atrocities committed against the Chinese and later smuggled the documentation out in the lining of an overcoat. After the Japanese defeat, Fitch testified at war crimes trials in Tokyo. He wrote two books about his China experiences, *To the Mecca of Inner Mongolia* and *My 80 Years in China,* and contributed articles to newspapers and periodicals. Obituaries and other sources: *New York Times,* January 23, 1979.

*   *   *

FITZGERALD, Nancy 1951-

PERSONAL: Born September 4, 1951, in Burbank, Calif.;

daughter of Earl E. (an engineer) and Marie (Wittak) Fitzgerald; children: Shaw Elizabeth. *Education:* Attended University of California, Los Angeles, 1969-70, and Reed College, 1970-71; University of California, Santa Barbara, B.A., 1973; graduate study at California State University, Northridge, 1973. *Home:* 7803 Genesta Ave., Van Nuys, Calif. 91406. *Agent:* Harvey Klinger, 250 West 57th St., New York, N.Y. 10019.

CAREER: High school English teacher in Burbank, Calif., 1973-74; secretary, 1974-78; writer. Member of creative writing faculty at University of California, Los Angeles, 1979. Teacher of pre-natal and post-natal exercise courses and childbirth preparation classes. *Member:* Popular Culture Association (West).

WRITINGS: St. Johns Wood, Doubleday, 1977; *Mayfair,* Doubleday, 1978.

WORK IN PROGRESS: A historical romance set in Victorian London; a book on "coaching" childbirth; a book on child-rearing in other cultures; a comprehensive book on formula fiction for women, including Gothics and Regencies.

SIDELIGHTS: Nancy Fitzgerald writes: "I've always been a storyteller and I love to read. I write to create the sort of books I like to read, and in the process I find I have learned more than I expected." *Avocational interests:* Dancing, Welsh literature, English peerage, pre-Raphaelites, jazz, mythology and symbolism, childbirth education, sewing.

* * *

FITZGERALD, Penelope 1916-

PERSONAL: Born December 17, 1916, in Lincoln, England; daughter of Edmund Valpy (editor of *Punch*) and Christina (Hicks) Knox; married Desmond Fitzgerald, August 15, 1941 (died, August, 1976); children: Edmund Valpy. *Education:* Somerville College, Oxford, received degree in English literature, with first class honors, 1939. *Religion:* Christian. *Office:* Westminster Tutors, Artillery Mansions, Victoria St., London S.W.1, England.

CAREER: Writer; teacher with Westminster Tutors, London, England.

WRITINGS: Edward Burne-Jones (biography), M. Joseph, 1975; *The Golden Child* (novel), Duckworth, 1977; *The Knox Brothers* (biography), Macmillan, 1977; *The Bookshop* (novel), Duckworth, 1978.

WORK IN PROGRESS: Research on William Morris's unpublished manuscripts, the Poetry Bookshop (Charlotte Mew, F. S. Flint), and novelist L. P. Hartley.

SIDELIGHTS: Penelope Fitzgerald comments: "I've begun to write at rather a late stage in life because I love books and everything to do with them. I believe that people should write biographies only about people they love, or understand, or both. Novels, on the other hand, are often better if they're about people the writer doesn't like very much."

* * *

FIX, William R. 1941-

PERSONAL: Born March 12, 1941, in Madison, Wis.; son of William J. (a printer) and Salome (Reuter) Fix; married Joanne E. Murray, January 9, 1968 (divorced, 1973). *Education:* University of Wisconsin—Madison, B.S., 1964; Simon Fraser University, M.A., 1968. *Politics:* "Monarchist." *Religion:* Christian.

CAREER: Motion picture cameraman and editor in New

York City, 1965-66; systems analyst in New York City, 1966-67; Canadian Broadcasting Corp., Vancouver, British Columbia, media consultant, 1968-69; writer.

WRITINGS: Pyramid Odyssey, Jonathan-James Books, 1978. Also author of a nonfiction book, *Star Maps,* 1979.

SIDELIGHTS: Fix writes: "I am particularly interested in the origin and nature of prehistoric civilizations, the causes of their declines, and their relevance to the fourth quarter of the twentieth century. *Star Maps* is an investigation of ancient Egyptian star maps, pyramid texts, initiation, out-of-body travel, and the celestial origin of man."

* * *

FLAHERTY, Gloria 1938-

PERSONAL: Born May 30, 1938, in Kearny, N.J.; daughter of John Robert and Jean (Bacenas) Flaherty. *Education:* Rutgers University, B.A., 1959; Johns Hopkins University, M.A., 1960, Ph.D., 1965. *Office:* Department of German, Bryn Mawr College, Bryn Mawr, Pa. 19010.

CAREER: Johns Hopkins University, Baltimore, Md., junior instructor in German, 1960-64; Northwestern University, Evanston, Ill., assistant professor of German, 1964-71; Bryn Mawr College, Bryn Mawr, Pa., associate professor of German, 1971—, chairman of department, 1971-77. *Member:* Modern Language Association of America, Comparative Literature Association, Renaissance Society of America, American Society for Eighteenth-Century Studies, Lessing Society, Association of Departments of Foreign Languages (member of executive committee, 1975-78), Germanistic Society of America (fellow), Phi Beta Kappa. *Awards, honors:* Julius Hoffmann Award, 1963, for excellence in German.

WRITINGS: (Contributor) David Daiches and Anthony Thorlby, editors, *Literature and Western Civilization,* Aldus Books, 1974; *Opera in the Development of German Critical Thought,* Princeton University Press, 1978. Contributor of articles and reviews to language journals. Consulting editor of *Modern Language Notes* and *Eighteenth-Century Life.*

WORK IN PROGRESS: Investigating theories of the performing arts and their relationship to the major literary genres.

SIDELIGHTS: Gloria Flaherty writes: "I am particularly concerned that the humanities regain the prestige they once had in the United States and that they be treated on an equal footing with the applied, theoretical, and social sciences.

"One of our major educational problems today is the excessive stress on vocationalism. Without deprecating the need for employability, I wonder whether training young people specifically for today's job market will equip them with the mental agility, imagination, and skills that they will need to have in order to adjust to the changes that will inevitably take place in the next twenty to forty years.

"As someone who has studied the relationship of money, technology, and utopian dreams in post-Renaissance literature, I believe that American educators should concentrate on teaching their students not merely to achieve some semblance of literacy, but more importantly to perceive the nuances, the rhetorical devices, the linguistic subtleties, the varying connotative values of what they read. And that means requiring them to select from a common core of courses that might not immediately add up to dollars and cents."

FLOYD, Lois Gray 1910(?)-1978

PERSONAL: Born in Larrabee, Wyo.; died December 22, 1978, in Woodland, Calif.; married William Floyd (deceased). *Education:* Texas Christian University, bachelor's degree in government, 1932; University of Texas, M.A. in psychology, 1939; New York University, earned Ph.D. in psychology. *Residences:* 111 East 85th St., New York, N.Y.; and Twilight Park, Haynes Fall, N.Y.

CAREER: Montclair State College, Upper Montclair, N.J., professor of psychology until 1976, professor emeritus, 1976-78.

WRITINGS: (With Bertha B. Quintana) *Que gitano!,* Holt, 1971. Contributor to *Reviews in Anthology.*

OBITUARIES: New York Times, December 25, 1978.*

* * *

FORD, Colin John 1934-

PERSONAL: Born May 13, 1934, in London, England; son of John William and Helene Martha Ford; married Margaret Elizabeth Cordwell (a film censor), August 12, 1961 (separated January 31, 1978); children: Richard John, Clare Michaela Elizabeth. *Education:* Oxford University, M.A., 1960. *Religion:* None. *Home:* 23 Gresley Rd., Islington N19 3LA, England. *Office:* National Portrait Gallery, London WC2H OHE, England.

CAREER: Manager and producer of Kidderminster Playhouse, 1958-60; general manager of Western Theatre Ballet, 1960-62; University of California Los Angeles, and California State University, Long Beach, visiting lecturer in English and drama, 1962-64; deputy curator of National Film Archive of England, 1965-72; National Portrait Gallery, London, England, 1972—, began as assistant keeper, became keeper of film and photography. Lecturer and broadcaster on film, theater, and photography; organizer of exhibitions. Director of Cinema City Exhibition, 1972; program director of London Shakespeare Film Festival, 1972. *Member:* British Academy of Film and Television Arts, Royal Photographic Society.

WRITINGS: (With Roy Strong) *An Early Victorian Album,* J. Cape, 1974, Knopf, 1977; *The Cameron Collection,* Van Nostrand, 1975; (editor) *Happy and Glorious: 130 Years of Royal Photographs,* Macmillan, 1977 (published in England as *Happy and Glorious: Six Reigns of Royal Photography,* Angus & Robertson, 1977); *Britain in the 1880's,* Penguin, 1980.

Radio and television writer. Contributor to magazines and to *Oxford Companion to Film.* Author of film "Masks and Faces."

WORK IN PROGRESS: Julia Margaret Cameron: Catalogue Raisonne, Completion expected in 1990; *Photography: The First Fifty Years.*

AVOCATIONAL INTERESTS: Travel, music, small boats.

* * *

FORD, Edmund Brisco 1901-

PERSONAL: Born April 23, 1901, in Papcastle, Cumberland, England; son of Harold Dodsworth and Gertrude Emma (Bennett) Ford. *Education:* Wadham College, Oxford, B.A., 1924, M.A., 1927, D.Sc., 1943. *Office:* Department of Zoology, Oxford University, South Parks Rd., Oxford, England.

CAREER: Oxford University, Oxford, England, researcher,

1924-27, demonstrator in zoology and comparative anatomy, then lecturer, 1928-38, reader, 1938-63, professor of ecological genetics, 1963-69, professor emeritus, 1969—, director of Genetics Laboratory, 1952-69, All Souls College, fellow, 1958-71, senior dean, 1958—. Galton Lecturer at University of London, 1939; Woodhall Lecturer at Royal Institution, 1957; Woodward Lecturer at Yale University, 1959, 1973. Past British member of International Committee of Genetics.

MEMBER: Royal Society (fellow), British Genetical Society (president, 1946-49), Nature Conservancy (founding member), Finnish Academy (foreign member), Somerset Archaeological Society (president, 1960-61). *Awards, honors:* Darwin Medal from Royal Society, 1954; Weldon Medal from Oxford University; 1959; D.Sc. from University of Liverpool, 1964; medal from University of Helsinki, 1967.

WRITINGS: Mendelism and Evolution, Methuen, 1931, 8th edition, Halsted, 1965; (with G.D.H. Carpenter) *Mimicry,* Methuen, 1933; *The Study of Heredity,* Home University Library, 1938, 2nd edition, Oxford University Press, 1950; *Genetics for Medical Students,* Chapman & Hall, 1942, 7th edition, 1973, Halsted, 1974; *Butterflies,* Collins, 1945, 4th edition, 1977; *British Butterflies,* Penguin, 1951; *Moths,* Collins, 1955, 3rd edition, 1972; *Ecological Genetics,* Chapman & Hall, 1964, 4th edition, Halsted, 1975; *Genetic Polymorphism,* Faber, 1965; *Evolution Studied by Observation and Experiment,* Oxford University Press, 1973, 2nd edition, in press; *Genetics and Adaptation,* Edward Arnold, 1976; *Understanding Genetics,* Faber, 1979. Contributor of about eighty articles to scientific journals.

WORK IN PROGRESS: Continuing research on ecological genetics and Iron Age archaeology.

SIDELIGHTS: Ford's genetic research, some of which was conducted with Julian Huxley, has covered evolution of dominance in wild material, growth of genetic controllers, defined genetic polymorphism, and predicting the association of human blood groups with disease.

* * *

FORD, Frank B(ernard) 1932-

PERSONAL: Born April 16, 1932, in New Haven, Conn.; son of William Francis (a printer) and Helena (Young) Ford; married Wilma Yocom (a puppeteer), October 25, 1961; children: Gregory, Paul. *Education:* University of Connecticut, B.A., 1958, M.A., 1960; post-graduate study at University of Delaware. *Home:* 741 South Franklin St., West Chester, Pa. 19380. *Office:* Department of English, West Chester State College, West Chester, Pa. 19380.

CAREER: West Chester State College, West Chester, Pa., assistant professor of English, 1960-62; Turkish Air Force Language School, Izmir, teacher of English and supervisor, 1962-64; West Chester College, assistant professor, 1965-77, associate professor of English, 1977. *Military service:* U.S. Army, 1952-54; became sergeant. *Member:* Associated Writing Programs. *Awards, honors:* Grant from Office of Advanced Drama Research, 1976.

WRITINGS—Plays: "Waterman" (one-act; first produced in Minneapolis at Guthrie 2, March 24, 1976), published in *Guthrie New Theater,* Volume I, Grove, 1977. Contributor of stories, poems, and an article to magazines, including *Nugget, Fine Arts, Delaware Literary Review,* and *Phantasm.*

WORK IN PROGRESS: "Texas," a three-act play commissioned by Guthrie 2; "Indignities," a one-hour radio drama commissioned by Earplay for National Public Radio; "Hamburger," a one-act play; "Tetzel," a play; a mystery novel; two short plays; "The History of the American Mind," a long poem; writing for television.

SIDELIGHTS: Ford writes: "I'm interested in where the mind can go, there being no absolute limit. In my unproduced play, "Texas," the protagonist thinks he has run past light. My own career goes more slowly in its split way—split in that the working out of problems on paper is a terrific upper; trying to reach an audience through various editors is a profound downer. But . . . I'm a twenty-year journeyman of all kinds of fiction and I don't intend to stop. Ever."

*   *   *

FORMAN, Celia Adler   1890(?)-1979

OBITUARY NOTICE: Born c. 1890; died January 31, 1979, in New York, N.Y. Actress. Forman was known as "the first lady of the Yiddish theatre." She first appeared on stage at the age of six months and went on to become one the most prominent champions of Jewish drama. In 1918, she helped open the first Yiddish Art Theatre, where the plays of Jewish playwrights were performed along with translations from the English, Russian, and German stage. Forman appeared throughout the world in Yiddish versions of the plays of Ibsen, Shakespeare, Chekhov, Shaw, Hauptmann, Sudermann, and others. In English language ventures, she won critical plaudits for her work in "Men in White," "Success Story," and "A Flag is Born." She wrote the two-volume *The Yiddish Theatre in America,* a study of the Yiddish theatre developed by her father, Jacob P. Adler, in the late nineteenth century. Obituaries and other sources: *New York Times,* February 2, 1979.

*   *   *

FORSYTH, Frederick   1938-

PERSONAL: Born in Ashford, England; married Carrie (a model), 1973; children: Frederick Stuart. *Residence:* County Wicklow, Ireland. *Address:* c/o Hutchinson Publishing Group, 3 Fitzroy Sq., London W1P 6JD, England.

CAREER: Correspondent in Paris, France, for Reuters News Service, and in Nigeria, for British Broadcasting Corp. (BBC); free-lance journalist in Biafra; free-lance writer. *Awards, honors:* Edgar Award from the Mystery Writers of America, 1972, for *The Odessa File.*

WRITINGS: The Biafra Story, Penguin, 1969, revised edition published as *The Making of an African Legend: The Biafra Story,* 1977; *The Day of the Jackal* (novel), Viking, 1971; *The Odessa File* (novel), Viking, 1972; *The Dogs of War* (novel), Viking, 1974; *The Shepherds* (juvenile), Hutchinson, 1975, Viking, 1976. Contributor of articles to newspapers and magazines.

WORK IN PROGRESS: The Devil's Alternative.

SIDELIGHTS: With a story based on actual events (the attempts to assassinate French President Charles de Gaulle) and with a precise, journalistic style, Frederick Forsyth created his first best-seller, the highly successful *The Day of the Jackal.* According to the *Washington Post,* Forsyth's story was so convincing that it actually caused French newspapers to send out their reporters to check on some episodes in the book. The credibility of the book is due to Forsyth's determination to work on background details; for *The Day of the Jackal,* he consulted with a professional assassin, a passport forger, and an underground armorer. He also relied on his experiences as a Reuters correspondent in Paris.

In addition to the startling success of his first novel, Forsyth's characterization of the meticulous and cold professional assassin surprisingly drew positive response from many critics and readers. Stanley Ellin of the *New York Times Book Review* recorded his reaction, "So plausible has Mr. Forsyth made his implausible villain, a professional assassin whose business card might well read 'Presidents and Premiers My Specialty,' and so excitingly does he lead him on his murderous mission against impossible odds, that even saintly readers will be hard put not to cheer this particular villain along his devious way." Forsyth, however, noted that he thought this positive response to his villain occurred largely in the United States where "there is this American trait of admiring efficiency, and the Jackal is efficient in his job."

Another part of the secret to the success of *The Day of the Jackal,* according to a *Times Literary Supplement* reviewer "is that real people move in and out of the plot. . . . The technique is not new, but Mr. Forsyth handles it with a mature confidence remarkable in a first novel, and reinforces the general aura of plausibility with a fanatical attention to what one might call the logistic details." Similarly, Forsyth strengthened the believability of his story by opening the novel with a factual account of De Gaulle signing the document that gave Algeria its independence. Following were the reactions of angry right-wing French colonists who were forced to leave the former territory, and the subsequent futile attempt on De Gaulle's life by a member of the Secret Army Organization (O.A.S.). Then Forsyth proceeded to include his own fictional account of another assassination attempt, and "did it with such verissimilitude that the reader is almost persuaded he is following the reconstruction of an actual event."

The Odessa File was Forsyth's second best-seller. Again Forsyth displayed a knack for mixing real-life events with fictional situations. Reportedly, he interviewed Nazi hunter Simon Wisenthal, and included as a character in his novel the former S.S. captain Eduard Roschmann who is said to be living in South America now. In the foreword to the book, Forsyth stated that ODESSA, the organization designed to aid former S.S. officers, does exist. By the end of the novel, the reader is inclined to believe him.

The Dogs of War, which was supposedly based on Forsyth's experiences as a correspondent during the Nigerian civil war, proved to be his most controversial book. In an article in the *London Times,* Forsyth was accused of financing an attempted coup in Equatorial Guinea which would have ousted President Francisco Marcias Nguema. He was said to have paid out two-hundred-thousand dollars in ammunition, supplies, and salaries for mercenaries. The attempt failed when the weapons could not be delivered and when Spanish authorities became suspicious and investigated the expedition that was part of an oil survey off the African coast. Forsyth at first denied the story, saying it was "a load of old codswallop." His former literary agent, Bryan Hunt, dismissed the allegations by implying that Forsyth was too cheap to finance such an operation. "To imagine Freddie giving anyone 10 pence would be amusing," remarked Hunt. Later, Forsyth admitted he needed some inside information about the logistics of starting a coup, and did not intend for an actual overthrow to occur.

The Dogs of War is perhaps Forsyth's least effective work. Donald Goddard of the *New York Times Book Review* observed that it "falls as far below 'Odessa' in its craftmanship as 'Odessa' fell short of *The Day of the Jackal.*" He also stated that the book "as a whole is informed with a kind of post-imperial condescension toward the black man that shows through not only in the bland assumption that five Europeans and six trusty native gunbearers are enough to deal with the mad dictator's palace guard of 40 to 60 elite troops and a back-up army of 400 men, but also in some openly patronizing references to the Africans' fear of fighting in the dark and their 'annoying habit' of shutting their eyes when firing automatic weapons.''

In a review of *The Dogs of War,* an *Atlantic* critic wrote: ''Forsyth gives little attention to characterization, preferring the chess master approach—that is, his people are defined by their movements on the board. The result of this style of doing things is a story in which no person arouses real sympathy on the readers' part, nor even the continuing interest based on solid dislike.''

Other critics disagree, and Forsyth has been accused of showing sympathy for mercenaries in his book. To these accusations, Forsyth was quoted in the *Washington Post* as saying: ''I don't have any affinity for mercenaries. They're just more interesting than most blokes, than streetsweepers or bartenders.'' Forsyth also stated that he intensely dislikes sweeping generalizations about mercenaries. He pointed out that European governments and African dictators had killed more people (in the millions) than the reported 40,000 deaths at the hands of mercenaries in the whole of Africa. Forsyth qualified his statements further: ''That's not an affinity with mercenaries though. It's a rejection of the hypocrisy of respectable society with its set-piece attitudes that can justify killing a million children by starvation in Biafra but can object vociferously to four or five mercenaries.''

About his work, Forsyth commented: ''I'm a writer with the intent of selling lots of copies and making money. I don't think my work will ever be regarded as great literature of classics. I'm just a commercial writer and I have no illusions about it.''

BIOGRAPHICAL/CRITICAL SOURCES: Observer, June 13, 1971, September 24, 1972, September 22, 1974; *Listener,* June 17, 1971, September 28, 1972; *Times Literary Supplement,* July 2, 1971, October 25, 1974, December 19, 1975; *New York Times Book Review,* August 15, 1971, December 5, 1971, November 5, 1972, July 14, 1974, October 16, 1977; *Washington Post,* August 19, 1971, September 26, 1971, December 12, 1978; *New York Times,* October 24, 1972, April 18, 1978; *Atlantic,* December, 1972, August, 1974; *Publishers Weekly,* September 30, 1974; *Contemporary Literary Criticism,* Gale, Volume 2, 1974, Volume 5, 1976; *Newsweek,* May 1, 1978.*

* * *

FOSBURGH, Lacey 1942-

PERSONAL: Born October 3, 1942, in New York, N.Y.; daughter of Hugh Whitney (a writer) and Helen (a public relations executive; maiden name, Edwards) Fosburgh; married Marc Libarle, August 10, 1973 (divorced, 1975); married David Harris (a journalist, writer, and politician), May 14, 1977. *Education:* Sarah Lawrence College, B.A., 1964. *Home:* 1937 Stockton St., San Francisco, Calif. 94133. *Agent:* Sterling Lord Agency, Inc., 660 Madison Ave., New York, N.Y. 10021.

CAREER: Fulbright study grant, New Delhi, India, 1964-66; *New York Herald Tribune,* New York City, news assistant, 1967; *New York Times,* New York City, staff correspondent, 1967-74; free-lance writer, 1974—. University of California, Berkeley, lecturer in journalism, 1974—. *Member:* National Women's Political Caucus, several women's jour-

nalism clubs. *Awards, honors:* Numerous publishers' prizes from *New York Times;* Edgar Allan Poe Special Award from Mystery Writers of America, 1978, for *Closing Time.*

WRITINGS: Closing Time (fictional biography; Literary Guild and Doubleday Book Club selection), Delacorte, 1977; *Four Quarters and the Moon* (novel), Doubleday, 1980. Contributor of articles to numerous magazines, including *New York Times Sunday Magazine, Ladies Home Journal,* and *Redbook.*

WORK IN PROGRESS: Research for a book on India.

SIDELIGHTS: Fosburgh, who speaks French, Hindi, Spanish, and Italian, has traveled extensively and lived in both India and Paris for periods of two years. As a journalist, she covered some of the nation's most conspicuous news stories, including the trials of Sirhan Sirhan and Patricia Hearst, and the 1973 Roseann Quinn murder case. It was the latter story, reportedly the basis for Judith Rossner's *Looking for Mr. Goodbar,* that led Fosburgh to develop her own interpretive account in *Closing Time.* Her study probes the internal and private lives of both the victim and her murderer, described by Joan Barthel as ''measured in pain, laced with a sense of dread.'' The assembled narrative, requiring three years of research, presents a series of eighty-four scenes that recreate the crime and the following police investigation. While one reviewer equated the book with Truman Capote's *In Cold Blood,* Capote himself remarked, ''Miss Fosburgh is a skillful, selective reporter and though it does not necessarily follow, she is also a literary artist, as *Closing Time,* with its beautifully constructed qualities—narrative tension, compassionate comprehension of lost souls, of curious minds in dangerous situations—abundantly proves.''

BIOGRAPHICAL/CRITICAL SOURCES: New York Times Book Review, November 20, 1977; *People,* January 30, 1978; *New Times,* May 15, 1978.

* * *

FOSTER, Elizabeth 1902-

PERSONAL: Born June 18, 1902, in Wilkes-Barre, Pa.; daughter of George E. (an educator) and Louise (Palmer) Vincent; married Maxwell E. Foster (a lawyer), June 9, 1926; children: Maxwell E., Jr., Vincent. *Education:* Bryn Mawr College, A.B., 1923. *Politics:* Independent.

CAREER: Director of Massachusetts Audubon Society, 1936-66.

WRITINGS: Lyrico, Gambit, 1970.*

* * *

FOSTER, Marian Curtis 1909-1978
(Mariana)

OBITUARY NOTICE—See index for *CA* sketch: Born in 1909 in Cleveland, Ohio; died October 27, 1978, in Long Island, N.Y. Artist, illustrator, and author of books for children. Many of Foster's books featured antique dolls as their main characters. Obituaries and other sources: *Authors of Books for Young People,* 2nd edition, Scarecrow, 1971; *Third Book of Junior Authors,* Wilson, 1972; *Publishers Weekly,* December 4, 1978.

* * *

FOSTER, Richard J(ames) 1942-

PERSONAL: Born May 3, 1942, in Albuquerque, N.M.; son of Lee Sherman and Marie (Temperance) Foster; married Alice Carolynn Kerr (a speech therapist), March 18, 1967;

children: Joel Timothy, Nathan Lee. *Education:* George Fox College, B.A., 1964; Fuller Theological Seminary, D.Th.P., 1970. *Politics:* Democrat. *Office:* 2100 University, Wichita, Kan. 67213.

CAREER: Youth minister at Friends church in Garden Grove, Calif., 1962-67; ordained clergyman of Society of Friends (Quakers), 1967; Family Counseling and Research Center, Garden Grove, counselor, 1967-68; associate pastor of Friends church in Arcadia, Calif., 1968-70, pastor in Canoga Park, Calif., 1970-74; Newberg Friends Church, Newberg, Ore., pastor, 1974-79; Friends University, Wichita, Kan., special lecturer in religion and philosophy and writer-in-residence, 1979—. Adjunct professor at George Fox College, 1974-79. Public lecturer. Member of publications board of California Yearly Meeting of Friends. *Awards, honors:* Named writer of the year by Warner Pacific College, 1978, for *Celebration of Discipline.*

WRITINGS: Quaker Concern in Race Relations: Then and Now, Martin Keller Associates, 1970; *Celebration of Discipline: The Path to Spiritual Growth,* Harper, 1978; (contributor) John L. Bond, editor, *Friends Search for Wholeness,* Friends United Press, 1978. Author of "Going Deeper," a column in *Faith and Work.* Contributor of more than thirty articles to magazines in the United States and Europe.

SIDELIGHTS: The premise for Richard Foster's *Celebration of Discipline* lies in its opening lines: "Superficiality is the curse of our age. . . . The desperate need today is not for a greater number of intelligent, or gifted people, but for deep people." Foster attempts to meet this need by introducing twelve basic Christian disciplines through four "inward disciplines" (meditation, prayer, fasting, study), four "outward disciplines" (simplicity, solitude, submission, service), and four "corporate disciplines" (confession, worship, guidance, celebration). The result, in reviewer Sister Ann Rita Murphy's words, is "a book which clearly illustrates the joy of the true Christian by demonstrating how a life of discipline has to be one of celebration."

Don Green examined the two major difficulties Foster believes confront those seeking "to explore the inner world." One problem lies in the "philosophic materialism" of the age, as Foster explains in his introduction: "Usually people will tolerate a brief dabbling in the 'inward journey,' but then it is time to go on with the *real* business in the *real* world." The second problem, continued Green, is that "modern seekers" often find themselves so immersed in the "clutter of our own existence" that "the call to a disciplined life only breeds frustration. Richard Foster is to be commended for the manner in which he clearly and simply nudges his readers into taking the steps."

Though Foster relied upon the thought of many past and present Christian writers in compiling his work, critics have maintained that *Celebration of Discipline* presents a remarkably fresh viewpoint. Such "Christian thinkers" as Soren Kierkegaard, J. H. Yoder, John Woolman, George Fox, and Agnes Sanford do indeed help Foster "illumine his ideas," declared Mark Silliman. But, as D. Elton Trueblood noted in his preface to *Celebration of Discipline,* "though the present volume demonstrates indebtedness to the Classics, it is not a book about them; it represents, instead, genuinely original work."

*   *   *

FOWLER, Raymond E(veleth) 1933-

PERSONAL: Born November 11, 1933, in Salem, Mass.; son of Raymond (a business administrator) and Doris (Eveleth) Fowler; married Margaret Pike; children: Sharon, Bethany, Raymond, David. *Education:* Gordon College of Liberal Arts, B.A. (magna cum laude), 1960. *Politics:* Independent. *Religion:* North American Baptist. *Home:* 13 Friend Court, Wenham, Mass. 01984. *Office:* General Telephone & Electronics Corp.—Sylvania, 189 B St., Needham Heights, Mass. 02194.

CAREER: General Telephone & Electronics Corp.—Sylvania, Needham Heights, Mass., administrative supervisor in Communications System Division, 1960—. Director of investigations for Mutual UFO Network; scientific associate at Center for UFO Studies; founder and director of Woodside Planetarium and Observatory. Guest on television and radio programs, including "Dick Cavett Show" and "Dave Garroway Show." Consultant to National Investigations Committee on Aerial Phenomena. *Military service:* U.S. Air Force, Security Service, 1952-56. *Member:* Phi Alpha Chi, Lambda Iota Tau.

WRITINGS: UFOs: Interplanetary Visitors, Exposition Press, 1974, Prentice-Hall, 1979; *The Andreasson Affair* (nonfiction), Prentice-Hall, 1979. Contributor to magazines and newspapers.

WORK IN PROGRESS: The Making of a UFO Investigator, publication expected in 1980.

SIDELIGHTS: Fowler comments: "I am very much interested in the question of the existence of extraterrestrial life and the resulting impact on science and theology if such is proven to exist. I am involved in UFO research and amateur astronomy. In 1970 I built and am now operating a private planetarium and observatory on my property for schools and clubs.

"There have been several motivating factors and circumstances that have been important to my involvement in investigating and documenting UFO sightings. Certain members of my family as far back as 1917 have had UFO experiences. Also, my father has had a lifelong private interest and experience with other extraordinary phenomena. He has taught me over the years that understanding and progress do not come by ignoring or ridiculing the inexplicable. Rather, they come by facing the problem squarely through investigation, acknowledgement and study. Apart from my scientific interest in unidentified flying objects, I am very interested in the implications from a theological aspect. Since my conversion to Christianity in 1950, I have become very involved in the Evangelical wing of the Christian church. I find a great need exists on the part of Evangelical theologians to expand, not necessarily change, their theological thinking from a geocentric to a universal viewpoint. I believe that UFOs are the product of extraterrestrial civilizations. It may be possible that certain Biblical accounts of aerial phenomena and contact with messengers from the sky are somehow relatable to the modern UFO phenomena. I consider this part of my interest to be highly speculative, yet worthy of study.

"My first book, *UFOs: Interplanetary Visitors,* presented my personal study of local UFO sightings as compared to the results of national studies by the government and civilian organizations. Step by step it eliminates the alternate hypotheses to the extraterrestrial hypotheses. It presents strong evidence that some UFOs cannot be explained away as hoaxes, hallucinations, misinterpretation of natural phenomena and misidentification of man-made objects. Documented evidence is also presented concerning government cover-up of significant UFO data from the public and lower echelons of the military.

"My second book, *The Andreasson Affair,* reflects the results of my twelve-month long investigation of an alleged close encounter of the third kind, including an abduction of one witness. It is based on a three-volume, 528 page report prepared for the Center for UFO Studies and the Mutual UFO Network. The results of character reference checks, lie detector tests, a psychiatric examination and months of hypnotic regression sessions indicate that the witnesses believe that the experience happened."

AVOCATIONAL INTERESTS: Church-related activities, fishing, canoeing, tennis, and gardening.

* * *

FOX, Ray Errol 1941-

PERSONAL: Born July 13, 1941, in Philadelphia, Pa.; son of D. Louis (a produce broker) and Jean B. (Levin) Fox; married Jean Thomas (a singer), August 26, 1966; children: Lauren Shay, Haley Wynn. *Education:* Attended Boston University, 1957-60, and Temple University, 1960-61. *Religion:* Jewish. *Home and office:* 88 Central Park W., New York, N.Y. 10023. *Agent* Betty Anne Clarke, International Creative Management, 40 West 57th St., New York, N.Y. 10019.

CAREER: Koppleman & Rubin (music publisher), New York City, staff writer, 1964-65; theatre and film lyricist, 1965-75; *Entertainment Spectrum,* New York City, theatre and dance critic, 1975-77; free-lance writer, 1977—. *Member:* Dutch Treat Club (member of board of governors).

WRITINGS: Angela Ambrosia (biography), Knopf, 1979.

Plays: "The Confidence Man" (script and lyrics; two-act musical), first produced in New York City at Manhattan Theatre Club, April 6, 1977. Also author of unproduced three-act comedy, "Footloose and Fancy Three," and unproduced screenplay, "The Keys."

Lyricist for theatre and films, including "The Sign in Sidney Brustein's Window," "Young Ben Franklin," "The Clowns," and "La Guerre Est Finie."

WORK IN PROGRESS: A novel; a musical drama.

SIDELIGHTS: Fox comments: "I don't believe in wasting words. Every word evokes a world of its own and modifies other worlds. The atmosphere varies. If a writer chooses well, he penetrates; if he is indiscriminate, no amount of verbiage can lift the fog.

"Writing lyrics, particularly theatre lyrics, was the best preparation I could have had for every other kind of writing I have done since. I learned how to make a word or two carry the weight of many, how to make every syllable count.

"Lyric writing also conditioned me to hear words sing, to expect them to sing. Sentences aren't composed only of words anymore, they are composed of syllables, and syllables have rhythm and meter and should scan. All is part of one big flow. I like to believe an entire book of mine could be scored.

"From regarding life as lyricist I learned my most valuable lesson—what *not* to write. Far too many songs have been written. Such superfluity applies to other kinds of writing as well. If I can't say something new, or say it differently, I shouldn't be writing it."

* * *

FRANCKE, Linda Bird 1939-

PERSONAL: Born March 14, 1939, in New York, N.Y.; daughter of S. Curtis (an insurance executive) and Janet (an organizer; maiden name, King) Bird; married G. David Mackenzie, January 6, 1961 (marriage ended, 1965); married Albert Francke III (a lawyer), October 7, 1967 (marriage ended, 1977); children: (first marriage) Andrew; (second marriage) Caitlin, Tapp. *Education:* Attended Bradford Junior College, 1958. *Politics:* Democrat. *Religion:* Presbyterian. *Home address:* Main St., Sagaponack, N.Y. 11962. *Agent:* Lynn Nesbitt, International Creative Management, 40 West 57th St., New York, N.Y. 10019. *Office:* Newsweek, 444 Madison Ave., New York, N.Y. 10022.

CAREER: Young & Rubicam, Inc., New York City, advertising copywriter, 1960-63; Ogilvy & Mather, Inc., New York City, advertising copywriter, 1965-67; *New York,* New York City, contributing editor, 1968-72; *Newsweek,* New York City, general editor, 1972—. Co-director of Writer's Resource Center, Southampton College. *Member:* Authors Guild of Authors League of America, Women's Media Group. *Awards, honors:* Awards from Cannes Film Festival, 1969, for a television commercial.

WRITINGS: The Ambivalence of Abortion, (nonfiction) Random House, 1978; *Fathers and Daughters* (nonfiction), Random House, 1980.

Work represented in several anthologies, including *Running Against the Machine,* 1969; *The Power Game,* 1970; *Women: A Book for Men,* 1979. Author of "Hers," a column in *New York Times,* 1977.

SIDELIGHTS: Since the 1973 Supreme Court ruling legalizing abortion in the first and second trimesters of pregnancy, the moral and emotional ambivalence towards abortion has not diminished. People have tended to align themselves as either for or against abortion, and neither of these camps have allowed much room for the expression of ambiguity. In her book, *The Ambivalence of Abortion,* Francke has addressed herself to this shadowy area of non-absolutes.

When, in May, 1976, the *New York Times* published an anonymous account of a woman's abortion, it was deluged with mail from women who described their own experiences with abortion. The author of that article was Francke, and she was compelled by the response her articles evoked to study the subject in greater depth. She interviewed women who had had abortions both before and after the Supreme Court decision, husbands and lovers of women who'd had abortions, parents of daughters who'd had abortions, and staff members of abortion clinics. The interviews are marked variously by anger, pain, guilt, and relief: Francke's conclusion is that few emerge from the experience of abortion without being scarred mentally and even physically. While some reviewers quibbled with her sampling technique, theorizing that she chose interview subjects with views similar to her own, most critics felt that Francke's conclusions were valid and important.

The criticism the book received was largely that Francke had not gone far enough in examining the difficult subject. Laurie Stone commented: "A book about the ambivalence and the abuses of abortion did need to be written, but Francke's effort doesn't suffice. There isn't enough material here for more than a long article. Most of the women Francke interviewed expected abortion to cause some physical and emotional pain, and Francke does not quote a single example of misleading or oversimplified proabortion propaganda. The feminist abortion counselors she interviewed are all sober and humane. So we are left with only Francke's word that misleading rhetoric exists."

Peter Skerry argued that Francke skirts the "question of abortion as an issue of public morality." He wrote: *"The*

Ambivalence of Abortion does make an effort to inform women more fully about the consequences of their decisions, and to tell one truth about abortion that is seldom heard—that it is psychologically and physically traumatic. Yet what the book offers in the end is little more than refined cost-benefit analysis.''

"The interviews are revelatory, painful, vivid,'' Barbara Grizzuti Harrison remarked. "But I would wish for more editorial comment. Francke addresses herself only to the emotional ambivalence surrounding abortion. She doesn't deal with moral ambiguity (or she chooses to regard morality and emotion as synonymous). . . . To read *The Ambivalence of Abortion* is to be convinced that the problems raised by abortion cannot be satisfied by right-on slogans. . . . I think the real message of Francke's book is something philosophers and moral logicians have always known: the most painful moral struggles are not those between the good and the evil, but between the good and the less good.''

Francke wrote to *CA*: "I am a woman, a condition that has become a plus only in the last ten years. Now I revel in being part of the social transition that is finally taking shape in America, and work extensively in areas of interest to women. We need to know more, expect more, gain more—and share it all.

"In writing *The Ambivalence of Abortion* I was shocked at the ignorance and misinformation sexually active people have about birth control. We need to spend more money—much more money—on sex education, especially among teenagers.''

BIOGRAPHICAL/CRITICAL SOURCES: New York Times, March 24, 1978; *New York Times Book Review*, April 2, 1973; *Village Voice*, April 3, 1978; *Washington Post Book World*, April 9, 1978; *Newsweek*, April 10, 1978; *Nation*, April 15, 1978; *Saturday Review*, May 13, 1978; *Ms.*, June, 1978; *New York Review of Books*, July 20, 1978; *Commentary*, July, 1978.

*   *   *

FRANK, Stanley B.   1908-1979

OBITUARY NOTICE—See index for *CA* sketch: Born April 22, 1908, in New York, N.Y.; died of a heart attack, January 6, 1979, in New York, N.Y. Known for his prolific output, Frank wrote more than 750 articles, 150 of which were for the *Saturday Evening Post*. He edited a collection of sports articles entitled *Sports Extra* and wrote *The Sexually Active Man Past Forty*. Obituaries and other sources: *New York Times*, January 9, 1979.

*   *   *

FRANKEL, Edward   1910-

PERSONAL: Born June 4, 1910, in New York, N.Y.; son of Morris and Sara (Gelerter) Frankel; married Helen Stawsky, May 26, 1939; children: Steven, Richard. *Education:* City College (now of the City University of New York), B.S., 1931; Columbia University, M.A., 1932; Yeshiva University, Ph.D., 1958. *Home:* 247 Parkview Ave., Bronxville, N.Y. 10708. *Office:* Department of Education, Herbert H. Lehman College of the City University of New York, Bedford Park Blvd. W., Bronx, N.Y. 10468.

CAREER: High school science teacher and guidance counselor in Bronx, N.Y., 1940-59; New York City Board of Education, Bureau of Educational Research, New York City, research assistant, 1959-65; Herbert H. Lehman College of the City University of New York, Bronx, N.Y., as-

sociate professor, 1965-72, professor of science education and educational research, 1972—, director of institutional and educational research, 1968-74. Member of executive committee of Bronx River Restoration Project. *Member:* National Science Teachers Association, American Fern Society, Torrey Botanical Club, New York Botanical Garden, Scarsdale Audubon Club (vice-president).

WRITINGS: DNA, Ladder of Life, McGraw, 1965, 2nd edition, 1979. Contributor of about seventy-five articles to education and environmental studies journals and newspapers.

WORK IN PROGRESS: The Bronx River: Past, Present, and Future, and *Fun With Ferns*.

SIDELIGHTS: Frankel comments: "I am currently engaged in environmental studies, particularly the natural history of the Bronx River Valley and the flora of Westchester. I recently listed about eight hundred of the vascular plants found in this area. I also lead field trips for conservation and botanical groups and teach field study courses at New York Botanical Garden.''

*   *   *

FRASER, Antonia (Pakenham)   1932-

PERSONAL: Born August 27, 1932, in London, England; daughter of Frank and Elizabeth (Harman) Pakenham; married Hugh Charles Patrick Joseph Fraser (member of British parliament), September 25, 1956 (marriage ended, 1977); children: Rebecca, Flora, Benjamin, Natasha, Damian, Orlando. *Education:* Oxford University, received degree, 1953. *Home:* 52 Campden Hill Sq., London W8, England. *Agent:* Curtis Brown Academic Ltd., 1 Craven Hill, London W2 3EW, England.

CAREER: Writer. Also worked as broadcaster and lecturer. Member of Arts Council, 1970-71. *Member:* Society of Authors (chairman, 1974-75). *Awards, honors:* James Tait Black Prize for biography, 1969, for *Mary, Queen of Scots*.

WRITINGS: Dolls, Putnam, 1963; *A History of Toys*, Delacorte, 1966, new edition, Springer Books, 1972; *Mary, Queen of Scots*, Delacorte, 1969; *King Arthur and the Knights of the Round Table*, (juvenile), Knopf, 1970; *Robin Hood* (juvenile), Knopf, 1971; *Cromwell, the Lord Protector*, Knopf, 1973 (published in England as *Cromwell, Our Chief of Men*, Weidenfeld & Nicolson, 1973); *King James VI of Scotland, I of England*, Weidenfeld & Nicolson, 1974, Knopf, 1975; (compiler) *Scottish Love Poems: A Personal Anthology*, Canongate, 1975, Taplinger, 1978; (editor) *The Lives of the Kings and Queens of England*, Knopf, 1975; (compiler) *Love Letters*, Weidenfeld & Nicolson, 1976, Knopf, 1977; *Quiet as a Nun*, Viking, 1977; *The Wild Island: A Mystery*, Norton, 1978. Translator of *Dior*, by Christian Dior, Weidenfeld & Nicolson. Also author of phonodisc, "Mary, Queen of Scots,'' National Portrait Gallery, 1971, and phonotape, "Sixteenth-Century Scotland,'' with Gordon Donaldson, Holt Information Systems, 1972.

SIDELIGHTS: Fraser received immediate acclaim in 1969 for her book *Mary, Queen of Scots*. Although Mary Stuart had already been the subject of numerous biographers, Fraser, according to a reviewer for *Economist*, managed to place "Mary in a far more favourable light than any historian of recent times.'' As Eric Forbes-Boyd noted, "Antonia Fraser takes the sympathetic view.'' Forbes-Boyd also observed that Fraser absolved Stuart of any participation in the murder of her husband, even though she later married the prime suspect in the case. C. V. Wedgewood felt that Fraser was able to justify her conclusions concerning Stuart's scandalous behavior. "Antonia Fraser has diligently compiled and sifted everything that is known to her," he wrote, "trying to reach the truth behind contemporary slanders and later legends. She has given particular attention to Mary's medical history, and is able to show that she was subject to periods of nervous collapse under stress, in which her vitality and her judgment forsook her and she fell into a kind of apathy."

Fraser impressed numerous reviewers with her extensive research for *Mary, Queen of Scots*. A critic for *Times Literary Supplement* claimed, "No source of information has been neglected." A reviewer for *Economist* called attention to the book's sound scholarship, another noted that Fraser's three years of research was evident throughout. Calling the book "a trustworthy chronicle," a writer for *Times Literary Supplement* proceeded to note: "One of the most valuable features of this book is its intensive study of Mary Stuart's health, based on more evidence than has perhaps been hitherto recognized as such. . . . It must be said that Lady Antonia shirks nothing. She has an answer, generally convincing, sometimes casuistical, but always well considered and presented to every charge that can be brought against her heroine."

Many critics were equally impressed with Fraser's abilities as a writer. Writing in *Book World*, Jean Stafford declared that Fraser "brings to this immense biography a vivid sense of the mores of the sixteenth century, so lucid a manner of presenting history that she succeeds in almost completely clarifying the muddied maelstrom in which Europe and the British Isles were thrashing and trumpeting, and a narrative dexterity that makes her sad tale seem told for the first time." Similarly, Helen Johnson wrote that *Mary, Queen of Scots* was "compulsively and poignantly readable."

Fraser invested much of herself in writing *Mary, Queen of Scots*. As one writer revealed, "Fraser's neck became dislocated from the constant typing but she remained so emotionally involved that she could weep while writing the execution scene." As Fraser explained, "I know it sounds affected, but after we had been together three years it seemed terrible that she had to go through all that." Even as a child Fraser had what she called an "identification with Mary, Queen of Scots. I would get some of my seven brothers and sisters to act out the execution scene, with me playing Mary and saying very dramatically, 'Don't cry, good people.'"

Prior to her success with *Mary, Queen of Scots*, Fraser had drawn some critics' attention with *A History of Toys*. However, the book was credited more for being attractively packaged than well written. A writer for *Best Sellers* called it "a handsome piece of publishing and well worth a library investment." However, the same writer also advised, "But do not expect this to be an exhaustive or even fully representative history of toys international." Writing in *New Statesman*, Gillian Freeman summed up *A History of Toys* as a "comprehensive, beautifully produced book."

After *Mary, Queen of Scots*, Fraser wrote a pair of children's books, *King Arthur and the Knights of the Round Table* and *Robin Hood*. Neither book was particularly well received by reviewers for *Times Literary Supplement*. *King Arthur and the Knights of the Round Table* "looks and reads like many versions current in the first half of this century," wrote one critic. "Her version of the stories depends, she herself says, on 'Malory and memory.' Is this quite good enough?" A reviewer of *Robin Hood* felt that it would "merely confuse those who have read it or are likely to read more authentic retellings." That same reviewer was, however, not unimpressed by its "speed and vigour."

Fraser followed her juvenile works with another impressive biography, *Cromwell*. The book bore many similarities to the previous biography, *Mary, Queen of Scots*. Fraser invested four years researching material on Cromwell which she hoped would "humanize" him. She was largely successful in accomplishing her task. A reviewer for *Economist* wrote that Fraser "has produced an exceedingly long but extremely well researched book. . . . The end product is important, very well-written and amply justifies the four years' work she has put into it." Paul Johnson felt that the book would "go a long way to redress the distortions from which Cromwell has suffered."

Some reviewers were dissatisfied with Fraser's approach to politics in *Cromwell*. "Her treatment of the political events which led to the constitutional crisis of the early 1640s is skimpy," wrote Johnson. "She pays far too little attention to the economic factors which contributed to the breakdown, and in general she is cursory in analysing the intellectual currents which galvanised the parliamentary party." And Jane Majeski found that Fraser's "emphasis on Cromwell as a typical country gentleman leaves one with the implausible impression that he stumbled on the throne of England by accident."

Fraser's third biography, *King James VI of Scotland, I of England*, was not as extensive a work as its predecessors. Called "part biography and part argument" by a writer for *New Yorker*, *King James VI of Scotland, I of England* offered, according to the critic, "entertaining portraits of James's sloppy courts, and, in emphasizing his staying powers, excites something like wonder." Alden Whitman agreed, finding the book "thoroughly readable as a character study. . . ." He also wrote, "on superficial levels . . . she has cleared away some of the unjust accusations leveled against James that have persisted over the years." By comparison, Majeski declared that Fraser would have produced a better biography if she'd followed the same steps taken for the previous books. She noted that *King James VI of Scotland, I of England* "lacks the thorough research and depth" of *Mary, Queen of Scots* and *Cromwell*. Majeski also believed that Fraser "would have done better to have written a thorough analysis of James's character . . . and to have left aside the political complications." After writing *King James VI of Scotland, I of England*, Fraser compiled *Love Letters*, which Frederic Raphael called, "A mixed post-bag, mostly from and to toppish people, Cromwell, Napoleon, Sir Thomas More, etc." Victoria Glendinning claimed that the selection was "admirably catholic" but concluded, "it is not fair to judge what love is from love-letters."

Love Letters was followed by Fraser's first novel, a mystery entitled *Quiet as a Nun*. Judging the book for its qualities as a mystery, many critics found it a poor contribution to the genre. Anna Quindlen noted, "Mystery lovers should be warned that who does what to whom is ridiculously easy to figure out. . . ." Daniel Coogan complained that *Quiet as a Nun* contained too many of the conventional mystery devices. "I hope her next investigation will reveal more of her," he wrote. "I hope also that the scene of the next crime will find a different use than to provide ruined towers, pseudo-ghosts and secret passages." While Coogan complained that Fraser did not invest enough of herself in the lead character of *Quiet as a Nun*, Jemima Shore, P. D. James found that the book contained "a heroine of whom, happily, it is promised that we shall know more." James also wrote that the book was "written with humour and sympathy." Jemima was also featured in a second mystery novel, *The Wild Island*.

BIOGRAPHICAL/CRITICAL SOURCES: Best Sellers, November 1, 1966; *New Statesman,* November 11, 1966, June 8, 1973, December 24, 1976; *Times Literary Supplement,* June 3, 1969, June 20, 1973, November 12, 1976; *Economist,* June 21, 1969, June 9, 1973; *Christian Science Monitor,* October 30, 1969; *Book World,* November 16, 1969; *New York Times Book Review,* November 23, 1969, March 30, 1975; *Saturday Review,* February 8, 1975; *New Yorker,* February 24, 1975; *Saturday Review/World,* October 23, 1975; *Authors in the News,* Volume 2, Gale, 1976.*

* * *

FRASER, G(eorge) S(utherland) 1915-

PERSONAL: Born November 8, 1915, in Glasgow, Scotland; married Eileen Lucy Andrew, 1946; children: one son, two daughters. *Education:* St. Andrews University, M.A., 1937. *Home:* 19 Guilford Rd., Stoneygate, Leicester, England. *Office:* University of Leicester, Leicester, England.

CAREER: Poet, critic, editor, biographer, translator, and travel writer. *Aberdeen Press and Journal,* Aberdeen, Scotland, journalist, 1937-39; free-lance journalist, 1946-59; cultural adviser to United Kingdom liaison mission in Japan, 1950-51; University of Leicester, Leicester, England, lecturer, 1959-63, reader in modern English literature, 1964—. Visiting professor at Rochester University, 1963-64. *Military service:* British Army, 1939-45; served in Middle East. *Awards, honors:* Hodder and Stoughton bursary, 1946.

WRITINGS—Poetry: Home Town Elegy, Editions Poetry, 1944; *The Traveller Has Regrets and Other Poems,* Harvill Press, 1948; *Leaves Without a Tree,* Hokuseido Press, 1956; *Conditions: Selected Recent Poetry,* Byron Press, 1969.

Criticism: *Post-War Trends in English Literature,* Hokuseido Press, 1950; *The Modern Writer and His World: Continuity and Innovation in Twentieth-Century English Literature,* Verschoyle, 1953, Criterion, 1955, revised edition, Deutsch, 1964, Praeger, 1965; *Vision and Rhetoric: Studies in Modern Poetry,* Faber, 1968, Dutton, 1969; *Metre, Rhythm, and Free Verse,* Methuen, 1970; *Essays on Twentieth-Century Poets,* Leicester University Press, 1977.

Other: *Vision of Scotland,* Elek, 1948; *News From South America,* Harvill Press, 1949, Library Publishers, 1952; *Scotland,* Studio Publications, 1955; *Ezra Pound,* Oliver & Boyd, 1960, Grove, 1961; (author of introduction) Donald B. Moore, *The Poetry of Louis MacNeice,* Humanities Press, 1972; *Alexander Pope,* Routledge & Kegan Paul, 1978.

Editor: (With J. Waller) *The Collected Poems of Keith Douglas,* Editions Poetry, 1951, revised edition with Waller and J. C. Hall, Faber, 1966, Chilmark Press, 1967; (with Ian Fletcher) *Springtime: An Anthology of Young Poets and Writers,* P. Owen, 1953; *Poetry Now: An Anthology,* Faber, 1956; *Selected Poems of Robert Burns,* Macmillan, 1960; Betty Parvin and others, *Vaughan College Poems,* University of Leicester, 1963; (with others) *British Writers and Their Work,* Volume 5, University of Nebraska Press, 1965; (with Hall and Waller) Keith Douglas, *Alamein to Zem Zem,* Faber, 1966, Chilmark Press, 1967; *John Keats: Odes, a Casebook,* Macmillan, 1971; Adi-Granth, *Selections From the Sacred Writings of the Sikhs,* Allen & Unwin, 1974.

Translator: Patrice de la Tour du Pin, *The Dedicated Life in Poetry, and the Correspondence of Laurent de Cayeux,* Harvill Press, 1948, reprinted, R. West, 1973; Gabriel Marcel, *The Mystery of Being,* Harvill Press, 1950; Marcel, *Men Against Humanity,* Harvill Press, 1952; Jean Mesnard, *Pascal: His Life and Works,* Harvill Press, 1952; (with E. de Mauny) S. Moreux, *Bela Bartok,* Harvill Press, 1953.

Contributor to periodicals, including *Times Literary Supplement, Observer, New Statesman, Listener, Partisan Review, Commentary, Poetry,* and *Chicago Critical Quarterly.*

SIDELIGHTS: Fraser is known for his compassionate approach to criticism. Norman MacCaig reported that Fraser's criticism "has been remarkable, not only for its perceptiveness, but for its civilised good manners and its consistent aim to see and enlarge on the best in whatever work he is dealing with." MacCaig noted that each of the twenty essays contained in *Essays on Twentieth-Century Poets* "has a clear light to shed." He continued, "On top of that, the blurb for once is right when it speaks of 'George Fraser's delight in discovering a good poem, a delight which he can convey to young and mature readers alike.'"

Fraser also distinguished himself when he continued to defend Ezra Pound at a point in the 1960's when the poet's popularity was waning. Fraser observed that Pound was "an innovator of the utmost importance, a superlative verse technician, a poet with from the beginning to the end of his work an impeccable ear, an explorer genius."

Fraser had similar praise for Lawrence Durrell in his critical study of that author. But his summation of Durrell as a "near-mystic, a near-image," was disputed by Edward Thomas. Of Durrell, Thomas wrote, "You can be a committed realist and yet be saved by your imagination; or you can believe in the supremacy of art and test this belief against the material of life. But somewhere there has to be interaction."

BIOGRAPHICAL/CRITICAL SOURCES: G. S. Fraser, *Ezra Pound,* Oliver & Boyd, 1960; *Spectator,* August 23, 1968; *London Magazine,* October, 1968; Fraser, *Essays on Twentieth-Century Poets,* Leicester University Press, 1977; *Listener,* January 19, 1978.*

* * *

FRAZIER, Shervert Hughes 1921-

PERSONAL: Born June 12, 1921, in Shreveport, La.; son of Shervert Hughes and Mary (Lowman) Frazier; married Gloria Barger, July 20, 1947; children: Elise Frazier Woodward, Alan, Rosalie, Stephen. *Education:* University of Illinois at Chicago Circle, B.S., 1941, M.D., 1943; University of Minnesota, M.S., 1957; Columbia College of Physicians and Surgeons, certificate, 1963. *Home:* 115 Mill St., Belmont, Mass. 02178. *Office:* McLean Hospital, Belmont, Mass. 02178.

CAREER: Intern, University of Illinois, Research and Educational Hospital, 1943-44; private practice of psychiatry in Harrisburg, Ill., 1946-50; Mayo Foundation Institute, Rochester, Minn., fellow in psychiatry, 1951-55; New York State Psychiatric Institute, New York, N.Y., chief research scientist, 1958-61; Ben Taub General Hospital, Houston, Tex., chief psychiatrist, 1962-68; New York State Psychiatric Institute, deputy director, 1968-72; McLean Hospital, Belmont, Mass., psychiatrist-in-chief, 1972—. Diplomate of American Board of Psychiatry and Neurology (member of board of directors, 1965; president, 1972); attending psychiatrist at New York City's Presbyterian Hospital, 1958-62, director of inpatient consultation service, 1961-62; director of Houston Psychiatric Institute, 1962-65; senior attending psychiatrist at Houston's Methodist Hospital, 1962-65. Professor and department head at Baylor University, 1965-68; professor at Columbia University College of Physicians and Surgeons, 1968-72; professor at Harvard University, 1972—. Administrator of Harrisburg Medical Foundation, 1948-51; member of board of directors of Kittay Scientific Foundation. Member of Commission for Mental Health and Mental

Retardation for Texas, 1965-67; member of President's Commission on Mental Health; consultant to Federal Aviation Administration and surgeon-general of U.S. Air Force. *Military service:* U.S. Naval Reserve, active duty in Medical Corps, 1944-46; served in Pacific theater; became lieutenant commander.

MEMBER: World Psychiatric Association (vice-president), American Medical Association, American College of Physicians, American Society of Human Genetics, American Psychiatric Association (head of Joint Commission on Public Affairs), American College of Psychiatrists (first vice-president), American Board of Family Practice, Association for Research in Nervous and Mental Diseases (president, 1972; head of board of trustees, 1976—), New York Academy of Medicine (fellow), Massachusetts Medical Association, Middlesex County Medical Society, Houston Psychiatric Society, Boston Psychoanalytic Society and Institute, Sigma Xi, Alpha Omega Alpha. *Awards, honors:* M.A. from Harvard University, 1972; Bowis Award from American College of Psychiatrists, 1978.

WRITINGS: (With A. C. Carr) *Introduction to Psychopathology,* Macmillan, 1964; (with A. P. Friedman and Dodi Schultz) *The Headache Book,* Dodd, 1973; (editor) *Aggression* (proceedings), Williams & Wilkins, 1974; (editor with R. H. Campbell, M. H. Marshall, and Arnold Werner) *A Psychiatric Glossary,* 4th edition (Frazier was not associated with earlier editions), American Psychiatric Association, 1975; (editor with J. O. Cole and A. F. Schatzberg) *Depression: Biology, Dynamics, and Treatment,* Plenum, 1978.

Contributor of about seventy-five articles to medical journals. Editor-in-chief of *McLean Hospital Journal;* member of editorial board of *Psychiatric Journal of the University of Ottawa, Psychiatric Annals, Psychiatrist's Bookshelf, Psychosomatics, Psychiatry,* and *Continuing Education in Psychiatry.*

WORK IN PROGRESS: Volume V of *Psychiatric Glossary,* with R. H. Campbell and Arnold Werner; a textbook in the behavioral sciences, publication by Little, Brown expected in 1980; research on violence and affective disorders.

SIDELIGHTS: Frazier told *CA:* "One of the most neglected areas of psychiatric research has been that of violence. In the process of planning my research, I started out to test the hypothesis of parental reinforcement owing to their gratification when their children acted out. This has led to a multifamily study of violent people inside and outside of prisons and state hospitals. Results so far have been informative and rewarding.

"The years of research into the causes and treatment of affective disorders is now beginning to pay off. I am exhilarated by the prospects of what we will find as we continue our work on blood levels, differential diagnosis and genetics."

*   *   *

FREED, Donald 1932-

PERSONAL: Born May 13, 1932, in Chicago, Ill. *Education:* Attended University of Illinois, 1950-51, Louisiana College, 1951-52, Art Institute of Chicago, 1952-54, and University of California, Los Angeles, San Fernando Valley State College, 1955-65. *Home:* 2337 Greenfield Ave., Los Angeles, Calif. 90064.

CAREER: Writer. Los Angeles Theatre Arts Foundation, Los Angeles, Calif., artistic director, 1957-65; Every Womans Village, Van Nuys, Calif., chairman of humanities department, 1965-68; Beverly Hills Adult School, Beverly Hills, Calif., chairman of humanities division, 1965-68. Dean of admissions and communication theory at Columbia School of Broadcasting, 1966, lecturer at University of California, Los Angeles, 1967, California State University at Long Beach, 1968. *Awards, honors:* John Larkin Award for "Faust"; Milton Lester Award for "Crime and Punishment"; finalist in International Gandhi Centennial at University of Southern Illinois, 1969, for "Bapu"; Office of Advance Drama Research grant from Rockefeller Foundation and University of Minnesota, 1970, for "Hogs Run Wild"; grant-in-aid from Russell Sage Foundation, 1972-73, for "The Police-Industrial Complex"; grant-in-aid from Citizens Against Crime of Silence Foundation, 1972-73, for "The Invisible Government."

WRITINGS: Freud and Stanislavsky: New Directions in the Performing Arts, Vantage Press, 1964; (with Joan Ross) *The Existentialism of Alberto Moravia,* Southern Illinois University Press, 1972; *Agony in New Haven: The Trial of Bobby Seale, Ericka Huggins, and the Black Panther Party,* Simon & Schuster, 1973; (with Mark Lane) *Executive Action: Assassination of a Head of State,* Dell, 1973; (with Barbara Morris Freed) *Big Brother and the Holding Company (the World Behind Watergate),* Ramparts, 1975; *The Killing of RFK,* Dell, 1975; *The Spymaster,* Arbor House, 1979. Also author, with Huey P. Newton, of *The War Against the Panthers.*

Plays: "Crime and Punishment" (adapted from the novel by Fyodor Dostoyevsky); *Inquest: The U.S. vs. Julius and Ethel Rosenberg,* first produced on Broadway at Music Box, 1970.

Editor: *The Glass House Tapes,* Avon, 1972; Kai Erickson and Huey P. Newton, *In Search of Common Ground,* Norton, 1973. Also editor of *To Die for the People,* 1972, and *Revolutionary Suicide,* 1973, both by Newton.

WORK IN PROGRESS: "Human Beings Without Fire"; a screenplay with Mark Lane, "The Murder of Martin Luther King."

*   *   *

FREEDMAN, Hy 1914-

PERSONAL: Born April 10, 1914, in Chelsea, Mass.; son of Frank (in business) and Bessie (Kanaber) Freedman; married Elizabeth Lipp, March, 1944 (divorced, February, 1961); children: Ross, Julie. *Education:* Attended Boston University, 1934-35. *Politics:* "Liberal and progressive Democrat." *Residence:* Los Angeles, Calif. *Agent:* Elaine Markson Literary Agency, Inc., 44 Greenwich Ave., New York, N.Y. 10011.

CAREER: Radio writer in Los Angeles, Calif., 1945-50; television writer in Hollywood, Calif. (including "Red Skelton Show" and "You Bet Your Life"), 1947-62. General manager of KVST-TV (public broadcasting affiliate), 1975. Member of board of directors of Western Industries, 1956-71. *Military service:* U.S. Navy, Seabees, 1942-45; received battle star. *Member:* Writers Guild of America (West; member of council, 1956-57, 1960-61; vice-president, 1961; president of television branch, 1961). *Awards, honors:* National radio and television awards, including Peabody Broadcasting Award from Academy of Television Arts and Sciences for "You Bet Your Life."

WRITINGS: Super Marriage—Super Sex, Ballantine, 1974; *Sex Link,* M. Evans, 1977. Contributor to *Forum.*

WORK IN PROGRESS: Another book.

SIDELIGHTS: Freedman writes: "I drifted into a writing career. After serving two years in the South Pacific in World War II I returned to the United States, got married, and learned that I was scheduled to be shipped out soon for another tour of duty. Preferring to remain in the States, at least for awhile, I considered the various possibilities for a job on base, and quickly concluded that writing was my best bet, if indeed not my only one.

"I wrote three articles for the base newspaper which were well received. This led directly to a job in the public relations office. There, one of my duties was the writing of a weekly half-hour radio show dramatizing the Seabee war experience overseas. This show was aired locally and to U.S. military bases overseas, and served as my introduction to broadcast writing.

"At the war's end, it was a short hop to Hollywood and network radio, for which I wrote several dramatizations. I soon turned to comedy writing, which seemed to offer more opportunities and greater rewards. In 1950 I began writing for television and was kept occupied in this medium for the next twenty years. It's only in recent years that I turned to writing for publication, while still keeping my hand in television.

"I've been attracted to sexuality, sociology, health and nutrition, and politics, have read widely in these areas, and have written about some of these subjects. Though always interested in the state of the nation and the world, my writing reflected these concerns only tenuously and obliquely. However, in my current writing my intention is to make this large subject the heart of my work."

*   *   *

FREEMAN, A. Myrick III 1936-

PERSONAL: Born February 6, 1936, in Plainfield, N.J.; son of A. Myrick, Jr. and Elisabeth L. Freeman; married; children: two. *Education:* Cornell University, A.B., 1957; University of Washington, Seattle, M.A., 1964, Ph.D., 1965. *Office:* Department of Economics, Bowdoin College, Brunswick, Me. 04011.

CAREER: Bowdoin College, Brunswick, Me., assistant professor of economics, 1965-69; Resources for the Future, Inc., Washington, D.C., visiting scholar, 1969-70; Bowdoin College, associate professor, 1971-75, professor of economics, 1975—, head of department, 1971-76. Visiting associate professor at University of Wisconsin—Madison, spring, 1973; fellow of Resources for the Future, Inc., 1976-78. Member of board of economic advisers of Public Interest Economics Center, 1972—. Participant in conferences and workshops; testified before U.S. Senate and House of Representatives; consultant to Environmental Defense Fund, Environmental Protection Agency, and Organization for Economic Cooperation and Development. *Military service:* U.S. Navy, 1957-63, assistant professor at University of Washington, Seattle, 1960-63; became lieutenant, 1961. *Member:* American Economic Association.

WRITINGS: International Trade: An Introduction to Method and Theory, Harper, 1971; (with Robert H. Haveman and Allen V. Kneese) *The Economics of Environmental Policy,* Wiley, 1973; (editor with Alain C. Enthoven, and contributor) *Pollution, Resources, and the Environment: A Book of Readings,* Norton, 1973; *The Benefits of Environmental Improvement: Theory and Practice,* Johns Hopkins Press, 1979.

Contributor: Julius Margolis and Haveman, editors, *Public*

Expenditures and Policy Analysis, Markham, 1970; Kenneth E. Boulding and Martin Pfaff, editors, *Transfers in an Urbanized Economy,* Wadsworth, 1972; Kneese and Blair T. Bower, editors, *Environmental Quality Analysis: Theory and Method in the Social Sciences,* Johns Hopkins Press, 1972; *The Costs of Pollution Control: A National Symposium,* North Carolina State University, 1972; Henry Peskin and Eugene Seskin, editors, *Cost-Benefit Analysis and Water Pollution Policy,* Urban Institute (Washington, D.C.), 1975; Richard Zeckhauser and others, editors, *Benefit Cost and Policy Analysis, 1974,* Aldine, 1975; F. Thomas Juster, editor, *The Distribution of Economic Well-Being,* Ballinger, 1977; Paul Portney, editor, *Current Issues in U.S. Environmental Policy,* Johns Hopkins Press, 1978; David Segal, editor, *The Economics of Neighborhood,* Academic Press, 1979. Contributor of about thirty articles and reviews to academic journals and popular magazines, including *New Republic,* and newspapers.

WORK IN PROGRESS: Research on environmental policy.

*   *   *

FREEMAN, Richard B(arry) 1944-

PERSONAL: Born June 29, 1944, in New Windsor, N.Y.; married Franziska Amacher. *Education:* Dartmouth College, B.A., 1963; Harvard University, Ph.D., 1968. *Home:* 10 Ellery St., Cambridge, Mass. 02138. *Office:* Department of Economics, 109 Littauer Center, Harvard University, Cambridge, Mass. 02138.

CAREER: Yale University, New Haven, Conn., assistant professor of economics, 1968-69; associated with Harvard University, Cambridge, Mass., 1969-70; University of Chicago, Chicago, Ill., assistant professor of economics, 1970-72; Harvard University, began as associate professor, 1973, became professor of economics.

WRITINGS: The Market for College-Trained Manpower, Harvard University Press, 1971; *Labor Economics,* Prentice-Hall, 1972, 2nd edition, 1978; (with Glen Cain and Lee Hansen) *Labor Market Analysis of Engineers and Technical Workers,* Johns Hopkins Press, 1973; *The Overeducated American,* Academic Press, 1976; *Black Elite,* McGraw, 1977.

*   *   *

FREEMAN, Susan Tax 1938-

PERSONAL: Born May 24, 1938, in Chicago, Ill.; daughter of Sol (a professor of anthropology) and Gertrude (Katz) Tax; married Leslie G. Freeman (a professor of anthropology), March 20, 1964; children: Sarah E. *Education:* University of Chicago, B.A., 1958; Harvard University, M.A., 1959, Ph.D., 1965. *Office:* Department of Anthropology, University of Illinois at Chicago Circle, P.O. Box 4348, Chicago, Ill. 60680.

CAREER: University of Illinois at Chicago Circle, assistant professor, 1965-70, associate professor, 1970-78, professor of anthropology, 1978—. Conducted some field studies in southern Mexico and extensive fieldwork in Spain. *Member:* American Anthropological Association, American Association for the Advancement of Science, Royal Anthropological Institute of Great Britain and Ireland. *Awards, honors:* Grants from Wenner-Gren Foundation, 1966, National Institute of Mental Health, 1967-71, and National Endowment for the Humanities, 1979.

WRITINGS: Neighbors: The Social Contract in a Castilian Hamlet, University of Chicago Press, 1970; *The Pasiegos:*

Spaniards in No Man's Land, University of Chicago Press, 1979. Contributor to anthropology journals. Associate editor of *American Anthropologist,* 1971-73, and *American Ethnologist,* 1974-76.

WORK IN PROGRESS: Exploring marginality in Spanish culture.

*   *   *

FRIAR, Kimon 1911-

PERSONAL: First name pronounced *Key*mun; born November 18, 1911, in Imrali, Turkey; came to United States in 1915, naturalized in 1920; son of James (a businessman) and Hrisoula (Hadjikonstandi) Friar; divorced. *Education:* Attended Art Institute of Chicago, 1929, and Yale University, 1932; University of Wisconsin, B.A. (with honors), 1934; University of Michigan, M.A., 1939; additional graduate study at State University of Iowa, 1940. *Politics:* Democrat. *Home:* Kallidromiou 10, Athens 706, Greece. *Agent:* Bertha Klausner International Literary Agency, Inc., 71 Park Ave., New York, N.Y. 10016.

CAREER: Poet; translator; editor; critic. Assistant professor at Adelphi College (now University), 1940-45, at Amherst College, 1945-46, at New York University, 1952-53, and at University of Minnesota, Duluth, 1953-54; regents lecturer, University of California, Berkeley, 1965; visiting professor at University of Illinois, and at University of Indiana, both summer, 1971; distinguished visiting professor, at Ohio State University, 1977-78, and at other universities and institutions in the United States, Greece, and South America. Director, costume and set designer, and translator of "The Bacchae," by Euripides, University of Wisconsin, 1932; editorial writer for *Michigan State Guide Book,* 1933-36; play reader, Detroit Federal Theater, 1936-37; Poetry Center, director, 1944-47, lecturer, 1944-47, 1952-53; director of Theater Circle at Circle-in-the-Square Theater, 1952-53. Presented weekly program, "Magic Casements of Prose and Poetry," WABF-Radio, 1952-53, program broadcast over WFMT-Radio, Chicago, 1952-53, and WKLK-Radio, Duluth, 1953-54; broadcast weekly radio program on cultural topics over Voice of America, 1958. *Awards, honors:* Zona Gale scholar, 1932-34; Hopwood Award, 1939, for essay on Yeats's "A Vision"; two Athens Academy awards and diplomas, 1976, for translation from the Greek and contribution to Greek letters; named honorary citizen of Iraklion, Crete, 1977; *Greek World* award, 1978.

Editor and translator from the Greek: Nikos Kazantzakis, *Odhisia* (epic poem), [Diphros, Athens], 1938, translation published as *The Odyssey: A Modern Sequel* (Book-of-the-Month Club, Book Find Club, and Seven Arts Club selections; adapted first four books as play entitled "The Reabduction of Helen," first produced at University of Michigan, 1970, produced at University of Wisconsin, May 14-16, 1971), Simon & Schuster, 1958; Kazantzakis, *The Saviours of God: Spiritual Exercises,* Simon & Schuster, 1961; *With Face to the Wall: The Selected Poems of Miltos Sahtouris,* Charioteer Press, 1961; Theodore Roubanis, *The Journey Continues* (poetry) bilingual edition, privately printed (Athens), 1970; *Modern Greek Poetry: From Cavafis to Elytis* (anthology), Simon & Schuster, 1973; *The Sovereign Sun: The Selected Poems of Odysseus Elytis,* Temple University Press, 1974; *Landscape of Death: The Selected Poems of Takis Sinopoulos,* bilingual edition, Ohio State University Press, 1979; (with Kostas Myrsiades) *Scripture of the Blind: Poems by Yannis Ritsos,* bilingual edition, Ohio State University Press, 1979; *The Target: The Selected Poems of Manolis Anagnostakis,* Pella, 1979; *Reinvestigation and the*

Descent From the Cross: Poems by Kostas Kindinis, North Central Publishing, 1979; *Two Plays by Nikos Kazantzakis,* North Central Publishing, 1979.

Editor only: *The Poetry Center Presents* (anthology), Gotham Book Mart, 1947; (with John Malcolm Brinnin) *Modern Poetry: American and British,* Appleton-Century-Crofts, 1951.

Translator only; all plays: Kazantzakis, "Sodom and Gomorrah" (two-act), first produced in Los Angeles, Calif., at University of California, Los Angeles, 1963, produced in New York City, at Jan Jus Playhouse, 1963; Kazantzakis, "Comedy: A Tragedy in One-Act," first produced in Ann Arbor, Mich., at University of Michigan, 1972. Also translator of selections from "Prometheus Bound," by Aeschylus, of "Oedipus the King," by Sophocles, and of "Hecuba," by Euripides, all for American Broadcasting Co. (ABC-TV) program on the Esso Theater, 1964.

Contributor: August Derleth and Raymond E. F. Larson, editors, *Poetry Out of Wisconsin,* Henry Harrison (New York, N.Y.), 1937; *The Nativity* (poetry), Pleias, 1974; *Landscape of Death: An Introduction to the Poetry of Takis Sinopoulos* (in Greek), Kedhros, 1978; *The Spiritual Odyssey of Nikos Kazantzakis,* North Central Publishing, 1979.

Author of introduction: Pandelis Prevelakis, *Nikos Kazantzakis and His Odyssey: A Study of the Poet and His Poem,* Simon & Schuster, 1961; *Six Poets* (anthology; in Greek), [Athens], 1970; Dylan Thomas, *Under Milkwood* (in Greek), Ermias (Athens), 1972; Roy Swanson, *Pindar's Odes,* Bobbs-Merrill, 1974; Dhimitris Kakavelakis, *Massa Confusa: Poems by Dhimitris* (in Greek), Pleis, 1977.

Also author of play "The Tragical History of Dr. Faustus" (adaptation of story by Christopher Marlow), first produced in Detroit, at Detroit Federal Theatre, 1937. Work represented in many anthologies, including: *New Directions 13,* New Directions, 1951; *Little Treasury of World Poetry,* edited by Hubert Creekmore, Scribner, 1952; and *Zero Anthology,* Zero Press, 1956. Author of weekly column, "Greek Letters and the Foreign Press," *Ta Nea* (Greek newspaper), 1975. Contributor of numerous articles, poems, and translations to American and Greek newspapers and periodicals, including *Poetry, Saturday Review, New Republic, New York Times Book Review, Quarterly Review of Literature, Books Abroad, Charioteer, Chicago Review, Greek Heritage,* and *Atlantic.*

Co-editor, *New Writing,* 1936; contributing critic, *New Republic,* 1952-54; *Charioteer,* founder, editor, 1960-62, Greek editor, 1967—; *Greek Heritage,* founder, editor, 1963-65; Greek editor, *World Literature Today,* 1966—; book review editor, *Athenian,* 1975—; Greek associate, *Paideuma* (a journal of Ezra Pound scholarship), University of Maine, 1976—.

*WORK IN PROGRESS—*Translating: *Beyond Lyricism: The Selected Poems of Eleni Vakalo; The Eye in the Mirror: The Selected Poems of Takis Varvitsiotis; The Danger Is Not Danger: The Selected Poems of Kostas Steryopoulos; The Selected Poems of Nikos Karousas; Bodyguards of the Odyssey: Poems by Nikos Kazantzakis; Contemporary Greek Poetry; The New Greek Poets; After the Metaphysical; Poems by Kostas Kindinis;* with Athena Dalla-Damis, *Buddha,* a play by Nikos Kazantzakis; *Ransom for Time: The Selected Poems of Andonis Decavalles;* into Greek, *Essays on Greek Subjects; The Stone Eyes of Medusa: Essays on English and American Subjects; Modern Greek Poetry;* an anthology, *Modern Greek Poetry: From Cavafis to the Present Day.*

SIDELIGHTS: Kimon Friar's most notable work to date is most likely his translation of Greek poet Nikos Kazantzakis' epic poem "Odhisia" as *The Odyssey: A Modern Sequel.* In a reader's report to the publisher, Friar told *CA,* Will Durant praised the translation highly, saying that it "is itself a work of art. Here is a book worthy of any Nobel Prize." John Ciardi voiced a similar opinion. He wrote in *Saturday Review:* "This is not a book of the year, nor a book of the decade, but a monument of the age. Kimon Friar has produced an English version that stamps him as a master translator." Accordingly, a *Time* reviewer called it "a masterpiece." Kimon Friar received from Kazantzakis the ultimate praise: that his translation was as good as the original." In 1960, Friar adapted *The Odyssey* into a film scenario for Twentieth-Century Fox.

Besides being a translator from the Greek, Friar is also an editor, and a poet in his own right. As an immigrant, Friar had difficulty with the English language even in high school, where he compensated for his lack of expertise in the subject by focusing his talents on art. It was not until he read John Keats's poem "Ode to a Grecian Urn" that Friar became fascinated by the English language. He became so absorbed in studying the works of Keats and came to identify with him so intensely that he even seemed to physically resemble the poet. Friar told *Athenian* reviewer Andy Horton, "I had sculpted myself from within and I made myself Keats." He even went so far as to read each letter written by Keats when he himself was the same age, to the day, of the author when he wrote it. Friar would then respond to these letters as if Keats were still living, commenting on his poetry, perhaps suggesting a grammatical or structural change in a poem. After studying Keats so completely, Friar became immersed in the writings of Ezra Pound, William Butler Yeats, T. S. Eliot, and other renowned poets.

With his friend John Malcolm Brinnin, Friar is co-editor of *Modern Poetry: American and British,* which is used in English classes at over three hundred universities. Robert Penn Warren, in a reader's report, called it "a very good anthology; the editors have shown excellent taste." Other critics have praised it as currently the best anthology of modern poetry to appear in English.

Friar has also demonstrated managerial abilities. As director of the Young Men's Hebrew Association Poetry Center in New York City, he developed more fully a program featuring prominent novelists, film directors, and playwrights, as well as poets. At the center such renowned artists as W. H. Auden, Anais Nin, James Agee, and e. e. cummings would read their writings for the public. Aspiring poets were also encouraged to participate in the readings. Similarly, Friar set up a variety of programs at Circle-in-the-Square, an Off-Broadway theatre. This time he produced operas, staged poetry readings, and concentrated on the plays of Arthur Miller (whom Friar had met when they were both attending the University of Michigan), Tennessee Williams, Archibald MacLeish, and Lillian Hellman, to name a few. These writers also read their own works.

Friar elaborated: "Because as a Greek immigrant from Turkey I at first could not express myself in language, I turned to painting during my grade school and high school days, later turned to poetry, then to drama as a medium combining many forms, and then back again to poetry. In order to make a living, I turned to teaching and lecturing on English and American literature at many universities and institutions, but in my mid-thirties I went to Greece to explore my heritage, found myself at last in my natural environment, and have ever since dedicated myself primarily to the translation and interpretation of modern Greek poetry. Although I have belief and hope in the destiny of the United States, I find myself, nevertheless, much more at home in Greece.

"Partly to learn the language, I began to meet and to translate the modern Greek poets, and to my delight found that their work could compare to any written in the world today. Wanting to be fair and not to favor one school or clique, I found myself gradually being trapped into translating some one hundred poets, only four of whom had died; with all the others I have translated their work in close collaboration, something, I think, rather unique. I have always resented the fact that nature made me only one person. I should have liked to live a thousand different lives. Translating so many poets has given me the opportunity of donning the mask, personalities, and styles of many creators. I can thus play many roles, and this is what, I believe, most attracts me to translation. Like an actor, I can interpret many dramas of contrasting styles, faithfully interpreting the author, and yet making my own voice and style heard also. I like to say that the poet in a translation should be heard, but the translator should be overheard. Now that I am finishing this self-imposed task, it remains to be seen whether or not I have anything to say on my own, apart from the long introductions I have written to all my books, my book reviews, articles, and sporadic poetry."

Friar has lived in Greece for twenty-five years. He has traveled in Canada, Mexico, France, England, Spain, Holland, Italy, Turkey, and Yugoslavia, and has toured throughout South America for ten months.

BIOGRAPHICAL/CRITICAL SOURCES: Saturday Review, December 13, 1957; *Time,* December 8, 1958; *Chicago Review,* Volume 21, number 2, 1969; *Books Abroad,* winter, 1971; *New York Times Book Review,* November 4, 1972; *Virginia Quarterly Review,* autumn, 1973; *Choice,* October, 1973; appendix to *Modern Greek Poetry: From Cavafis to Elytis,* Simon & Schuster, 1973; *Athenian,* October, 1974, November, 1974; *Translation Review,* Volume I, number 2, fall, 1978.

*   *   *

FRIEDMANN, John 1926-

PERSONAL: Born in 1926, in Vienna, Austria; came to the United States in 1940, naturalized citizen, 1944; son of Robert (a professor) and Susanne (Martinz) Friedmann; children: Manuela Christine. *Education:* University of Chicago, M.A., 1952, Ph.D., 1955. *Residence:* Los Angeles, Calif. *Office:* School of Architecture and Urban Planning, University of California, 405 Hilgard Ave., Los Angeles, Calif. 90024.

CAREER: Tennessee Valley Authority, Knoxville, industrial economist, 1952-55; Brazilian School of Public Administration, Rio de Janeiro, regional planning adviser and visiting professor of public administration, 1955-58; U.S. Operations Mission in Korea, Seoul, head of economic development section, 1958-61; Massachusetts Institute of Technology, Cambridge, associate professor of city and regional planning, 1961-65; Catholic University of Chile, Santiago, professor of urban development, 1966-69; University of California, Los Angeles, professor of planning, 1969—, head of urban planning program, 1969-75. Visiting professor at University of Bahia, 1955-58, University of Lund, summer, 1966, Hebrew University of Jerusalem, 1969, United Nations African Institute for Economic Development and Planning, 1971, Japan Center for Area Development Research, 1972, Institute of Social Studies (The Hague, Netherlands), 1973, and Centre for Environmental Studies (London, England), 1976; lecturer at universities all over the world; speaker at professional meetings. Director of Ford Foundation urban and regional development advisory program in Chile, 1965-69; founding member of INTERPLAN, 1963-66; member of board of directors of Urban Innovation Group, 1972-75; consultant to Organization of American States, Social Science Research Council, United Nations, Agency for International Development, and World Bank. *Military service:* U.S. Army, 1944-47; became first lieutenant.

MEMBER: Interamerican Planning Society, Phi Beta Kappa. *Awards, honors:* Honorary degree from Catholic University of Chile, 1969; commander of Order of Bernardo O'Higgins (Chile), 1969; Ford Foundation-Rockefeller Foundation grant, 1971-73; U.S. Office of Education grant, 1973-75; Guggenheim fellowship, 1975-76.

WRITINGS: The Spatial Structure of Economic Development in the Tennessee Valley (monograph), Department of Geography, University of Chicago, 1955; *Introducao ao planejamento democratico* (title means "Introduction to Democratic Planning"), Getulio Vargas Foundation, 1959; (editor with William Alonso, and contributor) *Regional Development and Planning: A Reader,* M.I.T. Press, 1964, revised edition published as *Regional Policy: Readings in Theory and Applications,* 1975; *Venezuela: From Doctrine to Dialogue,* Syracuse University Press, 1965; *Regional Development Policy: A Case Study of Venezuela,* M.I.T. Press, 1966; *Urban and Regional Development in Chile: A Case Study of Innovative Planning,* Ford Foundation, 1969; (editor and contributor) *Chile: Contribuciones a las Politicas Urbana, Regional y Habitacional* (title means "Chile: Contributions to Urban, Regional, and Housing Policies"), Centro de Desarrollo Urbana y Regional, 1970; *Urbanization, Planning, and National Development,* Sage Publications, 1973; *Retracking America: A Theory of Transactive Planning,* Doubleday, 1973; (with Robert Wulff) *The Urban Transition: Comparative Studies of Newly-Industrializing Societies,* Edward Arnold, 1976; (with Clyde Weaver) *Territory and Function: The Evolution of Regional Planning,* Edward Arnold, 1979; *The Good Society,* M.I.T. Press, 1979.

Contributor: W. R. Maki and B.J.L. Berry, editors, *Research and Education for Regional and Area Development,* Iowa State University Press, 1966; Bertram Gross, editor, *Action Under Planning,* McGraw, 1967; Lloyd Rodwin, editor, *Planning Urban Growth and Regional Development,* M.I.T. Press, 1969; Francine Rabinovitz and Felicity Trueblood, editors, *Latin American Urban Research,* Sage Publications, 1971; John Miller and Ralph Gakenheimer, editors, *Latin American Urban Policies and the Social Sciences,* Sage Publications, 1971; Niles Hansen, editor, *Growth Centers in Regional Economic Development,* Free Press, 1972; Donald McAllister, editor, *A New Focus for Land Use Planning,* National Science Foundation, 1973; Joseph S. DeSalvo, editor, *Perspectives on Regional Transportation Planning,* Heath, 1973; Christopher Board, editor, *Progress in Geography: International Reviews of Current Research,* Volume VIII, Edward Arnold, 1975; R. W. Burchell and G. Sternlieb, editors, *Planning Theory in the 1980's: A Search for Future Directions,* Transaction Books, 1978; Fu-chen Lo and Kamil Salih, editors, *Growth Strategy and Regional Development: Asian Experiences and Alternative Approaches,* Pergamon, 1978.

Contributor of about sixty-five articles and reviews to professional journals. Editor of special issue of *Journal of the*

American Institute of Planners, May, 1964; member of editorial board of *Journal of the American Institute of Planners,* 1961-75, *Revista Latinoamericana de Estudios Urbano-Regionales,* 1969-76, *Journal of the Interamerican Planning Society, Growth and Change, Development and Change* (the Netherlands), *Regional Studies* (England), and *Comparative Urban Research.*

WORK IN PROGRESS: The Recovery of Politics.

SIDELIGHTS: Friedmann writes: "My writing and teaching are closely intertwined. In academia, it is usually research, not writing, that is mentioned in this connection. Research, of course, is important, but writing—that is, communicating in a form appropriate to what is being said—is even more so. The inconsequential nature of much research is hidden behind an obscurantist style that is meant to suggest weightiness. But I regard writing as a form of communicating that, more than a vehicle for thought, is the form in which thought itself makes its appearance.

"Raised in the language of the social sciences, I am now trying to extricate myself from this language because it is too confining. How to achieve a style in which *anything* can be said: that is the question I confront and on which I am now working. *The Good Society* is my first attempt in this direction."

*   *   *

FRISCH, Karl von   1886-

PERSONAL: Born November 20, 1886, in Vienna, Austria; son of Anton Ritter von (a surgeon and urologist) and Marie (Exner) Frisch; married Margarethe Mohr (an artist), July 20, 1917; children: Johanna (Mrs. Theo Schreiner), Maria, Helen (Mrs. E. Pflueger), Otto. *Education:* University of Munich and Venice, Ph.D., 1910. *Home:* Ueber der Klause 10,8000, Munich 90, West Germany.

CAREER: University of Munich, Munich, Germany, teacher and research assistant, 1910-14, assistant professor, 1919-21; University of Rostock, Rostock, Germany, professor of zoology, 1921-23; University of Breslau, Breslau, Germany, professor of zoology, 1923-25; University of Munich, director of zoological institute and professor of zoology, 1925-46; University of Graz, Oesterreich, Germany, professor of zoology, 1946-50; University of Munich, professor of zoology, 1950-58. *Military service:* Served in various medical capacities, including bacteriology, during World War I. *Member:* American Entomological Society, American Physiological Society, Royal Society of London, Royal Entomological Society, Linnean Society, Academies of Science of Washington, Boston, Munich, Vienna, Goettingen, Uppsala, and Stockholm. *Awards, honors:* Honorary degrees from numerous universities, including University of Bern, 1949, Technische Hochschule, Zurich, 1955, University of Graz, 1957, Harvard University, 1963, and University of Rostock, 1969; Magellan Prize from American Philosophical Society, 1956; Kalinga Prize from United Nations Education, Scientific and Cultural Organization (UNESCO), 1959; Nobel Prize for Physiology or Medicine, 1973.

WRITINGS—In English: Aus dem Leben der Bienen, J. Springer, 1927, 9th edition, 1977, translation by Dora Ilse published as *The Dancing Bees: An Account of the Life and Senses of the Honey Bee,* Methuen, 1954, Harcourt, 1955; *Du und das Leben; Eine Moderne Biologie fuer Jedermann,* Ullstein, 1936, 19th edition, 1974, translation by Elsa B. Lowenstein published as *About Biology,* Oliver & Boyd, 1962, published as *Man and the Living World,* Harcourt, 1963; *Zehn kleine Hausgenossen,* E. Heimeran, 1940, published as *Zwoelf kleine Hausgenossen*, Rowohlt, 1976, translation by Margaret D. Senft published as *Ten Little Housemates*, Pergamon, 1960; *Bees: Their Vision, Chemical Senses, and Language*, Cornell University Press, 1950, revised edition, 1971; *Erinnerungen eines Biologen*, J. Springer, 1962, 3rd edition, 1973, translation by Lisbeth Gombrich published as *A Biologist Remembers*, Pergamon, 1967; *Tanzsprache und Orientierung der Bienen*, J. Springer, 1965, translation by Leigh E. Chadwick published as *The Dance Language and Orientation of Bees*, Harvard University Press, 1967; *Tiere alo Baumeister*, Ullstein, 1974, translation by Gombrich published as *Animal Architecture*, Helen and Kurt Wolf Books/Harcourt, 1974.

SIDELIGHTS: Frisch's scientific research has produced some surprising discoveries concerning the senses of sight and smell in various creatures. From 1900 to 1914, Frisch was involved in numerous tests which enabled him to conclude that fish were sensitive to color. Later, he also determined that fish could respond to sound.

Frisch also made a number of discoveries involving bees. In 1914, Frisch was able to prove that bees had a sense of color. He did this by training bees to associate food with a particular color. After placing the food on a different colored square, the bees would still return to the color they originally associated with the food. Frisch later used similar tests to prove that bees also possessed a sense of smell.

Frisch devoted most of his career as a sociobiologist to the study of bees. His years of studying the bee's environment resulted in the discovery that bees could communicate through dancing movements. He was able to analyze the bee's movements and determine how different motions could indicate where food could be found and how much there was. Frisch also observed that the movements were particular to each subspecies and that bees from one subspecies could not interpret another subspecie's "language."

For years, many scientists were skeptical of Frisch's claims because they felt his experiments lacked proper controls and allowances for variables. However, when they duplicated Frisch's tests, they found him to be accurate. Frisch's findings are now used for directing bees to honey and controlling pollination.

BIOGRAPHICAL/CRITICAL SOURCES: Karl von Frisch, *A Biologist Remembers*, Pergamon, 1967; *New York Times*, October 12, 1972.

*   *   *

FRISCH, Max (Rudolf) 1911-

PERSONAL: Born May 15, 1911, in Zurich-Hottingen, Switzerland; son of Franz Bruno (an architect) and Lina (Wildermuth) Frisch; married Gertrud Anna Constance von Meyenburg, July 30, 1942 (divorced, 1959); children: Ursula, Hans Peter, Charlotte. *Education:* Attended University of Zurich, 1931-33; Federal Institute of Technology, Zurich, diploma in architecture, 1940. *Home:* CH-6611 Berzona Tessin, Switzerland.

CAREER: Free-lance journalist for various Swiss and German newspapers, including *Neue Zuericher Zeitung* and *Frankfurter Zeitung*, began in 1933; architect in Zurich, Switzerland, 1945-55; full-time writer, 1955—. *Military service:* Swiss Army, 1939-45, served as cannoneer and later border guard on the Austrian and Italian frontiers. *Member:* Deutsche Akademie fuer Sprache und Dichtung, American Academy of Arts and Letters, P.E.N., Akademie der Kuenste, Comunita degli Scrittori. *Awards, honors:* Rocke-

feller Foundation grant, 1951; Schleussner-Schueller Prize from the Hessian radio network, 1955; Wilhelm Raabe Prize from the city of Brunswick, 1955; Georg Buechner Prize from the German Academy of Literature, 1958; Literature prize of the city of Zurich, 1958; Veillon Prize of Laussanne, 1958; Jerusalem Prize, 1965; Ehrenpreis des Schellergedaechtnispreises des Landes Baden-Wuerttemberg, 1965; Grosser Schillerpreis, 1974; honorary doctorate from the University of Marburg, Germany.

WRITINGS—Novels: *Juerg Reinhart*, Deutsche Verlags-Anstalt, 1934; *Eine sommerliche Schicksalsfahrt*, [Germany], 1934; *Antwort aus der Stille: Eine Erzaehlung aus den Bergen* (title means "Answer Out of Silence"), Deutsche Verlags-Anstalt, 1937; *Die Schwierigen; order, J'adore ce qui me brule* (title means "The Difficult Ones; or, J'adore ce qui me brule"), Atlantis (Zurich), 1943; *Bin; oder, Die Reise nach Peking* (title means "I am; or, The Trip to Peking"), Atlantis, 1945; *Stiller*, Suhrkamp (Frankfort on the Main), 1954, translation by Michael Bullock published as *I'm Not Stiller*, Abelard, 1958; *Homo Faber*, Suhrkamp, 1957, translation by Bullock published as *Homo Faber: A Report*, Abelard, 1959; *Mein Name sei Gantenbein*, Suhrkamp, 1964, translation by Bullock published as *A Wilderness of Mirrors*, Methuen, 1965, Random House, 1966; *Montauk*, Suhrkamp, 1975, translation by Geoffrey Skelton published as *Montauk*, Harcourt, 1976.

Plays: *Nun singen sie wieder: Versuch eines Requiems* (title means "Now They Are Singing Again: An Attempt at a Requiem"; two-act; first produced in Zurich at the Schauspielhaus, March 29, 1945), [Germany], 1946, Harrap, 1966; *Santa Cruz: Eine Romanze* (five-act; first produced in Zurich at the Schauspielhaus, March 7, 1946), Suhrkamp, 1946; *Die chinesische Mauer: Eine Farce* (first produced in Zurich at the Schauspielhaus, October 10, 1946), [Germany], 1947, revised version, Suhrkamp, 1955, translation of revised version by James L. Rosenberg published as *The Chinese Wall*, Hill & Wang, 1961; *Als der Krieg zu Ende war* (title means "When the War Was Over"; first produced in Zurich at the Schauspielhaus, January 8, 1948), Dodd, Mead, 1967.

Graf Oederland (title means "Count Oederland"; first produced in Zurich at the Schauspielhaus, February 10, 1951; produced in Washington, D.C., at Arena Stage as "A Public Prosecutor Is Sick of It All," 1973), Suhrkamp, 1951, Harcourt, 1966; *Don Juan; oder, Die Liebe zur Geometrie* (title means "Don Juan; or, The Love of Geometry"; five-act; first produced in Zurich at the Schauspielhaus, May 5, 1953), Suhrkamp, 1953; *Biedermann und die Brandstifter* (adapted from Frisch's radio play; first produced in Zurich at the Schauspielhaus, March 29, 1958; produced in London as *The Fire Raisers*, 1961; produced at the Maidman Playhouse as *The Firebugs*, February, 1963), Suhrkamp, 1958, translation by Bullock published as *The Fire Raisers*, Methuen, 1962, translation by Mordecai Gorelick published as *The Firebugs*, Hill & Wang, 1963; *Die grosse Wut des Philipp Hotz* (one-act; first produced in Zurich at the Schauspielhaus, March 29, 1958; produced at the Barbizon-Plaza Theatre as "The Great Fury of Philipp Hotz," November, 1969), translation published as *Philipp Hotz's Fury* in *Esquire*, October, 1962.

Andorra (adapted from Frisch's radio play; one-act; first produced in Zurich at the Schauspielhaus, November 2, 1961; produced on Broadway at the Biltmore Theatre, February 9, 1963; produced in London at the National Theatre, January, 1964), Suhrkamp, 1962, translation by Bullock published as *Andorra*, Hill & Wang, 1964; *Biografie: Ein Spiel* (two-act; first produced in Zurich at the Schauspielhaus,

February 1, 1968), Suhrkamp, 1967, translation by Bullock published as *Biography. A Game*, Hill & Wang, 1969. Also author of two plays, "Stahl" (title means "Steel"), 1927, and "Judith," 1948, as yet neither published nor produced.

Radio plays: *Rip van Winkle* (adapted from Washington Irving's story), 1953; "Herr Biedermann und die Brandstifter" (also see above), first produced on radio, 1953. Also author of two plays, "Herr Quixote," 1955, and "Andorra" (also see above), 1959, as yet neither published nor produced on radio.

Television plays: *Zurich Transit* (first produced on German television, January, 1966), Suhrkamp, 1966.

Collected plays: *Three Plays* (contains "The Fire Raisers," "Count Oederland," and "Andorra"), translated by Bullock, Methuen, 1962; *Three Plays* (contains "Don Juan," "The Great Rage of Philip Hotz," and "When the War Was Over"), translated by J. L. Rosenberg, Hill & Wang, 1967; *Four Plays* (contains "The Great Wall of China," "Don Juan," "Philipp Hotz's Fury," and "Biography"), translated by Bullock, Methuen, 1969.

Other: *Geschrieben im Grenzdienst 1939*, [Germany], 1940; *Blaetter aus dem Brotsack* (diary; title means "Pages From a Knapsack"), [Germany], 1940, reprinted, Atlantis, 1969; *Das Tagebuch mit Marion* (title means "Diary With Marion"), Atlantis, 1947, revised and expanded version published as *Tagebuch, 1946-1949*, Droemer Knaur (Munich), 1950, translation by Geoffrey Skelton published as *Sketchbook, 1946-1949*, Harcourt, 1977; *Ausgewaehlte Prosa*, Suhrkamp, 1961, Harcourt, 1968; *Stuecke*, two volumes, Suhrkamp, 1962; *Oeffentlichkeit als Partner* (essays), Suhrkamp, 1967; *Wilhelm Tell fuer die Schule*, Suhrkamp, 1971; *Tagebuch, 1966-1971*, [Germany], 1972, translation by Skelton published as *Sketchbook, 1966-1971*, Harcourt, 1974; *Dienstbuechlein*, Suhrkamp, 1974; *Stich-Worte*, Suhrkamp, 1975; *Gesammelte Werke in Zeitlicher Folge*, two volumes, Suhrkamp, 1976; *Frisch: Kritik, Thesen, Analysen*, Francke (Bern), 1977.

WORK IN PROGRESS: Triptychon, a play "that examines the mystification of death and the relationship between the living and the dead."

SIDELIGHTS: Although Max Frisch was born in Switzerland, he has never assumed the isolated and neutral stance of his native land. In both his plays and novels, Frisch excoriates the self-righteous attitude of those who refuse to accept responsibility for the evil in the world. Along with fellow Swiss dramatist Friedrich Duerrenmatt, he has been labeled "the conscience of the neutrals." But Frisch has done more than merely prick the conscience of his smug countrymen; his works have been translated into twenty languages and are considered to be powerful renderings of the dilemma of modern man. "The problem of identity, the problem of how man can find his true self, an authentic existence, is the central pivot around which most of Frisch's work revolves. . . . We create the others in the image we ourselves make of them," Martin Esslin explained. "And this for Frisch is the ultimate sin, the extinction of their authentic existence, the origin of all the troubles of our time. For the image that we thus make is a fixed, a dead thing, an imposition that can kill." Such an ardent champion of individual liberty is naturally also an opponent of totalitarianism; much of Frisch's literary output seeks to understand how authoritarian governments arise.

Frisch's extensive travels and his work as an architect helped to forge his moral and political conscience. When his father died, Frisch dropped out of the University of Zurich

and worked as a free-lance journalist. In this capacity, he traveled widely in central and Eastern Europe. During World War II he served as a gunner on the Austrian and Italian borders. When the war was over, he journeyed about the continent and saw for himself the ravages of war, including the Theresienstadt concentration camp in Czechoslovakia and the ruins of Goethe's house in Frankfort. In the years since, Frisch has traveled throughout the world, visiting the Soviet Union, the United States, Mexico, Japan and the Middle East. He feels that traveling helps him to avoid the insularity that develops when one remains rooted in a single country. It was his job as an architect that convinced him that socialism is the answer to society's ills. Frisch told an interviewer: "Then after I began to work as an architect and saw the problems of urbanization, I saw that there must be a change. The problems of urbanization can't be solved with present methods of unlimited economic growth. I became a socialist, though I hate to use that word because it means so many different things to so many people. . . . What I am talking about is a social contract where the emphasis is one of a better, more human, more meaningful life. We don't have a socialist country anyplace in the world."

Frisch drew some of his ideas on authentic existence from the works of such existential philosophers as Kierkegaard and Nietzsche. He also acknowledges that Bertolt Brecht, Franz Kafka, and Thomas Mann influenced his writing. Like Brecht, whom he knew personally, Frisch is concerned with morality, and he often employs the forms typical of Brecht's epic theater. Unlike Brecht and unlike most of the other German-speaking writers of his time, Frisch does not try to promote any type of ideology in his plays. He has been called "a Brecht without Marxism." Frisch's work also differs from that of Duerrenmatt. It is Frisch's humanity and involvement in his work that distinguishes him from Duerrenmatt, George Wellwarth maintained: "Frisch's two best plays, *Die Chinesische Mauer* and *Biedermann und die Brandstifter*, are consciously foredoomed pleas for a better world. The irony implicit in them no longer sounds like the scornful laughter of the gods we hear in Duerrenmatt; it sounds like the self-reproaching wailing of the damned."

The struggle of the individual to maintain his identity in a world that prefers the simplicity of stereotypes to the complexity of authentic existence is evident in a number of Frisch's plays. In *Don Juan; or, The Love of Geometry*, Frisch provides a new twist to the legend of Don Juan. The Don Juan whom he portrays does not wish to be a philanderer; he prefers geometry to women. However, he is forced into the role of womanizer by the demands and expectations of society. *Biography: A Game* also deals with the problem of establishing one's identity. In this play, a dying professor is given a chance to live his life over again. Even when he is given the opportunity to alter past events, he discovers that he cannot really change. "Perhaps it is in the nature of this complex nether world of what-might-have-been that few of the alternatives really come to life, that Frisch raises many questions and answers few," Eleanor Gurewitsch remarked. "But if 'Biography' is not a great play, it is at a minimum entertaining. It is also full of challenging ideas best appreciated by the playgoer who reads the play after he has seen it."

Frisch's novels as well are preoccupied with the question of identity. In *I'm Not Stiller*, a sculptor tries to assume a new identity because he feels that he is a failure both as an artist and as a husband, but his attempt is ultimately defeated. Esslin termed *I'm Not Stiller* "a remarkable tour de force . . . a deeply serious, searching, and philosophical work." The same theme is explored in *A Wilderness of Mirrors;* a reviewer for *Times Literary Supplement* noted that the book's central concern is with problems of identity, "a concern evident not only in the theme, plot, and characterization of the work, but also in its structure."

Society's tendency to categorize individuals has political ramifications, as Frisch demonstrates in a number of plays. In *Count Oederland,* Frisch's interests in identity and in totalitarianism are interwoven. In that play, a state prosecutor disappears (in a dream or in reality, the audience is never sure) while reviewing a case where a man has murdered a watchman with an ax for no apparent reason. The prosecutor turns to a life of crime and leads a revolution to overturn the established government. The revolution is successful, and the prosecutor prepares to become the country's new leader. But he comes to the realization that any power structure, even one that he heads, destroys his chance for freedom, and kills himself because he cannot find a way out of this predicament. Esslin claimed that *Count Oederland* brilliantly examines the question "Are we what we appear to be in our self-controlled, conscious waking hours; or are we the wild wishes and violent desires of our dreams?" Others have interpreted the play differently. *Count Oederland,* Diether H. Haenicke wrote, "has generally been understood as a rather inadequate explanation of the events of the Hitler era, which shows that every common man has a certain potential for violence and cruelty."

The potential that people have for violence and cruelty is realized in *Andorra.* "In *Andorra,*" Franz P. Haberl pointed out, "the image-making deteriorates from the level of the individual to racial prejudice by an entire nation and eventually to collective murder or at least acquiescence in it." In the play, Andorra is a mythical country somewhat like Switzerland. Andri, the illegitimate son of an Andorran schoolteacher, is mistakenly assumed to be a Jew. Because society has imposed this role upon him, he begins to think and behave as a Jew. Even when Andri learns that he is not Jewish, he is unable to shed his Jewish identity. When an anti-Semitic, totalitarian nation conquers Andorra, he is persecuted as a Jew and chooses to die as one. The townspeople are brought to trial for his murder. Although they deny any responsibility for Andri's death, their actions belie their words.

One of Frisch's most famous plays is *The Firebugs,* which Wellwarth called "a carefully worked out political allegory about the rise of totalitarian governments." The central character in *The Firebugs* is Biedermann, a weak-willed, middle-class man who prides himself on his moral righteousness, even though he has driven one of his employees to suicide. He and his wife are intimidated into inviting two arsonists into their house. Because it is easier to appease the firebugs than it is to oppose them, Biedermann gives them the matches they demand, the matches which ignite a fire that destroys his own home. "Among other things, *The Firebugs* says that society cannot be destroyed unless it collaborates actively with its destroyers. What it does most brilliantly, however, is analyze Biedermann's vulnerability, the reasons why he placates his destroyers, ignores his potential saviors, and even obstructs them," Robert B. Heilman stated.

The situation set forth in *The Firebugs* has been compared to numerous events in recent history. Some commentators have drawn parallels between the play and Hitler's assumption of power in Germany; others have compared it with the Communists' assumption of power in Czechoslovakia. The play is a parable about the development of the nuclear bomb,

still others contend. When *The Firebugs* was first produced in the United States in 1963, critics tended to dismiss it as irrelevant, but subsequent changes in American society have altered that opinion. After viewing a revival of the play in 1968, Vincent Canby noted that the director "has drastically changed it by giving it an unmistakable point of reference. The confrontation is no longer nebulous, but the specific confrontation between races in white and black America."

Another performance of *The Firebugs* in 1969 was also well received by American critics. Maria Becker offered a reason why: "This play is really more pertinent today in America than in Europe.... Until recently the American public seemed indifferent to the work of Frisch and Duerrenmatt and Guenter Grass as being too abstract and too remote to its experience. I believe that the complexity of America's problems, particularly the concern over the dehumanization of the Vietnam war, has changed all this." While visiting the United States in 1970, Frisch was asked about the dangers of totalitarianism developing in America. Frisch replied: "The protest against the war [Vietnam] and mankind's reliance on technology has transcended the young radicals. It seems to me there are enough healthy forces to contradict the radical fears that repression will gain the upper hand.... The very fact of a very active internal dissent ... belies the parallel of Germany, where the opposition to authoritarianism was minimal and helpless because too few people sensed the danger."

Although Frisch's plays and novels point out the defects in modern man, they offer little hope that change can be effected, either in the individual or in society. Many of Frisch's protagonists kill themselves in despair, and Frisch's work suggests that society is also on a suicidal course. The horrors of modern technology, particularly the development of the atomic bomb, are of great concern to Frisch. In *The Chinese Wall,* a contemporary intellectual is cast back into China at the time the Great Wall is being erected. The great conquerors of history are brought together there, and the modern man tries to alter the course of history by warning them of the dangers of nuclear war, but to no avail. One of Frisch's novels, *Homo Faber,* shows that scientists, even with all their technological advancements, are unable to control the course of events. "The image of Auschwitz, in which technological man could be seen as merely a more monstrous, because more powerful, repetition of the Stone Age savage, stands behind the subtle and delicate imagery of *Homo Faber,*" Esslin commented. After reading *Homo Faber,* Richard Plant declared, "Once in a while we feel that Max Frisch has captured that essential anguish of modern man which we find in the best of Camus."

Because Frisch's work is so highly esteemed, there is a great interest in his personal life and reflections. Frisch is a famous diarist. When his *Sketchbook, 1946-1949* was translated into English in 1977, it attracted favorable notices. V. S. Pritchett observed that the book "is not a hotchpotch of things and persons seen or of random ponderings but a coherent narrative, an ingenious mosaic. The fragments held together as the portrait of a sensitive moralist responding to the chaos in Europe." Another one of Frisch's journals, *Sketchbook, 1966-1971,* also earned kudos from critics. Richard Gilman noted that this sketchbook "shows us how the mind and imagination discover their themes and compulsions, and how writing is one means ... of being human."

Frisch's most recent work, *Montauk,* is his most controversial. Many commentators are uncertain as to which genre it belongs, autobiography or fiction. Frisch explained that he was experimenting with a new literary form when writing

Montauk: "I was bored with the form of writing which consists of half fiction, or pure invention, and half autobiography. I decided to be finished with this form once and for all. Thus I told the tale of 'Montauk' as a storyteller speaking about my life. It was a kind of therapy accompanying the acceptance of my own life." Opinions as to the merits of *Montauk* are divided. Laurie Stone called the book "very uneven going.... What rings true in *Montauk* reads like Frisch's fiction, and what does not read like fiction, does not ring true."

Francine du Plessix Gray, however, lavished praise on Frisch's inventiveness in his journals and *Montauk*. "Mr. Frisch's tour de force is that 'Montauk,' like 'Sketchbooks,' remains rigorously devoid of any confessionalism," Gray contended. "The author is in such control that these bluntly honest documents are infinitely less subjective and more elegantly impersonal than the thinly masked life histories that emerge in the fiction of Updike, Mailer and countless other contemporary novelists. The liberating effect of Mr. Frisch's rebellion against the tyranny of traditional genres, as well as the breadth of his human message, make him a more fitting candidate for the Nobel Prize than any other writer I can think of."

Homo Faber has been adapted for the screen by Paramount.

BIOGRAPHICAL/CRITICAL SOURCES: Spectator, April 11, 1958; *Saturday Review,* April 12, 1958, May 7, 1960, February 26, 1966; Hugh Frederic Garten, *Modern German Drama,* Methuen, 1959; *Tulane Drama Review,* March, 1962; George Wellwarth, *The Theater of Protest and Paradox: Developments in the Avant-Garde Drama,* New York University Press, 1964; *Times Literary Supplement,* November 11, 1965, January 25, 1968; *New York Times Book Review,* February 20, 1966, April 28, 1974, May 27, 1976, April 3, 1977, March 19, 1978; Frederick Lumley, *New Trends in 20th Century Drama,* Oxford University Press, 1967; Ulrich Weisstein, *Max Frisch,* Twayne, 1967; *Christian Science Monitor,* February 12, 1968; *New York Times,* July 2, 1968, November 27, 1969, May 17, 1970; *Village Voice,* July 11, 1968; *Books Abroad,* winter, 1968; Martin Esslin, *Reflections: Essays on Modern Theatre,* Doubleday, 1969; Brom Weber, editor, *Sense and Sensibility in Twentieth-Century Writing,* Southern Illinois University Press, 1970; Horst S. Daemmrich and Diether H. Haenicke, *The Challenge of German Literature,* Wayne State University Press, 1971; *Chicago Sun-Times,* May 5, 1974; *Biography News,* Gale, June, 1974; *Contemporary Literary Criticism,* Gale, Volume 3, 1975, Volume 9, 1978; *New Yorker,* May 24, 1976, July 11, 1977; *Nation,* July 3, 1976; *World Literature Today,* spring, 1977.*

*   *   *

FRYER, Jonathan 1950-

PERSONAL: Born June 5, 1950, in Manchester, England; adopted son of Harold (a company director) and Rosemary (a health visitor; maiden name, Bishop) Fryer. *Education:* Oxford University, B.A. (honors), 1973, M.A., 1977. *Politics:* Liberal. *Religion:* Quaker. *Home:* Seven Avenue de la Sauvagine, Box 95, B-1170, Brussels, Belgium. *Agent:* Michael Sissons, A. D. Peters Ltd., 10 Buckingham St., London, WC2N 6BU, England. *Office:* 23 Avenue d'-Auderghem, B-1040, Brussels, Belgium.

CAREER: Writer. Worked as journalist with Reuters News Agency in Brussels, Belgium, and London, England, 1973-74; visiting lecturer in modern Chinese studies at University of Nairobi, 1976. Also worked as interviewer for Mutual

Network, Canadian Broadcasting Corp., and Belgische Radio en Televisie. Executive secretary of Joint Task Force on Development Issues, 1978—; organising secretary of Non Governmental Organisation Liaison Committee to the European Communities, 1978-79. *Member:* Liberal International, National Union of Journalists, Writers Guild, P.E.N., Europe-China Association (member of board), Religious Society of Friends (clerk), Liberal Candidates' Association, Oxford University Liberal Club (secretary), North West Young Liberal Federation (vice-chairman), Foreign Residents' Consultative Assembly for Watermael-Boitsfort.

WRITINGS: The Great Wall of China, New English Library, 1975, A. S. Barnes, 1977; *Isherwood: A Biography,* New English Library, 1977, Doubleday, 1978; (editor) *China, Education and the West,* Europe-China Association, 1978; (with Rona Dobson) *Brussels as Seen by Native Painters,* 1979.

WORK IN PROGRESS: Violence, a novel; a biography of Lu Xun.

SIDELIGHTS: Fryer told *CA:* "Watching people is not alway taken kindly by the 'victim,' least of all in our WASP culture. The activity is nonetheless the kernel of my existence, finding expression not in voyeurism, but in moving from prolonged study to a relationship either literary (through the typewriter) or personal (through myself). Ever since I was a child, wondering who on earth my natural parents were, and what they looked like, I have scanned crowds and railway stations, drawing strength and happiness from the heterogeneous flood around.

"Travel has naturally been a major extension of this activity, taking me throughout Europe, Asia and Africa, and to a lesser extent North America. I relish pluralism, the variety of human form and nature, the unexpected and the expected, the beautiful and the ugly and the shifting balance between the two. Often the observer, I am led inevitably by fascination into hazardous participation.

"My politics stem also from this absurd concern for people, as does my religion. Liberalism and Quakerism are twin institutional pillars that hold up the roof that protects me from the world's storms, though each by definition allows individualism and even eccentricity.

"An impulse for communication has driven me to gobble up languages (English, French, German, Dutch, Spanish, Italian, basic Portuguese, Chinese, Japanese, rudimentary Arabic and Esperanto) like a gourmet determined to savour the special character of every dish, even if he goes out of his mind or bursts.

"I cherish the possibilities to be attracted to and to attract the minds and bodies of giving and receiving people of every colour, nationality and sex, for only through our love of humanity can we express our love of God."

Fryer's first book, *The Great Wall of China,* received lukewarm reviews. "The book is ... well informed," conceded a critic in *Choice:* "the author has done his homework. However, the repetition of much that is well known, the failure to provide page references for citations, the absence of any novel or potentially controversial thesis, and the pace at which the book proceeds through the centuries are all indications that it is meant for the general reader...." A reviewer for *Times Literary Supplement* agreed with the *Choice* critic. "The difficulties of writing about a subject which the author has hardly, if ever, seen are on the whole overcome," declared the writer for *Times Literary Supplement,* "and provided one is content with a historical rather than architectural angle, the book is an admirable popular account."

Isherwood, a biography of the famed novelist, was not reviewed as graciously as *The Great Wall of China.* Peter Stansky complained, "Isherwood deserves a much better biography. At best there are a few interesting ideas and perhaps a handy record of fact." Peter Conrad claimed that Fryer was "content to paraphrase Isherwood's own published accounts of events. . . . Some material of critical interest, concerning Isherwood's hesitations and alterations of emphasis while forming his works, lies abandoned in Fryer's book."

Fryer responded to critics of his books by telling *CA:* "What a terrible crime to write for the masses."

BIOGRAPHICAL/CRITICAL SOURCES: Times Literary Supplement, February 27, 1976, October 28, 1977; *Choice,* July/August, 1978; *New Republic,* October 14, 1978.

* * *

FUENTES MOHR, Alberto   1928(?)-1979

OBITUARY NOTICE: Born c. 1928; died January 25, 1979, in Guatemala City, Guatemala. Diplomat, economist, and political leader. Fuentes Mohr was Guatemala's foreign minister in 1970 when he was kidnapped by leftist guerrillas. He was eventually freed in exchange for the release of one of their members from prison. A few months later, he negotiated with the guerrillas for the life of American labor attache Sean Holly. Soon afterwards, though, he was arrested by the law-and-order ruler who replaced Guatemala's constitutional government. Recently, Fuentes Mohr was engaged in legislative efforts to curb the rampant violence of the extreme right when he was assassinated by submachine gun fire. In his book, *Kidnap and Capture,* Fuentes Mohr wrote about his encounters with extremists. Obituaries and other sources: *Washington Post,* January 27, 1979.

* * *

FUGARD, Athol   1932-

PERSONAL: Born June 11, 1932, in Middelburg, Cape Province, South Africa; son of Harold David (an owner of a general store) and Elizabeth Magdalena Frugard; married Sheila Meiring (a novelist, poet, and former actress), 1956; children: Lisa. *Education:* Attended Port Elizabeth Technical College, and University of Cape Town, 1950-53. *Address:* P.O. Box 5090, Walmer, Port Elizabeth, South Africa. *Agent:* William Morris Agency, 1350 Avenue of the Americas, New York, N.Y. 10019.

CAREER: Actor, director, and playwright. Crew member of a tramp steamer bound from Port Sudan, Sudan, to the Far East, 1953-55; Fordsburg Native Commissioner's Court, Johannesburg, South Africa, clerk, 1958; cleaning man, London, England, 1959-60; "The Blood Knot," New York City, actor, 1962; Serpent Company, Port Elizabeth, South Africa, director, 1965—; "The Trials of Brother Jero," London, director, 1966; "The Blood Knot," London, actor, 1966. Director of many of his own plays, including "The Blood Knot," "Hello and Goodbye," "People Are Living There," "Boesman and Lena," and "Statements After an Arrest Under the Immorality Act." Actor in most of his own plays in South Africa and in television film "The Blood Knot" for British Broadcasting Corp. (BBC), United Kingdom, 1968. *Awards, honors:* Obie Award for distinguished foreign play from *Village Voice,* 1971, for "Boesman and Lena."

WRITINGS—Plays: "No-Good Friday" (three-act), first produced in Cape Town, 1956; "Nongogo" (three-act), first produced in Cape Town, 1957; *The Blood Knot* (seven-scene; first produced in Johannesburg and London, 1961; produced Off-Broadway, 1964), Simondium, 1963, Odyssey, 1964, published in *New English Dramatists 13,* Penguin, 1968; *Hello and Goodbye* (two-act; first produced in Johannesburg, 1965; produced Off-Broadway at Sheridan Square Playhouse, September 18, 1969), A. A. Balkema, 1966, Samuel French, 1971; "The Occupation" (one-act), published in *Ten One Act Plays,* edited by Cosmo Pieterse, Heinemann, 1968; *Boesman and Lena* (two-act; first produced in Grahamstown, 1969; produced Off-Broadway at Circle in the Square, June 22, 1970; produced on West End at Royal Court Theatre Upstairs, July 19, 1971), Buren, 1969, revised and rewritten edition, Samuel French, 1971.

People Are Living There (two-act; first produced in Cape Town at Hofmeyr Theatre, June 14, 1969; produced on Broadway at Forum Theatre, Lincoln Center, November 18, 1971), Oxford University Press, 1970, Samuel French, 1976; (with Don MacLennan) *The Coat* [and] *Third Degree* (the former by Fugard, the latter by MacLennan), A. A. Balkema, 1971; *Statements* (contains three one-act plays: [with John Kani and Winston Ntshona] "Sizwe Bansi Is Dead," first produced in Cape Town, 1972, produced in New York City, 1974; [with Kani and Ntshona] "The Island," first produced in South Africa, 1972, produced on West End at Royal Court Theatre, December, 1973, produced in New York at Edison Theatre, November, 1974; and "Statements After an Arrest Under the Immorality Act," first produced in Cape Town, 1972, produced in London, 1974), Oxford University Press, 1974; "Dimetos" (two-act), first produced in Edinburgh, 1975, produced in London and New York City, 1976; "A Lesson From Aloes," first produced in Johannesburg, December, 1978.

Omnibus volumes: *Three Port Elizabeth Plays* (contains "The Blood Knot," "Hello and Goodbye," and "Boesman and Lena"), Viking, 1974; (with Kani and Ntshona) *Sizwe Banzi Is Dead and The Island,* Viking, 1976; *Boesman and Lena and Other Plays* (contains "The Blood Knot," "People Are Living There," "Hello and Goodbye," and "Boesman and Lena"), Oxford University Press, 1978. Screenplays: "Boesman and Lena," 1972. Also author of teleplay, "Mille Miglia," British Broadcasting Corp. (BBC), 1968.

Also author of (and actor in) films: "Boesman and Lena," 1972, "The Guest," 1976, and "Meetings With Remarkable Men," 1979.

WORK IN PROGRESS: A screenplay, "A Lesson From Marigolds."

SIDELIGHTS: South Africa's foremost playwright, Athol Fugard, has often been called "the conscience of his country" because of his compassionate portrayal of the treatment of nonwhites in South Africa. His concern for racial justice began at an early age and continually grew stronger as he became more personally involved. For a time Fugard worked with blacks and Orientals on a ship where he was the only white crew member. Later as a clerk at the Commissioner's Court he witnessed the cruel treatment of blacks who had broken the pass law. (In South Africa blacks are not allowed into urban white areas except "to minister to the needs of the white man," and are arrested if they are not carrying a pass to explain their presence in the restricted area.)

The pass laws are one example of the South African government policy of apartheid. This policy was begun in 1948 when the National Party gained control of the government. In the 1960's police cracked down on opponents of apartheid. On March 21, 1960, for example, seventy-two demonstrators were massacred near Johannesburg while protesting the pass laws. During this incident Fugard and his wife were in England, but returned home immediately to show their support of the anti-apartheid movement.

During his employment as a clerk, Fugard became friends with several blacks and began to visit them in their segregated shanty district. This area became the setting for his first play, "No-Good Friday," which, like all his other plays, deals with the bleak lives of people on the outskirts of South African society.

In 1962 Fugard helped form the Serpent Company, which became the first successful nonwhite theatre troupe in South Africa. The untrained actors battled difficult conditions. They could only rehearse after work until curfew. In addition, the government arrested several members and would not allow their plays to be performed publicly before white or mixed audiences.

Because of his sympathetic portrayal of minorities in his plays and his work with nonwhite theatre groups, Fugard was considered by the government to be an opponent of apartheid. None of his plays were banned, but in 1967 Fugard's passport was seized without any official reason being given; until 1971 he was not allowed out of the country. He told an Associated Press reporter, "the ironic thing about the whole business is that the state has made a considerable profit out of two of my plays which have been run at state-sponsored theaters."

Most of Fugard's plays are extended dialogues between two or three characters. Because there is little action critics often find the plays "boring" and "self-consciously literary," but definitely worth seeing. *New York* magazine's description of "Boesman and Lena" typifies the mixed feelings toward Fugard's works: "Even though short, the play seems slow and long-winded at first. . . . But slowly the language muddles through, the underlying humanity of these dehumanized beings creeps up on us. Against our will, we are drawn into compassionate kinship with them. . . . In the end, it is our sense of solidarity that makes a harsh experience rewarding."

"The Blood Knot" was Fugard's first play to be performed in America. It is the story of two colored half brothers, one dark-skinned, the other light-skinned and trying to pass for white. Edith Oliver called it "one of the best, and one of the best-performed, plays ever to be done Off Broadway."

"Hello and Goodbye" did not fare as well with critics. Marilyn Stasio commented: "Fugard has overwritten what is basically a one-act drama, which accounts for the repetitive dialogue, slack non-dramatic stretches, and bursts of bombast. But he has created compellingly absorbing people, and this accounts for the play's interest." This play deals with the reunion, after fifteen years, of a neurotic young man and his world-weary sister. The Off-Broadway production starred Colleen Dewhurst and Martin Sheen, who received tremendous acclaim for their performances and who, according to Catharine Hughes, "deserve all the more credit because the characters they are playing . . . just aren't that inherently interesting." On the other hand, Clive Barnes declared: "'Hello and Goodbye' is both unashamedly old-fashioned and, much more to the point, thoroughly engrossing. Mr. Fugard takes two not especially remarkable or unusual characters and by the sheer skill of his writing forces us to take an interest in them."

Another two-character play, "Boesman and Lena" is about a colored couple who, shut out of both the white and black communities, are living on the edge of despair. James Earl Jones and Ruby Dee were highly praised for their performances in the Off-Broadway production in 1970. The play itself, however, gathered mixed reviews. One *Stage* reporter was "bored . . . beyond belief" and observed that the writing "seemed dreary, repetitive, with little direction and little point." Conversely, Gerald Weales contended that the show itself was even more rewarding than the skillful acting and called Fugard "one of the best playwrights working in the theater today."

Termed "a disappointing play" by *Variety*, "People Are Living There" generally gained less recognition than Fugard's earlier plays. *Stage* magazine, however, assessed the play as "touching, amusing and sometimes brilliantly absurd in its comic effect."

AVOCATIONAL INTERESTS: Fishing.

BIOGRAPHICAL/CRITICAL SOURCES: Variety, July 9, 1969, September 24, 1969, November 7, 1971, December 1, 1971; *New York Times*, September 19, 1969, May 17, 1970, June 4, 1970, July 6, 1970, December 17, 1974, February 2, 1977; *Village Voice*, September 25, 1969, July 2, 1970, July 23, 1970; *New Yorker*, September 27, 1969, July 4, 1970, December 6, 1971, February 20, 1978; *Cue*, September 27, 1969, July 4, 1970, November 27, 1971; *Newsweek*, September 29, 1969, July 6, 1970; *Show Business*, October 4, 1969, July 4, 1970; *Nation*, November 10, 1969, February 20, 1978; *New York*, June 6, 1970, February 20, 1978; *Christian Science Monitor*, June 29, 1970; *Time*, July 13, 1970; *New Leader*, July 20, 1970; *Commonwealth*, October 9, 1970; *Newsday*, May 25, 1971; *Choice*, July, 1971, October, 1976; *Stage*, July 29, 1971, February 10, 1972; *Contemporary Literary Criticism*, Gale, Volume 5, 1976, Volume 9, 1978; *Booklist*, July 1, 1976.

*　　　*　　　*

FUSCO, Margie 1949-

PERSONAL: Born November 6, 1949, in Pittsburgh, Pa.; daughter of Nicholas S. (a railroad engineer) and Ruth (Fragale) Fusco; married Dennis Kovach (a lawyer), 1979. *Education:* University of Pittsburgh, B.A., 1970, M.A., 1978. *Home and office:* 100 North Front St., Milton, Pa. 17847.

CAREER: Kaufmann's Department Store, Pittsburgh, Pa., retail advertising copywriter, 1972-74; University of Pittsburgh, Pittsburgh, public relations specialist, 1974-76, associate director of news and publications, 1976-78; Mellon Bank, Pittsburgh, senior financial writer, 1978; Westinghouse (international power plants), Greentree, Pa., technical writer and editor, 1978-79; Geisinger Medical Center, Danville, Pa., news editor, 1979—. *Member:* Northeast Modern Language Association (head of poetry section, 1979).

WRITINGS: Putting Into Harbor (poems), West End Press, 1978. Contributor of poems and articles to literary journals and newspapers, including *road/house, Womanspirit, New England Review*, and *Backspace*.

WORK IN PROGRESS: "Poems of introspection."

SIDELIGHTS: Margie Fusco writes: "Although I write for a living and thoroughly enjoy my work in public relations, advertising, feature writing, and technical writing, it's only through poetry that I've found my own expression.

"After many years as a professional writer, I was guided into poetry when I entered University of Pittsburgh's graduate program in writing, where I was nurtured with much patience and love by two fine poets and teachers, Ed Ochester and Paul Zimmer.

"I am a city-dweller and have been in western Pennsylvania all my life but will be moving to an area of small towns and rural lands. Although I find it difficult to leave the place where all my roots are, I look forward to living with clean air and unpolluted rivers, and to beginning a family of my own in that relatively unspoiled setting.

"My poetry has been an exploration of my history: my Italian and Irish ancestors, their relationships with their environments, and the ways in which they have shaped me. My poetry since *Putting Into Harbor* is an attempt to move away from the city, study the new environment I will be entering, and focus more directly on my own relationships with both past and future environments."

G

GADAMER, Hans-Georg 1900-

PERSONAL: Born February 11, 1900, in Marburg an der Lahn, Germany; (now West Germany); son of Johannes (a university professor) and Johanna (Gewiese) Gadamer; married Kaete Lekebusch, 1950; children: Andrea. *Home:* Am Buechsenackerhang 53, 6900 Heidelberg, West Germany. *Office:* Philosophisches Seminar, University of Heidelberg, Heidelberg, West Germany.

CAREER: University of Marburg, Marburg an der Lahn, Germany (now West Germany), professor, 1937-39; University of Leipzig, Leipzig, Germany (now East Germany), professor, 1939-47; University of Frankfurt, Frankfurt, West Germany, professor, 1947-49; University of Heidelberg, Heidelberg, West Germany, professor of philosophy, 1949-68, professor emeritus, 1968—. Visiting professor at McMaster University, autumns, 1972-75, and Boston College, autumn, 1976. *Member:* Academy of Leipzig, Academy of Heidelberg, Academy of Athens, Academy of Rome, Boston Academy. *Awards, honors:* Reuchlin-Preis from Stadt Pforzheim, 1971; D.H.C. from University of Ottawa, 1977; Hegel-Preis from Stadt Stuttgart, 1979.

WRITINGS—In English: *Wahrheit und Methode: Grundzuege einer philosophischen Hermeneutik,* Mohr, 1960, 4th edition, 1975, translation published as *Truth and Method,* Seabury, 1975; *Hegels Dialektik: Fuent hermeneutische Studien,* Mohr, 1971, translation by P. Christopher Smith published as *Hegel's Dialectic: Five Hermeneutical Studies,* Yale University Press, 1976; (editor) *Truth and Historicity,* M. Nijhoff, 1972; *Philosophical Hermeneutics* (selected essays from *Kleine Schriften;* also see below), translation from the original German by David E. Linge, University of California Press, 1976.

Other: *Von geistigen Lauf des Menschen: Studien zu unvollendeten Dichtungen Goethes,* H. Kueper, 1949; *Kleine Schriften,* Mohr, Volume I: *Philosophie Hermeneutik,* 1967, Volume II: *Interpretationen,* 1967, Volume III: *Idee und Sprache, Platon, Husserl, Heidegger,* 1972, Volume IV: *Variationen,* 1977; *Werner Scholz,* A. Bongers, 1968; *Platos dialektische Ethik und andere Studien zur platonischen Philosophie,* F. Meiner, 1968; (with Max Mueller and Emil Staiger) *Hegel, Hoelderlin, Heidegger* (speeches), Badenia Verlag, 1971; *Wer bin ich und wer bist du?: Ein Kommentar zu Paul Celans Gedichtfolge Atemkristall,* Suhrkamp, 1973; *Vernunft im Zeitalter der Wissenschaft,* Suhrkamp, 1976;

Philosophische Lehrjahre, Klostermann, 1977; (with Werner Marx and Carl Christian Weizsaacker) *Heidegger: Freiburger Universitaatsvortraage zu seinem Gedenken,* Alber, 1977; *Poetica: Ausgewaahlte Essays,* Insel-Verlag, 1977.

Contributor: A. Giannaras, editor, *Convivium Cosmologicum,* Schwabe, 1973; H. Fahrenbach, editor, *Wirklichkeit und Reflexion,* Neske, 1973; H. F. Fulda and D. Henrich, editors, *Materialien zu Hegels "Phaenomenologie des Geistes,"* Suhrkamp Taschenb, 1973; I. Schuebler and W. Janke, editors, *Sein und Geschichtlichkeit,* Klostermann, 1974; L. J. Pongratz, editor, *Selbstdarstellungen,* Volume III, Felix Meiner, 1977. Contributor to philosophy journals.

Editor: Ernst Hoffmann, *Platonismus und christliche Philosophie,* Artemis-Verlag, 1961; *Hegel-Tage Royaumont 1964: Beitraage zur Deutung der Phaanomenologie des Geistes,* Bouvier, 1966; *Deutscher Kongress fuer Philosophie: Das Problem der Sprache,* Fink, 1967; (compiler) *Um die Begriffswelt der Vorsokratiker,* Wissenschaftliche Buchgesellschaft, 1968; *Idee und Zahl,* C. Winter, 1968; *Hegel-Tage,* Urbino, 1965, Bouvier, 1969; (compiler) *Philosophisches Lesebuch,* Fischer-Buecherei, 1969; *Hermeneutik und Dialektik,* Mohr, 1970; Kurt Riezler, *Parmenides,* Klostermann, 1970; Aristotle, *Metaphysik XII,* Klostermann, 1970.

WORK IN PROGRESS: Research on Plato and on literary hermeneutics.

*   *   *

GAFF, Jerry G(ene) 1936-

PERSONAL: Born February 5, 1936, in Dekalb County, Ind.; married wife, Sally S.; children: David, Amy. *Education:* DePauw University, A.B., 1958; Syracuse University, Ph.D., 1965. *Home:* 7504 Hamilton Spring Rd., Bethesda, Md. 20034. *Office:* Project on General Education Models, Society for Values in Higher Education, 1818 R St. N.W., Washington, D.C. 20009.

CAREER: Hobart and William Smith Colleges, Geneva, N.Y., instructor in sociology, 1962-64; University of the Pacific, University of California, Berkeley, 1967-72, began as assistant research psychologist at Center for Research and Development in Higher Education, became associate research psychologist; California State College, Sonoma, Rohnert Park, visiting professor of psychology, 1972-74; California State University and Colleges System, Los Angeles, director of Center for Professional Development, 1974-75; Society for Values in Higher Education, Washington, D.C., director of project on institutional renewal through the improvement of teaching, 1975-78, and project on general education models, 1978—. Visiting professor at University of Leyden, 1971-72; staff member of Canadian Community College Institute, Faculty Development Institute of Council for the Advancement of Small Colleges, and University of North Carolina's Institute for Undergraduate Curricular Reform. Participant and coordinator of workshops and conferences; consultant to private foundations and government agencies. *Member:* American Association for Higher Education, American Association for the Advancement of Science, American Association of University Professors, American Psychological Association, American Sociological Association, Professional and Organizational Development Network, Society for Values in Higher Education, Western Psychological Association. *Awards, honors:* Fellow of American College Testing Program, summer, 1971.

WRITINGS: Innovations and Consequences: A Study of Raymond College, University of the Pacific (monograph), University of the Pacific, 1967; *The Care of Identified Emotionally-Disturbed Children in Stanislaus County* (monograph), Stanislaus County Mental Health Association, 1968; *The Cluster College,* Jossey-Bass, 1970; (with J.B.L. Hefferlin, J. J. Bloom, and B. J. Longacre) *Inventory of Current Research on Postsecondary Education 1972,* Center for Research and Development in Higher Education, University of California, 1972; (with H.M.F. Crombag and T. M. Chang) *The University as an Environment for Learning: An Empirical Analysis* (monograph), Educational Research Center, University of Leyden, 1973; (with Wilson and others) *College Professors and Their Impact on Students,* Wiley, 1975; *Toward Faculty Renewal,* Jossey-Bass, 1975; (with wife, Sally S. Gaff, and C. Festa) *Resource Notebook* (monograph), Project on Institutional Renewal Through the Improvement of Teaching, Society for Values in Higher Education, 1976; (with S. S. Gaff and Festa) *Professional Development: A Guide to Resources,* Educational Change, in press. Also author of, with R. C. Wilson, *The Teaching Environment: A Study of Optimum Working Conditions for Effective College Teaching* (monograph), 1971. Contributor to *Encyclopedia of Education.* Contributor of about thirty articles and reviews to education journals and to *Change.*

* * *

GAGE, Edwin 1943-

PERSONAL: Born May 7, 1943, in Orlando, Fla.; son of Edwin (a realtor) and Kathryne (a realtor) Gage. *Education:* University of Michigan, B.A., M.A., 1969; also attended University College, London, 1969. *Home:* 777 North Camino de Oeste, Tucson, Ariz. 85705. *Agent:* Elaine Markson Literary Agency, Inc., 44 Greenwich Ave., New York, N.Y. 10011.

CAREER: University of Arizona, Tucson, instructor in English, 1970-74; Pima College, Tucson, Ariz., instructor in English, 1975—. Manager of Spear G Ranch, 1970-72. Psychiatric technician at St. Mary's Hospital, 1976. *Member:* Phi Beta Kappa. *Awards, honors:* National Endowment for the Humanities grant, 1976, for Stanford University; exchange fellowship from University of Michigan, 1978-79, for University College, London.

WRITINGS: Phoenix No More (novel), Harper, 1978.

WORK IN PROGRESS: Hostages to Fate, a novel.

SIDELIGHTS: Gage writes: "*Phoenix No More* was my

attempt to say in fiction what I felt needed to be said about the destruction of the Sonoran desert by greed; specifically the sort of greed which breeds with technology to give birth to toxic (for two-hundred-fifty-thousand years) nuclear waste material."

* * *

GALLIE, W(alter) B(ryce) 1912-

PERSONAL: Born October 15, 1912, in Lenzie, Scotland; son of Walter S. (a structural engineer) and Alice (a teacher; maiden name, Wormald) Gallie; married Menna Humphreys (a novelist, translator, and broadcaster), July 13, 1940; children: Charles D.W., Edyth M.V. Gallie Lewis. *Education:* Balliol College, Oxford, B.A. (first class honors), 1934, B.Litt., 1937, M.A., 1947; Cambridge University, M.A., 1967. *Home:* Cilhendre, Upper Saint Mary St., Newport, Dyfed, Wales.

CAREER: University of Wales, University College of Swansea, assistant lecturer, 1935-38, lecturer in philosophy, 1938-40, 1945-50; University of Keele, Keele, England, professor of philosophy, 1950-54; Queen's University of Belfast, Belfast, Northern Ireland, professor of logic and metaphysics, 1954-67; Cambridge University, Cambridge, England, professor of political science and fellow of Peterhouse, 1967-78, professor emeritus, 1978—, Wiles Lecturer, 1976. Visiting professor at New York University, 1962-63; Lewis Fry Memorial Lecturer at University of Bristol, 1964. *Military service:* British Army, 1940-45; became major; received Croix de Guerre. *Member:* Aristotelian Society (president, 1970-72).

WRITINGS: An English School, Cresset, 1949; *Peirce and Pragmatism,* Pelican Books, 1952, Dover, 1954, reprinted, Greenwood Press, 1975; (contributor) William R. Elton, editor, *Aesthetics and Language,* Philosophical Library, 1954; (contributor) Charles Frederick Carter, editor, *Uncertainty and Business Decisions: A Symposium,* Liverpool University Press, 1954; *A New University: A. D. Lindsay and the Keele Experiment,* Chatto & Windus, 1960; *Philosophy and the Historical Understanding,* Schocken, 1964, 2nd edition, 1968; *Philosophers of Peace and War: Kant, Clausewitz, Marx, Engels, and Tolstoy,* Cambridge University Press, 1978. Contributor to philosophy, political science, and French studies journals.

WORK IN PROGRESS: International Theory; Political Morality, publication expected in 1982.

AVOCATIONAL INTERESTS: Reading, travel.

* * *

GALLO, Max 1932-

PERSONAL: Born January 1, 1932, in Nice, France; son of Joseph (a clerk) and Mafalda Gallo. *Education:* Sorbonne, University of Paris, agrege de l'universite, docteur-es-lettres. *Address:* 216 boulevard Raspail, 75014 Paris, France.

CAREER: University of Nice, Nice, France, professor, 1960-70; Institut d'Etude Politique, Paris, France, professor, 1970-75; *L'Express,* Paris, reporter, 1970-77, columnist, 1977—. Consulting editor to Editions Robert Laffont.

WRITINGS—All published by Laffont, except as noted; novels: Le Cortege des vainqueurs, 1972, translation by Nancy Amphonx published as *With the Victors,* Doubleday, 1974; *Un pas vers la mer,* 1973; *L'Oiseau des origines,* 1974; *La Baie des anges,* Volume I: *La Baie des anges,* 1975, Volume II: *Le Palais des fetes,* 1976, Volume III: *La Prome-*

nade des anglais, 1976; *Que sont les siecles pour la mer*, 1977; *Les Hommes naissant tous le meme jour*, Volume I: *Aurore*, 1978, Volume II: *Crepuscule*, 1979.

Nonfiction: *L'Italie de Mussolini: vingt ans d'ere fasciste*, Librairie academique Perrin, 1964, translation by Charles Lam Markmann published as *Mussolini's Italy: Twenty Years of the Fascist Era*, Macmillan, 1973; *La Grande Peur de 1989*, 1966; *L'Affaire d'Ethiopie*, Centurion, 1967; *Gauchisme, reformisme et revolution*, 1968; *Maximilien Robespierre, histoire d'une solitude*, Librairie academique Perrin, 1968, translation by Raymond Rudorff published as *Robespierre the Incorruptible: A Psycho-Biography*, Herder & Herder, 1971; *Cinquieme Colonne 1939-1940*, Plon, 1970; *Tombeau pour la commune*, 1971; *Histoire de l'Espagne franquiste*, 1969, translation by Jean Stewart published as *Spain Under Franco: A History*, Dutton, 1973; *La Nuit des longs couteaux: 30 juin 1934*, 1970, translation by Lily Emmet published as *The Night of Long Knives*, Harper, 1972; *Au nom de tous les miens*, 1971, translation by Anthony White published as *For Those I Loved*, Little, Brown, 1972; *La Mafia, mythes et realities*, Seghers, 1972; *I manifesti nella storia e nel costume*, Mondadori (Milan), 1973, translation by Alfred Mayor and Bruni Mayor published as *The Poster in History*, American Heritage, 1974; *L'Affiche, miroir de l'histoire*, 1973; (with Regis Debray) *Demain l'-Espagne*, Seuil, 1974, published as *Dialogue on Spain*, Lawrence & Wishart, 1976.

WORK IN PROGRESS: A novel.

SIDELIGHTS: Gallo is both a historian and novelist. Although several of his numerous books on history have been translated into English from the French, *With the Victors* is his only novel to appear in English translation to date.

In *Robespierre the Incorruptible*, "Gallo has given us what he calls a psychobiography, something far more ambitious than a slice of conventional history and immensely less reliable," J. P. Reid observed in *Commonweal*. The author "has explored every likely corner of Robespierre's character and personality. The whole adds up to a compelling portrait." His "insights into the man's deepest sentiments and inspirations lift his narrative, finally, to lyrical heights." But a *New York Times Book Review* critic referred to the book as "a silly piece of French journalistic history," on the basis that Gallo is "neither biographer nor psychologist."

Spain Under Franco: A History is a good, idiomatic translation of the original French version, according to Elbridge Colby. Reviewing the book for the *Times Literary Supplement*, another critic wrote, "Gallo's powerful and absorbing book gives the most detailed account we have had so far of how Franco [had] remained in power" for so long.

The Night of Long Knives is a historical account of Hitler's purging of Ernst Roehn and other German Brown Shirt leaders. "The writing is vivid and suspenseful," R. E. O'Brien commented in *Best Sellers*. *Atlantic* critic Phoebe Adams noted that, overall, the book is "well organized."

Gallo has woven together both fiction and history in many of his novels. *La Baie des anges* is a three-volume saga set in France that follows the lives of various characters involved in major events of the era, beginning with the 1890's and ending in the present. The trilogy was praised by critics in noted French publications, including *Le Monde*, *L'Express*, and *Le Figaro*.

In writing a novel one tries to recapture something that has been lost, Gallo told one French interviewer. It is also a way of allowing the reader to vicariously experience the novel-ist's own memories. Gallo also expressed the hope that once someone picks up one of his books to read, he or she will want to go on and read all that he has written.

Gallo noted that he prefers writing novels to history books. He told *CA:* "A history book is written with the end of the fingers and a part of the brain. In a novel, I can express not only my intelligence but also my sensibility. Moreover, if a novel is successful, the reader and the author communicate together through reading and writing, which are, I believe, identical."

BIOGRAPHICAL/CRITICAL SOURCES: New York Times Book Review, September 26, 1971, October 6, 1974; *Atlantic*, August, 1972; *Best Sellers*, August 1, 1972, January 1, 1974; *Publishers Weekly*, November 26, 1973, August 19, 1974; *Washington Post Book World*, March 10, 1974; *Nation*, April 6, 1974; *Choice*, June, 1974, July, 1974, February, 1975; *French Review*, February, 1975; *Times Literary Supplement*, August 2, 1976.

*   *   *

GALLOIS, Claire   1938-

PERSONAL: Born November 11, 1938, in Paris, France; daughter of Pierre and Genevieve Gallois; married Bruno de Guillebon (an industrial financier), November, 1970; children: Swann. *Education:* Attended secondary school in Paris. *Politics:* None. *Religion:* "Born Catholic." *Home:* 28 rue de la Fontaine des Vaux, 78860 St. Nom la Breteche, France.

CAREER: Publicity editor for advertising agency, 1965-70; journalist for *Marie-Claire*, and *Elle*, 1970-72; radio and television work, 1972-73; free-lance writer, 1973—.

WRITINGS—In English: *Une fille consue de fil blanc* (novel), Buchet/Chastel, 1969, translation by Elizabeth Walter published as *A Scent of Lilies*, Stein & Day, 1971.

Other: *A mon seul desir* (novel; title means "To My Desire Alone"), Buchet/Chastel, 1964; *Des Roses plein les bras*, Buchet/Chastel, 1965; *Jeremie la nuit*, Buchet/Chastel, 1976; *La Vie n'est pas un roman*, Grasset, 1978; *A propos d'amour*, Grasset, in press. Contributor to magazines, including *Elle* and *Match*.

SIDELIGHTS: Claire Gallois writes: "Everything in life is important to me: every glance in the street, every word, every person, every book or paper I read.

"When my novels are finished they don't belong to me any more. They get their own life and I let them free. I never open again my finished novels."

*   *   *

GALLU, Samuel

EDUCATION: Recieved degrees from Pennsylvania State University and Columbia University; Boston College, Ph.D. *Residence:* Bucks County, Pa.

CAREER: Singer, television and film producer, director, and writer. Singer with Fred Waring's Pennsylvanians; worked on Voice of America radio broadcasts to Romania; formed Hollywood-based Gallu Productions, Inc., and produced 279 television programs, including "Navy Log" and "Border Patrol"; wrote and directed four theatrical films while residing in London, England; worked on children's television program, "Howdy Doody"; joined Metropolitan Opera Workshop and sang as tenor soloist with National Broadcasting Co. (NBC) Symphony under director Arturo Toscanini; became full-time writer. *Military service:* U.S. Navy, served in World War II.

SIDELIGHTS: After years of work in television and film production, Gallu has lately devoted most of his time to writing, particularly plays. Saying once that he was inspired by "the honesty of the guy," he wrote and produced a one-man show about former President Harry S Truman, "Give 'em Hell, Harry." The play, which starred James Whitmore in both the stage and film versions, has a "witty, blunt, enormously attractive text" and has been performed throughout the United States, as well as in England, West Germany, and Israel. Another play, "I'll Make You an Offer You Can't Refuse," is a satirical look at society from a gangster's point of view. "In it," Gallu remarked, "I'm drawing a parallel between companies who bribe countries, and Mafia-like characters who bribe people. Each gives people what they want." Philadelphia's Bicentennial Theatre also commissioned him to write a play for its celebration of America's two-hundredth birthday. Always fascinated by Romanian culture, Gallu wrote a historical novel about the stormy love affair between King Carol and Magda Lupescu for his doctoral thesis in Eastern European history.

BIOGRAPHICAL/CRITICAL SOURCES: Atlanta Constitution, September 27, 1975; *Atlantic Monthly,* November, 1975; *Authors in the News,* Volume 2, Gale, 1976.

*   *   *

GALUB, Jack   1915-
(Chuck Gant)

PERSONAL: Born December 6, 1915, in New York, N.Y.; son of Nathan and Esther (Sussman) Galub; married Marcelle Lubotsky (an employment counselor); children: Meg L. *Education:* New York University, B.S., 1937; also attended Michigan State College (now University) and Hunter College (now of the City University of New York). *Office:* Jack Galub, Inc., 27 West 96th St., New York, N.Y. 10025.

CAREER: In public relations, 1937-65; Jack Galub, Inc. (public relations firm), New York City, president, 1965—. Member of board of trustees of Overseas Press Club Foundation, 1976—. *Military service:* U.S. Army, in press and radio unit of Army Ground Forces, 1941-44; received three battle stars. *Member:* Overseas Press Club of America (member of board of governors, 1975-76), American Society of Journalists and Authors, Outdoor Writers of America, Road Runners Club of New York, Appalachian Trail Conference, National Jogging Association.

WRITINGS: The U.S. Air Force Academy Fitness Program for Women, Prentice-Hall, 1979. Author of corporate annual reports and marketing brochures. Author of "Yamaichi on Tokyo," a monthly report in *Investment Dealers' Digest,* 1973-76, and "A Review of Selected Financial Institutions," a weekly column in *Financial Chronicle,* 1975-76. Contributor of about seventy articles (some with photographs, some under pseudonym Chuck Gant) to a wide variety of national magazines, including *Glamour, Mothers' Manual, Outdoor Life, Popular Mechanics,* and *Retirement Living.* Editor and publisher of *Editorial Directory,* 1950-53.

WORK IN PROGRESS: Health-related books.

SIDELIGHTS: Jack Galub writes: "Looking back, it would appear that I had been preparing for the writing of *The U.S. Air Force Academy Fitness Program for Women* for most of my life.

"While still in grade school, I was awed by my brother Gaile's ability to captain the high school cross-country team, play football, and run the four-forty in record time. I wondered why I could not do likewise, but at that time there were no answers I could find or grasp. Those years may have contributed to a longstanding interest in the medical and physiological aspects of fitness, exercise, and sports.

"But between those early years and the past year when I began working on the book, there was a lengthy apprenticeship during which I mastered my approach to writing. Involved were many years of writing public relations materials and publicity stories for a highly diversified group of companies and associations, including Yamaichi Securities Co. Ltd., Toshiba, Datsun, Grolier Society, British Woollens, British West Indian Airways, Calvert, and Carstairs.

"After I established my own public relations firm I expanded my writing horizons. I started free-lancing for such magazines as *Woman's Day, Family Health, Mechanix Illustrated,* and *Runner's World.* I also wrote annual reports, speeches, and brochures for corporations, banks, and stock brokerage firms. I also write medical research-related materials for the United Cerebral Palsy Research and Educational Foundation. Recently I have been involved in the organization and production of public and press seminars featuring panels made up of prominent medical and health authorities.

"My writings for *Runner's World* and my consulting work with Cardio-Metrics Institute had a direct bearing on the fitness book. Both gave me new insights into training, athletic techniques, and cardiovascular enhancement. I could speak knowledgeably with physiologists, trainers, coaches, and doctors regarding the problems they face in the areas I was researching.

"This background and my ability to take publishable photographs (at one time *Look* talked to me about becoming a staff photographer) gave me an advantage over a number of writers in the sports and outdoors fields. But as I pointed out, my writing is not limited to these areas. Today I still write financial as well as other corporate copy and medical related materials.

"My writings reflect the desire that readers will find them informative as well as interesting. I want readers to feel they have learned something they can use in their own lives to enhance their enjoyment of living, better their health, improve their physical abilities, and learn more about the world surrounding us.

"I stress clear and simple—not simplistic—writing, even when presenting complex scientific material. I also want readers to enjoy, to appreciate, the light touch I interject when possible. They should not feel they are reading a textbook or a medical tome."

*   *   *

GAMMELL, Susanna Valentine Mitchell   1897(?)-1979
(S. Valentine Mitchell)

OBITUARY NOTICE: Born c. 1897 in Philadelphia, Pa.; died April 9, 1979, in Washington, D.C. Poet, author, and playwright. Mitchell was associated with J. Walter Thompson Co. in New York City until her marriage in 1925. In the 1930's, she edited the poetry magazine *Smoke.* Her writings, published under the name S. Valentine Mitchell, include a collection of poems, *Journey Taken by a Woman,* a collection of stories, *In This Bright April Weather,* and two novels, *No Second Spring* and *Make New Banners.* Her play is a dramatized version of *Make New Banners*. Obituaries and other sources: *Washington Post,* April 12, 1979; *New York Times,* April 13, 1979; *AB Bookman's Weekly,* May 21, 1979.

* * *

GANSBERG, Judith M. 1947-

PERSONAL: Born October 20, 1947, in Passaic, N.J.; daughter of Martin (a newspaper editor) and Agatha (Miller) Gansberg; married Robert J. Burger (a materials scientist), May 30, 1976. *Education:* University of Michigan, B.A., 1969; graduate study at Rutgers University, 1969-70; University of Maryland, M.A., 1973. *Religion:* Jewish. *Home:* 421 Glenbrook Rd., Stamford, Conn. 06906. *Agent:* Lewis Chambers, Lewischam Productions, Inc., 663 Fifth Ave., New York, N.Y. 10022.

CAREER: New York State Credit Union League, Inc., New York City, assistant director of education, 1970-71; free-lance writer, 1971—. Adjunct professor at Southeastern University, 1975-77; adjunct assistant professor at Sacred Heart University, 1978; adjunct assistant professor at College of New Rochelle, 1978—. Production assistant and associate producer for WRC-TV, 1972; independent filmmaker, director, and producer. Film consultant for "Summer of My German Soldier." *Member:* Authors Guild of Authors League of America, Independent Media Producers Association (member of executive committee, 1977), University of Michigan Alumni Association, Phi Kappa Phi. *Awards, honors:* Documentary award from American Film Festival and local Emmy Award from National Association of Television Arts and Sciences, both in 1974, for producing "When the Past Dries Up."

WRITINGS: Stalag, U.S.A.: The Remarkable Story of German POWs in America, Crowell, 1977; *Please Believe Us* (nonfiction), Walker & Co., 1979.

Films: "For Your Information: Children's Awareness of God's Love," WRC-TV, 1972; "The WIN II Tax Credit," Casey Associates, 1973; "Altruism: The Human Resource," Casey Associates, 1973; "The Lost Ancient Ruins: Masada," GL Productions, 1975; "Orientation to Pool Slide Safety Standard," Consumer Product Safety Commission, 1976; "Neiss Coding and Telecommunications," Consumer Product Safety Commission, 1976; "Nuclear Reactor Safety," NUS Corp., 1977.

Contributor to magazines, including *Omni,* and newspapers. Contributing editor of *Soap Box,* 1976-78; assistant editor of *Tennis,* 1978.

WORK IN PROGRESS: Television scripts.

SIDELIGHTS: Judith Gansberg writes: "While I have written mostly nonfiction, I want to get more into novels and dramatic (comedic) television scripts. What I really want to do is make some kind of a contribution through writing. Whether that means investigative reporting or just making people feel good through laughter is unimportant to me. I want to feel that I've added something to the quality of our lives through my talents, such as they are.

"I lived in Paris as a teenager and speak fluent French. I love to travel and never hesitate to take an assignment that requires seeing new places."

BIOGRAPHICAL/CRITICAL SOURCES: New York Times, February 1, 1978.

* * *

GARD, Robert Edward 1910-

PERSONAL: Born July 3, 1910, in Iola, Kan.; son of Samuel

Arnold and Louisa Maria (Ireland) Gard; married Maryo Kimball, June 7, 1939; children: Maryo Gwendolyn, Eleanor Copeland. *Education:* University of Kansas, B.A., 1934; Cornell University, M.A., 1938. *Home address:* 3507 Sunset Dr., Madison, Wis. 53705.

CAREER: Writer. University of Kansas, Lawrence, instructor, 1934-37; Cornell University, Ithaca, N.Y., instructor, 1940-43; University of Wisconsin, Madison, assistant professor, 1945-48, associate professor, 1948-55, professor, 1955—; Duell, Sloan, & Pearce, New York, N.Y., field director, 1958-60. Director of the New York State Playwriting Project, 1938-43, and of the Alberta, Canada, Folklore and Local History Project, 1943-45; participant in the Survey of Cultural Arts, Great Britain, 1953; trustee of the National Theatre Conference, 1958-62, and of the Foundation of Integrated Education, 1961—; Fulbright professor, University of Helsinki, 1959-60, visiting professor, 1963; U.S. delegate to the World Theatre Congress, Vienna, Austria, 1961; president, Wisconsin House Publications, Madison, 1969; co-founder, Dale Wasserman Professional Playwright Development Laboratory, Rhinelander, Wis., 1976. *Member:* National Theatre Conference, American Educational Theatre Association, American National Theatre and Academy, Wisconsin Academy of Sciences, Arts, and Letters (president, 1976-77), Wisconsin Arts Foundation and Council (president, 1957-59), Wisconsin Regional Writers Association (president, 1961-64), Pi Kappa Alpha. *Awards, honors:* Service award from Department of Speech, University of Kansas, 1958; Gold Medal of Honor from the Finnish Theatre, 1961; distinguished service award from the International Institute of Milwaukee, 1964; Governor's award for creativity, 1967; Wisconsin local history award; citation from the Wisconsin Academy of Sciences, Arts, and Letters.

WRITINGS: Raisin' th' Devil: A Comedy of Schoharie County, American Agriculturist, 1940; (editor with Alexander M. Drummond) *The Lake Guns of Seneca and Cayuga, and Eight Other Plays of Upstate New York,* Cornell University Press, 1942, reprinted, Kennikat, 1972; *Johnny Chinook: Tall Tales and True From the Canadian West* (legends), Longmans, Green, 1945, new edition, Tuttle, 1967; *Wisconsin Is My Doorstep: A Dramatist's Yarn Book of Wisconsin Lore* (legends), Longmans, Green, 1948; (with Drummond) *The Cardiff Giant,* Cornell University Press, 1949; *Midnight: Rodeo Champion* (juvenile), illustrated by C. W. Anderson, Duell, Sloan, 1951; *Grassroots Theater: A Search for Regional Arts in America,* University of Wisconsin Press, 1955; *A Horse Named Joe* (juvenile), illustrated by C. W. Anderson, Duell, Sloan, 1956; *Scotty's Mare* (juvenile), illustrated by Aaron Bohrod, Duell, Sloan, 1957; (contributor) David H. Stevens, editor, *Ten Talents in the American Theatre,* University of Oklahoma Press, 1957; *The Big One,* Duell, Sloan, 1958; *Run to Kansas* (juvenile), illustrated by Alan Moyler, Duell, Sloan, 1958; (with Gertrude S. Burley) *Community Theatre: Idea and Achievement,* Duell, Sloan, 1959, reprinted, Greenwood Press, 1975.

(With Leland G. Sorden) *Wisconsin Lore, Antics, and Anecdotes of Wisconsin People and Places,* Duell, Sloan, 1962; *Devil Red* (juvenile), illustrated by Richard W. Lewis, Duell, Sloan, 1963; *The Error of Sexton Jones,* Duell, Sloan, 1964; (with Spencer A. Gard) *The Early Background of the Gard Family in America,* [Iola, Kan.], 1965; (with Marston Balch and Pauline B. Temkin) *Theater in America: Appraisal and Challenge for the National Theatre Conference,* Dembar Educational Research Services, 1968; (with David

Semmes) *America's Players*, Seabury, 1967; (with Sorden) *The Romance of Wisconsin Place Names*, October House, 1968; *This Is Wisconsin*, Wisconsin House, 1969; (with others) *The Arts in the Small Community: A National Plan*, [Madison, Wis.], 1969; (with Helen O'Brien) *Act Nine: Plays for Youth*, Wisconsin House, 1970; *University Madison, U.S.A.*, Wisconsin House, 1970; *Down in the Valleys: Wisconsin Back Country Lore and Humor,*, Wisconsin House, 1971; *Wild Goose Marsh: Horicon Stopover*, Wisconsin House, 1972; (editor with Elaine Reetz) *The Trail of the Serpent: The Fox River Valley* (legends), Madison House, 1973; *Wisconsin Sketches*, edited by Mark E. Lefebvre, Wisconsin House, 1973; (with Allen Crafton) *A Woman of No Importance* (novel), Wisconsin House, 1974; *Wild Goose Country: Horicon Marsh to Horseshoe Island*, Wisconsin House, 1975; (editor with others) *We Were Children Then: Ninety Wisconsin Writers Age Sixty to Ninety-Six*, Wisconsin House, 1976. Also author of *A Time of Humanities*, edited by Robert Yahnke, 1976, *Innocence of Prairie*, 1978, and *My Land, My Home, My Wisconsin*, with Maryo Gard, 1978.

SIDELIGHTS: In reviewing Robert Gard's *Wisconsin Is My Doorstep: A Dramatist's Yarn Book of Wisconsin*, a *San Francisco Chronicle* critic observed: "*Wisconsin Is My Doorstep* is a collection of Wisconsin Folk Tales old and new. They are cast in a remarkably readable dramatic form that is closer to radio script than any other recognizable type of composition. In them, the author has retained the spirit and aim of folklore, which is to divert and often to amuse the audience...."

Gard's contributions to children's literature include *Midnight: Rodeo Champion*, which was reviewed by a *New York Herald Tribune Book Review* critic: "The style is crisp and authentic, the rodeo lore fascinating, the characterization excellent, and the illustrations by an expert [C. W. Anderson]."

BIOGRAPHICAL/CRITICAL SOURCES: San Francisco Chronicle, May 30, 1948; *New York Herald Tribune Book Review*, May 13, 1951.

* * *

GARFIELD, Patricia L(ee)   1934-

PERSONAL: Born August 31, 1934, in Erie, Pa.; daughter of Frederick Cameron (a lithographer) and Evelyn (Hahn) Goff; married Charles R. Darwin, September 10, 1955 (divorced, 1968); married Zalmon H. Garfield (a psychotherapist), April 26, 1969; children: (first marriage) Cheryl (Mrs. William Kaufman). *Education:* Temple University, B.A. (summa cum laude), 1963, M.A., 1964, Ph.D., 1968. *Residence:* San Francisco, Calif. *Agent:* Ruth Ann Waite, Paul R. Reynolds, Inc., 12 East 41st St., New York, N.Y. 10017.

CAREER: Temple University, Philadelphia, Pa., instructor in psychology, 1967-69; Philadelphia College of Textiles and Science, Philadelphia, assistant professor of psychology, 1969-71; California State College, Sonoma, Rohnert Park, instructor in psychology, 1973; University of California Extension, lecturer in psychology at various campuses. *Member:* American Psychological Association, Association for the Advancement of the Behavioral Therapies, Association for the Psychophysiological Study of Sleep, Western Psychological Association.

WRITINGS: Creative Dreaming, Simon & Schuster, 1974; (author of introduction) Robert Gumpertz, designer, *Dream Notebook*, San Francisco Book Co., 1976; (contributor) Herbert Otto and James Knight, editors, *Wholistic Healing:*

New Frontiers in the Treatment of the Whole Person, Nelson-Hall, 1979; *Pathway to Ecstasy: The Way of the Dream Mandala*, Holt, 1979. Contributor to psychology journals.

WORK IN PROGRESS: Research on dreams in different cultural groups and on *Chi* (Chinese word for energy flow).

SIDELIGHTS: Patricia Garfield comments: "I have been writing down my dreams since I was fourteen and am still fascinated with the wealth of self-understanding available from this inner source." *Avocational interests:* Travel, calligraphy, ethnic dance, *ch'i kung* (ancient Chinese movement system).

* * *

GARNER, Roberta   1943-
(Roberta Ash)

PERSONAL: Born November 10, 1943, in Urbana, Ill.; daughter of Henry R. (a professor of linguistics) and Renee (Toole) Kahane; married Larry Garner (a political scientist), November 27, 1976; children: (from previous marriage) Michael Ash. *Education:* University of Chicago, B.A., 1962, M.A., 1963, Ph.D., 1966. *Office:* Department of Sociology, DePaul University, 2323 North Seminary, Chicago, Ill. 60614.

CAREER: DePaul University, Chicago, Ill., assistant professor, 1971-73; associate professor of sociology, 1973—, head of department, 1978—. *Member:* American Sociological Association, American Association of University Professors.

WRITINGS: (Under name Roberta Ash) *Social Movements in America*, Markham, 1972, revised edition published under name Roberta Garner, Rand McNally, 1977; *Social Change*, Rand McNally, 1977; (with Peter Dreier) *Sociology: A Marxist Introduction*, Winthrop Publishing, 1979.

SIDELIGHTS: Roberta Garner writes: "My main interests are political sociology and Marxist theory. I am also interested in technological issues and have some experience in computer programming."

AVOCATIONAL INTERESTS: Travel (lived in Italy, 1978).

* * *

GATTY, Ronald   1929-

PERSONAL: Born July 9, 1929, in Long Beach, Calif.; son of Harold (a writer) and Elsie Louise (Limmex) Gatty. *Education:* Cornell University, M.Sc., 1952, Ph.D., 1957. *Home:* 20 East Ninth St., New York, N.Y. 10003. *Office:* Bernard M. Baruch College of the City University of New York, 17 Lexington Ave., New York, N.Y. 10010.

CAREER: Diver and fisherman in Fiji and Samoa, 1946-50; Rutgers University, New Brunswick, N.J., assistant professor of economics and statistics, 1957-62; Villanova University, Villanova, Pa., associate professor of economics and statistics, 1962-64; Bernard M. Baruch College of the City University of New York, New York, N.Y., professor of biometrics, 1964—. Director of research for New York State Joint Legislative Committee on Higher Education, 1965-66; financial consultant to New York City mayor's Temporary Commission on City Finances. *Military service:* U.S. Army, French and German translator and interpreter, 1952-55; served in France. *Member:* International Society for Chronobiology, American Statistical Association, American Association for Public Opinion Research, Pacific Science Association.

WRITINGS: The Body Clock Diet, Simon & Schuster, 1978. Contributor to academic journals, popular magazines, including *Cosmopolitan* and *New Woman*, and newspapers.

WORK IN PROGRESS: Research on ethnolinguistics of Fiji and on statistical algorithms of chronobiological times series.

SIDELIGHTS: Gatty comments: "Originally Australian, I was raised in the South Seas islands, mainly Fiji. This led to a life-long interest in Fijian lore and language. I try to spend several months each year in Fiji, which I consider 'home.' All this is leading to the major work of my life, already several years in progress, on the customs and traditions, as well as the language, of the Fijian people."

*   *   *

GAVIN, Thomas 1941-

PERSONAL: Born February 1, 1941, in Newport News, Va.; son of Donald James (in photo-finishing) and Virginia (Michael) Gavin; married Claire Ellen Campbell, April 15, 1967; children: Wendy Marie, Emily Sandra. *Education:* University of Toledo, B.A., 1969, M.A., 1972. *Politics:* "I cast my ballot for peace, solar energy, and organic agriculture, hoping to keep the planet habitable." *Religion:* "I aspire to the condition of Kierkegaard's knight of faith." *Home:* 81 Weybridge St., Middlebury, Vt. 05753. *Agent:* Georges Borchardt, Inc., 136 East 57th St., New York, N.Y. 10022. *Office:* Department of English, Middlebury College, Middlebury, Vt. 05753.

CAREER: Jackson Citizen-Patriot, Jackson, Mich., reporter, 1968; elementary school teacher in Jackson, 1968-69; high school English teacher in Toledo, Ohio, 1971-72; Delta College, University Center, Mich., lecturer in English, 1972-75; Middlebury College, Middlebury, Vt., assistant professor of English, 1975—.

WRITINGS: Kingkill (novel), Random House, 1977.

WORK IN PROGRESS: The Last Film of Emile Vico, a novel based on the circumstances climaxing the career of actor-director Emile Vico, publication by Random House expected in 1981.

SIDELIGHTS: Gavin writes: "In my professional career as a writer I owe much to the Bread Loaf Writers' Conference, which I attended as a contributor, 1973-74. I could not have had more wise and generous teachers than George P. Elliott and John Gardner, nor a colleague and friend more supportive than Robert Pack, the conference director.

"As a reader I admire the classic detective story. What fascinates me is the logic by which a rusty lock on the potting shed door, a sinister nun with a blue glass eye and pince-nez clad corpse in the vicar's bathtub are woven into a seamless pattern. My own writing begins when I stumble across an image from history or life that resonates with similar mystery. Why, for example, would a chess genius spend the last twelve years of his life playing the game he loves inside an airless box, letting the credit for his brilliant gambits go to a fraudulent automaton? In my novel, *Kingkill*, I tried to account for this mystery by creating a narrative that places fictional 'evidence' side by side with historical fact, and challenges the reader to test the truth of one against the other."

*   *   *

GEIGEL POLANCO, Vicente 1904-1979

OBITUARY NOTICE: Born in 1904 in Isabela, P.R.; died April 30, 1979, in San Juan, P.R. Writer, lawyer, and politi-

cian. Geigel Polanco was a former senator and an attorney general in the administration of Governor Luis Munoz Marin. He also headed the society of Puerto Rican authors, El Ateneo Puertoriqueno, and was a professor of law at the University of Puerto Rico. Among his writings are several books of poetry, including *Palabras de nueva esperanza, Canto de tierra adentro*, and *Canto del amor infinito*, and the books *El grito de Lares: Gesta de heroismo y sacrificio* and *Valores de Puerto Rico*. Obituaries and other sources: *Puerto Rican Authors: A Biobibliographic Handbook*, Scarecrow, 1974; *New York Times*, May 2, 1979; *Washington Post*, May 4, 1979.

*   *   *

GERHART, Gail M. 1943-

PERSONAL: Born July 3, 1943, in New York, N.Y.; daughter of Ernest E. and Dorothy (Scott) Gillam; married John D. Gerhart (an economist), June 1, 1968; children: Leslie, Nathaniel. *Education:* Radcliffe College, B.A., 1966; Columbia University, Ph.D., 1974. *Politics:* Democrat. *Home address:* P.O. Box 41081, Nairobi, Kenya.

CAREER: Worked as volunteer teacher in Tanzania, 1963-64; associated with Princeton University, Princeton, N.J., 1973-74; University of Botswana, Lesotho and Swaziland, Gabarone, Botswana, lecturer in history, 1975-76; International Rescue Committee, Nairobi, Kenya, representative, 1977—.

WRITINGS: (With Thomas G. Karis) *From Protest to Challenge: A Documentary History of African Politics in South Africa, 1882-1964*, Volumes III and IV (Gerhart was not associated with other volumes), Hoover Institution, 1977; *Black Power in South Africa: The Evolution of an Ideology*, University of California Press, 1978.

WORK IN PROGRESS: Continuing research on South African history and politics.

SIDELIGHTS: Gail Gerhart writes: "I have tried in my books to help South Africans come to grips with future change by enlarging their understanding of the past. Writing from an American perspective, I have tried to make the issue of racial oppression in South Africa intelligible and meaningful to Americans in the hope that more will eventually take a firmer stand on the side of justice."

BIOGRAPHICAL/CRITICAL SOURCES: New York Times Book Review, February 4, 1979.

*   *   *

GERROLD, David 1944-

PERSONAL: Born January 24, 1944, in Chicago, Ill.; son of Lewis Friedman (a photographer) and Johanna (Fleischer) Gerrold; *Education:* Attended University of Southern California; California State University at Northridge, earned B.A. degree. *Home and office address:* Box 1190, Hollywood, Calif. 90028. *Agent:* Henry Morrison, Inc., 58 West Tenth St., New York, N.Y. 10011.

CAREER: Science fiction writer, 1967—. *Awards, honors:* Hugo award nomination, 1968, for "The Trouble With Tribbles"; Nebula award nomination, 1972, for *In the Deadlands*, and, 1977, for *Moonstar Odyssey*; Hugo and Nebula award nominations, 1972, for *When Harlie Was One*, 1973, for *The Man Who Folded Himself*, and 1977, for *Moonstar Odyssey*; Skylark award, 1979.

WRITINGS: (With Larry Niven) *The Flying Sorcerers* (novel), Ballatine, 1971; (editor with Stephen Goldin) *Protostars*,

Ballantine, 1971; (editor with Goldin) *Generation*, Dell, 1972; *Space Skimmer* (novel), Ballantine, 1972; *When Harlie Was One* (Science Fiction Book Club selection), Doubleday, 1972; *With a Finger in My I* (short stories), Ballantine, 1972; *Yesterday's Children* (novel), Dell, 1972; *Battle for the Planet of the Apes* (novel; adapted from the screenplay by John William Corrington and Joyce Hooper Corrington), Universal Publishing & Distributing, 1973; *The Man Who Folded Himself* (Science Fiction Book Club selection), Random House, 1973; *The World of Star Trek*, Ballantine, 1973; (editor) *Alternities* (anthology), Dell, 1974; (editor) *Emphasis* (anthology), Ballantine, 1974; (contributor) Alan Dean Foster, editor, *Star Trek Log*, Corgi, 1976; (editor) *Ascents of Wonder*, Popular Library, 1977; *Moonstar Odyssey* (novel), New American Library, 1977; *Deathbeast* (novel), Popular Library, 1978.

Teleplays: *The Trouble With Tribbles* (first produced as episode of "Star Trek" television series by NBC-TV, telecast December 29, 1967), Ballantine, 1973. Also author of a revision of "I, Mudd," first produced in 1967, and "The Cloud Minders," first produced in 1968, both as episodes for "Star Trek", and of "More Troubles, More Tribbles," and "BEM," both for the animated "Star Trek" series. Columnist in *Starlog* and *Galileo*. Story editor of "Land of the Lost," 1974.

WORK IN PROGRESS: "It's bad luck to talk about them prior to completion."

SIDELIGHTS: Gerrold's science fiction novel, *Yesterday's Children*, is, according to the *Times Literary Supplement*, "that rare thing in the genre: a study of character." Aboard the starship *Burlingame*, a weak and tired captain contends with his mutinous crew, gives reluctant chase to an enemy space craft, and struggles with an ambitious, power-usurping officer for control of the ship. Like the *Caine Mutiny*, it examines the emotional and moral conflicts generated by the shifting balance of military authority. The *Times Literary Supplement* concluded: "*Yesterday's Children* remains a solidly worked-out SF novel with unusually good characterization."

Another book, *The Man Who Folded Himself*, looks at the paradoxical implications of time travel. With the aid of a special belt, a nineteen-year-old student confronts a half-dozen versions of himself at different ages. The awkward repercussions that follow gradually leave the narrator in complete loneliness and displacement. In the judgment of *Publishers Weekly*, "Gerrold is such a good writer that he keeps us reading through the most confusing shifts of time, space and character—right into pre-history." It is a story, noted the *Times Literary Supplement*, of "uncanny allegorical force" that explores the limits of self-knowledge being set by one's compulsive behavior. "Altogether most impressive."

BIOGRAPHICAL/CRITICAL SOURCES: Publishers Weekly, February 4, 1974, May 13, 1974; *Times Literary Supplement*, February 15, 1974, June 14, 1974; *Village Voice*, June 13, 1974; *Book World*, March 30, 1975.

*   *   *

GHELDERODE, Michel de   1898-1962

PERSONAL: Birth-given name, Adolphe-Adhemar-Louis-Michel Martens; name legally changed in 1929; born April 3, 1898, in Elsene, Belgium; died April 1, 1962, in Brussels, Belgium; son of Adolphe Martens (an official); married in 1924. *Education:* Studied art and music in Belgium. *Residence:* Belgium. *Religion:* Roman Catholic.

CAREER: Worked as archivist in Schaerboek, Belgium, for twenty years; poet, playwright, and journalist. Writer for *Journal de Bruges*, 1946-53. Principal playwright with Theatre Populaire Flamand. *Awards, honors:* Belgian Society author's prize, 1945; Malpertuis prize for drama, Belgian Royal Academy of Language and Literature, 1951; twice awarded Triennial prize, the second time in 1954; recipient of Picard award for dramatic literature.

WRITINGS—In English: *Mademoiselle Jaiere* (play), [published], 1942, translation by Derek Prouse published as *Miss Jairus*, 1958 (also see below); *Theatre*, five volumes, [Paris], 1950-57; *Seven Plays*, translated by George Hauger, Volume I (contains "The Ostend Interviews," "The Women at the Tomb," "Barabbas," "Three Actors and Their Drama," "Pantagleize," "The Blind Men," "Chronicles of Hell," and "Lord Halewyn"; also see below), Hill & Wang, 1960, Volume II (contains "Red Magic," "Hop Signor!," "The Death of Doctor Faust," "Christopher Columbus," "A Night of Pity," "Pint Bouteille," and "Miss Jairus"; also see below), McGibbin & Kee, 1966; *The Blind Men: In the Country of the Blind the One-Eyed Is King* (play), translated by Samuel Draper, Apiary Press, 1961; *The Strange Rider and Seven Other Plays*, translated by Draper, privately printed, 1964.

Plays: *Les Vieillards* (one-act; title means "The Old Men"), [published], 1924; *Oude Piet* (title means "Old Piet"; first produced in Antwerp at Ouvriers de la Renaissance, 1925), [published], 1925; *Le Mystere de la passion de notre Seigneur Jesus-Christ* (title means "The Mystery of the Passion of Our Lord Jesus Christ"; first produced in Brussels at Theatre des Marionnettes de Toone, March 30, 1934), [published], 1925; *La Mort du Docteur Faust* (three-act tragedy; title means "The Death of Doctor Faust"; first produced in Paris at Theatre Art et Action, January 27, 1928), [published], 1926; *Venus* (one-act tragi-farce), [published], 1927; *La Transfiguration dans le cirque* (title means "Transfiguration in the Circus"), [published], 1928; *Images de la vie de St. Francois d'Assise* (title means "Images of the Life of St. Francis of Assisi"; first produced in Brussels at Theatre Flamand, January 12, 1929), [published], 1928; *Don Juan, ou Les Amants chimeriques* (three-act; title means "Don Juan, or The Chimerical Lovers"), [published], 1928; *La Tentation de St. Antoine* (title means "The Temptation of St. Anthony"), [published], 1929; *Un Soir de pitie* (one-act; title means "A Night of Pity"), [published], 1929; *Le Massacre des innocents* (title means "The Slaughter of the Innocents"), [published], 1929; *Christophe Colomb* (three-scene; title means "Christopher Columbus"; first produced in Paris at Theatre Art et Action, October 25, 1929), [published], 1929; (with Jean Barleig) *Het meisje met de houten handen*, [published], 1929.

Duveloor, ou La Farce du diable vieux (title means "Duveloor, or the Farce of the Old Devil"), [published], 1931; *De zeven hoofdzonden* (title means "The Sleep of Reason"; first produced in Oudenaarde, December 23, 1934), [published], 1931; *De Sterrendief* (title means "The Star Thief"; first produced in Brussels at Vlaamse Volkstoneel, March 21, 1928), [published], 1932; *Arc-en-ciel*, Editions de l'Avant-poste, 1933; *Le Siege d'Ostende* (title means "The Siege of Ostend"; military farce), [published], 1933; *Les Femmes au tombeau* (one-act; title means "The Women at the Tomb"), [published], 1934; *Godelieve* (first produced in Ostend, September 4, 1932), [published], 1934; *La Balade du grand macabre: la grand kermesse* (three-act; title means "The Grand Macabre's Stroll"; first produced in Paris at Studio des Champs-Elysees, October 30, 1953), [published],

1934; *Pantagleize* (three-act; first produced in Brussels at Vlaamese Volkstoneel, April 24, 1930), [published], 1934; *Masques ostendais* (one-act pantomime; title means "Ostend Masks"), [published], 1935; *Le Menage de Caroline* (one-act; title means "Caroline's Place"; first produced in Brussels at Theatre Residence, January 19, 1952), [published], 1935; *La Pie sur le gibet* (one-act farce), [published], 1935; *Les Aveugles* (one-act; title means "The Blind Men"; first produced in Paris at Theatre de Poche, July 5, 1956), [published], 1936; *Hop, Signor!* (one-act; also see below), [published], 1938; *Le Cavalier bizarre* (one-act; title means "The Strange Rider"), [published], 1938.

Le Soleil se couche (nine scenes; title means "The Sun Sets"; first produced in Brussels at Theatre Royal Flamand, January 23, 1951), [published], 1942; *D'un diable qui precha merveilles* (three-act mystery for marionettes; title means "Of a Devil Who Preached Wonders"), [published], 1942; *La Farce des tenebreux* (three-act farce; title means "The Farce of the Band"), [published], 1942; *Le Club des menteurs* (one-act; title means "The Liars' Club"), [published], 1943; *Sire Halewyn* (fourteen scenes; title means "Lord Halewyn"; first produced in Brussels at Theatre Communal, January 21, 1938), [published], 1943; *Sortileges* (also see below), Marechal (Liege, Belgium), 1947.

Theatre (contains "Hop signor!," "Escurial," "Sire Halewyn," "Magie rouge," "Mademoiselle Jaire," and "Fastes d'enfer"), Gallimard, 1950-57; *Theatre d'ecoute* (contains three plays: "Le Singulier Trepas de messire Ulenspiegel" [eight-scene; title means "The Mysterious Death of Messire Ulenspiegel"], "Le Perroquet de Charles-Quint" [nine-scene; title means "Charles the Fifth's Parrot"], and "La Folie d'Hugo van der Goes" [three-scene; title means "The Madness of Hugo van der Goes"]), C.E.L.F., 1951; *La Farce de la mort qui faillit trepasser* (title means "The Farce About Death Who Almost Died"; first produced in Brussels at Vlaamse Volkstoneel, November 19, 1925), [published], 1952; *La Vie publique de Pantagleize* (one-act; title means "Pantagleize's Public Life"), [published], 1954; *Ultimes boutades*, Editions Dynamo, 1966.

Unpublished plays: "La Mort regarde a la fenetre" (title means "Death Looks at the Window"), first produced in 1918; "Les Repas des fauves" (title means "The Beasts' Meal"), first produced in 1919; "Trois acteurs, un drame" (one-act; title means "Three Actors and Their Drama), first produced in Brussels at Theatre Royal du Parc, April 2, 1931; "Piet Bouteille" (one-act), first produced in Brussels at Theatre Royal du Parc, April 2, 1931; "Marie la miserable" (six scene mystery; title means "Marie the Miserable"), first produced in Woluwe-St-Lambert before the St-Lambert Church, June 14, 1952.

Other works: *La Flandre est un songe*, Durendal (Brussels), 1953; Roger Iglesis and Alain Trutat, compilers, *Les Entretiens d'Ostende* (autobiographical; based on radio interviews broadcast by the Club d'Essai de la Radiodifusion Television Francaises), L'Arche, 1956; *Sortileges et autres contes crepusculaires* (contains "L'Ecrivain public," "Le Diable a Londres," "Le Jardin malade," "L'Amateur de reliques," "Rhotomago," "Sortileges," "Voler la mort," "Nuestra Senora de la Soledad," "Brouillard," "Un Crepuscule," "Tu fus pendu," and "L'Odeur du sapin"), Gerard (Verviers, Belgium), 1962; *Contes et dicts hors du temps*, L. Musin, 1975.

Also author of plays: "Sortie de l'acteur" (title means "Actor's Exit"), 1930; "D'un diable qui precha merveilles" (title means "Of a Devil Who Preached Marvels"), 1934; "Ars moriendi"; "Les Bourgeois de Gand" (title means "The Bourgeois of Ghent"); "Un caprice de Goya"; "Comte sans tete" (title means "The Headless Count"); "La Folie"; "Le Gest d'Onan" (title means "Onan's Gesture"); "La Nuit tombe sur la Flandre" (title means "Night Falls on Flanders"); and "Les Tribulations metaphysiques de Pantagleize" (title means "The Metaphysical Tribulations of Pantagleize").

Plays represented in anthologies, including *The Modern Theatre,* Volume V, edited by E. R. Bentley, translated by L. Abel, [Garden City, N.Y.], 1955-60, and *The New Theatre of Europe,* edited by R. W. Corrigan, translated by Hauger, [New York, N.Y.], 1962. Former co-editor of *Flandre Litteraire.*

SIDELIGHTS: Ghelderode made it his mission to remind playgoers of the inevitability of death in order to jolt them out of any complacency they might feel about life. A devout Catholic, he was also strongly influenced by his mother's obsession with the occult. "I have an angel on my shoulder and a devil in my pocket," he once confessed. His plays combine the presence of God and Satan with the vices of man.

As he abhorred the commonplace, Ghelderode gravitated toward the traditions of the medieval Flemish theatre, Elizabethan England, and ancient Spain. These traditions appealed to him because, as a self-described romantic, he felt the "theatre is an art of instinct and not reason." His interest was also captured by the paradoxical combination of the blasphemous with man's desire for atonement for his sins.

Marionette shows were often a part of the Flemish theatre and likewise are present in Ghelderode's plays. Marionettes fascinated him. It was his contention that there is often little difference between the movements of puppets and the wooden actions of real people. But he was not interested in analyzing this phenomenon; instead, he chose to characterize human action.

A former student of music and art, Ghelderode made up for what is considered a weak use of language by emphasizing visual and sound effects in his plays. "I discovered the world of shapes before the world of ideas," Ghelderode recalled. He was deeply affected by the paintings of his friend James Enson, but it was his keen interest in the works of Pieter Brueghel that prompted him to set some of his productions in the imaginary "Brueghelland." Similarly, "La Pie sur le gibet" and "Les Aveugles" are based on particular paintings by Brueghel. Some of the special sound effects used by Ghelderode to accent the macabre tone of his works are clanging bells, mournful cries, and cacophonous music.

Although Ghelderode wrote prolifically between World War I and World War II, public interest in his plays was not sparked until *Chronicles of Hell* scandalized Parisian audiences in 1949. They were shocked by his style of combining the "perversion of religious or political functions with scatological farce," as George Wellwarth put it. Wellwarth pointed out that "the theatre is just now beginning to catch up with him."

The first play by Ghelderode to be produced in the United States was *Pantagleize.* It is a "drama of Everyman," Robert W. Corrigan noted. At the onset of the play, Ghelderode wrote in a program note, Pantagleize, the protagonist, is "unfit for anything except love, friendship, and ardor—a failure, therefore, in our utilitarian age, which pushes out into the fringe everything that is productive, that does not pay dividends!" But, Corrigan added, "in that one day in which Pantagleize's destiny was fulfilled, he revealed the richness, the joy, the pain, the sadness, and the ludicrousness of each man's destiny, and in so doing he affirms the humanity of us all."

Ghelderode was considered an introvert, possibly because of ill health. As a child he had nearly died from a serious illness that left him partially paralyzed. When he was stricken with asthma many years later, he withdrew from society, surrounding himself with his puppets, masks, and marionettes. By that time he was already considered a master of his art.

AVOCATIONAL INTERESTS: Restoring forgotten texts used in medieval marionette productions.

BIOGRAPHICAL/CRITICAL SOURCES: Michel de Ghelderode, *Les Entretiens d'Ostende,* L'Arche, 1956; George Wellworth, *The Theatre of Protest and Paradox: Developments in the Avant-Garde Drama,* New York University Press, 1964; Robert W. Corrigan, editor, *The Theatre in Search of a Fix,* Delacorte, 1973; *Contemporary Literary Criticism,* Gale, Volume 6, 1976, Volume 11, 1979.*

*   *   *

GIBBS, Wolcott, Jr.   1935-
(Tony Gibbs)

PERSONAL: Born April 5, 1935, in New York, N.Y.; son of Wolcott (a writer) and Elinor (a writer; maiden name, Sherwin) Gibbs; married Elizabeth Villa, January 4, 1958 (divorced); married Elaine St. James (an entrepreneur), April 22, 1978; children: William, Eric. *Education:* Princeton University, B.A., 1957. *Religion:* None. *Office:* Yachting, 50 West 44th St., New York, N.Y. 10036.

CAREER: Doubleday & Co., Inc., New York City, publicity manager, 1958-63, editorial assistant, 1963-64; J. B. Lippincott Co., New York City, editor, 1966-68; *Motor Boating,* New York City, book editor, 1968-75; *Motor Boating and Sailing,* New York City, executive editor, 1975; *Yachting,* New York City, editor, 1975—. Member of Rules of the Road Advisory Commission. *Military service:* U.S. Army National Guard, 1957-63; U.S. Coast Guard Auxiliary.

WRITINGS—Under name Tony Gibbs: *Practical Sailing,* Hearst Books, 1971; *Pilot's Work Book,* Seven-Seas Press, 1972; *Pilot's Log Book,* Seven-Seas Press, 1972; *Powerboating,* Lippincott, 1973; *Sailing: A First Book* (juvenile), F. Watts, 1974; *Backpacking* (juvenile), F. Watts, 1975; *Navigation* (juvenile), F. Watts, 1975; *Advanced Sailing,* St. Martin's, 1975. Author of editor's page, and of "Rough Log," a column in *Yachting,* 1976-78. Contributor to boating magazines.

WORK IN PROGRESS: A book on cruising in small sailing yachts, publication by Norton.

*   *   *

GIBSON, D. Parke   1930-1979

OBITUARY NOTICE: Born October 8, 1930, in Seattle, Wash.; died May 12, 1979, in New York, N.Y. Businessman. Gibson was head of D. Parke Gibson International, a management consulting firm in New York City. He published *The Gibson Report,* a marketing guide on the black consumer market, and *Race Relations and Industry,* a periodic report on equal-opportunity compliance. He was also author of a comprehensive guide to the black consumer market, *$70 Billion in the Black,* and *The $30 Billion Negro.* Obituaries and other sources: *Who's Who in Public Relations (International),* 5th edition, PR Publishing, 1976; *New York Times,* May 14, 1979.

GIBSON, James J(erome)   1904-

PERSONAL: Born January 27, 1904, in McConnelsville, Ohio; son of Thomas Benton and Mary Gertrude (Stanbery) Gibson; married Eleanor Grier Jack, September 17, 1932; children: James Jerome, Jean Grier. *Education:* Princeton University, B.S., 1925, A.M., 1926, Ph.D., 1928. *Home:* 111 Oak Hill Rd., Ithaca, N.Y. 14850. *Office:* Department of Psychology, Cornell University, Ithaca, N.Y. 14853.

CAREER: Smith College, Northampton, Mass., instructor, 1928-29, assistant professor, 1929-36, associate professor of psychology, 1936-49; Cornell University, Ithaca, N.Y., professor of psychology, 1949—, head of department, 1961-64. Visiting professor at University of California, Berkeley, 1954-55, and Massachusetts Institute of Technology, 1973. Research associate at Yale University, 1935-36; member of Institute for Advanced Study, 1958-59; fellow of Center for Advanced Study in the Behavioral Sciences, 1963-64. *Military service:* U.S. Army Air Forces, director of aviation psychology research unit, 1942-46; became lieutenant colonel.

MEMBER: American Psychological Association (fellow; division president, 1954-55, 1958-59), Society of Experimental Psychologists, Society for the Psychological Study of Social Issues, American Association of University Professors, National Academy of Sciences, American Academy of Arts and Sciences, Eastern Psychological Association (president, 1959-60), Sigma Xi. *Awards, honors:* Howard Crosby Warren Medal from Society of Experimental Psychologists, 1952, for research on visual perceptions; senior Fulbright scholar at Oxford University, 1955-56; scientific contribution award from American Psychological Association, 1961, for experiments on vision; National Institutes of Health awards, 1964—; D.Sc. from University of Edinburgh, 1973; D.Phil. from University of Uppsala, 1976; D.Phil., from University of Padva, 1979.

WRITINGS: The Perception of the Visual World, Houghton, 1950, reprinted, Greenwood Press, 1974; *The Senses Considered as Perceptual Systems,* Houghton, 1966; *The Ecological Approach to Visual Perception,* Houghton, 1979. Contributor of articles and reviews to psychology journals.

WORK IN PROGRESS: "The nature of cognition and imagination."

SIDELIGHTS: Gibson told *CA:* "My first book has been translated into German and my second into German and Swedish. It appears that Europeans find my approach to psychology more plausible than do my fellow Americans. I have been moving toward a psychology of values instead of a psychology of stimulus."

*   *   *

GILFORD, Madeline Lee   1923-

PERSONAL: Born May 30, 1923, in New York, N.Y.; daughter of Max (a clothing designer) and Anna (a milliner; maiden name, Siegelbaum) Lederman; married Mitchell Fein, October 20, 1940 (divorced, November, 1948); married Jack Gilford (the actor), April 6, 1949; children: Lisa Lee Fein Smerling, Joseph Edward, Sam Max. *Education:* Attended high school in Bronx, N.Y. *Politics:* Socialist. *Religion:* Jewish. *Residence:* New York, N.Y. *Agent:* Helen Harvey, 410 West 24th St., New York, N.Y. 10001.

CAREER: Actress, 1926—. Has worked as casting director and consultant, producer, and teacher for radio, Broadway and Off-Broadway shows, films, television, and commercial advertising. Member of board of directors of WomanSchool,

1976-77. *Member:* Actors Equity Association, American Federation of Television and Radio Artists, Screen Actors Guild. *Awards, honors:* Award from *Show Business,* 1978, for *170 Years of Show Business.*

WRITINGS: (With Kate Mostel, Zero Mostel, and husband, Jack Gilford) *170 Years of Show Business,* Random House, 1978.

WORK IN PROGRESS: Left-Overs (tentative title), a sequel to her first book; theatrical adaptations, including an adaptation of *170 Years of Show Business.*

SIDELIGHTS: Madeline Gilford wrote: "I am and have been for most of my life a political activist on behalf of peace, disarmament, minority group rights, civil rights, feminist rights, the reorganization of society along more egalitarian principles: socialism, medical care for all, and subsidies for artists and arts programs."

With regard to her writing, Gilford reported that she was influenced by Anton Chekhov, James Joyce, Bernard Malamud, and Isaac Bashevis Singer. Gilford also stated that she does not consider herself a writer, and called *170 Years of Show Business* an "accident."

BIOGRAPHICAL/CRITICAL SOURCES: New York Times Book Review, May 21, 1978; *New York Times,* May 26, 1978.

* * *

GILGOFF, Alice 1946-

PERSONAL: Born December 18, 1946, in Far Rockaway, N.Y.; daughter of Herbert E. (a podiatrist) and Thelma (a pianist; maiden name, Friedman) Kottek; married Henry Gilgoff (a newspaper reporter), June 12, 1967; children: Hugh Lorin, Jon Noah, Matthew Dylan. *Education:* City College of the City University of New York, B.A., 1967. *Religion:* Jewish. *Home:* 40 East 89th St., New York, N.Y. 10028. *Agent:* Theron Raines, 475 Fifth Ave., New York, N.Y. 10017.

CAREER: Peace Corps, media specialist in Micronesia, 1967-69; WLIX-Radio, Islip, N.Y., copywriter, 1970; freelance writer, 1970—; *Newsday,* Garden City, N.Y., editor of question and answer column, 1975-76. *Member:* International Childbirth Education Association, American Society for Psycho-Prophylaxis in Obstetrics, National Association of Parents and Professionals for Safe Alternatives in Childbirth, National Organization for Women, La Leche League, Society for the Protection of the Unborn Through Nutrition, Authors Guild.

WRITINGS: Home Birth, Coward, 1978. Contributor of articles to magazines.

WORK IN PROGRESS: Research on childbirth and mothering.

SIDELIGHTS: Alice Gilgoff writes: "As I became more interested in my pregnancy and in methods of childbirth, I decided to feel out the editor of the local daily on my writing a story about the growth of childbirth preparation classes —then a new phenomenon. I did months of interviewing and research and completed a long feature article a little while after my first child was born. The story ended up on the first page of the daily feature magazine and got a good reaction. Since that time most of my writing has been related to health care and to having babies. Rather than prevent me from working in my profession, my children have always been the source of my writing."

Gilgoff also believes that childbirth is a feminist health care issue and takes a stand against those people who put home-makers and feminists on opposites sides of the fence. Often she is asked how she could possibly raise three children and work on the manuscript for her book, *Home Birth.* Gilgoff usually responds: "I have a husband who is a father to his children. He didn't 'help me' as some people put it; he just did what had to be done. On weekends he became the dominant parent. I once read about another week-end writer who complained that she had to remember to yell out to her husband things like 'Take the meat out of the freezer for dinner' even as she sat trying to concentrate at the typewriter. But luckily it wasn't like that for me. I had problems, but they passed when I realized Daddy would remember to bring along Pampers even if I didn't remind him. And even if he forgot, he would figure it out the same way I do when I forget."

* * *

GILHOOLEY, John 1940-
(Jack Gilhooley)

PERSONAL: Born June 26, 1940, in Philadelphia, Pa.; son of John Charles (an insurance executive) and Margaret (Cotter) Gilhooley. *Education:* Syracuse University, B.A., 1962; Villanova University, M.A. in theatre, 1964; University of Pennsylvania, M.A. in American civilization, 1966. *Home:* 639 West End Ave., New York, N.Y. 10025. *Agent:* Esther Sherman, William Morris Agency, 1350 Avenue of the Americas, New York, N.Y. 10019.

CAREER: Harcum Junior College, Bryn Mawr, Pa., instructor of theatre, 1963-65; Western Connecticut State College, Danbury, assistant professor of theatre, 1965-68; Jersey City State College, Jersey City, N.J., assistant professor of theatre and American literature, 1969-78; full-time writer, 1974—. Guest artist and lecturer at University of Kansas, 1973, Vassar College, 1973, University of New Hampshire, 1977, and Syracuse University, 1978. *Member:* American Federation of Teachers, Screen Actors Guild, Dramatists Guild, New Dramatists, Actors Equity Association. *Awards, honors:* Shubert Playwriting fellowship, 1972; Fenimore Playwriting Award, 1973; Jane L. Gilmore Award, 1976; MacDowell Colony fellowship, 1976; guest playwright at Eugene O'Neill Memorial Foundation, 1977; grant from the National Endowment for the Arts, 1978; guest playwright, Edward Albee Foundation, 1978; Millay Colony fellowship, 1979.

WRITINGS—Plays; all under name Jack Gilhooley: "The Last Act" (one-act), first produced Off-Off Broadway at 13th Street Theatre, 1971; "The Entrepreneurs of Avenue B" (one-act), first produced Off-Off Broadway at 13th Street Theatre, 1971; "Homefront Blues," (two-act), first produced in New York City at Manhattan Theatre Club, 1973; "The Last Christians," (two-act), first produced in New York City at The Open Space in Soho, 1975; "The Comeback" (one-act), first produced in New York City at Theatre for the New City, 1973; "The Time Trial" (two-act), first produced at the New York Shakespeare Festival, 1975; "The Competitors" (one-act), first produced Off Broadway at E.T.C. Co., 1976; "Mummer's End" (two-act), first produced in Washington, D.C., at the Folger Theatre, 1977; "The Elusive Angel" (two-act), first produced in Waterford, Conn., at the O'Neill Foundation, 1977, produced Off Broadway at the Phoenix Theatre, 1977; "Afternoons in Vegas" (two-act), first produced in Portsmouth, N.H., at Theatre by the Sea, 1977; "The Brixton Recovery" (two-act), first produced in Indianapolis, Ind., at Indiana Repertory Theatre, 1977; "Bankers' Hours" (one-act), first produced in Louisville, Ky., at Actors Theatre, May, 1979.

Also author of "Avenue B" (two-act), "The Ravelles' Comeback" (two-act), "Dancin to Caliope" (two-act), and "Descendants" (two-act), as yet neither published nor produced.

Radio plays: "Dancin to Caliope" (also see above), circulated by "Earplay" radio-drama producers, 1979. Also author of "The Comeback" (also see above), as yet neither published nor produced on radio.

Also author of screenplays, "The Last Mountain Man" and "Afternoons in Vegas."

WORK IN PROGRESS: Adaptations of "The Time Trial" and "The Elusive Angel" for the screen; "Shirley Basin," a two-act play.

SIDELIGHTS: In "Mummer's End," Jack Gilhooley uses the annual Mummer's Day parade held in Philadelphia to point up the divisions in one family and, by extension, the conflicts in American society as a whole. After viewing the play, Richard Eder wrote: "Mr. Gilhooley is ingenious in joining the reality of his engaging characters with the warring strands of American tradition that they represent. But the effect is uneven. Some of it is forced; the author has overpacked his symbols. More damaging: a lot of the comic dialogue is banal, about on the level of mediocre situation comedy. It is in the more serious moments . . . that the writing is most distinguished." Jonathan Takiff found "Mummer's End" delightful. He described it as "a wonderfully warm and funny piece, about a Kensington family steeped four generations in lore and traditions" and praised its mixture of "ethnocentric and everyman, satire and sincerity."

The plight of an impoverished couple who are ruthlessly exploited when they try to adopt a baby is explored in Gilhooley's "The Elusive Angel." Eder commented that "the incident portrayed is commonplace without the thought and reflection that would make it significant, and mildly grotesque without a spark of dramatic life." Nonetheless, he paid tribute to the "occasionally lively dialogue and several entertaining but familiar characters." Clive Barnes of the *New York Post* held "The Elusive Angel" in much higher esteem. Although Barnes found the plot quite obvious, he felt that the play was saved by Gilhooley's "skill at coloring in relevent [sic] details, his gift for the right turn of action, and his slow, but steady unveiling—not developing, for no one changes—characters. A domestic drama as sentimental as an O. Henry short story, the play has all the merits of its craftsmanship to commend it."

Gilhooley told *CA:* "I certainly don't know *how* I became a playwright although, on occasion, I wonder *why.* There's nothing in my background that would have warranted such a pursuit. James T. Farrell summed up the excruciating dilemma of the aspiring artist from a conservative Irish-Catholic background. In short, said vice should stay in the closet during the formative years. I suppose I simply had an aptitude for play reading in high school that carried over to my freshman year in college and was the primary reason for my almost immediate dismissal from the Wharton School of Commerce and Finance. Consequently, I still can't read the stock market (no great detriment to a playwright).

"I tend to write about subcultures and/or families. I don't know why and I wasn't aware of it until I looked back after my first couple of years of writing. I don't know if this will change and I don't know, at this point, if it should. I tend to stay as far away as possible from autobiographical inclusions. Initially, for me it is too painful. Secondly, for the audience it is too commonplace.

"My influences are Chekhov, then O'Neill and currently Sam Shepard and Lanford Wilson. My non-theatrical influences are Nelson Algren and Harry Crews."

Gilhooley also described some of his plays: "'Afternoons in Vegas' has to do with a group of bar women in Las Vegas. 'The Time Trial' deals with seven young adults in a small town who are drawn together by their fanatic interest in auto racing. 'Descendants' has to do with a working-class family reunion as the mother lies dying upstairs. 'Dancin to Caliope' explores a love triangle in a carnival."

BIOGRAPHICAL/CRITICAL SOURCES: New York Times, February 7, 1977, May 26, 1977, December 28, 1977; *Philadelphia Daily News,* March 4, 1977; *New York Post,* December 27, 1977.

* * *

GILMORE, Haydn   1928-

PERSONAL: Born December 13, 1928, in Wilkes-Barre, Pa.; son of Haydn and Anna (a teacher; maiden name, Lewis) Gilmore; married Jean Meitrott (a teacher), November 16, 1957; children: James, Dwight. *Education:* Temple University, B.A., 1950; Dallas Theological Seminary, Th.M., 1954; Syracuse University, M.A., 1970. *Religion:* Evangelical Protestant. *Home:* 16 Hilltop Dr., Tunkhannock, Pa. 18657. *Office:* 152 West High St., Nesquehoning, Pa. 18240.

CAREER: Ordained minister of American Baptist Church, 1955; U.S. Air Force, chaplain, 1959-68, served in Tachikawa, Japan, 1961-64, leaving service as captain; Keystone Junior College, La Plume, Pa., instructor in English and philosophy, 1968-69; Messiah College, Grantham, Pa., director of public information, 1970-71; *Montrose Independent,* Montrose, Pa., associate editor, 1972; *Runner's Gazette,* Lansford, Pa., associate editor, 1973—. Pastor of First Baptist Church, Lansford, 1977—. Director of community relations for Northeast Pennsylvania Health and Hospital Planning Council, 1973-74. Member of board of directors of Denver Christian Serviceman's Center (acting head of board of directors, 1967-68), and Sub-Area Council for Health Planning, Carbon County, Pa., 1978—. *Member:* Armed Forces Writer's League, American College Public Relations Association, Amateur Athletic Union, Pennsylvania Beekeepers Association, Toastmasters International. *Awards, honors:* George Washington Medal from Freedoms Foundation, 1967, for essay, "Safeguarding Freedom Keeps America."

WRITINGS: Jog for Your Life, Zondervan, 1974. Author of tract on golf. Contributor of about two hundred articles and reviews to magazines and newspapers.

WORK IN PROGRESS: A book about a marathon event, *Death One Fine Boston Afternoon,* publication expected in 1980; a book on beekeeping, publication expected in 1981.

SIDELIGHTS: Haydn Gilmore writes: "Wales is my father's and all my forebears' land of birth, with a few Scots slipping in. I have specialized in Anglo-Welsh poets: Dylan Thomas, Vernon Watkins, Roland Mathias. I have traveled in England and Wales and hope to return for an extended time." *Avocational interests:* Beekeeping.

* * *

GINNES, Judith S.
(Paige Mitchell)

PERSONAL: Born in New Orleans, La.; daughter of George J. (an engineer) and Esther (a teacher; maiden name,

Finerowsky) Segel; married Alvin M. Binder (an attorney), August 26, 1951 (divorced); married Abram S. Ginnes (a writer), June 30, 1969; children: (first marriage) Lisa, Mitch, Mike. *Education:* Attended Tulane University. *Religion:* Jewish. *Home:* 326 South Bentley, Los Angeles, Calif. 90049. *Agent:* Julian Bach Literary Agency, Inc., 3 East 48th St., New York, N.Y. 10017.

CAREER: Medical artist and writer.

WRITINGS—All under pseudonym Paige Mitchell: *A Wilderness of Monkeys,* Dutton, 1965; *Love Is Not a Safe Country,* Dutton, 1967; *The Covenant,* Atheneum, 1973; *Act of Love,* Knopf, 1976.

* * *

GINZBURG, Natalia 1916-
(Alessandra Tournimparte)

PERSONAL: Born July 14, 1916, in Palermo, Italy; daughter of Carlo (a novelist and professor of biology) and Lidia (Tanzi) Levi; married Leone Ginzburg (an editor and political activist), 1938 (died, 1944); married Gabriele Baldini, 1950. *Home:* 4 Via Ripense, Rome, Italy.

CAREER: Novelist, short story writer, dramatist, and essayist. Worked for Einaudi (publisher). *Awards, honors:* Marzotto Prize for European Drama, 1968, for *The Advertisement.*

WRITINGS: (Under pseudonym Alessandra Tournimparte) *La strada che va in citta* (two short novels), Einaudi (Turin, Italy), 1942, reprinted under own name, 1975, translation by Frances Frenaye published under own name as *The Road to the City* (contains "The Road to the City" and "The Dry Heart"), Doubleday, 1949; *E stato cosi,* Einaudi, 1947, reprinted, 1974; *Tutti i nostri ieri* (novel), Einaudi, 1952, translation by Angus Davidson published as *A Light for Fools,* Dutton, 1956, translation published as *Dead Yesterdays,* Secker & Warburg, 1956; (with Giansiro Ferrata) *Romanzi del 900,* Ediziono Radio Italiana (Turin), 1957; *Valentino* (short stories), Einaudi, 1957, published as *Sagittario,* 1975.

Le voci della sera, Einaudi, 1961, translation by D. M. Low published as *Voices in the Evening,* Dutton, 1963; *Le piccole virtu* (essays), Einaudi, 1962; *Lessico famigliare* (novel), Einaudi, 1963, translation by Low published as *Family Sayings,* Dutton, 1967; *Cinque romanzi brevi* (short novels and short stories), Einaudi, 1964; *Ti ho sposato per allegria* (plays), Einaudi, 1966; *The Advertisement* (play; translated by Henry Reed; first produced in London at Old Vic Theatre, September 24, 1968), Faber, 1969; *Teresa* (play), [Paris], 1970; *Mai devi domandarmi* (essays), Garzanti (Milan), 1970, translation by Isabel Quigly published as *Never Must You Ask Me,* Joseph, 1973; *Le voci della sera,* edited by Sergio Pacifici, Random House, 1971; *Caro Michele* (novel), Mondadori (Milan), 1973, translation by Sheila Cudahy published as *No Way,* Harcourt, 1974, published as *Dear Michael,* Owen, 1975; *Paese di mare e altre commedie,* Garzanti, 1973; *Vita immaginaria* (essays), Mondadori, 1974.

Also author of *Fragola e panna,* 1966, *La segretaria,* 1967, and "I Married You for the Fun of It," 1972.

SIDELIGHTS: Natalia Ginzburg is one of the best-known post-war Italian writers. Her cool, controlled, simple style of writing has impressed critics, and many have found her narrative gifts to be reminiscent of Chekov's. As Isabel Quigly commented on an early novel, *A Light for Fools,* "Inevitably, Chekhov comes to mind: not only because the long summer days, the endless agreeable but unrewarding

chat, the whole provincial-intellectual set-up, recall him, but because the Italian charm, and volatility, and loquacity, and unselfconscious egocentricity, and inability to move out of grooves, and so on, that Miss Ginzburg so brilliantly captures, are all Chekhovian qualities."

"Natalia Ginzburg is at her best when dealing with detail," Marc Slonim wrote of the book, "and her descriptions of children and adolescents have a definite poetic flavor. Most of the incidents and characters are seen through the eyes of an adolescent, and the book has much of the naivete and charm of a child's vision. This 'point of view' in the Jamesian sense gives a unity of diction to the whole narrative." Similarly, Quigly commented, "She has an extraordinary gift for what you might call cumulative characterization—a method that dispenses almost entirely with description and builds up solid and memorable people by the gradual mounting up of small actions, oblique glances, other people's opinions."

Other reviewers were critical of Ginzburg's method of characterization. Thomas G. Bergin commented that the characters in *Voices in the Evening* "are, for the most part, like excellent line drawings, quite real but somehow not 'filled in.' Their bone structure is magnificent, but there is no flesh." And although Otis K. Burger found the novel to be "crisp, brittle, entertaining, and informative," he also remarked that "the very coolness of the style tends to defeat the subtle theme of the death of a family (and a love) through sheer lack of gumption. The brevity of the book and its semi-comic treatment of a muted tragedy come to seem, not a strength but part of the general, fatal weariness. The 'voices in the evening' tend to cancel each other out—succeeding only too well in presenting people who, pallid to begin with, end as mere phantoms."

Although *Family Sayings* is on the surface a simple family tale, what is beneath and between the lines reveals the weight and worth of the novel. Raymond Rosenthal remarked that "what started as a simple family chronicle takes on the timeless, magnificent aspect of an ancient tale, a Homeric saga. It is magical, exhilarating. In the last pages, after all is accomplished and the deaths, the bereavements, the terrible losses of war and social struggle have been counted up, so to speak, the mere fact that Natalia's mother is still telling the same old stories, and that her father—the counter-muse, the rationalistic ogre—is still there to provide the antiphonic accompaniment of grumbles and complaints, becomes mythical in the truest sense. The surface of this book is also its depths."

Gavin Ewart also praised the book. He wrote: "A simple, distilled style, a reliance on the virtues of repetition, an awareness of the ridiculousness of human beings; a great love (reading between the lines) for both her father and her mother; the shadow of Proust. All these are in it. Dealing with more 'tragic' material, it has the control and the only slightly edited reality that one finds in *My Life and Hard Times* (remember Thurber?). Though this is verbal comedy and not farce, it still seems, like that masterpiece, to imply that life can be terrible, but also terribly funny."

No Way, Ginzburg's latest novel to appear in English translation, has as its main character Michael, a young revolutionary living in a basement apartment. Ginzburg develops the relationships between the characters through letters (most of which are written to Michael, few of which he answers). "While Michael is expending what turn out to be his last days," Martin Levin commented, "his father dies, his girlfriend Mara runs through a half dozen patrons, and his mother is jilted by her lover Philip. All of these relationships are assembled by epistolary connections that have the intricacy and the fragility of an ant city. The wit is mordant and comes directly out of paradox." Lynne Sharon Schwartz noted, "The contours of her sentences linger in the ear like phrases from great music, familiar, basic truths. Her characters, sad, thwarted, often drab types, are memorable in the manner of people one knew very long ago."

"What makes this book so wonderful," L. E. Sissman declared, "magical even—is that we are never bored by the imprisoned pacings and abortive flights of its people. They all become real and individual and fascinating through the technical gifts of the author.... *No Way* is a novel of the curdling of aspirations and the enfeebling of powers among those who heretofore held sway. Its quality lies in its reportorial accuracy, in its fine, warm, rueful equanimity, in its balance in the face of toppling worlds. It is a most remarkable book."

BIOGRAPHICAL/CRITICAL SOURCES: *Spectator*, August 24, 1956; *New York Times*, January 5, 1957, October 6, 1963; *Saturday Review*, September 21, 1963; *New Leader*, March 13, 1967; *London Magazine*, May, 1967; *Times Literary Supplement*, February 5, 1971, April 13, 1973, June 15, 1973, February 21, 1975, March 28, 1975, June 2, 1978; *New York Times Book Review*, September 1, 1974; *New Republic*, September 14, 1974; *New Yorker*, October 21, 1974; *New York Review of Books*, January 23, 1975; *Contemporary Literary Criticism*, Gale, Volume 5, 1976, Volume 11, 1979.*

*   *   *

GIOVENE, Andrea 1904-

PERSONAL: Born in 1904, in Naples, Italy. *Home:* Casa Rainone, Sant' Agata dei Go 82019, Bensvento, Italy.

CAREER: Writer. Affiliated with *Gazzettino de Venezia*, Venice, Italy, 1931-32, 1951-53, and *Mattino*, Naples, Italy, 1934-36; manager of *Il Mattino d' Italia*, 1950-52. Founder of *Vesuvia* (literary journal), 1928-29. *Awards, honors:* International Festival of Books Golden Pen award.

WRITINGS: Viaggio, Ricciardi, 1936; *Incanto*, Ricciardi, 1940, revised edition, Quaderni dell' Osservatore, 1969; *Fatti di Polonia e Germania*, Rossi (Naples), 1955; *L'autobiographia di Giuliano di Sansevero*, five volumes, Rizzoli (Milan), 1966-70, translation of Volume II by Marguerite Waldman published as *The Book of Sansevero*, Houghton, 1970 (published in England as *The Book of Giuliano Sansevero*, Collins, 1970), translation of Volume III and IV by Bernard Wall, Volume III published as *The Dilemma of Love*, Houghton, 1973, Volume IV published as *The Dice of War*, Houghton, 1974, Volume V: *El poder del silencio*.

SIDELIGHTS: Giovene's five-volume work, *L'autographia di Giulano di Sansevero*, is in fact an autobiographical novel that chronicles the author's life as a rebellious member of the Neopolitan aristocracy. "Characters, places and events are portrayed with loving, compassionate detail, but also with biting, incisive objectivity to reveal the conflict existing between the high romanticism of *fin de siecle* Naples and its squalid reality," wrote a *Publishers Weekly* reviewer. Although the story does contain good descriptions, "it fatally lacks any real grandeur," commented a critic for *Times Literary Supplement*. Giovene appears to aspire to a greatness he is incapable of achieving, reviewers said, and for this reason has been described as a "great writer *manque*."

Giovene's style of writing has been compared to that of Proust, Stendhal, and Lampedus. Disapproving of the com-

parison to Proust in particular, Jerry Mangione wrote in *Book World* that while Giovene "is nearly as narcissistic as Proust in his literary viewpoint, he has neither Proust's profundity nor his passionate involvement with other human beings." Other critics noted that Giovene lacks Proust's ability to write with humor. Nevertheless, as Stephen Wall concluded in the *Observer Review*, the most interesting aspect of the novel is in "the extensive glimpses of a presumable now vanished way of life."

L'autobiographia di Giulano di Sansevero has been translated into Finnish, French, Spanish, German, and Swedish. Over two hundred thousand copies of the set have been sold.

BIOGRAPHICAL/CRITICAL SOURCES: *Publishers Weekly*, July 27, 1970, June 10, 1974; *Kirkus Reviews*, August 1, 1970, April 1, 1973, June 1, 1974; *Observer Review*, August 9, 1970; *New Statesman*, August 14, 1970; *Listener*, August 20, 1970, January 18, 1973; *New Yorker*, October 10, 1970, December 9, 1974; *New York Times Book Review*, October 11, 1970, May 20, 1973; *Saturday Review*, November 21, 1970, November 28, 1970; *Book World*, November 22, 1970, April 15, 1973, September 15, 1974; *Times Literary Supplement*, January 26, 1973, February 8, 1974.*

*   *   *

GIRION, Barbara 1937-

PERSONAL: Born November 20, 1937, in New York, N.Y.; daughter of Sam and Blanche (Taub) Warren; married Heywood Jay Girion (a direct-mail advertising executive), November 27, 1957; children: Jeffrey, Eric, Laurie Sue. *Education:* Montclair State College, B.A., 1958; graduate study at Kean College and New School for Social Research. *Politics:* "I vote in every election." *Religion:* Jewish. *Home and office:* 25 Wildwood Dr., Short Hills, N.J. 07078. *Agent:* Marilyn Marlow, Curtis Brown Ltd., 575 Madison Ave., New York, N.Y. 10022.

CAREER: Junior high school teacher of history in Hillside, N.J., 1958-62; substitute teacher of retarded and emotionally-disturbed children, 1962-68; writer, 1968—. Engaged in community theater and public relations work, 1962-70. Guest lecturer at Hofstra University, 1978 and 1979; speaker of women's groups; workshop director. Member of Hillside Democratic Committee, 1962-67. President of Hillside Community Players, 1965-68. Member of board of governors of Jewish Community Federation of Metropolitan, N.J., 1973-78; member of board of directors of West Orange Young Men's-Young Women's Hebrew Association, 1973—; member of board of trustees of *Jewish News*, 1978—. *Member:* Society of Children's Book Writers (New York regional adviser). *Awards, honors:* National young leadership award from Council of Jewish Federations and Welfare Funds, 1973, for multi-media script "Like a Bridge."

WRITINGS—All juveniles: The Boy With the Special Face, Abingdon, 1978; *Joshua, the Czar and the Chicken Bone Wish*, Scribner, 1978; *A Tangle of Roots*, Scribner, 1979; *Misty and Me*, Scribner, 1979.

Author of scripts for children and adults, including "A Time to Love," 1973, and "Like a Bridge," 1975-76. Contributor to magazines, including *Seventeen*, *Co-Ed*, and *Young World*, and newspapers. Editor of Hillside *Democratic Newspaper*, 1961-66.

WORK IN PROGRESS: A Passing Shadow, a novel for adults; *The G.O. Corner*, a juvenile novel; *Like Everybody Else.*

SIDELIGHTS: Barbara Girion comments: "I guess the most exciting thing about being a writer is walking into a library and seeing a book you've written on the shelf. I'm still not used to it.

"For a while I wanted to be a singer-dancer-actress and studied dancing and drama. I appeared in many summer stock and community theater productions. I was also a junior high school teacher and even though I liked teaching, I kept writing. I combined my two loves, writing and theater, to write scripts and education programs for adults and children.

"I write about what I know. Most of my magazine stories come from real life. I eavesdrop a lot. My children try to hide in the closet when they talk on the telephone so I won't overhear them.

"It absolutely knocks me out to receive a letter from a kid in Arizona or Chicago telling me that characters in my books or stories think 'just like they do' and 'How did I know. . . .' All my life I've tried to communicate through the creative process so my words in print are intoxicating stuff. Add to this all the fantastic new people I've met and it makes all the pacing, sleepless nights, endless drafts, revisions and proof-reading well worth it."

*   *   *

GLANVILLE, Maxwell 1918-

PERSONAL: Born February 11, 1918, in Antigua, British West Indies; son of John A. and Caroline R. (George) Glanville; children: Arthur. *Education:* Attended New School for Social Research, 1942-43. *Politics:* "Universal." *Religion:* "Universal." *Home:* 775 Concourse Village E., Bronx, N.Y. 10451. *Office: Big Red,* 40 Empire Blvd., Brooklyn, N.Y. 11225; and Young Men's Christian Assoc., 180 West 135th St., New York, N.Y.

CAREER: Playwright and poet. Actor in New York City and on tour (stage, film, and television), 1946—; stage director in New York City, 1950—; drama teacher, 1959—; *Big Red* (newspaper), Brooklyn, N.Y., reporter and author of column, "Showbiz," 1977—. Acting trainer for CETA, 1975. Member of Frank Silvera Writers Workshop of Harlem Audelco (member of board of directors). Instructor and acting coach; artistic director of drama groups; director of community plays. Also worked as producer and stage manager; has given poetry readings. *Military service:* U.S. Army Air Forces, 1943-46; received sharpshooter medal. *Member:* Actors Equity Association, Screen Actors Guild. *Awards, honors:* Community award from Young Men's Christian Association, 1965; award from Bedford-Stuyvesant Civic Club and American Community Theatre, 1972, for community work in theatre and the arts.

WRITINGS—Plays: (Co-author) "Subway Sadie" (one-act comedy), first produced in New York City at Greenwich Mews Theatre, 1955; "The Bonus" (one-act comedy), first produced in New York City at American Community Theatre, 1961; "Cindy" (one-act; based on fairy tale "Cinderella"), first produced in New York City at American Community Theatre, 1962; (co-author) "Dance to a Nose-picker's Drum" (two-act), first produced at Clark Center Young Men's Christian Assoc., 1969. Also author of "Long Stretch—Short Haul" (three-act), first produced in New York City at American Community Theatre.

Unproduced scripts: "For Any Evil" (three-act play), 1960; "The Injectors" (one-act play), 1960; "A Walking Disorder" (screenplay), 1971; (co-author) "The Wire" (screen-play), 1973; (co-author) "Twit for Twat" (two-act musical comedy), 1979.

Author of column "Klub Klues" in New York edition of *Chicago Defender,* 1940, "90 Seconds or More With Maxwell Glanville" in *Amsterdam News,* 1942, and "Music Box" in several publications including *Negro Spotlight,* during 1940's and 1950's. Contributor of poems to magazines.

WORK IN PROGRESS: The Bitch, an autobiography; a one-act playlet, "The Martyr"; a two-act play, "Cindy"; short stories.

SIDELIGHTS: Glanville told *CA:* "My mother was a teacher who loved to write poetry and compositions. One day she challenged me. She implied that I couldn't write a poem, jokingly, because she knew the playful challenge would make me try. After I accepted, I was hooked. I hope to achieve a self-satisfaction, to relate my experiences and observations to help others in improving their efforts for a better world.

"When I attempt to write it is usually early morning hours. My pipe and living alone help my thinking! Keeping a diary while I enjoyed and experienced Broadway tours . . . provided initial material. My theatre background spurred the actual effort.

"On the contemporary scene, much of the writing uses the sensational or notorious for the market. There are other areas besides sex, violence, thievery, and the bizarre. Not that those things don't have a place in our literary archives, but the intellectual, the comedic, the ordinary-man-in-the-street who has not been married to a celebrity can be just as fascinating in his non-celebrated world. In other words, the attention-getter seems to have become more important than the literary achievement."

*   *   *

GLASS, David Victor 1911-1978

PERSONAL: Born January 2, 1911, in London, England; died September 23, 1978, in London; son of Philip and Dinah Glass; married Ruth Lazarus Durant (a sociologist), 1942; children: one son, one daughter. *Education:* Attended London School of Economics and Political Science, London. *Home:* 10 Palace Gardens Terrace, London, W.8, England.

CAREER: Population Investigation Committee, research secretary, 1936; London School of Economics and Political Science, London, England, reader in demography, 1946-48, professor of sociology, 1948-78. Chairman of United Nations working group on social demography of Europe. *Member:* International Union for Scientific Study of Population (honorary president). *Awards, honors:* D.Sc. from University of Michigan, 1967; honorary foreign member of American Academy of Arts and Sciences.

WRITINGS: The Town and a Changing Civilisation, John Lane, 1935; *The Struggle for Population,* introduction by A. M. Carr-Saunders, Clarendon Press, 1936; (with C. P. Blacker) *Population and Fertility,* Population Investigation Committee, 1939; *Population Policies and Movements in Europe,* Clarendon Press, 1940, second edition, A. M. Kelley, 1967; (editor) *Introduction to Malthus,* Wiley, 1953; (with E. Grebenik) *The Trend and Pattern of Fertility in Great Britain: A Report on the Family Census of 1946,* H.M.S.O., 1954; (editor) *Social Mobility in Britain,* Free Press, 1954; (editor) *The University Teaching of Social Sciences: Demography,* UNESCO, 1957; (editor with D.E.C. Eversley) *Population in History: Essays in Historical Demography,* Aldine, 1965; *London Inhabitants Within the*

Walls, London Record Society, 1966; (co-editor) *Population and Social Change,* Crane, 1972; (with P.A.M. Taylor) *Population and Emigration,* Irish University Press, 1976; *Numbering the People,* Heath, 1973; (compiler and author of introduction) *The Population Controversy,* Gregg, 1973; *The Development of Population Statistics,* Gregg, 1973. Also author of *A Discussion on Demography,* [London], 1963.

Joint editor: *Population Studies,* Cambridge University Press, 1947; *Society: Approaches and Problems for Study,* 1962; *British Journal of Sociology; Eugenics Review.*

SIDELIGHTS: A prominent economist and statistician, Glass was best known for his contributions to the field of current and historical population trends. Because of his expertise, he served as a United Kingdom representative to the United Nations and held several government positions in London and the United States. His most influential writings were *The Town and a Changing Civilisation* and *Population Policies and Movements in Europe.*

Population in History deals with the growth of western European populations during the eighteenth century. William Petersen complained about the book's organization: "The two editors contribute separate introductions which together take up the first 70 pages," followed by an unsystematic presentation of articles that give a "hodge-podge impression." *Times Literary Supplement,* however, commented that "the essays flash with ideas, relationships and questions needing further research, so that they should serve as an ideas book for historical demographers for some years to come."

Glass died a week before his scheduled retirement as professor of sociology at the London School of Economics and Political Science.*

* * *

GLOGAU, Lillian Flatow Fleischer 1925-

PERSONAL: Born February 15, 1925, in New York, N.Y.; daughter of Henry and Diana (Heller) Flatow; married F. E. Fleischer, 1948 (died, 1957); married Jerome N. Glogau, November 20, 1963; children: Jordan, Laurence, Alexander. *Education:* Brooklyn College (now of the City University of New York), B.A. (cum laude), 1946; Columbia University, M.A., 1949; New York University, Ed.D., 1969. *Home:* 515 Rehill Court, River Vale, N.J. 07675. *Office:* East Rampo Central School District #4, Spring Valley, N.Y. 10977.

CAREER: Public school teacher in New York, N.Y., 1946-49, and Plainview, N.Y., 1959-61, administrator, 1961-66; East Ramapo Central School District, Spring Valley, N.Y., superintendent of Spring Valley schools, 1966—. Director of Learning Center; president of Pragmatix, Inc. Leader of study-travel tours in Europe and the Middle East. Member of adjunct faculty of Fairleigh Dickinson University and Caldwell College. *Member:* American Association of School Administrators, American Society for Curriculum Development, Parent Teachers Association (life member), New York State School Administrators Association, Kappa Delta Pi, Pi Lambda Theta.

WRITINGS: (With Murray Fessel) *The Nongraded Primary School: A Case Study,* Parker Publishing, 1967; (with Edmund Krause and Max Rubinstein) *You and New York City* (juvenile), Benefic, 1968; (with Krause and Miriam Wexler) *Developing a Successful Elementary School Media Center,* Parker Publishing, 1972. Also author of *Let's See,* 1971. Contributor to education journals.

WORK IN PROGRESS: Television scripts.

GODWIN, Gaylord 1906(?)-1979

OBITUARY NOTICE: Born c. 1906 in Urich, Mo.; died May 14, 1979, in Elizabeth City, N.C. Journalist. Godwin was a reporter with United Press International for forty years. He began his career in UPI's Kansas City bureau, became bureau manager in Omaha, and later worked in Chicago. In 1948, he transferred to Washington, D.C., and covered the Agriculture and Interior departments. Godwin also worked as news editor of the *Coastland Times* newspaper in Manteo, N.C. Obituaries and other sources: *Washington Post,* May 17, 1979.

* * *

GOLDBERG, Lucianne Cummings 1935-

PERSONAL: Born April 29, 1935, in Boston, Mass.; daughter of Raymond and Jane (Moseley) Steinberger; married Sidney Goldberg (a news executive), April 10, 1966; children: Joshua, Jonah. *Education:* George Washington University, B.A., 1957. *Home and office:* 255 West 84th St., Apt. 6-A, New York, N.Y. 10024. *Agent:* Mary Yost Associates, Inc., 141 East 55th St., New York, N.Y. 10022.

CAREER: *Washington Post,* Washington, D.C., intern and member of promotion staff, 1957-60; Democratic National Committee, Washington, D.C., staff member, 1960; consultant to White House staff in Washington, D.C., 1961-62; Cummings & Associates, Washington, D.C., president, 1963-66; Women's News Service, New York City, news editor, 1966-72; Lucianne S. Goldberg, Inc. (literary agency), New York City, owner and president, 1972—.

WRITINGS: *Purr, Baby, Purr* (nonfiction), Hawthorne, 1970; (with Sondra Robinson) *Friends in High Places* (novel), Richard Marek Publishers, 1979; *Layla* (novel), Richard Marek Publishers, in press. Author of "Footlights of Broadway," a column syndicated by North American Newspaper Alliance, 1976—.

SIDELIGHTS: Goldberg writes: "When I started my career (the first being a journalist) as a literary agent I had to wade through mountains of bad writing. I began to wonder how a person could sit for perhaps years and produce hundreds of pages of work and thought that neither followed the basic rules of good solid writing nor told a simple, cohesive story. I found myself in the awkward position of telling people how to write fiction without having done it myself. The old aphorism 'Those who can do, those who can't teach' haunted me.

"I have led an interesting life, but so have most people. I knew it wouldn't sell as nonfiction. I hired the best fiction collaborator I could find, Sondra Till Robinson, and together we produced a novel about Washington in the sixties that subsequently sold hard cover to Richard Marek Publishing. The soft cover rights have just been sold to Bantam for an exhilarating (and vindicating) six-figures. Marek has signed me to do a second novel on the publishing industry on the strength of an outline and three sample chapters. This time out, thanks to the guidance and patience of Sondra Robinson, I will try to go solo. I now have the satisfaction of being able to tell the excellent writers I represent that I know the pain, the disappointment and the pure joy of producing the written word. If there is one single underlying theme in the fiction I have and hope to produce it is the many variations of the 11th Commandment: Thou Shalt Not Quit."

* * *

GOLDBERG, Nathan 1903(?)-1979

OBITUARY NOTICE: Born c. 1903 in Poland; died February 23, 1979, in New York, N.Y. Educator. Goldberg was emeritus professor of sociology at Yeshiva University. His writings include *The Classification of Jewish Immigrants and Its Implications* and *New Functional Hebrew-English, English-Hebrew Dictionary.* Obituaries and other sources: *New York Times,* February 27, 1979.

* * *

GOLDBERG, Philip 1944-

PERSONAL: Born December 5, 1944, in New York, N.Y.; son of Aaron (a businessman) and Ann (Manes) Goldberg. *Education:* City College of the City University of New York, B.B.A., 1966; graduate study at Northeastern University, 1967-68; Maharishi International University, M.A., 1974. *Politics:* "Uncommitted." *Religion:* "I like them all." *Home and office:* 348 West 11th St., New York, N.Y. 10014. *Agent:* John Cushman Associates, Inc., 200 West 57th St., New York, N.Y. 10019.

CAREER: Massachusetts Department of Mental Health, Boston, Mass., social worker with the mentally retarded, 1968-70; American lecturer in transcendental meditation and related subjects for Foundation for the Science of Creative Intelligence, 1971-74; Maharishi International University, Fairfield, Iowa, instructor in interdisciplinary studies and director of curriculum, 1974-76; writer and consultant, 1976—. Consultant to Institute for the Development of Consciousness.

WRITINGS: The TM Program: The Way to Fulfillment, Holt, 1976; (with Daniel Kaufman) *Natural Sleep: How to Get Your Share,* Rodale Press, 1978; *Executive Health: How to Manage Health Danger Signals and Manage Stress Successfully,* McGraw, 1978; (with Richard Rubin) *How to Borrow Money,* McGraw, 1979; (contributor) Sidney Lecker and Richard Winter, editors, *Health Passages,* Grosset, 1979.

WORK IN PROGRESS: Walk, Don't Run, "a tribute to walking as nature's best exercise"; *Athlete,* with Harty Platt, "an exploration of the life cycle of athletes"; a series on management with Christopher Hegarty, first book to be entitled *How to Manage Your Boss; Intuition,* "an exploration of nonrational ways of knowing"; *The Will,* a novel.

SIDELIGHTS: Goldberg writes: "I have been a word freak all my life, have read anything I could any time I could since my parents taught me to read at age three. My only vocational interest aside from wanting to change the world has always been writing, and I'm tickled to be able, finally, to do it full time. My abiding interest, one that influences all my work, is in how humans can live more harmoniously with nature. I believe we were meant to be happy; we are here to enjoy.

"Consciousness—its structure, dynamics, and potential—is the key to integrating the spiritual and material, the major task of man today and the new frontier of human inquiry. This subject is a consuming interest, one that will find its way into more and more of my work.

"I have been influenced by a variety of modern authors and by ancient writings usually associated with religions: the Christian mystics, the Cabalists, and especially Eastern sources such as the Taoist and Vedic seers. The modern authors—Salinger, Hemingway, Updike, and others—have influenced my style, even in nonfiction work, and the philosophers have influenced my thinking.

"I would like to see writing become less negative, celebrating life and human possibilities. Instead of darkness, I would like to see us reach for light."

GOLDMAN, Leo 1920-

PERSONAL: Born June 13, 1920, in Kingston, N.Y.; son of Morris (a woodworker) and Tillie (Kushner) Goldman; married Elsie Kamber, June 25, 1950; children: Deborah, Amy. *Education:* City College (now of the City University of New York), B.S., 1940; Columbia University, M.A., 1947, Ph.D., 1950. *Home:* 34 Cathay Rd., East Rockaway, N.Y. 11518. *Office:* Graduate School, City University of New York, 33 West 42nd St., New York, N.Y. 10038.

CAREER: University of Buffalo (now State University of New York at Buffalo), assistant professor, 1950-52, associate professor of education and psychology, 1952-58; Brooklyn College of the City University of New York, Brooklyn, N.Y., associate professor of education, 1958-64; City University of New York, Graduate School, New York, N.Y., professor of education, 1964—. Diplomate of American Board of Professional Psychology (member of board of directors, 1966-71). Fulbright lecturer at University of Amsterdam, 1965-66. Consultant to Hadassah Vocational Guidance Institute (Jerusalem). *Military service:* U.S. Army Air Forces, 1942-46; became staff sergeant. *Member:* American Psychological Association (fellow), Association for Measurement and Evaluation in Guidance (president, 1967-68), American Personnel and Guidance Association (member of executive council, 1966-68).

WRITINGS: Using Tests in Counseling, Appleton, 1961, 2nd edition, 1971; (editor) *Research Methods for Counselors,* Wiley, 1978. Contributor of about forty articles to psychology and counseling journals. Editor of *Personnel and Guidance Journal,* 1969-75; advisory editor for Wiley.

SIDELIGHTS: Goldman told CA: "In my books and articles I have tried to bridge theory and practice in the field of counseling psychology. This role developed gradually over a number of years; in fact, it was only after my first book and several articles had been published that I realized that this bridging process was indeed the theme of my writing and teaching.

"During the 1950's and 1960's I believed the main problems to be the practitioner's inadequate use of theory and research. I was critical of the level of professional work I saw in schools, colleges, and agencies, and tried to explain ways in which a firm foundation in research and theory could strengthen practice, even exhorting practitioners to do their own research.

"During the 1970's, however, I gradually came to the position that the available theory and research were not dealing with the problems facing practitioners and were in fact providing very little help in practical situations. My recent book and several articles in the latter 1970's have proposed that theorists and researchers abandon many of the research methods of the past, most of them borrowed from the physical sciences, and instead study contemporary problems with methods that are more likely to produce useful knowledge and insights."

* * *

GOLOMB, Louis 1943-

PERSONAL: Born February 9, 1943, in Pittsburgh, Pa.; son of Daniel Webster (in business) and Anne (a painter; maiden name, Temeles) Golomb; married Sylvia Yiung Lau (a teacher), May 6, 1977. *Education:* Attended Carnegie Institute of Technology (now Carnegie-Mellon University), 1961-63; Columbia University, B.S. (cum laude), 1968; Stanford University, A.M., 1971, Ph.D., 1976; postdoctoral study at University of Hawaii, 1977-79. *Home:* 6626 Darlington Rd., Pittsburgh, Pa. 15217. *Office:* Department of Anthropology, University of Hawaii, Honolulu, Hawaii 96822.

CAREER: U.S. Peace Corps, Washington, D.C., volunteer teacher of English and linguistics in Thailand, 1968-70; University of California, Los Angeles, anthropological consultant in psychiatry, 1975; Stanford University, Stanford, Calif., bibliographer in social and behavioral science collections, 1976; University of Hawaii, Honolulu, instructor in anthropology, 1977; conducted anthropological research and field work in Thailand and Malaysia, 1978. *Member:* American Anthropological Association, Linguistic Society of America, Association for Asian Studies, Phi Beta Kappa. *Awards, honors:* National Science Foundation travel grant, 1971; National Institute of Mental Health fellow, 1977-79.

WRITINGS: Brokers of Morality: Thai Ethnic Adaptation in a Rural Malaysian Setting, University Press of Hawaii, 1979. Contributor to *Journal of Southeast Asian Studies.*

WORK IN PROGRESS: Ethnicity, Communication, and Traditional Medical Systems in Thailand (tentative title).

SIDELIGHTS: Golomb speaks Thai, Malay, French, German, Italian, and some Spanish and Swedish. He spent several years in graphic design and has had works exhibited at various museums, including the Museum of Modern Art in New York City. He writes: "My teaching interests include linguistic anthropology (language and culture, cognitive anthropology, sociolinguistics, historical linguistics, descriptive linguistics, inter-cultural communication, and nonverbal social interaction), ethnicity, medical anthropology, peasant societies, and peoples of mainland Southeast Asia. My research interests include verbal and nonverbal communications between ethnic groups, symbolic maintenance of ethnic boundaries, pidginization of communication, the roles of minority healers in plural societies, and Thai and Malay ethnography and ethno-history.

"In academia we find marvelously complicated ways of describing simple, everyday human behavior. The real challenge for the scholar is to create a piece of work which meets the standards of his professional peers while remaining palatable for the casual reader."

*   *   *

GONZALEZ, Angel 1925-

PERSONAL: Born September 6, 1925, in Oviedo, Spain; son of Pedro and Maria (Muniz) Gonzalez-Cano. *Education:* University of Oviedo, licenciado en derecho, 1948. *Politics:* "Socialism in freedom." *Religion:* "None." *Office:* Department of Modern Languages, University of New Mexico, Albuquerque, N.M. 87131.

CAREER: Ministry of Public Works, Madrid, Spain, official, 1955-72; visiting professor at University of New Mexico, 1972, University of Utah, 1973, and University of Texas at Austin, 1974; University of New Mexico, Albuquerque, professor of contemporary Spanish literature, 1974—. *Awards, honors:* Antonio Machado poetry award, 1962.

WRITINGS: "Harsh World" and Other Poems (text in English and Spanish), English translation by Donald D. Walsh, Princeton University Press, 1977.

Other works: *Aspero mundo,* Adonais, 1956; *Sin esperanza, con convencimiento,* Literaturasa (Barcelona), 1961; *Grado elemental,* Ruedo Iberico (Paris), 1962; *Palabra sobre palabra,* Poesia para todos (Madrid), 1965, 3rd edition, Barral editores, 1977; *Tratado de urbanismo,* El bardo (Barcelona),

1967, 2nd edition, 1976; *Breves acotaciones para una biografia,* Inventarios (Las Palmas, Spain), 1969; *Procedimientos narrativos,* La Isla (Santander, Spain), 1972; *Juan Ramon Jimenez,* Jucar (Madrid), Volume I: *Estudio,* 1973, Volume II: *Antologia,* 1974; *Muestra de algunos procedimientos narrativos y de las actitudes sentimentales que habitualmente comportan,* Turner, 1976, revised and updated edition, 1977; (editor and author of introduction) *El grupo poetico de 1927,* Taurus (Madrid), 1976, 2nd edition, 1979; (editor and author of introduction) *Gabriel Celaya,* Alianza (Madrid), 1977.

Poetry represented in numerous anthologies. English translations of poetry have appeared in many periodicals, including *New Directions, Mundus Artium, Texas Quarterly, American Poetry Review,* and *New Republic.*

SIDELIGHTS: Gonzalez told *CA:* "Part of my poetry is determined by certain historical events: the Spanish Civil War, the long dictatorship of Franco. But I am not only an epic or civil poet—other more lyrical aspects of my poetry are equally defining. They are centered basically around the erotic-amorous theme and there is the preoccupation with the passage of time. I try to compose poetry from experience with a distancing tone by means of irony and a careful elaboration of the poetic language. I write little and slowly. Music and painting interest me as much as poetry."

Gonzalez added that he has "traveled extensively throughout Europe and America."

BIOGRAPHICAL/CRITICAL SOURCES: Jose Olivio Jimenez, *Diez anos de poesia espanola,* Insula (Madrid), 1972.

*   *   *

GOOD, Paul 1929-

PERSONAL: Born March 11, 1929, in Brooklyn, N.Y.; son of Paul Joseph (a realtor) and Evelyn (Boyd) Good; married Ruth Thompson (a poet), June 2, 1951; children: Sean, Regan. *Education:* Attended Brown University, 1947, and Boston University, 1948. *Politics:* Independent. *Religion:* "Born Roman Catholic; no religion now." *Home:* 119 Old Rd., Westport, Conn. 06880.

CAREER: World Telegram & Sun, New York City, rewriteman, 1953-56; National Broadcasting Co. (NBC), New York City, newswriter and editor, 1958-60; American Broadcasting Co. (ABC), New York City, newswriter, foreign and domestic correspondent, and Atlanta, Ga., bureau chief, 1961-64; free-lance writer, 1964—. Periodically wrote for the National Sharecroppers Fund for five years. *Military service:* U.S. Army, 1951-53.

WRITINGS: The American Serfs, Putnam, 1968; *Cycle to Nowhere* (monograph), U.S. Commission on Civil Rights, 1968; *Once to Every Man* (novel), Putnam, 1970; *Cairo, Illinois: Racism at Floodtide* (monograph), U.S. Commission on Civil Rights, 1973; *The Individual,* Time-Life, 1974; *The Trouble I've Seen: White Journalist/Black Movement,* Howard University Press, 1975. Author of column "The Old Sergeant," *Army Times,* for twelve years. Contributor of articles to *Nation, Harper's, Atlantic Monthly, Life, Reader's Digest,* and other periodicals.

WORK IN PROGRESS: Throwing Away Your Father, a novel; *Twelve Angry Judges,* a book with Emanuel Margolis examining lower court civil liberties decisions; a book on the life history of a compulsive gambler, for Harper.

SIDELIGHTS: Good's longer works reflect his "overriding serious commitment" to the concerns of race and civil rights in America. His first book, *The American Serfs,* examines the relationship between poverty and racism in the rural South. While Good partially blames governmental policies for the continuing problem of poverty, he asserts that racism contributes to its proliferation. "Racism," he remarked, "has blunted white sensibility to black poverty while the fact that the white poor have always been with us is converted into the dictum that they always should be." Another book, *Once to Every Man*, dramatizes the individual dreams and ambitions of people involved in a Florida freedom march. Good stated in a *Library Journal* interview that the book "tries to tell what happens to people when their ability to love is corrupted by racism or materialism." He continues his study of the civil rights movement in *The Trouble I've Seen*. Here Good provides an autobiographical account of what happened in the movement during 1964. The book, Pat Watters wrote, "probes deeper than any other I have seen" into the underlying, untold meanings of that time.

BIOGRAPHICAL/CRITICAL SOURCES: Saturday Review, November 16, 1969; *Nation,* January 13, 1969, April 10, 1976; *Library Journal,* June 15, 1970; *New York Times Book Review,* January 11, 1976.

* * *

GOODALL, Leonard E. 1937-

PERSONAL: Born March 16, 1937, in Warrensburg, Mo.; son of Leonard B. (in business) and Eula (a secretary; maiden name, Johnson) Goodall; married Lois Marie Stubblefield, August 16, 1959; children: Karla, Karen, Greg. *Education:* Central Missouri State University, B.A., 1958; University of Missouri, M.A., 1960; University of Illinois, Ph.D., 1962. *Religion:* Presbyterian. *Home:* 551 Golfcrest Dr., Dearborn, Mich. 48124. *Office:* Office of the Chancellor, University of Michigan—Dearborn, Dearborn, Mich. 48124.

CAREER: Arizona State University, Tempe, assistant professor of political science, 1962-67; University of Illinois at Chicago Circle, Chicago, associate professor of political science, 1967-71, associate dean of faculties, 1968-69, vicechancellor of university, 1969-71; University of Michigan—Dearborn, chancellor, 1971—. Member of board of directors of Metropolitan Fund, Inc. and Dearborn Chamber of Commerce, both 1973—; member of Wayne County Planning Commission, 1974—; consultant to Lilly Endowment. *Military service:* U.S. Army Reserve, 1958-64. *Member:* American Political Science Association, American Society for Public Administration, American Association for Higher Education, Economic Club of Detroit, Fair Lane Club of Dearborn. *Awards, honors:* A.A. from Schoolcraft College, 1977.

WRITINGS: (Editor) *The Office of Governor in Arizona,* Bureau of Government Research, Arizona State University, 1964; *State Regulation of Local Indebtedness in the United States,* Bureau of Government Research, Arizona State University, 1964; (editor) *Urban Politics in the Southwest,* Institute of Public Administration, Arizona State University, 1967; (with David Andrew Bingham) *Handbook for Mayors and Councilmen,* Institute of Public Administration, Arizona State University, 3rd edition, 1968; *The American Metropolis,* C. E. Merrill, 1968, 2nd edition (with Donald P. Sprengel), 1975; (editor) *State Politics and Higher Education: A Book of Readings,* LMG Associates, 1976. Contributor to education, social science, and political science journals, and *National Civic Review.*

WORK IN PROGRESS: A biography of former Dearborn mayor, Orville Hubbard.

GOODHART, Arthur Lehman 1891-1978

PERSONAL: Born March 1, 1891, in New York, N.Y.; died November 10, 1978, in London, England; son of Philip J. and Martha (Lehman) Goodhart; married Cecily M. Carter; children: Philip, William Howard, Charles Albert Eric. *Education:* Yale University, A.B., 1912; Cambridge University, earned law degree. *Residence:* London, England.

CAREER: Admitted to the bar in United States; served as assistant corporation counsel of New York City, 1915-17; called to the Bar, London, England; Cambridge University, Corpus Christi College, Cambridge, England, teacher and fellow for twelve years; Oxford University, University College, Oxford, England, professor of jurisprudence and chairman of faculty, beginning in 1937, master of college, beginning in 1951. Yale University, visiting professor, 1929, became associate fellow of Jonathan Edwards College. Editor of *English Law Quarterly Review,* until 1931. *Military service:* U.S. Army, served in World War I; became captain. *Member:* Member of many learned societies, including Phi Beta Kappa. *Awards, honors:* Received many honorary degrees and decorations from foreign governments, including knight commander of Order of the British Empire, 1948.

WRITINGS: Polland and the Minority Races, Brentano's, 1920, reprinted, Arno, 1971; *Essays in Jurisprudence and the Common Law* (collection of previously published essays), Cambridge University Press, 1931; *The British Constitution* (revision of article first published in *Outpost*), British Information Service (New York, N.Y.), 1946; *We of the Turning Tide,* F. W. Preece, 1947; *Five Jewish Lawyers of the Common Law,* Oxford University Press, 1949, enlarged edition, Books for Libraries Press, 1949; *The History of the 2/7 Australian Field Regiment,* Rigby, 1952; *English Law and Moral Law,* Stevens, 1953; (editor) Frederick Pollock, *Jurisprudence and Legal Essays,* Macmillan, 1961; *Law of the Land,* University Press of Virginia, 1966; *Lord Wright, 1869-1964,* Oxford University Press, 1967. Author of booklets on law.

Under name A. L. Goodhart: *The Legality of the General Strike in England,* W. Heffer & Sons, 1927, first published in *Yale Law Journal,* February, 1927; (contributor) *Problems of War and Peace,* Grotius Society (London), 1927; *Precedent in English and Continental Law: An Inaugural Lecture Delivered Before the University of Oxford,* Stevens & Sons, 1934; (author of foreword) *The Function of a University in a Modern Community,* Basil Blackwell, 1943. Also author of foreword of *The Definition of Law,* by Hermann U. Kantobowicz, 1958. General editor, with H. G. Hanbury, of "A History of English Law" series, by William Searle, Methuen.

SIDELIGHTS: While maintaining his United States citizenship, Goodhart became a prominent member of the British Bar and well-known figure at Oxford University. He achieved the status of Queen's counselor, one of the few Americans to have done so. At Oxford University, he was the first American to chair the law faculty and to direct one of the colleges.

OBITUARIES: New York Times, November 11, 1978.*

* * *

GOODRICH, David L(loyd) 1930-

PERSONAL: Born August 22, 1930, in New York, N.Y.; son of Lloyd (an art historian) and Edith (Havens) Goodrich; married Patricia Hurley, October 6, 1962; children: Adele Donham (stepdaughter). *Education:* Yale University,

B.A., 1952. *Home and office:* 123 East 94th St., New York, N.Y. 10028. *Agent:* Curtis Brown, Ltd., 575 Madison Ave., New York, N.Y. 10022.

CAREER: Writer. Doubleday, Inc., New York City, editorial assistant, 1952-57; Fawcett Publications, Inc., New York City, associate editor, 1957-59. *Military service:* U.S. Army, 1954-56; became specialist third class. *Member:* Authors Guild.

WRITINGS: Horatio Alger Is Alive and Well and Living in America (nonfiction), Cowles, 1971; *Art Fakes in America* (nonfiction), Viking, 1973; *Paint Me a Million* (novel), Putnam, 1978. Contributor of stories and articles to periodicals, including *Saturday Evening Post.*

WORK IN PROGRESS: Another novel.

BIOGRAPHICAL/CRITICAL SOURCES: Christian Science Monitor, November 23, 1973.

*   *   *

GORDON, Bernard K.   1932-

PERSONAL: Born July 12, 1932; children: four. *Education:* New York University, B.A. (honors), 1953, M.A., 1955; University of Chicago, Ph.D., 1959. *Home:* 113 Cutts Rd., Durham, N.H. 03824. *Office:* Department of Political Science, Social Science Center, University of New Hampshire, Durham, N.H. 03824.

CAREER: Library of Congress, Legislative Reference Service, Washington, D.C., national defense analyst, 1958-59; Vanderbilt University, Nashville, Tenn., assistant professor of political science, 1959-64; University of Singapore, Singapore, visiting professor of political science, 1964-65; George Washington University, Washington, D.C., adjunct associate professor of political science, 1965-71; University of New Hampshire, Durham, professor of political science, 1971—, head of department, 1971-74. Lecturer at Johns Hopkins University, 1967-71; visiting professor at American University, 1970-71; guest professor at Kyoto University, 1977-78. Head of Southeast Asian studies at Research Analysis Corp., 1966-71; member of Brookings Institution study group on U.S. policy in Asia, 1969-70. Participant at international professional meetings; expert witness for U.S. Senate; testified before U.S. House of Representatives; consultant to U.S. Senate, U.S. Secretary of Defense, and National Security Council. *Member:* International Institute for Strategic Studies, American Political Science Association, Association for Asian Studies. *Awards, honors:* Fulbright fellowships, 1955-56, 1977-78 (for Japan); Rockefeller Foundation fellowship, 1964-65; Ford Foundation fellowship, 1978-80.

WRITINGS: New Zealand Becomes a Pacific Power, University of Chicago Press, 1960; *The Dimensions of Conflict in Southeast Asia,* Prentice-Hall, 1966; (contributor) J. C. Wahlke and A. N. Dragnich, editors, *Government and Politics,* Random House, 1966, 2nd edition, 1971; (contributor) R. O. Tilman, editor, *Man, State, and Society in Southeast Asia,* Praeger, 1969; *Toward Dis-Engagement in Asia: A Strategy for American Foreign Policy,* Prentice-Hall, 1969.

(Contributor) L. J. Cantori and S. L. Spiegel, editors, *International Politics of Regions: A Comparative Approach,* Prentice-Hall, 1970; (contributor) P. A. Tharp, Jr., editor, *Regional International Organizations: Structures and Functions,* St. Martin's, 1971; (contributor) Zasloff and Goodman, editors, *Indochina in Conflict,* Heath, 1972; (contributor) H. B. Malmgren, editor, *Pacific Basin Development: The American Interests,* Lexington Books, 1972; (contribu-

tor) Y. C. Kim, editor, *Major Powers and Korea,* Research Institute on Korean Affairs, 1973; (contributor) G. Henderson, editor, *Divided Nations in a Divided World,* McKay, 1974; (editor with Kenneth J. Rothwell, and contributor) *The New Political Economy of the Pacific,* Ballinger, 1975. Contributor of about thirty articles to history, Asian studies, and scientific journals.

SIDELIGHTS: Gordon has conducted field studies in Australia, Burma, Cambodia, Indonesia, Japan, Malaysia, New Zealand, the Philippines, Singapore, Thailand, and Vietnam. His scholarly interests focus on international politics and Asian politics (especially East Asian international politics), the substance and process of American foreign policy, and U.S. defense and national security.

*   *   *

GORDON, Mildred   1912-1979
(The Gordons, a joint pseudonym)

OBITUARY NOTICE—See index for *CA* sketch: Born July 24, 1912, in Eureka, Kan.; died of cancer, February 3, 1979, in Tucson, Ariz. Magazine editor, screenwriter, and author. Gordon was editor of *Arizona* magazine before she began to free-lance for magazines. In 1950, she began writing full-time with her husband, and together they produced such books as *FBI Story* and *With This Ring,* and the filmscripts for the movies "That Darn Cat" and "Experiment in Terror." Obituaries and other sources: *The Author's and Writer's Who's Who,* 6th edition, Burke's Peerage, 1971; *Who's Who of American Women,* 9th edition, Marquis, 1975; *New York Times,* February 6, 1979; *AB Bookman's Weekly,* April 16, 1979.

*   *   *

GOULDING, Ray(mond Walter)   1922-

PERSONAL: Born March 20, 1922, in Lowell, Mass.; son of Thomas M. and Mary (Philbin) Goulding; married Elizabeth Leader, May 18, 1945; children: Raymond, Thomas, Barbara, Bryant, Mark, Melissa. *Office:* 420 Lexington Ave., New York, N.Y. 10017.

CAREER: Goulding, Elliot, Greybar Productions, Inc., New York, N.Y., president, 1954—. Member of comedy team "Bob and Ray," 1947—, with television series on all major networks; film and stage actor. *Military service:* U.S. Army, 1942-46; became first lieutenant. *Member:* American Federation of Television and Radio Artists, American Guild of Variety Artists, Screen Actors Guild. *Awards, honors:* Two Peabody Broadcasting Awards from Academy of Television Arts and Sciences; several awards for performances in television commercials.

WRITINGS—All with Bob Elliott: *Bob and Ray's Story of Linda Lovely and the Fleebus,* Dodd, 1960; *Bob and Ray: The Two and Only,* privately printed, 1970; *Write If You Get Work: The Best of Bob and Ray,* Random House, 1975.

*   *   *

GOULET, John   1942-

PERSONAL: Born December 18, 1942, in Boston, Mass.; son of John F. (in newspaper advertising) and Isabelle (Coquelin) Goulet; married Leslie Clark, September 20, 1965; children: Matthew. *Education:* St. John's University, Collegeville, Minn., B.A., 1964; San Francisco State College, M.A., 1969; University of Iowa, M.F.A., Ph.D., 1972. *Home:* 3000 North Maryland Ave., Milwaukee, Wis. 53211. *Agent:* Elaine Markson Literary Agency, Inc., 44 Greenwich Ave., New York, N.Y. 10011. *Office:* Department of English, University of Wisconsin, Milwaukee, Wis. 53201.

CAREER: Hanover College, Hanover, Ind., assistant professor of English, 1972-74; University of Wisconsin—Milwaukee, 1974—, began as associate professor, became professor of English.

WRITINGS: Oh's Profit (novel), Morrow, 1975.

WORK IN PROGRESS: Ahab's Wife, a novel.

SIDELIGHTS: Goulet comments: "My interest in contemporary linguistic theory and my experiments in teaching language to apes were important in writing *Oh's Profit,* which is about a gorilla who learns American sign language."

*   *   *

GOYTISOLO, Juan   1931-

PERSONAL: Born January 5, 1931, in Barcelona, Spain; immigrated to France, 1957. *Education:* Attended University of Barcelona and University of Madrid, 1948-52. *Residence:* Paris, France. *Office:* c/o Grove Press, 80 University Pl., New York, N.Y. 10003.

CAREER: Writer. Worked as reporter in Cuba, 1965; currently associated with Gallimard Publishing Co., France. Visiting professor at universities in the United States. *Awards, honors:* Received numerous awards for *Juegos de Manos.*

WRITINGS—Novels, unless otherwise indicated; in English: *Juegos de manos,* Ediciones Destino, 1954, translation by John Rust published as *The Young Assassins,* Knopf, 1959; *Duelo en el paraiso,* Editorial Planeta, 1955, translation by Christine Brooke-Rose published as *Children of Chaos,* Macgibbon & Kee, 1958; *Fiestas,* Emece Editores, 1958, translation by Herbert Weinstock published as *Fiestas,* Knopf, 1960; *La isla,* Seix Barral, 1961 , translation by Jose Yglesias published as *Island of Women,* Knopf, 1962 (published in England as *Sands of Torremolinos,* J. Cape, 1962); *Fin de fiesta; tentativas de interprefacion de una historia amorosa,* Seix Barral, 1962, translation by Yglesias published as *The Party's Over: Four Attempts to Define a Love Story* (stories), Weidenfeld & Nicolson, 1966, Grove, 1967; *Senas de identidad,* J. Mortiz, 1966, translation by Gregory Rabassa published as *Marks of Identity,* Grove, 1969; *Reivindicacion del Conde don Julian,* J. Mortiz, 1970, translation by Helen R. Lane published as *Count Julian,* Viking, 1974; *Juan sin tierra,* Editorial Seix Barral, 1975, translation by Lane published as *Juan the Landless,* Viking, 1977.

Other: *El circo,* Ediciones Destino, 1957; *La resaca,* Club del Libro Espanol, 1958; *Problemas de la novela,* Editorial Seix Barral, 1959; *Para vivir aqui,* Sur, 1960; *Campos de Nijar,* Seix Barral, 1960; *La Chanca,* Libreria Espanola, 1962; *Las mismas palabras,* Seix Barral, 1963; *Pueblo en marcha; instantaneas de un viaje a Cuba,* Libreria Espanola, 1963(?); *Plume d'hier, Espagne d'aujourd'hui,* compiled by Mariano Jose de Larra, Editeurs francais reunis, 1965; *El Furgon de cola,* Ruedo iberico, 1967; *Spanien und die Spanien,* M. Bucher, 1969; (author of prologue) Jose Maria Blanco White, *Obra inglesa,* Ediciones Formentor, 1972; *Obras completas,* Aguilar, 1977.

SIDELIGHTS: The literary world was greatly impressed when Goytisolo's first novel, *The Young Assassins,* was published in 1954. Later, when it was published in English, David Dempsey found that it "begins where the novels of a writer like Jack Kerouac leave off." Goytisolo was identified as a member of the Spanish "restless generation" but his first novel seemed as much akin to Dostoevski as it did to Kerouac. The plot is similar to Dostoevski's *The Possessed:* a group of students plot the murder of a politician but end up murdering the fellow student chosen to kill the politician. Dempsey wrote, "Apparently, he is concerned with showing us how self-destructive and yet how inevitable this hedonism becomes in a society dominated by the smug and self-righteous."

Children of Chaos was seen as a violent extension of *The Young Assassins.* Like Burgess's *A Clockwork Orange* and William Golding's *Lord of the Flies, Children of Chaos* focuses on the terror wrought by adolescents. The children have taken over a small town after the end of the Spanish Civil War causes a breakdown of order.

Fiestas begins a trilogy referred to as "The Ephemeral Morrow" (after a famous poem by Antonio Machado). Considered the best volume of the trilogy, it follows four characters as they try to escape life in Spain by chasing their dreams. Each character meets with disappointment in the novel's end. Ramon Sender called *Fiestas* "a brilliant projection of the contrast between Spanish official and real life," and concluded that Goytisolo "is without doubt the best of the young Spanish writers."

El circo, the second book in "The Ephemeral Morrow," was too blatantly ironic to succeed as a follow-up to *Fiestas.* It is the story of a painter who manages a fraud before being punished for a murder he didn't commit. The third book, *La resaca* was also a disappointment. The novel's style was considered too realistic to function as a fitting conclusion to "The Ephemeral Morrow."

After writing two politically oriented travelogues, *Campos de Nijar* and *La Chanca,* Goytisolo returned to fiction and the overt realism he'd begun in *La resaca.* Unfortunately, critics implied that both *Island of Women* and *The Party's Over* suffered because they ultimately resembled their subject matter. *The Party's Over* contains four stories about the problems of marriage. Although Alexander Coleman found that the "stories are more meditative than the full-length novels," he also observed, "But it is, in the end, a small world, limited by the overwhelming ennui of everything and everyone in it." Similarly, Honor Tracy noted, "Every gesture of theirs reveals the essence of the world, they're absolutely necessary, says another: we intellectuals operate in a vacuum. . . . Everything ends in their all being fed up."

Goytisolo abandoned his realist style after *The Party's Over.* "In *Marks of Identity,*" wrote Barbara Probst Solomon, "Goytisolo begins to do a variety of things. Obvious political statement, he feels, is not enough for a novel; he starts to break with form—using a variety of first, second and third persons, he is looking and listening to the breaks in language and . . . he begins to break with form—in the attempt to describe what he is really seeing and feeling, his work becomes less abstract." Robert J. Clements called *Marks of Identity* "probably his most personal novel," but also felt that the "most inevitable theme is of course the police state of Spain." Fusing experimentation with a firm political stance, Goytisolo reminded some critics of Joyce while others saw him elaborating his realist style to further embellish his own sense of politics.

Count Julian, Goytisolo's next novel, is widely considered to be his masterpiece. In it, he uses techniques borrowed from Joyce, Celine, Jean Genet, filmmaker Luis Bunuel, and Picasso. Solomon remarked that, while some of these techniques proved less than effective in many of the French novels of the 1960's, "in the hands of this Spanish novelist, raging against Spain, the results are explosive." Writing in the *New York Times Book Review,* Carlos Fuentes called *Count Julian* "an adventure of language, a critical battle against the language appropriated by power in Spain. It is also a search for a new/old language that would offer an alternative for the future." Throughout the book, there is a noticeable absence of punctuation which only serves to intensify the character of Julian, an outcast living in Africa. R. J. Thompson found *Count Julian* to be "a daring, shocking, savage, suicidally comic book." He concluded that it was "a book to be reckoned with."

With the publication of *Juan the Landless,* critics began to see his last three novels as a second trilogy. However, reviews were generally less favorable than those for either *Marks of Identity* or *Count Julian.* Anatole Broyard, calling attention to Goytisolo's obsession with sadistic sex and defecation, remarked, "Don Quixote no longer tilts at windmills, but toilets." A writer for *Atlantic* suggested that the uninformed reader begin elsewhere with Goytisolo.

BIOGRAPHICAL/CRITICAL SOURCES: Saturday Review, February 14, 1959, June 11, 1960, June 28, 1969; *New York Times Book Review,* January 22, 1967, May 5, 1974, September 18, 1977; *New Republic,* January 31, 1967; *Best Sellers,* June 15, 1974; *Nation,* March 1, 1975; *Contemporary Literary Criticism,* Gale, Volume 5, 1976, Volume 10, 1979; *Atlantic,* August, 1977.*

*   *   *

GRABER, Richard (Fredrick) 1927-

PERSONAL: Born April 23, 1927, in Minneapolis, Minn.; son of Robert Winfield and Ruth Alexandria Graber; married Barbara Ann Smith, April 16, 1954 (divorced May 23, 1972); children: Rebecca Ann, Nancy Elizabeth, John Fredrick. *Education:* University of Minnesota, B.A., 1951. *Politics:* Liberal. *Religion:* Liberal. *Home and office:* 36 North Ridge Rd., Old Greenwich, Conn. 06870. *Agent:* William Reiss, Paul R. Reynolds, Inc., 12 East 41st St., New York, N.Y. 10017.

CAREER: Cherokee Daily Times, Cherokee, Iowa, reporter, 1951-52; *Better Homes and Gardens,* Des Moines, Iowa, in book promotion, 1953-56; free-lance advertising and public relations writer in Minneapolis, Minn., 1957-61; *Edina-Morningside Courier,* Hopkins, Minn., editor, 1962-63; *Modern Medicine,* Edina, Minn., science writer, 1964-65; *Geriatrics,* Edina, editor, 1966-67; *Patient Care,* Darien, Conn., senior editor, 1968-72, managing editor, 1972-73; *Group Practice,* New York, N.Y., managing editor, 1973-75; free-lance writer, 1975—. *Military service:* U.S. Navy, 1945-46.

WRITINGS—Juveniles: *A Little Breathing Room,* Harper, 1978; *Pay Your Respects,* Harper, 1979. Contributor to medical journals.

WORK IN PROGRESS: Another novel, a book for young non-readers; research for a long novel set in the Midwest from 1940 to 1975.

SIDELIGHTS: Graber comments: "Without meaning to, I wrote a novel for young readers, *A Little Breathing Room.* It still reads well for adults. The second novel, *Pay Your Respects,* is a sequel issued for young readers and through regular trade channels. So far, I have not purposely slanted a novel for the younger readers because I don't know how, and I think it would be a serious mistake. I write what I have to write and hope for as many readers as possible, of any age (there aren't all that many). Writing an honest book of fiction

is the most demanding of all jobs. And the most rewarding. A writer has to be a little cockeyed to finish a novel, although *anyone* can start one. And from what I hear, 99 percent of the adults in the United States have started novels, or are about to. Precious few will complete one, or even want to."

*   *   *

GRABOSKY, Peter Nils 1945-

PERSONAL: Born July 21, 1945, in New York, N.Y.; son of Jack and Eleanor (Hall) Grabosky. *Education:* Colby College, B.A., 1966; Northwestern University, M.A., 1970, Ph.D., 1973. *Office:* Office of Crime Statistics, Department of Law, Government of South Australia, G.P.O. Box 464, Adelaide, South Australia 5001.

CAREER: University of Vermont, Burlington, assistant professor, 1973-77, associate professor of political science, 1977-78; Government of South Australia, Adelaide, director of Office of Crime Statistics, 1978—. Did field research in Sydney, Australia, 1972-73, and in Stockholm, Sweden, 1975. Member of Australian Criminology Research Council. *Military service:* U.S. Naval Reserve, active duty, 1966-69; became lieutenant junior grade. *Member:* American Political Science Association, Law and Society Association, American Judicature Society, Australian and New Zealand Society of Criminology (member of executive council). *Awards, honors:* Russell Sage fellow at Yale University, 1976-78.

WRITINGS: (With Ted Robert Gurr and Richard C. Hula) *The Politics of Crime and Conflict: A Comparative History of Four Cities,* Sage Publications, 1977; *Sydney in Ferment: Crime, Dissent, and Official Reaction, 1788-1973,* Australian National University Press, 1977.

WORK IN PROGRESS: Research on "measuring punishment and explaining variations in the severity of sanctions."

*   *   *

GRAMATKY, Hardie 1907-1979

OBITUARY NOTICE—See index for *CA* sketch: Born April 12, 1907, in Dallas, Tex.; died April 29, 1979, in Westport, Conn. Author and illustrator best known for his series about a tugboat called "Little Toot." Gramatky began the series in 1939; the final volume, *Little Toot Through the Golden Gate,* was published in 1975. He worked for Walt Disney Productions during the early 1930's, and later the Disney studios adapted *Little Toot* as a motion picture. His watercolors are now displayed in museums, including the Art Institute of Chicago and the Springfield Museum of Fine Art. Obituaries and other sources: *Books Are by People: Interviews With 104 Authors and Illustrators of Books for Young People,* Citation Press, 1969; *Authors of Books for Young People,* 2nd edition, Scarecrow, 1971; *Who's Who in the World,* 2nd edition, Marquis, 1973; *Authors in the News,* Volume 1, Gale, 1976; *New York Times,* May 1, 1979; *AB Bookman's Weekly,* May 21, 1979.

*   *   *

GRANICK, Harry 1898-
(Harry Taylor)

PERSONAL: Born January 23, 1898, in Nova Kraruka, Russia; came to the United States in 1905, naturalized citizen, 1918; son of Joseph (a worker) and Elizabeth (Tishkoffski) Granick; married Ray Weiss (a librarian), February 3, 1924; children: David. *Education:* "Like many writers of my generation, self-taught." *Home:* 100 La Salle St., New York, N.Y. 10027. *Agent:* Bertha Klausner, International Literary Agency, Inc., 71 Park Ave., New York, N.Y. 10016.

CAREER: Playwright. *Military service:* British Army, Jewish Legion, Royal Fusiliers, 1918-19; served in Palestine and Egypt. *Member:* Authors League of America, Dramatists Guild, American Society of Composers, Authors, and Publishers, New Playwrights Committee. *Awards, honors:* Peabody Broadcasting Award from Academy of Television Arts and Sciences, 1944, for radio series, "Great Adventure Series"; Sergel Prize from National Theatre Conference, 1949, and first prize from Five Arts Contest, 1952, both for "Witches' Sabbath."

WRITINGS: Run, Run (juvenile), Simon & Schuster, 1941; *Underneath New York,* Rinehart, 1947.

Plays: (Co-author) "Dear Mother" (three-act), first produced in New York City at Master Arts Theater, 1935; "Warsaw Ghetto" (tone poem), first produced in New York City at Carnegie Hall, February 10, 1946; "Reveille Is Always" (three-act), first produced in New York City at Young Men's Hebrew Association, 1947; "The Criminals" (three-act), first produced in Smithtown, N.Y., September, 1949; "Witches' Sabbath" (three-act), first produced in Syracuse, N.Y., at Syracuse University, May 2, 1951, produced Off-Broadway at Madison Avenue Playhouse, May, 1962; "The Guilty" (three-act), first produced in Dallas, Tex., at Margo Jones Theater, September, 1954; "The Hooper Law" (three-act), first produced in Dallas, Tex., at Margo Jones Theater, March 25, 1957; "The Bright and Golden Land" (two-act), first produced in Huntington, N.Y., at PAF Playhouse, March 27, 1977.

Unproduced plays: "Promenade and Around We Go" (three-act), 1968; "Hells of Dante" (three-act), 1968; "Pigeons" (three-act), 1972; "The Jew of Venice" (three-act), 1975; "Long Smoldering" (two-act), 1977; "Two for One," 1978.

Work represented in anthologies, including *American Stuff,* Viking, 1937, and *First Stage,* Purdue University, 1961-62.

Free-lance radio writer, 1934-46, and television writer, 1950-52. Contributor of poems, stories, and articles to magazines. Drama critic (under pseudonym Harry Taylor) for *Masses, Masses and Mainstream,* and *New Theater,* 1936-47.

WORK IN PROGRESS: Another play.

SIDELIGHTS: Granick writes: "I fought in Palestine and Egypt, and revisited Israel in 1965. My wife and I have visited England, France, Italy, Greece, Japan, the People's Republic of China, and the Soviet Union. My most consistent interest has been in the social and political environments of peoples everywhere and in the life of the individual coping with that and with his near ones.

"I have written five plays in the last five years. At eighty-one I am still being pushed to it and hopeful."

*   *   *

GRANOVETTER, Mark S.   1943-

PERSONAL: Born October 20, 1943, in Jersey City, N.J.; son of Sidney and Violet (Greenblatt) Granovetter; married Ellen Greenebaum, June 14, 1970. *Education:* Princeton University, A.B., 1965; Harvard University, A.M., 1967, Ph.D., 1970. *Home:* 103 Emerson St., Port Jefferson, N.Y. 11777. *Office:* Department of Sociology, State University of New York at Stony Brook, Stony Brook, N.Y. 11794.

CAREER: Johns Hopkins University, Baltimore, Md., assistant professor of social relations, 1970-73; Harvard University, Cambridge, Mass., assistant professor, 1973-75, associate professor of sociology, 1975-77; State University of New York at Stony Brook, associate professor of sociology, 1977—. Fellow of Center for Advanced Study in the Behavioral Sciences, 1976-77. *Member:* American Sociological Association.

WRITINGS: Getting a Job: A Study of Contacts and Careers, Harvard University Press, 1974. Contributor to sociology journals, including *American Journal of Sociology.*

WORK IN PROGRESS: Research on theories of income differences and threshold models of collective behavior.

*   *   *

GRANT, Charles L.   1942-

PERSONAL: Born September 12, 1942, in Newark, N.J.; son of Sydney E. (an Episcopalian priest) and Minerva (Clark) Grant; married Deborah Voss, June 14, 1973; children: Ian, Emily. *Education:* Trinity College, Hartford, Conn., B.A., 1964. *Home:* 44 Center Grove Rd., #H-21, Randolph, N.J. 07801. *Agent:* Kirby McCauley Ltd., 310 East 46th St., New York, N.Y. 10017. *Office:* 51-J Village Green, Budd Lake, N.J. 07828.

CAREER: High school teacher of English, drama, and history in public schools in New Jersey, 1964-74; writer, 1974—. Administrator of World Fantasy Awards. *Military service:* U.S. Army, Military Police,; served in Vietnam; received Bronze Star. *Member:* Science Fiction Writers of America (executive secretary, 1974-78; eastern regional director, 1978-81), Mystery Writers of America, Authors League of America. *Awards, honors:* Nebula Award from Science Fiction Writers of America, 1976, for story, "A Crowd of Shadows."

WRITINGS: The Shadow of Alpha, Berkley, 1976; *Ascension,* Berkley, 1977; *The Curse,* Major, 1977; *The Hour of the Oxrun Dead,* Doubleday, 1977; *The Ravens of the Moon,* Doubleday, 1978; *The Sound of Midnight,* Doubleday, 1978; (editor) *Shadows,* Doubleday, 1978; (editor) *Shadows #2,* Doubleday, 1979; (editor) *The Book of Horror,* Playboy Press, 1979; *A Phial of Stars* (science fiction novel), Berkley, 1979; *A Quiet Night of Fear* (science fiction novel), Berkley, in press. Contributor of more than thirty-five stories to science fiction and fantasy magazines.

WORK IN PROGRESS: A Night of Dark Intent, a horror novel, completion expected in 1981.

SIDELIGHTS: Grant writes: "I travel constantly for research/pleasure (in my case, indistinguishable), read two or three books a week when I can ... all of which (avocation/vocation, one and the same) are aimed at producing the best possible fantasy stories I can, the goal of which is simple: to provide my readers with some insight into their own fears and that of their society while, at the same time, giving them a hell of a good scare."

*   *   *

GRAY, Nigel   1941-

PERSONAL: Born April 9, 1941, in Augwafatten, Northern Ireland; married Yasmin Hamid, April 29, 1978; children: Sara, Jo. *Education:* University of Lancaster, B.A., 1971. *Politics:* Libertarian. *Religion:* Atheist. *Home:* 22 Gallfield Court, Northampton NN3 4AU, England.

CAREER: Actor, writer and editor, and photographer,

1971—. Also taught creative writing. Founder, editor, and publisher of *Firewood* (quarterly journal of socialist and working-class arts), 1975; writer-in-residence for East Midlands Arts, 1977 80. Formerly was a manual laborer. *Awards, honors:* Dickens Fellowship Award 1970, for a critical essay on Dickens in the centenary year.

WRITINGS: The Silent Majority (fiction), Vision Press, 1973; (withe David Craig) "The Battle Against the Giant" (two-act play), produced in London at Unity Theatre, 1974; (contributor) David Craig and Margot Heinemann, editors, *Experiments in English Teaching,* Edward Arnold, 1976; *Come Close* (poems), Journeyman Press, 1978; (with Craig) *The Rebels and the Hostage* (novel), Journeyman Press, 1978, first produced as a play in Northampton, England at Lings Theatre, April 6, 1979.

Juveniles: *My Cat,* Macmillan, 1975; (contributor) Sheila Elkin, editor, *More Stories From Playschool,* Pan Books, 1976, also produced as a television series by British Broadcasting Corp., 1976; *The Deserter* (novel), Harper, 1977; *It'll All Come Out in the Wash,* Harper, 1979; *Grannie's Holiday, A Visit to the Doctor.* [and] *Lunch Break* (three plays for slow readers), Hutchinson, 1979.

Work represented in anthologies, including *Winter's Tales 23,* edited by Peter Colenette, Macmillan, 1977.

WORK IN PROGRESS: Editing *Are You Working?,* memories of the Depression; *The Job,* a novel for young adults; *Tomorrow Belongs to Me,* a fantasy novel; *The Murder of Children,* a novel; *Shots,* a juvenile novel; texts for picture books.

SIDELIGHTS: Gray writes: "What British playwright Edward Bond said about *Come Close* sums up what I'm aiming for: 'Nigel Gray writes poetry as it ought to be written. . . . He knows the worst and loves the best. Now he writes sane poems for a mad world. They give me courage and hope and remind me again of the happiness it is to be human.' My poetry is meant to be spoken and I do a lot of readings, often working with musicians.

"I believe that we live in a world in which there is too much unnecessary hurt. My work is intended to help people to become more understanding of each other and of themselves. I write for children because I feel it's so important that future generations see more clearly than ours, and because I like them.

"I'd like to write poems like Brecht and novels like Vonnegut, but I don't have that sort of ability. I shall just continue to say the things that I think are important in the best way I can, and hope that, in practising my craft, I will become better at it."

The Deserter has been translated into German, Dutch, and Greek.

*   *   *

GRAYSON, Richard   1951-

PERSONAL: Born June 4, 1951, in Brooklyn, N.Y.; son of Daniel (a businessman) and Marilyn (a nutritionist; maiden name, Sarrett) Grayson. *Education:* Brooklyn College of the City University of New York, B.A., 1973, M.F.A., 1976; Richmond College of the City University of New York, M.A., 1975. *Home:* 1607 East 56th St., Brooklyn, N.Y. 11234.

CAREER: Fiction Collective, Brooklyn, N.Y., editorial assistant, 1975-77; Long Island University, Brooklyn, lecturer in English, 1975-78; Kingsborough Community College,

Brooklyn, lecturer in English, 1978-79; Brooklyn College of the City University of New York, Brooklyn, lecturer in English, 1979—. *Member:* Authors Guild, Mensa, Associated Writing Programs, Brooklyn College Alumni Association (member of board of directors, 1973—), Phi Beta Kappa. *Awards, honors:* Ottillie Grebanier Drama Award from Brooklyn College, 1973; scholarship from National Arts Club, 1977, to study at Bread Loaf Writer's Conference; scholarship from Santa Cruz Writing Conference, 1978; fellowship from Virginia Center for the Creative Arts, 1979.

WRITINGS: Disjointed Fictions, X Archives, 1978; *With Hitler in New York and Other Stories,* Taplinger, 1979. Contributor of short stories to more than one hundred magazines, including *Epoch, Texas Quarterly, Confrontation, Shenandoah, Carleton Miscellany,* and *Transatlantic Review.*

WORK IN PROGRESS: An Unauthorized Autobiography; a book-length study of the soap opera "Another World"; an anthology of fiction by writers under thirty.

SIDELIGHTS: Grayson told *CA:* "Writing has been the primary way I've defined myself; at first it was therapy, but now, I hope, it has become something more. I see the writer's first job as giving the lowdown on himself, and through himself, on humanity. As I reluctantly leave the longest adolescence in history, I find myself—happily—becoming less self-conscious, more patient. I would like to avoid becoming pompous, but I'm afraid statements like these are among the mine fields on the road to absurd self-importance. I have a lot to learn about writing (and other things)."

BIOGRAPHICAL/CRITICAL SOURCES: Kings Courier, August 7, 1978; *Aspect,* number 72/73, 1979.

*   *   *

GREALY, Desmond   1923(?)-1979

OBITUARY NOTICE: Born c. 1923 in Dublin, Ireland; died April 10, 1979. Journalist and television news producer. After World War II, Grealy worked for the *London Star,* the *London Daily Mirror,* and the *London Daily Herald.* He was an executive producer of the Independent Television News in London and later headed the news department of Irish Television in Dublin. In 1967, Grealy joined ABC news to become television assignment manager and since 1975 had worked as a CBS news producer. Obituaries and other sources: *New York Times,* April 13, 1979.

*   *   *

GRECO, Jose   1918-

PERSONAL: Original name, Costanzo Greco; born December 23, 1918, in Montorio nei Frentani, Italy; came to United States in 1928, naturalized citizen; son of Paolo Emilio (a laborer) and Carmela (Bucci) Greco; married Nila Amparo (a dancer), August 16, 1946; married third wife, Nana Lorca (a choreographer and dancer), 1972; children: (first marriage) Jose, Alexandria; (third marriage) Paolo. *Education:* Studied painting at Leonardo da Vinci Art School, New York, N.Y.; studied dance with Helene Veola. *Home:* 224 West 49th St., New York, N.Y. 10019. *Office:* c/o Kolmar-Luth Entertainment, Inc., 1776 Broadway, New York, N.Y. 10019.

CAREER: Dancer, choreographer, actor, and lecturer. Teacher of dance, 1936-45; made professional dance debut with New York Hippodrome Opera Company, in Carmen, N.Y., 1937; appeared with Spanish dancer, La Argentinita, in 1943, and subsequently toured with her company throughout the United States, 1943-45, making guest appearances at

Carnegie Hall, March, 1943, and at the Metropolitan Opera House, and performing in lead roles in such ballets as Ravel's "Bolero," and Granados's "Pictures of Goya"; following La Argentinita's death in 1945, he traveled to Spain and joined her sister, Pilar Lopez, in forming a dance group, Ballet Espanol; made debut with Ballet Espanol in Madrid, Spain, June 7, 1946; became choreographer and toured with the company in Spain and Portugal, 1946-48; choreographer and principal dancer for film, "Manolete," 1948; formed own dance company, Ballet y Bailes de Espana, and made public debut at Apollo Theatre in Barcelona, Spain, January, 1949; toured with the company in Europe, Great Britain, and South America, 1949-51, and gave a lecture-demonstration of Spanish dancing at Covent Garden Opera House, London, England; became choreographer, producer, director, and principal dancer of company, and made U.S. debut at the Schubert Theater, New York, N.Y., October 1, 1951; toured United States as principal dancer of Jose Greco and His Company of Spanish Dancers, Musicians, and Singers, 1951-75. Founded Jose Greco School of Spanish Arts at Northwood Institute, West Baden, Ind., 1968; established the Jose Greco Foundation for Hispanic Dance, Inc., 1971; founded Centro de Arte Espanol in Marbella, Spain, 1974. As an actor, he appeared in such films as "Around the World in 80 Days" and "Ship of Fools," and toured with such productions as "The Passion of Dracula." Made television appearances on variety shows, including "The Ed Sullivan Show" and "The Perry Como Show." *Awards, honors:* Cross of Knight of Civil Merit (Spain), 1962; Silver Bowl Award, International Platform Association, 1971; also received numerous honorary degrees, including doctorates from Northwood Institute and Fairfield University.

WRITINGS: (With Harvey Ardman) *The Gypsy in My Soul: The Autobiography of Jose Greco,* Doubleday, 1977.

SIDELIGHTS: When he decided to retire from his role as principal dancer of his own company, Jose Greco had been touring the United States as a dancer for twenty-four years. According to Greco, he began dancing as a child, responding to a natural "zest for music and dancing." Wanting at one point to become a painter, Greco studied at the Leonardo da Vinci Art School in New York City. However, after watching the Spanish dancer Vicente Escudero perform, his desire to paint soon acquiesced to what became his major love—dance. Greco's love for Spanish dancing inspired him to study Spanish culture: "I went to all the libraries, all the stores that had Spanish records, studied the history, philosophy, everything about the Spanish people. I didn't realize then how valuable all these academics would become later." It has also moved him to establish a foundation for the study of Hispanic dancing, and two schools for the study of Spanish art and culture.

The success that Greco has achieved through his dancing came largely as a surprise to his mother who objected to his efforts. In an article for the *Fort Lauderdale Sun-Sentinel,* he stated: "She opposed me going into show business. She realized it was a terrible challenge, one chance in a million that I could make it. I wasn't from absolute Spanish stock, I had none of the tradition, the culture or the past. She knew it was going to be a losing battle."

In his autobiography, *The Gypsy in My Soul,* Greco reveals much of his personal life: memories of a small Italian village; survival on the tough streets of Brooklyn; becoming the protege of the famous Spanish dancer La Argentinita; and the formation of his own dance company. Many critics have cited a lack of insight into the art of dance as a major flaw of the book. *New York Times Book Review* critic Jennifer Dun-

ning writes, "Mr. Greco makes no pretense at having been to the *zapateado* [Spanish tap dance] born, and though he was known for his personal elegance, what he brought to Spanish dance was flair for theatricality."

BIOGRAPHICAL/CRITICAL SOURCES: Miami Herald, March 28, 1975; *Fort Lauderdale Sun-Sentinel,* March 28, 1975; Jose Greco and Harvey Ardman, *The Gypsy in My Soul: The Autobiography of Jose Greco,* Doubleday, 1977; *Kirkus Reviews,* April 15, 1977; *New York Times Book Review,* July 10, 1977; *Choice,* November, 1977.

*   *   *

GREEN, Alan Singer   1907-

PERSONAL: Born December 6, 1907, in Chicago, Ill.; son of William G. and Malvine (Singer) Green; married Frances Katz, May 22, 1934 (died March 4, 1977); children: Jonathan, David. *Education:* Western Reserve University (now Case Western Reserve University), B.A., 1929, M.A., 1935; Hebrew Union College, New York, N.Y., rabbi, 1934, D.D., 1938; also attended Columbia University, 1930, and Hebrew University of Jerusalem, 1935-36. *Home:* 21949 Byron Rd., Cleveland, Ohio. *Office:* 2200 South Green Rd., Cleveland, Ohio.

CAREER: Rabbi of Jewish congregation in Troy, N.Y., 1937-44, first rabbi in Houston, Tex., 1944-47; Temple Emanu-El, Cleveland, Ohio, founder and rabbi, 1947—. President of Zionist district of Troy, N.Y., 1938, and local Council of Social Agencies, 1944; co-chairman of religious committee of Cleveland's Bonds for Israel, 1958-62; Jewish co-chairman of Cleveland Conference of Religion and Race, 1963-67; member of board of directors of Cleveland Council on Economic Opportunities, 1965-67. Member of alumni board of overseers of Hebrew Union College, 1968-70; treasurer, Central Conference of American Rabbis, 1970-72. *Member:* Phi Beta Kappa, Delta Sigma Rho, Zeta Beta Tau. *Awards, honors:* D.H.L. from Hebrew Union College, 1959.

WRITINGS: Facing the Issues of Contemporaneous Jewish Life, Hebrew Union College, 1935; *Teaching Modern Jewish History Through Fiction,* Union of American Hebrew Congregations, 1939; (with Jacob Golub) *A Short History of the Jewish People,* Union of American Hebrew Congregations, 1942; *Return to Prayer,* Union of American Hebrew Congregations, 1971; *Sex, God, and the Sabbath: The Mystery of Jewish Marriage,* Temple Emanu-El, 1979. Author of "The Jewish Scene," a column in *Reform Judaism,* 1938-44. Contributor to *Universal Jewish Encyclopedia.* Member of editorial board of *Reform Judaism.*

SIDELIGHTS: Green writes: "*Sex, God, and the Sabbath* sums up the inner motivation and essential faith of my forty-five years in the rabbinate. It blends Jewish basic teachings with modern thought and personal experience. It grows out of years of counseling young couples about to be married, and those seeking counsel already married, and sharing insight I gained in my own rewarding marriage.

"*Return to Prayer* has been called a 'starter set' on the road back to Jewish home observance, especially on the Sabbath, with motivation and interpretation. Hebrew charts help teach meaning and pronounciation of essential Sabbath, daily, and holiday devotions and songs to the home."

*   *   *

GREEN, Anita Jane   1940-
(Anita Bryant)

PERSONAL: Born March 25, 1940, in Barnsdall, Okla.;

daughter of Warren Gene and Lenora (Cate) Bryant; married Robert Einar Green (a professional manager), June 25, 1960; children: Robert Einar, Gloria Lynn, William Bryant, Barbara Elisabet. *Education.* Attended Northwestern University, 1959. *Home:* 4682 North Bay Rd., Miami Beach, Fla. 33140.

CAREER: Television performer, recording artist, and writer. Has performed with Bob Hope Christmas Tours, 1960-67, at White House functions, 1964-69, and with Billy Graham Evangelistic Crusades, 1965—. Actress in stage productions, including "Annie Get Your Gun," "Guys and Dolls," and "The Sound of Music." Performer on numerous recordings. Singer at conventions for Democratic and Republican parties, and at Super Bowl football games. Also appeared on numerous television shows and commercials. Commentator for National Broadcasting Co. (NBC-TV) during coverage of Orange Bowl parades. Spokeswoman for Coca-Cola Co., 1963-67, State of Florida Citrus Industry, 1968—, and Friedrich Air Conditioning Co., 1969—. Member of United States Organizations (USO) national council, 1961-66; member of board of Women's USO of New York. *Member:* American Orchid Society, Friends of Art Society, Project Survival (committee member), Florida Future Business Leaders of America, University of Tampa Alumni Association (honorary member).

AWARDS, HONORS: Named Miss Oklahoma and runner-up in Miss America contest, both 1959; 25th Anniversary Silver Medallion from United States Organizations, Gold Medal and citation from Veterans of Foreign Wars, and named to Oklahoma Hall of Fame, all 1966; nomination for Grammy Award from National Academy of Recording Arts and Sciences, 1968, for best religious recording of "How Great Thou Art"; Leadership Award from Freedoms Foundation at Valley Forge, 1969; Citizenship Gold Medal and citation from Veterans of Foreign Wars, 1978; named most admired woman in poll conducted by Good Housekeeping, and listed among top ten women in world in Gallup Poll, both 1977 and 1978; D.L., American Christian College; D.H.L., William Carey College; named one of the twenty-five most influential women in America by *World Almanac.*

WRITINGS—All under name Anita Bryant; all published by Revell, unless otherwise indicated: *Mine Eyes Have Seen the Glory* (autobiographical), 1970; *Amazing Grace* (autobiographical), 1971; *Bless This House* (inspirational), 1972; (with husband, Bob Green) *Fishers of Men* (inspirational), 1973; (with Green) *Light My Candle* (inspirational), 1974; *Bless This Food: The Anita Bryant Family Cookbook,* Doubleday, 1975; (with Green) *Running the Good Race* (inspirational), 1976; (with Green) *Raising God's Children* (inspirational), 1977; *The Anita Bryant Story: The Survival of Our Nation's Families and the Threat of Militant Homosexuality,* 1977; (with Green) *At Any Cost,* 1978.

WORK IN PROGRESS: A two hour "happening" for television; plans for a syndicated radio program entitled "The Anita Bryant Show"; plans for a weekly "musical/variety series" for television scheduled for 1980.

SIDELIGHTS: For years, Bryant has been a fixture in the entertainment world. Best known for her emotional and rousing versions of religious and patriotic songs, Bryant has performed on numerous television shows and toured many times with Bob Hope's troupe to entertain American soldiers overseas. She also gained prominence in the 1970's as a familiar performer in television orange juice commercials.

Bryant became the focus of national attention in 1977 when she made public her militant opposition to equal rights for homosexuals. In the spring of that year, Bryant began crusading throughout Dade County, Florida, urging the repeal of an ordinance that prohibited discrimination against homosexuals in employment and housing opportunities. She insisted that there was an imminent danger that homosexuals would obtain employment as teachers in public and private schools and encouraged local bureaucrats to put the repeal effort before voters in a special referendum. Bryant relied heavily on her wholesome Christian image to expand her following. She said that one reason she became so involved in the "gay rights" issue was because "God drew a circle and more or less asked me to step into it. . . ." But Bryant also feared for the safety of her own offspring, claiming that homosexuals "do much of their recruiting among children."

The repeal was eventually put on a special referendum in Dade County amid much publicity from both the local and national media. "We have created a national issue," declared a "gay rights" activist, "and we intend to stay with it." Bryant's detractors even found themselves counting the Dade County Democratic Party and the National Council of Churches among their allies, despite the fact that Bryant was insisting her beliefs were founded in religious fundamentals. "The Bible clearly says homosexuality is an abomination," she told reporters while citing the book of Leviticus as an example. The opposition retaliated by noting that the same book also prohibited shaving.

Meanwhile, Bryant was appearing at "Save Our Children" rallies held throughout Florida. The rallies brought in more money and people for her campaign. Finally, Bryant's efforts proved successful. The repeal was approved by the voters and Bryant celebrated: "The 'normal majority' have said, 'Enough! Enough! Enough!'" When informed of the outcome, she also remarked, "Tonight, the laws of God and the cultural values of men have been vindicated."

BIOGRAPHICAL/CRITICAL SOURCES: Anita Bryant, *Mine Eyes Have See the Glory,* Revell, 1970; Bryant, *Amazing Grace,* Revell, 1971; *Time,* May 2, 1977, June 13, 1977, June 20, 1977; *Newsweek,* June 5, 1977; *Ms.,* September, 1977.

*   *   *

GREEN, Ronald Michael 1942-

PERSONAL: Born December 16, 1942, in New York, N.Y.; son of Daniel David (in business) and Beatrice (a medical secretary; maiden name, Friedlander) Green; married Mary Jean Matthews (a college professor), June 25, 1965; children: Julie, Matthew. *Education:* Brown University, A.B. (summa cum laude), 1964; Harvard University, Ph.D., 1973. *Politics:* "Late 1960's radical turned Carter liberal." *Religion:* "Nominally Jewish." *Home address:* Sargent St., Norwich, Vt. 05055. *Office:* Department of Religion, Dartmouth College, Hanover, N.H. 03755.

CAREER: Dartmouth College, Hanover, N.H., instructor, 1969-73, assistant professor of religious ethics, 1973—. *Member:* American Academy of Religion, American Society for Political and Legal Philosophy, American Society of Christian Ethics, Society for Values in Higher Education. *Awards, honors:* Woodrow Wilson fellowship, 1964; Fulbright fellowship, 1965; Kent fellowship, 1965-69.

WRITINGS: *Population Growth and Justice,* Scholars' Press, 1975; *Religious Reason: The Rational and Moral Basis of Religious Belief,* Oxford University Press, 1978.

WORK IN PROGRESS: An extension of the theory proposed in *Religious Reason* to additional religious traditions, notably Islam and the religions of non-literate cultures.

SIDELIGHTS: Green writes: "As a student of religion and ethics, I have been privileged to witness the revolution in theory that, in the last decade, has made ethics a science and has helped us justify some key moral principles and judgments. Early on, however, I became convinced that this success in justifying principles actually made it harder to answer the personal question 'Why should I be moral?' Efforts to answer this question took me back to the philosophy of religion, to the work of Immanuel Kant, and to traditional religious belief. The result is my recent book and, I think, a very modern effort to demonstrate the rational intelligibility, even necessity, of religious belief as the basis of sustained moral commitment."

*   *   *

GREEN, William A., Jr. 1935-

PERSONAL: Born May 28, 1935, in Atlantic City, N.J.; son of William A. (a teacher) and June R. (Myers) Green; married wife, Karin Elizabeth (a psychologist), June 1, 1957; children: William, Kathryn, Jacqueline, Eric, Christopher. *Education:* University of Delaware, B.A., 1957; Harvard University, M.A., 1958, Ph.D., 1962. *Home:* 46 Walnut St., Holden, Mass. 01520. *Office:* Department of History, College of the Holy Cross, Worcester, Mass. 01610.

CAREER: Fresno State College, Fresno, Calif., assistant professor of history, 1963-64; College of the Holy Cross, Worcester, Mass., assistant professor, 1964-69, associate professor, 1969-75, professor of history, 1975—. *Military service:* U.S. Army, 1961-63; became captain. *Member:* American Historical Association, Conference on British Studies, Economic History Society, New England Historical Association, Phi Beta Kappa. *Awards, honors:* Ford-Batchelor fellowship from Holy Cross College, 1970; National Endowment for the Humanities fellow, summer, 1972; American Philosophical Society fellow, 1977; Rockefeller Foundation fellow, 1977-78; research fellow at University of London, 1977-78.

WRITINGS: British Slave Emancipation: The Sugar Colonies and the Great Experiment, 1830-1865, Clarendon Press, 1976. Contributor to history journals.

WORK IN PROGRESS: Europe, the Atlantic, and the Slave Trade, 1400-1800.

BIOGRAPHICAL/CRITICAL SOURCES: Times Literary Supplement, December 10, 1976; *American Historical Review,* April, 1977; *English Historical Review,* July, 1977.

*   *   *

GREENBERG, Ivan 1908-1973
(Philip Rahv)

PERSONAL: Birth-given name Ivan Greenberg; took the name Philip Rahv when he became a Communist; born March 10, 1908 in Kupin, Ukraine, Russia (now U.S.S.R.); came to the United States in 1922; died December 23, 1973, in Cambridge, Mass.; married Nathalie Swan (an architect), 1941 (marriage ended); married wife Theo (deceased); married again. *Education:* Attended high school in Providence, R.I. *Residence:* New York, N.Y.

CAREER: Editor and literary critic. Founding co-editor of *Partisan Review,* 1934-69; founding editor of *Modern Occasions,* 1970. Professor of English at Brandeis University, Waltham, Mass., 1957-73; taught at Adult Extension of New York University; senior fellow at Indiana University. *Awards, honors:* Guggenheim fellowship in criticism, 1950.

*WRITINGS—*All under name, Philip Rahv; criticism: *Image and Idea: Fourteen Essays on Literary Themes,* New Directions, 1949, revised and enlarged edition published as *Image and Idea: Twenty Essays on Literary Themes,* J. Laughlin (Norfolk, Conn.), 1957 (also see below); *The Myth and the Powerhouse,* Farrar, Straus, 1965 (also see below); *Literature and the Sixth Sense,* (includes *Image and Idea* and *The Myth and the Powerhouse*), Houghton, 1969; *Essays on Literature and Politics 1932-1972* (includes previously published and unpublished essays), edited by Arabel J. Porter and Andrew J. Dvosin, with a memoir by Mary McCarthy, Houghton, 1978.

Editor: *The Great Short Novels of Henry James,* Dial, 1944; Henry James, *The Bostonians,* Dial, 1945; Leo Tolstoy, *The Short Novels of Tolstoy,* Dial, 1946; (with William Phillips) *The Partisan Reader: Ten Years of the Partisan Review, 1934-1944,* Dial, 1946; *Discovery of Europe: The Story of American Experience in the Old World,* Houghton, 1947, revised edition, Doubleday, 1960; *Great Russian Short Novels,* Dial, 1951; (with Phillips) *The New Partisan Reader, 1945-1953,* Harcourt, 1953; (with Phillips) *The Avon Book of Modern Writing,* two volumes, Avon, 1953; (with Phillips) *The Berkley Book of Modern Writing,* Berkley, 1953; *Literature in America: An Anthology of Literary Criticism,* Meridian Books, 1958; *The Partisan Review Anthology,* Holt, 1962; *Eight Great American Short Novels,* Berkley, 1963; *Modern Occasions,* Farrar, Straus, 1965; Bernard Malamud, *Malamud Reader,* Farrar, Straus, 1967.

Contributor to periodicals, including *Nation, New Republic, New Masses, New Leader,* and *Southern Review.*

SIDELIGHTS: For thirty-five years Philip Rahv was the co-editor of *Partisan Review,* the prestigious journal T. S. Eliot once called "America's leading literary magazine." Rahv's influence on American literature was enormous and the majority of his literary criticism remains fresh and perceptive. Rahv was a complex man, but his most identifiable feature was his passion and respect for ideas. Mary McCarthy, a former colleague and friend, in a memoir written shortly after his death, recalled Rahv as "a powerful intellect, a massive, overpowering personality and yet shy, curious, susceptible, confiding." Alfred Kazin commented: "Though Rahv was inherently one of the narrowest men I knew, he was vividly authentic and stimulating as a critic of literature in society. . . . Literature for him came out of social tension, and to social tension it had to contribute—and Rahv's ideal aim was to add to it." The writer Delmore Schwartz punned that Rahv was a "manic impressive." Above all, Rahv remained a champion of literary and artistic modernism, even though towards the end of his life that was an unfashionable position.

Rahv was born in Russia, but left the country at an early age after the civil war. He immigrated with his family to Palestine. In 1922, he left, alone, to live with a brother in Providence, Rhode Island. He started his career as a junior advertising copywriter in Oregon, but during the Depression he moved to New York City. There, in the early 1930's, Rahv began to contribute criticism to such highly regarded leftist magazines as *Nation, New Masses, New Leader,* and *New Republic.*

Rahv joined the Communist party-affiliated John Reed Club in 1933, and the following year he and William Phillips convinced the editor of *New Masses* that the party needed a literary counterpart to its political magazine. *Partisan Review* began publication as an organ of the John Reed Club. However, in 1936, when the Moscow trials uncovered the terrors of Stalinism, Rahv broke with the party and the magazine disassociated itself from the club. It suspended publication for a few months, but resumed publication in 1937 with a new staff and a revised editorial policy. The list of contributors to the first issue of the new *Partisan Review* reads as a roster of many of the most important literary and artistic figures of the post-war generation. Included were works by Delmore Schwartz, James Agee, Edmund Wilson, James T. Farrell, Dwight Macdonald, Mary McCarthy, Sidney Hook, Lionel Trilling, Wallace Stevens, Pablo Picasso, and Rahv himself. Rahv dubbed the group, "The Truants." Others identified them collectively as "New York Intellectuals," "Old Left," or "The Family."

Although Rahv had broken with Stalin, Marxism remained influential to him both as a critic and as the formulator of *Partisan Review's* editorial policies. Rahv, commenting on the magazine's political reorientation, wrote that the staff's "own politics at the time might be summed up as a kind of independent and critical Marxism: independent of all party organizations and programs, and critical insofar as we were inclined to re-examine the entire course of socialism in order to understand its present plight. It goes without saying that we were intransigently anti-Stalinist."

In its heyday in the forties and fifties *Partisan Review* was a significant force in the development of American culture. The magazine provided a forum for intellectual debate and actively cultivated an audience for modernism. Many of the country's leading writers were frequent contributors, including Elizabeth Bishop, Randall Jarrell, Karl Shapiro, Robert Lowell, Eleanor Clark, Isaac Rosenfeld, Jean Stafford, and Saul Bellow. Frederick Crews wrote that there was "not only a recognizable *Partisan* style—wide-ranging, cutting, self-assured—but also a *Partisan* world view." He continued, "It was a complex of attitudes and positions derived in part from the debacle of the American left, in part from the concurrence of separatist and assimilationist impulses within the so-called 'New York Family,' and in part from the personality of Philip Rahv, by all accounts the ruling figure of *Partisan* during its most influential period."

That Philip Rahv was the cornerstone of *Partisan Review* is undisputed. Mark Shechner has written that Rahv sacrificed his own reputation as a writer in order to foster and promote the talents of other writers. Bellow, Jarrell, John Berryman, Bernard Malamud, and Elizabeth Hardwick were a few of Rahv's finds. "Discovering and promoting talent *was* his career," Shechner wrote. Rahv was known as an excellent editor and copy editor as well. "Philip's gifts as an editor were really those of a certain conservatism," remarked William Barrett, who was on the magazine's editorial staff for a time. "By this I don't mean any conservative ideology, but a certain conservatism of temperament. He had started out slowly and laboriously, a world for himself, and he wanted the magazine to live within it with him."

Rahv roughly divided his thirty-five year association with *Partisan Review* into three eras: what he termed the "socially oriented thirties," the "fundamentally conservative forties and fifties," and the "swinging sixties," which Rahv wrote at the end of his career, "is still with us." But throughout the cultural, political, social, and intellectual turbulence of these years, Rahv's voice remained constant. He was unwavering in his defense of modernism and in his denunciation of faddish literary trends. McCarthy wrote that for Rahv, "literature began with Dostoevsky and stopped with

Joyce, Proust, and Eliot; politics began with Marx and Engels and ended with Lenin."

McCarthy has written that Rahv played a critical part in the direction the nation's "intellectual life" would take at least three times: the first, when he and Phillips disaffiliated themselves and the magazine from the Communist party; the second, when he came out in favor of American radicals supporting the war against Hitler; and finally, when Rahv denounced Senator McCarthy while others in his circle were equivocating or actually supporting him.

Ideas were of paramount importance to Rahv. (McCarthy recalled in her memoir: "He was very much attached to the word 'ideas.' 'He has no *ideas*,' he would declare, discussing some literary claimant; to be void of ideas was, for him, the worst disaster that could befall an individual.") But while Rahv was concerned with ideas, he was decidedly non-ideological and practiced an intellectual ecclecticism that served him well.

In a review of *Image and Idea,* an early collection of Rahv's criticism, Richard Chase declared: "And what one admires most about Rahv's critical method is his abundant ability to use such techniques as Marxism, Freudian psychology, anthropology, and existentialism toward his critical ends without shackling himself to any of them. . . . Rahv is above all a political critic, in the sense that his criticism takes literature to be involved in the upshot of history and the practical transactions of men and public ideas. His skill in handling a complex criticism, which is only infrequently allowed to vanish away into the rigidities of a narrow technique, places these essays among the very best written by the leftist critics of the 1940's." Barrett stated that Rahv's understanding of the role of the critic allows him to wish to "establish some judgment that, even if it does not claim to be definitive, nevertheless marks out a path along which he wants to lead his readers. And it is because Rahv was so conscious of his public role, I think, that he has the critical virtues he does: his ability, at his best, was to bring together conflicting claims and strike some sort of judicious, sometimes even judicial, balance between them."

Abstraction was particularly alien to Rahv, according to many commentators. Barrett wrote: "The 'ideas' that concerned Philip were always concrete and intuitive, usually dramatic or colorful simplifications of already known but diffuse literary or political perceptions. He had little liking and in fact very little capacity for abstract ideas as such. This was a weakness, however which he turned into a strength, for it kept his feet on the ground and his mind attuned to the concrete."

An awareness of history (the "sixth sense" that Nietzsche found to be characteristic of the modern world) shaped Rahv's ideas and literary judgments, as he himself acknowledged. He titled a collection of his essays *Literature and the Sixth Sense,* and wrote that he "was struck . . . by the way in which my own strong interest in historical reason has in the long run affected my literary attitudes and judgments." If literature existed in a historical continuum, Rahv believed that he, as a critic, should play an active part in its evolvement. He described himself as "a prospective rather than retrospective critic," and defined the former as one who "conceives of literature as something and alive in his own time and relates himself to it by trying to affect its course of development here and now."

Rahv attributed most of his historical awareness to his early Marxist training. Although he broke with the Communist party line, he allowed, "I have nonetheless retained from

[Marxism] a certain approach, a measure of social and intellectual commitment and, I make bold to say, a certain kind of realism, not untouched with hope and expectancy, in my own outlook on society and the human potential as articulated in the constructs of the imagination."

"Rahv's sixth sense," reviewer John P. Sisk remarked, "has functioned since the mid-30's as a distant early warning system against the false promises of ideology—ideology understood as a natural enemy of historical insight. He has had the good fortune of discovering early in life that the ideologue's inevitable impulse in the presence of literature is to use it in the service of a 'higher cause.'" Frank Kermode made a similar assessment of Rahv's work. "His criticism has strength rather than ingenuity," he commented, "eloquence rather than wit. He mimics nobody, preferring his own voice with its certainty of timbre and its dynamic range (loud but controlled in polemic). . . . Apart from everything else, it was no small achievement to go on doing unfashionable things, to follow one's own road, when American criticism, for virtually a generation, was headed in quite a different direction. It called for sobriety and patience, for a sense of vocation and a sense of history."

And Rahv was often in opposition to the nation's critical consensus. In the forties and fifties when "New Criticism" was the rage in academic and literary circles, Rahv held his ground. This formalist, traditionalist school of criticism was decidedly ahistorical with its emphasis on myth and textual exegisis. In a well known essay, "The Myth and the Powerhouse," Rahv blasted the New Critics for being intimidated by history and cited their "reactionary inability to face the 'powerhouse' of social change." What he called the "swinging sixties" also revolted Rahv. "[Its] spokesman retain nothing more than the cultish mannerisms of the classic avant-garde," he complained. "They ape its dissidence and revolt while actually constituting themselves as a veritable academy, and a ruling academy at that, fawned upon in the most respectable quarters even as it turns out art objects as consumer goods."

According to several colleagues, Rahv always felt himself to be apart from the American experience. Nonetheless (or perhaps because of this alienation), he had keen insight into the nation's literature. Denis Donoghue declared that Rahv's criticism of American literature "amounted to a morality." He wrote, "He read the American novelists in the hope of discovering what forms American experience had taken and what forms it might still take. Whitman, James, and Hawthorne were indeed writers, but they were important to Rahv as indicating producible forms of experience, and at the same time for the price each of them paid for his characteristic form in its limitation or its exorbitance."

In "Paleface and Redskin," an early (1939) and still well-known essay, Rahv announced the "dichotomy between experience and consciousness" in American literature and divided authors into two distinct categories. The cultivated gentility of the "paleface" authors such as Hawthorne and Henry James was the opposite of the realism and anti-intellectualism of Cooper, Whitman, Dreiser, and other "redskins." Rahv argued that American writers were crippled by choosing one mode of expression over the other. The resulting literature was "fragmented" and "one-sided" and lacked the complexity and resonance of European literature. Thus, the isolationism of the "palefaces" and the exultation of experience of the "redskins" was equally damaging to their writing. Although Henry James was a long-time favorite author of Rahv's (he had been instrumental in the James revival) Rahv, near the end of his career, finally admitted

that James's overriding concern with consciousness was too narrow a perspective.

"Upon such a criticism of the American mind," Mark Shechner wrote, "Rahv founded the mission of *Partisan Review* to impart the experience and thought of Europe into the American consciousness, thereby enriching it and bringing it up to date." Rahv was responsible for introducing several European modernists to the United States. His essay on Kafka was one of the first on the writer to be published in this country. But he particularly loved the Russian writers Tolstoy and Dostoevsky. He wrote five essays on Dostoevsky in the course of his career and was working on a book about him at the time of his death. Shechner commented that Dostoevsky was so attractive to Rahv because he was the quintessential modernist and because his characters were so possessed by ideas. In his essays, Shechner noted, Rahv comes close to "if not defining himself through the novelist at least announcing an intellectual agenda for himself by examining what a life of ideas, pressed to its limits, might sound like." And Rahv praised Dostoevsky, Shechner wrote, "in terms that sounded like a veiled self-appraisal: 'The fact is that it is not in the construction of harmonies but in the uncovering of antimonies that his genius found its deeper expression.'"

The recently published collection, *Essays on Literature and Politics,* includes some of Rahv's most powerful early work and some previously uncollected essays. The latter essays are disappointing, according to many critics. "Set alongside Rahv's vigorous writing of earlier years they sound donnish and impersonal: the mastery of idiom has grown slack and the prose turned fussy and verbose as his classic muscularity of phrasing has faded into dreamy expositions punctuated by long-winded attacks on other critics." "Still," John Leonard wrote, "some Rahv is better than none. He must have been lonely at the end, estranged as much from the conservatism of *Commentary* magazine as from the new 'swinging' *Partisan Review* and disdainful of an age of what he called 'that orgastic self-glorification that you may find in our hipster writers who make do with the self (the ravenous, raging self of erotic fantasy and adolescent daydreams of power) when talent and moral intelligence failed them.'"

For Rahv was a man with "moral intelligence," and 'if his field of vision was sometimes narrow and his ideas occasionally derivative, most would agree with Donoghue's assessment: "On his chosen theme, which was more fated than chosen, his criticism has the grandeur, warmth and eloquence which make it a form of literature in its own right."

BIOGRAPHICAL/CRITICAL SOURCES: Commentary, July 22, 1949, April, 1970, June, 1974, May, 1979; *Nation,* July 23, 1949, November 8, 1965, November 11, 1978, November 18, 1978; *New York Times,* August 14, 1949, November 23, 1978; *New Republic,* September 26, 1949, November 29, 1969, December 2, 1978; *New York Review of Books,* December 9, 1965, July 12, 1970, November 23, 1978; Alfred Kazin, *Starting Out in the Thirties,* Little, Brown, 1965; *Observer,* March 12, 1967; *Times Literary Supplement,* March 16, 1967, September 24, 1971; *Listener,* March 23, 1967; *Cambridge Review,* May 7, 1971; *New York Times Book Review,* February 17, 1974; *Washington Post Book World,* January 7, 1979.

Obituaries: *New York Times,* December 24, 1973; *Newsweek,* January 7, 1974; *Time,* January 7, 1974; *Publishers Weekly,* January 21, 1974.*

GREENBERG, Polly 1932-

PERSONAL: Born April 21, 1932, in Milwaukee, Wis.; daughter of Lindsay (vice-president and editor-in-chief of *Milwaukee Journal*) and Margaret (an educator; maiden name, Pollitzer) Hoben; married Daniel S. Greenberg (a writer and editor), June, 1953 (divorced, 1964); children: Julie, Margaret, Cathryn, Ellen Elizabeth, Gwen. *Education:* Sarah Lawrence College, B.A., 1954; University of Delaware, M.Ed., 1957; further graduate study at University of Massachusetts. *Politics:* "Active grassrootist." *Religion:* "Ecumenical existential humanist." *Home:* 4914 Ashby St., Washington, D.C. 20007.

CAREER: Worked as an elementary school teacher in Maryland; employed by the U.S. Office of Education, 1963-64, Office of Economic Opportunity, 1964-65, Child Development Group of Mississippi, 1965-67, General Learning Corp., 1968-74, and Human Service Group, 1974-76; U.S. Department of Health, Education & Welfare, Office of Human Development Services, Washington, D.C., staff member, 1977—. Volunteer work includes counseling delinquent boys and teaching learning-disabled children and their parents. Public speaker; consultant.

WRITINGS: The Devil Has Slippery Shoes, Macmillan, 1969; *Oh, Lord, I Wish I Was a Buzzard* (juvenile), Macmillan, 1969; *Bridge-to-Reading: Comprehensive Early Childhood Curriculum,* Silver Burdett, 1973; *Day Care Do-It-Yourself Staff Growth Program,* Kaplan Press, 1975; *How To Convert the Kids From What They Eat To What They Oughta,* Kaplan Press, 1978; *Changes and Challenges: Our Children's Future,* Pergamon, 1979. Contributor to professional journals. Editor of *Dimensions,* 1974-76.

WORK IN PROGRESS: How to Be a Better Single Parent; Creative Coping: Single Parenting With Five Daughters, Two Careers, and a Serious Cash Flow Problem, an autobiography; a novel; a book "about peace, freedom, and love"; a book of short stories; four juvenile books.

SIDELIGHTS: Polly Greenberg comments: "I love to write because I have lots to say. I used to be crazy about working all the time; now I get enormous pleasure out of writing as a hobby, even if it is published.

"Over the past few years, however, I find it increasingly frustrating that publishing has become so commercialized and industrialized. An author has to write a 'proposal' almost as long as the book itself in order to get a manuscript read by an editor. Rules about length and other detail have come to outweigh public demand. And it is as time-consuming to 'sell' a manuscript to an agent as it is to sell it directly to a publisher.

"Because of all this, I tend to write, finish, and file books, not bothering with the incredible hassle and expense of marketing manuscripts or story ideas.

"The greatest frustration of all is getting my writing time funded up to the level of my family needs right now. When all my daughters are through college, I hope to buy a mountain farm, write at least three-quarters of the year, revel in nature, read novels, bask in my extended family, take care of my pets, and do challenging other jobs one-quarter of the year anywhere on earth.

"My passionate current interest is public policy pertaining to creating and assisting humane beings. I also want to write fiction."

AVOCATIONAL INTERESTS: Pets, nature, novels, travel, civic activities.

GREENBURGER, Francis 1949-

PERSONAL: Born February 13, 1949, in New York; son of Sanford Jerome (a literary agent) and Ingrid (Gruttefein) Greenburger. *Education:* Bernard M. Baruch College of the City University of New York, B.A., 1974. *Home:* 45 East 22nd St., New York, N.Y. 10010. *Office:* Sanford J. Greenburger Associates, Inc., 825 Third Ave., New York, N.Y. 10022.

CAREER: Sanford J. Greenburger Associates, Inc., New York, N.Y., literary agent and president, 1971—. President of Time Equities, Inc. (real estate firm), 1966—. *Member:* National Arts Club.

WRITINGS: (With Thomas Kiernan) *How to Ask for More and Get It: The Art of Creative Negotiation,* Doubleday, 1978.

SIDELIGHTS: Greenburger writes: "I enjoy working in fields where human ideas or circumstances can be developed and improved. I have applied my business acumen to two fields where I can derive great satisfaction from influencing diverse areas of human concern: housing and literature."

*   *   *

GREENLEAF, Peter 1910-

PERSONAL: Born July 29, 1910, in Brooklyn, N.Y.; son of Zelig and Tema (Uryash) Greenleaf; married Anne Schmukler, December 25, 1937; children: Eric, Tema L. Greenleaf Harnik. *Education:* New York University, B.A., 1931, M.A., 1939. *Home:* 13913-C Royal Palm Court, Palm Greens, Delray Beach, Fla. 33444 (winters); and Shunpike Rd., Sheffield, Mass. 01257 (summers).

CAREER: Board of Education, New York, N.Y., science teacher and department head in public schools, 1942-55, supervisor of audio-visual instruction and science specialist, 1950-72; writer, 1972—. Adjunct professor at Brooklyn College of the City University of New York, 1950-76; adjunct associate professor of astronomy at St. John's University. Film consultant. *Member:* Joint Association of Supervisors of the New York City Board of Education (president, 1968-69), New York Academy of Sciences, Science Council of New York City, Schoolmasters Club.

WRITINGS: Investigating Science (junior high school texts), three volumes, Random House, 1966; (with Paul Kahn and Sune Englebrectsen) *Exploring Outer Space,* Arco, 1972; (with Elliott Blaustein and Rose Blaustein) *Experiences in Science,* Globe Book Co., 1974; (with Blaustein and Blaustein) *Your Environment and You,* Oceania, junior high school edition, 1974, high school edition, 1978; (editor with M. N. Idelson and Joseph M. Oxenhorn) *Pathways to Science* (junior high school text), three volumes, Globe Book Co., 1975; (with Blaustein and Blaustein) *Insights Into Science,* Globe Book Co., 1977.

WORK IN PROGRESS: Revision of *Pathways of Science;* a laboratory manual for fifth and sixth grade science classes for Torres Book Co.

SIDELIGHTS: Greenleaf writes: "Our major objective in our science texts is to inculcate in children 'scientific literacy' so that the future of our democratic form of government will not be endangered, as it depends on informed judgments by the lay public. Our motto is 'Science without fears.' Therefore, our science texts are written with familiar faces, familiar places and without distorting the concepts of science, simple enough for all to understand."

GRIEVE, C(hristopher) M(urray)   1892-1978
(Isobel Guthrie, A. K. Laidlaw, Hugh
MacDiarmid, James MacLaren, Pteleon)

OBITUARY NOTICE—See index for *CA* sketch: Born August 11, 1892, in Langholm, Dumfriesshire, Scotland; died September 9, 1978, in Edinburgh, Scotland. Writer best known for his poetry written under pseudonym Hugh MacDiarmid. Grieve is considered by some critics to be the finest poet Scotland has produced since Robert Burns. His poetic style changed in many ways throughout his career: he began writing in English but later switched to Scots, his certainty was replaced by inquisitiveness, and his accessible lyricism gave way to an eclectic style that provoked comparisons with Joyce. Grieve also edited and translated many works. Obituaries and other sources: *The New Century Handbook of English Literature,* revised edition, Appleton, 1967; *Longman Companion to Twentieth Century Literature,* Longman, 1970; *The Author's and Writer's Who's Who,* 6th edition, Burke's Peerage, 1971; *Cassell's Encyclopaedia of World Literature,* revised edition, Morrow, 1973; *Contemporary Poets,* 2nd edition, St. Martin's, 1975.

*   *   *

GRIFFITHS, (Thomas) Mel(vin)   1910-

PERSONAL: Born September 6, 1910, in Wyandotte, Okla.; son of Arthur H. (a veterinarian) and Clara L. (George) Griffiths; married Rose Barbara Hitchings, May 7, 1942; children: Thomas David, Arthur Melvin. *Education:* Attended Sacramento Junior College, 1932-33, and George Washington University, 1942; University of Denver, A.B., 1947, M.A., 1948; Northwestern University, Ph.D., 1953. *Home:* 498 South Krameria St., Denver, Colo. 80224. *Office:* Department of Geography, University of Denver, Denver, Colo. 80208.

CAREER: University of Denver, Denver, Colo., instructor, 1950-51, assistant professor, 1951-58, associate professor, 1958-64, professor of geography, 1964-78, professor emeritus, 1978—, head of department, 1965-73. Consultant to legal firms trying cases before Indian Claims Commission. *Military service:* U.S. Army Air Forces, 1941-46; became captain. *Member:* Association of American Geographers, Royal Geographical Society (fellow), Westerners, Phi Beta Kappa, Sigma Xi, Explorers Club, Teknik Club. *Awards, honors:* National Science Foundation fellow at University of Stockholm, 1959-60.

WRITINGS: (Contributor) *America the Beautiful,* illustrations by John Pimlott, Reader's Digest Press, 1970; *San Juan Country,* Pruett, 1979; (with Lynell Rubright) *Colorado: A Geography,* Westview Press, 1979. Contributor to *Encyclopaedia Britannica.* Contributor to popular magazines, including *Natural History, Popular Mechanics,* and *Westways.*

SIDELIGHTS: Griffiths writes: "Academic training and field studies have brought me a unique understanding of the natural environment and man's relationship to it. All of my teaching and a large part of my popular writing has concentrated on giving my students, readers, and audiences a better understanding of the man-land symbiosis which has controlled man's short tenure on earth. Field work has taken me to such diverse environments as the Amazon rainforest, the Alto Plano of Mexico, sub-tropical Brazil, the Greenland icecap, the Sinai desert, the Dead Sea depression, North Cape, the Simpson Desert of central Australia, the Malay Peninsula, the summit of Alaska's Mount McKinley, and a good many thousand square miles between. I am drawing upon this storage bank of past experiences for the writing and consulting which comprises most of my current work load."

*   *   *

GRINDEL, Carl W(illiam)   1905-

PERSONAL: Born March 21, 1905, in Staten Island, N.Y.; son of Gustav W. and Catherine E. (Larkin) Grindel. *Education:* St. Joseph's College, Princeton, N.J., B.A., 1925, M.A., 1930; University of St. Tommaso, Ph.L., 1931, Ph.D., 1932. *Politics:* Independent. *Office:* Department of Philosophy, St. John's University, Jamaica, N.Y. 11439.

CAREER: Entered Congregation of the Mission (Vincentians), 1925, ordained Roman Catholic priest, 1930; St. Joseph's College, Princeton, N.J., professor of philosophy, 1932-35; St. John's University, Jamaica, N.Y., professor of philosophy, 1932-70, professor emeritus, 1970—, head of department, 1957-65. Consultant to Institute for the Advancement of Study in Catholic Doctrine. *Member:* Societe Internationale pour l'Etude de la Philosophie Medievale, American Philosophical Association, American Catholic Philosophical Association (president, 1961-62), Metaphysical Society of America. *Awards, honors:* Freedoms Foundation award, 1954.

WRITINGS: (Editor and contributor) *Concept of Freedom,* Regnery, 1955; (contributor) *Philosophy in a Technological Culture,* Catholic University Press, 1963; (editor) *God, Man, and Philosophy,* St. John's University Press, 1971. Author of proceedings of the Fifth International Thomistic Congress, 1960, and of the Thirteenth International Philosophy Congress, 1963.

WORK IN PROGRESS: Translation of works by R. P. Cornelio Fabro.

*   *   *

GROENBJERG, Kirsten A(ndersen)   1946-

PERSONAL: Born February 8, 1946, in Soenderborg, Denmark; came to the United States in 1965; daughter of Jens R. M. (a teacher) and Christine (Andersen) Groenbjerg; married Gerald D. Suttles (a professor of sociology), July 20, 1970. *Education:* Pitzer College, B.A., 1968; University of Chicago, M.A., 1971, Ph.D., 1974. *Office:* Department of Sociology, Loyola University, 6525 North Sheridan, Chicago, Ill. 60626.

CAREER: Hofstra University, Hempstead, N.Y., lecturer in sociology, 1971-73; State University of New York at Stony Brook, lecturer, 1973-74, assistant professor of sociology, 1974-76; Loyola University, Chicago, Ill., assistant professor, 1976-78, associate professor of sociology, 1978—. *Member:* International Sociological Association, American Sociological Association, American Public Welfare Association, American Political Science Association, Population Society of America, Midwest Sociological Association.

WRITINGS: Mass Society and the Extension of Welfare, 1969-70, University of Chicago Press, 1977; (with David Street and husband, Gerald Suttles) *Poverty and Social Change,* University of Chicago Press, 1978. Contributor to *Journal of Applied Social Sciences.*

WORK IN PROGRESS: The Interface Between Public and Private Welfare Systems in the United States.

SIDELIGHTS: Kirsten Groenbjerg writes: "The contrast between growing up in a welfare state (Denmark) and the controversies surrounding public welfare in the United

States has been the central issue behind my interest in welfare systems.''

* * *

GROH, George W. 1922-

PERSONAL: Born March 23, 1922, in Emporia, Kan.; son of George S. (a roofer) and Dorothy Groh; married Lynn Snowden (a newspaper reporter), December 22, 1950; children: Nancy, Barbara, Ellen. *Education:* College of Emporia, B.A., 1941; University of Missouri, B.J., 1946. *Politics:* Independent Democrat. *Home:* 30 Cooper Lane, Larchmont, N.Y. 10538. *Agent:* Jo Stewart, 201 East 66th St., New York, N.Y. 10021. *Office: MD,* 30 East 60th St., New York, N.Y.

CAREER: Corpus Christi Caller-Times, Corpus Christi, Tex., reporter, 1948-50; *Milwaukee Journal,* Milwaukee, Wis., reporter, 1950-52; free-lance writer in New York City, 1953-54; *MD* (magazine), New York City, senior staff writer, 1956—. *Military service:* U.S. Army, Glider Infantry, 1943-45; received Bronze Star and Purple Heart. *Awards, honors:* Western Heritage Award from National Cowboy Hall of Fame, 1966, for *Gold Fever.*

WRITINGS: Gold Fever (nonfiction) Morrow, 1966; *Black Migration,* Weybright, 1972. Contributor of about four hundred articles to magazines.

SIDELIGHTS: Groh comments: ''I grew up curious about the world, and was lucky enough to make curiosity my livelihood. My chief interests are history, biography, natural history, and science.''

* * *

GROOM, Winston 1943-

PERSONAL: Born March 23, 1943, in Washington, D.C.; son of Winston Francis (an attorney) and Ruth (Knudsen) Groom; married Ruth Noble, 1969 (divorced, 1974). *Education:* University of Alabama, A.B., 1965. *Agent:* Theron Raines, Raines & Raines, 475 Fifth Ave., New York, N.Y. 10017.

CAREER: Washington Star, Washington, D.C., staff writer, 1967-76; free-lance writer, 1976—. *Military service:* U.S. Army, 1965-67; served in Vietnam; became captain. *Member:* Authors Guild.

WRITINGS: Better Times Than These (novel), Summit Books, 1978.

WORK IN PROGRESS: A novel set on the southern coast of the Gulf of Mexico; a collection of stories.

SIDELIGHTS: Groom told *CA:* ''I tend to think of my writing as more traditional, in the sense that I want to tell a good story first, and any meanings assigned to it by anyone are pretty much incidental. Like most writers, I write about what I see and feel about the human race in the hope that it might help them understand their lives a little better.''

BIOGRAPHICAL/CRITICAL SOURCES: New York Times, June 28, 1978; *New York Times Book Review,* July 9, 1978; *People,* September 18, 1978.

* * *

GRYLLS, David (Stanway) 1947-

PERSONAL: Born February 19, 1947, in Newark, Nottinghamshire, England; son of Herman Francis (a headmaster) and Muriel (a matron at a home for the elderly; maiden name, Butler) Grylls. *Education:* Hendon College of Technology, B.A. (first class honors), 1969; King's College,

London, Ph.D., 1973. *Politics:* Labour. *Religion:* Atheist. *Home:* 5-A Redbourne Ave., London N3 2BA, England. *Office:* Department of Humanities, Middlesex Polytechnic, Hendon, London N4 4BT, England.

CAREER: Middlesex Polytechnic, London, England, lecturer, 1973-78, senior lecturer in English and American literature, 1978—.

WRITINGS: Guardians and Angels: Parents and Children in Nineteenth-Century Literature, Faber, 1978.

WORK IN PROGRESS: A book on nineteenth-century novelist George Gissing, publication expected in 1981.

SIDELIGHTS: Grylls writes: ''My first book was a combination of literary criticism and social history; it took me five years to write. I wrote the book because I wanted to correct certain stereotyped notions about the Victorian family. Likewise with my second book: I think George Gissing is unfairly neglected and I want to alter the received view of his work.

''As regards literary criticism in general, I suppose I have two main areas of interest. I'm interested in the social application of literature, but by this I don't mean going to literature to see how people in the past behaved. I believe such a method is unreliable. What I think a social historian may do, if he wants to turn to literature to supplement his findings, is treat it as a source of attitudes and values—how people thought and felt and made judgments, rather than what they did. This approach requires greater critical subtlety, but I think its results are more likely to be useful. My second main area of interest is the theoretical basis of literary criticism. A great deal, of course, has been written on this but there's still plenty of room for improvement.

''Among the contemporary writers I admire are Philip Larkin (poetry), Karl Popper (philosophy), Alison Lurie (fiction), and John Carey (criticism).''

Guardians and Angels was praised by Nicholas Tucker for presenting ''an excellent case for the 19th century as a time of really profound change in attitudes towards children,'' although he felt Grylls may have over-estimated the ''philosophical theory and baby-care advice'' found in the literature on which he based his conclusions.

BIOGRAPHICAL/CRITICAL SOURCES: New Society, May 25, 1978; *New Statesman,* June 9, 1978.

* * *

GUERNEY, Bernard Guilbert 1894-1979

OBITUARY NOTICE: Born in 1894 in Nicolaiev, Russia (now U.S.S.R.); died March 30, 1979, in State College, Pa. Book store proprietor, editor, and translator. Guerney operated the Blue Fawn bookstore in New York City since the 1920's. He was best known for his *Treasury of Russian Literature,* which included translations of works by Pushkin, Gogol, Tolstoy, and others. Obituaries and other sources: *New York Times,* April 2, 1979; *Publishers Weekly,* April 16, 1979.

* * *

GUSTAFSSON, Lars 1936-

PERSONAL: Born May 17, 1936, in Vasteraas, Sweden; son of Einar H. (a merchant) and Margareta (Carlsson) Gustafsson; married Madeleine Lagerberg (a literary critic), February 24, 1962; children: Joen, Lotten Marianne. *Education:* University of Uppsala, D.Phil., 1961. *Home:* Blaasbogatan 8, 72215 Vasteraas, Sweden.

CAREER: *Bonniers* (literary magazine), Stockholm, Sweden, editor-in-chief, 1961-72; free-lance writer, 1972—. Thord Gray Professor at University of Texas, 1979. Member of Akademie der Wissenschaften und der Literatur, 1971, and Akademie der Kuenste, 1973. Member of Swedish Copyright Law Commission.

WRITINGS—In English: *The Public Dialogue in Sweden: Current Issues of Social, Esthetic, and Moral Debate,* translated by Claude Stephenson, Norstedt, 1964; *Selected Poems,* translated by Robin Fulton, New Rivers Press, 1972; *Warm Rooms and Cold,* translated by Yvonne L. Sandstroem, Copper Beech Press, 1975; *Forays Into Swedish Poetry,* translated by Robert Rovinsky, University of Texas Press, 1978.

In Swedish: *Virtus politica: Politisk etik och nationellt svaermeri i den tidigare stormaktstidens litteratur,* Almqvist & Wiksells, 1956; *Jaerfaellaboken,* Jaerfaella kommunalfullmaektige, 1957; *Vaegvila: Ett mysteriespel paa prosa,* Siesta, 1957; *Poeten Brumbergs sista dagar och doed: En romantisk beraettelse,* Norstedt, 1959.

Broederna: En allegorisk beraettelse, Norstedt, 1960; (with Lars Baeckstroem) *Nio brev om romanen* (title means "Nine Letters on the Art of the Novel"), Norstedt, 1961; *Ballongfararna* (title means "The Aeronauts"), Norstedt, 1962; *Foeljeslagarna: En aeventyrsberaettelse* (title means "The Travel Company: An Adventure Story"), Norstedt, 1962; (editor with Hans Ylander) *Segla: Tretton beraettelser om segling i dikt och verklighet* (title means "Thirteen Stories About Sailing in Fiction and Reality"), Norstedt, 1963; *En foermiddag i Sverige: Dikter* (title means "A Morning in Sweden"), Norstedt, 1963; *Foerberedelser till flykt och andra beraettelser* (title means "Preparations for Flight and Other Tales"), Bonnier, 1963, new edition with new postscript, Norstedt, 1976; (editor) Ingemar Willgert, *Ur mitt inre: eller, Mellan mark och sky* (title means "From My Inner Life: Or Between Ground and Sky"), Bonnier, 1964; *Den egentliga beraettelsen om herr Arenander* (title means "The Essential Story of Mr. Arenander"), Norstedt, 1966; *En resa till jordens medelpunkk och andra dikter* (title means "A Journey to the Middle-Point of the Earth and Other Poems"), Norstedt, 1966; (editor with Daniel Hjorth) *Ny svensk beraettarkonst* (title means "New Swedish Prose"), Bonnier, 1966; *En privatmans dikter* (title means "The Poems of a Private Man"), PAN/Norstedt, 1967; *Broederna Wright uppsoeker Kitty Hawk: Och andra dikter* (title means "The Wright Brothers in Search of Kitty Hawk"), Norstedt, 1968; *Utopier och andra essaer om dikt och liv* (title means "Utopias and Other Lectures on Literature and Life"), PAN/Norstedt, 1969; *Konsten att segla med drakar och andra scener ur privatlivet* (title means "The Art of Sailing With Kiles and Other Scenes From Private Life"), Norstedt, 1969.

(Editor with Torkel Rasmusson) *Dikterna fraan 60-talet* (title means "The Poems of the Sixties"), Bonnier, 1970; *Kaerleksfoerklaring till en sefardisk dam* (title means "Declaration of Love to a Sephardic Lady"), Bonnier, 1970; *Tvaa maktspel: Tebjudningen som inte ville ta slut–Den nattliga hyllningen* (title means "Two Plays on Power: The Tea Party That Did Not Want to End [and] Celebration at Night"; the latter play first produced in Zurich in 1970), Bonnier, 1970; *Herr Gustafsson sjaelv* (novel; title means "Mr. Gustafsson Himself"), Bonnier, 1971; *Varma rum och kalla* (title means "Warm Rooms and Cold"), Bonnier, 1972; *Kommentarer* (title means "Comments"), Gidlund, 1972; *Yllet* (novel; title means "The Wool"), Bonnier, 1973; *Fosterlandet under jorden* (poems; title means "The Native

Country Under the Earth"), Bonnier, 1973; (with Jan Myrdal) *Den onoediga samtiden* (essays; title means "The Non-Necessary Contemporary World"), PAN/Norstedt, 1974; *Vaerldsdelar: Reseskildringar* (title means "Continents: Travels"), Norstedt, 1975; *Familjefesten* (novel; title means "The Family Meeting"), Bonnier, 1975; *Sigismund: Ur en polsk barockfurstes minnen* (novel; title means "Sigismund: From the Memories of a Polonian Baroque Prince"), Norstedt, 1976; *Strandhugg i svensk poesi: Femton diktanalyser* (title means "Forays Into Swedish Poetry: Fifteen Poetry Analyses"), FIB:s lyrikklubb, 1976.

Also author of *Den lilla vaerlden* (title means "The Small World"), 1977; *Tennisspelarna* (title means "The Tennis Players"), 1977; *Sonetter* (title means "Sonnets"), 1977; *En biodlares doed* (title means "The Death of a Beekeeper"), 1978; *Sprach och logn* (title means "Language and Lie"), 1978; and *Kinesisk hoest* (title means "Chinese Autumn"), 1978.

Unpublished plays: "Den nattliga hyllningen" (three-act), first produced on Swedish television, 1971; "Huset i Oneida," first produced on Swedish radio, 1972.

WORK IN PROGRESS: *The Giving of Sense: An Enquiry Into Friedrich Nietzsche's Philosophy,* publication by Norstedt expected in 1982; *The Anatomy of Failure,* completion expected in 1984; *The Public Lie in the Nineteenth Century,* completion expected in 1986.

SIDELIGHTS: Gustafsson commented: "My writing is mainly an inventory of the different layers of lies and truth in the society where I live."

* * *

GUTTRIDGE, Leonard F(rancis) 1918-

PERSONAL: Born August 27, 1918, in Wales; came to the United States in 1947; married Jean Stoddart (a secretary), August 25, 1956; children: Bruce, Vivien. *Education:* Attended school in Cardiff, Wales. *Politics:* "Moderate by Welsh standards, leftish on the American scale." *Religion:* "Of the open mind." *Home:* 616 Ripley St., Alexandria, Va. 22304.

CAREER: Indian Embassy, Washington, D.C., librarian, 1950-61; writer, 1961—. *Military service:* Royal Air Force, 1939-45; served in North Africa; became sergeant. *Member:* Royal Air Force Association.

WRITINGS: (With Jay D. Smith) *Jack Teagarden: Story of a Jazz Maverick,* Cassell, 1960, Capo Press, 1976; (with Smith) *The Commodores: The U.S. Navy in the Age of Sail,* Harper, 1969; (with George S. McGovern) *The Great Coalfield War,* Houghton, 1972. Contributor of stories and articles to magazines in England and the United States, including *Saga, Stag,* and *Melody Maker.*

WORK IN PROGRESS: Research on new findings concerning Abraham Lincoln's assassination, with Ray A. Neff.

SIDELIGHTS: Guttridge comments: "No matter how often produced under compulsions of necessity, my writing output has always reflected my interests. My principal instinctive addiction has been to jazz—ever since I heard Duke Ellington records via British Broadcasting Corp. on a neighbor's radio in 1934. I like many forms of music, but defy anyone to play me something, anything, more thrilling than the V-Disc 'Uncle Sam Blues' with its marvelous Lips Page vocal.

"I am addicted, too, to suspense stories and movies. I saw Hitchcock's 'Secret Agent' the day before I enlisted in the Royal Air Force, and disagree with those who do not list it among his best. I wrote some crime stories, managed to sell one to the last of the real pulps, *Popular Detective,* before the breed vanished.

"Power struggles of whatever description—between individuals in a mutually tight spot—intrigue me, and my love of the same took over in *The Commodores* so effectively that one reviewer called the book '*Executive Suite* on the high seas.' I maintain, indeed insist, that the best and most inexhaustible source for such dramatic staples as human conflict and the ironies of fate is true history, conscientiously researched.

My Welsh origins, I suppose, have determined my interest in fantasy. And they may also, given that country's historic association with coal, have led me to the story I wrote with Senator McGovern of this country's most dramatic labor war."

H

HADLEY, Morris 1894-1979

OBITUARY NOTICE: Born March 21, 1894, in New Haven, Conn.; died January 17, 1979, in Manhattan, N.Y. Lawyer and author. In 1922 Hadley founded the Webb, Patterson, & Hadley law firm, now Millbank, Tweed, Hadley, & McLoy. He was also associated with the New York School of Social Work for twenty-five years. Hadley wrote *Citizen and the Law* and *Arthur Twining Hadley*, a biography of his father, former president of Yale University. Obituaries and other sources: *The International Who's Who*, Europa, 1978; *Who's Who in America*, 40th edition, Marquis, 1978; *New York Times*, January 18, 1979.

*　　*　　*

HAEDRICH, Marcel (pseudonym) 1913-

PERSONAL: Born January 25, 1913, in Munster, France. *Home:* 35 Ave. Alphaud, Saint Mande 94160, France.

CAREER: Writer.

WRITINGS—In English: *Baraque 3, chambre 12: recit de captivite*, Les Editions Varietes, 1942, translation by Katherine Woods published as *Barrack Three, Room Twelve*, Reynal & Hitchcock, 1943; *Belle, de Paris* (novel), Editions de Trevise, 1958, translation by Marguerite Barnett published as *Belle, de Paris*, Heinemann, 1970; *Drame dans un miroir* (novel), Denoel, 1958, translation by Phyllis Johnson published as *The Crack in the Mirror*, Allen, 1960; *La Rose et les soldats* (novel), Grasset, 1961, translation by Monroe Stearns published as *The Soldier and the Rose*, Putnam, 1962; *Coco Chanel secrete*, Laffont, 1971, translation by Charles Lam Markham published as *Coco Chanel: Her Life, Her Secrets*, Little, Brown, 1972.

In French: (Editor) *R5*, 2nd edition, Bordas, 1945; *Les Petits Vaincus* (nonfiction), Bordas, 1946; *Si j'avais voulu* (novel), Laffont, 1952; *Les Evangiles de la vie* (novel; title means "Gospels of Life"), Laffont, 1953; *Je veux, tu veux, il veut* (essays; title means "I Want, You Want, He Wants"), Laffont, 1955; *Le Chemin de Damas* (four-act play; title means "The Road to Damascus"; first produced in Geneva, Switzerland at La Comedie, 1968), Laffont, 1956; *Le Vrai Proces de Monsieur Bill* (nonfiction; title means "The Real Trial of Mister Bill"), Grasset, 1960; *Le Patron* (novel; title means "The Boss"), Grasset, 1964; *L'Entre-deux dieux* (nonfiction; title means "The Period Between Two Gods"), Grasset, 1967; *Midi 25* (essays; title means "12:25"), Editions de

Trevise, 1969; *Et Moiese crea Dieu* (nonfiction; title means "And Moses Created God"), Laffont, 1970; *Seul avec tous* (nonfiction; title means "Alone With Everybody"), Laffont, 1973; (with Henriette Pascar) *Mariorca* (novel), Flammarion, 1973; *Les Jumeaux de Kissingen* (novel; title means "The Twins of Kissingen"), Laffont, 1975; *Le Marechal et la dactylo* (biography; title means "The Marshal and the Typist"), Laffont, 1977; *Une Enfance alsacienne ou le mal de Dieu* (nonfiction; title means "An Alsatian Childhood or a Sickness of God"), [Paris], 1978.

WORK IN PROGRESS: A novel, the saga of a great French family of Mauritzius Island; a new trial of Christ.

SIDELIGHTS: Haedrich told *CA*: "I am not a scholar. A widow of the war of 1914, my mother brought up three boys on her pension. She got me nevertheless to a commercial high school. Later I managed to convert to journalism, helped, I must say, by the circumstances: war.

"If you read the introduction to *Une Enfance alsacienne ou le mal de Dieu* you'll see how journalism and faith influence my writing. Faith is no longer to believe, but to understand. That is my credo. If you read the Bible with Darwin and Einstein in mind, you can follow the progress of God in man's train of thought, by the intermediary of words.

"My next book on God will be more direct and clearer. I was frightened to shock the "bien pensants." I'll have to go farther and, perhaps, recklessly. But right now I am finishing a very important novel about the saga of a great French family of Mauritzius, an island paradise. I hope it will be successful and solve forever my money problems."

*　　*　　*

HAEKKERUP, Per 1915-1979

OBITUARY NOTICE: Born December 25, 1915, in Ringsted, Denmark; died March 13, 1979, in Copenhagen, Denmark. Politician, editor, and author. Haekkerup had been a prominent figure in Danish politics since the end of World War II, serving as Foreign Minister, Finance Minister, and Minister of Economics and Trade. For five years he was legislative spokesman and floor leader of the Social Democratic Party. Haekkerup advocated a strong United Nations and actively encouraged its members to halt the Vietnam war and abolish apartheid in South Africa. He served as economic and political editor of *Aktuelt*, a Copenhagen daily newspaper, and in 1950 wrote *The Political Parties*. Obituaries and other sources: *The International Who's Who,* Europa, 1978; *Who's Who in the World,* 40th edition, Marquis, 1978; *New York Times,* March 14, 1979.

* * *

HAGG, G. Eric 1908(?)-1979

OBITUARY NOTICE: Born c. 1908; died April 28, 1979, in Illinois. Minister and author. Hagg was a member of the board of publications of the Lutheran Church in America and wrote several books on religion. Obituaries and other sources: *Chicago Tribune,* May 4, 1979.

* * *

HAGUE, William Edward, Jr. 1919-

PERSONAL: Born February 2, 1919, in Duquesne, Pa.; son of William Edward (a lawyer) and Edith (Osburn) Hague; married Margaret Cleland Anderson, July 22, 1950 (divorced). *Education:* Princeton University, A.B., 1940; graduate study at University of Pittsburgh, 1940-41. *Home:* 437 Pennsylvania Ave., San Francisco, Calif. 94107. *Agent:* Robert P. Mills Ltd., 156 East 52nd St., New York, N.Y. 10022.

CAREER: Associate editor of *Tide* (magazine), 1947-49; assistant account executive of Fitzgerald Advertising Agency, 1950-51; *Living for Young Homemakers,* copy editor, 1951-54, managing editor, 1954-61, editor of *Living's Guide to Home Planning,* 1958-61; Conde Nast Publications, New York, N.Y., senior editor of *House and Garden,* 1961, editor-in-chief of "House and Garden Guides," 1962-72; free-lance writer and real estate developer, 1972—. Associate of Zinkhon Communications (public relations firm), San Francisco, Calif., 1978-79. *Military service:* U.S. Naval Reserve, active duty, 1943-46; became lieutenant senior grade. *Member:* Potrero Hill Boosters and Merchants Association. *Awards, honors:* Dorothy Dawe Award from American Furniture Mart, 1969, for journalistic coverage in the home furnishing field.

WRITINGS—All published by Doubleday: How to Decorate with Color, 1964; *What You Should Know About Furniture,* 1965; *Planning Your Vacation Home,* 1968; *Planning Your Bathroom,* 1968; *How to Plan the Kitchen That Suits You,* 1969; *Making the Most of the One-Room Apartment,* 1969; *Outdoor Living,* 1970; *Your Vacation House: How to Plan It,* 1972; *The Complete Basic Book of Home Decorating,* 1976; *Know Your America: California,* 1978.

WORK IN PROGRESS: Waiting, a novel; "Casa Amarilla," a three-act play.

SIDELIGHTS: Hague writes: "My vocation and avocation have always merged. I have built or remodeled twenty-some houses and apartments in the last twenty-five years, doing the design and all the interior design myself. All of these projects have been featured in national magazines. I am presently restoring a Victorian house. I buy old homes, redesign, and sell them. It is profitable and stimulating.

"Of all the 'House and Garden Guides' which I edited—on building, decorating, garden, plans, kitchen, and bath—the remodeling guide was my favorite and it is still the area of most creative interest for me."

* * *

HAILEY, Sheila 1927-

PERSONAL: Born December 5, 1927, in London, England; daughter of James Watt (a tailor) and Beatrice (Willbourn) Dunlop; married Arthur Hailey (an author), July 28, 1951; children: Jane, Steven, Diane. *Education:* Attended Hendon Technical College, 1944-45. *Residence:* Lyford Cay, Nassau, Bahamas.

CAREER: George G. Harrap Ltd. (publishing company), London, England, editorial assistant, 1945-49; Maclean-Hunter Ltd. (publishing company), Toronto, Ontario, assistant editor, 1949-52; free-lance writer, 1952—.

WRITINGS: Bayard the Fearless (juvenile), A. Wheaton, 1952; *I Married a Best Seller,* Doubleday, 1978. Contributor of scripts to Canadian television programs, including "Morning Magazine," "Free and Easy," and "Take 30."

SIDELIGHTS: In *I Married a Best Seller,* Hailey chronicles her life with famed novelist Arthur Hailey. Although, as was noted in the *New York Times Book Review,* the Haileys were actually married years before Arthur produced a best seller, the book was praised for the insight it offered concerning his work habits.

Sheila Hailey told *CA:* "Details of my life and that of my husband's, including how he writes his books, my philosophy towards marriage, children, careers, etc., are contained in *I Married a Best Seller.* It is a frank, funny account of a twenty-eight-year-old marriage with all its ups and downs. I wrote it because I feel strongly about marriage and one's commitment to it, and because I think we live in an age where divorce has become too easy, almost fashionable. The divorce statistics of the 1970's are alarming and are setting an appalling example for younger generations.

BIOGRAPHICAL/CRITICAL SOURCES: New York Times Book Review, May 21, 1978.

* * *

HAINES, Max 1931-

PERSONAL: Born January 4, 1931, in Antigonish, Nova Scotia, Canada; son of Alex and Gussie Haines; married Marilyn Roll; children: Susan, Maureen, Eleanor. *Education:* Attended St. Francis Xavier University, and Dalhousie University. *Home and office:* 3 Deanecrest Rd., Islington, Ontario, Canada.

CAREER: Toronto Sun, Toronto, Ontario, author of columns "Crime Flashback" and "Max Haines Other Side," 1972—. *Member:* Quebec Society of Upper Canada.

WRITINGS: Bothersome Bodies, McClelland & Stewart, 1977; *Max Haines Calendar of Criminal Capers,* Virgo Press, 1978.

WORK IN PROGRESS: The Poisoners, a collection of true crime cases.

SIDELIGHTS: Haines' career has taken him to Jamaica, France, England, Ireland, Wales, Switzerland, Germany, the Netherlands, and Austria.

* * *

HALDEMAN, Linda (Wilson) 1935-

PERSONAL: Born July 14, 1935, in Washington, D.C.; daughter of John Barnett (an attorney) and Mildred (Beckwith) Wilson; married Harry Haldeman (a professor of English), August 8, 1959; children: Gene, John, Ruth, Elaine. *Education:* Loyola University, New Orleans, La., A.B., 1958; Pennsylvania State University, M.A., 1965. *Religion:* Anglo-Catholic. *Home and office address:* R.D. 5, Box 63, Indiana, Pa. 15701. *Agent:* McIntosh & Otis, Inc., 475 Fifth Ave., New York, N.Y. 10017.

CAREER: Columbus College of Art, Columbus, Ohio, instructor in English, 1959-60; writer, 1966—. *Member:* Authors Guild of Authors League of America.

WRITINGS: Star of the Sea (novel), Doubleday, 1978; *The Lastborn of Elvinwood* (novel), Doubleday, 1978. Contributor to *Opera News* and *Opera Journal*.

SIDELIGHTS: Linda Haldeman writes: "I am primarily a teller of tales. This is a profession that has fallen into disfavor with many critics. It is felt, it seems, that there are two kinds of fiction written, the good story and the literary novel, and it is assumed for some reason that they are mutually exclusive. It is my intention to remarry these two ideas of the novel after a too-long forced separation. An entertaining and absorbing plot ought not to exclude good writing style and sympathetic, well-developed characters.

"My interest in music and the theater, united in a passion for the musical theater of the opera, no doubt influences both the content and the form of my books.

"I came somewhat late in life to my profession, although it has been my intended vocation for the last thirty years. I have been a private storyteller since childhood, but not until recently have I been sufficiently satisfied with the workings of my imagination to expose them to the eyes of the world."

*   *   *

HALES, E(dward) E(lton) Y(oung)   1908-

PERSONAL: Born October 8, 1908, in Nottingham, England; son of James Elton (a civil servant) and Ethel (Burbidge) Hales; married Anne Porter, February 18, 1933; children: Barbara, Joseph, Christopher. *Education:* Oriel College, Oxford, B.A. (first class honors), 1930, M.A., 1936. *Politics:* "Whichever party seems to have the most suitable program." *Religion:* Roman Catholic. *Home:* Edburton House, Edburton, Henfield, West Sussex, England.

CAREER: Yale University, New Haven, Conn., instructor in history, 1931-34; Uppingham School, England, sixth form history master, 1935-39; Ministry of Education, London, England, inspector of schools, 1939-69. Writer. Information counselor at British Embassy in Washington, D.C., 1961-63. *Member:* Authors Club. *Awards, honors:* D.H.L. from Le Moyne College, 1962.

WRITINGS: Pio Nono, Kenedy, 1954; *Mazzini and the Secret Societies,* Kenedy, 1956; *The Catholic Church in the Modern World,* Doubleday, 1958; *Revolution and Papacy,* Doubleday, 1960; *The Emperor and the Pope,* Doubleday, 1961 (published in England as *Napoleon and the Pope,* Eyre & Spottiswoode, 1961); *Pope John and His Revolution,* Doubleday, 1965; *Chariot of Fire* (novel), Doubleday, 1977.

WORK IN PROGRESS: Studying social and religious groups in America and Europe in the nineteenth century, especially John Humphrey Noyes and Oneida Creek in the United States, Henry Prince in England, and Archdeacon Ebel in Germany: the people known as Perfectionists in all three countries.

SIDELIGHTS: Hales writes: "My interest in Italy and Italian art and culture was fostered by my mother and by my conversion to the Roman Catholic Church in 1949. These interests came together to produce my various books on the modern papacy.

"Hatred of airports, of waiting for flights, of filling in forms, and admiration for the Bible story of the woman of Samaria came together to inspire my recent satirical novel, *Chariot of Fire.*

"My American wife, from New Haven, Conn., has given me a lasting affection for New England and California.

"I think that all writing, whether it be history or fiction or poetry, is a form of escape because in it we move into a world of our own creation, which is not the everyday world that pushes itself upon us so relentlessly that we can't even think, let alone dream. Escape is not a vice but a necessity if we are to use our minds or our imaginations—the highest gifts we have been given—effectively at all. The scientist escapes to his microscope, the man of religion escapes to his prayers and meditations, the artist escapes to his studio, the writer escapes to his study. Unless they escape in this way they cannot fully live, or help others to do so."

*   *   *

HALIFAX, Joan (Squire)   1942-

PERSONAL: Born July 30, 1942, in Hanover, N.H.; daughter of John Raymond (a businessman) and Eunice (Spillane) Halifax; married Stanislav Grof (a psychiatrist), June 2, 1972 (divorced, 1977). *Education:* Tulane University, B.A., 1963; Union College and University, Ph.D., 1973. *Home and office:* 70 Barrow St., New York, N.Y. 10014. *Agent:* John Brockman Associates, Inc., Box 376, Planetarium Station, New York, N.Y. 10024.

CAREER: Columbia University, New York City, research assistant in department of anthropology, 1964-68; Musee de l'Homme, Paris, France, research assistant for Comite du Film Ethnographique, 1968-69; University of Miami, Miami, Fla., teacher, researcher, and clinical worker in departments of pediatrics and psychiatry, 1970-72; Maryland Psychiatric Research Center, Baltimore, Md., research associate, 1972-73; Esalen Institute, Big Sur, Calif., scholar-in-residence, 1973-77; New School for Social Research, New York City, member of faculty, 1977—. Lecturer on medical anthropology and psychiatry at many universities, institutes, and professional associations. Principal field work conducted in the Caribbean, 1966, 1972, 1974, United States, 1966, 1968, 1970-72, Africa, 1967, 1969, 1970, and Mexico, 1972, 1976, 1977-78. Film production assistant for "Peace Peddler," Dorfman, 1964, "Festival," Lerner, 1964-66, 1967, "Alcoa Presents," ABC-TV, 1967-68, and "I Can't Help It," Buggiani, 1968. Photographer, with exhibitions in New York, 1968, Paris, 1968, and London, 1969, a book jacket, and photographs in a film. Member of board of trustees of Fitzhugh Ludlow Memorial Library. Member of board of advisers of Huxley Hospice, Self Actualization Institute, Creative Growth Center, Dimele Center for Reconnective Psychotherapy, Human Dimensions West, and Biosynergy Foundation. Special consultant to the Comprehensive Health Planning Council, 1971-72; technical consultant to Columbia Pictures, 1978.

MEMBER: American Anthropological Association, American Academy of Psychoanalysis (scientific associate), Association of Humanistic Psychology, Society for Applied Anthropology, Society for Medical Anthropology, Society for the Anthropology of Visual Communication, Comite du Film Ethnographique, Office National pour le Commerce et l'Industrie. *Awards, honors:* National Science Foundation fellowship, 1972.

WRITINGS: (With Stanislaw Grof) *The Human Encounter With Death,* Dutton, 1977; *Shamanic Voices: A Survey of Visionary Narratives,* Dutton, 1979; *The Journey of Initiation,* Thames & Hudson, 1980.

Contributor: Alan Lomax, *Folk Song Style and Culture,* American Association for the Advancement of Science, 1968; Pierre Maranda and Elli Kongas Maranda, *Structural Analysis of Oral Tradition,* University of Pennsylvania

Press, 1971; *Cultural Impediments to Delivery of Health Care and Social Services in a Multi-Cultural Community*, Social Service Department, Jackson Memorial Hospital (Miami, Fla.), 1972; Richard Cox, editor, *Religious Systems and Psychotherapy*, C. C Thomas, 1973; *Human Quest*, Elysium Press, 1975; Arnold Toynbee, *Man's Concern With Life After Death*, Weidenfield & Nicolson, 1976, McGraw, 1977. Also contributor to *Phoenix: New Directions in the Study of Man*.

Screenplays: "Cages," 1968; "All the Way Home," 1968; "It Is for Us to See," University of Miami School of Medicine, Department of Pediatrics, 1970; "Kumquat Family," 1971.

Contributor of photographs: Kali Grosvenor, *Poems by Kali*, Doubleday, 1970.

Contributor of research or editorial assistance to books by other authors. Contributor to anthropological, medical, and psychological journals and magazines. Member of editorial board of *Journal of Humanistic Psychology* and *Journal of Consciousness and Culture;* consulting editor, McGraw-Hill, 1977—.

WORK IN PROGRESS: A World Survey of Shamanism, publication by McGraw-Hill expected in 1982; *The Secret Feast;* collaborating on research for Joseph Campbell's *Historical Atlas of World Mythology; Planet of the Gods*, "a botanical, biochemical, and anthropological study of visionary plants," with Richard Evans Schultes and Albert Hofmann; contributing a chapter, "Trance Induction in Indigenous American Churches," for *Danse du Possession*, edited by Jean Rouch, for Centre National de Recherche Scientifique.

SIDELIGHTS: Joan Halifax is a unique scholar—combining humanitarian aspects of Western and Eastern thought with careful scientific research processes. She collaborated on the basic text for song and dance style in *Cantometrics and Choreometrics*. She has worked in rigorously difficult situations internationally, directly benefiting those peoples she has studied in Africa, the Americas, and the Caribbean. At the Maryland Psychiatric Center, she pioneered new anthropological perspectives in the care of individuals dying of cancer, using herself as a research subject to discover how best to work with hallucinogens towards a conscious and masterful resolution of life crises. She was then invited to be scholar-in-residence at Esalen Institute, coordinating and directing training programs for health care professionals. While in Big Sur, she encountered five Huichol Indians from Mexico. In the ensuing close and unusual relationship with these extraordinary people, her life's orientation moved towards the lucidity of shamanism. This immersion in ritual life and sacred symbols was concurrent with her introduction to the subsequent practice of Rinzai Zen.

Numerous life experiences, ranging from temporary blindness and paralysis at the age of four to her work with Pentecostal churchgoers and her own spontaneous and often overwhelming visionary experiences, have awakened her to her own inner life and the personal relevance of altered states of consciousness in understanding the complementary relationship between living and dying. In her lectures, she states, "Death is the ornament of life."

Halifax's knowledge of psyche, myth, and symbol has led to a collaboration with the scholar Joseph Campbell on a historical atlas of world mythology and to her latest book, *Shamanic Voices*. She is presently creating another book on visions of the shaman's initiatory journey, and her third book on shamanism is scheduled for 1982. These books, she

writes, "will summarize the beginnings of religion at a time when the Paleolithic seed of all sacred impulses is still extant with us on this planet but will be gone in the next decade. They also are intended to give relevance to those visionary experiences which occur spontaneously in the lives of many individuals in Western culture at a time when such experiences are regarded as pathological."

Halifax once remarked that the most important experiences of her life were those that "emerged from the depths of the human soul in moments of extreme physical and mental anguish when the realization came that suffering can bring one into the field of compassion." Through her work with shamans and Buddhists she feels that "all people have a higher purpose in life—and that is to help in creating an abundant lifeway of the future—one that is characterized by physical, mental, and spiritual health, and one that supports the variety of forms of expression, be they biological, psychological, or cultural—this variety being the basis for survival."

BIOGRAPHICAL/CRITICAL SOURCES: Soho Weekly News, October 20, 1977.

* * *

HALL, George 1941-

PERSONAL: Born March 14, 1941, in Gary, Ind.; son of George (an architect) and Marion (Pripps) Hall. *Education:* Stanford University, B.A., 1963; University of California, Berkeley, graduate study, 1965-67. *Home and office:* 82 Macondray Lane, San Francisco, Calif. 94133.

CAREER: Writer and photographer, 1969—. *Military service:* U.S. Army, Intelligence Corps, 1963-65; became first lieutenant.

WRITINGS—All documentary photo books, except as noted: (With Baron Wolman and George Larson) *The Blimp Book*, Squarebooks, 1977; (with Robert S. Weider) *The Great American Convertible*, Doubleday, 1977; (with Ralph Story) *Secrets of Los Angeles* (travel guidebook), Story Books, 1978; (with Peter Garrison) *Carrier Pilot*, Presidio Press, 1979.

WORK IN PROGRESS: A book on the San Francisco Fire Department. *Avocational interests:* Flying, cooking, travel.

* * *

HALLMAN, Ruth 1929-

PERSONAL: Born June 30, 1929, in Hertford, N.C.; daughter of Edgar E. (a school superintendent) and Mattie (Reid) Bundy; married Robert E. Hallman (an advisory engineer), July 9, 1952; children: Bob, David, Robin, Lynn. *Education:* Winthrop College, B.A., 1951. *Politics:* Republican. *Religion:* Methodist. *Home and office:* 9602 Sudley Manor Dr., Manassas, Va. 22110.

CAREER: Elementary school teacher in Spartanburg, S.C., 1951-52, and Columbus, Ga., 1952-53; personnel secretary in Atlanta, Ga., 1953-55; remedial reading tutor in Atlanta, 1955-56; Wilson Memorial Hospital, Johnson City, N.Y., pediatrics program organizer, 1956-57; substitute teacher in Endicott, N.Y., 1957-58; Jennie F. Snapp School, Endicott, elementary school teacher, 1958-60; writer, 1971—. Volunteer teacher at hospitals and prisons; creative writing instructor; public speaker.

WRITINGS—All juveniles: *Secrets of a Silent Stranger*, Westminster, 1976; *I Gotta Be Free*, Westminster, 1977; *Gimme Something, Mister*, Westminster, 1978; *Midnight Wheels*, Westminster, 1979. Author of church school curriculum material.

WORK IN PROGRESS: A children's book about the U.S. Coast Guard; an adult mystery novel.

SIDELIGHTS: Ruth Hallman writes: "In everything I do—writing, teaching, speaking—there is the basic concern for children, people, who either have difficulty reading or who have never developed an interest in reading. I have spent my entire adult life working for such disadvantaged people.

"I am fortunate now to be working on a project of high interest/low vocabulary books for reluctant readers. These books have a very specific goal: to encourage, excite, and intrigue such readers to turn the next page, and the next, and the next. As a teacher and the mother of four children I say, with no reservation at all, that books of this type meet a very vital need for such reluctant readers as I have taught.

"In my books I deliberately use mysteries or adventures as my stories, having found that these will keep moving quickly enough to satisfy the shorter attention-span of reluctant readers. I have lived in many places in the United States, and different locations provide first-hand settings for my books. I try to incorporate interesting factual comments about the settings. If one child reads with more interest because of anything I write, I have achieved my goal."

BIOGRAPHICAL/CRITICAL SOURCES: Florida United Methodist, August 15, 1975; *Today,* August 23, 1975, August 31, 1976; *Binghamton Press,* October 21, 1977; *Raleigh News & Observer,* November 27, 1977; *Journal-Messenger* (Manassas, Va.), February 23, 1979.

* * *

HALPERIN, S(amuel) William 1905-1979

OBITUARY NOTICE: Born January 11, 1905, in Kaunas, Lithuania; died April 15, 1979, in La Jolla, Calif. Educator, historian, editor, and author. An internationally known specialist on European diplomatic history, Halperin was a professor at University of Chicago for over forty years. He was editor of the University of Chicago's *Journal of Modern History* and wrote several articles and books, including *Germany Tried Democracy.* Obituaries and other sources: *Directory of American Scholars,* Volume I: *History,* 7th edition, Bowker, 1978; *Chicago Tribune,* April 18, 1979, April 22, 1979; *New York Times,* April 19, 1979.

* * *

HALPRIN, Anna Schuman 1920-

PERSONAL: Born July 13, 1920, in Winnetka, Ill.; daughter of Isadore and Ida (Schiff) Schuman; married Lawrence Halprin (a landscape architect), September 19, 1940; children: Daria, Rana. *Education:* Attended Harvard University, 1940; University of Wisconsin—Madison, B.S., 1943. *Home:* 15 Ravine Way, Kentfield, Calif. 94904. *Office:* San Francisco Dancers' Workshop, 321 Divisadero St., San Francisco, Calif. 94117.

CAREER: Professional dancer and choreographer, 1945-48; co-owner of studio and teacher of modern dance, San Francisco, Calif., 1948-55; San Francisco Dancers' Workshop, San Francisco, founder and artistic director, 1956—. Founder and director of Marin Dance Cooperative. Member of faculty at Esalen Institute; guest teacher and performer at University of California, Berkeley, University of California, Los Angeles, University of Illinois, Reed College, Harvard University, San Francisco State University, and University of Michigan. Performer and lecturer in the United States and abroad. Organizer of workshops and classes. Performer in

films. Member of Gestalt Institute of San Francisco and San Francisco Arts Resource Development Committee. *Member.* Association for American Dance, Conscientious Artists of America, Regional Bay Area Arts Council. *Awards, honors:* Guggenheim fellowship, 1970-71; National Endowment for the Arts grant, 1976; National Education Association grant, 1977.

WRITINGS: (Contributor) Lawrence Halprin, editor, *The R.S.V.P. Cycles,* Braziller, 1969; *Collected Writings,* San Francisco Dancers' Workshop, 1973; (contributor) L. Halprin and Jim Burns, editors, *Taking Part,* M.I.T. Press, 1974; *Second Collected Writings,* San Francisco Dancers' Workshop, 1975; (with Burns and James Hurd Nixon) *Citydance 1977,* edited by Buck O'Kelly, San Francisco Dancers' Workshop, 1977. Also author of *A School Comes Home,* 1973; *Exit to Enter,* 1973; *Movement Ritual I;* with Nixon, *Dance as a Self-Healing Art* (booklet), 1977. Founder of *Impulse.*

WORK IN PROGRESS: A visual representation of the philosophy and life application of dance through music, slide show, and narration, with a book expected to result.

SIDELIGHTS: In 1955, Anna Halprin created her workshop for artists, architects, painters, dancers, poets, actors, and musicians to investigate the nature of dance. She writes that her own work in dance has been influenced in part by architect Walter Gropius and therapist Fritz Perls.

Halprin believes that everyone has the natural ability to dance, and she has developed a process to develop the natural sense of dance movement. She has also explored the connections between active imagination, imagery, visualizations, and movement. She has conducted numerous "public dance rituals" in the San Francisco area and, more recently, throughout the rest of the United States and abroad. She feels that her "events" afford people the opportunity to enact the communities they would like to create.

Her workshops and lectures have been commissioned by art festivals and museums, universities, religious organizations, community art centers, growth centers, and conferences in psychology, holistic health, humanities, and environmental awareness.

* * *

HAMILTON, Wallace 1919-

PERSONAL: Born August 17, 1919, in New York, N.Y.; son of B. Wallace (a physician) and Florence (a civic leader; maiden name, Durstine) Hamilton. *Education:* Harvard University, B.A. (cum laude), 1941. *Home:* 334 East 11th St., New York, N.Y. 10003. *Agent:* Lucianne Goldberg, 255 West 84th St., New York, N.Y. 10024.

CAREER: United Hospital Fund, New York City, publicity assistant, 1941; Greater New York Fund, New York City, publicity assistant, 1942; Massachusetts General Hospital, Boston, experimental subject for medical research on electrolytic balance in the human body, 1942-46; Committee on Educational Aid for Conscientious Objectors, Brooklyn, N.Y., executive director, 1946; World Council of Churches, New York City, secretary for publicity, 1947-51; KPFA radio station, Berkeley, Calif., director of public affairs programming, 1952-53, general manager, 1953-54; California Heart Association, San Francisco, director of public relations, 1955-62; Maryland Heart Association, Baltimore, director of public relations, 1962-63; Howard Research and Development, Baltimore, historian of Columbia City project, 1963-65; Rouse Company, Columbia, Md., director of institutional development, 1965-70; full-time writer, 1970—. Served as fund raiser for Emergency Committee of Atomic Scientists, 1946, and for Migrant Ministry, Home Missions Council, 1951-52. *Military service:* Registered as conscientious objector, 1941; served with Civilian Public Service as subject for medical research, 1942-46.

WRITINGS: Christopher and Gay: A Partisan's View of the Greenwich Village Homosexual Scene, Saturday Review Press, 1973; *Coming Out* (novel), New American Library, 1977; *David at Olivet* (novel), St. Martin's, 1979.

Produced plays: "The Burning of the Lepers" (three-act), first produced in Los Angeles at Kenmore Theatre, 1960; "The Midnight Cry" (three-act), first produced Off-Broadway at Folkesbeine Theatre, 1964; "Bunny Boy" (one-act), first produced in Baltimore, Md., at Center Stage, 1966; "Anthony in the Desert" (three-act), first produced in Bel Air, Md., at Hartford Community College, 1967; "Matinee" (one-act), first produced in Baltimore at Corner Theatre, 1970; "Bonus March" (two-act), first produced in Baltimore at Center Stage, 1968; "A Touch of Orpheus" (one-act), first produced in Baltimore at Corner Theatre, 1969; "Wanting" (one-act), first produced in Baltimore at Corner Theatre, 1969; "Tegaroon" (two-act), first produced in Baltimore at Corner Theatre, 1970; "Time Now" (two-act), first produced in Baltimore at Corner Theatre, 1970; "Rite for Bedtime" (one-act), first produced Off-Off Broadway at Omni Theatre Club, 1971; "A Month of Fridays" (two-act), first produced in New York City at Lambda Theatre Club, 1973; "The Transplants" (three-act), first produced in New York City at Sloane House, 1976; "The Queen's Will," first produced Off-Off Broadway at Dramatis Personae, 1978.

Unproduced plays: "Ajax" (three-act), 1958; "Sinai" (three-act), 1961; "Jolly Roger" (one-act), 1963; "Roxanna" (three-act), 1964; "Pygmalion" (one-act), 1968; "Legend of a Lady" (three-act), 1969; "Peppermint Straw" (two-act), 1971; "Hacking It" (two-act), 1971; "Cheney" (three-act), 1972; "Invitation to a Bear-Baiting" (two-act), 1974.

WORK IN PROGRESS: A novel about a male hustler for publication by St. Martin's Press; an American historical novel.

SIDELIGHTS: Hamilton commented: "In the course of my literary career I've written just about anything and everything. But for the past ten years I have concentrated, in both plays and books, on the gay experience. After all, straights have been writing about their trials and tribulations with enthusiastic prolixity for about three thousand years now. Since it now appears that gays are a biologically constant ten percent of the human species, it does seem time to start getting things in balance. We have our trials and tribulations, too!"

* * *

HAMMER, Kenneth M. 1918-

PERSONAL: Born June 29, 1918, in Nunda, S.D.; married wife, Alice E. (a teacher), April, 1955; children: Steven, Randall. *Education:* South Dakota State University, B.S., 1941, Ph.D., 1966; U.S. Air Force Institute of Technology, graduate, 1948. *Home:* 314 South High St., Fort Atkinson, Wis. 53538. *Office:* Department of Economics, University of Wisconsin—Whitewater, Whitewater, Wis. 53190.

CAREER: Associated with U.S. Air Force, 1941-61, retiring as major; University of Wisconsin—Whitewater, assistant professor, 1966-68, associate professor, 1968-74, professor of economics, 1974—.

WRITINGS: Test Bank for Economics, South-Western, 1970; *Men With Custer*, Old Army Press, 1972; (editor) *Custer in '76*, Brigham Young University Press, 1976. Contributor to history journals.

WORK IN PROGRESS: Research on early railroads.

SIDELIGHTS: Hammer's work has taken him to Finland, Poland, the Soviet Union, and England.

* * *

HANCE, Kenneth G(ordon) 1903-

PERSONAL: Born July 6, 1903, in Pasadena, Calif.; son of George Wallace (a photographer) and Lila Mae (Ives) Hance; married Winnifred D. Shattuck, June 15, 1928 (died, 1958); married Winifred Morse (a nurse), June 13, 1959; children: Kenneth G., Jr. *Education:* Olivet College, B.A., 1924, M.A., 1926; University of Michigan, Ph.D., 1937. *Religion:* Congregationalist. *Home:* 509 Ship St., St. Joseph, Mich. 49085.

CAREER: Olivet College, Olivet, Mich., instructor, 1924-26, assistant professor of speech, 1926-30; Albion College, Albion, Mich., assistant professor, then associate professor, 1937-40, professor of speech, 1937-40; University of Michigan, Ann Arbor, assistant professor, 1940-43, associate professor of speech, 1943-45; Northwestern University, Evanston, Ill., associate professor, 1945-48, professor of speech and assistant dean of the school of speech, 1948-56; Michigan State University, East Lansing, professor of speech, 1956-71, professor emeritus, 1971—. Acting academic dean at Olivet College, 1968-73. *Member:* Speech Association of America (honorary life member; past president; past executive vice-president), Religious Speech Communication Association, Central States Speech Association, Michigan Speech Association (distinguished life member), Phi Beta Kappa, Phi Kappa Phi. *Awards, honors:* L.H.D. from Olivet College, 1961.

WRITINGS: (Co-author) *Principles and Methods of Discussion*, Harper, 1937; (co-author) *Discussion in Human Affairs*, Harper, 1950; (editor) *Association Management*, U.S. Chamber of Commerce, 1958; (co-author) *Public Speaking and Discussion for Religious Leaders*, Prentice-Hall, 1961; (co-author) *Principles of Speaking*, Wadsworth, 1962, 3rd edition, 1974; (editor and contributor) *History of the Michigan Speech Association, 1925-1975*, Michigan Speech Association, 1975.

WORK IN PROGRESS: A history of Olivet College.

* * *

HANKS, Stedman Shumway 1889-1979

OBITUARY NOTICE: Born July 17, 1889, in Manchester, Mass.; died May 23, 1979, in Manhattan, N.Y. Airport engineer and author. A U.S. Air Force Colonel, Hanks was an avid supporter of air transportation. In 1936 he patented a flight strip and helped gain government appropriation for its construction throughout the country. He was founder and president of American Airports Corporation and executive director of the Massachusetts Aeronautics Commission. Hanks wrote *Frontiers Are Not Borders* and numerous other articles and books on aviation and foreign policy. Obituaries and other sources: *Who's Who in the East*, 16th edition, Marquis, 1977; *New York Times*, May 26, 1979.

* * *

HARBURG, E(dgar) Y(ipsel) 1896-
(Yip Harburg)

PERSONAL: Born April 8, 1896, in New York, N.Y.; son

of Lewis (a garment worker) and Mary (Ricing) Harburg; married Alice Richmond, February 23, 1923 (divorced, 1929); married Edelaine Roden, January 16, 1943; children: (first marriage) Ernest, Marjorie. *Education:* City College (now of the City University of New York), B.S., 1918. *Politics:* Liberal. *Religion:* None. *Home:* 262 Central Park W., New York, N.Y. 10024. *Agent:* International Creative Management, 40 West 57th St., New York, N.Y. 10019. *Office:* 551 Fifth Ave., New York, N.Y. 10017.

CAREER: Lyricist, playwright, poet. Owner of an electric appliance company, Brooklyn, N.Y., 1923-29. *Member:* American Society of Composers, Authors, and Publishers (ASCAP), American Guild of Authors and Composers, Dramatists Guild, Screen Writers Guild. *Awards, honors:* Academy Award, Academy of Motion Picture Arts and Sciences, 1938, for song "Over the Rainbow" from the motion picture "The Wizard of Oz"; Henderson Award for Best Musical Comedy, 1947-48, for "Finian's Rainbow"; Townsend Harris award for outstanding alumni, City College of the City University of New York, 1950; honorary doctor of letters, University of Vermont, 1971; James K. Hackett award, City College of the City University of New York, 1972; elected to Song Writer's Hall of Fame, 1973; nominee for induction into the Entertainment Hall of Fame, 1976; honorary doctor of arts, Columbia College, Chicago, 1978; citations from Academy of Motion Picture Arts and Sciences for song "Happiness is a Thing Called Joe" from screenplay "Cabin in the Sky," and for song "More and More" from screenplay "Can't Help Singing."

WRITINGS: (Author of book with Fred Saidy; author of lyrics with Burton Lane; music by Burton Lane) *Finian's Rainbow* (musical satire), Random House, 1947, Berkley Publishing, 1968; (author of lyrics; author of book with Saidy; music by Harold Arlen) *Jamaica* (first produced in New York at Imperial Theatre, October 31, 1957), Hart Stenographic Bureau, c.1957; (author of lyrics and story; book by Saidy and Henry Myers; music by Jacques Offenbach) *The Happiest Girl in the World* (first produced in New York at the Martin Beck Theatre, April 3, 1961), Hart Stenographic Bureau, 1961; *Rhymes for the Irreverent* (poems), Grossman, 1965; *At This Point in Rhyme: E. Y. Harburg's Poems,* Crown, 1976.

Lyricist for theatrical productions: "Earl Carroll's Sketchbook," 1929; "The Garrick Gaieties," 3rd edition, 1930; Carroll, "Vanities," 8th edition, 1930; "Shoot the Works," 1931; "Ballyhoo of 1932," 1932; "Americana," 3rd edition, 1932; "Walk a Little Faster," 1932; "Ziegfeld Follies," 1934; "Life Begins at 8:40," 1934; "Hooray for What!," 1937; "Hold on to Your Hats," 1940; "Bloomer Girl," 1944.

Lyricist and co-libretist for theatrical productions: (With Fred Saidy) "Flahooley," 1951; (with Saidy and Henry Myers) "Darling of the Day," 1968.

Lyricist for films: "The Sap of Syracuse," Paramount, 1930; "Queen High," Paramount, 1930; "Moonlight and Pretzels," Universal, 1933; "Leave it to Lester," Paramount, 1933; "The Count of Monte Cristo," Universal, 1934; "Take a Chance," Paramount, 1933; "The Singing Kid," First National, 1936; "Gold Diggers of 1937," First National, 1936; "Andy Hardy Gets Spring Fever," Metro-Goldwyn-Mayer (MGM), 1937; "The Wizard of Oz," MGM, 1939; "The Marx Brothers' Day at the Circus," MGM, 1939; "Babes on Broadway," MGM, 1941; "Ship Ahoy," MGM, 1942; "Cairo," MGM, 1942; "Rio Rita," MGM, 1942; "Song of Russia," MGM, 1943; "Cabin in the

Sky," MGM, 1943; "Meet the People," MGM, 1944; "Hollywood Canteen," Warner Bros., 1944; "Can't Help Singing," Universal, 1944; "Kismet," MGM, 1944; "Centennial Summer," Twentieth Century-Fox, 1946; "Stage Struck," Monogram, 1946; "California," Paramount, 1946; "Gay Purree," Warner Bros., 1962.

Author of numerous songs, including "Over the Rainbow," "Happiness Is a Thing Called Joe," "Brother Can You Spare a Dime," "April in Paris," "It's Only a Paper Moon," "What Is There to Say?," "Suddenly," "I'm Yours," "Isn't it Heavenly?," "You're a Builder Upper," "Ah But Is It Love," "More and More," "Right as the Rain," "Old Devil Moon," "On That Great Day Comin' Manana," "How Are Things in Glocca Morra?," and "We're Off to See the Wizard."

Contributor of light verse to newspapers and magazines.

WORK IN PROGRESS: "I Got a Song," an autobiographical play; "What a Day for a Miracle," a play based on the Children's Crusade of 1212.

SIDELIGHTS: Popularly known as Yip Harburg, this lyricist has written songs for some of the world's best-loved musicals, including "The Wizard of Oz," "Bloomer Girl," and "Finian's Rainbow." Harburg said that he was influenced by his teachers at City College and by authors George Bernard Shaw, Sir William Schwenk Gilbert, Jonathan Swift, Sean O'Casey, Oscar Wilde, and Mark Twain, all of whom were noted satirists.

Ira Gershwin was Harburg's classmate at Townsend Harris Hall, the prep school for City College. "There we wrote a humorous column for the high school paper entitled 'Much Ado,'" related Harburg, "and we collaborated on one Broadway show in 1934, 'Life Begins at 8:40,' for Bert Lahr. Ira and I have been close friends ever since school. I still visit him when I'm out on the coast."

When asked about his techniques for composing lyrics, Harburg told *CA:* "Anything goes, as long as it generates a song. Most ballad tunes are written first, and the lyrics fitted to the music. Sometimes the composer is given a title or possibly a line or two to work with. Most comedy songs start with several lines or possibly a whole verse. There are no formulas. Everything is geared to the particular psyches of composer and lyricist."

Harburg believes that musicals "have become a lost art for the newer generation that is undisciplined, without roots in poetry or literature." He called "The Wiz," a modern version of "The Wizard of Oz," "a theatrical disgrace in keeping with the ugliness of today's culture."

In Harburg's view, popular songs today "are not joyous. They're grim." He told Aljean Harmetz that songs are not written with "the craftsmanship, and the fine skill of the composers of the '20's and '30's. . . . Today even when there is no melody, the sound engineer can give you enough vibrations to make a song a hit."

Of his own songs, Harburg reflected, "It is hard to say which is my favorite, but I would rate 'Last Night When We Were Young' as a possible choice." Though the movie "The Wizard of Oz" has appeared on television each spring for many years, Harburg said he does not watch it every year, "but I do like to catch it every so often."

"What a Day for a Miracle," Harburg's new play, will be produced by the American Playwrights Company on university campuses. Since it costs one million dollars to open a show on Broadway, it would be too risky to attempt with a play about the Crusades. As he told Harmetz, "A show on the Crusades doesn't have sex."

Harburg appeared on the CBS television show "60 Minutes" on March 5, 1978.

AVOCATIONAL INTERESTS: Tennis, golf, swimming, travel.

BIOGRAPHICAL/CRITICAL SOURCES: David Ewen, *Great Men of American Popular Song,* Prentice-Hall, 1970; *Newsweek,* June 22, 1970; Max Wilk, *They're Playing Our Song,* Atheneum, 1973; Stanley Green, *World of Musical Comedy,* 3rd edition, Barnes, 1974; Lehman Engel, *Their Words Are Music,* Crown, 1975; *New York Times,* March 16, 1977; Aljean Harmetz, *The Making of the Wizard of Oz,* Knopf, 1977.

* * *

HARD, Edward W(ilhelm), Jr. 1939-
(T. W. Hard)

PERSONAL: Born October 6, 1939, in Buffalo, N.Y.; son of Edward W. (a geologist) and Mary Hazel (a librarian) Hard. *Education:* Yale University, B.A., 1962; Columbia University, M.D., 1966. *Home:* 200 Eleanor Dr., Woodside, Calif. 94062. *Agent:* Shirley Fisher, McIntosh & Otis, Inc., 475 Fifth Ave., New York, N.Y. 10017.

CAREER: Stanford University Hospital, Stanford, Calif., resident in surgery, 1972-75; Presbyterian Hospital, San Francisco, Calif., director of emergency services, 1975—. *Military service:* U.S. Navy, flight surgeon, 1967-72; became lieutenant commander. *Member:* American College of Emergency Physicians, Aerospace Medical Society.

WRITINGS—Under name T. W. Hard: *S.U.M. VII* (novel), Harper, 1979. Contributor of stories to *Saturday Evening Post.*

WORK IN PROGRESS: A novel on Victorian Africa.

SIDELIGHTS: Hard writes: "The novel *S.U.M. VII* was written from a germ of an idea first planted during a visit to Egypt in 1963. The story is about a team of medical researchers who discover a tomb south of the Valley of the Kings and uncover the extraordinary mummy of a high priest during the reign of Cheops in 2700 B.C.

"The body is brought back to the States under the code name S.U.M. VII and at a large university medical center is given a series of highly sophisticated medical tests. Here the researchers find some of the cells of the body are still capable of growth and the concept of reunification (resuscitation) is first entertained.

"A cardiopulmonary bypass operation is a success and for the first time in medical history a heart which has not beaten for five-thousand years springs to life. Yet radiocarbon dating indicates the body of S.U.M. VII predates the great pyramid and Pharoah Cheops by twenty-thousand years. Why are there certain elements in his blood found in no other members of the mammalian species? And why, too, does he speak a strange musical language which is indecipherable by the most sophisticated computers? Was S.U.M. VII really a high priest instrumental in the design of the great pyramid of Cheops, or was he someone much older, someone much more?

"The story was written to be entertaining, informative, and at the end to give the reader something to think about. It was fun to write and hopefully it will achieve these goals."

* * *

HARDER, Raymond Wymbs, Jr.

PERSONAL: Born October 25, 1920, in Mt. Vernon, N.Y.; son of Raymond Wymbs (an engineer) and Lucie (Belden Scott) Harder; married Eleanor Loraine Brown (a writer, composer, and teacher), September 4, 1949; children: Daniel W., Julia Ann. *Education:* Attended University of Missouri, 1940-41; University of California, Los Angeles, B.A., 1948. *Politics:* "Liberal independent." *Home:* 354E Military Ave., Los Angeles, Calif. 90034. *Office:* Michael-Sellers Advertising, 5900 Wilshire Blvd., Los Angeles, Calif. 90036.

CAREER: Euyart & Rose Advertising, Los Angeles, Calif., vice-president, 1960-68; Michael-Sellers Advertising, Los Angeles, senior accounting executive, 1968—; playwright. Advertising consultant. *Military:* U.S. Coast Guard; became lieutenant junior grade; received Bronze Star. *Member:* American National Theatre and Academy (western branch; first vice-president), American Society of Composers, Authors and Publishers, Dramatists Guild, Los Angeles Town Hall.

WRITINGS—Musical plays for children; all with wife, Eleanor Harder: *Annabelle Broom,* Music Theatre International (two-act; first produced in Los Angeles, Calif. at Players Ring Theatre, October, 1954), Music Theatre International, 1959; *Good Grief, a Griffin* (two-act; first produced at University of California at Los Angeles, May, 1962), Anchorage Press, 1968; *Sacramento Fifty Miles* (two-act; first produced in Los Angeles at California State Museum of Science & Industry, 1967), Anchorage Press, 1969; *Near Sighted Knight* (two-act; first produced in Pasadena, Calif., April, 1973), Anchorage Press, 1974.

Unpublished plays with wife, Eleanor Harder: "How Shall We Sing" (two-act musical), first produced in Missoula, Mont., October, 1976; "Rhumba-Tiya," first produced at Western Washington State College, February, 1978.

Contributor of articles and personality features to magazines.

WORK IN PROGRESS: A musical based on the west coast; a composite work comprised of several short plays.

SIDELIGHTS: Harder advised: "There is no short, easy road to success in the fields where I operate. Blessed as I am by being married to the only person with whom I believe I could collaborate, there are yet so many lessons to be learned, so many ideas to be worked out, that one lifetime simply isn't long enough to achieve the goals set up years ago."

* * *

HARDING, T(imothy) D. 1948-

PERSONAL: Born May 6, 1948, in London, England; son of Robert William (a teacher) and Sandra (a teacher; maiden name, Luce) Harding. *Education:* Pembroke College, Oxford, M.A. and B.Phil. *Home:* 45 Fitzwilliam Sq., Dublin 2, Ireland.

CAREER: Writer. *Member:* National Union of Journalists.

WRITINGS—All chess instruction manuals: (With R. G. Wade) *The Marshall Attack,* Batsford, 1974; (with George Botterill and Cerek Kottnauer) *The Sicilian Sozin,* Batsford, 1974; (with Peter Markland) *The Sicilian Richter-Rauzer,* Batsford, 1975; (with Bernard Cafferty) *Play the Evans Gambit,* R. Hale, 1976; *The Leningrad Dutch,* Batsford, 1976; (with Markland) *Sicilian E-5,* Batsford, 1976; (with Leonard Barden) *The Batsford Guide to Chess Openings,* Batsford, 1976; *Vienna Game,* Batsford, 1977; *Spanish-Marshall,* Batsford, 1977; (with Botterill) *The Scotch Game,* Batsford, 1977; (with Botterill) *The Italian Game,* Batsford, 1977; *Better Chess for Average Players,* Oxford University

Press, 1978; *Games of World Correspondence Chess Championships*, seven volumes, Batsford, 1979. Also author of *French-Advance and MacCutcheon Lines* and, with Wolfgang Herdenfeld, *French Classical Lines.*

Chess correspondent for *Irish Press* and *Sunday Press.* Contributor to chess journals.

WORK IN PROGRESS: More chess books.

* * *

HARDY, Alister C(lavering)   1896-

PERSONAL: Born February 10, 1896, in Nottingham, England; son of Richard (an architect) and Elizabeth (Clavering) Hardy; married Sylvia Garstang, December 3, 1928; children: Michael G., Belinda Hardy Farley. *Education:* Exeter College, Oxford, M.A., 1921, D.Sc., 1938. *Religion:* Unitarian-Universalist. *Home:* 7 Capel Close, Oxford, England.

CAREER: Ministry of Agriculture & Fisheries, England, scientific officer for fisheries, 1921-24; Royal Research Ship *Discovery,* chief zoologist of Antarctic expedition, 1925-27; University of Hull, Hull, England, professor of zoology and oceanography, 1928-41; University of Aberdeen, Aberdeen, Scotland, Regius Professor of Natural History, 1942-45; Oxford University, Oxford, England, professor of zoology, 1946-63, Linacre Professor of Zoology, 1946-61; writer, 1963-68; Oxford University, director of religious experience research at Manchester College, 1968-76; writer, 1976—. *Military service:* British Army, 1915-19; became captain. *Member:* Royal Society (fellow), Linnean Society, Zoological Society. *Awards, honors:* Knighted in 1957; LL.D. from University of Aberdeen; D.Sc. from University of Hull and University of Southampton; honorary fellow of Merton College, Oxford, 1946-63, and Exeter College, Oxford; award from American Lecompt du Nouey Foundation, 1968, for *The Living Stream;* science book award from Phi Beta Kappa, 1968, for *Great Waters.*

WRITINGS: (Editor with Julian Huxley and T.E.B. Firth) *Evolution as a Process,* Allen & Unwin, 1954; *The Open Sea,* Collins, Volume I: *The World of Plankton,* 1956, Volume II: *Fish and Fisheries,* 1959, one volume edition, Houghton, 1959; *The Living Stream: Evolution and Man,* Collins, 1965, Harper, 1966; *The Divine Flame: An Essay Toward a Natural History of Religion,* Collins, 1966; *Great Waters* (self-illustrated), Collins, 1967, Harper, 1968; (with R. Harvie and A. Koestler) *The Challenge of Chance,* Hutchinson, 1973, Random House, 1974; *The Biology of God,* J. Cape, 1975.

WORK IN PROGRESS: The Spiritual Nature of Man: A Study of Contemporary Religious Experience; Ponds, Pools, and Puddles: A Natural History of a Microscopic World.

SIDELIGHTS: Sir Alister Hardy's books fall into the category of popular science, readable and interesting to the general public, but they are not merely summaries or lay translations of scientific data.

Great Waters is the popular version of a journal he kept while sailing Atlantic and Antarctic waters on the square-rigger *Discovery* in the middle 1920's. The account is highly readable and full of factual information about whales, plankton, and oceanic biology and ecology in general.

Through all his writings, Hardy presents factual information, but does not hesitate to add and explain his own views of the natural world; for instance, his theory that natural selection is influenced, not only by physical and mechanistic development, but by the survival value of specific behavior

patterns, as well as habits which reinforce an animal's life-expectancy and general well-being.

His other books, especially in recent years, often go beyond "hard science" to the more controversial areas of telepathy and theology, but the subjects continue to be treated in a scientific manner. His studies in the area of natural theology have included anthropological, psychological, and philosophical research; while he has rejected many previously-established theories in these fields, he emphasizes that his own views represent not so much radical innovations as more simple changes of ideas and ways of thinking, and he calls for a more experimental approach by other researchers in these areas.

BIOGRAPHICAL/CRITICAL SOURCES: Times Literary Supplement, June 8, 1967; *Christian Century,* September 13, 1967; *New York Times Book Review,* March 17, 1968.

* * *

HARDY, Barbara (Gladys)

PERSONAL: Born in England; daughter of Maurice (a seaman) and Gladys (a barrister's clerk; maiden name, Abrahams) Nathan; married Ernest Hardy (a civil servant; died); children: two daughters. *Education:* University of London, B.A., 1947, M.A., 1949. *Residence:* London, England. *Office:* Birkbeck College, Malet St., London WC1E 7HX, England.

CAREER: University of London, Royal Holloway College, London, England, professor of English, 1965-70; University of London, Birkbeck College, London, professor of English, 1970—. *Member:* Modern Language Association (honorary member). *Awards, honors:* British Academy Rose Mary Crawshay Prize, 1962, for *The Novels of George Eliot: A Study in Form.*

WRITINGS—Criticism: *The Novels of George Eliot: A Study in Form,* Athlone Press, 1959, Oxford University Press, 1967; *Twelfth Night,* Basil Blackwell, 1962; *Wuthering Heights,* Basil Blackwell, 1963, Barnes & Noble, 1964; *The Appropriate Form: An Essay on the Novel,* Athlone Press, 1964, Northwestern University Press, 1971; *Jane Eyre,* Basil Blackwell, 1964, Barnes & Noble, 1965; *Charles Dickens: The Later Novels,* Longmans, Green, 1968; *The Moral Art of Dickens,* Oxford University Press, 1970; *The Exposure of Luxury: Radical Themes in Thackery,* University of Pittsburgh Press, 1972; *Tellers and Listeners: The Narrative Imagination,* Athlone Press, 1975, Humanities Press, 1976; *A Reading of Jane Austen,* P. Owen, 1975, New York University Press, 1976; *The Advantage of Lyric: Essays on Feeling in Poetry,* Indiana University Press, 1977.

Editor: *Middlemarch: Critical Approaches to the Novel,* Oxford University Press, 1967; George Eliot, *Daniel Deronda,* Penguin, 1967; *Critical Essays on George Eliot,* Barnes & Noble, 1970; Thomas Hardy, *The Trumpet Major,* Macmillan, 1974.

Contributor of reviews to periodicals, including *Daily Telegraph, Spectator,* and *Times Literary Supplement.*

WORK IN PROGRESS: A book, *Feeling in Victorian Literature;* a collection of essays and lectures on George Eliot; a study of the presentation of objects in fiction.

SIDELIGHTS: Much of Hardy's work has been devoted to the study of form in the novel, particularly in its moral and narrative aspects. Calling *The Moral Art of Dickens* an "economical and searching study," a *Washington Post* critic noted that "Hardy stresses the fundamentally moral enterprise which Dickens' career was, and with the fine instrument of her critical skill outlines the theme of moral transformation on various novels." Another book, *The Exposure of Luxury: Radical Themes in Thackery,* looks at the relationship between Thackery's rendering of surface appearances and his satiric purposes. "Reading [*The Exposure of Luxury*]," wrote a *Times Literary Supplement* critic, "is like being taken round a stately home by an incredibly knowledgeable and efficient guide. . . . Many of Thackery's finest scenes are recalled for us in a manner that greatly enhances our admiration for his psychological profundity."

Hardy's concern for narrative, a major consideration of all her criticism, is explored in *Tellers and Listeners: The Narrative Imagination.* The study examines several subsidiary forms of storytelling as demonstrated in the works of various fiction writers. Including such forms as reminiscences, boasts, gossip, daydreams, and jokes, observed John Cary, Hardy "shows not only how intricately and extensively the flesh of novels is composed of these small narrative cells, but also what a sharp instrument for distinguishing novelist from novelist the use of the storyteller, big and little, can amount to."

BIOGRAPHICAL/CRITICAL SOURCES: Times Literary Supplement, January 18, 1968, February 5, 1970, December 25, 1970, October 6, 1972, April 23, 1976, January 16, 1976; *New York Review of Books,* October 8, 1970; *Washington Post,* December 30, 1970; *Virginia Quarterly Review,* summer, 1971, winter, 1973; *New Statesman,* October 24, 1975; *Encounter,* July, 1977; *New York Times Book Review,* September 11, 1977.

*   *   *

HARLOW, LeRoy F(rancis) 1913-

PERSONAL: Born October 20, 1913, in Seattle, Wash.; son of Milton N. (a pharmacist) and Ruby Blanche (Robinson) Harlow; married Agda Gronbech (a university instructor), June 28, 1939; children: Steven G., John G., Christine G. (Mrs. Alan L. Allie), Thomas G., David G., Peter G., Julia G. (Mrs. John Taylor Doolittle). *Education:* Iowa State University, B.S., 1938; University of Minnesota, M.A., 1942. *Politics:* Republican. *Religion:* Church of Jesus Christ of Latter-day Saints (Mormons). *Home:* 1855 North Oak Lane, Provo, Utah 84601. *Office:* Institute of Public Management, 210 JKB, Brigham Young University, Provo, Utah 84602.

CAREER: U.S. Public Works Administration, Omaha, Neb., associate engineer, 1938-39; U.S. Social Security Board, Washington, D.C., field assistant in Des Moines, Iowa, and Lincoln, Neb., 1939-42; U.S. Bureau of the Budget, Washington, D.C., associate budget examiner, 1942-43; city manager of Sweet Home, Ore., 1943-45; Public Administration Service (management consultants), Chicago, Ill., staff consultant, 1945-46; city manager of Albert Lea, Minn., 1946-47; city manager of Fargo, N.D., 1947-49; Minnesota Efficiency in Government Commission, St. Paul, director, 1949-51; Village of Richfield, Minn., village manager, 1951-52; city manager of Daytona Beach, Fla., 1952-55; Booz, Allen & Hamilton (management consultants), Chicago, Ill., senior associate, 1955-61; New Mexico Revenue Structure Study Committee, Santa Fe, director, 1961-63; Greater Cleveland Tax Policy Study Commission, Cleveland, Ohio, director, 1963-64; Cuyahoga County Mayors and City Managers Association, Cleveland, Ohio, executive secretary, 1964-67; Brigham Young University, Provo, Utah, associate professor, 1967-76, professor of organization and management, 1976-79, professor emeritus, 1979—. Management

consultant, 1967—. Director of Utah Local Government Modernization Study, 1968-73; active in local political and civic affairs. Consultant to local, state, and federal government agencies. *Military service:* U.S. Army, Infantry, 1933-34.

MEMBER: International City Management Association, American Society for Public Administration (regional president, 1966, 1968), National Municipal League, Governmental Research Association, American Political Science Association, Society of American Military Engineers, Phi Kappa Phi, Commonwealth Club of California. *Awards, honors:* National awards from Governmental Research Association, 1965, 1970; certificate of merit from regional chapter of American Society for Public Administration, 1967.

WRITINGS: Handbook for the Study of State Government Administration, Minnesota Legislature, 1950; *How to Achieve Greater Efficiency and Economy in Minnesota's Government,* Minnesota Legislature, 1951.

Opportunities for Improving the New Mexico Revenue System, New Mexico Legislature, 1962; *Guides to Tax Policy Decisions in Greater Cleveland,* Greater Cleveland Tax Policy Study Commission, 1964; *Implementing the "Metropolitan Desk" Concept,* U.S. Department of Housing & Urban Development, 1966.

Local Government Modernization Study, five volumes, Bureau of Community Development, University of Utah, 1970; *Utah Local Government Finance Study,* five volumes, Bureau of Community Development, University of Utah, 1973; *Twelve Model Optional Plans of County Government,* twelve volumes, Bureau of Community Development, University of Utah, 1973; *Helping Utah's Local Governments Help Themselves,* Bureau of Community Development, University of Utah, 1973; *Without Fear or Favor: Odyssey of a City Manager,* Brigham Young University Press, 1977.

Contributor to management and administration journals, including *National Civic Review, Vital Speeches,* and *Western City.* Member of board of editors of *Public Administration Review.*

WORK IN PROGRESS: Without Fear or Favor Number Two (tentative title), for Brigham Young University Press; *Management for Everyman* (tentative title).

SIDELIGHTS: Harlow writes: "Because our society is complex and highly urbanized, I believe the secular organization most important to protection and enhancement of our individual social, economic, and personal well-being is our system of local governments. Yet, many of these governments are on the brink of financial, organizational, operational, and ethical bankruptcy.

"More than thirty years' experience as a city manager for five cities, and consultant to governments in nearly half the states and the Philippines persuades me that to reverse the current trend and establish 'good' local government requires the following: that although technical competence and efficient practices are essential, they must be built on a foundation of integrity, impartiality, and consistency; that proven principles of sound administrative organization and methods must be applied and maintained continuously; that citizens are entitled to be served by the best available people, whose selection is based on what they know and can do, not solely on whom they know and have politically supported; that every act of local government and all its records must be open to the public's watchdog, the American free press; and that citizens must not only be asked, but they must be assisted so far as time and energy permit, to be fully informed about all phases of local government business and to be involved in the overall management of that business.

"I also believe that the first prerequisite for administrative responsibility and authority in public employment is integrity. Honest mistakes, honestly made, can be tolerated and excused. But regardless of technical ability, the man or woman whose conduct has demonstrated beyond a question that he or she is not honest is, in my opinion, unfit to fill a public office. When the person in responsible charge of the organization has satisfied himself of this fact, it is not his choice but his duty to take necessary action. The degree and extent of evidence of dishonesty is not of major importance. The time to stop dishonesty in government is when it is first detected, not after it is well established."

* * *

HARRIS, Jay S(tephen) 1938-

PERSONAL: Born May 2, 1938, in Los Angeles, Calif.; son of Nathan (a film buyer) and Leah (a dental assistant; maiden name, Spector) Harris; married Marie Masters, April 16, 1967 (divorced, 1976); children: Jenny, Jesse. *Education:* Cornell University, A.B., 1961; New York University, LL.B., 1965. *Home:* 15 West 72nd St., New York, N.Y. 10023. *Office:* Weissberger & Harris, 120 East 56th St., New York, N.Y. 10022.

CAREER: County of New York, New York City, assistant district attorney, 1965-67; Phillips, Nizer, Benjamin, Krim & Ballon, New York City, associate, 1967-69; Weissberger & Harris, New York City, law partner, 1969—. Member of board of directors of American Theatre Wing. *Military service:* U.S. Army, 1961-63. *Member:* New York State Bar Association, Association of the Bar of the City of New York.

WRITINGS: TV Guide: The First Twenty-Five Years, Simon & Schuster, 1978.

* * *

HARRISON, Selig S(eidenman) 1927-

PERSONAL: Born March 19, 1927, in Pittsburgh, Pa.; son of Coleman (a lawyer) and Myrtle (Seidenman) Harrison; married Barbara Kathreen Johnston (a researcher), October 10, 1951; children: Coleman P., Kathreen G. *Education:* Harvard University, B.A. (cum laude), 1948. *Home:* 400 East 54th St., New York, N.Y. 10022. *Office:* Carnegie Endowment for International Peace, 30 Rockefeller Plaza, New York, N.Y. 10019.

CAREER: Associated Press, New York City, reporter in Detroit, Mich., 1949-51, foreign correspondent in New Delhi, India, 1951-54, on foreign desk in New York City, 1954; Columbia University, New York City, research associate at Language and Communication Research Center, 1955-56; *New Republic*, Washington, D.C., associate editor, 1956-59, managing editor, 1959-62; *Washington Post*, Washington, D.C., chief of New Delhi bureau, 1962-65, member of editorial board, 1965-67, chief of Tokyo bureau, 1968-72, assistant foreign editor, 1973, national reporter, 1974; Carnegie Endowment for International Peace, New York City, senior associate, 1974—. Professorial lecturer at Johns Hopkins School of Advanced International Studies, 1973; visiting professor at Amherst College, Smith College, Mt. Holyoke College, and University of Massachusetts, 1961; guest lecturer at Foreign Service Institute, 1959—; lecturer at colleges and universities throughout the United States. *Military service:* U.S. Navy, 1945-46. *Member:* Council on Foreign

Relations, Asia Society (head of India council, 1978—). *Awards, honors:* Nieman fellow at Harvard University, 1954-55; senior fellow of Brookings Institution, 1967-68, and East-West Center, 1972-73.

WRITINGS: The Most Dangerous Decades: An Introduction to the Comparative Study of Language Policy in Multilingual States (monograph), Language and Communication Research Center, Columbia University, 1957; (contributor) R. L. Park, editor, *Leadership and Political Institutions in India*, Princeton University Press, 1959; *India: The Most Dangerous Decades*, Princeton University Press, 1960; (editor and contributor) *India and the United States*, Macmillan, 1961; (contributor) K. A. Silvert, editor, *Expectant Peoples: Nationalism and Development*, Random House, 1963; *China, Oil, and Asia: Conflict Ahead?*, Columbia University Press, 1977; *The Widening Gulf: Asian Nationalism and American Policy*, Free Press, 1978.

Author of "India and America," a weekly column in *Hindustan Times*, 1959-61, and "The American Scene," in *Statesman*, 1966-68. Contributor to academic journals, including *Foreign Affairs* and *Foreign Policy*, and popular magazines, including *Harper's*.

WORK IN PROGRESS: A book on the conflict potential in the tribal borderlands overlapping the frontiers of Afghanistan, Pakistan, and Iran, for Carnegie Endowment for International Peace.

SIDELIGHTS: Harrison told *CA:* "My work represents a continuing attempt to unite the investigative techniques and intellectual perspectives of journalism and scholarship, thus achieving a richer result than the medium would separately permit. The unifying thread in my more serious work has been an interest in nationalism and the interplay between national and sub-national identities, especially in Asia, and I regard my latest effort, *The Widening Gulf: Asian Nationalism and American Policy*, as my most significant contribution."

BIOGRAPHICAL/CRITICAL SOURCES: John Hohenberg, *Between Two Worlds: Policy, Press, and Public Opinion in Asian-American Relations*, Praeger, 1967.

* * *

HART, Joseph 1945-

PERSONAL: Born May 1, 1945, in Brooklyn, N.Y.; son of John W. (in sales) and Loretta (a teacher; maiden name, McGrath) Hart; married Victoria Paley (an actress), September 18, 1969; children: Rebecca. *Education:* Fordham College (now University), B.A., 1966; New York University, M.A., 1967. *Home:* 155 North Sixth Ave., Highland Park, N.J. 08904. *Agent:* George Ziegler, 160 East 97th St., New York, N.Y. 10029. *Office:* Levin Theatre, Rutgers University, New Brunswick, N.J. 08903.

CAREER: Colonial Press, New York City, messenger, 1965-66; Police Athletic League, New York City, drama director, 1966-69; Rutgers University, New Brunswick, N.J., instructor, 1969-73, assistant professor, 1973-79, associate professor of drama, 1979—, also actor, director, and director of theatre workshop. Founder and director of Melting Pot Repertory Theatre; director for Popsickle Players Children's Theatre and Shoestring Players Children's Theatre. Playwright-in-residence at Cubiculo Theatre. *Awards, honors:* Fellow at New York University, 1967-69; Schubert fellow of Pittsburgh Playhouse, 1970; summer resident of Albee Foundation, 1977; resident of Aspen Playwrights Conference.

WRITINGS—Plays: *Ghost Dance: Drama and Theatre* (two-act; first produced in New Brunswick, N.J., at Rutgers University, April 30, 1971), Stage Magic Play Service, 1975.

Produced plays: "Absinthe" (three-act), first produced in New York City at New York University's Mainstage, April 19, 1969; "Sonata for Mott Street" (three-act), first produced in New York City at Cubiculo Theatre, February 23, 1970; "Brooklyn Bridge Is Falling Down" (two-act), first produced in New York City at Cubiculo Theatre, January 10, 1971; "Wiglaf: A Myth for Actors" (one-act), first produced in New York City at Cubiculo Theatre, December 20, 1973; "Window and Wall" (two-act), first produced in New York City at Cubiculo Theatre, December 6, 1974; "Dark Moon and the Full" (first produced in New York City at Irish Rebel Theatre, March 26, 1976), published in *Best Short Plays, 1977*, Chilton, 1977; "The Memoirs of Charlie Pops" (three-act), first produced in New York City at Cubiculo Theatre, September 12, 1979.

Unproduced plays: "Lot's Wife" (two-act), 1977; "Hit and Run" (one-act), 1978.

Contributor of plays, short stories, and poems to magazines, including *Drama and Theatre, Actor Training,* and *Prairie Schooner.*

SIDELIGHTS: Hart told *CA:* "My mother was a frustrated actress, my father was a frustrated novelist. I couldn't fight it, so I joined the two dreams and became a frustrated playwright.

"I began in realisms, moved into ensemble and experimentation, and lately have been revisiting realism. My interests are in our varying ideas of God, the influence of heredity and environment, and the possibility of classic tragic patterns in modern drama. I am interested in themes that don't make the theater shout 'me too!' and waddle off in the footsteps of movies, television, and the six o'clock news."

BIOGRAPHICAL/CRITICAL SOURCES: *Village Voice,* March 5, 1970; *Newark Star Ledger,* September 16, 1975; *New York Daily News,* September 16, 1975; *Cue,* October, 1975; *Woodbridge News Tribune,* April 23, 1977.

*   *   *

HASELER, Stephen Michael Alan 1942-

PERSONAL: Born January 9, 1942; son of Cyril P. (in sales) and Phyllis (Geggie) Haseler; married Roberta Alexander (an accountant), 1967. *Education:* London School of Economics and Political Science, B.Sc., 1963, Ph.D., 1967. *Home and office:* 4 Carlton Mansions, Holland Park Gardens, London W.14, England.

CAREER: Greater London Council, London, England, member of council and head of general purposes committee, 1973-77; writer. Labour candidate for Parliament, 1970. Political head of Greater London's Civil Service. Head of Labour Political Studies Centre, 1971—. *Member:* Wood Green Labour Club, Reform Club.

WRITINGS: *The Gaitskellites,* Macmillan, 1969; *The Death of British Democracy: A Study of Britain's Political Present and Future,* Prometheus Books, 1976; *Eurocommunism: Implications for East and West,* Macmillan, 1978. Also author of *Social Democracy: Beyond Revisionism,* 1971. Contributor to magazines and newspapers, including *Encounter, Commentary,* and *American Spectator.*

WORK IN PROGRESS: *Britain's Social Experiment,* for Basil Blackwell.

SIDELIGHTS: Haseler writes: "My main, and continuing,

interest remains the development of British 'socialism' and the health of the democratic system in Britain."

He describes *The Death of British Democracy* in its foreword: "I have attempted to expose some of the causes of the country's present political failure; to state the points at which the democratic pass has already been sold; to examine the weaknesses of the national response to the threats to British democracy; to speculate about the sort of future that can be expected if the present national decline is not arrested; and to suggest the broad outlines of a new political consensus which is now, in my opinion, the only way to salvage British democracy."

BIOGRAPHICAL/CRITICAL SOURCES: *New Statesman,* May 7, 1976; *Economist,* May 15, 1976; *Encounter,* January, 1977; *National Review,* July 22, 1977.

*   *   *

HASFORD, (Jerry) Gustav 1947-
(George Gordon)

PERSONAL: Born November 28, 1947, in Haleyville, Ala.; son of Hassell Gustave (a factory worker) and Hazel (a librarian; maiden name, Noblett) Hasford; married Charlene Broock (a librarian), September 1, 1978. *Education:* Attended Santa Monica City College, 1972. *Politics:* Socialist. *Religion:* "Beer." *Home:* 2099 Bayview, Morro Bay, Calif. 93442.

CAREER: Writer. Worked as hotel clerk in Longview, Wash., 1970-71. *Military service:* U.S. Marine Corp., 1966-68; became corporal; served as combat correspondent in Vietnam. *Member:* Vietnam Veterans Against the War.

WRITINGS: *The Short-Timers,* Harper, 1979. Contributor to periodicals under pseudonym George Gordon.

WORK IN PROGRESS: *Voodoo Dancer,* "a novel about a mountain sculptor in Africa"; *The Phantom Blooker,* "a novel about Vietnam veterans"; *The Undefeated,* "a novel about the life of a private in the Army of Virginia, a Confederate *Red Badge of Courage.*"

SIDELIGHTS: Hasford told *CA:* "Lao-Tze pointed out that nothing worth saying can be said with words. Words are crude and clumsy things, objects of ink, ultimately imprecise. And writing is as much fun as giving birth to a *Howard Johnson's.* Writers learn to live with that fact the way a soldier learns to live with fear or the way a doctor learns to live with death. When the battle is lost, the soldier attacks. When the case is hopeless, the doctor operates. So writers write. And whereas soldiers and doctors are allowed to bury their mistakes a writer is expected to publish his.

"Being a writer was not my first choice for a profession. I would much prefer to be an archaeologist, a sculptor, or a country-western singer. But then I had all these ideas for books which came to me in a vision. Since then, I have been convinced that there is no human problem which could not be solved if people would simply do as I say. Yet my work remains a personal statement—I speak for no groups or social factions. I have no goals beyond the completion of my next story. The praise I seek from my readers is that they finish my books. After being alternately damned and praised for equally invalid reasons, I am content to trade fame for accuracy of interpretation. Fame, for a writer, is like being a dancing bear with a little hat on your head."

Hasford's book, *The Short-Timers,* has met with both critical acclaim and derision. Walter Clemons called it "the best work of fiction about the Vietnam war I've read." He added, "*The Short-Timers* is a study of brutalization, narrated with a fastidious nonchalance that only a careless reader will mistake for lack of feeling." However, a critic for *New Republic* claimed, "*The Short-Timers* may be an effective purgation, but as a novel it not only fails to move but to interest." The same critic also cited Hasford for his excessive violence. "One reads on from morbid motives only," declared the *New Republic* writer.

BIOGRAPHICAL/CRITICAL SOURCES: Newsweek, January 1, 1979; *Chicago Tribune*, January 14, 1979; *New Republic*, January 27, 1979.

* * *

HATFIELD, Antoinette Kuzmanich   1929-

PERSONAL: Born January 17, 1929, in Portland, Ore.; daughter of Vincent and Josephine (Leovich) Kuzmanich; married Mark Odom Hatfield (a U.S. senator), July 8, 1958; children: Elizabeth, Mark Odom, Theresa, Charles Vincent. *Education:* University of Oregon, B.S., 1950; Stanford University, M.A., 1955. *Religion:* Baptist. *Home address:* P.O. Box 630, Newport, Ore. 97365.

CAREER: Junior high school English teacher and counselor in Salem, Ore., 1950-54; high school English teacher and counselor in Portland, Ore., 1956-57; Portland State College, Portland, Ore., counselor of women, 1957-58; realtor in Washington, D.C., 1975—. Member of Washington Board of Realtors. Member of Oregon Federation of Republican Women, 1957—, and Salem Assistance League, 1962—. *Member:* National Education Association, American Newspaper Women's Club (associate member), Daughters of the Nile, Delta Kappa Gamma, Alpha Phi.

WRITINGS: ReMarkable Recipes, Criterion, 1966; *More ReMarkable Recipes*, Criterion, 1970; *Food for Fellowship*, Word Books, 1971; *How to Help Your Child Eat Right*, Acropolis Books, 1973; *Food for Family and Friends*, Word Books, 1978.

* * *

HATZFELD, Helmut A(nthony)   1892-1979

OBITUARY NOTICE: Born November 4, 1892, in Bad-Duerkheim, Germany; died of kidney failure, May 18, 1979, in Washington, D.C. Educator and author. After the Nazis suspended him from his teaching career at the University of Heidelberg in 1935, Hatzfeld moved to Belgium and later to the United States, where he became professor of Romance languages at Catholic University. He was best known for his research on the baroque style in Spanish and French literature. Hatzfeld wrote over three hundred articles and twenty-five books in his field, including the prize-winning *Literature Through Art*. Obituaries and other sources: *Directory of American Scholars*, Volume III: *Foreign Languages, Linguistics, and Philology*, 7th edition, Bowker, 1978; *Who's Who in America*, 40th edition, Marquis, 1978; *Washington Post*, May 20, 1979.

* * *

HAUGHT, John F(rancis)   1942-

PERSONAL: Born November 12, 1942, in Buffalo, N.Y.; son of Paul (a farmer) and Angela (Swint) Haught; married Evelyn Pelligrino, September 4, 1967; children: Paul, Martin. *Education:* St. Mary's University, Baltimore, Md., B.A., 1964; Catholic University of America, M.A., 1968, Ph.D., 1970. *Home:* 1713 North Glebe Rd., Arlington, Va. 22207. *Office:* Department of Theology, Georgetown University, Washington, D.C. 20057.

CAREER: Georgetown University, Washington, D.C., assistant professor, 1970-76, associate professor of theology, 1976—. *Awards, honors:* Annual book award from College Theology Society, 1978, for *Religion and Self-Acceptance*.

WRITINGS: Religion and Self-Acceptance, Paulist/Newman, 1976. Contributor of articles and reviews to theology journals.

WORK IN PROGRESS: Research on science and religion.

SIDELIGHTS: Haught wrote: "My purpose in writing the above-mentioned book was to seek out the relationship between religion and self-knowledge, thus integrating concerns of thinkers from Socrates to contemporary psychology. My work now focuses on the problem of nature and purpose; a manuscript is now in its early phases."

* * *

HAUGHTON, Claire Shaver   1901-

PERSONAL: Born November 26, 1901, in Fairmount Springs, Pa.; daughter of Ziba Rice (a manufacturing supervisor) and Grace (a writer; maiden name, Taylor) Shaver; married Henry Osborne Haughton (an engineer), August 30, 1924; children: Anne Haughton Hansen, Henry Osborne, Jr., Alice Haughton Rice. *Education:* Attended Dickinson College, 1920-21, Pennsylvania State University, 1923-24, and University of Illinois, 1924-26; Southern Connecticut State College, B.A., 1954. *Politics:* Republican. *Religion:* Episcopalian. *Home:* 88 Pine St., Wallingford, Conn. 06942. *Agent:* Muriel Fuller, P.O. Box 193, Grand Central Station, New York, N.Y. 10017.

CAREER: Elementary school teacher in Delaware County, Pa., 1921-23; Yale University, New Haven, Conn., writer for American history film project, 1950-51; teacher of English to displaced foreign adults in Wallingford, Conn., 1951-52; elementary school teacher in Wallingford, 1952-69; public speaker and free-lance writer. *Member:* League of Women Voters, Wallingford Garden Club.

WRITINGS: Green Immigrants, Harcourt, 1978; *The Making of America's Garden*, Harcourt, in press. Contributor to *Teaching Foreign Children*, 1922.

WORK IN PROGRESS: Love Among the Ruins, a romance novel centered on plant-hunting in Mexico.

SIDELIGHTS: Claire Haughton writes: "A descendant of Pilgrims and Pennsylvania Quakers, I married a man whose ancestors founded Maryland and Virginia, and we moved to New England.

"World War II revealed that many soldiers knew little American history. To teach history more vividly in the public schools a project was organized to coordinate history textbooks with historical movies. I was assigned the early colonial years.

"My research immediately challenged me with the question: what did the first settlers eat? There were no gardens, no orchards. What seeds did they bring? How did they grow? The complete lack of information in this area interested me, and history and botany became an absorbing hobby. I visited botanical gardens here and in Mexico, Europe, and Hawaii. The result is *Green Immigrants*, the history of a hundred immigrant plants that have transformed America. Much of this material has been researched and organized for the first time."

* * *

HAUSER, Thomas   1946-

PERSONAL: Born February 27, 1946, in New York, N.Y.;

son of Simon J. (an attorney) and Eleanor (Nordlinger) Hauser. *Education:* Columbia University, B.A., 1967, J.D., 1970. *Home and office:* 11 Riverside Dr., #11-JE, New York, N.Y. 10023.

CAREER: Cravath, Swaine & Moore, New York, N.Y., attorney, 1971-77; writer, 1977—.

WRITINGS: The Execution of Charles Horman, Harcourt, 1978. Also author of *The Trial of Patrolman Thomas Shea* (nonfiction), 1979. Contributor to magazines and newspapers, including *New York.* Contributing editor of *McCall's.*

WORK IN PROGRESS: Brotherly Love, a psychological mystery novel.

*   *   *

HAVELOCK, Christine Mitchell   1924-

PERSONAL: Born June 2, 1924, in Cochrane, Ontario, Canada; came to United States in 1949; naturalized U.S. citizen; daughter of William W. (a banker) and Annie (Graham) Mitchell; married Eric A. Havelock (a professor), November 23, 1962. *Education:* University of Toronto, A.B., 1946; Harvard University, A.M., 1950, Ph.D., 1957. *Politics:* Democrat. *Religion:* Protestant. *Office:* Department of Art, Vassar College, Poughkeepsie, N.Y. 12601.

CAREER: Vassar College, Poughkeepsie, N.Y., 1957—, currently professor of art history, assistant to president of college, 1972-73, director of women's studies, 1978-79. Visiting professor, State University of New York at Buffalo, 1972. *Member:* College Art Association of America, American Institute of Archaeology, Women's Caucus for Art. *Awards, honors:* Fulbright fellow, 1951-52.

WRITINGS: Hellenistic Art, New York Graphic Society, 1971. Contributor to art and archaeology journals.

WORK IN PROGRESS: The Image of Women in Classical Art, publication expected in 1980.

SIDELIGHTS: Christine Havelock comments: "I have placed strong emphasis on style in Greek Art, which has led me to differ sometimes from conclusions reached by literary documentation, or by extrapolating from Roman copies. Recently I have come to enjoy areas of Greek art in which women are portrayed, so my interest in the feminist movement and my art history can be merged. I find this most satisfying."

*   *   *

HAVELOCK, Ronald G(eoffrey)   1935-

PERSONAL: Born March 21, 1935, in Toronto, Ontario, Canada; son of Eric Alfred (a professor of classics) and Ellen (Parkinson) Havelock; married Mary Morton Campbell, May 3, 1958 (divorced, 1975); children: Alice Mary, Laura Jeannette. *Education:* Harvard University, A.B., 1957; Boston University, A.M., 1962, Ph.D., 1965. *Home:* 1308 Fourth St. S.W., Washington, D.C. 20024. *Office:* Center for Technology and Administration, College of Public Affairs, 206 Hurst Hall, American University, Washington, D.C. 20016.

CAREER: Trainee in social psychology, Veterans Administration, 1962-65; United Nations Educational, Scientific, and Cultural Organization (UNESCO), Geneva, Switzerland, consultant to International Bureau of Education, 1974-76; University of Michigan, Ann Arbor, presently program director and research scientist at Center for Research on the Utilization of Scientific Knowledge, Institute for Social Research. Visiting fellow of National Institute of Education,

1976-78. Visiting professor and director of program for knowledge transfer and use at American University. Participant in national and international seminars, conferences, and workshops; consultant to National Science Foundation and National Academy of Sciences. *Awards, honors:* Grants from U.S. Air Force, 1966-68, U.S. Office of Education, 1966-69, 1968-71, 1972-73, Kellogg Foundation, 1968-71, U.S. Department of Transportation, 1968-71, U.S. Department of Labor, 1971-73, and U.S. Department of Health, Education & Welfare, 1972-73.

WRITINGS: Planning for Innovation Through Dissemination and Utilization of Knowledge, Institute for Social Research, University of Michigan, 1969; *Bibliography on Knowledge Utilization and Dissemination,* Institute for Social Research, University of Michigan, 1972; (with Mary C. Havelock) *Training for Change Agents,* Institute for Social Research, University of Michigan, 1973; *The Change Agent's Guide to Innovation in Education,* Educational Technology Publications, 1973; (with A. M. Huberman) *Solving Educational Problems: The Process of Educational Innovation in Developing Countries,* Praeger, 1978.

Contributor: G. Watson, editor, *Concepts for Social Change,* Volume I, National Training Laboratories, 1967; T. L. Eidell and J. M. Kitchel, editors, *Knowledge Production and Utilization in Educational Administration,* Center for the Advanced Study of Educational Administration, University of Oregon, 1968; *What Does Research Say About Getting Innovations Into Schools?,* Research for Better Schools, 1974; M. Kochen, editor, *Information for Action: Reorganizing Knowledge for Wisdom,* Academic Press, 1975; Kochen and J. Donohue, editors, *Information for the Communities,* American Library Association, 1975. Contributor of articles and reviews to education and psychology journals.

*   *   *

HAVEMANN, Joel   1943-

PERSONAL: Born July 16, 1943, in New York, N.Y.; son of Ernest C. (a writer) and Ruth (Bohle) Havemann; married Judith McIntosh (an editor), June 17, 1972; children: Terry Nicol (stepdaughter). *Education:* Harvard University, B.A., 1965. *Home:* 3809 Woodbine St., Chevy Chase, Md. 20015. *Office: National Journal,* 1730 M St. N.W., Washington, D.C. 20036.

CAREER: Chicago Sun-Times, Chicago, Ill., reporter, 1967-73; *National Journal,* Washington, D.C., reporter, 1973-78, deputy editor, 1978—. *Awards, honors:* Front Page Award from Chicago Newspaper Guild, 1968, for an article on the riots following the murder of Martin Luther King, Jr.

WRITINGS: Congress and the Budget, Indiana University Press, 1978.

SIDELIGHTS: Havemann is one of Washington's foremost non-governmental experts on the federal budget. He has written about the budget annually since 1973 in *National Journal.*

*   *   *

HAWKINS, Edward H.   1934-

PERSONAL: Born in 1934, in Wichita, Kan.; son of Edward H., Sr. (in insurance) and Martha E. (in insurance; maiden name, Cannon) Hawkins. *Education:* Attended San Francisco Art Institute, University of California, Berkeley, and University of Colorado. *Residence:* Denver, Colo.

CAREER: Independent motion picture producer and director (has made two hundred non-theatrical and advertising films), 1958—; writer, 1973—. *Member:* Colorado Authors League (past vice-president). *Awards, honors:* Award from San Francisco Film Festival for "The Eyes Have It"; citation from U.S. Air Force for film "Involvement: LIFE."

WRITINGS: Prisoners of Devil's Claw, Apollo, 1972; *Wellspring,* McGraw, 1978.

WORK IN PROGRESS: Two novels; three screenplays.

SIDELIGHTS: Hawkins writes: "I am a very private person. I prefer to write and hide away in the Colorado mountains, with mountain climbing and skiing. I have been a motion picture producer, writer, and director for a number of years and have, for the past five years, devoted all my time to writing professionally. My film career has taken me to all parts of the world; I have lived in Europe and the United Kingdom, and plan to return for locations for new novels and screenplays."

* * *

HAYMAN, LeRoy 1916-

PERSONAL: Born August 12, 1916, in Chicago, Ill.; son of Edward (a tailor) and Fannie (Treletsky) Hayman; married Anita Feder, June 29, 1941; children: Frances Hayman Froelich, Edward. *Education:* University of Illinois, B.A., 1937, M.A., 1940. *Home and office:* 2621 Southwest Natura Ave., Deerfield Beach, Fla. 33441.

CAREER: Teacher at military school in Boonville, Mo., 1940-42; *Compton's Encyclopedia,* Chicago, Ill., editor, 1946-61; Scholastic Magazines, Inc., New York, N.Y., editor, 1961-73; free-lance writer and editor, 1973—. Staff member at Pennsylvania State College (now University), 1942, Illinois Institute of Technology, 1946-51, and University of Chicago, 1952-53. *Military service:* U.S. Navy, 1942-45; became lieutenant junior grade. *Member:* Authors Guild of Authors League of America, Sigma Delta Chi. *Awards, honors:* Distinguished achievement award from Education Press, 1974.

WRITINGS: (Contributor) *People to Remember,* Scott, Foresman, 1960; *American Ambassador to the World: Adlai Stevenson,* Abelard, 1966; *What You Should Know About the U.S. Constitution,* Scholastic Book Services, 1966; *O Captain!: The Death of Abraham Lincoln,* Four Winds, 1968, reprinted as *Death of Lincoln; Book Notes: Tom Jones,* Barnes & Noble, 1968; *Harry Truman,* Crowell, 1969; *Leaders of the American Revolution,* Four Winds, 1970; *Road to Fort Sumter,* Crowell, 1971; *Assassinations of John and Robert Kennedy,* Scholastic Book Services, 1976; *Thirteen Who Vanished,* Messner, 1979; *Up, Up, and Away!,* Messner, in press. Editor of *Compton Yearbook, Junior Scholastic,* and *American Observer.*

SIDELIGHTS: Hayman writes: "Extensive travel in Europe and South America will be resumed when the dollar regains its dignity. Until then, I live and work in southern Florida, relishing the sun and the sea. I try to maintain a watch on the human condition all over the world, but I am a reporter, not a reformer. I've also been a teacher, full- or part-time, for most of my working life, rejoicing when my teaching has taken hold. Someday I'll write some kind of autobiography, but not yet."

* * *

HAYWARD, Max 1925(?)-1979

OBITUARY NOTICE: Born c. 1925 in London, England; died of cancer, March 18, 1979, in Oxford, England. Translator and author, best known for his work in contemporary Russian literature. Hayward's career as a translator began in his teens when he taught himself to read Russian. Later, during the Stalinist purges of artists and scholars after World War II, he dedicated himself to the preservation of Russian literature in the West. He translated works by major Russian authors, including Boris Pasternak, Aleksandr Solzhenitsyn, and Andrei Sinyavsky, and co-edited four books on Soviet literature. Obituaries and other sources: *New York Times,* March 20, 1979; *AB Bookman's Weekly,* April 16, 1979.

* * *

HEANEY, Seamus 1939-

PERSONAL: Born April 13, 1939, in County Derry, Ireland; married; children: two. *Education:* Attended St. Columb's College, Queen's University, B.A. *Home:* 16 Ashley Ave., Belfast 9, Northern Ireland.

CAREER: Poet. Worked as secondary school teacher, 1962-63; St. Joseph's College of Education, Belfast, Ireland, lecturer, 1963-66; Queen's University, Belfast, lecturer in English, 1966—. *Awards, honors:* Eric Gregory Award, 1966; Cholomondeley Award, 1967, Somerset Maugham Award, 1968, and Geoffrey Faber Memorial Prize, 1968, all for *Death of a Naturalist;* Denis Devlin Memorial Award, 1973, for *Wintering Out.*

WRITINGS—Poetry: Eleven Poems, Festival Publications, 1965; *Death of a Naturalist,* Oxford University Press, 1966; (with Dairo Hammond and Michael Longley) *Room to Rhyme,* Arts Council of Northern Ireland, 1968; *A Lough Neagh Sequence,* edited by Harry Chambers and Eric J. Morten, Phoenix Pamphlet Poets Press, 1969; *Door Into the Dark,* Oxford University Press, 1969; *Night Drive: Poems,* Credition, Devon, Richard Gilbertson, 1970; *Boy Driving His Father to Confession,* Sceptre Press, 1970; *Land,* Poem-of-the-Month Club, 1971; (editor with Alan Brownjohn) *New Poems: 1970-71,* Hutchinson, 1971; *Wintering Out,* Faber, 1972, Oxford University Press, 1973; (editor) *Soundings: An Annual Anthology of New Irish Poetry,* Blackstaff Press, 1972; *Soundings 2,* Blackstaff Press, 1974; *North,* Faber, 1975, Oxford University Press, 1976; *Bog Poems,* Rainbow Press, 1975. Also author of *Stations,* Ulsterman Publications.

Other: *The Fire i' the Flint: Reflections on the Poetry of Gerard Manley Hopkins,* Oxford University Press, 1975.

SIDELIGHTS: Heaney's first collection of poems, *Death of a Naturalist,* is among his most popular. Upon its publication in 1966, Heaney found himself in the forefront of a new generation of poets that also included Roger Hecht, Richard Frost, and James Whitehead. In a collective review of the already mentioned poets' first books, Samuel Marse noted, "In each of these books, there is evidence that the writer will achieve a real identity. Individual poems stick in the mind, not simply because they are well turned but because they suggest further and unusually individual developments."

In a review of *Door Into the Dark,* a writer for *Times Literary Supplement* referred to Heaney as one of the "tight-lipped poets...." The same writer also assessed Heaney's prose as "hard-edged: a punchy line travels about two inches." Another critic described Heaney's style as "clean and honest...."

Ranked among the best books in recent years when it came out, *Death of Naturalist* is almost exclusively devoted to depicting life in Northern Ireland. The book was highly praised for its keen insight into everyday life in the Irish countryside. David Galler declared that Heaney "leaves no doubt as to what he's seeing...." Similarly, Anthony Thwaite remarked, "It's impossible to fault the clean language, sensuous delight, concise and modest statements; and I'm sure it's all completely authentic."

Unfortunately, as some critics have noted, Heaney's gift for simplicity and clarity sometimes compromises his perception of the poem's subject. This leads to passages which, in attempting to compensate for the extreme simplicity, seem congested with descriptive terms. "The number of adjectives is daunting," wrote Galler; "they are huddled close by their nouns, for mutual safety.... Heaney's work is dense with exposition: if the level of simple metaphor is ever reached, it is all but obscured by a windmill of details." A reviewer for *Times Literary Supplement* echoed Galler's sentiments by commenting, "In Mr. Heaney's substantial and impressive *Death of a Naturalist* the most obvious surface fault is the rather glib or incongruous imagery stuck on in what seems to be an attempt to hit the required sophistication...."

Heaney's *Door Into the Dark* was reviewed by critics as a repeat of *Death of a Naturalist.* Alan Ross acknowledged that "*Door Into the Dark* scarcely extends his range, but it confirms his technical skill, his ability to enter into simple agricultural activities and give them resonance and depth." "At his best," Ross proceeded, "he persuades one of the sense of grace that craftsmanship, of whatever order, always gives off; at his more plodding, he still manages to make most urban verse of the instant-schools seem meretricious, vulgar and unskilled."

With *Wintering Out* and *North,* Heaney has grown as a poet and expanded his range to encompass, as a reviewer for *Sewanee Review* wrote, "a large, violent, and public landscape which is inhabited sometimes by Norsemen, sometimes by policemen, as well as by Mr. Heaney himself—now ready, it seems, to enter into a subtly nuanced dialogue with them on the subjects of politics, culture, and poetry." Helen Vendler stated: "Heaney, to my mind the best poet now writing in Ireland, seems the only one of his generation not in some way inhibited by the shadow of Yeats. Though he shares Yeats's love of the archaic, with its combination of the civilized and the stark, he unearths his archaism not in Celtic legends but in the bodies of long-dead Vikings, buried and preserved in Irish and Scandinavian bogs...."

BIOGRAPHICAL/CRITICAL SOURCES: Times Literary Supplement, January 17, 1967, July 17, 1969; *Kenyon Review,* January, 1967; *Virginia Quarterly Review,* summer, 1967; *Statesman,* June 27, 1969; *Punch,* July 2, 1969; *London,* October, 1969; *Contemporary Literature,* winter, 1968; *Sewanee Review,* winter, 1976; *New York Times Book Review,* April 18, 1976; *Contemporary Literary Criticism,* Gale, Volume 5, 1976, Volume 7, 1977.*

*　　*　　*

HEAPS, Willard A(llison) 1908-

PERSONAL: Born February 3, 1908, in Whiting, Iowa; son of Allison Ray (a clergyman) and Isabel (Warrington) Heaps. *Education:* Northwestern University, B.S., 1930; University of Michigan, A.B., 1931, M.A., 1934; Columbia University, M.A., 1940, Ed.D., 1942. *Home:* 2737 Barker Ave., Bronx, N.Y. 10467.

CAREER: Arizona State Teachers College, Tempe, assistant librarian and instructor in English, 1931-35; Pennsylvania State Teachers College, Kutztown, librarian and

director of library training, 1935-38; Columbia University, New York City, associate of School of Library Service, 1938-41; United Nations Educational, Scientific & Cultural Organization (UNESCO), Paris, France, assistant librarian, 1947-49; United Nations, New York City, chief of service to readers unit and acting chief of reference and documentation section, 1950-54; Carnegie Endowment for International Peace, New York City, librarian, 1954-55; free-lance indexer and writer, 1955—. *Military service:* U.S. Army, 1942-45; served in Europe; became lieutenant colonel.

WRITINGS: School Library Service in the United States, H. W. Wilson, 1940; *Book Selection for Secondary School Libraries,* H. W. Wilson, 1942; (with P. W. Heaps) *The Singing Sixties,* University of Oklahoma Press, 1960.

Juveniles: (Author of revision) Charles A. Browne, *The Story of Our National Ballads,* Crowell, 1960; *The Bravest Teenage Yanks,* Duell, Sloan & Pearce, 1963; (author of revision) Lydia Hoyt Farmer, *A Book of Famous Queens,* Crowell, 1964; *The Wall of Shame,* Duell, Sloan & Pearce, 1964; *Riots, U.S.A., 1765-1965,* Seabury, 1966; *The Story of Ellis Island,* Seabury, 1967; *Wandering Workers,* Crown, 1968; *Birthstones,* Meredith Corp., 1969; *Assassination: A Special Kind of Murder,* Meredith Corp., 1969; *Riots, U.S.A., 1965-1970,* Seabury, 1970; *Long Journeys,* Crown, 1970; *Taxation, U.S.A.,* Seabury, 1971; *Superstition!,* Thomas Nelson, 1972; *Juvenile Justice,* Seabury, 1974; *Psychic Phenomena,* Thomas Nelson, 1974.

Contributor of more than one hundred articles to education and library journals. Indexer of *Yearbook of the United Nations,* 1958-78. Book reviewer for *Library Journal,* 1956-63.

WORK IN PROGRESS: Murder by Poison, American Style; revision of *The Story of Ellis Island, Birthstones,* and *Assassinations: A Special Kind of Murder* as paperbacks.

SIDELIGHTS: Heaps writes: "Beginning an entirely new career of writing in middle age, more than twenty years ago, I chose the field of nonfiction for teenagers, both because of my pre-war experience in training high school librarians, and my competence in research acquired through my United Nations reference assignments. Locating sources of material might well be termed my avocation. Since my past books have been widely purchased for adult collections in public, college, and university libraries, my next book is to be issued as an adult trade title and will not bear the juvenile imprint and classification, but, I hope, will prove to be equally interesting to young adults."

*　　*　　*

HEARST, James 1900-

PERSONAL: Born August 8, 1900; son of Charles E. and Katharine (Schell) Hearst; married Meryl Norton, December 5, 1953. *Education:* Attended Iowa State Teachers College, Iowa State University, and University of Guanajuato. *Office:* Department of English, University of Northern Iowa, Cedar Falls, Iowa 50613.

CAREER: Operator of livestock farm; University of Northern Iowa, Cedar Falls, instructor in English, 1941—. Member of board of trustees of local public library. *Military service:* U.S. Army, Infantry, 1918. *Member:* United World Federalists, American Association of University Professors, American Civil Liberties Union, United Nations Association, Farm Bureau. *Awards, honors:* Award from Iowa Library Association; bicentennial award from governor of Iowa; award from Midwest Booksellers.

*WRITINGS—*All books of poems: *Country Men,* Prairie

Press, 1937; *The Sun at Noon,* Prairie Press, 1943; *Man and His Field,* Swallow Press, 1951; *Limited View,* Prairie Press, 1962; *Single Focus,* Prairie Press, 1967; *Dry Leaves,* Ragnarok, 1975; *Snake in the Grass,* Iowa State University Press, 1976. Contributor of articles and reviews to magazines, including *Nation.* Farm editor of *Midwest News.*

WORK IN PROGRESS: A book about his boyhood on an Iowa farm.

* * *

HEATH, Harry E(ugene), Jr. 1919-
(Kendall Hall)

PERSONAL: Born May 17, 1919, in Iola, Kan.; son of Harry Eugene (a machinist) and Lois Rebecca (McNally) Heath; married Audrey Joan Cass (a child development specialist), October 20, 1942; children: Harry Eugene III, Rebecca Jean Heath Brewer. *Education:* University of Tulsa, B.A., 1941; Northwestern University, M.S.J., 1947; Iowa State University, Ph.D., 1956; also attended University of Iowa and Oklahoma State University. *Religion:* Methodist. *Home:* 3512 North Washington, Stillwater, Okla. 74074. *Office:* Journalism and Broadcasting Building, Oklahoma State University, Stillwater, Okla. 74074.

CAREER: Tulsa Tribune, Tulsa, Okla., education writer, 1938-40; *Tulsa World,* Tulsa, sports writer, 1940-41; National Broadcasting Co., Chicago, Ill., news editor, 1941-42; University of Tulsa, Tulsa, instructor in journalism, assistant director of public relations, and director of News Bureau, 1946-47; University of Oregon, Eugene, instructor in journalism, 1947-48; Iowa State University, Ames, assistant professor, 1948-56, associate professor of journalism, 1956-61; Oklahoma State University, Stillwater, professor of journalism, 1961-65; University of Florida, Gainesville, professor of journalism, 1965-67; Oklahoma State University, professor of journalism and director of School of Journalism and Broadcasting, 1967—. Writer and producer for WOI-TV, Ames, Iowa, 1952. Lecturer at colleges, universities, and professional meetings. Consultant on public relations, typography, and design. *Military service:* U.S. Army, Chemical Corps, 1941-46, 1950-52; became major.

MEMBER: International Society for General Semantics, Society of Professional Journalists, Association for Education in Journalism (president of National Council on Radio and Television Journalism), Oklahoma Press Association, Oklahoma Education Association, Oklahoma Historical Society, Oklahoma Heritage Association, Phi Kappa Phi, Phi Delta Kappa, Pi Delta Epsilon, Theta Alpha Phi, Alpha Phi Omega, Gamma Sigma Delta, Kappa Tau Alpha.

WRITINGS: Guide to Newspaper Page Makeup (pamphlet), Iowa State University Press, 1950; (with Laurence R. Campbell and Ray Johnson) *A Guide to Radio-TV Writing,* Iowa State University Press, 1950; (with Louis I. Gelfand) *How to Cover, Write, and Edit Sports,* Iowa State University Press, 1951; (editor) *Directory of Journalism Films,* Iowa State University Press, 1954; (with Gelfand) *Modern Sportswriting,* Iowa State University Press, 1969; *Tell Me Now of Love* (poems), Journalistic Services (Stillwater, Okla.), 1973; *Pieces of String* (poems), Journalistic Services, 1977; *The Lonely Leaf* (poems), Journalistic Services, 1979.

Author of booklets and pamphlets. Author of "Critique," a monthly column in *Oklahoma Publisher,* 1964-65, 1967—. Correspondent for *Sporting News,* 1936-47; staff correspondent for *Daily Oklahoman,* 1946-47. Contributor to journalism and education journals, sometimes under pseudonym Kendall Hall, and to *Science of Mind.* Religion editor of

Stillwater News-Press, 1963-65; member of editorial advisory board, *Journalism Quarterly.*

WORK IN PROGRESS: Book-length poem; book of miscellaneous poems; book of real-life vignettes; research on journalistic interviewing and typography and design.

SIDELIGHTS: Heath wrote: "I believe in the therapeutic value of poetry, and would like to see both young and old encouraged to practice this creative art. Most people have the poetry locked up inside, and with a little instruction and encouragement it can be coaxed out. I favor free verse for this purpose."

* * *

HEBERT, Anne 1916-

PERSONAL: Born August 1, 1916, in Sainte-Catherine-de-Fossambault, Quebec, Canada; daughter of Maurice-Lang (a literary critic) and Marguerite Marie (Tache) Hebert. *Education:* Privately educated. *Residence:* Paris, France. *Address:* c/o Musson Book Co., 30 Lesmill Rd., Don Mills, Ontario, Canada M3B 2T6.

CAREER: Poet and novelist. Worked for Radio Canada, 1950-53, and for National Film Board, 1953-60. *Member:* Royal Society of Canada. *Awards, honors:* Grants from the Canadian government, 1954, Canadian Council of Arts, 1961, Guggenheim Foundation, 1963, and the province of Quebec, 1965; France Canada prize, 1957; Devernay prize, 1958; Governor General award, 1975; grand priz de Monaco, 1975; award from the French Academy, 1975; prix David of the province of Quebec, 1978.

WRITINGS: Les Songes en equilibre (poetry; title means "Dreams in Equilibrium"), Les Editions de l'arbre, 1942; *Le Tombeau des rois* (poetry), 1953, translation by Peter Miller published as *The Tombs of the Kings,* Contact Press (Toronto), 1967, augmented French edition published as *Poemes,* Editions du seuil, 1960, translation by Alan Brown published as *Poems,* Musson, 1975; *Les Chambres de bois* (novel), Editions du seuil, 1958, translation by Kathy Mezei published as *The Silent Rooms,* Musson, 1974; *Saint-Denys-Garneau and Anne Hebert* (selected works), Klanak Press (Vancouver, British Columbia), 1962; *Le Torrent: nouvelles,* Editions du seuil, 1963, new edition published as *Le Torrent, suivi de deux nouvelles inedites,* Editions HMH (Montreal), 1963, translation by Gwendolyn Moore published as *The Torrent: Nouvellas and Short Stories,* Harvest House (Montreal), 1973; *Le Temps sauvage, La Merciere assassinee, Les Invites au proces: Theatre* (plays), Editions HMH, 1967; *Kamouraska* (novels), Editions du seuil, 1970, translation by Norman Shapiro published under same title, Crown, 1973; *Les Enfants du sabbat* (novel), Editions du seuil, 1975, translation by Carol Dunlop-Hebert published as *Children of the Black Sabbath,* Musson, 1977.

SIDELIGHTS: Anne Hebert was born into an intellectually stimulating environment. Her father, Maurice-Lang Hebert, was a distinguished literary critic, and among his friends were some of the finest minds in Quebec. Due to a childhood illness Hebert was educated privately and spent most of her time at the family's country home in Sainte-Catherine-de-Fossambault.

She began writing poetry in her adolescence with the advice and guidance of her father and her cousin, the poet Hector de Saint-Denys-Garneau. Unlike Saint-Denys-Garneau, Hebert emerged from the spiritual struggle described in her first two books of poetry; her cousin remained in self-isolation until his death. *Le Songes en equilibre,* Hebert's first book of poetry, chronicled the experiences of a young woman who traveled from the easiness of childhood fun to the renunciation of pleasure and the pursuit and acceptance of a lonely life of spiritual and poetic duty. Hebert received a strict Roman Catholic training as a child, and believed the poet to be a spiritual force in man's salvation.

In her second book of poetry, Hebert revealed that the austere life she had chosen for herself was stifling her work. It is in this volume of her poetry that Hebert emerged from a dark and deep spiritual struggle. Samuel Moon observed: "[*The Tomb of the Kings*] is a book closely unified by its constant introspection, by its atmosphere of profound melancholy, by its recurrent themes of a dead childhood, a living death cut off from love and beauty, suicide, the theme of introspection itself. Such a book would seem to be of more interest clinically than poetically, but the miracle occurs and these materials are transmuted by the remarkable force of Mll. Hebert's imagery, the simplicity and directness of her diction, and the restrained lyric sound of her *vers libre*."

Although known primarily as a poet, Hebert has also written for the stage and television, and is the author of three published novels. Characteristic of Hebert's novels in the theme of the inhibiting burden of the past which binds any freedom for future actions. Many critics have noted that this theme is a French-Canadian phenomenon.

Kamouraska is Hebert's second novel and it has drawn praise from both Canadian and American critics. A *Choice* reviewer noted: "[This novel] conveys the same sense of mounting and almost unendurable excitement that one felt on first reading a Bronte novel—except that *Kamouraska* is modern in style and explicitness. The events are a stream-of-consciousness re-creation of a murder of passion that actually occurred in 1840. Hebert's poetic vision draws the thoughtful reader to be one with each of the frenzied characters." A *Canadian Forum* critic compared Hebert's "highly complex style and imagery" with that of Proust, Kafka, and Joyce, and stated that "the greatness of this work resides in the happy mixture of particularity and universality, unity and complexity, vitality and artistic orginality, and, above all, in the way the author makes simplistic moral judgment of the characters impossible."

Mel Watkins of the *New York Times* called Hebert a "stylist of the first rank" in his review of *Children of the Black Sabbath*. A novel that deals with a young novice who is possessed by the devil. Watkins observed that Hebert "both complements and heightens this eerie, aphotic atmosphere with the verity and density of her minor characters and with the restrained elegance of her prose. The result is an impressionistic tale that moves smoothly.... The vitality of the prose, of itself, makes it one of the best of its kind."

BIOGRAPHICAL/CRITICAL SOURCES: Poetry, June, 1968; *Choice*, September, 1973; *Canadian Forum*, November/December, 1973; *Contemporary Literary Criticism*, Gale, Volume 4, 1975; *New York Times*, September 7, 1977.

* * *

HECHT, Ben 1894-1964

PERSONAL: Born February 28, 1894, in New York, N.Y.; died April 18, 1964, in New York, N.Y.; son of Joseph and Sarah (Swernofsky) Hecht; married Marie Armstrong, 1915 (divorced, 1925); married Rose Caylor (a writer), 1925; children: (first marriage) Edwina. *Education:* Graduated from high school in Racine, Wisconsin. *Residence:* Nyack, New York.

CAREER: Journalist, novelist, playwright, and screenwriter. After high school graduation he worked for a time as an acrobat in Costello's Road Show in Wisconsin, then he owned and managed a theatre; worked for the *Chicago Journal,* Chicago, Ill., 1910 14; *Chicago Daily News*, Chicago, 1914-1923, began as writer, later founded a daily column, correspondent in Berlin, 1918-19; *Chicago Literary Times,* Chicago, founder and publisher, 1923-24. Founded a motion picture production company with Charles MacArthur in New York, 1934. *Awards, honors:* Received Academy Awards for "Underworld," 1927, and "The Scoundrel," 1935; received Academy Award nominations for "Viva Villa," 1934, "Wuthering Heights," 1939, "Angels Over Broadway," 1940, and "Notorious," 1946.

WRITINGS—Novels: *Erik Dorn*, Putnam, 1921, reprinted with an introduction by Nelson Algren, University of Chicago Press, 1963; *Fantazius Mallare: A Mysterious Oath,* drawings by Wallace Smith, Covici-McGee (Chicago), 1922, reprinted, Harcourt, 1978, published with *The Kingdom of Evil,* edited by R. Reginald and Douglas Menville, Arno, 1976 (also see below); *Gargoyles,* Boni & Liveright, 1922; *The Florentine Dagger: A Novel for Amateur Detectives,* Boni & Liveright, 1923; *The Kingdom of Evil: A Continuation of the Journal of Fantazius Mallare,* illustrations by Anthony Angarola, P. Covici, 1924, reprinted, Harcourt, 1978, published with *Fantazius Mallare: A Mysterious Oath,* edited by R. Reginald and Douglas Menville, Arno, 1976 (also see above); *Humpty Dumpty,* Boni & Liveright, 1924; *A Jew in Love,* Covici, Friede (New York), 1931; *Miracle in the Rain,* Knopf, 1943; *I Hate Actors,* Crown, 1944, published as *Hollywood Mystery,* Bartholomew, 1946; *The Cat That Jumped Out of the Story,* illustrations by Peggy Bacon, J. C. Winston, 1947. Also author of *Count Bruga,* 1926.

Nonfiction: *A Child of the Century* (autobiography), Simon & Schuster, 1954; *Charlie: The Improbable Life and Times of Charles MacArthur* (biography), Harper, 1957; *Perfidy,* Messner, 1961; *Gaily, Gaily* (correspondence and reminiscences), Doubleday, 1963, *Letters From Bohemia* (correspondence and reminiscences), Doubleday, 1964.

Short stories and sketches: *1001 Afternoons in Chicago,* illustrations by Herman Rosse, Covici-McGee, 1922; *Tales of Chicago Streets,* Haldeman-Julius (Girard, Kan.), 1924; *1001 Afternoons in New York,* illustrations by George Grosz, Viking, 1941; *Eleven Selected Great Stories,* Avon, 1943; *A Guide for the Bedevilled,* Scribner, 1944; *The Collected Stories of Ben Hecht,* Crown, 1945; *Concerning a Woman of Sin and Other Stories,* Avon, 1947; *A Treasury of Ben Hecht: Collected Stories and Other Writings,* Crown, 1959. Also author of *Cutie, A Warm Mama* (with Maxwell Bodenheim), c. 1924; *Broken Necks and Other Stories,* 1924; *Broken Necks: Containing More "1001 Afternoons,"* 1926; *Infatuation and Other Stories of Love's Misfits,* 1927; *Jazz and Other Stories of Chicago Life,* 1927; *The Sinister Sex and Other Stories of Marriage,* 1927; *The Unlovely Sin and Other Stories of Desire's Pawns,* 1927; *The Champion From far Away,* 1931; *Actor's Blood,* 1936.

Plays: *The Egoist* (first produced on Broadway, December 25, 1922) published, 1923; (with Charles MacArthur) *The Front Page* (three-act; first produced in New York at Times Square Theatre, August 14, 1928), Covici-Friede, 1928, acting edition, Samuel French, 1950; (with Gene Fowler) *The Great Magoo: A Love-Sick Charade in Three Acts and Something Like Eight Scenes, Recounting the Didoes of Two Young and Amorous Souls, Who Nigh Perished When They Weren't in the Hay Together,* illustrations by Herman Rosse, Covici-Friede, 1933; *To Quito and Back,* Covici-

Friede, 1937; (with MacArthur) *Ladies and Gentlemen* (three-act comedy; adapted from the drama "Twelve in A Box," by L. Bus-Fekete, [New York], 1939; (with MacArthur) *Fun to Be Free* (patriotic pageant), foreword by Wendell L. Wilkie, 1941. Also author of (with Maxwell Bodenheim) "The Master Poisoner" (one-act poetic play), included in Bodenheim's *Minna and Myself,* 1918; (with Kenneth Sawyer Goodman) "The Hero of Santa Maria: A Ridiculous Tragedy in One Act," 1920; (with Goodman) *The Wonder Hat and Other One Act Plays,* preface by Thomas Wood Stevens (contains "The Wonder Hat," "The Two Lamps," "An Idyll of the Shops," "The Hand of Siva," and "The Hero of Santa Maria"), 1925; "Christmas Eve: A Morality Play," 1928; (with MacArthur) "Twentieth Century," 1932; (with MacArthur, Richard Rodgers, and Lorenz Hart), "Jumbo" (musical), 1935; "Lily of the Valley," 1942; (with MacArthur) "Swan Song," 1946; "Winkleberg," 1958.

Screenplays: (With Charles MacArthur, and director) "Soak the Rich," Paramount, 1936; "Nothing Sacred" (based on "Letter to the Editor," a short story by James H. Street), United Artists, 1938; (author of screenstory with MacArthur) "Gunga Din" (based on the poem by Rudyard Kipling), RKO, 1939; "Goldwyn Follies," United Artists, 1938; "Lady of the Tropics," Metro-Goldwyn-Mayer, 1939; (with MacArthur) "Wuthering Heights," (based on the novel by Emily Bronte), United Artists, 1939; "It's a Wonderful World," Metro-Goldwyn-Mayer, 1939; "Let Freedom Ring," Metro-Goldwyn-Mayer, 1939; "Angels Over Broadway," Columbia Pictures, 1940; (wth Samuel Hoffenstein) "Lydia," United Artists, 1941; (with Charles Lederer) "Comrade X," Metro-Goldwyn-Mayer, 1940; (with others) "Tales of Manhattan," Fox, 1942; (with Seton I. Miller) "The Black Swan" (based on the novel by Rafael Sabatini), Fox, 1942; "China Girl," Fox, 1942; "Spellbound" (based on *The House of Dr. Edwardes,* a novel by Francis Beeding), United Artists, 1945; "Specter of the Rose" (based on the author's own short story), Republic, 1946; "Notorious," RKO, 1946; (with Lederer) "Her Husband's Affairs," Columbia Pictures, 1947; (with Lederer) "Kiss of Death," Fox, 1947; (with Lederer) "Ride the Pink Horse" (based on the novel by Dorothy B. Hughes), Universal, 1947; (with Quentin Reynolds) "The Miracle of the Bells" (based on the novel by Russell Janney), RKO, 1948.

(With Andrew Solt) "Whirlpool" (based on the novel by Guy Endore), Fox, 1950; "Where the Sidewalk Ends," (based on the novel by William L. Stuart), Fox, 1950; "Actors and Sin" (based on two of the author's own stories), United Artists, 1952; (with Lederer and I.A.L. Diamond) "Monkey Business," Fox, 1952; "Miracle in the Rain," (based on the author's own novel), Warner Bros., 1956; (with Frank Davis) "The Indian Fighter," United Artists, 1955; (with others) "Ulysses" (based on *The Odyssey* by Homer), Paramount, 1955; "The Iron Petticoat," Metro-Goldwyn-Mayer, 1956; (with Robert Presnell, Jr.) "Legend of the Lost," United Artists, 1957; "A Farewell to Arms" (based on the novel by Ernest Hemingway), Fox, 1957; (author of screenstory; screenplay by Charles Beaumont) "Queen of Outer Space," Allied Artists, 1958; (with Julian Halevy and James Edward Grant), "Circus World," Paramount, 1964. Also author of "Underworld," 1927; "Design for Living" (based on the play by Noel Coward), 1933; "Viva Villa," 1934; "The Scoundrel," 1935.

Other: *The Sensualists,* Messner, 1959; *In the Midst of Death,* Mayflower (London), 1964. Contributor to *Little Review, Smart Set,* and *PM* Magazine.

SIDELIGHTS: Hecht was associated with the Chicago "literary renaissance" in the years following World War I. Sherwood Anderson, Maxwell Bodenheim, and Pascal Covici were among his colleagues. Much of Hecht's early work was published in Margaret Anderson's *Little Review,* the literary organ of the "renaissance," and in *Smart Set.* Despite the fact that he literally fled from a college education, Hecht was an omnivorous reader and was particularly partial to the works of the French symbolists, including Gautier, Mallarme, Verlaine, and Baudelaire: he thought J. K. Huysmans was "the rajah of writing, his brain the splendid macaw of all literature."

Hecht's background in journalism was the single most important influence on his work. In the early days of his career he became known for his colorful sketches of Chicago lowlife. The city's back streets were his beat and, fascinated with the bizarre, he specialized in portraits of murders, brothels, and other urban maladies. James T. Farrell considers the collection of sketches Hecht wrote for the *Chicago Daily News* to be his best book. The collection is, Farrell wrote, "full of charm, color, and exciting phrases. Hecht's best talent is that of coining metaphors, and he was at his peak when he knocked off *1001 Afternoons in Chicago.* His subjects are usually grotesque. The grotesque has usually interested him and to it, he brings a sense of the mordant." These sketches still are well-known by reporters as models for the human interest story.

The Front Page, a play that Hecht collaborated on with Charles MacArthur has become known as a classic depiction of the newspaper business in the days when, according to William Albright, "nobody thought of going to journalism school, reporters would at least lease their mothers for a good story and the cry of 'Stop the presses!' was heard throughout the land. Reporter Hildy Johnson and managing editor Walter Burns are prototypes of the hard-boiled newsmen of the period. The play, first produced in 1928, was wildly successful and has been adapted as a film three times since then.

But if Hecht's newspaper stories were colorful, they were often gaudy, and sometimes even untrue. In his autobiography, *A Child of the Century,* Hecht confessed that his reputation as a reporter was "somewhat undeserved, for it was not my talents as a news gatherer that I offered my paper but a sudden fearless flowering as a fictioneer.... Tales of prodigals returned, hobos come into fortunes, families driven mad by ghosts, vendettas that ended in love feasts, and all of them full of exotic plot turns involving parrots, chickens, goldfish, serpents, epigrams and second-act curtains. I made them all up."

It is Marvin Felheim's contention that unlike other American novelists who served their apprenticeship as journalists to later write important novels, Hecht was never able to overcome his background. Felheim commented: "Always the reporter, with the mind set and the emotional make-up of the clever journalist out for a scoop or a good newspaper yarn, he never moved away from those preoccupations.... Hecht seems not to have learned anything from his days as a reporter.... [He] stands surprised by life, by brothels, homosexuals, lesbians, murders, vice and corruption; and he becomes a voyeur rather than a novelist, a point of view he never relinquished." While Felheim and other reviewers found his first novel, *Erik Dorn,* to be commendable in certain respects, Hecht's novelistic oeuvre has not been well received. As Felheim remarked: "No wonder Hecht's novels have not survived: in them he treats his times with a shallow contempt; he could neither rise to satire nor sense with sufficient passion the essential meanings. As readers, we respond as we do to newspaper accounts: that's the way of the world. We are left without either intellectual or emotional depth.''

Hecht's autobiography also met with little critical appreciation. Although some critics delighted in the warm portraits of his family and colleagues, most were put off by his tendentious long-windedness. Hecht wrote in the book that ''ideas lie on a perpetual rubbish heap.'' However, as Farrell pointed out, ''Hecht's iconoclasm about and his contempt for ideas does not mean that he is devoid of them. He isn't.'' Farrell continued: ''But generally his ideas are banal. They repeat what he has said in the yesterday of his own youth. His autobiography is a concoction, as improvised literary cocktail. Everything in life is an occasion for Hecht to sound off, and he fills too many pages with the wind of his prejudices.''

Hecht will probably remain best known as the screenwriter of more than sixty films. Ironically, he never took his work in the medium seriously and thought that his reputation as a novelist suffered for it. He wrote in his autobiography: ''Had I contented myself with writing books, as I started out to do when I was 17, I might have acquired a more definite identity than I seem to have, among literary critics if nowhere else. I can understand the literary critic's shyness toward me. It is difficult to keep praising a novelist or thinker who keeps popping up as the author of innumerable movie melodramas. It is like writing about the virtues of a preacher who keeps carelessly getting himself arrested in bordellos.''

Several critics have expressed the opinion that Hecht's talents were not in tune with his times, and that had he lived in another era, his work would have been more appreciated. In summation of Hecht's career, John Wain wrote: ''In a word, Mr. Hecht is a romantic. Not just any kind of romantic, but a Wildean romantic, a man of the nineties. If, instead of being a mid-twentieth century New Yorker, he had been a *fin de siecle* Londoner, he would have been faithfully present, week in and week out, at the Cheshire Cheese. His figure would have been a familiar one in the bars of Fleet Street, where he would have made an attentive listener to the monologues of Lionel Johnson. . . . That is Mr. Hecht's misfortune. Owing to an unaccountable kink in the time-corridor, he slipped sixty-five years and landed on the wrong side of the Atlantic into the bargain.''

BIOGRAPHICAL/CRITICAL SOURCES: Ben Hecht, *A Child of the Century* (autobiography), Simon & Schuster, 1954; Roy Newquist, *Counterpoint*, Simon & Schuster, 1964; Gilbert A. Harrison, editor, *The Critic as Artist: Essays on Books, 1920-1970*, Liveright, 1972; *Critique: Studies in Modern Fiction*, Volume XV, number 2, 1973; *Houston Post*, November 30, 1975; Jack Alan Robbins, editor, *Literary Essays, 1954-1974*, Kennikat, 1976; *Journal of Popular Culture*, spring, 1976; *Contemporary Literary Criticism*, Gale, Volume 8, 1978.*

*   *   *

HEINL, Robert Debs, Jr. 1916-1979

OBITUARY NOTICE—See index for *CA* sketch: Born August 12, 1916, in Washington, D.C.; died of a heart attack, May 5, 1979, in St. Barthelemy, French West Indies. Historian and writer best known for his books on the Marine Corps, including *Marines at Midway* and *Soldiers of the Sea*. A marine himself, Heinl was at Pearl Harbor during the Japanese attack in 1941 and later served in Guam and Iwo

Jima. In 1958, Heinl was appointed United States defense adviser to Haiti. Heinl departed after the Haitian government became displeased with his criticism of Haiti's uncooperative stance. He later penned a history of Haiti, *Written in Blood*, with his wife, Nancy Gordon. Obituaries and other sources: *Who's Who in the World*, 3rd edition, Marquis, 1976; *New York Times*, May 7, 1979; *Washington Post*, May 7, 1979; *Chicago Tribune*, May 8, 1979.

*   *   *

HELLEGERS, Andre E. 1926-1979

OBITUARY NOTICE: Born June 5, 1926, in Venio, Netherlands; died of a coronary attack, May 7, 1979, in Uithoorn, Netherlands. Physician and author. Hellegers was a pioneer in the field of medical ethics and was internationally known for his insight into population control, public health policies, and other ethical problems that had previously been ignored by most doctors. He was founder and director of the Kennedy Institute of Ethics at Georgetown University and was appointed to the presidental commission on population and birth control from 1968 to 1973. Hellegers was author of numerous articles for periodicals and worked on the four-volume *Encyclopedia of Bioethics* for the Kennedy Institute. Obituaries and other sources: *American Men and Women of Science*, 13th edition, Bowker, 1976; *Washington Post*, May 9, 1979.

*   *   *

HENEGAN, Lucius Herbert, Jr. 1902(?)-1979

OBITUARY NOTICE: Born c. 1902 in Paris, Tex.; died January 30, 1979, in Washington, D.C. Public affairs officer and journalist. Henegan worked for the federal government as a press officer in the Farmers Home Administration of the Agriculture Department and as a public affairs officer with the U.S. Information Agency (now International Communication Agency). One of the first formally trained black newspapermen, he began his career serving in editorial positions with the *Omaha Guide*, the *Kansas City Call*, and the *Baltimore Afro-American* newspapers. He was editor of the *Memphis World*. Obituaries and other sources: *Washington Post*, February 3, 1979.

*   *   *

HENNISSART, Martha
(R. B. Dominic, Emma Lathen, joint pseudonyms)

EDUCATION: Attended Harvard University. *Residence:* Boston, Mass. *Office:* c/o Victor Gollancz Ltd., 14 Henrietta St., Covent Garden, London WC2E 8QJ, England.

CAREER: Writer. *Awards, honors: Murder Against the Grain* named Best Crime Fiction Novel by the Crime Writers' Association, 1967.

WRITINGS—With Mary J. Latsis under joint pseudonym Emma Lathen: *Banking on Death*, Macmillan, 1961; *A Place for Murder*, Macmillan, 1963; *Accounting for Murder*, Macmillan, 1964; *Death Shall Overcome*, Macmillan, 1966; *Murder Makes the Wheels Go 'Round*, Macmillan, 1966; *Murder Against the Grain*, Macmillan, 1967; *Come to Dust*, Simon & Schuster, 1968; *A Stitch in Time*, Macmillan, 1968; *Murder to Go*, Simon & Schuster, 1969; *When in Greece*, Simon & Schuster, 1969; *Pick Up Sticks*, Simon & Schuster, 1970; *The Longer the Thread*, Simon & Schuster, 1971; *Ashes to Ashes*, Simon & Schuster, 1971; *Murder Without Icing*, Simon & Schuster, 1972; *Sweet and Low*, Simon & Schuster, 1974; *By Hook or by Crook*, Simon & Schuster,

1975; *Double, Double, Oil and Trouble,* Simon & Schuster, 1978.

With Latsis under joint pseudonym R. B. Dominic: *Murder, Sunny Side Up,* Abelard-Schuman, 1968; *Murder in High Place,* Doubleday, 1970; *There Is No Justice,* Doubleday, 1971; *Epitaph for a Lobbyist,* Doubleday, 1974; *Murder Out of Commission,* Doubleday, 1976.

SIDELIGHTS: Hennissart and Mary Jane Latsis, writing under the joint pseudonym Emma Lathen, have earned a high reputation in the field of detective novels. Lathen was lauded by Annette Grant as "a masterful plotter, an elegant stylist, a comic genius and an old-fashioned purist who never sacrifices logic for surprise effect." The Lathen books feature John Putnam Thatcher, the urbane vice-president of Sloan Guaranty Trust, who neatly solves white-collar homicides. "It is a pleasant world that Thatcher inhabits," noted Newgate Callendar, "and murder is only a passing, mildly irritating aberration. Life revolves around the functioning of Sloan Guaranty, and Thatcher is there to help make the function smooth."

The authors first met as graduate students at Harvard University and later discovered a mutual interest in detective novels. Between Hennissart's knowledge of law and Latsis's economic background, they found plenty of material for stories on corporate skullduggery. *Banking on Death,* their first book, was published after winning a contest at Macmillan, and it received positive reviews from *American Scholar* and other critics. The following novels were even more successful.

Hennissart and Latsis have an unusual writing technique. For each book the authors write a loose outline and then each writes alternate chapters. They told a *Forbes* interviewer: "We have discovered that it is essential that we agree on both the corpses and murderers and when the first corpse appears. You can't—when you hit a dull spot—kill somebody."

Most of Lathen's books have received high praise. Allen J. Hubin felt it was "her mischievous, sometimes biting choice of just the right word that elevates the commonplace to the sublime" in *Come to Dust.* And "if you think high finance in Wall Street can provide no very tempting background either for mystery or for human interest, you will change your mind when you [read *Death Shall Overcome*]," promised John Dickson Carr.

Murder Without Icing, in which Thatcher becomes involved with an ice hockey team, was a disappointment to some reviewers: H. C. Veit said, "The expected exciting plotting is there . . . but a weakness must be mentioned: Lathen has clearly never listened to an ice-hockey player, and some of the dialogue is painful." Newgate Callendar felt that in this book "her characters, even the murderers, now tend to be so damned civilized they end up merely icky instead of menacing."

The pseudonym Emma Lathen was constructed from parts of the authors' real names: the "M" of Mary and "Ma" of Martha for Emma, and "Lat" of Latsis and "Hen" of Hennissart form Lathen.

Hennissart and Latsis also write a series of mysteries about a congressman that are published under the joint pseudonym R. B. Dominic.

BIOGRAPHICAL/CRITICAL SOURCES: Harper's, July, 1967; *Times Literary Supplement,* July 27, 1967, December 21, 1967, December 11, 1969, December 26, 1975; *New York Times Book Review,* September 17, 1967, April 21, 1968,

July 7, 1968, October 20, 1968, September 7, 1969, March 1, 1970, December 27, 1970, March 14, 1971, March 26, 1972, November 26, 1972, September 22, 1974; *Books and Bookmen,* April, 1968; *Newsweek,* July 28, 1969; *New Yorker,* September 13, 1969, February 21, 1970, June 12, 1971, September 9, 1974; *Wall Street Journal,* December 3, 1970; *Saturday Review,* January 30, 1971; *Best Sellers,* April 1, 1971; *Library Journal,* November 1, 1972; *Critic,* March/April, 1973; (under pseudonym Emma Lathen) *Contemporary Literary Criticism,* Volume 2, Gale, 1974; *Christian Science Monitor,* June 4, 1975; *Forbes,* December 1, 1977.

*   *   *

HEPBURN, James Gordon   1922-

PERSONAL: Born December 13, 1922, in Montgomeryville, Pa.; son of William Wallace and Ethel Remington (Morton) Hepburn; married Margaret Mary Doorey, December 29, 1947; children: James. *Education:* Yale University, B.A., 1944; University of Pennsylvania, M.A., 1949, Ph.D., 1957. *Home:* 11 Mountain Ave., Lewiston, Me. 04240. *Office:* Department of English, Bates College, Lewiston, Me. 04240.

CAREER: Lafayette College, Easton, Pa., instructor in English, 1952-54; Cornell University, Ithaca, N.Y., instructor in English, 1957-61; University of Rhode Island, Kingston, assistant professor, 1961-64, associate professor of English, 1965-67; University of Leicester, Leicester, England, research fellow in English, 1969-72; Bates College, Lewiston, Me., Dana Professor of English and head of department, 1972—. *Military service:* U.S. Army, 1944-46.

WRITINGS: (Editor with Robert A. Greenberg) *Robert Frost: An Introduction,* Holt, 1961; (editor with Greenberg) *Modern Essays: A Rhetorical Approach,* Macmillan, 1962, 2nd edition, 1968; *The Art of Arnold Bennett,* Indiana University Press, 1963; *College Composition: Rhetoric, Grammar, Speech,* Macmillan, 1964; *Poetic Design: Handbook and Anthology,* Macmillan, 1966; (editor) *Letters of Arnold Bennett,* Oxford University Press, Volume I, 1966, Volume II, 1968, Volume III, 1970; *The Author's Empty Purse and the Rise of the Literary Agent,* Oxford University Press, 1968; *Confessions of an American Scholar,* University of Minnesota Press, 1971; *My Fierce Tiger* (juvenile), Platt, 1971; (editor) Edmund Gosse, *Father and Son,* Oxford University Press, 1974.

Plays: "Poor Dumb Animals" (three-act), first produced in Ealing, England, at Questors Theatre, June, 1971; "Time, Life, Sex, and You Know What" (three-act), first produced in Ealing, at Questors Theatre, June, 1972; "Magic 'n Tragic" (two-act), first produced in Ealing, at Questors Theatre, June, 1975; "Deaf, Dumb, and Blind" (two-act), first produced in Ealing, at Questors Theatre, June, 1975; "Moonship Moonshot" (three-act), first produced in Ealing, at Questors Theatre, May, 1977.

*   *   *

HETZELL, Margaret Carol   1917-1978

PERSONAL: Born July 9, 1917, in Vineland, N.J.; died of cancer, September 2, 1978, in Washington, D.C. *Education:* Received degree from Columbia Union College.

CAREER: Review and Herald Publishing Association, proofreader and copy editor, 1942-52, public relation department, assistant director, 1952-62, associate director, 1962-75, director of communications department, 1975-78. Conductor of public relations and writing workshops. Script writer and film director for Seventh-day Adventist Church. Editor of *Tell*. *Member:* Associated Church Press, Religious Public Relations Council.

WRITINGS: The Undaunted, Pacific Press, 1967. Also author of *Church PR Workbook*, 1969, and other religious books, film scripts, and articles.

SIDELIGHTS: For over twenty years Margaret Hetzell served as editor of *Tell*, the Seventh-day Adventist monthly journal. She also led writing and public relation workshops for the church in various countries, including Cyprus, Borneo, Africa, Iran, India, Canada, and the United States.*

* * *

HEWES, Hayden 1943-

PERSONAL: Born December 29, 1943, in Cape Girardeau, Mo.; son of E. E. (a teacher) and L. (Cooper) Hewes; married Kietha LaFlair (divorced January, 1975); children: Chris M. *Education:* Attended University of Oklahoma, 1962, and Oklahoma City University, 1963. *Politics:* "Individual, not party." *Religion:* Roman Catholic. *Home:* 3621 South Wynn Dr., Apt. 31, Edmond, Okla. 73034. *Agent:* Ruth Hagy Brod Literary Agency, 15 Park Ave., New York, N.Y. 10016. *Office address:* P.O. Box 441, Edmond, Okla. 73034.

CAREER: Central Merchandise Co., Oklahoma City, Okla., employee, 1964—. Director of International UFO Bureau, Inc., 1957—; vice-president of New Age Center Corp., 1968-78, of Institute of PSI, 1975-77, and of Sasquatch Investigations of Mid-America, 1976—; adviser with Roger Hight Productions. Guest on several hundred television and radio programs, discussing unidentified flying objects and related subjects. *Member:* Authors Guild, Authors League of America.

WRITINGS: The Truth About Flying Saucers, International UFO Bureau Press, 1966; (with Hal Crawford) *The Aliens*, International UFO Bureau Press, 1970; (with Crawford) *The Intruders*, International UFO Bureau Press, 1971; *Earthprobe*, International UFO Bureau Press, 1973; (editor with Brad Steiger) *UFO Missionaries Extraordinary*, Pocket Books, 1976.

Author of columns in *Saga UFO Report, The Hefley Report, Paranormal and Psychic Australia*, and *Canadian UFO Report*. Contributor of about two hundred-fifty articles to magazines and newspapers.

WORK IN PROGRESS: Sex and the Stargods, with James Maney; *The Immortal Cosmic Man; Immortal Cosmic Man Speaks Out; Space Age Religion 2001*, with Steiger; *Visions or Visitors*, with Maney and Bill Spaulding.

SIDELIGHTS: Hewes began his research on unidentified flying objects in 1957, and began writing in 1965, which was the year he made his own unidentified flying object sighting. His research compares data from hundreds of sightings from all over the world, including a report from President Jimmy Carter who was then governor of Georgia.

Hewes feels that the similarity of descriptions of vehicles, alien beings, and events from sightings lends credibility to the reports he has received. His lectures and writings cover such diverse subjects as religion, ancient history, evolution, and sex.

BIOGRAPHICAL/CRITICAL SOURCES: Robert Loftin, *Identified Flying Saucers*, McKay, 1968; *Oklahoma Journal*, May 1, 1977; *Edmond Evening Sun*, January 15, 1978.

HEWLETT, Dorothy (?)-1979

OBITUARY NOTICE: Died in 1979 in Richmond, Surrey, England. Scholar and author. Hewlett was a specialist in nineteenth-century literature and wrote several books on Keats and Elizabeth Barret Browning. She also wrote novels, including *Victorian House*, and edited the *Keats-Shelley Memorial Bulletin* with her husband, Norman Kilgour. Obituaries and other sources: *AB Bookman's Weekly*, April 16, 1979.

* * *

HEWLETT, Virginia B. 1912(?)-1979

OBITUARY NOTICE: Born c. 1912 in Danville, Va.; died May 7, 1979, in Washington, D.C. Author. In 1941 Hewlett moved to the Philippines with her husband, a reporter for the *United Press*. After the Japanese invaded the islands that same year, she worked at a medical aide station in Manila. Early in 1942, Hewlett was imprisoned by the Japanese and was not released until February, 1945, when the U.S. 1st Cavalry division liberated the camp. Hewlett's husband was with the division as a war correspondent at the time and found his wife near starvation. Later Hewlett wrote a partial account of her imprisonment, syndicated by Scripps-Howard in 1970. Obituaries and other sources: *Washington Post*, May 9, 1979.

* * *

HEYMANNS, Betty 1932-

PERSONAL: Born January 3, 1932, in Sheboygan, Wis.; daughter of Nick (a steamfitter) and Irma C. (a teacher and beautician; maiden name, Zimpel) Heymanns. *Education:* Attended Milwaukee Technical College, 1951-53, and University of Wisconsin, Milwaukee, 1968. *Religion:* Lutheran. *Home and office:* 10943 Glenway Court, Wauwatosa, Wis. 53222. *Agent:* Jackie M. Krill, 215 East Michigan St., Milwaukee, Wis. 53202.

CAREER: Professional portrait photographer, 1953—. Board member of United Cerebral Palsy of Wisconsin, 1977—; board member and secretary of United Cerebral Palsy of Southeastern Wisconsin, 1976—; member of Development Disabilities for Milwaukee County, 1978—. *Member:* Council for Wisconsin Writers.

WRITINGS: Bittersweet Triumph, Doubleday, 1977.

WORK IN PROGRESS: Flight of the Imperfect Butterfly.

SIDELIGHTS: Bittersweet Triumph is Betty Heymann's account of her life-long struggle to overcome cerebral palsy. Handicapped since birth, she learned to walk at age seven by clinging to ropes strung across the living room. She was unable to attend school at the usual age, so her mother began teaching her until a special school was found. Every day she faced new obstacles in the path of her ultimate goal—to be "normal."

At age nineteen Heymanns attended Milwaukee Area Technical College, where she learned film developing and portrait photography. With help she eventually built up a small but steady business in her parents' home. Though still handicapped, Heymanns is no longer subject to muscle spasms and is able to type, sew, prune the shrubbery in the yard, and run her photography studio.

In *Bittersweet Triumph* Heymanns writes: "Years ago . . . I had envisioned the story of my life as a mountain climb. There would be setbacks but eventually the peak of success would be reached—permanently. What a childish dream that was.

"Life is change—a crooked, uncertain path. What is success one day may be a failure the next day." By describing her struggles and adjustments to life as an adult with cerebral palsy, Heymann hopes to help others with the same problems and to share with them her realization that the normalcy she sought "does not exist. Not until a touch of madness reached my soul did I feel the true pulse of life."

BIOGRAPHICAL/CRITICAL SOURCES: Milwaukee Journal, March 20, 1977.

* * *

HEYNS, Barbara 1943-

PERSONAL: Surname is pronounced Hines; born July 17, 1943, in San Antonio, Tex.; daughter of Robert Ernest and Frances (Carpenter) Heyns; married Jeff A. Weintraub (a lecturer in sociology), December 19, 1976. *Education:* University of California, Berkeley, B.A., 1966; University of Chicago, M.A., 1969, Ph.D., 1971. *Home:* 1061 Keith Ave., Berkeley, Calif. 94708. *Office:* Department of Sociology, University of California, 410 Barrows Hall, Berkeley, Calif. 94720.

CAREER: Casa di Risparmio, Milan, Italy, research trainee and translator, summer, 1965; Office of Economic Opportunity, Washington, D.C., management intern, summer, 1967; Harvard University, Cambridge, Mass., assistant professor of education and research associate at Center for Educational Policy Research, 1970-72; University of California, Berkeley, assistant professor, 1972-76, associate professor of sociology, 1976—. Research associate with International Business Machines Corp., 1967. Staff member of McCarthy Presidential campaign, 1968. Consultant to National Opinion Research Center, Research Triangle, and Stanford Research Institute.

MEMBER: American Sociological Association, American Educational Research Association, Population Society of America, National Council on Measurement in Education, Sociologists for Women in Society, Pacific Sociological Association, North Dakota Study Group on Evaluation. *Awards, honors:* Grants from Spencer Foundation, 1972, Office of Economic Opportunity, 1972-75, and National Institute of Education, 1975-76; regents faculty research award, 1976.

WRITINGS: (Contributor) Scarvia Anderson, editor, *Sex Differences and Discrimination in Education,* Charles A. Jones Publishing, 1972; (with Christopher Jencks and others) *Inequality,* Basic Books, 1972; (contributor) Charles H. Reed, editor, *Conference Report: Sector Analysis of Elementary Education,* Agency for International Development, U.S. Government, 1976; *Summer Learning and the Effects of Schooling,* Academic Press, 1978. Contributor of about twelve articles and reviews to academic journals. Associate editor of *Sociology of Education,* 1975-78; guest editor of *Annual Review of Sociology,* April, 1975.

WORK IN PROGRESS: The Mandarins of Childhood, a comparative analysis of the organization and delivery of services to children.

SIDELIGHTS: Heyns told *CA:* "The focus of my research has involved education, sex roles, and social policy. My main interest is the extent to which social inequality can be linked, as either a cause or a consequence, to each of these areas."

* * *

HIBBARD, George Richard 1915-

PERSONAL: Born May 31, 1915, in Morton, Nottingham-shire, England; son of George Henry (a farmer) and Sydney Ann (Eaton) Hibbard; married Louise A. Higgitt, November 5, 1939; children: Sophia J. Hibbard Fisher. *Education:* University of London, B.A., 1936, M.A., 1938; further graduate study at University of Zurich, 1938-39. *Office:* Department of English, University of Waterloo, Waterloo, Ontario, Canada N2L 3G1.

CAREER: University of Southampton, Southampton, England, assistant lecturer in English, 1939-40; University of Nottingham, Nottingham, England, lecturer, 1946-54, senior lecturer, 1954-62, reader in English, 1962-70; University of Waterloo, Waterloo, Ontario, professor of English, 1970—. *Military service:* British Army, 1940-46. *Member:* International Shakespeare Association, Canadian Association of University Teachers, Association of Canadian University Teachers of English, Modern Humanities Research Association, Renaissance Society of America, Shakespeare Association of America.

WRITINGS: (Editor) *Three Elizabethan Pamphlets,* Harrap, 1951; *Thomas Nashe: A Critical Introduction,* Routledge & Kegan Paul, 1962; (editor) *Renaissance and Modern Essays,* Routledge & Kegan Paul, 1966; (editor) William Shakespeare, *Coriolanus,* Penguin, 1967; (editor) Shakespeare, *The Taming of the Shrew,* Penguin, 1968; (editor) Shakespeare, *Timon of Athens,* Penguin, 1970; (editor) Shakespeare, *The Merry Wives of Windsor,* Penguin, 1973; (editor) *The Elizabethan Theatre,* Macmillan (Canada), Volume IV (Hibbard was not associated with earlier volumes), 1974, Volume V, 1975, Volume VI, 1978, Volume VII, in press; (editor) Ben Jonson, *Bartholmew Fair,* Benn, 1977. Contributor to literature journals.

WORK IN PROGRESS: An edition of Shakespeare's *Hamlet,* publication by Oxford University Press expected in 1982.

SIDELIGHTS: Hibbard writes: "I have taken Candide's advice to heart, and grow vegetables."

* * *

HICKEY, Edward Shelby 1928(?)-1978

PERSONAL: Born c.1928, in San Benito, Tex.; died of a heart attack, November 14, 1978, in Alexandria, Va.; son of Thomas F. Hickey (a lieutenant general in the U.S. Army); married wife, Joan; children: Kevin, Joseph, Paul. *Education:* Attended West Point Military Academy, University of Vienna, and University of San Francisco.

CAREER/WRITINGS: Blue Danube network, Salzburg, Austria, editor and announcer, 1947-49; National Council of Catholic Men, Washington, D.C., radio director, 1954-56; Voice of America (VOA), newswriter, broadcaster, and anchorman, 1956-63, opened bureau in Lagos, Nigeria, 1963, foreign correspondent, 1963-70, deputy chief of news division in Washington, 1970-78. *Military service:* U.S. Army, 1950-54, served in Europe.

SIDELIGHTS: During his years with the Voice of America, Hickey served as anchorman for several space events, including the VOA live coverage of the first lunar landings. He also had extended assignments in Lagos, Nigeria, where he opened the first VOA West Africa bureau, and in Vietnam. From 1970 to 1978 Hickey was responsible for administration and planning in the VOA news division in Washington, D.C.*

* * *

HICKIN, Norman E(rnest) 1910-

PERSONAL: Born April 17, 1910, in Birmingham, England;

son of Ernest A. (a furniture manufacturer) and Alice (a pianist; maiden name, Priddey) Hicken; married Emma Fischer, October 10, 1936; children: Verney Hickin Naylor, Sari Hickin Quammie. *Education:* University of London, B.Sc., 1936, Ph.D., 1940. *Home and office:* Kateshill, Bewdley, Worcestershire DY12 2DR, England.

CAREER: Rentokil Ltd., East Grinstead, England, technical manager and director, 1944-57, scientific director, 1957-72, scientific consultant, 1972—. Visiting scientist at East African Fisheries Research Organization in Jinja, Uganda, 1954. Patron of West Midlands Conservation Corps. *Member:* International Trust for Zoological Nomenclature, Royal Entomological Society (fellow; member of council, 1950-51, 1961; vice-president, 1954, 1961), Institute of Biology (fellow; member of council, 1955, 1961; vice-president, 1960, 1961), Institute of Wood Science (fellow), Zoological Society (scientific fellow), British Wood Preserving Association (past member of council), Society for British Entomology, Freshwater Biological Association, Society of Wildlife Artists (founding member), Worcestershire Naturalists Trust, Shropshire Naturalists Trust. *Awards, honors:* Travel award from Nuffield Foundation for Uvira, Congo, and Jinja, Uganda, 1956.

WRITINGS—All self-illustrated: *Caddis: Field Study Books,* Methuen, 1952; *Woodworm: Its Biology and Extermination,* privately printed, 1954; *The Insect Factor in Wood Decay,* Hutchinson, 1963, 3rd edition, 1975; *The Woodworm Problem,* Hutchinson, 1963, 2nd edition, 1972; *The Dry Rot Problem,* Hutchinson, 1963; *Household Insect Pests,* Hutchinson, 1963, 2nd edition, 1975; *Forest Refreshed,* Hutchinson, 1965; *The Conservation of Building Timbers,* Hutchinson, 1967; *Caddis Larvae,* Hutchinson, 1967; *African Notebook,* Hutchinson, 1969; *Termites: A World Problem,* Hutchinson, 1971; *Bird Nest-Boxing,* Stanley Paul, 1971; *Wood Preservation: A Guide to the Meaning of Terms,* Hutchinson, 1971; *Natural History of an English Forest,* Hutchinson, 1971; *Beachcombing for Beginners,* David & Charles, 1975, Melvin Powers, 1976; *Irish Nature,* O'Brien Press, 1979; *Animal Life in the Galapagos,* Classey, 1979; *Building Surveyor's Guide to Buildings,* Godwin, 1979. Contributor of more than two-hundred-fifty articles and illustrations to scientific journals.

WORK IN PROGRESS: Irish Butterfly Book; Wyre Ways and Wildlife; The Woodworm Business; A Birmingham Boyhood.

SIDELIGHTS: Hickin told *CA:* "The great motivating factor in my career has been the study of insects. They have enthralled me since I was three years old. Most of my writing has been about wood-tunnelling insects and the purpose of my first books was to inform those people who should have known something of insect biology but didn't.

"Illustrating in black and white has always been an important part of my work and well over two thousand drawings have been published in my books, many having been used to illustrate textbooks on freshwater insects in Russia, Bulgaria, France, the United States and many other countries. The technique employed is that of scraperboard, i.e., using black ink on a chalk surface. The excess black is removed with fine needles and knives. I suppose that I should say that delineating the patterns of nature in black and white is my prime motivation for such drawings.

"I feel that it is essential that an author write something every day and in a highly disciplined manner. But the work should be carefully planned, both in the short and long term. It is only by adhering to this self-discipline that one can achieve high productivity."

HINTON, Nigel 1941-

PERSONAL: Born September 28, 1941, in London, England; son of Raymond George (a builder) and Eva (Blatchley) Hinton. *Education:* College of St. Mark and St. John, London, B.A., 1966; University of Kent at Canterbury, M.A., 1975. *Home and office:* Camellia Cottage, Leyswood, Groombridge, near Tunbridge Wells, Kent, England.

CAREER: Lintas Ltd., London, England, executive trainee in advertising, 1960-62; Kent Education Committee, Kent, England, English teacher and department head, 1966-74; professional actor, 1974—.

WRITINGS: Collision Course (novel), Thomas Nelson, 1976; *Getting Free* (novel), Thomas Nelson, 1978; (contributor) *The Book of Numbers,* Random House, 1978; (contributor) *Peel's Men,* Hamlyn, 1979.

Television plays: "The Reaper," Thames TV, 1979; "Burning the Boat," Thames TV.

WORK IN PROGRESS—All juveniles: *Beaver Towers,* a novel; *Something Beginning With "S".*

SIDELIGHTS: Hinton writes: "My first novel was written while I was still a teacher. I wanted to write something better for the kind of pupils I was teaching than what was generally available. When I received a letter about the book from a young American reader who signed himself 'Your new friend,' I found the urge to go on irresistible. I write for children and young adults because their world still has the dramatic clash between their personalities and social conventions (largely absent in adult Western society)."

* * *

HIPPS, Juanita Redmond 1913(?)-1979
(Juanita Redmond)

OBITUARY NOTICE: Born c. 1913 in Swansea, S.C.; died February 25, 1979, in St. Petersburg, Fla. Army nurse and author. A lieutenant colonel in the U.S. Army Nurses Corps, Hipps served at hospitals in Bataan, Corregidor, and Manila at the beginning of World War II. She was one of eight nurses evacuated to Australia just before the Japanese invaded the Philippine Islands. Hipps helped establish the Army Corps flight nurse program. Under her maiden name, Juanita Redmond, she wrote a best-selling story of Army nurses, *I Served on Bataan,* which was adapted by Paramount in 1943 as a film titled "So Proudly We Hail." Obituaries and other sources: *Washington Post,* March 1, 1979; *New York Times,* March 1, 1979.

* * *

HIRSCHMANN, Maria Anne
(Hansi)

PERSONAL: Known professionally as Hansi; born in Reichenberg, Czechoslovakia; came to United States in 1955, naturalized citizen, 1962; married; children: Christiane, Michael, Hanna, Maria, John. *Education:* Earned B.S., 1965, M.A., 1966. *Office:* Hansi Ministries, Inc., P.O. Box 552, Huntington Beach, Calif. 92648.

CAREER: Hansi Ministries, Inc., Huntington Beach, Calif., founder and chairman of the board, 1972—. Former elementary school and high school teacher. Public lecturer in the United States, Asia, Africa, the Middle East, and Latin America. *Awards, honors:* Americanism Medal from Daughters of the American Revolution, 1976; gold medal from Sons of the American Revolution, 1977; international distinguished service citation from International Society of Christian Endeavor Association, 1977.

WRITINGS: Hansi: The Girl Who Left the Swastika, Tyndale, 1973; *Hansi's New Life*, Revell, 1975; *Outposts of Love*, Revell, 1976; *I Am But a Child in Christ* (Bible study), with study guide, S.P.A.R.C. Publishing, 1978; *Please Don't Shoot, I'm Already Wounded*, Tyndale, 1979; *Will the East Wind Blow?*, S.P.A.R.C. Publishing, 1979.

WORK IN PROGRESS: Two bible studies, *Follow Me* and *Learn of Me*, both with Betty Pershing.

SIDELIGHTS: Maria Hirschmann came to the United States after serving time in a Communist labor camp. She escaped to West Germany, then to the United States. As a high school teacher she had a special interest in working with dropouts, juvenile delinquents, and other troubled teenagers.

*   *   *

HITCHCOCK, Raymond (John) 1922-

PERSONAL: Born February 9, 1922, in Calcutta, India; son of John Henry Frederick (a soldier) and Ruby (Rogers) Hitchcock; married Elizabeth Joyce Watts, August 27, 1949; children: Robyn, Lalage, Fleur. *Education:* Emmanuel College, Cambridge, M.A., 1955. *Politics:* Liberal. *Home and office:* Abbots Worthy Mill, Winchester, Hampshire, England. *Agent:* A. D. Peters & Co. Ltd., 10 Buckingham St., London W.C.2, England.

CAREER: Cable & Wireless Ltd., London, England, research and development engineer, 1949-60; free-lance writer, 1967—. *Military service:* British Army, Royal Engineers, 1940-45; served in Normandy; became lieutenant. *Member:* Institute of Electrical Engineers.

WRITINGS—Novels: *Percy*, W. H. Allen, 1969, Dodd, 1970; *Gilt-Edged Boy*, W. H. Allen, 1971; *Venus Thirteen*, W. H. Allen, 1972; *Attack the Lusitania*, M. Joseph, 1979. Author of radio plays and plays for British Broadcasting Corp. (BBC) and Anglia television. Contributor to magazines, including *Penthouse* and *World Medicine*.

WORK IN PROGRESS: A novel set in 1940.

SIDELIGHTS: "I started by writing satire," Hitchcock told *CA*, "but it was turned into a bit of a joke by the film industry. Now I just try to tell stories." *Avocational interests:* Humor and satire, stone-age architecture, Anglo-Saxon Britain, local history (especially history of sports and war).

*   *   *

HOAGLAND, Mahlon B(ush) 1921-

PERSONAL: Given name is pronounced *May*-lun; born October 15, 1921, in Boston, Mass.; son of Hudson (a scientist) and Anna (Plummer) Hoagland; married Elizabeth Stratton, May 8, 1943 (divorced); married Olley Jones (a bookseller), January 10, 1961; children: (first marriage) Judith Hoagland Hauck, Mahlon Bush, Jr., Robin. *Education:* Attended Williams College, 1940-41; Harvard University, M.D., 1948. *Home:* 234 Gulf St., Shrewsbury, Mass. 01545. *Office:* Worcester Foundation for Experimental Biology, Shrewsbury, Mass. 01545.

CAREER: Harvard Medical School at Massachusetts General Hospital, Cambridge, 1948-60, began as research fellow, became assistant professor of medicine; Harvard University, Cambridge, associate professor of bacteriology and immunology, 1960-67; Dartmouth College, Hanover, N.H., professor of biochemistry and head of Dartmouth Medical School, 1967-70; Worcester Foundation for Experimental Biology, Shrewsbury, Mass., president and scientific director, 1970—. Research associate at Carlsburg Laboratories, Copenhagen, Denmark, 1951-52, and at Cavendish Laboratories, Cambridge, England, 1957-58; research professor at the University of Massachusetts, 1970—. Executive secretary for the commission on research for Massachusetts General Hospital, 1954-57. Member of the board of directors of the Massachusetts division of the American Cancer Society Scholar cancer research; member of the board of science counsellors to the National Heart and Lung Institute, 1972-74. Consultant to National Institutes of Health, 1961-64, and the American Cancer Society, 1965-68.

MEMBER: American Academy of Arts and Sciences (fellow), American Society of Biological Chemists, American Society of Cell Biology, Association of Independent Research Institutes (president, 1976-77). *Awards, honors:* Sc.D. from Worcester Polytechnic Institute, 1973; Franklin Medal, 1976.

WRITINGS: The Roots of Life, Houghton, 1978. Contributor of more than fifty articles to scientific journals.

WORK IN PROGRESS: A science book for the layman.

SIDELIGHTS: Hoagland comments: "I have had a successful career in science and am now director of one of the country's largest free-standing independent research institutes devoted to fundamental studies of cancer, brain function, and hormone regulation. I believe that the public should know more about science and am now devoting more time to writing for the layman."

*   *   *

HOBBY, William P. 1932-

PERSONAL: Born January 19, 1932, in Houston, Tex.; son of William Pettus (a publisher) and Oveta (a publisher; maiden name Culp) Hobby; married Diana Stallings, September 11, 1954; children: Laura Poteat, Paul William, Andrew Purefoy, Katherine Pettus. *Education:* Rice University, B.A., 1953. *Politics:* Democrat. *Religion:* Protestant. *Home address:* P.O. Box 326, Houston, Tex. 77001. *Office:* 4747 Southwest Freeway, Houston, Tex. 77001.

CAREER: Houston Post Co., *Houston Post*, Houston, Tex., assistant secretary-treasurer, 1957-59, associate editor, 1959-60, managing editor, 1960-63, executive editor, 1963—, executive vice-president, 1963-65, president, 1965—; lieutenant governor of Texas, 1973—. Vice-chairman of Channel Two Television Co. and of KPRC Radio Co., 1970. Parliamentarian, Texas Senate, 1959; Child Guidance Center of Houston, member of board of directors, 1957-63, president, 1960-62. Vice-president of U.S. Equestrian, Inc., 1959-60. *Military service:* U.S. Naval Reserve; became lieutenant junior grade. *Member:* American Society of Newspaper Editors, Texas Hunter and Jumper Association (director, 1953—; president, 1959-61).

SIDELIGHTS: A conservative Democrat, Lieutenant Governor Hobby proposed a controversial bill that would have established separate presidential primary and state office elections in Texas. To prevent a vote on the bill, twelve dissenting state senators hid out for more than four days in May, 1979, in an Austin garage apartment. Meanwhile, Hobby ordered police to conduct a state-wide manhunt for the missing senators. The lieutenant governor finally yielded his stance on the bill and the senators returned to the capital.

BIOGRAPHICAL/CRITICAL SOURCES: Time, June 4, 1979.

HODEIR, Andre 1921-

PERSONAL: Born January 22, 1921, in Paris, France; son of Oidih and Angele (Guionnet) Hodeir; married Michele Bochm (a film editor); children: Catherine, Samantha. *Education:* Conservatoire National Superieur du Musique de Paris, 1942-47. *Home:* 66 rue du Colonel de Rochebrune, 92380 Garches, France.

CAREER: Jazz Hot, Paris, France, editor, 1947-50; free-lance writer, 1950—; *Panorama de la Musique,* Paris, editor, 1974-76. Visiting professor at Harvard University, 1976.

WRITINGS: Les Formes de la musique, Presses universi-taires de France, 1951, 7th edition, 1978, translation by Noel Burch published as *The Forms of Music,* Walker & Co., 1966; *Hommes et problemes du jazz: suivi de la religion du jazz,* Portulan, 1954, translation by David Noakes published as *Jazz: Its Evolution and Essence,* Grove, 1956; *La Musique depuis Debussy,* Presses universitaires de France, 1961, translation by Burch published as *Since Debussy: A View of Contemporary Music,* Grove, 1961; *Recueil d'articles sur le jazz* (selection of articles about jazz), translation by Burch published as *Toward Jazz,* Grove, 1962; (with Tomi Ungerer) *Les Trois Bouteilles de Warwick,* Ecole, 1976, translation by Richard Seaver published as *Warwick's Three Bottles* (juvenile), Grove, 1966; (with Ungerer) *Dame Cunegonde aux sports d'hiver,* translation by Richard Seaver published as *Cleopatra Goes Sledding* (juvenile), Grove, 1967; *Les Mondes du jazz,* Union generale d'-editions, 1970, translation by Burch published as *The Worlds of Jazz,* Grove, 1972.

In French: *Le Jazz, cet inconnu* (title means "This Unknown Jazz"), Editions France—Empire, 1945; *Introduction a la musique de jazz* (title means "An Initiation to Jazz"), Larousse, 1948; *La Musique etrangere contemporaine* (title means "Contemporary Music Out of France"), Presses universitaires de France, 1954, 3rd edition, 1971.

WORK IN PROGRESS: A novel; several stories for children.

SIDELIGHTS: Hodeir writes: "First I was just a musician writing about technical and aesthetic aspects of music. Then in *The Worlds of Jazz* I tried to be the voice of the music expressing itself in a literary and poetic way. Now in my un-finished novel I am trying my best to forget all about music, but I am not quite sure music isn't behind the stage during the play."

* * *

HOFFECKER, Carol E(leanor) 1938-

PERSONAL: Born December 29, 1938, in Wilmington, Del.; daughter of Ralph C. (an accountant) and Kathryn (Zebley) Hoffecker. *Education:* University of Delaware, B.A., 1960; Radcliffe College, M.A., 1962; Harvard University, Ph.D., 1967. *Religion:* Episcopalian. *Office:* Department of History, University of Delaware, Newark, Del. 19711.

CAREER: University of Delaware, Newark, assistant professor, 1973-75; associate professor of history, 1975—. *Member:* American Historical Association, Organization of American Historians, Historical Society of Delaware.

WRITINGS: Wilmington, Delaware: Portrait of an Industrial City, University Press of Virginia, 1974; *Brandy-wine Village: The Story of a Milling Community,* Old Brandywine Village, 1974; *Delaware: A Bicentennial History,* Norton, 1977.

WORK IN PROGRESS: Research for a book on twentieth-century Wilmington, Delaware.

* * *

HOGG, Oliver Frederick Gillian 1887-1979

OBITUARY NOTICE: Born December 22, 1887, in Bedford, England; died in 1979. Military historian, genealogist, and author. Hogg became a brigadier in the Royal Artillery and served in many military positions, including director of military administration for the Ministry of Supply from 1939 to 1946. He was the author of several books on military armaments and genealogy, including *Artillery: Its Origin, Heyday, and Decline* and *Further Light on the Ancestry of William Penn.* He contributed numerous historical and technical articles to army journals and to *Chamber's Encyclopedia.* Obituaries and other sources: *The Author's and Writer's Who's Who,* 6th edition, Burke's Peerage, 1971; *The Writers Directory, 1976-78,* St. Martin's, 1976; *Who's Who,* 131st edition, St. Martin's, 1979; *AB Bookman's Weekly,* April 16, 1979.

* * *

HOLLAND, Sheila 1937-
(Charlotte Lamb, Sheila Lancaster)

PERSONAL: Born December 22, 1937, in London, England; daughter of Ronald Francis and Florence Maud (Eve) Coates; married Richard Percy Holland (a writer), October 10, 1959; children: Michael, Sarah, Jane, Charlotte and David (twins). *Education:* Attended convent school in London, England. *Politics:* "I detest them (politicians, not people)." *Religion:* Christian. *Home and office:* Applegate, Port St. Mary, Isle of Man. *Agent:* Lisa Collier, Collier Associates, 280 Madison Ave., New York, N.Y. 10016.

CAREER: Bank of England, London, secretary, 1954-56; British Broadcasting Corp., London, secretary, 1956-58; writer, 1971—. *Member:* Society of Authors, Romantic Novelists Association, Crime Writers Association.

WRITINGS—All novels; under name Sheila Holland: Prisoner of the Heart, R. Hale, 1972; *Love in a Mist,* R. Hale, 1972; *A Lantern in the Night,* R. Hale, 1973; *Falcon on the Hill,* R. Hale, 1974; *Shadows at Dawn,* R. Hale, 1975; *The Growing Season,* R. Hale, 1975; *Gold of Apollo,* R. Hale, 1976; *Caring Kind,* R. Hale, 1976; *The Devil and Miss Hay,* R. Hale, 1977; *Eleanor of Aquitaine,* R. Hale, 1978; *Maiden Castle,* Playboy Press, 1978; *Love's Bright Flame,* Playboy Press, 1978; *Dancing Hill,* Playboy Press, 1978; *Folly by Candelight,* Playboy Press, 1979; *Shadows at Dawn,* Playboy Press, 1979; *Sophia,* Playboy Press, 1979; *The Masque,* Zebra Publications, 1979.

Under pseudonym Charlotte Lamb; all published by Mills & Boon: *Follow a Stranger,* 1973; *Carnival Coast,* 1973; *A Family Affair,* 1974; *Star-Crossed,* 1976; *Festival Summer,* 1977; *Florentine Spring,* 1977; *Hawk in a Blue Sky,* 1977; *Heron Quest,* 1977; *Kingfisher Morning,* 1977; *Master of Comus,* 1978; *Call Back Yesterday,* 1978; *Desert Barbarian,* 1978; *Disturbing Stranger,* 1978; *Autumn Conquest,* 1978; *The Long Surrender,* 1978; *The Cruel Flame,* 1978; *Duel of Desire,* 1978 *The Devil's Arms,* 1978; *Pagan Encounter,* 1978; *Forbidden Fire,* 1979; *The Silken Trap,* 1979; *Dark Dominion,* 1979; *Fever,* 1979; *Dark Master,* 1979; *Temptation,* 1979; *Twist of Fate,* 1979; *Possession,* 1979; *Love Is a Frenzy,* 1979; *Storm Centre,* 1979; *Frustration,* 1979.

Under pseudonym Sheila Lancaster: *Sweet Dark Wanton,* Hodder & Stoughton, 1979, Berkley, 1980; *The Tilthammer,* Hodder & Stoughton, 1980.

WORK IN PROGRESS: Two novels under name Sheila Holland, *Bells of the City* and *The Girl From Virginia*, both for Playboy Press.

SIDELIGHTS: Sheila Holland comments: "I love writing about people—the intricacies of character fascinate me, whether against a contemporary background or a historical one. Having been born in a country rich in the sediment of the past, it is not surprising that I find history fascinating. England is an odd mixture of bustle and nostalgia. Away from London's incredible packed streets lies an England still as green and beautiful as it was hundreds of years ago—and I love both faces of my country, although I have moved to a remote little island off England's coast. Here it is peaceful, wild, and very easy to write."

*   *   *

HOLLINGSWORTH, Dorothy Frances 1916-

PERSONAL: Born May 10, 1916, in Newcastle-upon-Tyne, England; daughter of Arthur (a pharmacist) and Dorothy (a teacher; maiden name, Coldwell) Hollingsworth. *Education:* University of Durham, B.Sc., 1937; Royal Infirmary, Edinburgh, Scotland, diploma in dietetics, 1939. *Home:* 2 Close, Petts Wood, Orpington, Kent BR5 1JA, England.

CAREER: Royal Northern Hospital, London, England, hospital dietitian, 1939-41; Ministry of Food, London, member of National Food Survey Division and Scientific Advisers Division, 1941-49; Ministry of Agriculture, Fisheries, and Food, London, principal scientific officer and scientific branch head, 1949-70; British Nutrition Foundation, London, director-general, 1970-77; International Union of Nutritional Sciences, member of council, 1975—, secretary-general, 1978—. State registered dietitian, 1963; chairman of International Committee of Dietetic Associations, 1961-65; member of National Food Survey Committee, 1951—, Committee on the Medical Aspects of Food Policy, 1970—, and Joint Agricultural Research Council-Medical Research Council Committee on Food and Nutrition Research, 1970-74; member of dietitians board of Council for Professions Support to Medicine, 1962-74; member of Medical Research Council's Physiological Systems and Disorders Board, 1974-77, and Environmental Medicine Research Policy Committee, 1975-76.

MEMBER: Independent Broadcasting Authority (member of medical advisory panel, 1970—), Royal Institute of Chemistry (fellow), Royal Society (member of National Committee for Nutritional Sciences, 1970—), British Dietetic Association (chairman, 1947-49), Institute of Biology (fellow; member of council, 1964-69; vice-president, 1978—), Nutrition Society (member of council, 1974-77), Institute of Food Science and Technology (fellow; vice-president, 1977-79), Society of Chemical Industry, University Women's Club, Arts Theatre Club. *Awards, honors:* Member of Order of the British Empire, 1958.

WRITINGS: (Editor of revision) J. C. Drummond and Anne Wilbraham, *The Englishman's Food*, J. Cape, 1957; (editor of revision with H. M. Sinclair) *Hutchison's Food and the Principles of Nutrition*, 12th edition (Hollingsworth was not associated with earlier editions), Edward Arnold, 1969; (editor with Margaret Russell) *Nutritional Problems in a Changing World*, Applied Science Publishers, 1973; (editor with Elisabeth Morse) *People and Food Tomorrow*, Applied Science Publishers, 1976. Contributor to scientific journals.

WORK IN PROGRESS: Studying trends in food consumption in relation to health.

SIDELIGHTS: Dorothy Hollingsworth writes that she believes in the "importance of good nutrition for good health." Her work in international nutrition has enabled her to travel extensively. Hollingsworth told *CA:* "Most of my writings are about the nutritional value of food supplies at different times and the relationships between food and health. *Nutritional Problems in a Changing World* is concerned with the nutritional problems of affluent society and *People and Food Tomorrow* is about the adequacy of food supplies to meet the needs of the future population of the world."

AVOCATIONAL INTERESTS: Music, theater, the countryside, gardening.

*   *   *

HONG, Yong Ki 1929(?)-1979

OBITUARY NOTICE: Born c. 1929 in Korea; died of kidney and liver failure, April 14, 1979, in Cheverly, Md. Radio commentator and journalist. Hong worked as a commentator for Christian Korean Radio and for Voice of America, and as anchorman for TBC radio. He was editor and writer for Korean newspapers, including Hapdong News Agency, Dong Hwa News Agency, and *Joong Age Ilbo* daily newspaper, and for Korean language newspapers in the United States. One month before his death he had been appointed managing editor of the New York City edition of the Korean daily newspaper, *Dong A*. Obituaries and other sources: *Washington Post*, April 18, 1979.

*   *   *

HOOPER, David (Vincent) 1915-

PERSONAL: Born August 31, 1915, in Reigate, England; son of Vincent (an architect) and Marjorie (Tatton-Winter) Hooper; married Joan Roma Rose, November, 1950. *Education:* Attended grammar school in Croydon, England. *Politics:* "All politicians are interested only in votes; none with the welfare of citizens." *Religion:* "Humanist." *Residence:* Dorset, England.

CAREER: Architect in England, 1945—; writer, 1959—. Chief architect for borough of Surrey Heath, 1974-79. *Member:* Royal Institute of British Architects.

WRITINGS—All chess books: (With Marc Euwe) *A Guide to Chess Endings*, Routledge & Kegan Paul, 1959, revised edition, Dover, 1976; *A Complete Defence to 1P-K4*, Pergamon, 1967, revised edition, 1973; *Steinitz*, Wildhagen of Hamburg, 1968; *A Pocket Guide to Chess Endgames*, G. Bell, 1970, revised edition, 1973; (with Dale Brandreth) *The Unknown Capablanca*, Batsford, 1975.

WORK IN PROGRESS: A book entitled *The Oxford Companion to Chess*.

*   *   *

HOPKINS, John (Richard) 1931-

PERSONAL: Born January 27, 1931, in London, England; married Prudence Balchin, 1954 (marriage ended); married Shirley Knight (an actress), 1970; children: two. *Education:* St. Catherine's College, B.A. *Home:* 24 Malamins Way, Bechenham, Kent, England. *Agent:* William Morris Agency, 4 Saville Row, London W.1., England.

CAREER: Worked as television studio manager; writer for television for British Broadcasting Co. (BBC-TV), 1962-64; free-lance writer, 1964—. *Military service:* National Service, 1950-51.

WRITINGS—Novels: *The Attempt*, Viking, 1967; *Tangier Buzzless Flies*, Atheneum, 1972.

Plays: *This Story of Yours* (first produced in London, 1968), Penguin, 1969; *Find Your Way Home* (first produced in London, 1970; first produced in New York City, 1974), Penguin, 1970, Doubleday, 1975; "Economic Necessity," first produced in Leicester, England, 1973; "Next of Kin," first produced in London, 1974.

Teleplays: "Break Up," 1958; "After the Party," 1958; "The Small Back Room," 1959; "Dancers in the Morning," 1959; "A Woman Comes Home," 1961; "A Chance of Thunder" (six-parts), 1961; "By Invitation Only," 1961; "The Second Curtain," 1962; "Look Who's Talking," 1962; "The Pretty English Girls," 1964; "I Took My Little World Away," 1964; "Parade's End" (adapted from the novel by Ford Madox Ford), 1964; "Time Out of Mind," 1964; "Houseparty" (ballet), 1964; "The Make Believe Man," 1965; "Fable," 1965; "Horror of Darkness," 1965; "A Man Like Orpheus," 1965.

"Some Place of Darkness," 1966; *Talking to a Stranger: Four Television Plays* (includes "Anytime You're Ready I'll Sparkle," "No Skill or Special Knowledge Is Required," "Gladly My Cross-Eyed Bear," and "The Innocent Must Suffer"), Penguin, 1967; (with others) *Z Cars: Four Scripts From the Television Series* (includes "A Place of Safety" by Hopkins), edited by Michael Marland, Longman, 1968; (with others) *Conflicting Generations: Five Television Plays* (includes "A Game—Like—Only a Game" by Hopkins), edited by Marland, Longman, 1968; "The Gambler" (adapted from the novel by Fyodor Dostoevsky), 1968; "Beyond the Sunrise," 1969.

"The Dolly Scene," 1970; "Some Distant Shadow," 1971; "That Quiet Earth," 1972; "Walk Into the Dark," 1972; "The Greeks and Their Gifts," 1972; "A Story to Frighten Children," 1976; "Double Dare," 1976. Also contributor of numerous scripts to the television series, "Z Cars."

Screenplays: (With Richard Maibaum) "Thunderball" (adapted from material by Kevin McClory and Jack Whittingham and the novel by Ian Fleming), United Artists, 1965; (co-author) "The Virgin Soldiers," 1969; (co-author) "Divorce—His, Divorce—Hers," 1972; (co-author) "The Offence," 1973.

SIDELIGHTS: Although he has also written plays and novels, Hopkins is best known for his work in television. He was a frequent contributor to the highly praised British television series, "Z Cars." In an age of fantasy and overt romanticism, "Z Cars" was acknowledged to be one of the more realistic police dramas.

Perhaps Hopkins' most striking teleplay is the four-part *Talking to a Stranger.* It contains four different perspectives of one day in a family. Some critics reacted strongly to Hopkins' apparent eagerness for melodrama but as many more alluded to his sure understanding of the various characters. The dialogue, much of which comes in the form of long monologues, exemplifies Hopkin's penchant for realism and expressive narrative.

Hopkins' plays have not met with as favorable a reaction as his teleplays. If his teleplays are realistic, his plays are even more so. *This Story of Yours* is about an overwrought police officer who, victimized by his own anguish, kills a child rapist. Less sordid is Hopkins' *Find Your Way Home* in which two homosexuals meet and take up housekeeping together. By portraying one as a prostitute and the other as a disgruntled husband, Hopkins' was able to create a realistic yet sensitive play.

Like his other writings, Hopkins' novels show a preference

for human emotion as opposed to action. Writing in *Book World*, J. R. Frakes observed: "In his first novel, *The Attempt*, Hopkins seemed to have gone as far as possible with the absolutely bone-dry, dispassionate fiction of pointless activity." However, Hopkins' second novel, *Tangier Buzzless Flies*, is less concerned with inactivity. The story of a man who sees his best friend die and considers suicide himself until he resolves his inner conflicts, *Tangier Buzzless Flies* was favorably reviewed by many critics. Comparing it to *The Attempt*, Frakes wrote: "Perhaps the change in locale from Peru to Africa accounts for the new quality . . . in *Tangier Buzzless Flies*, where, though the void still beckons, the rhythms of life beat triumphantly. . . ." Frakes concluded that "Albert Camus would have revered this novel." Jim Harrison wrote that "the writing is admirable and anyone who couldn't read the book with extreme interest is a dolt."

BIOGRAPHICAL/CRITICAL SOURCES: Book World, March 2, 1972; *New York Times Book Review,* May 14, 1972; *Contemporary Literary Criticism,* Volume 4, Gale, 1975.*

*   *   *

HOSFORD, Ray E. 1933-

PERSONAL: Born March 21, 1933, in Crosby, Minn.; son of Harry (a mill worker) and Melva (Bugh) Hosford; married Phyllis Hicks, December 17, 1955; children: Jeffrey Mark, Jacqueline Rae. *Education:* Central Washington State University, B.A. (cum laude), 1955, M.A., 1959; Stanford University, Ph.D., 1966. *Residence:* Goleta, Calif. 93017. *Office:* Graduate School of Education, University of California, Santa Barbara, Calif. 93106.

CAREER: Public school teacher in Aberdeen, Wash., 1955-56; Central Washington State University, Ellensburg, counselor, 1958-59; school teacher and counselor in Sunnyvale, Calif., 1959-65; Stanford University, Stanford, Calif., acting instructor in psychology, 1965-66; University of Wisconsin, Madison, assistant professor of counseling and behavioral studies, 1966-69; University of California, Santa Barbara, associate professor, 1969-74, professor of education, 1974—, associate dean of Graduate School of Education, 1970-73, member of Institute for Applied Behavioral Science. Participant in professional conventions and meetings; consultant to correctional facilities and Federal Bureau of Prisons. *Military service:* U.S. Air Force, 1956-58; became first lieutenant.

MEMBER: American Psychological Association, Association for the Advancement of Behavior Therapy, American Personnel and Guidance Association, American School Counselors Association, American Counselor Educators and Supervisors, Association for Counselor Education and Supervision, American Educational Research Association (member of executive committee, 1975), Wisconsin Counselor Educators Association, Kappa Delta Pi. *Awards, honors:* Grants from U.S. Office of Education, 1966, 1972, and from Federal Bureau of Prisons, 1975-79.

WRITINGS: Guidance Services in the Elementary Schools of Wisconsin, State Department of Instruction (Madison, Wis.), 1969; (with Louis A.J.M. de Visser) *Behavioral Approaches to Counseling: An Introduction,* American Personnel and Guidance Association, 1974; (editor with C. S. Moss, and contributor) *The Crumbling Walls: Counseling and Treatment of Prisoners,* University of Illinois Press, 1975; *Social Learning Approaches to Counseling,* Brooks-Cole, 1979.

Contributor: J. D. Krumboltz and C. E. Thoresen, editors, *Behavioral Counseling: Cases and Techniques,* Holt, 1969; T. A. Ryan and other editors, *Commitment to Action and Supervision: Report of a National Survey of Counselor Supervision,* Association for Counselor Education and Supervision, 1969; Ryan and other editors, *Systems Models for Counselor Supervision in School and Non-School Settings,* Association for Counselor Education and Supervision, 1970; James C. Hansen, editor, *Guidance Services in the Elementary School,* American Personnel and Guidance Association, 1970; M. M. Ohlsen, editor, *Counseling Children in Groups,* Holt, 1973; G. F. Farwell, N. R. Gamsky, and P. L. Mathieu-Coughlan, editors, *The Counselor's Handbook: Essays on Preparation,* Chandler Publishing, 1974; Ryan, editor, *Systems Model for the Counselor,* American Personnel and Guidance Association, 1978.

Films: "Helping the Shy Student," Counseling Films, Inc., 1967; "An Introduction to Behavioral Counseling," Counseling Films, Inc., 1969; "A Behavioral Counseling Seminar," Counseling Films, Inc., 1969; "Identifying the Problem," American Personnel and Guidance Association, 1974; "Observing and Recording Behavior," American Personnel and Guidance Association, 1974; "Formulating the Counseling Goal," American Personnel and Guidance Association, 1974; "Counseling Techniques: Reinforcement Procedures," American Personnel and Guidance Association, 1974; "Counseling Techniques: Social Modeling," American Personnel and Guidance Association, 1974; "Counseling Techniques: Desensitization," American Personnel and Guidance Association, 1974; "Counseling Techniques: Assertive Training," American Personnel and Guidance Association, 1974; "Counseling Techniques: Self-as-a-Model," American Personnel and Guidance Association, 1974.

Editor of media series published by American Personnel and Guidance Association, 1971—. Contributor of about twenty-five articles to psychology, education, and counseling journals. *Ad hoc* review editor of *Journal of Educational Research,* 1970.

WORK IN PROGRESS: Introduction to Counseling Psychology, with S. D. Brown and D. R. Atkinson; a monograph, *The Counseling Psychologist,* "a review of observational learning counseling strategies: modeling, self-observation, and self-as-a-model."

SIDELIGHTS: Hosford writes that his main research interest is "in investigating the effects of the self-as-a-model behavioral change strategy which I have been developing at the University of California, Santa Barbara. Many research ideas have emanated from therapy situations I have had with clients. I then evaluate their effectiveness under controlled conditions at the university."

*   *   *

HOSKING, Geoffrey A(lan)   1942-

PERSONAL: Born April 28, 1942, in Troon, Ayrshire, Scotland; son of Stuart (in banking) and Jean Ross (a teacher; maiden name, Smillie) Hosking; married Anne Lloyd Hirst (a teacher), December 19, 1970; children: Katya, Janet. *Education:* Attended school in Maidstone, England. *Home:* 113 Maldon Rd., Colchester, Essex CO3 3AX, England. *Agent:* Murray Pollinger, 4 Garrick St., London WC2E 9BH, England. *Office:* Department of History, University of Essex, Colchester, Essex CO4 3S4, England.

CAREER: University of Essex, Colchester, England, lecturer in government, 1966-71; University of Wiscon-

sin—Madison, visiting lecturer in political science, 1971-72; University of Essex, lecturer, 1972-76, senior lecturer in history, 1976-78, reader in Russian history, 1978—. *Member:* British Universities Association of Slavists, American Association for the Advancement of Slavic Studies.

WRITINGS: The Russian Constitutional Experiment: Government and Duma, 1907-14, Cambridge University Press, 1973; *Soviet Fiction Today: Studies in the New Russian Realism,* Holmes & Meier, in press.

WORK IN PROGRESS: A history of the Soviet Union.

SIDELIGHTS: Hosking told *CA:* "My interest in Russia goes back to my school days. We didn't study Russia or Communism at all at school; perhaps that's why I found it fascinating. I had the feeling then (and still have) that the great political, artistic, philosophical and religious issues of our day were somehow being decided in Russia. No one, of course, regards the Soviet Union any longer as a socialist paradise; few people think the country has anything particularly important to tell the world. But Russia's uniquely long experience in trying to fulfill the ideals of socialism makes it a country vitally important to study (whether or not one regards socialism as desirable). This is the viewpoint from which I have examined the contemporary novel in *Soviet Fiction Today.* The novelists (official and samizdat) are the most truthful and the profoundist historians of their own nation under Communist rule. They are both witnesses to and interpreters of that social reality. I hope to follow up this book with my own history of the U.S.S.R., largely based on more orthodox sources, but stressing internal social and cultural developments more than is usual in such general histories."

*   *   *

HOWARD, Edmund (Bernard Carlo)   1909-

PERSONAL: Born September 8, 1909, in Budapest, Hungary; son of Baron Howard of Penrith and Lady Isabella Giustiniana-Bandina; married Cecile Geoffroy-Dechaume, 1936; children: Anne (deceased), Esme, John, Anthony, Katherine. *Education:* New College, Oxford, B.A., 1929. *Home:* Jerome Cottage, Marlow Common, Buckinghamshire, England.

CAREER: Called to the Bar, 1932; practiced law on Northern Circuit in England, 1935-36; London Stock Exchange, London, England, secretary to board of trustees and managers, 1936-39; His Majesty's Diplomatic Service, London, England, foreign service officer in Rome, Italy, 1947-51, at Foreign Office in London, 1951-53; Her Majesty's Diplomatic Service, foreign service officer in Madrid Spain, 1953-57, Bogota, Colombia, 1957-59, Florence, Italy, 1960-61, and in Rome, 1961-65, consul-general in Genoa, Italy, 1965-69; writer, 1969—. *Military service:* British Army, King's Royal Rifle Corps, 1939-45, in psychological warfare, 1943-45; became major. *Member:* British-Italian Society (member of executive committee), Anglo-Colombian Society. *Awards, honors:* Member of Royal Victorian Order, 1961; companion of Order of St. Michael and St. George, 1969; commander of Order of Merit (Italy), 1973; Duchi di Galliera Prize from Genoa Chamber of Commerce, 1973, for *Genoa.*

WRITINGS: Genoa: History and Art in an Old Seaport, S.A.G.E.P., 1971, 2nd edition, 1978; (translator) Leon Poliakov, *The Aryan Myth,* Chatto & Windus, 1974.

SIDELIGHTS: Howard writes: "*Genoa* was written as a personal tribute to a fascinating city, in which I lived for years, and whose great achievements in statecraft, exploration, culture, and commerce do not command the interest they deserve." *Avocational interests:* Travel, gardening, walking.

* * *

HOWARD, James K(enton) 1943-

PERSONAL: Born June 30, 1943, in Ponca City, Okla.; son of Arthur R. (a life underwriter) and Dora (Utt) Howard; married wife, F. Kathryn, May 18, 1968 (divorced, November, 1975); children: Lara. *Education:* University of Oklahoma, B.A., 1965, M.A., 1979. *Politics:* Democrat. *Religion:* Disciples of Christ. *Home:* 1305 East Shawnee, Tahlequah, Okla. 74464. *Office:* Northeastern Oklahoma State University, Tahlequah, Okla. 74464.

CAREER: University of Oklahoma, Norman, assistant to president, 1967-68; Northland Press, Flagstaff, Ariz., editor, 1972-77; Oklahoma Department of Public Safety, Oklahoma City, research and publications consultant, 1977; Northeastern Oklahoma State University, Tahlequah, assistant dean of student affairs, 1978—. Head of board of trustees of Flagstaff Public Library, 1973-74; member of board of trustees of Friends of the Museum of Northern Arizona, 1974-77. *Military service:* U.S. Air Force, 1968-72; became captain. *Member:* National Association of Student Personnel Administrators, National Cowboy Hall of Fame and Western Heritage Center, Western History Association, University of Oklahoma Association, Sigma Delta Chi, Kappa Tau Alpha, Lambda Chi Alpha. *Awards, honors:* Award of merit from Rounce and Coffin Club, 1974, for *Color and Light: The Southwest Canvases of Louis Akin,* and 1975, for cover design of *Hang Gliding: The Flyingest Flying.*

WRITINGS: Ten Years With the Cowboy Artists of America, Northland Press, 1976; (editor) *History of the Oklahoma Department of Public Safety,* Oklahoma Department of Public Safety, *1977.*

WORK IN PROGRESS: Studying mass-media influence on statewide election results in Oklahoma.

SIDELIGHTS: Howard writes: "I had collected western books and works of art for a decade, and attended all of the annual exhibitions of the Cowboy Artists of America. My personal relationship with them and the phenomenal growth of interest in their work appeared worthy of documentation."

BIOGRAPHICAL/CRITICAL SOURCES: Harper's, December, 1974.

* * *

HOWARD, Richard 1929-

PERSONAL: Born October 13, 1929, in Cleveland, Ohio. *Education:* Columbia University, B.A., 1951, M.A., 1952. *Home:* 37 West 12th St., New York, N.Y. 10011.

CAREER: Poet, critic, and translator. Worked as lexicographer, 1953-57. *Awards, honors:* Pulitzer Prize for poetry, 1970, for *Untitled Subjects.*

WRITINGS—Poetry: Quantities, Wesleyan University Press, 1962; *The Damages: Poems,* Wesleyan University Press, 1967; *Untitled Subjects: Poems,* Atheneum, 1969; *Findings,* Atheneum, 1971; *Two-Part Inventions,* Atheneum, 1974; *Decade (for Hart Crane),* [Kent, Ohio], 1974; *Fellow Feelings: Poems,* Atheneum, 1976.

Other: *Alone With America: Essays on the Art of Poetry in the United States Since 1950,* Atheneum, 1969; (co-editor with Thomas Victor) *Preferences: Fifty-One American Poets Choose Poems From Their Own Work and From the Past,* Viking, 1974; (with Michael Filey) *Passenger's Must Not Ride on Fenders,* Green Tree, 1974.

Editor: Michel Butor, *Inventory: Essays,* Simon & Schuster, 1969; Charles Simic, *Dismantling the Silence* (poetry), Braziller, 1971; Carl Dennis, *A House of My Own* (poetry), Braziller, 1974; Jules Roy, *The War in Algeria,* Greenwood Press, 1975; E. M. Cioran, *The Trouble With Being Born,* Viking, 1976.

Translator: Alain Robbe-Grillet, *The Voyeur,* Grove, 1958; Claude Simon, *The Wind,* Braziller, 1959; Simon, *The Grass,* Braziller, 1960; Robbe-Grillet, *Two Novels (Jealousy and In the Labyrinth),* Grove, 1960; Andre Breton, *Najda,* Grove, 1961; Robbe-Grillet, *Last Year at Marienbad,* Grove, 1962; Butor, *Mobile,* Simon & Schuster, 1963; Michel Leiris, *Manhood,* Grossman, 1968; Simone de Beauvoir, *Force of Circumstance,* Simon & Schuster, 1963; Robbe-Grillet, *Erasers,* Grove, 1964; Robbe-Grillet, *For a New Novel: Essays on Fiction,* Grove, 1966; Jean Hytier, *The Poetics of Paul Valery,* Doubleday, 1966; Jules Renard, *Natural Histories,* Horizon Press, 1966; Maurice Nadeau, *History of Surrealism,* Macmillan, 1967; Simon, *Histoire,* Braziller, 1968.

Andre Gide, *The Immoralist,* Knopf, 1970; Jean Genet, *May Day Speech,* City Lights, 1970; Jean Cocteau, *Professional Secrets: An Autobiography,* Farrar, Straus, 1970; Cioran, *Fall Into Time,* Quadrangle, 1970; Simon, *The Battle of Pharsalus,* Braziller, 1971; Albert Camus, *A Happy Death,* Knopf, 1972; Roland Barthes, *Critical Essays,* Northwestern University Press, 1972; Maurice Pons, *Rosa,* Dial, 1972; Robbe-Grillet, *Project for a Revolution in New York,* Grove, 1972; Tzvetan Todorov, *The Fantastic,* 1973. Translator of the play by Fernando Arrabal, "The Automobile Graveyard," produced in New York City, 1961. Also translator of more than one hundred other works by French authors. Contributor to periodicals.

SIDELIGHTS: Howard is highly regarded in the literary community for his accomplishments as a poet, critic, and translator. As a translator, he is considered the person most responsible for introducing modern French fiction to American readers. As a critic, he produced *Alone With America,* a collection of essays on forty-one American poets that was described by one critic as "an awesomely ambitious book." And his work as a poet culminated in his acceptance of the Pulitzer Prize in 1970.

Published in 1962, *Quantities,* Howard's first book of poetry, was praised for its technical perfection but criticized for the lapses in many of the poem's narratives. Critics were most responsive to those poems which accompanied a high degree of technical skill with consistent narrative structure.

Howard's second collection, *The Damages,* fared better with critics. Writing in *Contemporary Literature,* Donald Sheehan found that Howard had resolved the weaknesses of his earlier collection. "Like Marianne Moore's, Howard's metric is syllabic, not accentual, and to the ear his lines thus move with the freedom, ease, and spontaneity of prose rhythms," declared Sheehan. "This syllabic metric is at once elaborately disciplined and immensely free. As a result, its discipline provides a perfect prosodic focus for Howard's powers of attention, while its prose freedom embodies his respect for reality."

Howard showed even more skill in his next collection, *Untitled Subjects.* The book is a series of monologues by fifteen writers from the past, including Sir Walter Scott, Ruskin, and William Thackeray. However, beyond being merely a series of monologues, *Untitled Subjects* contains, according to David Kalstone, "a deeper plot which makes this book exhilarating to read whole, rather than as detached or detachable poems: its awareness of the evasions and rigidities of history." Kalstone complimented Howard on his ingenious style. "He does, with his mixture of invented and real episodes, finally give the impression of voices in motion," he wrote. "Howard's is," summed up Kalstone, "in other words, an astounding book." A reviewer for *Harper's* echoed Kalstone's assessment, writing, "These fifteen long poems . . . are inspired blends of the historical and the wholly invented."

Two-Part Inventions is a variation on the style used in *Untitled Subjects*. "Howard has now moved on from the dramatic monologue to a new form . . . ," observed a writer for *New York Times Book Review*. But Howard's new form was not found praiseworthy by critics. "For all their wit and glitter, Mr. Howard's dialogues never really ignite as dialogues," wrote Christopher Ricks. However, J. D. McClatchy felt Howard's new style *was* successful at producing the desired effect. "The personalities . . . achieve a unique dramatic force which fulfills Howard's experiments to combine the structural intimacies of voice with the elaborate situations of speech."

Howard continued the style established in *Two-Part Inventions* in his most recent collection, *Fellow Feelings*. The title is derived from the concept of the poems in which Howard finds associations between himself and other writers, including Walt Whitman and Charles Baudelaire. Robert Phillips claimed that *Fellow Feelings* included many of Howard's finest poems. And a reviewer for *Choice* called Howard "a poet of intelligence who loves to play with language and his play often has charm."

Howard's enthusiasm for poetry and poets is also evident in his collection of essays, *Alone With America*. But critics did not exude the same enthusiasm for the essays. They did acknowledge the enormity of the project but felt that many of the essays were overwritten. A reviewer for *Antioch Review* found the book "terrifically *mannered* and *rife* . . . with *italicized gesture.* . . ." In *Virginia Quarterly Review*, a critic cautioned reader's who lacked sufficient knowledge of the subjects. The critic claimed that "a prior interest in the poets under discussion is essential: without it, there will not be an adequate background with which to plow through Howard's verbiage." Still, critics were not wholeheartedly against *Alone With America* and many felt that Howard exhibited considerable knowledge of the poets he chose for subjects.

Another result of Howard's affinity for poetry is *Preference*, in which he edited a collection of other poets' favorite poems. Included in the volume were James Dickey, W. H. Auden, and Mark Van Doren. James McKenzie complimented Howard's style for making "this volume both a delightfully instructive anthology and a valuable contribution to literary criticism. . . ."

BIOGRAPHICAL/CRITICAL SOURCES: Carleton Miscellany, fall, 1968; *Contemporary Literature*, spring, 1969; *Antioch Review*, winter, 1969-70; *Virginia Quarterly Review*, autumn, 1970; *Harper's*, October, 1969; *New York Times Book Review*, April 12, 1970, June 7, 1970, February 23, 1975; *Yale Review*, spring, 1975; *Choice*, June, 1976; *Commonweal*, September 10, 1976; *Authors in the News*, Volume 1, Coale, 1976; *Contemporary Literary Criticism*, Gale, Volume 7, 1977, Volume 10, 1979.*

HOWARD-HILL, Trevor Howard 1933-

PERSONAL: Born October 17, 1933, in Wellington, New Zealand; came to the United States in 1972; married Penelope Anne Din (a teacher), April 1, 1967; children: Miranda, Victoria. *Education:* Victoria University of Wellington, B.A., 1955, M.A., 1957, Ph.D., 1960; National Library School, Wellington, New Zealand, diploma, 1960; Oxford University, D.Phil., 1971. *Politics:* None. *Home:* 823 Poinsettia St., Columbia, S.C. 29205. *Office:* Department of English, University of South Carolina, Columbia, S.C. 29208.

CAREER: Alexander Turnbull Library, Wellington, New Zealand, head of cataloging, 1961-63; University of Birmingham, Birmingham, England, research associate and librarian at Shakespeare Institute, 1964; Oxford University, Oxford, England, fellow of National Institute for Research in Nuclear Science at Computing Laboratory, 1965-67, senior research fellow, 1967-70; University of Wales, University College of Swansea, Swansea, lecturer in English language and literature, 1970-72; University of South Carolina, Columbia, associate professor, 1972-77, professor of English, 1977—. Honorary lecturer at University of Leeds, 1972-75. *Member:* International Shakespeare Association, Bibliographical Society of America, Modern Language Association of America, American Association of University Professors, Shakespeare Association of America, Bibliographical Society (England), New Zealand Library Association, Virginia Library Association. Oxford Library Association, Cambridge Library Association. *Awards, honors:* British Academy grant, 1965; Huntington Library fellow, 1975; National Endowment for the Humanities fellow, 1979.

WRITINGS: (Editor) William Shakespeare, *Twelfth Night*, W. C. Brown, 1969; (editor) *Oxford Shakespeare Concordances*, thirty-seven volumes, Clarendon Press, 1969-73; *Bibliography of British Literary Bibliographies*, Clarendon Press, 1969, revised edition, 1980; *Index to British Literary Bibliography*, Clarendon Press, 1969.

(Editor) *Shakespearean Bibliography and Textual Criticism: A Bibliography*, Clarendon Press, 1971; (editor) *Julius Caesar: A Concordance to the Text of the First Folio*, Clarendon Press, 1971; (editor) *Pericles: A Concordance to the Text of the First Quarto of 1609*, Clarendon Press, 1972; *Ralph Crane and Some Shakespeare First Folio Comedies*, University Press of Virginia, 1972; (editor) *British Literary Bibliography, 1890-1969: An Index*, Clarendon Press, 1979; *Literary Concordances: A Guide to the Preparation of Manual and Computer Concordances*, Pergamon, 1979; (editor) *British Bibliography and Textual Criticism: A Bibliography*, two volumes, Clarendon Press, 1979; (editor) Fletcher and Massinger, *Sir John van Olden Barnavelt*, Malone Society, 1980. Contributor to academic journals.

WORK IN PROGRESS: A collection of studies on early English dramatic manuscripts; a book on the publication of English drama to 1642; editing Middleton's *Game at Chess for Revels* plays; textual studies of Shakespeare's First Folio; studies of British literary bibliography before 1890 and after 1969.

*   *   *

HOWLAND, Bette 1937-

PERSONAL: Born January 28, 1937, in Chicago, Ill.; daughter of Sam (a laborer) and Jessie (a counselor and social worker; maiden name, Berger) Sotonoff; married H. C. Howland, February 3, 1956 (divorced, September, 1962); children: Frank, Jacob. *Education:* University of Chicago,

B.A., 1955. *Religion:* Jewish. *Agent:* International Creative Management, 40 West 57th St., New York, N.Y. 10019.

CAREER: Writer. *Awards, honors:* Guggenheim Fellowship; fellowships from Rockefeller Foundation, and Marsden Foundation.

WRITINGS: W-3, Viking, 1974; *Blue in Chicago* (short stories), Harper, 1978. Contributor to *Commentary.*

WORK IN PROGRESS: The Life You Gave Me (contains three novellas), and a novel, *Grisha Lapidus: A Life*, both for Knopf.

SIDELIGHTS: Howland's first book, *W-3*, tells about life in a psychiatric ward. As Howland herself was hospitalized after an attempted suicide, many critics expected *W-3* to be a personal account. Instead, Howland opted for a detached stance and chose to simply chronicle daily life there. Eleanore Singer noted that Howland "writes in a mood of detachment, almost indifference, avoiding analysis and speculation and concentration on description with almost photographic clarity and detail." Sara Sanborn also called attention to Howland's lack of personal attention in *W-3*. She warned readers "hoping for the pornography of personal trouble...." Sanborn wrote that Howland "has the quality (rare among writers of memoirs) of being as interested in others as in herself. Here is no self-pity, sentimentality or special pleadings." Dorothy Rabinowitz expressed disappointment with Howland's account of life in the ward. "The gallery of portraits which makes up the bulk of *W-3* is less satisfactory than are the sections on herself and her family," wrote Rabinowitz. However, she did concede, "Because Miss Howland's book is the product of a hard eye and a moral sense sharpened by wit, grim as *W-3* is, there is much in it that gives pleasure."

Howland's collection of six stories, *Blue in Chicago*, also impressed critics. A reviewer for *New Yorker* wrote that the stories "are well worth reading, chiefly for the remarkable way the author transforms feelings of anger and loathing into something that serves as love." A critic for *Ms.* agreed. "Bette Howland's is a startling sensibility," the *Ms.* reviewer remarked. "With blunt honesty *and* affection she describes the horrific beauty of the lives of the people she knows...." Christopher Lehmann-Haupt observed that Howland's "prose zigzags, like a hound looking for a scent, in search of family, community, peace, a sense of self.... And always the prose with which she searches is arrhythmical, nervous, self-questioning, passionate."

Howland told *CA:* "I can't comment on my work—it's not for me to say. I loathe giving biographical details, possibly because they have of necessity appeared in my work."

BIOGRAPHICAL/CRITICAL SOURCES: Library Journal, September 15, 1974; *New Republic*, September 21, 1974; *New York Times Book Review*, October 6, 1974, February 19, 1978; *New Yorker*, April 24, 1978; *Ms.*, July, 1978.

*　　　*　　　*

HU, Shu Ming 1927-
(Shi Ming Hu)

PERSONAL: Born June 27, 1927, in Amoy, China; came to the United States in 1960, naturalized citizen, 1973; married; children: Shau-lay, Shau-nee. *Education:* National Amoy University, B.A., 1949; Taiwan Normal University, B.Ed., 1957; West Virginia University, M.A., 1962; Columbia University, Ed.D., 1967. *Office:* Department of Interdisciplinary Social Science, State University of New York at Stony Brook, Stony Brook, N.Y. 11794.

CAREER: Teacher in public schools in Tainan, Taiwan, 1950-51; director of instruction at girls' high school in Tainan, Taiwan, 1951-55; National Cheng Kung University, Tainan, Taiwan, instructor in languages, 1958-59; curriculum director at Chinese overseas high school in Sabah, Malaysia, 1959-60; teacher at private school in San Francisco, Calif., 1962-63; dean of girls at private school in Melbourne, Fla., 1963-64; teacher of Asian studies at high school in Melbourne, 1964-65; State University of New York at Stony Brook, assistant professor of social science, 1966—. Volunteer worker in Micronesia for U.S. Peace Corps, 1978-79. *Member:* U.S.-China People's Friendship Association, Royal Society for Asian Affairs. *Awards, honors:* Fellowship from University of Wisconsin, Summer Institute in Social Demography and Population Policy, 1973.

WRITINGS: Meiguo Jin Ershi Nian Lai De Jiaoyu Fazhan Gaikuang (title means "The Development of American Education in the Last Twenty Years"), Humanities, 1970; (editor with Eli Seifman; under name Shi Ming Hu) *Toward a New World Outlook: A Documentary History of Education in the People's Republic of China, 1949-1976*, AMS Press, 1976; *Education for Whom?: Revolutionary Education in the People's Republic of China*, University Press (Singapore), 1980. Author of reading-readiness student readers, for bilingual project in Yap District of Micronesia.

SIDELIGHTS: Toward a New World Outlook is a collection of documents that describe Chinese educational developments since 1949. The book contains transcriptions of tape-recorded personal interviews conducted by Shu Ming Hu and her co-editor, Eli Seifman, in their separate visits to China. *Choice* praised these interviews for their "special value" and noted that this "highly selected and well-documented ... volume complements Chang-tu Hu's *Chinese Education Under Communism*." One limitation of the book, however, is its lack of an index and bibliography.

BIOGRAPHICAL/CRITICAL SOURCES: Choice, September, 1977.

*　　　*　　　*

HUBBARD, P(hilip) M(aitland) 1910-

PERSONAL: Born November 9, 1910, in Reading, Berkshire, England; separated; children: one son, two daughters. *Education:* Jesus College, Oxford, B.A., 1933, M.A., 1940. *Residence:* Southwest Scotland. *Agent:* A. P. Watt Ltd., 26/28 Bedford Row, London WC1R 4HL, England.

CAREER: Civil servant in British India, mainly in northwest India (now Pakistan), 1934-47; administrator in London, England, 1948-60; writer, 1960—.

WRITINGS—Suspense novels: *Flush as May*, London House & Maxwell, 1963; *Picture of Millie*, London House & Maxwell, 1964; *A Hive of Glass*, Atheneum, 1965; *The Holm Oaks*, M. Joseph 1965, Atheneum, 1966; *The Tower*, Atheneum, 1967; *The Country of Again*, Atheneum, 1967, published as *The Custom of the Country*, Bles, 1969; *Cold Waters*, Atheneum, 1969.

High Tide, Atheneum, 1970; *The Dancing Man*, Atheneum, 1971; *The Whisper in the Glen*, Atheneum, 1972; *A Rooted Sorrow*, Atheneum, 1973; *A Thirsty Evil*, Atheneum, 1974; *The Graveyard*, Atheneum, 1975; *The Causeway*, Doubleday, 1976; *The Quiet River*, Doubleday, 1977; *Kill Claudio*, Doubleday, 1979.

Children's books: *Anna Highbury*, Cassell, 1963; *Rat Trap Island*, Cassell, 1964.

Work represented in anthologies, including *Dream of Fair*

Woman, edited by Charlotte Armstrong, A. & C. Black, 1966. Contributor of several hundred poems and stories to magazines, including *Punch*.

BIOGRAPHICAL/CRITICAL SOURCES: New York Times Book Review, May 28, 1967; *Book World*, May 5, 1968; *Punch*, May 7, 1969; *Spectator*, March 28, 1970; *Times Literary Supplement*, April 23, 1970, August 27, 1976; *New Yorker*, May 23, 1970; *Books*, June 1970; *Best Sellers*, April 15, 1971.

*   *   *

HUBLER, Herbert Clark   1910-

PERSONAL: Born July 26, 1910, in Portland, Ore.; son of William Herbert and Elsie (Clark) Hubler; married Reta Allison, June 12, 1934; children: Robert Keith, Bonnie Jean, Thomas Allin, Rowena Susan, Craig H. *Education:* Attended University of Washington, Seattle, 1934-36; Western Washington State College, B.A., 1937; Columbia University, M.A., 1946, Ed.D., 1949. *Politics;* Independent. *Religion:* Presbyterian. *Home and office:* 2102 Timlin Hill Rd., Portsmouth, Ohio 45662.

CAREER: Principal of public school in Elma, Wash., 1933-34; public school teacher in Aberdeen, Wash., 1934-37; junior high school science teacher in Seattle, Wash., 1937-45; Columbia University, Teachers College, New York, N.Y., demonstration teacher at campus school, 1945-47; Teachers College of Connecticut, New Britain, assistant professor of science education, 1947-49; Wheelock College, Boston, Mass., professor of science education, 1949-66; Ohio University, Portsmouth, on contract to South Vietnam as education adviser in science, 1966-69, professor, 1969-76, part-time professor of education, 1976—. Member of summer faculty at Washington State College, 1950, Bowling Green State University, 1953, Harvard University, 1954, University of Delaware, 1956, Bluefield State College, 1957, University of Maine and University of Rhode Island, both 1958, University of Alabama, 1959, University of California, Berkeley, 1960, and Western Washington State College, 1961; Fulbright lecturer in the Philippines, 1963-64.

MEMBER: Council on Elementary Science International (president, 1955-56), American Association for the Advancement of Science (fellow), National Science Teachers Association, Association for the Preparation of Teachers of Science, Scioto County Retired Teachers Association (vice-president), Masons (past master). *Awards, honors:* Science Education Recognition Award from National Association for Research in Science Teaching, 1957; national honor medal from government of South Vietnam, 1969.

WRITINGS: Working With Children in Science, Houghton, 1957; *Science for Children*, Random House, 1974.

WORK IN PROGRESS: Popular science books for adults and children, including *Some Say So*, on common beliefs and why we believe them; *More and More People*, on population and food supplies; picture books for reluctant readers.

SIDELIGHTS: Hubler writes: "As a recently retired professor of science education, I am continuing to seek public enlightenment regarding the implications of science in our modern way of life. To reach the general public necessitates a fascinating account in terms that are relevant and meaningful to the previously uninformed. Having spent many years doing just that, I am now attempting to continue the effort—one that is inherently fascinating and extremely important to the individual and to the public in general."

HUGHES, Shirley   1929-

PERSONAL: Born July 16, 1929, in Hoylake, near Liverpool, England; married; children: two sons, one daughter. *Education:* Attended Liverpool Art School and Ruskin School of Drawing and Fine Arts, Oxford. *Address:* 63 Lansdowne Rd., London W.11, England.

CAREER: Author and illustrator of books for children. *Awards, honors:* Other Award from the Children's Rights Workshop, 1976, for *Helpers*.

WRITINGS—All self-illustrated: *Lucy and Tom's Day*, W. R. Scott, 1960; *The Trouble with Jack*, Bodley Head, 1970; *Lucy and Tom Go to School*, Gollancz, 1973; *Sally's Secret*, Bodley Head, 1973; *Helpers*, Bodley Head, 1973, published as *George the Babysitter*, Prentice-Hall, 1977; *Lucy and Tom at the Seaside*, Gollancz, 1976; *Dogger*, Bodley Head, 1977; *It's Too Frightening for Me!*, Hodder & Stoughton, 1977.

Illustrator: Doris Rust, *Story a Day*, Faber, 1954; Rust, *All Sorts of Days*, Faber, 1955; Diana Ross, *William and the Lorry*, Faber, 1956; Edward H. Lang, *Curious Adventures of Tabby*, Faber, 1956; Rust, *Animals at Number Eleven*, Faber, 1956; Rust, *Animals at Rose Cottage*, Faber, 1957; Rust, *Mixed-Muddly Island*, Faber, 1958; Louisa May Alcott, *Little Women*, Blackie & Son, 1960; Dorothy Clewes, *The Singing Strings*, Collins, 1961; Hans Christian Andersen, *Fairy Tales*, Blackie & Son, 1961; Margaret McPherson, *The Shinty Boys*, Harcourt, 1963; Ruth Sawyer, *Roller Skates*, Bodley Head, 1964; Mabel E. Allan, *Mystery on the Fourteenth Floor*, Abelard, 1965; Helen Morgan, *A Dream of Dragons, and Other Tales*, Faber, 1965; Margaret Storey, *Kate and the Family Tree*, Faber, 1965; Storey, *The Smallest Doll*, Faber, 1966; Donald Bisset, *Little Bear's Pony*, Benn, 1966; Angela Bull, *Wayland's Keep*, Collins, 1966; Barbara Ireson, editor, *The Faber Book of Nursery Stories*, Faber, 1966; Margaret J. Baker, *Porterhouse Major*, Prentice-Hall, 1967; MacPherson, *The New Tenants*, Harcourt, 1968; John Randle, *Grandpa's Balloon*, Benn, 1968; Helen Cresswell, *A Day on Big O*, Follett, 1968; Ursula M. Williams, *A Crown for a Queen*, Meredith Press, 1968; Leonard Clark, compiler, *Flutes and Cymbals*, Crowell, 1969; Ann Thwaite, *The Holiday Map*, Follett, 1969; Williams, *The Toymaker's Daughter*, Meredith Press, 1969; Sara Corrin, editor, *Stories for Seven-Year-Olds, and Other Young Readers*, F. Watts, 1969.

Ruth Ainsworth, *The Ruth Ainsworth Book*, F. Watts, 1970; Morgan, *Satchkin Patchkin*, M. Smith, 1970; Helen Griffiths, *Moshie Cat*, Holiday House, 1970; Allan, *The Wood Street Secret*, Abelard, 1970; Jo Rice, *Robbie's Mob*, World's Work, 1971; Cresswell, *Rainbow Pavement*, Benn, 1971; Griffiths, *Federico*, Hutchinson Junior Books, 1971; Dorothy Edwards, *More Naughty Little Sister Stories*, Methuen, 1971; Williams, *The Three Toymakers*, Thomas Nelson, 1971; Corrin, editor, *Stories for Eight-Year-Olds, and Other Young Readers*, Faber, 1971; Morgan, *Mother Farthing's Luck*, Faber, 1971; Charles Perrault, *Cinderella; or, The Little Glass Slipper*, Walck, 1971; Barbara Sleigh, *The Smell of Privet*, Hutchinson, 1971; Nina Bawden, *Squib*, Gollancz, 1971; Elizabeth Goudge, *The Lost Angel: Stories*, Hodder & Stoughton, 1971; Julia Cunningham, *Burnish Me Bright*, Heinemann, 1971; Robina B. Willson, *Dancing Day*, Benn, 1971; Mary Stewart, *The Little Broomstick*, Brockhampton, 1971, Morrow, 1972; Frances M. Fox, *The Little Cat That Could Not Sleep*, Faber, 1971, Scroll Press, 1972; Morgan, *Mary Kate*, Thomas Nelson, 1972; Williams, *Malkin's Mountain*, Thomas Nelson, 1972.

Margaret Kornitzer, *The Hollywell Family*, Bodley Head, 1973; Storey, *The Family Tree*, Thomas Nelson, 1973; Edwards, *When My Naughty Little Sister Was Good*, Penguin, 1973; Mahy, *The Second Margaret Mahy Story Book*, Dent, 1973; Ruth Ainsworth, *Another Lucky Dip*, Penguin, 1973; Corrin, editor, *Stories for Five-Year-Olds, and Other Young Readers*, Faber, 1973; Ainsworth, *The Phantom Fisherboy: Tales of Mystery and Magic*, Deutsch, 1974; Edwards, *My Naughty Little Sister and Bad Harry*, Methuen, 1974; Jean Sutcliffe, *Jacko, and Other Stories*, Puffin, 1974; Jenny Overton, *The Thirteen Days of Christmas*, Thomas Nelson, 1974; Corrin, editor, *Stories for Under Fives*, Faber, 1974; Alison Farthing, *The Gauntlet Fair*, Chatto & Windus, 1974; Joan Drake, *Miss Hendy's House*, Brockhampton Press, 1974; Bisset, *Hazy Mountain*, Penguin, 1975; Marjorie Lloyd, *Fell Farm Campers*, Puffin, 1975; *Mahy, The Third Margaret Mahy Story Book*, Dent, 1975; M. E. Allan, *The Sign of the Unicorn: A Thriller for Young People*, White Lion, 1975.

Morgan, *Mrs. Pinny and the Blowing Day*, Puffin, 1976; Noel Streatfeild, *New Town: A Story about the Bell Family*, White Lion, 1976; Streatfeild, *The Painted Garden: A Story of a Holiday in Hollywood*, Puffin, 1976; Edwards, *My Naughty Little Sister Goes Fishing*, Methuen, 1976; Allan, *The Wood Street Rivals*, Methuen, 1976; Ruth Tomalin, *The Snake Crook*, Faber, 1966; Mahy, *The First Margaret Mahy Story Book: Stories and Poems*, Dent, 1976; Sara and Stephen Corrin, editors, *Stories for Six-Year-Olds, and Other Young Readers*, Penguin, 1976; Allan, *The Wood Street Helpers*, Methuen, 1976; Allan, *The Wood Street Group*, Methuen, 1976; Allan, *Away from Wood Street*, Methuen, 1976; Allan, *Fiona on the Fourteenth Floor*, Dent, 1976; Winifred Finlay, *Tattercoats, and Other Folk Tales*, Kaye & Ward, 1976, Harvey House, 1977; Alison M. Abel, editor, *Make Hay While the Sun Shines*, Faber, 1977.*

* * *

HUMPHREY, David C(hurchill) 1937-

PERSONAL: Born September 13, 1937, in Rochester, N.Y.; son of Harold J. (a business executive) and Vera E. (a teacher; maiden name, Paul) Humphrey; married Janet T. Gould, December 30, 1967; children: Justin G., Douglas C. *Education:* Princeton University, B.A., 1959; Harvard University, M.A.T., 1960; Northwestern University, M.A., 1962, Ph.D., 1968. *Home:* 405 Brady Lane, Austin, Tex. 78746. *Office:* Lyndon Baines Johnson Library, Austin, Tex. 78705.

CAREER: Carnegie-Mellon University, Pittsburgh, Pa., instructor, 1965-68, assistant professor of history, 1968-76, member of staff of social studies curriculum center, 1967-69; National Archives and Records Service, Washington, D.C., archivist at Office of Presidential Libraries in Washington, D.C., 1976-77, and Lyndon Baines Johnson Library in Austin, Tex., 1977—. Consultant to schools and the media. *Member:* Society of American Archivists, History of Education Society, Institute of Early American History and Culture, Texas State Historical Association. *Awards, honors:* National Endowment for the Humanities grant, 1971-72; William Adee Whitehead Award from New Jersey Historical Society, 1974, for article, "The Struggle for Sectarian Control of Princeton, 1745-1760"; certificate of commendation from American Association for State and Local History, 1977, for *From King's College to Columbia*.

WRITINGS: From King's College to Columbia, 1746-1800, Columbia University Press, 1976. Contributor of about fifteen articles and reviews to education and history journals.

WORK IN PROGRESS: Research on Austin, Tex., between the Civil War and World War I.

* * *

HUNT, Earl W(ilbur) 1926-

PERSONAL: Born March 12, 1926, in Brainerd, Minn.; son of Ralph Ernest (a farmer) and Alisemon (Harris) Hunt; married Vera Lorraine Knuppel (a cook), June 12, 1948; children: Valli Marie Hunt Arvig, Terry Earl. *Education:* Attended high school in Crosby, Minn. *Home:* 397 Sherrie Lane, Woodbury, Minn. 55119. *Office:* 3M Co., 3M Center, St. Paul, Minn. 55101.

CAREER: Manganese Chemical Corp., Riverton, Minn., technician, 1953-62; 3M Co., St. Paul, Minn., technologist, 1962—. *Military service:* U.S. Navy, 1944-46.

WRITINGS—All juveniles: *Lost in the Mountains*, Vantage, 1971; *The Living Wilderness*, Lerner, 1977.

WORK IN PROGRESS: Another nature book for young people.

SIDELIGHTS: Hunt told *CA:* "I write to help more of our young people get interested in nature, because I think it is one of the best ways of enriching their lives. I also feel that those who learn about nature and enjoy it will be more interested in helping to protect it.

"My interest in young people is shown on the front page of *Lost in the Mountains.* The book is 'dedicated to the teen-agers of today, in whom the author has a great deal of faith. Though they are often criticized, the vast majority of them are first-class citizens who will be leading the world of tomorrow.'

"The last page of *The Living Wilderness* further explains my thoughts: 'If, by our example, we teach our young people a deep respect for nature, I feel that we will make much progress toward the preservation of our earth. We will help to assure that our descendants will always be able to enjoy the brilliant colors of the leaves of autumn; the fresh morning air and the dew-coated grass of spring; the tracks of rabbits and deer in newly fallen snow; and the sight of wild geese as they fly in V-shaped formation to their breeding grounds in the Far North. We will enable future generations to experience the serenity of a quiet woods, to watch the unfolding of wild flowers, and to see ripples on the water as a fish breaks the surface of a still lake. All of these things, and many more, can be ours forever. All we need to do is enjoy them—and protect them.' "

* * *

HUNT, J(ohn) D(ixon) 1936-

PERSONAL: Born January 18, 1936, in Gloucester, England; son of Sydney H. and Marjorie (Dixon) Hunt; married Phyllis Marie DuBois (an academic librarian), February, 1973. *Education:* Attended English School of Languages, La Tour de Peliz, Switzerland, 1954; King's College, Cambridge, B.A. (honors), 1957, M.A., 1961. University of Bristol, Ph.D., 1964. *Residence:* Yorkshire, England. *Office:* Bedford College, University of London, Regent's Park, London N.W.1, England.

CAREER: Vassar College, Poughkeepsie, N.Y., instructor in English, 1960-62; University of Exeter, Exeter, England, assistant lecturer, 1962-63, lecturer in English, 1963-64; University of York, Heslington, England, lecturer in English, 1964-75, deputy provost of Langwith College, 1971-72; University of London, Bedford College, London, England, reader in English, 1975—. Visiting professor at Johns Hopkins University, summer, 1968, 1972-73, autumn, 1977; senior tutor at Open University, summer, 1971; lecturer at universities in the United States and France. Member of Institute for Advanced Study (Princeton, N.J.), 1977-78. Broadcaster for British Broadcasting Corp.—Third Programme. Participant in international conferences.

AWARDS, HONORS: Fulbright scholarship and English-Speaking Union fellowship, both 1959-60, for University of Michigan; Hopwood Awards from University of Michigan, all 1960, for poems, *All These Ithacas,* novel, *The Sad Probation,* and essays, *American Collage, and Other Pieces;* fellow of Folger Shakespeare Library, 1966, 1968; senior fellow of Leverhulme Trust, 1973-74, in Italy; British Academy European exchange grant, 1973-74.

WRITINGS: The Pre-Raphaelite Imagination, 1848-1900, Routledge & Kegan Paul, 1968; (editor and author of introduction) *Pope's "The Rape of the Lock": A Selection of Critical Essays,* Macmillan, 1968; *A Critical Commentary on Shakespeare's "The Tempest,"* Macmillan, 1968; (editor and author of introduction) *Tennyson's "In Memoriam": A Selection of Critical Essays,* Macmillan, 1970; (editor and contributor) *Encounters: Essays on Literature and the Visual Arts,* Studio Vista, 1971; (editor) Ronald Paulson, *Rowlandson: A New Interpretation,* Studio Vista, 1972; (editor) Wycherly, *The Country Wife,* Benn, 1973; (editor with Peter Willis) *The Genius of the Place: The English Landscape Garden, 1620-1820,* Elek, 1975; *The Figure in the Landscape: Poetry, Painting, and Gardening During the Eighteenth Century,* Johns Hopkins Press, 1976; *Andrew Marvell: His Life and Writings,* Elek, 1978; (editor and author of introductions) *The English Landscape Garden,* thirty volumes, Garland Publishing, 1980.

Contributor: A. E. Dyson, editor, *English Poetry: Select Bibliographical Guides,* Oxford University Press, 1971; Malcolm Bradbury and David Palmer, editors, *Victorian Poetry,* Edward Arnold, 1972; Bradbury and Palmer, editors, *Shakespearean Comedy,* Edward Arnold, 1972; Palmer, editor, *Tennyson and His Background,* G. Bell, 1973; J. B. Broadbent, editor, *John Milton: Introductions,* Cambridge University Press, 1973; A. D. Moody, editor, *The Waste Land in Different Voices,* Edward Arnold, 1974; James Sambrook, editor, *Pre-Raphaelites,* University of Chicago Press, 1974; C. A. Patrides, editor, *Aspects of Time,* University of Toronto Press, 1976; (author of introduction) William Gilpin, *Dialogue Upon the Gardens at Stowe,* Augustan Reprint Society, 1976; David Bevington and Jay H. Halio, editors, *Shakespeare: Pattern of Excelling Nature,* University of Delaware Press, 1978; Patrides, editor, *Approaches to Marvell: The York Tercentenary Lectures,* Routledge & Kegan Paul, 1978.

Work represented in anthologies, including *Modern European Poetry,* edited by Willis Barnstone, Bantam, 1966. Contributor of more than thirty articles, poems, and reviews to language and literature journals, literary magazines, including *Ambit* and *Michigan Quarterly Review,* and newspapers.

WORK IN PROGRESS: A biography of John Ruskin, publication by Dent expected in 1981; a book on the influence of Italian Renaissance gardens on English architecture and culture.

SIDELIGHTS: Hunt writes: "Trained in English literature, I have worked increasingly in the history of art and architecture, and firmly believe that literary studies need to reach out and relate words to images. I also think that academics need to use their expertise in larger arenas, which is why I have always enjoyed, for example, reviewing books in the London *Times* or for British Broadcasting Corp., and why I chose to write a life and works study of Andrew Marvell for non-specialists.

"I love travelling (especially in France, Italy, and Greece, all of which languages I speak more or less well—modern Greek painfully) and am fascinated by writers and artists who did travel—Marvell again, Ruskin, Turner, and the English travellers in the seventeenth and eighteenth centuries who visited Italy.

"My life is centred largely around my teaching and I resent even research work that takes me too far from those necessary classroom encounters; what is strangely called 'private work' feeds, for me, at least, directly into what I have to teach. I have always enjoyed teaching in the United States: both the students and courses are different and require different approaches—the changes they force in one stop the mental arteries from hardening.

"What spare time *is* left over goes into walking, especially in mountains, but not, positively *not,* into gardening, which I detest but engage in with manic abandon once in a while."

*   *   *

HUNTER, James H(ogg)   1890-

PERSONAL: Born December 30, 1890, in Maybole, Scotland; son of Archibald (a shoemaker) and Charlotte (Hogg) Hunter; married Margaret Elizabeth Diggins (a librarian), June 7, 1940; children: Bruce, Ian, Graeme. *Education:* Attended school in Scotland. *Religion:* Presbyterian. *Home:* 101 Cedar St., Orillia, Ontario, Canada L3V 2C6.

CAREER: Farm and Dairy, Peterborough, Ontario, reporter, 1914-19; *Toronto Globe,* Toronto, Ontario, reporter, 1919-29; *Evangelical Christian,* Toronto, editor, 1929-59; free-lance writer, 1959—. Member of board of directors of Scott Mission and Ontario Bible College. *Member:* Canadian Bible Society (member of board of directors). *Awards, honors:* LL.D. from Houghton College, 1950.

WRITINGS: The Mystery of Mar Saba, Evangelical Publishers, 1940; *The Great Deception* (nonfiction), Evangelical Publishers, 1945; *Banners of Blood,* Evangelical Publishers, 1947; *Thine Is the Kingdom* (novel), Zondervan, 1951; *Uncle Jim's Stories From Nature's Wonderland* (juvenile), Zondervan, 1953; *How Sleep the Brave: A Novel of Seventeenth-Century Scotland,* Zondervan, 1955; *A Flame of Fire: The Life and Work of R. V. Bingham,* Sudan Interior Mission, 1961; *Beside All Waters: The Story of Seventy-Five Years of Worldwide Ministry—The Christian and Missionary Alliance,* Christian Publishers, 1964; *The Hammer of God* (novel), Zondervan, 1965.

SIDELIGHTS: Hunter comments: "In both fiction and nonfiction, my Christian viewpoint is emphasized." *Avocational interests:* Travel (especially in the Middle East).

BIOGRAPHICAL/CRITICAL SOURCES: Moody Monthly, November, 1956.

*   *   *

HUNTER, Tim   1947-

PERSONAL: Born June 15, 1947, in Los Angeles, Calif.; son of Ian McLellan (a writer) and Alice (an executive; maiden name, Goldberg) Hunter; married Cynthis Janne duBois (a designer), July 15, 1977. *Education:* Harvard University, B.A., 1968. *Residence:* Los Angeles, Calif. *Agent:*

Phyllis Wender, Wender & Associates, 30 East 60th St., New York, N.Y. 10022.

CAREER: WGBH-TV, Boston, Mass., filmmaker, 1968-69; University of California, Santa Cruz, lecturer in film, 1970-74; unit publicist for a Public Broadcasting Service (PBS) television drama series, "Visions," 1975-77; writer, 1977—. *Awards, honors:* American Film Institute fellow, 1970.

WRITINGS—All with Charlie Haas; novels: *The Soul Hit* (mystery), Harper, 1977; *Over the Edge*, (based on own screenplay), Grove, 1979.

Screenplays: (With Charlie Haas) "Over the Edge," Warner Bros., 1979.

WORK IN PROGRESS: A mystery novel, *Pressure Drop*, with Charlie Haas.

SIDELIGHTS: "Charlie Haas and I enjoy collaborating on melodramas. Our only problem," Hunter says, "is that, for better or for worse, we can't make an original title stick. *Soul Hit*, a murder mystery about the record business was originally called 'Death Makes the Charts,' and the ambiguously named film and book, "Over the Edge,' was once 'Mousepacks' (which we got from a newspaper article about adolescent troublemakers in the Bay Area)."

* * *

HURST, G(eorge) Cameron III 1941-

PERSONAL: Born May 7, 1941, in Minneapolis, Minn.; son of G. Cameron, Jr. (in life insurance business) and Mary Jane (French) Hurst; married Carol Stoops (divorced); married Na Yop Pak; children: Ian Stuart. *Education:* Stanford University, B.A., 1963; University of Hawaii, M.A., 1966; Columbia University, Ph.D., 1972. *Office:* Department of History, University of Kansas, Lawrence, Kan. 66045.

CAREER: University of Kansas, Lawrence, assistant professor, 1969-75, associate professor, 1975-79, professor of history, 1979—, chairman of East Asian languages and cultures section, 1977—. Woodbridge distinguished scholar at Columbia University, 1969. *Member:* Association for Asian Studies. *Awards, honors:* Social Science Research Council grant, 1976; Fulbright fellow, 1978-79.

WRITINGS: (Translator from the Japanese, with David A. Dilworth) *An Outline of a Theory of Civilization*, Sophia University Press, 1971; (contributor) Dorothy Borg and Shumpei Okamoto, editors, *Road to Pearl Harbor*, Columbia University Press, 1972; (translator) Inoue Yasushi, *Ex-Emperor GoShirakawa*, Chikuma Shotso, 1972; (contributor) John W. Hall and Jeffrey P. Mass, editors, *Medieval Japan*, Yale University Press, 1974; *Insei: Abdicated Sovereigns in the Politics of Late Heian Japan, 1086-1185*, Columbia University Press, 1976. Contributor to *Monumenta Nipponica*, and to numerous newspapers. Editor for Japan of *Professional Review* (journal of Association for Asian Studies).

WORK IN PROGRESS: Research on Court and *Bakufu* in Kamakura, Japan; research on early history of the Koryo dynasty.

SIDELIGHTS: Hurst commented: "I am a scholar interested in the relationship between monarchies and aristocracies in ancient and medieval Japan and Korea. I am trained in those languages as well as Chinese, and find all facets of Japan and Korea, including modern politics, of interest. I lived for five years in Japan and one year in Korea. I hope to utilize my knowledge to write fiction, more popular material, and continue my academic writing."

HURSTON, Zora Neale 1903-1960

PERSONAL: Born January 7, 1903, in Eatonville, Fla.; died January 28, 1960, in Fort Pierce, Fla.; daughter of John (a preacher and carpenter) and Lucy (a seamstress; maiden name, Potts) Hurston; married Herbert Sheen, 1927 (divorced, 1931). *Education:* Attended Howard University, 1923-24; Barnard College, B.A., 1928; graduate study at Columbia University. *Residence:* Fort Pierce, Fla.

CAREER: Writer and folklorist. Collected folklore in the South, 1927-31; Bethune-Cookman College, Daytona, Fla., instructor in drama, 1933-34; collected folklore in Jamaica, Haiti, and Bermuda, 1937-38; collected folklore in Florida for the Works Progress Administration, 1938-39; Paramount Studios, Hollywood, Calif., staff writer, 1941; collected folklore in Honduras, 1946-48; worked as a maid in Florida, 1950; free-lance writer, 1950-56; Patrick Air Force Base, Fla., librarian, 1956-57; writer for *Fort Pierce Chronicle* and part-time teacher at Lincoln Park Academy, both in Fort Pierce, Fla., 1958-59. Was a librarian at the Library of Congress, Washington, D.C.; was professor of drama at North Carolina College for Negroes (now North Carolina Central University), Durham; was assistant to writer Fannie Hurst. *Member:* American Folklore Society, American Anthropological Society, American Ethnological Society, Zeta Phi Beta. *Awards, honors:* Guggenheim fellowship, 1936, 1938; Litt.D. from Morgan College, 1939; Annisfield Award, 1943, for *Dust Tracks on a Road*.

WRITINGS: (With Clinton Fletcher and Tim Moore) "Fast and Furious" (musical play), published in *Best Plays of 1931-32*, edited by Burns Mantle and Garrison Sherwood, 1931; (with Langston Hughes) "Mule Bone: A Comedy of Negro Life in Three Acts," 1931; *Jonah's Gourd Vine* (novel), with an introduction by Fanny Hurst, Lippincott, 1934, reprinted with a new introduction by Larry Neal, 1971; *Mules and Men* (folklore), with an introduction by Franz Boas, Lippincott, 1935, reprinted, Indiana University Press, 1978; *Their Eyes Were Watching God* (novel), Lippincott, 1937, reprinted, University of Illinois Press, 1978; *Tell My Horse* (nonfiction), Lippincott, 1938, published as *Voodoo Gods: An Inquiry Into Native Myths and Magic in Jamaica and Haiti*, Dent, 1939; *Moses, Man of the Mountain* (novel), Lippincott, 1939, reprinted, Chatham Bookseller, 1975; *Dust Tracks on a Road* (autobiography), Lippincott, 1939, reprinted, Chatham Bookseller, 1975; *Dust Tracks on a Road* (autobiography), Lippincott, 1942, reprinted with an introduction by Neal, 1971; (with Dorothy Waring) *Stephen Kelen-d'-Oxylion Presents Polk County: A Comedy of Negro Life on a Sawmill Camp With Authentic Negro Music* (three acts), [New York], c. 1944; *Seraph on the Suwanee* (novel), Scribner, 1948, reprinted, AMS Press, 1974. Also author of "The First One" (one-act play), published in *Ebony and Topaz*, edited by Johnson, and of "Great Day" (play).

Work represented in anthologies, including *Black Writers in America*, edited by Barksdale and Kinnamon; *Story in America*, edited by E. W. Burnett and Martha Foley, Vanguard, 1934; *American Negro Short Stories*, edited by Clarke; *The Best Short Stories by Negro Writers*, edited by Hughes; *From the Roots*, edited by James; *Anthology of American Negro Literature*, edited by Watkins. Contributor of stories and articles to periodicals, including *American Mercury*, *Negro Digest*, *Journal of American Folklore*, *Saturday Evening Post*, and *Journal of Negro History*.

WORK IN PROGRESS: *The Life of Herod the Great*, a novel.

SIDELIGHTS: Although Hurston was closely associated

with the Harlem Renaissance and has influenced such writers as Ralph Ellison, Toni Morrison, Gayl Jones, and Toni Cade Bambara, interest in her has only recently been revived after decades of neglect. Hurston's four novels and two books of folklore are important sources of black myth and legend. Through her writings, Robert Hemenway wrote, Hurston "helped to remind the Renaissance—especially its more bourgeois members—of the richness in the racial heritage; she also added new dimensions to the interest in exotic primitivism that was one of the most ambiguous products of the age."

Hurston was born and raised in the first incorporated all-black town in America, and was advised by her mother to "jump at de sun." At the age of thirteen she was taken out of school to care for her brothers's children. At sixteen, she joined a traveling theatrical troupe and worked as a maid for a white woman who arranged for her to attend high school in Baltimore. Hurston later studied anthropology at Barnard College and Columbia University with the anthropologist Franz Boas, which profoundly influenced her work. After graduation she returned to her hometown for anthropological study: The data she collected would be used both in her collections of folklore and her fictional works.

"I was glad when somebody told me: 'You may go and collect Negro folklore,'" Hurston related in the introduction to *Mules and Men*. "In a way it would not be a new experience for me. When I pitched headforemost into the world I landed in the crib of Negroism. From the earliest rocking of my cradle, I had known about the capers Br'er Rabbit is apt to cut and what the Squinch Owl says from the housetop. But it was fitting me like a tight chemise. I couldn't see it for wearing it. It was only when I was off in college, away from my native surroundings, that I could see myself like somebody else and stand off and look at my garment. Then I had to have the spyglass of anthropology to look through at that."

Hurston was an ambiguous and complex figure. She embodied seemingly antipodal traits, and Hemenway described her as being "flamboyant yet vulnerable, self-centered yet kind, a Republican conservative and an early black nationalist." Hurston was never bitter and never felt disadvantaged because she was black. Henry Louis Gates, Jr. explained: "Part of Miss Hurston's received heritage—and perhaps the traditional notion that links the novel of manners in the Harlem Renaissance, the social realism of the 30's, and the cultural nationalism of the Black Arts movement—was the idea that racism had reduced black people to mere ciphers, to beings who react only to an omnipresent racial oppression, whose culture is 'deprived' where different, and whose psyches are in the main 'pathological'.... Miss Hurston thought this idea degrading, its propagation a trap. It was against this that she railed, at times brilliantly and systematically, at times vapidly and eclectically."

Older black writers criticized Hurston for the frequent crudeness and bawdiness of the tales she told. The younger generation criticized her propensity to gloss over the injustices her people were dealt. According to Judith Wilson, Hurston's greatest contribution was "to all black Americans' psychic health. The consistent note in her fieldwork and the bulk of her fiction is one of celebration of a black cultural heritage whose complexity and originality refutes all efforts to enforce either a myth of inferiority or a lie of assimilation." Wilson continued, "Zora Neale Hurston had figured out something that no other black author of her time seems to have known or appreciated so well—that our homespun vernacular and street-corner cosmology is as valuable as the grammar and philosophy of white, Western culture."

Hurston herself wrote in 1928: "I am not tragically colored. There is no great sorrow dammed up in my soul, nor lurking behind my eyes. I do not mind at all. I do not belong to the sobbing school of Negrohood who hold that nature somehow has given them a lowdown dirty deal and whose feelings are all hurt about it.... No, I do not weep at the world—I am too busy sharpening my oyster knife."

Their Eyes Were Watching God is generally acknowledged to be Hurston's finest work of fiction. Still, it was controversial. Richard Wright found the book to be "counter-revolutionary." June Johnson praised the novel for its positiveness. She declared: "Unquestionably, *Their Eyes Were Watching God* is the prototypical Black novel of affirmation; it is the most successful, convincing, and exemplary novel of Blacklove that we have. Period. But the book gives us more: the story unrolls a fabulous, written-film of Blacklife freed from the constraints of oppression; here we may learn Black possibilities of ourselves if we could ever escape the hateful and alien context that has so deeply disturbed and mutilated our rightly efflorescence—*as people*. Consequently, this novel centers itself on Blacklove—even as *Native Son* rivets itself upon white hatred."

"She was full of sidesplitting anecdotes, humorous tales, and tragicomic stories," Langston Hughes wrote of Hurston, "remembered out of her life in the South as a daughter of a traveling minister of God. She could make you laugh one minute and cry the next....

"But Miss Hurston was clever, too—a student who didn't let college give her a broad 'a' and who had great scorn for all pretensions, academic or otherwise. That is why she was such a fine folklore collector, able to go among the people and never act as if she had been to school at all. Almost nobody else could stop the average Harlemite on Lenox Avenue and measure his head with a strange-looking, anthropological device and not get bawled out for the attempt, except Zora, who used to stop anyone whose head looked interesting, and measure it."

BIOGRAPHICAL/CRITICAL SOURCES: Langston Hughes, *The Big Sea*, Knopf, 1940; Zora Neale Hurston, *Dust Tracks on a Road* (autobiography), Lippincott, 1942; *Negro Digest*, February, 1962; Darwin T. Turner, *In a Minor Chord: Three Afro-American Writers and Their Search for Identity*, Southern Illinois University Press, 1971; *Negro American Literature Forum*, spring, 1972; *Black World*, August, 1972, August, 1974; *Village Voice*, August 17, 1972; Hughes and Arna Bontemps, *The Harlem Renaissance Remembered*, Dodd, 1972; Arthur P. Davis, *From the Dark Tower*, Howard University Press, 1974; *Ms.*, March, 1975, June, 1978; Robert Bone, *Down Home: A History of Afro-American Short Fiction From Its Beginnings to the End of the Harlem Renaissance*, Putnam, 1975; Robert E. Hemenway, *Zora Neale Hurston: A Literary Biography*, University of Illinois Press, 1977; *Contemporary Literary Criticism*, Volume 7, Gale, 1977; *New Republic*, February 11, 1978; *New York Times Book Review*, February 19, 1978; *Washington Post Book World*, July 23, 1978.

Obituaries: *New York Times*, February 5, 1960; *Newsweek*, February 15, 1960; *Publishers Weekly*, February 15, 1960; *Time*, February 15, 1960; *Wilson Library Bulletin*, April, 1960; *Current Biography*, Wilson, 1960; *Britannica Book of the Year*, 1961.*

*   *   *

HUTH, Angela 1938-

PERSONAL: Born August 29, 1938, in London, England;

daughter of Harold Edward (a film producer) and Bridget (Nickols) Huth; married Quentin Crewe, August 22, 1961 (divorced, November, 1970); married James Howard-Johnston (a university lecturer), June 24, 1978; children: (first marriage) Candida. *Education:* Attended schools in England and France. *Religion:* Church of England. *Home:* Pullens End, Pullens Lane, Headington, Oxford, England. *Agent:* Curtis Brown Ltd., 1 Craven Hill, London W.2, England.

CAREER: Journalist photographer, television reporter, and critic. Documentary reporter for British Broadcasting Corp. (BBC), 1966-68; Nightowls (shop), London, England, chairperson, 1970—. *Member:* International P.E.N., Society of Authors, Royal Society of Literature.

WRITINGS: Nowhere Girl (novel), Coward, 1970, published as *Somehow I Had to Find a Brass Band,* Coward, 1970; *Virginia Fly Is Drowning* (novel), Coward, 1972; *Sun Child* (novel), Collins, 1975; *South of the Lights* (novel), Collins, 1978; *Monday Lunch in Fairy Land and Other Stories,* Collins, 1979.

"Special Co-Respondent" (one-act teleplay), first produced for Canadian television, July 24, 1970. Author of plays for British Broadcasting Corp. and commercial television. Contributor to popular magazines, including *Vogue, Queen, Harper's, London Magazine,* and *Cosmopolitan,* and to national newspapers.

WORK IN PROGRESS: A novel; a stage play; an adaptation of *Virginia Fly Is Drowning* for BBC television.

SIDELIGHTS: Angela Huth comments: "I have no great message or burning philosophy—as a novelist I regard myself as a simple reporter, observing life with relish and transforming those observations into fictional matter. (I never use characters straight from life: it is much more interesting to invent. I do sometimes use places.) I am perhaps an 'old fashioned writer,' have been described as 'very English.' I look at small worlds in some detail and have hoped, in all my books, stories, and plays, that my readers will often smile, and often recognize poignant moments. Plot is my weakness, though I try to keep the narrative going. I like to write about all classes and ages, and find myself continually writing with great love of small corners of England. Contemporary themes such as feminism do not inspire me: tragi-comedies of manners and ordinary lives are what I strive to show. My greatest heroes are Jane Austen and Thomas Hardy."

AVOCATIONAL INTERESTS: The arts (especially painting), photography, ballet, reading.

BIOGRAPHICAL/CRITICAL SOURCES: Observer, June 28, 1970; *Variety,* July 1, 1970; *Times Literary Supplement,* July 16, 1970; *Stage,* July 30, 1970.

* * *

HUTSON, James H(oward)   1937-

PERSONAL: Born August 8, 1937, in Clarksburg, W.Va.; married in 1965. *Education:* Yale University, B.A., 1959, M.A., 1960, Ph.D., 1964. *Home:* 6681 McLean Dr., McLean, Va. 22101.

CAREER: Yale University, New Haven, Conn., instructor in history and assistant editor of "Papers of Benjamin Franklin," 1963-69; editor of publications, Institute for Early American History and Culture, 1969-72; Library of Congress, Washington, D.C., coordinator of American Revolution bicentennial program, 1972—.

WRITINGS: Pennsylvania Politics, 1746-1770, Princeton University Press, 1972; (editor with S. G. Kurtz) *Essays on*

the American Revolution, University of North Carolina Press, 1973; *A Decent Respect to the Opinions of Mankind,* U.S. Government Printing Office, 1976; *Letters from a Distinguished American,* U.S. Government Printing Office, 1978. Contributor to literary journals, including *William and Mary Quarterly* and *New England Quarterly.*

* * *

HUXLEY, Aldous Leonard   1894-1963

PERSONAL: Born July 26, 1894, in Godalming, Surrey, England; died November 22, 1963, in California; son of Leonard and Julia (Arnold) Huxley; married Maria Nys, 1919 (died, 1955); married Laura Archera, 1956; children: Matthew. *Education:* Balliol College, Oxford, B.A., 1916.

CAREER: Employed in government office during World War I; Eton College, Eton, England, schoolmaster, 1917-19; staff member of *Athenaeum* and *Westminster Gazette,* 1919-24; writer. *Member:* Athenaeum Club. *Awards, honors:* Award of Merit and Gold Medal, American Academy of Arts and Letters, 1959; D. Litt., University of California, 1959.

WRITINGS—Novels: *Crome Yellow,* Chatto & Windus, 1921, Doran, 1922, reprinted, Chatto & Windus, 1963, Harper, 1965; (translator) R. de Gourmont, *A Virgin Heart,* N. L. Brown, 1921; *Antic Hay* (also see below), Doran, 1923; *Those Barren Leaves,* Doran, 1925, reprinted, Avon, 1964; *Point Counter Point,* Doubleday, 1928, reprinted, Harper, 1969; *Brave New World* (also see below), Doubleday, 1932, reprinted, Bantam, 1960; *Eyeless in Gaza,* Harper, 1936, reprinted, Bantam, 1968; *After Many a Summer Dies the Swan,* Harper, 1939, reprinted, 1965; *Time Must Have a Stop,* Harper, 1944; *Ape and Essence,* Harper, 1948; *The Genius and the Goddess,* Harper, 1955; *Antic Hay and the Gioconda Smile* (also see below), Harper, 1957; *Brave New World and Brave New World Revisited* (also see below), Harper, 1960; *Island,* Harper, 1962.

Short stories: *Limbo: Six Stories and a Play,* Doran, 1920; *Mortal Coils: Five Stories* (also see below), Doran, 1922, reprinted, Chatto & Windus, 1968; *Little Mexican and Other Stories,* Chatto & Windus, 1924, reprinted, 1959; *Young Archimedes and Other Stories,* Doran, 1924; *Two or Three Graces: Four Stories,* Doran, 1925, reprinted, Chatto & Windus, 1963; *Brief Candles,* Doubleday, 1930, reprinted, Chatto & Windus, 1970; *The Gioconda Smile,* Chatto & Windus, 1938; *Collected Short Stories,* Harper, 1957; *The Crows of Pearblossom,* Random House, 1968.

Poetry: *The Burning Wheel,* B. H. Blackwell, 1916; *The Defeat of Youth and Other Poems,* Longmans, Green, 1918; *Leda and Other Poems,* Doran, 1920; *Selected Poems,* Appleton, 1925; *Arabia Infelix and Other Poems,* Fountain Press, 1929; *Apennine,* Slide Mountain Press, 1930; *The Cicadas and Other Poems,* Doubleday, 1931; Donald Watt, editor, *The Collected Poetry of Aldous Huxley,* Harper, 1971.

Plays: *Francis Sheridan's The Discovery, Adapted for the Modern Stage,* Chatto & Windus, 1924, Doran, 1925; *The World of Light: A Comedy in Three Acts,* Doubleday, 1931; *The Gioconda Smile* (adapted from the short story), Harper, 1948 (also published as *Mortal Coils,* Harper, 1948).

Nonfiction: *Along the Road: Notes and Essays of a Tourist,* Doran, 1925, reprinted, Books for Libraries Press, 1971; *Jesting Pilate: An Intellectual Holiday,* Doran, 1926 (published in England as *Jesting Pilate: The Diary of a Journey,* Chatto & Windus, 1957); *Essays New and Old,* Chatto &

Windus, 1926, Doran, 1927; *Proper Studies: The Proper Study of Mankind Is Man,* Chatto & Windus, 1927, Doubleday, 1928, reprinted, Chatto & Windus, 1957; *Do What You Will,* Doubleday, 1929, reprinted, Chatto & Windus, 1970; *Holy Face and Other Essays,* Fleuron, 1929.

Vulgarity in Literature: Digressions From a Theme, Chatto & Windus, 1930, Haskell House, 1966; *Music at Night and Other Essays,* Chatto & Windus, 1930, Doubleday, 1931, reprinted, Books for Libraries Press, 1970; *On the Margin: Notes and Essays,* Doran, 1932, reprinted, Chatto & Windus, 1971; *Beyond the Mexique Bay: A Traveller's Journal,* Harper, 1934, reprinted, Vintage, 1960; *1936 . . . Peace?,* Friends Peace Committee (London), 1936; *The Olive Tree and Other Essays,* Chatto & Windus, 1936, Harper, 1937, reprinted, Books for Libraries Press, 1971; *What Are You Going To Do About It? The Case for Constructive Peace,* Chatto & Windus, 1936; *An Encyclopedia of Pacifism,* Harper, 1937, reprinted, Garland, 1972; *Ends and Means: An Inquiry in the Nature of Ideals and Into the Methods Employed for Their Realization,* Harper, 1937, reprinted, Greenwood, 1969; *The Most Agreeable Vice,* [Los Angeles], 1938.

Words and Their Meanings, Ward Ritchie Press, 1940; *Grey Eminence: A Study in Religion and Politics,* Harper, 1941, reprinted, 1966; *The Art of Seeing,* Harper, 1942, reprinted, Chatto & Windus, 1964; *The Perennial Philosophy,* Harper, 1945, reprinted, Books for Libraries Press, 1972; *Science, Liberty and Peace,* Harper, 1946; (with Sir John Russell) *Food and People,* [London], 1949; *Prisons, With the 'Carceri' Etchings by G. B. Piranesi,* Grey Falcon Press, 1949.

Themes and Variations, Harper, 1950; (with Stuart Gilbert) *Joyce, the Artificer: Two Studies of Joyce's Method,* Chiswick, 1952; *The Devils of Loudun,* Harper, 1952; (with J. A. Kings) *A Day in Windsor,* Britannicus Liber, 1953; *The French of Paris,* Harper, 1954; *The Doors of Perception,* Harper, 1954, reprinted, 1970; *Heaven and Hell,* Harper, 1956, reprinted, 1971; *Tomorrow and Tomorrow and Tomorrow and Other Essays,* Harper, 1956 (published in England as *Adonis and the Alphabet and Other Essays,* Chatto & Windus, 1956); *A Writer's Prospect—III: Censorship and Spoken Literature,* [London], 1956; *Brave New World Revisited,* Harper, 1958; *Collected Essays,* Harper, 1959.

On Art and Artists: Literature, Painting, Architecture, Music, Harper, 1960; *Selected Essays,* Chatto & Windus, 1961; *The Politics of Ecology: The Question of Survival,* Center for the Study of Democratic Institutions (Santa Barbara), 1963; *Literature and Science* (also see below), Harper, 1963; *New Fashioned Christmas,* Hart Press, 1968; *America and the Future,* Pemberton Press, 1970.

Collections: *Texts and Pretexts: An Anthology With Commentaries,* Chatto & Windus, 1932, Harper, 1933, reprinted, Norton, 1962; *Rotunda: A Selection From the Works of Aldous Huxley,* Chatto & Windus, 1932; *Retrospect: An Omnibus of His Fiction and Non-Fiction Over Three Decades,* Harper, 1947, reprinted, Peter Smith, 1971; *The Letters of Aldous Huxley,* Chatto & Windus, 1969, Harper, 1970; *Great Short Works of Aldous Huxley,* Harper, 1969; *Collected Works,* Chatto & Windus, 1970; *Science, Liberty and Peace* (includes *Literature and Science*), Chatto & Windus, 1970.

Screenplays: (With others) "Pride and Prejudice," 1940; (with others) "Jane Eyre," 1944; "Woman's Vengeance" (based on own novel *The Gioconda Smile*), 1947. Also author, with others, of "Madame Curie."

Contributor to numerous periodicals, including *Life, Playboy, Encounter,* and *Daedalus.*

SIDELIGHTS: When Aldous Huxley was sixteen he was stricken with a disease of the eyes, which left him temporarily blind and which permanently disrupted his plan to enter the medical profession. Yet his scientific training remained a major force in all his future endeavors. He became a renowned and prolific man of letters, writing essays, fiction, and poetry, as well as criticism of painting, music, and literature, all of it touched by his scientific and analytic processes of thought and sense of detail.

Huxley's work is often seen as falling into two periods: his early work, much of it social satire, is arch and occasionally condescending; his later work, essentially mystical, is prophetic but in places self-righteous. The first period includes the novels like *Crome Yellow* (1921) and *Antic Hay* (1923), witty and sardonic dissections of British society, particularly the artists and aristocrats. It also includes the well known *Brave New World* (1932), which Andre Maurois once called "an exercise in pessimistic prognostication, a terrifying Utopia." The later period is marked by the publication in 1936 of the novel *Eyeless in Gaza,* which concerns the transformation of Anthony Beavis from cynic to mystic. A similar theme is explored in the novel *Time Must Have a Stop* (1944) as well as Huxley's later essays (especially *The Perennial Philosophy,* 1945) and his last novel, *Island* (1962).

Yet, at the chronological center of his career, Huxley balanced these two thrusts and produced the novel *Point Counter Point* (1928), which many critics regard as his most accomplished work of fiction. In it he confronted all of contemporary man's ideals—religion and false mysticism, science, art, sex, politics—and the disillusionment that their inadequacy invokes. In *Point Counter Point* Huxley achieved for the first time what he called the "musicalization of fiction." He shifted and juxtaposed moods, scenes and characters, and he modulated themes, creating through these variations a verbal counterpoint. As the character Philip Quarles puts it: "He shows several people falling in love, or dying, or praying in different ways—dissimilars solving the same problem." In this fashion, each of the characters (who are all representative of an idea or type) is enhanced and more clearly illuminated than he would be through a conventional presentation of events. Moreover, this breaking down of the story, relating the plot gradually and in pieces, parallels Huxley's theme: people who live for ideas and absolutes will be fragmented, unfulfilled human beings. He suggests that the world must be seen as a whole and accepted as it is, just as the novel, while being studied part by part from within, must be grasped in its entirety if any of the characters are to have significance.

As well as representing ideals, the characters in *Point Counter Point* are based on real people, for the book is a *roman a clef.* The most attractive of them is Mark Rampion, the whole man, who strongly resembles D. H. Lawrence, Huxley's life-long friend. In turn Rampion's friend Philip Quarles is suggestive of Huxley himself—a novelist concerned with point of view and a man whose problem is "to transform a detached intellectual scepticism into a way of harmonious all-round living."

In his search for such transformation Aldous Huxley went through many stages of mystical belief. His biographers and critics often cite his experiments with such hallucinogenic drugs as mescaline and lysergic acid (which he labelled "psychodelic") as means of discovering new capacities of the human psyche. But his brother Julian best explained his mystic inclinations in the 1965 *Memorial Volume.* Julian Huxley said that Aldous was equally fascinated by the hard facts of scientific discovery as by the facts of mystical experience. But, he added, the more science discovers and "the more comprehension it gives us of the mechanisms of existence, the more clearly does the mystery of existence itself stand out." That is, the more man may comprehend operative details, the more mysterious will seem the process itself. Hence, Aldous Huxley's mysticism was founded upon scientific training and his search for spiritual truth based on the urge, as Julian put it, "to achieve self-transcendence while yet remaining a committed social being."

Several of Huxley's novels have been adapted for the stage and for film. A collection of his original manuscripts is housed at the University of California.

Huxley was fluent in French, Italian, Spanish, and German, and read Latin. He traveled worldwide, most extensively throughout Italy and France.

AVOCATIONAL INTERESTS: Painting, walking, playing piano, "riding in fast cars."

BIOGRAPHICAL/CRITICAL SOURCES—Books: Jocelyn Brook, *Aldous Huxley,* Longmans, Green, 1954; Julian Huxley, *Aldous Huxley: A Memorial Volume,* Harper, 1965; Stephen J. Greenblatt, *Three Modern Satirists: Waugh, Orwell, and Huxley,* Yale University Press, 1965; Peter Bowering, *Aldous Huxley: A Study of the Major Novels,* Athlone (London), 1968; Ronald W. Clark, *The Huxleys,* McGraw, 1968; Laura Archera Huxley, *This Timeless Moment: A Personal View of Aldous Huxley,* Farrar, Straus, 1968; John Atkins, *Aldous Huxley,* Orion Press, 1968; Jerome Meckier, *Aldous Huxley: Satire and Structure,* Barnes & Noble, 1969; Laurence Brander, *Aldous Huxley: A Critical Study,* Bucknell University Press, 1970; Charles M. Holmes, *Aldous Huxley and the Way to Reality,* Indiana University Press, 1970; Milton Birnbaum, *Aldous Huxley's Quest for Values,* University of Tennessee Press, 1971; Peter Firchow, *Aldous Huxley: A Satirist and Novelist,* University of Minnesota Press, 1972; George Woodcock, *Dawn and the Darkest Hour: A Study of Aldous Huxley,* Viking, 1972; Peter Thody, *Huxley: A Biographical Introduction,* Scribner, 1973; Sybille Bedford, *Aldous Huxley: A Biography,* Knopf, 1974; *Contemporary Literary Criticism,* Gale, Volume 1, 1973, Volume 3, 1975, Volume 4, 1975, Volume 5, 1976.

Periodicals: *New Leader,* November, 1968; *New Statesman,* November 28, 1969; *Times Literary Supplement,* December 18, 1969; *Economist,* December 20, 1969; *Saturday Review,* May 2, 1970; *Newsweek,* May 4, 1970, December 9, 1974; *New Republic,* May 16, 1970, November 16, 1974; *Book World,* May 31, 1970; *Nation,* June 8, 1970; *New Yorker,* July 18, 1970, February 17, 1975; *Choice,* November, 1970; *Books and Bookmen,* March, 1971; *Saturday Review World,* November 16, 1974; *Time,* December 2, 1974; *Atlantic,* January, 1975; *National Review,* January 31, 1975; *Review America,* February 22, 1975; *Commonweal,* March 28, 1975; *Esquire,* April, 1975.*

*　　　*　　　*

HUZAR, Eleanor G(oltz)　1922-

PERSONAL: Born June 15, 1922, in St. Paul, Minn.; daughter of Edward Victor (a physician) and Clare (O'Neill) Goltz; married Elias Huzar, June 21, 1950 (deceased). *Education:* University of Minnesota, B.A., 1943; Cornell University, M.A., 1945, Ph.D., 1948. *Religion:* Roman Catholic. *Home:* 289 Gunson St., East Lansing, Mich. 48823. *Office:* Department of History, Michigan State University, East Lansing, Mich. 48824.

CAREER: Stanford University, Palo Alto, Calif., instructor in history, 1948-50; University of Illinois, Urbana, assistant professor of classics, 1951-55; Southeast Missouri State College, Cape Girardeau, associate professor of history, 1955-59; Carleton College, Northfield, Minn., associate professor of classics, 1959-60; Michigan State University, East Lansing, professor of history, 1960—. *Member:* American Historical Association, American Philological Association, Archaeological Institute of America, American Catholic Historical Association, Association of Ancient Historians, Classical Association of the Middle West and South.

WRITINGS: (Contributor) Max Savelle, editor, *A History of World Civilization,* Holt, 1957; *Mark Antony: A Biography,* University of Minnesota Press, 1978. Contributor of articles and reviews to history and classical studies journals.

WORK IN PROGRESS: Research on relations between the Roman Republic and Egypt.

*　　　*　　　*

HYMAN, Stanley Edgar　1919-1970

PERSONAL: Born June 11, 1919, in New York, N.Y.; died July 29, 1970; son of Moe (a paper merchant) and Lulu (Marshak) Hyman; married Shirley Jackson (a writer), August 13, 1940 (died, 1965); married Phoebe Pettingell, 1966; children: (first marriage) Laurence Jackson, Joanne Leslie, Sarah Geraldine, Barry Edgar; (second marriage) one. *Education:* Syracuse University, A.B., 1940. *Religion:* "Militant atheist." *Residence:* North Bennington, Vt.

CAREER: Literary critic. *New Republic,* New York City, editorial assistant, 1940; *New Yorker,* New York City, staff writer, 1940-70; *New Leader,* New York City, literary critic, 1961-65. Member of faculty at Bennington College, 1945-46, 1952-70; visiting professor at State University of New York at Buffalo, 1969-70. *Awards, honors:* American Council of Learned Societies fellowship, 1959; National Institute of Arts and Letters Award for criticism, 1967; Guggenheim fellowship, 1969.

WRITINGS—Criticism: *The Armed Vision: A Study in the Methods of Modern Literary Criticism,* Knopf, 1948, revised edition, Vintage Books, 1955; *Poetry and Criticism: Four Revolutions in Literary Taste,* Atheneum, 1961; *Nathaniel West,* University of Minnesota Press, 1962; *The Tangled Bank: Darwin, Marx, Fraser and Freud as Imaginative Writers,* Atheneum, 1962; (contributor) Howard Nemerov, *Poetry and Fiction: Essays,* Rutgers University Press, 1963; *The Promised End: Essays and Reviews, 1942-1962,* World Publishing, 1963; *Standards: A Chronicle of Books for Our Times,* Horizon Press, 1966; *Flannery O'Connor,* University of Minnesota Press, 1966; *Iago: Some Approaches to the Illusion of His Motivation,* Atheneum, 1970; *The Critic's Credentials: Essays and Reviews,* edited by wife, Phoebe Pettingell, Atheneum, 1978.

Editor: *The Critical Performance: An Anthology of American and British Literary Criticism of Our Century,* Knopf, 1956; *Darwin for Today: The Essence of His Works,* Viking, 1963; (with Barbara Karlmiller) Kenneth Burke, *Perspectives by Incongruity,* Indiana University Press, 1964; (with Karlmiller) Burke, *Terms for Order,* Indiana University Press, 1964; *The Magic of Shirley Jackson,* Farrar, Straus, 1966; William Troy, *Selected Essays,* Rutgers University Press, 1967; Shirley Jackson, *Come Along With Me,* Viking, 1968. Contributor to numerous periodicals.

SIDELIGHTS: Hyman enjoyed a great deal of notoriety from 1940 to 1970 as a literary critic for *New Yorker.* In retrospect, though, his reviews are considered timely and too short to have any lasting impact. Perhaps his best known work is *The Armed Vision,* a controversial volume which implied that modern literary criticism would be determined by the use of knowledge outside the field of literature. The book was widely read and discussed in its time but many critics now regard the work as a highly illogical proposal relying on unfounded principles.

Hyman applied his concept of interpreting literature from a variety of sources in *Iago.* Terry Eagleton was dissatisfied with the work. "The trouble with the book," wrote Eagleton, "is that it is neither particularly impressive as practical criticism nor particularly persuasive as a theoretical case. The practical criticism varies from the shallow and derivative to the painfully thin, and it is, in any case, a purely thematic critical method, which treats Othello as a casebook and leaves the whole poetic art of the play in curious suspension." Jerome Mazzaro disagreed with Eagleton. He declared, "The insights combine old and new readings, qualifying, rejecting, recommending, but always avoiding the diatribes of debate...." Mazzaro called *Iago* "a refreshing book, revolutionary in its generosity and sanity...."

The Critic's Credentials received similarly conflicting reviews. Wilfrid Sheed reported that if Hyman "were reviewing this collection himself, he would undoubtedly find at least a dozen major things wrong with it but wind up pronouncing it a very important book...." Sheed also remarked that Hyman's real intention with *The Critic's Credentials* was "to talk about ... his new discoveries: in cultural anthropology, psychology, comparative religion...." Sheed conceded that with his discoveries, Hyman worked "wonders with Joyce and Nabokov, not to mention such exotica as Japanese and African novels," but also warned readers to "skip him on Roth and Updike...." A reviewer for *New Yorker* observed that Hyman "admitted that he lacked practically all the gear he recommended...." However, the reviewer found that "Hyman had more than enough, as every article in this selection shows.... Like his personality, his style is forthright. It is also brisk, idiomatic, and idiosyncratic, so that reading him—no matter how serious his subject—is great fun."

BIOGRAPHICAL/CRITICAL SOURCES: Commonweal, October 30, 1970; *Nation,* November 30, 1970; *New York Times Book Review,* January 31, 1971, March 19, 1978; *New Yorker,* April 3, 1978.*

I

IACONE, Salvatore J(oseph) 1945-

PERSONAL: Born December 25, 1945, in Brooklyn, N.Y.; son of Salvatore G. and Stella (Raggio) Iacone; married Renee Adele Peterkin (an artist), May 27, 1972; children: Alexis. *Education:* Hunter College of the City University of New York, B.A., 1971; Oxford University, diploma, 1971; New York University, M.A., 1973; St. John's University, Jamaica, N.Y., Ph.D., 1979. *Residence:* Englewood, N.J. *Agent:* Susan Ann Protter, 156 East 52nd St., New York, N.Y. 10022.

CAREER: City University of New York, New York, N.Y., adjunct professor of English, 1972-77; Passaic County Community College, Paterson, N.J., assistant professor of English, 1977—.

WRITINGS: The Pleasures of Book Collecting, Harper, 1976. Literary editor of *Harper Book of World Mythology.* Contributor to *Esquire.*

WORK IN PROGRESS: The Remedial Reading Book; The Shakespeare Papers, a novel; a television dramatization of *The American,* by Henry James.

SIDELIGHTS: Iacone writes: "*The Pleasures of Book Collecting* grew out of my enthusiasm for collecting not only rare books and first editions, but books in general, as well as a desire to provide novice collectors with a modern guidebook that would be as entertaining to read as it would be practical and informative. For too many years, book collecting has been regarded as the province of the very rich, and many previous books have reflected that attitude as well as perpetuated it. I wanted my book to be informal yet useful, truthful and encouraging to collectors of all sizes of purses. As one reviewer stated, 'there is none of the implied snobbery and exclusiveness that has marred so many previous books on the subject.' This opinion, I feel, exactly captures the tone I intended to transmit to beginning collectors. Book collecting, like reading, is for anybody who develops a serious and enjoyable interest in it. It is, for certain, one of life's most pleasurable pursuits.

*   *   *

ICAZA CORONEL, Jorge 1906-1978

OBITUARY NOTICE: Born July 10, 1906, in Quito, Ecuador; died May 26, 1978, in Quito. Actor, playwright, and novelist. An active member of the Ecuadorian community, Icaza Coronel was a civil servant, founder of the Ecuadorian

Cultural Council, organizer of the Union of Artists and Writers, director of the National Library of Ecuador, and ambassador to the Soviet Union. He also lectured throughout the world and was a professor at the Universidad de Nuevo Mexico in Quito. Famed for his realistic descriptions of life in Ecuador, Icaza Coronel's best-known work is *Huasipungo,* which was translated as *The Villagers.* He turned from playwright to novelist when his version of Jules Romain's *Le Dictateur* was banned by the government of Ecuador. Obituaries and other sources: *Encyclopedia of World Literature in the Twentieth Century,* updated edition, Ungar, 1967; *Cassell's Encyclopaedia of World Literature,* revised edition, Morrow, 1973; *The International Who's Who,* Europa, 1978; *World Literature Today,* spring, 1979.

*   *   *

IKEDA, Daisaku 1928-

PERSONAL: Born January 2, 1928, in Tokyo, Japan; son of Nenokichi (a seaweed vendor) and Ichi (Komiya) Ikeda; married Kaneko Shiraki, May 3, 1952; children: Hiromasa, Shirohisa, Takahiro (all sons). *Education:* Graduated from Fuji Junior College. *Religion:* Nichiren Shoshu Buddhism. *Office:* Soka Gakkai, 32 Shinanomachi, Shinjuku-ku, Tokyo 160, Japan.

CAREER: Soka Gakkai (lay organization within Nichiren Shoshu sect of Buddhism, dedicated to peace, culture, and education), Tokyo, Japan, president, 1960—, founder of Komeito ("Clean Government Party"), 1964, Soka Junior and Senior High Schools, 1968, Soka University, 1971, and Soka Junior and Senior Girls High Schools, 1973; Nichiren Shoshu, Tokyo, head, 1964—; Soka Gakkai International, Tokyo, president, 1975—. Founder of Oriental Institute of Academic Research, 1962, Min-on Concert Association, 1962, and Fuji Art Museum, 1973. *Awards, honors:* Honorary doctorate, Moscow State University, 1975; named honorary citizen of forty-six cities in the United States and one in Japan.

*WRITINGS—*In English: *Lectures on Buddhism,* translated by Takeo Kamio, Seikyo Press, 1962; *Kagaku to Shukyo,* [Japan], 1965, translation published as *Science and Religion,* Sokagakkai, 1965; *Ningen Kakumei,* [Japan], 1966, translation from original Japanese manuscript published as *The Human Revolution,* Seikyo Press, 1965, abridged edition published in three volumes under same title, Weatherhill, 1972; *Guidance Memo,* Seikyo Press, 1966, translation by

George M. Williams published under same title, World Tribune Press, 1975; *Katei Kakumei,* [Japan], 1967, translation published as *The Family Revolution,* World Tribune Press, 1970; *Complete Works,* Seikyo Press, 1968.

The People: A Collection of Poetry, translated by Robert Epp, World Tribune Press, 1972; *Mirai o Hiraku Kimitachi e,* [Japan], 1972, translation by Epp published as *Advice to Young People,* World Tribune Press, 1976; *Watakushi no Bukkyo Kan,* [Japan], 1974, translation by Burton Watson published as *Buddhism: the First Millennium,* Kodansha International, 1977; *Buddhism: The Living Philosophy,* East Publications, 1974; *The Tide Toward the Twenty-First Century: Addresses,* Soka University Student International Center, c. 1975; *Hopes and Dreams* (poems), translated by Epp, World Tribune Press, 1976; *Yesterday, Today, and Tomorrow* (collection of essays), translated by Epp, World Tribune Press, 1976; (with Arnold Joseph Toynbee) *Choose Life,* Oxford University Press, 1976 (published in Tokyo as *The Toynbee-Ikeda Dialogue,* Kodansha International, 1976); *Watakushi no Shakuson Kan,* [Japan], 1975, translation published as *The Living Buddha: An Interpretive Biography,* Weatherhill, 1976; *Songs From My Heart,* Weatherhill, 1978.

Also author or editor of other works: *Kantogen, Kogishu,* 1962; (editor) Soka Gakkai, *Nichiren Shoshu Kyogaku Kaisetsu,* 1963, published as *Nichiren Shoshu Kyogaku Shojiten,* 1969; (editor) *Bukkyo Tetsugaku Daijiten,* 1964; *Ongi Kuden Kogi,* 1967-68; *Ikeda Kaicho Zenshu,* 1968; *Shido Yogen Shu,* 1968; *Seiji to Shukyo,* 1969.

Shonen ni Kataru, 1971; *Watakushi no Jinsei Zuiso,* 1971; *Joseisho,* 1971; *Gendai Bummei to Shukyo,* 1972; *Kino Kyo,* 1972; *Shishu Seinen no fu,* 1972; *Watakushi no Sahkuson Kan,* 1973; *Seimei o Kataru,* 1973; *Waga Tomo e,* 1973; *Kofu Dainisho no Shishin,* (speeches) 1973; *Chugoku no Ningen Kakumei,* 1974; *Fujinsho,* 1974; *Shonen to Sakura,* 1974; *Shonensho,* 1974; *Kyo no Kotoba Sambyaku-Rokujugo,* 1974.

Hokekyo o Kataru, 1975; *Koten o Kataru,* 1975; *Gosho to Shijo Kingo,* 1975; *Hyumaniti no Seiki e* (title means "Toward a Century of Humanity"), 1975; *Ikeda Daisaku Miyamoto Kenji Jinsei Taidan,* 1975; *Watakushi no Rirekisho,* 1975; *Watakushi no Tendai Kan,* 1975; *Soka Bunka Undo no Gendaiteki Yajuwari,* 1975; (with Arnold Joseph Toynbee) *Nijuisseiki e no Taiwa,* 1975; (with Konosuke Matsushita) *Jinsei Mondo,* 1975; (with Richard Nicolaus Garf von Coudenhove-Kalergi) *Bummei Nishi to Higasi,* 1975; *Joshibu e no Shishin,* 1976; *Waga Kokoro no Uta* (title means "Poems From My Heart"), 1976; *Ikeda Kaicho Koen Shu* (presidential addresses).

"Seikyo bunko" series: *Watakushi no Jinseikan,* 1970; *Watakushi no Zuisoshu,* 1970; *Watakushi no Teigen,* 1971; *Wakaki Tomo e Okuru,* 1973; *Watakushi wa ko Omou,* 1974; *Ongi Kuden Kogi,* 1974; *Kino kyo,* 1976; *Gosho to Shijo Kingo,* 1976; *Fujinsho,* 1977.

SIDELIGHTS: Daisaku Ikeda's career and writings are devoted to Soka Gakkai ("Value-creation Study Society"), a Buddhist layman's organization founded in 1930 by T. Makiguchi. Members follow the interpretations of Buddhism taught by Nichiren Shoshu, a thirteenth-century Japanese monk. He preached devotion to the Lotus Sutra, a Buddhist document, and believed that chanting the Daimoku would attune a person to all that the Lotus Sutra contained. He taught simplicity and unity, the realization of all potentialities into one moment that is the present.

Soka Gakkai has grown immensely under the leadership of J. Toda during the fifties, and under Daisaku Ikeda since 1960. Now there are more than ten million members in over thirty countries, including nearly two hundred thousand in America. Great emphasis is placed on gaining converts through members' testimonials and the aggressive evangelistic technique of Shakubuku, literally "break and subdue."

In addition to filling a spiritual void in Japan, Soka Gakkai has become a powerful force in the Japanese government with the formation of the Komeito ("Clean Government") party in 1964. Although the party is independent of the Soka Gakkai, most of its members are from the sect. Ikeda himself has become involved in politics, leading global missions for peace, urging a world food bank, nuclear disarmament, and "the creation of an international people-to-people crusade against war." He believes that "you have to have power to do anything at all meaningful," and he openly seeks this power for the Soka Gakkai.

BIOGRAPHICAL/CRITICAL SOURCES: Robert S. Ellwood, Jr., *Religious and Spiritual Groups in Modern America,* Prentice-Hall, 1973; *Time,* January 13, 1975.

* * *

IMMOOS, Thomas 1918-

PERSONAL: Born September 15, 1918, in Schwyz, Switzerland; son of Thomas (a banker) and Anna (Bueler) Immoos. *Education:* Attended Missionsseminar Schoeneck, 1938-45; School of Oriental and African Studies, London, B.A. (in classical Chinese), 1950; University of Zurich, Ph.D., 1960. *Home:* c/o Bethlehem Fathers, Shibuya Higashi 2-12-3, Tokyo 150, Japan. *Office:* Department of German Literature, Sophia University, Kioicho 7 Ban, Chiyoda-Ku, Tokyo 102, Japan.

CAREER: Entered Foreign Missionary Society of Bethlehem (Bethlehem Fathers), ordained Roman Catholic priest, 1945; Iwate University, Morioka, Japan, lecturer in German, English, and European literature, 1952-59; grammar school teacher of German literature and English in Immensee, 1960-62; Sophia University, Tokyo, Japan, professor of German literature and history of the theatre, 1962—. Lecturer at Tohoku University, 1958-59, and University of Tokyo, 1968-78. *Member:* Asiatic Society of Japan, German Asiatic Society, German Literature Society, Foreign Correspondent Club of Japan (Tokyo).

WRITINGS: *Asienreise* (poems; title means "Journey Through Asia"), Origo, 1963; *Gendai katorikku Sakka* (title means "Modern Catholic Writers"), Chuo Shuppan, 1964; *Faust und der deutsche Geist* (title means "Faust and the German Spirit"), Ikubundo Verlag, 1969; (with Erwin Halpern) *Japan: Tempel, Gaerten und Palaeste: Einfuehrung in Geschichte und Kultur–Begleiter zu den Kunststaetten in Japan* (travel guide; title means "Japan: Temples, Gardens and Palaces: Introduction to Japanese History and Culture—Companion to the Arts of Japan"), DuMont Schauberg, 1974; *Japanisches Theater,* Orel Fuessli, 1975, translation published as *Japanese Theatre,* Rizzoli International, 1977. Japanese correspondent for *Schweizerische Politische Korrespondenz, Rheinisher Merkur, Furche,* and *Salzburg Nachrichten.* Contributor to *Sophia.*

WORK IN PROGRESS: Editing a book on the shadow theatre of Japan with publication by Urs Baer Verlag expected in 1980; a book on how the Swiss discovered Japan, publication by Ostasiatische Gesellschaft expected in 1980; research projects on Japanese heroes on the European Baroque stage, and mystical and esoteric traditions in German literature from the Baroque period; two books, with working titles of *From Ritual to Art in the Japanese Theatre* and *Christian Literature in Japan.*

SIDELIGHTS: Immoos writes that his interests include comparative literature and religion, Jung's archetypes in literature and the theater, travel in Asia, and poetry and short stories.

He told *CA:* "Japan is the greatest museum of religious and theatrical traditions on earth. From prehistoric ritual to avant-garde experiments every stage of the history of theatre can be observed in a living social context. The Japanese phenomena are relevant for the interpretation of similar customs in ancient societies which have died out long ago. From the rituals and drama performances at Shinto festivals it is possible to deduce a theology of Shinto. Jung's archetypes are helpful for the understanding of many such performances."

*   *   *

IRGANG, Jacob 1930-

PERSONAL: Born October 27, 1930, in New York, N.Y.; son of Simon (a plumber) and Ruth (Tsirsch) Irgang. *Education:* Brooklyn College (now of the City University of New York), B.A., 1957; City College of the City University of New York, M.A., 1962. *Home:* 416 East 85th St., New York, N.Y. 10028. *Office:* Stuyvesant High School, 345 East 15th St., New York, N.Y. 10003.

CAREER: High school social studies teacher in New York City, 1958-64; Stuyvesant High School, New York City, social studies teacher, 1964—. *Military service:* U.S. Army, 1952-54; served in Korea. *Member:* American Historical Association, Association of Teachers of Social Studies. *Awards, honors:* Awards from Senior High School Joint Council on Economic Education and New York State Council on Economic Education.

WRITINGS: Using Economics, Sadlier, 1975; (with Howard L. Hurwitz and Frederick Shaw) *How to Prepare for the Social Studies Test: High School Equivalency,* McGraw, 1978. Contributor of music reviews to local newspapers in Nantucket, Mass.

SIDELIGHTS: "I have been teaching for twenty-one years only to discover that novels, newspaper reports, and movies concerning teaching consist of stereotyped versions of students and teachers," Irgang told *CA.* "I have had a number of interesting students in my classes who transcend these stereotypes. For example, one of my students in a history class refused to participate in shelter drills and was talking about the radical youth movement even before it became popular.

"During the sixties there was much downgrading of education. I firmly believed that we were losing a generation of young people who appeared to be drifting nowhere because of a lack of guidance in the home and in the school. These young believed what the politicians told them: that they were the greatest generation to have ever existed. However, I saw young people leaving high school bright but ignorant. I attempted to stick close to what were then called the 'old-fashioned' standards. It was a struggle for me to keep the students in school as it was difficult for them not to comply with the values of their peer group. There were times I wanted to write about learning and teaching in the sixties because there is definitely a human interest study to be told. Perhaps some day I will get an opportunity to write it up."

AVOCATIONAL INTERESTS: Travel (Europe and Japan), music.

IRVING, Clive 1933-

PERSONAL: Original surname, Bates; name legally changed; born February 2, 1933, in Luton, England; son of Alfred Ernest (a miller) and Grace (Beales) Bates; married Mimi Collette (a writer), March 6, 1958; children: Cindy, Saul. *Education:* Attended school in Luton, England. *Home:* 10 Rock Hill, London S.E.26, England. *Agent:* A. D. Peters, 10 Buckingham St., London W.C.2, England.

CAREER: London Sunday Times, London, England, managing editor, 1963-65; International Publishing Corp., London, executive editor of magazines, 1965-68; London Weekend Television, London, head of public affairs, 1968-70; *McCall's* (magazine), New York, N.Y., editorial adviser, 1970-71; *Newsday,* Garden City, N.Y., editorial adviser, 1971-72; free-lance writer, 1972—. *Military service:* Royal Air Force, 1949-52. *Member:* International P.E.N., British Institute of Persian Studies, Press Club (London).

WRITINGS: Anatomy of a Scandal, Morrow, 1963; *Pox Britannica,* Dutton, 1974; *The Crossroads of Civilisation,* Weidenfeld & Nicolson, 1979; *Axis,* Atheneum, in press.

WORK IN PROGRESS: Adapting *The Crossroads of Civilisation* into an eight-part television series.

SIDELIGHTS: Irving writes: "I am an eclectic in interests, a journalist by training, with no coherent pattern. My first book was a political study of the Profumo affair; the second polemic on British degeneration, written on return from two years in the United States. The third book represents three years' research and writing on the history of Persia, and I am now making it into an eight-part television series. The next book, my first novel, is about the pro-Nazi movement in England in the 1930's, part fiction and part based on extensive research.

"In the course of this work I have been intrigued by a number of dry trails. For example, how frequently in the official records accounts of meetings between Hitler and various public men in pre-war England have gone missing, both in the German archives and in London. Around 1945 somebody did a quick pruning operation. This pushed me to the part fact, part fiction solution: to extrapolate from known facts what *probably* was said, and thereby how disreputable it was likely to have been. There are many variations of 'faction,' according to the story, but in my case a strict self-imposed rule is: let nothing happen that could not really have happened. And that, it turns out, is quite enough to chill the liver."

*   *   *

ISMACH, Arnold H(arvey) 1930-

PERSONAL: Surname is pronounced *Iss*-mack; born December 28, 1930, in New York, N.Y.; son of Louis and Augusta (Lacher) Ismach; married Judith Daniels, June 20, 1959 (divorced, 1975); children: Richard, Theresa. *Education:* University of Oklahoma, B.A., 1951; University of California, Los Angeles, M.A., 1970; University of Washington, Seattle, Ph.D., 1975. *Politics:* Independent. *Home:* 3310 Northeast Roosevelt Court, Minneapolis, Minn. 55418. *Office:* 111 Murphy Hall, University of Minnesota, Minneapolis, Minn. 55455.

CAREER: Walla Walla Union-Bulletin, Walla Walla, Wash., news editor, 1954-55; *San Bernardino Sun-Telegram,* San Bernardino, Calif., city editor, 1955-69; University of Minnesota, Minneapolis, instructor, 1973-75, assistant professor, 1975-78, associate professor of journalism, 1978—. Consultant in public relations and opinion research. *Military service:* U.S. Army, information specialist, 1951-54; became sergeant first class. *Member:* Association for Education in Journalism, Society of Professional Journalists (local president, 1968; state president, 1977-78), Twin Cities Press Club (chairman, 1957), Citizens League of the Twin Cities. *Awards, honors:* Recipient of several newspaper contest prizes, 1955-70; American Political Science Association fellow in public affairs reporting, 1970-71.

WRITINGS: (With George Hage, Evevette Dennis, and Stephen Hartgen) *New Strategies for Public Affairs Reporting,* Prentice-Hall, 1976; (with Dennis and Donald Gillmor) *Enduring Issues in Mass Communication,* West Publishing, 1978; *The Media Society: Evidence About Mass Communication in America,* W. C. Brown, 1978; (editor with D. Grey and Gillmor) *No Law Means No Law: Hugo LaFayette Black and the First Amendment,* Iowa State University Press, 1978; (with Dennis) *Reporting Processes and Practices,* Wadsworth, in press.

WORK IN PROGRESS: An examination of "precision journalism" methods in American newspaper; *Puck, the Comic Weekly: America's First Humor Magazine,* with Chris Allen.

SIDELIGHTS: Ismach writes: "My principal interests are in the areas of the economics and sociology of the news media, and in the application of social science research methods to journalism." *Avocational interests:* Photography, music, tennis, hiking, camping.

J

JACKLIN, Anthony 1944-
(Tony Jacklin)

PERSONAL: Born July 7, 1944, in Scunthorpe, England; son of Arthur David and Doris (Pearce) Jacklin; married Vivien Murray, 1966; children: Bradley Mark, Warren, Tina. *Education:* Educated in England. *Home address:* Chestnut Lea, St. Mary, Jersey, Channel Islands. *Agent:* International Management Group, 58 Queen Anne St., London W1M 0DX, England.

CAREER: Professional golfer, 1962—. *Member:* Professional Golfers Association (life vice-president, 1970—), Potters Bar Golf Club, honorary member of more than twenty clubs. *Awards, honors:* Member of Order of the British Empire, 1970; won British assistant professional championship, 1965, Pringle Tournament and Dunlop Masters, 1967, Greater Jacksonville Open, 1968, 1972, British Open Championship, 1969, U.S. Open Championship, 1970, Benson & Hedges contest, 1971, British Professional Golfers Association contest, 1972, Dunlop Masters and Italian Open, 1973, Bogota Open, 1973, 1974, Scandinavian Open, 1975, Kerrygold International, 1976, and English National Professional Golfers Association Championship, 1977.

WRITINGS—All under name Tony Jacklin: *Golf, Step by Step,* Sterling, 1969; (with Jack Wood) *Golf with Tony Jacklin,* Dent, 1969; *Jacklin: The Champion's Own Story,* Hodder & Stoughton, 1970, Simon & Schuster, 1971; *One Hundred Jacklin Golfstrips: From the Daily Express,* edited by Iain Reid, Beaverbrook Newspapers, 1973.

AVOCATIONAL INTERESTS: Shooting.

* * *

JACOBSON, Cliff 1940-

PERSONAL: Born September 20, 1940, in Chicago, Ill.; son of Henry Jay (a mechanical engineer) and Clarissa (a singer; maiden name, Joffee) Jacobson; married Sharon Kay Roman, April 16, 1966; children: Clarissa, Peggy. *Education:* Purdue University, B.S., 1962; Indiana University, M.S., 1966. *Home:* 928 West Seventh St., Hastings, Minn. 55033. *Office:* Hastings Junior High School, Hastings, Minn. 55033.

CAREER: U.S. Bureau of Land Management, Coos Bay, Ore., forester, 1962; high school biology teacher in Indianapolis, Ind., 1968-71; Hastings Junior High School, Has-

tings, Minn., teacher of environmental science, 1971—. Professional canoe guide. *Military service:* U.S. Army, Artillery, 1962-64; served in Germany; became first lieutenant. *Member:* U.S. Canoe Association, National Rifle Association, National Education Association, Minnesota Canoe Association.

WRITINGS: Wilderness Canoeing and Camping, Doubleday, 1977; (contributor) Andrew Carra, editor, *The Complete Guide to Hiking and Backpacking,* Winchester Press, 1977. Contributor to outdoor magazines, including *Backpacker, Canoe, Camping Journal,* and *American Rifleman.*

WORK IN PROGRESS: A book on canoeing in the Arctic.

SIDELIGHTS: Jacobson writes: "Next to my family, wilderness is the most important thing in my life. My summer months are filled with one wilderness canoe trip after another. I seem never to get enough. Most of my writing is done in the fall and spring months. Winter is for cross-country skiing and wilderness ski touring. My outdoor writings come from first-hand experience, not from research into the ways of others. Only after I've tested the methods of others will I recommend them. I enjoy teaching young people, and am associated with a fifteen-day 'wilderness experience' canoeing/camping/rock-climbing summer program."

* * *

JACOBSON, Edith 1897(?)-1978

OBITUARY NOTICE: Born c. 1897 in Germany; died December 8, 1978, in Rochester, N.Y. Psychoanalyst, educator, and author. A practicing psychiatrist and psychoanalyst since 1929, Jacobson's special field of interest was depression and severe forms of mental disorder. Much of her training took place in Germany. She was imprisoned there by the Nazis shortly after Hitler came into power because she refused to divulge information about her patients to the Gestapo. Jacobson escaped from prison in 1938, but while there she wrote two papers about the behavior of her fellow prisoners. She was the author of *Depression.* Obituaries and other sources: *New York Times,* December 13, 1978.

* * *

JAEGER, Harry J., Jr. 1919(?)-1979

OBITUARY NOTICE: Born c. 1919 in Philadelphia, Pa.; died of a heart attack, January 16, 1979, in Washington, D.C. Minister, educator, and author. A former professor of theology at the Philadelphia College of Bible, Jaeger was pastor of Mount Vernon Presbyterian Church in Alexandria, Va., since 1972. He wrote four books, *Guide for Living, Hidden Rocks, The Easter Story,* and *The Shepherd's Psalm,* and contributed numerous articles to religious publications. Obituaries and other sources: *Washington Post,* January 20, 1979.

* * *

JAENEN, Cornelius John 1927-

PERSONAL: Born February 21, 1927, in Cannington Manor, Saskatchewan, Canada; son of John W. and Rosa A. (Minet) Jaenen; married Ina May Turner, July, 1948; children: Elizabeth, Anne, Margaret Rose, Jeannette, John, Suzanne, Mark, Michelle, Daniel. *Education:* University of Manitoba, B.A. (honors), 1947, M.A., 1950, B.Ed., 1958; Universite de Bordeaux, diplome de fin d'etudes, 1948; University of Ottawa, Ph.D., 1963. *Politics:* Liberal. *Religion:* Assemblies of Christians. *Home:* 9 Elma St., P.O. Box 963, R.R.4, Ottawa, Ontario, Canada K1G 3N2. *Office:* Department of History, University of Ottawa, Ottawa, Ontario, Canada K1N 6N5.

CAREER: High school assistant in Ashcroft, British Columbia, 1947-48; housemaster at boys' school in Fort Garry, Manitoba, 1948-52; curriculum adviser, member of ministry of Education, and history master at school in Addis Ababa, Ethiopia, 1952-55; high school history teacher in Winnipeg, Manitoba, 1955-58; Memorial University of Newfoundland, St. John's, assistant professor of history, 1958-59; University of Winnipeg, assistant professor, 1959-63, associate professor of history, 1963-67; University of Ottawa, Ottawa, Ontario, associate professor, 1967-69, professor of history, 1969—, head of department, 1970-72. Member of Manitoba advisory committee on bilingualism and biculturalism, 1963-64; co-head of historical committee of Manitoba Centennial Corp., 1964-66; organizer (and participant) of international congresses; consultant to Government of Ethiopia.

MEMBER: Canadian Institute of International Affairs (member of local council, 1965-67), Canadian Ethnic Studies Association (president, 1971-73), Society for French Historical Studies (vice-president, 1971-72), Manitoba Historical Society (member of council, 1951-52, 1963-67), Winnipeg Teachers Christian Fellowship (president, 1949-51). *Awards, honors:* Ronsard Medal from Government of France, 1947; award from National Council for Geographic Education, 1958, for an article on geography; grants from Canada Council, 1967, 1970, 1974, and 1976; grant from Government of France, 1968; Sainte-Marie Prize in Canadian History from Historical Sites Branch of Ontario Government, 1974, and prize from French Colonial Historical Society, 1976, both for *Friend and Foe;* grant from Social Sciences and Humanities Research Council of Canada, 1979.

WRITINGS: Some Thoughts on the Manitoba Mosaic (pamphlet), Ukrainian Voice (Winnipeg), 1964; *New Canadians and the Schools,* Ontario Institute for Studies in Education (Toronto), 1970; *Ethiopia Before the Congo: A Proposed Belgian Colony in Ethiopia, 1838-1856,* Institute for International Cooperation, 1974; *Friend and Foe: Aspects of French-Amerindian Cultural Contact in the Sixteenth and Seventeenth Centuries,* McClelland & Stewart, 1976; *The Role of the Church in New France,* McGraw, 1976; *Glimpses of the Franco-Manitoban Community* (in French and English), University of Winnipeg Press, 1976. Also editor of and contributor to *Slavs in Canada: Proceedings of the Third National Conference on Canadian Slavs,* Volume III, 1971.

Contributor: J. M. Bumsted, editor, *Documentary Problems in Canadian History,* Irwin-Dorsey International, 1969; *Report of Manitoba Mosaic,* Manitoba Secretariat on Dominion-Provincial Cultural Relations, 1971; Bumsted, editor, *Canadian History Before Confederation: Essays and Interpretations,* Prentice-Hall (Canada), 1972; Niall Byrne and Jack Quarter, editors, *Must Schools Fail?: The Growing Debate in Canadian Education,* McClelland & Stewart, 1972; Hugh A. Stevenson and J. Donald Wilson, editors, *Precepts, Policy, and Process: Perspectives on Contemporary Canadian Education,* Blake Associates, 1977; (author of introduction) W. W. Isajiw, editor, *Identities: The Impact of Ethnicity on Canadian Society,* Peter Martin, 1977; D. A. Muise, editor, *Approaches to Native History in Canada,* National Museums of Canada, 1977; M. L. Kovacs, editor, *Ethnic Canadians: Culture and Education,* Canadian Plains Research Center, 1978.

Editor of *Transactions* of the Historical and Scientific Society of Manitoba, Series III, 1964-66. Contributor to *Encyclopedia Americana.* Contributor of more than fifty articles to academic journals. Editor of *Canadian Ethnic Studies,* 1976, and *Canadian Ethnic Studies Bulletin.*

WORK IN PROGRESS: A book on the French regime in Ontario, publication by Champlain Society expected in 1981; a book on French-Amerindian relations in the eighteenth century.

SIDELIGHTS: Jaenen told *CA* he is a "popular and provocative public lecturer on subjects related to early Canadian history, ethnic and minority groups in Canada, and public education."

* * *

JAMES, Muriel

EDUCATION: Ph.D. from University of California, Berkeley. *Address:* c/o Addison-Wesley, Jacob Way, Reading, Mass. 01867.

CAREER: Transactional analysis therapist, 1958—. Director and vice-president of International Transactional Analysis Institute in California; licensed marriage and family counselor in private practice; ordained Protestant minister; instructor at University of California extension; consultant; guest on national television and radio programs. Adviser to California Commission on the Status of Women.

WRITINGS—All published by Addison-Wesley, except as indicated: (With Dorothy Jongeward) *Born To Win: Transactional Analysis With Gestalt Experiments,* 1971; (with Jongeward) *Winning With People: Group Exercises in Transactional Analysis,* 1973; *Born To Love: Transactional Analysis in the Church,* 1973; *What Do You Do With Them Now That You've Got Them? Transactional Analysis for Moms and Dads,* 1974; (with Louis M. Savary) *The Power at the Bottom of the Well: Transactional Analysis and Religious Experience,* Harper, 1974; *The People Book: Transactional Analysis,* text and teacher's editions, 1975; *The OK Boss,* illustrations by John Trotta, 1975; (with Savary) *The Heart of Friendship,* Harper, 1976; *A New Self: Self Therapy With Transactional Analysis,* 1977; *Marriage Is for Loving,* 1979. Also author of *Techniques in Transactional Analysis: For Psychotherapists and Counselors.*

BIOGRAPHICAL/CRITICAL SOURCES: Best Sellers, May, 1976.*

JASTAK, Joseph Florian 1901-1979

OBITUARY NOTICE—See index for CA sketch: Born March 19, 1901, in Gostyczyn, Poland; died May 26, 1979, in Wilmington, Del. Psychologist, researcher, and author of books on psychological testing and mental retardation. Jastak, long considered a pioneer in the field of psychological testing, published the Wide-Range Achievement Test in 1936, which was designed to identify people with learning disorders. During his years as chief psychologist at Delaware State Hospital, Jastak founded the Delaware Psychological Association and served as its president. Obituaries and other sources: American Men and Women of Science: The Social and Behavioral Sciences, 12th edition, Bowker, 1973; New York Times, May 28, 1979.

* * *

JAY, Karla 1947-

PERSONAL: Born February 22, 1947, in Brooklyn, N.Y.; daughter of Abraham N. (a marine carpenter) and Rhoda (Ginsberg) Jay. Education: Barnard College, A.B., 1968; New York University, Ph.D., 1973, M.Phil., 1978. Politics: "Radical matriarchist." Religion: "Dianic." Residence: Brooklyn, N.Y. Address: c/o Survey, P.O. Box 98, Orange, Mass. 01364. Agent: Berenice Hoffman, 215 West 75th St., New York, N.Y. 10023.

CAREER: Pace University, New York, N.Y., adjunct assistant professor of English, 1974—. Adjunct instructor, Brooklyn College of the City University of New York, 1974, LaGuardia Community College, 1975, and College of New Rochelle, 1975-77.

WRITINGS: (Editor with Allen Young) Out of the Closets: Voices of Gay Liberation, Douglas Books, 1972; (editor with Young) After You're Out: Personal Experiences of Gay Men and Lesbian Women, Links Books, 1976; (editor with Young) Lavender Culture, Harcourt, 1979; (with Young) The Gay Report, Summit, 1979. Contributor of articles and book reviews to magazines and newspapers, including Ms., Lesbian Tide, Majority Report, and Los Angeles Free Press.

WORK IN PROGRESS: Research on American lesbians in Paris from 1900 to 1920, especially Natalie Clifford Barney and Renee Vivien (Pauline Tarn); a novel.

SIDELIGHTS: Jay told CA: "When I was growing up in the fifties and sixties there were no positive books available to me about lesbians by lesbians. Most books were by heterosexist male psychologists with a vested interest in seeing homosexuals and lesbians as 'sick.' I was determined to spend at least part of my life collecting and writing material by gay people for gay people so that no one would ever have to grow up in the ignorance I did."

When Out of the Closets was first published, Jonathan Katz described it as "a collection of many of the most important writings to come out of the gay liberation movement in the last three years," and praised the book as "real and important for all of us." Jay's second book, After You're Out, was said by Choice to be "an indication of the arrival of the second phase both of gay liberation and the feminist movement—when the rhetoric diminishes and pragmatic suggestions are made about living openly and creatively as a gay person. . . . It is an excellent anthology for gay studies or for personal reading."

AVOCATIONAL INTERESTS: Vegetarianism, cooking, ecology.

BIOGRAPHICAL/CRITICAL SOURCES: Nation, July 2, 1973; Choice, October, 1976.

JAYNES, Roger W. 1946-

PERSONAL: Born March 6, 1946, in Iowa City, Iowa; son of Jens P. (a farmer) and Theodora M. (a beautician) Jensen; married Lanette F. Jaynes, June 18, 1967 (divorced September 12, 1978); children: Mickey Robert, Jeffrey Warren. Education: Ellsworth Junior College, A.A., 1965; University of Iowa, B.A., 1967. Office: Milwaukee Journal, 333 West State St., Milwaukee, Wis. 53201.

CAREER/WRITINGS: Miami Herald, Miami, Fla., sportswriter and editor, 1967-71; Rockford Newspapers, Rockford, Ill., author of sports column, 1971-73; Milwaukee Journal, Milwaukee, Wis., sportswriter and book reviewer, 1973—. Contributor to magazines, including Sports Illustrated, Insight, Stock Car Magazine, Basketball Weekly, and Sporting News. Awards, honors: Named sportswriter of the year by Florida Coaches Association, 1970, for a series on the importance of junior high athletics, by Illinois Associated Press, 1973, for "The Long Run: A Psychological Profile of the Long Distance Runner," and by Wisconsin Associated Press, 1976, for "Al McGuire: Past, Present, Future"; named top sports news writer of the year by Associated Press, 1977, for coverage of the N.C.A.A. basketball finals; first prize for national magazine writing from American Auto Racing Writers Association, 1977, for "Foyt, Unser, Johncock: The Hard-Chargers"; "Cheating: The Racers' Edge" was named Top Sports Story of the Year 1978 by the Milwaukee Press Club.

WORK IN PROGRESS: A novel dealing with the psychology of automobile racing.

SIDELIGHTS: Jaynes told CA: "The question that bothers man most is whether or not he is really in control. Can he decide his own fate, or has fate already decided what his life will be? And, if he doubts, can that doubt be controlled? It is, you see, a troublesome question, a whisper that creeps across his mind just before he shuts it off and falls asleep on steamy, still, summer nights. A dull pain that muddies his waters of decision and reflection.

"Doubt is an insidious little cancer that spreads and permeates every cell, every bit of his conscious and subconscious. It touches everything, spoils even the meat at the back of the cooler, unless the door of the mind is kept firmly locked.

"Hopefully, a writer can offer some answers, or intone a god who offers answers. But that is no good unless his reader is willing to believe that his god has clout, too. At best, perhaps, he can hope that the devil is merely a wardheeler in the corridors of heaven, a go-for who occasionally can screw up the works but is usually caught in the end.

"The saddest fact is that the American male seems to have given up, and those few that haven't have been slain by their respective Mrs. Macombers with the aide of those who switched sides. If the world is upside down today it is because there is no right, no wrong, no male, no female, no black, no white. Or a horribly sad, sonorous gray of mediocrity and garbage, the refuse of a society that bows to compromise and chases that old whore Egomania. . . .

"But, in certain professions, there are still a few men who put it on the line, who live the way they choose, and die the way they choose, and if some of them are race car drivers, so be it. A bunch of Don Quixotes, they are, all racing to see who gets to the windmill first.

"Few of them have trouble sleeping."

AVOCATIONAL INTERESTS: Collecting first editions.

JEFFARES, A(lexander) Norman 1920-

PERSONAL: Born August 11, 1920, in Dublin, Ireland; son of Cecil Norman (a university accountant) and Agnes (a civil servant; maiden name, Fraser) Jeffares; married Jeanne Agnes Calembert (a sculptor), July 29, 1947; children: Felicity Anne. *Education:* University of Dublin, B.A., 1943, Ph.D., 1945, M.A., 1946; Oriel College, Oxford, M.A., 1946, D.Phil., 1948. *Religion:* Church of Ireland. *Office:* Department of English Studies, University of Stirling, Stirling, Scotland; and Academic Advisory Services, Wester Moss, Rumbling Bridge, Kinross KY137QE Scotland.

CAREER: University of Dublin, Dublin, Ireland, lecturer in classics, 1943-44; University of Groningen, Groningen, Holland, lecturer in English, 1946-48; University of Edinburgh, Edinburgh, Scotland, lecturer in English, 1949-51; University of Adelaide, Adelaide, Australia, Jury Professor of English Language and Literature, 1951-56; University of Leeds, Leeds, England, professor of English literature, 1957-74, head of English department, 1957-64, chairman of School of English, 1961-64; University of Stirling, Stirling, Scotland, professor of English studies, 1974—. Lecturer; has lectured in the United States, Canada, India, Australia, the Middle East, France, Germany, Belgium, Italy, and Moscow, U.S.S.R. Vice-president, Film and Television Council of South Australia, 1951-56; secretary, Australian Humanities Research Council, 1954-57, and corresponding member for Great Britain and Ireland, 1958-70; director or managing director, Yeats International Summer School, 1969-71, Academic Advisory Services, 1972—, Colin Smythe, 1979—.

MEMBER: International Association for the Study of Anglo-Irish Literature (founding chairman, 1968-70; honorary co-chairman, 1970-73; honorary life president, 1973—), Australian Academy of Humanities (fellow), Association for Commonwealth Literature and Language Studies (chairman, 1966-69; honorary fellow, 1970—), Royal Society of Arts (fellow), Royal Society of Literature (fellow), Royal Commonwealth Society (fellow), Scottish Arts Council (chairman of literature committee, 1977—), Rucuhart Community Council, Athenaeum Club. *Awards, honors:* Honorary doctorate from University of Lille, 1977; honorary fellow of Trinity College, 1978.

WRITINGS: W. B. Yeats: Man and Poet, Yale University Press, 1949; *The Poetry of W. B. Yeats,* Barron's, 1961; (with Walter Fitzwilliam Starkie) *Homage to Yeats, 1865-1965,* University of California William Andrews Clark Memorial Library, 1966; *A Commentary on the Collected Poems of W. B. Yeats,* Stanford University Press, 1968; *George Moore's Mind and Art,* edited by Graham Owens, Oliver & Boyd, 1968, Barnes & Noble, 1970; *The Circus Animals: Essays on W. B. Yeats,* Stanford University Press, 1970; *W. B. Yeats,* Humanities Press, 1971; (with A. S. Knowland) *A Commentary on the Collected Plays of W. B. Yeats,* Stanford University Press, 1975; *Jonathan Swift,* Longman, 1976. Contributor to journals.

Editor: Maria Edgeworth, *Castle Rackrent and Other Stories,* Thomas Nelson, 1953; *Seven Centuries of Poetry: Chaucer to Dylan Thomas,* Longmans, Green, 1955, revised edition, 1960; Benjamin Disraeli, *Sybil,* Thomas Nelson, 1957; (with M. Bryn Davies) *The Scientific Background,* Pitman, 1958; *Poems of W. B. Yeats,* Macmillan, 1962; William Cowper, *Selected Poems and Letters,* Oxford University Press, 1963; *A Goldsmith Selection,* Macmillan, 1963; *Selected Plays of W. B. Yeats,* Macmillan, 1964; William Butler Yeats, *Selected Prose,* Macmillan, 1964; Yeats, *Selected Criticism,* Macmillan, 1964; (with K.G.W. Cross) *In Excited Reverie: A Centenary Tribute to William Butler Yeats, 1865-1939,* Macmillan, 1965; Walt Whitman, *Selected Poems and Prose,* Oxford University Press, 1966; William Congreve, "Incognita" and "The Way of the World," Edward Arnold, 1966, University of South Carolina Press, 1970; *Eleven Plays of William Butler Yeats,* Macmillan, 1967; Oliver Goldsmith, *She Stoops to Conquer,* St. Martin's, 1967; Congreve, *Love for Love,* St. Martin's, 1967; *Fair Liberty Was All His Cry: A Tercentenary Tribute to Jonathan Swift, 1667-1745,* St. Martin's, 1967; Richard Sheridan, *The School for Scandal,* St. Martin's, 1967; Sheridan, *The Rivals,* Macmillan, 1967; *Swift,* Macmillan, 1968; Thomas Crawford, *Scott's Mind and Art,* Oliver & Boyd, 1969, Barnes & Noble, 1970; George Farquhar, *The Beaux Stratagem,* Oliver & Boyd, 1972; Farquhar, *The Recruiting Officer,* Oliver & Boyd, 1973; *Restoration Comedy,* four volumes, Rowman & Littlefield, 1974; *Jonathan Swift,* Longman, 1976; *W. B. Yeats: The Critical Heritage,* Routledge & Kegan Paul, 1977.

General editor, *Writers and Critics,* 1960-73, *New Oxford English Series,* 1963—, and *Macmillan Histories of Literature,* 1978—. Editor, *A Review of English Literature,* 1960-67; *Ariel: Review of International English Literature,* 1970-72; joint editor, *Biography and Criticism,* 1963-73; literary editor, *Fountainwell Drama Texts,* 1968-75; (co-editor) *York Notes,* 1980—.

WORK IN PROGRESS: A History of Anglo-Irish Literature, publication expected in 1981; two other books, *The 1798 Revolution in Ireland* and *Companion to Yeats.*

SIDELIGHTS: Though Jeffares's scholarship ranges in interest from the poetry of Chaucer to twentieth-century literature, his principal concern is with the life and writings of William Butler Yeats. *W. B. Yeats: Man and Poet* is an introductory study of the Irish writer that chronologically examines Yeats's life and poetry. The insights gained, wrote one reviewer, "make a rich and meaningful, if somewhat kaleidoscopic, pattern." Another book, *A Commentary on the Collected Poems of W. B. Yeats,* presents a closer, disciplined reading of the poetry. Again including significant biographical data, Jeffares elaborates on the poems' literary allusions and parallels and the poet's use of mythology and symbolism. "This work of quiet and very great scholarship," a reviewer stated, "collects between two covers in the most matter of fact way all that the Yeats poems are about." Turning to the plays of Yeats, Jeffares provides an annotated guide to the poet's theatrical work in *A Commentary on the Collected Plays of W. B. Yeats.* He addresses the problems of the plays' obscurity and provides interpretation with glosses on difficult terms and names, summaries of various critical responses, and histories of production and publication. "It is a testimony to the success of the *Commentary,*" Edward Engelberg concluded, "that it leaves us with a very good idea of how much remains to be done with the plays."

AVOCATIONAL INTERESTS: Traveling, rebuilding old houses, drawing.

BIOGRAPHICAL/CRITICAL SOURCES: Economist, June 5, 1965; *Times Literary Supplement,* June 24, 1965, January 2, 1969, January 8, 1971, July 26, 1974, October 10, 1975; *Saturday Review,* December 11, 1965; *Poetry,* April, 1968; *Virginia Quarterly Review,* spring, 1969; *Criticism,* fall, 1969; *Sewanee Review,* winter, 1976; *Modern Language Review,* July, 1977; *Times Educational Supplement,* January 27, 1978.

JEFFERS, (John) Robinson 1887-1962

PERSONAL: Born January 10, 1887, in Pittsburgh, Pa.; died January 20, 1962, in Carmel, Calif.; son of William Hamilton (a Presbyterian minister and professor) and Annie Robinson (Tuttle) Jeffers; married Una Call Kuster, August 2, 1913 (died, 1950). children: Donnan Call, Garth Sherwood (twins). *Education:* Attended University of Western Pennsylvania; Occidental College, A.B., 1905; graduate study at University of Zurich, University of Southern California, and University of Washington. *Home:* Tor House, R.D. 2, Box 288, Carmel, Calif. 93921.

CAREER: Poet and playwright. *Member:* National Institute of Arts and Letters, American Academy of Arts and Letters, Authors League of America, Phi Beta Kappa, Sigma Chi, Nu Sigma Nu. *Awards, honors:* D.Litt., Occidental College, 1937; fellowship from Book-of-the-Month Club, 1937; L.H.D., University of Southern California, 1939; Levinson Prize, 1940; Eunice Tietjens Memorial Prize, 1951; Union League Civic and Arts Foundation Prize, 1952; Pulitzer Prize, 1954, for *Hungerfield and Other Poems;* fellowship from the Academy of American Poets, 1958; Shelley Memorial Award, 1961.

WRITINGS—Poetry: *Flagons and Apples,* Grafton Publishing, 1912, reprinted, Cayucos Books, 1970; *Californians,* Macmillan, 1916, reprinted, Cayucos Books, 1971; *Tamar and Other Poems,* P. G. Boyle, 1924; *Roan Stallion, Tamar and Other Poems,* Boni & Liveright, 1925; *The Women at Point Sur,* Boni & Liveright, 1927, reprinted, Liveright, 1977; *Poems,* The Book Club of California, 1928; *Cawdor and Other Poems,* Liveright, 1928, reprinted with *Medea,* New Directions, 1970; *Dear Judas and Other Poems,* Liveright, 1929, reprinted, 1977.

Descent to the Dead: Poems Written in Ireland and Great Britain, Random House, 1931; *Thurso's Landing and Other Poems,* Liveright, 1932; *Give Your Heart to the Hawks, and Other Poems,* Random House, 1933; *Solstice and Other Poems,* Random House, 1935; *Such Counsels You Gave to Me and Other Poems,* Random House, 1937; *The Selected Poetry of Robinson Jeffers,* Random House, 1938; *Be Angry at the Sun,* Random House, 1941; *The Double Axe and Other Poems,* Random House, 1948, reprinted, Liveright, 1977.

Hungerfield and Other Poems, Random House, 1954; *The Loving Shepherdess,* Random House, 1956; *The Beginning and the End and Other Poems,* Random House, 1963; *Selected Poems,* Vintage Books, 1965; *The Alpine Christ and Other Poems,* Cayucos Books, 1974; *Brides of the South Wind: Poems 1917-1922,* Cayucos Books, 1974.

Plays: *Medea* (based on Euripides's play of the same name; first produced on Broadway in 1948), Random House, 1946, reprinted with *Cawdor,* New Directions, 1970; "The Tower Beyond Tragedy" (based on Aeschylus's "Oresteia" and Jeffers's poem of the same name), first produced in 1950; "The Cretan Woman" (based on Euripides' *Hippolytus*), first produced in 1954.

Other: *Poetry, Gongorism, and a Thousand Years,* Ritchie, 1949, reprinted, Folcroft, 1974; *Themes in My Poems,* Book Club of California, 1956; Ann N. Ridgeway, editor, *The Selected Letters of Robinson Jeffers, 1897-1962,* Johns Hopkins Press, 1968.

SIDELIGHTS: Although Robinson Jeffers did graduate work in both forestry and medicine, his real ambition was to be a poet. A legacy from an uncle enabled him to devote himself to his chosen vocation. After he received his inheri-

tance, Jeffers moved with his wife to Carmel, California, where he built with his own hands a granite house and an observation tower. As he worked in his isolated stone tower, Jeffers could view the ocean and the mountains. This vista was to pervade nearly all the poetry that he produced. "Mr. Jeffers is . . . much admired by Californians for the beauty of his California landscape-painting," James G. Southworth pointed out. "What Wordsworth has done for the Lake District, Frost for New England, Shelley for the Italian sky, he, they feel, has done for California, particularly for the Monterey coastal mountain region."

Nature not only serves as a backdrop for Jeffers's verse; animals and natural objects are frequently compared to man, with man shown to be the inferior. "There is not one memorable person," Jeffers wrote in "Contrast," "there is not one mind to stand with the trees, one life with the mountains." Jeffers preferred nature to man because he felt that the human race was too introverted, that it failed to recognize the significance of other creatures and things in the universe. He termed his philosophy "inhumanism," which he explained was "a shifting of emphasis from man to not man; the rejection of human solipsism and recognition of the transhuman magnificence. . . . It offers a reasonable detachment as rule of conduct, instead of love, hate, and envy." Humanity had been spurned by an uncaring God, Jeffers believed, so each individual should rid himself of emotion and embrace an indifferent, nonhuman god.

To develop his philosophy of inhumanism, Jeffers drew on the ideas of others. Radcliffe Squires argued that Schopenhauer's philosophy had the biggest impact on Jeffers's thinking. He stated that "the essential concern in Schopenhauer, the relation of matter and idea, is an essential concern in Jeffers" and held that both men came to the same conclusion: "that there exists a superior reality behind appearance, a reality that is discoverable, though not easily so." Arthur B. Coffin refuted this thesis, maintaining that Nietzsche and Lucretius were Jeffers's primary influences: "Robinson Jeffers used the various concepts of Nietzsche's philosophy to clear away outworn intellectual traditions and religious preconceptions in order to develop his own doctrine of Inhumanism. That Nietzscheanism was a useful—though sometimes limited—tool for Jeffers is now obvious. That his Lucretian-derived Inhumanism and its insistence upon transhuman magnificence flourished from inception is equally clear." Ample evidence has been provided to show that the works of such cyclical historicists as Giambattista Vico, Oswald Spengler, and Flinders Petrie also had an effect on Jeffers's work.

Jeffers's pessimistic outlook was reinforced by his reading of Greek tragedy. As a child, Jeffers had been tutored by his father, a theologian and scholar, who familiarized him with ancient Greek and Biblical tales. Many of these tales are used in Jeffers's poetry. "Solstice," for example, is a retelling of the Medea legend set on the California coast, and "Tamar" is based on an Old Testament story. Many commentators feel that Jeffers misunderstood the nature of Greek tragedy. Kenneth Rexroth complained that Jeffers's "reworking of the plots of Greek tragedy make me shudder at their vulgarity, the coarsening of sensibility, the cheapening of the language and the tawdriness of the paltry insight into the great ancient meanings." Frederic I. Carpenter observed that there are contradictions between Jeffers's inhumanism and his use of tragedy: "The ideal Inhumanist . . . symbolically exorcises the human emotions of pity and terror, and this preserves him from reinvolvement in the tragic drama of history. But this exorcism seems to deny the efficacy and value of tragedy itself. For tragedy seeks not to destroy the emotions of pity and terror but to transmute and sublimate them."

In contrast, Robert Boyers felt that Jeffers did indeed achieve a tragic vision: "What is unmistakable . . . is the poet's steadfast refusal to counsel violence among men and his ability to achieve a perspective wherein the violence men would and did commit could be made tolerable, in a way even absorbed into the universe as an element of necessity. It is nothing less than a tragic vision; and if Jeffers in his poetry could not sufficiently examine and evoke the large potentialities of man within his limitations, as could a Shakespeare and a Yeats, he did at least project a vision worthy of our attention and capable of giving pleasure."

Certain motifs and symbols recur in Jeffers's poetry and serve to underline his belief in inhumanism. The incest motif prevalent in many of his poems emphasizes the danger of man's introversion. Hyatt H. Waggoner explained: "To love one's own kind is in effect to love within the human family, hence incestuous. Incest leads to perversions, mass murder, and finally to nameless and all-pervasive horrors, like those in a nightmare that are at once real and indefinable." To avoid the dangers of incest, Jeffers felt that humans should develop the qualities symbolized by the hawk and the rock. For him the hawk and the rock represented "bright power, dark peace; / Fierce consciousness joined with final / Disinterestedness."

Jeffers was not noted for his technical ingenuity, but he did develop a style that meshed with his philosophy. Boyers held that there were no paradoxes in Jeffers's "mature vision, so finely wrought, no telling nuances to qualify the poet's commitment; but everything is precisely placed, distributed its proper weight, and there are elements of style so subtly woven into the poem's basic structure that they largely escape observation." Louis Untermeyer praised Jeffers for his "gift of biting language and the ability to communicate the phantasmagoria of terror," while Selden Rodman noted that Jeffers wrote his poetry "with a one-dimensional straightforwardness that is almost Homeric. And the similes he uses, if not Homeric, are as primitively American as the flintlock and the Maypole."

Jeffers's favorite genre was the narrative poem, and exegesis has tended to center on his long, philosophic-dramatic poems. Some critics think that more attention should be paid to his shorter poems. Boyers acknowledged that none of Jeffers's long narratives succeed but felt that the shorter poems reveal Jeffers at his best, and thus deserve re-examination. The conflict that existed between Jeffers's commitment to inhumanism and his commitment to narrative realism interested John R. Alexander. "The doctrine of Inhumanism clearly advocates a rejection of all that can be considered human, while narrative realism by definition prescribes detailed attention to it," Alexander wrote.

Many readers have found Jeffers's philosophy, and consequently his poetry, repugnant. Rexroth echoed the opinions of others when he wrote of Jeffers: "His philosophy I find a mass of contradictions—high-flown statements indulged in for their melodrama alone, and often essentially meaningless. The constantly repeated gospel that it is better to be a rock than a man is simply an unscrupulous use of language." Untermeyer, however, cautioned readers that when approaching Jeffers's verse they must "separate the idea and its expression, remembering that the poem transcends the experience and the personality that prompted it. Between Jeffers the philosopher and Jeffers the poet there is a significant dichotomy. The philosophy is negative, repetitive, dismal. The poetry, even when bitterest, is positive as any creative expression must be."

Even those who are most bitterly opposed to Jeffers's ideology grant that he holds a unique place in modern American literature. James Dickey observed that Jeffers "fills a position in this country that would simply have been an empty gap without him: that of the poet as prophet, as large-scale philosopher, as doctrine-giver." Jeffers derived his belief that the poet should be a seer from Shelley, who held that poets are "the unacknowledged legislators of the world." Although one may dislike Jeffers's jeremiads, many of the terrors that he envisioned came true. "The vision of violence which he [Jeffers] first described in the 1920's has become the obsession of the 1960's," Carpenter declared. "His realization of the absolute absurdity of the historic idealism which would make the world safe for democracy by inventing the bomb which would destroy the world, was prophetic in every sense. His repeated warnings that violence is intrinsic in history, and that this unpleasant fact must be faced, rather than repressed, was prophetic."

Jeffers's last book, aptly entitled "The Beginning and the End," deals with many of the themes that had concerned him throughout his lifetime. The poems in this volume use such contemporary issues as the population explosion and the Cold War to support Jeffers's long-established opinions. When The Beginning and the End was published in 1963, a year after Jeffers's death, some critics felt that it would bolster his sagging reputation. "On its own merits and altogether apart from any pious atonement for the undeserved neglect he has suffered in his late years, this most modest of all his works should do much to make clear how remarkable his accomplishment was," Samuel French Morse stated. Joseph Bennet suggested that on the basis of The Beginning and the End "Jeffers' reputation might be in for a renaissance." Recently there has been a renewal of interest in Jeffers's work, but he still has both his ardent admirers and vehement detractors. The debate as to the nature and value of his achievement will probably continue for many years to come.

Some of Jeffers's work has been translated into Italian, German, Danish, and several Slavic languages.

AVOCATIONAL INTERESTS: Stone masonry, swimming, walking.

BIOGRAPHICAL/CRITICAL SOURCES: George Sterling, *Robinson Jeffers: The Man and the Artist*, Boni & Liveright, 1926; Alfred Kreymborg, *Our Singing Strength*, Coward, 1929; Lawrence Clark Powell, *Robinson Jeffers: The Man and His Work*, Primavera Press, 1934, revised edition, Haskell, 1940; Rudolph Gilbert, *Shine, Perishing Republic: Robinson Jeffers and the Tragic Sense in Modern Poetry*, Haskell, 1936; Melba Berry Bennett, *Robinson Jeffers and the Sea*, Gelber, Lilienthal, 1936, Norwood, 1976; William Van Wyck, *Robinson Jeffers*, Ward Ritchie, 1938; Gilbert, *Four Living Poets*, Unicorn Press, 1944; Louis Untermeyer, *Modern American Poetry*, Harcourt, 1950; James G. Southworth, *Some Modern American Poets*, Basil Blackwell, 1950; John Crowe Ransom, editor, *Kenyan Critics*, World Publishing, 1951; *Saturday Review*, January 16, 1954; *Poetry*, July, 1954; Radcliffe Squires, *The Loyalties of Robinson Jeffers*, University of Michigan Press, 1956.

M. L. Rosenthal, *The Modern Poets*, Oxford University Press, 1960; Kenneth Rexroth, *Assays*, New Directions, 1961; Frederic I. Carpenter, *Robinson Jeffers*, Twayne, 1962; *Virginia Quarterly Review*, summer, 1963; *Harvard*

Review, winter, 1963-64; Carpenter, *The Twenties,* Everett/Edwards, 1966; Melba Berry Bennett, *The Stone Mason of Tor House: The Life and Work of Robinson Jeffers,* Ward Ritchie, 1966; William Everson, *Robinson Jeffers: Fragments of an Older Fury,* Oyez, 1968; Hyatt H. Waggoner, *American Poets From the Puritans to the Present,* Houghton, 1968; James Dickey, *Babel to Byzantium,* Farrar, Straus, 1968; Randall Jarrell, *The Third Book of Criticism,* Farrar, Straus, 1969; *Sewanee Review,* summer, 1969, winter, 1972; David Littlejohn, *Interruptions,* Grossman, 1970; Charles I. Glicksberg, *Modern Literary Perspectivism,* Southern Methodist University Press, 1970; Jerome Mazzaro, editor, *Modern American Poetry: Essays in Criticism,* McKay, 1970; Arthur B. Coffin, *Robinson Jeffers: Poet of Inhumanism,* University of Wisconsin Press, 1971; Alex A. Vardamis, *Critical Reputation of Robinson Jeffers: A Bibliographical Study,* Shoe String Press, 1972; Robert J. Brophy, *Robinson Jeffers: Myth, Ritual and Symbol in His Narrative Poems,* Press of Case Western Reserve, 1973; *Contemporary Literary Criticism,* Gale, Volume 2, 1974, Volume 3, 1975.*

*   *   *

JELLICOE, (Patricia) Ann 1927-

PERSONAL: Born July 15, 1927, in Middlesborough, Yorkshire, England; daughter of John Andrea Jellicoe and Frances Jackson Henderson; married C. E. Knight-Clarke, 1950 (marriage dissolved, 1961); married David Roger Mayne, 1962; children: Katkin Ann Mayne, Thomas Jellicoe Mayne. *Education:* Attended Central School of Speech and Drama, 1943-47. *Agent:* Margaret Ramsey, Ltd., 14a Goodwins Court, St. Martins Lane, London WC2, England.

CAREER: Writer. Actress, stage manager, and director in and around London, England, 1947-51; Cockpit Theatre Club, London, founding director, 1950-53; Central School of Speech and Drama, London, lecturer and director, 1953-55; Royal Court Theatre, London, 1973-75. *Member:* League of Dramatists (committee member). Chair of the South West Arts Theatre Advisory Panel, 1979. *Awards, honors:* Elsie Fogarty Prize from Central School of Speech and Drama, 1947; co-winner of third prize in drama from *Observer,* 1956.

WRITINGS—Books: Some Unconscious Influences in the Theatre, Cambridge University Press, 1967; (with Roger Mayne) *Devon: A Shell Guide,* Faber, 1975.

Plays: "The Rising Generation" (first produced in London at Royal Court Theatre), published in *Ark* (magazine of Royal College of Art), Volume XXV, 1960, published in *Playbill 2,* edited by Alan Durband, Hutchinson, 1969; *The Knack* (three-act; first produced in Cambridge at Arts Theatre, 1961), S. French, 1962, published with *The Sport of My Mad Mother* as *The Knack and the Sport of My Mad Mother: Two Plays* (also see below), Dell, 1964; *The Sport of My Mad Mother* (three-act; first produced at Royal Court Theatre, 1958), Faber, 1964, published with *The Knack* as *The Knack and The Sport of My Mad Mother: Two Plays* (also see above), Dell, 1964; *Shelley: or, the Idealist* (first produced at Royal Court Theatre, 1965), Grove, 1966; *The Giveaway* (first produced in London at Garrick Theatre, 1969), Faber, 1970; *Three Jelliplays* (includes "You'll Never Guess," first produced at Arts Theatre, 1973, and "Clever Elsie, Smiling Jack, Silent Peter" and "A Good Thing and a Bad Thing," first produced together as "Two Jelliplays: Clever Elsie, Smiling Jack, Silent Peter, and A Good Thing and a Bad Thing," in London, 1974), Faber, 1975; "The Reckoning," first produced in Lyme Regis, England, 1978.

Adaptations and translations: Henrik Ibsen, *Rosmersholm* (first produced at Royal Court Theatre, 1960), Chandler (San Francisco), 1960; Ibsen, "The Lady From the Sea," first produced in London at Queen's Theatre, 1961; (with Ariadne Nicolaeff) Anton Chekhov, *The Seagull,* first produced at Queen's Theatre, 1963), Avon, 1975; Friedrich Kind, "Der Freishchuetz," first produced in London at Sadler Wells Theatre, 1964.

SIDELIGHTS: A fact often noted about Ann Jellicoe's work is that the printed texts of her plays are virtually meaningless. A playwright who came to the theater via acting and directing, she displays little interest in language and its content. Instead, she strives to make theater an emotional experience, as opposed to an intellectual exercise. She seeks to draw the audience into the drama, evoking the feelings rather than the understanding of the spectators. To this end, she makes vivid use of visual action, as well as sound, and employs dialogue more for its rhythm than its meaning.

In an interview in *New Theatre Magazine,* Jellicoe defined her purpose: "When I write a play I am trying to communicate with the audience. I do this by every means in my power—I try to get at them through their eyes, by providing visual action; I try to get at them through their ears, for instance by noises and rhythm. These are not loose effects; they are introduced to communicate with the audience directly through their senses, to reinforce the total effect of the play, and they are always geared to character and situation. The theatre is a medium which works upon people's imagination and emotion—not merely their intellect. And I am trying to use every possible effect that the theatre can offer to stir up the audience—to get at them through their emotions.... I write this way because—the image that everybody has of the rational, intellectual and intelligent man—I don't believe it's true. I think people are driven by their emotions, and by their fears and insecurities."

Jellicoe's first play, *The Sport of My Mad Mother,* illustrates her technique. Essentially plotless, the play portrays a group of teenagers in a sequence of episodes of arbitrary violence. Their leader, Greta, is associated with Kali, the Indian goddess of destruction and creation (the play's title is taken from a Hindu hymn: "All creation is the sport of my mad mother Kali"). As the critic John Russell Taylor explained, Jellicoe was trying in this play to do something completely. new to English theater: "to make her play primarily something which happened in front of its audience and made its effect as a totality, rather than a piece of neatly carpentered literary craftsmanship." Taylor compared the play's script to a score from which a musician can conjure a full orchestral sound or a ballet scenario awaiting a composer and choreographer to bring it to life. On the page, the script makes little sense and contains little conventional dialogue. Spoken parts are, to a large extent, monosyllabic—words and cries severed from their denotative meanings, uttered for the incantatory effect of their tone and rhythm.

Jellicoe spoke of this early play in the *New Theatre* interview: "You see, so many plays tell you what is happening the whole time. People don't act angry; they tell you they're angry. Now, my play is about incoherent people—people who have no power of expression, of analysing their emotions. They don't know why they're afraid; they don't even know that they are afraid. So they have to compensate for their fear by attacking someone else; they're insecure and frustrated, and they have to compensate for that by being big, and violent. And all this is directly shown, instead of being explained; if you're content to watch it without thinking all the time 'What is the meaning?' so that you don't even see or hear, you're so busy thinking—then you will get what it's about.''

The Knack is Jellicoe's best known and most successful play. Like *The Sport of My Mad Mother*, it contains minimal plot, but it is held together by a structure of emotional relationships rather than a series of episodes. It centers around three men—Tom, Tolen and Colin—who are, unlike the teenagers in the earlier play, normally intelligent and articulate. However, *The Knack* zeroes in on these men, in Taylor's words, "at precisely the point where the image of rational, intelligent man breaks down just because they are completely ruled by their emotions, their fears, and insecurities," i.e., their sex lives. The three men, living in one house, present sharp sexual contrasts: Tolen is the successful seducer, Colin the total failure, and Tom the one who seems to have placed his sexuality in a healthy perspective. The central conflict between them involves the arrival on the scene of the apparently innocent Nancy.

The resolution—who and how he gets the girl—occurs on the stage. But again Jellicoe's language, as printed in the text, does not sensibly follow the actions. Indeed, the dialogue is more ritualistic than realistic, often consisting of little more than a series of non sequiturs or repetitions. A frequently noted scene is a good example: when Tom and Colin gradually involve Nancy in their fantasy that the bed on stage is really a piano, the corresponding pages in the script are covered almost uninterruptedly with "pongs" and "plongs." What engages the audience are not the words but the actions, what Taylor called the play's sheer drive, verve, and ebullience.

The Knack was adapted for the screen as "The Knack . . . and How to Get It," and was released in 1965. In the film version, the play's actions were reinterpreted as slapstick humor by the director, Richard Lester. But a comment by *New York Times* film critic Bosley Crowther suggests that the film retained the play's essential flavor. Lester, Crowther wrote, "whips through this neo-Keystone business, flashing sight gags and throwaway lines so fast that it dazzles those accustomed to having their comedies milked and spelled out." The film, which Crowther also called "a wild and candid spoof of masculine sex drives," won the grand prize at the 1965 Cannes Film Festival.

BIOGRAPHICAL/CRITICAL SOURCES: New Theatre Magazine, Volume I, number 4, 1960; John Russell Taylor, *Anger and After,* Methuen, 1962, published as *The Angry Theatre: New British Drama,* Hill & Wang, 1969; *New York Times,* June 30, 1965; *Village Voice,* June 8, 1967; *Time,* February 23, 1970.

*   *   *

JENSEN, Albert C(hristian) 1924-

PERSONAL: Born January 26, 1924, in New York, N.Y.; son of Olaf E. and Beatrice M. (Horey) Jensen; married Patricia Lindeen (in sales), September 13, 1947; children: Chris, Jonathan, Laura. *Education:* State University of New York at Syracuse, B.S., 1951, M.S., 1954; further graduate study at University of Miami, Coral Gables, Fla., 1965-66, and State University of New York at Stony Brook, 1972-76. *Home address:* P.O. Box 223, Inglis, Fla. 32649.

CAREER: U.S. Fish & Wildlife Service, Woods Hole, Mass., research biologist, 1954-65; University of Miami, Marine Laboratory, Coral Gables, Fla., managing editor of *Bulletin of Marine Science,* 1965-67; New York State Department of Environmental Conservation, Stony Brook, assistant director, 1967-77; writer, 1977—. Adjunct assistant

professor at Long Island University, 1975-77; instructor at Central Florida Community College, 1978—. Head of Inglis town planning and zoning board, 1978—; member of coastal advisory committee of Withlacoochee Regional Planning Council, 1978—. Member of Civil Air Patrol. *Military service:* U.S. Army Air Forces, 1942-46. U.S. Air Force Reserve, 1949-79; became lieutenant colonel. *Member:* American Fishery Society, American Institute of Fishery Research Biologists (fellow), Gulf and Caribbean Fisheries Institute. *Awards, honors:* George Washington Honor Medal from Freedoms Foundation, 1973, for essay, "Human Goals—Values for Living."

WRITINGS: (Editor) *Proceedings of the International Conference on Tropical Oceanography,* University of Miami Press, 1966; *The Cod,* Crowell, 1972; *Wildlife of the Seas,* Chanticleer, 1979; *Nature's Notebook* (collection of newspaper columns), Deep Sea Press, 1980. Author of "Nature's Notebook," a weekly column in *New Bedford Standard Times,* 1960-66. Contributor to national magazines and newspapers, including *American Forests, Natural History, Organic Gardening, Yankee,* and *Sea Frontiers.* Managing editor of "Marine Resources of the Atlantic Coast," a fishery leaflet series, published by Atlantic States Marine Fisheries Commission, 1967—.

WORK IN PROGRESS: Sharks, Dolphin, and the Sea, publication by Deep Sea Press expected in 1981; *Billfish: Swordsmen of the Sea.*

SIDELIGHTS: Jensen writes: "Writing is my way of sharing with others events and ideas that I find interesting. I have traveled to Great Britain and Scandinavia, and made an oceanographic voyage along the west coast of Africa. The many African towns and villages I visited provided a great deal of background for magazine articles I have published.

"I believe it is extremely important for trained knowledgeable professional environmental scientists to write and publish in the popular media. The public needs to know the facts so they can make intelligent decisions about land clearing, power plants, sewage treatment facilities, ocean dumping, and all the other environmental matters that affect us and the natural world of which man is simply a part. This is particularly important for the seas of the world, the last frontier on Earth. When professionals publish only in technical journals, they are, in effect, talking only to their colleagues."

BIOGRAPHICAL/CRITICAL SOURCES: Newsday, July 1, 1973; *St. Petersburg Times,* April 6, 1978; *Tampa Tribune,* December 5, 1978.

*   *   *

JENSEN, Dwight 1934-

PERSONAL: Born September 4, 1934, in Malad, Idaho; son of Glenden Jacob (a railroad worker) and Lola (a teacher; maiden name, Nutting) Jensen; married Claudia Davison (a legal secretary), April 16, 1955; children: Leonard, Julia. *Education:* Idaho State University, B.A., 1955; also attended Western State College of Colorado, 1958-59; University of Washington, 1964, Stanford University, 1967, and Idaho State University, 1970-73. *Politics:* Democrat. *Religion:* Episcopal. *Office address:* P.O. Box 591, Boise, Idaho.

CAREER: KSEI-Radio, Pocatello, Idaho, reporter, 1959-60; *Delaware County Daily Times,* Chester, Pa., reporter, 1960-61; *Intermountain Observer,* Boise, Idaho, reporter, 1961-73; free-lance writer, 1974—. Reporter for KBOI-TV and Radio, 1961-74. Democratic candidate for U.S. Senate,

1978. Member of Idaho Commission on the Arts and Humanities, 1966-67; chairman of Idaho governor's advisory committee on Amtrak, 1974-75. *Military service:* U.S. Army, 1956-58; became first lieutenant. *Member:* Idaho Press Club (president, 1962-63).

WRITINGS: It's a Girl (three-act play; first produced in Pocatello, Idaho, on Idaho State University-TV, February, 1955), Art Craft Play Co., 1955; *Discovering Idaho,* Caxton, 1977; *There Will Be a Road* (novel), Doubleday, 1978. Contributor to magazines and newspapers. Editor and publisher of *Western Critic.*

WORK IN PROGRESS: Novels; research on Idaho history; social research.

SIDELIGHTS: Jensen told *CA:* "Most of my writing deals with Idaho or the West, or with Westerners transplanted to other locations. I engage in communications in several ways—as journalist, author, broadcaster, researcher, politician, and occasionally as an organizer. I began writing as soon as I was able to write; it has always been a major part of my life. In my books I hope to examine human problems and emotions. I spend most mornings writing. Once or twice a week I devote a morning to research and postpone the writing to the afternoon. I tend to have one priority project that I work on every day until it is done, and a number of other efforts that I advance slowly from time to time until they become priorities."

*   *   *

JOBB, Jamie 1945-
(Osh Kabibble)

PERSONAL: Surname is pronounced Jobe; born November 29, 1945, in Gallipolis, Ohio; son of James T. (in sales) and Hortense (Dillard) Jobb; married Marilyn Wylder (a writer, editor, and illustrator); children: e. Bo, Sach Magee. *Education:* Miami-Dade Junior College—North, A.A., 1966; University of Florida, B.S., 1968. *Politics:* "Gardening." *Religion:* "Nature." *Home:* 371 Irwin St., San Rafael, Calif. 94901.

CAREER: Miami Herald, Miami, Fla., sports writer and correspondent, 1965-69; *Gainesville Sun,* Gainesville, Fla., feature and entertainment writer and editor, 1969-70; Park South Teacher Center, San Francisco, Calif., editor of newsletter, 1971; Amazing Life Games (educational publisher), Sausalito, Calif., writer and editor, 1971-74; free-lance writer, 1974—. President of Diverse Unsung Miracle Plants for Healthy Evolution Among People (DUMP HEAP), 1978-79. *Member:* International Association of Lesser Known Food Plants and Trees, Friends of the Earth, San Francisco Media Alliance.

WRITINGS: My Garden Companion, Sierra Club-Scribner, 1977; *The Night Sky Book,* Little, Brown, 1977; *The Complete Book of Community Gardening,* Morrow, 1979. Also writer of television criticism for newspapers under pseudonym Osh Kabibble. Editor of *DUMP HEAP Journal.*

WORK IN PROGRESS: Books for garden innovators and people interested in uncommon plants, especially wild ones, for Diverse Unsung Miracle Plants for Healthy Evolution Among People.

SIDELIGHTS: Jobb writes: "As a journalist, I am trying to concentrate on stories that help people realize where they fit into their communities and how they can make positive contributions for the growth of all life around them. As a gardener I am learning to see what nature will grow for me and my family."

JOHNSON, Allen

PERSONAL: Born October 19, 1941, in Berkeley, Calif.; married Orna R. Johnson; children: David, Ilana. *Education:* University of California, Berkeley, B.A., 1963; Stanford University, M.A., 1965, Ph.D., 1968. *Home:* 1943 Greenfield, Los Angeles, Calif. 90025. *Office:* Department of Anthropology, University of California, Los Angeles, Calif. 90024.

CAREER: Columbia University, New York, N.Y., assistant professor of anthropology, 1968-75, director of training program in social anthropology, 1972-75; University of California, Los Angeles, associate professor of anthropology, 1975—, director of training program in behavioral anthropology, 1976-78. Faculty associate of University of Hawaii's training program in human ecology, summer, 1970; research clinical associate of Southern California Psychoanalytic Institute, 1977—. Conducted field work in Mexico, Brazil, and Peru. *Awards, honors:* National Science Foundation grants, 1972-76, 1976-78; National Institute of Mental Health grants, 1972-75, 1977-78.

WRITINGS: Sharecroppers of the Sertao: Economics and Dependence on a Brazilian Plantation, Stanford University Press, 1971; (contributor) George Dalton, editor, *Studies in Economic Anthropology,* American Anthropological Association, 1971; *Quantification in Cultural Anthropology: An Introduction to Ethnographic Research Design,* Stanford University Press, 1978; (contributor) Charles F. Cooper, editor, *Ecological Theory and Human Welfare,* Allenfold Osmun, in press. Contributor of about a dozen articles to scholarly journals, including *Human Nature.*

WORK IN PROGRESS: A book entitled *Machigrenga Ecology: Choice and Context in a Low-Energy Society.*

SIDELIGHTS: Johnson told *CA:* "The personal motive underlying much of my professional work is to gain some understanding of the paradox that people in modern, developed economies consume large quantities of produced goods, yet express dissatisfaction that they cannot have more; whereas people in primitive, low energy economies consume very little beyond their basic needs, yet express satisfaction with their level of consumption. By what processes do such differences in motivation and self-evaluation arise? Both ecological and psychological processes must be involved."

AVOCATIONAL INTERESTS: Tennis, classical piano, novels.

*   *   *

JOHNSON, Gerald White 1890-

PERSONAL: Born August 6, 1890, in Riverton, N.J.; son of Archibald (a country newspaper editor) and Flora Caroline (McNeill) Johnson; married Kathryn Hayward, April 22, 1922; children: two daughters. *Education:* Wake Forest College (now University), B.A., 1911. *Politics:* Democrat. *Home:* 217 Bolton Place, Baltimore, Md. 21217.

CAREER: Thomasville Davidsonian, Thomasville, N.C., founder and editor, 1910; *Lexington Dispatch,* Lexington, N.C., staff member, 1911-13; *Greensboro Daily News,* Greensboro, N.C., staff member, 1913-24; University of North Carolina, Greensboro, professor of journalism, 1924-26; *Baltimore Evening Sun* (now the *Baltimore Sun*), Baltimore, Md., editorial writer, 1926-43; free lance writer, 1943—. News commentator, WAAM-TV, Baltimore, 1952-54; contributing editor, *New Republic,* 1954—. *Military service:* U.S. Army, 321st Infantry, 81st Division, 1917-19;

served with American Expeditionary Force in France. *Member:* Phi Beta Kappa, West Hamilton Street Club, Century Club (New York City). *Awards, honors:* DuPont Commentators' award, 1953; Sidney Hillman Foundation Award, 1954; George Foster Peabody Award, 1954; gold medal of the state of North Carolina, 1964; Andrew White medal from Loyola College, Baltimore, 1969; runner-up for the Newbery medal, 1960, for *America Is Born,* and 1961, for *America Moves Forward;* Litt.D. from Wake Forest College, 1928, and Goucher College, 1969; LL.D. from College of Charleston, 1935, University of North Carolina, 1937, and University of North Carolina at Greensboro, 1966; D.C.L., University of the South, 1942.

WRITINGS: (With W. R. Hayward) *The Story of Man's Work,* Minton, Balch, 1925; *What Is News?,* Knopf, 1926; *Andrew Jackson: An Epic in Homespun,* Minton, Balch, 1927; *The Undefeated,* Minton, Balch, 1927; *Randolph of Roanoke: A Political Fantastic,* Minton, Balch, 1929; *By Reason of Strength,* Minton, Balch, 1930; *Number Thirty-Six,* Minton, Balch, 1933; *The Secession of the Southern States,* Putnam, 1933; *A Little Night Music: Discoveries in the Exploitation of an Art* (illustrated by Richard Q. Yardley), Harper, 1937, reprinted, Greenwood Press, 1970; *The Wasted Land,* University of North Carolina Press, 1937, reprinted, Books for Libraries, 1970; (with Frank R. Kent, H. L. Mencken, and Hamilton Owens) *The Sunpapers of Baltimore,* Knopf, 1937; *America's Silver Age: The Statecraft of Clay-Webster-Calhoun,* Harper, 1939.

Roosevelt: Dictator or Democrat?, Harper, 1941 (published in England as *Roosevelt: An American Study,* Hamish Hamilton, 1942); *American Heroes and Hero-Worship,* Harper, 1943, new edition, Kennikat, 1966; *Woodrow Wilson: The Unforgettable Figure Who Has Returned to Haunt Us,* Harper, 1944; *An Honorable Titan: A Biographical Study of Adolph S. Ochs,* Harper, 1946, reprinted, Greenwood Press, 1970; *The First Captain: The Story of John Paul Jones,* Coward, 1947; *Liberal's Progress,* Coward, 1948; *Our English Heritage,* Lippincott, 1949, reprinted, Greenwood Press, 1973; *Incredible Tale: The Odyssey of the Average American in the Last Half Century,* Harper, 1950; *This American People,* Harper, 1951; *The Making of a Southern Industrialist: A Biographical Study of Simpson Bobo Tanner,* University of North Carolina Press, 1952; *Pattern for Liberty: The Story of Philadelphia,* McGraw, 1952; *Mount Vernon: The Story of a Shrine,* Random House, 1953; *The Lunatic Fringe,* Lippincott, 1957, reprinted, Greenwood Press, 1973; *The Lines Are Drawn: American Life Since the First World War as Reflected in the Pulitzer Prize Cartoons,* Lippincott, 1958; *Peril and Promise: An Inquiry Into Freedom of the Press,* Harper, 1958, reprinted, Greenwood Press, 1974.

The Man Who Feels Left Behind, Morrow, 1961; *Hod-Carrier: Notes of a Laborer on an Unfinished Cathedral,* Morrow, 1964; *Politics: Party Competition, and the County Chairman in West Virginia,* Bureau of Information, University of Tennessee, 1970; *The Imperial Republic: Speculation on the Future, If Any, of the Third U.S.A.,* Liveright, 1972; *America-Watching: Perspectives in the Course of an Incredible Century,* Stemmer House, 1976.

For young people: *America: A History for Peter* (illustrated by Leonard E. Fisher), Morrow, Volume I: *America Is Born,* 1959, Volume II: *America Grows Up,* 1960, Volume III: *America Moves Forward,* 1960; *The Supreme Court* (illustrated by L. E. Fisher), Morrow, 1962; *The Presidency* (illustrated by Fisher), Morrow, 1962; *The Congress* (illustrated by Fisher), Morrow, 1963; *Communism: An Ameri-*

can's View, Morrow, 1964; *The Cabinet* (illustrated by Fisher), Morrow, 1966; *Franklin D. Roosevelt: Portrait of a Great Man* (illustrated by Fisher), Morrow, 1967; *The British Empire: An American View of Its History From 1776 to 1945,* Morrow, 1969.

SIDELIGHTS: Described by H. L. Mencken as "the best editorial writer in the South, a very excellent critic and a highly civilized man," Gerald White Johnson has been writing nearly six decades. One of his first books, *Andrew Jackson: An Epic in Homespun* was reviewed in *Saturday Review of Literature:* "No reader of this book is likely to complain that Mr. Johnson has failed to make the most of his dramatic material, or has suffered many of the dramatic silences in the play to go unabridged. . . . It is to Mr. Johnson's credit that, while he offers us no new facts, but turns on all the lights, works up a great color scheme, shifts the scenery with rapidity and skill, and keeps the orchestra hard at work, he remains a realist." This book made him famous and established him as an authority on American history and government.

The birth of his first grandson in 1950 was the stimulus for the trilogy *America: A History for Peter.* As a grandfather, Johnson thought it was his responsibility to make Peter aware of his American heritage. In a review of the first book, *America Is Born,* a *Horn Book* critic observed: "Humor and remarkable perspective on people as well as events are here and the story flows as easily as if Mr. Johnson were indeed telling it to Peter, with excitement and a steady interest that holds the reader as it would the listener." Added the *New York Herald Tribune Book Review:* "The outstanding qualities of this book are a humorous forthrightness that avoids the commonplace and the involved explanation, an ability to select the significant incident and give it color and reality, making it seem as fresh as if it were told for the first time." On the other hand the *New York Times Book Review* noted, "Mr. Johnson oversimplifies historical causes. Youngsters would appreciate his learning insight all the more if they do not suspect they are being patronized, just slightly." However, he also commented that it was "a really good book."

Of the second book in the trilogy, *America Grows Up,* a *Chicago Sunday Tribune* reviewer wrote, "Written by an experienced senior citizen for the youthful, this personalized essay is highly interpretative . . ., graphic and delightful . . ., [and] impartial and thoughtful. Much has been omitted, unfortunately, and incidental detail too often obscures the magnitude and magnificence of our story. . . . Over-simplification and archness of style limit the audience. The teen-age historian should and must cut his teeth on more historical bone and less interpretative meringue." According to a *New York Herald Tribune Book Review* critic, *America Moves Forward* is "Simple, fresh, and exciting enough for a child to read with pleasure yet heartily recommended for his elders, it is filled with his strongly expressed opinions presented candidly but fairly."

Encouraged by the success of the first trilogy, Johnson wrote a second, describing the three branches of the U.S. government. *The Presidency, The Congress,* and *The Supreme Court* received the same favorable reviews as the earlier trilogy. Three years later, Johnson added a fourth volume, *The Cabinet.* These books have been translated into more than thirty languages.

BIOGRAPHICAL/CRITICAL SOURCES: Saturday Review of Literature, November 5, 1927; *New York Times Book Review,* November 1, 1959; *New York Herald Tribune Book Review,* November 1, 1959, November 13, 1960; *Horn Book,* December, 1959; *Chicago Sunday Tribune,* May 8, 1960.*

JOHNSTON, Jennifer 1930-

PERSONAL: Born in Ireland. *Address:* c/o Doubleday & Co., 501 Franklin Ave., Garden City, N.Y. 11530.

CAREER: Writer.

WRITINGS—Novels: *The Captains and the Kings,* Hamish Hamilton, 1972; *The Gates,* Hamish Hamilton, 1973; *How Many Miles to Babylon?,* Doubleday, 1974; *Shadows on Our Skin,* Hamish Hamilton, 1977, Doubleday, 1978.

SIDELIGHTS: With her second novel, Johnston received praise for her subtle style. "For the most part," wrote a reviewer for *Times Literary Supplement, The Gates* "is cooly understated: a virtue, and one which supports the deliberately slight narrative, providing it with continuity and form where a more muscular handling would have left the impression of a series of isolated, sometimes unlikely, cameos." While dealing with a woman growing up in poverty and despair, Johnston manages to avoid an overemphasis on the romatic aspect of the novel. The *Times Literary Supplement* critic observed that "the lack of any grand or shattering passion is just what lends the novel its ability to move the reader without assailing him."

Annie Gottlieb called Johnston's third novel, *How Many Miles to Babylon?,* a "'Pilgrim's Progress' fable." This story of three soldiers in World War I focuses on Alexander Moore, an Irish lad who tells the story as he awaits execution for killing his fellow soldier, an act done to spare the other soldier execution for desertion. In the *Christian Science Monitor,* Pamela Marsh called *How Many Miles to Babylon?* "a brilliant book that won't go away. Its picture of boyhood spent in the Irish countryside and of enduring friendship hangs around in the memory long after the story has ended." Again, critics applauded Johnston's writing technique. "Her limpid, careful prose style," wrote Helen Rogan, "every word carrying its due weight, perfectly matches the character of her narrator."

Johnston's most recent novel, *Shadow on Our Skin,* was called "a story of violence and betrayal" by Frank Touhy. The instigator of the violence is Joe Logan, a North Irish Catholic who befriends Kathleen, an Irish teacher. When Joe's older brother, Brendan, discovers through an envious Joe that Kathleen is engaged to a British officer, he leads a physical assault against her. "There is, to be sure, something a bit too familiar about this story and the theme of a sensitive, poetic pre-adolescent boy who destroys his happiness while clawing desperately to save it," wrote Michael Mewshaw. "The characters remain vital, however, and the sense of mood is impeccable. *Shadows on Our Skin* is poignant, unpretentious and appealing." Valentine Cunningham referred to Johnston's writing as "deceptive fluency that only comes of the tightest control."

BIOGRAPHICAL/CRITICAL SOURCES: Times Literary Supplement, January 26, 1973, April 15, 1977; *Christian Science Monitor,* October 24, 1974; *New York Times Book Review,* October 27, 1974, January 12, 1975, March 26, 1978; *New Statesman,* April 15, 1977; *Contemporary Literary Criticism,* Volume 7, Gale, 1977.*

* * *

JOHNSTON, Randolph W. 1904-

PERSONAL: Born February 23, 1904, in Toronto, Ontario, Canada; son of Howard Addison (an inventor) and Gertrude (Wardell) Johnston; married Muriel G. Norman, 1926 (died, 1928); married wife, Margot (a sculptor), June 19, 1937; children: Marina E. Johnston Galarneaux, William W., Paul

Dennithone, Jeremy Peter. *Education:* Attended Ontario College of Art, 1921-23, Central School of Arts and Crafts, London, England, 1923-24, and University of Toronto, 1924-25. *Home address:* Box 530, Marsh Harbour, Bahamas.

CAREER: Professional sculptor, 1925—. Sculpture and drawing teacher at technical schools in Toronto, Ontario, 1926-31; designer of stage settings for private school in Deerfield, Mass., 1932-40; assistant professor at Smith College, 1940-50. Director of Deerfield Studios, 1932-38. Sculptures represented in private, public, and special collections in France, Germany, England, the Bahamas, and all over the United States.

WRITINGS: Country Craft Book, Countryman Press, 1937; *Book of Country Crafts,* Barnes & Yoseloff, 1964; *Artist on His Island,* Noyes Press, 1975. Contributor to museum publications and to *Rudder.*

WORK IN PROGRESS: Sculpture in bronze.

SIDELIGHTS: Johnston comments: "Writing is not my profession. I have been a sculptor all my life. I have my own fully-equipped bronze foundry on a desert island accessible only by water. I never exhibit and have no agent. My sculpture is always commissioned several years ahead. My work has been noted for its full range of emotional impact: love, courtship, death, war, man's inhumanity to man, and the joy of life."

* * *

JOHNSTON, William 1924-
(Susan Claudia, Heather Sinclair)

PERSONAL: Born January 11, 1924, in Lincoln, Ill.; son of John and Lucille (Shoap) Johnston; married Anne Korba (an executive secretary), October 24, 1954; children: Phillip, Susan, Peter, Thomas, Kelly. *Education:* Attended high school in Springfield, Ill. *Politics:* "Skeptic." *Religion:* "None." *Home and office:* 59 Chestnut St., Massapequa, N.Y. 11758. *Agent:* Scott Meredith Literary Agency, Inc., 845 Third Ave., New York, N.Y. 10022.

CAREER: WJOL-Radio, Joliet, Ill., news reporter, 1947-50; press agent, Tex McCrary Public Relations Agency, 1950-60; free-lance writer, 1960—. *Military service:* U.S. Navy, Air Corps; radio operator and gunner, 1942-45.

WRITINGS—Nonfiction: *Brand Name Versus Generic Drugs,* Lancer Books, 1965; *Resident,* Pyramid Publications, 1966; *Surgeon,* Pyramid Publications, 1966; *Grass Money,* Lancer Books, 1973; *The Winner's Guide to Dice,* Grosset, 1974.

Adult novels: *The Marriage Cage,* Lyle Stuart, 1960; *Save Her for Loving,* Monarch, 1962; *Dr. Starr,* Monarch, Book 1, 1962, Book 2: *Dr. Starr in Crisis,* 1963, Book 3: *Love Finds Dr. Starr,* 1964; *Girls on the Wing,* Monarch, 1962; *Two Loves Has Nurse Powell,* Nevada Publications, 1963; *Front Office,* Lancer Books, 1964; *The Power of Positive Loving,* Monarch, 1964; *The Roomer,* Tower, 1965; *Teenage Tramp,* Monarch, 1965; *Pride of Women,* Monarch, 1966; *Surgeon's Oath,* Lancer Books, 1968; *Come Love in My House,* Monarch, 1969; *Barney,* Random House, 1970; (under pseudonym Susan Claudia) *Clock and Bell,* Doubleday, 1974; *Mrs. Barthelme's Madness,* Putnam, 1976.

Gothic novels: *Madness at the Castle,* Signet, 1966; *The Silent Voice,* Lancer Books, 1967; *A Fear in Borzano,* Lancer Books, 1967; *Master of Foxhollow,* Beagle Books, 1973; *The Other Brother,* Beagle Books, 1974; (under pseudonym Heather Sinclair) *Remembered Kiss,* Signet, 1976; (under pseudonym Heather Sinclair) *Kiss a Stranger,* Signet, 1976; *Follow the Heart,* Signet, 1976.

Novels based on screenplays and television series: *Ben Casey*, Lancer Books, 1962; *Dr. Kildare*, Lancer Books, Book 1: *The Heart Has an Answer*, 1963, Book 2: *The Magic Key*, 1964, Book 3: *The Faces of Love*, 1963; *The New Interns*, Bantam, 1964; *The Swinger*, Dell, 1966; *Gilligan's Island*, Whitman Publishing, 1966; *The Munsters*, Whitman Publishing, 1966; *Get Smart*, Grosset, Book 1: *Get Smart!*, 1965, Book 2: *Sorry, Chief*, 1966, Book 3: *Get Smart Once Again*, 1966, Book 4: *Max Smart and the Perilous Pellets*, 1966, Book 5: *Missed It by That Much!*, 1967, Book 6: *And Loving It!*, 1967, Book 7: *Max Smart: The Spy Who Went Out to the Cold*, 1968, Book 8: *Max Smart Loses Control*, 1968, Book 9: *Max Smart and the Ghastly Ghost Affair*, 1969; *Captain Nice*, Grosset, 1967; *F Troop*, Whitman Publishing, 1967; *The Iron Horse*, Popular Library, 1967; *The Flying Nun*, Ace Books, Book 1: *Miracle at San Tanco*, 1968, Book 2: *The Littlest Rebels*, 1968, Book 3: *Mother of Invention*, 1969, Book 4: *The Little Green Men*, 1969, Book 5: *The Underground Picnic*, 1970; *The Brady Bunch*, Lancer Books, Book 1, 1969, Book 2: *Showdown at the PTA Corral*, 1969, Book 3: *Count up to Blast Down*, 1970, Book 4: *The Quarterback Who Came to Dinner*, 1970; *My Friend Tony*, Lancer Books, 1969; *The April Fools*, Popular Library, 1969; *Angel, Angel, Down We Go!*, Lancer Books, 1969; *Then Came Bronson*, Pyramid Publications, 1969; *Ironsides*, Whitman Publishing, 1969.

The New People, Grosset, 1970; *Room 222*, Grosset, Book 1: *What Ever Happened to Mavis Rooster?*, 1970, Book 2: *Monday Morning Father*, 1970, Book 3: *Love Is a Three-Letter Word*, 1970, Book 4: *Have You Heard About Kelly?*, 1973; *The Young Rebels*, Ace Books, Book 1: *The Hedgerow Incident*, 1970, Book 2: *The Seagold Incident*, 1971; *Nanny and the Professor*, Lancer Books, Book 1, 1970, Book 2: *What Hath Nanny Wrought?*, 1970, Book 3: *Nanny's Miracle*, 1970; *Dick Tracy*, Grosset, 1970; *The Monkees*, Whitman, 1970; *Matt Lincoln*, Lancer Books, Book 1: *The Revolutionist*, 1970, Book 2: *The Hostage*, 1971; *Chelsea Girls*, Lancer Books, 1971; *Uptight*, Lancer Books, 1971; *Mod Squad*, Pinnacle Books, 1971; *The Priest's Wife*, Lancer Books, 1971; *Klute*, Paperback Library, 1971; *Asylum*, Bantam, 1972; *Lieutenant Robinson Crusoe*, Whitman Publishing, 1972; *Happy Days*, Grosset, Book I: *Ready to Go Steady*, 1974, Book 2: *Fonzie Drops in*, 1974, Book 3: *The Invaders*, 1975, Book 4: *Fonzie, Superstar*, 1976, Book 5: *The Fonz and Lazonga*, 1976, Book 6-8, 1977; *Welcome Back, Kotter*, Grosset, Book 1: *The Sweathog Trail*, 1976, Book 2: *The Sweathog Newshawks*, 1976, Book 3: *The Super Sweathogs*, 1976, Book 4: *10-4 Sweathogs*, 1976, Book 5: *The Sweathog Sit-in*, 1977, Book 6: *Barbarino Drops Out*, 1977; *Medical Story*, Bantam, 1976; *Young Frankenstein*, Bantam, 1976; *Marcus-Nelson Murders*, Bantam, 1976; *Echoes of a Summer*, Ballantine, 1976; *King*, St. Martin's, 1978.

Juveniles: *Yogi Bear*, Whitman Publishing, 1963; *Snagglepuss the Lion*, Whitman Publishing, 1964; *The Flintstones*, Whitman Publishing, 1964; *Loopy De Loop*, Whitman Publishing, 1964; *The Funny Company*, Whitman Publishing, 1964; *Ricochet Rabbit*, Whitman Publishing, 1964; *Magilla Gorilla*, Whitman Publishing, 1965; *Swiss Family Duck*, Whitman Publishing, 1966; *Underdog*, Whitman Publishing, 1966; *Bozo the Clown*, Whitman Publishing, 1968; *The Fantastic Four*, Whitman Publishing, 1968; *Chitty Chitty Bang Bang*, Whitman Publishing, 1968; *Moby Dick*, Whitman Publishing, 1968; *Animal Stories*, Whitman Publishing, 1968; *Flossy Glossy*, Whitman Publishing, 1969; *Tom and Jerry*, Whitman Publishing, 1969; *Sam Wesket on the Planet

Framingham, Grosset, 1970; *Soul City Downstairs*, Pyramid Publications, 1970; *Bugs Bunny, Party Pest*, Whitman Publishing, 1978. Contributor of humor articles to national magazines and men's magazines, including *Holiday*, *Diners Club*, *Gentleman's Quarterly*, and *Cavalier*.

WORK IN PROGRESS: A fictional account of "American Revolution II."

SIDELIGHTS: Johnston writes briefly: "I am interested only in writing entertaining stories and remaining as anonymous as possible."

* * *

JOLLY, Hugh R. 1918-

PERSONAL: Born May 5, 1918, in Douglas, England; son of Reginald Bradley (a clerk in holy orders) and Muriel (a singer; maiden name, Crawshaw) Jolly; married Geraldine Mary Howard (a gynecologist), April 28, 1944; children: Christopher, Caryl, Paul. *Education:* Attended Marlborough College, 1931-36; Sidney Sussex College, Cambridge, B.A. (with honors), 1939, M.B. and B.Chir., 1942, M.A., 1943, M.D., 1951; received Diploma in Child Health, 1949. *Home:* Garden House, Warren Park, Kingston Hill, Surrey, England. *Office:* Department of Pediatrics, Charing Cross Hospital, Fulham Palace Rd., London W6 8RF, England.

CAREER: Served house posts at London Hospital, London, England, and at North Middlesex Hospital, Middlesex, England, 1943; Hospital for Sick Children, London, staff member, 1948-49, pathologist and senior medical registrar, 1950-51; Plymouth Clinical Area, Plymouth, England, consulting pediatrician, 1951-60; Charing Cross Hospital, London, consulting pediatrician, 1960—, physician in charge of department of pediatrics, 1965—. Professor at University of Ibadan, Nigeria, 1961-62; visiting professor at Ghana Medical School, 1967-69. Member of advisory board of Parents' Centres, Australia. *Military service:* British Army, Royal Army Medical Corps, dermatologist, 1944-47; served in Netherlands East Indies. *Member:* Royal College of Surgeons, Royal College of Physicians (fellow, 1965), Neonatal Society (founding member), Excerpta Medica (United Kingdom representative in pediatrics), Family Planning Association (vice-president), Royal College of Midwives (Kingston president), Old Achimotan Association (Ghana; guest member). *Awards, honors:* Raymond Horton-Smith' Prize from Cambridge University, 1951; medical journalists award, 1978.

WRITINGS: Sexual Precocity, C. C Thomas, 1955; *Diseases of Children*, Blackwell Scientific Publications, 1964, 3rd edition, 1976; *Common Sense About Babies and Children*, Times Newspapers, 1973; *Book of Child Care*, Allen & Unwin, 1975, revised edition, 1977; *More Commonsense About Babies and Children*, Pelham Books, 1978; (co-editor) *Mothercare Book*, Reader's Digest Press, 1978.

WORK IN PROGRESS: Care of the Handicapped Child; A History of Child Rearing.

SIDELIGHTS: Jolly's books have been published in Spanish, German, and Dutch.

* * *

JONES, (Gene) Donald 1931-

PERSONAL: Born February 3, 1931, in Cheyenne, Wyo.; son of Clarence A. (a business owner) and Margaret Ellen (a business associate; maiden name, Venables) Jones; married Karen Rudolf (a high school teacher), 1960; children: David Richard, Peter Donald. *Education:* Augustana College,

Sioux Falls, S.D., B.A., 1957; Drew University, M.Div., 1961, Ph.D., 1969. *Home:* 26 Hoyt St., Madison, N.J. 07940. *Office:* Department of Religion, Drew University, Madison, N.J. 07940.

CAREER: Drew University, Madison, N.J., instructor, 1967-69, assistant professor, 1969-74, associate professor, 1974-79, professor of religion, 1979—. Ordained United Methodist minister; pastor of United Methodist churches in Park Ridge, Ill. and Westfield, N.J. Member of board of trustees of New Jersey Shakespeare Festival. Member of local Democratic committee. *Military service:* U.S. Navy, 1951-55. *Member:* American Academy of Religion, American Society of Christian Ethics, Society for the Scientific Study of Religion, Society for Values in Higher Education, American Society of Church History, American Studies Association, Council on Religion and International Affairs. *Awards, honors:* Jesse Lee Prize, 1975.

WRITINGS: (Editor with Russell Richey, and contributor) *American Civil Religion,* Harper, 1973; *Bibliography of Business Ethics,* University Press of Virginia, 1976; *The Sectional Crisis and Northern Methodism: A Study in Piety, Politics, and Civil Religion,* Scarecrow, 1979; *Private and Public Ethics,* Edwin Mellen Press, 1979.

WORK IN PROGRESS: Editing *Selected Writings of Will Herberg,* with bibliography.

SIDELIGHTS: Jones writes: "My prime interest is relating religion and ethics to social issues. Current interests include business ethics, political ethics, and biomedical ethics. American religion and social issues are also an interest."

*   *   *

JONES, Harold 1904-

PERSONAL: Born February 22, 1904, in London, England; son of William Edward and Ethel Jones; married Mollie Merry, July, 1933; children: Stephanie Angela, Gabrielle Pamela. *Education:* Attended St. Dunstans College, 1914-20, Goldsmith's College, London, 1920-21, and Camberwell School of Arts and Crafts, 1922-23; Royal College of Art, diploma, 1929. *Home:* Doune Lodge, 27 Oxford Rd., Putney, London SW15 2LG, England. *Agent:* Laura Cecil, 10 Exeter Mansions, 106 Susxusbury Ave., London W1V 7DH, England.

CAREER: Writer and illustrator. Bermondsey Central School for Boys, London, England, teacher, 1930-34; Ruskin School of Drawing, Ashmolean Museum, Oxford, England, teacher, 1937-40; Working Men's College, London, head of evening art school, 1937-40; Chelsea School of Art, London, teacher, 1945-58; Sunningdale School of Ballet, Sunningdale, England, teacher, 1945-46. Has held exhibitions at the Royal Academy, Leicester Gallery, National Book League, Piccadilly Gallery, and Green & Abbott. *Military service:* Royal Engineers, lithographic draftsman, 1939-45.

WRITINGS—All self-illustrated: *The Visit to the Farm,* Faber, 1939; *The Enchanted Night,* Faber, 1947; *The Childhood of Jesus,* Gollancz, 1964; *There and Back Again,* Atheneum, 1977.

Illustrator: Cecil A. Joll, *Diseases of the Thyroid Gland,* Heinemann, 1932; M. E. Atkinson, *August Adventure,* J. Cape, 1936; Atkinson, *Mystery Manor,* Bodley Head, 1937; Walter de la Mare, *This Year: Next Year,* Holt, 1937; Atkinson, *The Compass Points North,* Bodley Head, 1938; Atkinson, *Smuggler's Gap,* Bodley Head, 1939; Atkinson, *Crusoe Island,* Bodley Head, 1947; John Pudney, *Selected Poems,*

Bodley Head, 1947; Kathleen Lines, *Four to Fourteen,* Oxford University Press, 1950; Lines, compiler, *Lavender's Blue,* Oxford University Press, 1954; Lines, compiler, *Once in Royal David's City,* Oxford University Press, 1956; Henry Fagen, *Nikya,* J. Cape, 1956; Donald Suddaby, *Prisoners of Saturn,* Bodley Head, 1957; Lines, compiler, *A Ring of Tales,* Oxford University Press, 1958; William Blake, *Songs of Innocence,* Faber, 1958; Elfrida Vipont, compiler, *Bless This Day,* Harcourt, 1958.

Lines, *Noah and the Ark,* Oxford University Press, 1961; *Songs From Shakespeare,* Faber, 1961; Charles Kingsley, *The Water Babies,* Gollancz, 1961, Watts, 1961; Robert Browning, *The Pied Piper of Hamelin,* Oxford University Press, 1962; Nathaniel Hawthorne, *The Complete Greek Stories of Nathaniel Hawthorne,* Gollancz, 1964; Lewis Carroll, *The Hunting of the Snark* (limited edition), Whittington Press, 1975; Oscar Wilde, *The Fairy Stories of Oscar Wilde,* Gollancz, 1976; Paul Ries Collin, *Calling Bridge,* Oxford University Press, 1976; Ruth Manning-Sanders, *The Town House and the Country Mouse,* Angus Robertson, 1977. Also designer of book jackets.

SIDELIGHTS: Jones's work has been purchased by the Tate Gallery, the Victoria and Albert Museum, and the London County Council.

BIOGRAPHICAL/CRITICAL SOURCES: Arts Guardian, December 6, 1974; *London Times,* August 27, 1975; William Feaver, *When We Were Young,* Thomas & Hudson, 1977.*

*   *   *

JONES, Howard 1940-

PERSONAL: Born October 21, 1940, in Lebanon, Tenn.; son of Howard Anderson and Louise (a secretary; maiden name, Collier) Jones; married Mary Ann Bumbera (a nursing home activities director), December 22, 1962; children: Deborah Ann, Howard, Sharise Lynn. *Education:* Indiana University, B.S., 1963, M.A., 1965, Ph.D., 1973. *Religion:* Church of Christ. *Home:* 12919 Northwood Lake, Northport, Ala., 35476. *Office:* Department of History, University of Alabama, University, Ala. 35486.

CAREER: High school history teacher in Gary, Ind., 1963-69; University of Nebraska, Lincoln, visiting assistant professor of U.S. foreign relations, 1972-74; University of Alabama, University, associate professor of U.S. foreign relations, 1974—. Part-time instructor at Indiana University Northwest, 1965-69. *Member:* Organization of American Historians, Society for Historians of American Foreign Relations, Society for Historians of the Early American Republic, Phi Alpha Theta. *Awards, honors:* Eli Lilly fellowship in American history, 1963-65; National Endowment for the Humanities summer stipend, 1974; University of Alabama summer faculty research fellowship, 1977; Pulitzer Prize nomination and Phi Alpha Theta Book Award, both 1978, both for *To the Webster-Ashburton Treaty;* research grant from the Truman Library, summer, 1979.

WRITINGS: To the Webster-Ashburton Treaty: A Study in Anglo-American Relations, 1783-1843, University of North Carolina Press, 1977; (contributor) Helen Delpar, editor, *The Discoverers,* McGraw, 1979; (contributor to revision) Samuel F. Bemis and Grace Griffin, editors, *Guide to the Study of American Foreign Relations* (revision edited by Richard Burns), two volumes, ABC-CLIO Press, 1980. Contributor of articles and reviews to history and foreign area studies journals.

WORK IN PROGRESS: Origins of the Truman Doctrine, 1945-1947, completion expected in 1982.

SIDELIGHTS: Jones told *CA:* "My goal always has been to write history based on thorough research in the primary sources. Past experience shows that publications grounded in this type of research survive the test of time far better than those built on rhetoric and emotion. Just as there had been no book-length study of the Webster-Ashburton Treaty of 1842, there is no comprehensive work on the formation of the Truman Doctrine of 1947. Treatises abound which accuse the United States of questionable motives in its post-1945 foreign policy, but there are insufficient numbers of careful studies stemming from documents and manuscripts housed in the National Archives, Library of Congress, presidential libraries, private collections of correspondence and papers, and other source materials derived from memoirs, diaries, interviews with contemporaries of the 1940's, and newspapers and periodicals.

"One has to agree that the vast amounts of government materials on the post-World War II era make it possible to 'prove' almost any thesis, yet it still seems feasible that research in these papers tempered with careful judgment can result in a reasonable explanation of the past. The difficult task, of course, is to gain a sense of the past without relying only upon the senses of the present. To judge policymakers of the 1940's through the advantage of post-Vietnam hindsight, for instance, would be unfair. In fact, to *judge* the past is to do it an injustice. The historian's responsibility is to facilitate *understanding* by getting as close as possible to the time span he is writing about. To do this, he must examine the documents of that time. Though it is impossible to present a definitive explanation of the motives of those people involved in making either the Webster-Ashburton Treaty or the Truman Doctrine, the satisfaction lies in trying to meet the challenge.

"In my work on the Webster-Ashburton Treaty, I have argued that the pact preserved peace between Great Britain and the United States by resolving many of the irritating problems in their relationship and thereby helping to establish a basis for mutual trust. Anglo-American affairs were not smooth following the War of 1812. The difficulties which confronted Secretary of State Daniel Webster and British Special Minister Lord Ashburton might have confounded lesser men. But they took advantage of their personal relationship as well as the desire in both the governments in Washington and London to avert war, and managed to secure a compromise that preserved the honor of both nations. It was no small task to remove animosities growing out of the long-standing Canadian-American boundary dispute, the serious yet comic-opera and bloodless 'Aroostook War,' the *Caroline* and Alexander McLeod crises, and the *Creole* slave revolt and related disagreements over the African slave trade, British visit-and-search policies, impressment, and extradition. And even though the questions rapidly rising over Oregon had not yet reached the danger stage, they had the potential of causing more trouble. Mutual suspicion meshed with entanglements over America's states' rights doctrine to frustrate earlier attempts to settle these Anglo-American issues. But finally, in the summer of 1842, the two negotiators met in Washington to prove once again that personal diplomacy still can overcome divisiveness threatening to lead nations into war. The diplomacy of Webster and Ashburton helped to make possible the development of perhaps the most significant international friendship in modern history.

"My work on the Webster-Ashburton Treaty emphasizes the importance of the interrelationship between foreign and domestic policy. Research in American, British, and Cana-

dian archives illustrates that international disputes oftentimes reflect political disputes at home. There is no way to write a comprehensive history based on diplomatic sources alone. Had I used this narrow approach there could have been no understanding of the intricate maneuverings followed by both Webster and Ashburton in securing their treaty. New evidence shows that the two men did not engage in disreputable tactics in working with the complicated and exasperating controversy involving the infamous 'red-line maps.' The documents do not suggest questionable exchanges of money during the negotiations, nor do they support the charge that Webster sacrificed his country's interests for personal gain. The men signed the treaty because they considered it the alternative to a disastrous third Anglo-American war.

"It is too early in my research on the Truman Doctrine to indicate what directions the book will take, but it seems clear that the story that already has appeared in various publications is not as accurate as it should be. What the documents ultimately will reveal remains a mystery at this time. Though the process of unraveling a story from a complex and seemingly unrelated pile of primary sources is slow and arduous, it is the only way to gain some understanding of the past."

*   *   *

JONES, Howard Mumford 1892-

PERSONAL: Born April 16, 1892, in Saginaw, Mich.; son of Frank Alexander and Josephine Whitman (Miles) Jones; married Clara Edgar McLure, July 13, 1918 (marriage ended); married Bessie Judith Zaban, June 11, 1927; children: (first marriage) Eleanor McLure. *Education:* Attended State Normal School (now University of Wisconsin—La Crosse), 1910-12; University of Wisconsin—Madison, B.A., 1914; University of Chicago, M.A., 1915. *Home:* 14 Francis Ave., Cambridge, Mass. 02138.

CAREER: University of Texas, Austin, adjunct professor of English, 1916-17; Montana State University, Missoula, assistant professor of English, 1917-19; University of Texas, associate professor of comparative literature and head of department, 1919-24; University of North Carolina, Chapel Hill, associate professor, 1924-27, professor of English, 1927-30; University of Michigan, Ann Arbor, professor of English, 1930-36; Harvard University, Cambridge, Mass., professor of English, 1936-60, Abbott Lawrence Lowell Professor of Humanities, 1960-62, Lowell Professor emeritus, 1962—, dean of Graduate School of Arts and Sciences, 1943-44, Rushton lecturer, 1946, editor-in-chief of John Harvard Library, 1959-62. Lecturer at University of Bristol, 1933; Messenger lecturer at Cornell University, 1948; lecturer at American Institute (Munich), 1950; visiting professor at Massachusetts Institute of Technology, 1962-63; lecturer at York University, 1962; Knapp Distinguished Professor at University of Wisconsin—Madison, 1963; Paley Visiting Professor at Hebrew University of Jerusalem, 1964; Weil lecturer at Hebrew Union College, 1967; Samuel S. Stratton lecturer at Middlebury College, 1967; Rockefeller Distinguished lecturer at University of Arkansas, 1975. Research associate at Henry E. Huntington Library; fellow of Center for Advanced Studies in the Behavioral Sciences, 1957-58. Head of American Council of Learned Societies, 1955-59, and Frank L. Weil Institute for Studies in Religion and the Humanities, 1959-61.

MEMBER: Modern Language Association of America (president, 1965), American Historical Association, American Philosophical Society, American Academy of Arts and

Sciences (president, 1944-51), American Antiquarian Society, Colonial Society of Massachusetts, Massachusetts Historical Society, Texas Philosophical Society, Phi Beta Kappa, Delta Sigma Rho. *Awards, honors:* Jusserand Medal from American Historical Association, 1934, for *America and French Culture;* honorary degrees include Litt.D. from Harvard University, 1936, University of Colorado, 1938, University of Wisconsin—Madison, 1948, Western Reserve University (now Case Western Reserve University), 1948, and Clark University, 1952, L.H.D. from Tulane University, 1938, D.H.L. from Ohio State University, 1960, Hebrew Union College, 1960, Northwestern University, 1966, Clarkson College of Technology, 1968, New York University, 1969, and University of Pennsylvania, 1976, and LL.D. from Colby College, 1962, University of Utah, 1966, and University of Windsor, 1969; Guggenheim fellowship, 1964-65; Pulitzer Prize in general nonfiction and Ralph Waldo Emerson Prize from Phi Beta Kappa, both 1965, both for *O Strange New World;* Hubbell Medal from Modern Language Association, 1970; Jaffe Medal from Phi Beta Kappa, 1973, and award from University of Chicago alumni, 1974, both for distinction in humanistic scholarship.

WRITINGS: The Masque of Marsh and River (play; first produced in La Crosse, Wis., at State Normal School, June 8, 1915), privately printed, 1915; *A Little Book of Local Verse,* privately printed, 1915; (translator) Heinrich Heine, *The North Sea* (poem), [Chicago], 1916, reprinted, Open Court, 1973; *Gargoyles and Other Poems,* Cornhill Co., 1918; *The King in "Hamlet",* University of Texas Press, 1918, reprinted, Folcroft, 1973; (with R. H. Griffith) *A Bibliography of the Works and Manuscripts of Byron,* University of Texas Press, 1924; *America and French Culture, 1750-1848,* University of North Carolina Press, 1927, reprinted, Greenwood Press, 1973; *Contemporary Southern Literature: An Outline for Individual and Group Study,* University of North Carolina Press, 1928, reprinted, Richard West, 1977; (with Philip Schuyler Allen) *The Romanesque Lyric,* University of North Carolina Press, 1928, reprinted, Barnes & Noble, 1969; (editor) *The Selected Poems of Edgar Allan Poe,* Spiral Press, 1929.

(Contributor of translation) T. H. Dickinson, editor, *Chief Contemporary Dramatists* (includes Jones's translation of Sem Benelli's *The Love of Three Kings*), 3rd edition, Houghton, 1930; *The Life of Moses Coit Tyler,* University of Michigan Press, 1933; (editor with Ernest E. Leisy) *Major American Writers,* Harcourt, 1935, 3rd edition (with Leisy and Richard M. Ludwig), 1952; (editor with Robert Morss Lovett) *The College Reader,* Houghton, 1936; *They Say the Forties* (poems), Holt, 1937; *The Harp That Once–: A Chronicle of the Life of Thomas Moore,* Holt, 1937, reprinted, Russell, 1970; (editor with S. I. Hayakawa) *Oliver Wendell Holmes,* American Bank Co., 1939; (Editor) Tobias Smollett, *The Expedition of Humphry Clinker,* Dutton, 1943; *Ideas in America,* Harvard University Press, 1944; *Education and World Tragedy,* Harvard University Press, 1946; *The Theory of American Literature,* Cornell University Press, 1948, revised edition, 1965; (editor with Ludwig and Marvin B. Perry) *Modern Minds: An Anthology of Ideas,* Heath, 1949, 2nd edition, 1954; (editor) *Primer of Intellectual Freedom,* Harvard University Press, 1949.

The Bright Medusa, University of Illinois Press, 1952, reprinted, Greenwood Press, 1977; *Guide to American Literature and Its Backgrounds Since 1890,* Harvard University Press, 1953, 4th edition (with Ludwig), 1972; *The Pursuit of Happiness,* Harvard University Press, 1953; (editor with Walter B. Rideout) *Letters of Sherwood Anderson,* Hough-

ton, 1953; *The Frontier in American Fiction: Four Lectures on the Relation of Landscape to Literature,* Magness Press, 1956; *American Humanism: Its Meaning for World Survival,* Harper, 1957; *Reflections on Learning,* Rutgers University Press, 1958; *Our Great Society: Humane Learning in the United States,* Harcourt, 1959; (editor with Dougald MacMillan) *Plays of the Restoration and Eighteenth Century,* Holt, 1959.

Humane Traditions in America: A List of Suggested Readings, Harvard University Press, 1961; (with David Riesman and Robert Ulrich) *The University and the New World,* University of Toronto Press, 1962; (editor with I. Bernard Cohen) *A Treasury of Scientific Prose: A Nineteenth-Century Anthology,* Little, Brown, 1963, (published in England as *Science Before Darwin: A Nineteenth-Century Anthology,* Deutsch, 1963); (editor with Edwin H. Sauer) *Short Stories: An Anthology for Secondary Schools,* Holt, 1963; *History and the Contemporary: Essays in Nineteenth-Century Literature,* University of Wisconsin Press, 1964; *O Strange New World: American Culture—The Formative Years,* Viking, 1964; (editor) Ralph Waldo Emerson, *Emerson on Education: Selections,* Columbia University Press, 1966; (editor) Emerson, *English Traits,* Harvard University Press, 1966; *Jeffersonianism and the American Novel,* Columbia University Press, 1967; *Belief and Disbelief in American Literature,* University of Chicago Press, 1967; *The Shrine of the Word,* Spiral Press, 1967; (translator) Thomas of Celano, *Dies Irae,* Spiral Press, 1967; (author of foreword) William Charvat, *The Profession of Authorship in America, 1800-1870,* Ohio State University Press, 1968; (editor) Harriet Beecher Stowe, *Uncle Tom's Cabin; or, Life Among the Lowly,* C. E. Merrill, 1969; *Violence and Reason: A Book of Essays,* Atheneum, 1969.

The Age of Energy: Varieties of American Experience, 1865-1915, Viking, 1971; *Revolution and Romanticism,* Harvard University Press, 1974; (editor with wife, Bessie Zaban Jones) *The Many Voices of Boston: A Historical Anthology, 1630-1975,* Little, Brown, 1975; (editor) Herman Melville, *Moby-Dick,* Norton, 1976; *Autobiography,* University of Wisconsin Press, 1979.

Also author of "The Shadow" (one-act play; first produced in Milwaukee, Wis.), represented in anthology *Wisconsin Plays II,* 1918. Author of three bilingual German-English pamphlets introducing American history, government, and schools, printed in 1945 for the U.S. Army. Contributor of articles, stories, poems, and reviews to literary journals and popular magazines, including *New Republic, Saturday Review of Literature,* and *Yale Review.* Literary editor of *Boston Evening Transcript,* 1938-41.

WORK IN PROGRESS: The Great West in American Literary History.

SIDELIGHTS: In Jones's *Theory of American Literature,* "the meat of the book . . . is a survey of the rise and development of literary nationalism and American literary scholarship in the nineteenth-century," wrote reviewer Frank Lentricchia, Jr. "As a guide to certain basic issues in American literary and cultural history, Jones's scholarship inspires confidence. But here and there throughout the book . . . we meet disappointing evasions of responsibility . . . and frequent expressions of taste that seem to have no relevance whatsoever to the issues at hand."

Jones's *Belief and Disbelief in American Literature* concentrates on eight authors from the American Revolution to the twentieth century—Paine, Irving, Bryant, Cooper, Emerson, Whitman, Twain, and Frost. "This book could be a model for all scholarly writing," said Thomas Lask. He felt Jones's problem "was not to determine how close each writer was to orthodox belief ... [but] how these men felt about those questions that are the subject of religious teachings: man's place in the universe, his relation to a Supreme Being and what moral sanctions can be drawn from this relationship." "Every essay," concluded Lask, "is full of suggestions for further reading and exploration. ... Mr. Jones has, in short, set up a small feast for the mind." Edward E. Ericson, meanwhile, made several objections to the book in light of its purpose. He saw Jones "ostensibly" charting the historical development of "the belief and disbelief in Christianity by American men of letters," and felt those authors studied were "weighted heavily on the side of disbelief." Secondly, Ericson continued, "there are too few authors treated to allow the sweeping conclusions which Jones makes."

In *Jeffersonianism and the American Novel,* Jones examined the affinity between Jeffersonian philosophy and the themes of American novelists while looking "at culture in general, and at literature in particular, from a utilitarian standpoint: does it 'make for rationality, the strengthening of the moral sense, or civic responsibility?'" Ernest Redekop gave an example of how Jones linked William Howells to Jefferson "by his distrust of the passions, by his dislike of snobbery, by his life in egalitarianism and by the innate moral sense." Twain, too, was linked by his "'wide humanity. ...'" However, "Twain's pessimism and disbelief in the autonomy of the will make him anti-Jeffersonian." The 1920's marked a turning point in American fiction when such novelists as Hemingway, O'Hara, Anderson, Farell, and Steinbeck and their portrayals of "somewhat less than models of human uprightness" no longer created, in Jones's words, "a responsible work of art in a democracy struggling to achieve its ideals in a world that seems leagued against the existence of the democratic republic in the Jeffersonian sense." In Jones's view, very few novels published since that time respond affirmatively to contemporary culture and human life.

Jones commented for *CA* on the future of life in America: "If the world survives, I note the steady decline of the humanities so far as literary expression is concerned, 'mass culture' replacing them; and the steady increase in mechanization, much of which seems to me non-human and often inhumane. I do not believe, if we survive, that a country whose population is guessed to be 220 million by the end of the century can indefinitely continue to be governed competently by an eighteenth-century constitution, but I look with dread to a possible new constitutional convention."

BIOGRAPHICAL/CRITICAL SOURCES: Poetry, May, 1967; *Canadian Forum,* December, 1967; *New York Times,* December 23, 1967; *Encounter,* autumn, 1968; *Georgia Review,* autumn, 1968; Howard Mumford Jones, *Autobiography,* University of Wisconsin Press, 1979.

*   *   *

JONES, Jack 1924-
(Jay Edmond)

PERSONAL: Born June 14, 1924, in El Paso, Tex.; son of John Edmund (in insurance) and Gladys (Scott) Jones; married Barbara Stewart (a teacher), January, 1954; children: Scott T. *Education:* University of Southern California, B.A., 1949. *Residence:* La Jolla, Calif. *Agent:* Arthur Pine Associates, Inc., 1780 Broadway, New York, N.Y. 10019. *Office: Los Angeles Times*—San Diego Edition, 225 Broadway, San Diego, Calif. 92101.

CAREER: Los Angeles Daily News, Los Angeles, Calif., reporter, 1949-54; *Los Angeles Times,* Los Angeles, reporter, 1954-78, with San Diego edition, 1978—.

WRITINGS—Novels: *Journey Into Death,* Gold Medal, 1954; *The Animal,* Morrow, 1975. Writer for radio series, "Jason and the Golden Fleece," NBC-Radio, 1953-54. Contributor of about fifteen stories to men's magazines, under pseudonym Jay Edmond.

*   *   *

JONES, Royston Oscar 1925-1974

PERSONAL: Born October 28, 1925; died, 1974; son of David and Gwladys Mary (Williams) Jones; married Elvira Diez de Artazcoz, 1948; children: three. *Education:* King's College, London, B.A. (first class honors), 1946, M.A., 1949.

CAREER: University of Aberdeen, Aberdeen, Scotland, assistant lecturer in Spanish, 1948; University of St. Andrews, St. Andrews, Scotland, lecturer in Spanish, 1949; University of London, London, England, lecturer in Spanish at King's College, 1950-56, reader in Spanish and head of department at Queen Mary College, 1956-63, Cervantes Professor of Spanish at King's College, 1963-73, fellow of King's College, 1972; Cambridge University, Cambrdige, England, professor of Spanish and fellow of Downing College, 1973-74.

WRITINGS: (editor) *La vida de Lazarillo de Tormes y de sus fortunas y adversidades,* Manchester University Press, 1963; (editor) Luis de Gongora y Argote, *Poems,* Cambridge University Press, 1966; (editor) *A Literary History of Spain,* Barnes & Noble, Volume II: *The Golden Age: Prose and Poetry, the Sixteenth and Seventeenth Centuries,* 1971, Volume VIII, 1972; (editor) Antonio de Guevara, *Arte de marear,* University of Exeter, 1972; (editor) *Studies in Spanish Literature of the Golden Age,* Tamesis, 1973; (editor) Juan del Encina, *Poesia lirica y cancionero musical,* Castalia, 1975. General editor of *A Literary History of Spain,* Barnes & Noble, 1971-72. Contributor to language and Spanish studies journals.*

*   *   *

JONES, Sandy 1943-

PERSONAL: Born August 16, 1943, in Atlanta, Ga.; daughter of James Lauren and Virginia (a social worker; maiden name, McWhorter) Freeman; married Paul Eugene Jones (a professor), August 23, 1969; children: Marcie. *Education:* Furman University, B.A., 1965; Appalachian State University, M.A., 1972. *Religion:* Society of Friends (Quakers). *Home and office:* 220-C Donnybrook Lane, Baltimore, Md. 21204.

CAREER: Mecklenburg Association for the Blind, Charlotte, N.C., social worker, 1967-68; Belk Department Store, Charlotte, advertising copywriter, 1970; Mental Health Association of Baltimore, Baltimore, Md., director of public information and education, 1971-72; writer and consultant, 1972—. *Member:* Association for Childhood Education International, National Association for the Education of Young Children.

WRITINGS: Good Things for Babies, Houghton, 1976; *Learning for Little Kids,* Houghton, 1979. Contributor to consumer publications and women's magazines.

WORK IN PROGRESS: A book on parent-baby attachment in infancy; a book on product design and safety for infants and young children.

SIDELIGHTS: Sandy Jones writes: "My religious background as a Southern Baptist and my intense involvement in the Red Cross youth movement as a youngster and teenager led me to feel that the main purpose of my life was to be of a wide social service to others. As a senior in high school, I traveled to Europe as part of a 'young U.S. scholars abroad' program sponsored by the American Red Cross. Through this opportunity to identify with people of other cultures I came to a strong sense of the crucial need for human understanding and cultural openness.

"The years after college were spent in one dismal unsatisfying social work position after another, until I retreated to Pendle Hill, a Quaker adult study center, where I began to become aware of my longing to be creative. I tried painting and poetry unsuccessfully. It wasn't until I married in my late twenties that I began to ponder the possibility of being creative through writing, although at that time I was only aware of fiction as the medium for creative writing.

"My writing began in earnest when I accepted a job as an advertising copywriter. My first meaningful writing position was as director of public information and education for a mental health association. I wrote news releases, brochures, and a monthly newsletter. At last I was doing something that came naturally and easily to me.

"*Good Things for Babies* arose about a year after I had given birth to Marcie. In our loneliness in a stark apartment complex in Baltimore—away from family and friends—I began a mother-baby group. From our discussions and my incessant mailing of requests for catalogues in order to get mail, the book emerged, a sourcebook of safety and consumer advice for parents.

"At last! I had found a way to be of service to others by communicating through my book to mothers and fathers. Letters from parents thanking me for my book and giving me suggestions for new editions began to come in from Missouri, Texas, and all over the United States and Canada.

"Several years after beginning my first book, I undertook the second, a sourcebook for parents of three-to-eight-year-olds. It was conceived as a follow-up to the first book, but the result was much more massive than the first. I asked parents to write articles about their own experiences with their youngsters. I gathered together all that was known in the area of early childhood education and translated it into terms that could be easily understood by most parents. I reviewed hundreds of products in order to list mail-order items for parents who wanted something more than the neighborhood toy shop offered. The second book was three times larger than the first.

"Now I am busily writing articles about consumer concerns for major magazines, while planning a new book that will use my photographic skills as well as my writing ability. It will focus on the delicate and sensuous relationship between parents and their babies, and will probably take several years of work.

"Always, my goal is to help young children and their parents. I feel if I can free them to love one another—taking away the restrictions that keep them from engaging fully with one another—then my work is infinitely meaningful."

BIOGRAPHICAL/CRITICAL SOURCES: Family Safety, spring, 1978; *Baltimore Sun,* April 25, 1978.

* * *

JORDAN, Wayne 1903(?)-1979

OBITUARY NOTICE: Born c. 1903 in Lower Salem, Ohio;

died of a heart attack, March 16, 1979, in Buffalo, N.Y. Historian, educator, and journalist. During his newspaper career, Jordan served as reporter for the *Toledo Times,* news editor of the *Detroit Free Press,* managing editor of the *Philadelphia Inquirer,* assistant to the managing editor of the *Buffalo Evening News,* editor of the *Lorain Journal,* and associate editor of *Business Week.* He was also a professor at University of Maine and established the journalism department there in 1948. Obituaries and other sources: *New York Times,* March 18, 1979.

* * *

JOUHANDEAU, Marcel Henri 1888-1979
(Marcel Provence)

OBITUARY NOTICE: Born July 26, 1888, in Gueret, France; died April 7, 1979, in Rueil-Malmaison, France. Educator and author. A prolific French writer known for his purity of style, Jouhandeau wrote most often about his home town, his marriage, his homosexuality, and his religion. Among his 127 published works were many novels and memoirs, including *Marcel and Elise, Un Monde,* and *La Jeunesse de Theophile.* Obituaries and other sources: *The Author's and Writer's Who's Who,* 6th edition, Burke's Peerage, 1971; *World Authors, 1950-1970,* Wilson, 1975; *The International Who's Who,* Europa, 1978; *Who's Who in the World,* 40th edition, Marquis, 1978; *New York Times,* April 10, 1979.

* * *

JOYCE, William W(alter) 1934-

PERSONAL: Born July 11, 1934, in Appleton, Wis.; son of Donald M. and Elizabeth (Breitenstein) Joyce; married Mary Bosser, August 25, 1956; children: Sean, Kevin, Elizabeth, William. *Education:* Lawrence College, B.A., 1956; Northwestern University, M.A., 1960, Ed.D., 1964. *Religion:* Lutheran. *Home:* 2941 Colony Dr., East Lansing, Mich. 48823. *Office:* Department of Elementary and Special Education, Michigan State University, East Lansing, Mich. 48824.

CAREER: Teacher at public schools in Waukegan, Ill., 1961-62; Michigan State University, East Lansing, assistant professor, 1964-66, associate professor, 1967—. Visiting professor at Indiana University, summer, 1967. Member of social studies textbook evaluation committee of Michigan Department of Education, 1973—; consultant to film companies, book publishers, and U.S. Department of Defense. *Member:* National Council for the Social Studies, National Council for Geographic Education, American Educational Research Association, John Dewey Society, Phi Delta Kappa (faculty adviser, 1972-77).

WRITINGS: (With W. R. Houston, S. D. Lee, and H. Gross) *Exploring Regions of Latin America and Canada,* with teacher's editions, Follett, 1968, 4th edition, 1977; (with Houston and R. G. Oana) *Elementary Education in the Seventies: Implications for Theory and Practice,* Holt, 1970; (with J. C. MacLendon and John R. Lee) *Readings on Elementary Social Studies: Emerging Changes,* Allyn & Bacon, 1970; (editor with J. A. Banks) *Teaching Social Studies to Culturally Different Children,* Addison-Wesley, 1971; (contributor) *A Symposium on the Development of Human Intelligence,* Department of Sociology and Anthropology, Ohio University, 1972; (editor with F. L. Ryan) *Social Studies and the Elementary Teacher: Promises and Practices,* National Council for the Social Studies, 1978; (with J. Alleman-Brooks) *Teaching Elementary Social Studies Through the*

Human Experience, Holt, 1979. Author of teacher education material for Edison Institute. Contributor of articles and reviews to education and social science journals. Elementary education editor of *Social Education,* 1973-79.

* * *

JUDD, Robert 1939-

PERSONAL: Born June 16, 1939, in Ohio; son of Clarence H. and Cora H. Judd. *Education:* Williams College, B.A. (honors), 1961. *Politics:* "Skeptic." *Home address:* Hatch Pond, South Kent, Conn. 06785. *Agent:* Jay Acton, Edward J. Acton, Inc., 17 Grove St., New York, N.Y. 10014. *Office:* J. Walter Thompson Co., 543 Hudson St., New York, N.Y. 10014.

CAREER: J. Walter Thompson Co. (advertising agency), New York, N.Y., creative director and vice-president, 1961—.

WRITINGS: (With Deborah Phillips) *How to Fall Out of Love,* Houghton, 1978.

WORK IN PROGRESS: An alternative to sex manuals, with Deborah Phillips; a novel.

* * *

JUHASZ, Suzanne 1942-

PERSONAL: Born April 12, 1942, in Chicago, Ill.; daughter of Philip Julius (a sales manager) and Janet (a teacher; maiden name, Rosenthal) Hecht; married Joseph Boris Juhasz (a professor), June 18, 1963; children: Alexandra, Jennifer, Antonia. *Education:* Bennington College, B.A., 1963; University of California, Berkeley, M.A., 1967, Ph.D., 1970. *Home:* 1081 Lincoln Place, Boulder, Colo. 80302. *Office:* Department of English, University of Colorado, Boulder, Colo. 80309.

CAREER: Bucknell University, Lewisburg, Pa., lecturer in English, 1971-73; San Jose State University, San Jose, Calif., lecturer in English, 1973-74; University of Colorado, Boulder, assistant professor of English, 1974—. Lecturer at University of California, Santa Cruz, winter, 1974. *Member:* Modern Language Association of America (member of Women's Caucus), Philological Association of the Pacific Coast. *Awards, honors:* Florence Howe Award for Feminist Criticism, 1978, for "Towards a Theory of Form in Feminist Autobiography."

WRITINGS: Metaphor and the Poetry of Williams, Pound, and Stevens, Bucknell University Press, 1974; *Naked and Fiery Forms: Modern American Poetry by Women, a New Tradition,* Harper, 1976; *Benita to Reginald: A Romance* (poems), Out of Sight Press, 1978. Contributor to academic and literary journals, including *International Journal of Women's Studies, Frontiers, Southern Poetry Review,* and *Nimrod.*

WORK IN PROGRESS: The *"Undiscovered Continent":* *Emily Dickinson and the Space of the Mind;* a novel; poems.

* * *

JUNGK, Robert 1913-

PERSONAL: Birth-given name, Robert Baum; name legally changed; born November 5, 1913, in Berlin, Germany (now West Berlin, West Germany); naturalized U.S. citizen; emigrated to Austria; son of Max and Elli (Bravo) Jungk; married Ruth Suschizky, April 21, 1948; children: Peter, Stefan. *Education:* Attended University of Berlin, 1932-33; received degree from Sorbonne, University of Paris; University of

Zurich, Ph.D., 1945. *Home:* Steingasse 31, Salzburg A5090, Austria. *Agent:* The Lantz Office, Inc., 114 East 55th St., New York, N.Y. 10022.

CAREER: Journalist; writer of documentary films for television, 1933, 1935, and 1960-62; Technical University of Berlin, West Berlin, West Germany, professor, 1968—. Cofounder of International Future Research Conferences, Oslo, Norway, 1967, Kyoto, Japan, 1970, and Bucharest, Hungary, 1972. *Member:* P.E.N. Club (West Germany branch), Gesellschaft fuer Zukunftsfragen (co-founder), Zentrum Berlin fuer Zukunftsforschung (co-founder). *Awards, honors:* Hachette Prize (Paris), 1958; publicist prize (West Germany), 1960; Prix de la Resistance (Liege), 1960; International Peace Prize, 1961; Golden Bolsche Medal (Stuttgart), 1970; German conservation prize, 1978.

WRITINGS—In English: Die Zukunft hat schon begonnen: Amerika's Allmacht und Ohnmacht (also see below), Scherz & Goverts, 1952, new edition, Scherz, 1969, translation by Marguerite Waldman published as *Tomorrow Is Already Here: Scenes From a Man-Made World,* Simon & Schuster, 1954; (author of introduction) Jean Pierhal, *Albert Schweitzer: das Leben eines guten Menschen,* Kindler, 1955, translation by Pierhal published as *Albert Schweitzer: The Story of His Life,* Philosophical Library, 1957; *Heller als tausend Sonnen: das Schicksal der Atomforscher* (also see below), Scherz & Govertz, 1956, translation by James Cleugh published as *Brighter Than a Thousand Suns: A Personal History of the Atomic Scientists,* Harcourt, 1958; *Strahlen aus der Asche: Geschichte einer Wiedergeburt* (also see below), Scherz, 1959, translation by Constantine Fitzgibbon published as *Children of the Ashes: The Story of a Rebirth,* Harcourt, 1961; *Die grosse Maschine,* Scherz, 1966, translation by Grace Marmor Spruch and Traude Wess published as *The Big Machine,* Scribner, 1968; (editor) *International Future Research Conference, 1st, Oslo, 1967,* Universitetsforlaget, 1969; *China and the West: Mankind Evolving,* Humanities Press, 1970; *The Challenge of Life: Biomedical Progress and Human Values,* Editiones Roche, 1972; *The Everyman Project: A World Report on the Resources From Humane Society,* Liveright, 1977; *The New Tyranny: How Nuclear Power Enslaves Us,* translated from the German by Christopher Trump, Grosset, 1979.

Other: Die Schweiz unter dem Pressekonklusum von 1823 bis 1829, Druckerei Mueh-Leroux, 1947; *Die Zunkunft hat schon begonnen, Heller als tausend Sonnen,* [and] *Strahlen aus der Asche* (also see above), Scherz, 1963; (editor with Hans Josef Mundt) *Modelle fuer eine neue Welt,* Desch, 1964; (editor with Mundt) *Der Griff nach der Zukunft: Planen und Freiheit,* Desch, 1964; (editor with Mundt) *Deutschland ohne Konzeption? Am Beginn einer neuen Epoche,* Desch, 1964; (editor) *Wege ins neue Jahrtausend: Wettkampf der Planungen in Ost und West,* Desch, 1964; (editor with Mundt) *Das umstrittene Experiment, der Mensch, Siebenundzwanzig wissenschaftler Diskutieren die Elemente einer biologischen Revolution,* Desch, 1966; *Bergedorfer Gespraechskreis zu Fragen der Freien Industriellen Gesellschaft,* Moegliche & Wuenschbare Zukuenfte, 1968; *Menschheitstraeume: Visionen veraendern die Wirklichkeit,* Schwann, 1969.

Technologie der Zukunft, Springer, 1970; (with Werner Filmer) *Terassentum und Sonnenhuegel,* Schwann, 1970; (with Hellmut Maurer) *Staedtebau-Alternativen '73,* Dipa, 1973; *Der sanfte Weg,* Verlag-Anstalt, 1976; *Die Grenzen der Resignation,* Hammer, 1977. Also author of phonorecord, "Models for the Future."

WORK IN PROGRESS: The Experts, a critique of the corruption of science.

SIDELIGHTS: In *Brighter Than a Thousand Suns,* Jungk described the development of the atomic bomb, going back to the very science-oriented Germany of the 1920's. "The extraordinary atmosphere of this idyllic time in modern science was beautifully evoked in Dr. Jungk's book," observed Jeremy Bernstein in the *New Yorker.* Jungk was harshly criticized, however, for inaccurately describing the way in which the atom bomb is built.

The Big Machine was different. In this book, Bernstein "found that [Jungk] has done a remarkable job—in terms of accuracy, soundness of observation, and even a sense of poetry in creating for the general reader a feeling of what doing modern physics is like." The "big machine" of the title refers to the proton synchroton, a twenty-eight-billion-electron-volt accelerator used to create the high energy nuclear particles that are necessary for controlled scientific study of the universe. The accelerator was built by the Conseil Europeen pour la Recherch Nuclcairc (CERN), a multinational science institute located near Geneva, Switzerland. The book gives the historical background of CERN and contains sketches of scientists involved in its projects. E. E. Morison described *The Big Machine* as a "concise textbook in the sociology of the new physics community and, in some sort, of all the communities of modern science."

Jungk told *CA* he "had to leave Germany in 1933 for racial and political reasons." He has been in exile ever since. His primary purpose, he wrote, is "to bridge nationalities, ideologies, science, and the arts."

BIOGRAPHICAL/CRITICAL SOURCES: New York Times Book Review, September 1, 1968; *Scientific American,* November, 1968; *New Yorker,* October 4, 1969; *Times Literary Supplement,* July 17, 1969; *New York Times,* June 8, 1979, July 6, 1979.

K

KAESTLE, Carl F(rederick) 1940-

PERSONAL: Born March 27, 1940, in Schenectady, N.Y.; son of Francis L. (an electrical engineer) and Regina (Perreault) Kaestle; married Elizabeth Mackenzie (an instructor in nursing), June 6, 1964; children: Frederika, Christine. *Education:* Yale University, B.A. (magna cum laude), 1962; graduate study at Columbia University, 1966-67; Harvard University, M.A.T., 1964, Ph.D., 1971. *Home:* 610 South Prospect Ave., Madison, Wis. 53711. *Office:* Department of Educational Policy Studies, University of Wisconsin, 223 Education Building, Madison, Wis. 53706.

CAREER: High school English teacher in Newton, Mass., 1962-63; American School of Warsaw, Warsaw, Poland, principal, 1964-66; University of Wisconsin—Madison, assistant professor, 1970-73, associate professor, 1973-77, professor of educational policy studies and history, 1977—, head of department of educational policy studies, 1978-79. Visiting fellow at Princeton University's Shelby Cullom Davis Center for Historical Studies, 1971-72, and Harvard University's Charles Warren Center for Studies in American History, 1974-75. Participant in seminars and conferences. *Member:* History of Education Society (member of board of directors, 1974-77), Social Science History Association (member of program committee, 1979). *Awards, honors:* National Institute of Education grant, 1973; Spencer Fellowship from National Academy of Education, 1974-79; Guggenheim fellowship, 1977-78; H. I. Romnes faculty fellowship, 1979—.

WRITINGS: The Evolution of an Urban School System: New York City, 1750-1850, Harvard University Press, 1973; *Joseph Lancaster and the Monitorial School Movement: A Documentary History,* Teachers College Press, 1973; (contributor) Lawrence Stone, editor, *Schooling and Society,* Johns Hopkins Press, 1976; (contributor) Tamara Hareven, editor, *Family Transitions and the Life Course in Historical Perspective,* Academic Press, 1978; (with Maris A. Vinovskis) *Education and Social Change in Nineteenth-Century Massachusetts,* Cambridge University Press, 1979; *Education in the New Republic: Schooling and American Society, 1780 to 1860,* Hill & Wang, in press. Contributor of articles and reviews to education, sociology, and history journals. Member of national advisory board, *School Review,* 1974—.

SIDELIGHTS: Kaestle told *CA:* "I am involved in local educational affairs, including support for an open classroom program in the public shcools. I play amateur jazz piano and am a relatively ignorant but enthusiastic opera enthusiast. After ten years of studying different aspects of schooling in early industrial England and America, I plan to indulge some other research interests, including the history of the nineteenth-century American family and the history of federal involvement in public education since 1940."

*   *   *

KAHNWEILER, Daniel-Henry 1884-1979
(Daniel Henry)

OBITUARY NOTICE—See index for *CA* sketch: Born June 25, 1884, in Mannheim, Germany; died January 11, 1979, in Paris, France. Art dealer, art historian, publisher, and author. Although educated for a career in banking, Kahnweiler became an art dealer in Paris in 1907. By 1914 he had become a reputable dealer in the work of such artists as Georges Braque, Andre Derain, and Pablo Picasso. It was Kahnweiler's friendship with Picasso, which lasted from 1907 until the artist's death in 1973, that gave his endeavors financial stability. Kahnweiler also established himself as a publisher of the work of young writers when he financed the printing of the first book by the French poet Guillaume Apollinaire. He was the author of numerous books on art and biographies of artists with whom he was associated through his galleries. Obituaries and other sources: *Art and Artists,* July, 1971; *International Who's Who,* Europa, 1978; *Who's Who in the World,* 4th edition, Marquis, 1978; *New York Times,* January 13, 1979.

*   *   *

KAISARI, Uri 1899(?)-1979

OBITUARY NOTICE: Born c. 1899 in Jaffa, Israel; died January 10, 1979, in Tel Aviv, Israel. Editor and journalist. Originator of the term "sabra" for Israel-born youths, Kaisari held editorial posts for several Israeli newspapers, including that of managing editor for *Doar Hayom.* He founded a social-political weekly in 1937 called *Nine in the Evening,* which was later sold and the name was changed to *Hoalam Hazeh.* Obituaries and other sources: *Detroit Jewish News,* January 19, 1979.

*   *   *

KAISER, Otto 1924-

PERSONAL: Born November 30, 1924, in Prenzlau, Germany; son of Oskar and Bertha (Boettcher) Kaiser; married Gertrud Stracke (a physician), August 31, 1962; children: Joachim, Marianne, Hans-Gerhard. *Education:* University of Tuebingen, D.Th., 1956, habilitation, 1957. *Religion:* Lutheran. *Home:* Auf dem Wuesten 10, Marburg 7, West Germany. *Office:* Faculty of Evangelical Theology, University of Marburg, Marburg, West Germany.

CAREER: Vicar in Baden-Wuerttemberg, West Germany, 1952-54; ordained Lutheran minister, 1953; University of Tuebingen, Tuebingen, Baden-Wuerttemberg, member of assistant faculty of evangelical theology, 1958-61; University of Marburg, Hess, West Germany, professor of Old Testament, 1961—, dean of theology faculty, 1963-64, 1969-70, 1970-71, 1976-77, head of faculty of evangelical theology, 1965-66. *Military service:* German Army, 1943-45; became lieutenant.

WRITINGS: Der Prophet Jesaja: Uebersetzt und erklaert (also see below), three volumes, Vandenhoeck & Ruprecht, 1963-73, translation by R. A. Wilson published in two volumes as *Isaiah 1-12: A Commentary,* Westminster, 1972, and *Isaiah 13-39: A Commentary,* Westminster, 1974; (with Werner Georg Kuemmel and Gottfried Adam) *Einfuerung in die exegetischen Methoden,* Christian Kaiser Verlag, 1963, 6th edition, 1979, translation by E.V.N. Goetchius published as *Exegetical Method: A Student's Handbook,* Seabury, 1963; *Einleitung in das Alte Testament: Eine Einfuerung in ihre Ergebnisse und Probleme,* Guetersloher Verlaghaus G. Mohn, 1969, 5th edition, 1978, translation by John Sturdy published as *Introduction to the Old Testament: A Presentation of Its Results and Problems,* Augsburg, 1975.

Other: *Die mythische Bedeutung des Meeres in Aegypten, Ugarit und Israel* (title means "The Mythical Signification of the Sea in Egypt, Ugarit and Israel"), A. Toepelmann, 1959, 2nd edition, 1962; *Der koenigliche Knecht: Eine traditionsgeschichtlich—exegetische Studie ueber die Ebed-Jahwe—Lieder bei Deuterojesaja* (title means "The Kingly Servant: An Exegetical Study on the Ebed-Yahwe-Songs in Deutero-Isaiah"), Vandenhoeck & Ruprecht, 1959, 2nd edition, 1962; (editor with Ernst Wuerthwein) *Tradition und Situation* (title means "Tradition and Situation"), Vandenhoeck & Ruprecht, 1963; (editor) *Theologische Wissenschaft* (title means "Theological Science"), Kohlhammer, 1972; (editor) *Denkender Glaube: Festschrift fuer Carl Heinz Ratschow* (title means "Thinking Belief"), de Gruyter, 1976; (with Eduard Lohse) *Tod und Leben* (title means "Death and Life"), Kohlhammer, 1977; (editor) *Gedenken an Rudolf Bultmann* (title means "Remembrance of Rudolf Bultmann"), Mohr, 1977; *Klagelieder* (title means "Lamentations"), publication by Vandenhoeck & Ruprecht, in press; *Jesaja 1-12* (title means "Isaiah Chapters 1-12"; also see above), Vandenhoeck & Ruprecht, in press. Also editor of *Mitherausgebar Juedisches Schriftum in hellenistisch-roemischer Zeit* (title means "Jewish Scriptures From Hellenistic and Roman Times"), 1973, and *Das Alte Testament Deutsch* (title means "The Old German Testament"), 1978. Contributor of nearly forty articles to theology and philosophy journals. "Kommentar zum Alten Testament" (title means "Commentary on the Old Testament"), co-editor, 1971, editor, 1977.

SIDELIGHTS: An English translation of *Tod und Leben* is expected to be published by Abingdon.

*   *   *

KALCHEIM, Lee 1938-

PERSONAL: Born June 27, 1938, in Philadelphia, Pa. *Edu-*

cation: Trinity College, B.A.; also attended Yale University Drama School. *Home:* 31 West Ninth St., New York, N.Y. 10011. *Agent:* Audrey Wood, International Creative Management, 40 West 57th St., New York, N.Y. 10019.

CAREER: Playwright. *Awards, honors:* Rockefeller grant, 1953; Emmy Award from Academy of Television Arts and Sciences, 1973.

WRITINGS—Plays: "A Party for Divorce," first produced in New York City, 1963; "Match Play" (first produced in New York City, 1964), published in *New Theatre in America,* edited by Edward Parone, Dell, 1965; "... And the Boy Who Came to Leave" (first produced in Minneapolis, 1965; produced in New York City, 1973), published in *Playwrights for Tomorrow: A Collection of Plays, Volume 2,* edited by Arthur H. Ballet, University of Minnesota Press, 1966; "An Audible Sigh," first produced in Waterbury, Conn., 1968.

"The Surprise Party," first produced in New York City, 1970; "Who Wants to Be the Lone Ranger," first produced in Los Angeles, 1971; (with Jeremiah Morris and Susan Perkins) "Hurry, Hurry," first produced in New York City, 1972; "The Prague Spring," first produced in Providence, 1975, produced in New York City, 1976; "Win With Wheeler," first produced in Waterford, Conn., 1975; "Winning Isn't Everything," first produced Off-Broadway at Hudson Guild Theatre, December 3, 1978.

Teleplays: "Reunion," 1967; "Let's Get a Closeup of the Messiah," 1969; "Trick or Treat," 1970; "Is (This) Marriage Really Necessary?," 1972; "The Class of '63," 1973; "The Bridge of Adam Rush," 1974. Contributor of scripts to the television series, "All in the Family," 1971-72.

SIDELIGHTS: Although many of Kalcheim's plays are noted for their accounts of human needs and emotions, his most recent play, "Winning Isn't Everything," is a comedy. Mel Gussow wrote, "With sight gags, one-liners, double-takes and more 'business' than at a checkout counter in a supermarket, 'Winning Isn't Everything' is programmed to please." He concluded that the "comedy is likable but undistinguished."

BIOGRAPHICAL/CRITICAL SOURCES: New York Times, December 4, 1978.*

*   *   *

KALLIFATIDES, Theodor 1938-

PERSONAL: Born March 12, 1938, in Molai, Greece; son of Dimitrios (a teacher) and Antonia (Kiriazakou) Kallifatides; married Gunilla Ander (a sociologist); children: Markus, Johanna. *Education:* University of Stockholm, B.A., 1967. *Home:* Bjoerkvaegen 12, Huddinge, Sweden 141 44. *Office:* Svenska Dagbladet, Raalambsvaegen 7, Stockholm, Sweden.

CAREER: University of Stockholm, Stockholm, Sweden, lecturer in philosophy, 1969-72; *Bonniers Litteraera Magazin,* Stockholm, Sweden, editor-in-chief, 1972-76; *Svenska Dagbladet,* Stockholm, Sweden, critic, 1976—. *Military service:* Greek Army, 1960-62. *Member:* International P.E.N., Union of Swedish Writers.

WRITINGS: Boender och Herrar, Bonniers, 1973, translation by Thomas Teal published as *Masters and Peasants,* Doubleday, 1977.

Other works: *Minnet i exil* (title means "Memory in Exile"), Bonniers, 1969; *Utlaenningar* (title means "Foreigners"), Bonniers, 1970; *Tiden aer inte oskyldig* (title means "Time Is not Innocent"), Bonniers, 1971; *Plogen och Svaerdet* (title means "The Plough and the Sword"), Bonniers, 1975; *Den Grymma Freden* (title means "The Atrocious Peace"), Bonniers, 1977; *Kaerleken* (title means "Love"), Bonniers, 1978. Editor of *Dikten finns oeverallt Prisma* (title means" Poetry Is Everywhere"), 1974.

Author of "Vad haender sedan, Ali?" (play; title means "What Happened Then, Ali?"), for Radio Sweden, 1971; "Jag heter Stelios" (screenplay; title means "My Name Is Stelios"), Swedish Filminstitutet, 1973.

WORK IN PROGRESS: A screenplay adapted from *Kaerleken.*

SIDELIGHTS: Kallifatides writes: "I emigrated to Sweden from Greece in 1964. I decided to write in Swedish instead of Greek, and that had a very significant impact on my work. I speak English, French, Greek, Swedish, Danish, and Norwegian. I have written more about my childhood and early youth in Greece than my adult life in Sweden. I have tried to understand the Greek way of thinking and living which among other things produced so many saints, heroes, torture experts, and dictators. I have had the dubious benefit of experiencing a world war, a civil war, and a couple of dictatorships. Writing in another language than my mother tongue was for me a means to greater freedom emotionally and to intellectual objectivity, and of course it was too a kind of intellectual challenge, I suppose."

AVOCATIONAL INTERESTS: Chess, prize-fighting.

* * *

KAMMAN, Madeleine M(arguerite Pin)   1930-

PERSONAL: Born November 22, 1930, in Courbevoie, France; came to United States in 1960; daughter of Charles Georges (an optometrist) and Simone Louise (Labarriere) Pin; married Alan B. Kamman (a business executive), February 15, 1960; children: Alan Daniel, Neil Charles. *Education:* Sorbonne, University of Paris, certificate, 1951; Paris Cordon Bleu, diploma, 1964; Ecole des Trois Gourmandes, diploma, 1968. *Home:* 454 Ward St., Newton Centre, Mass. 02159. *Agent:* Curtis Brown Ltd., 575 Madison Ave., New York, N.Y. 10022. *Office:* Modern Gourmet, Inc., 81-R Union St., Newton Centre, Mass. 02159.

CAREER: Hotel de voyageurs, Chateau la Valliere, Indre-et-Loire, France, cook's apprentice, 1940-55; Suissair, Paris, France, reservations manager, 1952-60; teacher of classic French cuisine in Cheltenham, Pa., 1962-64; owner and operator of Madeleine Kamman School of Traditional French Cuisine, 1964-69; Modern Gourmet, Inc. (cooking school and restaurant), Newton Centre, Mass., president, 1970—. Member of faculty at Northeastern University. *Member:* International Wine and Food Society, Escoffier Society Foundation, American Culinary Federation, Association des Restauratrices Cuisinieres. *Awards, honors:* Restaurant awards from *Holiday,* 1977, 1978, 1979.

WRITINGS: The Making of a Cook, Atheneum, 1971; *Dinner Against the Clock,* Atheneum, 1973; *When French Women Cook,* Atheneum, 1977. Contributor to *Family Circle* and to newspapers.

WORK IN PROGRESS: Chez la Mere Madeleine, a book on new cuisine in America, including recipes for all the dishes offered at Modern Gourmet's Restaurant.

SIDELIGHTS: Kamman told *CA:* "I have made it my mission to prove Paul Bocuse wrong in his statement that there is no place for women in professional kitchens. I also insist on the fact that chefs are nothing unless they are first and foremost gifted cooks or, if not naturally gifted, at least well-trained.

"My interest in *Cuisine de Femmes* (food prepared by women) is almost as old as I am. I have been trained by an extremely gifted woman cook and raised by another one. I have studied the food of French and Italian women all over the map of France and Italy in great depth and I insist that creativity in the kitchen comes not only in the masculine, but also in the feminine. Let women get the formal technical kitchen education that has been reserved for men for the three centuries that classic cuisine lasted and one will see their creativity develop. They have not done so badly after all with natural instinct. Anyone who knows the wealth of ideas of French provincial cooking will vouch for that."

AVOCATIONAL INTERESTS: Collecting eighteenth-century French porcelain and earthenware.

* * *

KAO, Charles C. L.   1932-

PERSONAL: Born February 29, 1932, in Kaohsiung, Taiwan; came to the United States in 1967; naturalized citizen, 1974; married; children: one. *Education:* Tainan Theological College, B.Th. (summa cum laude), 1955; graduate study at St. Andrew's College, Selly Oak, England, 1959-60, and Westminster College, Cambridge, England, 1960-61; Union Theological Seminary, New York, N.Y., S.T.M., 1962; Boston University, Ph.D., 1969; postdoctoral study at Harvard University, 1969-70. *Home:* 145 Winthrop Rd., Brookline, Mass. 02146.

CAREER: Tainan Theological College, Tainan, Taiwan, professor of religion, 1957-59, 1963-67; Emerson College, Boston, Mass., lecturer in philosophy, 1970, 1976; independent research scholar and writer, 1971—. Member of Hastings Center Institute of Society, Ethics, and the Life Sciences. Delegate to ecumenical gatherings in the United States and abroad. *Member:* Society for Health and Human Values, American Academy of Religion. *Awards, honors:* Cabot research grant, 1973-74.

WRITINGS: Search for Maturity, Westminster, 1975. Contributor to theology journals and religious magazines, including *Upper Room.*

WORK IN PROGRESS: A book about problems of pluralism, equality, and human rights based on psychological understanding of reality perception; a book on stages, themes, and experiences in the growing process, based on personal interviews, biographical studies, and established theories.

* * *

KAPLAN, Bess   1927-

PERSONAL: Born July 1, 1927, in Winnipeg, Manitoba, Canada; daughter of Jacob (a butcher) and Rachel (Dickter) Olin; married Phil Kaplan, February 11, 1951 (died August 12, 1976); children: Gerry, Allan, Elaine, Sheldon. *Education:* Attended junior high school in Winnipeg, Ontario. *Religion:* Jewish. *Home and office:* 9 O'Meara St., Winnipeg, Manitoba, Canada R2W 3Z1.

CAREER: Factory worker, 1943-51; writer, 1959—. *Member:* Canadian Authors Association (Winnipeg president, 1969-71), Penhandlers (president, 1973), B'nai B'rith. *Awards, honors:* Centennial award from Winnipeg branch of the Canadian Authors Association, 1969, for story "Rainy Day"; award, 1972, for article, "The Magic of Fiction"; Kathleen Strange Memorial Award from Winnipeg branch of the Canadian Authors Association, 1973; grant from Manitoba Arts Council, 1977.

WRITINGS: Corner Store (novel), Queenston House, 1976,

published as *The Empty Chair,* Harper, 1977; *Malke, Malke* (novel), Queenston House, 1977. Author of "The Better Years," a weekly humor column in *Winnipeg Free Press,* 1959-64. Contributor of articles and stories to Canadian magazines and newspapers, including *Chatelaine* and *Montrealer.* Editor of *Jewish Post,* 1973, 1974, and 1975.

WORK IN PROGRESS: Some Call Me God, a novel.

SIDELIGHTS: Bess Kaplan writes: "Some people go through life resisting writing. I have been a writer since the age of six. Of course I didn't know then that I was researching my subject—human beings—but when I began my first novel in 1964, it was all there in my head. That doesn't mean I find writing easy. It's a kind of madness of which I do not want to be cured.

"What motivates me? Sometimes anger. My third novel began when the United Nations passed a resolution that Zionism is racism. It will be my only angry novel—if I can only stop fiddling with it and decide it's finished.

"All my novels have a Jewish viewpoint. I feel I have a calling to speak up for my people. My parents were a young bride and groom when they fled the Ukraine in 1921, when pogroms against the Jews were a common and regular occurrence. My grandparents were killed in the Ukraine when their village burned to the ground during the Holocaust years.

"I am preoccupied with young writers. I set up the Young Writers Short Story Contest for my branch of the Canadian Authors Association in 1971, and have been its judge since that time. Each year I think: 'That's it. Now someone else has to do it.' But I keep doing it. I've also gone into classrooms, when invited, and talked with students about writing.

"When I was small, I dreamed of being a famous and rich author when I grew up. I'm grown up now and still dreaming of it."

AVOCATIONAL INTERESTS: Oil painting, travel (including Israel).

BIOGRAPHICAL/CRITICAL SOURCES: Winnipeg Tribune, December 13, 1975, June 23, 1976; *Winnipeg Guide,* March 9, 1977; *Regina Leader-Post,* June 15, 1977; *Winnipeg Free Press,* July 22, 1977; *Star-Phoenix,* August 5, 1977; *Canadian Jewish News,* December 16, 1977.

*   *   *

KAPLAN, Sidney 1913-

PERSONAL: Born March 1, 1913, in New York, N.Y.; son of Henry and Dora (Kuhl) Kaplan; married Emma Nogrady (a librarian), May 6, 1933; children: Cora Lotte Kaplan Lushington, Paul H. D. *Education:* City College (now of the City University of New York), B.A., 1940; Boston University, M.A., 1947; Harvard University, Ph.D., 1960. *Home:* 10 Hampton Terrace, Northampton, Mass. 01060.

CAREER: University of Massachusetts, Amherst, instructor, 1946-51, assistant professor, 1951-56, associate professor, 1956-60, professor of American literature and black studies, 1960-68; writer. Fulbright lecturer and visiting lecturer at University of Thessaloniki, Greece, University of Zagreb, Yugoslavia, and University of Kent, England. Consultant to National Portrait Gallery and Smithsonian Institution. *Military service:* U.S. Army, 1942-45; became first lieutenant. *Awards, honors:* Bancroft Award from Association for the study of Negro life and history, 1950, for article "The Miscegenation Issue of the Election of 1864."

WRITINGS: (Editor) Edgar Allan Poe, *The Narrative of A.*

Gordon Pym, Hill & Wang, 1960; (editor) Herman Melville, *Battle-Pieces and Aspects of the War,* Scholar's Facsimiles & Reprints, 1960, revised edition, University of Massachusetts Press, 1972; *The Portrayal of the Negro in American Painting,* Bowdoin College, 1964; (contributor) J. E. Hardy and S. L. Gross, editors, *The Image of the Negro in American Literature,* University of Chicago Press, 1967; (editor) Samuel Sewall, *The Selling of Joseph: A Memorial,* Gehenna Press, 1968; (editor with Jules Chametzky, and contributor) *Black and White in American Culture: An Anthology From the Massachusetts Review,* University of Massachusetts Press, 1969; *The Black Presence in the Era of the American Revolution, 1770-1800,* Smithsonian Institution Press, 1973. Contributor of about forty articles and reviews to history, literature, and black studies journals.

WORK IN PROGRESS: With wife, Emma Nogrady Kaplan, "The Black Presence in the U.S.A.: Constitution to Emancipation," an exhibition for the National Portrait Gallery.

SIDELIGHTS: Kaplan commented: "The inter-relationships of society, literature, and art in the United States have been my continuing scholarly concern."

*   *   *

KAPOOR, Ashok 1940-

PERSONAL: Born November 21, 1940, in Lahore, India; came to United States in 1960, naturalized citizen, 1970; son of Chaman Lal (in business) and Rani (Mehra) Kapoor; married Catherine Murray (an art collector), April 15, 1967; children: Sonya, Celina. *Education:* St. Stephen's College, Delhi, India, B.A. (honors), 1960; graduate study at Davidson College, 1961; University of North Carolina, M.B.A., 1962, Ph.D., 1966. *Home:* 65 Philip Dr., Princeton, N.J. 08540. *Office:* Graduate School of Business Administration, New York University, 100 Trinity Pl., New York, N.Y. 10006.

CAREER: New York University, New York, N.Y., assistant professor, 1966-70, associate professor, 1970-73, professor of marketing and international business, 1974—. Member of board of directors of International Schools Services; speaker at professional meetings all over the world; consultant to business, public, and government institutions, including United Nations, World Bank, and Agency for International Development. *Member:* Academy of International Business.

WRITINGS: International Business Negotiations: A Study in India, New York University Press, 1970; (with Robert McKay) *Managing International Markets,* Darwin Press, 1971; (with Philip D. Grub) *The Multinational Enterprise in Transition,* Darwin Press, 1972; (with Jean Boddewyn) *International Business-Government Relations,* American Management Association, 1973; (with Boddewyn, John Fayerweather, and others) *World Business Systems and Environment,* International Textbook Co., 1973; *The New Middle East and Foreign Investments,* Darwin Press, 1975; (with Boddewyn and Jack N. Behrman) *International Business-Government Communication,* Heath, 1975; (with Felipe Alfonso, Seijiro Matsumura, and Masaru Sakuma) *Planning for International Business Negotiations,* Ballinger, 1975; (with Fayerweather) *Strategy and Negotiation for the International Corporation,* Ballinger, 1976; (editor) *Asian Business and Foreign Investments,* Darwin Press, 1976; (editor and contributor) *International Business Development and the Middle East,* Westview Press, 1978. Contributor to business journals.

WORK IN PROGRESS: Negotiating With Governments:

U.S. Corporate Experience in the Developing Countries, research on the emergence of non-traditional flows of trade and investment, and on negotiating with governments of developing countries.

SIDELIGHTS: Kapoor writes: "It is imperative that we attempt to understand the many and complex forces influencing motivations of individuals in different countries. At a minimum it requires viewing a situation from a perspective of a person from a particular society."

* * *

KAPUR, Harish 1929-

PERSONAL: Born February 21, 1929, in Jhelum, Pakistan; son of Trikol Chand and Yashoda (Khanna) Kapur; married Carmen Stofer (separated); children: Sunita. Education: University of Bombay, B.A., 1947, M.A., 1949, LL.B., 1951; University of Geneva, Ph.D., 1965. Religion: Hindu. Residence: Switzerland. Office: Graduate Institute of International Studies, 132 Rue de Lausanne, Geneva, Switzerland.

CAREER: United Nations, New York, N.Y., assistant legal adviser to the high commissioner for refugees in Geneva, Switzerland, 1957-61; Harvard University, Cambridge, Mass., research associate at Russian Research Center, 1961-62; Graduate Institute of International Studies, Geneva, Switzerland, 1962—, began as assistant professor, became associate professor, then professor of international studies, director of Asian Centre, 1977—. Special adviser to United Nations high commissioner for refugees, 1971-72. President of scientific council of Asian Documentation and Research Center, 1972-77.

WRITINGS: (Contributor) Kurt London, editor, A Half Century of Soviet Policy, [Baltimore], 1962; Soviet Russia and Asia, 1917-1927: A Study of Soviet Policy Towards Turkey, Iran, and Afghanistan, M. Joseph, 1966; The Soviet Union and the Emerging Nations: A Case Study of Soviet Policy Toward India, M. Joseph, 1972; The Embattled Triangle: Moscow, Peking, New Delhi, Abhinav Publications, 1973; China in World Politics, India International Centre, 1977; (contributor) Sijthoff and Noordhoff, International Relations in a Changing World, [Leiden], 1977. Contributor to history and international studies journals.

WORK IN PROGRESS: The Awakening Giant: China's Ascension in World Politics, publication expected in 1979; China and the Third World, publication expected in 1980; The Third World in the International System, publication expected in 1981.

SIDELIGHTS: Kapur writes: "My general interest in history and international affairs has marked my academic career. Though with the passage of time I have developed a particular interest in literature, my principal interest is international politics."

* * *

KARLIN, Muriel Schoenbrun

PERSONAL: Born in New York, N.Y.; daughter of Henry B. and Frieda (Berger) Schoenbrun; married Leonard Karlin, September 5, 1945; children: Henry Edward, Lisa Yvonne. Education: Brooklyn College (now of the City University of New York), B.A., 1945; New York University, M.A., 1946. Home: 63 Haven Esplanade, Staten Island, N.Y. 10301.

CAREER: Junior high school teacher of general science in Staten Island, N.Y., 1958-63, education and vocational counselor, 1963-66, assistant principal, 1966; writer and consultant, 1966—. Director of Muriel S. Karlin Counseling Services.

WRITINGS: (With Regina Berger) Successful Methods for Teaching the Slow Learner, Parker Publishing, 1969; (with Berger) Survival Instructions for the Teacher, Cawther Press, 1970; (with Berger) Experiential Learning: An Effective Teaching Program for Elementary Schools, Parker Publishing, 1971; (with Berger) The Effective Student Activities Program, Parker Publishing, 1971; (with Berger) Discipline and the Disruptive Child: A Practical Guide for Elementary Teachers, Parker Publishing, 1972; Administrator's Guide to a Practical Career Education Program, Parker Publishing, 1974; (with Berger) Individualizing Instruction: A Complete Guide for Diagnosis, Planning, Teaching, and Evaluation, Parker Publishing, 1974; Administering and Teaching Sex Education in the Elementary School, Parker Publishing, 1975; (with M. Margolis) Pathways to Careers, Globe Book Co., 1975; Classroom Activities Desk Book for Fun and Learning, Parker Publishing, 1975; Solving Your Career Mystery (juvenile), Richards Rosen, 1975; Teacher's Handbook of Special Learning Problems and How to Handle Them, Parker Publishing, 1977; Illustrated Treasury of Classroom Activities, Parker Publishing, 1980. Author of "Focus on Education," a column in Staten Island Advance. Contributor to education journals. Editor of Career Education Workshop.

SIDELIGHTS: Karlin told CA: "My prime interest at this time is in careers, career counseling, and guidance. I also write travel material for the Staten Island Advance, having toured many parts of the world."

* * *

KARNES, Merle B(riggs) 1916-

PERSONAL: Born August 5, 1916, in Chaffee, Mo.; divorced; children: two. Education: Southeast Missouri State College, B.S., 1937; University of Missouri, M.S., 1941, Ed.D., 1949; postdoctoral study at University of Illinois, 1949. Home: 2105 Grange Dr., Urbana, Ill. 61801. Office: Institute for Child Behavior and Development, College of Education, University of Illinois at Urbana-Champaign, 403 East Healey St., Champaign, Ill. 61820.

CAREER: Elementary school teacher in Chaffee, Mo., 1937-38, Leadwood, Mo., 1938-40, and Webster Groves, Mo., 1941-42; high school teacher in Elizabethtown, Ky., 1943-45; elementary school teacher in Monterey, Calif., 1945-46, and Champaign, Ill., 1948-50; director of preschool program for the mentally handicapped in Champaign, Ill., 1950-53, director of special services, 1953-65; University of Illinois at Urbana-Champaign, Champaign, professor of education, 1965—, director of research and development program for culturally disadvantaged preschool children and their families, 1965-69, director of precise early education of children with handicaps, 1970, director of retrieval and acceleration of promising young disadvantaged, 1971-73, and retrieval and acceleration of promising young handicapped and talented, 1975, director of resource access project, 1976. Member of advisory board of Educational Resources Information Center for the Handicapped, 1973-74.

MEMBER: Council for Exceptional Children (member of executive board; governor-at-large; chairman of publications committee), National Council for Administrators of Special Education (president), American Educational Research Association, National Association for the Education of Young Children, Association for the Gifted (TAG), National Association for Gifted Children, American Association for the Education of the Severely/Profoundly Handicapped, Illinois Council for Exceptional Children (president), Illinois Council of Administrators of Special Education (president). *Awards, honors:* Citation from University of Missouri, 1959; special award from American Psychological Association, 1970; J. E. Wallace Wallin Award from Council for Exceptional Children, 1973; citation from Illinois Association of School Administrators, 1973; Caritas Award from Caritas Society, 1976; H.D.L. from Eastern Kentucky University, 1977.

WRITINGS: (With G. Drennen, I. Garrison, and others) *A Guide: Directing the Education for Exceptional Children in Local School Systems,* Illinois State Department of Education, 1956; *Prevocational Services for Handicapped Youth,* Division of Public Instruction, State of Illinois, 1961; (co-author) *A Guide to Supervision of Special Education,* Illinois Council of Administrators of Special Education, 1965; (co-author) *A Guideline for Cooperative Vocational Service for Handicapped Youth at the High School Level,* Illinois Commission on Children, 1965; *An Approach for Working With Parents of Disadvantaged Children: A Pilot Project,* Institute for Research on Exceptional Children, 1966; (with J. P. Wollersheim, R. L. Stoneburger, and A. S. Hodgins) *A Comparative Study of Two Preschool Programs for Culturally Disadvantaged Children: A Highly Structured and a Traditional Program,* Institute for Research on Exceptional Children, 1966; (with S. A. Kirk and W. D. Kirk) *You and Your Retarded Child,* revised edition, Pacific Books, 1968.

Early Childhood Enrichment Series, Volume I: *Development of Perceptual Skills,* Volume II: *Development of Language Skills,* Volume III: *Development of Number Readiness,* Volume IV: *Development of Reading Readiness,* with educational toys and games, Milton Bradley Co., 1970; (with R. R. Zehrbach and G. R. Jones) *The Culturally Disadvantaged Student and Guidance* (monograph), Houghton, 1971; *GOAL: Language Development,* Milton Bradley Co., 1972; (co-author) *Helping Young Children Develop Language Skills: A Handbook of Activities,* revised edition, Council for Exceptional Children, 1973; *GOAL: Mathematical Concepts,* Milton Bradley Co., 1973; *Karnes Early Language Activities,* GEM, Inc., 1975; (editor with A. H. Hayden, J. B. Jordan, and M. M. Wood, and contributor) *Early Childhood Education for Exceptional Children: A Handbook of Ideas and Exemplary Practices,* Council for Exceptional Children, 1977; *Creative Games for Learning: Games for Parents and Teachers to Make,* Council for Exceptional Children, 1977; *Learning Language at Home,* Council for Exceptional Children, 1977; *GOAL II: Language Development,* Milton Bradley Co., 1977; (with R. Lee) *What Research and Experience Tells the Teacher of Exceptional Children: Early Childhood* (monograph), Council for Exceptional Children, 1978.

Contributor: E. Paul Torrance and Robert D. Strom, editors, *Mental Health and Achievement,* Wiley, 1965; Anne Adams, editor, *Threshold Learning Abilities,* Macmillan, 1972; R. K. Parker, editor, *The Preschool in Action: Exploring Early Childhood Programs,* Allyn & Bacon, 1972, revised edition (edited by Parker and Mary Carol Day), 1977; June B. Jordan and Rebecca F. Daily, editors, *Not All Little Wagons Are Red: The Exceptional Child's Early Years,* Council for Exceptional Children, 1973; Julian C. Stanley, editor, *Compensatory Education for Children, Ages Two to Eight,* Johns Hopkins Press, 1973; Sally Ryan, editor, *A Report on Longitudinal Evaluations of Preschool Programs,* Volume I, Children's Bureau, Office of Child Development,

U.S. Department of Health, Education & Welfare, 1974; Lynn Gunn, editor, *Outreach: Replicating Services for Young Handicapped Children,* Technical Assistance Development System, 1975; J. J. Gallagher, editor, *The Application of Child Development Research to Exceptional Children,* Council for Exceptional Children, 1975; *Alternatives for Teaching Exceptional Children: Essays from Focus on Exceptional Children,* Love Publishing, 1975; M. L. Maehr and W. M. Stallings, editors, *Culture, Child, and School-Socio-Cultural Influences on Learning,* Brooks/Cole, 1975; Bernard Spodek and Herbert Walberg, editors, *Early Childhood Education: Issues and Insights,* McCutchan, 1977; (author of foreword) C. J. Maker, *Providing Programs for the Gifted Handicapped,* Council for Exceptional Children, 1977. Author of readers, workbooks, and teacher's manuals. Contributor of more than fifty articles and reviews to education, special education, and psychology journals.

* * *

KASTNER, Joseph 1907-

PERSONAL: Born March 28, 1907, in Brooklyn, N.Y.; son of Aron (a restaurateur) and Fani (Blutreich) Kastner; married Barbara Harris, August 25, 1934; children: Jonathan Barth, Matthew Harris. *Education:* Attended City College (now of the City University of New York), 1924-26; Yale University, Ph.B., 1930. *Politics:* Democrat. *Religion:* Jewish. *Home and office:* 199 River Rd., Grandview, N.Y. 10960.

CAREER: Worked as copy boy in New York City, 1924; *New York World,* New York City, reporter, 1930; *New Yorker,* New York City, reporter, 1930; staff writer for *Fortune,* 1930-36; *Life,* New York City, staff writer, 1936-44, copy editor, 1944-69, consulting editor, 1969-71; free-lance writer, 1971—. *Member:* Authors Guild of Authors League of America. *Awards, honors:* National Book Award nomination in history, 1978, for *A Species of Eternity.*

WRITINGS: (With James Crockett) *Evergreens,* Time-Life, 1975; *Hector Berlioz,* Time-Life, 1976; *A Species of Eternity,* Knopf, 1977, published in England as *A World of Naturalists,* J. Murray, 1978. Contributor to magazines, including *Smithsonian* and *Horticulture,* and newspapers.

WORK IN PROGRESS: A History of Maize; Three Nineteenth-Century Diarists.

BIOGRAPHICAL/CRITICAL SOURCES: *Library Journal,* October 1, 1977; *Christian Science Monitor,* December 8, 1977; *New York Times Book Review,* January 22, 1978, March 27, 1978.

* * *

KATZ, Jane B(resler) 1934-

PERSONAL: Born December 18, 1934, in New York, N.Y.; daughter of Harvey J. (a teacher and writer) and Blix (an actress; maiden name, Ruskay) Bresler; married S. Jack Katz (a lawyer), February, 1959; children: Marc, Mari. *Education:* Adelphi College (now University), B.A., 1955; University of Minnesota, B.S., 1961. *Home:* 817 North Tyrol Tr., Minneapolis, Minn. 55416.

CAREER: Free-lance writer. Writer of magazine copy and publicity for radio and television, 1955-60; high school English teacher in Robbinsdale, Minn., 1961-66; high school teacher in Minneapolis, Minn., 1966-69. *WRITINGS:* (Editor) *We Rode the Wind: Recollections of Nineteenth-Century Tribal Life,* Lerner, 1975; *Let Me Be a Free Man: A Documentary History of Indian Resistance,*

Lerner, 1975; *I Am the Fire of Time: The Voices of Native American Women*, Dutton, 1977, 2nd edition, 1978. Author of radio scripts for "People Worth Hearing About," a series of documentary plays on the lives of American Indian leaders of the past and present, aired by KUOM-Radio, 1971.

WORK IN PROGRESS: This Song Remembers: Self-Portraits of Native Americans in the Arts, publication expected in 1980; oral history of American Indians, Aleuts, and Eskimos.

SIDELIGHTS: Katz writes: "I'm interested in oral history and ethnic literature. Oral history provides insight into an individual's and a people's traditions, emotional and spiritual life, their experiences and response to experience. It is as important as written history. The Indian's voice has been too long unheard.

"This is a multi-ethnic society. The most honest, and often the most lyrical, writing is coming from ethnic writers. I'd like to see them included in the mainstream of American literature. My role is to give them that recognition.

"I love a multi-media approach. My recent books interweave poetry, prose, oral history, and visual material."

* * *

KATZ, Jonathan 1938-

PERSONAL: Born February 2, 1938, in New York, N.Y.; son of Bernard (an advertising art director) and Phyllis (a magazine editor; maiden name, Brownstowne) Katz. *Education:* Attended Antioch College, 1956-57, City College of New York (now City College of the City University of New York), 1957-60, and New School for Social Research. *Home:* 51 Bank St., New York, N.Y. 10014. *Agent:* Joan Raines, Raines & Raines, 475 Fifth Ave., New York, N.Y. 10017.

CAREER: Prince Studio, New York City, free-lance textile designer, 1960-65; New Group, Inc., New York City, partner and free-lance textile designer, 1965-70; Henry Glass, Inc., New York City, textile designer 1970-72, 1976. Writer, 1967—. *Member:* National Gay Archives and Library Committee, Gay Academic Union. *Awards, honors:* Two Louis M. Rabinowitz Foundation grants, one to research and write a play ("Inquest at Christiana") for radio, 1967, and another to continue research on the American history of homosexual oppression and resistance, 1976; annual gay book award from American Library Association, 1975, for general editorship of "Homosexuality: Lesbians and Gay Men in Society, History, and Literature."

WRITINGS—Plays: "The Dispute Over the Ownership of Anthony Burns," produced on WBAI-FM, New York City, 1967; "Inquest at Christiana," produced on WBAI-FM, New York City, 1968; *Coming Out! A Documentary Play About Gay Life and Liberation in the U.S.A.* (two-act; first produced in New York at the Gay Activists' Alliance, June 16, 1972; produced Off-Broadway at Nighthouse Theatre, June, 1973), Arno, 1975.

Books: (With father, Bernard Katz) *Black Woman: A Fictionalized Biography of Lucy Terry Prince* (story of an eighteenth-century slave), Pantheon, 1973; *Resistance at Christiana: The Fugitive Slave Rebellion, Christiana, Pennsylvania, September 11, 1851; A Documentary Account*, Crowell, 1974; *Gay American History: Lesbians and Gay Men in the U.S.A.; A Documentary*, Crowell, 1976.

Also researcher and editor of phonograph record scripts, including "Black Pioneers, Volumes I and II," Caedmon Records, 1968-69, and an unproduced record, "Red Man/White Man: Documents of Conflict," Caedmon Records. General editor of "Homosexuality: Lesbians and Gay Men in Society, History, and Literature" series, Arno, 1975. Contributor of reviews to *Nation* and *Body Politic*.

WORK IN PROGRESS: A second volume on lesbian and gay male American history.

SIDELIGHTS: Katz's approach to history has favored the documentary method. His *Resistance at Christiana* examines a major but not well-known episode in black American history—the 1851 confrontation between fugitive slaves and a Maryland slave owner and his posse. Relying heavily on the words and observations of those involved, Katz produced what one reviewer called "the best account of the collective and successful resistance by black people to fugitive slave hunters following passage of the infamous Fugitive Slave Act of 1850.... [He] has added an important, though long neglected chapter to the scholarly recreation of black history." His next book, *Gay American History*, anthologizes large amounts of primary historical documents about homosexuality in the United States. The book incorporates hundreds of letters, diaries, interviews, and legal documents, most of which were previously buried in libraries and archives. Katz reconstructs, among other histories, a 400-year period of conflict between homosexuals and American society, homosexuality in American Indian culture, and the resistance mounted by early organizations in the homosexual emancipation movement. Regina Kahney wrote: "By limiting his scope to material relevant to gay *American* history, Katz has avoided duplication of past works and compiled a uniquely contemporary volume of invaluable reference."

BIOGRAPHICAL/CRITICAL SOURCES: Best Sellers, July 15, 1974; *Choice*, October, 1974; *American History Review*, February, 1976; *Publishers Weekly*, June 21, 1976; *Village Voice*, December 6, 1976; *Book World*, January 30, 1977; *Booklist*, October 15, 1977.

* * *

KATZ, William 1940-

PERSONAL: Born March 18, 1940, in New York, N.Y.; son of Herbert (a sales executive) and Sylvia (Dulberg) Katz; married Jane Reckseit (a researcher), December 11, 1966; children: Sharon Elizabeth, Abigail Eve. *Education:* University of Chicago, A.B., 1961; Columbia University, M.S., 1962. *Residence:* New York, N.Y. *Agent:* Peter Lampack, Peter Lampack Agency, 551 Fifth Ave., Room 2015, New York, N.Y. 10017.

CAREER: U.S. Central Intelligence Agency, McLean, Va., intelligence officer, 1962-63; Hudson Institute, Harmon-on-Hudson, N.Y., assistant to director, 1964-65; *New York Times*, New York, N.Y., assistant to associate editor and member of editorial staff of *New York Times Magazine*, 1965-70; free-lance writer, 1970—. *Military service:* U.S. Army Reserve, 1963-69. *Member:* Writers Guild of America, Authors League of America, Dramatists Guild.

WRITINGS—Novels: *North Star Crusade*, Putnam, 1976; *Death Dreams*, Ballantine, 1979; *Ghost Flight*, Dell, 1980.

Television scripts: (With Edward Adler) "Nicky's World," Columbia Broadcasting System (CBS-TV), 1974; "The Spy Who Returned From the Dead," American Broadcasting Companies (ABC-TV), 1974; "Nightmare at 43 Hillcrest," ABC-TV, 1974.

WORK IN PROGRESS: Visions of Terror, the second in the "Death Dreams" series; a political thriller, centered around a Russian attempt to neutralize an American technological breakthrough.

SIDELIGHTS: William Katz's novels have been published in Spanish, Italian, Norwegian, Swedish, Japanese, and French. The motion picture rights to *North Star Crusade* have been acquired by Sir Lew Grade.

Katz writes: "My novels usually involve events that 'can't happen,' according to the presumed experts. In *North Star Crusade* a small group seizes a nuclear submarine, although its security system is considered foolproof. In *Death Dreams* the evidence that a woman is hovering in a spiritual afterlife is rejected by every 'respected' physician. My next book deals with a historical figure whose demise has been certified by all important scholars. He suddenly reappears. Thus the suspense operates on two levels: determining whether an event is actually happening, then dealing with the threat it represents.

"I'm primarily a storyteller. I write stories for their intrinsic value, not as vehicles for profound messages. However, my own point of view is usually expressed by one of the characters. I do not hesitate to put my opinion in the mouth of an unpopular character if that will serve the story.

"One thread that has coincidentally run through my books is the fallacy that anyone can be fully 'trained' to handle a crisis. Education and experience have their places, but my heroes (and heroines) are usually those who have added heavy doses of imagination, common sense, and the human spirit to their university degrees. As I saw in my brief government service, and later in journalism, education and wisdom are not necessarily related, and this observation has affected the behavior of my characters."

AVOCATIONAL INTERESTS: Politics (especially international relations and strategic studies), history (especially twentieth-century history), music, ballet, photography, travel (Europe, the Middle East).

*   *   *

KAUFMAN, Daniel 1949-

PERSONAL: Born May 4, 1949, in New York, N.Y.; son of Matthew (an orthodontist) and Ruth (a writer; maiden name, Lyons) Kaufman; married Jane Goldstein (a therapist), September, 1977. *Education:* Amherst College, B.A., 1973. *Home:* 103 Church St., Watertown, Mass. 02172. *Agent:* Helen Merrill, 337 West 22nd St., New York, N.Y. 10011.

CAREER: Photographer for Polaroid Corp., 1970-78; freelance photographer and writer, 1978—. *Awards, honors:* Fulbright grant, 1977.

WRITINGS: Natural Sleep, Rodale Press, 1978; *How to Get Out of Debt,* Pinnacle Books, 1978.

SIDELIGHTS: Kaufman writes that he is a specialist in stress-release techniques, natural healing, and drugless treatments.

*   *   *

KEINZLEY, Frances 1922-

PERSONAL: Surname is pronounced *Kinz*-ley; born May 26, 1922, in Portadown, Ireland; daughter of Thomas (a soldier) and Mary Jane Keinzley; married Arthur Allan Hunt (an electrical engineer), March 2, 1945; children: Alannah, Regan, Clancy, Shannon. *Education:* Attended parochial schools in Auckland, Australia. *Religion:* Roman Catholic. *Residence:* Auckland, New Zealand. *Agent:* Curtis Brown Ltd., 1 Craven Hill, London, England.

CAREER: Writer, 1960—. *Military service:* New Zealand Women's Army Auxiliary Corps, 1944; served in Pacific

theater. *Awards, honors:* New Zealand Award of Achievement, 1960, for *Tangahano.*

WRITINGS: Tangahano (novel), P. Davies, 1960; *A Time to Prey* (novel), W. H. Allen, 1969, Stein & Day, 1970; *Illusion* (novel), W. H. Allen, 1970; *Cottage at Chapelyard* (novel), Bobbs-Merrill, 1975. Also author of *The Toymaker.* Author of "Touche," a column.

WORK IN PROGRESS: Studying eighteenth-century Spain.

SIDELIGHTS: Frances Keinzley's books have been published in eight countries in Finnish, Norwegian, Danish, Swedish, German, and Spanish.

She writes: "I'm an ordinary person living an ordinary life to the best of my ability. I probably couldn't cope with any earth-shaking excitements even if they happened. I have travelled extensively, but prefer the quiet predictable life. From the time I could think independently my tastes have been flexible, and my standards rigid. Between these two poles lie vast encompassing latitudes of mental, intellectual, and creative freedoms.

"It is my opinion that a novelist who can claim his or her book is a spotlight on any particular facet of Life in a modern society is an extraordinarily clever person. I lean to the belief that one has to stand off at a distance to see anything in its true perspective—as an artist has to do when he stands off from his easel; as a woman trying on a special dress has to do when she stands off from her mirror; as any viewer has to do who goes to the top of the hill to see the valley below. One cannot stand close to an object or era and say categorically: 'I see this clearly when I stand in the centre of it.' One, with the best will in the world, can give only a blurred-edged impressionist account.

"Personally, as a novelist, if I start to put a book together I do so because I believe I have the ingredients of a good story. I believe most writers start off with this conception and that it is the reviewers and the critics who turn it into a literary 'baby' to be adored and indulged—or abandoned.

"As a writer I have been very surprised at what some reviewers have read between the lines of my writing. I like to think those readers who pay me the compliment of reading me, read their own significances and insignificances in what I write. After all, the writer and the reader are the parents, and reviewer the midwife at the birth and as such is bound to give a clinical account of an otherwise very personal happening.

"I truly cannot take writing books as seriously as it seems conventional to do."

*   *   *

KEITH, Jean E. 1921-1979

OBITUARY NOTICE: Born January 11, 1921, in Elizabethtown, Ky.; died of cancer, March 16, 1979, in Louisville, Ky. Historian and author. Keith was actively involved in the preservation of historic landmarks in Alexandria, Va., and in several of the city's civic organizations, including the Alexandria Bicentennial Commission. For twenty-three years he served as historian with the U.S. Army Corps of Engineers and co-authored a book on the army's official history of World War II. He also wrote several books, including *Historic Alexandria, Virginia, Street by Street* and *Sand Mountains and Sawgrass Marshes.* Obituaries and other sources: *Directory of American Scholars,* Volume I: *History,* 7th edition, Bowker, 1974; *Washington Post,* March 18, 1979.

KELCH, Ray Alden 1923-

PERSONAL: Born September 13, 1923, in Logan, Ohio; son of Albert Robison and Clara (Lindsey) Kelch. *Education:* Ohio State University, A.B., 1947, M.A., 1949, Ph.D., 1955. *Politics:* Democrat. *Religion:* Episcopalian. *Home:* 171 Melrose Ave., San Francisco, Calif. 94127. *Office:* Department of History, San Francisco State University, San Francisco, Calif. 94132.

CAREER: Stephens University, Columbia, Mo., instructor in history, 1953-57; San Francisco State University, San Francisco, Calif., 1957—, began as assistant professor, became professor of history, 1964, head of department, 1964-70. Visiting professor at Arizona State University, Tempe, 1970-71. *Military service:* U.S. Army, 1943-46. *Member:* American Historical Association, Conference on British Studies, American Association of University Professors.

WRITINGS: Newcastle, a Duke Without Money: Thomas Pelham-Holles, 1693-1768, University of California Press, 1974.

WORK IN PROGRESS: A biography of Edmund Herbert (1684-1769), deputy paymaster of the Royal Marines.

BIOGRAPHICAL/CRITICAL SOURCES: Economist, March 9, 1974; *Times Literary Supplement,* March 29, 1974.

*   *   *

KELLY, Emmett (Leo) 1898-1979

OBITUARY NOTICE: Born December 9, 1898, in Sedan, Kan.; died of a heart attack, March 28, 1979, in Sarasota, Fla. Clown, cartoonist, and author. Emmett Kelly was known the world over as Weary Willie, the mournful clown. Dressed in a tattered suit, tie, and hat, and wearing a sad smile under a growth of beard, bushy eyebrows, and unkempt hair, Willie would make audiences laugh at his pathetic condition. Among his favorite acts were competition with the elusive spotlight and staring at someone in the audience while he sat munching a cabbage leaf. Kelly created the character of Weary Willie while working as a cartoonist with an advertising film company in Kansas City. Though he had also worked in circuses as a trapeze artist, Kelly finally concentrated on being a clown in 1931, when he began to develop the character of Willie. He was instantly popular and worked with the Ringling Brothers and Barnum & Bailey Circus from 1942 to 1956. Later he appeared in nightclubs, musicals, and movies, and became one of the most familiar clowns in America. Kelly wrote an autobiography, *Clown,* in 1954. Obituaries and other sources: *Current Biography,* Wilson, 1954; *Who's Who in America,* 40th edition, Marquis, 1978; Lowell Swortzell, *Here Come the Clowns,* Viking, 1978; *New York Times,* March 29, 1979.

*   *   *

KEMPNER, S. Marshall 1898-

PERSONAL: Born December 30, 1898, in New York, N.Y.; son of Adolph K. and Addie (Oppenheimer) Kempner; married Charlotte Kempner, November 7, 1929; children: Charlotte Davis (Mrs. R. W. Beyers), Phyllis A. *Education:* Columbia University, A.B., 1919; graduate study at Harvard University, 1919-20. *Home:* 2 Fifth Ave., San Francisco, Calif. 94118. *Office:* French Bank of California, 235 Montgomery St., San Francisco, Calif. 94104.

CAREER: Heidelbach Ickelheimer & Co. (international bankers), New York City, managing executive, 1920-28; Stern, Kempner & Co. (now Stern, Lauer & Co.), New York City, partner, 1929-38; Industrial Capital Corp., San Francisco, Calif., president and member of board of directors, 1946-65; investment counselor, 1965—. Chairman of French Bank of California, 1971—. Founder, past vice-president, and past member of board of directors of French-American Bilingual School; past founder and member of board of directors of San Francisco's International Hospitality Center; co-founder of Geneva School of International Studies, Geneva, Switzerland. Past member of board of directors of Hampton House Financial Corp. and F. H. Lenway & Co.; member of board of directors of National Refugee Service, Inc., 1940-41. Member of board of trustees of World Affairs Council of Northern California, 1961—; head of Business Friends of France, San Francisco. *Military service:* U.S. Army, in finance department, 1939-45; became lieutenant colonel.

MEMBER: Phi Beta Kappa, Columbia Alumni of Northern California, Harvard Club, Banker's Club, Commonwealth Club, Stock Exchange Club. *Awards, honors:* Officer of Ordre National du Merite (France), 1940-41; citation from Army Service Forces, 1945; chevalier of Order of Leopold II (Belgium), 1959, and Ordre National de la Legion d'Honneur (France), 1960.

WRITINGS: Inside Wall Street, 1920-1942, Hastings House, 1973.

SIDELIGHTS: Kempner told *CA:* "I was prompted to write *Inside Wall Street, 1920-1942* because I thought the aspects of Wall Street in that era might be of interest to those currently engaged in it. The whole character of Wall Street was different in the period about which I wrote. The First National Bank of the City of New York and J. P. Morgan & Co. were, in my view, the dominant figures; dominant because the leading corporations of the country banked with them. As I recall it, the First National Bank only had 500-600 accounts in total, and I was informed that the average deposit balance was $500,000. This institution, although shunning publicity, wielded enormous power. To be amongst its depositors was to be amongst the elite. Furthermore, it could be very rewarding because of the contacts it afforded. Through it one might gain access to the large corporations. I shall not forget the instance when I asked the bank as a favor whether they would accept a deposit which was much smaller than the usual balances. They agreed to do so. As a young man I was thrilled when one of the senior officers of the bank said, 'Well, you are a member of the family now.' This indeed proved to be an invaluable asset because of the accesses that it afforded. An instance was when I asked the bank for an introduction to General Motors in Detroit. This was promptly supplied, and when I arrived in Detroit, to my astonishment, I was immediately given an office and a secretary was put at my disposal. I had come merely on a fact-finding errand and was overwhelmed by the reception.

"Another aspect of Wall Street in the former period was that the large member firms tended to be dominated by a single family or a single person. J. P. Morgan & Co. and Lehman Brothers are examples that come to my mind. In the former period, the capital of a firm was generally concentrated in the hands of a few wealthy partners. Today, a firm's capital is more evenly distributed amongst many partners.

"Wall Street at the period about which I wrote was somewhat like a club. There were the 'ins' and the rest. By the 'ins' are meant those fortunate enough to be friendly with the First National Bank or J. P. Morgan & Co. Through those two institutions access might be had to the prominent corporations of the country.

"The club-like atmosphere has completely changed today, and to a degree, the power of some of the institutions. The large corporations tend to distribute their deposits and maintain relationships at several banks. Moreover, amongst the member firms there has been a democratization with capital distributed among several partners rather than concentrated in the hands of a very few.

"Perhaps the single most important influence in Wall Street has become the dominant role of the Securities and Exchange Commission. It properly exercises the role of policeman. At the time of which I wrote there were moral standards imposed by custom and the 'Street' was, I believe without exaggeration, controlled by the First National Bank and J. P. Morgan. When I use the word controlled, I do not mean dictated to, but rather that the favorable disposition of those two institutions could prove most helpful. Friendliness of the big banks can still be most helpful, but their influence was far greater in former periods."

* * *

KEMSLEY, William George, Jr. 1928-

PERSONAL: Born April 11, 1928, in Detroit, Mich.; son of William George and Verna (Smith) Kemsley; married Marcella Bennis Myers, September 10, 1966; children: Diane Amelia, Molly O. (adopted), Katie, William George III, Andrew Dae Sung (adopted), Maggie Mi Sook (adopted). *Education:* Attended Columbia University, 1948-49, and Wayne State University, 1949-52. *Religion:* Episcopalian. *Home:* 83 Adams St., Bedford Hills, N.Y. 10507. *Office:* Backpacker, 65 Adams St., Bedford Hills, N.Y. 10507.

CAREER: Archives of American Art, Detroit, Mich., administrative director, 1958-60; Detroit Bolt & Nut Co., Detroit, assistant to president, 1960-61; free-lance writer and consultant, 1961-64; Corporate Annual Reports, Inc., New York City, executive vice-president, 1964-68; William Kemsley Associates, Inc., New York City, owner, 1968-72; WKA Corporate Graphics, Inc., Greenwich, Conn., owner, 1972—. Owner and publisher of *Backpacker*, 1973—. Editor. *Military service:* U.S. Naval Reserve, active duty, 1945-46.

MEMBER: American Hiking Society (chairman), Outdoor Writers of America, Wilderness Society, National Wildlife Federation, Friends of the Earth, Explorers Club, Sierra Club, Audubon Society, Appalachian Mountain Club, Adirondack Mountain Club, Swiss Alpine Club. *Awards, honors:* Award of Merit for graphic design from Society of Publication Designers, 1971, for *Progress;* award for design from *Art Direction* and one show award of distinction for copy and graphics design from Art Director's Club of New York, both 1972, both for the 1971 Washington Post Company annual stockholder report; one show award of distinction for copy and graphics design from Copy Club of New York, 1972, for Servomation Corporation annual stockholder report; award of distinction as one of ten best designed magazines of the year from *Folio,* 1974, for *Backpacker;* award of merit for graphic design from Society of Publication Designers, certificate of distinction for creativity from *Art Direction,* and certificates of distinction for photography and graphic design from *Communication Arts,* all 1976, all for *Backpacker.*

WRITINGS: Backpacking Equipment Buyers Guide, Macmillan, 1975; (contributor) Alma Deane MacConomy, editor, *Wildlife Country,* National Wildlife Federation, 1978; *Whole Hikers Handbook,* Morrow, 1979. Contributor of travel and sport articles to newspapers and to national magazines, including *Audobon, Holiday,* and *Success.*

WORK IN PROGRESS: An autobiographical book on wilderness travel techniques.

SIDELIGHTS: Kemsley comments: "I have worked on all aspects of writing, publicity and advertising copy, free-lance magazine and newspaper articles, product and descriptive brochures, sales letters and annual reports.

"Luck ran with me when I got the hair-brained idea in 1972 to start my own magazine about a subject I loved passionately—backpacking. Now I own the only significant magazine in the field, and am able to live the kind of life I really enjoy. I spend about a week per month outdoors backpacking, ski touring, mountain climbing, or hiking.

"My greatest joys come from being with my wife and children. We try to go on as many trips as possible so that we can spend time together as a family. We do this not because we 'ought to do it' but because we don't want to miss out on any of the good times, and don't want to have to look back and regret that we didn't do these things before it was too late.

"I have hiked in forty of the states, five provinces of Canada, in England, Scotland, Wales, Norway, Japan, and the islands in the Caribbean. I have hiked forests, tundra, glaciers, wilderness beaches, canyons, swamps, and deserts in most of our national parks and a number of our wilderness areas. For several years of my life, while living in Manhattan, getting off for a weekend backpacking trip two or three times a month saved my sanity. Our children would rather hike than have a party.

"Next to my family and my work, my most important concern is for the preservation of the wilderness experience. There is still a surprisingly great amount of untrammeled scenic land left in America. I am concerned about preserving enough of it to provide the kind of character-building experience that my generation has been fortunate to have had. Our nation's wilderness provides its citizens with a spiritual sanctuary. I spend as much time as I can spare engaged in activities that will help to preserve these lands."

* * *

KENEALLY, Thomas (Michael) 1935-

PERSONAL: Born October 7, 1935, in Sydney, Australia; married Judith Martin, 1965; children: two. *Education:* Attended St. Patrick's College, New South Wales. *Home:* 5 The Grange, Wimbledon, London S.W. 19, England.

CAREER: Novelist. High school teacher in Sydney, Australia, 1960-64; University of New England, New South Wales, Australia, lecturer in drama, 1968-70. *Military service:* Served in Australian Citizens Military Forces. *Awards, honors:* Miles Franklin Award, 1967, 1968; Captain Cook Bi-Centenary Prize, 1970; Heinemann Award for literature, 1973, for *The Chant of Jimmie Blacksmith.*

WRITINGS—Novels: *The Place at Whitton,* Cassell, 1964, Walker & Co., 1965; *The Fear,* Cassell, 1965; *Bring Larks and Heroes,* Cassell Australia, 1967, Viking, 1968; *Three Cheers for the Paraclete,* Angus & Robertson (Sydney), 1968, Viking, 1969; *The Survivor,* Angus & Robertson, 1969, Viking, 1970; *The Dutiful Daughter,* Viking, 1971; *The Chant of Jimmie Blacksmith,* Viking, 1972; *Blood Red, Sister Rose: A Novel of the Maid of New Orleans,* Viking, 1974 (published in England as *Blood Red, Sister Rose,* Collins, 1974); *Gossip From the Forest,* Collins, 1975, Harcourt, 1976; *Moses the Lawgiver,* Harper, 1975; *Season in Purgatory,* Collins, 1976, Harcourt, 1977; *A Victim of the Aurora,* Collins, 1977, Harcourt, 1978; *Passenger,* Harcourt, 1979.

Plays: "Halloran's Little Boat," first produced in Sydney, Australia, 1966; "Childermass," first produced in Sydney, 1968; "An Awful Rose," first produced in Sydney at Jane Street Theatre, June 1, 1972. Also author of television play, "Essington," produced in United Kingdom, 1974.

SIDELIGHTS: Thomas Keneally's novels have been most notably characterized by their sensitivity to style, their objectivity, their suspense, and their diverse subject matter. Whether he is writing a murder mystery or a historical novel, this "honest workman" has consistently demonstrated to critics that he deserves consideration among "the most talented of current Australian writers."

While discussions of Keneally often consider his years spent as a seminary student, only one of his novels focuses directly on the subject. In *Three Cheers for the Paraclete* his protagonist is a "doubting priest," Father James Maitland, who "runs afoul of the local taboos" in a Sydney seminary. He pseudonymously writes a book called "The Meanings of God," and then is asked by the local archbishop to attack it; he invites a cousin and his wife to spend a night in the seminary and is sternly reminded that it is "a house for celibates"; he advises a "psychotic seminarian to consult a psychiatrist." Despite these transgressions, Maitland remains committed to his vocation, at one point saying, "The essential is that I remain in the church." "More anchored to the old order than he realizes," he accepts suspension from the church until he is later allowed to assume a minor post.

As in many of his novels, Keneally presents the characters in *Three Cheers for the Paraclete* objectively and compassionately. "The author does not exaggerate his character portrayals," wrote reviewer Thomas L. Vince. "Neither the Archbishop nor Bishop-Elect Costello are portrayed as vicious or single-minded men. Nor is Fr. Maitland shown to be a paragon of all virtues brutally exploited by an out-dated Church. What is refreshing about this novel is that the priests and bishops are seen in the fullness of their humanity and that neither Maitland nor his friend, Egan, desert the Church." Richard Sullivan shared this view: "Though this admirably sustained novel makes it clear that some structures are too rigid, that the Church is not unflawed in its members, both clerical and lay, and that more windows need opening, at the same time it reveals with fine objectivity that it is human beings who are at fault, each in his own way, Maitland as much as any."

A similar example of Keneally's desire for objectivity is evident in his account of the St. Joan of Arc story, *Blood Red, Sister Rose.* Bruce Cook claimed Keneally's "intent, in fact, seems to be to reduce her and her legend to recognizably human dimensions." Placing Keneally's Joan of Arc in a historical perspective, *Time's* Melvin Maddocks saw her standing between the "Joan-too-spiritual" of the original legend and the "Joan-too-earthy" of George Bernard Shaw: She is "less spectacular than the first two but decidedly more convincing and perhaps, at last, more moving."

Though the subjects of Keneally's novels are diverse, ranging from an eighteenth-century British penal colony in Australia to a World War II medical unit in Yugoslavia, war is often used as a backdrop in his work. After *Blood Red, Sister Rose,* wherein he "seemed determined to write a sort of antihistorical novel, one that would expose the pettiness of war's political basis," Keneally followed with two more wartime novels, *Season in Purgatory* and *Gossip From the Forest.* The first book told the story of a young English surgeon transferred to a Yugoslavian medical unit in World War II. There, Doctor Pelham confronts assorted horrors of war—wounded soldiers, Nazi bombs, "suicidal attacks" ordered by "lunatic brigadiers,"—while being transformed "into a mature, compassionate, politically disenchanted paladin" by his lover, Moja. Again, Keneally's skill in character portrayal earned praise; but it was not the main characters who captured Jane Miller's attention. "Keneally is interesting about almost everything but his hero and heroine," she wrote. "His language falters into cliche whenever he confronts them. Yet they are surrounded by clusters of men and women, some of whom are startlingly understood and visualized." Margo Jefferson also commended Keneally for perceiving "astutely but not harshly that the most wrenching experiences can leave habits of mind and upbringing intact. The horrors survived in 'Season in Purgatory' are all the sharper for not leading to catharsis."

Gossip From the Forest, one of Keneally's most highly applauded works, combines fiction and historical event—the signing of the armistice ending World War I. As the delegations from France, England, and Germany convene near Compiegne, France, Keneally's "immediate concern," said a *Times Literary Supplement* reviewer, "is to convey the isolation of each man in [the] group, the absolute indifference they feel towards each other." P. S. Prescott explained that "the delegates dream, tell stories, write letters, quarrel among themselves. Keneally is a patient, exploratory writer, content to poke at his characters, to let antagonisms develop. His forest is a fateful place, fit to get lost in, and his characters are all lost one way or another—in stupidity, delusion, desperation. His book is about the crushing effects past attitudes have upon present emergencies. It is not a cheerful story." Ultimately, wrote Paul Fussell, *Gossip From the Forest* "is a study of the profoundly civilian and pacific sensibility beleaguered by crude power. Erzberger [the pacifist and liberal member of the Reichstag who led the German delegation] is intelligent, hopeful, studious, unpretentious, absent-minded and easily bored, and Keneally depicts him as a doomed negotiator with no leverage but personal decency, a knack at sympathy and a flair for language. . . . By the end of the novel we are deeply sympathetic with Erzberger's fate and with Keneally's point, that the 20th century will not tolerate Matthias Erzbergers. They are civilized, and they are sane."

Those familiar with Keneally's historically-based novels might be surprised by an earlier work, *The Dutiful Daughter.* The surrealism in this novel is obvious: Barbara and Damian Glover's parents "have been afflicted by a horrifying physical metamorphosis which has left them half animal, half human." Melvin Maddocks took a cynical view of Keneally's intent: "Observing that 'absolutely millions of people' are mad with 'family pride,' he concludes that 'the only way for them to get humility is through learning they're—you know—beasts.' Accordingly, like a Greek mythologist with the heart of a gloomy seminary student, Keneally makes an original sin literal by turning Father and Mother Glover into bull and cow from the waist down." Despite this and other objections to the book, including the author's "suggestion that family is another name for incest," Maddocks applauded Keneally for "forcefully raising an ancient question: What is the demon in man that so often makes him a monster to those condemned to love him—including himself?" Muriel Haynes, too, concentrated on theme while focusing on the religious questions raised in the book: "The narrative is modeled loosely on the Christian legend of redemption, the course of the savior who assumes the suffering and fate of man, including, in the author's view, his carnality. If we are to be restored to human wholeness, our animality must be accepted without a sense of sin and admitted to the province of divine grace. . . . Keneally's theme is not naive optimism but hope as an affirmation of a state that is yet to be.''

Critics have continually cited Keneally's strength and ability in weaving his subjects into lively fiction. In *Bring Larks and Heroes* he made his story "fresh as blood." In *The Chant of Jimmie Blacksmith* he used "great skill in blending psychology and adventure." Jonathan Yardly thought Keneally "not merely an entertainer telling a bloody and exciting story. He is also a writer of formidable skills and resources; . . . he has a visceral feeling for physical action and his prose conveys it powerfully."

Keneally has also impressed reviewers by making seemingly impossible ideas work. In *Blood Red, Sister Rose*, A. G. Mojtabai thought "it would seem fool-hardy to attempt to revive these worn tales [of the Joan of Arc legend] again. Yet . . . Keneally has done it and carried it off with aplomb." Likewise, the *Times Literary Supplement* praised *The Dutiful Daughter* for showing "Keneally's skill in using to his advantage a subject which in less capable hands might have looked merely grotesque, or even ridiculous."

Style and language are often discussed in treatments of Keneally's work. One critic proclaimed him "Australia's most individual stylist since Patrick White." His prose style has evidently improved since an early novel, *Bring Larks and Heroes*, where his presentation was viewed as "overwrought" by one reviewer and further challenged by another: "The style is awkward, disjointed and lacking in rhythms," wrote David Halliwell. "Mr. Keneally beats up a phrase until it dies of dislocation." As soon as his next novel, though, he was writing in a "fluent style," and by *Gossip From the Forest* Keneally's presentation had become, in George Steiner's words, "as stylized as a Balinese dance-drama."

Keneally's control of language has been variously respected for being rich, concise, and aggressively determined. One aspect that has troubled readers, though, is his tendency to use modern dialogue in novels set in past centuries. John S. Phillipson observed how in *Bring Larks and Heroes* "only plot details peculiar to the 18th century belong to that era historically; as far as language goes, the time of this story could be 1968." And, according to Neil Hepburn, Keneally had the same problem in *Blood Red, Sister Rose*. "What imprisons this book," he remarked, "is the Keneally trade mark—the use of modern, and transatlantic modern, colloqualism for dialogue."

In his latest novel, *Victim of the Aurora*, Keneally returned to the Antarctic setting he had previously explored in *The Survivor*. The similarities between the two works immediately struck Anne Tyler. "In fact," she wrote in the *New York Times Book Review*, "it almost seems that Thomas Keneally, on a slow day, picked up a copy of 'The Survivor' . . . turned the plot over in his mind awhile, and decided to rework it with a few new twists. In 'The Survivor' a middle-aged man reflected upon the disaster that overcame the leader of his South Pole expedition, and tried to deal with his own guilt, which grew out of his brief affair with the leader's wife. In 'Victim of the Aurora,' an old man in a nursing home reflects on the disaster that occurred to *his* South Pole expedition (this time a murder)." In addition, Tyler felt *Victim of the Aurora* "lacks a sense of depth." Jonathan Keates might have challenged her statement. He believed "its virtues, those of a continuing alertness to points of landscape and historical background, an exemplary lucidity in the unfolding of theme and the ability to give a full perspective to

even the most negligible figure, are what we can expect from a writer as consistently good as Keneally.''

BIOGRAPHICAL/CRITICAL SOURCES: Punch, February 28, 1968; Spectator, March 1, 1968, November 25, 1972, September 7, 1974, November 15, 1975, September 4, 1976, September 3, 1977; Books and Bookmen, April, 1968, October, 1972, March, 1974; Best Sellers, July 15, 1968, April 1, 1969, July 1, 1971, August 15, 1972, February 1, 1975, August, 1976, August, 1978; Time, August 16, 1968, June 7, 1971, August 28, 1972, February 10, 1975; Saturday Review, April 12, 1969, July 24, 1971; Washington Post Book World, April 27, 1969, April 19, 1970, August 29, 1971, August 13, 1972, January 26, 1975, February 20, 1977, March 26, 1978; Commonweal, October 24, 1969.

New York Times, April 4, 1970, September 9, 1972; Times Literary Supplement, May 7, 1970, April 23, 1971, September 15, 1972, October 26, 1973, October 11, 1974, September 19, 1975, September 3, 1976, October 14, 1977; New York Times Book Review, September 27, 1970, September 12, 1971, January 16, 1972, July 27, 1972, December 3, 1972, February 9, 1975, April 11, 1976, February 27, 1977, October 14, 1977; Kirkus Reviews, March 15, 1971, July 1, 1972, February 1, 1976, November 1, 1976; Observer, April 25, 1971, September 10, 1971, November 24, 1974, September 21, 1975, December 14, 1975, September 5, 1976, September 4, 1977; New Statesman, September 1, 1972, October 26, 1973, October 11, 1974, September 19, 1975, September 3, 1976, September 9, 1977; Nation, November 6, 1972; New Yorker, February 10, 1975, July 23, 1976, May 23, 1977, May 8, 1978; Contemporary Literary Criticism, Gale, Volume 5, 1976, Volume 8, 1978, Volume 10, 1979; Guardian Weekly, March 7, 1976, September 12, 1976, Newsweek, April 19, 1976, February 7, 1977, June 18, 1979; America, November 13, 1976, May 28, 1977; World Literature Today, winter, 1977, autumn, 1977; National Review, April 29, 1977; West Coast Review of Books, July, 1978.*

* * *

KENNEDY, William 1928-

OFFICE: c/o Viking Press, 625 Madison Ave., New York, N.Y. 10022.

CAREER: Writer. Worked as movie critic and reporter for *Albany Times-Union.*

WRITINGS: The Ink Truck, Dial, 1969; *Legs*, Coward, 1976; *Bill Phelan's Greatest Game*, Viking, 1978. Contributor to *National Observer.*

SIDELIGHTS: Kennedy's first novel, *The Ink Truck*, deals with a prolonged newspaper strike. "It is," said Kennedy, "perhaps, a metaphor for commitment, a survival handbook for failures, a study in resistance, a comedy of metaphysical lust, a report on the willful pursuit of disaster." Kennedy has long been revered by critics for his original comic style. Wrote Doris Brumbach, "No one writing in America today . . . has Kennedy's rich and fertile gift of gab; his pure, verbal energy; his love of poeple, and their kitsch and kin. Like his characters, he too is a wonder." Brumbach also declared that "Kennedy's pitch is perfect. His is the true comic spirit, conveyed by a tumult of fierce and wonderful language."

Legs is Kennedy's novelization of the life of noted gangster Jack "Legs" Diamond. In a review of *Legs*, a *Newsweek* critic called the book "a peculiarly seductive portrait and *Legs* is a very skillful story, full of bounce and wit." Kennedy's most recent work, *Billy Phelan's Greatest Game*, was sized up by one reviewer as "a series of vivid and isolated scenes in the joints of Albany's Broadway, where his incidental characters, seedy and doomed, endlessly gamble, drink, and whore in pools of artificial light." The reviewer also wrote, "It's a world of hustlers and suckers in a perennially fascinating era; Kennedy recreates both with an energetic, argot-flavored style that is hard to resist."

BIOGRAPHICAL/CRITICAL SOURCES: Library Journal, October 1, 1969; *Newsweek*, June 23, 1975; *Contemporary Literary Criticism*, Volume 6, Gale, 1976; *Saturday Review*, April 29, 1978; *Atlantic*, June, 1978.*

* * *

KENT, John Wellington 1920-
(Jack Kent)

PERSONAL: Born March 10, 1920, in Burlington, Iowa; son of Ralph Arthur (in sales) and Marguerite (Bruhl) Kent; married June Kilstofte, June 9, 1954; children: John Wellington, Jr. *Education:* Attended high school in Dallas, Tex. *Politics:* Conservative. *Religion:* Episcopalian. *Home and office:* 103 West Johnson St., San Antonio, Tex. 78204.

CAREER: Free-lance commercial artist, 1935-41, and cartoonist, 1935-50; McClure Newspaper Syndicate, New York, N.Y., author of comic strip "King Aroo," distributed internationally, 1950-65; free-lance cartoonist, 1965-68; writer and illustrator of children's books, 1968—. *Military service:* U.S. Army, Field Artillery, 1941-45; became first lieutenant. *Member:* National Cartoonists Society, American Institute of Graphic Arts, Authors Guild, Authors League of America. *Awards, honors:* Awards from Chicago Graphics Associates, 1969, for *Just Only John*, and Chicago Book Clinic, 1971, for *Mr. Meebles.*

WRITINGS—All self-illustrated children's books, except as noted; all under name Jack Kent: *King Aroo* (collection of comic strip cartoons), Doubleday, 1952; *Just Only John*, Parents' Magazine Press, 1968; *Clotilda*, Random House, 1969; *Fly Away Home*, McKay, 1969; *The Grown-Up Day*, Parents' Magazine Press, 1969; *Mr. Elephant's Birthday Party*, Houghton, 1969; *The Blah*, Parents' Magazine Press, 1970; *Mr. Meebles*, Parents' Magazine Press, 1970; *The Fat Cat*, Parents' Magazine Press, 1971; *The Wizard of Wallaby Wallow*, Parents' Magazine Press, 1971; *Jack Kent's Fables of Aesop*, Parents' Magazine Press, 1972; *Dooly and the Snortsnoot*, Putnam, 1972; *Mrs. Mooley*, Golden Press, 1973; *Jack Kent's Twelve Days of Christmas*, Parents' Magazine Press, 1973; *More Fables of Aesop*, Parents' Magazine Press, 1974; *Jack Kent's Hop, Skip and Jump Book*, Random House, 1974; *The Egg Book*, Macmillan, 1975; *There's No Such Thing as a Dragon*, Golden Press, 1975; *The Christmas Pinata*, Parents' Magazine Press, 1975; *Jack Kent's Happy-Ever-After Book*, Random House, 1976; *Jack Kent's Merry Mother Goose*, Golden Press, 1977; *The Funny Book*, Golden Press, 1977; *Cindy Lou and the Witch's Dog*, Random House, 1978; *Supermarket Magic*, Random House, 1978; *Socks for Supper*, Parents' Magazine Press, 1978; *Jack Kent's Hokus-Pokus Bedtime Book*, Random House, 1979; *Hoddy Doddy*, Greenwillow, 1979; *Piggy Bank Gonzales*, Parents' Magazine Press, 1979.

Illustrator: Polly Berends, *Jack Kent's Book of Nursery Tales*, Random House, 1970; Ruth Gross, *The Bremen-Town Musicians*, Scholastic Book Services, 1974; Sarah Barchas, *I Was Walking Down the Road*, Scholastic Book Services, 1975; Carla Stevens, *How to Make Possum's Honey Bread*, Scholastic Book Services, 1975; Stevens, *The Magic Carrot Seeds*, Scholastic Book Services, 1976; Freya Littledale, *Seven at One Blow*, Scholastic Book Services,

1976; Rita Gelman, *Why Can't I Fly?*, Scholastic Book Services, 1976; Gelman, *More Spaghetti, I Say*, Scholastic Book Services, 1977; Gross, *The Emperor's New Clothes*, Scholastic Book Services, 1977; Barchas, *Janie and the Giant*, Scholastic Book Services, 1977; Jane Yolen, *The Simple Prince*, Parents' Magazine Press, 1978; Bonnie Bishop, *No One Noticed Ralph*, Doubleday, 1979; Beatrice de Regniers, *Laura's Story*, Atheneum, 1979.

WORK IN PROGRESS: Knee-High Nina; Floyd, the Tiniest Elephant; a riddle, rhyme, and joke book; a book of three dog tales.

SIDELIGHTS: Kent writes: "I must confess that my motivation for writing and illustrating children's books is the selfish desire to make a living doing what I enjoy. I love books and hope that, by concocting amusing stories for wee folk, I can woo them into reading as a habit; that my fluff will create an appetite for more nourishing fare."

AVOCATIONAL INTERESTS: Art and archaeology, architecture (designed his own home), languages, travel (the people and the places), music and dance (symphony, opera, and ballet), nature.

* * *

KENYON, Ernest M(onroe) 1920-

PERSONAL: Born August 24, 1920, in Philadelphia, Pa.; son of Ernest Monroe (a naval officer) and Mabel (Brown) Kenyon; married Florence B., August 23, 1942 (died, February, 1971); married Priscilla Hersey; children: Virginia C. Kenyon McNulty, David M. *Education:* Massachusetts Institute of Technology, S.B., 1942, Ph.D., 1949. *Politics:* "Conservative-ish." *Religion:* Episcopalian. *Home and office:* 5 Kearsarge Woods, North Conway, N.H. 03860. *Agent:* Sanford J. Greenburger Associates, Inc., 825 Third Ave., New York, N.Y. 10022.

CAREER: U.S. Army, career officer, 1949-72, worked as food processing engineer, retiring as lieutenant colonel; writer, 1972—.

WRITINGS: Rogue Golem (science fiction novel), Popular Library, 1977. Contributor of more than one hundred articles, stories, and reviews to professional journals and magazines, including *Astounding Science Fiction* and *Blue Book*.

WORK IN PROGRESS: The Last God Going Home, a sequel to *Rogue Golem;* two other science fiction novels, *House of Angels* and *The Drunks*.

SIDELIGHTS: Kenyon writes: "My first book represents the theme of man's apparent helplessness in a world of forces and pressures over which he seems to have little or no control. It is an attempt to show one possible reason for this predicament and to indicate that the universe is at once greater, stranger, and more meaningful than we even dream. The 'rat race' syndrome is only apparent and has developed from our own limited and entirely erroneous view of the universe, of what it is, and how it is put together. We can escape it only if we are willing to 'turn the corner,' look at it from a different point of view, see it, at least a little of it, as it is. This of course requires struggle, effort, inquiry, but not along the blind alley of Newtonian or even Einsteinian physics. It requires a 'rogue' mind, willing to suspend belief, awake from 'Newton's sleep.' In the sequel to *Rogue Golem* this theme is even further developed.

"The hero of these books, Josh Billings, is 'everyman' who had the courage to look at himself and his world and to call it what it was, not what someone in authority told him it was. In doing so, painful as it was, he found significance and meaning."

AVOCATIONAL INTERESTS: Travel (Mexico, the Caribbean).

* * *

KEPPLER, Herbert 1925-

PERSONAL: Born April 21, 1925, in New York, N.Y.; son of Victor (a photographer) and Josephine T. (Windmann) Keppler; married Louise M. Lyman, June 7, 1956; children: Kathryn Louise, Thomas Victor. *Education:* Harvard University, B.A., 1945. *Home:* 119 North Highland Pl., Croton-on-Hudson, N.Y. 10520. *Office: Modern Photography,* 130 East 59th St., New York, N.Y. 10022.

CAREER: New York Sun, New York City, reporter, 1948-49; *Modern Photography,* New York City, associate, 1950-67, editorial director and publisher, 1967-74; ABC Leisure Magazines, New York City, vice-president in photography, 1974—; author of column, "Keppler's SLR Notebook," for *Modern Photography. Military service:* U.S. Naval Reserve, active duty as commanding officer, 1945-46. *Member:* Rolls Royce Owners Club.

WRITINGS: Official 35mm Camera Rating Guide, Amphoto, 1957; *Keppler on the Eye Level Reflex,* Amphoto, 1960; *How to Make Better Pictures in Your Home,* Amphoto, 1962; *124 Ways to Test Cameras, Lenses, and Equipment,* Amphoto, 1962; *The Pentax Way,* Focal Press, 1966; *The Nikon-Nikkormat Way,* Focal Press, 1977.

SIDELIGHTS: Keppler writes: "I write travel columns with photographs, emphasizing the Orient, Asia, Africa, and Caribbean areas."

* * *

KERMAN, Sheppard 1928-

PERSONAL: Born August 26, 1928, in Brooklyn, N.Y.; son of Louis (a businessman) and Leila (a poet; maiden name, Benowitz) Kerman; married Ilona Murai (a ballet teacher), January 19, 1957; children: Christina. *Education:* City College (now of the City University of New York), B.S.S., 1950. *Home:* 102-10 66th Rd., Forest Hills, N.Y. 11375. *Agent:* Bret Adams, 36 East 61st St., New York, N.Y. 10019. *Office:* In-Perspective Communications, 205 Lexington Ave., New York, N.Y. 10016.

CAREER: Kenyon & Eckhardt Advertising, New York City, writer and producer, 1964-69; Charisma Organization, New York City, writer and producer, 1969-71; Stage Right (multi-media producers), New York City, creative director, 1971-72; In-Perspective Communications, Inc., New York City, president and creative director, 1973—. Actor in films, including "Boss Tweed," industrial and army training films, and in Broadway plays, including "All for Love," 1950-51, "The Prescott Proposals," 1953, "Tonight in Samarkand," 1954, "The Great Sebastians," 1956, and "The Sound of Music," 1959-63; producer and director of "Mr. Simian," 1963-64; narrator of television commercials. Creator of multi-media works for industry, including speeches, motivational pieces, and musicals such as "Seesaw," 1973. *Member:* American Federation of Television and Radio Artists, American Society of Composers, Authors and Publishers, Dramatists Guild, Screen Actors Guild, Actors Equity, Players Club. *Awards, honors:* Best radio play, WNYC student awards, 1946, for "Jacob Rils"; best actor award, *Show Business,* 1950, as Everyman in "All for Love," and 1951, as Marc Antony in "All for Love"; Obie award, 1964, for "Mr. Simian"; Los Angeles Drama Critics Circle award, 1978, for overall visual design concept in "Beatlemania."

WRITINGS—Plays: "The Dark and the Day" (three-act), first produced in New York City at New Dramatists Committee, 1952; "Bilby's Doll" (two-act), first produced in New York City at New Dramatists Committee, 1953; *Cut of the Axe* (two-act; first produced on Broadway at Ambassador Theatre, February 1, 1960), Samuel French, 1961; "Players on a Beach" (one-act), first produced in New York City at Masters' Institute Theatre, 1961; "Mr. Simian" (three-act), first produced Off-Broadway at Astor Place Playhouse, October, 1963; "The Tune of the Time" (two-act), first produced in Atlanta at Civic Theatre, October, 1969. Also author of "Nine Rebels" (two-act), 1962, and "The Husband-In-Law" (three-act), 1968.

Author of scripts for television shows, including "Danger," "Matinee Theater," "Studio One," and "Camera 3." Lyricist for songwriters Marvin Hamlisch, Lee Pockriss, and John Strauss. Also author of unpublished volume of poetry, *The Candy Man.*

WORK IN PROGRESS: "Distant Relations," a multi-media musical; "Peter, Paul, and the Piper," a play.

SIDELIGHTS: Kerman commented: "My plays, poems, operas, and television scripts have somehow placed emphasis on the survival of the individual in a world of contradictory philosophies. Today my primary work is in the area of mixed and multi-media presentations for industry and theatre. My unique background as writer, lyricist, director, and producer has been the source of my own creative survival and has fortunately led me into a new art form in which the disciplines of the media I previously performed in, wrote for, and directed, still apply. It has allowed me to innovate and set a standard in visual projections for the theatre. (At least, that has been the attempt since "Seesaw," in 1973, through "Beatlemania," in 1977, and "Platinum," in 1978.)

"The writer draws images in words. I am now able to draw words, characters, and emotions in images—images that can perform in harmony with all aspects of a staged performance and can communicate deeper aspects of character and theatricality. If survival—coping—has, and continues to be the thread that runs through my written work, the visual media has become both needle and fabric."

Kerman has combined his knowledge of theatre and corporate business to produce important audio-visual effects in both areas. As Olga Barrekette explained, "Kerman uses every aspect of graphic art, live action, film, video, photography, sound, original music, AVL machines and computer programming of as many as 3-5 thousand slides to meet the specific needs of his client."

In the Broadway musical "Seesaw" the effects were achieved by projecting pictures onto tall vertical panels on stage. The projection of the pictures had to be precisely coordinated with the movement of the screens from backstage. Kerman and his crew took over three thousand pictures for the play, including night panoramas, double exposures, and dissolves, of which 158 were used in "Seesaw."

BIOGRAPHICAL/CRITICAL SOURCES: Atlantic City Sunday Press, June 10, 1973; *Back Stage,* November 17, 1978.

* * *

KERN, Jean B(ordner) 1913-

PERSONAL: Born April 30, 1913, in Bristol, Ind.; daughter of John S. (a botanist) and Stanta (Lung) Bordner; married Alexander C. Kern (a professor), June 27, 1936; children: John R., Antonia Curtze Mills. *Education:* University of

Wisconsin—Madison, B.A. and M.A., both 1933, Ph.D., 1936. *Home:* 1639 Ridge Rd., Iowa City, Iowa 52240. *Office:* Department of English, Coe College, Cedar Rapids, Iowa 52402.

CAREER: University of Wisconsin—Madison, instructor in English, 1942-43; Iowa State University, Ames, instructor in English, 1946-47, 1957-58; Georgetown University, Washington, D.C., assistant professor of English in Ankara, Turkey, 1958-60; Grinnell College, Grinnell, Iowa, lecturer in English, 1960-61; Coe College, Cedar Rapids, Iowa, assistant professor of English, 1961-64; American University of Cairo, Cairo, Egypt, associate professor of English, 1964-66; Coe College, associate professor, 1966-70, professor of English, 1970-75, professor emeritus, 1975—. Guest lecturer at University of Tubingen, West Germany, 1966; lecturer at University of Nis, Yugoslavia, 1976-77. Member of board of Iowa Humanities, 1975—. *Member:* International Association of University Professors of English, Modern Language Association of America, American Society for Eighteenth-Century Studies, Midwest Modern Language Association. *Awards, honors:* Fellowship from Newberry Library, summer, 1962; grant from Huntington Library, summer, 1963; Associated Colleges of the Midwest Faculty fellow, 1971-72.

WRITINGS: (Author of introduction) Charles Macklin, *Introduction to Charles Macklin's Covent Garden Theatre,* Augustan Reprint Society, 1965; (author of introduction) Charles Macklin, *A Will and No Will and The New Play Criticized,* Augustan Reprint Society, 1967; *From Chaucer to Gibbon,* University of Iowa Press, 1975; *Dramatic Satire in the Age of Walpole,* Iowa State University Press, 1976. Contributor to language and humanities journals.

WORK IN PROGRESS: Family, Sex, and Marriage in Eighteenth-Century Novels by Women (tentative title).

SIDELIGHTS: Kern comments briefly: "My interest in women's studies is evident in my work in progress on neglected women authors of the eighteenth century."

* * *

KERSHAW, Gordon Ernest 1928-

PERSONAL: Born May 5, 1928, in Sanford, Maine; son of Clifford (a textile worker) and Violet (a nursing home proprietor; maiden name, Gilpin) Kershaw; married Carolyn Groves (a professor of English), July 21, 1976; children: Christina Elizabeth. *Education:* University of Maine at Orono, A.B., 1950; Boston University, A.M., 1954; University of Pennsylvania, A.M., 1964, Ph.D., 1971. *Religion:* Episcopalian. *Home:* 17 Dogwood Circle, Frostburg, Md. 21532. *Office:* Department of History, Frostburg State College, Frostburg, Md. 21532.

CAREER: Frostburg State College, Frostbrug, Md., assistant professor, 1971-72, associate professor, 1972-74, professor of American history, 1974—, head of department, 1973—. *Military service:* U.S. Army, 1951-53; became first lieutenant. *Member:* American Historical Association, Organization of American Historians, Maine Historical Society.

WRITINGS: The Kennebeck Proprietors: Gentlemen of Property and Judiciuos Men, 1749-1775, New Hampshire Publishing, 1975; (with David M. Dean, Harry I. Stegmaier, Jr., and John B. Wiseman) *Allegany County: A History,* McClain Printing Co., 1976; *James Bowdoin: Patriot and Man of the Enlightenment,* Museum of Art, Bowdoin College, 1976. Contributor of articles and reviews to history and literary journals, including *American Neptune, New England Quarterly,* and *William and Mary Quarterly.*

WORK IN PROGRESS: A Biography of James Bowdoin II.

SIDELIGHTS: Kershaw writes: "For me, the great lure and fascination in the writing of history is the attempt to determine men's motivations. This is usually an elusive quest, but in a few very rare and satisfying instances I have been fortunate enough to find all of the pieces of a particular puzzle."

BIOGRAPHICAL/CRITICAL SOURCES: William and Mary Quarterly, April, 1976; *American Historical Review,* December, 1976.

* * *

KERTESZ, Andre 1894-

PERSONAL: Born July 2, 1894, in Budapest, Hungary; came to United States in 1936, naturalized citizen, 1944; son of Leopold and Ernestine (Hoffman) Kertesz; married Elizabeth Sali, June 17, 1933. *Education:* Attended high school in Budapest, Hungary. *Home and office:* 2 Fifth Ave., New York, N.Y. 10011.

CAREER: Photographer, with solo shows in New York City, Chicago, Paris, and Venice. *Member:* American Society of Magazine Photographers. *Awards, honors:* Commander of French Order of Arts and Letters; gold medal from Venice Biennale, 1976; New York City mayor's award, 1977.

*WRITINGS—*All collections of photographs by author: *A. Kertesz, Photographer,* Museum of Modern Art, 1964; *On Reading,* Grossman, 1971; Nicolas Ducrot, editor, *Andre Kertesz: Sixty Years of Photography,* Grossman, 1972; Ducrot, editor, *J'aime Paris: Photographs Since the Twenties,* Grossman, 1972; *Washington Square,* Grossman, 1975; *Of New York,* Knopf, 1976; *Andre Kertesz,* Aperture, 1976; Ducrot, editor, *Distortions,* Knopf, 1976.

Other: *Soixante Photographies d'enfants* (title means "Children"), Plon, 1933; Pierre MacOrlan, *Paris vu par Andre Kertesz* (title means "Paris Seen by Andre Kertesz"), [Paris], 1934; Jaboune, *Nos amis des betes* (title means "Our Friends the Animals"), [Paris], 1936; Hamp, *Les Cathedrales du vin* (title means "The Cathedrals of Wine"), [Paris], 1937; *Paragraphic,* Grossman, 1966; *Andre Kertesz munkassaga* (title means "The Work of Andre Kertesz"), Corvina, 1972. Also photographer of *Day of Paris,* text by George Davis, 1945.

SIDELIGHTS: Kertesz told CA: "Officially, I am the creator of the literary reportage. I made my first photos in 1912 and my reportage was always an interpretation of my feelings about what I had seen. At the time when I came to the United States, this was a sin and I was punished. The photography in America at that time wanted only to see documentation: I did not accept that. In my opinion, the reportage in America today is still only documentation. Eugene Smith, the photographer, was the only one who tried to interpret his feelings through his reports. He was also punished: *Life* magazine fired him."

* * *

KETCHUM, Carlton Griswold 1892-

PERSONAL: Born February 17, 1892, in Yankton, S.D.; son of Lester (a newspaper journalist) and Luna L. (a teacher; maiden name, Beard) Ketchum; married Mildred Caroline Storey, October 8, 1914; children: David Storey. *Education:* University of Pittsburgh, B.S., 1916. *Politics:* Republican. *Religion:* Presbyterian. *Home:* 530 Glen Arden Dr., Pittsburgh, Pa. 15208.

CAREER: Ketchum, Inc. (public relations company), Pittsburgh, Pa., president and member of board of directors, 1919-66, chairman of board of directors, 1966-78, chairman emeritus, 1978—. Vice-president of One Hundred Thousand Pennsylvanians. Finance director of Republican National Committee, 1937-41, 1949-57. *Military service:* U.S. Army, 1917-19; became second lieutenant. U.S. Army Air Forces, 1942-45; served in European and Mediterranean theaters; became colonel. *Member:* American Legion (past commander), Western Pennsylvania Historical Society (member of executive committee, 1971—), Pittsburgh Chamber of Commerce (past member of board of directors), University of Pittsburgh Alumni Council (past chairman), Omicron Delta Kappa, Duquesne Club, University Club, Masons.

WRITINGS: The Recollections of Colonel Retread, U.S.A.A.F., 1942-45, Hart Publishing, 1976.

*   *   *

KEVLES, Daniel Jerome 1939-

PERSONAL: Surname is pronounced *Kev*-less; born March 2, 1939, in Philadelphia, Pa.; son of David (a teacher) and Anne (Rothstein) Kevles; married Bettyann Holtzmann (a writer), May 18, 1961; children: Beth, Jonathan. *Education:* Princeton University, B.A., 1960, Ph.D., 1964; graduate study at Oxford University, 1960-61. *Politics:* Liberal. *Home:* 575 La Loma Rd., Pasadena, Calif. 91105. *Office:* Division of Humanities and Social Sciences, California Institute of Technology, 1201 East California Blvd., Pasadena, Calif. 91125.

CAREER: California Institute of Technology, Pasadena, assistant professor, 1964-68, associate professor, 1968-78, professor of history, 1978—. Visiting research fellow at University of Sussex, 1976; visiting professor at University of Pennsylvania, 1979. Member of White House staff in Washington, D.C., 1964; member of National Science Foundation fellowship panel, 1978. *Member:* Organization of American Historians, History of Science Society (president of West Coast branch, 1978-80), American Association for the Advancement of Science, British Society for the History of Science, Phi Beta Kappa. *Awards, honors:* National Science Foundation fellowship for Oxford University, 1960-61, grants, 1965, 1973-74, 1978-80; Woodrow Wilson fellowship, 1961-62; American Council of Learned Societies grant, 1973.

WRITINGS: The Physicists: The History of a Scientific Community in Modern America, Knopf, 1978. Contributor of articles and reviews to academic journals, popular magazines, and newspapers, including *Scientific American,* and *Harper's.*

WORK IN PROGRESS: Genetics and Society (tentative title), a history of genetics and eugenics in the United States and England from 1890, publication by Knopf expected in 1984.

SIDELIGHTS: Kevles writes: "In my writing I generally aim to interpret scientists, who are as human as anyone else, science, which is one of man's greatest intellectual achievements, and their combined role in society, both contemporary and historical. I like to dramatize my subjects as much as possible, to include anecdote along with analysis. Books about science should be as readable and as accessible as books about, say, politics or culture, especially since science and technology affect our lives in so many ways. I'm an old Jeffersonian: the healthiest way to deal with even abstruse issues of public policy is not by courts of experts alone but through an informed public."

AVOCATIONAL INTERESTS: Competitive swimming, playing guitar and piano, "cooking, eating, and drinking with good company," restoring his 1956 Jaguar XK-140.

*   *   *

KEYES, Evelyn 1919(?)-

PERSONAL: Born in Port Arthur, Tex.; married Barton Bainbridge (died); married Charles Vidor (a film director; divorced); married John Huston (a film director; divorced); married Artie Shaw (a bandleader and clarinetist), 1957 (separated). *Education:* Attended public schools in Atlanta, Ga. *Residence:* Hollywood, Calif. *Agent:* Irving Paul Lazar Agency, 211 South Beverly Dr., Beverly Hills, Calif. 90212.

CAREER: Worked as a dancer in night clubs; actress; has appeared in forty-four films, including "Gone With the Wind," "Here Comes Mr. Jordan," "A Thousand and One Nights," "The Jolson Story," "The Mating of Millie," "The Seven Year Itch," and "Around the World in 80 Days"; writer, 1971—. Toured with the National Company of "No, No Nanette," 1973.

WRITINGS: I Am a Billboard (novel), Lyle Stuart, 1971; *Scarlett O'Hara's Younger Sister: My Lively Life In and Out of Hollywood* (autobiography), Lyle Stuart, 1977.

SIDELIGHTS: "I'm an American product, the American dream of a few million people, the 17-year-old girl who came to Hollywood and starred in movies and wanted to marry a prince," Evelyn Keyes told an interviewer for the *New York Times.* The world that Keyes discovered in Hollywood, however, was disillusioning. She found that most of the directors and producers were concerned only with sex: "It was simply that a female was the product, the Fuller Brush, the shiny new car they were selling that year. They were obsessed by cleavage—how to show it, how to hide it. If you were going to be in their picture, they wanted you to be a sexual object. I played the girl who gets the boy. Producers have to find you sexually attractive or they feel their picture is going to go out the window." Off the screen, sex was also an obsession. Keyes claimed that her refusal to grant sexual favors to a Columbia studios chief was responsible for his withdrawing support from her career. As a result, she was never able to become a really famous celebrity.

If she had to do all over again, Keyes once remarked, she would never have gone to Hollywood: "It was a dumb thing to do. The trouble is that all the real decisions in our lives are made before we know what to do." Instead of being an actress, Keyes wishes that she had become a writer. Her ambition to be a writer was realized later in life, when she wrote *I Am a Billboard* and *Scarlett O'Hara's Younger Sister: My Lively Life In and Out of Hollywood.*

Despite its title, *Scarlett O'Hara's Younger Sister* is not chiefly interested in examining Keyes's roles in motion pictures. "I wasn't writing a book about the movies," Keyes explained. "I was writing about survival." Among the things that Keyes had to survive were four unsuccessful marriages and several love affairs. Some readers considered *Scarlett O'Hara's Younger Sister* to be indiscreet because Keyes gives the names of her lovers and also describes the physical quality of their relationships. But Keyes defended her decision to tell all: "The days are gone when people could write sweet little ladylike books. . . . Look at *People* magazine. This whole country is one big gossip column."

BIOGRAPHICAL/CRITICAL SOURCES: James Robert Parish and Lennard DeCarl, *Hollywood Players: The Forties,* Arlington House, 1976; Evelyn Keyes, *Scarlett*

O'Hara's Younger Sister: My Lively Life In and Out of Hollywood, Lyle Stuart, 1977; *New York Times,* July 28, 1977.*

* * *

KIMURA, Jiro 1949-

PERSONAL: Name pronounced *Ji*raw Kim*ur*ah; born August 28, 1949, in Osaka, Japan; son of Masao (in insurance) and Masako (an insurance salesperson; maiden name, Shimizu) Kimura; married Kazue Matsumura (a writer for television), May 31, 1978. *Education:* Pace University, B.A., 1973. *Home:* 52 Barrow St., New York, N.Y. 10014.

CAREER: Writer. Consultant to *EQ* (Japanese edition of *Ellery Queen's Mystery Magazine*). *Member:* Mystery Writers of America.

WRITINGS: Hand-to-Mouth New York Life, Sanshu-Sha (Japan), 1976; (with Nobumitsu Kodaka) *Complete New York Guide,* Sanshu-Sha, 1976; (translator) Roger L. Simon, *The Big Fix,* Hayakawa (Japan), 1976; (translator) Edward D. Hock, *Enter the Thief,* Hayakawa, 1976; (translator) Simon, *Wild Turkey,* Hayakawa, 1977; (translator and editor) Hoch, *Hoch's Dozen,* Hayakawa, 1978; *The Second International Congress of Crime Writers Picture Book,* Kikugoro (Japan), 1979. Also translator of *The Brass Rainbow,* by Michael Collins, Hayakawa, 1979. Contributor of regular columns to *EQ* and to *Hayakawa's Mystery Magazine,* both published in Japan.

WORK IN PROGRESS: Interrogation and Confession, a collection of interviews with mystery writers.

AVOCATIONAL INTERESTS: Reading mystery stories, listening to jazz, viewing films.

* * *

KING, Joe 1909(?)-1979

OBITUARY NOTICE: Born c. 1909; died April 16, 1979, in Ridgewood, N.J. Journalist. A sportswriter for forty years, King wrote for several New York papers, including the *New York Telegram* and the *New York World-Telegram.* He later joined the Ridgewood newspaper chain, beginning as assistant managing editor and becoming executive editor. Obituaries and other sources: *New York Times,* April 17, 1979.

* * *

KINGSLEY, Sidney 1906-

PERSONAL: Birth-given name, Sidney Kieschner; born October 18, 1906, in New York, N.Y.; son of Robert and Sonia (Smoleroff) Kieschner; married Madge Evans (an actress), July 25, 1939. *Education:* Cornell University, B.A., 1928. *Home:* 79 Glengray Rd., Oakland, N.J. 07436. *Office:* 108 Fifth Ave., New York, N.Y. 10011.

CAREER: Actor, director, producer, and playwright. *Military service:* U.S. Army, 1939-43; became lieutenant. *Awards, honors:* Pulitzer Prize for best American play, and Theatre Club award for best play, both in 1934, both for "Men in White"; Theatre Club award, 1936, for "Dead End"; New York Drama Critics Circle Award for best play, 1943, Newspaper Guild Page One Award, 1943, Theatre Club award, 1943, all for "The Patriots"; Edgar Allen Poe Award, 1949, for "Detective Story"; New York Drama Critics Circle Award, and Donaldson Award for outstanding achievement in theatre, both in 1951, both for "Darkness at Noon"; medal of merit for outstanding drama, American Academy of Arts and Letters, 1951.

WRITINGS—Plays: *Men in White* (three-act; first produced on Broadway at Broadhurst Theatre, September 26, 1933), Covici Friede, 1933; *Dead End* (three-act; first produced on Broadway at Belasco Theatre, October 28, 1935), Random House, 1936; "Ten Million Ghosts," first produced on Broadway at St. James Theatre, October 23, 1936; "The World We Make" (adapted from novel, *The Outward Room,* by Millen Brand), first produced in New York at Guild Theatre, November 20, 1939; (with wife, Madge Evans) *The Patriots* (three-act; first produced in New York at National Theatre, January 29, 1943), Random House, 1943; *Detective Story* (three-act; first produced Off-Broadway at Hudson Theatre, March 23, 1949), Random House, 1949; *Darkness at Noon* (three-act; adapted from the novel by Arthur Koestler; first produced on Broadway at Alvin Theatre, January 13, 1951), Random House, 1951; "Lunatics and Lovers," first produced on Broadway at Broadhurst Theatre, December 13, 1954; *Night Life* (three-act; first produced on Broadway at Brooks Atkinson Theatre, October 23, 1962), Dramatists Play Service, 1964; "The Art Scene" (part one of a trilogy; first produced on Broadway in 1969).

Translator of *Napoleon the First,* written by Theodor Tagger under pseudonym Ferdinand Bruckner. Also author of original story for the film "Homecoming," Metro-Goldwyn-Mayer (MGM), 1946.

SIDELIGHTS: Best known for his Pulitzer Prize-winning play, *Men in White,* Kingsley is one of the few Broadway playwrights to successfully deal with serious social issues in his plays. Joseph Wood Krutch commented: "I know no contemporary American who can take a topic—slum children in *Dead End* or doctors and nurses in *Men in White*—and then turn out a more stage-worthy piece, full of shrewd if not too profound observation crisply and humorously embodied in recognizable types." His often melodramatic plays have been especially noted for their realism and accuracy of detail.

Kingsley's first Broadway hit, *Men in White,* is the story of a doctor who must choose between a satisfying personal life and service to humanity in the hospital. It was an immediate success, running 351 performances. Walter Prichard Eaton declared: "*Men in White* captures reality with almost a passion of sincerity and breathes a spirit of idealism—the idealism of the medical profession at its best, which is probably one of the reasons for its great popular success." The story was adapted as a film of the same title by Metro-Goldwyn-Mayer (MGM) in 1934.

Movie rights were assigned for two other Kingsley plays. The first was *Dead End,* a story of crime in the slums filmed by United Artists in 1937. The other was *Detective Story,* a 1951 Paramount film starring Kirk Douglas as a detective whose ethics have become twisted after years of working with criminals.

Perhaps Kingsley's most controversial play was *The Patriots,* a dramatization of the struggle of Thomas Jefferson and Alexander Hamilton over the nature of good government. Kingsley and his wife spent months researching and writing the play, yet critics and audiences argued over its historical accuracy and dramatic merit. But no matter what their conclusions, large crowd attended the play, and it won several awards, including the New York Drama Critics Circle Award in 1943.

His serious plays achieved the greatest success at the box office. When Kingsley turned to less lofty topics, however, his plays did not fare as well. *Lunatics and Lovers* was "romantic dribble" according to Allan Lewis. "What might have been a riotous travesty of con men conning themselves turns into a collection of gags and artificial situations in a fabricated play aimed at commercial success,'' Lewis wrote.

''The Art Scene'' was scheduled to be part one of a trilogy dealing with what Kingsley described as ''the phenomenon of change in our time as reflected in and influenced by the various segments of the art world.''

BIOGRAPHICAL/CRITICAL SOURCES: New York Herald Tribune, April 1, 1934; Nation, April 9, 1949; Saturday Review, February 3, 1951; Allan Lewis, American Plays and Playwrights of the Contemporary Theatre, Crown, 1965; New York Times, May 28, 1969, July 12, 1979; Show Business, June 7, 1969; National Observer, August 18, 1969; Variety, December 10, 1969.*

*   *   *

KINNEY, Richard   1924(?)-1979

OBITUARY NOTICE: Born c. 1924; died February 19, 1979, in Evanston, Ill. Educator, lecturer, poet, and author. Blind at age seven and totally deaf by age twenty, Kinney became the second blind-deaf person in the world, after Helen Keller, to earn a doctorate degree. He served as a faculty member and later as executive director and president at the Hadley School for the Blind in Winnetka, Ill., for twenty-five years. He earned numerous awards, including the Helen Keller Gold Medal for Literary Excellence and a citation for meritorious service from President Dwight D. Eisenhower. Kinney wrote four books of poetry and a textbook on the deaf-blind. Obituaries and other sources: Chicago Tribune, February 21, 1979.

*   *   *

KLAIBER, Jeffrey L.   1943-

PERSONAL: Born January 11, 1943, in Indianapolis, Ind.; son of Keith Velmar (in business) and Katherine (a nurse; maiden name, Lockwood) Klaiber. Education: Loyola University, Chicago, Ill., M.A., M.Th.; Catholic University of America, Ph.D. Home: 751 Jiron Chancay, Lima, Peru 10226.

CAREER: Entered Society of Jesus (Jesuits), ordained Roman Catholic priest; Catholic University, Lima, Peru, professor of history, 1976—. Priest and counselor for Santo Toribio Parish in Lima, Peru; professor at University of the Pacific, Lima, 1977—.

WRITINGS: Religion and Revolution in Peru, 1824-1976, University of Notre Dame Press, 1977.

WORK IN PROGRESS: Research on the history of the Roman Catholic church in Peru.

SIDELIGHTS: Klaiber commented: ''I am a Jesuit priest, committed to the creation of a Christian social order in Peru. In my activities as a teacher or writer I aim to influence leftist thinkers to humanize their search for justice, and to awaken the social conscience of others, especially the young, who have not yet seen the need for social justice. Fundamentally, I want to create the conditions of a revolution without violence in Latin America.''

*   *   *

KLEIN, Joseph   1946-
(Joe Klein)

PERSONAL: Born September 7, 1946, in New York; son of Malcolm (a printer) and Miriam (Warshauer) Klein; married Janet Eklund, February 8, 1967 (divorced, 1975); children: Christopher, Terry. Education: University of Pennsylvania,

A.B., 1968. Home: 54 Morton St., New York, N.Y. 10014. Agent: Elizabeth McKee, Harold Matson Co., Inc., 22 East 40th St., New York, N.Y. 10016.

CAREER/WRITINGS: Beverly/Peabody Times, Beverly, Mass., reporter, 1969-72; WGBH-TV, Boston, Mass., reporter, 1972; Real Paper, Boston, Mass., news editor, 1972-74; Rolling Stone, New York, N.Y., associate editor, 1974-78, Washington bureau chief, 1974-76; free-lance television and magazine writer, 1978—. Notable assignments include coverage of the 1976 presidential campaign, the Israeli invasion of Lebanon, 1978, the Carter administration, and busing in Boston. Contributor to magazines, under name Joe Klein, including Mother Jones. Awards, honors: Robert Kennedy Journalism Award, 1973; finalist for National Magazine Award from Columbia University School of Journalism, 1977, for ''The Plastic Coffin of Charlie Arthur''; Deems Taylor Award from American Society of Composers, Authors & Publishers, 1978, for ''Notes on a Native Son.''

WORK IN PROGRESS: A biography of Woody Gutline, to be published by Alfred Knopf.

SIDELIGHTS: Klein writes: ''I've generally specialized in reporting on 'unfamous' people—a worker dying of cancer caused by his job, a union official, a grocer in Florida, the marketing executive who decided to sell granola in boxes—as well as profiles of politicians, ranging from George Wallace, to Jerry Brown, to Jimmy Carter's top young aides, to Fidel Castro.''

*   *   *

KLIGERMAN, Jack   1938-

PERSONAL: Born August 28, 1938, in Atlantic City, N.J.; son of Samuel K. (in sales) and Ethel (a receptionist; maiden name, Schreiber) Kligerman; married Anne Barbara Kane (an audiologist), June 5, 1960; children: Jonathan, Rachel. Education: Syracuse University, B.A., 1960, M.A., 1962; University of California, Berkeley, Ph.D., 1967. Religion: Jewish. Home: 64 Rutgers St., Closter, N.J. 07624. Agent: Richard Curtis Literary Agency, 156 East 52nd St., New York, N.Y. 10022. Office: Department of English, Herbert H. Lehman College of the City University of New York, Bronx, N.Y. 10468.

CAREER: Herbert H. Lehman College of the City University of New York, Bronx, N.Y., assistant professor, 1967-75, associate professor of English, 1975—. Member: John Burroughs Memorial Association (member of board of directors, 1979-82).

WRITINGS: (With Michael Paull) Invention: A Course in Pre-Writing and Composition, Winthrop Publishing, 1973; (editor and author of introduction) The Birds of John Burroughs: Keeping a Sharp Lookout, Hawthorn, 1976; A Fancy for Pigeons, Hawthorn, 1978. Contributor to philosophy and literature journals and popular magazines, including Smithsonian and New Jersey Outdoors.

SIDELIGHTS: Kligerman writes: ''I have been working my way from teaching literature and linguistics toward teaching photography and nonfiction/prose writing. I've been enrolled in a photography workshop with Ralph Weiss since the beginning of 1978. I want to keep integrating my writing and photography.''

*   *   *

KLINE, Thomas J(efferson)   1942-

PERSONAL: Born July 16, 1942, in Washington, D.C.; son of Oral Lee (a biochemist) and Susan (an archivist; maiden name, White) Kline; married Katherine Gordon (a journalist), August 28, 1965; children: Ethan, Chloe. *Education:* Oberlin College, B.A. (cum laude), 1964; Columbia University, M.A., 1966, Ph.D., 1969. *Home:* 44 Harrison St., Newton, Mass. 02161. *Office:* Department of Modern Languages, Boston University, 718 Commonwealth Ave., Boston, Mass. 02215.

CAREER: Columbia University, New York, N.Y., assistant professor, 1969-70; State University of New York at Buffalo, Buffalo, an associate dean, 1970-79; currently associated with Boston University, Boston, Mass. Singer with Cantata Singers, Canby Singers, and Buffalo Collegium Musicum. *Member:* Modern Language Association of America, American Association of Teachers of French, Midwest Modern Language Association. *Awards, honors:* Woodrow Wilson fellowship.

WRITINGS: Andre Malraux and the Metamorphosis of Death, Columbia University Press, 1973. Contributor to language and psychology journals.

WORK IN PROGRESS: A monograph on the films of Bernardo Bertolucci.

SIDELIGHTS: Kline writes: "My major interests include psychoanalysis and cinema, particularly the films of Bertolucci. I have traveled in Europe and North Africa, and have lived in France."

AVOCATIONAL INTERESTS: Running.

* * *

KLOPFER, Peter H(ubert) 1930-

PERSONAL: Born August 9, 1930, U.S. citizen born in Berlin, Germany; son of Hubert Robert K. (an economist) and Edith (a sculptress; maiden name, Brauer); married Martha Smith (a farmer and teacher), in 1955; children: Erika, Lisa, Margarete. *Education:* University of California, Los Angeles, B.A. (honors), 1952; Yale University, Ph.D., 1957. *Office:* Department of Zoology, Duke University, Durham, N.C. 27706.

CAREER: High school science teacher in Lenox, Mass., 1952-53, head of department, 1955-56; Duke University, Durham, N.C., assistant professor, 1958-63, associate professor, 1963-67, professor of zoology, 1967—, director of Field Station for Animal Behavior Studies, 1968-73. Visiting professor at Tel-Aviv University, spring, 1970. U.S. representative on International Ethology Committee, 1967-77. Member of regional executive committee of American Friends Service Committee, 1967-74. Carolina Friends School, Durham, chairman of board, 1970-75, member of board executive committee, 1979-80.

MEMBER: American Association for the Advancement of Science (fellow), Animal Behavior Society (fellow), Organization for Tropical Studies (member of board of directors, 1967—), North Carolina Academy of Science. *Awards, honors:* Fellow of U.S. Public Health Service at Cambridge University, 1957-58; National Institute of Mental Health grants, 1965-70, 1970-80; Humboldt Award from West Germany, 1979-80.

WRITINGS: Behavioral Aspects of Ecology, Prentice-Hall, 1962, 2nd edition, 1973; (with Jack P. Hailman) *Introduction to Animal Behavior: Ethology's First Century,* Prentice-Hall, 1967, revised edition, 1974; *Territories and Habitats: A Study of the Use of Space by Animals,* Basic Books, 1969; (editor) *Behavioral Ecology,* Dickenson, 1970; (editor with Hailman) *An Historical Sample From the Pens of Ethologists,* Addison-Wesley, Volume I: *Function and Evolution*

of Behavior, 1972, Volume II: *Control and Development of Behavior,* 1973; (with Robert Barnett and Lee McGeorge) *Maternal Care* (monograph), Addison-Wesley, 1973; *Instinct Is a Cheshire Cat: A Primer on Animal Behavior,* Lippincott, 1973; (editor with Patrick P.G. Bateson) *Perspectives in Ethology,* Plenum, Volume I, 1973, Volume II, 1977, Volume III, 1978; (editor with Robert Wallace) *Readings in Sociobiology,* Holt, 1980; (editor with David Gubernick) *Parental Behavior,* Plenum, 1980. Also author of *Girls and Horses: A Sex Difference in Attachments,* with wife, Martha Klopfer and Jackie Etemad, in press.

Contributor: David Lehrman, Robert Hinde, and Evelyn Shaw, editors, *Advances in the Study of Behavior,* Academic Press, 1965; Thomas Sebeok, editor, *Animal Communication,* Indiana University Press, 1968; Allen W. Stokes, editor, *Laboratory Studies of Animal Behavior,* W. H. Freeman, 1968; Adolph Barash, editor, *Methods in Teaching Biology,* University of Tel Aviv, 1971; Gordon Bermant, editor, *Perspectives in Animal Behavior,* Scott, Foresman, 1973; Edward Simmel and Michael Hahn, editors, *Communication, Behavior, and Evolution,* Academic Press, 1976; Klaus Immelmann, editor, *Animal Behavior,* Kindler Publishing, 1978; Gerald A. Doyle and Robert D. Martin, editors, *The Study of Prosimian Behavior,* Academic Press, 1978; Aaron Roy, editor, *Species Identification,* Garland Publishing, 1978. Also contributor to *Social Behavior on Islands,* edited by Robert Wallace, in press.

Contributor to *International Encyclopedia of Neurology, Psychiatry, Psychoanalysis, and Psychology.* Contributor of more than sixty articles and reviews to scientific journals and popular science magazines in the United States and abroad, and to *Churchman* and *Friends Journal.* Associate editor of *Journal of Experimental Zoology,* 1970-76; member of editorial board of *American Naturalist,* 1972-76; editorial adviser to Springer-Verlag, 1970—.

WORK IN PROGRESS: Numerous writings.

* * *

KNICKMEYER, Steve 1944-

PERSONAL: Born April 2, 1944, in Cassville, Mo.; son of W. L. (a writer) and Louise (a writer; maiden name, Reed) Knickmeyer; children: Ragan Cash. *Education:* University of Oklahoma, B.A., 1967. *Politics:* "Yes." *Religion:* "No." *Home:* 1100 East 18th, No. 330, Box 24, Ada, Okla. 74820. *Agent:* Albert Zuckerman, Writer's House, Inc., 132 West 31st St., New York, N.Y. 10001. *Office:* Ada Evening News, 116 North Broadway, Ada, Okla. 74820.

CAREER: City of Industry, Calif., sign painter, 1966; Tinker Air Force Base, Midwest City, Okla., inventory manager, 1968-71; *Ada Evening News,* Ada, Okla., reporter and book editor, 1971—. Member of board of directors of General Motors and American Telephone & Telegraph.

WRITINGS: Straight (mystery novel), Random House, 1976; *Cranmer* (mystery novel), Random House, 1978.

WORK IN PROGRESS: Waiver (tentative title), the third mystery novel in the "Cranmer/Maneri" series, for Random House.

SIDELIGHTS: Knickmeyer writes: "I started writing in 1973 because my dad, a short-story writer before the magazine markets collapsed, died in that year without completing a novel he'd fooled with for years. I didn't want that to happen to me. I plan to write more ambitious novels when I become established enough with mysteries to earn eating money. I'm a police/court reporter for my newspaper, which fits nicely with writing mysteries. I'm also a compulsive gambler—blackjack and sporting events—which might explain why I enjoy the uncertainties of writing fiction.''

*   *   *

KNIGHT, Doug(las E.) 1925-

PERSONAL: Born September 9, 1925, in Massachusetts; son of Douglas Euart (a sales manager) and Eleanor (Leitch) Knight; married Marjorie Reed (a secretary), March 25, 1950; children: Douglas, Linda, Gregory, Steven. *Education:* Tufts University, B.A., 1949; graduate study at Boston University, 1950-51. *Politics:* Independent. *Religion:* "Pantheist." *Home address:* Hominy Pot Rd., North Sutton, N.H. 03260. *Agent:* Lurton Blassingame, 60 East 42nd St., New York, N.Y. 10017.

CAREER: Writer. Developed an in-house newspaper, for International Business Machines (IBM), 1965. Public speaker on outdoor survival, survival foods, and camping; guest on radio and television programs, including "Speaking of Sports" and "Monitor." *Military service:* U.S. Navy, 1943-46; became lieutenant junior grade. *Member:* American Society for Cybernetics (director and vice-president in public affairs and publications), Society of Journalists and Authors, Outdoor Writers Association of America. *Awards, honors:* Medal and scholarship from Stern Foundation, awards from Mason-Dixon Outdoor Writers Competition.

WRITINGS: (Co-editor) *Cybernetics, Simulation, and Conflict Resolution,* Spartan Books, 1971; (co-editor) *Cybernetics, Ecology, and Artificial Intelligence,* Spartan Books, 1972; (contributor) *The Experts Book on Freshwater Fishing,* Simon & Schuster, 1974. Contributor to outdoor, sport, and men's adventure magazines, including *True, Outdoor Life, Field and Stream, Guns,* and *Safari.* Senior editor of *Journal of Cybernetics.*

SIDELIGHTS: Knight writes: "My travels have taken me from the northernmost reaches of Alaska to the tip of Argentina; through the British Isles—Scotland, England, Ireland, across the breadth of Canada. I specialize in hunting, fishing, travel, conservation, and ecology-oriented articles. I have hunted big game over much of the world, with Boone & Crockett mule deer from New Mexico and B & C class Canadian moose, as well as Alaskan book caribou.

"In the 1965 Eastern Outdoor Writers Trapshooting Competition in Maryland, I took first place against some of the toughest competitors in the outdoor field. At my first Winchester invitational Outdoor Editors' Shoot in Connecticut, 1970, I took first place in trap and entered the Winners' Circle in 1971."

*   *   *

KNIGIN, Michael Jay 1942-

PERSONAL: Born December 9, 1942, in Brooklyn, N.Y., *Education:* Temple University, B.F.A., 1966. *Home:* 832-34 Broadway, New York, N.Y. 10003.

CAREER: Painter and lithographer, 1966—. Work represented in more than fifty galleries and collections, including Whitney Museum of American Art, Smithsonian Institution, and Museum of Graphic Art; work shown in more than eighty exhibitions in the United States and abroad, 1970—, including Japan, Colombia, Israel, Taiwan, and Hong Kong; made costumes for Metropolitan Opera. Instructor at Pratt Institute and Pratt Graphics Center, 1968-74, assistant professor, 1974, 1976-78; instructor at Yale University, 1971; guest instructor at Indiana University, 1971. Owner of li-

thography workshop in New York, N.Y., 1968-72; co-owner and director of Chiron Press, 1968-71; builder and director of Burston Graphics Center, Jerusalem, Israel, 1974, art and technical director, 1975; art director for Cinetudes Film Productions Ltd., 1977. Production and set designer for "Thursday Night Woman," released by American Film Institute, 1973; photographer for "Tunnelvision," released in 1975. *Awards, honors:* Ford Foundation grant, 1964, for Tamarind Lithography Workshop; Experiments in Art and Technology grant, 1969, for Lithographic Technical Institute.

WRITINGS: (With Murray Zimiles) *The Technique of Fine Art Lithography,* Van Nostrand, 1969; (with Zimiles) *Contemporary Lithographic Workshops Around the World,* Van Nostrand, 1974, revised edition, 1977.

Creator and director of "On the Rocks," an animated film, released in 1974. Contributor of articles, artwork, and reviews to magazines, including *Ambiance* and *Artist's Proof,* and newspapers.

*   *   *

KNOWLER, John 1933(?)-1979

OBITUARY NOTICE: Born c. 1933 in London, England; died March 4, 1979, in London. Editor and author. Knowler worked in the publishing field as London editor for Holt, Rinehart, and Winston, editorial director of the New Fiction Collective, editorial scout in England for Saturday Review Press and Bantam Books, managing director of Rupert Hart-Davis, and editor of hardcover books at Allen Lane/Penguin Books. He wrote several works of fiction, including *The Trap* and *Divinitas.* Obituaries and other sources: *Publishers Weekly,* March 19, 1979.

*   *   *

KNOWLES, John H(ilton) 1926-1979

OBITUARY NOTICE: Born May 23, 1926, in Chicago, Ill.; died of cancer, March 6, 1979, in Boston, Mass. Physician, medical administrator, educator, and author. A well-known and controversial figure in American medicine, Knowles had been president of the Rockefeller Foundation since 1972. He strongly advocated preventive medicine and comprehensive prepaid health insurance for all Americans and was concerned with the rising costs of medical care. Knowles was the youngest doctor ever to serve as general director of the Massachusetts General Hospital, where his innovations included the installation of coronary-care and other specialized-care units. In 1969 he was proposed as a nominee for the position of assistant secretary of Health, Education, and Welfare under President Nixon, but lost the post because many American Medical Association officials would not back him. Among Knowles's writings were *Respiratory Physiology and its Clinical Application* and *Doing Better and Feeling Worse: Health in the United States.* Obituaries and other sources: *Time,* July 4, 1969; *Life,* July 11, 1969; *Current Biography,* Wilson, 1970; *Who's Who in America,* 40th edition, Marquis, 1978; *New York Times,* March 7, 1979; *Washington Post,* March 8, 1979.

*   *   *

KOCH, Charlotte
(Charles Raymond; joint pseudonym with husband, Raymond Koch)

PERSONAL: Married Raymond Koch (a carpenter and writer). *Home:* 1116 West North Shore Ave., Chicago, Ill. 60626.

CAREER: Writer. Worked as office worker. *Member:* Authors Guild, Authors League of America. *Awards, honors:* Best juvenile novel award from Friends of American Writers, 1968, for *Jud.*

WRITINGS—All with husband, Raymond Koch, under joint pseudonym Charles Raymond: *Up from Appalachia,* Follett, 1966; *The Trouble with Gus,* Follett, 1968; *Jud* (juvenile), Houghton, 1968; *Enoch* (juvenile), Houghton, 1969.

* * *

KOCH, Raymond
(Charles Raymond, a joint pseudonym)

PERSONAL: Son of Herman and Frieda Koch; married Charlotte (a writer). *Home:* 1116 West North Shore Ave., Chicago, Ill. 60626.

CAREER: Writer. Self-employed carpenter, 1950-72. *Member:* Authors Guild, Authors League of America, Childrens Reading Round Table. *Awards, honors:* Best juvenile novel award from Friends of American Writers, 1968, for *Jud.*

WRITINGS—All with wife, Charlotte Koch, under joint pseudonym Charles Raymond: *Up From Appalachia* (juvenile novel), Follett, 1966; *The Trouble With Gus* (juvenile novel), Follett, 1968; *Jud* (juvenile novel), Houghton, 1968; *Enoch* (juvenile novel), Houghton, 1969; *Educational Commune,* Schocken, 1972.

SIDELIGHTS: Parts of *Up From Appalachia* have been included in school readers. *Enoch* was translated and published in German.

* * *

KOEHLER, Margaret (Hudson)
(Meg Hudson; Russell Mead, pseudonym)

PERSONAL: Born in New York, N.Y.; daughter of Erastus Mead (a physician) and Margaret (a nurse; maiden name, Giffen) Hudson; married Charles Russell Koehler (a journalist), May 24, 1947; children: Stephen Hudson, Richard Hudson. *Education:* Attended Syracuse University; also studied languages, harp and piano privately. *Religion:* Protestant. *Residence:* Orleans, Mass. *Agent:* Emilie Jacobson, Curtis Brown Ltd., 575 Madison Ave., New York, N.Y. 10022.

CAREER: Worked as newspaper reporter in Georgia, New Jersey, New York, and Washington, D.C., and as writer for a Washington, D.C., public relations firm; free-lance writer, 1960—. Active in local community work. *Member:* American Society of Journalists and Authors, Authors Guild, Authors League of America, National Press Club.

WRITINGS Under name Margaret Koehler: *Visitors Guide to Cape Cod National Seashore,* Chatham Press, 1973; *Recipes From the Portuguese of Provincetown,* Chatham Press, 1973; *Recipes From the Russians of San Francisco,* Chatham Press, 1974.

Under name Meg Hudson: *The House on Kettle Hole Pond,* Bantam, 1979.

Author of fact detective stories under pseudonym Russell Mead for such magazines as *True Detective, Master Detective,* and *Official Detective.* Contributor to more than thirty magazines and newspapers, including *Gourmet, Travel/ Holiday, Boston Herald American,* and *Carte Blanche.*

WORK IN PROGRESS: Four novels, *Behold the Turtle, The C Factor, The Jasper Stone,* and *Boardwalk.*

SIDELIGHTS: Margaret Koehler writes: "I speak Spanish and French, and would like to speak twenty other languages as well; I feel that communication is probably the most vital thing in the world today, and in this respect professional writers must stand at and remain at the helm. Thus, travel is my favorite hobby, and is indulged in as much as is economically possible. Places visited are inevitably springboards for articles and books; fortunately this is an enthusiasm my husband shares.

* * *

KOHL, Marvin 1932-

PERSONAL: Born May 19, 1932, in New York, N.Y.; son of Jesse and Mollie (Wenzel) Kohl; married Phylia Joyce Wurman (a Head Start program director), September 2, 1955; children: Richard, Rhiana, Matthew, Maura. *Education:* City College (now of the City University of New York), B.A., 1954; New York University, M.A., 1958, Ph.D., 1966. *Home:* 168 Temple St., Fredonia, N.Y. 14063. *Office:* Department of Philosophy, State University of New York College at Fredonia, Fredonia, N.Y. 14063.

CAREER: Long Island University, Greenvale, N.Y., Mitchell College, lecturer, 1959-61, Brooklyn Center, instructor in philosophy, 1961-65; State University of New York College at Fredonia, assistant professor, 1965-68, associate professor, 1968-73, professor of philosophy, 1973—. Visiting lecturer in medical ethics, Mount Sinai School of Medicine, City University of New York, 1968-73. *Military service:* U.S. Army, 1954-56. *Awards, honors:* National Institute of Mental Health fellowship, 1970-71.

WRITINGS: The Morality of Killing: The Sanctity of Life, Abortion, and Euthanasia, Humanities, 1974; (editor) *Beneficent Euthanasia,* Prometheus Books, 1975; (editor) *Infanticide and the Value of Life,* Prometheus Books, 1978.

WORK IN PROGRESS: A book on the foundations of ethics, tentatively entitled *The Grounds and Limits of the Right to Life,* publication expected in 1981.

SIDELIGHTS: Marvin Kohl told *CA:* "In *The Morality of Killing* and other writings, I outline a moral theory which maintains that, generally, basic needs should be minimally satisfied; that every defacto basic need claim creates a right on the part of the individual and an obligation on the part of society; that man has both the prima facie right of life and to relinguish life; and that the right to relinguish life allows for certain types of abortion, suicide, and active and passive euthanasia. In recent essays I also explore the implications of the concept of having a meaningful life and suggest that, when a life is irrevocably meaningless, it may be permissible to end or to allow that life to end.

"The purpose of my new work is to explain how a richly endowed but limited right to life can be, and indeed is, a primary moral rule. My analysis and explanation will be based on issues drawn from ethical theory, chiefly, however on the questions of why one human ideal is preferable to another, why and to what extent the human community is obligated to help others, and why a theory of rights is necessary. My own view may be described as that of beneficent ideal utilitarianism."

* * *

KOHT, Halvdan 1873-1965

PERSONAL: Surname rhymes with "root"; born July 7, 1873, in Tromsoe, Norway; died December 12, 1965, in Oslo, Norway; son of Paul Steenstrup (a professor) and Betty (Giaever) Koht; married Karen Elisabeth Grude, September 29, 1898 (died, July 10, 1960); children: Aase Gruda Skard, Paul Gruda. *Education:* Attended University of Copenhagen, 1897, University of Leipzig, 1897-98, and Sorbonne, University of Paris, 1898-99; University of Oslo, Dr. Philos., 1908. *Politics:* Labour Party. *Home:* Fjellveien 2, Lysaker, Norway.

CAREER: University of Oslo, Oslo, Norway, assistant professor, 1900-07, associate professor, 1908-10, professor of history, 1910-35, dean of faculty for humanities, 1915-17; Norwegian Minister of Foreign Affairs, 1935-41. Visiting professor at Harvard University, 1930-31. Member of Baerum Community Council, 1917-19, 1929-35. Member of Norwegian Nobel Committee, 1919-45. *Member:* Comite International des Sciences Historiques (president, 1926-33), Union Academique International (vice-president, 1927-30), member of academies of Caen, Copenhagen, Helsingfors, London, Lund, Prague, Venice, Warzaw, and Oslo, Norwegian Historial Association (president, 1912-27, 1932-36), American Historical Association (honorary member), National Institute of Historical Sources (president, 1918-27), Norwegian Genealogical Association (president, 1928-40), Noregs Maallag (president, 1921-25). *Awards, honors:* Litt.D. from Cambridge University, 1930; D. Hum. Litt. from University of Chicago, 1941, and University of Warzaw, 1958; officer of Legion d'Honneur, 1928; Gunnerus Medal from Det Kongelige Videnskabers Selskab (Trondheim), 1952.

WRITINGS—In English: *Henrik Ibsen: Eit diktarliv*, Aschehoug (Oslo), 1928, revised edition, 1954, translation by Ruth Lima McMahon and Hanna Astrup Larsen published as *The Life of Ibsen*, Norton, 1931, translation by Einar Haugen and A. E. Santaniello published as *Life of Ibsen*, Blom, 1971; *The Old Norse Sagas*, Norton, 1931, reprinted, Kraus, 1971; *Norway Neutral and Invaded*, Macmillan, 1941; (with Sigmund Skard), *The Voice of Norway*, Columbia University Press, 1944; *The American Spirit in Europe: A Survey of Transatlantic Influences*, University of Pennsylvania Press, 1949; *Historikar i laere: Utgjevi ab den Norske historiske forening*, I kommisjon hos Groendahl (Oslo), 1951, translation and notes by Erik Wahlgren published as *Education of an Historian*, R. Speller, 1957; *Drivmakter i historia*, Aschehoug, 1959, translation by Haugen published as *Driving Forces in History*, Belknap Press, 1964.

Other works: *Henrik Ibsen: Samlede vaerker*, Volume X (Halvdan was not associated with earlier volumes), Gyldendal (Copenhagen), c. 1902; *Henrik Wergeland: Ei folkeskrift*, Aschehoug, 1908; *Die stellung Norwegens und Schwedens im deutschdaenischen konflikt: Zumal waehrend der jahre 1863 und 1864*, [Copenhagen], 1908; *Volksheros und weltheros*, Weidmann (Berlin), 1909; *Abraham Lincoln: Et hundredaarsminde*, [Kristiania (now Oslo)], 1909; *Folkestyre*, Mallingske bogtrykkeri (Kristiania), 1909; *A. O. Vinje: Stutt livsskildring*, Aschehoug, 1909; (editor) *Henrik Ibsen: Efterladte skrifter*, Gyldendal (Kristiania), 1909; *Pengemagt og arbeid i Amerika*, Aschehoug, 1910; *Bismark: Statsmanden*, Aschehoug, 1911; *Prisar og politikk i norsk historie*, Mallingske bogtrkkeri, 1913; *Den amerikanske nasjonen i upphav og reising*, Aschehoug, 1920; *Amerikansk kultur i det nittende aarhundred*, Gyldendal (Copenhagen), 1920; *Innhogg og utsyn i norsk historie*, Aschehoug, 1921; *Norsk bondereising: Fyrebuing til bondepolitikken*, Aschehoug, 1926; (editor) *Vaare hoevdinger*, [Trondheim], 1929, selections published as *Norske hoevdinger: Livsskildringer redigert*, Nordisk tidende (Brooklyn), c. 1940; *Stortings opploeysinga i 1836: Opplyst med nye aktstykke* [Oslo], 1937;

Saga litteraturen: Populaere foerelesningar, Det Norske samlaget (Oslo), 1938.

Fraa skanse til skanse: Minne fraa krigsmaanadene i Noreg, 1940, Tiden (Oslo), 1947; *Norsk utanriks politikk fram til 9, april 1940: Synspunkt fraa hendings tida*, Tiden, 1947; *Revolusjonsaaret, 1848*, Tiden, 1948; (author of new edition) *Oversigt over middelalderens historie: Udgivet som grundlag for eksaminatorier og forelaesninger*, Gyldendal, 1949; *Vincens Lunge contra Henrik Krummedige, 1523-1525*, Aschehoug, 1950; *Olav Engelbriktsson og sjoelvstende-tapet, 1537*, Aschehoug, 1951; *Baerum arbeiderparti, 1902-1952*, Oslo, 1952; *Kong Sverre*, Aschehoug, 1952; *Paa leit etter liner i historia*, Aschehoug, 1953; *Harald Haarfagre og rikssamlinga*, Aschehoug, 1955; (editor) Ann Margret Holmgren, *Norske Brev: Saerlig fra 1905*, Gyldendal, 1955; *Dronning Margareta og Kalmar-unionen*, Aschehoug, 1956; *For fred og fridom i krigstid, 1939-40*, Tiden, 1957; (editor and author of introduction) Sars Johan Ernst Welhaven, *Brev, 1850-1915*, Gyldendal, 1957. *Fraa norsk midalder: Tre foerelesningar for Universitetet i Bergen, November, 1958*, Universitetsforlaget i kommisjon (Bergen), 1959.

Inn i einveldet, 1657-1661, Aschehoug, 1960; *Verda og Noreg: Historie fraa skilde tider*, Aschehoug, 1962; *Kongesoger: Sverre-soga, Baglarsoger*, Det Norske samlaget, 1962; *Menn i historia*, Aschehoug, 1963; *Nye innhogg og utsyn*, Aschehoug, 1964; *Minnearv og historie: Gamle og nye artiklar*, Aschehoug, 1965; *Minne fraa unge aar*, Aschehoug, 1968; (with Francis Bull and Didrik Arup Seip) *Innledninger til Hundraarsutgaven av Henrik Ibsens Samlede verker*, Gyldendal, 1972.

Author of more than three thousand articles for journals, encyclopedias, and newspapers. Editor of *Syn og Segn*, 1901-08.

SIDELIGHTS: Koht was the Foreign Minister of Norway's Labor Government when the country was invaded by the Nazis in 1940. A strong proponent of neutrality, Koht led Norway's government-in-exile until he was forced to retire in 1941 due to ill health.

OBITUARIES: New York Times, December 13, 1965, December 14, 1965.*

*   *   *

KOJECKY, Roger 1943-

PERSONAL: Surname is pronounced Ko-*yet*-ski; born January 29, 1943, in London, England; son of Miroslav (an army officer) and Sheila (Watson) Kojecky; married Marie-Christine Dieudonne, July 2, 1977. *Education:* University of Aberdeen, M.A. (honors), 1966; Lincoln College, Oxford, D.Phil., 1969. *Politics:* Liberal Democrat. *Religion:* Evangelical Christian. *Home:* 42 Nursery Rd., Cuckoo Hill, Pinner, Middlesex HA5 2AP, England.

CAREER: British Council lecturer in English literature at Tokyo University of Education and Keio University, 1970-72; International Business Machines Ltd. (IBM), London, England, executive, 1974—. Lecturer at University of London. *Member:* Conference on Christianity and Literature, Shaftesbury Project Political Action Study Group (convener, 1974-78). *Awards, honors:* George Adam Smith Prize from University of Aberdeen, 1973, for *T. S. Eliot's Social Criticism*.

WRITINGS: T. S. Eliot's Social Criticism, Farrar, Straus, 1972. Editor of *Intercom*, 1975-77.

WORK IN PROGRESS: The Plays of Noel Coward, a critical study; a collection of short stories.

SIDELIGHTS: Roger Kojecky pointed out that his book, *T. S. Eliot's Social Criticism,* contained the first publication of a paper, "On the Place and Functions of the Clerisy," by Eliot and a discussion of its context. Frank Kermode in *New York Times Book Review* described the book as "maturely critical and intelligent.... and excellent on the adaptation of the Coleridgean notion of the clerisy." Robert Nye called it "a contribution to serious understanding of the poet's general position."

Kojecky also noted that the settings for his short stories "draw on my observations in Japan, Czechoslovakia, France, and Britain."

BIOGRAPHICAL/CRITICAL SOURCES: *Scotsman,* January 22, 1972; *New York Times Book Review,* March 26, 1972.

* * *

KOMODA, Beverly 1939-

PERSONAL: Born November 26, 1939, in Seattle, Wash.; daughter of Robert R. (a dentist) and Mary (Uno) Higashida; married Kiyoaki Komoda (an art director and free-lance illustrator), July, 1962; children: Paul, Daniel, Kurt. *Education:* Attended Chouinard Art Institute, 1957-61. *Religion:* Protestant. *Home:* 14 Maple Stream Rd., East Windsor, N.J. 08520.

CAREER: Free-lance writer and illustrator, 1963—. *Member:* Authors Guild, Authors League of America.

WRITINGS: *Simon's Soup* (children's book; self-illustrated) Parents' Magazine Press, 1978.

Illustrator—All children's books: Richard Jackson, *Douglas Saves the Day,* Macmillan, 1964; Carole Vetter, *The Wishing Night,* Macmillan, 1966; Carol G. Hogan, *Eighteen Cousins,* Parents' Magazine Press, 1968; Miriam Young, *Jelly Beans for Breakfast,* Parents' Magazine Press, 1968; Winifred E. Wise, *The Revolt of the Darumas,* Parents' Magazine Press, 1970; Mary Blount Christian, *The First Sign of Winter,* Parents' Magazine Press, 1973.

WORK IN PROGRESS: Picture books.

SIDELIGHTS: Beverly Komoda comments: "I wish to depict various world-wide truths via the humorous picture book story. In *Simon's Soup* the theme was the importance of perseverance to reach a goal. The story themes I use in *Simon's Soup* and in my works in progress are ones that I feel very strongly about in my own life. Portraying them humorously makes it fun.

"I have a large affection for the books that I read when young. My favorites became an integral part of me. I hope to give back in some small measure some of the enjoyment I experienced (and still do) as a 'bookworm,' through my work."

* * *

KONRAD, Gyoergy 1933-
(George Konrad)

PERSONAL: Born in 1933, in Hungary. *Religion:* Jewish. *Address:* c/o Helen and Kurt Wolff Books, Harcourt Brace Jovanovich, Inc., 757 Third Ave., New York, N.Y. 10017.

CAREER: Social worker and novelist.

WRITINGS: (With Ivan Szelenyi) *Az uj lakotelepek szociologiai problemai* Akademiai Kiado, 1969; *A latogato,* Magveto, 1969, translation by Paul Aston published (under name George Konrad) as *The Case Worker,* Harcourt, 1974; (under name George Konrad) *The City Builder,* translation by

Ivan Sanders, Harcourt, 1977. Also author of *A Varosalapito.*

WORK IN PROGRESS: A book about his adventures in New York City; a book about an old peasant couple.

SIDELIGHTS: Konrad grew up in a small village in eastern Hungary. During the Nazi occupation in 1944 his parents were arrested. Eleven-year-old Konrad had heard about the mass deportation of Jews that was taking place and knew that he and his younger sister must leave town, but Jews were not allowed to travel on trains. Konrad found his father's hidden money and bribed the local police to give them passes to Budapest, where his aunt lived. The day after they left all the Jews from his village were deported. The women and children were sent to concentration camps in Auschwitz, where nearly all of them died, and the men were sent as forced laborers to the Ukrainian front.

When Konrad and his sister returned home in 1945, they found many of the Jewish men waiting for their families to return. Konrad told Patricia Blake: "These men kept staring at us, and you could see they were thinking 'It's good you're alive, but what about *our* children?' ... I don't think I am exaggerating when I say that I had the thought that I must live in place of my old school friends. I felt I had to substitute for those dead Jewish children. I am not only myself."

In 1974 Konrad and fellow author Ivan Szelenyi were arrested and imprisoned in Budapest. Police had found hidden in Szelenyi's apartment a manuscript of their sociological study called "The Intelligentsia on the Road to Class Power" and charged them with subversive agitation. After six days in jail they were released because the manuscript had never been available to the public. The book was banned and Konrad was told he could leave the country if he felt he could not obey the law. However, said Konrad, "it would have been rather cowardly to emigrate as a result of a case that turned out not to be so serious after all.... If he isn't forced to it, a writer should not emigrate, should not turn away from the risks of his profession. He must accept those risks and live with them; he must be free wherever he finds himself."

Praised by many critics as a "stunning first novel," *The Case Worker* is a first-person narrative about the life of a social worker cracking under the strain of the wretchedness and cruelty he must deal with each day. "Such raw human suffering as is depicted here is infrequently the subject of works of fiction," said the *New Yorker,* "and even more infrequently the theme of a writer as skilled, brilliant, and willing to take risks as Mr. Konrad. This is an almost unbearable book to read, but it should not be missed." Neal Ascherson, however, felt that there was "much to make reservations about: his violent, remorseless battering of the feelings causes monotony, his rhetorical seizures which spatter the reader with a hundred hot adjectives in a few sentences are, it seems to me, the easy but wrong way to the effect he wants."

The City Builder, the second of Konrad's books to be translated into English, received mixed reviews. The book is divided into ten chapters, which Susan Lardner described as "interwoven fragments that range in tone from grim irony to nostalgia, and include reminiscence, indecipherable dreams, panoramic description, invective, and exhortation." Frances Taliaferio commented that "the fault of this novel is its terrible abundance, its bombardment with sensory and symbolic details. There are certainly pity and terror in many of Konrad's furious visions, but they are mixed with the ennui of his relentless tone." Nevertheless, Jascha Kessler called

The City Builder "a beautiful, brave book, a work of the stoic imagination."

BIOGRAPHICAL/CRITICAL SOURCES: Books Abroad, autumn, 1970; *New York Times Book Review,* January 27, 1974, December 1, 1974; *Village Voice,* February 28, 1974; *New Yorker,* March 11, 1974, April 10, 1978; *New Republic,* March 16, 1974; *New York Review of Books,* August 8, 1974, March 9, 1978; *Choice,* September, 1974; *Contemporary Literary Criticism,* Gale, Volume 4, 1975, Volume 10, 1979; *Times Literary Supplement,* January 31, 1975; *Time,* November 28, 1977.*

*   *   *

KOSOF, Anna 1945-

PERSONAL: Born May 22, 1945, in Hungary; daughter of Andor and Clara (Biro) Forgach; married Carl Kosof (a public relations agent), January 22, 1965 (divorced); married J. Richard Holmes (a professor), May 12, 1972; children: (first marriage) Stefan. *Education:* Attended Connecticut College, summers, 1962-64; City College of the City University of New York, B.A., 1974; Hunter College of the City University of New York, M.A., 1975; further graduate study at New School for Social Research. *Home:* 345 East 81st St., New York, N.Y. 10028. *Office:* Interscience, 20 East 49th St., New York, N.Y. 10017.

CAREER: Narcotics Institute, New York City, researcher, 1966-67; Addicts Rehabilitation Center, New York City, counselor and supervisor, 1967-68; "Night Call" (radio program), New York City, associate producer, 1968-69; Harlem Hospital, New York City, counselor for "Narco I" program, 1969-71; Infinity (residential drug treatment center for young people), New York City, director of education and cultural affairs, 1971-72; National Drug Abuse Training Center, Silver Springs, Md., consultant, 1973; associate producer for "Realidades," WNET-TV, 1973; La Guardia Community College of the City University of New York, Long Island City, N.Y., adjunct instructor in social science and anthropology, 1975—. General manager of WBAI-Radio, 1976—; currently vice-president of Interart. Assistant to owner of Melvin Van Peebles Production Company, 1969-73.

MEMBER: American Anthropological Association, Society for the Anthropology of Visual Communication, New York Women's Anthropological Caucus.

WRITINGS: The Run-Aways, F. Watts, 1977. Contributor to *Third Press Review.*

WORK IN PROGRESS: Women in the Addicted Society; research on youth problems, Africa, anthropology, and broadcasting.

SIDELIGHTS: Kosof's first book is based on research concentrated on the East Coast, dealing with teenagers, parents, police, teenage prostitutes, and directors of centers for runaways. She has studied dance with leading professionals, including Martha Graham and Merce Cunningham.

BIOGRAPHICAL/CRITICAL SOURCES: Time, August 23, 1968; *Newsweek,* May 12, 1969; *Saturday Review,* August 26, 1969; Michael Zwerin, *The Silent Sound of Needles,* Prentice-Hall, 1969.

*   *   *

KRAKOWSKI, Lili 1930-

PERSONAL: Born July 24, 1930, in Berlin, Germany; came to United States in 1941, naturalized citizen, 1946; daughter of Menko Max (a scholar) and Sophia (Prins) Hirsch; married M. E. Krakowski (in business), November 21, 1956. *Education:* Rochester Institute of Technology, A.A.S., 1953. *Politics:* Republican. *Religion:* Jewish. *Home and office address:* P.O. Box 1, Constableville, N.Y. 13325. *Agent:* James Oliver Brown Associates, 25 West 43rd St., New York, N.Y. 10036.

CAREER: County Center, White Plains, N.Y., teacher of pottery, 1954-56; World Publishing, New York City, promotion assistant in library sales, 1960-61; Sussman & Sugar, New York City, account executive and writer, 1961-62; Macmillan Publishing Co., Inc., New York City, senior copywriter, 1962-65; McGraw-Hill Book Co., New York City, copy chief, then advertising manager in trade book department, 1965-68; March Advertising, Inc., New York City, director of book promotion, 1968-73; free-lance writer, 1973—.

WRITINGS: (Translator from the German) Friedel Stoetzner, *The Transplanted* (novel), McGraw, 1966; *Starting Out: The Guide I Wish I'd Had When I Left Home,* Stein & Day, 1973. Contributor of articles and reviews to magazines.

WORK IN PROGRESS: The Pottery Teacher; Picture Puzzle, a mystery novel; *The Return,* a Utopian novel.

SIDELIGHTS: Lili Krakowski writes: "I believe that knowledge is freedom and freedom happiness. I believe man must have total freedom from other men in order to perfect his direct relationship to God. What we owe each other is help and support in that search.

"My book on pottery is directed at people who, for want of good teachers, must teach themselves. All my writing reflects my beliefs in one way or the other—even the mysteries. In an age when television gives us all the entertainment we can use, the written word must operate at a more serious level. My Utopian novel illustrates my viewpoints very clearly."

*   *   *

KRAMER, Victor A. 1939-

PERSONAL: Born October 21, 1939, in Youngstown, Ohio; son of Edward L. (a furniture restorer) and Leota (an antiques dealer; maiden name, Feuerstein) Kramer; married Dewey E. Weiss (a professor), September 6, 1963; children: Jerome Victor. *Education:* St. Edward's University, A.B., 1961; University of Texas, M.A., 1963, Ph.D., 1966. *Politics:* Democrat. *Religion:* Roman Catholic. *Home:* 1748 Vickers Circle, Decatur, Ga. 30030. *Office:* Georgia State University, Atlanta, Ga. 30303.

CAREER: Marquette University, Milwaukee, Wis., assistant professor, 1966-69; Georgia State University, Atlanta, assistant professor, 1969-76, associate professor of literature, 1976—. Fulbright senior lecturer at University of Regensburg, 1974-75; lecturer at professional meetings in Germany and the United States.

MEMBER: Modern Language Association of America, National Council of Teachers of English, American Studies Association, American Association of University Professors, South Atlantic Modern Language Association. *Awards, honors:* Grants from Georgia State Foundation, 1972, American Philosophical Society, 1973, Emory University, 1973, and Georgia State Urban Life Center, 1978.

WRITINGS: (Editor) *Studies in the Literary Imagination: The Harlem Renaissance,* Georgia State University, 1974; *James Agee,* Twayne, 1975; (contributor) Jac Tharpe, editor, *Tennessee Williams: A Tribute,* University Press of

Mississippi, 1977; (co-editor and contributor) *Olmsted South,* Greenwood Press, 1979; (editor) *Studies in the Literary Imagination: Literary Theory,* Georgia State University, 1979. Also contributor to *The 1930's,* University of Alabama Press. Contributor of more than forty articles and reviews to academic journals.

WORK IN PROGRESS: A book on Thomas Merton for publication by G. K. Hall; a book on James Agee, Walker Percy, and Peter Taylor; a bibliography of Agee's and Flannery O'Connor's literary manuscripts, for Garland Publishing; a critical edition of Agee's *A Death in the Family;* editing *The Development of Agee's Career as a Writer: Documents of Twenty Years;* research on Hemingway, Frost, Pynchon, Merton, and Caroline Gordon.

*　*　*

KRASNER, Stephen D(avid) 1942-

PERSONAL: Born February 15, 1942, in New York, N.Y.; son of Jack and Lillian (Weiss) Krasner. *Education:* Cornell University, B.A., 1963; Columbia University, M.A., 1967; Harvard University, Ph.D., 1971. *Office:* Department of Political Science, University of California, Los Angeles, Calif. 90024.

CAREER: Harvard University, Cambridge, Mass., assistant professor of government, 1971-75; University of California, Los Angeles, associate professor of political science, 1976—.

WRITINGS: Defending the National Interest, Princeton University Press, 1978. Contributor to political science journals.

WORK IN PROGRESS: The Political Economy of North-South Relations.

*　*　*

KRAUSS, Herbert Harris 1940-

PERSONAL: Born June 13, 1940, in Philadelphia, Pa.; son of Leon and Ethel (Cohen) Krauss; married Beatrice Joy Osgood (a psychologist), August 28, 1965; children: Michael Conal, Daniel Avram. *Education:* Pennsylvania State University, B.S., 1961, M.S., 1962; Northwestern University, Ph.D., 1966. *Home:* 5 Willow St., Irvington, N.Y. 10533. *Office:* Department of Psychology, Hunter College of the City University of New York, 695 Park Ave., New York, N.Y. 10021.

CAREER: University of Oregon, Eugene, intern in medical psychology at Medical School, 1963-63; University of Kansas, Lawrence, assistant professor of psychiatry, 1966-67; Ohio State University, Columbus, assistant professor of child psychiatry and chief psychologist, 1967-69; University of Georgia, Athens, associate professor of psychology, 1969-71; Hunter College of the City University of New York, New York, N.Y., associate professor, 1971-73, professor of psychology, 1973—. *Member:* American Psychological Association, New York Academy of Science, Sigma Xi.

WRITINGS: (Contributor) H. D. Werner, editor, *New Understandings of Human Behavior,* Association Press, 1970; (with wife, Beatrice Krauss) *Living With Anxiety and Depression,* Thomas More Press, 1973; (contributor) B. B. Wolman, editor, *Between Survival and Suicide,* Gardener, 1978. Contributor of more than forty articles to psychology journals.

WORK IN PROGRESS: Classics in Psychology; a textbook on abnormal psychology; a book of short character studies.

KREIN, David F(rederick) 1942-

PERSONAL: Born April 14, 1942, in Mauston, Wis.; son of Gideon I. (a clergyman) and Dorothy (Bibb) Krein; married Louise Hall (a teacher), December 19, 1964. *Education:* University of Dubuque, B.A. (magna cum laude), 1963; Duke University, M.A., 1965; further graduate study at University of Wisconsin—Madison, 1964-65; University of Iowa, Ph.D., 1974. *Home:* 6304 Scott St., Davenport, Iowa 52806. *Office:* Department of Social Science, Palmer Junior College, 1000 Brady St., Davenport, Iowa 52803.

CAREER: Washburn University of Topeka, Topeka, Kan., instructor in history, 1965-67; Clarke College, Dubuque, Iowa, assistant professor of history, 1967-69; University of Iowa, Iowa City, adjunct instructor in history, 1974-76; Palmer Junior College, Davenport, Iowa, associate professor of history, 1976—, head of department of social science, 1976—, and head of Division of Behavioral and Social Sciences, 1978—. Adjunct instructor at Black Hawk College, 1974-76. *Member:* American Historical Association, Phi Alpha Theta.

WRITINGS: The Last Palmerston Government: Foreign Policy, Domestic Politics, and the Genesis of "Splendid Isolation", Iowa State University Press, 1978. Contributor to history journals.

WORK IN PROGRESS: The Vienna Congress, 1814-1815; Britain and the World Since 1485.

SIDELIGHTS: Krein told *CA:* "*The Last Palmerston Government* was originally my doctoral dissertation, but had to be cut in half for publication. My interest is foreign relations, especially the ways in which domestic politics affect them. My present work on the Vienna Congress will take five to seven years to complete, as it is a multi-archival project and will require at least a year's research in Europe. The other project, *Britain and the World Since 1945,* should be done in two years as it is really an interpretive essay based on secondary sources. I have also been working on a novel about life in the sixties for several years, but I don't know if or when that will be finished as I find writing fiction an intensely painful experience. Writing history is a sheer joy for me."

*　*　*

KROUT, John Allen 1896-1979

OBITUARY NOTICE: Born October 3, 1896, in Tiffin, Ohio; died April 3, 1979, in Tiffin. Educator, administrator, and author. Krout began his career at Columbia University as an instructor in history, rose to professor, and retired as provost and vice president thirty-six years later. He also served as chairman of the national education division of the President's Committee for Hungarian Relief and as trustee of the New York State Historical Association. Formerly an editor of the *Political Science Quarterly,* Krout wrote several books, including *Approaches to Social History.* Obituaries and other sources: *Directory of American Scholars,* Volume I: *History,* 6th edition, Bowker, 1974; *Who's Who in America,* 39th edition, Marquis, 1976; *New York Times,* April 5, 1979.

*　*　*

KUBINYI, Laszlo 1937-

PERSONAL—Education: Attended Boston Museum School and Art Students League, New York, N.Y. *Residence:* New York, N.Y.

CAREER: Author and illustrator of children's books. Traveled throughout the world, particularly the Middle East; played the dumbek (a Middle Eastern drum) in an Armenian orchestra.

WRITINGS: The Cat and the Flying Machine (self-illustrated), Simon & Schuster, 1970; Zeki and the Talking Cat Shukru (self-illustrated), Simon & Schuster, 1970.

Illustrator: Cristoforo Columbo, Across the Ocean Sea: A Journal of Columbus's Voyage, edited by George Sanderlin, Harper, 1966; Coralie Howard, What Do You Want to Know?, Simon & Schuster, 1968; Martin Gardner, Perplexing Puzzles and Tantalizing Teasers, Simon & Schuster, 1969; Jeanne B. Hardendorff, Witches, Wit, and a Werewolf, Lippincott, 1971; Betty Jean Lifton, The Silver Crane, Seabury, 1971; Adrien Stoutenburg, Haran's Journey, Dial, 1971; Tony Hillerman, The Boy Who Made Dragonfly: A Zuni Myth, Harper, 1972; Maureen Mollie Hunter McIlwraith, The Haunted Mountain, Harper, 1972; F. N. Monjo, Slater's Mill, Simon & Schuster, 1972; Peter Putnam, Peter the Revolutionary Tsar, Harper, 1973; Felice Holman, I Hear You Smiling, and Other Poems, Scribner, 1973; Maia Wojciechowska, Winter Tales From Poland, Doubleday, 1973; Natalia Maree Belting, editor, Our Fathers Had Powerful Songs, Dutton, 1974; Lloyd Alexander, The Wizard in the Tree, Dutton, 1975; Margaret Greaves, The Dagger and the Bird: A Story of Suspense, Harper, 1975; Ellen Pugh, The Adventures of Yoo-Lah-Teen: A Legend of the Salish Coastal Indians, Dial, 1975; Miriam Anne Bourne, Patsy Jefferson's Diary, Coward, 1976.*

*   *   *

KUHLMAN, James A(llen)   1941-

PERSONAL: Born September 4, 1941, in Chicago, Ill.; son of David Luther (a contractor) and Gertrude Anne (an investment analyst; maiden name, Brushmoore) Kuhlman; married M. Braden Kleibacker (a speech therapist), September 3, 1966; children: Ann Braden, Lara Kathryn. Education: Northwestern University, B.S., 1963, M.A. (political science), 1968, Ph.D., 1971; George Washington University, M.A. (public and international affairs), 1966. Home address: Route 1, Box 224, Lake Point District, Chapin, S.C. 29036. Office: Department of Government, University of South Carolina, Columbia, S.C. 29208.

CAREER: University of South Carolina, Columbia, assistant professor, 1969-72, associate professor, 1972-78, professor of government and head of department, 1978—. President of Institute for Public Policy Development. Member of policy board of Republican National Committee's Council on National Security and International Affairs. Member: International Political Science Association, International Studies Association (executive director, 1978—), American Political Science Association, American Academy of Political and Social Science, American Association for the Advancement of Slavic Studies, American Association for the Advancement of Science, Academy of Political Science, Southern Political Science Association. Awards, honors: Outstanding civilian service medal from U.S. Department of the Army, 1977.

WRITINGS: (With Louis J. Mensonides) The Future of Inter-Bloc Relations in Europe, Praeger, 1974; (with Mensonides) Changes in European Relations, Sijthoff, 1976; (with Mensonides) American and European Security, Sijthoff, 1977; (editor) Strategies, Alliances, and Military Power, Sijthoff, 1977; (editor) The Foreign Policies of Eastern Europe, Sijthoff, 1978; (with Andrew Gyorgy) Innovations in Communist Systems, Westview Press, 1978; (with Richard

P. Farkas) Regional Integration: Theory and Research on Eastern Europe, Sijthoff, 1979; (editor) Hemispheric Security: Issues in Inter-American Relations, Sijthoff, 1979.

Contributor: Charles Gati, editor, International Politics of Eastern Europe, Praeger, 1976; James N. Rosenau, Kenneth Thompson, and Gavin Boyd, editors, World Politics, Free Press, 1976; Dennis Clark Pirages, editor, Sustainable Society, Praeger, 1977.

General editor of "East-West Perspectives" and "Studies in U.S. National Security," both series published by Sijthoff.

WORK IN PROGRESS: Editing The Global Strategic Balance; editing The Warsaw Pact: Strengths and Weaknesses; editing Military Policy: Analysis and Evaluation.

SIDELIGHTS: Kuhlman comments: "The vehicle of scientific inquiry as a transnational communication process remains the single most promising activity in the pursuit of peace in the contemporary international system. The subjects of my written work, my professional endeavors and travels, and my personal contacts world-wide are all elements keyed to this belief and conceived to reinforce cross-cultural dissemination of knowledge and information."

*   *   *

KUHLMANN, Susan   1942-

PERSONAL: Born June 23, 1942, in Goshen, N.Y. Education: Radcliffe College, A.B., 1964; Stanford University, M.A., 1966; New York University, Ph.D., 1970. Office: Department of English, University of Iowa, Iowa City, Iowa 52240.

CAREER: Ohio State University, Columbus, visiting assistant professor of English, 1972-73; University of Iowa, Iowa City, assistant professor, 1973-77, associate professor of English, 1977—. Member: Modern Language Association of America.

WRITINGS: Knave, Fool, and Genius, University of North Carolina Press, 1973.

*   *   *

KULTERMANN, Udo   1927-

PERSONAL: Born October 14, 1927, in Stettin, Germany (now part of Poland); came to the United States in 1967; son of Georg and Charlotte (Schultz) Kultermann; married Judith Danoof, 1975; children: (previous marriage) Martin, Andreas, Eva. Education: Attended University of Greifswald, 1946-50; University of Muenster, Ph.D., 1953. Home: 6833 Kingsbury, St. Louis, Mo. 63130. Office: School of Architecture, Washington University, Lindell-Skinker Blvd., St. Louis, Mo. 63130.

CAREER: Museum Schloss Morsbroich, Leverkusen, West Germany, director, 1959-64; Washington University, St. Louis, Mo., professor of architecture, 1967—. Awards, honors: Most beautiful book of the year award in Germany, 1969, for Neue Formen des Bildes.

WRITINGS—In English: Baukunst der Gegenwart, Wasmuth, 1958, translation by E.H.W. Priefert published as Architecture of Today, Universe Books, 1959; Neues Bauen in Japan, Wasmuth, 1960, translation published as New Architecture in Japan, Thames and Hudson, 1961; Neues Bauen in Afrika, Wasmuth, 1963, translation by Ernst Flesch published as New Architecture in Africa, Universe Books, 1964; Neues Bauen in der Welt, Wasmuth, 1965, 2nd edition, 1976, translation by Flesch published as New Architecture in the World, Universe Books, 1966, 2nd edition,

1977; *Neue Dimensionen der Plastik,* Wasmuth, 1967, 2nd edition, 1972, translation by Stanley Baron published as *The New Sculpture,* Praeger, 1968; *Neue Formen des Bildes,* Wasmuth, 1969, 2nd edition, 1975, translation by Gerald Onn published as *The New Painting,* Praeger, 1970, 2nd edition, Westview Press, 1978; *New Directions in African Architecture,* Braziller, 1969; (with Werner Hofmann) *Baukunst in unserer Zeit: Die Entwicklung seit 1850,* Heyer, 1969, translation by Peter Usborne published as *Modern Architecture in Color,* Viking, 1970; *Kenzo Tange: Architecture and Urban Design* (trilingual, in German, English, and French), Artemis, 1970, revised edition, 1978; *Leben und Kunst: Zur Funktion der Intermedia,* Wasmuth, 1970, translation by John William Gabriel published as *Art and Life,* Praeger, 1971; *Radikaler Realismus,* Wasmuth, 1972, translation published as *New Realism,* New York Graphic Society, 1972; *Ernest Trova,* Abrams, 1978.

In German: *Dynamisch Architektur* (title means "Dynamic Architecture"), Lucas Cranach Verlag, 1958; *Wassili und Hans Luckhardt: Bauten und Projekte* (title means "Wassili and Hans Luckhardt: Buildings and Projects"), Wasmuth, 1959; *Junge deutsche Bildhauer* (title means "Young German Sculptors"), Kupferberg, 1963; *Der Schluessel zur Architektur von Heute* (title means "The Key to Architecture of Today"), Econ Verlag, 1963; *Geschichte der Kunstgeschichte: Der Weg einer Wissenschaft* (title means "History of Art History: The Formation of a Science"), Econ Verlag, 1966; *Architektur der Gegenwart* (title means "Contemporary Architecture"), Holle, 1967; *Gabriel Grupello,* Deutscher Verlag fuer Kunst-Wissenscheft, 1968; *Die Architektur im Zwanzigsten Jahrhundert* (title means "Architecture in the Twentieth Century"), DuMont, 1977; *Contemporary Sculpture,* Mondadori, 1979; *The Basilica of Maxentius,* Gebr. Mann, 1979; *Architecture of the Seventies,* Architectural Press, 1980; *The Renaissance of Contemporary Architecture in the Arab States,* Architectural Press, 1980; *The Body of Woman,* Fischer, 1980; *Architects of the Third World,* DuMont, 1980.

SIDELIGHTS: Kultermann's books have been published in Dutch, French, Spanish, Serbo-Croatian, Finnish, Romanian, and Italian.

*　　　*　　　*

KUNDERA, Milan 1929-

PERSONAL: Born April 1, 1929, in Brno, Czechoslovakia; immigrated to France, 1975; son of Ludvik (a pianist) and Milada (Janosikova) Kundera; married Vera Hrabankova, September 30, 1963. *Education:* Attended Film Faculty, Academy of Music and Dramatic Arts, Prague, 1956. *Address:* c/o Gallimard, Rue Sebastien Botin, Paris, France.

CAREER: Writer. Film Faculty, Academy of Music and Dramatic Arts, Prague, Czechoslovakia, assistant professor of film, 1958-70; University of Rennes, Rennes, France, professor of comparative literature, 1975—. *Member:* Union of Czechoslovak Writers (member of central committee, 1963-70). *Awards, honors:* Czechoslovak Writers' Publishing House Prize, 1961 and 1969; Klement Gottwald State Prize, 1963; Union of Czechoslovak Writers' Prize, 1967; Prix Medicis, 1973, for *La Vie est ailleurs;* Prix Mondello, 1978, for *The Farewell Party.*

WRITINGS—Novels: *Zert,* Czechoslovak Writers' Union Publishers, 1967, translation by David Hamblyn and Oliver Stallybrass published as *The Joke,* Coward, 1969; *Zivot de jinde,* translation from the original Czech manuscript by Francois Kerel published as *La Vie est ailleurs,* Gallimard

(Paris), 1973, translation from the original Czech manuscript by Peter Kussi published as *Life Is Elsewhere,* Knopf, 1974; *Valcik na rozloucenou,* translation from the original Czech manuscript by Kerel published as *La Valse aux adieux,* Gallimard, 1976, translation from the original Czech manuscript by Kussi published as *The Farewell Party,* Knopf, 1976; *Kniha smichu a zapomneni,* translation from the original Czech manuscript by Kerel published as *Le Livre du rire eb de l'oubli,* Gallimard, 1979.

Short stories: *Smesne lasky,* Czechoslovak Writers' Union Publishers, 1969, translation by Suzanne Rappeaport published as *Laughable Loves,* Knopf, 1974.

Poetry: *Clovek zahrada sira* (title means "Man: A Broad Garden"), Czechoslovak Writers' Union Publishers, 1953; *Posledni maj* (title means "The Last May"), Czechoslovak Writers' Union Publishers, 1955, revised edition, 1963; *Monology* (title means "Monologues"), Czechoslovak Writers' Union Publishers, 1957.

Plays: *Majitele klicu* (one-act; title means "The Owners of the Keys"; first produced in Prague at the National Theatre, 1962), Czechoslovak Writers' Union Publishers, 1962; *Ptakovina* (two-act), first produced in Prague at Divadlo Na Zabradli, 1968. Also author of *Dve usi dve svatby.*

Nonfiction: *Umeni romanu,* Czechoslovak Writers' Union Publishers, 1960.

Contributor of short stories to magazines, including *Esquire.* Member of the editorial board of *Literarni noviny,* 1956-59 and 1963-68, and of *Listy,* 1968-69.

SIDELIGHTS: "All my life long," Czech author Milan Kundera once wrote, "I have been protesting against the mutilation of works of art in the name of an ideological doctrine as practiced in the socialist countries of Europe." The Soviet invasion of Czechoslovakia in August, 1968, dashed Kundera's hopes that censorship might be abolished. He lost his job at the Prague Film Faculty, his plays were no longer produced, and his books were banned. His books were receiving substantial royalties from sales abroad, but a repressive tax law allowed him to receive only a small percent of the money. When the University of Rennes in France offered him a job in 1975, he obtained permission to move to that country, where he now lives.

Because his works may no longer be published in Czechoslovakia, Kundera writes his manuscripts in his native tongue and then turns them over to a French translator. The books are first published in France and then in other countries. Although some authors might find such a situation frustrating, Kundera has discovered that there are some benefits in the arrangement: "Czech is a vivid, suggestive, sensuous language, sometimes at the expense of a firm order, logical sequence and exactitude.... Writing my last two novels, I particularly had my French translator in mind. I made myself—at first unknowingly—write sentences that were more sober, more comprehensible. A cleansing of the language." Not having his books published in Czechoslovakia has also taught Kundera that great writing must have a universal application: "To depict human situations in a way which makes it impossible for them to be understood beyond the frontiers of any single country is a disservice to the readers of that country too. By so doing we prevent them from looking further than their own backyard, we force them into a straitjacket of parochialism."

Ironically, Kundera's first novel to be published in the West, *The Joke,* was "censored" by his British publisher. In an effort to make the novel more appealing to the reading public, the publisher omitted one chapter all together and juggled several others around. Enraged, Kundera fired off a letter to the *Times Literary Supplement.* While he had no doubt that the editing had been done in good faith, he observed that it had the same effect as Soviet censorship had. He compared the mentality of a London publisher to that of a Communist censor: "The depth of their contempt for art is equally unfathomable."

Although he is an ardent foe of censorship, Kundera does not advocate any particular political stance in his writings, and he despises the term "dissident." He was surprised to discover that in the West "people write about the literature of the so-called East European countries as if it were indeed nothing more than a propaganda instrument, be it pro- or anti-Comunist. I must confess I don't like the word 'dissident,' particularly when applied to art. It is part and parcel of that same politicizing, ideological distortion which cripples a work of art."

Kundera's writing is free of political cant, but neither readers nor critics can completely ignore the political import of his novels and short stories. In *The Joke,* Ludvik Jahn sends a prank postcard to his serious-minded girlfriend on which he writes, "Optimism is the opium of the people! The healthy atmosphere stinks! Long live Trotsky!" Ludvik's joke results in his being ousted from the Communist party, expelled from college, and thrown into jail. When Ludvik finally is released from prison, he seeks revenge by cuckolding an old enemy, another joke that backfires. The American publisher of *The Joke* ballyhooed the novel as an exposé of "the brutal regime in Czchoslovakia today." Critics hastened to point out, however, that *The Joke* is not a political tract. "This book is a living argument, neither communist nor anticommunist," D.A.N. Jones contended. Clive Jordan observed that although Kundera satirizes "communist reasoning and rituals from Ludvik's standpoint," he also provides other points of view: "The multiplicity of viewpoints is intellectually demanding but mirrors life's complexities; and they have the effect of commenting on or correcting Ludvik's ironic assumptions." According to Michael Berman, *The Joke* supplies "a miniature social history of Czechoslovakia during the past 20 years," but its primary empahasis is on the inner world and personal problems of Ludvik.

The publication of *Life Is Elsewhere* renewed the debate about the political nature of Kundera's writings. Paul Theroux contended that Kundera's humor is dependent upon "the ridiculous strictures set up by a Socialist government. . . . One can't imagine his particular situations growing out of anything but a combined anger and fascination with the cut-price Stalinists who have the whip-hand in Prague." A reviewer for *Time* had a different opinion: "There is a Czech tradition of satirizing mindless officialdom that goes back to Kafka's *The Trial* and Jaroslav Hasek's *The Good Soldier Svejk.* But this is not Kundera's main theme, and there is no reason to think that his work would be wholly different if this country's absentee landlords were still the Habsburgs, not the Soviets."

"*Life Is Elsewhere* is not a political novel, but the fictional biography of a lyric poet," Charles Nicol asserted. The lyric poet is Jaromil, a young man who has been encouraged by his doting mother to display an artistic temperament. In actuality, Jaromil is untalented, stupid, and given to romantic posturing, although he is not entirely without charm. Walter Clemons explained, "Jaromil is a deluded and tragic-farcical figure, his mother a pathetic gorgon. Kundera's achievement is to engage our sympathy in their misadventures instead of

inviting our contempt." *Life Is Elsewhere* "is a sly and merciless lampoon of revolutionary romanticism," a *Time* reviewer stated. He went on to remark that "Kundera commits some of the funniest literary savaging since Evelyn Waugh polished off Dickens in *A Handful of Dust.*" Jane Larkin Crain found *Life Is Elsewhere* to be "an altogether extraordinary work, complex, chilling, and brilliantly executed."

Other critics were not so enthusiastic about *Life Is Elsewhere.* "It seems to me that the novel is only half-successful because it looks so much as if Kundera is shooting a clumsy fish in a very small barrel," Theroux commented. "And it is not a very convincing rebuttal of the heroics of Byron and Shelley or the poetic mind in general." Pearl K. Bell asked, "Is the book an attack on the romantic poet's unspeakable ego, with its treacherous confusion of poetry and politics? One can only make a half-hearted guess, for in the end *Life Is Elsewhere* remains an unenticing mystery, overweeningly arch and coy, a long-winded and unamusing joke without discernible point or punchline."

Unlike *Life is Elsewhere, Laughable Loves* was allowed to be published in Czechoslovakia. Obviously, authorities did not feel the collection of short stories was of a political nature. Some Western reviewers agreed with this assessment. Bell noted that "the corrosive irony of *Laughable Loves* . . . touches barely at all upon politics; it is directed almost entirely at the characters' sexual foibles." In contrast, Ivan Sanders wrote, "Of course even the stories contained in *Laughable Loves* seem apolitical only on the surface. In many of them, sexual experimentations and strategies become metaphors for personal and political freedom." Whether or not they considered Kundera's short stories to be political allegories, commentators esteemed *Laughable Loves.* Clemons applauded the short stories for being "buoyantly energetic and virtuosic." A *Time* reviewer called *Laughable Loves* "light, wry and wise," while Theroux declared, "I would be very surprised if a better collection of stories appeared this year."

Sexual farce is also an important element in *The Farewell Party.* The novel takes a satiric look at a government health spa for infertile women, but beneath its slapstick surface many critics discerned a serious intent. Ross Feld pointed out that Kundera's "whirling plot and matchstick characters are obligations—ethics is his real game. Large and often nasty underchords sit in this novel, and they're refreshingly stripped of chic: imprisonment, suicide, sperm-banking, abortion." While granting that *The Farewell Party* does try to grapple with ethical problems, R.Z. Sheppard found the novel shallow: "The novel's bright comic surfaces compensate for its lack of depth. But not enough. With its clinical setting and the circle of didactic characters intended to illustrate moral predicaments, *The Farewell Party* seems like a molehill version of *The Magic Mountain.*" D. J. Enright also found *The Farewell Party* lacking when he compared it to Thomas Mann's *The Magic Mountain:* "The world of *The Magic Mountain* could go somewhere, anywhere—the world of *The Farewell Party* and *The Joke* doesn't look to be going anywhere at all. Many readers will be ready to accept this as inevitable and commiserate with its truthful author. I am not sure about this response. Perhaps literature needs to be something more than simply and solely true to the facts."

Some of Kundera's works have been translated into German, Dutch, Swedish, Finnish, Hebrew, Japanese, Italian, Spanish, Danish, Norwegian, Yugoslavian, Greek, and Turkish.

BIOGRAPHICAL/CRICITAL SOURCES: *Saturday Review*, February 1, 1969, December 20, 1969, July 27, 1974, September 4, 1976; *Time*, July 25, 1969, August 5, 1974, August 30, 1976; *New Statesman*, September 26, 1969; *Times Literary Supplement*, October 2, 1969, July 21, 1978; *New Leader*, January 5, 1970, August 5, 1974; *New York Times Book Review*, January 11, 1970, July 28, 1974, December 1, 1974, September 6, 1976, November 27, 1977, January 8, 1978; *Washington Post Book World*, January 18, 1970; *New York Review of Books*, May 21, 1970, August 8, 1974, September 16, 1976; *Books Abroad*, spring, 1974; *Esquire*, April, 1974; *Newsweek*, July 29, 1974; *New Republic*, September 7, 1974, August 30, 1975, September 6, 1975; *National Review*, October 25, 1974; *Contemporary Literary Criticism*, Gale, Volume 4, 1975, Volume 9, 1978; *Nation*, October 2, 1976; *Le Monde*, January 23, 1976; *Index on Censorship*, November/December, 1977; *Spectator*, June 10, 1978.

*   *   *

KUNHARDT, Philip B(radish) Jr.   1928-

PERSONAL: Born February 5, 1928, in New York, N.Y.; son of Philip Bradish (in wool business) and Dorothy (Meserue) Kunhardt; married Katharine Trowbridge; children: Philip III, Peter, Jean, Sandra, Sarah, Michael. *Education:* Princeton University, B.A. *Agent:* Paul Reynolds, 12 East 41 St., New York, N.Y. 10017. *Office:* Time, Inc., Rockefeller Center, New York, N.Y.

CAREER: Writer. Worked as managing editor of *Life.* Member: Century Club.

WRITINGS: *Twenty Days,* Harper, 1965; *My Father's House,* Random House, 1971; *Mathew Brady and His World,* Time-Life, 1977.

WORK IN PROGRESS: A book on Abraham Lincoln, for Little, Brown.

SIDELIGHTS: Kunhardt told *CA:* "I have worked for Time, Inc., for twenty-nine years and so my book writing has been done at nights, on weekends and vacations, or on sabbaticals. Motivation comes from needing the money, getting satisfaction from writing; I never read a book I've written once it's published."

*   *   *

KUNICZAK, W(iselaw) S(tanislaw)   1930-

PERSONAL: Born February 4, 1930, in Lwow, Poland; came to United States in 1950, naturalized citizen, 1957; son of Stanislaw Bronislaw (a soldier) and Maria Helena (Georgeon) Kuniczak; married Kathryn Stein, January 28, 1960 (died, December, 1976); married Amy Wallin (a ballerina), June, 1979. *Education:* London School of Economics and Political Science, B.Sc., 1949; Alliance College, B.A., 1954; Columbia University, M.S., 1955. *Politics:* Independent Democrat. *Religion:* Roman Catholic. *Residence:* New York, N.Y., and London, England. *Agent:* Max Gartenberg, 331 Madison Ave., New York, N.Y. 10017.

CAREER: *Auburn Citizen-Advertiser,* Auburn, N.Y., reporter, feature writer, assistant telegraph editor, assistant city editor, and copy editor, 1954-55; *Cleveland Plain Dealer,* Cleveland, Ohio, reporter, feature writer, military editor, and columnist, 1957-60; staff writer for public relations firms and advertising agencies, including Griwold-Eschelman Co., and Standard Oil Co. of Ohio, both Cleveland, Ketchum McLeod & Grove, and Burson-Marstelller, Inc., both Pittsburgh, Pa., 1960-68; *Pittsburgh Post-Gazette,* Pittsburgh, rewriter and feature writer, 1968-69; Allied Press Enterprises, Kyrenia, Cyprus, managing editor and feature columnist on Middle East affairs, 1972-74; free-lance writer, 1974—. Lecturer at Carnegie-Mellon University, 1968; lecturer for adult education program in Chagrin Falls, Ohio, 1960-61. *Military service:* U.S. Army, Infantry, 1955-58; served in Korea; became sergeant.

MEMBER: Polish Institute of Arts and Sciences in America. *Awards, honors:* Photojournalism award from Associated Press, 1955; nominated for Pulitzer Prize in investigative reporting, 1956; award from Cleveland Newspaper Guild, 1957; gold medal from Pittsburgh Advertising Club, 1968, for print campaign, silver medal, 1968, for radio campaign.

WRITINGS: *The Thousand Hour Day* (novel; Book-of-the-Month Club selection), Dial, 1966; *The Sempinski Affair* (novel), Doubleday, 1969; *My Name Is Million: An Illustrated History of the Poles in America,* Doubleday, 1978; *The March* (novel), Doubleday, 1979; *The Hazardous Road to Rome: The Life and Writings of Pope John Paul II,* Doubleday, 1979. Also editor of *The Glass Mountain: An Anthology of Polish Folk Tales, Fables, and Legends.* Contributor to *American Heritage.*

WORK IN PROGRESS: *Journeys,* a novel, publication by Doubleday expected in 1981; editing and translating *The Trilogy* by Henryk Sienkiewicz.

SIDELIGHTS: Kuniczak, who has been writing since childhood, once commented that he was "a novelist who finds himself doing more nonfiction than he wants to." *My Name Is Million* is one of Kuniczak's nonfiction works and he hopes that "it may encourage other American writers to pay some attention to historical truth in their treatment of Poland and the Poles in the United States." Subtitled *An Illustrated History of the Poles in America, My Name Is Million* covers "the Polish story in America" from the early 1600's to the twentieth century. Discussed in the book are the wide range of contributions to American life made by Poles, including such notables as Casimir Pulaski, Thaddeus Kosciuszko, Dr. Jacob Bronowski, Dr. Zbigniew Brzezinski, Arthur Rubinstein, Czeslaw Milosz, Senator Edmund Muskie, and Stan "The Man" Musial. Kuniczak concluded: "There have been no significant movements in American history in which the Poles have not played a part, no area of American life in which they have not left an imprint of their own. They are today a vital and energetic community of Americans, of many talents and considerable material resources."

Kuniczak's books have been published in seventeen languages and in twenty-two countries. He is fluent in French and Spanish, and understands Greek, Turkish, and Arabic. Kuniczak is a world traveler who has lived mainly in Mexico, Europe, and the Middle East. During the October War of 1973, he served as a volunteer ambulance driver in Israel.

*   *   *

KUNST, David W(illiam)   1939-

PERSONAL: Born July 16, 1939, in Minnesota; son of Al T. (a corporation manager) and Augusta (Onstead) Kunst; married Jan Wabner (a secretary), May 19, 1959 (divorced); married Jenny Samuel (a teacher), May 1, 1976; children: Debbie, Brad, Dan. *Education:* Attended Mankato State College, 1967-69, University of Minnesota, 1968-69, and Coastline Community College, 1977-79. *Home:* 2035 Fullerton A-2, Costa Mesa, Calif. 92627. *Agent:* Sanford J. Greenburger Associates, Inc., 825 Third Ave., New York, N.Y. 10022.

CAREER: County Engineer's Surveyor, Waseca, Minn., surveyor, 1959-70; walked around the world, 1970-74; writer and lecturer, 1975—. Multi-cultural school consultant. *Member:* Australia Kangaroo Club, Horse Thief Detectives, Turtles. *Awards, honors:* Kunst Brothers Day proclamation by governor of Minnesota, 1973.

WRITINGS: The Man Who Walked Around the World, Morrow, 1979.

WORK IN PROGRESS: Cracker Jack, completion expected in 1984; *Confrontation,* completion expected in 1986; *Panacea.*

SIDELIGHTS: Kunst told *CA:* "To be free and to do what no other had done, I quit my job of eleven years as an engineering surveyor, walked out of town, and around the world. Walking and experiencing for the four years, three months, and sixteen days it took me to circle the earth was the most rewarding, exciting, and inspirational high of my life to date."

According to a *Time* magazine feature, Kunst began his foot-odyssey in Waseca, Minnesota, accompanied by his brother John and a mule. Said Mrs. Kunst: "I kept expecting him to call from La Crosse and say 'Come over and pick us up.'" But Kunst and his caravan continued on to Manhattan where they lodged for a week as guests of a Holiday Inn. Upon their arrival, the mule was quickly ushered out of the lobby, but not before he relieved himself at the hotel's front entrance.

While the Kunst brothers often received the hospitality of the road, they also met with misadventure. As *Time* reported, they were mistaken for smugglers in Spain, rudely chased away by the mayor of a French village, and stoned by anti-Americans in Iran and Turkey. The saddest moment of the journey, however, occurred near Kabul, Afghanistan. Having read in a local newspaper that the Kunsts were collecting money for UNICEF, bandits attacked the brothers. Actually, they had only been collecting pledges, not cash. In the ambush, John was shot dead and David suffered a bullet hole in one lung. After a three-month recuperation in Waseca, though, Kunst resumed his 15,000-mile walk around the world with his older brother Peter.

On the final leg of his walk, Kunst's hometown began preparations to welcome its new hero. But in Nebraska, Kunst complained to newsmen of the "hypocrisy, pettiness, self-righteousness and narrow-mindedness" found among Wasecans. Furthermore, *Time* related, the townsfolk were offended by "his announcements that he often enjoyed female companionship along the way" and that he had "no intention of resuming his marriage or living in Waseca again." As a result, the town's mayor, the local Congressman, and Senator Hubert Humphrey decided to boycott the ceremonies.

"I'm a social deviate," Kunst later remarked, "a radical, even a little crazy. I don't fit into anybody's pattern and I never will."

Kunst ended his trek where it began at the Waseca Cinema. Welcomed by a crowd of 5,000 people, he swigged from a bottle of champagne and toasted the U.S. as "the best damn country I've ever been in." Reflecting on the experience and his current occupation, Kunst told *CA:* "The year I spent writing and remembering the first recorded walk around the world was the most challenging, stimulating, and demanding of my life. The hand won over the foot. So I write."

BIOGRAPHICAL/CRITICAL SOURCES: Time, October 14, 1974; *National Enquirer,* October 17, 1974.

*   *   *

KYPER, Frank 1940-

PERSONAL: Born April 16, 1940, in Marlboro, Mass.; son of Ralph E. (a clergyman) and Mary (a nurse; maiden name, Schaible) Kyper; married Norma-Jean Blodgett, June, 1971 (died March 2, 1974); married Mary Montville, October 12, 1974; children: Kristin, Kathleen. *Education:* Boston University, B.S., 1963. *Home:* 20 Hilltop Dr., Burlington, Mass. 01803. *Office:* New England Truck World, 27 Muzzey St., Lexington, Mass. 02173.

CAREER: Massachusetts Port Authority, Boston, public relations executive, 1968-70; Boston & Maine Railroad, Boston, crossing tender, 1970-73; *New England Construction,* Lexington, Mass., feature editor, 1973—, *New England Truck World,* Lexington, editor, 1975—. Excursion director for Railroad Enthusiasts, 1970-74. *Military service:* U.S. Army, Intelligence Corps, 1963-66; served in Germany; became sergeant. *Member:* Railway and Locomotive Historical Society, National Railway Historical Society, Light Railway Transport League, Railways to Yesterday, Canadian Railroad Historical Association, Seashore Trolley Museum, 470 Railroad Club.

WRITINGS: The Railroad That Came Out at Night, Stephen Greene Press, 1977; (with Lee Rainey) *East Broad Top,* Golden West, 1979. Contributor to railway journals. Editor of *Railroad Enthusiast,* 1966-75.

WORK IN PROGRESS: Books on railroading in New Hampshire and Vermont, and on the Boston, Revere Beach & Lynn Railroad.

SIDELIGHTS: Kyper comments: "My professional career has revolved around writing and publishing, and, when combined with a deep and long-standing interest in railroading, it seemed natural to turn to writing books. Much of my writing career has been devoted to transportation—railroads, highways, aviation, and maritime."

L

LaBRECQUE, Claude X.

PERSONAL: Born in Berlin, N.H.; son of Henri Louis (a logging contractor), and Julia (Lauzon) LaBrecque, *Education:* Attended University of Ottawa. *Politics:* "According to the issues." *Religion:* "Nostalgic Roman Catholic." *Home:* 25 Rue Elm, Granby, Quebec, Canada.

CAREER: Storyteller, lecturer in storytelling, songwriter, and "wandering minstrel." *Member:* Canadian Association of Publishers, Authors and Composers, Canadian Society of Children's Authors, Illustrators, and Performers, Canadian Folk Music Society, Society of Children's Book Writers. *Awards, honors:* Robert Wyndham scholar at Hofstra University, 1974; fellow of Academy of Canadian Writers, 1978.

WRITINGS—For children: *Worms for Sale,* Thomas Nelson, 1974; *How Big Will It Be?,* Highway Book Shop, 1975. Contributor to textbooks. Contributor to magazines and newspapers in Canada and the United States. Publisher of *Open Diary.*

WORK IN PROGRESS: The Magic of Storytelling; "Bubble-Gum," a recording of his songs and stories.

SIDELIGHTS: LaBrecque comments: "I feel very strongly that an author's job is not done when he finishes his book. If he believes in what he has written, it is up to him to dramatize his message."

* * *

LAGERKVIST, Paer (Fabian) 1891-1974

PERSONAL: Born May 23, 1891, in Vaexjoe, Sweden; died July 11, 1974; son of Anders Johan (a railway linesman) and Johanna (Blad) Lagerquist; married Karen Dagmar Johanne Soerensen, 1918 (marriage dissolved, 1925); married Elaine Luella Hallberg, 1925. *Education:* Attended University of Uppsala, 1911-12. *Residence:* Lidingoe, Sweden.

CAREER: Writer. Theater critic for *Svenska Dagbladet* (newspaper), Stockholm, Sweden, 1919. *Awards, honors:* Literary prize from Samfundet De Nio, 1928; elected to Swedish Academy of Literature, 1940; Ph.D. from University of Gothenburg, 1941; Nobel Prize for Literature, 1951.

WRITINGS—Novels: *Det eviga leendet,* [Stockholm], 1920, reprinted, Bonnier, 1969, translation by Denys W. Harding and Erik Mesterton published as *The Eternal Smile,* Gordon Fraser, 1934 (also see Collections); *Boedeln,* [Stockholm], 1933, reprinted, Bonnier, 1966 (also see Plays and Collec-

tions); *Dvaergen,* Bonnier, 1944, translation by Alexandra Dick published as *The Dwarf,* L. B. Fisher, 1945; *Barabbas,* Bonnier, 1950, translation by Alan Blair with a preface by Lucien Maury and a letter by Andre Gide published as *Barabbas,* Random House, 1951 (also see Plays and Other); *Sibyllan,* Bonnier, 1956, translation by Naomi Walford published as *The Sibyl,* Random House, 1958; *Ahasverus doed,* Bonnier, 1960, translation by Walford published as *The Death of Ahasuerus,* Random House, 1962 (also see Collections); *Pilgrim paa havet,* Bonnier, 1962, translation by Walford published as *Pilgrim at Sea,* Random House, 1964 (also see Collections); *Det Heliga landet,* Bonnier, 1964, translation by Walford published as *The Holy Land,* Random House, 1966 (also see Collections); *Mariamne,* Bonnier, 1967, translation by Walford published as *Herod and Mariamne,* Knopf, 1968. Also author of *Maenniskor,* 1912, and *Tva sagor om livet,* 1913.

Plays: *Sista maenskan* (three-act), Bonnier, 1917; *Teater: Den svaara stunden* [and] *Modern teater: Synpunkter och angrepp* (three one-act plays and essays; first produced together in Duesseldorf at Schauspielhaus, 1918), Bonnier, 1918 (also see Nonfiction and Collections); *Himlens hemlighet* (one-act; produced in Stockholm at Intimate Theatre, 1921), originally published in *Kaos,* [Stockholm], 1919 (also see Collections); *Den osynlige* (three-act; first produced in Stockholm at Royal Dramatic Theatre, 1924), Bonnier, 1923 (also see Collections); *Han som fick leva om sitt liv* (three-act; first produced at Royal Dramatic Theatre, 1928), Bonnier, 1928 (also see Collections); *Konungen* (three-act; first produced in Malmoe at City Theatre, 1950), [Stockholm], 1932 (also see Collections); *Boedeln* (one-act), first produced in Stockholm at Vasa Theatre, 1934 (adapted from Lagerkvist's novel of the same name; also see Novels and Collections); *Mannen utan sjael* (five-act; first produced at Royal Dramatic Theatre, 1938) [Stockholm], 1936, translation by H. Koekeritz published in *Scandinavian Plays of the Twentieth Century,* Volume I, [Princeton, N.J.], 1944 (also see Collections); *Seger i moerker* (four-act; first produced at Royal Dramatic Theatre, 1940), Bonnier, 1939 (also see Collections).

Misommardroem i fattighuset (three-act; first produced in Stockholm at Blanche Theatre, 1941), [Stockholm], 1941, translation by Alan Blair published as *Midsummer Dream in the Workhouse,* Hodge, 1953 (also see Collections); *Den Vises sten* (four-act; first produced at Royal Dramatic

Theatre, 1948), [Stockholm], 1947; *Laat maenniskan leva* (one-act; first produced in Goeteborg at City Theatre, 1949), Bonnier, 1949, translation by H. Alexander and L. Jones published in *Scandinavian Plays of the Twentieth Century*, Volume III, [Princeton, N.J.], 1951; *Barabbas* (two-act; first produced at Royal Dramatic Theatre, 1953) Bonnier, 1953 (adapted from Lagerkvist's novel of the same name; also see Novels and Other).

Poetry: *Motiv* (with prose pieces), Bonnier, 1914; *Aangest*, Bonnier, 1916, reprinted, 1966; *Hjaertats saanger*, 1926, reprinted, 1962; *Vid laegereld*, [Stockholm], 1932; *Genius*, [Stockholm], 1937; *Saang och strid*, Bonnier, 1940; *Dikter*, Bonnier, 1941; *Hemmet och stjaernan*, Bonnier, 1942; *Aftonland*, Bonnier, 1953, translation by W. H. Auden and Leif Sjoeberg with an introduction by Sjoeberg published as *Evening Land*, Wayne State University Press, 1975; *Dikter*, Bonnier, 1958; *Valda dikter*, Bonnier, 1967; *Dikter*, Bonnier, 1974. Also author of *Den lyckliges vaeg*, 1921.

Nonfiction: *Teater: Den svaara stunden* [and] *Modern teater: Synpunkter och angrepp* (essays and plays), Bonnier, 1918 (also see Plays and Collections); *Gaest hos verkligheten* [and] *Det besegrade livet* (autobiography), Bonnier, 1925, *Det besegrade livet* published separately, Bonnier, 1927, *Gaest hos verkligheten* published separately, Bonnier, 1967, translation of *Gaest hos verkligheten* by Erik Mesterton and Denys W. Harding published as *Guest of Reality*, J. Cape, 1936 (also see Collections); *Den knutna naeven* (essays), [Stockholm], 1934; *Antechnat: Ur efterlaemnade dagboecker och anteckningar* (diary), Bonnier, 1977.

Other: *Onda Sagor* (title means "Evil Tales"), [Stockholm], 1924, reprinted, Aldus, 1965 (also see Collections); *Den Befriande maenniskan*, [Stockholm], 1939; *Verner von Heidenstam: Intraedestal i Svenska akademien den 20 december 1940*, Bonnier, 1940; (with Gunnar De Frumerie) *Frya saanger* (songs), Foereningen svenska tonsaettare (Stockholm), 1945; (with De Frumerie) *Tre saanger*, Foereningen svenska tonsaettare, 1946; *Sugor, satiere och noveller*, Bonnier, 1957; (with Christopher Fry) *Barabbas* (screenplay; adapted from own novel), produced by Columbia Pictures, c. 1960 (also see Novels and Plays); *Sjaelarnas maskerad*, Aldus, 1962; *Pilgrimen*, Bonnier, 1966.

Collections: *Jaern och maenniskor* (short stories), Bonnier, 1915; *Teater: Den svarra stunden* [and] *Modern teater: Synpunkter och angrepp* (plays and essays), Bonnier, 1918, portions included in the translation by Thomas R. Buckman published with other plays by Lagerkvist as *Modern Theatre: Seven Plays and an Essay* (includes "Modern Theatre: Points of View and Attack," "The Difficult Hour" [three one-act plays], "The Secret of Heaven," "The King," "The Hangman," and "The Philsopher's Stone"), University of Nebraska Press, 1966 (also see Plays); *Kaos* (includes stories, poems, and a play, "Himlens hemlighet"), [Stockholm], 1919 (also see Plays and below); *Gaest hos verkligheten* [and] *Det besegrade livet* (autobiography), Bonnier, 1925 (also see Nonfiction and below).

Kaempande ande (short stories and prose sketches), [Stockholm], 1930; *Skrifter*, three volumes, [Stockholm], 1932; *The Eternal Smile: Three Stories* (includes "The Eternal Smile," "Guest of Reality," and "The Executioner"), translated from the Swedish by Erik Mesterton, Denys W. Harding, and David O'Gorman, Gordon Fraser, 1934, Hill & Wang, 1971 (also see Novels, Nonfiction, and below); *I den tiden* (short stories), [Stockholm], 1935; *Prosa*, [Stockholm], 1945, published in five volumes, 1949; *Dramatik* (includes "Modern teater," "Sista maenskan," "Den

svaara stunden," "Himlens hemlighet," "Den osynlige," "Han som fick leva om sitt liv," "Konungen," "Boedeln," "Mannen utan sjael," "Seger i moerker," and "Midsommardroem i fattighuset"), Bonnier, 1946 (also see Plays and Nonfiction); *The Eternal Smile and Other Stories*, translated from the Swedish by Alan Blair and others, Random House, 1954 (also see Novels and above); *The Marriage Feast and Other Stories*, translated from the Swedish by Blair and Carl Eric Lindin, Chatto & Windus, 1955, Hill & Wang, 1973; *Boedeln, Den knutna naeven, I den tiden*, [and] *Den befriande maenniskan*, Bonnier, 1956 (also see Novels); *Prosastycken ur aangest, Den fordringsfulla gaesten, Det eviga leendet, Morgonen*, [and] *Onda sagor*, Bonnier, 1962 (also see Novels and Other); *Ahasverus doed, Pilgrim paa havet*, [and] *Det Heliga landet*, Bonnier, 1966 (also see Novels).

SIDELIGHTS: Born into a strongly religious and conservative family, Lagerkvist abandoned his early training and, after a year of studying humanities at the University of Uppsala, left for an extended trip to Paris. There he became acquainted with the modern art movement and was especially influenced by the Fauvist, cubist, and naivist movements that were in vogue at the time. His early writings reflected the artistic principles he was exposed to. Lagerkvist's own artistic principles were delineated in a controversial essay, "Modern Theatre: Points of View and Attack," published in 1918. In the essay Lagerkvist denounced the Scandinavian playwright Ibsen and the naturalism he espoused and turned to the playwright Strindberg as his literary mentor. *Anguish*, Lagerkvist's early book of poetry, has been called the first expressionistic work in Swedish literature, and its publication established his reputation as an important Scandinavian writer and his connection to the German expressionist movement.

Lagerkvist's early work was dark, lyrical, and pessimistic. World War I deeply disturbed him and Holger Ahlenius characterized his writings of this era as "one single cry of despair over the bestiality of man." The conflict between the traditional Christian and the modern scientific-determinist views became a departure point for his writing: Lagerkvist's works were largely concerned with man's relationship to God, with the meaning of life, and with the conflict between good and evil. In the thirties, in response to the brutalities of Nazism and fascism, Lagerkvist became, according to Alrik Gustafson, "the most eloquent and rigidly uncompromising Swedish critic of totalitarianism." He became known as a defender of the values of "heroic humanitarian idealism." Lagerkvist described himself as "a believer without faith—a religious atheist." Andre Gide wrote: "It is a measure of Lagerkvist's success that he managed so admirably to maintain his balance on a tightrope which stretches across the dark abyss that lies between the world of reality and the world of faith."

Although Lagerkvist's later works were thematically similar to his earlier works, they became more accessible, less pessimistic and more realistic. Whereas, his earlier writings had reeked of despair, his later view was of "love, sublimated into a Christian-Platonic mysticism," Ahlenius commented. Eventually Lagerkvist came to believe that good and love could triumph over evil. His play *Han som fick leva om sitt* published in 1928 is generally regarded to be the beginning of the more mature, optimistic period of his writing.

Lagerkvist was virtually unknown in the United States until the publication of the English translation of *Barabbas* in 1951, the same year he received the Nobel Prize for Literature. The novel is the story of the condemned thief whose place Christ took on the cross. In a review of the novel,

Graham Bates remarked: "The work combines the utmost physical realism with an intensity of spiritual conflict not often equaled in the retelling of Biblical tales. Paer Lagerkvist has taken a man barely mentioned in the New Testament and has built him into a character as real, as evil, and as good as he must have been to the men who knew him those centuries ago. This is no outline sketch in black and white but a deeply conceived and richly colored portrait of a man driven beyond the powers of his endurance by a force he could never actually believe in."

Charles Rollo called *Barabbas* a "small masterpiece" and commented: "In a prose style that is swift, sparing, limpid, and hauntingly intense in its effects—a style whose energy and beauty the translator, Alan Blair, has magnificently preserved—Lagerkvist evokes the early Christian era with a selective realism more telling than any ponderously detailed reconstruction of the past. Every image sustains the feeling, 'That is the way things were'; every movement in the story has an unerring rightness." Harvey Breit praised Lagerkvist for taking "a complex moral theme" and constructing the tale "with a craftsman's complete mastery and simplicity," synthesizing "an elaborate, moral vision and austere poetic style."

"All his [Lagerkvist's] fiction is freighted with philosophy, but in the best of it narrative structure and scene finely support the burden," critic Richard M. Ohmann wrote. "And in the best of his fiction that burden is overwhelmingly one of doubt and brooding evil, not of reassurance. Uncertainty and suffering are woven into the very fabric of experience as Lagerkvist most powerfully feels it; affirmation in his world is like a candle in the outer darkness." Michele Murray, however, complained that Lagerkvist's writing lacked intensity and specificity, which left his characters without individuality. In a review of *Pilgrim at Sea,* she declared: "Lagerkvist's characters are not even characters, but mere spokesmen, mouthpieces of Good or Evil or Lust or Cupidity, whose sins and virtues are as pallid as they are. Deprived of the density which sustains fiction and summons the power of evocation, Lagerkvist has written, not a Profound Statement of Mankind's Struggle With Good and Evil, . . . but merely a philosophical melodrama, in which phantoms wrestle with vague concepts devoid of both significance and vitality."

Adele Bloch was more appreciative of Lagerkvist's use of archetypal characters and situations. She compared him to Thomas Mann, "whose heroes fashion their natures and destinies according to certain legendary prototypes." She continued: "Fuller recognition of identification with mythical figures is slowly attained by certain individuals, as the generations move towards more civilized levels of conscience. In the case of Lagerkvist's fictional characters, complete self-realization can be gained only after a lifetime of guilt, struggles and re-enactment of some original sins."

Winston Weathers reviewed Lagerkvist's last novel, *Herod and Mariamne,* which he termed "another religious-psychological parable." "At that novel's end," he wrote, "Lagerkvist reminds the reader once more that Herod is representative of a mankind 'that replenishes the earth but whose race shall one day be erased from it, and . . . will leave no memorial.' *Herod and Mariamne* is a bitter novel, a brief, brilliant, haunting work. Yet its bitterness may be a challenge: its chilling 'no' may stimulate the 'yes' of faith."

Lucien Maury summed up by Lagerkvist's career in the preface he wrote to the English translation of *Barabbas.* He wrote: "There is scarcely a single aesthetic problem in the realm of literature which Lagerkvist has not striven to define and resolve—not only theoretically, but in the practice of his art—whether in the theatre, the short story, or works of meditation, and verse. . . . It has been a far cry with him from anguish to serenity, to that interior joy which triumphs over all despair; from early revolt to an acceptance which has never been mere resignation, though often it is not far removed from a mood of burning adoration, from a religious sense at one with reason, from faith in the existence of a principle to be found at the source of all our human destiny."

BIOGRAPHICAL/CRITICAL SOURCES: Paer Lagerkvist, *Guest of Reality,* translated from the Swedish by Erik Mesterton and Denys W. Harding, J. Cape, 1936; *American-Scandinavian Review,* December, 1940; *Saturday Review of Literature,* October 27, 1951; *American-Swedish Monthly,* November, 1951; *New York Times,* November 16, 1951; *New York Times Book Review,* November 25, 1951; *Atlantic,* December, 1951, October, 1975; Lucien Maury, preface to *Barabbas,* Randon House, 1951; Andre Gide, prefatory letter in *Barabbas,* Randon House, 1951; *Commonweal,* May 11, 1962, April 3, 1964, January 10, 1969; Winston Weathers, *Paer Lagerkvist: A Critical Essay,* Eerdmans, 1968; Robert Donald Spector, *Paer Lagerkvist,* Twayne, 1973; *International Fiction Review,* January, 1974; Leif Sjoeberg, *Paer Lagerkvist,* Columbia University Press, 1976; *Contemporary Literary Criticism,* Gale, Volume 7, 1977, Volume 10, 1979.

Obituaries: *New York Times,* July 12, 1974; *Newsweek,* July 22, 1974; *Time,* July 22, 1974; *Current Biography,* September, 1974.*

*   *   *

LAGERWERFF, Ellen Best   1919-

PERSONAL: Born June 4, 1919, in Soerabaia, Java; came to the United States in 1959; daughter of Jan Willem (a physician and professor) and Anna Ch.M. Mulder (a psychiatrist and plastic surgeon; maiden name, Van de Graaf) Best; married John M. Lagerwerff (a specialist in aerospace medicine), July 2, 1954 (died June 15, 1978); children: Karen A. deVries Perlroth. *Education:* Mensendieck Institute, Amsterdam, Netherlands, graduated, 1940; graduate study at Rheumatology Hospital, Rotterdam, Netherlands, 1949-50, and Le Systeme le Bon Depart, The Hague, Netherlands, 1953. *Religion:* Protestant. *Home and office:* 2345 Cornell, Palo Alto, Calif. 94306.

CAREER: Certified specialist in Mensendieck System of Functional Exercises, 1940; private practice as teacher of Mensendieck in the Netherlands, 1940-59, St. Paul, Minn., 1959-61, Van Nuys, Calif., 1961-63, La Jolla, Calif., 1963-66, and Palo Alto, Calif., 1966—. Public lecturer; guest on television and radio programs. Member of Nederlandse Mensendieck Bond; founder and coordinator of Academy of Mensendieck Specialists, 1973; has worked in hospitals. *Member:* American Corrective Therapy Association, American Society of Allied Health Professions, Sabian Assembly.

WRITINGS: Houding—Gezondheid—Elegance (booklet; title means "Posture—Health—Elegance"), L.J.C. Boucher, 1956; (with daughter, Karen A. Perlroth) *Mensendieck Your Posture and Your Pains,* Doubleday, 1973. Contributor to medical journals.

WORK IN PROGRESS: "Working on a philosophical-subject book for Doubleday."

SIDELIGHTS: Ellen Lagerwerff is one of six Mensendieck specialists currently practicing in the United States. Her

1973 book explains the Mensendieck method of body education and/or reconditioning, which involves logical body movements applied habitually to all daily activities. Her method is popular with the aged and ill because it does not involve strenuous activity, and with younger and more active people for its effect of correcting posture problems and promotion of general well-being.

Lagerwerff told *CA:* "The circumstances which made me decide to write the book, *Mensendieck Your Posture and Your Pains,* were that I observed the great need for Americans to develop their kinaesthetic sense, and I was so fortunate to possess a wealth of knowledge and experience to help them. I concentrated on the most basic techniques, explained and instructed succinctly, so that every reader could immediately apply them. Now, eight years after starting the manuscript, I still would not know how I could have written it any better."

AVOCATIONAL INTERESTS: Weaving, knitting, philosophical studies, riding, skiing, sailing, swimming.

BIOGRAPHICAL/CRITICAL SOURCES: American Corrective Therapy Journal, July-August, 1974.

* * *

LAGO, Mary M(cClelland) 1919-

PERSONAL: Surname is pronounced *Lay*-go; born November 4, 1919, in Pittsburgh, Pa.; daughter of Clark (a teacher) and Olive (a teacher; maiden name, Malone) McClelland; married Gladwyn Lago (a professor of electrical engineering), March 4, 1944; children: Jane Hazel, Donald Russell. *Education:* Bucknell University, B.A., 1940; University of Missouri, M.A., 1965, Ph.D., 1969. *Home:* 834 Greenwood Court, Columbia, Mo. 65201. *Agent:* Curtis Brown Ltd., 1 Craven Hill, London W.2, England. *Office:* Department of English, University of Missouri, Columbia, Mo. 65211.

CAREER: Friendship Press, New York City, assistant to promotion director, 1941-43; Missions Council of Congregational Christian Churches, New York City, assistant to publications director, 1943-47; University of Missouri, Columbia, instructor, 1964-69, lecturer, 1970-74, associate professor of English, 1975—. *Member:* Modern Language Association of America, Association for Asian Studies, Virginia Woolf Society, William Morris Society, Society of Authors (England), Midwest Modern Language Association, Midwest Victorian Studies Association, Phi Beta Kappa. *Awards, honors:* Research grants from American Philosophical Society, 1967-68, 1972, American Council of Learned Societies, 1972, and National Endowment for the Humanities, 1976; faculty-alumni award, University of Missouri, Columbia, 1978.

WRITINGS: (Translator with Tarun Gupta) Rabindranath Tagore, *The Housewarming and Other Selected Writings,* edited by Amiya Chakravarty, New American Library, 1965; (translator with Supriya Sen Bari, and author of introduction) Tagore, *The Broken Nest,* University of Missouri Press, 1971; (editor) *Imperfect Encounter: Letters of William Rothenstein and Rabindranath Tagore, 1911-1941,* Harvard University Press, 1972; (editor with Karl Beckson, and author of introduction) *Max and Will, Max Beerbohm and William Rothenstein: Their Friendship and Letters, 1893-1945,* Harvard University Press, 1975; *Rabindranath Tagore,* Twayne, 1976; (editor of abridgment) Rothenstein, *Men and Memories: Recollections, 1872-1938,* University of Missouri Press, 1978.

Work represented in anthologies, including *The Contemporary World Poets,* edited by Donald Junkins, Harcourt, 1976.

Author of "Mrs. Max: Florence Beerbohm, in Her Letters," a radio script broadcast by British Broadcasting Corp. Radio 3, November 21, 1974. Contributor of more than twenty articles, translations, and reviews to literature and Asian studies journals and newspapers. Member of editorial board of *Literature East and West* and *Twentieth Century Literature.*

WORK IN PROGRESS: Editing and writing introduction for Thomas M. Rooke's journals of Sir Edward Burne-Jone's studio conversations, 1894-98; editing and writing introduction for selections from the diaries of Stopford A. Brooke, 1888-1916; a study of the problems of cultural exchange between England and India, 1900-1920, as embodied in the work of Edward J. Thompson and Christiana Herringham; editing letters of E. M. Forster, with P. N. Furbank.

SIDELIGHTS: Lago commented: "I am always asked how I became interested in Tagore, Rothenstein, Beerbohm, and Forster. The chain began with efforts to learn Rabindrasangit—Tagore's songs—which led to learning the language, which led to translations and to the discovery that it was William Rothenstein who was the prime mover of Tagore's career in the West and remained his friend and correspondent for thirty years. Interest in Rothenstein led to interest in Max Beerbohm; their friendship endured for more than fifty years. Interest in Tagore and in Bengali literature led to Forster, picking up along the way others in the Rothenstein-Tagore-Forster circle such as Stopford Brooke and Christiana Herringham.

"As a teacher, I am often asked about the relation between teaching and research: Which predominates? The answer is neither. They nourish each other."

AVOCATIONAL INTERESTS: Travel (especially England), languages (including Bengali), music (choral singing).

* * *

LAGUERRE, Andre 1916(?)-1979

OBITUARY NOTICE: Born c. 1916 in London, England; died January 18, 1979, in New York, N.Y. Journalist. Laguerre was best known for his longstanding career as managing editor of *Sports Illustrated.* He took over the magazine in 1959, four years after its introduction, and turned it into Time, Inc.'s most popular and profitable periodical by switching its format to coverage of professional athletics. Laguerre also helped establish *Classic—The Magazine About Horses and Sport* in 1976 and served as its editor and publisher. Obituaries and other sources: *Newsweek,* October 22, 1973; *Time,* December 8, 1975; *New York Times,* January 19, 1979.

* * *

LAMBERG-KARLOVSKY, Clifford Charles 1937-

PERSONAL: Born October 2, 1937, in Prague, Czechoslovakia; son of Karl (a lawyer) and Bellina (a lawyer; maiden name, Karlovsky) Lamberg; married Martha Veale, 1959; children: Karl, Christopher. *Education:* Dartmouth College, A.B., 1959; graduate study at Yale University, 1962; University of Pennsylvania, A.M., 1964, Ph.D., 1965. *Politics:* Democrat. *Religion:* Protestant. *Home:* 22 Stevens Rd., Melrose, Mass. 02138. *Office:* Department of Anthropology, Harvard University, Cambridge, Mass. 02138.

CAREER: Franklin and Marshall College, Lancaster, Pa., assistant professor of anthropology, 1964-65; Harvard University, Cambridge, Mass., assistant professor, 1965-69, professor of anthropology and curator of Near Eastern archaeology, 1969—. Director of research for American School of Prehistoric Research; director of archaeological expeditions to Syria, Saudi Arabia, and Iran. Member of board of trustees of American Institute of Iranian Studies, American Institute of Yemeni Studies, and American Schools of Oriental Research. *Member:* American Anthropological Association (fellow), American Oriental Society (fellow), Society of Antiquaries (fellow), Explorers Club, Columbia University Seminar (associate in archaeology). *Awards, honors:* National Science Foundation grants, 1969-76.

WRITINGS: Metallurgical Technology and Archaeology of India-Pakistan, American Anthropological Association, 1965; (editor) *Foundations of Civilization,* Scott, Foresman, 1972; (editor) *Ancient Civilizations and Trade,* University of New Mexico Press, 1974; *Hunters, Farmers, and Civilization,* Scott, Foresman, 1978; *Ancient Civilizations,* Cummings, 1979. Contributor to anthropology and Oriental studies journals.

WORK IN PROGRESS: A book about archaeological excavations in Iran, three volumes, publication by Peabody Museum of Archaeology and Ethnology, Harvard University.

AVOCATIONAL INTERESTS: Skiing.

* * *

LAMBERT, Sheila 1926-

PERSONAL: Born August 27, 1926, in West Hartlepool, England; married G. R. Elton (a historian), August 30, 1952. *Education:* University of London, B.A., 1947, M.A., 1949. *Home:* 30 Millington Rd., Cambridge CB3 9HP, England.

CAREER: Beaverbrook Foundations, London, England, executive secretary and archivist of Bonar Law and Lloyd George papers, 1954-67; writer, 1950—.

WRITINGS: List of House of Commons Sessional Papers, 1701-50, List and Index Society, 1968; *Bills and Acts: Legislative Procedure in Eighteenth-Century England,* Cambridge University Press, 1971; (editor) *The House of Commons Sessional Papers of the Eighteenth Century,* 147 volumes, Scholarly Resources, 1975-76. Contributor to history and library journals. Member of advisory committee of "Papers of James Boswell," Yale University Press.

WORK IN PROGRESS: Continuing research on British parliamentary history, especially in the seventeenth century.

* * *

LAMBTON, Anne (Patricia St. Clair) 1918-

PERSONAL: Born August 18, 1918, in London, England; daughter of Lawrence W. W. (in business) and Gwendoline (Daniell) Lees; married Charles Coghill (a military officer; deceased); married David Rawnsley (deceased); married Edward Lambton (a race horse owner), November 2, 1956. *Education:* Attended private girls' school in Tetbury, England. *Politics:* Conservative. *Religion:* Church of England. *Home:* Villa Palma, Vieille Montagne, Tangier, Morocco. *Office:* c/o Anthony Furman, 527 Madison Ave., New York, N.Y. 10022.

CAREER: Model and fashion promoter, 1939—; writer, 1960—. Public relations organizer for international hotels and casinos and for Greek and Lebanese tourist offices. Fundraiser for United Nations.

WRITINGS: (With Heather Seyler) *The Seventeen-Twenty Book,* Arthur Barker, 1965; *The Sisters,* Coward, 1975; *The Daughters,* Berkley Publishing, 1978; *The Lebanese Heiress,* Berkley Publishing, 1979. Also co-author of *The Mancatcher's Manual.* Contributor to popular magazines and newspapers in England and the United States, including *Vogue* and *Woman's Own.*

WORK IN PROGRESS: The Courtesan, "a jet-set saga."

SIDELIGHTS: Anne Lambton writes: "I am an exjet-setter who has settled in Morocco, and visits New York City in the spring and fall. I am now writing about the world in which I have lived. While commencing a career in popular fiction, I have filled in the time by building up a garden and converting a run-down house into a showplace." *Avocational interests:* Cats, prevention of cruelty to animals.

* * *

LAMMING, George (William) 1927-

PERSONAL: Born June 8, 1927, in Barbados; came to England, 1950. *Education:* Attended Combermere High School in Barbados. *Home:* 14-A Highbury Place, London N 5, England. *Office:* c/o Holt, Rinehart & Winston, 383 Madison Ave., New York, N.Y. 10017.

CAREER: Writer. Worked as schoolmaster in Trinidad, 1946-50; factory worker in England, 1950; broadcaster for British Broadcasting Corp. (BBC) Colonial Service, 1951. *Awards, honors:* Guggenheim Fellowship, 1955; Somerset Maugham Award, 1957.

WRITINGS: In the Castle of My Skin (novel), McGraw, 1953; *The Emigrants* (novel), M. Joseph, 1954, McGraw, 1955; *Of Age and Innocence* (novel), M. Joseph, 1958; *Season of Adventure* (novel), M. Joseph, 1960; *The Pleasures of Exile,* M. Joseph, 1960; (editor) *New World: Guyana Independence Issue,* New World Group Associates, 1966; *Water With Berries* (novel), Holt, 1972; *Natives of My Person* (novel), Holt, 1972; (editor) *Cannon Shot and Glass Beads: Modern Black Writing,* Pan Books, 1974. Work represented in anthologies, including *West Indian Stories,* edited by Andrew Salkey, Faber, 1960, and *Stories From the Caribbean,* edited by Salkey, Elek, 1965.

SIDELIGHTS: With his first novel, *In the Castle of My Skin,* Lamming was hailed as a refreshing new talent. The novel covers the growth of a village in Barbados through the years of colonial imperialism into industrial development. Lamming incorporates both a first- and third-person narrative into the novel and four adolescent males share the reader's attention. However, Lamming reveals much of the action through his narrator. In the novel, Lamming exposes the underside of imposed education and class distinction. Writing in what Jan Carew called a "prose that was dazzlingly original," Lamming, according to Carew, "brings a private vision to bear on time and space, uniting them into an inseparable entity and islanding this entity in his own fertility."

Lamming's second novel, *The Emigrants,* was described by Carew as "the work of a brilliant but detached narrator accompanying a shipload of nomadic West Indians to Britian." Many critics consider *The Emigrants* to be Lamming's most depressing novel. Through the shifting narrative, he reveals the hopelessness felt by the West Indians as they prepare for their arrival in England. Unfortunately, some critics claimed *The Emigrants* marked a decline in quality compared to *In the Castle of My Skin.* Probably due in part to the multiple narrative, critics found *The Emigrants* to be misshapen and often overwritten.

Wilson Harris called *Of Age and Innocence* "a novel which somehow fails . . . but its failure tells us a great deal." Harris felt that Lamming's "energies" had been spread too thin in the novel and pointed to his unique narrative style as the reason for the "diffusion." "The book seems to speak with a public voice," wrote Harris, "the voice of a peculiar orator, and the compulsions which inform the work appear to spring from a verbal sophistication rather than a visual, plastic and conceptual imagery." Harris claimed that a greater concentration on Lamming's part to enhance the experiences in the novel would have improved its quality. Harris advised Lamming "to work for the continuous development of a main individual character in order to free himself somewhat from the restrictive consolidation he brings about which, unfortunately . . . blocks one's view of essential conflict."

Season of Adventure, Lamming's fourth novel, was praised by Michael Cook for its devotion to "characters' at least trying to discover their roots and natures." Unlike Lamming's other novels, *Season of Adventure,* according to Cook, is not victimized by an antithetical writing style. "Only two of the novels—the very first, *In the Castle of My Skin,* and the fourth, *Season of Adventure*—manage to escape this malaise of tendentiousness . . . ," wrote Cook.

Lamming's most recent novels, *Water With Berries* and *Natives of My Skin,* were seen by critics as successful fusions of his difficult prose style with his anguished subject matter. *Water With Berries,* the story of three West Indians exiled to England and how they are consumed with despair and self contempt was called "incredible" by Paul Theroux in *Encounter.* Theroux wrote that "the poetic prose of the narrative has a perfect dazzle. . . ." He also noted, "It is when expatriation is defined and dramatised that *Water With Berries* takes on a life of its own, for Mr. Lamming is meticulous in diagnosing the condition of estrangement."

Oddly enough, critics expressed more disappointment with the melodrama of *Water With Berries* than with Lamming's style. A reviewer for *Times Literary Supplement* found that the novel, parts of which suggest Shakespeare's *The Tempest,* "flounders between realism and fantasy." But the same critic also noted that "Mr. Lamming writes very well. . . ."

Published the same year as *Water With Berries, Natives of My Person* was reviewed less favorably. In reviewing Lamming's saga of the slave market and colonization, Theroux wrote, "More historical detail might have made it more comprehensible; too much of it is shadowy action and vaguely poetical momentousness." In comparison, Thomas Lask found *Natives of My Person* well researched. He wrote that "the author has done such a fine job establishing the authenticity of his background that it takes the reader a while to realize that what he is expecting simply isn't there. . . ." But Lask too noted that *Natives of My Person* may turn back some readers because of its highly evolved prose.

BIOGRAPHICAL/CRITICAL SOURCES: Michael G. Cooke, *Modern Black Novelists: A Collection of Critical Essays,* Prentice-Hall, 1971; *Book World,* January 23, 1972; *Times Literary Supplement,* February 11, 1972; *New York Times Book Review,* February 27, 1972; *New York Review of Books,* March 9, 1972; *Encounter,* May, 1972; *Yale Review,* summer, 1973.*

*   *   *

LANDER, Louise 1938-

PERSONAL: Born March 1, 1938, in New York, N.Y.; daughter of William H. (a journalist) and Margaret (a department store executive; maiden name, Slade) Lander; divorced. *Education:* University of Chicago, B.A., 1959; University of Michigan, J.D., 1969. *Home:* 509 West 110th St., New York, N.Y. 10025.

CAREER: Center on Social Welfare Policy and Law, New York City, staff attorney, 1969-70; University of Pennsylvania, Philadelphia, staff attorney on Health Law Project, School of Law, 1970-72; MFY Legal Services, Inc., New York City, staff attorney, 1972-73; Health Policy Advisory Center, New York City, staff analyst, 1973-76; writer, 1976—. Adjunct professor at Union Graduate School, 1977-78. Member of community board of Bellevue Hospital Center, 1973-74. *Member:* National Health Lawyers Association, Authors Guild.

WRITINGS: (Contributor) David Kotelchuck, editor, *Prognosis Negative: Crisis in the Health Care System,* Vintage, 1976; *Defective Medicine: Risk, Anger, and the Malpractice Crisis,* Farrar, Straus, 1978; (contributor) Marcus G. Raskin, editor, *The Federal Budget and Social Reconstruction,* Transaction Books, 1978; (contributor) Ruth Roemer and George A. McKray, editors, *Issues in Health Law: A Resource Handbook,* Greenwood Press, 1979. Contributor to health care journals.

WORK IN PROGRESS: Research on health policy and health law.

SIDELIGHTS: In a review of *Defective Medicine* Fitzuh Mullan wrote: "The Lander book takes one of the mastodons [of American life] . . . and dissects it carefully. Her examination is thorough and telling. The problem as she sees it has little to do with the simple question of competence in the profession. Rather, the massive dissatisfaction with American medicine that is reflected in the increased frequency of litigation against doctors is a product of a calling gone awry, a social function that has, in large part, lost touch with society. . . . *Defective Medicine* spends relatively little time talking about the actual malpractice crisis but moves quickly to the question of reform. . . . Lander's criticisms are far more crisp than her solutions."

BIOGRAPHICAL/CRITICAL SOURCES: Washington Post Book World, September 10, 1978.

*   *   *

LANDESMAN, Charles 1932-

PERSONAL: Born December 17, 1932, in Brooklyn, N.Y.; son of Charles (a lawyer) and Rose (Bernstein) Landesman; married Arlyne Diller (a teacher), June 19, 1955; children: Erica, Jennifer, Peter. *Education:* Wesleyan University, Middletown, Conn., A.B., 1954; Yale University, M.A., 1956, Ph.D., 1959. *Home:* 57 Walbrooke Rd., Scarsdale, N.Y. 10583. *Office:* Department of Philosophy, Hunter College of the City University of New York, 695 Park Ave., New York, N.Y. 10021.

CAREER: Yale University, New Haven, Conn., instructor in philosophy, 1957-59; University of Kansas, Lawrence, assistant professor, 1959-62, associate professor, 1962-65, professor of philosophy, 1965-66; Hunter College of the City University of New York, New York, N.Y., associate professor, 1965-70, professor of philosophy, 1970—, head of department, 1967-71. Visiting professor at Wayne State University, 1963. *Member:* American Philosophical Association, American Association of University Professors, American Federation of Teachers, Society for Philosophy and Public Affairs, Phi Beta Kappa. *Awards, honors:* Woodrow Wilson fellow, 1954-55; Mellon Foundation grant, 1977-78.

WRITINGS: (Editor with Norman Care, and author of introduction) *Readings in the Theory of Action*, Indiana University Press, 1968; (editor and author of introduction) *The Foundations of Knowledge*, Prentice-Hall, 1970; (editor and author of introduction) *The Problem of Universals*, Basic Books, 1971; *Discourse and Its Presuppositions*, Yale University Press, 1972; *Philosophy: An Introduction to the Central Issues*, Random House, in press. Contributor to *Encyclopedia of Philosophy*. Contributor of about twenty-five articles and reviews to philosophy journals.

* * *

LANE, Michael (John) 1941-

PERSONAL: Born June 11, 1941, in Kent, England; son of Bert Henry John (a naval officer) and Iris Mabel (Waldegrave) Lane; children: Lindsay Ruth. *Education:* Jesus College, Cambridge, B.A., 1964; University of Kent, M.A., 1967. *Politics:* Socialist. *Religion:* Atheist. *Home:* Netherwood, West Bergholt, Essex, England. *Agent:* Deborah Rogers Ltd., Goodge St., London, England. *Office:* University of Essex, Colchester, Essex, England.

CAREER: Worked as executive director of stage management, 1958-61, 1964-66; currently associated with University of Essex, Colchester, England. Media consultant. *Member:* British Sociological Association, Ipswich Town Supporters Club.

WRITINGS: *Structuralism*, J. Cape, 1970; *Commerce Against Culture*, Basic Books, 1978. Author of radio talks. Contributor to journals.

WORK IN PROGRESS: The community story of an Umbrian town; a history of post-war culture in the Western world; a study of book publishing.

* * *

LANGLEY, Bob 1936-

PERSONAL: Born August 28, 1936, in Newcastle, England; son of Robert Gerald and Corol (McCormack) Langley; married Patricia Kelly, May 14, 1975. *Residence:* Keswick, England. *Agent:* A. P. Watt & Son, 26/28 Bedford Row, London WC1R 4HL, England. *Office:* British Broadcasting Corp.—Television. Pebble Mill, Birmingham, England.

CAREER: Television scriptwriter, reporter, and interviewer; British Broadcasting Corp., Birmingham, England, host of television program.

WRITINGS: *Walking the Scottish Border*, R. Hale, 1976; *Lobo*, R. Hale, 1977; *Death Stalk*, Doubleday, 1978; *War of the Running Fox*, Scribner, 1979. Also author of *Warlords*, 1979.

WORK IN PROGRESS: Traverse of the Gods.

* * *

LAPIN, Jackie 1951-

PERSONAL: Born December 17, 1951, in Los Angeles, Calif.; daughter of Milton A. (a sales manager) and Lillian (Weinman) Lapin. *Education:* University of Southern California, B.A. (magna cum laude), 1974. *Home and office:* 4727 Orion #B, Sherman Oaks, Calif. 91423.

CAREER: Associated with Los Angeles News Agency, Los Angeles, Calif.; worked as reporter for Associated Press, *Detroit Free Press*, and *Washington Post*; worked in public relations at J. Walter Thompson, Daniel J. Edelman, and Bea Miller & Associates; worked as editorial assistant at *Swimming World*; free-lance writer. Presented "Dodger Dugout" on KTTV-TV. Instructor of journalism at California State University, Northridge. *Member:* American Society of Journalists and Authors. *Awards, honors:* Awards from Greater Los Angeles Press Club, 1974, for best college feature, and 1974, 1977, for best sports story; awards from Valley Press Club, 1975; mark of excellence from Sigma Delta Chi; received two William Randolph Hearst Awards.

WRITINGS: *The Woman in Athletic Administration*, Goodyear Publishing, 1979. Author of column in *PSA California*. Contributor to sports and popular magazines, including *Sports Illustrated*, *Playgirl*, *Bon Appetit*, and *WomenSports*, and to newspapers. Contributing editor of *Women's Sports*. Past contributing editor of *Volleyball*, *Sportswoman*, and *Southern California Sports Guide*.

WORK IN PROGRESS: Women Exercising Their Rights in Sports.

SIDELIGHTS: Lapin writes: "I have specialized in sports writing and sports public relations. However, I am currently seeking more general public relations free-lance work."

AVOCATIONAL INTERESTS: Travel (Europe, the Caribbean), outdoor activities (rafting, hiking).

* * *

LAPP, John Clarke 1917-1977

PERSONAL: Born December 25, 1917, in Ottawa, Ontario, Canada; died September 19, 1977; son of Charles Albert and Margaret (Waddell) Lapp; married Margaret Smail, September 12, 1941 (deceased); married Danielle Cauquil, February 28, 1969; children: (first marriage) Harvey. *Education:* Queen's University, Kingston, Ontario, B.A., 1939, M.A., 1940; Cornell University, Ph.D., 1942.

CAREER: University of Illinois, Champaign-Urbana, instructor in French, 1942-43; Bucknell University, Lewisburg, Pa., assistant professor of French, 1945-47; Oberlin College, Oberlin, Ohio, assistant professor, 1947-49, associate professor, 1949-55, professor of French, 1955-56; University of California, Los Angeles, professor of French, 1956-63, head of department, 1956-61; Stanford University, Stanford, Calif., professor of French, 1963-68, William H. Bonsall Professor of French, 1968-77, executive head of department of French and Italian, 1963-68. Fulbright lecturer in France, 1961-62. *Military service:* U.S. Naval Reserve, active duty, 1943-45.

AWARDS, HONORS: Officer d'Academie, 1955; chevalier of Legion d'Honneur, 1961; Fulbright grant, 1966-67; Guggenheim fellowship, 1966-67, 1973-74.

WRITINGS: (Editor) Pontus de Tyard, *The Universe*, Cornell University Press, 1950; (editor) *Contes divers de trois siecles*, Houghton, 1950, 2nd edition, 1963; (with H. A. Grubbs) *French Reviewed for Colleges*, Houghton, 1952; *Notes and Commentary on Madame Bovary*, Oberlin Press of the Times, 1952; *Aspects of Racinian Tragedy*, University of Toronto Press, 1955, revised edition, 1964; (translator) Pierre Corneille, *Le Cid*, Appleton, 1955.

Zola Before the Rougon-Macquart, University of Toronto Press, 1964; (editor) Pontus de Tyard, *Oeuvres poetiques completes*, Didier, 1966; (editor) de Tyard, *Modeles de phrases, suivis d'un recueil de Modeles de lettres d'amour* (critical edition), University of North Carolina Press, 1967.

The Esthetics of Negligence: La Fontaine's Contes, Cambridge University Press, 1971; *The Brazen Tower: Essays in Mythological Imagery, 1550-1670*, Stanford University Press, 1977. Contributor to language journals.

[Sketch verified by wife, Danielle C. Lapp]

LARKEY, Patrick Darrel 1943-

PERSONAL: Born November 10, 1943, in San Antonio, Tex.; son of Isaac Farend (an Air Force colonel and corporation executive) and Carrie (Traugh) Larkey; married Janet Hogan; children: Stephanie Lynn. *Education:* Stanford University, B.A., 1969; University of Michigan, M.P.P., 1971, Ph.D., 1975. *Home:* 126 Hawthorne St., Pittsburgh, Pa. 15218. *Office:* Department of Social Science, Carnegie-Mellon University, Pittsburgh, Pa. 15213.

CAREER: City of Ann Arbor, Mich., program manager, 1971-72; University of British Columbia, Vancouver, assistant professor of commerce, 1975-77; Carnegie-Mellon University, Pittsburgh, Pa., assistant professor of public policy and social science, 1977—. Principal of Policy Analysts, Inc. Member of Ann Arbor's committee on community development. *Military service:* U.S. Coast Guard, 1962-66. *Member:* National Tax Association, American Economic Association, Public Choice Society, American Society of Public Administration, Operations Research Society of America.

WRITINGS: Evaluating Public Programs: The Impact of General Revenue Sharing on Municipalities, Princeton University Press, 1979. Contributor to political science and tax journals.

WORK IN PROGRESS: Research on urban fiscal crises, behavioral theories of regulatory processes, relative capabilities of military organizations, a behavioral theory of public finance, and federal regulation of local education.

SIDELIGHTS: Larkey comments: "My primary research motivation is to develop theories of economic decision processes that are both dynamic and grounded empirically. These are the theories required to address practical economic questions effectively."

* * *

LARRABEE, Harold A(tkins) 1894-1979

OBITUARY NOTICE:—See index for *CA* sketch: Born August 20, 1894, in Melrose, Mass.; died February 2, 1979, in Austin, Tex. Educator, translator, editor, and author of books on philosophy. A professor of philosophy, Larrabee was the editor of the *Humanist* and the *New England Quarterly.* He was the author of two books of poetry and the translator of several works by the French scientist Charles Mayer. Obituaries and other sources: *Who's Who in America,* 39th edition, Marquis, 1976; *New York Times,* February 6, 1979.

* * *

LARSON, Bruce L(lewellyn) 1936-

PERSONAL: Born January 10, 1936, in Hawley, Minn.; son of Wendell Garfield (a farmer and trucker) and Agnes (Herzog) Larson. *Education:* Concordia College (Moorhead, Minn.), B.A., 1959; University of North Dakota, M.A., 1961; University of Kansas, Ph.D., 1971. *Home:* 1102 Warren, Mankato, Minn. 56001. *Office:* Department of History, Mankato State University, Mankato, Minn. 56001.

CAREER: University of Kansas, Lawrence, assistant instructor in history, 1961-62; Concordia College, Moorhead, Minn., instructor in history, 1962-63; University of Kansas, assistant instructor in history, 1963-65; Mankato State University, Mankato, Minn., assistant professor, 1965-72, associate professor, 1972-76, professor of hisotry, 1976—, faculty member in Scandinavian studies program, 1974—. Field representative, Minnesota Historical Society, 1973, 1977.

Narrator and consultant to "Just Plain Slim: The St. Louis Years," a television documentary on Charles A. Lindbergh, produced by KTVI-TV, St. Louis, Mo., 1977. *Member:* American Historical Association, Organization of American Historians, American Aviation Historical Society, Agricultural History Society, Swedish Pioneer Historical Society, Minnesota Historical Society. *Awards, honors:* Elmer L. and Eleanor J. Andersen Foundation fellowship, 1972-73; Minnesota Historical Society grant, 1974; national merit award from Pi Gamma Mu, 1977.

WRITINGS: Lindbergh of Minnesota: A Political Biography, foreword by Charles A. Lindbergh, Jr., Harcourt, 1973; (contributor) Byron Nordstrom, editor, *The Swedes in Minnesota,* Denison, 1976; (contributor) Burton J. Williams, editor, *Essays on Kansas History in Honor of George L. Anderson,* Coronado Press, 1977; (contributor) Nils Hasselmo, editor, *Perspectives on Swedish Immigration,* Swedish Pioneer Historical Society, 1978. Contributor of articles and reviews to professional journals, including *American Historical Review, Journalism Quarterly,* and *Minnesota History.*

WORK IN PROGRESS: The North Star State: A Documentary History of Minnesota, with Russell W. Fridley and David L. Nass, for Eerdmans; research on Charles A. Lindbergh and early American aviation.

SIDELIGHTS: "Contacts with Charles A. Lindbergh, Jr. during the last decade of his life were especially meaningful, including participation with him at the 1973 dedication of the Lindbergh Interpretive Center at Little Falls, Minnesota," Larson recalled. Larson enlisted the aid of the younger Lindbergh for his biography of Charles A. Lindbergh, Sr., a progressive Republican U.S. representative from Minnesota from 1907 to 1917. The elder Lindbergh, who was vilified by his constituents for vigorously opposing U.S. entry into World War I, identified with the Nonpartisan League and the Farmer-Labor party in his later career.

Larson interviewed Lindbergh, Jr. extensively and spent ten years working on the biography of his father. Lindbergh, Jr. praised Larson's effort, as Wesley Pruden, Jr. reported: "It's as accurate as it can be made. Usually I'm highly critical, from a standpoint of accuracy, of most publications, books, magazines, newspapers. On the average, they're inaccurate. But here, in this book, I know of no instance of inaccuracy. It's an excellent picture of my father. It's very objective."

AVOCATIONAL INTEREST: Travel, golf.

BIOGRAPHICAL/CRITICAL SOURCES: Time, April 29, 1966; *National Observer,* June 30, 1973; *Journal of American History,* September, 1974.

* * *

LARSON, Robert W. 1927-

PERSONAL: Born March 20, 1927, in Denver, Colo.; son of Walter S. (a banker) and Helen (Leafgren) Larson; married Carole Barrett Lang, September 14, 1959 (divorced, 1972); children: Helen E. Larson Carlson, Matthew R. *Education:* University of Denver, A.B., 1950, A.M., 1953; University of New Mexico, Ph.D., 1961. *Politics:* Democrat. *Religion:* Presbyterian. *Home:* 2101 22nd Ave., #304, Greeley, Colo. 80631. *Office:* Department of History, University of Northern Colorado, Greeley, Colo. 80639.

CAREER: Public school teacher in Denver, Colo., 1950-58; University of Northern Colorado, Greeley, assistant professor, 1960-64, associate professor, 1964-68, professor of history, 1968—. *Military service:* U.S. Navy, 1945-46. *Mem-*

ber: American Historical Association, Organization of American Historians, Rocky Mountain Social Science Association (past member of board of directors), Western History Association. *Awards, honors:* American Philosophical Society grants, 1963, 1964, 1969; Newberry fellowship from Newberry Library (Chicago), 1977.

WRITINGS: New Mexico's Quest for Statehood, 1846-1912, University of New Mexico Press, 1968; *New Mexico Populism: A Study of Radical Protest in a Western Territory,* Colorado Associated University Press, 1974. Contributor to *Reader's Encyclopedia of the American West.* Contributor to history journals.

WORK IN PROGRESS: A book on the Populist movement in the front-range states of the Rocky Mountains; a novel for teenagers on the Butterfield Express in the Southwest; a children's history of mail transportation in America.

SIDELIGHTS: Larson writes: "My books are a result of an intense interest in the history of the American Southwest from 1846 to 1912. Beginning with my first trip down the Taos Valley to Santa Fe some twenty years ago, I have had a continuing fascination with this area. New Mexico has been particularly interesting to me because of the unique blend of three cultures found there: Hispanic, Indian, and Anglo. This interest in New Mexico has motivated me to do some serious historical research and writing about the state, as well as write a historical novel for young people, using pre-Civil War New Mexico as a background."

* * *

LATHAM, Roger M. 1914(?)-1979

OBITUARY NOTICE: Born c. 1914; died May 15, 1979, in Interlaken, Switzerland. Journalist. Outdoors editor for the *Pittsburgh Press* since 1957, Latham had previously worked as research chief of the Pennsylvania Game Commission. He died when he fell down a mountain in Switzerland, where he and several others had been photographing mountain goats. Obituaries and other sources: *New York Times,* May 17, 1979.

* * *

LATSIS, Mary J(ane)
(R. B. Dominic, Emma Lathen, joint pseudonyms)

EDUCATION: Attended Harvard University. *Residence:* Boston, Mass.

CAREER: Economic analyst and author. Worked for United Nations, New York, N.Y.; also worked as author of bank letters. *Awards, honors: Murder Against the Grain* named Best Crime Fiction Novel by the Crime Writers' Association, 1967.

WRITINGS—With Martha Hennissart under joint pseudonym Emma Lathen: *Banking on Death,* Macmillan, 1961; *A Place for Murder,* Macmillan, 1963; *Accounting for Murder,* Macmillan, 1964; *Death Shall Overcome,* Macmillan, 1966; *Murder Makes the Wheels Go 'Round,* Macmillan, 1966; *Murder Against the Grain,* Macmillan, 1967; *Come to Dust,* Simon & Schuster, 1968; *A Stitch in Time,* Macmillan, 1968; *Murder to Go,* Simon & Schuster, 1969; *When in Greece,* Simon & Schuster, 1969; *Pick Up Sticks,* Simon & Schuster, 1970; *The Longer the Thread,* Simon & Schuster, 1971; *Ashes to Ashes,* Simon & Schuster, 1971; *Murder Without Icing,* Simon & Schuster, 1972; *Sweet and Low,* Simon & Schuster, 1974; *By Hook or by Crook,* Simon & Schuster, 1975; *Double, Double, Oil and Trouble,* Simon & Schuster, 1978.

With Martha Hennissart under joint pseudonym R. B. Dominic: *Murder, Sunny Side Up,* Abelard-Schuman, 1968; *Murder in High Place,* Doubleday, 1970; *There Is No Justice,* Doubleday, 1971; *Epitaph for a Lobbyist,* Doubleday, 1974; *Murder Out of Commission,* Doubleday, 1976.

SIDELIGHTS: "Emma Lathen is probably the best living American writer of detective stories," proclaimed C. P. Snow. Perhaps the author's greatest mystery, however, has been her own identity, which was a well-kept secret for many years. Lathen is actually a joint pseudonym of Mary Jane Latsis and Martha Hennissart. The authors constructed the pseudonym Emma Lathen from parts of their real names: the "M" of Mary and "Ma" of Martha form Emma, and "Lat" of Latsis and "Hen" of Hennissart form Lathen.

The authors met while attending graduate school at Harvard University. They later discovered a mutual enjoyment of mystery stories, and collaborated to write one of their own. This led to more Lathen novels, all featuring the "anamalous detective, John Putnam Thatcher—a middle-aged, pin-striped Wall Street banker—[who] deals with crime in a neat, businesslike manner, never leaving clots of blood spattered around," according to Annette Grant. Thatcher is constantly described as "urbane," and Anthony Boucher commented: "I keep saying 'urbane, witty, faultless, delightful'; what other adjectives is one to use for Lathen's precise blends of formal detection and acute social satire?"

Latsis, an economist, and Hennissart, a lawyer, glean ideas and information for stories from their professional activities and careful reading of financial journals. They hid their own identities for so long, according to *New York Times Book Review,* because "they prefer not to have their clients worrying that a pending matter will end up as a *corpus delicti* in a future Lathen mystery."

Many critics would agree with P. D. James that "a new novel by Emma Lathen is like luncheon at Bertorelli's: the ambience and the characters may be familiar but value and satisfaction are guaranteed." Perhaps the best-loved Lathen novel was *Murder Against the Grain,* which involves the theft of a million dollars during a U.S./Soviet wheat deal. *Times Literary Supplement* said, "Miss Lathen's touch with the international relations is perfectly balanced, and her light asides . . . are charming. Also, this is good proper detection."

Some of Lathen's other books received mixed reviews. While *Ashes to Ashes* was described by *New Yorker* as having "very little movement and very little bite," it was praised by Leo Fleming for its "sudden flashes of wit and a deep insight into people."

Latsis and Hennissart also write a series of mysteries about a congressman that are published under the joint pseudonym R. B. Dominic.

BIOGRAPHICAL/CRITICAL SOURCES: Harper's, July, 1967; *Times Literary Supplement,* July 27, 1967, December 21, 1967, December 11, 1969, December 26, 1975; *New York Times Book Review,* September 17, 1967, April 21, 1968, July 7, 1968, October 20, 1968, September 7, 1969, March 1, 1970, December 27, 1970, March 14, 1971, March 26, 1972, November 26, 1972, September 22, 1974; *Books and Bookmen,* April, 1968; *Newsweek,* July 28, 1969; *New Yorker,* September 13, 1969, February 21, 1970, June 12, 1971, September 9, 1974; *Wall Street Journal,* December 3, 1970; *Saturday Review,* January 30, 1971; *Best Sellers,* April 1, 1971; *Library Journal,* November 1, 1972; *Critic,* March/April, 1973; (under pseudonym Emma Lathen) *Contemporary Lit-*

erary Criticism, Volume 2, Gale, 1974; *Christian Science Monitor,* June 4, 1975; *Forbes,* December 1, 1977.

* * *

LAUER, Jean-Philippe 1902-

PERSONAL: Born May 7, 1902, in Paris, France; son of Philippe (a librarian) and Marie (Eclancher) Lauer; married Marguerite Jouguet; children: Pierre, Daniel, Florence Lauer Chappey. *Education:* Attended Ecole Militaire des Genie at Versailles, 1922; Ecole Nationale Superieure des Beaux-Arts, dipl. architecture, 1926. *Religion:* Roman Catholic. *Home:* 5 chemin Chancelier Seguier, L'Etang-le-Ville, France F-78620.

CAREER: Service des Antiquites a Saqqara, Saqqara, Egypt, architect, 1926-31, director of operations, 1932-39; Service des Antiquites a Saqqara, director of operations, 1945-56; Centre National de la Recherche Scientifique, Paris, France, chief of research, 1957-65, director of research, 1965-73, honorary director of research, 1973—. *Military service:* French Army, Engineers, 1939-40; became lieutenant.

MEMBER: Academie des Inscriptions et Belles-Lettres (corresponding member), Francaise d'Egyptologie (vice-president), Institut d'Egypte (vice-president), Institut d'Archeologie de Berlin, Institut Tcheco-Slovaque de l'Universite Charles (associate member), Fondation Egyptologique Reine Elisabeth (corresponding member). *Awards, honors:* Officer of Legion d'Honneur; commander of Ordre National du Merite; commander of Ordre des Palmes Academiques; Prix Bordin, 1937; gold medals from Salon des Artistes Francais, 1938, and Academie des Inscriptions et Belles-Lettres; Prix Noel des Vergers et Gaston Maspers, 1977.

*WRITINGS—*In English: *Saqqara: The Royal Cemetery of Memphis–Excavations and Discoveries Since 1850,* Scribner, 1976.

In French: *Fouilles a Saqqarah: La Pyramide a degres,* Institut francais d'archeologie orientale, Volumes I-II: *L'Architecture,* 1939, Volume III: *Complements,* 1939; *Etudes complementaires sur les monuments du roi Zoser a Saqqarah,* Institut francais d'archeologie orientale, 1948; *Le Probleme des pyramides d'Egypte: traditions et legendes, exploration, description, theories, science et croyances des constructeurs,* Payot, 1948; (with Charles Picard) *Les Statues ptolemaiques du Sarapieion de Memphis,* Presses universitaires de France, 1955; *Observations sur les pyramides,* Institut francais d'archeologie orientale, 1960; *Les Pyramides de Saqqarah: The Pyramids of Sakkarah* (bilingual edition), Institut graphique egyptien, 1961, 4th edition, Institut francais d'archeologie orientale, 1972; *Histoire monumentale des pyramides d'Egypte,* Institut francais d'archeologie orientale, 1962; *Les Pyramides a degres, troisieme dynastie,* Le Caire, 1962; (with Jean Leclant) *Mission archeologique de Saqqarah,* Institut francais d'archeologie orientale, 1972; (with Leclant) *Le Temple haut du complexe funeraire de le pyramide du roi Teti,* Institut francais d'archeologie orientale, 1972; *Le Mystere des pyramides,* Presses de la Cite, 1974; (with Leclant) *Le Temple haut du complexe funeraire de le pyramide du roi Ounar,* Institut francais d'archeologie orientale, 1977. Contributor of about one hundred-fifty articles to scholarly journals.

WORK IN PROGRESS: Le Temps des pyramides, de la prehistoire aux Hyksos, publication by Gallimard.

LAUERSEN, Niels H(elth) 1936-

PERSONAL: Born September 10, 1936, in Copenhagen, Denmark; came to the United States in 1967, naturalized citizen, 1972; son of Hans B. and Maria (Helth) Lauersen. *Education:* University of Copenhagen, B.S., 1962, M.D., 1967. *Home:* 75 East End Ave., New York, N.Y. 10021. *Agent:* Gael Greene, 280 West End Ave., New York, N.Y. 10023. *Office:* Department of Obstetrics, Medical Center, Cornell University, 1300 York, New York, N.Y. 10021.

CAREER: New York Hospital, New York City, associate professor of obstetrics and gynecology, 1972; Cornell University, Medical Center, New York City, associate professor of obstetrics and gynecology, 1972—, researcher, 1972—. *Military service:* Danish Air Force, 1956-59. *Member:* Literary Guild of America, Society of Gynecological Investigation.

WRITINGS: It's Your Body: A Woman's Guide to Gynecology, Grosset, 1978.

WORK IN PROGRESS: A childbirth manual.

* * *

LAURIE, Rona

PERSONAL: Born in Derby, England; daughter of Alan Rupert (a physician) and Alexandrina (Ross) Laurie; married Edward Lewis Neilson (a commander in the Royal Navy), August 28, 1961. *Education:* University of Birmingham, B.A. (honors); also attended Royal Academy of Dramatic Art. *Home:* 2 New Quebec St., London W1H 7DD, England. *Office:* Department of Drama in Education, Guildhall School of Music and Drama, John Carpenter St., London EC4Y OAR, England.

CAREER: Professional actress in London, England, 1939-58; Guildhall School of Music and Drama, London, examiner and lecturer in drama, 1958—, head of department of drama in education, 1970—. Drama tutor for Studio 68 and Arts Education School. *Member:* Guild of Drama Adjudicators (chairperson, 1969-72), Society of Teachers of Speech and Drama (chairperson, 1977—), British Federation of Music Festivals (adjudicator, 1958—), Poetry Society. *Awards, honors:* Fellowship from Guildhall School of Music and Drama, 1967.

WRITINGS: (Editor with Edita Maisie Cobby) *Speaking Together,* Books I and II, Pitman, 1964; (editor with Daniel Roberts) *The Eighth Anthology,* Guild Hall School of Music and Drama, 1964; (editor) *A Hundred Speeches From the Theatre,* Evans Brothers, 1966, revised edition published in America as *One Hundred Speeches From the Theater,* Crowell-Collier Press, 1973; (editor) *Scenes and Ideas,* Pitman, 1967; (with Cobby) *Adventures in Group-Speaking,* Pitman, 1967; (editor with John Holgate) *The Eleventh Anthology,* Guild Hall School of Music and Drama, 1969; (editor with Holgate) *The Thirteenth Anthology,* Guild Hall School of Music and Drama, 1973; *Festivals and Adjudication,* Pitman, 1975. Contributor to *Speech and Drama.*

WORK IN PROGRESS: Dramatization of a children's classic, publication expected in 1980.

SIDELIGHTS: Rona Laurie writes: "I regard all my work, whether it be writing, acting, verse-speaking, directing, adjudicating, or teaching, as a seamless garment. My interest is in language, written or spoken, and its power of communicating ideas, stirring the imagination and heart, and stimulating thought in an increasingly materialistic age."

LAURI-VOLPI, Giacomo 1893(?)-1979

OBITUARY NOTICE: Born c. 1893 in Rome, Italy; died March 17, 1979, in Valencia, Spain. Opera singer and author. Lauri-Volpi was a leading tenor with the Metropolitan Opera from 1923 to 1934. He was popular with the audiences and had a large repertory, including Spontini's "La Vestale," Rossini's "William Tell," and the standard Verdi and Puccini operas. Lauri-Volpi had a longlasting career, singing in Italian opera houses until he was nearly seventy years old. One of his books was *L'Equivoco,* an autobiography. Obituaries and other sources: Harold Simpson, *Singers to Remember,* Oakwood Press, 1974; *Musicians Since 1900,* Wilson, 1978; *New York Times,* March 20, 1979.

* * *

LAWRENCE, Marjorie 1907-1979

OBITUARY NOTICE: Born February 17, 1907, in Melbourne, Australia; died January 13, 1979, in Little Rock, Ark. Singer, singing teacher, and author of her autobiography. Lawrence was a leading Wagnerian soprano at the Metropolitan Opera in the 1930's. In 1941, while on tour in Mexico, she was stricken with polio, but later made a successful comeback. Her autobiography, *Interrupted Melody,* was made into a film of the same name in 1955. Lawrence taught singing at several colleges and universities. Obituaries and other sources: *Current Biography,* Wilson, 1940; *Who's Who in Music and Musicians' International Directory,* 6th edition, Hafner, 1972; *Biography News,* Volume I, Gale, 1974; *Who's Who,* 126th edition, St. Martin's, 1974; *Musicians Since 1900,* Wilson, 1978; *Chicago Tribune,* January 15, 1979; *New York Times,* January 15, 1979.

* * *

LAYE, Camara 1928-

PERSONAL: Family name, Kamara; personal name, Laye; born January 1, 1928, in Kouroussa, French Guinea (now Guinea), West Africa; son of Kamara Komady (a goldsmith) and Daman Sadan; children: four. *Education:* Attended Central School of Automobile Engineering, Ecole Ampere, Conservatoire des Arts et Metiers, and Technical College for Aeronautics and Automobile Construction, all near Paris, France.

CAREER: Worked in a market and at various other jobs in Paris, France, before becoming a motor mechanic for Simca Corp. in a Paris suburb, c. 1953; served as attache at ministry of youth in Paris; returned to Guinea, 1956; worked as engineer for the French colonial regime in Guinea, 1956-58; government of Guinea, Conakry, diplomat in Liberia, Ghana, and other African countries, beginning 1958; became director of Centre de Recherche et d'Etudes in Conakry; exiled self from Guinea, 1965; lived for a time in Ivory Coast; research fellow in Islamic Studies at Dakar University, Senegal, c. 1971; associated with the Institut Francais d'Afrique Noire in Dakar; became a university teacher in Senegal. *Awards, honors:* Prix Charles Veillon, 1954, for *L'Enfant noir.*

WRITINGS: L'Enfant noir (autobiography), Plon, 1953, translation by James Kirkup, Ernest Jones, and Elaine Gottlieb published as *The Dark Child,* Noonday Press, 1954 (published in England as *The African Child,* Collins, 1959); *Le Regard du roi* (novel), Plon, 1954, translation by Kirkup published as *The Radiance of the King,* Collins, 1956, Collier, 1971; *Dramouss* (autobiographical novel), Plon, 1966, translation by Kirkup published as *A Dream of Africa,* Collins, 1968, Collier, 1971. Contributor of articles and short stories to publications, including *African Arts, Black Orpheus, Presence Africaine,* and *Paris-Dakar.*

SIDELIGHTS: Camara Laye's books focus on his Guinea homeland while featuring the perspective of the outsider. Laye himself developed his view of Guinea from without by spending nearly six years as a student in Paris. After leaving his native tribal village, Laye first learned of urban life in his high school town, Conakry, the capitol of Guinea. After high school he accepted a scholarship to study engineering in the Paris suburb of Argenteuil, France. Predictably, the young Laye met difficulty in transferring from culture to culture. His birthplace, Kouroussa, rested within the anachronistic traditions of ancient African empires far different from the world's modern cities. A belief in magic sustained these people as exemplified by Laye's father, a goldsmith, who was assumed to have held supernatural abilities.

Laye did earn a professional certificate in Paris, but decided to continue his education by pursuing his own interests in study. Working part-time during the day and attending school at night, Laye began to write remembrances of his native land to help relieve the pain of his loneliness and poverty. The result of these first writing efforts appeared in his autobiography, *L'Enfant noir* ("A Dark Child"). In this book, Laye recreated his life in his tribal homeland and followed by recounting his exposure to urban life in Conakry and his first impressions as a student in Paris. One conflict Laye expressed was the difficulty in maintaining the life style of his traditional culture when aware of modern life outside that society. Thomas Lask outlined the culture's expectations for those like Laye, and its inevitable disappointment: "The clever boy with his learning will bring honor and fulfillment to his people. But in the process of harnessing that learning he must move further and further from the society that nurtured him. A final sundering troubles the consciousness of the boy and all those who love him. 'Hasn't he learned enough?' the mother asks, unwilling to contemplate the long voyage to France for her teen-age African son. The answer is bound to be no. Perhaps he never will."

A common complaint surrounding *L'Enfant noir* centered on Laye's apparent unwillingness to attack the evils of colonialization. At the same time, however, Laye earned praise for contributing to the negritude movement by heightening awareness of traditional African life and values.

Lifted from his poverty by the financial success of *L'Enfant noir,* Laye soon published his next work, *Le Regard du roi* ("The Radiance of the King"). Here Laye reversed the pattern of his own experience, an African lost in an alien European culture, by forcing his hero, Clarence, to adapt to the strange African culture surrounding him. He, too, is poor, and has no means for a living until he finds work in the king's court. "But this is not as easy as one would have thought," declared Jeanette Macaulay, "because every task has its spiritual significance. . . . He has to adapt himself to a new society, a society which does not need him in any way, a society whose conceptions of life, of the value of life and the values in life are completely different from his own. In the end, Clarence's search for the king with whom he hopes to hold an audience becomes an obsession. It's the mirage which lures him on through dark forests with people he doesn't feel anything for, with people who do not understand him."

Le Regard du roi has met interpretations on two levels: religious and cultural. On the religious level, as Janheinz Jahn observed, "it is usually considered as an ingenious allegory about man's search for god." Despite his worries about conforming to African society, Clarence "can only be redeemed after he has learned that his moral problems are not essential," wrote Jahn. "This is one of the strongest arguments against the Christian interpretation of the end of the book." David Cook, meanwhile, admitted Clarence's journey "might be compared to the quest for the holy grail—the great myth of early Christendom," and noted Clarence's questions: "What is an adequate god figure? What is the relationship between the human and the superhuman? What are we to understand by worthiness?" Ultimately, Cook believed, Laye is concerned to re-establish a true link between the idea of love and the idea of religion. . . . The concept of love with which Camara Laye is concerned is the monopoly of no particular religion and no particular race."

This theme of assimilation was shared by those interpreting *Le Regard du roi* on a cultural level. Jahn thought "the end of the novel, often misunderstood, means that even the white man in Africa can be redeemed and accepted when he shows his will to learn and not only to teach." In this novel, "the white man may be the protagonist but Africa is the antagonist," wrote Charles R. Larson. "It is the hero's ability to comprehend the magnitude and the complexity of the African experience—to realize that his own culture has little significance at all—which leads us to a basic aspect of what Senghor has seen as the final evolutionary stage of cultural syncretism—'reformed negritude,' a kind of world culture which embodies the best of all cultures. . . . Clarence, who is archetypal of Western man in particular, is symbolic of everyman and his difficulties in adjusting not only to a different culture, but to life itself."

Laye left Paris and returned to his homeland two years before it gained its independence in 1958. Although he did diplomatic work for the new regime, by 1960 his desire to escape public service and his increasingly critical writings strained his relationship with President Sekou Toure. Larson reported that Toure "gave the option either of altering the manuscript of his third work and remaining in the country, or living in exile if his French publisher brought out the book as written." Laye chose to flee and, with his wife and children, managed to escape the country.

These bitter experiences in Guinea were reflected in Laye's only book published since 1954, *Dramouss* ("A Dream of Africa"). The book was much harsher in tone than *L'Enfant noir* and much more political: Macaulay called it "mainly a diatribe against the political errors of President Sekou Toure." *Dramouss* begins near the time when *L'Enfant noir* left off as the narrator, Fatoman, returns from a six-year exile in Paris. Flashback serves to reveal the incidents of the Paris years before Fatoman discovers Guinea laden with shallow slogans and an influx of materialism as it approaches independence. His father, for example, once a revered artisan, now carves wooden objects for tourists instead. Bickering political parties convince Fatoman further of impending trouble for his country, and he warns a political meeting of the need for order in the establishment of the new government: "Someone must say that though colonialism . . . was an evil thing for our country, the regime you are now introducing will be a catastrophe whose evil consequences will be felt for decades. Someone must speak out and say that a regime built on spilt blood through the activities of incendiaries of huts and houses is nothing but a regime of anarchy and dictatorship, a regime based on violence." After going back to Paris and returning again to Guinea, Fatoman discovers, as reported by the *Times Literary Supplement*, "his fears of the regime are confirmed, his friends murdered and he is

anxious for his own life. The book ends with a small parable in which, after Fatoman's father says some prayers, a hawk returns to the family compound a chicken it seized. Those who get God on their side . . . The Black Lion of Allah will eventually help eternal Africa take revenge on an unscrupulous present."

The ten year gap between the publication of *Le Regard du roi* and *Dramouss* aroused the anticipation of those impressed with Laye's first two works. Though his most recent book confused some with its use of allegory, its overwhelming impact was its severity. "*A Dream of Africa*," wrote Larson in *Books Abroad*, "contains some of the bitterest criticism an African intellectual has ever leveled against his own country. One wonders what kind of book Camara Laye will write next." Sketchy details of Laye's life since his exile increase that wonder. One report states that in 1970, the Guinea government seized Laye's wife while she was visiting her ill mother in Conakry and has kept her imprisoned as an enemy of the state.

BIOGRAPHICAL/CRITICAL SOURCES: Camara Laye, *The Dark Child*, Noonday Press, 1954; Ulli Beier, editor, *Introduction to African Literature: An Anthology of Critical Writings From "Black Orpheus,"* Northwestern University Press, 1967; *Times Literary Supplement*, May 4, 1967; *Observer Review*, February 4, 1968; *Books Abroad*, spring, 1969, spring, 1971; *New York Times*, September 16, 1969; Laye, *A Dream of Africa*, Collier, 1971; Christopher Haywood, editor, *Perspectives on African Literature*, Africana Publishing, 1971; Charles R. Larson, *The Emergence of African Fiction*, Indiana University Press, 1971; Michael G. Cooke, editor, *Modern Black Novelists: A Collection of Critical Essays*, Prentice-Hall, 1971; *Books and Bookmen*, February, 1971; *Contemporary Literary Criticism*, Volume 4, Gale, 1975.*

* * *

LaZEBNIK, Edith 1897-

PERSONAL: Born January 1, 1897, in Russia; came to the United States in 1913, naturalized citizen, 1913; daughter of David and Rachel (Lutz) Eisenberg; married Samuel LaZebnik, December 16, 1913 (died, 1979); children: Zelda LaZebnik Gerow, William Lannik, Herbert, Jeanette LaZebnik Bernhard, Jack, Robert. *Education:* "Self-taught." *Religion:* Jewish. *Home:* Van Buren Apartments, #115, 625 North Van Buren, Tucson, Ariz. 85711.

CAREER: Writer, 1978—.

WRITINGS: Such a Life (autobiography), Morrow, 1978; *I Love America*, Morrow, 1980.

SIDELIGHTS: Edith LaZebnik writes: "My book compares life in the United States to life in Russia. My motivation is to show young people how fortunate they are to live here and to appreciate what they have. I have traveled to Europe and Israel several times for research, and to confirm my own views and observations.

"I had hoped to be an entertainer when I came to this country. Now my grandchildren are doing what I had dreamed about."

BIOGRAPHICAL/CRITICAL SOURCES: Edith LaZebnik, *Such a Life*, Morrow, 1980.

* * *

LEACH, Bernard Howell 1887-1979

OBITUARY NOTICE: Born January 5, 1887, in Hong Kong;

died May 6, 1979, in St. Ives, Cornwall, England. Potter and author of several books on pottery. An internationally known potter, Leach was strongly influenced by Oriental pottery. He traveled throughout China and Japan before settling in a coastal resort town in Cornwall, where he established his studio in 1920. Obituaries and other sources: *The Author's and Writer's Who's Who,* 6th edition, Burke's Peerage, 1971; *Who's Who in the World,* 2nd edition, Marquis, 1973; *Who's Who,* 126th edition, St. Martin's, 1974; *Ceramics Monthly,* November, 1974, June, 1977; *Country Life,* March 3, 1977; *Art & Artists,* March, 1977; *Time,* April 4, 1977; *New York Times,* May 7, 1979.

* * *

LEADER, Mary (Bartelt)

PERSONAL: Born in Milwaukee, Wis.; daughter of Arthur Herman (an attorney) and Mabel Hall (a teacher; maiden name, Duncan) Bartelt; married Eric Siegfried Leader (a research technician). *Education:* University of San Antonio, A.A.; University of Texas, B.A.; University of Wisconsin—Milwaukee, M.A., 1972; also studied drama privately. *Religion:* Presbyterian. *Home and office:* 10412 West Sunset Woods Lane, Mequon, Wis. 53092. *Agent:* Emilie Jacobson, Curtis Brown Ltd., 575 Madison Ave., New York, N.Y. 10022.

CAREER: Milwaukee Journal, Milwaukee, Wis., reporter during World War II; actress in touring company of "Women of Destiny," 1955-70; news and feature writer and theatre reviewer for *Cedarburg News Graphic,* 1961-68. Silhouettist for stage production "The King and I." *Member:* Actors Equity Association, Council of Wisconsin Writers (member of board of directors), Milwaukee Press Club, Gamma Phi Beta. *Awards, honors:* Certificate of commendation from Allstate Safety Crusade, 1962, for "Where to Beware," a column in *Cedarburg News Graphic.*

WRITINGS: Triad (novel), Coward, 1973; *Salem's Children* (novel), Coward, 1979. Author of "Women of Destiny" (program of monodramas).

Author of "Where to Beware," safety column in *Cedarburg News Graphic,* 1962-66. Contributor to *Milwaukee Journal,* 1960—.

WORK IN PROGRESS: A novel with a background of Celtic folklore, featuring a current social problem with a supernatural twist.

SIDELIGHTS: Mary Leader writes: "My first two novels have had elements of the supernatural. I believe the best tales of the supernatural are those which present the latter as a natural thing, because that is what the supernatural is—an extension of the natural, as the unknown is merely an extension of the known. With every new invention or discovery a little bit more of the supernatural or unknown becomes commonplace to us: flying, radio, television, nuclear energy, outer space, et cetera. To those who object to supernatural fiction on religious grounds, I counter with 'What is religion, if not a belief in the supernatural?'

"My novels are multi-layered. Beneath the surface story lie psychological motivations, universal mythology, and allegory. My heroes and heroines are 'Everyperson' and my most hateful villain is Cruelty Personified. In *Salem's Children,* the citizens of isolated Peacehaven all carry a chip on their shoulders because their ancestors were executed as witches in Salem in 1692. In their effort to vindicate their ancestors these descendants become the worst witchhunters of all. The question proposed is—should the present be liable for the sins of the past?

"Years ago I discovered to my horror that I am descended from William Stoughton, chief justice of the appellate court of oyer and terminer in Salem, which sent twenty people (most of them innocent, I believe) to their deaths. He was also the only judge who in later years did not recant. At length I resolved to study that episode in history for a better understanding, since I felt I had much to make up for. I hope that *Salem's Children* will do the job.

"The recent tragedy at Jonestown in Guyana has held a particular horror for me, as it has made *Salem's Children* almost prophetic—though on a small scale. Here too, in the character of Lucian, one has the charismatic figure of a false prophet—one who poses as a 'born-again' minister doing good works, who drives a wedge between children and their parents, who inevitably assumes a god role, and who, when his power and divinity are threatened, brings down disaster. I have always been distrustful of super-charismatics, both in politics and religion, particularly if their mission is to make their followers throw away their previous moral standards and beliefs, and especially their own judgment, will, and power of decision."

AVOCATIONAL INTERESTS: Art (painting, sketching, and design), reading, gardening, drama, her dogs and cat, silhouettes.

* * *

LEDDEROSE, Lothar 1942-

PERSONAL: Born July 12, 1942, in Munich, Germany (now West Germany); son of Georg (a professor of music) and Maria (a professor of music; maiden name, Freundlieb) Ledderhose; married Doris Croissant (a university teacher), May 26, 1975; children: Julia. *Education:* Attended University of Cologne, University of Bonn, and University of Paris; University of Heidelberg, Ph.D., 1969; postdoctoral study at Princeton University and Harvard University, both 1969-71, and University of Tokyo, 1972-75. *Religion:* Roman Catholic. *Home:* Merianstrasse 16, 6900 Neckargemuend, West Germany. *Office:* Kunsthistorisches Institut, Universitaet Heidelberg, Seminarstrasse 4, 6900 Heidelberg, West Germany.

CAREER: Museum fuer Ostasiatische Kunst, Berlin, West Germany, researcher, 1975-76; University of Heidelberg, Heidelberg, West Germany, professor of East Asian art history, 1976—. *Member:* Deutsche Morgenlaendische Gesellschaft (deputy chairman).

WRITINGS: Die Siegelschrift (chuan-shu) in der Ch'ing-Zeit: Ein Beitrag zue Geschichte der chinesischen Schriftkunst, Franz Steiner, 1970; *Mi Fu and the Classical Tradition of Chinese Calligraphy,* Princeton University Press, 1978. Contributor to art and museum journals.

WORK IN PROGRESS: Catalogue of the Chinese Paintings in the Museum fuer Ostasiatische Kunst, Berlin.

* * *

LEE, Elsie 1912-

(Elsie Cromwell, Jane Gordon; Lee Sheridan, a joint pseudonym with Michael Sheridan)

PERSONAL: Born January 24, 1912, in Brooklyn, N.Y.; daughter of Samuel Byron (an engineer) and Helen (Bogert) Williams; married Morton Lee, December 27, 1941 (deceased). *Education:* Attended Swarthmore College, 1929-32, and Pratt Institute, 1932-33. *Religion:* Society of Friends (Quakers). *Home and office:* 160 West 95th St., New York, N.Y. 10025. *Agent:* Bill Berger Associates, Inc., 444 East 58th St., New York, N.Y. 10022.

CAREER: Price, Waterhouse & Co., New York, N.Y., librarian, 1937-42; Reeves Laboratories, New York City, office manager, 1942-45; Gulf Oil Co., New York City, librarian, 1947-51; Andrews, Clark & Buckley, New York City, executive secretary, 1951-53; writer, 1945—. *Member:* Authors Guild of Authors League of America, Mensa.

WRITINGS—Novels: *The Blood Red Oscar*, Lancer Books, 1962; *Comedy of Terrors* (adapted from the screenplay by Richard Matheson), Lancer Books, 1964; *The Doctor's Office*, Lancer Books, 1965; (under pseudonym Jane Gordon) *Season of Evil*, Horwitz Publications, 1966; *Fulfillment*, Lancer Books, 1968; (under pseudonym Elsie Cromwell) *The Governess*, Paperback Library, 1969; (under Cromwell pseudonym) *Ivorstone Manor*, Paper Books, 1970; *The Diplomatic Lover*, Dell, 1971; *Star of Danger*, Dell, 1971; *Silence Is Golden*, Dell, 1971; *The Passions of Medora Graeme*, Arbor House, 1972; *The Spy at the Villa Miranda*, Dell, 1973; *The Curse of Carranca*, Dell, 1973; *Prior Betrothal*, Arbor House, 1973; *The Wicked Guardian*, Dell, 1973; *Second Season*, Dell, 1973; *Sinister Abbey*, Dell, 1973; *An Eligible Connection*, Cedric Chivers, 1974, Dell, 1975; *Roomates*, Dell, 1976; *Mansion of Golden Windows*, Dell, 1976; *Dark Moon, Lost Lady*, Dell, 1976; *Nabob's Widow*, Delacorte, 1976; *Mistress of Mount Fair*, Dell, 1977; *The Drifting Sands*, Dell, 1978; *Satan's Coast*, Dell, 1978; *Clouds Over Vellanti*, Dell, 1979. Also author of *Barrow Sinister*.

Other: *The Exciting World of Rocks and Gems*, Trend Books, 1959; (under pseudonym Lee Sheridan) *The Bachelor's Cookbook*, Collier, 1962; *Easy Gourmet Cooking*, Lancer Books, 1962; *At Home With Plants: A Guide to Successful Indoor Gardening*, Macmillan, 1966; *Second Easy Gourmet Cookbook*, Lancer Books, 1968; *Elsie Lee's Book of Simple Gourmet Cookery*, Arbor House, 1971; *Elsie Lee's Party Cookbook*, Arbor House, 1974.

Contributor to periodicals with Michael Sheridan under joint pseudonym Lee Sheridan.

WORK IN PROGRESS: A novel.

SIDELIGHTS: Lee told *CA*: "I write fairy tales for grownups, principally women, but many husbands find them bearable for the day they're in bed with a cold. I am better at characterizations than plots, and best with cats who are unanimously adored by my readers.... Life has taught me that I may be highly individual but am definitely not unique. Anything I understand will be equally understood by at least a million other Americans. Therefore I will not compromise on the quality of vocabulary and grammar in my books: if a word is unknown to the reader, let him look it up.

"I believe that a writer's responsibility is to TEACH subtly through entertainment. Even the flimsiest, sleaziest story should use good English that will encourage a reader to broaden his own knowledge. Punctuation, grammar, and spelling should reinforce what was learned in school. Historical dates and incidents should be accurate, even in a paperback."

AVOCATIONAL INTERESTS: Cats, cooking, music, bridge and two-pack solitaire games, word games, old-fashioned jigsaw puzzles.

*   *   *

LEE, Mabel Barbee 1886(?)-1978

OBITUARY NOTICE: Born c. 1886; died December 12, 1978, in Santa Barbara, Calif. Author and educator. Lee wrote several books, including *Cripple Creek Days*. Obituar-

ies and other sources: Mabel Barbee Lee, *Gardens in My Life: An Intimate Memoir*, Doubleday, 1970; *Publishers Weekly*, February 26, 1979.

*   *   *

LEE, Susan Dye 1939-

PERSONAL: Born September 4, 1939, in Cincinnati, Ohio; daughter of Griffith deRush (a stockbroker) and Sara (a teacher; maiden name, Earls) Dye; married John Robert Lee (a professor), January 11, 1968 (deceased). *Education:* Attended DePauw University, 1957-59; University of Kentucky, A.B. (summa cum laude), 1961; Northwestern University, M.A., 1966, doctoral candidate, 1978—. *Politics:* Independent. *Home and office:* 2300 Sherman Ave., Evanston, Ill. 60201.

CAREER: Elementary school teacher in Bath, Mich., 1961-62; high school English teacher in Lansing, Mich., 1962-64; Evanston Township High School, Evanston, Ill., history teacher, 1966-67; writer and consultant (on books and audio-visual materials), 1967—. *Member:* American Historical Association, Organization of American Historians, Women Historians of the Midwest.

WRITINGS: (With others) *Exploring Regions of Latin America and Canada* (elementary school text), with teacher's guide, Follett, 1969; *Law in a New Land* (elementary school text), Houghton, 1970; (contributor) Lindley J. Stiles and Bruce D. Johnson, editors, *Morality Examined*, Princeton Book Co., 1977; *Abigail Adams* (juvenile), Childrens Press, 1977; *Eliza Pinckney* (juvenile), Childrens Press, 1977; *Abraham Lincoln* (juvenile), Childrens Press, 1978; *Jefferson Davis* (juvenile), Childrens Press, 1978; *Robert E. Lee* (juvenile), Childrens Press, 1978.

With husband, John R. Lee—All juveniles; all published by Childrens Press: *John Paul Jones*, 1974; *George Washington*, 1974; *Thomas Jefferson*, 1974; *John Hancock*, 1974; *Benjamin Franklin*, 1974; *Sam and John Adams*, 1974; *Charlestown*, 1975; *New York*, 1975; *Philadelphia*, 1975; *Williamsburg*, 1975; *Yorktown*, 1975; *George Rogers Clark: War in the West*, 1975; *The Fall of the Quaker City*, 1975; *The Road to Lexington and Concord*, 1975; *Battle for Quebec*, 1975; *The Battle for Long Island and New York*, 1975; *Boston*, 1976.

Also author of *Case Studies in United States History*, 1966, and *Ulysses S. Grant* (juvenile), Childrens Press.

Contributor of articles and reviews to history and women's studies journals.

WORK IN PROGRESS: Research on the Women's Christian Temperance Union.

SIDELIGHTS: Susan Lee writes: "My motivation is a need to communicate. I need to write; it is an effective way of talking with large numbers of people. Being in touch with others is the essence of life." *Avocational interests:* Travel, playing piano, patronizing the arts.

*   *   *

LEESE, Elizabeth 1937-

PERSONAL: Born September 26, 1937, in Yorkshire, England; daughter of Mark and Marie Jose (Carlton) Leese. *Education:* Attended school in London, England. *Home:* Flat 12, 2 Gliddon Rd., London W.14, England.

CAREER: National Film Archive, London, England, information assistant, 1962-78; free-lance researcher, 1978—. Participant in exchange program, British Film Institute,

1977. *Member:* British Academy of Film and Television Arts.

WRITINGS: Costume Design in the Movies, Barnden, Castell & Williams, 1976, Ungar, 1977.

WORK IN PROGRESS: Cataloging the Ernst Dryden Collection, which consists of costume designs, film and theatre fashion designs, and advertising and fashion illustrations.

SIDELIGHTS: Leese told *CA:* "I wrote *Costume Design in the Movies* because at the time there was no reference book on film costume and I felt that there should be a quick source for information on that subject. When I was well into the project I realised why no one had ever produced a book on the subject of costume design: there were hardly any written sources in published form and I had to go back to original sources for most of the information. It took a great deal of spare time."

* * *

LEGVOLD, Robert 1940-

PERSONAL: Born February 26, 1940, in Minneapolis, Minn.; son of Oscar E. (in business) and Hazel (Anderson) Legvold; married Gloria D. Welch (a teacher); children: Nancy D., Nathan C. *Education:* University of South Dakota, A.B., 1962; Fletcher School of Law and Diplomacy, earned M.A., M.A.L.D., and Ph.D. *Home:* 11 Fenwick Rd., Winchester, Mass. 01890. *Office:* Council on Foreign Relations, 58 East 68th St., New York, N.Y. 10021.

CAREER: Tufts University, Medford, Mass., associate professor of political science, 1967-77; Council on Foreign Relations, New York, N.Y., senior fellow, 1978—. Visiting associate professor at Columbia University, 1977—. Consultant to U.S. Department of Defense and U.S. Department of State. *Member:* International Institute of Strategic Studies, Council on Foreign Relations, American Council of Germany.

WRITINGS: Soviet Policy in West Africa, Harvard University Press, 1970. Contributor to political science journals.

WORK IN PROGRESS: The Soviet Union and the Contemporary International Order.

* * *

LEHMAN, Ernest Paul 1915-

PERSONAL: Born in New York, N.Y.; married wife, Jacqueline; children: Roger, Alan. *Education:* City University of New York, B.A.

CAREER: Screenplay writer, film producer, and author. Has also worked as a radio comedy writer, Broadway press agent, free-lance short story writer, and as copy editor for a Wall Street financial magazine. *Member:* Writers Guild of America West (member of council, 1965-69), Screenwriters Guild (member of executive board). *Awards, honors*—All for best screenplay: Nomination from Writers Guild, 1954, for "The Executive Suite"; Writers Guild award and Academy Award nomination from Academy of Motion Picture Arts and Sciences, both 1954, both for "Sabrina"; Writers Guild Award, 1956, for "The King and I"; Writers Guild nomination and Academy Award nomination, both 1959, both for "North by Northwest"; Writers Guild award and Academy Award nomination, both 1961, both for "West Side Story"; Writers Guild award, 1965, for "The Sound of Music"; Writers Guild award and Academy Award nomination, both 1966, both for "Who's Afraid of Virginia Woolf?"

WRITINGS: The Comedian and Other Stories, New American Library, 1957; *Sweet Smell of Success and Other Stories,* New American Library, 1957; *North by Northwest* (screenplay; also see below), Viking, 1972; *The French Atlantic Affair* (novel), Atheneum, 1977.

Screenplays: (Author of screen story, with Geza Harcseg) "The Inside Story," Republic, 1948, re-released as "The Big Gamble," Republic, 1954; "Executive Suite" (adapted from the novel by Cameron Hawley), Metro-Goldwyn-Mayer, 1954; (with Billy Wilder and Samuel Taylor) "Sabrina" (adapted from the play, "Sabrina Fair," by Taylor), Twentieth Century-Fox, 1954; "The King and I" (adapted from the play by Richard Rodgers and Oscar Hammerstein), Twentieth Century-Fox, 1956; "Somebody Up There Likes Me" (adapted from the autobiography by Rocky Graziano written with Rowland Barber), Metro-Goldwyn-Mayer, 1956; (with Clifford Odets) "Sweet Smell of Success" (adapted from own novella, "Tell Me About It Tomorrow"), United Artists, 1957; "North by Northwest," Metro-Goldwyn-Mayer, 1959.

"From the Terrace" (adapted from the novel by John O'-Hara), Twentieth Century-Fox, 1960; "West Side Story" (adapted from the play by Arthur Laurents), United Artists, 1961; "The Prize" (adapted from the novel by Irving Wallace), Metro-Goldwyn-Mayer, 1963; "The Sound of Music" (adapted from the play by Howard Lindsay and Russel Crouse), Twentieth Century-Fox, 1965; "Who's Afraid of Virginia Woolf?" (adapted from the play by Edward Albee), Warner Brothers, 1966; "Hello Dolly" (adapted from the play, "The Matchmaker," by Thorton Wilder), Twentieth Century-Fox, 1969; (and director) "Portnoy's Complaint" (adapted from the novel by Philip Roth), Warner Brothers, 1972; "Family Plot" (adapted from the novel, *The Rainbird Pattern,* by Victor Canning), Universal, 1976; (with Kenneth Ross and Ivan Moffat) "Black Sunday" (adapted from the novel by Thomas Harris), Paramount, 1977.

Contributor of articles and short stories to numerous publications, including *Esquire, Redbook, Collier's, Harper's, Liberty, Town and Country, Cosmopolitan,* and *American Mercury.*

SIDELIGHTS: After a luminous screenwriting career, Lehman returned to fiction with the suspense-filled *The French Atlantic Affair.* His screenwriting experience apparently was reflected in this first novel: Metro-Goldwyn-Mayer bought the movie rights before the book was even released.

A synopsis of the plot reveals its adaptability to the screen. The "tightly woven" story is of two unemployed aerospace engineers and their partners in crime—seventy-four married couples—as they attempt to "shipjack" a France-bound ocean liner and demand $35 million in ransom. While the three thousand other passengers are unaware of the scheme, the conspirators promise authorities they'll bomb the ship within forty-eight hours if their demands aren't met. When an irate wife complains to the ship's captain about her husband's smuggled ham radio, the ship's crew is able to renew its communication with land. Eventually, the plot spans the Atlantic as the Presidents of France and the United States, the French police, the U.S. Navy, French and American media personalities, and an American think tank work to avoid the looming disaster.

An unbelievable plot? Reviewers seemed to think so—but still commended Lehman's skills in making it work. "The plot itself seems so monstrously unreal that it couldn't possibly happen," wrote Joseph McCaffrey. "But then it is put together so logically and skillfully that it begins to seem real and the reader is hooked." Richard Freedman shared the opinion: "For all its absurdities, this is a highly successful, literately written thriller."

Other critics remained unimpressed by Lehman's depiction of sex. Richard Shahan thought "the book focuses on sex and sensationalism" and wondered if all the "profanity" is "so necessary." From a different perspective, Thomas Cullinan compared Lehman to some contemporaries when he noted "the book is overloaded with sex, much too bizarre for the the imagination of a Harold Robbins or an Irving Wallace." Meanwhile, Freedman offered a more positive interpretation of sex as protrayed in this "'Moby Dick' of ransom capers": "Lehman . . . can churn out as luridly convincing a sex scene as any in the business to spark interest when the plot shows signs of buckling under its own weight. He just as adroitly shifts the action from ship to shore just before attention begins to flag from sheer claustrophobia."

Lehman's narrative abilities also earned him praise in his most recent screenwriting effort, "Black Sunday." In this story of a terrorist attack on the Super Bowl, Lehman, together with Kenneth Ross and Ivan Moffat, "fashioned a shrewd screenplay from Thomas Harris's novel." As part of the film's total effect, the screenwriting was applauded by Judith Christ, who believed "Black Sunday" to be "the finest espionage thriller of recent years, that rare action-adventure melodrama that unflaggingly sustains both its suspense and the truth of its topicality while coping with characters as complex as its plot."

BIOGRAPHICAL/CRITICAL SOURCES: Newsweek, April 4, 1977; *Saturday Review*, April 30, 1977; *Kirkus Reviews*, June 1, 1977; *Cleveland Plain Dealer*, August 7, 1977; *Houston Chronicle*, August 8, 1977; *New York Times Book Review*, September 4, 1977; *Denver Post*, September 18, 1977; *Christian Science Monitor*, September 23, 1977; *Philadelphia Sunday Bulletin*, November 13, 1977.*

* * *

LEHMANN, Linda 1906-

PERSONAL: Surname is pronounced *Lay*-man; born August 14, 1906, in Chicago, Ill.; daughter of Alois Julius (a woodworker) and Matilda (Kull) Bernhart; married Kenneth F. Lehmann (a structural engineer and architect), July 20, 1940; children: Scott K., Ronald A. *Education:* Rockford College, A.B., 1927; University of Illinois, M.A., 1930. *Politics:* Independent. *Religion:* United Church of Christ. *Residence:* Nathrop, Colo. 81236.

CAREER: High school and junior high school English teacher in Valley Junction, Iowa, 1927-29; high school English teacher in Wauwatosa, Wis., 1930-38, and Niles Township, Ill. (also head of department), 1938-40; substitute high school and junior college teacher in Hibbing, Minn., 1940-41; writer, 1962—. *Member:* American Association of University Women (local president, 1966-68), League of Women Voters, Hinsdale Community Artists, Delta Sigma Rho. *Awards, honors:* Creative writing awards from American Association of University Women, 1970, for juvenile story "Endure for a Night," and 1973, for poem "Spaceling."

WRITINGS: Better than a Princess (juvenile), Thomas Nelson, 1978. Editor of column, "Village Vagaries," in *Hinsdale Doings*, 1962-73. Contributor to English and education journals.

WORK IN PROGRESS: A sequel to *Better than a Princess; Lucky Kurt* (tentative title), a novel for children.

SIDELIGHTS: Linda Lehmann writes: "My book was written partly to preserve something of my mother's story and partly to encourage others to cherish and save the anecdotes of their families before they are forgotten. I'd like to write of the ordinary, steady elements in our country, as I think they act as a kind of cultural ballast. There are plenty of writers (too many?) who are so eager to keep ahead of even the vanguard of trends that I can't consider the mores and people described as typical. That's age, partly, I know!"

AVOCATIONAL INTERESTS: "I call myself a dabbler, since I don't do anything exceptionally well, but I enjoy music and choir, watercolor and oil painting, reading, church and civic affairs, travel (bicycled in the British Isles; lived in the Canal Zone), domesticities like cooking and sewing, and outdoor sports like swimming and hiking."

* * *

LEHMANN, Paul Louis 1906-

PERSONAL: Surname is pronounced *Lay*-man; born September 10, 1906, in Baltimore, Md.; son of Timothy (a clergyman) and Martha (Menzel) Lehmann; married Marion Nelle Lucks (a teacher), August 29, 1929; children: Peter Michael (deceased). *Education:* Ohio State University, B.A. (honors) and B.Sc., both 1927; Union Theological Seminary, New York, N.Y., B.D., 1930, Th.D., 1936. *Politics:* "Left of center." *Home and office:* 176 77th St., New York, N.Y. 10021.

CAREER: Ordained minister of United Church of Christ, 1937, and Presbyterian Church of the United States of America, 1946; pastor of Evangelical and Reformed church in Garwood, N.J., 1927-29; pastor's assistant at Lutheran church in New York City, 1929-31; Elmhurst College, Elmhurst, Ill., assistant professor, 1933-37, associate professor of religion and philosophy, 1937-40; Eden Theological Seminary, Webster Groves, Mo., associate professor of Biblical and systematic theology, 1940-41; Wellesley College, Wellesley, Mass., associate professor of Biblical history, 1941-46; Princeton Theological Seminary, Princeton, N.J., lecturer, 1946-47, assistant professor, 1947-49, Stephen Colwell Professor of Applied Christianity, 1949-56, director of graduate studies, 1952-56; Harvard University, Cambridge, Mass., Parkman Professor of Theology, 1956-57, Florence Corliss Lamont Professor of Divinity, 1957-63; Union Theological Seminary, New York City, Auburn Professor of Systematic Theology, 1963-68, Charles A. Briggs Professor of Systematic Theology, 1968-74, professor emeritus, 1974—. Visiting professor at Union Theological Seminary, Richmond, Va., 1974-76, Bryn Mawr College, autumn, 1976, San Francisco Theological Seminary, spring, 1976, spring, 1977, and Moravian Theological Seminary, autumn, 1977; lecturer at colleges, universities, and seminaries all over the United States. Delegate to international theological conferences. Founder and chairman of National Emergency Civil Liberties Committee, 1951-53 (now member of executive committee); head of American Committee for the protection of the Foreign-Born, 1970—.

MEMBER: American Theological Society (vice-president, 1960-61; president, 1969-70), Duodecim Theological Society, Phi Beta Kappa. *Awards, honors:* D.D. from Lawrence College (now University), 1949; M.A. from Harvard University, 1956; LL.D. from Elmhurst College, 1967, and Colorado College, 1973; D.Th. from University of Tuebingen, 1971.

WRITINGS: Forgiveness: Decisive Issue in Protestant Thought, Harper, 1940; (translator) Werner Richter, *Re-Educating Germany*, University of Chicago Press, 1945;

(contributor) Joseph Fletcher, editor, *Christianity and Property*, Westminster, 1947; (contributor) John Hutchinson, editor, *Christian Faith and Social Action*, Scribner, 1953; (contributor) Charles Kegley and Robert Bretall, editors, *Reinhold Niebuhr: His Political, Religious, and Social Thought*, Macmillan, 1956; (contributor) Walter Leibrecht, editor, *Theology and Culture*, Harper, 1959.

Ethics in a Christian Context, Harper, 1963; (contributor) Thomas W. Ogletree, editor, *Openings in Christian-Marxist Dialogue*, Abingdon, 1968; (contributor) John C. Wynn, editor, *Sexual Ethics and Christian Responsibility*, Association Press, 1970; *The Transfiguration of Politics*, Harper, 1975. Associate editor of Westminster Press, 1946-47.

WORK IN PROGRESS: The Shaping of Responsible Freedom (tentative title), publication expected in 1981.

BIOGRAPHICAL/CRITICAL SOURCES: Theology Today, April, 1972; Alexander J. McKelway and E. David Willis, editors, *The Context of Contemporary Theology: Essays in Honor of Paul Lehmann*, John Knox, 1974.

* * *

LEIBOWITZ, Irving 1922-1979

OBITUARY NOTICE—See index for *CA* sketch: Born August 5, 1922, in New York, N.Y.; died of cancer April 29, 1979, in Cleveland, Ohio. Journalist, educator, and author of a book on the state of Indiana. Leibowitz was associated with the *Indianapolis Times* for nearly twenty years, serving as its managing editor from 1960-66. He was the editor of the *Lorain (Ohio) Journal* at the time of his death. Obituaries and other sources: *Who's Who in America*, 40th edition, Marquis, 1978; *New York Times*, April 30, 1979; *Chicago Tribune*, May 6, 1979.

* * *

LENDVAI, Paul 1929-

PERSONAL: Born August 24, 1929, in Budapest, Hungary; son of Andor (a lawyer) and Edith (Polecsek) Lendvai; married Gizella Lustig, 1952 (divorced); married Margaret Pollock, July 17, 1962. *Education:* Attended Diplomatic Academy, 1948. *Office:* Bank-Gasse 8, Vienna A-1010, Austria.

CAREER: Financial Times, London, England, correspondent from Vienna, 1960—. *Member:* Austrian P.E.N. *Awards, honors:* Karl Renner Prize for Journalism, 1974.

WRITINGS: Eagles in Cobwebs: Nationalism and Communism in the Balkans, Doubleday, 1969; *Anti-Semitism Without Jews: Communist East Europe*, Doubleday, 1971; (with Karl Heinz Ritschel) *Kreisky: Portraet eines Staatsmannes* (title means "Kreisky: Portrait of a Statesman"), Econ-Verlag, 1972; *Die Grenzen des Wandels: Spielarten des Kommunismus im Donauraum*, Europaverlag, 1977. Author of *Egypt*, 1952, and *Greece*, 1954. Correspondent for *Die Tat*, 1962—. Editor of *Europaeische Rundschau*, 1975—.

* * *

LENGYEL, Jozsef 1896-1975

PERSONAL: Born in Marczali, Hungary; died July 14, 1975, in Budapest, Hungary; married Olga Kirillova; children: one daughter. *Education:* Attended University of Budapest and University of Vienna. *Residence:* Budapest, Hungary.

CAREER: Novelist and short story writer. In 1915, joined a group of avant-garde poets; later became a founding member of the Hungarian Communist party; member of editorial board of *Voros ujsag* ("Red Gazette"), official newspaper of the Hungarian Soviet Republic, 1919; left Hungary after the collapse of the Communist government in 1919; lived in Vienna until 1927, and later in Berlin, writing articles and screenplays; moved to Moscow in 1930 and worked as a journalist until his arrest in 1937; arrested, sentenced and deported to Siberia where he spent eighteen years in labor camps, 1937-55; released in 1955, and returned to Hungary. *Member:* P.E.N. *Awards, honors:* Received numerous awards for his work, including the Kossuth Prize by the Hungarian Council of Ministers.

WRITINGS—In English: *Prenn Ference banyatott elete avagy minden tovabb mutat* (novel), Szepirodalmi Konyvkiado, 1959, translation by Ilona Duczynska published as *Prenn Drifting*, P. Owen, 1966; *Elevult tartozas* (stories and two novellas, "Igezo" and "Elejetol vegig"), Szepirodalmi Konyvkiado, 1964, translation of "Elejetol vegig" and "Igezo" by Duczynska published as *From Beginning to End and The Spell*, P. Owen, 1966, published as *From Beginning to End*, Prentice-Hall, 1968; *Ujra a kezdat* (novel), Magveto Kiado, 1970, translation by Duczynska published as *The Judge's Chair*, P. Owen, 1968; *Acta Sanctorum, and Other Tales*, translated from the original Hungarian by Duczynska, P. Owen, 1970; *Confrontation* (novel), translated from the original Hungarian by Anna Novotny, Citadel, 1973.

In Hungarian; all published by Szepirodalmi Konyvkiado, except as noted: *Visegradi utca* (memoirs), [Moscow], 1932, Kossuth Konyvkiado, 1957; *Kulcs* (stories), 1956; *Harom hidepito: elbeszeles egy alkotas eloeleterol* (stories), 1960; *Igezo*, 1961; *Keresem Kina kozepet* (travel diary), 1963; *Mit bir az ember* (novel), 1965; *Tukrok* (essays), 1967; *A tudas faja* (stories), Kozmosz, 1968; *Ezsau mondja*, 1969; *Besci portyak*, Magveto Kiado, 1970; *Trend Richard vallomasai* (novella; title means "Richard Trend's Confessions"), Magveto Kiado, 1970; *Hidepitok* (title means "Caisson"), Magveto Kiado, 1971; *Igezo*, two volumes, Magveto Kiado, 1971; *Isten ostora* (novel), Magveto Kiado, 1972; *Levelek arisztophaneszhez*, Magveto Kiado, 1972; *O hit-Jeruzalem* (poems), Magveto Kiado, 1973.

SIDELIGHTS: Jozsef Lengyel, who began writing expressionistic poetry as a young student in 1915, is considered "in some ways a paradox in Hungarian literature." As George Gomori in *Books Abroad* explained, "few writers began their career three times in forty years, each time in a different country, and even rarer is the writer who suddenly springs to fame at the age of sixty-five after a lifetime of relative obscurity."

Lengyel's literary career had its roots in those early years in Hungary, where he joined a circle of avant-garde poets who had rejected bourgeois society. Lengyel's first poems were published with the works of other members of the group, most notably those of the leader Lajos Kassak. Lengyel soon left the group to become a Communist and later vigorously supported the Hungarian Soviet Republic of Bela Kun. According to Gomori, Lengyel at this time believed in the effectiveness of terror, "not only against the enemies of the revolution but also against those fellow socialists who had certain scruples about pulling the trigger." In 1919, the short-lived Kun regime collapsed and Lengyel fled first to Vienna, then later to Berlin, where he wrote articles and screenplays in German. Lengyel switched literary careers again in 1930, when he moved to Moscow where he worked as a journalist. It was during this period in Moscow that Lengyel wrote *Visegradi utca*, his memoirs about the Hungarian Communist party and the revolution and regime of

Bela Kun. Although published in Moscow in 1932, *Visegradi utca* did not appear in Hungary until 1957.

The majority of Lengyel's work, and certainly the most important, began to appear several years after his release from Siberia and return to Hungary. Arrested in Moscow during one of Stalin's purges, Lengyel was tried, sentenced, and sent to Siberia—to the place that Solzhenitsyn called the "Gulag Archipelago." For eighteen years Lengyel lived in hard-labor camps and as "a free settler confined to certain areas." It was his stories about camp experiences that brought Lengyel out of literary obscurity. Gomori remarked that "without his Russian and in particular his Siberian cycle of stories he would not be regarded as an important writer today."

It would be an understatement to say that Lengyel's eighteen years in Siberia had a profound effect upon his work. As the *Times Literary Supplement* noted, "the outstanding experience of his life was prison and it is only natural that his most important work should describe prison experience." According to Irving Howe of the *New York Times Book Review,* "since then [his imprisonment] Lengyel has been writing fiction about the ordeal of Communists who discover that their belief has been false—or has been falsified by those who speak in its name."

Much of Lengyel's work has been classified by numerous critics as part of the "genre of prison-camp literature"; or, as Howe stated, "'the literature of the survivors,' the testimony of those who have gone through the hell of the concentration camps and now offer us their memories, their reflections, their wounds." It is in this way that Lengyel has been compared to the Russian Solzhenitsyn. Indeed, he has been called the "Hungarian Solzhenitsyn." A *New Statesman* critic noted that "Jozsef Lengyel forms an obvious parallel with the Russian dissident: as a writer who has served a large part of his life . . . in detention and labour camps in the Soviet Union." Like that of his Russian contemporary, Lengyel's works are primarily about experiences in Soviet labor camps, a system which both authors morally opposed. Lengyel differed from Solzhenitsyn in numerous ways, and not the least of which was style. While his "basic methodological assumptions may also be 'realistic,'" Gomori observed, "his approach to reality is less broadly descriptive than jerkily episodic, less analytical than cinematographic." Also absent from Lengyel's prose is the "emotional attachment to Russian soil" that Solzhenitsyn so strongly expressed. While exile from Russia was a tragedy for Solzhenitsyn, Lengyel's return to Hungary, his "creative source," was "a recovery of his real self."

Critics have also agreed that Lengyel's style of writing changed from his earlier, pre-Siberian work, and all have lauded the difference. A *Times Literary Supplement* reviewer emphasized that Lengyel had "lost all signs of his early dogmation: his prose is simple, lucid, realistic." Paul Varnai in *Books Abroad* praised Lengyel for his "tense dialogue . . . [and] sensuous descriptions." Gomori observed that Lengyel's "early stories are marred by a gap between perception and artistic expression; experience seems to have been forced through a filter of abstractions." He admitted, however, that in Lengyel's later works, specifically *The Spell* and *From Beginning to End* "the immediacy and authenticity of experience are overwhelming."

Raymond Sokolov in the *New York Times Book Review* suggested that the years in Siberia had "left him [Lengyel] with an almost religious feeling for things concrete and basic to life. Bread is the real theme of *From Beginning to End*."

Sokolov also stated that "unlike most personal records of concentration camps or forced labor, Lengyel's story does not shriek and rage at the undeniable obscenity he suffered for so long. The horror is all there . . . but the tone is detached and ruminative."

Other critics also noticed the detachment in Lengyel's work and Gomori attributed the possible achievement of "a certain distance and objectivity in describing people" to Lengyel's "basic strangeness." As a Hungarian in a Russian labor camp, Lengyel considered himself a stranger, and the character of the stranger is the central hero in his writings. In his description of this character, Gomori quoted from Lengyel's *The Spell:* "'He was a stranger, gloomy-eyed, past forty years perhaps. His papers were in order. But only the village recorder knew his name.'" In *From Beginning to End* Lengyel introduced one of his favorite "alter egos": Nekersdi Gyorgy, or, Nameless George. Like Lengyel, Nameless George is a Hungarian and also a former camp inmate. Gomori noted that Nameless George is in double exile, both as a Hungarian and as a Communist tortured and imprisoned by other Communists.

Both *The Spell* and *From Beginning to End* are considered part of the Siberian or Russian cycle of Lengyel's work. In addition, another "international" cycle has been identified within his prose. Included in this classification are the novels *Prenn Drifting, The Judge's Chair,* and *Trend Richard vallomasai* ("Richard Trend's Confessions"). Although referred to as "international" in themes by Gomori, these novels are bound by their characters to the Hungarian revolution of 1919. Ferenc Prenn, the hero of *Prenn Drifting,* is a former soldier of the Hungarian Red Army who turns "crafty vagabond in later years." Richard Trend of *Trend Richard vallomasai* is a leftist architect deported by the Germans to a concentration camp. In the camp his life is saved by Istvan Banicza, a Communist engineer, who appears in both *The Judge's Chair* and *Confrontation.* It is in the novel *Confrontation* that both the Russian and international cycles merge.

Officially banned by the Hungarian government, *Confrontation* was issued in a kind of "samizdat" edition for party officials and literary heirarchy in about 1968 or 1969. Because Lengyel refused to make the changes "suggested" by the Hungarian Writers Union, the novel was stamped: "To be regarded as a manuscript." "What makes *Confrontation . . .* an unusual and important book," wrote a *Listener* critic, "is that it dramatises the mental conflict of two life-long Communists, Banicza, once in a Nazi concentration camp . . . and Lassu who escaped from pre-war Hungary only to be imprisoned by Stalin." A *Times Literary Supplement* reviewer described the book as "essentially a dialogue between two good and honest communists, one representing Lengyel and one representing his opponents but also his doubts." Lengyel is represented by Enge Lassu, a Communist who unsuccessfully struggles to "overcome his sense of betrayal by the Party." Released from a camp in Siberia and forbidden to enter the city of Moscow, Lassu, nevertheless, secretly makes his way throough the city to the Hungarian Embassy where a former compatriot, Banicza, works as first secretary. He tells Banicza,"' I can only be a Communist if it will be admitted, before the whole world, that the ones who did these things to us were no Communists.'" According to Ivan Sanders in *Books Abroad,* "their confrontation is one between a disillusioned, beaten political prisoner and a confident representative of the brand new Hungarian People's Republic." Lassu suggests to Banicza that both the Nazi and Stalinist camps are similar. Banicza "rejects Lassu's equation between the two forms of barbarism, voicing the old argument—that it is the system that is different." Lassu however, declared Sanders, "even believes that Stalin's victims were far worse off: 'It was the enemy torturing you. Me? I was tortured by my own.'" Susan Knight of *New Statesman* noted that Lassu (and Lengyel) found Hitler's camps "preferable for one cogent reason: 'black was not white in the Nazi camps; you knew right was on your side. But if the light of faith is put out, if your own side turns against you, the darkness soon drives you mad.'"

The terror of those years under Stalin overshadowed Lengyel's novel about Attila the Hun, *Isten ostora*. Planned originally as a film scenario and then reworked into a novel, *Isten ostora* was, in Varnai's view, "a strong indictment of and a warning against any cult of personal power." Attila the Hun has been nostalgically considered a glorious figure from Hungary's past. Lengyel, according to Varnai, portrayed Attila "as a forerunner of modern tyrants whose autocracy is based on force, intimidation and mistrust. . . . Loyalty can bring about one's downfall just as much as treachery or the expression of the slightest doubt in the Master's vision." Varnai found Lengyel's "choice of Attila as subject . . . significant," and observed that "among those novels in which the present is projected into a real or fictitious past or future, *Isten ostora* stands out with its coherence, clarity or purpose and natural flow."

Acta Sanctorum, and Other Tales is a collection of Lengyel's work representing three different periods in his life: the thirties prior to his arrest, the Russian cycle, and work from recent years. Gomori noticed in Lengyel's more recent work "a new anxiety about the present; he castigates the spiritual minimalism of the consumer society and watches with growing alarm the politician's conjuring tricks in the shadow of gigantic nuclear missiles."

In spite of the fact that he was both a witness and a victim of the brutalities of Stalinist Communism, Lengyel remained an optimist. As Knight recorded in her review of *Confrontation*, "Lengyel wouldn't write, he says, if he didn't believe that things would improve."

BIOGRAPHICAL/CRITICAL SOURCES: Times Literary Supplement, January 21, 1965, April 28, 1972, December 21, 1973, November 20, 1977; *New York Times Book Review*, April 14, 1968, March 24, 1974; *Listener*, October 22, 1970, December 13, 1973; *Books Abroad*, spring, 1973, winter, 1975, summer, 1975; *Washington Post Book World*, January 6, 1974; *New Statesman*, January 25, 1974; *Contemporary Literary Criticism*, Volume 7, Gale, 1977.

OBITUARIES: New York Times, July 16, 1975.*

*   *   *

LEONARD, Richard Anthony   1900(?)-1979

OBITUARY NOTICE: Born c. 1900 in San Francisco, Calif.; died April 12, 1979, in Wilton, Conn. Radio programmer and producer and author. Leonard was associated with the National Broadcasting Company and was involved for many years with the production of "NBC Symphony of the Air." He wrote several books, including *The Stream of Music* and a history of Russian music. Obituaries and other sources: *New York Times*, April 14, 1979.

*   *   *

LERMAN, Eleanor   1952-

PERSONAL—Home: 161 Charles St., New York, N.Y. 10014.

CAREER: Poet. *Awards, honors:* Juniper Prize from University of Massachusetts, for *Come the Sweet By and By*.

WRITINGS—All poetry: Armed Love, Wesleyan University Press, 1973; *Come the Sweet By and By*, University of Massachusetts Press, 1975. Contributor to periodicals.

SIDELIGHTS: Lerman has developed a reputation as an x-rated poet. Her subjects usually include, according to one critic, "glimpses of life in a drug-torn Lesbian ghetto. . . ." Other bizarre facets of Lerman's first book, *Armed Love*, include suicide threats, Lesbian infidelity, and torture, both physical and mental. For one who depicts the rather sordid side of life, Lerman writes with "wit and polemic skill. . . ." X. J. Kennedy observed of Lerman's style, "At its clearest, its tone is absolute candor."

Lerman is also adept at presenting herself in a variety of moods. "Fresh resilience rather than wry weariness is her hallmark," declared Sally M. Gall. "Sometimes she flaunts a heroic Lesbianism in the fatuous face of the establishment. At other times she reveals all the vulnerability and romanticism of a sensitive girl in her very, very early twenties. She can be lighthearted, toughminded, fierce, tender, mystical, and romantic. . . ."

Lerman's blatant baring of both emotions and surroundings has disturbed some critics and impressed others. "Such terrifying simplicity, such hunger for love are bound to unnerve us and stir us. . . . ," wrote Kennedy. "Much of the time, though, the raw facts just remain on their page like meat left in its butcher's paper, untouched by deep understanding or by art." In a contrasting review, Mark Halliday expressed favor for that which Kennedy disdained. "There is a raw meat quality to Lerman's work: it shows no signs of academic curing, no workshop seasoning, nor does it smell like any dish cooked in the kitchen of a major American poet past or present," claimed Halliday. "But what lies thick and red on the page is not a catalogue of facts—Lerman's poetry is too (literally) fantastic for that—but of emotions, volatile and potentially volatile."

While *Armed Love* drew comparisons with Rimbaud, Jerome McGann found parallels with Emily Dickinson evident in Lerman's second collection, *Come the Sweet By and By*. "The traumatized settings are familiar enough," observed McGann. "What distinguishes her work in this mode is its humaneness, as if ordinary people in very typical American places, doing commonplace things, had unexpectedly discovered themselves and their environment to be possessed. The poems record how people try to maintain their most basic human feelings—love in particular—despite the fearful sense that the world they live in is out of their control."

BIOGRAPHICAL/CRITICAL SOURCES: New York Times Book Review, February 17, 1974; *Shenandoah*, fall, 1974; *Poetry*, October, 1975, September, 1977; *Parnassus: Poetry in Review*, spring-summer, 1976; *Times Literary Supplement*, December 10, 1976; *Contemporary Literary Criticism*, Volume 9, Gale, 1978.*

*   *   *

LESKY, Albin (Hans)   1896-

PERSONAL: Born July 7, 1896, in Graz, Austria; son of Albin (an educator) and Maria (Stolz) Lesky; married Erna Lesky-Klingenstein (a college professor), November 11, 1939; children: Peter. *Education:* University of Graz, Dr. phil., 1920; additional study at University of Marburg an der Lahn, 1921. *Home:* Alserstrasse 69/17, A-1080, Vienna, Austria.

CAREER: High school teacher of classics, Graz, Austria, 1920-32; University of Graz, Graz, lecturer in classics, 1924-

32; University of Vienna, Vienna, Austria, professor of classics, 1932-36; University of Innsbruck, Innsbruck, Austria, professor of classics, 1936-49; University of Vienna, professor of classics, 1949-67, professor emeritus, 1967—. President of International Commission on Latin Language Thesaurus, 1958-67. *Military service:* Austrian Army, 1915-18. *Member:* Austrian Academy of Sciences (vice-president, 1963-69; president, 1970), Royal Irish Academy (honorary member), Bayerische Academy, Heidelberger Academy, British Academy, Academy of Athens, Academy of Stockholm, Academy of Gent, Academie des Sciences Politiques. *Awards, honors:* Wilhelm Hartel Prize from Austrian Academy of Science, 1959; Purkyne medal from University of Brno, 1963; Austrian award for science and art, 1964; Order of Merit award, 1971; City of Vienna award, 1972; Dr. phil. honoris causa, University of Innsbruck, University of Athens, University of Gent, and University of Glasgow.

WRITINGS—In English: *Die griechische tragoedie,* Kroener, 1938, translation by H. A. Frankfort published as *Greek Tragedy,* Barnes & Noble, 1965, 3rd edition, 1978; *Geschichte der griechischen Literatur,* Francke, 1957-58, 3rd edition, 1971, traslation of 2nd edition by James Wills and Cornelias de Heer published as *A History of Greek Literature,* Crowell, 1966.

Other: (Contributor) *Jahresberichte ueber die fortschritte der Klassischen altertumswissenschaft* (title means "New Publications in Classics"), [Leipzig], 1937; *Der Kommos der Choephoren* (title means "Aeschylus Choephoroe"), Hoelder-Pichler-Tempsky, 1943; *Erziehung, Verfall und Aufban der Schule* (title means "The Evolution of Austrian School After Nazi-time"), Tyrolia, 1946; *Thalatta: Der Weg der Griechen zum Meer* (title means" The Sea in Greek Poetry"), Rohrer, 1947, reprinted, Arno, 1973; *Die Homerforschung in der Gegenwart* (title means "New Research in Homer"), Sexl, 1952; *Die tragische Dichtung der Hellenen* (title means "The Tragic Poetry of the Greeks"), Vandenhoeck & Ruprecht, 1956, 3rd edition, 1972.

Goettliche und menschliche Motivation im homerischen Epos (title means "The Motivation of Gods and Men in Homer"), C. Winter (Heidelberg), 1961; (with Hans Diller) *Gottheit und Mensch in der Tragoedie des Sopokles* (title means "Gods and Men in the Tragedy of Sophocles"), Wissenschaftliche Buchgesellschaft, 1963; *Herakles und das Ketos* (pamphlet; title means "The Adventure of Heracles With Ketos"), Boehlau in Kommission, 1967; *Homeros,* Druckenmueller, 1967; *Der Kampf um die Rechtsidee im griechischen Denken* (pamphlet; title means "The Greek Ideas of Justice), [Athens], 1968.

SIDELIGHTS: In Lesky's words, his works "are intended to preserve the heritage of the classical antiquity which remains an integrated element of Western civilization. Notwithstanding ample detailed research, these books are devoted to a synthesis which tries to make its contents available to a wide public."

A *Choice* critic called Lesky's *Greek Tragedy* "a model of thoroughness, clarity, and critical insight"; it is "a work that can and should be used by everyone from the beginning student to the advanced scholar, and is an essential reference work in the field of Greek tragedy." In the opinion of a *Times Literary Supplement* writer, Lesky's "chapters on Aeschylus, Sophocles and Euripides could not be better.... Main weight is naturally given to the chief problems of each play, particularly the relation of man to the gods or the relation of man to his fellows, but it is remarkable how much Professor Lesky manages to include about structure, choral technique, language, [and] scenic problems."

Critics' views on Lesky's *A History of Greek Literature* clashed. D. M. Glixon considered the book a "masterwork," and the *Economist* described it as a "very readable literary history in the purer sense, full of wit and wisdom, accessible to the nonspecialist, brilliantly written and ... brilliantly translated from the German." A reviewer for the *Times Literary Supplement,* however, disagreed entirely, saying Lesky is more adept at "writing historical rather than literary criticism." His "critical appraisal tends to get buried under a mass of otiose summarizing, bibliographical detail, and scholarly exegis." Furthermore, the reviewer classified the book as "near-unreadable," and definitely not for the nonspecialist.

BIOGRAPHICAL/CRITICAL SOURCES: Times Literary Supplement, December 23, 1965, November 24, 1966; Walther Kraus, editor, *Gesammelte Schriften: Aufsaetze und Reden zu antiker und deutscher Dichtung und Kultur,* Francke, 1966; *Saturday Review,* March 19, 1966; *Economist,* April 9, 1966; *Choice,* May, 1966, September, 1966.

*   *   *

LESLIE, Josephine Aimee Campbell   1898-1979
(R. A. Dick)

PERSONAL: Born June 8, 1898, in Wexford, Ireland; died April 28, 1979; daughter of Robert-Abercromby (a captain) and Josephine (Rosling); married Melville Eric Leslie, June 1, 1927; children: Penelope Ann Josephine, Martin Rowley Melville. *Education:* Attended Princess Helena's College, Ealing, England. *Religion:* Church of England. *Home:* Hawes Brae, Rosemarkie, Ross-shire, Scotland. *Agent:* Bolt & Watson, Chandos House, Buckingham Gate, London S.W.1, England; Margery Vosper, International Copyright Bureau Ltd., Suite 8, 26 Charing Cross Rd., London WC2H 0D6, England.

CAREER: Writer, 1945-79. *Military service:* Member of Voluntary Aid Detachment (V.A.D.), 1916-19. *Member:* Society of Authors.

WRITINGS—All under pseudonym R. A. Dick: *The Ghost and Mrs. Muir,* Ziff-Davis, 1945, reprinted, Pocket Books, 1974; *Adventures of Jama,* Museum Press, 1949; *She Walked to the Wedding,* Hodder & Stoughton, 1953; *Unpainted Portrait,* Hodder & Stoughton, 1954; *Light and Shade,* Hodder & Stoughton, 1956; *The Second Blessing,* Hodder & Stoughton, 1958; *A King Will Come* (one-act play; first produced in Burghead, Moreyshire, at Village Hall), Evans Brothers, 1959; *Witch Errant: An Improbable Comedy in Three Acts* (first produced in Glasgow, Scotland, at Citizens Theatre, March 22, 1954), Evans Brothers, 1959; *Duet for Two Hands,* R. Hale, 1960; *Wanted,* R. Hale, 1962; *The Devil and Mrs. Devine,* Pocket Books, 1974. Contributor to magazines, including *Blackwoods, Woman's Journal, Argosy,* and *Scots.*

WORK IN PROGRESS: "The Tree," a three-act play.

SIDELIGHTS: "The Ghost and Mrs. Muir," a feature film starring Rex Harrison, was first released by Twentieth-Century Fox in 1947. The story later served as the basis of an American television series of the same name, "for which [Leslie] never received a half-penny!," Meville Leslie told *CA.* Translations of *The Ghost and Mrs. Muir* have appeared in Spanish, Portuguese, and French.

AVOCATIONAL INTERESTS: Gardening, travel, reading.

*   *   *

LESLIE, S(amuel) Clement   1898-

PERSONAL: Born July 15, 1898, in Perth, Australia; son of

Joseph and Amy Leslie; married Doris Frances Falk (a Christian Science practitioner), January 10, 1924; children: David Clement, Jocelyn Frances, Alison Mary. *Education:* University of Melbourne, M.A., 1920; Balliol College, Oxford, D.Phil., 1923. *Politics:* "Flexible." *Religion:* Christian Scientist. *Home:* 9 Southwood Heights, London N.6, England.

CAREER: University of Wales, University College of North Wales, Bangor, lecturer in philosophy, 1922-23; University of Melbourne, Parkville, Victoria, Australia, senior lecturer in philosophy, 1924-26; publicity manager for Gas, Light & Coke Co., 1936-40; Ministry of Supply, London, England, director of public relations, 1940; director of public relations at Home Office and Ministry of Home Security, 1940-43; principal assistant secretary at Home Office, 1943-45; director of Council of Industrial Design, 1945-47; British Treasury, London, head of Information Division, 1947-59; writer and consultant, 1959—. Chairman of *Round Table,* 1967—. Member of Northern Ireland Development Council, 1955-65; adviser to Runnymede Trust. *Military service:* Australian Army, 1918.

MEMBER: Royal Institute of International Affairs, Reform Club. *Awards, honors:* Rhodes Scholar at Oxford University, 1920-22; commander of Order of the British Empire, 1946.

WRITINGS: The Rift in Israel: Religious Authority and Secular Democracy, Schocken, 1971. Also author of *Front Line, 1940-41,* 1942. Contributor of articles and reviews to magazines and newspapers.

SIDELIGHTS: Leslie writes: "A tourist visit to Israel in 1967 interested me in the phenomenon of a Jewish state with a secular or near-secular majority. I studied this for several years, then wrote *The Rift in Israel.*

"The approach of the book is as detached and yet sympathetic as I could make it, and it seems to me that very little appears in today's dramatic newspaper headlines that seriously faults what I wrote in 1970-71. This shows either that I succeeded in getting well below the surface (as a good many critics said) or that the character of life in Israel is fixed and firm—or possibly both."

* * *

LEVER, Janet 1946-

PERSONAL: Born December 5, 1946, in St. Louis, Mo.; daughter of Harry H. (an accountant) and Sophia (Goldberg) Lever. *Education:* Washington University, St. Louis, Mo., B.A., 1968; Yale University, Ph.D., 1974. *Agent:* Patricia Berens, Sterling Lord Agency, Inc., 660 Madison Ave., New York, N.Y. 10021. *Office:* Department of Sociology, Northwestern University, Evanston, Ill. 60201.

CAREER: Northwestern University, Evanston, Ill., assistant professor of sociology, 1974—. *Member:* International Sociological Association, American Sociological Association.

WRITINGS: (With Pepper Schwartz) *Women at Yale,* Bobbs-Merrill, 1971. Contributor to sociology journals and popular magazines, including *Ms.*

WORK IN PROGRESS: The Experience of Sport, with Stanton Wheeler.

SIDELIGHTS: Janet Lever has interviewed two hundred men of Rio de Janeiro, in Portuguese, about their leisure interests. She told *CA:* "More can be learned about people from their leisure than from their work—because it's more a matter of free choice and because they invest more of their emotional selves in it." Lever is also an expert on Brazilian soccer.

* * *

LEVERING, Ralph (Brooks) 1947-

PERSONAL: Born February 27, 1947, in Mount Airy, N.C.; son of Samuel R. (an orchardist) and Miriam (Lindsey) Levering; married Patricia Webb (a librarian), June 3, 1967; children: Matthew, Brooks. *Education:* University of North Carolina, B.A., 1967; Princeton University, M.A., 1969, Ph.D., 1972. *Home:* 518 Geneva Dr., Westminster, Md. 21157. *Office:* Department of History, Western Maryland College, Westminster, Md. 21157.

CAREER: George Mason University, Fairfax, Va., lecturer in history, 1971-72; Western Maryland College, Westminster, assistant professor, 1972-78, associate professor of history, 1978—. *Member:* American Historical Association, Organization of American Historians, Society of Historians of American Foreign Relations. *Awards, honors:* National Endowment for the Humanities fellow, 1976-77.

WRITINGS: American Opinion and the Russian Alliance, 1939-1945, University of North Carolina Press, 1976; (with Nancy M. Warner and Margaret Taylor Woltz) *Carroll County, Maryland: A History, 1837-1976,* Carroll County Bicentennial Committee, 1976; *The Public and American Foreign Policy, 1918-1978,* Morrow, 1978.

WORK IN PROGRESS: The Press and John F. Kennedy's Foreign Policy; The Cold War, 1945-1972, publication expected in 1981.

SIDELIGHTS: Levering told *CA:* "My major interest is in the role of public opinion and the press in the formation of American foreign policy. I believe that most writers on international relations focus too narrowly on interactions between officials of the nations involved and thereby tend to slight the role of public opinion, the press, and opposition politicians in shaping foreign policy issues. I also believe that inadequate attention has been paid to the efforts of such groups as religious bodies, corporations, and labor unions in their attempt to influence foreign policy. In both my published and forthcoming books I try to bring attention to the importance of non-governmental influence on the making of American foreign policy.

"My interest in public involvement in foreign policy issues derives in part from my parents' lifelong work in such organizations as the United World Federalists and the Friends Committee on National Legislation, both of which have given major emphasis to foreign affairs. Like my parents, I have been concerned about improving relations between the United States and the major Communist powers and, more importantly, about convincing the American people that their government must take the lead in slowing the potentially catastrophic arms race."

* * *

LEVINE, Edna S(imon)

PERSONAL: Born in New York, N.Y.; daughter of Jacob and Esther Simon; married Matthew Levine (a psychiatrist; deceased). *Education:* New York University, received B.A., M.A. in clinical psychology, 1939, Ph.D., 1948; Columbia University, M.A. in special education, 1941. *Home:* 170 East 78th St., New York, N.Y. 10021.

CAREER: Psychometrician at Bureau of Statistics and Research, New York City; consulting psychologist in mental health clinic, Hospital for Joint Diseases, New York City; research assistant in psychology at Bellevue Hospital, New York City; teacher, and founder and director of psychological service program, at Lexington School for the Deaf; founder and associate research scientist with mental health project for the deaf, New York State Psychiatric Institute, 1956-59; New York University, New York City, adjunct professor, 1960-61, professor of educational psychology, 1961-75, professor emeritus, 1975—, founder and director of Center for Research and Advanced Training in Deafness Rehabilitation, 1966-70; writer and lecturer, 1975—. Diplomate of American Board of Examiners in Professional Psychology; affiliated with Hunter College (now of the City University of New York). Founder and director of Foundation for the Deaf, beginning in 1948; organizer and director of Deaf Repertory Theatre, 1960-61; head of auditory committee for New York State Board of Regents' Office of State-Wide Planning for Vocational Rehabilitation; president of World Federation of the Deaf's Psychology Commission; president of United Nations international task force on organization of services for the deaf; head of public information and education committee of Friends and Relatives of the Institutionalized Aged, Inc.; member of board of consultants of Volta Bureau; consultant to Vocational Rehabilitation Administration.

MEMBER: National Association of the Deaf (honorary life member), American Professional Society of the Deaf (honorary member), American Psychological Association (fellow; past member of executive council), American Hearing Society (member of board of directors), Inter-Branch Library Association of New York (member of board of directors), Phi Beta Kappa, Kappa Delta Pi, Phi Lambda Theta. *Awards, honors:* Fellow of U.S. Department of Health, Education & Welfare's Office of Vocational Rehabilitation, 1959; woman of the year award from Phi Zeta Epsilon, 1968; D.Litt. from Gallaudet College, 1969; award from New York State Department of Education, 1969; Estelle A. Samuelson Award from New York League for the Hard of Hearing, 1974; children's book of the year award from Child Study Association of America, 1974, for *Lisa and Her Soundless World;* International Solidarity Merit Award (first class) from World Federation of the Deaf, 1975.

WRITINGS: Youth in a Soundless World, New York University Press, 1956; *The Psychology of Deafness: Techniques of Appraisal for Rehabilitation,* Columbia University Press, 1960; (editor with James F. Garrett) *Psychological Practices With the Physically Disabled,* Columbia University Press, 1962; (editor with Garrett) *Rehabilitation Practices With the Physically Disabled,* Columbia University Press, 1973; *Lisa and Her Soundless World* (juvenile), Behavioral Publications, 1974; *Spartanburg Conference Proceedings,* Professional Rehabilitation Workers with the Adult Deaf, 1976.

Contributor: B. Bolton, editor, *Measurement and Evaluation in Rehabilitation,* University Park Press, 1976; R. Frisina, editor, *Hearing Impairment: Trends in the U.S.A.—A Bicentennial Monograph,* Volta Bureau, 1976.

Contributor to hearing and education journals. Member of editorial advisory board of *Volta Review, American Annals of the Deaf, Mental Health in Deafness,* New York League for the Hard of Hearing, and Action for Children's Television.

SIDELIGHTS: Edna Levine was working in the field of clinical psychology when she began to be aware of and involved in the problems of the deaf. Eventually her work-load re-

quired that she limit herself to one speciality. She chose work with the deaf, and has devoted the rest of her life to it. She has worked toward advanced educational programs for the deaf and their teachers all over the world. Requests for her guidance have come from India, the Far East, the Middle East, Africa, Europe, and Australia. Her books have been published in Serbo-Croatian, Polish, and Czech.

In 1972 Levine was granted a papal audience at the Vatican.

AVOCATIONAL INTERESTS: Shopping, detective novels, art (collecting, especially Impressionist paintings) and visiting art museums, cooking and entertaining, "roaming the streets of New York City," and the countryside.

BIOGRAPHICAL/CRITICAL SOURCES: Silent Worker, November, 1963.

*   *   *

LEVINE, Maurice   1902-1971

PERSONAL: Born June 10, 1902, in Cincinnati, Ohio; died May 1, 1971; son of Louis (in business) and Esther (Goldstein) Levine; married Diana Bailen, August 12, 1934; children: Ann Levine Meyers, Ellen Levine Ebert, Martha Levine Dunkelman. *Education:* University of Cincinnati, B.A., 1923, M.A., 1924; Johns Hopkins University, M.D., 1928; University of Vienna, certificate in neurology, 1928; postdoctoral study at Graduate Institute for Psychoanalysis, 1937.

CAREER: University of Cincinnati, Cincinnati, Ohio, lecturer in psychology, 1923-24; Notre Dame Bay Hospital, Twillingate, Newfoundland, junior intern in surgery, 1927; Johns Hopkins Hospital, Baltimore, Md., intern in internal medicine, 1928-29, resident in psychiatry at Phipps Psychiatric Clinic, 1929-32, became chief resident; Johns Hopkins University, Baltimore, instructor in psychiatry, 1929-32; University of Cincinnati, assistant professor, 1933-44, associate professor, 1944-46, professor of psychiatry and director of department, 1947-71, fellow of Graduate School, 1971. Diplomate of American Board of Psychiatry and Neurology, 1940. Faculty member at Chicago Institute for Psychoanalysis, 1942-71; visiting professor at University of Washington, Seattle, summer, 1944; Samuel D. Gross Lecturer at University of Louisville, 1945; Eli Moschowitz Lecturer at Mount Sinai Hospital (New York, N.Y.), 1952; Frank L. Weil Lecturer in Religion and the Humanities at Hebrew Union College (Cincinnati), 1968-69. Neuropsychiatrist at Armed Forces Induction Center, 1942-44; director of psychiatry service at Cincinnati General Hospital and Children's Hospital, both 1947-71; director of Central Psychiatric Clinic of local Community Chest, 1947-71. Head of Mental Hygiene Council of Public Health Federation, 1936-37; examiner for American Board of Psychiatry and Neurology, 1945-50; member of executive council of National Committee for Mental Hygiene, 1947-50; president of American delegation to First International Congress of Psychiatry, 1950. Speaker at professional gatherings; consultant to surgeons-general of U.S. Army and U.S. Public Health Service. *Member:* Institute for Intercultural Studies (member of board of directors, 1965-71).

WRITINGS: Psychotherapy in Medical Practice, Macmillan, 1942, reprinted, 1966; (co-editor) *Psychiatry and Medical Education,* American Psychiatric Association, 1952; *Psychiatry and Ethics* (Behavioral Science Book Service main selection), introduction by Margaret Mead, Braziller, 1972.

Contributor: Groves and Blanchard, editors, *Readings in*

Mental Hygiene, Holt, 1937; Alcxander and French, editors, *Studies in Psychosomatic Medicine*, Ronald, 1948; E. Weiss and O. S. English, editors, *Psychosomatic Medicine*, 2nd edition, Saunders, 1949; Alexander and Ross, editors, *Dynamic Psychiatry*, University of Chicago Press, 1952; Alexander and Ross, editors, *Twenty Years of Psychoanalysis*, Norton, 1953; *Psychiatric Treatment*, Williams & Wilkins, 1953; *The Psychiatrist: His Training and Development*, American Psychiatric Association, 1953; *Steps Forward in Mental Hospitals*, American Psychiatric Association, 1953; Alexander, editor, *Psychoanalysis and Psychotherapy*, Norton, 1956; (author of preface) W. Donald Ross, *Practical Psychiatry for Industrial Physicians*, C. C Thomas, 1956; (author of foreword) Michael Balint, *The Doctor, His Patient, and the Illness*, International Universities Press, 1957; Linscott and Stein, editors, *Why You Do What You Do*, Random House, 1957.

James Titchener, editor, *Surgery as a Human Experience*, Oxford University Press, 1960; (author of foreword) Hofling and Leininger, editors, *Basic Psychiatric Concepts in Nursing*, Lippincott, 1960; Alexander and Ross, editors, *The Impact of Freudian Psychiatry*, University of Chicago Press, 1961; *Training in Psychosomatic Medicine*, Hafner, 1964; Freedman and Kaplan, editors, *Comprehensive Textbook of Psychiatry*, Williams & Wilkins, 1967; (author of foreword) Louis Gottschalk and Goldine Gleser, *The Measurement of Psychological States Through the Content Analysis of Verbal Behavior*, University of California Press, 1969; (author of foreword) Milton Kramer, editor, *Dream Psychology and the New Biology of Dreaming*, C. C Thomas, 1969; E. Mansell Pattison, editor, *The Experience of Dying*, Prentice-Hall, 1977.

Contributor to *American Handbook of Psychiatry* and to medical journals. Member of editorial board of *Journal of the American Psychoanalytic Association*, 1951-53; member of editorial advisory board of *Journal of Nervous and Mental Disease*, 1960-66; member of international editorial board of "Mind and Medicine," a monograph series, Tavistock Publications, 1962-71.

SIDELIGHTS: In her introduction to Levine's posthumously published *Psychiatry and Ethics*, Margaret Mead wrote: "[The book's] major contribution is to a style of intellectual conduct, a generous and concerned inclusiveness in which the reader becomes almost as much a part of the argument as the writer. This is the way Maurice Levine always wanted it to be."

Another passage from the book illustrates Levine's attraction to "psychiatry and ethics": "The study of ethics is fascinating, on its own. The study of the contribution of psychiatry to ethics makes it even more so. But when one adds that such a study may lead to additional ways of coping with the dangers facing the world, in the present and the future, the urgency of such a study becomes compelling."

BIOGRAPHICAL/CRITICAL SOURCES: Comprehensive Psychiatry Journal, July, 1968, January-February, 1976; Maurice Levine, *Psychiatry and Ethics*, Braziller, 1972.

[Sketch verified by wife, Diana Levine]

*   *   *

LEVINE, Norman D(ion)   1912-

PERSONAL: Surname rhymes with "vine"; born November 30, 1912, in Boston, Mass.; son of Max and Adele (Daen) Levine; married Helen Marie Saxon, March 2, 1935. *Education:* Iowa State College (now University), B.S.,

1933; University of California, Berkeley, Ph.D., 1937. *Home:* 702 LaSell Dr., Champaign, Ill. 61820. *Office:* College of Veterinary Medicine, University of Illinois, Urbana, Ill. 61801.

CAREER: University of Illinois, Urbana, assistant animal parasitologist at experiment station, 1937-41, associate animal pathologist, 1941-46, assistant professor, 1946-47, associate professor, 1947-53, professor of veterinary parasitology and veterinary research, 1953—, professor of zoology, 1965-77, head of Parasitology Division in department of veterinary pathology and hygiene, 1946—, senior member of Center for Zoonoses Research, 1960—, member of its executive committee, 1961—, director of Center for Human Ecology, 1968-74 (senior member, 1965-69; member of executive committee, 1965-74). Visiting professor at University of Hawaii, summer, 1962. Diplomate of American Board of Microbiology, 1959-64, and member of its governing board. Member of National Academy of Sciences-National Research Council, 1956-62; director of National Science Foundation Summer Institute in General Parasitology, 1967. Organized International Conference on Protozoology, 1965, and International Congress of Parasitology, 1964, 1974, 1978; member of veterinary medicine advisory committee of Illinois Board of Higher Education, 1969—; member of Metropolitan Chicago task force on environmental health and comprehensive health planning, 1969—. Consultant to U.S. Department of Agriculture. *Military service:* U.S. Army, parasitologist in Sanitary Corps, 1942-46; served in Pacific theater; became major; received Bronze Star.

MEMBER: World Federation of Parasitologists (member of council, 1960-65), American Academy of Microbiology (charter fellow; member of board of governors, 1963-66), American Association for the Advancement of Science (member of council, 1963-66, 1969), American Institute of Biological Sciences (member of governing board, 1970-71), American Microscopical Society (honorary member; president, 1968-69), American Society of Parasitologists (committee head, president-elect, 1979), American Society of Professional Biologists (president-elect, 1965-66; president, 1966-68), Society of Nematologists (member of executive committee, 1963-64), Society of Protozoologists (honorary member; vice-president, 1958-59; president, 1959-60; member of executive committee, 1960-71), American Society of Zoologists, Society for Experimental Biology and Medicine, Wildlife Disease Association, American Society of Tropical Medicine and Hygiene, American Veterinary Medical Association, American Association of University Professors, U.S. Livestock Sanitary Association, Society of Systematic Zoologists, Midwestern Conference of Parasitologists, Illinois Academy of Science (member of executive committee, 1961—; first vice-president, 1965-66; president, 1966-67), Helminthological Society of Washington, Sigma Xi (vice-president, 1962-63; president, 1963-64), Phi Sigma, Gamma Sigma Delta, Phi Kappa Phi (president, 1961-62), Phi Mu Alpha, Sinfonia, Phi Zeta.

WRITINGS: Protozoan Parasites of Domestic Animals and of Man, Burgess, 1961, 2nd edition, 1973; (with Virginia Ivens) *The Coccidian Parasites (Protozoa, Sporozoa) of Rodents* (monograph), University of Illinois Press, 1965; *Nematode Parasites of Domestic Animals and of Man*, Burgess, 1968; (with Ivens) *The Coccidian Parasites (Protozoa, Sporozoa) of Ruminants* (monograph), University of Illinois Press, 1970; (with others) *Human Ecology*, Duxbury, 1975; *Textbook of Veterinary Parasitology*, Burgess, 1978; (with Ivens and Daniel L. Mark) *Principal Parasites of Domestic Animals in the United States: Biological and Diagnostic In-*

formation, Colleges of Agriculture and Veterinary Medicine, University of Illinois, 1978.

Editor: *Malaria in the Interior Valley of North America*, University of Illinois Press, 1964; *Pavlovsky's Natural Nidality of Transmissible Diseases with Special Reference to the Landscape Epidemiology of Zooanthroponoses* (translated from Russian by F. K. Plous, Jr.), University of Illinois Press, 1966; *Natural Nidality of Diseases and Questions of Parasitology* (translated from Russian by Plous), University of Illinois Press, 1968; N. P. Naumov, *The Ecology of Animals* (translated from Russian by Plous), University of Illinois Press, 1972.

Contributor: H. E. Biester and L. H. Schwarte, editors, *Diseases of Poultry*, Iowa State University Press, 1943, 5th edition, 1965; J. B. Coates, Jr., E. C. Hoff, and P. M. Hoff, editors, *Preventive Medicine in World War II*, Volume VI: *Communicable Diseases—Malaria*, Office of the Surgeon General, U.S. Department of the Army, 1963; G. D. Schmidt, editor, *Problems in Systematics of Parasites*, University Park Press, 1969; R. J. Flynn, editor, *Parasites of Laboratory Animals*, Iowa State University Press, 1973; D. M. Hammond and P. L. Long, editors, *The Coccidia*, University Park Press, 1973; E. C. Melby, Jr. and N. H. Altman, editors, *CRC Handbook of Laboratory Animal Science*, CRC Press, 1974.

Contributor of more than four hundred articles and reviews to scientific and medical journals. Contributor to *Handbook of Biological Data*. Editor of *Journal of Protozoology*, 1965-71, book review editor, 1972—; member of editorial board of *American Journal of Veterinary Research, Transactions of the American Microscopical Society*, and *American Midland Naturalist;* member of advisory board of *Advances in Veterinary Medicine and Comparative Medicine*, 1972—.

WORK IN PROGRESS: Research on protozoan and helminth parasites of domestic animals and man (including invertebrates, vertebrates, and wild animals).

SIDELIGHTS: Levine writes: "Learning, writing, and teaching pass the time between birth and death. Life would be boring without them."

*   *   *

LEWIS, Robert T(urner) 1923-

PERSONAL: Born June 17, 1923, in Taft, Calif.; son of D. Arthur (an accountant) and Amy (Turner) Lewis; married Jane Badham, March 23, 1946; children: Jane, William, Richard. *Education:* University of Southern California, B.A., 1947, M.A., 1950; University of Denver, Ph.D., 1952. *Home:* 107 Opal Ave., Balboa Island, Calif. 92662. *Agent:* Francis Greenburger, Sanford J. Greenburger Associates, Inc., 825 Third Ave., New York, N.Y. 10022. *Office:* Department of Psychology, California State University, 5151 State University Dr., Los Angeles, Calif. 90032.

CAREER: California State University, Los Angeles, assistant professor, 1952-58, associate professor, 1958-64, professor of psychology, 1964—. Chief psychologist at Hollywood Presbyterian Hospital's Psychiatric Clinics, 1953-59; director of psychological services at Salvation Army Men's Social Center (Pasadena, Calif.), 1958-66; director of Pasadena Psychological Center, 1964-74; associate director of Cortical Function Laboratories, 1972—. *Military service:* U.S. Naval Reserve, active duty, 1943-47. *Member:* American Psychological Association, California State Psychological Association, Los Angeles County Psychological Association.

WRITINGS: (With Louis Thorpe and Barney Katz) The

Psychology of Abnormal Behavior, Ronald, 1961; (with Hugh Petersen) *Human Behavior: An Introduction to Psychology*, Ronald, 1974; (with Herb Goldberg) *Money Madness*, Morrow, 1978; *Taking Chances: The Psychology of Losing and How to Profit From It*, Houghton, 1979.

WORK IN PROGRESS: Two novels.

SIDELIGHTS: Lewis comments: "As a practicing psychologist for more years than I care to admit, I have a profound interest in people and what makes them tick, both consciously and unconsciously. I have found great satisfaction in sharing my understanding of human behavior with students I have taught over the years in classes and through textbooks. Now I hope to broaden that audience by writing popular psychology books and fiction.

"In *Money Madness* we attacked the 'lab taboo,' personal involvement with money, a subject often considered off limits even for discussion in psychotherapy. Today, in most circles, it is more acceptable to talk about one's intimate sex life than how much money one makes or has in the bank. We attempted to look at why this is so and how money becomes an extension of our basic personality.

"In undertaking the writing of *Taking Chances* I experienced something akin to what since appeared in a column by Erma Bombeck. She stated that she was in a book store and found 187 books on winning but none on losing. I somehow felt compelled to do something to reduce the odds. Now there are 187 books on winning and *1* on losing. It attempts to provide an alternative to the win at all costs philosophy and to help people overcome the fear of losing so they might better enjoy the fruits of competing and getting involved in life."

*   *   *

LEWIS, Sasha Gregory 1947-

PERSONAL: Born May 12, 1947, in San Francisco, Calif.; daughter of a sailor in the merchant marine and a business manager. *Residence:* San Jose, Calif. *Agent:* Mary Yost Associates, Inc., 141 East 55th St., New York, N.Y. 10022. *Office:* P.O. Box 7091, Menlo Park, Calif. 94025.

CAREER: Peninsula Electronic News, Los Altos, Calif., editor, 1971; *Electronic News*, San Francisco, Calif., staff writer, 1971-72; free-lance writer in Hawaii, 1973; *San Mateo Advocate*, San Mateo, Calif., senior editor, 1974-78; free-lance investigative journalist, 1978—. *Military service:* U.S. Coast Guard Reserve. *Member:* Media Alliance, Interchange (member of advisory board, 1978-79).

WRITINGS: Sunday's Women: A Report on Lesbian Life Today, Harper, 1979; *Slave Trade: Illegal Aliens Today*, Beacon Press, 1979.

WORK IN PROGRESS: America's New Right.

SIDELIGHTS: Sasha Lewis has completed more than a year of research on the contemporary American Right. She is one of a half-dozen top American experts on the political Right and the radical Right. Her research on a group of political organizations headed by a California state senator has resulted in the largest fines yet assessed by the Federal Elections Commission for violation of election laws. Her published reports on the new Right political organizations affiliated with Richard A. Viguerie have been cited and reprinted by dozens of publications and organizations, most recently Americans for Democratic Action. She has also reported on other right-wing organizations now under investigation by federal authorities.

Lewis writes: "My motivation, since my first days as a stringer for a California daily newspaper at age sixteen, has always been to translate the realities of the larger world (national politics, macro-economics, scientific technology) into the effects they have on individual people in their daily lives.

"My primary concerns are that basic human rights be assured to all people, and that freedom of expression and opinion be maintained in the United States and extended throughout the world. As world economics, politics, and science advances, people as individuals are excluded from access to much of the information affecting their lives by virtue of the fact that these fields have become so complex *and* so specialized. I am either a relic of the past or an omen of the future—a generalist. I believe that specialization of areas of knowledge has led to dogmatism—liberal and conservative dogmatism—that limits not only our ability to improve human rights, but to an extent restricts freedom of expression and opinion. My writings, therefore, tend to adhere to no 'party line,' but attempt to be unfettered explorations of the world around us. In political circles I have been attacked by both extreme Right and Left. This, in my view, is high praise of my success in these explorations.

"It is my hope, in the near future, to be able to expand from nonfiction into fiction. I am, once again, either a relic or an omen, in that I believe in the future of the written word as a bearer of ideas, human ideals, and aspirations that will always have an important role to play. This belief grows stronger the more I hear the doomsayers of print media."

*   *   *

LI, Hui-Lin 1911-

PERSONAL: Born July 15, 1911, in Soochow, China; naturalized U.S. citizen; married in 1946; children: two. *Education:* Soochow University, B.S., 1930; Yenching University, M.S., 1932; Harvard University, Ph.D., 1942. *Office:* Department of Biology, University of Pennsylvania, Philadelphia, Pa. 19174.

CAREER: Soochow University, Soochow, China, instructor in biology, 1932-40; Harvard University, Cambridge, Mass., technical assistant at Arnold Arboretum, 1941-43; Soochow University, professor of biology, 1946-47; National Taiwan University, Taipei, professor of biology and head of department, 1947-50; University of Virginia, Charlottesville, research fellow at Blandy Farm, 1950-51; Smithsonian Institution, Washington, D.C., visiting research scholar, 1951-52; University of Pennsylvania, Philadelphia, research associate of Morris Arboretum, 1952-54, taxonomist, 1954-70, director, 1970-74, associate professor, 1958-64, professor of botany, 1964-73, John Bartram Professor of Botany and Horticulture, 1973—. Professor and director of biological studies at Chinese University of Hong Kong, 1964-65.

MEMBER: International Association for Plant Taxonomy, International Dendrological Society, American Institute of Biological Sciences, Botanical Society of America, Society for Economic Botany, American Society of Plant Taxonomists, American Association for the Advancement of Science, Academia Sinica, Washington Academy of Sciences, Sigma Xi, Phi Tau Phi. *Awards, honors:* Harrison research fellowship from University of Pennsylvania, 1943-46; research associate of Academy of Natural Sciences of Philadelphia, 1945-46, 1973—; Guggenheim fellowship, 1961-62; Fulbright fellowship for National Taiwan University, 1968; grants from National Science Foundation, National Institutes of Health, American Philosophical Society, and American Council of Learned Societies.

WRITINGS: *Chinese Flower Arrangement*, Hedera House, 1956, new edition, Van Nostrand, 1959; *The Garden Flowers of China*, Ronald, 1959; *The Origin and Cultivation of Shade and Ornamental Trees*, University of Pennsylvania Press, 1964; *Woody Flora of Taiwan*, Livingston, 1964; *Floristic Relationships Between Eastern Asia and Eastern North America* (monograph), Morris Arboretum, University of Pennsylvania, 1971; *Trees of Pennsylvania, the Atlantic States, and the Lake States*, University of Pennsylvania Press, 1972; (editor with T. S. Liu, and contributor) *Flora of Taiwan*, Volume I, Epoch Publishing, 1975. Also author of a book in Chinese, with an English summary, on the origin of cultivated plants in South-East Asia, published by Chinese University of Hong Kong, 1966.

Contributor of nearly two hundred articles and reviews to scientific journals in the United States and abroad. Editor of *Morris Arboretum Bulletin*, 1973-75; translation editor of *Acta Botanica Sinica*, 1974-75; head of editorial committee of *Flora of Taiwan*, 1973—.

*   *   *

LIEBERMAN, Gerald F. 1923-

PERSONAL: Born March 16, 1923, in Brooklyn, N.Y.; son of Abraham Isidore (a house painter) and Frieda (a dress operator; maiden name, Bernstein) Lieberman; married Sylvia Beatrice Kwintner (a purchasing agent), April 11, 1948; children: Mona Helene (Mrs. Melvin Loeser), Laurie Jo. *Education:* Attended University of Hawaii, 1943-44. *Religion:* Jewish. *Home:* 2325 Ocean Ave., Brooklyn, N.Y. 11229. *Agent:* Ann Elmo Agency, Inc., 60 East 42nd St., New York, N.Y. 10017.

CAREER: Shipping clerk, laborer in New York City's garment district and at Brooklyn Navy Yard, 1941-43; U.S. Naval Installation, Pearl Harbor, Hawaii, electrical technician, 1943-44; U.S. Maritime Service, radio officer on troop transport vessels, 1944-47; in advertising copywriting, 1948-49, and automotive chemicals sales in New York City, 1950-78; free-lance writer, 1950-68; Radiator Specialty Co. (chemical company), Charlotte, N.C., sales manager for New York district, 1968-78; free-lance writer, 1978—. Reporter for *New York Times*, 1971-78.

WRITINGS: *Off the Cuff* (joke book), Pocket Books, 1956; *The Laff Parade*, Pocket Books, 1957; *The Greatest Laughs of All Time*, Doubleday, 1961; *The Sea Lepers* (novel), Doubleday, 1971; *3500 Good Jokes for Speakers*, Doubleday, 1975. Contributor of stories and articles to magazines and newspapers, including *Variety*.

WORK IN PROGRESS: *The Last Assignment*, a novel dealing with the moral dilemma of an investigative reporter, completion expected in 1980 or 1981.

SIDELIGHTS: Lieberman writes: "It was about 1950 that I started to do some soul searching. I was twenty-seven and not at all pleased with the idea of spending the rest of my life in American industry. The depression had put college out of reach and mind.

"During World War II I had written for a Navy newspaper and the *Honolulu Star-Bulletin*. I wanted desperately to write sea stories, but I lived in New York, which was the hub of American comedy at that time. A former shipmate recommended me to a quiz show producer who gave me my first free-lance assignment writing quiz show questions. This led directly to comedy work for such people as Jackie Gleason and Paul Winchell. I wrote a very successful parody of 'Dragnet,' which locked me into the comedy field. I had hoped to be able to make enough money to write fiction, but it didn't happen. I also wrote column quips and publicity material for celebrities, including Liberace, and for awhile worked as ghostwriter for a syndicated music column.

"My first joke book was published in 1956, but I was tired of comedy and even more tired of show business, which I had never liked.

"I have always felt that the only profession open to someone with limited formal education is the writing field. I came into it naive, pleased that I could sell almost anything I wrote, and looking forward to growing as a writer through experience. I still don't know if I was correct.

"I am quite adamant in saying that I will not do another joke book. For several months now I have been concentrating on *The Last Assignment,* and I hope to be able to write a book a year, for survival purposes.

"Off in the distance somewhere there is that flicker of hope that probably will never die—that somehow I will be able to go back to writing about the sea and ships."

*   *   *

LIEBESCHUETZ, Hans 1893(?)-1978(?)

OBITUARY NOTICE: Born c. 1893; died c. 1978 in Liverpool, England. Historian, educator, and author of books in his field. Liebeschuetz taught at the University of Liverpool and wrote on medieval intellectual history and Judaism. Obituaries and other sources: *AB Bookman's Weekly,* February 5, 1979.

*   *   *

LIEDERMAN, Judith 1927-

PERSONAL: Born December 5, 1927, in New York, N.Y.; daughter of Abe (a realtor) and Yetta (Samuels) Ellis; married Arthur M. Marks, October 25, 1952 (died, 1962); married Donald E. Liederman (a utilities executive), June 1, 1968; children: (first marriage) Melissa Marks Castle, Madeleine Jill. *Education:* Attended Syracuse University and Hunter College (now of the City University of New York). *Religion:* Jewish. *Home:* 1025 Ridgedale Dr., Beverly Hills, Calif. 90210. *Agent:* Arthur Pine Associates, Inc., 1780 Broadway, New York, N.Y. 10019.

CAREER: Advertising copywriter in New York, N.Y., 1957-60; writer. *Member:* Anti-Defamation League of B'nai B'rith (member of regional board of directors; member of executive committee). *Awards, honors:* John Chapman Award from *New York Times,* 1944.

WRITINGS: The Moneyman (novel), Houghton, 1978. Contributor to *Saturday Review* and *Writer's Digest.*

WORK IN PROGRESS: Research for *The Resort* (tentative title), a novel about an important American resort and the family who owned it.

SIDELIGHTS: Judith Liederman comments: "To write has been a lifelong ambition, a driving force, a luxury in which only lately I've had the time and the peace to indulge. I admire writers with a strong identifiable 'style'; there is entirely too little style in fiction today. Perhaps out of a fear of over-writing, I find many writers are *under*-writing, leaving the reader with a sense of impoverishment. I want to involve the reader's emotions, to appeal to his senses. It is emotions I care about in my writing, not concepts or story lines. Strong characterizations are what count, what stay with the reader long after the book is closed."

AVOCATIONAL INTERESTS: Travel (especially England).

LINCOLN, W(illiam) Bruce 1938-

PERSONAL: Born September 6, 1938, in Stafford Springs, Conn.; son of William Albert and Ruth (a nurse; maiden name, Drake) Lincoln; married Patricia O'Keefe, May 19, 1976. *Education:* College of William and Mary, B.A. (cum laude), 1960; University of Chicago, M.A. (honors), 1962, Ph.D., 1966. *Agent:* Helen Barrett, William Morris Agency, 1350 Ave. of the Americas, New York, N.Y. 10019. *Office:* Department of History, Northern Illinois University, DeKalb, Ill. 60115.

CAREER: Memphis State University, Memphis, Tenn., assistant professor of history, 1966-67; Northern Illinois University, DeKalb, assistant professor, 1967-70, associate professor, 1970-78, professor of history, 1978—. Visiting associate professor at University of Illinois at Chicago Circle, 1971-72, and University of Chicago, 1977-78; associate of University of Illinois Russian and East European Studies Center, summers, 1975-77. Speaker on Russian and Soviet affairs.

MEMBER: American Association for the Advancement of Slavic Studies, Mid-West Slavic Association (member of executive committee, 1976-77), Phi Beta Kappa. *Awards, honors:* Dissertation exchange research fellowship from Inter-University Committee on Travel Grants, 1964-65, for the Soviet Union; grant from American Council of Learned Societies and Social Science Research Council, 1967; visiting scholar at Columbia University's Russian Institute, summer, 1967, senior fellowship, 1978; grants from American Philosophical Society, 1968, 1970; exchange research fellowship from International Research and Exchanges Board, 1970-71, for the Soviet Union, senior fellowships, 1973-74, 1978-79; Fulbright-Hays fellowship, 1970-71, 1974 (for Poland), 1978-79; American Council of Learned Societies grants, 1973, 1978, 1978-79.

WRITINGS: (Editor) *Documents in World History, 1945-1967,* Chandler Publishing, 1968; *Nikolai Miliutin: An Enlightened Russian Bureaucrat,* Oriental Research Partners, 1977; *Nicholas I: Emperor and Autocrat of All the Russias,* Indiana University Press, 1978; *Petr Semenov-Tian-Shanskii: A Life for Science in Russia,* Oriental Research Partners, 1979; *The Romanovs: Autocrats of All the Russias,* Dial Press, in press.

WORK IN PROGRESS: The Tsar's Most Loyal Servitors: Russia's Enlightened Bureaucracy.

SIDELIGHTS: Lincoln told *CA:* "My work has been most influenced by the writings and personalities of three great contemporary historians whose vast knowledge about Russia's past cannot but inspire awe in one who knows them and has read their works: professors Leopold Haimson, Marc Raeff, and Petr Andreevich Zaionchkovskii. It was more years ago that I care to remember when they taught me that the writing of history is an all-consuming craft that demands not sporadic attention but daily devotion. This is the dictum I have sought to follow since I began to study Russia's history nearly two decades ago. More recently, I have become convinced that the historian who writes only for other specialists neglects an important part of an historian's broader task. Therefore, beginning with my book about Nicholas I, I have begun to write for a broader audience in the hope that my efforts to explain Russia's past may enable readers to better understand Russia's present."

BIOGRAPHICAL/CRITICAL SOURCES: New Statesman, July 7, 1978; *Birmingham Post,* August 17, 1978; *British Book News,* September, 1978; *History Today,* September, 1978; *Times Literary Supplement,* October 6, 1978.

LINDERMAN, Gerald F(loyd) 1934-

PERSONAL: Born September 13, 1934, in Marshfield, Wis.; son of Floyd Merrill (a bank officer and corporate cost analyst) and Leonore Schell (Luenzmann) Linderman; married Barbara Silliman (a yoga teacher), December 22, 1956; children: Karen Elizabeth, Kathryn Rebecca. *Education:* Yale University, B.A., 1956; Northwestern University, M.A., 1964, Ph.D., 1971. *Home:* 2618 Essex Rd., Ann Arbor, Mich. 48104. *Office:* Department of History, Haven Hall, University of Michigan, Ann Arbor, Mich. 48109.

CAREER: U.S. Department of State, Washington, D.C., vice-consul in Kaduna, Northern Nigeria, 1959-61, consul in Madras, India, 1961-63, political officer and second secretary of embassy in Leopoldville, Congo, 1964-65; Northwestern University, Evanston, Ill., instructor in history, 1968-69; University of Michigan, Ann Arbor, lecturer, 1969-71, assistant professor, 1971-74, associate professor of history, 1974—. *Military service:* U.S. Army, 1958. U.S. Army Reserve, 1958-64. *Member:* American Historical Association, Organization of American Historians. *Awards, honors:* Ruth M. Sinclair Memorial Prize, 1972, for contributions to University of Michigan's Honors Program; Class of 1923 Literary and Educational Award from University of Michigan, 1977, for excellence in teaching; Smithsonian Institution fellow, 1977-78.

WRITINGS: Mirror of War: American Society and the Spanish-American War, University of Michigan Press, 1974.

WORK IN PROGRESS: A study of the social and political effects of changing perceptions of Civil War combat, 1865-1900, with a book expected to result.

* * *

LINN, Charles F. 1930-

PERSONAL: Born August 19, 1930, in Beaver, Pa.; son of Charles Scott and Helen (Dickson) Linn; married Nancy Rankin, October 28, 1952; children: Jeff, Jenny, Holly, Heather, Susan. *Education:* Colgate University, B.A., 1952; Wesleyan University, Middletown, Conn., M.A.T., 1957, C.A.S., 1963. *Politics:* "Vote the rascals out!" *Home:* 163 East Mohawk St., Oswego, N.Y.

CAREER: High school teacher of mathematics in Connecticut, 1956-65; State University of New York College at Oswego, instructor in mathematics education, 1965—. *Military service:* U.S. Navy, 1952-55; became lieutenant junior grade.

WRITINGS: Puzzles, Patterns, and Pastimes, Doubleday, 1967; *Odd Angles,* Doubleday, 1967; *Estimation,* Crowell, 1971; *Probability,* Crowell, 1973; *The Golden Mean* (Junior Literary Guild selection), Doubleday, 1976; *The Ages of Mathematics,* Volume II, Doubleday, 1977. Author of mathematics booklets. Author of a column in *Current Science,* and mathematics pages in *Science and Math Weekly.* Mathematics editor for American Education Publications, 1960-66.

WORK IN PROGRESS: "A genuine alternative to the traditional high school mathematics program"; material for a course on mathematics as recreation; material for a mathematics clinic for "alleged mathephobes."

SIDELIGHTS: Linn writes: "Since the most pressing need, in the mathematics business, seems to be for good materials that kids can use in schools, I have made valiant efforts in that direction. However, I discovered long ago that textbook publishers are wary (to indulge in an outrageous understate-ment) of that which is different. So, seeing little prospect for saving the world, I've confined my efforts to the local scene. I cannot report any startling successes, but the customers seem generally satisfied.

"I have worked with prospective math teachers for fourteen years here, figuring that was the best way to change what goes on in the schools. I believe the hypothesis is valid, but either I am not the person to do it, or this is not the place to do it, or this is not the time, or some of the above."

* * *

LIPE, Dewey 1933-

PERSONAL: Born February 10, 1933, in Lincoln, Neb.; son of Carl Edgar (a farmer) and Clara Elsie (Schoenleber) Lipe; married Nancy Ellen Dewar (an artist), June 6, 1959; children: Mi Ae (adopted). *Education:* Nebraska Wesleyan University, A.B., 1954; graduate study at Garrett Graduate School of Theology, 1954-59, University of Geneva, 1956-57, University of Wisconsin, Madison, 1959, and University of California, Los Angeles, 1959-60; Ohio State University, M.A., 1964, Ph.D., 1966. *Home address:* P.O. Box 8088, Stanford, Calif. 94305. *Agent:* Lambert Wilson, 8 East 10th St., New York, N.Y. 10003. *Office:* American Institutes for Research, P.O. Box 1113, Palo Alto, Calif. 94302.

CAREER: American Institutes for Research, Palo Alto, Calif., research psychologist, 1966—. Psychotherapist with Behavior Therapy Associates, 1969—. Director of Self-Management Schools, 1972-74; member of board of directors of Educational Evaluation and Research, Inc., 1975—; psychology consultant. *Member:* Mensa. *Awards, honors:* First prize at art show at Holbrook Palmer Park, Atherton, Calif., 1973, for "Butterfly-Moth and Cocoon"; award from San Jose Art League regional competition, 1974, for "Victorian Mourning Cradle"; merit award from Bay Area Arts and Crafts Guild annual show, 1975, for "Perchance to Dream."

WRITINGS: (Contributor) H. B. Pepinsky and M. J. Patton, editors, *The Psychological Experiment: A Practical Accomplishment,* Pergamon, 1971; (with Menko Rose and John Marquis) *A Program for Learning Deep Muscle Relaxation With a Relaxation Training Tape,* Self-Management Schools, 1972; (with Jurgen Wolff) *Slimmanship,* Nelson-Hall, 1975; (with Wolff) *Help for the Overweight Child,* Stein & Day, 1978; (with Peter Dahl and Judith Appleby) *Mainstreaming Guidebook for Vocational Educators,* Olympus, 1978. Contributor to psychology and education journals.

WORK IN PROGRESS: Research on the psychology of health, including self-management of childhood asthma and spontaneous recovery from cancer; a fiber mushroom tree sculpture.

SIDELIGHTS: Lipe writes: "A persistent theme throughout my research and writing career has been motivation and self-management. This theme concerns the vital life force that propels and the imagery and imagination that direct the evolution of our personality and character. It may seem strange, but the sidelight that has profoundly influenced this research has been my twenty years of partnership with artist Nancy Lipe, who taught me to perceive subtleties of color, form, and texture and their interrelationships.

"As the photographer of our fiber sculptures that have appeared in various books and magazines, I have learned the power of the lens to highlight sublime elements of the subject at hand. The artists, photographers, therapists, and researchers create in their minds of today the forms that will constitute the environment of tomorrow."

BIOGRAPHICAL/CRITICAL SOURCES: San Jose Mercury, August 17, 1973; Palo Alto Times, October 3, 1974; Jean Ray Laury, New Uses for Old Laces, Doubleday, 1974; Westart, January 10, 1975, June 13, 1975; Open Chain, August, 1975; Country Almanac, August 27, 1975; Alyson Smith Gonsalves, editor, Macrame Techniques and Projects: A Sunset Book, Lane, 1975; Laury and Ruth Milliken Law, Handmade Toys and Games, Doubleday, 1975; Visual Dialog, Volume II, number 1, 1976; Anna Ballarian, Fabric Collage: Contemporary Stitchery and Applique, Davis Publications (New York), 1976; Elyse and Mike Sommer, Wearable Crafts: Creative Clothing, Body Adornments, and Jewelry From Fabrics and Fibers, Crown, 1976; E. Sommer and M. Sommer, A New Look at Knitting, Crown, 1977; E. Sommer, Textile Collector's Guide, Monarch, 1978; Bucky King and Jude Martin, Ecclesiastical Crafts, Van Nostrand, 1978.

*   *   *

LIPSCOMB, James 1926-

PERSONAL: Born March 8, 1926, in Tulsa, Okla.; son of Joseph Karnes (in oil industry) and Ethel (a teacher; maiden name, Chapman) Lipscomb; married Roberte Monnard (a professor), April 13, 1949; children: John Harris. Education: University of Miami, A.B. (magna cum laude), 1947; University of Iowa, M.F.A., 1949. Home: 58 Heritage Hill, Tarrytown, N.Y. 10591. Agent: Julian Bach Literary Agency, Inc., 3 East 48th St., New York, N.Y. 10017. Office: 56 West 45th St., New York, N.Y. 10036.

CAREER: University of Miami, Coral Gables, Fla., instructor, 1950-51; Life, New York City, staff writer, 1953-61; film producer for Drew Associates, 1961-65; James Lipscomb, Inc., New York City, film producer, 1965—. Military service: U.S. Navy; served as aviation cadet.

WRITINGS: So You Think You Know the Rules of Yacht Racing, Norton, 1963; Cutting Loose, Little, Brown, 1972. Contributor to magazines.

*   *   *

LITOFF, Judy Barrett 1944-

PERSONAL: Born December 23, 1944, in Atlanta, Ga.; daughter of John and Dorothy (Wooddall) Barrett; married Hal Litoff (a writer), September 30, 1966; children: Nadja Barrett, Alyssa Barrett. Education: Emory University, B.A., 1967, M.A., 1968; University of Maine, Ph.D., 1975. Home: 248 Morris Ave., Providence, R.I. 02906. Office: Department of History, Bryant College, Smithfield, R.I. 02917.

CAREER: Bryant College, Smithfield, R.I., assistant professor of history, 1975—. Member of local American Friends Service Committee; television and film consultant. Member: American Historical Association, Organization of American Historians, American Association of University Women, National Trust for Historic Preservation, Coordinating Committee on Women in the Historical Profession, Southern Association of Women Historians, Women Educators of Rhode Island, Rhode Island Black Heritage Society, Phi Kappa Phi, Phi Alpha Theta, Pi Sigma Alpha.

WRITINGS: (With husband, Hal Litoff) Recognitions: A Sourcebook of Working Women in Maine, Bureau of Labor Education (Orono, Me.), 1974; American Midwives, 1860 to the Present, Greenwood Press, 1978. Contributor to history journals.

WORK IN PROGRESS: Continuing research on the history of American midwives.

SIDELIGHTS: Judy Litoff writes: "The circumstances surrounding the birth of my daughter in 1972, who was delivered by an obstetrician in a hospital, made me especially curious about the history of the American midwife and the forces which brought about her near-elimination. My interest in midwives, coupled with a larger commitment to uncovering woman's past, convinced me that the changing role of the midwife in American society would make an appropriate study."

In her book, American Midwives: 1860 to the Present, Litoff traces the decline of midwife-assisted births in the United States. The rapid replacement of midwives, she found, can be attributed to the development of obstetrics and the popular demand for painless delivery. "American Midwives," commented James Reed, "provides a balanced narrative of the twentieth-century debate over the role of the midwife in childbirth. . . . The strength of Litoff's study is her even-handed presentation of a wide spectrum of opinion . . . , and will provide an accurate introduction for future investigators."

BIOGRAPHICAL/CRITICAL SOURCES: American Historical Review, February, 1979.

*   *   *

LITTKE, Lael J. 1929-

PERSONAL: Born December 2, 1929, in Mink Creek, Idaho; daughter of Frank George and Ada Geneva (Petersen) Jensen; married George C. Littke (a college professor), June 29, 1954; children: Lori S. Education: Utah State University, B.S., 1952; attended City College (now of the City University of New York), 1955-59, and University of California, Los Angeles, 1968. Politics: Democrat. Religion: Church of Jesus Christ of Latter-day Saints (Mormons). Home: 1345 Daveric Dr., Pasadena, Calif. 91107. Agent: Larry Sternig, 742 Robertson, Milwaukee, Wis. 53213.

CAREER: Writer, 1963—. Gates Rubber Co., Denver, Colo., secretary, 1952-54; Life Insurance Association of America, New York City, secretary, 1954-60; employed as a medical secretary by a physician in New York City, 1960-63. Member: P.E.N. International, Mystery Writers of America, Science Fiction Writers of America, Society of Children's Book Writers, California Writer's Guild, Southern California Council on Literature for Children and Young People.

WRITINGS: Wilmer the Watchdog, Western, 1970; Tell Me When I Can Go, Scholastic Book Services, 1978. Story represented in anthology, Best Short Stories of 1973, edited by Martha Foley, Houghton, 1973. Contributor of short stories to Ellery Queen's Mystery Magazine, Seventeen, Ladies Home Journal, and Co-ed.

WORK IN PROGRESS: Jigsaw, a young people's mystery novel.

SIDELIGHTS: Littke told CA: "I find association with other professional writers to be very valuable and stimulating because non-writers never quite understand what we do. They think all you have to do is have the time.

"One of my major interests is travel. I have seen most of the United States, the eastern parts of Canada, and part of Mexico. I have had one trip to Europe. I speak a smattering of Spanish and Danish."

BIOGRAPHICAL/CRITICAL SOURCES: Pasadena Star-News, September 2, 1976; Preston Citizen (Preston, Idaho), March 23, 1978.

LIU, Da 1910-

PERSONAL: Born August 10, 1910, in Kiang-Su, China; came to United States in 1956, naturalized citizen, 1977; son of Liu Te Fu. *Education:* Attended National University of China, 1930-34, Columbia University, 1957-58, and New School for Social Research, 1958-61. *Religion:* Taoist. *Home:* 520 West 110th St., Apt. 7-A, New York, N.Y. 10025. *Office:* T'ai Chi Society of New York, 1047 Amsterdam Ave., New York, N.Y. 10025.

CAREER: Teacher of T'ai Chi Chu'an and writer. Teacher and president of T'ai Chi Society of New York, New York City, 1959—; president of Computerized I Ching Horoscope Co., New York City, 1970-78. Member of staff in Chinese section at United Nations, 1961-71. President of Taoist Institute International. Lecturer at China Institute and Southern Methodist University; teacher at churches and church-sponsored institutions; leader of workshops.

WRITINGS: T'ai Chi Ch'uan and I Ching: A Choreography of Body and Mind, Harper, 1972; *Taoist Health Exercise Book,* Links Books, 1974; *I Ching Coin Prediction,* Harper, 1975; *The Tao of Health and Longevity,* Schocken, 1978; *I Ching Numerology,* Harper, 1978; *The Tao and Chinese Culture,* Schocken, 1979. Contributor to *New York Scholar.*

WORK IN PROGRESS: The I Ching and Chinese Culture, a scholarly study, and *T'ai Chi Sword,* publication of both expected in 1980; *T'ai Chi Ch'uan and Meditation.*

SIDELIGHTS: Liu comments: "In my writings I have tried to convey the importance of Taoist ideals for everyday life. T'ai Chi Ch'uan has been my interest for more than fifty years. It is a martial art, but more important, it is a method through which one can gain health and longevity. Coupled with its sister art of meditation, it can help one truly attain harmony in life. I have taught this for many years, both in China and the United States. Recently I have been writing books to share my knowledge and experience of the Tao with readers of the Western world."

BIOGRAPHICAL/CRITICAL SOURCES: Dallas Morning News, August 6, 1971.

*   *   *

LOCHER, Richard 1929-
(Dick Locher)

PERSONAL: Surname is pronounced *Lo*-ker; born June 4, 1929, in Dubuque, Iowa; son of Joseph John (a dentist) and Lucille (Jungk) Locher; married Mary Therese Cosgrove, June 15, 1957; children: Steve, John, Jana. *Education:* Attended Loras College and University of Iowa; Chicago Academy of Fine Arts, graduated, 1951; Los Angeles Art Center, graduated, 1955. *Home:* 921 Heatherton Dr., Naperville, Ill. 60540. *Office: Chicago Tribune,* 435 North Michigan Ave., Chicago, Ill. 60611.

CAREER: U.S. Air Force, career officer, 1951-71, test pilot, 1952-53, in aircraft design, 1953-64, retired as major; *Chicago Tribune,* Chicago, Ill., editorial cartoonist, 1972—. Assistant artist and writer for comic strip "Dick Tracy," 1958-62. Art director in sales promotion at Hansen Company, Chicago, 1962-68; owner and president of Novamark Corp. (art studio), 1968-73. Painter and sculptor, 1960—. Instructor at Chicago Academy of Fine Arts. *Member:* Association of American Editorial Cartoonists. *Awards, honors:* Award from Scripps Howard Institute, 1975, for conservation; Dragonslayer Award from National Educational Society, 1976, 1977, 1978; runner-up for Overseas Press Club award, 1978.

WRITINGS—Under name Dick Locher: *Dick Locher Draws Fire* (cartoons), Chicago Tribune Books, 1979. Writer for "Buck Rogers" comic strip, 1953-55. Contributor of articles and drawings to magazines and newspapers in the United States and abroad, including *U.S. News and World Report, Forbes, Playboy,* and *National Review.*

WORK IN PROGRESS: Sculptures in bronze of U.S. presidents Carter, Nixon, Ford, and Johnson.

SIDELIGHTS: Locher's paintings and sculptures are represented in galleries, showrooms, and corporate offices all over the world, and in the White House and Kremlin. A game he invented, "Poker Face," patented in 1971, accompanied astronauts on "Apollo 14" to the moon.

His interviews include meetings with Henry Kissinger, President Gerald Ford, Presidents Jose Portillo of Mexico and Carlos Andres Perez of Venezuela. He has also interviewed Russian cartoonists in Moscow.

Essentially Locher's work favors the small businessman and depicts the absurdities of political life and big government.

Locher writes: "Comments come by mail from all over the world—Europe, Russia, Australia, Israel—from unknown people, farmers, business men, senators, representatives, Presidents, and kids. Some agree with and some take issue with my cartoons, but all are informative and interesting.

"My philosophy, quoted from Ding Darling, is: 'You can let just as much hot air out of a balloon with a needle as you can with an ax.' Cartoons reflect the world as it is with no false statements and nothing imagined. They are a mirror of our society, a true reflection of history as it is happening."

*   *   *

LOCKRIDGE, Richard 1898-

PERSONAL: Born September 26, 1898, in St. Joseph, Mo.; son of Ralph David L. and Mary Olive (Notson) Lockridge; married Francis Davis (a writer), March 4, 1922 (died, 1963); married Hildegarde Dolson (a writer), May 26, 1965. *Education:* Attended Kansas City Junior College, 1916-18, and University of Missouri, 1920. *Residence:* Tryon, N.C. *Office:* J. B. Lippincott, East Washington Sq., Philadelphia, Pa. 19105.

CAREER: Writer. *Kansas City Kansan,* Kansas City, Kan., reporter, 1921-22; *Kansas City Star,* Kansas City, reporter, 1922; *New York Sun,* New York, N.Y., reporter, 1923-29, drama critic, 1929-42. *Military service:* U.S. Naval Reserve Force, 1918. U.S. Naval Reserve, 1942-45; became lieutenant. *Member:* International P.E.N., Authors League of America, Players Club.

WRITINGS—All published by Lippincott, unless otherwise indicated: *Darling of Misfortune: Edwin Booth, 1833-1893,* Century Co., 1932, reprinted, Benjamin Blom, 1971; *Mr. and Mrs. North,* Frederick A. Stokes, 1936; *Death in the Mind,* Dutton, 1945; *A Matter of Taste,* 1949; *The Empty Day,* 1964; *Squire of Death,* 1965; *Encounter in Key West,* 1966; *Murder for Art's Sake,* 1967; *One Lady, Two Cats,* 1967; *Murder in False-Face,* 1968; *A Plate of Red Herrings,* 1968; *Die Laughing,* 1969; *Troubled Journey,* 1970; *Twice Retired,* 1970; *Preach No More,* 1971; *Death in a Sunny Place,* 1971; *Write Murder Down,* 1972; *Death on the Hour,* 1974; *Or Was He Pushed?,* 1975; *A Streak of Light,* 1976; *The Tenth Life,* 1977.

"Captain Heimrich" series; all published by Lippincott: *Murder Can't Wait,* 1964; *Murder Roundabout,* 1966; *With Option to Die,* 1967.

"Inspector Heimrich" series; all published by Lippincott: *A Risky Way to Kill*, 1969; *Not I, Said the Sparrow*, 1973; *Dead Run*, 1976.

"Captain Heimrich" series; all with wife, Frances Lockridge; all published by Lippincott: *I Want to Go Home*, 1948; *Spin Your Web, Lady!*, 1949; *Foggy, Foggy Death*, 1950; *A Client Is Cancelled*, 1951; *Death by Association*, 1952; *Stand Up and Die*, 1953; *Death and the Gentle Bull*, 1954; *Burnt Offering*, 1955; *Let Dead Enough Alone*, 1956; *Practice to Deceive*, 1957; *Accent on Murder*, 1958; *Show Red for Danger*, 1960; *–With One Stone*, 1961; *First Come, First Kill*, 1962; *The Distant Clue*, 1963.

"Mr. and Mrs. North" series; all with Frances Lockridge; all published by Lippincott, unless otherwise indicated: *Death Takes a Bow*, Avon, 1948; *Murder Is Served*, 1948; *Murder Comes First*, 1951; *Curtain for a Jester*, 1953; *Killing the Goose*, 1958; *The Long Skeleton*, 1958; *The Judge Is Reversed*, 1960; *Murder Has its Points*, 1961.

Other; all with Frances Lockridge; all published by Lippincott: *Think of Death*, 1947; *The Dishonest Murder*, 1949; *Cats and People*, 1950; *Murder in a Hurry*, 1950; *The Lucky Cat*, 1953; *Death Has a Small Voice*, 1953; *A Key to Death*, 1954; *The Nameless Cat*, 1954; *Death of an Angel*, 1955; *The Cat Who Rode Cows*, 1955; *The Faceless Adversary*, 1956; *Murder! Murder! Murder!!!*, 1956; *Voyage Into Violence*, 1956; *The Tangled Cord*, 1957; *Catch as Catch Can*, 1958; *The Innocent House*, 1959; *Murder and Blueberry Pie*, 1959; *Murder Is Suggested*, 1959; *The Golden Man*, 1960; *And Left for Dead*, 1961; *The Drill Is Locked*, 1961; *The Ticking Clock*, 1962; *Night of Shadows*, 1962; *Murder by the Book*, 1963; *The Devious Ones*, 1964; *Quest of the Bogeyman*, 1964.

WORK IN PROGRESS: Another mystery.

* * *

LOLLI, Giorgio 1905-1979

OBITUARY NOTICE—See index for *CA* sketch: Born October 4, 1905, in Ancona, Italy; died May 14, 1979, in Rome, Italy. Psychiatrist, researcher, educator, and author. Lolli was medical director of the Yale University Clinic for Alcoholics and the Connecticut Commission on Alcoholism. He was also the founder and director of the International Center for Psychodietetics, which had branches in both New York City and Rome. The center conducted research into human eating and drinking habits and, at the time of his death, Lolli was working on a study of the American teenager's drinking habits. Lolli was the author of more than eleven books and hundreds of scientific articles. Obituaries and other sources: *New York Times*, May 22, 1979.

* * *

LONG, James M. 1907-1979

OBITUARY NOTICE: Born in 1907 in Des Moines, Iowa; died March 20, 1979, in Rome, Italy. Foreign correspondent and editor. Long was a correspondent from Rome, Italy, for the Associated Press for twenty-three years. For five years after his retirement he was the managing editor of the English-language newspaper, *Rome Daily American*. Obituaries and other sources: *New York Times*, March 21, 1979.

* * *

LONGHURST, Henry Carpenter 1909-1978

PERSONAL: Born March 18, 1909, in Bromham, Bedfordshire, England; died July 23(?), 1978, in Sussex, England;

son of Henry William (a justice of the peace) and Constance Longhurst; married Claudine Marie Sier, 1938; children: one son, one daughter. *Education:* Clare College, Cambridge, B.A. *Home:* Clayton Windmills, Hassocks, Sussex, England.

CAREER: Journalist, golf commentator, and writer, 1932-78. Golf correspondent for *Sunday Times of London* for forty years. Golf commentator for American Broadcasting Companies, Inc. (ABC-TV), Columbia Broadcasting System, Inc. (CBS-TV), and British Broadcasting Corp. (BBC-TV). Member of Parliament, Acton division of Middlesex, 1943-45. *Awards, honors:* Won German amateur title in golf, 1937; journalist of the year special award, 1969; Walter Hagen Award for contributions to Anglo-American golf relations, 1973.

WRITINGS: Golf, McKay, 1937; *It Was Good While It Lasted*, Dent, 1941; *I Wouldn't Have Missed It*, Dent, 1945; *You Never Know Till You Get There*, Dent, 1949; *Golf Mixture*, Laurie, 1952; *Round in Sixty-Eight*, Laurie, 1953; *The Borneo Story: The History of the First 100 Years of Trading in the Far East by the Borneo Company Limited*, Newman Neame, 1956; *Adventure in Oil: The Story of British Petroleum*, Sidgwick & Jackson, 1959; *Spice of Life*, preface by Lord Brabazon of Tara, Cassell, 1963; *Only on Sundays*, Cassell, 1964; (with Geoffrey Cousins) *The Ryder Cup*, Stanley Paul, 1965; (author of foreword) A. S. Graham, *Graham's Golf Club*, Stanley Paul, 1965; *Talking About Golf*, Macdonald & Co., 1966; *Never on Weekdays*, Cassell, 1968; *My Life and Soft Times* (autobiography), Cassell, 1971; *The Best of Henry Longhurst*, edited by Mark Wilson, Simon & Schuster, 1978. Also author of *Candid Caddies*, 1936. Contributor to *Golf Illustrated* and *Sports Illustrated*.

SIDELIGHTS: Henry Longhurst became a golf commentator toward the end of his years as a journalist. He covered the Masters, U.S. Open, British Open, and PGA Championship, along with other golf events. Characterized by his dry wit and understatement, Longhurst was praised by the *New York Times* for bringing "a civilized, literary style to television golf commentary."

A golfer himself, Longhurst was captain of the golf team at Cambridge University in 1930 and won the German amateur title in 1937.

AVOCATIONAL INTERESTS: Fishing, travel.

OBITUARIES: New York Times, July 24, 1978.*

* * *

LONGWORTH, Richard C(ole) 1935-

PERSONAL: Born March 13, 1935, in Des Moines, Iowa; son of Wallace H. (a physician) and Helen (Cole) Longworth; married Barbara Bem (a researcher), July 19, 1958; children: Peter, Susan. *Education:* Northwestern University, B.S.J., 1957; graduate study at Harvard University, 1968-69. *Home:* 2617 Lincolnwood Dr., Evanston, Ill. 60201. *Office: Chicago Tribune*, 435 North Michigan Ave., Chicago, Ill. 60611.

CAREER/WRITINGS: Chicago City News Bureau, Chicago, Ill., police reporter, 1957-58; United Press International, Chicago, foreign and diplomatic correspondent in Chicago, London, Moscow, Vienna, and Brussels, 1958-76; *Chicago Tribune*, Chicago, economic writer, 1976—. Contributor to magazines, including *Saturday Review, Reader's Digest, Atlantic*, and *European Community*. *Member:* Chicago Council on Foreign Relations. *Awards, honors:* Nieman fellowship at Harvard University, 1968; University of Missouri award for economic writing, 1979, for series on world trade; Inter-American Press Association News award, 1979, for series on South America.

SIDELIGHTS: Longworth writes: "I specialize in international and economic reporting. I spent sixteen years abroad for United Press International, writing on oil and dollar crises and other world economic upheavals. Since joining the *Tribune* I have continued to travel widely and co-authored a series on world trade, on inflation, and on South America. I have covered the news in fifty-eight nations on five continents."

*　　*　　*

LORD, Mary Stinson Pillsbury   1904-1978

PERSONAL: Born November 14, 1904, in Minneapolis, Minn.; died July 21, 1978, in New York, N.Y.; daughter of Charles Stinson and Nellie Pendleton (Winston) Pillsbury; married Oswald Bates Lord (a textile manufacturer), December 7, 1929; children: Charles Pillsbury, Winston. *Education:* Smith College, B.A. (cum laude), 1927. *Religion:* Congregationalist. *Home:* 425 East 58th St., New York, N.Y. 10022.

CAREER: Volunteer social worker, Minneapolis, Minn., 1927; family welfare worker, Minneapolis, 1927-29; Charity Organization Society, New York City, volunteer case worker, 1930-31; Junior League of New York, president, 1936-38; East Side Settlement House, New York City, vice-president and director, 1939-43; New York World's Fair, chairman of national advisory committee on women's participation and director of hospitality program, 1939-40; New York City Defense Recreation Committee, co-chairman, 1941-42; Civilian Defense, Region II, assistant director, 1941-43; Women's Council of the Greater New York Fund, 1943; New York War Fund, chairman of women's division, 1943; National War Fund, member of board of directors, chairman of women's activities, 1944; Civilian Advisory Committee for the Women's Army Corps (WAC), national chairman, 1944; New York Woman's Council, member of board, 1945; United States Committee for the International Children's Emergency Fund, chairman, 1948; National Commission of Secretary of Defense, adviser, 1950; National Health Council, president, 1952; Citizens for Eisenhower-Nixon, co-chairman, 1952; United Nations, U.S. alternate representative to U.N. General Assembly, 1953-59, U.S. representative to U.N. Commission on Human Rights, ECOSOC, UN, 1953-61, U.S. delegate to U.N. General Assembly, 1958, 1960; New York Committee on Education and Employment of Women, 1963; International Rescue Committee, president, 1971-78.

Member of board of directors of People-to-People Committee, U.S. Committee on Refugees, National Committee for International Development, Johns Hopkins School of Advanced International Studies, Atlantic Council U.S.A., and Women's Africa Committee. Member of Committee for Winning the Peace, President's Commission for Observation of the 25th Anniversary of the United Nations. Trustee of Smith College, Town Hall, Inc., and American University in Cairo. Vice-chairman of Citizens Committee for Peace with Freedom in Viet Nam. Honorary governor of Atlantic Institute, Paris.

MEMBER: Planned Parenthood Federation of America, National Society of Colonial Dames of America, Women's National Republican Club, Cosmopolitan Club, Women's City Club (vice-president, 1940-42), Phi Beta Kappa. *Awards, honors:* Twelve honorary degrees, including L.L.D. from Smith College, 1953, Syracuse University, 1954, Temple University, 1956, and Wilmington College, 1961; L.H.D. from Wheaton College, 1953, Russell Sage College, 1954, Western College, 1962, Pratt Institute, 1967, and Tufts University, 1966. Office of Civilian Defense ribbon for five thousand hours of volunteer service, 1943; woman of the month, American Woman's Association, May, 1946; citation from General Omar Bradley, 1948; named among "Friends of Children," *Parents Magazine,* March, 1950.

WRITINGS: A New Human Rights Action Program, U.S. Government Printing Office, 1953; *New U.S. Action Program for Human Rights,* U.S. Government Printing Office, 1953; (with husband, Oswald Bates Lord) *Exit Backward, Bowing,* Macmillan, 1970. Author of articles on human relations.

SIDELIGHTS: Heir to the Pillsbury flour fortune, Mary Lord devoted her life to work in public health and social welfare. During her career she held chairmanships of many national committees. As chairman of the Civilian Advisory Committee for the Women's Army Corps (WAC), Lord traveled extensively throughout Europe and the Middle East, touring WAC installations and studying the needs of WACs. She also helped with legislation that made the Women's Army Corps part of the U.S. Army rather than an auxiliary.

In 1953, President Dwight D. Eisenhower appointed Lord to succeed Eleanor Roosevelt as U.S. representative to the United Nations Commission on Human Rights, a post she held for eight years.

OBITUARIES: New York Times, July 23, 1978; *Time,* August 7, 1978.*

*　　*　　*

LORION, R(aymond) P(aul)   1946-

PERSONAL: Born May 19, 1946, in Worcester, Mass.; son of Edmond G. (in insurance sales) and Irene (Brodeur) Lorion; married Shelia C. O'Connor, November 24, 1967; children: Jennifer Irene, Matthew Raymond. *Education:* Tufts University, B.S. (summa cum laude), 1968; University of Rochester, Ph.D., 1972. *Residence:* Knoxville, Tenn. *Office:* Department of Psychology, University of Tennessee, Knoxville, Tenn. 37916.

CAREER: University of Rochester, Rochester, N.Y., research associate, 1972-74, assistant professor of psychology, 1973-74; Temple University, Philadelphia, Pa., associate professor of psychology, 1974-79; University of Tennessee, Knoxville, professor of psychology and director of school/community psychology, 1979—. Research associate of Irving Schwartz Institute. Member of local mayor's advisory committee on mental health. *Member:* American Psychological Association, Eastern Psychological Association, Phi Beta Kappa.

WRITINGS: (With E. L. Cowen, M.A. Trost, and others) *New Ways in School Mental Health: Early Detection and Prevention of School Maladaption,* Behavioral Publications, 1975; (with Fred McKinney and Melvin Zax) *Effective Behavior and Human Development,* Macmillan, 1976; (translator) Pierre Oleron, *Language and Mental Development,* Lawrence Erlbaum Associates, 1977; (editor) *Ajuriaguerra's Handbook of Pediatric Psychiatry,* Masson, 1979.

Contributor: H. H. Barten and Leopold Bellak, editors, *Progress in Community Mental Health,* Volume III, Human Sciences Press, 1975; Barry Pless and Gilbert Graves, editors, *Measurement of Outcome,* U.S. Government Printing Office, 1976; Ira Iscoe, Bernard L. Bloom, and Charles Spielberger, editors, *Community Psychology in Transition,* Hemisphere Publishing, 1977; P. Whitten, editor, *Psychotherapy: Current Perspectives,* F. Watts, 1978; P. J. Woods, editor, *The Psychology Major: Training and Employment Strategies,* American Psychological Association, 1978. Also contributor to *Handbook of Psychotherapy and Behavior Change,* edited by S. L. Garfield and A. Bergin.

Contributor of about thirty articles and reviews to psychology and mental health journals. Member of editorial board of *American Journal of Community Psychology* and *International Journal of Mental Health.*

WORK IN PROGRESS: Six scientific papers.

SIDELIGHTS: Lorion told *CA:* ''The major focus of my research and writing is upon the design and analysis of mental health treatment approaches for the disadvantages and the design and evaluation of primary and secondary prevention programs for the alleviation of psychosocial disorders. A related area of interest is the training of community psychologists and evaluation research professionals.''

* * *

LORRANCE, Arleen 1939-

PERSONAL: Born February 26, 1939, in New York, N.Y.; daughter of Irving and Rose (Karpincas) Udoff; married Richard Lorrance (marriage ended). *Education:* Brooklyn College of the City University of New York, B.A., 1963, M.F.A., 1971; further graduate study at U.S. International University, 1971-73. *Politics:* ''Voter.'' *Religion:* ''Love.'' *Home address:* P.O. Box 7601, San Diego, Calif. 92107.

CAREER: Professional actress, 1953-71; drama teacher, 1957-71; Love Project, San Diego, Calif., executive director, 1970—. *Member:* American Federation of Television and Radio Artists, Actors Equity Association, Screen Actors Guild.

WRITINGS: The Love Project, LP Publications, 1972, revised edition, 1978; (with Diane K. Pike) *Channeling Love Energy,* LP Publications, 1974, revised edition, 1976; *Buddha from Brooklyn,* LP Publications, 1975; *Musings for Meditation,* LP Publications, 1976; *Why Me?: How to Heal What's Hurting You,* Rawson Associates, 1978. Contributor to *Equals One, Education Today,* and *Seeker Newsletter.*

WORK IN PROGRESS: Born of Love, poems; *Leaves of Love,* poems; *Love Works,* with Diane K. Pike.

SIDELIGHTS: Arleen Lorrance writes: ''My greatest motivating force is love: receiving people as beautiful, exactly as they are. I am inspired by kindness, by gentleness, by honesty, by inner strength. My writing is the gift of my life process to all humankind.''

* * *

LOW, Joseph 1911-

PERSONAL: Born August 11, 1911, in Coraopolis, Pa.; son of John Routh and Stella (Rent) Low; married Ruth Hull, October 21, 1940; children: Damaris, Jennifer. *Education:* Attended University of Illinois, 1930-32; Art Students League, New York City, studied with George Grosz, 1935. *Address:* Box 129, Cruz Bay, St. John, Virgin Islands 00830; and Box 362, Chilmark, Mass. 02535.

CAREER: Began his art career in 1933 by typesetting and printing his own work; free-lance designer in New York City, 1941; Indiana University, Bloomington, instructor in

design and graphic art, 1942-45, also established the university's Corydon Press; worked for advertising agencies and editorial offices in Morristown, N.J., 1946-54; Eden Hill Press, South Norwalk, Conn., founder, 1959, and owner; author and illustrator of books for children. *Awards, honors: Mother Goose Riddle Rhymes* was one of the *New York Times* Best Illustrated Children's Books of the Year, 1953; *New York Herald Tribune* Children's Spring Book Festival Award, 1962, for *Adam's Book of Odd Creatures; The Mouse and the Song* by Marilynne K. Roach was selected as one of the American Institute of Graphic Arts Fifty Books of the Year in 1974, and was also chosen for the Children's Book Showcase in 1975; *Trust Reba* and *The Land of the Taffeta Dawn* (the latter written by Natalia M. Belting and illustrated by Low) were exhibited in the American Institute of Graphic Arts Children's Book Show, 1973-74.

WRITINGS—All self-illustrated: (With wife, Ruth Low) *Mother Goose Riddle Rhymes,* Harcourt, 1953; *Adam's Book of Odd Creatures,* Atheneum, 1962; *Smiling Duke,* Houghton, 1963; *There Was a Wise Crow,* Follett, 1969; *Trust Reba,* McGraw, 1974; *Boo to a Goose,* Atheneum, 1975; *Five Men Under One Umbrella, and Other Ready-to-Read Riddles,* Macmillan, 1975; *Little Though I Be,* McGraw, 1976; *What If . . .? 14 Encounters—Some Frightful, Some Frivolous—That Might Happen to Anyone,* Atheneum, 1976; *A Mad Wet Hen and Other Riddles,* Morrow, 1977; *The Christmas Grump,* Atheneum, 1977; *Benny Rabbitt and the Owl,* Greenwillow, 1978; *My Dog, Your Dog,* Macmillan, 1978; *The Devil Himself,* McGraw, 1978.

Illustrator: Wendell William Wright and Helene Laird, *Rainbow Dictionary,* World Publishing, 1947, reprinted as *The Rainbow Dictionary for Young Readers,* Collins & World, 1972; Milton Allan Rugoff, editor, *Harvest of World Folk Tales,* Viking, 1949; Olivia E. Coolidge, *Egyptian Adventures,* Houghton, 1954; Maurice Machado Osborne, *Rudi and the Mayor of Naples,* Houghton, 1958; Miriam Schlein, *The Big Cheese,* W. R. Scott, 1958; Walter de la Mare, *Jack and the Beanstalk,* Knopf, 1959; Helene Jamieson Jordan, *How a Seed Grows,* Crowell, 1960; Rose Laura Mincieli, *Pulcinella; or, Punch's Merry Pranks,* Knopf, 1960; *The Wren-Boy's Rhyme,* Eden Hill Press, 1961; Brian Burland, *St. Nicholas and the Tub,* Holiday House, 1964; Augusta R. Goldin, *Spider Silk,* Crowell, 1964; Jonathan Swift, *Directions to Servants,* Pantheon, 1964.

Clyde Robert Bulla, *More Stories From Favorite Operas,* Crowell, 1965; Marguerite Harmon Bro, *How the Mouse Deer Became King,* Doubleday, 1966; Maria Elena De La Iglesia, *The Cat and the Mouse, and Other Spanish Tales,* Pantheon, 1966; Judy Hawes, *Shrimps,* Crowell, 1967; Lloyd Frankenberg, editor, *Poems of Robert Burns,* Crowell, 1967; Bernice Kohn, *Telephones,* Coward, 1967; Barbara K. Walker and Mine Suemer, *Stargazer to the Sultan,* Parents' Magazine Press, 1967; Nathan Zimelman, *To Sing a Song as Big as Ireland,* Follett, 1967; Constance B. Hieatt, *The Knight of the Lion,* Crowell, 1968; Howard Liss, *Friction,* Coward, 1968; Paul Showers, *Hear Your Heart,* Crowell, 1968; Alvin R. Tresselt, *The Legend of the Willow Plate,* Parents' Magazine Press, 1968; Daisy Aldan, editor, *Poems From India,* Crowell, 1969; Countee Cullen, *The Lost Zoo,* Follett, 1969; Sophia Harvati Fenton, *Greece,* Holt, 1969; George Mendoza, *A Beastly Alphabet,* Grosset, 1969; Mendoza, *Flowers and Grasses and Weeds,* Funk, 1969; *The Compleat Gamester* (limited edition), Barre, 1969.

Mark Twain, *The Notorious Jumping Frog and Other Stories,* edited by Edward Wagenknecht, Heritage Press, 1970; Myra Cohn Livingston, editor, *Speak Roughly to Your Little*

Boy: A Collection of Parodies and Burlesques, Harcourt, 1971; Padraic Colum, *The White Sparrow,* McGraw, 1972; Sigmund Kalina, *Your Bones Are Alive,* Lothrop, 1972; Natalia Maree Belting, *The Land of the Taffeta Dawn,* Dutton, 1973; Mary Ann Hoberman, *The Raucous Auk: A Menagerie of Poems,* Viking, 1973; Henry Wadsworth Longfellow, *Paul Revere's Ride,* Windmill Books, 1973; Russell E. Erickson, *The Snow of Ohreeganu,* Lothrop, 1974; Marilynne K. Roach, *The Mouse and the Song,* Parents' Magazine Press, 1974; Franklyn Mansfield Branley, *Roots Are Food Finders,* Crowell, 1975; Dorothy O. Van Woerkom, *Meat Pies and Sausages,* Greenwillow Books, 1976; Livingston, *A Lolligag of Limericks,* Atheneum, 1978.

SIDELIGHTS: Low's works have been exhibited throughout the United States, Europe, and South America. Several of his designs are represented in permanent collections at numerous museums, libraries, and universities, including the Boston Museum of Fine Arts, the Library of Congress, and Princeton University. *Avocational interests:* Sailing.

BIOGRAPHICAL/CRITICAL SOURCES: New York Times, November 1, 1953; *Saturday Review,* November 14, 1953.*

* * *

LOWITZ, Sadyebeth Heath 1901-1969

PERSONAL: Born December 3, 1901, in Richmond, Mich.; died November 13, 1969 in Greenwich, Conn.; daughter of J. Alexander and Sadie (Allington) Heath; married Anson C. Lowitz (an advertising executive and author), September 12, 1925 (died January 22, 1978); children: Roberta Frances (Mrs. John Ross Hamilton). *Education:* University of Michigan, B.A., 1925; Columbia University, M.A., 1927. *Religion:* Congregationalist. *Residence:* Greenwich, Conn.

CAREER: Author of children's books. Dean of Finch Junior College, 1947-48. Trustee of Knox School and Greenwich (Conn.) Historical Society; member of board of governors, University of Michigan; president of Round Hill Church Guild, Greenwich.

WRITINGS—With husband, Anson C. Lowitz; all "Really Truly Story" juvenile series: *The Pilgrims' Party,* Stein & Day, 1931, revised edition, Lerner, 1967; *General George the Great,* Stein & Day, 1932, revised edition, Lerner, 1967; *The Cruise of Mr. Christopher Columbus,* 1932, revised edition, Lerner, 1967; *The Magic Fountain,* Stein & Day, 1936, revised edition, Lerner, 1967; *Mr. Key's Song,* Stein & Day, 1937, revised edition, Lerner, 1967; *Barefoot Abe,* Stein & Day, 1938, revised edition, Lerner, 1967; *Tom Edison Finds Out,* Stein & Day, 1940, revised edition, Lerner, 1967.

OBITUARIES: New York Times, November 16, 1969; *Publishers Weekly,* January 5, 1970.*

* * *

LUARD, Nicholas 1937-
(James McVean)

PERSONAL: Born June 26, 1937, in London, England; son of James McVean and Susan (Spencer) Luard; married Elisabeth Baron Longmore (a wildlife painter), February 25, 1963; children: Caspar, Francesca, Poppy, Honey. *Education:* Attended Winchester College, 1951-54, and Sorbonne, University of Paris, 1954-55; Cambridge University, M.A., 1960; University of Pennsylvania, M.A., 1961. *Home:* 10 Wilbraham Pl., London SW1, England. *Agent:* Jonathan Clowe Ltd., 14 Jeffreys Pl., London NW1, England.

CAREER: Writer. Worked in theatre and publishing; also associated with North Atlantic Treaty Organization

(NATO). Founder of Establishment theatre club. *Military service:* Coldstream Guards, 1955-57; became 2nd lieutenant.

WRITINGS: (With Dominick Elwes) *Refer to Drawer* (humor), A. Barker, 1964; *The Warm and Golden War* (novel), Secker & Warburg, 1967, Pantheon, 1968; *The Robespierre Serial* (novel), Harcourt, 1975; *Travelling Horseman* (novel), Weidenfeld & Nicolson, 1975; *The Orion Line* (novel), Secker & Warburg, 1976, Harcourt, 1977; (under pseudonym James McVean) *Blood Spoor* (novel), Dial, 1978; *The Dirty Area* (novel), Harcourt, 1979.

WORK IN PROGRESS: A novel under the pseudonym James McVean, *The White Falcon; The Last Wilderness,* "a portrait of the Kalahari Desert and its wildlife," with illustrations by wife, Elisabeth Baron Luard.

SIDELIGHTS: Most of Luard's writings are espionage novels. "Luard knows his spy literature," wrote Newgate Callendar. "The hero of his books is not without sensitivity, and that is *de rigueur* today in the better spy novels. . . ." In a review of *The Robespierre Serial,* Callendar described the plot as "familiar." However, he added that "Luard writes very well, and the reader will be swept along. Good storytelling and logical plotting can compensate for almost anything."

Patrick Cosgrave cited *Travelling Horseman* for its familiar structure, too. Cosgrave's major complaint was that Luard relied too heavily on data. "It is a good, strong story," Cosgrave conceded, "but the presentation and, again, all the technical detail, consign it irrevocably to the world of 'faction,' a mixture of documentary and story-telling."

Cosgrave was less harsh in his review of *The Orion Line.* "The theme is well-worn," he wrote, "but Mr. Luard's treatment is sensitive, exciting, and often brilliant. Cosgrave noted "the influence of Hemingway" in *The Orion Line* and claimed the novel was Luard's "best thriller so far. . . ."

Luard told *CA:* "I am a specialist in espionage and counter-intelligence. I am attracted in novels to the theme of 'the man alone.' I am also a naturalist and explorer, travelling widely in remote places." Luard speaks French, Spanish, German, and other languages.

BIOGRAPHICAL/CRITICAL SOURCES: New York Times Book Review, April 6, 1975; *Spectator,* January 17, 1976, October 16, 1976.

* * *

LUBBOCK, Percy 1879-1965

PERSONAL: Born June 4, 1879, in London, England; died August 1, 1965; son of Frederic and Catherine (Gurney) Lubbock; married Sybil Cuffe, 1926 (died, 1943). *Education:* Attended Eton College and King's College, Cambridge.

CAREER: Writer. Cambridge University, Magdalene College, Cambridge, England, curator of Pepys Library, 1906-08. *Military service:* Served with British Red Cross during World War I. *Awards, honors:* James Tate Black Prize, 1922; *Femina-Vie Heureuse* Prize, 1923; Royal Society of Literature Benson Medal, 1926; named Commander of Order of the British Empire, 1952.

WRITINGS: Elizabeth Barrett Browning in Her Letters, Smith & Elder, 1906, reprinted, AMS Press, 1974; *Samuel Pepys,* Scribner, 1909, reprinted, Folcroft Library Editions, 1974; *The Craft of Fiction* (criticism), Scribner, 1921, reprinted, Scribner, 1955; *George Calderon: A Sketch From Memory,* Richards Press, 1921; *Earlham* (history and biography), Scribner, 1922, reprinted, Greenwood Press, 1974; *Roman Pictures* (novel), Scribner, 1923; *The Region Cloud* (novel), Scribner, 1925; *Mary Cholmondeley: A Sketch From Memory*, J. Cape, 1928; *Shades of Eton* (autobiography), Scribner, 1929; *Portrait of Edith Wharton*, Appleton Century, 1947, reprinted, Kraus Reprints, 1969; Marjory Gane Harkness, editor, *Percy Lubbock Reader*, Bond Wheelwright, 1957.

Editor: *A Book of English Prose*, two volumes, Cambridge University Press, 1913; Henry James, *The Ivory Tower*, Scribner, 1917; James, *The Middle Years*, Scribner, 1917; James, *The Sense of the Past*, Scribner, 1917, reprinted, 1971; *The Letters of Henry James*, two volumes, Scribner, 1920, reprinted, Octagon Books, 1970; *The Novels and Stories of Henry James*, thirty-five volumes, Scribner, 1923; *The Diary of Arthur Christopher Benson*, Longman, 1926.

SIDELIGHTS: Lubbock is best known for his critical work, *The Craft of Fiction*, for which he borrowed from literary concepts of Henry James. James claimed that a novelist must possess a sense of reality and then compliment that with the ability to discern a unique subject from life. Lubbock assessed this ability as "the power that recognizes the fruitful idea and seizes it as a thing apart." After choosing a subject, the novelist, according to James, must define the form of the novel. James insisted that the form of the novel must be that the illusion of reality is obtained.

Lubbock pursued James's "novel as reality" concept still further. He suggested that an ideal shape existed by which the novel best lent itself to the illusion of reality. Lubbock proposed that the best way for a novelist to achieve this illusion in the work was with the dramatic (as opposed to narrative) form. In short, Lubbock favored enactment over description. "As for intensity of life . . . ," he wrote, "the novelist has recourse to his other arm, the one that corresponds with the single arm of the dramatist. Inevitably, as the plot thickens and the climax approaches—inevitably, whenever an impression is to be emphasized and driven home—narration gives place to enactment, the train of events to the particular episode, the broad picture to the dramatic scene."

Lubbock also refuted the first-person narrative style. Referring to the narrator, he wrote that "he can only recall the past and tell us what he was, only *describe* his emotion; and he may describe very vividly . . . but it would necessarily be more convincing if we could get behind this description and judge for ourselves." In support of his earlier case for "enactment," Lubbock concluded, "Drama we want, always drama, for the central, paramount affair, whatever it is."

However, Lubbock does not insist that all novelists should ascribe to his own preference for drama without regard for subject or theme. "Such is the progress of the writer towards drama," he noted; "such is his method of evading the drawbacks of a mere reporter and assuming the advantages, as far as possible, of a dramatist. How far he may choose to push the process in his book—that is a matter to be decided by the subject; it entirely depends upon the kind of effect that the theme demands. It may respond to all the dramatization it can get, it may give all that it has to give for less. The subject dictates the method."

Critical assessments of *The Craft of Fiction* have been mixed. Gilbert Seldes wrote, "I can think of few contemporary writers and no critics who can afford to disregard *The Craft of Fiction*, and if there are readers who are still capable of taking esthetic pleasure in the novel . . . , I urge them, in the interest of 'creative reading,' to disregard the occasional

obscurity of Dr. Lubbock's presentation and learn from him nearly all that can be learned, except from the novelists themselves, of the art." A reviewer for *Outlook*, though, was unimpressed with Lubbock's criticism. The reviewer wrote that "if there are any who desire to be called critics without exercising a critical judgement, they should study Mr. Lubbock carefully." The same critic noted sarcastically, "It only remained to invent a jargon and turn literary criticism into studio gossip." Taking offense with Lubbock's obsession with form, the writer mused, "The time may yet come when even a Tolstoy will be superciliously challenged: 'Are you crystallised?'"

Derek Stanford, attending to Lubbock's own writing style, observed, "Like the subtle smoke of a long-extinct cigar, Mr. Lubbock's style preserves the illusion that things are with us which have since passed away." Quoting Cyril Connolly, Stanford called Lubbock a "'mandarin' author, a master of English in its literary rather than vernacular form."

BIOGRAPHICAL/CRITICAL SOURCES: Percy Lubbock, *The Craft of Fiction*, Scribner, 1921, reprinted, Scribner, 1955; *Dial*, March 1922; *Outlook*, March 4, 1922; *London Mercury*, February, 1923; Lubbock, *Shades of Eton*, Scribner, 1929; *Month*, December, 1952.*

* * *

LUCAS, C. Payne 1933-

PERSONAL: Born September 14, 1933, in Spring Hope, N.C.; son of Russell and Minnie (Hendricks) Lucas; married Freddie Hill, August 29, 1964; children: Therese, C. Payne, Hillary. *Education:* Maryland State College, B.A. (summa cum laude), 1959; American University, M.A., 1961. *Home:* 4241 Mathewson Dr. N.W., Washington, D.C. 20011. *Office:* Africare, Inc., 1601 Connecticut Ave. N.W., Washington, D.C.

CAREER: Game specialist for Montgomery City Recreation Department, 1959-60; worked as police and citizens corp. junior consultant, 1960-61; Office of the Secretary of Defense, Washington, D.C., executive trainee, 1961; Democratic National Committee, Washington, D.C., research assistant, 1961-62; U.S. Peace Corps, Washington, D.C., operations and training officer for Africa, 1962-63, associate director in Togo, 1963, deputy director, 1964, official in Uganda and Kenya, 1964, director in Niger, 1964-66, deputy director for Africa, 1966-67, director for Africa, 1967-68, director of office of returned volunteers, 1969-71; Africare, Inc., Washington, D.C., executive director, 1971—. Member of board of directors of New Directions, Overseas Development Council, International Voluntary Services, District of Columbia Institute of Mental Hygiene, Washington Metropolitan Junior Citizen Police Corps, and Trans-Africa. *Military service:* U.S. Air Force, airborne radio technician, 1954-57. *Member:* Pi Sigma Alpha, Cosmos Club. *Awards, honors:* Distinguished Federal Service Award, 1967; LL.D. from University of Maryland, 1975.

WRITINGS: (With Kevin Lowther) *Keeping Kennedy's Promise*, Westview Press, 1978. Contributor to newspapers.

SIDELIGHTS: Lucas was instrumental in establishing Peace Corps programs in Uganda and Kenya. Later he was responsible for the agency's antidiscrimination policies and he eventually controlled agency operations in twenty-three African countries. His last responsibilities included career opportunity and voluntary action programs for Peace Corps veterans, aimed at keeping them actively involved in problem-solving situations in the United States.

LUDLAM, Charles

ADDRESS: 55 Morton, New York, N.Y. 10014.

CAREER: Playwright, actor, and director of stage productions. Actor in plays, including "Big Hotel," 1967, and "Eunuchs of the Forbidden City," 1972; actor in motion pictures, including "Lupe," 1966. Co-founder of Play-House of the Ridiculous, 1966; founder of Ridiculous Theatrical Co. *Awards, honors:* Obie Award for acting from *Village Voice,* 1973.

WRITINGS—Plays: "When Queens Collide," first produced in New York City, 1967; "Big Hotel," first produced in New York City, 1967; "Conquest of the Universe," first produced in New York City, 1967; (and director) "Bluebird" (first produced in New York City, 1970, revised version produced in New York City, 1975), published in *More Plays From Off-Off Broadway,* edited by Michael Smith, Bobbs-Merrill, 1972; "The Grand Tarot," first produced in New York City, 1972; (and director) "Eunuchs of the Forbidden City" (five-act), first produced in New York City at the Theater for the New City, April, 1972; (and director) "Corn," first produced in New York City, 1972; (and director) "Camille: A Tear Jerker" adapted from the play by Alexander Dumas, "Camille"), first produced in New York City, 1973; (and director) "Stage Blood," first produced in New York City, 1974; (and director) "Hot Ice," first produced in New York City, 1974; (and director) "The Ventriloquist's Wife," first produced in New York City at Reno Sweeney's, December 26, 1977; (and director) "Utopia Inc.," first produced in New York City at Ridiculous Theater, December, 1978; "The Enchanted Pig," first produced Off-Broadway at Sheridan Square Playhouse, April 22, 1979. Co-contributor with Bill Vehr of the play "Turds in Hell," to *Drama Review,* September, 1970.

SIDELIGHTS: "If Charles Ludlam had lived fifty years ago," wrote Mel Gussow, "he might have been a vaudeville headliner, but he would have never lost his sense of the Ridiculous." This "sense of the Ridiculous" is readily evident in most of Ludlam's work. "Bluebeard" is about a mad scientist bent on creating a third genital. "Ventriloquist's Wife" concerns an actor who is upstaged and dominated by his dummy, and "Eunuchs of the Forbidden City" embraces a host of bizarre characters, including an empress who kills her son and triggers the Boxer Rebellion, an emperor who impregnates a concubine, and numerous eunuchs mouthing lines like "We have no power to love. . . . We must love power."

Ludlam's dialogue is punctuated with numerous puns and sincerely delivered cliches. Some of his more notorious lines are referred to as "Ludlamisms." "Boredom is absence of yumyum," declares a character in "Eunuchs of the Forbidden City." Another announces, "I don't think of myself as being castrated—I think of myself as being extremely well circumcised." In "The Ventriloquist's Wife," a performer preparing to saw a woman in half remarks, "The last woman I sawed in half is living in Paris and London."

Ludlam's most recent plays have been praised by Gussow in the *New York Times.* He called "Eunuchs of the Forbidden City "an exuberant and robust work, one of Ludlam's most polished and comic inventions." Gussow also observed, "'The Ventriloquist's Wife' raises ventriloquism to a high comic art." He was less impressed with "Utopia Inc." "It lacks the monstrous lunacy of . . . 'Bluebeard,'" claimed Gussow, who also noted the absence of "the blissful virtuosity of 'The Ventriloquist's Wife.'" Gussow suggested that Ludlam, who acts in most of his plays, was also less impres-

sive. "The role straitjackets his comic impulse," Gussow lamented, "and cheats the audience of a prime Ridiculous delectation."

Ludlam seems to have summed up his attitude towards his art when he spoke before a presentation of "Utopia Inc. "Don't look for deeper meaning," he warned. "Just take it at face value."

BIOGRAPHICAL/CRITICAL SOURCES: New York Times, April 7, 1972, December 28, 1977, December 5, 1978, April 24, 1979.*

*   *   *

LUSTBADER, Eric Van   1946-

PERSONAL: Born December 24, 1946, in New York, N.Y.; son of Melvin Harry (a state social security bureau director) and Ruth (Aaronson) Lustbader. *Education:* Columbia University, B.A., 1968. *Home:* 575 Grand St., New York, N.Y. 10002. *Agent:* Henry Morrison, Inc., 58 West 10th St., New York, N.Y. 10011.

CAREER: CIS-TRANS Productions (music producers), New York City, owner, 1963-67; elementary school teacher in New York City, 1968-70; *Cash Box* (music trade journal), New York City, associate editor, 1970-72; Elektra Records, New York City, director of international artists and repertory, and assistant to the president, 1972-73; Dick James Music, New York City, director of publicity and creative services, 1974-75; Sweet Dream Productions, New York City, owner, 1975-76; NBC-TV, New York City, writer and field producer of news film on Elton John, 1976; CBS Records, New York City, designer of publicity and album covers and manager of media services, 1976-78. Free-lance writer, 1973—. *Member:* Science Fiction Writers of America, Author's Guild, Museum of Modern Art, South Street Seaport Museum.

WRITINGS—Novels: *The Sunset Warrior,* Doubleday, 1977; *Shallows of Night,* Doubleday, 1978; *Dai-San,* Doubleday, 1978; *Beneath an Opal Moon,* Doubleday, 1980.

WORK IN PROGRESS: Four novels, *The Ninja, Convention, Sirens,* and *The Seer.*

AVOCATIONAL INTERESTS: Japanese and Mayan history, history of pre-war Shanghai, music, ballet.

*   *   *

LUSTGARTEN, Karen   1944-

PERSONAL: Born April 12, 1944, in Boston, Mass.; daughter of Ben (a pharmacist) and Sophie (Lipofsky) Lieberson; married Bernie Lustgarten (a photographer), July, 1972 (divorced May, 1978). *Education:* University of California, Berkeley, B.A., 1966; California State College (now University), Los Angeles, elementary teaching credential, 1968; attended Instituto de Cultura Hispanica, Madrid, Spain, 1971; San Jose State University, graduate study, 1973-74. *Residence:* San Francisco, Calif. *Agent:* Larsen/Pomada, 1029 Jones St., San Francisco, Calif. 94109. *Office:* The Lustgarten of San Francisco, 715 Harrison, San Francisco, Calif. 94107.

CAREER: Teacher of "The Lustgarten Technique of Body Conditioning" and disco dance classes both in private studios and through numerous college and adult education programs; director of The Lustgarten of San Francisco (a disco-spa), San Francisco, Calif., 1978—. Elementary teacher in Van Nuys, Calif., 1968; social worker for Los Angeles County Department of Public Social Services, 1968-70;

adult probation officer in San Francisco, 1974; creator of exercise program for an obesity study clinic at University of California, Berkeley, 1975; performer and writer of exercise segments for television program, "The Evening Magazine Show," 1976-77. Lecturer and choreographer. Member of board of directors of Bay Area Benefit Concerts, Inc. *Member:* American Federation of Television and Radio Artists.

WRITINGS: The Complete Guide to Disco Dancing, Warner Books, 1978. Author of syndicated newspaper column, "The Dynamic Body," 1975—; disco consultant to *Rolling Stone* magazine. Contributor of articles to *Discoworld, Dancing Madness, City Sports,* and *Horse Lovers* magazine.

WORK IN PROGRESS: The Dynamic Body, a book based on the author's technique of body conditioning; *Secret Exercises: Sexy Exercises;* a script for an exercise television show; compiling music tapes for a corresponding exercise book.

SIDELIGHTS: Karen Lustgarten, who was nominated for a Northern California Emmy Award for her performance and writing of exercise segments for "The Evening Magazine Show," has studied dance for twelve years in Boston, Los Angeles, and San Francisco. She has also done several years of research into the many areas of body conditioning. Described by *San Francisco* magazine as "a disco dance 'pioneer' exercise lady," Lustgarten began teaching disco dancing when it was still referred to as "fast" dancing. She writes in the introduction to her first book, *The Complete Guide to Disco Dancing:* "When I first began teaching disco dancing in March, 1973, no one knew what the word 'disco' meant. . . . I had to devise my own way of translating seemingly amorphous writing into something that made dance sense to my students. I didn't realize it then, but I was researching a dance form that had never been studied or written about before. . . . I hope this book will help to legitimize disco dancing as a unique and liberating dance form."

In the introduction to her forthcoming book, *The Dynamic Body,* Karen Lustgarten states: "I have attempted to produce the most beautiful exercise book ever written. It is my feeling that a toned, healthy body is a work of art tantamount to other natural and man-made artworks. I have never considered exercise to be a drugery; instead, I find it to be a *joyous* expression and release of my physical, mental, and emotional self. The effort has its visible rewards: creating a refined, live sculpture out of your own body.

"I first taught disco dance and exercise as a way to put myself through a master's program in public health. I always danced as an avocation, but never before drew upon this dance talent for income. By combining academic skills of research and writing, with my dance and teaching talent, and an ability to make these subjects entertaining, quite by serendipity I developed and wrote a disco dance book. To me a good writer must be thoroughly knowledgeable about a subject(s), feel a passion to communicate that knowledge, and have a creative talent to express knowledge in an original, entertaining, and articulate way."

BIOGRAPHICAL/CRITICAL SOURCES: San Francisco, February, 1975, June, 1978; *Chic,* January, 1978; *San Francisco Examiner,* June, 1978.

* * *

LUXTON, Leonora Kathrine 1895-
(Nona Howard)

PERSONAL: Born November 16, 1895, in Kansas City, Mo.; daughter of Charles F. and Kathrine (Bradford) Show-

alter; married David N. Ross, June 14, 1914 (deceased); married Earl R. Luxton (a compositor), January 2, 1947; children: (first marriage) Kathrine Ross Shaw, David H., Leonora Ross Galloway. *Education:* Attended high school in Kansas City, Mo. *Politics:* None. *Home and office:* 1922 Mangoe St., Charlotte Harbor, Fla. 33950.

CAREER: Indianapolis Times, Indianapolis, Ind., reporter, beginning in 1922; *Indianapolis Star,* Indianapolis, reporter, until 1926; *New York American,* New York, N.Y., feature writer and administrator of social services, 1926-36; *Miami Daily News,* Miami, Fla., reporter and magazine writer, 1936-38; free-lance magazine writer, 1938-41; *Boston Globe,* Boston, Mass., reporter and feature writer, 1942-50; professional astrologer and teacher of the occult, 1950—. Freelance writer, 1926—. Administrator of social services for Hearst newspapers in New York. Speaker in Chicago, Boston, Washington, and Miami, for the American Federation of Astrologers. *Member:* American Federation of Astrologers.

WRITINGS: (Under pseudonym Nona Howard) *Follow Your Lucky Stars,* Penn Publishing, 1939; *Astrology: Key to Self-Understanding,* Llewellyn, 1978. Contributor, sometimes under pseudonym Nona Howard, to popular magazines and astrology journals, including *McCall's, Redbook, Mademoiselle, Horoscope, American, Hollywood,* and *Silver Screen.*

WORK IN PROGRESS: Ten books, based on her lectures; collecting "occultly-dictated material" on life after death, after-life conditions, world religions, and philosophical teachings.

SIDELIGHTS: Luxton told *CA* that her first position as a society editor came about as a result of "an impassioned speech made in Indianapolis in 1922 on the need of an animal shelter there." Since about that time, too, Luxton's "interests have been divided between the very practical business of building more houses than any non-professional builder (not less than fifteen in Florida and Massachusetts) and personally testing the truth of astrology as a practical guide to the best and worst times for such ventures."

Luxton wrote: "At age eighty-three, I still do much writing but not for profit as I think that occultly-received dictation must be given freely in books or personally to those interested. The varied nature of my work is shown in the very different material of the first book on astrology, published in 1939, and the latest book, in which almost all of the material came through in occult dictation or automatic writing (typing). *Follow Your Lucky Stars* (originally published as a series of lessons in *Horoscope* magazine), dealt with the specific effects of planetary transits upon many persons who were then prominent in public life, so is now outdated. Then, however, it was on library lists. In contrast, the second book, *Astrology: Key to Self-Understanding,* concerns the spiritual meaning of the planets as well as the way their transits bring about the changes of conditions in human life and influence the personality of individuals. While definitely for advanced students or teachers of astrology, the book can be studied by non-astrological readers interested in the serious aspects of astrology rather than the lighter personal interpretations found in most books today.

"Most of my feature writing is in a very light and somewhat humorous style, if subject matter permits. In more than a half century of such writing almost every kind of non-technical matter was covered. In astrology I have been considered one of the older and most published writers since 1936, with articles in most of the periodical publications on astrology from that date. The Nona Howard name was dropped after my present marriage because my interests at that time turned to the more serious aspects of this science.

"In view of my present age, my future information on after life conditions must be occultly conveyed through my husband, in the hope that he will continue his interest in this study and record whatever information I may be able to transmit from some other plane!"

The proceeds from *Astrology* will go to Luxton's favorite charity, a local animal shelter. She and her husband have owned as many as twelve dogs at one time and currently own seven of them, along with two parrots, "a very intelligent macaw and two deodorized skunks."

* * *

LYDON, Michael 1942-

PERSONAL: Born September 14, 1942, in Boston, Mass.; son of Patrick J. and Auce (Joyce) Lydon; married; children: Shuna. *Education:* Yale University, B.A. (cum laude), 1965.

CAREER: Free-lance writer; musician. *Newsweek,* bureau correspondent in San Francisco, Calif., and London, England, 1965-68. *Awards, honors:* American Library Association notable book award for *Rock Folk.*

WRITINGS: Rock Folk: Portraits From the Rock 'n' Roll Pantheon, Dial, 1971; *Boogie Lightning,* Dial, 1974.

WORK IN PROGRESS: A book on contemporary show business; an introduction to music; many songs and musical compositions.

SIDELIGHTS: Rock Folk is comprised of articles on various aspects of rock music, previously written for *Rolling Stone,* the *New York Times,* and *Ramparts.* Ellen Sander described Lydon's writing as "piquant and full of incidental delight. . . . Lydon always uses his subject as an opportunity to illuminate the scene in general and his insights are always right on."

BIOGRAPHICAL/CRITICAL SOURCES: Saturday Review, July 31, 1971.*

* * *

LYNCH, John 1927-

PERSONAL: Born January 11, 1927, in Boldon, England; son of John Patrick and Teresa (Collins) Lynch; married Wendy Kathleen Norman, August 6, 1960; children: Kathleen, Madeleine, Caroline, Jonathan, Mark. *Education:* University of Edinburgh, M.A., 1952; University of London, Ph.D., 1955. *Religion:* Roman Catholic. *Home:* 8 Templars Cres., London N3 3QS, England. *Office:* Institute of Latin American Studies, University of London, 31 Tavistock Sq., London WC1H 9HA, England.

CAREER: University of Liverpool, Liverpool, England, lecturer in modern history, 1954-61; University of London, London, England, lecturer, 1961-64, reader, 1964-70, professor of Latin American history, 1970—, director of Institute of Latin American Studies, 1974—. *Military service:* British Army, 1945-48. *Member:* Royal Historical Society (fellow), Academia Nacional de la Historia (Argentina; fellow).

WRITINGS: Spanish Colonial Administration, 1782-1810, Athlone Press, 1958; *Spain Under the Habsburgs,* Oxford University Press, Volume I, 1964, Volume II, 1969; (with R. A. Humphreys) *The Origins of the Latin American Revolutions, 1808-1826,* Knopf, 1965; *The Spanish American Revolutions, 1808-1826,* Norton, 1973.

WORK IN PROGRESS: Research on Argentine *caudillo*

John Manuel de Rosas, Spain and America in the sixteenth through the eighteenth centuries, and on River Plate countries, 1750-1850.

SIDELIGHTS: Lynch told *CA:* "The profession of historian has greatly changed in recent years under the influence of social science and statistics. At a time when measurement and conceptualization are paramount, I consider that the historian still has a duty to be readable, not least outside of the profession, and that the virtues of pragmatism, intuition, and a sense of style are as important as ever.

"I first became interested in Latin American history out of ignorance and curiosity, eager to discover a new world of sources and events. Since then I have tried to remove a few academic blind spots in Britain by teaching and writing in this field, and also to contribute the views of an outsider to Latin Americans. It is a matter of particular pleasure not only that I have been invited to lecture in their countries but that my books have been translated into Spanish and received a sympathetic reception in the Hispanic world. It is a challenging world, though the challenge for the historian is a limited one. The historian would not claim to resolve the problems of the present, only to reveal the past that lies behind the present."

* * *

LYONS, Augusta Wallace

PERSONAL: Born in Prospect, Oldham County, Ky.; daughter of Tom (a journalist and newspaper editor) and Augusta (French) Wallace; married Leo Handel, January 27, 1942 (divorced, May, 1948); married Edward Lyons (a novelist), July 14, 1954 (divorced, 1978); children: (first marriage) Tom, Albert, Leslie (adopted daughter). *Education:* Educated in Kentucky; attended college. *Politics:* "Usually loyal dissent." *Religion:* Unitarian-Universalist. *Home and office:* 321 Zorn Ave., Louisville, Ky. 40206. *Agent:* Mary Yost Associates, Inc., 141 East 55th St., New York, N.Y. 10022.

CAREER: Began as chorus girl and actress, including Broadway performances; also worked as photographer's model; *Louisville Times,* Louisville, Ky., associate editor, 1945-50; free-lance writer, 1950—. Speaker at colleges and on radio and television programs. Active participant in civil rights and other protest movements. *Member:* Mystery Writers of America, Sierra Club, National Association for the Advancement of Colored People, Adoptive Parents Committee, Society for a Sane Nuclear Policy, Kentucky Youth Advocates.

WRITINGS: Season of Desire (novel), Signet, 1961; *Murder in Prospect, Kentucky* (suspense novel), Putnam, 1967; *All the Lovely Possibilities* (novel), Redbook, 1968; *Dancing on Sand* (novel), Putnam, in press. Also author of *Three Women.*

Work represented in anthologies, including *Best American Short Stories of 1956,* Houghton, 1956; *Teenage Treasury of Imagination and Discovery,* Funk, 1962; *Sometimes Magic,* Platt, 1966. Contributor of stories and articles to magazines, including *New Renaissance, Parents' Magazine, Nature,* and *Redbook.*

WORK IN PROGRESS: A book on the Vietnamese "boat people," publication expected in 1981.

SIDELIGHTS: Augusta Lyons describes *Dancing on Sand* as "a novel about women who like and love men, but also feel their fathers, brothers, sons, and they themselves are heirs to traditions that need revising."

Her interest in the Vietnamese "boat people" is illustrated by the fact that she has recently "adopted" a family of three adults and an infant to share her home.

She comments: "The most useful thing I do is to nurse snakes wounded on highways. They are the best and cheapest known pesticide, and they don't pollute land, rivers, or seas.

"When my mother complained about finding one of my recuperating snakes in a bureau drawer on top of her best lingerie, my father told her the snake was worth three hundred seventy-five dollars a year to the American farmer as a pesticide. This was in the depression when you could get a steak dinner in a nice restaurant for fifty cents.

"My father won many of his battles, or lived to see competent younger men and women take up where he had to leave off, but he felt he never succeeded in diminishing people's 'hard-headed, confounded stupidity' about snakes. So I'm still trying.

"I also work as a private duty nurse to groundhogs, raccoons, tortoises, and one skunk."

*   *   *

LYONS, Catherine 1944-

PERSONAL: Born October 15, 1944, in Grove City, Pa.; daughter of Alexander Johnston (a physician) and Martha (an educator; maiden name, Leech) Lyons. *Education:* Southern Seminary Junior College, A.A.B., 1965; Western College for Women, B.A., 1967; Northwestern University, M.A., 1970; also attended Garrett-Evangelical Theological Seminary, 1967-70. *Politics:* Democrat. *Religion:* Lutheran. *Home:* 200 West 79th St., New York, N.Y. 10024. *Office:* Board of Global Ministries, Room 350, 457 Riverside Dr., New York, N.Y. 10027.

CAREER: American Medical Association, Chicago, Ill., executive in department of medical ethics, 1969-70; Board of Global Ministries, Health and Welfare Ministries Division, New York, N.Y., research assistant, 1970-74, assistant general secretary, 1974—. Member of Hastings Center for the Study of Society, Ethics, and the Life Sciences, founding member of board of trustees of Garrett-Evangelical Theological Seminary.

WRITINGS: Organ Transplants: The Moral Issues, Westminster, 1970, 2nd edition, S.C.M.P., 1971. Contributor to magazines, including *Spectrum, Colloquy, Christianity and Crisis,* and *New World Outlook.*

SIDELIGHTS: Catherine Lyons writes: "All my writing, past and anticipated, pertains to the fields of death and dying, biomedical ethics, and women's issues."

*   *   *

LYSAGHT, Averil M(argaret)

PERSONAL: Born in New Zealand; daughter of Brian (a farmer) and Emily (Stowe) Lysaght. *Education:* Victoria University of Wellington, M.Sc., 1929; University of London, Ph.D., 1935. *Home:* 6 Cumberland Gardens, Great Percy St., London W.C.1, England. *Office:* c/o *Lyon Playfair Literary,* Level 4, Imperial College of Science and Technology, University of London, London SW7 2AZ, England.

CAREER: University of London, Imperial College of Science and Technology, London, England, working with natural history collections made during voyages of Captain James Cook and studying the life of Sir Joseph Banks, 1948—.

MEMBER: British Ornithological Society, Zoological Society, Royal Horticultural Society, Society for the Bibliography of Natural History (fellow), Society of Authors. *Awards, honors:* Frantz Chapman Award, American Museum of Natural History, 1965, for research on the birds of Sir Joseph Banks; American Philosophical Society grant, 1965; Doctor of Letters, Memorial University of St. John's (Newfoundland), 1979.

WRITINGS: Joseph Banks in Newfoundland and Labrador, 1766, Faber, 1971; *Book of Birds,* Phaidon, 1975; (contributor) *The Journal of A.M.S. Endeavour,* Genesis, 1978. Contributor to British Museum yearbook and to scientific journals. Assistant zoology editor of *Chambers's Encyclopaedia,* 1945-48.

WORK IN PROGRESS: Continuing research on the life of Sir Joseph Banks and the lives of his artists.

AVOCATIONAL INTERESTS: Painting, gardening.

*   *   *

LYSONS, Kenneth 1923-

PERSONAL: Born October 16, 1923, in Buxton, Derbyshire, England; son of Joseph (a farmer) and Beatrice (Bunting) Lysons; married Audrey Dutton, September 21, 1946; children: Michael, Jeffrey, Edith. *Education:* University of Liverpool, diploma in public administration, 1961, M.A., 1965; Brunel University, Ph.D., 1973; University of Manchester, M.Ed., 1975. *Religion:* Methodist. *Home:* Lathom, Scotchbarm Lane, Whiston, near Prescot, Merseyside, England.

CAREER: Naylor Brothers Ltd., Engineers, Golborne, Lancashire, England, industrial purchaser, 1945-54; St. Helens College of Technology, England, lecturer, 1959-64, senior lecturer, 1964-67, principal lecturer, 1967-71, head of department of business and administrative studies, 1971—. Held teaching post at Warrington Technical College, 1954-59. Member of board of governors of schools for the mentally handicapped; member of St. Helens Preparation for Retirement Committee; former member of Education Committee of Institute of Purchasing and Supply; member of Joint Industrial Training Board Committee on Industrial Purchasing, Ministry of Labour, 1971-73.

MEMBER: Chartered Institute of Secretaries (fellow), Institute of Purchasing and Supply (fellow), Institute of Personnel Management (associate member). *Awards, honors:* Diploma in Municipal Administration, Local Government Examining Board; diploma in Management Studies, British Institute of Management and Ministry of Education.

WRITINGS: Your Hearing Loss and How to Cope with It, David & Charles, 1978; *The Development of Training for Workers With the Adult Deaf* (pamphlet), British Deaf Association, 1978; *Money and Retirement,* David & Charles, 1979; *Purchasing Handbook,* Macdonald & Evans, 1979. Contributor to purchasing, social service, and church magazines.

WORK IN PROGRESS: Leisure and Retirement.

SIDELIGHTS: Lysons writes: "I write about problems of the handicapped, especially the blind, deaf, and hard of hearing; business, including commercial education; and religion and the relevance of religion to contemporary problems. I write because I like research, especially the people one meets, and because I like writing. I believe that if work is looked upon as a hobby the labor disappears." *Avocational interests:* Music, reading, rugby football.

M

MacCORMAC, Earl Ronald 1935-

PERSONAL: Born April 26, 1935, in Jamaica, N.Y.; son of Earl C. (in business) and Katherine (Kissel) MacCormac; married Nancy M. Hamilton (a politician), August 23, 1958; children: Ann Fletcher, Susan Hamilton. *Education:* Yale University, B.E., 1955, B.D., 1958, M.A., 1959, Ph.D., 1961; postdoctoral study at University of Minnesota, 1964-65. *Office:* Department of Philosophy, Davidson College, Davidson, N.C. 28036.

CAREER: Davidson College, Davidson, N.C., assistant professor of religion and philosophy, 1961-64; University of Minnesota, Minneapolis, administrative intern, 1964-65; Davidson College, associate professor, 1965-72, professor of philosophy, 1972—, dean of Center for Honor Studies, 1973-76. Advisory director of First Union National Bank, Charlotte, N.C. *Military service:* U.S. Naval Reserve, 1956-65; became lieutenant senior grade. *Member:* American Philosophical Association, Philosophy of Science Association, Hume Society, Southern Society for Philosophy and Psychology. *Awards, honors:* Grant from Phillips Foundation, 1964-65; visiting fellow at Mansfield College, Oxford, 1968-69; Thomas Jefferson Award from McConnell Foundation, 1971.

WRITINGS: Metaphor and Myth in Science and Religion, Duke University Press, 1976. Contributor to philosophy journals.

WORK IN PROGRESS: Another book on metaphor.

AVOCATIONAL INTERESTS: Tennis, jogging, philately.

* * *

MACK, Stan(ley)

EDUCATION: Attended the Rhode Island School of Design.

CAREER: Worked as art director for *New York Times Book Review* and *New York Herald Tribune Book Week;* author and illustrator of children's books. *Awards, honors: One Dancing Drum* was listed among the *New York Times* Choice of Best Illustrated Children's Books of the Year in 1971, and was chosen by the Children's Book Showcase in 1972; *The Preposterous Week* was one of the books chosen as part of the American Institute of Graphic Arts Children's Book Show in 1971-72; honors from Society of Illustrators and from the Art Directors Club.

WRITINGS—All self-illustrated: (With Gail Kredenser) *One Dancing Drum,* S. G. Phillips, 1971; *Ten Bears in My Bed: A Goodnight Countdown,* Pantheon, 1974; *The King's Cat Is Coming!,* Pantheon, 1976; *Where's My Cheese?* (a Junior Literary Guild selection), Pantheon, 1977.

Illustrator: Gail Kredenser, *The ABC of Bumptious Beasts: Poems,* Crown, 1966; Edward Lear, *The Story of the Four Little Children Who Went Round the World,* Crown, 1967; Carolyn Wolff, *Three People,* Quist, 1968; Marguerita Rudolph, *Star Bright,* Lothrop, 1969; Ennis Rees, *Potato Talk,* Pantheon, 1969; Robert M. Jones, compiler, *Can Elephants Swim?,* Time-Life, 1969; Erich Kaestner, *The Little Man and the Big Thief,* Knopf, 1969; Thomas Roberts, *The Magical Mind Adventure of Hannah and Coldy Coldy,* Knopf, 1971; Matt Robinson, *A Lot of Hot Water,* Random House, 1971; George Keenan, *The Preposterous Week,* Dial, 1971; Paula Scher, *The Brownstone,* Pantheon, 1973; Arnold Sundgaard, *Jethro's Difficult Dinosaur,* Pantheon, 1977.*

* * *

MacKAYE, Milton 1902(?)-1979

OBITUARY NOTICE: Born c. 1902 in Redfield, Iowa; died March 21, 1979, in Miami, Fla. Reporter, free-lance magazine writer, and author of books. MacKaye worked as a reporter for several newspapers in the 1920's, as a screenwriter for Paramount Pictures, and as chief of the London office of what later became the Office of War Information. He was best known for the political profiles he wrote for such magazines as *New Yorker, Saturday Evening Post,* and *Reader's Digest.* He also wrote four books, including *Dramatic Crimes of 1927* and *Tin Box Parade.* Obituaries and other sources: *Washington Post,* March 23, 1979; *New York Times,* March 24, 1979.

* * *

MACKERRAS, Colin Patrick 1939-

PERSONAL: Born August 26, 1939, in Sydney, Australia; son of Alan Patrick (a university teacher) and Catherine Brearcliffe (a writer; maiden name, MacLaurin) Mackerras; married Alyce Barbara Brazier, June 29, 1963; children: Stephen, Lucy, Martin, Veronica, Josephine. *Education:* University of Melbourne, B.A., 1961; Australian National University, B.A. (honors), 1962, Ph.D., 1970; Cambridge University, M.Litt., 1964. *Politics:* Australian Labor party.

Home: 19 Allambee Cres., Capalaba, Queensland 4157, Australia. *Office:* School of Modern Asian Studies, Griffith University, Nathan, Queensland 4111, Australia.

CAREER: Peking Institute of Foreign Languages, Peking, China, foreign expert and teacher of English, 1964-66; Australian National University, Canberra, research scholar, 1966-69, research fellow, 1969-73, senior research fellow in Far Eastern history, 1973; Griffith University, Nathan, Australia, professor of modern Asian studies, 1974—, chairman of school, 1979—. *Member:* Asian Studies Association of Australia (member of council, 1976—), Australian Society of Authors, Australian Institute of International Affairs, Australian and New Zealand Association for the Advancement of Science, American Academy of Political and Social Science, Asian Studies Association, Queensland History Teachers Association. *Awards, honors:* International visitor of U.S. Department of State, 1977.

WRITINGS: (With Neale Hunter) *China Observed, 1964/67,* Nelson (Australia), 1967; *The Uighur Empire According to the T'ang Dynastic Histories,* Faculty of Asian Studies, Australian National University, 1968, University of South Carolina Press, 1973, revised edition published as *The Uighur Empire According to the T'ang Dynastic Histories: A Study in Sino-Uighur Relations, 744-840,* 1972; *The Rise of the Peking Opera, 1770-1870: Social Aspects of the Theatre in Manchu China,* Clarendon Press, 1972; *Amateur Theatre in China,* Australian National University Press, 1973; (editor with Donald D. Leslie and Wang Gungwu) *Essays on the Sources for Chinese History,* Australian National University Press, 1973; *The Chinese Theatre in Modern Times,* Thames & Hudson, 1975; (editor and contributor) *China: The Impact of Revolution,* Longman, 1976; (with Robert Chan) *Chronology of Modern China From 1842 to the Present Day,* Thames & Hudson, in press. Contributor to Asian studies journals. Editor of *Papers on Far Eastern History,* 1970-73.

WORK IN PROGRESS: Editing a book on Asian music, publication expected by the Curriculum Development Centre, Australian Government; editing a book on Chinese theater history, publication expected by University of Hawaii Press; *Chinese Theatre Since Mao,* completion expected in 1981.

SIDELIGHTS: Mackerras writes: "Coming from a musical family, I have always been interested in European music and opera. The most interesting experience of my life has been to live in Peking teaching English at a time when very few Westerners did so. This developed a fascination with Chinese opera, history, politics, and society, supplemented both before and after by intensive university training.

"I was generally very impressed with China, despite some misgivings, and came to feel that the West should do more to develop good relations with the Chinese. I have believed this with increasing strength since the mid-1960's and have been greatly pleased to see my own hopes and expectations realized through recent developments. The largest of my books on China is a classified chronology of major events since 1842, the beginning of Western impact. This includes not only political, but also cultural and economic events." In addition, Mackerras has covered "natural disasters and the births and deaths of famous people," in his writings.

BIOGRAPHICAL/CRITICAL SOURCES: Sydney Bulletin, February 6, 1979.

MacNEICE, (Frederick) Louis   1907-1963
(Louis Malone)

PERSONAL: Born September 12, 1907, in Belfast, Ireland; died September 4, 1963, in London, England; son of John Frederick (a Protestant bishop) and Elizabeth Margaret (Clesham) MacNeice; married Giovanna Marie Therese Ezra, 1930 (divorced, 1946); married second wife, Hedli Anderson (a singer); children: one son, one daughter. *Education:* Attended Merton College, Oxford University, 1926-30.

CAREER: University of Birmingham, Birmingham, England, lecturer in classics, 1930-36; University of London, Bedford College, London, England, lecturer in Greek, 1936-40; British Broadcasting Corp. (BBC), London, feature writer and producer, 1940-49, 1950-63. Special lecturer in English, Cornell University, spring, 1940; lecturer, British Institute, Athens, Greece, 1949-50. *Awards, honors:* Commander of the Order of the British Empire, 1957.

WRITINGS—Poetry: Blind Fireworks, Gollancz, 1929; *Poems,* Faber, 1935, Random House, 1937; *The Earth Compels,* Faber, 1938; *Autumn Journal,* Random House, 1939; *Poems, 1925-1940,* Random House, 1940; *The Last Ditch,* Cuala Press (Dublin), 1940, reprinted, Irish University Press (Shannon), 1971; *Plant and Phantom,* Faber, 1941; *Springboard, 1941-1944,* Faber, 1944, Random House, 1949; *Holes in the Sky,* Faber, 1948, Random House, 1949; *Collected Poems, 1925-1948,* Faber, 1949; *Ten Burnt Offerings,* Faber, 1952; *Autumn Sequel,* Faber, 1954; *The Other Wing,* Faber, 1954; *Visitations,* Faber, 1957, Oxford University Press (New York), 1958; *Eighty-Five Poems,* Faber, 1959; *Solstices,* Oxford University Press, 1961; *The Burning Perch,* Faber, 1963; *Round the Corner,* Faber, 1963; *Selected Poems,* selected by W. H. Auden, Faber, 1964; *Collected Poems,* edited by E. R. Dodds, Faber, 1966, Oxford University Press, 1967; *The Revenant: A Song Cycle for Hedli Anderson,* Cuala Press, 1975.

Plays: *One for the Grave: A Modern Morality Play,* Faber, 1921, reprinted, 1968, Oxford University Press, 1968; *Persons From Porlock and Other Plays for the Radio,* British Broadcasting Corp., 1938, reprinted, 1969; *Out of the Picture* (two-act; first produced in London by the English Group Theatre), Faber, 1937, reprinted, 1956, Harcourt, 1938; *Christopher Columbus* (radio play), Faber, 1944; *The Dark Tower,* Faber, 1948, Random House, 1949; "The March Hare Reigns," published in *The Smith,* 1959; *The Mad Islands, and The Administrator* (two radio plays), Faber, 1964.

Translations: *The Agamemnon of Aeschylus* (first produced in London by the English Group Theatre, 1936), Faber, 1936, reprinted, 1967; *Goethe's Faust,* Faber, 1951, Oxford University Press, 1953.

Other: (Under pseudonym Louis Malone) *Roundabout Way* (novel), Putnam, 1932; (with W. H. Auden) *Letters From Iceland,* Random House, 1937, reprinted, 1969; *I Crossed the Minch,* Longmans, Green, 1938; *Modern Poetry: A Personal Essay,* Oxford University Press, 1938, reprinted, Haskell House (New York), 1969; *Zoo,* M. Joseph, 1938; *The Poetry of W. B. Yeats,* Oxford University Press, 1941, reprinted, 1969; *Meet the U.S. Army,* Ministry of Information (London), 1943; *The Penny That Rolled Away,* Putnam, 1954 (published in England as *The Sixpence That Rolled Away,* Faber, 1956); *Astrology,* edited by Douglas Hill, Doubleday, 1964; *Varieties of Parable,* Cambridge University Press, 1965; *The Strings Are False: An Unfinished Autobiography,* Oxford University Press, 1966.

Sound recordings: *Louis MacNeice Reading His Own Poetry* (with commentary), Harvard College Library, 1953; *Collected Poems,* Harvard College Library, 1953.

Contributor to numerous periodicals, including *Spectator, New Statesman and Nation, London Mercury, Criterion, Times Literary Supplement,* and *New Verse.*

SIDELIGHTS: In the 1930's, MacNeice was associated with the group of English poets that included W. H. Auden, Stephen Spender, and C. Day Lewis. Theirs was a Freudian-Marxian verse that shared, in M. L. Rosenthal's words, "a sense of the historical moment that was sometimes as violent as a physical sensation." They also shared a discursive, allusive and, at the same time, pointed manner. Yet MacNeice is distinguished from these thirties poets: his tone was more colloquial than that of the others, his manner more casual. Too, he refrained from following, in his poetry, the dictates of any political party. As Martin S. Day explained, MacNeice remained "the sensitive intellectual protesting the world's disorder but offering no panacea."

During the forties and fifties, MacNeice's youthful renown lagged. In 1959, Anthony Thwaite wrote: "His work is very readable, he is never boring, he is an excellent craftsman, and has many of the virtues of a good journalist—a 'reporter of experience' with sharp, vivid, precise phrases. But he seldom has much depth or penetration." Thus has MacNeice's reputation suffered, for it is only recently that critics have begun again to see his work and his attention to detail as more than poetic journalism.

Thomas Blackburn has insisted that MacNeice was not a shallow writer. He "is always implicated in whatever he writes about. He is not the detached reporter . . . but a poet who writes with open heart and mind . . . [about] his own humanity." Donald Best Moore has counted among MacNeice's gifts "an acute sensory, and especially visual, perception" that is an integral part of the emotional or intellectual feeling being poetically expressed: "Colour, shape, light and shade, sound, smell, touch and taste, lend to his verse an immediacy closely connected with time and place."

Furthermore, Terence Brown has recognized MacNeice's maturity and assurance of voice: "His poetic contribution to our literature is the embodiment of a creative scepticism in a verse, and therefore in a voice, which is nearly always recognisably and maturely his own." John Press has even ranked MacNeice with Shakespeare, Jenson, Herrick, Burns, Byron, Tennyson and Browning, the few poets who "have managed to make poetry out of the enjoyment which they have distilled from the minor pleasures of life."

Upon his death, MacNeice's other work—especially his translations of Horace and Goethe and his pioneering work in radio drama—were much praised along with the poetry. But Walter Allen summed it up: "If his poetry was minor poetry it was of a kind we can never have too much of and that was particularly rare in our time. . . . His poetry was a poetry of comment, and the whole of his life, and the life of his times, was his subject matter."

BIOGRAPHICAL/CRITICAL SOURCES: J. Southworth, *Sowing the Spring,* Oxford University Press, 1940; *Times Literary Supplement,* October 28, 1949; Anthony Thwaite, *Contemporary English Poetry,* Heinemann, 1959; Thomas Blackburn, *The Price of an Eye,* Longmans, Green, 1961; *New York Times,* September 22, 1963; Martin S. Day, *History of English Literature 1837 to the Present,* Doubleday, 1964; John Press, *Louis MacNeice,* Longmans, Green, 1965; M. L. Rosenthal, *Chief Modern Poets of England and America,* Volume I, MacMillan, 1966; Derek Stanford,

MacNeice, Spender, Day Lewis: The Pylon Poets, Erdmans, 1969; Donald Best Moore, *The Poetry of Louis MacNeice,* Leicester University Press, 1972; *Encounter,* August, 1972; *Contemporary Literary Criticism,* Gale, Volume 1, 1973, Volume 4, 1975, Volume 10, 1979; Terence Brown, *Louis MacNeice: Sceptical Vision,* Barnes & Noble, 1975; Dan David, *Closing Time,* Oxford University Press, 1975.*

*　　*　　*

MAGGIOLO, Walter A(ndrew)   1908-

PERSONAL: Born June 26, 1908, in Bronx, N.Y.; son of Charles and Alice Virginia (Rovere) Maggiolo. *Education:* College of the Holy Cross, A.B. (cum laude), 1930; Harvard University, LL.B., 1933; further graduate study at St. John's University, Jamaica, N.Y., and Columbia University. *Religion:* Roman Catholic. *Home:* 1619 North Nicholas St., Arlington, Va. 22205.

CAREER: Admitted to the bar of New York State, 1934; private law practice in New York City, 1933-39; New York State Labor Relations Board, New York City, trial attorney, 1939-43; Federal Mediation and Conciliation Service, Washington, D.C., U.S. conciliation commissioner, 1943-52, regional representative for the Northeast, 1945-49, general counsel and assistant to the director, 1952-57, director of mediation activity, 1957-72; lecturer and arbitrator, 1972—. Associate member of faculty at College of the Holy Cross, Cornell University, and Fordham University; lecturer at Crown Heights School of Industrial Relations and Xavier Institute of Industrial Relations; professor at Georgetown Law Center. Director of industrial relations for Toledo Blade Co., 1949; member of arbitration panel of New York State Mediation Board. *Member:* American Arbitration Association, American Bar Association, Federal Bar Association, Catholic Lawyers Guild, Industrial Relations Society, District of Columbia Bar Association, Harvard Alumni Association, Holy Cross Alumni Association, Royal Arcanum (past regent), Knights of Columbus. *Awards, honors:* Crusader Award from College of the Holy Cross, 1945, for contributions to education in labor and industrial relations.

WRITINGS: Techniques of Mediation in Labor Disputes, Oceana, 1973. Contributor to labor and industrial relations journals.

*　　*　　*

MAGNUSON, Warren G(rant)   1905-

PERSONAL: Born April 12, 1905, in Moorhead, Minn.; son of William G. and Emma Carolina (Anderson) Magnuson; married Jermaine Elliot Peralta, October 4, 1964; children: Juanita Peralta (Mrs. Donald Garrison). *Education:* Attended University of North Dakota, 1923, and North Dakota State University, 1924; University of Washington, B.A., 1925, J.D., 1929. *Politics:* Democrat. *Religion:* Lutheran. *Residence:* Seattle, Wash. *Office:* 127 Russell Senate Office Building, Washington, D.C. 20510.

CAREER: Admitted to the Bar of Washington State, 1929; general practice of law, Seattle, Wash., 1929-31; Stern & Schermer, Seattle, attorney, 1931-32; special prosecuting attorney, King County, Wash., 1932; member of Washington state legislature, 1933-34; assistant U.S. district attorney, 1934; prosecuting attorney, King County, Wash., 1934-36; U.S. House of Representatives, congressman from 1st Washington district, 1937-44, serving on the Alaskan International Highway Commission, Naval Affairs Committee, and Special House Committee on Post-War Military Policy; U.S. Senate, senator from Washington, 1944—, serving on

Commerce Committee, Appropriations Committee, Budget Committee, Democratic Policy Committee, and Democratic Senatorial Campaign Committee. *Military service:* U.S. Navy, 1941, served aboard U.S.S. *Enterprise* in South Pacific; became lieutenant commander.

MEMBER: International Oceanographic Foundation (life fellow), American Legion, Veterans of Foreign Wars, American Veterans of World War II, Sons of Norway, Elks, Eagles, Theta Chi, Order of the Coif, Washington Athletic Club of Seattle, Burning Tree, City Club. *Awards, honors:* Maritime man of the year award from Maritime Press Association, 1955; Chapter award, 1960, national board of directors award, 1961, and national man of the year award, 1962, all from National Defense Transportation Association; world trade award from Metropolitan Board of Trade, 1961; award from American Cancer Society, 1962; man of the year award from National Fisheries Institute, 1964; outstanding service award from Pacific Lutheran University, 1966; Wright brothers memorial trophy from National Aeronautic Association, 1968; distinguished service award from American College of Cardiology, 1972; Albert Lasker Award from Albert and Mary Lasker Foundation for public service in health, 1973; excalibur award for auto safety from National Motor Vehicle Advisory Council, 1974; admiral of the ocean sea award from Admiral of the Ocean Sea Awards Committee, 1975; award from National Science Foundation, 1975; named consumer of the year by National Consumers League, 1977. Honorary doctorates from Gonzaga University, 1966, Seattle University, 1967, St. Martin's College, 1967, University of Puget Sound, 1967, University of the Pacific, 1970, Gallaudet College, 1972, and University of Alaska, 1973.

WRITINGS: (With Jean Carper) *The Dark Side of the Marketplace,* Prentice-Hall, 1968; (with Elliot A. Segal) *How Much for Health?,* Luce, 1974.

SIDELIGHTS: Now the senior member of the Senate, Magnuson has been referred to by columnist Jack Anderson and consumer advocate Ralph Nader as one of the two most effective men in the Senate. He has long been recognized as a leader in such fields as health, consumer protection, the environment, human rights, education, transportation, and energy. His strong interest in consumer affairs and health-related issues generated two books, *The Dark Side of the Marketplace* and *How Much for Health?*

Magnuson's legislative accomplishments include bills that created the National Cancer Institute, the National Science Foundation, the Corporation for Public Broadcasting (PBS), the Agency for Consumer Advocacy, and the National Railroad Passenger Corporation (AMTRAK). Often referred to as "Mr. Oceanography," he has sponsored most of the ocean-related legislation in Congress, authoring the Ports and Waterways Safety Act of 1972, the Safe Drinking Water Act of 1974, and a 200-mile fishing limit bill. His ongoing activities concern the passage of a national no-fault auto insurance program, a national health insurance program, and continuing efforts to protect whales and other endangered species of animals.

Magnuson's two books demonstrate his special concern for consumer exploitation and national health care. Morton C. Paulson noted that *The Dark Side of the Marketplace* "could be the most important piece of consumer literature since Ralph Nader's *Unsafe at Any Speed.*" The book exposes several forms of fraudulent business practices, including bait-and-switch advertising, chain-referring selling, and costly auto repair flim-flams. *How Much for Health?,* his

second book, intends to "stimulate the people of this country to demand of their government those actions necessary to secure for each individual the right to reasonable health care." Magnuson proposes a six-part health program organized around research, prices, health care delivery systems, quality medical services, manpower and facility increases, and environmental health.

BIOGRAPHICAL/CRITICAL SOURCES: National Observer, July 18, 1968; *Dun's Review,* April, 1972; *Atlantic Monthly,* May, 1972; George Douth, *Leaders in Profile: The U.S. Senate,* Sperr & Douth, 1972.

*   *   *

MAHAN, William Allen   1930-

PERSONAL: Born July 9, 1930, in Port Townsend, Wash.; son of Leroy J. (a postal worker) and Madge (an executive secretary; maiden name, Allen) Mahan; married, April 20, 1955; divorced, April 3, 1973; children: Kerrigan Patrick, Colleen Shannon, Erin Kelly. *Education:* Attended State College of Washington (now Washington State University), 1948-49. *Home and office:* 3904 Berryman Ave., Los Angeles, Calif. 90066.

CAREER: Child actor in the Jones Family movies for Twentieth-Century-Fox, 1935-40, appearing in twenty-one films; associate film producer for Twentieth Century-Fox, 1963-65, producing "Take Her She's Mine" (1963), "What a Way to Go" (1964), and "Dear Brigitte" (1965); newspaper columnist for *Register* and *Tribune* syndicate, 1971-75; United Media Enterprises, Inc., Los Angeles, Calif., executive director of talent management division, 1979 —. Has also worked as a part-time literary agent, independent film producer, and as a film distribution negotiator in Central and South America. Lecturer. *Military service:* U.S. Navy, 1951-55. *Member:* Writers Guild of America, West, Film Editors Guild.

WRITINGS: What Is Your Name and Telephone Number?, Ashley Books, 1975; (with sister, Colleen Mahan) *The Moviola Man* (novel), Doubleday, 1979. Author of syndicated columns, "Inside the Tube," and "Outside Hollywood," 1971-75. Writer for television show, "Emergency," 1970.

WORK IN PROGRESS: The Boy Who Looked Like Shirley Temple.

SIDELIGHTS: After spending most of his life in the entertainment industry, William Mahan began writing quite by accident. One day while his wife and some other women were discussing the writing talents of columnist Jack Smith, Mahan challenged them by insisting anyone could write like that. Though he had no journalism experience, Mahan set out to prove his point by writing and submitting some columns of his own to various newspapers. After one paper agreed to print his column—for free—other papers accepted it too. Eventually it evolved into his two syndicated columns, "Inside the Tube" and "Outside Hollywood." Mahan's wife again spurred his writing career, in 1973, in a radically different way: by leaving him. Two years and many frustrated dates later, Mahan wrote of his experiences as a father of three in search of a mate in his first book, *What Is Your Name and Telephone Number?*

Mahan's newspaper columns, said Marinelle Duggan, are "centered around an interview with one celebrity, but spiced with anecdotes and adventures from his own life." In one column, for example, he recalled an incident when he, a nineteen-year-old disillusioned college student, and a friend, the then-aspiring actor David Janssen, tried unsuccessfully to enthuse two girls about "parking in a lonely spot, looking at the moon (there wasn't one) and playing soft music on the radio." Years later, though Janssen had made a name in television, he hadn't done the same in the movies. Mahan's column explained why. "Everyone thought he was the coming new Gable," Mahan quipped, "but I always knew better. Any guy that couldn't make two girls give a damn in a car at Lake Arrowhead could never be able to fill Rhett Butler's ears."

What Is Your Name and Telephone Number? is a sometimes comical, sometimes serious guidebook for the "newly available male." "Particularly," said Dave Nicolette, "one who is forty-two and hasn't dated in twenty years." Mahan's own search dragged him through "the gamut of personalities from swinger to feminist to tight wad to hooker to childhood sweetheart to Cosmo(politan) girl," wrote Patricia deLuna. Though he never succeeds in finding a wife for himself and a mother for his children, he "ends his story on a hopeful note," according to the *Los Angeles Herald Examiner*. "He is convinced the woman he is seeking is out there somewhere under the blazing California sun and as long as his verility and stamina—and bankroll—holds out he is determined to find her."

Mahan warned in his preface, however, that "this is a serious book. Although the experiences may seem funny to you, let me assure you that they were not funny to me. The point is, I overcame, I think." There is also a therapeutic aspect of the book, as Mahan continued: "It will serve to assure you ['the newly separated or divorced man'] that you're not a freak, a sex maniac nor ready for a trailer in some senior citizens' trailer park. It will lessen your anticipation, nerve strain, confusion, your hopes, dreams, agony and ultimate despair you are bound to face when you take on the world singlehanded, in that first year."

Mahan's varied background in entertainment and journalism is ideally suited for his new job at United Media Enterprises. The company has recently expanded, now scouting talent for book publishers and motion picture and television producers as well as for newspapers. Mahan is well aware of the need for such a service. "As a writer, a former actor and a producer, I've been on the other side of the desk," he said. "I know how tough it is for creative people—even the most gifted of them— to get agents and/or connections to realize their potentials. We want to be that agency—that connection."

BIOGRAPHICAL/CRITICAL SOURCES: Fort Worth Star-Telegram, August 18, 1971; *Richmond Times-Dispatch*, March 15, 1973; William Allen Mahan, *What Is Your Name and Telephone Number?*, Ashley Books, 1975; *Grand Rapids Press*, July 13, 1975; *Los Angeles Herald-Examiner*, August 31, 1975; *Long Beach Independent Press-Telegram*, August 31, 1975; *Editor & Publisher*, March 24, 1979.

*   *   *

MAJOR, Geraldyn Hodges 1894-
(Gerri Major)

PERSONAL: Born July 29, 1894, in Chicago, Ill.; daughter of Herbert and Mae (Powell) Hodges; married H. Bing A. Dismond, December 17, 1917 (divorced December 22, 1939); married John R. Major, June 6, 1946 (deceased). *Education:* University of Chicago, Ph.B., 1915; Chicago Teachers College, graduate degree in education, 1917; also attended Columbia University and New York University. *Politics:* Democrat. *Religion:* Episcopalian. *Home:* 2235 Fifth Ave., #10-C, New York, N.Y. 10037. *Office:* Johnson

Publishing Co., 1270 Avenue of the Americas, New York, N.Y. 10020.

CAREER: Pittsburgh Courier, Pittsburgh, Pa., New York society editor, 1924-27; *Interstate Tattler*, New York City, managing editor, 1927-32; women's editor, *Daily Citizen*, 1933-34; Bureau of Public Health Education and Information, New York City, administrative assistant, 1934-46; *New York Amsterdam News*, New York City, women's editor, 1948-53; Johnson Publishing Co., New York City, associate editor, 1953-67, head of Paris bureau, 1967-68, senior staff editor, 1967—. Director of Geraldyn Dismond Bureau of Specialized Publicity, 1924-34. Member of Northside Center for Child Development and Vocational Guidance and Workshop Center. Member of advisory board of Freedom National Bank.

MEMBER: Centro Studi e Scambi Internazionali, Academia Internazionale Leonardo da Vinci, National Association of Media Women (honorary life member), National Council of Negro Women, American Women in Radio and Television, National Association for the Advancement of Colored People (life member), Negro Actors Guild, Urban League of Greater New York, Capital Press Club, Alpha Kappa Alpha (founding member of Beta chapter). *Awards, honors:* Citations from Frontiers of America, 1950, Media Women, 1953, Dominican Press Association, 1959, African Cultural Society of the Dominican Republic, 1959, National Association of Fashion and Accessory Designers, 1962, Negro Business and Professional Women's Foundation, 1963, Alpha Kappa Alpha, 1966, and National Association of Colored Women's Clubs, 1966; received medal of honor from Centro Studi e Scambi Internazionali; honneur et merite decoration from Republic of Haiti, 1952; named honorary citizen of Boys' Town, 1952.

WRITINGS: (With Doris E. Saunders) *Gerri Major's Black Society*, Johnson Publishing (New York, N.Y.), 1976. Author of "Gerri Major's Society World," a column in *Jet*. Contributor to popular magazines, including *Black World*, *Ebony*, and *Black Stars*.

*   *   *

MAMLEYEV, Yuri 1931-

PERSONAL: Listed in some sources as Yury Mamleev; born December 11, 1931, in Moscow, U.S.S.R.; came to United States, 1975, naturalized U.S. citizen, 1980; son of Vitaly I. (a psychologist) and Zinaida P. (a translator; maiden name, Romanova) Mamleyev; married Farida Abidova (an assistant librarian), April 7, 1973. *Education:* Moscow Forestry Institute, M.S., 1955. *Politics:* Independent. *Home:* 705 East Seneca St., Ithaca, N.Y. 14850.

CAREER: Writer. Worked as teacher of mathematics at high schools in Moscow, U.S.S.R., 1959-70; private tutor of mathematics in Moscow, 1970-74; Cornell University, Ithaca, N.Y., lecturer in Russian literature, 1976-77.

WRITINGS: A Collection of Short Stories, translated by Bill Tjalsma, Taplinger, 1979. Also author of unpublished novels, *Shatuny* and *Sky Above Hell*. Contributor to periodicals, including *New Review, Gnosis, Russian Literary Triquarterly*, and *Question de*.

WORK IN PROGRESS: "The Unknown Russia, for Taplinger, which will be a study of dissident spiritual movements in contemporary Russia. They include mystical and occult movements oriented towards Eastern religions, old religious sects, new religious sects, spiritual movements among youth, the groups of Gurdjeff, etc."

SIDELIGHTS: Writing in the *New York Review of Books,* Carl Proffer called Mamleyev's prose "decadent" and "fantastic." He noted: "Mamleev writes about such Soviet *bizarreries* as a psychopathic vampire, a kind of bloodoholic, who is trying to stay on the wagon, or at least on the Moscow bloodmobile. . . . Crude scatalogical detail and spoofs of metaphysical fiction are also typical of Mamleev's work. . . ."

Mamleyev told *CA:* "I started to write in 1953. Still, before my emigration to the U.S. in 1975, I wrote three novels (one of them unfinished), about one hundred stories, a book of poems, and works of metaphysics. However, it was impossible to publish this in the Soviet official press for my writings were far away from the obligatory standards for Soviet art. Because of it, they were circulated in the Samisdat. Other kinds of my contact with the public were readings in private apartments.

"In my creative writings I combine the metaphysical problems with reflections on our modern life. I see in my writings the combination of the Eastern metaphysical approach with the tradition of display of 'the abyss of human soul' arising from Gogol and Dostoevski. On the other hand, some of my works simply reflect the sides of life in contemporary Russia unknown to the West: the life of unorthodox religions, mystical and erotical groups and sects, and their interconnection with the world of nonconformist artists and writers.

"At the same time, art for me is the way of world-knowledge and self-knowledge which is close to classical meditation and contemplation. In this sense, art, in my opinion, means the journey to unknown reality which, however, often has the mask of our usual reality. It is not 'fantastic' realism but penetration into hidden reality. Typical of such writing among my works is the chapter 'The Infernal Firmament' from my novel, 'Sky Above Hell.'"

BIOGRAPHICAL/CRITICAL SOURCES: New York Review of Books, February 19, 1976; *Times Literary Supplement,* May 6, 1977.

*   *   *

MANLEY, Michael Norman 1923-

PERSONAL: Born December 10, 1923, in Kingston, Jamaica; son of Norman W. (premier of Jamaica) and Edna (a sculptress and painter; maiden name, Swithenbank) Manley; married Beverly Anderson, 1972; children: Rachel Manley Ennevor, Joseph, Sarah, Natasha. *Education:* London School of Economics and Political Science, London, B.Sc., 1949. *Office:* Office of the Prime Minister, P.O. Box 272, Kingston 6, Jamaica.

CAREER: Journalist and broadcaster on "Caribbean News," British Broadcasting Corp., 1949-51; associate editor, *Public Opinion,* 1952; National Workers Union, Kingston, Jamaica, sugar supervisor, 1953-55, island supervisor and first vice-president, 1955-62; Government of Jamaica, Kingston, member of Senate, 1962-67, member of House of Representatives from central Kingston, 1967-72, prime minister, 1972—, minister of external affairs, 1972-75, economic affairs, 1972-75, defense, 1972—, youth and community development, 1974-75, and national mobilization and human resources development, 1977—. Jamaican representative to executive council of Caribbean Congress of Labour. President of People's National party, 1969—. President of Caribbean Bauxite Mineworkers and Metal Workers Federation, 1964-74. *Military service:* Royal Canadian Air Force, 1942-45. *Awards, honors:* Order of the Liberator (Venezuela), 1973; LL.D. from Morehouse College, 1973; Order of Jose

Marti (Cuba), 1975; gold medal from United Nations, 1978, for work against apartheid.

WRITINGS: The Politics of Change, Deutsch, 1974; *A Voice at the Workplace,* Deutsch, 1975; *The Search for Solutions,* Maple House Publishing, 1976.

AVOCATIONAL INTERESTS: Reading, music, gardening, boxing, tennis, cricket.

*   *   *

MANLEY, Seon

PERSONAL: Born in Connecticut; married Robert Manley (a management consultant); children: Shivaun (daughter). *Education:* Attended Wellesley College. *Home:* Greenwich, Conn.

CAREER: Writer and editor; has been employed in bookstores and in a publishing company.

WRITINGS: Adventures in Making: The Romance of Crafts Around the World, Vanguard, 1959; *Rudyard Kipling, Creative Adventurer,* Vanguard, 1965; *Long Island Discovery: An Adventure Into the History, Manners, and Mores of America's Front Porch,* Doubleday, 1966; *My Heart's in the Heather* (autobiography), Funk & Wagnalls, 1968; *Nathaniel Hawthorne: Captain of Imagination,* Vanguard, 1968; (with husband, Robert Manley) *Beaches: Their Lives, Legends, and Lore,* Chilton, 1968; *My Heart's in Greenwich Village* (autobiography), Funk & Wagnalls, 1969; (with R. Manley) *Islands: Their Lives, Legends, and Lore,* Chilton, 1970; (with Susan Belcher) *O Those Extraordinary Women; or, The Joys of Literary Lib,* Chilton, 1972; *Dorothy and William Wordsworth: The Heart of a Circle of Friends,* Vanguard, 1974; *The Ghost in the Far Garden, and Other Stories,* Lothrop, 1977.

Editor: *James Joyce: Two Decades of Criticism,* Vanguard, 1948, reprinted, 1963; *Teen-Age Treasury for Girls,* Funk & Wagnalls, 1958; *Teen-Age Treasury of Good Humor,* Funk & Wagnalls, 1960; (with R. Manley) *The Age of the Manager: A Treasury of Our Times,* Macmillan, 1962.

Editor, with sister Gogo Lewis: *Teen-Age Treasury of Our Science World,* Funk & Wagnalls, 1961; *Teen-Age Treasury of Imagination and Discovery,* Funk & Wagnalls, 1962; *Mystery! A Treasury for Younger Readers,* Funk & Wagnalls, 1963; *Teen-Age Treasury of the Arts,* Funk & Wagnalls, 1964; *Merriment! A Treasury for Young Readers,* Funk & Wagnalls, 1965; *Suspense: A Treasury for Young Adults,* Funk & Wagnalls, 1966; *The Oceans: A Treasury of the Sea World,* Doubleday, 1967; *Magic: A Treasury for Young Readers,* Funk & Wagnalls, 1967; *Polar Secrets: A Treasury of the Arctic and Antarctic,* Doubleday, 1968; *High Adventure: A Treasury for Young Adults,* Funk & Wagnalls, 1968; *To You With Love: A Treasury of Great Romantic Literature,* M. Smith, 1969; *Shapes of the Supernatural,* Doubleday, 1969.

A Gathering of Ghosts: A Treasury, Funk & Wagnalls, 1970; *Ladies of Horror: Two Centuries of Supernatural Stories by the Gentle Sex,* Lothrop, 1971; *Grande Dames of Detection: Two Centuries of Sleuthing Stories by the Gentle Sex,* Lothrop, 1973; *Mistresses of Mystery: Two Centuries of Suspense Stories by the Gentle Sex,* Lothrop, 1973; *Bewitched Beings: Phantoms, Familiars, and the Possessed in Stories From Two Centuries,* Lothrop, 1974; *Baleful Beasts: Great Supernatural Stories of the Animal Kingdom,* Lothrop, 1974; *Masters of the Macabre: An Anthology of Mystery, Horror, and Detection,* Doubleday, 1975; *Ladies of the Gothics: Tales of Romance and Terror by the Gentle Sex,*

Lothrop, 1975; *Ladies of Fantasy: Two Centuries of Sinister Stories by the Gentle Sex*, Lothrop, 1975; *Sisters of Sorcery: Two Centuries of Witchcraft Stories by the Gentle Sex*, Lothrop, 1976; *Women of the Weird: Eerie Stories by the Gentle Sex*, Lothrop, 1976; *Ghostly Gentlewomen: Two Centuries of Spectral Stories by the Gentle Sex*, Lothrop, 1977; *Masters of Shades and Shadows*, Doubleday, 1978.

SIDELIGHTS: Seon Manley's literary success has been very diverse. A *Young Readers Review* critique of *Nathaniel Hawthorne: Captain of the Imagination* noted that "one strength of the book lies in Manley's evocation of the times during which Hawthorne lived. But its main strength is in its picture of the creative artist as he struggles to put his inward vision on paper. This struggle to create, regardless of 'outside' influences and distractions, is yet dependent upon those very same 'outside' influences. This interaction between the environment and the creative spirit, which transmutes the artist's experiences into a work of art, is shown to the reader so that an appreciation of the difficulties and mysteries involved is inevitable. . . ."

Manley's autobiography, *My Heart's in the Heather*, was reviewed in the *New York Times Book Review:* "The structure of Seon Manley's book is as episodic as memory. Each episode is a delight. Mama is wholly Americanized, a dedicated admirer of the Revolutionary War heroine Molly Pitcher. Papa's heart remains in the heather. He never does take out naturalization papers, though he gives the United States credit for two world bargains: the Bill of Rights and the five-and-ten. The dialogue, especially between the children is superb."

Manley has edited several anthologies with her sister. In reviewing *Teen-Age Treasury of Our Science World*, a *Chicago Sunday Tribune* critic wrote, "This bright anthology . . . is not a series of dry articles on the state of various sciences today. It is instead, a collection of the warm and witty, live and lively things that have been said about science and scientists and about the people who enlarge the boundaries of knowledge." The *New York Times Book Review* added, "An unconventional, immensely provocative anthology. . . . Certain of the selections seem a little far-fetched, but the volume succeeds admirably in prodding the reader, who may have thought of science as a remote field for geniuses, into a realization of its breadth and immediacy."

BIOGRAPHICAL/CRITICAL SOURCES: New York Times Book Review, October 8, 1961, May 5, 1968; *Chicago Sunday Tribune*, November 12, 1961; *Young Readers Review*, May, 1969; *Children's Literature Review*, Volume 3, Gale, 1978.*

* * *

MANN, John H. 1928-

PERSONAL: Born July 15, 1928, in New York, N.Y.; son of Harvey T. and Edna (Brand) Mann; married Carola Honroth, August 18, 1955 (divorced January, 1970); children: Susan Elizabeth, Karen Patricia, Robert Christopher, Lisa Christina. *Education:* Harvard University, B.A., 1949; City College (now of the City University of New York), M.A., 1954; Columbia University, Ph.D., 1956. *Home:* 26 Linden St., Livonia, N.Y. 14487. *Office:* Department of Sociology, State University of New York College at Geneseo, Geneseo, N.Y. 14454.

CAREER: Market researcher for James M. Vicary, Inc., 1950; assistant director of Moreno Psychodramatic Institute, 1952-55; Columbia University, Teachers College, New York City, instructor in psychology, 1955-56; Russell Sage

Foundation, New York City, resident, 1956-57; New York University, New York City, assistant professor, 1957-60, associate professor of sociology, 1960-68; State University of New York College at Geneseo, professor of sociology, 1968—, head of department, 1968-72. Instructor at City College (now of the City University of New York), 1953-54; visiting professor at University of Wyoming, summer, 1954. Program coordinator for Columbia University's Center for the Improvement of Group Procedures, 1954-55; research associate of National Training Laboratories, summer, 1957; research coordinator for Jewish Board of Guardians, 1964-65; director of Center for the Exploration of Human Potential, 1966—; consultant to U.S. Children's Bureau and Stanford Research Institute.

MEMBER: American Psychological Association, American Sociological Association, American Academy of Psychotherapists, New York State Psychological Association, New York Society of Clinical Psychologists. *Awards, honors:* National Institute of Mental Health grants, 1957-58, 1964-66; U.S. Air Force grant, 1957-59; Russell Sage Foundation grant, 1959-61; Office of Vocational Rehabilitation grant, 1961-63; grant from United Cerebral Palsy, Inc. 1962.

WRITINGS: Frontiers of Psychology, Macmillan, 1963; *Sigmund Freud*, Macmillan, 1964; *Louis Pasteur, Father of Bacteriology*, Scribner, 1964; *Behavioral Effects of Leadership Training*, National Center for the Exploration of Human Potential, 1966; *Changing Human Behavior*, Scribner, 1965; (contributor) B. Biddle and E. J. Thomas, editors, *Social Role: Readings in Theory and Application*, Wiley, 1966; (editor with Herbert Otto) *Human Potentialities: The Challenge and the Promise*, Warren Green, 1967; (editor with Otto) *Ways of Growth*, Grossman, 1968.

Encounter: A Weekend With Intimate Strangers, Grossman, 1970; *Learning to Be*, Free Press, 1972; (with M. Richard) *Exploring Social Space*, Free Press, 1973; *Students of the Light*, Grossman, 1973; (contributor) D. L. Ford, editor, *Minority Group Problems: An Experiential Handbook*, University Associates, 1974. Contributor of more than twenty articles to psychology and sociology journals.

WORK IN PROGRESS: Before the Sun.

* * *

MARCEAU, Marcel 1923-

PERSONAL: Born March 22, 1923, in Strasbourg, France; son of Charles (a butcher) and Anne (Werzberg) Mangel; married Huguette Mallet (an actress; divorced); married Ella Jaroszewicz, June 16, 1966; children: Michel, Baptiste. *Education:* Attended School of Dramatic Art of Sarah Bernhardt Theatre, 1946. *Home:* 28 Bercheres-sur vesgre, France. *Agent:* Ronald A. Wioford Associates, Inc., 119 West 57th St., New York, N.Y. 10019. *Office:* Theatre de la Musique, 70 rue Reaumur, Paris 3, France.

CAREER: Actor and pantomimist. Actor in stage productions for Barrault-Renaud, Co., including "Baptiste," 1946, and "Praxitele and the Golden Fish," 1946, and for Compagnie de Mime Marcel Marceau, including "Bip Goes to the Park," 1947, and "Un Pierrot de Montmartre," 1951; actor in motion pictures, including "Mic-Mac," 1950, "The Overcoat," 1951, "Pantomimes," 1954, and "Un jardin public," 1955; appeared on television shows, including "The Ed Sullivan Show," 1956, and "The Victor Borge Show," 1963. Has toured with own mime company throughout the world. *Military service:* Served in French Underground, 1944; also served in French Army. *Awards, honors:* Deburan Prize, 1948, for "Mort avant L'Aube"; Emmy Award from Academy of Television Arts and Sciences, 1955.

WRITINGS: (With Jean Dorcy, Etienne Decroux, and Jean-Louis Barrault) *A la rencontre de la mime et des mimes*, Neuilly-sur-Seine, 1958, translation by R. Speller and Pierre de Fontnouvelle published as *The Mime*, R. Speller, 1961; (and illustrator) *The Story of Bip* (juvenile), Harper, 1976.

SIDELIGHTS: Marceau was first inspired to become a mime when only a child. His mother had taken him to see some of Charlie Chaplin's films and soon afterward, he began mimicking birds and even vegetation. During World War II, Marceau performed before troops and in 1946, he enrolled in an acting school. There he learned mime under the tutelage of Etienne Decroux, who had earlier taught the famous mime and actor Jean-Louise Barrault.

In a company of actors studying with Barrault, Marceau achieved success for his interpretation of Arlequin, a role taken from one of Barrault's most successful films, "The Children of Paradise." The high praise Marceau received persuaded him to pursue a career in mime. In 1947, a performance of his own act, "Praxitele and the Golden Fish," also garnered favorable reviews and Marceau's career was underway.

By 1947, Marceau had developed his own mime persona, a character named Bip who was inspired from Pip in Charles Dickens's *Great Expectations*. As Bip, Marceau toured Switzerland, Belgium, Italy, and Holland. When he returned to France for a number of performances in 1951, his audience began to grow beyond the cult following he'd developed outside the country. He eventually played in Israel and on television in England.

When Marceau finally performed in the United States in 1956, he limited his shows to brief pantomimes (as opposed to the more elaborate, lengthier stories he'd been acting out in Europe). Marceau justified this change in the show by claiming that American audiences would have to appreciate and understand mime at its simplest before they'd be able to enjoy the more complex performances.

In the last twenty years, Marceau has solidified his reputation as the world's greatest mime. He has toured North America fifteen times, often playing at universities which he calls "the flower of America." And in Mel Brooks's film, "Silent Movie," Marceau had the only speaking part. So far, Marceau has shown no sign of easing his pace. "I feel much more exhausted when I don't play," he told *Horizon* magazine. "I am at my strongest point now. If I wouldn't perform, my physical ability would slow down. At my age I have to be in my mime world all the time. When I sense that I am not as strong as I am now, I will stop."

Marceau sees himself as a performer, not an entertainer. "The difference between an entertainer and a performer is that the performer imprints a deep dramatic effect on the public's mind. If I do the fish, I become the fish, I breathe the water. It's no more to show; it's to live." He also revealed that his profession is much more demanding than one would think. "I am not frustrated as a mime, but I am anxious. The craft is there, the possibility of perfection. Mime, for me is an art that captures without words the essence of man. I don't like mime to look nice or cute. It must be tense."

BIOGRAPHICAL/CRITICAL SOURCES: Dance, July, 1975; *Horizon*, April, 1978; *People*, February 12, 1979.*

* * *

MAREMAA, Thomas 1945-

PERSONAL: Born September 3, 1945, in Austria; son of Edgar and Elsa (Lasu) Maremaa; married Mollyanne Brewer (a graphic designer), October 23, 1971. *Education:* Dartmouth College, A.B., 1967; graduate study at University of Zurich, 1967-68; University of California, Berkeley, M.A., 1970. *Home address:* P.O. Box 768, Bolinas, Calif. 94924. *Agent:* Perry H. Knowlton, Curtis Brown Ltd., 575 Madison Ave., New York, N.Y. 10022.

CAREER: U.S. Peace Corps, Washington, D.C., English teacher in Turkey, beginning in 1969. *Awards, honors:* James B. Reynolds fellowship for Zurich, 1967-68.

WRITINGS: Studio (novel), Morrow, 1978; *1937* (novel), Morrow, 1980. Contributor to newspapers.

SIDELIGHTS: Maremaa comments: "I write novels—and to me, novels are history, a way of passing on what we know to those coming after us. My concern, as it must be for any writer now, is with the survival of the species."

* * *

MARESCA, Thomas Edward 1938-

PERSONAL: Born February 5, 1938, in Jersey City, N.J.; married. *Education:* St. Peters College, B.A., 1959; Johns Hopkins University, M.A., 1961, Ph.D., 1963. *Home:* 30 Fifth Ave., New York, N.Y. 10011. *Office:* Department of English, State University of New York at Stony Brook, Stony Brook, N.Y. 11790.

CAREER: Ohio State University, Columbus, assistant professor of English, 1965-67; State University of New York at Stony Brook, associate professor, 1968-75, professor of English, 1975—. *Member:* Modern Language Association of America, American Society for Eighteenth-Century Studies, Northeast Modern Language Association, New York Eighteenth-Century Seminar. *Awards, honors:* Fellow of Humanities Center at Johns Hopkins University, 1967-68.

WRITINGS: Pope's Horatian Poems, Ohio State University Press, 1967; *Epic to Novel*, Ohio State University Press, 1974; (contributor) *Essays in Honor of Earl R. Wasserman*, Johns Hopkins Press, 1975; (with E. G. Schreiber) *Bernardus Silvestris's Commentary on the Aeneid: A Translation and Introduction*, University of Nebraska Press, 1979; *Three English Epics* (studies of *Troilus and Criseyde, The Faerie Queene*, and *Paradise Lost*), University of Nebraska Press, 1979. Contributor of articles and reviews to language and humanities journals.

* * *

MARIL, Nadja 1954-

PERSONAL: Born March 24, 1954, in Baltimore, Md.; daughter of Herman (an artist) and Esta (a psychiatric social worker; maiden name, Cook) Maril; married Cyril J. Patrick (in business), August 26, 1978. *Education:* Attended Smith College, 1972-73; University of California, Santa Barbara, B.A. (cum laude), 1975. *Home:* 12-A Howland St., Provincetown, Mass. 02657. *Office:* J. C. Patrick Ltd., P.O. Box 657, Provincetown, Mass. 02657.

CAREER: Community Council, Isla Vista, Calif., communications coordinator, 1975-76; Tres Condados Girl Scout Council, Santa Barbara, Calif., secretary, 1976-77; freelance writer in Baltimore, Md., 1977-78; Gryphon Gifts and Gallery, Provincetown, Mass., manager, 1979—. Manager of antiques, gifts, and art work at J. C. Patrick Ltd.; director of Cottage Gallery, summer, 1979. Literary secretary to Kenneth Rexroth, 1976. Member of board of directors of Isla Vista Food Cooperative, 1974; secretary of Provincetown Democratic Town Committee, 1979—. *Member:*

Women Writers Guild, Lower Cape League of Women Voters (member of board of directors, 1978-79).

WRITINGS: Me, Molly Midnight, the Artist's Cat (juvenile), Stemmer House, 1977; *Molly's Adventures Out-of-Doors,* Stemmer House, in press. Contributor to newspapers.

WORK IN PROGRESS: The Truth According to Hilary and Carlos, a novel, publication expected in 1981.

SIDELIGHTS: Maril comments: "*Me, Molly Midnight* is a true story inspired by my interest in conveying the artist's point of view in formulating his work—in this case, paintings. My goal in writing for children is to instruct and entertain at the same time.

"My current novel, *The Truth According to Hilary and Carlos,* presents a series of events from two different people's perspectives at different times. The time periods are merely illusionary since I believe all events occur simultaneously. As three dimensional creatures we experience time in a linear fashion. The characters in my novel are somewhat aware of their limited prospective of time but they are not aware of the entirely different conceptions of reality each of them have painted."

BIOGRAPHICAL/CRITICAL SOURCES: Baltimore Sun, December 18, 1977.

*   *   *

MARITAIN, Jacques 1882-1973

PERSONAL: Born November 18, 1882, in Paris, France; died April 28, 1973, in Toulouse, France; son of Paul (a lawyer) and Genevieve (Favre) Maritain; married Raissa Oumanoff (a poet and writer), November 26, 1904 (died, 1960). *Education:* Sorbonne, University of Paris, agrege and docteur en philosophie, 1905; studied biology at University of Heidelberg, 1905-08; studied philosophy of Thomas Aquinas with Pere Clerissac. *Home:* Residence provinciale des Dominicains, avenue Lacordaire, 31, Toulouse, France.

CAREER: French philosopher and Roman Catholic theologian; writer. Did editorial work for Maison Hachette (publishing company), Paris, France, c. 1908-11; Institut Catholique, Paris, professor of modern history and philosophy, 1913-39; visiting professor at Columbia University, New York City, and Princeton University, Princeton, N.J. and professor at Institute of Mediaeval Studies, Toronto, Ontario, 1940-44; French ambassador to the Vatican, 1945-48; Princeton University, professor of philosophy, 1948-53, professor emeritus, 1953-73. Teacher at College Stanislas, Paris, 1912-14, 1915-16, and at Petit Seminaire, Versailles, France; guest lecturer at University of Chicago, 1938; vice-president of Ecole Libre des Hautes Etudes (Franco-Belgian University), New York City. Lectured widely in Europe, North America, and South America. *Awards, honors:* Grand prix de litterature from the Academie Francaise, 1961; Grand prix national des lettres, 1963; commander of the Legion of Honor and of the Order of St. Gregory the Great; medal of the French Resistance; Grand Cross of the Order of Pius IX; Doctor ad honorem from Congregation of Studies in Rome.

WRITINGS: La Philosophie bergsonienne (essays), M. Riviere, 1914, revised and augmented edition, 1930, translation by Mabelle Louise Andison and J. Gordon Andison published as *Bergsonian Philosophy and Thomism,* Philosophical Library, 1955; *Art et scholastique,* Librarie de l'art catholique, 1920, translation by J. O'Connor published as *The Philosophy of Art,* 1923, translation of revised French edition by J. F. Scanlan published as *Art and Scholasticism,*

Scribner, 1930, published with translation of "Frontieres de la poesie" by Joseph W. Evans as *Art and Scholasticism, and The Frontiers of Poetry* (also see below); (with wife, Raissa Maritain) *La Vie d'oraison,* privately printed, 1922, translation by Algar Thorold published as *Prayer and Intelligence,* Sheed & Ward, 1928; *Antimoderne,* Editions de la revue des jeunes, 1922; *Theonas; ou, Les Entretiens d'un sage,* [Paris], 1925, translation by F. J. Sheed published as *Theonas: Conversations of a Sage,* Sheed & Watson, 1933, reprinted, Books for Libraries Press, 1969; *Trois Reformateurs: Luther–Descartes–Rousseau,* Plon-Nourrit, 1925, revised and augmented edition, 1939, translation published as *Three Reformers: Luther–Descartes–Rousseau,* Sheed & Ward, 1928, Crowell, 1929, reprinted, Greenwood Press, 1970; *Response a Jean Cocteau,* Stock, 1926; *Primaute du spirituel,* Plon, 1927, translation by Scanlan published as *The Things That Are Not Caesar's,* Scribner, 1930; (author of preface) Leon Bloy, *Lettres a ses filleuls,* [France], 1928.

Religion et culture, Desclee de Brouwer, 1930, translation by Scanlan published as *Religion and Culture,* Sheed & Ward, 1931; *Le Docteur angelique,* Bruges, 1930, translation by Scanlan published as *The Angelic Doctor: The Life and Thought of Saint Thomas Aquinas,* Dial Press, 1931, published as *St. Thomas Aquinas, Angel of the Schools,* Sheed & Ward, 1933, published as *St. Thomas Aquinas,* Sheed & Ward, 1938, newly translated and revised edition by Evans and Peter O'Reilly, Meridian Books, 1958; *Elements de philosophie,* 2nd edition, [Paris], 1930, Volume I: *Introduction generale a la philosophie,* translation by E. I. Watkin published as *An Introduction to Philosophy,* Sheed & Ward, 1930, Volume II: *L'Ordre des concepts,* translation by Imelda Choquette published as *An Introduction to Logic,* Sheed & Ward, 1937, revised edition published as *Formal Logic,* c. 1960; *Descartes: textes suivas de debats au Studio franco-russe,* Cahiers de la quinzaine, 1931; *Reflexions sur l'intelligence et sur sa vie propre,* Desclee de Brouwer, 1931; *Le Songe de Descartes, suivi de quelques essais,* R. A. Correa, 1932, translation by Andison published as *The Dream of Descartes, Together With Some Other Essays,* Philosophical Library, 1944; *Distinguer pour unir; ou, Les Degres du savoir,* Desclee de Brouwer, 1932, 6th edition, revised and augmented, 1959, translation of second edition by Margot Adamson and Bernard Wall published as *The Degrees of Knowledge,* G. Bles, 1937, translation of fourth edition by Geraldddd B. Phelan published as *Distinguish to Unite; or, The Degrees of Knowledge,* Scribner, 1959; (editor) George Ghislain Dandoy, *L'Ontologie du Vedanta,* Desclee de Brouwer, 1932; *Du Regime temporel et de la liberte,* Desclee de Brouwer, 1933, translation by Richard O'Sullivan published as *Freedom in the Modern World,* Sheed & Ward, 1935, reprinted, Gordian Press, 1971; *De las philosophie chretienne,* Desclee de Brouwer, 1933, translation by Edward H. Flannery published as *An Essay on Christian Philosophy,* Philosophical Library, 1955; *Some Reflections on Culture and Art* (bilingual edition), University of Chicago Press, 1933; *Sept Lecons sur l'etre et les premiers pincipes de la raison speculative,* Pierre Tequi, 1934, translation published as *A Preface to Metaphysics: Seven Lectures on Being,* Sheed & Ward, 1939, reprinted, Books for Libraries Press, 1971.

Frontieres de la poesie et autres essais (essays; contains "Frontieres de la poesie," "Dialogues," "Trois Peintres: George Rouault, Gino Severini, Marc Chagall," and "La Cief des chants"), L. Rouart, 1935, translation of "Trois Peintres," "Dialogues," and "La Cief des chants" by E. de P. Matthews published as *Art and Poetry,* Philosophical Library, 1943, translation of "Frontieres de la poesie" by Evans published with *Art and Scholasticism* as *Art and Scholasticism, and The Frontiers of Poetry*, Scribner, 1962 (also see above); *Science et sagesse, suivi d'eclaircissements sur la philosophie morale*, Labergerie, 1935, translation by Wall published as *Science and Wisdom*, G. Bles, 1940; *La Philosophie de la nature; essai critique sur ses frontieres et son objet*, Peirre Tequi, 1935, translation by Imelda C. Bryne published as *The Philosophy of Nature*, Philosophical Library, 1951; *Lettre sur l'independance*, [Paris], 1935; *Humanisme integral: problemes temporels et spirituels d'une nouvelle chretienne*, F. Aubier, 1936, translation by Adamson published as *True Humanism*, Scribner, 1938, reprinted, Books for Libraries Press, 1970, revised translation by Evans published as *Integral Humanism: Temporal and Spiritual Problems of a New Christendom*, Scribner, 1968; *Questions de conscience: essais et allocutions*, Desclee de Brouwer, 1938; *Les Juifs parmi les nations*, Editions de cerf, 1938, translation published as *A Christian Looks at the Jewish Question*, Longmans, Green, 1939, reprinted, Arno Press, 1973 (published in England as *Antisemitism*, G. Bles, 1939); (with Raissa Maritain) *Situation de la poesie*, Desclee de Brouwer, 1938, 3rd edition, 1964, translation by Marshall Sutler published as *The Situation of Poetry: Four Essays on the Relations Between Poetry, Mysticism, Magic, and Knowledge*, Philosophical Library, 1955; *Quatre Essais sur l'esprit dans sa condition charnelle*, Desclee de Brouwer, 1939, revised edition, Al-Satie, 1956.

De la Justice politique: notes sur la presente guerre, Plon, 1940; *Scholasticism and Politics*, tranlation edited by Mortimer J. Adler, Macmillan, 1940, 3rd edition, G. Bles, 1954; *Ransoming the Time*, translated from the original French by Harry Lorin Bensse, Scribner, 1941, reprinted, Gordian Press, 1972 (published in England as *Redeeming the Time*, G. Bles, 1943); *Confession de foi*, Editions de la Maison francaise, 1941; (editor) *The Living Thoughts of Saint Paul*, Longmans, Green, 1941; *A Travers le desastre*, Editions de la Maison francaise, 1941, translation published as *France, My Country, Through the Disaster*, Longmans, Green, 1941; *Le Crepuscule de la civilisation*, 2nd edition, Editions de l'arbre, 1941, 3rd edition, 1944, translation by Lionel Landry published as *The Twilight of Civilization*, Sheed & Ward, 1943; *Les Droits de l'homme et la loi naturelle*, Editions de la Maison francaise, 1942, translation by Doris Anson published as *The Rights of Man and Natural Law*, Scribner, 1943, reprinted, Gordian Press, 1971; *Saint Thomas and the Problems of Evil*, translated from the original French by Mabelle Andison, Marquette University Press, 1942; *The Natural Law and Human Rights*, Christian Culture Press, 1942; *Education at the Crossroads* (lectures), Yale University Press, 1943; *Christianisme et democratie*, Editions de la Maison francaise, 1943, translation by Anson published as *Christianity and Democracy*, Scribner, 1944, reprinted, Books for Libraries Press, 1972; *Messages (1941-1944)*, Editions de la Maison francaise, 1945; *A Travers la victoire*, P. Hartmann, 1945; *The Person and the Common Good*, translated from the original French by John J. Fitzgerald, Scribner, 1947; *De Bergson a Thomas d'Auin* (essays), [Paris], 1947; *Court traite de l'existence et de l'existant*, P. Hartmann, 1947, translation by Lewis Galantiere and Gerald B. Phelan published as *Existence and the Existent*, Pantheon, 1948, new edition, 1964; *Raisons et raison: essais detaches*, Egloff, 1948, translation, with additional essays, published as *The Range of Reason*, Scribner, 1952; *La Signification de l'atheisme contemporain*, Desclee de Brouwer, 1949; *The Meaning of Human Rights* (lectures), [Philadelphia], 1949.

Neuf Lecons sur les notions premieres de la philosophie morale, Pierre Tequi, 1951; *Man and the State* (lectures), University of Chicago Press, 1951; (editor) Leon Bloy, *Pages*, Mercure de France, 1951; (contributor) Pierre Angel, editor, *Lettres inedites sur l'inquietude moderne*, Editions universelles, 1951; *George Rouault*, H. N. Abrams, 1952; *Creative Intuition in Art and Poetry* (lectures), Pantheon Books, 1953; *Approches de Dieu*, Alsatia, 1953, translation by Peter O'Reilly published as *Approaches to God*, Harper, 1954; *L'Homme et l'etat*, Presses universitaires de France, 1953; *On the Philosophy of History*, edited by Evans, Scribner, 1957; *Truth and Human Fellowship*, Princeton University Press, 1957; *Reflexions sur l'Amerique*, A. Fayard, 1958, translation published as *Reflections on America*, Scribner, 1958; *Sociologie et religion*, Librairie Artheme Fayard, 1958; *The Sin of the Angel: An Essay on a Re-Introduction of Some Thomistic Positions*, translated from the original French by William L. Rossner, Newman Press, 1959; (with Raissa Maritain) *Liturgie et contemplation*, Desclee de Brouwer, 1959, translation by Evans published as *Liturgy and Contemplation*, P. J. Kenedy, 1960; *Pour une philosophie de l'education*, Librairie Artheme Fayard, 1959.

La Philosophie dans la cite, Alsatia, 1960; *La Philosophie morale*, Gallimard, 1960, translation published as *Moral Philosophy: An Historical and Critical Survey of the Great Systems*, Scribner, 1964; *The Responsibility of the Artist*, Scribner, 1960; *Man's Approach to God*, Archabbey Press, 1960; *On the Use of Philosophy: Three Essays*, Princeton University Press, 1961; (author of introduction) Bruno de Jesus-Marie, *Saint Jean de la Croix*, Desclee de Brouwer, 1961; *The Education of Man: Educational Philosophy*, edited by Donald Gallagher and Idella Gallagher, Doubleday, 1962; *La Fine del Machiavellismo*, La Locusta, 1962; *Dieu et la permission du mal*, Desclee de Brouwer, 1963, translation by Evans published as *God and the Permission of Evil*, Bruce Publishing Co., 1966; *Saint Paul*, McGraw, 1964; *Carnet de notes*, Desclee de Brouwer, 1965; *Le Paysan de la Garenne, un view laic s'interroge a propose du temps present*, Desclee de Brouwer, 1966, translation by Michael Cuddihy and Elizabeth Hughes published as *The Peasant of the Garonne: An Old Layman Questions Himself About the Present Time*, Holt, 1968; *De la Grace et de l'humanite de Jesus*, Desclee de Brouwer, 1967, translation by Evans published as *On the Grace and Humanity of Jesus*, Herder & Herder, 1969.

De l'Eglise du Christ: la personne de l'eglise et son personnel, Desclee de Brouwer, 1970, translation by Evans published as *On the Church of Christ: The Person of the Church and Her Personnel*, University of Notre Dame Press, 1973; *Approches san entraves*, Fayard, 1973; *Jacques Maritain, Emmanuel Mounier, 1929-1939* (correspondence), Desclee de Brouwer, 1973.

Collected works: Joseph W. Evans and Leon R. Ward, editors, *Challenges and Renewals: Selected Readings*, University of Notre Dame Press, 1966; Donald Gallagher and Idella Gallagher, editors, *A Maritain Reader: Selected Writings*, Image Books, 1966; Henry Bars, editor, *Oeurves, 1912-1939*, Desclee de Brouwer, 1975.

SIDELIGHTS: Jacques Maritain, considered one of the most important and influential philosophers and Catholic theologians, was born into a family of liberal Protestants. His father was a prosperous Burgundian lawyer and his mother was the daughter of Jules Favre, the French lawyer and politician who played an important role in the formation of the Third Republic. Although Paul Maritain was a Catholic, he left the education of young Jacques to his wife who brought up her son in the rationalist, republican, and humanist traditions of her own Protestant family.

Following his graduation from Lycee Henri IV, Maritain attended the Sorbonne where he pursued the study of literature and philosophy. It was at the Sorbonne that Maritain met Raissa, his future wife and colleague, in one of his classes. Raissa, a Russian Jewess, was also a student of philosophy and the arts and shared Maritain's own disillusionment with the trends in philosophy. Together they searched for "a framework of beliefs" that offered more meaning to life than that given by the schools of relativism and rationalism. A mutual friend at the university persuaded Jacques and Raissa to attend a lecture by Henri Bergson at the College de France. Bergson, whom Maritain would later oppose, spoke of a philosophy of intuition mixed with a belief in socialism. He offered a definite contrast to the rationalist and relativisitic explanations of life, but as Jacques later realized, did not explain "eternal verities."

Raissa and Jacques were married in 1904. Of his years at the Sorbonne, Jacques Maritain once said, "The best thing I owe to my studies at that time is that they brought me into touch with the woman who, ever since, in all my work, has always been at my side in a perfect and blessed union." But Raissa and Jacques were still disheartened by their inability to regain their lost faith and decided to make a suicide pact. They soon met Leon Bloy, a philosopher who was fiercely Catholic. Jacques persuaded Bloy to spend some time with them and after numerous sessions Raissa and Jacques decided to convert to Catholicism. In 1906, Raissa and Jacques were baptized along with Raissa's sister, Vera.

After Jacques received his agrege from the Sorbonne he went to Heidelberg to study biology under the direction of Hans Driesch, a scientist who was regarded by his colleagues as anti-materialist. Three years later Jacques and Raissa returned to Paris where he accepted a position with the publishing firm of Maison Hachette. Although Jacques was entitled to teach because of his degree, he recognized the anti-clericism in the academic world at the time and anticipated that he would not be free to teach according to his own beliefs.

It was Raissa who first discovered Thomas Aquinas. Jacques followed her lead and immersed himself in a study of the *Summa Theologica*. He began years of serious study of Aquinas with Pere Clerissac and emerged one of the leading proponents of Thomistic thought and Christian humanism. "Christian humanism, as Mr. Maritain elaborated it, was a subtle philosophy, an application of the principles of Thomas Aquinas, the 13-century scholastic, to 20th-century problems of art, science and society," wrote a *New York Times* columnist. It was Jacques Maritain's application of Thomistic doctrine to contemporary problems that branded him as a liberal and left-wing Catholic.

Maritain held that Catholic dogma was "eternally true," but that it needed to focus on the world and society in its present condition. His endorsement of the worker-priest movement in France after the Second World War caused an uproar among Vatican officials and theologians alike. But Maritain firmly held to his belief that "the church should open itself to the world as it is," and saw the worker-priest movement as the exemplification of "pastoral Catholicism."

Maritain taught Thomistic thought and doctrine at numerous colleges and universities throughout the United States and Europe, both Catholic and non-Catholic. He began his academic career in 1913 with a post at the Institut Catholique in

Paris. In 1940, Maritain began a lecture tour in the United States and was forced to cancel his return to France because of World War II. During the war Jacques and Raissa lived mainly in Greenwich Village. There Jacques attended daily mass at the nearby parish, St. Joseph, and, in the evening, gave parties with Raissa during which "lofty conversation flowed easily in both French and English as the guests and hosts consumed peanuts and sipped ginger ale."

During his lifetime Jacques Maritain wrote more than seventy books on philosophy, most of which addressed some facet of Thomistic thought. His first book, *Bergsonian Philosophy and Thomism,* was a criticism of Henri Bergson's philosophy of intuition. His next book, *Art and Scholasticism,* was a compilation of essays and articles on the academic attitude toward art. Included in this volume is the essay *The Frontiers of Poetry* which considered the possibility of a Christian revival for the aesthetics instead of the existing materialistic and degenerate attitudes toward contemporary art.

According to a *Times Literary Supplement* critic, Maritain in *Art and Scholasticism* "writes with a detachment which is as flawless as his sincerity; he never confuses theory and practice, or preaches when he has undertaken to explain. His perfect manners, his penetrative and subtly ramifying exposition, exercise a Circean charm on the emancipated reader." But a *New Statesman* reviewer disagreed: "Maritain has thrown off humility and in donning the raiment of pride he has led the world towards falsehood and the abyss. Yet when the modern artist, or even the Oriental artist, happens to accomplish a good piece of work, M. Maritain claims him as one of his elect. He builds up his theory of distinction, but refuses to say where it begins or ends. He is at once exclusive, and when it serves his purpose, all embracing. He weakens his argument by attempting to be on both sides at the same time."

Maritain followed *Art and Scholasticism* with the publication of *Antimoderne,* a collection of magazine articles on the problems of modern thought written during the early 1900's. In that same year, 1922, Raissa's and Jacques's first collaboration, *Prayer and Intelligence,* was published. His book *Three Reformers: Luther—Descartes—Rousseau,* an examination of the characters and the beliefs of the three reformers, caused somewhat of an uproar and was labeled controversial from the outset.

M. M. Colum observed: "No one can call this book of Maritain's an easy or a simple book; there flow through it the currents of a dozen streams of high intellectual contemporary thought. The author is profoundly religious, with that mystical and intellectual Catholicism backed by philosophy that seems almost the peculiar property of the Latin-peoples. His mind is totally unlike any other mind that I know of in writing today." A *Christian Century* reviewer called *Three Reformers* "a brilliant, provocative . . . interpretation of the characters and influences of the three reformers named, and incidentally of the course of civilization from the reformation to the French revolution." "While the author's major argument," the critic continued, "is completely vitiated by his devotion to the idea of ecclesiastical authority as the criterion of truth and of solidarity under the guidance of the church as the formula for the organization of society, many of the details of his criticism are penetrating and suggestive."

The controversial nature of the work stemmed from Maritain's analysis of the reformers through the eyes of a fervent, albeit left-wing, Catholic. Dino Ferrari found that "there is some wisdom to be garnered from his book, but it is, unfortunately, clouded by the controversial character of the writing.'' In spite of the biased nature of the work, a *Times Literary Supplement* critic determined that ''his essays are worth reading both for their individual merit and because they indicate a very significant current of contemporary thought.''

An Introduction to Philosophy is one of the books Maritain wrote during his employment with Institut Catholique at the request of his superiors. Described as an outline for beginners, *Introduction* has drawn praise from numerous critics. According to a *Catholic World* reviewer, ''One cannot imagine a clearer and more helpful guide for the beginner wishing to obtain his bearings in the subject and to work towards a complete and proportioned view of the whole system. The section on pure metaphysics—ontology—is a triumph of lucid exposition and a stimulating lesson in clear thinking.'' John Bakeless stated: ''It is a work typical of the best French scholarship—that is, it is accurate, logical, clear and charmingly written. Severe orthodoxy has not had such a defender for some years, formidable at once in his vigor and his ability to win a sympathetic comprehension for his point of view. Those who cannot agree with M. Maritain—and they will be many, including me—will at least be grateful to him for an admirable statement of the chief problems of all thought, and a clear indication where those who do not like his solutions can go to get others.''

Considered one of his major works, *The Degrees of Knowledge* is pure and heavy Maritain. As E. A. Moody noted: ''Among contemporary philosophers who draw inspiration from the writings of St. Thomas Aquinas, Jacques Maritain is outstanding for his courage, his intellectual vitality, and his contagious enthusiasm for the pursuit of wisdom. In *The Degrees of Knowledge* these qualities are apparent on every page. The book is not easy to read . . . and its metaphysical orientation will no doubt seem anachronistic to many readers. But it is the work of a truly philosophic mind, and he who passes it by because he is sure of disagreeing with it, closes the door to an illuminating intellectual adventure.''

''I have no space,'' wrote C.E.M. Joad of *Degrees*, ''in which to indicate the scope and grandeur of this book. I do not agree with its premises or with many of its conclusions, and it moves within a universe of discourse different from mine. Yet it is impossible to read it without realising that one is making contact with the mind of a great man expressing with noble dignity and eloquence the conclusions of an intelligence of uncommon power.''

True Humanism is another work which ranks as the best of Maritain. It is in this book that Maritain firmly states that the spiritual and temporal planes of man's existence are distinct, ''as the things which are Caesar's and the things which are God's.'' But he warned: ''They are distinct, they are not separate. To make Christianity an abstraction, to put God and Christ on one side while I work in things of the world, is to cut myself in two halves: one Christian half for the things of eternal life—and one for things of time, a pagan or semi-Christian or ashamedly Christian or neutral half.''

''In its essential humility and in the integrity of its endeavour,'' wrote Desmond Hawkins, ''*True Humanism* is a deeply challenging book. Even in disagreement, and abetted by an uncomfortable translation, it would be impossible not to be impressed by the nobility and lucidity of M. Maritain's argument. Those who wish to understand the Christian attitude to contemporary politics will find it here, expressed with an exacting precision which must spur the reader to clarify and sharpen his own beliefs.'' W. N. Pittenger

agreed: ''Sometimes a book comes to one's attention, and on first glancing through it one thinks it is 'just another volume to be read.' Then one begins to get into it, and soon one feels that one should stand up and cheer, so stimulating is its reading. That is the way the present book impressed the reviewer. It is so sane, so clear, so profound, so brave, and with all the qualifications one may make at point after point.''

Maritain's *The Peasant of the Garonne* is perhaps his most controversial book and a disappointment to most liberals. As Daniel Callahan of *New Republic* observed, this book ''is likely to send his old admirers looking for a new exemplar.'' In this work Maritain criticized another important theologian, Pierre Teilhard de Chardin, for his questioning of accepted Catholic beliefs. *Garonne* also ''decried what Mr. Maritain regarded as dangerous consequences of Vatican II, especially a spirit of restiveness over church dogmas,'' the *New York Times* related. According to Callahan, *Garonne* ''is arrogant, unpleasantly coy at times, badly written and boring. Maritain draws on three main sources for his critique of the 'modernizers': his own earlier works, those of his poetess Raissa, and the Bible, in about that order of precedence. The result is a book which suggests that the main fault of the new theology is that it has forgotten Jacques Maritain.''

Reviewing one of Maritain's final works, *On the Church of Christ*, a *Christian Century* critic stated: ''Many will regret these late, rather cramped and crabby thoughts about the church by a Catholic giant of the century. But hidden in them is a love letter to the church, a search for what is enduring, and a sometimes misguided or misleading attempt to sort out its true friends from its enemies. The accent is on church as persona—an infallible persona, that is.''

Maritain retired from public life in 1960 after the death of Raissa, but he still continued to exert influence over the Catholic Church where he was considered ''a pressure group of his own,'' and over the world at large. Francois Mauriac, Jean Hugo, Georges Rouault, and Jean Cocteau counted themselves among his admirers. Maritain was often consulted by church fathers, including Pope Pius XI and Pope Pius XII. In addition, his name appeared along with the names of cardinals and other members of church hierarchy in the encyclical *Populorum Progressio*. His books have appeared in numerous languages, including Spanish, Portuguese, German, Italian, Polish, and Vietnamese. Reinhold Niebuhr, the Protestant theologian, once said, ''Maritain belongs to that small company of great spirits in any age from whom one may learn.'' Pope Paul VI echoed these sentiments when he declared, ''I am a disciple of Maritain. I call him my teacher.''

BIOGRAPHICAL/CRITICAL SOURCES—Periodicals: *Times Literary Supplement*, November 8, 1928, April 10, 1930, May 22, 1930, January 22, 1938, January 28, 1939, March 12, 1971, April 5, 1974; *Catholic World*, September, 1929, November, 1930, January, 1931, September, 1933, May, 1939; *New York Evening Post*, May 11, 1929, August 30, 1930; *Books (New York Herald Tribune)*, May 19, 1929, July 6, 1930, July 10, 1938, April 9, 1939; *Saturday Review of Literature*, June 8, 1929; *Christian Century*, September 11, 1929, October 5, 1938, March 22, 1967, March 20, 1968, May 12, 1973, December 19, 1973; *New York Times*, December 22, 1929, August 10, 1930, March 24, 1967, November 14, 1971; *Saturday Review*, April 5, 1930, March 9, 1968; *Spectator*, April 5, 1930, August 16, 1930; *New Statesman*, April 26, 1930, May 10, 1930; *New Republic*, May 21, 1930, October 5, 1938, November 30, 1938, March 2, 1968; *Yale Re-*

view, autumn, 1930; *New Statesman & Nation,* March 12, 1938, April 22, 1939; *Commonweal,* March 23, 1934, June 1, 1934, July 13, 1934, December 7, 1934, December 28, 1934, May 27, 1938, December 23, 1938, October 13, 1939, November 24, 1939, April 12, 1968, August 15, 1975; *Journal of Philosophy,* December 22, 1938; *Best Sellers,* March 1, 1968; *Washington Post Book World,* March 24, 1968; *Books & Bookmen,* May, 1968; *Commentary,* September, 1968; *Manchester Guardian,* November 11, 1968; *New York Times Book Review,* November 14, 1971; *America,* May 12, 1973, February 23, 1974, June 14, 1975, April 8, 1978; *Time,* May 14, 1973; *Thought,* December, 1975; *Christianity Today,* October 6, 1978.

Books: Raissa Maritain, *Les Grandes Amities,* [New York], 1941, translation by Julie Kernan published as *We Have Been Friends Together,* Longmans, Green, 1942; R. Maritain, *Adventures in Grace,* translated from the original French by Kernan, Longmans, Green, 1945; John Howard Griffin and Yves R. Simon, *Jacques Maritain: Homage in Words and Pictures,* foreword by Anthony Simon, Magi Books, 1974; Joseph Amato, *Mounier and Maritain: A French Catholic Understanding of the Modern World,* University of Alabama Press, 1975; Kernan, *Our Friend, Jacques Maritain: A Personal Memoir,* Doubleday, 1975; Brooke Williams Smith, *Jacques Maritain: Anti-Modern or Ultramodern?,* Oxford University Press, 1976.

OBITUARIES: New York Times, April 29, 1973; *Newsweek,* May 7, 1973; *Time,* May 7, 1973; *Commonweal,* May 18, 1973; *Christianity Today,* May 25, 1973; *National Review,* May 25, 1973.*

*   *   *

MARKS, Eli S(amplin) 1911-

PERSONAL: Born December 15, 1911, in New York, N.Y.; son of Philip (an insurance agent) and Lizzie (Samplin) Marks; married Lily Brunschwig (a clinical psychologist), December 23, 1940; children: Phyllis Marks Maris, Judith Marks Marks, Alan. *Education:* Columbia University, A.B., 1932, M.A., 1933, Ph.D., 1935. *Politics:* Democrat. *Religion:* Jewish. *Home:* 4178 Suitland Rd., Suitland, Md. 20023. *Office:* U.S. Bureau of the Census, Washington, D.C. 20233.

CAREER: Fisk University, Nashville, Tenn., assistant professor of statistics and director of Statistics Laboratory, 1935-42; War Production Board, Washington, D.C., economist and statistician, 1942-43; Office of Price Administration, Washington, D.C., economist and statistician, 1943-46; National Office of Vital Statistics, Washington, D.C., sampling statistician, 1946-47; U.S. Bureau of the Census, Washington, D.C., head of response research unit, 1947-53; National Opinion Research Center, Chicago, Ill., senior study director of disaster project, 1953-56; National Analysts, Inc., Philadelphia, Pa., mathematical statistician, 1956-61; Case Institute of Technology (now Case Western Reserve University), Cleveland, Ohio, associate professor of behavior science, 1961-64; University of Pennsylvania, Philadelphia, research professor of statistics and operations research, 1964-72; U.S. Bureau of the Census, chief census research and technical adviser, 1972—. Associate professor at University of Chicago, 1953-56; lecturer at U.S. Department of Agriculture Graduate School, University of Michigan, and University of Alberta; visiting professor at Columbia University, spring, 1967. Technical assistant for Organization of American States missions to Chile, 1960, 1970, and U.S. Agency for International Development mis-

sions to Korea, 1970, 1973-74, and Paraguay, Venezuela, El Salvador, Colombia, Costa Rica, Honduras, Malaysia, Indonesia, the Philippines, and Vietnam; consultant to United Nations Food and Agriculture Organization and Population Council.

MEMBER: International Association of Survey Statisticians, International Statistical Institute, Inter-American Statistical Institute, American Psychological Association, American Statistical Association (member of board of directors), American Association for the Advancement of Science, American Public Health Association, American Association for Public Opinion Research, American Population Association.

WRITINGS: (With E. L. Hartley) *Psychology Work-Book,* Harper, 1933; *Housing Survey of Nashville, Tennessee, 1940,* Nashville Housing Authority, 1940; (with Charles S. Johnson and others) *Statistical Atlas of Southern Counties,* University of North Carolina Press, 1941; (with Frederick Mosteller, Herbert Hyman, and others) *The Pre-Election Polls of 1948,* Social Science Research Council, 1949; (with William Seltzer and Karol J. Krotki) *Population Growth Estimation: A Handbook of Vital Statistics Measurement,* Population Council, 1974; (contributor) Krotki, editor, *Developments in Dual System Estimation of Population Size and Growth,* University of Alberta Press, 1978. Contributor of about thirty articles to statistics journals and periodicals in the behavioral sciences.

*   *   *

MARQUAND, John P(hillips) 1893-1960

PERSONAL: Born November 10, 1893, in Wilmington, Del.; died July 16, 1960, in Newbury, Mass.; son of Philip (a civil engineer) and Margaret (Fuller) Marquand; married Christina Davenport Sedgwick, September 8, 1922 (divorced, May 19, 1935); married Adelaide Ferry Hooker, April 16, 1937 (divorced, 1958); children: (first marriage) John P., Jr., Christine; (second marriage) Blanche Ferry, Timothy Fuller, Elon Huntington Hooker. *Education:* Harvard University, B.A., 1915. *Residence:* Newbury, Mass.

CAREER: Boston Transcript, Boston, Mass., reporter and magazine writer, 1916; *New York Herald Tribune,* New York City, Sunday magazine feature writer, 1919-20; J. Walter Thompson (advertising agency), New York City, copywriter, 1921-22; writer, 1922—. Special consultant to the secretary of war, 1944-45. *Military service:* U.S. Army, Artillery, 1916-17; became first lieutenant. *Awards, honors:* Pulitzer Prize, 1938, for *The Late George Apley.*

WRITINGS—All novels, unless otherwise indicated: *The Unspeakable Generation,* Scribner, 1922; *Four of a Kind* (short stories and the short novel, *Only a Few of Us Left*), Scribner, 1923; *Lord Timothy Dexter of Newburyport, Mass.: First in the East, First in the West, and the Greatest Philosopher in the Western World* (biography), Milton, Balch, 1925, extensive revision with added commentary published as *Timothy Dexter Revisited,* Little, Brown, 1960; *The Black Cargo,* Scribner, 1925, reprinted, AMS Press, 1976; *Warning Hill,* Little, Brown, 1930, reprinted, Pyramid, 1964; *Haven's End* (short stories), Little, Brown, 1933, reprinted, Arno, 1977; *Ming Yellow,* Little, Brown, 1935; *No Hero,* Little, Brown, 1935, published as *Your Turn, Mr. Moto,* Berkley, 1963; *Thank You, Mr. Moto,* Little, Brown, 1936, reprinted, Popular Library, 1977 (also see below); *Think Fast, Mr. Moto,* Little, Brown, 1937, reprinted, Popular Library, 1977; *The Late George Apley: A Novel in the Form of a Memoir,* Little, Brown, 1937, reprinted, Franklin

Library, 1977 (also see below); *Mr. Moto Is So Sorry*, Little, Brown, 1938, reprinted, Popular Library, 1977 (also see below); *Mr. Moto's Three Aces* (omnibus), Little, Brown, 1938; *Wickford Point*, Little, Brown, 1939 (also see below).

Don't Ask Questions, R. Hale, 1941; *H. M. Pulham, Esquire*, Little, Brown, 1941 (also see below); *Last Laugh, Mr. Moto*, Little, Brown, 1942, reprinted, Popular Library, 1977; *So Little Time*, Little, Brown, 1943 (also see below); *It's Loaded, Mr. Bauer*, R. Hale, 1943; *Repent in Haste*, Little, Brown, 1945; (with George S. Kaufman) *The Late George Apley* (play, based on Marquand's novel of the same name; first produced in 1946), Dramatists Play Service, 1946 (also see above); *B. F.'s Daughter*, Little, Brown, 1946; *Point of No Return*, Little, Brown, 1949 (also see below); *Melville Goodwin, USA*, Little, Brown, 1951; *Thirty Years* (nonfiction and short stories), Little, Brown, 1954; *Sincerely, Willis Wayde*, Little, Brown, 1955; *North of Grand Central: Three Novels of New England* (omnibus; contains *The Late George Apley*, *Wickford Point*, and *H. M. Pulham, Esquire*, Little, Brown, 1956 (also see above); *Stopover: Tokyo*, Little, Brown, 1957; *Life at Happy Knoll* (short stories), Little, Brown, 1957; *Women and Thomas Harrow*, Little, Brown, 1958; *So Little Time* [and] *Point of No Return* (omnibus), Little, Brown, 1961 (also see above); *Thank You, Mr. Moto and Mr. Moto Is So Sorry: From the Saturday Evening Post* (omnibus), Curtis Publishing, 1977 (also see above).

Stories represented in anthologies, including *O. Henry Memorial Award Prize Stories*, 1932, and *Fifty Best American Short Stories*, edited by Edward J. O'Brien, 1939. Contributor of numerous stories to magazines, including *Saturday Evening Post*, *Ladies' Home Journal*, *Collier's*, *Harper's*, *Atlantic*, and *Sports Illustrated*. Member of editorial board of Book-of-the-Month Club, 1944-60.

SIDELIGHTS: Marquand is perhaps the most successful novelist of manners of mid-twentieth century America. His novels, which were immensely popular with the public and critics alike, are largely concerned with upper-class life in Boston and New England. Called by Charles A. Brady a "Martini-Age Victorian," Marquand gently satirized the nascent business and consumer oriented society. Randall Jarrell wrote, "It is romantic, miraculous almost, that Marquand should be here, straight out of *The Age of Innocence*, to observe this new age of adjusting to one's group, and sharing the experience of one's generation, and getting divorced because the president of one's corporation doesn't approve of one's wife, and all the rest of it."

Marquand wrote in the tradition of such social novelists as Ellen Glasgow, Edith Wharton, James Gould Cozzens, John O'Hara, and, most notably, Sinclair Lewis. Marquand repeatedly expressed his admiration for Lewis and once said: "I would hesitate to rank myself with Lewis; I don't think I have nearly the same stature. But I am working in his vineyard."

Marquand was born into the culture he satirized and throughout his works the paradoxical qualities of identification with the culture and distance from it are evident. Among his New England ancestors were former governors of the Massachusetts Bay Colony and the bluestocking Margaret Fuller. His early years were spent in New York City where his father was a wealthy broker. The senior Marquand's holdings were wiped out in the Panic of 1907, though, and he moved with his wife to Panama to work as an engineer on the canal construction. John was sent to the family home at Curzon's Mill, Massachusetts, to be raised by maiden aunts. For many generations the Marquand men had been educated

at Harvard University and John entered the class of 1915. Because of his family's reduced wealth, he had gone to a public high school and consequentially was at a disadvantage socially at Harvard.

In 1921, after working for a few years as a newspaper feature writer and as an advertising copywriter, Marquand began what would become a fifteen year apprenticeship in the craft of commercial writing with the publication of a short story in the *Saturday Evening Post*. Many of the stories he contributed to popular periodicals were published as serials and later relased as books. He learned his craft extremely well and by 1931, he had published fifty-nine short stoires and five serials in such mass-circulation magazines as *Ladies' Home Journal*, *Collier's* and *Saturday Evening Post*.

While the stories were seldom praised for their artistry, many of them are estimable works of entertainment. Marquand grew increasingly aware of the artistic limitations inherent in the genre and became "restless" to fuse the popular elements of his short stories with what he deemed to be the more significant elements of novels. In the foreword to a collection of his early stories Marquand explained why he was unhappy with some of the stories. He wrote: "Unfortunately there is no such thing as writing acceptable fiction, or even what are called 'pot-boilers,' with one's tongue in one's cheek. I have no desire to apologize for any of the stories that appear here, because each was the best I could do at the time I wrote it. Many show that I strove in various ways to reconcile popular writing with art, and I often overstrained myself in the process. Of necessity these stories lack depth and significance, qualities popular periodicals customarily avoid, and almost inevitably they reach a happy ending."

After an extended trip to the Far East, Marquand started writing his first "serious" novel—*The Late George Apley*. It first appeared as a serial in the *Saturday Evening Post* in 1936 and the following year it was published as a book. The novel was a huge success and Marquand received the Pulitzer Prize for it in 1938. His reputation as a serious novelist won, Marquand went on to write nine more major novels, each of them well-received.

The heroes of Marquand's mature novels were well-to-do businessmen, doctors, lawyers, or writers. He was unequaled in his depiction of the lives of the very rich. "None of our writers seems to know this milieu as intimately as does Marquand," Fadiman declared. "He has cut out for himself a specialty in which he is unrivaled." Bernard Dekle stated: "John P. Marquand was an author whose destiny compelled him to do only what he could do well. He was an acute and brilliant observer of upper-class manners. He had the sharp eye of the born reporter, the sensitive ear for speech, the gift of creating atmosphere and of projecting social types."

But Marquand's ambivalence towards the upper-class of his own origins is evident in his writing. While his perception was sharp, his depiction was not caustic. John Gross commented that Marquand's "satirical portraits were never etched in acid," and that "his judgments always tended to be highly tentative." He indentified with and had affection for many of the characters he satirized. The "Harvard Man," for example, figured in many of Marquand's novels and he portrayed him with gentle humor. Fadiman explained this in terms of Marquand's ambivalence. He wrote: "He understands the admirable loyalty, linking often with dazzling personal courage, that moves his prep-school boys and his Harvard golden lads. He understands too that this loyalty and this courage, like all virtues not mortised in philosophy, are limited because barren of attachment to a larger world.'"

Marquand regularly used the technique of flashback to tell the story of his main character's life. As he explained to a *Cosmopolitan* interviewer, "What interests me personally in fiction is to take my central character, not in his youth or early manhood, but when he is nearly through, when he is faced with an important decision in his life. I then prefer to have him go back to his early past."

Dekle characterized the typical Marquand novel and its hero. "It is usually the tale of an affluent half-disillusioned man searching his past trying to unravel his present, to extricate himself from the web in which accident and circumstance have entangled him," he remarked. "A Marquand hero is usually middle-aged, a conformer who, although he hates the rules, knows he must abide by them, for only by following accepted standards of belief and behavior can he function as the kind of human being he wants to be."

Because of the similarity of his work, Marquand has been accused of writing formula novels. Leo Gurko, for example, contended that the novels are "almost exactly alike. They deal with a fixed problem, and pass through identical stages in the course of working it out. Marquand's technical skill conceals this fact for a time creating the illusion of variety and change. But when it becomes plain, one realizes that here is the restricting element that has kept Marquand—and will probably always keep him—from reaching the level of his great predecessors."

Gross, however, argued that "what looks like formula is really more precisely a kind of compulsion which grows from a personal need to refigure the same sum again and again (and by 'sum' we mean a highly personal reading of life), always with the eternally undying hope that eventually a different result may be achieved." And according to Fadiman, Marquand's return to the same artistic ground was the basis for his growth as an artist. He declared: "Marquand's whole writing career may be thought of as a series of enlargements. Each of these enlargements stops short of complete escape. Thus the hallmark of his art is the tension resulting from the play between his precise memory of a smaller experience and his growing understanding of a larger one."

While the critic Alfred Kazin admired Marquand's talents as a social novelist and found his portraits to be drawn with "ease and skill," he was convinced that toward the end of his career Marquand suffered from the fate that writers of that genre are particularly susceptible to. He commented: "What has happened to Marquand's novels is perhaps due to the fact that the local traditions which have always represented class in this country have increasingly disappeared under the pressures of a technological society. The novelist of manners, like Marquand . . . who has always depended on a tradition stable enough to include the satirist himself, now finds himself angrily crying out against the absence of values themselves. . . . The social novelist in America pays for his lack of ideas when he is left without the social traditions on which he has depended so long for his sustenance as a man and for his achievement as an artist."

Gross suggested that Marquand's popularity rests with the fact that he was a preserver of traditional values in an era when they were rapidly disappearing. "It seems not unlikely that Marquand has won and retained a large following in the United States as a result of his rather stubborn insistence that some standards may be maintained in a world which appears willing to reject any such possibility," he wrote. "If, as has been asserted, it is in our day quite impossible to proclaim the absolute dedication to a moral code, Marquand provides the next best possibility—something, to be sure,

less than a moral code with absolute finality; but in lieu of a code, we have at least a sense of fidelity to standards reaffirmed, even if often more honored in the breach than in the observance."

Marquand's "Mr. Moto" novels were the basis for a popular series of motion pictures featuring Peter Lorre as the Japanese secret agent.

BIOGRAPHICAL/CRITICAL SOURCES—Selected books: Philip Hamburger, *J. P. Marquand, Esquire*, Houghton, 1952; Harold C. Gardiner, editor, *Fifty Years of the American Novel: A Christian Appraisal*, Scribner, 1952; introduction and foreword to *Thirty Years*, Little, Brown, 1954; Alfred Kazin, *Contemporaries*, Little, Brown, 1958; Maxwell Geismar, *American Moderns: From Rebellion to Conformity*, Hill & Wang, 1959; John J. Gross, *John P. Marquand*, Twayne, 1963; Walter Allen, *The Modern Novel: In Britain and the United States*, Dutton, 1964; Bernard Dekle, *Profiles of Modern American Authors*, Tuttle, 1969; Stephen Birmingham, *Late John Marquand: A Biography*, Lippincott, 1972; *Contemporary Literary Criticism*, Gale, Volume 2, 1974, Volume 10, 1979.

Selected periodicals: *Life*, July 31, 1944; *Cosmopolitan*, March, 1947, August, 1959; *New York Times Book Review*, April 24, 1949; *Commentary*, May, 1950; *American Scholar*, October, 1952; *Harper's*, November, 1954; *Atlantic*, September, 1956, October, 1960; *Newsweek*, June 19, 1972.*

* * *

MARQUES, Rene 1919-1979

OBITUARY NOTICE: Born in 1919 in Arecibo, Puerto Rico; died March 22, 1979, in San Juan, Puerto Rico. Writer. Marques was one of Puerto Rico's best-known and most widely acclaimed authors. Among his works are the play, "The Oxcart," the novel, *The Evening of Man*, and the short story collection, *Another Day of Ours*. Obituaries and other sources: *Who's Who in the World*, 2nd edition, Marquis, 1973; *New York Times*, March 25, 1979.

* * *

MARSDEN, Lorna R(uth) 1942-

PERSONAL: Born March 6, 1942, in British Columbia, Canada; daughter of J. E. and Grace (Simister) Bosher; married in 1961. *Education:* University of Toronto, B.A., 1968; Princeton University, Ph.D., 1972. *Office:* Department of Sociology, University of Toronto, 563 Spadina Ave., Toronto, Ontario, Canada.

CAREER: University of Toronto, Toronto, Ontario, assistant professor, 1972-76, associate professor of sociology, 1976—, head of department, 1977—. Vice-president of Liberal Party of Canada, 1975—. Member of Ontario Committee on the Status of Women, 1971—; president of National Action Committee on the Status of Women, 1975-77; founding member of Canadian Research Institute for the Advancement of Women, 1975—.

MEMBER: Canadian Sociology and Anthropology Association, Canadian Population Society, Women in Canadian Anthropology and Sociology, American Sociological Association, Population Association of America, University of Toronto Faculty Association (vice-president, 1976-77).

WRITINGS: Population Probe, Copp, 1972; (editor with Edward B. Harvey) *Canadian Population Concerns*, Population Research Foundation, 1977; (with Harvey) *The Fragile Federation: Social Change in Canada*, McGraw, 1979.

Contributor: E. B. Harvey, editor, *Perspectives in Modernization*, University of Toronto Press, 1972; B. Schlesinger, editor, *Family Planning in Canada*, University of Toronto Press, 1974; Patricia Marchak, editor, *The Working Sexes*, Institute of Industrial Relations, University of British Columbia, 1977; Audrey Whipper, editor, *Collection in Honour of Oswald Hall*, McClelland & Stewart, 1979.

Contributor of about twenty articles to professional and popular journals, including *Canadian Forum, Atlantis*, and *Ontario Naturalist*. Editor of *Bulletin* of Canadian Sociology and Anthropology Association, 1974-76; member of editorial board of *Journal* of Addiction Research Foundation, 1978-80.

WORK IN PROGRESS: Research on the medical profession in Canada.

SIDELIGHTS: Marsden has concentrated her writing activities in the areas of population studies, female participation in the labor force, and social movements in Canada. But she has also written about such diverse subjects as air and noise pollution, community library use, alcoholism among women, and preventive dental health education in public schools. Her research includes work with Chilean refugees, and the fertility of immigrant women in Canada.

*   *   *

MARSH, Jeri 1940-

PERSONAL: Born August 16, 1940, in Mansfield, Ohio; daughter of Robert E. (a teacher) and Geraldine (a teacher; maiden name, Hostetler) Lee; divorced; children: Rob, Randy, Rusty, Dinah. *Education:* Pacific University, Forest Grove, Ore., B.A., 1962, M.A., 1966. *Religion:* Christian. *Home address:* Route 3, Box 580, Cornelius, Ore. 97113.

CAREER: High school teacher, 1961-64 and 1968-70; college teacher, 1965-66; staff member at a shelter/home for battered women in Washington County, Ore., 1978—. Teacher of creative writing classes; public speaker; professional photographer.

WRITINGS: Hurrah for Alexander (juvenile), Carolrhoda, 1977. Author of "If I Hold His Hands in Mine" (one-act play; first produced in Omaha, Neb., at Grace Brethren Bible Church, Easter Sunday, 1972), Baker's Plays, 1972. Contributor of more than one hundred stories and articles, some under pseudonyms, to national magazines, including *Better Camping, Young World, Woman's Life, Power for Living*, and *Guideposts*.

WORK IN PROGRESS: A historical novel, based on the life of her great-grandmother, Louisa Hochstetter Basinger; research on aging, women's rights, the women's movement, and "what women are doing to help themselves."

*   *   *

MARSHALL, Alan 1902-

PERSONAL: Born May 2, 1902, in Noorat, Victoria, Australia; son of William Bertred (a horse-breaker, drover, and store manager) and Adameina Henrietta (Leister) Marshall; married Olive Dixon, May 30, 1941 (divorced, 1957); children: Catherine, Jennifer Marshall O'Mara. *Education:* Graduate of a city business college in Victoria, Australia. *Religion:* Agnostic. *Home and office:* "Gurrawilla," 13a Potter St., Black Rock, Victoria, Australia 3193. *Agent:* Gwen Hardisty, 20 Potter St., Black Rock, Victoria, Australia 3193.

CAREER: Accountant, clerk, night watchman, and fortune teller, 1922-39; writer, journalist, and lecturer, 1939—. *Member:* Australian Folklore Society, Fellowship of Australian Writers, Australia-U.S.S.R. Society (national president, 1973—), Crippled Children's Societies. *Awards, honors:* Australian Literature Society prize for best short story, 1933, for "A Little Son"; Commonwealth Literary Fund Fellowship, 1954 and 1961; Officer of the Order of the British Empire, 1972; LL.D. from Melbourne University, 1972; Order of Friendship of Peoples from the Presidium of the Supreme Soviet of the U.S.S.R., 1977, for activities in strengthening ties between the peoples of Australia and the Soviet Union.

WRITINGS: These Are My People (travel), F. W. Cheshire, 1944, 5th edition, 1957; *Tell Us About the Turkey, Jo* (short stories), Angus & Robertson, 1946; *Ourselves Writ Strange* (travel), F. W. Cheshire, 1948, 3rd edition published as *These Were My Tribesmen*, Lansdowne, 1965; *Pull Down the Blind* (humorous sketches), F. W. Cheshire, 1949; *How Beautiful Are Thy Feet* (novel), Chesterhill Press, 1949; *Bumping Into Friends* (humorous sketches), F. W. Cheshire, 1950; *People of the Dreamtime* (aboriginal myths), F. W. Cheshire, 1952, Hyland House, 1978; *I Can Jump Puddles* (autobiographical novel), F. W. Cheshire, 1955, World Publishing, 1956; *How's Andy Going* (short stories), F. W. Cheshire, 1956; *The Gay Provider: The Myer Story* (history of Australia's famed retail department store), F. W. Cheshire, 1961; *This Is the Grass* (autobiographical novel), F. W. Cheshire, 1962; *In Mine Own Heart* (autobiography), F. W. Cheshire, 1963; *Whispering in the Wind*, Thomas Nelson, 1969; *Pioneers and Painters: 100 Years of Eltham and Its Shire* (history), Thomas Nelson, 1971; *Fight for Life*, Cassell, 1972; (compiler with Sretan Bozic) *Aboriginal Myths*, Gold Star Publications, 1972; *Short Stories*, Thomas Nelson, 1973, published as *Wild Red Horses*, 1976; *Hammers Over the Anvil*, Thomas Nelson, 1975; *Four Sunday Suits and Other Stories*, Thomas Nelson, 1975; *Complete Stories of Alan Marshall*, Thomas Nelson, 1977; *Alan Marshall Talking*, Longman Cheshire, 1978. Writer of advice column for the lovelorn, "Alan Marshall's Casebook," in *Melbourne Argus*, 1938-58. Contributor of hundreds of humorous sketches to various magazines, literary journals, and newspapers.

WORK IN PROGRESS: Writing short stories for publication.

SIDELIGHTS: Though crippled by polio when he was six, Marshall unreservedly dismisses the polite attempts by anyone to extend him special consideration or assistance. If it occurs, he will ignore any reference to a handicap, explaining to a friend once that "to help a cripple rise by taking hold of his arm is the same as trying to help an ordinary man by taking hold of his legs." As John Hetherington noted, he has traveled unaccompanied throughout Australia's outback, venturing as far as Arnhem Land, where he exchanged stories with the primitive tribesmen there who dubbed him Gurrawilla, "the Singing Man."

Whatever the endeavor, Marshall has determined to meet it on his own terms. He knew at eight years old that he would someday write books like those of W. H. G. Kingston and R. M. Ballantyne, authors of boys' adventure tales, but he would not see his first book, *These Are My People*, published until 1944. During the intervening and often difficult years between his young ambitions and eventual success, he worked briefly as an accountant in the shire office at Kangaroo Ground, after which he held any number of odd jobs. "Probably the cushiest of them," Hetherington said, "was in a Brunswick coffin factory, where Marshall doubled as a clerk by day and a watchman by night, drawing two weekly pay envelopes, and living, sleeping and eating in a room on the premises, surrounded by coffins." While working again as an accountant in the 1930's, the shoe company that employed him closed down, and Marshall resolved to forsake his tentative career as a businessman for one as a writer.

Marshall wrote constantly. Despite periods of hunger, repeated rejections in the literary market place, and his own dissatisfaction with what he wrote, a few of his short stories were published. One of them, "A Little Son," won the Australian Literature Society's prize for the best short story of 1933. Hetherington added: "He did not, like some writers of talent, scorn journalism in his struggling days. In 1938 he launched, of all things, a newspaper column of advice to the lovelorn . . . [which] continued to be published, with some interruptions, for nearly twenty years . . . and gained Marshall a large following among women." Moreover, he wrote hundreds of humorous sketches for various Australian magazines and newspapers, many of which were later collected and published as *Bumping Into Friends* and *Pull Down the Blind*. Marshall labored for recognition, and when well past thirty, he established a literary reputation for himself.

Marshall's serious books, Hetherington observed, "are Australian to the last syllable. Nobody but an Australian with a consuming love of his own country and its people—the dark-skinned as well as the light-skinned people—could have written them." His special affinity for the Australian landscape was shaped during his childhood years in Noorat. There, in the western district of Victoria, he discovered a lasting love of the bush and bush people. He learned from his father, "a bushman to the fingertips," more about the outback than from anyone else, and characters drawn from its people and fauna flourish in his stories. When writing *This Is the Grass,* an autobiographical novel, he retreated to the bush for several months where he knew he could retain the "high emotional level" necessary for the project. Living and working in a caravan, Marshall wrote the closing words believing it to be the best of his books.

Marshall's books, however, demonstrate an enthusiasm for more than remote environments. He is a writer who believes that literature should be based on the lives of people, exhibiting both their weaknesses and strengths. As his father used to say: "I like books that tell the truth. I'd sooner be sad with the truth than happy with a lie, blowed if I wouldn't." Marshall regards this observation as the principle upon which all his writing depends. He once said: "As a writer, I want to record my experiences, or rather to record what I have learnt from them, but to do this truthfully and courageously one must first of all establish himself as a man. That is the most difficult task of all."

Marshall told *CA:* "I think that the motivating factor behind most of my stories is intense indignation against exploitation and injustice. I seek to change those conditions and circumstances that prevent people from realizing their full potential. Since I began writing when I was a youth, when the crusading side of my craft was strong within me, my books became a way of expressing this indignation.

"I view my country as if it is the custodian of some secret it is withholding from me. I sometimes have the feeling that I am destined to break through this barrier and so describe my country and its people so that it lives and they live, fully created, breathing and living with all the intensity I feel exists within myself.

"I wrote my autobiography in three volumes and regard these as my best books. These books and my short stories have been translated into twenty-seven different languages. Several of my short stories have been filmed in Australia.

"My advice to aspiring writers is to take no notice of criticism unless it confirms a doubt you already have in your mind, then alter the part that has aroused this doubt.

"The power some writers have to evoke a scene so that it becomes real to me has always roused my envy. Joseph Conrad could do this. He and Maxim Gorky had a big influence on my writing.

"I feel that one is a product of the era in which one lives and at his best is a spokesman for that era. I feel that a lot of modern writers step out of the era with which they are familiar and thus destroy their value to those writers seeking a lead in giving a picture of their time."

BIOGRAPHICAL/CRITICAL SOURCES: John Hetherington, *Australians: Nine Profiles,* F. W. Cheshire, 1960; Hetherington, *Forty-two Faces,* Angus & Robertson, 1963; *In Mine Own Heart,* F. W. Cheshire, 1963; Harry Marks, *I Can Jump Oceans,* Thomas Nelson, 1976.

*   *   *

MARTIN, Valerie   1948-

PERSONAL: Born March 14, 1948, in Sedalia, Mo.; daughter of John Roger (a sea captain) and Valerie (Fleischer) Metcalf; married Robert M. Martin (an artist), December 10, 1970; children: Adrienne Metcalf. *Education:* University of New Orleans, B.A., 1970; University of Massachusetts, M.F.A., 1974. *Agent:* Jed Mattes, International Creative Management, 40 West 57th St., New York, N.Y. 10019. *Office:* New Mexico State University, Box 3-E, Las Cruces, N.M. 88003.

CAREER: Writer. New Mexico State University, Las Cruces, visiting lecturer in creative writing, 1978-79. *Member:* Authors Guild of Authors League of America.

WRITINGS: Set in Motion (novel), Farrar, Straus, 1978; *Alexandra* (novel), Farrar, Straus, 1979.

WORK IN PROGRESS: Documents, an epistolary novel set in New Orleans.

SIDELIGHTS: Valerie Martin's first novel, *Set in Motion,* won the admiration of Anatole Broyard. "While Miss Martin knows how to cut through the fat, this has not made her book thin and self-conscious as some acute books are," Broyard commented. "She writes as if she felt that, now that we know the worst about ourselves, we might as well sit back and enjoy it."

BIOGRAPHICAL/CRITICAL SOURCES: New York Times, June 23, 1978.

*   *   *

MARVIN, Burton Wright   1913-1979

OBITUARY NOTICE: Born December 23, 1913, in Somerville, Mass.; died of cancer, March 8, 1979, in Syracuse, N.Y. Educator, journalist, and co-author of books in his field. After working as a newspaper reporter in the 1930's and 1940's, Marvin served as an administrator and professor of journalism at several universities. Most recently, he was assistant dean at Syracuse University's School of Public Communications. He co-wrote two books, *The Training of Journalists* and *Modern Journalism.* Obituaries and other sources: *Directory of American Scholars,* Volume II: *English, Speech, and Drama,* 6th edition, Bowker, 1974; *Who's Who in America,* 40th edition, Marquis, 1978; *New York Times,* March 10, 1979.

MASON, Gabriel Richard 1884-1979

OBITUARY NOTICE: Born October 6, 1884, in Minsk, Russia; died May 28, 1979, in New York, N.Y. Educator and novelist. Mason was with the New York City public school system for fifty-two years. After retiring, he taught philosophy at Brooklyn College and acted in an Off-Broadway play. Mason also wrote a novel, *Above Destiny.* Obituaries and other sources: *Directory of American Scholars,* Volume IV: *Philosophy, Religion, and Law,* 6th edition, Bowker, 1974; *New York Times,* May 30, 1979.

*   *   *

MASON, Herbert Warren, Jr. 1932-

PERSONAL: Born April 20, 1932, in Wilmington, Del.; son of Herbert Warren (a paper manufacturer) and Mildred Jane (a paper manufacturer; maiden name, Noyes) Mason; married Mary Stauffer Grimley (a professor of English), September 11, 1954; children: Cathleen, Paul, Sarah. *Education:* Harvard University, A.B., 1955, A.M., 1965, Ph.D., 1969. *Politics:* "Registered Democrat, unofficial Thoreauvian." *Religion:* Roman Catholic. *Home:* 227 Payson Rd., Belmont, Mass. 02178. *Office:* Department of University Professors, Boston University, Boston, Mass. 02215.

CAREER: Wentworth Institute, Boston, Mass., teacher of English, 1950-57; American School of Paris, Paris, France, teacher of English, 1959-60; St. Joseph's College, North Windham, Me., instructor in English, 1960-62; Simmons College, Boston, instructor in comparative literature, 1962-63; Tufts University, Medford, Mass., visiting professor of Islamic history, 1966-67; worked as translator on series project for Bollingen Foundation, New York, 1968-72; Boston University, Boston, university professor of religion and Islamic history, 1972—. Member of faculty at University of Maine in Gorham, spring, 1962, and in Portland, summer, 1967; resident of Cummington Community for the Arts, autumn, 1978. Has given readings at colleges and universities all over the United States; conducted writing and translating workshops. Semi-professional baseball player, summer, 1950; crew member on a schooner, 1951; actor for summer theater, 1951, 1952; private detective, 1956. Member of board of trustees of Board of the Charity of Edward Hopkins; member of Boston Athenaeum.

MEMBER: International P.E.N., International Congress of Orientalists, Mediaeval Academy of America, American Oriental Society, American Academy of Religion, Society for Values in Higher Education (fellow). *Awards, honors:* Award from Kittredge Fellowship, 1957, for play, "Empty Houses"; National Book Award nomination, 1971, for *Gilgamesh.*

WRITINGS: (Editor) *Reflections on the Middle East Crisis,* Mouton, 1970; (author of adaptation) *Gilgamesh: A Verse Narrative,* Houghton, 1971; *Two Statesmen of Medieval Islam,* Mouton, 1974; *The Death of al-Hallaj: A Dramatic Narrative* (poem), University of Notre Dame Press, 1979; (editor and translator) Louis Massignon, *The Passion of al-Hallaj,* four volumes, Princeton University Press, 1980. Author of adaptations for theater and films. Contributor of articles, stories, and poems to magazines, including *American Poetry Review, American Scholar,* and *Psychology Today.* Co-editor of *Humaniora Islamica,* 1973, 1974.

WORK IN PROGRESS: Where the Rivers Meet, a novella; *Summer Light,* a novella; *Moments in Passage,* memoirs and travel accounts; a novel; a book on Islamic mysticism; a biography of French orientalist Louis Massignon; "Alexan-der," a verse play based on a Persian legend about Alexander the Great's quest for eternal life.

AVOCATIONAL INTERESTS: Travel (Europe, the Middle East, Turkey, Egypt, North Africa), sailing, walking, baseball, music (Mozart to "soft" rock).

*   *   *

MATTHEWS, Ralph 1904(?)-1978

PERSONAL: Born c. 1904, in Harford County, Md.; died of pneumonia August 30, 1978, in Washington, D.C.; married wife, Inez D.; children: Ralph, Jr.; stepchildren: John M. Braxton, Phyllis Braxton, Shirley A. Fonseca. *Education:* Attended Morgan State College and Columbia University.

CAREER:/WRITINGS: Afro-American newspaper chain, Baltimore, Md., reporter, 1924-35, Washington, D.C., editor, 1935-47, Newark, N.J., editor, 1947-51, Washington, editor, 1951-54; *Cleveland Call and Post,* Cleveland, Ohio, 1954-59; *Afro-American,* Philadelphia, Pa., editor, 1959-64, Washington, associate editor, 1964-68. *Member:* Capital Press Club. *Awards, honors:* Wendell L. Willkie public leadership award for national political reporting; citation from National Newspaper Publishers Association, 1977.

SIDELIGHTS: During his years with the *Afro-American* newspapers, Matthews covered stories on civil rights, politics, the Korean conflict, and the coronation of King George VI of Britain in 1936. For sixteen years he also ran the New Faces Guild, a variety show sponsored by *Afro-American* for the benefit of Children's Hospital and other charities.

Matthews received a citation from the National Newspaper Publishers Association in 1977 for his writing and his "ability to establish great newspapers and watch them make their mark in history as fighters for the black cause."

*   *   *

MAUNDER, Elwood R(ondeau) 1917-

PERSONAL: Born April 11, 1917, in Bottineau, N.D.; son of Henry Langham (a clergyman) and Florence (a pastoral assistant; maiden name, Blackmore) Maunder; married Margaret Edna Fornell, September 19, 1941 (divorced); married Eleanor Louise Arge (an executive secretary), February 14, 1973; children: Jean Michele, Martha Ellen, Elizabeth Ann. *Education:* University of Minnesota, B.A., 1939; Washington University, St. Louis, Mo., M.A., 1947; further graduate study at London School of Economics and Political Science, 1947-48. *Politics:* Independent Democrat. *Religion:* Protestant. *Home and office:* 407 Gay Rd., Aptos, Calif. 95003.

CAREER: Minneapolis Times-Tribune, Minneapolis, Minn., reporter and feature writer, 1939-40; *Minneapolis Star-Journal,* Minneapolis, sports reporter and feature writer, 1940-41; Methodist Board of Missions, New York, N.Y., director of public relations, 1948-50; Methodist Church, Ohio Area, Columbus, director of public relations, 1950-52; Forest History Society, Santa Cruz, Calif., executive director in St. Paul, Minn., 1952-64, in New Haven, Conn., 1964-69, and in Santa Cruz, 1969-78, founding editor of *Journal of Forest History,* 1957-68, editor-in-chief, 1968-78, editor and senior historian, 1978-79; writer. *Military service:* U.S. Coast Guard Reserve, active duty as public relations specialist and combat correspondent, 1941-45, editor of *Soundings,* 1945; served in European and Mediterranean theaters. *Member:* Forest History Society (fellow), Society of American Foresters (honorary member), Society of American Archivists, American Historical Association, Organization of American

Historians, Oral History Association, American Forestry Association, Commonwealth Club of California.

WRITINGS—All published by Forest History Society (Santa Cruz, Calif.), except as noted: *Clarence F. Korstian: Forty Years of Forestry,* Forest History Society, Yale University, 1969; *J. P. Kinney and the Office of Indian Affairs: A Career in Forestry,* Forest History Society, Yale University, 1969; *C. H. Kreienbaum: The Development of a Sustained Yield Industry, The Simpson-Reed Interests in the Pacific Northwest, 1920's to 1960's,* 1972; *J. Herbert Stone: A Regional Forester's View of Multiple Use,* 1972; *Verne L. Harper: A Forest Service Research Scientist and Administrator Views Multiple Use,* 1972; *Frederick W. Grover: Multiple Use in Forest Service Land Planning,* 1972; (with Amelia R. Fry) *Emanuel Fritz: Teacher, Editor and Forestry Consultant,* 1972; *Joseph E. McCaffrey: Go South, Young Man,* 1973; *Walter Samuel Johnson: Twentieth Century Businessman,* 1974; *Lieutenant General Milton A. Reckord: A Personal Memoir of Ninety-Five Years,* 1974; *Clinton R. Gutermuth: Pioneer Conservationist and the Natural Resources Council of America,* 1974; *Alfred C. Redfield: Reflections of an Ecologist on the Origins of the Natural Resources Council of America,* 1974.

Harold M. Stilson: The Shingle Weaver's Story in Western Red Cedar, 1975; *Charles Plant: A Canadian Manufacturing Executive Discusses Western Red Cedar Shingle Industry,* 1975; *Paul R. Smith: The Western Red Cedar Industry, 1910 to the Present,* 1975; *Virgil G. Peterson: The Red Cedar Shingle & Handsplit Shake Bureau's Role in the Red Cedar Industry,* 1975; *Dr. Richard E. McArdle: An Interview With the Former Chief, U.S. Forest Service, 1952-1962,* 1975; *George L. Drake: A Forester's Log, Fifty Years in the Pacific Northwest,* 1975; *Charles A. Connaughton: Forty-Three Years in the Field With the U.S. Forest Service,* 1976; (with John R. Ross) *Eunice Remington Wardwell, Louise E. Richter and Harold S. Sutton: Three Memoirs on St. Regis Paper Company History,* 1976; (with Ross) *Homer A. Vilas and James E. Kussmann: Evolution of a Paper Company, the Carlisle-Ferguson Years at St. Regis,* 1977; *William G. Reed: Four Generations of Management, the Simpson-Reed Story,* 1977; *Henry E. Clepper: Conservation's Communicator,* 1977; *James Greeley McGowin: South Alabama Lumberman, the Recollections of His Family,* 1977; *Robie M. Evans: Memoirs of a Pioneering Forester in the West,* 1977; *Verne L. Harper, George M. Jemison, Clarence L. Forsling: Early Forest Service Research Administrators,* 1978; *Inman F. Eldredge, Elwood L. Demmon, Walter Damtoft and Clinton H. Coulter: Voices From the South,* 1978. Contributor of articles to forestry journals.

WORK IN PROGRESS: A history of the St. Regis Paper Company.

SIDELIGHTS: Maunder told *CA:* "My interests are now turned to further exploration of opportunities for writing and publishing works of oral history which will have both popular and academic appeal. As one of the pioneers in the oral history movement and one of the founders of the Oral History Association, I am keenly interested in finding new uses for oral history as a tool in historical research, writing and archival preservation. Following retirement from the Forest History Society in May, 1979, after more than twenty-seven years service as executive director and senior historian, I intend to set up my own consultancy in oral history. In this new phase of my career I shall extend my conduct of oral history interviewing, editing and publishing into other areas than forest and conservation history which has been the focus of my work up to now."

MAURINA, Zenta   1897-1978

OBITUARY NOTICE: Born December 15, 1897, in Grobnia, Latvia; died April 25, 1978. Writer of novels, short stories, essays, critical biographies, and autobiographies in German and Latvian. Maurina's books include *Die weite Fahrt, Denn das Wagnis ist schoen,* and *Die eisernen Riegel zerbrachen.* Obituaries and other sources: *Encyclopedia of World Literature in the Twentieth Century,* updated edition, Ungar, 1967; *Cassell's Encyclopaedia of World Literature,* revised edition, Morrow, 1973; *World Literature Today,* spring, 1979.

*   *   *

MAXWELL, Kenneth (Robert)   1941-

PERSONAL: Born March 2, 1941, in Wellington, Somersetshire, England; came to the United States in 1964; son of Kenneth Bruce and Jean (Anderson) Maxwell. *Education:* St. John's College, Cambridge, B.A., 1963, M.A., 1967; Princeton University, M.A., 1967, Ph.D., 1970. *Office:* Research Institute on International Change, School of International Affairs, Columbia University, 420 West 118th St., New York, N.Y. 10027.

CAREER: University of Kansas, Lawrence, assistant professor of history, 1969-71; Institute for Advanced Study, Princeton, N.J., member of School of Historical Studies, 1971-75; Columbia University, New York, N.Y., associate professor of history, 1976—, senior research fellow at Research Institute on International Change, 1978-80. Executive director of Conference on Political Culture and Communications, 1978; consultant to Tinker Foundation, Inc., 1978—. *Member:* American Historical Association, Conference on Latin American History, Latin American Studies Association. *Awards, honors:* Gulbenkian fellow, 1964; Newberry Library fellow, 1968-69; Rockefeller Foundation fellow, 1974-76; Guggenheim fellow, 1976-77.

WRITINGS: Conflicts and Conspiracies: Brazil and Portugal, 1750-1808, Cambridge University Press, 1973. Contributor to newspapers and journals, including *Dissent, New York Times, New York Review of Books,* and *Foreign Affairs.*

WORK IN PROGRESS: Research on Portugal and Angola, revolution and decolonization, the role of the mass media in advanced societies, and eighteenth-century Portugal and Brazil.

SIDELIGHTS: Maxwell writes: "After graduating from Cambridge I spent a year in Europe, eventually living some months both in Madrid and Lisbon where I learned the languages and wrote for local newspapers. At graduate school I studied Portuguese-Brazilian relations during the period leading up to Brazilian independence. I then spent two years researching *Conflicts and Conspiracies,* which when translated became a best seller in Brazil (1978). I had visited Portugal many times since 1963 and covered the Portuguese Revolution and decolonialization of the Portuguese territories in Africa.

"I continue to be interested in historical studies and teach colonial Latin American history at Columbia, but I also work and write on contemporary international affairs, especially on relationships between the developed and the developing world. Journalism and history, though separate types of enterprises which require different methodologies, nonetheless can strengthen one another. I have certainly found this to be the case."

AVOCATIONAL INTERESTS: Travel (Europe, South

America, the Middle East, Eastern Europe, Africa), Art (especially drawing and painting).

*   *   *

MAY, Allan 1923-

PERSONAL: Born July 15, 1923, in Chicago, Ill.; son of Meredith Russell (a designer) and Jane (an educator; maiden name, Kennedy), May; married Eleanor Brown (a public health nurse), August 24, 1946; children: Elizabeth, Martha, Meredith, Melinda. *Education:* University of Illinois, B.S., 1949; University of Washington, Seattle, M.A., 1968. *Religion:* Roman Catholic. *Home:* 21614 86th Pl. W., Edmonds, Wash. 98020. *Office: Everett Herald*, Everett, Wash. 98206.

CAREER: Worked for *New York Times*, 1946, *Wenatchee World* (Washington), 1949-51, *Seattle Times*, 1952, and Geiser Hardware, 1952-54; *Everett Herald*, Everett, Wash., journalist, 1954—. *Military service:* U.S. Marine Corps, 1943-46. *Member:* Sigma Delta Chi (member of chapter board of directors; treasurer), Kiwanis (local president, 1970).

WRITINGS—All include photographs by author: *Up and Down the North Cascades National Park*, Pacific Northwest National Parks Association, 1973; *Sea People of Ozette*, B & E Publishing, 1975; *A Voice in the Wilderness*, Nelson-Hall, 1978. Contributor to magazines and newspapers, including *National Observer*.

WORK IN PROGRESS: Novels on World War II and on community pressure groups; nonfiction books on newspaper practices and on the effect of the loss of the American frontier.

SIDELIGHTS: May commented to *CA:* "Essentially I am a journalist and reporter. My books, so far, have all devolved from long term assignments for my paper. The first two were descriptive and fun to do. The third was controversial and even more fun, as well, I believe, as more important. Though the subjects vary widely, all my books reflect a basic concern of mine regarding the relationship of men and their environment and the effects of technology—or the lack of it.

AVOCATIONAL INTERESTS: Hiking, backpacking, history, sociology, photography.

*   *   *

MAYER, Arno J. 1926-

PERSONAL: Born June 19, 1926, in Luxembourg; came to the United States in 1941; naturalized citizen in 1944; son of Frank J. (a business executive) and Ida (Lieben) Mayer; divorced; children: Carl, Daniel. *Education:* City College (now of the City University of New York), B.B.A., 1949; Yale University, M.A., 1950, Ph.D., 1953; also attended New School for Social Research and Graduate Institute of International Studies, Geneva, Switzerland. *Home:* 58 Battle Rd., Princeton, N.J. 08540. *Office:* Department of History, Princeton University, Princeton, N.J. 08540.

CAREER: Brandeis University, Waltham, Mass., assistant professor of politics, 1954-58; Harvard University, Cambridge, Mass., assistant professor of history, 1958-61; Princeton University, Princeton, N.J., associate professor, 1961-63, professor of history, 1963—. Visiting professor at Columbia University, 1966-70, 1973-74, and New York University, 1970-71. Research associate of Columbia University's Institute of War and Peace Studies, 1971-72; director of associated studies at Ecole Pratique des Hautes Etudes, spring, 1973.

AWARDS, HONORS: Fellow of Foundation for World Government, 1953-54, American Council of Learned Societies, 1960-61, Rockefeller Foundation, 1963-64, Guggenheim Foundation, 1967-68, Princeton's Institute for Advanced Study, spring, 1968, and Lehrman Institute, 1976-77; George Louis Beer Prize from American Historical Association, 1959, for *Political Origins of the New Diplomacy;* Social Science Research Council grant, 1962; Herbert Baxter Adams Prize from American Historical Association, 1968, for *Politics and Diplomacy of Peacemaking.*

WRITINGS: Political Origins of the New Diplomacy, 1917-1918, Yale University Press, 1959; *Politics and Diplomacy of Peacemaking: Containment and Counter-Revolution at Versailles, 1918-1919*, Knopf, 1967; *Dynamics of Counterrevolution in Europe, 1870-1956*, Harper, 1971; (editor) Felix Gilbert, *History: Choice and Commitment*, Harvard University Press, 1977.

Contributor: Francis L. Loewenheim, editor, *The Historian and the Diplomat*, Harper, 1967; C. Vann Woodward, editor, *The Comparability of American History*, Basic Books, 1967; J. Barrington Moore and Kurt Wolff, editors, *The Critical Spirit: Essays in Honor of Herbert Marcuse*, Beacon Press, 1967; Leonard Krieger and Fritz Stern, editors, *The Responsibility of Power: A Festschrift for Hajo Holborn*, Doubleday, 1967; Florian Stuber and Michael Mooney, editors, *Humanists on Public Policy*, Columbia University Press, 1977; Charles L. Bertrand, editor, *Revolutionary Situations in Europe, 1917-1922*, Interuniversity Center for European Studies (Montreal, Quebec), 1977. Contributor to history journals. Advisory editor of *Annales: Economies, Societes, Civilisations, Gesellschaft und Geschichte*, and *Journal of Peace Research.*

WORK IN PROGRESS: Europe as an Ancient Regime, 1848-1917; Domestic Causes and Purposes of War, 1870-1940.

*   *   *

MAYER, Mercer 1943-

PERSONAL: Born in 1943, in Little Rock, Ark.; married wife, Marianna (an author).

CAREER: Worked as an art director in an advertising agency; full-time author and illustrator of children's books. *Awards, honors: Everyone Knows What a Dragon Looks Like* was selected as one of the *New York Times* Choice of Best Illustrated Books of the Year, and was part of the American Institute of Graphic Arts Book Show, both in 1976; Irma Simonton Black Award from the Bank Street College of Education, 1977, for *Everyone Knows What a Dragon Looks Like; While the Horses Galloped to London* was selected as part of the Children's Book Showcase, 1974; Brooklyn Art Books for Children Citation, 1977, for *Frog Goes to Dinner.*

WRITINGS—All self-illustrated: *A Boy, a Dog, and a Frog*, Dial, 1967; *There's a Nightmare in My Closet*, Dial, 1968; *Terrible Troll*, Dial, 1968; *If I Had . . .* , Dial, 1968; *I Am a Hunter*, Dial, 1969; *Frog, Where Are You?*, Dial, 1969; *A Special Trick*, Dial, 1970; (with wife, Marianna Mayer) *Mine*, Simon & Schuster, 1970; *The Queen Always Wanted to Dance*, Simon & Schuster, 1971; (with M. Mayer) *A Boy, a Dog, a Frog, and a Friend*, Dial, 1971; (with M. Mayer) *Me and My Flying Machine*, Parents' Magazine Press, 1971; *A Silly Story*, Parents' Magazine Press, 1972; *Frog on His Own*, Dial, 1973; *Bubble, Bubble*, Parents' Magazine Press, 1973; *Mrs. Beggs and the Wizard*, Parents' Magazine Press, 1973; *What Do You Do With a Kangaroo?*, Four Winds,

1974; *One Monster After Another,* Golden Press, 1974; *Two Moral Tales,* Four Winds, 1974; *Two More Moral Tales,* Four Winds, 1974; *Walk, Robot, Walk,* Ginn, 1974; *You're the Scaredy-Cat,* Parents' Magazine Press, 1974; *Frog Goes to Dinner,* Dial, 1974.

Just for You, Golden Press, 1975; (with M. Mayer) *One Frog Too Many,* Dial, 1975; *The Great Cat Chase: A Wordless Book,* Four Winds, 1975; *Professor Wormbog in Search for the Zipperump-a-Zoo,* Golden Press, 1976; *Liza Lou and the Yeller Belly Swamp,* Parents' Magazine Press, 1976; *Ah-Choo,* Dial, 1976; *Four Frogs in a Box,* Dial, 1976; *Hiccup,* Dial, 1976; *There's a Nightmare in My Cupboard,* Dent, 1976; *Just Me and My Dad,* Western Publishing, 1977; *Little Monster's Word Book,* Western Publishing, 1977; *Oops,* Dial, 1977; *Professor Wormbog's Gloomy Kerploppus: A Book of Great Smells,* Western Publishing, 1977; (editor) *The Poison Tree, and Other Poems,* Scribner, 1977; *Appelard and Liverwurst,* Scholastic Book Services, 1978; *Little Monster at Work,* Western Publishing, 1978; *Little Monster You-Can-Make-It Book,* Western Publishing, 1978.

Illustrator: John D. Fitzgerald, *The Great Brain,* Dial, 1967; Liesel M. Skorpen, *Outside My Window,* Harper, 1968; George Mendoza, *The Gillygoofang,* Dial, 1968; Sidney Offit, *The Boy Who Made a Million,* St. Martin's, 1968; Mendoza, *The Crack in the Wall, and Other Terribly Weird Tales,* Dial, 1968; Sheila LaFarge, *Golden Butter,* Dial, 1969; Fitzgerald, *More Adventures of the Great Brain,* Dial, 1969; Kathryn Hitte, *Boy, Was I Mad!,* Parents' Magazine Press, 1969; Warren Fine, *The Mousechildren and the Famous Collector,* Harper, 1970; Jean R. Larson, *Jack Tar,* M. Smith, 1970; Barbara Wersba, *Let Me Fall Before I Fly,* Atheneum, 1971; Jane H. Yolen, *The Bird of Time,* Crowell, 1971; Jan Wahl, *Margaret's Birthday,* Four Winds, 1971; Fitzgerald, *Me and My Little Brain,* Dial, 1971.

Candida Palmer, *Kim Ann and the Yellow Machine,* Ginn, 1972; Mildred Kantrowitz, *Good-Bye Kitchen,* Parents' Magazine Press, 1972; Wahl, *Grandmother Told Me,* Little, Brown, 1972; Fitzgerald, *The Great Brain at the Academy,* Dial, 1972; Mabel Watts, *While the Horses Galloped to London,* Parents' Magazine Press, 1973; Fitzgerald, *The Great Brain Reforms,* Dial, 1973; Wersba, *Amanda Dreaming,* Atheneum, 1973; Fitzgerald, *The Return of the Great Brain,* Dial, 1974; Fitzgerald, *The Great Brain Does It Again,* Dial, 1975; John Bellairs, *The Figure in the Shadows,* Dial, 1975; Jay Williams, *Everyone Knows What a Dragon Looks Like,* Four Winds, 1976; *Mercer's Monsters,* Western Publishing, 1977; Williams, *The Reward Worth Having,* Four Winds, 1977.*

*   *   *

MAYFIELD, Sara (Martin)   1905-1979

OBITUARY NOTICE—See index for *CA* sketch: Born September 10, 1905, in Tuscaloosa, Ala.; died January 10, 1979, in Tuscaloosa. Journalist, editor, playreader, and theatre casting director. As a journalist for the *Birmingham* (Ala.) *News* Mayfield covered the Inter-American Conference in Mexico and the formation of the United Nations. In addition to her biography of H. L. Mencken, *The Constant Circle,* Mayfield wrote *Exiles in Paradise,* a book about her college classmate, Zelda Sayre (Mrs. F. Scott Fitzgerald). She was also the author of *Mona Lisa,* a historical novel. Obituaries and other sources: *New York Times,* January 15, 1979.

*   *   *

MAYNARD, Fredelle (Bruser)   1922-

PERSONAL: Born July 9, 1922, in Foam Lake, Saskatche-

wan, Canada; daughter of Bernard (a merchant) and Rona (Slobinsky) Bruser; married Max S. Maynard, March 20, 1948 (marriage ended, 1973); children: Rona Maynard Jones, Joyce Maynard Bethel. *Education:* University of Manitoba, B.A. (honors), 1943; University of Toronto, M.A., 1944; Harvard University, Ph.D., 1947. *Home:* 25 Metcalfe St., Toronto, Ontario, Canada M4X 1R5; and 78 Madbury Rd., Durham, N.H. 03824. *Agent:* Curtis Brown Ltd., 575 Madison Ave., New York, N.Y. 10022.

CAREER: Wellesley College, Wellesley, Mass., instructor in English, 1948-49; University of New Hampshire, Durham, instructor in English, part-time, 1949-65; writer, 1965—. National examiner in English for College Entrance Examination Board, 1969-74; writer in residence at University of Illinois, 1974. Educational consultant to National Assessment of Educational Progress. *Member:* Writers Union (Canada), Phi Beta Kappa. *Awards, honors:* Fellow of Radcliffe Institute, 1968-69; Penney-Missouri Award, 1973, for distinction in women's journalism.

WRITINGS: Raisins and Almonds, Doubleday, 1972; *Guiding Your Child to a More Creative Life,* Doubleday, 1973. Contributor to literary journals and popular magazines, including *Reader's Digest, Woman's Day,* and *New Republic.*

WORK IN PROGRESS: A book on problem-solving.

SIDELIGHTS: Fredelle Maynard observed: "I write about everything that interests me. Since I'm interested in education, child care and development, current medical research, family and personal relationships, and cultural trends, my writing covers a wide range. I travel a great deal, observe and experience, and try to give my experience a shape, a pattern, that will have meaning for others."

*   *   *

MAZER, Milton   1911-

PERSONAL: Born March 5, 1911, in New York, N.Y.; son of Martin (a tailor) and Rose (Orman) Mazer; married Virginia O'Leary (a free-lance writer), January 29, 1949; children: Mark F. *Education:* University of Pennsylvania, B.A., 1932, M.D., 1935; William A. White Psychoanalytic Institute, certificate, 1951. *Politics:* Independent Democrat. *Home address:* P.O. Box 95, West Tisbury, Mass. 02575. *Office:* Martha's Vineyard Mental Health Center, Edgartown, Mass. 02539.

CAREER: Mount Sinai Hospital, Philadelphia, Pa., intern, 1935-36; Montefiore Hospital, Bronx, N.Y., resident in internal medicine, 1936-37; Mount Sinai Hospital, Philadelphia, clinical assistant, 1937-39; Veterans Administration, Washington, D.C., ward surgeon, 1939-41, associate chief of cardiovascular research unit, 1941-43, chief of unit, 1942-43; Veterans Hospital, Bronx, N.Y., resident in psychiatry, 1946-49; private practice in psychoanalysis and psychotherapy, 1949—. Supervisory analyst in clinical services and training analyst at William A. White Psychoanalytic Institute, 1951—; director of Martha's Vineyard Mental Health Center, 1961—; assistant psychiatrist at Massachusetts General Hospital, 1963—. Lecturer at New York University, 1949-54, adjunct associate professor, 1955-60; member of faculty, research associate, and fellow of William Alanson White Institute of Psychiatry, Psychoanalysis, and Psychology, 1953—; research associate at Harvard University, 1968-69, instructor, 1969-72, assistant clinical professor, 1972—. Town moderator of West Tisbury, Mass., 1968-78. *Military service:* U.S. Army Air Forces, 1943-46; served in England; became captain. *Member:* American Psychiatric Association, American Academy of Psychoanalysis (charter fellow). *Awards, honors:* National Institute of Mental Health grant, 1964-69.

WRITINGS: (Editor with Clara Thompson and Earl G. Witenberg) *The Outline of Psychoanalysis,* Random House, 1955; *People and Predicaments,* Harvard University Press, 1976.

Contributor: Jules H. Masserman, editor, *Science and Psychoanalysis,* Grune, 1965; J. H. Merin, editor, *Etiology of the Neuroses,* Science and Behavior Books, 1966; C. Scott Moss, editor, *The Hypnotic Investigation of Dreams,* Wiley, 1967; Henry Grunebaum, editor, *The Practice of Community Mental Health,* Little, Brown, 1970. Contributor to *Collier's Encyclopedia Yearbook* and *American Handbook of Psychiatry.* Contributor of articles to medical and mental health journals, and of short stories to *New Yorker* and *Esquire.*

SIDELIGHTS: Mazer writes: "*People and Predicaments* is a result of my work at the Martha's Vineyard Mental Health Center and my life on Martha's Vineyard. It is based on my clinical work on the island and the findings of my psychiatric epidemiological studies and what I have learned about the nature of the community from my fellow islanders. It owes much to the subtle intimations that came to me day by day as I became more and more a part of the community, joining in its everydayness, sharing its joys and sorrows, knowing of each birth and death, reacting to its tensions and changes, and participating in its social and political life."

*   *   *

McCARDLE, Dorothy Bartlett   1904-1978

PERSONAL: Born July 25, 1904, in Jonesboro, Tenn.; died November 1, 1978, in McClean, Va.; daughter of George Edwin (in lumber business) and Kate (Deaderick) Bartlett; married Carl Wesley McCardle (a reporter and government official), September 15, 1934 (died, 1972); children: Marcia (Mrs. Sterling R. Maddox, Jr.). *Education:* Attended Smith College, 1922-23; University of Pennsylvania, B.A., 1927. *Home:* 6109 Ramshorn Pl., McClean, Va. 22101. *Office:* 1150 15th St. NW, Washington, D.C. 20005.

CAREER/WRITINGS: Philadelphia North American, Philadelphia, Pa., started in classified advertising department, became a reporter, 1923; *Philadelphia Inquirer,* Philadelphia, reporter, 1924-37; free-lance writer, 1937-78; wrote for North American Newspaper Alliance (NANA), 1940-60; *Washington Post,* Washington, D.C., social events columnist and reporter, 1951-78. Contributor to magazines, including *McCall's* and *Saturday Review. Member:* Alpha Omicron Pi, Washington Press Club.

SIDELIGHTS: Before she moved to Washington, D.C., McCardle was a "hard news" reporter. She covered such top stories of the day as the Hindenberg disaster and the Lindbergh kidnapping. However, when McCardle began writing for the *Washington Post,* she was assigned to the women's section, with the White House as one of her main beats. In the *Post's* obituary, J. Y. Smith recalled: "But hers was social reporting with a difference. There was a 'hard news' side—the fortunes of political figures, who was 'in' and who was 'out,' what people discussed and thought about as well as what they wore and what they ate."

In 1972 and 1973 McCardle was barred from covering White House social events by Richard Nixon. She was never told why she was barred, but the action was apparently in response to the *Post's* unfavorable articles about Nixon's presidency in general.

OBITUARIES: Washington Post, November 3, 1978; *Newsweek,* November 13, 1978.*

*   *   *

McCARY, James Leslie   1919-1978

PERSONAL: Born April 5, 1919, in Winkler, Texas; died August 31, 1978; son of Frank Leslie (a barber) and Mary Lucille (Ferguson) McCary; married LaVirle Precise, August 15, 1938; children: Mary Lesley McCary Schlumberger, Stephen P. *Education:* North Texas State University, B.S., 1940; University of Houston, M.S., 1942; University of Texas, Ph.D., 1948; also attended University of Pittsburgh, Cornell University, and U.S. Naval Academy.

CAREER: Intern and resident at Medical Center, University of Pittsburgh, Pittsburgh, Pa., and Western State Psychiatric Institute, 1946-47; Austin State Hospital, Austin, Tex., psychologist, 1947-48; Oak Place Hospital, Houston, Tex., chief psychologist, 1948-65; University of Houston, Houston, associate professor, 1948-51; professor of psychology, 1951-78, director of clinical training program in psychology, 1948-62; psychologist in private practice at Almeda Clinic, 1948-78. Instructor at University of Texas, Main University (now University of Texas at Austin), 1947-48; lecturer at University of Texas Medical Branch at Galveston, 1958-78; speaker to professional and lay audiences. Certified by American Board of Examiners in Professional Psychology, Texas State Board of Examiners of Psychologists, American Board of Examiners in Psychological Hypnosis, and by American Association of Sex Educators, Counselors, and Therapists. Member of Sex Information and Education Council of the United States (member of board of directors, 1970-72); member of certification board of American Association of Sex Educators, Counselors, and Therapists, 1974-78. *Military service:* U.S. Naval Reserve, active duty, 1942-45; became lieutenant commander.

AWARDS, HONORS: President's teaching excellence award, University of Houston, 1970; Piper Professor Award for outstanding and academic achievement, Minnie Stevens Piper Foundation, 1971; national award for outstanding contributions to education in psychology, American Psychological Foundation, 1972, honorable mention, 1973, for *Human Sexuality;* national award, American Association of Sex Educators, Counselors, and Therapists, 1977.

WRITINGS: (Editor with Daniel E. Sheer) *Six Approaches to Psychotherapy,* Dryden, 1955; (editor) *Psychology of Personality: Six Modern Approaches,* Logos International, 1956; *Physiological and Psychological Factors of Sexual Behavior* (workbook), Pierre St. Le Macs, 1965; *Introduction to Sexology* (workbook), Pierre St. LeMacs, 1966; *Human Sexuality: Physiological, Psychological, and Sociological Factors of Sexual Behavior,* including workbooks and instructor's manuals, Van Nostrand, 1967, abridged edition, 1978, 3rd edition published as *McCary's Human Sexuality,* 1978.

(With Mark McElhaney) *The Abbreviated Bible, With the Apocrypha,* Van Nostrand, 1971; *Sexual Myths and Fallacies,* Van Nostrand, 1971; *Human Sexuality: A Course for Young Adults,* including teacher's guide, American Book Co., 1972; *A Complete Sex Education for Parents, Teenagers, and Young Adults,* Van Nostrand, 1973; *Teaching Human Sexuality,* including instructor's guide, Van Nostrand, 1973; *Freedom and Growth in Marriage,* including instructor's manual, Hamilton Publishing, 1975; (editor with Donna Copeland) *Modern Views of Human Sexual Behavior,* Science Research Associates, 1976; (editor with Copeland and others) *Advanced Readings in Human Sexuality*, Science Research Associates, in press.

Contributor: I. Rubin and L. Kirkendall, editors, *Sex in the Adolescent Years*, Associated Press, 1968; D. Grummon, editor, *Sexuality: A Search for Perspective*, Van Nostrand, 1971; R. L. Clard and R. W. Cumley, editors, *The Book of Health*, 3rd edition, Van Nostrand, 1973; E. S. Morrison and V. Borosage, editors, *Human Sexuality: Contemporary Perspectives*, National Press, 1973; C. Gordon and G. Johnson, editors, *Readings in Human Sexuality: Contemporary Perspectives*, Harper, 1976; O. K. Buros, editor, *The Eighth Mental Measurements Yearbook*, Gryphon Press, 1978; H. Otto, editor, *The New Sex Education*, Follett, 1978.

Contributor to *World Encyclopedia*, and of nearly eighty articles and reviews to psychology journals. Past member of editorial boards of *Journal of Marriage and Family Counseling, Journal of Sex Education and Therapy, Journal of Rehabilitation and Sexuality*, and *Family Coordinator*. Editorial consultant to *Current Health*.

[Sketch verified by secretary, Carmen Perez]

*   *   *

McCLELLAND, Charles A.   1917-

PERSONAL: Born April 25, 1917, in Oakley, Idaho; son of Carl A. and Mae (Poulton) McClelland; married; children: three. *Education:* San Jose State College (now University), A.B. (honors), 1938; University of California, Berkeley, M.A., 1939, Ph.D., 1942. *Home:* 28507 Robinview Lane, Rancho Palos Verdes, Calif. 90274. *Office:* School of International Relations, University of Southern California, Los Angeles, Calif. 90007.

CAREER: San Francisco State College (now San Francisco State University), San Francisco, Calif., 1946-64, began as instructor, became assistant professor, then associate professor, then professor of international relations, head of department, 1954-58, and Division of Social Sciences, 1958-62, dean of instruction, 1962-63, director of Institute for Research on International Behavior, 1962-64; University of Southern California, Los Angeles, professor of international relations, 1964—, director of China Lake studies in deterrence, 1965, world event interaction survey, 1967-73, and threat recognition and analysis project, 1973-76, Annenbergh scholar-in-residence at Center for the Study of the American Experience, 1978. Visiting professor and research associate of Institute for Communication Research at Stanford University, 1961-62; professor and director of center for Research on Conflict Resolution at University of Michigan, 1966-67. *Member:* Society for General Systems Research (president, 1961-63), International Studies Association (vice-president, 1962), American Political Science Association (member of council, 1966-68).

WRITINGS: Nuclear Weapons, Missiles and Future War: A Problem for the Sixties, Howard Chandler, 1960; *The United Nations: The Continuing Debate*, Howard Chandler, 1960; *The College Teaching of International Relations*, Institute for Research on International Behavior, San Francisco State College, 1962; *Theory and the International System*, Macmillan, 1966; *The Communist Chinese Performance in Crisis and Non-Crisis: Quantitative Studies of the Taiwan Straits Confrontation, 1950-1964*, U.S. Naval Ordnance Test Station (China Lake, Calif.), 1967; *The Management and Analysis of International Event Data: A Computerized System for Monitoring and Projecting Event Flows*, World Event Interaction Survey, University of Southern California, 1971.

Contributor: F. A. Cave, editor, *Causes and Consequences of World War II*, Dryden, 1948; James N. Rosenau, editor, *International Politics and Foreign Policy: A Reader in Research and Theory*, Free Press, 1961, 2nd edition, 1969; Elton McNeil, editor, *The Nature of Human Conflict*, Prentice-Hall, 1964; J. David Singer, editor, *Quantitative International Politics: Insights and Evidence*, Free Press, 1968; Albert Lepawsky, Edward H. Buehris, and Harold D. Lasswell, editors, *The Search for World Order: Studies by Students and Colleagues of Quincy Wright*, Appleton, 1971; Rosenau, Vincent David, and Maurice A. East, editors, *The Analysis of International Politics: Essays in Honor of Harold and Margaret Sprout*, Free Press, 1972; Charles F. Hermann, editor, *International Crisis: Insights from Behavioral Research*, Free Press, 1972; Willard A. Beling, editor, *The Middle East: Quest for an American Policy*, State University of New York Press, 1973.

Contributor to *Encyclopaedia Britannica, International Encyclopedia of the Social Sciences*, and *Dictionary of Political Science*. Contributor of about twenty articles to political and social science journals and to *Saturday Review of Literature*. Editor of *Background: Journal of the International Studies Association*, 1962-66.

WORK IN PROGRESS: Current World Stress Studies, publication by International Relations Research Institute, University of Southern California; *Democracy World Watch*, Center for the Study of the American Experience, University of Southern California.

*   *   *

McCONNELL, Jean   1928-

PERSONAL: Born November 18, 1928, in London, England; daughter of E. J. (a London transport officer) and Elizabeth (MacDonald) Fox; married Terence McConnell, January 13, 1945 (divorced, 1976); children: Karen. *Education:* Attended Jesmond College. *Religion:* Atheist. *Politics:* "Uncommitted." *Home:* 9 Hadlow Rd., Tonbridge, Kent, England.

CAREER: Writer, lecturer, theatrical producer, and reporter for *Northern Whig and Belfast Post* (newspaper), 1945-48; professional actress with repertory theatres at various places, including West End and Stratford, England; performer touring with Glyndbourne Theatre Co.; television and radio performer, 1947-51; drama instructor, lecturer, and producer for various institutes, including Northern Polytechnic, City Literary Institute, and Central London Institute, 1951—; currently drama instructor at West Kent Further Education College. Producer for Cork Operatic Society, National Westminster Bank, and other companies. Director on board of Churchill Theatre, Bromley, England. Volunteer worker with community youth groups. *Military service:* Women's Royal Naval Service, 1943-45. *Member:* Writers Guild of Great Britain, Crime Writers' Association.

WRITINGS: (With Eric Newton) *Drama in the Making*, University of London Press, 1956; (with Newton) *The Legend of Carcassonne*, University of London Press, 1962, revised edition, 1962; *The Detectives: Turning Points in Criminal Investigation*, David & Charles, 1976.

Plays: *Haul for the Shore* (three-act; first produced in London at British Broadcasting Corp. (BBC-TV), 1951; also see below), Kenyon-Deane, 1953; *The Red Cloak* (one-act; first produced in Tonbridge at Tonbridge Theatre and Arts Club, 1952), Kenyon-Deane, 1955; *The Pick of the Season* (three-act; first produced in London at BBC-TV, 1955), Kenyon-Deane, 1956; *One Man Banned* (three-act; first produced in

Tonbridge at Theatre Club, 1954), Kenyon-Deane, 1957; *Look Out for the Catch* (three-act; first produced in Tunbridge Wells at Assembly Hall Theatre, 1960), Walter H. Baker, 1961; *Money's No Object* (three-act; first produced in Bromley at Repertory Theatre, 1960), Walter H. Baker, 1961; *Chord on the Triangle* (three-act; first produced in London at BBC-Radio, 1961), Walter H. Baker, 1961; *It's a Gift* (one-act; first produced in London at BBC-Radio, 1962), Samuel French, 1964; *Wine in a Venetian Goblet* (one-act; first produced in Tonbridge at Hildenborough Community Centre, 1968), Kenyon-Deane, 1968; *Blush Pink* (one-act; first produced in London at BBC-Radio, 1966), Kenyon-Deane, 1968; *Ripe for Conversation* (one-act; first produced in Tonbridge at Oast Theatre, 1973), English Theatre Guild, 1975; *A Memory of Frank Danby* (one-act; first produced in Tonbridge at Oast Theatre, 1976), English Theatre Guild, 1976. Also author of "Fear of the Panther" (three-act), first produced in London at Richmond Theatre, 1964, and "Poor Poor Janey," first produced in Tonbridge at Oast Theatre, 1977.

Author of unpublished radio plays for BBC-Radio, including "Transport of Delight," 1960, "A Lovesome Thing," 1965, and "The Emancipation of Eddie Burling," 1968. Author of radio documentaries, including "Dead Giveaway," 1976, "The Menials," 1976, "Final Checkup," 1977, and "For You the War Is Over," 1977. Author of teleplays for BBC-TV, including "The Coelacanth," 1957, "The Henpecked Murderer," 1969, and "Haul for the Shore" (also see above), 1953. Contributor to television series, including "Tell it to the Marines," "Dr. Finlay's Casebook," and "Woman's World." Author of television serials "Smugglers Cove," "The Skewbald," and "Twins at Number Twelve."

WORK IN PROGRESS: Articles and short stories for women's magazines.

SIDELIGHTS: McConnell told *CA:* "My main occupation has been in the field of drama, as an actress, playwright, and producer. In this respect I have worked in the United Kingdom, Eire, and Zambia. Several of my plays have a crime theme and most recently I have been concerned with documentary work on crime."

*   *   *

McCORMICK, Jack (Sovern) 1929-1979

OBITUARY NOTICE—See index for *CA* sketch: Born January 19, 1929, in Indianapolis, Ind.; died February 12, 1979, in Bethesda, Md. Author, ecologist, and president of environmental consulting firm. McCormick began his career with the American Museum of Natural History in New York City, where he designed the hall of North American forests. He later served as a consultant in ecology at the Kalbfleisch Field Research Station and, in 1971, he formed his own environmental consulting firm. McCormick wrote several books in his field, including *The Living Forest, The Life of the Forest,* and *The Pine Barrens.* Obituaries and other sources: *American Men and Women of Science,* 13th edition, Bowker, 1976; *Washington Post,* February 15, 1979.

*   *   *

McCRARY, (James) Peyton 1943-

PERSONAL: Born June 22, 1943, in Danville, Va.; son of Giles Mebane (a pharmacist) and Virginia (Motley) McCrary; married Patricia Fitzgerald (a legal secretary), August 24, 1963; children: Ellen, Justin. *Education:* University of Virginia, B.A. (honors), 1965, M.A., 1966; Princeton University, Ph.D., 1972. *Politics:* Democrat. *Religion:*

Presbyterian. *Home:* 5459 Suwannee Circle, Mobile, Ala. 36608. *Office:* Department of History, University of South Alabama, Mobile, Ala. 36688.

CAREER: University of Minnesota, Minneapolis, instructor, 1969-71, assistant professor of history, 1972-76; Vanderbilt University, Nashville, Tenn., assistant professor of history, 1976-78; University of South Alabama, Mobile, associate professor of history, 1978—.

WRITINGS: Abraham Lincoln and Reconstruction: The Louisiana Experiment, Princeton University Press, 1978. Contributor to *Journal of Interdisciplinary History.*

WORK IN PROGRESS: Research on voting behavior and policy transformation in the Civil War party system, 1854-76, on the revolutionary dimensions of the American Civil War (an essay in comparative history), and on the relationship between academic professionalization and social criticism in the South (a case study of the "Bassett affair," 1903).

SIDELIGHTS: McCrary writes: "The major thrust of my research and writing lies in an effort to comprehend the larger significance of the American Civil War, the nation's most important experience, with the phenomenon of revolutionary change. Because I believe that the richest insights can often be obtained through intensive examination of a particular case, I elected in my first book to dwell on the effort to reconstruct the pivotal state of Louisiana during the presidency of Abraham Lincoln. Case studies are most revealing, however, when illuminated by more general concerns. Thus the book has much to say about the debate between president and Congress over reconstruction, the distinctive characteristics of the Civil War party system, the ideological conflicts which dominated political discourse during the war, and the transformation of slaves into free men. At present I am pursuing the implications of my findings in several essays dealing with the nineteenth-century party system and with the revolutionary characteristics of the war against slavery.

The moral commitment which initially prompted my work was a concern for the civil rights of Southern blacks; this dates me, I suppose, as an intellectual product of the early 1960's. My decision to become a historian in 1963 coincided with a decision to reject the racial values of my Southern white childhood. My conversion experience, so to speak, was the result of encountering the work of C. Vann Woodward, whose humane scholarship made him the folk hero of a generation of young Southerners. I have preferred the quieter path of writing history to the more difficult road of direct action, because I am by nature a writer rather than an organizer. I take solace, however, in the hope that what I have to say about the past will contribute something of value in coping with our present dilemma."

*   *   *

McCUEN, Jo Ray 1929-

PERSONAL: United States citizen born abroad; born November 19, 1929; daughter of Walter R. (a clergyman) and Gladys (Corley) Beach; married David H. Cotton (divorced); married John T. McCuen (a vice-chancellor of a community college), July, 1972; children: (first marriage) David B. *Education:* Pacific Union College, B.A., 1950; University of Southern California, M.A., 1968, Ph.D., 1968. *Home:* 39 Glenflow Court, Glendale, Calif. 91206. *Office:* Department of English, Glendale Community College, Glendale, Calif. 91208.

CAREER: Glendale Community College, Glendale, Calif., professor of English, 1966—.

WRITINGS: (With Anthony Winkler) *Rhetoric Made Plain,* Harcourt, 1974, 2nd edition, 1978; (with Winkler) *Readings for Writers,* Harcourt, 1974, 3rd edition, 1979; (with Winkler) *From Idea to Essay,* Science Research Associates (SRA), 1977, 2nd edition, 1979; *Research Paper Handbook,* Harcourt, 1979.

SIDELIGHTS: Jo Ray McCuen writes: "Because of my deep interest in Biblical history and Biblical literature, I have come to see this field as my academic speciality. I like to think that I have awakened in my students an appreciation for the imaginative, dynamic, melancholy, tragic, and even humorous quality of Hebrew literature.

"In writing books about how to write, I have always tried to remain open to modern pedagogy without discarding time-tested techniques. I believe this philosophy is responsible for the success of Winkler-McCuen books."

AVOCATIONAL INTERESTS: Skiing (especially downhill racing).

*   *   *

McDERMOTT, Gerald 1941-

PERSONAL: Born in 1941, in Detroit, Mich.; married Beverly Brodsky (an artist), 1969. *Education:* Degree from the Pratt Institute of Design. *Residence:* Hudson River Valley, N.Y.

CAREER: Worked as a graphic designer for New York City's public television station; filmmaker; illustrator and reteller of folk tales. *Awards, honors:* American Film Festival Blue Ribbon, 1970, for film version of "Anansi the Spider"; Caldecott Medal, 1975, for *Arrow to the Sun.*

WRITINGS—All retold folk tales; all created from animated films by author; all self-illustrated: *Anansi the Spider: A Tale From the Ashanti,* Holt, 1972; *The Magic Tree: A Tale From the Congo,* Holt, 1973; *Arrow to the Sun: A Pueblo Indian Tale,* Viking, 1974; *The Stonecutter: A Japanese Folk Tale,* Viking, 1975; *The Voyage of Osiris: A Myth of Ancient Egypt,* Dutton, 1977; *The Knight of the Lion,* Four Winds, 1978; *Papagayo the Mischief Maker,* Dutton, 1978.

SIDELIGHTS: Gerald McDermott's career has been influenced by various people and events throughout his life. At the age of four his parents enrolled him in Saturday classes for children at the Detroit Institute of Arts. Several years later, he became involved in local radio programs where he gained experience in music, sound effects, and other areas that proved to be invaluable in his filmmaking career.

As a teenager, McDermott's artistic style was influenced by the Bauhaus principles incorporated in the special curriculum at the public high school he attended in Detroit. By the time he was a high school senior, McDermott was experimenting with graphics on film. The future illustrator continued his art training at the Pratt Institute. During his summer vacation, McDermott made his first animated film, "The Stonecutter." This film (and all the films that followed) was created by painstakingly drawing 6,000 frames in synchronization with prerecorded music and assigning one picture for each note.

All of McDermott's works are based on old folktales. His friendship with Jungian mythologist, Joseph Campbell, played an important role in this aspect of his career. Through Campbell, McDermott became aware of the relationship between symbols and mythology. This new insight provided McDermott with additional material for his stories.

In the late 1960's McDermott was working on several films, but found little support or enthusiasm for his artistic endeavors. The discouraged filmmaker and his wife decided to move to southern France for a change of environment. Before leaving the country, however, McDermott struck up an acquaintance with George Nicholson, now editorial director of Viking Junior Books. Nicholson was impressed with McDermott's cinematic approach to the African myth "Anansi the Spider" and offered the filmmaker a multi-book contract to transfer his works from celluloid to paper. The McDermotts lived and worked in France for two years before returning to the United States.

BIOGRAPHICAL/CRITICAL SOURCES: New York Times Book Review, May 5, 1974; *Authors in the News,* Volume 2, Gale, 1976.*

*   *   *

McDOWELL, Virginia (Duncan) H(ecker) 1933-

PERSONAL: Born June 16, 1933, in Chicago, Ill.; daughter of Andrew Duncan (in advertising) and Virginia (a pianist; maiden name, Powell) Duncan Hecker; married Warren E. McDowell (a surveyor), September 11, 1954; children: Thomas Kenneth, Mathew Edward, Mary Lou, Ann Elizabeth. *Education:* Attended Marquette University, 1951-52, and De Anza College, 1969-70; University of California, Santa Cruz, B.A. (honors), 1972, Ph.D., 1976; graduate study at University of California, San Francisco, 1972-75. *Politics:* Independent. *Religion:* "None now." *Home:* 7974 Pumpkin Dr., Cupertino, Calif. 95014. *Office:* Department of Human Development, California State University, Hayward, Calif. 94542.

CAREER: Lakewood City Hospital, Lakewood, Ohio, medical technologist, 1953-54; Columbus City Hospital, Columbus, Ga., medical technologist, 1955-56; University of California, San Francisco, research associate at Langley-Porter Neuropsychiatric Institute, 1975; California State University, Hayward, lecturer in human development, 1975—, acting head of human development department, 1977. Instructor at West Valley College, 1975-76, Foothill College, 1976, and De Anza College, 1976. Speaker at professional meetings. *Member:* American Psychological Association, Association for Humanistic Psychology.

WRITINGS: Re-Creating: The Experience of Life Change and Religion, Beacon Press, 1978.

WORK IN PROGRESS: Research on women's reentry into colleges and universities.

SIDELIGHTS: Virginia McDowell writes: "I wrote *Re-Creating* as a doctoral thesis, and the motivation was the deadline. I also wrote it as part of a personal agenda: it was my way of dealing with my origins and traditions in a way that would permit them to be put to rest—kindly. I would not write the same book now. It is of value because of where I have been. I was deeply fascinated with the people I was interviewing and remain so."

*   *   *

McELHANEY, James W(illson) 1937-

PERSONAL: Born December 10, 1937, in New York, N.Y.; son of Lewis Keck and Sara (Hess) McElhaney; married Maxine Dennis Jones, August 17, 1961; children: David, Benjamin. *Education:* Duke University, A.B., 1960, LL.B., 1962. *Home:* 2842 East Overlook, Cleveland Heights, Ohio 44118. *Office:* School of Law, Case Western Reserve University, 11075 East Blvd., Cleveland, Ohio 44106.

CAREER: Admitted to Bar of Wisconsin, 1962; Wickham, Borgelt, Skogstad & Powell, Milwaukee, Wis., law associate, 1966; University of Maryland—Baltimore County, Baltimore, assistant professor, 1966-69, associate professor, 1969-72, professor of law, 1972-73; Southern Methodist University, Dallas, Tex., visiting professor, 1973-74, professor of law, 1974-76; Case Western Reserve University, Cleveland, Ohio, visiting Joseph C. Hostetler Professor of Trial Practice and Advocacy, 1976-77, Joseph C. Hostetler Professor of Trial Practice and Advocacy, 1977—. Special faculty member of National Institute for Trial Advocacy, 1975—; visiting professor at University of Tulsa, summer, 1977; member of summer faculty at Washington University, St. Louis, Mo., 1978. Director of conferences and workshops; executive producer of video tape series for National Institute for Trial Advocacy; consultant to National College of District Attorneys. *Military service:* U.S. Army, Judge Advocate General's Corps, 1963-65; became captain. *Member:* American Bar Association, Association of American Law Schools (head of trial advocacy section, 1974-75, and evidence section, 1978-79), Federal Bar Association.

WRITINGS: Effective Litigation: Trials, Problems, and Materials, with teacher's manual, West Publishing, 1974; *Readings in Trial Advocacy,* National Institute for Trial Advocacy, 1978.

Author of manuals. Author of "Trial Notebook," a column in *Litigation,* 1977—. Editor of monograph series, published by litigation section of American Bar Association, 1975-77. Contributor of more than twenty articles and reviews to law journals. Associate editor of *Litigation.*

WORK IN PROGRESS: Editor of *The Best of Litigation;* contributor to *Criminal Defense Techniques,* publication by Matthew Bender expected in 1979 or 1980.

SIDELIGHTS: McElhaney comments: "Awkward language is not precision and obscurity is not great insight. New ideas may be expressed plainly, and the better the author understands them, the more likely it is they will be understandable to others."

AVOCATIONAL INTERESTS: Music ("I have made my own harpsichord which someday I may be able to play"), building and flying radio-controlled airplanes, theatre.

* * *

McFADDEN, Robert D(ennis) 1937-

PERSONAL: Born February 11, 1937, in Milwaukee, Wis.; son of Frank Joseph (in business) and Violet (Charleston) McFadden; married Elizabeth Hathaway, June, 1963 (divorced, 1968); married Judith Silverman, June 20, 1971; children: (second marriage) Nolan. *Education:* Attended University of Wisconsin—Eau Claire, 1955-57; University of Wisconsin—Madison, B.S., 1960. *Residence:* New York, N.Y. *Office:* New York Times, 229 West 43rd St., New York, N.Y. 10036.

CAREER/WRITINGS: Wisconsin Rapids Daily Tribune, Wisconsin Rapids, Wis., reporter, 1957-58; *Wisconsin State Journal,* Madison, reporter, 1958-59; *Cincinnati Enquirer,* Cincinnati, Ohio, reporter, 1960-61; *New York Times,* New York, N.Y., reporter, 1961—. *Military service:* U.S. Army, 1960-61. U.S. Army Reserve, 1961-68. *Awards, honors:* Journalism awards include spot news story award from Uniformed Firemen's Association, 1967, for covering a Brooklyn Heights fire in a home for the elderly; byline award from New York Press Club, 1973, for covering killings of police officers by radical fugitives, 1974, for covering a police siege

of gunmen in a sporting goods store; Pulitzer Prize nomination, 1977, for reporting on New York City's blackout; spot news story award from New York Society of Silurians, 1977, for blackout coverage and follow-up; Page One Award from Newspaper Guild of New York, 1978, for blackout coverage.

* * *

McFARLAND, Carl 1904-1979

OBITUARY NOTICE: Born October 6, 1904, in Washington, D.C.; died of cancer, May 16, 1979, in Charlottesville, Va. Attorney, educator, government official, and author of books in his field. McFarland served as an assistant attorney general during the Roosevelt administration. He was a specialist in administrative law and was the principal drafter of the Federal Administrative Procedure Act in 1946. McFarland was a professor emeritus of law at the University of Virginia. Obituaries and other sources: *Directory of American Scholars,* Volume IV: *Philosophy, Religion, and Law,* 7th edition, Bowker, 1978; *Who's Who in America,* 40th edition, Marquis, 1978; *Washington Post,* May 18, 1979.

* * *

McFARLAND, Gerald Ward 1938-

PERSONAL: Born November 7, 1938, in Oakland, Calif.; son of Frank E. (a bookbinder) and Marguerite (a teacher; maiden name, Ward) McFarland; married Dorothy Tuck (a writer and teacher), August 15, 1964. *Education:* University of California, Berkeley, A.B., 1960; Columbia University, M.A., 1962, Ph.D., 1965. *Office:* Department of History, University of Massachusetts, Amherst, Mass. 01002.

CAREER: University of Massachusetts, Amherst, instructor, 1964-65, assistant professor, 1965-70, associate professor, 1970-75, professor of history, 1975—. *Member:* American Historical Association, Organization of American Historians, Society for Values in Higher Education. *Awards, honors:* American Council of Learned Societies grant, 1971-72; Guggenheim fellowship, 1978-79.

WRITINGS: Mugwumps, Morals and Politics, 1884-1920, University of Massachusetts Press, 1975; (editor) *Moralists or Pragmatists? The Mugwumps, 1884-1900,* Simon & Schuster, 1975. Contributor to *McGraw-Hill Encyclopedia of World Biography,* McGraw, 1973. Contributor to periodicals, including *Soundings, Historian, Journal of American History,* and *Political Science Quarterly.*

WORK IN PROGRESS: Families on the Move: Family and Migration in Nineteenth-Century America.

SIDELIGHTS: McFarland told *CA:* "The focus of my scholarly career to date has been the study of American political history. I was first drawn to this field while in graduate school at Columbia University in the early 1960's. It was a time when Richard Hofstadter's writings challenged many of us. . . .

"The publication of my book on the Mugwumps, I felt, marked a turning point in my career. For a dozen years prior to 1975 I had focused on research in political history. Now I felt eager to explore new subjects, especially such topics as family history and social mobility that had long figured in my teaching and reading, but had not been especially evident in my published work. The present research proposal for a case study of the impact of westward migration on selected nonelite families reflects these recent scholarly concerns."

McFARLAND, M(alcolm) Carter 1912-

PERSONAL: Born February 4, 1912, in Fleeton, Va.; son of Malcolm V. (a Navy officer and marine engineer) and Nina (Carter) McFarland; married Jean Long, June, 1939 (deceased); children: Diana McFarland DelVecchio, Anne Carter Kirtley. *Education:* Spring Hill College, Ph.B. (magna cum laude), 1933; Georgetown University, M.A., 1938, Ph.D., 1946. *Religion:* Roman Catholic. *Home:* 1200 North Nash St., Apt. 835, Arlington, Va. 22209. *Office:* National Housing Conference, 1126 16th St. N.W., Washington, D.C. 20036.

CAREER: Washington Gas & Light Co., Washington, D.C., assistant advertising manager, 1934-40; Federal Housing Administration, Washington, D.C., training officer, 1940-41, chief of marketing section, 1941-42, chief of radio and motion picture section, 1942-44; U.S. National Housing Agency, Washington, D.C., training officer, 1944-47; College of St. Thomas, St. Paul, Minn., associate professor of economics, 1947-50; U.S. Housing and Home Finance Agency, Washington, D.C., director of operations analysis, 1950-54, assistant administrator for plans and programs, 1954-58, director of Division of Economics and Program Studies, 1958-61; Department of Housing and Urban Development, Washington, D.C., assistant Federal Housing Administration commissioner for programs, 1961-70, assistant commissioner for rehabilitation, 1970-72; American Institute of Architects, Washington, D.C., director of urban and housing programs, 1972-74; writer and consultant, 1974-76; National Housing Conference, Washington, D.C., resident scholar, 1977-78; executive vice president of Center for Housing Policy, 1978—. Adjunct lecturer at American University, 1946, adjunct professor, 1970-74; visiting lecturer at University of Minnesota, 1949, Hill Foundation visiting professor, 1965; lecturer at George Washington University and about twenty other American universities. Consultant to International Center for Social Gerontology, the U.S. Department of Housing and Urban Development, Library of Congress, and National Bureau of Standards.

MEMBER: American Economic Association, Society for the Preservation and Encouragement of Barbershop Quartet Harmony (past local president), Lambda Alpha. *Awards, honors:* Distinguished service award from U.S. Housing and Home Finance Agency, 1959.

WRITINGS: The Challenge of Urban Renewal, Urban Land Institute, 1958, 2nd edition, 1962; *Residential Rehabilitation in Harlem Park,* U.S. Housing and Home Finance Agency, 1962; *FHA Experience with Mortgage Foreclosures and Property Acquisitions,* U.S. Housing and Home Finance Agency, 1963; *FHA Multi-Family Rehabilitation Guide,* U.S. Department of Housing and Urban Development, 1965; (editor with Walter Vivrett) *Residential Rehabilitation,* University of Minnesota Press, 1966; *Report on the FHA Section 221 (d) (3) Below-Market Interest Rate Program,* U.S. Department of Housing and Urban Development, 1966; *Residential Rehabilitation: The State of the Art and Its Potential,* U.S. Department of Housing and Urban Development, 1966; *Study of FHA-Assisted Nursing Homes,* U.S. Department of Housing and Urban Development, 1966; *Goals and Accomplishments in Residential Rehabilitation,* U.S. Government Printing Office, 1967; *Housing Elderly Pennsylvanians,* International Center for Social Gerontology, 1976; *Government Supported Residential Rehabilitation,* U.S. Department of Commerce, 1977; *Federal Government and Urban Problems,* Westview Press, 1978; *Urban Housing,* McGraw, 1979.

Contributor: Clark Tibbetts and Wilma Donahue, editors, *Social and Psychological Aspects of Aging,* Columbia University Press, 1962; W. L. C. Wheaton, Grace Milgrim, and Mary Ellin Meyerson, editors, *Urban Housing,* Free Press, 1966; James Gillies, editor, *Essays in Urban Land Economics,* University of California Press, 1966; Eugene Morris and Henry Halprin, editors, *Urban Renewal and Housing,* Practicing Law Institute, 1969; Stanley Smiegel, editor, *Housing and Urban Development in Sweden,* U.S. Department of Housing and Urban Development, 1972; Morton Schussheim, editor, *Subsidized Housing,* U.S. Government Printing Office, 1977.

Contributor to *Encyclopedia Americana.* Contributor of more than twenty articles to professional journals.

SIDELIGHTS: McFarland comments: "My primary motivations are to learn (and teach what I learn) and to improve the quality and relevance of public programs aimed at improving our cities.

"I began writing in college where I contributed articles to college newspaper and edited the yearbook of my class. My interest in writing was stimulated by much reading as a youth and by a high school English teacher who followed the unusual but effective practice of simply reading great literature to his classes. After graduation I took a job writing advertising copy for newspapers, direct mail, and radio. This experience further whetted my interest in the writing of clear, vivid prose. During my years as a government executive I did much writing both for myself and for cabinet secretaries and presidents. Probably the most-discussed speech I ever wrote was delivered by a cabinet secretary.

"I never write about any subject I do not know thoroughly, either from personal experience or from research, or both. To write well requires the discipline of steady application to the job at hand. A book may require this kind of sustained application for a year and a half. One must organize his ideas, put them in clear English, then rewrite and polish until he is satisfied that the end product is the best he can do."

AVOCATIONAL INTERESTS: Music, literature, art, architecture, science, history, philosophy, government, jogging.

*   *   *

McGRATH, William J(ames) 1937-

PERSONAL: Born May 19, 1937, in Butte, Mont.; son of Murel James (an engineer) and Fernella (a civil servant; maiden name, Pierce) McGrath; married Juliet, August 19, 1961 (divorced, 1976); married Stephanie Frontz (a librarian), May 14, 1978; children: Jennifer. *Education:* Rice University, B.A., 1959, M.A., 1961; University of California, Berkeley, Ph.D., 1965. *Home:* 451 Park Ave., Rochester, N.Y. 14607. *Office:* Department of History, University of Rochester, Rochester, N.Y. 14627.

CAREER: University of Chicago, Chicago, Ill., assistant professor of history, 1965-71; University of Rochester, Rochester, N.Y., assistant professor, 1971-74, associate professor of history, 1974—. *Member:* American Historical Association, American GO Association. *Awards, honors:* Woodrow Wilson fellowship, 1962-63; Fulbright fellowship, 1963-64; grant from Leo Baeck Institute, 1968; grant from National Endowment for the Humanities, 1977, fellowship, 1978-79.

WRITINGS: Dionysian Art and Populist Politics in Austria, Yale University Press, 1974. Contributor to history journals.

WORK IN PROGRESS: An intellectual and psychological biography of the young Sigmund Freud.

SIDELIGHTS: McGrath commented: "I am particularly interested in studying the historical origins of creativity and artistic innovation, and the socio-political context within which important thinkers live and work. In my first book I attempted to demonstrate this with regard to the compositions of Gustav Mahler and in my current book I hope to show how Freud's basic discoveries were shaped by the political forces of his time."

*   *   *

McHUGH, Mary 1928-

PERSONAL: Born December 5, 1928, in Orange, N.J.; daughter of John W. (an engineer) and Ida Mae (Snyder) Kennard; married Earl J. McHugh (an attorney), November 21, 1953; children: Karen, Kyle. *Education:* Wheaton College, Norton, Mass., B.A., 1950; also attended Sorbonne, University of Paris. *Politics:* Independent. *Religion:* Agnostic. *Home:* 556 West Wayne Ave., Wayne, Pa. 19087.

CAREER: George Fry & Associates (management consultants), New York City, psychologist's assistant, 1950-53; David McKay Co., Inc. (publisher), New York City, assistant to publicity director, 1953-55; Pendray & Co. (public relations firm), New York City, secretary, 1955-56; writer. Member of board of directors of National Council on Crime and Delinquency. *Member:* League of Women Voters (member of board of directors).

WRITINGS: The Woman Thing, Praeger, 1973; *Law and the New Woman,* F. Watts, 1975; *Psychology and the New Woman,* F. Watts, 1976; *Veterinary Medicine and Animal Care Careers,* F. Watts, 1977; *Careers in Engineering and Engineering Technology,* F. Watts, 1978; *Young People Talk About Death,* F. Watts, 1979. Contributor to *Cosmopolitan.*

SIDELIGHTS: Mary McHugh writes: "My life has changed a lot since the women's movement. I learned to respect myself and to take time to do things I considered important. I've been a writer all my life, but I was forty-three before my first book was published. That gave me my confidence to spend most of my time writing, and life is at its most rewarding for me now."

*   *   *

McKENNA, F(rancis) E(ugene) 1921-1978

OBITUARY NOTICE: Born July 29, 1921, in Globe, Ariz.; died November 10, 1978, in New York, N.Y. Chemist, librarian, technical information specialist, and editor. McKenna was the president and executive director of Special Libraries Association. He was the head of its publication department and editor of *Special Libraries.* Obituaries and other sources: *Current Biography,* Wilson, 1966, February, 1979; *American Men and Women of Science,* Bowker, 1976; *Wilson Library Bulletin,* December, 1978.

*   *   *

McKIMMEY, James 1923-
(Benjamin Swift)

PERSONAL: Born September 5, 1923, in Holdrege, Neb.; son of James, Sr. and Viola (Carlson) McKimmey; married Martha Nell Nicol, April 4, 1947. *Education:* University of San Francisco, B.S., 1950. *Home address:* P.O. Box 8756, South Lake Tahoe, Calif. 95731. *Agent:* Joseph Elder, 150 West 87th St., New York, N.Y. 10024.

CAREER: Writer. Guest lecturer at Lake Tahoe Community College, 1977. *Military service:* U.S. Army, Infantry, 1942-46. *Member:* Mystery Writers of America (vice-president, 1963), Sigma Alpha Epsilon.

WRITINGS: The Perfect Victim, Dell, 1957; *Winner Take All,* Dell, 1959; *Cornered,* Dell, 1960; *The Satyr,* Monarch, 1960; *24 Hours to Kill,* Dell, 1961; *The Wrong Ones,* Dell, 1961; *The Long Ride,* Dell, 1961; *Run if You're Guilty,* Lippincott, 1963; *A Circle in the Water,* Morrow, 1965; *Blue Mascara Tears,* Ballantine, 1965; *Never Be Caught,* Boardman, 1966; *The Hot Fire,* Dell, 1968; *The Man With the Gloved Hand,* Random House, 1972; (under pseudonym Benjamin Swift) *Play-Off,* Fearon, 1979; *Buckaroo,* Scholastic, 1979.

Stories represented in numerous anthologies, including *Best Detective Stories of the Year,* Dutton, 1963, 1968, 1970, 1973, and 1978; and *Crimes and Misfortunes,* edited by J. Francis McComas, Random House, 1970. Contributor of more than one hundred-fifty short stories and articles to periodicals, including *Good Housekeeping, Cosmopolitan, Alfred Hitchcock's Mystery Magazine,* and *Redbook.*

WORK IN PROGRESS: Last Gathering, a long novel.

SIDELIGHTS: McKimmey commented: "The motive of writing is to entertain, to enlighten in small fashion, and to stay at home at the typewriter rather than going out to what is popularly considered more appropriate employment for a mature individual. When I do get out of my office at home, it is often as a photojournalist, which is a professional reason to pursue photography and travel."

BIOGRAPHICAL/CRITICAL SOURCES: Writer, September, 1970; *New York Times Book Review,* September 3, 1972; *Washington Post Book World,* September 17, 1972.

*   *   *

McKINNEY, Gordon B(artlett) 1943-

PERSONAL: Born June 6, 1943, in Whitefield, N.H.; son of Bartlett (an executive) and Marcella (Finley) McKinney; married Martha McCreedy (an executive), August 30, 1969. *Education:* Bates College, B.A., 1965; Northwestern University, M.A., 1969, Ph.D., 1971. *Home:* 2 Circle Dr., Clyde, N.C. 28721. *Office:* Department of History, Western Carolina University, Cullowhee, N.C. 28723.

CAREER: Valdosta State College, Valdosta, Ga., assistant professor, 1970-75, associate professor of history, 1975-78; Western Carolina University, Cullowhee, N.C., associate professor of history, 1978—. *Member:* American Historical Association, Organization of American Historians, American Association of University Professors, Southern Historical Association.

WRITINGS: Southern Mountain Republicans: Politics and the Appalachian Community, 1865-1900, University of North Carolina Press, 1978. Member of editorial board of *Appalachian Journal.*

WORK IN PROGRESS: A biography of Senator Henry W. Blair.

*   *   *

McLENNAN, Barbara N(ancy) 1940-

PERSONAL: Born March 25, 1940, in New York, N.Y.; daughter of Sol and Gertrude (Rochkind) Miller; married Kenneth McLennan (an economist), August 14, 1962; children: Gordon, Laura. *Education:* City College of the City University of New York, B.A. (magna cum laude), 1961; University of Wisconsin—Madison, M.A., 1962, Ph.D., 1965. *Home:* 6950 Duncraig Court, McLean, Va. 22101. *Office:* Committee on the Budget, U.S. House of Representatives, Washington, D.C. 20515.

CAREER: Temple University, Philadelphia, Pa., assistant professor, 1965-72, associate professor of political science, 1972-79; U.S. House of Representatives, Washington, D.C., human resources specialist and budget analyst for Committee on the Budget, 1978—. Senior political scientist at Stanford Research Institute, 1972-74; consultant to UNESCO. *Member:* International Studies Association, American Political Science Association, Association for Asian Studies, American Association of University Professors, Northeast Political Science Association, Phi Beta Kappa.

WRITINGS: (Contributor) K. Ishwaran, editor, *Politics and Social Change*, E. J. Brill, 1966; (editor and contributor) *Crime in Urban Society*, Dunellen, 1970; (editor and contributor) *Political Opposition and Dissent*, Dunellen, 1973; *Comparative Political Systems*, Duxbury, 1975, 2nd edition, 1980. Author of monographs. Contributor to political science journals.

WORK IN PROGRESS: A revised edition of *Comparative Political Systems*.

SIDELIGHTS: McLennan wrote: "The thrust of most of my political science writings has been toward an attempt to develop a system of thought by which different political events and systems can be compared with a minimum of preconceived bias. Thus I have focused on the idea of political systems, grouping them by category of actual style of practice not by traditional geographic or economic considerations. My aim has been to isolate the essence of politics and to focus on that—not on side issues or the propaganda normally implied by dividing countries into developed and developing categories."

* * *

McMANUS, James Kenneth 1921-
(Jim McKay)

PERSONAL: Began using professional name of Jim McKay in 1950; born September 24, 1921, in Philadelphia, Pa.; son of Joseph Francis (a real estate appraiser) and Florence (Gallagher) McManus; married Margaret Dempsey (a syndicated newspaper feature writer), October 2, 1948; children: Mary Edwina, Sean Joseph. *Education:* Loyola College, Baltimore, Md., B.A., 1943. *Politics:* Democrat. *Religion:* Roman Catholic. *Residence:* Westport, Conn. *Agent:* Roberta Pryor, International Creative Management, 40 West 57th St., New York, N.Y. 10019. *Office:* ABC Sports, 1330 Avenue of the Americas, New York, N.Y. 10019.

CAREER: Baltimore Evening Sun, Baltimore, Md., police and general assignment reporter and aviation editor, 1946-47; WMAR-TV, Baltimore, news and sports commentator, 1947-50; Columbia Broadcasting System, Inc. (CBS), New York City, variety show host, weather and sports commentator, and radio interviewer, 1950-61; American Broadcasting Companies, Inc. (ABC), New York City, host of "ABC's Wide World of Sports" program, 1961—. Sports commentator for both the winter and summer Olympics, 1960, 1964, 1968, 1972, and 1976; also host of such events as the Kentucky Derby, the Indianapolis "500," and golf tournaments. *Military service:* U.S. Navy, 1943-46; became lieutenant. *Awards, honors:* Emmy Award from the Academy of Television Arts and Sciences, 1968 and 1970, both for "outstanding achievement in sports programming," two awards, 1973, one for coverage of Olympic games and the other for commentary on the deaths of the Israeli Olympic team, 1974, 1975, 1976; George Polk Memorial Award for journalism, 1972; Officer's Cross, Order of Merit (West Germany), 1974.

WRITINGS—Under professional name Jim McKay: *My Wide World* (autobiographical), Macmillan, 1973. Contributor of articles to periodicals.

SIDELIGHTS: As host for "ABC's Wide World of Sports," McManus has traveled around the world visiting such places as the Lenin Stadium in Moscow, the Melbourne Cricket Grounds in Dublin, and covering such events as ski racing in the Alps and the mountains of Chile, Le Mans, and the Olympics. It was his coverage of the 1972 Olympic games in Munich that added a new dimension to McManus's career as a sports commentator. Following the Arab terrorist attack on the dormitory of Israeli athletes, McManus remained on location for fifteen hours providing Americans with on-the-spot commentary.

In his book, *My Wide World*, McManus discussed his feelings about that switch from sports coverage to news: "Reporting, I think, is simply the communication to someone not on the scene of a given event, a happening. The reporter's job is to tell as clearly and accurately as he can the facts of the situation and, in the case of television, to explain the meaning of the visual image on the screen. More subtly, I think the reporter must communicate the mood of the moment.

"Assuming a fairly wide range of interests on the part of the reporter, it does not really matter whether the subject matter is sports or news. If the event is given its proper perspective, if the facts and the feelings are reported accurately and promptly, then the reporter is doing his job."

AVOCATIONAL INTERESTS: Golf, tennis, skiing, photography, singing.

BIOGRAPHICAL/CRITICAL SOURCES: Jim McKay, *My Wide World*, Macmillan, 1973.

* * *

McMILLAN, Constance (VanBrunt Johnson) 1949-

PERSONAL: Born July 29, 1949, in Los Angeles, Calif.; daughter of Godwin Augustus (a photographer) and Vida (a professor of education; maiden name, Milton) VanBrunt; married Don L. Johnson, September 3, 1971 (divorced March 14, 1974); married Robert F. McMillan (a project manager), September 14, 1975; children: (second marriage) Ayisha Nell. *Education:* Sarah Lawrence College, B.A., 1971; Harvard University, M.A.T., 1972. *Home:* 2631 Kyle Ave. N., Golden Valley, Minn. 55422. *Office:* EMC Corp., 180 East Sixth St., St. Paul, Minn. 55422.

CAREER: Tutor in Lincoln, Mass., 1971-72; Johnson Publishing Co., Chicago, Ill., creator and managing editor of *Ebony Jr.*, 1972-76; currently associated with EMC Corp. (publisher), St. Paul, Minn. Program assistant at African American Institute (New York City), summers, 1968-75. Member of board of directors of National Black Child Development Institute. *Member:* Business and Professional Women National Federation, Children's Reading Roundtable. *Awards, honors:* Earth Theater Award, 1975, for service to children's theater; SAY Children's Theater Award, 1975, for service to children's literature.

WRITINGS—For young people: *Donny and Marie Osmond: Breaking All the Rules*, EMC Corp., 1977; *Nadia Comaneci: Enchanted Sparrow*, EMC Corp., 1977; *Jockey Steve Cauthen: Million Dollar Baby*, EMC Corp., 1977; *Randy and Janet Johnson: Ready and Right!*, EMC Corp., 1977. Also editor of *Champions and Challenges*, Volumes I-II, EMC Corp. Contributor to academic journals and popular magazines, including *Ebony*.

WORK IN PROGRESS—Screenplays: "History of Maggie Lena Walker"; "History of Mamie Pleasant"; "History of Madam C. J. Walker."

SIDELIGHTS: Constance McMillan writes: "It is most important that we capture moments of laughter—positive experiences in contemporary writing. Success stories and the like are too often overlooked for drollery. Literature is often depressing—and a good piece of journalistic commentary too hard to find. I enjoy writing positive commentaries."

*   *   *

McMILLAN, James B. 1907-

PERSONAL: Born August 24, 1907, in Talladega, Ala.; son of William C. (an industrialist) and Celeste (Miller) McMillan; married Antoinette Brannon, August 29, 1931; children: Cynthia McMillan Lanford. *Education:* Attended Davidson College, 1925-26; Alabama Polytechnic Institute, B.S., 1929; University of North Carolina, M.A., 1930; University of Chicago, Ph.D., 1946; also attended Johns Hopkins University and Columbia University. *Home:* 7 North Pinehurst, Tuscaloosa, Ala. 35401.

CAREER: University of Alabama, University, professor of English linguistics, 1931-75; writer, 1975—. Visiting professor at University of Florida, 1947, University of Chicago, 1948, Georgetown University (also director of English-language program in Turkey), 1958-59, and University of Ankara, 1958-59. Managing editor of *Alabama Review,* 1947-63, and *Publication of the American Dialect Society,* 1964—. Member of board of directors of University of Alabama Press, 1945-62. *Member:* Modern Language Association of America, National Council of Teachers of English, Linguistic Society of America, American Dialect Society (president, 1950-53), Southeastern Conference on Linguistics, South Atlantic Modern Language Association, Phi Beta Kappa, Omicron Delta Kappa.

WRITINGS: (With Norman Foerster and J. M. Steadman) *Writing and Thinking,* Houghton, 1952; (with L. Boone and others) *Communicative Arts,* Colonial Press, 1961; *Annotated Bibliography of Southern American English,* University of Miami Press, 1971. Contributor to language and speech journals. Member of editorial board of *American Speech,* 1944-45, 1949-50, 1969-70, *National University Extension News,* 1953-55, *College Composition and Communication,* 1954-56, *Dictionary of American Regional English,* 1964—, *Abstracts of English Studies,* 1964-76, and *Harcourt-Brace School Dictionary,* 1969.

WORK IN PROGRESS: Research on phonology, lexis, semantic change, and pornolinguistics.

SIDELIGHTS: McMillan writes: "After nearly a half century of studying, teaching, and writing about English linguistics, I am still irritated by widespread myths and misconceptions about language, for example the television and movie characters' *anythin'* (invented in Hollywood by false analogy with native and respectable *somethin'* and *nothin'*), and broadcasters who say *Louisiana* as if the state had been named for a King Louise rather than King Louis."

BIOGRAPHICAL/CRITICAL SOURCES: I. Willis Russell and James C. Raymond, editors, *James B. McMillan: Essays in Linguistics by His Friends and Colleagues,* University of Alabama Press. 1978.

*   *   *

McNALLY, Tom 1923-

PERSONAL: Born March 8, 1923, in Berlin, N.H.; son of Frank X. (an accountant) and Lena (Cassidy) McNally; married Phyllis Gibson Brown, December 31, 1949; children: Thomas Robert, Marc Francis. *Education:* Loyola College, Baltimore, Md., B.S., 1949. *Home:* 2506 Harrison St., Glenview, Ill. 60025. *Office:* Chicago Tribune, 435 North Michigan Ave., Chicago, Ill. 60611.

CAREER: Montgomery Ward & Co., Baltimore, Md., management trainee, 1949-52; *Baltimore Sun,* Baltimore, Md., outdoor editor, 1952-56; *Chicago Tribune,* Chicago, Ill., outdoor editor, 1956—. *Military service:* U.S. Army, 1942-45; became sergeant. *Member:* Outdoor Writers Association of America, American Fisheries Society, Association of Great Lakes Outdoor Writers, Chicago Press Club.

WRITINGS: (Editor) *Fishermen's Digest,* John, Paul, 1958; *Fishing for Boys* (juvenile), Follett, 1962, reprinted as *Fishing,* 1972; *Hunting for Boys* (juvenile), Follett, 1962, reprinted as *Hunting,* 1972; *The Young Sportsman's Guide to Spinning* (juvenile), Thomas Nelson, 1964; *Camping for Boys and Girls* (juvenile), Follett, 1966; *Tom McNally's Fishermen's Bible,* Follett, 1970, 3rd edition, Jolex, 1976; *Camping* (juvenile), Follett, 1972; *Mostly About Dogs,* J. Philip O'Hara, 1972; *Tom McNally's Complete Book of Fishermen's Knots,* J. Philip O'Hara, 1975; *Tom McNally on Camping,* Jolex, 1978. Also author of *The Joys of Fishing* and *Ultra-Light Spinning.*

Author of a column in *Fishing World.* Contributor to outdoor magazines. Senior editor and associate publisher of *Fly Fisherman;* Midwest editor of *Field and Stream.*

*   *   *

McNAMARA, Jo Ann 1931-

PERSONAL: Born May 7, 1931, in Janesville, Wis.; daughter of James A. (an automobile company comptroller) and Chloe C. (Christman) McNamara; married Eldon R. Clingan, April 25, 1959 (marriage ended, 1972); children: Edmund. *Education:* Columbia University, B.S., 1956, M.A., 1959, Ph.D., 1967. *Home:* 500 West 111th St., New York, N.Y. 10025. *Office:* Hunter College of the City University of New York, 695 Park Ave., New York, N.Y. 10021.

CAREER: Hunter College of the City University of New York, New York, N.Y., associate professor of medieval history, 1963—. *Member:* American Historical Association, Mediaeval Academy of America, Coordinating Committee of Women in the Historical Profession, Berkshire Conference, Institute for Research in History.

WRITINGS: Gilles Aycelin: Servant of Two Masters, Syracuse University Press, 1973; (contributor) Lois W. Banner and Mary S. Hartmann, editors, *Clio's Consciousness Raised,* Harper, 1974; (contributor) Susan Stuard, editor, *Women in Medieval Society,* University of Pennsylvania Press, 1975; (contributor) Renate Bridenthal and Claudia Koonz, editors, *Becoming Visible,* Houghton, 1976; (translator) Pierre Riche, *Daily Life in the World of Charlemagne,* University of Pennsylvania Press, 1978. Contributor to history and feminist studies journals.

WORK IN PROGRESS: Contributing editor of a textbook for an interdisciplinary course in women's studies; research on the influence of the church in shaping the European family in the Middle Ages.

*   *   *

McNICKLE, (William) D'Arcy 1904-1977

OBITUARY NOTICE—See index for CA sketch: Born January 18, 1904, in St. Ignatius, Mont.; died December, 1977.

Educator, administrator, and writer. Beginning in 1936, McNickle held several posts in Washington, D.C., with the Bureau of Indian Affairs, where he last served as director of tribal relations. In 1952 he left that post to direct American Indian Development, Inc., in Boulder, Colo. His books deal mostly with Indian affairs and include *The Indian Tribes of the United States: Ethnic and Cultural Survival* and *Indian Man: A Life of Oliver La Farge*. Obituaries and other sources: *American Men and Women of Science: The Social and Behavioral Sciences*, 12th edition, Bowker, 1973; *World Literature Today*, spring, 1979.

* * *

McPHAIL, (Michael) David 1940-

PERSONAL: Born June 30, 1940, in Newburyport, Mass.; son of Bernard E. and Rachel (Cutter) McPhail; married wife, Janis (marriage ended); married wife, Mickey; children: Tristian, Joshua, Gabrian. *Education:* Attended Vesper George University and Boston Museum of Fine Arts School. *Home:* Granite St., Pigeon Cove, Mass. 01966.

CAREER: Artist and writer.

WRITINGS—All self-illustrated children's books: *The Bear's Toothache*, Little, Brown, 1972; *The Cereal Box*, Little, Brown, 1974; *Henry Bear's Park*, Little, Brown, 1976; *The Train*, Little, Brown, 1977; *The Magical Drawings of Moony Finch*, Doubleday, 1978.

WORK IN PROGRESS: Writing and illustrating *Stanley*, a children's book.

SIDELIGHTS: McPhail writes: "I wanted to be a 'fine artist,' and it took several years for me to realize and accept that illustrating books *is* a fine art. Sometimes it's an agony, often a joy—usually a lot of work."

* * *

McVICKER, Daphne Alloway 1895-1979

OBITUARY NOTICE: Born in 1895; died May 24, 1979, in New York, N.Y. Free-lance writer. Vicker wrote *The Queen Was in the Kitchen* in 1944. She also wrote for *Cosmopolitan* magazine. Obituaries and other sources: *New York Times*, May 27, 1979.

* * *

MEAD, William B(owmar) 1934-

PERSONAL: Born April 1, 1934, in St. Louis, Mo.; stepson of Beelis O. (a manufacturer) and Charlotte (Bowmar) Burkitt; married Jennifer Hilton (an independent filmmaker), June 9, 1956; children: Christopher, Andrew, Meagan. *Education:* Northwestern University, B.A., 1955. *Home and office:* 7520 Radnor Rd., Bethesda, Md. 20034. *Agent:* Peter Skolnik, Sanford J. Greenburger Associates, Inc., 825 Third Ave., New York, N.Y. 10022.

CAREER: United Press International, Richmond, Va., newswriter, 1958-60; Reynolds Metals Co., Richmond, in public relations, 1960-64; United Press International, newswriter in Chicago, Ill., 1964-65, Michigan news manager in Detroit, 1965-67, correspondent in Washington, D.C., 1968-72; *Money*, New York, N.Y., correspondent in Washington, D.C., 1972-76; free-lance writer, 1976—. *Military service:* U.S. Army, 1955-57. *Member:* Washington Independent Writers. *Awards, honors:* American Political Science Association Congressional fellow, 1967-68; John Hancock award for excellence, 1973, for article on how to deal with inflation; award from J. C. Penney Co. and University of Missouri

School of Journalism, 1975, for article on how to compare store-brand and nationally advertised grocery products.

WRITINGS: Even the Browns: The Zany, True Story of Baseball in the Early Forties, Contemporary Books, 1978. Contributor to *Washingtonian*.

WORK IN PROGRESS: Two books.

SIDELIGHTS: Reviewing *Even the Browns*, a critic for *Sports Illustrated* commented that the book is "a thoroughly diverting and occasionally surprising exploration of a slice of baseball history heretofore largely ignored," adding that it is "marvelously informative and fun to read." "Mr. Mead describes the Browns and baseball's war years with wit and irony," wrote a *New York Times* reviewer. "The tone is chatty, informal and humorous."

BIOGRAPHICAL/CRITICAL SOURCES: Philadelphia Inquirer, March 26, 1978; *Sports Illustrated*, April 3, 1978; *New York Times*, April 23, 1978; *Boston Globe*, April 28, 1978; *Minneapolis Tribune*, May 7, 1978; *Chicago Tribune*, May 21, 1978; *Sporting News*, May 27, 1978; *Time*, July 23, 1978; *Washington Post*, September 9, 1978.

* * *

MEDALIA, Leon S. 1881-

PERSONAL: Born December 5, 1881, in Palestine; son of Abraham Isaac (a merchant) and Pessie (Rabinowitz) Medalia; married Eugenia Zeitlan, September 1, 1908 (died, 1956); married second wife, Mabel, January 12, 1958; children: (first marriage) Nahum Zeitlan, Avram Izak. *Education:* Tufts University, M.D., 1905; postdoctoral study at Massachusetts Institute of Technology, 1919-21. *Politics:* Republican. *Religion:* Jewish. *Home:* 39 Cornet Stetson Rd., Scituate, Mass. 02066. *Office:* 78 Baystate Rd., Boston, Mass.

CAREER: Private practice of internal medicine in Boston, Mass., 1905—. Instructor at Tufts University, 1905-10. Pathologist at Mount Sinai Hospital and Beth Israel Hospital (both in Boston), 1908-20; cancer researcher at Palmer Memorial Hospital and City Health Laboratory, 1908-20. Member of national board of directors of Palestine Foundation Fund, 1920-27; president of Bureau of Jewish Education, 1920-28; founder and president of Hebrew University of Jerusalem, 1920-31 (also member of board of trustees); member of board of trustees of Association of Jewish Philanthropies. *Military service:* U.S. Army, laboratory chief for Infectious Disease Service, 1917-19, pathologist and laboratory chief, 1941-45; became colonel. U.S. Army Reserve, 1925—.

MEMBER: American Medical Association, American Public Health Association, Society of American Bacteriologists, American Association for the Advancement of Science, American Gerontological Society, American Heart Association, Reserve Officers Association of the United States, Military Order of the World War (life member), Association of Military Surgeons of the United States, Military Order of Foreign Wars of the United States, Royal Society of Health (fellow), Massachusetts Medical Association, Massachusetts Public Health Association, State Dental Society of New Hampshire (honorary member), Greater Boston Medical Association, Boston Medical Association (honorary member), Boston Medical Library Association, Masons, New Century Club, Army and Navy Club. *Awards, honors:* Citation from Hebrew University of Jerusalem, 1970.

WRITINGS: My First Ninety Years, Fountainhead, 1976. Contributor to medical journals.

MELLANBY, Kenneth 1908-

PERSONAL: Born March 26, 1908, in Barrhead, Scotland; son of Alexander Lawson (a professor of engineering) and Anne (Maunder) Mellanby; married Helen Nielson Dow, 1933 (divorced); married Jean Copeland (a writer), May 15, 1949; children: Jane Mellanby Impey, Alexander. *Education:* King's College, Cambridge, B.A., 1929, Sc.D., 1942. *Politics:* "Floating voter." *Religion:* Unitarian. *Home:* Hill Farm, Wennington, Huntingdon PE17 2LU, England.

CAREER: London School of Hygiene and Tropical Medicine, London, England, research worker, 1930-36; Royal Society of London, London, Sorby Research Fellow, 1936-45; University of London, London, reader in entomology, 1945-47; University of Ibadan, Nigeria, school principal, 1947-54; Rothamsted Experimental Station, England, head of entomology department, 1955-61; Monks Wood Experimental Station, Huntingdon, England, director, 1961-74; research fellow of Natural Environment Research Council, 1974-76. Professor at University of Leicester, 1969-76; consultant to conservation agencies. *Military service:* British Army, Medical Corps, 1942-45; became major. *Member:* Institute of Biology (president, 1970-72), Bedfordshire Hunting Institute, Naturalist Trust (president), Athenaeum Club. *Awards, honors:* Wandsworth fellowship, 1934; Commander of Order of the British Empire, 1954; D.Sc. from University of Ibadan, 1965, University of Bradford, 1969, and University of Leicester, 1972; honorary professor of biology from University of Leicester; honorary professorial fellow from University of Wales.

WRITINGS: Scabies, Oxford University Press, 1944, revised edition, Merlin, 1972; *Human Guinea Pigs,* Gollancz, 1945, revised edition, Merlin, 1973; *The Birth of Nigeria's University,* Methuen, 1958; *Pesticides and Pollution,* Collins, 1967; *The Mole,* Collins, 1972; *The Biology of Pollution,* Arnold, 1972; *Can Britain Feed Itself?,* Merlin, 1975; *Talpa,* Collins, 1976. Also author of scientific papers. Editor of "New Naturalist" series, Collins, 1969—. Author of column in *Nature,* 1975—. Editor of *Environmental Pollution,* 1969—.

SIDELIGHTS: Mellanby told *CA:* "Most of my life has been spent in scientific research and administration. My scientific papers have dealt with the details of research. My books have mostly dealt with subjects on which I have done scientific work and problems arising from it. Thus during the 1939-45 war I worked on the human parasitic disease Scabies, and wrote a clinical textbook on the subject. I had used human volunteers for this work, hence my book *Human Guinea Pigs.*

"Later I became involved in ecological problems, including pollution. I wrote two books, one in the "New Naturalist" series, *Pesticides and Pollution,* and a textbook entitled *The Biology of Pollution.* This latter has been translated into French and Spanish.

"As a result of research, I wrote a scientific monograph entitled *The Mole.* I thought that this subject would make a children's book so I produced *Talpa, The Story of a Mole.* This has been translated into Dutch, Danish, Finnish, and Greek." Mellanby added that although he spent ten years researching the book, he wrote it in less than two weeks, working only in the evenings.

AVOCATIONAL INTERESTS: Gardening, wine, food.

*   *   *

MELSON, Robert 1937-

PERSONAL: Born December 27, 1937, in Warsaw, Poland; came to the United States in 1947, naturalized citizen, 1952; son of William (in business) and Nina (Ponczek) Melson; married Gail Freedman (a professor); children: Sara, Joshua. *Education:* Massachusetts Institute of Technology, B.S., 1959, Ph.D., 1967; graduate study at Yale University, 1959-60. *Office:* Department of Political Science, Purdue University, West Lafayette, Ind. 47907.

CAREER: Michigan State University, East Lansing, assistant professor of political science, 1967-71; Purdue University, West Lafayette, Ind., associate professor of political science, 1971—. Fellow of Center for Advanced Studies, University of Illinois, 1969-70. *Member:* American Political Science Association (chairman of ethnic and cultural pluralism award committee).

WRITINGS: (Editor with Howard Wolpe) *Nigeria: Modernization and the Politics of Communism,* Michigan State University Press, 1971. Contributor to *American Political Science Review.*

WORK IN PROGRESS: Communalism and Genocide in Comparative Perspective; False Papers: A Memoir of World War II.

*   *   *

MELVILLE, Joy 1932-

PERSONAL: Born May 21, 1932, in Surrey, England; daughter of Lawrence Roy (a sugar broker) and Elyse (Johnson) Melville. *Education:* Educated in England. *Home:* 72 St. George's Sq., London S.W.1, England. *Agent:* A. D. Peters Ltd., 10 Buckingham St., London W.C.1, England. *Office: New Society,* 30 Southampton St., London W.C.1, England.

CAREER: Punch, London, England, assistant editor, 1959-71; *New Society,* London, England, assistant editor, 1971—.

WRITINGS: Phobias and Obsessions, Coward, 1977; (contributor) J. P. Martin, editor, *Violence and the Family,* Wiley, 1978. Contributor to psychology journals, popular magazines, and newspapers.

WORK IN PROGRESS: A book on mental health.

*   *   *

MENDELSOHN, Michael John 1931-

PERSONAL: Born January 30, 1931, in Cleveland, Ohio; son of Milton L. and Evelyn (Rosenberg) Mendelsohn; married Tiba Sladen, 1952; children: Lynn, Lori. *Education:* University of Pittsburgh, B.A., 1951; Trinity University, San Antonio, Tex., M.A., 1954; University of Colorado, Ph.D., 1962. *Office:* University of Tampa, Tampa, Fla. 33606.

CAREER: U.S. Air Force, career officer, assignments in San Antonio and Okinawa, 1951-58, instructor at U.S. Air Force Academy, Colorado Springs, Colo., 1958-59, assistant professor, 1959-63, associate professor, 1963-70, professor of English, 1970-72, retiring as lieutenant colonel; University of Tampa, Tampa, Fla., professor of English, vice-president of academic affairs, and dean of faculty, 1972—. Overseas extension lecturer for University of California, 1956; overseas extension professor for University of Maryland, 1956-58; lecturer at University of Colorado, Colorado Springs, 1963-68. *Member:* Modern Language Association of America, Rocky Mountain Modern Language Association.

WRITINGS: Clifford Odets, Humane Dramatist, Everett/ Edwards, 1969. Contributor to theater journals.

MENDELSON, Mary Adelaide (Jones) 1917-

PERSONAL: Born August 13, 1917, in Grand Rapids, Mich.; daughter of Paul Walton and Florence (Diamond) Jones; married Ralph Richard Mendelson, February 22, 1941; children: Walton Louis, Phillip Heath. *Education:* Radcliffe College, B.A., 1939; University of Michigan, M.A., 1940; Fenn College, teaching certificate, 1959. *Home:* 3137 Fairmount Blvd., Cleveland Heights, Ohio 44118. *Office:* Nursing Home Advisory and Research Council, Inc., 1001 Huron Rd., Columbus, Ohio 44115.

CAREER: Children's Aid Society, Detroit, Mich., case worker, 1940-41; American Red Cross, Home Service, case worker in Cleveland, Ohio, 1941-42, assistant director in Grand Rapids, Mich., 1942-46; high school history teacher in Shaker Heights, Ohio, 1959-63; Cuyahoga Community College, Cleveland, instructor in political science, 1963-64; Federation for Community Planning, Cleveland, staff director of nursing homes, 1964-72, nursing homes consultant, 1972-73; writer and lecturer, 1973-76; Nursing Home Advisory and Research Council, Inc., Columbus, Ohio, executive director, 1976—. Member of board of directors of Cuyahoga County Office of Price Stabilization, 1946, and Citizens League of Cleveland, 1967; candidate for Cleveland Heights City Council, 1961, 1963. Member of Ohio governor's task force on nursing homes, 1971-72, Ohio Board of Regents' advisory committee on geriatric medicine and gerontology, 1978—, and committee on older persons, of Federation for Community Planning, 1978—. Testified before U.S. Senate; consultant to U.S. Department of Health, Education & Welfare.

MEMBER: League of Women Voters (local president, 1952; member of state board of directors, 1958), Cleveland College Women's Association (member of board of directors, 1951), Radcliffe Club (local president, 1951). *Awards, honors:* George Polk Memorial Award from Long Island University, 1975; Frances Payne Bolton Award, 1975; achievement award from Young Women's Christian Association, 1978.

WRITINGS: Tender Loving Greed: How the Incredibly Lucrative Nursing Home "Industry" Is Exploiting America's Old People and Defrauding Us All, Knopf, 1974. Author of a column in *Insight,* 1976—. Contributor to magazines and newspapers, including *Washington Monthly, Annals,* and *Business and Society Review.*

* * *

MENSOIAN, Michael G(eorge), Jr. 1927-

PERSONAL: Born June 24, 1927, in Providence, R.I.; son of Michael George (owner of a furniture manufacturing company) and Alice (Ogassian) Mensoian; married Sirvart Gregorian (a registered nurse), July 5, 1969; children: Martha Alice, Christopher Michael. *Education:* Clark University, A.B., 1949; Boston University, M.Ed., 1951, C.A.G.S., 1959, M.A., 1964; Worcester State College, M.Ed., 1956; University of Connecticut, Ph.D., 1962; University of Pittsburgh, C.L.A.S., 1970. *Politics:* Independent. *Religion:* Armenian Apostolic. *Home:* 607 Commonwealth Ave., Newton Centre, Mass. 02159. *Office:* Department of Regional Studies, Boston State College, 625 Huntington Ave., Boston, Mass. 02115.

CAREER: Fitchburg State College, Fitchburg, Mass., assistant professor of education, 1954-56; Boston State College, Boston, Mass., assistant professor, 1956-59, associate professor, 1960-69, professor of geography, 1970—, director of Latin American studies program, 1969-74, 1978—, head of department of regional studies, 1970—. Lecturer at American Schools in Brazil, 1978. Director of graduate program for teachers in American schools overseas, and director of graduate programs in geography, earth science, and planning. Consulting geography editor for Catholic textbook division of Doubleday & Co.; consultant with Center for International Education. *Military service:* U.S. Navy, 1945-47. U.S. Naval Reserve, 1947-50. Massachusetts National Guard, 1950-70; became lieutenant colonel, U.S. Army National Guard, 1970—; became major.

MEMBER: Association of American Geographers, Asian Geographers, Conference of Latin Americanist Geographers, Society for Armenian Studies, Armenian Students' Association of America (member of board of directors), Friends of Armenian Culture Society (member and secretary of board of trustees), New England-St. Lawrence Valley Geographical Society, Armenian Educational Council.

WRITINGS: (With J. P. Jones and R. W. Spayne) *Manual for Physical Geography,* W. C. Brown, 1968; (with Hugh Brooks) *Arab World, New Africa,* Sadlier, 1968; (with Brooks, Clark Crain, and others) *Arab World, New Africa: Oriental and Ocean Worlds,* Sadlier, 1972; (with William Norris and David Dicker) *People of the Middle East and North Africa,* Sadlier, 1972; (with Norris and others) *The People of Africa and Asia,* Sadlier, 1974; (contributor) Richard P. Momsen, editor, *Geographical Analysis for Development in Latin America and the Caribbean,* Conference of Latin Americanist Geographers, 1975. Contributor to *World Book Encyclopedia.* Contributing editor of *Armenian Quarterly,* 1970-75.

WORK IN PROGRESS: Studying migrational behavior of Spanish-speaking people in Boston, Mass.; research on population growth and associated socioeconomic problems, especially in Latin America, the Middle East, and North Africa.

SIDELIGHTS: Mensoian writes: "The underlying theme whenever I write about Latin America or the arabized world is the essential unity between society and the environment within which it functions. Although the environmentalism of classical antiquity and that of the late 19th century has proven untenable, man's activity is still circumscribed by the character of his environment and paradoxically, by the ramifications of his advancing technology which is supposed to free him from those constraints.

"It is very satisfying to know that my work serves as an introduction for many young readers in their formative years to two of the largest and imperfectly known culture regions in the world.

"My efforts are motivated by a firm conviction that in our rapidly contracting world where ideas and events may have almost instantaneous impact, our failure to appreciate and accommodate legitimate demands from third world nations throughout Latin America, the Middle East, Northern Africa or elsewhere for a more equitable sharing of the world's resources and the rising expectations of their populations could easily prevent the development of a functional global system to assist mankind in his 21st century.

"Unfortunately, the ideological confrontations between East and West, manifested in both the political and economic arenas, have preempted concern for the potentially explosive relationship evolving between the developed nations on the one hand and those of the third world on the other.

"The differences in perspective, priorities, and values between the two must yield to the greater need for cooperative effort to solve the basic areas of concern such as population-resource imbalance, resource distribution, consumption patterns, etc.

"Not only for humanitarian reasons, but for purely pragmatic or national reasons as well, the United States and other developed nations must provide the leadership and the example needed to develop more effective political and socioeconomic delivery systems on a global scale.

"The more I view the world and write about its people and problems, the more firmly convinced I become that the diversity gives way to a fundamental sameness.

"If my work produces any message for the reader, at any level, it is that people and places and things are more alike than different and that the well-being of a nation or a society is inextricably related to the well-being of the world system of which it forms a part."

AVOCATIONAL INTERESTS: Travel (Caribbean, Mexico, Venezuela, Brazil), woodworking, HO-scale railroading.

* * *

MEREDITH, Richard C(arlton) 1937-

PERSONAL: Born October 21, 1937, in Alderson, W. Va.; son of Joseph Thompson (a pipefitter) and LaVon (Butcher) Meredith; married Joy Cecilia Gates, October 5, 1963; children: Kira, Derek, Rand. *Education:* Attended West Virginia State College, 1955-56, and Pensacola Junior College, 1960-61; University of West Florida, B.A., 1972. *Politics:* "Libertarian (more than anything else)." *Religion:* None. *Home:* 510 Queens Court (Pace), Milton, Fla. 32570. *Agent:* Scott Meredith Literary Agency, Inc., 845 Third Ave., New York, N.Y. 10022.

CAREER: Grice Electronics, Inc., Pensacola, Fla., advertising manager, 1962-69; *Milton Press-Gazette,* Milton, Fla., cartoonist and author of column "Spinoffs," 1972-75; *Santa Rosa Free Press,* Milton, editor, 1975; *National Enquirer,* Lantana, Fla., copy editor, 1976-77; free-lance writer, illustrator, and graphic designer, 1977—. *Military service:* U.S. Army, 1957-60, 1962. *Member:* Authors Guild of Authors League of America. *Awards, honors:* Phoenix Award from Southern Science Fiction Convention, 1970, for *We All Died at Breakaway Station.*

WRITINGS—All science fiction, except as noted: *The Sky Is Filled With Ships,* Ballantine, 1969; *We All Died at Breakaway Station,* Ballantine, 1969; *At the Narrow Passage,* Putnam, 1973; *Run, Come See Jerusalem,* Ballantine, 1976; *No Brother, No Friend,* Doubleday, 1976; *Vestiges of Time,* Doubleday, 1978; *The Awakening* (occult novel), St. Martin's, 1979; *The Timeliner Trilogy,* Playboy Press, 1979. Contributor to science fiction magazines.

WORK IN PROGRESS: The Beast (tentative title), an occult novel, for St. Martin's; two other novels; a book on muscular dystrophy, based on his own experiences as a father; a book on oddities of human clothing through the ages.

SIDELIGHTS: Meredith comments: "Until comparatively recently I considered myself exclusively a science fiction writer, but now believe I am expanding into a wider realm and consider this a rather significant stage of my own personal growth. In childhood and adolescence my interests were essentially scientific; my aim was to be an astronomer, but high school mathematics classes proved to me I didn't have the prerequisites. From pure science, my interest shifted to science fiction. Later I wandered into fantasy and 'occult' fiction, not so much as a writer, but as a reader. My first effort at writing an 'occult' novel (really an old-fash-

ioned ghost story along the lines of some of the things Shirley Jackson used to do or similar to some of Richard Matheson's early work) has all the earmarks of being more successful than my science fiction, and will probably generate several more, one of which is already underway, and another which I've only outlined.

"Like most science fiction fans who began reading in the 1940's or 1950's, I see Robert A. Heinlein as the single most important writer in the field, and would cite him, along with several other science fiction writers, as having been influential on my own writing. Outside science fiction, I believe Hemingway, Faulkner, and Thomas (not Tom) Wolfe have been most influential, though I'm not suggesting my work can be compared to theirs!

"One of the most interesting periods of my life, and one about which I may someday write a novel, was the year 1962, when, as an Army reservist, I was called back into active duty following the so-called Berlin Crisis, and was assigned, with a handful of fellow reservists, to augment an undertrained and under-strength unit of the Mississippi National Guard that had also been called up. During the ten months I spent at Fort Bragg, N.C., playing soldier, I witnessed some of the most bizarre and improbable incidents I've ever encountered in my life, and still look back on it all with a certain amount of disbelief. If the state of Mississippi has a reputation for backwardness, I can only say that it's fully justified.

"An equally interesting period was the year and a half I spent on the staff of the *National Enquirer,* in its own way as improbable as the Mississippi National Guard, but since I am still contributing material to the *Enquirer* on occasion, I will say nothing more about it now. There's another novel in that if I ever work up the courage to do it."

* * *

MERRITT, Raymond H(arland) 1936-

PERSONAL: Born March 29, 1936, in Sioux Falls, S.D.; son of Harland D. (a parts foreman) and Gertrude (Hansen) Merritt; married LaDonna Anenson, August 18, 1956; children: Cindy Rae, Michele Denise, Heidi Jo. *Education:* St. Olaf College, B.A., 1958; Luther Theological Seminary, B.D., 1962; University of Minnesota, M.A., 1963, Ph.D., 1968. *Politics:* Liberal. *Religion:* Lutheran. *Home:* 544 North Falls, River Falls, Wis. 54022. *Office:* Cultural and Technological Studies Program, University of Wisconsin, E-385 EMS Building, Milwaukee, Wis. 53201.

CAREER: Slovik, Mathre & Associates, Northfield, Minn., architectural draftsman, 1955-58; Department of Streets, Watertown, S.D., clerk, 1959; Village of Brooklyn Center, Minn., building inspection clerk, 1960; intern at Lutheran church in Seattle, Wash., 1960-61; G. T. Schjeldahl Co., Northfield, mechanical draftsman, 1961-62; Northfield Foundry, Northfield, mechanical draftsman, 1963; South Dakota School of Mines and Technology, Rapid City, instructor in social sciences, 1963-64; Wisconsin State University (now University of Wisconsin—River Falls), River Falls, instructor in history, 1964-66; North Dakota State University, Fargo, assistant professor of history, 1966-69, chairman of department, 1969; University of Wisconsin—Milwaukee, assistant professor, 1969-71, associate professor of history and systems design, 1971—, director of Urban History Institute, summers, 1970-72, director of cultural and technological studies program, 1972—. Associated with Hugel, Blatherwick & Fritzel, summer, 1955, and with William E. Broderson (architect), summer, 1958. Member of board of directors of Lutheran Campus Ministry, 1969-72. Director of educational tours; public lecturer; consultant (including National Endowment for the Humanities).

MEMBER: American Historical Association, Organization of American Historians, American Society for Engineering Education, American Studies Association of Northern Illinois and Wisconsin (president, 1972-73), Society for the History of Technology (member of advisory council; head of committee on technical studies and education, 1977—), Public Works Historical Society (member of board of trustees, 1975-80; vice-president, 1977-78; president, 1978—). *Awards, honors:* National Science Foundation grant, 1969; visiting scholar at Smithsonian Institution, 1972; National Endowment for the Humanities grants, 1973, 1977, 1978; Sloan Foundation grants, 1974, 1975; historic preservation grants, 1978, 1979.

WRITINGS: (Editor with Bill Reid) *One Soakers in American History,* Berkeley, 1968; *Engineering in American Society, 1850-1875,* University Press of Kentucky, 1969; *Conflict, Controversy, and Creativity: A History of the St. Paul District Corps of Engineers, 1866-1976,* U.S. Government Printing Office, 1979. Contributor of articles and reviews to history and education journals.

WORK IN PROGRESS: A history of municipal engineering; research on historical preservation in Wisconsin.

SIDELIGHTS: Merritt's efforts at University of Wisconsin—Milwaukee have concentrated on providing a wide range of humanities and social sciences courses for engineering students. The result of his work so far has been the cultural and technological studies program, which not only presents such varied courses as communication, comparative literature, English, geography, history, philosophy, political science, sociology, urban affairs, and anthropology, but makes a concentrated effort to relate these subjects directly to technological development and to the world of the engineering and science major. The success of his program can be measured by its continuation and rapid growth, and the fact that more than half the program's participants have come from disciplines outside engineering. The program has recently expanded into the area of historic preservation research and evaluation.

Merritt writes: "Technology has permeated our whole existence. It seems to be the source of our many problems, as well as the key to proposed solutions. This Promethean god should not be worshipped, but studied and understood. My professional life has been devoted to exploring the meaning of technology as it has affected our values, relationships, and ultimate concerns."

BIOGRAPHICAL/CRITICAL SOURCES: Journal of General Education, summer, 1977.

* * *

MERTENS, Lawrence E(dwin) 1929-

PERSONAL: Born March 6, 1929, in New York, N.Y.; son of John H. (an architect) and Marie (Loehr) Mertens; married Margarete Anna Waider, July 8, 1975; children: Oliver Larry, Thomas John. *Education:* Columbia University, B.S.E.E., 1951, M.S.E.E., 1952, D.Eng. Sci., 1955. *Home:* 649 Southeast Elm Dr., Palm Bay, Fla. 32905. *Office:* RCA Aerostat Systems, RCA Service Co., P.O. Box 4008, Patrick Air Force Base, Fla. 32925.

CAREER: Radio Corp. of America (now RCA Corp.), Camden, N.J., manager, 1952-62; RCA Service Co., Patrick Air Force Base, Fla., manager and chief scientist for RCA

Aerostat Systems, 1962—. Adjunct professor at Florida Institute of Technology. President of Photoquatics, 1967-72. *Member:* Institute of Electrical and Electronic Engineers, Society of Photo-Optical Instrumentation Engineers, Marine Technology Society.

WRITINGS: In-Water Photography, Wiley, 1970. Contributor to scientific and skin diving magazines. Guest editor of *Ocean Optics.*

WORK IN PROGRESS: Measuring the propagation of light in the sea and its application to long-range underwater television.

SIDELIGHTS: Mertens told *CA:* "Most of the techniques and equipment for underwater photography were developed by a handful of pioneers using trial and error methods. *In-Water Photography* attempts to establish a scientific framework for improving performance and designing new systems. A number of the old and widely believed theories are shown to be incorrect or to have only limited applicability. Methods of applying lasers and image processing are shown."

AVOCATIONAL INTERESTS: Tennis, boating, scuba diving, underwater photography.

* * *

MESTON, John 1915(?)-1979

OBITUARY NOTICE: Born c. 1915 in Pueblo, Colo.; died March 24, 1979, in Tarzana, Calif. Writer for television and films. Meston created and wrote almost 200 scripts for the long-running television series, "Gunsmoke." He created several other series for CBS television. Obituaries and other sources: *Chicago Tribune,* March 28, 1979; *New York Times,* March 28, 1979.

* * *

METZ, Mary Haywood 1939-

PERSONAL: Born October 2, 1939, in Zurich, Switzerland; daughter of Richard Mansfield (a classicist) and Margaret (a librarian; maiden name, Mowbray) Haywood; married Donald L. Metz (a sociologist), July 31, 1965; children: David Haywood, Michael Lehman. *Education:* Radcliffe College, A.B., 1960; graduate study at University of Freiburg and Free University of Berlin, 1960-61; University of California, Berkeley, M.A., 1966, Ph.D., 1971. *Religion:* United Church of Christ. *Home:* 2952 North Stowell Ave., Milwaukee, Wis. 53211. *Office:* Department of Behavioral Science, Mount Mary College, 2900 North Menomonee Parkway, Milwaukee, Wis. 53222.

CAREER: Earlham College, Richmond, Ind., intern, 1969-70, assistant professor of sociology, 1970-76; Mount Mary College, Milwaukee, Wis. lecturer in sociology, 1976—. Lecturer at Marquette University, spring, 1978. *Member:* American Sociological Association, American Educational Research Association, Society for Values in Higher Education (member of central committee, 1971-74; member of board of directors, 1972-74), Midwest Sociological Association, Phi Beta Kappa, Alpha Kappa Delta. *Awards, honors:* Fellowship from German Academic Exchange Commission, 1960-61; Woodrow Wilson fellowship, 1961-62; Kent Fellow, 1965-69; National Institute of Education grant, 1974-75.

WRITINGS: Classrooms and Corridors: The Crisis of Authority in Desegregated Secondary Schools, University of California Press, 1978. Contributor to sociology and education journals. Member of editorial board of *Soundings: An Interdisciplinary Journal,* 1974-77.

WORK IN PROGRESS: A study of public schools in a large city which are under court order to desegregate, completion expected in 1981.

SIDELIGHTS: Metz wrote: "A sociologist who does ethnographic work such as mine must be a lover of vicarious participation. The heart of the task of field work lies in an effort to comprehend each person's perspective with its social roots. Empathetic comprehension of persons in the varied roles in a social context provides an understanding of the clashes and harmonies in their interaction which none of the actors alone possesses.

"*Classrooms and Corridors* is a study of two schools with carefully matched desegregated student bodies each of which included a wide social and academic range of students. The book reports the variety of ways in which teachers and students understood the moral order of the classroom and the way these understandings shaped their daily interaction—in cooperation and conflict.

"The book then explores the extensive differences between the schools despite their similar student bodies and location in a single district. The diversity of the student bodies, especially their diversity in social background, academic skill, and consequent understanding of the character of relationships in a school, presented dilemmas for the school staffs. These dilemmas pushed them to choose, in practice, between effective education and reliable order. They did so despite the fact that external audiences and the staffs themselves considered both goals essential. The histories, faculty cultures, and values of the principals lead to different choices in the two schools, with the result that, their formal similarity notwithstanding, they created very different school experiences for their students.

"The study draws upon the sociological theory developed in the study of organizations other than schools for much of its analysis. However, it is written for the practitioner and involved parent as well as for an academic audience.

"When I did the field research for *Classrooms and Corridors* as a young woman without children I arrived on the scene with something of the freshness and objectivity of an anthropologist visiting a new culture. Now as I start on a new study of desegregated public schools, I am no longer such an outsider. My own children are in the primary grades in the desegregated schools of a large city. As president of the parent organization of a citywide desegregated school I have engaged in political struggle with the school board. I have learned much that I did not know before from the intimate involvement which parents' emotions create in situations involving their children. But I look forward to withdrawal once more into the role of an observer who must of necessity empathize with all parties. The alternation of detached consideration and wholehearted involvement can, I hope, contribute to wisdom in both roles."

*   *   *

MEYER, Armin Henry   1914-

PERSONAL: Born January 19, 1914, in Fort Wayne, Ind.; son of Armin Paul (a clergyman) and Leona (Buss) Meyer; married Alice James (a journalist), April 23, 1949; children: Kathleen Meyer White. *Education:* Lincoln College, A.A., 1933; Capital University, A.B., 1935; Ohio State University, M.A., 1941. *Religion:* Lutheran. *Home:* 4610 Reno Rd. N.W., Washington, D.C. 20008. *Office:* School of Foreign Service, Georgetown University, Washington, D.C. 20057.

CAREER: Capital University, Columbus, Ohio, assistant professor of mathematics and director of admissions and public relations, 1935-41, dean of men, 1939-41; affiliated with Office of War Information, 1943-46, and U.S. Information Agency, 1946-52; U.S. Foreign Service, Washington, D.C., Officer in Baghdad, 1944-48, Washington, D.C., 1948-52, Beirut, 1952-55, and in Kabul, Afghanistan, 1955-57, deputy director of South Asian Affairs, 1957-58, deputy director of Near Asian Affairs, 1958-59, director, 1959-60, deputy assistant secretary of state for Near Eastern and South Asian Affairs, 1960-61, ambassador to Lebanon, 1961-65, Iran, 1965-69, and Japan, 1969-72; chairman of cabinet committee to combat terrorism, 1972-73; American University, Washington, D.C., visiting professor, 1974-75; Georgetown University, Washington, D.C., adjunct professor of diplomacy and director of Ferdowsi project, 1975—. *Awards, honors:* Honorary degrees from Capital University, 1957, Lincoln College, 1969, South Dakota School of Mines and Technology, 1972, Ohio State University, 1972, and Wartburg College, 1972.

WRITINGS: Assignment Tokyo: An Ambassador's Journal, Bobbs-Merrill, 1974.

*   *   *

MEYER, Heinrich   1904-1977

OBITUARY NOTICE—See index for *CA* sketch: Born May 17, 1904, in Nuremberg, Germany (now West Germany); died October 10, 1977, in Bellingham, Wash. Author and professor. Meyer taught German at Muhlenberg College, University of Hamburg, and at Rice, Princeton, and Vanderbilt Universities. The author of biographies, criticism, novels, and historical studies, he also edited *German Studies in America* and contributed hundreds of articles to newspapers and journals. Obituaries and other sources: *Cassell's Encyclopaedia of World Literature,* revised edition, Morrow, 1973; *World Literature Today,* spring, 1979.

*   *   *

MICHAUX, Henri   1899-

PERSONAL: Born May 24, 1899, in Namur, Belgium; immigrated to France; naturalized French citizen; married Marie Louise Ferdiere, 1943 (died, 1948). *Education:* Attended University of Brussels for one year. *Religion:* Roman Catholic. *Residence:* Galerie le Point Cardinal, 3 rue Jacob, Paris 75006, France.

CAREER: Poet; writer; painter. Sailor in French Merchant Marines, 1920, 1938-39; *Hermes,* Paris, France, director, 1937-39. Artwork exhibited at Guggenheim Museum, September, 1978, and at Pompidou Center, National Museum of Modern Art of Paris, April-May, 1978.

WRITINGS—In English: *Ecuador: journal de voyage,* [France], 1929, revised edition, Gallimard, 1968, translation by Robin Magowan published as *Ecuador: A Travel Journal,* University of Washington Press, 1968; *Un barbare en Asie* (travel notes), Gallimard, 1933, revised edition, Gallimard, 1967, translation by Sylvia Beach published as *A Barbarian in Asia,* New Directions, 1949; *L'Espace du dedans* (poetry), Gallimard, 1944, revised and enlarged edition, 1966, translation by Richard Ellmann published as *Selected Writings: The Space Within,* New Directions, 1951; (self-illustrated) *Miserable miracle,* Rocher, 1956, revised and enlarged edition, Gallimard, 1972, translation by Louise Varese published as *Miserable Miracle: Mescaline,* City Lights, 1963; *L'Infini turbulent,* Mercure, 1957, revised and enlarged edition, Gallimard, 1967, translation by Michael Fineberg published as *Infinite Turbulence,* Calder & Boyars,

1975; *Connaissance par les gouffres*, Gallimard, 1961, revised edition, Gallimard, 1967, translation by Haakon Chevalier published as *Light Through Darkness*, Orion Press, 1963; *Les Grandes Epreuves de l'esprit et les innombrables petites* (autobiography), Gallimard, 1966, translation by Richard Howard published as *The Major Ordeals of the Mind and the Countless Minor Ones*, Harcourt, 1974; *Michaux*, translation from the French by Teo Savory, bilingual edition, Unicorn Press, 1967; Peter Broome, editor, *Au pays de la magie* (text in French; introduction and commentaries in English), Athlone Press, 1977.

Other: *Mes proprietes* (poetry and prose), J. D. Fourcade, 1929; *La Nuit remu* (poetry), Gallimard, 1935, revised edition, 1967; *Voyage en Grande Garbagne*, Gallimard, 1941; *Liberte d'action* (poetry), Fontane, 1945; *Ici, Poddema* (excerpt from *Livre du voyager*; also see below), Mermod (Lausanne, Switzerland), 1946; *Epreuves, exorcismes, 1940-44* (poetry; title means "Tests, Exorcisms"), Gallimard, 1946; Rene Bertele, editor, *Henri Michaux*, Seghers, 1946, revised and enlarged edition, 1957; *Peintures et dessins*, Editions du point du jour, 1946; *Nous deux encore*, Lanbert, 1948; *Arriver a se reveiller*, L'Air du temps, 1948; *Henri Michaux*, P. Drouin, 1948; *Ailleurs* (poetry), Gallimard, 1948, revised edition, 1969; *La Vie dans les plis* (poetry), Gallimard, 1949, new edition, 1965.

Passages, 1937-1950, Gallimard, 1950, revised and enlarged edition, NRF, 1963; (self-illustrated) *Mouvements* (poetry), Gallimard, 1951; *Nouvelles de l'etranger*, Mercure, 1952; *Face aux verrous* (poetry; title means "Facing the Bolts"), Gallimard, 1954, revised edition, 1967; *Quatre cents hommes en croix*, P. Bettencourt, 1956; *Plume; precede de Lointaine interieur* (poetry), Gallimard, 1957, revised edition, 1967; (self-illustrated) *Paix dans les brisements* (poetry), Flinker, 1959; Galerie Daniel Cordier, compiler, *Henri Michaux*, [Paris], 1959.

La Psilocybine, [Paris], 1960; *Situations-gouffres*, [Paris], 1960; *Vents et poussieres, 1955-1962*, Flinker, 1962; *Henri Michaux, oeuvres recentes*, presented by Cordier, text by Genevieve Bonnefoi, [Paris], 1962; *Vers la completude* (poetry), GLM, 1966; *L'Espace du dedans, pages choisies (1927-1959)*, Gallimard, 1966; *Henri Michaux*, [Paris], 1966; Bertele, compiler, *Parcours: Suite de douze eaux-fortes originales*, Le Point cardinal, 1966; K. Leonard, editor and compiler, *Henri Michaux*, [London], 1968; *Facons d'endormi, facons d'eveille*, Gallimard, 1969.

Poteaux d'angle, Herne, 1971; *En revant a partir de peintures enigmatiques*, Fata Morgana (Montpellier, France), 1972; *Emergence-resurgences*, Skira, 1972; *Quand tombent les toits* (play), GLM, 1973; *Moments; traversees du temps* (poetry), Gallimard, 1973; *Bras casse*, Fata morgana, 1973; *Par la voie des rythmes*, Fata morgana, 1974; *Ideogrammes en Chine*, Fata morgana, 1975; *Moriturus*, Fata morgana, 1976; *Choix de poemes*, Gallimard, 1976. Also author of *Livre du voyager, Ailleurs, Liberte d'action* (title means "Freedom of Action"), 1947, and of poetry including *Que je fus*, 1927, *Un Certain Plume*, 1931, and *Apparitions*, 1946.

Exhibition catalogs: Asger Oluf Jorn, editor, *Henri Michaux*, Silkeborg Museum (Denmark), 1962; *Amsterdam. Stedelijk Museum. Henri Michaux*, Staatsdrukkerij, 1964; *Henri Michaux*, Musee national d'art moderne (Paris), 1965; *Henri Michaux: choix d'oeuvres des annees 1946-1966*, Le Point cardinal, 1967; *Michaux a Venezia centro internazionale delle arti e del costume, Palazzo Grassi, 1967*, Rizzoli grafica (Milan), 1967; *Exposition Henri Michaux: peintures, 1946-67*, text by Bonnefoi, [Rouen, France], 1968; *Henri Michaux*, bilingual edition, W. Girardet, 1969; *Henri Michaux*, Kestner Gesellschaft, 1972; *Henri Michaux: oeuvres nouvelles, 26 novembre 1974-fin janvier 1975*, Le Point cardinal, 1974.

SIDELIGHTS: Michaux is a poet of unique style, one that is particularly difficult to pinpoint. He most closely resembles the surrealists, but cannot even accurately be grouped with them. Frederic Sepher pointed out that much of his poetry reads like short stories, although most of it does rhyme. He stated that while Michaux is probably the "least lyric of all contemporary French poets," and employs few metaphors, "he is brilliantly imaginative, inventive and rythmic. He even verges on the musical in his haunting, desperate litanies with their repetitions and developments."

Haunting, too, is Michaux's emphasis on "the strangeness of natural things and the naturalness of strange things," as Andre Gide once described Michaux's philosophy. Like Swift, Flaubert, and Lautreament, Michaux created imaginary lands inhabited by equally chimerical creatures. The royal spider, the Hacs, the Emanglons, and the Gaurs are just a few of the inhabitants in what are considered his best works, including *Voyage en Grande Garbagne, Au Pays de la magie*, and *Ici, Poddema*. These creatures are portrayed as being more real than human beings. So are their worlds seen as being far less fantastic and less absurd than the one in which Michaux himself lives. As a *Times Literary Supplement* critic put it, "It is surprising how true much of his poetry is even at the most superficial level." What has really happened in the thirty-odd years since the publication of *Voyage en Grande Garbagne* seems more strange than what is in the book, the critic asserted.

Michaux's world is filled with aggression and hostility. Through his writings he emphasizes fears and anxieties that are most often suppressed by others. As Sepher pointed out, Michaux's poetry is a form of self-analysis: it exorcises the terrible demons that reside within him. And to absorb blows that life meant for him, he invented a character named Plume. Plume is a weak, pathetic, yet humorous person, resembling Charlie Chaplin, who is constantly being bullied by his more intrepid associates. He embodies the weakness Michaux sees in himself, and in all men.

Michaux's works are imbued with a sense of alienation not only from others, but from himself as well. He warns that twentieth-century life is dangerous: one must be perpetually on guard for it is too easy to lose oneself, a frightening feeling he often describes. There is an ever-present conflict between one's inner and outer lives. Michaux contends that by developing stringent social mores that lead to the suppression of the individual by society, it is man himself who is responsible for this conflict. But man's condition is not hopeless. Michaux combats his own struggle between inner thoughts and the outside world by practicing strict self control, and with a sense of humor that is "one of his most salient characteristics," as Sepher observed.

While Michaux's writings are read worldwide and his poetry is currently popular among young people in France, the man himself remains somewhat of an enigma. Introverted and introspective, Michaux has screened much of his private life, especially his early years, from public view. It is known, however, that he felt alienated from his parents from the beginning. He voraciously read the works of mystics, and later was influenced by the writings of Lautreament, Ruysbroeck, Kafka, and Ernst Hello. He also painted, inspired by the modernist artists, most notably Paul Klee.

In his youth, Michaux had hoped to join the priesthood but

was dissuaded from doing so by his father. Instead, he pursued medical studies but eventually abandoned them to sail with the merchant marines. As a sailor, Michaux traveled to the United States, South America, and England, and later, on his own, to Asia, where he accumulated material used in writing travel books, such as *Ecuador* and *Un barbare en Asie.* But the travels he described were not all physical: even then, Michaux also wrote of the journeys within himself. In *New Republic,* a critic commented: "Coming upon *Ecuador* today one cannot, except by an act of imagination, appreciate the revolutionary thing it was when it was first published, nor the risk that Michaux took in those days. But the risk and the kind of adventure in which he engaged deserves to be compared with that of other great innovative writers of our time. Like them, he is powerful, incomplete, shifting, strangely satisfying and dissatisfying."

Like Aldous Huxley, Michaux experimented with hallucinogenic drugs, primarily mescaline, in exploration of his inner self and of further awareness. He was fifty-seven when he embarked on his first drug-induced voyage. At sixty-seven he gave up drugs at his doctor's advice, believing he had already experienced all that he could with them anyway. Some of his experiences are mirrored in *The Major Ordeals of the Mind and the Countless Minor Ones, Miserable Miracle, L'Infini turbulent, Connaissance par les gouffres,* and *L'Espace du dedans.* The latter is "not the kind of book to be read from cover to cover, but one to be dipped into, a little at a time," a *Times Literary Supplement* critic noted. Michaux's "poetry is the result of exploring and, in its most liberal sense, analysing the 'space within', the infinite universe of the inner self where the galaxies move and revolve according to laws whose mathematics may be forever beyond our comprehension."

In recent years, Michaux has devoted most of his talents to painting. That, for him, is another form of exorcism. He has said that he can better express himself through this medium. Many of his books include original drawings and paintings.

BIOGRAPHICAL/CRITICAL SOURCES—Books: Kurt Leonhard, *Henri Michaux,* translated by Anthony Kitzinger, Thames & Hudson, 1968; Malcolm Bowie, *Henri Michaux: A Study of His Literary Works,* Clarendon Press, 1973; Henri Michaux, *The Major Ordeals of the Mind and Countless Minor Ones,* translated by Richard Howard, Harcourt, 1974; Peter Broome, *Henri Michaux,* Athlone Press, 1977.

Articles: *L'Express,* January 5-11, 1970; *Times Literary Supplement,* September 25, 1970, August 6, 1971, May 4, 1973, February 15, 1976; *Modern Language Journal,* October, 1970; *Choice,* November, 1970, October, 1974; *Art in America,* March, 1971; *Books Abroad,* winter, 1974; *Encounter,* July, 1977; *World Literature Today,* winter, 1977; *Contemporary Literary Criticism,* Volume 8, Gale, 1978.

*   *   *

MICHEL, Anna   1943-

PERSONAL: Born December 12, 1943, in Mishawaka, Ind.; daughter of Raymond (a contractor) and Yolanda Rossi; married Robert Michel (a teacher of English), August 4, 1973. *Education:* Indiana University, B.A., 1967; Bank Street College, M.S., 1975. *Residence:* Linden, N.J. *Office:* First Presbyterian Nursery School, 12 West 12th St., New York, N.Y. 10011.

CAREER: Actress in summer stock and repertory and on tour, 1967-69; substitute teacher, 1970-72, remedial reading teacher, 1972-74, assistant teacher, 1974-75, all at schools in

New York City; International Play Group, New York City, co-teacher, 1975-76; First Presbyterian Nursery School, New York City, head teacher, 1976—. Volunteer art teacher at a day care center, 1972; volunteer teacher of American sign language at Columbia University, 1975-77. Marketing research interviewer for Commerical Analysts, 1968-69.

WRITINGS: Little Wild Chimpanzee (juvenile), Pantheon, 1978; *Little Wild Elephant* (juvenile), Pantheon, 1979; *Little Wild Lion* (juvenile), Pantheon, 1980; *Nim: The True Story of a Research Chimpanzee* (about a chimpanzee who learned sign language), Knopf, 1980; (with husband, Robert Michel, and Alan Barwiolek) *Living in Silence,* Pantheon, in press.

SIDELIGHTS: Anna Michel writes: "If there are books available on subjects that really interest children, teachers can stimulate reading. I have seen that most children are interested in animals, so animal life seemed like a good general area to write about. I want to present accurate and interesting information without diluting it in the fashion of some textbooks, so it was necessary for me to narrow down the subject as much as possible. I had read Jane Goodall's *In the Shadow of Man* and was fascinated by the behavior of the wild chimpanzees she had studied. I liked the idea of doing further research on chimpanzees and then sharing it.

"I believe it is important for children to realize that animals are not the property of human beings to be put at their service. If life on earth is to survive, children must grow into responsible adults who respect all life. I want to tell them that chimpanzees and other wild animals live more fulfilled and natural lives apart from humans. For this reason, I chose to write about wild chimpanzees, rather than captive ones, and to include no people in the book."

AVOCATIONAL INTERESTS: Travel.

*   *   *

MILLER, J(oseph) Hillis   1928-

PERSONAL: Born March 5, 1928, in Newport News, Va.; son of Joseph Hillis and Nell (Critzer) Miller; married Dorothy Marian James, April 2, 1949; children: Robin Leigh, Matthew Hopkins, Sarah Elizabeth. *Education:* Oberlin College, B.A., 1948; Harvard University, M.A., 1949, Ph.D., 1952. *Home:* Sperry Rd., Bethany, Conn. 06525. *Office:* Department of English, Yale University, New Haven, Conn. 06520.

CAREER: Literary critic. Williams College, Williamstown, Mass., instructor in English, 1952-53; Johns Hopkins University, Baltimore, Md., assistant professor, 1953-59, associate professor, 1959-63, professor of English, 1963-68, chairman of department, 1964-68, professor of English and humanistic studies, 1968-72; Yale University, New Haven, Conn., professor of English, 1972—, Gray Professor of Rhetoric, 1975—, chairman of department, 1976—. Visiting professor at University of Hawaii, summer, 1956, Harvard University, summer, 1962, 1972, Swarthmore College, 1967, University of Virginia, 1968, University of Washington, summer, 1971, and University of Zurich, 1972. Danforth Seminar lecturer at University of Chicago, 1959; teacher at Harvard University, summer, 1962; Ward-Phillips Lecturer at Notre Dame University, 1967. Member of supervisory committee of English Institute, 1968-71; fellow of Center for Humanities at Wesleyan University, 1971; trustee of Keuka College, 1971—.

MEMBER: American Academy of Arts and Sciences (member of research committee, 1968-69, executive council, 1970-73), Society for Religion in Higher Education (fellow), Phi

Beta Kappa. *Awards, honors:* Guggenheim Fellowship, 1959, 1965; Harbison Distinguished Teaching Award from Danforth Foundation, 1968; fellowship from Wesleyan Center for the Humanities, 1971.

WRITINGS—All criticism, except as noted: *Charles Dickens: The World of His Novels,* Harvard University Press, 1958; *The Disappearance of God: Five Nineteenth-Century Writers,* Harvard University Press, 1963; *Poets of Reality: Six Twentieth-Century Writers,* Harvard University Press, 1965; (editor with Roy Harvey Pearce) *The Act of the Mind: Essays on the Poetry of Wallace Stevens,* Johns Hopkins University Press, 1965; (editor) *William Carlos Williams: A Collection of Critical Essays,* Prentice-Hall, 1966; (contributor) James Thorpe, editor, *Relations of Literary Study: Essays on Interdisciplinary Contributions,* Modern Language Association, 1967; (contributor) Pearce, editor, *Experience in the Novel,* Columbia University Press, 1968; *The Form of Victorian Fiction: Thackeray, Dickens, Trollope, George Eliot, Meredith, and Hardy,* University of Notre Dame Press, 1968; *Thomas Hardy: Distance and Desire,* Harvard University Press, 1970; *Charles Dickens and George Cruikshank,* University of California, 1971; (editor) *Aspects of Narrative,* Columbia University Press, 1971; (editor) Thomas Hardy, *The Well-Beloved* (novel), Macmillan, 1976.

Contributor to periodicals and journals, including *Virginia Quarterly Review, Daedalus, New Literary History, Critical Inquiry,* and *Georgia Review.*

SIDELIGHTS: Miller is often referred to as one of the Geneva critics, a group that also includes Georges Poulet, Marcel Raymond, Albert Beguin, and Jean-Pierre Richard. The Geneva group proposes that literature is a key to the consciousness of the writer whose literature is being appraised. Primarily interested in the subjectivity with which a writer writes, the Geneva group has maintained that most efficient means of grasping a writer's subjective nature is by attending to the writer's entire body of works.

John Fowles found Miller's critical approach insufficient in *Thomas Hardy.* "On occasion," wrote Fowles, "one feels Mr. Miller is altogether too much the structural anthropologist on loan to literature. There is no literary criticism proper." He also declared, "I find Mr. Miller's approach one-sided. In too much academic analysis nowadays one methodology—in this case, an anatomical or structural interpretation—occludes others that are just as vital." Lionell Stevenson agreed with some of Fowles observations. He contended that Miller "dwells on Hardy's use of the past tense as though this were unusual rather than customary in fiction. Indeed, much of his discussion of Hardy might be applied with little or no modification to other novelists." However, Fowles did find some advantages in Miller's critical style. "Hardy's writing has been very thoroughly dismantled by the end of this book," Fowles wrote. "We learn a lot about how Hardy 'worked' as a creative 'machine.'" Regarding the book, Fowles concluded that "Hardy-lovers . . . must certainly read it; for if it has some of the defects of the narrow angle, it has also a high proportion of its virtues."

Sverre Lyngstad also had praise for Miller's style. "A sympathetic reader," noted Lyngstad, Miller "recreates the patterns of Hardy's writing in terms of its own imagery, especially weaving, and his book has the formal beauty of a work of art in its own right." He summed up the work as "a high level accomplishment."

In other works, notably *Poets of Reality* and *The Form of Victorian Fiction,* Miller's criticism revolves around notions of God. Concerning *Poets of Reality,* Kingsley Weatherhead wrote, "Hillis Miller's thesis is that the nihilism that followed the disappearance of God and the absorption of the creation into man's consciousness has been escaped in turn by the abandonment of the independence of the ego and its dispersal among things of an exterior nature." Dudley Flamm contended that Miller's preoccupation with nihilism as a vehicle in his criticism flawed *The Form of Victorian Fiction.* "Much too exclusively," wrote Flamm, "Miller relies on the idea of the death of God." However, he also noted that "even a rejection of this part of his thesis will not rob what he says about the novels themselves of its ability to assist readers toward the goal of achieving full 'consciousness of the consciousness' of the novelists."

BIOGRAPHICAL/CRITICAL SOURCES: Times Literary Supplement, February 10, 1966; *Partisan Review,* winter, 1967; *Comparative Literature,* fall, 1968; *Prairie Schooner,* summer, 1969; *Virginia Quarterly Review,* winter, 1969; *New York Times Book Review,* June 21, 1970; *Yale Review,* October, 1970; *Books Abroad,* winter, 1971.*

*   *   *

MILLER, Walter M(ichael, Jr.)   1923-

PERSONAL: Born January 23, 1923, in New Smyrna Beach, Fla.; son of Walter Michael and Ruth Adrian (Jones) Miller; married Anna Louise Becker, May 1, 1945; children: Margaret Jean (Mrs. Husam Arafat), Walter Michael III, Cathryn Augusta, Alys Elaine (Mrs. Earl Tracy). *Education:* Attended University of Tennessee, 1940-42, and University of Texas, 1947-49. *Home:* 403 Lenox Ave., Daytona Beach, Fla. 32018.

CAREER: Writer. *Military service:* U.S. Army Air Forces, 1942-45, served in Europe; received Air Medal with two Oak Leaf Clusters. *Awards, honors:* Hugo Award for best novelette, 1955, for "The Darfstellar"; received best novel award, 1961, for *A Canticle for Leibowitz.*

WRITINGS: A Canticle for Leibowitz (novel; Catholic Digest Book Club selection, Science Fiction Book Club selection), Lippincott, 1960, 3rd edition, 1973; *Conditionally Human* (collection of three science fiction stories), Ballantine, 1962; *The View From the Stars,* Ballantine, 1964. Author of scripts for television shows. Contributor of numerous stories to science fiction and other periodicals, including *American Mercury* and *Amazing.*

SIDELIGHTS: Primarily a science fiction writer, Miller is best known for *A Canticle for Leibowitz.* This book is unusual in that it combines religious concepts with futuristic fiction. Walker Percy explained: "Like a cipher the book has a secret. But unlike a cipher the secret can't be told. Telling it ruins it. . . . The peculiar nature of the secret is that the book cannot be reviewed. For either the reviewer doesn't get it or, if he does, he can't tell."

Among the critics who did review *A Canticle for Leibowitz* were Lois and Stephen Rose, who observed: "Miller . . . is always true to the story. His characters happen to be concerned with theological questions, but when they speak they always remain within the context of the story. Thus the theological conclusions are drawn by the characters and not by the author speaking directly to the reader." Percy contended that while Miller's prose may not be "distinguished," the novel is still "of more moment than the better known sci-fi futuristic novels, *1980* and *Brave New World.*"

A Canticle for Leibowitz was also published in French, Finnish, Hebrew, Italian, and Portuguese. Film rights for the novel were purchased by Sidney Beckerman in 1969.

BIOGRAPHICAL/CRITICAL SOURCES: Variety, November 6, 1968; Show Business, March 1, 1969; Lois Rose and Stephen Rose, The Shattered Ring: Science Fiction and the Quest for Meaning, John Knox, 1970; David Madden, editor, Rediscoveries, Crown, 1971; Contemporary Literary Criticism, Volume 4, Gale, 1975; Best Sellers, August, 1975.*

* * *

MILLS, James R(obert) 1927-

PERSONAL: Born June 6, 1927, in San Diego, Calif.; son of William S. (a contractor) and Beatrice (Wrighton) Mills; married Joanna Rohrbough, January 9, 1959; children: Beatrice, William, Eleanor. *Education:* San Diego State University, B.A., 1950, M.A., 1960. *Religion:* Baptist. *Office:* California Senate, State Capitol, Sacramento, Calif. 95814.

CAREER: Public school teacher in San Diego, Calif. 1950-54; San Diego Historical Society, San Diego, curator of Serra Museum, 1955-60; California Assembly, Sacramento, Democratic member of state assembly, 1961-66; California Senate, Sacramento, state senator, 1967—, president *pro tempore*, 1971—. Head of transportation committee of National Conference of State Legislatures; member of California Transportation Commission; member of board of directors of Amtrak, 1977—. Member of California Policy Seminar. *Military service:* U.S. Army, 1950-53. *Member:* Maritime Museum Association, Maritime Research Society, County and Municipal Employees Association, Urban League, American Legion, Veterans of Foreign Wars, Masons. *Awards, honors:* More than thirty-five awards for work in government and politics.

WRITINGS: Historic Landmarks of San Diego County, San Diego Historical Society, 1958; *San Diego: Where California Began,* San Diego Historical Society, 1960; *The Gospel According to Pontius Pilate,* Revell, 1978; *Poems of Inspiration From the Masters,* (religious poems), Revell, 1979. Contributing editor of *San Diego,* 1957-61.

SIDELIGHTS: Mills's major efforts as a state senator have been directed toward opening the activities of the state legislature to public scrutiny, by requiring roll-call voting procedures and permitting public and news media access to senate and committee meetings, and toward improving public transportation in California. He also has an active interest in improving state support of education.

* * *

MINGUS, Charles 1922-1979

OBITUARY NOTICE: Born April 22, 1922, in Nogales, Ariz.; died of a heart attack, January 5, 1979, in Cuernavaca, Mexico. Musician, composer, and author of his memoirs. Mingus distinguished himself as one of the finest bassists in jazz music. During the 1940's he played with such notables as Louis Armstrong and Lionel Hampton; after moving to New York in 1951, his fellow musicians included Charlie Parker, Stan Getz, and Duke Ellington. Some of his own bands were termed "Jazz Workshops," for Mingus was always changing his style and experimenting with new forms of music. He also had a reputation for being a less-than amicable performer: he would call abrupt halts in mid-song to lecture audiences on their disturbing behavior; sometimes he would become so irritated by the audience's and musicians' actions that he would leave the stage, and, on one occasion, he was involved in a fracas over racial slurs. He remained popular in the 1970's with recording contracts and performances in Europe and at the annual Newport Jazz Festival.

However, he suffered from a degenerative muscle disease which by 1977 had left him unable to play. He composed up until his death, and one of his final projects was a collaboration with singer and songwriter Joni Mitchell. In 1971, Mingus's autobiography, *Beneath the Underdog,* was published. Obituaries and other sources: *Newsweek,* May 17, 1971; *New Yorker,* May 29, 1971; *Current Biography,* Wilson, 1971; *Down Beat,* January 12, 1978; *Chicago Tribune,* January 9, 1979; *New York Times,* January 9, 1979; *Washington Post,* January 9, 1979.

* * *

MINSKY, Hyman P(hilip) 1919-

PERSONAL: Born September 23, 1919, in Chicago, Ill.; son of Sam (a clothing designer) and Dora (Zakon) Minsky; married Esther De Pardo, November 9, 1955; children: Diana, Alan. *Education:* University of Chicago, B.S., 1941; Harvard University, M.P.A., 1948, Ph.D., 1954. *Politics:* "Self-styled 'Man of the Left'." *Home:* 541 Warren Ave., St. Louis, Mo. 63130. *Agent:* Jean Steinberg, 175 West 93rd St., New York, N.Y. 10025. *Office:* Department of Economics, Washington University, St. Louis, Mo. 63130.

CAREER: Brown University, Providence, R.I., associate professor, 1949-57; University of California, Berkeley, assistant professor, 1957-59, associate professor, 1959-65; Washington University, St. Louis, Mo., professor of economics, 1965—. Visiting lecturer or professor at Carnegie Institute of Technology, 1947, University of California, 1956-57, and Harvard University, 1966. Director of Mark Twain Bankshares, St. Louis. Consultant to Unicorn Fund (New York), Pakistan Institute for the Development of Economics, and the board of governors of the Federal Reserve System and Federal Deposit Insurance Corporation. *Military service:* U.S. Army, 1943-46. *Member:* American Economics Association, Royal Economic Society.

WRITINGS: (Contributor) Irwin Friend and others, *Private Capital Markets,* Prentice-Hall, 1964; (editor) *California Banking in a Growing Economy, 1946-1975,* Institute of Business and Economic Research, 1965; (contributor) G. Horwich, editor, *Monetary Process and Policy: A Symposium,* Irwin, 1967; *Financial Instability Revisited: The Economics of Disaster,* Federal Reserve Board of Governors, 1972; *John Maynard Keynes,* Columbia University Press, 1975; *Financial Instability and the Strategy of Economic Policy,* Twentieth Century Fund, 1979.

WORK IN PROGRESS: Financial Instability and the Strategy of Economic Policy (tentative title); *The Twentiety Century Fund,* completion expected in 1979.

SIDELIGHTS: Minsky has written extensively on financial institutions, practices, and the effects of financial institutions in the American and other capitalist economies. He has also served as an economic consultant to banks and has testified before Congress on many occasions. Minsky told *CA* that "to date the advice offered business has been followed, but the advice offered Congress has never been followed."

Praising Minsky's *John Maynard Keynes* as "a wonderful little book . . . [and] a delight to read," Sidney Weintraub commented that "it is mind-boggling that in returning to the best covered figure in the history of economics Minsky has been able to capture Keynes's vision in a fresh, timely perspective."

BIOGRAPHICAL/CRITICAL SOURCES: Choice, May, 1976; *American Academy of Political and Social Science. Annals,* July, 1976.

MITCHAM, Carl 1941-

PERSONAL: Born September 20, 1941, in Dallas, Tex. *Education:* University of Colorado, B.A. (summa cum laude), 1967, M.A., 1969, further graduate study, 1969-70. *Office:* Department of Philosophy and Psychology, St. Catharine College, St. Catharine, Ky. 40061.

CAREER: Berea College, Berea, Ky., instructor in philosophy, 1970-72; St. Catharine College, St. Catharine, Ky., instructor in philosophy and psychology, 1972—. *Member:* American Catholic Philosophical Association, Society for the History of Technology, Kentucky Philosophical Association. *Awards, honors:* Abbott Payson Usher Prize from Society for the History of Technology, 1974, for *Bibliography of the Philosophy of Technology;* National Science Foundation-National Endowment for the Humanities grant, 1978-80.

WRITINGS: (Editor with Robert Mackey) *Philosophy and Technology: Readings in the Philosophical Problems of Technology,* Free Press, 1972; (with Mackey) *Bibliography of the Philosophy of Technology,* University of Chicago Press, 1973; (contributor) Paul T. Durbin, editor, *Research in Philosophy and Technology,* Volume I, Jai Press, 1978; (contributor) George Bugliarello and Dean B. Doner, editors, *The History and Philosophy of Technology,* University of Illinois Press, 1979. Contributor to *Encyclopedia of Bioethics.* Contributor of articles, poems, translations, and stories to scholarly journals and literary magazines. Review and bibliography editor of *Research in Philosophy and Technology.*

*   *   *

MITCHELL, Marianne Helen 1937-

PERSONAL: Born April 8, 1937, in Toledo, Ohio; daughter of Frank H. and Helen (Metzger) Mitchell. *Education:* University of Toledo, B.A., 1958 M.A., 1961, Ed.D., 1964. *Office:* School of Education, Indiana University, Bloomington, Ind. 47401.

CAREER: High school English teacher in Toledo, Ohio, 1958-60; Central Michigan University, Mount Pleasant, assistant professor of counselor education, 1964-66; Indiana University, Bloomington, associate professor of counselor education, 1966—. *Member:* American Personnel and Guidance Association, Phi Kappa Phi, Pi Lambda Theta, Pi Beta Phi, Delta Kappa Gamma.

WRITINGS: *The Counselor and Sexuality,* Houghton, 1973; (with Robert L. Gibson and Robert E. Higgins) *The Development and Management of School Guidance Programs,* W. C. Brown, 1973; (with Gibson) *An Introduction to Guidance,* Macmillan, 1980. Also author of *The High School Dropout: Can He Succeed in College?*

*   *   *

MITCHELL, Peter M(cQuilkin) 1934-

PERSONAL: Born October 15, 1934; married Lou Harden, September 16, 1961; children: Andrew, Thomas. *Education:* Marquette University, B.A., 1956; University of Colorado, M.A., 1960, Ph.D., 1965 *Home:* 42 Lessing Rd., West Orange, N.J. 07052. *Office:* Seton Hall University, South Orange, N.J. 07079.

CAREER: Seton Hall University, South Orange, N.J., assistant professor, 1963-67, associate professor of history, 1967—, vice-president for academic affairs, 1973—. Intern with American Council on Education, 1972-73. Member of board of trustees of Children's Institute. *Awards, honors:* Fellow of Colonial Williamsburg, 1967.

WRITINGS: (Editor with John B. Duff) *The Nat Turner Rebellion: The Historical Event and the Modern Controversy,* Harper, 1971.

*   *   *

MITCHELL, Yvonne 1925-1979

OBITUARY NOTICE—See index for *CA* sketch: Born July 7, 1925, in London, England; died of cancer, March 24, 1979, in London. Author and actress, best known for her award-winning film roles in "The Divided Heart," 1954, and "Woman in a Dressing Gown," 1957. In 1960, Mitchell appeared with George C. Scott in the highly acclaimed Broadway production of "The Wall." She also directed plays and wrote "Here Choose I" (published as *The Same Sky*), which won the 1951 Festival Britain Prize for best new play. Among her other writings are books for children and novels, including *The Bedsitter, Frame for Julian,* and *A Year in Time.* Obituaries and other sources: *The Author's and Writer's Who's Who,* 6th edition, Burke's Peerage, 1971; *Who's Who in the Theatre,* 16th edition, Pitman, 1977; *International Motion Picture Almanac,* Quigley, 1979; *Who's Who,* 131st edition, St. Martin's, 1979; *New York Times,* March 31, 1979.

*   *   *

MIZUMURA, Kazue

PERSONAL: Born in Kamakura, Japan; came to the United States in 1955; married Claus Stamm (a writer); children: one daughter (deceased). *Education:* Attended Women's Art Institute, Tokyo, Japan, and Pratt Institute, Brooklyn, N.Y. *Home:* Stamford, Conn.

CAREER: Began working in Japan as a commercial artist and instructor of Japanese sumi-e painting shortly after World War II; employed in the United States as a textile designer for four years; illustrator, 1959—; author of children's books, 1966—. *Awards, honors:* Outstanding Picture Book award, *New York Times,* 1968, for *If I Were a Mother.*

WRITINGS—All self-illustrated; all published by Crowell: *I See the Winds,* 1966; *If I Were a Mother . . . ,* 1968; *The Emperor Penguins,* 1969; *The Way of an Ant,* 1970; *The Blue Whale,* 1971; *If I Built a Village . . . ,* 1971; *If I Were a Cricket . . . ,* 1973; *Opossum,* 1974; *Flower Moon Snow: A Book of Haiku,* 1977.

Illustrator: Elizabeth Vining Gray, *The Cheerful Heart,* Viking, 1959; Patricia Miles Martin, *Suzu and the Bride Doll,* Rand McNally, 1960; Masako Matsuno, *A Pair of Red Clogs,* World Publishing, 1960; Claus Stamm, *The Very Special Badgers,* Viking, 1960; Janet Lewis, *Keiko's Bubble,* Doubleday, 1961; Rachel E. Carr, *The Picture Story of Japan,* McKay, 1962 Matsuno, *Taro and the Tofu,* World Publishing, 1962; Stamm, *Three Strong Women,* Viking, 1962; Yoshiko Uchida, *Rokubei and the Thousand Rice Bowls,* Scribner, 1962; Valdine Plasmati, *Algernon and the Pigeons,* Viking, 1963; Uchida, *The Forever Christmas Tree,* Scribner, 1963; Roma Gans, *It's Nesting Time,* Crowell, 1964; Martin, *The Greedy One,* Rand McNally, 1964; Stamm, *The Dumplings and the Demons,* Vikings, 1964; Uchida, *Sumi's Prize,* Scribner, 1964.

Matsuno, *Chie and the Sports Day,* World Publishing, 1965; Frank Bonham, *Mystery in Little Tokyo,* Dutton, 1966; Nancy Serage, *The Prince Who Gave Up a Throne,* Crowell, 1966; Uchida, *Sumi's Special Happening,* Scribner, 1966; Aileen Lucia Fisher, *My Mother and I,* Crowell, 1967; Jean Craighead George, *The Moon of the Winter Bird,* Crowell,

1969; Uchida, *Sumi and the Goat and the Tokyo Express,* Scribner, 1969; Bernice Freschet, *Jumping Mouse,* Crowell, 1971; John Frederick Waters, *Neighborhood Puddle,* Warne, 1971; Joanna Cole, *Plants in Winter,* Crowell, 1973; Freschet, *Skunk Baby,* Crowell, 1973; Sigmund Kalina, *Air, the Invisible Ocean,* Lothrop, 1973; Laurence P. Pringle, *Water Plants,* Crowell, 1975; Judy Hawes, *Fireflies in the Night,* Crowell, 1976; May Sarton, *A Walk Through the Woods,* Harper, 1976; Lorie K. Harris, *Biography of a Whooping Crane,* Putnam, 1977.

SIDELIGHTS: Although Mizumura's interest in art began when she was a child, she never thought of pursuing it as a career. For the young Japanese girl, it was enough of a dream to lead the life of a happy wife and mother. Her ideal life came to a disruptive end however, when World War II took the lives of her husband and infant daughter. Forced to earn her own living, Mizumura relied on her artistic talents to provide her with a source of income.

Until the mid 1960's, Mizumura was limited to illustration assignments with Japanese themes. Publishers assumed the work of a Japanese artist would be a credible addition to their books with an Oriental setting. Mizumura provided the publishers with kind of art work they were seeking, but the jobs gave her little opportunity to use other drawing techniques. Artistic limitations and encouragement from Elizabeth Riley of the publishing company of Thomas Y. Crowell soon led Mizumura to write and illustrate her own books.

BIOGRAPHICAL/CRITICAL SOURCES: Doris De Montreville and Donna Hill, *Third Book of Junior Authors,* H. W. Wilson, 1972.*

* * *

MODIANO, Patrick Jean 1945-

PERSONAL: Born July 30, 1945, in Boulogne-Billancourt, France; son of Albert (a financier) and Luisa (an actress; maiden name, Colpyn) Modiano; married Dominique Zehrfuss, 1970; children: Zenaide, Maria. *Education:* Attended high school in Thones, France. *Residence:* Paris, France. *Agent:* Georges Beaume, 3 quai Malaquais, 75006 Paris, France.

CAREER: Novelist, 1968—. *Awards, honors:* Prix Roger Nimier, 1968, and Prix Felix Feneon, 1969, both for *La Place de l'Etoile;* Grand Prix Roman from L'Academie Francaise, 1972, for *Ring Roads;* Prix Goncourt, 1978, for *Rue des boutiques obscures.*

WRITINGS: *La Place de l'Etoile* (novel), Gallimard, 1968; *La Ronde de nuit,* Gallimard, 1969, translation by Patricia Wolf published as *Night Rounds,* Knopf, 1971; *Les boulevards de ceinture,* Gallimard, 1972, translation by Caroline Hillier published as *Ring Roads,* Gollancz, 1974; (with Louis Malle) *Lacombe Lucien* (screenplay; released by Louis Malle, 1974), Gallimard, 1974, translation by Sabine Destree published as *Lacombe Lucien,* Viking, 1975; *Villa Triste* (novel), Gallimard, 1975, translation by Hillier published as *Villa Triste,* Gollancz, 1977; (with Emmanuel Berl) *Interrogatoire par Patrick Modiano suivi de Il fait Beau, allons au cimetiere* (title means "Examination" and "The Weather Is Fine, To the Cemetery"), Gallimard, 1976; *Livret de Famille* (novel; title means "Family Book"), Gallimard, 1977; *Rue des boutiques obscures* (novel; title means "Dark Shops' Street"), Gallimard, 1978.

* * *

MOFFATT, (Marston) Michael 1944-

PERSONAL: Born February 8, 1944, in Connecticut; son of E. Marston (an engineer) and Aileen (a teacher; maiden name, Threewit) Moffatt. *Education:* Reed College, B.A., 1966; Oxford University, B. Litt., 1968; University of Chicago, Ph.D., 1975. *Religion:* "Bokononist." *Office:* Department of Sociology and Anthropology, Rutgers University, New Brunswick, N.J. 08903.

CAREER: Rutgers University, New Brunswick, N.J., assistant professor of sociology and anthropology, 1975—. Consultant with Cantor Associates. *Member:* American Anthropological Association, Association of Asian Studies. *Awards, honors:* Junior fellow of Foreign Area Fellowship Foundation, in India, 1970-72.

WRITINGS: An Untouchable Community in South India: Structure and Consensus, Princeton University Press, 1978.

WORK IN PROGRESS: Research on student culture in New Jersey.

* * *

MOFFETT, (Anthony) Toby 1944-

PERSONAL: Born August 18, 1944, in Holyoke, Mass.; son of Anthony John (a beer salesman) and Mary (Romenius) Moffett; divorced; children: Julia. *Education:* Syracuse University, B.A., 1966; Boston College, M.A., 1968. *Politics:* Democrat. *Office:* 2 Cannon House Office Building, Washington, D.C. 20515; 160 Farmington Ave., Bristol, Conn. 06010.

CAREER: Public school teacher in Boston, Mass., 1967-68; U.S. Commissioner of Education, Washington, D.C., liason to urban street gangs, 1968-69; U.S. Department of Health, Education, and Welfare, Washington, D.C., director of Office of Students and Youth, 1969-70; aide to Senator Walter F. Mondale in Washington, D.C., 1970-71; Center for the Study of Responsive Law, Washington, D.C., director of Connecticut Citizen's Action Group (CCAG) in Hartford, Conn., 1971-74; U.S. House of Representatives, congressman from 6th Connecticut district, 1975—, serving on Interstate and Foreign Commerce Committee and Government Operations Committee, also member of several subcommittees. Member of educational board of Kettering Foundation. *Awards, honors:* Nationwide testimonial from International Association of Machinists, 1979, for work helpful to consumers on energy bill.

WRITINGS: The Participation Put-On: Reflections of a Disenchanted Washington Youth Expert, Delacorte, 1970; *Nobody's Business: The Political Intruder's Guide to Everyone's State Legislature,* Chatham Press, 1973.

SIDELIGHTS: In *The Participation Put-On* Congressman Toby Moffett analyzed the office he directed for more than a year, HEW's Office of Students and Youth. Under this Nixon administration outpost, director Moffett controlled $100,000 worth of grants for the new office—an office created, in Stephen Schlesinger's view, "to probe the headaches of restless teenagers and develop a style and rhetoric designed to appease their demands." According to *Publishers Weekly,* Moffett, too, soon realized he headed a bogus outlet for youth participation "whose real purpose was to make young people *think* they were participating to keep them from making real demands." He resigned in 1970 in protest against the U.S. invasion of Cambodia and the president's handling of the Kent State affair.

Schlesinger made several objections to *The Participation Put-On* before praising it for its honesty. On a stylistic level, Schlesinger termed the book an "overdrawn, belabored description" burdened by "loose" organization. He also made note of several inconsistencies seen in Moffett's championship of civil rights. For example, Schlesinger claimed Moffett fought "for funds for ghetto street gangs and for the civil rights of students; yet he never protested the softening of the desegregation guidelines by his own agency." Part of the reason for Moffett's problem in the book, continued Schlesinger, rested in the insubstantial nature of his job and the administration's "superficial" attitude towards it. Thus, "only when we catch glimpses of the crass politics of the Nixon administration, and the bewilderment of Moffett's own life, does his account begin to intrigue."

Apparently, Moffett's experience with the Office of Students and Youth led him to reanalyze the need for separate youth programs. While working for Ralph Nader's Connecticut Citizen's Action Group (CCAG) he reflected on the role of the young in our society. "What I'm doing now is removing myself from the illusion that young people are something special," he said. "That's a myth. . . . Our work is setting precedent for young people, to show them that you can overturn, you can challenge, you can research and expose." Moffett also explained why there was no student group to parallel the CCAG: "My response was no, why should there be a separate student group? The kids are involved and they're there and they're dealing with older people and working people and there's no talk about participation, they're just doing it."

Under Nader's auspices, the CCAG offered a much more viable outlet for change than the government program. Free to pursue environmental, safety, and other concerns without governmental or political ties, the group became "the prototype for citizen lobbies." In addition to his fights against utility rate hikes and incessant highway expansion, Moffett spearheaded the investigation of test cheating charges against the manufacturers of the M-16 rifle and helped organize state high school students in a conference on the politics of ecology. He also used the CCAG to compile information for his second book, *Nobody's Business,* a collection of in-depth profiles on every Connecticut State legislator running for reelection that year.

The CCAG's influence undoubtedly helped Moffett in his campaign for a congressional seat. Boosted by the "instant support" of fellow "raiders," he appealed to a constituency eager for change and posted convincing primary and final election victories.

Christopher Scanlan probed the personality that won the 1974 congressional election and cited Moffett's "natural charm" as a key element in his political image. He called Moffett an "obvious" politician—"and a good one"—though at times he "comes across just a bit too slick." This image evidently is not new to Moffett. While an undergraduate at Syracuse University one reporter called him "a slick opportunist . . . a guy on the make with whomever was in power." Moffett has shown, however, that he will risk isolation and side with himself when necessary. In a 1975 house vote he lived up to his defense-cut campaign promise as he voted against the construction of twelve F-11 bombers—planes which would have been built in Hartford and would have provided employment for several hundred constituents. His was the only no vote heard from a Connecticut legislator.

Moffett's other House activities have been varied, focusing most notably on his membership with the Interstate and Foreign Commerce Committee and the Government Operations Committee. He has also served on a transportation subcommittee where he advocated improved passenger and freight rail service. One highlight of his legislative career occurred in 1977, when House speaker Tip O'Neill appointed Moffett to serve on the ad hoc energy committee to draft the House version of President Carter's energy policy. Locally, he has stressed personal accessability to his constituents and has even held "office hours" in shopping malls and in other public places.

BIOGRAPHICAL/CRITICAL SOURCES: Publishers Weekly, November 22, 1971; *Saturday Review,* January 1, 1972; *New Republic,* January 29, 1972; *America,* March 4, 1972; *Best Sellers,* April 15, 1972; *Choice,* July, 1972, March, 1974; *Connecticut,* May, 1975.

* * *

MOJTABAI, A(nn) G(race)   1938-

PERSONAL: Surname is pronounced "much-to-buyee"; born in 1938, in Brooklyn, N.Y.; married in 1960; children: Chitra (daughter), one son. *Education:* Earned degree from Antioch College; graduate degrees from Columbia University. *Office:* c/o Nan Talese, Simon & Schuster, 1230 Avenue of the Americas, New York, N.Y. 10020.

CAREER: Copyperson at *Cleveland Press,* Cleveland, Ohio; archaeological assistant at Field Museum of Natural History, Chicago, Ill.; worked in a mental hospital in Maryland; presently a cataloguer at Cohen Library, City College of the City University of New York, New York City.

WRITINGS: Mundome (novel), Simon & Schuster, 1974; *The 400 Eels of Sigmund Freud* (novel), Simon & Schuster, 1976.

SIDELIGHTS: Ann Mojtabai's first novel, *Mundome,* received tremendous acclaim from the critics. Described by *New Yorker* as a "first novel of extraordinary originality and purity," it deals with the relationship between Richard, a librarian, and his sister Meg who has just returned home from a mental hospital. Richard's narration makes him seem a devoted brother, and, as Timothy Foote explained, he "is well past jagged recollections of Meg's ominous girlhood and into an account of her relapse . . . before the reader, by now totally in the grip of the author, really admits that Richard the good may in fact be Richard the bad, a brother whose sexual advances perhaps drove Sister Meg insane in the first place." Calling *Mundome* "brief, enigmatic, and fascinating," Jonathan Yardley declared that "madness . . . has been widely used as a metaphor in postwar fiction, . . . but rarely has it been as effectively—indeed devastatingly—employed as in this novel."

The 400 Eels of Sigmund Freud earned mixed reviews. In comparing it to Mojtabai's first book, a *New Yorker* critic reflected that while "'Mundome' had a mysterious, disturbing quality about it, this one seems merely unthought-out and disconnected." Similarly, Pearl K. Bell remarked: "Mrs. Mojtabai is spare and cryptically suggestive to a fault. In her ruthless trimming of anything that smacks of fatty excess, she has also shorn away some of the living tissue as indispensable to her story as the eels of Sigmund Freud." Nevertheless, Doris Grumbach contended that "the novel works well . . . [and is] a fine, intelligent and moving book."

Ann Mojtabai lived abroad for several years in Teheran, Iran, and then in Pakistan, where her husband was head of the Iranian cultural mission.

BIOGRAPHICAL/CRITICAL SOURCES: New York Times Book Review, May 12, 1974, May 30, 1976; *New Republic,* May 18, 1974; *Time,* May 20, 1974; *New Yorker,* June 3, 1974, July 5, 1976; *America,* June 15, 1974; *Sewanee Review,* summer, 1974; *Contemporary Literary Criticism*, Gale, Volume 5, 1976, Volume 9, 1978; *Newsweek*, June 7, 1976; *New Leader*, June 7, 1976; *New York Review of Books*, June 10, 1976; *Saturday Review*, June 12, 1976; *Nation*, July 31, 1976, August 7, 1976.*

* * *

MONNET, Jean   1888-1979

OBITUARY NOTICE: Born November 9, 1888, in Cognac, France; died March, 1979, near Monfrot-l'Amaury, France. Government official, economist, and author. Known as the "father of Europe," Monnet had been involved in the reorganization of Europe since World War I. He was a coordinator of war efforts for both world wars, served as a League of Nations official, was active in international financial affairs, and managed his family's brandy business. In 1946 Monnet developed a plan to revive the post-war French economy by modernizing French industry. The Monnet Plan encouraged French participation in the Marshall Plan and the Schuman Plan, which Monnet also drafted. In the 1950's Monnet established the European Coal and Steel Community and the Action Committee for the United States of Europe. Both organizations led the way for the establishment of the European Common Market and the European Community, which sought to integrate the countries of Europe politically and economically. Monnet wrote an autobiography, *Memoirs*, which was published in 1978. Obituaries and other sources: *Current Biography*, Wilson, 1947; Merry Bromberger and Serge Bromberger, *Jean Monnet and the United States of Europe*, Coward, 1969; *Newsweek*, May 5, 1975; *Foreign Affairs*, April, 1977; Jean Monnet, *Memoirs*, translated from the French by Richard Mayne, Doubleday, 1978; *New York Times Biographical Service*, November, 1978; *Who's Who*, 131st edition, St. Martin's, 1979; *Chicago Tribune*, March 23, 1979; *Time*, March 26, 1979.

* * *

MONSEY, Derek   1921-1979

OBITUARY NOTICE—See index for *CA* sketch: Born March 28, 1921, in Bridlington, Yorkshire, England; died in 1979 in London, England. Novelist and journalist. Monsey was a theatre critic in London for the *Picture Post, Spectator*, and the *Sunday Express*. His books include *The Hero Observed, The Affair*, and *August in the Family*. Obituaries and other sources: *AB Bookman's Weekly*, April 16, 1979.

* * *

MONTAGUE, Peter Gunn   1938-

PERSONAL: Born November 6, 1938, in Westport, Conn.; son of John Tyree and Margaret Abbott (Jones) Montague; married Katherine Karassik, October 18, 1970; children: (first marriage) Tyree Gunn, Timothy Gunn, Jessica Lee. *Education:* University of the Americas, B.A., 1962; Indiana University, M.A., 1967; University of New Mexico, Ph.D., 1971. *Home and office address:* P.O. Box 4524, Albuquerque, N.M. 87106.

CAREER: University of New Mexico, Albuquerque, associate professor of architecture and planning, 1972—, director of Center for Environmental Research and Development, 1977—. Consultant to U.S. Congress. *Member:* Authors Guild of Authors League of America, Society of Magazine Writers, National Association of Science Writers, American Studies Association.

WRITINGS: (With wife, Katherine Montague) *Mercury*, Sierra Club Books, 1971; (with K. Montague) *No World Without End*, Putnam, 1975. Contributor to popular magazines, including *Audubon, Ramparts*, and *Saturday Review*.
WORK IN PROGRESS: Studying radioactive waste disposal.

* * *

MONTHERLANT, Henry (Milon) de   1896-1972

PERSONAL: Born April 21, 1896, in Paris, France; died September 21, 1972, by his own hand in Paris; son of Joseph Milon and Marguerite Camuset (de Riancey) de Motherlant. *Education:* Attended Ecole Sainte-Croix de Neuilly. *Residence:* Paris, France.

CAREER: Sportsman, bullfighter, novelist, and playwright. Secretary of construction fund for Douaumont Cemetary honoring the war dead, 1921-24; traveled and lived in Italy, Spain, and North Africa, 1925-32; war correspondent for right-wing weekly, *Marianne*, c. 1940. *Military service:* French Army, 1914-18; war correspondent with French infantry, 1930-40; worked with Swiss Red Cross, 1942-45; received Croix de Guerre and Medaille des Combattants Volontaires. *Awards, honors:* Grand Prix de Litterature of the Academie Francaise, 1934, for *Lament for the Death of an Upper Class;* elected to the Academie Francaise , 1960.

WRITINGS—Novels: Le *Songe*, Grasset, 1922, translation by Terence Kilmartin published as *The Dream*, Weidenfeld & Nicholson, 1962, Macmillan, 1963; *Les Bestiaires*, Grasset, 1926, revised edition, Plon, 1929, translation by Peter Wiles published as *The Matador*, Elek, 1957, reprinted French edition, Gallimard, 1972; *Les Celibataires*, Grasset, 1934, reprinted, Gallimard, 1967, translation by Thomas McGreevy published as *Lament for the Death of an Upper Class*, J. Miles, 1935, and as *Perish in Their Pride*, Knopf, 1936, translation by Terence Kilmartin published as *The Bachelors*, Macmillan, 1960, reprinted, Greenwood Press, 1977; *Les Jeunes Filles* (first volume in tetralogy), Grasset, 1936, translation by McGreevy published as "Young Girls" contained in *Pity for Women*, G. Routledge, 1937, Knopf, 1938, reprinted French edition, Gallimard, 1972; *Pitie pour les femmes* (second volume in tetralogy), Grasset, 1936, translation by John Rodker published as *Pity for Women* contained in *Pity for Women* (see above), reprinted French edition, Gallimard, 1972; *Le Demon du bien* (third volume in tetralogy), Grasset, 1937, translation by Rodker published as "The Demon of Good" contained in *Costals and the Hippogriff*, Knopf, 1940 (published in England as *The Lepers*, G. Routledge, 1940), reprinted French edition, Gallimard, 1972; *Les Lepreuses* (fourth volume in tetralogy), Grasset, 1939, translation by Rodker published as *The Lepers* contained in *Costals and the Hippogriff* (see above; published in England as *The Lepers* [see above]), reprinted French edition, Gallimard, 1972; *L'Histoire d'amour de la Rose de Sable* (novelette), Plon, 1954, translation by Alec Brown published as *Desert Love*, Noonday, 1957, full French text published as *La Rose de sable*, Gallimard, 1968; *Le Chaos et la nuit*, Gallimard, 1963, translation by Kilmartin published as *Chaos and Night*, Macmillan, 1964; *Les Garcons*, Gallimard, 1969, translation by Kilmartin published as *The Boys*, Weidenfeld & Nicholson, 1974.

Fiction: *Histoire de la petite 19*, Grasset, 1924; *La Peri*, A. Rey, 1930; *Serge Sandrier*, Droin, 1948; *Pages d'amour de "La Rose de sable*," Laffont, 1949; *La Cueilleuse de branches*, Horay, 1951; *Une aventure au Sahara*, Archant, 1951; *Les Auligny* (extracts from *La Rose de sable;* see above), Amiot-Dumont, 1956.

Plays: *L'Exil* (three-act; title means "The Exile"), Editions du Capitole, 1929; *Pasiphae* (one-act; first produced in Paris at Theatre Pigalle, December 6, 1938), Editions des Cahiers de Barbarie, 1936, also published with *Demin il fera jour* (see below); *La Reine morte; ou, Comment on tue les femmes* (three-act; first produced in Paris at Comedie-Francaise, December 8, 1942), Gallimard, 1942, revised edition published as *La Reine morte*, 1947, published under same title with introduction by H. R. Lenormand, Macmillan, 1951, translation by Jonathan Griffin published as "Queen After Death" in *The Master of Santiago and Four Other Plays*, Knopf, 1951, reprinted French edition, Gallimard, 1971; *Fils de personne; ou, Plus que le sang* (four-act; first produced in Paris at Theatre Saint-Georges, December 18, 1943), Laffont, 1943, translation by Griffin published as "No Man's Son" in The *Master of Santiago and Four Other Plays* (see above), edition published under French title edited by France Anders, Macmillan, 1964, reprinted French edition, Gallimard, 1973; *Un incompris* (one-act title means "Misunderstood"; first produced in Paris at Theatre Saint-Georges, December 18, 1943), Gallimard, 1944; *Fils de personne* [and] *Fils des autres* [and] *Un incompris*, Gallimard, 1944.

Malatesta (four-act; first produced in Paris at Theatre Marigny, December 19, 1950), Marguerat, 1946, translation by Griffin published under same title in *The Master of Santiago and Four Other Plays* (see above), translation by Griffin published as *Malatesta*, Routledge and Kegan Paul, 1962, reprinted French edition, Gallimard, 1966; *Le Maitre de Santiago* (three-act; first produced in Paris at Theatre Hebertot, May 9, 1949), Gallimard, 1947, edition published under same title edited by Lucille Becker and Alba della Fazia, Heath, 1965 (edition published in England under same title edited by J. Marks, G. G. Harrap, 1960), translation by Griffin published as *The Master of Santiago*, Routledge & Kegan Paul, 1962, and contained in *The Master of Santiago and Four Other Plays* (see above), reprinted French edition, Gallimard, 1966; *Demain il fera jour* [and] *Pasiphae* (former in three acts; first produced in Paris at Theatre Hebertot, May 9, 1949), Gallimard, 1949, translation of former by Griffin published as "Tomorrow the Dawn" contained in *The Master of Santiago and Four Other Plays* (see above); *Celles qu'on prend dans ses bras* (three-act; first produced in Paris at Theatre de la Madeleine, October 20, 1950; title means "Women One Takes in One's Arms"), Wapler, 1949, revised edition, Editions de Paris, 1957.

La Ville dont le Prince est un enfant (three-act; title means "The City Whose Prince Is a Child"), Gallimard, 1951, revised edition, 1957, reprinted, 1973; *Port-Royal* (one-act; first produced in Paris at Comedie-Francaise, December 8, 1942), Lefebvre, 1954, critical edition with notes in English by Richard Griffiths, Blackwell, 1976 (see below); *Broceliande* (three-act; first produced in Paris at Comedie-Francaise, October 24, 1956), Gallimard, 1956; *Don Juan* (three-act; first produced in Paris at Theatre de l'Athenee, November 4, 1958), Gallimard, 1958, revised edition published as *La Mort qui fait le trottoir*, 1972; *Le Cardinal d'Espagne* (three-act; first produced in Paris in 1960; title means "The Cardinal of Spain"), Gallimard, 1960, edition published under same title edited by Robert B. Johnson and Patricia J. Johnson, Houghton, 1972; *La Guerre civile* (three-act; title means "The Civil War"), Gallimard, 1965.

Essays: *La Releve du matin* (title means "Morning Exaltation"), Societe litteraire, 1920, revised edition, Grasset, 1933, reprinted, Gallimard, 1972; *Premiere Olympique: le paradis a l'ombre des epees*, Grasset, 1924; *Deuxieme Olympique: les onze devant la porte doree*, Grasset, 1924; *Aux fontaines du desir* (title menas "At the Fountains of Desire"), Grasset, 1927; *Chant funebre pour les morts de Verdun*, Grasset, 1924; *Earinus*, E. Hazan, 1929; *Hispano-Moresque*, Emile-Paul Freres, 1929; *Pour une vierge noire*, Editions du Cadran, 1930; *Mors et vita*, Grasset, 1932; *Service inutile* (title means "Useless Service"), Grasset, 1935, reprinted, Gallimard, 1973; *La Possession de soi-meme*, Flammarion, 1938; *L'Equinoxe de septembre*, Grasset, 1938; *Paysage des "Olympiques,"* photographs by Karel Egermeier, Grasset, 1940; *Le Solstice de juin*, Grasset, 1941; *La Paix dans la Guerre*, Ides et Calendes, 1941; *Savoir dire non*, Lardanchet, 1941; *Sur les femmes*, Sagittaire, 1942; *D'aujourd'hui et de toujours*, Hachette, 1944; *Croire aux ames*, Vigneau, 1944; *Unvoyageur solitaire est un diable*, Lefebvre, 1946; *La Deesse Cypris*, Colas et Rousseau, 1946; *L'Eventail de fer*, Flammarion, 1944; *L'Art et la vie*, Denoel, 1947; *L'Etoile du soir*, Lefebvre, 1949; *Notes sur mon theatre* (contains "Notes de theatre," "La Reine morte," "Malatesta," and "Fils de personne"), L'Arche, 1950; *Coups de soleil*, La Palantine, 1950, reprinted, Gallimard, 1976; *Espana sagrada*, Wapler, 1951; *Le Fichier parisien*, Plon, 1952, second revised edition, Gallimard, 1974; *Le Plaisir et la peur*, Chez l'Artiste, 1952; *Textes sous une occupation (1940-44)*, Gallimard, 1953; *La Redemption par les betes*, Fequet and Bandier, 1959; Peter Quennell, editor, *Selected Essays*, translated by John Weightman, Weidenfeld & Nicolson, 1960, Macmillan, 1961; *Le Treizieme Cesar*, Gallimard, 1970.

Notebooks: *Carnets XXIX a XXXV, du 19 fevrier 1935 au 11 janvier 1939*, La Table Ronde, 1947; *Carnets XLII a XLIII, du 1 janvier 1942 au 31 decembre 1943*, La Table Ronde, 1948; *Carnets XXII a XXVIII, du 24 avril 1932 au 22 novembre 1934*, La Table Ronde, 1955; *Carnets XIX a XXI, du 19 septembre 1930 au 26 avril 1932*, La Table Ronde, 1956; *Carnets, annees 1930 a 1944*, Gallimard, 1957; *Va jouer avec cette poussiere (carnets, 1958-1964)*, Gallimard, 1966; *La Maree du soir (carnets, 1968-1971)*, Gallimard, 1972; *Tous feux eteints: carnets 1965, 1966, 1977, carnets sans dates, carnets 1972*, Gallimard, 1975.

Other: *La Lecon de football dans un parc*, Grasset, 1924; *Lettre sur le serviteur chatie*, Editions des Cahiers Libres, 1927; *La Mort de Peregrinos*, E. Hazan, 1927; *Sans remede*, M. P. Tremois, 1927; *Barres s'eloigne*, Grasset, 1927; *Pour le delassement de l'auteur*, E. Hazan, 1928; *Un desir frustre mime l'amour*, Lapina, 1928; *Pages de tendresse*, Grasset, 1928; *La Petite Infante de Castille* (short story), Grasset, 1929, reprinted, Gallimard, 1973; *Les Iles de la felicite*, Grasset, 1929; *Le Genie et les fumisteries du divin*, Societe Nouvelle des Editions, 1929; *Sous les drapeaus morts*, Editions du Capitole, 1929; *Le Chant des amazones*, Govone, 1931; *Histoire naturelle imaginaire*, Trianon, 1933; *Encore un instant de bonheur* (poetry; title means "Still a Moment of Happiness'), Grasset, 1934, revised edition, 1938; *Il y a encore des paradis: Images d'Alger, 1928-1931*, P. & G. Soubiron, 1935; *Mariette Lydis*, Editions des artistes d'aujourd'hui, 1938.

Les Nouvelles Chevaleries, Jean Vigneau, 1942; *La Vie en forme de proue*, Grasset, 1942; *Le Meme*, Nouvelle Revue Francaise, 1944; *Notes de la guerre seche: somee-oise, mai-juin 1944*, Editions litteraires, 1944; *La Vie amoureuse de M. de Guiscart*, Les Presses de la Cite, 1946; *Trois Romans*, Grasset, 1946; Marya Katerska, compiler, *Pages catholiques*, Plon, 1947; *Saint-Simon*, L'Originale, 1948; *L'Infini est du cote de Malatesta*, Gallimard, 1951; *Theatre choisi*, Hachette, 1953; *Montherlant par lui-meme*, Editions du

Seuil, 1953; *Monuments et memories,* Gallimard, 1956; *La Muse libertine,* Editions de Paris, 1957; *Discours de reception a l'Academie francaise et reponse de M. le duc de Levis Mirepoix* (speech), Gallimard, 1963; *Un assassin est mon maitre* (title means "An Assassin Is my Master"), Gallimard, 1971; *La Tragedie sans masque: notes de theatre,* Gallimard, 1972; *Mais aimons-nous ceux que nous aimons?,* Gallimard, 1973.

Omnibus volumes: *Les Olympiques* (contains *Premiere Olympique: le paradis a l'ombre des epees* and *Deuxieme Olympique: les ouze devant la porte doree*), Gres, 1926, revised edition, Grasset, 1938, reprinted, Gallimard, 1965; *Les Jeunes Filles* (tetralogy of novels; contains *Les Jeunes Filles, Pitie pour les femmes, Le Demon du bien,* and *Les Lepreuses*), Gallimard, 1943, reprinted, Club des libraires de France, 1961, translation by Terence Kilmartin published as *The Girls,* two volumes, Harper, 1968; *Le Chant de Minos* [*and*] *Pasiphae,* M. Fabianc, 1944, reprinted, Editions L.C.L., 1967; *Fils de personne: ou, Plus que le sang* [*and*] *Un incompris,* Gallimard, 1944, reprinted, 1973; *L'Exil* [*and*] *Pasiphae,* La Table Ronde, 1946.

Le Theatre complet [*de Montherlant*] (contains "Malatesta," "La Reine morte," "Fils de personne," "Un Incompris," "Le Maitre de Santiago," "Demain il fera jour," "Pasiphae," and "Celles qu'on prend dans ses bras"), five volumes, Ides et calendes, 1950; *Aux fontaines du desir* [*and*] *La Petite Infante de Castille,* Gallimard, 1954; *Mors et vita* [*and*] *Service inutile,* Gallimard, 1954; *Port-Royal* [*and*] *Notes de theatre,* Gallimard, 1954; *Theatre,* preface by J. De Laprade, Gallimard, 1955, enlarged edition, 1965, new edition published as *Theatre* [*de*] *Montherlant,* 1968; *Broceliande* [*and*] *L'Art et la vie,* Gallimard, 1956; *Romans et oeuvres de fiction non theatrales,* preface by R. Secretain, Gallimard, 1959.

Essais, Gallimard, 1963; *Oeuvre romanesque,* Editions Lidis, Volume 1: *Le Songe,* 1963, Volume II: *Les Olympiques,* 1963, Volume III: *Les Bestiaires,* 1964, Volume IV: *La Petite Infante de Castille* and *Encore un instant de bonheur,* 1964, Volume V: *Les Celibataires,* 1964, Volume VI: *Les Jeunes Filles* [*and*] *Pitie pour les femmes,* 1963, Volume VII: *Le Demon du bien,* 1964, Volume VIII: *Le Chaos et la nuit,* 1964; *Theatre,* Editions Lidis, 1965.

Contributor: (Author of preface) Henri-Louis Dubly, *Les Mains tendues,* [Paris], 1926; (author of preface) Edouard Des Courrieres, *Physionomie de la boxe,* Editions de Paris, 1929; F. Masereel, editor, *Juin 1940,* Somogny, 1942; (author of preface) Arlette Davids, *Rock Plants,* Hyperion Press, 1948; (editor) *Dictionnaire encyclopedique Lidis,* Lidis, 1971.

SIDELIGHTS: Despite the often controversial attitudes displayed in Montherlant's writings, many critics and several distinguished men of letters have praised his works. In 1961, Justin O'Brien wrote: "Many articulate Frenchmen had seen him as the greatest living writer of France. Gide had spoken of his 'undeniable authenticity,' and Camus had been stirred by his essays. Romain Rolland and Louis Aragon, both Marxists, declared him to be as thoroughly French as one could possibly be; and Malraux saw him as reflecting the same heroic tradition that he himself embodied." In 1964, O'Brien added: "However much he feels himself to be out of harmony with our time, Henry de Montherlant will live as one of the outstanding writers of the century."

Montherlant began his writing career at an early age, having already written a book on the life of Scipio by the time he was ten years old. Judith Greenberg declared that his early

essays contained in *Coups de soleil* "are so well written, so perfectly put, that it is hard to refrain from quoting nearly every page." Many of his first novels, such as *Le Songe* and *Les Bestiaires,* dealt with war, bullfighting, and sports, all of which played an important part in his life. His novels on these topics exalted the masculine qualities of virility, violence, and sensual enjoyment, and Lucille Becker noted that "they reflect, as a whole, the basic *joie de vivre* of youth, which sees before it infinite possibilities for self-fulfillment. They transcribe the author's passion for life and his confidence in the joys it will afford him."

After enlisting in the army during World War I, Montherlant was seriously wounded. Then after the war, when he returned to the bullfighting he had enjoyed since the age of fifteen, he was gored by a bull. In addition to these injuries, Montherlant contracted typhoid fever and had two attacks of pneumonia, all within two years. It is not surprising that he wrote: "In *Service Inutile,* the reader will find not more than five or six pages dating from the years 1925-27. I was too preoccupied with myself, too busy worrying and trying to save myself from despair, to give much attention to anything else."

Even after his illness and injuries, Montherlant's writings maintained a generally optimistic view of life. Martin Turnell, however, believed that "in spite of the emphasis that [Montherlant] places on life, happiness and pleasure in his essays and *Notebooks* ... neither his style nor his psychological acumen can blind us to the profoundly destructive attitude which underlies an apparently positive approach to experience." His later plays, notebooks, and the novel *Le Chaos et la nuit* most noticeably demonstrate Montherlant's cynicism, his rejection of unmanly qualities such as pity, sentimentality, tenderness, or mediocrity, his belief in the bitterness of useless service, and his nihilistic tendencies.

Though Montherlant served in the French army, he also adulated the enemy during World War II and welcomed the swastika as heralding a new era of grandeur. This caused him to be placed on a list of writers who had allegedly betrayed France. The case against him was based mainly on comments contained in *L'Equinoxe de septembre* and *Le Solstice de juin.*

In his *Carnets XLIII* Montherlant remarked, "I have never written anything without, at some time or other, feeling the urge to write the opposite." He often succumbed to this urge, leaving the reader with contrasting and paradoxical views of the author. Greenberg summarized this attitude: "Montherlant celebrates and identifies with all he finds: various dualities, *alternance* and *syncretisme,* innocence and sensuality, discipline and liberty, openness, honesty and the possible hypocrisy of 'truth,' gravity and humor, and always passion." Turnell agreed that Montherlant "is a man of contradictions: Catholic and pagan; a soldier who now detests modern warfare; a patriot who enjoys belaboring the fatherland; and—most important of all for an understanding of his work—a womaniser who at bottom hates women."

Montherlant never married. In his foreword to *Service Inutile* he explained that if he married, "either my wife would be neglected and would suffer, or the deepest part of myself—my soul—would be ruined, or more probably still both would be seriously damaged.... And once married (given my ideas, I could obviously only marry someone poor) I should be lost; by 'lost' I mean, obliged to earn money." This he believed would not allow him the freedom to be open to new adventures.

Ben Ray Redman described Montherlant's attitude toward

women: "Their only excuse for their inferior existence is that they are essential to what he likes to call The Act." Some critics believe that *Les Jeunes Filles* expresses most eloquently Montherlant's view of the opposite sex. Costals, the main character of this tetralogy, studiously avoids entanglements with women. He thinks men are embarrassed and ashamed at the passive role a man who is loved must play. "For a man to allow himself to be embraced, caressed, held hands with, looked at with swimming eyes—ugh! . . . A man who is loved is a prisoner."

Another novel, *Desert Love*, also contains interesting observations on male/female relationships. One character, Guiscart, was an artist who devoted his whole life to chasing women: "In his room or his studio it was a rare hour, the sixty mintues of which could get by without the explosive prompting, jerking him to his feet, to hurry to the window and, at sight of the first skirt passing by, storm at himself: 'There goes another littledollop of love and I'm missing it.'" Yet Guiscart played by certain rules. He coveted only women whose conquest seemed doubtful, refusing to bother with any who made the first advance. He did not care about keeping the women, but rather found discarding them as pleasing as taking them on. Guiscart "had never taken anything seriously which had originated in a women's mind or a woman's heart" and declared that "there was nothing to know [about women] and that if by any chance there were, it was not worth a man's understanding."

While these views reveal some insight into the author's minds, it is not to be automatically assumed that Montherlant believed as his characters do. In the foreword to *The Girls* he pointed out that "in Costals he has deliberately painted a character whom he intended to be disquieting and even, at times, odious; and that this character's words and actions cannot in fairness be attributed to its creator. . . . One might well wonder whether the critics and the public, on reading *La Rose de sable*, would attribute to the author the same abundance of virtues as they attributed to him of vices after reading *The Girls*."

Montherlant's writings touch upon various other aspects of sexuality in addition to man/woman relationships. The play *Pasiphae* is a dramatic representation of Pasiphae, a character in Greek mythology, describing her vacillating emotions of passion and shame just before having sexual relations with a bull, an act which resulted in the birth of the Minotaur. Another play, *La Ville dont le Prince est un enfant*, deals with the intimate friendship of two boys, Servrais and Soubrier, at a Catholic secondary school, and the jealousy of the school's Abbe, who is also passionately attached to Soubrier.

Reflecting upon his personal life, Montherlant once wrote: "I believe that very few contemporary French authors . . . avoid the limelight more than I do, or are keener to remain in the background. I claim no credit for this; it is a matter of taste." He had no concern with the usual social amenities, and accepted visitors so seldom that he was considered a recluse. This did not affect his writing career, however. In fact, he was elected to the Academie Francaise "without his making a single, traditional visit to the voting members and . . . [had] the unique privilege of giving his acceptance speech before a regular, private session of the members rather than in public, beneath the famous *Coupole*," noted Henri Kops.

Although he began his career as a novelist, Montherlant achieved his greatest success as a playwright. His first play, *La Reine morte*, was an immediate success and ran for 825

performances. His other plays were also well received in Paris except for *Broceliande, Don Juan*, and *Le Cardinal d'Espagne*. Most of his plays are psychological studies, often with historical and religious themes, reminiscent of the classical tradition of Racine and Corneille. *Le Maitre de Santiago*, declared Lucille Becker, "is the closest to French classical tragedy, not only by reason of the purity and sobriety of the dramatic line, but also because all of the action takes place within the characters." Henri Peyre remarked that "it is unlikely that Montherlant's plays will ever be performed on Broadway . . . [because] they deride with haughty sarcasm not only the materialistic values of money and success, but also the religious delusions, the democratic consolations, the effeminacy of the modern world."

Suicide was a prominent theme in Montherlant's writings, especially in his notebooks of 1958 to 1964, titled *Va jouer avec cette poussiere. Times Literary Supplement* observed that in *Le Treizieme Cesar* "Montherlant pleads for a greater understanding of suicide and of those who take their own lives. He sympathizes with suicide promoted by fear of suffering or old age, as well as with suicide as an alternative to the compromising of one's principles." Montherlant regarded suicide as "the last act by which a man can show that he dominated life and was not dominated by it."

In 1972, the seventy-six year old author had been blind in the left eye for four years, had recently suffered a heart attack, and had been in generally bad health for several years. It is not surprising under these circumstances that Montherlant took his own life. *New York Times* reporter Andreas Freund said Montherlant had hinted to friends about his suicide. He was found in his favorite chair at home where he had shot himself in the throat. Even the date of his death seemed to have been deliberately chosen by the novelist. *Times Literary Supplement* commented, "He committed suicide on September 21, 1972 and we know that *L'Equinoxe de september*—the title of a collection of essays published in 1938—had a special place in his private mythology." Montherlant's forword to *Service Inutile* contains an ominous prediction of his fate: "Aedificabo et destruam; I shall build, and then I shall destroy that which I have built. There we have an epigraph for this book—an epigraph for my life."

BIOGRAPHICAL/CRITICAL SOURCES: Henry de Montherland, *Service Inutile*, Grasset, 1935; *Saturday Review*, October 12, 1940, September 29, 1951, August 26, 1961; *New York Times*, October 20, 1940; Montherlant, *Carnets XXIX a XXXV, du 19 fevrier 1935 au 11 janvier 1939*, La Table Ronde, 1947; Montherlant, *Carnets XLII a XLIII, du 1 janvier 1942 au 31 decembre 1943*, La Table Ronde, 1948; Montherlant, *Desert Love*, translated by Alec Brown, Noonday Press, 1957; Henri Perruchot, *Montherlant*, Gallimard, 1959; Friedrich Lemley, editor, *Trends in Twentieth Century Drama*, Barrie & Rockliff, 1960; *Commonweal*, May 12, 1961; *Reporter*, September 14, 1961; John Cruickshank, *Montherlant*, Oliver & Boyd, 1964; *New York Times Book Review*, November 8, 1964, January 19, 1969; *New York Review of Books*, January 14, 1965; Montherlant, *Va jouer avec cette poussiere (carnets, 1958-1964)*, Gallimard, 1966; John Batchelor, *Existence and Imagination: The Theatre of Henry de Montherlant*, University of Queensland Press, 1967; *Books Abroad*, spring, 1967, summer, 1968, summer, 1969, spring, 1970, winter, 1974; Montherlant, *The Girls*, translated by Terence Kilmartin, introduction by Peter Quennell, Harper, 1968; *Listener*, January 11, 1968, August 15, 1968; *Books & Bookmen*, October, 1968; *Book World*, January 26, 1969; *Time*, February 7, 1969; *New Re-*

public, February 8, 1969; *National Review,* February 11, 1969; *Nation,* March 31, 1969; *Punch,* April 2, 1969.

Lucille Becker, *Henry de Montherlant: A Critical Biography,* preface by Harry T. Moore, Southern Illinois University Press, 1970; *Times Literary Supplement,* September 25, 1970, May 25, 1973, October 4, 1974, September 3, 1976, May 6, 1977; *Plays: Players,* March, 1971; *Stage,* April 1, 1971; *Spectator,* April 20, 1974; *World Literature Today,* summer, 1977; *Contemporary Literary Criticism,* Volume 8, Gale, 1978.

OBITUARIES: New York Times, September 23, 1972; *L'-Express,* September 25-October 1, 1972; *Newsweek,* October 2, 1972; *Antiquarian Bookman,* October 16, 1972.*

*   *   *

MOON, Michael E(lliott) 1948-

PERSONAL: Born January 22, 1948, in Missoula, Mont.; son of Gareth C. (a state forester) and Marjory (Elliott) Moon; married Chara Boehm, March 22, 1967 (divorced August 12, 1976); married Joy McIntyre (an artist), November 24, 1978; children: Matthew Elliott, Amy Isobel, Joshua Gareth-Carl. *Education:* Attended Montana State University, 1967-68; University of Montana, B.A., 1974. *Politics:* "No affiliation." *Religion:* Christian. *Home and office address:* P.O. Box 8934, Missoula, Mont. 59807. *Agent:* John Hartnett, Brann-Hartnett Agency, 14 Sutton Pl. S., New York, N.Y. 10022.

CAREER: Montana Department of Natural Resources and Conservation, Helena, public information specialist, 1974-77; writer, 1977—. Also worked as logger, forest firefighter, and timber cruiser.

WRITINGS: John Medicinewolf (novel), Dial, 1979. Contributor to magazines.

WORK IN PROGRESS: The Misfits (tentative title), a sequel to *John Medicinewolf.*

SIDELIGHTS: Moon writes: "The setting for all my work is the Pacific Northwest, particularly the woods. The main theme of my work is the role of technology in the life of personkind, and I am primarily interested in fiction. I have wanted to write since I was about fourteen but, sidetracked by alcoholism, I didn't publish anything until I was thirty. I admire Camus, Twain, Melville, and Dinesen from the past, and contemporary writers Piercy, Vonnegut, Brautigan, Vidal, and Rossner.

"My advice to young writers is to read everything in sight, study the classics for ten years, and then forget it all and write from personal experience. The most important thing a writer owns is not his reputation nor his typewriter—it's his faith in himself."

*   *   *

MOORE, Gary T(homas) 1945-

PERSONAL: Born March 13, 1945, in Calgary, Alberta, Canada; came to the United States in 1962; son of J. Thomas and Grace I. Moore; married Kristine Gunther (an artist); children: Mindan J. Gunther-Moore. *Education:* University of California, Berkeley, B.Arch. (honors), 1968; Clark University, M.A., 1973, doctoral candidate, 1975. *Home:* 2561 North Prospect Ave., Milwaukee, Wis. 53211. *Office:* Department of Architecture, University of Wisconsin—Milwaukee, Milwaukee, Wis. 53201.

CAREER: University of Wisconsin—Milwaukee, assistant professor of architecture, 1976—, coordinator of environmental-behavior studies graduate option, 1977—, Urban Research Center, scientist, 1978—. Principal of Cohen/Moore Associates, 1978—. Founder and chair of Design Methods Group, 1966-70; co-founder, Environmental Design Research Association, 1968. *Member:* American Psychology Association, Society for Research in Child Development. Environmental Design Research Association (co-founder; member of steering committee, 1968-70; member of board of directors, 1978—). *Awards, honors:* Eisner Prize for Creativity in Architecture, 1966; Woodrow Wilson fellowship, 1968; Canada Council doctoral fellowship, 1969-72; design award for *Emerging Methods in Environmental Design and Planning,* 1971; two citations from *Progressive Architecture* for research, 1978 and 1979.

WRITINGS: (Editor) *Emerging Methods in Environmental Design and Planning,* M.I.T. Press, 1970; (editor with Reginald G. Golledge) *Environmental Knowing: Theories, Research, and Methods,* Dowden, 1976; (with U. Cohen, J. Oertel, and L. van Ryzin) *Designing Environments for Handicapped Children,* Educational Facilities Laboratories, 1979. Also author of ten monographs. Contributor of numerous papers and short articles to journals and books on environmental psychology and architecture.

WORK IN PROGRESS: Research on children's outdoor recreation behavior; two books with U. Cohen, T. McGinty, and others, monographs, and two interim research reports, all based on a national study of children's play areas and child care facilities, for U.S. Government Printing Office and academic publisher.

SIDELIGHTS: Moore wrote: "My work within the university has been addressed to the development of a research tradition within architecture. More specifically, I have been interested in the relations between architecture and human behavior. In this regard, I have been actively involved in helping to shape the new field of environment-behavior studies, both its research arm in the social sciences (for example, environmental psychology) and its applied arm in the professions concerned with the environment (such as research applications in architecture). Before working on architecture/behavior questions, I spent some years helping to develop the sister area of design methodology. The overriding concern has been to find a more rational and humanistic basis for making architectural and planning decisions (based on human needs, behavior, and preferences) and a more rational process for making such decisions (design methodology).

"It is clear to me that architecture and planning are applied disciplines the goals of which are to envelope and facilitate human behavior, not to thwart people's needs. Sadly, this has not been the tradition of modern architecture. The new field of environment-behavior studies, with which I have been associated since its inception, is an attempt to base architecture on empirical research about behavior/space relations and to see this translated into better planning and design."

Environmental Knowing: Theories, Research, and Methods is a collection of thirty papers and nine commentaries written by American and British specialists in a variety of fields related to design. Moore and co-editor Golledge have blended papers on aspects of psychology, geography, anthropology, and the use of computers to explain "how humans come to know their environment," as *Human Ecology* reviewer Briavel Holcomb put it.

"The editors note that the acquisition of environmental knowledge involves a complicated series of processes—sensation, perception, imagery, retention, recall, reasoning, problem solving, judgment, and evaluation," wrote Holcomb. They make the point that although each person has a unique perception of his or her environment, some aspects are viewed in the same way by others. This makes possible "environmental communication," which is an essential step in getting to know the environment.

In the *American Institute of Planners Journal*, Donald Appleyard described the book as a "thorough and carefully wrought work." Reviewers in *Contemporary Psychology* cautioned, "The reader should be on guard ... for unwarranted conclusions, faulty designs, inappropriate statistics, and the like." But they also called the editors' introductions "excellent," using the same term to describe their "discussion of the historical roots, development and future prospects for the field.... Perhaps the book's strongest point is the diversity of ideas it presents."

BIOGRAPHICAL/CRITICAL SOURCES: Progressive Architecture, May, 1971, January, 1979; *Journal of the Royal Town Planning Institute*, November, 1971; *Architectural Science Review*, Volume 16, number 2, 1973; *American Institute of Planners Journal*, April, 1977; *Contemporary Psychology*, Volume 22, number 9, 1977; *Human Ecology*, Volume V, number 3, 1977; *Geographical Analysis*, January, 1979.

*   *   *

MOORE, Honor 1945-

PERSONAL: Born October 28, 1945, in New York, N.Y.; daughter of Paul (an Episcopal bishop) and Jenny (a writer; maiden name, McKean) Moore. *Education:* Radcliffe College, B.A. (cum laude), 1967; attended Yale University, 1967-69. *Home and office:* 100 Hudson St. 5E, New York, N.Y. 10013. *Agent:* Wendy Weil, Julian Bach Literary Agency, 3 East 48th St., New York, N.Y. 10013; Audrey Wood (play agent), International Creative Management, 40 West 57th St., New York, N.Y. 10019.

CAREER: Writer. Has given numerous poetry readings at libraries, colleges, and women's centers throughout the United States. Lecturer in women, theatre, and creativity. Teacher of writing and theatre workshops. Founder of the Poetry Series at Manhattan Theatre Club. Member of the board of directors of Poets and Writers, Inc., Manhattan Theatre Club (ex officio), and Jenny McKean Moore Fund for Writers. Member of Columbia University Seminar: Women and Society. *Member:* P.E.N., Poetry Society of America, Dramatists Guild. *Awards, honors:* CAPS fellowship from New York State Council on the Arts, 1975.

WRITINGS—Plays: *Mourning Pictures* (two-act; first produced in Lenox, Mass., at Lenox Arts Center, 1974; produced on Broadway at Lyceum Theatre, 1974), included in *The New Women's Theatre: Ten Plays by Contemporary American Women*, Random, 1977. Also author of four-act play, "Years," which received a staged reading at the American Place Theatre, 1978.

Collections: (Editor, author of introduction, and contributor) *The New Women's Theatre: Ten Plays by Contemporary American Women* (includes "Mourning Pictures"), Random, 1977.

Poetry: *Leaving and Coming Back* (chapbook), Effie's Press, 1979.

Contributor of poems to anthologies, including: *The New Woman's Survival Sourcebook*, edited by Susan Rennie and Kirsten Grimstad, Knopf, 1975; *We Become New*, edited by Lucille Iverson and Kathryn Ruby, Bantam, 1975; *The Lesbian Reader*, edited by Gina Covina and Laurel Galana, Amazon Press, 1976; *Tangled Vines: Poems About Mothers and Daughters*, edited by Lyn Lifshin, Beacon Press, 1978.

Contributor of poems to magazines, including *Yardbird, Nation, Chrysalis, Thicket, American Review, Sunbury, Hudson River Anthology, Black Box, Amazon Quarterly.* Contributor of articles and reviews to magazines, including *Ms.* and *Harper's Weekly.* Contributing editor to *Chrysalis.*

WORK IN PROGRESS: A collection of poems; a theatre piece, as yet untitled, directed by Victoria Rue; a biography/memoir of her grandmother, Margarett Sargent, "a painter who stopped painting after twenty years as a professional. In addition to being a biography and memoir, this book will also be an exploration of the difficulties of female creativity."

SIDELIGHTS: Susan Braudy described *Mourning Pictures* as "a stunning first play about the exploration of what a daughter and a mother say to each other and to themselves when the mother is dying ... it gives us a deep sounding of one woman's development as a daughter, a woman and a writer." Honor Moore's drama also earned words of praise from Brendan Gill. "Miss Moore is a very good writer, and there is scarcely a word too many in her text," Gill wrote. "She has pruned it and left room within it for silences that put me in mind of passages in Eliot's *Four Quartets.*"

Moore told *CA:* "I began writing in about 1968 just as the women's movement was beginning. That movement and the community of women writers that it encouraged have nurtured me as a writer. Writers, especially writers working with risky and controversial subject matter, need community and context. I write out of the women's movement. The journalist Annie Gottlieb once said that she defined the women's movement as 'women in movement'; it is this movement, both in myself and in women around me (friends, family—I have five sisters) that energizes my art.

"I am a poet first, and then a playwright and prose writer. My poems are charts of where I am, psychically and spiritually. *Mourning Pictures* is a play, but it is also a long poem. My new play 'Years' is the chronicle of a friendship between two women in their twenties. Norah and Rachel were best friends in high school and see each other four or five times during their twenties. The play begins with Rachel's college graduation and ends with Norah's thirtieth birthday. It is a play about commitment to friendship and commitment to art: Rachel is an orchestra conductor, Norah a poet. The play does not explore the idea that if 'one sings the other doesn't' but rather asks, 'if both sing, what happens?'"

Moore knows Latin, Greek, and French. Her poem, "I Have a War With My Mother," was recited in Claudia Weill's motion picture, "Girlfriends," produced by Warner Bros. in 1978. Some of her poems are recorded on a long playing record, "A Sign I Was Not Alone," produced by Out and Out Books in 1978.

AVOCATIONAL INTERESTS: Travel (Europe, Asia, and the Soviet Union).

BIOGRAPHICAL/CRITICAL SOURCES: Ms., November, 1974; *New Yorker*, November 18, 1974.

*   *   *

MORANTE, Elsa 1918-

PERSONAL: Born August 18, 1918, in Rome, Italy; married Alberto Moravia (a writer), 1941 (marriage ended). *Residence:* Rome, Italy. *Office:* c/o Alfred A. Knopf, Inc., 201 East 50th St., New York, N.Y. 10022.

CAREER: Writer. *Awards, honors:* Viareggio Prize, 1948, for *Mensogna e sortilegio;* Strega Prize, 1966, for *L'isola di Arturo.*

WRITINGS—In English: *Menzogne e sortilegio,* Einaudi, 1948, abridged translation by Adrienne Foulke published as *House of Liars,* Harcourt, 1951; *L'isola di Arturo,* Einaudi, 1957, translation by Isabel Quigly published as *Arturo's Island,* Knopf, 1959; *La storia,* Einaudi, 1974, translation by William Weaver published as *History: A Novel,* Knopf, 1977.

Other: *Alibi* (poems), Longanesi, 1958; *Le straordinarie avventure di Caterina,* Einaudi, 1959; *Lo scialle andaluso* (title means "The Andalusian Shawl"), Einaudi, 1963; *Il monce salvato dai ragazzini e altri poemi* (title means "The World Saved by Little Children"), Einaudi, 1968. Also author of *Le bellisime avventure di cateri dalla trecciolina,* 1941, *Il gioco segreto,* 1941, and *Botteghe oscure,* 1958. Translator of *Il libro degli appunti,* Rizzoli, 1945, and *Il meglio di Katherine Mansfield,* 1957. Work anthologized in *Modern Italian Stories,* 1955, and *Wake,* Volume 12.

SIDELIGHTS: Morante's first novel, *House of Liars,* though published in the United States only in an abridged version, is considered by some critics to be one of the great twentieth-century Italian novels. It is the story of a woman, Elisa, and her attempts to discover the history of her parents and grandparents. "At first glance," wrote Serge Hughes, "the novel would appear to be a belated realistic novel of the late nineteenth century. But it does not require much reading to become aware that the psychology which motivates the characters is completely, darkly modern, and that in using a somewhat dated setting and technique, the author has achieved a horror effect...." Frances Keene called *House of Liars* "a cross between a Gothic tale and a picaresque novel," but also felt that Morante had overextended herself in combining the two styles. She noted that "Morante is writing out of her epoch." Still, Paolo Milano found Morante to be a "visionary teller" and Keene declared, "The writer is an observant, stick-to-itive young woman: nothing escapes her."

Arturo's Island is similar to *House of Liars.* The main character, Arturo, recalls his childhood of being raised by a friend of his father. Arturo, who worships his father although he sees him only infrequently, discovers that his father has remarried. He transfers his adoration for his father to his stepmother. Eventually, Arturo leaves both the island and his past behind. Pamela Hansford Johnson deemed *Arturo's Island* "a poetic story, with all the charm the improbable has when it is told in the tone of probability." Johnson believed that the "theme of the book is remoteness; the remoteness of the island from the world of politics and war, the remoteness of the child from the parent...." Granville Hicks found many similarities between *Arturo's Island* and *Huckleberry Finn.* He discovered that both books shared a penchant for "idyllic passages" but also noted, "Both boys are exposed to evil in varied and terrible forms, but Arturo is profoundly changed, whereas Huck isn't."

Frederic Morton claimed that *Arturo's Island* was "a much more successful creation" than *House of Liars.* Although he thought that both novels had "an impressionistic rather than a dramatic style, as well as a theme dealing with the fraying-away of human ties," he also found Morante's style in the earlier novel "too cluttered with tiny virtuosities...."

Morante's most recent novel, *History,* is the result of six years of work. It covers the lives of several people in Europe during the 1940's. "The plot is a progress of disasters," as-

sessed Robert Alter. He added that "Morante's compassion . . . frequently spills over into pathetic excess, and her tough realism breaks down into a tediously proliferated series of disasters rigged by the novelist against her own creations." Because of the "pathetic excess," Alter decided that *History* "does not really support the weight of all its encrusted details, though if it fails as a whole, it nevertheless has a good many arresting moments." Paul Gray commented, "Morante continually makes old tricks fresh—not as a paring down of life's complexity but as short cuts into the absurdities of conflict and the urgencies of peace."

Stephen Spender felt that *History* succeeded in presenting an ideological viewpoint. "The tragedy of politics, as seen in History," wrote Spender, "is the inability of men to make politics human." He also noted, "The tragic end is of course inevitable, imposed by Elsa Morante's view of History and perhaps also by the nineteenth-century form she has chosen. The great virtue of her novel however is that although the reader accepts the inevitable ending, the life conveyed works as much against tragedy as for it. . . ."

Although Alter believed that "the very title of this enormous novel . . . is something of a provocation," Spender cautioned readers who might misinterpret the title of *History.* He wrote that "to try to extract a message or lesson from Elsa Morante's book is to follow too literally the clue hinted at in the title. The story that she has to tell stands marvelously on its own."

BIOGRAPHICAL/CRITICAL SOURCES: *New York Times,* October 7, 1951, August 16, 1959; *Saturday Review,* October 20, 1951, August 15, 1959; *Nation,* October 27, 1951; *New Statesman and Nation,* May 23, 1959; *New York Times Book Review,* April 24, 1977; *New York Review of Books,* April 28, 1977; *Time,* May 2, 1977; *Contemporary Literary Criticism,* Volume 8, Gale, 1978.*

*　　*　　*

MORRIS, David 1945-

PERSONAL: Born September 24, 1945, in New York, N.Y.; son of Augustus (an accountant) and Lottie (a teacher; maiden name, Levine) Morris. *Education:* Cornell University, B.S., 1966; University of Florida, M.A., 1967; Union Graduate School, Ph.D., 1973. *Home:* 3025 Ontario Rd. N.W., #307, Washington, D.C. 20009. *Office:* Institute for Local Self-Reliance, 1717 18th St. N.W., Washington, D.C. 20009.

CAREER: University of the District of Columbia, Washington, D.C., associate professor of political science, 1968-72; Institute for Local Self-Reliance, Washington, D.C., director, 1974—. Fellow of Institute for Policy Studies, 1968. Member of board of directors of National Center for Appropriate Technology; member of national advisory board of Energy Extension Services. *Member:* Mid-Atlantic Solar Energy Association (member of board of directors).

WRITINGS: *We Must Make Haste–Slowly,* Random House, 1973; (with Karl Hess) *Neighborhood Power,* Beacon Press, 1975; (with Gil Friend) *Kilowatt Counter,* Alternative Sources of Energy, 1975; *The Dawning of Solar Cells,* Environmental Action of Colorado, 1975. Author of column in *Solar Age.* Contributor to *Collier's Encyclopedia Yearbook.*

WORK IN PROGRESS: *The New City States; Energy Self-Reliance for the District of Columbia; Decentralized Electrical Generation.*

SIDELIGHTS: Morris comments: "My background is in Latin American development and neighborhood development, and I have a deep interest in technology and electronics. I am motivated by a desire to see citizens become planners. Cities as nations and local self-reliance are the underpinnings of my work."

AVOCATIONAL INTERESTS: Information systems, science fiction.

BIOGRAPHICAL/CRITICAL SOURCES: Mother Earth News, summer, 1976.

*   *   *

MORRISON, Donald George   1938-

PERSONAL: Born August 29, 1938, in Beverly, Mass.; son of Kenneth Cross (a pharmacist) and Helen Morrison; married Gretchen Hegemann, June 17, 1963 (divorced, September, 1972); married Jean Marie Borgatti (an art historian), August 11, 1975; children: Angus Anthony Borgatti. *Education:* Massachusetts Institute of Technology, B.S. (astronautics), 1961, B.S. (economics and politics), 1961, Ph.D., 1979. *Politics:* None. *Religion:* None. *Home:* 33 Clearwater Rd., Chestnut Hill, Mass. 02167. *Office:* Department of Political Science, Massachusetts Institute of Technology, Cambridge, Mass. 02139.

CAREER: Northwestern University, Evanston, Ill., research associate and instructor in management science, 1966-70; York University, Toronto, Ontario, member of faculty of environmental studies, 1970-71, Institute for Behavioural Research, director of research, 1970-71, research associate, 1974-75; Massachusetts Institute of Technology, Cambridge, professor of political science, 1975—. Visiting professor at University of Ibadan, Ibadan, Nigeria, 1971-74. *Military service:* U.S. Marine Corps, 1961-62. U.S. Marine Corps Reserve, 1962-67. *Member:* American Political Science Association, American Economic Association, American Sociological Association, African Studies Association, Econometric Society, Psychometric Society.

WRITINGS: Black Africa: A Comparative Handbook, Free Press, 1972, 2nd edition, 1979. Contributor to professional journals.

WORK IN PROGRESS: Books on African politics and statistics.

*   *   *

MORTON, John (Cameron Andrieu) Bingham (Michael)   1893-1979 (Beachcomber)

OBITUARY NOTICE: Born June 7, 1893, in London, England; died May 10, 1979, in Worthington, England. Writer. Although Morton wrote numerous novels, biographies, and histories, he was best known as Beachcomber, the author of a humorous column that ran in the *London Daily Express* for fifty years until his retirement in 1975. Obituaries and other sources: *World Authors, 1950-1970,* Wilson, 1975; *Chicago Tribune,* May 13, 1979.

*   *   *

MOSELEY, Ray   1932-

PERSONAL: Born December 2, 1932, in Marshall, Tex.; son of William C. (a grocer) and Veta (Blanton) Moseley; married Jenepher Wolff (in public relations), October 26, 1966; children: John Patrick, Ann Elizabeth. *Education:* North Texas State University, B.A., 1952. *Home:* 1519 Central Ave., Wilmette, Ill. 60091. *Office: Chicago Tribune,* 435 North Michigan Ave., Chicago, Ill. 60611.

CAREER/WRITINGS: Wichita Falls Record-News, Wichita Falls, Tex., reporter, 1952; *Dallas Times-Herald,* Dallas, Tex., state editor, 1952-56; *Arkansas Gazette,* Little Rock, reporter, 1956-59; *Detroit Free Press,* Detroit, Mich., reporter, 1959-61; *Rome Daily American,* Rome, Italy, managing editor, 1961-62; United Press International, reporter in Rome, Italy, 1962-64, bureau manager in Cairo, Egypt, 1964-66, Belgrade, Yugoslavia, 1966-67, and Rome, Italy, 1968-70, reporter in Washington, D.C., 1970-71; *Philadelphia Evening Bulletin,* Philadelphia, Pa., diplomatic correspondent in Washington, 1971-72; United Press International bureau manager in Moscow, Soviet Union, 1972-74, editor for Europe, Africa, and the Middle East in Brussels, Belgium, 1974-77; *Chicago Tribune,* Chicago, Ill., reporter, 1977-79, correspondent in Africa, 1979—. *Awards, honors:* Edward Scott Beck Award from *Chicago Tribune,* and award from Chicago Headline Club, both 1977, both for series of articles on child pornography.

SIDELIGHTS: Moseley's stories include the Little Rock integration crisis, 1957-58, the Indo-Pakistan war, 1965, Middle East war, 1967, and Iranian revolution, 1978-79. He also covered such Vatican stories as the deaths of Popes John XXIII and John Paul I and elections of Popes Paul VI and John Paul II.

*   *   *

MOSES, Wilson Jeremiah   1942-

PERSONAL: Born March 5, 1942, in Detroit, Mich.; son of William Heard and Ida Mae (a nurse; maiden name, Johnson) Moses; married Maureen Joan Connor (a librarian), November 30, 1963; children: William Joseph, Jeremiah Showers. *Education:* Wayne State University, A.B., 1965, M.A., 1967; Brown University, Ph.D., 1975. *Politics:* Social Democrat. *Religion:* Roman Catholic. *Office:* Department of History, Southern Methodist University, Dallas, Tex. 74275.

CAREER: Wayne State University, Detroit, Mich., instructor of English, 1969-70; Brown University, Providence, R.I., teaching associate, 1970-71; University of Iowa, Iowa City, assistant professor of history, 1971-76; Southern Methodist University, Dallas, Tex., associate professor of history and director of black studies, 1976—. *Member:* National Council for Black Studies, Organization of American Historians, African Heritage Studies Association, Association for the Study of Afro-American Life and History. *Awards, honors:* Fellowships from National Endowment for the Humanities, 1978, and Southern Fellowships Fund, 1978-79.

WRITINGS: The Golden Age of Black Nationalism, 1850-1925, Shoe String, 1978. Contributor to history, literature, and black studies journals.

WORK IN PROGRESS: Afro-American Messianism From Phyllis Wheatley to Andrew Young; The Madonna of the Street: Black Nationalism Religious and Literary; a biography of Alexander Crummell.

SIDELIGHTS: Moses told *CA:* "I believe that most of America's problems stem from the abandonment of the Puritan ethic. If we turn our young women into bunnies, it is not long before the young men become bunnies also.

"Black studies must teach the values of sacrifice, self-denial, and restraint. Iron will, iron discipline, correct diet, physical fitness, and other warrior virtues will place black people in a position to retrieve the day when the sun sets on the Western lands and they sink into the sea."

MOSHER, Arthur Theodore 1910-

PERSONAL: Born October 4, 1910, in Ames, Iowa; son of Martin L. (a professor) and Elva Katherine Mosher; married Alice Wynne Hall, February 1, 1936; children: William E., Arthur Theodore, Alice Anne Mosher Wimsatt, Richard W. *Education:* University of Illinois, B.S., 1932, M.S., 1941; University of Chicago, Ph.D., 1946. *Home:* 118 North Sunset Dr., Ithaca, N.Y. 14850.

CAREER: Allahabad Agricultural Institute, Allahabad, India, instructor in agricultural engineering, 1933-40, head of extension department, 1946-50, principal, 1948-53; University of Chicago, Chicago, Ill., visiting professor of economics and cultural change, 1953-55; Cornell University, Ithaca, N.Y., visiting professor of rural education, 1955-57; Agricultural Development Council, New York, N.Y., president, 1957-73, associate in Sri Lanka, 1974-76; writer, 1976—. *Member:* American Agricultural Economics Association (fellow), Society for International Development, University Club (New York, N.Y.).

WRITINGS: Technical Cooperation in Latin American Agriculture, University of Chicago Press, 1957; *Getting Agriculture Moving,* Praeger, 1966; *Creating a Progressive Rural Structure,* Agricultural Development Council, 1969; *To Create a Modern Agriculture,* Agricultural Development Council, 1971; *Thinking About Rural Development,* Agricultural Development Council, 1976; *An Introduction to Agricultural Extension,* Agricultural Development Council, 1978.

SIDELIGHTS: Mosher writes: "My major interest throughout my career has been international agricultural development, especially in Asia and Latin America. My writings have all been primarily for practitioners in that field rather than for the academic community. Brevity and easy readability are the characteristics I have sought to add to technical accuracy."

*　　　*　　　*

MUHEIM, Harry Miles 1920-

PERSONAL: Surname is pronounced *Mew*-hime; born February 17, 1920, in San Francisco, Calif.; son of Emile Francis (a civil engineer) and Anna (Kleinhammer) Muheim; married Jane Curtze; children: Heidi (Mrs. William Guilfoyle), Mark. *Education:* Stanford University, B.A., 1941, M.A., 1949; further study at University of Colorado, 1942-43. *Politics:* Democrat. *Home and office:* 8601 Sundale Dr., Silver Spring, Md. 20910. *Agent:* Gloria Safier, 667 Madison Ave., New York, N.Y. 10021.

CAREER: New York University, New York City, associate professor of speech and drama, 1950-58; Walter Reed Army Medical Center, Washington, D.C., staff writer for television division, 1958-60; independent writer, 1960—. *Military service:* U.S. Navy, 1942-46; became lieutenant; received Bronze Star. *Member:* Writers Guild of America, East, National Press Club, Dramatists Guild, Authors Guild, Phi Beta Kappa. *Awards, honors:* Guggenheim fellowship to write play "Lightfinger," 1956; awards for various films from American Film Festival, Fifth International New York and TV Film Festival, Columbus Film Festival, Information Film Producers of America, and Freedom Foundation.

WRITINGS: Vote for Quimby—and Quick! (novel), Macmillan, 1978. Author of feature film scripts, including "The Cable Car Caper," 1968, (with Art Buchwald) "Puhkow! Puhkow!," 1969, "The Greatest Man in the World" (adaptation of James Thurber short story), 1970, and "The War-

Movie War," 1971. Author of many industrial, educational, and documentary films, including "The Leisure Boom," 1961, "The Marvelous Mousetrap," 1962, "Sound and Light at Ford's Theatre," 1968, "Never Trust. E" 1970, *"Where Do We Go From Here?,"* 1972, "Big Apple," 1976, and *"The Eye of Thomas Jefferson,"* 1977. Also author of numerous speeches and promotional material for political events, including Robert F. Kennedy's presidential primary campaign, 1968, Hubert Humphrey's presidential campaign, 1968, E. G. Marshall's Democratic pre-election speech on CBS-TV, 1970, four ballot propositions for the State of Ohio, 1975, and Jay Rockefeller's West Virginia governorship campaign, 1976. Author of dramas and comedies for television programs "Philco Television Playhouse," "Kraft Television Theatre," "Alfred Hitchcock Presents," and others, 1952-60.

WORK IN PROGRESS: L.A. and the Yellow Peril, a novel based on the screenplay "The War-Movie War," dealing with events that took place during the first two weeks of World War II in Beverly Hills, Calif.

SIDELIGHTS: Muheim's ambition has always been to write for the movies and the stage. Although his feature films never reached the screen and his last successful play was during college, he has come close to his goals by writing numerous scripts for television theatre programs and various types of films.

Muheim wrote his first novel at age fifty-eight at his wife's urging: "It's too late for the Nobel, but if you're aiming for a Pulitzer, you better get off your ass." *Vote for Quimby—and Quick!* went to nineteen publishers before Macmillan accepted it.

Howard Kissel described *Quimby* as "a delightful amalgam of political savvy, fantasy sex and some poignant moments of reflection on the American system." Much of the material in the novel is taken from certain true political events and speeches that Muheim found to be great sources of humor. Other parts of the book are based on Muheim's speechwriting experience with politicians. He told Genevieve Stuttaford: "Politicians I've worked with are basically honorable men. . . . You can always tell whether you're working for a bum."

Muheim also remarked that he doesn't expect his first novel to "go echoing down the corridors of the 20th century." *Quimby* has received mixed reviews. Alan Ryan called it "a thoughtless and sloppy book" and commented: "It is hard to laugh either at or with a narrator who makes unfortunate and unfunny cracks about 'ethnics,' who 'belts' Manhattans, smokes cigars after sex, and says 'Boss!' a lot. The slang is outdated, the personalities unattractive, the attitudes incongruously paunchy." Stuttaford, however, asserted that this "funny, poignant, upbeat novel . . . has been receiving impressive reviews."

Muheim told *CA:* "My profile is generally low except among my friends, where I am regarded as a caution—and fairly funny. I prize uncontrollable laughter as a rich, capricious, and rare gift. I think that the capacity to enjoy it is an interesting character trait—a trait that links to others. My father would fall occasionally into these fits of laughter—never at entertainment or at something that was *planned* to be funny, but always at something gone wrong in life itself. Our phrase for that would be: 'Look at Joe. He's got a red boy.' The reference was simply to the fact that his face grew so red when he laughed so hard. The source of the phrase is no clearer than that. It was, in any case, no reference to a young Indian.

"I think that politics today is pretty much as it always has been. Knowledge of the political process is minimal. Interest in the process is moribund. Cynicism about the process is high. And yet the system remains foolproof here in America because it does not depend on people growing more intelligent or more moral or more interested. Its real success emanates from that remarkable clause in the Constitution that causes all federal public officials to come up for re-election *on schedule*. The states and localities copied that rule, though they did not have to, and it insures a simple and wonderful thing: the new person elected may not be better than the person thrown out, but at least he or she is new. And he or she too can be thrown out on schedule. And of course, the fact that two hundred million people believe in and act upon this fragile system is the true miracle.

"I got started in speechwriting by flying to Miami and writing a speech. The invitation came after six years of work in political media, and it turned out to be a good one. I suppose you do not *have* to enjoy and understand politics to be a speechwriter, but most people who are do. As with brain surgery, the more you understand, the more likely you are to do a good job."

BIOGRAPHICAL/CRITICAL SOURCES: Worcester Telegram, June 4, 1978; *Women's Wear Daily,* June 14, 1978; *Publishers Weekly,* June 19, 1978; *New York Times Book Review,* June 25, 1978.

*   *   *

MUILEMAN, Kathryn Saltzman 1946-

PERSONAL: Born January 4, 1946, in Los Angeles, Calif.; daughter of Marvin L. (a writer, news reporter, editor, and publisher) and Barbara (a publisher; maiden name, Freed) Saltzman; married Anton Muileman (a cartographer), July 24, 1974. *Education:* Attended public schools in Los Angeles, Calif. *Office:* 27540 Pacific Coast Highway, Malibu, Calif. 90265.

CAREER: Writer, 1971—.

WRITINGS: (With father, Marvin L. Saltzman) *Eurail Guide: How to Travel Europe and All the World by Train,* Saltzman Co., 1971, 9th edition, 1979.

WORK IN PROGRESS: Annual revision of *Eurail Guide;* a historical novel; two nonfiction books.

SIDELIGHTS: Muileman writes: "I love travel and receive much satisfaction from making worldwide travel easier, safer, and more pleasant for others. The annually-revised book to which I have devoted the past ten years also fulfills my interest in consumer protection. It describes every train ride in the world (115 countries) a tourist might want to take, with complete details as to departure and arrival times, discount rail passes offered all over the world, notable scenery en route, what to see in more than 700 interesting cities, train services (eating, sleeping, air-conditioning), current ticket prices for more than 700 European train rides, descriptions of such exotic rail trips as the Trans-Siberian Express route and crossing the Arctic Circle by train in Norway, a unique travel language system (French, German, Italian, Spanish), and other information I would have liked to have when I toured Europe by train for many months in 1970. The book has grown from 96 pages in 1971 to its present 768 pages as we continue to add our own travel experiences and also those of thousands of our readers who tell us about their adventures."

AVOCATIONAL INTERESTS: Wildlife and travel photography, culinary arts, gardening, theatre arts, music, and book collecting.

MUIR, Malcolm 1885-1979

OBITUARY NOTICE: Born July 19, 1885, in Glen Ridge, N.J.; died January 30, 1979, in New York, N.Y. Government official and editor. Muir presided over McGraw-Hill Publishing Co. from 1928 to 1937. During the 1920's he also founded *Business Week.* After leaving McGraw-Hill, Muir became editor-in-chief and eventually president of *Newsweek.* He also served under President Franklin Roosevelt as an administrator of the National Recovery Administration. Obituaries and other sources: *Current Biography,* Wilson, 1953, February, 1979; *Newsweek,* May 6, 1968; *Who's Who in America,* 38th edition, Marquis, 1974; *New York Times,* January 31, 1979; *Washington Post,* January 31, 1979; *Chicago Tribune,* February 1, 1979.

*   *   *

MULKEEN, Thomas P(atrick) 1923-

PERSONAL: Born May 28, 1923, in New York, N.Y.; son of Patrick J. (a grocery chain executive) and Katherine (Mannix) Mulkeen; divorced; children: two. *Education:* Harvard University, A.B., 1943; Long Island College of Medicine, M.D., 1948. *Home:* 9949 Shore Rd., Brooklyn, N.Y. 11209.

CAREER: Kings County Hospital, Brooklyn, N.Y., intern, 1948-51; Long Island College Hospital, Brooklyn, surgical resident, 1951-52; Queens General Hospital, Jamaica, N.Y., surgical resident, 1952-55; Mount Morris Tuberculosis Hospital, Mt. Morris, N.Y., staff surgeon, 1956; private practice in surgery in New York City, 1957-66; Office of the Chief Medical Examiner, New York City, investigator, 1961-73; writer, 1973—. Diplomate of American Board of Surgery, 1958. *Military service:* U.S. Army Reserve, Medical Corps, 1953-57; became captain.

WRITINGS: Honor Thy Godfather (detective novel), Stein & Day, 1973; *My Killer Doesn't Understand Me* (detective novel), Stein & Day, 1973.

WORK IN PROGRESS: An autobiographical novel about a crucial year in a surgeon's life.

SIDELIGHTS: Mulkeen writes: "The facts of my biography are misleading. It's true that I went to many schools and became a surgeon. It's also true I had a few unique experiences, such as riding in a bootlegger's car during Prohibition, pitching a baseball game against Groton School, investigating a few murders for the New York City Police Department, and renting Stephen Spender's house in London. On an overall basis, however, I feel I've never done much and that my life has been lacking in breadth.

"What it does have is depth. I never shared the mobility of my generation. I stayed in Brooklyn close to my relatives. In the end it paid off. I have the memory of what happened to a family and a city. Someone has said that life is best viewed through one window, after all.

"Putting it another way, I was finally able to distinguish between action and drama—and to see that they are apt to be antithetical. I like action books and the rare book that contains real drama. What I dislike are the hybrids in which a synthetic moral crisis is grafted on in order to make the book 'meaningful.'

"It seems to me that the ultimate aim of a writer is to produce a drama—a book with a sense of causality—a book in which the plot is the theme. It's not easy. Many years ago Aristotle observed that the young Greek poets were having a difficult time doing just that."

MULLEN, Barbara 1914-1979

OBITUARY NOTICE: Born June 9, 1914, in Boston, Mass.; died March 9, 1979, in London, England. Actress and author of an autobiography, *Life Is My Adventure.* Mullen began her acting career at the age of three and thereafter appeared on stage and screen. She was best known for her leading role in the British film, ''Jeannie,'' in 1943. Obituaries and other sources: *Who's Who in the Theatre,* 16th edition, Pitman, 1977; *New York Times,* March 10, 1979.

*   *   *

MURAVIN, Victor 1929-

PERSONAL: Born June 16, 1929, in Vladivostok, U.S.S.R.; came to United States in 1973; adopted son of Roman (an agronomist) and Serafina Muravin; married Irina Khrabrova, 1968 (marriage ended, 1972); married Mezy Gutierrez, 1976. *Education:* Attended Merchant Navy College, Vladivostock, Extra-Mural English Course, Moscow, Teachers' Training College, Archangel, and Political University, Krasnoyarsk; Long Island University, United Nations graduate certificate and M.A., both 1976; New School for Social Research, Ph.D., 1978. *Politics:* ''Realistic (anti-Marxist).'' *Religion:* Russian Orthodox. *Home:* 63-93 Alderton St., Rego Park, N.Y. 11374.

CAREER: Worked as a shepherd, ploughman, and cowboy in Russian countryside, 1939-44; joined merchant marine and served as a sailor and chief radio officer in Soviet Pacific and Arctic, 1945-54; was a longshoreman, technical college teacher of English, translator, university lecturer in English and American studies in Krasnoyask, and associate professor of applied linguistics and head of department of English at a college in eastern Russia, 1954-66; lecturer in American studies at a college east of Moscow, 1967-71; writer, 1970—; private tutor in English and Russian, Moscow, 1971-72; Chilewich Corp., New York City, translator, 1973-78; radio officer aboard merchant vessel, 1978; Language Guild Institute, New York City, director of translation department, 1978—. Teacher of Russian at Franklin D. Roosevelt Institute of Maritime Studies, New York City, 1973-75.

WRITINGS: Aurora Borealis (biographical novel; part II of Vikenty Angarov trilogy), translated from the Russian by Alan Thomas, privately printed, 1975, published as *The Diary of Vikenty Angarov,* Newsweek, 1978. Also author of two English textbooks for Russian technical colleges, published in U.S.S.R., 1964, 1965, and of a collection of short stories in Russian, 1974. Contributor of fifteen articles and stories to Russian newspapers in Paris and New York, 1973-75.

WORK IN PROGRESS: The Typhoon, the first part of the Vikenty Angarov trilogy, being translated; *The Last Trip,* the final third of the trilogy; *The Rubicon: The Fate of a Soldier in Russia; Intelligence Agent; The Hard Way,* a book about Stalin; *The Second Christ,* about Karl Marx; *The Departing World,* about the West; *The Russian Steppe,* a trilogy.

SIDELIGHTS: A member of the first generation of Russians brought up entirely under Stalinism, a young Victor Muravin believed his adopted father, ''a non-party Bolshevik,'' to be an ''enemy of the people'' when the man was arrested and charged as a German spy in 1937. The boy's love for the Red Army continued as he became a member of the Pioneers and the Young Communist League (Komsomol). This loyalty to Stalin's regime was tested, however, during Muravin's service as a merchant marine. Practically a slave himself, living hungry and working hard on politically disciplined ships,

Muravin saw semi-starved convicts in the Kolyma gold mine and Arctic concentration camps. A Russian nationalist rather than a dissident, the young Muravin's belief in Marxism-Leninism faded as he continually observed the enslaved in prison ships and camps; but he still maintained his loyalty to the land and its Communist regime.

Persistently troubled by the many flaws he saw in the system, Muravin turned to the study of Russian and European history for an answer to his great concern for his struggling country and its many deprived and suffering citizens. These studies, combined with his first-hand experience of the nation's ills, led him to conclude that Russia's troubles had come from the West, along with Marxism. Later, he abandoned his belief in Communism—a ''disaster-inviting doctrine.''

After his dismissal from several jobs during the 1950's, Muravin's relationship with his country by the end of the decade was, at best, strained. His two English textbooks, the first to be published outside Moscow since the Revolution and the first ever to bring his college a profit, were the cause of three ''book trials'' with the local KGB.

In 1966, Muravin returned to Krasnoyarsk to help his mother earn a visa to visit her brother in the United States. During this time, however, the KGB became suspicious of his intentions and declared him ''an enemy of the Soviet power.'' Before being sentenced to a lunatic asylum, a fate he would have avoided by taking a self-made cyanide pill, several friends persuaded the KBG to alter their decision.

Exhausted from these conflicts, Muravin began to think of emigrating. ''I did not want to emigrate,'' he recalls. ''I loved Russia. It is my land. I tilled it, suffered with it. It saved me twice from starvation. I left my sweat on it. But on this land I lived my life in poverty and serfdom. I decided to emigrate in order to go back to sea and regain my personal freedom.'' After waiting a year for Soviet authorities to approve his request for exile, Muravin left for Italy.

Once in Italy, Muravin continued the writings he began in Moscow—writings that were either burned or buried to escape the attention of the KGB. His ''pent-up hatred for the Communist system'' was heightened when some chapters of his first book were sent to Moscow (with the clandestine influence of the KGB) instead of to a German publisher. Advised to leave Italy for his own safety, Muravin was denied a visa by Australia and Canada before being accepted by the United States.

''I began writing my books motivated by anti-Communism,'' Muravin told *CA.* ''I will complete and publish them all as a memory to Russia's past tragedy and as a contribution to man's political wisdom and for the survival of Western democracy.'' His first published effort, *The Diary of Vikenty Angarov,* chronicles the years 1937-54, all but one of which Angarov (a friend of the author) spent in Soviet slave labor camps. Containing elements of history and biography, this account is based, according to the author, on events that occurred in those seventeen years.

Muravin's depiction of Angarov's strength of character has been highly praised. The *New Yorker* admired in the author's ''shatteringly effective'' writing ''the peculiarly Russian qualities that were necessary for survival in those camps in those demented years: self-possession, endurance, courage, a deep-rooted patriotism, a compassionate sense of brotherhood, and an unflagging hatred of Stalin, with a total absence of such Western indulgences as bitterness, irony, self-pity, and despair.'' Scott Sanders compared Angarov to ''a Hemingway hero, he survives by obeying a personal code that is at once honorable and ruthless.'' In fact, ''Angarov is determined not only to survive but also to outlive Stalin,'' said Deam W. Given. ''He yearns for the day when he can spit on Stalin's grave.''

Despite Angarov's hatred of Stalin, Muravin is somewhat less critical of the leader whose policies caused an estimated eighteen million deaths during his reign. ''Muravin never blames the reign of terror on Stalin alone,'' commented Sanders. ''He makes it clear that Stalin only rode historical currents that had been set in motion long before the Bolshevik Revolution in 1917, back in the era of czarist terror.'' Alla Burago agreed: ''This human drama is played out against a refrain common in Russia's literature of the underground—psychological probings into the nature of Stalin. Strangely compassionate—familiarly Russian—the outcome of this soul-searching reveals Stalin himself 'a prisoner of history and of Russia.'''

If Muravin's intention in writing Angarov's story was to bring his readers ''close to the warm beating heart of humanity,'' criticism indicates he has succeeded. ''There is every emotion here but humor; the victim's plight is too terrible for even black humor at even its bottomless blackest,'' wrote the *New Yorker*. The *West Coast Review of Books* added: ''This book is sure to touch every heart, inflame every mind and inspire commitment to every reader to the basic concept of human rights.'' Mitzi M. Brunsdale cited the comment of Solzhenitsyn (to whom Muravin has been favorably compared) that world literature is ''a certain common body and a common spirit, a living heartfelt unity reflecting the growing unity of mankind.'' She then concluded, ''If this is true . . . then Victor Muravin's *Diary of Vikenty Angarov* lies very close to the warm beating heart of humanity.''

Muravin reflected on his role as a writer amid the competing Soviet and Western worlds: ''Despite the terrible losses in human lives and material wealth in the last war, Communism has recovered and is successfully competing with the West for the minds of men the world over. It is offering a peaceful solution to the modern world's main problem: which system will be accepted by humanity within the next twenty to twenty-five years, mutli-party democracy of one-party Communism? Both systems have their advantages and disadvantages. The West is ready to accept the convergence of both systems, Communism insists on converting the West and the world to Communism. The West will be able to survive the competition only if it adds ideology and propaganda to its old commercial advertising. You cannot keep advertising goods and keep losing human minds forever; there is an end to everything under the moon. The Western book world should switch some of its resources from publishing for money to publishing for ideas, which always brings money as well.

''It is to the peaceful solution of this basic problem of both worlds that I devote my books. Stories of human sufferings and happiness, of weakness and strength, cowardice and courage, of human life as it is and as it should be, have no limit in time and serve humanity as a whole, 'very close to the warm beating heart of humanity.'''

BIOGRAPHICAL/CRITICAL SOURCES: Kirkus Reviews, February 1, 1978; *Houston Post,* February 26, 1978, *Houston Chronicle,* April 9, 1978; *Chicago Tribune Book World,* May 21, 1978; *Chicago Sun-Times,* May 21, 1978; *Washington Post Book World,* May 21, 1978; *New Yorker,* May 22, 1978; *Grand Rapids Press,* June 11, 1978; *San Diego Evening Tribune,* June 16, 1978; *Buffalo Evening News,* June 25, 1978; *Baltimore News American,* July 2, 1978; *Tampa*

Tribune-Times, August 13, 1978; *Montreal Gazette,* August 26, 1978; *West Coast Review of Books,* September, 1978; *Arizona Daily Star,* September 17, 1978; Victor Muravin, *The Diary of Vikenty Angarov,* Newsweek, 1978.

*   *   *

MURPHY, Gardner   1895-1979

OBITUARY NOTICE: Born July 8, 1895, in Chillicothe, Ohio; died March 18, 1979, in Washington, D.C. Psychologist, educator, and author best known for his work in parapsychology, personality, and social behavior. One of Murphy's research interests was a study of how psychology could prevent wars. He also urged his peers to postulate on ''potentialities utterly different from those that can be extrapolated from man's present and past behavior.'' He wrote more than twenty books, including *In the Minds of Men, Personality,* and *Human Potentialities.* Obituaries and other sources: *Current Biography,* Wilson, 1960; *American Men and Women of Science: The Social and Behavioral Sciences,* 12th edition, Bowker, 1973; *Who's Who in America,* 40th edition, Marquis, 1978; *New York Times,* March 21, 1979; *Washington Post,* March 21, 1979.

*   *   *

MURPHY, William M(ichael)   1916-

PERSONAL: Born August 6, 1916, in New York, N.Y.; son of Timothy Francis and Florence (McDonald) Murphy; married Evelyn Harriet Doane (in educational administration), September 2, 1939; children: David Timothy Michael, Susan Doane Murphy Thompson, Christopher Ten Broeck. *Education:* Harvard University, B.A., 1938, M.A., 1941, Ph.D., 1947. *Politics:* Democrat. *Religion:* Unitarian-Universalist. *Home:* 1077 Glenwood Blvd., Schenectady, N.Y. 12308. *Office:* Department of English, Union College, Schenectady, N.Y. 12308.

CAREER: Union College, Schenectady, N.Y., assistant professor, 1946-48, associate professor, 1948-60, professor of English, 1960—, Thomas Lamont Professor of Ancient and Modern Literature, 1978—. Member of local Municipal Housing Authority, 1950-51, and county board of supervisors, 1956. *Military service:* U.S. Naval Reserve, active duty, 1943-46; became lieutenant. *Member:* Modern Language Association of America, American Committee on Irish Studies, Nova Scotia Bird Society, Cape Sable Historical Society.

WRITINGS: David Worcester (1907-1947): A Memorial, privately printed, 1953; *The Yeats Family and the Pollexfens of Sligo,* Dolmen, 1971; *Letters from Bedford Park,* Cuala, 1972; (editor with Richard J. Finneran and George M. Harper) *Letters to W. B. Yeats,* Columbia University Press, 1977; *Prodigal Father: The Life of John Butler Yeats (1839-1922),* Cornell University Press, 1978.

WORK IN PROGRESS: Editing letters and documents of the family of John Butler Yeats.

*   *   *

MURRAY, Walter I(saiah)   1910-1978

PERSONAL: Born May 22, 1910, in New Orleans, La.; died January 10, 1978, in New York, N.Y.; son of Cecilia Murray; married Barbara Worthy, October 2, 1954; children: Walter Isaiah, Jr., Daniel Andrew. *Education:* Indiana State College (now Indiana State University), bachelor's degree, 1939; Indiana University, master's degree, 1942; University of Chicago, Ph.D., 1947. *Home:* 143-15 170th St., Springfield Gardens, N.Y. 11434.

CAREER: Elementary school teacher in Robbins, Ill., 1932; Gary public schools, Gary, Ind., mathematics teacher, 1934-37; Southern University and Agricultural and Mechanical College, Baton Rouge, La., instructor, 1953-54; Dunbar Elementary School, Phoenix, Ariz., principal, 1954-57; Agricultural and Technical College of North Carolina (now North Carolina Agricultural and Technical State University), Greensboro, instructor, 1955-56; Brooklyn College of the City University of New York, Brooklyn, associate professor of education, 1956-67, professor of education, 1969-78. Director of Search for Education, Elevation and Knowledge (SEEK), 1966. Appointed by Mayor John V. Lindsay to Civilian Complaint Review Board, 1966. Chairman of Institute for the Advancement of Criminal Justice, 1973. Consultant to Human Affairs Research Center, U.S. Office of Education. *Member:* Opportunities Industrialization Centers of America, Association for Supervision and Curriculum Development, Omega Psi Phi (former president of Queens chapter). *Awards, honors:* Plaque from Tau Omega, 1958, and from Beta Tau, 1961, both for service as faculty adviser; service key award from Phi Delta Kappa, 1974.

WRITINGS: (Contributing editor) Lester D. Crow, editor, *Teaching in the Elementary School: Readings in Principles and Methods,* McKay, 1961; (with Crow and Hugh Smythe) *Educating the Culturally Disadvantaged,* McKay, 1966; (with Crow and Irving Bloom) *Teaching Language Arts in the Elementary School,* W. C. Brown, 1968. Contributor of articles to professional journals.

SIDELIGHTS: Murray was an educator, author, and civic leader. As a professor of education at Brooklyn College, he specialized in training teachers to instruct children from the slums. He said once that a major failure in school systems was that teachers did not believe that black students could learn. His concern for the problem generated, among other publications, the book *Educating the Culturally Disadvantaged.* Murray's civic work included his service on New York City's short-lived Civilian Complaint Review Board in 1966. Appointed by Mayor John V. Lindsay, he was one of two black members on the civilian-dominated panel that investigated charges of police brutality and discourtesy. Following a city-wide referendum, however, the board was abolished after four months of operation. Other civic work brought him several awards for distinguished community service.

OBITUARIES: New York Times, January 11, 1978.

[Sketch verified by wife, Barbara Worthy Murray]

* * *

MYASSIN, Leonid Fedorovich   1895-1979
(Leonide Massine)

OBITUARY NOTICE: Born August 9, 1895, in Moscow, Russia (now U.S.S.R.); died March 15, 1979, in Borken, West Germany. Dancer, choreographer, and author. Massine was known as one of the greatest ballet dancers and choreographers of the century. His dancing career spanned six decades, and he was a choreographer almost as long. Massine was the principal dancer with Serge Diaghilev's Ballet Russe in Paris and was enormously influenced by the master. Massine created numerous ballets in the modern mode, including "Parade," "La Boutique Fantasque," "Le Tricorne," and "Pulcinella." He danced and taught ballet throughout Europe, in South America, and was associated with companies in New York City as well. After World War II he worked in films. His performance in "The Red Shoes," a film based on Diaghilev's career, was a tremen-

dous success. Massine wrote *My Life in Ballet,* an autobiography, in 1968, and *Massine on Choreography* in 1974. Obituaries and other sources: *Current Biography,* Wilson, 1940; *Who's Who in the World,* 2nd edition, Marquis, 1973; *Biography News,* Volume II, Gale, 1975; *The International Who's Who,* Europa, 1978; *Who's Who,* 131st edition, St. Martin's, 1979; *New York Times,* March 17, 1979; *Washington Post,* March 18, 1979.

* * *

MYERS, Charles A(ndrew)   1913-

PERSONAL: Born June 10, 1913, in State College, Pa.; son of Charles Emory (a professor) and Christine (Bidelspacher) Myers; married Nancy Nash, June 15, 1937; children: Charles Nash, Anne Howard Myers Forsyth, Tamson Elizabeth Myers Ely. *Education:* Pennsylvania State University, B.A., 1934; University of Chicago, Ph.D., 1939. *Politics:* Independent. *Religion:* Society of Friends (Quakers). *Residence:* Cataumet, Mass. *Office:* Sloan School of Management E52-454A, Massachusetts Institute of Technology, Cambridge, Mass. 02139.

CAREER: Beloit College, Beloit, Wis., instructor in economics, 1938-39; Massachusetts Institute of Technology, Cambridge, instructor, 1939-40, assistant professor, 1941-45, associate professor, 1945-49, professor of industrial relations, 1949-64, professor of economics and management, beginning 1964, Sloan Fellows Professor of Management, 1967-78, professor emeritus, 1978—, director of industrial relations section of Sloan School of Management, 1948—. Staff member of national rubber survey committee, 1942; hearing officer for War Production Board (Boston), 1944-45. Member of Social Science Research Council committee on labor market research, 1949-56; public member of President's Railroad Commission, 1960-62; National Manpower Policy Task Force, chairman of task force, 1969-71, member.

MEMBER: American Academy of Arts and Sciences (fellow), National Academy of Arbiters (charter member), Industrial Relations Research Association (member of executive board, 1952-55; president, 1962). *Awards, honors:* Cardinal Cushing Award from Labor Guild of Boston Roman Catholic Archdiocese, 1977.

WRITINGS: (With W. Rupert Maclaurin) *The Movement of Factory Workers,* Wiley, 1943; *Industrial Relations in Sweden,* M.I.T. Press, 1951; (with George P. Shultz) *The Dynamics of a Labor Market,* Prentice-Hall, 1953, reprinted, 1977; *Labor Problems in the Industrialization of India,* Harvard University Press, 1958, published in India as *Industrial Relations in India,* Asia Publishing House, 1959; (with Frederick Harbison) *Management in the Industrial World,* McGraw, 1959.

(With Clark Kerr, John T. Dunlop, and Harbison) *Industrialism and Industrial Man,* Harvard University Press, 1960; (with Paul Pigors) *Personnel Administration,* McGraw, 1947, 9th edition, in press; (with Pigors and F. T. Malm) *Management of Human Resources,* McGraw, 1965, 3rd edition, 1973; (with Harbison) *Education, Manpower, and Economic Growth,* McGraw, 1964; (editor with Harbison) *Manpower and Education,* McGraw, 1965; (editor) *The Impact of Computers on Management,* M.I.T. Press, 1967; *Computers in Knowledge-Based Fields,* M.I.T. Press, 1970; *The Role of the Private Sector in Manpower Development,* Johns Hopkins Press, 1971; (with Kerr, Dunlop, and Harbison) *Industrialism and Industrial Man Reconsidered,* Industrial Relations Section, Princeton University, 1975.

SIDELIGHTS: Myers comments: "Many of my books with Clark Kerr, John T. Dunlop, and especially the late Professor Frederick Harbison of Princeton, grew out of an inter-university study of labor problems in economic development, on which we worked for more than twenty-two years. With them, or with my wife, or alone, I have been in Sweden, India, around the world twice, in South America, Western Europe, and parts of Africa."

When asked to describe his changing views on industrialism and industrial man, Myers told *CA* that "the final report of *Industrialism and Industrial Man Reconsidered* was more pessimistic about a worldwide spread of industrialism than was suggested in the original 1960 book."

*   *   *

MYERS, Mary Ruth   1947-

PERSONAL: Born August 5, 1947, in Warrensburg, Mo.; daughter of Jessie J. (an Air Force colonel) and Mavourneen (a teacher; maiden name, Cross) Parsons; married Henry W. Myers (a horologist), June 19, 1970; children: Jessica Louise. *Education:* University of Missouri, B.J., 1969. *Politics:* Democrat. *Religion:* Unitarian-Universalist. *Home and office:* 1333 Corry St., Yellow Springs, Ohio 45387. *Agent:* Emilie Jacobson, Curtis Brown Ltd., 575 Madison Ave., New York, N.Y. 10022.

CAREER: Saginaw News, Saginaw, Mich., reporter, 1969-70; *Journal Herald,* Dayton, Ohio, feature writer, 1970-72; free-lance writer, 1972—. *Awards, honors:* First prize from *Mademoiselle* playwriting contest, 1966, for "Cookbook."

WRITINGS: "Cookbook" (one-act play; first produced in Columbia, Mo., at University Theatre, spring, 1967), published in *Mademoiselle,* 1966; *He Lured Her to the Primrose Path* (one-act western melodrama; first produced in Cheyenne, Wyo., at Francis E. Warren Air Force Base, August, 1967), Pioneer Drama Service, 1967; *A Journey to Cuzco* (novel), Coward, 1979. Contributor to *Writer.* Alumni editor of Alpha Gamma Delta *Quarterly,* 1972-73.

WORK IN PROGRESS: Conquistador's Purchase, a historical romance set in Lima, Peru, 1544-1548; *Malinalco,* a contemporary romantic suspense novel set in a small Mexican village.

SIDELIGHTS: Myers writes: "I am an avid fan of all things pertaining to Latin America, both current and historical. My husband and I have traveled throughout South America and Mexico, as well as Canada, whose Bruce Peninsula especially charms us. I speak Spanish well enough to get us by without a guide. I feel North Americans have a terrible misconception of the Spanish conquest and the incredible hardships and valor which accompanied it, two centuries before the founding of our own country. Similar misconceptions exist regarding Latin American society today."

N

NABOKOV, Nicolas 1903-1978

PERSONAL: Born April 4, 1903, near Minsk, Russia; came to United States in 1933, naturalized in 1939; died April 6, 1978 in New York, N.Y.; son of Dimitry and Lydia (von Falz-Fein) Nabokov; married fourth wife, Dominique Cibiel, March 23, 1970; children: (by previous marriages) Ivan, Peter, Alexander. *Education:* Attended Stuttgart Conservatory; attended Music Academy of Berlin, 1920-23; Sorbonne, University of Paris, License es Lettres, 1924. *Residence:* Paris, France; and New York, N.Y.

CAREER: Wells College, Aurora, N.Y., professor of music history, composition, and theory, head of music department, 1936-41; St. John's College, Annapolis, Md., professor of music, 1941-44; Peabody Conservatory, Baltimore, Md., professor of composition, 1943-45; U.S. Military Government, Germany, adviser for cultural affairs, 1945-47; Peabody Conservatory, professor of composition, 1947-51; Congress for Cultural Freedom, secretary general, 1951-63; head of the Berlin Festival, 1963-67; Aspen Institute of Humanistic Studies, Aspen, Colo., composer in residence and adviser to the president on arts, 1969; New York University, New York, N.Y., staff member of history department, c.1970-78. Vice-chief for the Voice of America to Russia, 1947; adviser for internal cultural affairs to mayor of West Berlin, 1963. Adviser to the Festival of Israel and other international festivals. *Member:* National Institute of Arts and Letters, Berlin Academy of Arts and Letters.

WRITINGS: Old Friends and New Music, Little, Brown, 1951, reprinted, Greenwood Press, 1974; *Igor Stravinsky,* Colloquium Verlag, 1964; (editor with Anna Kallin) *Twentieth-Century Composers,* Weidenfeld & Nicolson, 1970, Holt, 1971; (author of introduction) Frederik Goldbeck, *France, Italy and Spain,* Weidenfeld & Nicolson, 1974; *Bagazh: Memoirs of a Russian Cosmopolitan,* Atheneum, 1975.

Composer of scores: "Ode" (ballet), for Serge Diaghilev's Ballets Russes, 1928; Archibald MacLeish, "Union Pacific" (ballet), for Col. de Basil's Ballets Russes, first produced in Philadelphia, 1934; Stephen Spender, "La Morte di Rasputin" (opera; title means "Rasputin's End"), Ricordi, 1963; George Balanchine, "Don Quixote," first produced in New York by the New York City Ballet, 1965; W. H. Auden, "Love's Labor's Lost" (opera version of Shakespeare's play of the same title), first performed at the 25th Edinburgh International Festival, Scotland, 1971. Also composer of three symphonies, several concert works for voice and orchestra, and concertos for piano and flute.

SIDELIGHTS: Although remembered as composer of the musical score for "Don Quixote," Nicolas Nabokov was better known for his organization of three international music festivals during his years with the Congress for Cultural Freedom. The first, "Masterpieces of the 20th Century," took place in Paris in 1952, the second, "Music in Our Time," in Rome in 1954, and the third, "East-West Music Encounter," in Tokyo in 1961. Although Nabokov was unaware of it at the time, these festivals were largely funded by the Central Intelligence Agency (CIA). The money was channeled through various American foundations to the Congress for Cultural Freedom, which Stephen Koch proclaimed to be "by far the best-funded and -organized anti-Communist cultural-exchange program of the Fifties." When the source of its funds was revealed, the congress fell into disgrace because of its role as "a secretly funded instrument of U.S. foreign policy, posing as something else."

In addition to being the cousin of novelist Vladimir Nabokov, Allen Hughes said the composer "seemed to have met virtually everybody worth knowing in the arts in his lifetime." His books *Old Friends and New Music* and *Bagazh* contain prize anecdotes about such notables as Isadora Duncan, W. H. Auden, Isaiah Berlin, Harry Kessler, and Igor Stravinsky.

Before his death, Nabokov had nearly completed a third volume of memoirs and had been making plans for a Stravinsky Festival to be held in Venice in 1980.

BIOGRAPHICAL/CRITICAL SOURCES: Old Friends and New Music, Little, Brown, 1951, reprinted, Greenwood Press, 1974; *High Fidelity,* April, 1968, April, 1973; *Bagazh: Memoirs of a Russian Cosmopolitan,* Atheneum, 1975; *Saturday Review,* November 15, 1975; *Atlantic Monthly,* January, 1976.

OBITUARIES: New York Times, April 7, 1978; *Time,* April 17, 1978.*

*   *   *

NAFZIGER, E(stel) Wayne 1938-

PERSONAL: Born August 14, 1938, in Bloomington, Ill.; son of Orrin (a farmer) and Beatrice (a teacher; maiden name, Slabaugh) Nafziger, married Elfrieda Toews (a teacher), August 20, 1966; children: Brian, Kevin. *Education:* Goshen College, B.A., 1960; University of Michigan, M.A., 1962; University of Illinois, Ph.D., 1967. *Politics:* "Democratic socialist." *Religion:* Protestant. *Home:* 232 Summit, Manhattan, Kan. 66502. *Office:* Department of Economics, Kansas State University, Manhattan, Kan. 66506.

CAREER: Kansas State University, Manhattan, assistant professor, 1966-73, associate professor, 1973-78, professor of economics, 1978—. Fulbright professor at Andhra University, 1970-71. Research associate at University of Nigeria, 1964-65; fellow of University of Hawaii's East-West Center, 1972-73, and University of Birmingham's Centre of West African Studies, 1976; visiting scholar at Cambridge University, 1976; lecturer at Soviet Academy of Sciences and U.S. State Department. Member of board of overseers of Hesston College. *Member:* Society for International Development, American Economic Association, American Association of University Professors, African Studies Association, Association for Asian Studies, Association for Comparative Economic Studies, Nigerian Economic Society, Omicron Delta Epsilon.

WRITINGS: African Capitalism, Hoover Institution, 1977; (with Henry Bernstein and Donal Cruise O'Brien) *Development Theory: Three Critical Essays,* Frank Cass, 1978; *Class, Caste, and Entrepreneurship,* University Press of Hawaii, 1978.

Contributor: Peter Kilby, editor, *Entrepreneurship and Economic Development,* Free Press, 1971; *Teaching of the Social Sciences,* Andhra University Press, 1971; Sayre P. Schatz, editor, *South of the Sahara: Development in African Economies,* Macmillan, 1972; Robin Higham, editor, *Civil Wars in the Twentieth Century,* University of Kentucky Press, 1972; Frances Stewart, *Employment, Income Distribution and Development,* Frank Cass, 1975. Contributor to economic and social science journals.

WORK IN PROGRESS: Economic Development, a text book, publication by Wadsworth expected in 1981; *The Economics of Political Violence: The Nigerian-Biafran War.*

SIDELIGHTS: In a review of Nafziger's *African Capitalism,* John J. Metzler stated: "*African Capitalism* raises the standard for the black entrepreneurs who have risked their fortunes on the economic wheel of fate. Some succeed and some don't; the purpose of this heavily researched volume aims to show why.... Interestingly, education provides a positive as well as a negative stimulus to the individual firms—better education generally proved that the firm will have higher productivity although the profit level will tend to be lower. The author feels that lower profits are assumed because the higher educated entrepreneur has less practical and technical experience.... *African Capitalism* ... provides one with some very sound bases for analyzing entrepreneurial growth in Nigeria; such knowledge can apply to much of the Third World."

Nafziger told *CA:* "My works focus on capitalism, poverty, income inequality, class differences, and political instability in the Third World. *Class, Caste, and Entrepreneurship,* which focuses on the origins of manufacturing entrepreneurs in a newly industrializing city in southern India, offers a perspective on vertical socio-economic mobility, and the differences in economic opportunities between the privileged and underprivileged portions of the population. A highly disproportional number of the entrepreneurs (especially successful ones) are from high castes and from families with a high economic status. Members of the dominant castes, leading classes, and large business houses can avert the threat of democratization, industrialization, and modernization to the positions of their families by using the advantages of the past—property, influence, status and so forth—to obtain the concessions, experience, education, training, and industrial capital usually essential for successful industrial undertakings. Contrary to a widelyheld viewpoint, this low degree of socio-economic class mobility is found not only in India but also in the United States and most of the rest of the nonsocialist world.

"Although it has become fashionable in recent years to offer sweeping critiques of the theory of development and underdevelopment of the Third World, these are too often made from a narrow point of view and directed at a superficial reading of the literature. The three essays by Bernstein, Cruise O'Brien, and me are distinguished by their exhaustive treatment of the subject, and by a clarity of style and focus. They treat, in turn, the sociology (Bernstein), politics (Cruise O'Brien) and economics (Nafziger) of development."

BIOGRAPHICAL/CRITICAL SOURCES: World Research INK, December, 1978.

* * *

NAGLE, James J. 1909-1978

PERSONAL: Born in 1909, in New York; died November 23, 1978, in Bronx, N.Y.; married Velma Stanek; children: Nancy. *Education:* Attended Columbia University. *Residence:* Bronx, New York.

CAREER/WRITINGS: New York Times, New York City, 1927-78. He was a secretary in the commercial department, 1927-33, secretary on the news desk beginning in 1933, became a reporter in 1946, first in real estate news, then in business and financial news. Also wrote a daily report on trading on the American Stock Exchange and was a copy editor and makeup editor for the Sunday financial-business section. *Member:* New York Financial Writers Association (member of board of governors).

OBITUARIES: New York Times, November 23, 1978.*

* * *

NAPOLITANE, Catherine A(nn) Durrum 1936-

PERSONAL: Surname is pronounced Na-*pol*-i-tan; born December 31, 1936, in Muskogee, Okla; daughter of Francis Edward and Kitty Lou (Moore) Durrum; married Andrew Nicholas Napolitane (president of an advertising company), June 12, 1955 (divorced, November, 1973); children: Andrew Nicholas, Jr., Christina Ann. *Education:* Adelphi University, B.S., 1978. *Religion:* Protestant. *Home:* 146 Pine St., Garden City, N.Y. 11530. *Agent:* Rhoda A. Weyr, William Morris Agency, 1350 Avenue of the Americas, New York, N.Y. 10019.

CAREER: NEXUS Organization, Inc. (self-help agency for formerly married women), Garden City, N.Y., president, 1971—. Member of B. J. Spoke Art Gallery; has had solo exhibitions of her work.

WRITINGS: Living and Loving After Divorce, Rawson Associates, 1977.

WORK IN PROGRESS: A step-by-step manual for organizing NEXUS chapters all across the United States.

SIDELIGHTS: Catherine Napolitane writes: "Although my first love is art, I want to help all of us who have fallen into the 'second-class citizen' position accidentally, through no fault of our own.

"The most important issue to me today is that of helping women to make a good life. I want much change to come about in women's lives. I want all women to be able to be confident and proud of their lives and, most important, *not* to be afraid of banding together as a group of divorced women and speaking out as a viable and valid body of people.

"Through working with thousands of NEXUS women I have learned how valuable support is, from a group, from family, from friends. Since NEXUS is a supportive group I believe in 'spreading the word.' Many women shy away from joining a group or really accepting their divorced state and thereby close themselves off from valuable and comforting lifelines. I have learned that pain and panic can be lessened and coped with through sharing. My first desire to write a book about this came out of observing the women who came to NEXUS. I wanted so badly to share the experiences of women who came to me and to NEXUS, and also to share my own experience with the 'stages' of divorce in order to help the next person through this trying time with some concrete ideas, some recommendations to lessen the pain, some maps (road maps of the things to come) to follow, and to feel more relaxed about the confusion that surrounds this trauma."

BIOGRAPHICAL/CRITICAL SOURCES: Newsday, July, 1972; *New York Times,* February 18, 1978; *New York,* October 16, 1978.

*   *   *

NASH, Bruce M(itchell)   1947-

PERSONAL: Born August 14, 1947, in Brooklyn, N.Y.; son of Murray A. (a jeweler) and Lucille (Schweitzer) Nash (a teacher); married Sophie Mitchell, May 12, 1967; children: Robyn Debra, Jennifer Alicia. *Education:* Florida State University, B.S., 1969, M.S., 1970. *Home and office:* 2288 Gabriel Lane, West Palm Beach, Fla. 33406. *Agent:* Sanford J. Greenburger Associates, Inc., 825 Third Ave., New York, N.Y. 10022; and Bret Adams Ltd., 36 East 61st St., New York, N.Y. 10021.

CAREER: Florida State University, Tallahassee, director of North Carolina branch office and research associate of Southeastern Correctional and Criminological Research Center, 1970-73; North Carolina Department of Correction, Raleigh, N.C., director of planning and research, 1973-76; writer, 1976—. Head of corrections programs for North Carolina governor's committee on law and order, 1973.

WRITINGS: Thirty Years of Television, Drake, 1976; *The Fifties Nostalgia Quizbook,* Drake, 1977; *The World Championship Boxing Quizbook,* Drake, 1977; *The Elvis Presley Quizbook,* Warner Books, 1978; *Whatever Happened to Blue Suede Shoes?,* Grosset, 1978; *The Official Superman Quizbook,* Warner Books, 1978; *The Thumbs Up, Thumbs Down Pun Book,* Grosset, 1979; *Tubeteasers: The Official Television Quiz and Puzzle Book,* A. S. Barnes, 1979; *Do You Remember the Shook-Up Sixties?,* Dale Books, 1979; *Sports Computer Matchups,* Grosset, 1979; *The Official Comic and Cartoon Trivia Quizbook,* Dale Books, 1979.

WORK IN PROGRESS: Numerous books, including *The Road to Hollywood, Americans All: Who Are We?, The Three-D Book,* several books on screenplays, and two novels; composing and writing songs for four record albums for children.

SIDELIGHTS: Nash told *CA:* "I write to give pleasure and enjoyment to people of all ages and persuasions. I hope my creative abilities enable me to enrich their lives in some way. If I can entertain people with my work, I will have succeeded as a writer.

"Many of my books have a nostalgic flavor. People are beset with many pressures and problems today. They yearn to escape, if but momentarily, back into a period in their lives that they remember as being more carefree and devoid of troubles. My books offer readers the opportunity to relive their 'happy days,' whether it be reminiscing about the 1950's (*Whatever Happened to Blue Suede Shoes?*), fondly recalling vintage TV programs (*Tubeteasers: The Official Television Quiz and Puzzle Book*), or remembering the joys of reading comic book adventures (*The Official Superman Quizbook*). I do not view these books in the category of 'trivia' but rather as 'nostalgia.' Trivia implies that the item is of little consequence. My books are popular because they conjure up 'nostalgic' feelings in the minds and hearts of readers.

"My writing goal is to create motion picture properties. Already, I have written detailed treatments for four feature films. I have always been in love with the movies. To move people emotionally with a film creation is a tremendous talent. I have always respected the creative skills of those artists who have developed motion pictures that truly entertained and captured the imagination of the viewing public. I hope to join the ranks of these filmmakers in the not-so-distant future."

AVOCATIONAL INTERESTS: Jogging, baseball, collecting boxing films, composing music for children, viewing movies.

*   *   *

NASH, N. Richard   1913-
(N. Richard Nusbaum)

PERSONAL: Birth-given name, Nathan Richard Nusbaum; born June 7, 1913, in Philadelphia, Pa.; son of S. L. (a bookbinder) and Jennie (Singer) Nusbaum; married Helena Taylor, 1935 (divorced, 1954); married Janice Rule, March, 1956 (divorced, 1956); married Katherine Copeland, November, 1956; children: (first marriage) one son; (third marriage) two daughters. *Education:* University of Pennsylvania, B.S., 1934. *Address:* c/o Atheneum Publications, 122 East 42nd St., New York, N.Y. 10017.

CAREER: Playwright, screenwriter, television writer, and novelist. Producer of musical "Wildcat," with Michael Kidd, first produced on Broadway at Alvin Theatre, December 16, 1960. *Wartime service:* Office of War Information, World War II. *Member:* Authors League of America, Writers Guild of America, West, Academy of Motion Picture Arts and Sciences, Dramatists Guild. *Awards, honors:* Maxwell Anderson Verse Drama Award, 1940, for "Parting at Imsdorf"; International Drama Award (Cannes, France) and Prague Award, both 1954, both for "See the Jaguar"; Karl Gosse Award, 1957, for "The Rainmaker"; Archer Award, 1960, for "Handful of Fire"; also recipient of Orbeal Award, Cannes Theatre Laurel, and Europa Prize for Literature.

WRITINGS—Plays: (Under name N. Richard Nusbaum) *So Wonderful! (In White)* (one-act), Samuel French, 1937; (under name N. Richard Nusbaum) *Incognito* (three-act), Samuel French, 1941; (under name N. Richard Nusbaum) *Parting at Imsdorf* (one-act), Samuel French, 1941; (under name N. Richard Nusbaum) *Sky Road: A Comedy of the Airways* (three-act), Row, Peterson & Co., 1941; "Second Best Bed," first produced on Broadway at Ethel Barrymore Theatre, June 3, 1946; "The Young and Fair," first produced in New York City at Fulton Theatre, November 22, 1948; *See the Jaguar* (three-act; first produced on Broadway at Court Theatre, December 3, 1952), Dramatists Play Service, 1953; *The Rainmaker* (three-act; first produced on Broadway at Court Theatre, October 28, 1954), Random House, 1955, musical adaptation produced as "110 in the Shade" on Broadway at Broadhurst Theatre, October 24, 1963; *Girls of Summer* (three-act; first produced on Broadway at Longacre Theatre, November 19, 1956), Samuel French, 1957; *Handful of Fire* (three-act; first produced on Broadway at Martin Beck Theatre, October 1, 1958), Samuel French, 1959; "Wildcat," musical adaptation first produced on Broadway at Alvin Theatre, December 16, 1960; *The Happy Time* (two-act musical adaptation; first produced on Broadway at Broadway Theatre, January 18, 1968), Dramatic Publishing Co., 1969; "Echoes" (two-act), first produced in New York City at Bijou Theatre, February 26, 1973; "Sarava" (musical based on "Dona Flor and Her Two Husbands," by Jorge Amado), first produced in New York City at Mark Hellinger Theater, 1979.

Novels: *Cry Macho*, Delacorte, 1975; *East Wind, Rain*, Atheneum, 1977; *The Last Magic*, Atheneum, 1978.

Also author of two books on philosophy, *The Athenian Spirit* and *The Wounds of Sparta*.

Screenplays: "Nora Prentiss," Warner Bros., 1946; (author of adaptation with Arthur Sheekman) "Welcome Stranger," Paramount, 1946; (with Harry Clork) "The Sainted Sisters" (adapted from the short story, "The Sainted Sisters of Sandy Creek," by Elisa Bialk), Paramount, 1948; (with Sheekman) "Dear Wife" (sequel to the play, "Dear Ruth," by Norman Krasna), Paramount, 1950; "The Vicious Years," Film Classics, 1950; author of screen story with Harvey S. Haislip) "The Flying Missile," Columbia, 1951; (with Gertrude Berg) "Molly" (adapted from the radio serial, "The Goldbergs," by Berg), Paramount, 1951; "Maru Maru," Warner Bros., 1952; (with John D. Klorer) "Top of the World," United Artists, 1955; "The Rainmaker" (adapted from own play), Paramount, 1956; "Porgy and Bess" (adapted from the folk opera by George Gershwin), Columbia, 1959.

Teleplays: "House in Athens," National Broadcasting Co. (NBC); (adapter of own play) "The Rainmaker," NBC; "The Brownstone," NBC; "The Happy Rest," NBC; (adapter of own play) "The Young and Fair," NBC; "The Arena," NBC; "Welcome Home," American Broadcasting Co. (ABC); "The Joker," ABC.

SIDELIGHTS: Perhaps known best for his immensely popular "The Rainmaker," in recent years Richard Nash has concentrated on novel writing. His seriousness about this new genre is exemplified by his diligence: he spent seven years researching and writing *East Wind, Rain.*

In "The Rainmaker," a "con man" brings rain to a drought-stricken land while awakening the potential for love in a spinster. Understandably, Nash's first novel, *Cry Macho*, brought a comparison to the famous romantic comedy. Arthur Ramirez wrote in *Southwest Review*: "In ... *Cry Macho*, Nash returns to a dusty setting and spiritually and emotionally drained characters. In both works the characters are colorful, the backdrop is picturesque, the action and narrative focus outrageously larger than life, and the message ultimately positive and reassuring. But the touch of artistry in connecting various threads is absent, nor is there a hypnotic presence in *Cry Macho* equal to the intriguing rainmaker-conman." But, Ramiriz continued, "psychoanalysis and Women's Lib ... cause Nash to move away from his portrait of a spinster in distress ... to a more modern union of strength and kindness, giving and taking."

Nash drew upon both experience and diligent research in creating his best selling Pearl Harbor novel, *East Wind, Rain.* "I first got interested in the Japanese," he told *Publishers Weekly*, "when I served with OWI on the West Coast in World War II. Then after the war I went to Hawaii, and what do you think I became? A bum. Literally, I looked and behaved like a wreck. And do you know what stopped me from being a bum? Sheer terror. I lived a hand-to-mouth existence. I actually lived in the wilderness—the Big Island of Hawaii. The experience obviously stuck even though I went back to Hawaii nine times to do research on the book." In addition, Nash says he "made a thorough and complete pest of myself at the Naval library at Pearl Harbor.... I must have interviewed at least 100 Navy people, starting with ex-admirals on down to sailors who served at the base before the Japanese attack and who have retired in Hawaii."

Joe David Bellamy termed the novel a combination of "a love story with a saga of revenge with the mysteries of espionage in an exotic locale at a historic moment." In addition to this setting, "Nash ... shows he has a fairly impressive grasp of both [character and plot] and the initiative to put them to work on a mixture of sure fire recipes for clearing out bookstore windows." "It is undoubtedly a rarity to find a novel of entertainment that is this well written."

While enjoying the praise surrounding *East Wind, Rain,* Nash found that critics have made some disturbing distinctions in their treatment of the book. "What annoys me," he said, "is how critics treat a book like 'East Wind, Rain.' First they call it popular entertainment—that's OK with me—then they say, 'Isn't it amazing that the book is so beautifully written.' I think critics who make a distinction between popular entertainment and good writing are helping to popularize bad fiction."

An *Observer* reviewer, however, questioned the good writing label. Citing faults in plot control and language use, he believed that "Nash declines [the] ... simple, direct approach. Instead he lashes his narrative with dollops of ethical pondering until it barely trickles to its climax—lengthy excursions into traditional Japanese moral imperatives, for instance, that are confused, unpersuasive, and fatal to the story's flow." Bellamy, too, admitted "Nash does not always steer completely clear of improbabilities or stereotypes. But, believe me—I couldn't help myself—I enjoyed this book."

Nash crossed half the globe to treat a new subject in *The Last Magic. Kirkus Reviews* described the plot: "The pope is dying, radical terrorists are attacking Catholic clergy (an excessively gory crucifixion of a cardinal), and liberal Father Michael Farris, a favorite of the pope, is eager to do whatever he can to hold the Church together." The plot thickens with the aid of "much heavy-breathing revelations of dull secrets," but is plagued by "a strange absence of action or momentum."

James Walt, meanwhile, remained convinced that Nash is a "suspense novelist" and explained his focus on violence: "Today's violence plays into his hands and lends an air of truth to episodes in his novels that a quieter age would have dismissed as lunatic or diabolic." "In *The Last Magic,*" Walt expanded, "Nash lets up on the sensationalism—a trifle. His theme, all the same, betokens the ambitious writer: the ability of Catholicism to survive.... It is a flawed but powerful book. Nash makes his point about universal violence too well; but ideas underlie his melodrama, and his lowest and loftiest characters illustrate his mastery of dialogue."

BIOGRAPHICAL/CRITICAL SOURCES: New York Times Book Review, July 13, 1975, March 6, 1977; *Southwest Review*, autumn, 1976; *Kirkus Reviews*, December 1, 1976, July 15, 1978; *New York Times*, February 11, 1977, February 12, 1979; *Observer*, March 19, 1977; *Saturday Review*, March 19, 1977; *Publishers Weekly*, June 6, 1977; *Virginia Quarterly*, autumn, 1977; *New Republic*, September 30, 1978; *West Coast Review of Books*, November, 1978; *New Yorker*, November 6, 1978.*

*   *   *

NASH, William (Wray), Jr.   1928-

PERSONAL: Born November 25, 1928, in Brooklyn, N.Y.; son of William Wray (an engineer) and Janet (Fobes) Nash; married Dorothy Westerberg, December 23, 1950; children: Meryl, Wendy, Janet, Joseph. *Education:* Harvard University, A.B., 1950; University of Pennsylvania, M.C.P., 1956, Ph.D., 1961. *Politics:* Democrat. *Religion:* Episcopal. *Home:* 3086 Cascade Rd. S.W., Atlanta, Ga. 30311. *Office:* College of Urban Life, Georgia State University, University Plaza, Atlanta, Ga. 30303.

CAREER: Philadelphia Urban Traffic and Transportation Board, Philadelphia, Pa., planning analyst, 1954-56; American Council to Improve Our Neighborhoods (ACTION), research analyst in Philadelphia, Pa. and Cambridge, Mass., 1956-58; Harvard University, Cambridge, instructor, 1958-60, assistant professor, 1960-63, associate professor, 1963-69, professor of city and regional planning, 1969-71, director and research associate of Joint Center for Urban Studies (with Massachusetts Institute of Technology), 1962-66, head of department of city and regional planning, 1965-70, director of Center for Environmental Design Studies, 1969-71; Georgia State University, Atlanta, professor of urban life, 1971—, associate director of Urban Public Services, 1971-75, dean of College of Urban Life, 1977—. Technical adviser at Bandung Institute of Technology, 1961-62; research adviser to Georgia Department of Transportation, 1975-77. Member of Atlanta Zoning Review Board, 1974-76. Member of board of directors of Central Atlanta Progress, 1971-74, and I-20 Coalition, 1974-75; consultant with Nash-Vigier, Inc., 1962-66, principal, 1969-71; consultant to Arthur D. Little, Inc., Virgin Islands Planning Board, and Ford Foundation. *Military service:* U.S. Army, Artillery, 1950-53; became first lieutenant; received Bronze Star.

MEMBER: American Institute of Planners, American Academy of Political and Social Sciences, National Academy of Sciences, Georgia Planning Association (member of board of directors, 1963-64; president, 1973-74), Sigma Xi, Tau Sigma Delta, Phi Kappa Phi. *Awards, honors:* Grant from Education Commission of the States, 1975-77.

WRITINGS: Residential Rehabilitation: Private Profits and Public Policy, McGraw, 1959; *The Emerging Metropolis*, Doubleday, 1967; (contributor) H. Wentworth Eldridge, editor, *Taming Megalopolis*, Doubleday, 1967; (editor with Bernard J. Freidan) *Shaping an Urban Future*, M.I.T. Press, 1969; *Four Days, Forty Hours*, edited by Riva Poor, Bursk & Poor, 1970. Contributor to *Collier's Encyclopedia Yearbook*. Contributor to professional journals.

WORK IN PROGRESS: Essays in City Planning; The Urban Imps; Multiple Sclerosis: A Personal Experience; research on benefit-cost, reserve sharing, governmental reorganization, citizen participation, zoning, housing, transportation analysis, and urban model building.

SIDELIGHTS: Nash comments: "My book titles speak for themselves, with the possible exception of *The Urban Imps,*

which I am writing because I have been professionally appalled at the apparent contretemps encountered in obtaining desirable social or political action, which could be attributed to the evil acts of public figures or private businessmen."

*   *   *

NATHAN, James A.   1942-

PERSONAL: Born May 1, 1942, in Chicago, Ill.; son of Samuel A. (in sales) and Dorothy (in sales; maiden name, Goldsmith) Nathan. *Education:* Indiana University, A.B. (honors), 1964; Johns Hopkins School for Advanced International Studies, M.A., 1966, Ph.D., 1972; also studied at London School of Economics and Political Science, 1962-63, Johns Hopkins University center in Bologna, Italy, 1965-66, and University of Madrid, 1965. *Office:* Department of Political Science, University of Delaware, Newark, Del. 19711.

CAREER: U.S. Department of State, Washington, D.C., vice-consul and third secretary of embassy, 1967-68, second secretary of embassy, 1968-1970; University of Delaware, Newark, assistant professor, 1972-75, associate professor of political science, 1975—. Visiting professor at University of the Americas, 1967; scholar-in-residence at Naval War College, 1979. Research assistant at Institute for Defense Analysis and Washington Center for Foreign Policy Research, both 1968-69. Participant in professional meetings in the United States and abroad. *Awards, honors:* Grants from National Science Foundation, 1969-71, Spencer Foundation, 1972-73, National Institute of Education, 1974-75, and Naval War College, 1974-77.

WRITINGS: (With Richard Remy, James Becker, and Judith Tourney) *International Education in a Global Age*, National Council for the Social Studies, 1975; (with James Oliver) *United States Foreign Policy and World Order*, Little, Brown, 1976; (with Oliver) *The Future of Sea Power*, Indiana University Press, 1979; (contributor) Thomas Paterson, editor, *A Guide to the Foreign Relations of the United States' Society for Historians of American Foreign Relations*, Society of History of American Foreign Relations, 1980. Contributor to *Handbook of the Social Sciences*. Contributor of about twenty-five articles to periodicals, including *Futures, World Politics*, and *Washington Monthly*. Associate editor of *USA Today*, 1976—.

WORK IN PROGRESS: International Relations and a New World Order, with James Oliver, publication by Little, Brown, expected in 1981; a revision of *United States Foreign Policy and World Order*, for Little, Brown; several articles, including "one on the moral basis of international society, another on Frederick the Great and the balance of power, an article on American 'vulnerabilities' in the Indian Ocean, an article on the utility of military power, and a draft for an article on the diplomatic tradition and world order and the changing nature of international law."

SIDELIGHTS: Nathan commented: "I intend to write a novel soon about life and love in the American Foreign Service. I don't have a well defined ideological position beyond subscribing to Isiahu's injunction to 'seek truth, love justice and mercy. . . .' For fun, I dive, box—less now with advancing years—play racquet sports and the like."

*   *   *

NEAL, Arminta Pearl   1921-

PERSONAL: Born August 12, 1921, in El Paso, Tex.; daughter of John Robert (a physician) and Edith Pearl (Ald-ridge) Neal. *Education:* University of California, Los Angeles, B.A., 1943; attended Los Angeles Art Center School, 1946-47; University of Denver, M A , 1971. *Home:* 4960 West Oregon Place, Denver, Colo. 80219. *Office:* Denver Museum of Natural History, City Park, Denver, Colo. 80205.

CAREER: Douglas Aircraft Co., Santa Monica, Calif., production illustrator in engineering division, 1943; Los Angeles County Museum, Los Angeles, Calif., volunteer worker, 1946-47; Denver Art Museum, Denver, Colo., preparator in Indian and native arts department, 1947-49; University of Denver, Denver, Colo., adjunct professor of anthropology, 1949; Colorado State Historical Society Museum, Denver, member of staff in exhibit department, 1949; Denver Museum of Natural History, Denver, preparator in archaeology department, 1950-57, designer of exhibits in archaeology, geology, and paleontology, 1957-59, curator of department of graphic design, 1959-71, curator of anthropology and graphic design, 1971-74, assistant director of exhibits and collections, planning, and development, 1974—. Free-lance illustrator. Guest lecturer at University of Colorado and University of Denver; participant in conferences and workshops. Participated in field studies in the southwestern United States. Member of Smithsonian Institution advisory council for the administration of the National Museum Act, 1973-76; adviser to National Endowment for the Humanities; consultant on exhibit design and construction. *Military service:* Women's Army Corps, researcher for Army Signal Corps, 1944-46.

MEMBER: International Council of Museums (member of U.S. executive committee, 1974-79), American Association of Museums (member of council, 1974-77; vice-president, 1977-79), American Association for State and Local History, American Anthropological Association (fellow), Mountain-Plains Museum Conference, Colorado-Wyoming Association of Museums (member of board of directors, 1972-73), Art Directors Club of Denver (past member of executive council). *Awards, honors: Cherokee Dance and Drama* was named one of fifty best books of the year by American Institute of Graphic Design, 1951; bronze medals from *Display World,* 1968, 1970, for displays in competitions; award of merit from American Association for Conservation Information, 1970; professional award from Mountain-Plains Museum Conference, 1973; Top Hand Award from Colorado Authors League, 1976, for *Exhibits for the Small Museum;* professional award from Big Sisters of Colorado, 1978.

WRITINGS—All self-illustrated: (With H. M. Wormington) *The Story of Pueblo Pottery,* Denver Museum of Natural History, 1951; *Cigar Box Dioramas* (booklet), privately printed, 1958, revised edition published by NASCO (Ft. Atkinson, Wisc.), 1977; *Twelve Authentic Western Houses* (portfolio), privately printed, 1960; *Help! For the Small Museum: A Handbook of Exhibit Ideas and Methods,* Pruett, 1969; *Exhibits for the Small Museum,* American Association for State and Local History, 1976.

Illustrator: Frank Speck and Leonard Broom, *Cherokee Dance and Drama,* University of California Press, 1951; Ruth Underhill, *Red Man's America,* University of Chicago Press, 1953; Walter Goldschmidt, *Ways of Mankind,* Beacon Press, 1954; Underhill, *First Came the Family,* Morrow, 1958; Doris Samford, *Ruffles and Drums,* Pruett, 1967. Contributor of about twenty articles to scientific and museum journals, and to *Rocky Mountain Life.*

WORK IN PROGRESS: Natural History Exhibits for Small Museums, completion expected in 1982.

SIDELIGHTS: Arminta Neal writes: "Museums today are powerful communicators—whether large and national in scope or smaller and more regional. My work is to encourage the small-museum professional in the development of effective communication through exhibits that help to create understanding rather than a negative or culturally-biased reaction."

*   *   *

NEAVE, Airey (Middleton Sheffield)   1916-1979

PERSONAL: Born January 23, 1916; died March 30, 1979, in London, England; son of Sheffield Airey Neave (a scientist); married Diana Josceline Barbara Giffard, December 29, 1942; children: Marigold Neave Webb, Patrick, William. *Education:* Merton College, Oxford, B.A. (with honors), 1938, M.A., 1955. *Religion:* Church of England. *Agent:* John Farquharson Ltd., Bell House, Bell Yard, London W.C.2, England. *Office:* House of Commons, London S.W.1, England; and Clarke Chapman Services Ltd., NEI Ltd., Tavistock House E., Woburn Walk, London WC1H 9HU, England.

CAREER: Called to the Bar at Middle Temple, 1943; barrister-at-law, 1943-79; Conservative member of Parliament from Abingdon Division of Berkshire, 1953-79, Parliamentary private secretary to minister of transport and civil aviation, 1954, and secretary of state for the colonies, 1954-56, joint Parliamentary secretary to minister of transport and civil aviation, 1957-59, Parliamentary under-secretary of state for air, 1959, member of select committee of House of Commons on science and technology, 1965-75, head of committee, 1970-74, deputy chairman of Parliamentary and scientific committee, 1971-74, head of leader of the opposition's private office, 1975-79, opposition spokesman on Northern Ireland, 1975-79. Director of Clarke Chapman Services Ltd., 1971-79. British delegate to United Nations high commissioner for refugees, 1970-75; head of standing conference of British organizations for aid to refugees, 1972-74. Member of board of governors of Imperial College of Science and Technology, London, 1963-71. *Military service:* British Army, Royal Artillery, 1939-51, prisoner of war, 1940-42, with Military Intelligence, 1942-44, and Army Group, 1944-45, with British War Crimes Executive, 1945-46, commissioner for criminal organizations at International Military Tribunal in Nuremberg, 1946, commanding officer of Territorial Army intelligence school, 1949-51; served in France; became lieutenant colonel; received Military Cross, French Croix de Guerre, American Bronze Star, companion of Distinguished Service Order; mentioned in dispatches. *Member:* Carlton Club. *Awards, honors:* Officer of Order of Orange Nassau (Netherlands), 1945; member of Order of the British Empire, 1947; companion of Order of St. Michael and St. George; commander of Order Polonia Restituta, 1971, knight of order, 1977.

WRITINGS: They Have Their Exits, Little, Brown, 1953; *Little Cyclone,* Hodder & Stoughton, 1954; *Saturday at M.1.9: A History of Underground Escape Lines in North-West Europe in 1940-45,* Hodder & Stoughton, 1969, published in the United States as *The Escape Room,* Doubleday, 1970; *The Flames of Calais: A Soldier's Battle, 1940,* Hodder & Stoughton, 1972; *Nuremberg,* Little, Brown, 1979.

SIDELIGHTS: A much decorated World War II hero, Airey Neave was captured by the Nazis in 1940 and imprisoned in maximum-security Colditz Castle in Saxony. He escaped from the prison by impersonating a German officer, but he still was faced with a long and dangerous trek across Europe before he could reach safety at Gibraltar. With the help of underground guides, Neave eventually returned to Great Britain. Upon his return, he supervised a highly successful operation to rescue other British and American prisoners of war. After the German surrender, Neave served as an official of the International Military Tribunal in Nuremberg.

Neave's wartime exploits provided the material for many of his books. In *They Have Their Exits,* he recounts his escape from the Nazis and describes his work at Nuremberg. A reviewer for the *Times Literary Supplement* said of the book, "This is an escape story and a good one, but its success is owed not to the artifice of mingling post-war trials with war-time thrills but to the way in which the author tells his own story." In another real-life adventure story, *Saturday at M.1.9.,* Neave writes about the network of underground escape routes established in Nazi-occupied Europe. J. C. Dougherty noted that the book "reads more like a James Bond thriller than non-fiction. The only criticism this reviewer can think of is that Airey Neave speaks too much of himself. His role was, in truth, overshadowed by on-the-scene operatives who took the most daring of risks." A critic for the *Times Literary Supplement* assessed Neave's role differently: "In the age of the non-hero, it is a joy to be able to recommend a book which is written by one who not only bears the insignia but expresses also the reality of heroism. [The book] will lift the hearts of everyone for whom the virtues of courage and self-sacrifice still have meaning." In 1969, Willis World Wide Productions acquired the motion picture rights for *Saturday at M.1.9.*

Ironically, Neave survived many harrowing experiences during World War II only to meet a violent end in his own country. After the war, Neave served as a member of Parliament for more than twenty-five years. A Conservative, he was one of Margaret Thatcher's closest political allies and served as the shadow cabinet's minister to Northern Ireland. Neave abhorred the tactics of the Irish Republican Army (IRA) and advocated the reinstatement of the death penalty for convicted terrorist killers. His hard line probably led to his death. On March 30, 1979, Neave was driving his car out of the Parliament's underground parking garage when a bomb exploded under the hood. He died shortly afterwards. In an anonymous telephone call, the IRA claimed responsibility for planting the bomb.

BIOGRAPHICAL/CRITICAL SOURCES: Airey Neave, *They Have Their Exits,* Little, Brown, 1953; *Times Literary Supplement,* April 3, 1953, September 25, 1969; *Spectator,* April 3, 1953; *New York Herald Tribune Book Review,* August 30, 1953; *Christian Science Monitor,* October 10, 1953; *New Yorker,* October 17, 1953; *San Francisco Chronicle,* October 25, 1953; Neave, *Saturday at M.1.9.,* Hodder & Stoughton, 1969, published in the United States as *The Escape Room,* Doubleday, 1970; *Best Sellers,* October 1, 1970; *Newsweek,* April 9, 1979; *Time,* April 9, 1979.

OBITUARIES: Publishers Weekly, April 16, 1979.

*   *   *

NEHRU, Jawaharlal 1889-1964

PERSONAL: Name Pronounced *Ja-wa-har-*lal Nay-*roo;* Born November 14, 1889, in Allahabad, India; died May 27, 1964, of a heart attack, in New Delhi, India; son of Motilal (a lawyer) and Swarup Rani Nehru; married Kamala Kaul, March, 1916 (died, 1936); children: Indira Nehru Gandhi. *Education:* Trinity College, Cambridge, earned degree (second class honours), 1910; Inner Temple, London, law degree, 1912. *Residence:* New Delhi, India.

CAREER: Admitted to Bar of Inner Temple, England, 1912; barrister in high court of Allahabad, India; member of all-India congress, 1918-64; member of Mahatma Gandhi's non-violence movement, 1920-67; Government of India, president of national congress, 1929, 1936, 1937, 1946, 1951-54, minister of external affairs, 1946-64, first prime minister of independent India, 1947-64. Delegate of Bankepore Congress, 1912. *Awards, honors:* Doctor of Laws, Osmania University (Hyderabad, India), 1948.

WRITINGS: Statements, Speeches, and Writings, [Allahabad], 1929; Principal R. Dwivedi, editor, *The Life and Speeches of Pandit Jawahar Lal Nehru,* National Publishing (Delhi, India), 1930(?); *Glimpses of World History* (juvenile), two volumes, Kitabistan (Bangladesh), 1934-35 (also see below); *India and the World* (essays), Allen & Unwin, 1936; *Jawaharlal Nehru,* John Lane, 1936, enlarged edition, Bodley Head, 1955, published as *Toward Freedom,* John Day, 1941 (also see below); *Recent Essays and Writings on the Future of Indian Communalism, Labour and Other Subjects,* Kitabistan, 1937; *Letters From a Father to His Daughter* (for children), Kitabistan, 1938; *Nehru-Jinnah Correspondence,* J. B. Kripalani, 1938; *Eighteen Months in India, 1936-1937,* Kitabistan, 1938.

The Parting of the Ways and the Viceroy-Gandhi Correspondence, Lindsay Drummond for India League, 1940; *The Quintessence of Nehru,* introduction by K. T. Narasimha Char, Allen & Unwin, 1941; *Points of View* (extracts from *Toward Freedom*), John Day, 1941 (also see above); V. K. Krishna Menon, *The Unity of India: Collected Writings 1937-1940,* Lindsay Drummond, 1941; J. P. Gupta, editor, *Nehru Flings a Challenge,* foreword by P. S. Wadia, Hamara Hindustan Publications, 1943; *Prison Humours,* New Literature, 1944; *Important Speeches of Jawaharlal Nehru,* Indian Printing Works, 1945, revised and enlarged edition published as *Important Speeches,* Indian Printing Works; *The Discovery of India,* John Day, 1946; Bright, editor, *India on the March,* Indian Printing Works, 1946, published as *Selected Writings,* Indian Printing Works, 1960; (contributor) *India: Constituent Assembly,* [New Delhi], 1947; D. R. Bose, compiler, *New India Speaks,* A. Mukherjee, 1947; *Nehru on Gandhi,* John Day, 1948; *Sri Ramakrishna and Swami Vivekananda,* Advarta Ashrama, 1949; *Mahatma Gandhi,* Signet Press, 1949.

Independence and After: A Collection of Speeches, 1946-49, John Day, 1950 (later published as Volume I of *Speeches;* also see below); Bright, editor, *Before and After Independence,* Indian Printing Works, 1950; *Inside America: A Voyage of Discovery,* National Book Stall, c. 1950; *Visit to America,* John Day, 1950; *Talks With Nehru: India's Prime Minister Speaks out on the Issues of Our Time,* John Day, 1951; *The Story of the World* (for children), sketches by Richard Albany, John Day, 1951; *Speeches, 1949-1953,* Ministry of Information and Broadcasting, Government of India, 1954 (later published as Volume II of *Speeches;* also see below); *India and the Arab World,* [Bombay], 1955; (author of introduction), Kanaiyalal Maneklal Munshi, *Indian Temple Sculpture,* A. Goswami, 1956; S. K. Narain, editor, *Selections From Jawaharlal Nehru,* Oxford University Press, 1956; *Planning and Development: Speeches of Jawaharlal Nehru (1952-56),* Ministry of Information and Broadcasting, 1956; *Towards a Socialistic Order,* revised edition, All Congress Committee, 1956; *Speeches in Parliament, November 16-December 7, 1956,* Information Service of India, c. 1957; *Speeches,* Ministry of Information and Broadcasting, Government of India, 1957, Volume I: *Independence and After: A Collection of Speeches, 1946-49* (also see above), Volume II: *Speeches: 1949-1953* (also see above), Volume III: *1953-57* (all part of *Jawharlal Nehru: Speeches;* also see below); *A Bunch of Old Letters,* Asia, c. 1958; Basant Kumar Chatterjee, editor, *Etam aura Nehrau,* [India], 1958; *On Community Development,* Ministry of Information and Broadcasting, Government of India, 1958; (contributor) *Official Correspondence Between the Central Government of the People's Republic of China and the Government of India,* Foreign Languages Press (Peking), 1959.

Social Welfare in India, revised and abridged edition, Planning Commission, 1960; *The Wit and Wisdom of Gandhi,* New Book Society of India, 1960; *Documents on the Sino-Indian Boundary Question,* Foreign Languages Press, 1960; *Itihasa ke mahapuruba* (in Hindi), [India], 1960; T. K. Mahadevan, editor, *Freedom From Fear: Reflections on the Personality and Teachings of Gandhi,* Gandhi Smarak Nidhi, 1960; N. B. Sen, editor, *Wit and Wisdom,* New Book Society of India, 1960; R. K. Karanjia, interviewer, *The Mind of Mr. Nehru,* foreword by Radhakrishnan, Allen & Unwin, 1960; C. D. Narasimhaiah, *India's Spokesman: From Speeches and Addresses,* Macmillan, (Madras, India), 1960; *India Today and Tomorrow,* Indian Council for Cultural Relations, Orient Longman, 1960; *The Quintessence of Nehru,* Allen & Unwin, 1961; (with Lopez Mateos) *Mexico y la Indio* (in Spanish), Editorial "La Justicia", 1961; *Prime Minister Nehru's Visit to U.S.A.,* [New Delhi], c. 1961; *The Prime Minister Comes to America,* Information Service of India (Washington, D.C.), 1961; *India's Foreign Policy: Selected Speeches, September 1946-April 1961,* Ministry of Information and Broadcasting, Government of India, 1961; *Ardishah hayi Nihru,* [India], c.1961; *Prime Minister on Sino-Indian Relations,* four parts, Ministry of External Affairs, Government of India, 1961-62.

Jawaharlal Nehru on Co-operation, Ministry of Information and Broadcasting, 1962; *Nehru Writes to Heads of States,* [New Delhi], 1962; *Synopsis of the Nehru-Fateh Singh Talks,* [Amritsar, India], 1962; *Nehru's Letter to Cho-En-Lai, November 14, 1962,* [New Delhi], 1962; *Prime Minister of Goa,* Ministry of External Affairs, 1962; *India's Freedom,* Barnes & Noble, 1962; *Jawaharlal Nehru: Speeches,* five volumes, Ministry of Information and Broadcasting, 1963 (also see above); *Prime Minister on Chinese Aggression,* Ministry of External Affairs, 1963; *Al-Udwan al-Sini fi al-harb wa-al-silm* (title means "Sino-Indian Border Dispute"), [India], 1963; *India's Quest, Being Letters on Indian History* (excerpts from *Glimpses of World History*), Asia, 1963 (also see above); *Nehru Souvenir,* Review Publications (Meerut, India), 1964; Jastin Vijayavardhana, compiler, *Tibbataye Bauddha manava samharaya,* [India], 1964; *Nehru on Socialism,* Perspective Publication, 1964; *Nehru and Africa: Extracts From Jawaharlal Nehru's Speeches on Africa, 1946-1963,* Indian Council for Africa, 1964; Ramnarayan Chandhary, editor, *Nehru, in His Own Words,* translated from the Hindi, Navajivan Publishing House, 1964; *Zindah dil Javahir* (in Urdu), [India], 1964; *Jawaharlal Nehru: Excerpts From His Writings and Speeches,* Ministry of Information and Broadcasting, 1964; Sen, editor, *Glorious Thoughts of Nehru,* New Book Society of India, 1964, revised and enlarged edition, 1968; *Azadi de satraha kadama* (in Hindi), [India], 1964.

Sita Ram Jayaswal, editor and compiler, *Nehru on Society, Education and Culture,* foreword by Radhakamal Mukerjee, Vinod Pustak Maudir, 1965; Dorothy Norman, editor, *Nehru, the First Sixty Years,* two volumes, John Day, 1965; (contributor) S. Chellaswamy, compiler, *Letters From Late Prime Minister Mr. Jawaharlal Nehru and Other Statesmen*

on National Issues, [Madras], 1965; *Vneshniaia politika Indii: izbrannye rechi i vystupleniia, 1946-1961,* Progress, 1965; N. L. Gupta, editor, *Nehru on Communalism,* Sampradayikta Virodhi Committee, 1965; Sita Ram Jayaswal, editor and compiler, *Nehru on Society, Education and Culture,* foreword by Radhakamal Mukerjee, Vinod Pustak Maudir, 1965; *Mahatma Gandhi,* Asia, 1966; H. D. Malaviya, *Congressman's Primer for Socialism,* foreword by Indira Gandhi, introduction by Gulzari Lal Nanda, Socialist Congressman, 1965; *The Philosophy of Mr. Nehru,* foreword by Zakir Husain, Allen & Unwin, 1966; K. Rames, editor, *Nehrusuktislu* (in Telugu), [India], 1966; B. N. Mullik, compiler, *Nehru on Police,* Dehra Dun, Palit & Dutt, 1970. Also author of *Thoughts from Nehru,* Allied Publishers (Bombay), and *Important Speeches,* edited by Bright, Indian Printing Works. Also author of numerous booklets on political issues.

SIDELIGHTS: For thirty-one years, Nehru was in the forefront of India's nationalist movement as the principal protege of spiritual leader Mohandes (Mahatma) Gandhi. Then from 1947 until his death, he served as the first prime minister of independent India, the largest democracy in the world.

It was surprising that two men as diverse as Nehru and Gandhi fought together so long for the same cause: freeing India from British supremacy. While both Nehru and Gandhi were considered "practical idealists," as Nehru once termed it, and both believed in reaching political goals via passive resistance, the basic ideology of the two men clashed. Nehru was an avid proponent of democracy while Gandhi believed in a single ruler as long as he or she was "spiritually emancipated," noted P. N. Pandy. In addition, Gandhi was adamantly against industrialization just as Nehru was fervently for it.

Nehru was "the epitome of modern man," wrote his sister, Krishna Nehru Hutheesing. Committed to developing India into a self-sufficient world power, he ardently supported science and technology, certain that research in these areas could mitigate "the harsh circumstances of the natural environment and triumph over illness, hunger and war," in Hutheesing's words. Acting toward the industrial development of India, Nehru established numerous institutes to study a wide-range of fields, including agriculture, medicine, the causes of cancer, nutrition, fuel, and textiles. Through his endeavors, national scientific laboratories were set up in several of India's major cities. In addition, he brought India into the atomic age by creating a national atomic energy commission with institutes in Bombay and Calcutta. He himself headed the ministry of atomic energy.

Nehru "envisioned a world of equal opportunity, education, and living standards for all mankind, made safe and just by an enlightened government operating on socialistic principles," Hutheesing pointed out. With these ends in mind, he first undertook the formidable task of unifying a country diverse in religious belief, language, and custom. In September of 1926, Nehru declared that "religion as practiced in India has become the old man of the sea for us and it has not only broken our backs but stunted and almost killed all originality of thought and mind. Like Sinbad the Sailor we must get rid of this terrible burden before we can aspire to breathe freely or do anything useful." Nehru also believed that of the fourteen languages spoken in India, one should be chosen as the country's official tongue. It was he who directed the gradual transition to Hindi.

As India's prime minister, Nehru brought about radical social and economic changes. He fought the iniquities of the

Hindu caste system by promulgating the Untouchability Act of 1955, forbidding the practice of untouchability. In addition, he proscribed the custom of bigamy and gave widows the right of inheritance.

Profoundly influenced by his 1926 and 1938 visits to Europe, Nehru's nationalistic political stance grew to include a strong feeling of internationalism as well. In leading India, Nehru sought peaceful co-existence between his country and the rest of the world. In December, 1952, he stated, "As in the world today, so also in our country, the philosophy of force can no longer pay and our progress must be used on peaceful co-operation and tolerance of each other." He was the first of any Asian or African leader to espouse a policy of nonalignment with any world power.

Nehru was harshly criticized for his leniency in dealing with Red China. It was the only major country with which he could not reach his goal of peaceful co-existence. Even after signing the Sino-Indian Treaty on Tibet, China entered the northern border of India, a fact that Nehru kept hidden from parliament until five years later.

It is perhaps ironic that such a powerful head of state had been only mildly interested in government affairs at the onset of his career. As a young lawyer Nehru had joined the moderate party, representing it at the Bankepore Congress as a delegate. He then saw the congress as "a theatre where well-to-do English-educated Indians were playing the role of gentlemen politicians in their 'morning coats and well-pressed trousers,'" wrote Pandy.

Then in 1919, Gandhi organized the Satyagraha Sabha ("truthful effort") in reaction to the Rowlatt Bill just passed by the ruling British. The bill enabled the English to "short-circuit the processes of law in dealing with terrorists," Pandy explained, a bill that seemed to leave much room for interpretation. It was this movement of peaceful noncooperation with the British raj that spurred Nehru's interest in politics. In *Toward Freedom,* Nehru stated: "I was afire with enthusiasm and wanted to join the Satyagraha Sabha immediately. I hardly thought of the consequences—law breaking, jail going, etc."

In 1920, Nehru visited the inhabitants of the Jumna River in Allahabad, an experience that furthered his commitment to politics. A Brahman, or member of the wealthy class, himself, Nehru had been unaware of just how wretched the conditions under which many of his countrymen survived. "That visit was a revelation to me," he wrote. "A new picture of India seemed to rise before me, naked, starving, crushed and utterly miserable. And their faith in us, casual visitors from the distant city, embarrassed me and filled me with a new responsibility that frightened me."

Nehru's sense of responsibility and firm commitment to Gandhi's philosophy of civil disobedience resulted in jail sentences many times throughout his life. In all, Nehru was imprisoned nine times for a total confinement of nine years. While in jail he became immersed in study, especially of writings on Marxism and Taoism. A prolific author, he also accomplished most of his writing while behind bars. In the preface to *Toward Freedom,* an autobiography, he wrote: "The primary object in writing these pages was to occupy myself with a definite task, so necessary in the long solitudes of jail life, as well as to review past events in India, with which I had been connected, to enable myself to think clearly about them. I began the task in a mood of self-questioning . . . [and] if I thought of an audience, it was one of my own countrymen and countrywomen."

Reviewing *Toward Freedom,* Margaret Marshall observed

in *Nation:* "It is the impact of this double play of forces upon an intelligent, sensitive, and genuinely noble being which makes his remarkable autobiography one of the most absorbing personal histories of modern times." Concerning the writing itself, Charles Fleischer commented in the *New York Times:* "Since the style is the man, let it be promptly recorded that Nehru's autobiography is written in lucid, purest English, his deepest thoughts expressed in simplest speech. In a word, his style is so obviously sincere that the man's integrity is absolutely unquestionable." Clifton Fadiman noted in *New Republic* that while "his is not an autobiography of universal appeal . . . Nehru's book is one of the few available to English readers that really make clear history and meaning of the Indian Nationalist movement during the last thirty years."

The Discovery of India is Nehru's second autobiography. Isaac Rosenfelt commented, "There is a turgid feeling to *The Discovery of India* which must be attributed to the great gloom and greater injustice of Nehru's wartime imprisonment. . . ." John Bicknell described it as "A profound and illuminating document, not only in its exploration of the Indian heritage but especially for the light it throws on the character of a remarkably brilliant and complex personality."

Nehru was the father of former Prime Minister of India Indira Gandhi.

AVOCATIONAL INTERESTS: Yoga, horseback riding, swimming, spinning yarn, reading, "mountains, running water, children, glaciers, good conversation, all animals except bats and centipedes."

BIOGRAPHICAL/CRITICAL SOURCES—Books: Jawaharlal Nehru, *Toward Freedom,* John Day, 1941; Nehru, *Glimpses of World History,* John Day, 1942; Nehru, *The Discovery of India,* John Day, 1946; Frank Moraes, *Jawaharlal Nehru: A Biography,* Macmillan, 1956; Vincent Sheean, *Nehru: The Years of Power,* Random House, 1959; R. K. Karanjia, *The Mind of Mr. Nehru: An Interview,* Allen & Unwin, 1960; K. T. Narasimha Char, *The Quintessence of Nehru,* Allen & Unwin, 1961; Michael Edwardes, *Nehru: A Pictorial Biography,* Viking, 1962; Dorothy Norman, *First Sixty Years,* Bodley Head, 1965; Krishna Nehru Hutheesing, *We Nehrus,* Holt, 1967; Atulananda Chakrabarti, *Lonesome Pilgrim,* foreword by Hugh Tinker, Allied Publications, 1969; Rao, *Nehru Legacy,* Popular Prakashan, 1971; Elizabeth Manchline Roberts, *Gandhi, Nehru and Modern India,* Methuen, 1974; John B. Alphonso Karkala, *Jawaharlal Nehru,* Twayne, 1975; Sarvepalli Gopal, *Jawaharlal Nehru: A Biography,* Volume I: *1889-1947,* Harvard University Press, 1976; Bishwa Nath Pandey, *Nehru,* Macmillan, 1976; B. R. Nanda, editor, *Indian Foreign Policy: The Nehru Years,* University of Hawaii, 1976; Bishwa Nath Pandey, *Nehru,* Stein & Day, 1976; *Encyclopedia Americana,* Americana, 1977.

Articles: *New Yorker,* February 22, 1941, August 17, 1946, November 11, 1967; *New York Times,* February 23, 1941, July 28, 1946, May 28, 1964; *Nation,* March 1, 1941; *New Republic,* September 23, 1946, January 28, 1967, June 19, 1971; *Washington Post,* December 19, 1962; *Times Literary Supplement,* September 21, 1973; *Foreign Affairs,* April, 1974; *English Historical Review,* April, 1974; *American Historical Review,* April, 1976.*

*   *   *

NEUMANN, Jonathan 1950-

PERSONAL: Born April 14, 1950, in New York, N.Y.; son

of Richard (a musician) and Anci (a dancer; maiden name, Ackersman) Neumann. *Education:* City College of the City University of New York, B.A. (cum laude), 1971. *Politics.* Independent. *Religion:* Jewish. *Home:* 602 South Washington Sq., Philadelphia, Pa. 19106. *Office: Philadelphia Inquirer,* 400 North Broad St., Philadelphia, Pa. 19101.

CAREER/WRITINGS: New York Post, New York, N.Y., copyboy, 1969; *Daily Hampshire Gazette,* Northampton, Mass., reporter, 1972-76; *Philadelphia Inquirer,* Philadelphia, Pa., reporter, 1976—. Notable assignments include coverage of an academic/financial scandal at University of Massachusetts, convicted killers who've been found innocent, interrogation techniques of Philadelphia Police Dept., and cigarette smuggling. *Awards, honors:* Pulitzer Prize for public service, 1978.

SIDELIGHTS: Neumann told *CA:* "As a reporter, when I come across a situation which seems particularly unjust or outrageous—and when nobody seems to be interested in doing anything to correct the problem—I am generally motivated to begin investigating, digging and reporting until the problem is recognized and, with luck, solved."

BIOGRAPHICAL/CRITICAL SOURCES: New York Times, April 18, 1978; *Time,* April 24, 1978; *Penthouse,* April, 1978.

* * *

NEVILLE, Richard F. 1931-

PERSONAL: Born September 6, 1931, in Brooklyn, N.Y.; married Roselyn R. Bryson; children: Richard F., Jr., Shannon, Elizabeth, John, Mary, Heather, Barbara. *Education:* Central Connecticut State College, B.S., 1953; Columbia University, M.A., 1957; University of Connecticut, Ph.D., 1963. *Home:* 13319 Tamworth Lane, Silver Spring, Md. 20904. *Office:* Division of Education, University of Maryland—Baltimore County, 5401 Wilkens Ave., Baltimore, Md. 21228.

CAREER: Elementary school teacher in Greenwich, Conn., 1953-56, high school basketball coach, 1955-56; Central Connecticut State College, New Britain, demonstration teacher and instructor in education, 1956-58; principal of elementary school in Berlin, Conn., 1958-60; University of Connecticut, Storrs, instructor in education, 1960-64; University of Maryland, College Park, associate professor of education, 1964-69; University of Maryland—Baltimore County, Baltimore, professor of education, 1969—, head of Division of Education, 1969-71, dean of Division of Education, 1972-77. Visiting professor at University of Puerto Rico, summer, 1967, State University of New York College at Plattsburg, summers, 1974, 1977, and University of Georgia, summer, 1976; guest lecturer at University of New Hampshire. Member of national evaluation board of National Council for Accreditation of Teacher Education, 1970-74. Director of workshops.

MEMBER: National Education Association, Association for Supervision and Curriculum Development, National Society for the Study of Education, American Association of University Professors, American Association for the Advancement of Science, Maryland State Association for Teacher Education, Maryland Association for Supervision and Curriculum Development (first vice-president, 1965-67; president, 1967-68), Phi Delta Kappa.

WRITINGS: (Co-author) *The Foundations of Elementary School Teaching,* Ronald, 1963; (co-author) *The Faculty as Teachers: A Perspective on Evaluation* (monograph), ERIC, 1971; (with Robert J. Alfonso and Gerald R. Firth) *Instruc-*

tional Supervision: A Behavior System, Allyn & Bacon, 1975, 2nd edition, 1978. Contributor to education journals.

* * *

NEY, Virgil 1905-1979

OBITUARY NOTICE: Born February 19, 1905, in Omaha, Neb.; died May 14, 1979, in Washington, D.C. Military historian, educator, and author. During World War II Ney was a member of General Douglas MacArthur's staff. After the war he established a school of military history in Korea. He was also involved in various government projects. His writings include *Notes on Guerrilla Warfare* and *Fort on the Prairies.* Obituaries and other sources: *Directory of American Scholars,* Volume 1: *History,* 6th edition, Bowker, 1974; *Washington Post,* May 18, 1979.

* * *

NIETHAMMER, Carolyn 1944-

PERSONAL: Born May 21, 1944, in Illinois; daughter of George H. and Maxine (Mick) Niethammer; married Ford Burkhart (a professor of journalism), February 4, 1978. *Education:* University of Arizona, B.A., 1966. *Home:* 604 East First St., Tucson, Ariz. 85705.

CAREER: Arizona Daily Star, Tucson, reporter, 1966-67; *Tucson Daily Citizen,* Tucson, reporter, 1969; Arroyo Seco Ski Dormitory, Taos, N.M., cook, 1970; University of Arizona, Tucson, faculty member in creative writing, 1975—. Teacher at Tucson Public Library, 1978; gives private seminars on gathering and cooking wild desert foods. Member of board of directors of Our Sonoran Heritage. *Member:* Western Writers of America, Tepary Burrito Society.

WRITINGS: American Indian Food and Lore, Macmillan, 1974; *Daughters of the Earth,* Macmillan, 1977. Editor of archaeological and anthropological reports.

WORK IN PROGRESS: A novelized biography of Nellie Cashman, an Irish immigrant known throughout the Western mining frontier for her cooking, ability as a miner, and charitable activities.

SIDELIGHTS: Carolyn Niethammer writes: "My present work on Nellie Cashman will fall into that gray area between fiction and nonfiction. It allows me to combine my enjoyment of historical research with the development of my skills in fiction, a new field of endeavor."

* * *

NINEHAM, Dennis (Eric) 1921-

PERSONAL: Born September 27, 1921, in Southampton, England; son of Stanley Martin and Bessie Elizabeth (Gain) Nineham; married Ruth Corfield Miller, August 13, 1946; children: Elizabeth Nineham Clark, Clare Nineham Drury, Hugh, Christopher. *Education:* Queen's College, Oxford, (first class honors), 1944; graduate study at Lincoln Theological College, 1944-45. *Religion:* Anglican. *Home and Office:* The Warden's Lodgings, Keble College, Oxford University, Oxford OX1 3PG, England.

CAREER: Oxford University, Queen's College, Oxford, England, fellow, 1946-54; University of London, King's College, London, England, professor of Biblical and historical theology, 1954-58, professor of divinity, 1958-64, fellow, 1963—; Cambridge University, Cambridge, England, Regius Professor of Divinity and fellow of Emmanuel College, 1964-69; warden at Oxford University, Keble College, 1969-79; professor of theology at Bristol University, England,

1980—. Member of general synod of Church of England, 1970-76. *Awards, honors:* M.A. from Oxford University, 1946; B.D. from Oxford University, 1964, and Cambridge University, 1964; D.D. from Yale University, 1965, University of Birmingham, 1972, and Oxford University, 1978.

WRITINGS: (Editor) *Studies in the Gospels,* Basil Blackwell, 1955, 2nd edition, 1957; *A New Way of Looking at the Gospels,* S.P.C.K., 1962; *Commentary on St. Mark's Gospel,* Penguin, 1963, new edition, 1978; (editor) *The Church's Use of the Bible,* S.P.C.K., 1963; (contributor) W. M. Pettinger, editor, *Christ for Us To-day,* S.C.M. Press, 1968; *The Use and Abuse of the Bible: A Study of the Bible in an Age of Rapid Cultural Change,* Macmillan, 1976; *Explorations in Theology,* S.C.M. Press, 1977; (contributor), J. H. Hick, editor, *The Myth of God Incarnate,* S.C.M. Press, 1977.

WORK IN PROGRESS: "Commentary on arts after Apostles."

BIOGRAPHICAL/CRITICAL SOURCES: Times Literary Supplement, April 8, 1977.

*   *   *

NOCK, O(swald) S(tevens) 1905-

PERSONAL: Born January 21, 1905, in Sutton, Coldfield, England; son of Samuel James (a bank manager) and Rose (a teacher; maiden name, Stevens) Nock; married Olivia Hattie Ravenall, May 15, 1937; children: Jill Stevens Nock Crocker, Trevor Stevens. *Education:* Imperial College of Science and Technology, London, A.C.G.I., 1924, B.Sc., 1924, D.I.C., 1925. *Politics:* Conservative. *Religion:* Church of England. *Home:* 28 High Bannerdown, Bath BA1 7JY, England.

CAREER: Westinghouse Brake & Signal Co. Ltd., London, England, 1925-68, trainee, 1925, worked in various departments, 1926-35, draftsman, 1935-37, senior design draftsman, 1937-45, mechanical engineer, 1945-49, chief draftsman in brake department, 1949-57, chief mechanical engineer, 1959-65, planning manager, 1965-68; writer, 1968—. *Member:* Institution of Civil Engineers (fellow), Institution of Mechanical Engineers (fellow), Institution of Railway Signal Engineers (honorary fellow; past president).

WRITINGS: The Locomotives of Sir Nigel Gresley, Longmans, Green, 1945; *Locomotives of the L.N.E.R.: Standardisation and Renumbering,* 2nd edition, London & North Eastern Railway, 1947; *The Railways of Britain, Past and Present,* Batsford, 1948, 3rd edition, 1962; *Scottish Railways,* Thomas Nelson, 1950, revised edition, 1961; *British Locomotives From the Footplate,* Ian Allan, 1950; *British Trains, Past and Present,* Batsford, 1951; *The Great Western Railway: An Appreciation,* Heffer, 1951; *The Premier Line: The Story of London and North Western Locomotives,* Ian Allan, 1952; *Four Thousand Miles on the Footplate,* Ian Allan, 1952; *Fifty Years of Western Express Running,* Everard, 1954; *Locomotives of the North Eastern Railway,* Ian Allan, 1954.

The Railway Engineers, Batsford, 1955; *British Railways in Action,* Thomas Nelson, 1956; *Steam Locomotive: The Unfinished Story of Steam Locomotives and Steam Locomotive Men on the Railways of Great Britain,* Allen & Unwin, 1957, 2nd edition, Augustus M. Kelley, 1968; *Branch Lines,* Batsford, 1957; *Father of Railways: The Story of George Stephenson,* Thomas Nelson, 1958; *The Great Northern Railway,* Ian Allan, 1958; *The Railway Race to the North,* Ian Allan, 1959; *Historical Steam Locomotives,* A. & C. Black, 1959.

(With Eric Treacy) *Main Lines Across the Border,* Thomas Nelson, 1960; *The London and North Western Railway,* Ian Allan, 1960; *British Steam Railways,* A. & C. Black, 1961; *The South Eastern and Chatham Railway,* Ian Allan, 1962, revised edition, 1971; *Fifty Years of Railway Signalling,* Institution of Railway Signal Engineers, 1962; *The Caledonian Railway,* Ian Allan, 1962; *British Railways in Transition,* Thomas Nelson, 1963; *The Great Western Railway in the Nineteenth Century,* Ian Allan, 1963; *Continental Main Lines, Today and Yesterday,* Allen & Unwin, 1963; *History of the Great Western Railway,* Volume 3 (Nock was not associated with previous volumes), Ian Allan, 1964; *The Midland Compounds,* Augustus M. Kelley, 1964; *The Pocket Encyclopedia of British Steam Locomotives in Colour,* Blandford, 1964; *Sir William Stanier: An Engineering Biography,* Ian Allan, 1964.

Railway Holiday in Austria, David & Charles, 1965; *The Highland Railway,* Ian Allan, 1965; *Britain's New Railway: Electrification of the London-Midland Main Lines from Euston to Birmingham, Stoke-on-Trent, Crewe, Liverpool, and Manchester,* Ian Allan, 1965; *The British Steam Railway Locomotive, 1926-65,* Ian Allan, 1966; *Historic Railway Disasters,* Ian Allan, 1966, 2nd edition, 1969; *The L.N.W.R. Precursor Family: The Precursors, Experiments, Georges, Princes of the London and North Western Railway,* Augustus M. Kelley, 1966; *The London and South Western Railway,* Ian Allan, 1966; (editor) *Single Line Railways: A Handbook of Management, Engineering, and Operation,* David & Charles, 1966; *Southern Steam,* David & Charles, 1966; *Steam Railways in Retrospect,* A. & C. Black, 1966; *Steam Railways of Britain in Colour,* Blandford, 1967; *The G.W.R. Stars, Castles, and Kings,* David & Charles, 1967; *British Steam Locomotives at Work,* Allen & Unwin, 1967; *The Caledonian Dunalastairs and Associated Classes,* Augustus M. Kelley, 1968; *North Western: A Saga of the Premier Line of Great Britain, 1846-1922,* Ian Allan, 1968; *The Railway Enthusiast's Encyclopedia,* Hutchinson, 1968; *The Lancashire and Yorkshire Railway: A Concise History,* Ian Allan, 1969; *L.N.E.R. Steam,* Augustus M. Kelley, 1969; *British Railway Signalling: A Survey of Fifty Years' Progress,* Augustus M. Kelley, 1969.

Railways at the Zenith of Steam, 1920-40, Macmillan, 1970; *Rail, Steam, and Speed,* Allen & Unwin, 1970; *Britain's Railways at War, 1939-1945,* Ian Allan, 1971; *L.M.S. Steam,* David & Charles, 1971; *Railways in the Years of Pre-Eminence, 1905-1919,* Macmillan, 1971; *Railways of Australia,* A. & C. Black, 1971; *Railways of Southern Africa,* A. & C. Black, 1971; *Speed Records on Britain's Railways,* David & Charles, 1971; *G.W.R. Steam,* David & Charles, 1972; *Engine 6000: The Saga of a Locomotive,* David & Charles, 1972; *The Dawn of World Railways, 1800-1850,* Macmillan, 1972; *The Golden Age of Steam: A Critical and Nostalgic Memory of the Last Twenty Years Before Grouping on the Railways of Great Britain,* A. & C. Black, 1973, St. Martin's, 1974; *The Gresley Pacifics,* David & Charles, 1973; (with George Heiron) *The Majesty of British Steam,* Ian Allan, 1973; *Railways in the Formative Years, 1851-1895,* Macmillan, 1973; *Underground Railways of the World,* St. Martin's, 1973; *Railways of Canada,* A. & C. Black, 1973; *Railways in the Transition From Steam, 1940-1965,* Macmillan, 1974; *Electric Euston to Glasgow,* Ian Allan, 1974.

Algoma Central Railway, A. & C. Black, 1975; *Locomotion: A World Survey of Railway Traction,* Scribner, 1975; *Railways of the Modern Age Since 1963,* Blandford, 1975, Macmillan, 1976; *Railways Then and Now: A World History,* Crown, 1975; *Out the Line* (autobiography and bibliography), Elek, 1976; *Sixty Years of West Coast Express Running*, Ian Allan, 1976; *Great Steam Locomotives of All Times*, Blandford, 1976, Arco, 1977; (editor) *Encyclopaedia of Railways*, Octopus Books, 1977; *World Atlas of Railways*, Intercontinental Book Productions, 1978; *Railways of the U.S.A.*, A. & C. Black, 1979; *150 Years of Competitive Locomotive Testing*, Ian Allan, 1980; *Two Miles a Minute: A Definitive Study of the British High Speed, and Advanced Passenger Trains*, Patrick Stephens, 1980; *150 Years of British Main Line Railways*, David & Charles, 1980.

WORK IN PROGRESS: Editing, with a team of experts from the Institution of Railway Signal Engineers, a textbook on modern railway signalling practices in the United Kingdom, publication by A. & C. Black; *A Centenary History of the Westinghouse Brake Company in England*, publication expected in 1981.

SIDELIGHTS: Nock told *CA:* "I have been interested in railways from my cradle, and from a very early age determined I would have a career in railway engineering. After completing my training, I was fortunate in obtaining employment with a firm having world-wide interests. My work for and experience in railways became infinitely wider than if I had joined one railway. Since retirement from regular day-to-day business my writing activities have greatly increased, extending to all the latest techniques. I was recently in Hong Kong seeing progress on their new mass transit railway."

AVOCATIONAL INTERESTS: Travel (Europe, India, Africa, Australia, New Zealand, United States, Canada), photography, natural history, painting, gardening.

*   *   *

NOONAN, John Ford 1943-

PERSONAL: Born October 7, 1943, in New York, N.Y.; married Marcia Lunt, 1962 (divorced, 1965); children: three. *Education:* Brown University, A.B., 1964; Carnegie Institute of Technology, M.A., 1966. *Home:* Apartment 5, 233 West Fourth St., New York, N.Y. 10014. *Agent:* Joan Scott Inc., 162 West 56th St., New York, N.Y. 10019.

CAREER: Playwright and actor. Buckley Country Day School, Long Island, N.Y., teacher of Latin, English, and history, 1966-69; Fillmore East Rock Theatre, New York City, stagehand, 1969-71; E. F. Hutton Co., New York City, stockbroker, 1971-72; Villanova University, Villanova, Pa., professor of drama, 1972-73. Actor in stage productions and motion pictures. *Awards, honors:* Rockefeller grant, 1973.

WRITINGS—Plays: *The Year Boston Won the Pennant* (two-act; first produced in New York City, 1969), Grove, 1970; "Lazarus Was a Lady," first produced in New York City, 1970; "Rainbows for Sale" (first produced in New York City, 1971), published in *The Off-Off Broadway Book*, edited by Albert Poland and Bruce Mailman, Bobbs-Merrill, 1972; "Concerning the Effects of Trimethylchloride," first produced in New York City, 1971; "Monday Night Varieties," first produced in New York City, 1972; (and director) "Older People," first produced in New York City, 1972; "Good-By and Keep Cold," first produced in New York City, 1973; "A Noonan Night," first produced in New York City, 1973; "A Sneaky Bit to Raise the Blind, and Pick Pack Pock Puck," first produced in New York City, 1974.

Screenplays: "Septuagenarian Substitute Ball," 1970; "The Summer the Snows Came," 1972.

SIDELIGHTS: Noonan's best known work is "The Year Boston Won the Pennant," the story of a baseball pitcher,

Marcus Sykowski, and his efforts to earn enough money to buy an artificial arm to replace his glove arm, which he lost in an unexplained accident. After some obscure episodes, including a fraudulent kidnapping plot and involvement with an underworld character, Sykowski obtains a prosthetic limb. But things turn out badly for the revitalized athlete. After his return to baseball, he suffers a nervous breakdown and his comeback is abbreviated by assassination.

Many critics found the play confusing. A reviewer for *New Yorker* wrote, "I found much of it extremely puzzling." Harold Clurman reported, "The loose-jointed awkwardness of the script, the unevenness of its style, the meagerness of emotion and scenic invention in the production rob the event of some of its potential effect and contribute to an impression of obscurity." Similarly, Harry Gilroy confessed: "It's a strange play. What it is all about—except for a somewhat remote relationship to baseball—is hard to say." *Variety* described the play as "a surrealistic, satirical, symbol-crammed attempt to illuminate the subconscious strains in American life, which the author represents as cruel, ugly, exploitative—in short, inhuman."

Another play of Noonan's to receive attention from critics was "Older People." It consists of several unrelated sketches exploring the frustrations encountered by the elderly. John Simon wrote that "if we are to believe Mr. Noonan, a good three-quarters of old people's time is spent on vainly trying to have intercourse, or on vainly trying to avoid having intercourse." Simon also noted, "What makes these lay figures 'older' is their uncomfortable similarity to persons in older plays (chiefly by Beckett and Ionesco); what makes them 'people,' I cannot for the life of me discover." Marilyn Stasio echoed Simon's feelings: "The situations range from a sexually sterile marriage to the sterile reunion of an aging Hollywood star and his first love to the sterile existence of the inmates of an old folk's home." Writing about the characters, Stasio noted "Noonan's contempt for them, and the lack of insight or wit with which he conveys this disdain."

Despite the severe criticism received by some of Noonan's plays, Joyce Tetrick observed that the playwright "is happily endowed with a wild theatrical imagination." He has been considered by some a promising playwright because of the potential shown in his writing. *Variety* noted that "Noonan has a fecund imagination and an interesting technical approach that augurs well for his future work."

BIOGRAPHICAL/CRITICAL SOURCES: New York Times, May 22, 1969, May 23, 1969; *Variety*, May 28, 1969; *Village Voice*, May 29, 1969; *Show Business*, May 31, 1969; *New Yorker*, May 31, 1969; *Nation*, June 9, 1969; *Cue*, May 29, 1972; *New York*, May 29, 1972.*

*   *   *

NOSS, John Boyer 1896-

PERSONAL: Born October 5, 1896, in Sendal, Japan; came to the United States in 1912; son of Christopher (an American missionary) and Lura (a missionary; maiden name, Boyer) Noss; married Mary Williamson Bell, June 14, 1922 (died April 4, 1968); married Flora Balch Rudisill, April 14, 1976; children: (second marriage) Nevin L. Harner, Philip B. Harner (stepsons). *Education:* Franklin and Marshall College, A.B., 1916; Theological Seminary of the Reformed Church in the United States, B.D., 1922; University of Edinburgh, Ph.D., 1928. *Home:* 509 North President Ave., Lancaster, Pa. 17603.

CAREER: Ordained minister of United Church of Christ,

1922; pastor of United Church of Christ in Ephrata, Pa., 1922-26; Franklin and Marshall College, Lancaster, Pa., 1928-63, began as faculty member, became professor of religion, 1931-45, professor of philosophy, 1945-63, head of department of philosophy, 1945-63; writer, 1963—. Lecturer at Union Theological Seminary (New York, N.Y.), 1952-65; adjunct professor at Lancaster Theological Seminary, 1958—, Garvin Lecturer, 1977; visiting lecturer at University of California, Santa Barbara, 1963-64. *Member:* American Philosophical Association, Phi Beta Kappa, Torch Club. *Awards, honors:* D.D. from Franklin and Marshall College, 1964.

WRITINGS: Man's Religions, Macmillan, 1949, 5th edition, 1974; *Living Religions,* United Church Press, 1962, revised edition, 1967. Contributor to *Encyclopaedia Britannica* and *Funk and Wagnalls Encyclopedic Dictionary.* Editor of "Research Abstracts in History of Religions," published by *Journal of the Bible and Religion,* 1955-63.

WORK IN PROGRESS: Man's Religions, 6th edition, for Macmillan.

* * *

NOSSACK, Hans Erich 1901-1978

OBITUARY NOTICE: Born January 30, 1901, in Hamburg, Germany; died in 1978 in Hamburg. Author. Nossack's books are often concerned with existential themes. His style is a blend of realism and mythical elements. Included among his writings are *The Impossible Proof* and *To the Unknown Hero.* Nossack also wrote short stories and plays. Obituaries and other sources: *Encyclopedia of World Literature in the Twentieth Century,* updated edition, Ungar, 1967; *The Penguin Companion to European Literature,* McGraw, 1969; *Cassell's Encyclopaedia of World Literature,* revised edition, Morrow, 1973; *World Authors, 1950-1970,* Wilson, 1975; *The Oxford Companion to German Literature,* Clarendon Press, 1976; *World Literature Today,* spring, 1979.

* * *

NOVACK, Evelyn Reed 1906(?)-1979

OBITUARY NOTICE: Born c. 1906; died of cancer, March 22, 1979, in New York, N.Y. Marxist anthropologist and feminist best known for her involvement in the Socialist Workers Party. Novack wrote *Problems of Women's Liberation* and *Women's Evolution: From Matriarchal Clan to Patriarchal Family.* Obituaries and other sources: *Publishers Weekly,* April 16, 1979.

* * *

NOVAK, Stephen R(obert) 1922-

PERSONAL: Born June 30, 1922, in Passaic, N.J.; son of Stephen (a salesman) and Elizabeth (Etl) Novak; married Mary June Pellitere, April 3, 1948 (died October 8, 1973). *Education:* Attended Pace University, 1939-43; Lehigh University, B.S., 1948. *Politics:* Democrat. *Religion:* Roman Catholic. *Home:* 329 Parish Dr., Wayne, N.J. 07470.

CAREER: Manager of family tire business, Hackensack, N.J., 1948-64; co-owner of a retail tire and phonograph record business, Middletown, N.Y., 1966-69; managing field auditor in Paterson, N.J., 1969-74; free-lance writer, 1974—. Part-time employee at American Institute of Certified Public Accountants, New York City. *Military service:* U.S. Army, Field Artillery and Infantry, 1943-46; became sergeant major. Received Bronze Star. *Member:* American Institute of Certified Public Accountants, Mystery Writers of America,

New Jersey Society of Certified Public Accountants, New York Poetry Society.

WRITINGS: Accounting Desk Book, fifth edition, Institute for Business Planning, 1977; *Field Auditors Manual and Guide,* Institute for Business Planning, 1979; "Less Than Angels" (one-act play), first produced in New York, N.Y., March, 1976. Short story represented in anthology, *Tricks and Treats,* Doubleday, 1976.

WORK IN PROGRESS: A political mystery novel; a three-act play; various short stories, business articles and poems, "completed and making the mail-rounds."

SIDELIGHTS: Novak remarks: "My interest in writing was sparked in the Thirties when I was in grammar school —when I read Thomas Wolfe and realized that a huge man could use such a little thing as a pen to produce wondrous words. My idols now are Norman Mailer (for his use of the language) and Ernest Hemingway (for his editorial brevity). My interests (and skills, I think) are quite broad (mystery, business, drama, etc.); and I hope my writing reflects some kind of combination between my Catholicism and the Democratic, constitutional concepts of the rights of man. The pursuit of happiness, business ethics, too much governmental control, high-pressure living, transportation mania, high taxes, lack of leadership and trust in government; and one man's nobility—all motivate me."

* * *

NOXON, James Herbert 1924-

PERSONAL: Born January 13, 1924, in Oshawa, Ontario, Canada; son of Gerald Jones and Lela (Fox) Noxon; married Irena Danuta, May, 1956 (divorced, May, 1972); children: Barbara Jolante, Christopher James, Andrew Gerald. *Education:* Queen's University, Kingston, Ontario, B.A., 1952, M.A., 1954; University of Edinburgh, Ph.D., 1958. *Religion:* None. *Home:* 466 Dundurn St. S., Hamilton, Ontario, Canada 8LP 4L9. *Office:* Department of Philosophy, McMaster University, Hamilton, Ontario, Canada.

CAREER: McMaster University, Hamilton, Ontario, lecturer, 1956-59, assistant professor, 1960-64, associate professor, 1964-70, professor of philosophy, 1970—, head of department, 1963-66, 1978—. *Military service:* Royal Canadian Air Force, 1942-46. *Member:* Amnesty International, Canadian Philosophical Association.

WRITINGS: Hume's Philosophical Development, Oxford University Press, 1973. Contributor to philosophy and literature journals. Member of editorial board of *Hume Studies.*

WORK IN PROGRESS: Philosophical Aspects of Biography.

* * *

NOYLE, Ken(neth Alfred Edward) 1922-

PERSONAL: Born June 16, 1922, in London, England; came to the United States; son of Ernest (an entertainer) Noyle; married Yoko Shimoyana, July, 1963 (divorced); children: Ric, Cherry. *Education:* Attended elementary school. *Politics:* None. *Religion:* "All." *Home:* 7962 K Mission Center Ct., San Diego, Calif. 92108. *Agent:* Peri Winkler, 535 Evelyn Pl., Beverly Hills, Calif. 90210.

CAREER: Entertainer, 1928—. Performed on Springbok Radio (South Africa), Australian Broadcasting Corp., and British Broadcasting Corp., as well as radio stations in India and Luxembourg; hosted "The Ken Noyle Show" in Australia; producer, narrator, and director for Twentieth

Century-Fox television productions. *Military service:* Served in Royal Air Force.

WRITINGS: *Here Today: Zen Inspired Poetry,* Tuttle, 1960; *Gone Tomorrow: Zen Inspired Poetry,* Tuttle, 1966; *The Geisha Diary* (novel), Putnam, 1976. Also author of "Sights-and-Sounds of the World" series, children's books, film scripts, and television and radio scripts. Composer of more than a hundred songs (both music and lyrics). Contributor to magazines, including *Saturday Evening Post.*

WORK IN PROGRESS: "Children Are Tomorrow," a series; *The Avatar,* a novel set in India; *The Slum Flower,* a novel set in Puerto Rico; *The Race,* a novel set in Africa; *The Second Coming Bit,* a novel set in Hollywood; *The Sound of Samisens,* a novel set in Japan; *Make Money in Your Sleep,* nonfiction; *Sex; It's All in Your Mind,* nonfiction; *What to Do If Your Mind Is Pregnant,* nonfiction; *Cook Book for Lovers;* "Yen for Murder," a screenplay set in Japan; "Sounds of Israel"; "Sounds of Rome"; "Sounds of the Holy Land."

SIDELIGHTS: Noyle made his debut as an entertainer at the age of six, as a magician, and two years later was a featured performer on the radio series "The Ovaltines." Since then, he has circled the globe sixty-four times, visiting 127 countries, and has appeared in nearly every area of the performing arts.

As a professional magician, using sleight of hand, comedy magic, illusions, extra-sensory perception, and hypnotism, Noyle has appeared with circuses, ice and aqua shows, in vaudeville, music halls, and repertory. He has entertained military personnel during the Battle of Britain, the siege of Malta, and operations in the North African desert, Burma, Korea, and Vietnam.

Noyle has worked as a stand-up comic, sometimes performing in Japanese, Chinese, Swahili, and Afrikaans. Television and radio performances as actor, guest, interviewer, magician, fashion commentator, and comic include appearances in France, Germany, Hong Kong, Thailand, the Soviet Union, and the United States. His film work has involved writing, producing, directing, and narrating documentaries, and he has made hundreds of commercial short films. He is also a prolific photographer.

The Geisha Diary was written after Noyle lived with one of Japan's most famous geishas. But this is only one facet of his repertoire for talk show appearances. He considers himself a leading psychometrist, and this subject is a popular one with his audiences. He is an artist whose paintings have been published on covers of Japanese national magazines, an inventor, and designer.

Noyle writes: "I have no political leanings but might run for King in 1984. Religion, if any: Zen, I shave my head. I am intrigued with animals and their relationship with man. I adore women and children. My pet hates: bigots and people who use religion as a cover-up. I am totally intolerant of intolerance."

AVOCATIONAL INTERESTS: "Playing golf badly," gourmet cooking, karate-ka (brown belt), comparative religions, psychic experiences.

* * *

NUSSBAUM, Al(bert F.) 1934-
(Lee Frederick, Doris Hiller, Albert Martin, A. F. Oreshnik)

PERSONAL: Born April 9, 1934, in Buffalo, N.Y.; son of Albert F. (a restaurateur) and Margaret (Martin) Nussbaum; married Alicia Majchrowicz, June 21, 1960 (divorced, 1964); children: Alison. *Education:* Highland Community Junior College (Kansas), A.A., 1970. *Agent:* Knox Burger, 39½ Washington Sq. S., New York, N.Y. 10012; and H. N. Swanson, Inc., 8523 Sunset Blvd., Los Angeles, Calif. 90069. *Office address:* P.O. Box 2590, Hollywood, Calif. 90028.

CAREER: Writer. Worked as draftsman and aircraft mechanic. *Military service:* U.S. Army, 1955-57. *Member:* Mystery Writers of America, Writers Guild of America, West.

WRITINGS—All published by Fearon-Pitman, excepted as noted: *Gypsy,* 1977; (under pseudonym A. F. Oreshnik) *The Demeter Star,* 1977; (under pseudonym Doris Hiller) *Black Beach,* 1977; (under pseudonym Lee Frederick; with D. Bromley) *Crash Dive,* 1977; (under pseudonym Albert Martin) *The Secret Spy,* 1978; (under Oreshnik pseudonym) *The Bad Joke,* 1978; (contributor) Brian Garfield, editor, *I, Witness,* Times Books, 1978; *Little Big Top,* 1979. Scriptwriter for television series "Switch," 1977. Hollywood correspondent for "Take One." Contributor to periodicals, including *The Writer, Alfred Hitchcock's Mystery Magazine,* and *American Scholar.*

WORK IN PROGRESS: *Coup d'etat; The Fox,* "black humor"; *Escape to Tomorrow,* a "prison fantasy."

SIDELIGHTS: Nussbaum told *CA:* "I began writing while serving a 40-year sentence for multiple bank robberies."

BIOGRAPHICAL/CRITICAL SOURCES: *Writer's Digest,* February, 1978; Brian Garfield, editor, *I, Witness,* Times Books, 1978.

* * *

NUTTER, G(ilbert) Warren 1923-1979

OBITUARY NOTICE—See index for *CA* sketch: Born March 10, 1923, in Topeka, Kan.; died of cancer, January 15, 1979, in Charlottesville, Va. Educator, government official, and author. In addition to his university teaching posts, Nutter held several governmental positions during his career. As assistant secretary of defense under President Richard M. Nixon, he was a staunch supporter of U.S. involvement in Vietnam. He criticized Henry Kissinger's detente policy with the Soviet Union, which he attacked in his 1975 book, *Kissinger's Grand Design.* A specialist on the Soviet Union and in the economics of defense, Nutter wrote several other books, including *The Strange World of Ivan Ivanov, The Extent of Enterprise Monopoly in the United States,* and *Growth of Government in the West.* Obituaries and other sources: *Who's Who in America,* 40th edition, Marquis, 1978; *New York Times,* January 16, 1979; *Washington Post,* January 17, 1969.

* * *

NYE, Miriam (Maurine Hawthorn) Baker 1918-
(Miriam Hawthorn Baker)

PERSONAL: Born June 14, 1918, in Castana, Iowa; daughter of Horace Boies (a professor) and Hazel Dean (a teacher; maiden name, Waples) Hawthorn; married Carl Edmund Baker, June 21, 1941 (died May 12, 1970); married John Arthur Nye (a clergyman and church historian), December 25, 1973; children: (first marriage) Kent Alfred, Dale Hawthorn; (second marriage) Mary Nye Morris, Ella Nye Lass, Hazel Nye Beckerbauer (stepdaughters). *Education:* Morningside College, B.A., 1939, graduate study, 1957-58; also attended University of Arizona, New College, Edinburgh, and University of South Dakota. *Religion:* United Methodist. *Home and office address:* Route 2, Box 193, Moville, Iowa 51039.

CAREER: Language teacher at public school in Rock Falls, Ill., 1939-41; junior high school teacher of social studies in Moville, Iowa, 1957-62, and Climbing Hill, Iowa, 1962-64; Hillside Turkey Farm, Moville, owner and manager, 1970—. Area counselor for Iowa State University, 1973—. Member of Siouxland Health Planning Council, 1971-73, and Woodbury Extension Council, 1972-75. *Member:* American Association of University Women, American Farm Bureau, Common Cause, Iowa Federation of Women's Clubs (creative writing chairman of 8th district, 1978—), Alpha Kappa Delta, Sigma Tau Delta, Moville Woman's Club (president, 1948-49). *Awards, honors:* Poetry awards, including first prize from Iowa Federation of Women's Clubs, 1943, for "The Advent."

WRITINGS: Recipes and Ideas From the Kitchen Window, General Publishing, 1973; *But I Never Thought He'd Die: Practical Help for Widows,* Westminster, 1978. Author of "From the Kitchen Window," a column in *Sioux City Journal,* 1953—. Contributor of poems and articles, usually under name Miriam Hawthorn Baker, to magazines and newspapers.

WORK IN PROGRESS: Scarlet Point, a juvenile historical novel; *Marrying After Fifty.*

SIDELIGHTS: Miriam Nye writes: "Writing has been my favorite activity since childhood. Earliest verse was dictated to my mother before I could push the pencil effectively. Throughout school days and college days writing and editing were important to me. A book might have been attempted sooner, but there were always projects, such as a church Christmas pageant, a community history, a poem for a special occasion, or a magazine article, to drain off my time and energy for written expression.

"For more than twenty-five years I have written a weekly column for homemakers, with considerable freedom to express my thought on a wide range of subjects. Along the way I have researched and written several magazine articles on western Iowa history. Now and then I have written news features, won poetry prizes, and sold pageants for publication.

"In 1973 I was urged to compile a book of the recipes which had appeared in my column, and some excerpts from pieces written on such subjects as use of marginal moments, the art of forgetting, disliking a person, safety belts, shortening the business meeting, building world peace through international friendship. The enthusiastic acceptance of my little book was a happy surprise.

"The book of practical help for widows grew out of my own realization of the need for such help in 1970. Had it been written in 1972 and 1973, it would have been strictly a 'personal experience of widowhood,' not so different from a good many others which have appeared. Research during independent graduate study, and several years' gathering of ideas from other widows, broadened the scope of the book.

"Now, at age sixty, I look forward to doing further writing. Even some fiction may be attempted."

AVOCATIONAL INTERESTS: Travel (including Europe).

BIOGRAPHICAL/CRITICAL SOURCES: Sioux City Journal, August 19, 1973, October 27, 1978.

O

OATES, Wayne Edward 1917-

PERSONAL: Born June 24, 1917, in Greenville, S.C.; son of Joseph A. (a textile worker) and Lula (a textile worker; maiden name, Cappell) Oates; married Pauline Rhodes, May 31, 1942; children: William Wayne, Charles Edwin. *Education:* Attended Mars Hill Junior College, 1938; Wake Forest College (now University), B.A., 1940; graduate study at Duke University; Southern Baptist Theological Seminary, B.D., 1945, Th.D., 1947; postdoctoral study at Union Theological Seminary, New York, N.Y., and University of Louisville. *Politics:* Democrat. *Home:* 3500 Winchester Rd., Louisville, Ky. 40207. *Office:* School of Medicine, University of Louisville, Box 1055, Louisville, Ky. 40201.

CAREER: Ordained Baptist minister, 1940; pastor of Baptist churches in Nash County, N.C., 1940-43, Union City, Ky., 1943-45, and Louisville, Ky., 1945-48; Southern Baptist Theological Seminary, Louisville, assistant professor, 1948-51, associate professor, 1951-55, professor of psychology of religion, 1955-74; University of Louisville, Louisville, professor of psychiatry and behavioral sciences, 1974—, associate of department of pediatrics. Visiting professor at Union Theological Seminary, New York, N.Y., 1952, 1961, and Princeton Theological Seminary, 1961. Chaplain at Kentucky State Hospital and Kentucky Baptist Hospital. Member of board of advisers of Earlham School of Religion. Diplomate of American Association of Pastoral Counselors.

MEMBER: Association of Clinical Pastoral Education (supervisor), American Association of Marriage and Family Therapy (supervisor). *Awards, honors:* Litt.D. from Wake Forest University, 1962; distinguished service award from American Association of Pastoral Counselors, 1969; distinguished service award from College of Chaplains, American Protestant Hospital Association, 1974.

WRITINGS: Introduction to Pastoral Counseling, Broadman, 1954; *What Psychology Says About Religion,* Association Press, 1955; *Religious Factors in Mental Illness,* Association Press, 1955; *Religious Dimensions of Personality,* Association Press, 1958; *The Revelation of God in Human Suffering,* Westminster, 1958; *Christ and Selfhood,* Association Press, 1961; *Protestant Pastoral Counseling,* Westminster, 1962; *The Christian Pastor,* Westminster, 1964; *Alcohol: In and Out of the Church,* Broadman, 1965; *On Becoming the Children of God,* Westminster, 1969; *Pastoral Care in Crucial Human Situations,* Judson Press, 1969; *New Dimensions in Pastoral Care,* Fortress, 1969; *On Becoming the Children of God,* Westminster, 1969.

When Religion Gets Sick, Westminster, 1970; *Where to Go for Help,* Westminster, 1971; *Anxiety in Christian Experience,* Word Books, 1972; *The Bible in Pastoral Care,* Baker Book, 1972; *The Holy Spirit and Contemporary Man,* Baker Book, 1972; *Pastoral Counseling and Social Problems,* Baker Book, 1972; *Confessions of a Workaholic,* Abingdon, 1972; *The Psychology of Religion,* Word Books, 1973; *Life's Detours,* Upper Room, 1974; *Pastoral Counseling,* Westminster, 1974; (with Wade Rowatt) *Before You Marry Them,* Broadman, 1975; *Pastoral Care in Grief and Separation,* Westminster, 1976; *Workaholics: Make Laziness Work for You,* Doubleday, 1978; *The Religious Care of Psychiatric Patients,* Westminster, 1978; *Nurturing Silence in a Noisy Heart,* Doubleday, 1979.

Also author of *Premarital Pastoral Counseling,* Broadman. Member of board of advisers of *Pastoral Psychology Journal, Catalyst,* and Religious Book Club.

*   *   *

O'BRIEN, Tim 1946-

PERSONAL: Born October 1, 1946, in Austin, Minn.; *Education:* Macalester College, B.A. (summa cum laude); graduate study at Harvard University. *Home:* 49 Irving St., Apt. 3, Cambridge, Mass. 02138. *Agent:* Lynn Nesbit, International Creative Management, 40 West 57th St., New York, N.Y. 10019.

CAREER: Writer. National affairs reporter for *Washington Post,* Washington, D.C. *Military service:* U.S. Army, served in Vietnam; became sergeant. *Member:* Phi Beta Kappa. *Awards, honors:* National Book Award, 1978, for *Going After Cacciato.*

WRITINGS: If I Die in a Combat Zone, Box Me Up and Ship Me Home (anecdotes), Delacorte, 1973; *Northern Lights* (novel), Delacorte, 1974; *Going After Cacciato* (novel), Delacorte, 1978. Contributor to magazines, including *Playboy, Esquire,* and *Redbook.*

SIDELIGHTS: The Vietnam war is the informing principle of all three of Tim O'Brien's books, though only two are directly about the war itself. *If I Die in A Combat Zone, Box Me Up and Ship Me Home* is a personal narrative, a collection of anecdotes about the author's tour of duty in Vietnam.

The other two volumes are novels; *Going After Cacciato* is also about American soldiers in Vietnam while the earlier novel, *Northern Lights*, concerns a returned Vietnam veteran and his relationship with his brother.

The sketches in *If I Die in a Combat Zone* were originally published in *Playboy* and two midwestern newspapers. Critics speculate that the book must convey the feelings of many Vietnam veterans, particularly those "who did their traditional duty in a war which they privately despised." To Annie Gottlieb, it "brilliantly and quietly evokes the footsoldier's daily life in the paddies and foxholes, evokes a blind, blundering war": the numbers of U.S. casualties, the attitude of rebellion among the troops, the agony of human atrocities, and the pathos of human contact.

Perhaps inevitably, any writer so steeped in the war experience will be compared to two other American "war novelists," Ernest Hemingway and Joseph Heller, both of whose works strongly influenced O'Brien. Roger Sale pointed out some parallels between *Northern Lights* and Hemingway's *The Sun Also Rises:* the similarities between Addie and Lady Brett Ashley, between Grace and Hadley Hemingway, and between the ski races at Grand Marais and the bull fights in Pamplona. Richard Freedman, praising O'Brien's "crisp, authentic and grimly ironic" writing in *Going After Cacciato,* noted that "as the characters are making their separate peace, their farewell to arms, Hemingway rhythms emerge." The terms in which other critics describe O'-Brien's work similarly suggest Hemingway. B. M. Firestone appreciated his "precise and highly evocative writing style." Gottlieb observed that he "writes—without either pomposity or embarrassment—with the care and eloquence of someone for whom communication is still a vital and serious possibility."

Several aspects of *Going After Cacciato* recall Heller's *Catch-22.* O'Brien's book centers around a dream-vision in which a soldier decides to walk away from Vietnam and make it on foot to Paris, pursued by a squad of other soldiers sent to bring him back. This prompted Christopher Lehmann-Haupt to explain that "the whole of 'Going After Cacciato' is triggered by the incident that concludes 'Catch-22,' namely the decision of a soldier with an innocent face to leave the war by simply taking off." Beyond this, there are similarities of style and structure between the two novels, the careful intertwining of fantasy and reality to communicate the madness and horror of war. Likening O'Brien's work to the "magical realism" of contemporary South American novelists, Freedman lauded O'Brien's ability to counterpoint "the gritty realism of combat against a dream-like state." He concluded: "To combine the two and make the result esthetically convincing is a major achievement and possibly the only way to deal with the truths of Vietnam."

BIOGRAPHICAL/CRITICAL SOURCES: Atlantic, May, 1973; *New Republic,* May 12, 1973, February 7, 1976; *Washington Post Book World,* May 27, 1973, June 3, 1973, June 30, 1974, February 19, 1978; *New York Times Book Review,* July 1, 1973, December 2, 1973, October 12, 1975, February 12, 1978; *New Yorker,* July 16, 1973, March 27, 1978; *America,* September 1, 1973, November 17, 1973; *Times Literary Supplement,* October 19, 1973, April 23, 1976; *Guardian Weekly,* October 20, 1973; *Books and Bookmen,* December, 1973; *New Statesman,* January 4, 1974; *New York Review of Books,* November 13, 1975; *Commonweal,* December 5, 1975; *Listener,* April 1, 1976; *Spectator,* April 3, 1976; *Nation,* January 29, 1977, March 25, 1978; *Library Journal,* December 18, 1977; *Contemporary Literary Criticism,* Volume 7, Gale, 1977; *New York Times,* February 12, 1978,

March 19, 1979, April 24, 1979; *Saturday Review,* February 18, 1978, May 13, 1978; *Newsweek,* February 20, 1978; *Christian Science Monitor,* March 9, 1978; *Harper's,* March, 1978; *Antioch Review,* spring, 1978; *Virginia Quarterly Review,* summer, 1978; *Los Angeles Times,* March 22, 1979.*

*   *   *

OCAMPO, Victoria 1891-1979

OBITUARY NOTICE: Born c. 1891; died January 27, 1979, in San Isidro, Argentina. Argentine writer of avant-garde works and publisher of *Sur,* an international literary periodical. A collection of her work entitled *Testimonios* contains essays, memoirs, and criticism. Obituaries and other sources: *Who's Who in the World,* 2nd edition, Marquis, 1973; *International Who's Who,* Europa, 1974; *Ms.,* January, 1975; *A Dictionary of Contemporary Latin American Authors,* Center for Latin American Studies, Arizona State University, 1975; *Americas,* May, 1976; *Publishers Weekly,* February 26, 1979.

*   *   *

O'COLLINS, Gerald Glynn 1931-

PERSONAL: Born June 2, 1931, in Melbourne, Australia; son of P. Francis (a lawyer) and Joan (Glynn) O'Collins. *Education:* University of Melbourne, B.A., 1957, M.A., 1958; Heythrop College, London, S.T.L., 1967; Cambridge University, Ph.D., 1968. *Home and office:* Universita Gregoriana, Piazza della Pilotta 4, 00187 Rome, Italy.

CAREER: Entered Society of Jesus (Jesuits), 1950, ordained Roman Catholic priest, 1963; external lecturer at Heythrop College, 1966-67, and University of Leicester, 1967; Cambridge University, Pembroke College, Cambridge, England, research fellow, 1967-69; Jesuit Theological College, Melbourne, Australia, lecturer in theology, 1969-73; Gregorian University, Rome, Italy, professor of theology, 1974—. *Member:* Studiorum Novi Testamenti Societas. *Awards, honors:* Traveling fellowship from University of Melbourne, 1965-67.

WRITINGS: Patrick McMahon Glynn (biography), Melbourne University Press, 1965; *Theology and Revelation,* Mercier Press, 1968; *Man and His New Hopes,* Herder & Herder, 1969; *The Resurrection of Jesus Christ,* Judson, 1973, published in England as *The Easter Jesus,* Darton, Longman & Todd, 1973; *Theology of Secularity,* Mercier Press, 1974; *Patrick McMahon Glynn: Letters to His Family,* Polding Press, 1974; *Faith Under Fire,* Polding Press, 1974; *The Case Against Dogma,* Paulist Press, 1975, published in England as *Has Dogma a Future?,* Darton, Longman & Todd, 1975; *The Calvary Christ,* Westminster, 1977; *What Are They Saying About Jesus?,* Paulist Press, 1977; *What Are They Saying About the Resurrection?,* Paulist Press, 1978; *The Second Journey,* Paulist Press, 1978, enlarged edition, Villa Books (Dublin), 1979; *A Month With Jesus,* Dimension Books, 1978; (editor and contributor) *The Cross Today,* Paulist Press, 1978; *Problems and Perspectives in Fundamental Theology,* Queriniana, in press. Contributor to theology journals.

SIDELIGHTS: O'Collins writes: "I am another expatriate Australian professor and writer—this time in theology, and the first Australian to hold a position at Gregorian University, the premiere theological center in the Roman Catholic Church. Teaching and writing theology here, as well as simply living in Rome, have become an even more exciting and worthwhile project after one election of a vigorous, Polish Pope."

ODETS, Clifford   1906-1963

PERSONAL: Born July 18, 1906, in Philadelphia, Pa.; died August 14, 1963, in Los Angeles, Calif.; son of Louis J. (a printer and company vice-president) and Pearl (Geisinger) Odets; married Luise Rainer (an actress), January 8, 1937 (divorced May, 1940); married Bette Grayson (an actress), May 14, 1943 (died, 1954); children: (second marriage) Nora, Walt. *Education:* Attended secondary school in New York, N.Y. *Religion:* Jewish.

CAREER: Playwright. Left school at age fourteen; worked as actor in local New York City theatre groups, vaudeville performer, radio play and gag writer, and as radio broadcaster; acted character parts in traveling stock theatre productions and small parts in Broadway plays, 1923-28; played juvenile roles in New York Theatre Guild productions, 1928-30; founding member and actor with Group Theatre, New York City, 1930-35; screenwriter in Hollywood, Calif., 1935-37; returned to New York and remained associated with Group Theatre, 1937-41; screenwriter and producer in Hollywood, 1941-61; worked in television, beginning 1961. Theatre director. *Member:* League of American Writers, Actors' Equity Association, Dramatists Guild, Screen Writers Guild. *Awards, honors:* New Theatre League award and Yale Drama Prize, both 1935, both for "Waiting for Lefty"; Award of Merit Medal from American Academy of Arts and Letters, 1961.

WRITINGS—Plays: *Awake and Sing* (three-act; first produced on Broadway at Belasco Theatre, February 19, 1935; copyrighted in 1933 under title "I Got the Blues"), Covici-Friede, 1935 (also see below); *Waiting for Lefty [and] Till the Day I Die: Two Plays* (the former, one-act; the latter, seven scene; both first produced on Broadway at Longacre Theatre, March 26, 1935), Covici-Friede, 1935 (also see below); *Paradise Lost* (three-act; first produced on Broadway at Longacre Theatre, December 9, 1935), Random House, 1936 (also see below); *Golden Boy* (three-act; first produced on Broadway at Belasco Theatre, November 4, 1937), Random House, 1937 (also see below); *Rocket to the Moon* (three-act; first produced on Broadway at Belasco Theatre, November 24, 1938), Random House, 1939 (also see below).

Night Music: A Comedy in Twelve Scenes (three-act; first produced on Broadway at Broadhurst Theatre, February 24, 1940), Random House, 1940; *Clash by Night* (two-act; first produced on Broadway at Belasco Theatre, December 27, 1941), Random House, 1942; "The Russian People," (three-act; adapted from the play by Konstantin Simonov), first produced in New York, N.Y., at Guild Theatre, December 29, 1942; *The Big Knife* (three-act; first produced on Broadway at American National Theatre and Academy, February 24, 1949), Random House, 1949 (also see below); *The Country Girl* (three-act; first produced on Broadway at Lyceum Theatre, November 10, 1950), Viking, 1951, published as *Winter Journey*, Samuel French, 1955; "The Flowering Peach" (three-act), first produced on Broadway at Belasco Theatre, December 28, 1954. Also author of unproduced plays, "9-10 Eden Street," "The Silent Partner," "The Law of Flight," "By the Sea," "The Seasons," and "The Tides of Fundy."

Omnibus volumes: *Three Plays* (contains "Awake and Sing," Waiting for Lefty," and "Till the Day I Die"), Covici-Friede, 1935; *Six Plays of Clifford Odets* (contains "Awake and Sing," "Waiting for Lefty," "Till the Day I Die," "Paradise Lost," "Golden Boy," and "Rocket to the Moon"), Modern Library, 1939, reprinted, 1963; *Golden Boy, Awake and Sing, [and] The Big Knife*, Penguin, 1963.

Screenplays: "The General Died at Dawn" (adapted from the novel by Charles G. Booth), Paramount, 1936, (and director) "None but the Lonely Heart" (adapted from the novel by Richard Llewellyn), RKO, 1944; "Deadline at Dawn" (adapted from the novel by William Irish), RKO, 1946; (with Zachary Gold) "Humoresque" (adapted from the short story by Fannie Hurst), Warner Brothers, 1946; (with Ernest Lehman) "Sweet Smell of Success" (adapted from the novella, "Tell Me About It Tomorrow," by Lehman), United Artists, 1957; (and director) "The Story on Page One," Twentieth Century-Fox, 1960; "Wild in the Country" (adapted from the novel, *The Lost Country,* by J. R. Salamanca), Twentieth Century-Fox, 1961. Also author of unproduced screenplays, "Gettysburg" and "The River is Blue."

SIDELIGHTS: A writer of the depression, Clifford Odets became an idol of the proletariat in the mid-1930's. Yet his own roots in the working class he treated so sympathetically in his works were not very deep: "I was a worker's son until the age of twelve," Odets once recalled. His father originally worked as a printer, but eventually came to own his own printing plant. When he moved his family to Philadelphia, the senior Odets continued to prosper in business. In contrast, young Clifford remained intent on pursuing a less conventional life by writing, giving poetry recitals, and acting in various companies. His refusal to pursue the family business combined with his devotion to writing at times provoked conflict in his family. Once Odet's obviously irate father smashed Clifford's typewriter. (Later, he replaced it.)

By 1930, Odets lived alone in New York City. There he grew increasingly aware of the destructive impact of the Great Depression as he observed the city's suffering masses. R. Baird Shuman reported that "as the depression continued, Odets grew more and more concerned about the plight of the working and middle classes. He looked about him for ways of ameliorating the widespread suffering and privation of the masses." Drawing on this sympathy, a sympathy he claimed first developed after reading Hugo's *Les Miserables* in 1918, Odets wrote his first play, "9-10 Eden Street." Upon reading the play, Group Theatre associate Harold Clurman noticed most of the pain emitted from the work came from Odets himself. "Something in his past life had hurt him," Clurman speculated. "He was doubled up in pain, now, and in his pain he appeared to be shutting out the world." Whatever the source of his pain, Odets could not have been too encouraged about succeeding in acting or in writing—he "was not generally considered a gifted actor"; "9-10 Eden Street" was never produced.

Even Odets's association with the Group Theatre did not provide him enough influence to get his next play, "Awake and Sing," staged. Despite its interest in the work, the financially weak organization could not risk the chance of introducing an unproven playwright. Undaunted by this rejection, Odets wrote his next play, "Waiting for Lefty," for a New Theatre League play contest. It won, and was soon being played by the awarding organization on Sunday nights. This brief exposure precipitated a glorious introduction into the New York Theatre world: within a year the most talked about playwright since Eugene O'Neill has three plays running on Broadway.

"Waiting for Lefty" is "undoubtedly the most angry play which Clifford Odets had ever produced," claimed Shuman. Based on the incidents of the 1934 New York City cab strike, it is set on a practically bare stage, a meeting hall where the taxi drivers' union is gathered to take a strike vote. As the strike talks progress the union members, who have been seated among the audience, come forth to defend their position. In the process, flashback reveals the hardship in each of their financially desperate lives. With word that the absent Lefty, their militant representative, has been killed by an assailant, the workers fervently join together in chanting "Strike! Strike! Strike!" The plays's impact is made even more shattering by Odets's skillful manipulation of events as they lead to a climax. As Joseph Wood Krutch pointed out, "The pace is swift, the characterization is for the most part crisp, and the points are made, one after another, with bold simplicity."

In judging "Waiting for Lefty," Krutch felt "there is no denying its effectiveness in achieving all it sets out to achieve." He conceded, however, that the play's "simplicity must be paid for at a certain price. The villains are mere caricatures and even the very human heroes occasionally freeze into stained glass attitudes.... No one, however, expects subtleties from a soap-box, and the interesting fact is that Mr. Odets invented a form which turns out to be a very effective dramatic equivalent of soap-box oratory."

Encouraged by the success of "Waiting for Lefty," the Group Theatre finally decided to run "Awake and Sing." Their decision was hardly a mistake: many critics include it among Odets's finest plays. "Awake and Sing" presented, with an "extraordinary freshness," the story of Ralph Berger as he frees "himself from his obsession with a purely personal rebellion against poverty which separates him from his girl and determines to throw himself with enthusiasm into the class struggle." Odets's ability in bringing life into his play fascinated Alfred Kazin: "In Odets's play there was a lyric uplifting of blunt Jewish speech, boiling over and explosive, that did more to arouse the audience than the political catch words that brought the curtain down. Everybody on that stage was furious, kicking, alive—the words, always real but never flat, brilliantly authentic like no other theater speech on Broadway, aroused the audience to such delight that one could feel it bounding back and uniting itself with the mind of the writer."

The Broadway success of Odets's proletariat themes brought him sudden critical attention. One critic called him "one of the few American playwrights who is worth thinking about at all." Many did think about him, but not so receptively; "Waiting for Lefty" was banned in seven cities. His suspected affiliations with the Communist party only increased the controversy surrounding him. Although Odets had belonged to the party for an eight-month span in 1934, he later quit, claiming it interfered with his freedom to write. He also joined in a delegation traveling to Cuba in 1935 to investigate conditions there. The group was deported by the Cuban government after the first day. Such activities helped create a "Communist" stigma around Odets which continued for many years: in the 1950's he testified at the Senate McCarthy hearings.

The much anticipated fourth Odets's play, "Paradise Lost," marked an unexpected turning point in his career. It failed miserably, but not before the success of his earlier works had made him an attractive candidate for a Hollywood screenwriting job. The decision racked Odets: he saw the lure of Hollywood and its promise of financial success shadowed by his devotion to the Group Theatre and its atmosphere of artistic freedom. Moved by the reasoning that he could help finance the Theatre with his Hollywood earnings, Odets decided to leave. In doing so, he incurred the scorn of many who accused him of abandoning his proletarian ideals for Hollywood's big money. Response to his first screenplay, "The General Died at Dawn," was made in the light of

his plays. One disappointed critic asked, "Odets, where is thy sting?"

While the impact of the Hollywood move on Odets's career has been debated, at least one change is certain: his next plays gained a much broader audience. In "Golden Boy," Odets continued to probe the themes of his previous plays but kept his political and economic theories in the background. The story of a young Italian boy who abandons the fiddle for a fighting career, "Golden Boy" re-established Odets's reputation as a leading dramatist. Stark Young felt "his theatrical gift most appears . . . in the dialogue's avoidance of the explicit. The explicit, always to be found in poor writers trying for the serious, is the surest sign of a lack of talent.... Mr. Odets is the most promising writer our theatre can show." Viewing his career in retrospect, Walter Kerr affirmed that Hollywood had at least not stolen Odets's playwrighting sting: "Odets wrote *Golden Boy* at the height of his powers as an angry, moralizing neo-realist, and it remains his most successful play."

Drawing on his belief that "the more talented the Marxian dramatist the less sharply his plays are set from the best work of writers holding different political opinions," Krutch felt that in many respects Odets's next play, "Rocket to the Moon," was his finest. It was the last play to evoke major comparisons with his earlier Marxist works and their view of American life. Barry Hyams felt it similiar to "Waiting for Lefty" and "Golden Boy," for these plays "did not attempt to speak *for* America. They spoke of America, of its indestructible good nature.... The shipping clerk could feel like Paul Bunyan. His nature was wedded to Walt Whitman.... His testament was that the human being not be nullified."

Odets's later plays were marked by moments of genuine praise but failed to capture the critical acclaim of the earlier works. "Night Music" was a "lyric improvisation . . . on the basic homelessness of the little man in the big city," wrote Harold Clurman. "It is charmingly sentimental, comically poetic, airy and wholly unpretentious." But, Clurman continued, "in *Night Music* Odets is far more wistful than angry." In "The Big Knife," a portrait of life in Hollywood, John Gassner thought Odets proved he "had lost none of his theatrical vigor and that no one writing realistic drama . . . can surpass his power to write with an explosive force and with a wild and swirling poetry of torment and bedevilment.... If *The Big Knife* is not a successfully realized play, . . . it is because Odets, a product of the agitated left-wing theatre of the 1930's, is heir to its major faults—to the tendency to put too much of the blame on society and too little on the individual." Another play, "The Country Girl," enjoyed tremendous success on Broadway and had "a certain honesty and considerable power." But still, said Clive Barnes, it was "by no means, a great play."

"The Flowering Peach," Odets's last play, marked a significant conclusion to his playwriting career as it confronted the author's declining political commitment. Shuman found in the play, a retelling of the Noah's ark story, evidence that "Odets seemed to find again the proper vehicle for what he wanted to say: . . . beyond hope and despair lies the desperate idea of *hope*." Gassner, on the other hand, expressed disappointment in these "doubts and vacillations.... It seemed as if Odets, with the example of generations of men before him, had given up hopes for a better world and is ready to accept humanity on its own second-best terms." Gerald Rabkin demonstrated, however, that the tone of acceptance inherent in "The Flowering Peach" can be interpreted differently. He believed "the significance of the play lies in the fact that Odets finally attempted to come to terms with the esthetic consequences of the loss of his political commitment.... The essence of *The Flowering Peach* is the acceptance of the loss of political faith.... Odets is basically concerned with man's reaction to cosmic injustice, his attempt to construct a means whereby he can *accept* this injustice. It is this concept of acceptance which dominates *The Flowering Peach*."

In general, whatever faults there have been in Odets's plays have been transcended by his writing skill, especially in character presentation and language. "What has been impressive in Mr. Odets's plays," declared *Commonweal* reviewer Grenville Vernon, has not been their ideas, which are pretty confused, or their structure, which has been pretty melodramatic, but the fact that the characterizations and the dialogue have a bite and an originality of turn which set them apart from the somewhat pallid characters and dialogues of most modern plays." Edith Isaacs, too, noticed "each of Odets's faults has almost its counterpart in creative quality. Against his extreme subjectiveness can be placed his wise desire to express the nature and the problems of the people that he knows.... Against the fact that he himself does most of the talking in his plays, there is the fact that the talk is exceptionally alive and theatrical, speech for an actor's tongue. Against the fact that the majority of his characters are cliches, the recognition that in almost every play there is at least one that is a real creation ... one that has three dimensions and a soul."

While most critics at least respect Odets's contribution to the American theatre, there are some who feel he barely deserves that. John Simon called Odets "a well-meaning, mildly skillful hack, like the rest of our thirties dramatists. A hack who had lost his nerve." In a similar opinion, Brendan Gill declared: "The fact is that Odets has always been an absurdly overpraised playwright, and it is odd, looking back over his career, to recall the wringing of hands that took place when he seemed to abandon a lofty purpose on Broadway for the fleshpots of Hollywood; the dream factory was his proper milieu, and if he did not prosper there as an artist it is because there was little of the artist in him capable of prospering anywhere."

Undoubtedly, the events of the 1930's spurred Odets to write his plays of social impact. In a time when America thirsted for some sort of hope, his romanticism in plays offering hope for the individual mattered more than the inconsistencies inherent in them. As Allan Lewis noted, "These final exhilarating but inconsistent affirmations were requirements of the play of the depression, for actuality was full of heartbreak and terror." Inevitably, then, as the despair of the depressed thirties faded, a force that had provided the impact for Odets's plays was lost. "It is true that Odets took up other issues in certain works," admitted Malcom Goldstein, "particularly in his late plays; but whether subsidary or paramount, class-consciousness is never absent, regardless of the year and the remoteness of his characters' concerns from money worries. Having taken a stand with the destitute proletariat, he could not recognize the fact of a rising employment index. After the first six plays ... Odets's work dwindled in relevance to the age, until finally, after 1954, he could give the stage nothing at all."

BIOGRAPHICAL/CRITICAL SOURCES: Nation, March 13, 1935, April 3, 1972; *New Republic,* November 17, 1937, September 27, 1939, April 30, 1951; *New Yorker,* January 22, 1938, March 25, 1972; *Commonweal,* December 16, 1938, March 28, 1952, December 3, 1971; *Theatre Arts,* April, 1939, October, 1954, September, 1955; Harold Clurman, *The Fervent Years,* Knopf, 1945, Harcourt, 1975; *Commentary,* May, 1946; *Forum,* May, 1949; *Saturday Review of Literature,* December 9, 1950; Joseph Wood Krutch, *The American Drama Since 1918: An Informal History,* Braziller, 1957.

John Gassner, *Theatre at the Crossroads,* Holt, 1960; Winifred Loesch Dusenbury, *The Theme of Loneliness in American Drama,* University of Florida Press, 1960; R. Baird Shuman, *Clifford Odets,* Twayne, 1962; *American Quarterly,* winter, 1963; *Drama Survey,* fall, 1963; Gerald Rabkin, *Drama and Commitment,* Indiana University Press, 1964; Alan S. Downer, editor, *American Drama and Its Critics,* Chicago University Press, 1965; Allan Lewis, *American Plays and Playwrights of the Contemporary Theatre,* Crown, 1965; Alfred Kazin, *Starting Out in the Thirties,* Little, Brown, 1965; Jean Gould, *Modern American Playwrights,* Dodd, 1966; *Time,* June 8, 1970; *South Atlantic Quarterly,* winter, 1970, spring, 1972; *New York Times,* December 24, 1971; March 16, 1972; *Contemporary Literary Criticism,* Volume 2, Gale, 1974; John Simon, *Singularities: Essays on the Theatre, 1964-73,* Random House, 1975.*

*   *   *

O'GARA, James Vincent, Jr.   1918-1979

OBITUARY NOTICE—See index for *CA* sketch: Born March 26, 1918, in Brooklyn, N.Y.; died of cancer, January 10, 1979, in Hempstead, N.Y. Editor and columnist. O'Gara served as news editor at the Religious News Service for four years before joining *Advertising Age* in 1950 as a writer. Beginning in 1958, he held a series of editing positions there and helped make *Advertising Age* one of the most respected trade publications in its field. O'Gara also taught communication arts at Fordham University. Obituaries and other sources: *Who's Who in Advertising,* 2nd edition, Redfield, 1972; *Who's Who in America,* 40th edition, Marquis, 1978; *New York Times,* January 11, 1979.

*   *   *

OHKAWA, Kazushi   1908-

PERSONAL: Born November 16, 1908, in Numazu City, Japan; son of Kyusaku and Yoshiko (Uda) Ohkawa; married Sachiko Tokime, December 29, 1936; children: Hisashi, Eiko Ohkawa Nozawa, Hiroshi. *Education:* Imperial University of Tokyo, B.S., 1933; University of Tokyo, Ph.D.,1952. *Home:* 3903 Jindaiji, Mitaka-Shi, Tokyo 181, Japan.

CAREER: Utsunomiya Agricultural College, Utsunomiya, Japan, professor of agriculture, 1936-47; Economic Stabilization Board, Tokyo, Japan, chief of production cost section in Price Bureau, 1947-49; Hitotsubashi University, Tokyo, professor of agriculture, 1949-72, professor emeritus, 1972—. Visiting professor at Yale University, 1973. Director-general of Economic Planning Agency's Economic Research Institute, 1959-64, member of Economic Deliberation Council, 1964-69; training and research director at International Development Center of Japan, 1974—. Co-chairman of consultative committee of Asian Agricultural Survey, for Asian Development Bank; participant in international conferences.

WRITINGS: (With Miyohei Shinohara, Mataji Umemura, and others) *The Growth Rate of the Japanese Economy Since 1878,* Kinokuniya, 1957; (editor with Shinohara and Umemura) *Estimates of Long-Term Economic Statistics of Japan Since 1868,* Toyokezai-Shinposha, Volume I: *National Income,* 1974, Volume III: *Capital Stock,* 1966, Volume IV: *Capital Formation,* 1971, Volume VI: *Personal*

Consumption Expenditure, 1967, Volume VII: *Government Expenditure,* 1966, Volume VIII: *Prices,* 1967, Volume IX: *Agriculture and Forestry,* 1966, Volume X: *Mining and Manufacturing,* Volume XII: *Railroads and Electric Utilities,* 1965; (editor with Lawrence Klein) *Economic Growth: The Japanese Experience Since the Meiji Era,* Irwin, 1968; (editor with B. F. Johnston and Hiyomitsu Kanada) *Agriculture and Economic Growth: Japan's Experience,* Princeton University Press, 1970; *Differential Structure and Agriculture,* Kinokuniya, 1972; (with Henry Rosovsky) *Japanese Economic Growth: Trend Acceleration in the Twentieth Century,* Stanford University Press, 1973; (editor with Shinohara) *Patterns of Japanese Development: A Quantitative Appraisal,* Yale University Press, 1979. Contributor to economics journals.

* * *

OLESHA, Yuri (Karlovich)   1899-1960

PERSONAL: Born March 3, 1899, in Elisavetgrad (now Kirovograd), Ukraine, Russia (now U.S.S.R.); died May 10, 1960, of heart failure in Moscow, U.S.S.R.

CAREER: Novelist, playwright, journalist, poet, film scenarist, short story writer, adapter of novels for the stage, and author of plays for children's puppet theatres. Began career as journalist for railway newspaper, *Gudok. Military service:* Soviet Red Army, served in Russian Civil War.

WRITINGS—In English: *Zavist,* [Moscow], 1928, Pergamon Press, 1969, Ardis, 1977, translation by Anthony Wolfe published as *Envy,* L. & V. Woolf, 1936, translation by P. Ross contained in *Envy* [and] *The Unknown Artist* (the latter by V. Kaverin), Westhouse, 1947, translation contained in *The Embezzlers and Envy* (the former by Valentin Kataev), Ardis, 1975 (also see below); *Tri Tolstyaka,* [Moscow], 1928, reprinted, 1969, translation by Fainna Glagoleva published as *The Three Fat Men,* Foreign Languages Publishing House (Moscow), 1964 (also see below); *The Wayward Comrade and the Commissars* (includes "Envy," "Love," and "Lyompa"), translated by Andrew R. MacAndrew, New American Library, 1960; *Ni dnya bez strochki* (reminiscences and correspondences), [Moscow], 1965, translation published as *No Day Without a Line,* Ardis, 1978; *Envy and Other Works* (includes "Love," "Lyompa," "The Cherry Stone," and "A List of Assets"; also see below), translation and introduction by MacAndrew, Anchor Books, 1967; *Love and Other Stories* (includes "Envy," "Liompa," and "The Cherry Stone"; also see below), translation and introduction by Robert Payne, Washington Square Press, 1967; *The Complete Short Stories and The Three Fat Men,* Ardis, 1978. Work represented in anthologies, including *Avant Garde Drama: Major Plays and Documents,* edited by B. F. Dukore and D. C. Gerould, Bantam, 1970.

Other: *Lyubov* (short stories; title means, "Love"), [Moscow], 1928; *Vishnevaya kostochka* (short stories; title means "The Cherry Stone"), [Moscow], 1930; *Kine,* [U.S.S.R.], 1931; *Izbrannoe* (selected works), [Moscow], 1935, Russian Language Specialists, 1973; *Izbrannye sochineniya,* [Moscow], 1956; *Povesti i rasskazy* (novels and stories), [Moscow], 1965; *Pyesy,* [Moscow], 1968; *Rasskazy* (selected stories), Prideaux Press, 1971; *Legenda* (selected stories), introduction in English, Bradda Books, 1974.

Also author of plays "Spisok blagodeyany" (title means " A List of Assets"), 1931, "Strogy yunosha" (title means " A Strict Young Man"), 1934, "Walter," 1937, and "Zagovar chuvstu" (based on own novel, *Zavist;* title means "The Conspiracy of Feelings"). Film scenarios include "Cherny

chelovek" (title means "The Black Man"), 1932, and "Strogy yunosha" (based on own play), 1934.

SIDELIGHTS: For a writer whose career was to be aborted by Stalinist oppression, the success of Yuri Olesha's first novel, *Zavist* ("Envy"), is surprising: the government controlled Soviet press endorsed it as did a spectrum of Soviet literary journals. Apparently, though, this endorsement came from a misreading of the novel; soon this comic parody of Soviet officials was denounced for its anti-Soviet overtones. The reaction against the work precipitated a trend which saw Olesha mollified into a writer of little more daring than children's puppet plays. By 1934, essentially all of what he would be remembered for had been written.

Zavist viewed Soviet society in transition and gloomily presented a choice of two sterile worlds: "the old order, with its romantic escapism, and the new, with its cult of technology and contempt for human values." Writing at the time of Stalin's rise to power, Olesha envisioned a world void of human feelings. More specifically, he focused on "the plight of 'the superfluous man,' a figure of hesitation and sensitiveness destroyed by a rationalistic world," declared Irving Howe.

Olesha explored his theme by attempting "to disclose the moral and emotional shortcomings of the materialist plan of salvation," said a *Times Literary Supplement* reviewer. In doing so, he pitted a dreamer (Kavalerov) and an anarchist (Ivan Babichev) against the forces of mechanization and collectivization, represented by Ivan's sausage-maker brother and his adopted soccer player son. Kavalerov and Ivan join in a "conspiracy of feelings" against what Gleb Struve described as the "new mechanized, planned, totalitarian society which has discarded all ethical ballast and has proclaimed that the end justifies the means." The irony of their scheme is that, in fighting mechanization, these romantics rely on a machine ("Ophelia") designed to destroy machines. "Needless to say," wrote Maurice Friedburg, "Ophelia proves no match for the opposition's weapons: indices of labor productivity (in this case, the manufacture of sausages) and goal scores."

Olesha's bleak view of the Soviet world in transition is demonstrated by an essential incongruity in the book. "For all their vulgarity and meanness the two 'negative' characters of *Envy* are human, while the two main spokesman of the 'new world,' the world of sausages, machines, and model canteens, are both vulgar *and* inhuman," explained Struve. Still, Olesha made clear which of the two evils he sympathized with. "Though Kavalerov and Ivan are defeated," reasoned Edward J. Brown, "Olesha has so contrived the telling of his story that the reader identifies himself with their disreputable human feelings, and never with the Buddha-shaped businessmen in nose spectacles. The bizarre form of the novel conceals a defense of human values which Olesha felt were being trampled upon in the name of building socialism, and a plea for the right to existence of love, a sense of personal honor, and respect for oneself."

Without a doubt, Olesha devoted extraordinary attention to his craft. Though estimates vary, scholars contend he wrote up to three hundred revisions of the first page of *Zavist.* Several elements of Olesha's style, too, have been praised by critics of his first novel. Rich in imagery and yet simple in style, *Zavist* demonstrated "Olesha was one of the few . . . in Russia who knew what an undercurrent in a text and its role in a prose work were, [and] who had a mastery of prose rhythm, grotesque fantasy, hyperbole, sound effects, and unexpected turns of the imagination," commented Nina Berberova. Perhaps most notable in Olesha's presentation is his use of slapstick. Robert Payne saw this technique as a "comedy of the most wanton kind, gay and impenitent, happily indiscreet and wonderfully invigorating. . . . Its purpose was to question the foundations of the Soviet state, and if possible, to laugh it out of existence. . . . Slapstick was merely the sugar coating of a deliberate and reasoned apparatus of the state." This reliance on slapstick is not surprising: Payne revealed that Olesha "had a special reverence, amounting almost to adoration, for Charlie Chaplin."

Olesha continued his social criticism in this next novel, *Tri tolstyaka* ("The Three Fat Men"). A fairy-tale version of the Russian revolution, this celebration of the proletarian victory enjoyed tremendous popularity, seeing over thirty editions published in the thirty years after its first printing. It was also made into a play, a ballet, and, in 1966, a film. Victor Pertsov took a comparatively innocent view of the book when he wrote *"Three Fat Men* is a tale beautifully told in the tradition of the French romanticists. Although the scene is laid in an imaginary country and the tone is humorous, Olesha deals with serious matters, helping his young readers to see the victory of the people as the victory of health, beauty and life." Meanwhile, Payne wondered how this "explicit denunciation of the regime disguised as a fairy tale" was ever published and how Olesha survived its publication. Obviously, the Soviet government interpreted the book differently than did Payne.

The charges of "formalism," "naturalism," "objectivism," and "cosmopolitanism," which Soviet literary critics hurled at *Zavist,* also met Olesha's short stories, according to Andrew R. MacAndrew. Pertsov cited these works to demonstrate his belief that "Olesha's artistic vision is remarkable." He noted their philosophical and experimental nature while insisting Olesha was not prompted by a search for new forms. Beyond the "artistic touches which make a 'gem' of the simplest of these stories," stated Pertsov, is "the author's sharpness of vision [which] serves a profoundly modern purpose: Olesha seeks in his stories to reveal and affirm the material nature of the world, to convey in tangible form the primary nature of being in relation to mind." In one of Olesha's more popular stories, "Liompa," the death of an old man is described lucidly through the eyes of a child. Another, "Love," "shares a similar theme and a similar contrast of characters" with *Envy,* Anthony Hippisley pointed out. "But due to a complex system of symbolic images the meaning of this story is not immediately apparent."

Olesha continued to write into the mid 1930's, concentrating on short stories, plays, and film scenarios. The play "Spisok blagodeyany" ("A List of Assests") told the story of an actress who loses her idealized vision of the West (Paris) by finding it decadent and corrupt. But the publication of anti-Western works did not, however, mean the end of conflict with the Soviet state. His 1934 film scenario, "Strogy yunosha" ("A Strict Young Man"), was banned. Despite Olesha's plea at the First Congress of Soviet Writer's for greater humanism in Soviet letters, he never returned to the forefront of his country's literary scene. Only during the "thaw" following Stalin's death in 1953 did his works see publication there again.

Two arrests and increasing Stalinist oppression limited Olesha's literary output to adapting novels for the stage and writing children's puppet plays. The man who once said "I write about how life triumphs over everything—yes, over everything," was forced to write "for the basket": "I do write—every morning," he said later. "And every night I tear it up." Olesha's perfectionist habits account, in part, for the thinness of his collected writings; Soviet restrictions play

a much larger role. "Of Mandelshtam, Essenin, and Mayakovsky, the most famous of the literary victims of the Soviet state, it can be said with some confidence that at the time of their death they had written nearly all the work that was in them," observed Payne. "The tragedy of Olesha was that he was silenced when he had just begun to write."

BIOGRAPHICAL/CRITICAL SOURCES: Times Literary Supplement, August 16, 1947; Gleb Struve, *Soviet Russian Literature 1917-1950,* University of Oklahoma Press, 1951; *Soviet Literature,* November, 1956; Vera Alexandrova, *A History of Soviet Literature,* Doubleday, 1963; Edward J. Brown, *Russian Literature Since the Revolution,* Crowell-Collier, 1963; *Slavic Review,* September, 1966; Yuri Olesha, *Envy and Other Works,* translated by Andrew R. MacAndrew, Doubleday, 1967; Olesha, *Love and Other Stories,* translated by Robert Payne, Washington Square Press, 1967; *Saturday Review,* December 23, 1967; *Nation,* January 15, 1968; *Harper's,* January, 1968; Robert A. Maguire, *Red Virgin Soil,* Princeton University Press, 1968; Nina Berberova, *The Italics Are Mine,* Harcourt, 1969; *Studies in Short Fiction,* summer, 1973; *Contemporary Literary Criticism,* Volume 8, Gale, 1978.*

*   *   *

OLIPHANT, J(ames) Orin   1894-1979

OBITUARY NOTICE: Born March 23, 1894, in Elberton, Wash.; died February 24, 1979, in Salem, Ore. Historian and author of *The Rise of Bucknell University.* Oliphant was Bucknell University's first archivist. He specialized in the history of the American West. Obituaries and other sources: *Directory of American Schools,* Volume I: *History,* 6th edition, Bowker, 1974; *New York Times,* February 28, 1979.

*   *   *

OLKOWSKI, Helga   1931-

PERSONAL: Born December 15, 1931, in Detroit, Mich.; daughter of David and Tosia (a dancer; maiden name, Mundstock) Martin; married Earl Williamson, 1950 (divorced); married William Olkowski (a pest management specialist), November, 1969; children: (first marriage) David. *Education:* Columbia University, B.A. (magna cum laude), 1953; graduate study at University of California, Berkeley, 1953-54; Antioch College (West), M.S., 1976. *Office:* Center for the Integration of the Applied Sciences, John Muir Institute, 1307 Action St., Berkeley, Calif. 94706.

CAREER: Teacher at private school in Oakland, Calif., 1955; Oakland Public Museum, Oakland, teacher, 1957; Institute of Human Abilities, Oakland, teacher, 1968-69; Urban Studies Project, Oakland, teacher, 1970; Antioch College (West), San Francisco, Calif., member of core faculty in ecology and natural systems program, 1971-75; John Muir Institute, Napa, Calif., research associate, 1975-78, co-director of Center for the Integration of the Applied Sciences in Berkeley, 1977—. Partner of Environmental Research Associates, 1972—. Member of board of directors of Transnational Network of Appropriate Technologists; vice-chairman of board of directors of National Center for Appropriate Technology. Director of education and research at Integral Urban House, of Fallarones Institute, 1974-77; research associate in biological control at University of California, Berkeley, 1973-78; counselor for Saratoga Horticultural Foundation. Consultant to Environmental Protection Agency. *Member:* American Association for the Advancement of Science, Association of Applied Insect Ecologists.

WRITINGS: How Not to Use Toxic Pesticides in Home and

Garden (pamphlet), Consumers Cooperative of Berkeley, 1970; *Common Sense Pest Control* (booklet), Consumers Cooperative of Berkeley, 1971; *Gardening in the City* (pamphlet), Rodale Press, 1971; *Backyard Composting* (booklet), Ecology Center Press, 1975; (with husband, William Olkowski) *The City People's Book of Raising Food*, Rodale Press, 1975; (contributor) Richard Merrill, editor, *Radical Agriculture*, Harper, 1976; (contributor) D. Pimental, editor, *Pest Control Strategies*, Academic Press, 1978; (contributor) J. W. Frankie and C. S. Koehler, editors, *Perspectives in Urban Entomology*, Academic Press, 1978; (with W. Olkowski) *Common Sense Pest Control for the Home and Garden*, Environmental Protection Agency, 1978; (with W. Olkowski) *Integrated Pest Management of City Shade Trees*, Environmental Protection Agency, 1978; (with W. Olkowski and T. Javits) *The Integral Urban House*, Sierra Club Books, 1978.

Author of "Ecology Corner," a column in *Berkeley Citizen*, 1966, and "Book Reviews: Ecology," a column in *Freedom News*, 1971. Contributor of more than thirty articles to scientific journals, horticulture magazines, and newspapers. Contributing editor of *Horticulture*, 1976-77; associate editor of *IPM Practitioner*.

BIOGRAPHICAL/CRITICAL SOURCES: Garden Annual, Time-Life, 1978.

*   *   *

OLLMAN, Bertel 1935(?)-

PERSONAL: Married; children: one. *Education:* University of Wisconsin, Madison, B.A. (political science), 1956, M.A. (political science), 1957; Oxford University, B.A. (politics, philosophy, and economics), 1959, M.A. (political theory), 1963, D.Phil., 1967. *Office:* Department of Politics, New York University, 25 Waverley Pl., New York, N.Y. 10003.

CAREER: University of Maryland, College Park, assistant professor of government for Overseas Division in England and France, 1958, 1962-63; University of the West Indies, Kingston, Jamaica, lecturer in government, 1963-66; New York University, New York, N.Y., 1967—, began as assistant professor, currently associate professor of politics, director of Center for Marxist Studies, 1975—. Senior research fellow at Columbia University's Institute on Communist Affairs, 1971-72, visiting professor, 1972; visiting professor at Union College, 1974; lecturer on Marxist theory at colleges and universities in the United States, Canada, England, and Europe. President of Class Struggle, Inc. (producers of Marxist board game "Class Struggle"), 1978—. Educational director for International Institute for Education's Council on Student Travel, 1959-63; member of policy planning committee of People's National Party of Jamaica (research director, 1964-66); trainee at Metropolitan Academy of Psychoanalytic Training, 1969-71. *Member:* American Political Science Association, Modern Language Association of America, Caucus for a New Political Science, Union of Radical Political Economists, East Coast Socialist Sociologists, Phi Beta Kappa.

WRITINGS: (Contributor) *Dialectique Marxiste et pensee structurale*, Centre d'Etudes Socialistes, 1968; *Alienation: Marx's Conception of Man in Capitalist Society*, Cambridge University Press, 1971; (contributor) Dick Howard and Karl Klare, editors, *The Unknown Dimension: European Marxism Since Lenin*, Basic Books, 1971; (author of introduction) Wilhelm Riech, *Sex-Pol: Marxist Writings, 1929-1934*, Random House, 1973; (contributor) Ira Katznelson, editor, *The Best of "Politics and Society"*, McKay, 1975; (contributor)

Severyn Bialer, editor, *Theory and Practice of Radical Movements*, Praeger, 1977; (editor with Ted Norton) *Studies in Socialist Pedagogy*, Monthly Review Press, 1978; *Social and Sexual Revolution*, South End Press, 1978. Contributor of articles and reviews to scholarly and radical journals. Member of board of editors of *Kapitalistate*, 1973-76.

WORK IN PROGRESS: A book on Marx's method; a book on Marx's theory of class consciousness; a collection of his previously published articles; editing a book on Marx's method, with Waldo Mazelis; editing a book on Marx's critique of capitalist ideology, with Mazelis; editing a collection of Marxist writings on American government, with Jim Robinson; research on the materialist conception of history, Marx's theory of the state and critique of capitalist ideology.

*   *   *

O'NEILL, E. Bard 1941-

PERSONAL: Born July 21, 1941, in Poughkeepsie, N.Y.; son of Andrew Thomas (a truck driver) and Edith May (Brown) O'Neill; married Nancy Gallagher (a nurse), January 9, 1965; children: Suzanne, Andrew, Sarah. *Education:* St. Michael's College, B.A., 1963; San Diego State College (now San Diego State University), M.A., 1968; University of Denver, Ph.D., 1972. *Politics:* Independent. *Religion:* Roman Catholic. *Home:* 6604 Greenview Lane, Springfield, Va. 22152. *Office:* Department of National Security Affairs, National War College, Fort L. J. McNair, Washington, D.C. 20319.

CAREER: U.S. Air Force, career officer, 1963—, intelligence officer with Strategic Air Command in Wyoming, 1963-65, intelligence officer in South Vietnam, 1965-66, instructor at U.S. Air Force Academy, 1967-69, associate professor of political science, 1972-76, member of faculty at National War College, 1976—, director of Middle East studies, senior research fellow at National Defense University, 1976—, present rank, lieutenant colonel. Visiting associate professor at University of Denver, 1975; visiting lecturer at University of Colorado, 1975-76, and Catholic University of America, 1977-79. Participant (and director) in scholarly conferences; gives lectures to civil, religious, business, and military groups. *Member:* International Studies Association, American Political Science Association, Middle East Studies Association, Middle East Institute, Pi Sigma Alpha, Delta Epsilon Sigma. *Awards, honors:* National Security Education fellow, 1973.

WRITINGS: (Contributor) Richard Head and E. J. Rokke, editors, *American Defense Policy*, 3rd edition (O'Neill was not included in earlier editions), Johns Hopkins Press, 1973, 4th edition, 1977; *Revolutionary Warfare in the Middle East*, Paladin Press, 1974; (editor with D. J. Alberts and Steven J. Rossetti, and contributor) *Political Violence and Insurgency: A Comparative Approach*, Phoenix Press, 1974; (contributor) John Endicott and Roy W. Stafford, editors, *Comparative Defense Policy*, Johns Hopkins Press, 1974; (editor with Joseph S. Szyliowicz, and contributor) *The Energy Crisis and U.S. Foreign Policy*, Praeger, 1975; (with Szyliowicz) *Petropolitics and the Atlantic Alliance* (monograph), National Defense University, 1976; *Petroleum and Security: The Limitations of American Military Power in the Persian Gulf* (monograph), National Defense University, 1977; *Armed Struggle in Palestine*, Westview Press, 1978; (editor and contributor) *Insurgency in the Modern World*, Westview Press, 1979. Contributor to military and foreign area studies journals.

WORK IN PROGRESS: Contributing material to *Collection*

of Teaching Modules on National Security Affairs, edited by James Harf and William Trout; research on Egyptian and Israeli defense policies and on terrorism in the context of insurgency.

SIDELIGHTS: O'Neill writes: "My principal area of research is the Israeli-Palestinian Arab conflict. My overriding view is that there is right and wrong on both sides—it is necessary to de-emphasize polemics. Additionally, it is possible that under carefully negotiated conditions, which assure Israel's security from violent attacks, a Palestinian state could resolve the Palestinian problem. Such a state could include among its leaders pragmatic elements in the PLO that will recognize Israel. This will require compromise on the part of both sides."

AVOCATIONAL INTERESTS: Youth athletic programs.

* * *

O'NEILL, Timothy P. 1941-

PERSONAL: Born April 9, 1941, in Tullamore, Ireland; son of Stephen and Brigid (Conroy) O'Neill; married Carmel A. MacGarry, 1965; children: Eoin, Aine, Sheila, Bairbre. *Education:* Attended University College of National University of Ireland, 1959-65. *Office:* Department of History, Carysfort College of Education, Blackrock, County Dublin, Ireland.

CAREER: Teacher, 1962-65; National Museum of Ireland, Dublin, ethnologist, 1965-73; Carysfort College of Education, Blackrock, Ireland, teacher of history and head of department, 1972—.

WRITINGS: Ireland: A Junior Historical Atlas, Educational Company of Ireland, 1971; *Life and Tradition in Rural Ireland,* Dent, 1977. Also writer of television scripts. Contributor to history, ethnology, and antiquarian journals.

WORK IN PROGRESS: A social history of modern and early modern Ireland; a book on poverty; television scripts for "Search," a series on Radio Telefis Eireann.

AVOCATIONAL INTERESTS: Bicycling, fishing, photography.

* * *

ONETTI, Juan Carlos 1909-

PERSONAL: Born July 1, 1909, in Montevideo, Uruguay; son of Carlos and Honoria (Borges) Onetti; married Dolly Muhr, November, 1955; children: Jorge, Isabel. *Home:* Gonzalo Ramfrez 1497, Montevideo, Uruguay.

CAREER: Writer. Worked as editor for Reuter Agency in Montevideo, Uruguay, 1942-43, and in Buenos Aires, Argentina, 1943-46; manager of advertising firm in Montevideo, 1955-57; director of libraries in Montevideo, 1957—. *Awards, honors:* National literature prize of Uruguay, 1963; Ibera-American award from William Faulkner Foundation, 1963.

WRITINGS—In English: La vida breve, Editorial Sudamericana, 1950, translation by Hortense Carpentier published as *A Brief Life,* Grossman, 1976; *El astillero,* Compania General Fabirl Editora, 1961, translation by Rachel Caffyn published as *The Shipyard,* Scribner, 1968.

Other: *Tierra de nadie* (novel), Editorial Losada, 1941; . . . *Para esta noche . . . ,* Editorial Poseidon, 1943; *Un sueno realizado, y otros cuentos,* Numero, 1951; *Los adioses,* Sur, 1954; *Una tumba sin nombre,* Marcha, 1959.

La cara de la desgracia (novella), Editorial Alfa, 1960; *El infierno tan temido,* Editorial Asir, 1962; *Tan triste como*

ella, Editorial Alfa, 1963; *Juntacadaveres,* Editorial Alfa, 1964; *El pozo* [and] *Seguido de origen de un novelista y de una generacion literaria* (the latter by Angel Rama), Editorial Alfa, 1965, reprinted as *El pozo* [and] *para una tumba sin nombre* [and] *Seguido de origen de un novelista y de una generacion literaria,* Editorial Calicanto, 1977 (also see below); *Jacob y el otro: Un sueno realizado y otros cuentos,* Ediciones de la Banda Oriental, 1965; *Cuentos Completos,* Centro Editor de America Latina, 1967, revised edition, Corregidor, 1974; *Novelas cortas completas* (contains *El pozo, Los adioses, La cara de la desgracia, Tan triste como ella,* and *Para una tumba sin nombre*), Monte Avila Editores, 1968; *La novia robada y otros cuentos,* Centro Editor de America Latina, 1968.

Obras completas, Aguilar, 1970; *La muerte y la nina,* Corregidor, 1973; *La novia robada,* Siglo Veintiuno Argentina Editores, 1973; *Onetti* (articles and interview), Troisi y Vaccaro, 1974; *Tiempo de abrazar y los cuentos de 1933 a 1950* (collected stories), Arca, 1974; (with Joacquin Torres-García and others; author of report) *Testamento artistico,* Biblioteca de Marcha, 1974; *Para una tumba sin nombre,* Libreria del Colegio, 1975 (also see above); *Requiem por Faulkner,* Arca, 1975; *Tan triste como ella y otros cuentos* (collected stories), Lumen, 1976.

Editor of *Marcha,* 1939-42, and *Vea y Lea,* 1946-55.

SIDELIGHTS: Although Onetti is considered by many critics to be among the finest novelists in South America, only two of his books have been translated into English. *The Shipyard,* though written after *A Brief Life,* was published first. It tells the story of Larsen, a shipyard worker who seeks to improve his social status by attaching himself to the shipyard owner's daughter. He is unable to see that the society he aspires to has disintegrated. The novel ends with his death. "Larsen moves through Onetti's pages as a figure virtually doomed to disaster," declared James Nelson Goodsell. "He carries a revolver almost all the time . . . as if to give the impression that it will be the vehicle of his own demise." The gun, however, is not the cause of Larsen's death. He dies of pneumonia incurred after he deserts a pregnant woman going into labor. As David Gallagher explained, Larsen would "not be trapped into aiding and abetting the birth of a new creature, for that would be to accept the continuation of a game, a farce, that served him just a bit too ill." Gallagher also excused Onetti for his apparent excesses. "Some may think it disheartening that so many worms and so many spiders should come out of an 'undeveloped country,'" wrote Gallagher. But he endorsed *The Shipyard* as "a book which, for all its portentuousness, few Latin American novelists have equaled."

The plot of *A Brief Life* is much more fantastical than that of *The Shipyard.* It concerns Juan Carlos Brausen, referred to as a "sort of Argentine Walter Mitty" by Emir Rodriguez Monegal. Brausen is preoccupied with his neighbor, a prostitute. Eventually he acts on his dreams and approaches her. After becoming her pimp, Brausen imagines a screenplay within which he creates an entire town of characters. By the novel's end, Brausen has reneged on his commitment to film the imaginary screenplay and he escapes to another town. Hugo J. Verani called *A Brief Life* "one of the richest and most complex novelistic expressions in Spanish-American fiction."

Because of its unique unfolding of plot, *A Brief Life* received inevitable comparisons with the work of William Faulkner. Luys A. Diez noted that "much of Faulkner's rich, dark sap flows through the meandering narrative." Diez also contended, "Onetti's novelistic magic, like Faulkner's, requires a certain amount of perseverance on the reader's part." And Monegal remarked, "In *A Brief Life*, Onetti's love for Faulknerian narrative is already evident."

Several critics expressed their high regard for Onetti's skillful use of experimental narration. Zunilda Gertel wrote that "Onetti's narrative does not postulate an ideology or an intellectual analysis of the ontological. Instead, the existential projection of the 'I' is shown as a revelation within the signs imposed on him by literary tradition considered as ritual, not as reconciliation." John Deredita claimed that *A Brief Life* "exhaustively tests the power of fantasy and fictional imagination as a counter to the flow of time...." And Verani concluded, "Onetti does not emphasis the mimetic quality of narrative. The aim of his fiction is not to reflect an existent reality, a factual order, but ... to create an essentially fabulated reality invested with mythic significance."

BIOGRAPHICAL/CRITICAL SOURCES: New York Times Book Review, June 16, 1968, January 11, 1976; *Christian Science Monitor*, October 8, 1968; *Review 75*, winter, 1975; *Nation*, April 3, 1976; *Contemporary Literary Criticism*, Gale, Volume 7, 1977, Volume 10, 1979.*

*   *   *

ORAISON, Marc 1914-

PERSONAL: Born July 7, 1914, in Ambares, France; son of Jules (a surgeon) and Marie (La Croix) Oraison. *Education:* Faculte de Medecine, Bordeaux, docteur en medecine, 1942; Catholic Institute (Paris), docteur en theologie, 1951. *Religion:* Catholic. *Home:* 3 rue de la Trinite, Paris 75009, France.

CAREER: Surgeon and psychotherapist. Ordained Roman Catholic priest, 1948; priest of diocese of Bordeaux, France, 1948—. Writer. *Military service:* French military, 1939-40; served in Indochina, 1945-46; member of French Reserve. *Member:* Societe des Gens de Lettres, Ecrivains Croyants d'Expression Francaise.

WRITINGS—In English: *L'Union des epoux*, Fayard, 1956, translation by Andre Humbert published as *Union in Marital Love*, Macmillan, 1958 (published in England as *Man and Wife: The Physical Foundations of Marriage*, Longmans, Green, 1959); *Amour ou constrainte? Quelques aspects psychologiques de l'education religieuse*, Spes (Paris), 1957, translation by Una Morrissey published as *Love or Constraint? Some Psychological Aspects of Religious Education*, Kenedy, 1959.

L'Harmonie du couple humain, Ouvrieres, 1960, translation by Albert J. La Mothe, Jr., published as *The Harmony of the Human Couple*, Fides, 1967; *La Peche*, Desclee de Brouwer (Paris), 1959, translation published as *Sin*, Macmillan, 1962; *Amour, peche, souffrance*, Fayard, 1961, translation by William Barrow published as *Love, Sin, and Suffering*, Macmillan, 1964; *Devant l'illusion et l'angoisse*, Fayard, 1958, translation by Bernard Murchland published as *Illusion and Anxiety*, Macmillan, 1963; *Savoir aimer: pour une claire information sexuelle*, Fayard, 1963, translation by Humbert published as *Learning to Love: Frank Advice for Young Catholics*, Hawthorn, 1965; *Une morale pour notre temps*, Fayard, 1964, new edition, Seuil, 1970, translation by Nels Challe published as *Morality for Our Time*, Doubleday, 1968; *Learning to Love*, Paulist Press, 1966; *Le Celibat: aspect negatif, realites positives*, Centurion, 1966, translation by Leonard Mayhew published as *The Celibate Condition and Sex*, Sheed & Ward, 1967; *Le Mystere humain de la sexualite*, Seuil, 1966, translation published as *The Human*

Mystery of Sexuality, Sheed & Ward, 1967; *La Mort, et puis apres?*, Fayard, 1967, translation by Theodore DuBois published as *Death, and Then What?*, Newman Press, 1969; *Etre avec ... la relation a autrui ...*, Centurion, 1968, translation by Rosemary Sheed published as *Being Together: Our Relationships With Other People*, Doubleday, 1970; *Tete dure* (autobiography), Seuil, 1969, translation by J. F. Bernard published as *Strange Voyage: The Autobiography of a Non-Conformist*, Doubleday, 1969.

Pour une education morale dynamique: changements d'optique necessaires, Fayard, 1970, translation by Bernard published as *Morality for Moderns*, Doubleday, 1972; *La Transhumance*, Seuil, 1970, translation published as *The Wound of Mortality: A Meditation on the Human Condition*, Doubleday, 1971; *Le Hasard et la vie*, Seuil, 1971, translation by Murchland published as *Chance and Life: Faith as the Living Reality*, Doubleday, 1972; *La Question homosexuelle*, Seuil, 1975, translation published as *The Homosexual Question*, Harper, 1977.

Other: *Vie chretienne et problemes de la sexualite*, P. Lethielleux, 1952; *Medecine et guerisseurs*, P. Lethielleux, 1955; *Problemes de psychanalyse*, Fayard, 1957; (with others) *Les Enfants produgues: problemes des bandes asociales et essai de solutions*, Fayard, 1962; *Psychologie et sens du peche*, revised and enlarged edition, Desclee De Brouwar, 1968; *Actualites: Vietnam, Israel, Prague, l'argent, les greffes, l'amour, les groupes*, Fayard, 1969; (with Bruno Lagrange) *Ailleurs existe, la resurrection*, Fayard, 1969.

Les Conflits de l'existence: s'affronter et s'entendre, Centurion, 1970; *Vocation: phenomene humain*, Desclee De Brouwer, 1970; *Depasser la peur*, Desclee De Brouwar, 1972; *Le temps des alibis*, Seuil, 1973; *Le Couple en question: dialogue entre Marc Oraison et J. de Boubon Busset*, Beauchesne (Paris), 1973; *Jesus Christ, ce more vivent*, Grasset, 1973; *La Culpabilite*, Seuil, 1974; *Vivre en adulte*, Centurion, 1974; *L'Apprenti sorcier*, Seuil, 1976; *Au point ou j'en suis ...* (autobiography), Seuil, 1978.

Contributor to *Le Monde, Revue Nouvelle* (Belgium), *Informations Catholique internationales, Cahiers laennec*, and *Supplement de la vie spirituelle*.

WORK IN PROGRESS: La Prostitution ... et alors?, for Seuil.

SIDELIGHTS: Oraison, a surgeon turned priest and psychotherapist, links the scientific with the spiritual in his many writings. In *Illusion and Anxiety*, which caused some controversy when it first appeared in France, Oraison explored the internal conflict from which human beings suffer as a result of dealing with other people, with God, and with other aspects of their existence. The book contains a "particularly perceptive passage on the problem of homosexuality," stated a reviewer in *Christian Century*. In *America*, Father Sebastian described it as "an excellent basic text for those interested in the problems of spiritual maturity."

The Human Mystery of Sexuality is concerned with the role sex plays in the lifelong development of the personality. "Appealing and delightful in its style," wrote a *Choice* critic, it is "significant in its linking of many areas of psychological research with biological and sociological theory." It is unique in its "profound consideration of human love." In *Christian Century*, E. V. Stein noted too that "this is a book deserving of a studied consideration, not for any new data but for the author's ability to recast the familiar in a light that breeds reverence rather than contempt and that suggests new connections between Freud's 'genital character' and the *imago dei*."

In *Being Together: Our Relationships With Other People,* Oraison supported the premise that the only perfect relationship an individual can have is with God and again emphasizes that our relationships with one another at best fall short of this perfection. In the book Oraison focused on the negative aspects of sexuality, according to critic W. P. Ryan. He commented in the *New York Times Book Review,* "This is certainly a book to be read but needs to be read with rose-colored glasses to make its coloration normal." F. J. Braceland concluded in *America* that although "brilliant in some places, the book is marred in others by tiresome verbiage. Nevertheless, it is in general an interesting and timely work."

Oraison's autobiography, *Strange Voyage: The Autobiography of a Non-Conformist,* was described by T. H. Clancy as "an immensely heartening book for those who love the Church." Oraison "has been a great force in awakening the Church to the need for a renewal of moral theology, especially in the realm of sex, and in demonstrating the help that modern medicine and psychotherapy can provide in religious and sacerdotal formation." One flaw of the book, in *Commentary* critic Philip Deasy's opinion, is that the reason the author calls himself a non-conformist is not revealed until fairly late in the narrative. Deasy did add, however, that "the highlights of Father Oraison's intellectual life receive eloquent emphasis throughout *Strange Voyage.*"

Ultimately, it is love that human beings seek. This is Oraison's message in his *Morality for Moderns.* "In this all too short but very readable book, Fr. Oraison once again revealed the wealth of his understanding of human behavior," wrote G. L. Chamberlain. "He breaks new ground in Catholic moral thinking and unearths fresh insights." But Rosemary Haughton, in *Commonweal,* said the book is "simple to the point of naivete, and its patient explanations of basic positions in psychology since Freud are breathtakingly banal."

Another *America* reviewer called *The Wound of Mortality: A Meditation on the Human Condition* "the sleeper 'spiritual' book of the year (1971). Rooted in the psychological reality of Jesus Christ, this practically unreviewed book of self-discovery is like a 'Catholic' Kierkegaardian leap into faith." It is "strong stuff, not for casual weekend retreats," he advised. Opposing this view, Edward Gannan commented in *Best Sellers:* "It is difficult to find anything to credit in this jumble, except maybe to suggest it as a gold mine for the logic professor in search of howling fallacies."

BIOGRAPHICAL/CRITICAL SOURCES: Christian Century, August 14, 1963, June 14, 1967, October 25, 1972; *America,* February 15, 1964, March 28, 1970, September 12, 1970, February 12, 1972, May 27, 1972; *Critic,* April, 1967; *Choice,* November, 1967; Marc Oraison, *Strange Voyage: The Autobiography of a Non-Conformist,* Doubleday, 1969; *New York Times Book Review,* March 15, 1970, March 5, 1972; *Best Sellers,* October 15, 1970, December 1, 1970; *Commonweal,* December 18, 1970, September 8, 1972.

*   *   *

ORBACH, Susie 1946-

PERSONAL: Born November 6, 1946, in London, England; daughter of Maurice (a member of Parliament) and Ruth (a teacher; maiden name, Huebsch) Orbach. *Education:* Attended University of London, City University of New York, and State University of New York at Stony Brook. *Politics:* "Socialist-Feminist." *Religion:* Jewish. *Office:* Women's Therapy Centre, 19-A Hartham Rd., London N. 7, England.

CAREER: New York Law Commune, New York, N.Y., in city planning, 1969-71; psychotherapist, 1972—. Faculty member at Richmond College of the City University of New York, 1971-73. Co-founder and director of Women's Therapy Centre, 1976—. Consultant in psychotherapy training.

WRITINGS: Fat Is a Feminist Issue, Paddington, 1978. Also author, with Luise Eichenbaum, of *Inside Out and Outside In: A Developmental View of Female Psychology,* 1979. Contributor to *Science for the People.*

WORK IN PROGRESS: The Myth of Intelligence, with Joseph Schwarz.

SIDELIGHTS: Susie Orbach writes: "I do not see myself as a writer. In fact I find it excruciating work, but I think it is important to share ideas that are nurtured in the women's liberation movement to a mass audience. I think it is important to give a different view of ways to see and change the world than we learn through conventional channels. Hence I write from the perspective of one who is attempting to change our ways of doing and seeing."

*   *   *

ORLINSKY, Harry M(eyer) 1908-

PERSONAL: Born March 14, 1908, in Owen Sound, Ontario, Canada; came to the United States in 1931; naturalized citizen in 1938; son of Isaac Moses and Libby Elizabeth (Ardy) Orlinsky; married Donya Fein, September 2, 1934; children: Walter Sidney, Seymour Ivan. *Education:* University of Toronto, B.A., 1931; graduate study at University of Pennsylvania, 1931-35; Dropsie College, Ph.D., 1935; postdoctoral study at Hebrew University of Jerusalem, 1935-36. *Office:* Hebrew Union College—Jewish Institute of Religion, 40 West 68th St., New York, N.Y. 10023.

CAREER: American Schools of Oriental Research, Jerusalem, Israel, Nies scholar, 1935-36; Baltimore Hebrew College, Baltimore, Md., professor of Biblical literature and Jewish history, 1936-44; Hebrew Union College—Jewish Institute of Religion, New York, N.Y., assistant professor, 1944-45, professor of Bible, 1945—. Fellow of Johns Hopkins University, 1936-41; visiting instructor at Hebrew Union College—Jewish Institute of Religion, 1943-44; lecturer at New School for Social Research, 1947-49; visiting professor at Dropsie College, summers, 1951, 1953, and 1955, Brandeis University, summers, 1959 and 1960, Hebrew University of Jerusalem, 1962, and Graduate Theological Union, Berkeley, Calif., 1969; Grinfield Lecturer at Oxford University, 1973-75; Horace Kallen Lecturer at Herzlia Hebrew Teachers Institute—Jewish Teachers Seminary, 1976; Albright Memorial Lecturer at Johns Hopkins University, 1977. Past associate trustee of American Schools of Oriental Research; member of Yivo Institute of Jewish Research; committee member of Pseudepigraphique Grecque d'Ancient Testament, 1967—; member of Herausgeberkollegium of Arbeiten zur Literatur und Geschichte des Hellenistischen Judentums; member of Hebrew University of Jerusalem excavations at Ramat Gan, 1936.

MEMBER: International Organization for Septuagint and Cognate Studies (co-founder; president, 1968-73), International Organization for Masoretic Studies (founder; president, 1972—), American Oriental Society (member of executive committee, 1953), Society of Biblical Literature (vice-president, 1969; president, 1970), Academy for Jewish Research (fellow), Jewish Book Council (delegate at large), Old Testament Society, American Standard Bible Committee (Revised Standard Version), Jewish Academy of Arts and Sciences, British Society for Old Testament Studies, American Friends of Israel Exploration Society (co-founder; president, 1953—), American Friends of Hebrew University (member of board of directors). *Awards, honors:* Frank L. Weil Award from National Jewish Welfare Board, 1959; Guggenheim fellow, 1968-69; fellow of Princeton University Council of the Humanities, 1965—; Harry M. Orlinsky Institute of Biblical and Archaeological Research at Baltimore Hebrew College, 1979. D.H.L. from Baltimore Hebrew College, 1972, and Spertus College of Judaica, 1979.

WRITINGS: The Septuagint: The Oldest Translation of the Bible, Union of American Hebrew Congregations, 1949; (translator with A. ben Isaiah and B. Sharfman), *The Pentateuch and Rashi's Commentary: A Linear Translation,* 5 volumes, S.S. & R. Publishing Co., 1949-50; (translator with other members of American Standard Bible Committee) *The Holy Bible, Revised Standard Version,* Thomas Nelson, 1952; *Ancient Israel,* Cornell University Press, 1954, 2nd edition, 1960; (editor) Solomon Goldman, *From Slavery to Freedom,* Abelard, 1958.

(Editor-in-chief) *The Torah: The Five Books of Moses,* Jewish Publication Society of America, 1962, 2nd edition, 1967; (author of prolegomenon) C. D. Ginsburg, *Introduction to the ... Hebrew Bible,* Ktav, 1965; *Genesis* (New Jewish Version), Harper Torchbook, 1966; (editor) *Notes on the New (Jewish) Translation of "The Torah",* Jewish Publication Society, 1969; (editor and author of prolegomenon) A. B. Ehrlich, *Mikre ki-Pheschuto* (title means "The Bible According to Its Literal Meaning"), 3 volumes, Ktav, 1969; (with others) *The Five Megilloth and Jonah,* Jewish Publication Society, 1969; (editor and co-author) *Interpreting the Prophetic Tradition,* Hebrew Union College Press and Ktav, 1969; *Understanding the Bible Through History and Archaeology,* Ktav, 1972; *Essays in Biblical Culture and Bible Translation,* Ktav, 1974; (with others) *The Prophets,* Jewish Publication Society, 1978; *Israel Exploration Journal Reader,* 2 volumes, Ktav, 1980.

Contributor: Edward C. Hobbs, editor, *A Stubborn Faith: Papers on Old Testament and Related Subjects Presented to Honor William Andrew Irwin,* Southern Methodist University Press, 1956; G. E. Wright, editor, *The Bible and the Ancient Near East: Essays in Honor of W. F. Albright,* Doubleday, 1961; P. Ramsey, editor, *Religion,* Prentice-Hall, 1965; *Studies on the Second Part of the Book of Isaiah,* E. J. Brill, 1967; *Interpreter's Dictionary of the Bible,* supplementary volume, Abingdon, 1976.

Editor of *Library of Biblical Studies,* Ktav, 1966— and of *Septuagint and Cognate Studies* and *Masoretic Studies,* Society of Biblical Literature and Scholars Press, 1974—. Contributor to theology journals. Member of editorial board of *Journal of Biblical Literature, Israel Exploration Journal, Jewish Apocryphal Literature, Jewish Quarterly Review,* and *Old Testament Abstracts.*

WORK IN PROGRESS: "The Septuagint and Its Hebrew Text," to be published in Volume II or III of *The Cambridge History of Judaism; The Canonization of the Hebrew Bible and the Exclusion of the Apocrypha; The Holy Land: The Biblical View; Male-Oriented Language in the New Bible Translations; The Hebrew Covenant.*

SIDELIGHTS: Orlinsky is a leading Biblical scholar who has given much of his time to translating ancient texts for both Jewish and Protestant readers. He strives for accuracy and faithfulness to the original texts in all his work, but has made a great effort to gear his work to the sensitivities of today's readers. His public and professional lectures have dealt with the use of nonsexist language in current transla-

tions as well as the difficulty of translating from a rich expressive language to English, which he considers inadequate for the purpose.

Orlinsky is the first and only Jewish scholar who has been a full participating member of a committee that made an official Christian translation of the Hebrew Bible, the Protestant Revised Standard Version. In 1966 the Catholic Biblical Association of Great Britain produced an official Bible, the Revised Standard Version: Catholic Edition, thus making him the first and only Jew to participate in the making of an authorized Catholic translation of the Bible. As editor-in-chief of the New Jewish Version of the Bible, Orlinsky is the only person to have participated fully in the making of a Jewish, Protestant, and Catholic translation of the Bible.

"In the attempt to comprehend Biblical concepts and history," Orlinsky told *CA,* "I have been careful to let the Hebrew text speak for itself (exegesis) and to exclude the many later interpretations that were read back into it (eisegesis). Thus I have argued that it is simply 'wind' rather than traditional 'Spirit' (or 'spirit') that correctly renders the Hebrew *ru'ah* in Genesis 1:2, and that it is 'young woman' rather than traditional 'virgin' that correctly reproduced the meaning of the Hebrew *almah* in Isaiah 7:14. Scholarly concensus had opted since the twenties for an amphictyony in the period preceding the rise of the Hebrew monarchy (10th century B.C.E.), the period of the so-called 'Judges' (actually military chieftains). I was the first scholar to argue against this notion in detail, and the theory is now all but rejected. Most scholars still hold that the prophets and other biblical writers conceived of the God of Israel as an international God; I have long held that He was both a national God (of Israel alone) and a Universal God (sole creator, master of all the universe and its natural phenomena and inhabitants—in the sky and on the earth and in the seas); but He was never conceived as an international God.

"There is a long-held scholarly belief that the Second Isaiah (author of chapters 40-55 and much of 56-66), especially in chapter 53, speaks of a 'Servant of the Lord who suffered vicariously for sinful Israel and mankind'; I have argued in detail that this belief is a post-Jesus innovation (Philip to the Ethiopian eunuch, chapter 8 of the Book of Acts) that was read back into the Bible. Scholars have long asserted that the Hebrew text of the Bible was fixed in the first millennium by Jewish scribes known as Masoretes, and hence the term "the Masoretic text." I have argued that the Hebrew text of the Bible was never fixed, and that the definite article 'the' in 'the Masoretic text' is a scholarly fiction; many Masoretes were responsible for many Hebrew manuscripts of the Bible coming into being, each manuscript containing *a* masoretic text. None of these texts can lay claim to ultimate authority."

Orlinsky was selected to examine the four Dead Sea scrolls that the Israeli Government purchased in 1954. He discusses the story of the scrolls in *Essays in Biblical Culture and Bible Translation.* He commented: "I have published a number of articles in which I have argued against the sensational claims made by the majority of scholars for the value of the text of the scrolls, especially the complete Isaiah text of the Bible; this is the burden of my chapter on 'The Textual Criticism of the Old Testament' in *The Bible and the Ancient Near East.*"

AVOCATIONAL INTERESTS: Classical music, sports, humor, and independent thinking.

BIOGRAPHICAL/CRITICAL SOURCES: New York Times, May 21, 1973, November 26, 1977; *Jerusalem Post,*

August 4, 1965; *Baltimore Jewish Times,* April 23, 1976; *Baltimore Sun,* May 17, 1976, November 15, 1977; *Johns Hopkins Magazine,* March, 1978; *New Orleans Times-Picayune,* November 19, 1978.

*   *   *

ORMOND, Leonee (Jasper) 1940-

PERSONAL: Born August 27, 1940, in Kingston-upon-Thames, Surrey, England; married Richard Ormond (deputy director of National Portrait Gallery), May 11, 1963; children: Augustus Jasper, Marcus Conrad. *Education:* St. Anne's College, Oxford, B.A., 1962; University of Birmingham, M.A., 1965. *Religion:* Church of England. *Residence:* London, England. *Office:* Department of English, King's College, University of London, London W.C.2, England.

CAREER: Birmingham College of Education, Birmingham, England, assistant lecturer in English, 1963-65; University of London, King's College, London, England, assistant lecturer, 1965-68, lecturer in English, 1968—. *Member:* University Women's Club.

WRITINGS: George du Maurier, Routledge & Kegan Paul, 1969; (contributor) Ian Fletcher, editor, *Meredith Today,* Routledge & Kegan Paul, 1971; (contributor) Isabel Armstrong, editor, *Writers and Their Background: Robert Browning,* G. Bell, 1972; (with husband, Richard Ormond) *Lord Leighton,* Yale University Press, 1975. Contributor to magazines, including *Burlington* and *Apollo.*

WORK IN PROGRESS: Literary Subjects in Victorian Painting.

SIDELIGHTS: Leonee Ormond writes: "I am particularly interested in writing biography, and in the relationship between literature and the arts. George du Maurier, about whom I wrote my first biography, was both an artist (a cartoonist for *Punch*) and a novelist. Lord Leighton was an artist only, but his close friendship with Robert Browning again carried me into a world where the arts were fruitfully connected. My current project is a study of the literary subject-picture, considering which subjects were popular at which dates, and why. Biography is my real love, however, and I hope to find a good subject for one in the near future."

AVOCATIONAL INTERESTS: Travel (especially Europe).

*   *   *

ORSO, Kathryn Wickey 1921-1979

OBITUARY NOTICE—See index for *CA* sketch: Born July 19, 1921, in Fargo, N.D.; died of cancer, April 24, 1979, in Towson, Md. Educator, consultant, and speaker on religious education. After working as a parent educator in Baltimore's public schools, Orso became an assistant in continuing education for Baltimore's Essex Community College. A member of the League of Women Voters and the Religious Education Association, she also contributed articles to the *Lutheran Church Women* of the Lutheran Church in America. Her books include *Manual for Christian Parents, Double Your Fun and Effectiveness Through Team Teaching,* and *It's Great to Pray.* Obituaries and other sources: *Washington Post,* April 29, 1979.

*   *   *

ORTON, John Kingsley 1933-1967
(Joe Orton)

PERSONAL: Born in 1933 in Leicester, England; murdered August 9, 1967. *Education:* Attended Royal Academy of Dramatic Art. *Residence:* London, England.

CAREER: Actor; playwright. *Awards, honors:* London critics variety award, 1964, for *Entertaining Mr. Sloane,* "Loo" named best play of 1966 by *Evening Standard.*

WRITINGS—All under name Joe Orton; all plays, except as noted: *Entertaining Mr. Sloane* (first produced in London at New Arts Theatre, May 6, 1964), Hamilton, 1964, Grove Press, 1965; *Loot,* Grove Press, 1967; *Crimes of Passion: The Ruffian on the Star* [and] *The Erpingham Camp* (both one-act plays; first produced in New York at Astor Place Theater, October 26, 1969), Methuen, 1967; *What the Butler Saw,* Samuel French, 1969; *Funeral Games* [and] *The Good and Faithful Servant,* Methuen, 1970; *Head to Toe* (novel), Blond, 1971; *The Complete Plays,* Methuen, 1976, Grove Press, 1977. Also author of "Until She Screams," 1970, a sketch for Kenneth Tynan's *Oh! Calcutta.*

WORK IN PROGRESS: A film script for the Beatles.

SIDELIGHTS: While Orton was being hailed by critics as the best modern writer of farce in English, audiences were walking out on performances of his plays. For Orton was an iconoclast who dramatized the hypocrisy and perverseness of contemporary morality. As John Lahr wrote, "Orton's plays offend in order to instruct and heal.... [His] farces make an audience confront the schizophrenic patterns of their lives, rather than evade them." In this respect, he has been compared to Oscar Wilde, George Bernard Shaw, and Noel Coward.

The subject matter of Orton's plays is what viewers found offensive. For example, *Entertaining Mr. Sloane* is about a middle-aged brother and sister who protect their father's murderer because he is attractive and young and they want to sleep with him. In *Loot,* a mother's corpse is carefully guarded because also in the coffin is the plunder from a robbery. However, John Russell Taylor pointed out that "the key to Orton's dramatic world is to be found in the strange relationship between the happenings of his plays and the manner in which the characters speak of them." That is, while the occurrences on stage may be morally or conventionally outrageous, "the primness and propriety of what is said hardly ever breaks down."

Other critics have observed the same phenomenon. Keath Fraser noted Orton's knack for parodying "the manners which spring from an abyss between the characters' decorous language and their indecorous actions." Katharine J. Worth called this "the cool convention": the ability of style to keep feeling, or more particularly, violence and brutality, in its place. Harold Pinter described his work as "brilliant and truly original. He has an instinctive grasp of construction."

That language is central to Orton's world view is confirmed by his imprisonment at one time for defacing library books. But language is central to his talent, too. Harold Clurman observed his ability to create dialogue "at once traditionally elegant and nasally obscene," and went on to say, "If you open your mouth in laughter at an Orton play, a spoonful of acid is dashed into it. His jokes are a preamble to murder."

Ironically, Orton himself was brutally murdered at the pinnacle of his career: he was thirty-four. As a result of his newly acquired success, Orton had been growing apart from Kenneth Halliwell, also a writer, with whom he had lived for fifteen years. Desperate, Halliwell killed Orton with a hammer, just as the character Pringle had put an end to his wife in Orton's own *Funeral Games,* noted Lahr. Then Halliwell took his own life with an overdose of nembutals. Lahr wrote: "Their deaths confirmed the vision of Orton's comedy, that reality is the ultimate outrage. Their epitaph was Orton's plays: a heritage of laughter created out of a lifetime's hunger for revenge.''

BIOGRAPHICAL/CRITICAL SOURCES: Time, September 15, 1967; *Nation,* November 17, 1969, August 6, 1977; *London Sunday Times,* November 22, 1970; John Russell Taylor, *The Second Wave,* Hill & Wang, 1971; F. Joseph, editor, *Behind the Scenes,* Holt, 1971; Katharine J. Worth, *Revolutions in Modern English Drama,* Bell, 1972; *Modern Drama,* February, 1972; John Lahr, *Astonish Me,* Viking, 1973; *Contemporary Literary Criticism,* Volume 4, Gale, 1975; Lahr, *Prick Up Your Ears: The Biography of Joe Orton,* Knopf, 1978; *New York Times,* March 9, 1979; *New Boston Review,* April/May, 1979.*

*   *   *

OSGOOD, Lawrence 1929-

PERSONAL: Born January 24, 1929, in Buffalo, N.Y. *Education:* Harvard University, B.A. (cum laude), 1950; University of Michigan, M.A., 1952. *Agent:* Samuel French, Inc., 25 West 45th St., New York, N.Y. 10036. *Office:* Department of Dramatic Arts, University of Connecticut, Storrs, Conn. 06268.

CAREER: Poets' Theatre, Cambridge, Mass., founding member, 1950, director of experimental productions, 1956; Haithcock School, Greenwich, Conn., head of English department, 1958-59; Bard College, Annandale-on-Hudson, N.Y., librarian, 1959-60; McGraw-Hill Book Co., New York City, editor, 1960-63; Actors Studio, New York City, member of Playwrights Unit, 1960-66, member of Playwrights Committee, 1962-64; Richard Barr-Edward Albee Playwrights Unit, New York City, member, 1962-65; free-lance editor for New York publishers, 1964-71; Loft Theatre Workshop, New York City, member, 1971; Teenage Theatre Workshop, New York City, director, 1971; director of plays at a theatre in Storrs, Conn., including ''Krapp's Last Tape,'' ''Les Batisseurs d'Empire,'' and ''The Double Dealer,'' 1971-72; University of Connecticut, Storrs, assistant professor of dramatic arts, 1971—.

WRITINGS—All plays, unless otherwise indicated: ''The Ox on the Roof,'' first produced in Annandale-on-Hudson, N.Y., 1960, also produced on Broadway; *Pigeons* (first produced in 1963; also produced on Broadway), published in *New American Plays,* edited by Robert W. Corrigan, Hill & Wang, 1965; *The Rook* (first produced in 1964; also produced on Broadway), published in *New Theatre in America,* edited by Edward Parone, Dell, 1965; ''Soap,'' first produced in Stockbridge, Mass., 1970, produced on Broadway, 1971; (contributor) *How I Write,* Harcourt, 1972. Also writer of screenplays for ''Love of Life'' television series, 1966.

*   *   *

OSIS, Karlis 1917-

PERSONAL: Born December 26, 1917, in Riga, Latvia; came to the United States in 1950, naturalized citizen, 1959; son of August and Olga (Linde) Osis; married Klara Zale (a poet), 1951; children: Gunta Alexander, Ulvids, Saija. *Education:* University of Munich, Ph.D., 1951. *Home:* 10 Douglas Rd., Glen Ridge, N.J. 07028. *Office:* American Society for Psychical Research, Chester F. Carlson Research Laboratory, 5 West 73rd St., New York, N.Y. 10023.

CAREER: Duke University, Durham, N.C., research associate in parapsychology, 1951-57; Parapsychology Foundation, New York City, director of research, 1957-62; American Society for Psychical Research, New York City, director of research, 1962—. *Member:* American Psychological Association, Parapsychological Association (past president), Society for the Scientific Study of Religion, American Association for the Advancement of Science.

WRITINGS: Deathbed Observations by Physicians and Nurses, Parapsychology Foundation, 1961; (with Erlendur Haraldsson) *At the Hour of Death,* Avon, 1977. Contributor to psychic research journals.

WORK IN PROGRESS: Laboratory research and ''real-life'' studies of out-of-body experiences in the United States and India; studies in creativity and extra-sensory perception in artists.

*   *   *

OWEN, Frank 1907(?)-1979

OBITUARY NOTICE: Broadcaster and writer. Owen was editor of two newspapers and a member of the British Parliament. His writings include *Peron: His Rise and Fall* and *The Fall of Singapore.* Obituaries and other sources: *AB Bookman's Weekly,* April 16, 1979.

*   *   *

OZAWA, Terutomo 1935-

PERSONAL: Born January 17, 1935, in Yokohama, Japan; came to the United States in 1959, naturalized citizen, 1972; son of Hanjiro and Tsuru Ozawa; married Hiroko Aoyama, November 4, 1967; children: Edwin T., Clare R. *Education:* Tokyo University of Foreign Studies, B.A., 1958; Columbia University, M.B.A., 1962, Ph.D., 1966. *Home:* 648 Heather Court, Fort Collins, Colo. 80521. *Office:* Department of Economics, Colorado State University, Fort Collins, Colo. 80523.

CAREER: University of Northern Colorado, Greeley, assistant professor of economics, 1966-68; Colorado State University, Fort Collins, assistant professor, 1968-70, associate professor, 1970-74, professor of economics, 1974—. Visiting research associate at Center for Policy Alternatives, of Massachusetts Institute of Technology, 1975-76; consultant to World Bank. *Member:* American Economic Association.

WRITINGS: Transfer of Technology From Japan to Developing Countries, United Nations Institute for Training and Research, 1971; *Japan's Technological Challenge to the West, 1950-1974: Motivation and Accomplishment,* M.I.T. Press, 1974; *Multinationalism, Japanese Style: The Political Economy of Outward Dependency,* Princeton University Press, 1979. Contributor to economic, business, and international studies journals.

WORK IN PROGRESS: U.S.-Japan Trade Relations, publication expected in 1980.

SIDELIGHTS: Ozawa commented: ''Economic events affect our everyday life; yet economics is considered to be a very difficult subject for the average person to comprehend—in fact, it is still known to be 'a dismal science.' In writing books, I strive to erase this stigma.''

P

PALMER, Arnold (Daniel) 1929-

PERSONAL: Born September 10, 1929, in Latrobe, Pa.; son of Milfred Jerome (a golf teacher and greenskeeper) and Doris (Morrison) Palmer; married Winifred Walzer, December 20, 1954; children: Margaret Ann (Mrs. Douglas Reintgen), Amy (Mrs. Robert L. Saunders). *Education:* Attended Wake Forest University, 1947-50, 1953. *Politics:* Republican. *Religion:* Presbyterian. *Home and office address:* Box 52, Youngstown, Pa. 15696. *Agent:* International Literary Management, Inc., 767 Fifth Ave., New York, N.Y. 10022.

CAREER: Professional golfer. Arnold Palmer Enterprises, Youngstown, Pa., president, 1960—; Arnold Palmer Cadillac, Charlotte, N.C., president, 1974—. President and owner of Latrobe Country Club, Latrobe, Pa.; president and part-owner of Bay Hill Club and Lodge, Orlando, Fla. Member of board of directors of Pro Group, Inc., Chattanooga, Tenn., and of Latrobe Area Hospital, Latrobe, Pa. Business associate of Ironwood Country Club, Palm Desert, Calif. Member of Westmoreland Airport Authority, Westmoreland, Pa. Honorary national chairman and member of the board of trustees of the March of Dimes, National Foundation. *Military service:* U.S. Coast Guard, 1950-53.

MEMBER: Professional Golfers Association of America, Laurel Valley Golf Club (Ligonier, Pa.), Rolling Rock Club (Ligonier), Duquesne Club (Pittsburgh, Pa.), Oakmont Country Club (Oakmont, Pa.), Quail Hollow Country Club (Charlotte, N.C.), Cherry Hills Country Club (Denver, Colo.), Lakeside Country Club (Hollywood, Calif.), Wilshire Country Club (Los Angeles, Calif.), Indian Wells Country Club (Palm Desert, Calif.). *Awards, honors:* LL.D., Wake Forest University, 1970; honorary doctor of humanities, Thiel College. Golf awards include: PGA Player of the Year, Professional Golfers Association of America, 1960, 1962; charter inductee, World Golf Hall of Fame (Pinehurst, N.C.); inductee, American Golf Hall of Fame (Foxburg, Pa.); Bob Jones Award, U.S. Golf Association; William D. Richardson and Charles Bartlett Awards, Golf Writers Association of America; Gold Tee Award, Metropolitan Golf Writers Association (New York); Man of Silver Era, *Golf Digest;* Vardon Trophy winner, 1961, 1962, 1964, 1967; U.S. Ryder Cup team member, 1961, 1963, 1965, 1967, 1971, 1973, captain, 1963, 1975. Sports awards include: Associated Press Athlete of the Decade, 1960-69; Hickok Athlete of the Year, 1960; Sportsman of the Year, *Sports Illustrated,* 1960.

WRITINGS: Arnold Palmer's Golf Book: Hit It Hard!, Ronald, 1961; *Portrait of a Professional Golfer,* Golf Digest, 1964; *My Game and Yours,* Simon & Schuster, 1965; *Situation Golf,* illustrated by Jesus J. Gutierrez, McCall Publishing Co., 1970; (with William Barry Furlong) *Go for Broke,* Simon & Schuster, 1973; (with Bob Drum) *Arnold Palmer's Best 54 Golf Holes,* Doubleday, 1977.

WORK IN PROGRESS: Book to be developed from series of instructional articles published in *Golf.*

SIDELIGHTS: A golfer since the age of three, Arnold Palmer learned almost everything he knows about the sport from his father, who was a greenskeeper and teaching professional at the Latrobe Country Club. During high school he was first player on the golf team for four years and lost only one match. During these years he also won the Western Pennsylvania Junior three times and the Western Pennsylvania Amateur five times.

Palmer's golfing talent enabled him to get a golf scholarship at Wake Forest University. Although he majored in business administration, Palmer spent most of his energy on golf, winning many tournaments, including the Southern Intercollegiate. During his senior year his roommate, Bud Worsham, brother of golfer Lew Worsham, was killed in an automobile accident. Palmer became restless and quit school to join the U.S. Coast Guard. Although he later returned to Wake Forest, he never obtained his degree.

Upon his return to civilian life, Palmer continued to golf and won the U.S. Amateur championship. His dream was to win the four major amateur golf tournaments in one year, but it was financially impossible to support himself while putting in the necessary practice time to meet his goal. Instead Palmer turned professional by signing with Wilson Sporting Goods Co. in 1954.

In the following years Arnold Palmer was the winner of numerous national and international tournaments, including the Masters title in 1958, 1960, 1962, and 1964, the U.S. Open championship in 1960, the British Open championship in 1961 and 1962, the Tournament of Champions in 1966, and the Bob Hope Classic in 1971 and 1973. In 1963 he became the first man ever to win more than $100,000 in official money in one year, and has earned the record of being one of golf's leading money winners.

Each of Palmer's books deals with some aspect of golf. *My Game and Yours* was praised by Rex Lardner as "the best-natured of all golf-instruction books . . . [which] should do readers a lot of good." His next book, *Situation Golf,* which describes golf strategy, contains "much good reading but not much help in striking the ball better," according to *Choice.* *Arnold Palmer's Best 54 Golf Holes* includes a physical description of each hole, directions on how to best play it, and reminiscences of events that occurred there.

Palmer told *CA* that while some people have learned to golf using golf instruction books, "the best way to learn is a combination of personal instruction by a teaching professional and reading of qualified written instruction." He also noted: "I receive a constant flow of advice through the mail from many well-meaning fans and have throughout my career. Much of the advice has been sound, too."

Arnold Palmer is fully certified as a business jet pilot and travels in a Cessna Citation, which he owns.

BIOGRAPHICAL/CRITICAL SOURCES: New York Times Book Review, April 11, 1965, May 1, 1977; *Sports Illustrated,* June 27, 1966, April 4, 1966, December 19, 1966, March 6, 1967, October 30, 1967, October 14, 1968, August 3, 1970, June 11, 1973, February 18, 1974, June 20, 1977, June 19, 1978; M. H. McCormack, *Arnie,* Simon & Schuster, 1967; *Choice,* October, 1970; *Time,* March 1, 1971; *Newsweek,* August 9, 1971; F. Bisher, *The Birth of a Legend: Arnold Palmer's Golden Year,* Prentice-Hall, 1972.

* * *

PANZARELLA, Joseph John, Jr. 1919-

PERSONAL: Born February 21, 1919, in Brooklyn, N.Y.; son of Joseph John (a barber) and Mamie (Lambrosa) Panzarella; married Josephine Seminar, June 17, 1945; children: Jeanine (Mrs. Joseph Sanfilippo), Joseph John III, Jacqueline (Mrs. Richard Safrath), Jennifer (Mrs. Joseph Vilacci), Judy Ann, James, Jeffrey (deceased). *Education:* St. Francis College, Brooklyn, N.Y., B.A. (cum laude), 1942; Long Island College of Medicine, M.D., 1945. *Religion:* Roman Catholic. *Residence:* Setauket, N.Y. *Office:* 366 Broadway, Amityville, N.Y. 11701.

CAREER: St. Mary's Hospital, Brooklyn, N.Y., intern, 1945-46; Mary Immaculate Hospital, Jamaica, N.Y., resident in anesthesiology, 1946-48, assistant attending anesthesiologist, 1948-54; New York University, New York, N.Y., fellow at Institute of Physical Medicine and Rehabilitation, 1955-57, assistant attending physician at University Hospital, 1957-72, associate attending physician, 1972-73, associate attending physician in out-patient department of Institute of Physical Medicine and Rehabilitation, 1957-73, instructor at Bellevue Medical School, 1957-62, assistant clinical professor at Postgraduate Medical School, 1962—. Certified by American Board of Physical Medicine and Rehabilitation, 1960, and American Academy of Physical Medicine and Rehabilitation, 1961. Associate attending director of department of physical medicine and rehabilitation at Beth Israel Hospital, 1957-65, Jamaica Hospital, 1960-70, and Mercy Hospital, Rockville Center, N.Y., 1963-65; attending director of physical medicine and rehabilitation at Mary Immaculate Hospital, 1957-68; attending physician at St. Mary's Hospital, 1960-64; director of Brunswick Hospital Center, Rehabilitation Hospital, Amityville, N.Y., 1968—; director of physical medicine and rehabilitation at Franklin General Hospital, 1964—, and rehabilitation at Ozanam Hall of Residence, 1972—. Professor at Nassau Community College and Suffolk Community College, both

1970—. Member of Nassau and Suffolk Stroke Coordinating Council. Guest on about twenty television and radio programs, including "Today Show" and news broadcasts. Consultant to Continental Insurance Co. *Military service:* U.S. Army, 1943-45.

MEMBER: International Society for the Rehabilitation of the Disabled, Pan American Medical Association, American Medical Association, American Congress of Physical Medicine and Rehabilitation, American Academy of Compensation Medicine (member of board of directors, 1977), National Rehabilitation Association, American Society of Law and Medicine, American Academy of Physical Medicine and Rehabilitation, Association of Medical Rehabilitation Directors and Coordinators (honorary life member), Disabled American Veterans (life member), National Paraplegic Foundation (branch organizer, 1959; vice-president, 1959-60), Insurance Rehabilitation Study Group (charter member; group head, 1966), New York State Medical Society, Queens County Medical Society, Suffolk County Medical Society, Alpha Omega Alpha. *Awards, honors:* Outstanding disabled veteran award from State of New York, 1966; presidential citations, 1967 and 1973, for employment of the handicapped; Frank L. Babbott Memorial Award from State University of New York Downstate Medical Center, 1975; physicians' award from U.S. President Gerald Ford, 1975; named handicapped American of the year by President's Committee on Employment of the Handicapped, 1977; D.Sc. from St. Francis College, Brooklyn, N.Y., 1977, and St. John's University, Staten Island Campus, 1978; plaque from Long Island Rehabilitation Association, 1977; Human Dignity Award from Kessler Rehabilitation Institute, 1979.

WRITINGS: Spirit Makes a Man, Doubleday, 1978. Contributor to medical journals.

SIDELIGHTS: Panzarella writes: "My main interests are medicine, and the care of the disabled, including the elimination of architectual barriers, the maintenance of the dignity of the disabled, the establishment of suitable living quarters, and the elimination of fear and intolerance of society towards the disabled."

* * *

PARENTEAU, Shirley Laurolyn 1935-

PERSONAL: Surname is pronounced Pur-*ahn*-toe; born January 22, 1935, in Garibaldi, Ore.; daughter of Howard Paul (a logger) and Olive (a writer and doll maker; maiden name, Stanbrough) Brunson; married George Parenteau (a sheet metal foreman), October 9, 1954; children: David, Scott, Cherie. *Education:* Attended high school in Taft, Ore. *Religion:* United Church of Christ. *Home:* 9815 Emerald Park Dr., Elk Grove, Calif. 95624. *Office:* P.O. Box 336, Elk Grove, Calif. 95624.

CAREER: Allstate Insurance Co., Salem, Ore., insurance rater, 1955-56; Fairview (home for the mentally retarded), Salem, Ore., dictaphone transcriber, 1959-60; writer, 1961—. *Member:* Society of Children's Book Writers, California Writers Club, Democratic Women's Club.

WRITINGS—All juveniles: Blue Hands, Blue Cloth, Childrens Press, 1978; *Crunch It, Munch It, and Other Ways to Eat Vegetables,* Coward, 1978; *Secrets of Scarlet,* Childrens Press, 1979; (with Barbara Douglass) *A Space Age Cookbook for Kids,* Prentice-Hall, 1979; *Jelly and the Spaceboat,* Coward, in press. Author of "Outdoor Wife," a column in *Elk Grove Citizen,* 1972—. Contributor to boating and other outdoor magazines and regional periodicals, including *Sacramento, Boating,* and *Field and Stream,* and newspapers.

WORK IN PROGRESS: Holly and the Star Gang, a juvenile science fiction novel; *The Talking Coffins of Cryo-City* (tentative title), a novel for teenagers on cryonics; research for an adult book on the Oriental hobby of *suiseki,* or collection and display of natural rocks which resemble mountains, figures, and other sculptures by nature.

SIDELIGHTS: Shirley Parenteau comments: "Our family has camped across the United States in tent and travel trailer and camped the length of the Alcan Highway. With our small cruiser we've camped on Kootenaye Lake in British Columbia, the Canadian Gulf Islands, and the Sacramento Delta, among other waters. Most of my interest and writing has revolved around the outdoors. Three years ago, I became interested in writing for children and now devote most writing time to that.

"I believe in humor, optimism, and enjoyment of nature. Through our years of outdoor recreation, my family has become close to nature and through my column and other writings, I try to remind readers of the beauty, fun, and sense of renewal to be found in the outdoors.

"In writing books for children, I hope to share with readers my own love for books and adventure, and to keep them turning pages by offering humor and suspense. *Blue Hands, Blue Cloth* and *Secrets of Scarlet* are the first two books in a series on the history of natural color from plants, insects, and snails. Both are fiction based on fact. *Crunch It, Munch It* gives anecdotes in the history of nineteen vegetables as well as nutritional information and easy recipes. *Jelly and the Spaceboat* is a science-fiction novel for 8-12 year-olds, set in the Sacramento Delta with the theme that it's not where you're from, but who you are that matters.

"Science-fiction is a long-time love of mine and I'm particularly enjoying writing it for children. I believe it is a vehicle in which one can deliver solid information and a viewpoint on life while entertaining the reader.

"Barbara Douglass and I had a lot of fun writing *A Space Age Cookbook for Kids.* We added space stories, space jokes, space riddles and space fact to recipes revised for children and given space names.

"Part of the pleasure in writing is in research. You never know what field you'll explore next. I have almost as much fun learning about a subject such as cryonics for *The Talking Coffins of Cryo-City,* as in working it into a story."

*   *   *

PARKER, Joan H.   1932-

PERSONAL: Born October 16, 1932, in Pittsfield, Mass,; daughter of David Clark (a telephone company executive) and Emma (Klink) Hall; married Robert Parker (a novelist), August 16, 1956; children: David, Daniel. *Home:* 636 Man, Lynnfield, Mass. 01940. *Agent:* John Hawkins. *Office:* State Department of Education, 1551 Osgood St., North Andover, Mass.

CAREER: Has worked as instructor at Salem College, Salem, Mass., as supervisor of student teaching at Tufts University, Medford, Mass., and as assistant professor at Endicott College, Beverly, Mass.; State Department of Education, North Andover, Mass., staff development specialist, 1976—. Member of Lynnfield Conservation Commission.

WRITINGS: (With husband, Robert Parker) *Three Weeks in Spring,* Houghton, 1978.

WORK IN PROGRESS: A book on running and jogging; a book on cooking.

PARRA, Nicanor   1914-

PERSONAL: Born September 5, 1914, in Chillan, Chile; son of Nicanor P. (a teacher) and Clara S. (Navarette) Parra; married Ana Troncoso, 1948 (marriage ended); married Inga Palmen; children: seven. *Education:* Attended University of Chile, Brown University, and Oxford University. *Address:* c/o Julia Bernstein, Parcela 272, Lareina, Santiago, Chile. *Office:* Instituto Pedagogico, Avenida Macul 774, Santiago, Chile.

CAREER: Poet and scientist. University of Chile, Santiago, professor of theoretical physics, 1947—. Visiting professor at Louisiana State University, 1966-67; has given poetry readings in many countries, including the United States, Russia, Venezuela, Cuba, Peru, and Argentina. *Awards, honors:* Premio municipal de poesia, 1937, for *Cancionero sin nombre,* and 1954, for *Poemas y antipoemas;* premio nacional de literatura, 1969, for *Obra gruesa.*

WRITINGS—In English translation: *Poemas y antipoemas,* Nascimento, 1954, translation of selected poems by Jorge Elliot published as *Anti-poems,* City Lights, 1960, 3rd Spanish edition, Nascimento, 1972; *Poems and Antipoems* (bilingual selection of poems from other works), edited by Miller Williams, New Directions, 1967; *Obra gruesa,* Editorial Universitaria, 1969, translation by Miller Williams of selected poems published as *Emergency Poems,* New Directions, 1972.

Other writings: *La cueca larga,* Editorial Universitaria, 1958, 2nd edition, 1966; *Versos de salon,* Nascimento, 1962; (with Pablo Neruda) *Discursos,* Nascimento, 1962; *La cueca larga y otros poemas,* edited by Margarita Aguirre, Editorial Universitaria de Buenos Aires, 1964; (editor) *Poesia sovietica rusa,* Editorial Progreso, 1965; *Canciones rusa,* Editorial Universitaria, 1967; *Poemas,* Casa de las Americas, 1969; *Poesia rusa contemporanea,* Ediciones Nueva Universidad, Universidad Catolica de Chile, 1971; *Los profesores,* Antiediciones Villa Miseria, 1971; *Antipoemas: Antologia (1944-1969),* Seix Barral, 1972; *Artefactos/Nicanor Parra,* Ediciones Nueva Universidad, Universidad Catolica de Chile, 1972, enlarged edition, 1972.

Also author of *Cancionero sin nombre,* 1937, *La evolucion del concepto de masa,* 1958; *Deux poemas,* 1964, *De varios libros,* 1965, *Tres poemas,* 1965, *Defensa de Violeta Parra,* 1967, (translator from the English) R. D. Lindsay and Henry Margenau, *Fundamentos de la fisica* (title means "Foundations of Physics"), 1967, and *Muyeres,* 1969. Author of *Ejercicios respiratorios.*

SIDELIGHTS: "Parra," declared Alexander Coleman, "is an antipoet. Antipoets . . . dread the very idea of Poetry and its attendant metaphors, inflated diction, romantic yearning, obscurity and empty nobility." His antipoems, Miller Williams noted, seek to "break the mold" of a poetry grown stale and academic. "I always associated Poetry with the voice of a priest in the pulpit," Parra remarked. And though poets may sing, he reflected, man talks. "Let the birds do the singing." Accordingly, his poetry is rooted in daily life and ordinary speech; he attempts to focus again, as with the eye of a camera, "on the flesh and blood man in all his dimensions, positive as well as negative." As Coleman related, Parra intends to "take poetry back out into the streets and crack our heads with it. The weapons? Irony, burlesque, an astringent barrage of cliches and found phrases, all juxtaposed in a welter of dictions that come out in a wholly original way, laying open everybody's despair."

"[Parra's] vision of reality," wrote Hernan Vidal, "is that of the lower sectors of the bourgeoisie. . . . [His] world is an 'enormous sewer' of shabby *pensiones,* dirty soda fountains, rundown offices, trashy cemeteries." Its inhabitants, he reported, are frustrated teachers, bored office clerks, hysterical old ladies, gangsters, oversexed women, and "boxers fighting by moonlight." But though images of despair and death have their place in his poetry, Parra claims that his verses "aim at the negation which is necessarily implied in every emotional, categorical affirmation. They amount to a joyous acceptance of life and a humorous condemnation of death." Donald Schier added: "Most of what Parra says does not seem very upsetting. . . . He returns several times to cemeteries and thoughts of death, but always, of course, avoids the temptation to be serious, let alone elevated or sublime."

Humor, as Vidal observed, is both an effect of Parra's language and a hopeful response to life. Writing poems that are very narrative, casual and conversational in style, Parra makes his antipoems from the language of an impoverished world; he uses cliches, graffiti, news clippings, slogans, advertisements, songs, and pseudo-letters to reflect the world he sees. "This world," Vidal commented, "has no language to express itself except the mechanical, worn-out, stale cliche. In Parra's hands the cliche becomes both the means to portray the gray mediocrity that permeates everything, and, through humor, a tool of resistance. Humor undermines the tragedy of a senseless existence by presenting it as a joke in bad taste. It also gives Nicanor Parra's poetry its original flavor and stature."

Several critics have offered their overall impression of Parra's work. In his review of *Poems and Antipoems,* Mark Strand commented: "Parra's poems are hallucinatory and violent, and at the same time factual. The well-timed disclosure of events—personal or political—gives his poems a cumulative, mounting energy and power that we have come to expect from only the best fiction. . . . It is the difference between Parra's antipoems and anybody else's that is significant. He sounds like nobody else and yet he sounds contemporary." Hayden Carruth added: "Free, witty, satirical, intelligent, often unexpected (without quite being surrealistic), mordant and comic by turns, always rebellious, always irreverent—it is all these and an ingratiating poetry too." Concluding his discussion of *Emergency Poems,* Coleman remarked: "It is an extraordinary experience reading these pieces, and I can't imagine anyone even vaguely interested in new poetry that won't devour [these poems]. . . . Nicanor Parra is a poet (or an antipoet or whatever) of total command and total grandeur."

BIOGRAPHICAL/CRITICAL SOURCES: Arizona Quarterly, summer, 1967; *New York Times Book Review,* December 10, 1967, May 7, 1972; *Carleton Miscellany,* spring, 1968; *Books Abroad,* summer, 1968; *Poetry,* September, 1968; *Hudson Review,* autumn, 1968, winter, 1972-73; *New Statesman,* November 8, 1968; *Nation,* August 7, 1972; *National Observer,* March 24, 1973; *Partisan Review,* summer, 1974; *Contemporary Literary Criticism,* Volume 2, Gale, 1974.*

*   *   *

PARSONS, Talcott   1902-1979

OBITUARY NOTICE—See index for *CA* sketch: Born December 13, 1902, in Colorado Springs, Colo.; died May 8, 1979, in Munich, West Germany. Sociologist and author. Internationally renowned for his analyses of social systems, Parsons believed that all societies, both primitive and advanced, "have a common pulse and a stable and enduring structure." The social theorist began teaching at Harvard in

1927 and spent the rest of his career there, becoming professor emeritus in 1973. A prolific writer, Parsons's books include *The Social System, The Economy and Society,* and *Toward a General Theory of Social Action.* He died while on a European speaking tour. Obituaries and other sources: *Current Biography,* Wilson, 1961; *The Author's and Writer's Who's Who,* 6th edition, Burke's Peerage, 1971; *American Men and Women of Science: The Social and Behavioral Sciences,* 12th edition, Bowker, 1973; *International Who's Who,* Europa, 1978; *Who's Who in America,* 40th edition, Marquis, 1978; *Washington Post,* May 12, 1979; *Newsweek,* May 21, 1979.

*   *   *

PARTNER, Peter (David)   1924-

PERSONAL: Born July 15, 1924, in Little Heath, Hertfordshire, England; son of David and Bertha E. (Partridge) Partner; married Leila M. Fadil (a teacher), October 24, 1953; children: David Michael, Simon Christopher, Sumaya Mary. *Education:* Magdalen College, Oxford, B.A., 1950, earned M.A. degree, D.Phil., 1956. *Home:* 9-A Kingsgate St., Winchester S023 9PD, England. *Agent:* Brandt & Brandt, 101 Park Ave., N.Y. 10017; and A. M. Heath, 4042 William IV St., London WC2N 4DD, England.

CAREER: Winchester College, Winchester, England, assistant master of history, 1955—. Member of Princeton Institute for Advanced Study, 1976-77. *Military service:* Royal Naval Volunteer Reserve, 1942-46; became lieutenant. *Member:* Society for Italian Studies, Athenaeum Club.

WRITINGS: The Papal State under Martin V, British School at Rome, 1958; *A Short Political Guide to the Arab World,* Praeger, 1960; *The Lands of St. Peter: The Papal State in the Middle Ages and the Early Renaissance,* University of California Press, 1972; *Renaissance Rome, 1500-1559: A Portrait of a Society,* University of California Press, 1976. Italian correspondent for *Observer,* 1953-55. Contributor to history journals, popular magazines in the United States and England, including *Spectator, Harper's,* and *Twentieth Century,* and to newspapers.

WORK IN PROGRESS: The Templars and Their Myth: Magical Politics and the Making of a Magical Identity, publication by Oxford University Press expected in 1980.

SIDELIGHTS: Partner told *CA:* "My main academic interests are in medieval and Renaissance European history, with a special interest in the history of Italy and the Papacy. My current interests are in the history of magic and its influence on literary taste. I have a long-standing interest in the modern Middle East, including North Africa. I have also written quite widely on educational policy in Britain, especially on private secondary schools."

Partner further commented that while researching *The Templars and Their Myth* he "became much impressed by the long history of the modern myth of the Knights Templar, which began with Masonic and neo-chivalric revival ideas in the eighteenth century, and continued as an Illuminist and Romantic theme into the nineteenth and even the twentieth centuries. The transmission of symbolic myths through history is something I have studied in art history in the work of Wittkower, Wind, Panofsky, Seznec, and others. My book on the Knights Templar has thus ceased to deal only with the actual history and physical end of the real military order concerned, and has come to deal also with the transmutation of these events into a modern myth which forms part of the mythologizing and magical strands in the Romantic and Symbolist views of life. Modern anthropological theory, such as that represented in the United States by Clifford Geertz, has helped me to bridge the gap between the strict historical empiricism in which I was trained, and the broader aesthetic interpretations of life which are so important, in my view, to our contemporary culture."

*   *   *

PARTRIDGE, Eric (Honeywood) 1894-1979

OBITUARY NOTICE—See index for *CA* sketch: Born February 6, 1894, in Poverty Bay, New Zealand; died in 1979 in Devon, England. Lexicographer. Partridge abandoned teaching and novel writing to devote his life to the study of words. He concentrated much of his attention on the speech of common people, and published his findings in such books as *A Dictionary of Cliches* and *A Dictionary of Slang and Unconventional English*. As an advocate of plain and popular language use, Partridge believed language "was created by people, not in a laboratory." Characterized by a scholar's insight and an entertaining style, his other writings include *English: A Course for Human Beings* and *Usage and Abusage: A Guide to Good English*. Obituaries and other sources: *Current Biography*, Wilson, 1963; *The New Century Handbook of English Literature*, revised edition, Appleton, 1967; *Longman Companion to Twentieth Century Literature*, Longman, 1970; *The International Who's Who*, Europa, 1978; *Who's Who in the World*, 4th edition, Marquis, 1978; *Who's Who*, 131st edition, St. Martin's, 1979; *Time*, June 11, 1979.

*   *   *

PASSES(-PAZOLSKI), Alan 1943-

PERSONAL: Born January 12, 1943; son of Monty and Betty (Glicksman) Passes; married Esther Cukierman, 1965 (divorced, 1969); married Jane Darling, 1972; children: (first marriage) Emmanuelle; (second marriage) Daniel. *Education:* Attended schools in Switzerland and France. *Politics:* Radical. *Home:* 50 Hamilton Rd., London, England. *Agent:* (Drama) Harvey Unna, 14 Beaumont Mews, Marylebone High St., London W. 1, England; (literature) Murray Pollinger Ltd., 4 Garrick St., London W.C.2, England.

CAREER: Has worked as a technician in a film laboratory, as a translator and writer of film subtitles in Paris, France, for *Presence Africaine* (magazine), and as an assistant film director in Paris and London, England; free-lance writer, 1976—. *Member:* Association of Cinematograph and Television Technicians, Theatre Writers Union. *Awards, honors:* Arts Council of Great Britain bursaries, 1976, 1977.

WRITINGS: Big Step (novel), Allison & Busby, 1977.

Plays: "Effects" (three one-acts), first produced at Oval Theatre, 1970; "Sic," first produced in 1973; "Barricadoodah" (three-act fantasy), first produced in London, England, at Royal Court Theatre Upstairs, 1974; "The Holy Cost," first produced in 1974; "Gum and Nail," first produced in 1975; "A Load of Zlocki" (comedy), first produced in 1975; "And," first produced in London at Soho-Poly Theatre, 1976; "Mystic of the Western World" (one-act), first produced in London at Soho-Poly Theatre, 1976; "No Sheep on the Bush," first produced in London at Common Stock Theatre, 1976; "Death Raise," first produced in London at Soho-Poly Theatre, 1977; "Spellbound," first produced in London at Common Stock Theatre, 1977.

Author of feature films, including translation and adaptation of Jean Cocteau's play "Le Bel indifferent" for a film, 1975. Contributor of a story to *New Worlds*.

WORK IN PROGRESS: Bits, a novel; "Karel," a filmscript; two plays, "The Hunter-Gatherers" and "Gregor Samsa Is Alive But Not So Well and Living with Jemima Puddleduck."

SIDELIGHTS: Passes writes: "Being a product of French education but writing in English, with the additional inheritance of Jewish culture (though not in the purely religious sense), has given me a background comprising both emotional and intellectual conflict and synthesis which naturally extend into my work.

"The protagonist of my novel *Big Step* is an archangel who becomes a human being. A poor Jewish peddler, the hero of my play 'And' works through his own conditioned caricature of himself with an awareness of his true humanity. The hero of Kafka's 'Metamorphosis,' Gregor Samsa, instead of dying as a beetle (as in the story), self-resurrects in another play of mine back to manhood, through pain, experience, and intercourse (both social and sexual).

"This process toward 'full' humanity is of the utmost importance for me in all my writing. What I am searching for (and I am certainly not alone) is the clearer definition and expression of that part of man which is social and political; and that which is biological, physiological, and spiritual. My instinct, understanding, and hopefully, artistic impulse toward these parts which have been falsely and forcibly segregated, is to try to show how they fuse together. And belong together."

*   *   *

PATEMAN, Carole 1940-

PERSONAL: Born December 11, 1940, in Sussex, England; daughter of Ronald and Beatrice Kate (Horscroft) Bennett; married Roy Pateman, February 27, 1960. *Education:* Attended Ruskin College, Oxford, 1963-65; Lady Margaret Hall, Oxford, B.A., 1967, M.A., 1971, D.Phil., 1971. *Politics:* "Feminist." *Religion:* None. *Office:* Department of Government, University of Sydney, Sydney, New South Wales, Australia 2006.

CAREER: Clerical worker in England and Kenya, 1957-63; Oxford University, Somerville College, Oxford, England, Mary Ewart research fellow, 1970-72; University of Sydney, Sydney, Australia, lecturer, 1972-76, senior lecturer in government, 1976—. Visiting fellow at Australian National University, 1975. *Member:* Political Studies Association (United Kingdom), Australasian Political Studies Association.

WRITINGS: Participation and Democratic Theory, Cambridge University Press, 1970; *The Problem of Political Obligation,* Wiley, 1979. Contributor to political science journals.

WORK IN PROGRESS: Research on political theory and feminism and on problems in democratic theory.

SIDELIGHTS: Pateman writes: "If I had not had the good fortune to go to Ruskin College, Oxford, an adult education college, I would not have had an academic career. I am the only member of my family to have had a university education. More colleges like Ruskin are needed, especially for women."

*   *   *

PATRIS, Louis 1931-
(Louis Patsouras)

PERSONAL: Born May 5, 1931, in Steubenville, Ohio; son of William (a worker) and Helen (Stratoudakis) Patsouras;

married Sandra Lee Dickinson (a social worker), June 2, 1978; children: Patricia. *Education:* Kent State University, B.A., 1953, M.A., 1959; Ohio State University, Ph.D., 1966. *Politics:* Socialist. *Religion:* Humanist. *Home:* 494 Moore Rd., Akron, Ohio 44319. *Office:* Department of History, Kent State University—Stark Campus, 6000 Frank Ave. N.W., Canton, Ohio 44720.

CAREER: Kent State University—Stark Campus, Canton, Ohio, instructor, 1963-67, assistant professor, 1967-72, associate professor of history, 1972—. *Military service:* U.S. Army, 1954-56. *Member:* American Historical Association.

WRITINGS—All under name Louis Patsouras: (Editor with Jeffrey R. Orenstein) *The Politics of Community,* Kendall/Hunt, 1973; *Jean Grave and French Anarchism,* Kendall/Hunt, 1978; *Varieties and Problems of Twentieth-Century Socialism,* Nelson-Hall, 1979.

WORK IN PROGRESS: Leon Blum and French Socialism.

*   *   *

PATTERSON, Paul 1909-

PERSONAL: Born March 28, 1909, in West, Tex.; son of John D. (a fence builder) and Noda E. (Pollard) Patterson; married Marjorie V. Mixon (a teacher), December 1, 1939. *Education:* Sul Ross State University, B.A.; also attended University of Texas; studied in Mexico, Spain, and Switzerland. *Politics:* Liberal Democrat. *Religion:* Methodist. *Home address:* P.O. Box 993, Crane, Tex. 79731.

CAREER: Elementary school teacher in Marfa, Tex., 1935-37, and Sanderson, Tex., 1938-40; Crane High School, Crane, Tex., teacher of Spanish, journalism, history, sociology, and civics, c. 1950-77. Collected oral history of the Southwest for Texas Tech University, summers, 1964-74. Also worked on ranches and oil fields, as rodeo announcer and performer, and as announcer for KFJZ-Radio. *Military service:* U.S. Army Air Forces, cryptographer, 1942-45; served in Italy and Africa; became sergeant. *Member:* National Education Association (life member), Western Writers of America, Texas Folklore Society, Permian Basin Historical Society, Lions Club. *Awards, honors:* Plaque from National Cowboy Hall of Fame and Oklahoma Western Heritage Center, 1964.

WRITINGS: Sam McGoo and Texas Too, Mathis, Van Nort & Co., 1947; *Pecos Tales,* Encino Press, 1967; *Crazy Women in the Rafters,* University of Oklahoma Press, 1976. Author of "Ups and Downs of Crane Town" (play), first produced in Crane, Tex. Contributor to regional magazines and religious periodicals.

WORK IN PROGRESS: Sheepherder, a novel; *The Saga of a Slow Yet Steadfast Lover,* a novel; *Tour's a Crowd,* a novel; *Noah's Prairie Ark,* a juvenile; *A Picture of Life's Other Side,* an autobiography.

SIDELIGHTS: Patterson writes: "As a child our family moved thirty-six times in a covered wagon. I saw lots of hard times, suffered many set-backs and privations, but never realized it until it was too late. I learned that the greatest gift is the gift of forgiveness. As a consequence we all had more friends (real friends) than most people.

"I have traveled widely in Mexico and Europe. I have given more than two hundred talks in Texas, touching upon the Old West and the current scene, and made serious sermons at churches of various denominations, but all my speeches are in the lighter vein. I say this in modesty and humility (*Texas* humility): in March, 1943, I was nominated by *Reader's Digest* as one of the biggest liars in the Army, Navy, and Marines."

PATTERSON, Richard North 1947-

PERSONAL: Born February 22, 1947, in Berkeley, Calif., son of Richard W. (a business executive) and Marjorie Frances (North) Patterson; married Judith Anne Riggs (a teacher and editor), January 12, 1974; children: Shannon Heath, Brooke North. *Education:* Ohio Wesleyan University, B.A., 1968; Case Western Reserve University, J.D., 1971. *Politics:* Independent. *Religion:* None. *Home:* 4758 Tarton Dr., Santa Rosa, Calif. 95405. *Agent:* Hy Cohen Literary Agency, Ltd., 111 West 57th St., New York, N.Y. 10019. *Office:* U.S. Securities and Exchange Commission, 450 Golden Gate Ave., San Francisco, Calif. 94102.

CAREER: Admitted to Ohio State Bar, 1971, District of Columbia Bar, 1973, and Alabama State Bar, 1975; Office of the Attorney General, Columbus, Ohio, assistant attorney general, 1971-73; U.S. Securities and Exchange Commission, Washington, D.C., trial attorney, 1973-75; Berkowitz, Lefkovits & Patrick (law firm), Birmingham, Ala., partner in firm, 1975-78; U.S. Securities and Exchange Commission, San Francisco, Calif., attorney, 1978—. Writer. *Member:* Mystery Writers of America.

WRITINGS: The Lasko Tangent (novel), Norton, 1979. Contributor of short story to *Atlantic Monthly.*

WORK IN PROGRESS: A second novel, tentatively entitled *The Outside Man;* researching a third novel, tentatively entitled *Missing Person.*

SIDELIGHTS: Patterson explained to *CA* that "the circumstances of my first novel, *The Lasko Tangent,* were somewhat unusual." The events of his past certainly did not point to any interest in writing: he had been educated in history and in law, had worked as a trial lawyer, and had been forced by his career to largely abandon serious reading. It was not until he read several novels by Ross Macdonald, creator of the Lew Archer series, that he began "to realize that Macdonald had crystalized a vague impulse to write that I'd felt for several years. I admired his conciseness, his gift for mood and setting, his eye for detail. More than that, it seemed Macdonald had made the detective novel humane and compassionate, with the insight of psychology. Clearly, Macdonald cared about his characters and their situations, and that inspired me to try. So, I evolved a mystery plot which meant something to me in terms of my own experience, and began."

With the aid of a University of Alabama course in creative writing, within six months Patterson had completed the first draft for his novel. But, as he revealed, "the next six months were harder. With the advice of friends I revised *The Lasko Tangent* three times, tightening and complicating the plot to make it more effective. This effort—at times quite discouraging—concluded with astonishing good luck: the sale of my final version to W. W. Norton & Co. as an unsolicited submission, the first such sale at Norton in about five years.

"Since then, I've worked at learning the craft of writing. Of immense value was a year of study under Jesse Hill Ford, a truly great writer who was more generous with his time and talents than his students had any right to expect. Because of Ford's comprehensive understanding of the writer's work, I gained a much deeper appreciation of what writing is about, in the process doing the four drafts necessary to complete my first short story, "The Client," and sell it to *Atlantic Monthly.*

"My experience with my second novel has thus far been the same: eleven months and four drafts to evolve half a book that I can tolerate. In this third project my goals are different than in my first. I believe in taking risks, in trying to do more; that each day, one defines (or redefines) oneself. So I let my writing go where my interests take me, hoping that writing will in turn expand my interests and sympathies."

Patterson often regrets that he did not write sooner, but realizes that his career as a lawyer has given him interesting and valuable experience (including work with the Watergate Special Prosecutor in Washington, D.C.). He feels his involvement with complex securities cases has taught him patience. In addition, his work in law has given him the opportunity to live and work in all regions of the country and "has led to deeper involvement with lives other than my own."

"Of course," he adds, "there can never be enough. To paraphrase an old thought, when you consider writing, the writing considers you. The act of writing can make one intensely aware of his own shallowness, prejudice, insensitivity, or plain lack of knowledge. Almost always I feel woefully illprepared. But perhaps this enforced humility can lead the writer to a more sincere desire to learn and to a heightened understanding of others. And, certainly, writing forces one to confront people and ideas otherwise unknown."

Patterson insists he has "no real philosophy of writing," but does offer these opinions on the subject: "A writer should at least consider the moral issues presented by his times, and compassion alone does not make good writing—but writing without it will less surely succeed." And, as he told *Library Journal,* "Unavoidably, writers are preservers of language and grace of expression in an increasingly less literate society.... At its best, fiction can be as enlightening as psychology and anthropology because, in rendering the minds and passions of his characters, the writer illuminates the whole. In this sense, good writing is a weave of fabrications which are ultimately 'true.'"

One event that has had a "profound" effect on Patterson was the 1968 assassination of Robert Kennedy. "In all three of my projects," he reflected, "I find some glancing allusion to Kennedy or the event, which I suspect has some symbolic importance to me in terms of absurdity and loss. To some degree my work seems to reflect the individual's necessary effort to make sense of his situation in a world which is often absurd and hostile, and which may lack any ultimate meaning. Underlying this is the belief that each person must respect the individual freedom of action and speculation which belongs to every person. I believe one must question one's own motives—aware of our limitations of vision and insight—while respecting the possibilities for a different vision and insight in others.

"I should add that such themes are certainly not new, and their reflection in my own writing is imperfect. In all cases, the paramount goal of my work has been simply to entertain.... One of the best things about writing is that there's almost no experience that isn't useful, and I hope writing will eventually give me more time for new places and people, as well as to more deeply enjoy my family."

AVOCATIONAL INTERESTS: Tennis, racquetball, jogging, film, reading, theatre, ballet, "most music, particularly contemporary rock."

BIOGRAPHICAL/CRITICAL SOURCES: Birmingham Post Herald, May 9, 1978; *Library Journal,* February 1, 1979.

*   *   *

PATTERSON, Wayne 1946-

PERSONAL: Born December 20, 1946, in Philadelphia, Pa.; son of George M. (a roofing contractor) and Marjorie (an elementary school teacher; maiden name, Kief) Patterson; married Marlene Babal, August 13, 1977. *Education:* Swarthmore College, B.A., 1968; University of Pennsylvania, M.A. (international relations), 1969, M.A. (history), 1974, Ph.D., 1977. *Home:* 808 North Henry St., Green Bay, Wis. 54302. *Office:* Department of History, Saint Norbert College, De Pere, Wis. 54115.

CAREER: University of Maryland, College Park, lecturer in history and political science, 1974-75; Saint Norbert College, De Pere, Wis., assistant professor of history, 1977—. Lecturer at colleges, universities, and scholarly meetings. *Member:* International Studies Association, American Historical Association, Association for Asian Studies, Immigration History Society, Conference on Peace Research in History, Interchange for Pacific Scholarship, Society for Historians of American Foreign Relations, National Association for Interdisciplinary Ethnic Studies, Delta Tau Kappa.

WRITINGS: (Contributor) Thomas E. Hachey, editor, *The Problem of Partition: Peril to World Peace,* Rand McNally, 1972; (author of introduction) William Ballis, *The Legal Position of War,* Garland Publishing, 1973; (editor with Hyungchan Kim) *The Koreans in America, 1882-1974: A Chronology and Fact Book,* Oceana, 1974; (author of revision) Woodbridge Bingham, Hilary Conroy, and Frank W. Ikle, *A History of Asia,* Allyn & Bacon, 1974; (with Kim) *The Koreans in America,* Lerner, 1977; (contributor) Kim, editor, *The Korean Diaspora: Historical and Sociological Studies of Korean Immigration and Assimilation in North America,* ABC Clio Press, 1977; (contributor) Andrew C. Nahn, editor, *The United States and Korea,* Western Michigan University Press, 1979; (editor with Conroy and Sandra Davis, and contributor) *The Meiji Mind in Thought and Action,* University of Pennsylvania Press, 1980. Contributor of about fifteen articles and reviews to academic journals. Member of editorial board of Interchange for Pacific Scholarship.

WORK IN PROGRESS: A book on Korean immigration to Hawaii, 1896-1910; a book on Koreans in Hawaii; editing a bibliography, *The Koreans in North America,* for Balch Institute.

SIDELIGHTS: Patterson comments: "I did research on Korean immigration to the United States because there seemed to be plenty of material on Chinese and Japanese immigration, but none on Korean. I hope I have filled this void. I have done research all over the country, including two years in Hawaii, and have spent time in Taiwan, Japan, Korea, Hong Kong, Singapore, Nepal, Malaysia, Burma, the Philippines, Thailand, Laos, and Vietnam. I can speak or read Chinese, Japanese, Korean, Latin, and German."

*   *   *

PECHMAN, Joseph Aaron 1918-

PERSONAL: Surname is pronounced *Peck*-man; born April 2, 1918, in New York, N.Y.; son of Gershon and Lena Pechman; married Sylvia Massow, September 29, 1943; children: Ellen Massow, Jane Elizabeth. *Education:* City College (now of the City University of New York), B.S., 1937; University of Wisconsin (now University of Wisconsin—Madison), M.A., 1938, Ph.D., 1942. *Home:* 7112 Wilson Lane, Bethesda, Md. 20034. *Office:* Brookings Institution, 1775 Massachusetts Ave. N.W., Washington, D.C. 20006.

CAREER: National Research Project, Philadelphia, Pa.,

statistician, 1937; assistant director of state income tax study, Wisconsin Tax Commission, 1938-39; Office of Price Administration, Washington, D.C., economist, 1941-42; U.S. Department of the Treasury, Washington, D.C., assistant director of tax advisory staff, 1946-53; Massachusetts Institute of Technology, Cambridge, associate professor of finance, 1953-54; Council of Economic Advisers, Washington, D.C., economist, 1954-56; Committee for Economic Development, Washington, D.C., economist, 1956-60; Brookings Institution, Washington, D.C., executive director of studies of government finance, 1960-70, director of economic studies program, 1962—. Irving Fisher Research Professor at Yale University, 1956-66; fellow of Center for Advanced Study in the Behavioral Sciences, 1975-76. *Military service:* U.S. Army, meteorologist, 1942-45.

MEMBER: American Finance Association (president, 1971), American Economic Association (vice-president, 1978), National Tax Association, Phi Beta Kappa. *Awards, honors:* LL.D. from University of Wisconsin—Madison, 1978.

WRITINGS: (With Frank Allan Hanna) *Analysis of Wisconsin Income,* National Bureau of Economic Research, 1948; (with Herbert Stein) *Essays in Federal Taxation,* Committee for Economic Development, 1959.

Financing State and Local Government, Brookings Institution, 1965; *Individual Income Tax Provisions of the Revenue Act of 1964,* Brookings Institution, 1965; *A New Tax Model for Revenue Estimating* (pamphlet), Brookings Institution, 1965; *Federal Tax Policy,* Brookings Institution, 1966, 3rd edition, 1977; (with James Tobin) *Is a Negative Income Tax Practical?,* Brookings Institution, 1967; (with Walter W. Heller) *Questions and Answers on Revenue Sharing,* Brookings Institution, 1967; *Report of the Canadian Royal Commission on Taxation: A Summing Up* (pamphlet), Brookings Institution, 1967; (with Henry J. Aaron and Michael K. Taussig) *Social Security: Perspectives for Reform,* Brookings Institution, 1968; (with Aaron and Taussig) *The Objectives of Social Security* (pamphlet), Brookings Institution, 1968; *The Rich, the Poor, and the Taxes They Pay* (pamphlet), Brookings Institution, 1969.

Distribution of Federal and State Income Taxes by Income Classes, Brookings Institution, 1972; (with Benjamin A. Okner) *Individual Income Tax Erosion by Income Classes,* Brookings Institution, 1972; *International Trends in the Distribution of Tax Burdens: Implications for Tax Policy,* Institute for Fiscal Studies (London, England), 1973; (with Okner) *Who Bears the Tax Burden?,* Brookings Institution, 1974, reprinted as *How Fair Is the American Tax System?,* 1975; (with George F. Break) *Federal Tax Reform: The Impossible Dream?,* Brookings Institution, 1975; (editor with Michael Timpane) *Work Incentives and Income Guarantees: The New Jersey Negative Income Tax Experiment,* Brookings Institution, 1975; *Federal Tax Reform for 1976,* Fund for Public Policy Research, 1976; (editor) *Comprehensive Income Taxation,* Brookings Institution, 1977; *Setting National Priorities: The 1978 Budget,* Brookings Institution, 1977. Contributor of articles and reviews to economic and finance journals. Member of board of editors of American Economic Association, 1960-63.

WORK IN PROGRESS: Studying distribution of tax burdens and federal budget policy.

*   *   *

PECHTER, Edward 1941-

PERSONAL: Born February 12, 1941, in New York, N.Y.; son of Israel (an attorney) and Mildred (a teacher; maiden name, Schneider) Pechter; married Lesley Wynne (an art consultant), May 19, 1971; children: David. *Education:* Cornell University, B.A., 1962; University of California, Berkeley, M.A., 1964, Ph.D., 1968. *Office:* Department of English, Concordia University, Montreal, Quebec, Canada H3G 1M8.

CAREER: Concordia University, Montreal, Quebec, assistant professor, 1968-73, associate professor of English, 1974—. *Member:* Association of Canadian University Teachers of English, Modern Language Association of America, Shakespeare Association of America.

WRITINGS: Dryden's Classical Theory of Literature, Cambridge University Press, 1975. Contributor to literature and history journals.

WORK IN PROGRESS: A book on Shakespeare, "about the way his plays engage their audience's expectations for dramatic closure."

*   *   *

PECK, Richard 1934-

PERSONAL: Born April 5, 1934, in Decatur, Ill.; son of Wayne M. (a merchant) and Virginia (Gray) Peck. *Education:* Attended University of Exeter, 1954-55; DePauw University, B.A., 1956; Southern Illinois University, M.A., 1959; further graduate study at Washington University, 1960-61. *Home:* 10 Mitchell Pl. #4A, New York, N.Y. 10017. *Agent:* Sheldon Fogelman, 10 East 40th St., New York, N.Y. 10016.

CAREER: Southern Illinois University, Carbondale, instructor in English, 1958-60; high school teacher of English in Northbrook, Ill., 1961-63; Scott, Foresman Co., Chicago, Ill., textbook editor, 1963-65; Hunter College and Hunter College High School, New York, N.Y., instructor in English and education, 1965-71; writer, 1971—. Assistant director of Council for Basic Education, Washington, D.C., 1969-70. *Military service:* U.S. Army, 1956-58; served in Stuttgart, Germany. *Member:* Author's Guild. *Awards, honors:* National Council for the Advancement of Education Writing Award, 1971; Friends of American Writers Award, 1976, for *The Ghost Belonged to Me;* Edgar Allen Poe Award from Mystery Writers of America for best juvenile mystery novel, 1976, for *Are You in the House Alone?;* named Illinois Writer of the Year, 1977, by Illinois Association of Teachers of English.

WRITINGS: (With Norman Strasma) *Old Town, A Complete Guide: Strolling, Shopping, Supping, Sipping,* 2nd edition, [Chicago], 1965; (editor with Ned E. Hoopes) *Edge of Awareness: 25 Contemporary Essays,* Dell, 1966; (editor) *Sounds and Silences: Poetry for Now,* Delacorte, 1970; (editor) *Mindscapes: Poems for the Real World,* Delacorte, 1971; (editor) *Leap Into Reality,* Dell, 1972; *Don't Look and It Won't Hurt,* (young adult), Holt, 1973; (with Stephen N. Judy) *The Creative Word,* Volume II (Peck was not associated with other volumes), Random House/Singer School Division, 1973; (compiler) *Transitions: A Literary Paper Casebook,* Random House, 1974; *Dreamland Lake* (young adult), Holt, 1974; *Through a Brief Darkness* (young adult), Viking, 1975; *Representing Super Doll* (young adult), Viking, 1975; *The Ghost Belonged to Me* (young adult), Viking, 1976; *Are You in the House Alone?* (young adult), Viking, 1976; (editor) *Pictures That Storm Inside My Head* (poems), Avon, 1976; *Monster Night at Grandma's House* (juvenile), illustrated by Don Freeman, Viking, 1977; *Ghosts I Have Been* (young adult), Viking, 1977; *Father Figure* (young adult), Viking, 1978; *Secrets of the Shopping Mall* (young adult), Delacorte, 1979; *Amanda/Miranda* (novel), Viking, 1980.

Author of column on the architecture of historic neighborhoods for *New York Times*. Contributor of poetry to several anthologies, *Saturday Review*, and *Chicago Tribune Magazine*. Contributor of articles to periodicals including *American Libraries*, *PTA Magazine*, and *Parents Magazine*.

SIDELIGHTS: Peck commented on his writing career: "I never was one of those young people determined to be a writer at all costs. I didn't write a 600-page autobiographical novel in the bowels of Greenwich Village at the age of twenty. If I had, I'd be in another line of work today. And, fortunately, I never had one of those creative writing teachers who say, 'Write what you know!' 'Write from your heart!' 'Express yourself!' "

"I didn't start writing seriously until I'd identified my potential readership. And for me they were the students I'd been teaching after my return to civilian life. Correction: they were the students who were willing and able to spend a part of their leisure time with books. As a teacher, I'd already learned that you can only teach those who are willing to be taught. I'd learned, too, that the best, most independent, most promising students were the thoughtful, quiet ones—students who will reach for a book in search of themselves—who often get overlooked in our crisis-oriented society and the schools that mirror it.

"One day, years later, I gave up teaching. I didn't want to, but it seemed to me that teaching had begun to turn into something that looked weirdly like psychiatric social work—a field in which I was not trained or interested. I turned in my pension and hospitalization plan and my attendance book—which was, come to think of it, the first work of fiction I ever wrote. I moved my typewriter out into the garden of the brick barn in Brooklyn where I live. And I began writing a novel to some of the young people I'd left behind in the classroom."

In his article "In the Country of Teenage Fiction," Peck explained the importance of good books for teenagers. "It seems to me," he said, "that trying to write a valid novel for a young reader—let's say a thirteen-year-old who is at a sensitive and troubled point in his life—is at least as important and far more challenging than writing a 'real, adult novel.'

"It's a harder job because of the pitfalls. No one who has passed through adolescence can re-enter it with a vision unblurred by personal nostalgia and the kind of publicity the current youth scene receives. It's a great temptation to preach, to patronize, to pander, to placate, and especially to propagandize."

Peck outlined some important elements of young adult fiction for an *English Journal* interviewer. First of all, he said, the "signal factor" of the genre is "unreality masked as realism. One way or another, the protagonist has to do something that the reader cannot do." Whether "deadly serious" or "melodramatically absurd," the protagonist should "act on behalf of the reader in a particularly direct way." For this reason, travel is an important event for Peck's characters. "We have to remember that our readers are institutionalized twice—in homes and in schools. They set store in great mobility." Finally, Peck claimed comedy is "a major lack in young adult fiction today. We have a great deal of diversity in subject matter and approach and style, but we don't have enough humor. We need more because the young don't generate it themselves."

BIOGRAPHICAL/CRITICAL SOURCES: American Libraries, April, 1973; *Psychology Today*, September, 1975; *English Journal*, February, 1976; *Times Literary Supplement*, March 25, 1977.

*   *   *

PELTA, Kathy 1928-

PERSONAL: Born October 18, 1928, in Madrid, Iowa; daughter of Edwin H. (an engineer) and Kathryn (Zenor) Birdsall; married Edmond Pelta (an engineer), February 22, 1957; children: Brian, Meg. *Education:* San Diego State College (now University), A.B., 1949; graduate study at University of California, Berkeley, 1949-51.

CAREER: U.S. Foreign Service, Bonn, Germany, staff member, 1951-54; Voice of America, Washington, D.C., secretary, 1954-55; RAND Corp., Santa Monica, Calif., technical writer, 1956-57; System Development Corp., Santa Monica, technical writer, 1957-60; free-lance writer, 1960—.

WRITINGS—For children: *What Does a Lifeguard Do?*, Dodd, 1977; *What Does a Paramedic Do?*, Dodd, 1978. Also editor and illustrator of various books.

WORK IN PROGRESS: Additional juvenile books for the career series for Dodd.

SIDELIGHTS: Kathy Pelta comments: "Writing is my first love, art my second. I enjoy working in silkscreen, woodblock, and pen and ink."

*   *   *

PELTZ, Mary Ellis 1896-

PERSONAL: Born May 4, 1896, in New York, N.Y.; daughter of Leonard E. (a translator) and Edith (Bell) Opdycke; married John DeWitt Peltz (a social worker), June 6, 1924 (deceased); children: John D., Jr., Henry S., Mary Ellis Nevius. *Education:* Barnard College, B.A., 1920. *Religion:* Protestant Episcopal. *Home:* 169 East 78th St., New York, N.Y. 10021. *Office:* Metropolitan Opera, Lincoln Center, New York, N.Y. 10023.

CAREER: New York Evening Sun, New York City, assistant music critic, 1920-24; *Opera News*, New York City, founder and editor, 1936-57; Metropolitan Opera, New York City, archivist, 1957—. Vice-chairman of Bar Harbor, Me., Historical Society; member of board of directors of Mt. Desert Island Hospital and Jessup Memorial Library. *Member:* Junior Leagues of America (president of Junior League of New York City, 1928-30; committee chairman of national organization, 1930-32), Colony Club.

WRITINGS: (With Robert Lawrence) *The Metropolitan Opera Guide*, Modern Library, 1939; *Spotlights on the Stars: Intimate Sketches of Metropolitan Opera Personalities*, Metropolitan Opera Guild, 1943; *Metropolitan Opera Milestones*, Metropolitan Opera Guild, 1944; (editor) *Opera Lover's Companion*, Ziff-Davis, 1948; *Behind the Gold Curtain: The Story of the Metropolitan Opera, 1883-1950*, Farrar, Straus, 1950; (with Boris Goldovsky) *Accents on Opera: A Series of Brief Essays Stressing Known and Little Known Facts and Facets of a Familiar Art*, Farrar, Straus, 1953; (editor) *Introduction to Opera*, Barnes & Noble, 1956; *The Magic of The Opera: A Picture Memoir of the Metropolitan*, Praeger, 1960; (editor with Gerald Fitzgerald) *Metropolitan Opera Annuals: Third Supplement, 1966-76*, James T. White, 1978. Contributor of articles and poems to *Harper's*, *Vogue*, *Poetry*, *New Republic*, and *Musical America*.

PENROSE, Roland (Algernon) 1900-

PERSONAL: Born October 14, 1900, in London, England; son of James Doyle and Elizabeth Josephine (peckover) Penrose; married Valentine Andree Boue, 1925 (marriage ended); married Lee Miller, 1947 (died, May, 1978); children: one son. *Education:* Queen's College, Cambridge, B.A., 1922. *Home:* 11-A Hornton St., London W.8, England. *Agent:* A. P. Watt Ltd., 26/28 Bedford Row, London WC1R 4HL, England.

CAREER: Painter in France, 1922-34; painter in London, England (with exhibitions in London and Paris), 1935-39; Institute of Contemporary Arts, London, founding member and chairman, 1947—, president, 1969—. British Council in Paris, fine arts officer, 1956-59, Fine Arts Council member, 1959-67; Tate Gallery, member of board of trustees, 1959-66, organized Picasso Exhibition, 1960; organized International Surrealist Exhibition in London, 1936. *Military service:* Home Guard, 1940-42. British Army, 1943-45; became captain. *Member:* Garrick Club. *Awards, honors:* Commander of Order of the British Empire, 1961; knighted, 1966.

WRITINGS: The Road Is Wider Than Long (poems), London Gallery Editions, 1939; *Home Guard Manual of Camouflage,* Routledge & Sons, 1941; *In the Service of the People* (pamphlet on French wartime resistance), Heinemann, 1945; (author of introduction) *Homage to Picasso on His 70th Birthday,* Efron, 1951; *Portrait of Picasso,* Lund, Humphries, 1956, Museum of Modern Art, 1957, revised and enlarged edition, 1971; *Henry Moore: Sculpture et dessins,* [Paris] 1957; *Picasso: His Life and Work,* Gollancz, 1958, Harper, 1959, revised edition, 1973.

Picasso, Arts Council of Great Britain, 1960; (author of introduction and notes) Pablo Picasso, *Four Themes,* Folio Society, 1961; *Picasso: Modern Sculpture,* Universe Books, 1961; (with R. H. Wilenski) *Picasso,* two volumes, Faber Gallery, 1961; *Picasso at Work,* with photographs by Edward Quinn, Doubleday, 1964 (published in England as *Picasso at Work: An Intimate Photographic Study,* W. H. Allen, 1965); *Staedtische Kunstgalerie: Englische Kunst der Gegenwart,* Bochum, 1964; *McWilliam, Sculptor,* Transatlantic, 1964; *Study for an Exhibition of Violence in Contemporary Art,* Institute of Contemporary Arts, 1964; *Picasso Sculptures,* Tudor, 1965; *Creacion en el espacio de Joan Miro,* Wittenborn, 1966, translation published as *Creation in Space of Joan Miro,* 1966; *The Sculpture of Picasso,* Museum of Modern Art, 1967.

Miro, Abrams, 1970; *Picasso,* Dutton, 1971; (editor with John Golding) *Picasso: In Retrospect,* Praeger, 1973 (published in England as *Picasso, 1881-1973,* Elek, 1973); *Man Ray,* New York Graphic Society, 1975; *Tapies,* Rizzoli International, 1978. Also author of *R. A. Augustinci presente Martin Bradley: Peintures et totems,* 1966.

AVOCATIONAL INTERESTS: Gardening.

* * *

PENZEL, Frederick 1948-

PERSONAL: Born September 9, 1948, in Cortland, N.Y.; son of Irwin (a teacher) and Harriet (a teacher; maiden name, Feinstein) Penzel. *Education:* State University of New York at Albany, B.A., 1970; Yale University, M.F.A., 1973. *Home:* 45 Stetson Rd., Apt. K, Williamstown, Mass. 01267. *Office:* Department of Theatre, Williams College, Williamstown, Mass. 01267.

CAREER: Adelphi University, Garden City, N.Y., assistant professor of theatre, technical director, and lighting designer, 1973-75; Nassau Community College, Garden City, N.Y., assistant professor of theatre, technical director, and lighting designer, 1975-76; Williams College, Williamstown, Mass., lecturer in theatre, technical director, and lighting designer, 1976—. Technical director and lighting designer at State University of New York at Albany, summer, 1977; technical director for Yale Cabaret, 1971-73; member of technical staff of Santa Fe Opera Company, 1970.

WRITINGS: Theatre Lighting Before Electricity, Wesleyan University Press, 1978.

WORK IN PROGRESS: A textbook on stagecraft; research on the history of stage machinery and scenic devices.

SIDELIGHTS: Penzel comments: "My work bridges both the academic study of theatre and the practical aspects of theatrical production."

* * *

PERES, Shimon 1923-

PERSONAL: Surname legally changed; born August 16, 1923, in Wolozyn, Poland; came to Palestine in 1933; naturalized Israeli citizen; son of Isaac and Sarah Persky; married Sonia Gelman; children: Zvia (daughter), Jonathan, Nechemia (son). *Education:* Attended New York University and Harvard University. *Politics:* Labour party of Israel. *Religion:* Jewish. *Home:* 12 Oppenheimer St., Ramat-Aviv, Tel-Aviv, Israel. *Office:* Labour Party of Israel, 110 Hayarkon St., Tel-Aviv, Israel.

CAREER: Member of Haganah movement, 1947, and secretary of Hano'ar Ha'oved movement (working youth movement), both in Israel; government of Israel, Tel-Aviv, Israel, head of Ministry of Defence's naval service and of defense mission to United States, 1948-52, deputy director-general of Ministry of Defence, 1952-53, director-general, 1953-59, member of Knesset (Israeli parliament), 1959—, deputy minister of defense, and member of Mapai secretariat, 1959-65, founding member and secretary-general of Rafi party, 1965, minister for economic development in the administered areas and for immigrant absorption, 1969-70, minister of transport and communication, 1970-74, minister of information, 1974, minister of defense, 1974-77, acting prime minister, 1977. Member of Israeli Labour party, 1968—, chairman of party and leader of the opposition, 1977—. Mapai delegate to World Zionst Congress in Basel, Switzerland, 1966; chairman of Yad Ben-Gurion. *Awards, honors:* French Legion of Honor, 1957.

WRITINGS: Ha-Shalav ha-ba, translation published as *The Next Phase,* Weidenfeld & Nicholson, 1965; *Kela' David,* translation published as *David's Sling,* Random House, 1970. Also author of another book in Hebrew, "Tomorrow Is Now," 1978. Author of unpublished poetry. Contributor of many articles to periodicals, mainly on politics.

WORK IN PROGRESS: A book on seven eminent personalities in the modern history of Isreal.

SIDELIGHTS: A protege of Israel's founding father David ben-Gurion, Shimon Peres is a leading figure in Israeli politics today. When Premier Yitzhak Rabin was forced to relinquish his post in April of 1977 as a result of a scandal, Peres took over as acting prime minister. In the following month the divided Labour party became unified when it named Peres as its choice for the premiership. His chief opponent, right-wing Likud (Hebrew for "Unity") party leader Menachim Begin unexpectedly won the election. Peres then became opposition leader and chairman of the Labour party.

Peres had been up for the Labour party nomination twice

before, both times unsuccessfully. Some politicians say former Prime Minister Golda Meir's animosity toward him has hindered his chances of victory. This feeling of dislike was allegedly aroused when Meir served as foreign minister and Peres held the post of minister of defense: Peres's unconventional method of privately negotiating with leaders of other countries was the source. Nevertheless, he narrowly missed winning the nomination over Rabin in 1974.

Much of Peres's political career has taken place under Israel's ministry of defense where he has held several major posts. During the time that he held the top position of director-general, appointed by then-Premier ben-Gurion, he was responsible for the formation of the Israel Defence Forces, the development of the country's own arms industry, and progress in the field of nuclear research. In 1955 Peres negotiated with France to obtain more up-to-date military weapons as a precautionary measure: the U.S.S.R. was supplying arms to Egypt, Israel's main adversary, via Czechoslovakia. This step led to Israel's victory over Egypt in the Sinai Campaign in 1956. Although firm in his belief in the country's eventual autonomy, Peres was forced to look to the United States for additional support. By the Six Day War against Jordan, Syria, Iraq, and Egypt, Israel's defense arsenals had become more sophisticated with the addition of fighter planes and missiles—all Peres's doing.

In 1974, Peres followed Moshe Dayan as defense minister, the Knesset's key position after premier. Under his leadership, Israel's defense budget has tripled and its arsenal, having suffered great losses in the Yom Kippur War of 1973, has been rebuilt and markedly improved. *Newsweek* reporter Kim Willenson wrote that Peres was also a strong figure behind Israel's rescue of prisoners held in Entebbe, Uganda (on which the teleplay "Raid on Entebbe" was based).

Willensen called Peres "a disciplined intellectual," by virtue of the fact that he writes his own speeches and tenaciously reserves two hours nightly for reading books on subjects other than politics. His book *David's Sling* evoked conflicting responses from reviewers. David Schoenbrun praised it highly by saying, "Of all the works on the Middle East struggle in general, and the Israeli view of it in particular, the most comprehensive, lucid, objective, and sophisticated is *David's Sling*." On the other hand, a critic for the *Times Literary Supplement* wrote that Peres's account is seldom very specific, and more than half the book is didactic rather than narrative."

The Labour party leader is currently involved in Arab-Israeli peace negotions, having met several times with Egyptian President Anwar Sadat. In a *Time* interview with Dean Fischer and David Halevy, he said: "There are times when leadership has to represent the wishes of the people and other times when the leadership has to lead. The peace negotiations are the overriding consideration of our people and this is guiding us."

BIOGRAPHICAL/CRITICAL SOURCES: Times Literary Supplement, December 25, 1970; *Saturday Review,* February 6, 1971; *New York Times Book Review,* February 28, 1971; *Midstream,* June-July, 1974; *Israel Magazine,* May, 1975; *Time,* March 3, 1975, November 8, 1976, April 18, 1977, April 25, 1977, August 7, 1978; *Newsweek,* January 10, 1977, February 28, 1977, April 18, 1977, May 16, 1977; *Nation,* May 14, 1977.

*   *   *

PERLIS, Vivian 1928-

PERSONAL: Born April 26, 1928, in Brooklyn, N.Y.; daughter of Charles R. (in business) and Frances (Platzer) Goldberger; married Sanford James Perlis (a physician), August 28, 1949; children: Michael, Lauren, Jonathan. *Education:* University of Michigan, B.Mus., 1949, M.Mus., 1952. *Religion:* Jewish. *Home:* 139 Goodhill Rd., Weston, Conn. 06883. *Office:* Yale University, 3282 Morse College, New Haven, Conn. 06520.

CAREER: Yale University, New Haven, Conn., reference librarian, 1969-72, lecturer in American studies, 1972-78, and music, 1978—, director of oral history project, 1972—, research associate, 1972-77, senior research associate, 1977—. Co-producer of a film, "A Good Dissonance Like a Man," released by Theodore Timreck, 1976, and of recordings for Columbia Broadcasting Co., "The 100th Anniversary of Charles Ives," 1974, "Old Songs Deranged," 1975, and "The Music of Leo Ornstein," 1977. Harpist and teacher of harp, 1957-73. Consultant. *Member:* American Musicological Association, Music Library Association, American Studies Association, Sonneck Society, Ives Society. *Awards, honors:* Award from American Academy of Arts and Letters, 1971, for an oral history of Charles Ives; Kinkelday Award from American Musicological Society, and award from Connecticut Book Publishers, both 1975, both for *Charles Ives Remembered: An Oral History;* Grammy nomination, 1975; grants from National Endowment for the Humanities, 1971-72, and 1976-79, Rockefeller Foundation, 1972-74, Martha Baird Rockefeller Fund for Music, 1977-79, Hindemith Foundation, 1975-78, and Columbia Broadcasting System Foundation, 1978-80; Peabody Award for the film, "A Good Dissonance Like a Man."

WRITINGS: Charles Ives Remembered: An Oral History, Yale University Press, 1974; (co-editor) *An Ives Celebration,* University of Illinois Press, 1977; *Two Men for Modern Music* (monograph), Institute for Studies in American Music, 1978. Contributor of articles to periodicals.

WORK IN PROGRESS: A biography of Aaron Copland, with Copland, publication expected in 1981; an oral history of Steinway & Sons; an oral history of Duke Ellington; a television special on Eubie Blake.

SIDELIGHTS: Vivian Perlis writes: "I am founding director of the first and only continuing oral history project in American music. My first documentary project, on Charles Ives, became the motivation for my change in career from a performing harpist to my full-time research activities and the establishment of 'Oral History, American Music.' This project is housed at Yale University, sponsored by the School of Music, and funded from various sources. Its aim is to collect and preserve source material by means of tape-recorded interviews and video tapes with important figures of twentieth-century music. In addition to the biographical project, research includes several other units of work such as the Steinway & Sons history, a study of film music, and a history of electronics in music."

*   *   *

PERRUCCI, Robert 1931-

PERSONAL: Born November 11, 1931, in New York, N.Y.; son of Dan (a cab driver) and Inez (Mucci) Perrucci; married Carolyn Cummings (a professor), August, 1965; children: Mark, Celeste, Chris, Alissa, Martin. *Education:* State University of New York College at Cortland, B.S., 1958; Purdue University, M.S., 1959, Ph.D., 1962. *Office:* Department of Sociology and Anthropology, Purdue University, West Lafayette, Ind. 47906.

CAREER: Purdue University, West Lafayette, Ind., assistant professor, 1962-65, associate professor, 1965-67, professor of sociology, 1967—, head of department, 1978—. Visiting Simon Professor and senior research fellow at University of Manchester, 1968-69. Member of board of directors of Indiana Center on Law and Poverty, 1973-76. Consultant to National Science Foundation and National Academy of Sciences. *Military service:* U.S. Marine Corps, 1951-53.

MEMBER: American Sociological Association (member of council, 1974-75), Society for the Study of Social Problems, North Central Sociological Association (president, 1973-74). *Awards, honors:* National Science Foundation grants, 1966-68, 1969-70, 1976-78; National Institute of Mental Health grant, 1969-72; U.S. Public Health Service grant, 1973-74.

WRITINGS: (Editor with Marc Pilisuk, and contributor) *The Triple Revolution,* Little, Brown, 1968, 2nd edition published as *The Triple Revolution Emerging,* 1971; (with Joel Gerstl) *Profession Without Community,* Random House, 1969; (editor with Gerstl, and contributor) *The Engineers and the Social System,* Wiley, 1969; *Circle of Madness: On Being Insane and Institutionalized in America,* Prentice-Hall, 1974; (with Dean Knudsen and Russell Hamby) *Sociology: Basic Structures and Processes,* W. C. Brown, 1977.

Contributor: G. K. Zollschan and W. Hirsch, editors, *Explorations in Social Change,* Houghton, 1964; H. Meissner, editor, *Poverty in the Affluent Society,* Harper, 1966; D. Hansen, editor, *Essays in Sociology and Education,* Wiley, 1967; M. Lefton and others, editors, *Approaches to Deviance,* Appleton, 1968; J. Roach and others, editors, *Social Stratification in the United States,* Prentice-Hall, 1969; Hansen, editor, *Explorations in Sociology and Counseling,* Houghton, 1969; P. Meadows and E. H. Mizruchi, editors, *Urbanization and Change,* Addison-Wesley, 1969; G. L. Maddox, editor, *The Domesticated Drug: Drinking Among Collegians,* College and University Press, 1970; I. Morrissett, editor, *Social Science in the Schools,* Holt, 1971; E. Friedson, editor, *Professions and Their Prospects,* Sage Publications, 1972; Joel Gerstl and Glen Jacobs, editors, *Professions for the People: The Politics of Skill,* Schenkman, 1976; William M. Evan, editor, *Interorganization Relations,* Penguin, 1977; L. Senesh, editor, *The Organic Curriculum,* Columbia University Press, in press.

Contributor of about thirty articles and reviews to social science journals. Associate editor of *American Sociological Review,* 1969-72, *Social Problems,* 1971-75, *Sociological Focus,* 1972—, and *Sociological Quarterly,* 1975—; consulting editor of *Behavioral Science Teacher,* 1972-77.

WORK IN PROGRESS: Divided Loyalties: A Study of Whistle-Blowing; Paths to the Mental Hospital.

AVOCATIONAL INTERESTS: Running.

*   *   *

PETERS, Christina   1942-

PERSONAL: Born May 4, 1942, in San Pedro, Calif.; daughter of Donald Cecil (a dock worker) and Adelle Jean (Buckman) Giertz; married Douglas Allan Cunha, November 31, 1967 (divorced, February, 1976); children: Adams (deceased), Lynn (deceased), Teri. *Education:* Cabrillo College, L.V.N., A.S.N. *Religion:* "My own." *Home:* 192 Bean Creek Rd., Scotts Valley, Calif. 95066. *Agent:* Dominick Abel Literary Agency, 498 West End Ave., #12-C, New York, N.Y. 10017. *Office:* Rawson-Wade Associates, 630 Third Ave., New York, N.Y. 10017.

CAREER: Restaurant owner, 1959-64; electronics supervisor, 1964-67; currently a nurse specializing in acute alcohol-

ism care and metabolic nutrition. Volunteer worker at a Santa Cruz alcohol detoxification center.

WRITINGS: (With Ted Schwartz) *Tell Me Who I Am Before I Die,* Rawson, 1978.

WORK IN PROGRESS: God's Nightmare, metaphysical and parapsychological research applicable to multiple personality; *Count Time,* on women in prison.

SIDELIGHTS: Christina Peters comments: "I firmly believe that my autobiographical book has a definite message: that help and hope for multiple personality victims can and must be brought into the open."

BIOGRAPHICAL/CRITICAL SOURCES: Coins, March, 1977; *Family Circle,* September 1, 1978.

*   *   *

PETERS, Daniel (James)   1948-

PERSONAL: Born July 24, 1948, in Milwaukee, Wis.; son of John A. (a pharmacist) and Arla (a teacher; maiden name, Langdon) Peters; married Annette Kolodny (a feminist critic and writer), June 14, 1970. *Education:* Yale University, B.A. (cum laude), 1970; graduate study at University of British Columbia, 1970-71. *Politics:* "Neo-Wobbly." *Religion:* "Moon worshiper." *Home address:* R.F.D. 1, Lee Hook Rd., Newmarket, N.H. 03857. *Agent:* Susan Lescher, Robert Lescher, 155 East 71st St., New York, N.Y. 10021.

CAREER: Writer, 1971—. *Member:* Authors Guild.

WRITINGS: Border Crossings (novel), Harper, 1978.

WORK IN PROGRESS: A long historical novel "about the Aztecs of Mexico, code-named 'Montezuma's Galoshes,' indicating its blend of serious fiction and strict ethnographic accuracy."

SIDELIGHTS: Peters writes: "I started working in my father's drug store when I was fourteen, worked in factories during the summers while in college, and as a donut salesman, busboy, and office clerk during the school year. I was a conscientious objector in the Vietnam Resistance. I did a one-year stint teaching freshman English and six months as a child care worker, proving lousy at both.

"I've been writing full-time since 1971, and it is still the only work worth doing. I have two operating premises: life is a fiction and the truth is good manners. Beyond that, I wing it."

*   *   *

PETERS, Ronald M., Jr.   1947-

PERSONAL: Born September 8, 1947, in Muncie, Ind.; son of Ronald M. and Helene (Loughlin) Peters; married Glenda May, November 28, 1975; children: John Michael. *Education:* Indiana University, A.B., 1969, M.A., 1972, Ph.D., 1974. *Residence:* Norman, Okla. *Office:* Department of Political Science, University of Oklahoma, Norman, Okla. 73019.

CAREER: University of Oklahoma, Norman, assistant professor of political science, 1975—.

WRITINGS: The Massachusetts Constitution of 1780: A Social Compact, University of Massachusetts Press, 1978.

WORK IN PROGRESS: The Modern Speaker, on the speaker of the U.S. House of Representatives.

*   *   *

PETRONI, Frank A.   1936-

PERSONAL: Born February 4, 1936, in Boston, Mass.;

marricd; children: two. *Education:* Emerson College, B.S., 1961; University of Arizona, M.A., 1963; University of Minnesota, Ph.D., 1968. *Office:* Behavioral Research Associates, 2030 East Speedway Blvd., Tucson, Ariz. 85719.

CAREER: University of Minnesota, Duluth, instructor in sociology, 1963-65; University of Minnesota, Minneapolis, trainee in medical sociology, 1965-68; Menninger Foundation, Topeka, Kan., research social psychologist, 1968-70; University of Arizona, Tucson, assistant professor of sociology, 1970-75; Behavioral Research Associates, Tucson, Ariz., senior associate, 1972—. Certified psychologist. Speaker at schools, churches, and clubs; consultant.

MEMBER: American Psychological Association, American Orthopsychiatric Association, American Personnel and Guidance Association. *Awards, honors:* National Institute of Mental Health grant, 1968-69; grant from Kansas Department of Social Welfare, 1969-70.

WRITINGS: (Contributor) K. W. Taylor and James Frideres, editors, *Readings in Medical Sociology,* Simon & Schuster, 1970; (with Lillian Petroni and Ernest Hirsch) *Two, Four, Six, Eight, When You Gonna Integrate?,* Behavioral Publications, 1971; (contributor) I. R. Stuart and L. E. Abt, editors, *Interracial Marriages,* Grossman, 1972; (contributor) Norman Denzin, editor, *Children and Their Caretakers,* Transaction Books, 1973. Contributor to psychology and social science journals.

*   *   *

PEYREFITTE, Alain Antoine   1925-

PERSONAL: Born August 26, 1925, in Najac, France; son of Jean and Augustine (Roux) Peyrefitte; married Monique Luton, December 14, 1948; children: Florence, Christel, Veronique, Emmanuelle, Benoit. *Education:* Attended University of Montpellier, Ecole Normale Superieure, Ecole Nationale d'Administration, and Centre National de la Recherche Scientifique; Sorbonne, University of Paris, earned diploma. *Home:* 111 rue de Ranelagh, Paris 16e, France. *Office:* Assemblee nationale, Paris 7e, France.

CAREER: Secretary, French Ministry of Foreign Affairs, 1947; embassy secretary, Bonn, Germany, 1949; served on mission to Poland, 1954; assistant director, European Organization, 1956; member, French delegation, Brussels Conference on the Common Market and Euratom, 1956-57; counselor, Foreign Affairs, 1958; deputy, Seine-et-Marne Department, 1958, 1962, 1967, 1968, 1973, 1978; French representative, European Parliament, 1959-62; minister for the repatriated, 1962; minister of information, 1962-66; minister of scientific research, atomic and space-related questions, 1966-67; minister of national education, 1967-68; president, committee on cultural, home and social problems, National Assembly, 1968-72; minister of administrative reforms and planning, 1973-74; minister of cultural affairs and environment, 1974; president, committee on violence and criminality, 1976; minister of justice, 1977—. French delegate, United Nations General Assembly, 1959-60, 1968-72; counsellor general, Bray-sur-Seine canton, 1964, 1970, 1976; mayor of Provins, 1965, 1971, 1976. *Member:* Union of Democrats for the Republic (secretary general, 1972-73). *Awards, honors:* Chevalier de la Legion d'honneur; Commandeur des Palmes academiques et de Arts et de Lettres; elected to the French Academy, 1977.

WRITINGS: Les Roseaux froisses (title means "The Bruised Reeds"), Gallimard, 1948, reprinted, 1977; *Le Mythe de Penelope* (title means "The Myth of Penelope") Gallimard, 1949, reprinted, 1977; *Rue d'Ulm, chroniques de la vie normalienne* (title means "Rue d'Ulm, Chronicles of Normalien Life"), J. Vigneau, 1950, Flammarion, 1963; *Faut-il partager l'Algerie?* (title means "Must Algeria Be Divided?") Plon, 1961; *Quand la Chine s'eveillera ... le monde tremblera,* Fayard, 1973, translation by Graham Webb published as *The Chinese: Portrait of a People,* Bobbs-Merrill, 1977; *Le Mal Francais* (title means "The French Sickness"), Plon, 1976.

SIDELIGHTS: Trained in anthropology and philosophy, Alain Peyrefitte has been a diplomat and government minister. As president of the French National Assembly's Commission of Cultural and Social Affairs, he led a study mission to the People's Republic of China in 1971. *The Chinese: Portrait of a People* grew out of the trip and is, according to Jerome Alan Cohen, "a comprehensive effort written in the tradition of Edgar Snow, to describe and assess the Promethean human adventure presided over by Mao Tse-tung for a generation." A critic for the *New Yorker* also lauded *The Chinese*: "M. Peyrefitte puts what he saw and heard into a first-rate intellectual framework: Chinese history, Mao's theory, and his own wise detachment when considering an alien culture." In contrast, Robert Shaplen discerned a bias in the book: "The worship of Mao and what he accomplished colors almost all of Peyrefitte's opinions, and he repeatedly quotes the parroted adulation of others."

BIOGRAPHICAL/CRITICAL SOURCES: Saturday Review, June 25, 1977; *New York Times Book Review,* July 17, 1977; *New Yorker,* July 25, 1977.

*   *   *

PHILLIPS, Charles F(ranklin, Jr.)   1910-

PERSONAL: Born May 25, 1910, in Nelson, Pa.; son of Charles Franklin Phillips. *Education:* Colgate University, A.B., 1931; Harvard University, Ph.D., 1934. *Home address:* Maple Hill Lane, Auburn, Maine 04210.

CAREER: Hobart College (now Hobart College and William Smith College), Geneva, N.Y., staff member in department of economics, 1933-34; Colgate University, Hamilton, N.Y., staff member in department of economics, 1934-41; National Defense Advisory Commission, Washington, D.C., economist; Office of Price Administration, Washington, D.C., economist, deputy administrator for rationing, 1944; Bates College, Lewiston, Maine, president of college, 1944-67, president emeritus, 1967—. Head of board of directors of Central Maine Power Co. and Hannaford Brothers Co.; member of board of directors of Union Mutual Life Insurance Co., Sperry & Hutchinson Co., and Allied Maintenance Corp. Past public governor of American Stock Exchange; past president and past head of board of directors of New England Council. Member of U.S. State Department mission to India and Pakistan, 1953-54; speaker and adviser in Switzerland, Puerto Rico, Poland, Finland, the Soviet Union, the Far East, Australia, New Zealand, Portugal, and Eastern Europe.

AWARDS, HONORS: Honorary degrees from Colgate University, Colby College, Bowdoin College, Northeastern University, University of Maine, Western New England College, Nasson College, Morehouse College, Shaw University, and Bates College.

WRITINGS: Marketing, edited by Edgar S. Furniss, Houghton, 1938, 6th edition, with Delbert J. Duncan, published as *Marketing: Principles and Methods,* Irwin, 1968, 7th edition, edited by James M. Carman and Kenneth P. Uhl, published as *Phillips and Duncan's Marketing: Principles and Methods,* 1973; (with J. V. Garland) *Government Spending and Economic Recovery,* H. W. Wilson, 1938; (with Garland) *The American Neutrality Problem,* H. W. Wilson, 1939; *Competition in the Synthetic Rubber Industry,* University of North Carolina Press, 1963; (with George Robert Hall) *Bank Mergers and the Regulatory Agencies,* Board of Governors, Federal Reserve System, 1964; *The Economics of Regulation: Theory and Practice in the Transportation and Public Utility Industries,* Irwin, 1965, revised edition, 1969; *Retailing: Principles and Methods,* 6th edition, Irwin, 1968; (editor) *Competition and Monopoly,* Department of Economics, Washington and Lee University, 1974; (editor) *Telecommunications, Regulation, and Public Choice,* Department of Economics, Washington and Lee University, 1975. Also author of *Marketing by Manufacturers,* and *A Tax Program to Encourage the Further Economic Growth of Puerto Rico.* Contributor to journals in education, economics, business, and political science, and to *Reader's Digest.*

* * *

PHILLIPS, Hiram Stone 1912(?)-1979

OBITUARY NOTICE: Born c. 1912; died of a heart attack, in February, 1979, near St. Petersburg, Fla. Consultant to businesses and government organizations and author. Phillips specialized in Latin America-related projects, including one for the Agency for International Development. He also worked as a public administrator in Costa Rica. Phillips wrote *Guide for Development: Institution-Building and Reform.* Obituaries and other sources: *Washington Post,* February 19, 1979.

* * *

PICKFORD, Mary 1893-1979

OBITUARY NOTICE: Birth-given name Gladys Smith; born April 8, 1893, in Toronto, Ontario, Canada; died May 29, 1979, in Santa Monica, Calif. Actress and author best known for her performances in such silent films as "The Poor Little Rich Girl," "Rebecca of Sunnybrook Farm," and "Pollyanna." While still in her teens, Pickford wed frequent co-star Owen Moore. She later divorced him to marry actor Douglas Fairbanks. Although during the silent era Pickford enjoyed the same celebrity as Charlie Chaplin, she chose to retire when sound was added to films. Among her writings are two memoirs, *Why Not Try God* and *My Rendezvous With Life,* and a novel, *The Demi-Widow.* In her later years, Pickford became a recluse; she lived with her third husband, Buddy Rogers, in the home she had once shared with Fairbanks. Obituaries and other sources: *Current Biography,* Wilson, 1945; *The Canadian Who's Who,* Volume 12, Who's Who Canadian Publications, 1972; *Celebrity Register,* 3rd edition, Simon & Schuster, 1973; *New York Times,* May 30, 1979; *Chicago Tribune,* May 31, 1979; *Time,* June 11, 1979.

* * *

PIERCE, Lawrence C(olman) 1936-

PERSONAL: Born December 24, 1936, in Seattle, Wash.; son of Lawrence J. and Isabel (Colman) Pierce; married Robin Gaffner (a writer), September 26, 1961; children: Eric. *Education:* Yale University, B.A., 1959; Cornell University, M.P.A., 1965, Ph.D., 1969. *Home:* 2066 University St., Eugene, Ore. 97403. *Office:* Department of Political Science, University of Oregon, Eugene, Ore. 97403.

CAREER: University of Oregon, Eugene, assistant professor, 1969-74, associate professor, 1974-78; professor of political science, 1978—.

WRITINGS: The Politics of Fiscal Policy Formation, Goodyear Publishing, 1971; *The Freshman Legislator,* Binfords & Mort, 1972; *The State School Finance Alternatives,* Center for Educational Policy and Management Information, University of Oregon, 1975; (with Walter Garms and James W. Guthrie) *School Finance: The Economics and Politics of Public Education,* Prentice-Hall, 1978.

WORK IN PROGRESS: A second edition of *The Freshman Legislator;* a manuscript on collective bargaining in public education.

* * *

PIERSON, Stanley 1925-

PERSONAL: Born January 1, 1925, in Torrance, Calif.; son of Daniel and Pearl (Frost) Pierson; married Joan Mimnaugh (a teacher), September 19, 1953; children: Michael, George, Paul. *Education:* University of Oregon, B.A., 1950; Harvard University, A.M., 1951, Ph.D., 1957. *Home:* 1800 Fairmount, Eugene, Ore. 97403. *Office:* Department of History, University of Oregon, Eugene, Ore. 97403.

CAREER: Wesleyan University, Middletown, Conn., instructor in history, 1954-57; University of Oregon, Eugene, assistant professor, 1957-64, associate professor, 1964-70, professor of history, 1970—, head of department, 1969-71. *Military service:* U.S. Army, 1943-46. *Member:* American Historical Association, American Association of University Professors. *Awards, honors:* Book prize from Pacific Coast branch of American Historical Association, 1974, for *Marxism and the Origins of British Socialism.*

WRITINGS: Marxism and the Origins of British Socialism, Cornell University Press, 1973; *British Socialists: The Journey From Fantasy to Politics,* Harvard University Press, 1979.

WORK IN PROGRESS: Research on the role of the middle classes in the German socialist movement, 1890-1920.

* * *

PINGET, Robert 1919-

PERSONAL: Born July 19, 1919, in Geneva, Switzerland; immigrated to France, 1946. *Education:* Earned law degree; studied at Ecole des Beaux-Arts. *Home:* 4 rue de l'Universite, Paris 7e, France.

CAREER: Writer, 1951—. Formerly practiced law, painted, and taught French in England. *Awards, honors:* Ford Foundation grant, 1960; Prix des Critiques for *L'Inquisitoire,* 1963; Prix Femina for *Quelqu'un,* 1965.

WRITINGS: Entre Fantoine et Agapa (short stories), Laffont, 1950; *Mahu ou le materiau* (novel), Laffont, 1952, translation by Alan Sheridan-Smith published as *Mahu or the Material,* Calder & Boyars (London), 1966; *Le Renard et la boussole* (novel), Gallimard, 1953; *Graal flibuste,* Editions de minuit, 1956, unexpurgated edition published under same title, 1966, published with *Robert Pinget ou le palimpseste* by Olivier de Magny, Union generale d'editions, 1963; *Baga* (novel), Editions de minuit, 1958, translation by John Stevenson published as *Baga,* Calder & Boyars, 1967; *Le Fiston* (novel), Editions de minuit, 1959, translation by Richard N. Coe published as *No Answer,* J. Calder, 1961, translation by Richard Howard published as *Monsieur Levert,* Grove, 1961, author's own dramatic adaptation published as *Lettre Morte* (two-act; first produced in Paris, 1960), Editions de minuit, 1959, published with an English version of *La Derniere Bande* by Samuel Beckett, Editions de minuit, 1960 (also see below).

La Manivelle (radio script; bilingual edition; translated as "The Old Tune" by Samuel Beckett), Editions de minuit, 1960 (also see below); *Ici ou ailleurs: Suivi de Architruc et de L'Hypothese* (three plays), Editions de minuit, 1961; *Clope au dossier* (novel), Editions de minuit, 1961; *L'Inquisitoire* (novel), Editions de minuit, 1962, translation by Donald Watson published as *The Inquisitory*, Grove, 1966; *Autour de Mortin* (radio script), Editions de minuit, 1965, French text with English introduction and notes edited by Anthony Cheal Pugh published under same title, Methuen, 1971 (also see below); *Quelqu'un* (novel), Editions de minuit, 1965; *Le Libera*, Editions de minuit, 1968, translation by Barbara Wright published as *The Libera me Domine*, Calder & Boyars, 1972, Red Dust, 1978; *Passacaille* (novel), Editions de minuit, 1969, translation by Wright published as *Recurrent Melody: Passacaille*, Calder & Boyars, 1975, translation by Wright published as *Passacaglia*, Red Dust, 1978; *Fable*, Editions de minuit, 1971; *Identite: Suivi de Abel et Bela*, Editions de minuit, 1971; *Paralchimie: Suivi de Architruc, L'Hypothese*, [and] *Nuit*, Editions de minuit, 1973; *Cette voix*, Editions de minuit, 1975.

Collections: *Plays*, translated by Barbara Bray, except as indicated, Volume I (contains *The Old Tune* [translated and adapted by Samuel Beckett], *Clope*, and *Dead Letter*), J. Cape, 1963, published as *Three Plays*, Hill & Wang, 1966, Volume II (contains *Architruc*, *About Mortin*, and *The Hypothesis*), Calder & Boyars, 1967, published as *Three Plays*, Hill & Wang, 1968; *Lettre mort: Suivi de la Manivelle, piece radio-phonique* (bilingual edition with English translation by Beckett), Editions de minuit, 1970.

Translator into French of Samuel Beckett's *All That Fall*, 1964. Work represented in the anthology *Voix et silences: Les Meilleures Pieces radiophoniques francaises*, edited by Anna Otten, Irvington, 1968.

WORK IN PROGRESS: A novel and radio plays.

SIDELIGHTS: Pinget has been identified with the "new novelists" of France, a group which includes Alain Robbe-Grillet, Nathalie Sarraute, Claude Simon, and Michel Butor. As Peter Broome has described it, "The French *nouveau roman* has a pronounced self-destructive urge. It puts the novel on trial, denies its own innocence, exposes the novelist himself as the chief suspect, incriminates him in his inadequate and self-contradictory evidence, and condemns the two of them together to a life sentence of fruitless forced labors." However, Pinget's approach to the "new novel" differs from that of other "new novelists" in that, according to Bettina L. Knapp, he is "far more personal."

Pinget once stated: "One thing alone interests me in the novel: *to capture the tone of a voice*. This tone is, in actuality one of the components of my own voice which I try to isolate, then to objectify." Knapp explained her interpretation of Pinget's literary goals. "His search consists mainly in discovering the right tone (tonality or voice) of his novels' narrators," she wrote. "Only after this initial task has been accomplished can he (author-narrator) really be himself and so express the feelings, ideas and atmosphere of his contemporaries and the world in which they live. Pinget is not interested in the symbolism involved or in the psychology of his characters or even in the themes or deeper meanings of their discourses which are never clearly delineated."

Pinget has rejected the subjective limitations of plot, anecdotage, and sometimes even punctuation and has instead attempted to create with pure objectivity. The minutely detailed description of characters and settings is the most frequently discussed element of his style. Pinget's description are so finely drawn, John Updike wrote in a discussion of *The Inquisitory*, that "an attentive reader with pencil in hand could probably draw, from the various textual indications, a map of the entire region."

The Inquisitory is Pinget's best known work in the United States. The novel consists entirely of the police interrogation of an old deaf man who has supposedly witnessed a crime. Samuel Beckett has called it "one of the most important novels of the last ten years." Updike was impressed with the novel and saw it in the continuum of French literature. "Pinget's very avant-garde novel of the absurd incorporates the full French novelistic tradition," he wrote. "Like Proust, he has a cure who dabbles in the etymology of place names; like Balzac, he avidly traces the fortunes of little provincial shops through all their vicissitudes of gossip. The number of anecdotes, or miniature novels, caught in his nets of description cannot be counted; presumably some are expanded elsewhere in Pinget's *oeuvre*.... [By] the novel's end this district, into which enough historical allusion has been insinuated to render it an analogue of France, serves as a model of the world, with all human possibilities somewhere touched upon."

Reviewer Thomas Bishop commented: "*The Inquisitory* is, beyond the literal and metaphoric levels, a novel about the writing of a novel. In essence the old man dictates his story, prodded by questions which may be his own. In this sense Pinget's work focuses on the impossibility of writing. Despite the multitude of details—or rather because of it—the overall picture constantly shifts, and no solid texture is allowed to develop out of uncertainty. The reality so carefully constructed in its minute components explodes in its totality. By accumulating countless characters, streets, and place-names, Pinget causes them all to lose meaning as they blend into an overwhelming mass."

"At the end," critic Robert Garis wrote, "no discernable structure of meaning has been achieved. This failure is the book's meaning.... Pinget crams his novel with the deliberate false substantiality of denotation without connotation—proper names of people, towns, streets; descriptions of furniture; unconnected and undeveloped fragments of events and relations. With none of these are we allowed, much less enabled, to make meaningful contact: life, then, is information without order."

Nigel Dennis also found the novel to be inaccessible and had reservations about its structure. He declared: "Faced with this sort of novel, one is obliged to ask: Was it the only way in which it could have been written? Would it have been as good or better written in a more ordinary way? Does M. Pinget's way add depth to the subject? Does it bring out the characters more completely? Does it show us aspects of life that would be more concealed if the writing were more orthodox? In short, does the experiment justify anything except the right to declare experiment a capital crime?" Davis admitted that some readers thought so, noting that the book was a best-seller in France and had won an important literary prize. His own assessment, though, was that the novel "is only a deliberate struggle—maintained with incredible stamina—to ride a one-wheeled bicycle for 399 miles. It is hardly surprising, then, that the total effect is immensely involved, generally unreadable, and appallingly boring."

Bishop disagreed. "*The Inquisitory* is, in fact, a disturbing, bewildering book," he wrote. "But its very confusion dazzles rather than dazes; it creates a compulsive effect on the reader. Once caught in Pinget's maze, he will not want to put it down until he has heard the old servant out."

BIOGRAPHICAL/CRITICAL SOURCES: Laurent LeSage, *The French New Novel: An Introduction and a Sampler,* Pennsylvania State University Press, 1962; *Saturday Review,* February 11, 1967; *New York Review of Books,* March 23, 1967; *Hudson Review,* summer, 1967; *London Magazine,* October, 1967; *New Yorker,* November 4, 1967; *Observer,* August 27, 1972; *Times Literary Supplement,* September 29, 1972, March 1, 1974, May 2, 1975; *Books Abroad,* Volume 46, number 3, summer, 1972; Martin Esslin, *The Theatre of the Absurd,* Overlook Press, 1973; *International Fiction Review,* July, 1974; *Contemporary Literary Criticism,* Gale, Volume 7, 1977.

*   *   *

PINNEY, Thomas 1932-

PERSONAL: Born April 23, 1932, in Ottawa, Kan.; son of John J. and Lorene (Owen) Pinney; married Sherrill Ohman, September 1, 1956; children: Anne, Jane, Sarah. *Education:* Beloit College, B.A., 1954; Yale University, Ph.D., 1957. *Home:* 228 West Harrison, Claremont, Calif. 91711. *Office:* Department of English, Pomona College, Claremont, Calif. 91711.

CAREER: Hamilton College, Clinton, N.Y., instructor in English, 1957-61; Yale University, New Haven, Conn., instructor in English, 1961-62; Pomona College, Claremont, Calif., assistant professor, 1962-67, associate professor, 1967-73, professor of English, 1973—. *Awards, honors:* Guggenheim fellow, 1966; American Council of Learned Societies grant, 1973; Mellon fellowship from Pomona College, 1974.

WRITINGS: (Editor) *Essays of George Eliot,* Columbia University Press, 1963; (editor with John Clive) *Selected Writings of Thomas Babington Macaulay,* University of Chicago Press, 1972; *A Short Handbook and Style Sheet,* Harcourt, 1977. Editor of *Letters of Thomas Babington Macaulay,* Cambridge University Press, 1974—.

WORK IN PROGRESS: A History of Wine in America.

*   *   *

PLATER, Alan (Frederick) 1935-

PERSONAL: Born April 15, 1935, in Jarrow on Tyne, Northumberland, England; son of Herbert Richart (an engineer) and Isabella (Scott Plunkett) Plater; married Shirley Ann Johnson (a former architect), April 12, 1958; children: Stephen, Janet, David. *Education:* Attended King's College, Durham, 1953-57 and University of Newcastle. *Home:* 5 Hull Rd., Cottinghamshire, North Humberside HU16 4PA, England. *Agent:* Margaret Ramsey Ltd., 14-A Goodwin's Ct., St. Martin's Lane, London WC2N 4LL, England.

CAREER: Employed in architect's office in Hull, England, 1957-60; qualified as architect in 1961; playwright for radio, television, and theatre; writer of screenplays, poet, broadcaster, and theatre critic; free-lance writer, 1961—. Member of British Broadcasting Company general advisory council; co-founder and member of council of Humberside Theatre. *Member:* Writers Guild of Great Britain, Dramatists Club (London). *Awards, honors:* Writers Guild of Great Britain Award, 1972, for radio play, "Close the Coalhouse Door."

WRITINGS: (Contributor) Alfred Bradley, editor, *Worth a Hearing: A Collection of Radio Plays* (includes "The Mating"; also see below), Blackie & Sons, 1967; (contributor) Michael Marland, editor, *Z Cars: Four Scripts From the Television Series* (includes "A Quiet Night"; also see below), Longmans, Green, 1968; (author of introduction) Sid

Chaplin, *Close the Coalhouse Door,* Methuen, 1969; (contributor) *Playbill Three* (plays), Hutchinson, 1969; (contributor) Marland, editor, *Theatre Choice: A Collection of Modern Short Plays* (includes "See the Pretty Lights"; also see below), Blackie & Sons, 1972; *Collected Plays* (includes "Excursion," "Christmas Day in the Morning," "And a Little Love Besides," and "Seventeen Per Cent Said Push Off"; also see below), Blackie & Sons, 1973; *The Trouble With Abracadabra* (children's play), Macmillan, 1975; *The Fosdyke Saga* (dramatized version of Bill Tidy's cartoon strip; also see below), Samuel French, 1978.

Plays: "Ted's Cathedral," first produced in Stoke on Trent, 1963; "The Referees" (also see below), first produced in Stoke on Trent, 1963; "The Rainbow Machine" (also see below), first produced in Stoke on Trent, 1963; "A Smashing Day," music by Ken Kingsley and Robert Powell, first produced in Stoke on Trent, 1965; "Charlie Came to Our Town" (revised version of teleplay, "The Nutter"; also see below), music by Alex Glasgow, first produced in Harrogate, Yorkshire, at the Harrogate Festival, 1966; "The What on the Landing?" (also see below), first produced in Scarborough, Yorkshire, 1968; "Close the Coalhouse Door," music by Glasgow, first produced in Newcastle upon Tyne, 1968; "Don't Build a Bridge, Drain the River!," music by Glasgow, first produced in Hull, 1970; "Simon Says!," music by Glasgow, first produced in Leeds at Leeds Playhouse, 1970; "And a Little Love Besides," first produced in Hull at Hull Arts Centre, October 13, 1970; (with others) "King Billy Vaudeville Show," first produced in Hull, 1971; "Seventeen Per Cent Said Rush Off" (also see below), first produced, 1972; "The Tigers Are Coming-O.K.?" first produced in Hull, 1972; "Swallows on the Water," first produced in Hull, 1973; (with Glasgow) "Trinity Tales," first produced in Birmingham, 1975; (with Jim Bywater) "Tales of Humberside," first produced in Hull, 1975; "Our Albert," first produced in Hull, 1976; "The Fosdyke Saga," music by Bernard Wrigley, first produced at Bush Theatre, 1977; "Well Good Night Then," first produced in Hull, 1978.

Teleplays: "The Referees," 1961; "A Smashing Day," 1962; "A Quiet Night," 1963; "See the Pretty Lights," 1963; "So Long Charlie," 1963; "Z Cars" series (18 episodes), 1963-65; "Ted's Cathedral," 1964; "Fred," 1964; "The Incident," 1965; "The Nutter," 1965; "Softly Softly" series (22 episodes), 1966-72; "To See How Far It Is" (trilogy), 1968; "The First Lady" series (4 episodes), 1968-69; "Rest in Peace, Uncle Fred," 1970; "Seventeen Per Cent Said Push Off," 1972; "The Land of Green Ginger," 1973; "It Must Be Something in the Water" (documentary), 1973; "Willow Cabins," 1976; "Trinity Tales," 1976; "Night People," 1978.

Radio Plays: "The Smokeless Z One," 1961; "Counting the Legs," 1961; "The Mating Season," 1962; "The Rainbow Machine," 1962; "The Seventh Day of Arthur," 1963; "Excursion," 1966; "The What on the Landing?" 1967.

Screenplays: "The Virgin and the Gypsy," 1970; "Juggernaut," 1974; "All Things Bright and Beautiful" (adaptation of the book by James Herriot), 1976.

Also author of many other single plays and contributor to series, documentaries, and comedy shows.

WORK IN PROGRESS: Adapting *The Good Companions,* by J. B. Priestly, as a nine-part television series; working on new stage play entitled "Bernie's Tunes."

SIDELIGHTS: "I generally take refuge in the Peter De Vries dictum that you don't ask a cow to analyse milk," Plater told *CA*. "I write because I'm endlessly curious about humanity, especially when it's eccentric, not necessarily in a noisy or flamboyant way. I look for the ordinary man, so-called, and seek to reveal the extraordinary that dwells within. Generally the plays come out more-or-less comic, which means laughter beats the tears by a short head in a photo-finish. On any scale, individual and parochial, or collective and cosmic, that seems about right."

The ordinary man that Plater looks for usually comes from northeastern England's industrial region: the same area where he was born and still lives. A prolific writer considered to be one of the leading dramatists of this part of England, Plater speaks for the working class.

Plater's work has received mixed reviews. His play "Close the Coalhouse Door" proved very successful. Donald Bryden called it "a warmly funny, boisterous and moving show" focusing on the industrial age. "The terrible thing about history, said Orwell, is how few names of its slaves have been preserved. Tenderly and furiously, 'Close the Coalhouse Door' does a little to redress the injustice." A *London Magazine* reviewer, however, disagreed. He wrote that "all Mr. Plater's energy and craftmanship seems to have been expanded on the interior charade which is the heart of his piece, and the framework—the family celebration and a love affair—is both soppy and clumsy."

"And a Little Love Besides" prompted this response from a *Stage and Television Today* critic: "Mr. Plater made his points very obviously and occasionally with a great deal of humour. . . . Funny sequences were interspersed in a heavy-handed manner with some very heavy opinions. Conversely, moments which seemed to have dramatic impact were cut short by seemingly out of place funny lines."

Plater's film version of the well-loved Yorkshire veterinarian James Herriot's third book, "All Things Wise and Wonderful" is "dowdy, underfinanced, yet irresistably appealing," in *Washington Post* critic Gary Arnold's estimation. John Alderton stars as Herriot with Lisa Harrow playing his wife, Helen. In spite of the wide success of Herriot's books, none of the prominent film companies in the United States opted to import the screenplay. Arnold attributed this lack of interest to the fact that even the seemingly likely candidate, Metro-Goldwyn-Mayer (MGM), "obviously can't distinguish the heart-warming from the hateful." An independent company owned by Albert Schwartz could and did.

In the film, Plater "retains Herriot's structure while soft-pedaling his pronounced episode rythm," wrote Arnold. The advent of World War II, he continued, is "subtly used to enhance the value of life that absorbs the Herriots. The movie closes on a wonderful lyric note as Dr. Herriot goes out for a stroll with his infant son minutes after listening to war declared over the wireless." The result is "exceptionally stirring."

AVOCATIONAL INTERESTS: Reading, jazz, watching soccer.

BIOGRAPHICAL/CRITICAL SOURCES: Plays and Players, October, 1968; *Observer Review*, October 27, 1968, September 13, 1970; *London Magazine*, January, 1969; *Punch*, February 11, 1970; *The Stage and Television Today*, September 24, 1970, October 15, 1970; *Washington Post*, September 15, 1978.

*   *   *

PLATER, William M(armaduke) 1945-

PERSONAL: Born July 26, 1945, in East St. Louis, Ill.; son

of Everett Marmaduke (a trucker) and Marguerite (a banker; maiden name, McBride) Plater; married Gail Maxwell (a teacher), October 16, 1971; children: Elizabeth Rachel. *Education:* University of Illinois, B.A., 1967, M.A., 1969, Ph.D., 1973. *Home:* 201 West Washington, Urbana, Ill. 61801. *Office:* School of Humanities, University of Illinois, 112 English Building, Urbana, Ill. 61801.

CAREER: University of Illinois, Urbana-Champaign, assistant dean of College of Liberal Arts and Sciences, 1973-74, assistant director of School of Humanities, 1974-77, associate director, 1977—, assistant professor of humanities, 1977—. Committee member of Urbana Council on Teacher Education for Innovative and Experimental Curricula, 1974—. *Member:* Modern Language Association of America, Midwest Modern Language Association.

WRITINGS: Man and the Multitude: A Symposium (monograph), College of Liberal Arts and Sciences, University of Illinois, 1967; *The Grim Phoenix: Reconstructing Thomas Pynchon*, Indiana University Press, 1978.

Poems anthologized in *I/73*, Finial Press, 1973; *Shape*, Ginn, 1973; *Response: Rhetoric for Action*, Allyn & Bacon, 1973. Contributor to academic journals.

WORK IN PROGRESS: Research for a book on metaphor in American literature.

*   *   *

POETKER, Frances Jones 1912-

PERSONAL: Surname is pronounced *Pet*-ker; born April 16, 1912, in Ohio; daughter of Charles Benjamin (a florist) and Louise (Johnston) Jones; married Joseph G. Poetker (manager of a florist shop), August 10, 1937. *Education:* Vassar College, B.A., 1933; University of Cincinnati, M.A., 1934. *Religion:* Lutheran. *Home:* 1059 Celestial, Cincinnati, Ohio 45202. *Office:* Jones the Florist, 1037 East McMillan, Cincinnati, Ohio 45206.

CAREER: Vice-president of Nikko Inn, Cincinnati, Ohio; buyer for Mabley & Carew, Cincinnati; currently associated with Jones the Florist, Cincinnati. Member of advisory board of Garden Center of Cincinnati. Member of board of directors of Bethesda Hospital and Cincinnati Bell Telephone Co.; member of policies board of Cincinnati Symphony; member of president's council of Xavier University and honors committee of University of Cincinnati. *Member:* Society of American Florists (member of board of directors), Garden Club of America, American Academy of Florists, American Horticultural Society (member of board of directors), Cincinnati Chamber of Commerce, Bankers Club. *Awards, honors:* Award from U.S. Department of Agriculture; Sylvia Award from American Academy of Florists, (annual grand trophy for orchid arrangements); named to Floricultural Hall of Fame.

WRITINGS: (With Marion R. Becker, Paul Sears, and Janet Forberg) *Wild Wealth*, Bobbs-Merrill, 1971. Author of "Fun with Flowers," a syndicated column appearing in sixty-eight newspapers. Wrote a syndicated television course on plant ecology and a local radio and television series on the history of music. Contributor to magazines, including *American Horticulturist* and *Executive Housekeeper*.

WORK IN PROGRESS: A guidebook to the world's botanical gardens, with Everett Conklin; identifying plants depicted on Chinese porcelains in Taft Museum.

SIDELIGHTS: Frances Poetker writes: "I am interested in plants native to a certain area and their ecological potential. For many years I traveled widely as a commentator for Florists Transworld Delivery. Now I lecture on historical gardens and the history of flower arrangements. The florist shop is my principal career, but I wish to continue writing and working in the field of ecology.''

* * *

POGGI, Gianfranco 1934-

PERSONAL: Born February 28, 1934, in Modena, Italy; son of Enrico (a judge) and Maria (Vigo) Poggi; married Patricia Lipscomb (a weaver), July 21, 1962; children: Maria Linda. *Education:* University of Padua, laurea, 1956; University of California, Berkeley, M.A., 1959, Ph.D., 1963. *Home:* 34 Braid Cres., Edinburgh EH10 6AU, Scotland. *Office:* Department of Sociology, University of Edinburgh, 18 Buccleuch Pl., Edinburgh EH8 9LN, Scotland.

CAREER: University of Edinburgh, Edinburgh, Scotland, lecturer, 1964-68, reader, 1968-74, professor of sociology, 1974—. *Member:* British Sociological Association, American Sociological Association.

WRITINGS: Catholic Action in Italy, Stanford University Press, 1965; *Images of Society,* Stanford University Press, 1972; *The Development of the Modern State,* Stanford University Press, 1978.

* * *

POLANSKY, Norman A. 1918-

PERSONAL: Born October 22, 1918, in Carbondale, Pa.; son of Joseph Joel (a merchant) and Cecelia (Kaplan) Polansky; married wife, Grace H., March 8, 1944 (divorced, 1964); married Nancy Finley, February 7, 1964; children: Vaughn, Jonathan. *Education:* Harvard University, A.B., 1940; graduate study at University of Iowa, 1940-41; Case Western Reserve University, M.S.S.A., 1943; University of Michigan, Ph.D., 1951. *Politics:* Democrat. *Religion:* Jewish. *Home:* 210 Great Oak Dr., Athens, Ga. 30605. *Office:* Department of Social Work, University of Georgia, Athens, Ga. 30602.

CAREER: Austen Riggs Center, Stockbridge, Mass., psychologist, 1952-55; Case Western Reserve University, Cleveland, Ohio, professor of social work, 1955-60; Highland Hospital, Asheville, N.C., psychologist and director of Social Service, 1960-64; University of Georgia, Athens, Regents' Professor of Social Work, 1964—. Member of faculty at Smith College; consultant to National Institute of Mental Health and U.S. Department of Health, Education and Welfare. *Military service:* U.S. Army, 1943-46; became staff sergeant. *Member:* American Orthopsychiatric Association (member of board of directors, 1961-63), National Association of Social Workers (member of board of directors, 1957-59), Council on Social Work Education, Phi Beta Kappa, Sigma Xi, Psi Chi.

WRITINGS: (Editor) *Social Work Research,* University of Chicago Press, 1960, 2nd edition, 1975; *Ego Psychology and Communication,* Aldine, 1971; (with C. DeJaix and S. Sharlin) *Child Neglect,* Child Welfare League of America, 1972; (with DeJaix and R. D. Bergman) *Roots of Futility,* Jossey-Bass, 1972. Member of editorial board of *Social Work, American Journal of Orthopsychiatry, Merrill-Palmer Quarterly of Behavior and Development,* and *Journal of Social Science Research.*

WORK IN PROGRESS: Continuing research on child neglect.

SIDELIGHTS: Polansky comments: ''My intent has been to draw on behavioral science to improve the practice of social work. In this I have had some success, while also teaching and doing therapy.'' *Avocational interests:* Playing the violin, sailing, swimming.

* * *

POLING, David 1928-

PERSONAL: Born October 15, 1928, in Spring Lake, N.J.; son of Paul Newton and Olive (Tomlinson) Poling; married Ann Reid, September 5, 1950; children: John, Lesley Poling Kempes, Andrew, Charles. *Education:* College of Wooster, B.A., 1950; Yale University, M.Div., 1953. *Home:* 3735 Manchester N.W., Albuquerque, N.M. 87107. *Office:* First United Presbyterian Church, 215 Locust N.E., Albuquerque, N.M. 87102.

CAREER: Ordained Presbyterian minister; pastor of Presbyterian churches in Leroy, N.Y., 1953-57, Buffalo, N.Y., 1957-62, and Bartlesville, Okla., 1962-64; *Christian Herald,* New York, N.Y., 1964-68, began as associate editor, became president; Synod of New Mexico and Synod of the Southwest, Albuquerque, director of Southwest Mission Foundation, 1971-75; First United Presbyterian Church, Albuquerque, N.M., pastor, 1975—. President of Golden Rule Foundation and Memorial-Home Community (Penny Farms, Fla.); member of board of trustees of College of Wooster, Presbyterian Hospital Center, and Ghost Ranch Foundation. *Member:* Humane Association of the United States (member of board of directors), Yale Club, Union League of New York, Rotary International. *Awards, honors:* L.H.D. from Willamette University, 1969; D.D. from Hope College, 1970.

WRITINGS: The Last Years of the Church, Doubleday, 1969; *They Walked With Christ,* Enterprise Press, 1971; (with George Marshall) *Schweitzer,* Doubleday, 1971; (editor) *This Great Company,* Keats Publishing, 1976; *Songs of Faith, Signs of Hope,* Word, Inc., 1976; *Why Billy Graham?,* Zondervan, 1977. Author of a column syndicated by National Education Association, 1966—. Contributor to religious periodicals, popular magazines, and newspapers, including *Saturday Review, McCall's,* and *Reader's Digest.*

* * *

POLLOCK, Ted 1929-

PERSONAL: Born September 3, 1929, in Hazleton, Pa.; son of Harry (in business) and Esther (Liberman) Pollock; married Barbara Gore, January 13, 1957; children: Jill Rachel. *Education:* Brooklyn College (now of the City University of New York), B.A., 1949; Duke University, M.A., 1950; Columbia University, Ph.D., 1959. *Residence:* Old Tappan, N.J. *Agent:* Wieser & Wieser, Inc., 60 East 42nd St., New York, N.Y.

CAREER: Nasson College, Springfield, Maine, assistant professor of English, 1955-56; free-lance writer, 1957-61; Institute for Business Research, Inc., Englewood, N.J., president, 1961-68; International Business Machines Corp., North Tarrytown, N.Y., program manager, 1968—. *Military service:* U.S. Army, 1953-55. *Member:* Authors Guild, Mystery Writers of America.

WRITINGS: The Professional Salesman's Guide, Prentice-Hall, 1964; *Managing Creatively,* two volumes, Cahners, 1971; *The Rainbow Man* (suspense novel), McGraw, 1979; *Moving on Up,* Hawthorn, 1979. Contributor to business and management journals.

WORK IN PROGRESS: Research for a suspense novel set in the United States.

SIDELIGHTS: Pollock has written that his first novel was begun simply to see if he could do it. The idea of writing a novel came about before the story line evolved. He wrote late at night for more than a year, with music in the background to set the mood, aiming at a book which would provide entertainment and suspense.

Pollock comments: "Although I've been writing professionally for more than twenty years, my first work of fiction has been my most personally rewarding work to date. I find that I enjoy the challenges of the thriller *genre* and, while I certainly do not plan to limit myself to it, my next novel will be a thriller, too. Then I plan to take a fling at a play, probably a comedy. As you might surmise from that, I am basically an optimistic person."

BIOGRAPHICAL/CRITICAL SOURCES: Library Journal, February 1, 1979; *Writer,* June, 1979.

* * *

POLUNIN, Oleg 1914-

PERSONAL: Born November 28, 1914, in Reading, England; son of Vladimir (an artist) and Elizabeth (an artist; maiden name, Hart) Polunin; married Lorna Mary Venning, June 7, 1943; children: Ivan, Natasha Polunin Hilton. *Education:* Magdalen College, Oxford, M.A., 1942. *Home:* 2 Lockwood Court, Knoll Rd., Godalming, Surrey GU7 2EP, England.

CAREER: Charterhouse School, Godalming, England, assistant master, 1938-72; writer, 1972—. Conducted botanical explorations in Nepal, 1949-52, Turkey, 1954-56, Pakistan, 1960, Kashmir, Iraq, and Lebanon. Lecturer and guide on tours of Greece, Turkey, Iran, India, and other countries. Founding member and former head of Surrey Naturalists' Trust. *Military service:* British Army, Intelligence Corps, 1940-46; became captain. *Member:* Royal Horticultural Society, Linnean Society, Alpine Garden Society. *Awards, honors:* Veitch Memorial Medal from Royal Horticultural Society, 1962, for introducing new horticultural species.

WRITINGS: (With A. J. Huxley) *Flowers of the Mediterranean,* Chatto & Windus, 1965; *Flowers of Europe,* Oxford University Press, 1969; *Concise Flowers of Europe,* Oxford University Press, 1972; (with B. E. Smythies) *Flowers of South-West Europe,* Oxford University Press, 1973; *Trees and Bushes of Europe,* Oxford University Press, 1976; *Flowers of Greece and the Balkans,* Oxford University Press, 1980.

WORK IN PROGRESS: Field Guide to the Flowers of the Himalayas, publication by Oxford University Press expected in 1982; *Atlas of the Vegetation of Europe,* Oxford University Press, 1983.

SIDELIGHTS: Polunin writes: "As an educator and former schoolmaster I am now very happy to be able to 'educate' a much wider public. My books are meant to be used in the field as a means of identifying plants, and are for amateurs and professionals alike. They have been translated into seven western European languages, and the demand for them is continuous.

"I have undertaken many plant-hunting expeditions in Europe and Asia; my collections are represented in the British Museum. I have amassed a large collection of plant photographs taken in the field. I have also acted as a tour leader for botanical tourist parties, and am able to appreciate what information and books are required in the field by the ordinary traveller. I have to fulfill the difficult task of adapting expert taxonomic botanical knowledge to a more popular format acceptable to the amateur as well as the professional biologist."

AVOCATIONAL INTERESTS: Making stoneware pottery.

* * *

POMERANTZ, Charlotte 1930-

PERSONAL: Born July 24, 1930, in Brooklyn, N.Y.; daughter of Abraham L. (an attorney), and Phyllis (Cohen) Pomerantz; married Carl Marzani (a writer), November 12, 1966; children: Gabrielle Rose, David Avram. *Education:* Sarah Lawrence, B.A., 1953. *Home and office:* 260 West 21st St., New York, N.Y. 10011.

CAREER: Writer.

WRITINGS: (Editor) *A Quarter-Century of Un-Americana, 1938-1963: A Tragicomical Memorabilia of HUAC, House Un-American Activities Committee,* foreword by H. H. Wilson, Marzani & Munsell, 1963.

All fiction for children: *The Bear Who Couldn't Sleep,* illustrations by Meg Wohlberg, Morrow, 1965; *The Moon Pony,* illustrations by Loretta Trezzo, Young Scott Books, 1967; *Ask the Windy Sea,* illustrations by Nancy Grossman and Anita Siegel, Young Scott Books, 1968; *Why You Look Like You Whereas I Tend to Look Like Me,* pictures by Rosemary Wells and Susan Jeffers, Young Scott Books, 1969; *The Day They Parachuted Cats on Borneo: A Drama of Ecology* (play in rhyme), scenery by Jose Aruego, Young Scott Books, 1971; *The Piggy in the Puddle,* pictures by James Marshall, Macmillan, 1974; *The Princess and the Admiral,* drawings by Tony Chen, Addison-Wesley, 1974; *The Ballad of the Long-Tailed Rat,* illustrations by Marian Parry, Macmillan, 1975; *Detective Poufy's First Case; or, The Missing Battery-Operated Pepper Grinder,* pictures by Marty Norman, Addison-Wesley, 1976; *The Mango Tooth,* pictures by Marylin Hafner, Greenwillow Books, 1977; *The Downtown Fairy Godmother,* illustrations by Susanna Natti, Addison-Wesley, 1978; *The Tamarindo Puppy* (poems in English and Spanish), Greenwillow Books, 1979.

SIDELIGHTS: Most of Pomerantz's books, often described as "zany," are aimed at children from three to fourteen. Her play, *The Day They Parachuted Cats on Borneo,* is didactic, based on a true incident of ecological imbalance precipitated by the use of the chemical spray DDT on the island of Borneo. DDT was sprayed to put an end to malaria-carrying mosquitos, but in the process killed other more desirable creatures, including the cats. Rats then ran rampant until more felines were dispatched via parachute to rescue the island. "It is a complicated chain superbly presented in an amusing verse-play format and excellent illustrations," observed Randolph Hogan in the *New York Times.*

BIOGRAPHICAL/CRITICAL SOURCES: New York Times Book Review, August 15, 1971, May 5, 1974; *Language Arts,* March 15, 1974, February 2, 1976, February 1, 1977, September, 1977, November 1, 1978.

* * *

POMEROY, William J(oseph) 1916-

PERSONAL: Born November 25, 1916, in Waterloo, N.Y.; son of William Charles (a metalworker) and Bertha Louella (Jetto) Pomeroy; married Celia Bautista Mariano (a teacher), May 28, 1948. *Education:* Attended University of the Philippines, 1948-50; Soviet Union Academy of Sciences, Ph.D., 1972. *Politics:* Communist. *Religion:* None. *Home:* 15 Roseleigh Close, Cambridge Park, Twickenham TW1 2JT, England.

CAREER: Writer, 1946—. Also worked as metal grinder, foundry worker, punch-press operator, and construction worker. *Military service:* U.S. Army Air Forces, historian, 1942-46; served in Pacific theater; became staff sergeant. *Member:* International Organization of Journalists.

WRITINGS: Born of the People, International Publishers, 1953; *The Forest,* International Publishers, 1963; *Beyond Barriers* (poems), Pedro Ayuda & Co., 1963; *Guerrilla and Counter-Guerrilla Warfare,* International Publishers, 1964; *Half a Century of Socialism: Soviet Life in the Sixties,* International Publishers, 1967; *Chelobek na doroge* (stories; title means "Man on the Road"; translated into Russian by K. Zhukovski and others), Creative Literature Publishers, 1968; (editor and author of introduction) *Guerrilla Warfare and Marxism,* International Publishers, 1968; *American Neo-Colonialism: Its Formation in the Philippines and Asia,* International Publishers, 1970; *Apartheid Axis: The U.S. and South Africa,* International Publishers, 1971; *Trail of Blame* (stories), International Publishers, 1971; *An American-Made Tragedy: Neo-Colonialism and Dictatorship in the Philippines,* International Publishers, 1974; *Soviet Reality in the Seventies,* Progress Publishers, 1979.

Contributor: Arturo G. Roseburg, editor, *Essays: English, American, Filipino,* Bardavon, 1950; Leo Huberman and Paul M. Sweezy, editors, *Regis Debray and the Latin American Revolution,* Monthly Review Press, 1968; Alister Taylor, editor, *Peace, Power, and Politics in Asia,* [Wellington, New Zealand], 1969; Jessica Smith, editor, *A Family of Peoples,* New World Review, 1973; Mark Selden, editor, *Re-Making Asia,* Random House, 1974; Marilyn Bechtel, David Laibman, and Smith, editors, *Six Decades That Changed the World,* New World Review, 1978.

Work anthologized in *Poets of Today,* International Publishers, 1964; *Puls zemli* (title means "Pulse of the Earth"), Creative Literature Publishers, 1973; *Philippineskie novelli* (title means "Philippine Stories"), Zhazushi, 1973.

Author of political pamphlets and textbooks in the Philippines. Correspondent from the Philippines for *Allied Labor News,* 1947-50; staff correspondent for *National Guardian,* 1963-68, and *Daily World,* 1968—. Contributor of about twenty-five-hundred articles, stories, poems, and reviews to magazines and newspapers all over the world, including *Daily Worker, Monthly Review, Science and Society,* and *American Dialogue.* Member of editorial board of *Labour Monthly,* 1969—.

WORK IN PROGRESS: Research for a book on the history of the left-wing movement in the Philippines.

SIDELIGHTS: Pomeroy writes: "The most important factor in the shaping of my career as a writer has been my participation in the Communist movement in the United States, the Philippines, and elsewhere in the world. This began in 1937, the most immediate reason being identification with the anti-fascist struggles in many countries, and especially in Spain, at that time.

"While in the U.S. Army during World War II, I was in the Pacific theater, in campaigns from Australia all the way to Japan. I came in contact with the Communist-led anti-Japanese guerrilla movement in the Philippines known as the Huk movement. After the war, I worked in the United States long enough to earn my passage by ship and returned to the Philippines at the end of 1946 as a free-lance writer, intending to write about the Huk movement. When I arrived there the movement was being brutally suppressed and was fighting back; it was the start of a long armed liberation struggle. I managed to contact the underground movement

and to travel extensively with the guerrilla forces, interviewing leaders and members. The result was my first book, *Born of the People,* published as the autobiography of Huk leader Luis Taruc.

"In 1948 I married a Filipina who was a leading member of the Huk movement, and while I was enrolled as a student at the University of the Philippines, we were both active in the Manila underground of the movement. In April, 1950, we both accepted an assignment to join the guerrilla forces of the movement in the mountains of Luzon island, to conduct the political schools of the movement and to supervise its propaganda activities. As chief of the propaganda department, I produced a vast amount of written material, in pamphlet, leaflet, magazine, and textbook forms. I was also chief editor of the theoretical magazine of the movement. Our experiences in the guerrilla struggle were recounted in my book *The Forest.*

"In April, 1952, my wife and I were both captured in battle. We were tried and sentenced to life imprisonment under the charge of 'rebellion complexed with murder, arson, robbery, and kidnapping.' This unreal and illegal charge was later declared or ruled unlawful by the Philippine Supreme Court. However, we were in prison as political prisoners for ten years until, at the end of 1961, we were both released on presidential pardon, due to a campaign for our release conducted internationally by American friends. I was deported to the United States, but my wife was barred from joining me by the McCarran-Walter Immigration Act. Due to the fact that neither of us can go to the other's country for political reasons, we have lived in more tolerant England since 1963.

"I mention this background because it has a bearing on my writing. While in prison I did a considerable amount of writing, including short stories, poems, and the manuscript of *The Forest.* Many of the short stories written in prison were later published in magazines in various countries and in books. Many of the poems were published in *Beyond Barriers* a year after our release. The manuscript of *The Forest* could not be taken out of prison when I was released, so when I reached the United States after deportation, I secluded myself in a rented room in New York City and rewrote the entire manuscript from memory in one month.

"During forty years or more of writing, I have been more or less successful with short stories, poetry, history, biography, essays (both personal and formal), book reviews, literary criticism, humor, propaganda, and political journalism; in the latter I have specialized in writing about international affairs."

AVOCATIONAL INTERESTS: "I have a deep love for classical music, which I like to have playing while I write, and a general love for all the arts—painting, ballet, drama, and the cinema in particular. Reading has been a passion for all my conscious life. Military matters have also fascinated me, and I have written a good deal about guerrilla warfare. An interest in sports has declined with age, but I do a great deal of walking (I do not own and never have owned a car). One of my greatest enjoyments is traveling: I am endlessly interested in new places. I have traveled in Asia and Europe, both east and west. I have been in the Soviet Union frequently, and twelve out of the fifteen Soviet republics, with special interest in central Asia. Additional interests: cooking, gardening, talking with friends, cats, sea voyages. In truth, I must confess to being interested in just about everything under the sun."

PONGE, Francis (Jean Gaston Alfred) 1899-

PERSONAL: Surname is pronounced ponzh; born March 27, 1899, in Montpellier, France; son of Armand (a bank director) and Juliette (Saurel) Ponge; married Odette Chabanel, July 4, 1931; children: Armande. *Education:* Educated in France. *Residence:* Paris, France.

CAREER: Poet and essayist. Editions Gallimard (publisher), Paris, France, secretary, 1923; Hachette (publisher), Paris, France, secretary, 1931-37; Progress de Lyon, Bourg-en-Bresse, France, head of center, 1942; Alliance Francaise, Paris, France, professor, 1952-64. Editor of *Progres* (newspaper), Lyon, France. Political traveler for National Committee of Journalists, 1942-44. Literary and artistic director of *Action*, 1944-46. Virginia C. Gildersleeve Visiting Professor at Barnard College and Columbia University, 1966-67. Lecturer; has made many lecture tours in France and abroad. *Military service:* Member of French Resistance during World War II. *Member:* Bayerischen Akademie der Schoenen Kuenste. *Awards, honors:* Officer of Legion d'honneur; international poetry prize, 1959; international Ingram Merrill Foundation award, 1972; International Books Abroad Literature Prize, 1974.

WRITINGS—In English: *La Savon* (poetry), Gallimard, 1967, translation by Lane Dunlop published as *Soap*, J. Cape, 1969; *Two Prose Poems*, translated from the French by Peter Hoy, Black Knight Press, 1968; *Rain: A Prose Poem*, translated from the French by Hoy, Poet & Printer, 1969; *Things*, translation by Cid Corman of selected poems, Grossman, 1971; (with Pierre Descargues and Andre Malraux) *G. Braque, de Draeger*, Draeger, 1971, translation by Richard Howard and Lane Dunlop published as *G. Braque*, Abrams, 1971; *The Voice of Things*, translation by Beth Archer of selected poems, McGraw, 1972.

Other writings: *Le Parti pris des choses* (poetry), Gallimard, 1942; *L'Oeillet, le guepe, le mimose* (poetry), Mermod, 1946; *Le Carnet du bois de pins*, Mermod, 1947; *Liasse: Vignt-et-un Textes suivis d'une bibliographie*, Ecrivains reunis, 1948; *Le Peintre a l'etude*, Gallimard, 1948; *Proemes*, Gallimard, 1948; *La Seine*, Guilde du livre, 1950; *La Rage de l'expression*, Mermod, 1952.

Le Grand Recueil, Gallimard, Volume I: *Lyres*, 1961, Volume II: *Methodes*, 1961, Volume III: *Pieces*, 1961; *Francis Ponge*, edited by Philippe Sollers, P. Seghers, 1963; *De La Nature morte et de Chardin*, Hermann, 1964; *Pour un Malherbe*, Gallimard, 1965; *Tome premier*, Gallimard, 1965; *Nouveau Recueil*, Gallimard, 1967; *Ponge*, edited by Jean Thibaudeau, Gallimard, 1967; *Le Parti pris des choses, precede de douze petits ecrits et suivi de proemes*, Gallimard, 1967.

Entretiens de Francis Ponge avec Philippe Sollers, edited by Sollers, Gallimard, 1970; *La Fabrique du "pre"*, Albert Skira, 1971; *Ici haute*, R. G. Cadou, 1971; (with Pierre Descargues and Edward Quinn) *Picasso de Draeger* Draeger, 1974; (contributor) *A Phillipe Jaccottet*, La Revue de belles-lettres, 1976; *L'Atelier contemporaine/Francis Ponge*, Gallimard, 1977; *Ponge: Inventeur et classique*, Union generale d'editions, 1977; *Comment une figue de paroles et pourquoi/Francis Ponge*, Flammarion, 1977.

Also author of *The Sun Placed in the Abyss and Other Texts*, SUN; *Douze Petits Ecrits*, 1926; *La Crevette dans tous ses etats*, 1948; *L'Araignee*, 1952; *Des Cristaux naturels*, P. Bettencourt.

Contributor of poems and essays to literary journals.

SIDELIGHTS: Ponge has been called the poet of things; a plant, a shell, a cigarette, a pebble, a piece of soap become the objects of his attention. "What has an imperious fascination for him," observed Betty Miller, "is the essence of the interior life of the plant or shell, so that we feel in reading him almost as though it were the plant which spoke to express miraculously, without human intervention, its personality." Many critics note that his poems are an attempt to strip away some of the stereotypes and abstractions that have been imposed on things, to restore some sense of their "isolated yet radiant" existence. "The thrill in reading Ponge," remarked Michael Lally, "is in discovering the wealth of revelations, and extensions of them, to be found in the careful and accurate descriptions of things." The *Times Literary Supplement* added: "The almost fetichist excitement which Ponge clearly feels in the precise delineation of scenes and things seems to be his essential gift."

BIOGRAPHICAL/CRITICAL SOURCES: Nouvelle Revue Francaise, September, 1956; *Times Literary Supplement*, May 4, 1962, September 30, 1965, September 12, 1968; Alexander Aspel and D. R. Justice, editors, *Contemporary French Poetry: 14 Witnesses of Man's Fate*, University of Michigan, 1965; *New York Times*, October 28, 1971, October 30, 1971; *National Observer*, December 18, 1971; *Time*, December 20, 1971; *New York Review of Books*, November 30, 1972; *World Literature Today*, autumn, 1974, spring, 1978; *Contemporary Literary Criticism*, Volume 6, Gale, 1976; *Book World*, March 12, 1978.*

* * *

POOL, Eugene (Hillhouse) 1943-

PERSONAL: Born May 9, 1943, in New York, N.Y.; son of J. Lawrence (a neurosurgeon) and Angeline (James) Pool; married Priscilla Choate, February 24, 1968; children: Nathan Beekman. *Education:* Harvard University, A.B. (cum laude), 1964; Boston University, M.A., 1973. *Office:* Buckingham Browne & Nichols School, Cambridge, Mass. 02138.

CAREER: Buckingham Browne & Nichols School, Cambridge, Mass., teacher of English, 1964—. *Military service:* U.S. Army Reserve, 1967-73.

WRITINGS: The Captain of Battery Park (novel for children), Addison-Wesley, 1978.

WORK IN PROGRESS: A children's book.

SIDELIGHTS: Pool writes: "*The Captain of Battery Park* is about an eleven-year-old girl who lives in New York City. She rescues an Arctic tern and meets Dr. William Kidd, a man who lives in an old warehouse full of birds of all kinds and who does everything he can to live up to the reputation of his namesake, the notorious pirate. All of my books will have animals in them.

"I am a long-distance runner of many years' experience. My best time for a marathon is 2:45:28."

* * *

PORTER, Peter (Neville Frederick) 1929-

PERSONAL: Born February 16, 1929, in Brisbane, Australia; son of William Ronald (a businessman) and Marion (a nurse; maiden name, Main) Porter; married Jannice Henry (a nurse), 1961 (died, 1974); children: two daughters. *Education:* Educated in Brisbane, Australia, and Toowoomba, Australia. *Home:* 42 Cleveland Sq., London, England.

CAREER: Poet and free-lance writer. Worked as journalist, bookseller, clerk, and in advertising. Compton Lecturer in poetry at University of Hull, 1970-71; visiting lecturer in English at University of Reading, fall, 1972, at Sydney University, summer, 1975, and at University of New England, Armidale, autumn, 1977.

WRITINGS: Once Bitten, Twice Bitten: Poems, Scorpion Press, 1961; (with Kingsley Amis and Dom Moraes) *Penguin Modern Poets 2*, Penguin, 1962; *Poems, Ancient and Modern*, Walker, 1964; *Words Without Music* (poetry), Sycamore Press, 1968; *A Porter Folio: New Poems*, Scorpion Press, 1969; *The Last of England* (poetry), Oxford University Press, 1970; (editor) Alexander Pope, *A Choice of Pope's Verse*, Faber, 1971; (editor) *New Poems, 1971-72: A P.E.N. Anthology of Contemporary Poetry*, Hutchinson, 1972; *After Martial* (poetry), Oxford University Press, 1972; *Preaching to the Converted* (poetry), Oxford University Press, 1972; (with Arthur Boyd) *Jonah*, Secker and Warburg, 1973; *A Share of the Market* (poetry), Ulsterman Publications, 1973; (editor with Anthony Thwaite) *The English Poets: From Chaucer to Edward Thomas*, Secker and Warburg, 1974; (with Roloff Beny) *Roloff Beny in Italy*, Harper, 1974; (with Boyd) *The Lady and the Unicorn*, Secker and Warburg, 1975; *Living in a Calm Country* (poetry), Oxford University Press, 1975; *The Cost of Seriousness* (poetry), Oxford University Press, 1978.

Also author of radio plays, including "The Siege of Munster," 1971, "The Children's Crusade," 1973, and "All He Brought Back From the Dream," 1978. Contributor to periodicals and newspapers, including *Encounter, New Statesman, Observer,* and *London Magazine*.

WORK IN PROGRESS: Narcissus, with W. Arthur Boyd, completion expected in 1980; *Collected Poems*, completion expected in 1981; an untitled volume of new poems, completion expected in 1981.

SIDELIGHTS: Porter's early work shows the influence of W. H. Auden. A critic for *London Magazine*, in a review of *Poems, Ancient and Modern*, noted, "Porter has a lot in common with Auden: love of theories and ideas as such (even theology), love of unusual words. . . ." He also hinted that Auden's influence was too evident in Porter's first volumes. "Indeed," wrote the *London Magazine* reviewer in reference to *Poems, Ancient and Modern*, "Spot the Auden is a game that can too easily be played with this book. . . ." However, the reviewer found Porter's second collection to be an improvement over *Once Bitten, Twice Bitten*. "*Poems, Ancient and Modern* has, I think, more successful poems in it than *Once Bitten, Twice Bitten*," he declared. "The props, historical, scenic and cultural, do not get in the way of the poetry. . . ."

By the time *A Porter Portfolio* was published, Porter had shown an inclination to master various poetic techniques. Although Brian Jones remarked that the resemblance to Auden was still evident, the same reviewer felt that Porter had created "a volume . . . in which achievement and experiment make interesting bedfellows. . . ." Jones called *A Porter Portfolio* "an interim book, full of promise for the next period."

Porter's affection for Auden was still evident in *The Last of England*. Again, as John Fuller observed, "Porter acknowledges the influence . . . and sometimes indeed it shows very directly. . . ." But Fuller also asserted that Porter was "consciously enlarging and varying his approach." And he concluded that "most of the time the Audenesque modes are productive, and Porter's voice speaks clearly and individually from them, shrewd, tart and chasteningly funny." Porter's reputation as a "sensuous" poet also began flourishing

with *The Last England*. "In the past," wrote Alan Brownjohn, "he hasn't always moved with complete success from the detached, satirical voice to the personal, but in the new volume his more intimate, ruminative poems are among the best, pointing towards a promising development of a more sensuous side to his immensely resourceful and intelligent talent."

After the publication of *Preaching to the Converted*, Porter was hailed by David Selzer as a "major poet." Selzer had expressed disappointment with Porter's previous work, *After Martial*, writing, "I know that *After Martial* will be more widely read than *Preaching to the Converted*, but, generally good though the former is, it does poorly, in comparison, as a measure of us." But he also conceded, "There is a richness of texture in all of Mr. Porter's work, a richness of metrical forms, content, metaphor. . . ." Douglas Dunn believed that in *Preaching to the Converted* Porter had successfully fused his sensuousness with his satiric wit. "He laments contemporary horrors as if he were the maestro of a famous Carnival shut down because of plague," wrote Dunn. "Porter is more than just a 'social poet.' He is a tragedian who can't stop laughing."

Porter's continual growth as a poet received Dunn's attention again with *Living in a Calm Country*. "Rhythmically," wrote Dunn, "he is more assured; he is altogether closer to the mastery of idiom his ambitious work has been demanding." Russell Davies was another critic impressed by Porter's sensuous yet satiric style. "Porter strikes me as one of the very few modern poets who can communicate distress without giving the feeling that he is congratulating himself on being able to live with himself," revealed Davies. A reviewer for *Choice* seemed to think that Porter had not yet fulfilled his promise as a poet with *Living in a Calm Country*. "One is not convinced that the poet has fully come to terms with his own experience," claimed the *Choice* critic, "but he makes engaging poems out of a strongly identified European cultural heritage and keenly ironic observation. . . ."

Porter's most recent collection, *The Cost of Seriousness*, shows a marked preoccupation with death. As a critic for *Encounter* noted, "Peter Porter has always been . . . interested in death: in his earlier collections he frequently reflected upon the deaths of others or contemplated his own. . . ." "Now," continued the reviewer, "in this fine new collection death is at the centre." However, Fuller found *The Cost of Seriousness* "no less varied than usual. . . ." He particularly praised "Roman Incident," finding it "the penultimate poem in the book." "Roman Incident," contended Fuller, "provides a characteristic . . . culmination of the uncomfortable self-appraisal in this book."

BIOGRAPHICAL/CRITICAL SOURCES: London Magazine, February, 1965, October, 1969; *New Statesman*, September 25, 1970, October 24, 1975, June 2, 1978; *Listener*, December 24, 1970; *Encounter*, March, 1973, February, 1976, August, 1978; *Phoenix*, July, 1973; *Choice*, March, 1976; *Contemporary Literary Criticism*, Volume 5, Gale, 1976.

* * *

PORTER, Raymond J(ames) 1935-

PERSONAL: Born January 3, 1935, in Mt. Vernon, N.Y.; son of James Joseph (a plumbing contractor) and Gertrude (Kirchoff) Porter; married Lilyann Mitchell, November 19, 1960; children: Alison, Elaine, Colin. *Education:* College of the Holy Cross, B.A., 1957; Columbia University, M.A.,

1963, Ph.D., 1970. *Politics:* Independent. *Religion:* Roman Catholic. *Home:* 46 Revere Rd., Larchmont, N.Y. 10538. *Office:* Department of English, Iona College, 715 North Ave., New Rochelle, N.Y. 10801.

CAREER: Iona College, New Rochelle, N.Y., professor of English, 1961—. Part-time professional musician. *Member:* Modern Language Association of America, American Committee for Irish Studies, James Joyce Society.

WRITINGS: (Editor with James D. Brophy) *Modern Irish Literature: Essays in Honor of W. Y. Tindall*, Twayne, 1972; *Brendan Behan*, Columbia University Press, 1973; *P. H. Pearse*, Twayne, 1973. Contributor to literature journals and *Eire-Ireland*.

WORK IN PROGRESS: The Novels of Brian Moore.

* * *

POSPELOV, Pyotr Nikolayevich 1898-1979

OBITUARY NOTICE: Born June 20, 1898, in Konakovo, Russia (now U.S.S.R.); died in 1979. Soviet Communist Party theoretician and editor. Pospelov gained recognition for his outspoken manner regarding Soviet-American relations. In 1951 he predicted that the United States would suffer a fate similar to Nazi Germany if it instigated war or interfered with activities in the Soviet Union. A staunch party supporter, Pospelov often quoted Lenin; he accused Stalin of being responsible for the lack of Soviet accomplishments during his years in power. Pospelov also spoke favorably of Khrushchev during that leader's tenure as party chief. He edited a history of the Soviet involvement in World War II as well as an account of the Communist Party during the 1930's. Obituaries and other sources: *International Who's Who*, Europa, 1978; *New York Times*, April 24, 1979.

* * *

POST, Austin 1922-

PERSONAL: Born March 16, 1922, in Chelan, Wash. *Office:* U.S. Geological Survey, Tacoma, Wash. 98402.

CAREER: Research hydrologist, U.S. Geological Survey, Tacoma, Wash.

WRITINGS: Effects of the March 1964 Alaska Earthquake on Glaciers, U.S. Government Printing Office, 1967; (with Edward R. LaChapelle) *Glacier Ice*, University of Toronto Press, 1971; *Inventory of Glaciers in the North Cascades*, U.S. Government Printing Office, 1971.

* * *

POULTON, Edith Eleanor (Diana) Chloe 1903-

PERSONAL: Surname is pronounced *Pole*-ton; born April 18, 1903; daughter of Gilbert (a farmer) and Ethel (a painter; maiden name, Curtis) Kibblewhite; married Thomas Leycester Poulton (an illustrator), April 9, 1923 (deceased); children: Alethea Virginia (deceased), Celia Poulton Clayton. *Education:* Attended Slade School of Fine Art; studied the lute privately. *Politics:* Labour. *Home:* 5 Wilton Sq., Islington, London N1 3DL, England.

CAREER: Performer on the lute. Professor at Royal College of Music, 1969—. Broadcaster on radio and television in France, Sweden, and England, 1926—; gives lectures and recitals. *Member:* Lute Society (co-founder; president), Society for Renaissance Studies, Incorporated Society of Musicians, Viola da Gamba Society, Society of Genealogists, Dolmetsch Foundation, Lute Society of America. *Awards, honors:* H.R.C.M., Royal College of Music, 1970.

WRITINGS: An Introduction to Lute Playing, Schott & Co., 1961; (editor) *English Ballad Tunes for the Lute*, Gamut Publications, 1965; *John Dowland*, Faber, 1972; (editor with Basil Lam) *Collected Lute Music of John Dowland*, Faber, 1974, 2nd edition, 1978. Also editor of the revision of Ernst Meyer's, *English Chamber Music*.

Co-author of "John Dowland" (radio play). Contributor to *New Grove's Dictionary of Music and Musicians*. Contributor to music journals.

WORK IN PROGRESS: A book on the lute and its music; editing four songbooks by John Dowland; revising *An Introduction to Lute Playing*.

SIDELIGHTS: Diana Poulton writes that her special interest is sixteenth-century Spanish music.

* * *

POVEY, John F. 1929-

PERSONAL: Born April 5, 1929, in London, England; son of Frederick (a surveyor) and Muriel (Lambert) Povey; married Gail Enslow, November 27, 1960. *Education:* University of South Africa, B.A., 1954, M.A., 1956; Michigan State University, Ph.D., 1962. *Politics:* None. *Religion:* None. *Home:* 20651 Seaboard Rd., Malibu, Calif. 90265. *Office:* Department of English, University of California, Los Angeles, Calif. 90074.

CAREER: University of California, Los Angeles, professor of English, 1964—. *Member:* African Studies Association, Teachers of English to Speakers of Other Languages.

WRITINGS: Ray Campbell, Twayne, 1977. Editor of *African Arts*.

WORK IN PROGRESS: Research on contemporary South African literature.

* * *

POWELL, Neil 1948-

PERSONAL: Born February 11, 1948, in London, England. *Education:* University of Warwick, B.A., 1969, M.Phil., 1975. *Office:* c/o Carcanet Press, Ltd., 330 Corn Exchange, Manchester M4 3BG, England.

CAREER: Teacher of English at a school in Huntingdon, England, 1971-74; St. Christopher School, Letchworth, England, teacher of English, 1974—. *Member:* Society of Authors. *Awards, honors:* Gregory Award from Society of Authors, 1969.

WRITINGS: Suffolk Poems, Mandeville, 1975; *At the Edge* (poems), Carcanet Press, 1977; *Carpenters of Light* (criticism), Carcanet Press, 1979.

Work anthologized in *Ten English Poets*, Carcanet Press, 1976. Contributor to magazines, including *London*, *Encounter*, and *New Statesman*.

WORK IN PROGRESS: Windows (tentative title), poems; *The End of English*, essays; *Shakespeare and the Turn of a Century* (tentative title), criticism.

SIDELIGHTS: Powell writes: "My obsessional interests are music (mostly early) and gardening (mostly shrubs); I'm bound to admit that these strike me as, in many ways, more noble and satisfying skills than literature. Otherwise, such statements as I care to make—or can't help making—about myself are in my poems."

POWELL, Philip Wayne   1913-
(Philip Wayne)

PERSONAL: Born October 30, 1913, in Chino, Calif.; son of Robert Chester and June (Holcomb) Powell; married Maria Luisa Vanegas Guarin, January 22, 1942; children: Diana Linda Powell Fornas, Lilia Patricia Powell Rochester. *Education:* Attended Occidental College, 1930-32; University of California, Berkeley, A.B., 1936, Ph.D., 1941. *Home:* 1216 Shoreline Dr., Santa Barbara, Calif. 93109. *Office:* Department of History, University of California, Santa Barbara, Calif. 93106.

CAREER: U.S. Department of State, Washington, D.C., divisional assistant, 1941-43; University of Pennsylvania, Philadelphia, visiting professor of history, 1943-44; Northwestern University, Evanston, Ill., assistant professor of history, 1944-48; University of California, Santa Barbara, associate professor, 1948-54, professor of history, 1954—, head of department, 1958, 1962-64, director of study center, University of Madrid, 1964-66. National head of U.S. Conference on Latin American History, 1947; adviser to International Conference of American States, Bogota, 1948; member of United States-Spain Fulbright Committee, 1965-66. *Military service:* U.S. Marine Corps Reserve, active duty, 1942-43.

MEMBER: American Academy of Franciscan History (associate), Western History Association, Westerners, Instituto de Cultura Hispanica (Spain; honorary member), Phi Beta Kappa, Phi Gamma Delta. *Awards, honors:* Rockefeller Foundation fellow, 1938-39; American Philosophical Society fellow, 1944; Del Amo Foundation fellow, 1950, 1955, 1961; commander, Order of Isabel la Catolica (Spain), 1974.

WRITINGS: Soldiers, Indians, and Silver: The Northward Advance of New Spain, 1550-1600, University of California Press, 1952, reprinted as *Soldiers, Indians, and Silver: North America's First Frontier War,* Center for Latin American Studies, Arizona State University, 1975; (under pseudonym Philip Wayne) *Ponzona en Las Nieves* (historical novel; title means "The Conspiracy at Nieves"), Porrua, 1966; *Tree of Hate: Propaganda and Prejudices Affecting United States Relations With the Hispanic World,* Basic Books, 1971; (editor) *War and Peace on the North Mexican Frontier: A Documentary Record,* Volume I: *Crescendo of the Chichimeca War, 1551-1585,* Porrua, 1971; *Mexico's Miguel Caldera: The Taming of America's First Frontier, 1548-1597,* University of Arizona Press, 1977. Advisory editor of *Americas.*

WORK IN PROGRESS: The Guns of San Juan, a book on the 1568 Hawkins-Drake defeat in Mexico and its global consequences.

SIDELIGHTS: Powell told CA: "Early in life, during elementary and secondary schooling in southern California, I became much aware of the wide chasm of cultural prejudice between Anglo- and Spanish-Americans as a schoolground witness of 'Gringo'-Mexican antagonisms. This experience led, with strong parental encouragement, to my deep interest in Spanish language and in Mexican culture and, from there, into the broader field of Latin American and Iberian studies (including much dedication to the literatures of those countries).

"Much of my writing, both nonfiction and fiction, carries some message of sympathy for Hispanic cultures and peoples and, simultaneously, attempts to correct erroneous views and harmful misconceptions pertaining to these peoples as so often held in the Nordic and Anglo-American mind, a deep historical prejudice that I explain in my *Tree of Hate,* a kind of history of the origins and growth of this hispanophobia that is known to scholars as the 'Black Legend.' In my forthcoming *Guns of San Juan,* a book concerning the origin of Spanish-English fighting on the seas and in European-American diplomacy, there is much corrective writing designed to dissipate the strong hispanophobic roots that come to us through English literature.

"I have traveled and lived in Europe and Latin America. I chose a career in historical research and writing for the sheer enjoyment of these pursuits; salary, royalties, and professional activities are secondary, in most ways, to the fun of it."

AVOCATIONAL INTERESTS: Music, tennis.

*   *   *

POWERS, Joseph M(ichael)   1926-

PERSONAL: Born February 27, 1926, in Rochester, N.Y.; son of Thomas James (a tool and die worker) and Florence (a medical secretary; maiden name, Armour) Powers. *Education:* Attended University of Santa Clara, 1945-47; Gonzaga University, earned B.A. and M.A., 1950; Pontifical Gregorian University, S.T.D., 1962. *Politics:* "Democrat leaning to socialist." *Residence:* Berkeley, Calif. *Office:* Jesuit School of Theology, 1735 Le Roy Ave., Berkeley, Calif. 94709.

CAREER: Entered Society of Jesus (Jesuits), 1943, ordained Roman Catholic priest, 1958; instructor in humanities at Bellarmine College Prep, 1950-52; Loyola High School, Los Angeles, Calif., instructor in Latin rhetoric, 1952-55; Alma College, Los Gatos, Calif., assistant professor of theology, 1962-69; Jesuit School of Theology, Berkeley, Calif., associate professor, 1969-80, professor of theology, 1980—. Visiting lecturer at Villanova University, University of Washington, Seattle, Loyola University, New Orleans, La., and Boston College. *Member:* North American Academy of Liturgy, Catholic Theological Society of America, American Academy of Religion, Pacific Coast Theological Society.

WRITINGS: (Contributor) J. Schall and D. Wolf, editors, *Current Trends in Theology,* Doubleday, 1965; *Eucharistic Theology,* Herder & Herder, 1967; *Spirit and Sacrament: The Humanizing Experience,* Seabury, 1973; (contributor) F. A. Eigo and Silvio Fittopaldi, editors, *American Spirituality: Independence and Interdependence,* Villanova University Press, 1976; (contributor) Paul Bernier, editor, *Bread From Heaven,* Paulist/Newman, 1977; (contributor) Fittopaldi, editor, *Christian Spirituality in the United States: Independence and Interdependence,* Villanova University Press, 1978. Contributor to *Encyclopedia Americana* and *New Catholic Encyclopedia.* Contributor of about twenty articles and reviews to scholarly journals.

WORK IN PROGRESS: A study of the interface between theology of faith and psychology of creativity.

SIDELIGHTS: Powers's languages include Italian, Dutch, German, French, Latin, and some Greek and Spanish; his writings have been translated into German, Spanish, and Italian.

Powers writes: "Although my field is usually characterized as 'systematic' or 'philosophical' theology, I usually refer to it as 'whimsical' theology—to the horror of more serious colleagues. When I was far more 'religious' than I am now, a wise old man answered my worried questions about the state of my soul and the world in general with the words, 'You're taking this religion business entirely too seriously.' It was the best piece of advice I ever had. Eventually it led me to believe that fidelity to a religious tradition can only be a creative fidelity, a reason for finding an intellectual father in Gabriel Marcel.

"On and off for about seven years I was a choral conductor—in spite of the fact that I could barely read music. That, along with the amateur theatrical experience I have had, has contributed to my own artistic endeavors as a teacher and writer.

"I guess that a lot of optimism, compassion, and megadoses of Vitamin B-Complex keep me rolling along."

*　　*　　*

POWYS, John Cowper   1872-1963

PERSONAL: Surname is pronounced *Po*-is; born October 8, 1872, in Shirley, Derbyshire, England; came to United States, 1928; died June 17, 1963, in Merionethshire, Wales; son of Charles Francis (an Anglican clergyman) and Mary Cowper (Johnson) Powys; married Margaret Alice Lyon, 1896 (died, 1947); children: one son. *Education:* Corpus Christi College, M.A. *Residence:* Blaenau-Festiniog, Wales.

CAREER: Educator, critic, novelist, and poet. Lecturer in literature at universities in England, including Oxford University and Cambridge University; lecturer at universities in the United States, winters c. 1904-34; lived in New York, 1928-34; returned to Wales, 1934; full-time writer, c. 1934-60. *Awards, honors:* Honorary doctor of letters from University of Wales.

WRITINGS: Odes and Other Poems, Rider & Co., 1896; *Poems,* Rider & Co, 1899; *The War and Culture: A Reply to Professor Muensterberg,* G. A. Shaw, 1914 (published in England as *The Menace of German Culture: A Reply to Professor Muensterberg,* Rider & Co., 1915); *Visions and Revisions: A Book of Literary Devotions,* G. A. Shaw, 1915, reprinted, CORE Collection, 1978; *Wood and Stone: A Romance,* G. A. Shaw, 1915; *Wolf's-Bane Rhymes* (poems), G. A. Shaw, 1916; *Confessions of Two Brothers,* Manas Press, 1916, reprinted, Scholarly Press, 1971; *One Hundred Best Books,* G. A. Shaw, 1916; *Rodmoor: A Romance,* G. A. Shaw, 1916, revised edition with preface by G. Wilson Knight, Colgate University Press, 1973; *Suspended Judgments: Essays on Books and Sensations,* G. A. Shaw, 1916, reprinted, Norwood Editions, 1977; *Mandragora* (poems), G. A. Shaw, 1917.

The Complex Vision, Dodd, 1920; *Samphire, T. Seltzer,* 1922; *The Art of Happiness,* Haldenian-Julius, 1923, reprinted, Village Press, 1974; *Psychoanalysis and Morality,* J. Colbert, 1923, reprinted, Village Press, 1975; *Ducdame* (novel), Doubleday, 1925; *The Religion of a Sceptic* (essays), Dodd, 1925, reprinted, Village Press, 1975; *The Secret of Self Development,* Haldeman-Julius, 1926, reprinted, Village Press, 1974; *The Art of Forgetting the Unpleasant,* Haldeman-Julius, 1928, reprinted, Village Press, 1974; *The Meaning of Culture* (essays), Norton, 1929, reprinted, 1957; *Wolf Solent* (novel), Simon & Schuster, 1929, reprinted, Scholarly Press, 1971.

The Owl, the Duck, and—Miss Rowe! Miss Rowe! (short stories), Black Archer Press, 1930, reprinted, Village Press, 1975; *In Defence of Sensuality* (essays), Simon & Schuster, 1930, reprinted, Village Press, 1974; *Dorothy M. Richardson,* Joiner and Steele, 1931; *A Glastonbury Romance* (novel), Simon & Schuster, 1932, reprinted, Pan Books, 1975; *A*

Philosophy of Solitude (essays), Simon & Schuster, 1933, reprinted, Village Press, 1974; *Weymouth Sands* (novel), Simon & Schuster, 1934, reprinted with an introduction by Angus Wilson, Rivers Press, 1973; *Autobiography,* Simon & Schuster, 1934, reprinted, New Directions, 1960, revised edition with introduction by J. B. Priestley and notes by R. I. Blackmore, Colgate University Press, 1968; *Jobber Skald* (novel), John Lane, 1935; *Maiden Castle* (novel), Simon & Schuster, 1936, reprinted, Colgate University Press, 1966; *Morwyn; or, The Vengeance of God* (novel), Cassell, 1937, reprinted, Sphere, 1977; *Enjoyment of Literature* (essays), Simon & Schuster, 1938 (published in England as *The Pleasures of Literature,* Cassell, 1938).

Owen Glendower (novel), Simon & Schuster, 1940, reprinted, Chivers, 1974; *Mortal Strife,* J. Cape, 1942, reprinted, Village Press, 1974; *The Art of Growing Old* (essays), J. Cape, 1944; *Dostoievsky* (essays), John Lane, 1946, reprinted, Haskell House, 1973; *Pair Dadeni; or, The Cauldron of Rebirth,* Druid Press, 1946; *Obstinste Cymric: Essays 1935-47,* Druid Press, 1947, reprinted, Village Press, 1973; *Rabelais: His Life, the Story Told by Him, Selections Therefrom Here Newly Translated, and an Interpretation of His Genius and His Religion,* Bodley Head, 1948, reprinted, Philosophical Library, 1951, reprinted, Village Press, 1974.

The Inmates (novel), Philosophical Library, 1952; *In Spite Of: A Philosophy for Everyman* (essays), Philosophical Library, 1953; *Atlantis* (essays), Macdonald, 1954, reprinted, Chivers, 1973; *The Brazen Head* (novel), Colgate University Press, 1956; *Lucifer: A Poem,* Macdonald, 1956; *Up and Out* (contains "Up and Out" and "The Mountains of the Moon"), Macdonald, 1957, reprinted, Village Press, 1974; *Ichiro Hara,* editor, *Culture and Nature,* Hokuseido Press, c. 1958; *Letters of John Cowper Powys to Louis Wilkinson, 1935-1956,* Colgate University Press, 1958; Hara, editor, *Culture and Life,* Hokuseido Press, c. 1958; *Homer and the Aether,* Macdonald, 1959.

All or Nothing, Macdonald, 1960, reprinted, Village Press, 1974; Kenneth Hopkins, editor and author of introduction, *John Cowper Powys: A Selection From His Poems,* Colgate University Press, 1964; Bernard Jones, editor, *Letters From John Cowper Powys to Glyn Hughes,* Ore Publications, 1971; Arthur Uphill, editor, *Letters to Nicholas Ross,* Bertram Rota, 1971; *William Blake,* Village Press, 1974; Iorwerth C. Peate, editor and author of introduction and notes, *John Cowper Powys: Letters, 1937-1954,* University of Wales Press, 1974; Bernard Jones, editor, *Romer Mowl and Other Stories* (contains "Romer Mowl," "The Spot on the Wall," and "The Harvest Thanksgiving"), Toucan Press, 1974; *Two and Two,* Village Press, 1974; *An Englishman Up-State,* Village Press, 1974; *Real Wraiths,* Village Press, 1974; Malcolm Elwin, editor, *Letters of John Cowper Powys to His Brother Llewelyn,* Village Press, 1975; *You and Me,* Village Press, 1975.

Also author of: (With Bertrand Russell) *Debate: Is Modern Marriage a Failure?,* 1930; *Porius: A Romance of the Dark Ages* (novel), 1951. Contributor to periodicals, including *Dial, American Mercury,* and *Century.*

SIDELIGHTS: John Cowper Powys belonged to a very literary family. His mother was collaterally related to the British poets William Cowper and John Donne. Of Powys's immediate family, six of his ten brothers and sisters also published books, although only two others, Llewelyn and Theodore Francis, achieved literary prominence.

It has been said of Powys's lectures and writings that they reveal more about him than about the intended subject. No matter how odd the characters, "nobody in a novel by Mr. Powys is ever as interesting as the author himself," observed Mark Van Doren. "His best book is still his 'Autobiography,' which is completely and frankly about himself, and where to be sure he confesses that he has made an art out of acting as if he were even more interesting than he is." But despite the autobiographical nature of all his work, Glen Cavaliero insisted that "far from being narrowly egoistic and inward-turning, [it] is a projection of the self into an autonomous world of the imagination which is accessible to everyone."

Powys published his first novel when he was forty-three years old, and continued a prolific writing career until his eighties. Many of his works deal with myths, cosmic fantasies, and the elemental forces of nature. *A Glastonbury Romance,* for example, is an adaptation of the myth that Joseph of Arimathea possessed the Holy Grail. In his writings Powys seeks to convey his personal philosophies and as a result the characters often seem to soliloquize instead of talk.

An important theme in Powys's writing is man's sexual nature. G. Wilson Knight assessed his treatment of the subject as "both unorthodox and traditional." Powys clearly presents man's obsession with the "bisexual . . . vision which, though transmitted through human figures, speaks from a dimension beyond the biological." His handling of human sexuality is strangely impersonal in that "there is a divergence from ordinary desire to a more refined but impersonal and cerebral fascination." In Knight's opinion, "probably his [Powys's] most important contribution to our religious tradition is his insistence that 'no religion that doesn't deal with sex-longing in some kind of way is much use to us.'"

Powys tells us that he himself is half a woman and thus he can understand sexual matters from a woman's point of view. But as Knight pointed out, Powys's fictional women are generally presented as stereotypical "normal" girls and are less individualized than the male characters. The only in-depth female characters are "those who have, or touch, boy-like attributes, such as Gladys in *Wood and Stone,* Philippa in *Rodmoor,* and Persephone Spear in *A Glastonbury Romance.*"

Most of Powys's novels are extremely long, and as Knight explained, "his mastery of the long sentence, like the wielding of a giant's club, tempts him, on occasion, too far." *Times Literary Supplement* called Powys a "self-indulgent writer . . . [who was] never fully master of the pace and cohesion of an entire novel," and complained about his "coyness or archness, his literary echoes, his use of capital letters, italics, hyphens, and exclamation marks to draw attention to what should be sufficiently challenging in itself."

On the other hand, many of the same critics who panned Powys also praised him as a genius for his eloquence, humor, and cunning irony. *Times Literary Supplement* explained this paradox: "Powys is rather like life itself: you can object strongly to parts of it, and be often baffled for a meaning, but the sum total impresses."

BIOGRAPHICAL/CRITICAL SOURCES: John Cowper Powys, *Confessions of Two Brothers,* Manas Press, 1916, reprinted, Scholarly Press, 1971; John Cowper Powys, *Autobiography,* Simon & Schuster, 1934, reprinted, New Directions, 1960, revised edition, Colgate University Press, 1968; Mark Van Doren, *The Private Reader: Selected Articles and Reviews,* Holt, 1942; George Wilson Knight, *Saturnian Quest,* Methuen, 1964, reprinted, Harvester Press, 1978; Harold P. Collins, *John Cowper Powys: Old Earth-*

man, Barrie & Rockliff, 1966; Kenneth Hopkins, *Powys Brothers: A Biographical Appreciation,* Fairleigh Dickenson University Press, 1967; Richard Breckon, *John Cowper Powys: The Solitary Giant,* K. A. Ward, 1969; Belinda Humtrey, *Essays on John Cowper Powys,* University of Wales Press, 1972; *Times Literary Supplement,* March 24, 1972, February 8, 1974, May 16, 1975; Jeremy Hooker, *John Cowper Powys,* University of Wales Press, 1973; Glen Cavaliero, *John Cowper Powys, Novelist,* Clarendon Press, 1973; Henry Miller, *Immortal Bard,* Village Press, 1973; *London Magazine,* February/March, 1973; Oloff De Wet, *A Visit to John Cowper Powys,* Village Press, 1974; *Books and Bookmen,* February, 1974, February, 1977, March, 1977; *Choice,* June, 1975 *Modern Fiction Studies,* summer, 1976; *Contemporary Literary Criticism,* Gale, Volume 7, 1977, Volume 9, 1978.*

*   *   *

PRESHING, W(illiam) A(nthony) 1929-

PERSONAL: Born April 24, 1929, in Edmonton, Alberta, Canada; son of John (a laborer) and Teresa (Steiner) Preshing; married Lillian Jane Linell, June 27, 1959; children: William David, Susan Marian, Carolyn Jane. *Education:* University of Alberta, B.Ed., 1952, B.A., 1957; University of Western Ontario, M.B.A., 1956; University of Illinois, Ph.D., 1965. *Religion:* Roman Catholic. *Home:* 13908 86th Ave., Edmonton, Alberta, Canada T5R 4A9. *Office:* Office of Institutional Research and Planning, 116 University Hall, University of Alberta, Edmonton, Alberta, Canada T6G 2E8.

CAREER: Dittrich Men's Shop, Edmonton, Alberta, in sales (also furnishing manager), 1948-50; Farwil Corp., Edmonton, Alberta, in sales, 1956-57; University of Alberta, Edmonton, 1957-63, began as instructor, became associate professor of commerce; University of Calgary, Calgary, Alberta, associate professor of commerce, 1965-69; University of Alberta, Edmonton, director of institutional research and planning, 1969-78, director of community relations, 1978—. President of William A. Preshing & Associates (development consultants), 1966—. Head of conciliation and arbitration boards. Member of board of directors of Calgary Catholic Family Services, 1966-68; head of Calgary Institute for the Development of Manpower, 1966-68; head of Alberta Classification Appeals Board, 1972-74. Co-chairman of contest committee for Commonwealth Games and head of its Public Affairs and Awareness Division, 1977— (also coordinator of university games, vice-president in marketing, and attache for Tanzania).

MEMBER: Institute for Public Administration (executive member of local chapter, 1976—), American Marketing Association (northern Alberta president, 1970-71), Edmonton Symphony Society (member of board of directors, 1973-77), Edmonton Sierra Club (president, 1976-77). *Awards, honors:* Economics-in-action fellow of University of Wisconsin—Madison, 1960; James Webb Young fellow of University of Illinois, 1964-65.

WRITINGS: (Contributor) F. J. Bridges and J. M. Chapin, editors, *Case Study in Critical Incidents in Management,* Irwin, 1963, revised edition, 1969; *Cases for Managerial Decision,* Gage, 1964; (contributor) E. J. Mock, R. E. Schultz, and other editors, *Basic Financial Management,* International Textbook, 1968; (contributor) J. G. Longenecker, editor, *Principles of Management and Organizational Behavior,* C. E. Merrill, 1969; (contributor) W. W. Haynes and J. L. Massie, editors, *Management: Analysis,*

Concepts, and Cases, 2nd edition (Preshing was not associated with 1st edition), McGraw, 1969.

(Contributor) William J. Stanton, editor, *Fundamentals of Marketing,* McGraw, 1971; (contributor) *Auditing for Systems Improvement,* Association for Systems Management, 1972; (with J. A. Murray and E. G. Yaworsky) *Concepts and Canadian Cases in Marketing,* Longmans, Canada, 1973; *Business Management in Canada: An Introduction,* Wiley of Canada, 1974, revised edition, 1979. Editor of "The Book Mill," a column in *Western Catholic Reporter,* 1960-65, and "By the Book," 1973-78. Contributor to *Intercollegiate Bibliography of Cases.* Contributor of about eighty articles to professional journals. Member of board of directors of *Western Catholic Reporter,* 1975—, head of board of directors, 1976-78.

WORK IN PROGRESS: A supplementary casebook to accompany *Business Management in Canada.*

AVOCATIONAL INTERESTS: Skiing, skating, swimming.

* * *

PREUS, Herman Amberg 1896-

PERSONAL: Born July 28, 1896, in Spring Prairie, Wis.; son of Christian Keyser and Louise Augusta (Hjort) Preus; married Florence Nesbitt, July 30, 1930; children: Suzanne Preus Dahl, James, Mary. *Education:* Luther College, B.A., 1916; University of Minnesota, LL.B., 1920; Luther Theological Seminary, C.T., 1925, M.Th., 1925; University of Edinburgh, Ph.D., 1928; also attended University of Oslo, 1923-24, University of Leipzig, 1924, and University of Paris, 1927-28. *Politics:* Republican. *Home:* 2340 Valentine Ave., St. Paul, Minn. 55108. *Office:* 2375 Como Ave., St. Paul, Minn. 55108.

CAREER: Ordained Lutheran minister, 1928; pastor of Lutheran church in Minneapolis, Minn., 1928-36; Luther Theological Seminary, St. Paul, Minn., professor of theology, 1936-67, professor emeritus, 1967—; University Lutheran Church of Hope, Minneapolis, associate pastor, 1967-77; writer, 1977—. Fulbright lecturer at University of Oslo, 1953-54. Member of International Congress for Luther Research, 1956, 1960, 1966; advisory member of Lutheran World Federation's Theological Commission, 1956. *Military service:* U.S. Navy, 1917-18; became ensign.

MEMBER: Society for Reformation Research, Norwegian-American Historical Association, Nordmanns-Forbundet, Phi Delta Phi. *Awards, honors:* Fulbright fellow at University of Oslo, 1960-61; D.D. from Concordia Seminary, 1967.

WRITINGS: Communion of Saints, Augsburg, 1948; (editor with Martin Chemnitz and translator) *The Doctrine of Man,* Augsburg, 1962; *A Theology to Live By,* Concordia, 1977. Also co-author of *More About Luther,* 1958. Contributor to theology journals.

SIDELIGHTS: Preus is competent in Hebrew, Greek, Latin, German, Norwegian, Swedish, Danish, and French.

* * *

PRICE, Garrett 1896-1979

OBITUARY NOTICE: Born in 1896 in Bucyrus, Kan.; died April 8, 1979, in Norwalk, Conn. Illustrator and cartoonist best known for his cover work for *New Yorker* and *Colliers.* Price's drawings were featured in the collection *Drawing Room Only* and in various editions of *The New Yorker Anniversary Album.* Obituaries and other sources: *Illustrators of Books for Young People,* Scarecrow, 1975; *New York Times,* April 10, 1979; *Washington Post,* April 11, 1979.

PRYOR, Lawrence A(llderdice) 1938-
(Larry Pryor)

PERSONAL: Born May 1, 1938, in New York, N.Y.; son of Samuel Frazier, Jr. (an executive) and Mary Taylor (Allderdice) Pryor; married Gabrielle Greer, June 9, 1962; children: Benjamin S., William R. *Education:* Stanford University, A.B., 1961; Columbia University, B.A., 1962. *Home:* 50 Acacia Tree Lane, Irvine, Calif. 92715. *Agent:* Harold Ober Associates, Inc., 40 East 49th St., New York, N.Y. 10017. *Office:* Los Angeles Times, Times-Mirror Sq., Los Angeles, Calif. 92715.

CAREER: Louisville Courier-Journal, Louisville, Ky., staff writer, 1964-68; *Los Angeles Times,* Los Angeles, Calif., copy editor for Orange County edition, 1968-70, staff writer in Los Angeles, 1970-78, assistant metropolitan editor, 1978—. Instructor at California State University, Long Beach, 1974-75, and University of Southern California, 1975-76. *Member:* Sigma Delta Chi.

WRITINGS: The Viper (a novel), Harper, 1978. Contributor under penname Larry Pryor to journalism magazines, *Glimpses,* and newspapers.

WORK IN PROGRESS: A suspense novel; a movie script and television play.

SIDELIGHTS: Pryor writes: "My expertise as a journalist has been in the areas of energy, the environment, and labor. I continue to follow these areas closely. My chief interest is in the impact that technology has on man and the environment. I have followed and written about nuclear safety and other issues involving sophisticated and potentially catastrophic technology, including the liquefied gases. Low-level radiation, in particular, strikes me as being the most important public health issue of the 1970's and I have done a number of stories on this topic, including a series for the *Los Angeles Times* that I wrote from the Pacific Test Range in the Marshall Islands. Microwave radiation is looming as an equally important topic, particularly in terms of its long-term effects on the brain and an individual's thought processes. My next novel deals with this topic in a fictional setting."

AVOCATIONAL INTERESTS: Ornithology, music, photography, golf.

* * *

PUHARICH, Henry (Andrija) Karl 1918-

PERSONAL: Born February 19, 1918, in Chicago, Ill.; *Education:* Northwestern University, A.B., 1942, M.B., 1946, M.D., 1947; postdoctoral study at Pratt Institute, 1962-63. *Home:* 87 Hawkes Ave., Ossining, N.Y. 10562.

CAREER: Permanente Foundation Hospital, Oakland, Calif., intern, 1946-47, chief resident in medical research, 1947-48; Round Table Foundation, Glen Cove, Maine, founder and director of research, 1948-58; General Foods Corp., N.Y., animal researcher and manager of animal care facility, 1949-52; researcher and consultant in Carmel, Calif., 1958-61; Intelectron Corp., New York City, founder, president, and director of medical research, 1961-71; Stanford Research Institute, Stanford, Calif., researcher on the nature of paranormal powers in human beings, 1972-73; Essentia Research Associates, New York City, president, 1973—. Licensed physician in California, Maine, and New York; physician in private practice, until 1961; member of cardiovascular research team at New York University. Vice-president of Lab Nine Ltd. Conducted scientific field studies in Mexico, Hawaii, Brazil, and Israel. Designed research programs for Tel Aviv University, Rochester Institute of Technology, American Academy for Human Development, National University of Mexico, University of Southern California, University of Pennsylvania, and Sweden's Royal Institute of Technology. Guest on television and radio programs; appeared in films; lecturer worldwide. Consultant to Belk Research Foundation, Mind Science Foundation, and Consciousness Research Foundation. *Military service:* U.S. Army, head of outpatient service at Army Chemical Center, 1953-55, chief of emergency service at Fort Ord, 1958-59; became captain.

MEMBER: Pan American Medical Association, American Association for the Advancement of Science, American Association for Humanistic Psychology, American Medical Association (Space Medicine Branch), American Academy of General Practice, American Geriatric Society, American Society for Cybernetics, American Academy of Political and Social Science, American Society for Artificial Internal Organs, National Geographic Society, Aerospace Medical Association, Columbian Society of Angiology, New York Academy of Sciences, New York Zoological Society, Mycological Society of San Francisco, Eta Sigma Phi. *Awards, honors:* LL.D. from Emerson College; General Foods Corp. fellow, 1949-52.

WRITINGS: The Sacred Mushroom, Doubleday, 1959; *Beyond Telepathy,* Doubleday, 1962; (with J. L. Lawrence) *Electrostimulation Techniques of Hearing,* Defense Documentation Center (Alexandria, Va.), 1964; *Signal Detection: Zero to Infinity* (monograph), Parapsychology Foundation, 1969; *Uri: A Journal of the Mystery of Uri Geller,* Doubleday, 1974; (with John G. Fuller) *Arigo,* Crowell, 1974; (contributor) John White, editor, *Psychic Exploration: A Challenge for Science,* Putnam, 1974; (contributor) Rick J. Carlson, editor, *The Frontiers of Science and Medicine,* Wildwood House, 1975.

Author of "The Sacred Mushroom," a film aired on ABC-TV, January 24, 1961. Contributor of about fifteen articles to professional journals.

SIDELIGHTS: In 1972 Puharich visited Israel to study Uri Geller. A year later he was able to test Geller's paranormal powers at Stanford Research Institute. Puharich writes: "The resulting publications and attendant publicity triggered a wide-spread serious interest in the phenomena in many countries. I was involved in initiating many of these research projects, for example in Germany at Max Planck Institute, in England at University of London, as well as leading universities and institutes in Canada, France, Denmark, Italy, the United States, and Mexico.

"This renewed research effort in the paranormal led to a call for a conference to exchange data, techniques, and views in the rapidly growing effort. I took the lead in organizing the Tarrytown Conference held in 1975 in New York. At this conference twenty-seven scientists pooled data and discussed the theoretical implications of the findings.

"Perhaps the most fruitful aspect of my work during the past four years occurred on November 23, 1973, during a BBC-TV broadcast on the 'Dimbleby Show' performed by Uri Geller, John Taylor, and Lyall Watson. During the course of this broadcast, while Geller was demonstrating psychokinetic feats, thousands of people in the British Isles reported that spontaneous psychokinetic effects occurred in their homes while they were watching him. Many of these people were subsequently studied at University of London, and found to have retained their new-found paranormal powers. The same phenomenon was repeated during the following year in twenty-three countries, wherever Geller demon-

strated on television. There is still no scientific explanation for this phenomenon, although much research has been carried out by many workers." His book, *Uri,* has been published in fourteen languages in twenty-two countries.

But Puharich's research has not been limited to studies of the paranormal. His earliest research dealt with electrical recording of neural activity in animals during taste responses. This led to an interest in sonic transmission phenomena and problems of deafness. He also carried out research in other sensory modalities, notably vision and touch, but the greater part of his research was in audiology and electronic engineering, aimed at rehabilitation of hearing in the clinically totally deaf. He has patented nearly fifty inventions in the United States, Argentina, Brazil, Sweden, Australia, Italy, Switzerland, Norway, Canada, the Netherlands, India, Pakistan, France, England, Germany, Belgium, and Japan.

Other research includes field expeditions, financed in part by the U.S. Army Chemical Corps, to gather hallucinogenic botanicals. *The Sacred Mushroom* describes his studies in Mexico. Botanical specimens discovered in Hawaii were presented and catalogued at Bishop Museum in Honolulu. In Brazil, he studied primitive surgical techniques, and use of plants and drugs for healing.

Other professional interests, perhaps less colorful, but no less important, include cardiovascular research, design and analysis of medical experiments in humans and animals, neuropsychiatry, psychiatry, hypnosis, and communications research. His communications research resulted in a simple technique for enhancing human sensitivity for extra-sensory perception. Human information transfer (of a non-sensory nature) was carried out with gifted subjects from all over the world. It was concerned with devising environmental control systems, drug experiments, anesthetic gas experiments, and electronic systems, with at least some interest in the use of such methods for psychological warfare.

*   *   *

PULMAN, Jack 1928(?)-1979

OBITUARY NOTICE: Born c. 1928; died of a heart attack, May 20, 1979, in London, England. Author of adaptations for television. Pulman was best known for "I, Claudius," a televised adaptation of the novel by Robert Graves. Prior to "I, Claudius," he had adapted Tolstoy's *War and Peace,* Thomas Mann's *Buddenbrooks,* and some of the works of Henry James. At the time of his death, Pulman was adapting Herman Wouk's *Winds of War.* Obituaries and other sources: *New York Times,* May 22, 1979.

*   *   *

PUTNAM, Peter B(rock) 1920-

PERSONAL: Born June 11, 1920, in Fort Ogelthorpe, Ga.; son of Brock and Margaret (Faber) Putnam; married Durinda Dobbins, August 12, 1944; children: Brock, Barbara Durinda, John Gerry. *Education:* Princeton University, B.A., 1942, Ph.D., 1950. *Home:* 48 Roper Rd., Princeton, N.J. 08540. *Agent:* James Brown Associates, Inc., 25 West 43rd St., New York, N.Y. 10036.

CAREER: Princeton University, Princeton, N.J., lecturer in history, 1944-55; free-lance writer, 1955—. President of Chaplin School, 1961-63. Member of executive committee of Princeton Alumni Council, 1972-76; vice-president and member of board of directors of Recording for the Blind, 1955-76, president, 1976—. *Member:* International P.E.N.,

Authors League of America, Unitarian-Universalist Association (president, 1954-57; vice-president, 1965-67), Massachusetts Association for the Blind (member of board of directors, 1967-71), Cottage Club, Princeton Triangle Club (member of board of trustees).

WRITINGS: Seven Britons in Imperial Russia, 1698-1812, Princeton University Press, 1952; *"Keep Your Head Up, Mr. Putnam!",* Harper, 1952; (translator) Marc Bloch, *Apologie pour l'histoire* (title means "The Historian's Craft"), Knopf, 1953; *Cast Off the Darkness,* Harcourt, 1957; *The Triumph of the Seeing Eye* (juvenile; edited by Walter Lord), Harper, 1963; *Peter, The Revolutionary Tsar* (juvenile), Harper, 1973; *Love in the Lead,* Dutton, 1979.

WORK IN PROGRESS: Possessed by Memory, an autobiography.

SIDELIGHTS: "I had always had vague Walter Mitty dreams of being a writer, but until my attempted suicide shortly before my twenty-first birthday, I had nothing to write about," Putnam told *CA.* "Then in a ten-day sleep I cannot remember, I had a miraculous awakening to life and a sense of my own selfhood previously lacking. Near death and totally blind, I was more alive than I had ever been.

"When I first began to write my story, it was as a novel, and I was soon stuck in it. Then the grind of completing college and graduate school without sight forced me into other kinds of writing, a senior thesis on Dostoevsky with whose characters I strongly identified, and because that led to an interest in Russia, a doctoral dissertation on Russia.

"During a week when I was blocked on the Ph.D., I began to write a part of my story as straight autobiography—my experience at the Seeing Eye school in the fall of 1941. I wrote feverishly all week and got so much on paper that I had the confidence to finish it later. At this writing, *"Keep Your Head Up, Mr. Putnam!"* is still in print, twenty-seven years later. It was dramatized on television on the Robert Montgomery show, and it led to the next book.

Hugh Kahler, the marvelous editor at *Ladies Home Journal,* shrewdly surmised that *Keep* was not the whole story. I had not revealed my suicide attempt. With his reassuring encouragement, I began a further autobiography, and although I had not meant to when I started, I found I had to confess my suicide attempt in order to explain the central experience of my life. *Cast Off the Darkness* is certainly my best book and is the only one out of print.

"The Triumph of the Seeing Eye was written as a juvenile, but the juvenile label is too narrow for *Peter, the Revolutionary Tsar.* Charlie Price, a first rate writer, once told me that an American writer must assume that his reader is both ignorant and intelligent. He knows nothing, but he catches on very fast. That was the premise on which I wrote *Peter.* I

assumed that American readers, adult as well as adolescent, knew nothing about Peter or his period, and I sought to explain them from the ground up, but I had no thought that the book had an upper age limit. The label restricted readership needlessly.

"Love in the Lead, which E. P. Dutton is about to bring out, is a comprehensive history of the Seeing Eye on its fiftieth anniversary. To me it is a dramatic and moving story of vivid and colorful personalities, unexpected twists, and the miraculous partnerships forged between humans and dogs by love.

"Writing history and autobiography has driven home the truth of Wright Morris's insight that anything processed by memory is a work of fiction, and a mishearing of that remark has given me the title of my next book, *Possessed by Memory.* It will be a comprehensive family memoir and autobiography written with my own possessed memory at the center. I have sometimes thought that it could be subtitled 'Northern WASPS have roots, too.' But I mean that in no sense to deprecate the many fine books written about Southern, black, Jewish, and other minority families."

*   *   *

PYNN, Ronald   1942-

PERSONAL: Born September 11, 1942, in Eau Claire, Wis.; son of Willard E. (an educator) and Mary A. Pynn; married Scharlene L. Broker, September 16, 1961; children: Suzanne, Stephen, Karen. *Education:* Wisconsin State University—Eau Claire (now University of Wisconsin, Eau Claire), B.S., 1964; University of Michigan, M.A., 1965, Ph.D., 1970. *Politics:* Democrat. *Religion:* United Church of Christ. *Home:* 2713 Olive, Grand Forks, N.D. 58201. *Office:* Department of Political Science, University of North Dakota, Grand Forks, N.D. 58201.

CAREER: Lake Superior State College, Sault Sainte Marie, Mich., assistant professor of political science, 1970-71; University of North Dakota, Grand Forks, assistant professor, 1971-74, associate professor, 1974-78, professor of political science, 1979—. *Member:* American Political Science Association, Midwest Political Science Association.

WRITINGS: Watergate and the American Political Process, Praeger, 1975.

WORK IN PROGRESS: Changing Expectations: American Government, publication by Van Nostrand expected in 1981.

SIDELIGHTS: Pynn told *CA:* "My writing seeks to provide a comprehensive but balanced framework for students to organize and evaluate information. I do most of the writing in my office during the day, in between students and classes; I jealously guard my evenings as free time for my family and other activities."

Q

QUINDERPUNTE, Raoul (Cornelius) 1907-

PERSONAL: Born March 1, 1907, in New Rutherford, Conn.; son of Elwood Reagan (a used auto salesman) and Rita Chen (an artist; maiden name, Lo-San) Quinderpunte; married Jill Bryce (a pedicurist), 1943 (died, 1966); married Nina Barnes (an auctioneer), June 10, 1976; children: Carl, Johann, Chunga-Wai, Yarletta, Bryan. *Education:* Attended New Rutherford Community College, 1926-27, 1936, 1972. *Politics:* "Hoover was always underrated—I'd vote for him tomorrow." *Religion:* Buddhist. *Home:* 221 Lewiston Rd., Grosse Pointe Farms, Mich. 48236.

CAREER: Writer and taxidermist. Worked as used auto salesman for Elwood's Garage and Fine Machinery, 1924-36; librarian in Harlem, N.Y., 1967; cement salesman, 1972. *Member:* American Society of Authors, Poets, and Taxidermists (ASAPT), American Animal Lovers and Authors (AALA), Wallace Beery Fan Club. *Awards, honors:* Bronze Squirrel from American Society of Authors, Poets, and Taxidermists (ASAPT), 1952, for successfully stuffing a hummingbird; Gold Elk from ASAPT, 1974, for "most realistic eyes in a mammal" (lightweight division); Iron Bookmark from American Animal Lovers and Authors, 1975, for *Formaldehyde Is My Ink.*

WRITINGS: For Better Scissors (essays), New Thoughts Press, 1929; *Eyes That Glow Like Headlights: A Nighttime Deerhunter's Guide,* New Thoughts Press, 1944; *Squirrels and Girls: One Taxidermist's Weekend in Las Vegas,* Snake-Eyes Books, 1949; *Mammal Brethren,* Wildlife Readings, 1952; *Shoot to Preserve: Why I Favor Wholesale Slaughter,* privately printed, 1958; *Seek Not the Grizzly,* Barren Books, 1960; *Why Prairie Dogs Burrow and Other Essays,* Wildlife Readings, 1964; *Campfire Logbook,* Wildlife Readings, 1967; *Sing, Cougar, Sing: An African Journal,* Bongo Books, 1970; *Formaldehyde Is My Ink* (autobiography), Wildlife Readings, 1975.

WORK IN PROGRESS: "Revising a journal I kept while camping in the Badlands."

SIDELIGHTS: Quinderpunte told *CA:* "I'd guess that in my seventy-odd years, I've done more and seen more and been to more places (seen more people) than just about any other writing taxidermist. During the 1940's, I was a part of the first expedition to see the print of Bigfoot. It was quite a spectacle. The toeprints alone could seat five comfortably (with leg-room).

"But through everything, I've learned one steadfast rule: Always keep your sense of humor. Without that, you might as well quit living because laughing is what *really* makes everything seem okay, even when you're staring into the faces of starving wolves (which I did in 1962 when I undertook a one-man expedition to Isle Royale, Michigan, to test wind resistence for poodle-fur parkas I'd planned on marketing).

"Dead animals will always be my first love. I began stuffing my sister's shredded dolls when I was still in my teens and soon moved on to animals. I'll never forget the tears my mother cried when she came home and found Mounty (our terrier) perched proudly on the mantle. From then on, I knew where my fate was. Since then, I've stuffed just about every North American animal in existence and hunted also abroad.

"To sum up my life so far (and I plan on going a whole lot farther), I'd say I've seen better and I've seen better still but I wouldn't have it any other way. Life's been good to me and if I can remind others of how good it is by preserving what used to be alive—well, so be it."

AVOCATIONAL INTERESTS: Camping, swimming, yodeling, riding wild animals.

R

RA, Jong Oh 1945-

PERSONAL: Born August 23, 1945, in Seoul, Korea; came to United States in 1957, naturalized citizen, 1967; son of Iong Gwyn and Gwee (Nye) Ra; married Carol Fae Hawn (a professor), June, 1962; children: Stephanie Susan, Alison Emily. Education: Indiana State University, A.B., 1961, M.S., 1962; University of Illinois, M.S., 1965, Ph.D., 1972. Religion: Protestant. Home: 1523 June Dr. N.W., Roanoke, Va. 24019. Office: Department of Political Science, Hollins College, Hollins College, Va. 24020.

CAREER: Hollins College, Hollins College, Va., assistant professor, 1969-75, associate professor of political science, 1975—, head of department, 1977—. Visiting associate professor at University of Illinois, 1976-77. Member: American Political Science Association, Southern Political Science Association, Midwest Political Science Association. Awards, honors: Grants from National Science Foundation, 1969, 1973, National Endowment for the Humanities, 1975, and Mellon Foundation, 1972, 1978.

WRITINGS: Labor at the Poll: Union Voting in Presidential Elections, 1952-1976, University of Massachusetts Press, 1978. Contributor to Youth and Society.

WORK IN PROGRESS: Religion and Politics: A Comparative Historical Analysis, completion expected in 1981.

SIDELIGHTS: Ra summarized his two books: "Labor at the Poll is an attempt to build a theory of union voting behavior based on plural levels of support from philosophical (or normative), historical (or descriptive), and social psychological (or behavioral) perspectives. The presidential election results of 1952, 1956, 1960, and 1964 are used to test the theory, and the election data from the 1968, 1972 and 1976 elections are used to re-evaluate some of the theoretical propositions.

"Religion and Politics is an in-depth analysis of two prominent religious revolts that occurred in the late nineteenth and the early twentieth century in Korea. It is an effort to critically reevaluate and, if possible, build a theory of religion and politics."

*   *   *

RABE, David (William) 1940-

PERSONAL: Born March 10, 1940, in Dubuque, Iowa; son of William (a meatpacker) and Ruth (a department store worker; maiden name, McCormick) Rabe; married Elizabeth Pan (a laboratory technician), 1969 (marriage ended); married Jill Clayburgh (an actress), March, 1979; children: (first marriage) Jason. Education: Loras College, B.A.; Villanova University, M.A. Agent: Ellen Neuwald, Inc., 905 West End Ave., New York, N.Y. 10025.

CAREER: Playwright. Worked various jobs, 1963-65; New Haven Register, New Haven, Conn., feature writer, 1969-70; Villanova University, Villanova, Pa., assistant professor, 1970-72, consultant, beginning 1972. Military service: U.S. Army, 1965-67; served in Vietnam. Member: Philadelphia Rugby Club. Awards, honors: Associated Press award, 1970, for series of articles written on Daytop addict rehabilitation program; Obie Award for distinguished playwriting from Village Voice, Drama Desk Award, and Drama Guild Award, all 1971, all for "The Basic Training of Pavlo Hummel"; Elizabeth Hull-Kate Warriner Award from Dramatists Guild, 1971, Variety poll award, 1971, Outer Circle Award, 1972, and Antoinette Perry (Tony) Award for best play of 1971-72 season on Broadway, 1972, all for "Sticks and Bones"; New York Drama Critics Circle Citation, 1972; New York Drama Critics Circle Award for best American play, 1976, for "Streamers"; National Institute and American Academy Award in Literature, 1976; Guggenheim fellowship, 1976.

WRITINGS—Plays: Two Plays by David Rabe (contains "Sticks and Bones" [two-act], produced in New York City at Anspacher Theatre, November 7, 1971, produced on Broadway at John Golden Theatre, August 1, 1972; and "The Basic Training of Pavlo Hummel," first produced in New York City at Newman Stage of The Public Theatre, May 20, 1971), Viking, 1973; "The Orphan," produced in New York City at Anspacher Theatre, April 18, 1973; In the Boom Boom Room (three-act; produced on Broadway at Vivian Beaumont Theatre, November 8, 1973), Knopf, 1975; Streamers (produced in New Haven at Long Wharf Theater, 1976; produced on Broadway at Mitzi Newhouse Theater, 1976), Knopf, 1977. Also author of "The Crossing" (one-act).

SIDELIGHTS: Though Rabe's award-winning plays "The Basic Training of Pavlo Hummel," "Sticks and Bones," and "Streamers" deal with the effects of the Vietnam war on his characters' lives, the playwright was quick to dispel the "antiwar" label. "I don't like to hear them called antiwar plays," he said. "Works like that, like some of the social-action plays of the thirties, are designed for immediate effect. All I'm trying to do is *define the event* for myself and for other people. I'm saying, in effect, 'This is what goes on,' and that's all.''

Rabe should know "what goes on." He originally thought of his service in Vietnam (in a hospital support unit) "as a cause," but the experience soon changed his life. He was shocked by what he saw there, particularly American soldiers ("kids, just kids") "standing around some bar like teenagers at a soda fountain, talking coldly about how many of their guys got killed in the last battle." Rabe continued: "You don't think of it; you can't. The way I tried to keep a journal over there but couldn't do it—it resulted in a kind of double vision that made everything too intense. Anyway, I don't think it was until I got back and saw the tremendous indifference at home that I started to view the whole thing as decadent, really corrupt."

Like David in "Sticks and Bones," Rabe returned home alienated from American society. "It wasn't just that I couldn't reach my family," he explained, "I couldn't reach *anybody*. People would listen attentively, but not understand a thing. It was the *impossibility* of understanding that got to me, caused not so much by a lack of awareness on the part of most people, but by the quality of what awareness there was."

Rabe admitted he felt "tremendous hostility—no, *mistrust*—about the antiwar movement," "I agreed with the radicals intellectually, but I couldn't get emotionally involved because of the experience thing." He tried desperately to get a job as a Vietnam war correspondent to help change America's limited awareness of the war. Unsuccessful, he decided to resume graduate study at Villanova—where he also wrote his first two plays.

It was not until Joseph Papp, the director of the New York Shakespeare Festival's Public Theatre, read "Pavlo Hummel" that the play was produced. The story of a "cipher" who dismally attempts to create a new identity for himself as a soldier, "Pavlo Hummel" was praised by Catharine Hughes as "one of the best plays to come out of America's Vietnam nightmare." But, Hughes pointed out, "Rabe does not make anything—apart from the hell and absurdity of war—*that* black and white. He avoids both easy sentimentality and facile point-scoring and . . . he realizes that horror and comedy, like tragedy and comedy, are seldom far apart. His Vietcong are no more heroic than his Americans (which by now seems almost refreshing)."

When "Sticks and Bones" joined "Pavlo Hummel" at the Anspacher in 1971, Rabe became the only playwright, other than Shakespeare, to have two plays performed concurrently in New York's Public Theatre. Director Papp enthusiastically praised his new talent: "He is the most important writer we've ever had. There's a great link between him and O'Neill, not so much in style but in that he's so painfully honest. I think he's in pain. He's dealing with things so deep."

Rabe's thrust on the American family in "Sticks and Bones" is made apparent by the names of his main characters: Ozzie, Harriet, David, and Rick. In contrast to the security provided by Harriet's fudge, Ozzie's possessions, and Rick's guitar, David, when he speaks, reminds his family of the atrocities of Vietnam or his love for a "yellow girl." Henry Hewes gave this interpretation of the play's end: "Since David is unchangeable, the family must get rid of him and the memories he brought from the war. They do this by strangling the personification of the Vietnamese girl, who has been silently appearing throughout the play, and by helping David to kill himself. But the suggestion at the end of the play is that David will not entirely die, and that America will never quite exorcise the ghosts of Vietnam."

Variety objected to "Sticks and Bones" as "wordy and repetitious" and suffering from the inarticulateness of its hero. Despite these reservations, the reviewer applauded the "shattering impact" of Rabe's play—"a work of passion by a gifted writer." Clive Barnes cited "this interestingly flawed play" as being "far less confident in its style and texture" than "Pavlo Hummel," claiming Rabe's inexperience must "take the rap" for "the occasionally ponderous symbolism." Nonetheless, "Sticks and Bones" "has a moral force that neither flinches nor sermonizes. This is surely all too unusual in our theater."

Once called "the Neil Simon of desperation and death," Rabe is unsure himself as to the roots of his pain. "I don't know where the pain comes from," he told *Newsweek*. "It can't be just the war." He took a lighter approach to his "fate" with another reviewer: "I didn't plan to be against the grain, you know. It just happened that way." As desperation and death are serious subjects, so is Rabe's devotion to the theatre. "Theater is very serious to me, and I'm serious about it," he said. "If I see a play that is totally frivolous, I almost get sick to my stomach. On the other hand, if *Sticks and Bones* is done right, it should be very funny. And its stylization should insulate the audience a little. If that doesn't happen, it can seem totally overbearing and self-righteous."

Rabe's third play, "The Orphan," was an ambitious attempt to link modern violence with Greek mythology. John Simon believed the author's "parallel between the Manson 'family' and the House of Atreus preposterous." "Rabe hits out against both secular and religious authorities," Simon continued, "indeed, against God himself in the person of a slippery and unsavory Apollo; but, much as I sympathize with his thesis, it falls between parallels as surely as if they were stools." Walter Kerr saw unfulfilled possibilities in the play as he concluded, "If *The Orphan* were a cohesive work for the theatre, it would be one of the most despairing plays ever written."

Upon the production of "In the Boom Boom Room," Rabe denied that his new play broke away from the pattern set in his earlier works. "It's not about the war," he noted, "but then *Sticks and Bones* wasn't either. . . . People are liable to think it's very different from what I've been doing but essentially it isn't."

In Stanley Kauffmann's words, this play "is a semi-realistic, semi-expressionist work about a Philadelphia go-go girl, daughter of a casual criminal father and a vapid mother, sexual prey of dozens of men, how she got that way and how she declines to a new nadir." The theme, "the ravaging of a female-social-sexual victim" Kauffmann believed "so familiar that one *counts* on the familiarity," met a different interpretation from Marilyn Stasio: "The remarkable quality about David Rabe is his willingness to confront the alien culture of the Boom Boom Room and the level of society it represents. Not only does he face it head on, and attempt to understand and communicate the dynamics of the people who live in it, but he also finds amidst the wretchedness and ugliness a good deal of character and dignity."

Like Stasio, who felt "In the Boom Boom Room" lacked the vivid surrealism necessary to create "a dramatic vision of a woman's personal hell," many reviewers found some faults in the play but still gave praise to the total effect. Harold Clurman thought "the whole is uneven, at times forced and crude, but its power is unmistakable." In his *Commonweal* review Gerald Weales explained that "although much of *In the Boom Boom Room* is overextended and overexplained, at his best Rabe has an oblique style which is attractive because it suggest more than it defines, because it opens the audience to possibility."

Rabe returned to the backdrop of war and again found award-winning acclaim with "Streamers" in 1976. The barracks room set in a Virginia army camp was described as "a microcosm for some of the most explosive tensions in U.S. society—racial, sexual, social." In Rabe's story a homosexual (Richie), a professed anti-homosexual (Billy), and an indifferent black (Roger) make "considerable . . . adjustment to the sexual and racial differences in each other's personalities" until a newcomer (Carlyle), "a black draftee churning with bottled-up violence, . . . becomes a human bomb that blasts the utopia into blood and death."

Weales found that in "Streamers" (the "most realistic of the Rabe plays") "it is obvious that Billy's interfering impulses, his failure to understand Richie or Carlyle, the violence hidden in his angry innocence provide a workable analogy for the American presence in Southeast Asia." "But," he continued, "Rabe clearly does not intend that his play should have a narrowly political reference." Clurman seemed to agree when he felt a "universal" inference invoked in "Steamers": "Humanity is composed of poor forked animals caught in a trap of which they can never understand the exact identity or the way out."

Among other criticism of "Streamers," Kauffmann questioned the meaning of its title. "But what does it symbolize?" he asked. "What does the symbol of an unopened parachute mean to anything we have seen?" Weales had an answer: "'Steamers' offers a world . . . in which, eventually, everyone's parachute refuses to open." Meanwhile, in drawing the composite figure pervading Rabe's plays, T. E. Kalem summarized Rabe's "heroes": "In classic term his protagonists are all undergoing initiation rites. But the lack of catharsis in his dramas means that after the initiation, no induction into full manhood occurs. Nothing like wisdom is reached, or even stoic serenity." If Kalem's assessment is accurate, then the unopened parachute is an appropriate metaphor for the whole of Rabe's work.

BIOGRAPHICAL/CRITICAL SOURCES: *New York Times,* May 30, 1971, November 3, 1971, November 8, 1971, December 12, 1971, April 19, 1973, April 29, 1973, November 9, 1973, May 8, 1977; *New Yorker,* May 29, 1971, March 11, 1972, May 3, 1976, May 2, 1977; *Saturday Review,* November 27, 1971, April 17, 1976; *Cue,* December 4, 1971, December 3, 1973; *New York Times Biographical Edition,* December 12, 1971; *Newsweek,* December 20, 1971, February 23, 1976; *Newsday,* March 2, 1972; *Variety,* March 8, 1972; *New York Post,* March 11, 1972; *After Dark,* August, 1972; *New York Sunday News,* April 1, 1973; *New Republic,* May 26, 1973, December 1, 1973, June 12, 1976; *New York,* September 17, 1973; *Village Voice,* November 15, 1973; *Nation,* November 26, 1973, December 3, 1973, May 8, 1976, May 14, 1977; *Commonweal,* December 14, 1973, May 21, 1976; Catharine Hughes, *Plays, Politics and Polemics,* Drama Book Specialists, 1973; John Simon, *Uneasy Stages: A Chronicle of the New York Theater, 1963-73,* Random House, 1975; *Contemporary Literary Criticism,* Gale, Volume 4, 1975, Volume 8, 1978; *Time,* May 3, 1975, May 9, 1977; *America,* May 15, 1976; *Commentary,* July, 1976; *Atlantic,* December, 1976.*

RACKIN, Phyllis 1933-

PERSONAL: Born September 15, 1933, in Newark, N.J.; daughter of Milton Philip (a civil engineer) and Ethel (a teacher; maiden name, Shulman) Finkelstein; married Donald Rackin (a professor of English), January 1, 1954; children: Rebecca Jane, Ethel Elizabeth Rackin Gussie. *Education:* Rutgers University, B.A., 1954; Auburn University, M.A., 1957; University of Illinois, Ph.D., 1962. *Home:* 405 West Price St., Philadelphia, Pa. 19144. *Office:* General Honors Program, University of Pennsylvania, Philadelphia, Pa. 19104.

CAREER: University of Pennsylvania, Philadelphia, instructor, 1962-64, assistant professor, 1964-75, associate professor of English, 1975—. Member of local Democratic Committee, 1975—. *Member:* Modern Language Association of America, Shakespeare Association of America, Northeast Modern Language Association. *Awards, honors:* Lindback Award from Lindback Foundation, 1977, for distinguished teaching.

WRITINGS: *Shakespeare's Tragedies,* Ungar, 1978. Contributor to literature journals.

WORK IN PROGRESS: Studying Shakespearean metadrama and Shakespeare's *Coriolanus* and *Richard II.*

SIDELIGHTS: Phyllis Rackin writes: "Feminism, Shakespeare, literary theory, liberal education, and liberal politics are my main commitments—I'm not sure in what order. My book on Shakespeare's tragedies grew out of my teaching."

*　　　*　　　*

RADOFF, Morris L(eon) 1905-1978

PERSONAL: Born January 10, 1905, in Houston, Tex.; died December 2, 1978, in St. Margaret's, Maryland, after several strokes; married May Conkling. *Education:* Attended University of Texas, 1922-24; University of North Carolina, A.B., 1926, A.M., 1927; Johns Hopkins University, Ph.D., 1932. *Residence:* St. Margaret's, Md. *Office address:* State of Maryland Hall of Records Commission, P.O. Box 828, Annapolis, Md. 21404.

CAREER: Archivist and writer. Johns Hopkins University, Baltimore, Md., instructor, 1933-36; archivist of Maryland, 1939-75. Member of St. Mary's city commission. *Member:* Society of American Archivists (vice-president, 1946, president, 1954-55), Maryland Historical Trust (trustee).

WRITINGS: *Buildings of the State of Maryland at Annapolis,* Hall of Records Commission [Maryland], 1954; (editor) *The Old Line State, a History of Maryland,* Historical Records Association, 1956; *The State House at Annapolis,* Hall of Records Commission [Maryland], 1972. Editor of *Maryland Historical Record Survey,* 1936-38; regional editor of *Historical Record Survey,* 1938-39.

OBITUARIES: *Washington Post,* December 3, 1978.*

*　　　*　　　*

RADVANYI, Netty 1900-
(Anna Seghers)

PERSONAL: Maiden name, Reiling; known professionally as Anna Seghers; born November 19, 1900, in Mainz, Germany (now West Germany); married Ladislaus Radvanyi (a sociologist), 1925; children: Peter, Ruth. *Education:* Attended University of Cologne; Heidelberg University, Ph.D., 1924. *Religion:* Jewish. *Residence:* East Berlin, East Germany.

CAREER: Novelist, essayist, and short story writer. Joined

German Communist Party and Union of Proletarian and Revolutionary Writers, 1928; emigrated from Germany to Paris, France, to escape Nazi oppression, 1933; fled from Paris to Spain upon German invasion of France, 1940; settled in an anti-fascist colony in Mexico City, Mexico, 1940; returned to East Germany, 1947. Helper of Republicans in Spanish Civil War. Member of Lenin Peace Prize committee. *Member:* German Writer's Association (elected president, 1950), Deutsche Academie der Kunste, Heinrich Heine Club for Free German Culture (founding member). *Awards, honors:* Kleist Prize, 1929, for *Aufstand der Fischer von St. Barbara;* National Prize, 1951, 1959; Lenin Peace Prize.

WRITINGS—All under name Anna Seghers; in English: *Aufstand der Fischer von St. Barbara* (novel), Kiepenheuer, 1929, Suhrkamp Verlag, 1966 (also see below), translation by Margaret Goldsmith published as *The Revolt of the Fishermen*, Mathews & Marrot, 1929, Longmans, Green, 1930, translation by Jack Mitchell and Rene Mitchell published as *Revolt of the Fisherman of Santa Barbara*, contained in *Revolt of the Fisherman of Santa Barbara [and] A Price on His Head*, Seven Seas Publishers, 1960 (also see below); *Der Kopflohn* (novel), Querido Verlag (Amsterdam), 1933, Luchterhand, 1976 (also see below), translation by Eva Wulff published as *A Price on His Head*, contained in *Revolt of the Fisherman of Santa Barbara [and] A Price on His Head* (also see above); *Das siebte Kreuz* (novel), D. F. Editorial (Mexico), 1942, Luchterhand, 1973 (also see below), translation by James A. Galston published as *The Seventh Cross* (Book-of-the-Month Club selection), Little, Brown, 1942; *Transit*, translation by Galston from original German manuscript, Little, Brown, 1944, original manuscript published under same title, Aufbau-Verlag, 1962 (also see below); *Die Toten bleiben jung* (novel), Aufbau-Verlag, 1949 (also see below), translation published as *The Dead Stay Young*, Little, Brown, 1950; *Benito's Blue and Nine Other Stories*, translation by Joan Becker, Seven Seas Publishers, 1973.

Other works: *Auf dem Wege zur amerikanischen Botschaft, und andere Erzahlungen* (title means "'On the Way to the American Embassy' and Other Stories"), Kiepenheuer, 1930 (also see below) *Die Gefahrten* (novel; title means "Companions of the Road"), Kiepenheuer, 1932 (also see below); *Die Rettung* (novel; title means "The Rescue"), Querido Verlag, 1937, Luchterhand, 1965; *Der Ausflug der toten Madchen, und andere Erzahlungen* (title means "'The Excursion of the Dead Girls' and Other Stories"), Aurora Verlag, 1946 (also see below); *Sowjetmenschen, Lebensbeschreibungen nach ibren Berichten* (travel description of Russia) Verlag Kultur und Fortschritt, 1948.

Frieden der Welt: Ansprachen und Aufsatze, 1947-53 (essays and lectures on peace), Aufbau-Verlag, 1953; *Die grosse Veranderung und unsere Literatur* (essays and lectures), Aufbau-Verlag, 1956; *Der Bienenstock*, Aufbau-Verlag, 1956; *Brot und Salz* (three stories), Aufbau-Verlag, 1958; *Chrisanta: Mexikanische Novelle* (novella), Insel-Verlag, 1958 (also see below); *Die Entscheidung* (novel; title means "The Decision"), Aufbau-Verlag, 1959 (also see below); *Der Weg durch den Februar* (historical novel), Verlag des Ministeriums fur Nationale Verteidigung, 1959 (also see below); *Die Hochzeit von Haiti*, Reclam, 1959, Macmillan (London), 1970 (also see below).

Die Linie (three stories), Aufbau-Verlag, 1960; *Der erste Schritt*, Aufbau-Verlag, 1960; *Das Licht auf dem Galgen: eine karibische Geschichte aus der Zeit der Franzosichen Revolution* (title means "The Light of the Gallows"), Afbau-Verlag, 1961 (also see below); *Uber Tolstoi, Uber Dostojewskij*, Aufbau-Verlag, 1962; *Erzahlungen* (includes "Auf dem Wege zur amerikanischen Botschaft," "Der Ausflug der toten Madchen," "Die Hochzeit von Haiti," "Wiedereinfuhrung der Sklaverei in Guadeloupe," "Crisanta," and "Das Licht auf dem Galgen"), two volumes, Luchterhand, 1964 (also see below); *Sagen von Artemis*, Insel-Verlag, 1965; *Die Kraft der Schwachen* (nine stories; title means "The Strength of the Weak"), Aufbau-Verlag, 1965; *Wiedereinfuhrung der Sklaverei in Guadeloupe*, Suhrkamp, 1966 (also see above); *Das wirkliche Blau [and] Eine Geschichte aus Mexiko*, Aufbau-Verlag, 1967 (also see below); *Das Vertrauen* (novel; title means "The Confidence"), Aufbau-Verlag, 1968 (also see below); *Das Schilfrohr*, Signal-Verlag, 1968; *Glauben an Irdisches: Essays aus vier Jahrzehnten*, Reclam, 1969; *Ausgewahlte Erzahlungen*, Rowohlt, 1969.

Geschichten aus Mexiko (includes "Der Ausflug der toten Madchen," "Das wirklich Blau," and "Crisanta"), Aufbau-Verlag, 1970; *Briefe an Leser*, Aufbau-Verlag, 1970; *Aufstellen eines Maschinengewehrs im Wohnzimmer der Frau Kamptschik*, Luchterhand, 1970; *Uber Kunstwerk und Wirklichkeit*, Akademie-Verlag, 1971; *Die Uberfahrt* (title means "The Crossing"), Luchterhand, 1971; *Sonderbare Begegnungen* (three stories), Luchterhand, 1973; *Funf Erzahlungen*, Reclam, 1975; *Die schonsten Sagen bom Rauber Woynok*, Suhrkamp, 1975; *Willkommen Zukunft!*, Kurbiskern und Tendenzen Damnitz, 1975.

Omnibus volumes: *Der Kopflohn [and] Der Weg durch den Februar*, Aufbau-Verlag, 1961; *Aufstand der Fischer von St. Barbara, Die Gefahrten, Das wirkliche Blau, [and] Erzahlungen*, Luchterhand, 1968; *Werke in zehn Banden* (contains "Aufstand der Fischer von St. Barbara," "Die Gefahrten," "Das siebte Kruz," "Transit," "Die Toten bleiben jung," "Die Entscheidung," "Das Vertrauen," and "Erzahlungen"), ten volumes, Luchterhand, 1977.

SIDELIGHTS: The dominant thrust behind Anna Segher's works, her unflinching humanism, grew even stronger in the 1930's as she fled from country to country to escape Nazi oppression. Having already established her reputation as an anti-fascist author, Seghers, a Jew, faced a double handicap when Hitler seized German power in 1933. She countered by escaping to Paris with her husband and two children. World War II made living in France equally precarious, however, as anti-Nazi refugees were sought out by the German influenced French government. When the Nazis stormed Paris, Seghers succeeded on her second attempt to escape the French capital, and finally, the country. Reunited with her husband, who had been captured in Paris, she lived in Mexico for a time before returning to settle in East Berlin in 1947.

From her earliest work Seghers has demonstrated her reverence for unoppressed human life while evincing a belief in the common man as guardian of that freedom. "Invariably, Anna Seghers's heroes are the lowly, the poor, and the slow-witted," declared Theodore Huebener. "She is fond of portraying simple beings who think very little and feel very deeply, who have an unshakable belief and never doubt." In *Aufstand der Fischer von St. Barbara* ("The Revolt of the Fisherman") she stated the case for a generation of revolutionary, socially conscious individuals by describing exploited fishermen and their revolt against their capitalistic ship owners. Likewise in *Die Toten bleiben jung* ("The Dead Stay Young") and *Die Kraft der Schwachen* ("The Strength of the Weak") the energies of the typical, non-elite members of the human community were presented as a nation's source of vitality.

Seghers's belief that historical progress is based on the efforts of all individuals, not just a select few, helps explain her lifelong commitment to Communism. Her attraction to the party, however, was based on "emotional rather than intellectual considerations," reported Huebener. "On her sixtieth birthday she confessed that methodical thinking was foreign to her; intellectual processes to her were always something strange, erratic, and mysterious. . . . For her, communism is not a philosophical or a political program, but rather a matter of faith and feeling." Seghers joined the Communist party before the rise of the Nazi power in Germany; as late as 1971, she was still "recognized as one of the most representative writers of the Communist state."

In one of her most famous works, *Das siebte Kruz* ("The Seventh Cross"), Seghers revealed her belief that transcendence of a totalitarian system is dependent upon communal activity. The story deals with seven men and their escape from a Nazi concentration camp. The twist from a conventional escape novel, and the root in this novel's theme, is that the key to freedom, in Harold Rosenberg's analysis, "is not dependent upon the relative skills of the fugitive and his professional pursuers but upon the behavior of society itself." Rosenberg demonstrated that while two men in particular are the most likely to escape (one, Wallau, is "an expert in the psychology of escape"; the other, Belloni, is an acrobat), more than physical skill is needed to succeed. Belloni and Wallou are captured because they get no help from the community surrounding them. Meanwhile, another escapee (George) "manages to hold out long enough to allow several strangers . . . to join together on his side."

According to Rosenberg, "the escape takes on tremendous importance as a test of how much courage, resourcefulness, and desire for freedom still exist in the country." Seghers allows few of her readers or characters to avoid confronting at least the thought of what the fugitives represent to the possibilities for freedom. Said Rosenberg: "*The Seventh Cross* shows how the approach of the fugitive, or even the mere appearance of his picture in the newspapers, forces scores of people to go over their pasts and to make a decision that will determine the character of their entire future existence." Hope for the prisoners' existence in the immediate future is symbolically preserved by the seventh cross. While each captured escapee is tied to one of the seven crosses erected as a deterrant to other prisoners, one cross—George's—remains empty. "The seventh cross," theorized Diether H. Haenicke, "becomes the symbol of hope for the inmates of the camp, since, day by day, the vacant cross exemplifies the impotence of the regime."

Another novel of exile, *Transit*, has not been considered a characteristic Seghers work. Though the escape motif of *Das siebte Kruz* is mirrored in the struggle of German refugees as they attempt to get the visas and certificates needed for emigration, there is little of the same hope offered in *Transit*. Huebener called it "practically existentialist" before noting that Seghers later rewrote the final chapters to create a much more optimistic finish. In relation to *Das siebte Kruz*, *Transit* was uncharacteristic in another way, at least according to William Dubois. He thought "readers of *The Seventh Cross* will begin *Transit* with hope and finish it (if they can bear its vagaries that long) with a complete sense of let-down. . . . *Transit* is one of the dullest failures this reviewer has encountered in a long, long time."

The *Times Literary Supplement* used the three stories in *Sonderbare Begegnungen* as evidence that Seghers has not recently matched the artistic success of her earlier works. "Their one-dimensional framework and self-conscious naiv-

ety of plot and characterization appeal little to either the imagination or the intellect." Yet Segher maintained some of her common themes with a piece of "socialist realism" and an attack on the "inhumanity of war." The third story, "Die Reisebegegnung," is a more unique Seghers story. It pictures a literary discussion between Franz Kafka, Nikolai Gogol, and Ernst Theodor Hoffmann. "Their conversation," commented the *Times Literary Supplement,* "covers such questions as the relationship between realism and fantasy in literature and the social responsibilities of the writer."

Seghers's reputation has declined among others too. Her writing, long noted for its sharp simplicity, has been criticized for becoming weak and nebulous. Her political thinking, too, has been criticized as she is now considered by some to be too closely linked to the East German "establishment" while her staunch Communist stance has allegedly drifted into shallow ideology. Regardless of her loss of prominence in the West, the *Times Literary Supplement* reminded readers that Seghers is "still the doyenne of East German letters. . . . The reverential tone of the official reviews of *Sonderbare Begegnungen* in the East German press testifies to the high esteem in which she is held there."

BIOGRAPHICAL/CRITICAL SOURCES: *New York Times Book Review,* September 20, 1942, May 14, 1944; Jurgen Ruhle, *Literature and Revolution,* Praeger, 1969; Theodore Huebener, *The Literature of East Germany,* Ungar, 1970; Horst S. Daemmrich and Diether H. Haenicke, editors, *The Challenge of German Literature,* Wayne State University Press, 1971; *Booklist,* February 1, 1973, March 1, 1975; Harold Rosenberg, *Discovering the Present: Three Decades in Art, Culture, and Politics,* University of Chicago Press, 1973; *Times Literary Supplement,* March 8, 1974; *Books Abroad,* winter, 1974; *Contemporary Literary Criticism,* Volume 7, Gale, 1977.*

* * *

RAINE, Kathleen (Jessie) 1908-

PERSONAL: Born June 14, 1908, in London, England; daughter of George (a schoolmaster) and Jessie (a teacher) Raine; married Hugh Sykes Davies (a Cambridge don; divorced); married Charles Madge (a poet and professor; divorced); children: (second marriage) one daughter, one son. *Education:* Girton College, Cambridge, M.A., 1929. *Home:* 47 Paultons Sq., London S.W.3, England.

CAREER: Poet, critic, editor, and translator. Lecturer at Morley College, London; Andrew Mellon lecturer at National Gallery of Art, Washington, D.C., 1962. *Member:* University Women's Club. *Awards, honors:* Harriet Monroe Memorial Prize, 1952; Arts Council award, 1953; Oscar Blumenthal Prize, 1961; Cholmondeley Award, 1970; Smith Literary Award, 1972; D. Litt., Leicester University, 1974; Chapelbrook Award.

WRITINGS: Stone and Flower: Poems, 1935-43, Nicholson & Watson, 1943; (translator) Denis de Rougemont, *Talk of the Devil,* Eyre & Spottiswoode, 1945; *Living in Time* (poems), Editions Poetry, 1946; (compiler with Max-Pol Fouchet) *Aspects de la litterature anglaise,* Fountaine, 1947; (translator) Honore de Balzac, *Cousin Bette,* Hamish Hamilton, 1948; (translator) Paul Foulquie, *Existentialism,* Dobson, 1948; *The Pythoness and Other Poems,* Hamish Hamilton, 1948, Farrar, Straus, 1952.

(Translator) Balzac, *Lost Illusions,* Lehmann Books, 1951; (editor and author of introduction) Samuel Taylor Coleridge, *The Letters of Samuel Taylor Coleridge,* Grey Walls Press,

1952; *Selected Poems,* Weekend Press, 1952; *The Year One* (poems), Farrar, Straus, 1953; *Collected Poems,* Hamish Hamilton, 1956, Random House, 1957; (editor and author of introduction) Coleridge, *Selected Poems and Prose of Coleridge,* Penguin (London), 1957.

Christmas: An Acrostic (poem), privately printed, 1960; (author of introduction) William Butler Yeats, *Letters on Poetry From W. B. Yeats to Dorothy Wellesley,* Oxford University Press, 1964; *The Hollow Hill and Other Poems, 1960-64,* Hamish Hamilton, 1965; *Defending Ancient Springs,* Oxford University Press, 1967; *Blake and Tradition,* two volumes, Princeton University Press, 1968; *Ninfa Revisited* (poems) Enitharmon, 1968; *Six Dreams and Other Poems,* Enitharmon, 1968; (translator with R. M. Nadal) Pedro Calderon de la Barca, *Life's a Dream,* Hamish Hamilton, 1968, Theatre Arts, 1969; (editor) Coleridge, *Letters,* Folcroft, 1969; (editor with George Mills Harper) *Thomas Taylor the Platonist: Selected Writings,* Princeton University Press, 1969.

William Blake, Thames & Hudson, 1970, Praeger, 1971; *The Lost Country* (poems), Dolmen Press, 1971; *Faces of Day and Night* (autobiography), Enitharmon, 1972; *Yeats, the Tarot, and the Golden Dawn,* Dolmen Press, 1972, revised edition, Humanities Press, 1976; *Farewell Happy Fields: Memories of Childhood* (autobiography), Hamish Hamilton, 1973, Braziller, 1977; *On a Deserted Shore* (poems), Hamish Hamilton, 1973; *Death-in-Life and Life-in-Death: "Cuchulain Comforted" and "News for the Delphic Oracle,"* Oxford University Press, 1974; (editor) William Blake, *A Choice of Blake's Verse,* Faber, 1974; (editor) Percy Bysshe Shelley, *Shelley,* Penguin (London), 1974; *The Land Unknown* (autobiography), Braziller, 1975; *The Oval Portrait and Other Poems,* Enitharmon, 1977; *The Lion's Mouth: Concluding Chapters of Autobiography,* Hamish Hamilton, 1977.

SIDELIGHTS: Though she was born in London and has lived there much of her life, Raine has said she stills feels exiled from the Northumberland countryside where she spent her youth. At the outset of World War I, Raine's parents sent her to live with her maternal grandmother and an aunt in a northern England hamlet. There she spent the years she claims to be the epitome of all she's ever loved. A return to her parents' home in an "ugly" London suburb at the age of ten only heightened her longing for the bucolic north; but she remained in the city until she left for Cambridge on a scholarship. Two short-lived marriages followed her college career, the second of which haunted her deeply: "That I hurt a man so fine by marrying him for inadequate, indeed for deeply neurotic, reasons, lies heavily on my conscience." Helen Bevington reported that "at this point of distress she began to write poems, 'a few grains of gold calcinated from all that dross of life in the fires of an overwhelming physical passion.'" In addition, Bevington believed Raine's impulse to devote many years to the study of William Blake was rooted in a personal searching. Together, her poems, her criticism, and her autobiographies form the essence of Raine's written work.

Raine's attraction to the natural world and her introspective nature are reflected in her poetry. Babette Deutsch observed from Raine's verse that she "is a woman whose pity tends to lapse into self-pity. But, she holds with [Edwin] Muir that 'the ever-recurring forms of nature mirror an eternal reality.' . . . Raine's poems gain in depth and subtlety because they keep returning to the actualities that embody the mystery of the physical universe and of conscious selfhood." This response to nature also impressed Ralph J. Mills: "She is, first

of all, gifted with an intuitive sense of the relationship existing between human beings and the surrounding world of nature, a relationship so foreign to our habitual modern ways of thinking about ourselves and the urbanized, technological environment in which most of us live that its very simplicity jars us. . . . Like Blake, Wordsworth, and Coleridge, she is concerned with deciphering the secret hints of the larger scheme of being embodied in the visible surface of the natural world."

Many critics feel Raine's poetry is closely associated with the Romantic tradition in another way, language. A *Spectator* reviewer questioned the "resolutely archaic diction" in *The Lost Country:* "Who else could offer us so many examples of a vocabulary long since fossilised. . . . There's only the occasional hint to suggest that English poetry has progressed at all since the Georgians." A *Listener* critic, meanwhile, heard a similar "slightly dated" diction in *The Oval Portrait* but found it effective: "Miss Raine writes of old age, its losses and memories, without making concessions to modernism other than to use a free-flowing verse form which gives her poems a dream-like quality." Howard Nemerov also felt Raine quite consciously instills her work with the language of the past: "Kathleen Raine's poems are unfashionable on purpose, unworldly, traditional, meditative, belonging to memory and dream, to solitude and silence. . . ." A key influence on Raine's poetry has been the literary tradition to which she closely associates herself. As Nemerov noted, Raine "is one of the great poetic inheritors" in a tradition "given intellectual form by Plato and mediated to us chiefly . . . by Blake and his contemporary Thomas Taylor." Raine has been variously called a Wordsworthian, a Shelleyan Platonist, and a Christian Metaphysical, but she holds her closest alliance with Blake. Mills cited "certain spiritual affinities" she has with Blake, and Deutsch said "close as she seems to Blake, she appears to have escaped his confusions." Her devotion to Blake, though prevalent in her poetry, can be more accurately measured in her critical work, *Blake and Tradition.*

The purpose behind *Blake and Tradition* was to establish "that Blakes's thought, including much of his symbolic imagery, belongs to the classical tradition of anti-materialist philosophy since Plotinus," declared J. Bronowski. *Books Abroad* reviewer John E. Rexine defined the work more specifically, claiming it to be a demonstration of "how much he owes to Jewish mysticism, alchemy, and mythology, particularly classical, as well as to show the relation of Blake's work to Orphic, Neoplatonic, Gnostic, and Hermetic writings, and to Swedenborgian theology, to mention only the most obvious." Ants Oras described the amount of scholarship entailed by this monumental task: "Twenty years of labor involving an examination of everything Blake is known or supposed to have read, a meticulous scrutiny of his engravings as to their bearing on his thought, and of nearly everything written about him, are embodied in more than eight hundred pages of lucid, closely reasoned text." Not surprisingly, Rexine cautioned that "this is not a book for the masses but for the serious scholar and student."

This one aspect, the "examination of everything Blake is known or supposed to have read," has posed a problem for reviewers of *Blake and Tradition.* "Raine is at constant pains to try to establish Blake's detailed knowledge of specific texts," argued Robert F. Gleckner. Bronowski voiced a similar reservation, arguing "not everything in Blake is an echo or an analogue of old beliefs and symbols; and when Kathleen Raine seems to labor to find it so, she must make many wonder whether she really is sensitive to Blake's endlessly springing originality." And, Oras stated simply, "Reading Miss Raine, one occasionally feels that Blake cannot have been so completely immersed in what he read in Boehme, Porphyry, Plotinus and the others . . . as not to respond in a more impulsively personal, eruptive fashion." Jerome McGann, on the other hand, felt Raine did not overestimate the need to establish Blake's tradition so completely. He insisted "she hardly exaggerates when she says that we must recover the sources of his special symbolic language in order to understand much of his poetry."

Aside from this problem, many critics heralded the undeniable significance of Raine's *magnum opus*. This product of an obvious "labor of love" helped Kathleen Nott understand Blake's "curious" and formerly "deeply boring" "Prophetic Books." "Now, with Miss Raine's intricate and efficient key, I shall find out what they really mean and will never permit myself to be bored by them again." Oras was also lured to this "epic feat" by a personal awareness of Blake made possible by Raine's efforts. "The skill with which Kathleen Raine unravels these threads of traditions, and yet manages to reconstitute them in our minds as components of very living, very personal art, is remarkable from the start," he said. Others raised *Blake and Tradition* to an eminent position in the realm of Blake scholarship. McGann, for example, included Raine's work as "certainly one of the four most important books yet written on Blake's ideas" (along with those by Northrop Frye, David Erdman, and Peter Fisher).

Raine again concentrated on the importance of a writer's literary tradition in another major work, *Defending Ancient Springs*. In this book, "Miss Raine argues that the authentic poet draws his inspiration from such a source as Plato's world of Ideas, or Yeats's *Anima Mundi*," summarized Wallace Fowlie. M. L. Rosenthal shared this view: "Miss Raine's whole argument, in fact revolves around the idea of 'the learning of the poets,' a traditional symbolic language in which they are expert that is the key to 'the beautiful order of "eternity"' as grasped by Blake, Shelley, Yeats, St. John Perse, Muir, and others." Though *Defending Ancient Springs* has been criticized for being dogmatic and having a narrowly focused vision, Rosenthal contended that, overall, it instructs with a voice "warmly engaged with its subject." "When Miss Raine writes in this way we can only be grateful, and forgive her efforts elsewhere to disdain the opposition out of existence, and rebuke ourselves for any impatience with the merely local and petulant side of her argument."

A highlight of Raine's more recent work has been the three-volume publication of her autobiography. The first volume, *Farewell Happy Fields*, covers the years before her entrance to Cambridge. One striking aspect of the book is the early sense of isolation felt by Raine. Despite her idyllic love for Northumberland, she still longed for something more—Scotland, "the place of poetry." She was, in Bevington's terms, "happy in paradise, yet unhappy in exile." One specific incident, reported V. S. Pritchett, intensified this sense of isolation and marked a turning point in a predominantly happy childhood. Pritchett recalled an early love affair broken when Raine's father threatened to kill the boy and forced the young couple to separate: "The dazed girl accepted her situation without question. But from this date begins the open war with her father about his politics, and a hatred of the timidity and meanness of suburban life." Such experiences, evidently, were as crucial to Raine's development as were her fond childhood memories. For Victor Howes, they symbolized a universal meaning: "Her twin themes of innocence and experience, of a magical world almost carelessly thrown aside in exchange for an asphalt jungle, seem not merely to recapitulate the story of a single life, they seem in some Proustian way to encapsulate the history of our time."

The second segment of Raine's autobiography, *The Land Unknown*, examined the literary and social culture of the twenties and thirties while continuing to explore her developing sensibilities. Jane Larkin Crain found some "marvelous moments here: a sketch of William Empson, a poet's description of English landscape, [and] clear-headed speculation on matters literary and philosophical." Though Crain did object to "all the self-absorption" in the autobiography, others welcomed Raine's explanation of "where she went wrong in her life." Without self-pity but in penitential tones, the chronicle includes reflections on her two marriages, the World War II years, her brief conversion to Roman Catholicism, and her longing for what Bevington called "some higher vision of radiance and joy"—a void eventually filled by Blake. Robert Nye appreciated Raine's candor: "What is beautiful and remarkable about 'The Land Unknown' is the way in which a great deal of messy material is given shape and substance by Miss Raine's truthfulness."

In the last segment of her autobiography, *The Lion's Mouth*, Raine described the "central event" of her life, her relationship with writer and artist Gavin Maxwell. The *New Yorker* explained the intensity of the relationship: "Whether they saw one another or not, wherever they went (she lectured and taught), whatever they did (he married briefly and disastrously), they could not break off, and they remained the most important, terrifying, and beloved figures in each other's lives until his death in 1971."

With the varied publication of poetry, criticism, editings, and autobiographies, Raine has made the 1970's her most productive decade ever. Now more than seventy years old, she shows no sign of abating her lifelong devotion to literature and writing.

BIOGRAPHICAL/CRITICAL SOURCES: Babette Deutsch, *Poetry in Our Time,* Doubleday, 1963; Ralph J. Mills, *Kathleen Raine: A Critical Essay,* Eerdmans, 1967; *Listener,* January 4, 1968, January 3, 1974, September 29, 1977, October 13, 1977; *Sewanee Review,* July, 1968, January, 1972, July, 1972; *Virginia Quarterly Review,* autumn, 1968, summer, 1969; *Poetry,* May, 1969, October, 1970; *New Statesman,* July 18, 1969, October 1, 1971, November 23, 1973, February 15, 1974, July 11, 1975, October 21, 1977; *Observer Review,* August 17, 1969; *New York Review of Books,* October 23, 1969, December 13, 1973; *Nation,* December 22, 1969.

Books Abroad, winter, 1970; *Times Literary Supplement,* January 29, 1970, December 10, 1971, January 7, 1972, June 1, 1973, December 14, 1973, May 3, 1974, February 14, 1975, August 8, 1975, July 29, 1977, October 21, 1977; *Hudson Review,* spring, 1970; *American Literature,* May, 1970; *Modern Philology,* August, 1970; *Guardian Weekly,* December 12, 1970, January 8, 1973, July 19, 1975; *Observer,* December 13, 1970, November 18, 1973, May 5, 1974, August 3, 1974, July 27, 1975, October 2, 1977; *Books and Bookmen,* February, 1971, February, 1974, July, 1977, November, 1977; *Review of English Studies,* February, 1971; *Journal of Aesthetics and Art Criticism,* spring, 1971; *Philological Quarterly,* July, 1971; *Spectator,* December 25, 1971, October 22, 1977; *New York Times Book Review,* October 12, 1975, May 1, 1977; *New Yorker,* October 13, 1975, April 18, 1977, April 17, 1978; *Christian Science Monitor,* October 23, 1975, May 18, 1977; *Saturday Review,* November 1, 1975,

March 19, 1977; *Contemporary Literary Criticism*, Volume 7, Gale, 1977.*

* * *

RANDOLPH, A(sa) Philip   1889-1979

OBITUARY NOTICE: Born April 15, 1889, in Crescent City, Fla.; died May 16, 1979, in New York, N.Y. Civil rights leader and editor best known for his work relating to labor unions. Randolph helped organize the Brotherhood of Sleeping Car Porters and later became the first black vice-president of the American Federation of Labor-Congress of Industrial Organizations (AFL-CIO). Randolph also pressured President Truman into abolishing segregation in the armed forces. Later, he led marches to Washington, D.C., to protest the treatment of blacks. From 1917 to 1925, Randolph edited the black-oriented socialist publication, *The Messenger*, which he co-founded with Chandler Owen. Obituaries and other sources: *Ebony*, May, 1969; Russell L. Adams, *Great Negroes, Past and Present*, Afro-American Publishing Co., 1969; James J. Flynn, *Negroes of Achievement in Modern America*, Dodd, 1970; *Who's Who in America*, 39th edition, Marquis, 1976; *International Who's Who*, Europa, 1978; *Washington Post*, May 18, 1979.

* * *

RAPHAEL, Chaim   1908-
(Jocelyn Davey)

PERSONAL: Born July 14, 1908, in Middlesbrough, England; married, 1934 (divorced, 1963); children: one son, one daughter. *Education:* Oxford University, M.A. (honors), 1930, graduate study, 1931. *Home:* 27 Langdale Rd., Hove, East Sussex, England. *Agent:* Georges Borchardt, Inc., 136 East 57th St., New York, N.Y. 10022.

CAREER: Oxford University, Oxford, England, lecturer in Hebrew at Exeter College and Cowley Lecturer in post-Biblical Hebrew, 1932-39, Kennicott fellow, 1934-37; British Government, liaison officer for internment camps in Britain, 1940-41, in Canada, 1941-42, economic adviser for British Information Services in New York, N.Y., 1942-45, economic director, 1945-57, head of Information Division of British Treasury, 1957-69, head of Information Division of civil service department, 1969-70; University of Sussex, Brighton, England, fellow in Jewish social history, 1970—. *Member:* Reform Club. *Awards, honors:* Member of Order of the British Empire, 1951, Commander, 1965.

WRITINGS: Memoirs of a Special Case, Knopf, 1962; *The Walls of Jerusalem: An Excursion Into Jewish History*, Knopf, 1968; *A Feast of History*, Simon & Schuster, 1972; *The Passover Haggadah*, Behrman, 1978; *Encounters With the Jewish People*, Behrman, 1979 (published in England as *A Coat of Many Colours*, Chatto & Windus, 1979).

Mystery novels; under pseudonym Jocelyn Davey: *A Capitol Offence: An Entertainment*, Knopf, 1956 (published in England as *Undoubted Deed*, Chatto & Windus, 1956); *The Naked Villany*, Knopf, 1958; *A Touch of Stagefright*, Chatto & Windus, 1962; *A Killing in Hats*, Chatto & Windus, 1966; *A Treasury Alarm*, Chatto & Windus, 1976.

Contributor to magazines in the United States and England, including *Commentary*, *Atlantic Monthly*, *New Yorker*, and *Encounter*.

SIDELIGHTS: The Walls of Jerusalem began as an English translation of the Midrash, completed before World War II, and was finally published as a history for the educated layman. Enlivened with anecdote and analogy, it has been well received on both sides of the Atlantic.

BIOGRAPHICAL/CRITICAL SOURCES: Washington Post, May 7, 1968; *Reporter*, June 13, 1968; *Commentary*, September, 1968; *New Statesman*, December 13, 1968; *Jewish Quarterly*, summer, 1969.

* * *

RATNER, Joseph   1901(?)-1979

OBITUARY NOTICE: Born c. 1901 in London, England; died of a heart attack, August 21, 1979, in New York, N.Y. Philosopher, educator, and writer best known for his works on Spinoza, including *The Philosophy of Spinoza* and *Spinoza on God*. Ratner, who studied under and befriended philosopher Thomas Dewey, edited Dewey's articles for *Characters and Events*. Obituaries and other sources: *New York Times*, August 22, 1979.

* * *

RATTIGAN, Terence (Mervyn)   1911-1977

PERSONAL: Born June 10, 1911, in London, England; died November 30, 1977, in Hamilton, Bermuda; son of William Frank Arthur (a diplomat) and Vera (Houston) Rattigan. *Education:* Attended Trinity College, Oxford, 1930-1933. *Office:* c/o Dr. Jan van Loewen Ltd., 81/83 Shaftesbury Ave., London W1V 8BX, England.

CAREER: Playwright and screenwriter, 1934-77. *Military service:* Royal Air Force, Coastal Command, 1940-45; became flight lieutenant. *Awards, honors:* Ellen Terry award, 1947, and New York Drama Critics Circle award, 1948, both for "The Winslow Boy"; Ellen Terry award, 1948, for "The Browning Version"; Commander of the Order of the British Empire (C.B.E.), 1958; knighted, 1971.

WRITINGS—Plays: (With Philip Heimann) "First Episode," first produced in London, 1933, produced in New York City, 1934; *French Without Tears* (first produced in London, 1939; produced in New York City, 1934; revised version produced as "Joie de Vivre" in London, 1960), Hamish Hamilton, 1937, Farrar & Rinehart, 1938; *After the Dance* (produced in London, 1939), Hamish Hamilton, 1939; (with Anthony Maurice) "Follow My Leader," produced in London, 1940; (with Hector Bolitho) "Grey Farm," produced in New York City, 1940, produced in London, 1942; *Flare Path* (first produced in London, 1942; produced in New York City, 1942), Hamish Hamilton, 1942; *While the Sun Shines* (first produced in London, 1943; produced in New York City, 1944), Samuel French, 1945; *Love in Idleness* (produced in London, 1944), Hamish Hamilton, 1945, revised version published as *O Mistress Mine* (produced in New York City, 1946), Samuel French, 1949; *The Winslow Boy* (first produced in London, 1946; produced in New York City, 1947), Dramatists Play Service, 1946; *Playbill: "The Browning Version" and "Harlequinade"* (first produced in London, 1948; produced in New York City, 1949), Hamish Hamilton, 1949, published in two volumes by Samuel French, 1950.

Adventure Story (produced in London, 1949), Samuel French, 1950; *Who is Sylvia?* (produced in London, 1950), Hamish Hamilton, 1951; *The Deep Blue Sea* (produced in London, 1952; produced in New York City, 1952), Hamish Hamilton, 1952, Random House, 1953; *The Sleeping Prince* (two-act; produced in London, 1953; produced in New York City, 1956), Hamish Hamilton, 1954, Random House, 1957; *Separate Tables: Two Plays* (produced in London, 1954; produced in New York City, 1956), Hamish Hamilton, 1955, Random House, 1957; *"The Prince and the Showgirl": The Script for the Film*, New American Library, 1957; *Variation on a Theme* (produced in London, 1958), Hamish Hamilton, 1958.

Ross: A Dramatic Portrait (produced in London, 1960; produced in New York City, 1961), Hamish Hamilton, 1960, Random House, 1962; *Man and Boy* (produced in London, 1963; produced in New York City, 1963), Samuel French, 1963; *A Bequest to the Nation* (televised as "Nelson," 1966; revised version produced in London at the Haymarket Theatre on September 23, 1970, as "A Bequest to the Nation"), Hamish Hamilton, 1970; "All on Her Own" (televised, 1968; produced in London, 1974; produced in London as "Duologue," 1976), published in *The Best Short Plays 1970,* edited by Stanley Richards, Chilton, 1970; "High Summer" (televised, 1972), published in *The Best Short Plays 1973,* edited by Richards, Chilton, 1973; *In Praise of Love: "Before Dawn", and "After Lydia"* (produced in London, 1973; "After Lydia" produced as "In Praise of Love" on Broadway at Morosco Theatre, 1974), Hamish Hamilton, 1973, Samuel French, 1975; "Cause Celebre," first produced on the West End at Her Majesty's Theatre, July 14, 1977.

Collections: *Collected Plays,* Hamish Hamilton, Volume I (contains "French Without Tears," "Flare Path," "While The Sun Shines," "Love in Idleness," and "The Winslow Boy"), 1953, Volume II (contains "The Browning Version," "Harlequinade," "Adventure Story," "Who is Sylvia?," and "The Deep Blue Sea"), 1953, Volume III (contains "The Sleeping Prince," "Separate Tables," "Variation on a Theme," "Ross," and "Heart to Heart"), 1964.

Screenplays: (With Anatole de Grunwald and Ian Dalrymple) "French Without Tears" (based on Rattigan's play of the same name), Paramount, 1939; (with de Grunwald) "Quiet Wedding," Universal, 1941; "The Day Will Dawn," 1941; (with de Grunwald, Patrick Kirwin, and Frank Owen) "The Avengers," 1942; (with Rodney Ackland) "Uncensored," Twentieth Century-Fox, 1943; (with de Grunwald) "English Without Tears," 1944; (with de Grunwald) "Johnny in the Clouds," United Artists, 1946; "Journey Together," 1946; (with de Grunwald) "While the Sun Shines" (based on Rattigan's play of the same name), 1947; (with de Grunwald) "Her Man Gilbey," Universal, 1949.

(With de Grunwald and Anthony Asquith) "The Winslow Boy" (based on Rattigan's play of the same name), Eagle Lion, 1950; (with Ackland) "Bond Street," 1950; (with Graham Greene) "Young Scarface" (based on Greene's novel, *Brighton Rock*), Mayer-Kingsley, 1952; "The Browning Version" (based on Rattigan's play of the same name), Universal, 1952; "Breaking the Sound Barrier," United Artists, 1952; "The Final Test," J. Arthur Rank Organisation, 1954; "The Deep Blue Sea" (based on Rattigan's play of the same name), Twentieth Century-Fox, 1955; "The Man Who Loved Redheads," United Artists, 1955; "The Prince and the Showgirl" (based on Rattigan's play, "The Sleeping Prince"), Warner Bros., 1957; (with John Gay) "Separate Tables" (based on Rattigan's play of the same name), United Artists, 1958; "The V.I.P.s," Metro-Goldwyn-Mayer (MGM), 1963; "The Yellow Rolls Royce," MGM, 1965; "Goodbye, Mr. Chips" (based on James Hilton's novel of the same name), MGM, 1969; "A Bequest to the Nation," 1973; "Conduct Unbecoming"; "Mr. Burke and Mr. Wills," Veric Production Ltd. and British Lion.

Television plays: "The Final Test," 1951; "Heart to Heart," 1962; "Ninety Years On," 1964; "Nelson," 1966; "All on Her Own," 1968; "High Summer," 1972.

Radio plays: "A Tale of Two Cities" (based on Charles Dickens's novel of the same name), 1950; "Cause Celebre," 1975.

SIDELIGHTS: Stagestruck as a youngster, Terence Rattigan decided at an early age that he wanted to be a dramatist. While he was still in college, Rattigan wrote a play, "First Episode," that had brief and disastrous runs in London and New York City. Rattigan was undaunted by the failure and quit college to pursue a career in the theatre. His father disapproved of his career plans but agreed to finance the aspiring playwright for two years. As his part of the bargain, Rattigan promised his father that if he was still unsuccessful after the two years had elapsed he would begin a career in diplomacy or banking. Shortly before the probationary period expired, Rattigan's "French Without Tears" became a smash hit in London. More success was to follow. Rattigan is the only dramatist to have written two plays that ran for more than one thousand performances apiece in London. In addition to his popular plays, he wrote a number of original movie scripts, including "The V.I.P.s," "The Yellow Rolls Royce," and "Conduct Unbecoming."

Rattigan's predilection for bourgeois characters and middle class values aroused the disdain of some critics and the approbation of others. Reviewing productions of "The Winslow Boy" and "A Bequest to the Nation," Hilary Spurling noted that "both plays are designed to take one back . . . to the days when one was proud to be an Englishman. . . . Pain and fear are discreetly underplayed in favour of the soothing virtues, courage, loyalty and perseverance in face of frightful odds." Ronald Bryden also remarked upon the traditional values espoused in "The Winslow Boy": "Rattigan's surface self-congratulation is part of an argument that British society is strong enough to tolerate questioning, dissent, individuality. Today we can see that the quantity of reassurance was a measure of British insecurity in those post-war years. . . . But it's possible to envy the confidence still underlying the play that tolerance is something we can afford, that our sameness is sufficient to permit differences."

Characters rather than ideas are emphasized in Rattigan's plays. "I rejoice," he wrote in an article for the *New York Herald Tribune* in 1956, "in the death of the cult of the play of ideas and the re-emergence since the war, in Europe as in America, of the play that unashamedly says nothing—except possibly that human beings are strange creatures, and worth putting on the stage where they can be laughed at or cried over, as our pleasure takes us." Rattigan contended that "character makes the play" not only in serious plays but also in farce. John Russell Taylor observed that "French Without Tears" "is under the bright, bustling surface, a gentle comedy of character, in which each seems for a moment to be faced with what he has most desired and finds that it is in fact what he most fears." While granting the effectiveness of farces like "French Without Tears," Frederick Lumley asserted that Rattigan failed in his serious plays of character: "In his farces we do not ask that his characters should be complete individuals, whereas in a serious play that character must be a creation. The main criticism of Rattigan's work, then, is a fundamental criticism, namely, that his characters are wishy-washy creatures with neither nobility in their thoughts nor individuality in their actions. They are types we know exist, and though we might recognise them, they are certainly not people we would want as our friends."

Whatever the defects in Rattigan's characterization, virtually all commentators concede that he was a master craftsman. "Terence Rattigan has been turning out neatly turned-out comedies and dramas since the 1930s, and is still writing

1930s plays," Stanley Kauffman wrote in 1975. "He finds his little idea, for comedy or poignance, and he stitches his little script about it with considerable craft and no unnecessary nuisance." In *The Rise and Fall of the Well-Made Play*, John Russell Taylor examined in detail the quality of Rattigan's craftsmanship. Taylor offered "The Winslow Boy" and "The Browning Version" as examples of plays that were expertly constructed, but he regarded "The Deep Blue Sea" as the play in which Rattigan "most happily constructed a fully articulated plot according to well-made principles without too obviously showing his hand." After viewing a performance of "A Bequest to the Nation," Spurling also paid tribute to Rattigan's craftsmanship: "Mr Rattigan's lightness of touch belongs with much else—his knack of smuggling serviceable information in small, discreetly wrapped and easily assimilated packages; his manner of sewing a scene together and finishing off with an exit line, which snaps it shut like a press-stud; his habit, when approaching troubled emotional waters, of quoting Shakespeare—all these belong to a style of playwriting long neglected, but by no means to be sneezed at."

Rattigan's style of playwriting has indeed been long neglected. Although he had exulted in 1956 that the play of ideas was dead, later that same year the showing of John Osborne's "Look Back in Anger" ushered in a new era in British theatre, one in which plays of craftsmanship and character were distinctly unfashionable. Rattigan took this turn of events philosophically. "Fashion is ephemeral," he once told an interviewer. "Someday we'll get back to the state in which a curtain goes up on a sitting room where the maid is on the phone saying 'Lady Silversmith is out.'" Although drawing-room drama has not yet come back into vogue, Rattigan's reputation has gained considerable luster in recent years. A reviewer for *Newsweek* remarked in 1974: "The plays of Terence Rattigan are precisely the kind of thing that Britain's Angry Young Men were supposed to have swept off the stage in the '50s, led by John Osborne on first broom.... But how would history judge between Rattigan and Osborne right now? Angry shmangry. Rattigan the 'drawing-room dramatist' has almost certainly written more good plays . . . than Osborne."

AVOCATIONAL INTERESTS: Golf and squash, watching cricket games.

BIOGRAPHICAL/CRITICAL SOURCES: George Jean Nathan, *The Theatre Book of the Year 1944-45: A Record and an Interpretation*, Knopf, 1945; *New Statesman and Nation*, March 4, 1950; *New York Herald Tribune*, September 23, 1956; John Russell Taylor, *The Rise and Fall of the Well-Made Play*, Methuen, 1967; Frederick Lumley, *New Trends in 20th Century Drama: A Survey Since Ibsen and Shaw*, Oxford University Press, 1967; *Christian Science Monitor*, November 29, 1969; *New York Times*, September 25, 1970; *Variety*, October 14, 1970; *Observer Review*, September 27, 1970, November 8, 1970; *Plays and Players*, November, 1970, December, 1970, November, 1973; *New Yorker*, April 1, 1974; *Newsweek*, December 23, 1974; *Nation*, December 28, 1974; *New Republic*, January 4 & 11, 1975; *Contemporary Literary Criticism*, Volume 7, Gale, 1977.

OBITUARIES: New York Times, December 1, 1977; *Washington Post*, December 1, 1977; *Newsweek*, December 12, 1977; *Time*, December 12, 1977; *AB Bookman's Weekly*, February 6, 1978.*

RAYNOR, Henry (Broughton) 1917-

PERSONAL: Born January 29, 1917, in Manchester, England; married Elli Gertrude Friedrich, January 6, 1946. *Education:* Attended secondary school in Manchester, England. *Politics:* "Vaguely central." *Home:* 4 Fairhall, Colley Lane, Reigate, Surrey RH2 9JA, England.

CAREER: Teacher of English and history at schools in Whitchurch, England, 1941-43, Southport, England, 1943-48, Liverpool, England, 1948-55, London, England, 1956-71, and in Guildford, England, 1972—. Free-lance broadcaster and correspondent. *Member:* Critics Circle.

WRITINGS: Joseph Haydn, Boosey & Hawkes, 1962; *Radio and Television*, Edward Arnold, 1971; *A Social History of Music From Beethoven to the Middle Ages*, Barrie & Jenkins, 1972, Schocken, 1972; *Mahler*, Macmillan, 1974; *Music and Society Since 1815*, Barrie & Jenkins, 1976, Schocken, 1976; *The Orchestra: A History*, R. Hale, 1978, Scribner, 1978; *Mozart*, Macmillan, 1978; *Music in England: A Social and Stylistic History*, R. Hale, 1980.

Author of "The Long Spoon" (one-act play), first produced in London, England at New Gateway Theatre, September, 1955. Contributor to *Grove's Dictionary of Music and Musicians, Concise Illustrated Encyclopedia of Music*, and *Outline of Music*. Contributor to magazines and newspapers in the United States and England, including *Observer, Music Review*, and *Tempo*.

WORK IN PROGRESS: Farewell, Manchester, an autobiography.

SIDELIGHTS: Henry Raynor writes: "I was born in a working class family with a passion for books, music, and the theatre. I wrote verse and impossibly intellectual half-baked plays, and found myself writing about music and actually finding readers. I wrote about music and musicians, the theatre and television, and won some attention as an occasional broadcaster. The British Broadcasting Corp. produced my radio drama-documentary, 'There Was a Child Went Forth" in 1956, and I had a play produced. I lecture from time to time, and conduct extra-mural and other adult education classes, notably on music, occasionally on creative writing.

"It seemed to me, some twenty-five years ago, that the work of most historians of music is incomplete because an enormous musicological concentration on the development of styles makes it impossible for authors to deal with the extremely important questions of the influence of patrons and outside authorities like municipalities and churches, on the growth of audiences, the development of musical organizations, and consequently on the composers themselves.

"*A Social History of Music* and *Music and Society Since 1815* were an attempt to write music history without stylistic considerations, but dealing with the influences of society on music. *Music in England* attempts to be both social and stylistic."

*   *   *

RAZZELL, Arthur (George) 1925-

PERSONAL: Born October 17, 1925, in Welling, Kent, England; son of William Lewis (a designer) and Alice (Wakefield) Razzell; married Daphne Jean Patten (a dress designer), August 12, 1950; children: Philip, Simon, Margaret. *Education:* Attended University of London, 1949-51. *Politics:* Liberal. *Religion:* Anglican. *Home:* The Olives, Buxted, Sussex, England. *Office:* County Hall, Lewes, East Sussex, England.

CAREER: University of London, Institute of Education, London, England, lecturer in education, 1964-69; University of Lancaster, Lancaster, England, senior researcher, 1969-72; Scholastic Publication Ltd., London, director, 1965-75; Ravenscote County Middle School, Frimley, England, headmaster, 1972-78; county adviser on teacher training, East Sussex County Council, 1979—. Consultant to Macmillan Publishers. *Military service:* Royal Navy, 1942-45. Served on staff of Admiral Lord Fraser, 1973-76; became lieutenant. *Member:* William Morris Society, Society of Authors.

WRITINGS: *Circles and Curves,* Doubleday, 1964; *Symmetry,* Doubleday, 1964; *Probability,* Doubleday, 1964; *A Question of Accuracy,* Doubleday, 1964; *Four and the Story of Four,* Doubleday, 1964; *Three and the Story of Three,* Doubleday, 1964; *Juniors,* Penguin, 1967; *Have We Got Time?,* Hart-Davis, 1968; *Signs and Symbols,* Hart-Davis, 1968; *The Lie of the Land,* Hart-Davis, 1968; *Shapes and Numbers,* Hart-Davis, 1968; *A Postscript to Plowden,* Penguin, 1968; (with Alec Ross) *The Middle Years of Schooling,* Schools Council, 1969; *Education for Democracy,* Penguin, 1970; (with Ross) *The Curriculum for the Middle Years,* Schools Council, 1975; *Ways of Knowing,* Macmillan, 1976; *Awareness One,* Macmillan, 1976; *Awarenesses Two,* Macmillan, 1976; *You Need to Know Your Tables,* Macmillan, 1976. Television scriptwriter for twenty-two programs in series "Summing It Up," broadcast in the United Kingdom by Independent Television, and for forty programs in Primary Mathematics Programs, 1959-63. Member of "New Education," 1964-67.

SIDELIGHTS: Razzell told *CA:* "Having now passed the ripe age of fifty, I have purchased an old Tudor house, built in 1550 and set in rural Sussex. The thick oak beams are rich in woodworm, death-watch beetle, dry-rot and wet-rot. All this can be dealt with, and in my old age I can sit surrounded by my books and papers in front of a twelve-foot-long inglenook fireplace. Opposite the house there is a village store, a small post office, a local garage and a pub. The way of life has changed little over the past three hundred years and as the atmosphere soaks into my bloodstream I look forward to a flush of truly creative writing!"

*   *   *

READ, Herbert Edward 1893-1968

PERSONAL: Born December 4, 1893, in Kirbymoorside, Yorkshire, England; died June 12, 1968; married Evelyn Roff, 1919 (marriage ended); married Margaret Ludwig; children: (first marriage) one son; (second marriage) three sons, one daughter. *Education:* Attended University of Leeds.

CAREER: Critic, poet, essayist, writer on art, editor, and publisher. Government Treasury Office, London, England, assistant principal, 1919-22; Victoria and Albert Museum, London, assistant keeper, 1922-31; University of Edinburgh, Edinburgh. Scotland, professor of fine arts, 1931-33; *Burlington Magazine,* London, editor, 1933-39. Lecturer at Liverpool University and at Harvard University; lecturer in poetry and art in Great Britain and abroad. *Military service:* British Army, World War I; served in France and Belgium; received Distinguished Flying Order and Military Cross. *Awards, honors:* Leon fellow, University of London, 1940-42; created Knight of the Order of the British Empire, 1953; Royal College of Art fellow.

WRITINGS—Poems: *Songs of Chaos,* Elkin Mathews, 1915; *Eclogues: A Book of Poems,* Beaumont, 1919; *Naked Warriors,* [London], 1919; *Collected Poems, 1913-1925,*

Faber & Gwyer, 1926; *The End of the War,* Faber, 1933; *Poems, 1914-1934,* Harcourt, 1935; *Thirty-Five Poems,* Faber, 1940; *A World Within a War,* Faber, 1944, Harcourt, 1945; *Collected Poems,* Faber, 1946, New Directions, 1951; *Moon's Farm, and Poems Mostly Elegaic,* Faber, 1955, Horizon Press, 1956; *Selected Writings: Poetry and Criticism,* foreword by Allen Tate, Faber, 1963, Horizon Press, 1964; *Collected Poems,* Horizon Press, 1966.

Other works: *In Retreat: A Journal of the Retreat of the Fifth Army From St. Quentin, March 1918,* L. & V. Woolf, 1925 (also see below); *English Stained Glass,* Putnam, 1926, reprinted, Kraus Reprint, 1973; *Reason and Romanticism: Essays in Literary Criticism,* Faber & Gwyer, 1926, Haskell House, 1974 (also see below); *English Prose Style,* Holt, 1928, revised edition, Beacon Press, 1966; *Phases of English Poetry,* L. & V. Woolf, 1928, Harcourt, 1929, revised edition, New Directions, 1950, 1st edition reprinted, Richard West, 1976; *The Sense of Glory: Essays in Criticism,* Cambridge University Press, 1929, Richard West, 1977 (also see below); *Staffordshire Pottery Figures,* Duckworth, 1929.

Wordsworth, J. Cape, 1930, J. Cape & H. Smith, 1931, new edition, Faber, 1965; *Ambush,* Faber, 1930, Haskell House, 1974; *The Meaning of Art,* Faber, 1931, published as *The Anatomy of Art: An Introduction to the Problems of Art and Aesthetics,* Dodd, 1932, revised edition published as *The Meaning of Art,* Praeger, 1972; *Form in Modern Poetry,* Sheed & Ward, 1932, Richard West, 1977 (also see below); *The Innocent Eye,* Faber, 1933 (also see below); *Art and Industry: The Principles of Industrial Design,* Faber, 1934, Horizon Press, 1954, 5th edition, Faber, 1966; *Art Now: An Introduction to the Theory of Modern Painting and Sculpture,* Faber, 1933, Harcourt, 1937, 5th edition, Pitman, 1968; *The Green Child: A Romance* (novel), Heinemann, 1935, introduction by Kenneth Rexroth, New Directions, 1948, reprinted, introduction by Graham Greene, Chatto & Windus, 1970; *In Defence of Shelley and Other Essays,* Heinemann, 1936, Books for Libraries Press, 1968 (also see below); *Art and Society,* Macmillan, 1937, new edition, Schocken, 1966; *Poetry and Anarchism,* Faber, 1938, new edition, Freedom Press, 1947, Norwood, 1977; *Collected Essays in Literary Criticism* (two parts; part one, "General Theories," part two, "Particular Studies," also see below; includes "The Sense of Glory," "Form in Modern Poetry," "In Defence of Shelley," and essays from "Reason and Romanticism"), Faber, 1938, 2nd edition, 1951, published as *The Nature of Literature,* Horizon Press, 1956.

Annals of Innocence and Experience, Faber, 1940, revised edition (includes "In Retreat" and "The Innocent Eye"), 1946, Haskell House, 1974; *The Philosophy of Anarchism,* Freedom Press, 1940, Norwood, 1975; *To Hell With Culture: Democratic Values Are New Values,* Paul, Trench, Trubner, 1941 (also see below); *The Politics of the Unpolitical* (includes "To Hell With Culture"), Routledge, 1943; *Education Through Art,* Faber, 1943, 3rd edition, Pantheon, 1974; *The Education of Free Men,* Freedom Press, 1944; *A Coat of Many Colors* (essays) Routledge, 1945, new edition, Horizon Press, 1956; *The Grass Roots of Art: Four Lectures on Social Aspects of Art in an Industrial Age,* Wittenborn, 1947, revised edition, 1955; (author of notes and introduction) *Klee, 1879-1940,* Faber, 1948, Pitman, 1949; (author of introduction) Ben Nicholson, *Paintings, Reliefs, Drawings,* Lund, Humphries, 1948; *Aristotle's Mother: An Imaginary Conversation* (radio play; first produced by British Broadcasting Corp., November, 1946), Secker & Warburg, 1948; *Coleridge as Critic,* Faber, 1949, Haskell House, 1964; *Existentialism, Marxism, and Anarchism: Chains of Freedom,*

Freedom Press, 1949; *Education for Peace,* Scribner, 1949; (contributor of prints) *Atelier 17,* Wittenborn, 1949.

Contemporary British Art, Penguin (Middlesex), 1951, revised edition (Baltimore), 1964; (author of notes and introduction) *Gauguin, 1848-1903,* Pitman, 1951; *Art and the Evolution of Man,* Freedom Press, 1951; *The Philosophy of Modern Art: Collected Essays,* Faber, 1952, Horizon Press, 1953; *The True Voice of Feeling: Studies in English Romantic Poetry,* Pantheon, 1953; (author of introduction) *Australia: Aboriginal Paintings, Arnhem Land,* New York Graphic Society, 1954; *Anarchy and Order: Essays in Politics,* Faber, 1954, Beacon Press, 1971, revised edition, Souvenir Press, 1974; *Icon and Idea: The Function of Art in the Development of Human Consciousness,* Harvard University Press, 1955; *The Art of Sculpture,* Pantheon, 1956, 2nd edition, Princeton University Press, 1969; *The Tenth Muse: Essays in Criticism,* Routledge & Kegan Paul, 1957, Horizon Press, 1958; *The Significance of Children's Art,* University of British Columbia Press, 1957; *A Concise History of Modern Painting,* Praeger, 1959, 3rd edition, 1975.

The Forms of Things Unknown: Essays Towards an Aesthetic Philosophy, Horizon Press, 1960; *The Parliament of Women* (three-act play), Vine Press, 1960; *A Letter to a Young Painter* (essays), Horizon Press, 1962; *To Hell With Culture and Other Essays on Art and Society,* Schocken, 1963; *Lord Byron at the Opera* (radio play), P. Ward, 1963; *The Contrary Experience: Autobiographies* (includes "The Innocent Eye" and part two of *Annals of Innocence and Experience*), Horizon Press, 1963, revised edition, foreword by Graham Greene, 1974; *A Concise History of Modern Culture,* Praeger, 1964; *The Origins of Form in Art,* Horizon Press, 1965; *Henry Moore: A Study of His Life and Work,* Thames & Hudson, 1965, Praeger, 1966; *The Redemption of the Robot: My Encounter With Education Through Art,* Trident, 1966; *Poetry and Experience,* Horizon Press, 1967; *Art and Alienation: The Role of the Artist in Society,* Horizon Press, 1967; *The Cult of Sincerity,* Faber, 1968, Horizon Press, 1969; *The Art of Jean Arp,* Abrams, 1968 (published in England as *Arp,* Thames & Hudson, 1968); *Essays in Literary Criticism: Particular Studies* (part two of *Collected Essays in Literary Criticism*), Faber, 1969.

Editor: Thomas Ernest Hulme, *Speculations: Essays on Humanism and the Philosophy of Art,* Harcourt, 1924, new edition, Humanities Press, 1971; (with Bonamy Dobree) *The Anthology of English Prose,* Viking, 1931 (published in England as *The London Book of English Prose,* Eyre & Spottiswoode, 1931), 2nd edition published as *The London Book of English Prose,* Macmillan, 1949; *Unit 1: The Modern Movement in English Architecture, Painting, and Sculpture,* Cassell, 1934; *The English Vision: An Anthology,* Eyre & Spottiswoode, 1933; (and author of introduction) *Surrealism,* Faber, 1936, Praeger, 1971; *The Knapsack: A Pocket-Book of Prose and Verse,* Routledge, 1939; (and author of introduction) Alistair Morton, and others, *The Practice of Design,* Humphries, 1946; (with Dobree) *The London Book of English Verse,* Macmillan, 1949, 2nd edition, 1965; *This Way, Delight: A Book of Poetry for the Young,* Pantheon, 1956; (and translator) Wilhelm Worringer, *Form in Gothic,* Schocken, 1964; (and author of introduction) *The Styles of European Art,* Thames & Hudson, 1965; *Encyclopaedia of the Arts,* Meredith, 1966; (with Michael Fordham and Gerald Adler) Carl Gustav Jung, *Collected Works,* 2nd edition, Pantheon, 1966.

SIDELIGHTS: As a literary and art critic, Herbert Read possessed a "keen and vital intellect" equal to his "open-eyed unbiased judgement," observed H. W. Hausermann.

And, in Henry Treece's view, as a poet Read "represented more phases of human recognition than any other writer living today." Read combined his sharpness of perception with his commitment to "searching life at a very great depth" to produce writing after writing in a career that spanned six decades. "Only [Ezra] Pound's creative lifetime," wrote Marius Bewley, "has been longer and more representative in our time."

Critics have cited several distinct traits in Read's poems. Like Hausermann's response to Read's criticism, Bewley believed "one cannot read the . . . *Collected Poems* without a sharp awareness of the writer's informed intelligence." Read also wrote a distinctively modern verse, with Imagism being, in Kathleen Raine's analysis, "the first of several movements with which Herbert Read was to associate himself. From the regionalism which inspired his first and enduring poetic loyalty to Wordsworth he moved . . . into the American expatriate *ethos* which . . . introduced into English letters that internationalism which changed, perhaps permanently, the course of its native current." James Dickey commented further on the influence of Wordsworth when he said: "The poems I think of most persuasively as Read's ('A World Within a War,' 'Moon's Farm') are about land, and its relationship to those who live on it. These poems have more of the feudal (and older) sense of *belonging* to the land than any I know since Wordsworth's."

Read's development as a poet, critic, and thinker owed itself to the influence of several important mentors. Besides Wordsworth, other poets in his literary tradition, most of them Imagists, included T. E. Hulme, F. S. Flint, Pound, Hilda Doolittle, Marianne Moore, William Carlos Williams, and his lifetime friend and closest literary associate, T. S. Eliot. As a critic, Read depended heavily upon Coleridge's *Biographia Literaria,* as well as the *Letters* of John Keats. Among others who shaped Read's mind (long known for its anarchist convictions) are John Ruskin, Sigmund Freud, Soren Kierkegaard, and Carl Jung.

While the intellectual aspects of Read's poetry are apparent, some feel this quality has adversely affected his presentation. "There is too much of the will, here [in *Moon's Farm*], and not enough of the carrying flow of passion," argued Dickey. "Read's verse has over it, still, a strong cast of the would-be poet, the straining articulateness of the amateur." Geoffrey Moore also recognized a burdening will when he declared: "Yet for all his hard work and seriousness Sir Herbert has, but for a handful of poems, always seemed more of a thinker expressing himself in verse than a true poet."

Critics agree that Read evinced a different character as a poet than as a critic. In a 1926 review of a critical work, *Reason and Romanticism,* D. S. Mirsky claimed "Read is an anti-Romantic and a champion of the intellectual revival." But others have shared the view that Read is "anti-romantic in his criticism only." "Read divided his activities between the spontaneous, lyrical approach of the poet and the logical, discursive approach of the essayist," wrote George Woodcock. "His views on poetry tended to the romantic; his practice in prose was inclined to the classical." Graham Greene, too, noticed the distinction, and seemed more moved by his "creative" work: "The result of separating Mr. Read's creative from his critical work has an odd effect—there is color, warmth, glow, the passion which surrounds the 'sense of glory,' and we seem far removed from the rather dry critic with his eyes fixed on the distinctions between the ego and the id."

Read's criticism has surprised many because of its tolerance. Raine saw Read's open-armed approach to others' works bound in a desire to "relate his criticism to system after system. Under the compulsive necessity always to have a theory, he was almost naively uncritical of ideas as long as they were new." John Berger, meanwhile, looked for explanations in his personality: "If he is over-tolerant towards nonsense, it is because he credits everyone with his own sincerity." Treece also felt Read's critical attitude rested in "his very nature, his lability, his tolerance and breadth.... For Read's humility is only the obverse of his honest solidity; it is the humanity of the man who can recognise, probe and still respect the multiplicity of the world in which he walks."

Though Read concentrated mainly on poetry and criticism, one of his most widely read books is a novel. Worth T. Harder considered *The Green Child* a "masterpiece, a work as extraordinary now as it was when first published in 1935. Seductive, complex, self-contained, it appears at once to invite and to forbid analysis.... What seems to have happened in *The Green Child* was that he combined his ideas in such unexpected ways and embodied them in a fantasy so entrancing as to render his readers unable or unwilling to grasp the meaning of his allegory. Yet it is the matching of image with idea in this work that is, finally, most extraordinary of all." Similarly, Woodcock thought it "no ordinary novel" and "full of intrinsic symbolic suggestiveness." He also felt that although by nature Read was more a poet and essayist than a novelist, "*The Green Child* would not have been the small and unique classic it has now become if Read had not used in writing it his poet's complex sensitivity to words and the essayists power to control and manipulate ideas."

Read's ultimate contribution as a writer lay in his "reasonable romantic championship of art to others," praised David D. Harvey. He believed art to be a seminal force in education and industry, as exemplified by such works as *Art and Industry* and *The Redemption of the Robot: My Encounter With Education Through Art*. Woodcock believed Read's most influential book, *Education Through Art*, succeeded in this way because it reached beyond his special audience and "influenced many of the very people he had hoped to convert—the teachers and the instructors in colleges of education." In his lifetime Read saw Britain's Society of Education Through Art and an International Society for Education Through Art founded on the basis of his work, but these accomplishments formed only a foundation for his great hope. As Woodcock emphasized, "Read died believing that his philosophy of life—the aesthetic philosophy—was valid, and that some day, if the world was not destroyed by technicians, mankind would come to live by it, through true education and a life in which work and art would become indistinguishable."

One of Read's sons, Piers Paul, is the author of several novels.

BIOGRAPHICAL/CRITICAL SOURCES: London Mercury (now *Life and Letters Today*), November, 1926, September, 1928; Henry Treece, editor, *Herbert Read: An Introduction to His Work by Various Hands*, Faber, 1944, reprinted, Kennikat, 1969; Graham Greene, *The Lost Childhood*, Viking, 1951; Geoffrey Moore, *Poetry Today*, Longmans, Green, 1958; Francis Berry, *Herbert Read*, Longmans, Green, 1961, *Manchester Guardian Weekly*, May 30, 1963; Peter Orr, editor, *Poet Speaks*, Barnes & Noble, 1966; *Burlington Magazine*, August, 1968; James Dickey, *Babel to Byzantium*, Farrar, Straus, 1968; *Southern Review*, winter,

1969; *Sewanee Review*, summer, 1969, autumn, 1973; Arlene Zekowski, *Seasons of the Mind: With the Correspondence of Sir Herbert Read*, Wittenborn, 1969.

Robin Skelton, editor, *Herbert Read: A Memorial Symposium*, Methuen, 1970; *Spectator*, May 9, 1970, November 21, 1970; *Encounter*, June, 1970; *Times Literary Supplement*, July 2, 1970, January 29, 1971; *Economist*, November 21, 1970; *Books and Bookmen*, February, 1971; *Christian Century*, April 28, 1971; *America*, June 5, 1971; George Woodcock, *Herbert Read: The Stream and The Source*, Faber, 1972; *American Artist*, March, 1973, April 1976; *American Political Science Review*, June, 1973; *Art News*, February, 1974; *Childhood Education*, February, 1975; *Observer*, April 13, 1975; *Contemporary Literary Criticism*, Volume 4, Gale, 1975; *Washington Post Book World*, December 25, 1977.*

*　　*　　*

REAGAN, Ronald 1911-

PERSONAL: Born February 6, 1911, in Tampico, Ill.; son of John Edward (a shoe salesman) and Nellie (Wilson) Reagan; married Jane Wyman (an actress), January 24, 1940 (divorced, 1948); married Nancy Davis (an actress), March 4, 1952; children: (first marriage) Maureen Elizabeth, Michael Edward; (second marriage) Patricia Ann, Ronald Prescott. *Education:* Eureka College, B.A., 1932. *Residence:* Pacific Palisades, Calif.

CAREER: WHO-Radio, Des Moines, Iowa, sports announcer and editor, 1932-37; actor in more than fifty feature films, 1937-64, including "Dark Victory," Warner Bros., 1939, "Angels Wash Their Faces," Warner Bros., 1939, "Knute Rockne—All American," Warner Bros., 1940, "Kings Row," Warner Bros., 1941, "The Hasty Heart," Warner Bros., 1950, "Storm Warning," Warner Bros., 1950, "She's Working Her Way Through College," Warner Bros., 1952, and "The Killers," Universal, 1964; actor and production supervisor on the weekly television program, "General Electric Theater," and speaker throughout the United States for General Electric's personnel relations program, 1954-62; host and actor in the "Death Valley Days" television series, 1962-65; governor of the state of California, 1966-75; host of a nationally syndicated radio commentary program and author of a nationally syndicated weekly newspaper column, 1975, 1977—; campaigned for the U.S. Republican presidential nomination, 1976. Lecturer and public speaker. Owner and operator of a horse breeding and cattle ranch. Chairman, Republican Governors' Association, 1969; presidential appointee to advisory commission on intergovernmental relations, 1970; member of human resources committee of National Governors' Conference, 1972; presidential appointee to commission investigating the Central Intelligence Agency (CIA), 1974-75; member of board of directors of Committee on Present Danger, 1977—, Committee on Fundamental Education, and St. John's Hospital; served on board of trustees, Eureka College; member of California Republican State Central Committee and national advisory board, Young Americans for Freedom. *Military service:* U.S. Army, 1942-45; became captain.

MEMBER: Screen Actors Guild (member of board of directors, 1946-60, president, 1947-52), Motion Picture Industry Council (president and member of board of directors), American Federation of Radio and Television Artists, California Thoroughbred Breeders Association, Young Men's Christian Association (YMCA), Friars Club, Rancheros Visitadores, Bohemian Club, Tau Kappa Epsilon. *Awards, honors:* Recipient of numerous awards, including: National Safety Council Public Interest Award, 1954; National Humanitarian Award from National Conference of Christians and Jews, 1962; George Washington Honor Medal Award from Freedoms Foundation, 1971, for a public address, and 1973, for a published article; Medal of Valor from the state of Israel, 1971; award from American Newspaper Guild.

WRITINGS: (With Richard G. Hubler) *Where's the Rest of Me?* (autobiography), Duell, Sloan & Pearce, 1965; (with Charles Hobbs) *Ronald Reagan's Call to Action,* Warner Books, 1976. Columnist. Contributor of articles to periodicals.

SIDELIGHTS: In an era when political campaigns are waged as media wars, Ronald Reagan is the first professional media-bred candidate. His career as a movie actor, television host, and personnel relations speaker spanned more than twenty-five years when Reagan entered politics as a candidate for governor of the state of California in 1965.

Concurrent with his career as a grade-B actor (usually playing the part of the All-American boy), Reagan became involved in film industry politics. During his tenure as president of the Screen Actor's Guild (an AFL-affiliated union representing motion picture performers), he cooperated with efforts to purge the industry of suspected Communists, and in 1947 he testified before the House Committee on Un-American Activities in its investigation into the alleged Communist infiltration of the motion picture industry. Although he appeared as a cooperative witness, Reagan did admonish the Committee: "I hope that we are never prompted by our own fear of Communism into compromising any of our democratic principles." In 1959 he led a Guild strike to win salary increases and medical benefits for its members.

In the years following World War II, Reagan, who originally considered himself to be a New Deal Democrat, was active in liberal causes. He wrote about this involvement in his autobiography, *Where's the Rest of Me?:* "I was a near-hopeless hemophiliac liberal. I bled for causes: I had voted Democratic, following my father, in every election. . . . I was blindly and busily joining every organization I could find that would guarantee to save the world." Although he supported Harry S Truman for president in 1948 and the liberal senatorial candidate Helen Gahagan Douglas (who lost the election to Richard Nixon) in 1950, Reagan's politics became increasingly conservative during the 1950's. He campaigned for Dwight Eisenhower in 1952 and 1956, and for Nixon in 1960. It wasn't until 1962, however, that he officially switched to the Republican party.

Reagan attributes his conversion to conservatism to the speeches he gave as personnel relations speaker for General Electric. From 1954 to 1962 he toured all 135 General Electric plants and spoke to an estimated quarter of a million employees about the evils of big government. Reagan related how his political orientation shifted during this period: "Eventually what happened to me was because I always did my own speeches and did the research for them, I just woke up to the realization one day that I had been going out and helping to elect the people who had been causing the things I had been criticizing. So it wasn't any case of some mentor coming in and talking me out of it. I did it in my own speeches."

Reagan burst onto the national political scene when his fundraising speech for Republican presidential candidate Barry Goldwater was nationally televised in October, 1964. "A Time for Choosing"—a litany of complaints about federal bureacracy—"drew more contributions than any other single speech in political history," the *New York Times* stated. Buoyed by his success and urged by friends and advisers to pursue a career in politics, Reagan announced his candidacy for the governorship of California the next year.

Billing himself as a "citizen politician," Reagan based his campaign on such issues as slashing taxes and welfare expenses and halting bureaucratic growth and the student revolt at the University of California. "The campaign was backlash politics all the way," Larry Agran commented. But Reagan was an effective speaker and campaigner and, with over one million votes more than the incumbent Edmund G. "Pat" Brown, Sr., he was elected governor in 1966. Simplicity was to be the cornerstone of Reagan's term in office and he set the tone in his inaugural address. He told the people of California: "For many years now, you and I have been shushed like children and told there are no simple answers to the complex problems which are beyond our comprehension. Well, the truth is, there *are* simple answers."

According to Richard J. Whalen, Reagan had inherited a "fiscal mess" from former governor Brown. The budget deficit was $194 billion when Reagan took office: He left office with a $500 million surplus. Some of the cuts were highly controversial. Reagan's first official acts were aimed at clearing up what he called "the mess at Berkeley," and included the firing of the president of the University of California and the slashing of the 1967 university operating budget. However, while general state spending increased 50 percent during his two terms, state funds for colleges and universities rose 100 percent. The same year, Reagan reduced the state budget by 10 percent by severely pruning the state mental health program. He eliminated 4,000 state jobs—3,700 of which were out of the state Department of Mental Hygiene. But Reagan was unable to hold down state spending for his entire term. By 1975, state spending had increased at a rate one and one-half times greater than personal income had risen. Although he made several dramatic and popular gestures like the one-time tax rebate given when the huge 1967 tax increase produced far more revenues than were needed, taxes doubled during Reagan's two terms.

In 1971, what Whalen and others regard as Reagan's "outstanding accomplishment" as governor was passed into law—The Welfare Reform Act of 1971. Reagan had referred to welfare as "this cancer eating at our vitals," and had made reform a top priority. The success of the welfare reform bill is still hotly disputed; admirers claimed that it saved the state $2 billion, and critics claimed that it cost the state $100 million the first full year of operation. The present governor of California, Edmund "Jerry" Brown, Jr., assessed the plan recently: "The Reagan welfare program is holding up and considering today's high unemployment, it is amazing that it has kept welfare down as much as it has."

Generally, Reagan's governorship was criticized for its lack of positive direction. One of Reagan's former political directors told Jules Witcover and Richard M. Cohen: "He's a great counterpuncher, but he can't throw a punch. He can react, but he can't act. He would be incapable of creating any kind of plan in his own head and carrying it through. He's just not a leader, and it has nothing to do with his conservatism." Tom Goff was also uneasy with Reagan's tendency to offer "surface solutions" to complex problems. He wrote: "He was interested in the quick and dramatic solution—the Sunday punch—that would turn things around right now. In his first year Reagan offered an across-the-board reduction of 10 per cent in all government expenditures. He ended up that year supporting an overall increase of that much or more. His final effort, late in his second term, was to sponsor an initiative which once and for all, he hoped, would put a permanent lid on government spending by placing a mandatory limit on the state's taxing power. The people turned him down. In sum, he offered surface solutions to deep-seated government ills and the amorphous mass that is modern state government simply oozed out from under him.''

Whalen, however, found that Reagan had ''proved an innovative and surprisingly able executive. Some of his major reforms have survived. By contrast to other large states, California's fiscal condition is outstanding, a legacy of the Reagan years.'' Near the end of Reagan's second term of office, Agran commented that he had ''been unable to alter the fundamental character or direction of state government or to cure the social and economic ills he so loudly deplored before he came into power. . . . By any objective standard, and measured by his own promises, the Governor has been an across-the-board failure. Yet curiously, Ronald Reagan does not leave office stigmatized by failure. On the contrary, he has managed to survive it all by relying increasingly on what he understands and practices best: media politics and public relations. By these means, Reagan has demonstrated his durability as a political quantity and his attractiveness as a Presidential candidate.''

So attractive was Reagan as a presidential candidate that in 1976 he won more primary votes than did the Republican incumbent, Gerald Ford. Reagan's campaign was nominally based on a program of ''creative federalism,'' but its real strength lay in ''The Speech,'' a carefully honed and successful showpiece of rhetoric. Witcover and Coehn described it: ''Rather than a static thing worked ragged by repetition, The Speech is more like the seasons—constantly changing, constantly infused with the nourishment of new phrases, one-liners, comfortable homilies, biting sarcasm that thrills true believers and even some skeptics. But if you ask for a copy of The Speech, Reagan would have to tell you that there isn't one. It exists on hundreds of index cards, never used in precisely the same order. As a result, The Speech comes in as many versions as Reagan can produce by shuffling his deck. He will not use a text. He does not do well with one and he feels it robs him of audience eye contact. So he works the index cards like worry beads.'' John Osborne discussed the contents of The Speech: ''Most of these stories are peopled by misty characters whose identities and adventures tend to go unverified even by newspapers in the areas concerned. There is 'the man in New Jersey' who was told by Social Security that he was dead, proved he wasn't, and after prolonged haggling was given $700 to pay for his funeral. There are the police and prosecuters in San Bernardino, California, who convicted a couple of hiding heroin in their baby's diaper and lost the case on appeal because the baby had not consented to be searched. There is Chicago's 'Welfare Mary' (an actual person, somewhat enlarged by Reagan) who according to him drew $150,000 a year from fraudulent welfare claims and sported two Lincoln Continentals.''

But while Reagan's performance ''has maximum impact on first viewing, [it] subsequently discloses more of the actor's contrivance and political packaging,'' Whalen wrote. ''Political success has come almost too easily for Reagan, subtly undermining his professional discipline. His long experience in addressing friendly audiences has bred a streak of self-indulgence. He often contradicts himself. He has a weakness for theorizing aloud. He shoots from the lip, as in his initial bellicose comments on Angola. Sometimes, he seems

a script-reader who is reading lines he hasn't really thought about or perhaps even seen before.''

One costly error of rhetorical judgment came when Reagan declared his intention to cut $90 billion out of Ford's budget by transferring authority for certain programs from the federal government to the state and local level. On the recommendation of his advisers, he listed specific programs to be dropped or transferred. The public outcry that followed this declaration caused him to recant on the specific figure and the specific programs, while stressing that he thought the concept was still sound.

Although as governor of California he had had no experience in foreign policy, Reagan perceived that the area was Ford's most vulnerable, and he made criticism of Ford's foreign policy the keystone of his campaign. Reagan protested the administration's stand on the Panama Canal and criticized Ford for allegedly allowing U.S. defense strength to fall behind the Soviet Union's. Osborne claimed that Reagan distorted facts about the Panama Canal and the U.S.-Soviet arms race. He contended: ''Ronald Reagan is a master, the greatest master in this reporter's experience, of distortion that generally (but not always) contains a core of truth that makes it impossible or at least chancy to call the man a liar.'' Barry Goldwater called his ideas on the Panama Canal ''dangerous.'' George F. Will, however, was more appreciative of Reagan's stance on the canal issue. He wrote: ''Reagan's argument, like much political argument, involves simplification, even caricature. But however flawed, it at least is a *political* argument, an attempt at public pedagogy. Reagan hopes the canal issue will cause a vague anxiety to crystallize into an idea. That is the first step in manufacturing a national resolve. He is using the canal issue as Andrew Jackson used the national-bank issue, as a piece of sand around which he hopes nacre will form, producing in time a pearl beyond price, a broad new consensus about national purpose.''

When the race for the presidential nomination was down to the wire and the tussle for uncommitted delegates became seemingly deadlocked, Reagan, acting on the advice of his campaign manager, John P. Sears, and the chairman of Citizens for Reagan, Senator Paul Laxalt, made the bold and unprecedented move of announcing Richard Schweiker as his running mate. Never before had a candidate announced his vice-presidential choice before actually winning the nomination. The selection of Schweiker, a liberal Republican senator from Pennsylvania who held no apparent ideological common ground with Reagan, came as a shock to Reagan supporters who, as *Newsweek* reported, ''were stunned and outraged by the choice—and seemed initially on the brink of mutiny.'' Reagan's strategy, *Time* wrote, was ''a bold reach to the left in hopes that he might pick up some of the 'soft' Ford delegates in such states as Pennsylvania, New York, and New Jersey. The calculated risk was that Reagan's conservative idealogues would grumble, but finally stay with him, while moderates would drift away from Ford. By the end of a tumultuous week, it was clear that the last-gasp Reagan strategy had failed.'' Some of Reagan's previously announced supporters switched their allegiance to Ford; other fence-straddling delegates also turned to Ford after Reagan's selection was announced.

At the Republican convention in August, 1976, Reagan tried one last gamble to win the nomination by offering two amendments to the party platform. The first—requiring a presidential candidate to name his running mate the morning before nomination night—lost after a heated struggle with the Ford opposition. The second—the so-called ''morality in foreign policy amendment,'' which criticized Ford's handling of U.S.-Soviet relations and praised dissident Soviet writer Alexander Solzhenitsyn whom Ford had neglected to invite to the White House—was approved by a voice vote after the Ford delegation decided to acquiesce.

Although Ford won the nomination on the first ballot with 1,187 votes to Reagan's 1,070, Reagan had led an impressive challenge. ''He deserves,'' wrote Murray Kempton, ''when you consider the weight assigned, to be counted as one of the great candidates in our memory, perhaps the greatest who never got his chance.'' Certainly, Reagan had a large and loyal following. Elizabeth Drew described the adulation of Reagan's supporters when his name was placed in nomination at the convention, even though Ford's victory at that point was virtually assured. She wrote: ''As Paul Laxalt . . . finishes his speech, the band swings into 'California, Here I Come' and 'Dixie,' and the Reagan supporters break into a loud, raucous demonstration. It is the emotion of people with something in their hearts. They are a movement. Reagan. The idea of Reagan stirs excitement in them. He spoke to their emotions. There are things they are after—and against. They won't win the nomination, but they came close enough to show 'em. I may have seen a more emotional demonstration somewhere, but I don't remember it. The long, low sound of the horns goes on and on.''

According to numerous political observers, Reagan will campaign for the presidency in 1980, and the consensus is that he is likely to win the Republican nomination. There are indications that he is broadening his political base in an attempt to appeal to more than far-right, conservative voters. *New Times* wrote of Reagan that ''in reality he is a conservative, not a caricature. . . . His relative moderation reflects a belief that conservatism does not have to be so pure that it becomes a permanent political suicide pact. This time around, Ronald Reagan is the conservative candidate who would rather be president than far right.''

BIOGRAPHICAL/CRITICAL SOURCES: New York Times Magazine, November 14, 1965, October 16, 1966, February 22, 1976, June 6, 1976; Ronald Reagan and Richard G. Hubler, *Where's the Rest of Me?,* Duell, Sloan & Pearce, 1965; *New York Times,* June 9, 1966, January 3, 1967; *Nation,* June 22, 1974, January 10, 1976; *Los Angeles Times,* November 21, 1975; *U.S. News and World Report,* February 9, 1976, August 9, 1976; *Harper's,* February, 1976, November, 1976; *Esquire,* March, 1976; *Newsweek,* May 17, 1976, August 9, 1976, August 16, 1976, August 30, 1976; *New Republic,* June 12, 1976; *Time,* August 2, 1976, August 9, 1976, August 30, 1976; *New York Times Book Review,* August 15, 1976; *New Yorker,* October 18, 1976, October 25, 1976; Reagan and Charles Hobbs, *Ronald Reagan's Call to Action,* Warner Books, 1976; Edmund G. Brown and Bill Brown, *The Political Chameleon,* Praeger, 1976; *New Times,* October 2, 1978.

*   *   *

REGARDIE, (Francis) Israel 1907-

PERSONAL: Born November 17, 1907, in London, England; came to United States, 1920(?). *Education:* Attended Columbia Institute of Chiropractic and Los Angeles College of Chiropractic. *Office:* c/o Llewellyn Publications, P.O. Box 43383, St. Paul, Minn. 55164.

CAREER: Chiropractor; writer; occultist. Traveled through Europe as a companion to occultist Aleister Crowley, 1928-34; later practiced chiropractic medicine and a form of psychotheraphy based on the work of Dr. Wilhelm Reich in Cal-

ifornia. *Military service:* U.S. Army, served in World War II.

WRITINGS: The Art of True Healing: A Treatise on the Mechanism of Prayer, and the Operation of the Law of Attraction in Nature, Leaf Studio, 1932, Helios, 1964; *A Garden of Pomegranates: An Outline of the Qabalah,* Rider, 1932, Llewellyn, 1971; *The Tree of Life: A Study in Magic,* Rider, 1932, Weiser, 1969; *My Rosicrucian Adventure,* Aries Press, 1936, Llewellyn, 1971; *The Golden Dawn: An Account of the Teachings, Rites, and Ceremonies of the Order of the Golden Dawn,* Aries Press, 1937, Hazel Hills Corp., 1969; *The Philosopher's Stone,* Rider, 1938, Llewellyn, 1970; *The Middle Pillar,* Aries Press, 1938, Llewellyn, 1970; *The Romance of Metaphysics: An Introduction to the History, Theory, and Psychology of Modern Metaphysics,* Aries Press, 1947.

The Art and Meaning of Magic, Helios, 1964, new edition, 1969; *Be Yourself: A Guide Book to the Art of Relaxation,* Helios, 1965; *Roll Away the Stone: An Introduction to Aleister Crowley's Essays on the Psychology of Hashish,* Llewellyn, 1968; *Twelve Steps to Spiritual Enlightenment,* Sangreal Foundation, 1969; (contributor) Aleister Crowley, *Aha,* Sangreal Foundation, 1969; *The Eye in the Triangle: An Interpretation of Aleister Crowley,* Llewellyn, 1970; *How to Make and Use Talismans,* Weiser, 1972; (contributor) Aleister Crowley, *The Vision and the Voice,* Sangreal Foundation, 1972; *A Practical Guide to Geomantic Divination,* Weiser, 1972.

SIDELIGHTS: In addition to his reputation as a psychotherapist, Regardie is noted for his scholarly writings on occultism and is regarded as a leading authority on the life and teachings of occultist Aleister Crowley. After his association with Crowley between 1928 and 1934, Regardie concentrated on his own psychotherapeutic activities, especially a technique derived from the work of Wilhelm Reich. He returned to public discussion of occultism in the 1950's as a reaction to the treatment of Crowley by other writers. Since that time, many of Regardie's writings have been concerned with Crowley and his beliefs. ''I think there's no doubt that Crowley had considerable greatness as a teacher and writer,'' Regardie once said. ''True, he was certainly a very difficult man, but nothing like the monster of depravity and evil that the gutter press of his day made him out to be. . . . I'd say he was a Victorian hippie.''

BIOGRAPHICAL/CRITICAL SOURCES: Nat Freeland, *The Occult Explosion,* Putnam, 1972.*

*   *   *

REGGIANI, Renee 1925-

PERSONAL: Born November 16, 1925, in Milan, Italy; daughter of Ergisto (a foundry worker) and Maria (Colli) Reggiani; married Luciantonio Ruggieri (a playwright), December 29, 1955. *Education:* National Academy of Theatre, Rome, Italy, received diploma; University of Aix-en-Provence, received degree. *Home:* Via Trau 3 (Corso Trieste), 00698, Rome, Italy. *Agent:* Nina Froud, 14 Beaumont Mews, Marylebone High St., London W1N 4HE, England. *Office:* Televisione Italiana, Viale Mazzini 14, Rome, Italy.

CAREER: Writer; creator and producer of television programs. Televisione Italiana, Rome, writer, 1955—. *Awards, honors:* Premio ente nazionale biblioteche popolari e scolastiche, 1956, and Hans Christian Andersen Award, 1962, both for *Le avventure di cinque ragazzi e un cane;* Premio laura orvieto, 1964, for *Domani dopodomani;* Europa-Dralon Award, 1965, for *Il treno del sole;* Premio villa Taranto, 1966, for *Lo spaventapasseri;* Premio internazionale Europeo citta di caorle, 1968, for *Carla degli scavi.*

WRITINGS—In English: *Le avventure di cinque ragazzi e un cane,* L. Cappelli, 1960, translation by Mary Lambert and Anne Chisholm published as *Five Children and a Dog,* Coward, 1965, new Italian edition published as *Quando i sogni non hanno soldi* (title means "When Dreams Have No Money"), F. lli Fabbri, 1971; *Il treno del sole,* Garzanti, 1961, translation by Patrick Creagh published as *The Sun Train,* Coward, 1966; *Domani dopodo mani,* Vallecchi, 1964, translation by Chisholm published as *Tomorrow and the Next Day,* Coward, 1967.

In Italian: *Strane avventure di una meravigliosa estate* (juvenile; title means "Strange Adventures of a Wonderful Summer"), Cappelli, 1963; *Lo spaventapasseri* (juvenile; title means "The Scarecrow"), L'Ariete, 1966; *Carla degli scavi* (title means "Carla of the Archeological Excavations"), Garzanti, 1968; *Hanno rapito il papa* (title means "The Pope Has Been Kidnapped"), Garzanti, 1976; (with husband, Luciantonio Ruggieri) *Processo alla guerra: Il teatro contro* (essay; title means "Trial Against the War: The Theatre in Opposition"), Bulzoni, 1976; (with Ruggieri) *La resistenza e la guerriglia* (essay; title means "Resistance and Guerrilla"), Venezia, 1977.

* * *

REHFUSS, John Alfred 1934-

PERSONAL: Born December 3, 1934, in Salem, Ore.; son of Herman J. (a farmer) and Naoma (Fleet) Rehfuss; married Carol Litchfield (a teacher), June 15, 1957; children: Debbie, Brent, Todd. *Education:* Willamette University, B.A. (honors), 1956; University of Southern California, M.S., 1958, D.P.A., 1965. *Politics:* Independent. *Religion:* Methodist. *Home:* 1831 Wayside Lane, Sacramento, Calif. 95825. *Office:* Department of Public Administration, California State University, Sacramento, Calif. 95819.

CAREER: City Administrative Office, Los Angeles, Calif., intern and junior budget analyst, 1956-59; City of Pico Rivera, Calif., administrative assistant to city manager, 1959-62; City of Palm Springs, Calif., assistant city manager, 1962-65, acting city manager, 1964; San Jose State University, San Jose, Calif., assistant professor of political science, 1965-67; U.S. Civil Service Commission, Executive Seminar Center, Berkeley, Calif., associate director, 1967-69; Northern Illinois University, DeKalb, associate professor, 1969-77, professor of political science, 1977-78, director of Center for Governmental Studies, 1972-76; California State University, Sacramento, professor of public administration and department chair, 1978—. Member of advisory committee of Illinois State Department of Local Government Affairs, 1974-76. Organizer and participant in professional meetings; consultant to National Science Foundation. *Military service:* California National Guard, 1958-59.

MEMBER: International City Management Association, National Association of Schools of Public Affairs and Administration (national conference chairman, 1975), American Society for Public Administration (Chicago chapter president, 1975-76; member of national council, 1976-79), Lions Club International.

WRITINGS: (Editor) *Middle Management Issues in Local Government,* Northern Illinois University Press, 1970; *Public Administration as Political Process,* Scribner, 1973; (with Thomas P. Murphy) *Urban Politics in the Suburban Era,* Dorsey, 1976. Contributor of about thirty articles and re-

views to professional journals. Contributing editor of *Ripon Forum,* 1973-76.

WORK IN PROGRESS: The Job of the Public Executive, publication expected in 1981.

SIDELIGHTS: Rehfuss comments: "I believe strongly that better and stronger management is the key to better public services. Management cannot be taught, but it can be explained to those who have or will have such management tasks in such a way that they will understand their job better and become more effective on the job. True, along with better management, government requires better incentive systems for managers and changes in the structural arrangements under which they work. These are important, but a simple focus on improving the public manager, even under the present conditions, can substantially improve government performance."

AVOCATIONAL INTERESTS: Playing bridge, bicycling.

* * *

REICH, Peter M(aria) 1929-

PERSONAL: Born June 9, 1929, in Vienna, Austria; came to United States in 1937, naturalized citizen, 1943; son of Hanns Leo (a writer and actor) and Nelly Reich; married Betty Jane Kosberg, February 16, 1952 (divorced May 15, 1969); children: Carol, Holly, James. *Education:* Attended U.S. Military Academy, 1948; Northwestern University, B.S., 1951, graduate study, 1952. *Politics:* Independent. *Religion:* Methodist. *Office: Chicago Tribune,* Chicago, Ill. 60611.

CAREER: Chicago Today (formerly *Chicago American*), Chicago, Ill., general assignment reporter, rewrite man, movie critic, aviation writer, aviation/space editor, 1952-74; *Chicago Tribune,* Chicago, national/foreign writer and editorial page columnist, 1974—. Lecturer with Redpath Bureau, 1959-74, and Associated Clubs (Topeka, Kan.), 1960—. *Military service:* U.S. Army, 1948.

MEMBER: Aviation/Space Writers Association, Chicago Press Veterans, South Pole Society, Sigma Delta Chi. *Awards, honors:* More than twenty-five journalism awards, including Pulitzer Prize nominations, 1962, for Continental Air Lines jetliner bombing stories, 1966, for series on Chicago draftees, 1970, for preview and coverage of "Apollo 11" moon landing, and 1973, for stories about a fatal collision between two jetliners at Chicago's O'Hare Airport; National Citation of Honor from U.S. Air Force Association, 1966, for distinguished aerospace reporting; named cancer communicator of the year by American Cancer Society, 1974, for series of articles on cancer; James J. Strebig Memorial Award from Aviation/Space Writers Association, 1977, for columns on national defense.

WRITINGS: (Contributor) C. D. MacDougall, editor, *Reporters Report Reporters,* Iowa State University Press, 1968; (contributor) Emerson Clarke and Vernon Root, editors, *Your Future in Technical and Science Writing,* Richards Rosen, 1972.

WORK IN PROGRESS: Writing on the U.S. space program.

SIDELIGHTS: Reich's assignments have taken him all over the world, including Antarctica, South America, Europe, the Mediterranean, Fiji, New Zealand, Labrador, Iceland, Mexico, and the Caribbean. His search for news stories has placed him aboard the "Concorde" supersonic jetliner, in an astronaut's training place on a zero-gravity mission, on a global mission in a jet bomber, at the South Pole, and in basic training at Fort Leonard Wood, Mo. *Avocational interests:* Photography, travel, shooting, swimming, tennis.

REICHEK, Morton A(rthur) 1924-

PERSONAL: Born November 2, 1924, in New York, N.Y.; son of Meyer (a salesman) and Katherine (Rabinowitz) Reichek; married Sybil R. Green (a high school teacher), June 13, 1953; children: Amy, Marjorie (deceased), James. *Education:* New York University, B.S., 1948; graduate study at American University, 1948-50. *Politics:* Independent. *Religion:* Jewish. *Home:* 16 Bromley Dr., Parsippany, N.J. 07054. *Agent:* Max Gartenberg, 331 Madison Ave., New York, N.Y. 10017. *Office:* Business Week, 1221 Avenue of the Americas, New York, N.Y. 10020.

CAREER/WRITINGS: Business Week (magazine), New York City, correspondent in Washington, D.C., 1952-63; Newhouse Newspapers, New York City, correspondent in Washington, D.C., 1963-65; *Forbes* (magazine), New York City, associate editor, 1965-66; *Business Week,* associate editor, 1966-76; Gulf & Western Industries, Inc., New York City, director of editorial services, 1976-78; *Business Week,* senior writer, 1978—. Notable assignments include coverage of Kennedy assassination, Cuban missile crisis, corporate activities, and "the war on poverty." Contributor to numerous magazines, including *New York Times Sunday Magazine, New York Times Book Review, New Republic, Present Tense, Columbia Journalism Review, Saturday Evening Post, New Leader, Harper's, Bookletter, Midstream,* and *Book Digest. Military service:* U.S. Army, 1943-46; became staff sergeant. *Member:* American Society of Journalists and Authors, National Press Club, New York Financial Writers Association. *Awards, honors:* Grant from U.S. State Department to participate in North Atlantic Treaty Organization (NATO) journalist program, 1957; journalist fellow in Carnegie-Mellon University's Graduate School of Industrial Administration executive program, 1979.

SIDELIGHTS: Reichek told *CA:* "The primary challenge for the journalist is to remain a generalist, always eager to pursue new subject matter areas. In my own career, I have reported on and written about subjects ranging from politics, business, foreign affairs, and wildlife conservation, to labor unions, military affairs, and science and technology. The opportunity to examine such wide-ranging facets of contemporary society and to become conversant with so many specialized fields—and the personalities who dominate them—makes journalism a profession that keeps one constantly in the mainstream of life."

AVOCATIONAL INTERESTS: Business, economics, biography, ethnic and religious affairs, military affairs, social issues.

*   *   *

REID, William 1926-

PERSONAL: Born November 8, 1926, in Glasgow, Scotland; son of Colin Colquhoun and Mary Evelyn (Bingham) Reid; married Nina Frances Brigden, 1958. *Education:* Attended Trinity College. *Home:* 66 Ennerdale Rd., Richmond, Surrey, England.

CAREER: Tower of London, Armouries, London, England, senior museum assistant, 1956-65, assistant keeper, 1965-70; National Army Museum, London, director, 1970—. Member of British national committee of International Council of Museums, 1973—. *Military service:* Royal Air Force, 1945-48. *Member:* International Association of Museums of Arms and Military History (secretary-general, 1969—), Society of Antiquaries (fellow; member of council, 1975-76), Museums Association (fellow), Chelsea Society (member of council, 1978—).

WRITINGS: Arms Through the Ages, Harper, 1976 (published in England as *The Lore of Arms,* Mitchell Beazley, 1976). Contributor to professional journals and popular magazines, including *Connoisseur* and *Guildhall Miscellany.*

WORK IN PROGRESS: Articles on history and art.

SIDELIGHTS: Reid told *CA:* "Throughout my writing career I have only achieved any satisfaction from articles published to disseminate knowledge which I believed was held by me alone. The commissioned book or article has rarely, if ever, been satisfying. There were some exceptions to this rule in *The Lore of Arms* where I had an opportunity to publish newly discovered facts which were insufficient to form a basis of an article. *Avocational interests:* Music, ornithology.

*   *   *

REINERT, Paul C(lare) 1910-

PERSONAL: Born August 12, 1910, in Boulder, Colo.; son of Francis J. and Emma (Voegtle) Reinert. *Education:* St. Louis University, A.B., 1933, A.M., 1934, S.T.L., 1941; University of Chicago, Ph.D., 1944. *Home and office:* St. Louis University, 221 North Grand Blvd., St. Louis, Mo. 63109.

CAREER: Entered Society of Jesus (Jesuits), 1927, ordained Roman Catholic priest, 1940; Creighton University High School, Omaha, Neb., instructor, 1934-37; St. Louis University, St. Louis, Mo., assistant, 1937-38, instructor in education, 1938-41, dean of College of Arts and Sciences, 1944-48, academic vice-president, 1948-49, president of university, 1949-74, chancellor, 1974—. Registrar at St. Mary College, Leavenworth, Kan., 1938-41. Member of executive committee of American Council on Education, 1953-57, member of its Federal Relations Commission, 1963-67, member of board of directors, 1965-68; head of Conference of Jesuit Presidents, 1960-62; president of National Council of Independent Colleges and Universities, 1973; member of board of trustees of Educational Testing Service, 1969-73; member of Regis College Educational Corp., 1973—; member of board of directors of Council for Financial Aid to Education, 1962-69, Midwest Research Institute, 1962—, and Central Midwestern Regional Educational Laboratory, 1966-69. Member of Catholic Commission on Intellectual and Cultural Affairs, 1958—; delegate to Jesuit Congregation in Rome, 1965-66. President of Midtown, Inc., 1972—; head of New Town/St. Louis, Inc., 1974—; member of board of directors of Civic Progress, Inc., 1958—, St. Louis City Art Museum, 1961-74, and St. Louis Civic Alliance for Housing, 1969-71; member of St. Louis Educational Television Commission, 1953-66 (head of commission, 1955-57). Member of National Commission on Accrediting, 1950-58, Missouri State Commission for Humanities, 1975—, and Missouri Compensation Commission, 1977.

MEMBER: Association of American Colleges (member of board of directors, 1970-74; head of board of directors, 1972-73), Association of Urban Universities (president, 1950-51), National Catholic Educational Association (member of executive board, 1956-65; vice-president, 1964-65), National Education Association (member of executive committee of its Association for Higher Education, 1954-57; vice-president, 1956-57), Jesuit Educational Association (president, 1966-70), North Central Association of Colleges and Secondary Schools (member of executive committee, 1955-61; president, 1956-57), Missouri Association of Colleges and Universities (president, 1965-67), Independent Colleges and Universities of Missouri (president, 1974), Missouri Academy of Squires, Phi Beta Kappa, Phi Delta Kappa. *Awards, honors:* Honorary degrees include LL.D. from St. Ambrose College, 1951, Loyola University, Chicago, Ill., 1957, Xavier University, 1954, Washington University, St. Louis, Mo., 1955, Colorado College, 1956, University of Missouri, 1957, John Carroll University, 1961, University of Notre Dame, 1964, St. Joseph's College, 1964, St. Anselm's College, 1967, College of Mount St. Joseph on the Ohio, 1970, Loyola University, New Orleans, La., 1973, Southern Illinois University, 1973, and Creighton University, 1976, Ped.D. from Bradley University, 1956, L.H.D. from Manhattan College, 1963, Lindenwood College, 1972, DePaul University, 1973, Carroll College, 1974, St. Francis College, 1974, Canisius College, 1975, Brandeis University, 1975, Wittenberg University, 1976, Ursuline College, 1976, University of Portland, 1977, and Tarkio College, 1977, Litt.D. from McKendree College, 1966, and St. Norbert College, 1975, Ed.Admin.D. from Drury College, 1973, D.Public Service from Regis College, 1977, and S.T.D. from Providence College, 1978; leadership award from B'nai B'rith, 1954; interracial justice award from Catholic Interracial Council of St. Louis, 1960; Creighton Award from Creighton College, 1962; Eleanor Roosevelt Humanities Award, 1964; chancellors award from Rockhurst College, 1966; Simon LeMoyne Medal from LeMoyne College, 1972; distinguished service award from National Council of Independent Colleges and Universities, 1973; higher education award from Academy of Educational Development, 1977.

WRITINGS: (Contributor) *The University in a Developing Society,* University of Notre Dame Press, 1967; (contributor) *The Catholic University: A Modern Appraisal,* University of Notre Dame Press, 1970; *The Urban Catholic University,* Sheed, 1970; *To Turn the Tide,* Prentice-Hall, 1972. Contributor of about a dozen articles to professional journals, and to *Change.* Member of board of advisers of *College Management,* 1973.

SIDELIGHTS: Reinert writes: "Several years ago the Carnegie Commission, after an intensive study of urban institutions of higher learning, identified St. Louis University as one of only a few universities that 'have long been not only in, but *of* and *for* their cities.' I would be correct in saying, I believe, that my thirty-five year career here has been devoted almost entirely to the justification of that statement. In earlier years my major efforts were devoted to upgrading the stature of the university, expanding its physical facilities, and stabilizing its financial operations—all intended to make the university a greater resource for enhancing the quality of urban life. More recently, as chairman of Newtown/St. Louis, Inc., as well as chancellor of the university, I have broadened my objectives to include the 600 city-block area enveloping both mid-town campuses of the university."

Reinert was among the first administrators of Catholic universities to give laymen a majority on their boards of trustees. He continues with active membership in a score of civic organizations and community institutions, many of which he has served for at least thirty years.

* * *

REISS, Johanna (de Leeuw) 1929(?)-

PERSONAL—Children: Two daughters. *Religion:* Jewish.

CAREER: Writer of books for young people. *Awards, honors:* Charles and Bertie G. Schwartz Juvenile Award from the Jewish Book Council, 1972, Newbery Medal Honor Book, 1973, and Buxtehuder Bulle for outstanding children's book promoting peace, 1976, all for *The Upstairs Room.*

WRITINGS: The Upstairs Room, Crowell, 1972; *The Journey Back,* Crowell, 1976.

SIDELIGHTS: The Nazi occupation of the Netherlands during World War II forced Reiss to become separated from her family when she was ten years old. The young girl and her sister hid for almost three years in the attic of a sympathetic Christian family to escape the horrors of a concentration camp. Nearly thirty years later, Reiss recounted her childhood memories in *The Upstairs Room.* A critic for the *New York Times* wrote: "This admirable account is as important in every aspect as the one bequeathed to us by Anne Frank.... In the end, we are grateful to fate for having spared a child who can reminisce with neither hate nor bitterness but a kind of gentleness that leaves us with a lump in our throats."

BIOGRAPHICAL/CRITICAL SOURCES: New York Times Book Review, November 5, 1972, January 16, 1977; *Saturday Review,* June 12, 1976.*

* * *

REITEMEYER, John Reinhart 1898-1979

OBITUARY NOTICE: Born April 14, 1898, in Elizabeth, N.J.; died April 21, 1979, in Barkhamsted, Conn. Publisher and journalist responsible for the success of Connecticut's most circulated newspaper, the *Hartford Courant.* He rose quickly during the 1920's from night city editor to Sunday editor and then city editor. From 1947 to 1968 Reitemeyer was both president and publisher of the *Courant.* Obituaries and other sources: *New York Times,* April 23, 1979.

* * *

RENNER, Beverly Hollett 1929-

PERSONAL: Born June 26, 1929, in Danville, Ill.; daughter of Kenneth James (an oil company executive) and Clara (a teacher; maiden name, Creighton) Hollett; married Dick Arnold Renner (a professor of English), June 22, 1952; children: Sherrie, Amy, Paul. *Education:* University of Madison, Wisconsin, B.A., 1951. *Politics:* Independent. *Religion:* Presbyterian. *Home and office address:* Route 1, Box 144-A, Ridgeville, Ind. 47380.

CAREER: Dubuque Telegraph-Herald, Dubuque, Iowa, general assignments reporter, 1951-54; writer, 1976—. Founding member and co-director of Midwest Writers' Workshop, 1977. *Member:* National Audubon Society, Whitewater Woodland Association, Mortar Board Alumni Association (local president, 1977).

WRITINGS: The Hideaway Summer (juvenile nonfiction), Harper, 1978.

WORK IN PROGRESS: Mr. Mugalumpy, a children's book; research for a dog story set during the Civil War.

SIDELIGHTS: Renner writes: "Writing for children has been my main interest because I'm a story teller, and there can be no more satisfying listener than one who is young or young at heart, who still believes anything is possible.

"My goal is to write the kind of books the reader hates to put down, and hates to see coming to an end—the beloved book that is read more than once.

"I did not begin to write regularly until our youngest child started school. As a late bloomer in this profession, I was grateful that I did not have to send my book to more than one publisher. There are so many stories that I want to tell that I find myself worrying about having the time to tell them all the way they should be told."

AVOCATIONAL INTERESTS: "I'm an amateur naturalist."

* * *

RENOIR, Jean 1894-1979

OBITUARY NOTICE: Born September 15, 1894, in Paris, France; died of a heart attack, February 12, 1979, in Los Angeles, Calif. French filmmaker best known for his two masterpieces, "Grand Illusion" and "Rules of the Game." The son of famed impressionist painter Pierre-August Renoir, he began his career in 1924 when he wrote the script for an obscure film that featured his wife. Renoir was disappointed in the direction of the film and decided he would direct his own screenplays henceforth. Although less than popular at first, by 1931 he was developing a reputation with his sympathetic but ironic films. "Toni," a 1935 effort, featured amateur actors in natural settings; this film later had a profound effect on "New Wave" filmmakers such as Francois Truffaut and Jean-Luc Godard. His 1937 anti-war film, "Grande Illusion," is considered by many to be among the finest films ever made. "Rules of the Game," a study of French high society, was elevated to similar status upon its release. Renoir came to the United States in 1942 and continued to make highly regarded films, including "Diary of a Chambermaid" and "The Southerner." After World War II he commuted between his homes in Los Angeles and Paris. His last film, "The Little Theatre of Jean Renoir," was released in 1969; a novel, *The Englishman's Crimes,* is to be published posthumously. Obituaries and other sources: Leo Braudy, *Jean Renoir: The World of His Films,* Doubleday, 1972; Andre Bazin, *Jean Renoir,* edited by Francois Truffaut, translation by W. W. Halsey II and William H. Simon, Simon & Schuster, 1973; *International Who's Who,* Europa, 1978; *Chicago Tribune,* February 14, 1979; *New York Times,* February 14, 1979; *Time,* February 26, 1979.

* * *

REPP, Ed Earl 1900(?)-1979

OBITUARY NOTICE: Born c. 1900; died February 14, 1979, in Paradise, Calif. Writer best known for his science fiction and his screenplays, including the westerns "Rawhide Ranger" and "Guns of Hate." He also wrote for television. Obituaries and other notices: *International Motion Picture Almanac,* Quigley, 1978; *Publishers Weekly,* April 9, 1979.

* * *

RHYS, Jean 1894-1979

OBITUARY NOTICE—See index for *CA* sketch: Born August 24, 1894, in Roseau, Dominica, West Indies; died May 14, 1979, in Exeter, England. Novelist. Encouraged by her mentor, Ford Maddox Ford, Rhys published five moderately successful books between 1927 and 1939 before she retired to private life in Devonshire, England. The reclusive Rhys dispelled rumors about her own death in 1958 when she personally answered a radio broadcaster's request for information about her. With the 1966 publication of *Wide Sargasso Sea,* her first book in nearly forty years, Rhys continued to explore her favorite theme: the lonely woman alienated in a male-dominated society. The fictional biography of the mad wife of Mr. Rochester in Charlotte Bronte's *Jane Eyre,* the successful *Wide Sargasso Sea,* spurred the reprinting of all Rhys's earlier books. Her later books include *My Day* and *Sleep It Off, Lady.* Obituaries and other sources: *Current Biography,* Wilson, 1972; *Encyclopedia of World Literature in the Twentieth Century,* Volume IV supplement, Ungar, 1975; *World Authors, 1950-70,* Wilson, 1975; *Who's Who in Twentieth Century Literature,* Holt, 1976; *Who's Who,* 131st edition, St. Martin's, 1979; *New York Times,* May 17, 1979; *Washington Post Book World,* May 18, 1979; *Time,* May 28, 1979; *Newsweek,* May 28, 1979.

* * *

RICHARDS, Dorothy B(urney) 1894-

PERSONAL: Born April 7, 1894, in Little Falls, N.Y.; daughter of James Gordon (a merchant) and Laura (Crouse) Burney; married Allison M. Richards, November 30, 1920 (deceased). *Education:* Attended high school in Little Falls, N.Y. *Politics:* Liberal. *Religion:* Agnostic. *Home and office:* Beaversprite Sanctuary, R.D. #1, Dolgeville, N.Y. 13329.

CAREER: Beaversprite Sanctuary, Dolgeville, N.Y., founder, and director, 1932—. Director of Defenders of Wildlife, 1948-76, honorary director, 1976—. *Member:* National Audubon Society, Humane Association of the United States, Fund for Animals, Nature Conservancy, Wilderness Society.

WRITINGS: (With Hope Sawyer Buyukmihci) *Beaversprite: My Years Building an Animal Sanctuary,* introduction by Cleveland Amory, Chronicle Books, 1977.

WORK IN PROGRESS: A sequel to *Beaversprite* based on observations of the nocturnal activity of beavers.

SIDELIGHTS: Dorothy Richards comments: "I established Beaversprite in 1932 by buying fifty acres. My husband and I enlarged it to about nine hundred acres and were especially interested in beavers. I have sat by a beaver pond every evening since 1934, except during winter months when ponds are frozen over.

"After my husband died I donated the sanctuary to the F. W. Erdman Estate as the only forseeable way to perpetuate it. The Erdman Trust has since enlarged the acreage to about twelve hundred. They made me director and have been very cooperative in establishing a nature center.

"My home has been open to visitors by appointment and I attempt to dispel some of their ignorance by talking and allowing close contact with live beavers. This procedure has made many beaver fans and keeps me busy."

Beaversprite is the story of Richards's involvement with animal conservation, particularly with regard to the growth of the beaver community in the state of New York. When she and her husband began their conservation efforts there were no beavers on their land and very few in the state. They had to import a pair, Samson and Delilah, but were told by a conservation officer that there was little hope for a beaver population. Through the Richards's diligent efforts, and also those of Samson and Delilah, the beaver population at Beaversprite increased. In *Beaversprite,* Richards provides new data on animal behavior as well as information about founding a wildlife sanctuary.

Richards continued: "Knowing beavers is to be hooked entirely and to consider them superior to any other species. My life for the last forty-five years has convinced me they are next to humans in intelligence. What amazes and discourages me is that they are so little known although their structures and engineering feats are the most elaborate of any creature except man and could not possibly be attributed to instinct. To provide the ponds which mean safety to them they frequently change a landscape so it is unrecognizable. Their outstanding characteristics, like gentleness, patience, and a well developed sense of humor, are most endearing. Imagine sensitive creatures that contribute so much to the wilderness being sacrificed to the whims of stupid humans. What a world!''

Numerous articles have been written about Dorothy Richards and her work at Beaversprite. In addition, a documentary for CBS-TV was shown nationally in 1972.

* * *

RICHMAN, Saul 1917(?)-1979

OBITUARY NOTICE: Born c. 1917; died of cancer, January 14, 1979, in San Diego, Calif. Press agent who developed a reputation for flamboyant promotion. His publicity stunts included dressing up as an astronaut to promote the play ''Moonchild.'' On another occasion, he instructed Brazilian singer Carmen Miranda to answer all questions during interviews with the words ''men and money.'' Richmond also wrote *Guy: The Life and Times of Guy Lombardo.* Obituaries and other notices: *New York Times,* January 16, 1979.

* * *

RIDDEL, Frank S(tephen) 1940-

PERSONAL: Surname is accented on first syllable; born October 25, 1940, in Sistersville, W.Va.; son of James Franklin (a service manager for an automobile agency) and Mary (a secretary; maiden name, Poole) Riddel; married Maria Carmen Fayos (a teacher), June 28, 1964; children: Ana, Niles. *Education:* Marshall University, A.B., 1962, M.A., 1965; Ohio State University, Ph.D., 1971. *Home:* 1323 13th St., Huntington, W.Va. 25701. *Office:* Department of Social Studies, Marshall University, Huntington, W.Va. 25701.

CAREER: High school social studies teacher in Gallipolis, Ohio, 1962-63, and Barboursville, W.Va., 1963-68; Marshall University, instructor, 1968-69, assistant professor, 1971-78, associate professor of social studies, 1978—. *Member:* National Council for the Social Studies, Society for Spanish and Portuguese Historical Studies.

WRITINGS: Related Aspects of the Social and Economic Problems, Cultural Tradition, and Educational System of Rural Appalachia, Clearinghouse on Rural Education and Small Schools, New Mexico State University, 1973; (editor) *Appalachia: Its People, Heritage, and Problems,* Kendall/Hunt, 1974. Contributor to history and political science journals.

WORK IN PROGRESS: Research on the political socialization of Spanish children during the Franco era.

SIDELIGHTS: Riddel writes: ''My interest in Appalachia stems from the fact that I was born and raised in West Virginia and have observed the social and economic problems of the region at close range. My marriage to a Spaniard has resulted in my learning Spanish and traveling widely in Spain. The Spanish political scene has become my major research interest.''

AVOCATIONAL INTERESTS: Travel (especially Spain and Latin America).

* * *

RIFKIND, Carole 1935-

PERSONAL: Born June 23, 1935, in New York, N.Y.; daughter of Julius and Eva (Pifko) Lewis; married Richard Allen Rifkind (a professor), June 24, 1956; children: Barbara, Nancy. *Education:* Barnard College, B.A., 1956; New York University, M.S., 1964; Columbia University, M.A., 1974. *Home:* 445 Riverside Dr., New York, N.Y. 10027. *Office:* Municipal Art Society, 30 Rockefeller Plaza, New York, N.Y. 10020.

CAREER: Hudson River Museum, Yonkers, N.Y., coordinator, 1973-74; Columbia University, New York City, adjunct assistant professor of architecture and planning, 1976-78; Municipal Art Society, New York City, director of information exchange. Consultant to Partners for Livable Places. *Member:* National Trust for Historic Preservation, Association for Preservation Technology, Victorian Society of America, Preservation League of New York State, Columbia University Seminar on the City.

WRITINGS: (With Carol Levine) *Mansions, Mills, and Main Streets,* Schocken, 1975; *Main Street: The Face of Urban America,* Harper, 1977; *A Field Guide to American Architecture,* New American Library, 1979. Editor of Columbia University's *Preservation Bulletin.*

WORK IN PROGRESS: A History of Travel and Tourism in America.

* * *

RIPLEY, Theresa M(argaret) 1944-

PERSONAL: Born September 24, 1944, in Pontiac, Ill.; daughter of William Raymond (a farmer) and Blanche (Phillips) Ripley. *Education:* Illinois State University, B.S. (honors), 1966; Indiana University, M.S., 1968; University of Oregon, Ph.D., 1971. *Home:* 1000 West 28th, Eugene, Ore. 97405. *Office:* Department of Counseling Psychology, University of Oregon, Eugene, Ore. 97403.

CAREER: Indiana University, Bloomington, assistant head counselor, 1967-68; University of Portland, Portland, Ore., program coordinator, 1968-69; University of Oregon, Eugene, assistant professor of education in counseling and coordinator of career planning, 1972—. Director of Career Services Division of United Learning Corp., 1974—. Member of state advisory board for research and exemplary career education, 1972-75; workshop coordinator and public speaker. *Member:* American Personnel and Guidance Association, American Association of University Professors, National Vocational Guidance Association, Kappa Delta Pi, Kappa Delta Epsilon. *Awards, honors:* Fulbright grant for Sweden, 1979.

WRITINGS: (With John W. Loughary) *This Isn't Quite What I Had in Mind: A Career Planning Program for College Students,* United Learning Corp., 1974; (with Loughary) *Career Survival Skills,* C. E. Merrill, 1974; (with Loughary) *Career and Life Planning Guide,* Follett, 1976; (with Loughary) *Helping Others Help Themselves: A Guide to Counseling Skills,* McGraw, 1979. Contributor to education and counseling journals and to *Dynamic Years.* Co-founder of *Lifespan.*

WORK IN PROGRESS: A book on leisure planning; a book on ''managing transitions through self-empowerment''; a businesswoman's guide to traveling alone.

SIDELIGHTS: Theresa Ripley told *CA:* ''To do effective career planning, each person must plan in three areas. These areas are: 1) Your job—what you do to earn a living; 2) Your vocation—what you do to feel a sense of self worth or fulfillment; and 3) Your leisure—what you do that is fun, relaxing, and pleasing to do. I am concerned with helping people do effective planning in all three of these areas.'' *Avocational interests:* Making furniture, genealogy, photography, collecting fine art prints, crafts.

RITCHIE, (John) Andrew 1943-

PERSONAL: Born August 21, 1943, in Edinburgh, Scotland. *Education:* Fitzwilliam College, Cambridge, B.A., 1966. *Politics:* "Social democrat/socialist." *Religion:* None. *Home:* 1923 Stuart St., Berkeley, Calif. 94703. *Agent:* Michael Larsen/Elizabeth Pomada, 1029 Jones St., San Francisco, Calif. 94109.

CAREER: Has variously worked as a teacher, researcher, radio announcer, program writer, and translator.

WRITINGS: (With Alex Pravda and Andrew Ochey) *Czechoslovakia: The Party and the People,* Allen Lane, 1973; *King of the Road: A Social History of Cycling,* Ten Speed Press, 1975.

WORK IN PROGRESS: A biography of black athlete Major Taylor; a history of the bicycle in America; a novel about the colonization of the universe.

* * *

RITZ, David 1943-
(Esther Elizabeth Pearl)

PERSONAL: Born December 2, 1943, in New York, N.Y.; son of Milton M. (a stockbroker) and Pearl (Graver) Ritz; married Roberta Plitt (a comedienne); children: Alison and Jessica (twins). *Education:* University of Texas, B.A., 1966; State University of New York at Buffalo, M.A., 1969. *Religion:* Jewish. *Residence:* Los Angeles, Calif. *Agent:* Aaron M. Priest Literary Agency, 150 East 35th St., New York, N.Y. 10016.

CAREER: Bloom Advertising, Dallas, Tex., copywriter, 1961-70; Houston/Ritz/Cohen/Jagoda (advertising agency), New York, N.Y., owner, 1971-75; writer, 1975—. Teacher at University of Pennsylvania, 1969. *Awards, honors:* Fulbright scholar, 1968.

WRITINGS: (With Ray Charles) *Brother Ray,* Dial, 1978; *Glory* (novel), Simon & Schuster, 1979.

WORK IN PROGRESS: A novel, *Jerusalem the Passionate,* under pseudonym Esther Elizabeth Pearl.

* * *

RIVERS, Conrad Kent 1933-1968

PERSONAL: Born in Atlantic City, N.J.; deceased. *Education:* Wilberforce University, A.B., 1955; also studied at Temple University and Chicago Teachers College.

CAREER: Poet and writer. Also teacher in Chicago (Ill.) schools; served in U.S. Armed Forces. *Awards, honors:* Annual Conrad Kent Rivers Poetry Award was established by *Black World* Magazine.

WRITINGS—All poems: *Perchance to Dream, Othello,* Wilberforce University, 1959; *The Black Bodies and This Sunburnt Face,* Free Lance Press (Cleveland, Ohio), 1962; *The Still Voice of Harlem,* Paul Breman (London), 1968, 2nd edition, 1972; *The Wright Poems,* introduction by Ronald L. Fair, Paul Breman, 1972. Also author of short stories and play "Dusk at Selma," 1965.

Work represented in numerous anthologies, including: *For Malcolm: Poems on the Life and Death of Malcolm X,* edited by Dudley Randall and Margaret G. Burroughs, 2nd edition, Broadside Press, 1969; *Afro-American Literature: Poetry,* edited by William Adams, Houghton, 1970; *Black Literature in America,* edited by H. A. Baker, McGraw, 1971; *Black Writers of America: A Comprehensive Anthology,* edited by Richard Barksdale and Kenneth Kinnamon,

Macmillan 1972; *Understanding the New Black Poetry: Black Speech and Black Music as Poetic References,* edited by Stephen Henderson, Morrow, 1973. Contributor of literary criticism and nonfiction to *Negro Digest.*

SIDELIGHTS: Don L. Lee described Rivers as "not only a world traveler but a word-traveler too." In *Dynamite Voices,* published After Rivers' death, Lee eulogized: "Bodies pass on but words endure. Even though Rivers didn't have a long runway, his plane was able to lift off and it will always be in flight, dropping a still voice in Harlem and on the Southside of Chicago."

BIOGRAPHICAL/CRITICAL SOURCES: Robert Hayden, *Kaleidoscope,* Harcourt, 1967; *Negro Digest,* August, 1968; H. A. Baker, editor, *Black Literature in America,* McGraw, 1971; Don L. Lee, *Dynamite Voices: Black Poets of the 1960's,* Broadside Press, 1971; *Contemporary Literary Criticism,* Volume 1, Gale, 1973.*

* * *

ROARK, Albert E(dward) 1933-

PERSONAL: Born April 6, 1933, in Nogales, Ariz.; son of James Larson and Mary (Valdez) Roark; married Anne Borders (a school system supervisor); children: Vivian, Albert, Stephen, Jacque, James. *Education:* Arizona State University, B.A., 1959, M.A., 1962; University of Arizona, Ph.D., 1966. *Office:* School of Education, University of Colorado, Campus Box 249, Boulder, Colo. 80309.

CAREER: High school social studies teacher in Phoenix, Ariz., 1959-63, head of department, 1962-63, guidance counselor, 1962-64; Tucson Child Guidance Clinic, Tucson, Ariz., psychologist, 1965-66; University of Colorado, Boulder, assistant professor, 1966-69, associate professor, 1969-73, professor of education, 1973—. Interviewer and research associate of Human Interaction Research Institute, 1966-67. Member of state committee on the role and functions of elementary school counselors, 1968-69. Conductor and participant in workshops and training programs; speaker at public and professional meetings; consultant in the United States and Nicaragua.

MEMBER: American Personnel and Guidance Association, National Education Association, Rocky Mountain Association for Counselor Education and Supervision (president, 1976), Colorado Personnel and Guidance Association (president, 1975), Colorado Education Association, Colorado Association for Counselor Education and Supervision, Boulder Personnel and Guidance Association (president, 1969-71). *Awards, honors:* Clifford Houston Award from Colorado Personnel and Guidance Association, 1975.

WRITINGS: (With Gene Stanford) *Human Interaction in Education,* Allyn & Bacon, 1974; (with Stanford, Chester R. Cromwell, and William Ohs) *Becoming,* Lippincott, 1975; (contributor) Ray Eiben and Al Milliren, editors, *Educational Change: A Humanistic Approach,* University Associates, 1976. Also author with Jim Rose and Gerald Lundquist, of *Organization Development in the Schools,* Love Publishing. Contributor of about thirty articles to professional journals and to *Arizona and the West.* Editor of *Awareness* (of Colorado Personnel and Guidance Association), 1971-73.

WORK IN PROGRESS: Research and writing in interpersonal conflict management.

* * *

ROARK, James L. 1941-

PERSONAL: Born September 28, 1941, in Eunice, La.; son

of Clayco B. and Elouise (Pritchard) Roark; married Martha Wire (a teacher), August 11, 1963; children: Michael James, Benjamin William. *Education:* University of California, Davis, B.A., 1963, M.A., 1964; Stanford University, Ph.D., 1973. *Home:* 7451 Bland Dr., Clayton, Mo. 63105. *Office:* Department of History, University of Missouri, St. Louis, Mo. 63121.

CAREER: University of Nigeria, Nsukka, lecturer in history, 1965-67; University of Missouri, St. Louis, began as assistant professor, 1971, currently associate professor of history. Fulbright professor at University of Nairobi, 1976-77. *Member:* Organization of American Historians, Society for Values in Higher Education, Southern Historical Association. *Awards, honors:* Allan Nevins Award from Society of American Historians, 1977, for *Masters Without Slaves;* National Endowment for the Humanities fellowship, 1978-79.

WRITINGS: Masters Without Slaves: Southern Planters in the Civil War and Reconstruction, Norton, 1977. Contributor to *Encyclopedia of Southern History.* Contributor to history journals.

WORK IN PROGRESS: A history of three generations of the Wade Hampton family of South Carolina.

SIDELIGHTS: Roark writes: "Born in the South of southern parents, trained in the West by two of this nation's most perceptive interpreters of the South, I am an American historian with a special interest in southern history. The distinctive history of the South deserves study in and of itself; but in addition, because it so often offers a counterpoint to national trends, it also provides insight into the broader course of American development. I want to provide a window through which to view the changing perceptions and conditions of the southern aristocracy in the nineteenth century."

BIOGRAPHICAL/CRITICAL SOURCES: New York Times, June 25, 1977; *New York Times Book Review,* October 16, 1977.

* * *

ROBB, Inez (Callaway)   1901(?)-1979

OBITUARY NOTICE: Born c. 1901 in Middletown, Calif.; died April 4, 1979, in Tucson, Ariz. Writer. Robb worked as a war correspondent for International News Service during the 1940's and later became associated with both Scripps-Howard Newspapers and United Features Syndicate. She wrote *Don't Just Stand There.* Obituaries and other sources: *Current Biography,* Wilson, 1958, June, 1979; *New York Times,* April 6, 1979; *Washington Post,* April 6, 1979; *Chicago Tribune,* April 8, 1979.

* * *

ROBERGE, Earl   1918-

PERSONAL: Born July 11, 1918, in Waterbury, Vt.; son of Alcide (a sculptor) and Cora (Hetu) Roberge; married Gertrude Veronica Coughlin (an office manager), October 18, 1945; children: Mildred Anne Roberge Gordon. *Education:* Attended St. Michael's College, 1935-39. *Politics:* Independent. *Religion:* Roman Catholic. *Home and office:* 764 Bryant Ave., Walla Walla, Wash. 99362.

CAREER: Roberge Studio, Walla Walla, Wash., owner, 1946-72; Earl Roberge, Inc., Walla Walla, owner, 1970—. *Military service:* U.S. Army Air Forces, 1942-45. *Member:* American Society of Magazine Photographers, Walla Walla Chamber of Commerce (head of publicity committee). *Awards, honors:* Award of merit from Washington State Photographers Association, 1959, 1962, 1967.

WRITINGS: (Photographer) Bill Gulick, *Snake River Country,* Caxton, 1970; *Timber Country* (with own photographs), Caxton, 1973; *Napa Wine Country* (with own photographs), Graphic Arts Center (Portland, Ore.), 1975. Contributor of articles and photographs to national magazines, including *Audubon, American Weekly, Argosy, Fortune,* and *Wines and Vine.*

WORK IN PROGRESS: Columbia: Great River of the West, with his own photographs.

SIDELIGHTS: Roberge comments: "I am basically a photographer who, after working with an author, discovered that writers get more credit (and money) than photographers. So I became a writer. *Columbia* involved more than three years' work, sixty thousand miles, and fifty-eight-hundred photographs. I travel extensively, especially in areas of the world where French, Italian, Spanish, German, and English are spoken."

AVOCATIONAL INTERESTS: Skiing, kayaking, mountain-climbing, flying his own plane, Judo, Karate, tennis, gun collecting.

* * *

ROBERTS, Arthur Sydney   1905(?)-1978

PERSONAL: Born c.1905, in Liverpool, England; came to United States, 1920; naturalized U.S. citizen, 1939; died September 27, 1978, in Orange Park, Fla.; married Kathryn White.

CAREER/WRITINGS: Journalist. *Savannah News,* Savannah, Ga., police reporter, 1927-35; Associated Press, New York City, reporter, 1935-42, member of Washington bureau, 1942-44, editor, 1944-70. *Member:* The Fossils (Washington, D.C.), Wheaton Presbyterian Church board of deacons (trustee and president).

SIDELIGHTS: Before becoming an editor, Roberts served the Associated Press as a regional reporter in the South and also covered the House of Representatives.

OBITUARIES: Washington Post, September 29, 1978.*

* * *

ROBERTS, John M(orris)   1928-

PERSONAL: Born April 14, 1928, in Bath, England; son of Edward Henry and Dorothy Julia (Hallett) Roberts; married, 1960 (marriage ended); married, 1964; children: one son, two daughters. *Education:* Oxford University, B.A. (first class honors), 1949, M.A., 1952, D.Phil., 1953. *Agent:* A. D. Peters Ltd., 10 Buckingham St., London W.2, England. *Office:* Vice-Chancellor's Office, University of Southhampton, Highfield, Southampton S09 5NH, England.

CAREER: Oxford University, Merton College, Oxford, England, fellow and tutor, 1953-79, acting warden, 1969-70, 1977-79; University of Southampton, Southampton, England, vice-chancellor, 1979—. Member of Princeton University's Institute for Advanced Study, 1960-61; visiting professor at University of South Carolina, 1961, and Columbia University, 1963. Council of Taunton School, member, 1964—, president of council, 1978—; member of Royal Literary Fund, 1975—; member of board of trustees of Doulton Educational Trust and Longman Educational Trust, both 1978—. Member of British Film Institute committee on film archives, 1975—. *Member:* Royal Historical Society (fellow; member of council, 1974-77). *Awards, honors:* Commonwealth Fund fellowship for study at Princeton University and Yale University, 1953-54.

WRITINGS: (Contributor) A. Goodwin, editor, *The European Nobility in the Eighteenth Century,* A. & C. Black, 1953; (contributor) *Art and Ideas in Eighteenth-Century Italy,* [Rome], 1960; (editor) *French Revolution Documents,* Barnes & Noble, Volume I (with R. C. Cobb), Volume II (with John Hardman), 1966-73; *Europe, 1880-1945,* Holt, 1967, revised edition, Longman, 1970; (editor) *Europe in the Twentieth Century,* four volumes, Taplinger, 1970; *The Mythology of the Secret Societies,* Scribner, 1972; (with others; also adviser) *Journey to the Modern World,* CRM Books, 1973; *The Paris Commune From the Right,* Longman, 1974; *The Age of Revolution and Improvement: The Western World, 1775-1847,* University of California Press, 1975; (special adviser) Nathaniel Harris, *The Forties and Fifties,* Macdonald & Co., 1975; (special adviser) Harris, *The Sixties,* Macdonald Educational, 1975; *History of the World,* Knopf, 1976 (published in England as *The Hutchinson History of the World,* Hutchinson, 1976).

Editor of "History of the Twentieth Century" series, Purnell, 1968-70, and of "The Short Oxford History of the Modern World" series and "Oxford History of England" series, both for Oxford University Press. Editor of *English Historical Review,* 1967-77. Contributor to *New Cambridge Modern History.* Contributor to history journals.

WORK IN PROGRESS: A historical television series.

* * *

ROBERTS, Keith   1937(?)-1979

OBITUARY NOTICE: Art historian and editor of *Burlington* magazine. Roberts was also an editorial adviser for Phaidon Press. Obituaries and other sources: *AB Bookman's Weekly,* April 16, 1979.

* * *

ROBICHAUD, Gerald A(laric)   1912-1979

OBITUARY NOTICE: Born March 19, 1912, in Chicopee Falls, Mass.; died February 12, 1979, in Oaxaca, Mexico. Journalist best known for his correspondence from Washington, D.C., and his association with *Chicago Daily News* and *Chicago Sun-Times.* Obituaries and other sources: *Who's Who in America,* 40th edition, Marquis, 1978; *Chicago Tribune,* February 15, 1979.

* * *

ROCKS, Lawrence   1933-

PERSONAL: Born August 27, 1933, in New York, N.Y.; son of Charles and Frieda (Goldberg) Rocks; married Marlene Gerber (a teacher), April 7, 1968; children: Burton Evan. *Education:* Queens College (now of the City University of New York), B.S., 1955; Purdue University, M.S., 1957; Technische Hochschule, Vienna, Austria, D.Sc., 1964. *Home:* 29 Seville Lane, Stony Brook, N.Y. 11790. *Office:* Department of Chemistry, C. W. Post College, Long Island University, Greenvale, N.Y. 11548.

CAREER: Long Island University, C. W. Post College, Greenvale, N.Y., assistant professor, 1958-73, associate professor of chemistry, 1973—. Lecturer; guest on radio and television programs in the United States and Australia, including "Mike Douglas Show," "Living Easy," and "Today Show." Member of board of directors of Enercon Corp. Consultant to Research Media, Inc. *Member:* American Chemical Society, American Association for the Advancement of Science.

WRITINGS: (With Richard P. Runyon) *The Energy Crisis,*

Crown, 1972; *Developing Your Chemistry Fundamentals* (textbook), PPC Books, 1979. Author of "Our Energy Crisis," a column distributed by King Features Syndicate, 1973-76. Contributor to scientific journals and popular magazines, including *National Review* and *Newsday,* and newspapers.

SIDELIGHTS: Rocks writes: "Energy will be a major factor for decades in international politics, technological development of nations, and the life-style of people. Personally, I see the ultimate future of energy systems in the biophotolysis of water: sunshine can split water into versatile and clean hydrogen fuel through the action of enzymes present in many species of microorganisms. Biophotolysis is the alternative to both fossil fuels and nuclear power. Such a system would be the most long-lived, environmentally safe and economically feasible energy system possible." Rocks's energy book has been translated into Japanese, French, and Spanish.

* * *

RODGERS, W(illiam) R(obert)   1909-1969

PERSONAL: Born in 1909, in Belfast, Ireland; died in 1969. *Education:* Queens University, earned degree.

CAREER: Poet. Worked as minister of Loughgall Presbyterian Church, 1939-46; scriptwriter for British Broadcasting Corp., 1946-52. *Member:* Irish Academy of Letters.

WRITINGS: Awake! and Other Wartime Poems, Secker & Warburg, 1941; *Europa and the Bull, and Other Poems,* Farrar, Straus, 1952; (author of introduction and notes) *Ireland in Colour; a Collection of Forty Colour Photographs,* Studio Publications, 1957; *Collected Poems of W. R. Rodgers,* Oxford University Press, 1971; (editor) *Irish Literary Portraits: W. B. Yeats, James Joyce, George Moore, J. M. Synge, George Bernard Shaw, Oliver St. John Gogarty, F. R. Higgins, A. E.; W. R. Rodgers's Broadcast Conversations With Those Who Knew Them,* Taplinger, 1972. Also author of *Ulstermen and Their Country,* 1947. Contributor to *New Statesman.*

SIDELIGHTS: As an initial volume, Rodgers's *Awake! and Other Wartime Poems* impressed many critics. Since that time, much of his work has been compared with that of Gerard Manley Hopkins and W. H. Auden. Louise Bogan referred to Rodgers as possessing "a contemporaneous and candid spirit. . . ." She also noted, "He uses the packed directness of alliterative Anglo-Saxon of Hopkins' and Auden's experiments and gives it surprising Celtic turns." "What is best about this poet," she surmised, "is his glance into the future and his realization that more than a casual peace must be demanded. . . ."

George Barker claimed that the poems in Rodger's first book, *Awake! and Other Wartime Poems,* were "noisy, verbose, eloquent and intellectually rather adolescent. . . ." He also asserted that Rodgers "is at present obsessed with assonance to the point where it sticks like a plum in his throat and impedes almost all utterance. . . ." But Barker also believed that Rodgers's "obsession with the word as machinery is acknowledgedly the healthiest of propensities in the young poet. . . ." Barker then concluded that Rodgers "has only to take a deep breath and clear his throat of technical matter in order to say things both comprehensibly and memorably."

Although Mark Van Doren has called Rodgers "the war poet of the war," David Daiches preferred to think of Rodgers as simply a poet. In a review of *Awake! and Other Wartime Poems,* Daiches noted that "quite a number of these poems were written before the war started." Daiches also refused to accept the notion that Rodgers was an experimental poet. "Now Mr. Rodgers," wrote Daiches, "though these are his first poems, doesn't sound like an experimentalist at all; nevertheless his poetry is fresh and original." Daiches also found that Rodgers's "ideas are simple but not silly, his verse limpid but not trite."

Patrick Stevenson discovered much to be treasured in Rodgers's *Collected Poems.* "His *Collected Poems* are . . . memorable for some remarkable refurbishings of classical myths and for poems on music," declared Stevenson. "By any standards 'Europa and the Bull' . . . is a notable achievement. All his many qualities are here displayed to perfection and the nature descriptions—light and shadow, movement, texture, sound, scent, and sensuality—are exquisite." Stevenson also remarked, "The few poems on music show the author to have had a deep feeling for that art and in particular for the timbre and character of orchestral instruments."

Writing in *Poetry,* Thomas Shapcott lamented Rodgers's creative lapse during the last twenty years of his life. "For his last project," wrote Shapcott, "Rodgers had chiselled his technique down finely, and apparently had a theme particularly suited to his aims and his language. But between 1949, when it was first proposed, and his death in 1969, he had written only seventy-six lines. His *Collected Poems* . . . do not excuse the dead man that failure."

Irish Literary Portraits, published after Rodgers's death, was deemed "an important book for literary historians" by a reviewer for *Choice.* The reviewer also recommended the book to "general readers and those interested in media. . . ." A writer for *Virginia Quarterly Review* also found it to be a worthy volume. "Glimpses into the literary process of mythmaking," the reviewer stated, "petty rivalries, and the atmosphere of Dublin make this an informative as well as a delightful book."

BIOGRAPHICAL/CRITICAL SOURCES: New Republic, April 13, 1942; *Poetry,* May, 1942, April, 1973; Louise Bogan, *Selected Criticism: Poetry and Prose,* Noonday Press, 1955; *Phoenix,* July, 1973; *Virginia Quarterly Review,* autumn, 1973; *Choice,* November, 1973; *Contemporary Literary Criticism,* Volume 7, 1977.*

*   *   *

ROGERS, Kenneth Ray
(Kenny Rogers)

PERSONAL: Born in Houston, Tex.; son of Floyd and Lucille (Hester) Rogers; married Marianne Gordon (an actress), October 2, 1977. *Education:* Attended University of Houston. *Residence:* Los Angeles, Calif. *Office:* Management Three, 9744 Wilshire, Beverly Hills, Calif. 90212.

CAREER: Member of singing groups, including Bobby Doyle Trio, until 1966, New Christy Minstrels, 1966-67, and Kenny Rogers and the First Edition, 1967-76; associated with United Artists, 1976—. Also actor in syndicated television series, "Rollin'." *Awards, honors:* Grammy Award for best male vocalist (country) and awards from Academy of Country Music for best single and best song, all 1977, all for "Lucille"; named "Cross-Over Artist of the Year" by *Billboard,* 1977; Academy of Country Music Award for best male vocalist, 1977; three awards from America's Juke Box Operators Association (AMOA), 1978; recipient of numerous other honors, including two from Country Music Association, 1977, and five nominations for various awards, 1978.

WRITINGS—Under name Kenny Rogers: (With Len Epand) *Making It With Music,* Harper, 1978.

Also author of recordings, including the United Artists releases "Daytime Friends," "Kenny Rogers," "Ten Years of Gold," (with Dottie West) "Everytime Two Fools Collide," and "Love or Something Like It." Author of numerous songs, including "Sweet Music Man."

WORK IN PROGRESS: Recording another album with Dottie West.

SIDELIGHTS: A tireless performer, Rogers devotes equal time to touring and recording. He has recorded numerous gold records as well as given concerts throughout the United States, Canada, New Zealand, and Scotland. And his many awards testify to his talents as both a singer and songwriter.

Rogers's career took off after he formed Kenny Rogers and the First Edition with other members of the New Christy Minstrels. A basic rock 'n' roll group, the First Edition peaked in the late 1960's with a string of hits, including "Just Dropped in to See What Condition My Condition Was In," "Ruby (Don't Take Your Love to Town)," and "Something's Burnin'." "I loved the First Edition," recalled Rogers. "There never was one minute I didn't feel proud of its success." Rogers soon tired of the repetition involved in touring and recording with the group, though, so they disbanded. "One day we realized doing the same thing over and over just didn't excite us," he said. "There were no hard feelings. We just left the stage one night and never came back."

Embarked on a solo career, Rogers seemed content to stay out of the limelight for a while. Within two years, however, he was back with another popular song, "Lucille." "I was going along just fine with my quiet little career," Rogers mused, "when someone screwed up and got me a hit."

"Lucille" was not his first solo hit, though. He'd already made the country music charts with three singles, "Homemade Love," "Laura," and "While the Feeling's Good."

Rogers followed the success of "Lucille" with another popular tune, "Every Time Two Fools Collide." From the album of the same name, "Every Time Two Fools Collide" was recorded with another country music artist, Dottie West. "Dottie is a very good friend of mine and the thing I enjoyed most about doing the album is that it was all so genuine," claimed Rogers. "It was done for the right reason; we really enjoy singing together." The resulting collaboration was such a success with music fans that Rogers and West decided to record a second album together.

While working with West, Rogers also was busy writing his book, *Making It With Music.* "The reason I decided to write the book is that I've been barraged constantly, throughout my career, with questions from aspiring young musicians," said Rogers. "The book heavily stresses what one should do to get started in the business. It's not designed to make a star out of someone who is not capable of or interested in becoming a star. It's designed to help a person with an average amount of talent who just wants to make a decent living in a very lucrative business."

Rogers has done more than just make a living for himself, though. He reached the top of his field in two distinctly different forms of music, country and rock 'n' roll. Although he never regreted his years playing rock 'n' roll, Rogers noted, "It's interesting. I had to become a country artist to buy a tuxedo."

AVOCATIONAL INTERESTS: Softball, tennis.

*   *   *

ROGERS, Pat   1938-

PERSONAL: Born March 17, 1938, in Beverley, Yorkshire,

England; married Pauline Turner (a painter), August 16, 1969; children: Becky, Gabriel Alexander. *Education:* Fitzwilliam College, Cambridge, B.A., 1961, M.A., 1965, Ph.D., 1968. *Residence:* Bristol, England. *Office:* Department of English, University of Bristol, 40 Berkeley Sq., Bristol BS8 1HY, England.

CAREER: Cambridge University, Cambridge, England, fellow, 1964-69; University of London, London, England, lecturer in English, 1969-73; University of Wales, Bangor, professor of English, 1973-76; University of Bristol, Bristol, England, professor of English, 1977—. *Military service:* Royal Air Force, 1956-58. *Member:* British Society for Eighteenth-Century Studies (secretary, 1972-74). *Awards, honors:* Member's prize from Cambridge University, 1962, for essay "Sociology and Literature"; Le Bas prize from Cambridge University, 1969, for "Grub Street: An Historical Essay."

WRITINGS: (Editor) Daniel Defoe, *A Tour Through the Whole Island of Great Britain,* Penguin, 1971; *Grub Street: Studies in a Subculture,* Harper, 1972; (editor) *Defoe: The Critical Heritage,* Routledge & Kegan Paul, 1972; *The Augustan Vision,* Barnes & Noble, 1974; *An Introduction to Pope,* Harper, 1975; (editor) *Contexts of English Literature: The Eighteenth Century,* Holmes & Meier, 1978; *Henry Fielding: A Biography,* Elek, 1979; *Robinson Crusoe,* Allen & Unwin, in press; (editor) *Complete Poems of Jonathan Swift,* Penguin, in press. Editor of *Granta,* 1972-73, *Cambridge Review,* 1973-74, and *Scriblerian,* 1979—.

WORK IN PROGRESS: Studies of Samuel Johnson and James Boswell; *A Preface to Swift;* a study of the life of Joshua Reynolds.

SIDELIGHTS: Rogers is a specialist in eighteenth-century literature. His *Grub Street: Studies in a Subculture* reconstructs the factual and literary history of one of London's most famous streets. In this "excellent book," wrote an *Economist* critic, "[Rogers] walks down the labyrinth of myth, metaphor and city slum with a certain step and every evidence of intellectual satisfaction.... He extracts the maximum information from the evidence: it is a brilliant piece of detection, for Grub Street no longer exists." Another book, *The Augustan Vision,* is an attempt to view the whole of English culture in order to gain a greater insight into this particular period of English literature. "Among the well-known general introductions to the period ... Roger's book belongs with the best," commented Claude Rawson. "There is more intellectual vitality, more thought-provoking power [in this volume] than in many a book which prides itself on never putting a foot wrong."

AVOCATIONAL INTERESTS: "My interests focus on a small number of subjects: the eighteenth century, particularly in Britain, France, and North America; music, especially Mozart and Haydn, and also English music of the sixteenth, seventeenth, and eighteenth centuries; and the British landscape. My family and I enjoy exploring wooded countryside; otherwise my recreations are staying at home and listening to Mozart."

BIOGRAPHICAL/CRITICAL SOURCES: Economist, May 27, 1972, December 9, 1972; *Observer,* May 28, 1972, October 13, 1974; *Spectator,* June 3, 1972; *Times Literary Supplement,* June 23, 1972, January 5, 1973, October 4, 1974; *New Statesman,* June 23, 1972; *Philological Quarterly,* July, 1973; *Modern Philology,* February, 1975.

ROHLEN, Tom 1940-

PERSONAL: Born October 29, 1940, in Evanston, Ill. *Education:* Princeton University, B.A. (magna cum laude), 1962; University of Pennsylvania, Ph.D., 1971. *Address:* P.O. Box 1341, Ross, Calif. 94957.

CAREER: U.S. Department of State, Washington, D.C., foreign service officer in Japan, 1962-65; University of California, Santa Cruz, assistant professor, 1971-75, associate professor, 1975—. Program coordinator at Aspen Institute; consultant to business, government, and private foundations. *Member:* American Anthropological Association, Association for Asian Studies, Japan Society. *Awards, honors:* Citation from governor of American Samoa, 1978.

WRITINGS: For Harmony and Strength: Japanese White-Collar Organization in Anthropological Perspective, University of California Press, 1974. Contributor to a variety of academic and popular journals, including *Human Nature, Daedalus,* and *New York Times Book Review.* Associate editor of *Journal of Japanese Studies.*

WORK IN PROGRESS: A book on Japanese high school education for University of California Press; editing a book on modern Japan with Dan Okimoto for McGraw-Hill; editing a book on conflict in Japanese society for Princeton University Press.

SIDELIGHTS: Rohlen comments: "Having begun studying Japanese on a bet in college, I have never ceased being drawn further down a fated path trying to understand Japanese culture. I try to apply anthropological methods and insights, especially in-depth field research, to modern Japanese society. Being gregarious and enjoying Japanese sake have helped immensely.

"Lately I am concentrating on Japanese business, as it is the most dynamic element not only of Japanese society but of the entire Asian and Pacific region."

*   *   *

ROLLESTON, James Lancelot 1939-

PERSONAL: Born December 5, 1939, in Lyndhurst, England; came to United States in 1961, became permanent resident in 1967; son of William Lancelot (a military colonel) and Audrey Joy (Upton) Rolleston; married Priscilla Mae Schnake, 1962; children: Christopher, Victoria. *Education:* Cambridge University, B.A., 1961; University of Minnesota, M.A., 1962; Yale University, Ph.D., 1968. *Home:* 3238 Pickett Rd., Durham, N.C. 27705. *Office:* Department of German, Duke University, Durham, N.C. 27706.

CAREER: Yale University, New Haven, Conn., acting instructor, 1966-68, instructor, 1968-69, assistant professor, 1969-72, associate professor of German, 1972-75; Duke University, Durham, N.C., associate professor of German, 1975—. Director of National Endowment for the Humanities summer seminar for college teachers, 1976. *Member:* Modern Language Association of America.

WRITINGS: Rilke in Transition: An Exploration of His Earliest Poetry, Yale University Press, 1970; *Kafka's Narrative Theatre,* Pennsylvania State University Press, 1974; (editor) *Twentieth-Century Interpretations of Kafka's "The Trial",* Prentice-Hall, 1976.

WORK IN PROGRESS: A book on modern Germanic poetry and poetic theory; preparing articles on Nietzsche, Expressionism, and the poetics of the 1950's.

SIDELIGHTS: Rolleston writes: "I am increasingly involved in comparative literature, not for theoretical reasons (although the revival of literary theory is a source of strength to a teacher), but because the field attracts students to whom literature really matters. I find teaching and research converging more and more as we move into a world which, in part because of its urge to dispense with the imaginative role of literature, is increasingly permeated with conceptual and textural instability."

* * *

ROMAINS, Jules 1885-1972
(Louis Farigoule)

PERSONAL: Birth-given name Louis-Henri-Jean Farigoule; name legally changed in 1953; born August 26, 1885, in Cevannes, France; died August 14, 1972, in Paris, France; son of Henri (a teacher) and Marie (Richier) Farigoule; married Gabrielle Gaffe, 1912 (divorced, 1936); married Lisa Dreyfus, 1936. *Education:* Attended Lycee Condorcet, 1897-1905; Ecole Normale Superiure, agregation de philosophie, 1909. *Residence:* Paris, France.

CAREER: Writer, poet, dramatist, essayist. Teacher of philosophy in Brest, France, 1909, in Laon, France, 1910-17, and in Nice, France, 1917-19; full-time writer, 1919-72. Member of Academie Francaise, beginning in 1946. *Member:* International P.E.N. Club (president, 1938-41). *Military service:* French Army, 1914-15.

WRITINGS—In English: *Mort de quelqu'un* (novel), [Paris], 1911, translation by Desmond McCarthy and Sydney Waterlow published as *The Death of a Nobody,* B. W. Huebsch, 1914, new edition, New American Library, 1961; *Les Copains,* [Paris], 1913, reprinted, Gallimard, 1962, translation by Jacques Le Clercq published as *The Boys in the Back Room,* R. M. McBride, 1937; (under name Louis Farigoule) *La Vision extra-retinienne et le sens paraptique: recherches de psycho-psysiologie experimentale et de physiologie histologique,* Nouvelle revue francaises, 1920, new edition, Gallimard, 1964, translation by Charles Kay Ogden published as *Eyeless Sight: A Study of Extra-Retinal Vision and the Paroptic Sense,* Putnam, 1964; *Psyche* (contains "Lucienne," "Le Dieu des corps," and "Quand le navire"; also see below), [Paris], 1922-29, translation by John Rodker published as *The Body's Rapture* (contains "Lucienne's Story," "The Body's Rapture," and "Love's Questing"), Liveright, 1933; *Lucienne* (also see above), Nouvelle revue francaise, 1922, translation by Waldo Frank, Boni & Liveright, 1925; *Knock, ou Le Triomphe de la medecine* (three-act comedy; first produced in Paris at La Comedie des Champs-Elysees, December 15, 1923), Imprint de l'illustration, 1924, reprinted, 1956, revised edition with notes in English edited by J. B. Alton, Longman, 1973, translation by Harley Granville-Barker published as *Doctor Knock,* [London], 1925; *Le Dieu des corps* (also see above), Gallimard, 1928, reprinted, 1966, translation by John Rodker published as *The Lord God of the Flesh,* Pocket Books, 1953.

A Letter to My American Readers, Knopf, 1935; *Sept mysteres du destin de l'Europe,* Editions de la maison francaise (New York, N.Y.), 1940, translation by Germaine Bree published as *Seven Mysteries of Europe,* Knopf, 1940, reprinted, Books for Libraries Press, 1971; *Stefan Zweig: grand europeen,* Editions de la maison francaise, 1941, translation by James Whitall published as *Stefan Zweig: Great European,* Viking, 1941; *Salsette decouvre l'Amerique,* Editions de la maison francaise, 1942, translation by Lewis Galantiere published as *Salsette Discovers America,* Knopf, 1942.

Tussles With Time, translation of original French manuscript entitled "Violation de frontieres" by Gerard Hopkins, Sidgwick & Jackson, 1952; *Examen de conscience des Francais,* Flammarion, 1954, translation by Cornelia Schaeffer published as *A Frenchman Examines His Conscience,* Essential Books, 1955; *Une femme singuliere* (novel), Flammarion, 1957, translation by A. Pomerans published as *The Adventuress,* Muller (London), 1958; *As It Is On Earth,* translation of original French manuscript entitled "Situation de la terre" by Richard Howard, Macmillan, 1962; (editor) *Napoleon I, Emperor of the French, 1769-1821: Napoleon par lui-meme* (in English and French), Librairie academique Perrin, 1963; *Lettre ouverte contre une vaste conspiration,* A Michel, 1966, translation by Harold J. Salemson published as *Open Letter Against a Vast Conspiracy,* J. H. Heineman, 1967.

"Les Hommes de bonne volonte" series, Flammarion, 1932-46; translation published as "Men of Good Will" series, Volumes 1-3 translated by Warre Wells, Volumes 2-14 translated by Gerard Hopkins, all published by Knopf, 1933-46: Volume 1: *Les Hommes de bonne volonte,* translation published as *Men of Good Will,* Book 1: *Le Six octobre,* translation published as *The Sixth of October,* Book 2: *Crime de Quinette,* translation published as *Quinette's Crime;* Volume 2, translation published as *Passion's Pilgrims,* Book 3: *Les Amours enfantines,* translation published as *Childhood's Loves,* Book 4: *Eros de Paris,* translation published as *Eros in Paris;* Volume 3, translation published as *The Proud and the Meek,* Book 5: *Les Superbes,* translation published as *The Proud,* Book 6: *Les Humbles,* translation published as *The Meek;* Volume 4, translation published as *The World From Below,* Book 7: *Recherche d'une eglise,* translation published as *The Lonely,* Book 8: *Province,* translation published as *Provincial Interlude;* Volume 5, translation published as *The Earth Trembles,* Book 9: *Montee des perils,* translation published as *Floor Warning,* Book 10: *Les Pouvoirs,* translation published as *The Powers That Be;* Volume 6, translation published as *The Depths and the Heights,* Book 11: *Recours a l'abime,* translation published as *To the Gutter,* Book 12: *Les Createurs,* translation published as *To the Stars;* Volume 7, translation published as *Death of a World,* Book 13: *Mission a Rome,* translation published as *Mission to Rome,* Book 14: *Le Drapeau noir,* translation published as *The Black Flag;* Volume 8, translation published as *Verdun,* Book 15: *Prelude a Verdun,* translation published as *The Prelude,* Book 16: *Verdun,* translation published as *The Battle;* Volume 9, translation published as *Aftermath,* Book 17: *Vorge contre Quinette,* translation published as *Vorge Against Quinette,* Book 18: *La Douceur de la vie,* translation published as *The Sweets of Life;* Volume 10, translation published as *The New Day,* Book 19: *Cette grande lueur a l'est,* translation published as *Promise of Dawn,* Book 20: *Le Monde est ton aventure,* translation published as *The World Is Your Adventure;* Volume 11, translation published as *Work and Play,* Book 21: *Journees dans la montagne,* translation published as *Mountain Days,* Book 22: *Les Travaux et les joies,* translation published as *Work and Play;* Volume 12, translation published as *The Wind Is Rising,* Book 23: *Naissance de la bande,* translation published as *The Gatherings of the Gangs,* Book 24: *Comparutions,* translations published as *Offered in Evidence;* Volume 13, translation published as *Escape in Passion,* Book 25: *Le Tapis magique,* translation published as *The Magic Carpet;* Volume 14, translation published as *The Seventh of October,* Book 26: *Francoise,* translation published as *Francoise,* Book 27: *Le Sept octobre,* translation published as *The Seventh of October.*

Other—All published in Paris, except as noted: *Odes et Prieres*, 1913, *Le Voyage des amants* (poetry), 1920; *Cromedeyre-le-vieil* (drama in verse), 1920; *Donogoo Tonka; ou, Les Miracles de la science* (also see below), Nouvelle revue francaise, 1920; *Le Bourg regenere* (also see below), 1920; *Le Mariage de le Trouhadec* (four-act comedy), 1921; (author of introduction) *La Fanconnier: vingt-deux reproductions de peintures*, [Amieus, France], 1921; *Amour couleur de Paris* (poetry), 1921; *M. Le Trouhadec caisi par la debauche* (five-act comedy), Repertoire du Vieux-Colombier, 1922; (with Georges Chenneviere) *Petit traite de versification*, Nouvelle revue francaise, 1923; *Le Vin blanc de la villette*, 1923; *Theatre*, 1924-35; *Le Dictateur* (four-act play), Imprimerie de l'illustration, 1926, reprinted, 1959; *Jean le Maufranc: mystere* (five-act play), Imprimerie de l'illustration, 1927; *Chants des dix annees*, 1928; *Boen, ou La Possession des biens* (three-act comedy), Imprimerie de l'illustration, 1929.

Problemes d'aujourd'hui, Editions KRA, 1931; *Le roi masque* (three-act comedy), 1932; *Visite aux Americains*, 1936; *Pour l'esprit et la liberte*, 1937; *Une vue des choses*, Editions de la maison francaise, 1941; *Grace encore pour la terre!* (three-act play), Editions de la maison francaise, 1941; *Messages au francais*, Editions de la maison francaise, 1941; *Mission ou demission de la France?*, D. F. Ediciones Quetzal, 1942; *Bertrand de Ganges* (also see below), Editions de la maison, francaise, 1944, new edition edited by A. G. Lehman, G. G. Harrap (London), 1961; *Choix de poemes*, 1948; *Le Moulin et l'hospice*, 1949.

Portrait de Paris, Perrin, 1951; Pierre Toulze, editor, *Pages choisies*, Hachette, 1953; *Passagers de cette planete ou allons-nous?*, B. Grasset, 1955; Fernand Vial and Santina C. Vial, editors, *Le Petit Charles*, Dryden (Hinsdale, Ill.), 1956; *Le Roman des douze*, Julliard, 1957; *Souvenirs et confidences d'un ecrivain*, 1958.

Les Hauts et les bas de la liberte: Supremes avertissements: Retrouver la foi: Nouvelles Inquietudes (collection), 1960; *Hommage a Alfonso Reyes, 1889-1959*, [Cahors, Coueslant], 1960; *Landowski: la main et l'esprit*, photography by Pierre Berdoy, Biblioteque des Arts, 1961; *Alexandre Le Grand*, Hachette, 1962; *Ai-je fait ce que j'ai voulu?*, Wesmael-Charlier (Namur, Belgium), 1964; *Richesses theatrales et Knock la scintillante*, 1972.

All published by Gallimard: *Europe* (poetry), 1916, reprinted, 1960; *Quand le navire*, 1929; (author of epilogue with S. Zweig) Ben Jonson, *Volpone* (five-act comedy), 1929; *Pieces en un acte* (title means "One-Act Plays"; contains "La Scintillant," "Amedee et les messieurs en rang," "Demetrios," and "Le Dejeuner morocain"), 1930, reprinted, 1956.

All published by Flammarion: *Problemes europeens*, 1933; *Le Couple France-Allemagne*, 1934; *Zola et son exemple: discours de Medan*, 1935; *Cela depend de vous*, 1939; *Le Colloque de novembre, discours de Jules Romains a l'Academie francaise et response de Georges Duhamel de l'Academie francaise, sept novembre 1946*, 1946; *Bertrand de Ganges, suivi de Nomentames le refuge* (also see above), 1947; *Le Moulin et l'hospice*, 1949; *Paris des hommes de bonne volonte*, illustrations by Pierre Belves, 1949.

Le fils de Jerphanion (novel), 1956; *Pierres levees, suivi de Maisons* (poetry), 1957; *Le Besoin de voir clair; deuxieme rapport Antonelli* (novel), 1958; *Examen de conscience des Francais*, 1958; *Memoires de Madame Chauverel* (novel), 1959; *Hommes, medecins, machines*, 1959; *Pour raison garder*, three volumes, 1960-67; *Les Hauts et les bas de la lib-*
erte, 1960; *Un grand honnete homme*, 1961, new edition, Harrap, 1963; *Portraits d'inconnus*, 1962; *Recherche d'une eglise*, 1926; *Lettres a un ami*, Part I, 1964, Part II, 1965; *Un etre en marche* (poetry), 1967; *Marc-Aurele; ou, l'Empereur du bonne volonte*, 1968; *Amities et rencontres* (autobiography), 1970. Columnist in *Aurore*.

SIDELIGHTS: "The idea of a vast novel, composed of a great number of volumes, and in which I would try to present a sort of epic from the beginning of the 20th century all over the world, and especially in France . . . existed in my mind from earliest youth, from the very time when I began to write," Romains recalled. He was referring to the conception of his most extensive and notable work, "Men of Good Will." Written in twenty-seven parts, the novel has been compared to Balzac's "Comedie Humaine," Zola's "Rougon-Macquart," and Proust's "A la recherche de temps perdu."

Described by Alden Whitman as "one of the most intricately-designed and most majestic of modern novels," "Men of Good Will" encompasses twenty-five years of western European history. It chronicles the lives of four hundred characters caught up in the events of the time and in the lives of one another. "Their brilliant talk and [the] artful blend of imagination and history combine to create the illusion of reading the inside biography of an age in all its tortuosity," Whitman pointed out.

In setting the beginning and end of the novel on historically unexceptional days (October 6, 1908, and October 7, 1933), Romains underlines his belief that *every* day is in fact replete with action. He further emphasizes that all aspects of life, such as work, love, art, and politics, are intertwined.

The protagonists of the novel, Jeraphanion and Jallez, both aspire to change the world, but through different means. The former is action-oriented while the latter promotes change through his writing. Regardless of the method, Romains asserts, good will alone can never overcome the power of fate. Andre Maurois concluded that Romains "has written an epic that, however pessimistic in its facts, remains inspiring in its love of freedom and its deep sympathy for the adventure of the human race."

Maurois has described Romains as a "great novelist, greater essayist and poet." But Romains was disappointed that he was not more widely known as a poet. Nevertheless, Georges Duhamel, who had known him for many years, assured him, "In your poems, you have painted the world, you have painted your own times, and your own self." In *Europe*, Romains's poetry reflects his defiance over World War I.

"Unanism" is the term Romains used to describe his belief in a single, universal spirit, a "tremendous conception of giving a picture of life that would encompass all classes of society and types of people, with emphasis on the group," O'Brien explained. Romains himself pointed out that *La Vie Unanime* reveals "a new vision of human groups in themselves and not, as was most often the case before them, of the individual elements that compose them."

Although Romains was considered aloof by his peers in France, he was revered for his story-telling talents in the United States, where he was exiled during World War II. He enjoyed talking with people, mainly to store material for future writings. An acquaintance once accused him of "always sizing up people with the eye of a professional psychiatrist."

Romains was fluent in German, Italian, and Spanish, and could speak some English.

BIOGRAPHICAL/CRITCAL SOURCES: Germaine Bree and Otis Guiton, *The French Novel: From Gide to Camus,* Harcourt, 1962; Andre Maurois, *From Proust to Camus: Profiles of Modern French Writers,* translated by Carl Morse and Renaud Bruce, Weidenfeld & Nicolson, 1967; Henri Peyre, *French Novelists of Today,* Oxford University Press, 1967; Denis Boak, *Jules Romains,* Twayne, 1974; *Contemporary Literary Criticism,* Volume 7, Gale, 1977.

OBITUARIES: New York Times, August 18, 1972; *Newsweek,* August 28, 1972; *Time,* August 28, 1972.*

* * *

RONAY, Gabriel Ernest 1930-

PERSONAL: Born June 4, 1930, in Oradea, Transylvania, Romania; son of Ernest (a writer) and Klara (Lorincz) Ronay; married Lois Elspeth Neale (a researcher), May 21, 1966; children: Clare Gabrielle, Christian Anna, Catherine Lois. *Education:* University of Budapest, B.A., diploma in education; University of Edinburgh, M.A. (honors), 1960. *Politics:* "A *Liberal* believer in parliamentary democracy." *Religion:* "Once Catholic." *Home:* 7 Orchard Rd., Highgate, London N6 5TR, England. *Agent:* Richard Simon Scott, 32 College Cross, London N1 1PR, England. *Office: Times,* London W.C.1, England.

CAREER: Reuters News Agency, London, England, radio reporter, 1960-64, sub-editor and foreign correspondent, 1965-67; *Times,* London, foreign news sub-editor, 1967—. *Member:* Society of Authors.

WRITINGS: (With Colin Chapman) *The Rape of Czechoslovakia,* Lippincott, 1968; *The Dracula Myth,* W. H. Allen, 1972; *The Truth About Dracula,* Stein & Day, 1972; *The Tartar Khan's Englishman,* Cassell, 1978. Also author of *Romanian Foreign Policy Since the Second World War,* 1970. Author of column in *New Statesman,* 1965-70. Contributor to magazines and newspapers.

WORK IN PROGRESS: The Anglo-Saxon Connection, "a new vital historical discovery of English efforts to keep the crown in Anglo-Saxon hands and ward off the 1066 Norman Conquest," with publication by Cassell.

SIDELIGHTS: Ronay writes: "Research on our past helps me to understand present trends and attitudes; medieval history is an excellent antidote for one writing about the present political scene professionally. Apart from salvaging a part of our common European heritage, my books are intended to shed some fresh light on people, events, and situations which—if dispassionately viewed—have some relevance to our present problems."

AVOCATIONAL INTERESTS: The environment, defense of nature, travel, chess, skiing, music.

* * *

ROOME, Katherine Ann Davis 1952-

PERSONAL: Born June 3, 1952, in Mt. Kisco, N.Y.; daughter of Jerome (a consultant) and Mildred (a writer of mystery novels) Davis; married Hugh Reinagle Roome III (a consultant), August 5, 1977. *Education:* Attended Tufts University, 1970-72; Williams College, B.A. (summa cum laude), 1974; Cornell University, J.D., 1977. *Residence:* Bedford, N.Y. *Agent:* Scott Meredith Literary Agency, Inc., 845 Third Ave., New York, N.Y. 10022.

CAREER: Chadbourne, Parke, Whiteside & Wolff, New York, N.Y., law associate, 1977—. *Member:* Authors Guild, Authors League of America, Phi Beta Kappa.

WRITINGS: (With mother, Mildred Davis) *Lucifer Land* (historical novel), Random House, 1977; *Letter of the Law* (novel), Random House, 1979.

WORK IN PROGRESS: A novel about a law firm in New York City.

SIDELIGHTS: Katherine Roome writes: "There is no doubt that my interest in writing dates back more than twenty years to an age when I was still climbing onto my mother's lap while she was trying to write mystery novels. Sheer competitive spirit keeps us both scribbling when all other inspiration fails." *Avocational Interests:* Riding, sailing, skiing.

* * *

ROOT, Oren 1911-

PERSONAL: Born June 13, 1911, in New York, N.Y.; son of Oren (a railroad executive) and Aida (a foundation executive; maiden name, de Acosta) Root; married Daphne Skouras, February 15, 1946; children: Oren, Jr., Spyros, Dolores Root Simpson, Anthony. *Education:* Princeton University, A.B., 1933; University of Virginia, LL.B., 1936. *Politics:* Republican. *Religion:* Roman Catholic. *Home address:* P.O. Box 565, Bedford, N.Y. 10506. *Agent:* Sterling Lord Agency, Inc., 660 Madison Ave., New York, N.Y. 10021. *Office:* Barrett, Smith, Shapiro, Simon & Armstrong, 26 Broadway, New York, N.Y. 10004.

CAREER: Root, Barrett, Cohen, Knapp & Smith, New York City, attorney, 1946-65; Irving Trust Co., New York City, executive, 1965-72; Barrett, Smith, Shapiro, Simon & Armstrong, attorney, 1972—. Superintendent of banks for State of New York in Albany, 1961-64. Member of board of directors of Vera Institute of Justice and International Rescue Committee. *Member:* American Arbitration Association (member of board of directors), Council on Foreign Relations, Century Association.

WRITINGS: Persons and Persuasions, Norton, 1974. Contributor to magazines and newspapers, including *Saturday Review, Atlantic Monthly, America,* and *New York Times Magazine.*

* * *

RORVIK, David M(ichael) 1946-
(Michael Davidson)

PERSONAL: Born November 1, 1946, in Circle, Mont.; son of Alan and Frances (Ferch) Rorvik. *Education:* University of Montana, B.A. (with high honors), 1966; Columbia University, M.S. (with highest honors), 1967. *Residence:* San Francisco, Calif. *Agent:* Barbara Lowenstein, 250 West 57th St., New York, N.Y. 10019.

CAREER: Time magazine, New York, N.Y., reporter, 1967-70; free-lance science writer, 1970—. Lecturer for Future Presentations, Inc., 1978-79. *Awards, honors:* Pulitzer traveling fellowship, 1968, for studying the press and the politics of apartheid in white-dominated countries; Alicia Patterson Foundation fellowship, 1976-77, for studying the politics of cancer research.

WRITINGS: (With Landrum B. Shettles) *Your Baby's Sex: Now You Can Choose,* Dodd, 1970, revised edition published as *Choose Your Baby's Sex: The One Sex-Selection That Works,* 1977; *Brave New Baby: Promise and Peril of the Biological Revolution,* Doubleday, 1971; *As Man Becomes Machine: The Evolution of the Cyborg,* Doubleday, 1971; (under pseudonym Michael Davidson) *The Sex Surrogates,* Geis, 1972; (with O. S. Heyns) *Decompression Ba-*

bies, Dodd, 1973; (with Eleanor Easley and others) *Good Housekeeping Woman's Medical Guide*, Goodhousekeeping Books, 1974, revised edition, edited by David Devlin, published in England under same title, Ebury Press, 1975; *In His Image: The Cloning of a Man* (Literary Guild selection), Lippincott, 1978. Author of column, "Present Shock," in *Esquire*. Contributor to numerous periodicals, including *Esquire, Good Housekeeping, Playboy, Science Digest, New York Times Magazine*, and *Ladies Home Journal*.

SIDELIGHTS: A telephone call from an eccentric millionaire led to the events which David M. Rorvik recounts as fact in *In His Image: The Cloning of a Man*. Rorvik claims that he was contacted by a wealthy old man, identified only as "Max" in the book, who longed to have a baby—not just any baby, but an exact genetic duplicate of himself. According to Rorvik, Max was familiar with Rorvik's articles on genetic engineering and asked the writer if he could locate a scientist willing to try cloning a human being. After securing a scientist with the necessary expertise, Rorvik had carried out his part of the bargain, but he insisted that Max allow him to follow the progress of the experiments. Although Rorvik was not present during many of the important steps in the cloning process, he alleges that after several attempts the experiment succeeded and that Max now has an heir who is a replica of himself.

No documentation is offered to support Rorvik's story. The real names of the characters are not revealed, nor is the location of the laboratory disclosed. In an afterword to the text, Rorvik writes: "I entertain absolutely no expectation that anyone, scientist or layman, will accept this book as proof of the events described herein.... I hope, however, that many readers will be persuaded of the possibility, even the probability, of what I have described and will benefit by this preview of an astonishing development whose time at least in terms of some of the emotional and ethical issues it raises, has apparently not quite yet come." J. B. Lippincott, publisher of *In His Image*, stresses in a publisher's note that it cannot vouch for the book's authenticity: "The account that follows is an astonishing one. The author assures us it is true. We do not know. We believe simply that he has written a book which will stimulate interest and debate on issues of the utmost significance for our immediate future."

Many readers were willing to accept *In His Image* on this basis. "Whether Rorvik's story is fact or fiction," observed M. Stanton Evans, "it makes plain for us the moral challenge presented by the idea of cloning and genetic engineering generally and, even more important, the ethical path by which we have brought ourselves to the brink of so horrendous a development." Robert Bacon echoed these sentiments when he wrote, "It may be worthwhile having this book appear at this time to start us thinking about the very important implications of the cloning process in the future of mankind."

Questions about the book's veracity have inevitably arisen. Some unbelievers note that in 1970 Rorvik told an interviewer for the *Great Falls Tribune* that he wished to write a novel called *The Clone*; they suggest *In His Image* is that novel, masquerading as truth. Rorvik, however, denies that he ever seriously proposed writing such a novel. Thus far, only one commentator, Max Lerner of the *New York Post*, has stated publicly that he believes the book to be a true account. "At the risk of being a laughingstock for the rest of my life I want to say that I take seriously the recent book on human cloning," Lerner declared.

The scientific community by and large considers *In His Image* to be a hoax, but opinion is divided as to whether it would have been possible for a human baby to have been cloned in 1976, as Rorvik claims. In an article in the *New York Times*, several scientists point out a number of technical difficulties that must be surmounted before a human being can be cloned. Others express doubt that such an accomplishment could take place without other researchers in the field being aware of it. Such opinions are in marked contrast with the views of Clifford Grobstein, a molecular biologist and former dean of the School of Medicine at the University of California, San Diego. "Few knowledgeable biologists would dispute the possibility that human cloning might be achieved by concentrated effort, whether in 1976, 1984, or 2076.... No step he [Rorvik] describes strains the bounds of credulity," Grobstein asserted. "Most of the procedures flow directly from recent actual advances in reproductive biology. If the alleged result—a cloned human—is not scientifically convincing, it is not because the steps described are unreasonable. It is because objective evidence of success is totally lacking."

Judith Randal also contended that it may have been possible for an infant to have been cloned in 1976. "Like pieces of a jigsaw puzzle, the scientific and technological elements of a baby-cloning experiment have been lying around—some of them for years—waiting to be assembled," she pointed out. If a human has not been cloned, it is not because technical expertise is lacking, Randal argued. Rather, scientists have been reluctant to perform such experiments because of political and moral considerations. Randal made another important point: If Max and his baby do exist, and if they ever come forward, it would be quite simple to prove the authenticity of their relationship. Tests could determine whether or not their fingerprints, blood and tissue chemistries, and skin are genetically identical.

Moral and scientific issues aside, is *In His Image* a literary work of merit? Even on this point the book as aroused controversy. "'In His Image' is an engrossing book written in a readable, non-technical style," declared a reviewer for the *Youngstown Vindicator*. Robert Bacon also felt the book was "good reading." In contrast, Michael Crichton, author of *The Andromeda Strain*, found *In His Image* to be "stupefyingly dull. The plot is highly unlikely, the characters sketchy and improbably motivated, and the narrator himself is by turns dimwitted and melodramatic."

Some of Rorvik's books have been translated into Spanish, French, German, Norwegian, Portuguese, Japanese, Chinese, Arabic, Italian, Finnish, Danish, Polish, Indian, and Dutch.

BIOGRAPHICAL/CRITICAL SOURCES: David M. Rorvik, *In His Image*, Lippincott, 1978; *New York Times*, March 4, 1978, March 11, 1978, March 23, 1978, July 11, 1978; *Washington Post*, March 12, 1978, March 31, 1978; *New York Post*, March 29, 1978; *San Francisco Chronicle*, April 3, 1978; *Youngstown Vindicator*, April 16, 1978; *New York Times Book Review*, April 23, 1978; *Portland Oregonian*, April 23, 1978; *Springfield Union*, May 17, 1978; *Time*, July 24, 1978.

* * *

ROSE, Leo E. 1926-

PERSONAL: Born in Hanford, Calif. *Education:* University of California, Berkeley, A.B., 1949, Ph.D., 1960. *Office:* Department of Political Science, University of California, Berkeley, Calif. 94720.

CAREER: University of California, instructor in Far East

studies, 1954-55; Human Relations Area Files Project, Berkeley, Calif., research associate, 1955-56; University of California, Berkeley, director of Himalayan border countries project at Institute of International Studies, 1960-69, lecturer in political science, 1969—. Visiting professor at University of Oregon, 1961, and University of California, Los Angeles, 1970; research fellow at University of London, 1970. Conducted field studies in Japan, Korea, England, India, Nepal, Sikkim, Southeast Asia, Sri Lanka, and Bhutan.

MEMBER: American Political Science Association, Association for Asian Studies. *Awards, honors:* Hildegarde Millar Award in International Relations; Ford Foundation grants, 1973, 1974; American Council of Learned Societies fellow, 1975-76; Sherman Fairchild distinguished scholar at California Institute of Technology, 1976-77; Canada Council grant for McGill University, 1978-79.

WRITINGS: Nepal: Government and Politics, Human Relations Area File Press, 1956; (with Stanley Maron and Julie Heyman) *A Survey of Nepal Society,* Human Relations Area File Press, 1956; (with Margaret W. Fisher and Robert A. Huttenbach) *Himalayan Battleground: Sino-Indian Rivalry in Ladakh,* Praeger, 1963; (with Bhuwan Lal Joshi) *Democratic Innovations in Nepal: A Case Study of Political Acculturation,* University of California Press, 1966; (with Fisher) *The North-East Frontier Agency of India,* U.S. Department of State, 1967; *Sikkim as a Factor in Himalayan Area Politics,* RAND Corp., 1969; (with Fisher) *The Politics of Nepal: Persistence and Change in an Asian Monarchy,* Cornell University Press, 1970; *Nepal: Strategy for Survival,* University of California Press, 1971; (editor with Wayne Wilcox) *Asia and the International System,* Winthrop Publishing, 1972; *The Politics of Bhutan,* Cornell University Press, 1977; *An Introduction to Nepal,* Westview Press, 1979.

Contributor: *Resources for South Asian Area Studies in the United States,* University of Pennsylvania Press, 1962; Robert A. Scalapino, editor, *The Communist Revolution in Asia,* Prentice-Hall, 1965, 2nd edition, 1969; Allan A. Spitz, editor, *Contemporary China,* Washington State University Press, 1967; Donald Smith, editor, *Religion and Political Modernization,* Princeton University Press, 1974; James Rosenau, Kenneth Thompson, and Gavin Boyd, editors, *World Politics,* Free Press, 1976; B. N. Pandey, editor, *Leadership in South Asia,* Vikas Publishing House, 1977; S. D. Muni, editor, *Nepal Under an Assertive Monarchy,* Chetana Publications, 1977; Ram M. Roy, editor, *Democracy in Crisis in India,* California State University Foundation, 1977; James Fisher, editor, *Himalayan Anthropology,* Aldine, 1978; Lawrence Ziring, editor, *The Subcontinent in World Politics,* Praeger, 1978. Contributor to *Encyclopedia Americana* and *Encyclopaedia Britannica.* Contributor of about fifteen articles to academic journals. Editor of *Asian Survey,* 1962—.

WORK IN PROGRESS: Research on India as a regional power, Indian decision-making during the 1971 Indo-Pakistan war, and Kashmir political development in the modern period.

*   *   *

ROSENBLATT, Roger 1940-

PERSONAL: Born September 13, 1940, in New York, N.Y.; son of Milton B. (a physician) and Mollie (a teacher; maiden name, Spruch) Rosenblatt; married Virginia Jones (a teacher), June 15, 1963; children: Carl Becker, Amy Eliza-

beth, John Milton. *Education:* New York University, A.B. (honors), 1962; Harvard University, A.M., 1963, Ph.D., 1968. *Home:* 3252 N St. N.W., Washington, D.C. 20007. *Agent:* A. Watkins, Inc., 77 Park Ave., New York, N.Y. 10016. *Office: Washington Post,* 1150 15th St. N.W., Washington, D.C. 20071.

CAREER: Harvard University, Cambridge, Mass., assistant professor of English and American literature, 1968-73; National Endowment for the Humanities, Washington, D.C., director of education, 1973-75; *New Republic,* Washington, D.C., literary editor and author of column "The Back of the Book," 1975-78; *Washington Post,* Washington, D.C., editorial writer and author of weekly column, 1978—. *Member:* National Book Critics Circle (member of board of directors), Century Club, Cosmos Club. *Awards, honors:* Fulbright scholar, 1965-66.

WRITINGS: Black Fiction, Harvard University Press, 1974. Contributor to popular magazines, including *Harper's* and *Saturday Review,* professional journals, and newspapers.

WORK IN PROGRESS: A book on Washington, D.C., publication by Harper expected in 1980.

*   *   *

ROSENFELD, Lulla 1914-
(Lulla Adler)

PERSONAL: Born March 3, 1914; daughter of Joseph (an actor) and Frances Adler (an actress); married Paul M. Rosenfeld (a lawyer), May 14, 1932 (divorced, 1952); children: Josephine Rosenfeld Oppenheim. *Education:* Studied at Civic Repertory Theatre, 1930-32, and at Artef Theatre, 1936, both in New York, N.Y. *Home:* 55 West 11th St., New York, N.Y. 10011. *Agent:* Curtis Brown Ltd., 575 Madison Ave., New York, N.Y. 10022.

CAREER: Actress; writer. Began acting in 1921, on tour in New York City, Chicago, and South America with family; acted in Yiddish Art Theatre, beginning 1933; acted in Theatre Group Production "Gentle People," 1939, in motion picture "Reunion in France," 1943, in theatre production "Enemy of People," 1947, and in other plays on stage, radio, and television. Writer of radio and television programs. *Member:* Authors Guild. *Awards, honors:* National Endowment for the Humanities, 1975-76.

WRITINGS: Bright Star of Exile: Jacob Adler and the Yiddish Theatre, Crowell, 1977, new edition, Barrie & Jenkins, 1979. Author of screenplay, "Paris Blues" (adaptation of the book), and of several promotional films for United Jewish Appeal. Contributor of book reviews to *Saturday Review of Literature,* all under name Lulla Adler.

WORK IN PROGRESS: Selected Yiddish Plays of the Yiddish Theatre, "a collection of heretofore untranslated plays. The accompanying essays will throw some light on the history of the Yiddish theatre and on some of the influences, historical and cultural, that shaped its development."

SIDELIGHTS: Rosenfeld wrote: "The Yiddish theatre, now in its decline, was once described by an important American critic as 'the best in New York, both in stuff and in acting.' While it is remembered with much affection, very little is known about this extraordinary stage. The warm folk aspect of Yiddish theatre is the subject of innumerable reminiscences; the breadth of its subject matter, the seriousness of its artistic aims, are being forgotten.

"Contrary to the view now prevalent, it was not a folk theatre, but in the best sense, a national theatre where, in addition to marvellous studies of Jewish life by Jacob Gordin, Sholem Aleichem, Sholem Asch, and others, a mass immigrant audience saw world classics performed by magnificent actors. And it is a fact that many plays of Tolstoy, Gorki, Hauptmann, Ibsen, Strindberg, and Shaw had their first American productions on the Yiddish stages of the Lower East Side.

"It was to make all this clear, to correct misconceptions that have grown up over the years, that I wrote the book *Bright Star of Exile: Jacob Adler and the Yiddish Theatre.* What had begun as the relatively simple biography of a great actor soon widened into a work of far larger scope. My earliest researches uncovered a world so extraordinary, so theatrically and humanly *meaningful,* that I realized I must set down not only Adler's life, but the whole story. While Adler's career and personal history remained central, the book was broadened to encompass the entire saga of the Yiddish theatre from its beginnings one hundred years ago to the present day. Portraits of other great actors, portraits of major playwrights, fascinating lesser figures, the successes and the failures, the tragedies and the absurdities—all this against the backdrop of tremendous historic events—became an integral part of the book.

"I was perhaps uniquely fitted for this somewhat formidable task. Growing up in the Yiddish theatre, I had a living connection. I could understand its personalities and events form the *inside.* As a member of the Adler family (Jacob Adler was my grandfather), I had access to a wealth of personal and theatrical data unknown to the world at large. Lastly, my years of professional experience as a writer enabled me to organize all the diffused and scattered research material, and to create from it a living picture of Adler and the great personalities around him.

"The book was six years in the making. It was the culmination of my lifelong passion for literature and for the theatre, and on the whole I feel it succeeds in doing what I wanted it to. Isaac Bashevis Singer wrote of *Bright Star of Exile:* 'The book is a masterpiece. I consider it one of the greatest books ever written about this period.'" A *New Yorker* critic praised the book as well, commenting, "The entire cast of the book is volatile, passionate, reckless, intense and glamorous—as hugely entertaining offstage as on." And Murray Schumach wrote in the *New York Times* that the book "captures what may be the greatest romance of all illegitimate theatre—the 60-year romance of the audience and the Yiddish theatre they followed through poverty and pogrom to build a great theatre among New York tenements and sweat shops. A book with rewards for anyone who has ever found joy in any theatre."

In 1977 the *Philadelphia Inquirer* named *Bright Star of Exile* one of the Hundred Best Books of the Year. The book is currently being considered for a television series.

Rosenfeld is now working on a second book entitled *Selected Great Plays of the Yiddish Theatre.* She told *CA,* "The book will be a continuation of my effort to provide a truer picture of a great, but neglected epoch in theatre history."

BIOGRAPHICAL/CRITICAL SOURCES: New York Times, July 1, 1977, July 8, 1977; *New Yorker,* August 22, 1977; *Book World (Washington Post),* October 9, 1977.

*   *   *

ROSENSTIEL, Leonie 1947-

PERSONAL: Born December 28, 1947, in New York, N.Y.; daughter of Raymond (an investor) and Annette (an anthropologist; maiden name, Bitterman) Rosenstiel. *Education:* Juilliard School of Music, certificate, 1964; Barnard College, B.A., 1968; Columbia University, M.A., 1970, M.Phil., 1973, Ph.D., 1974. *Home:* 4 Old Mill Rd., Manhasset, N.Y. 11030.

CAREER: Barnard-Columbia Chamber Music Society, New York City, founder and director, 1965-67; *Current Musicology,* New York City, associate editor, 1969-71, special projects editor, 1971-73; instructor in music at adult school in Manhasset, N.Y., 1974-76; Caribbean Network System, New York City, associate producer, 1977. Director of Manhasset Chamber Ensemble, 1975. Alumni trustee of Professional Children's School.

MEMBER: International Musicological Society, Authors Guild, Authors League of America, American Musicological Society, Music Library Association, Sonneck Society, Project for the Oral History of Music in America. *Awards, honors:* Honorary diploma from Instituto de Bellas Artes (Mexico); honorable mention from Mesa de Trabajo de los Medios Masivos de Communicacion, 1975, for article "Music and Communication in Colombia, 1800-1936"; American Philosophical Society grant; American Council of Learned Societies grant; Rockefeller Foundation grant.

WRITINGS: (Translator) *Music Handbook,* Colorado College Music Press, 1976; *The Life and Works of Lili Boulanger,* Fairleigh Dickinson University Press, 1978; (contributor) *Twentieth-Century Music,* J. Calder, 1979; (contributor) *The First International Conference on Music and Communication,* UNESCO, 1979; (editor and contributor) *The Schirmer History of Music,* E. C. Schirmer, in press. Contributor to *Women's Work,* edited by Marnie Hall; also contributor of articles and translations to musicology journals.

WORK IN PROGRESS: A biography of Nadia Boulanger; research on the sociology of music, Latin American and North American music, the history of French music, and diffusion of musical styles and attitudes toward music and musicians.

SIDELIGHTS: Leonie Rosenstiel writes: "I have traveled widely throughout the United States, Canada, Latin America, and Europe, observing people and customs rather than simply seeing places. My first book was a translation from medieval Latin into English. Now I am beginning to study Russian.

"Formative influences have included my father's humanistic approach to economics and my mother's training in anthropology, but extend outward to my maternal grandfather's gift for languages (he knew more than ten fluently) and the attitudes of my master teachers of violin, Louis Persinger and Sandor Vegh. The result has been a desire to meet people on their own terms and to analyze situations from as many different points of view as possible."

AVOCATIONAL INTERESTS: Reading, yoga, listening to people, writing letters, good conversation.

*   *   *

ROSOW, Irving 1921-

PERSONAL: Born August 24, 1921, in Cleveland, Ohio; son of Eli (in laundry work) and Mary (in laundry work; maiden name, Chait) Rosow; married wife, Ursula, September, 1949 (divorced, September, 1969); children: Cordula, Ben. *Education:* Wayne State University, B.A., 1943, M.A., 1948; Harvard University, Ph.D., 1955. *Residence:* San Francisco, Calif. *Office:* Langley Porter Institute, University of California, San Francisco, Calif. 94143.

CAREER: Harvard University, Cambridge, Mass., staff analyst at Russian Research Center, 1951-54; Belmont Hospital, Sutton, England, senior sociologist, 1954-57; Purdue University, West Lafayette, Ind., associate professor of sociology, 1957-58; Case Western Reserve University, Cleveland, Ohio, professor of sociology and director of aging study, 1958-69; University of California, Langley Porter Institute, San Francisco, professor of sociology, 1969—. Consultant to National Research Council, National Institute on Aging, National Institute of Health, and National Institute of Mental Health. *Military service:* U.S. Army Air Forces, 1943-45; became sergeant; received Fouraguerre Belgique.

MEMBER: International Sociological Association, International Association of Gerontology, American Sociological Association, Gerontological Society (member of executive council, 1978-81; vice-president, 1979; head of behavioral and social science section, 1979). *Awards, honors:* Annual award from San Francisco Senior Citizens Centers, 1971; Prochovnik Annual Award from Israel Gerontological Society, 1975.

WRITINGS: (With Alex Inkeles and Raymond Bauer) *Soviet Citizen,* Harvard University Press, 1959; (with Rhona Rapoport and Robert Rapoport) *Community as Doctor,* Tavistock Publications, 1960; *Social Integration of the Aged,* Macmillan, 1967; *Socialization to Old Age,* University of California Press, 1974; *Authority in Emergencies,* Disaster Research Center, Ohio State University, 1977.

Contributor: Richard Williams, Clark Tibbitts, and Wilma Donahue, editors, *Process of Aging: Social and Psychological Perspectives,* Atherton, 1963; *Age With a Future,* Munksgaard, 1964; Ethel Shanas and Gordon Streib, editors, *Social Structure and Family,* Prentice-Hall, 1965; Frances Carp, editor, *Patterns of Living and Housing of Middle-Aged and Older People,* National Institute of Child Health and Human Development, 1967; Carp, editor, *Retirement Process,* National Institute of Child Health and Human Development, 1968; Frances Jeffers, editor, *Proceedings of Seminars, 1965-69,* Duke University Center for Study of Aging and Human Development, 1969; Thomas Byerts, editor, *Environmental Research and Aging,* Gerontological Society, 1974; Klaus Riegel and John Meacham, editors, *The Developing Individual in a Changing World,* Mouton, 1976; Robert Binstock and Ethel Shanas, editors, *Handbook of Aging and the Social Sciences,* Van Nostrand Reinhold, 1976; Corinne Nydegger, editor, *Measuring Morale,* Gerontological Society, 1977; Steve Zarit, editor, *Readings in Aging and Death,* Harper, 1977; Peter Ostwald, editor, *Communication and Social Interaction,* Grune, 1977. Also contributor to *Social Theory and Social Intervention,* edited by Herman Stein, 1968.

Contributor of more than thirty articles to scientific journals.

WORK IN PROGRESS: Criteria of Adult Socialization.

BIOGRAPHICAL/CRITICAL SOURCES: Gerontologie 71, October, 1971.

*　　　*　　　*

ROSS, Helen 1890(?)-1978

PERSONAL: Born c. 1890, in Independence, Mo.; died August 9, 1978, in Washington, D.C. *Education:* Graduated from University of Missouri; studied at Vienna Institute of Psychoanalysis in the 1930's. *Residence:* Washington, D.C.

CAREER: Taught Latin and French in high schools in Missouri before World War I; worked for Federal Railway Administration in Washington, D.C., during the war; Chi-

cago Institute for Psychoanalysis, Chicago, Ill., began as research associate in 1934, administrative director, 1941-56; moved to New York in 1956; Washington Psychoanalytic Institute, Washington, D.C., faculty member in child development and analysis, 1966-1978. Visiting instructor and administrator in child analysis programs in Washington, D.C., New York, and Pittsburgh; conducted seminars on child development. Director of Freud Archives and Hampstead clinic, London; honorary trustee of Chicago Institute for Psychoanalysis; member of board of directors of Field Foundation. *Member:* American Psychoanalytic Association, Washington Psychoanalytic Society.

WRITINGS: (With Adelaide M. Johnson) *Psychiatric Interpretations of the Growth Process,* Family Service Association of America, 1949; *Fears of Children* (booklet), illustrated by Janet La Salle, Science Research Associates, 1951, revised edition, illustrated by Marc Belenchia, 1970; (editor with Franz Gabriel Alexander) *Dynamic Psychiatry,* University of Chicago Press, 1952; (editor with Alexander) *Twenty Years of Psychoanalysis,* Norton, 1953; *The Shy Child* (pamphlet), Public Affairs Committee (New York), 1956; (with Bertram David Lewin) *Psychoanalytic Education in the United States,* Norton, 1960; (editor with Alexander) *The Impact of Freudian Psychiatry,* University of Chicago Press, 1961; (with Lillian Ross) *The Player: A Profile of an Art,* Simon & Schuster, 1962; (editor) August Aichhorn, *Delinquency and Child Guidance: Selected Papers,* International Universities Press, 1964. Author of the column, "Your Child," in *Chicago Sun-Times* in the 1950's.

SIDELIGHTS: When Ross consulted Franz Alexander, the renowned psychoanalyst at the University of Chicago, about her desire to study analysis, he told her to go to Vienna. She enrolled at Sigmund Freud's Vienna Institute of Psychoanalysis and was associated with Anna Freud and Helen Deutsche.

The Helen Ross Professorship in Social Welfare Policy was established by the University of Chicago in 1976.

OBITUARIES: Washington Post, August 11, 1978.*

*　　　*　　　*

ROSS, Michael 1905-

PERSONAL: Born June 14, 1905, in Newcastle upon Tyne, England; son of Sir Archibald John Campbell (a marine engineer) and Maria (Gousseva) Ross; married Simone Elise Axelle Brocard, June, 1937 (died August 29, 1978); children: Katya. *Education:* Attended Marlborough College, 1917-21, and University of London. *Politics:* Independent. *Religion:* Roman Catholic. *Home:* 11 Castlenau Mansions, London S.W.13, England. *Agent:* Campbell-Thomson & McLaughlan, 31 Newington Green, London N16 9PU, England.

CAREER: Artist; paintings and drawings represented in museums in the United States, Canada, and England, including National Gallery of Canada; work exhibited in galleries, including Royal Academy and Decre Gallery. Worked in London, England, as an art teacher and as an advertising executive for J. Walter Thompson Co. Has also worked for British Secret Service and as a writer and script reader for British Broadcasting Corp. *Military service:* British Army, Royal Engineers, 1939-45; served in Germany; became major; mentioned in dispatches. *Member:* Royal Geographical Society (fellow), Society of Authors (fellow), Royal Society of Artists (fellow), Berlioz Society. *Awards, honors:* Diploma from Exhibition of Decorative Artists in Monza, Italy, 1937.

WRITINGS: People of the Mirage, Barrie & Rockliff, 1953; (editor and translator) *Scourge of the Eagle* (translation of *L'Opposition a Napoleon*), Sidgwick & Jackson, 1974; *Banners of the King: The War of the Vendee, 1793*, Hippocrene, 1975; *The Reluctant King* (biography of Joseph Bonaparte), Sidgwick & Jackson, 1976; *Cross the Great Desert* (biography of Rene Caillie), Gordon Cremonesi, 1977; *Bougainville, A Biography*, Gordon Cremonesi, 1978.

WORK IN PROGRESS: A biography of Alexandre Dumas the elder; a book on the Acadians of Nova Scotia and their ultimate fate.

SIDELIGHTS: Ross comments: "I am interested in history in general, and French literature and history in particular. I feel that all politicians (including presidents) would benefit from a greater knowledge of history. I am fascinated by Napoleon, much as I dislike him."

Ross enjoys traveling, especially in the more primitive areas of France and northern Spain. He has lived in the Balkans and has also crossed the Sahara desert.

AVOCATIONAL INTERESTS: Classical music.

* * *

ROSS, Wilda 1915-

PERSONAL: Born October 23, 1915, in Santa Barbara, Calif.; married Edward S. Ross, 1942 (divorced, 1971); children: Martha Ross Gauthier, Clark. *Education:* University of California, Berkeley, A.B., 1941. *Home:* 328 Las Casitas Court, Sonoma, Calif. 95476.

CAREER: Technician for Bureau of Insect Identification, Washington, D.C. Developed natural history programs for schools and junior museums. *Member:* Sierra Club, Audubon Society, California Native Plant Society (local co-founder). *Awards, honors:* Golden Junior Literary Guild award, for *Can You Find the Animal?*.

WRITINGS—All for children: *Who Lives in This Log?*, Coward, 1971; *What Did Dinosaurs Eat?*, Coward, 1972; *Can You Find the Animal?*, Coward, 1974; *Cracks and Crannies: What Lives There?*, Coward, 1975; *The Rain Forest: What Lives There?*, Coward, 1977. Editor of local newsletter of California Native Plant Society.

WORK IN PROGRESS: A children's book about tigers born in an animal park.

SIDELIGHTS: Wilda Ross writes: "I am presently establishing a garden of native plants used by California Indians and *padres* at Sonoma Mission. I have traveled on all the continents, collecting insects for a museum, with self-contained research expeditions."

* * *

ROSSITER, (Percival) Stuart (Bryce) 1923-

PERSONAL: Born February 25, 1923, in London, England; son of George Percival (a company secretary) and Mary Louise (Stuart) Rossiter. *Education:* King's College, Cambridge, B.A., 1948, M.A., 1953. *Residence:* London, England.

CAREER: Westminster Reference Library, London, England, assistant librarian, 1950-53; Kent County Library, England, senior assistant at Deal branch, 1954; writer, 1954—. *Military service:* Royal Air Force, fighter controller, 1942-46; became flying officer. *Member:* Guild of Travel Writers, Royal Geographical Society (fellow), Royal Philatelic Society (fellow), Society of Postal Historians (fellow; president, 1977). *Awards, honors:* National and international awards for philatelic exhibitions, including gold medal from Capex in Toronto, Ontario, 1978.

WRITINGS: The London Quiz Book, Benn, 1957; *Blue Guide to Greece*, Rand McNally, 1967, 3rd edition, 1977; *Blue Guide to Malta*, Rand McNally, 1968; *Blue Guide to Yugoslavia: The Adriatic Coast*, Rand McNally, 1972; *Blue Guide to Crete*, Rand McNally, 1973, 2nd edition, 1977; *Postal Communications in the Second World War*, Proud-Bailey, 1980.

Editor—Rossiter was not associated with earlier editions: *Rome and Central Italy*, Benn, 2nd edition, 1964; *Denmark*, Benn, 2nd edition, 1965; (with Litellus Russell Muirhead) *England*, Benn, 7th edition, 1965, 9th edition, 1979; *The South of France: Provence and the French Alps*, Benn, 1966; *Paris*, Rand McNally, 3rd edition, 1968; *Wales*, Rand McNally, 5th edition, 1969; *Rome and Environs*, Rand McNally, 1971; *Northern Italy: From the Alps to Rome*, Benn, 6th edition, 1971; *London*, Rand McNally, 10th edition, 1973, 11th edition, 1978. Contributor to *Postal History International*. Honorary editor of *London Philatelist*, 1975—.

WORK IN PROGRESS: An atlas for stamp collectors, publication by Paddington Press expected in 1980; an autobiography; research for a detailed guide book to Turkey.

* * *

ROTHENBERG, Polly 1916-

PERSONAL: Born March 14, 1916, in Miamisburg, Ohio; daughter of Jerry S. (an engineer) and Maude (a teacher; maiden name, Kessler) Swank; married Maurice Rothenberg, May 8, 1936; children: Carol Rothenberg Oxner, Joan Rothernberg Martin. *Education:* Miami University, Oxford, Ohio, B.A., 1966; also attended Penland School of Art, 1969, Eastern Connecticut State College, 1972, and Georgian College of Applied Art and Science, 1973. *Residence:* Dayton, Ohio.

CAREER: Ceramist, 1966—; writer and photographer, 1969—. *Member:* International Guild of Craft Journalists, Authors, and Photographers, World Crafts Council.

WRITINGS—All self-illustrated; all published by Crown: *Metal Enameling*, 1969; *The Complete Book of Ceramic Art* (Book-of-the-Month Club selection), 1972; *Creative Stained Glass*, 1973; *The Complete Book of Creative Glass Art*, 1974; *Decorating Glass*, 1977. Contributor of articles to *Ceramics Monthly* and *Design*.

WORK IN PROGRESS: Research in archaeology, geology, and geography related to the processes and history of vitreous enamels, ceramic clays, and borosilicates.

SIDELIGHTS: Rothenberg told *CA:* "After returning to Miami University to complete work on my degree, I became discouraged at the lack of good instructive books on the techniques of the art crafts that interested me and vowed to write my own books. I began writing articles on metal enameling and ceramics that formed the nucleus of my first book, *Metal Enameling*. My second, *The Complete Book of Ceramic Art*, is the best-selling and I feel the best of my books.

"The success of all my books is, I think, due to my extensive research and painstaking experimentation in all my processes and to the detailed and complete explanations and illustrations of them in the books. All photographed sequences are executed by me. Extensive travels to photograph artists working in their own studios and their finished work are included as illustrations in my books, along with my own work-in-process. Books showing only an author's work can be monotonous, in my opinion."

AVOCATIONAL INTERESTS: Politics ("My interest in political science led me to realize and appreciate that the pulling and tugging between political groups is very much a part of and important to the democratic process. A strong two-party government is vital to the health and strength of our nation's system.").

* * *

ROTHMAN, Tony 1953-

PERSONAL: Born April 29, 1953, in Philadelphia, Pa.; son of Milton A. (a physicist) and Doris (a psychotherapist; maiden name, Weiss) Rothman. *Education:* Swarthmore College, B.A., 1975; graduate study at Cambridge University, 1975; University of Texas, Ph.D., 1980. *Home:* 1687 Lawrence Rd., Lawrenceville, N.J. 08648. *Office:* Department of Physics, University of Texas, Austin, Tex. 78712.

CAREER: National Radio Astronomy Observatory, Green Bank, W.Va., research assistant, 1974, 1976; University of Texas, Austin, assistant instructor in mathematics, 1978—.

WRITINGS: The World Is Round (science fiction novel), Ballantine, 1978. Contributor to *Isaac Asimov's Science Fiction Magazine* and *ANALOG Science Fact and Fiction.*

WORK IN PROGRESS: Cosmos: The Scenic Route to Heaven, a novel, publication expected in 1981; "The Magician and the Fool," a three-act historical play; research on primordial black hole formation.

SIDELIGHTS: Rothman writes: "I have a great interest in music and once considered a career as an oboist. Although I am now studying general relativity, I still play music as much as possible. My first novel was science fiction, but I think my varied interests will tend to make my future work more eclectic.

"I regard my work in relativity not so much as a career, but as a basis for a world view. Training in physics gives one a methodology useful in almost any endeavor where problem solving is required. The realization that, in physics, one always deals with models rather than 'reality' (whatever that is), has given me the flexibility to examine life situations from various points of view (models). General relativity interests me in particular because it comes closest, of the various subfields in physics, to satisfying a vague religious impulse that most physicists would admit underlies their work.

"Science fiction interests me frankly in terms of its philosophic possibilities, not so much as an adventure-gadget genre. This point of view unfortunately runs counter to sound business sense. How the two will be resolved by me is as yet unclear."

* * *

RUBINS, Jack L(awrence) 1916-

PERSONAL: Born February 25, 1916, in New York, N.Y.; son of Charles Russell (in sales) and Eva (Rubin) Rubins; married Tamara Kreinine, June 8, 1943; children: Rosette Ellen Rubins Boyer, Marlene Linda Rubins Pick. *Education:* City College (now of the City University of New York), B.S. (cum laude), 1937; University of Geneva, B.M.S., 1942, M.D., 1943; American Institute of Psychoanalysis, certificate in psychoanalysis, 1955. *Politics:* Democrat. *Religion:* Jewish. *Home:* 82-15 234th St., Queens Village, N.Y. 11427. *Office:* 125 East 87th St., New York, N.Y. 10028.

CAREER: Internships and residencies in psychiatry and neurology, Geneva, Switzerland, and New York City, 1942-48; private practice of psychiatry and psychoanalysis, 1948—. Member of faculty at New School for Social Research, 1955-68; lecturer at American Institute for Psychoanalysis, 1955-77; associate clinical professor at New York Medical College, 1960—. Attending psychoanalyst at Karen Horney Clinic, 1955—; chief of psychiatry and director of Mental Health Clinic at Flushing Hospital, 1974—. *Wartime service:* Free French Forces, volunteer physician, 1944.

MEMBER: International Federation of Psychotherapy, International Association of Social Psychiatry (fellow), American Psychiatric Association (fellow) American Academy of Psychoanalysis (fellow), American Association for Social Psychiatry (fellow), Association of American Medical Colleges (fellow), Royal Society of Health (fellow), Association for the Advancement of Psychoanalysis (past president), Swiss Psychiatric Society (honorary member), New York State Medical Society, New York County Medical Society, Queens County Psychiatric Society (past president), Queens County Mental Health Society. *Awards, honors:* Gralnick Award from American Institute of Psychoanalysis, 1957.

WRITINGS: (Editor) *New Developments in Horney Psychoanalysis,* Robert E. Krieger, 1974; *Karen Horney: Gentle Rebel of Psychoanalysis,* Dial, 1978.

Contributor: H. English and A. English, editors, *Dictionary of Psychological and Psychoanalytic Terms,* Longmans, Green, 1958; J. Masserman, editor, *Science and Psychoanalysis,* Grune, Volume VII, 1963, Volume XI, 1967; H. Kelman, editor, *New Perspectives in Psychoanalysis,* Norton, 1967; A. Freedman and H. Sadock, editors, *Comprehensive Textbook of Psychiatry,* Williams & Wilkins, 1967; D. Siva-Sankar, editor, *Schizophrenia: Current Concepts and Research,* Plenum, 1969. Contributor of about one hundred-twenty articles to medical journals.

WORK IN PROGRESS: Holistic-Dynamic Psychoanalysis: The Horney Theories Today, three volumes, publication expected in 1982.

SIDELIGHTS: Rubin writes: "I am most qualified to write on the use of the Horney theories of psychoanalysis, a subject which is not well-known or accurately known in the public and professional world. Since I have studied and worked in Switzerland, I would like to see the theories spread to Europe."

"My last biographical book was not only the story of Karen Horney's life, but an attempt to place her life in the context of the historical events of the period 1885-1950 and to show how her ideas were the product of both her personal development and certain social changes. Because her theories take into account the influence of social forces—in contrast to the classical Freudian analytic theories—I believe they are most relevant to what most people are experiencing in today's troubled times. My new work will be devoted to clarifying these theories and to showing how they are applicable to the psychological problems of the present."

Karen Horney: Gentle Rebel of Psychoanalysis was described by Robert Kirsh as "a thoughtful and readable biography." Other critics noted Rubin's unbiased description of the factional quarrels among New York psychiatrists and his avoidance of speculations on Horney's personal life. *Manchester Guardian* commented: "Between the lines of his conscientious book, the patient reader can discern the firm profile of an outstanding doctor and an impressive, if poignantly contradictory, human being."

BIOGRAPHICAL/CRITICAL SOURCES: Los Angeles

Times, August 9, 1978; *Newsweek,* August 21, 1978; *Newsday,* October 22, 1978; *Manchester Guardian,* March 9, 1979.

* * *

RULFO, Juan 1918-

PERSONAL: Born May 16, 1918, in Sayula, Jalisco, Mexico. *Education:* Attended University of Guadalajara, and University of Mexico City. *Residence:* Mexico City, Mexico. *Office:* Centro Mexicano de Escritores, Valle Arizpe, 18 Mexico D.F. 12, Mexico.

CAREER: National Institute for Indigenous Studies, Mexico City, Mexico, director of editorial department. Adviser to young writers at Centro Mexicano de Escritores. *Member:* Centro Mexicano de Escritores (fellow).

WRITINGS: El llano en llamas y otros cuentos, Fondo de Cultura Economica, 1953, translation by George D. Schade published as *The Burning Plain and Other Stories,* University of Texas Press, 1967, 2nd Spanish edition, corrected and augmented, Fondo de Cultura Economica, 1970; *Pedro Paramo* (novel), Fondo de Cultura Economica, 1955, translation by Lysander Kemp published under same title, Grove, 1959; (contributor) Abelardo Gomez Benoit, editor, *Antologia contemporanea del cuento hispano-americano* (title means "A Contemporary Anthology of the Hispanic-American Story"), Instituto Latinoamericano de Vinculacion Cultural, 1964; (contributor) *Cronicas de Latinoamericano,* Editorial Jorge Alvarez, 1968; Reina Roffe, compiler, *Autobiographia armada,* Ediciones Corregidor, 1973. Collaborator with Juan Arreola on the review *Pan.*

SIDELIGHTS: Two works of fiction, *The Burning Plain and Other Stories* and *Pedro Paramo,* have earned Rulfo his international reputation as perhaps the best of Latin America's writers. In *The Burning Plain,* Rulfo depicts the harsh relationship between a parched and primitive Mexican landscape and the bitter, tragic lives of its inhabitants. "To live, in Rulfo, is to bleed to death," remarked Luis Harss and Barbara Dohmann. "The pulse of the days beats hard, carrying off hope, gutting life at the core, spilling forces, emptying illusions. . . . It is the ability to close in suddenly and strike home that at moments gives Rulfo the dignity of a tragedian." The force of his fiction, they continued, derives from a discipline and economy of language that often blurs the distinction between prose and poetry. James Nelson Goodsell added: "Along with his fellow Mexicans, Carlos Fuentes and Rosario Castellanos, Rulfo is more concerned with technique and vigorous description than with large social ills." The novel *Pedro Paramo,* however, reveals a depth of vision that can accomodate both the artistic concerns of the novelist and the particular and universal implications of Mexican history.

The story of *Pedro Paramo* tells of Paramo's feudal dominance over the life of the town Comala and its people. A powerful political boss and landowner, Paramo exploits the townspeople for years until they finally starve to death. We learn half-way through the novel, surprisingly, that all the characters are dead; the story all along has been the remembered history of ghosts conversing beneath the grave. It is an indication of the technical difficulties Rulfo confronts—flashbacks, interior monologues and dialogues, atemporal time sequences—to creat what Kessel Schwartz described as "an ambiguous and magical world, a kind of timeless fable of life and death." In his discussion of Rulfo's technique, Luis Leal observed: "The transitions between the scenes are not carried out by formal linking elements,

but, like the stanzas of a poem, the scenes are juxtaposed, united only by the central theme and lyrical motifs." The implications of Paramo's life, Schwartz reflected, reverberate deep within the Mexican soul. "Pedro Paramo, even though he is dead, still lives just as the good and the bad and fear and sorrow still live on in Mexican towns and in the Mexican spirit." It is a life, he explained, that by its example confirms a fatalistic and pessimistic view of the universe and, as Rulfo wrote, demonstrates the "futility of all history in its ineffectual consequences and its essentially barbaric nature." The novel's tragic hope, Schwartz noted, is for a new dawn of life, "if nowhere else than beyond death."

BIOGRAPHICAL/CRITICAL SOURCES: Luis Harss and Barbara Dohmann, *Into the Mainstream: Conversations With Latin-American Writers,* Harper, 1967; *Christian Science Monitor,* January 4, 1968; *Hispania,* December, 1971, September, 1974, March, 1975; Kessel Schwartz, *A New History of Spanish American Fiction,* Volume II, University of Miami Press, 1971; *National Observer,* March 24, 1973; *English Journal,* January, 1974; Merlin H. Forster, editor, *Tradition and Renewal: Essays on Twentieth Century Latin American Literature and Culture,* University of Illinois Press, 1975; *Contemporary Literary Criticism,* Volume 8, Gale, 1978.*

* * *

RUSINOW, Dennison I. 1930-

PERSONAL: Born October 29, 1930, in Newark, N.J.; son of Sydney I. and Eulalie (a social worker and executive; maiden name, Menuez) Rusinow; married Mary Worthington, June 19, 1965; children: Alison Lucy, Tamara Craig. *Education:* Duke University, B.A., 1952; New College, Oxford, B.A., 1954, M.A., 1959; St. Antony's College, Oxford, D.Phil., 1963. *Home:* Baumgartenstrasse 91, Vienna, Austria A-1140. *Office:* American Universities Field Staff, P.O. Box 150, Hanover, N.H. 03755.

CAREER: American Universities Field Staff, Hanover, N.H., associate for Southeast Europe, 1963—, associate director, 1973-76. Adjunct lecturer at California Institute of Technology, 1971; adjunct professor of Dartmouth College, 1975-76. Member of board of governors and board of trustees of Institute of Current World Affairs, 1967-71, 1975-79. *Military service:* U.S. Navy, 1955-58. U.S. Naval Reserve; became lieutenant junior grade. *Awards, honors:* Rhodes scholar at Oxford University, 1952; fellow of Institute of Current World Affairs, 1958-63.

WRITINGS: Italy's Austrian Heritage, Clarendon Press, 1969; *The Yugoslav Experiment, 1948-1974,* University of California Press, 1977. Contributor of more than fifty articles to professional journals and journals in the arts, including *Common Ground* and *Antioch Review,* and to newspapers.

WORK IN PROGRESS: Research on nationalism and the life and times of the nation-state in today's world, and on development, life, and mores in Danubian and Adriatic Europe.

SIDELIGHTS: Rusinow comments that his goal is "observation and scholarly journalism from an important, complex, and fascinating part of the world, with equal emphasis on political and social developments, and on human lives and hopes, motivated by America's manifest need for more interest in and information about the world at large, and by the fun of living in and observing these parts of the world."

RYCKMANS, Pierre 1935-
(Simon Leys)

PERSONAL: Born September 28, 1935, in Brussels, Belgium; married Han-Fang; children: four. *Education:* University of Louvain, received Ph.D. and LL.D. *Office address:* Department of Chinese, Australian National University, Box 4, Canberra Australian Capital Territory, 2600 Australia.

CAREER: Art historian; sinologist. Previously taught history of art at Chinese University of Hong Kong; currently teacher of Chinese literature at Australian National University.

WRITINGS: La Vie et l'oeuvre de Su Renshan, rebelle, peintre, et fou, 1814-1849?, two volumes, 1970, translation by Angharad Pimpaneau published as *The Life and Work of Su Renshan: Rebel, Painter, and Madman, 1814-1849?*, Centre de publication de l'U. E. R. Extreme-Orient-Asie du Sud-Est de l'Universite de Paris, 1970; *Les "Propos sur la peinture" de Shitao* (title means "A Study of Shitao's *Treatise on Painting*"), Institut belge des hautes etudes chinoises (Brussels), 1970; (under pseudonym Simon Leys) *Les Habits neufs du president Mao, chronique de la revolution culturelle*, Champ, 1971, translation by Carol Appleyard and Patrick Goode published as *The Chairman's New Clothes: Mao and the Cultural Revolution*, St. Martin's, 1977; (under pseudonym Simon Leys) *Ombres chinoises*, Union general d'editions, 1975, revised and enlarged edition with preface by Jean-Francois Revel, Laffont, 1978, translation published as *Chinese Shadows*, Viking, 1977; (under pseudonym Simon Leys) *Images brisees*, Laffont, 1976, translation published as *Broken Images*, Allison & Busby, 1979. Contributor to periodicals, including *Newsweek, New Republic, Dissent*, and *L'Express*.

WORK IN PROGRESS: Research on modern Chinese literature and on Chinese painting and aesthetics; translating literary works from Chinese into French.

SIDELIGHTS: Chinese Shadows was widely reviewed and especially well received among sinologists in France. In the book, Ryckmans blames Maoism for "having destroyed the cultural and human values of the past only to retain its vices; it prolongs in its own interest the habits of feudalism and military bureaucracy." Yet visitors to China, many of whom are intellectuals, often return home raving about the country and its people. Ryckmans decided to write *Chinese Shadows* to speak up against this "indiscriminate and ill-informed piety toward all things Chinese."

John Updike commented in the *New Yorker* that *Chinese Shadows* "lacks the depth that shadows give; Mr. Leys sounds a thin note of personal rejection, in these jottings of a frustrated lover of a vanished civilization." But F. B. Randall countered in *Nation*: "Leys might have written a less rambling and more comprehensive book. He might have had more charity for sinners and fools. He might have made greater efforts to keep his spleen from overmastering his balance. But then he would not have been so effective a barrier in a time of great need." *Newsweek* critic Russell Watson called *Chinese Shadows* an "engagingly cranky work" which is essentially an "iconoclastic guidebook."

Ryckmans defended his book against some of its critics when he told *CA:* "The purpose and meaning of *Chinese Shadows* have been largely misunderstood in the United States. The book actually is *not* concerned with tourism nor with cultural nostalgias. It is an attempt to criticize Maoism from a leftist point of view. Starting from first-hand observation, it raises questions regarding the very nature of the Maoist regime: instead of calling it 'socialist' and 'revolutionary,' would it not be more aptly qualified as 'bureaucratic' and 'totalitarian'?

"What I wrote has since been vindicated by the official press in the People's Republic, which is now exposing far more thoroughly and far more ferociously the dark side of Maoism. A Chinese translation of *Chinese Shadows* (in excerpts) was officially distributed in China last year, in ten million copies."

Earlier in the decade, Ryckmans had surmised that officials in Peking would not readmit him to China if they were aware of his true identity. Consequently, he chose to use a pseudonym, Simon Leys, when writing books critical of the country. In a review of the first book written under that name, *Chairman Mao's New Clothes*, John Fairbank called it "one of the most caustic exposes by a Sinologist of the Cultural Revolution's basically anti-intellectual attack on China's cultural heritage." Ryckmans's identity as author of the books written under the Leys pseudonym has since become known.

Ryckmans lived for ten years in East Asia: Taiwan, Singapore, Japan, Hong Kong, and China. His experiences formed the basis of *Chinese Shadows*.

BIOGRAPHICAL/CRITICAL SOURCES: Nation, July 2, 1977; *New Republic*, August 6-13, 1977; *New York Times Book Review*, August 28, 1977; *Newsweek*, September 12, 1977; *New York Review of Books*, September 29, 1977; *New Yorker*, October 24, 1977; *National Review*, October 28, 1977; *Christian Science Monitor*, November 15, 1977; Simon Leys, *Chinese Shadows*, Viking, 1977; *Commentary*, January, 1978.

*　　*　　*

RYDER, Rowland (Vint) 1914-

PERSONAL: Born March 5, 1914, in Birmingham, England; son of Rowland Vint (a county cricket secretary) and Cicely (Matthews) Ryder; married Margaret Eileen Baker (a teacher). *Education:* Exeter College, Oxford, M.A., 1946. *Home:* 14 North Dr., Edgbaston, Birmingham 5, England.

CAREER: Free-lance writer and assistant schoolmaster, 1937—. *Military service:* British Army, Royal Armoured Corps, 1940-45; received Africa Star. *Member:* Old Edwardians Association, Warwickshire County Cricket Club.

WRITINGS: Edith Cavell, Stein & Day, 1975; *Ravenstein: Portrait of a German General*, Hippocrene, 1978.

Author of documentary play, "Patriotism Is Not Enough," broadcast by BBC-4 Radio, 1975.

WORK IN PROGRESS: "Various writings."

S

SABAROFF, Rose Epstein 1918-

PERSONAL: Born September 4, 1918, in Cleveland, Ohio, daughter of Hyman Israel (in business) and Bertha (in politics; maiden name, Glaser) Epstein; married Bernard J. Sabaroff (a college professor), December 28, 1940; children: Ronald Asher, Nina Katya. *Education:* University of Arizona, B.A., 1941; San Francisco State College (now University), M.A., 1954; Stanford University, Ed.D., 1957. *Home:* 2501 Capistrano St., Blacksburg, Va. 24060. *Office:* Department of Curriculum and Instruction, College of Education, Virginia Polytechnic Institute and State University, 315 WMG, Blacksburg, Va. 24061.

CAREER: Elementary school teacher in San Francisco, Calif., 1951-55; Stanford University, Stanford, Calif., supervisor of student teachers, 1956-57; Oregon State University, Corvallis, assistant professor of education, 1958-61; Harvard University, Cambridge, Mass., lecturer in education, 1961-66; Virginia Polytechnic Institute and State University, Blacksburg, associate professor, 1967-69, professor of education, 1969—. *Member:* International Reading Association, American Educational Research Association, National Education Association, Virginia Professors of Reading (president, 1975-77), Gamma Theta Upsilon, Pi Lambda Theta, Phi Delta Kappa. *Awards, honors:* Award from National Geographic Society, 1968, for articles in *Journal of Geography;* research award from Virginia Educational Research Association, 1977.

WRITINGS: Integrated Linguistic Approach to Reading, Silver Burdett, 1966; (with R. P. Hanna and others) *Geography in the Teaching of Social Studies,* Houghton, 1966; (with M. A. Hanna) *The Open Classroom,* Scarecrow, 1974; *Teaching Reading With a Linguistic Approach,* Virginia Polytechnic Institute and State University Press, 1978; *Cognitive Style and Reading Behavior,* Reading Improvement, 1979; *Diagnosis and Treatment of Reading Disabilities: A Resource Guide,* Virginia Polytechnic Institute and State University Press, 1979. Contributor to education and geography journals.

WORK IN PROGRESS: Games to Play for Reading With a Linguistic Approach; comparative research on education in Norway, Romania, Yugoslavia, and Bavaria.

SIDELIGHTS: Rose Sabaroff writes: "I have always been interested in finding ways to help children with learning problems—particularly in reading. I have conducted research with Mexican-American children in Arizona, urban black children in Boston, and Appalachian white children in southwest Virginia. I find many of the problems to be related to cultural differences and poverty. Much of my professional writing has been to help teachers find better ways of teaching children to read."

*   *   *

SACHS, (Stewart) Harvey 1946-

PERSONAL: Born June 8, 1946, in Cleveland, Ohio; son of Milton William (a postal clerk) and Bella (a secretary; maiden name, Bloom) Sachs; married Barbara Gogolick (a harpsichordist), September 30, 1967. *Education:* Attended Cleveland Institute of Music, 1960-64, Oberlin College, 1964-65, Mannes College of Music, 1965-66, and University of Toronto, 1968-71. *Home:* 47 Glenhill Close, Finchley, London N.3, England.

CAREER: Lake Erie Opera Theatre, Cleveland, Ohio, rehearsal assistant, 1964; WCLV-FM Radio, Cleveland, Ohio, guest writer, 1964-66; piano teacher and instrumental ensemble instructor, Toronto, Ontario, 1967-70; Peterborough Symphony Orchestra, Peterborough, Ontario, conductor and musical director, 1972-75. Guest conductor of ensembles and orchestras in Canada and Italy, 1970—; guest lecturer at Canadian and Italian universities and schools of music, 1972—. Radio writer for Canadian Broadcasting Corp., 1973. *Awards, honors:* First prize from Heinz Unger Conducting Competition in Toronto, Ontario, 1970; Canada Council grants, 1971, 1972, 1974.

WRITINGS: Toscanini, Lippincott, 1978.

WORK IN PROGRESS: A book on some famous conductors of the first half of the twentieth century, publication by Weidenfeld expected in 1981.

SIDELIGHTS: Sachs wrote to *CA:* "My interest in Toscanini, which began when I was fifteen, grew out of a very intense interest in music that had begun several years earlier. Even then he seemed to me a model of artistic and human integrity; and he remains for me now not just another highly competent baton wielder, but someone who maintained and lived up to some very firm convictions regarding his position as an artist and as a member of society.

"My second book will examine the working methods of a few of the most important conductors of this century. It will be based on filmed and recorded documentation and on the testimony of instrumentalists, singers, and others who worked with these people. My hope is that my twenty years experience in watching conductors great and small in rehearsal, and my own practical conducting experience, will help me to explain to musicians and laymen alike the conductor's profession as conceived by some of that profession's leading exponents."

* * *

St. JAMES, Bernard

PERSONAL: Born in Berlin, Germany; came to the United States. *Education:* City College (now of the City University of New York), received B.A.; University of California, Los Angeles, received M.A.. *Agent:* Wieser & Wieser, Inc., 52 Vanderbilt Ave., Room 1402, New York, N.Y. 10017.

CAREER: Writer. Worked as an electrical worker, driver for a television news truck, teacher, and record company president. *Military service:* U.S. Army, Signal Corps. *Member:* Mystery Writers of America.

WRITINGS: April Thirtieth (novel), Harper, 1978; *The Scrapfaggot Witch* (novel), Harper, 1979.

WORK IN PROGRESS: Another novel; a documentary script for public television; a treatment for a motion picture script.

SIDELIGHTS: St. James writes: "I was born in Berlin, Germany, of Romanian parents, grew up in Paris, and then in New York City. I have lived in Hollywood, California, and Cambridge, Massachusetts. My dream and ambition has long been to breed race horses in Ireland (where I hope to live)." *Avocational interests:* Listening to jazz.

* * *

SALOMON, Irving 1897-1979

OBITUARY NOTICE: Born August 23, 1897, in Chicago, Ill.; died January 7, 1979, in San Diego, Calif. Author and businessman who helped develop both the Peace Corps and public television. Salomon wrote *Retire and Be Happy.* Obituaries and other sources: *Who's Who in World Jewry,* Pitman, 1972; *Who's Who in America,* 40th edition, Marquis, 1978; *Chicago Tribune,* January 9, 1979.

* * *

SALTZMAN, Marvin L(ouis) 1922-

PERSONAL: Born March 29, 1922, in Omaha, Neb.; son of Samuel (a merchant) and Dorette (Adler) Saltzman; married Barbara Freed (a publisher), May 7, 1944; children: Kathryn Saltzman Muileman, Stephen. *Education:* Attended University of California, Los Angeles, 1939-42, U.S. Coast Guard Academy, 1943, Loyola University, Los Angeles, Calif., 1966, and Loyola Law School, 1966-68; University of West Los Angeles, J.D., 1970. *Office:* 27540 Pacific Coast Highway, Malibu, Calif. 90265.

CAREER: Omaha Eagle, Omaha, Neb., editor and publisher, 1934; *Los Angeles Herald-Express,* Los Angeles, Calif., assistant radio editor, 1935-36; *Blue & White Daily,* Los Angeles, editor, 1939; *Media Agencies Clients,* Beverly Hills, Calif., founder, editor, and publisher, 1951-65; writer of travel books, 1971—. President of Saltzman Co. (publishing company), 1971—. *Member:* Zeta Beta Tau, Alpha Delta Sigma, Phi Alpha Delta. *Awards, honors:* Named man of the year by Western States Advertising Agencies Association, 1963.

WRITINGS: (With daughter, Kathryn S. Muileman) *Eurail Guide: How to Travel Europe and All the World by Train,* Saltzman Co., 1971, 9th edition, 1979.

WORK IN PROGRESS: Annual revisions of *Eurail Guide;* a contemporary novel; a nonfiction book.

SIDELIGHTS: Saltzman writes: "In 1973, my wife and I became the first people to make the longest (8,013 miles) train ride in the world, from Lisbon to Moscow, and then across Siberia to Khabarovsk. We have traveled by train across the Arctic Circle and across the equator.

"Travel is the only way to comprehend the universality of religion, history, economics, politics, culture, sociology, and the human personality. Travel writing makes it easier for others to acquire knowledge of the world and mankind by providing them with the information needed in order to travel widely."

AVOCATIONAL INTERESTS: Orchid genealogy, gardening, deep sea fishing, philology, collecting matchbooks, swizzle sticks, and last editions of once-prominent newspapers and magazines.

* * *

SAND, Margaret 1932-

PERSONAL: Born November 2, 1932, in St. Louis, Mo.; daughter of Henry John (a compiler of catalogs) and Anna Andres (Koopmann) Kollenberg. *Education:* Attended St. Louis University, 1950-51, and Washington University, St. Louis, Mo., 1951-53; also studied at American Theatre Wing, 1954-55. *Residence:* St. Louis, Mo. *Agent:* Anita Diamant, Writer's Workshop, Inc., 51 East 42nd St., New York, N.Y. 10017. *Office:* Storz Instrument Co., 3365 Tree Court Industrial Blvd., St. Louis, Mo. 63122.

CAREER: Secretary in New York, N.Y., 1954-58; secretary and office manager in St. Louis, Mo., 1959-60; Wagner Electric Corp., St. Louis, Mo., export correspondent, 1960-68; worked as legal secretary, 1968-70; Storz Instrument Co., St. Louis, Mo., export correspondent, 1970—. Active in local amateur drama productions.

WRITINGS: The Chanting of Children (novel), Coward, 1978.

WORK IN PROGRESS: Another novel.

SIDELIGHTS: Margaret Sand writes: "As a child I preferred reading to playing or doing anything else, and I have been addicted to reading ever since. I was quite young when I decided I wanted to write myself. I speak and write Spanish (necessary in my work). I am not much of a joiner, but I support Women's Liberation in every way I can.

"My book took many years to grow from the germ of an idea planted in my imagination by a play I heard on the radio as a child. I was so young, in fact, that when I try to recall the dual-sister relationship presented in that play, I don't think I was able to understand whether there really were two sisters or whether the sinister, mysterious one was the 'extremely articulate alter ego' I had the psychiatrist speak of in my book.

Subsequently I knew two real sisters, one of whom was an invalid and eventually died. I never knew what the relationship was between them, but I found it more and more fascinating to speculate about it, until finally the book was ready to be written."

AVOCATIONAL INTERESTS: The theater.

* * *

SANDERS, D(onald) G(len) 1899-

PERSONAL: Born October 17, 1899, in Hemlock, Ohio;

son of John F. (a miner) and Leota Sanders; married Irene Lennon, June 1, 1927; children: Jane Sanders Curie, Sandra Sanders Breuer. *Home:* 525 South Walnut St., Orrville, Ohio 44667. *Agent:* John Schaffner Literary Agency, 425 East 51st St., New York, N.Y. 10022.

CAREER: Worked as telegrapher for Pennsylvania Railroad, 1915-65; writer, 1978—. *Member:* Brotherhood of Railway, Airline and Steamship Clerks, Freight Handlers, Express and Station Employees.

WRITINGS: The Brasspounder, Hawthorn, 1978.

SIDELIGHTS: Sanders told *CA:* "Morse telegraphy was the missing link that would tie together the vast railroad systems of the U.S.A. and Canada some 125 years ago. In railroad, communications were and are both vital and viable. Without the all-out efforts of railroads on this continent, the outcome of World Wars I and II might have been something quite different, and history thus rewritten. On the railroads telegraphing was an around-the-clock job, and thus did not attract too many women—who would be relegated to night work in their beginning years, due to the rules of seniority. But those who did make the grade were quite as capable as anyone else. It might be added here that telegraphers fell into two general categories—the 'op' and the 'ham.' Telegraphing was obviously my lifework. It was not just a job but a career—a fascinating one. I think I can safely add that the 'monotony of the assembly line' never touched the Morse man. On the contrary he was afforded a certain measure of respect and acclaim. My book, *The Brasspounder,* was written at the insistence of my family. Perhaps I should add here that the Morse man was known on the wire by his 'sine'—of one or two letters. I 'sined' GS."

* * *

SANDERS, Scott Russell 1945-

PERSONAL: Born October 26, 1945, in Memphis, Tenn.; son of Greeley Ray (in farming and industrial relations) and Eva (Solomon) Sanders; married Ruth Ann McClure (a teacher), August 27, 1967; children: Eva Rachel, Jesse Solomon. *Education:* Brown University, B.A. (summa cum laude), 1967; Cambridge University, Ph.D., 1971. *Home:* 1113 East Wylie St., Bloomington, Ind. 47401. *Office:* Department of English, Indiana University, Bloomington, Ind. 47401.

CAREER: Indiana University, Bloomington, assistant professor, 1971-74, associate professor of English, 1975—. *Member:* War Resisters International, Science Fiction writers of America, Friends of the Earth, Sierra Club, Phi Beta Kappa. *Awards, honors:* Woodrow Wilson fellow, 1967-68; Danforth fellow, 1967-71; Marshall Scholar, 1967-71; Bennett fellow in creative writing, 1974-75.

WRITINGS: D. H. Lawrence: The World of the Major Novels, Viking, 1974. Author of film guides. Author of "One Man's Fiction," a column in *Chicago Sun-Times,* 1977—. Contributor of stories, articles, and reviews to literary journals, including *Transatlantic Review, Telos,* and *Ohio Review.* Fiction editor of *Cambridge Review,* 1969-71, and *Minnesota Review,* 1976—; advisory editor of *Indiana Writes;* member of editorial board of *Structuralist Review.*

WORK IN PROGRESS: Fetching the Dead, a collection of previously-published stories; *Wilderness Plots,* stories on the settlement of the Ohio Valley; *Warchild,* a novel linking the anti-Vietnam movement to the space program; *Bad Man Ballad,* a novel; *The Imagination of Nature,* nonfiction; a book on science fiction films; *Terrarium,* a science fiction novel.

SIDELIGHTS: Sanders writes: "I have long been divided, in my life and in my work, between science and the arts. Early on, in graduate study, this took the form of choosing literary studies rather than theoretical physics. My novel, *Warchild,* concerns the images of science alive in the minds of persons growing up in the 1950's and 1960's. My other fiction has alternated between historical studies of the settlement of the Ohio Valley and science fictional studies of the twenty-first century.

"In all of my fiction, regardless of period or style, I am concerned with the ways in which human beings come to terms with the practical problems of living on the planet, in nature. I am also concerned with the life of communities, more than with the life of isolated individuals: a concern not much in fashion in our time.

"My criticism, heavily influenced by the work of the British scholar, Raymond Williams, is sociological: I am concerned with the ways in which ideas and literary forms emerge in relation to specific social/historical conditions. In my nonfiction I am concerned with the ways in which authors have represented nature.

"I have been active in working on little magazines, and feel their health is a good gauge of the health of literature at any given time. I have also worked against the Vietnam war, in favor of environmental protection and wilderness preservation. Marriage and childrearing are important influences on the shaping of my imagination."

AVOCATIONAL INTERESTS: Building, hiking, running, wild flowers, voyaging.

* * *

SANDLER, Benjamin P. 1902(?)-1979

OBITUARY NOTICE: Born c. 1902; died in 1979, in Asheville, N.C. Nutrition expert and author of books in his field. During the 1940's, Sandler theorized that tuberculosis and polio were related to the amount of sugar and starches in diets. His writings include *Diet Prevents Polio* and *How to Prevent Heart Attacks.* Obituaries and other sources: *New York Times,* May 23, 1979.

* * *

SANDROF, Ivan 1912(?)-1979

OBITUARY NOTICE: Born c. 1912 in Gardner, Mass.; died February 1, 1979, in Worcester, Mass. Writer who was literary editor of *Worcester Telegram* from 1960 to 1976. He was the founder of the National Book Critics Circle. His own writings include history books and pieces for *New Yorker* and *Esquire.* Obituaries and other sources: *New York Times,* February 3, 1979; *Publishers Weekly,* May 5, 1975, February 12, 1979.

* * *

SANGER, Richard H. 1905(?)-1979

OBITUARY NOTICE: Born c. 1905; died March 20, 1979, in Solana Beach, Calif. Author and Foreign Service associate specializing in the Middle East. Sanger's work took him to Lebanon, Jordan, Africa, and the Soviet Union, where he helped construct Moscow's subway. His writings include *The Arabian Peninsula* and *Where the Jordan Flows.* Obituaries and other sources: *Washington Post,* March 30, 1979.

* * *

SANGREY, Dawn 1942-

PERSONAL: Born February 11, 1942, in Lancaster, Pa.;

daughter of Abram W. (a minister) and Dorothy (Herr) Sangrey; married Paul McKenna Fargis (a book publisher), April 23, 1977. *Education:* Mount Holyoke College, B.A., 1963; Johns Hopkins University, M.A.T., 1964. *Home and office:* 200 Haines Rd., Bedford Hills, N.Y. 10507. *Agent:* Elaine Markson Literary Agency, Inc., 44 Greenwich Ave., New York, N.Y. 10011.

CAREER: High school English teacher in Pelham, N.Y., 1964-66, and Scarsdale, N.Y., 1966-72; D. Van Nostrand Co., New York City, textbook editor, 1972-74; Latham Publishing Co., New York City, textbook editor, 1974-76; freelance writer and editor, 1976—. Adjunct lecturer at Manhattan Community College of the City University of New York, 1974. Member of board of directors of long-termers committee at Bedford Hills Correctional Facility; member of National Organization of Victim Assistance.

WRITINGS: (With Morton Bard) *The Crime Victim's Book,* Basic Books, 1979.

WORK IN PROGRESS: A book about the impact of the women's movement on contemporary marriage, completion expected in 1981.

SIDELIGHTS: Sangrey commented: "Being human is a difficult business that is made easier when we tell each other what it is like for us. My work is focused on the ways in which people manage and explain their lives, how we adjust to the things that change and affirm the things that remain constant. Conversations with (extra) ordinary people are the greatest resource for this work; they understand more deeply than any self-styled expert."

In writing *The Crime Victim's Book,* Sangrey and her coauthor, psychology professor Martin Bard, intended to meet the emotional needs of crime victims. The authors contend "that much of the victim's suffering is unnecessary, that there are strategies for dealing with it," wrote Anatole Broyard. Victims often become disoriented after the event, unable to explain the crime and the seemingly chaotic world in which it occurred. What they need, according to the authors, is sympathy and a chance to air their feelings. "Ventilation is often the only expression of his feelings that he will get," continued Broyard. "For even if the criminal is caught, he may not be convicted.... The victim needs to be reassured that he is not a loser or a failure who has been 'used' by a smarter, stronger criminal. He needs to realize that his feeling of contamination, of being stigmatized, is an expression of social aversion to the crime, and not to him." *The Crime Victim's Book* gives the often forgotten victim some long overdue help towards his own rehabilitation.

BIOGRAPHICAL/CRITICAL SOURCES: New York Times, February 3, 1979.

* * *

SATPREM 1923-

PERSONAL: Name originally Bernard Enginger; known as Satprem since 1957; born October 30, 1923, in Paris, France; son of Maurice (a chemical engineer) and Marie-Louise (Le Gloahec) Enginger. *Education:* Educated in Paris, France. *Residence:* New Delhi, India. *Mailing address:* Institut de Recherches Evolutives, 32 Ave. de l'Oberservatoire, 75014 Paris, France.

CAREER: French Colonial Government, Pondicherry, India, chief of information service, 1946-49; editor, writer, and translator, 1953—.

WRITINGS: L'Orpailleur (novel), Editions du Seuil, 1960; *Sri Aurobindo; ou, L'Aventure de la conscience,* Buchet/Chastel, 1964, translation by Tehmi published as *Sri Aurobindo; or, The Adventure of Consciousness,* Harper, 1968, 3rd edition, Sri Aurobindo Ashram, 1970; *Le Grand Sens* (monograph), Ashram Press, 1969, translation by Sujata Nahar published as *The Great Sense,* Ashram Press, 1969; *Sri Aurobindo et l'avenir de la terre* (radio broadcast), Ashram Press, 1973, translation by Maggi Lichi published as *Sri Aurobindo and the Earth's Future,* Ashram Press, 1973; *La Genese du surhomme: Essai d'evolution experimentale,* Ashram Press, 1971, translation by Roger Toll published as *On the Way to Supermanhood,* in press; *Par le corps de la terre; ou, Le Sannyasin* (novel), R. Laffont, 1974, translation by Marianna Fitzpatrick published as *By the Body of Earth,* Harper, 1978; *Mere,* Volume I: *Le Materialisme divin,* Volume II: *L'Espece nouvelle,* Volume III: *La Transformation de la mort,* R. Laffont, 1976, translation by M. De La Foret published as *Mother; or, The Divine Materialism,* Mother's Institute of Research (New Delhi), 1977; *L'-Agenda de l'Action Supramentale sur la Terre,* thirteen volumes, Institute of Evolutionary Research, 1978-82, translation published as *The Agenda of the Supramental Action on Earth,* 1979-83.

SIDELIGHTS: During World War II Satprem was active in the French Resistance movement. He was arrested by the Gestapo at the age of twenty and imprisoned in concentration camps for nearly two years. After his release he traveled to Egypt, then India. In Pondicherry he met the Indian sage Sri Aurobindo and the sage's French collaborator, "the Mother."

In 1949 Satprem began a series of adventures and explorations in the jungles of South America, which later formed the basis of his first novel, and in Africa. In 1953 he returned to India and became a *sannyasi,* or wandering monk, which served as the basis of his second novel. He has lived in Pondicherry since 1958, devoting himself to Sri Aurobindo and, until her death, to "the Mother."

* * *

SAUERHAFT, Stan 1926-

PERSONAL: Born November 25, 1926, in New York, N.Y.; son of Al and Rae Sauerhaft; married Rosalie Tolkin, October 28, 1951; children: Richard Craig, Douglas Clark, Robert James. *Education:* University of Michigan, B.A., 1948, M.A., 1949. *Home:* 21 Windmill Pl., Armonk, N.Y. 10504. *Office:* Hill & Knowlton, Inc., 633 Third Ave., New York, N.Y. 10017.

CAREER: McCann-Erickson, Inc., New York City, vice-president and head of creative plans board for Communications Counselors, Inc., 1954-59; Chase & Sauerhaft Associates, Inc., New York City, president, 1959-65; Hill & Knowlton, Inc. (public relations firm), New York City, executive vice-president and director of management committee, 1965—. Lecturer at Columbia University, 1961-64; member of public relations advisory committee at Pace University. Member of board of directors of Gardner-Jones, Inc. (Chicago, Ill.). *Military service:* U.S. Army, 1944-46; became staff sergeant. *Member:* Public Relations Society of America, Authors Guild of Authors League of America, Union League Club, Burning Tree Country Club.

WRITINGS: (Contributor) *Top Management Handbook,* Maynard, 1960; *Critical Thoughts on Public Relations,* M. W. Lads, 1968; *The Merger Game,* Crowell, 1971; (contributor) Max Ways, editor, *Critical Issues in Public Relations,* Prentice-Hall, 1975. Contributor to business and public relations journals and popular magazines, including *New Yorker, Business Week,* and *Dun's Review.*

WORK IN PROGRESS: A novel dealing with contemporary business and public relations.

SIDELIGHTS: Sauerhaft writes: *"The Merger Game* grew out of my experiences helping companies defend themselves against hostile takeovers. It was written in a semi-novelistic style to enable me to comment on characters that could have seemed similar to some well-known persons."

*   *   *

SAWYER, Charles   1887-1979

OBITUARY NOTICE—See index for *CA* sketch: Born February 10, 1887, in Cincinnati, Ohio; died April 7, 1979, in Palm Beach, Fla. Lawyer, civic leader, and former presidential aide. Active in local, state, and national government, Sawyer served as Cincinnati City Council member, lieutenant governor of Ohio, U.S. Ambassador to Belgium, and as secretary of commerce under President Harry S Truman. Sawyer also owned a number of Ohio radio stations and at one time owned eighteen Ohio newspapers. He outlined his political persuasions in his 1968 book, *Concerns of a Conservative Democrat.* Obituaries and other sources: *Current Biography,* Wilson, 1948; *Who's Who in America,* 39th edition, Marquis, 1976; *Who's Who in American Politics,* 6th edition, Bowker, 1977; *Who's Who,* 131st edition, St. Martin's, 1979; *New York Times,* April 9, 1979; *Washington Post,* April 9, 1979.

*   *   *

SCHAFFNER, Nicholas   1953-

PERSONAL: Born January 28, 1953, son of John Valentine (a literary agent) and Perdita (MacPherson) Schaffner. *Education:* Attended New College, Sarasota, Fla., 1970-73; State University of New York Empire State College at State Springs, B.A., 1977. *Home:* 19 Grove St., New York, N.Y. 10014. *Agent:* John Schaffner Literary Agency, 425 East 51st St., New York, N.Y. 10022.

CAREER: Writer, composer, and performer in New York, N.Y.

WRITINGS: The Beatles Forever, Cameron House, 1977.

Co-author of "The Harlequin" (musical play), first produced in New York, N.Y., at Open Space Experimental Theater Festival, March, 1978. Contributor of articles and poems to magazines, including *Panache* and *Rolling Stone,* and newspapers.

WORK IN PROGRESS: Stories of fantasy and the supernatural.

SIDELIGHTS: Schaffner comments: "As far as my writing goes, my two main interests are fantastic literature and pop music. I combine these in my own musical compositions."

*   *   *

SCHAU, Michael   1945-

PERSONAL: Born September 19, 1945, in St. Louis, Mo.; son of Peter E. and Ruth (employed by U.S. Postal Service; maiden name, Froning) Schau; married Carole Beiser, August 19, 1967 (divorced February 15, 1978). *Education:* University of Missouri, B.A., 1968. *Politics:* Independent. *Home and office:* 173 Riverside Dr., New York, N.Y. 10024.

CAREER: Billboard Publications, New York City, reporter, 1968-70; *Motion Picture Daily,* New York City, film reviewer, 1970-71; *Where* (magazine), New York City, editor, 1974—. *Awards, honors:* Prize from Art Directors Club of New York, 1975.

WRITINGS: J. C. Leyendecker, Watson-Guptill, 1974; *All-American Girl: The Art of Coles Phillips,* Watson-Guptill, 1975; (editor and author of introduction) *The Norman Rockwell Poster Book,* Watson-Guptill, 1976; *The Second Norman Rockwell Poster Book,* Watson-Guptill, 1977. Contributor of articles and reviews to magazines and newspapers.

WORK IN PROGRESS: A book on American artist Howard Chandler Christy.

*   *   *

SCHEADER, Catherine   1932-

PERSONAL: Born August 25, 1932, in Astoria, N.Y.; daughter of Peter M. and Bridget (O'Reilly) O'Reilly; married Edward C. Scheader (a civil engineer), July 6, 1957; children: Barbara Jean, John, Susan. *Education:* Hunter College (now of the City University of New York), B.A.; Rutgers University, M.Ed. *Politics:* Independent. *Religion:* Roman Catholic. *Home:* 45 Inglewood Lane, Matawan, N.J. 07747.

CAREER: Reading specialist in public schools in Marlboro, N.J., 1971-77; curriculum consultant in public schools in Manasquan, N.J., 1977-78; East Brunswick Board of Education, East Brunswick, N.J., reading specialist, 1978—. *Member:* International Reading Association, National Education Association, New Jersey Education Association, Kappa Delta Pi.

WRITINGS—All juveniles: *Charles Drew,* C. E. Merrill, 1972; *Robert Smalls,* C. E. Merrill, 1972; *Matthew Henson,* C. E. Merrill, 1972; *Harriet Tubman,* C. E. Merrill, 1972; *Frederick Douglass,* C. E. Merrill, 1972; *Mary Cassatt,* Childrens Press, 1978; *Lorraine Hansberry,* Childrens Press, 1978.

WORK IN PROGRESS: Antonia Brico, a juvenile, for Childrens Press; *My Brother the Cat,* for children; fiction for adults.

SIDELIGHTS: Catherine Scheader writes: "I began to write in response to the needs of a young black student for whom I could not locate material offering appropriate role models that were on his reading level. My next objective was to write the same kind of books for young girls who were interested in the arts. I am now writing a contemporary fantasy for pre-teens. In the planning stage is a novel for adults about the nurturing roles that women play. The need to examine affirmative directions taken by human beings in unusual circumstances is an important part of my motivation and my work."

*   *   *

SCHEELE, Carl H(arry)   1928-

PERSONAL: Born June 19, 1928, in Cleveland, Ohio; son of Carl August (a commercial artist) and Frances (Standring) Scheele; married Joanne Brewer (a painter), June 21, 1954; children: Martha, August. *Education:* Cleveland Institute of Art, diploma, 1952; University of Illinois, B.F.A., 1953; Western Reserve University (now Case Western Reserve University), M.A., 1956. *Politics:* Independent. *Home:* 2912 North 22nd St., Arlington, Va. 22201. *Office:* Division of Community Life, National Museum of History and Technology, Smithsonian Institution, Washington, D.C. 20560.

CAREER: Baltimore & Ohio Railroad, Cleveland, Ohio, telegrapher and agent, 1944-46; Carl A. Scheele Studio, Cleveland, commercial artist, 1946-48; elementary school teacher in Cleveland, 1957-59; Smithsonian Institution, Washington, D.C., curator of Divisions of Postal History and Community Life at National Museum of History and Technology, 1959—. *Military service:* U.S. Army, information specialist, 1954-56; served in Japan. *Member:* American Historical Association.

WRITINGS: A Short History of the Mail Service, Smithsonian Institution Press, 1970; *Neither Snow nor Rain: The Story of the United States Mails,* Smithsonian Institution Press, 1970; (contributor) Peter C. Marzio, editor, *A Nation of Nations,* Harper, 1976; *American Post Offices,* Smithsonian Institution Press, 1977. Contributor to *Fleetwood's Standard First Day Cover Catalog.*

WORK IN PROGRESS: Research on the recording careers of Bert Williams, Henry Burr, Nora Bayes, and Lewis James, on popular music, popular singers and recording artists in America, 1895-1925, and on American vaudeville.

SIDELIGHTS: Scheele has conducted research and planning for several major museum exhibits, and has created two record albums—"Come Josephine in My Flying Machine: Inventions and Topics in Popular Song, 1910-1929," New World Records, 1977, and "Praise the Lord and Pass the Ammunition: Songs of World War I and World War II," New World Records, 1978.

He writes: "Varied experiences in my pre-museum career helped to shape my interests in historical material culture. Similarly, I have remained deeply motivated in the field of collecting because the collecting activities of my father and his father were sources of profound inspiration. My orientation is both visual and historical, and a career as a curator in one of the world's outstanding history museums has remained stimulating and rewarding. The exhibition of and writing about historical objects and processes, historical performances on record, and the images of the American past continue to challenge and fascinate. Even my avocation of building model railroad equipment and my personal collections of books and phonograph records reflect my thorough preoccupation with historical processes."

*   *   *

SCHENKEN, Howard   1904(?)-1979

OBITUARY NOTICE: Born c. 1904; died of a brain tumor, February 20, 1979, in Palm Springs, Calif. Bridge player and author of books, including *Four Aces System of Contract Bridge* and *Howard Schenken's Big Club.* Schenken won numerous tournaments in his career of more than fifty years. He also wrote an autobiography, *Education of a Bridge Player.* Obituaries and other sources: *New York Times,* February 21, 1979; *Chicago Tribune,* February 22, 1979; *Washington Post,* February 22, 1979.

*   *   *

SCHERE, Monroe   1913-
(Jessica Howard, J. K. Summerhill, Abigail Winter)

PERSONAL: Surname is pronounced like "sheer"; born February 26, 1913, in New York, N.Y.; son of Joseph and Ray (Liman) Schere; married Janet Housman, August 20, 1935 (divorced, 1976); married Jean Karsavina (a novelist), May 27, 1976; children: Jonathan, Ivan. *Education:* Attended University of Alabama, 1929-31. *Home and office:* 115 East 87th St., New York, N.Y. 10028. *Agent:* Henry Morrison, Inc., 58 West 10th St., New York, N.Y. 10011.

CAREER: Weil, Gotshal & Manges, New York City, law clerk, 1931-35; free-lance writer, 1935-52; Maxwell Sackheim Agency, New York City, mail order copywriter, 1952-

54; Prentice-Hall, Inc., Englewood Cliffs, N.J., advertising copywriter, 1954-57; free-lance writer, 1957—. *Military service:* U.S. Maritime Service, 1945; U.S. Coast Guard Reserve, 1945. *Member:* Authors Guild, Authors League of America. *Awards, honors:* First prize from *True Story,* 1954, for story "The Santa Claus Without a Heart."

WRITINGS: Work Wonders From Within Yourself, Prentice-Hall, 1964; *Parker Prosperity Program,* Prentice-Hall, 1967; *Take Charge of Your Life,* Hawthorn, 1968; *Your Changing City* (juvenile), Prentice-Hall, 1969; *The Story of Maps* (juvenile), Prentice-Hall, 1969.

Under pseudonym Abigail Winter: *Whispering Caverns* (novel), Simon & Schuster, 1974; *The Smiling Dragon* (novel), Dell, 1976; *Olivia's Story* (novel), Dell, 1976; *Savage Embrace* (novel), Warner, 1978.

Contributor of numerous short stories to science fiction and western magazines, and of articles on health. Also writes under pseudonyms Jessica Howard and J. K. Summerhill.

WORK IN PROGRESS: A historical novel about John Brown, publication by Jove Books.

SIDELIGHTS: Schere told *CA:* "When I was in high school I read all of that era's science fiction. Since I didn't want a nine-to-five job, and since (smile, everybody!) a writer's life looked like a bed of roses, I wrote science fiction. At length, when I was sixteen, my first published story, "The Meteoric Magnet," appeared in Hugo Gernsback's *Air Wonder Stories* for April, 1929. When Hugo neglected to send me a check, I went to see him about it: he smiled feebly and gave me twenty-five dollars." That experience taught Schere to write with a particular market in mind and to never forget that an author "write[s] for money."

"Nevertheless," Schere continued, "I do sometimes write fancy bits for nonpublication—but not during my working hours. I have profited by a determination to work. And by developing certain habits, such as going straight from the breakfast table to my typewriter, every morning. True, some writers create as many words at night, after coming home from a job, as I do in my preferred six daylight hours of writing next to a window. The important thing is to make sure that when you're supposed to be writing, you do nothing else.

"Anyway, that first sale did not lead me to an instantaneous career, so I became a nine-to-five law clerk. Then I began to sell short-short stories to newspaper syndicates for about ten dollars a story. I found I could sell confession stories for a couple of hundred bucks, so I quit my job and wrote confessions and some science fiction, westerns, action stories and such for the old pulp markets now dead and gone. Eventually I hit a dry spell. And I had kids in school and mortgage payments to meet.

"So I went into nine-to-five mail-order advertising, then into the advertising of self-improvement books and a sideline of ghostwriting such books and other sorts. Eventually I took a fresh start in at-home free-lancing, and it has worked out. One of my major markets for a time was the Gothic novel, strictly for women. Now I have settled into historical romances, being one of the several male authors in the field who—writing for women—find it advisable to use female pen names. Why do some men write for women? None of us know.

"You can see that this dithyramb speaks for a commercially slanted fiction writer: one who writes to be published where the money is. I respect those who write to please themselves, but the public's taste is my criterion. Take note that some excellent writing thunders through the ages because some great authors were naturally attuned to public taste. Balzac, whose work has taught me a great deal, wrote about sex (that is, various aspects of the male-female relationship), about making and losing money, about getting rich, about joys and sorrows in family life, about the lives of people whom his readers might like to be, i.e., the aristocracy, for whom these days we can substitute *jet set.* Modern fiction is different in style, but still deals with exactly the same topics. Write for the public taste (like Balzac, Shakespeare . . .), add the masters' terrific talent, and your work will never be forgotten.

"Most writers, however, know that their work will definitely be forgotten. Some can't face that truth and I've heard them wail, "What am I writing for?" How about writing to make a living? And at the same time, whether you write for *Lurid Love* or *Harvard Business Review*—whether you write fiction or articles or poetry—you still can be an honest craftsman. You don't have to be a genius to tune your work to human nature, knowing your readers will be grateful for it. You still can return to the classics for basic grounding, then go to successful modern writing for a briefing on modern style. Nor need you ever copy anyone else, nor ever "write down," nor ever submit a careless sentence. Writing gives you a wonderful chance to express yourself. In fact, you can't help expressing yourself, and you're miles ahead of people who never found a way.

"Let alone that once you make your living at writing—and I mean a living that includes not only bread but also plenty of cake—you join a small elite. Human-nature-wise, this is pleasant. Anyone who'd like to kick around more of the whys and wherefores is cordially invited to get in touch. Of all the varieties of people in the world, I most enjoy talking to other writers."

AVOCATIONAL INTERESTS: Sailing, sculpting in wood, astronomy, philosophy.

*   *   *

SCHICKELE, Peter 1935-
(P.D.Q. Bach)

PERSONAL: Born July 17, 1935, in Ames, Iowa; son of Rainer (an agricultural economist) and Elizabeth (a biothermologist) Schickele; married Susan Sindall (a dance instructor), 1962; children: Karla, Matthew. *Education:* Swarthmore College, B.A., 1957; Juilliard School of Music, M.S., 1960. *Office:* Vanguard Records, 71 West 23rd St., New York, N.Y. 10010.

CAREER: Composer-in-residence for public schools in Los Angeles, Calif., 1960-61; Swarthmore College, Swarthmore, Pa., instructor in music, 1961-62; Juilliard School of Music, New York City, member of music faculty, 1961-65; composer and performer, 1965—. Co-founder of Composers Circle, 1959, and Open Window, 1967.

WRITINGS: The Definitive Biography of P.D.Q. Bach, Random House, 1976. Composer and arranger (sometimes under pseudonym P.D.Q. Bach), including scores for films and plays such as "Silent Running" and "Oh! Calcutta!" and songs for such well-known performers as Joan Baez and Buffy St.-Marie.

SIDELIGHTS: Schickele was interested in theater long before he began his studies in music and his performances as the discoverer of P.D.Q. Bach indicate that his interest in that medium has not waned.

His early career, however, was as a serious composer for orchestra, band, and voice, including chamber music, dance scores, and music for theater and films. His recordings include "Good Time Ticket" and "The Open Window" for Vanguard Records, "Silent Running" for Decca, and "Oh! Calcutta!" for United Artists, and he has appeared with major symphony orchestras.

In 1965, feeling more and more restricted by the attitudes of serious musicians and the academic world in general, Schickele began moving toward a less rigid milieu. He had been arranging music for popular dance bands and jazz groups, and had performed in a rock band. In 1965 he presented his most unorthodox approach to music in the guise of P.D.Q. Bach.

P.D.Q. Bach (1807-1742) was introduced as the youngest and oddest of the sons of Johann Sebastian Bach, and by far "history's most justly neglected composer." Through the efforts of Peter Schickele, P.D.Q. Bach's unusual compositions have entertained audiences and enthusiastic reviewers all over the United States.

His repertoire includes such works as "Fanfare for the Common Cold," "Hansel and Gretel and Ted and Alice," "Schleptet," and "Toot Suite," and utilizes a wide variety of instruments ignored by more conventional composers, such as left-handed sewer flute, shower hose, bicycle, and foghorn.

This eclectic combination of sounds has been preserved by Vanguard Records on seven albums: "An Evening With P.D.Q. Bach," "An Hysteric Return: P.D.Q. Bach at Carnegie Hall," "The Intimate P.D.Q. Bach," "Report From Hoople: P.D.Q. Bach on the Air," "P.D.Q. Bach's Half-Act Opera, 'The Stoned Guest,'" "The Wurst of P.D.Q. Bach," and "Portrait of P.D.Q. Bach."

Schickele now spends about half of each year on P.D.Q. Bach and the other half writing and performing other kinds of music ranging from symphonic works to pop songs. "It's all part of the same continuum," he said.

*   *   *

SCHMIDERER, Dorothy 1940-

PERSONAL: Born October 26, 1940, in New York, N.Y.; daughter of Simon (an architect) and Mary (an art teacher; maiden name, Burlingham) Schmiderer. *Education:* Bryn Mawr, A.B., 1963; further study at Parson School of Design, 1964-66. *Home and office:* 238 East 58th St., New York, N.Y. 10022.

CAREER: Scholastic Magazines, Inc., New York City, designer, 1966-69; Harper & Row Publishers, Inc., New York City, book designer, 1970-76; Viking Press, Inc., book designer, 1977-78; free-lance book designer, 1978—. *Awards, honors:* Children's Book Council Showcase Award, 1972, for *The Alphabeast Book;* award from American Institute of Graphic Arts, 1975, for design of *Honkytonk Heroes.*

WRITINGS: (Self-illustrated) *The Alphabeast Book: An Abecedarium,* Holt, 1971.

*   *   *

SCHMIDT, Fred H(artz) 1918-

PERSONAL: Born March 7, 1918, in Cuero, Tex.; son of Fred Hartz (in sales) and Bertha (Frobese) Schmidt; married Venola Morgan, June 26, 1941 (divorced, 1974); married Sonia Portales (an executive secretary), November 12, 1974; children: Eric, Sandra Schmidt Pollard, Kurt. *Education:* University of Texas, B.A., 1939, graduate study, 1940; graduate study at U.S. Department of Agriculture Graduate School, 1962. *Politics:* "Vacillate between Democrat and Socialist." *Religion:* "Insignificant." *Home and office address:* P.O. Box 362, Tehachapi, Calif. 93561.

CAREER: Employed as cotton mill worker, dishwasher, and district union director (for Textile Workers Union of America and Oil, Chemical & Atomic Workers Union), 1941-55; Texas State Congress of Industrial Organizations, Austin, executive secretary, 1955-57; Texas State American Federation of Labor-Congress of Industrial Organizations, Austin, secretary-treasurer, 1957-61; administrative assistant to U.S. Congressman Henry B. Gonzalez in Washington, D.C., 1961-63; University of California, Los Angeles, research economist at Institute of Industrial Relations, 1963-74, senior lecturer in management, 1965-74; writer and artist, 1974—. Member of national board of directors of American Veterans Committee, 1946-50, and regional U.S. Wage Stabilization Board, 1947-48; consultant to U.S. Department of Labor, U.S. Department of Commerce, Equal Employment Opportunity Commission, and Office of Economic Opportunity, 1965-74. *Military service:* U.S. Army, 1942-45; became master sergeant. *Member:* Beta Gamma Sigma.

WRITINGS: After the Bracero, Institute of Industrial Relations, University of California, Los Angeles, 1964; (with Paul Bullock) *Hard-Core Unemployment and Poverty in Los Angeles,* U.S. Government Printing Office, 1964; *Spanish-Surnamed American Employment in the Southwest,* U.S. Government Printing Office, 1970; (contributor) Gus Tyler, editor, *Mexican-Americans Tomorrow,* University of New Mexico Press, 1975; (with Vernon Briggs and Walter Fogel) *The Chicano Worker,* University of Texas Press, 1977. Contributor to social science and industrial relations journals.

WORK IN PROGRESS: A novel; epic poems.

SIDELIGHTS: Schmidt writes: "Cesar Chavez has me teaching every week at La Paz, ten miles down the mountain: teaching farm workers what I know about negotiating and administering union contracts—a rejuvenating activity for me. I've got to be the only CIO organizer who ever made Beta Gamma Sigma, the scholarship society for business administration students (I made radicals out of some of my students and they elected me).

"I am also one of the world's greatest undiscovered stone sculptors, but when it gets cold outside in these mountains, I come inside and try oil paintings, some of which I sell, and occasionally I write. Between the writings, paintings, sculptures, and my meager pension from University of California, along with my wife's income from her ceramics and her part-time job ramrodding the local school's Indian program, we have a good life.

"All this means that I'm not a driven writer, but I do have a folder full of pregnant articles on economics which should devastate the Carter or any other administration in power."

BIOGRAPHICAL/CRITICAL SOURCES: Texas Observer, January 28, 1961; *Ramparts,* September, 1965; *Christian Science Monitor,* August 19, 1967; *Los Angeles Times.* February 5, 1968, December 17, 1972; *Reporter,* January 25, 1968; *Arizona Republic,* January 25, 1968; *Austin American,* May 18, 1970; *San Antonio Light,* May 29, 1970; *New York Times,* May 29, 1970, January 1, 1971; *Washington Post,* May 29, 1970.

*   *   *

SCHNEPPER, Jeff A(lan)   1947-

PERSONAL: Born September 25, 1947, in Brooklyn, N.Y.; son of Simon (a plumber) and Doris (Shapiro) Schnepper; married Barbara Spradlin (a historian), May 26, 1974; children: Brandy Rebecca. *Education:* Brooklyn College of the City University of New York, B.A. (cum laude), 1968; New York University, M.B.A., 1970, LL.M., 1977; State University of New York at Buffalo, J.D. (honors), 1976. *Politics:* Independent. *Religion:* Jewish. *Home:* 224 Mimosa Dr., Cherry Hill, N.J. 08003. *Agent:* Martin H. Pine, Arthur Pine Associates, Inc., 1780 Broadway, New York, N.Y. 10019. *Office:* Graduate School of Financial Sciences, American College, Bryn Mawr, Pa. 19010.

CAREER: Ford Motor Co., Livonia, Mich., financial analyst, 1970; Allied Supermarkets, Detroit, Mich., cash manager, 1971; Pace University, New York, N.Y., instructor in accounting and finance, 1972-73; State University of New York College at Geneseo, assistant professor of accounting, 1973-75; Rutgers University, New Brunswick, N.J., assistant professor of economics, 1975-78; American College, Bryn Mawr, Pa., associate professor of accounting and finance, 1978—. Accredited public accountant in New Jersey; practicing attorney in New York and New Jersey. Participant in U.S. Department of State scholar-diplomat program; speaker at professional gatherings; has testified before U.S. Congressional committees; consultant in the United States and Brazil.

MEMBER: National Society of Public Accountants, National Association of Accountants for Educational Projects (local associate director), American Bar Association, Federal Bar Association, Federal District Bar Association, National Legal Aid and Defender Association, American Arbitration Association, National Association of Securities Dealers, Mensa, Eastern Economic Association, Western Economic Association, New Jersey Bar Association, New York Bar Association, Camden County Bar Association, Delta Tau Kappa, Omicron Delta Epsilon.

WRITINGS: Inside the I.R.S.: How It Works (You Over), Stein & Day, 1978; *Financial and Tax Planning: Transactions, Tables, and Worksheets,* Warren, Gorham & Lamont, 1979. Contributor of about thirty-five articles to law, economic, tax, and finance journals. Associate economic editor of *Intellect: National Review of Professional Thought* and *U.S.A. Today.*

WORK IN PROGRESS: Charitable Remainder Trusts and the Tax Reform Act of 1969; A Taxpayer's Guide Through Judicial Audit Appeal.

BIOGRAPHICAL/CRITICAL SOURCES: Washington Post, September 22, 1978; *Vogue,* November, 1978; *San Francisco Examiner,* November 3, 1978; *Barron's,* November 6, 1978.

*   *   *

SCHOEFFLER, Oscar E(dmund)   1899-1979

OBITUARY NOTICE—See index for *CA* sketch: Born March 5, 1899, in Alton, Ill.; died May 6, 1979, in Sarasota, Fla. Authority on men's fashions. Schoeffler was fashion editor of *Esquire* magazine for a number of years before retiring as fashion director and vice-president in 1971. He also was the fashion director of *Gentleman's Quarterly* and wrote a syndicated column, "Esquire's Avenues of Fashion." Schoeffler co-wrote *Esquire's Encyclopedia of Twentieth Century Men's Fashion* in 1973. Obituaries and other sources: *New York Times,* May 11, 1979.

SCHOENBERG, Bernard 1927-1979

OBITUARY NOTICE—See index for *CA* sketch: Born April 6, 1927; died of cancer, April 25, 1979, in New York, N.Y. Psychiatrist and professor. As professor of psychiatry at Columbia University College of Physicians and Surgeons, Schoenberg devoted much of his work to the psychological and social aspects of patient care. Along with Dr. Austin H. Kutscher he founded the Foundation of Thanatology, the first U.S. organization "devoted to the study of the dying and the improvement of medical education in the treatment of the dying patient." His approaches to the subject have been widely imitated. Editor of the *Journal of Health and Society* and the *Journal of Thanatology,* Schoenberg also co-edited several books, including *Psychosocial Aspects of Terminal Care* and *Loss and Grief: Psychological Management in Medical Practice.* Obituaries and other sources: *New York Times,* April 26, 1979.

*   *   *

SCHOENFIELD, Allen 1896(?)-1979

OBITUARY NOTICE: Born c. 1896; died January 19, 1979, in Ann Arbor, Mich. Science writer who was a staff member of the *Detroit News* for more than forty years. He received the Distinguished Service Award from the University of Michigan following his retirement in 1962. Obituaries and other sources: *Detroit Jewish News,* January 26, 1979.

*   *   *

SCHORR, Alan Edward 1945-

PERSONAL: Born January 7, 1945, in Bronx, N.Y.; son of Herbert (a power foreman) and Regina (Fingerman) Schorr; married Debra Genner, June 11, 1967; children: Zebediah Genner. *Education:* Hunter College of the City University of New York, B.A., 1966; Syracuse University, M.A., 1967; graduate study at University of of Iowa, 1967-72; University of Texas at Austin, M.S., 1973. *Home address:* P.O. Box 944, Auke Bay, Alaska 99821. *Office:* University Library, University of Alaska, Box 1447, Juneau, Alaska 99802.

CAREER: University of Alaska, Fairbanks, assistant professor of library science and government publications and map librarian, 1973-78; University of Alaska, Juneau, assistant professor of library science and director of university library, 1978—. *Member:* American Library Association (member of governing council, 1977—), Pacific Northwest Library Association, Alaska Library Association, Special Libraries Association, Explorers Club of New York.

WRITINGS: (Editor) *Directory of Special Libraries in Alaska,* Special Libraries Association, 1975; *Alaska Place Names,* University of Alaska Press, 1975; (compiler and author of annotations) *Government Reference Books 74/75,* Libraries Unlimited, 1976; *Government Documents in the Library Literature,* Pierian, 1976; (compiler and author of annotations) *Government Reference Books 76/77,* Libraries Unlimited, 1978. Contributor to library and history journals. Editor of *Sourdough: Journal of the Alaska Library Association,* 1974-75; associate editor of *SLA Geography and Map Bulletin,* 1975-76.

WORK IN PROGRESS: A novel, tentatively entitled *The Gatkis Connection,* about life in the environs of Woodlawn Cemetary in Bronx, N.Y.

SIDELIGHTS: Schorr told *CA:* "In the past few years I have written nearly one hundred book reviews for approximately twenty library and history journals and have come to realize that with the incredible increase of new books each year such reviews and critiques play an important part in determining what winds up on the shelves in public and academic libraries. Selection of appropriate titles for libraries is a difficult and complex task and is made considerably easier by the availability of well written reviews by informed individuals. Another area of concern is the production of reference works which permit individuals access to the vast storehouse of information hiding on the shelves in most libraries. My basic belief, enhanced by a recent visit to the Peoples Republic of China, is that all people have a right to use libraries and other information resources and that librarians should take an active part in producing guides, directories, handbooks, etc., to this data."

*   *   *

SCHORSKE, Carl E(mil) 1915-

PERSONAL: Born March 15, 1915, in New York, N.Y.; son of Theodore A. (a banker) and Gertrude (Goldschmidt) Schorske; married Elizabeth Rorke, June 14, 1941; children: Theodore, Anne Schorske Edwards, Stephen, John, Richard. *Education:* Columbia University, A.B., 1936; Harvard University, M.A., 1937, Ph.D., 1950. *Home:* 106 Winant Rd., Princeton, N.J. 08540. *Office:* Department of History, Princeton University, Princeton, N.J. 08540.

CAREER: Wesleyan University, Middleton, Conn., assistant professor, 1946-50, associate professor, 1950-55, professor of history, 1955-60; University of California, Berkeley, professor of history, 1960-69; Princeton University, Princeton, N.J., Dayton-Stockton Professor of History, 1969—, director of European cultural studies, 1973—. Visiting lecturer at Harvard University, 1951-52, and at Yale University, 1952-53. Political analyst for Office of Strategic Services, 1941-46; member of German studies group and Council on Foreign Relations, 1946-50. Member of board of trustees of Institute of Architecture and Urban Studies and Institute of Humanities. Fellow at Center on Advanced Studies in Behavioral Sciences, 1959-60, and at the Institute of Advanced Studies, Princeton University, 1967-68, and 1969-72. *Military service:* U.S. Naval Reserve, active duty, 1943-46; became lieutenant junior grade. *Member:* American Academy of Arts and Sciences, American Historical Association (member of council, 1964-68), Phi Beta Kappa.

AWARDS, HONORS: Award from Social Sciences Research Council, 1946; Toppan Prize from Harvard University, 1950. Harvard University fellow, 1938-41; Rockefeller fellow, 1949; Guggenheim fellow, 1954-55. D.L.H. from Wesleyan University, Middletown, Conn., 1967.

WRITINGS: (With Hoyt Price) *The Problem of Germany,* [New York], 1947; *German Social Democracy, 1905-1917,* Harvard University Press, 1955, reprinted, Russell & Russell, 1970; (editor with wife, Elizabeth Schorske) William L. Langer, *Explorations in Crisis,* Harvard University Press, 1969; *Fin de siecle Vienna: Politics and Culture,* Knopf, in press. Member of editorial board of *Central European History,* 1972-75, *Philosophy and Public Affairs,* and *Daedalus.*

*   *   *

SCHRADER, Richard James 1941-

PERSONAL: Born August 24, 1941, in Canton, Ohio; son of A. W. (a machinist) and Margaret (Karcher) Schrader. *Education:* University of Notre Dame, B.A., 1963; Ohio State University, M.A., 1965, Ph.D., 1968. *Office:* Department of English, Boston College, Chestnut Hill, Mass. 02167.

CAREER: Princeton University, Princeton, N.J., instructor, 1968-69, assistant professor of English, 1969-75, John Witherspoon Bicentennial Preceptor, 1972-75; Boston College, Chestnut Hill, Mass., assistant professor, 1975-78, associate professor of English, 1978—. *Member:* Modern Language Association of America, Mediaeval Academy of America, Mencken Society, Association for Scottish Literary Studies, Society for American Baseball Research.

WRITINGS: (Editor) *The Reminiscences of Alexander Dyce,* Ohio State University Press, 1972. Contributor to literature and medieval and Renaissance studies journals.

WORK IN PROGRESS: Research for a book on *Beowulf* and the literary epic.

* * *

SCHULTZ, Theodore William 1902-

PERSONAL: Born April 30, 1902, in Arlington, S.D.; son of Herry E. (a farmer) and Anna E. (a farmer; maiden name Weiss); married Esther Florence Werth; children: Elaine Schultz Olfson, Margaret, Theodore Paul. *Education:* South Dakota State College (now University), B.S., 1928; University of Wisconsin, M.S., 1928, Ph.D., 1930. *Home:* 5620 Kimbark Ave., Chicago, Ill. 60637. *Office:* Department of Economics, University of Chicago, 1126 East 59th St., Chicago, Ill. 60637.

CAREER: Iowa State College of Agriculture and Mechanic Arts (now Iowa State University of Science and Technology), Ames, assistant professor, 1930-31, associate professor, 1931-35, professor of agricultural economics, 1935-43, head of department of economics and sociology, 1934-43; University of Chicago, Chicago, Ill., professor of economics, 1943-72, chairman of department, 1946-61, Charles L. Hutchinson Distinguised Service Professor of Economics, 1952—. Conducted studies of agricultural development in Central Europe and Russia, 1929, and in Scandinavian countries and Scotland, 1936; chairman of Agricultural Development Mission in Argentina, Brazil, and Uruguay, 1941; director of studies of technical assistance in Latin America, 1953-57. Advisor to U.S. government organizations, including President's Economic Council, Federal Reserve Board, Peace Corps, Agency of International Development, Departments of Agriculture, Commerce, Defense, State, and Health, Education, and Welfare. Consultant to United Nations agencies, including Department of Economic Development, Food and Agriculture Organization, and International Bank for Reconstruction and Development, and to private organizations, including Ford Foundation, Rockefeller Foundation, Carnegie Corporation, RAND Corporation, and Brookings Institution. National Bureau of Economic Research, member of board of directors, 1949-67, vice-president, 1958, chairman of conference on investment in human beings, 1962, chairman of conference on new economic approaches to fertility, 1972, chairman of conference on marriage, family, human capital, and fertility, 1973. Chairman of research advisory board of Committee for Economic Development, 1957-59; guest of Soviet Academy of Sciences, 1960; co-chairman of consultive committee, Asian Development Bank, 1967; governor of board of International Development Research Center, Canada, 1973-78. Trustee of Institute of Current World Affairs, 1935-58, Population Council, 1957—, and International Agricultural Development Service, 1975—.

MEMBER: American Agricultural Economics Association (fellow), American Economic Association (distinguished fellow; vice-president, 1949; president, 1960), American Planning Association, American Academy of Arts and Sciences (fellow), American Philosophical Association (fellow), National Academy of Sciences, National Academy of Education (founding member, 1965). *Awards, honors:* LL.D. from Grinnell College, 1949, Michigan State University, 1962, University of Illinois, 1968, University of Wisconsin, 1968, and Catholic University of Chile, 1979; Fellow of Center for Advanced Study in the Behavioral Sciences, 1956-57; D.Sc. from South Dakota State College, 1959; Francis A. Walker Medal from American Economic Association, 1972, for "a contribution of the highest distinction to economics"; distinguised service award from American Agricultural Editors Association, 1973; Leonard Elmhirst Medal from International Agricultural Economics Association, 1976, for contributions to the economics of world agriculture.

WRITINGS: *Redirecting Farm Policy,* Macmillan, 1943; *Agriculture in an Unstable Economy,* McGraw, 1945; *Production and Welfare of Agriculture,* Macmillan, 1949; (with others) *Measures for Economic Development of Underdeveloped Countries,* United Nations Department of Economic Affairs, 1951; *The Economic Organization of Agriculture,* McGraw, 1953; *The Economic Value of Education,* Columbia University Press, 1963; *Transforming Traditional Agriculture,* Yale University Press, 1964; *Economic Crises in World Agriculture,* University of Michigan Press, 1965; *Economic Growth and Agriculture,* McGraw, 1968; *Investment in Human Capital: The Role of Education and of Research,* Free Press, 1971; *Human Resources/Human Capital: Policy Issues and Research Opportunities,* National Bureau of Economic Research, 1972.

Editor: *Food for the World,* University of Chicago Press, 1945 reprinted, Arno, 1976; *Investment in Human Beings,* University of Chicago Press, 1962; *Investment in Education: Equity-Efficiency Quandry,* University of Chicago Press, 1972; *New Economic Approaches to Fertility,* University of Chicago Press, 1973; *Marriage, Human Capital, and Fertility,* University of Chicago Press, 1974; *Economics of the Family: Marriage, Children, and Human Capital,* University of Chicago Press, 1975; *Distortions of Agricultural Incentives,* Indiana University Press, 1978.

Contributor: N. B. Henry, editor, *Social Forces Influencing American Education,* University of Chicago Press, 1961; Leo Fishman, editor, *Poverty Amid Affluence,* Yale University Press, 1966; Walter L. Fishel, editor, *Resource Allocation in Agricultural Research,* University of Minnesota Press, 1971; *Poverty Symposium,* University of Florida, 1975; *Contemporary Issues in Agricultural and Economic Development of Developing Nations,* East African Literature Bureau, 1977; Jerome Karabel and A. H. Halsey, editors, *Power and Ideology in Education,* Oxford University Press, 1977; *Lectures in Agricultural Economics,* Economic Research Service, U.S. Department of Agriculture, 1977; (author of forward) B. N. Ghosh, *Disguised Unemployment in Under-Developed Countries,* Heritage Publishers, 1977; Theodor Dams and others, editors, *Decision-Making and Agriculture,* Alden Press, 1977; William H. McNeill and Ruth Adams, editors, *Human Migration,* Indiana University Press, 1978; (contributor with Rati Ram) *Economic Development and Cultural Change,* University of Chicago Press, 1979.

Contributor to *Journal of Political Economy, American Journal of Agricultural Economics,* and other journals in his field. Editor of *Journal of Farm Economics,* 1939-42.

SCHULZE, Gene 1912-

PERSONAL: Surname is pronounced *Shul*-zee; born April 6, 1912, in Roscoe, Tex.; son of Adolph, Jr. and Martha (Wemken) Schulze; married Ruth Reinke, July 13, 1935 (divorced, 1958); children: James Gene, Michael Gene, Kathryn Ann Schulze Moser. *Education:* University of Texas, Austin, B.A., 1932; University of Texas, Galveston, M.D., 1936. *Politics:* "Liberal for persons, conservative for money." *Religion:* "Every living thing is God." *Home address:* P.O. Box 409, Flatonia, Tex. 78941. *Agent:* Helen Barrett, William Morris Agency, 1350 Ave. of the Americas, New York, N.Y. 10017. *Office:* 3916 Gramercy, Houston, Tex. 77025.

CAREER: Englewood Hospital, Chicago, Ill., intern, 1936-37; private practice of medicine in Schulenberg, Tex., 1937-50; Austin State Hospital, Austin, Tex., staff physician, 1950-52; Veterans Administration Hospital, Houston, Tex., staff psychiatrist, 1952-54; private practice of psychiatry in Houston and Flatonia, Tex., 1954-69; Camarillo State Hospital, Camarillo, Calif., staff psychiatrist, 1970-72. *Awards, honors:* Carr P. Collins Award, 1970, for *Third Face of War.*

WRITINGS: Third Face of War, Jenkins Publishing, 1970; *Yesterday's Seasons,* Hawthorn, 1978. Contributor of stories to magazines.

WORK IN PROGRESS: How Do I Grow?, on his work with Albert Schweitzer; a biography of German-American sculptress Elizabet Ney; a book of fables; two books on mental hospitals.

SIDELIGHTS: Schulze writes: "Working for short periods of time as an on-and-off ship's surgeon, I have traveled all over the world, excepting Russia and mainland China. During each two-month off-period I'd work in some small hospital as a volunteer doctor. Therefore I have worked in such places as Hong Kong, Guadalupe, British Honduras, Jerusalem, Transkei (South Africa), Ethiopia, Taiwan, and Molokai."

*   *   *

SCHWAB, John J. 1923-

PERSONAL: Born February 10, 1923, in Cumberland, Md.; son of Joseph L. and Eleanor (Cadden) Schwab; married Ruby Baxter, August 4, 1945; children: Mary E. Schwab Seligman. *Education:* University of Kentucky, B.A., 1946; University of Louisville, M.D., 1946; University of Illinois, M.S., 1949. *Religion:* Protestant. *Home:* 6217 Innes Trace, Louisville, Ky. 40222. *Office:* P.O. Box 35260, Louisville, Ky. 40232.

CAREER: Holzer Clinic, Gallipolis, Ohio, internist, 1954-59; University of Florida, Gainesville, professor of psychiatry and medicine, 1967-74; University of Louisville, Louisville, Ky., professor of psychiatry, 1974—, also currently head of department. *Military service:* U.S. Army, Medical Corps, 1949-54; became captain. *Member:* American Association for Social Psychiatry (president, 1971-73), Academy of Psychosomatic Medicine (president, 1970-71), American Medical Association, Pavlovian Society, Foundation of Thanatology, American College of Psychiatrists, Alpha Omega Alpha.

WRITINGS: Handbook of Psychiatric Consultation, Appleton, 1968; (with J. H. Masserman) *Serial Handbook of Modern Psychiatry,* Volume I, Intercontinental Medical Book Corp., 1974; (with daughter, M. E. Schwab) *Sociocultural Roots of Mental Illness,* Plenum, 1978; (with wife, R. B. Schwab, R. A. Bell, and G. J. Warheit) *Social Order and Mental Health,* Brunner, 1978. Contributor to medical journals.

WORK IN PROGRESS: Research on the epidemiology of mental illness and health, and on consultation-liaison psychiatry.

*   *   *

SCHWARTZ, Paula 1925-
(Elizabeth Mansfield, Libby Mansfield)

PERSONAL: Born March 13, 1925, in New York, N.Y.; daughter of Samuel and Hilda (Horowitz) Reibel; married Ira A. Schwartz (a metallurgical engineer), May 29, 1956; children: Wendy Elizabeth (Mrs. Jonathan Strong), David Saul. *Education:* Hunter College (now of the City University of New York), B.A., 1945; City College (now of the City University of New York), M.A., 1950; further graduate study at American University, 1969-70. *Residence:* Annandale, Va. *Agent:* Collier Associates, 280 Madison Ave., New York, N.Y. 10016.

CAREER: High school English teacher in New York, N.Y., 1947-65; George Washington University, Washington, D.C., lecturer in English, 1966-67; Dunbarton College, Washington, D.C., assistant professor of English, 1967-73; Northern Virginia Community College, Annandale, part-time lecturer in English, 1974—. Lecturer at New York University, 1963-64; guest lecturer and theater director at colleges. Director for community theater productions.

MEMBER: Authors Guild, Authors League of America, Dramatists Guild. *Awards, honors:* Pauline Eaton Oak Award from District of Columbia Recreation Department, 1971, for direction and production of "You're a Good Man, Charlie Brown"; Sallie Shepherd Prize from Irene Leache Memorial, 1974, for light verse, "Fragmented, and the Fanny Rogers Curd Prize," 1976, for essay, "The Last Secret Vice," and 1978, for essay, "To the One Who Ripped Off My Purse"; first prize from *Dramatics* one-act play contest, 1974, for "Parcel Pick-Up"; first prize from Delaware Theater Association bicentennial play contest, 1975, for "The Tory Spinster"; first prize from Wilmette Children's Theater national children's play competition, 1978, for "Sensible Sam and the Noodleheads."

WRITINGS: Historical novels; all under pseudonym Elizabeth Mansfield, except as noted: (Under pseudonym Libby Mansfield) *Unexpected Holiday,* Dell, 1978; *My Lord Murderer,* Berkley, 1978; *The Phantom Lover,* Berkley, 1979; *A Very Dutiful Daughter,* Berkley, 1979; *The Viscount From Virginia,* Berkley, 1979.

Plays: "Parcel Pick-Up" (one-act), produced in 1976; "The Tory Spinster" (two-act musical), first produced in Dover, Del., by the Kent County Theatre Guild, April, 1976; "Afterwords" (three one-act plays), produced in Abingdon, Va., at Barter Theater, July, 1977; "Sensible Sam and the Noodleheads" (one-act children's musical), first produced in Wilmette, Ill., at Wilmette children's Theater, March, 1979.

Contributor of articles, a play, stories, and poems to magazines, including *Good Housekeeping, Seventeen, Reader's Digest,* and *Today's Family.*

SIDELIGHTS: Schwartz commented: "Since I only recently (less than five years ago) began to write, and even more recently (for the last year or two) dared to consider myself a 'writer,' I hesitate to pontificate on this strange and wonderful profession. As a teacher of literature, I viewed writers with a respect bordering on awe, and I was able to try my hand at it only when it dawned on me that I didn't have to be Tolstoy to make a living at writing. I've greatly enjoyed all my life's work, but writing is, for me, the most fulfilling occupation. Of course, I'd feel even more fulfilled if I could be a Tolstoy even momentarily.''

*   *   *

SCHWARTZ, Richard B. 1941-

PERSONAL: Born October 5, 1941, in Cincinnati, Ohio; son of Jack J. (an attorney) and Marie (a banker; maiden name, Schnelle) Schwartz; married Judith Lang (a teacher and writer), September 7, 1963; children: Jonathan. *Education:* University of Notre Dame, A.B., 1963; University of Illinois, A.M., 1964, Ph.D., 1967. *Religion:* Roman Catholic. *Office:* Department of English, University of Wisconsin, 6147 White Hall, Madison, Wis. 53706.

CAREER: National Council of Teachers of English, Urbana, Ill., staff assistant, 1966; U.S. Military Academy, West Point, N.Y., instructor in English, 1967-69; University of Wisconsin—Madison, assistant professor, 1969-72, associate professor, 1972-78, professor of English, 1978—, associate dean of Graduate School, 1977. *Military service:* U.S. Army, 1967-69; became captain. *Member:* Modern Language Association of America, American Society for Eighteenth-Century Studies, Johnson Society (Central Region). *Awards, honors:* National Endowment for the Humanities grant, 1970; American Council of Learned Societies fellow, 1978-79; H. I. Romnes fellowship, 1978—.

WRITINGS: Samuel Johnson and the New Science, University of Wisconsin Press, 1971; *Samuel Johnson and the Problem of Evil,* University of Wisconsin Press, 1975; *Boswell's Johnson: A Preface to the Life,* University of Wisconsin Press, 1978; (editor) *The Plays of Arthur Murphy,* four volumes, Garland Publishing, 1979. Contributor of articles and reviews to language and literature journals and literary magazines, including *New Rambler, Genre,* and *Georgia Review.*

WORK IN PROGRESS: The Texture of Life in Johnson's London (tentative title).

*   *   *

SCHWARTZ, Stephen (Lawrence) 1948-

PERSONAL: Born March 6, 1948, in New York, N.Y.; son of Stanley L. (a businessman) and Sheila (a teacher; maiden name, Siegal) Schwartz; married Carole Ann Piasecki, June 6, 1969; children: Scott Lawrence, Jessica Lauren. *Education:* Attended Juilliard School of Music, 1964; Carnegie Institute of Technology (now Carnegie-Mellon University), B.F.A., 1968. *Residence:* Ridgefield, Conn. *Agent:* Shirley Bernstein, Paramuse Associates, 1414 Avenue of the Americas, New York, N.Y. 10019.

CAREER: Composer, lyricist, director, and author. *Member:* National Academy of Recording Arts & Sciences (national trustee), American Society of Composers, Authors & Publishers, Dramatists' Guild, Society of Stage Directors & Choreographers. *Awards, honors:* Two Grammy Awards from National Academy of Recording Arts & Sciences, 1971, for ''Godspell'' original cast recording; Drama Desk Awards, 1971, for ''Godspell'' music and lyrics and 1978, for direction of ''Working''; Trendsetter Award from *Billboard,* 1971, for ''Godspell'' and ''Mass''; award from National Theatre Arts Conference, 1971, for ''Godspell.''

WRITINGS: The Perfect Peach (juvenile), Little, Brown, 1977.

Composer and lyricist for title song of ''Butterflies Are Free,'' 1969; composer of music and new lyrics for ''Godspell,'' 1971; author, with Leonard Bernstein, of English texts for Bernstein's ''Mass,'' 1971. Composer and lyricist for plays: ''Pippin,'' 1972; ''The Magic Show,'' 1974; ''The Baker's Wife,'' 1976. Adapter, director, composer, and lyricist of four songs for a play, ''Working,'' 1978.

BIOGRAPHICAL/CRITICAL SOURCES: Horizon, April, 1978.

*   *   *

SCHWEITZER, Gertrude 1909-

PERSONAL: Born January 10, 1909, in New York, N.Y.; daughter of Harry (in advertising) and Bessie (a store manager; maiden name, Adler) Kaufman; married Stanley Schweitzer (an attorney), March 1, 1929; children: Carol S. (Mrs. George Goldberg), John. *Education:* Attended Columbia University, 1926, New York University, 1950-53, and New School for Social Research, 1953-55. *Politics:* Independent. *Religion:* Unitarian-Universalist. *Home address:* P.O. Box 185, Armonk, N.Y. 10504. *Agent:* Sterling Lord Agency, Inc., 660 Madison Ave., New York, N.Y. 10021.

CAREER: National Bellas Hess, New York City, catalog copywriter, 1926-27; D. H. Ahrend, New York City, direct mail copywriter, 1928-30; free-lance writer, 1942—. *Member:* Amnesty International, Authors Guild of Authors League of America, Audubon Society. *Awards, honors:* Award from Bureau of Intercultural Relations, 1947, for short story, ''Moment of Glory,'' published in *Saturday Evening Post.*

WRITINGS: The Young People (fiction), Crowell, 1953; *Born* (fiction), Doubleday, 1960; *So Many Voices* (fiction), Prentice-Hall, 1964; *The Ledge* (fiction), Delacorte, 1972; *Shadows on the Left Bank* (fiction), Dell, 1973; *Before Honor* (fiction), Doubleday, 1974; *The Herzog Legacy* (fiction), Doubleday, 1976. Contributor of about three hundred stories to national magazines, including *Good Housekeeping, Ladies Home Journal, McCalls, Redbook,* and *Saturday Evening Post.*

WORK IN PROGRESS: A mystery novel; short stories.

SIDELIGHTS: Gertrude Schweitzer comments: ''I believe the main purpose of fiction is to tell a good story through interesting and believable characters.''

AVOCATIONAL INTERESTS: Gardening, birds, fishing, cross country skiing, international travel (especially France).

*   *   *

SCIASCIA, Leonardo 1921-

PERSONAL: Born January 8, 1921, in Racalmuto, Sicily; came to Italy. *Home:* Via Redentore 131, Caltanissetta, Italy.

CAREER: Writer. *Awards, honors:* Premio Crotone; Premio Libera Stampa Lugano; Premio Prato.

WRITINGS—In English: Le parrocchie di Regalpetra (essays), Laterza, 1956, translation published as *Salt in the Wound* (includes *Death of the Inquisitor*), Orion Press, 1969; *Il giorno della civetta* (novel), Einaudi, 1961, translation by Archibald Colquhoun and Arthur Oliver published as *Mafia Vendetta,* J. Cape, 1963, Knopf, 1964; *Il consiglio d'Egitte,* Einaudi, 1963, translation by Adrienne Foulke published as *The Council of Egypt,* Knopf, 1966; *A ciascuno il suo,* Einaudi, 1966, translation by Foulke published as *A Man's Blessing,* Harper, 1968; *Il contesto,* Einaudi, 1971, translation by Foulke published as *Equal Danger,* Harper, 1973; *Todo modo,* Einaudi, 1974, translation by Foulke published as *One Way or Another,* Harper, 1977.

Other; all published by Einaudi unless otherwise indicated: *Gli zii di Sicilia,* 1958; *Morte dell'inquisitore* (biography; title means "Death of the Inquisitor"), Laterza, 1964; *Feste religiose in Sicilia,* Leonardo da Vinci editrice, 1965; *L'onorevole, dramma in tre atti* (play; three-act), 1965.

La corda pazza. Scrittori e cose della Sicilia, 1970; (with Rosario La Duca) *Palermo felicissima,* Il punto, 1973; *Il mare colore del vino,* 1973; (with others) *Mostra retrospettiva della opere di Christian Hess: Palermo Palazzo del turismo, 26 novembre–10 dicembre 1974,* Cassa centrale di risparmio Vittorio Emanuele per le province siciliane, 1974; *La scomparsa di Majorana,* 1975; *L'onorevole; Recitazione della controversia liparitana; I mafiosi* (collected works), 1976; *I pugnalatori,* 1976; *Candido: ovvero, Un sogno fatto in Sicilia,* 1977. Author of *Favole della dittatura,* 1950, and *La Sicilia, il suo cuore,* 1952. Also author of the play "Story of the Lipari-tana Controversy."

Contributor to periodicals, including *New York Times.*

SIDELIGHTS: In Italy, Sciascia is considered one of the finest novelists writing today. Herbert Mitgang reported, however, that Sciascia "was puzzled and saddened when I told him that in the United States his books sometimes fall into the mystery bin." But Sciascia replied, "At least I hope they will be regarded as metaphysical mysteries." Sciascia has succeeded in winning over many American critics. As Mitgang observed, "Sciascia is a careful and slow writer who has turned out a unified body of work in the last 20 years." He also described Sciascia as "a novelist respected by his peers and readers for grappling with old themes that reach down to the condition of life and justice."

Sciascia's first work to appear in English translation was *Salt in the Wound,* a collection of essays referred to by a *Book World* critic as the "social biography of an imaginary Sicilian town." The book chronicles the suffering of peasants through "centuries under the combined forces of the rich and the Church, later to be joined by the Fascist and Christian Democratic parties and the Mafia." A. Mario Rotondaro called *Salt in the Wound* "a truly enjoyable volume, one that can be reread with pleasure," but the reviewer for *Book World* was less impressed. "What finally disappoints about the work," noted the *Book World* critic, "is the author's sense of hopelessness about the conditions he describes. For all its concern, *Salt in the Wound* is a cry of protest against seemingly immovable forces rather than an angry demand that they be removed."

Millicent Bell summed up *Mafia Vendetta* as "not so much a stripped-down novel as an achieved movie-script." She added, "His novel . . . is built almost entirely of stretches of dialogue to which the barest minimum of narrative and description is added." Essentially the story of a policeman's efforts to solve a murder, *Mafia Vendetta,* as Bell stated, "also succeeds beyond its end as social accusation. All along the way we are shown the human beings who are made to play their roles by all that they are, all that their lives have been."

Bell found *The Council of Egypt* "somewhat labored and pallid by comparison [with *Mafia Vendetta*]." She further declared that *The Council of Egypt* "lacks the advantage of Sciascia's main asset, his gift for recording the behavior and speech of his contemporaries." It is the story of a forger who creates a law which grants priorities to royalty as opposed to

aristocracy in the event of inheritance disputes. Anthony West called the novel "a very cooly ironic and detached piece of storytelling concerned mainly with social hypocrisy in the manner of Voltaire or Anatole France."

In comparison to *The Council of Egypt,* West remarked that *A Man's Blessing* was a "homage of imitation to Graham Greene." Similar to Greene's *The Man Within, A Man's Blessing* concerns one man's attempt to solve the murder of a friend. However, as his search takes him into the criminal world, he learns less and less. Eventually, he is absorbed into the underworld and in an ironic ending, the townspeople reveal that throughout the story they knew the solution to the murder. West wrote: "This graceful piece of storytelling is in fact a savagely expressed cry of despair. Sciascia has moved on from the belief that life is a comedy, which would be much more enjoyable for the actors if they would only be a little more reasonable and a little less emotional, to discover its tragic essence. This account of his discovery, in the form of a novel, is at once moving and horrifying, and may well in time win itself recognition as one of the minor classics of extreme pessimism."

Writing in *Critic,* Dick Datchery called *Equal Danger* "an intellectual suspense novel." Datchery found the story of Inspector Rogas and his search for the murderer of several judges to be "a serious parody, complex and sometimes vague, but always rewarding." In *Newsweek,* P. S. Prescott lamented the fact that too often Sciascia is mistakenly classified as a mystery writer. He called this misconception of Sciascia "an appalling irony that perhaps even Sciascia cannot stomach." Datchery noted, "The crimes in his stories do not demand solutions; they serve, rather, as vehicles for social comment: to show how justice can be removed to a plateau where it is concerned only with its forms." Phoebe Adams agreed with Datchery. She observed that the chase in the novel "turns into a fable about power exercised for its own sake regardless of the purposes for which it was conferred and therefore spreading universal criminality."

Sciascia's most recent work to be published in the U.S. is *One Way or Another.* It is the story of a curious driver who decides to investigate a mysterious sign on the road. He discovers a secret religious order run by Don Gaetano who wears spectacles similar to those of Satan in a painting. John Ahern called Don Gaetano "one of the strongest, most intriguing characters that Sciascia has ever created. A brilliant intellect, a widely read, cynical master of paradox, a scornful, ruthless manipulator of the rich and powerful for his own ends." Prescott, however, was not as impressed. He claimed that *One Way or Another* "lacks the wit, the aphorisms and the scathing cynicism that distinguished the author's earlier books." Prescott also found the characters "familiar" and added that "their arguments are tiresome."

BIOGRAPHICAL/CRITICAL SOURCES: Best Sellers, April 15, 1968, June 1, 1969; *New Yorker,* May 3, 1969; *Book World,* September 7, 1969; *Partisan Review,* fall, 1972; *Newsweek,* June 16, 1973, May 9, 1977; *New York Times Book Review,* September 16, 1973; *Critic,* November/December, 1973; *New Republic,* September 17, 1977; *Contemporary Literary Criticism,* Gale, Volume 8, 1978, Volume 9, 1978.*

* * *

SCOTT, James B(urton) 1926-

PERSONAL: Born November 24, 1926, in Niagara Falls, N.Y.; son of Ethel (Scanlan) Scott; married Pauline Villnave, November 10, 1950; children: James, Ann, Sally,

Geoffrey, Philip, Greg, Brian, Mark. *Education:* State University of New York at Buffalo, B.A., 1951, M.A., 1958; Syracuse University, Ph.D., 1964. *Residence:* Fairfield, Conn. *Office:* Department of English, University of Bridgeport, South Hall, Bridgeport, Conn. 06602.

CAREER: State University of New York at Buffalo, instructor in English, 1953-58; Syracuse University, Syracuse, N.Y., instructor, 1958-64; University of Bridgeport, Bridgeport, Conn., 1964—, began as assistant professor, currently professor of English. Publicity director for Polka Dot Playhouse, 1970-73. *Military service:* U.S. Army, Corps of Engineers, 1944-46; served in Pacific theater. *Member:* American Association of University Professors.

WRITINGS: William Golding, Barrister, 1970; *Djuna Barnes,* Twayne, 1976. Assistant state editor of *Syracuse Herald-Journal,* 1959-64.

WORK IN PROGRESS: Experimental fiction.

*   *   *

SCOTT, Otto J.   1918-

PERSONAL: Born May 26, 1918, in New York, N.Y.; son of Otto F. (a broker) and Katherine (McGivney) Scott; married; children: one daughter. *Politics:* "Skeptical party." *Religion:* Presbyterian. *Residence:* San Diego, Calif.

CAREER: Affiliated with United Feature Syndicate, New York City, 1939-40, and Diamond & Sherwood, San Francisco, Calif., 1948-53; Globaltronix de Venezuela, Caracas, vice-president, 1954-56; Mohr Associates, New York City, vice-president, 1957-59; Becker, Scott & Associates, New York City, vice-president, 1960-63; *Rubber World,* New York City, editor, 1964-67; Ashland Oil, Inc., Ashland, Ky., assistant to chairman, 1968-69; writer, 1969—. *Military service:* U.S. Merchant Marine, 1941-47. *Member:* Authors Guild, Overseas Press Club.

WRITINGS: The Exception: The History of Ashland Oil, McGraw, 1968; *Robespierre: The Voice of Virtue,* Mason & Lipscomb, 1974; *The Creative Ordeal: The Story of Raytheon,* Atheneum, 1974; *James I,* Mason & Lipscomb, 1976; *The Professional: A Biography of J. B. Saunders,* Atheneum, 1976; *The Secret Six: John Brown and the Abolitionist Movement,* Times Books, 1979.

SIDELIGHTS: Scott writes: "I am a descendant of a long line of businessmen whom I regard as having been productive, creative, and decent men of their times, and I hope to see a world in which we are all able to enjoy liberty without being forced into obeying the blueprints of fanatics.

"My historical books are part of a quartet that opens in the Reformation when the fool James I betrayed the Protestant cause, moves on to the French Revolution and Robespierre, and is now at the time before the American Civil War when six New England idiots armed, financed, encouraged, and hailed John Brown of Harper's Ferry fame. Those accustomed to the usual historical versions will find in all three of these works a pair of eyes that look at the world from a singular vantage: mine. I do not share common views, and have the deepest contempt for persons who follow mass-cults, are parts of coteries, believe what they read in newspapers, and expect, in Will Durant's pithy phrase, 'a world in which the dull will be protected from the clever.' I do not, nor do I fear the world as it is. In my research I find the past to be fascinating mainly where it overlaps, or continues to intrude upon or influence the present.

"I also think it is the duty of writers to expand the knowledge of their readers and to point, from special vantages,

toward elements of life and society that they have not before noticed, considered, or properly judged."

*   *   *

SEBESTA, Sam L(eaton)   1930-

PERSONAL: Born April 4, 1930, in Ellsworth, Kan. *Education:* University of Kansas, B.S., 1953; Northwestern University, M.A., 1960; Stanford University, Ed.D., 1963. *Home:* 1546 Northeast 92nd, Seattle, Wash. 98195. *Office:* University of Washington, 122 Miller Hall, Seattle, Wash. 98195.

CAREER: Teacher and principal at public elementary schools in Kansas, 1950-57; teacher at public junior high school in Illinois, 1958-60; University of Washington, Seattle, assistant professor, 1963-66, associate professor, 1966-70, professor of reading, 1970—. *Military service:* U.S. Air Force, 1956-58. *Member:* International Reading Association, National Council of Teachers of English.

WRITINGS: Ivory, Apes, and Peacocks, International Reading Association, 1968; (with Carl J. Wallen) *The First R: Readings on Teaching Reading,* Science Research Associates, 1972; (with William J. Iverson) *Literature for Thursday's Child,* Science Research Associates, 1975; (with Robert Ruddell) *Time and Beyond,* Allyn & Bacon, 1978.

AVOCATIONAL INTERESTS: Ballet, opera, swimming.

*   *   *

SEEGER, Charles Louis   1886-1979

OBITUARY NOTICE: Born December 14, 1886, in Mexico City, Mexico; died of a heart attack, February 7, 1979, in Bridgewater, Conn. Musicologist and author of works in his field. Seeger, according to the *New York Times,* "taught the first course in musicology in the United States." Seeger was founder of both the American Musicological Society and the American Society for Comparative Musicology. He wrote *Studies in Musicology* and at the time of his death was working on *Principia Musicologica* and an autobiography. In 1977, numerous musicologists gathered at the University of California to pay tribute to Seeger. His son is folksinger Pete Seeger. Obituaries and other sources: *Encyclopedia of Folk, Country, and Western Music,* St. Martin's, 1969; *Directory of American Scholars,* Volume 1: *History,* 6th edition, Bowker, 1974; *Who's Who in America,* 40th edition, Marquis, 1978; *New York Times,* February 8, 1979.

*   *   *

SEEMAN, Ernest Albright   1887-

PERSONAL: Born November 13, 1887, in Durham, N.C.; son of Henry (a printer) and Betty (Albright) Seeman; married Julia Henry (divorced); married Elizabeth Brickel (a commercial artist and writer); children: (first marriage) William Henry. *Education:* Attended elementary school in Durham, N.C. *Politics:* Liberal Democrat. *Religion:* Agnostic. *Home address:* R.D.2, Erwin, Tenn. 37650. *Agent:* Bernice Hoffman, 215 West 75th St., New York, N.Y. 10023.

CAREER: Worked as a clarinetist, a composer, and for King Features; Seeman Printing, Durham, N.C., began as member of staff, later became president; Duke University Press, Durham, manager of press, 1924-34; writer, 1934—. *Military service:* U.S. Navy, World War I.

WRITINGS: American Gold (novel), Dial, 1978. Contributor of about thirty articles to magazines, including *New Re-*

public, Harper's, National Guardian, and *Parents' Magazine.* Past editor of *Character and Personality,* Duke University.

WORK IN PROGRESS: Two novels.

SIDELIGHTS: Seeman began his novel in the 1930's, but more than forty years passed before it could be published. It is an epic novel of a family and a mythical North Carolina tobacco town, and it spans the decades between the Civil War and the 1920's.

Seeman's multi-faceted career began long before he ventured into writing. Barely into his teens, he went on a tour of England to study birds, and made the acquaintance of naturalist John Burroughs. At the age of fourteen he worked for awhile with Samuel Langley, who is credited with inventing the first airplane.

Most of his formal employment was in the printing business, where he met writer Thomas Wolfe. Seeman remained at Duke University Press until his so-called radical ideas and outspoken views on labor practices forced his untimely retirement.

After visiting some of the larger urban areas of the North, notably New York City and Chicago, he and his wife settled down permanently in Tennessee, in a small cabin far back on Bald Mountain, where he continued writing novels (unpublished) and magazine articles until his health failed.

Seeman's wife, Elizabeth, writes: "[In his earlier years] Ernest had an original mind. He studied the handwriting of identical twins, the earliest drawings of young children, and personality problems." She describes him further as "a man with great insight, tender, kind, and sympathetic, with a curious original wit—a great storyteller, with almost total recall."

BIOGRAPHICAL/CRITICAL SOURCES: Elizabeth Seeman, *In the Arms of the Mountain,* Crown, 1961; *New York Times,* August 6, 1978.

*   *   *

SEIGEL, Jerrold (Edward) 1936-

PERSONAL: Born June 9, 1936, in St. Louis, Mo.; son of William and Katherine (Ginsburg) Seigel; married Jayn Rosenfeld (a musician), August 28, 1966; children: Micol, Jessica. *Education:* Harvard University, A.B., 1958; Princeton University, Ph.D., 1963. *Home:* 151 Hartley Ave., Princeton, N.J. 08540. *Office:* Department of History, Princeton University, Princeton, N.J. 08540.

CAREER: Princeton University, Princeton, N.J., instructor, 1961-64, assistant professor, 1964-68, associate professor, 1968-78, professor of history, 1978—. *Member:* American Historical Association, American Association of University Professors.

WRITINGS: Rhetoric and Philosophy in Renaissance Humanism, Princeton University Press, 1968; (editor with T. K. Rabb) *Action and Conviction in Early Modern Europe,* Princeton University Press, 1969; *Marx's Fate: The Shape of a Life,* Princeton University Press, 1978. Contributor to *Dictionary of the History of Ideas,* Scribners, 1973. Contributor of articles and reviews to scholarly journals, including *American Scholar* and *Journal of Interdisciplinary History.*

WORK IN PROGRESS: A book on Bohemianism in nineteenth-century France; studies on modern social theory.

*   *   *

SEILHAMER, Frank Henry 1933-

PERSONAL: Born September 4, 1933, in Pittsburgh, Pa.;

son of Robert and Nancy (Paravate) Seilhamer; married wife, Rosemarie, June 21, 1952; children: Frank, Dora, Darrell, Kimberly. *Education:* Thiel College, B.A., 1956; Lutheran Theological Seminary of Gettysburg, B.D., 1959, S.T.M., 1966; graduate study at University of Pittsburgh, 1959-62, and Johns Hopkins University, 1966-67; Dropsie University, Ph.D., 1971. *Office:* Department of Old Testament, Trinity Lutheran Seminary, 2199 East Main St., Columbus, Ohio 43209.

CAREER: Ordained Lutheran minister; pastor of Lutheran churches in Dubois, Pa., 1959-61, Greensburg, Pa., 1961-64, and Marysville, Pa., 1964-68; Dropsie University, Philadelphia, Pa., assistant to president, 1968-69; Hamma School of Theology, Springfield, Ohio, assistant professor, 1969-72, associate professor, 1972-73, professor of Old Testament and president of school, 1973-78; Trinity Lutheran Seminary, Columbus, Ohio, professor of Old Testament and provost, 1978—. *Member:* Society of Biblical Literature, American School of Oriental Research.

WRITINGS: And God Spoke, CSS Publishing, 1971; *Here Am I,* CSS Publishing, 1972; *Words for Living,* CSS Publishing, 1972; *Tongues as of Fire,* CSS Publishing, 1974; *The New Covenant in Jeremiah,* NWP, 1976; *Prophets and Prophecy,* Fortress, 1977; *Justice Now,* Fortress, 1977; *New Lives for Old,* Augsburg, 1979. Contributor to *New Pulpit Digest.*

WORK IN PROGRESS: Lift Up Your Eyes, a guidebook on the Middle East; *Songs From the Soul,* a commentary on the Psalms.

SIDELIGHTS: Seilhamer writes: "The linking of the presence of God to life here and now is my consuming passion. Probing all of its dimensions and its implications for justice, compassion, and individual and corporate renewal is the focal point of my work in my own country and abroad. With the Middle East as a second home the 'third world' is an integral part of my life and concern, an area to which I return at least once or twice every year."

*   *   *

SEIXAS, Judith S. 1922-

PERSONAL: Born August 7, 1922, in New York, N.Y.; daughter of Irving Abraham (a stockbroker) and Edythe (Carr) Sartorious; married Frank A. Seixas (a physician), September 29, 1946; children: Peter, Abigail Seixas Horowitz, Noah. *Education:* Carleton College, B.A., 1944; Columbia University, M.A., 1945; Rutgers School of Alcohol Studies, certificate, 1969. *Home and office:* 2 Summit Dr., Hastings-on-Hudson, N.Y. 10706.

CAREER: Hunter Model School, New York City, member of psychological testing staff, 1946; Children's Court, White Plains, N.Y., psychologist, 1947; National Opinion Research Center, New York City, interviewer, 1967; Westchester Council on Alcoholism, Westchester County, N.Y., counselor and director of educational services, 1969-75; Alcoholism Services (consulting and educational firm), Hastings-on-Hudson, N.Y., director, 1975—; *Reader's Digest,* Pleasantville, N.Y., counselor in employee alcoholism program, 1976-79. Faculty member, San Diego Summer School of Alcohol Studies, 1972. American Field Service, member of Americans Abroad committee, 1960-72, president, 1962. *Member:* International Council on Alcoholism, National Council on Alcoholism, Alcohol and Drugs Problems of North America, American Orthopsychiatric Association, New York State Federation of Professional Health Educators.

WRITINGS: Alcohol–What It Is, What It Does (for young people), Greenwillow, 1977; (contributor) Nada J. Estes and M. Edith Heinemann, editors, *Alcoholism: Development, Consequences, and Interventions,* Mosby, 1977; *Living With a Parent Who Drinks Too Much* (for young people), Greenwillow, 1979.

SIDELIGHTS: Seixas told *CA:* "My work is basically with alcoholics and their families: counseling, treatment, and referral. I have lived in Hastings for twenty-eight years and feel very involved with this community and, of late, with teen-age drinking problems."

* * *

SELDES, Marian (Hall) 1928-

PERSONAL: Born August 23, 1928, in New York, N.Y.; daughter of Gilbert (a writer and critic) and Alice (Hall) Seldes; married Julian Arnold Claman, November 3, 1953 (divorced August 17, 1961); children: Katharine. *Education:* Studied at School of American Ballet, 1941-44; Neighborhood Playhouse School of the Theatre, graduated, 1947. *Home:* 125 East 57th St., New York, N.Y. 10022. *Office:* Drama Division, Juilliard School, Lincoln Center, New York, N.Y. 10023.

CAREER: Professional actress, 1947—. Performed in more than fifty stage plays, including "The Ginger Man," "Medea," "Crime and Punishment," "Equus," and "Deathtrap"; appeared in feature films, including "The Lonely Night," "Mr. Lincoln," and "The Greatest Story Ever Told," as well as television programs. Artist-in-residence at Stanford University, 1955. Member of faculty and drama director at Juilliard School, 1969—.

MEMBER: Actors Equity Association, American Federation of Television and Radio Artists, Screen Actors Guild. *Awards, honors:* Obie Award from *Village Voice,* 1963, for "The Ginger Man"; Antoinette Perry Award from League of New York Theatres, 1967, for "A Delicate Balance"; Drama Desk Award, 1971, for "Father's Day"; nomination for Antoinette Perry Award from League of New York Theatres, 1971, for "Father's Day," and 1978, for "Deathtrap"; Obie Award from *Village Voice,* 1978, for "Isadora Duncan."

WRITINGS: The Bright Lights, Houghton, 1978.

WORK IN PROGRESS: "A book about being an actress in the theatre."

* * *

SEMENOV, Julian Semenovich 1931-

PERSONAL: Born October 8, 1931, in Moscow, U.S.S.R.; son of Semen Alexandrovich and Galina Nicolaevna Semenov; married Katerina Michalkova, November 8, 1956; children: Dunia, Olga. *Education:* Attended Moscow Institute of Oriental Languages and Moscow State University, both 1954. *Home:* Suvorovsky Blvd., Apt. 6, Moscow, U.S.S.R. *Agent:* V.A.A.P., 6A Bronnaia, Moscow K104, U.S.S.R. *Office:* Union of Soviet Writers, 52 Vokovsky, Moscow, U.S.S.R.

CAREER: Writer. *Literaturnaya Gazeta* (literary newspaper), Moscow, special correspondent in Chile, Australia, Portugal, the United States, Borneo, and China, 1958-68, permanent special correspondent, 1967—; *Pravda* (newspaper), Moscow, U.S.S.R., war correspondent in Vietnam, 1967, permanent special correspondent, 1967—. *Military service:* Entered Soviet Army, 1945; became captain, 1954. *Member:* Union of Soviet Writers (member of the board),

Union of Russian Writers (chairman of International Literature Commission). *Awards, honors:* Lenin's Medal, 1970; Prize of Russian Soviet Republic, 1976, for "Seventeen Moments of Spring" (television film).

WRITINGS—In English: *Pri ispolnenii sluzhebnykh obiazennostei,* [Moscow], 1962, translation by Robert Daglish published as *In the Performance of Duty,* Foreign Languages Publishing (Moscow), 1963; *Petrovka 38: Povesti i rasskazy,* Molodaia gavardiia, 1964, translation by Michael Scammel published as *Petrovka 38,* Stein & Day, 1965; *Semnadtsat mgnovenii vesny* (novel), Molodaia gvardiia, 1970, translation by Katherine Judelson published as *Seventeen Moments of Spring,* Progress Publishers (Moscow), 1973, translation by H. W. Chalsma published as *The Himmler Ploy,* Popular Library, 1978.

Other writings: *Diplomaticheskii agent: Povest* (title means "Ambassador"), Molodaia gvardiia, 1959; (with Natalia Konchalovskaia) *Chzhungo, nin khao* (title means "Good Day, China"), [Moscow], 1959; *Sorok deviat chasov 25 minut* (title means "49 Hours, 25 Minutes"), Molodaia gvardiia, 1960; *Ukhodiat, chtoby vernutsia: Rasskazy i povest,* Sovetskii pisatel, 1961; *Novelly* (title means "Short Stories"), [Moscow], 1966; *Parol ne nuzhen* (title means" No Password Needed"), [Moscow], 1966; *Shifrovka dlia Bliukhera* (title means "Secret Letter for Marschall Bluecher"), [Moscow], 1966; *Maior Vikhr* (title means "Captain Storm"), Voenizdat, 1967; *V'etnam, Laos,* [Moscow], 1969.

On ubil menia pod Luang-Prabangoin (title means "He Killed Me Near Luang Prabang"), [Moscow], 1970; *Marshrut SP-15–Borneo* (title means "Route 15—North Pole to Borneo"), 1971; *Brillianty dlia diktatury proletariata* (title means "Diamonds for Dictatorship of the Proletariat"), Molodaia gvardiia, 1972; *Ogareva, shest* (title means "Six Ogareva"), [Moscow], 1973; *Na "kozle" za volkom,* [Moscow], 1974; *Tainaia voina Maksima Maksimovicha Isaeva* (title means "Secret War of Isaev"), [Moscow], 1974; *Vozvrashchenie v fiestu* (title means "Return to the Fiesta"), [Moscow], 1975.

WORK IN PROGRESS: "Alternative"; "Moscovsky Ra Bochiy"; research on the world political situation and journalism.

SIDELIGHTS: Semenov has been called one of the founders of the new political novel in the U.S.S.R. When asked about this type of writing he told *CA* that "it's necessary for everybody to know history because history is an instrument of progress and peace." Semenov feels that in order to write a political novel "it's necessary to know the subject and be objective."

* * *

SEROFF, Victor I(ilyitch) 1902-1979

OBITUARY NOTICE—See index for *CA* sketch: Born October 14, 1902, in Batoum, Russia (now U.S.S.R.); died May 10, 1979, in New York, N.Y. Pianist and biographer. Seroff studied with Moritz Rosenthal in Vienna and Theodore Szanto in Paris before coming to the United States. In addition to other books on music, Seroff wrote a series of books on Chopin, Mozart, Liszt, and Berlitz for Macmillan. His latest book, *The Real Isadora,* is a biography of Isadora Duncan. Obituaries and other sources: *Who's Who in Music and Musicians' International Directory,* 6th edition, Hafner, 1972; *New York Times,* May 17, 1979.

SHAFFER, Helen B. 1909(?)-1978

PERSONAL: Born in c.1909, in Washington, D.C.; died July 18, 1978, in Washington, D.C., of cancer; married Samuel Shaffer (a journalist); children: Joan, Karen Baskin, Susan Clark. *Education:* George Washington University, earned two bachelor's degrees; also studied at Art Students League in New York. *Residence:* Washington, D.C.

CAREER: Journalist. *Washington Daily News,* Washington, D.C., culture critic and assistant city editor during 1930's; member of Washington, D.C., staff of *Look* magazine; editor for Raymond Gram Swing; associated with Editorial Research Reports, 1952-74, began as senior writer. Notable assignments include coverage of current news topics. *Military service:* Writer with Office of War Information during World War II.

OBITUARIES: Washington Post, July 19, 1978.*

*   *   *

SHALHOPE, Robert E. 1941-

PERSONAL: Born February 24, 1941, in Kansas City, Mo.; son of Lee F. (in trucking) and Cecile (Marshall) Shalhope; married Emma T. Simmons (a travel agent), August 18, 1962; children: Adelaide, Robert. *Education:* DePauw University, B.A., 1963; University of Missouri, M.A., 1964, Ph.D., 1967. *Home:* 500 Terrace Pl., Norman, Okla. 73069. *Office:* Department of History, University of Oklahoma, Norman, Okla. 73069.

CAREER: University of Oklahoma, Norman, assistant professor, 1967-71, associate professor of history, 1971—. *Member:* Organization of American Historians, Institute of Early American History and Culture.

WRITINGS: Sterling Price: Portrait of a Southerner, University of Missouri, 1971. Contributor to history journals.

WORK IN PROGRESS: John Taylor of Caroline: Pastoral Republican; a study of American political culture, 1815-1840.

*   *   *

SHANGE, Ntozake 1948-

PERSONAL: Original name Paulette Williams; name changed in 1971; name pronounced En-to-zaki Shong-gay; born October 18, 1948, in Trenton, N.J.; daughter of Paul T. (a surgeon) and Eloise (a psychiatric social worker and educator) Williams; married second husband, David Murray (a musician), July, 1977. *Education:* Received undergraduate degree from Barnard College (with honors), 1970; received degree from University of Southern California, Los Angeles. *Home:* 203 West 23rd St., No. 1016, New York, N.Y. 10011.

CAREER: Writer and performer. Faculty member in women's studies, California State College, Sonoma; lecturer at Douglass College, 1978. Has given poetry readings.

WRITINGS: For Colored Girls Who Have Considered Suicide/When the Rainbow Is Enuf (choreopoem; first produced in New York City at Studio Rivbea, July 7, 1975; produced Off-Broadway at Anspacher Public Theatre, 1976; produced on Broadway at Booth Theatre, September 15, 1976), Shameless Hussy Press (San Lorenzo, Calif.), 1975, Macmillan, 1976; *Sassafras* (novella), Shameless Hussy Press, 1976; "A Photograph: A Study of Cruelty" (poem-play), first produced in New York City at Public Theatre, December, 1977; (with Thulani Nkabinda and Jessica Hagedorn) "Where the Mississippi Meets the Amazon," first

produced in New York City at Public Theatre Cabaret, 1977; *Natural Disasters and Other Festive Occasions* (prose and poems), Heirs, 1977; *Nappy Edges* (poems), St. Martin's, 1978.

Contributor to periodicals, including *Black Scholar, Third World Women, Ms.,* and *Yardbird Reader.*

WORK IN PROGRESS: A play, "In the Middle of a Flower"; a film adaptation of her novella *Sassafras.*

SIDELIGHTS: "Being alive, being a woman and being colored is a metaphysical dilemma I haven't yet solved," Ntozake Shange told an interviewer. The dilemma has been central to both Shange's life and her writing, and its expression has often been in the form of anger. Laura Berman discussed Shange's rage: "Now, she says, she doesn't know whether the injustices she has suffered because she's black, or those suffered because she's a woman, are greater. She doesn't know whether the angers are separate or whether they converge at some point. But they fuel her work, they account for the intensity with which she speaks, and she feels no desire to escape from them."

Shange's anger wasn't always so evident. "I was always what you call a nice child," she told Jean Vallely. "I did everything nice. I was the nicest and most correct. I did my homework. I was always on time. I never got into fights. People now ask me, 'Where did all this rage come from?' And I just smile and say it's been there all the time, but I was just trying to be nice."

Shange's childhood was filled with music, literature, and art. Dizzy Gillespie, Miles Davis, Chuck Berry, and W.E.B. Du Bois were among the frequent guests at her parents' house. On Sunday afternoons Shange's family held variety shows. She recalled them in a self-interview published in *Ms.:* "my mama wd read from dunbar, shakespeare, countee cullen, t. s. eliot. my dad wd play congas & do magic tricks. my two sisters & my brother & i wd do a soft-shoe & then pick up the instruments for a quartet of some sort: a violin, a cello, flute & saxophone. we all read constantly. anything. anywhere. we also tore the prints outta art books to carry around with us. sounds/images, any explorations of personal visions waz the focus of my world."

However privileged her childhood might have seemed, Shange felt that she was "living a lie." As she explained to Allan Wallach: "[I was] living in a world that defied reality as most black people, or most white people, understood it—in other words, feeling that there was something that I could do, and then realizing that nobody was expecting me to do anything because I was colored and I was also female, which was not very easy to deal with."

One act of protest was Shange's name change from Paulette Williams to the Zulu words Ntozake ("she who comes with her own things") Shange ("she who walks like a lion"). She told Berman: "A name means a lot more than just a signature on your Master Charge. It's who you are. I didn't want to be defined by a heritage that infuriates me. I didn't want any kind of Anglo-Saxon name, because European culture has nothing to do with me. And I didn't want my first name, because I was named after my father—I didn't want a man's name either." And she explained to another interviewer, "I had a violent resentment of carrying a slave name. Poems and music come from the pit of myself, and the pit of myself isn't a slave."

Writing poetry became an outlet for Shange's enraged feminism and a means of expressing her dissatisfaction with the role of black women in society. She and a group of friends, including various musicians and the choreographer-dancer Paula Moss, would create improvisational works comprised of poetry, music, and dance, and would frequently perform them in bars in San Francisco and New York. Moss described their performances, which would eventually develop into "For Colored Girls Who Have Considered Suicide/When the Rainbow Is Enuf": "She (Shange) had this poetry and I had this dance and so we just started to put it out there and see if it would work. At first we had no idea that we would ever be paid or that anyone would ever really look at this as a piece of theatre; we just did this so we would have an outlet. We would go to small bars or schools or something and give a workshop and Ntozake would read and then we would combine the two together. And I guess that's why she calls it a 'choreopoem'; she likes movement to her work because her work is something of a song. I used to use her voice as music; I would just dance to her reading, her poetry, and that would be my music."

Shange told an interviewer about the genesis of "For Colored Girls": "I wanted to be very clear and very honest in these poems. That's why I used the words '*Colored* Girls' in the title. That's a word my grandmother would understand. It wouldn't put her off and turn her away. I wanted to get back to the brass tacks of myself as a child; I was a regular colored girl, with a family that was good to me."

"Shange's poems aren't war cries," Jack Kroll wrote in a review of the Public Theatre production of "For Colored Girls." "They're outcries filled with a controlled passion against the brutality that blasts the lives of 'colored girls'—a phrase that in her hands vibrates with social irony and poetic beauty. These poems are political in the deepest sense, but there's no dogma, no sentimentality, no grinding of false mythic axes." Critic Edith Oliver remarked: "The evening grows in dramatic power, encompassing, it seems, every feeling and experience a woman has ever had; strong and funny, it is entirely free of the rasping earnestness of most projects of this sort. The verses and monologues that constitute the program have been very well chosen—contrasting in mood yet always subtly building." T. E. Kalem noted that "the tension of the evening stems from two separate strands of emotion. On the one hand, these monologues are portraits in embittered pain, the basic proposition being, 'He done her wrong.' On the other hand, they demonstrate the concentric power of love in a woman's life."

While critic Michele Wallace was not completely satisfied with "For Colored Girls," and complained of the occasional "worn-out feminist cliches," she was still able to commend Shange. She wrote: "There is so much about black women that needs retelling; one has to start somewhere, and Shange's exploration of this aspect of our experience, admittedly the most primitive (but we were all there at some time and, if the truth be told, most of us still are) is as good a place as any. All I'm saying is that Shange's 'For Colored Girls' should not be viewed as the definitive statement on black women, but as a very good beginning." She continued: "Very few have written with such clarity and honesty about the black woman's vulnerability, and no one has ever brought Shange's brand of tough humor and realism to it."

Shange's next production, "A Photograph: A Study of Cruelty," received less positive reviews, although critics were generally impressed with the poetic quality of her writing. "Miss Shange is something besides a poet but she is not—at least not at this stage—a dramatist," Richard Eder declared. "More than anything else, she is a troubadour. She declares her fertile vision of the love and pain between black women and black men in outbursts full of old malice and young

cheerfulness. They are short outbursts, song-length; her characters are perceived in flashes, in illuminating vignettes." Martin Gottfried concurred with this assessment and commented: "Shange is a wonderful poet, but she is not yet a playwright and does not create playable characters. Stretches of 'A Photograph' are outright recitations, beautiful soliloquies, but you listen to them as if at a recital, not as dialogue." Oliver's comments were more positive. "[Shange's] own poetic talent and passion carry the show, and her characters are given flesh and blood by the author," she wrote.

Addressing the fact that her writing has been almost entirely woman-centered, Shange wrote: "you haveta remember there's an enormous ignorance abt women's realities in our society. we ourselves suffer from a frightening lack of clarity abt who we are. my work attempts to ferret out what i know & touch in a woman's body. if i really am committed to pulling the so-called personal outta the realm of non-art.... we must learn our common symbols, preen them and share them with the world."

BIOGRAPHICAL/CRITICAL SOURCES: New York Post, June 12, 1976; *Newsweek,* June 14, 1976; *New Yorker,* June 14, 1976, August 2, 1976, January 2, 1978; *Time,* June 14, 1976, July 19, 1976; *New York Daily News,* June 15, 1976; *New York Times,* June 16, 1976, December 22, 1977; *Cue,* June 26, 1976; *Washington Post,* June 29, 1976; *New Leader,* July 5, 1976; *Village Voice,* August 16, 1976; *Newsday,* August 22, 1976; *Christian Science Monitor,* September 9, 1976; *New York Amsterdam News,* October 9, 1976; *Ebony,* August, 1977; *Horizon,* September, 1977; *Ms.,* December, 1977; *Saturday Review,* February 18, 1978; *Washington Post Book World,* October 15, 1978; *Detroit Free Press,* October 30, 1978; *Contemporary Literary Criticism,* Volume 8, Gale, 1978.*

*   *   *

SHAPIRO, Cecile

PERSONAL: Born in New York, N.Y.; daughter of Bernard Cowan Peyser (a jeweler) and Irene (a membership director; maiden name, Roth) Gould; married David Shapiro (an artist and professor of art), June 18, 1944; children: Deborah Shapiro Krasner, Anna Roberta. *Education:* Adelphi University, B.A., 1961; Columbia University, M.A., 1965. *Home:* 124 Susquehanna Ave., Great Neck, N.Y. 11021; (summers) R.D. 77, Cavendish, Vt. 05142. *Agent:* Anita Diamant, Writer's Workshop, Inc., 51 East 42nd St., New York, N.Y. 10017.

CAREER: Hofstra University, Hempstead, N.Y., part-time instructor in English, 1963-64; Herbert H. Lehman College of the City University of New York, Bronx, N.Y., part-time instructor in English, 1965-66; Norwalk Community College, Norwalk, Conn., instructor in English, 1966-68; Harcourt, Brace, Jovanovich, Inc., New York City, textbook editor, 1968-69; free-lance editor and writer, 1969-71; Adelphi University, Garden City, N.Y., supervisor of student teachers in English, 1971-74; free-lance writer, 1974—. *Member:* Authors Guild of Authors League of America, American Society of Journalists and Authors (member of board of directors), Victorian Society, National Book Critics Circle.

WRITINGS: (With Lauris Mason) *Fine Prints: Collecting, Buying, and Selling,* Harper, 1976; (editor with husband, David Shapiro) *Abstract Expressionism: A Record of the Search,* B. Franklin, 1980. Contributor to education and art journals and popular magazines, including *Saturday Review,*

American Preservation, and *Artnews.* Book review editor for "House and Garden" special publications.

WORK IN PROGRESS: "There are always one or two works progressing, but the current ones seem still too fragile for exposure to these pages."

SIDELIGHTS: Shapiro wrote: "My interests include twentieth-century fiction, the decorative and fine arts, architecture and preservation, cooking and gardening, and I write about all of these as well as other subjects as they present themselves. I am perhaps most interested in other women and men, the reason I write personality pieces for magazines and occasionally add to my stack of unpublished fiction."

* * *

SHEEDY, Alexandra Elizabeth 1962-

PERSONAL: Born June 13, 1962, in New York, N.Y.; daughter of John J. (an executive) and Charlotte (a writer and literary agent; maiden name, Baum) Sheedy. *Education:* Attends high school in New York City. *Home:* 145 West 86th St., New York, N.Y. 10024. *Agent:* Charlotte Sheedy, 145 West 86th St., New York, N.Y. 10024.

CAREER: Writer and actress.

WRITINGS: She Was Nice to Mice (for children), illustrated by Jessica Ann Levy, McGraw, 1975. Contributor of articles to periodicals, including *New York Times, Seventeen, Ms.,* and *Village Voice.*

WORK IN PROGRESS: A book, *Yours Truly, Mandy.*

SIDELIGHTS: Sheedy, who wrote her first published book when she was twelve, told *CA:* "I started writing because I used to tell stories to the children who lived nearby and when I was six I started writing them down. I write poetry and plays, too, and writing is important to me. It is important for me to express my feelings and thoughts. If I'm feeling angry or wonderful or upset or happy I just write it out and reread the feelings over and over again. When I'm depressed I read something I wrote when I was happy and I can feel a great lift in my spirits. I love writing!

"I am really close to my parents. My mother and my father do not live together. We children spend half of the week at one house and half of the week at the other house. We have been living as we do for six years. I get along well with my brother Patrick, who is ten, and my sister Meghan, who is thirteen. We have an iguana and rabbit as pets."

* * *

SHELDON, Eleanor Bernert 1920-
(Eleanor H. Bernert)

PERSONAL: Born March 19, 1920, in Hartford, Conn.; daughter of M. G. and Fannie (Myers) Bernert; married James Sheldon (a television film director), March 19, 1950 (divorced); children: James, Jr., John Anthony. *Education:* Colby Junior College, A.A., 1940; University of North Carolina, A.B., 1942; University of Chicago, Ph.D., 1949. *Home:* 630 Park Ave., New York, N.Y. 10021. *Office:* 630 Park Ave., New York, N.Y. 10021.

CAREER: Office of Population Research, Princeton, N.J., assistant demographer in Washington, D.C., 1942-43; U.S. Department of Agriculture, Washington, D.C., social scientist, 1943-45; University of Chicago, Chicago, Ill., associate director of Chicago community inventory, 1947-50; Social Science Research Council, New York City, social scientist, 1950-51; United Nations, New York City, social scientist, 1951-52; University of California, Los Angeles, lecturer in

sociology, 1955-61, research associate, 1955-61, associate research sociologist, 1957-61; Russell Sage Foundation, New York City, sociologist and executive associate, 1961-72; Social Science Research Council, president, 1972—. Research associate at Columbia University, 1950-51, lecturer, 1951-52, visiting professor, 1969-71; visiting professor at University of California, Santa Barbara, winter, 1971. Member of National Science Foundation advisory committees; member of board of scientific counselors, National Institute of Mental Health, 1973-77, head of board, 1975-77; member of National Center for Education Statistics advisory council; member of advisory panel of U.S. Congress, 1976-77; member of national advisory council of University of Texas' Hogg Foundation for Mental Health, 1976-79. Member of board of directors of Equitable Life Assurance Society of the United States, Citicorp and Citibank, Mobil Corp., and United Nations Research Institute for Social Development; member of board of trustees of RAND Corp., American Assembly, Colby-Sawyer College, and Rockefeller Foundation.

MEMBER: International Sociological Association, International Union for the Scientific Study of Population, American Association for the Advancement of Science (fellow), American Association for Public Opinion Research, American Sociological Association (fellow), American Statistical Association (fellow), Population Society of America (second vice-president, 1970-71), Society for Research in Child Development, American Academy of Arts and Sciences (fellow), Sociological Research Association (president, 1971-72), Council on Foreign Relations, Eastern Sociological Society.

WRITINGS—Under name Eleanor H. Bernert: (Contributor) E. W. Burgess, editor, *Methods of Personality Study,* Department of Sociology, University of Chicago, 1946; (with Louis Wirth) *Chicago Community Fact Book,* University of Chicago Press, 1949; (contributor) Paul Hatt and A. J. Reiss, Jr., editors, *Reader in Urban Sociology,* Free Press, 1951; *America's Children,* Wiley, 1958; (contributor) Eli Ginzberg, editor, *The Nation's Children,* Volume I: *The Family and Social Change,* Columbia University Press, 1960; (contributor) N. B. Henry, editor, *Social Forces Influencing American Education,* University of Chicago Press, 1961.

Under name Eleanor Bernert Sheldon; (with R. A. Glazier) *Pupils and Schools in New York City,* Russell Sage, 1965; (contributor) A. J. Reiss, Jr., editor, *The School in a Changing Society,* Free Press, 1965; (contributor) Leonard Goodman, editor, *Economic Progress and Social Welfare,* Columbia University Press, 1966; (editor with W. E. Moore, and contributor) *Indicators of Social Change: Concepts and Measurements,* Russell Sage, 1968; (contributor) *Federal Statistics: Report of the President's Commission,* Volume II, U.S. Government Printing Office, 1971; (editor) *Family Economic Behavior,* Lippincott, 1973; (contributor) R. L. Clewett and J. C. Olson, editors, *Social Indicators and Marketing,* American Marketing Association, 1973; (contributor) *Evaluating Governmental Performance: Changes and Challenges for GAO,* U.S. Government Printing Office, 1975; (contributor) Jules Backman, editor, *Social Responsibility and Accountability,* New York University Press, 1975.

Contributor to *Encyclopedia of Social Work* and *International Encyclopedia of the Social Sciences.* Contributor of about twenty articles to professional journals.

WORK IN PROGRESS: Corporate Social Responsibility.

SIDELIGHTS: Sheldon told *CA:* "From almost the very

beginning of my academic work, I have been interested in specialized types of cross-disciplinary research. Over the years, this has taken the form of an examination of the determinants and consequences of population change, having been a demographer, and followed by research in the general fields of medical sociology and child studies.

"In more recent years, I have devoted my attention to problems in the conceptualization and measurement of social change, again drawing not only on my demographic and sociological training, but on my interests in economics, urbanization, and statistics.

"These activities have coalesced into my present commitment to the field of social indicators, concerned predominantly with the causes, measurement, and potential prediction of large-scale social change and its effects on the quality of human life."

* * *

SHERIDAN, Anne-Marie 1948-

PERSONAL: Born January 11, 1948, in Paris, France; daughter of James Selwyn (a diplomat) and Jane (Sherlock) Sheridan. *Education:* Newnham College, Cambridge, B.A., 1970. *Religion:* Church of England. *Agent:* Georges Borchardt, Inc., 136 East 57th St., New York, N.Y. 10022.

CAREER: Secretary and companion to businesswomen, 1966-70; free-lance writer, 1974—.

WRITINGS: The Far-Off Rhapsody (novel), Simon & Schuster, 1976; *Summoned to Darkness* (novel), Simon & Schuster, 1978.

WORK IN PROGRESS: Another novel.

SIDELIGHTS: Anne-Marie Sheridan writes: "Having a private income, I am not strongly motivated to work, even if I were not a hedonist. But when I do get around to it, I take a tremendous amount of pain and trouble. Hedonists are always perfectionists."

* * *

SHERRIFF, R(obert) C(edric) 1896-1975

PERSONAL: Born June 6, 1896, in Kingston-on-Thames, England; died November 13, 1975; son of Herbert Hankin (an insurance agent) and Constance (Winder) Sherriff. *Education:* Attended New College, Oxford, 1931-34.

CAREER: British playwright, novelist, and scriptwriter for films, television, and radio. Claims adjuster for Sun Insurance Office, 1914, 1918-28. *Military service:* British Army, c.1915-18, served in East Surrey Regiment; became captain. *Member:* Royal Society of Literature (fellow), Society of Antiquaries (fellow).

WRITINGS—Plays: Journey's End (three-act; first produced on the West End at Apollo Theatre, December 9, 1928; produced on Broadway at Henry Miller's Theatre, March 22, 1929), Gollancz, 1929, Samuel French, 1931; *Badger's Green* (three-act; first produced in London, 1930), Gollancz, 1930, Samuel French, 1934, revised edition, 1962; *Two Hearts Doubled* (playlet), Samuel French, 1934; (with Jeanne De Casalis) *St. Helena* (twelve-scene; first produced on the West End at Old Vic Theatre, February 4, 1936; produced on Broadway at Lyceum Theatre, October 6, 1936), Gollancz, 1934, Stokes Publishing, 1935; *Miss Mabel* (three-act; first produced on the West End at Duchess Theatre, November 23, 1948), Gollancz, 1949.

Home at Seven (three-act; first produced on the West End at Wyndham's Theatre, March 7, 1950), Gollancz, 1950; "The

Kite," contained in *Action: Beacon Lights of Literature*, edited by Georgia G. Winn and others, Iroquois, 1952; *The White Carnation* (two-act; first produced on the West End at Globe Theatre, March 20, 1953), Samuel French, 1953; *The Long Sunset* (three-act; first produced off the West End at Mermaid Theatre, November 3, 1962), Elek, 1956, Samuel French, 1958; *The Telescope* (three-act; first produced on the West End at Prince of Wales' Theatre, April 20, 1960), Samuel French, 1961. Also author of: "Profit and Loss," 1923; "Mr. Bridie's Finger," 1926; "Windfall," first produced in London, 1933; "Dark Evening," 1949.

Novels: (With Vernon Bartlett) *Journey's End* (adapted from the play by Sherriff; see above), Gollancz, 1930, reprinted, 1968; *The Fortnight in September,* Gollancz, 1931, Stokes Publishing, 1932; *Greengates,* Stokes Publishing, 1936; *The Hopkins Manuscript,* Macmillan, 1939, reprinted with introduction by John Gassner, 1963, revised edition published as *The Cataclysm,* Pan Books, 1958; *Chedworth,* Macmillan, 1944; *Another Year,* Macmillan, 1948; *The Wells of St. Mary's,* Heinemann, 1962, Hutchinson, 1973; *The Siege of Swayne Castle,* Gollancz, 1973.

Screenplays: "The Invisible Man," Universal, 1933; (with Charles Kenyon) "The Road Back," Universal, 1937; "Goodbye, Mr. Chips," Metro-Goldwyn-Mayer (MGM), 1939; "Four Feathers," United Artists, 1939; "That Hamilton Woman," United Artists, 1941; "This Above All," Twentieth Century-Fox, 1943; (with F. L. Green) "Odd Man Out," Universal, 1947, contained in *Three British Screen Plays,* edited by Roger Manvell, Methuen, 1950; *Quartet: Stories by W. Somerset Maugham, Screenplays by R. C. Sherriff* (Eagle Lion, 1949), Heinemann, 1948, Doubleday, 1949; *Trio: Stories by W. Somerset Maugham, Screen Adaptations by W. Somerset Maugham, R. C. Sherriff, and Noel Langley* (Paramount Pictures, 1950), Doubleday, 1950; "No Highway in the Sky," Twentieth Century-Fox, 1951; "The Night My Number Came Up," Continental, 1955; "The Dam Busters," Warner Brothers, 1955; "Storm Over the Nile," Columbia, 1956.

Other: *King John's Treasure* (juvenile), Macmillan, 1954; *No Leading Lady* (autobiography), Gollancz, 1968. Also author of radio plays, "The Long Sunset," 1955, and "Cards With Uncle Tom," 1958, and television play, "The Ogburn Story," 1963.

SIDELIGHTS: Though R. C. Sherriff gained fame as a novelist and a screenwriter, he is best known for his play *The Journey's End,* which has been considered one of the most influential war dramas of its time.

Sherriff did not plan to become a writer. He began writing plays for the Kingston Rowing Club to perform in order to earn money for the club. The seventh year he ran out of comedy ideas for a new play and instead jotted down some notes on conversations and characters from his experiences during World War I. The resulting play, *The Journey's End,* was a success not only locally, but nationally and internationally as well. Sherriff sent the play for criticism to George Bernard Shaw, who helped launch it on its prosperous West End run.

Rebecca West commented that *The Journey's End* is "enormously impressive and stirring, and in the matters of dialogue and selection it is beyond praise," although the play's obsession with youth and immaturity makes it "a sad play, sadder even than a war play ought to be." In 1929, A. G. Macdonell declared: "The Peace Societies of England ought to join together and send *Journey's End* on tour throughout the length and breadth of the country. It is worth fifty times more than all their propaganda."

Sherriff's next play, *Badger's Green,* had a disappointing reception in London. He therefore determined to become a schoolmaster and entered New College, Oxford at the age of thirty-five. He seemed to excel at his rowing rather than his studies, however, and when he had an attack of pleurisy it ended his rowing career and his chances of earning a degree as well.

Fortunately, Sherriff's writing talents came to his aid. He wrote a novel, *The Fortnight in September,* which was an instant success despite the fact that he had originally had no intention of publishing the book. Sherriff often commented that he seemed to write best when he wasn't trying, and this maxim proved true throughout his career.

In 1933, James Whale, a Hollywood director, invited Sherriff to help write a screenplay for H. G. Wells's *The Invisible Man.* Others had attempted unsuccessfully to write the script, but by sticking to the original plot Sherriff managed it adeptly. In the following years he returned to Hollywood often to work on such screenplays as "Goodbye, Mr. Chips," "That Hamilton Woman," and "The Night My Number Came Up."

Several of Sherriff's plays have been adapted as films, including: "The Journey's End," Tiffany, 1930; "Badger's Green," Highbury, 1949; and *Home at Seven,* filmed as "Murder on Monday," Mayer-Kingsley, 1953.

AVOCATIONAL INTERESTS: Rowing, cricket, archaeology.

BIOGRAPHICAL/CRITICAL SOURCES: London Mercury, January, 1929; Rebecca West, *Ending in Earnest,* Doubleday, 1931; R. C. Sherriff, *No Leading Lady* (autobiography), Gollancz, 1968; *Observer Review,* July 28, 1968; *Punch,* August 7, 1968; *Books and Bookmen,* September, 1968; *Times Literary Supplement,* September 19, 1968; *Observer,* January 11, 1970; *Guardian Weekly,* January 20, 1973.

OBITUARIES: New York Times, November 18, 1975; *AB Bookman's Weekly,* January 5, 1976.*

* * *

SHOSTECK, Robert 1910-1979

OBITUARY NOTICE—See index for *CA* sketch: Born April 25, 1910, in Newark, N.J.; died of a heart attack, March 18, 1979, in Bethesda, Md. Museum curator and writer on nature. Shosteck was a forest ranger and outdoors editor for the *Washington Post* before joining B'nai B'rith, the Jewish service organization, in 1941. He directed research in the vocational services bureau there until 1957, when he became curator of the organization's museum. A lover of the outdoors, Shosteck worked as a consultant to the National Park Service, founded hiking clubs, and wrote several books on nature, including *Potomac Trail Book* and *Flowers and Plants: An International Lexicon.* Obituaries and other sources: *Who's Who in World Jewry,* Pitman, 1972; *Who's Who in the South and Southwest,* 13th edition, Marquis, 1973; *Washington Post,* March 20, 1979.

* * *

SHOWELL, Ellen Harvey 1934-

PERSONAL: Born October 26, 1934, in Kingsport, Tenn.; daughter of Clarence B. and Elizabeth (a teacher; maiden name, Hudson) Harvey; married John S. Showell; children: Michael D. H. *Education:* Berea College, A.B., 1957. *Religion:* Unitarian-Universalist. *Home:* 1200 North Cleveland St., Arlington, Va. 22201. *Agent:* McIntosh & Otis, Inc., 475 Fifth Ave., New York, N.Y. 10017.

CAREER: Advertising and public relations writer for housing and light construction industry, Washington, D.C., 1961-63; Office of Economic Opportunity and Action, Washington, D.C., feature story writer for VISTA program, 1963-71; free-lance writer, 1971—.

WRITINGS: The Ghost of Tillie Jean Cassaway (juvenile), Four Winds Press, 1978.

WORK IN PROGRESS: A children's novel about a commune in Appalachia.

SIDELIGHTS: Ellen Showell writes: "I wanted to write a ghost story for children that had a real element of mystery in it, to tell a good story but to leave the reader with a respect for what is not known. Having grown up in the mountains, I know they excite a sense of mystery and wonder and beauty."

* * *

SIBLEY, Celestine 1917-

PERSONAL: Born May 23, 1917, in Holly, Fla.; daughter of W. R. (in lumber business) and Evelyn (Barber) Sibley; married James W. Little (deceased); children: James W., Susan Little Bazemore, Mary Little Vance. *Education:* Attended Spring Hill College and University of Florida. *Politics:* Democrat. *Religion:* Presbyterian. *Home address:* Route 1, Woodstock, Ga. 30188. *Agent:* Edward J. Acton, Inc., 17 Grove St., New York, N.Y. 10014. *Office: Atlanta Constitution,* 72 Marietta St., Atlanta, Ga. 30302.

CAREER: Atlanta Constitution, Atlanta, Ga., currently reporter and author of column; writer. Member of board of directors of United Nations Children's Fund (UNICEF); past member of board of directors of Atlanta Child Service and local Legal Aid Society. *Awards, honors:* Three awards from Associated Press for news stories; two awards from Georgia Conference on Social Work for stories contributing to human welfare; radio and television awards from Pall Mall; awards from Dixie Council of Authors and Journalists, for *Small Blessings;* Green Eyeshadow Award from Sigma Delta Chi.

WRITINGS—All published by Doubleday unless otherwise indicated: *The Malignant Heart* (mystery novel), 1957; *Peachtree Street, U.S.A.: An Affectionate Portrait of Atlanta,* 1963; *Christmas in Georgia* (stories), 1964; *A Place Called Sweet Apple,* 1967; *Dear Store: An Affectionate Portrait of Rich's,* 1967; *Especially at Christmas,* 1969; *Mothers Are Always Special,* 1970; *The Sweet Apple Gardening Book,* 1972; *Day by Day With Celestine Sibley,* 1975; (author of introduction) *The Compleat Vegetable Book,* Oxmoor House, 1976; *Small Blessings,* 1977; *Jincey,* Simon & Schuster, 1979.

* * *

SILVER, Alfred 1951-

PERSONAL: Born March 13, 1951, in Brandon, Manitoba, Canada; son of Gerald J. and Margerita Silver. *Education:* Attended vocational high school in Winnipeg, Manitoba. *Office address:* P.O. Box 462, Winnipeg, Manitoba, Canada R3C 2J3.

CAREER: Actor, 1971—; musician, 1972—; cab driver, 1976; guitar teacher, 1977—. *Awards, honors:* Sir Barry Jackson Trophy from Dominion Drama Festival, 1970, for "Mad Jack's Escape."

WRITINGS: Good Time Charlie's Back in Town Again (novel), Avon, 1978.

Plays: "Mad Jack's Escape" (three-act), first produced in Winnipeg, Manitoba at Manitoba Theatre School, 1969; "Volka Sane" (two-act), first produced in Regina, Saskatchewan at University of Saskatchewan, 1978; "Dud Shuffle" (three-act), first produced at Manitoba Theatre Workshop, 1978; "More of a Family" (one-act), first produced at Manitoba Theatre Workshop, 1978.

Radio scripts: "Spaw," Canadian Broadcasting Corp. (CBC), 1978; "U.I.C.," CBC, 1979.

WORK IN PROGRESS: The Murder of Jack Marchon (tentative title), a novel about a hypothetical society that exists without laws; research on the life of Xenophon and on early Iron Age civilizations.

SIDELIGHTS: Silver writes: "Whatever I've learned has been learned from experience. Whatever I have to say can only be communicated by taking someone through an experience, which is to say, by telling a story."

*   *   *

SIMENON, Georges (Jacques Christian) 1903-
(Bobette, Christian Brulls, Germain d'Antibes, Jacques Dersonnes, Georges d'Isly, Luc Dorsan, Jean Dorsange, Jean Dossage, Jean du Perry, Georges Martin Georges, Gom Gut, Kim, Plick et Plock, Georges Sim, Gaston Vialis, G. Violis)

PERSONAL: Born February 13, 1903, in Liege, Belgium; son of Desire (an insurance clerk) and Henriette (Brull) Simenon; married Regine Renchon, March 24, 1923 (divorced, June 21, 1950); married Denise Ouimet, June 22, 1950; children: Marc, Jean, Marie-Georges, Pierre. *Education:* Educated in Liege, Belgium. *Address:* 12 Avenue des Figuiers, 1007, Lausanne, Switzerland.

CAREER: Worked as a baker's apprentice and bookstore clerk in Liege, Belgium; *Liege Gazette,* Liege, began as police reporter, became comic columnist; wrote first novel *Au pont des arches* (a satire), 1921; went to Paris, France, 1922, and became full-time writer of pulp fiction under various pseudonyms; traveled in Europe during late 1920's on his yacht, *Ostrogot;* wrote first "Maigret" novel while in the Netherlands, 1931, and produced nineteen "Maigret" mysteries, 1931-33; abandoned "Maigret" character and turned to psychological novels, 1933-73; continued "Maigret" series, 1940; came to the United States following World War II and traveled and lived in the United States and Canada; moved to Switzerland, 1955—; retired from writing novels, 1973; currently writing diaries and nonfiction. *Wartime service:* Worked with refugees in Vichy, France during World War II. *Member:* Acadame Royale de Langue et Litterature Francaise (Brussels). *Awards, honors:* Received Grand Masters Award from Mystery Writers of America.

WRITINGS—All novels in "Maigret" series: *Pietr-le-Letton,* Fayard, 1931, translation published as *The Strange Case of Peter the Lett,* Covici-Friede, 1933, translation by Anthony Abbott published as "The Case of Peter the Lett" in *Inspector Maigret Investigates,* Hurst & Blackett, 1934, translation by Daphne Woodward published as *Maigret and the Enigmatic Lett,* Penguin, 1963; *Au rendez-vous des terre-neuvas,* Fayard, 1931, translation by Margaret Ludwig published as "The Sailors Rendezvous" in *Maigret Keeps a Rendezvous,* George Routledge, 1940, Harcourt, 1941; *Le Charretier de la "Providence,"* Fayard, 1931, translation published as *The Crime at Lock 14* [with] *The Shadow on the Courtyard,* Covici-Friede, 1934, translation by Robert Baldick published as *Maigret Meets a Milord,* Penguin, 1963;

Le Chien jaune, Fayard, 1931, translation by Geoffrey Sainsbury published as "A Face for a Clue" in *The Patience of Maigret,* George Routledge, 1939, Harcourt, 1940, published as *A Face for a Clue* [with] *A Crime in Holland,* Penguin, 1952; *La Danseuse du Gai-Moulin,* Fayard, 1931, translation by Sainsbury published as "At the Gai-Moulin" in *Maigret Abroad,* Harcourt, 1940, published as *At the Gai-Moulin* [with] *A Battle of Nerves,* Penguin, 1951; *M. Gallet decede,* Fayard, 1931, translation published as *The Death of Monsieur Gallet,* Covici-Friede, 1932, translation by Anthony Abbott published as "The Death of M. Gallet" in *Introducing Inspector Maigret,* Hurst & Blackett, 1933, translation by Margaret Marshall published as *Maigret Stonewalled,* Penguin, 1963.

La Nuit du carrefour, Fayard, 1931, translation published as *The Crossroad Murders,* Covici-Friede, 1933, translation by Abbot published as "The Crossroad Murders" in *Inspector Maigret Investigates,* Hurst & Blackett, 1933, published as *La Nuit de carrefour,* edited and adapted by P. W. Packer, Oxford University Press, 1935, translation by Robert Baldick published as *Maigret at the Crossroads,* Penguin, 1963; *Le Pendu de Saint-Phiolien,* Fayard, 1931, translation by Abbot published as *The Crime of Inspector Maigret,* Covici-Friede, 1933, published as "The Crime of Inspector Maigret" in *Introducing Inspector Maigret,* Hurst & Blackett, translation by Tony White published as *Maigret and the Hundred Gibbets,* Penguin, 1963, published as *Maigret et le Pendu de Saint-Pholien,* edited by Geoffrey Goodall, St. Martin's, 1965; *Un Crime en Hollande,* Fayard, 1931, translation by Geoffrey Sainsbury published as "A Crime in Holland" in *Maigret Abroad,* Harcourt, 1940, published as *A Crime in Holland* [with] *A Face for a Clue,* Penguin, 1952; *La Tete d'un homme (L'Homme de la Tour Eiffel),* Fayard, 1931, translation by Sainsbury published as "A Battle of Nerves" in *The Patience of Maigret,* George Routledge, 1939, Harcourt, 1940, published as *A Battle of Nerves* [with] *At the Gai-Moulin,* Penguin, 1950.

L'Affaire Saint Fiacre, Fayard, 1932, translation by Margaret Ludwig published as "The Saint-Fiacre Affair" in *Maigret Keeps a Rendezvous,* George Routledge, 1940, Harcourt, 1941, translation by Robert Baldick published as *Maigret Goes Home,* Penguin, 1967; *Chez les Flamands,* Fayard, 1932, translation by Geoffry Sainsbury published as "The Flemish Shop" in *Maigret to the Rescue,* George Routledge, 1940, Harcourt, 1941; *Le Fou de Bergerac,* Fayard, 1932, translation by Sainsbury published as "The Madman of Bergerac" in *Maigret Travels South,* Harcourt, 1940; *La Guinguette a duex sous,* Fayard, 1932, translation by Sainsbury published as "Guinguette by the Seine" in *Maigret to the Rescue,* George Routledge, 1940, Harcourt, 1941; *Liberty Bar,* Fayard, 1932, translation by Sainsbury published as "Liberty Bar" in *Maigret Travels South,* Harcourt, 1940; *L'Ombre Chinoise,* Fayard, 1932, translation published as *The Shadow in the Courtyard* [with] *The Crime at Lock 14,* Covici-Friede, 1934, published in England as "The Shadow in the Courtyard" in *The Triumph of Inspector Maigret,* Hurst & Blackett, 1934, translation by Jean Stewart published as *Maigret Mystified,* Penguin, 1965; *Le Port des brumes,* Fayard, 1932, translation by Stuart Gilbert published as "Death of a Harbormaster" in *Maigret and M. L'Abbe,* George Routledge, 1941, Harcourt, 1942; *L'Ecluse no. 1,* Fayard, 1933, translation by Margaret Ludwig published as "The Lock at Charenton" in *Maigret Sits It Out,* Harcourt, 1941; *Maigret,* Fayard, 1934, translation by Ludwig published as "Maigret Returns" in *Maigret Sits It Out,* Harcourt, 1941.

Cecile est morte, Gallimard, 1942, translation by Eileen Ellenbogen published as *Maigret and the Spinster*, Harcourt, 1977; *Maigret et les caves du Majestic*, [published], 1942, translation by Caroline Hiller published as *Maigret and the Hotel Majestic*, Hamish Hamilton, 1977, Harcourt, 1978; *Maigret a New York*, Presses de la Cite, 1947, translation by Adrienne Foulke published as *Maigret in New York's Underworld*, Doubleday, 1955, published as *Inspector Maigret in New York's Underworld*, New American Library, 1956; *Maigret se fache*, Presses de la Cite, 1947; *La Pipe de Maigret*, Presses de la Cite, 1947; *Maigret et son morte*, Presses de la Cite, 1948, translation by Jean Stewart published as *Maigret's Dead Man*, Doubleday, 1964 published as *Maigret's Special Murder*, Hamish Hamilton, 1964; *Les Vacances de Maigret*, Presses de la Cite, 1948, translation by Geoffrey Sainsbury published as *Maigret on Holiday*, Routledge & Kegan Paul, 1950, published as *No Vacation for Maigret*, Doubleday, 1953; *Maigret chez le coroner*, Presses de la Cite, 1949; *Maigret et la vieille dame*, Presses de la Cite, translation by Robert Brain published as *Maigret and the Old Lady*, Hamish Hamilton, 1958; *Mon ami Maigret*, Presses de la Cite, 1949, translation by Nigel Ryan published as *My Friend Maigret*, Hamish Hamilton, published as *The Methods of Maigret*, Doubleday, 1957; *La Premier Enquette de Maigret, 1913*, Presses de la Cite, 1949, translation by Robert Brain published as *Maigret's First Case*, Hamish Hamilton, 1965.

L'Amie de Mme Maigret, Presses de la Cite, 1950, translation by Helen Sebba published as *Madame Maigret's Own Case*, Doubleday, 1959 published as *Madame Maigret's Friend*, Hamish Hamilton, 1960; *Les Petits Cochons sans queues*, Presses de la Cite, 1950, published as *Maigret et les petits cochons sans queues*, 1957; *Maigret en mueble*, Presses de la Cite, 1951, translation by Robert Brain published as *Maigret Takes a Room*, Hamish Hamilton, 1960, published as *Maigret Rents a Room*, Doubleday, 1961; *Maigret et la grande perche*, Presses de la Cite, 1951, translation by J. Maclaren-Ross published as *Maigret and the Burglar's Wife*, Hamish Hamilton, 1955, published as *Inspector Maigret and the Burglar's Wife*, Doubleday, 1956; *Les Memories de Maigret*, Presses de la Cite, 1951, translation by Jean Stewart published as *Maigret's Memories*, Hamish Hamilton, 1963.

Maigret, Longnon et les gangsters, Presses de la Cite, 1952, translation by Louise Varese published as *Maigret and the Killers*, Doubleday, 1954, published as *Maigret and the Gangsters*, Hamish Hamilton, 1974; *Le Revolver de Maigret*, Presses de la Cite, 1952, translation by Nigel Ryan published as *Maigret's Revolver*, Doubleday, 1956; *Maigret et l'homme du banc*, Presses de la Cite, 1953, translation by Eileen Ellenbogen published as *Maigret and the Man on the Bench*, Harcourt, 1975, published in England as *Maigret and the Man on the Bench*, Harcourt, 1975, published in England as *Maigret and the Man on the Boulevard*, Hamish Hamilton, 1975; *Maigret a peur*, Presses de la Cite, 1953, translation by Margaret Duff published as *Maigret Afraid*, Hamish Hamilton, 1961, *Maigret se trompe*, Presses de la Cite, 1953, translation by Alan Hodge published as "Maigret's Mistake" in *Maigret Right and Wrong*, Hamish Hamilton, 1957; *Maigret a l'ecole*, Presses de la Cite, 1954, translation by Daphne Woodward published as *Maigret Goes to School*, Hamish Hamilton, 1957; *Maigret chez le ministre*, privately printed, 1954, translation by Moura Budberg published as *Maigret and the Calme Report*, Harcourt, 1969, published in England as *Maigret and the Minister*, Hamish Hamilton, 1969; *Maigret et la jeune morte*, Presses de la Cite, 1954,

translation by Woodward published as *Inspector Maigret and the Dead Girl*, Doubleday, 1955, published as *Maigret and the Young Girl*, Hamish Hamilton, 1955.

Maigret et le corps sans tete, privately printed, 1955, translation by Eileen Ellenbogen published as *Maigret and the Headless Corpse*, Hamish Hamilton, 1967, Harcourt, 1968; *Un Echec de Maigret*, Presses de la Cite, 1956, translation by Daphne Woodward published as *Maigret's Failure*, Hamish Hamilton, 1962; *Maigret s'amuse*, Presses de la Cite, 1957, translation by Richard Brain published as *Maigret's Little Joke*, Hamish Hamilton, 1957, published as *None of Maigret's Business*, Doubleday, 1958; *Maigret voyage*, Presses de la Cite, 1958, translation by Jean Stewart published as *Maigret and the Millionaires*, Harcourt, 1974; *Les Scrupules de Maigret*, Presses de la Cite, 1959, translation by Robert Eglesfield published as *Maigret Has Scruples*, 1959, Hamish Hamilton, published as "Maigret Has Scruples" in *Versus Inspector Maigret*, Doubleday, 1960, published as *Maigret Has Scruples* [with] *Maigret and the Reluctant Witness*, Ace Books, 1962; *Une Confidence de Maigret*, Presses de la Cite, 1959, translation by Lyn Moir published as *Maigret Has Doubts*, Hamish Hamilton, 1968; *Maigret et les temoins recalcitrants*, Presses de la Cite, 1959, translation by Daphne Woodward published as "Maigret and the Reluctant Witness" in *Versus Inspector Maigret*, Doubleday, 1960.

Maigret aux assises, Presses de la Cite, 1960, translation by Robert Brain published as *Maigret in Court*, Hamish Hamilton, 1961; *Maigret et les vieillards*, Presses de la Cite, 1960, translation by Robert Eglesfield published as *Maigret in Society*, Hamish Hamilton, 1962; *Maigret et le voleur paresseux*, Presses de la Cite, 1961, translation by Daphne Woodward published as *Maigret and the Lazy Burglar*, Hamish Hamilton, 1963; *Maigret et les braves gens*, Presses de la Cite, 1962, translation by Helen Thompson published as *Maigret and the Black Sheep*, Harcourt, 1976; *Maigret et le client du samedi*, Presses de la Cite, 1962, translation by Tony White published as *Maigret and the Saturday Caller*, Hamish Hamilton, 1964; *Maigret et l'inspecteur malgracieux*, Presses de la Cite, 1962; *La Colere de Maigret*, Presses de la Cite, 1963, translation by Robert Eglesfield published as *Maigret Loses His Temper*, Hamish Hamilton, 1965, Harcourt, 1974; *Maigret et le clochard*, Presses de la Cite, translation by Jean Stewart published as *Maigret and the Bum*, Harcourt, 1973, published as *Maigret and the Dosser*, Hamish Hamilton, 1973; *Maigret et le fantome*, Presses de la Cite, 1964, translation by Eileen Ellenbogen published as *Maigret and the Apparition*, Harcourt, 1976, published as *Maigret and the Ghost*, Hamish Hamilton, 1976; *Maigret se defend*, Presses de la Cite, 1964, translation by Alistair Hamilton published as *Maigret on the Defensive*, Hamish Hamilton, 1966, *La Patience de Maigret*, Presses de la Cite, translation by Alistair Hamilton published as *The Patience of Maigret*, Hamish Hamilton, 1966; *Maigret et l'affair Nahour*, Presses de la Cite, 1966, translation by Alistair Hamilton published as *Maigret and the Nahour Case*, Hamish Hamilton, 1967; *Le Voleur de Maigret*, Presses de la Cite, 1967, translation by Nigel Ryan published as *Maigret's Pickpocket*, Harcourt, 1968; *L'Ami d'enfance de Maigret*, Presses de la Cite, 1968, translation by Eileen Ellenbogen published as *Maigret's Boyhood Friend*, Harcourt, 1970; *Maigret a Vichy*, Presses de la Cite, 1968, translation by Ellenbogen published as *Maigret in Vichy*, Harcourt, 1969, published as *Maigret Takes the Waters*, Hamish Hamilton, 1969; *Maigret hesite*, Presses de la Cite, 1968, translation by Lyn Moir published as *Maigret Hesitates*, Harcourt, 1970;

Maigret et le tueur, Presses de la Cite, 1969, translation by Moir published as *Maigret and the Killer,* Harcourt, 1971, published as *Le Meurtre d'un etudiant,* edited by Frederick Ernst, Holt, 1971.

La Folle de Maigret, Presses de la Cite, 1970, translation by Eileen Ellenbogen published as *Maigret and the Madwoman,* Harcourt, 1972; *Maigret et le marchand de vin,* Presses de la Cite, 1970, translation by Ellenbogen published as *Maigret and the Wine Merchant,* Harcourt, 1971; *Maigret et l'homme tout seul,* Presses de la Cite, 1971, translation by Ellenbogen published as *Maigret and the Loner,* Harcourt, 1975; *Maigret et l'indicateur,* Presses de la Cite, 1971, translation by Lyn Moir published as *Maigret and the Informer,* Harcourt, 1972, published as *Maigret and the Flea,* Hamish Hamilton, 1972; *Maigret et Monsieur Charles,* Presses de la Cite, 1972, translation by Marianne A. Sinclair published as *Maigret and Monsieur Charles,* Hamish Hamilton, 1973. Also author of: *Maigret au "Picratts,"* Presses de la Cite, translation by Cornelia Schaffer published as *Inspector Maigret and the Strangled Stripper,* Doubleday, 1956, translation by Daphne Woodward published as "Maigret in Montmartre" in *Maigret Right and Wrong,* Hamish Hamilton, 1954.

All novels; all published by Fayard, except as indicated: *Le Relais d'Alsace,* 1931, translation by Stuart Gilbert published as "The Man From Everywhere" in *Maigret and M. Labbe,* George Routledge, 1941, Harcourt, 1942, published as *The Man From Everywhere* [with] *Newhaven-Dieppe,* Penguin, 1952; *Le Passageur du "Polarlys,"* 1932, translation by Gilbert published as "The Mystery of the 'Polarlys'" in *Two Latitudes,* George Routledge, 1942, Harcourt, 1943, translation by Victor Kosta published as "Danger at Sea" in *On Land and Sea,* Hanover House, 1954; *Les Treize Coupables,* 1932; *Les Treize Enigmes,* 1932; *Les Treize Mysteries,* 1932; *L'Ane rouge,* 1933; *Le Coup de lune,* 1933, translation by Gilbert published as "Tropic Moon" in *Two Latitudes,* George Routledge, 1942, Harcourt, 1943, published as *Tropic Moon,* Berkeley, 1958; *Les Fiancailles de M. Hire,* 1933, translation by Daphne Woodward published as "Mr. Hire's Engagement" in *The Sacrifice,* Hamish Hamilton, 1958; *Les Gens d'en face,* 1933, translation by Geoffrey Sainsbury published as *The Window Over the Way* [with] *The Gendarme's Report,* Routledge & Kegan Paul, 1951, translation by Victor Kosta published as "Danger Ashore" in *On Land and Sea,* Hanover House, 1954, translation by Robert Baldick published as *The Window Over the Way,* Penguin, 1966; *Le Haut-mal,* 1933, translation by Stuart Gilbert published as "The Woman in the Grey House" in *Affairs of Destiny,* George Routledge, 1942, Harcourt, 1944; *La Maison du Canal,* 1933, translation by Geoffrey Sainsbury published as *The House by the Canal* [with] *The Ostenders,* Routledge & Kegan Paul, 1952; *Les Suicides,* Nouvelle Revue Francaise, 1934, translation by Gilbert published as "One Way Out" in *Escape in Vain,* George Routledge, 1943, Harcourt, 1944; *L'Homme de Londres,* 1934, translation by Gilbert published as "Newhaven-Dieppe" in *Affairs of Destiny,* George Routledge, 1942, Harcourt, 1944, published as *Newhaven-Dieppe* [with] *The Man From Everywhere,* Penguin, 1952; *Le Locataire,* Nouvelle Revue Francaise, 1934, translation by Gilbert published as "The Lodger" in *Escape in Vain,* George Routledge, 1943, Harcourt, 1944.

All published by Nouvelle Revue Francaise, except as indicated: *Les Clients d'Avrenos,* 1935; *Les Pitard,* 1935, translation by Geoffrey Sainsbury published as *A Wife at Sea* [with] *The Murderer,* Routledge & Kegan Paul, 1949; *Quar-tier Negre,* 1935; *Les Demoiselles de Concarneau,* 1936, translation by Stuart Gilbert published as "The Breton Sisters" in *Havoc by Accident,* Harcourt, 1943; *L'Evade,* 1936, translation by Sainsbury published as *The Disintegration of J.P.G.,* George Routledge, 1937; *Long Cours,* 1936; *45° a l'hombre,* 1936; *L'Assassin,* 1937, translation by Sainsbury published as *The Murderer* [with] *A Wife at Sea,* Routledge & Kegan Paul, 1947; *Le Blanc a lunettes,* 1937, translation by Gilbert published as "Tatala" in *Havoc by Accident,* Harcourt, 1943; *Faubourg,* 1937, translation by Gilbert published as "Home Town" in *On the Danger Line,* Harcourt, 1944; *Le Testament Donadieu,* 1937, translation by Gilbert published as *The Shadow Falls,* Harcourt, 1945.

Ceux de la soif, 1938; *Chemin sans issue,* 1938, translation by Gilbert published as *Blind Alley,* Reynal & Hitchcock, 1946, published as "Blind Alley" in *Lost Moorings,* George Routledge, 1946; *Le Cheval blanc,* 1938; *L'Homme qui regardait passer les trains,* 1938, translation by Gilbert published as *The Man Who Watched the Trains Go By,* Musson, 1942, Reynal & Hitchcock, 1946; *La Marie du port,* 1938, translation by Sainsbury published as *A Chit of a Girl* [with] *Justice,* Routledge & Kegan Paul, 1949, published as *The Girl in Waiting* [with] *Justice,* Pan Books, 1957; *La Mauvaise Etoile,* 1938; *Monsieur La Souris,* 1938, translation by Sainsbury published as *Monsieur La Souris* [with] *Poisoned Relations,* Routledge & Kegan Paul, 1950, translation by Robert Baldick published as *The Mouse,* Penguin, 1966; *Les Rescapes du "Telmaque,"* 1938, translation by Stuart Gilbert published as *The Survivors* [with] *Black Rain,* Routledge & Kegan Paul, 1949; *Les Soeurs Lacroix,* 1938, translation by Sainsbury published as *Poisoned Relations* [with] *Monsieur La Souris,* Routledge & Kegan Paul, 1950; *Le Suspect,* 1938, translation by Gilbert published as "The Green Thermos" in *On the Danger Line,* Harcourt, 1944; *Touriste de bananes (ou, Les Dimanches de Tahiti),* 1938, translation by Gilbert published as "Banana Tourist" in *Lost Moorings,* George Routledge, 1946; *Les Trois Crimes de mes amis,* 1938; *Le Bourgmestre de Furnes,* 1939, translation by Sainsbury published as *The Bourgomaster of Furnes,* Routledge & Kegan Paul, 1952; *Chez Krull,* 1939, translation by Daphne Woodward published as "Chez Krull" in *A Sense of Guilt,* Hamish Hamilton, 1955, published as *Chez Krull,* New English Library, 1966; *Le Coup de vague,* 1939.

Les Inconnus dans la maison, 1940, translation by Geoffrey Sainsbury published as *Strangers in the House,* Routledge & Kegan Paul, 1951, Doubleday, 1954; *Malempin,* 1940; *Bergelon,* 1941; *Cour d'Assises,* 1941, translation by Sainsbury published as *Justice* [with] *A Chit of a Girl,* Routledge & Kegan Paul, 1949; *Il pleut bergere,* 1941, translation by Sainsbury published as *Black Rain,* Reynal & Hitchcock, 1947, published as *Black Rain* [with] *The Survivors,* Routledge & Kegan Paul, 1949; *La Maison des sept jeunes filles,* Gallimard, 1941; *L'Outlaw,* Gallimard, 1941; *Le Voyageur de la Toussaint,* 1941, translation by Sainsbury published as *Strange Inheritance,* Routledge & Kegan Paul, 1970; *Le Fils Cardinaud,* 1942, translation by Richard Brain published as "Young Cardinuad" in *The Sacrifice,* Hamish Hamilton, 1956, published as *Young Cardinaud,* New English Library, 1966; *Once Charles s'est enferme,* 1942; *La Verite sur Bebe Donge,* 1942, translation by Sainsbury published as *The Trial of Bebe Donge,* Routledge & Kegan Paul, 1952, translation by Louise Varese published as "I Take This Woman" in *Satan's Children,* Prentice-Hall, 1953; *La Veuve couderc,* 1942, translation by Robert J. P. Hewitton (under pseudonym John Petrie) published as *Ticket of Leave,* Routledge & Kegan Paul, 1954, published as *The Widow* [with] *Magi-*

cian, Doubleday, 1955; *La Rapport du gendarme*, 1944, translation by Sainsbury published as *The Gendarme's Report* [with] *Window Over the Way*, Routledge & Kegan Paul, 1951.

L'Aine des ferchaux, Gallimard, 1945, translation by Geoffrey Sainsbury published as *Magnet of Doom*, George Routledge, 1948, published as *The First Born*, Reynal & Hitchcock, 1949; *Le Fenetre des Rouet*, Editions de la Jeune Parque, 1945, translation by Robert J. P. Hewitton (under pseudonym John Petrie) published as *Across the Street*, Routledge & Kegan Paul, 1954; *La Fruite de Monsieur Monde*, Editions de la Jeune Parque, 1945, translation by Jean Stewart published as *Monsieur Monde Vanishes*, Hamish Hamilton, 1967, Harcourt, 1977; *Je me souviens*, Presses de la Cite, 1945; *Le Cercle des Mahe*, Gallimard, 1946; *Les Noches de Poitiers*, Gallimard, 1946; *Trois Chambres a Manhattan*, Presses de la Cite, 1945, translation by Lawrence G. Blochman published as *Three Beds in Manhattan*, Doubleday, 1964.

Au Bout du rouleau, Presses de la Cite, 1947; *Le Clan des Ostendais*, Gallimard, 1947, translation by Sainsbury published as *The Ostenders* [with] *The House by the Canal*, Routledge & Kegan Paul, 1952; *Lettre a mon juge*, Presses de la Cite, 1947, translation by Louise Varese published as *Act of Passion*, Prentice-Hall, 1952; *Le Passager clandestin*, Editions de la Jeune Parque, 1947, translation by Nigel Ryan published as *The Stowaway*, Hamish Hamilton, 1957; *Le Bilan maletras*, Gallimard, 1948; *Le Destin des Malou*, Presses de la Cite, 1948, translation by Dennis George published as *The Fate of the Malous*, Hamish Hamilton, 1962; *La Jument perdu*, Presses de la Cite, 1948; *La Neige etait sale*, Presses de la Cite, 1948, translation by Louise Varese published as *The Snow Was Black*, Prentice-Hall, 1950, translation by Robert J. P. Hewitton (under pseudonym John Petrie) published as *The Stain on the Snow*, Routledge & Kegan Paul, 1953; *Pedigree*, Presses de la Cite, 1948, translation by Robert Baldick published as *Pedigree*, Hamish Hamilton, 1962; *Les Fantomes du chapelier*, Presses de la Cite, 1941, translation by Nigel Ryan published as "The Hatter's Ghost" in *The Judge and the Hatter*, Hamish Hamilton, 1956, translation by Willard Trask published as *The Hatter's Phantoms*, Harcourt, 1976; *Le Fond de la bouteille*, Presses de la Cite, 1949, translation by Cornelia Schaffer published as "The Bottom of the Bottle" in *Tidal Wave*, Doubleday, 1954, published as *The Bottom of the Bottle*, Hamish Hamilton, 1977; *Les Quatre Jours du pauvre homme*, Presses de la Cite, 1949, translation by Louise Varese published as "Four Days in a Lifetime" in *Satan's Children*, Prentice-Hall, 1953, published as *Four Days in a Lifetime*, Hamish Hamilton, 1977.

All published by Presses de la Cite, except as indicated: *L'Enterrement de Monsieur Bouvet*, 1950, translation by Eugene MacCowan published as "The Burial of Monsieur Bouvet" in *Destinations*, Doubleday, 1955, published as *Inquest on Bouvet*, Hamish Hamilton, 1958; *Un Nouveau dans la ville*, 1950; *Tante Jeanne*, 1950, translation by Geoffrey Sainsbury published as *Aunt Jeanne*, Routledge & Kegan Paul, 1953; *Les Volets verts*, 1950, translation by Louise Varese published as *The Heart of a Man*, Prentice-Hall, 1951, published as "The Heart of a Man" in *A Sense of Guilt*, Hamish Hamilton, 1955; *Marie qui louche*, 1951, translation by Varese published as *The Girl With a Squint*, Harcourt, 1978; *Le Temps d'Anais*, 1951, translation by Varese published as *The Girl in His Past*, Prentice-Hall, 1952; *Une Vie comme neuve*, 1951, translation by Joanne Richardson published as *A New Lease on Life*, Doubleday,

1963; *Les Freres Rico*, 1952, translation by Ernst Pawel published as "The Brothers Rico" in *Tidal Wave*, Doubleday, 1954, published in England as "The Brothers Rico" in *Violent Ends*, Hamish Hamilton, 1964; *La Morte de Belle*, 1952, translation by Louise Varese published as "Belle" in *Tidal Wave*, Doubleday, 1954, published as "Belle" in *Violent Ends*, Hamish Hamilton, 1954.

Antoine et Julie, 1953, translation by Helen Sebba published as *Magician* [with] *The Widow*, Doubleday, 1955, published as *Magician*, Berkeley, 1956, published in England as *The Magician*, Hamish Hamilton, 1974; *L'Escalier de fer*, 1953, translation by Eileen Ellenbogen published as *The Iron Staircase*, Hamish Hamilton, 1963, Harcourt, 1977; *Feux Rouges*, 1953, translation by Norman Denny published as "The Hitchhiker" in *Destinations*, Doubleday, 1955, published as *The Hitchhiker*, Signet, 1957, published as "Red Lights" in *Danger Ahead*, Hamish Hamilton, 1955; *Crime impuni*, 1954, translation by Louise Varese published as *Fugitive*, Doubleday, 1955, translation by Tony White published as *Account Unsettled*, Hamish Hamilton, 1962; *Le Grand Bob*, 1954, translation by Eileen Lowe published as *Big Bob*, Hamish Hamilton, 1969; *L'Horloger d'Everton*, 1954, translation by Norman Denny published as "The Watchmaker of Everton" in *Danger Ahead*, Hamish Hamilton, 1955, published as *The Watchmaker of Everton* [with] *Witnesses*, Doubleday, 1956; *Les Temoins*, privately printed, 1954, translation by Moura Budberg published as *Witnesses* [with] *The Watchmaker of Everton*, Doubleday, 1956, published as "The Witnesses" in *The Judge and the Hatter*, Hamish Hamilton, 1956.

La Boule noire, 1955; *Les Complices*, 1955, translation by Bernard Frechtman published as *The Accomplices* [with] *The Blue Room*, Harcourt, 1964, published as *The Accomplices*, Hamish Hamilton, 1966, Harcourt, 1977; *En Case de malheur*, 1956, translation by Helen Sebba published as *In Case of Emergency*, Doubleday, 1958; *Le Fils*, 1957, translation by Daphne Woodward published as *The Son*, Hamish Hamilton, 1958; *Le Negre*, 1957, translation by Sebba published as *The Negro*, Hamish Hamilton, 1959; *Le Petit Homme d'Arkhangelsk*, 1957, translation by Nigel Ryan published as *The Little Man From Arkangel*, Hamish Hamilton, 1957, published as *The Little Man From Arkangel* [with] *Sunday*, Harcourt, 1966; *Le Passage de la Ligne*, 1958; *Le President*, 1958, translation by Woodward published as *The Premier*, Hamish Hamilton, 1961, published as *The Premier* [with] *The Train*, Harcourt, 1966; *Strip-Tease*, 1958, translation by Robert Brain published as *Striptease*, Hamish Hamilton, 1959; *Dimanche*, 1959, translation by Nigel Ryan published as *Sunday*, Hamish Hamilton, 1960, published as *Sunday* [with] *The Little Man From Arkangel*, Harcourt, 1966; *La Vieille*, 1959.

L'Ours en pluche, 1960, translation by John Clay published as *Teddy Bear*, Hamish Hamilton, 1971, Harcourt, 1972; *Le Veuf*, 1960, translation by Robert Baldick published as *The Widower*, Hamish Hamilton, 1961; *Betty*, 1961, translation by Alistair Hamilton published as *Betty*, Harcourt, 1975; *Le Train*, 1961, translation by Baldick published as *The Train*, Hamish Hamilton, 1964, published as *The Train* [with] *The Premier*, Harcourt, 1966; *Les Autres*, 1962, translation by Hamilton published as *The House on Quai Notre Dame*, Harcourt, 1975, published as *The Others*, Hamish Hamilton, 1975; *La Porte*, 1962, translation by Woodward published as *The Door*, Hamish Hamilton, 1964; *Les Anneaux de Bicetre*, 1963, translation by Jean Stewart published as *The Patient*, Hamish Hamilton, 1963, published as *The Bells of Bicetre*, Harcourt, 1964; *La Chambre bleue*, 1964, translation by Eileen Ellenbogen published as *The Blue Room* [with] *The Accomplices*, Harcourt, 1964, published as *The Blue Room*, Hamish Hamilton, 1965; *L'Homme au petit chien*, 1964, translation by Stewart published as *The Man With the Little Dog*, Hamish Hamilton, 1965.

Le Petit Saint, 1965, translation by Bernard Frechtman published as *The Little Saint*, Harcourt, 1965; *Le Train de Venise*, 1965, translation by Alistair Hamilton published as *The Venice Train*, Harcourt, 1974; *Le Confessional*, 1966, translation by Jean Stewart published as *The Confessional*, Hamish Hamilton, 1967, Harcourt, 1968; *La Mort d'Auguste*, 1966, translation by Bernard Frechtman published as *The Old Man Dies*, Harcourt, 1967; *Le Chat*, 1967, translation by Frechtman published as *The Cat*, Harcourt, 1967; *Le Demenagement*, 1967, translation by Christopher Sinclair-Stevenson published as *The Move*, Harcourt, 1968, published as *The Neighbors*, Hamish Hamilton, 1968; *La Main*, 1968, translation by Moura Budberg published as *The Man on the Bench in the Barn*, Harcourt, 1970; *La Prison*, 1968, translation by Lyn Moir published as *The Prison*, Harcourt, 1969; *Il y a encore des noisetiers*, 1969; *Novembre*, 1969, translation by Jean Stewart published as *November*, Harcourt, 1970.

Le Riche Homme, 1970, translation by Jean Stewart published as *The Rich Man*, Harcourt, 1971; *Le Cage de verre*, 1971, translation by Antonia White published as *The Glass Cage*, Harcourt, 1973; *La Disparition d'Odile*, 1971, translation by Lyn Moir published as *The Disappearance of Odile*, Harcourt, 1972, *Les Innocents*, 1972, translation by Eileen Ellenbogen published as *The Innocents*, Hamish Hamilton, 1973, Harcourt, 1974.

All under pseudonym Georges Sim: *Au pont des arches* (title means "Aboard the Ark"), Benard (Liege), 1921; *Les Ridicules* (title means "The Ridiculous Ones"), Benard, 1921; *Les Larmes avant le bonheur* (title means "Tears Before Happiness"), Ferenczi, 1925; *Le Feu s'eteint* (title means "The Fire Is Out"), Fayard, 1927, reprinted, 1954; *Les Voleurs de bavires* (adventure; title means "The Ship Robbers"), Tallindier, reprinted, 1954; *Defense d'aimer* (title means "Defense of Loving"), Ferenczi, 1927; *Le Cercle de la soif* (adventure; title means "The Circle of Thirst"), Ferenczi, 1927, published as *Le Cercle de la mort* (title means "The Circle of Death"), 1933; *Paris-Leste*, Editions Paris-Plaisirs, 1927; *Un Monsieur libidineux* (title means "A Libidinous Gentleman"), Editions Prima, 1927; *Les Coeurs perdus* (title means "The Lost Hearts"), Tallandier, 1928; *Le Secret des Lamas* (adventure; title means "The Secret of the Lamas"), Tallandier, 1928, reprinted, 1954; *Les Maudits du Pacifique* (adventure; title means "The Damned of the Pacific"), Tallandier, 1928, reprinted, 1954; *Le Monstre blanc de la terre de feu* (title means "The White Monster of the Land of Fire"), Ferenczi, 1928, published (under pseudonym Christian Brulls) as *L'Ile de la desolation* (title means "Desolation Island"), 1933; *Miss Baby*, Fayard, 1928; *Le Semeur de larmes* (title means "Sower of Tears"), Ferenczi, 1928; *Le Roi des glaces* (adventure), Tallandier, 1928, reprinted, 1954; *Le Sousmarin dans la foret* (title means "The Submarine in the Forest"), Tallandier, 1928, reprinted, 1954; *La Maison sans soleil* (title means "The House Without Sunshine"), Fayard, 1928, reprinted, 1954; *Aimer d'amour* (title means "In Love With Love"), Ferenczi, 1928; *Songes d'ete* (title means "Summer Dreams"), Ferenczi, 1928; *Les Nains des cataractes* (adventure), Tallandier, 1954; *Le Lac d'angoisse* (adventure; title means "The Lake of Agony"), Ferenczi, 1928, published (under pseudonym Christian Brulls) as *Le Lac des esclaves* (title means "The Lake of the Slaves"), 1933; *Le Sang des gitanes* (title means "The Blood of the Gipsies"), Ferenczi, 1928; *Chair de beaute*, (title means "Beautiful Flesh"), Fayard, 1928; *Les Memoires d'un prostitute* (title means "Memoirs of a Prostitute"), Editions Prima, 1929; *En Robe de mariee*, Tallandier, 1929; *La Panthere borgne* (adventure; title means "The Blind Panther"), Tallandier, 1929; *La Fiancee aux mains de glace* (title means "The Fiancee and the Sea of Ice"), Fayard, 1929; *Les Bandits de Chicago* (adventure; title means "The Outlaws of Chicago"), Fayard, 1929; *L'Ile des hommes roux* (adventure; title means "The Island of the Red Men"), Tallandier, 1929; *Le Roi du Pacifique* (adventure; title means "The Kind of the Pacific"), Ferenczi, 1929, abridged edition published as *Le Bateau d'or* (title means "The Boat of Gold"), Ferenczi, 1955; *Le Gorille-Roi* (title means "The Gorilla King"), Tallandier, 1929; *Les Contrabaniers de l'alcool* (adventure; title means "The Rum Runners"), Fayard, 1929; *La Femme qui tue* (title means "The Dead Woman"), Fayard, 1929; *Destinees* (title means "Destinies"), Fayard, 1929, reprinted, 1954; *L'Ile des maudits* (adventure; title means "Island of the Damned"), Ferenczi, abridged edition published as *Naufrage du "Pelican"* (title means "The Shipwreck of the Pelican"), 1933; *La Femme en deuil* (title means "The Wife in Mourning"), Tallandier, 1929.

L'Oeil de l'Utah (adventure; title means "The Eye of Utah"), Tallandier, 1930; *L'Homme qui tremble* (adventure; title means "The Shaky Man"), Fayard, 1930; *Nez d'argent* (adventure; title means "The Scent of Money"), Ferenczi, 1930, abridged edition published as *Le Paria des bois sauvages* (title means "The Outcast of the Wild Woods"), 1933; *Mademoiselle Million* (title means "Miss Million"), Fayard, 1930, published as *Les Ruses de l'amour* (title means "The Tricks of Love"), 1954; *Le Pecheur de bouees* (adventure; title means "The Fisherman of the Buoys"), Tallandier, 1930; *Le Chinois de San-Francisco* (title means "The Chinese of San Francisco"), Tallandier, 1930; *La Femme 47* (title means "The Woman 47"), Fayard, 1930; *Katia, Acrobate* (title means "Katia Acrobat"), Fayard, 1931; *L'Homme a la cigarette* (title means "The Man With the Cigarette"), Tallandier, 1931; *L'Homme de poire* (title means "The Victim"), Fayard, 1931, reprinted, 1952; *Les Errants* (title means "The Ramblers"), Fayard, 1931, reprinted, 1954; *La Maison de l'inquietude* (crime novel; title means "The House of Anxiety"), Tallandier, 1932; *L'Epave* (title means "The Slave"), Fayard, 1932, reprinted, 1952; *Matricule 12* (crime novel; title means "Ledger 12"), Tallandier, 1932; *La Fiance du diable* (title means "The Devil's Intended"), Fayard, 1932; *La Femme rousse* (crime novel; title means "The Redheaded Woman"), Tallandier, 1933; *Le Chateau des sables rouges*, Tallandier, 1933; *Le Yacht fantome* (adventure; title means "The Phantom Yacht"); originally published (under pseudonym Christian Brulls) as *Le Desert du froid qui tue* [title means "The Loneliness as Cold as Death"], Ferenczi, 1928), Ferenczi, 1933; *Deuxieme Bureau* (crime novel; title means "Second Bureau"), Tallandier, 1933.

All novels under pseudonym Jean du Perry: *Le Roman d'une dactylo* (title means "The Romance of a Typist"), Ferenczi, 1924; *Amour d'exile* (title means "Love of an Exile"), Ferenczi; *L'Oiseau blesse* (title means "The Wounded Bird"), Ferenczi, 1925; *L'Heureuse fin* (title means "Precious Happiness"), Ferenczi, 1925; *Pour la sauver* (title means "For the Rescue"), 1925; *Ceux qu'on avait oubles . . .*, 1925; *Pour qu'il soit heureux*, 1925; *Amour Afrique* (title means "African Love"), 1925; *A l'assaut d'un coeur* (title means "Assault on a Heart"), 1925; *L'Orgueil d'aimer* (title means "The Pride of a Lover"), 1926; *Celle qui est aimee* (title means "One Who is Loved"), 1926; *Les Yeux qui ordonnent* (title means "The Commanding Eyes"), 1926; *Que ma mere l'ignore* (title means "What My Mother Didn't Know"), 1926; *De la rue au bonheur* (title means "On the Street of Happiness"), 1926; *Un Peche de jeunesse* (title means "A Sin of Youth"), 1926.

Lili Tristesse (title means "Lili Sadness"), 1927; *Un Tout petit coeur* (title means "Every Little Heart"), Editions du Livre National, 1927; *Le Fou d'amour* (title means "The Madman of Love"), 1928; *Coeur Exalte* (title means "Exalted Heart"), 1928; *Trois Coeurs dans la tempete* (title means "Three Hearts in a Storm"), 1928; *Les Amants de la mansarde* (title means "The Attic Lovers"), 1928; *Un Jour de soleil* (title means "A Sunny Day"), 1928; *La Fille de l'autre* (title means "The Other's Daughter"), 1929; *L'Amour et l'argent* (title means "Love and Money"), 1929; *Coeur de poupee* (title means "The Heart of a Doll"), 1929; *Une Femme a tue* (title means "A Wife to Murder"), 1929; *Deux Coeurs de femme* (title means "Two Hearts of a Woman"), 1929; *L'Epave d'amour* (title means "The Wreckage of Love"), 1929; *Le Mirage de Paris* (title means "The Illusion of Paris"), 1929; *Celle qui passe* (title means "Those Who Pass"), 1930; *Petite Exile* (title means "Little Exile"), 1930; *Les Amants de malheur* (title means "Lovers of Trouble"), 1930; *La Femme ardent* (title means "The Passionate Woman"), 1930; *La Porte close* (title means "The Closed Door"), 1930; *Le Poupee brisee* (title means "The Broken Doll"), 1930; *Pauvre Amante* (title means "Poor Lover"), 1931; *Le Reve qui meurt* (title means "The Murderous Dream"), F. Rouff, 1931; *Marie-Mystere* (title means "Mysterious Marie"), Fayard, 1931.

All novels under pseudonym Georges-Martin Georges; all published by Ferenczi, except as indicated: *L'Orgueil qui meurt* (title means "The Pride That Murdered"), Editions du Livre National, 1925; *Un Soir de veritage* (title means "An Evening of Truth"), 1928; *Brin d'amour* (title means "Quality of Love"), 1928; *Les Coeurs vides* (title means "The Empty Hearts"), 1928; *Cabotine . . .* , 1928; *Amier, Mourir* (title means "To Love, To Murder"), 1928; *Voleuse d'amour* (title means "The Thief of Love"), 1929; *Une Ombre dans la nuit* (title means "A Shadow in the Night"), 1929; *Nuit de Paris* (title means "Parisian Night"), 1929; *La Victime* (title means "The Victim"), 1929; *Un Nid d'amour* (title means "A Love Nest"), 1930; *Bobette, mannequin* (title means "Bobette, Model"), 1930; *La Puissance du souvenir* (title means "The Power to Remember"), 1930; *Le Bonheur de Lili* (title means "Lili's Happiness"), 1930; *Le Double Vie* (title means "The Double Life"), 1931.

Novel under pseudonym Georges d'Isly: *Etoile de cinema* (title means "Movie Star"), F. Rouff, 1925.

All novels under pseudonym Christian Brulls: *La Pretresse des vaudoux* (adventure; title means "The Voodoo Priestess"), Tallandier, 1925; *Nox l'insaissable* (crime novel), Ferenczi, 1926; *Se Ma Tsien, le sacrificateur* (adventure), Tallandier, 1926; *Le Desert du froid qui tue* (adventure; title means "The Loneliness as Cold as Death"), Ferenczi, 1928, published (under pseudonym Georges Sim) as *Le Yacht fantome* (title means "The Phantom Yacht"), 1933; *Mademoiselle X . . .* (title means "Miss X"), Fayard, 1928; *Annie, danseuse* (title means "Annie, Dancer"), Ferenczi, 1928; *Dolorosa* (title means "Delores"), Fayard, 1928; *Les Adolescents passionnes* (title means "The Passionate Teenagers"), Fayard, 1929; *L'Amant sans nom* (title means "The Nameless Lover"), Fayard, 1929; *Un Drame au Pole Sud* (adventure; title means "A Drama at the South Pole"),

Fayard, 1929; *Les Pirates du Texas* (adventure; title means "The Texas Pirates"), Ferenczi, 1929, published as *La Chasse au whiskey* (title means "The Shot of Whiskey"), 1934; *Capitan S.O.S.* (adventure; title means "Captain S.O.S."), Fayard, 1929.

Jacques d'Antifer, roi des Iles du Vent (adventure; title means "Jacques d'Antifer, King of the Windy Islands"), 1930, published as *L'Heritier du Corsaire*, 1934; *L'Inconnue* (title means "The Stranger"), Fayard, 1930; *Train de nuit* (title means "Night Train"), Fayard, 1930; *Pour venger son pere* (title means "To Avenge One's Father"), Ferenczi, 1931; *La Maison de la haine* (title means "The House of Hatred"), Fayard, 1931; *La Maison des disparus*, Fayard, 1931; *Les Forcats de Paris* (title means "The Convicts of Paris"), Fayard, 1932; *La Figurante* (title means "The Figurehead"), Fayard, 1932; *Fievre* (title means "Fever"), Fayard, 1932; *L'Ile de la desolation* (adventure; title means "The Island of Misery"; originally published [under pseudonym Georges Sim] as *Le Monstre blanc de la terre de feu* [title means "The White Monster of the Land of the Dead"], 1928) Ferenczi, 1933; *Le Lac des esclaves* (title means "The Lake of the Slaves"; originally published [under pseudonym Georges Sim] as *Le Lac d'angoisse* [title means "The Lake of Agony"], 1928), Ferenczi, 1933; *L'Evasion* (title means "The Escape"), Fayard, 1934; *L'Ils empoisonne* (adventure; title means "The Poisoned Island"), Ferenczi, 1937; *Seul parmi les gorilles* (adventure; title means "Alone Among the Gorillas"), Ferenczi, 1937.

All novels under pseudonym Gom Gut; all published by Editions Prima: *Un Viol aux q'uat'z arts*, 1925; *Perversites frivoles*, 1925; *Au grand 13*, 1925; *Plaisirs charnes*, 1925; *Aux vingt-huit negresses*, 1925; *La Noche a Montmartre*, 1925; *Liquettes au vent*, 1926; *Une Petite tres sensuelle*, 1926; *Orgies bourgoise*, 1926; *L'Homme aux douze etreintes*, 1927; *Entreintes passionnees*, 1927; *Une Mome dessalee*, 1927; *L'Amant fantome*, 1928; *L'Amour a Montparnasse*, 1928; *Les Distractions d'Helene*, 1928.

Novels under pseudonym Plick et Plock; published by Editions Prima: *Voluptueues Etreintes*, 1925; *Le Cheri de Tantine*, 1925.

All novels under pseudonym Luc Dorsan; all published by Editions Prima, except as indicated: *Histoire d'un pantalon*, 1926; *Nini violce*, 1926; *Nichonnette*, 1926; *Memoires d'un vieux suiveur*, 1926; *Nuit de noces, doubles noces, les noces ardents*, 1926; *Le Pucelle de Benouville*, Ferenczi, 1928.

Under pseudonym Bobette: *Bobette et ses satyres*, Ferenczi, 1928.

Under pseudonym Kim: *Un Petit Poison*, Ferenczi, 1928.

Novels under pseudonym Jacques Dersonnes; published by Ferenczi: *Un Seul Basier* (title means "A Single Kiss"), 1928; *La Merveilleuse Adventure* (title means "The Marvelous Adventure"), 1929; *Les Etapes du Mensonge*, 1930; *Baisers mortels* (title means "Deadly Kisses"), 1930; *Victime de son fils* (title means "Victim of His Son"), 1931.

Novels under pseudonym Jean Dorsange; published by Ferenczi: *L'Amour meconnu* (title means "Misunderstood Love"), 1928; *Celle qui revient*, 1929; *Coeur de jeune fille* (title means "Heart of a Young Girl"), 1930; *Soeurette* (title means "Little Sister"), 1930; *Les Chercheurs de bonheur* (title means "The Fortune Hunters"), 1930.

Novels under pseudonym Gaston Vialis; published by Ferenczi: *Un Petit Corps blesse* (title means "A Small Wounded Body"), 1928; *Hair a force d'amier* (title means "Hate and the Power of Love"), 1928; *Le Parfum du passe* (title means "The Perfume of the Past"), 1929; *Lili-sourire* (title means "Smile, Lili"), 1930; *Folie d'un soir* (title means "Madness of an Evening"), 1930; *Ame de jeune fille* (title means "Soul of a Young Girl"), 1931.

Novel under pseudonym Germain d'Antibes: *Helas!* (title means "Alas!"), Ferenczi, 1929.

Novel under pseudonym Jean Dossage: *Les Deux Maitresses* (title means "The Two Mistresses"), Ferenczi, 1929.

Novel under pseudonym G. Violis: *Trop belle pour elle!* (title means "Very Good for Her!"), Ferenczi, 1929.

Short stories and omnibus volumes: *Les Sept Minutes* (short stories; title means "The Seven Minutes"), Nouvelle Revue Francaise, 1938; *Maigret revient* (short stories; title means "Maigret Returns"), Nouvelle Revue Francaise, 1942; *Le Petit Docteur* (short stories; title means "The Little Doctor"), Nouvelle Revue Francaise, 1943; *Les Nouvelles Enquetes de Maigret* (short stories; title means "The New Cases of Maigret"), Nouvelle Revue Francaise, 1944; *Les Dossiers de l'Agence O* (short stories; title means "The Files of the O Agency"), Nouvelle Revue Francaise, 1945; *Le Commissaire Maigret et L'Inspecteur Malchanceaux* (four novellas; title means "Commissioner Maigret and Inspector Malchanceaux"), Presses de la Cite, 1947. Also author of *Signe Picpus* (short stories), Nouvelle Revue Francaise, 1944, translation by Geoffrey Sainsbury published as *To Any Lengths*, Penguin.

Un Noel de Maigret (short stories), Presses de la Cite, 1951, translation by Jean Stewart published as *Maigret's Christmas*, Hamish Hamilton, 1976, Harcourt, 1977; *Omnibus Simenon* (collection of novels), ten volumes, Gallimard, 1951-52; *Les Tournants dangereux* (four novellas), Appleton, 1953; *Le Bateau d'Emile* (short stories; title means "Emile's Boat"), Gallimard, 1954; *The Short Cases of Inspector Maigret* (short stories), Doubleday, 1959.

La Rue aux trois poussins (short stories), Presses de la Cite, 1963; *A Maigret Omnibus* (includes "Maigret's Mistake," "Maigret Has Scruples," "Maigret and the Reluctant Witnesses," "Maigret in Montmartre," and "Maigret Goes to School"), Hamish Hamilton, 1962, published as *Five Times Maigret*, Harcourt, 1964; *A Maigret Quartet* (includes "Maigret's Failure," "Maigret in Society," "Maigret and the Lazy Burglar," and "Maigret's Special Murder"), Hamish Hamilton, 1964; *The Second Maigret Omnibus* (includes "Maigret and the Old Lady," "Maigret and the Young Girl," "Maigret's Little Joke," "Maigret's First Case," and "Maigret Takes a Room"), Hamish Hamilton, 1964, published as *Maigret Cinq*, Harcourt, 1965; *A Simenon Omnibus* (includes "Mr Hire's Engagement," "The Man from Archangel," "In Case of Emergency," "Sunday," and "The Premier"), Hamish Hamilton, 1965; *Trois Nouvelles* (title means "Three New Works"), edited by Frank W. Lindsay and Anthony Nazarro, Appleton, 1966; *Les Enquetes du Commissaire Maigret* (title means "The Cases of Commissaire Maigret"), Presses de la Cite, Volume I, 1966, Volume II, 1967; *An American Omnibus* (includes "The Hitchhiker," "Belle," "The Watchmaker of Everton," and "The Brothers Rico"), Harcourt, 1967; *Ouevres completes* (title means "Complete Works"), compiled by Gilbert Sigaux, Editions Rencontre (Lausanne), forty-one volumes, 1967-70; *Ouevres Completes Maigret* (title means "Complete Maigret"), compiled by Sigaux, Editions Rencontre, twenty-five volumes, 1967-70; *Maigret Triumphant* (includes "Maigret and the Burglar's Wife," "Maigret's Revolver," "My Friend Maigret," "Maigret Afraid," and "Maigret in Court"), Hamish Hamilton, 1969.

The Simenon Omnibus, thirteen volumes, Penguin, 1970-78; *Choix de Simenon* (textbook edition; short stories; title means "Choice Simenon"), edited by F. W. Lindsay and A. M. Nazzaro, Appleton, 1972; *A Maigret Trio* (includes "Maigret's Failure," "Maigret in Society," and "Maigret and the Lazy Burglar"), Harcourt, 1973; *La Piste du Hollandais* (short stories), Presses de la Cite, 1973; *Maigret: A Fifth Omnibus* (includes "Madame Maigret's Friend," "Maigret on the Defensive," "The Patience of Maigret," and "Maigret Takes the Waters"), Hamish Hamilton, 1973; *Maigret Victorious* (includes "Maigret's Memoirs," "Maigret and the Headless Corpse," and "Maigret and the Saturday Caller"), Hamish Hamilton, 1975; *Complete Maigret Short Stories*, two volumes, Hamish Hamilton, 1976, Harcourt, 1977.

Other: *Je me souviens* (title means "I Remember"), Presses de la Cite, 1945, reprinted, 1970; *Long Cours dur les rivieres et canaux* (illustrated nonfiction), Editions Dynamo (Liege), 1952; *Le Roman de l'homme* (lectures and essays), Presses de la Cite, 1959, translation by Bernard Frechtman published as *The Novel of Man*, Harcourt, 1964; *La Femme en France* (illustrated nonfiction; title means "The Woman in France"), Presses de la Cite, 1960; *Entretien avec Roger Stephanie* (interview), Radio Television Francaise, 1963; *Ma Conviction profonde* (unedited writings), Callier, 1963; *Le Paris de Simenon* (illustrated nonfiction), Tehou, 1969, translation published as *Simenon's Paris*, Dial, 1970.

Quand j'etais vieux (autobiography), translation by Helen Eustis published as *When I Was Old*, Harcourt, 1971; *Lettre a ma mere* (autobiography), Presses de la Cite, 1974, translation by Ralph Manheim published as *Letter to My Mother*, Harcourt, 1976; *Un Homme comme un autre* (biography; title means "A Man Like any Other"), Presses de la Cite, 1975; (with Francis Lacassin and Gilbert Sigaux) *A la decouverte de la France*, Union General d'Editions, 1976; (with Lacassin and Sigaux) *A la recherche de l'homme nu*, Union General d'Editions, 1976.

Diaries; all published by Presses de la Cite: *Des Traces de pas*, 1975; *Vent du nord, vent du sud*, 1976; *Les Petits Hommes* (title means "The Little Men"), 1976; *De la cave au grenier;* 1977; *A l'abri de notre arbre*, 1977; *Un Banc au soleil*, 1977; *Tant que je suis vivant*, 1978.

WORK IN PROGRESS: Publication of diaries and miscellaneous writings.

SIDELIGHTS: Georges Simenon is one of the world's most prolific writers, having produced novels, stories, and other works numbering in the hundreds over a span of five decades. Although he writes exclusively in French, his work is available world-wide in more than forty languages. It has been said that at the peak of his writing career, when he was regularly producing four or more books per year, a new Simenon translation was appearing somewhere in the world on the average of once every three days. But of all his writing, he is best known as the creator and chronicler of the cases of his detective—Inspector Jules Maigret.

Simenon was born in Liege, Belgium, where as a youth he was already determined to become a writer of some sort. His schooling was cut short as a result of the death of his father. Accordingly, he was apprenticed to a pastry chef to learn a trade. Simenon abandoned his apprenticeship after one year, and at the age of seventeen he began his career as a writer by taking a newspaper job with the *Leige Gazette* as an assistant night police reporter. His writing began in earnest: also at age seventeen he published his first novel, *Au pont des arches* ("Aboard the Ark").

In 1922 Simenon left Belgium for Paris to concentrate on a career as a full-time writer of fiction. His early attempts met with rejection and led him to consult Colette, the renowned novelist, who was at that time the editor of *Le Matin*. Colette, too, rejected Simenon's material for publication and suggested that his writing was "too literary" for the mass market. She advised him to simplify and clarify his writing. Simenon's efforts in this direction resulted in the development of his skills as a storyteller of the first rank. He began writing pulp fiction at the rate of eighty pages per day. Simenon published hundreds of books and stories under various pseudonyms during the next several years and soon found that he was able to afford such luxuries as a chauffeur-driven car and, finally, a yacht, the *Ostrogot*.

In 1929, while traveling throughout Europe aboard his yacht, Simenon wrote *The Strange Case of Peter the Lett,* which was the first novel to feature Inspector Maigret. Simenon's creation of Inspector Maigret represented a departure from the conventional portrayal of a super-sleuth. When Simenon presented his first Maigret manuscript to the editors at Fayard, his sometime publishers, they were doubtful of the novel's chances for success with the reading public. Trudee Young wrote: "They [the Maigrets] were not like other detective novels. The main character, Inspector Maigret—a heavy-set, pipe-smoking detective—did not use scientific means to solve his cases, only his intuition; there were no love affairs; there were no truly good guys and bad guys; and, finally, the story ended neither bad nor good."

Simenon's Inspector Maigret is a real cop, unlike Sherlock Holmes, consulting detective, or Hercule Poirot, Agatha Christie's eccentric little Belgian detective with the egg-shaped head. Although Maigret rose through the ranks of the Paris Police Department, he is, in many of the novels, the highest ranking working cop in France. His actual position is chief superintendent, in charge of the homicide division of the police judiciaire, but he is generally demoted in translation and referred to as "Inspector." Because of his high official position, Maigret is often photographed and quoted in the Parisian press. He is, despite his personal modesty, a very well known personage.

Inspector Maigret also differs from most famous fictional crime fighters (particularly his American counterparts) in that he rarely carries a gun, rarely throws a punch or takes one, and hardly ever is involved in a chase either on foot or in a car. In fact, Maigret does not know how to drive. Although in the later novels he owns a car, his wife, Madame Maigret, drives him to Meung-sur-Loire for quiet weekends at their country house.

As Otto Penzler points out in his *The Private Lives of Private Eyes* . . . , the fact that Maigret does not call his wife by her given name, Louise, but Madame Maigret, and that she calls him Maigret rather than Jules, "should not be considered as even the slightest evidence to indicate a lack of affection for either one for the other." The Maigrets are a devoted, solidly middle-class Parisian couple.

If to all outward appearances Maigret is an ordinary man, of ordinary habits and tastes (although while on a case, he can and does consume inordinate amounts of alcohol), the opposite is true of his abilities and methods as a policeman. Maigret's outstanding traits are his unerring intuition, his compassion for both victim and murderer, and his extraordinary patience. While investigating a murder, Maigret spends hours, and more often days, in watchful waiting—seeking insights into the lives and minds of both the victim and his assassin. Only when he finally and thoroughly understands

the reasons why the crime came to be committed does he arrest his suspect. About Maigret and his methods of investigation, Penzler states that "unlike most of the great detectives of literature, Maigret does not have immense powers of deduction. He cannot obtain a few clues, consider their ramifications, then swoop down like an avenging hawk of justice and triumphantly carry away a killer to stand trial.

"Maigret's powers are intuitive. . . . He attempts to slip into the skin of his quarry and think like him, act like him—indeed become him as nearly as possible. When he has practically assumed his suspect's identity, he is sure of his man and is able to arrest him."

S. K. Oberbeck summed up the character of Jules Maigret in a review for *Newsweek*. Oberbeck wrote: "In Inspector Maigret, Simenon has created the minimal hero, a Gallic gumshoe as renowned as Sherlock Holmes or Perry Mason—but with none of their flamboyant traits. He exhibits no flashing forensics, slight deductive genius, rarely encounters personal violence and never steps out with the dolls. If anything, Maigret is utterly bourgeois, egoless, sympathetic and understanding toward criminals, a man whose home life is unruffled domesticity and who wearily laments his shortcomings."

In the same way that Inspector Maigret is unlike most famous fictional sleuths, Simenon's crafting of the stories themselves differ from the traditional form of the mystery and detection genre. Anthony Boucher observed that Simenon's work in this area departed "from the well-shaped plot and the devious gimmick (though he could be very good at these when he chose) to lay stress on the ambiance and milieu of the crime and on the ambivalent duel . . . between the murderer and Maigret."

In the opinions of devotees of mystery and detection fiction, the Maigret stories do not strictly adhere to all the usual requirements of the genre. In the introduction to their *Catalogue of Crime,* Jacques Barzun and W. H. Taylor state that "anyone who says, 'I can't bear detective stories, but I love Simenon' is saying that he prefers the art which is farthest from the center of detection properly so called. To make this judgement is not to deprecate the taste or deprecate the art, which is often of the highest order. But it is not detection. True, Maigret, like any other cop, wants to get his man, and he knows where to wait for him—he has had previous information. But what he contributes is the patience of a god. And what his readers enjoy is his boredom, fatigue, wet feet, and hunger."

Similarly, Edward Galligan makes a distinction between traditional mystery fiction and Simenon's Maigret stories. According to Galligan, the Maigrets "are, in a sense, fables demonstrating the ways of the creative, or intuitive intelligence. They most definitely are not mere mystery stories. They are free of the gimmicks and cliches that make most mystery stories tedious to all but the addicts of the genre. Much more concerned with the why's of murder than with the who's, the Maigrets are perceptive about the realities of human behavior. And like all of his work, they are written in a beautifully spare, unpretentious style that Simenon developed in his twenties, when he trained himself as a writer by grinding out an incredible number of commercial fictions."

Also attesting to the uniqueness of Simenon's mystery fiction, novelist and critic Julian Symons wrote in his *Mortal Consequences:* "The Maigret stories stand quite on their own in crime fiction, bearing little relation to most of the other work done in the field. (Simenon is not much interested in crime stories and has read few of them.) . . . There are no great feats of ratiocination in them and the problems they present are human as much as they are criminal.... Maigret's detached sympathy becomes our own, and like him we do not care to dig too deeply into the roots of crime.... Simenon is an undoubted master of the crime story, but his mastery rests primarily in the creation of Jules Maigret."

As much as Maigret is admired and enjoyed by readers of crime fiction, Simenon himself has not always been one of the Inspector's fans. After completing nineteen Maigret novels, Simenon gave up the series for a number of years to concentrate on writing more serious novels, which he termed *romans-crise,* or novels of crisis. His serious novels focus on the psychological motivations of the characters as they approach and experience a crisis in their lives. These novels, like the Maigrets, often involve crime—not the solution of crime, as in the Maigrets—but rather, in the examination of the events in the lives and psyches of the characters which lead them inexorably and inevitably to commit a crime—usually murder. Edward Galligan wrote: "The serious novels are individually more complex and as a group more varied than the Maigrets. They deal with characters from all walks of life, though usually with a preference for those who are in or who have come from obscure positions in society. The novels are set in all sorts of places, for Simenon has traveled widely and has lived for extended periods in a number of different countries, including the United States. And they confront, in one way or another, all of the fundamental problems in individual lives. There are very few descriptive generalizations to be made about them which are both valid and useful. They are short.... They nearly all involve acts of violence ... because they are concerned with people who are driven to their limits."

Andre Gide, an admirer and long-time critical correspondent of Simenon, wrote of what he called the "profound psychological and ethical interest" of his subjects. Gide stated: "This is what attracts and holds me in him. He writes for 'the vast public,' to be sure, but delicate and refined readers find something for them too as soon as they begin to take him seriously. He makes one reflect; and this is close to being the height of art; how superior he is in this to those heavy novelists who do not spare us a single commentary! Simenon sets forth a particular fact, perhaps of general interest; but he is careful not to generalize; that is up to the reader."

Claude Mauriac feels that although "the reader may be easily disappointed by a given book of Simenon's ... surprise and admiration often come with the last pages, which renew, renovate and clarify the preceeding chapters retrospectively.... The very last lines of Georges Simenon's novels most always have the greatest value: it is there that in a few very simple words, insignificant in appearance, he reveals what he knows about *the secrets of men.*"

In an article entitled "Simenon on Simenon" for the *Times Literary Supplement,* Simenon revealed to his readers some of his thoughts about himself, not as a writer, but as a man. "Simenon," he wrote, "is truly a modest man. He knows his own limitations and does not make for himself the claims that have sometimes been made for him by some of his more florid admirers. He describes himself as a craftsman, has a healthy distrust of intellectuals, of *belle-lettriens,* of literary occasions and intellectual conversations, feels ill at ease at social functions, and is quite unambitious in conventional terms: recognition, decorations, and so on. He can, it is true, well afford to be...."

BIOGRAPHICAL/CRITICAL SOURCES—Books: Andre

Gide, *The Journals of Andre Gide,* Volume IV: *1938-1949,* translated by Justin O'Brien, Knopf, 1951; Thomas Narcejac, *The Art of Simenon,* translated by Cynthia Rowland, Routledge & Kegan Paul, 1952; Claude Mauriac, *The New Literature,* translated by Samuel I. Stone, Braziller, 1959; Georges Simenon, *Pedigree,* translated by Robert Baldick, Hamish Hamilton, 1962; Brigid Brophy, *Don't Never Forget: Collected Views and Reviews,* Holt, 1966; Harry T. Moore, *Twentieth Century French Literature Since World War II,* Southern Illinois University Press, 1966; John Raymond, *Simenon in Court,* Hamish Hamilton, 1968; O. A. Hagen, *Who Done It? A Guide to Detective, Mystery and Suspense Fiction,* Bowker, 1969; Frederick Frank, *Simenon's Paris,* Dial, 1970; Jacques Barzun and W. H. Taylor, *Catalogue of Crime,* 1971; Simenon, *When I Was Old,* translated by Helen Eustis, Harcourt, 1971; Julian Symons, *Mortal Consequences: A History—From the Detective Story to the Crime Novel,* Harper, 1972; *Contemporary Literary Criticism,* Gale, Volume 1, 1973, Volume 2, 1974, Volume 3, 1975, Volume 8, 1978; Simenon, *Letter to My Mother,* translated by Ralph Manheim, Harcourt, 1976; Trudee Young, *Georges Simenon,* Scarecrow, 1976; Dilys Winn, editor, *Murder Ink,* Workman, 1977; Otto Penzler, *The Private Lives of Private Eyes, Spies, Crime Fighters and Other Good Guys,* Grosset, 1977; Lucille Frackman Becker, *Georges Simenon,* Twayne, 1977.

Periodicals: *Spectator,* March 23, 1951; *Saturday Review,* February 21, 1953; *New York Times Book Review,* August 25, 1957; March 16, 1969, February 25, 1973, November 4, 1973, November 21, 1976, May 22, 1977, July 1, 1979; *South Atlantic Quarterly,* Autumn, 1967; *Adam International Review,* Autumn, 1969; *Life,* May 9, 1969; *Time,* March 14, 1969; *Newsweek,* April 27, 1970, February 19, 1973; *Armchair Detective,* January, 1971; *Washington Post,* September 17, 1972; *World,* May, 1973; *Critic,* January/February, 1974; *National Review,* April 30, 1976, December 10, 1976; *New Yorker,* April 24, 1978, April 2, 1979; *New York Review of Books,* October 12, 1978.

* * *

SINCOFF, Michael Z(olman)   1943-

PERSONAL: Born June 28, 1943, in Washington, D.C.; son of Murray Paul and Anna Frances (Jaffe) Sincoff. *Education:* University of Maryland, B.A., 1964, M.A., 1966; Purdue University, Ph.D., 1969. *Office:* Celanese Corp., 1211 Avenue of the Americas, New York, N.Y. 10036.

CAREER: University of Tennessee, Knoxville, instructor in English, summer, 1968; Ohio University, Athens, assistant professor, 1969-74, associate professor of interpersonal communication, 1974-76, director of Center for Communication Studies, 1972-76; Celanese Corp., New York, N.Y., director of personnel development for Chemical Group, 1976—. Visiting professor at University of Minnesota, spring, 1974. Management Training Institute (Tulsa, Okla.), senior staff consultant, 1970-71, vice-president, 1971-72, executive vice-president, 1972-74, president, 1974-76; associate and member of board of directors of Public Systems Associates, Inc. (Durham, N.C.), 1975—.

MEMBER: International Communication Association (life member; business manager, 1970-72; executive secretary, 1970-73; member of board of directors and executive committee, 1970-73), American Arbitration Association, American Association for the Advancement of Science, American Association of University Professors, Council of Communication Societies, Academy of Management, Central States

Speech Association, Speech Communication Association of Ohio (member of executive council, 1974-76; head of Organizational Communication Division, 1974-76), Blue Key. *Awards, honors:* Outstanding teacher award from Central States Speech Association, 1971; university professor award from Ohio University, 1973-74; systems design fellowships from National Aeronautics & Space Administration (NASA) and American Society for Engineering Education, 1973, 1974, 1975, 1976.

WRITINGS: (Editor with Calvin R. Dyer and Paul D. Cribbins, and contributor) *The Energy Dilemma and Its Impact on Air Transportation,* Old Dominion University, 1973; (editor with Jarir S. Dajani and Curtis M. Brooks, and contributor) *Urban Transportation: Perspectives on Mobility and Choice,* Old Dominion University, 1974; (editor with Dajani, and contributor) *General Aviation and Community Development,* Old Dominion University, 1975; (editor with Dajani, and contributor) *Planning and Evaluation Parameters for Offshore Complexes,* Old Dominion University, 1976; (with Robert S. Goyer) *Interviewing Methods,* Kendall/Hunt, 1977, revised edition, 1980. Contributor to a wide variety of academic journals. Editor of newsletter of International Communication Association, 1970.

WORK IN PROGRESS: Police Interviewing and Criminal Interrogation; Student Personnel Administration, completion expected in 1980.

*   *   *

SINKLER, George 1927-

PERSONAL: Born December 22, 1927, in Charleston, S.C.; son of Moses (a laborer) and Mary Etta (Jones) Sinkler; married Albertha Amelia Richardson, August 19, 1949; children: Gregory, Kenneth, Georgette. *Education:* Augustana College, Rock Island, Ill., A.B., 1953; Columbia University, M.A., 1954, Ed.D., 1966. *Politics:* Democrat. *Religion:* Methodist. *Home:* 821 Beaumont Ave., Baltimore, Md. 21212. *Office:* Department of History, Morgan State University, Coldspring and Hillen Rd., Baltimore, Md. 21239.

CAREER: Prairie View A & M College (now University), Prairie View, Tex., associate professor of history, 1955-66; Morgan State University, Baltimore, Md., professor of American history, 1966—. Visiting associate professor at Amherst College, 1969; lecturer at colleges and universities. *Military service:* U.S. Navy, steward's mate, 1946-49. *Member:* American Historical Association, Organization of American Historians, American Association of University Professors, Phi Beta Kappa, Phi Alpha Theta, Kappa Delta, Kappa Delta Pi. *Awards, honors:* Fellow of Institute for Southern History at Johns Hopkins University, 1972-73.

WRITINGS: The Racial Attitudes of American Presidents: From Lincoln to Theodore Roosevelt, Doubleday, 1971. Contributor to history and black studies journals and newspapers.

WORK IN PROGRESS: The Racial Attitudes of American Presidents Before the Civil War, completion expected in 1983.

SIDELIGHTS: Sinkler comments: "I have always had an intense urge to *be* somebody because of the Caucasian charge of Negro racial inferiority. I *have* always been interested in the racial views of white people, and that is why I chose the subject for my research. I sincerely believe that, if black and white could only live together and mix from the diaper stage, they could get along and America could be great. I believe in the brotherhood of man and man's capacity to transcend race if he tries hard enough."

SINYAVSKY, Andrei (Donatevich) 1925- (Abram Tertz)

PERSONAL: Born October 8, 1925, in Moscow, U.S.S.R.; immigrated to France, 1973; married; wife's name, Masha (an art historian); children: Yegor (son). *Education:* Moscow University, degree, 1949, kandidat, 1952. *Residence:* Bourg-la-Reine, France. *Office:* Sorbonne, University of Paris, 12 Place du Pantheon, 75231 Paris, France.

CAREER: Writer. Gorki Institute of World Literature, Moscow, U.S.S.R., senior research fellow, until 1966; Moscow University, Moscow, lecturer on Russian literature, until 1966; tried and sentenced to seven years' hard labor for alleged anti-Soviet writings, 1966; released from prison, 1971; Sorbonne, University of Paris, Paris, France, 1973—, began as assistant professor, currently professor of Slavic studies. *Military service:* Soviet Army. *Member:* Union of Soviet Writers (expelled, 1966). *Awards, honors:* Bennett Award from the Grolier Club, 1978.

WRITINGS—Novels; under pseudonym Abram Tertz: *Sud idyot,* [published], 1960, translation by Jozef Lobodowski from original Russian manuscript published as *Sad idzie,* Instytut Literacki (Paris), 1959, translation by Max Hayward from original Russian manuscript published as *The Trial Begins,* Pantheon, 1960; *Lyubivom,* [published], 1964, translation by Lobodowski from original Russian manuscript published as *Lubimow,* Instytut Literacki, 1963, translation by Manya Harari published as *The Makepeace Experiment,* Pantheon, 1965.

Short stories; under pseudonym Abram Tertz: *Fantasticheskie povesti,* Instytut Literacki, 1961, translation by Hayward and Ronald Hingley published as *Fantastic Stories,* Pantheon, 1963 (published in England as *The Icicle, and Other Stories,* Collins & Harvill, 1963). Work also represented in *Soviet Short Stories 2,* edited by Peter Reddaway, 1968.

Nonfiction: (With I. N. Golomshtok) *Pikasso* (title means "Picasso"), Znanie (Moscow), 1960; (with A. N. Menshutin) *Poeziya pervykh let revolyutsii, 1917-20,* (title means "The Poetry of the First Years of the Revolution"), Nauka (Moscow), 1964; (author of introduction) Anna Akhmatova, *Selected Poems of Anna Akhmatova,* translated by Richard McKane, Oxford University Press, 1969; *For Freedom of Imagination* (collection of essays), translated by Laszlo Tikos and Murray Peppard, Holt, 1971. Also author of *Istoriya russkoy sovetsky literatury* (title means "History of Soviet Russian Literature"), Volume III, 1961.

Nonfiction; under pseudonym Abram Tertz: "Chto takoe sotsialisticheski realizm," published in *L'Esprit* magazine, 1959, translation by George Dennis published as *On Socialist Realism,* Pantheon, 1960; *Mysli vrasplokh,* [published], 1966, translation from original Russian manuscript by Lobodowski published as *Mysli niespodziewane,* Instytut Literacki, 1965, translation by R. Szulkin and A. Field published as "Thought Unaware" in *New Leader,* July 19, 1965, translation by Harari published as *Unguarded Thoughts,* Collins & Harvill, 1972; *Golos iz khora,* [published], 1973, translation by Hayward and Kyril FitzLyon published as *A Voice From the Chorus,* Farrar, 1976; *Progulki s Pushkinym* (criticism; title means "Strolling With Pushkin"), Overseas Publications Exchange, 1975; *V teni Gogolia* (criticism), Overseas Publications Interchange, 1975. Works collected in *Fantasticheski mir Abrama Tertsa* (title means "Fantastic World of Abram Tertz"), 1967. Contributor of essays and book reviews to *Novy mir.* Founder of literary journal, *Syntaxis.*

SIDELIGHTS: For many years Andrei Sinyavsky was forced to maintain two identities. On one hand, he was an esteemed literary critic at the Gorki Institute of World Literature in Moscow. A friend and protege of Boris Pasternak, Sinyavsky was particularly interested in Soviet poetry and wrote many highly regarded books and articles on that subject. Although he had argued for greater freedom of expression in some of his essays, he had never incurred the wrath of Soviet authorities. On the other hand, Sinyavsky was also a renegade writer who secretly published works outside of the Soviet Union. His fiction, written in a style reminiscent of Gogol and Dostoevksi, diverged sharply from the standards upheld by government censors.

As a student, Sinyavsky had been an active member of Komsomol, the Young Communists League. According to one friend, the young Sinyavsky "could not conceive of his country having any other structure than that created by 1917. The very word 'revolution' . . . had for him an emotional quality, the ring of something holy which portended the coming of a more just social system, a new humanism which would bring renewal to the universe." His allegiance to Marxism began to waver, however, when his father was arrested in 1951 in a Stalinist purge. Khrushchev's famous speech in 1956, which revealed some of the atrocities of the Stalin years, deeply disturbed Sinyavsky and many other Soviet intellectuals. Sinyavsky could no longer accept the idea of unquestioning faith in the Soviet system and began to forge for himself a new style of writing. It was about this same time that he began smuggling some of his works abroad, using a former French student, Madame Helene Peltier-Zamoyska, as a messenger.

Sinyavsky published in the West under the pen name Abram Tertz. Many years later he explained why he had selected Tertz as his *nom de plume:* "For my part, though I am not a Jew, I have deliberately taken a Jewish pseudonym. Abram Tertz was a gangster in the Odessa of Balel's era; there is an underworld song about him. As a writer I feel I am a Jew—in Russia anyone today who does not conform to Socialist Realist standards is in effect an outcast, a Jew." Abram Tertz first came to the attention of the world in 1959, when an essay entitled "On Socialist Realism" appeared in the French magazine *L'Esprit.* In it Sinyavsky attacked the official Soviet line that the purpose of art is to glorify socialism; he argued that art which serves as a propaganda instrument is trite and simplistic, and that is does not capture the essence of modern life. "I put my hope in a phantasmagoric art, with hypotheses instead of a Purpose, an art in which the grotesque will replace realistic descriptions of ordinary life," he wrote. "Such an art would correspond best to the spirit of our time." "On Socialist Realism," which was translated into several languages, aroused the admiration and the curiosity of many commentators. The original essay had been unsigned, but later versions appeared under the name Abram Tertz. Interest in this mysterious Russian writer was intensified when some of his novels and short stories were published in the West—*The Trial Begins, The Makepeace Experiment,* and *Fantastic Stories.*

"Whoever 'Tertz' may be, he deals with universal human questions with an excitement that indicates that there exists in Russia today a black market in religious ideas," a *Time* reviewer wrote in a critique of *The Trial Begins.* Other critics were also impressed by the novel, which follows the life of Vladimir Globov, a Soviet official who plays a key role in the persecution of the Jews during the last days of Stalin's reign. Michael Frayn hailed Tertz as a "writer of the greatest freshness, technical skill, passion, and self-discipline,"

while Harry Schwartz praised the novel's intermingling of humor and horror: "The first reading of 'The Trial Begins' is bound to produce chuckle after chuckle. It is only after a second reading or reflection on what one has read that the full horror of the story sinks in." Although several reviewers pointed out that *The Trial Begins* would never have been permitted to be published in the Soviet Union, Phoebe Adams observed: "It would be a mistake, I think, to take this acidly funny and demurely unpleasant little book as evidence of Communist disaffection in Russia. The author is not attacking Communism in the classic sense, but merely the hysterical excesses of the last days of Stalin's regime."

Tertz' short story collection, *Fantastic Stories,* did not arouse so much enthusiasm as *The Trial Begins* did. "The stories seem mechanical and willed, more a reaction to Communist dogma than the result of a style organically nurtured," Irving Howe declared. A critic for *Virginia Quarterly Review* was more generous: "Although he lacks the technical brilliance and startling insights of such writers as Vladimir Nabokov and Jorge Luis Borges, Tertz's stories are consistently interesting and engaging. Through an apparent disassociation with reality, he creates a new reality—not one of allegory or political satire as many readers might expect, but one of new vision caused by the fusion of limited reality and unlimited imagination."

Sinyavsky also put his unlimited imagination to work in *The Makepeace Experiment,* a novel about a Russian mechanic who gains ascendancy over the minds of his townspeople. *The Makepeace Experiment,* George Feifer wrote, is "a work of splendid craftsmanship, imagination, scope and power, a tour de force of truth-through-distortion." Martin Levin was equally admiring. "Mr. Tertz's witty comments on Soviet society are visible enough. But they are embedded in a whimsical context, created out of narrative, fable, cryptical Joycean associations and telescoping characters, that leave the reader as exhilarated and bemused as four jiggers of vodka on an empty stomach," Levin noted. He concluded, "Abram Tertz, whoever he is, has a splendidly baroque imagination and a gift for high and low comedy, whatever the import one chooses to read into it."

By the time *The Makepeace Experiment* was published in 1963, many critics were trying to guess who Tertz really was. They eventually got their answer, but the revelation of Tertz's true identity came at considerable cost to the author and had international repercussions. In September of 1965 Sinyavsky was accused of being Tertz and was arrested by Soviet authorities. Arrested at the same time was Yuri Daniel, a translator of poetry who was accused of publishing short stories in the West under the pseudonym Nikolai Arzhak. Both writers were placed in prison pending trial. Several weeks later dispatches from Moscow announced that Sinyavsky and Daniel had admitted that they had published books abroad under pseudonyms. This fact was confirmed by Jerzy Giedroyc, a Polish publisher who owned the international publishing rights for the works of Tertz and Arzhak. The case of Sinyavsky and Daniel quickly became a *cause celebre.* In the United States, eighteen leading writers sent a missive to Aleksei Kosygin, the Soviet Premier, protesting the arrest of Sinyavsky and Daniel and assuring him that it would be far too simplistic to merely dismiss their writings as "anti-Soviet."

The two writers were brought to trial in February, 1966. It is not a crime in the Soviet Union to publish books abroad; Sinyavsky and Daniel were accused of violating article 70 of the Russian criminal code, which covers anti-Soviet propaganda and agitation. Most observers felt that the trial was a sham. Before Sinyavsky and Daniel even entered the courtroom, Soviet newspapers had accused the pair of publishing treasonous, immoral, and pornographic literature. Although it was supposed to be an open trial, no foreign correspondents were allowed in the courtroom and the majority of the onlookers were members of the secret police. Sinyavsky's and Daniels's supporters were forced to wait outside the building while the trial progressed. Several people had offered to testify on the writers' behalf, but only one was allowed to take the stand, and he was quickly dismissed.

Because a transcript of the trial was smuggled out of the country, a record does exist of what transpired in the courtroom. Both Sinyavsky and Daniel pleaded not guilty to the accusation that their literary works "contain slanderous statements against the Soviet system and are used by reactionary propaganda against the Soviet State." Although the prosecution cited a number of cases in which Western reviewers had described Tertz as an enemy of the Soviet regime, Sinyavsky pointed out that a number of other Western critics, including Andrew Field and Czeslaw Milosz, had expressed the opinion that Tertz was not anti-Soviet. Sinyavsky contended that he had not written with the intent of denigrating the U.S.S.R. He was motivated, he told the court, by concern for the Russian people: "I wanted to tell people about the nation's spiritual needs. I am not a political writer. I am far removed from politics."

In his final plea, Sinyavsky summarized his case: "The most rudimentary thing about literature—it is here that one's study of it begins—is that words are not deeds, and that words and literary images are conventions: authors are not identical with the characters they create.... The question arises: what is propaganda, and what is literature? The viewpoint of the prosecution is that literature is a form of propaganda, and that there are only two kinds of propaganda: pro-Soviet or anti-Soviet. If literature is simply un-Soviet, it means that it is anti-Soviet. It is a poor business if writers are judged and categorized by such standards." The prosecution, however, argued that "both defendants have acted intentionally and deliberately. The very content of the works of Sinyavsky and Daniel attests to the hostility of their authors toward the Soviet people, the state, and the Communist party. The works are a mockery of everything that is dear and sacred to a Soviet person: the motherland, the Communist ideal, the Soviet way of life, the morality of the Soviet people." Both writers were convicted. Sinyavsky was sentenced to seven years in a labor camp, Daniel to five.

Within the Soviet Union, reaction to the conviction of Sinyavsky and Daniel was mixed. Not long after the trial was over, *Literaturnaya Gazeta,* the newspaper of the Union of Soviet Writers, printed a letter signed by eighteen members of the philology department at Moscow University. The professors castigated Sinyavsky for posing as a loyal Marxist while he was sending anti-Soviet materials out of the country to be published. An even harsher condemnation came from Mikhail Sholokhov, a Soviet novelist who won the Nobel Prize for Literature in 1965. In an address before the twenty-third congress of the Soviet Communist party, Sholokhov said, "Had these rascals with black consciences [Sinyavsky and Daniel] been caught in the memorable nineteen hundred twenties, when judgment was not by strictly defined articles of the criminal code but was guided by 'a revolutionary sense of justice,' the punishment meted out to these turncoats would have been different." Other Soviet intellectuals were more sympathetic to the plight of their compatriots. A petition by sixty-three Moscow writers sent to the same assembly which Sholokhov addressed urged the release of Sinyavsky and Daniel. "Although we do not approve the means by which these writers published their work abroad, we cannot accept the view that their motives were in any way anti-Soviet, which alone could have justified the severity of the sentence," they asserted. "At the same time," they went on, "the condemnation of writers for the writing of satirical works creates an extremely dangerous precedent and threatens to hold up the progress of Soviet culture."

The Sinyavsky-Daniel case attracted so much attention because it was unprecedented in modern Soviet history. Although other intellectuals who had crossed the Communist regime had been persecuted, none had ever been held criminally responsible for the political effects of their literary works. The trial also seemed to point up a growing dissatisfaction with the restrictive policies of the Soviet Communist party. "The point of the present cultural tug of war, with its fulcrum in the Sinyavsky-Daniel case, is one of freedom of expression under mature Communism.... If the advocates of neo-Stalinist dogmatism really held the upper hand, unchallenged, there would be no tug of war, no reservation or dissent, even whispered, in the corridors of the Writers Union," Peter Grose observed. "And Mr. Sinyavsky's students would not mill around outside his trial chambers, if Mr. Sinyavsky was even honored with a trial."

Despite all the protests, Sinyavsky and Daniel remained in prison. Sinyavsky turned the situation to his advantage. His term in prison, he recalled, was "the hardest time of my life but, in another way, the happiest. Speaking as an artist, I found the camp a fantastic existence—a fairytale world terrifying but fascinating. It is a distillation of the whole world outside—the worst and the best kinds of people all together—people who collaborated with the Nazis and killed a lot of Jews; saintly people who were there for their religious beliefs—even members of the underworld, although it was supposed to be a political prison. Knowing I was a writer, they came and told me their stories, some of which were fascinating." Sinyavsky continued to write at the labor camp. He wrote a study of Pushkin as well as the material that he shaped into *A Voice From the Chorus* after he was released.

A Voice From the Chorus is comprised of notes and letters that Sinyavsky mailed to his wife while he was incarcerated. Interspersed with Sinyavsky's philosophical and literary meditations are comments from the other prisoners, or the "chorus." Their utterances are variously vulgar, annoying, wise, and banal. Many reviewers found these interruptions of Sinyavsky's thoughts to be the most remarkable aspect of the book. Harvey Fireside wrote that "the uniqueness of the work ... resides in the relationship of the 'voice' of this Ishmael to the 'chorus' of his shipmates—the common criminals whose boasts, ballads and curses counterpoint the musings of the solitary survivor."

A Voice From the Chorus does not attempt to document the horrors of the Soviet labor camp, nor is it a political tract. Dan Jacobson praised Sinyavsky's understated treatment of the physical conditions in which he was writing: "His extreme abstemiousness or frugality in this regard has a double effect: it puts into particularly sharp focus those sudden details of his daily existence which do appear; and it lends an extraordinary deliberateness and intensity to the reflections on other topics of which the book is largely composed." Fireside lauded Sinyavsky for refusing to enter into political discussions or to give a realistic portrayal of the labor camp: "While Solzhenitsyn disturbs us by his polemical revision of history, Sinyavsky deliberately avoids politics in the journals of his six years in a prison camp to leave us with a sense of wonder at an artist's ability to transmute suffering into self-knowledge. . . . Sinyavsky's chronicle of internal exile is, finally, a tour de force demonstrating the author's esthetic of fantasy as a more adequate response to the mindless horrors of our age than was the realism still constricting the scope of Solzhenitsyn.''

In 1973 Sinyavsky and his family received permission to immigrate to France, where he had been offered a professorship at the Sorbonne. Since moving to the West, he has shunned publicity, although recently he has become more amenable to interviewers. While on a trip to the United States in 1978 to receive the Bennett Award, Sinyavsky talked with reporters about conditions in the Soviet Union. Although he was not hopeful that political repression would cease, he did express optimism about the spiritual growth of the Soviet people. This optimism stemmed from his term in the labor camp: "I observed ordinary people, in spite of destruction and oppression maintain an artistic vein, a vein that lives in the most primitive people.'' He echoed this thought in a speech later the same evening: "An author is destined to vanish, to perish; whereas the art associated with him survives and triumphs, even though it be labeled criminal. . . . It is not we who possess art; rather, it is art that sometimes takes possession of people and in part manifests itself through them.''

Sinyavsky's books have been translated into Polish, German, Spanish, French, and Portuguese.

In 1966 BBC-Television screened a reconstruction of the trial of Sinyavsky and Daniel.

BIOGRAPHICAL/CRITICAL SOURCES: Times Literary Supplement, April 29, 1960, June 28, 1963; *Guardian,* April 29, 1960; *New York Herald Tribune Book Review,* September 11, 1960; *Atlantic,* October, 1960, January, 1962, February, 1979; *Time,* October 3, 1960, April 12, 1963, July 30, 1965, July 19, 1968; *New York Times Book Review,* October 16, 1960, November 26, 1961, July 11, 1965, September 18, 1966, June 27, 1976, October 30, 1977; *Chicago Sunday Tribune,* October 30, 1960; *Saturday Review,* November 5, 1960, November 11, 1961, April 13, 1963, July 24, 1965, February 27, 1971; *New Republic,* December 5, 1960, May 11, 1963, September 25, 1976; *Commonweal,* January 5, 1962, December 3, 1976; *Slavic Review,* September, 1962, December, 1970; *Virginia Quarterly Review,* summer, 1963; *New Yorker,* September 21, 1963, October 11, 1976.

Encounter, July, 1965, April, 1966, February, 1974, August, 1976; *Newsweek,* July 26, 1965, February 25, 1974, July 12, 1976; *Christian Science Monitor,* August 5, 1965; *Book Week,* August 22, 1965; *New York Review of Books,* October 14, 1965, August 5, 1976; *New York Times,* December 8, 1965, January 13, 1966, February 11, 1966, February 13, 1966, February 15, 1966, February 16, 1966, April 2, 1966, November 19, 1966, November 17, 1978; Max Hayward, editor and translator, *On Trial: The Soviet State Versus Abram Tertz and Nikolai Arzhak,* Harper, 1966, revised edition, 1967; *Harper's,* February, 1966; *Le Monde,* April 17, 1966; *New York Times Magazine,* April 17, 1966; *Listener,* August 31, 1967, November 23, 1967, December 14, 1967; *Canadian Slavic Studies,* fall, 1967; *Esquire,* March, 1968; Helen Muchnic, *Russian Writers,* Random House, 1971; *Washington Post Book World,* May 16, 1971; Richard Lourie, *Letters to the Future: An Approach to Sinyavsky-Tertz,* Cornell University Press, 1975; *Nation,* September 4, 1976; *Commentary,* November, 1976; *Contemporary Literary Criticism,* Volume 8, Gale, 1978; *Washington Post,* November 20, 1978; *World Literature Today,* spring, 1979.*

SKELLY, James R(ichard)   1927-

PERSONAL: Born May 23, 1927, in Evansville, Ind.; son of Kenneth (a manufacturer) and Lydia (Scheips) Skelly. *Education:* Attended Ohio State University, 1947-48; Case Western Reserve University, B.A., 1955. *Politics:* Conservative. *Religion:* Conservative. *Home and office address:* P.O. Box 23734, Fort Lauderdale, Fla. 33308.

CAREER: Cleveland Aquarium, Cleveland, Ohio, curator, 1953-55; Cleveland Museum of Natural History, Cleveland, staff biologist, 1955-56, registrar, 1956-60; Holy Cross Hospital, Fort Lauderdale, Fla., chemist, 1963-66; Artists and Writers Press, New York City, assistant editor in Florida, 1966-68; free-lance writer, 1968—. Part-time chemist with Laboratory for Research in Ophthalmology, Case Western Reserve University Medical School, 1956-61. *Military service:* U.S. Merchant Marine, 1944-46. U.S. Army, 1949-52. *Member:* Writers Guild.

WRITINGS—All with Herbert Spencer Zim; all juveniles; all published by Morrow: *Machine Tools,* 1969; *Hoists, Cranes, and Derricks,* 1969; *Trucks,* 1970; *Cargo Ships,* 1970; *Telephone Systems,* 1971; *Tractors,* 1972; *Metric Measure,* 1974; *Pipes and Plumbing Systems,* 1974; *Eating Places,* 1975.

WORK IN PROGRESS: "I rarely talk about the things I'm working on and this is not one of those rare occasions. I find you expend your talent when you do that, and you should receive something when you tell what you're discovering or have discovered in the past. It's all an author has to sell.''

SIDELIGHTS: Skelly commented: "After the first blushes of being published, I think the main motivation to writing is the intense interest in an idea that doesn't seem to have been expressed as well as I can do it. Of course, one must also keep an eye on the market, unless one is very well-heeled. *Avocational interests:* Fishing, sailing, and writing novels ("but publishers reject them'').

*   *   *

SLATER, Ian   1941-

PERSONAL: Born December 1, 1941, in Queensland, Australia; son of David James (in trade) and Mavis (Horton) Slater; married Marian Ella Johnston (a technician), December 18, 1968. *Education:* University of British Columbia, B.A., 1972, M.A., 1973, Ph.D., 1977. *Religion:* Anglican. *Home:* 4074 West 17th Ave., Vancouver, British Columbia, Canada V6S 1A6. *Agent:* McClelland & Stewart, 25 Hollinger Rd., Toronto, Ontario, Canada M4B 392.

CAREER: Commonwealth Bank of Australia, Brisbane, clerk, 1961; Australian Department of the Navy, Canberra, medals clerk, 1961; Australian Department of External Affairs, Canberra, cipher clerk, 1961-62; Australian Department of Defence, Joint Intelligence Bureau, Canberra, defense officer, 1962-63; Australian Bureau of Meteorology, Melbourne, clerk, 1963-64; associated with New Zealand Department of the Treasury and New Zealand Oceanographic Institute, Wellington, 1964-66; University of British Columbia, Vancouver, oceanographic technician, 1966-69, lecturer, 1978—. *Member:* Writers Union of Canada, Canadian Political Science Association. *Awards, honors:* Mack Eastman United Nations Award from United Nations (Vancouver branch), 1971, for essay, "The United Nations: Its Problems as Reflected in a Comparative History of the League of Nations and the United Nations''; Canada Council grant for doctoral study on George Orwell at University of London, 1974.

WRITINGS: Firespill (novel), Bantam, 1977; *Sea Gold* (novel), Bantam, 1979.

Plays: "The Van Don Soldier" (radio play), Canadian Broadcasting Corp. (CBC), 1971; "Black Lion" (radio play), CBC, 1972; "Sea Gold" (radio play), CBC, 1972; "The Factory" (radio play), CBC, 1973; "Flash Point" (ten-minute animation), National Film Board of Canada, 1978; "The Far Garden" (one-act), first produced in Vancouver, British Columbia, at DuMaurier Festival of One-Act Plays, 1979.

Work represented in anthologies, including *Under Twenty-Five*, Jacaranda Press, 1966. Contributor of poems, stories, articles, and reviews to journals, including *Fiddlehead* and *Prism*, and newspapers.

WORK IN PROGRESS: An "adventure-thriller-espionage" novel.

SIDELIGHTS: Slater's first novel, *Firespill*, has been published in Italian, Norwegian, French, Spanish, Portuguese, Swedish, Dutch, Turkish, and Danish, and will soon be published in German.

He writes: "*Firespill*, about a massive oil spill which catches fire off the northwest coast of North America, was written in part because I am sure that such a catastrophe will happen. I am interested in alerting people to the fact that in the sleek world of automation—in this case, the supertanker—Murphy's Law often runs riot, aided very largely by human error. For all this, however, *Firespill* was written primarily as entertainment. *Sea Gold* is a story about what I believe will be the mounting crisis over who owns what in the deep sea. The sea bed in places is vastly rich in minerals and we have now developed the technology to exploit it. The Law of the Sea Conference, I believe, has failed dismally to come to grips with the problem and what we are about to see are unilateral decisions to exploit the deep oceans based not on the Law of the Sea but on corporate need and greed. *Sea Gold* is an adventure story based on this premise. Although not autobiographical, many of the technical details and the feeling for the sea which went into writing this novel came from my varied oceanographic experience in the Tasman Sea, the southwest Pacific, northeast Pacific, and southern ocean during my time as an oceanographic technician."

BIOGRAPHICAL/CRITICAL SOURCES: Canadian Fiction, autumn, 1977.

*   *   *

SLAUGHTER, Carolyn   1946-

PERSONAL: Born January 7, 1946, in New Dehli, India; daughter of Gerald Columba (a colonial civil servant) and Marian (Webb) Ryan; married Denis Pack-Beresford (a public relations director; divorced); married Daniel Cromer (a company director); children: Alice Eliza, Daniel Thomas. *Education:* Educated in South Africa and England. *Home:* 6 Ashburn Gardens, London S.W.7, England. *Agent:* Richard Scott Simon, 32 College Cross, London N.1, England.

CAREER: Novelist. Advertising copywriter in London, England, for advertising agencies, including Garland Compton, Ltd., 1966-68, Norman Craig & Kummel, 1969-71, Collett, Dickenson & Pearce, 1971-72, Nadler, Larimer & Cromer, 1972-74; free-lance writer, 1974-76. *Awards, honors:* Geoffrey Faber Memorial Prize from Faber & Faber, 1977, for *The Story of the Weasel*.

WRITINGS: The Story of the Weasel (novel; Literary Guild selection), Hart-Davis, 1976, published as *Relations*, Mason-Charter, 1978; *Columba* (novel), Hart-Davis, 1977, Panther House, 1979; *Magdalene* (novel), Hart-Davis, 1978.

WORK IN PROGRESS: A novel set in the Kalahari Desert, publication by Hart-Davis expected in 1980.

SIDELIGHTS: Slaughter writes: "My greatest area of interest is childhood, specifically the years between birth and pre-puberty. Nothing happens after that, cycles only repeat.

"In my novels I always seem to be drawn to situations of great stress—violence, insanity. I keep returning to these themes because they are, for me, haunting, and because I believe that by exploring them fully in fiction one can reduce their terror. The danger of this is that the work can easily become sombre, and I have to work harder all the time to change the mood and pace of my novels as they tend to be claustrophobic, somewhat linear. I am happiest writing in the present tense, in the first person, and will try to find a way of making that form work effectively in the future. I don't think books should be nice cosy things to curl up with—some should be more like a kick in the guts."

*   *   *

SMALL, George L(eroy)   1924-

PERSONAL: Born March 27, 1924, in Malden, Mass.; son of George Arthur (a banker) and Alice (Weston) Small; married Geraldine Henrietta Koepke, July 4, 1970; children: Elizabeth Mary. *Education:* Attended Sorbonne, University of Paris, 1948-49; Brown University, B.A., 1950; Columbia University, M.I.A., 1952, Ph.D., 1968; also attended University of Geneva, 1952-53. *Office:* Department of Geography, Staten Island College of the City University of New York, Staten Island, N.Y. 10301.

CAREER: Herbert H. Lehman College of the City University of New York, Bronx, N.Y., instructor in geography, 1964-66; Hunter College of the City University of New York, New York, N.Y., instructor in geography, 1966-68; Richmond College of the City University of New York, Staten Island, N.Y., assistant professor, 1968-72, associate professor of geography, 1972-79; Staten Island College of the City University of New York, Staten Island, N.Y., professor of geography, 1979—. Adviser to conservation groups; television consultant in Switzerland. *Military service:* U.S. Army, 1942-46; served in European theater. *Member:* Association of American Geographers, American Geographical Society. *Awards, honors:* National Book Award from National Book Committee, 1972, for *The Blue Whale*.

WRITINGS: The Blue Whale, Columbia University Press, 1972.

*   *   *

SMITH, James   1904-1972

PERSONAL: Born June 17, 1904, in Batley, Yorkshire, England. *Education:* Trinity College, Cambridge, B.A. (first class honours), 1924.

CAREER: Literary critic. Teacher at Percivel Whitley College of Further Education, Halifax, England, and King Edward VII School, Sheffield, England, 1931-33; inspector of schools, 1934-37; Roman Catholic University of Friebourg, Switzerland, professor of English, 1947-69. Examiner for Cambridge Local Examiners Syndicate; lecturer in English, Instituto Pedagogico, Caracas, Venezuela, 1940; director of British-Venezuelan Cultural Centre, Caracas. *Awards, honors:* Elizabeth Proctor visiting fellow, 1928-30.

WRITINGS: Edward M. Wilson, editor, *Shakespearian and Other Essays*, Cambridge University Press, 1974. Contributor of criticism to *Scrutiny, Essays in Criticism*, and *English*.

WORK IN PROGRESS: A collection of critical essays beginning with the works of T. S. Eliot and ending with *Beowulf.*

SIDELIGHTS: In writing the pieces collected in the posthumously published *Shakespearian and Other Essays,* Smith focused primarily on Shakespeare's comedies, but also included criticism of the metaphysical poetry of Baudelaire, Wordsworth, Empson, and Crose. Many of the essays had been previously published separately in journals. Of the twelve or more essays Smith had written specifically for the book, only seven were recovered. Martin Dodsworth noted the "classic quality" of these, pointing out that they "fundamentally question conventional readings of comedies, relating art to other human interests and activities." Philip Brockbank added, "The earlier essays on the comedies remain among the best of their kind, civilised, lucid, judicious and precise, with much close observation that does not too much attempt to do our reading for us."

Referring to Smith's "colloquial metaphors," F. W. Bateson noted that "their almost continuous subtlety distinguished his comments from those of any other Shakespearian critic since Coleridge." And, because of Smith's unique style of criticism, he has been counted among the few masters since Samuel Johnson.

BIOGRAPHICAL/CRITICAL SOURCES: Encounter, June 15, 1974; *Times Literary Supplement,* August 30, 1974; *Choice,* September, 1974; *Essays in Criticism,* Volume 26, 1976.*

* * *

SMITH, Joanmarie 1932-

PERSONAL: Born June 20, 1932, in New York, N.Y.; daughter of Charles J. (a musician) and Gertrude (in business; maiden name, Conroy) Smith. *Education:* St. John's University, Jamaica, N.Y., B.S., 1963; Fordham University, M.A., 1966, Ph.D., 1971. *Religion:* Roman Catholic. *Home:* 189 Chestnut St., Brooklyn, N.Y. 11208. *Office:* Department of Philosophy, St. Joseph's College, 245 Clinton Ave., Brooklyn, N.Y. 11205.

CAREER: Teacher of religion at private school in Jamaica, N.Y., 1964-65; Brentwood College, Brentwood, N.Y., assistant professor of philosophy, 1965-70; St. Joseph's College, Brooklyn, N.Y., associate professor of philosophy, 1970—. Adjunct associate professor at Boston College, New York University, Creighton University, St. John's University (Jamaica, N.Y.), Barry College, Providence College, and Molloy College. *Member:* American Association of Professors and Researchers in Religious Education, American Academy of Religion, American Catholic Philosophical Society, Religious Education Association.

WRITINGS: (With Gloria Durka) *Modeling God,* Paulist/Newman, 1976; (editor with Durka) *Emerging Issues in Religious Education,* Paulist/Newman, 1976; (editor with Durka) *The Aesthetic Dimension of Religious Education,* Paulist/Newman, 1979.

WORK IN PROGRESS: Research on the influence of the sociology of knowledge on religious phenomena, especially conversion.

SIDELIGHTS: Joanmarie Smith writes: "I am interested in the conclusions of the philosophers of science that science is not the objective, value-free discipline it was once considered to be. I am especially interested in exploring the ramifications of these conclusions for religion."

SMITH, Julia Floyd 1914-

PERSONAL: Born January 30, 1914, in Savannah, Ga.; daughter of Marmaduke Hamilton (a writer) and Julia Frances (a musician; maiden name, Heidt) Floyd; married Henry Garden Strachan, January 15, 1935 (died, 1940); married Albert Franklin Smith (a retirement board district manager), December 12, 1957; children: (first marriage) Henry Garden (deceased); (second marriage) Julia Frances (deceased). *Education:* Florida State University, B.S., 1951, M.S., 1954, Ph.D., 1964. *Home:* 23 West Perry St., Savannah, Ga. 31401. *Office:* Department of History, Georgia Southern College, Statesboro, Ga. 30458.

CAREER: Georgia Southern College, Statesboro, associate professor of history, 1967—. *Member:* American Association of University Professors, Southern Historical Association, Florida Historical Society, Georgia Historical Society, Georgia Association of Historians (member of executive council, 1974-76), Savannah Historic Research Association (president, 1969-72). *Awards, honors:* Rembert W. Patrick Memorial Book Award from Florida Historical Society, 1973, for *Slavery and Plantation Growth in Antebellum Florida, 1821-1860;* National Endowment for the Humanities senior fellowship, 1975-76.

WRITINGS: Slavery and Plantation Growth in Antebellum Florida, 1821-1860, University of Florida Press, 1973. Contributor of articles and reviews to history journals.

WORK IN PROGRESS: Tidewater Culture and Slavery in Antebellum Georgia; continuing research on the economics of rice culture before 1865 along the Georgia and South Carolina coast.

SIDELIGHTS: Julia Smith writes: "My major area of vocational interest is restoration and preservation of historic houses in Savannah; I have recently restored one of four row houses built in 1854 by John Stoddard, and hope to continue this work."

* * *

SMITH, Martin (Cruz) 1942-
(Simon Quinn)

PERSONAL: Born November 3, 1942, in Reading, Pa.; son of John Calhoun (a musician) and Louise (an Indian rights leader; maiden name, Lopez) Smith; married Emily Arnold (a chef), June 15, 1968; children: Ellen Irish, Luisa Cruz. *Education:* University of Pennsylvania, B.A., 1964. *Agent:* Knox Burger Associates Ltd., 39½ Washington Sq. S., New York, N.Y. 10012.

CAREER: Writer. Worked for *Philadelphia Daily News,* 1965, and Magazine Management, 1966-69.

WRITINGS: The Indians Won (novel), Belmont-Tower, 1970; *Gypsy in Amber* (mystery novel), Putnam, 1971; *Canto for a Gypsy* (mystery novel), Putnam, 1972; *The Human Factor* (novel), Dell, 1975; *Nightwing* (suspense novel), Norton, 1977; *The Analog Bullet* (novel), Belmont-Tower, 1978.

Under pseudonym Simon Quinn: *His Eminence, Death* (novel), Dell, 1974; *Nuplex Red,* Dell, 1974; *The Midas Coffin,* Dell, 1975; *Last Rites for the Vulture,* Dell, 1975.

BIOGRAPHICAL/CRITICAL SOURCES: New York Times Book Review, October 23, 1977; *Washington Post,* November 3, 1977.

* * *

SMITH, Stan(ley Roger) 1946-

PERSONAL: Born December 14, 1946, in Pasadena, Calif.;

son of Charles Kenneth (a realtor) and Rhoda (Widmer) Smith; married Marjory Logan Gengler, November 23, 1974. *Education:* University of Southern California, B.A., 1969. *Politics:* Republican. *Religion:* Presbyterian. *Home:* 706 Schooner Ct., Sea Pines Plantation, Hilton Head Island, S.C. 29928. *Agent:* Don Dell and Frank Craighill, 888 17th St. N.W., Suite 1200, Washington, D.C. 20006. *Office:* 888 17th St. N.W., Suite 1200, Washington, D.C. 20006.

CAREER: Professional tennis player; member of U.S. Davis Cup Team, 1969-74. Instructor at tennis clinics throughout the world. Adviser to President's Council on Physical Fitness, 1971-75; consultant to numerous businesses, including Wilson Sporting Goods Co. and Adidas. *Military service:* U.S. Army, 1970-72; received Distinguished Service Medal. *Member:* Association of Tennis Professionals, Athletes in Action, Big Brothers of America (member of board of directors of Greater Los Angeles chapter, 1966-71), Beta Theta Pi. *Awards, honors:* Ranked number one in U.S. doubles, 1968, 1969, 1970, 1971, 1972, 1974, number one in U.S. singles, 1969, 1971, 1972, 1973, world's number one tennis player, 1973; holder of twenty-three U.S. singles and doubles titles, including U.S. Open doubles, 1968, 1974, and U.S. Open singles, 1971; named Martini and Rossi Tennis Player of the Year, 1971, 1972; winner of Wimbledon singles title, 1972, and six World Championship tennis titles in 1973, including World Championship of Tennis Finals in singles and Rothman's World Doubles; L.H.D., 1974, from Greenville College.

WRITINGS: Stan Smith's Six Tennis Basics, edited by Larry Sheehan, Atheneum, 1974; (with Tom Valentine) *Inside Tennis,* Regnery, 1974; (with Sheehan) *Stan Smith's Guide to Better Tennis,* Grosset, 1975; *Pass the Ammunition,* Manor, 1976; (with Bob Lutz and Sheehan) *Modern Tennis Doubles,* Atheneum, 1977; *It's More Than Just a Game,* Revell, 1977. Also author of *The Executive Tennis Diary,* 1975. Author of syndicated column, "Better Tennis."

SIDELIGHTS: A late bloomer by tennis standards, at sixteen Stan Smith was not even accepted as a ball boy at the Los Angeles Tennis Club. "I really thought it would be great to be on the same court with McKinley, Ralston, and Osuana," he later recalled, "but I was turned down. The fellow in charge of the ball boys said I was too awkward and that I'd clomp around and bother the players. It took me a while to learn how to manage my size-13 feet." A year later the "awkward" Smith won the U.S. National Junior Championship.

Aside from his success in tennis, Smith is well known for his conscientiously helpful and courteous nature. Frank Deford characterized him as "deeply religious, God-fearing, temperate and disciplined, a true sportsman, a respectful loving son and a self-made champion whose 'corny dream' is to build and manage his own YMCA. John Calvin would have been proud of him." Smith took a lighter view of himself. "Listen, I act up too," he said. "Sometimes I sneak an after-dinner mint before dinner."

Even when "at the top of the tennis world" in the early 1970's, Smith humbly reasoned that his "good salary . . . really isn't everything, . . . people I know who have done well financially may not be happy, and . . . some people who haven't done well financially really have fine homes and fine families. There's a meaning in their lives you can really see." Meanwhile, "Christ has been the reigning influence" in his life.

BIOGRAPHICAL/CRITICAL SOURCES: Sports Illustrat-

ed, September 1, 1969, February 28, 1972; *Time,* September 27, 1971, March 13, 1972, October 30, 1972; *New York Times Biographical Edition,* May 26, 1973; *Saturday Evening Post,* January, 1974; *Biography News,* September/October, 1975.

*   *   *

SMITH, Woodruff D(onald) 1946-

PERSONAL: Born March 22, 1946, in Missoula, Mont.; son of Donald Howard (a lawyer and Air Force officer) and Ernestine (a nurse; maiden name, Grindatti) Smith; married Jane Helen Lobred (an editor), August 26, 1967; children: Rebecca, Anthony. *Education:* Harvard University, A.B., 1967; University of Chicago, A.M., 1968, Ph.D., 1972. *Residence:* San Antonio, Tex. *Office:* Division of Social Sciences, University of Texas, San Antonio, Tex. 78249.

CAREER: Roosevelt University, Chicago, Ill., assistant professor of history, 1968-69; Sparcom, Inc., Alexandria, Va., senior analyst, 1972-73; University of Texas, San Antonio, assistant professor, 1973-77, professor of history, 1977—. *Military service:* U.S. Navy, 1969-72; became lieutenant junior grade. *Member:* Cheiron: International Society for the History of the Behavioral and Social Sciences, American Historical Association. *Awards, honors:* Woodrow Wilson fellow, 1967-68; National Endowment for the Humanities grant, 1974; American Philosophical Society grant, 1976; German Academy Exchange Service grant, 1978.

WRITINGS: The German Colonial Empire, University of North Carolina Press, 1978. Contributor to history, social science, and archaeology journals.

WORK IN PROGRESS: Research on German imperialist ideology, 1890-1910, and German social science in the late nineteenth century.

*   *   *

SNOW, Donald Clifford 1917-
(Thomas Fall)

PERSONAL: Born in 1917. *Home:* New York, N.Y.

CAREER: Author of books for young adults.

WRITINGS—All under pseudonym Thomas Fall: Prettiest Girl in Town, Harper, 1950; *The Justicer,* Rinehart, 1959; *Eddie No-Name,* illustrations by Ray Prohaska, Pantheon, 1963; *Edge of Manhood,* illustrations by Henry C. Pitz, Dial, 1964; *My Bird Is Romeo,* illustrations by Louise Gordon, Dial, 1964; *Wild Boy,* illustrations by Pitz, Dial, 1965; *The Profit and the Loss,* McKay, 1965; *Canalboat to Freedom,* illustrations by Joseph Cellini, Dial, 1966; *Dandy's Mountain,* illustrations by Juan Carlos Barberis, Dial, 1967; *Goat Boy of Brooklyn,* illustrations by Fermin Rocker, Dial, 1968; *Jim Thorpe,* illustrations by John Gretzer, Crowell, 1970; *The Ordeal of Running Standing,* McCall, 1970; *Emily and the Killer Hawk,* Scholastic Book Services, 1976.

SIDELIGHTS: Donald Snow's Cherokee heritage is reflected in many of his writings. Barbara Wersba, writing in the *New York Times Book Review,* had the following comments about *Edge of Manhood:* "[The author] has let the facts speak for themselves, and by leaving them unstressed, has made a deeper statement than any treatise on the subject. Misguided by images of television 'redskins,' our children know all too little of the American Indians' culture, suffering, or decline."

Reviewing *The Ordeal of Running Standing,* a critic observed in the *New York Times Book Review:* "If there is any truth in Snow's celebrated quip that America went directly from savagery to decadence, it can be found in the crisis of the Indian.... [His] super-Western dramatizes a bitter chapter of this larcenous history and enlivens it with frontier humor...."

One critic has described Snow as having "a rare talent for writing about adolescence." His book, *Dandy's Mountain* is an example. According to *Book World*, "In the hands of a less skillful writer, the preoccupation with the dictionary could have become an exercise in cleverness, but [the author] has made Dandy a believable girl.... [He has depicted her] mother and father as real people with a relationship between themselves as well as with their children.... [He] sees adults as an important part of young people's lives, primarily giving them help when they need it, but otherwise lending quiet strength to young people who must learn to accept responsibility for their own actions...."

BIOGRAPHICAL/CRITICAL SOURCES: New York Times Book Review, November 1, 1964, November 29, 1970; *Book World,* September 24, 1967.*

*   *   *

SNYDER, Carol 1941-

PERSONAL: Born August 11, 1941, in Brooklyn, N.Y.; daughter of Irving (in business) and Shirley (in business; maiden name, Silver) Glasberg; married Michael Snyder (a consulting electronics engineer), September 21, 1961; children: Amy, Linda. *Education:* Brooklyn College of the City University of New York, B.A., 1962; also attended New York University, 1972, and Rutgers University, 1976, 1977. *Residence:* Bridgewater, N.J. *Agent:* Dorothy Markinko, McIntosh & Otis, Inc., 475 Fifth Ave., New York, N.Y. 10017.

CAREER: Elementary school teacher in Brooklyn, N.Y., 1962-63; Bridgewater Raritan Schools, Raritan, N.J., teacher of children with learning disabilities, 1974-78; writer, 1978—. Member of board of directors of Martin Luther King Youth Center, 1969—; member of play therapy program at Somerset Hospital, 1970-72; writing consultant to New Jersey Young Author's Program, 1978—. *Member:* Authors Guild of Authors League of America, Society of Children's Book Writers, National Organization for Women, National Council of Jewish Women (head of community issues section, 1972-73), Somerset Art Association, Patricia Lee Gauch Writers Workshop. *Awards, honors:* Shared with husband in Hannah G. Solomon Award for Service to Children from local chapter of National Council of Jewish Women, 1973.

WRITINGS—All for children: *Ike and Mama and the Once-a-Year Suit,* Coward, 1978; *Ike and Mama and the Block Wedding,* Coward, 1979; *Ike and Mama and the Once-in-a-Lifetime Movie,* Coward, 1980. Contributor to *Scholastic Sprint.*

SIDELIGHTS: Snyder writes: "Along with my writing, I teach children with learning disabilities, which I prefer to call learning possibilities.

"In order to get a feeling for the times of Ike and Mama in 1918, as well as the speech patterns, I tape-recorded interviews with relatives and freinds in New York City, Baltimore, and Fort Lauderdale. I believe that generations have much to learn from each other and that the wisdom of past generations of families is a gift waiting to be unwrapped by present and future children.

"I love writing for children. Every day is interesting. When you spend your time listening and hearing how children speak, you regain some of the wonder and curiosity of the child. I have strong feelings about family, and the need for people from different ethnic backgrounds to get along together. It's the concept of the *maven* (expert): each person contributing his or her own talent or expertise."

AVOCATIONAL INTERESTS: Volunteer community work, painting, reading, camping.

BIOGRAPHICAL/CRITICAL SOURCES: Bernardsville News, October 19, 1978.

*   *   *

SOFFER, Reba N(usbaum) 1934-

PERSONAL: Born December 22, 1934, in Nashville, Tenn.; daughter of Phillip (a scholar) and Ida (Finesilver) Nusbaum; married Bernard H. Soffer (a physicist), January 28, 1956; children: Roger Phillip. *Education:* Brooklyn College (now of the City University of New York), B.A., 1955; Wellesley College, M.A., 1957; Harvard University, Ph.D., 1962. *Home:* 665 Bienveneda Ave., Pacific Palisades, Calif. 90272. *Office:* Department of History, California State University, Northridge, Calif. 91300.

CAREER: California State University, Northridge, instructor, 1961-62, assistant professor, 1962-65, associate professor, 1965-70, professor of history, 1970—. Visiting lecturer at University of California, Los Angeles, 1969. Member of board of directors of Pacific Palisades Property Owners Association, 1978-83. Senior consultant to National Endowment for the Humanities.

MEMBER: American Historical Association, Institute of Historical Research, Conference on British Studies (associate executive secretary, 1978-83), Pacific Coast Conference on British Studies (president, 1976-78), Phi Beta Kappa, Kappa Delta Phi, Phi Alpha Theta. *Awards, honors:* National Endowment for the Humanities fellowship, 1971; American Council of Learned Societies fellowship, 1972; American Philosophical Society grant, 1974; award from Pacific Coast Branch of American Historical Association, 1978, for *Ethics and Society in England.*

WRITINGS: Ethics and Society in England: The Revolution in the Social Sciences, 1870-1914, University of California Press, 1978. Contributor to historical and British studies journals.

WORK IN PROGRESS: What is Intellectual History?, on the traditions of writing and interpreting intellectual history in the twentieth century.

SIDELIGHTS: Reba Soffer writes: "As an intellectual historian, I am interested in the relationship between ideas as they emerge within the compelling world of experience. Modern social science developed before World War I in response to a radically transformed society, increasingly urban and industrial, and to altered perceptions of that society by theorists and reformers. *Ethics and Society* discusses the independent revolution in the methodology and purposes of social science that, in England from the 1870s to 1914, led to a fundamental rethinking of social concepts and practices directed towards a widespread improvement in the quality of life. In the process of studying the origins, assumptions, and purposes of modern social science, I have come to believe that there are no models generally applicable to the history of ideas. The circumstances, the way people understand them, the urgency of their own need to remedy those circumstances, as well as the pressing contingency of objective and remorseless events, all contribute differently in different situations. In my new work on the traditions of intellectual history, I examine with a critical eye the failures of this genre of history. It seems to me that the history of ideas should be as intellectually and emotionally compelling as any humanistic discipline and as immediately practical as any social science.''

*   *   *

SOKOLOV, Raymond 1941-

PERSONAL: Married; wife's name, Margaret. *Office:* c/o Alfred A. Knopf, Inc., 201 East 50th St., New York, N.Y. 10022.

CAREER: Writer.

WRITINGS: (Translator with wife, Margaret Sokolov) Pierre Jalee, *Imperialism in the Seventies*, Third Press, 1971; *Great Recipes From the New York Times*, Quadrangle, 1973; *Native Intelligence* (novel), Harper, 1975; *The Saucier's Apprentice: A Modern Guide to Classic French Sauces for the Home*, Knopf, 1976. Book reviewer for *Newsweek;* restaurant critic for *New York Times.* Contributor to periodicals.

SIDELIGHTS: Sokolov is best known for his food-related writings in the *New York Times.* However, his sole work as a novelist has been hailed by many critics as a highly imaginative piece of fiction. *Native Intelligence* is the story of Alan Casper, a Peace Corp volunteer who is sent to indoctrinate an obscure tribe into Western ways. Although he succeeds at first, Casper eventually becomes a member of the Xixi community. Greil Marcus called *Native Intelligence* ''one of those unusual books that captures a time with nerve and precision, with neither condescension nor nostalgia.'' Sokolov explained his unusual choice for a first novel to *Library Journal.* ''When I left the *New York Times* to write this novel,'' he claimed, ''I wanted to explore, fictionally, the atmosphere of the pre-Vietnam period, when the 'best and the brightest,' giddy with the grasp of power, thought they could bring America and the rest of the world up to their standard.''

Many critics have cited *Native Intelligence* for its perceptive humor. Michael Mewshack called it ''an appealing parody of a certain jejune liberalism and a barbed perception of national naivete.'' Marcus declared that *Native Intelligence* was ''an inventive, convincing book.'' He also wrote that the novel was ''full of ideas and yet saved from strain at every turn by its humor.'' And Charles R. Larson noted ''Sokolov's ability to parody almost everything that falls within his sight: modern-day anthropology, official government documents, linguistic studies of obscure languages, traditional folk tales of exotic people, even gourmet recipes.''

Both of Sokolov's cookbooks have also been praised for their originality. Miriam Ungerer called *Great Recipes From the New York Times*, ''An eclectic anthology of recipes.'' But Ungerer also warned readers that most of the recipes in the book were for ''experienced cooks with well-padded wallets.'' Two critics for the *New York Times* wrote that *The Saucier's Apprentice* ''comes at just the right time.'' The book details three essential sauces and then covers numerous other variations on the original three. The *New York Times* reviewers summed up *The Saucier's Apprentice* as ''a little classic, a book fraught with good sense instead of emotion. Because it fills a gap . . . it can be used by professionals and non-professionals alike for years to come.''

BIOGRAPHICAL/CRITICAL SOURCES: *Saturday Review/World*, November 20, 1973; *Library Journal*, February 1, 1975; *New York Times Book Review*, May 11, 1975,

November 21, 1976; *New Republic*, June 28, 1975; *Rolling Stone*, February 12, 1976; *Contemporary Literary Criticism*, Volume 7, Gale, 1977.*

*   *   *

SOLOMON, Ezra 1920-

PERSONAL: Born March 20, 1920, in Rangoon, Burma; came to United States in 1947, naturalized citizen, 1951; son of Ezra and Emily (Rose) Solomon; married Janet Lorraine Cameron, May 7, 1949; children: Catherine Shan, Janet Ming, Lorna Cameron. *Education:* University of Rangoon, A.B. (honors), 1940; University of Chicago, Ph.D., 1950. *Home:* 775 Santa Ynez, Stanford, Calif. 94305. *Office:* Graduate School of Business, Stanford University, Stanford, Calif. 94305.

CAREER: University of Chicago, Chicago, Ill., instructor, 1948-51, assistant professor, 1951-55, associate professor, 1955-57, professor of finance, 1957-61; Stanford University, Stanford, Calif., Dean Witter Professor of Finance, 1961-71, director of International Center for Management Education, 1961-64; member of the President's Council of Economic Advisers in Washington, D.C., 1971-73; Stanford University, Dean Witter Professor of Finance, 1973—. Consultant to major U.S. business corporations. *Military service:* Royal Naval Volunteer Reserve, Burma Division, 1942-47; became lieutenant. *Member:* American Economic Association, American Finance Association.

WRITINGS: *Money and Banking*, Holt, 5th edition, 1968; *Metropolitan Chicago: An Economic Analysis*, Free Press, 1958; *The Management of Corporate Capital*, Free Press, 1960; *The Theory of Financial Management*, Columbia University Press, 1963; *The Anxious Economy*, San Francisco Book Co., 1976. Editor of *Journal of Business*, 1953-57; member of board of editors of *Journal of Finance*, 1965-66, *Journal of Business Finance*, 1969—, and *Journal of Quantitative and Financial Analysis*, 1969-71.

*   *   *

SONTAG, Alan 1946-

PERSONAL: Born May 2, 1946, in Brooklyn, N.Y.; son of Louis (a cab driver) and Rose (Radin) Sontag. *Education:* Attended Queens College of the City University of New York, 1963-68. *Politics:* None. *Religion:* Jewish. *Home:* 301 East 79th St., New York, N.Y. 10021. *Agent:* Collier Associates, 280 Madison Ave., New York, N.Y. 10016.

CAREER: Professional bridge player and writer, 1977—. *Awards, honors:* Named bridge sportsman of the year by International Bridge Press Association, 1975; won London *Sunday Times* Invitational Bridge Tournament, 1973 and 1975.

WRITINGS: *The Bridge Bum* (autobiography), Morrow, 1977; *Power Decisions* (book on bridge), Morrow, 1979. Coauthor of ''Oswald Jacoby and Alan Sontag,'' a bridge column syndicated by Newspaper Enterprises Assoc., to more than five hundred outlets in the United States, 1978—.

SIDELIGHTS: Sontag writes: ''I have traveled all over the world teaching and playing bridge. Most important to my career have been the five national bridge championships I have won, plus the fact that I am the only player ever to win the London *Sunday Times* Invitational twice.''

BIOGRAPHICAL/CRITICAL SOURCES: *Best Sellers*, October, 1977.

SORSBY, Arnold 1900-

PERSONAL: Born June 10, 1900, in Bialystock, Poland; son of Jacob Sourasky and Elka Slomiansky; married Charmaine V. Guinness, 1943. *Education:* University of Leeds, M.B., 1921, M.D., 1928; also attended University of London, 1924, and University of Edinburgh, 1927. *Home:* 19 Parham Court, Grand Ave., Worthing, Sussex BN11 5AH, England.

CAREER: Royal Eye Hospital, London, England, surgeon, 1931-66, dean of Medical School, 1934-38. Hunterian Professor at Royal College of Surgeons, England, 1933, 1941, research professor of opthalmology, 1943-66, professor emeritus, 1966—; Montgomery Lecturer at Royal College of Surgeons, Dublin, Ireland, 1941. Ophthalmic surgeon at London Jewish Hospital, 1927-43, Hampstead General Hospital, 1928-43, and West End Hospital for Nervous Diseases, 1933-38; director of medical ophthalmology unit at Lambeth Hospital, 1963-66. Vice-president of International League Against Trachoma, 1951-68; member of World Health Organization's expert advisory panel on trachoma, 1954-69. Honorary director of Medical Research Council's Wernher Group for Research in Ophthalmological Genetics Research, 1953-66; honorary adviser to Royal National Institute for the Blind, 1963-66; consultant to Ministry of Health, 1966-71. *Member:* Royal College of Surgeons (England; fellow). *Awards, honors:* Middlemore Prize from British Medical Association, 1936; commander of Order of the British Empire, 1966; Keith Medal from Royal College of Surgeons, 1966; Grimshaw Award from National Federation of the Blind, 1967.

WRITINGS: (Editor) *Tenements of Clay* (essays), Julian Friedmann, 1974, Scribner, 1976; (editor) *All Men Are Created Equal* (poems), Quartet Books, 1979.

Medical books: *A Short History of Ophthalmology*, J. Bale, 1933; (editor) *Modern Trends in Ophthalmology*, Hoeber, Volume I, 1940, Volume II, 1949, Volume III, 1955, Volume IV, 1967, Volume V, 1973; *Medicine and Mankind*, Faber, 1941, 2nd edition, 1948; *Genetics in Ophthalmology*, Mosby, 1951, 2nd edition published as *Ophthalmic Genetics*, Appleton, 1970; (editor) *Systemic Ophthalmology* (also see below), Mosby, 1951, 2nd edition, 1958; (editor) *Clinical Genetics*, Mosby, 1953, 2nd edition, Butterworth & Co., 1973; *Blindness in England, 1951-1954*, H.M.S.O., 1956; (with B. Benjamin, M. Sheridan, and Janet Stone) *Emmetropia and Its Aberrations: A Study in the Correlation of the Optical Components of the Eye*, H.M.S.O., 1957; (with Joseph Ungar) *Antibiotics and Sulphonamides in Ophthalmology*, Oxford University Press, 1960; (with Stone and G. A. Leary) *Refraction and Its Components During the Growth of the Eye From the Age of Three*, H.M.S.O., 1961; (editor) *Modern Ophthalmology*, Butterworth & Co., Volume I: *Basic Aspects*, 1963, Volume II: *Systemic Aspects* (a revision of *Systemic Ophthalmology;* also see above), 1963, Volumes III-IV: *Topical Aspects*, 1963, 2nd edition, Lippincott, 1972; *The Incidence and Causes of Blindness in England and Wales, 1948-1962*, H.M.S.O., 1966; *The Incidence and Causes of Blindness in England and Wales, 1963-1968*, H.M.S.O., 1972; *Diseases of the Fundus Oculi*, Butterworth & Co., 1975.

Editor of "Pocket Monographs on Practical Medicine," published by J. Bale, 1933-37. Contributor to ophthalmology, genetics, and medical history journals. Editor of *Journal of Medical Genetics*, 1964-69.

WORK IN PROGRESS: The Biology of Moral Deficiency.

SOUTHWORTH, Herbert Rutledge 1908-

PERSONAL: Born February 6, 1908, in Canton, Okla.; son of Walton Rutledge (a banker) and Lulah (Shoemaker) Southworth; married Suzanne Maury (a lawyer), October 1, 1948. *Education:* Attended University of Arizona, summer, 1930; Texas Tech University, B.A., M.A.; further graduate study at Columbia University, 1941; Sorbonne, University of Paris, D.E.H., 1975. *Religion:* None. *Home:* Chateau de Roche, Concremiers, 36300 Le Blanc, Indre, France.

CAREER: Library of Congress, Washington, D.C., staff member, 1934-37; Spanish Information Bureau, New York, N.Y., editor, 1938-39; writer and analyst for Office of War Information, 1941-46; Sociedad africana de radiodifusion, Tangier, Morocco, general manager, 1946-61; free-lance writer, 1961—. Professor at University of Vincennes, 1969; Regents Professor at University of California, San Diego, 1974. *Member:* Society for Spanish and Portuguese Historical Studies.

WRITINGS: El mito de la cruzada de Franco, Editions Ruedo Ibarico, 1963; *Antifalango*, Editions Ruedo Ibarico, 1967; *Guernica! Guernica!*, University of California Press, 1977.

WORK IN PROGRESS: An Analytical History of Spanish Fascism; Bibliography of the Spanish Civil War and the Franco Era.

*　　*　　*

SPICER, Jack 1925-1965

PERSONAL: Born in 1925, in Hollywood, Calif.; died in 1965.

CAREER: Poet and linguist.

WRITINGS: After Lorca (translations of poems by Federico Garcia Lorca with additional material; limited edition), White Rabbit Press (San Francisco), 1957, reprinted, Coach House Press (Toronto), 1974; *Billy the Kid* (poem), Enkidu Surrogate (Stinson Beach, Calif.), 1959; *Lament for the Makers* (poems), White Rabbit Press, 1962; *The Heads of the Town up to the Aether*, lithographs by Fran Herndon, Auerhahn Society (San Francisco), 1962; *The Holy Grail*, White Rabbit Press, 1964; (with Lawrence Ferlinghetti) *The Spicer/Ferlinghetti Correspondence. Dear Jack*, White Rabbit Press, c. 1964.

Language (poems), White Rabbit Press, 1965; *Book of Magazine Verse*, edited by Stan Persky, White Rabbit Press, 1966; *The Day Five Thousand Fish Died in the Charles River* (limited edition), Kriya Press (Pleasant Valley, N.Y.), 1967; *The Red Wheelbarrow* (limited edition), Hove, Sussex, Peter Riley, c. 1968, reprinted, Arif (Berkeley, Calif.), 1971; *A Book of Music*, White Rabbit Press, 1969; *Some Things From Jack* (poems; limited edition), Plain Wrapper Press (Verona, Italy), 1972; (with Robert Duncan) *An Ode & Arcadia*, Small Press Distribution, 1974; *Admonitions* (poems), Adventures in Poetry (New York), c.1974; *15 False Propositions About God*, ManRoot Books (San Francisco), 1974; *The Collected Books of Jack Spicer*, edited and with a commentary by Robin Blaser, Black Sparrow Press, 1975.

Also author of *Homage to Creeley* (poems), c. 1950's, and *The Ballad of the Dead Woodcutter*. Contributor to *The San Francisco Capitalist Bloodsucker-N: An Amalgam of the San Francisco Capitalist Bloodsucker, a Journal of Marxist Opinion and N—The Magazine of the Future.*

SIDELIGHTS: Spicer was a Beat poet, an associate of Robert Duncan and Allen Ginsberg, who spent his life in California. His poetry has influenced the younger generation of poets with its "seeming openness to inner and outer experiences and to the wobble between," critic Richard Elman declared.

Samuel Charters has noticed that the methods of surrealism are central to Spicer's poetry. He wrote: "Surrealism, as it breaks up the sense of movement within the poem, could be considered even anti-poetic, but in his questioning of poetry Spicer still moves as a poet. He uses the method—the sound—of surrealism—the limitless tying together of unlikes that is implicit in surrealist technique—but in the larger outlines of the poem he is still thinking through image to idea. The materials of the poem seem to come from the subconscious, but the structuring of the materials is done by a conscious poetic intelligence."

In an assessment of Spicer's work, Ross Feld commented: "Even in a self-conscious century . . . no contemporary poet seems more art-occupied than Jack Spicer. Or more elusive. What he giveth in self-review he taketh away in a sort of holy thundering shyness that's more Jerome than Frances. What's more, self-consciousness leads also to sorrows, in particular loneliness—who else but me is looking?—and here also Spicer is no more fully satisfying: he's the poet's poet par excellence, no reference points except the very poem, yet he refuses to console us with homilies and buck-up, trade-union sermons. Wonderfully likable in his muscular, no-bullshit manner, and yet in a second he's gone, just as he originally intended. Is it, then, all worth it? Yes. Spicer is something new and valuable, extremely so."

Elman concluded: "Jack Spicer's poems are always poised just on the face side of language, dipping all the way over toward that sudden flip, as if an effort were being made through feeling strongly in simple words to sneak up on the event of a man ruminating about something, or celebrating something, without rhetorical formulae, in his own beautiful inept awkwardness. It's that poised ineptitude and awkwardness of the anti-academic teacher, the scholar of linguistics who can't say what he knows in formal language, and has chosen to be very naive and look and hear and do. Spicer was not a very happy poet. He was obsessed with possibilities he could only occasionally realize, and too aware of contemporary life to settle for anything less in his work than what he probably could not achieve. He must have been a great spirit."

BIOGRAPHICAL/CRITICAL SOURCES: Some Poems/ Poets: Studies in American Underground Poetry Since 1945, Oyez, 1971; James Herndon, *Everything as Expected: A Remembrance of Jack Spicer,* Small Press Distribution, 1973; *New York Times Book Review,* November 23, 1975; *Parnassus: Poetry in Review,* spring/summer, 1976; *Contemporary Literary Criticism,* Volume 8, Gale, 1978.*

* * *

SPICER, James 1928(?)-1979

OBITUARY NOTICE: Born c. 1928; died of cancer, January 27, 1979, in New York, N.Y. Organizer of plays and jazz presentations and editor. Spicer arranged performances by saxophonist Bobo Shaw, pianist Cecil Taylor, and The Paul Taylor Dance Company. He edited Julien Beck's *The Life of the Theater* and Judith Malina's *The Enormous Despair.* Obituaries and other sources: *New York Times,* January 30, 1979.

SPINGARN, Natalie Davis 1922-

PERSONAL: Born in New York, N.Y.; married Jerome H. Spingarn; children: Jeremy Davis, Jonathan Edward. *Education:* Attended Vassar College. *Home:* 1409 29th St. N.W., Washington, D.C. 20007. *Office:* 1211 Connecticut Ave. N.W., Suite 504, Washington, D.C. 20007.

CAREER: Free-lance writer on health and welfare subjects, 1945-61; U.S. Department of Health, Education & Welfare, Washington, D.C., staff assistant to Secretary of Health, Education & Welfare, 1961-62; executive assistant to U.S. Senator Abraham Ribicoff in Washington, D.C., 1962-67; U.S. Department of Health, Education & Welfare, assistant director of Center for Community Planning, 1967-69; free-lance writer and consultant, 1969—. Executive director of National Commission on Confidentiality of Health Records, 1976—. Reporter for television.

WRITINGS: (Contributor) Mary A. Stites, editor, *History of the American Association of Medical Social Workers,* American Association of Medical Social Workers, 1955; *The Volunteer and the Psychiatric Patient,* American Psychiatric Association, 1959; *To Save Your Life,* Little, Brown, 1963; (contributor) Joseph Newman, editor, *People Helping People,* U.S. News & World Report, 1971; (contributor) Morton Levitt and Ben Rubenstein, editors, *On the Urban Scene,* Wayne State University Press, 1972; *Heartbeat: The Politics of Health Research,* Luce, 1976.

Contributor to professional and popular magazines, including *New Republic, Parents' Magazine,* and *Harper's,* and newspapers. Assistant editor of *Chronicle of Higher Education,* 1974.

* * *

SPITZ, David 1916-1979

OBITUARY NOTICE—See index for *CA* sketch: Born December 13, 1916, in New York, N.Y.; died March 23, 1979, in Locust Valley, N.Y. Educator and author. Spitz taught political science at Ohio State University for more than twenty years before coming to Hunter College and the Graduate Center of the City University of New York in 1970. A member of the American Civil Liberties Union, Spitz wrote and edited a number of books, including *Democracy and the Challenge of Power* and *The Liberal Idea of Freedom.* Obituaries and other sources: *American Men and Women of Science: The Social and Behavioral Sciences,* 12th edition, Bowker, 1973; *New York Times,* March 25, 1979; *AB Bookman's Weekly,* April 16, 1979.

* * *

SPLAVER, Sarah

PERSONAL: Born in New York, N.Y.; daughter of Morris and Rose (Farber) Splaver. *Education:* New York University, Ph.D., 1953. *Religion:* Jewish. *Home and office:* 3310 Rochambeau Ave., Bronx, N.Y. 10467.

CAREER: U.S. War Department, Washington, D.C., personnel supervisor, 1943-46; high school guidance director in New York City, 1946-50; private practice as counseling psychologist and guidance consultant in New York City, 1950—. Editor and publisher of Occu-Press, 1953-70. Lecturer to professional and lay audiences, including children; consultant to International Business Machines Corp., New York Life Insurance Co., and federal government agencies.

MEMBER: International Council of Psychologists (fellow), American Personnel and Guidance Association (life member), American Rehabilitation Counseling Association,

American School Counselor Association, American Association for the Advancement of Science, American Psychological Association, National Vocational Guidance Association, Authors Guild of Authors League of America, Academy of Religion and Mental Health, New York Personnel and Guidance Association, Metropolitan Association for Applied Psychology, B'nai B'rith (vice-president of educators' chapter). *Awards, honors:* Recipient of certificate from mayor of New York City.

WRITINGS: Opportunities in Vocational Guidance, Vocational Guidance Manuals, 1949, revised edition published as *Opportunities in Guidance,* 1961; *Occupational Books, an Annotated Bibliography: An Analysis of Recommended Occupational Books Published From 1946 to 1951,* Biblio Press, 1952; *High School Students and Occupational Books,* Occu-press, 1953.

Careers in Personnel Administration, Walck, 1962; *Your Career if You're Not Going to College* (juvenile), Messner, 1963, revised edition, 1971; *Your College Education: How to Pay for It* (juvenile), Messner, 1964, revised edition, 1968; *Your Personality and You,* Messner, 1965; *Your Handicap: Don't Let It Handicap You,* Messner, 1967, revised edition, 1974; *The High School Student's Guide to Summer Jobs, 1967* (juvenile), Edwin House Publishers, 1967; *Some Day I'll Be a Doctor* (juvenile), Hawthorn, 1967; *Some Day I'll Be a Librarian* (juvenile), Hawthorn, 1967; *Some Day I'll Be an Aerospace Engineer* (juvenile), Hawthorn, 1967; *You and Today's Troubled World: A Psychologist Talks to Urban Youth* (juvenile), Messner, 1970; *Paraprofessions: Careers of the Future and the Present* (juvenile), Messner, 1972; *Nontraditional Careers for Women* (juvenile), Messner, 1973; *Nontraditional College Routes to Careers,* Messner, 1975; *Career Choices in Psychology* (juvenile), Messner, 1976; *Your Personality and Your Career* (juvenile), Messner, 1977; *Your Mind and Breast Diseases* (adult), Veritas Press, 1978.

Author of career guidance pamphlets for young people. Organizer of "Socio-Guidrama Series" (playlets for teenagers). Contributor to professional journals and popular magazines. Editor-in-chief of *Guidance Exchange,* 1960—; book review editor of *School Counsel.*

AVOCATIONAL INTERESTS: Photography, golf.

*   *   *

SPOONER, Frank (Clyffurde) 1924-

PERSONAL: Born March 5, 1924, in Cleveland, Australia; son of Harry Gordon Morrison and Ethel Beatrice (Walden) Spooner. *Education:* Christ's College, Cambridge, B.A., 1947, M.A., 1949, Ph.D., 1953. *Home:* 145 Gilesgate, Durham DH1 1QQ, England. *Office:* Department of Economic History, University of Durham, 23 Old Elvet, Durham DH1 3HY, England.

CAREER: Centre National de la Recherche Scientifique, Paris, France, charge de recherches, 1949-50; Cambridge University, Cambridge, England, Allen scholar, 1951, and fellow of Christ's College, 1951-57; Oxford University, Oxford, England, lecturer in history, 1958-59; Harvard University, Cambridge, Mass., visiting lecturer in economics, 1961-62; Yale University, New Haven, Conn., Irving Fisher Professor of Economics, 1962-63; University of Durham, Durham, England, lecturer, 1963-64, reader, 1964-66, professor of economic history, 1966—. Reader at Ecole Pratique des Hautes Etudes, 1957-61; resident tutuor of Lumley Castle, 1965-70; director of Institute of European Studies, 1969-76. *Military service:* Royal Naval Volunteer Reserve, 1942-46; became sub-lieutenant.

MEMBER: Royal Economic Society (life member), Economic History Society, Economic History Association (life member), Royal Historical Society (fellow), Anglo-Austrian Society, Hakluyt Society, American Economic Association (life member), English-Speaking Union, Association Marc Bloch, Societe Francaise de Numismatique (corresponding member), Vereniging het Nederlandsch Economisch-Historisch Archief, United Oxford and Cambridge University Club. *Awards, honors:* Commonwealth Fund fellowship for the United States, 1955-57; Laureats de l'Academie from Academie des Sciences Morales et Politiques, 1957; Leverhulme Fund fellowship, 1976-78; West Europe Award from British Academy, 1978-79.

WRITINGS: L'economie mondiale et les frappes monetaires en France, 1493-1680, Sevpen (Paris), 1956, translation of revised edition published as *The International Economy and Monetary Movements in France, 1493-1725,* Harvard University Press, 1972. Contributor to professional journals.

WORK IN PROGRESS: Research in libraries and archives in France, the Netherlands, Spain, Italy, and West Germany.

SIDELIGHTS: Spooner commented: "My work has concentrated on the continuities of historical structures in a changing world. The long-known evolution of monetary systems and attitudes to wealth form a part of these developments. As communities converge in industrial activity and generations outlive the technologies in which they grew up, it would appear that instability and upheaval are the prevailing themes. However, I prefer to think that when studied in depth, historical change serves to emphasize the unity of the centuries and the persistent optimism of the human spirit."

*   *   *

SPRAGENS, Thomas A(rthur), Jr. 1942-

PERSONAL: Born March 27, 1942, in Frankfort, Ky.; son of Thomas A. (a college president) and Catharine (Smallwood) Spragens; married Ann Stephanie Wood (a lawyer), September 5, 1970; children: Jacqueline Ann. *Education:* Wesleyan University, Middletown, Conn., A.B. (high honors), 1963; Duke University, Ph.D., 1968. *Office:* Department of Political Science, Duke University, Durham, N.C. 27706.

CAREER: Duke University, Durham, N.C., associate professor of political science, 1968—, acting head of department, 1978-79, fellow of Few Federation, 1974-77. *Member:* American Political Science Association, Southern Political Science Association, Phi Beta Kappa. *Awards, honors:* National Endowment for the Humanities younger humanist fellow, 1974; Rockefeller Foundation fellow, 1977-78.

WRITINGS: The Dilemma of Contemporary Political Theory: Toward a Post-Behavioral Science of Politics, Dunellen, 1973; *The Politics of Motion: The World of Thomas Hobbes,* University Press of Kentucky, 1973; *Understanding Political Theory,* St. Martin's, 1976. Contributor of articles and reviews to political science and social science journals. Member of board of editors of *Journal of Politics,* 1977—.

WORK IN PROGRESS: The Irony of Liberal Reason.

*   *   *

STABILE, Toni

PERSONAL: Born in New York, N.Y.; daughter of Nicola and Rosina (Tramontano) Stabile. *Education:* University of Kentucky, A.B.; graduate study at Columbia University.

Agent: Shirley Fisher, McIntosh and Otis, 475 Fifth Ave., New York, N.Y. 10017. *Office:* 411 East 53rd St., New York, N.Y. 10022.

CAREER: Writer. Investigative reporter and consultant for *Consumer Advocate.* Lecturer at professional gatherings; expert witness for U.S. Senate hearings; consultant to television stations in the United States, Canada, and Italy. *Member:* American Society of Journalists and Authors, Women in Communications, Authors Guild, Authors League of America, National Academy of Television Arts and Sciences, National Press Club, Theta Sigma Phi. *Awards, honors:* Award from WPIX-TV, 1974, for service to consumers.

WRITINGS: Cosmetics: Trick or Treat?, Hawthorn, 1966, 3rd edition, Arco, 1969; *Cosmetics: The Great American Skin Game,* Ballantine, 1973, revised edition, Charter Books, 1979. Contributor to cosmetic journals, popular magazines, including *Reader's Digest, Redbook, Nation, Today's Health,* and *Modern Miss,* and newspapers.

SIDELIGHTS: Toni Stabile comments: "My first book was dedicated to the seven years that went into its research and writing, and to the many people who helped along the way. The second book was dedicated to the hope that an alerted Congress will act swiftly to close the legislative loopholes which now permit the marketplace to be used as a laboratory where the entire population unwittingly pays to take trick-or-treat risks. Both books have become source books for ongoing cosmetic reforms and legislation, and have pioneered in the resultant ingredient labeling on cosmetic products."

*   *   *

STAFFORD, Jean   1915-1979

OBITUARY NOTICE—See index for *CA* sketch: Born July 1, 1915, in Covina, Calif.; died March 26, 1979, in White Plains, N.Y. Novelist and author of short stories. Long admired for her literary craftmanship and her deft characterization, Stafford had written three novels and several short story collections when she received the 1970 Pulitzer Prize in fiction for her *Collected Stories.* Her works commonly featured women and children as protagonists who battled alienation and isolation in their imprisoned worlds. Among her best-known writings are two of her novels, *Boston Adventure* and *The Mountain Lion,* and her 1953 short story collection, *Children Are Bored on Sunday.* She also wrote juvenile books and a book based on interviews with the mother of Lee Harvey Oswald, *A Mother in History.* Stafford was married three times to writers: poet Robert Lowell, Oliver Jensen, and *New Yorker* critic A. J. Liebling. Obituaries and other sources: *Current Biography,* Wilson, 1951, June, 1979; *Encyclopedia of World Literature in the Twentieth Century,* updated edition, Ungar, 1967; *The Reader's Adviser: A Layman's Guide to Literature,* Volume I: *The Best in American Fiction, Poetry, Essays, Literary Biography, and Reference,* 12th edition, Bowker, 1974; *Contemporary Novelists,* 2nd edition, St. Martin's, 1976; *Who's Who in Twentieth Century Literature,* Holt, 1976; *Who's Who in America,* 40th edition, Marquis, 1978; *Chicago Tribune,* March 29, 1979; *Washington Post,* March 29, 1979; *Time,* April 9, 1979; *Newsweek,* April 9, 1979; *Publishers Weekly,* April 9, 1979; *AB Bookman's Weekly,* April 16, 1979.

*   *   *

STAGG, Albert   1903-

PERSONAL: Born July 5, 1903, in Santiago de Guayaquil, Ecuador; son of Leonard Charles (a planter) and Francisca

(Caamano) Stagg; married Cynthia Ross-Lowe (a painter), April 15, 1933; children: Anne Belle, Michael Leonard. *Education:* Attended private secondary school in Concord, Mass. *Home:* 106 West Sherwood Dr., Payson, Ariz. 85541.

CAREER: Cocoa planter in Ecuador, 1920-24; traveled in Europe and the United States, 1924-28; oil field manager in Venezuela, 1928-31; rancher in Chile and Ecuador, 1933-44; livestock exporter in Toronto and Oakville, Ontario, 1945-58; lived for four years in Italy and six years in France before settling in Arizona in 1969. Also lived in New York City and Tangier, Morocco.

WRITINGS: The First Bishop of Sonora, Antonio de los Reyes, O.F.M., University of Arizona Press, 1976; *The Almadas and Alamos, 1783-1867,* University of Arizona Press, 1978.

SIDELIGHTS: Stagg writes: "My ancestors were actively engaged in the history of Latin America: two *conquistadores,* one viceroy of Peru, the founder and first president of Ecuador, two later presidents of Ecuador, churchmen, explorers, and statesmen. After I became an Arizona resident in 1969 and discovered that my mother's maternal ancestors, the Almadas, had been prominent in Sonora, research came naturally." Stagg speaks Spanish, French, and Italian.

*   *   *

STAGG, Evelyn   1914-

PERSONAL: Born July 9, 1914, in Ruston, La.; daughter of William Thomas (an insurance manager) and Myrtie (Matthews) Owen; married Frank Stagg (a professor), August 19, 1935; children: Ted, Robert, Virginia Stagg Shane. *Education:* Attended Judson College, 1930-32; Louisiana College, A.B., 1934; WMU School, M.R.E., 1938. *Religion:* Baptist. *Residence:* Louisville, Ky.

CAREER: Writer. Associated with Southern Baptist Theological Seminary, Louisville, Ky.

WRITINGS: (With husband, Frank Stagg) *Woman in the World of Jesus,* Westminster, 1978.

*   *   *

STAHL, Norman   1931-

PERSONAL: Born October 11, 1931, in Brooklyn, N.Y.; son of Walter John (a banker) and Josephine (Chiara) Stahl; married Flaye Arline Hallenbeck, January 20, 1957; children: Matthew Walter, Walter John, Glenn Christopher. *Education:* Brooklyn College of the City University of New York, B.A., 1961. *Politics:* Republican. *Religion:* Roman Catholic. *Home:* 80 Seventh St., Bayshore, N.Y. 11706. *Agent:* Julian Bach Literary Agency, Inc., 3 East 48th St., New York, N.Y. 10017. *Office:* Ted Bates & Co., Inc., New York, N.Y. 10036.

CAREER: Batten, Barton, Durstine & Osborn, Inc. (advertising agency), New York City, copy group head, 1956-65; Ted Bates & Co. (advertising agency), New York City, creative director and senior vice-president, 1965—.

WRITINGS: The Assault on Mavis A. (novel), Random House, 1978.

WORK IN PROGRESS: Another novel.

AVOCATIONAL INTERESTS: Flying (private license).

BIOGRAPHICAL/CRITICAL SOURCES: Washington Post, October 20, 1978.

STALLWORTH, Anne Nall 1935-

PERSONAL: Born September 30, 1935, in Birmingham, Ala.; daughter of John Martin (a farmer and bookkeeper) and Lida (a writer; maiden name, Crump) Nall; married Clarke Stallworth (a newspaper editor), September 3, 1955; children: Carole Anne, Clarke III. *Education:* Attended Birmingham-Southern College, 1948-49. *Home:* 148 Glenhill Dr., Birmingham, Ala. 35213. *Agent:* Curtis Brown Ltd., 575 Madison Ave., New York, N.Y. 10022.

CAREER: Birmingham News, Birmingham, Ala., in advertising department, 1951-58; writer. In charge of publicity and promotion for Birmingham Music Club. *Awards, honors:* First prize for fiction from Alabama Library Association, 1973, for *This Time Next Year.*

WRITINGS: This Time Next Year (novel), Vanguard, 1971; *Where the Bright Lights Shine* (novel), Vanguard, 1977. Contributor of short story to *McCall's.*

WORK IN PROGRESS: A novel about the South in the 1960's.

SIDELIGHTS: Anne Stallworth writes: "I am motivated to write because of the great pleasure it gives me and because it rounds out my life. I cannot imagine not writing, since I have been writing since high school. Being published is wonderful, but I would write if I were never published again. I think fiction is the highest form in writing; this is where the great truths are found (not in nonfiction as so many people think). I do not travel much because it takes time from writing. Eveything I need to write about is here in the South: the people, the events, the place. I could write for the next hundred years and never run out of material."

*   *   *

STANFORD, William Bedell 1910-

PERSONAL: Born January 16, 1910, in Belfast, Northern Ireland; son of Bedell (a clergyman) and Susan (Jackson) Stanford; married Dorothy Isobel Wright, March 21, 1935; children: Danae Stanford O'Regan, Philip, Melissa Stanford Webb, William. *Education:* Trinity College, Dublin, received B.A., M.A., and Litt.D. *Religion:* Church of Ireland. *Home:* 2 Mount Salus, Dalkey, County Dublin, Ireland. *Office:* 5033 Arts Building, Trinity College, University of Dublin, Dublin 2, Ireland.

CAREER: University of Dublin, Dublin, Ireland, fellow of Trinity College, 1934-62, senior fellow, 1962—, tutor, 1938-54, Regius Professor of Greek, 1940—, deputy public orator, 1958-60, public orator, 1970-71, pro-chancellor. Sather Professor of Classical Literature at University of California, Berkeley, 1966; visiting professor at McGill University, 1968, Wayne State University, 1971, Princeton University, and University of Texas. Head of Irish National Committee for Greek and Latin Studies, 1968-72; head of council of Dublin Institute for Advanced Studies. Representative from University of Dublin to Irish Senate, 1948-69; Irish representative to Council of Europe, 1951, European Parliamentary Conference, 1956, and Inter-Parliamentary Conference, 1959. Past member of Irish Radio Advisory Council; member of board of governors of Erasmus Smith's School. *Member:* Royal Irish Academy (vice-president, 1969), Hellenic Society (member of council, 1965-68), Classical Association (Birmingham president, 1968), Trinity College, Dublin, Association, Royal Irish Yacht Club.

WRITINGS: Greek Metaphor, Basil Blackwell, 1936; *Ambiguity in Greek Literature,* Basil Blackwell, 1939; *Aeschylus in His Style,* Basil Blackwell, 1942; (editor) *Homer's Odys-*

sey, Macmillan, Volume I, 1947, 2nd edition, 1961, Volume II, 1948, 2nd edition, 1962; *The Ulysses Theme,* Basil Blackwell, 1954, 2nd edition, 1963; (editor) *The Frogs of Aristophanes,* Macmillan, 1958, 2nd edition, 1963; (editor) *Sophocles' Ajax,* Macmillan, 1963; *The Sound of Greek,* University of California Press, 1967; (with R. B. McDowell) *Mahaffy,* Routledge & Kegan Paul, 1971; (with J. V. Luce) *The Quest for Ulysses,* Phaidon, 1974; (with R. Fagles) *The Oresteia of Aeschylus,* Viking, 1975; *Ireland and the Classical Tradition,* Figgis, 1977. Also editor of *Livy XXIV,* 1942. Contributor to literature, theology, and history journals, and literary magazines. Editor of *Hermathena,* 1942-62.

*   *   *

STANTON, Will 1918-

PERSONAL: Born October 16, 1918, in Cleveland, Ohio; son of Frank W. (a lawyer) and Marie (Seelbach) Stanton; married June Porter, August 25, 1946 (died May 1, 1956); married Elizabeth Kain, June 1, 1958; children: Edward, Donald, Linda Stanton Foflygen, Timothy, Tobias, Bartholomew, Benjamin. *Education:* Princeton University, A.B., 1941. *Home and office:* 1001 Ocean Ave., New London, Conn. 06320. *Agent:* Curtis Brown Ltd., 575 Madison Ave., New York, N.Y. 10022.

CAREER: Writer. Also worked as farmer, construction worker, and house painter. *Military service:* U.S. Army Air Forces, 1942-45; became flight officer; received Air Medal.

WRITINGS: Once Upon a Time Is Enough, Lippincott, 1969; *The Golden Evenings of Summer,* McCall's, 1971; *The Old Familiar Booby Traps of Home,* Doubleday, 1977. Contributor of stories, poems, and articles to magazines in the United States and abroad, including *Reader's Digest, Life, Look, Saturday Review,* and *Redbook.*

*   *   *

STARR, S(tephen) Frederick 1940-

PERSONAL: Born March 24, 1940, in New York, N.Y.; married Nancy Lee Hines, September 13, 1963; children: Anna Edmondson, Elizabeth Hines. *Education:* Yale University, B.A., 1962; King's College, Cambridge, M.A., 1964; Princeton University, Ph.D., 1968. *Office:* Kennan Institute for Advanced Russian Studies, Woodrow Wilson International Center for Scholars, Smithsonian Institution Building, Washington, D.C. 20560.

CAREER: Princeton University, Princeton, N.J., instructor, 1968-69, assistant professor, 1969-74, associate professor of history, 1974-76; Kennan Institute for Advanced Russian Studies, Washington, D.C., secretary of institute and assistant director of Wilson International Center, 1975—. Vice-chairman, National Council for Soviet and East European Research, 1978—; special adviser to President's Commission on Foreign Languages and International Studies, 1978-79. Member of selection board of International Research and Exchange Board, 1973-75; member of Yale University Council, 1977—; Harvard University, member of visiting committee, Russian Research Center, 1978—, member of visiting committee, department of Slavic Languages and Literature, 1978—; member of international advisory board, United Auto Workers, 1979—.

MEMBER: American Historical Association, American Association for the Advancement of Slavic Studies. *Awards, honors:* Ehrman studentship for King's College, Cambridge, 1962-64; Fulbright-Hays grant, 1966-67; fellow of International Research and Exchange Board, 1971-72; National

Book Award nomination, 1973, for *Studies on the Interior of Russia;* National Endowment for the Humanities younger humanist fellow, 1973; Mellon fellow of Aspen Institute for Humanistic Studies, 1974-75.

WRITINGS: The Archaeology of Hamilton County, Ohio, Cincinnati Museum of Natural History, 1960, 2nd edition, 1967; (editor) *Studies on the Interior of Russia* (biography of August von Haxthausen), translated from German by Eleanore L. Schmidt, University of Chicago Press, 1972; *Decentralization and Self-Government in Russia, 1830-1870,* Princeton University Press, 1972; (with Cyril E. Black and others) *Modernization of Japan and Russia: A Comparative Study,* Free Press, 1975; *Konstantin Melnikov: Solo Architect in a Mass Society,* Princeton University Press, 1978.

Contributor: *Art and Architecture: U.S.S.R., 1917-1932,* Wittenborn, 1971; George Gibian, editor, *The Russian Avant-Garde, 1908-1922,* [Ithaca, N.Y.], 1974; Michael Hamm, editor, *The City in Russian History,* University Press of Kentucky, 1976; Sheila Fitzpatrick, editor, *The Cultural Revolution in Russia, 1928-1931,* Indiana University Press, 1977; Jeremy Azrael, editor, *The Non-Russian Peoples of the U.S.S.R.,* [New York], 1978. Contributor of more than forty articles and reviews to scholarly journals, popular magazines, including *Smithsonian,* and newspapers.

WORK IN PROGRESS: An edition of diplomatic memoirs of Hans von Herwarth.

SIDELIGHTS: Starr conducted archaeological research in Turkey in 1959 and 1961. He is also an active clarinetist.

*   *   *

STEENE, Birgitta 1928-

PERSONAL: Born October 7, 1928, in Uddevalla, Sweden; daughter of Ragnar (in business) and Katrine (Kassow-Jensen) Steene; children: Mikael. *Education:* University of Uppsala, B.A., 1951; further graduate study at Sorbonne, University of Paris, 1949-50, and University of Kansas, 1951-52; University of Washington, Seattle, M.A., 1955, Ph.D., 1960. *Office:* Scandinavian Department, University of Washington, Seattle, Wash. 98195.

CAREER: University of Louisiana, New Orleans, instructor in English, 1959-60; University of Calgary, Calgary, Alberta, assistant professor, 1960-62; University of Pennsylvania, Philadelphia, assistant professor of Scandinavian and general literature, 1962-65; Temple University, Philadelphia, Pa., associate professor of English, 1967-73; University of Washington, Seattle, professor, 1973—, head of Scandinavian department, 1973-78, director of cinema studies program, 1974-76, 1978—. *Member:* International Association of Scandinavian Studies (member of council), Modern Language Association of America, Society for the Advancement of Scandinavian Studies, Society for Cinema Studies (member of council). *Awards, honors:* National Endowment for the Humanities grant, 1976-77.

WRITINGS: Ingmar Bergman, Twayne, 1968, revised edition, 1980; *The Greatest Fire: A Study of August Strindberg,* Southern Illinois University Press, 1972; (editor) *Focus on the Seventh Seal,* Prentice-Hall, 1972. Contributor to literature and Scandinavian studies journals.

WORK IN PROGRESS: Reference Guide to Ingmar Bergman, for G. K. Hall; a biography of Ingmar Bergman.

SIDELIGHTS: Birgitta Steene comments: "The anti-feminist attitude in American academic circles in the 1950's, when I came over from Europe as a graduate student, was appalling. As someone involved in academic life throughout her career, it has been rewarding for me to see a gradual change come about for (and in) American women *vis-a-vis* professional careers. Traditional male attitudes are still depressingly strong and unconscious, however, in the higher echelons of university administrations.

"As a young woman in the late 1940's and early 1950's I used to hitch-hike throughout Europe and Africa. It was very safe. I stopped doing it on this continent because in the United States everyone treated me as a prostitute of the road."

AVOCATIONAL INTERESTS: Skiing, her summer home in Sweden, the island of Crete.

*   *   *

STEINBACH, Alexander Alan 1894-1978

PERSONAL: Born February 2, 1894, in Baltimore, Md.; died November 12, 1978, in Hollywood, Fla.; son of Abraham and Sarah (Wolfe) Steinbach; married Sadye Silberstein, June 8, 1919; children: Ruthanne Steinbach Greenspan. *Education:* Johns Hopkins University, B.A., 1917; Atlantic University, M.A., 1930; Hebrew Union College, Rabbi, 1930. *Residence:* Hollywood, Fla.

CAREER: Rabbi of Congregation Ahavath Sholom, Bluefield, W.Va., 1921-22, and Temple Beth El, Norfolk, Va., 1922-34; Temple Ahavath Sholom, Brooklyn, N.Y., rabbi, 1934-66, rabbi emeritus, 1966-78. Former president and member of board of New York Board of Rabbis; member of board of Brooklyn Board of Rabbis. Member of board of directors of National Home for Asthmatic Children, Denver, Colo., beginning 1935, and Brooklyn Juvenile Guidance Center, beginning 1936. Honorary chairman of National Poetry Day, 1958, 1959; honorary president of Jewish Book Council of America. *Military service:* U.S. Army, 1943-46; became captain. *Member:* Synagogue Council of America, Central Conference of American Rabbis, Brooklyn Association of Reform Rabbis, Eugene Field Society. *Awards, honors:* First prize, Bookfellow Poetry Annual, 1940, and American Poetry League Contest, 1949; D.D. from Hebrew Union College, 1956; Frank L. Weil Award for Distinguished Contributions to the Advancement of Jewish Culture in America from Jewish Welfare Board, 1970.

WRITINGS: Sabbath Queen: Fifty-Four Bible Talks to the Young, Behrman's Jewish Book House, 1936; *What Is Judaism?: A Guide for Young People,* Behrman's Jewish Book House, 1937; *When Dreamers Build* (poetry), Kaleidograph Press, 1937; *Musings and Meditations,* Wings Press, 1941; *In Search of the Permanent, and Other Essays,* Wings Press, 1946; *Bitter-sweet: Prose-Poems, Sonnets, Lyrics,* Library Publishers, 1955; *Faith and Love,* Philosophical Library, 1959; *Through Storms We Grow, and Other Sermons, Lectures, and Essays,* Bloch Publishing, 1964. Also author of *Treatise Baba Mezia,* 1929. Editor of New York Board of Rabbis *Bulletin,* 1950-60, *Jewish Book Annual,* 1954-76, and *In Jewish Bookland,* beginning 1960.

AVOCATIONAL INTERESTS: Music.

OBITUARIES: New York Times, November 15, 1978.*

*   *   *

STEINHOFF, William (Richard) 1914-

PERSONAL: Born February 13, 1914, in Chicago, Ill.; son of William Richard and Nellie (Mulligan) Steinhoff; married Rosannah Cannon (an editor), January 6, 1940. *Education:* University of California, Berkeley, A.B., 1938, M.A., 1940, Ph.D., 1948. *Home:* 519 Onondaga, Ann Arbor, Mich.

48104. *Office:* Department of English Language and Literature, University of Michigan, Ann Arbor, Mich. 48104.

CAREER: University of Michigan, Ann Arbor, instructor, 1948-52, assistant professor, 1952-57, associate professor, 1957-63, professor of English, 1963—. Ford Foundation faculty fellow, 1954-55; visiting professor at University of Aix-Marseille, France, 1964-65. Head of Michigan Commission on Teacher Certification, 1961-62. *Military service:* U.S. Army, 1943-46; became second lieutenant. *Member:* National Council of Teachers of English, Modern Language Association of America, Conference on College Composition and Communication (member of executive committee, 1959-60). *Awards, honors:* University of Michigan Press Award, 1976.

WRITINGS: (Editor) *Modern Short Stories,* Oxford University Press, 1951; (editor) *The Image of the Work,* University of California Press, 1952; (editor with Arthur Japheth Carr) *Points of Departure: Essays and Stories for College English,* Harper, 1960; *George Orwell and the Origins of 1984,* University of Michigan Press, 1975 (published in England as *The Road to 1984,* Weidenfeld & Nicolson, 1975).

*   *   *

STELLMAN, Steven D(ale) 1945-

PERSONAL: Born May 7, 1945, in Toronto, Ontario, Canada; son of Samuel D. (a professor) and L. Mandy (a lawyer; maiden name, Mandlsohn) Stellman; married Jeanne Mager (an occupational health specialist), October 10, 1967; children: Andrew, Emma. *Education:* Attended Massachusetts Institute of Technology, 1962-64; Ohio State University, B.Sc., 1966; New York University, Ph.D., 1971. *Religion:* Jewish. *Home:* 117 St. Johns Pl., Brooklyn, N.Y. 11217. *Office:* American Health Foundation, 320 East 43rd St., New York, N.Y. 10017.

CAREER: Princeton University, Princeton, N.J., Department of Biochemical Sciences, research associate, 1971-73; University of Colorado, Denver Center, Denver, Colo., instructor in chemistry, 1973-74; American Health Foundation, New York, N.Y., chief of Division of Computing and Biostatistics, 1975—. *Member:* Society for Epidemiologic Research, American Chemical Society, Association for Computing Machinery.

WRITINGS: (With S. S. Epstein) *The Politics of Cancer,* Sierra Club Books, 1978.

WORK IN PROGRESS: Research on cancer and cardiovascular disease epidemiology.

SIDELIGHTS: Stellman told *CA:* "The main causes of disease in American society are to be found in our environment. For some causes, like smoking, behavioral modification (for example, cessation) is the most effective solution. For involuntary exposures, however, arising from industrial sources, strict regulation is needed, which can only be effective when an informed public becomes involved on a personal and societal level."

*   *   *

STEPHENSON, Jean 1892-1979

OBITUARY NOTICE: Born August 29, 1892, in Waco, Tex.; died January 22, 1979, in Frostburg, Md. Genealogist and author of books in her field. Stephenson was involved in numerous geneological projects, including a research program which trained college students in methodology. Obituaries and other sources: *Washington Post,* January 26, 1979.

STEPHENSON, Maureen 1927-

PERSONAL: Born February 14, 1927, in Manchester, England; daughter of Joseph (a tailor) and Anne (Byrom) Duffy; married Louis John Stephenson (an engineer), August 21, 1954; children: William, David, Sarah. *Education:* Attended high school in London, England. *Religion:* Roman Catholic. *Home:* Ansley Mill Farm, Ansley, North Warwickshire CV10 0QT, England. *Agent:* Collier Associates, 280 Madison Ave., New York, N.Y. 10016.

CAREER: Shepperton Studios, London, England, in film continuity, 1944-47; Pinewood Studios, London, in film continuity, 1948-50; Denham Studios, London, in film continuity, 1950-52; Ealing Studios, London, in film continuity, 1952-54; writer, 1977—.

WRITINGS: Ride the Dark Moors (Gothic novel), Zebra Books, 1977; *The House on Wath Moor* (Gothic novel), Zebra Books, 1979.

WORK IN PROGRESS: Research for a novel set in eighteenth-century Warwickshire.

SIDELIGHTS: Maureen Stephenson writes: "Born into a second generation Irish immigrant family, I was never conscious of the lack of money; my father, having a deep love of literature, music, and art, gave a richness to my life which I have always kept.

"My father gave me the idea of writing and bought me a correspondence course in fiction writing. In my opinion, such courses are the best way to start. Then for ten years I worked in the film business, and found working on film scripts invaluable in learning how to build up a story and a character.

"I wrote short stories from time to time, and the best I achieved was encouraging letters from fiction editors. Then about ten years ago we bought a historic cottage in a Yorkshire dale that fired my imagination and I wrote my first novel. From this experience I feel one must live in surroundings that stimulate.

"The authors who have had the greatest influence on me are the Bronte sisters. They achieve a mystical other-worldliness that I admire."

*   *   *

STERN, Laurence (Marcus) 1929-

PERSONAL: Born June 16, 1929, in New York, N.Y.; son of August L. (a journalist) and Mary (Markusfeld) Stern; married Joan Davis, June 20, 1951 (divorced); married Turri Herndon, (divorced); children: Gunther, Marc, Catherine, Christopher. *Education:* Attended Brooklyn College (now of the City University of New York), 1946, and New School for Social Research, 1949; University of Missouri, A.B., 1951. *Home:* 1706 21st St. N.W., Washington, D.C. 20009. *Office:* 1150 15th St. N.W., Washington, D.C. 20005.

CAREER: Editor and writer for U.S. Information Agency (USIA), 1951-52; *Washington Post,* Washington, D.C., 1952—, national affairs reporter, 1962-65, national editor, 1965-68, assistant managing editor, 1968-70, Saigon bureau chief, 1970-72, foreign and national affairs correspondent, 1972-77, assistant managing editor for national affairs, 1977—. *Military service:* U.S. Army, 1946-47. *Member:* Federal City Club. *Awards, honors:* Newspaper Guild Front Page Award, 1958, 1962; National Headliners Award and American Political Science Association Award, both 1962; Carnegie Endowment for International Peace senior fellow, 1974-75.

WRITINGS: The Wrong Horse: The Politics of Intervention and the Failure of American Diplomacy, Times Books, 1977; (with Charles A. Krause, Richard Harwood, and the staff of the *Washington Post*) *Guyana Massacre: The Eyewitness Account,* Berkley, 1978.

WORK IN PROGRESS: A Washington novel.

SIDELIGHTS: Stern's *The Wrong Horse* examines American foreign policy in the eastern Mediterranean during the post-World War II era. It specifically analyzes the effects of interventionist U.S. policies in Greece at the time of the 1967 "Colonel's Coup" in Athens and the Cyprus crisis of 1974. This latter episode precipitated a string of diplomatic explosions as Turkey invaded Cyprus, the Greek government dissolved, the U.S. Congress rebelled against the Ford administration by cutting off aid to Turkey, and Turkey closed U.S. bases.

"The essence of Stern's study," wrote Yale historian Gaddis Smith, is "that animosities on Cyprus between Greece and Turkey might have receded had not the United States backed 'the wrong horse' in Athens, i.e., the despicable junta [of Papadopoulos] rather than Papandreous and democracy." This "Greek dictatorship," reasoned author Stern, "was seen by most of its opponents as an almost inevitable consequence of both the massive and continuing U.S. investment in the military sector of Greek society and Washington's open disapproval of the civilian leaders who stressed economic reform and development as well as disengagement from Cold War entanglements."

Especially noteworthy for his role in the "failure of American diplomacy" is former Secretary of State Henry Kissinger. Smith felt Stern's "primary criticism of Kissinger is philosophical." Not only does the author condemn Kissinger for helping "sustain the odious junta," and ignoring its intentions on Cyprus, "Stern faults Kissinger on method: for reacting too late to the overthrow of Makarios, for appearing to accept Sampson and thus hastening the Turkish invasion of Cyprus, for disingenuous manipulation of the press, for leaving subordinate officials in the dark while he bungled away by telephone." Alex Beam took another opinion of Stern's indictment of Kissinger: "Stern views the Greece-Turkey-Cyprus confrontation as 'a metaphor for American foreign policy failure under the leadership of Henry Kissinger.' His choice is appropriate, for a military 'client' dictatorship gummed up the foreign policy machinery, is repeated in Vietnam, Cambodia and elsewhere during the Kissinger years."

A common complaint among reviewers of *The Wrong Horse* was that Stern did not go far enough in offering his own assessment of the situation. "By focusing so closely on the minutiae of U.S. action," argued Harrison E. Salisbury, "Stern almost misses the basics. What is the United States doing in the eastern Mediterranean anyway?" While acknowledging that "the material is fascinating," Ronald Steel felt "too often the detail seems extraneous, and one is left in the underbrush without a clear view of the forest. . . . The impact would have been greater had Stern not confined his analytical skills to his brief introduction and epilogue. In this case the author was too modest."

Stern's "clear, taut study" enlightened readers by bringing to light an issue lost in the shadow of Vietnam and Watergate. As Beam claimed, "Stern has created a minor masterpiece, a tightly knit account of a crucial foreign policy vignette based on extensive post-mortem interviews with all of the participants." Likewise, this "is a short book with a strong message," declared Salisbury. "As a case history in

recent American policy . . . it is probably as good a one as can be selected to dramatize the fatuity and the painting-into-a-corner which have come to characterize so many of our foreign interventions."

A different type of foreign affair, the 1978 mass murder/suicide ritual at Jonestown's People's Temple, prompted *The Guyana Massacre.* Almost miraculously, the 210-page chronicle saw publication within two weeks after the incident. *Washington Post* South America correspondent Charles Krause had been among the group of reporters who accompanied California Congressman Leo Ryan to investigate Jim Jones's religious commune. Krause managed to survive the ambush on the entourage and afterwards returned to Jonestown to witness the scene where more than nine hundred poisoned cult members lay dead. Summoned back to Washington by *Post* executive editor Benjamin Bradlee, Krause joined senior editors Stern and Richard Harwood in a suite at the Madison Hotel and the three wrote the sixty-thousand-word manuscript in five days. As Stern told *CA,* "It was an experiment in full professional concentration, notwithstanding the horse race aspect of a book on a singularly gruesome episode in our history."

BIOGRAPHICAL/CRITICAL SOURCES: Washington Post Book World, December 18, 1977; *New York Times Book Review,* February 12, 1978, January 7, 1979; *The Progressive,* May, 1978; *New Yorker,* May 1, 1978; *Nation,* May 20, 1978; *Time,* December 12, 1978.

*   *   *

STETSON, Damon 1915-

PERSONAL: Born August 1, 1915, in Hanover, Mass.; son of Bernard L. and Marion (Mitchell) Stetson; married Shirley Parker (a college administrator), 1949; children: Nancy Stetson Remsen, David. *Education:* Bates College, A.B., 1936; Columbia University, M.S., 1937. *Home:* 55 Sunset Ave., Verona, N.J. 07044. *Office: New York Times,* 229 West 43rd St., New York, N.Y. 10036.

CAREER: Newark Evening News, Newark, N.J., reporter, 1937-40, bureau chief, 1940-41; *New York Times,* New York City, labor writer, 1953—, Detroit bureau chief, 1955-63. Member of board of trustees of Bates College. *Military service:* U.S. Navy, 1942-46; became lieutenant senior grade; received Bronze Star.

WRITINGS: Aircraft Engines, U.S. Navy, 1943; *Airplane Structures,* U.S. Navy, 1944; (contributor) Edward W. Barrett and Robert F. Hewes, editors, *Journalists in Action,* Channel Press, 1963; *Starting Over* (on second careers), Macmillan, 1971. Contributor to periodicals.

WORK IN PROGRESS: Writing on labor-management relations.

SIDELIGHTS: Stetson commented: "Most of my writing is currently topical—related to labor-management relations and the field of work.

"I did some research awhile back for an article for the *New York Times* on second careers. Out of this came a request from Macmillan for a book which finally emerged as *Starting Over.*

"A man in his middle years may realize that he will never become president of his company, be appointed top account executive, win a Pulitzer Prize, head a bank, or make a million. Many women, too, having raised a family, or because of financial pressures or the desire for personal expression may be ready for a change. I found an epidemic of career changing in the early seventies and put the story together with scores and scores of case histories. Life can begin again.''

* * *

STEVENS, Rosemary (Anne) 1935-

PERSONAL: Born March 18, 1935, in Bourne, England; came to the United States in 1961, naturalized citizen, 1968; daughter of William E. and Mary A. (Tricks) Wallace; married Robert B. Stevens (an academic administrator), January 28, 1961; children: Carey, Richard. *Education:* Oxford University, B.A., 1957; Victoria University of Manchester, diploma, 1959; Yale University, M.P.H., 1963, Ph.D., 1968. *Office:* Department of History and Sociology of Science, University of Pennsylvania, 215 South 34th St., Philadelphia, Pa. 19104.

CAREER: Yale University, New Haven, Conn., research associate, 1962-68, assistant professor, 1968-71, associate professor, 1971-74, professor of public health, 1974-76; Tulane University, New Orleans, La., professor of health systems management, 1976-78; University of Pennsylvania, Philadelphia, professor of history and sociology of science, 1979—.

WRITINGS: Medical Practice in Modern England, Yale University Press, 1966; *American Medicine and the Public Interest,* Yale University Press, 1971; (with Joan Vermeulen) *Foreign Medical Graduates in American Medicine,* U.S. Government Printing Office, 1972; (with husband, Robert Stevens) *Welfare Medicine in America,* Free Press, 1974; (with Louis Wolf Goodman and Stephen S. Mick) *The Alien Doctors,* Wiley, 1978. Contributor to professional journals.

WORK IN PROGRESS: Research on the social history of medicine, the medical profession, and politics and policies of American health services.

* * *

STEVENSON, Charles 1908(?)-1979

OBITUARY NOTICE: Born c. 1908; died March 14, 1979, in Bennington, Vt. Educator and author. Stevenson was professor of philosophy at the University of Michigan for thirty-one years. He wrote *Ethics and Language* and *Facts and Values.* Obituaries and other sources: *New York Times,* March 19, 1979.

* * *

STEWART, J(ohn) I(nnes) M(ackintosh) 1906-
   (Michael Innes)

PERSONAL: Born September 30, 1906, in Edinburgh, England; son of John (in education) and Eliza Jane (Clark) Stewart; married Margaret Hardwick (a physician), 1932; children: three sons, two daughters. *Education:* Oriel College, Oxford, B.A., 1928. *Home:* Fawler Copse, Kingston Lisle, Wantage, Berkshire, England.

CAREER: Writer. University of Leeds, Yorkshire, England, lecturer in English, 1930-35; University of Adelaide, Adelaide, South Australia, jury professor of English, 1935-45; Queen's University, Belfast, Ireland, lecturer, 1946-48; Oxford University, Oxford, England, reader in English literature, 1969—. Student of Christ Church College, Oxford, 1949—; Walker Ames Professor at University of Washington, 1961. *Awards, honors:* Matthew Arnold Memorial Prize, 1929; D.Litt., from University of New Brunswick, 1962.

WRITINGS—Novels; published by Norton unless otherwise indicated: *Mark Lambert's Supper,* Gollancz, 1954; *The Guardians,* Gollancz, 1955, Norton, 1957; *A Use of Riches,* 1957; *The Man Who Won the Pools,* 1961; *The Last Tresilians,* 1963; *An Acre of Grass,* 1965; *The Aylwins,* 1966; *Vanderlyn's Kingdom,* 1967; *Avery's Mission,* 1971; *A Palace of Art,* 1972; *Mungo's Dream,* 1973; *The Gaudy,* Gollancz, 1974, Norton, 1975; *Young Pattullo,* Gollancz, 1975, Norton, 1976; *A Memorial Service,* 1976; *The Madonna of the Astrolab,* 1977; *Full Term,* 1978.

Other: (Editor) Michel Eyquem de Montaigne, *Montaigne's Essays: John Florio's Translation,* Random House, 1931; *Educating the Emotions,* [Adelaide], 1944; (contributor) Raynor Heppenstall, editor, *Imaginary Conversations: Eight Radio Scripts,* Secker & Warburg, 1948; *Character and Motive in Shakespeare: Some Recent Appraisals Examined,* Longman, 1949; *The Man Who Wrote Detective Stories and Other Stories,* Norton, 1959; *Eight Modern Writers,* Oxford University Press, 1963; *Rudyard Kipling,* Dodd, 1966; (author of introduction) J. B. Priestley, *Thomas Love Peacock,* Penguin, 1966; (editor) Colin Wilkie, *Moonstone,* Penguin, 1966; (editor and author of introduction) William Makepeace Thackeray, *Vanity Fair,* Penguin, 1968; *Joseph Conrad,* Dodd, 1968; *Cucumber Sandwiches and Other Stories,* Norton, 1969; *Thomas Hardy: A Critical Biography,* Dodd, 1971; *Shakespeare's Lofty Scene,* Oxford University Press for the British Academy, 1971.

Novels under pseudonym Michael Innes: *Death at the President's Lodging,* Gollancz, 1936, reprinted, Penguin, 1964, published as *Seven Suspects,* Dodd, 1937, reprinted, Doubleday, 1962; *Hamlet, Revenge!,* Dodd, 1937, reprinted, Penguin, 1976; *Lament for a Maker,* Dodd, 1938, reprinted, New English Library, 1964; *The Spider Strikes Back,* Dodd, 1939 (published in England as *Stop Press,* Gollancz, 1939).

The Secret Vanguard, Gollancz, 1940, Dodd, 1941; *A Comedy of Terrors,* Dodd, 1940 (published in England as *There Came Both Mist and Snow,* Gollancz, 1940, reprinted, Gollancz, 1972); *Appleby on Ararat,* Dodd, 1941, reprinted, Greenwood Press, 1971; *The Daffodil Affair,* Dodd, 1942, reprinted, Garland Publishing, 1976; *The Weight of the Evidence,* Gollancz, 1943, Dodd, 1944; *Appleby's End,* Dodd, 1945, reprinted, Greenwood Press, 1970; *Unsuspected Chasm,* Dodd, 1946 (published in England as *From London Far,* Gollancz, 1946); *What Happened at Hazelwood,* Gollancz, 1944, Dodd, 1947, reprinted, Gollancz, 1973; *Night of Errors,* Gollancz, 1947, Dodd, 1948, reprinted, Gollancz, 1974; *The Case of the Journeying Boy,* Dodd, 1949 (published in England as *The Journeying Boy,* Gollancz, 1949).

Paper Thunderbolt, Dodd, 1951 (published in England as *Operation Fox,* Gollancz, 1951); *One Man Show,* Dodd, 1952 (published in England as *A Private View,* Gollancz, 1952); *Christmas at Candleshoe,* Dodd, 1953; *The Man From the Sea,* Dodd, 1955; *A Question of Queens,* Dodd, 1956 (published in England as *Old Hall, New Hall,* Gollancz, 1956); *Death on a Quiet Day,* Dodd, 1957 (published in England as *Appleby Plays Chicken,* Gollancz, 1957); *The Long Farewell,* Dodd, 1958; *Hare Sitting Up,* Dodd, 1959.

The Case of Sonia Wayward, Dodd, 1960 (published in England as *The New Sonia Wayward,* Gollancz, 1960); *Silence Observed,* Dodd, 1961; *The Crabtree Affair,* Dodd, 1962 (published in England as *A Connoisseur's Case,* Gollancz, 1962); *Money From Holme,* Gollancz, 1964, Dodd, 1965; *The Bloody Wood,* Dodd, 1966; *A Change of Heir,* Dodd, 1966; *Death by Water,* Dodd, 1968; *Appleby at Allington,* Dodd, 1968; *Picture of Guilt,* Dodd, 1969 (published in England as *A Family Affair,* Gollancz, 1969).

Death at the Chase, Dodd, 1970; *An Awkward Lie,* Dodd, 1971; *The Open House,* Dodd, 1972; *Appleby's Answer,* Dodd, 1973; *Appleby's Other Story,* Gollancz, 1973, Dodd, 1974; *The Mysterious Commission,* Gollancz, 1974, Dodd, 1975; *The Gay Phoenix,* Gollancz, 1976, Dodd, 1977; *Honeybath's Haven,* Gollancz, 1977, Dodd, 1978.

Other; under Innes pseudonym: (With Heppenstall) *Three Tales of Hamlet,* Gollancz, 1950; *Dead Man's Shoes,* Dodd, 1954 (published in England as *Appleby Talking: Twenty-Three Detective Stories,* Gollancz, 1954); *Appleby Talks Again: Eighteen Detective Stories,* Gollancz, 1956, Dodd, 1957; *Appleby Intervenes: Three Tales From Scotland Yard* (contains *One Man Show, A Comedy of Terrors,* and *The Secret Vanguard*), Dodd, 1965; *The Appleby File: Detective Stories,* Gollancz, 1975, Dodd, 1976.

SIDELIGHTS: Stewart has distinguished himself as both a novelist and literary scholar. His mysteries, written under the pseudonym Michael Innes, have been acknowledged by critics for their intellectual tone and erudite quality; and critics, notably Rayner Heppenstall, have compared some of his other novels to those of Henry James. His scholarly work, *Thomas Hardy,* is considered by many reviewers to be a valuable source of information on that particular author.

Stewart's first two biographies, *Rudyard Kipling* and *Joseph Conrad,* were not as successful as the later *Thomas Hardy. Rudyard Kipling* was viewed by one writer for *Times Literary Supplement* as a "useful introduction" to the British author. However, the same writer also complained about the lack of fresh information in Stewart's book. The critic warned that "for those for whom introductions are no longer needed its pleasures are rather those of reading about the familiar than of deeper exploration or critical enlightenment."

Stephen Miller held *Joseph Conrad* in a more favorable light. Citing Bertrand Russell's lament that "Conrad, I suppose, is in process of being forgotten . . . ," Miller claimed that Stewart's book would renew appreciation for the novelist. But Heppenstall was less enthusiastic. Although he conceded that *Joseph Conrad* "will meet, I feel sure, a need," he also remarked that the book "somehow has the effect of putting him back into the nonsense world" where too much theorizing is done on certain novelists. Heppenstall voiced his disappointment by writing, "Now, I thought, people would just have to stop talking and writing nonsense about Hardy, James, Shaw, Conrad, Kipling, Yeats, Joyce, and Lawrence."

Stewart's third biography, *Thomas Hardy,* received many enthusiastic reviews. A critic for *Economist* wrote, "Anyone who enjoys reading Hardy's fiction will get a great deal of pleasure and stimulation from reading the commentaries on the novels. . . ." The same critic declared that Stewart's "familiarity with the whole file of Hardy studies is abundantly evident, but his contribution differs from most of the worthy discourses in its relaxed and often humorous tone. . . ." John Boyley called *Thomas Hardy* "concise, elegant, and witty. . . ." James Gindin was similarly impressed, calling it "a highly praiseworthy and provocative book." Gindin also admired Stewart's approach to Hardy, deeming it "biographical, but biographical in an intelligent and flexible way that avoids the dogma implicit in the set of consistent philosophy or structural criticism. . . ."

Stewart's novel, *Vanderlyn's Kingdom,* also received a great deal of critical attention, although not always of a positive nature. R. G. G. Price compared Stewart to "a great journalist," and commented that "he can fill a paragraph with things never noticed before; but people and places lose substantiality as events roll." A critic for *Times Literary Supplement* described the novel as "basically about the dangers of trying to organize and direct the creative life of an artist when one has no intrinsic feeling for the end product," but noted that "it falls short of complete achievement." Alan Pryce-Jones blamed the novel's failure on a lack of significant characters. He wrote that Stewart "has omitted to populate his places with people." Guy Davenport was ambivalent about *Vanderlyn's Kingdom.* "The result is not bad," he observed, "but is less than convincing."

Critics were in disagreement concerning Stewart's *Mungo's Dream.* His story of a friendship shrouded in impending doom was called "a stilted demonstration of what a novel should not be" by Jeanne Kinney. In a difference of opinion, a reviewer for *Times Literary Supplement* wrote, "Mr. Stewart, in true detective style, keeps everyone guessing to the final chapter. And he spins out his illusion with a good deal of light-hearted literary cavorting. . . ." Martin Amis noted both the flaws and fine points of *Mungo's Dream* in his review. "It appears that Mr. Stewart has . . . fallen victim to the diversity of his own talents," he wrote. After observing that there is some of both the mystery-writer and academic imposed in the work, Amis did assert that "there is a lot going on in *Mungo's Dream;* the interest never flags and Mr. Stewart's sharp eye makes up for his cauliflower ear."

The Gaudy concerns Duncan Pattullo, an alumnus of Oxford University who has returned after twenty years to attend a reunion. Melody Hardy wrote that Stewart "captures the romance of an Oxford education and its impact on the men who experience it. . . ." She further remarked, "In telling this tale, reminiscent of C. P. Snow, Stewart has captured an environment. . . ." A reviewer for *Times Literary Supplement,* taking into account that *The Gaudy* is the first of five novels featuring Pattullo, was less impressed. "The present reviewer . . . ," it was noted, "hopes to be spared the next four installments." The writer added, "One feels that Mr. Stewart would have written better if he had known Christ Church, Oxford, less well."

Young Pattullo is the second of five novels featuring Duncan Pattullo. Victoria Glendinning wrote, "There is nostalgia on every page, expressed in elegant, well-made sentences. . . ." She called the novel "an educated, subtle discourse for readers whom the writer is courteous enough to suppose as educated and subtle as himself." Lalage Pulvertaft agreed with Glendinning that *Young Pattullo* contains "wonderful accounts of undergraduate life. . . ." However, like the critic who wrote on *The Gaudy* for *Times Literary Supplement,* Pulvertaft felt that Stewart was too close to his subject. "The trouble," she wrote, "is that Mr. Stewart's highly wrought, tense tangential style mirrors this society all too closely."

Stewart's third novel in the Duncan Pattullo series, referred to collectively as "A Staircase in Surrey," is *A Memorial Service.* While both Julian Barnes and Susan Kennedy found the novel enjoyable, they both also pointed out Stewart's use of a serial-convention. "One of the drawbacks of the serial novel is the need to remind the reader . . . of people and events introduced in earlier volumes," wrote Kennedy. "Mr. Stewart's way of handling this is to take up old threads in after-dinner conversations or on leisurely, companionable walks. . . ." And Barnes wrote that *A Memorial Service* "has pleasures analogous to those of the high-table dinners [Stewart] so regularly describes. . . ."

Aside from his scholarly works and novels, Stewart also

penned a collection of short stories, *Cucumber Sandwiches.* The tales, often reminiscent of Henry James shorter works, were deemed "perfect" by a critic for *New York Times Book Review.* Neil Millar noted that *Cucumber Sandwiches* "exhales the drama of every battle between flesh and spirit. It flesh never undresses in public, and nearly always dresses for dinner. Its spirit rarely raises—and never lowers—its kindly, cultured, understanding voice." The writer for *New York Times Book Review* also noted that Stewart "shapes and polishes each sentence with respectful craftsmanship. The same writer added, "Little enough is left us these days. Let us give deep thanks to J.I.M. Stewart for his intellect, his respect for undecayed English, and his preservative humor."

Stewart has also written numerous mysteries under the pseudonym of Michael Innes. Many of the novels feature Sir John Appleby, a resourceful crime-solver who rose in rank to become chief police commissioner before retiring. Even in retirement, though, he has been present in Stewart's recent mysteries such as *The Gay Phoenix.* The novels have been praised for their Victorian style although some critics have found them exceedingly erudite and, according to one critic, "boring." However, the character of Appleby is a popular one with both British and American readers.

BIOGRAPHICAL/CRITICAL SOURCES: Times Literary Supplement, January 19, 1967, September 21, 1967, December 25, 1969, February 2, 1973, October 25, 1974, June 6, 1975, May 7, 1976; *Spectator,* September 22, 1967; *New York Times Book Review,* April 7, 1968, June 19, 1970, May 29, 1977; *National Review,* April 9, 1968; *New Leader,* September 9, 1968; *New Statesman,* December 20, 1968, September 24, 1971, February 9, 1973, June 13, 1975, April 30, 1976; *Christian Science Monitor,* June 13, 1970; *Book World,* November 28, 1971; *Economist,* January 15, 1972; *Virginia Quarterly Review,* winter, 1972; *Best Sellers,* June, 1975; *Contemporary Literary Criticism,* Volume 7, Gale, 1977.*

*   *   *

STEWART, Walter Bingham 1913-

PERSONAL: Born August 15, 1913, in Evanston, Ill.; son of Walter Morgan and Elizabeth (Bingham) Stewart; married Jane Sinclair, July 3, 1938; children: Sinclair Bingham, Donald James. *Education:* Attended University of Illinois, 1932-33; University of North Carolina, Chapel Hill, A.B., 1938; attended Northwestern University, 1939-40, University of Wisconsin, 1961-63, and Upper Iowa University, 1962-63; Radford College, M.A., 1965; further study at University of Florida, 1968-69. *Home:* 2828 North Atlantic Ave., Daytona Beach, Fla. 32018.

CAREER: Raleigh News & Observer, Raleigh, N.C., wire editor, 1935-37; Parker Pen Co., Janesville, Wis., advertising manager, 1939-43; Louis Melind Co., Chicago, Ill., sales and advertising manager, 1943-47; Reynolds Pen Co., Chicago, advertising manager, 1947-50; H. W. Gossard Co., Chicago, advertising manager, 1950-61; Travelmats-Press Publishing Co., Prairie du Chien, Wis., manager, 1961-63; Radford College, Radford, Va., chairman of journalism department, 1965-78; *Radford Messenger,* Radford, editor, 1973-78. Correspondent for *Roanoke Times,* 1970-72. Notable assignments include interviews of Elizabeth Taylor, Spiro Agnew, Nelson Rockefeller, John Mitchell, and Eric Sevareid. Consultant. *Member:* Society for Collegiate Journalists (vice-president, 1975-77), Rotary Club, Kappa Delta Pi, Phi Delta Kappa, Phi Gamma Delta.

WRITINGS: Do You Pass the Model Test, Gale Publishing,

1957; *Do You Dress Like a Model,* Gale Publishing, 1958; *Do You Have a Model Figure,* Gale Publishing, 1959; *The Complete Book of Modeling,* Collegiate Press, 1974. Also author of *Adventures in Travel.*

*   *   *

STOCK, Phyllis H(artman) 1930-

PERSONAL: Born May 17, 1930, in New York, N.Y.; daughter of Alexander (an accountant) and Helene (Morse) Hartman; married Robert W. Stock, 1976 (divorced); children: Barbara, David. *Education:* Attended New York University, 1947-48; University of Bridgeport, B.A., 1960; Yale University, M.A., 1961, Ph.D., 1965. *Home:* 54 Riverside Dr., New York, N.Y. 10024. *Office:* Department of History, Seton Hall University, South Orange, N.J. 07079.

CAREER: Bridgeport Sunday Post, Bridgeport, Conn., journalist, 1950-58; Seton Hall University, South Orange, N.J., assistant professor, 1965-69, associate professor, 1969-78, professor of history, 1978—. Chair of the Coordinating Committee on Women in the Historical Profession, 1978-79. *Member:* American Historical Association, Association for French Historical Studies, Authors Guild of Authors League of America, Institute for Research in History (member of board of directors, 1978-79), Conference Group on Women's History, Coordinating Committee for Women in the Historical Profession (head of New York region, 1978-79).

WRITINGS: Better Than Rubies: A History of Women's Education, Putnam, 1978.

WORK IN PROGRESS: A biography of Comtesse d'Agoult; a monograph on secular morality in nineteenth-century France.

SIDELIGHTS: Phyllis Stock comments: "I have been working in women's history for six years now, and consider it a study vital to women's understanding of their position in society. If you don't know how you got here, you haven't much chance of changing the conditions that put you here. So I am a historian and a feminist."

*   *   *

STONE, David K(arl) 1922-

PERSONAL: Born March 24, 1922, in Reedsport, Ore.; son of Karl R. (a planning director) and Genevieve (Rogers) Stone; married Peggy Lee Barker (a model), February 14, 1952; children: Kelly, Jamie. *Education:* University of Oregon, B.A., 1947; graduate study at Art Center College of Design, Los Angeles, 1948, and University Michoacan de San Nicolas de Hidalgo, Mexico, 1949. *Home and office:* 6 Farm View Rd., Port Washington, N.Y. 11050.

CAREER: Farm laborer in Thurston, Ore., 1937-39; Springfield Creamery, Springfield, Ore., truck driver, 1939-40; Westfir Lumber Co., Oakridge, Ore., lumber stacker, 1940-41; illustrator and painter, 1950—. Professional artist (civilian) for U.S. Air Force in Washington, D.C., 1960—; vice-president of Craven Evans & Stone Graphics Studio, New York, N.Y., 1973-75. Vice-chairman of Art Advisory Council, 1969-79. Member of village board of governors of Flower Hill, N.Y., 1969-70; member of board of directors of Port Washington-Manhasset Coalition for Racial Concern. *Military service:* U.S. Army, Infantry, 1941-46; became first lieutenant. *Member:* Society of Illustrators (president, 1968-69), Graphic Arts Guild (member of board of directors). *Awards, honors:* Certificate of merit from Society of Illustrators, 1964, 1966, 1969, 1971, 1974, 1976, 1978; Society of Illustrators Artist and Book Show gold medal, 1965; St.

Louis Art Directors Club medal, 1969; U.S. Air Force plaque, 1970; Graphic Arts Guild commendation, 1975.

WRITINGS: Art in Advertising (self-illustrated), Pitman, 1961; *Thanksgiving,* Holt, 1968.

Illustrator: Dorothea J. Snow, *The Mystery of Ghost Burro Canyon,* Bobbs-Merrill, 1962; Neola Tracy Lane, *Secret of the Silver Spoons,* Bobbs-Merrill, 1963; Louisa May Alcott, *Little Women,* Whitman Publishing, 1965; Alcott, *Little Men,* Whitman Publishing, 1965; Gladys Baker Bond, *Patrick Will Grow,* Whitman Publishing, 1966; Katherine J. Hardie and Pauline P. Meek, *The Birth of God's People,* CLC Press, 1968; Kenneth Grahame, *The Wind in the Willows,* Golden Press, 1968; Glenn P. Crone, *There Really Is a Santa Claus,* John Knox, 1968; Louise Munro Foley, *The Caper Club,* Singer, 1969; Veronica Nash, *Carlito's World: A Block in Spanish Harlem,* Rutledge Books, 1969; *Three Little Pigs,* Platt, 1969; Robert F. Burgess, *Where Condors Fly,* World Publishing, 1969; Walt Whitman, *Miracles: The Wonders of Life,* Rand McNally, 1969.

Tom McGowen, *Hammett and the Highlanders,* Follett, 1970; Eleanor L. Clymer, *We Lived in the Almont,* Dutton, 1970; Lois Johnson, editor, *Christmas Stories Round the World,* Rand McNally, 1970; Wayne Carley, *Mixed-Up Magic,* Garrard, 1971; Carley, *Percy the Parrot Strikes Out,* Garrard, 1971; Eleanor Harder, *Darius and The Dozer Bull,* Abingdon, 1971; John A. McKinnes, *Goodnight Painted Pony,* Garrard, 1971; Lee Cooper, *The Pirate of Puerto Rico,* Putnam, 1972; Ewan Clarkson, *The Running of the Deer,* Dutton, 1972; Clymer, *Me and the Eggman,* Dutton, 1972; Ernest Hemingway, *For Whom the Bell Tolls,* Shogo Ku Kan (Tokyo), 1972; Bernard Max Garfinkel, *The Champions,* Platt, 1972; Dion Henderson, *Algonquin,* Whitman Publishing, 1972; Clarkson, *In the Shadow of the Falcon,* Dutton, 1973; Frank Martin, *How Do You Say It? In English, Spanish and French,* Platt, 1973; Bernice W. Carlson and Ristina Wigg, *We Want Sunshine in Our Houses,* Abingdon, 1973; Norman Mailer, *The Naked and the Dead,* Shogo Ku Kan, 1973; Morton Grosser, *The Snake Horn,* Atheneum, 1973; June L. Shore, *What's the Matter With Wakefield?,* Abingdon, 1974; William MacKellar, *Alfie and Me and the Ghost of Peter Stuyvesant,* Dodd, 1974; Marcia Polese, *Frankie and the Fawn,* Abingdon, 1974.

Clarkson, *Wolf Country: A Wilderness Pilgrimage,* Dutton, 1975; Elizabeth Rider Montgomery, *Duke Ellington: King of Jazz,* Dell, 1975; Mary Burg Whitcomb, *Tee-bo the Talking Dog on the Trail of the Persnickety Prowler,* Western Publishing, 1975; MacKellar, *The Cat That Never Died,* Dodd, 1976; Jeannie Hagy, *And Then Mom Joined the Army,* Abingdon, 1976; MacKellar, *The Kid Who Owned Manhattan Island,* Dodd, 1976; Dianne Glaser, *The Case of the Missing Six,* Holiday House, 1978.

*   *   *

STONE, Robert 1937(?)-

PERSONAL: Born in 1937(?), in Brooklyn, N.Y.; married; children: two. *Residence:* Amherst, Mass. *Office:* Amherst College, Amherst, Mass. 01002.

CAREER: Writer. Currently associated with Amherst College, Amherst, Mass. *Awards, honors:* William Faulkner Foundation Award for "notable first novel," 1968, for *A Hall of Mirrors;* National Book Award, 1974, for *Dog Soldiers.*

WRITINGS—Novels: A Hall of Mirrors, Houghton, 1967; *Dog Soldiers,* Houghton, 1974.

Screenplays: "WUSA" (adapted from the novel by Stone, *A Hall of Mirrors*), Paramount, 1970; (with Judith Rascoe) "Who'll Stop the Rain" (adapted from the novel by Stone, *Dog Soldiers*), United Artists, 1978.

Also contributor to periodicals, including *Harper's.*

SIDELIGHTS: With only two novels to his credit, Stone has been hailed as one of the finest writers in the United States. Richard Locke called him "one of our best novelists under forty," and Raymond Sokolov wrote that "Stone, of all the new writers, has gone farthest into the other America and the dark side of his own mind."

Stone's first novel, *A Hall of Mirrors,* was considered the finest first novel by an American writer in 1968 by voters for the William Faulkner Award. L. Hugh Moore agreed with the selection, writing that "no recent novel has more contemporary relevance nor more radical themes." Donald Newlove summed up the novel's main character, Rheinhardt, as "a matchless juicehead, an unregenerate rogue genius of the bottle, a 29-year-old alky-and-pothead disc-jockey who is the soul of the hip '60s, shipwrecked in Dixie." In the book, Rheinhardt meets up with Geraldine; a destitute woman whose husband and child have died and who's recently been scarred by her boyfriend. Rheinhardt and Geraldine become roommates and he obtains a job as a radio announcer. In the finale, Rheinhardt wreaks havoc at a political rally in which he is the master of ceremonies. Ivan Gold wrote that this scene "outstripped" the famous "finale of Nathanael West's most ambitious book," *The Day of the Locust.* Following the turmoil at the rally, during which explosions and a murder occur, Geraldine is imprisoned. She then hangs herself and Rheinhardt prepares to leave for another town.

Moore called Stone's view of modern society "a profoundly pessimistic one." A writer for *Time* wrote, "Stone's theme is the inextricable grip of the under-world on its inhabitants; he draws a sure-handed diagram of brutal power and its victims." Yet another critic, David Thorbun, wrote, "In its earned hopelessness, *A Hall of Mirrors* sees, and dramatizes with terrible conviction, a truth which has afflicted men at all times but which presses upon us in this moment with particular intensity: that we are all prisoners, our humanity imperiled, and in the grip of monsters." Moore was even more pessimistic. "What disturbs and what makes the novel contemporarily relevant is the fact that Stone offers no melioristic possibility," he declared. "To survive in the new ice age is immoral; neither work, bitter humor, nor withdrawal is humanly possible. 'Despair and die' is the final message of the novel."

The film adaptation of *A Hall of Mirrors,* "WUSA," was not as successful as the novel. Paul Zimmerman blamed many of the film's flaws on director Stuart Rosenberg. Zimmerman wrote that "'WUSA' . . . fails to solve its structural problems" and claimed that "Rosenberg has aggravated the problem by cluttering his already overpopulated narrative with symbolic but extraneous and predictable minor characters." Zimmerman also found fault with Stone's screenplay. "These failings could be forgiven as cinematic shorthand if the principals were drawn with clarity and point," he observed. "But in his screenplay Stone has failed to liberate them from his own novel. As a result, they carry heavy but vague burdens. . . ."

Stone turned to the world of drugs for his second novel, *Dog Soldiers,* for which he received the National Book Award. It is the story of a naive American journalist in Vietnam who smuggles heroin into the U.S. and involves his wife and an unknowing friend in a harrowing attempt to sell the narcotic. P. S. Prescott called the novel, "Part melodrama, part morality play." He added, "It is a world in which innocence or vestigial remnants of decent behavior prove fatal to their owners...." Writing in the *New York Times Book Review,* Richard Locke observed, "This new book is even more violent and despairing, less sympathetic, than the first, but it is much more tightly written, more ironic."

Several critics called attention to the lack of "likeable" characters in *Dog Soldiers.* Locke wrote, "Stone's books are strong stuff: he is not hostile or self-pitying or an angry sentimentalist, but he's hardly giving aid and comfort to his readers...." He also suggested, "Stone's characters are always losers: men troubled and angry and conscience-poor, not simply macho, and women who are certainly more real and important to him (as are children) than they are for most young male writers today...." And L. L. Hill lamented that "the reader is not likely to encounter a human being in this novel whose fate he can really care about." William Pritchard noted that Stone's characters seem inclined "to speed up the trip towards death." He added that the environment in *Dog Soldiers* is "a claustrophobic world; barely a moment of impulse allowed in the direction of a better life.... Everybody is tainted, even the old people round the television in a cheap hotel . . . have 'reptile faces.'"

Reviewers had similar words for the film adaptation of *Dog Soldiers,* "Who'll Stop the Rain," although there were still complaints about the nature of the characters. David Ansen called it "a hard-hitting movie about the moment when the dreams of a generation turned into a nightmare." Penelope Gilliatt wrote that "Who'll Stop the Rain" is, "in the guise of an adventure thriller, a fine film about the rising temperature of delirium in a society that voluntarily soaks itself in stimulants and soporifics...." She also noted that the film "is stocked with a populace of beings made somnolent by drugs, drink, fear, shell shock, who gather the tatters of their outward lives around them as if the scraps were robes." But Richard Schickel seemed in agreement with some critics of the novel when he wrote, "The trouble is that the movie deals predictably with an ugly milieu (drug dealing) and with characters whom one cannot, in the end, even pity."

Despite critical acclaim, "Who'll Stop the Rain," failed to draw sizable audiences. And Stone himself complained that director Karel Reisz tampered too much with the screenplay co-written by Stone and Judith Rascoe. "I'm pleased with the film," he told Leigh Charlton, "even though I disagree with the changes in Marge's character and I'm furious about the title change. Hool? Who Will? You can't start a title like that...." Stone's disagreement with the character of Marge in the film stems from the fact that, in the book, she is already a drug-user. In "Who'll Stop the Rain," though, Marge is an innocent victim of her husband's scheme. "There's no question that Tuesday Weld could have delivered the whole character," said Stone, "but Karel felt there was not enough time to establish her prior involvement with drugs and her motivation for smuggling heroin. I didn't agree, and I would not traduce my own book." Finally, Stone conceeded that "the film is 'faithful' to the novel, but the important thing is, they are entirely separate entities."

BIOGRAPHICAL/CRITICAL SOURCES: Best Sellers, September 1, 1968; *Time,* September 8, 1967, November 11, 1974, August 21, 1978; *New York Times Book Review,* September 24, 1967, November 3, 1974; *Times Literary Supplement,* February 8, 1968; *Village Voice,* February 22, 1968, August 28, 1978; *Statesman,* February 16, 1968; *Nation,* April 1, 1968; *Commonweal,* April 5, 1968; *Newsweek,* July

22, 1968, November 9, 1970, November 11, 1974, August 21, 1978; *Critique,* Volume XI, number 3, 1968; *Hudson Review,* spring, 1975; *New York Review of Books,* April 3, 1975; *Contemporary Literary Criticism,* Volume 5, Gale, 1976; *New Yorker,* September 4, 1978.*

* * *

STONEQUIST, Everett Verner　1901-1979

OBITUARY NOTICE: Born October 5, 1901, in Worcester, Mass.; died of a heart attack, March 22, 1979, in Glens Falls, N.Y. Sociologist and author best known for his books on race relations. Stonequist explored the problems of minorities in the United States in his book *The Marginal Man.* He was chairman of the sociology department of Skidmore College for forty years. Obituaries and other sources: *New York Times,* March 28, 1979.

* * *

STOREY, Robert F(ranklin)　1945-

PERSONAL: Born October 2, 1945, in Louisville, Ky.; son of Leonard Isaac (a furniture worker) and Marjorie (Hamm) Storey; married Chompunut Bunnag (an economist), September 21, 1974. *Education:* University of Louisville, B.A., 1967; University of California, Los Angeles, M.A., 1968, Ph.D., 1972. *Politics:* None. *Religion:* None. *Home:* 119 West Stratford Ave., Lansdowne, Pa. 19050. *Office:* Department of English, Temple University, Philadelphia, Pa. 19122.

CAREER: Temple University, Philadelphia, Pa., assistant professor of English, 1972-73; University of Pennsylvania, Philadelphia, assistant professor of English, 1973-78; Temple University, assistant professor of English, 1978—.

WRITINGS: Pierrot: A Critical History of a Mask, Princeton University Press, 1978. Contributor to language and literature journals, including *Denver Quarterly* and *Mask, Mime, and Marionette.*

WORK IN PROGRESS: Pierrot Partout: A Study of Nineteenth-Century Pantomime; Games and Endgames: A Psychoanalytic Study of Three Absurdists.

SIDELIGHTS: Storey comments: "The great work of Arnold Schoenberg stands behind whatever is of value in my book on Pierrot."

* * *

STOTT, Jane　1940-

PERSONAL: Born February 21, 1940, in Rockville Centre, N.Y.; daughter of Thomas Arthur (an insurance broker) and Eula (a teacher; maiden name, Reeves) Kielty; married William Merrell Stott (a teacher and writer), June 16, 1962; children: Molly Alexander, Gordon Kielty. *Education:* Attended Wheaton College, Norton, Mass., 1958-60; Sarah Lawrence College, B.A., 1962; Stanford University, M.A., 1964. *Home:* 1213 Red Bud Trail, Austin, Tex. 78746.

CAREER: Yale University, Library, New Haven, Conn., secretary and archivist, 1962-63; Radio Senegal, Dakar, broadcaster, 1965-66; U.S. Information Agency, Fes, Morocco, instructor in English, 1966-67; Southwest Center for Educational Television, Austin, Tex., researcher, 1976; writer, 1976—. District water director in Austin, Tex., 1978—.

WRITINGS: (With husband, William Stott) *On Broadway,* University of Texas Press, 1978.

WORK IN PROGRESS: Another book with husband, William Stott.

SIDELIGHTS: Stott told *CA:* "I did *On Broadway* for the same reason I do anything: to try and make something beautiful, of course."

*   *   *

STRAUB, Peter (Francis) 1943-

PERSONAL: Born March 2, 1943, in Milwaukee, Wis.; son of Gordon Anthony and Elvena (Nilsestuen) Straub; married Susan Bitker (a counselor), August 22, 1966; children: Benjamin Bitker. *Education:* University of Wisconsin, Madison, B.A., 1965; Columbia University, M.A., 1966; further graduate study at University College, Dublin, Ireland, 1969-72. *Politics:* "Mainstream Undecided." *Home:* 79 Hillfield Ave., London N.8, England. *Agent:* Carol Smith, 2 John St., London W.1, England.

CAREER: University School, Milwaukee, Wis., teacher of English, 1966-69; writer, 1969—. *Member:* International P.E.N., Writer's Action Group, Author's Guild.

WRITINGS: Ishmael (poems), Turret Books, 1972; *Open Air* (poems), Irish University Press, 1972; *Marriages* (novel), Coward, 1973; *Julia* (novel), Coward, 1975; *If You Could See Me Now* (novel), Coward, 1977; *Ghost Story* (novel), Coward, 1979.

WORK IN PROGRESS: Shadowland, a novel, publication by Coward expected in 1981.

SIDELIGHTS: Straub comments: "I am just ending a ten-year period of living outside the United States, which was and is of great value in seeing my own country from the viewpoint of an outsider. At the moment, my chief literary aim is to explore the qualities inherent in narrative and story, which has come to seem more important to me with every book. I am interested in placing the unreal in a real context as closely defined and described as possible, and in writing lyrical and suspenseful books which might do for the supernatural story what Chandler did for the crime story."

AVOCATIONAL INTERESTS: Jazz music.

*   *   *

STRESHINSKY, Shirley G. 1934-

PERSONAL: Born October 7, 1934, in Alton, Ill.; daughter of Thomas C. (a railroad trainman) and Edna (Brinker) Gaghen; married Theodore Streshinsky (a photographer), June 16, 1966; children: Mark Theodore, Maria Ingrid. *Education:* University of Illinois, B.S., 1956. *Home address:* Box 674, Berkeley, Calif. 94701. *Agent:* Betty Anne Clarke, International Creative Management, 40 West 57th St., New York, N.Y. 10019.

CAREER: Jackson & Moreland Engineering Co., Boston, Mass., proofreader, 1956-57; *Welding Engineer* (magazine), Chicago, Ill., writer, 1957-59; First Western Bank, San Francisco, Calif., magazine editor, 1959-61; free-lance writer, 1961—. *Awards, honors:* Society of Magazine Writers Award for Excellence, 1969; National Council for Advancement of Education Writing award, 1969; Education Press award, 1969.

WRITINGS: (With Lauren Elder) *And I Alone Survived* (nonfiction), Dutton, 1978. Contributor of articles to numerous magazines, including *Ladies Home Journal, McCall's, Glamour, Redbook, Ms., Parents' Magazine,* and *Readers Digest,* and to newspapers, including *Los Angeles Times.*

WORK IN PROGRESS: A "California" novel for Putnam.

SIDELIGHTS: Streshinsky's book, *And I Alone Survived,* describes the ordeal her co-author Lauren Elder faced when the plane in which Elder was traveling crashed in the mountains en route to Death Valley, California. The pilot and other passenger, both friends of Elder, were killed. The injured survivor struggled down the mountains and ten miles further to reach safety. Even though human survival against terrific odds has been the subject of many recent books and films, wrote P. J. Earl in *Best Sellers,* "it is interesting reading, written in a breezy, conversational style. For further insight into the happening, many chapters are devoted to the emotions and feelings of Elder's family and friends as the ordeal was occurring."

In suspense, *School Library Journal* reviewer Jack Forman compared the story to *Alive,* by Piers Paul Reed, an account of the experiences of survivors of a plane crash in the Andes mountains, saying *And I Alone Survived* is "less complex and easier to read." Even though the book "begins slowly and self-consciously," he said, "it gains momentum, becoming an involving saga of heroism."

Streshinsky told *CA:* "My magazine work has covered a gamut of subjects—I've written about suicide and murder; I've written about boxers and movie stars; I've also written about the pleasures of being a parent, as well as some of the problems of working mothers (a category I happen to fall into).

BIOGRAPHICAL/CRITICAL SOURCES: Best Sellers, August, 1978; *School Library Journal,* September, 1978.

*   *   *

STRICK, Ivy 1952-

PERSONAL: Born January 5, 1952, in New York, N.Y.; daughter of Louis (in business) and Racelle (an artist; maiden name, Kessler) Strick; married J. William Keyser, September 5, 1971 (divorced November, 1978). *Education:* Attended St. John's College, Annapolis, Md., 1970-72; New York University, B.S., 1975. *Home:* 1436 Lexington Ave., #2-A, New York, N.Y. 10028.

CAREER: Jeweler, 1968-74; actress, 1975-77; writer and free-lance designer of book jackets, 1977—.

WRITINGS: Scot Free (novel), Taplinger, 1979; *The Home Makers* (novel), Taplinger, 1979; *Smitten* (novel), Taplinger, 1980.

SIDELIGHTS: Ivy Strick writes: "I didn't begin to mature until forced to give up the idea, at the age of twenty-five, that I would be a Movie Star. It was a difficult time. Life looked bleak. I began to entertain myself writing short, barbed sketches of some people I once knew. Then I linked the scenes together, thought up an exciting ending, and gave it the title *Scot Free.* I think I was alone in the belief that the novel would be completed, but discipline was never a problem because I was writing from the heart.

"Twenty-five was old for a failing actress, but twenty-seven is notably young for a novelist. I feel like I've been given a fresh start, with no penalty to pay.

"My hopes for the future include learning to be more adventurous, perhaps traveling to England or Canada. I'd like to make some friends outside my family. I often think of moving to Nashville."

*   *   *

STRINGFIELD, Leonard H(arry) 1920-

PERSONAL: Born December 17, 1920, in Cincinnati, Ohio; son of Leonard R. (a supervisor) and Mildred (Ringenberger) Stringfield; married Dell R. Romero, June 13, 1947;

children: Colette Stringfield Stegmaier, Denise Stringfield Sparks, Camille. *Education:* Attended University of Cincinnati, 1940-41. *Politics:* Conservative. *Religion:* Protestant. *Home:* 4412 Grove Ave., Cincinnati, Ohio 45227. *Office:* DuBois Chemicals, DuBois Tower, Cincinnati, Ohio 45202.

CAREER: DuBois Chemicals, Cincinnati, Ohio, director of public relations and marketing services, 1951—. Public relations director, member of board of directors, and state section director for Mutual UFO Network; investigator for Center for UFO Studies; Ohio investigator for Ground Saucer Watch. Worked on unidentified flying objects projects with Air Defense Command, U.S. Air Force, 1953-57; director of Civilian Research, Interplanetary Flying Objects, 1953-57; member of public relations staff for National Investigation Committee on Aerial Phenomena, 1957-70; early warning coordinator for Colorado Project (on unidentified flying object activity), 1967-69; adviser on unidentified flying objects to nation of Grenada, 1977-78. Teacher of ufology at high school in Cincinnati, 1969. *Military service:* U.S. Army Air Forces, Intelligence Corps, 1942-45; served in Pacific theater. *Member:* Public Relations Society of America.

WRITINGS: Inside Saucer Post, 3-0 Blue, privately printed, 1957; *Situation Red, the UFO Siege,* Doubleday, 1977. Editor and publisher of *Orbit,* 1953-57.

WORK IN PROGRESS: Continuing research on unidentified flying objects.

SIDELIGHTS: Stringfield told *CA:* "My penchant for creative writing began during my teens, when I began to feel that words and sentences should be rhetorically apt to create a mood or atmosphere for the reader with special emphasis on foreshadowing. I have a probing, curious feel for the abstract and unexplained, and following World War II, the mystery of the UFO (coupled with a firsthand experience during the war) triggered me to research. The data collected from the earliest fifties provided me with a vast archive of knowledge that I believe should be shared with the world public. Since publication of *Situation Red, The UFO Siege,* more vital data have come my way.

"This new information involves the prevalence of an official secrecy lid that conceals the fact that alien craft and humanoid entities have been recovered by our military. Intact craft, and deceased alien bodies, I am told by reliable sources, are held at Wright-Patterson Air Force Base and other security areas. My sources include medical people who relate that secret studies continue on the bodies. I have much biological data, most of which was released in a paper I presented at a research symposium on July 29, 1978 in Dayton, Ohio. The paper's title was "Retrievals of the Third Kind". I will pursue this phase of research as new data reaches me from reliable sources."

*   *   *

STROBER, Gerald S.   1935-

PERSONAL: Born October 11, 1935, in Brooklyn, N.Y.; son of Philip (in business) and Faye (Cogert) Strober; children: Robin, Jonathan, Lori. *Education:* Gordon College, B.A. (magna cum laude), 1961; New York University, M.A., 1962. *Religion:* Jewish. *Agent:* Aaron M. Priest Literary Agency, 150 East 35th St., New York, N.Y. 10016.

CAREER: Worked as private social worker, 1962-67; National Conference of Christians and Jews, New York City, research consultant, 1967-68; American Jewish Committee, New York City, human relations executive, 1968-74; Noah

Productions, New York City, vice-president, 1977—. Member of executive board of Herut-United Zionist Revisionists.

WRITINGS: (With Lowell Streiker) *Religion and the New Majority,* Association Press, 1972; *Portrait of the Elder Brother* (monograph), American Jewish Committee, 1972; *American Jews: Community in Crisis,* Doubleday, 1974; *Graham: A Day in Billy's Life,* Doubleday, 1976; *Billy Graham: His Life and Faith,* Word Books, 1977; *Aflame for God: The Jerry Falwell Story,* Thomas Nelson, 1979.

SIDELIGHTS: Strober told *CA:* "I am interested in the sociology of American religion with particular emphasis on the evangelical and fundamentalist movements. I am particularly concerned with the social and political outworkings of these movements and I am also keenly interested in tracing the careers and significance of the evangelical/fundamentalist leadership. My books on Billy Graham and Jerry Falwell have also provided the opportunity for me to obtain a close-up view of the movements these men represent."

*   *   *

STURGEON, Wina
(Cory Moore)

PERSONAL: Born in New York, N.Y.; daughter of Ralph and Florence (Price) Golden; married Theodore Sturgeon, April 16, 1969 (divorced, 1976); children: Andros. *Education:* Attended New York University and University of California, Los Angeles. *Politics:* "Humanism." *Agent:* Arthur Pine Associates, 1780 Broadway, New York, N.Y. 10019. *Office:* KBIG-Radio, 7755 Sunset, Los Angeles, Calif. 90048.

CAREER: Writer. Worked as wing rider for air shows, 1961-62; associated with International Publishing Co., 1966-69; KFWB, Hollywood, Calif., consumer reporter, 1971-77; consumer reporter for KHJ-TV and KBIG-Radio, 1977—. Also worked as dancer in Italy and as reporter for KTTV. *Awards, honors:* Emmy Award from Academy of Television Arts and Sciences, 1976; commendation from Los Angeles Board of Supervisors, 1977, for service to community.

WRITINGS: Depression: How to Recognize It, Treat It, Grow From It, Prentice-Hall, 1979. Contributor to newspapers and periodicals, often under pseudonym Cory Moore, including *Los Angeles Times.* Editor of *Teen Screen* magazine.

WORK IN PROGRESS: A book, tentatively titled *Variel;* research on mind over aging and symptoms of aging; research on "using the mind to correct chemical defects which may cause emotional disturbances."

SIDELIGHTS: Sturgeon told *CA:* "My personal belief is that the mind is the key to the problems which plague mankind. Learning more about the brain and how it functions will allow us to control certain ills such as cancer, mental illness, etc., which currently baffle medical science. Books which have impressed me include Bleibtrau's *Parable of the Beast,* and the work of Dr. Nathan Kline of New York. I have worked as a writer in London, a dancer in Italy, and a free-lance reporter in Jamaica. All of my work goes towards helping mankind understand the workings of the mind."

*   *   *

SULEIMAN, Ezra N.   1941-

PERSONAL: Born November 20, 1941, in Basra, Iraq; son of N. R. (in business) and Sophie (Jiji) Suleiman; married; wife's name, Susan (a professor of French); children: Michael, Daniel. *Education:* Harvard University, A.B. (cum laude), 1964; graduate study at University of Paris, 1963-64, and University of London, 1964; Columbia University, M.A., 1966, Ph.D., 1971. *Home:* 174 South Westgate Ave., Los Angeles, Calif. 90049. *Office:* Department of Political Science, University of California, Los Angeles, Calif. 90024.

CAREER: City University of New York, New York, N.Y., assistant professor of political science, 1971-73; University of California, Los Angeles, associate professor, 1973-76, professor of political science, 1976—. Visiting professor at University of Grenoble, 1973, and Sorbonne, University of Paris, 1973-74. *Member:* International Political Science Association, American Political Science Association, Council on European Studies, French Political Science Association. *Awards, honors:* French Government fellow, 1968-69; travel grant from European Institute at Columbia University, 1970; Ford Foundation grant, 1972-74; American Philosophical Society grant, 1973; American Council of Learned Societies fellow, 1973-74, grant, 1975; Fulbright senior scholar in France, 1977; Guggenheim fellow, 1977-78; German Marshall Fund fellow, 1978-79.

WRITINGS: (Contributor) Andrew Cordier, editor, *Columbia Essays in International Affairs: The Dean's Papers,* Columbia University Press, 1967; *Politics, Power, and Bureaucracy in France,* Princeton University Press, 1974; (editor with S. Warnecke, and contributor) *Industrial Policies in Western Europe,* Praeger, 1975; *Elites in French Society: The Politics of Survival,* Princeton University Press, 1978. Also contributor to *Two Decades of Gaullism,* edited by Stanley Hoffmann and W. G. Andrews. Contributor of articles and reviews to American and European journals in political and social sciences, and to newspapers. Member of editorial committee of *Comparative Politics,* 1973—, editor, October, 1977.

WORK IN PROGRESS: The Transformation of French Society in the Postwar Period, publication by Knopf; editing *Organizing Political Leadership,* with Richard Rose, American Enterprise Institute.

SIDELIGHTS: Suleiman comments: "My research to date bears largely on the development of European political institutions and elites. My current work attempts to examine Western European societies in a comparative perspective. Approximately half my time is spent traveling, teaching, and conducting research in Western Europe."

* * *

SUSSKIND, Charles 1921-

PERSONAL: Surname is pronounced *Zees*-kin; born August 19, 1921, in Prague, Czechoslovakia; came to the United States in 1945, naturalized citizen, 1946; son of Bruno B. (an accountant) and Gertruda (a pianist; maiden name, Seger) Susskind; married Thelma Gabriel (a publisher), May 1, 1945; children: Pamela, Peter, Amanda. *Education:* California Institute of Technology, B.S., 1948; Yale University, M.Eng., 1949, Ph.D., 1951. *Politics:* Republican. *Office:* College of Engineering, University of California, Berkeley, Calif. 94720.

CAREER: Stanford University, Stanford, Calif., research associate and lecturer in engineering, 1951-55; University of California, Berkeley, assistant professor, 1955-58, associate professor, 1958-64, professor of engineering science, 1964—. Member of board of directors of San Francisco Press. *Military service:* U.S. Army Air Forces, 1942-45. *Member:* American Association for the Advancement of Science, Society for the History of Technology (member of advisory

council), History of Science Society, Institute of Electrical and Electronics Engineers (fellow), Bioengineering Society, Institution of Electronic and Radio Engineers (England). *Awards, honors:* Clark Maxwell Premium from British Institution of Radio Engineers, 1952; National Science Foundation senior faculty fellow, 1968-69.

WRITINGS: (Editor) *Encyclopedia of Electronics,* Van Nostrand, 1962; (with Marvin Chodorow) *Fundamentals of Microwave Electronics,* McGraw, 1964; (with Lynn Shell) *Exporting Technical Education,* Institute of International Education, 1968; *Understanding Technology,* Johns Hopkins Press, 1973; *Twenty-five Engineers and Inventors,* San Francisco Press, 1976. Contributor to *Encyclopaedia Britannica.* Contributor of more than one hundred articles to journals.

WORK IN PROGRESS: With Friedrich Kurylo, a biography of physicist and Nobel Prize winner Ferdinand Braun, for M.I.T. Press; *History of Electricity in Medicine,* with Margaret Rowbottom, publication expected in 1980; a history of radar; a biography of Heinrich Hertz, who discovered electromagnetic-wave propagation.

SIDELIGHTS: Susskind comments: "I have a somewhat unusual career as a research engineer and educator whose avocation (history of science and technology) has become a major professional interest, and has led to the establishment of pioneering courses at Berkeley on the historical and social aspects of technology. Relatively few books about technology are written by engineers, who are generally put down as inarticulate—a stereotype I am doing my best to controvert."

* * *

SUTHERLAND, Elizabeth 1926-

PERSONAL: Born August 24, 1926, in Kemback, Fife, Scotland; daughter of Kenneth (a clergyman) and Mary Coventry (Aitken) Sutherland-Graeme; married John Dixon Marshall (a clergyman), December 31, 1946; children: Michael, Jeremy, Alison. *Education:* University of Edinburgh, certificate, 1946. *Politics:* "Liberal to Labour." *Religion:* Episcopal Church in Scotland. *Home:* 21 Swinton Rd., Baillieston, Glasgow 69, Scotland. *Agent:* Murray J. Pollinger, 4 Garrick St., London WC2E 9BH, England.

CAREER: Scottish Episcopal Church, Edinburgh, assistant social worker, 1974—. *Member:* Scottish P.E.N., Glasgow Writers Club, Arts Centre Group. *Awards, honors:* Constable trophy, 1972, for *Lent Term;* book award from Scottish Arts Council, 1976, for *Hannah Hereafter.*

WRITINGS: The Black Isle: A Portrait of the Past (guidebook), Prothero Books, 1973; *Lent Term* (novel), Constable, 1973; *The Seer of Kintail* (historical novel), Constable, 1974; *Hannah Hereafter* (novel), Constable, 1976, Harcourt, 1978; *The Eye of God* (historical novel), Constable, 1977; (author of notes), Alex Mackenzie, *The Prophecies of the Brahan Seer,* Constable, 1977. Contributor to history journals.

WORK IN PROGRESS: A novel about the Scottish highland clearances of the eighteenth and nineteenth centuries, publication by Constable; a contemporary novel on changes brought about by oil explorations off the Scottish coast.

SIDELIGHTS: Sutherland commented: "I like to explore a theme in my novels. For example, in *Lent Term* I was interested in comparing sexual and marital love. For a clergy wife to have tackled such a subject caused a small furor in Scotland at the time! In *Hannah Hereafter,* I wanted to think about death. As a result, I was able to examine my own thoughts at a far deeper level than before and this is one of the bonuses I enjoy most about writing novels. Although the *Eye of God* and the *Seer of Kintail* were about witchcraft and second sight in the Highlands, the themes were 'judgement' and 'precognition' in all their different aspects, and in my most recently completed book about the Highland clearances by the nineteenth century, the theme is 'roots.' How much does it change and affect a personality to be forcibly transferred from one piece of territory to another. In my next book, which will have a strong supernatural flavour, I want to think about 'change.'

"Although I've written all my life, I have served a long apprenticeship writing articles, children's stories, poetry, and short stories which have appeared in a variety of papers and magazines. I finally achieved publication with my fifth novel. I like to write early in the morning when my mind is fresh and uncluttered by the problems of families connected with my work. One of my chief joys in life is the company of children. I passionately believe in the importance of a happy childhood and my work as a social worker in the east end of Glasgow is mainly directed to this end."

AVOCATIONAL INTERESTS: Walking, country life, good food, conversation ("gossip!"), people.

*   *   *

SUTTLES, Gerald   1932-

PERSONAL: Born November 11, 1932, in Madison County, N.C. *Education:* Reed College, B.A., 1959; University of Illinois, M.A., 1962, Ph.D, 1966. *Home:* 5850 North Drake, Chicago, Ill. 60659. *Office:* Department of Sociology, University of Chicago, Chicago, Ill. 60637.

CAREER: Intern at National Training School, 1962; Institute for Social Research, Chicago, Ill., field associate, 1963-66; University of Michigan, Ann Arbor, assistant professor of sociology, 1966-67; University of Chicago, Chicago, Ill., associate professor of sociology, 1967-71; State University of New York at Albany, associate professor, 1971-72, professor of sociology, 1972-76; University of Chicago, professor of sociology, 1976—. *Military service:* U.S. Navy, 1951-55. *Member:* American Sociological Association, Society for the Study of Social Problems, Phi Beta Kappa. *Awards, honors:* Woodrow Wilson fellow; C. Wright Mills Award, 1969; Lating Award from University of Chicago Press, 1970.

WRITINGS: (Contributor) Klein and Myerhoff, editors, *Juvenile Gangs in Context: Theory Research and Action,* University of Southern California Press, 1963; *The Social Order of the Slum,* University of Chicago Press, 1968; (contributor) Daniel Glaser, editor, *Crime in the City,* Harper, 1970; (contributor) George McCall, editor, *Social Relations,* Aldine, 1970; (contributor) Laumann, Seigle, and Hodge, editors, *The Logic of Social Hierarchies,* Markham, 1970; *The Social Construction of Communities,* University of Chicago Press, 1972; (contributor) A. Hawley and V. Rock, editors, *Metropolitan America: A Contemporary Perspective,* Sage Publications, 1975; (contributor) A. Inkeles, J. Coleman, and N. Smelser, editors, *Annual Review of Sociology,* Sage Publications, 1976; (author of introduction) Ellsworth Faris, *The Nature of Human Nature,* University of Chicago Press, 1977; (with Kirsten A. Groenbjerg and David P. Street) *Poverty and Social Change,* University of Chicago Press, 1978; (contributor) Street, editor, *Handbook of Urban Life,* Jossey-Bass, 1978.

General editor of "The City and Society," a series, Sage Publications. Contributor to journals in the behavioral sciences. Associate editor of *American Journal of Sociology,* 1969-71, member of editorial board, 1976—; associate editor of *American Sociological Review,* 1976—; consulting editor of *Urban Life,* 1972—.

*   *   *

SUTTON, Walter   1916-

PERSONAL: Born January 25, 1916, in Milwaukee, Wis.; son of Walter Evender and Maud (Farrington) Sutton; married Vivian Irene Ryan, December 22, 1941; children: Catherine Beth Sutton Penner. *Education:* Heidelberg College, B.A., 1937; Ohio State University, M.A., 1938, Ph.D., 1946. *Office:* Department of English, Syracuse University, 203 Hall of Languages, Syracuse, N.Y. 13210.

CAREER: University of Rochester, Rochester, N.Y., instructor in English, 1946-47; Syracuse University, Syracuse, N.Y., assistant professor, 1948-52, associate professor, 1952-59, professor of English, 1959-71, distinguished professor of humanities, 1971—, director of graduate studies, 1968-71, head of department of English, 1971-74. Visiting professor at University of Minnesota, University of Washington, Seattle, Princeton University, Colgate University, and University of Hawaii. Lecturer at universities and meetings in England, Germany, the Netherlands, and Romania. *Military service:* U.S. Coast Guard, 1942-45.

MEMBER: Modern Language Association of America, American Studies Association, American Society for Aesthetics, American Association of University Professors. *Awards, honors:* Howald Fellow at Ohio State University, 1947-48; senior visiting fellow of Council of the Humanities at Princeton University, 1960-61; Ohioana Book Award, 1963, for *The Western Book Trade.*

WRITINGS: The Western Book Trade, Ohio State University Press, 1961; *Modern American Criticism,* Prentice-Hall, 1963; (editor) *Ezra Pound: A Collection of Critical Essays,* Prentice-Hall, 1963; (editor with Richard Foster) *Modern Criticism: Theory and Practice,* Odyssey, 1963; (editor with wife, Vivian Sutton) *Plato to Alexander Pope: Backgrounds of Modern Criticism,* Odyssey, 1966; (editor with Harrison Meserole and Brom Weber) *American Literature: Tradition and Innovation,* two volumes, Heath, 1969, revised edition, four volumes, 1974; *American Free Verse: The Modern Revolution in Poetry,* New Directions, 1973.

Contributor: Roy Harvey Pearce, editor, *Whitman: A Collection of Critical Essays,* Prentice-Hall, 1962; Irvin Ehrenpreis, editor, *American Poetry,* Edwin Arnold, 1965; *Humanistic Scholarship in America,* Princeton University Press, 1966; Jiri Levy, editor, *Zapadni Literarni Veda a Estetika,* Ceskoslovensky Spisovatel, 1966; *Proceedings of the Fifth International Congress of Aesthetics, Amsterdam, 1964,* Mouton, 1968; Joseph Katz, *The Blue Hotel,* Merrill, 1969; Haskell S. Springer, editor, *Studies in Billy Budd,* Merrill, 1970; Brom Weber, editor, *Sense and Sensibility in Twentieth-Century Writing,* Southern Illinois University Press, 1970; John Engels, editor, *Studies in Paterson,* Merrill, 1971; Linda W. Wagner, editor, *Interviews With William Carlos Williams,* New Directions, 1976; Louis J. Budd and Edwin H. Cady, editors, *The New American Literary History,* Duke University Press, in press.

Contributor to professional journals and literary magazines. Head of editorial committee at Syracuse University Press, 1962-67; member of advisory board of *Style,* 1966—; member of board of editors of *American Literature,* 1973-76.

WORK IN PROGRESS: Research on the epic tradition in American literature and the relationship between contemporary American criticism and poetry.

SIDELIGHTS: Sutton told *CA:* "I consider myself fortunate to be a university teacher of literature both because of the nature of my subject (a privilege to talk and write about) and because of the opportunity my work affords for continuing contact with younger people embarking on the same career. Each year, as eager new students appear in classes, I am reminded of Carl Sandburg's felicitous autobiographical title 'Always the Young Strangers.' In my teaching and writing I have always attempted to resist hermetic formalism of whatever fashion, and to relate literature in the broadest possible way to its social environment, the soil from which it grows."

AVOCATIONAL INTERESTS: Traveling.

* * *

SWAIN, Martha H(elen) 1929-

PERSONAL: Born June 21, 1929, in Cape Girardeau, Mo.; daughter of Jim Henry (a civil engineer) and Verna (Welborn) Swain. *Education:* Mississippi State University, B.S., 1950; Vanderbilt University, M.A., 1953, Ph.D., 1975. *Politics:* Democrat. *Religion:* Presbyterian. *Home:* 613 Grove St., Denton, Tex. 76201. *Office:* Department of History and Government, Texas Woman's University, Denton, Tex. 76204.

CAREER: Public school teacher in Vardaman, Miss., 1950-53, and Natchez, Miss., 1953-56; high school teacher of social studies in Pensacola, Fla., 1956-63; Florida State University, Tallahassee, assistant professor of social studies education, 1963-64; high school teacher in Pensacola, 1963-69; Texas Woman's University, Denton, instructor, 1974-75, associate professor of history, 1975—, head of department of history and government, 1978—. Summer instructor at Stetson University, 1959-64, and Rutgers University, 1965. Member of Denton County Historical Commission. *Member:* American Historical Association, National Council for the Social Studies, American Association of University Women (local vice-president, 1975-77), Southern Historical Association, Mississippi Historical Society, Delta Kappa Gamma, Phi Delta Kappa, Phi Alpha Theta. *Awards, honors:* Award from *Journal of Mississippi History,* 1976, for "The Lion and the Fox: President Franklin D. Roosevelt and Senator Pat Harrison"; research grant from Eleanor Roosevelt Institute, 1976.

WRITINGS: Pat Harrison: The New Deal Years, University Press of Mississippi, 1978. Contributor to history and regional studies journals.

WORK IN PROGRESS: The New Deal and Women's Relief Work; research on twentieth-century Mississippi social issues.

SIDELIGHTS: Martha Swain writes: "I am happy that I am old enough to remember many of the personalities, problems, and issues in Mississippi history that interest me. I am also vastly interested in all twentieth-century southern political figures and research in the rich manuscript collections that are open to research. I feel that the greatest simulus for my research came from the professional training that I had at Mississippi State and at Vanderbilt. I hope that my future publications will help elevate a number of southern political figures to the recognition they deserve among historians and the general public."

* * *

SWEET, Robert Burdette 1930-

PERSONAL: Born February 21, 1930, in Chicago, Ill.; son of Arthur Burdette (in insurance sales) and Helen (Rippe) Sweet. *Education:* Cornell College, Mt. Vernon, Iowa, B.A., 1951; graduate study at Northwestern University, 1953; Middlebury College, M.A., 1958; University of Denver, Ph.D., 1969. *Home:* 649 Partridge, Menlo Park, Calif. 94025. *Agent:* John Schaffner Literary Agency, 425 East 51st St., New York, N.Y. 10022. *Office:* Department of English, San Jose State University, San Jose, Calif. 95192.

CAREER: High school teacher of English in Winnetka, Ill., 1953-59; Wright Junior College, Chicago, Ill., member of faculty, 1961-63; Kendall College, Evanston, Ill., member of faculty, 1963-68; San Jose State University, San Jose, Calif., associate professor of English, 1970—. *Member:* National Council of Teachers of English (member of Commission on Composition, 1967-68). *Awards, honors:* First prize from Evanston Drama Club, 1966, for "Memory of Fire."

WRITINGS: Memory of Fire (stories and a play, "Memory of Fire"; three-act; first produced in Evanston, Ill., at Kendal College, 1966), East West Publications, 1967; *The Mambo* (novel), Echo Publishers West, 1975; *Dame America* (story cycle), Barlenmir, 1978; *Akbar* (novel), Heinemann, 1979.

Work anthologized in *Mixed Bag,* edited by Helene Hutchinson, Scott, Foresman, 1970, and *The Far Side of the Storm: New Ranges of Western Fiction,* edited by Gary Elder, San Marcos Press, 1975. Contributor of stories and poems to literary journals, including *Chicago Review, Western Humanities Review, New York Quarterly,* and *Occident.*

WORK IN PROGRESS: The Lord of the Mayas, a historical novel.

SIDELIGHTS: Sweet writes: "I have traveled in India, Yucatan, Malaysia, Greece, Bali, and the West Indies, where many of my stories, poems, and plays are set. Years after the event they can be recalled as places of impossible transformations, dreams of fire, where the unconscious is revealed." *Avocational interests:* Painting, piano, composing music, mountain hiking.

BIOGRAPHICAL/CRITICAL SOURCES: Small Press Review, January, 1975; *Spartan Daily,* November 4, 1975.

* * *

SWINTON, George 1917-

PERSONAL: Born April 17, 1917, in Vienna, Austria; married; children: two. *Education:* McGill University, B.A., 1946; also attended Montreal School of Art and Design, 1946-47, and Art Students' League of New York, 1949-50. *Religion:* "Non-denominational Christian." *Office:* Carleton University, Ottawa, Ontario, Canada.

CAREER: Saskatoon Art Centre, Saskatoon, Saskatchewan, curator, 1947-49; associated with Smith College, Northampton, Mass., 1950-53; Queen's University, Kingston, Ontario, artist-in-residence, 1953-54; National Gallery of Canada, Ottawa, assistant chief of industrial design, 1954; University of Manitoba, Winnipeg, member of faculty, 1954-68, professor of art, 1968-74, adjunct professor of anthropology, 1970-74; Carleton University, Ottawa, Ontario, sessional lecturer, 1973-74, professor of art history, 1974—. Artist, with more than thirty solo shows in Canada and the United States; represented in public and private collections, including National Gallery of Canada and Smith College Museum. Associated with television shows, including "Art in Action," Canadian Broadcasting Corp. (CBC), 1959-62, "Telescope," (CBC), 1965, "School TV," (CBC), 1970, "Eskimo Art and Culture," (CBC), 1970-71, and "Sweet Are the Uses of Adversity," (CBC), 1974; guest on television and radio programs. Visiting lecturer at Walter Vincent Smith Museum, 1950-53, University of Massachusetts, 1951-53, and Hillyer College, 1952-53; visiting professor at Simon Fraser University, 1972, University of Wisconsin, Madison, 1974; speaker at major U.S. and Canadian schools, art centers, galleries, and museums. Member of Canadian Eskimo Arts Council, 1967-73. Member of board of governors of Winnipeg Art Gallery, 1972-73; consultant to Christies of Canada, Canadian Postal Services, and Inuit Cultural Institute. *Military service:* Canadian Army, Intelligence Corps; became captain. *Member:* Canadian Society for Graphic Arts (western representative, 1960-63). *Awards, honors:* Canada Council senior fellow, 1959-60, grants, 1965, 1972; first prizes from Philadelphia Print Club, 1951, and Winnipeg Show, 1960; purchase prizes from two Canadian Biennials and from Hamilton Winter Exhibition, 1963; grant from Donner Canadian Foundation, 1974-76.

WRITINGS: (With Donald Buchanan) *What Is Good Design?,* NIDC, 1954; *Painting in Canada's Prairie Provinces Today,* Dallas Museum of Contemporary Arts, 1957; *Eskimo Sculpture,* McClelland & Stewart, 1965; *Tiktak: Sculptor From Rankin Inlet, N.W.T.,* University of Manitoba Press, 1970; *Eskimo Fantastic Art,* Gallery, University of Manitoba, 1972; *Sculpture of the Eskimo,* New York Graphic Society, 1972; *The Inuit: Cultures and Art,* McClelland & Stewart, 1979.

Contributor: (Illustrator) Thomas Saunders, *Red River of the North,* Peguis Publishers, 1970; (author of introduction) *Life With the Esquimaux,* new edition (Swinton was not associated with 1st edition), M. G. Hurtig, 1970; *Sculpture/Inuit: Masterworks of the Canadian Arctic,* University of Toronto Press, 1971; (author of introduction) *Baker Lake Prints, 1972,* Sanavik Co-Operative, 1972; (author of introduction) *Arctic Quebec Prints,* La Federation des cooperatives du Nouveau Quebec, 1972; (author of introduction) Armand Tagoona, *Shadows,* Oberon, 1975; *New Perspectives in Canadian Archaeology,* Royal Society of Canada, 1977. Also contributor to *Art, Artisans and Society,* 1978, and *Eskimo Games and Play,* 1978.

Author of a weekly column in *Saskatoon Star Phoenix,* 1947-49; art critic for *Winnipeg Tribune,* 1954-58. Contributor to *Collier's Encyclopedia.* Contributor of about forty articles to art journals, popular magazines, including *Natural History* and *Canadian Forum,* and newspapers.

WORK IN PROGRESS: "Form, Content and Technology in Prehistoric Canadian Eskimo Art," to be included in *Primitive Technology and Art.*

* * *

SWORD, Wiley 1937-

PERSONAL: Born December 7, 1937, in Mexico, Mo.; son of Winfield E. (a manufacturer's representative) and Genevieve (Johnson) Sword; married Marianne Cusenza, January 20, 1968; children: Greg, Andy. *Education:* University of Michigan, B.B.A., 1959. *Home:* 5640 Kolly Rd., Birming-

ham, Mich. 48010. *Office:* Techni-Cast, Inc., 24001 Southfield Rd., Southfield, Mich. 48075.

CAREER: Techni-Cast, Inc., Southfield, Mich., manufacturer's agent for automotive and industrial supplies, 1960—. *Military service:* Michigan Air National Guard, 1960-66; became lieutenant.

WRITINGS: Shiloh: Bloody April (nonfiction), Morrow, 1974. Contributor to magazines.

WORK IN PROGRESS: Bitter Victory, "the first comprehensive study of a largely unknown American war—the Indian-American War of 1790-1795."

SIDELIGHTS: Sword writes: "A strong interest in American military history initiated my work on Shiloh. My perspective in writing has been to emphasize the personal aspects in interpreting the dramatic events of our past. By means of primary research I plan to continue the quest to explain in popular terms some of the significant, if often overlooked, aspects of our history."

AVOCATIONAL INTERESTS: Golf, collecting military antiquities.

* * *

SYMONS, (Dorothy) Geraldine 1909-
(Georgina Groves)

PERSONAL: Born August 13, 1909, in Newara Elya, Ceylon; daughter of Frank Albert (a military physician) and Dorothy (Bennett) Symons. *Education:* Attended school in Salisbury, England. *Politics:* Conservative. *Religion:* Anglican. *Home:* 4 De Vaux Pl., Salisbury, England. *Agent:* Curtis Brown Ltd., 1 Craven Hill, London, England.

CAREER: Writer. Guide to historic homes, 1950-69. *Wartime service:* Red Cross, 1939-42; ambulance driver, 1940-42. Y.W.C.A., with Voluntary Aid Detachment, 1943-46.

WRITINGS: All Souls (novel), Longmans, Green, 1950; *French Windows* (novel), Longmans, Green, 1952; *Children in the Close* (biography), Batsford, 1959; *The Suckling* (novel), Macmillan, 1969.

Juveniles: *The Rose Window,* Heinemann, 1964; *The Quarantine Child,* Heinemann, 1966; (under pseudonym Georgina Groves) *Morning Glory,* Whiting & Wheaton, 1966; *The Workhouse Child,* Macmillan, 1969; *Miss Rivers and Miss Bridges,* Macmillan, 1971; *Mademoiselle,* Macmillan, 1973; *Now and Then,* Faber, 1977, published as *Crocuses Were Over, Hitler Was Dead,* Lippincott, 1978; *Second Cousins Once Removed,* Macmillan, 1978.

WORK IN PROGRESS: Mrs. Trog, a sequel to *Second Cousins Once Removed.*

SIDELIGHTS: The Suckling was adapted for a radio program for the British Broadcasting Corp., 1972. *The Workhouse Child* is presently being adapted for television.

BIOGRAPHICAL/CRITICAL SOURCES: Times Literary Supplement, April 6, 1973.

T

TAAFFE, Edward James 1921-

PERSONAL: Born December 11, 1921, in Chicago, Ill.; son of Edward James and Julia Loretta (Murphy) Taaffe; married Marialyce Dunne, September 8, 1948; children: Maura Joan, Edward James, Michael Robert, Julie Ann, Susan Deirdre, Brian Thomas, Karen Elizabeth, David Matthew. Education: New York University, B.S. (meteorology), 1944; University of Illinois, B.S. (journalism), 1945; University of Chicago, S.M., 1949, Ph.D., 1952. Home: 4314 Olentangy Blvd., Columbus, Ohio 43214. Office: Department of Geography, Ohio State University, Columbus, Ohio 43210.

CAREER: University of Illinois at Chicago Circle, Chicago, instructor in geography, 1948-51; Loyola University, Chicago, Ill., assistant professor of geography and economics, 1951-56; Northwestern University, Evanston, Ill., 1956-63, began as assistant professor, became associate professor of geography; Ohio State University, Columbus, currently professor of geography and head of department. Member of board of directors of Social Science Research Council, 1971-72; member of geography and earth science committee of National Academy of Sciences-National Research Council, 1964. Military service: U.S. Army Air Forces, 1943-46. Member: Association of American Geographers (vice-president, 1970-71; president, 1972-73), American Geographical Society, Regional Science Association, Sigma Xi.

WRITINGS: (With Barry J. Garner and Maurice H. Yeates) The Peripheral Journey to Work: A Geographical Consideration, Northwestern University Press, 1963; (editor with Robert Henry Tufrey Smith) Readings in Economic Geography, Rand McNally, 1968; (editor) Geography, Prentice-Hall, 1970; (with Howard L. Gauthier, Jr.) Geography of Transportation, Prentice-Hall, 1973.

*　　*　　*

TACHAU, Mary K(atherine) Bonsteel 1926-

PERSONAL: Born June 8, 1926, in Cleveland, Ohio; daughter of Max Kilbourne (a teacher and insurance agent) and Ruth McKee (a social worker; maiden name, Neitzel) Bonsteel; married Eric S. Tachau (an insurance executive), September 6, 1947; children: Katherine Hutchins, Susan McKee, David Brandeis. Education: Oberlin College, A.B., 1948; University of Louisville, M.A., 1958; University of Kentucky, Ph.D., 1972. Politics: "Democratic. A knee-jerk liberal; leftish." Religion: Unitarian-Universalist. Home:

3710 Fairway Lane, Louisville, Ky. 40207. Office: Department of History, University of Louisville, 101-B Gottschalk Hall, Louisville, Ky. 40208.

CAREER: University of Louisville, Louisville, Ky., lecturer, 1958-61, instructor, 1961-65, assistant professor, 1965-72, associate professor of history, 1972—, head of department, 1974-77, ombudsman, 1972-74, member of board of trustees of the university, 1976-77. Co-administrator of Kentucky Federal Judicial Selection Commission, 1977—; member of advisory committee on Kentucky Constitution, 1978—; co-ordinator of Legislative Action for Women, 1978—. Member of executive committee of Allied Organizations for Civil Rights, 1964-68.

MEMBER: American Historical Association, Organization of American Historians, American Society for Legal History, Society for Historians of the Early American Republic, American Association of University Professors (local president, 1975-76), Filson Club, Southern Historical Association. Awards, honors: American Bar Foundation fellow, 1977-78.

WRITINGS: Federal Courts in the Early Republic: Kentucky, 1789-1816, Princeton University Press, 1978. Contributor of articles and reviews to scholarly journals.

WORK IN PROGRESS: Judicial Federalism, a study of the Pennsylvania federal and state courts, 1789-circa 1820; Congress Shall Make No Law, on the original intent of the free speech provision of the First Amendment to the Constitution; Andrew Jackson and the Law; Whiskey Rebellion; Hidden and Covered Up.

SIDELIGHTS: Mary Tachau comments: "Like many women of my generation, I spent ten years doing what the culture expected me to do: having babies, keeping house, engaging in volunteer community work. Through the latter I discovered that I love to teach. Because I have a wise husband and responsible children, I was able to build a career that, as it happened, converged with the women's movement. I am committed to civil liberties and civil rights, and to securing equal opportunities for all so that they can develop their full human potential."

*　　*　　*

TAITZ, Emily 1937-

PERSONAL: Born May 5, 1937, in New York; daughter of Max (an architect) and Sylvia (a bookkeeper; maiden name,

Leinseider) Siegel; married Isaac Taitz (a real estate investor), December 21, 1958; children: Daniel, Tamar, Miriam, Ariel. *Education:* Queens College (now of the City University of New York), B.A., 1958. *Religion:* Jewish. *Home and office:* 2 Sycamore Dr., Great Neck, N.Y. 11021.

CAREER: Louis Harris Poll, New York City, secretary, 1958-59; Empress Travel, New York City, travel agent, 1959-60; writer, 1970—. Lecturer; teacher of adult education classes in Jewish studies; member of Women's Center of Nassau County. *Member:* Jewish Feminist Organization (founding member of local branch).

WRITINGS: (With Sondra Henry) *Written Out of History: A Hidden Legacy of Jewish Women as Revealed Through Their Writings and Letters,* Bloch Publishing, 1978, study guide, 1979. Contributor to *Jewish Digest* and *Outlook.* Literary editor of *Light.*

WORK IN PROGRESS: We Also March for Freedom, a juvenile novel based on Jewish holidays; research on Jewish women in history since 1800; *A Real Jewish Princess and Other Stories.*

SIDELIGHTS: Taitz writes: "My immediate motivation for writing my book was the shocking lack of information in history books on Jewish (or any) women, and the considerable contributions of women to the human race and the Jewish people.

"I first became interested in Jewish law involving women through my activities with the Women's Center Speakers Bureau and the Jewish Feminist Organization. I soon began writing articles on this subject, then books. I expect to continue writing, and do not rule out other subject areas for the future.

"I have traveled extensively in Europe. We travel to Israel frequently, not only because my husband grew up there, but also because it is a country in which I feel very much at home culturally. I speak Hebrew and this, as well as my cultural interest in Judaism, has channeled my writing interests."

* * *

TAMMUZ, Benjamin 1919-

PERSONAL: Name legally changed, 1939; born July 11, 1919, in Kharkov, Russia; emigrated to Israel, 1924; son of Joseph and Sophia (Segal) Kammerstein; married Miriam Solberg, November 5, 1946; children: On, Jonathan. *Education:* Attended Herzlia College, 1936, and Sorbonne, University of Paris, 1950-51. *Religion:* Jewish. *Home:* 13 Levy Izhak, Tel-Aviv, Israel.

CAREER: Sculptor, 1938-39; member of "Palmah" underground, 1942-43; newspaper censor, 1946-47; *Yom-Yom* (daily newspaper), Tel-Aviv, Israel, editor, 1948-50; *Ha'aretz Shelana* (weekly newspaper), Tel-Aviv, editor, 1950-65; *Ha'aretz* (daily newspaper), Tel-Aviv, editor of literary supplement, 1965-78; free-lance writer, 1978—. Sculptor. Cultural affairs counselor at Israel's embassy in London, England, 1971-75. *Military service:* Liaison officer with Armed Forces in Middle East, 1944-45.

MEMBER: Israel Writers Association, Painters and Sculptors Association. *Awards, honors:* Talpir Literary Prize, 1966, for "Elyakum" trilogy; literary prize from Israel's Ministry of Culture, 1968, for children's books; literary prize from Prime Minister of Israel, 1977, for body of work; Jena literary prize from Mexico, 1979, for *Requiem for Na'aman.*

WRITINGS: (Editor with Max Wykes-Joyce) *Art in Israel,*

Massada Publishing, 1965, Chilton, 1967; *Be-sof ma'arov,* 1966, translation by Joseph Schachter published as *Castle in Spain,* Bobbs-Merrill, 1973; (editor with Leon Yudkin) *Meetings With the Angel,* Deutsch, 1973; (editor) *The Story of Art in Israel,* Massada Publishing, 1979; *Requiem for Na'aman* (novel), translation by Richard Flantz, New American Library, 1979.

Holot zahav (stories; title means "Sands of Gold"), 1950; *Gan Naul* (stories; title means "A Garden Enclosed"), 1957; *A Boat Sails to Sea,* 1958; *Night on the Western Bank* (novel for children), 1959; *Sipur Anton ha-Armeni ve-sipurim aberim* (stories; title means "Anton the Armenian and Other Stories"), 1964; *Laylah be-Roma* (title means "A Night in Rome"), 1964; *Hayei Elyakum* (novel; title means "The Life of Elyakum"), 1965; *Kat shel kelavim* (title means "Pack of Dogs"), 1968; *Sefer Hahazayoth* (title means "Book of Hallucinations"), 1969; *Ya'akov* (novel; title means "Jacob"), 1971; *Ha-Pardes* (title means "The Orchard"), 1971; *Rizi the Dog* (novel for children), 1971; *Ang'iyoksil: Terufah nedirah* (title means "Angioxyl, A Rare Cure"), 1973; *Bottle Parallels* (novel), 1975; *The King Sleeps Four Times a Day* (novel for children), 1979; *The Scent of Geranium* (stories), 1979; *The Second Soul* (novel for children), 1979; *Alexander Abrmov* (novel), 1980.

Art critic for *Ha'aretz,* 1948-58.

* * *

TANNER, Tony 1935-

PERSONAL: Born, 1935, in Richmond, Surrey, England; *Education:* Jesus College, Cambridge, B.A. *Office:* Department of English, King's College, Cambridge University, Cambridge, England.

CAREER: Literary critic. Cambridge University, King's College, Cambridge, England, director of English studies, 1964—. Visiting professor at Northwestern University, Emory University, and Stanford University. *Awards, honors:* Harkness Fellowship; fellowship from American Council of Learned Societies.

WRITINGS: Conrad: Lord Jim (criticism), Barron's Educational Guide, 1963; *The Reign of Wonder: Naivety and Reality in American Literature,* Cambridge University Press, 1965; *Saul Bellow* (criticism), Oliver & Boyd, 1965, Barnes & Noble, 1967; (editor) Jane Austen, *Mansfield Park,* Penguin, 1966; (editor) *Henry James: Modern Judgments,* Macmillan, 1968; (editor) Henry James, *Hawthorne,* St. Martin's Press, 1968; *City of Words: American Fiction, 1950-1970,* Harper, 1971; *Problems and Roles of the American Artist as Portrayed by the American Novelist,* Oxford University Press for the British Academy, 1971; (editor) Austen, *Pride and Prejudice,* Penguin, 1972. Also editor of *Sense and Sensibility* by Austen.

SIDELIGHTS: Tanner's most recent work that received a great deal of critical attention is *City of Words,* an investigation into the stylistic innovations and dilemmas of more than twenty modern American writers. In reference to Tanner's variety of subjects, B. F. Dick noted, "One expected Tanner to be familiar with Bellow, Roth, Malamud, Mailer, Updike, et al.; but he has conserved his best writing for Thomas Pynchon, John Hawkes, and William Gaddis...." Dick added that Tanner's "style is dazzling...." Jonathan Raban also praised Tanner's style. He wrote that *City of Words* "has all the flash and parry, the taste for provocative intellectual games and puzzles, the passionate enthusiasm for what's new, of a packed undergraduate course in the hands of a hard-headed good talker."

However, Raban was dissatisfied with Tanner's "readings of almost every novelist in the book. . . ." Raban wrote that Tanner was "very good at detecting and admiring precision engineering but disappointingly inept at seeing why the structure was needed in the first place." A critic in *Times Literary Supplement* was similarly dismayed by Tanner's undecisive summations of the authors discussed in the book. The critic did acknowledge that the book contained "some interesting passages on Mailer, Bellow and Heller," but concluded that "otherwise the book is a disappointment." The reviewer blamed the flaws on Tanner's "uncritical approach—a suspension of judgment which he justifies as essential to the appreciation of diversity and variety. . . ."

BIOGRAPHICAL/CRITICAL SOURCES: New Statesman, March 19, 1971; *Times Literary Supplement,* July 16, 1971; *Saturday Review,* August 28, 1971.*

*   *   *

TATAR, Maria M. 1945-

PERSONAL: Born May 13, 1945, in Pressath, Germany; came to the United States in 1951, naturalized citizen, 1956; daughter of Joseph (a physician) and Elizabeth (Demeter) Tatar. *Education:* Denison University, B.A., 1967; Princeton University, M.A., 1969, Ph.D., 1971. *Home:* 143 Walden St., Cambridge, Mass. 02140. *Office:* Department of Germanic Languages and Literatures, Harvard University, 422 Boylston Hall, Cambridge, Mass. 02138.

CAREER: Harvard University, Cambridge, Mass., assistant professor, 1971-77, associate professor of German, 1977—. *Member:* Modern Language Association of America, American Association of Teachers of German, Phi Beta Kappa. *Awards, honors:* Fulbright fellow, 1969-70; National Endowment for the Humanities fellow, 1974-75; Radcliffe Institute fellow, 1977-79.

WRITINGS: Spellbound: Studies on Mesmerism and Literature, Princeton University Press, 1978. Contributor to language and literature journals.

WORK IN PROGRESS: A book on German Romanticism.

*   *   *

TATE, (John Orley) Allen 1899-1979

OBITUARY NOTICE—See index for *CA* sketch: Born November 19, 1899, in Winchester, Ky.; died February 9, 1979, in Nashville, Tenn. Poet, critic, editor, novelist, biographer, and educator. Tate began his literary career in the 1920's when he and several friends, including Robert Penn Warren and John Crow Ransom, founded the literary magazine, *The Fugitive.* He published his first poetry in that decade while writing free-lance criticism in New York and later while living among the expatriates in Paris. His erudite verse is at once classical in its allusions and modern in its style, closely allied with the tradition of T. S. Eliot, his strongest influence. Tate's own Southern background influenced him as well, and the Civil War is a favorite theme: in addition to biographies of Jefferson Davis and Stonewall Jackson, his only novel, *The Fathers,* is set in that era, and one of his most famous poems is "Ode to the Confederate Dead." Though Tate built his reputation as a poet, his essays, his editings, and his various other writings form the bulk of his literary output. In the background of his written work is a teaching career which spanned more than thirty years, most of them spent at the University of Minnesota. A witty man, Tate was also a popular public speaker. Tate's award-winning *Collected Poems* was published in 1977; he had been

working intermittently on his memoirs in the years before his death. Obituaries and other sources: *Current Biography,* Wilson, 1940, April, 1979; *Encyclopedia of World Literature in the Twentieth Century,* updated edition, Ungar, 1967; *The Reader's Adviser: A Layman's Guide to Literature,* Volume I: *The Best in American and British Fiction, Poetry, Essays, Literary Biography, Bibliography, and Reference,* 12th edition, Bowker, 1974; *Contemporary Poets,* 2nd edition, St. Martin's, 1975; *Contemporary Novelists,* 2nd edition, St. Martin's, 1976; *Who's Who in America,* 40th edition, Marquis, 1978; *New York Times,* February 10, 1979; *Washington Post,* February 10, 1979; *Chicago Tribune,* February 10, 1979; *Time,* February 19, 1979; *Publishers Weekly,* February 26, 1979.

*   *   *

TAVERNE, Dick 1928-

PERSONAL: Born October 18, 1928, in Sumatra; son of Nicholas Jacobus (a geologist) and Louise (Koch) Taverne; married Janice Hennessey (an immunologist), August 5, 1955; children: Suzanna, Caroline. *Education:* Balliol College, Oxford, L.H. (first class honors), 1951. *Politics:* Independent Social Democrat. *Home:* 60 Cambridge St., London S.W.1, England. *Office:* Institute for Fiscal Studies, 2 Castle Lane, London S.W.1, England.

CAREER: Called to the bar, Middle Temple, 1954, appointed Queen's Counsel, 1965; British Government, House of Commons, London, England, member of parliament, representing Lincolnshire, 1962-72, Parliamentary under-secretary of state at Home Office, 1966-68, minister of state at Treasury, 1968-69, financial secretary to Treasury, 1969-70, independent member of Parliament, representing Lincolnshire, 1973-74; Institute of Fiscal Studies, London, director, 1971—. Television and radio broadcaster. Member of board of directors of Equity and Law Assurance Co., 1972—, and BOC International, 1975—.

WRITINGS: Economic and Monetary Union in Europe (monograph), European Movement, 1971; *The Future of the Left,* J. Cape, 1974. Contributor to magazines and newspapers in England, the Netherlands, and Germany.

*   *   *

TAYLOR, Gordon Rattray 1911-

PERSONAL: Born January 11, 1911, in Eastbourne, England; son of Frederick Robert and Adele (Baker) Taylor; married Lysbeth Morley Sheaf, 1945 (deceased); married Olga Treherne Anthonisz, 1962; children: (first marriage) two daughters. *Education:* Attended Trinity College, Cambridge. *Home:* The Hall, Freshford, Bath BA3 6EJ, England.

CAREER: Worked for *Morning Post,* 1933-36; free-lance writer, 1936-38; leader and feature writer for *Daily Express,* 1938-40; affiliated with Monitoring Service and European News Broadcasts of British Broadcasting Corp., 1940-44; staff member in Psychological Warfare Division of Supreme Headquarters of Allied Expeditionary Force, 1944-45; free-lance writer and broadcaster, 1945-50; employed as director of social research organization, 1950-54; British Broadcasting Corp., writer for television science programs, 1958-66, chief science adviser, 1963-66; writer, 1966—. Devised British pavilion display for Turin Fair, 1961. Gives lecture tours in the United States.

MEMBER: International Science Writers Association (founder; past president), Conservation Society (member of council), Society of Authors, Savile Club, Roy Club. *Awards, honors:* Ondas Award, 1961, for series "Eye on Research"; Brussels Award, 1961, for program "Machines Like Men"; book of the year award from *Yorkshire Post*, 1970, for *The Doomsday Book*.

WRITINGS: Economics for the Exasperated, John Lane, 1947; *Conditions of Happiness*, Bodley Head, 1949, Houghton, 1951; *Industry and Society*, Ashridge, 1949; (editor) *Nationalised Industry*, Acton Society Trust, 1950; *Are Workers Human?*, Falcon Press, 1950, Houghton, 1952; *Sex in History*, Thames & Hudson, 1953, 3rd edition, Philips Park Press, 1965, Vanguard, 1970; *The Angel-Makers: A Study in the Psychological Origins of Historical Change, 1750-1850*, Heinemann, 1958, revised edition, Secker & Warburg, 1973, Dutton, 1974.

Eye on Research, J. Murray, 1960; (editor) Robert Briffault, *The Mothers* (abridged edition), Universal Library, 1963; *The Science of Life: A Picture History of Biology*, McGraw, 1963; (with James Mourilyan Tanner) *Growth*, Time, Inc., 1965, revised edition, 1968; *The Biological Time Bomb*, World Publishing, 1968; *The Doomsday Book: Can the World Survive?*, World Publishing, 1970; *Rethink: A Paraprimitive Solution*, Secker & Warburg, 1972, Dutton, 1973, reprinted as *Rethink: Radical Proposals to Save a Disintegrating World*, Penguin, 1974; *How to Avoid the Future*, Secker & Warburg, 1975; *A Salute to British Genius*, Secker & Warburg, 1977.

Television and radio scripts for British Broadcasting Corp. include "Eye on Research" (television series), "The Science of Life," "Science International Series" (for television), and "Science International Challenge" (for television). Author of "Focus," a feature in *Science Journal*. Contributor to periodicals, including *Encounter*, *New Statesman*, *Observer*, and *Futures*. Editor of *Horizon*, 1964-66.

Taylor's books have been published in French, Spanish, German, and Italian.

AVOCATIONAL INTERESTS: Wine, gardening, baroque music.

* * *

TAYLOR, James Spear 1897(?)-1979

OBITUARY NOTICE: Born c. 1897, in Rochester, N.Y.; died February 19, 1979, in Washington, D.C. Economist, energy consultant, and author of the best-seller *How to Own Your Own Home*. Taylor was an adviser to Presidents Hoover and Eisenhower, serving also as speech writer for the former. He assisted in the planning for re-integration of World War II veterans. Obituaries and other sources: *Washington Post*, February 21, 1979.

* * *

TAYLOR, Mildred D.

PERSONAL: Born in Jackson, Miss. *Education:* Degree from University of Toledo; graduate study at University of Colorado. *Address:* c/o Dial Press, 1 Dag Hammarskjold Plaza, 245 East 47th St., New York, N.Y. 10017.

CAREER: Writer. English and history teacher with the Peace Corps in Ethiopia for two years. *Awards, honors: Song of the Trees* named Outstanding Book of the Year by the *New York Times*; American Library Association Notable Book, 1976, National Book Award finalist, 1977, and Newbery Medal, 1977, all for *Roll of Thunder, Hear My Cry*.

WRITINGS—Juvenile books: *Song of the Trees*, Dial, 1975; *Roll of Thunder, Hear My Cry*, Dial, 1976.

WORK IN PROGRESS: Two more books on the Logan family which will follow the children presented in her two earlier books into adulthood and through World War II.

SIDELIGHTS: Mildred Taylor wrote: "From as far back as I can remember my father taught me a different history from the one I learned in school. By the fireside in our Ohio home and in Mississippi, where I was born and where my father's family had lived since the days of slavery, I had heard about our past. . . . It was a history of ordinary people, some brave, some not so brave, but basically people who had done nothing more spectacular than survive in a society designed for their destruction. Some of the stories my father had learned from his parents and grandparents as they had learned them from theirs; others he told first-hand, having been involved in the incidents himself. There was often humor in his stories, sometimes pathos, and frequently tragedy; but always the people were graced with a simple dignity that elevated them from the ordinary to the heroic.

"In those intervening years spent studying, traveling, and living in Africa and working with the Black student movement, I would find myself turning again and again to the stories I had heard in my childhood. I was deeply drawn to the roots of that inner world which I knew so well. . . . In this new book *Roll of Thunder, Hear My Cry* I included the teachings of my own childhood, the values and principles by which I and so many other Black children were reared, for I wanted to show a different kind of Black world from the one so often seen. I wanted to show a family united in love and self-respect, and parents, strong and sensitive, attempting to guide their children successfully, without harming their spirits, through the hazardous maze of living in a discriminatory society.

"I also wanted to show the Black person as heroic. In my own school days, a class devoted to the history of Black people in the United States always caused me painful embarrassment. This would not have been so if that history had been presented truly, showing the accomplishments of the Black race both in Africa and in this hemisphere. . . . It is my hope that to the children who read my books, the Logans will provide those heroes missing from the schoolbooks of my childhood, Black men, women, and children of whom they can be proud."

Roll of Thunder, Hear My Cry was adapted for television, 1978.

BIOGRAPHICAL/CRITICAL SOURCES: New York Times Book Review, November 16, 1975, November 21, 1976; *Kirkus Reviews*, September 15, 1976; *Commonweal*, November 19, 1976.*

* * *

TEBBEL, John (William) 1912-

PERSONAL: Born November 16, 1912, in Boyne City, Mich.; son of William Farr and Edna Mae Tebbel; married Kathryn Carl (a copy editor), April 29, 1939; children: Judith Elaine Tebbel Acuna. *Education:* Central Michigan University, A.B., 1935; Columbia University, M.S., 1937. *Politics:* Independent. *Home:* 876-A Heritage Village, Southbury, Conn. 06488. *Agent:* Harold Matson Co., Inc., 22 East 40th St., New York, N.Y. 10016.

CAREER: Times-News, Mt. Pleasant, Mich., city editor, 1935-36; *Detroit Free Press*, Detroit, Mich., reporter, 1937-39; *Providence Journal*, Providence, R.I., feature writer and

Sunday music editor, 1939-41; *American Mercury,* New York City, managing editor, 1941-43; *New York Times,* New York City, Sunday staff writer, 1943; E. P. Dutton & Co., Inc., New York City, associate editor, 1943-46; New York University, New York City, assistant professor, 1949-52, associate professor, 1952-54, professor of journalism, 1954-76, head of department, 1954-65, director of Graduate Institute of Book Publishing, 1958-62. Part-time instructor at Columbia University, 1941-46. Free-lance writer, 1943—. Member of board of directors of Public Interest Public Relations, 1975-78; consultant to Ford Foundation. *Member:* Society of Professional Journalists, Authors Guild of Authors League of America, Players Club, New York University Club. *Awards, honors:* Litt.D. from Central Michigan University, 1948; alumni award from Journalism Alumni Association of Columbia University, 1975.

WRITINGS: An American Dynasty: The Story of the McCormicks, Medills, and Pattersons, Doubleday, 1947, reprinted, Greenwood Press, 1968; *The Marshall Fields,* Dutton, 1947; *George Horace Lorimer and the Saturday Evening Post,* Doubleday, 1948; (editor) Francis Parkman, *The Battle for North America,* Doubleday, 1948.

(With Kenneth N. Stewart) *Makers of Modern Journalism,* Prentice-Hall, 1950; *Your Body: How to Keep It Healthy,* Harper, 1951; *The Conqueror* (novel), Dutton, 1951; *Touched With Fire* (historical novel), Dutton, 1952; *The Life and Good Times of William Randolph Hearst,* Dutton, 1952; *George Washington's America,* Dutton, 1954; *A Voice in the Streets* (novel), Dutton, 1954; *The Magic of Balanced Living: A Man's Key to Health, Well-Being, and Peace of Mind,* Harper, 1956.

(With Keith Jennison) *The American Indian Wars,* Harper, 1960; *The Inheritors: A Study of America's Great Fortunes and What Happened to Them,* Putnam, 1962; (editor with Ann Seranne) *The Epicure's Companion,* McKay, 1962; *The Human Touch in Business: The Story of Charles R. Hook, Who Rose From Office Boy to Internationally-Known Business Leader,* Otterbein Press, 1963; *David Sarnoff: Putting Electrons to Work* (juvenile), Encyclopaedia Britannica, 1963; *Paperback Books: A Pocket History,* Pocket Books, 1963; *The Compact History of the American Newspaper,* Hawthorn, 1963, revised edition, 1969; *From Rags to Riches: Horatio Alger, Jr. and the American Dream,* Macmillan, 1964; *Red Runs the River: The Rebellion of Chief Pontiac* (juvenile), Hawthorn, 1966; *The Compact History of the Indian Wars,* Hawthorn, 1966; *Open Letters to Newspaper Readers,* James Heineman, 1968; *The Compact History of American Magazines,* Hawthorn, 1969; (with Ramon Eduardo Ruiz) *South by Southwest: The Mexican-American and His Heritage* (juvenile), Doubleday, 1969.

The Battle of Fallen Timbers, August 20, 1974: President Washington Secures the Ohio Valley (juvenile), F. Watts, 1972; *A History of Book Publishing in the United States,* Bowker, Volume I: *The Creation of an Industry, 1630-1865,* 1972, Volume II: *The Expansion of an Industry, 1865-1919,* 1975, Volume III: *The Golden Age: Between Two Wars, 1920-1940,* 1978, Volume IV: *A Great Period of Growth: 1940-1980,* Bowker, 1980; *The Media in America: A Social and Political History,* Crowell, 1974; *Opportunities in Publishing Careers,* Vocational Guidance Manuals, 1975; *Opportunities in Journalism,* Vocational Guidance Manuals, 1977.

Author of about forty ghostwritten books. Contributor of more than five hundred articles to popular magazines, including *Saturday Review.*

WORK IN PROGRESS: The Press and the Presidency, publication by Indiana University Press expected in 1982.

SIDELIGHTS: Tebbel told *CA:* "I agree with Samuel Johnson that no man but a blockhead ever wrote for anything but money. Yet Johnson knew, as every writer knows, that he also writes because there is no alternative. At ten, living on a farm in the middle of Michigan, with Manhattan as remote from me as the moon, I told inquiring relatives that when I grew up I intended to go to New York and be a writer. A dozen or so years later, I was doing just that. I could not then, nor could I now, conceive of any other kind of life—except for music, a life I sampled briefly with my violin, but fortunately had sense enough to realize was not my real talent. The experience, however, gave me a lifetime of listening enjoyment, as well as an opportunity to write about music on occasion.

"Newspapers were the springboard I used to attain the literary life, as so many others have done, from Dickens onward, and I still regard it as an ideal preparation. The news is life itself, the same materials the writer uses for nonfiction or, enhanced, as fiction. Reporting as I did, from the small town to the big city, gives a writer basic perspectives and perceptions about life that stay with him always. (I use "he" and "him" generically, of course; as we all know by now, women respond in the same way.) When I became a writer of books and magazine articles, I found that newspapers had taught me how to organize, how to dig for facts, and in many cases how to separate illusion from reality. I had one other advantage: a year spent with Douglas Southall Freeman as a once-a-week professor. He taught me the research methods I have used ever since, methods of the utmost value.

"A year spent at the Graduate School of Journalism, Columbia University, was the turning point in my life. It translated me from a Michigan small town to life on metropolitan dailies, besides subjecting my writing for the first time to the critical eye of top-flight professionals, and demonstrating to me that although I had been writing for money since I was fourteen, I had a great deal to learn about the craft. I am still learning.

"Another turning point came in 1949. I had topped off a career on newspapers and magazines with four years as a publisher's editor, a job I had enjoyed more than anything I'd ever done. After ghostwriting a few books for the publisher, E. P. Dutton, I had quit with a two-book contract from Doubleday and freelanced for three years—enough time to convince me I could never cope with the constant anxiety of the freelancer's life. Then my Columbia classmate, Vance Packard, who has been my good friend for forty years, helped me get a job in the journalism department at New York University. As so many other writers have discovered, I found that teaching and writing made an ideal combination as a way of life, particularly since teaching gave me nearly as much satisfaction.

"I am a compulsive writer—that is, I'm not really happy unless I'm writing. I work a regular business day, more or less, at the typewriter (an Olympia office standard electric), stopping for lunch and for tea. I work best under deadline pressure, and intersperse writing bouts with spells of travel, another addiction. I write to the constant accompaniment of a New York good music station, and I hear a great deal of music, both classic and jazz, at other times, often from a very large recorded library of both. I'm also an obsessive magazine reader, and consequently don't read as many books as I'd like to, but I would never be able to do that in any case. Another interest is sports, which I follow avidly on television. I see as much theatre as possible, and in fact have never met an art I didn't like.

"My books have had reasonably good sales, for the most part, and one (*The Inheritors*) was on the *New York Times* best-seller list for a week. Some have been translated and distributed in the U. K., Spain, West Germany, Sweden, Italy, Brazil, and Australia. Of them all, my greatest satisfaction has come from the four-volume *A History of Book Publishing in the United States.* For me, it has been not only a rewarding part-time absorption for the past twenty years, but extremely satisfying in the sense that I have created something unique that will outlast me and be useful to future generations. No writer could ask for more.

"As for advice to aspiring writers, Epictetus said it all in his *Discourses,* and I repeated it for twenty years in my fiction workshop at N.Y.U.: 'If you would be a writer, write.'"

* * *

TEMPERLEY, Howard 1932-

PERSONAL: Born November 16, 1932, in England; son of Fred (a bank clerk) and Eva (Holland) Temperley; married June Flambert, September 27, 1957 (divorced, 1966); married Rachel Hooper (a teacher), September 29, 1966; children: Alison Lynn, Rebecca Caroline, Nicholas Rowley. *Education:* Oxford University, B.A., 1956; Yale University, earned M.A. degree, Ph.D., 1960. *Agent:* Curtis Brown Ltd., 1 Craven Hill, London W.2, England. *Office:* School of English and American Studies, University of East Anglia, Norwich, England.

CAREER: University of Manchester, Manchester, England, lecturer, 1961-67; University of East Anglia, Norwich, England, senior lecturer in English and American studies, 1967—. *Military service:* British Army, 1951-53; became second lieutenant.

WRITINGS: British Antislavery, 1833-1870, University of South Carolina Press, 1972. Contributor to American studies journals. Editor of *Journal of American Studies.*

WORK IN PROGRESS: Research on the political economy of abolition and the economic thinking behind the antislavery movement, with a book expected to result.

* * *

TENPAS, Margaret (Susan Lyon) 1923-

PERSONAL: Born October 14, 1923, in Pittsburgh, Pa.; daughter of John Boyd (a dentist) and Ethel (a teacher; maiden name, Peterson) Lyon; married Emerson Tenpas (in sales administration), July 19, 1947; children: Barbara (Mrs. Jun-ichi Meguro), Nancy, Janet, Ronald. *Education:* University of Pittsburgh, B.S., 1945; Gannon College, M.A., 1970. *Politics:* Republican. *Religion:* Methodist. *Residence:* Erie, Pa. *Office:* Department of English, Gannon College, Perry Sq., Erie, Pa. 16541.

CAREER: High school school teacher of shorthand, typing, and bookkeeping in Bethel, Pa., 1945-47, and Mill Creek, Pa., 1948-50; adult education teacher in Erie, Pa., 1953-58; Mercyhurst College, Erie, substitute teacher, 1965-67; high school teacher of English in Erie, 1971-75; Gannon College, lecturer in English, 1975—. Member of Erie Playhouse board of directors and Mill Creek Township Recreation Commission. *Member:* American Association of University Women, Erie Family Campers.

WRITINGS: Bridge to Blue Hill (juvenile fantasy), Carolrhoda, 1972; *Erie: From Forest Trail to Port City* (juvenile),

Erie Branch, American Association of University Women, 1976. Contributor of articles, stories, and poems to magazines for children and adults, including *Scholastic, Trails,* and *Pet Life.* Editor of *Prism* and newsletter of Erie Family Campers.

WORK IN PROGRESS: Research on reading programs.

SIDELIGHTS: Margaret Tenpas comments: "Much of my writing is about my children or for them, as I read picture books for at least twelve years during my family's younger days. I'm interested in personalities and enjoy information based on history and stories that have an ironic twist. I write because working with words allows me to be creative and communicate ideas. Working on the high school newspaper gave me the delight of seeing myself in print."

AVOCATIONAL INTERESTS: "Baking cookies, canning tomatoes, whipping together a new skirt, packing the trailer to go camping, attending swimming meets, taking a course in belly dancing—all provide diversions from writing. . . ."

* * *

TERRY, Arthur 1927-

PERSONAL: Born February 17, 1927, in York, England; son of Arthur (an insurance official) and Beatrice (Hardisty) Terry; married Mary Gordon Sellar (a librarian), June, 1955; children: Richard, Sally, Philip. *Education:* Trinity Hall, Cambridge, B.A., 1947, M.A., 1950. *Home:* 11 Braiswick, Colchester CO4 5AU, England. *Office:* Department of Literature, University of Essex, Wivenhoe Park, Colchester CO4 3SQ, England.

CAREER: Queen's University of Belfast, Belfast, Northern Ireland, assistant lecturer, 1950-54, lecturer, 1954-60, senior lecturer, 1960-62, Musgrave Professor of Spanish and head of department, 1962-72; University of Essex, Colchester, England, professor of literature, 1973—. *Military service:* British Army, Royal Education Corps, 1947-49; became sergeant. *Member:* Associacio Internacional de Llengua i Literatura Catalanes (vice-president, 1973—), Association of British Hispanists, British Comparative Literature Association, Anglo-Catalan Society (president, 1962-66). *Awards, honors:* Bonay i Carbo Prize from Institut d'Estudis Catalans (Barcelona), 1966, for *La Poesia de Joan Maragall.*

WRITINGS: La Poesia de Joan Maragall, Editorial Barcino, 1963; *Two Views of Poetry,* Queen's University of Belfast, 1964; (editor) *An Anthology of Spanish Poetry, 1500-1700,* Pergamon, Part I, 1965, Part II, 1968; (translator) Gabriel Ferrater, Salvador Espriu, and Pere Quart, *A Small War* (pamphlet), Festival Publications, 1966; (translator) Luis Cernuda, Jose Angel Valente, Claudio Rodriquez, and Angel Crespo, *The Sacrifice* (pamphlet), Festival Publications, 1967; *Catalan Literature,* Benn, 1972; *Antonio Machado: "Campos de Castilla,"* Grant & Cutler, 1973; (editor and translator) Ausias March, *Selected Poems,* Edinburgh University Press, 1976; (with Joaquim Rafel) *Introduccion a la lengua y la literatura catalanas* (title means "Introduction to Catalan Language and Literature"), Ariel, 1977. Contributor of about one hundred articles, translations, and reviews to journals and to *Listener.*

WORK IN PROGRESS: A book of essays on modern Catalan poetry, for Edicions 62, publication expected in 1981; a critical book on seventeenth-century Spanish poetry, publication by Cambridge University Press expected in 1981.

SIDELIGHTS: Terry told *CA:* "As a university teacher, I believe that teaching and research are two halves of a single activity: teaching keeps one's research from becoming trivial, and the experience of doing research prevents one's teaching from becoming dogmatic.

"'Every critic,' said Matthew Arnold, 'should try and possess one great literature, at least, besides his own; and the more unlike his own, the better.' Conversely, someone who is concerned in the first place with foreign literatures is likely to remain an incomplete critic insofar as he fails to think seriously about the literature of his own language. Hence my growing interest in comparative literature.

"A critic, if he is not himself an original writer, needs to be as conscious as possible of what is involved in the creation of a literary work. Translation, particularly of verse, is one way of ensuring this; one's successes may be minimal, but at least the frustrations are genuine.

"My involvement with Spanish poetry dates from so far back that it's difficult now to reconstitute the various stages; one important factor, certainly, was the presence in Cambridge of Luis Cernuda—one of the finest modern Spanish poets—at the beginning of my undergraduate career. The origins of my interest in Catalan literature and culture can be traced quite specifically to one man: Dr. J. M. Batista i Roca, a great scholar and patriot, who also taught me at Cambridge. It was he who enabled me to spend a year in Barcelona as a research student, in the course of which I came to know a number of writers and artists, some of whom were to become close friends. Writing about Catalan poetry has, I suspect, been my way of identifying myself with a culture I greatly admire and which continues to produce writers of outstanding quality."

AVOCATIONAL INTERESTS: Music (playing the piano; chamber music).

*   *   *

THEROUX, Alexander Louis   1939-

PERSONAL: Born in 1939, in Medford, Mass.; and son of Albert (a salesman) Anne Theroux. *Education:* Attended St. Francis College, Biddeford, Me.; University of Virginia, Ph.D., 19 . *Residence:* Cape Cod, Mass.

CAREER: Worked for Longwood College, Farmville, Va., and Harvard University, Cambridge, Mass.; currently associated with Phillips Academy, Andover, Mass., 1978—. *Awards, honors:* Fulbright fellowship; Guggenheim fellowship.

WRITINGS: Three Wogs (novel), Gambit, 1972, reprinted with an additional essay, David R. Godine, 1975; *The Great Wheedle Tragedy* (for children), illustrated by Stan Washburn, David R. Godine, 1975; *The Schinocephalic Waif* (for children), illustrated by Washburn, David R. Godine, 1975.

Author of column in *Boston* magazine. Contributor of articles to periodicals, including *Esquire* and *National Review.*

SIDELIGHTS: Theroux's highly stylized first novel, *Three Wogs* ("wogs" are foreigners who have moved to England), met with great critical enthusiasm. "Once the reader has become accustomed to the flamboyancies of Mr. Theroux' extravagant, bombastic style, he can settle down to the feast spread before him and enjoy bit by bit the coruscations, the precisions, and the persuasiveness of an acute playful intelligence all too ready to cozen the unwary," a reviewer for the *Virginia Quarterly Review* wrote. "As a striking tour de force the book is incomparable."

Calling Theroux a "certified, grade A, major, new talent," D. Keith Mano commented, *"Three Wogs* is an incredible performance: hilarious, moving, incisive and flamboyant

beyond description. . . . I'd love to spend six days and seven nights bus-touring the Beckford Gothic garden of his vocabulary: never mind the meanings—that much I don't ask. *Clooms, lampion, barrikin, furibund,* and yes . . . *mormoops.* . . . His metaphors have East and West wings, cul-de-sac staircases, a gazebo on the hill. The syntax taxes. Yet—be sure of this—at no time is "Three Wogs" abstruse or unreadable. It is overwritten, certainly, but that is the book's premise: joy and fun its sanction."

Critic Diane Johnson had some reservations, though. She found that the three novellas or long stories that make up the book are "successful in varying degrees, given the initial romantic proposition that all Wogs are good, because they are uncorrupted by civilization. And all Englishmen, supposedly civilized, are bad, premises one doesn't really bother to challenge in a comic and highly stylized work like this. Because English bigots are uncomfortably like American ones, it is alarming enough without trying to be believable."

Theroux is a somewhat eccentric member of the literary Theroux family (his younger brother Paul has written thirteen books). He lives in an old farmhouse on Cape Cod with a magnificent library of rare books and first editions. Theroux has a passion for obscure poets and acknowledges that his literary mentor is the nineteenth-century English writer Baron Corvo. He shares Corvo's aspiration to make his opponents "smart, wince and squirm" with his writing, James Atlas has noted. "His prose and conversation are enriched by profane, ornate invective," Atlas wrote of Theroux. Having been jilted by the woman he planned to marry, "he includes a veiled reference to her in virtually everything he writes," Atlas commented.

Theroux once entered a Trappist monastery, but after two years of silence he left to become a novice in a Franciscan seminary. He subsequently left the seminary and took a construction job in Boston until he enrolled in college. "I could have been a saint," he told Atlas, "but I became a man of letters."

BIOGRAPHICAL/CRITICAL SOURCES: New York Times Book Review, August 8, 1971, April 16, 1972, June 4, 1972, December 3, 1972; *Washington Post Book World,* February 13, 1972; *Virginia Quarterly Review,* summer, 1972; *Times Literary Supplement,* July 6, 1973; *Observer,* July 6, 1973; *New Statesman,* July 20, 1973; *Contemporary Literary Criticism,* Volume 2, Gale, 1974; *National Review,* October 24, 1975; *New York Times* magazine, April 30, 1978.*

*   *   *

THOM, Robert   1929-1979

OBITUARY NOTICE—See index for *CA* sketch: Born July 2, 1929, in New York, N.Y.; died May 8, 1979, in Malibu, Calif. Poet, playwright, and screenwriter. Though Thom had some success as a poet while in college, his writings went largely unnoticed until his 1957 play, "Compulsion," appeared on Broadway. Starring Roddy McDowall and Dean Stockwell, the play ran for 140 performances. Thom broadened his career in the 1960's when he began writing screenplays. Such films as "All the Fine Young Cannibals" and "The Subterraneans" dealt with youth and its problems. Thom also wrote a number of television scripts, including a 1963 Emmy Award-winning episode of "The Defenders." Obituaries and other sources: *New York Times,* May 12, 1979.

THOMAS, Edison H(ugh) 1912-

PERSONAL: Born June 5, 1912, in Cadiz, Ky.; son of Robert H. and Ora Agnes (Bridges) Thomas; married Thelma Waits Garrett, January 27, 1956; stepchildren: Barbara Garrett Read, Ronald L. Garrett, Dwayne R. Garrett, Sue Garrett Manahan. *Education:* Attended Western Kentucky University, 1931-33, and University of Louisville, 1949-52. *Politics:* Democrat. *Religion:* "Born-again Baptist." *Home:* 9402 Janna Dr., Louisville, Ky. 40272.

CAREER: Stringer for daily newspapers in Kentucky and Tennessee, 1933-37; *Record,* Cadiz, Ky., editor, 1938-42; *Louisville Courier-Journal,* Louisville, Ky., on copy desk, 1946-47; did public relations work for War Assets Administration, Reynolds Metals Co., Kentucky Baptist Convention, and Southern Baptist Home Mission Board, 1947-52; Louisville & Nashville Railroad, Louisville, staff member of *L & N* (magazine), 1952-61, manager of railroad's news bureau, 1961-77; free-lance writer, 1977—. *Military service:* U.S. Navy, 1942-45; served in Pacific-Asiatic Theater, combat correspondent in the Philippines, 1945.

MEMBER: Sons of the American Revolution, Sons of the Confederacy, Thomas-Bridges Association (honorary life member; past president), Filson Club, Kentucky Historical Society.

WRITINGS: The Great Locomotive Chase (monograph), Louisville & Nashville Railroad, 1962; (with Charles B. Castner) *Great Builders of L & N Steam,* Louisville & Nashville Railroad, 1967; *The Thomas and Bridges Story, 1540-1840,* T & E Publishers, 1972; *John Hunt Morgan and His Raiders,* University Press of Kentucky, 1975.

Author of film script "Here Comes the General," Louisville & Nashville Railroad, 1962, and historical pageant "Goodbye, Carolina," first produced in 1974. Author of booklets and brochures. Contributor to transportation magazines.

WORK IN PROGRESS: A historical novel about the migration of a pioneer family from North Carolina to Kentucky after the American Revolution, completion expected in 1980; a series of sketches on pioneer life in Western Kentucky; an article on the assassination of William Gobel, an early-day governor of Kentucky.

SIDELIGHTS: Thomas writes: "Graduating from high school in the middle of the Great Depression brought little but honors. Attending college was also somewhat of a struggle. I did odd jobs to keep going, and once borrowed fifty dollars from a cousin on which I went an entire semester. After college I took jobs where I could find them, including work as a waiter and later a night cook on a Mississippi River steamboat. I can still fry some of the best bacon and eggs even today.

"I began my writing career while still in high school, later writing plays for amateur production and short stories for magazines. In the mid-1930's I moved into newspaper work, a career that was interrupted by World War II.

"When the war ended I returned to Kentucky and joined the copy desk of the *Louisville Courier-Journal.* In 1952, I joined the staff of the Louisville & Nashville Railroad. Assignments took me throughout the thirteen states served by the railroad. It was a plush job and included free travel and plenty of expense money while I wrote rail-oriented stories about everything from a new stretch of track to appearances of the current Miss America in the territory.

"In 1962, during the Civil War centennial, I wrote a series of stories about the part the railroad played in that conflict. At the same time, the railroad refurbished the historic Civil War steam locomotive 'General,' of Great Locomotive Chase fame, and sent it on tour. I handled the publicity for these tours, which extended over a period of almost four years. This ended when the railroad gave the engine to the State of Georgia.

"I retired from railroading in 1977, but writing and printer's ink apparently will never be completely purged from my system. I love research, and have spent many delightful hours digging into my ancestral lines in North Carolina and Virginia. I eventually wound up at Jamestown, Va., where my Thomas ancestors landed in 1610. A trip to England and Wales helped me to wrap up family historical data.

"I've taken some ten thousand thirty-five millimeter color slides during my lifetime and probably will take ten thousand more before the end of my world. My current project is to put together a series of color prints I have made, for a 'traveling exhibit.' For retirement I blew a considerable amount of money for a new camera and lenses (I could have gone through college in 1931 on that amount) and I am enjoying life to the fullest."

AVOCATIONAL INTERESTS: Travel in England, Europe, Brazil, Greece.

*   *   *

THOMAS, Elizabeth Ann 1952-
(Liz Thomas)

PERSONAL: Born May 14, 1952, in London, England; daughter of Clifford William (a salesman) and Joan Florence (Dobson) Thomas; married John Hunter Bloomfield, (a property valuer), June 10, 1978; *Education:* Middlesex Hospital (London), received state certification in nursing, 1972. *Religion:* Pentecostal. *Home:* 72 Kensington High St., London W84PE, England. *Agent:* Giles Gordon, Anthony Shiels Associates, 2-3 Morwell St., London WCIB 3AR, England.

CAREER: Worked at various nursing jobs in homes and in hospitals in London, England, 1968-70; state enrolled nurse, 1972; volunteer worker among the poor in Saigon, South Vietnam (now Ho Chi Minh City, Socialist Republic of Vietnam), 1972-75; British Council for Aid to Refugees, London, worker with Vietnamese refugees, 1976—. Member of Middlesex Hospital League. *Awards, honors:* Member of the Order of the British Empire, 1976, for nursing services to children in South Vietnam.

WRITINGS: (Under name Liz Thomas) *Dust of Life: Children of the Saigon Streets,* Hamish Hamilton, 1977.

SIDELIGHTS: After witnessing and living in the unbelievably impoverished surroundings of South Vietnam's slums, Liz Thomas knows first hand the taste of the "dust of life." Her three-year stay there began in 1972, when she left England to do volunteer work in a Saigon orphanage. She later worked in a miserably overcrowded hospital before opening up her own home for girls—mostly prostitutes. Thomas's memoirs of these extremely difficult—and rewarding—years appear in her book, *The Dust of Life: Children of the Saigon Streets.*

One wonder of these memoirs is how the author even survived the horrors she met in Vietnam. Thomas witnessed and worked with lice-infested children fighting with rats for their food on the orphanage floors, the same floors where "the nurses would cook and urinate." She visited prisoners in the Saigon jails. She aided the drug addicts on Le Lai Street—"a district where few foreigners dared to walk." At her home for girls she abandoned her Western dress and lived as the girls did: poorly. Her and her friends' hunger drove them to eat their pet dog. She lost thirty pounds, became infested with head lice, and was hospitalized for exhaustion.

If Thomas's survival in these conditions is amazing, her success in her mission is miraculous. "Of all the millions of foreigners who went to South Vietnam during the civil war, few could have done more good or less harm than Liz Thomas," wrote Richard West. She washed over thirty babies each day in the orphanage, while Vietnamese women would simply watch. She befriended the young in the jails. Her refuge for prostitutes offered food (at least at first), a home, and a new course for life: "No smoking, no drugs, no stealing, no prostitution." Though limited, her reputation did spread beyond those she helped. West, who also lived in Vietnam, claimed she "really was just as famous and popular in the slums of Saigon as she was unknown in the posh quarter where we journalists lived."

The Communist victory and the fall of Saigon imperiled both Thomas and the poor with whom she worked. In addition to her fear that "she would be mistaken for an American and killed," Communism promised no improvement for her Vietnamese friends. "She ably tells of the dramatic days surrounding the fall of Saigon," reported Marjorie Margolies, "—how the takeover affected 'her' people, and how communism did little more than bring worse, in some cases even more corrupt, poverty.... She came to realize that under the new regime her hands were tied, so she reluctantly left the country she had come to call home."

Though she now lives in England, Thomas has continued her devotion to the Vietnamese by working with refugees, the "boat people." Still, spurred by her memories and her love for Vietnam's people, the twenty-seven-year-old nurse envisions a return. As she told CA, she and her husband "hope to return to Southeast Asia where I can continue working amongst the poor."

BIOGRAPHICAL/CRITICAL SOURCES: Spectator, January 29, 1977; New Statesman, February 4, 1977; Listener, February 10, 1977; Observer, February 13, 1977; Guardian Weekly, February 13, 1977; Kirkus Reviews, November 15, 1977; Washington Post Book World, January 31, 1978.

*   *   *

THOMAS, Lewis 1913-

PERSONAL: Born November 25, 1913, in Flushing, N.Y.; son of Joseph S. (a surgeon) and Grace Emma (Peck) Thomas; married Beryl Dawson, January 1, 1941; children: Abigail, Judith, Eliza. Education: Princeton University, B.S., 1933; Harvard University, M.D., 1937. Home: 333 East 68th St., New York, N.Y. 10021. Office: Memorial Sloan-Kettering Cancer Center, 1275 York Ave., New York, N.Y. 10021.

CAREER: Boston City Hospital, Boston, Mass., intern, 1937-39; Neurological Institute, New York City, resident in neurology, 1939-41; Boston City Hospital, Tilney Memorial Fellow at Thorndike Laboratory, 1941-42; Rockefeller Institute for Medical Research, New York City, visiting investigator, 1942-46; Johns Hopkins University, Baltimore, Md., assistant professor of pediatrics, 1946-48; Tulane University, New Orleans, La., associate professor, 1948-50, professor of medicine, 1950, director of Division of Infectious Disease, 1948-50; University of Minnesota, Minneapolis, professor of pediatrics and medicine and director of pediatric research laboratories at Heart Hospital, 1950-54; New York University, New York City, professor of pathology, 1954-

69, head of department, 1954-58, director of University Hospital, 1959-66, dean of School of Medicine, 1966-69; Yale University, New Haven, Conn., professor of pathology and head of department, 1969-72, dean of School of Medicine, 1971-73; Memorial Sloan-Kettering Cancer Center, New York City, president, chief executive officer, and member of Sloan-Kettering Institute, 1973—.

Professor at Cornell University; adjunct professor at Rockefeller University (also member of board of trustees); member of board of overseers of Harvard University, 1976—; member of scientific advisory board of C. V. Whitney Laboratory for Experimental Marine Biology and Medicine, at University of Florida, 1976—; member of council of visitors of Bank Street College of Education, 1975—; associate fellow of Ezra Stiles College, Yale University. Pediatrician at Harriet Lane Home for Invalid Children, of Johns Hopkins University, 1946-48; director of medical divisions at Bellevue Hospital, 1958-66, president of Medical Board, 1963-66; chief of pathology at Yale-New Haven Hospital, 1969-73; attending physician at Memorial Hospital; member of scientific advisory committee of Massachusetts General Hospital, 1969-72; member of scientific advisory board of Scripps Clinic and Research Foundation, 1973-78. Member of board of directors of New York City Public Health Research Institute, 1960-69; member of board of trustees of C. S. Draper Laboratory, 1974—, Cold Spring Harbor Laboratory, 1974—, and Hellenic Anticancer Institute (Athens), 1977—; member of scientific advisory committee of Fox Chase Institute for Cancer Research, 1976—; member of scientific council of International Institute of Cellular and Molecular Pathology (Brussels), 1977—. Member of Commission on Streptococcal and Staphylococcal Diseases, of U.S. Department of Defense's Armed Forces Epidemiological Board, 1950-62; member of New York City Board of Health, 1955-60, and Health Research Council, 1974-75 (head of narcotics advisory committee, 1961-63); member of National Advisory Health Council, 1958-62, and National Advisory Child Health and Human Development Council, 1963-67; member of President's Science Advisory Committee, 1967-70; head of National Academy of Sciences committee to review national cancer plan, 1972; member of special medical advisory group to U.S. Veterans Administration. Member of board of trustees of Guggenheim Foundation, 1975—, and board of directors of Squibb Corp., 1969—, and Josiah Macy, Jr. Foundation, 1975—. Military service: U.S. Naval Reserve, Medical Corps, active duty, 1941-46; became lieutenant commander.

MEMBER: International Academy of Pathology, Association of American Physicians, American Pediatric Society, American Association of Immunologists, Society for Experimental Biology and Medicine, American Academy of Microbiology (charter member), American Rheumatism Association, American Society for Clinical Investigation, National Academy of Sciences Institute of Medicine (member of council, 1973-76), American Philosophical Society, American Academy of Arts and Sciences, American Association of University Professors, Peripatetic Clinical Society, Practitioners Society, Harvey Society, Interurban Clinical Club, Phi Beta Kappa, Alpha Omega Alpha, Century Association, Harvard Club. Awards, honors: Honorary degrees include M.A. from Yale University, 1969, Sc.D. from University of Rochester, 1974, Princeton University, 1976, Medical College of Ohio, 1976, and Columbia University, 1978, LL.D. from Johns Hopkins University, 1976, L.H.D. from Duke University, 1976, and Reed College, 1977; National Book Award in Arts and Letters, 1974, for The Lives *of a Cell;* distinguished achievement award from *Modern Medicine,* 1975; visiting scholar of Phi Beta Kappa, 1977-78.

WRITINGS: The Lives of a Cell: Notes of a Biology Watcher, Viking, 1974; *The Medusa and the Snail: More Notes of a Biology Watcher,* Viking, 1979.

Contributor: *Rheumatic Fever: A Symposium,* University of Minnesota Press, 1952; Gregory Schwartzman, editor, *The Effects of ACTH and Cortisone Upon Infection and Resistance,* Columbia University Press, 1953; Russell Cecil and R. F. Loeb, editors, *A Textbook of Medicine,* Saunders, 1953; H. S. Lawrence, editor, *Cellular and Humoral Aspects of the Hypersensitive States,* Paul B. Hoeber, 1959; *Biological Problems of Grafting,* Les Congres et Colloques de L'Universite de Liege, 1959; *Streptococcus, Rheumatic Fever, and Glomerulonephritis,* Williams & Wilkins, 1964; W. Braun and M. Landy, editors, *Bacterial Endotoxins,* Rutgers University, Institute of Microbiology, 1964; *The Inflammatory Process,* Academic Press, 1965; *The Modern Hospital,* McGraw, 1967; P. A. Miescher, C. Henze, and R. Schett, editors, *The Modern University: Structure, Functions, and Its Role in the New Industrial State,* Georg Thieme Verlag, 1969; *Microbial Toxins,* Volume III, Academic Press, 1970; G. J. Gallagher, editor, *Immunological Disorders of the Nervous System,* Williams & Wilkins, 1971; J. Z. Bowers and E. F. Purcell, editors, *Advances in American Medicine: Essays at the Bicentennial,* Josiah Macy, Jr. Foundation, 1976.

Contributor of a poem to *New Yorker.* Contributor of about two hundred articles to medical and scientific journals, including *Science, Nature, Daedalus,* and *Saturday Review of Science.* Author of column, "Notes of a Biology Watcher," in *New England Journal of Medicine,* 1971—. Member of editorial board of *Human Pathology, Journal of Immunology, American Journal of Pathology, Cellular Immunology, Journal of Medicine and Philosophy, Inflammation, Perspectives in Biology and Medicine, Human Nature, Journal of Developmental and Comparative Immunology,* and *Daedalus.*

SIDELIGHTS: The observation of the natural world has long been Thomas's vocation and avocation. Although his medical specialty is pathology, Thomas's interest has been captured by the range of natural phenomena from the unit of the cell to human social patterns. In 1971 he began contributing a popular column, "Notes of a Biology Watcher," to the prestigious *New England Journal of Medicine.* Some of these essays were collected and published in 1974 as *The Lives of a Cell: Notes of a Biology Watcher.* The book, which according to a *Time* reviewer combined "wit" and "imagination" with a "bold, encouraging vision of both man and nature," received a National Book Award the same year. Critics were dazzled with Thomas's accomplishment, but he was somewhat embarrassed by his newfound status as a book author. "I mean it's not really fair to have a book with a cover and everything when you never wrote a book, except in such little tiny bits," he told Barbara Yuncker. "I *love* having it, but it doesn't seem as though I'd earned it."

Symbiosis—the mutually beneficial relationship between organisms—is the main theme of the book. "There is a tendency for living things to join up, establish linkages, live inside each other, return to earlier arrangements, get along whenever possible. This is the way of the world," Thomas stated in one essay. He decries man's attempt to remove himself from nature, and concludes that, "The whole dear notion of one's own self—marvelous old free-willed, free-enterprising, autonomous, independent, isolated island of a Self—is a myth."

John Updike noted that Thomas's "absorption in the marvels of symbiotic interconnection intoxicates this scientist, and leads him into flights of what must be fantasy." Some of his ideas, Updike commented, seem "more mystical than demonstrable." He continued: "Dr. Thomas has the mystic's urge toward total unity. He views the earth as a single cell in its membrane of atmosphere.... Not that he professes any use for old-fashioned supernaturalist religion. Yet his doctrine of universal symbiosis soars with an evangelical exultation, and it is interesting that even his careful prose lapses into the grammar of teleology."

Joyce Carol Oates pondered what tack to take in praising Thomas's work. She remarked: "A reviewer who concentrates upon Dr. Thomas's effortless, beautifully-toned style, even to the point of claiming that many of the twenty-nine essays in this book are masterpieces of the 'art of the essay,' would direct attention away from the sheer amount of scientific information these slender essays contain. A reviewer who deals with the book as 'science' would be forced, by Dr. Thomas's marvelous use of paradox, to admit that the book might not yield its wisdom at a single reading." She continued: "One might as well rise to the higher speculation that [this book] anticipates the kind of writing that will appear more and more frequently, as scientists take on the language of poetry in order to communicate human truths too mysterious for old-fashioned common sense."

Most of Thomas's essays end on the upbeat, which critics found to be refreshing. The title essay of *The Lives of a Cell* succinctly expresses Thomas's perception of man's place in the universe and his belief in the continued existence of that universe. He wrote: "We are told that the trouble with Modern Man is that he has been trying to detach himself from nature. He sits on the topmost tiers of polymer, glass, and steel, dangling his pulsing legs, surveying at a distance the writhing life of the planet. In this scenario, Man comes on as a stupendous lethal force, and the earth is pictured as something delicate, like rising bubbles at the surface of a country pond, or flights of fragile birds. But it is an illusion to think that there is anything fragile about the life of the earth; surely this is the toughest membrane imaginable in the universe, opaque to probability, impermeable to death. We are the delicate part, transient and vulnerable as cilia."

BIOGRAPHICAL/CRITICAL SOURCES: New York Times Book Review, May 26, 1974; *Newsweek,* June 24, 1974; *Village Voice,* June 27, 1974; *New York Post,* June 29, 1974; *New Yorker,* July 15, 1974; *Time,* July 22, 1974, May 14, 1979; *New York Review of Books,* November 28, 1974.

*   *   *

THOMAS, Lowell Jackson, Jr. 1923-

PERSONAL: Born October 6, 1923, in London, England; son of Lowell Jackson (the journalist) and Frances (Ryan) Thomas; married Mary Taylor Pryor, May 20, 1950; children: Anne Frazier, David Lowell. *Education:* Dartmouth College, B.A., 1948; Princeton University, graduate study, 1951-52. *Politics:* Republican. *Religion:* Protestant. *Home:* 7022 Tanaina Dr., Anchorage, Alaska 99502.

CAREER: Fox Movietone News, assistant cameraman in South America, 1939, member of Bradford Washburn Alaskan mountaineering expedition, 1940; lecturer, 1946—; assistant economist and photographer with Max Weston Thornburg, Turkey, 1947, Iran, 1948; worked in film production, Iran, 1949; organized the Tibet expedition with father, Lowell Thomas, Sr., 1949; Cinerama, Inc., field work in South America, Africa, and Asia, 1951-52, assistant producer, 1952-54; with wife, Mary, wrote and filmed their travels by small plane through Europe, Africa, and the Middle East, 1954-55; producer of "Flight to Adventure" television series, National Broadcasting Co., 1956; producer and writer of "High Adventure" television series, 1957-59; producer of several documentary films, including "Adaq, King of Alaskan Seas," 1960, a film on the University of Alaska, 1964, and a film on Arctic oil exploration for Atlantic-Richfield Co., 1969; member of the Rockwell Polar Flight (first flight around the world over both poles), 1965; Alaska state senator, 1967-75; lieutenant governor of Alaska, 1975—; writer. President of Western Alaska Council of the Boy Scouts of America; member of board of directors, Salvation Army, Anchorage Unit; member of Alaska Chamber of Commerce. *Military service:* U.S. Army Air Forces, Southeast Training Command, 1943-45; became first lieutenant.

MEMBER: Screen Actors Guild, Aircraft Owners and Pilots Association, Delta Kappa Epsilon, Marco Polo Club, Explorers' Club and Dutch Treat Club (both New York City), Bohemian Club (San Francisco), Rotary Club and Press Club (both Anchorage). *Awards, honors:* D. Litt., Scottsbluff College, 1969.

WRITINGS: Out of this World: Across the Himalayas to Tibet, Greystone Press, 1950; (with wife, Mary P. Thomas) *Our Flight to Adventure,* Doubleday, 1956; *The Silent War in Tibet,* Doubleday, 1959, reprinted, Greenwood Press, 1973; *The Dalai Lama,* Duell, Sloan, 1961; (editor) *The Trail of Ninety-Eight,* Duell, Sloan, 1962; (editor with father, Lowell Thomas, Sr.) *More Great True Adventures,* Hawthorn, 1963; *Lowell Thomas Jr.'s Adventures in National Country: A Guide to Florida,* Popular Library, 1966; (with L. Thomas, Sr.) *Famous First Flights That Changed History,* Doubleday, 1968.

SIDELIGHTS: At the age of fifteen, Lowell Thomas, Jr. acquired a job as an assistant cameraman for the Fox Movietone News and embarked on a career that has taken him from South America to Alaska. The world traveler has written several books about his expeditions around the globe, but his most recent book, *Famous First Flights That Changed History,* highlights the adventures of some of the early pioneers of air travel. The book covers events from the first flight over the English Channel in 1909 to the 1965 jet flight over both poles.*

*   *   *

THOMPSON, Anne Armstrong   1939-

PERSONAL: Born September 28, 1939, in Lexington, Ky. *Education:* University of Kentucky, B.S., 1960; Fletcher School of Law and Diplomacy, M.A., 1961. *Agent:* James Brown Associates, Inc., 25 West 43rd St., New York, N.Y. 10036.

CAREER: Writer.

WRITINGS—Novels: *The Swiss Legacy,* Simon & Schuster, 1974; *Message From Absalom,* Simon & Schuster, 1975; *The Romanov Ransom,* Simon & Schuster, 1978; *The Man Caine,* Crowell, 1979.

*   *   *

THOMPSON, Arthur A., Jr.   1940-

PERSONAL: Born February 2, 1940, in Jonesboro, Ark.; son of Arthur A. Thompson. *Education:* University of Tennessee, B.S., 1961, Ph.D., 1965. *Home:* 7604 Lakeview Ave. N.E., Tuscaloosa, Ala. 35401. *Office:* P.O. Box J, University, Ala. 35486.

CAREER: Virginia Polytechnic Institute and State University, Blacksburg, assistant professor of economics, 1964-67; University of Alabama, Tuscaloosa, professor of business administration, 1967—. *Member:* American Economic Association, Western Economic Association, Southern Economic Association, Southern Case Research Association, Midsouth Academy of Economists.

WRITINGS: Economics of the Firm: Theory and Practice, Prentice-Hall, 1973, 2nd edition, 1977; *Strategy and Policy: Concepts and Cases,* Business Publications, 1978. Contributor of more than fifty articles to business and economics journals.

*   *   *

THOMPSON, Earl   1931(?)-1978

PERSONAL: Born c.1931; died November 9, 1978, in Sausalito, Calif.; married; children: three. *Education:* Attended University of Missouri and Columbia University. *Residence:* Brooklyn, N.Y.

CAREER: Thompson once listed his various occupations as: "thief, roughneck, gandy dancer, laborer, driver, sailor, tank commander, cartoonist, reporter, editor, commercial artist and novelist." He and his wife operated a graphics studio in Brooklyn, N.Y. *Military service:* Served in U.S. Navy and U.S. Army. *Awards, honors:* National Book Award nomination for *A Garden of Sand;* two Mahan Short Story Awards from University of Missouri.

WRITINGS—Novels: *A Garden of Sand,* Putnam, 1970; *Tattoo,* Putnam, 1974; *Caldo Largo,* Putnam, 1976.

WORK IN PROGRESS: The third and fourth books in the series that included *A Garden of Sand* and *Tattoo.*

SIDELIGHTS: Despite its touchy subject—incest between a mother and son—Earl Thompson's first novel was widely praised by critics and earned a National Book Award nomination. *A Garden of Sand,* Thompson told an interviewer, "is a story about pathetic people, but I don't think it is at all tragic. Given the identical condition, I consider them ahead of those whose striving for some kind of pleasure and happiness result in experiences less rich. These are people who are the victims of an arbitrary morality of a repressive society. It is also an effort to show these people how almost everything they have ever been told officially has been a pack of goddamn lies. Yet, I hope to indicate that even on this desperate level three essential virtures pertain: courage, generosity, and magnanimity."

"This is a rare novel," a reviewer for *Newsday* wrote, "tough, honest, uncompromising and yet somehow heartening: a frank look at a boy's growing up in a world where his only mainstay is his sexuality. To read it is to realize that 90 per cent of all books about sexuality are phony and mechanical. This one is real, to the utmost, frightening degree."

Critics have noted that there are flaws in the novel; however, they do not seriously damage the work. "Earl Thompson's first novel has plenty of things wrong with it," Walter Clemons wrote, "but none of them fatally effect its openness of feeling and its forlorn believability." Clemons cited Thompson's "unshakable feeling for character," and concluded, "Earl Thompson is on many pages a shaky writer, but where it counts, making you see through the page to what he's describing and making you believe him, he has made something indelible."

Thompson explained that he is "of the people of whom I write and will never truly be of any other." He continued: "My persisting values are those of that class which is trapped between poverty that is a personal moral failure and the lure of material reward for citizenship they can never achieve. A class that is a persistent pain in the ass to all representative societies, whatever their ism. People who are so early frightened by violence anything short of death is a personal victory. And all have been wounded.''

Caldo Largo, Thompson's most recent novel, was also successful. The book is about arms smuggling in the Gulf of Mexico: Martin Levin called it "a richly rewarding trip." Christopher Lehmann-Haupt found that Thompson's descriptive powers were strong. "He makes his Gulf waters positively seethe with wildlife, about which he has interesting lore to impart that even Melville forgot to mention," Lehmann-Haupt commented. "But most of all," the critic continued, "what saves 'Caldo Largo' from being merely an exciting yarn—assuming that it has to be rescued from such a state at all—is Mr. Thompson's refreshingly skeptical view of the American system, which serves to make entirely plausible the desperate pitch of his characters' behavior. It is by no means propagandistic social realism that Mr. Thompson serves up. He couldn't write that drearily even if he set out to."

BIOGRAPHICAL/CRITICAL SOURCES: Library Journal, June 15, 1970; *Esquire,* September, 1970; *New York Times,* January 6, 1971, January 28, 1977; *Best Sellers,* January 15, 1971; *Newsday,* January 16, 1971; *Hudson Review,* spring, 1975; *New York Times Book Review,* March 13, 1977.

OBITUARIES: Publishers Weekly, November 27, 1978.*

*   *   *

THOMPSON, Kay 1912(?)-

PERSONAL: Born November 9, 1912(?), in St. Louis, Mo.

CAREER: Author, actress, singer, pianist, and songwriter. Worked as pianist with St. Louis Symphony, St. Louis, Mo., 1928; singer in St. Louis, 1928; diving instructor in California, 1929; singer with Mills Brothers for radio; singer and arranger with Fred Waring's Band, New York City; co-producer with Jim Backus of ''Kay Thompson and Company'' radio show for Columbia Broadcasting Systems (CBS); arranger and songwriter of motion pictures for Metro-Goldwyn Mayer, including ''The Ziegfeld Follies,'' ''The Harvey Girls,'' and ''The Kid from Brooklyn,'' Hollywood, Calif., 1942-46; nightclub performer with Williams Brothers, 1947-53; entertainer in New York City, 1954; actress in motion pictures, including ''Funny Face,'' 1956, and ''Tell Me That You Love Me Junie Moon,'' 1970, and on television. Founder of Eloise Ltd.

WRITINGS: Eloise: A Book for Precocious Grown Ups, illustrations by Hilary Knight, Simon & Schuster, 1955; *Eloise in Paris,* illustrations by Knight, Simon & Schuster, 1957; *Eloise at Christmastime,* illustrations by Knight, Random House, 1958; *Eloise in Moscow,* illustrations by Knight, Simon & Schuster, 1959; *Kay Thompson's Miss Pooky Peckinpaugh and Her Secret Private Boyfriends Complete with Telephone Numbers,* illustrations by Joe Eula, Harper, 1970.

SIDELIGHTS: Thompson accounted for her diverse talents by telling a *McCall's* interviewer, "If artistically you are able to do one thing, you are more than likely able to do them all."

Eloise, the character in her books, was born sometime during her nightclub act with the Williams Brothers. In apologizing for being late for a rehearsal, Thompson responded in a high, childish voice that her name was Eloise and she was

six. The other performers each invented a juvenile identity and joined the game. Illustrator Hilary Knight brought Eloise to life. The first Eloise book had sold over 150,000 copies at the time its sequel was published two years later.

Eloise is a brat who lives at the Plaza Hotel in New York, the location chosen because Thompson stayed there and performed there often. At the height of her popularity Eloise became identified with the Plaza Hotel. Her portrait hung in a place of honor, and a room was named after her, with all the furnishings and decor taken directly from book illustrations. For a time, the hotel received calls from little girls wanting to talk to Eloise. Thompson spoke with many of the callers when she was there until she realized that Eloise's calls outnumbered her own.

Kay Thompson also founded Eloise Ltd., which produced records and post cards among other Eloise-related items. In addition, the character has inspired a line of children's fashions, as well as dolls and hotel kits.

BIOGRAPHICAL/CRITICAL SOURCES: McCall's, January, 1957; *Publishers Weekly,* May 12, 1969; *Harper's Bazaar,* November, 1972.*

*   *   *

THOMPSON, Susan O(tis) 1931-

PERSONAL: Born August 9, 1931, in Nashville, Tenn.; daughter of Lawrence Jennings (a paper broker) and Pauline Nell (a nurse; maiden name, Roberts) Otis; married John Anderson Thompson (a professor of English), December 29, 1962; children: Louise, Keeler, Peter (stepchildren). *Education:* Sweet Briar College, A.B. (summa cum laude), 1952; Columbia University, M.S., 1963, D.L.S., 1972. *Politics:* Democrat. *Religion:* Agnostic. *Home:* 418 Central Park W., Apt. 71, New York, N.Y. 10025. *Office:* School of Library Service, Columbia University, New York, N.Y. 10027.

CAREER: Columbia University, New York, N.Y., assistant professor, 1972-78, associate professor of library science, 1978—. *Member:* American Library Association, American Printing History Association (member of national board of trustees, 1974-78), Private Libraries Association, Association of American Library Schools, Bibliographical Society of America, American Library History Roundtable, Center for the Book Arts, New York Library Association, Phi Beta Kappa, Beta Phi Mu (president of Nu chapter, 1977-78), Typophiles, Friends of the Columbia Libraries, Grolier Club.

WRITINGS: (With Robert J. Clark, Martin Eidelberg, and David A. Hanks) *The Arts and Crafts Movement in America, 1876-1916,* Princeton Art Museum, 1972; (editor) *Caxton: An American Contribution to the Quincentenary Celebration,* Typophiles, 1976; *American Book Design and William Morris,* Bowker, 1977; (contributor) Jean Peters, editor, *Book Collecting: A Modern Guide,* Bowker, 1977. Contributor to library and printing history journals. Editor of *Printing History.*

WORK IN PROGRESS: Reader in Rare Book Librarianship, for Information Handling Service; *Turn-of-the-Century Graphic Art in Britain and America,* with Joseph Dunlap, for Dover; *Preservation of Library Materials: A Guide to Information Sources,* with Paul Banks, for Gale.

SIDELIGHTS: Susan Thompson writes that her main interests are "history of the book and other graphic communication, especially from the design point of view; history of libraries, librarianship, publishing, book-selling, and book-collecting; preservation of library materials; and current book arts. I disagree strongly with those pundits who predict the demise of the book. But it is true that the technology of printing is changing. It seems important to me to keep alive the traditional book arts and to increase our historical understanding of them.''

* * *

THOMSON, Peggy 1922-

PERSONAL: Born November 6, 1922, in St. Louis, Mo.; daughter of Jules (a chemical engineer) and Helen (Gilli) Bebie; married John Seabury Thomson (a government employee), May 11, 1945; children: Christopher, Hilary, David. *Education:* Swarthmore College, B.A. (with high honors). *Politics:* Democrat. *Religion:* Unitarian-Universalist. *Home and office:* 23 Grafton St., Chevy Chase, Md. 20015.

CAREER: Life, New York, N.Y., researcher, 1943-47; *Washington Post,* Washington, D.C., writer for magazine section, 1964-67; free-lance writer. *Member:* American Society of Journalists and Authors, Washington Independent Writers (member of board of directors, 1976, 1978).

WRITINGS: On Reading Palms (juvenile), Prentice-Hall, 1974; *Museum People, Collectors and Keepers at the Smithsonian,* Prentice-Hall, 1977. Contributor of articles and reviews to magazines and newspapers, including *Smithsonian* and *American Education.*

WORK IN PROGRESS: Research on museum and natural history subjects.

SIDELIGHTS: Peggy Thomson writes: ''I aspire to heavy research with a light touch. My subjects are kids, curators, and horseshoe crabs. *Museum People* consists of interviews with the animal freeze-drier, a hanger of airplanes, a collector of First Lady dresses, neon signs, and Presidential memorabilia, the special effects technician, and curators of volcanology, postal history, and graphic arts. It also has chapters on collecting, keeping track of things, conserving, and exhibiting.

''I have written articles about kids, dealing with bilingual education, migrants' day care, learning through filmmaking, the arts, outdoor programs, hands-on science, an environmental living program, and Foxfire.''

* * *

THORNTON, Francis John 1938-

PERSONAL: Born October 28, 1938, in Mahanoy City, Pa.; son of Francis J. (a police officer) and Helen (a nurse; maiden name, Maher) Thornton; married Mary Margaret Fullwood (a teacher), November 6, 1976. *Education:* Villanova University, B.S., 1962, M.A., 1964; further graduate study at University of Pittsburgh, 1966-69, and Duquesne University, 1970-74. *Politics:* Democrat. *Religion:* Roman Catholic. *Home:* 4834 Hobaugh St., Murrysville, Pa. 15668. *Office:* Department of Speech & Theater, Duquesne University, Pittsburgh, Pa. 15219.

CAREER: High school English teacher in Philadelphia, Pa., 1962-63; College of Great Falls, Great Falls, Mont., member of English department, 1963-66; Duquesne University, Pittsburgh, Pa., currently member of English department, director of theater, 1970-77. Commentator on KDKA-TV; training director at WDVQ-FM Radio, 1972—.

WRITINGS: The Snake Harvest (novel), Coward, 1978.

WORK IN PROGRESS: Incident at El Morro (tentative title), a novel.

THURSTON, Robert (Donald) 1936-

PERSONAL: Born October 28, 1936, in Lockport, N.Y.; son of Donald and Ruth (Stearns) Thurston; married Joan K. Sullivan (a college teacher and administrator), June, 1964; children: Jason. *Education:* State University of New York at Buffalo, B.A., 1959, M.A., 1967. *Home and office:* 200 Cabrini Blvd., Apt. 19, New York, N.Y. 10033.

CAREER: Lockport Union-Sun and Journal, Lockport, N.Y., reporter, 1959; Alliance College, Cambridge Springs, Pa., assistant professor of English, 1967-68; bookstore manager in Williamsville, N.Y., 1968-71; writer, 1969—. *Military service:* U.S. Army, 1960-62. *Awards, honors:* First prize from Clarion Science Fiction Writers Workshop, 1960, for story, ''Wheels.''

WRITINGS: (With Glen A. Larson) *Battlestar Galactica* (adaption of film script), Berkley, 1978; *Alicia II* (science fiction novel), Putnam, 1978; (with Larson) *Battlestar Galactica II: The Cylon Death Machine,* Berkley, 1979. Also author of seven introductions to science fiction books reprinted by Gregg.

Work represented in anthologies including *New Dimensions Five,* edited by Robert Silverberg, *New Voices,* edited by George R. R. Martin, and *Rod Sterling's Other Worlds.* Contributor of stories to science fiction and fantasy magazines, including *Magazine of Fantasy and Science Fiction, Analog,* and *Fantastic.*

WORK IN PROGRESS: One more ''Galactica'' novel for Berkley; *A Set of Wheels* (tentative title), a novel based on previously published stories.

SIDELIGHTS: Robert Thurston writes: ''*Alicia II* is an attempt to portray certain contemporary social problems and emotional dilemmas in science fictional terms. By depicting a society in which people literally use the bodies of other people to continue their own lives, it may say something figuratively about how people use other people in several other respects.

''The major difference between *Alicia II* and the Galactica novelizations is the amount of time necessarily spent on each work. While I worked on *Alicia* at intervals over a number of years, the books in the Galactica series were produced for a deadline. This means that (ideally) a writer's novels represent the best kind of prose he/she can offer, while a novelization (again, ideally) represents his/her best second or third draft of the material.

''The novelization seems to demand a highly denotative prose style, while the novel, I think, works better in textured and connotative language. In adapting episodes from the 'Battlestar Galactica' television series, I tried to adapt stories conceived by Glen A. Larson and his colleagues for the visual medium into narratives more appropriate to the 'litarary' form of science fiction. My purpose was to write a book which would have specific reference to space opera as practiced within the genre, while the filmed sequences' references tended more toward the cinematic traditions of science fiction.''

* * *

TIERNEY, Paul Ambrose 1895(?)-1979

OBITUARY NOTICE: Born c. 1895; died March 3, 1979, in Port Washington, N.Y. Editor best known for his work with the *New York Post.* He also worked for numerous other newspapers, including *New York Globe, Newark News,* and *Long Island Star-Journal.* Tierney was decorated during World War I for replacing a wounded ambulance driver and driving wounded soldiers to safety. Obituaries and other sources: *New York Times,* March 6, 1979.

* * *

TIKHONOV, Nikolai Semyonovich 1896-1979

OBITUARY NOTICE: Born December 4, 1896, in St. Petersburg, Russia (now Leningrad, U.S.S.R.); died February 8, 1979. Writer. Tikhonov wrote short stories, essays, and verse, including *Leningrad Accepts the Challenge* and *The Fiery Year.* He had been chairman of the Soviet Peace Committee since 1949. Obituaries and other sources: *The Reader's Encyclopedia,* 2nd edition, Crowell, 1965; *Encyclopedia of World Literature in the Twentieth Century,* updated edition, Ungar, 1967; *The Penguin Companion to European Literature,* McGraw, 1969; *Cassell's Encyclopaedia of World Literature,* revised edition, Morrow, 1973; *International Who's Who,* Europa, 1978; *Washington Post,* February 13, 1979.

* * *

TINDALL, George Brown 1921-

PERSONAL: Born February 26, 1921, in Greenville, S.C.; son of Goin Roscoe and Nellie Evelyn (Brown) Tindall; married Carliss Blossom McGarrity, June 29, 1946; children: Bruce McGarrity, Blair Alston Mercer. *Education:* Furman University, A.B., 1942, LL.D., 1971; University of North Carolina, M.A., 1948, Ph.D., 1951. *Home:* 305 Burlage Circle, Chapel Hill, N.C. 27514. *Office:* Department of History, University of North Carolina, Chapel Hill, N.C. 27514.

CAREER: Eastern Kentucky State College (now University), Richmond, assistant professor of history, 1950-51; University of Mississippi, University, assistant professor of history, 1951-52; Women's College of the University of North Carolina (now University of North Carolina at Greensboro), Greensboro, assistant professor of history, 1952-53; Louisiana State University, Baton Rouge, assistant professor of history, 1953-58; University of North Carolina at Chapel Hill, associate professor, 1958-64, professor of history, 1964-69, Kenan Professor, 1969—. Member of Princeton University's Institute for Advanced Study, 1963-64; Fulbright professor at University of Vienna, 1967-68; visiting professor at Kyoto American Studies Summer Seminar, 1977; Eugenia Dorothy Blount Lamar lecturer at Mercer University, 1970; Walter Lynwood Fleming lecturer at Louisiana State University, 1973; Ralph Brown Draughon lecturer at Auburn University, 1974; lecturer at institutions in the United States, Germany, and Scotland. *Military service:* U.S. Army Air Forces, 1942-46; became second lieutenant.

MEMBER: American Historical Association, Organization of American Historians, Society of American Historians, American Society of History Associations (president, 1973), Southern Historical Association (member of executive committee, 1964-68; vice-president, 1972; president, 1973), Historical Society of North Carolina, North Carolina Literary and Historical Society. *Awards, honors:* Guggenheim fellow, 1957-58; Social Science Research Council fellow, 1959-60; Charles S. Sydnor Award from Southern Historical Association, 1968; Lillian E. Smith Award from Southern Regional Council, 1968; Mayflower Cup from North Carolina Society of Mayflower Descendants, 1968; Litt.D. from Furman University, 1971.

WRITINGS: South Carolina Negroes, 1877-1900, University of South Carolina Press, 1952; (editor) *The Pursuit of Southern History: Presidential Addresses of the Southern*

Historical Association, Louisiana State University Press, 1964; (editor) *A Populist Reader,* Harper, 1966; *The Emergence of the New South, 1913-1945,* Louisiana State University Press, 1970; *The Disruption of the Solid South,* University of Georgia Press, 1972; *The Persistent Tradition in New South Politics,* Louisiana State University Press, 1975; *The Ethnic Southerners* (essays), Louisiana State University Press, 1976.

Contributor: Charles G. Sellers, editor, *The Southerner as American,* University of North Carolina Press, 1960; Frank E. Vandiver, editor, *The Idea of the South: Pursuit of a Central Theme,* University of Chicago Press, 1964; Arthur S. Link and Rembert W. Patrick, editors, *Writing Southern History: Essays in Historiography in Honor of Fletcher M. Green,* Louisiana State University Press, 1965; Edgar T. Thompson, editor, *Perspectives on the South: Agenda for Research,* Duke University Press, 1967; Arthur M. Schlesinger, Jr., editor, *History of U.S. Political Parties,* Volume II, Chelsea House, 1973; Louis D. Rubin, Jr. and C. H. Holman, editors, *Southern Literary Study: Problems and Possibilities,* University of North Carolina Press, 1975; Joab Thomas and Donald Noble, editors, *The Rising South,* University of Alabama Press, 1976; *The People of the South: Heritages and Futures,* Southern Regional Conference, 1976.

Contributor of more than forty articles and reviews to professional and popular history journals, including *American Heritage.* Member of board of editors of *American Historical Review,* 1970-74.

BIOGRAPHICAL/CRITICAL SOURCES: New York Times, January 16, 1977.

* * *

TIUSANEN, Timo 1936-

PERSONAL: Born April 13, 1936, in Viipuri, Finland; son of Miikka (a civil engineer) and Kaisu (a headmistress of a secondary school; maiden name, Blom) Tiusanen; married Ritva Tuulikki, 1958; children: Mikko, Jukka. *Education:* University of Helsinki, M.A., 1959, L.Lit., 1965, Ph.D., 1969; also attended Yale University, 1963-64. *Home:* Vironkatu 4 C 19, 00170 Helsinki 17, Finland. *Office:* Institute of Comparative Literature and Theatre Research, University of Helsinki, Hallituskatu 11-13, 00100 Helsinki 10, Finland.

CAREER: Helsingin Sanomat (daily newspaper), Helsinki, Finland, literary critic, 1958-63; University of Helsinki, Helsinki, instructor, 1964-67, acting associate professor, 1967-68, private docent, 1969-77, professor of theater research, 1977—. Visiting stage director at Helsinki City Theater, 1963-68, general manager, 1970-74; third manager of Finnish National Theater, 1969; vice-chairman of Helsinki Theater Museum, 1970—. Research assistant at Academy of Finland, 1970, senior research fellow, 1974-77.

MEMBER: International P.E.N. (Finnish president, 1968-69), Finnish Theater Managers' Union (member of board of directors, 1968-74), Aleksis Kivi Society (vice-chairman, 1969—), Finnish Poetry Readers' Union (president, 1977—). *Awards, honors:* Vaaskivi Medal from University of Tampere, Finland, 1962, for work as a literary critic; grants from America's Loan to Finland, 1963-64, Finnish Cultural Foundation, 1964-66, British Academy, 1976, and American Council of Learned Societies, 1978-79.

WRITINGS: Tapa puhua (title means "A Way of Speaking"), Kirjayhtymae, 1963; (editor) *Suomalaista huumoria* (title means "Finnish Humor"), Tammi (Helsinki), 1963;

O'Neill's Scenic Images, Princeton University Press, 1968; *Teatterimme hahmottuu* (title means "Our Theater Finds Its Shape"), Kirjayhtymae, 1969; (contributor) Ingrid Luterkort, editor, *Theater in the Five Scandinavian Countries,* Nordiska Teaterunionen (Stockholm), 1971; *Duerrenmatt: A Study in Plays, Prose, Theory,* Princeton University Press, 1977; *Linjoja* (title means "Lines of Development"), Otava (Helsinki), 1977.

Work represented in anthologies, including: *Eugene O'Neill,* edited by Ernest G. Griffin, McGraw, 1976; *O'Neill: A World Citizen,* edited by Virginia Floyd, Ungar, 1979; *O'-Neill,* edited by Horst Frenz, Southern Illinois University Press, 1980. Contributor to *Reader's Encyclopedia of World Drama* and *Crowell's Handbook of Contemporary Drama.* Contributor to magazines and newspapers.

WORK IN PROGRESS: A book on playwright Arthur Miller.

SIDELIGHTS: Tiusanen writes: "My work as a stage director with professional theater companies includes 'Long Day's Journey into Night,' 'The Beaux' Stratagem,' 'The Wild Duck,' and 'An Enemy of the People.' I have made four record albums, reading Finnish poetry and prose.

"Coming into academic teaching and research from journalism and practical theatre work, I should like to emphasize that drama should be connected with the stage, and we should try to write in such a vigorous and lively style that our books belong to literature, too, in the best meaning of the word."

BIOGRAPHICAL/CRITICAL SOURCES: News from the Finnish Theatre, June, 1978; *Choice,* June, 1978.

* * *

TOMLINSON, Gerald (Arthur) 1933-

PERSONAL: Born January 24, 1933, in Elmira, N.Y.; son of Arthur W. (a factory worker) and Margaret D. (a secretary; maiden name, Loomis) Tomlinson; married Alexis Usakowski (an editor), August 19, 1966; children: Eli Theodore, Matthew Akim. *Education:* Marietta College, A.B., 1955; studied law at Columbia University, 1959-60. *Address:* Box 432A, R.D.1, Lake Hopatcong, N.J. 07849. *Office:* Silver Burdett Co., 250 James St., Morristown, N.J. 07960.

CAREER: Teacher of social studies and English in Horseheads, N.Y., and Watkins Glen, N.Y., 1955-56; Prentice-Hall, Inc., Englewood Cliffs, N.J., associate editor, 1960-63; Harcourt, Brace, Jovanovich, Inc., New York City, associate editor, 1963-66; Holt, Rinehart & Winston, Inc., New York City, senior editor, 1966-69; executive editor of Silver Burdett Co., 1969—; writer, 1974—. *Military service:* U.S. Army, 1956-58; served as intelligence specialist. *Member:* International Reading Association, Mystery Writers of America, National Council of Teachers of English.

WRITINGS: On a Field of Black (novel), Nellen, 1979.

Contributor: *Best Detective Stories of the Year, 1976,* Dutton, 1976; *When Last Seen,* Harper, 1977; *Cop Cade,* Doubleday, 1978. Work represented in anthologies, including *Ellery Queen's Anthology #37,* Davis, 1979. Also contributor of stories to mystery magazines including *Ellery Queen's Mystery Magazine, Alfred Hitchcock's Mystery Magazine, Mystery Monthly,* and *Mike Shayne Mystery Magazine.* Contributor of an article to *The Armchair Detective* and verse to *London Mystery* and *Ellery Queen's Mystery Magazine.*

WORK IN PROGRESS: Bulletman, a comic mystery novel, publication expected in 1980.

SIDELIGHTS: Tomlinson writes: "As a textbook editor I ought to mention that it was a textbook—*How I Write/ 1* (Harcourt, 1972)—that sparked my interest in short story writing; specifically, a piece in it by Judson Phillips, 'The Short Story.' I followed Phillips's ten-point summary assiduously, and the resulting story, 'The Perfectionist,' was purchased by *Ellery Queen's Mystery Magazine.* Since then the story has been anthologized, bought by a scholastic magazine, and has been reprinted in Sweden, Denmark, Norway, and the Netherlands. Good advice from a textbook!"

* * *

TOOMER, Jean 1894-1967

PERSONAL: Born December 26, 1894, in Washington, D.C.; died March 30, 1967; married Marjory Latimer, 1932 (deceased); married Marjorie Content, 1934. *Education:* Attended University of Wisconsin, 1914, and City College of New York (now of the City University of New York), 1917-18; also attended Gurdjieff Institute (France). *Religion:* Quaker. *Residence:* Bucks County, Pa.

CAREER: Writer. Worked as teacher in Georgia, 1920-21; associated with Gurdjieff Institute in Harlem, N.Y., 1925, and Chicago, Ill., 1926-33.

WRITINGS: Cane (novel comprised of poems and short stories), Boni & Liveright, 1923, reprinted, Harper, 1969; *Essentials* (aphorisms and apothegms), Lakeside Press, 1931, reprinted, Xerox University Microfilms (Ann Arbor, Mich.), 1975; *The Flavor of Man* (lecture), Young Friends Movement of the Philadelphia Yearly Meetings, 1949, reprinted, Young Friends Movement of the Philadelphia Yearly Meetings, 1974; Darwin Turner, editor, *The Wayward and the Seeking: A Miscellany of Writings,* Howard University Press, 1978. Author of plays, including "Natalie Mann." Author of unpublished works, including "Portage Potential," 1931, "Eight-Day World," 1932, and an autobiography, "Outline of Autobiography," 1934. Novella "York Beach" included in anthology *The New American Caravan,* Macaulay, 1929; short stories and poetry included in numerous anthologies.

Contributor of short stories, poetry, and criticism to periodicals, including *Broom, Crisis, Liberator, Little Review, Modern Review, Nomad, Prairie,* and *Adelphi.*

SIDELIGHTS: Toomer's major contribution to literature is *Cane,* a novel comprised of poetry and prose which Robert Bone hailed as the product of a "universal vision." Upon the publication of *Cane* in 1923, Toomer was ranked with Ralph Ellison and Richard Wright as a leading figure in the Harlem Renaissance. In his introduction to *Cane,* Waldo Frank wrote that "a poet has arisen among our American youth who has known how to turn the essences and material of his Southland into the essences and materials of literature."

Cane's structure is of three parts. The first third of the book is devoted to the black experience in the Southern farmland. As Bernard W. Bell noted, "Part One, with its focus on the Southern past and the libido, presents the rural thesis." Houston A. Baker, Jr., called Toomer's style "Southern psychological realism." The characters inhabiting this portion of the book are faced with an inability to succeed. Citing the story "Fern" as an example, Baker wrote: "The temptations and promises presented by Fern's body are symbolic of the temptations and promises held out by the road of life . . . which stretches before the rural black American, and the frustration experienced by men in their affairs with Fern is symbolic of the frustration of the life journey. Men are willing to give their all, but the result is simply frustration, haunting memory, and hysteria.'' Toomer infused much of the first part with poetry. ''In the sketches, the poet is uppermost,'' wrote Robert Littell. ''Many of them begin with three of four lines of verse, and end with the same lines, slightly changed. The construction here is musical.''

The second part of *Cane* is more urban oriented and concerned with Northern life. The writing style throughout is much the same as the initial section with poetry interspersed with stories. Charles W. Scruggs noted that Toomer revealed the importance of the second section in a letter to the author's brother shortly before the publication of *Cane*. ''From three angles, Cane's design is a circle,'' Scruggs quoted Toomer as writing. ''Aesthetically, from simple forms to complex ones, and back to simple forms. Regionally, from the South up into the North, and back into the South again.'' But Toomer, in the same letter, also cited the completion of the ''circle'' as the story ''Harvest Song,'' which is contained in the second section. As Scruggs explained, ''Toomer is describing *Cane* in organic terms, and therefore it never really ends.'' Scrugg noticed the acceleration of the narrative as the novel's focus moved from South to North. ''The spiritual quest which gains momentum in the agrarian South 'swings upward' in the electric beehive of Washington,'' he declared. ''The 'cane-fluted' world does not die in the North. It continues to haunt the dreams and lives of those who have strayed far from their roots to dwell in the cities.''

The concluding third of the novel is a prose piece entitled ''Kabnis.'' Bell called this final part ''a synthesis of the earlier sections.'' The character of Kabnis, Bell claimed, represented ''the Black writer whose difficulty in reconciling himself to the dilemma of being an Afro-American prevents him from tapping the creative reservoir of the soul.'' Littell, as opposed to seeing ''Kabnis'' as a ''synthesis'' of the earlier portions, called it a ''strange contrast to the lyric expressionism of the shorter pieces.'' Earlier he'd written that of the three sections, ''Kabnis'' was by ''far the most direct and most living, perhaps because it seems to have grown so much more than been consciously made. There is no pattern in it, and very little effort at poetry.''

Many critics have offered interpretations of the title *Cane*. ''Toomer uses Cain as a symbol of the African in a hostile land,'' wrote Scruggs, ''tilling the soil of the earth, a slave, without enjoying her fruits. Yet strangely enough, this Cain receives another kind of nourishment from the soil, spiritual nourishment, which the owners of it are denied.'' Bell owned a slightly different perspective regarding the title. He wrote: ''Equally important as a symbol of the rural life is sugar cane itself. Purple in color, pungently sweet in odor, mysteriously musical in sound, and deep-rooted in growth, cane represents the beauty and pain of living close to nature. It also represents the Gothic qualities of the Black American's African and southern past, especially his ambivalent attitude toward this heritage.'' Baker acknowledged the validity of the *Cane* image in the Northern portion of the novel. He contended that ''even when Toomer deals with the life of the urban black American . . . , he still presents the rhythms and psychological factors that condition life in the land of sugar cane, a land populated by the 'sons of Cane.'''

Praise for Toomer's writing is extensive. Baker cited his ''mysterious brand of Southern psychological realism that has been matched only in the best work of William Faulkner.'' Kenneth Rexroth was no less impressed. ''Toomer is the first poet to unite folk culture and the elite culture of the white avant-garde,'' he contended, ''and he accomplishes

this difficult task with considerable success. He is without doubt the most important Black poet.'' Critics such as Bell and Gorham Munson preferred to dwell on Toomer's use of language. ''There can be no question of Jean Toomer's skill as a literary craftsman,'' asserted Munson. ''Toomer has found his own speech, now swift and clipped for violent narrative action, now languorous and dragging for specific characterizing purposes, and now lean and sinuous for the exposition of ideas, but always cadenced to accord with an unusually sensitive ear.'' Bell attributed *Cane*'s ''haunting, illusive beauty'' to ''Toomer's fascinating way with words.'' He wrote, ''The meaning of the book is implicit in the arabesque pattern of imagery, the subtle movement of symbolic actions and objects, the shifting rhythm of syntax and diction, and the infrastructure of a cosmic consciousness.''

After the publication of *Cane*, Toomer continued writing prodigiously. However, most of his work was rejected by publishers. He became increasingly interested in the teachings of George I. Gurdjieff, a Greek spiritual philosopher, and turned to teaching Gurdjieff's beliefs in America. Finally, Toomer embraced the Quaker religion and lived his last decade as a recluse. S. P. Fullwinder summed up Toomer's life as ''a story of tragedy.'' He wrote: ''As long as he was searching he was a fine creative artist; when the search ended, so did his creative powers. So long as he was searching his work was the cry of one caught in the modern human condition; it expressed modern man's lostness, his isolation. Once Toomer found an identity-giving absolute, his voice ceased to be the cry of modern man and became the voice of the schoolmaster complacently pointing out the way—his way.''

BIOGRAPHICAL/CRITICAL SOURCES: Jean Toomer, *Cane*, Boni & Liveright, 1923, reprinted, Harper, 1969; *New Republic*, December 26, 1923; *Crisis*, February, 1924; *Opportunity*, September, 1925; Robert A. Bone, *The Negro Novel in America*, Yale University Press, 1965; *Phylon*, winter, 1966; Howard A. Baker, Jr., *Black Literature in America*, McGraw, 1971; Kenneth Rexroth, *American Poetry in the Twentieth Century*, Herder, 1971; Darwin T. Turner, *In a Minor Chord: Three Afro-American Writers and Their Search for Identity*, Southern Illinois University Press, 1971; *American Literature*, May, 1972; Arna Bontemps, editor, *The Harlem Renaissance Remembered*, Dodd, 1972; *Contemporary Literary Criticism*, Gale, Volume 1, 1973, Volume 4, 1975; *Black World*, September, 1974.*

*   *   *

TOURAINE, Alain 1925-

PERSONAL: Born August 3, 1925, in Hermanville, France; son of Albert (a physician) and Odette (Cleret) Touraine; married Adriana Arenas Pizarro, February 9, 1957; children: Marisol, Philippe. *Education:* Ecole Normale Superieure, agrege d'histoire, 1950, docteur es lettres, 1965. *Home:* 32 boulevard de Vaugirard, 75015 Paris, France. *Office:* Centre Etude Mouvements Sociaux, 54 boulevard Raspail, 75006 Paris, France.

CAREER: Centre National de la Recherche Scientifique, Paris, France, member of research staff, 1950-57; Ecole Pratique des Hautes Etudes (now Ecole des Hautes Etudes en Sciences Sociales), Paris, acting director of studies, 1958-60, director of L.S.I. Laboratory of Industrial Sociology, 1958-70, director of studies, beginning in 1960, founder and director of Center for the Study of Social Movements, 1970—; University of Paris, Nanterre, France, professor of sociology, 1966—, head of department, 1966-69. Member of advisory committee to United Nations University Human and Social Development Program, 1977-79. *Member:* International Society of Political Psychology (Los Angeles), Association Internationale de Sociologie (vice-president, 1974-78), Societe Francaise de Sociologie (president, 1968-70).

WRITINGS—In English: *Sociologie du travail: Classes sociales et pouvoir politique en Amerique latine*, Seuil, 1961, translation published as *Working-Class Consciousness and Economic Development in Latin America*, Washington University (St. Louis), 1967; (with Claude Durand and others) *Les Travailleurs et les changements techniques*, Organisation de cooperation et developpement economique, 1965, translation published as *Workers' Attitudes to Technical Change: An Integrated Survey of Research*, Organization for Economic Cooperation and Development (O.E.C.D.; Paris), 1965; *Le Mouvement de mai ou le communisme utopique*, Seuil, 1968, translation by Leonard F. S. Mayhew published as *May Movement: Revolt and Reform: May 1968—The Student Rebellion and Workers' Strikes—The Birth of a Social Movement*, Irvington, 1971; *La Societe post-industrielle*, Denoel, 1969, translation by Mayhew published as *The Post-Industrial Society: Tomorrow's Social History: Classes, Conflicts, and Culture in the Programmed Society*, Random House, 1971; *Universite et societe aux Etats-Unis*, Seuil, 1972, published as *The Academic System in American Society*, McGraw-Hill, 1974; *Production de la societe*, Seuil, 1973, translation by Derek Coltman published as *The Self-Production of Society*, University of Chicago Press, 1977.

Other: *L'Evolution du travail ouvrier aux usines Renault*, preface by Georges Friedmann, Centre national de la recherche scientifique, 1955; *Ouvriers et syndicats d'Amerique Latine*, Seuil, 1961; (editor) *La Civilisation industrielle T. IV de l'histoire generale du travail*, Nouvelle Librarie France, 1961; (with Orietta Ragazzi) *Ouvriers d'origine agricole*, Seuil, 1961; *Sociologie de l'action*, Seuil, 1965; (editor with N. Cleuziou and F. Lentin) *Le H.L.M.: Une Societe petite bourgeoise*, Centre Recherche Urbaine, 1966; (with T. D. Tella and others) *Huachipato et Lota: Etude sur la conscience ouvriere dans deux entreprises chiliennes*, Centre National Recherche Scientifique, 1966; *La Conscience ouvriere*, Seuil, 1966; (with J. B. Dofny) *Les Ouvriers et le progres technique*, Colin, 1967; (editor with V. Ahtik and others) *Mobilite des enterprises industrielles dans la region parisienne*, Institut Amenagement Urbain Regim Parisienne, 1968.

Production de la societe, Seuil, 1973; *Vie et mort du Chili populaire: Journal sociologique, juillet-septembre 1973*, Seuil, 1973; *Lettres a une etudiante*, Seuil, 1974; *Pour la sociologie*, Seuil, 1974; *Les Societes dependantes: essais sur l'Amerique latine*, Duculot, 1976; (with Birnbaum and others) *Au dela de la crise*, Seuil, 1976; *La Societe invisible: Regards 1974-1976*, Seuil, 1977; *Un desir d'histoire*, Stock, 1977; *Sociologie permanente*, Volume I: *Le Voix et le regard*, Volume II: (with F. Dubet, Z. Hegedus, and M. Wieviorka) *Lutte etudiante*, Seuil, 1978.

WORK IN PROGRESS: Research on the antinuclear movement and on the Occitan movement; five more volumes of *Sociologie permanente.*

SIDELIGHTS: Critics' opinions vary as to the worth of Alain Touraine's many books on sociology. *The May Movement*, Peter Steinfels pointed out, "has the merit of recognizing and relating the pro-modernization and anti-modernization elements that were a central feature in the French

events." But *Saturday Review* critic Emile Capouya said he found Touraine's "expository method utterly defeating."

While some reviewers said reading *The Self-Production of Society* was somewhat difficult, a *Choice* critic described Touraine's latest book as "a beautifully reasoned and tightly written volume somewhat outside of the ordinary vein of American sociology." The book is aimed, however, at "the more sophisticated scholar; it is full of ideas and insights but on a rather abstract level."

BIOGRAPHICAL/CRITICAL SOURCES: International Labour Review, August, 1970; *New York Times Book Review*, May 9, 1971; *Saturday Review*, May 15, 1971; *Choice*, April, 1972, September, 1977; *New York Review of Books*, April 6, 1972; *Times Literary Supplement*, February 1, 1974, February 8, 1974; *Encounter*, October, 1974; *American Journal of Sociology*, May, 1976.

* * *

TRAVIS, Dempsey J. 1920-

PERSONAL: Born February 25, 1920, in Chicago, Ill.; son of Mittie (Strickland) Travis; married Moselynne Hardwick. *Education:* Roosevelt University, B.A., 1949; Northwestern University, certificate, 1969. *Home:* 8001 South Champlain, Chicago, Ill. 60619. *Office:* Travis Realty Co., 840 East 87th St., Chicago, Ill. 60619.

CAREER: Travis Realty Co., Chicago, Ill., president, 1949—. President of Sivart Mortgage Corp., 1953—, and Urban Research Institute, 1969—. Member of board of directors of Sears Bank & Trust Co. and National Housing Conference; member of board of trustees of Northwestern Memorial Hospitals. Member of local mayor's advisory committee on building code amendments and of Operation PUSH. *Military service:* U.S. Army, Ordnance Corps, 1942-46. *Member:* United Mortgage Bankers of America (president), Mortgage Bankers of America, Chicago Council on Foreign Relations, Economic Club, Cliff Dwellers, Metropolitan Club. *Awards, honors:* D.B.A. from Daniel Hale Williams University, 1976.

WRITINGS: Don't Stop Me Now (autobiography), Children's Press, 1970. Contributor to *Ebony*. Financial editor of *Dollars and Sense.*

WORK IN PROGRESS: Research on problems of low-income black displacement from center cities.

AVOCATIONAL INTERESTS: Travel (Latin America, Africa, Europe, Soviet Union).

BIOGRAPHICAL/CRITICAL SOURCES: John Seder and Berkeley Burrell, *Getting It Together: Black Businessmen in America*, Harcourt, 1971; *Famous Blacks Give Success Secrets*, Johnson Publishing Co., 1973.

* * *

TREDEZ, Alain 1926-
(Alain Trez)

PERSONAL: Born February 2, 1926, in Berck-sur-Mer, Pas-de-Calais, France; married Denise Laugier (a children's author), 1950; children: Isabelle, Corinne, Florence. *Education:* Attended the University of Paris and Ecole des Sciences Politiques. *Residence:* Paris, France.

CAREER: Dominique (children's magazine), Paris, France, co-editor with wife, 1952—; author and illustrator of books for children, 1958—. *Military service:* Served in the 25th Airborne Division of the French Army as a paratrooper, 1949-50. *Awards, honors: Sophie* received an honorable mention in the *New York Herald Tribune* Children's Book Festival, 1964.

WRITINGS—Under pseudonym Alain Trez: *La Preuve*, Denoel, 1965; *L'Amour de A a Z*, A. Michel, 1969.

All under pseudonym Alain Trez, with wife Denise Tredez under pseudonym Denise Trez; all self-illustrated: *Circus in the Jungle*, World Publishing, 1958; *Fifi*, World Publishing, 1959; *The Butterfly Chase*, World Publishing, 1960; *Le Petit Chien*, World Publishing, 1961, translation by Douglas McKee and Donine Mouche published as *The Little Dog*, Faber, 1962; *The Magic Paintbox*, World Publishing, 1962; *The Little Knight's Dragon*, World Publishing, 1963; *Sophie*, translation from the French by McKee, World Publishing, 1964; *Sophie Runs Away*, translation from the French by McKee, Faber, 1965; *The Royal Hiccups*, translation from the French by McKee, Viking, 1965; *Le Vilain Chat*, World Publishing, 1965, translation by McKee published as *The Mischievous Cat*, Faber, 1966; *Rabbit Country*, translation from the French by McKee, Viking, 1966; *Good Night, Veronica*, translation from the French by McKee, Viking, 1968; *The Three Little Mermaids*, World Publishing, 1969; *Maila and the Flying Carpet*, translation from the French by McKee, Viking, 1970; *The Smallest Pirate*, translation from the French by McKee, Viking, 1970; *Pourquoi Pas?*, L'Ecole des Loisirs, 1971; *The Three Little Mermaids*, Faber, 1977.

SIDELIGHTS: Alain Tredez's artistic career has been very diverse and has included cartooning, book illustrating, advertising, and serious painting. Paris was the site of the first major exhibition of his works in 1968.

Tredez enjoys creating books for children with his wife. After working out a story line together, Denise writes the text while Alain does the illustrations. *Circus in the Jungle* was their first such effort, and a *New York Times* critic noted, "Such an extravaganza could be merely silly, but French cartoonist Alain Trez and his wife deftly shape it into a brief, smartly paced, surprising romp into fantasy." Added *Booklist:* "Not a distinguished picture book, but a diverting one with its childlike imaginings, breezy action, and gaily colored, amusing pictures."

Fifi was described by the *Chicago Sunday Tribune* as, "Impish, implausible adventure, told with delightful deadpan...." *Kirkus* observed: "The unabashed manner in which the text and cartoon-like illustrations flirt with nonsense give rise to a humor which is most refreshing." A *Christian Science Monitor* critic made the following comments on *The Butterfly Chase:* "The Trez team pay a delightful tongue-in-cheek tribute to the perserverance of a French butterfly hunter with his honor at stake.... The illustrations, like the text, are bizarre and winsome." Noted the *Chicago Sunday Tribune:* "The authors show an uncanny knack of proceeding from the logical to the illogical to the utterly absurd, all with aplomb and delightful deadpan. Their drawings add to the delight of a captivating book."

Of *The Royal Hiccups*, a *Book Week* reviewer commented: "Stories [by the Tredezes] are above all, animated: a lot happens, the pace never drags—one might even say it is melodramatic—and the gay, airy cartoon art by Monsieur Trez deftly complements the brisk narrative.... That the story's revolution is not really satisfactory is small price to pay for the splendidly decorative art. Each drawing is edged like a rug to give it an oriental tone, and no opportunity is lost to embellish the scene in eye-filling detail."

BIOGRAPHICAL/CRITICAL SOURCES: Booklist, November 15, 1958; *New York Times*, January 18, 1959; *Kirkus*,

August 1, 1959; *Chicago Sunday Tribune*, November 1, 1959, November 6, 1960; *Christian Science Monitor*, November 3, 1960; *Book Week*, September 12, 1965; Doris De Montreville and Donna Hill, editors, *Third Book of Junior Authors*, H. W. Wilson, 1972.*

* * *

TREMAIN, Ruthven 1922-

PERSONAL: Born June 13, 1922, in New York, N.Y.; daughter of Edwin Ruthven (a sales manager) and Emily (a registered nurse; maiden name, Ninde) Tremain. *Education:* Wellesley College, B.A., 1943. *Politics:* Republican. *Religion:* Episcopal. *Home and office:* 44 West Tenth St., New York, N.Y. 10011.

CAREER: Wesleyan University, Middletown, Conn., teaching fellow in physics, 1943-45; *Time* magazine, New York, N.Y., researcher, 1946-49; free-lance artist, soap and package designer, 1950-67; writer and illustrator of children's books, 1962—.

WRITINGS—All self-illustrated: (With Joel Rothman) *Secrets With Ciphers and Codes*, Macmillan, 1969; *Summer Diary*, Macmillan, 1970; *My Friends*, Macmillan, 1971; *Fooling Around With Words*, Greenwillow, 1976; *Teapot, Switcheroo, and Other Silly Word Games*, Greenwillow, 1978. Also creator of *1964 Chin Up Calendar*, Macmillan, 1963, and *Calendar for Children*, Macmillan, 1963, 1965-76, Doubleday, 1977, 1978.

SIDELIGHTS: "I simply like to read and write and draw," Ruthven Tremain told *CA*. "I enjoy trying to present material to kids in an interesting and entertaining way. My favorite nonworking activities are reading, talking to friends, gambling (stock market, poker, backgammon, blackjack), and traveling, especially to casinos."

Tremain's book *Fooling Around With Words* is a collection of puzzles and word and picture games for children. It has been praised by the University of Chicago's Center for Children's Books as "one of the better collections of word games for this reading level" because "almost every entry can teach a child, painlessly, something about the language."

BIOGRAPHICAL/CRITICAL SOURCES: Bulletin of the Center for Children's Books, University of Chicago, January, 1977.

* * *

TRILLIN, Calvin 1935-

PERSONAL: Born December 5, 1935, in Kansas City, Mo.; son of Abe and Edyth (Weitzman) Trillin; married Alice Stewart, August 13, 1965; children: Abigail, Sarah. *Education:* Yale University, B.A., 1957. *Home:* 12 Grove St., New York, N.Y. 10014. *Office: New Yorker*, 25 West 43rd St., New York, N.Y. 10036.

CAREER: Time magazine, New York City, reporter, 1960-63; *New Yorker*, New York City, staff writer, 1963—, author of the column, "U.S. Journal."

WRITINGS: An Education in Georgia (nonfiction), Viking, 1964; *Barnett Frummer Is an Unbloomed Flower, and Other Adventures of Barnett Frummer, Rosalie Mondle, Roland Magruder, and Their Friends* (short stories), Viking, 1969; *U.S. Journal* (nonfiction), Dutton, 1971; *American Fried: Adventures of a Happy Eater* (nonfiction), Doubleday, 1974; *Runestruck* (novel), Little, Brown, 1977; *Alice, Let's Eat: Further Adventures of a Happy Eater* (nonfiction), Random House, 1978. Author of the column, "Variations," in *Na-*

tion. Contributor to periodicals, including *Atlantic, Harper's, Life, Esquire, New York Times* Magazine, and *Travel and Leisure.*

SIDELIGHTS: "Calvin Trillin is to be blessed for having written so engaging and witty and entertaining a book," Joyce Carol Oates commented on his first book, *Barnett Frummer.* In the collection of related short stories, Trillin poked fun at the major concerns of New York's Upper West Side crowd—anti-war protest, race relations, art, and cooking. The major character, Barnett Fummer, tries to be with-it for the sake of his elusive love, Rosalie Mondle. She gets invited to all the right parties: Barnett does not. "I can't understand it," he complains. "I don't like to blow my own horn, but I do think I'm as guilty as anybody."

Thomas Lash praised Trillin's "deft way of exposing the rickety scaffolding of lofty causes and the habit of party givers to run in packs. He can smell a fishy canape long before anyone else has gotten a whiff of it." Melvin Maddocks stated: "Mr. Trillin is almost too tentative and understated to be a satirist. He does not so much prick the snob's balloon as loosen the neck and let a little air leak out on the sly. But he does make the basic distinction that exposes the snob. There is a world of difference, he reminds us, between taking life seriously and taking seriously one's opinions about it. We need all the reminding we can get."

U.S. Journal is a collection of thirty-two vignettes that originally appeared in *New Yorker.* Trillin traveled across the country and recorded his impressions in these essays, which reviewers found to be refreshingly free of the cant that often pervades journalistic accounts of this type. Noting the wide range of the subjects Trillin considered, Walter Goodman commented: "He reminds us of what the Big Idea men tend to overlook, that life still goes on along its varied and peculiar course in towns around the country. He is a professional, too, in not letting his hard work show. It is evident from this collection that he asks a lot of questions of a lot of people, then takes pains to compose an article rather than give us his notes embellished with higher thoughts; but no strain shows. . . . Instead of force-feeding us conclusions, he invites us to share his observations. He is pleasant company."

Virginia Hall was similarly appreciative. She declared: "Trillin writes as if he sees with his memory—which is, I suppose, a round about way of suggesting that he is a master of perspective, fitting circumstantial odds and ends together in a pattern of past and present that gives the weight of continuity or the feel of irony to events that might otherwise occur as 'peculiarities' on the American scene. His view is tragi-comic; silliness is touched with sadness and sadness, with the absurd. It is a viewpoint that evokes strange moods in the reader—a 'mixed bag' of emotions that can't be aroused by front-page news stories, however politically momentous or socially relevant."

"Irony is the province of satire, generally, or polite conversation, and Trillin's essays share the qualities of both," John Seelye wrote. "His journalist's instincts lead him to the freaks and follies of American life, those grotesques which the tradition of Mark Twain, Sherwood Anderson, and Ernest Hemingway (two of whom were also journalists) has told us are symbolic of the quality of American life, the bizarrerie of life along Walt Whitman's 'Road.'" But Seelye suggested that Trillin's social consciousness was underdeveloped and that his "most sympathetic expression—for exploited poor whites and struggling black people of the South—scarcely rises above an alliterative, 'tch, tch!'" According to E. S. Connell though, Trillin's "scales are

usually balanced; he is a judicious journalist and has presented an agreeable collection. More important, several passages show compelling depth. As cautious as he is, he can create a wave of emotion in the reader—usually a wave of rage at the bigots, paralytic bureaucrats and myopic hucksters who infest 'U.S. Journal.' His account of desperate people in South Carolina is guaranteed to spoil your lunch."

R. Z. Sheppard concluded: "Wherever he goes, Trillin resists the temptation to put his pulse on the finger of the nation. There is never any doubt about where his sympathies lie but, like his late colleague, *The New Yorker*'s A. J. Liebling, Trillin exhibits great technical control and a quiet passion for fairness and precision. He is, to use a phrase that Liebling reserved for high praise, 'a careful writer.'"

For his next book, *American Fried,* Trillin continued to travel around the United States, but this time his subject was food. Carefully eschewing restaurants offering "Continental cuisine," Trillin set out on the backroads to discover good food—as much of it as possible. He ate crawfish in Louisiana, crab cakes and sausage in Baltimore, chili in Cincinnati, delicatessen in New York City, and reserved his highest praise for the barbecue at Arthur Bryant's restaurant in Kansas City, Missouri ("the single best restaurant in the world"). "The result," Raymond A. Sokolov wrote, "is a loosely-structured gorge cooked up by my favorite underground glutton. Trillin glories in over-eating and in eating over the counter at unknown hamburger joints and chili parlors and barbecue pits that have somehow survived in an era committed to the insipid catastrophes of industrialized fast-food and deracinated 'gourmet' restaurants."

David Sanford decided to investigate Trillin's claim that Kansas City (Trillin's hometown) has four or five of the best restaurants in the world. So Sanford traveled, via Greyhound bus, to Kansas City in pursuit of the ultimate cuisine. He concluded that Arthur Bryant "puts together one fantastic barbecue beef sandwich "and that the hamburger Trillin recommended was "sublime." As for the chocolate shake—he "liked it a lot." ("What does one say about a milkshake?").

Dorothy Rabinowitz was delighted with the book and described it as "composed of a blend of waspish sociology and a sensuality so explicit as to border on the prurient." She continued: "Mr. Trillin is one of that rare breed of humor writers to whom literacy is not a burden. He is a man with a gift for the right rhythms of a prose passage, a man with an ear for when a line should end. Indeed, so far as humor is concerned, Mr. Trillin has here performed one of the most admirable and elegantly ordered entertainments to have come by in years."

"I can tell you why I had trouble reading Calvin Trillin's first novel, *Runestruck,*" Christopher Lehmann-Haupt wrote. "The print wouldn't hold still because the book made me shake so with laughter." This novel is set in the small Maine Coast town of Berryville, which becomes chaotic when a Viking runestone is discovered—proof, according to residents, that Leif Erikson landed there. A Viking Village and Beach Area is quickly constructed: The Yankee Cafe changes its name to Leif's Lair.

Robert Strozier found that the book was "fairly predictable," and added that "there are some running gags and bits of business in there that do run on." Still, he wrote, "I enjoyed the book, it's amusing; and Trillin, . . . who probably knows more about small towns than anybody has this nice, easy-going, amiable way of poking fun where fun should be poked." Lehmann-Haupt cited Trillin's "perfect sense of timing, not to mention the effortlessness with which he has worked them into this fable." He continued, "Suffice it to say then that in 'Runestruck' Mr. Trillin has created an ideal fictional version of his particular brand of humor—a quality that should be well known by now from his previous books."

In his latest book, *Alice, Let's Eat,* Trillin again stalks the country for good food. Reviewer Ben Yagoda, judging the book by a friend's criterion that the more and better food scenes a book has, the better the book is, wrote, *"Alice, Let's Eat* may represent some kind of ideal. Never, I am quite sure, has there been so much sheer *relishing* in print."

Trillin's wife, Alice, who generally only consumes three meals a day and suffers from what Trillin describes as "seemingly uncontrollable attacks of moderation," is set up as his foil in this book. Alice has somewhat redeemed herself in Trillin's eyes, though, by never having failed to order dessert in a restaurant since "the spring of 1965, in a Chinese restaurant that offered only canned kumquats." She gets taken along on Trillin's culinary adventures, sometimes against her will, as in the New England church game supper debacle, in which both Trillins decided that they were not particularly fond of beaver. As a conciliatory gesture, Trillin took her to Paul Bocuse's little out-of-the-way place in Lyons, France to celebrate her fortieth birthday.

Reviewers smacked their lips. Lehmann-Haupt wrote of Trillin: "The persona he creates of himself is an extremely appealing one. He isn't just very funny; beneath the clown and self-deprecator lies a serious crusader for the virtues of regional American cuisines and against the pretentiousness and downright badness of American Continental restaurants that are modeled on the continent of Antarctica, where everything starts out frozen." Yagoda was worried that readers might be so overcome with "the pleasure they take in reading descriptions of Arthur Bryant's ambrosia-like burnt edges," that they might "overlook how wonderful a comic essayist Trillin is." He continued, "Most important, he knows precisely how much of himself to reveal. His persona is composed of what must be real characteristics—for instance, to put it bluntly, a tendency toward gluttony—which are stripped of anything tiresome, intimate, or complex, and turned into recurring comic motifs."

BIOGRAPHICAL/CRITICAL SOURCES: Washington Post Book World, October 26, 1969, May 16, 1971, June 2, 1974, September 25, 1978, October 19, 1978; *Time,* October 31, 1969, March 22, 1971, September 18, 1978; *Life,* November 7, 1969; *New York Times,* November 7, 1969, May 12, 1977, January 5, 1979; *Christian Science Monitor,* November 13, 1969, April 22, 1971; *New York Times Book Review,* January 25, 1970, April 22, 1971, May 16, 1971, June 2, 1974, March 6, 1977; *Best Sellers,* April 15, 1971; *New Republic,* April 17, 1971, September 13, 1975, October 7, 1978; *Saturday Review,* May 8, 1971, May 18, 1974, March 19, 1974; *New Leader,* May 17, 1971; *New York Review of Books,* August 12, 1971; *Commentary,* August, 1971; *Authors in the News,* Volume 1, Gale, 1976; *Village Voice,* September 25, 1978; *Chicago Tribune,* November 12, 1978.

*   *   *

TRUESDELL, Leon E.   1881(?)-1979

OBITUARY NOTICE: Born c. 1881; died January 12, 1979. Demographer and author of works in his field. Truesdale worked for the Agriculture Division of the Census Bureau from 1925 to 1955. He also wrote poetry. Obituaries and other sources: *Washington Post,* January 22, 1979.

TUANN, Lucy H(siu-mei) C(hen)   1938-
(Chen Jo-hsi)

PERSONAL: Born November 15, 1938, in Taipei, Taiwan; daughter of Ah-chuan Chen and Ni Chan; married Shih-yu Tuann (a researcher), September 18, 1964; children: Peter, Tom. *Education:* National Taiwan University, B.A., 1961; Mount Holyoke College, certificate, 1963; Johns Hopkins University, M.A., 1965. *Religion:* Christian. *Home:* 7411 Stirling St., Vancouver, British Columbia, Canada V5P 4H7.

CAREER: Modern Literature Bimonthly, Taipei, Taiwan, editor, 1958-62; Johns Hopkins University, Baltimore, Md., librarian, 1965-66; Huatung Institute of Hydraulic Engineering, Nanking, China, lecturer in English, 1969-73; New Method College, Hong Kong, 1973-74; bank teller, 1975-77; Hoover Institution on War, Revolution and Peace, Stanford, Calif., resident scholar, 1978—; free-lance writer, 1979—. *Awards, honors:* Wu's Art and Literary Prize, 1978, for *Yin Hsienchang; The Execution of Mayor Yin and Other Stories From the Great Proletarian Cultural Revolution* was selected as a Notable Book of 1978 by the American Library Association.

WRITINGS—All under pseudonym Chen Jo-hsi: *Spirit Calling* (stories about Taiwan), Heritage Press, 1962; *Yin Hsienchang,* Horizon Press, 1976, translation published as *The Execution of Mayor Yin and Other Stories from the Great Proletarian Cultural Revolution,* Indiana University Press, 1978; *Chen Jo-hsi Zixuanji* (title means "Selected Stories of Chen Jo-hsi"), Linking Press, 1976; *Lao Ren* (stories; title means "The Old Man"), Linking Press, 1978; *Kuei* (novel; title means "The Repatriates"), Ming Pao Monthly, 1979. Contributor of stories and articles to periodicals in the United States, France, the Netherlands, Japan, Germany, and Norway.

WORK IN PROGRESS: Wenge zayi (title means "Memoirs of the Cultural Revolution"), publication expected in 1980.

SIDELIGHTS: In 1966, Lucy Tuann moved with her husband to the People's Republic of China, living first in Peking and later in Nanking. Prior to 1966 Ms. Tuann had spent some years in the United States working on a graduate degree. According to David Lattimore of the *New York Times Book Review,* for Tuann, "as for many from Taiwan; discovering America meant discovering China—the country's great writers of the first half of the century and the great national accomplishments, under the People's Republic, of the second half—all kept from view in the Kuomintang-ruled province."

Tuann arrived on the mainland during Mao's "Cultural Revolution"; she left "disillusioned" seven years later, and after the government permitted her departure. As Lattimore observed, the revolution "had no use for their talents (Tuann had achieved a literary reputation in Taiwan) and, in fact, jeopardized the very accomplishments that had aroused their admiration and devotion." During those seven years on the mainland, Tuann never wrote, not even a line. But since her departure she has produced a novel and three collections of stories, including *The Execution of Mayor Yin and Other Stories From the Great Proletarian Cultural Revolution.*

Based on Tuann's experiences during the Cultural Revolution, *The Execution of Mayor Yin* is, according to Richard Bernstein, "in the great tradition of Orwell and Solzhenitsyn; its true subject is the survival—and sometimes the defeat—of the human spirit in its lonely quest for integrity." In his review, Bernstein also noted that "were it not for [Tuann's] collection of poignant stories set in the China of the '60s and early '70s, it is very likely that the entire epoch, during which the lives of hundreds of millions of people were profoundly shaken, would never have found its way into contemporary literature." Lattimore agreed: "While actual Chinese *samizdat* remains beyond reach of readers of English, here for the first time in translation is something close to it."

A *Times Literary Supplement* reviewer described Tuann as "concerned with what has happened to human life under communism, but not . . . anti-communist. . . . A feeling of suffocation, bewilderment, and helplessness floats like a mist through all the stories, but through it there emerges, strong and solid, the Chinese gift for dignity, endurance, affection, and consideration under adversity."

BIOGRAPHICAL/CRITICAL SOURCES: *New York Times,* December 13, 1977; *Times Literary Supplement,* June 9, 1978; *Time,* June 26, 1978; *New York Times Book Review,* July 30, 1978.

* * *

TUCHMAN, Gaye 1943-

PERSONAL: Surname is pronounced *Tuck*-man; born February 4, 1943, in Passaic, N.J.; daughter of Jack (a merchant) and Evelyn (Sugarman) Tuchman. *Education:* Brandeis University, B.A. (cum laude), 1964, M.A., 1967, Ph.D., 1969; also attended State University of New York at Buffalo, 1964-65. *Religion:* Jewish. *Residence:* New York, N.Y. *Office:* Department of Sociology, Queens College of the City University of New York, Flushing, N.Y. 11367.

CAREER: State University of New York at Stony Brook, assistant professor of sociology, 1969-72; Queens College of the City University of New York, Flushing, N.Y., assistant professor, 1972-76, associate professor of sociology, 1977—. Visiting assistant professor at Queens College of the City University of New York, summers, 1970-71, and Columbia University, summers, 1972-73 (seminar associate, 1975—); visiting adjunct assistant professor at New School for Social Research, 1971-72. Participant in international seminars and conferences.

MEMBER: American Sociological Association, Sociologists for Women in Society (national co-founder; member of national executive board, 1970-73; executive vice-president, 1975-77; regional president, 1970-73), Society for the Study of Social Problems (member of board of directors, 1976-79), Association of Public Opinion Researchers, Eastern Sociological Society. *Awards, honors:* National Institute of Mental Health grant, 1972-73; Russell Sage Foundation grant, 1976; Ford Foundation grant, 1978-79; National Endowment for the Humanities grant, 1979-80.

WRITINGS: (Editor and contributor) *The TV Establishment: Programming for Power and Profit,* Prentice-Hall, 1974; (contributor) Marcia Millman and Rosabeth Moss Kantor, editors, *Another Voice: Feminist Perspectives on Social Life and Social Science,* Doubleday, 1975; (contributor) Ann Foote Cahn, editor, *Women in a Full-Employment Economy: A Compendium Prepared for the Use of the Joint Economic Committee of Congress,* U.S. Government Printing Office, 1977; (contributor) Paul Hirsch, Peter Miller, and Gerald Kline, editors, *Strategies for Communications Research: Annual Review of Communications Research,* Volume VI, Sage Publications, 1977; (editor with Arlene Kaplan Daniels and James Benet, and contributor) *Hearth and Home: Images of Women in the Mass Media,* Oxford Uni-

versity Press, 1978; *Making News: A Study in the Construction of Reality,* Free Press, 1978. Contributor of about twenty articles and reviews to journals in the behavioral and social sciences. Associate editor of *Urban Life,* 1975—, *Journal of Broadcasting,* 1977-79, and *Pacific Sociological Review,* 1977-79.

WORK IN PROGRESS: *Women's Careers in Culture: A Social History of Artists and Writers.*

SIDELIGHTS: Tuchman told *CA:* "I rarely see myself as a writer, but rather as a sociologist who enjoys telling other people what I've learned, and to disseminate ideas as widely as possible. . . ."

* * *

TUGWELL, Rexford Guy 1891-

PERSONAL: Born July 10, 1891, in Sinclairville, N.Y.; son of Charles Henry and Edessa (a teacher; maiden name, Rexford) Tugwell; married Florence E. Arnold, 1914 (divorced, 1938); married Grace Falke, 1938; children: Tanis, Marcia, Tyler, Franklin. *Education:* University of Pennsylvania, B.S., 1915, M.A., 1916, Ph.D., 1922. *Religion:* Unitarian. *Address:* P.O. Box 4068, Santa Barbara, Calif. 92705.

CAREER: University of Washington, Seattle, Wash., assistant professor of economics, 1917-18; manager of American University Union in Europe, 1918; Columbia University, New York City, instructor, 1920-22, assistant professor, 1922-26, associate professor, 1926-31, professor of economics, 1931-37; U.S. Department of Agriculture, Washington, D.C., assistant secretary, 1933, under secretary, 1934-37; chairman of New York City Planning Commission, 1938; chancellor of University of Puerto Rico, 1941; governor of Puerto Rico, 1941-46; University of Chicago, Chicago, Ill., professor of political science and director of Institute of Planning, 1946-57, professor emeritus, 1957. Visiting professor of economics at London School of Economics, 1949-50; Hillman lecturer at Howard University, 1959; professor at Columbia University, 1962-63; associated with Center for Study of Democratic Institutions, 1964-65, senior fellow of political science, 1966—; research professor of political science, University of Southern Illinois, 1965-66.

MEMBER: International Institute of Planners, American Political Science Association, Delta Upsilon, Cosmos. *Awards, honors:* Litt. D. from University of New Mexico, 1933; LL.D. from University of Puerto Rico, 1953; award from Woodrow Wilson Foundation, 1958; Silver Medal from American Association of Planning Officials, 1967; Bancroft Prize, 1969.

WRITINGS: *The Economic Basis of Public Interest,* George Banta, 1922, A. M. Kelley, 1968; (editor) Morris Albert Copeland, Sumner Hubert Slichter, and others, *The Trend of Economics,* Knopf, 1924, Kennikat, 1971; (with Thomas Munro and Roy E. Stryker) *American Economic Life and the Means of Its Improvement,* Harcourt, 1925, 3rd edition, 1930; *Industry's Coming of Age,* Harcourt, 1927; (with Munro, Stryker, and Donald J. Henderson), *Teaching American Economic Life and A Manuel of Questions,* Harcourt, 1928, 3rd edition, 1930; *Soviet Russia in the Second Decade,* John Day, 1928.

Mr. Hoover's Economic Policy, John Day, 1932; *The Industrial Discipline and the Governmental Arts,* Columbia University Press, 1933; *Our Economic Society and Its Problems: A Study of American Levels of Living and How to Improve Them,* Harcourt, 1934; (editor) *Redirecting Education,* Columbia University Press, 1934, Books for Libraries

Press, 1971; *Agriculture and the Consumer,* [Washington, D.C.], 1934; *The Battle for Democracy,* Columbia University Press, 1935, Greenwood Press, 1969.

Changing the Colonial Climate: The Story, From His Official Messages, of Governor Rexford Guy Tugwell's Efforts to Bring Democracy to an Island Possession Which Serves the United Nations as a Warbase, [San Juan], 1942, Arno, 1970; *Puerto Rican Public Papers of R. G. Tugwell, Governor of Puerto Rico,* [San Juan], 1945, Arno, 1970; *The Stricken Land: The Story of Puerto Rico,* Doubleday, 1947; *A Chronicle of Jeopardy,* University of Chicago Press, 1955; *The Democratic Roosevelt: A Biography of Franklin D. Roosevelt,* Doubleday, 1957; *The Place of Planning in Society: Seven Lectures on the Place of Planning in Society With Special Reference to Puerto Rico,* [San Juan], 1958; *The Art of Politics as Practiced by Three Great Americans: Franklin Delano Roosevelt, Luis Munoz Marin, and Fiorello H. LaGuardia,* Doubleday, 1958.

The Enlargement of the Presidency, Doubleday, 1960; (with Joseph Dorfman) *Early American Policy: Six Columbia Contributors,* Columbia University Press, 1960; *The Light of Other Days,* Doubleday, 1962; *How They Became President: Thirty-Five Ways to the White House,* Simon & Schuster, 1965; *F.D.R.: Architect of an Era,* Macmillan, 1967; *The Brains Trust,* Viking, 1968; *Grover Cleveland,* Macmillan, 1968.

A Model Constitution for a United Republics of America, Center for the Study of Democratic Institutions, 1970; *Off Course: From Truman to Nixon,* Praeger, 1971; *In Search of Roosevelt,* Harvard University Press, 1972; (editor) *The Presidency Reappraised,* Praeger, 1974; *The Emerging Constitution,* Harper Magazine Press, 1974; *Tugwell's Thoughts on Planning,* edited by Salvador M. Padilla, University of Puerto Rico Press, 1975; *The Compromising of the Constitution (Early Departures),* University of Notre Dame Press, 1976; *Roosevelt's Revolution: The First Year, a Personal Perspective,* Macmillan, 1977.

Also author of phonorecords, including "Memoirs of the New Deal," and "Beyond the Smoke Filled Room."

SIDELIGHTS: Tugwell was a key figure in the Roosevelt administration during the 1930's and 1940's. Many of the innovative concepts he urged Roosevelt to implement were decisive in combating the economic depression which spread throughout the United States. And in a political, as well as advisory capacity, he was instrumental in stabilizing Puerto Rico's unenviable economic plight.

As a child, Tugwell led a rather mild life. Stricken by asthma at an early age, he took to reading as a means of solace. But he was a mediocre student and preferred activities such as fishing and swimming. He worked in a factory during the summer months and the wage discrimination left a marked impression on him. Tugwell drifted through high school and began to examine economic principles more closely. Disillusioned by the inability of the political machinery to help the working class, Tugwell was determined to fight the economic injustices.

After earning a doctorate, Tugwell turned to teaching economics. Several books written by him during his years at Columbia University forced others to acknowledge him as a talent in his field. In 1927, Tugwell was part of a delegation which visited the Soviet Union to study aspects of its economy. Shortly after returning to the United States, he took a position within the Roosevelt administration. Tugwell became one of the major forces behind Roosevelt's New Deal economic package. Encouraging restrictive crop harvesting

and soil conservation, Tugwell changed the face of agriculture in America. He helped resituate farmers whose land turned barren and pushed for and helped create the Civilian Conservation Corps (CCC).

Like Roosevelt, Tugwell's radical measures invited accusations that he was a communist. But the measures worked to turn back the Depression and inspire the American people. After receiving a great deal of recognition for his role in the government's battle against the Depression, Tugwell found his services in demand. He chose to work in New York City with Mayor LaGuardia. For two years he prepared the annual budget for the "Big Apple." Then, in 1940, Tugwell responded to a request by U.S. Secretary of the Interior Harold Ickes to investigate enforcement procedures in Puerto Rico regarding corporate land-purchasing limitations.

Once in Puerto Rico, Tugwell befriended Luis Munoz Marin, who was influential in the application of the corporate limitations law. With Marin's assistance, Tugwell was named chancellor of the University of Puerto Rico. However, the position was not to be a lasting one. In 1941, Tugwell accepted Roosevelt's offer of the Puerto Rican governorship.

Tugwell served in his capacity as governor for six years. During that time, he established many rectifying programs. He formed a budget bureau and was equally important in updating administrative structure. Many of Tugwell's writings deal with his years in Puerto Rico, including *The Stricken Years* and *The Place of Planning in Society.* Finally, in 1946, Tugwell resigned as governor of Puerto Rico, leaving the memory of vigilant service behind.

He returned to the academic life when he arrived in the United States again. Accepting a position with the University of Chicago, Tugwell taught political science and lent his considerable skills to government agencies and corporations that requested them. At the age of sixty-six, Tugwell chose to retire from the academic world as well as the political front.

*   *   *

TUNG, William L(ing) 1907-
(Ling Tung)

PERSONAL: Born September 29, 1907, in Shanghai, China; came to the United States in 1950, naturalized citizen, 1962; son of Zu-cha and Kuanvon (Wang) Tung; married Yueh-chiung Pu, January 23, 1932. *Education:* Fuh Tai University, B.A., 1928; University of Illinois, M.A., 1937, Ph.D., 1939; postdoctoral study at Yale University, 1939-40. *Home:* 150-67 87th Ave., Jamaica, N.Y. 11432. *Office:* Department of Political Science, Queens College of the City University of New York, Flushing, N.Y. 11367.

CAREER: Northwestern University, Sian, China, lecturer in government and law, 1928-30; Hangchow University, Hangchow, China, professor of political science, 1940-42; Western China Industrial and Commercial College, Chungking, China, acting president, 1942-43; Ministry of Information, Chungking, secretary-general, 1943-44; Chinese Embassy, The Hague, Netherlands, ambassador, 1945-47; Ministry of Foreign Affairs, Nanking, China, director of department of American affairs, 1947-49, vice-minister of foreign affairs, 1949-50; Chester Supply Corp., New York, N.Y., president, 1950-57; St. John's University, Jamaica, N.Y., professor of political science and head of department, 1957-62; Queens College of the City University of New York, Flushing, N.Y., professor of political science,

1962—. Vice-chairman of Queens Charter Revision Committee, 1960-61. *Member:* International Political Science Association, American Society of International Law, American Political Science Association, China Law Society, Phi Beta Kappa. *Awards, honors:* Received decorations for distinguished contributions to international diplomacy from China, 1945, and Chile, 1947.

WRITINGS: (Under name Ling Tung) *China and Some Phases of International Law,* Oxford University Press, 1940; *Cases and Other Readings in International Law,* Evans Book Co. (Shanghai), 1940; *The Political Institutions of Modern China,* Nijhoff, 1964; *International Law in an Organizing World,* Crowell, 1968; *International Organization Under the United Nations System,* Crowell, 1969; *China and the Foreign Powers: The Impact of and Reaction to Unequal Treaties,* Oceana, 1970; *Revolutionary China: A Personal Account, 1926-1949* (autobiography), St. Martin's, 1973; (editor) *The Chinese in America, 1820-1973: A Chronology and Fact Book,* Oceana, 1974; *V. K. Wellington Koo and China's Wartime Diplomacy,* Center of Asian Studies, St. John's University (Jamaica, N.Y.), 1977.

In Chinese: *Ti kuo chu i yu Chung-hua min tsu* (title means "Imperialism and China"), Kwaimin Press (Shanghai), 1930; *Chung-kuo Cheng-fu* (title means "The Chinese Government"), two volumes, World Book Co. (Shanghai), 1941; *Chan-Ch'ien Chih Chung-kuo Hsien-cheng Chih-tu* (title means "The Constitutional and Political Systems of Prewar China"), World Book Co. (Taipei), 1968; *Chung-wai Yueh-tse P'ing-chia Tung-Ling Chung-kuo Yu Kuo-chi Wen-t'i Lun-chu Hsien-chi* (title means "Selected Essays on International Problems"), Hwa Kang Press (Taipei), 1975. Contributor to political science journals.

WORK IN PROGRESS: Research on government and politics in China, Japan, and Korea.

SIDELIGHTS: Tung comments that his major interest is "promotion of rule of law in the international community."

*　　*　　*

TUNNARD, Christopher 1910-1979

OBITUARY NOTICE—See index for *CA* sketch: Born July 7, 1910, in Victoria, British Columbia, Canada; died of cancer, February 13, 1979, in New Haven, Conn. Architect, educator, and urban and regional planner. Tunnard was a professor at Yale University in the 1950's when he became noted for his concept of the "regional city." After studying the 600-mile "Atlantic Urban Region" from Portland, Maine, to Norfolk, Virginia, he warned urban planners of the need to concentrate less on the individual cities and to focus more on the area as a whole. Tunnard also believed that the economic life of a city depended largely upon its aesthetic appeal. Among his books on such subjects are *Gardens in the Modern Landscape, The Modern American City,* and *Man-Made America: Chaos or Control?* Obituaries and other sources: *Current Biography,* Wilson, 1959, May, 1979; *Who's Who in America,* 40th edition, Marquis, 1978; *New York Times,* February 15, 1979.

*　　*　　*

TWOMBLY, Robert C(harles) 1940-

PERSONAL: Born November 16, 1940, in Boston, Mass.; son of L. Stewart (a chemical technician) and Ruth (a secretary; maiden name, Richardson) Twombly; children: Jonathan, David. *Education:* Harvard University, B.A., 1962; University of Wisconsin, Madison, M.A., 1964, Ph.D.,

1968. *Politics:* Socialist. *Home:* 17 Old Mill Rd., West Nyack, N.Y. 10994. *Office:* Department of History, City College of the City University of New York, New York, N.Y. 10031.

CAREER: University of Wisconsin—Madison, instructor in history, 1968-69; City College of the City University of New York, New York, N.Y., assistant professor, 1969-74, associate professor of history, 1974—. *Member:* Society of American Historians, Institute of Early American History and Culture, Mid-Atlantic Radical Historians Organization. *Awards, honors:* City University Research Foundation grant, 1975-76; American Philosophical Society grant, 1976-77; National Endowment for the Humanities grant, 1977.

WRITINGS: Blacks in White America Since 1865, McKay, 1971; *Frank Lloyd Wright: An Interpretive Biography,* Harper, 1973; *Frank Lloyd Wright: His Life and His Architecture,* Wiley, 1978. Contributor of articles and reviews to architecture and history journals and to newspapers. Member of editorial board of *Marxist Perspectives.*

WORK IN PROGRESS: Colonial Communities: Towns in Pre-Revolutionary America, publication by Hill & Wang expected in 1981; *Architecture in Three Stages of American Capitalism,* publication by University of Chicago Press expected in 1983.

SIDELIGHTS: Twombly commented: "It becomes more important for me to explore the ways in which corporate and state policies affect architectural design. My scholarship is more and more influenced by my politics, so my new work on architecture will actually be an analysis of American political culture. Since architecture is created and purchased by individuals and groups from the dominant classes, it embodies class experiences—ideology, objectives, perspectives. Design history is least of all the history of style or technology, most of all the history of ideas. Although architectural space is consciously composed by clients and designers, most people—including intellectuals—think nothing of it, indeed, take it for granted, even though we all live most of our lives inside buildings. This is but another example of the ways in which people are constantly manipulated by powers over which they have no control. The role of the scholar is to illuminate these phenomena in hopes that people, becoming more aware, will attempt to gain more influence over their situations."

*　　*　　*

TYMON, Dorothy

PERSONAL: Born in Jackson, Mich.; daughter of Edward (a builder) and Esther (Hymen) Tymon. *Education:* University of Alaska, B.A., 1943; New York University, M.A., 1953. *Office:* 67-53 Woodhaven Rd., Rego Park, N.Y. 11374.

CAREER: Real estate broker, New York City, 1974—; Neighborhood Housing Rehabilitation Organization, Long Island, N.Y., executive director, 1978—. Part-time professor of real estate brokerage and property law, Long Island University, Greenvale, N.Y., and Hofstra University, Hempstead, N.Y., 1974—. Rehabilitation and urban specialist. President of Queens chapter of Long Island Board of Realtors. *Member:* American Society of Journalists and Authors, National Press Club, Chamber of Commerce. *Awards, honors:* Distinguished service award, Long Island Board of Realtors, 1977-78; neighborhood housing preservation award, New York State Division of Housing.

WRITINGS: America Is for Sale, Farnsworth Publishing,

1973; *The Condominium: A Guide for the Alert Buyer,* Golden-Lee, 1976, revised edition, 1978. Contributor to magazines, including *American Way, Family Weekly, Ms., Real Estate Today,* and *Mortgage Banker.*

WORK IN PROGRESS: A book on converting rental buildings into condominiums and cooperatives.

SIDELIGHTS: Tymon's work and writing covers a wide variety of subjects in the field of consumer advocacy, but her specialty is rehabilitating urban neighborhoods. One of Tymon's major projects is the redevelopment of buildings in Ridgewood, a southwest Queens community on Long Island that has recently been plagued by building abandonment and neglect. Plans include repairs to neglected structures and the changeover from apartments and private homes to cooperative living arrangements.

BIOGRAPHICAL/CRITICAL SOURCES: New York Daily News, February 17, 1978, March 9, 1979; *New York Post,* August 5, 1978; *Money,* March 19, 1979.

TYRRELL, R(obert) Emmett, Jr.   1943-

PERSONAL: Surname is accented on first syllable; born December 14, 1943, in Chicago, Ill.; son of Robert Emmett (a research chemist) and Patricia (a musician; maiden name, Rogers) Tyrrell; married Beverly Parsons, December 11, 1968 (died January 30, 1969); married Judy Mathews (a writer), February 12, 1972; children: Patrick Daniel, Kathryn Mathews. *Education:* Indiana University, A.B., 1965, M.A., 1967. *Home:* 102 West Sixth St., Bloomington, Ind. 47401. *Office:* P.O. Box 877, Bloomington, Ind. 47401.

CAREER: American Spectator, Bloomington, Ind., editor-in-chief, 1967—. Consultant to White House. *Member:* Saturday Evening Club, Pumpkin Papers Irregulars. *Awards, honors:* Award from American Institute for Public Service, 1975; American Eagle Award from Invest in America, Inc., 1975; named one of Ten Outstanding Men in America, U.S. Jaycees, 1977.

WRITINGS: The Future That Doesn't Work: Social Democracy's Failures in Britain, Doubleday, 1977; *Public Nuisances,* Basic Books, 1979. Contributor to magazines and newspapers, including *Commentary, National Review, Harper's,* and *New York.*

U

URRY, David (Laurence) 1931-

PERSONAL: Born January 24, 1931, in London, England; son of Alfred and Esmeralda (Christmas) Urry; married Katherine Judith Broadbelt (a photographer). *Education:* Chelsea College, London, B.S.C., 1960, Ph.D., 1963. *Religion:* Christian. *Home:* 4 The Drive, Reydon, Southwold, Suffolk, England.

CAREER: Hatfield Polytechnic, Hatfield, England, assistant lecturer, 1963-65, lecturer in zoology, 1965-67, research director in marine ecology, 1965-69, senior lecturer in ecology, 1967-69; free-lance photographer, writer, and filmmaker, 1969—. *Member:* Royal Photographic Society (fellow). *Awards, honors:* Gold medal from British Film Festival, 1976, for "Look Again at Gulls."

WRITINGS: (With wife, K. J. Urry) *Flying Birds,* Harper, 1970; (contributor) D.M.T. Ettlinger, editor, *Natural History Photography,* Academic Press, 1974. Author of documentary film script, "Look Again at Gulls," released by Royal Society for the Protection of Birds, 1975. Contributor to scientific journals and popular magazines.

WORK IN PROGRESS: "Seabirds" (tentative title), a documentary film script for Royal Society for the Protection of Birds.

SIDELIGHTS: Urry told *CA:* "I resigned my senior lectureship in marine ecology in protest over a decision of my college to allow students to train at a germ warfare establishment. To have continued in an executive position under this policy would have been irreconcilable with my interpretation of the Christian Gospel. I have now developed a former spare time interest in wildlife photography, and since leaving formal zoology, I have been a free-lance photographer, writer and film-maker, specialising in wildlife subjects.

"Although my film work has been almost exclusively as director/cameraman and scriptwriter for the Royal Society for the Protection of Birds (including, as well as the films mentioned above, 'Flying Birds', a wordless, lyrical celebration of the beauty of bird flight), it is not concerned primarily with details of conservation. I am more concerned to arouse an interest in, and understanding of, wildlife; I hope to remove scientific and technical concepts from the realms of jargon, placing them within the grasp of the lay audience, so that they may be helped to gain some further insight into the complex beauty and brilliance of the natural world. It is a sadness to me that scientific understanding and poetic insight are so frequently regarded as antipathetic."

BIOGRAPHICAL/CRITICAL SOURCES: British Birds, December, 1973.

V

VANAUKEN, Sheldon

PERSONAL: Born in Indiana; son of Glenn and Grace Vanauken; married Jean Palmer Davis (deceased). *Education:* Wabash College, B.A.; Yale University, M.A.; Oxford University, B.Litt. *Religion:* Anglican. *Residence:* Lynchburg, Va. *Office:* Lynchburg College, Lynchburg, Va. 24504.

CAREER: Lynchburg College, Lynchburg, Va., currently professor of history and English. *Military service:* U.S. Navy and U.S. Naval Reserve; became lieutenant commander. *Awards, honors:* National Religious Book Award, Gold Medallion Award from Evangelical Publishers, Mark of Excellence award from *Campus Life,* certificate of merit from Wheaton College, and "best of the year award" from *Eternity,* all 1978, for *A Severe Mercy.*

WRITINGS: A Severe Mercy (autobiography and poetry), Harper, 1977. Contributor of articles, stories, and poems to scholarly journals and to *Christianity Today* and *New Oxford Review.*

WORK IN PROGRESS: Novel, *Gateway to Heaven.*

SIDELIGHTS: Vanauken writes: "In all my books, I hope to serve Christ." *Avocational interests:* Sailing.

*   *   *

van LAWICK, Hugo   1937-

PERSONAL: Born April 10, 1937, in Soerabata, Indonesia; son of Hugo (a naval officer) and Isabella (van Ittersum) van Lawick; married Jane Goodall (an animal behaviorist), March 25, 1964 (divorced); children: Hugo Eric Louis. *Education:* Educated in the Netherlands. *Residence:* Serengeti, Tanzania, East Africa. *Agent:* William Collins & Sons, 14 St. James's Pl., London SW1A 1PS, England.

CAREER: Gombe Stream Research Center, Tanzania, East Africa, administrative director, 1962-74; free-lance writer and photographer, 1974—. *Military service:* Netherlands Army, 1957-58; became second lieutenant. *Awards, honors:* Two Emmy Awards from the Academy of Television Arts and Sciences, both 1973; Golden Hugo from Chicago Film Festival, 1973; Golden Eagle, 1973, for television special "The Wild Dogs of Africa"; Atlanta Silver Star, 1973; Bradford Washburn Award from the Boston Museum of Science, 1974, for "bringing science to the public"; Order of Merite of Senegal for contributions to wildlife conservation.

WRITINGS: (Contributor of photographs) Jane Goodall, *My Friends, the Wild Chimpanzees,* National Geographic Society, 1967; (with Goodall) *Innocent Killers,* Houghton, 1971; (contributor of photographs) Goodall, *In the Shadow of Man,* Houghton, 1971; (with Goodall) *Grub: The Bush Baby,* Houghton, 1972; *Solo, the Story of an African Wild Dog,* Houghton, 1974; *Savage Paradise,* with own photographs, Morrow, 1978.

WORK IN PROGRESS: Serengeti, a book on the animals of the Serengeti and also of the Ngorongoro Crater, publication expected in 1980.

SIDELIGHTS: Savage Paradise has been described by one critic as "one of the biggest coffee table books of the season, with almost 200 pages of photographs, double spreads . . . of the Serengeti's predatory birds and beasts." This same *Washington Post Book World* critic also observed that "in this case, Big is Beautiful. The book's size along with its unifying range of tawny colors, contributes to a sense of plains and sky—and wonder. Text comes at the front; captions, keyed to mini-photos, come at the back. In between are the fine pictures of animals—singly and in great numbers—stalking, hunting, at play."

A *Time* reviewer also praised van Lawick's photographs and noted: "Having spent some 16 years observing and photographing wild animals in Africa, van Lawick has a scientist's understanding of beastly behavior and a raconteur's way with anecdotes. But his long suit is photography: studies of sociable lions coping with the problems of love life and day care, graceful leopards stalking their prey, packs of hyenas engaging in gang warfare, and endearing cheetah families at play—all unique glimpses of the harsh beauty of a wild and fragile paradise."

BIOGRAPHICAL/CRITICAL SOURCES: Times Literary Supplement, November 9, 1973; *Christian Science Monitor,* February 27, 1974; *Washington Post Book World,* March 3, 1974, March 16, 1975, December 3, 1978; *New York Times Book Review,* May 4, 1975; *Time,* December 11, 1978.

*   *   *

Van PEEBLES, Melvin   1932-

PERSONAL: Born August 21, 1932, in Chicago, Ill. *Education:* Graduated from Ohio Wesleyan University. *Office:* c/o Ballantine Books, Div. of Random House, 201 East 50th St., New York, N.Y. 10022.

CAREER: Writer, director of motion pictures, and composer. Worked as operator of cable cars in San Francisco, Calif. Director of motion pictures, including "Watermelon Man," 1970. *Military service:* U.S. Air Force; served as navigator-bombardier. *Member:* Directors Guild of America, French Directors Guild. *Awards, honors:* First Prize from Belgian Festival for "Don't Play Us Cheap."

WRITINGS: Un ours pour le F.B.I. (novel), Buchet-Chastel, 1964; translation published as *A Bear for the F.B.I.,* Trident, 1968; *Un Americain en enfer* (novel), Editions Denoel, 1965, translation published as *The True American: A Folk Fable,* Doubleday, 1976; *Le Chinois du XIV* (short stories), Le Gadenet, 1966; *La Fete a Harlem. La Permission* (two novels; former adapted from the play by Van Peebles, "Harlem Party"; also see below), J. Martineau, 1967, translation of *La Fete a Harlem* published as *Don't Play Us Cheap: A Harlem Party,* Bantam, 1973; *Sweet Sweetback's Baadasssss Song* (adapted from the screenplay by Van Peebles; also see below), Lancer Books, 1971; *The Making of Sweet Sweetback's Baadasssss Song* (nonfiction), Lancer Books, 1972; *Aint Supposed to Die a Natural Death* (play; produced in New York City at the Ethel Barrymore Theatre, 1971; adapted from the recordings by Van Peebles, "Brer Soul" and "Aint Supposed to Die a Natural Death"), Bantam, 1973; *Just an Old Sweet Song,* Ballantine, 1976.

Other: "Harlem Party" (play), produced in Belgium, 1964, later performed as "Don't Play Us Cheap," produced in New York City at the Ethel Barrymore Theatre, 1972; (and director) "The Story of a Three Day Pass" (screenplay), Sigma III, 1968; (and director) "Sweet Sweetback's Baadasssss Song" (screenplay), Cinemation Industries, 1971; (and director) "Don't Play Us Cheap" (adapted from the play by Van Peebles). Also creator of short films, including "Sunlight," Cinema 16, and "Three Pick Up Men for Herrick," Cinema 16.

Composer for recordings, including "Brer Soul," "Aint Supposed to Die a Natural Death," "Watermelon Man" (soundtrack for the motion picture), "Serious as a Heart Attack," "Sweet Sweetback's Baadasssss Song" (soundtrack for the motion picture), and "Don't Play Us Cheap" (soundtrack for the motion picture).

SIDELIGHTS: Van Peebles began his career as an artist by creating short films. He had hoped that his first film efforts would lead to a filmmaking opportunity in Hollywood but moguls there were unimpressed. Instead of obtaining a position as a director or even assistant director, he was offered a job as an elevator operator. Seemingly at a dead end, Van Peebles suddenly received word from Henri Langlois, an associate of the French Cinematheque film depository who'd been impressed with Van Peebles's films. Langlois invited Van Peebles to come to Paris. There, Van Peebles enjoyed brief celebrity as an avant-garde filmmaker. But he had no opportunities to pursue filmmaking.

Van Peebles worked for some time as an entertainer in cafes until he discovered a means by which he could once again take up filmmaking. In France, one could gain entry into the Directors Guild if he wished to adapt his own French writings. So Van Peebles, in self-taught French, began writing novels. His first work, *A Bear for the F.B.I.,* concerned events in the life of an American middle-class black. Critical response was favorable, with Martin Levy remarking that "Van Peebles crystallizes the racial problem with rare subtlety." However, Van Peebles noted that the subtlety of the novel hindered his chances of being published in the United States. "I wrote the first work and my 'calling card,' to es-

tablish my reputation so I could get my 'black' novels published," Van Peebles claimed. "But the publishers aren't interested unless you either lacerate whites or apologize to them."

American publishers displayed a similar lack of interest towards Van Peebles next novel, *The True American,* which was written in 1965 but not published in the United States until 1976. It is the story of George Abraham Carver, a black prisoner who is accidently killed by falling rocks. Carver arrives in Hell and learns that blacks are treated well there. This is because the majority of Hell's residents are white and, supposedly, the preferential attention the blacks receive causes the white residents more grief. Despite the "promising" premise, the novel was reviewed unfavorably in *New Yorker.* "Unfortunately," wrote the critic, "the book never really lives up to its promise, largely because of its pasteboard characters, its meandering plot, and its author's tendency to use a two-ton sledgehammer to drive home every point he makes about racist America."

Van Peebles continued to write, though, and produced in rapid succession a collection of short stories, *Le Chinois du XIV,* and two short novels, *La Fete a Harlem* and *La Permission.* At the same time, he was also arranging another film project. With the financial assistance of the French Ministry of Cultural Affairs and a private citizen, Van Peebles made "The Story of a Three Day Pass," a film about a black soldier's encounter with a French woman. "The Story of a Three Day Pass" attracted substantial audiences in France and, upon its release in the United States, Van Peebles was in demand in Hollywood.

In 1969, after returning to the United States, Van Peebles agreed to direct a film written by Herman Raucher entitled "Watermelon Man." This film deals with a white insurance agent who awakens one morning to discover that he's turned into a black man. "It's authentic stuff," related Van Peebles, "that laughs *with,* not at people." Later, he insisted, "I thought I had to make 'Watermelon Man' in order to do the films I really wanted to do."

Van Peebles's next film, "Sweet Sweetback's Baadasssss Song," is probably his best known work to date. He made the film in three weeks, using nonunion crews while keeping union officials disinterested by spreading rumors that he was making a pornographic film, something unworthy of their attention. Hollywood had refused to finance the film after a reading of the screenplay failed to impress studio officials. Fortunately, Van Peebles received a sizeable loan from Bill Cosby which enabled him to complete the film. There was also difficulty promoting the film. Distributors declined to present it, theatres refused to book it, and talk shows refused to host Van Peebles. Eventually, he resorted to promoting it himself by passing out leaflets on street corners. Such determination ultimately payed off for Van Peebles. As a writer for *Time* noted, "Van Peebles fast talk, plus audience word of mouth, made it a limited success. But that was enough." After the initial success of the film, it was mass-released to more than one hundred theatres and enjoyed brief status as the top money-making film in *Variety.*

The film elicited a variety of critical responses. The story of a black sex-show performer who avenges a youth's beating at the hands of two policemen by murdering them and eventually escapes to Mexico enraged some reviewers. Robert Hatch accused him of relying "on rather irresponsible contemporary emotionalism to revitalize stock films he must have seen in his childhood." Vincent Canby claimed, "Instead of dramatizing injustice, Van Peebles merchandizes it.'' He also declared that ''the militancy of 'Sweet Sweetback' is of a dull order, seemingly designed only to reinforce the prejudices of black audiences without in any way disturbing those prejudices.'' Clayton conceded, ''The film is an outrage,'' but then observed that it was ''designed to blow minds.'' He wrote, ''Through the lens of the Van Peebles camera comes a very basic Black America, unadorned by faith, and seething with an eternal violence.'' In the same review, Rily contended, ''It is a terrifying vision, the Blood's nightmare journey through Watts, and it is a vision Black people alone will really understand in all of its profane and abrasive substance.''

Van Peebles told a *Time* reporter that the film was not just for black audiences. ''If films are good,'' he expressed, ''the universality of the human experience will transcend the race and creed and crap frontiers.'' But he also noted that the film does have some specific messages for blacks. ''Of all the ways we've been exploited by the Man, the most damaging is the way he destroyed our self-image,'' he asserted. ''The message of 'Sweetback' is that if you can get it together and stand up to the Man, you can win.'' In another interview, Van Peebles asked a writer, ''When's the last time you saw a film in which the black man won in the end?'' He then declared, ''In my film, the black audience finally gets a chance to see some of their own fantasies acted out—about rising out of the mud and kicking ass.''

After the success of ''Sweet Sweetback,'' Van Peebles was inundated with filmmaking offers from Hollywood studios. However, he insisted that he maintain his independence. ''I'll only work with them on my terms,'' he stated. ''I've whipped the man's ass on his own turf. I'm number one at the box office—which is the way America measures things—and I did it on my own. Now they want me, but I'm in no hurry.'' In a similar interview, Van Peebles remarked, ''I am what I am, man. You don't like? That's your problem.''

Van Peeble's most recent work has been as a playwright. ''Aint Supposed to Die a Natural Death,'' his first play to be produced in the United States, proved to be a popular one with Broadway audiences. Marilyn Stasio called it a ''tremendously vital musical with a dynamic new form all its own.'' She also wrote, ''The show is an electrifying piece of theatre without having songs, a book, a story line, choreography, or even standard production numbers—and yet all these elements are on the stage, skillfully integrated into a jolting new experience.''

A writer for *Variety* was impressed with Van Peebles's other U.S. production, ''Don't Play Us Cheap.'' The reviewer noted that ''this new show does not seem to be infused with hate, and it offers what appears to [be] a racial attitude without foul language, deliberate squalor or snarling ugliness.'' The same critic observed that ''points are made with humor rather than rage and are probably more palatable for general audiences.'' ''Don't Play Us Cheap' is a somewhat special show,'' concluded the writer for *Variety*, ''probably with greater meaning and appeal for black audiences than for whites.'' Van Peebles later adapted the play for film.

BIOGRAPHICAL/CRITICAL SOURCES: New York Times Book Review, October 6, 1968; *Best Sellers*, October 15, 1968; *New York Times*, May 18, 1969, April 23, 1971, May 9, 1971; *Newsweek*, June 6, 1969, June 21, 1971; *Nation*, May 24, 1971; *Time*, August 16, 1971; *Cue*, October 30, 1971; *Variety*, May 24, 1971; *Contemporary Literary Criticism*, Volume 2, Gale, 1974; *New Yorker*, March 1, 1976.*

Van ZWIENEN, Ilse Charlotte Koehn 1929-
(Ilse Koehn)

PERSONAL: Born August 6, 1929, in Berlin, Germany; came to United States, 1958; naturalized U.S. citizen, 1976; daughter of Frite Wilhelm (an electrician) and Charlotte Martha (a master tailor; maiden name, Sckrabei) Koehn; married John Herman Van Zwienen (an art director), May 24, 1969. *Education:* Attended Hochschuele Fuer Bildende Kuenste, 1948-54. *Home:* 50 Sound Beach Ave., Old Greenwich, Ct. 06870. *Agent:* Janet Loranger, P.O. Box 113, West Redding, Ct. 06896.

CAREER: Free-lance illustrator and writer, 1954; designer for exhibitions and industrial fairs, 1958; J. Walter Thompson Co., New York, N.Y., associate art director, 1959-64; art director for Campbell-Downe Advertising Agency, 1965-68; free-lance book designer and illustrator, 1968—. *Member:* Author's Guild. *Awards, honors:* Horn Book Award for nonfiction from *Boston Globe*, Book Award for children's literature, and Jane Addams Peace Award Honor Book, all 1978, all for *Mischling, Second Degree*.

WRITINGS—Under name Ilse Koehn: *Mischling, Second Degree: My Childhood in Nazi Germany*, Greenwillow Books, 1977.

WORK IN PROGRESS: ''Funny and sad stories of love in post-World War II Berlin.''

SIDELIGHTS: Koehn told *CA:* ''At the end of 1958, I came to New York with the very first commercial jet . . . I was the only German passenger. . . . I found a job with J. Walter Thompson Co., and worked there until 1964.''

After leaving J. Walter Thompson Co. for a position with Campbell-Downe, Koehn ''began free-lancing, doing bookjackets and illustrations. The smartest move I ever made, since one free-lance job from Dell made me not only meet the art director but, after due course and preliminaries, we married. We married on a sailboat. We have been sailing happily ever since.''

In a review of *Mischling, Second Degree: My Childhood in Nazi Germany*, Naomi Bliven called it ''a remarkable book in good plain English prose.'' Claiming that the book ''haunts the imagination,'' Bliven also noted that Koehn's ''memoir, in registering what a child learns as it grows, shows her experiencing corruption, hypocrisy, and intimidation before she was quite old enough to know what they were.'' Bliven observed that Koehn's grandmother plays the role of ''savior'' in the book ''because it is a story of a historic era so terrible that only a prehistoric personage could rescue its narrator: as if Merlin had saved an English child.''

AVOCATIONAL INTERESTS: Gardening, sewing.

BIOGRAPHICAL/CRITICAL SOURCES: Washington Post, November 3, 1977; *Publishers Weekly*, November 21, 1977; *San Francisco Chronicle*, January 15, 1978; *Chicago Tribune*, February 5, 1978; *New Yorker*, May 1, 1978; *Economist*, May 6, 1978; *Observer*, June 4, 1978; *Times Educational Supplement*, June 16, 1978.

* * *

VAUGHAN, Roger 1937-

PERSONAL: Born July 9, 1937, in Manchester, N.H.; son of Frank Ivan (a physician) and Helen (O'Neil) Vaughan; married second wife, Karen Possum Helgesen (a set designer), November 9, 1967; children: (first marriage) Roger, Jr., Kimberly Vancil (stepdaughter). *Education:* Brown University, B.A., 1959. *Religion:* ''Unorganized.'' *Home address:*

West Main Rd., Little Compton, R.I. 02837. *Agent:* Rhoda A. Weyr, William Morris Agency, 1350 Avenue of the Americas, New York, N.Y. 10019.

CAREER: Worked as fisherman, carpenter, and photographer; reporter for *Saturday Evening Post,* 1961-65; *Life,* New York, N.Y., editor and writer, 1965-69; director of Brown News Bureau, 1972-75; free-lance writer, 1975—. *Member:* Little Compton Athletic Association (vice-president).

WRITINGS: The Grand Gesture (nonfiction), Little, Brown, 1975; *Ted Turner, the Man Behind the Mouth,* Norton, 1978. Member of editorial board of *Brown Alumni Monthly.*

WORK IN PROGRESS: "Working on nonfiction novel with basic smuggling plot circa 1968."

SIDELIGHTS: Vaughn comments: "I am motivated by the need to write, probably an ego trip, and by the need to work for myself. This is necessary as I am probably otherwise unemployable. The only thing I consider really vital is the need for people to laugh, mainly at themselves. I work toward that end. I also think trying to tell the truth is important, even if you don't always succeed."

* * *

VAUGHN, Jack A(lfred) 1935-

PERSONAL: Born December 26, 1935, in Snohomish, Wash.; son of James Alfred and Carolyn (Hall) Vaughn. *Education:* University of Washington, Seattle, B.A., 1957; University of Hawaii, M.F.A., 1960; University of Denver, Ph.D., 1964. *Home:* 565 Esplanade, Redondo Beach, Calif. 90277. *Office:* Theatre Arts Program, California State University—Dominguez Hills, Carson, Calif. 90747.

CAREER: Jamestown College, Jamestown, N.D., assistant professor of English, 1964-66, associate professor of theatre and speech, 1966-68; California State University, Dominguez Hills, Carson, assistant professor, 1968-72, associate professor, 1972-77, professor of theatre arts, 1977—. Guest professor at Morningside College, 1967, and World Campus Afloat, 1967-68. Regional head of American College Theatre Festival, 1976-78. *Member:* American Theatre Association, California Educational Theatre Association, Southern California Educational Theatre Association (member of advisory board, 1976-78). *Awards, honors:* National Endowment for the Humanities grant, summer, 1975; distinguished professor award, California State University—Dominguez Hills, 1977; award of excellence for college theatre, AMOCO Company, 1979.

WRITINGS: (Editor) *Two Comedies by Thomas D'Urfey,* Fairleigh Dickinson University Press, 1976; *Drama A to Z: A Handbook,* Ungar, 1978; *Shakespeare's Comedies,* Ungar, in press. Contributor to philology and speech journals.

WORK IN PROGRESS: An anthology, *The Annotated Playreader,* with Peter Lach.

* * *

VESTLY, Anne-Cath(arina) 1920-

PERSONAL: Born February 15, 1920, in Rena, Norway; daughter of Aagot and Mentz Schulerud; married Johan Vestly. *Education:* Studied acting at Studioteatret, Oslo. *Home:* Noeklesvingen 36, Oslo 6, Norway.

CAREER: Actress and writer. *Member:* Norwegian Authors' Association, Norwegian Dramatists' Association, Association of Authors of Children's Books. *Awards, honors:* Awards from Norwegian Ministry of Education, 1955,

for *Ole Aleksander faar skjorte,* 1957, for *Aatte smaa, to store og en lastebil,* and 1958, for *Mormor og de aate ungene i skogen.*

WRITINGS—Children's books; in English: *Aatte smaa, to store og en lastebil,* Tiden Norsk Forlag, 1957, translation published as *Eight Children and a Truck,* Methuen, 1973; *Mormor og de atte ungene i skogen,* Tiden Norsk Forlag, 1958, translation by Patricia Crampton published as *Eight Children Move House,* Methuen, 1974; *Aurora i blokk z,* Tiden Norsk Forlag, 1966, translation by Eileen Amos published as *Hallo Aurora!,* Longman Young Books, 1973, adaption by Jane Fairfax published as *Hello, Aurora,* Crowell, 1974; *Aurora og Sokrates,* Tiden Norsk Forlag, 1969, translation published as *Aurora and Socrates,* Crowell, 1973.

Other—all published by Tiden Norsk Forlag, except as noted: *Ole Aleksander Fili-bom-bom-bom,* 1953; *Ole Aleksander paa farten* (title means "Ole Aleksander on the Run"), 1954; *Ole Aleksander far skjorte* (title means "Ole Aleksander Has a Shirt"), 1955; *Ole Aleksander og Bestemor til vaers* (title means "Ole Aleksander and Grandmother in the Air"), 1956; *Ole Aleksander paa flyttefot* (title means "Ole Aleksander Moves House"), 1958; *Marte og mormor og mormor og Motten,* 1959.

En liten takk fra Anton, 1960; *Mormors promenade,* 1961; *Acht Kleine, swei Grosse und ein Lastauto,* Rascher, 1962; *Barnas store sangbok* (title means "Children's Big Songbook"), J. W. Cappelen, 1962; *Lillebror og knerten* (title means "Lillebror and 'Rooty'"), 1962; *Trofaste Knerten* (title means "Faithful Knerten"), 1963; *Grossmutter und die acht Kinder im Walde* (title means "Grandmother and the Eight Children in the Woods"), Rascher, 1963; *Marten, Morten und Grossmutter,* Rascher, 1964; *Knerten gifter seg* (title means "Knerten Marries"), 1964; *Knerten i Bessby* (title means "Knerten in Bessby"), 1965; *Aurora og pappa* (title means "Aurora and Daddy"), 1967; *Aurora og den vesle blaa bilen* (title means "Aurora and the Little Blue Car"), 1968.

Aurora i Holland (title means "Aurora in Holland"), 1970; *Aurora paa burtigruten* (title means "Aurora on the Express Liner"), 1971; *Aurora fra Fabelvik* (title means "Aurora from Fabelvik"), 1972; *Knerten og Forundringskpakken* (title means "Knerten and the Surprise Packet"), 1973; *Knerten paa sykkeltur* (title means "Knerten on Bicycle Tour"), 1974; *Guro,* 1975; *Guro og nokkerosene* (title means "Guro and the Water Lilies"), 1976.

WORK IN PROGRESS: Third volume of "Guro" series.*

* * *

VIANSSON-PONTE, Pierre 1920-1979

OBITUARY NOTICE: Born August 2, 1920, in Clisson, France; died of cancer, May 7, 1979, in Paris, France. French writer best known for his documentation of the de Gaulle years. In 1953 Viansson-Ponte co-founded *L'Express.* Later he became a chief editor and analyst for *Le Monde.* He authored six books on the Gaullists and one on cancer entitled *Changer la Mort.* Obituaries and other sources: *Who's Who in the World,* 3rd edition, Marquis, 1976; *New York Times,* May 8, 1979.

* * *

VILLET, Barbara 1931-

PERSONAL: Surname is pronounced Vill-*et;* born February 6, 1931; daughter of Thomas L. (a film news editor) and Cecilia (a nurse; maiden name, Fitzpatrick) Cummiskey; married Grey Villet (a photographer), May, 1963; children: Ann Cecilia; Stephanie, John (stepchildren). *Education:* Middlebury College, B.A., 1952; Harvard University, A.M.T., 1953. *Home and office:* R.F.D. 1, Shushan, N.Y. 12873. *Agent:* Joan Foley, Foley Agency, 34 East 38th St., New York, N.Y. 10016.

CAREER: Radio Free Europe, New York City, writer at news desk, 1953-55; high school teacher in Valley Stream, N.Y., 1955-56; *Life,* New York City, researcher, reporter, and staff writer, 1957-71; free-lance writer, 1971—. Alumnae trustee of Middlebury College. *Awards, honors:* Best of *Life* Award from *Life* Magazine.

WRITINGS: (With husband, Grey Villet) *Those Whom God Chooses,* Viking, 1967; *Head Nurse,* Doubleday, 1976. Contributor to popular magazines, including *Atlantic, Quest, Country Journal,* and *McCall's.*

WORK IN PROGRESS: A book on Afrikaners, with publication by Everest House.

SIDELIGHTS: Barbara Villet comments: "My husband and I have just returned from a second extensive trip to South Africa on assignment. We have also worked as a photojournalistic team in South America, throughout the United States and Southeast Asia, and have done advertising work as a sideline in the Middle East, Canada, Egypt, Greece, and Africa. In fact, my only solo work is *Head Nurse,* based on an essay originally executed for *Life.*"

* * *

VINEBERG, Ethel (Shane) 1902-

PERSONAL: Born June 5, 1902, in Moncton, New Brunswick, Canada; daughter of Jacob (a manufacturer) and Emma (Shapiro) Shane; married Solomon Vineberg, August 29, 1929 (died, 1966); children: Sarah Ellen Vineberg Winston. *Education:* Attended McGill University, 1923; McGill University, diploma. *Religion:* Jewish. *Home:* 5025 MacDonald Ave., #305, Montreal, Quebec, Canada H3X 2V2.

CAREER: Children's Memorial Hospital, Montreal, Quebec, assistant in social service department, 1923-27; Neighbourhood House of Montreal, Montreal, Quebec, head social worker, 1927-29, and 1932-34; writer, 1967—. Honorary member of board of directors of National Council of Jewish Women of Canada (Montreal vice-president).

WRITINGS: Grandmother Came from Dworitz, Tundra Books, 1969, 2nd edition, 1978, Scribner, 1978. Also author of *History of the National Council of Jewish Women,* edited by May Cutler, 1967.

WORK IN PROGRESS: Judy Remembers, set in a small New Brunswick community, 1900-1910.

SIDELIGHTS: Ethel Vineberg comments: "I wrote my second book so that my only daughter's children would know something of their forebears, of their standards and ways of life."

* * *

von FRANZ, Marie-Louise 1915-

PERSONAL: Born January 4, 1915, in Munich, Germany; daughter of Erwin (a baron and an Austrian colonel) and Margaret (Schoen) von Franz. *Education:* University of Zurich, Ph.D. (classical languages), 1940; studies with Carl Gustav Jung. *Religion:* Reformed. *Home:* Lindenbergstrasse 15, 8700 Kunsmacht, Switzerland.

CAREER: Jungian analyst, 1948—, and teacher at C. G.

Jung Institute, Zurich, Switzerland. Also former teacher of Greek and Latin in Zurich. Lecturer at universities and colleges throughout the world.

WRITINGS: (Contributor) Carl Gustav Jung, *Aion. Untersuchungen zur Symbolgeschichte* (title means "Aion: Researches Into the Phenomenology of the Self"), Rascher Verlag, 1951; (editor and author of commentary) Thomas Aquinas, *Aurora consurgens; ein dem Thomas von Aquin zugeschriettbenes Dokument der alchemistischen Gegensatzproblematik,* Rascher Verlag, 1957, translation by R.F.C. Hull and A.S.B. Clover published as *Aurora consurgens: A Document Attributed to Thomas Aquinas on the Problem of Opposites in Alchemy,* Pantheon Books, 1966; *Die Visionen des Niklaus von Fluee,* Rascher Verlag, 1959.

(With Emma Jung) *Die Graalslegende in psychologischer Sicht,* Rascher Verlag, 1960, translation by Andrea Dykes published as *The Grail Legend,* Putnam for C. G. Jung Foundation for Analytical Psychology, 1970; (editor with C. G. Jung and others) *Man and His Symbols,* Doubleday, 1964; (contributor) C. G. Jung, *Mysterium coniunctionis; Untersuchungen ueber die Trennung und Zusammensetzung der seelischen Gegensatze in der Alchemie,* Rascher Verlag, 1968, translation by Hull published as *Mysterium Coniunctionis: An Inquiry Into the Separation and Synthesis of Psychic Opposites in Alchemy,* Princeton University Press, 1970.

Zahl und Zeit: Psychologische Uberlegungen zu einer Annaeherung von Tiefenpscyhologie und Physik, E. Klett, 1970, translation by Dykes published as *Number and Time: Reflections Leading Toward a Unification of Depth Psychology and Physics,* Northwestern University Press, 1974; *A Psychological Interpretation of the Golden Ass of Apuleius,* Spring Publications (New York), 1970; *The Problem of the Puer Aeternus,* Spring Publications (New York), 1970; (with Ulrich Mann and Hans-W. Heidland) *C. G. Jung und die Theologen,* Radius Verlag, 1971; *Lecture on Jung's Typology,* edited by James Hillman, Spring Publications, 1971; *Problems of the Feminine in Fairytales,* Spring Publications, 1972; *C. G. Jung, Sein Mythos in unserer Zeit,* Huber, 1972, translation by William H. Kennedy published as *C. G. Jung, His Myth in Our Time,* Putnam for C. G. Jung Foundation for Analytical Psychology, 1975; *Patterns of Creativity Mirrored in Creation Myths,* Spring Publications, 1972; *An Introduction to the Psychology of Fairy Tales,* Spring Publications, 1970, 2nd edition, 1973; *Shadow and Evil in Fairy Tales* (lectures), Spring Publications, 1974; *Time: Patterns of Flow and Return,* Thames & Hudson, 1978.

WORK IN PROGRESS: A book on the resurrection body in alchemy.

SIDELIGHTS: Von Franz commented: "I worked for 28 years with C. G. Jung in analysis and cooperated in his work on Western alchemy and also on folk-tales. I like to connect the symbolism of these fields with the actual problems of modern man for they contain the healing archetypal foundations of his soul."

Von Franz lectures in three languages, French, German, and English, in the United States, England, France, Canada, Germany, and Switzerland. She also noted that her writings are mostly "applying his [Jung's] basic ideas to new fields."

* * *

VRYONIS, Speros (P.), Jr. 1928-

PERSONAL: Born July 18, 1928, in Memphis, Tenn.; son of Speros P. (in business) and Helen (Touliatou) Vryonis;

divorced; children: Speros Basil, Demetrios, Nikolas. *Education:* Southwestern College at Memphis, B.A., 1950; Harvard University, M.A., 1954, Ph.D., 1956. *Office:* Department of History, University of California, Los Angeles, Calif. 90024.

CAREER: Harvard University, Cambridge, Mass., instructor in history, 1956-60; University of California, Los Angeles, assistant professor, then associate professor, 1960-67, professor of history, 1967—, director of Center for Near Eastern Studies, 1972-76. *Member:* Mediaeval Academy of America, American Philosophical Society, Middle East Studies Association, American Academy of Arts and Sciences, Macedonian Society of Thessaloniki (corresponding member), Ionian Academy, Islamic Institute of India. *Awards, honors:* Guggenheim fellowship, 1969; Kokkinos Award from academy of Athens; Haskins Award from Mediaeval Academy of America; Fulbright fellowship.

WRITINGS: Byzantium and Europe, Harcourt, 1967; (editor) *Readings in Medieval Historiography,* Houghton, 1968; *The Decline of Medieval Hellenism in Asia Minor and the Process of Islamization From the Eleventh Through the Fifteenth Century,* University of California Press, 1971; (editor) *Byzantium: Its Internal History and Relations With the Muslim World,* Varorium Reprints, 1971; (editor) *Aspects of the Balkans: Continuity and Change,* Mouton, 1972; *Islam and Cultural Change in the Middle Ages,* Harrassowitz, 1975; *Individualism and Conformity in Classical Islam,* Harrassowitz, 1977. Contributor to scholarly journals.

W

WAKIL, S(heikh) P(arvez)   1935-

PERSONAL: Born December 16, 1935, in Gujrat, West Pakistan; son of Sheikh Abdul and Bintul (Fatah) Wakil; married Farkhanda A. Shah (a librarian), September 30, 1960; children: Salman. *Education:* University of Punjab, B.Sc. (with distinction), 1956, B.A., 1957, M.A. (with distinction), 1959; Washington State University, M.A., 1974. *Home:* 105 Poplar Cres., Saskatoon, Saskatchewan, Canada S7M 0A7. *Office:* Department of Sociology, University of Saskatchewan, Saskatoon, Saskatchewan, Canada S7N 0W0.

CAREER: University of the Punjab, Lahore, Pakistan, assistant professor of sociology, 1963-64; University of Saskatchewan, Saskatoon, instructor, 1964-66, lecturer, 1966-67, assistant professor, 1967-73, associate professor of sociology, 1973—, head of department, 1976-78. Visiting faculty member of Wayne State University, 1970-71. Acting director of research at Sind University's Institute of Scientific Study and Research, 1976; associate director of research at Northwest Institute of Research, 1976-77. Speaker at international professional meetings and at public gatherings; guest on television and radio programs. Adviser to Pakistan's Ministry of Education and Pakistan Environmental Protection Agency.

MEMBER: International Sociological Association, Canadian Sociology and Anthropology Association, Canadian Association for South Asian Studies (member of board of directors, 1973-78), Canadian Ethnic Studies Association, Canadian Civil Liberties Association, Canadian Association for Asian Studies, Canada-Pakistan Cultural Association (president, 1971-74; member of executive committee, 1977—), American Sociological Association, National Council on Family Relations, Western Association of Sociologists and Anthropologists, Vanier Institute of the Family, John Howard Society (member of board of directors, 1974-76), Islamic Association of Saskatchewan (president, 1971-72). *Awards, honors:* Canada Council grants, 1967-68, 1968-69.

WRITINGS: (Contributor) K. Ishwaran, editor, *The Canadian Family,* Holt, 1971, revised edition, 1976; (editor) *Marriage, Family, and Society: Canadian Perspectives,* Butterworth & Co. (Toronto), 1975; (contributor) R. P. Mohan and Don Martindale, editors, *Handbook of Contemporary Developments in World Sociology,* Greenwood Press, 1975;

Marriage and Family in Canada (monograph), Department of Sociology, University of Calgary, 1976; (editor) *South Asia: Perspectives and Dimensions,* Canadian Association for South Asian Studies, 1977. Contributor to sociology journals. Editor of *Newsletter* of Canadian Association for South Asian Studies, 1973-78; associate editor of *International Journal of Sociology of the Family,* 1971—, and *Sind Journal of Political Studies and Modern History,* 1976—; book review editor of *International Review of Modern Sociology,* 1971—.

WORK IN PROGRESS: Research on violence in the family, contradictions in role expectations within marriage, demographic and cultural analysis of the Canadian family, and ethnographic aspects of Punjabi society (including the status of women, stratification, family systems, mate selection, role analysis within the family, thematic analysis of folklore and folk songs, and analysis of values relevant to socio-economic development.

*   *   *

WALDERS, Joe   1948-

PERSONAL: Born January 30, 1948, in Sharon, Pa.; son of Joseph B. (a restaurant-tavern owner) and Amelia (O'-Shaney) Walders; married Joni Browne (an actress), February 18, 1978; children: Kevin (stepson). *Education:* Attended Pennsylvania State University and Kent State University; Syracuse University, B.S. (magna cum laude), 1971. *Office:* 1081 Westwood Blvd., Suite 216, Los Angeles, Calif. 90024.

CAREER: Free-lance writer, 1975—. Also has worked as television newsfilm photographer. *Military service:* U.S. Air Force, motion picture production officer, 1968-72; became first lieutenant. *Member:* Writers Guild of America (West).

WRITINGS: The World's Most Challenging TV Quiz, Doubleday, 1978; (contributor) Jay Harris and others, editors, *TV Guide: The First Twenty-Five Years,* Simon & Schuster, 1978.

Scripts: (Co-author) "Death Machines," Crown International Pictures, 1976. Author of educational and industrial scripts. Contributor to magazines and newspapers, including *Popular Science, Grit,* and *TV Guide.*

WORK IN PROGRESS: A science series for television, "How About. . . ."

SIDELIGHTS: Walders writes: "As a matter of financial survival, I've developed the twin attributes of writing for many different media and writing rapidly. Switching between media, say from television to magazines, keeps me refreshed and constantly challenged. I hope it makes me a better writer."

* * *

WALDO, Anna Lee 1925-

PERSONAL: Born February 16, 1925, in Great Falls, Mont.; daughter of Lee William (a railroad auditor) and Cecelia Anna (Prayzek) Van Artsdale; married Willis H. Waldo (a chemist), August 27, 1949; children: Judith Ann Waldo Helm, Sara Sally K., Dale F., Patricia G., Richard K. *Education:* Montana State University, B.S., 1947; University of Maryland, M.S., 1950. *Politics:* Independent. *Religion:* Presbyterian. *Residence:* St. Louis, Mo. *Office:* St. Louis Community College—Meramec, St. Louis, Mo. 63122.

CAREER: Worked as toxicologist for Dayton, Ohio, Police Dept.; Miami Valley Hospital, Dayton, Ohio, research biochemist, 1950-56; worked as instructor in biochemistry at Midwest Medical Institute, Kirkwood, Mo.; Physicians and Surgeons Group, Kirkwood, clinical chemist, 1956-65; Mercy Junior College, St. Louis, Mo., instructor in organic chemistry, 1965-69; St. Johns Mercy Hospital, Creve Coeur, Mo., biochemist and instructor in biochemistry, 1969-74; St. Louis Community College—Meramec, St. Louis, Mo., instructor in chemistry and physical science, 1974—. Abstractor for Chemical Abstracts Service. Member of St. Louis Dance Theatre-Ballet Company. *Member:* American Chemical Society, Southwestern Oklahoma Historical Society.

WRITINGS: Sacajawea: Savage to Saint (novel), Avon, 1979. Contributor to scientific journals.

WORK IN PROGRESS: Research on North American Indians and organic chemistry.

SIDELIGHTS: Anna Waldo writes: "In addition to raising five children, I am most interested in science, both experimental research and teaching, North American archaeology, and actual digs. I have followed the Lewis and Clark Trail as a book project in order to study a small segment of American history and to become thoroughly acquainted with it and thus appreciate our heritage! My concern for the Lewis and Clark expedition and my awareness of the importance of St. Louis as the gateway to the West was only natural since I have lived most of my married life in St. Louis."

Called "an epic" by its publisher, Waldo's novel, *Sacajawea,* is the story of an American Indian who actually accompanied Lewis and Clark on their expeditions. Over one thousand pages, the novel covers Sacajawea's life from the age of eleven to her death in 1884 when she was almost one-hundred years old. Waldo told an interviewer that the novel was well researched. "It's fact," she said, "as much as I could find. The background is authentic. Only the story is made up where facts didn't exist." In the same interview, she related, "I used library sources, history societies and people who were experts. I wrote to universities all over the country—and even in Germany. That's where Sacajawea's son went."

As part of research, Waldo also turned to the St. Louis Westerners, an organization before which a descendent of Clark once spoke. Although women are not allowed to attend meetings of the St. Louis Westerners, Waldo persuaded her husband to visit. "My husband wasn't interested at all when he first went to the St. Louis Westerners," she declared. Eventually, he not only joined but became vice-president and Waldo was even granted her own interview with Clark's descendent.

Clark devoted much time to writing *Sacajawea.* "I wrote every day," she related. "I'm not a housekeeper, so if things piled up, they didn't bother me. There was always something much more interesting happening in the book." Still, Waldo did have other activities. "I taught chemistry part time . . . but wrote about five or six hours a day," she noted. "When my children would come home from school, I'd usually be in the middle of something creative." She noted that her creative drive often diverted her from distractions. "They could have yelled," she mused. "I still wouldn't have heard them."

Despite the enormous volume of the novel, it is still only slightly more than half of its original length. After the extensive editing, Waldo consoled herself by observing, "I'll use it in something else."

BIOGRAPHICAL/CRITICAL SOURCES: Publishers Weekly, December 4, 1978.

* * *

WALEY, Arthur (David) 1889-1966

PERSONAL: Birth-given name, Schloss, adapted mother's maiden name, 1914; born August 19, 1889, in London, England; died June 27, 1966. *Education:* Attended King's College, Cambridge, and School of Oriental and African Studies (London). *Residence:* London, England.

CAREER: Writer and translator. Worked as assistant keeper of Department of Prints and Drawings at British Museum, 1912-1930; lecturer at University of London School of Oriental Studies. *Military service:* Associated with Ministry of Information during World War II. *Member:* British Academy (companion of honour). *Awards, honors:* Queen's Medal for Poetry, 1953.

WRITINGS: The No Plays of Japan, Allen & Unwin, 1921, Knopf, 1922, reprinted, C. E. Tuttle, 1976; *An Introduction to the Study of Chinese Painting,* Scribner, 1923, AMS Press, 1974; *Three Ways of Thought in Ancient China* (contains excerpts from works of Chuang Chou, Mencius, and others), Allen & Unwin, 1939, reprinted, Allen & Unwin, 1963; *The Life and Times of Po Chue-i, 772-846 A.D.,* Allen & Unwin, 1949; *The Poetry and Career of Li Po, 701-762 A.D.,* Macmillan, 1950; *The Real Tripitaka, and Other Pieces,* Macmillan, 1952; *Yuan Mei, Eighteenth Century Chinese Poet,* Grove, c. 1956; *The Opium War Through Chinese Eyes,* Macmillan, 1958; *Zen Buddhism and Its Relation to Art,* Luzac, 1959; *The Secret History of the Mongols, and Other Pieces,* Allen & Unwin, 1963, Barnes & Noble, 1964.

Editor and translator, unless otherwise indicated: *Chinese Poems,* Lowe Bros., 1916, reprinted, Rutgers University Library, 1965; *One Hundred and Seventy Chinese Poems* (also see below), Constable, 1918, Knopf, 1919, reprinted, J. Cape, 1969; *Japanese Poetry: The 'Uta,'* Clarendon, 1919, reprinted, University Press of Hawaii, 1976; *More Translations From the Chinese* (also see below), Knopf, 1919; *The Temple and Other Poems* (also see below), Knopf, 1923; *Translations From the Chinese* (contains selections from *One Hundred and Seventy Chinese Poems* and *More Translations From the Chinese;* also see above), Knopf, 1941, reprinted, Vintage Books, 1971; *Chinese Poems* (contains selections from *One Hundred and Seventy Chinese Poems, More Translations From the Chinese,* and *The Temple and Other Poems;* also see above), Allen & Unwin, 1946; Yüean Ch'ii, *The Nine Songs: A Study of Shamanism in Ancient China,* Allen & Unwin, 1955; Confucius, *The Analects of Confucius,* Allen & Unwin, 1956; Lao-Tzu, *The Way and Its Power: A Study of the Tao Te Ching and Its Place in Chinese Thought,* Grove, 1958; *Tun-huang Manuscripts: Ballads and Stories From Tun-huang,* Macmillan, 1960; (editor only) Li Chih-ch'ang, *The Travels of an Alchemist,* Routledge & Kegan Paul, 1963.

Also translator and author of introduction for numerous works. Editor of *The Yearbook of Oriental Art and Culture, 1924-25* (and subsequent editions).

SIDELIGHTS: Waley is best known for his translations of Japanese and Chinese poetry. Many of his translations show the influence of the Imagist poets, including Ezra Pound. Among Waley's other notable accomplishments is the translation of the six-volume *The Tale of Genji.*

AVOCATIONAL INTERESTS: Skiing.*

* * *

WALFORD, Lionel Albert 1905-1979

OBITUARY NOTICE: Born May 29, 1905, in San Francisco, Calif.; died of cancer, April 9, 1979, in Atlantic Highlands, N.J. Marine biologist and author of books in his field. Walford was associated with various government agencies, including United States Fish and Wildlife Service, and was consultant to numerous fishery commissions. He wrote *Game Fishes of the Pacific Coast From Alaska to the Pacific.* Obituaries and other sources: *American Men and Women of Science: The Physical and Biological Sciences,* 12th edition, Bowker, 1971-73; *Who's Who in the East,* 16th edition, Marquis, 1973; *New York Times,* April 10, 1979; *Washington Post,* April 11, 1979.

* * *

WALKER, Bruce (James) 1944-

PERSONAL: Born July 25, 1944, at Edwards Air Force Base, Calif.; son of Frank L. (in sales) and Helen (an office worker; maiden name, Mohr) Walker; married Pamela Carlson, April 30, 1966; children: Therese, Stephen, Scott. *Education:* Seattle University, B.A., 1966; University of Colorado, M.B.A., 1968, D.B.A., 1971. *Home:* 421 East Erie, Tempe, Ariz. 85282. *Office:* Department of Marketing, Arizona State University, Tempe, Ariz. 85281.

CAREER: University of Kentucky, Lexington, assistant professor of business administration, 1970-74; Arizona State University, Tempe, associate professor, 1974-79, professor of marketing, 1979—, research associate at Bureau of Business and Economic Research, 1975-78. Member of board of directors of Enercom, Inc. Participant in professional meetings and training programs; marketing consultant. *Member:* American Marketing Association, Southern Marketing Association, Retail Financial Executives of Arizona. *Awards, honors:* Grants from Kentucky Research Foundation, 1971, 1972, Arizona Commission for Postsecondary Education, 1975-76, and Arizona Solar Energy Research Commission, 1977.

WRITINGS: (Editor) *Directory of Colorado Manufacturers,* Business Research Division, University of Colorado, 1967, 1968-69, and 1970; (co-editor) *Marketing Channels and Institutions: Readings on Distribution Concepts and Practices,* Grid Publishing, 1973, revised edition, 1978; (with Joel B.

Haynes) *Retailing Today: An Introduction,* Harcourt, 1975; (with Don L. James and Michael J. Etzel) *Minority Small Businessmen in Arizona and Available Entrepreneurial Aids,* Bureau of Business and Economic Research, Arizona State University, 1976; (contributor) V. A. Musselman and E. H. Hughes, *Introduction to Modern Business,* 7th edition (Walker was not included in earlier editions), Prentice-Hall, 1977. Contributor of about thirty articles and reviews to business and marketing journals. Member of editorial staff of "Marketing Abstracts," published by *Journal of Marketing,* 1972-76.

WORK IN PROGRESS: Revising *Retailing Today,* publication by Harcourt expected in 1981; articles on retailing, franchising, and distribution channels.

SIDELIGHTS: Walker told *CA:* "My textbook development has been motivated by my desire to provide improved teaching materials in specialized areas of business administration. I have also found that writing textbooks is an excellent way to stay current in—perhaps even to get ahead of—my main areas of teaching and research."

Regarding research projects that have led to published articles, Walker said: "As an academician, my research efforts have been part of my job description. I have tried—as much as possible—to conduct research that will make a contribution to the body of knowledge in the field of marketing as well as be useful to marketing practitioners. In an applied field, such as marketing, the criterion of practicality is particularly important. It has also been gratifying that research leading to publication ordinarily supplements (or complements) the material I use in my class lectures and discussion."

* * *

WALKER, D(aniel) P(ickering) 1914-

PERSONAL: Born June 30, 1914, in London, England; son of Frederick Pickering (in business) and Miriam (Crittall) Walker. *Education:* Oxford University, B.A., 1935, D.Phil., 1940. *Politics:* None. *Religion:* None. *Home:* 2 Regents Park Ter., London N.W.1, England. *Office:* Warburg Institute, University of London, Woburn Sq., London WC1H 0AB, England.

CAREER: British Foreign Office, London, England, staff member, 1943-45; University of London, London, reader, 1945-61, professor at Warburg Institute, 1961—. *Military service:* British Army, 1940-43. *Member:* British Academy (fellow).

WRITINGS: Spiritual and Demonic Magic, Warburg Institute, 1958; *The Decline of Hell,* Routledge & Kegan Paul, 1964; *Ancient Theology,* Duckworth, 1972; *Studies in Musical Science,* Warburg Institute, 1978.

WORK IN PROGRESS: Research on exorcism in sixteenth-century France and England.

AVOCATIONAL INTERESTS: Chamber music, gardening.

* * *

WALKER, Franklin (Dickerson) 1900-1979

OBITUARY NOTICE—See index for *CA* sketch: Born November 13, 1900, in Republic, Mich.; died in 1979 in San Francisco, Calif. Educator and author. A Rhodes scholar, Walker spent most of his academic career at California universities. In addition to biographies of Frank Norris and Ambrose Bierce, Walker wrote books on the literature of California, including *A Literary History of Southern Califor-*

nia and *San Francisco's Literary Frontier.* Obituaries and other sources: *Who's Who in America,* 38th edition, Marquis, 1974; *AB Bookman's Weekly,* April 16, 1979.

* * *

WALKER, Morton 1929-

PERSONAL: Born October 1, 1929, in Brooklyn, N.Y.; son of Louis T. (a shoe merchant) and Rae (a shoe merchant; maiden name, Goodman) Walker; married Joan Bloom (a lecturer and radio commentator), December 31, 1950; children: Mark, Randall, Jules. *Education:* Attended New York University, 1947-49; Illinois College of Podiatric Medicine, D.P.M., 1953; also attended University of Bridgeport, 1960, and University of Connecticut, 1967-68. *Religion:* Jewish. *Home and office:* 484 High Ridge Rd., Stamford, Conn. 06905. *Agent:* Richard Curtis Associates, Inc., 156 East 52nd St., New York, N.Y. 10022.

CAREER: Doctor of podiatric medicine in Stamford, Conn., 1953-69; WSTC-Radio, Stamford, scriptwriter and producer, 1970-71; University of Connecticut, Stamford, instructor in fiction and nonfiction writing, 1971-74; writer, 1974—. President of Connecticut Natural Foods Associates. *Member:* American Medical Writers Association, American Society of Journalists and Authors, Association for Cardiovascular Therapies (president). *Awards, honors:* Ten medals from American Podiatry Association, 1958-68, for research, writing, and exhibits; eight awards from *Current Podiatry Journal,* 1969-79; Jesse H. Neal Editorial Achievement Award from American Business Press, 1975, for twelve-part magazine series "The Making of Malpractice," 1976, for special issue "Coping with Crisis in the Office: Special Report."

WRITINGS: Your Guide to Foot Health, Follett, 1964, revised edition, Arco, 1972; (with wife, Joan Walker) *Think and Grow Thin,* Arco, 1973; (with Marvin Fogel) *Medical School Admission Adviser,* Hawthorn, 1976; *Sport Diving: The Instructional Guide to Skin and Scuba,* Contemporary Books, 1977; (with Abram Hoffer) *Orthomolecular Nutrition,* Keats Publishing, 1978; (with J. Walker) *Help Your Mate Lose Weight,* Jove, 1978; (with J. Walker) *Lose Weight/Gain Health/Live Longer,* Arco, 1978; (with Bernice Yoffe and Parke Gray) *The Complete Book of Birth,* Simon & Schuster, 1979; *Advertising and Promoting the Professional Practice,* Hawthorn, 1979; *Total Health,* Everest House, 1979; (with son, Mark Walker) *Self-Test Your Health,* Hawthorn, 1980; (with Hoffer) *Nutrients to Age Without Senility,* Keats Publishing, 1980; (with Carol Cush) *Carol Cush's Book on Total Body Awareness,* Rawson/Wade, 1980; (with Beverly Johnson) *Beverly Johnson's Book of Health and Beauty,* Times Books, 1980; (with Charles Walsh) *The Medical Practice Management Desk Book,* Prentice-Hall, 1980; *How Not to Have a Heart Attack,* F. Watts, 1980.

Ghost writer for other physicians. Feature writer for *Forum,* 1969-73. Contributor of about six hundred articles to professional journals and popular magazines, including *McCall's, Writer's Digest, Today's Health,* and *Skin Diver.* Editor of *Scrivener,* 1971-75.

WORK IN PROGRESS: How to Find Health in an Unhealthy World, with Laurence Lother, and *Doctor, Will My Child Ever Act Normal?,* with Abram Hoffer; magazine articles on health, nutrition, and psychology.

SIDELIGHTS: In *Writer's Digest* Walker commented on his motivation for writing, especially for the popular media: "I write ... because it is more rewarding in many ways than receiving money. I find it more fun and a greater challenge. Here I act as a reporter writing about people in need of help rather than describing products, techniques and conditions. To me, turning out publishable medical copy for the popular market is a good time.

"There's another reason, too. Because good newspaper and magazine medical writing is increasingly concerned with evaluating medical results, people now want real knowledge. No more are they willing merely to accept the opinion of a lecturer. They demand evidence. Just as physicians are facing Professional Standards Review Organizations to provide better medical care, lay medical writers are answering questions from the galleries of consumers—should drugs be sold generically or by brand name? How should I take nutritional supplements? What should I take to prevent a cold? Physicians are dependent on medical writers to be cautious and accurate. After all, readers eventually become patients!"

AVOCATIONAL INTERESTS: Scuba diving, fitness, travel (especially the Caribbean).

BIOGRAPHICAL/CRITICAL SOURCES: Writer's Digest, January, 1976.

* * *

WALKER, Samuel 1942-

PERSONAL: Born December 19, 1942, in Indianapolis, Ind. *Education:* University of Michigan, B.A., 1965; University of Nebraska at Omaha, M.A., 1970; Ohio State University, Ph.D., 1973. *Home:* 4015 Burt St., Omaha, Neb. 68131. *Office:* Department of Criminal Justice, University of Nebraska, Box 688, Omaha, Neb. 68101.

CAREER: University of Nebraska, Omaha, faculty member of department of criminal justice, 1974—.

WRITINGS: A Critical History of Police Reform: The Emergence of Professionalism, Lexington Books, 1977; *Popular Justice: A History of American Criminal Justice,* Oxford University Press, 1979.

WORK IN PROGRESS: A history of federal assistance programs related to juvenile justice.

* * *

WALLACE, Bruce 1920-

PERSONAL: Born May 18, 1920, in McKean, Pa.; son of George Egbert and Rose Irma (Paterson) Wallace; married Miriam Jane Covalla, November 3, 1945; children: David Bruce, Roberta Scott. *Education:* Columbia University, B.A., 1941, Ph.D., 1949. *Home:* 416 Mitchell St., Ithaca, N.Y. 14850.

CAREER: Carnegie Institution of Washington, Cold Springs Harbor, N.Y., associated with department of genetics, 1947-49, associated with biological laboratories, 1949-58; Cornell University, Ithaca, N.Y., associate professor, 1958-61, professor of genetics, 1961—. *Military service:* U.S. Army Air Forces, 1943-46. *Member:* American Society of Naturalists (president, 1971), Genetic Society of America (vice-president, 1973; president, 1974), Society for the Study of Evolution (president, 1974), American Academy of Arts and Sciences.

WRITINGS: (With Theodosius Grigorievich Dobzhansky) *Radiation, Genes, and Man,* Holt, 1959, revised edition published as *Radiation, Genes, and Man: Biological Aspects of Radiation Hazards* (edited by Frank N. Paparello), 1963; (with Adrian M. Srb) *Adaptation,* Prentice-Hall, 1961, 2nd edition, 1964; *Chromosomes, Giant Molecules, and Evolu-*

tion, Norton, 1966; *Topics in Population Genetics,* Norton, 1968; *Genetic Load: Its Biological and Conceptual Aspects,* Prentice-Hall, 1970; (editor) *Essays in Social Biology,* Volume I: *People, Their Needs, Environment, Ecology,* Volume II: *Genetics, Evolution, Race, Radiation Biology,* Volume III: *Disease, Sex, Communication, Behavior,* Prentice-Hall, 1972. Contributor to scholarly journals.

* * *

WALSH, John Evangelist 1927-

PERSONAL: Born December 27, 1927, in New York, N.Y.; son of Thomas (in sales) and Ann (Cunny) Walsh; married Dorothy Schubis, November, 1957; children: John, Timothy, Ann, Matthew. *Education:* Iona College, B.A., 1953. *Religion:* Roman Catholic. *Residence:* Dumont, N.J. *Office: Reader's Digest,* Pleasantville, N.Y. 10570.

CAREER: Worked as senior editor at Simon & Schuster, New York, N.Y.; senior editor at Prentice-Hall, Englewood Cliffs, N.J.; *Reader's Digest,* Pleasantville, N.Y., senior editor, 1972—. *Military service:* U.S. Army, reporter and editor for Army newspaper, 1946-48; served in Italy. *Awards, honors:* Edgar Award from Mystery Writers of America, 1969, for *Poe the Detective.*

WRITINGS: The Shroud (nonfiction), Random House, 1963; *Strange Harp, Strange Symphony,* biography of Francis Thompson), Hawthorn, 1967; *Poe the Detective* (PMLA Book Club selection), Rutgers University Press, 1968; *The Hidden Life of Emily Dickinson,* Simon & Schuster, 1971; *One Day at Kitty Hawk* (*Psychology Today* Book Club selection), Crowell, 1975; *Night on Fire* (on John Paul Jones), McGraw, 1978.

Juvenile: *The Sinking of the "U.S.S. Maine",* F. Watts, 1969; *The Mayflower Compact,* F. Watts, 1971; *The Philippine Insurrection,* F. Watts, 1973.

Also editor of *Letters,* by Thompson, Hawthorn. Contributor to periodicals, including *Sports Illustrated* and *Catholic Digest.*

WORK IN PROGRESS: Nonfiction.

SIDELIGHTS: Walsh told *CA:* "I find fascination in *facts*—their recovery and interpretation—and though I've written several books, perhaps my fondest memory involves my being able to prove that Babe Ruth *did* actually call his shot in the 1932 World Series. Not far behind is my discovery of the true identity of Emily Dickinson's great love."

* * *

WALSTER, G. William 1941-

PERSONAL: Born April 13, 1941, in Palo Alto, Calif.; son of Don Bernard (an Episcopal priest) and Alda (Lehman) Walster; married Elaine C. Hatfield, April 26, 1962 (divorced, 1978). *Education:* Stanford University, B.A., 1963; University of Minnesota, Ph.D., 1968. *Religion:* None. *Home:* 2207 East 34th St., Minneapolis, Minn. 55407. *Agent:* Timothy Seldes, Russell & Volkening, Inc., 551 Fifth Ave., New York, N.Y. 10017. *Office:* Control Data Corp., P.O. Box O, Minneapolis, Minn. 55440.

CAREER: University of Wisconsin, Madison, assistant professor of educational psychology, 1968-71; University of Mannheim, Mannheim, Germany, research professor, 1972; University of Wisconsin, Madison, associate professor, 1972-77, professor of sociology, 1977-78; Control Data Corp., Minneapolis, Minn., senior research analyst, 1978—. *Member:* Institute of Mathematical Statistics, Society of

Industrial and Applied Mathematics, American Mathematical Society, American Statistical Association, Society of Experimental Social Psychology.

WRITINGS: (With E. Berscheid and wife, Elaine Walster) *Equity: Theory and Research,* Allyn & Bacon, 1978; (with E. Walster) *A New Look at Love,* Addison-Wesley, 1978.

WORK IN PROGRESS: Statistics for Mortals, completion expected in 1985; research on the development of new inferential statistical techniques.

SIDELIGHTS: Walster writes: "I am constantly amazed at how unwilling people are to accept new revolutionary ideas. To persist in creative activities one must continue to ignore criticism and ridicule. It is too bad that we cannot reward creative people during their lifetimes. Yet this is no cause for bitterness, which is self-destructive."

* * *

WALTERS, Ronald G(ordon) 1942-

PERSONAL: Born April 23, 1942, in Sacramento, Calif.; son of Russell Goodrum (a government employee) and Arville (Scholfield) Walters; married Charlotte Higgins (a designer), July 25, 1965; children: Nathaniel. *Education:* Stanford University, A.B., 1963; University of California, Berkeley, M.A., 1965, Ph.D., 1971. *Home:* 3300 Beech Ave., Baltimore, Md. 21211. *Office:* Department of History, Johns Hopkins University, Baltimore, Md. 21218.

CAREER: Johns Hopkins University, Baltimore, Md., instructor, 1970-72, assistant professor, 1972-75, associate professor of history, 1975—. *Member:* American Historical Association, Organization of American Historians, Southern Historical Association, Phi Beta Kappa. *Awards, honors:* Younger humanist fellow of National Endowment for the Humanities, 1974-75; Rockefeller Foundation fellow, 1977-78.

WRITINGS: (Editor) *Primers for Prudery: Sexual Advice to Victorian America,* Prentice-Hall, 1974; *The Antislavery Appeal: American Abolitionism After 1830,* Johns Hopkins Press, 1976; *American Reformers, 1815-1860,* Hill & Wang, 1978. Contributor of articles and reviews to history journals. Member of board of editors of *Journal of Family History.*

WORK IN PROGRESS: A book on the evolution of the American popular entertainment industry, 1800-1913, publication expected in 1981.

SIDELIGHTS: Walters comments: "Coming of intellectual age in the conformist days of the 1950's and the ferment of the 1960's, I have been primarily concerned to discover what lies behind the changing perceptions Americans have of themselves and their society. My work has treated such diverse topics as early New England law, black newspapers, Victorian sexuality, reform movements, and popular entertainment, but running through it all is a desire—very much a product of the 1960's—to understand the relationship between belief and action, and to uncover the sources of moral behavior."

* * *

WARD, Craig 1892-1979
(Hugh MacCraig)

OBITUARY NOTICE: Born July 4, 1892, in San Francisco, Calif.; died March 25, 1979, in New York, N.Y. Astrologer and author of reference books in his field. Ward began his career as an actor on stage and in silent films. In the late 1930's, however, he became a professional astrologer and writer, using the name Hugh MacCraig. Among his best-known works are *The 200 Year Ephemeris* and its companion volume, *The Ephemeris of the Moon.* Obituaries and other sources: *New York Times,* April 1, 1979; *AB Bookman's Weekly,* April 16, 1979.

* * *

WARD, Fred 1935-

PERSONAL: Born July 16, 1935, in Huntsville, Ala.; son of Newman Ellis (in government) and Bess (Church) Ward; married Charlotte Mayes (a writer), June 8, 1958; children: Kimberly, Christopher, Laura, David. *Education:* University of Florida, B.A., 1957, M.A., 1959. *Politics:* Democrat. *Religion:* Protestant. *Home and office:* 7106 Saunders Court, Bethesda, Md. 20034.

CAREER: WKNO-TV, Memphis, Tenn., film director, 1959; St. Petersburg Junior College, St. Petersburg, Fla., instructor in television production, 1959-60; free-lance writer and photographer, 1960-79; Fred Ward Productions, Inc., Washington, D.C., president, 1968—. Owner of Photographic Seminars (Washington, D.C.), 1975-78. Member of board of directors of Adler Communications, Inc.; consultant in photography. *Military service:* U.S. Naval Reserve, 1954-62. *Member:* National Press Photographers Association, White House News Photographers Association, Sigma Delta Chi, Beta Theta Pi.

WRITINGS: Golden Islands of the Caribbean, Crown, 1972; (with Hugh Sidey) *Portrait of a President,* Harper, 1975; (with wife, Charlotte Ward) *The Home Birth Book,* Inscape, 1976; *Inside Cuba Today,* Crown, 1978. Contributor to *National Geographic.*

WORK IN PROGRESS: A book about diamonds; articles for *National Geographic* on Dominica, fiber optics, agri-chemicals, and Libya.

SIDELIGHTS: Ward writes: "My nonfiction writing is an outgrowth of a deep interest in world travel and the assignments I undertake for principal international publications. For instance, it is becoming somewhat of a pattern that I transform my articles for *National Geographic* into books. Other writing is based on topics that hold great interest for me. After having three children at home, my wife and I wrote *The Home Birth Book.* When present writing and photography commitments are completed, I plan to begin my first fiction book."

* * *

WATJEN, Carolyn L. T.
(Caroline Stafford)

PERSONAL: Born in Greensboro, N.C.; daughter of James Clifton, Jr. (in business) and Pearle (Linville) Teachey; married John Wheaton Watjen (a chemical engineer); children: Melinda, David. *Education:* University of North Carolina, Greensboro, B.A.; University of Pennsylvania, M.A. *Religion:* Protestant. *Residence:* Greenville, Del. *Agent:* Julie Fallowfield, McIntosh & Otis, Inc., 475 Fifth Ave., New York, N.Y. 10017.

CAREER: Writer and historian. Also worked as librarian for Associated Press in New York, N.Y. *Member:* American Association of University Women (member of board of directors), Mystery Writers of America, Rolls-Royce Owners' Club.

WRITINGS—All Gothic novels; all under pseudonym Caroline Stafford: *The House by Exmoor,* Simon & Schuster, 1975; *Moira,* Simon & Schuster, 1976; *The Teville Obses-*

sion, Simon & Schuster, 1978; *The Honour of Ravensholme,* Simon & Schuster, 1979. Also author of "The Tryst" (three-act play).

WORK IN PROGRESS: Research for books set in Northumberland, Bermuda, and medieval England.

SIDELIGHTS: Caroline Watjen writes: "I have been a voracious reader, enjoying nonfiction as well as fiction, though historical novels have always been a particular favorite. History has fascinated me, and the blending of fact and conjecture is intriguing. It was natural for me to turn to historical novels myself.

"Writing comes easily to me, a pleasure rather than an effort. If I do try to force it, it immediately becomes stale. I do not use people I have known in my work. This is never successful. My characters and the setting in which they live dictate the story line and action in my books. The story line is sometimes as much of a revelation to me as it is to the reader. I never outline.

"Because I research my books and actually visit the setting, atmosphere is an important factor and a central feature of my style. Action scenes are exciting and challenging to write.

"Travel is a passion—I've seen much of Europe by car—and we always take hundreds of photographs for my reference later. Britain is my spiritual home, I suppose. I love it as a visitor and a writer. I have an ear for languages and accents, which has been very useful in my books. My education was thorough, with a grounding in science, philosophy, history, literature, the arts, and languages. This has given me an exceptional range of interests from which to draw both in plotting and in character development.

"I have enjoyed writing Gothics, for they are pure entertainment. However, I do not plan to limit my career to this genre by any means."

AVOCATIONAL INTERESTS: Gardening, oil painting, brass rubbings from England, studying languages, travel, reading.

* * *

WATMOUGH, David 1926-

PERSONAL: Born August 17, 1926, in London, England; son of Gerald and Ethel (Bassett) Watmough. *Education:* Attended King's College, London, 1945-49. *Politics:* Independent. *Religion:* Anglican. *Home:* 3358 West First Ave., Vancouver, British Columbia, Canada V6R 1G4. *Agent:* Charlotte Sheedy Literary Agency, 145 West 86th St., New York, N.Y. 10024.

CAREER: Writer. British Broadcasting Corp., London, talks producer for Third Program, 1956; *San Francisco Examiner,* San Francisco, Calif., feature writer and reviewer, 1958-60; editor for Ace Books, 1957; *Vancouver Sun,* Vancouver, British Columbia, drama and art critic, 1963-66. Broadcaster for British Broadcasting Corp., Canadian Broadcasting Corp., and KPFA-Radio. *Military service:* Royal Navy, 1944-45. *Member:* Writers Union of Canada (British Columbia representative). *Awards, honors:* Canada Council bursary awards, 1968, and 1970, both for writing for theatre; Canada Council senior arts grant, 1976.

WRITINGS: A Church Renascent, S.P.C.K., 1951; *Names for the Numbered Years* (plays; contains "Friedhof," "My Mother's House Has Too Many Rooms," and "Do You Remember One September Afternoon?"), Bau-Xi Press, 1967; *Ashes for Easter* (short stories), Talonbooks, 1972; *Love and the Waiting Game* (short stories), Oberon Press,

1975; *No More Into the Garden* (novel), Doubleday, 1978; *Unruly Skeletons,* Doubleday, in press.

Work anthologized in *Cornish Short Stories,* Penguin, and *CBC Encounter.*

SIDELIGHTS: Watmough writes: "All my three volumes of fiction to date (and these are my primary concerns) center upon my first-person protagonist, Davey Bryant. This character is Cornish-born, is homosexual, and so far in his early forties, he has become a Canadian citizen. My goal is, through an open-ended sequence of novels, to come up with the portrait of a particular man living through his particular twentieth-century times. This has/will cover(ed) a French period, a New York period, San Francisco, and Vancouver, and so far extends from 1926 to 1969, with gaps still to be filled in forthcoming volumes.

"I make a substantial part of my income from giving professional readings, more than a thousand in the past ten years." Watmough has also recorded his poems on "Pictures From a Dying Landscape," Kanata Records, 1972.

BIOGRAPHICAL/CRITICAL SOURCES: Canadian, November 18, 1972; *Canadian Fiction,* winter, 1976.

* * *

WATTS, Al(bert) L. 1934-

PERSONAL: Born November 20, 1934, in Randolph, Iowa; son of Albert Q. and Irene D. (Gier) Watts. *Education:* Washington State University, B.A., 1959. *Home:* 5348 Southwest Lander, Seattle, Wash. 98116. *Office:* Seattle *Post-Intelligencer,* Sixth and Wall Sts., Seattle, Wash. 98111.

CAREER/WRITINGS: Walla-Walla Union-Bulletin, Walla-Walla, Wash., sports editor, 1962-64; *Oregonian,* Portland, Ore., sports writer and columnist, 1964-66; Boeing Co., Seattle, Wash., public relations representative and editor of employee newspaper, 1966-69; *Seattle Post-Intelligencer,* Seattle, aviation, transportation, and military writer, 1969—, author of column, "Airspace," 1978—. *Military service:* U.S. Army, 1959-62. *Member:* Pacific Northwest Newspaper Guild. *Awards, honors:* Regional award from Sigma Delta Chi, 1975, for story on the impact of airport noise and its cost; Blethen Award from Washington Newspaper Publishers, 1976, for story on community impacts of Trident nuclear submarine base on Puget Sound; awards from Aviation/Space Writers Association, 1977, 1978.

WORK IN PROGRESS: Various free-lance transportation and travel articles; a novel.

SIDELIGHTS: Watts writes: "I am motivated by the need to inform the public about what large companies and public agencies are doing, about actions that affect the man and woman on the street. In this connection, I try to remain aloof from offered statements, so as not to be a mouthpiece for companies' or agencies' public relations departments. I also try to put things in clear, concise language, and to battle the growing bastardization of English; *communication* is my game."

AVOCATIONAL INTERESTS: Physical fitness (running, weight training), travel (Europe, the Far East), books, good music, most sports, the sun.

* * *

WAUGH, Evelyn (Arthur St. John) 1903-1966

PERSONAL: Born October 28, 1903, in Hampstead, London, England; died April 10, 1966, in Taunton, Somerset, England; son of Arthur (a writer and publisher) and Catherine Charlotte (Raban) Waugh; married Evelyn Gardner, 1928 (divorced, 1930; marriage annulled, 1936); married Laura Herbert, 1937; children: (second marriage) Auberon, Margaret, Teresa, Harriet, two other sons. *Education:* Attended Hertford College, Oxford, and Heatherley's Art School. *Religion:* Roman Catholic.

CAREER: Satirical novelist and essayist. Worked for a short time as schoolmaster, as journalist for *London Daily Express,* and as war correspondent in Abyssinia. *Military service:* Royal Marines and Commandos, c.1939-45; became major. *Awards, honors:* Catholic literary award from Gallery of Living Catholic Authors, 1945, for *Brideshead Revisited;* honorary degree from Loyola College.

WRITINGS: The World to Come (poetry), Westminster Press, 1916; *Rossetti: His Life and Works,* Dodd, 1928, reprinted, Norwood, 1978; *Decline and Fall* (novelette), Chapman & Hall, 1928, Doran, 1929, reprinted, Little, Brown, 1977; *A Bachelor Abroad: A Mediterranean Journal,* J. Cape & H. Smith, 1930, (published in England as *Labels: A Mediterranean Journal,* Duckworth, 1930, new edition, 1974); *Vile Bodies* (novel), J. Cape & H. Smith, 1930, reprinted, Little, Brown, 1977; *Black Mischief* (novel), Farrar & Rinehart, 1932, new edition, Hutchinson, 1968, reprinted, Little, Brown, 1977; *Remote People,* Duckworth, 1931, published as *They Were Still Dancing,* Farrar & Rinehart, 1932; *Ninety-two Days: The Account of a Tropical Journey Through British Guiana and Part of Brazil,* Farrar & Rinehart, 1934; *A Handful of Dust* (novel), Farrar & Rinehart, 1934, reprinted, Little, Brown, 1977; *Edmund Campion* (biography), Sheed, 1935, reprinted, Penguin, 1957; *Waugh in Abyssinia,* Longmans, 1936; *Mr. Loveday's Little Outing and Other Sad Stories,* Little, Brown, 1936; *Scoop* (novel), Little, Brown, 1938 (published in England as *Scoop, A Novel About Journalists,* Chapman & Hall, 1938), reprinted, 1977; *Mexico: An Object Lesson,* Little, Brown, 1939 (published in England as *Robbery Under Law: The Mexican Object-Lesson,* Chapman & Hall, 1939).

Work Suspended: Two Chapters of an Unfinished Novel, Chapman & Hall, 1942; *Put Out More Flags* (novel), Little, Brown, 1942, new edition, Hutchinson Educational, 1968; *Brideshead Revisited: The Sacred and Profane Memories of Captain Charles Ryder* (novel), Little, Brown, 1945, revised edition, Harlow, Longmans, 1968; *When the Going Was Good* (contains portions of *Labels, Remote People, Ninety-two Days,* and *Waugh in Abyssinia*), Duckworth, 1946, Little, Brown, 1947, reprinted, Greenwood Press, 1976; *Edmund Campion* (biography), Little, Brown, 1946, 3rd edition, Longmans, 1961; *Scott-King's Modern Europe,* Chapman & Hall, 1947, Little, Brown, 1949; *Wine in Peace and War,* Saccone & Speed, 1947; *The Loved One: An Anglo-American Tragedy* (novel), Chapman & Hall, 1948, Random House, 1958, new edition with introduction, glossary, and notes by Linton Stone, Heinemann, 1967.

Helena (novel), Little, Brown, 1950; *Men at Arms* (first novel in trilogy; also see below), Little, Brown, 1952; *Men at War,* Little, Brown, 1952; *Love Among the Ruins: A Romance of the Near Future,* Chapman & Hall, 1953; *Tactical Exercise* (short stories), Little, Brown, 1954; *Officers and Gentlemen* (second novel in trilogy; also see below), Little, Brown, 1955; *The Ordeal of Gilbert Pinfold: A Conversation Piece* (novel), Little, Brown, 1957; *The World of Evelyn Waugh,* edited by Charles J. Rolo, Little, Brown, 1958; *Monsignor Ronald Knox, Fellow of Trinity College, Oxford, and Protonotary Apostolic to His Holiness Pope Pius XII,* Little, Brown, 1959 (published in England as *The Life of the*

Right Reverend Ronald Knox, Fellow of Trinity College, Oxford, and Pronotary Apostolic to His Holiness Pope Pius XII, Chapman & Hall, 1959).

Tourist in Africa, Little, Brown, 1960; *Unconditional Surrender* (third novel in trilogy; also see below), Chapman & Hall, 1961, published as *The End of the Battle*, Little, Brown, 1962; *Basil Seal Rides Again; or, the Rake's Regress*, Little, Brown, 1963; *A Little Learning: An Autobiography; the Early Years*, Little, Brown, 1964 (published in England as *A Little Learning: The First Volume of an Autobiography*, Chapman & Hall, 1964); *Sword of Honour* (trilogy; includes *Men at Arms, Officers and Gentlemen*, and *Unconditional Surrender*), Chapman & Hall, 1965, Little, Brown, 1966; *Work Suspended and Other Pieces, Including Basil Seal Rides Again*, Penguin, 1967; *The Private Diaries of Evelyn Waugh*, edited by Michael Davie, Observer magazine, 1973; *The Diaries of Evelyn Waugh*, Little, Brown, 1976; *A Little Order*, edited by Donat Gallagher, Eyre Methuen, 1977.

Omnibus volumes: *Vile Bodies* [and] *Black Mischief*, Dell, 1960; *Scoop* [and] *Put Out More Flags*, Dell, 1961; *Men at Arms* [and] *Officers and Gentlemen*, Dell, 1961; *The Ordeal of Gilbert Pinfold* [and] *Tactical Exercise* [and] *Love Among the Ruins*, Penguin, 1962; *A Handful of Dust* [and] *Decline and Fall*, Dell, 1966; *The Ordeal of Gilbert Pinfold and Other Stories* (contains *Mr. Loveday's Little Outing, Scott-King's Modern Europe, Love Among the Ruins*, and *The Ordeal of Gilbert Pinfold*), Chapman & Hall, 1973; *Decline and Fall* [and] *Black Mischief* [and] *A Handful of Dust* [and] *Scoop* [and] *Put Out More Flags* [and] *Brideshead Revisited*, Heinemann, 1977.

SIDELIGHTS: A noted satirist, novelist, and essayist, Evelyn Waugh was the most prominent author of a talented literary family. His father, Arthur, was an editor and publisher at Chapman & Hall, a small but prestigious London publishing house. His children Auberon and Harriet have published books, and his brother Alec was a novelist as well.

Waugh wrote his first book at age seven. It was a five-hundred word novel entitled "The Curse of the Horse Race." Chapter one, "Betting," began: "I bet you 500 pounds I'll win. The speaker was Rupert a man of about 25 he had a dark bushy mistarsh and flashing eyes." Waugh commented that of his early works this, his earliest, was the only one to show some imagination.

Waugh's writing style is characterized by its sharp satire and sophisticated wit. R. Z. Sheppard declared, "It is . . . never too late to read or reread Waugh. His vitality, matchless craftmanship, audacious imagination and stinging perceptions . . . have not dated." *Decline and Fall, Vile Bodies*, and his other early novels manifest most clearly Waugh's biting sarcasm. Frederick R. Karl believed these early writings to be Waugh's "most effective work, [because] Waugh is defending no one and nothing."

Robert Murray Davis describes Waugh's central theme as "the individual in retreat from a chaotic and menacing society." In *A Handful of Dust*, Brenda and Tony Last inhabit a world of mad but unchangeable social rules. Tony lives in the past, putting all his energies into the restoration of his country home. Brenda seeks relief from her boring life in the country by having an affair with one of London's social parasites, unwittingly setting into motion a chain of events ending in destruction of herself and her husband. Davis feels this book is the "most penetrating of Waugh's novels" because "it traces more vividly and uncompromisingly the effects of seeking refuge from the world without adequate re-

sources for the retreat or an ordered, enduring place of withdrawal."

A Handful of Dust presents a particularly ridiculous view of divorce proceedings. Though it was Brenda who was unfaithful, she could not receive alimony payments unless she was the plaintiff in the case. Always the helpful husband, Tony agreed to provide evidence of his own infidelity by spending the weekend with another woman at a seaside hotel. His divorce lawyer made the arrangements: "'We always send our clients there. The servants are well accustomed to giving evidence.'"

Waugh's own first marriage to Evelyn Gardner was disastrous and short-lived: she ran off with a future baronet. This undoubtedly influenced Waugh's portrayal of women. Sheppard notes that "betrayal by women is recurrent in much of his fiction. The ladies are usually charming and never malicious, but . . . their egoism, stupidity, conceit and self-regard become the causes for both cruelty and comedy."

Waugh converted to Catholicism in 1930, and thereafter religion became very important to him. Although he continued to write scathing remarks that often seemed far from Christian, Waugh once told a friend, "You have no idea how much nastier I would be if I was not a Catholic."

In later years religious themes crept into Waugh's writings. His first religious novel was *Brideshead Revisited*, a serious story of Catholic aristocracy published in 1945. While this was one of his most popular novels and was on the best-seller list, some critics questioned its literary merit. Wilfred Sheed remarked about the book: "He'd tried to be serious and he'd made a fool of himself. . . . It must have hurt him deeply that he explained . . . [his religion] so badly."

Brideshead Revisited was also the first novel in Waugh's trend toward a more tolerant and sympathetic view of society, as opposed to the indiscriminant cruelty displayed earlier. Critics generally prefer his earlier work. For example, Gene Kellogg declared that "the comparison between early and late Waugh invariably reminds one of a rapier which by the continual addition of weight has turned into a sledgehammer." Likewise, Karl observed, "When he could lampoon all ideas, his own as well, Waugh had secure purchase on ground that was his alone; but when either because of age, success, or artistic belief he let down the comic mask and spoke personally, then his novels lost their style."

In *The Loved One*, published in 1948, Waugh returned briefly to the sarcasm he was noted for. This novel satirizes America's commercialized burial customs. In A. C. Ward's opinion: "The theme is in reality so grotesque and nauseating that an exceptional degree of literary discipline and tact is required to treat it. Waugh exhausts the theme in the first dozen or so pages and the book thereafter becomes contaminated by prolonged gnawing at its own material. It must be noted, however, that reviewers gave *The Loved One* unmeasured praise."

Before settling down as a full-time writer, Waugh attempted a teaching career. In *A Little Learning* he describes his miserable failure at a boys' school in Flintshire. He had no credentials for teaching and did not know how to handle the students. "I was from the first an obvious dud," Waugh wrote. Having failed to impress the boys on their first meeting, he had little chance to improve his reputation with them. "I had forgotten . . . that a schoolmaster can only commend himself by boasting."

In his personal life, Evelyn Waugh is "neither what the public takes him for nor what he gives himself out to be," reported *Times Literary Supplement.* He appeared to the public as pessimistic, cynical, disdainful, and rude, a class-conscious, self-made aristocrat, full of contempt for lower classes. His writings generally confirm that view. As R. Z. Sheppard noted, "the reader who is unaware of Waugh the artist might easily believe that . . . [he] was simply an overly educated snob, a widely traveled glutton and a dipsomaniac."

Frances Donaldson provides a more pleasant insight into Waugh's personality in *Evelyn Waugh: Portrait of a Country Neighbor.* Donaldson and her husband became close friends with the Waugh family, and her anecdotes reveal Waugh's charm, wit, ebullience, and generosity. Waugh was "extremely hospitable" and loved to entertain, Donaldson informs us. He would often invite people to stay for the weekend, but this was "a highly dangerous procedure, because Evelyn who looked forward excitely to the visit all the week before, could seldom endure anyone for so long a period." His fear of boredom and love of privacy outweighed his hospitality long before the visit ended.

Though Waugh yearned for companionship, "between his prejudices and his inability to enjoy ordinary society, Evelyn was very much cut off." When he met new people, Donaldson related, he would make an effort to be amusing, but often his jokes were so stylized that people didn't find them funny. He also "had the faculty of pulverising other people, reducing them to silence," and with one cutting remark could lose a friend of many years.

Waugh's novel, *The Loved One,* was adapted as a film produced by Metro-Goldwyn-Mayer in 1965 and *Decline and Fall* was filmed as "Decline and Fall of a Bird Watcher" by Twentieth-Century Fox in 1969.

BIOGRAPHICAL/CRITICAL SOURCES: Times Literary Supplement, May 16, 1960, September 3, 1976, February 3, 1978; Frederick R. Karl, *A Reader's Guide to the Contemporary English Novel,* Farrar, Straus, 1962; Evelyn Waugh, *A Handful of Dust,* Little, Brown, 1962; A. C. Ward, *Twentieth-Century English Literature 1901-1960,* Methuen, 1964; Waugh, *A Little Learning,* Little, Brown, 1964; *Papers on Literature and Language,* summer, 1967; Frances Donaldson, *Evelyn Waugh: Portrait of a Country Neighbor,* Weidenfeld & Nicolson, 1967; Alec Waugh, *My Brother Evelyn and Other Portraits,* Farrar, Straus, 1968; *Contemporary Literary Criticism,* Gale, Volume 1, 1973, Volume 3, 1975, Volume 8, 1978; *Newsweek,* January 22, 1968, May 7, 1973, November 24, 1975; Gene Kellogg, *The Vital Tradition: The Catholic Novel in a Period of Convergence,* Loyola University Press, 1970; *New York Times Book Review,* July 1, 1973, February 10, 1974, Ocotber 16, 1977; *Esquire,* September, 1973; Christopher Sykes, *Evelyn Waugh: A Biography,* Little, Brown, 1975; *Time,* December 8, 1975, October 17, 1977, February 12, 1979; *Critic,* fall, 1976; *Saturday Review,* November 12, 1977; *New York Review of Books,* December 8, 1977; *New Yorker,* January 16, 1978; *New Republic,* May 12, 1979.

OBITUARIES: New York Herald Tribune, April 11, 1966; *New York Times,* April 11, 1966; *Illustrated London News,* April 16, 1966; *Publishers Weekly,* April 18, 1966; *Time,* April 25, 1966; *Newsweek,* April 25, 1966; *Antiquarian Bookman,* May 2, 1966; *National Review,* May 3, 1966; *Books Abroad,* spring, 1967.*

* * *

WAUGH, Harriet 1944-

PERSONAL: Daughter of Evelyn (a writer) and Laura (Herbert) Waugh.

CAREER: Writer and editor. Worked as a technician in the London Planetorium.

WRITINGS: Mirror, Mirror: A Novel, Weidenfeld & Nicolson, 1973, Little, Brown, 1975; *Mother's Footsteps* (novel), Weidenfeld & Nicolson, 1978.

SIDELIGHTS: The central character of Harriet Waugh's first novel, *Mirror, Mirror,* is a man so hideously ugly that people want to gouge his eyes out. His visage is transformed by plastic surgery, but the beautification takes place only on the surface. The character, Godfrey Pettlement, becomes a preacher, vengefully founds a cult of death, and is ultimately murdered himself. Some reviewers were put off by the grisliness of the work. Others, like Peter Ackroyd, found the novel legitimized by Waugh's "gift for lyricism."

Still, the book was not particularly well-received by reviewers who felt that its excesses and flaws outweighed its admirable features. A *Times Literary Supplement* critic wrote: "Rather too much of Harriet Waugh's first novel consists of competent but directionless reportage from [a] too-familiar waste-land. To sharpen the impact, however, she spikes it with horror-fantasy and theological allegory." Dorothy Rabinowitz judged that despite some worthwhile moments—"notably some scathing assaults on evangelistic piety"—the book fell short of its promise. Waugh, wrote Rabinowitz, "dissipates her energies on a good many characters, none of them as interesting as Godfrey."

The unevenness of the novel bothered many critics. Timothy Mo noted: "Two novels of differing quality have been crammed into one: a novel about that self-regarding, flat-sharing brigade of middle-class young Londoners too often written about, and at the same time a very fine piece of black fantasy. To be fair, Miss Waugh is very amusing when she is flaying sacred cows, like guilt about the Third World, or satirising glib young revolutionaries. But if she had spared us her girls industriously scrambling eggs in their flatlets it might have been better. This is an uneasy, neurotic book, but the obsessions give it a lot of drive."

Peter Ackroyd, who found the book to be generally well-written, remarked, ". . . Miss Waugh has a perceptiveness that is all the more attractive because it seems so casual. I only wish that it had been employed within a less conventional and personal context. It is bitterness and world-weariness which ruin the book." And Susan S. McDonald commented: "*Mirror, Mirror* has its mild successes—it is, for example, a fresh refurbishing of some old symbolic material—but Miss Waugh's satire doesn't work as well as it should. She is an intelligent writer, but she lacks enough delicacy of style to detract from the seams and contrivances of the story, and her occasionally awkward narration lurches forward when she feels she must get us somewhere."

Waugh is a member of the literary Waugh family—Evelyn is her father, Alec is her uncle, Auberon is her brother—and while critics have not compared her favorably to her relatives, they have found similarities in their work. According to *Time,* "Evelyn satirized his peers and times by following sane characters through a giddy world. Harriet uses the much less engaging converse: crazy people, sane society. The father's unremittingly inhospitable view of humanity lent his books bite and pace. The daughter, so far at least, clearly shares his disdain for British foible, but cannot sustain it; when she lapses into tolerance, the novel drags. Even so," he admitted, "*Mirror, Mirror* reflects a provocative and steely talent." And a *Times Literary Supplement* writer commented, "[She] displays, in a reasonably new version, her family's characteristic liveliness of mind and pen: once she has mastered the laborious art of economy, she should be able to delight us all.''

Waugh's latest novel, *Mother's Footsteps*, is also concerned with the macabre and suffers from unevenness. The *Times Literary Supplement* reviewer cited its ''uncertainty of purpose,'' and its implausible ending. Francis King, though, thought that the book contained some splendid scenes, and wrote: ''Throughout all of this Harriet Waugh shows that she can write with exceptional skill, if also with exceptional carelessness.... The result is a book that, despite minor exasperations of style, is singularly impressive in its mixture of devastating cynicism and grudging compassion.''

BIOGRAPHICAL/CRITICAL SOURCES: Spectator, January 12, 1974, May 20, 1978; *Times Literary Supplement,* January 18, 1974, July 14, 1978; *New Statesman,* January 18, 1974; *Listener,* February 7, 1974; *Saturday Review,* March 22, 1975; *Time,* April 14, 1975; *New York Times Book Review,* June 8, 1975; *National Review,* July 18, 1975; *Contemporary Literary Criticism,* Volume 6, Gale, 1976; *Observer,* June 4, 1978.*

*　　　*　　　*

WAX, Judith　1932(?)-1979

OBITUARY NOTICE: Born c. 1932; died May 25, 1979, in an airplane crash in Chicago, Ill. Author of *Starting in the Middle,* a book on middle-aged people. Wax, who was bunny director for *Playboy,* wrote ''Waterbury Tales,'' a satirical poem about Watergate. Obituaries and other sources: *Chicago Tribune,* May 27, 1979; *Publishers Weekly,* June 4, 1979.

*　　　*　　　*

WAX, Sheldon　1928(?)-1979

OBITUARY NOTICE: Born c. 1928; died May 25, 1979, in an airplane crash in Chicago, Ill. Managing editor of *Playboy.* Wax also edited several magazines on the automobile industry during the 1950's. Obituaries and other sources: *Chicago Tribune,* May 27, 1979; *Publishers Weekly,* June 4, 1979.

*　　　*　　　*

WAYNE, John　1907-1979

PERSONAL: Birth-given name Marion Michael Morrison; took name John Wayne, 1929; born May 26, 1907, in Winterset, Iowa; died June 11, 1979, in Los Angeles, Calif., son of Clyde L. (a druggist) and Mary Margaret (Brown) Morrison; married Josephine Saenz, June 24, 1933 (divorced); married Esperanza Baur (an actress and dancer), January 17, 1946 (divorced, 1953) married Pilar Palette, November 1, 1954 (separated, November 19, 1973); children: Michael, Toni (Mrs. Don La Cava), Patrick, Melinda (Mrs. Gregory Munoz), Aissia, John Ethan, Marisa. *Education:* Attended University of Southern California, 1925-27. *Politics:* Republican. *Residence:* Newport Beach, Calif. *Office:* Batjac Productions Inc., 5451 Marathon St., Hollywood, Calif. 90038.

CAREER: Actor in more than one hundred-fifty motion pictures, including ''Stagecoach,'' 1939, ''Red River,'' 1948, ''The Quiet Man,'' 1951, ''The Searchers,'' 1956, ''Rio Bravo,'' 1959, ''The Man Who Shot Liberty Valance,'' 1962, ''Hatari,'' 1962, ''The Green Berets,'' 1968, ''True Grit,'' 1969, and ''The Cowboys,'' 1972. Director of motion pictures, including ''The Alamo,'' 1960, and ''The Green Berets,'' 1968. Co-founder of Motion Picture Alliance for the Preservation of American Ideals, 1944; president of

Theatre for Freedom, Inc., 1950; founder of Batjac Productions Inc. *Member:* Academy of Motion Picture Arts and Sciences. *Awards, honors:* Nomination for Academy Award for best actor from Academy of Motion Picture Arts and Sciences, 1950, for ''Sands of Iwo Jima''; Academy Award for best actor, 1969, for ''True Grit.''

WRITINGS: America, Why I Love Her, Simon & Schuster, 1977.

SIDELIGHTS: Wayne began his career as an actor in the late 1920's when he obtained a summer job as a stuntman for Twentieth Century-Fox. After a speaking part in ''Men Without Women,'' Wayne hired on as a prop man for the film ''The Big Trail.'' Unfortunately his large frame hindered his work and he periodically broke things and knocked equipment over. Then, acting on a tip from fellow director John Ford, Raoul Walsh decided to cast Wayne as one of the film's characters. They rushed him through a crash-course in acting but the turn of events was too sudden. Even though Wayne toured in western garb to help promote the film, ''The Big Trail'' failed to turn a profit.

Wayne next appeared in two long-forgotten films, ''Girls Demand Excitement'' and ''Three Girls Lost,'' then was induced by producer Leon Schlesinger to star in a series of low-budget westerns. Since westerns were considered an inferior genre, they were generally allotted much less time for filming and editing than other films. Consequently, from 1930 to 1939, Wayne appeared in more than seventy films.

For years while Wayne was acting in grade-B westerns, John Ford had toyed with the idea of directing a quality western. However he was repeatedly turned away by producers when he insisted that Wayne be cast as the Ringo Kid, a gunfighter in search of his parents' murderers. Finally, producer Walter Wanger accepted Ford's terms and ''Stagecoach'' was filmed. This motion picture was given all the attention usually reserved for more respectable genres and the results justified the care. ''Stagecoach'' was nominated for several Academy Awards and proved to the Hollywood moguls that westerns could be taken seriously.Shortly after ''Stagecoach,'' Wayne achieved ''leading man'' status. But though he starred opposite actresses such as Joan Crawford and Marlene Dietrich, most of his films from the early 1940's are regarded as inferior. Some exceptions are those made under the direction of Ford, notably ''The Long Voyage Home.'' Widely considered by critics as one of the best adaptations of an O'Neill play, it contained a subtle performance by Wayne as a lonely, dumb-but-friendly Swede. The quality of Wayne's films seemed to be steadily declining until he again teamed with Ford in ''They Were Expendable,'' a true-to-life war drama. His previous film, ''Tall in the Saddle,'' had rekindled public interest in him and ''They Were Expendable'' proved to be an appropriate follow-up.

During the late 1940's, Wayne made a series of fine films. He followed a stellar performance in ''Sands of Iwo Jima'' with two more in John Ford's ''Fort Apache'' and ''Rio Grande.'' Critics now refer to both films as classics of the western genre. ''Red River,'' made under the direction of Howard Hawks, contained a fine performance by Wayne in what would become for him a patented role: the aging gunfighter.

While an attempt by Wayne to move beyond war dramas and westerns had backfired in the 1940's, a similar attempt in the 1950's resulted in a number of memorable roles. His performances in both ''Big Jim McLain'' and ''The Quiet Man'' were acknowledged for showing a sensitivity unexpected from an actor typecast into a standard ''rough 'n' ready'' character. But Wayne also continued to make westerns during the 1950's. Among his most notable films were "Hondo," "The Searchers," ranked with "Stagecoach" as one of the great American films, and "Rio Bravo," which was Wayne and Howard Hawks's answer to "High Noon," a film both Hawks and Wayne felt was a tainting of the American hero myth.

Wayne made his debut as a director in 1960 with "The Alamo"; however, the film was heavily criticized for its slow pace and excessive rhetoric. Wayne eventually consulted with Ford who did provide some assistance, but the film was massacred by critics and Wayne waited eight years before directing his second film, "The Green Berets." It, too, was roundly panned by critics for being blatantly pro-Vietnam War and for containing such oversights as a Vietnam-viewed ocean sunset!

In the sixties, Wayne delivered another string of outstanding performances in films such as "North to Alaska," "Hatari," "El Dorado," and "The Man Who Shot Liberty Valance." He capped the decade by receiving an Academy Award for his "True Grit" portrayal of Rooster Cogburn, a one-eyed, drunken gunfighter who helps a young woman fight off a band of evil-doers. Wayne later repeated the role opposite Katherine Hepburn in a failed sequel.

Although his detractors have implied that Wayne refuses to extend himself as an actor, he has still performed admirably in the 1970's. "The Cowboys" was praised for its refreshing story about an old rancher forced to employ young boys as ranch hands and Wayne received special praise for his convincing death scene. "The Shootist" made several best-film lists for 1977. In it, Wayne played an aging gunfighter dying of cancer. The film was cited for Wayne's touching performance because he'd undergone operations for cancer in the past.

For more than forty years and two hundred films, Wayne has typified the American spirit of strength, honesty, and determination. He is now regarded with Humphrey Bogart, Errol Flynn, and a few others, as one of the great heroes of American cinema. His films have grossed more than any other performer's and for years he was a top box-office draw. Although many of his admirers insist that Wayne never received the credit he deserved as an actor, he has endured to become a legend in American culture.

BIOGRAPHICAL/CRITICAL SOURCES: J. A. Place, *Western Films of John Ford,* Citadel, 1974; Alan G. Barbour, *John Wayne,* Harcourt, 1974; George Carpozi, Jr., *The John Wayne Story,* Dell, 1974; David Paige, *John Wayne,* Popular Library, 1976; Allen Eyles, *John Wayne and the Movies,* A. S. Barnes, 1976; Charles Silver, *Western Film,* Harcourt, 1976; Andrew Sarris, *John Ford Movie Mystery,* Indiana University Press, 1976; Andrew Sinclair, *John Ford: The Waning of the Great West,* Dial, 1979.

OBITUARIES: Time, June 25, 1979; *Newsweek,* June 25, 1979; *People,* June 25, 1979.*

* * *

WEAVER, Peter 1925-

PERSONAL: Born November 19, 1925, in Cleveland, Ohio; son of Robert A. (in business) and May (Tuthill) Weaver; married Vida Barrera, April 10, 1955; children: Paul, Michael. *Education:* Kenyon College, B.A., 1950. *Politics:* Independent. *Religion:* Roman Catholic. *Home:* 5102 Cammack Dr., Washington, D.C., 20016. *Office:* 5100 Cammack Dr., Washington, D.C. 20016.

CAREER: Cleveland Plain Dealer, Cleveland, Ohio, reporter, 1950-55; correspondent from New York, Brazil, Mexico, and Washington, D.C., for *Business Week* magazine, 1955-64; chief of Washington Bureau for *Forbes* magazine, 1964-69; author of columns, "Mind Your Money" and "Your Retirement Dollar," syndicated by King Features, 1969—. Commentator for WJLA-TV, 1974—. *Military service:* U.S. Navy, radioman, 1944-46; served in Pacific theater; received two battle stars. *Member:* National Press Club. *Awards, honors:* Fairchild Award from Overseas Press Club, 1959, for best business story from abroad; Interstate Natural Gas Association of America Award from University of Missouri, 1968, for "The Mess in Medicine."

WRITINGS: You, Inc. (nonfiction), Doubleday, 1972. Author of television series for the elderly, aired by South Carolina Educational Television, 1975.

WORK IN PROGRESS: Books on the costs of education and the revolution in retirement.

SIDELIGHTS: Weaver comments: "I received considerable coaching and enormous motivation to write from professors at Kenyon College (such as John Crowe Ransom and Robert Hillyer). The 'Great Fire' at Kenyon College in 1949, which killed nine students, launched me into a career of journalism. I have always felt that everyone should consider not having to work for someone else all their lives, and that thought motivated my book, *You, Inc.,* which shows how to escape organization life."

* * *

WEBBER, Thomas L(ane) 1947-

PERSONAL: Born July 14, 1947, in Minot, N.D.; son of George W. (a clergyman) and Helen (a social activist) Webber; married Andrea Bertocci (a physician), June 8, 1968; children: Aili, Matthew. *Education:* Harvard University, B.A., 1969; Columbia University, Ph.D., 1976. *Home:* 315 East 106th St., #18-B, New York, N.Y. 10029.

CAREER: College for Human Service, New York, N.Y., coordinator and teacher of American history, social science research, and systems analysis, 1974—.

WRITINGS: Deep Like the Rivers: Education in the Slave Quarter Community, 1831-1865, Norton, 1978.

WORK IN PROGRESS: A semi-autobiographical novel, "the story of a young man returning from college to his home in East Harlem during the late 1960's. It explores how the black and Puerto Rican power movements affected the lives of one young, small family."

SIDELIGHTS: Webber told *CA:* "My first book, *Deep Like the Rivers,* tries to present the world as it was understood and lived in by American slaves. As much as possible it describes this 'world view' in the words of slaves or ex-slaves themselves."

"Although I began writing in order to meet the various requirements of an undergraduate and graduate education, it has now become for me a kind of therapy. By writing about social and personal issues that concern me I am able to deal with them more directly and honestly in my life. Writing is also an outlet for my imagination. Like acting, writing is a way for me to experience people and events that I am not able to experience, and sometimes would not care to experience, in real life."

* * *

WEEDEN, Robert B(arton) 1933-

PERSONAL: Born January 8, 1933, in Fall River, Mass.;

son of Robert H. and Doris B. Weeden; married Judith Stenger (a potter), June 13, 1959; children: Robert, Bristol, Kimberly. *Education:* University of Massachusetts, B.Sc., 1953; University of Maine, M.Sc., 1955; University of British Columbia, Ph.D., 1959. *Office:* School of Agriculture and Land Resources Management, University of Alaska, Fairbanks, Alaska 99701.

CAREER: Alaska Department of Fish and Game, Fairbanks, research biologist, 1959-69; University of Alaska, Fairbanks, professor of resource management, 1970—. Visiting professor at University of California, Santa Cruz, 1972-73. Member of Alaska Environmental Advisory Board, 1972-74, and National Marine Fisheries Advisory Committee, 1975-78; director of Alaska governor's Division of Policy Development, 1975-76; member of scientific advisory board of Marine Mammal Commission, 1977—. *Member:* Wildlife Society (director of council, 1972-74), National Audubon Society (member of board of directors, 1976—), American Ornithologists Union, Cooper Ornithological Society, Alaska Conservation Society (past president). *Awards, honors:* Conservation award from American Motors Corp., 1968.

WRITINGS: Alaska: Promises to Keep, Houghton, 1978. Contributor of articles and a poem to conservation and wildlife magazines.

WORK IN PROGRESS: A new program in wildlife conservation for Alaska Department of Fish and Game.

SIDELIGHTS: Weeden wrote: "My career in ornithological research has evolved since 1968 into a career of teaching and advocating resource and environmental policies. My book was begun early in this transition period, and completed in 1978 at the height of involvement in my role as a political activist-adviser at national and state levels. I don't consider myself a writer; probably my readers don't either. I do have a vision of the kind of life Alaskans can create for themselves out of the natural character of the land, our frontier history, and our responses to modern imperatives. I write in hopes that reading about my perceptions will help people articulate their own."

*   *   *

WEEKS, Edward (Augustus) 1898-

PERSONAL: Born February 19, 1898, in Elizabeth, N.J.; son of Edward Augustus and Frederika (Suydam) Weeks; married Frederica Watriss, May 28, 1925 (died July, 1970); married Phoebe Adams, February 19, 1971; children: Sara Weeks Thomson, Edward Francis. *Education:* Attended Cornell University, 1915-17; Harvard University, B.S., 1922; graduate study at Cambridge University, 1922-23. *Politics:* Democrat. *Religion:* Episcopalian. *Home:* 59 Chestnut St., Boston, Mass. 02108. *Office:* 8 Arlington St., Boston, Mass. 02116.

CAREER: Horace Liveright, Inc., New York, N.Y., reader and salesman, 1923; Atlantic Monthly Co., Boston, Mass., associate editor of *Atlantic Monthly* (magazine), 1924-28, editor of Atlantic Monthly Press, 1928-38, editor of *Atlantic Monthly,* 1938-66, senior editor and consultant of Atlantic Monthly Press, 1966—. Head of Massachusetts Committee to Reform Book Censorship, 1929-30. American Field Service, member of board of directors, 1960-70, life member of board of trustees; member of board of directors of United Negro College Fund, 1944-74; member of board of trustees of Wellesley College, 1947-65, and Colonial Williamsburg, Inc., 1958-69; honorary trustee of University of Rochester. *Military service:* French Army, Field Service, 1917. U.S.

Army, ambulance driver, 1917-19; received volunteer's medal and Croix de Guerre.

MEMBER: Phi Beta Kappa, Zeta Psi, Tavern Club, Anglers Club, Century Club. *Awards, honors:* Twenty-one honorary degrees, including Litt.D. from Northeastern University, 1938; Henry Johnson Fisher Award, 1968, for distinguished service to Magazine Publishers' Association; Irita Van Doren Award from American Booksellers Association, 1970.

WRITINGS: This Trade of Writing, Little, Brown, 1935; (editor) *Great Short Novels,* Doubleday, 1941; *The Schooling of an Editor,* New York Public Library, 1950; (with Esther A. Richards) *Letters Analyzed and Spaced,* Exposition Press, 1952; *The Open Heart,* Little, Brown, 1955; (editor with Emily Flint) *Jubilee: One Hundred Years of the "Atlantic",* Little, Brown, 1957 (published in England as *New England Oracle,* Collins, 1958); *Mazo de la Roche,* Little, Brown, 1958; *In Friendly Candor,* Little, Brown, 1959 (published in England as *In Friendly Candour,* Hutchinson, 1960).

Breaking Into Print: An Editor's Advice on Writing, Writer, Inc., 1962; (author of text) Fritz Busse, *Boston, Cradle of Liberty* (sketches), Arts, Inc., 1965; *The Lowells and Their Institute,* Little, Brown, 1966; *Fresh Waters,* Little, Brown, 1968; *The Moisie Salmon Club: A Chronicle,* Barre Publishers, 1971; *My Green Age* (memoirs), Little, Brown, 1973; *Myopia, 1875-1975,* Stinehour Press, 1975; (with Leverett Saltonstall) *Salty: Recollections of a Yankee in Politics,* Boston Globe, 1976. Editor of *The Pocket Atlantic,* 1946. Contributor of articles and reviews to magazines.

WORK IN PROGRESS: Memoirs.

*   *   *

WEGLYN, Michi(ko Nishiura) 1926-

PERSONAL: Born November 29, 1926, in Stockton, Calif.; daughter of Tomojiro (a farmer) and Misao (Yuasa) Nishiura; married Walter M. Weglyn (a perfume chemist), March 5, 1950. *Education:* Attended Mount Holyoke College, 1944-45, and Barnard College, 1947-48. *Residence:* New York, N.Y. *Agent:* Paul R. Reynolds, Inc., 12 East 41st St., New York, N.Y. 10017.

CAREER: As "Michi," designer of theatrical costumes for ice shows, night clubs, Broadway, and television, including the Roxy Theatre, 1952-53, "Skating Vanities of 1953," Kraft Television Theater, 1954, "The Tony Bennett Show," 1956, and "The Perry Como Show," 1957-66; founder and head of costume manufacturing and design studio, Michi Associates, Ltd., 1964-67; writer, 1967—. *Member:* Authors Guild, Academy of Television Arts and Sciences, Japanese American Citizens League, Association of American Indian Affairs, National Association for the Advancement of Colored People (NAACP). *Awards, honors:* Hattie M. Strong Foundation grant, 1945; Japanese American of the Biennium award from Japanese American Citizens League, 1974-76; Anisfield-Wolf Award in Race Relations, 1976, for *Years of Infamy.*

WRITINGS: Years of Infamy: The Untold Story of America's Concentration Camps, introduction by James A. Michener, Morrow, 1976; (editor with Betty E. Mitson) *Valiant Odyssey,* Brunks, 1978.

WORK IN PROGRESS: Voices From the Internment Years

SIDELIGHTS: In 1941, when war with Japan seemed inevitable, President Franklin Roosevelt commissioned State Department investigator Curtis B. Munson to determine the loyalty of West Coast Japanese Americans. Munson returned in November of that year to confirm the conclusions of various intelligence sources, certifying "a remarkable, even extraordinary degree of loyalty among this generally suspect ethnic group." He concluded: "There is no Japanese-American problem on the West Coast." Nonetheless, within three months after war's outbreak, the U.S. Army (under Executive Order 9066) ordered 112,000 civilians—more than 70,000 of them native-born American citizens—removed from their homes and herded into barbed wire rung "relocation centers." Among them was Michi Weglyn, who, thirty-five years later, would release her account of a long-neglected era of American history in her book, *Years of Infamy*.

Weglyn's work is more than an eyewitness account of the internment experience. Spurred by Attorney General Ramsey Clark's statement during the heat of the civil rights turbulence of the 1960's that "we have never had, do not now have and will not ever have concentration camps here," Weglyn says she "felt compelled to codify *the truth* by exposing documents which would speak for themselves." In 1975, after eight years of research, she had finished. Relying extensively on hitherto secret files from the FDR Library, the National Archives, and other repositories, she sought the source of this "rash, deliberate violation of the constitution." As James M. Martin notes, "Weglyn does not flinch from direct attribution of the whole Japanese internment program to where it has always belonged: squarely on the doorstep of President Roosevelt. For once the standard liberal evasion of blaming it all on 'public opinion' in California, the Army colonel who wrote the executive order authorizing it, and the entire category of diversionary figures which might divert attention from the White House, is bypassed."

Though the government backed its action with a "protective custody rationalization," Weglyn offers a radically different reason. The government argument was that Japanese Americans needed protection from the ever-mounting public hysteria following the Pearl Harbor attack. Weglyn, in contrast, contends the United States actually formed hostage colonies which could have been used, if needed, as leverage to ensure better treatment of American civilian and military prisoners held by the Japanese, even as possible trade bait for their return. This "reprisal reserve" theory, reports Robert Perkins, "was based on the 'racist' notion that an American of Japanese ancestry would be more loyal to Japan than to America." In fact, the plan affected more than just the Japanese minority in the United States. "The State Department," declares Weglyn, "persuaded various Central and South American governments to kidnap Japanese immigrants, and even progenies who were citizens of these nations, to bring them for internment in alien detention camps in the United States."

Aside from her analysis of the politics behind the program, Weglyn outlines details of camp life itself. Small families, like her own, were forced to share the same one-room barrack "apartment," a small dimly lit room with no running water. Amid these abrasive circumstances, those seventeen or over were compelled to take loyalty oaths "telling you to choose between Japan and the United States," recollects Weglyn. "It was presented, absurdly, to our parents who, as Asians, were denied American citizenship. It was also forced on children who were born in the United States." Most internees, however, accepted their treatment with remarkable restraint. Weglyn explains why: "Though Americans, we were torn asunder by the trauma of being helplessly stereotyped as 'Japs'—a contemptuous racial slur directed against us as well as the enemy. We felt ashamed for what we then believed was a wholly dastardly attack on Pearl Harbor. In our utter naivete (the vast majority of us were school-age children not yet of voting age) we felt that we were atoning for that by being in the camps. There had been wild rumors of Japanese American treachery—later proved to be lies. We felt responsible." Only recently, she claims, have ex-internees begun to talk openly of their camp experiences, of its effect on individuals and lives "so cataclysmically disarranged."

Among Weglyn's goals in writing her book was the need "to expiate our honor, our self-esteem," and to help undo the psychic damage which she describes as "castration": a deep consciousness of personal inferiority, a proclivity to non-communication and a shying away from exposure which might subject us to further hurt." As she told *CA:* "Japanese Americans have long been reluctant to talk about that time of America's betrayal. So much shame had been heaped upon them, so much public revulsion by cruel stereotyping, so much guilt. In *Years of Infamy* I wanted to transfer that guilt, that shame, where it rightfully belongs: on FDR who, by a mere sweep of the pen—by executive fiat—established those camps of infamy. And I wanted to force fellow Americans to face up to realities, of the utter fragility of rights in a democratic society. Especially when fear-promoting racist hysteria against a minority is politically expedient and becomes a calculated campaign embarked upon and manipulated by the government."

Judging by the response of her fellow ethnics to *Years of Infamy*, Weglyn has succeeded. Since its publication, Japanese Americans have been vigorously protesting their wartime treatment; and during recent observances of "Executive Order 9066 Day" (February 19, 1979), the nation's media reported a ground swell of special commemoration activities and calls throughout the nation that redress legislation be enacted by Congress—a move spearheaded by the Japanese American Citizens League.

Weglyn has also succeeded in arousing the American conscience to this previously obscure event by way of the extensive critical response to *Years of Infamy*. United States Ambassador to Japan Mike Mansfield calls Weglyn's contribution "a conscience-wrenching book of major significance.... Every American concerned with human liberty should know of this bleak period of our national history." Civil libertarian Edison Uno believes "no other book on the subject contributes so many new facts: the shameful conspiracies, the official deceptions and cover-ups.... It is a masterful contribution to the rewriting of that part of our history too long distorted and misrepresented." And former U.S. Ambassador to Japan Edwin O. Reischauer concludes: "It is a terrible story that Michi Weglyn lays out with clarity and precision.... This is a story Americans need to know more about and to keep fresh in their minds. It happened only a generation ago, and the attitudes that lay behind it still have considerable currency in our land."

Undoubtedly, Weglyn is much aware of their currency, as her own experience as an oppressed minority and her work among others have heightened her awareness of all oppressed peoples. "In my early teens I worked as a farm hand and crop picker alongside the 'Oakies,' 'Arkies,' Filipino, and Chicano migrant workers," she says. "Perhaps this shared experience with the deprived and downtrodden explains, in part, my empathy for the disinherited. The wartime internment experience also has helped to enlarge my understanding of those among us assigned to a lesser status, who continue to be scapegoated and shortchanged. It distresses me deeply that racism rages on wildly as ever and continues to treat our minority peoples—Blacks, Chicanos, Native Americans, Asians—as aliens in their own land. My concern for Native Americans on whose sun-scorched reservation land we languished together in dreary exile runs especially deep. To think they are trapped in that howling, dust-whipped hellhole still!''

Years of Infamy has been published in Japanese.

BIOGRAPHICAL/CRITICAL SOURCES: New York Daily News, December 11, 1957, July 22, 1976; *New York Post,* January 9, 1958; *New York Times,* December 16, 1961, May 10, 1976; *St. Louis Post-Dispatch,* February 5, 1965; *Detroit News,* March 25, 1965; *Pacific Citizen,* December 19-26, 1975; *New Canadian,* February 20, 1976, April 20, 1976; *Los Angeles Times,* May 2, 1976, May 27, 1976; *Saturday Review,* May 15, 1976; *Chicago Tribune,* May 16, 1976; *Bookletter,* June 7, 1976; *Sacramento Bee,* June 27, 1976; *Best Sellers,* July, 1976; *New York Nichibei,* July 1, 1976; *Minneapolis Tribune,* July 11, 1976; *People,* December 6, 1976; *Gnomes and Knots,* Harper, 1977; *Springfield Union,* March 11, 1977; *American Historical Review,* June, 1977; *Journal of American History,* June, 1977; *Libertarian Review,* November, 1978.

*   *   *

WEINSTEIN, Martin E. 1934-

PERSONAL: Born July 23, 1934, in Brooklyn, N.Y.; married Erika Marianne, May, 1958; children: Ingrid, Felix, Sonjia. *Education:* University of Southern California, B.A. (magna cum laude), 1958; Yale University, certificate, 1960; Columbia University, M.A., 1965, Ph.D., 1969. *Home:* 307 West Vermont, Urbana, Ill. 61801. *Office:* Department of Political Science, University of Illinois, Urbana, Ill. 61801.

CAREER: Columbia University, New York, N.Y., assistant director of East Asian Institute, executive editor, and research associate, 1969-70; University of Illinois, Urbana, 1970—, currently associate professor of political science. Research associate at Brookings Institution, 1973-74; special assistant to American embassy in Tokyo, 1975-77. *Military service:* U.S. Army, Infantry, 1954-56. U.S. Air force, Counterintelligence, 1958-63. *Member:* Council on Foreign Relations, Phi Beta Kappa, Phi Kappa Phi.

WRITINGS: Japan: The Risen Sun (monograph), Foreign Policy Association, 1970; *Japan's Postwar Defense Policy, 1947-1968,* Columbia University Press, 1971; (contributor) James W. Mordley, editor, *Forecast for Japan: Security in the 1970's,* Princeton University Press, 1972; (contributor) Frank B. Horton and others, editors, *Comparative Defense Policy,* Johns Hopkins Press, 1974; *The U.S.-Japan Alliance: Is There an Equivalent for Mutual Indispensability?* (monograph), California Arms Control Seminar, 1975; (contributor) Bernard K. Gordon and Kenneth J. Rothwell, editors, *The New Political Economy of the Pacific,* Ballinger, 1975. Contributor to scholarly journals and newspapers.

WORK IN PROGRESS: "Trends in Japanese Foreign and Defense Policy," to be included in *New Directions in Japan and in Japanese-American Relations.*

AVOCATIONAL INTERESTS: Travel (Europe, Asia).

*   *   *

WELCH, James 1940-

PERSONAL: Born in 1940, in Browning, Mont. *Education:* University of Montana, earned B.A.; attended Northern Montana College. *Home:* 231 Wylie St., Missoula, Mont. 59801.

CAREER: Poet and novelist. *Awards, honors:* National Endowment for the Arts grant, 1969.

WRITINGS: Riding the Earthboy 40: Poems, World Publishing, 1971; *Winter in the Blood* (novel), Harper, 1974. Contributor of poetry to periodicals.

SIDELIGHTS: A *Saturday Review* critic made this prediction in a review of Welch's first book of poetry, *Riding the Earthboy 40:* "His poems are alert, sorrowful, and true. For a young man he is very strong. . . . If Welch stays put in his own life, I think his strengths should develop: his voice is clear, laconic, and it projects a depth in experience of landscape, people, and history that conveys a rich complexity. You realize he is not looking at a thing, but seeing into it—which is vision.''

Welch's promise was realized in his first novel, *Winter in the Blood,* the story of a young Indian living on a reservation in Montana. The unnamed narrator is, like Welch, part Blackfeet and part Gros Ventre Indian. He describes himself as a "servant to a memory of death.'' Both his father and brother are dead: in the course of the novel, his beloved grandmother dies as well. Reynolds Price described the narrator's life as a "black sack tied firmly shut.'' But just as the story "threatens to die in its crowded sack,'' Price wrote, "it opens onto light—and through natural, carefully prepared, but beautifully surprising narrative means: a recovery of the past; a venerable, maybe lovable, maybe usable past. . . . Enough to say that it involves the narrator's late discovery of long-suppressed facts about his own heritage—the names and history of his grandparents—and that Welch's new version of the central scene in all narrative literature (the finding of lost kin) can stand proudly with its most moving predecessors in epic, drama and fiction.''

It is the tone of the novel that Charles R. Larson found to be most noteworthy. Likening the novel to John Steinbeck's early works and Ernest Hemingway's short stories, Larson wrote, "An elegiac quietness bridges the scenes between the present and the past, juxtaposing the events in the narrator's present life with those of his youth. . . . These scenes recapturing the past are beautifully controlled by the skillful use of nuance, by balancing flashbacks against the events in the present.''

A *New Yorker* reviewer felt the novel was flawed by a main character who is simply too "callow and unappealing,'' but his fault finding was uncharacteristic of reviewers. Paul Gray remarked that Welch "neatly juggles despair and hope; the book's surfaces convey both a sad seediness and a tumbledown vitality. . . . With remarkable force, *Winter in the Blood* brings its experiences home to others. Its prose is as dry and tough as pemmican. It turns a long historic outrage into a short, relentlessly unsentimental elegy.''

"*Winter in the Blood* is a beautiful book,'' Larson wrote, "put together with loving care, an unforgettable story of life on the reservation, close to the land. From common events and situations Welch has chiseled a work of perfect unity and finish. For some readers this will be the most significant piece of Indian writing they have yet encountered; for others, it will be simply a brilliant novel—independent of any racial context.''

Price concluded his review with this encomium: "Few books in any year speak so unanswerably, make their own local terms so thoroughly ours. 'Winter in the Blood'—in its young crusty dignity, its grand bare lines, its comedy and mystery, its clean pathfinding to the center of hearts—deserves more notice than good novels get. Mere true stories.''

BIOGRAPHICAL/CRITICAL SOURCES: *Saturday Review*, October 2, 1971, December 14, 1974; *Village Voice*, October 24, 1974: *New York Times*, October 30, 1974; *New York Times Book Review*, November 10, 1974; *Newsweek*, November 11, 1974; *Time*, December 9, 1974; *New York Review of Books*, December 12, 1974; *New Republic*, December 14, 1974; *New Yorker*, December 23, 1974; *Hudson Review*, summer, 1975; *Contemporary Literary Criticism*, Volume 6, Gale, 1976.*

* * *

WELCH, Richard Edwin, Jr. 1924-

PERSONAL: Born June 16, 1924, in Newburyport, Mass.; son of Richard Edwin (a manufacturer of women's shoes) and Helen (Hale) Welch; married Christina S. Marquand (a writer of children's books), September 4, 1948; children: Catherine Helen, Richard Edwin III, Christina S., Elizabeth M., Margaret Curzon. *Education:* Dartmouth College, A.B., 1948; Harvard University, M.A., 1949, Ph.D., 1952. *Politics:* Democrat. *Religion:* Episcopalian. *Home:* 848 Paxinosa Ave., Easton, Pa. 18042. *Office:* Department of History, Lafayette College, Easton, Pa. 18042.

CAREER: Colgate University, Hamilton, N.Y., instructor in history, 1952-53; Virginia Military Institute, Lexington, assistant professor of history, 1953-58; Lafayette College, Easton, Pa., assistant professor, 1958-62, associate professor, 1962-70, professor, 1970—, Charles A. Dana Professor of History, 1978—, head of department, 1977—. *Military service:* U.S. Army, 1942-46. *Member:* American Historical Association, Organization of American Historians, Society of Historians of American Foreign Relations, Phi Beta Kappa, Phi Alpha Theta. *Awards, honors:* American Philosophical Society grant, 1971-72.

WRITINGS: Theodore Sedgwick, Federalist: A Political Portrait, Wesleyan University Press, 1965; (contributor) Daniel M. Smith, editor, *Major Problems in American Diplomatic History*, Heath, 1966; *George Frisbie Hoar and the Half-Breed Republicans*, Harvard University Press, 1971; *Imperialists Versus Anti-Imperialists: The Debate Over Expansion in the 1890's*, F. E. Peacock, 1972; (contributor) T. G. Paterson, editor, *American Imperialism and Anti-Imperialism*, Crowell, 1973; *Response to Imperialism: The United States and the Philippine-American War*, University of North Carolina Press, 1979. Contributor to *Dictionary of American History* and *Encyclopedia of American Foreign Policy*. Contributor of articles and reviews to history journals and newspapers.

WORK IN PROGRESS: A book on the U.S. response to four twentieth-century social revolutions (Mexican, Russian, Chinese, Cuban).

* * *

WELCH, Timothy L. 1935-
(Patrick Cake)

PERSONAL: Born December 25, 1935, in Yuba City, Calif.; married; wife's name, Jacque; children: Timothy, Nicole, Dominie, Susan. *Education:* Stanford University, B.A., 1958, M.A., 1961; University of California, Berkeley, Ph.D., 1973. *Home:* 250 Thunderbird Dr., Aptos, Calif. 95003. *Agent:* Arnold P. Goodman, 500 West End Ave., New York, N.Y. 10024. *Office:* Cabrillo College, 6500 Soquel Dr., Aptos, Calif. 95003.

CAREER: Information officer, U.S. Army, 1958-59; *Los Gatos Times-Observer*, Los Gatos, Calif., reporter, 1961-62;

Fresno City College, Fresno, Calif., journalism instructor, 1963-67; Cabrillo College, Aptos, Calif., administrative dean of community services, 1967—. Member of Santa Cruz County Arts Commission, 1971-73, and Santa Cruz County Planning Commission, 1973-75. Also director of Cabrillo Suspense Writers Conference. *Member:* California Community Colleges Community Services Association (president, 1971-73), California Community and Junior College Association (chairman, 1971-75), Rio Del Mar Tennis Club, Commonwealth Club.

WRITINGS: The Tennis Murders, Popular Library, 1976; (under pseudonym Patrick Cake) *The Pro Am Murders*, Proteus Press, 1979. Contributor to *Community Services Catalyst* and *New Directions for Community Colleges*. Editor of *Community Services Catalyst*, 1971-74.

WORK IN PROGRESS: Colombian Blue, a suspense adventure set in South America.

SIDELIGHTS: Welch told *CA:* "I suppose I am most pleased, in my two-book career, to have introduced photographs into suspense fiction with *The Pro Am Murders*. It seems clear that the novel needs to take on the visual character of our times, and I hope to be able to work out effectively the relationship between text and photo images; this is the key to the successful integration of the two. The attempt in this 'photo-fiction' is to find a useful new literary form, and should be distinguished from the 'foto-novels' out, which are comic books made from popular films, and the 'novelizations' of screenplays to capitalize on movie releases. In my present work, I am using archival material and good advice from a man who photographed South America extensively for *National Geographic* in the late 1930's when *Colombian Blue* is set.

"The first attempt, in *The Pro Am Murders*, was not successful in the eyes of the critics; they liked the photos, but found them irrelevant. Perhaps. Certainly the internal logic of 'why this photo and not another?' needs more thought. But the photographs have a resonance of the time and place for the writer of the text, and this has its own usefulness. The first question in photo-fiction is this: Who is taking the pictures? Is it a character in the story? If so, why is this person doing so, and how did they get in the hands of the author? (Does this imply that all photo-fiction must be first person?) The second question in this: Are the pictures of characters in the story, or of dramatic moments, or of handsome scenery, or what? Does one hire models and shoot layouts, or look for candid 'moments?'" Concerning his readers and the writer's vocation, Welch writes: "I suppose I hope to have readers laugh, on occasion, and get goose pimples, on others, and once in a great while to say, 'Yes, that's the way it is.' To persuade them, maybe, that all our fantasies are funny, but necessary. Advice to aspiring writers from a two-book gunslinger comes close to felonious offense; but let's say that I thought Brian Garfield was correct when he said to find the master(s) who moved you most, and read them and re-read them until the bones of the skeleton begin to emerge. Every writer has been influenced by other writers. This is given. The question is to untangle the whole pile of noodles and find the right ones in the right proportions—and not to leave anyone out! And, of course, write."

* * *

WELLEN, Edward (Paul) 1919-
(Paul Felder, Lew Gellert, Larry Killian)

PERSONAL: Born October 2, 1919, in New Rochelle, N.Y.; son of Hyman Levy (a tailor) and Lillian (an office worker; maiden name, Wilensky). *Education:* Attended Shrivenham American University (England), 1945, and City College of New York (now of the City University of New York), 1951-55. *Home:* 167 Centre Ave., New Rochelle, N.Y. 10805. *Agent:* Scott Meredith, 845 Third Ave., New York, N.Y. 10022.

CAREER: Writer. Worked as mail-order stamp dealer in New Rochelle, N.Y., 1946-52, and advertising consultant in New Rochelle, 1950-52. *Military service:* U.S. Army, 1942-45; served in Chemical Warfare Service; received European-African-Middle Eastern Service Medal with seven battle stars. *Member:* Mystery Writers of America, Science Fiction Writers of America. *Awards, honors:* First prize from Birmingham Festival of the Arts, 1964, for television script "The Hubert Otis."

WRITINGS: Hijack, Beagle Books, 1971. Also author of television episode "Bourbon Street Beat," American Broadcasting Co., 1959, and unproduced teleplay "Swamp Fire (Fea Follet)." Contributor of short stories under pseudonyms Paul Felder, Lew Gellert, and Larry Killian to periodicals, including *Mike Shayne Mystery Magazine* and *The Executioner Mystery Magazine.*

WORK IN PROGRESS: The L'chayim War, "Israel must blitz the U.S.S.R. to avert Holocaust II"; *The Understander,* "protagonist switches between alternate worlds."

SIDELIGHTS: Wellen told *CA:* "I hope I maintain an ironically empathetic attitude toward the world and my characters. Call it 'Seeing the Lion's Point of View,' after Huck Finn's remark upon having soared out of the lion's reach."

Wellen explained his introduction to writing: "One of my grade school teachers would hand me tear sheets of her favorite magazine stories as a reward (and maybe as a quietener) when I finished classwork early. Of these stories I remember only Richard Connell's 'The Most Dangerous Game,' which has since become a classic of the suspense genre, but this would have been more than enough to turn me on."

Wellen also reported that "[James] Joyce has influenced me—too much. And now *Writer's Digest* School uses my stories as examples in its correspondence course. It's better for the ego to be an influence than to be influenced." Wellen told *CA* that he didn't believe that writing has diminished in importance as an art form. "Trouble is," he declared, "it's more and more addressed to 'Occupant,' which is to say that this is a rapidly changing, increasingly complex world looking for easy answers and living on fast foods."

*   *   *

WELLER, Michael 1942-

PERSONAL: Born September 26, 1942, in New York, N.Y.; son of Paul (a photographer) and Rosa (an artist; maiden name, Rush) Weller. *Education:* Attended Manchester University, 1964; received degree from Brandeis University, 1965. *Residence:* New York, N.Y. *Agent:* Howard Rosenstone, 850 Seventh Ave., New York, N.Y. 10019; and Michael Imison, Jan Van Loewen Ltd., 18-83 Shaftesburn Ave., London WIV 8BX, England.

CAREER: Playwright. *Awards, honors:* Drama Desk Award, 1971, for most promising playwright; Rockefeller fellowship, 1973; Creative Artists Public Service grant, 1976.

WRITINGS—Plays: (Adapter and composer) "Fred" (two-act; from the novel *Malcolm* by James Purdy), first produced in Waltham, Mass., at Brandeis University, 1965;

"Cello Days at Dixais Place," first produced in Cambridge, Mass., at Loeb Theatre Experimental Annex, 1965; (and composer) "How Ho-Ho Rose and Fell in Seven Short Scenes," first produced in Manchester, England, at University of Manchester, 1966; (adapter and composer) "The Making of Theodore Thomas, Citizen" (three-act; from the play "Johnny Johnson" by Paul Green), first produced in London at Stepney Institute, 1968; "Happy Valley" (two-act), first produced in Edinburgh at Fringe Theatre, 1969; "The Bodybuilders" and "Now There's Just the Three of Us" (two one-acts; first produced in London at Open Space Theatre, 1969), published in *The Bodybuilders, and Tira Tells Everything There Is to Know About Herself,* Dramatists Play Service, 1972, and in *Off-Broadway Plays 2,* Penguin, 1972 (also see below); "Poison Come Poison" (sketch), first produced in London, 1970.

Cancer (two-act; first produced in London at Royal Court Theatre, September 15, 1970), Faber, 1971, produced and published as *Moonchildren* (first produced in Washington, D.C., at Arena Stage, September, 1971; produced on Broadway at Royale Theatre, February 21, 1972), Delacorte, 1972; "Grant's Movie" (one-act; first produced in London at Open Space Theatre, 1971), published in *Grant's Movie, and Tira: One-Act Plays,* Faber, 1972 (also see below); "Tira Tells Everything There Is to Know About Herself" (one-act; first produced in London at Open Space Theatre, 1971), published in *The Bodybuilders, and Tira Tells Everything There Is to Know About Herself,* Dramatists Play Service, 1972, produced and published as "Tira" (first produced in New York City at W. P. A., 1975), published in *Grant's Movie, and Tira; One-Act Plays,* Faber, 1972 (also see below); *The Bodybuilders and Tira Tells Everything There Is to Know About Herself,* Dramatists Play Service, 1972 (also see above); *Grant's Movie, and Tira: One-Act Plays,* Faber, 1972 (also see above); (author of lyrics with Jim Steinman) "More Than You Deserve" (two-act musical), first produced in New York City at Public Theatre, 1973; "Twenty-Three Years Later," first produced in Los Angeles at Mark Taper Forum, 1973; *Fishing* (two-act; first produced in New York City at Public Theatre, 1975), French, 1975; "Alice" (sketch), first produced in London as part of "After Calcutta," 1976; "Split" (one-act), first produced in New York City at Ensemble Studio Theatre, 1978; "Loose Ends" (two-act), first produced in Washington, D.C., at Arena Stage, 1979, produced in New York City at Circle in the Square Theatre, 1979. Also author of the unpublished, unproduced play, "The Greatest Little Show on Earth."

Screenplays: (Adapter) "Hair" (from the play by Gerome Ragni and James Rado), United Artists, 1979; (adapter) "Ragtime" (from the novel by E. L. Doctorow), 1980.

WORK IN PROGRESS: "Dwarfman," a two-act play to be produced in New York City, 1980.

SIDELIGHTS: Moonchildren, Weller's most popular play, provides "an epitaph for its time," according to critic Clive Barnes, who compared the play to Chekhov's *Cherry Orchard.* Weller's play is set in the mid-sixties in a college town and is about a group of seniors—five men and two women—who share an apartment. Weller drew on his own college experiences to write the play. He explained: "My college education ended in 1965. During my last year I shared a house with several people. I managed to learn very little about them. Most of the things they did baffled me. What I did no doubt baffled them. We were best of friends. We graduated and drifted apart. I am still baffled. This play is not an explanation. It is not about why. It is perhaps a description of a puzzle.''

'''Moonchildren' is a sort of mood piece,'' a *Variety* reviewer wrote, ''a group character study of sensitive, subtle, articulate and irrepressibly jocular young people, plus several scornful portraits of coarse, obtuse, hypocritical middleaged fringe people. The situations are funny, the dialog is witty in the gutter language of today, and the play holds attention, though its popularity may be limited.'' The same reviewer noticed flaws, including a ''lack of a clear story line'' and the ''absence of a strong central character,'' although Weller has commented that this was deliberate.

The portrait Weller draws of his own generation is far from sentimental. Another *Variety* reviewer praised the playwright because he was ''able to make comic use of the naivete of a group of college students without patronizing them and [was] able to show their seriousness without succumbing to a flood of sentimentality.'' Acclaiming *Moonchildren* as ''one of the better plays written about American youth,'' critic Tom Prideaux remarked: ''But though they read James Joyce and Ho Chi Minh, they still dwell in a nursery Utopia, prattling taboo words, concocting fantasies, spinning ironic yarns about their pregnant cat (there is no cat). The ultimate irony is that for all the free utterance and free fancies, they can't free their own feelings. A death in a boy's family, a seriously bruised love affair are hushed up or tossed off. And when the group disbands, even the last goodbyes go unsaid, leaving us with the sad feeling that most of these bright, valuable kids have somehow misfired and left the world poorer.''

Marilyn Stasio declared that Weller's ''nostalgia is laced with bitterness.'' The play's major drawback, she noted, was its ''pseudo-naturalism.'' She wrote, ''The characters are obviously meant to be realistic, but the intensity of Weller's scorn for their selfishness and their superficiality turns them into little monsters—altogether too monstrous to be true.'' Clive Barnes disagreed. ''Mr. Weller's skill is twofold,'' he claimed. ''He writes dialogue that is both believable and yet surprising, which is no easy trick. He also relates a man to his setting. There are a hundred and one stories in this play, but what is important is that every single character rings totally true.''

John Simon thought that the play was promising and cited Weller's gift for capturing college banter and the admirable casting as its major attributes. On the other hand, he complained that in the play Weller is ''on to some tricks —almost, I regret to say, mannerisms—and milks them mercilessly.'' The playwright, Simon declared, doesn't know ''when to let go of something.'' He ''seems to think it infinitely clever to take something and keep turning it around, like a coin in a nervous man's hand. . . . But the most infelicitous thing about *Moonchildren*,'' Simon declared, ''is that it tries, at times, to go serious.'' Other reviewers mentioned that problem, particularly noting the last scene in which one of the characters makes a long speech about his mother's death from cancer.

Clive Barnes demurred. ''There are two kinds of comedy,'' he wrote. ''The comedy that makes you laugh and then lets you go, and the comedy that makes you laugh and then, for an encore, makes you think. Eventually the latter plays are the better value for your money. 'Moonchildren' is fascinatingly and dazzlingly one of those.''

Weller dislikes being restricted to writing his plays according to the strict definition of a genre. To construct plays in that rigid manner, he told interviewer Chris Chase, ''denies the variety that happens in life where things can be hysterically funny in the middle of something extremely depressing. You're sad, and you go out and spend half the day in a daze, and then it's all invalidated by a phone call or a letter and you're elated and that's all the way it is. And the more spacious you can make a work, the more all-encompassing you can make a work, the more jubilantly you're celebrating the voices that are in your head.''

Despite its mostly positive critical reception and a successful production in Washington, D.C., when *Moonchildren* was moved to Broadway by David Merrick with the original cast it closed after only sixteen performances. It later reopened at Theatre de Lys and ran for a year. Since then it has had over 1,000 productions worldwide.

Characterizations are still Weller's strong suit in *Fishing,* one of his more recent plays. Barnes commented: ''Mr. Weller's ear for dialogue is as convincing as ever, and his good-natured wit (his characters are rarely waspish; irony or violence is the nearest they get to nastiness) is always appealing. Despite a slow, rather poor beginning, and a joking, pseudo-melodramatic ending that doesn't quite come off, the play is neatly constructed. You get to know the people and they are interesting.''

Walter Kerr was less sympathetic to Weller's work. Commenting that the characters in the later play are reminiscent of the characters in *Moonchildren,* he remarked: ''The remnants of that captivating college crew now speak of themselves, baldly, as 'a lost generation in search of roles in a century without meaning,' announce that 'Life is a freak show, right?' (This of course gives the *whole* show away; we used to deduce such things, beneath the cock-crows, to our delight.) When one of the friends is told he's moody, he snaps 'You're not supposed to notice, and if you notice you're not supposed to say anything, and if you say anything it's supposed to be a joke.' In 'Fishing' they *do* notice, and they *do* say, and it's not a joke.''

John Simon thought that Weller covered the same ground in *Moonchildren* as in *Fishing,* and that the former was a better play. Nonetheless, he wrote, ''*Fishing* is a play of texture. It captures accurately, I think, the sound and feel of whimsical, aimless, not yet uncontented lives, some of which will wander into usefulness, some into chronic dissatisfaction and dilettantism, and some perhaps, into suicide. But except for this texture, the play gives us little else. It is as if a tailor showed us an expertly woven and ingeniously patterned piece of cloth, but teasingly refused to comply with our request to cut it into a suit.'' While admitting that *Fishing* shows Weller at less than his best, Catharine Hughes remarked that even so, '' . . . Weller is invariably worth watching.''

''Loose Ends'' is another play that deals with life during the 1960's. Weller documents the changes of Paul and Susan, a pair of idealists who meet in the sixties and marry, only to see their relationship disintegrate along with their ideals. After exhibiting bitter feelings about careers and the possibility of having children, Paul and Susan divorce. They unite towards the play's end but it is only a half-hearted reunion, for both of them are now involved in other relationships. Richard Eder wrote that ''Weller's message seems to be that life for the idealists and flower children of a decade ago has become very flat as they settled into the pragmatic privacies of prosperity.''

Walter Kerr called ''Loose Ends'' ''fascinating'' and ''engrossing.'' He noted, ''Perhaps Mr. Weller's own candor has compelled him to look uncertainty straight in the face again, to take us back to where the 'Moonchildren' were before they managed to invent their own demanding code." Eder contended that "Weller has managed to suggest that even at the start their grace was superficial, owing most of its strength to their youth and beauty." In the end, according to Eder, Paul and Susan "become case-histories."

BIOGRAPHICAL/CRITICAL SOURCES: New Statesman, September 18, 1970; *Listener,* September 24, 1970; *Variety,* September 30, 1970, November 24, 1971, February 23, 1972; *New York Times,* October 22, 1971, February 22, 1972; March 5, 1972, November 5, 1973, February 13, 1975, February 23, 1975, June 7, 1979, June 8, 1979, June 17, 1979; *Washington Post,* December 8, 1971, February 23, 1972; *Playbill,* February, 1972; *Cue,* March 4, 1972; *New York,* March 6, 1972, March 10, 1975; *Life,* April 7, 1972; *Plays and Players,* May, 1975; *Contemporary Literary Criticism,* Volume 10, Gale, 1979.

*   *   *

WELLS, Dee (Alberta) 1925-

PERSONAL: Born March 19, 1925, in Providence, R.I.; daughter of John W. and Hazel (Young) Chapman; married Alfred W. Wells, September, 1949 (divorced, 1955); married Sir Alfred Ayer (a professor), July, 1960; children: (first marriage) Alexandra Wells Foges; (second marriage) Nicholas. *Education:* Attended Sorbonne, University of Paris. *Home:* 10 Regent's Park Ter., London N.W.1, England.

CAREER: Free-lance writer, 1954-60; *Sun,* London, England, author of column, "Dee Wells Says," 1960-70; free-lance writer, 1970—. Television and radio broadcaster. *Member:* Abortion Law Reform Association (vice-president). *Awards, honors:* Named columnist of the year by Granada Television, 1966, for "Dee Wells Says."

WRITINGS: Jane (novel), Viking, 1974. Contributor to magazines and newspapers, including *Punch.*

SIDELIGHTS: Susan Jenks describes Wells's first novel: *Jane* "is the story of a 34-year-old American woman living in London, who has not one, but three lovers that drop by her apartment on different days of any given week. . . . The inevitable complications arise when Jane becomes pregnant and neither she, nor her trio of weekday paramours, knows whose baby it might be." Wells commented that writing this novel was "just giggle, giggle the whole time," and admitted that *Jane* had its share of literary loopholes. Nevertheless, she sought to make the plot believable and culturally plausible without resorting to those "lovely, literary-type sentences" found in most novels.

BIOGRAPHICAL/CRITICAL SOURCES: Philadelphia Bulletin, January 23, 1974; *Authors in the News,* Volume 1, Gale, 1976.

*   *   *

WELLS, Merle William 1918-

PERSONAL: Born December 1, 1918, in Lethbridge, Alberta, Canada; U.S. citizen born abroad; came to United States in 1930; son of Norman Danby (a farmer) and Minnie Muir (a teacher; maiden name, Huckett) Wells. *Education:* Boise Junior College, A.A., 1939; College of Idaho, A.B., 1941; University of California, Berkeley, M.A., 1947, Ph.D., 1950. *Religion:* Presbyterian. *Home:* 1325 Longmont, Boise, Idaho 83706. *Office:* Idaho State Historical Society, 610 North Julia Davis Dr., Boise, Idaho 83706.

CAREER: College of Idaho, Caldwell, instructor in history, 1942-46; Alliance College, Cambridge Springs, Pa., associate professor of history, 1950-58; Idaho State Historical Society, Boise, historian and archivist, 1959—, state historic preservation officer, 1968—. Visiting professor at College of Idaho, 1959; lecturer at Boise State University, 1963—. Member of board of directors of National Conference of State Historic Preservation Officers, 1968—. Member of Idaho State Commission on the Arts and Humanities, 1966-67, and Idaho State Bicentennial Commission, 1971-76. Chairman of Southern Idaho Migrant Ministry; member of general board of Idaho Council of Churches, 1966-75; member of board of directors, History Department, General Assembly of the United Presbyterian Church, 1978—.

MEMBER: American Historical Association, Society of American Archivists, American Association for State and Local History (member of council, 1973-77), American Association of University Professors, Western History Association (member of council, 1973-76), Pacific Northwest Library Association, Idaho Library Association. *Awards, honors:* Society of American Archivists fellow, 1971.

WRITINGS: Rush to Idaho, Idaho Bureau of Mines & Geology, 1961; *Gold Camps and Silver Cities,* Idaho Bureau of Mines & Geology, 1964; *A Short History of Idaho,* Idaho State Historical Society, 1974; *Anti-Mormonism in Idaho, 1872-1892,* Brigham Young University Press, 1978. Contributor to *Encyclopaedia Britannica, American Oxford Encyclopedia, World Book Encyclopedia,* and *Crowell-Collier Encyclopedia.* Also contributor of about forty articles to history journals. Regional editor of *Journal of the West;* member of editorial board of *Pacific Northwest Quarterly.*

WORK IN PROGRESS: Research on the Western Federation of Miners in Idaho and British Columbia, labor history, mining history in Idaho, gold and silver in U.S. history, and Pacific Northwest political history and public administration, church history, Snake Country exploration.

SIDELIGHTS: Wells told *CA:* "My writing has been affected mostly by long and varied experience in college teaching and, in the past decade or two, by extensive experience in public administration. Historical interpretation of the Pacific Northwest has been my primary interest in publication, which now extends over forty years. Professional experience in state archives and in historic preservation has also had a substantial impact upon my research and publication activities.

"My primary interest in historical interpretation comes from teaching logic and philosophy as well as history. This approach has led me to avoid letting traditional preconceptions (and misconceptions) obscure an understanding of interesting events of the past. I am not inclined toward historical revision, but generally approach subjects that have been neglected—or misunderstood through lack of basic research. To a great extent, my attitude towards historical investigation derives from early exposure to comparative history as a fourth generation Canadian, as well as third generation in the United States. Most of my research has been concentrated on complex subjects that have resisted simple analysis and have required close attention over a long period of time. My investigation of Idaho's anti-Mormons took most of forty years and still is subject to revision. So are most of my other specialties."

*   *   *

WELLS, Rosemary

EDUCATION: Studied at the Museum School in Boston, Mass. *Address:* c/o Dial Press, 1 Dag Hammarskjold Plaza, New York, N.Y. 10017.

CAREER: Author, illustrator, and designer. Awards, honors: The American Institute of Graphic Arts selected Impossible Possum by Ellen Conford for their 1971-72 children's book show, and Two Sisters and Some Hornets by Beryl Epstein and Dorrit Davis and Noisy Nora for their 1973-74 children's book show; Noisy Nora was also selected for the children's book showcase in 1974; Brooklyn art books for children citation, 1975 and 1977, for Benjamin and Tulip; Irma Simonton Black Award, 1976, for Morris's Disappearing Bag.

WRITINGS: John and the Rarey (self-illustrated), Funk, 1969; Michael and the Mitten Test (self-illustrated), Bradbury, 1969; The First Child (self-illustrated), Hawthorne, 1970; Martha's Birthday (self-illustrated), Bradbury, 1970; Miranda's Pilgrims (self-illustrated), Bradbury, 1970; The Fog Comes on Little Pig Feet, Dial, 1972; Unfortunately Harriet, Dial, 1972; Benjamin and Tulip (self-illustrated), Dial, 1973; Noisy Nora (self-illustrated), Dial, 1973; None of the Above, Dial, 1974; Abdul (self-illustrated), Dial, 1975; Morris's Disappearing Bag: A Christmas Story (self-illustrated), Dial, 1975; Don't Spill It Again, James, Dial, 1977; Leave Well Enough Alone, Dial, 1977.

Illustrator: William Schwenck Gilbert and Arthur Sullivan, A Song to Sing (from the Yeomen of the Guard), Macmillan, 1968; Gilbert and Sullivan, W. S. Gilbert's the Duke of Plaza Toro (from The Gondoliers), Macmillan, 1969; Paula Fox, Hungry Fred, Bradbury, 1969; Charlotte Pomerantz, Why You Look Like You Whereas I Tend to Look Like Me, Young Scott Books, 1969; Robert William Service, The Shooting of Dan McGrew and The Cremation of Sam McGee, Young Scott Books, 1969; Rudyard Kipling, The Cat That Walked by Himself, Hawthorne, 1970; Winifred Rosen, Marvin's Manhole, Dial, 1970; Ellen Conford, Impossible Possum, Little, Brown, 1971; Marjorie Weinman Sharmat, A Hot Thirsty Day, Macmillan, 1971; Beryl Williams and Dorrit Davis, Two Sisters and Some Hornets, Holiday House, 1972; Virginia A. Tashjian, editor, With a Deep Sea Smile, Little, Brown, 1974.

BIOGRAPHICAL/CRITICAL SOURCES: Bulletin of the Center for Children's Books, June, 1975.*

*   *   *

WENGERT, Norman Irving 1916-

PERSONAL: Born November 7, 1916, in Milwaukee, Wis.; son of Eugene F. and Lydia (Semmann) Wengert; married Janet Mueller, October 9, 1940; children: Eugene Mark, Christine Ann, Timothy John. Education: Attended Concordia College, Milwaukee, Wis., 1930-36; University of Wisconsin, Madison, B.A., 1938, J.D., 1942, Ph.D., 1947; Fletcher School of Law and Diplomacy, M.A., 1939. Home: 1225 Teakwood Dr., Fort Collins, Colo. 80521.

CAREER: Associated with Tennessee Valley Authority, 1941-48; City College (now of the City University of New York), New York, N.Y., faculty member, 1948-51; U.S. Department of the Interior, Washington, D.C., member of Secretary's program staff, 1951-52; North Dakota State University, Fargo, professor of social science and head of department, 1952-56; Resources for the Future, Inc., Washington, D.C., research associate, 1956; University of Maryland, College Park, professor of public administration, 1956-59; National Outdoor Recreation Resources Review Committee, Washington, D.C., deputy director, 1959-60; Wayne State University, Detroit, Mich., professor of political science and head of department, 1960-68; Pennsylvania State University, University Park, visiting professor of public

administration, 1968-69; U.S. Army Corps of Engineers, Institute for Water Resources, Fort Belvoir, Va., research associate, 1969-70; Colorado State University, Fort Collins, professor of political science, 1970—. Member of Wisconsin Bar. Special adviser to Government of India, 1959. Visiting research professor at U.S. Army Corps of Engineers Institute of Water Resources, 1969-70. Member of policy analysis staff of U.S. Department of Agriculture Forest Service, 1978-79. Summer fellow at Fonds fuer Umweltstudien, 1973. Consultant to Thorne Ecological Institute and National Water Quality Commission. Military service: U.S. Naval Reserve, active duty, 1944-45.

MEMBER: American Political Science Association, American Society for Public Administration, American Water Resources Association, Midwest Political Science Association, Western Political Science Association, Sigma Xi, Coif.

WRITINGS: Valley of Tomorrow: TVA and Agriculture, Bureau of Public Administration, University of Tennessee, 1952; Natural Resources and the Political Struggle, Doubleday, 1955; (with others) India's Food Crisis and Steps to Meet It, Indian Ministries of Food & Agriculture and Community Development, 1959; The Administration of Natural Resources: The American Experience, Indian Institute of Public Administration, 1961; (with George M. Walker, Jr.) Urban Water Policies and Decision-Making in the Detroit Metropolitan Region, Office of Research Administration, University of Michigan, 1970; Urban-Metropolitan Institutions for Water-Planning, Development, and Management: An Analysis of Usages of the Term "Institutions", Environmental Resources Center, Colorado State University, 1972; (editor and contributor) Institutions for Urban-Metropolitan Water Management: Essays in Social Theory, Environmental Resources Center, Colorado State University, 1972; (with Fred Nogge) Searching the Social Science Literature on Water: A Guide to Selected Information Storage and Retrieval Systems, Environmental Resources Center, Colorado State University, 1972; Oil Shale Country Fact Book: Garfield, Mesa, Moffat and Rio Blanco Counties, Colony Development Operation, 1973; Property Rights in Land: A Comparative Exploration of German and American Concepts and Problems, Department of Political Science, Colorado State University, 1974; (with others) Fort Collins Utility Services and Growth Management, Environmental Resources Center, Colorado State University, 1975; The Political Allocation of Benefits and Burdens: Economic Externalities and Due Process in Environmental Protection, Institute of Governmental Studies, University of California, Berkeley, 1976.

Contributor: Phillip O. Foss, editor, Education in Natural Resources, Colorado State University, 1965; Adapting Institutions to the Conditions of Economic Growth, Montana State University, 1966; Environmental Studies: Political Dynamics of Environmental Control, Institute of Public Administration, Indiana University, 1967; John R. Moore, editor, The Economic Impact of TVA, University of Tennessee Press, 1967; Maynard M. Hufschmidt, editor, Regional Planning: Challenge and Prospects, Praeger, 1969; Leslie L. Roos, Jr., editor, The Politics of Eco-Suicide, Holt, 1971; National Land Use Policy: Objectives, Components, Implementation, Soil Conservation Society of America, 1972; Leonard B. Dworsky, David J. Allee, and Sandor C. Csallany, editors, Social and Economic Aspects of Water Resources Development, American Water Resources Association, 1972; Phillip O. Foss, editor, Politics and Ecology, Duxbury, 1972; Dennis L. Thompson, editor, Politics, Policy, and Natural Resources, Free Press, 1972; Joseph S.

DeSalvo, editor, *Perspectives on Regional Transportation Planning,* Heath, 1973; David W. Hendricks and other editors, *Environmental Design for Public Projects,* Water Resources Publications, 1975; John A. Quinn, editor, *Land Resources: A Rationale for Policy, Planning, and Procedures,* Department of Urban and Regional Planning, University of Illinois, 1975; Thomas E. Dickinson, editor, *Agriculture in the Future and Its Implications for Land Use Planning,* Division of Environmental Studies, University of California, Davis, 1975; Albert E. Utton, W. R. Derrick Sewell, and Timothy O'Riordan, editors, *Natural Resources for a Democratic Society: Public Participation in Decision-Making,* Westview Press, 1976; John C. Pierce and Harvey R. Doerksen, editors, *Water Politics and Public Involvement,* Ann Arbor Science Publishers, 1976.

Also editor of *The Energy Crisis: Reality or Myth,* 1973. Also author of *Land Use Planning and Control in the German Federal Republic,* 1975.

Contributor of about thirty-five articles to professional journals. Editor of *Annals of the American Academy of Political and Social Science,* January, 1960, co-editor, November, 1973; associate editor of *Bulletin* of American Water Resources Association.

WORK IN PROGRESS: Research on land use policy, selection of power plant sites, constitutional doctrines, forest policy history, and federal reserved water rights.

SIDELIGHTS: Wengert mentions that his vocational interests include environment and resource policy and policy processes, as well as environmental and land use planning and control law.

*   *   *

WERNER, Herma 1926-
(Eve Cowen, Joma Pinner)

PERSONAL: Born November 12, 1926, in New York, N.Y.; daughter of Alexander (a florist) and Gertrude (Eisenberg) Cohen; married Harry Werner (a sales representative), January 31, 1952. *Education:* Cooper Union, B.F.A., 1976. *Home:* 4818 43rd St., Woodside, N.Y. 11377. *Agent:* Sanford J. Greenburger Associates, Inc., 825 Third Ave., New York, N.Y.

CAREER: Writer; artist. Paintings exhibited at galleries and libraries in New York, N.Y. and environs; one-person show at Stamford, Connecticut museum. *Member:* Mystery Writers of America.

WRITINGS: (Under pseudonym Joma Pinner; with John Piniat) *The Magic Arm,* Educational Challenges, Inc., 1978; (with Piniat) *Going for the Win,* Scholastic Book Services, 1978; *The Dragster,* Scholastic Book Services, 1979; (under pseudonym Eve Cowen) *Jungle Jenny,* Fearon-Pitman, 1979. Contributor of short stories to *Alfred Hitchcock Mystery Magazine, Readers Digest* (educational division), and other magazines.

WORK IN PROGRESS: Time and the World, a romance book; *Cranberry Witch,* a teen mystery; *Sarah Dippity,* a children's book with illustrations.

SIDELIGHTS: Werner told *CA:* "I write adventure material and mysteries particularly for the reluctant reader market which is used in school remedial reading programs. I consider it work of redeeming social value, and more than enough reason for getting up in the morning. I still paint and have begun to do illustrations for children's books, being circulated among publishers now."

Werner further commented: "All my published material to date has been accomplished without a literary agent, and I am continuing to circulate teen, young adult and children's books on my own, without the benefit of an agent. This, of course, is because it is a market that makes itself directly accessible to the writer without an agent."

*   *   *

WESBERRY, James Pickett 1906-

PERSONAL: Born April 16, 1906, in Bishopville, S.C.; son of William McLeod and Lillian Ione (Galloway) Wesberry; married Ruby Lee Perry, September 5, 1929 (died, December, 1941); married Mary Sue Latimer, June 1, 1943; children: (first marriage) James Pickett, Jr. *Education:* Mercer University, A.B., 1929, M.A., 1930; Newton Theological Institute, B.D., 1931; Andover Newton Theological Institute, M.S.T., 1934; further graduate study at Harvard University, 1931, Union Theological Seminary, New York, N.Y., summers, 1935, 1965, Yale University, 1946, and Southern Baptist Theological Seminary, 1957. *Home:* 1715 Merton Rd. N.E., Atlanta, Ga. 30306. *Office:* Baptist Center, 2930 Flowers Rd. S., Suite 107, Atlanta, Ga. 30341.

CAREER: Ordained Baptist minister, 1926; pastor of Baptist churches in Soperton, Ga., 1928-30, Medford, Mass., 1930-31, Kingstree, S.C., 1931-33, and Bamberg, S.C., 1933-34; Morningside Baptist Church, Atlanta, Ga., pastor, 1944-75, pastor emeritus, 1975—; evangelist, counselor, chaplain, and writer, 1975—. Professor at Mercer University (Atlanta, Ga.), 1944-53. President of Highview Nursing Home, 1947-60 (chaplain, 1975—), and National Youth Courtesy Foundation, 1971—. President of Georgia Baptist Convention, 1956-57; member of executive committee of Southern Baptist Convention, 1959-65; member of board of managers of Lord's Day Alliance of America, 1971—, executive director, 1975—; chaplain of Yaarab Temple. Head of Georgia Literature Commission, 1953-75; member of Georgia governor's Citizens Penal Reform Commission, 1968; member of board of directors of Atlanta Fund Review Board, 1964-70; member of honorary board of directors of Dogwood Association Festival, 1970-71, and Atlanta Union Mission, 1972—. Member of board of trustees of Mercer University, 1944-49, 1954-57, 1972-74 (member of president's council, 1974—), Atlanta Baptist College (now Mercer University at Atlanta), 1964-72, and Truett McConnell College, 1960-65.

MEMBER: Atlanta Area Military Chaplains Association (honorary member), Masons, Shriners, Lions, Atlanta Harvard Club, Atlanta Athletic Club, Atlanta Amateur Movie Club. *Awards, honors:* LL.D. from Atlanta Law School, 1946; D.D. from Mercer University, 1957; L.H.D. from LaGrange College, 1962; Litt.D. from Bolen-Draughan College, 1967; named man of the South by *Dixie Business,* 1972; member of the South's Hall of Fame, 1972.

WRITINGS: Rainbow Over Russia, privately printed, 1963; *Baptists in South Carolina Before the War Between the States,* R. L. Bryan, 1966; *Evangelistic Sermons,* Broadman, 1973; *Meditations for Happy Christians,* Broadman, 1973; *When Hell Trembles, and Other Sermons for Revival,* Baker Book, 1974. Also author of *Prayers in Congress,* 1949, *Every Citizen Has a Right To Know,* 1954, and *The Life and Work of William Screven.* Staff correspondent for *Christian Century,* 1951-58. Editor of "The People's Pulpit," a column in *Atlanta Times,* 1964-65. Editor of *Sunday,* 1975—, and *Basharet.*

WEST, Eugenia Lovett

PERSONAL: Born in Boston, Mass.; daughter of Sidney (a minister and teacher) and Esther (an artist; maiden name, Parker) Lovett; married Eric F. West (a business executive), September 20, 1944; children: Eugenia, George, Eric F., Jr., Victoria. *Education:* Attended Sarah Lawrence College, 1940-42. *Politics:* Independent. *Religion:* United Church of Christ. *Home address:* Sterling City Rd., Lyme, Conn. 06371.

CAREER: Writer, 1967—. Volunteer community worker.

WRITINGS: The Ancestors Cry Out (novel), Doubleday, 1979. Contributor to local newspapers. Editor of *Playhouse Square Gazette,* 1973-74.

WORK IN PROGRESS: A historical novel.

SIDELIGHTS: Eugenia West wrote, for *Library Journal:* "My aim as I wrote *The Ancestors Cry Out* was solely to entertain. So often, after a tiring day, or when starting a trip, I really long for a book with suspense, an interesting background, and appealing characters. But this type of story should, in my opinion, do more than provide a few hours of escape reading. Georgette Heyer, for example, gave us a vivid picture of Regency clothes, manners, wit. I believe that there is a need today, as there always has been, for the well-written book that adds to a reader's general knowledge in a light-hearted way."

BIOGRAPHICAL/CRITICAL SOURCES: Library Journal, February 1, 1979.

* * *

WEST, Uta 1928-
(Renee Auden)

PERSONAL: Given name is pronounced *You*-ta; born January 13, 1928, in Gdansk, Poland; came to the United States in 1941, naturalized citizen, 1945; daughter of Morris (in business) and Nadia (in business; maiden name, Goldberg) Gorki; married Arthur Wesley West, Jr. (an artist and entrepreneur), March 12, 1961; children: Nina Felicia. *Education:* Brooklyn College (now of the City University of New York), B.A. (honors), 1949; graduate study at Columbia University, 1949-50. *Politics:* "Disenchanted; the less government the better." *Religion:* "The lease common denominator of all major faiths." *Home address:* P.O. Box 689, Wellfleet, Mass. 02667. *Agent:* Elaine Markson Literary Agency, Inc., 44 Greenwich Ave., New York, N.Y. 10011.

CAREER: College of the Virgin Islands, St. Thomas, instructor in Romance languages, 1967; Olympia Press, New York City, editor, 1968-69; Bee-Line Press, New York City, editor, 1969; full-time writer, 1969-78; Cape Cod Community College, Barnstable, Mass., instructor in magazine writing, 1978—. Also worked as ballroom dancing teacher and nightclub singer in Mexico. *Awards, honors:* Fellowship for Yaddo Colony, 1958.

WRITINGS: (Editor) *Women in a Changing World,* McGraw, 1975; *If Love Is the Answer, What Is the Question?,* McGraw, 1977. Also author of three paperback novels, under pseudonym Renee Auden, for Bee-Line Press and Olympia Press, 1970-74. Author of "Mirrors," a column in *New Dawn.* Contributor to popular magazines, including *Viva, Penthouse, Pageant, Countdown,* and *Cosmopolitan.*

WORK IN PROGRESS: Bar Life (tentative title), on patterns of social drinking in public places.

SIDELIGHTS: Uta West comments: "My interests have evolved from an appraising look at feminism to an examina-tion of how contemporary relationships have been affected by recent cultural upheavals, to an analysis of other aspects of current life. My purpose in writing about the changing, conflicting values of our society was, first of all, to sort out my own confusions, and then to see if I could get an echo back: 'Hello out there! Is it the same for you, too?' Now that I know I am not alone, I am ready for the next step—the distillation of experience into story form. I hope to return to writing novels, my first and true love.''

AVOCATIONAL INTERESTS: Travel, dancing, gardening, movies, "lively conversation."

* * *

WESTBIE, Constance 1910-

PERSONAL: Born October 5, 1910, in Pierre, S.D.; daughter of Albert George and Adelaide (a musician; maiden name, Sebree) Loveall; married John Merryll Westbie (a physician), April 5, 1941 (deceased); children: John Arthur, Donald Kaelber. *Education:* Attended University of California, Berkeley. *Home:* 5033 Russell Dr., Paradise, Calif. 95969. *Agent:* Reece Halsey Agency, 8733 Sunset Blvd., Los Angeles, Calif. 90069.

CAREER: Legal secretary and private secretary, 1930-41; writer. Piano teacher, 1930—; church organist, 1962—. Lecturer on creative writing. *Member:* National Writers Club, California Federation of Chaparral Poets, California Writers Club, Ina Coolbrith Circle of California, Paradise Guild of Arts and Crafts. *Awards, honors:* Writing awards include grand prize from Ina Coolbrith Circle of California, 1977, for "Olivia," and nonfiction award from National Writers Club, 1977, for *Night Stalks the Mansion.*

WRITINGS: The Birdcage Murders (mystery novel), Bouregy, 1964; (with Harold Cameron) *Night Stalks the Mansion* (nonfiction), Stackpole, 1978. Contributor to confession magazines and poetry magazines.

WORK IN PROGRESS: The Beloved and the Betrayed, a biography of educator Ione Swan; *Sing a Song of Murder* (tentative title); *Moon Madness and Other Poems,* serious poems; *Once Over Lightly,* light verse.

SIDELIGHTS: Constance Westbie writes: "As a legal secretary in Oakland, I started writing confession stories. I can't even remember the names of the periodicals now, but I broke into print via this medium 'way back in the thirties. I never liked this type of thing and discontinued it when it had served my purpose.

"After my husband retired and we moved to Paradise I started writing again. I published my first mystery in 1964. I had a disastrous fire in which all my current manuscripts were destroyed and stopped writing for several years, except for poetry.

"After another several years of community service work and secretarial work in the local school district, I decided to go back to writing as a career."

* * *

WESTIN, Jeane Eddy 1931-

PERSONAL: Born July 3, 1931, in Oklahoma City, Okla.; daughter of Henry Franklin (a pipefitter) and Anna Blanche (a department store buyer; maiden name, Barnes) Eddy; married Gene Theodore Westin (an editor and photographer), April 28, 1962; children: Cara Marlene. *Education:* Attended Fairmont State College, 1958, American River College, 1960-62, 1970-74, and University of California,

Davis, 1979. *Politics:* Democrat. *Agent:* Jane Jordan Browne Multimedia Product Development, Inc., 410 South Michigan Ave., Chicago, Ill. 60605.

CAREER: Humane Society of the United States, Washington, D.C., director of education, 1961-68; Animal Protection Institute, Sacramento, Calif., director of public relations, 1968-70; Schwalbe Associates, San Francisco, copy writer, 1970-73; writer, 1970—. Member of board of directors of Animal Protection Institute, 1978—. *Military service:* Women's Army Corps, 1951-57. *Member:* Authors Guild, Authors League of America, American Society of Journalists and Authors. *Awards, honors:* Literary achievement award from Sacramento Arts Council, 1974.

WRITINGS: Making Do: How Women Survived the Thirties, Follett, 1976; *Finding Your Roots,* J. P. Tarcher, 1977; *The Thin Book,* CompCare, 1978; *Break Out of Your Fat Cell,* CompCare, 1979. Contributor of about two-hundred-fifty articles to magazines and newspapers in the United States and England, including *Woman's Day, True, Modern Maturity, Ms.,* and *Discovery.*

WORK IN PROGRESS: The Coming Parent Revolution (tentative title), publication by Lippincott expected in 1981; a novel set during the Bar Kocheba rebellion in Judea, 135 A.D.

SIDELIGHTS: Jeane Westin writes: "My work reflects the enthusiasms of my own life. At present, I am interested in what is happening to the contemporary family. I see so many angry parents who have lost faith in their native ability to parent and as many angry children looking for parents who are sure of themselves. I cannot imagine any other life; I have a good relationship with my typewriter."

*   *   *

WETMORE, Alexander 1886-1978

PERSONAL: Born June 18, 1886, in North Freedom, Wis.; died December 6, 1978, in High Point, Md., of congestive heart failure; son of Nelson Franklin (a physician) and Emma Amelia (Woodsworth) Wetmore; married Fay Holloway, October 13, 1912 (died, February, 1953); married Beatrice Thienen, December 16, 1953; children: Margaret Fenwick Harlan. *Education:* University of Kansas, A.B., 1912; George Washington University, M.S., 1916, Ph.D., 1920. *Home:* 5901 Osceola Rd., Washington, D.C. 20016. *Office:* c/o Smithsonian Institution, Washington, D.C. 20560.

CAREER: Ornithologist and writer. Department of Agriculture, Washington, D.C., agent, 1910-12, assistant biologist, 1913-23, biologist, 1924; National Zoological Park, Washington, D.C., superintendent, 1924-25; Smithsonian Institution, Washington, D.C., assistant secretary and director of United States National Museum, 1925-44, secretary, 1945-52, research associate, 1953-78. Trustee of Textile Museum, 1928-52, and George Washington University Wildlife Institute; director of Gorgas Memorial Institute of Tropical Medicine; member of advisory committee of International Wild Life Protection; member of International Commission for Bird Preservation (joint Latin-American study); member of Committee for Protection of Cult Treasures in War Areas, 1942-46; vice-chairman of National Advisory Committee on Aeronautics, 1945-52; member of national advisory committee of State Department of Education, Science, and Cultural Cooperation, 1946-52; member of commission of Institute of National Parks in Belgium Congo, 1946-52; member of advisory board of Arctic Research Laboratories, 1948-52; delegate to International Ornithological Congress, 1930, 1934, chairman of United States delegation, 1938, president of

United States delegation, 1950; secretary-general of Eighth American Scientists Congress; United States representative to International-American Commission of Experts on National Protection of Wildlife Preserves, 1940. *Member:* National Academy of Scientists (home secretary, 1951-55), American Ornithologists Union (vice-president, 1923-25, president, 1926-29), American Philosophers Society, and numerous other organizations. *Awards, honors:* Isidore Geoffroy St. Hilaire Medal from Society of National d'Acclimation (France), 1927; Otto Herman Medal from Hungarian Ornithological Association, 1931; Order of Merit from Carlos Manuel de Cespedes (Cuba), 1948; Brewster Medal from American Ornithological Union, 1959; Coues Award, 1972; and other awards.

WRITINGS: Birds of Puerto Rico, U.S. Government Printing Office, 1916; *The Migration of Birds,* Harvard University Press, 1926; *Observations on the Birds of Argentina, Paraguay, Uruguay, and Chile,* U.S. Government Printing Office, 1926; *The Birds of Haiti and the Dominican Republic,* U.S. Government Printing Office, 1931; *A Check-List of the Fossil Birds of North America,* Smithsonian Institution, 1940; *The Birds of San Jose and Pedro Gonzalez Islands, Republic of Panama,* Smithsonian Institution, 1946; *The Birds of Isla Coiba, Panama,* Smithsonian Institution, 1957; (with others) *Songs and Garden Birds of North America,* National Geographic Society, 1964; (with others) *Water, Prey, and Game Birds of North America,* National Geographic Society, 1965; *The Birds of Panama,* Smithsonian Institution, Volume I: *Tinamidae to Rynchopidae,* 1965, Volume II: *Columbidae to Picidae,* 1968, Volume III: *Passeriformes: Dendrocolaptidae to Oxyruncidae,* 1972. Also author of numerous reports, articles, and pamphlets on birds.

WORK IN PROGRESS: Volume IV of *The Birds of Panama.*

SIDELIGHTS: Wetmore devoted most of his life to the study of birds. He helped define 189 newly discovered species and subspecies. At one time, he had accumulated more than four thousand different bird skins and more than two hundred different eggs. He later donated both collections to the Smithsonian Institution.

In honor of Wetmore's ninetieth birthday, S. Dillon Ripley penned, "Truly the incessant and intensive zeal which he has single-mindedly given to the study of birds over the years, often at very considerable personal expenditure in time and energy, will mark the career of Alexander Wetmore as one of the most memorable in the entire history of American ornithology."

OBITUARIES: Washington Post, December 9, 1978.*

*   *   *

WETZEL, Richard D(ean) 1935-

PERSONAL: Born December 27, 1935, in Pitman, Pa.; son of Myles H. (a carpenter) and Violet (Witmer) Wetzel; married Arlene M. Ranshaw (a public school music teacher), December 29, 1956; children: Richard D., Jr., Erika, John, Dara. *Education:* Indiana University, Indiana, Pa., B.Mus.Ed., 1957; University of Pittsburgh, M.Mus., 1968, Ph.D., 1970; studied under Roland Leich, Joseph Esposito, Robert Snow, and Theodore Finney. *Home address:* P.O. Box 206, Chesterhill, Ohio 43728. *Office:* Department of Music, Ohio University, Athens, Ohio 45701.

CAREER: Free-lance musician and teacher, 1956-70; Ohio University, Athens, professor of music history and musicology, 1970—; composer; music has appeared in *Worshipbook* and the hymnal of the United Church of Christ. President of Chesterhill village council, 1975-79. *Member:* American Musicological Society, American Society of Composers, Authors, and Publishers, Sonneck Society. *Awards, honors:* Mellon fellowships from University of Pittsburgh; research grants from Harmonie Associates Foundation; Sinfonia Foundation award, 1972.

WRITINGS: Frontier Musicians: A History of the Music and Musicians of George Rapp's Harmony Society, 1805-1906, Ohio University Press, 1976. Contributor to *Grove's Dictionary of Music and Musicians,* 6th edition. Contributor to numerous professional journals and magazines.

WORK IN PROGRESS: The Life and Works of William Cumming Peters.

SIDELIGHTS: Wetzel writes that his special interests are American music in general and the music of German Americans in particular.

* * *

WHITE, James 1913-

PERSONAL: Born September 16, 1913, in Dublin, Ireland; son of Thomas John (an accountant) and Mary Florence (Coffey) White; married Agnes Bowe, April 30, 1941; children: Mary, Catherine, Peter, Patrick, Mark. *Education:* Attended high school in Dublin, Ireland; studied privately in Europe. *Politics:* None. *Religion:* Roman Catholic. *Home:* 15 Herbert Park, Dublin 4, Ireland. *Office:* National Gallery of Ireland, Merrion Sq., Dublin 2, Ireland.

CAREER: Art critic for *Standard,* 1940-50; *Irish Press,* Dublin, Ireland, art critic, 1950-59; *Irish Times,* Dublin, art critic, 1959-62; Municipal Gallery of Modern Art, Dublin, curator, 1960-64; National Gallery of Ireland, Dublin, director, 1964—. Professor at Royal Hibernian Academy, 1968—; external lecturer at University College, Dublin and Trinity College, Dublin, 1955—. Visiting lecturer at schools and broadcaster on radio and television in England, Italy, the United States, and Canada. Member of Irish Arts Council and Irish Advisory Committee on Art and Architecture. Organized art exhibitions in Dublin and Paris.

MEMBER: International Council of Museums (head of Irish committee), Irish Art Historians (chairman), Friends of National Collections of Ireland (vice-president), Kildare Street Club. *Awards, honors:* French Legion of Merit; Italian Order of Merit; silver medal from Italian Department of Foreign Affairs, 1967; Arnold K. Henry Medal from Irish RCS; LL.D. from National University of Ireland, 1970.

WRITINGS: (With Michael Wynne) *Irish Stained Glass,* Gills, 1963; *The National Gallery of Ireland,* Thames & Hudson, 1968; (with Hilary Pyle) *Jack B. Yeats: Centenary Exhibition,* Thames & Hudson, 1971; *John Butler Yeats and the Irish Renaissance,* Dolmen Press, 1972. Contributor to *Encyclopedia of Art.* Contributor to art journals and popular magazines in Europe and the United States, including *Apollo, Connoisseur,* and *Art Notes,* and newspapers.

WORK IN PROGRESS: Research on the history of Irish painting and on paintings of Vicente Masip.

AVOCATIONAL INTERESTS: Golf, swimming, gardening, bridge.

* * *

WHITE, Patrick C. T. 1924-

PERSONAL: Born August 21, 1924, in Vancouver, British

Columbia, Canada; son of Arthur Edwin (a teacher) and Elise (a musician; maiden name, Telfer) White; married Jane Dennis Seymour, August 6, 1949; children: Christopher, Alison. *Education:* University of British Columbia, B.A., 1946; Cambridge University, M.A., 1950; University of Minnesota, Ph.D., 1954. *Religion:* Anglican. *Home:* 183 Glenview Ave., Toronto, Ontario, Canada M4R 1R4. *Office:* Department of History, University of Toronto, Smith Hall, Toronto, Ontario, Canada.

CAREER: University of Toronto, Toronto, Ontario, lecturer, 1953-59, assistant professor, 1959-63, associate professor, 1963-69, professor of history, 1969—. *Military service:* Royal Canadian Navy. *Member:* Organization of American Historians.

WRITINGS: (Editor) *Lord Selkirk's Diary,* Champlain Society, 1959; *America and the War of 1812,* Wiley, 1965; *The Critical Years,* Wiley, 1970; *Conducting the Diplomacy of the New Nation,* Pitman, 1971. Editor for Champlain Society, 1955-62.

WORK IN PROGRESS: A history of Canadian-American relations; research on American foreign policy.

AVOCATIONAL INTERESTS: Travel, music, fishing, shooting.

* * *

WHITNEY, Cornelius Vanderbilt 1899-

PERSONAL: Born February 20, 1899, in New York, N.Y.; married Marie Louise Hosford, 1958; children: five. *Education:* Attended Yale University, 1922.

CAREER: Mine worker for Metal Exploration Co., 1923-25; founder and head of board of directors of Pan American Airways, 1927-41; president of Whitney Industries, Inc. (lumber company), 1931—. Founder and head of board of directors of Hudson Bay Mining & Smelting Co., 1928-64 (member of board of directors, 1964—), and Marine Studios, Inc., 1937—. Associated with A. Parker Bryant, Inc. (real estate and insurance firm). Assistant secretary of U.S. Air Force, 1947-49, under-secretary of commerce, 1949-50, special envoy of President Truman to England, Luxembourg, Italy, and Spain, 1950. Co-producer of film classics "A Star Is Born," "Rebecca," and "Gone with the Wind." Member of board of directors of Performing Arts Center of Saratoga Springs, N.Y.; member of board of trustees of American Museum of Natural History, Whitney Museum of Modern Art, and Philharmonic Society. Active in civic and business affairs in New York and Kentucky. *Military service:* U.S. Army Air Forces; served in India, Africa, and Japan; became colonel; received Distinguished Service Medal and Legion of Merit with two battle stars. *Member:* Kentucky Colonels.

WRITINGS: High Peaks (autobiography), University Press of Kentucky, 1977.

SIDELIGHTS: Since 1959, Whitney has divided his time between New York and Kentucky. In 1970 he bought property in Mallorca, and since then has been engaged in restoring the ancient section of Trujillo in the Estremadura section of Spain.

* * *

WIDEMAN, John Edgar 1941-

PERSONAL: Born June 14, 1941, in Washington, D.C.; married Judith Ann Goldman; children: Daniel Jerome, Jacob Edgar. *Education:* University of Pennsylvania, B.A., 1963; New College, Oxford, B.Phil., 1966.

CAREER: Howard University, Washington, D.C., teacher of American literature, summer, 1965; University of Pennsylvania, Philadelphia, Pa., associate professor of English and director of Afro-American studies program, beginning in 1967. Has also served as administrator/teacher in a curriculum planning, teacher-training institute sponsored by National Defense Education Act. National Humanities Faculty consultant in numerous states. *Member:* National Humanities Faculty, Association of American Rhodes Scholars (member of board of directors), Rhodes Scholar Selection Committee for Pennsylvania (Middle Atlantic States Final), Phi Beta Kappa. *Awards, honors:* Ben Franklin Scholar, University of Pennsylvania, 1959; Rhodes Scholar, Oxford University New College, 1963; Kent fellow, University of Iowa, 1966, to attend creative writing workshop; received Thouron fellowship for two years study in England; received creative writing prize, University of Pennsylvania.

WRITINGS—All novels: *Glance Away,* Harcourt, 1967; *Hurry Home,* Harcourt, 1970; *The Lynchers,* Harcourt, 1973. Contributor of articles, short stories, and poetry to periodicals, including *Negro Digest, Black World,* and *American Scholar.*

SIDELIGHTS: Harry Roskolenko has described Wideman as "a novelist of high seriousness and depth . . . with a poet's flair for a taut, meaningful, emotional language." Wideman's first book, *A Glance Away,* focuses on a day in the life of a young black drug addict and a middle-aged white professor dominated by homosexuality and alcoholism. Illustrating the themes of homecoming and salvation, the story probes each man's struggle to overcome and understand his personal compulsions. What moves the reader, S. F. Caldwell wrote, "is Wideman's artistry, his one- and two-paragraph evocations of joy and sorrow . . . echoed time and again through the course of the book." Roskolenko found the novel "tight, compact and shining with verbal and dramatic skill. . . . Wideman has written a powerfully inventive novel."

In his second novel, *Hurry Home,* Wideman presents a black law school graduate's quest for self and an exhausted, guilt-ridden white writer's search for the mulatto son he's never seen. The writer, Webb, hopes to have his son's forgiveness, whereas Cecil Braithwaite hopes to resolve his sense of alienation in a predominantly white society. "Braithwaite's struggle," according to John Leonard, "is not only with a divided self . . . [but] also with Western culture, white history, painting, architecture, literature, music." His search for origins, identity, and home takes him to Europe and Africa, only to discover that "there is no Africa" and that he must return home again. "Many of [the book's] pages," remarked Joseph Goodman, "are packed with psychological insight, and nearly all reveal Mr. Wideman's formidable command of the techniques of fiction." Wideman employs flashbacks, varying points of view, journals, letters, dreams, and puns to tell Braithwaite's story. "It is a dazzling display," Goodman concluded.

Another book, *The Lynchers,* is about four black men who, as representatives of black frustration and anger, plot the lynching of a white cop. The act is to be the symbolic inauguration of "a new dispensation," a new day for blacks in America. But the book, observed R. P. Brickner, "suggests that it does not believe the plan will work, suggests that its story is, in fact, about an unbearable dilemma—die or suffer." Discussing the author's style, Brickner noted that "the revelations of atmosphere, physical sensation, peculiar perception, have a great deal of impact—newness and rightness." F. L. Ryan commented: "Wideman obviously has many of the qualities essential for becoming a fine novelist.

He has a keen ear for dialect, a hungry curiosity about the low life in a big city, a rich awareness of the necessity for symbolic structure, and a passion for a cause."

BIOGRAPHICAL/CRITICAL SOURCES: Journal of Negro History, January, 1963; *Negro Digest,* May, 1963; *New York Times Book Review,* September 10, 1967, April 19, 1970, April 29, 1973; *Best Sellers,* September 15, 1967, June 1, 1973; *American Scholar,* autumn, 1967; *Saturday Review,* October 21, 1967; *New York Times,* April 2, 1970; *Newsweek,* May 7, 1970; John O'Brien, editor, *Interviews With Black Writers,* Liveright, 1973; *Contemporary Literary Criticism,* Volume 5, Gale, 1976.*

*   *   *

WIEDER, Robert S(hannon) 1944-
(Robert Shannon)

PERSONAL: Born July 2, 1944, in Los Angeles, Calif.; son of William G. (in automobile parts business) and Marjorie (Lyon) Wieder; married Robin P. Brooks (a physician), September 4, 1977. *Education:* University of California, Berkeley, B.A., 1966, M.A., 1969. *Politics:* "Anarcho-Republican." *Religion:* "Pantheist." *Home and office:* 2519 Alva Ave., El Cerrito, Calif. 94530.

CAREER: ABC-TV, Hollywood, Calif., producer, writer, and director, 1965, 1966; KTVU-TV, Oakland and San Francisco, Calif., public relations and publicity director, 1967; Lennen & Newell Advertising, San Francisco, Calif., copywriter, 1968-70; Richardson, Siegel, Rolfs & McCoy, Seattle, Wash., copy chief, 1971; Dakis Concern, Orinda, Calif., creative director, 1972-73; free-lance writer, 1973—; comedian. *Member:* National Organization for Reform of Marijuana Laws (charter member). *Awards, honors:* Best humor award from *Playboy,* 1975, for "Clark Ghent's School Days."

WRITINGS: (With George Hall) *The Great American Convertible,* Doubleday, 1977. Contributor of more than ninety articles (one under pseudonym Robert Shannon) to popular journals, including *Playboy, Penthouse, New West,* and *Lampoon.* Contributing editor of *Oui,* 1976-78, *WomenSports,* 1974-77, and *Chic,* 1978—.

WORK IN PROGRESS: "Dumb Is Beautiful," for *Penthouse.*

SIDELIGHTS: Wieder writes: "My major focus is humorous fiction, humorous essays, and pop-sociology. My motivation: a congenital compulsion to write. Philosophy: if it's not funny, who needs it? Interests: drugs, politics, stand-up comedy, medicine, media, sports. I have six unpublished novels, written while starving and living in my station wagon, about a Japanese restaurant, and in an anarchist collective. All are For Sale, cheap."

*   *   *

WIENER, Martin J. 1941-

PERSONAL: Born June 1, 1941, in New York, N.Y.; son of Harold H. (in business) and Eva (Richter) Wiener; married Carol Zisowitz, September 27, 1964 (marriage ended, 1977); children: Wendy June, Julie Milton. *Education:* Brandeis University, B.A., 1962; Harvard University, M.A., 1963, Ph.D., 1967. *Politics:* "Skeptic." *Religion:* Jewish. *Home:* 1700 Herman Dr., #1009, Houston, Tex. 77006. *Office:* Department of History, Rice University, Houston, Tex. 77001.

CAREER: Rice University, Houston, Tex., assistant professor, 1967-72, associate professor of history, 1972—. *Mem-*

ber: American Historical Association, Conference on British Studies. *Awards, honors:* National Endowment for the Humanities fellow, 1973-74.

WRITINGS: Between Two Worlds: The Political Thought of Graham Wallas, Oxford University Press, 1971. Contributor to history journals.

WORK IN PROGRESS: Cultural Resistance to Economic Growth in Britain, 1850-1975; research on moral ideas and moral reform in nineteenth-century England and on nineteenth-century urban history.

SIDELIGHTS: Wiener comments: "My chief research interest since my undergraduate days has been the modernization of society over the past century and a half, and its intellectual, psychological, and cultural consequences."

*   *   *

WILBUR, C(larence) Martin 1908-

PERSONAL: Born May 13, 1908, in Dayton, Ohio; son of Hollis A. (employed by Young Men's Christian Association) and Mary (Matteson) Wilbur; married Kathryn Edson, July 17, 1932; children: John Hollis, Ann Wilbur MacKenzie. *Education:* Oberlin College, A.B., 1931; graduate study at College of Chinese Studies, 1932-34; Columbia University, M.A., 1932, Ph.D., 1941. *Politics:* Liberal. *Religion:* Unitarian-Universalist. *Home:* 77 Nannahagan Rd., Pleasantville, N.Y. 10570. *Office:* The Eastern Asian Institute, Columbia University, 420 West 118th St., New York, N.Y. 10027.

CAREER: Field Museum of Natural History, Chicago, Ill., curator of Chinese archaeology, 1936-42; Office of Strategic Services, Washington, D.C., research analyst, 1943-45; U.S. Department of State, Washington, D.C., researcher in Washington and China, 1945-47; Columbia University, New York, N.Y., associate professor, 1947-57, professor, 1957-76, George Sansom Professor Emeritus of Chinese history, 1976—, director of East Asian Institute, 1957-63. Member of advisory council of China Institute. *Member:* Association for Asian Studies (member of board of directors; president, 1971-72), Asia Society (past member of board of directors), Columbia University Faculty Club. *Awards, honors:* Social Science Research Council grant, 1934-35; Foreign Area training fellow, Japan and South Asia, 1954-55; Fulbright grant for Taiwan, 1961-62; East-West Center grant, 1967-68.

WRITINGS: Slavery in China During the Former Han Dynasty, Field Museum of Natural History, 1943; (with Julie Lien-ying How) *Documents on Communism, Nationalism, and Soviet Advisers in China, 1918-1927,* Columbia University Press, 1956, revised edition, 1980; (editor and author of introduction) Chen Kung-po, *The Communist Movement in China,* Octagon, 1966; *Sun Yat-sen, Frustrated Patriot,* Columbia University Press, 1976.

Contributor: *Japan Between East and West,* Harper, 1957; Ping-ti Ho and Tang Tsou, editors, *China in Crisis: China's Heritage and the Communist Political System,* University of Chicago Press, 1968; M. Searle Bates, *Change in China: An Approach to Understanding,* Friendship Press, 1968; John Wilson Lewis, editor, *Party Leadership and Revolutionary Power in China,* Cambridge University Press, 1970; Ramon H. Myers, *Two Chinese States: U.S. Foreign Policy and Interests,* Hoover Institution Press, 1978; John K. Fairbank, editor, *Cambridge History of China,* Cambridge University Press, 1980.

Contributor of about fifty articles and reviews to scholarly journals and popular magazines. Member of editorial board of *Asian Survey* and *Contemporary China.*

SIDELIGHTS: Wilbur writes: "Having grown up in China, I naturally turned to a career in Chinese studies. Interested first in China's early history and archaeology, I changed my interest to the modern period as a result of research work in the Office of Strategic Services during World War II. I have traveled extensively in Asia—China, Korea, Japan, Taiwan, India; I read and speak Chinese.

"I have attempted to be as objective as possible in my scholarly writing about recent and contemporary China, since the subject is controversial, especially in its political aspects. Particularly I have delved for reliable documentary sources, preferably archival materials, and have worked in the Kuomintang Archives in Taiwan, the British Foreign Office Archives, and the archives of the U.S. Department of State. I also organized an oral history project at Columbia to interview in depth eminent Chinese who had careers during the Republican period, 1912-49, and the result was about a dozen carefully edited life histories that add historical perspective. A by-product was valuable collections of papers, diaries, etc., available for scholarly research. Objectivity, I believe, must also be accompanied with sympathetic imagination for the times and the people under study."

AVOCATIONAL INTERESTS: Gardening, theater, music, art.

BIOGRAPHICAL/CRITICAL SOURCES: Perspectives on Changing China: Essays in Honor of C. Martin Wilbur, Westview Press, 1979.

*   *   *

WILDSMITH, Brian 1930-

PERSONAL: Born January 22, 1930, in Penistone, Yorkshire, England; son of Paul and Annie Elizabeth (Oxley) Wildsmith; married Aurelie Janet Craigie Ithurbide, 1955; children: Claire, Rebecca, Anne, Simon. *Education:* Attended Barnsley School of Art and the Slade School of Fine Art, University College, London, 1949-52. *Home:* 11 Castellaras, 06370 Mouans-Sartoux, France.

CAREER: Selhurst Grammar School for Boys, art teacher, 1954-57; free-lance artist and illustrator of books for children, 1957—. *Military service:* National Service, 1952-54. *Awards, honors:* Kate Greenaway medal, 1962, for *Brian Wildsmith's ABC,* runner-up in 1964 and 1967; *Brian Wildsmith's ABC* received the Brooklyn Art Books for Children Citation, 1973; *Brian Wildsmith's Birds* was listed among the *New York Times* Choice of Best Illustrated Children's Books of the Year in 1967.

WRITINGS—All self-illustrated: A Brian Wildsmith Portfolio, F. Watts, 1962-66; *Brian Wildsmith's ABC,* Oxford University Press, 1962, F. Watts, 1963; *Brian Wildsmith's Mother Goose,* F. Watts, 1964; *Brian Wildsmith's 1, 2, 3's,* F. Watts, 1965; *Brian Wildsmith's Wild Animals,* F. Watts, 1967; *Brian Wildsmith's Birds,* F. Watts, 1967; *Brian Wildsmith's Fishes,* F. Watts, 1968; *Brian Wildsmith's Circus,* F. Watts, 1970; *Brian Wildsmith's Puzzles,* Oxford University Press, 1970, F. Watts, 1971; *The Owl and the Woodpecker,* Oxford University Press, 1971, F. Watts, 1972; *The Twelve Days of Christmas,* F. Watts, 1972; *The Little Wood Duck,* Oxford University Press, 1972, F. Watts, 1973; *The Lazy Bear,* Oxford University Press, 1973, F. Watts, 1974; *Brian Wildsmith's Squirrels,* Oxford University Press, 1974, F. Watts, 1975; *Python's Party,* Oxford University Press, 1974, F. Watts, 1975; *Maurice Maeterlinck's Blue Bird,* F. Watts, 1976; *The True Cross,* F. Watts, 1978.

Illustrator: Eileen O'Faolain, *High Sang the Sword,* Oxford

University Press, 1959; Rene Guillot, *Prince of the Jungle,*
S. G. Phillips, 1959; Frederick Grice, *The Bonny Pit Laddy,*
Oxford University Press, 1960, published as *Out of the
Mines,* F. Watts, 1961; Nan Chauncy, *The Secret Friends,*
Oxford University Press, 1960, F. Watts, 1962; Eleanor
Graham, *The Story of Jesus,* Hodder & Stoughton, 1960;
Chauncy, *Tangara,* Oxford University Press, 1960; Made-
leine Polland, *The Town Across the Water,* Constable, 1961;
Veronique Day, *Landslide!,* Bodley Head, 1961; *Arabian
Nights, Tales from the Arabian Nights,* Oxford University
Press, 1961, F. Watts, 1962; Roger L. Green, *Myths of the
Norsemen,* Bodley Head, 1962.

Jean de La Fontaine, *The Lion and the Rat: A Fable,* F.
Watts, 1963; Geoffrey Trease, *Follow My Black Plume,*
Macmillan, 1963; Edward Blishen, editor, *Oxford Book of
Poetry for Children,* F. Watts, 1963; Charlotte Morrow, *The
Watchers,* Hutchinson, 1963; Trease, *A Thousand for Sicily,*
Macmillan, 1964; Mother Goose, *Nursery Rhymes,* Oxford
University Press, 1964; de La Fontaine, *The North Wind
and the Sun,* F. Watts, 1964; Kevin Crossley-Holland, *Hav-
elok the Dane,* Macmillan, 1964, Dutton, 1965; de La Fon-
taine, *The Rich Man and the Shoemaker,* F. Watts, 1965;
Charles Dickens, *Barnaby Rudge,* Ginn, 1966; Robert L.
Stevenson, *A Child's Garden of Verses,* F. Watts, 1966; de
La Fontaine, *The Hare and the Tortoise,* F. Watts, 1967;
Philip Turner, *Brian Wildsmith's Illustrated Bible Stories,*
F. Watts, 1968; de La Fontaine, *The Miller, the Boy, and the
Donkey,* F. Watts, 1969.

SIDELIGHTS: Brian Wildsmith's kaleidoscopic drawings
have delighted children for nearly two decades. Wildsmith,
who works mostly in full color, thinks that the relationship of
the illustration and the printed text to be similar to a marriage—they complement one another, but can also exist separately. His first effort, *Brian Wildsmith's ABC,* was praised
by the *New York Herald Tribune Books:* "Bold, original pictures drawn in the individual style of an artist provide an
excellent beginning for a child's education. Children should
have a variety of books with this sort of picture, pictures that
are paintings and not merely illustrations."

Besides retelling *Maurice Maeterlinck's Blue Bird* in what a
Publishers Weekly critic called, "bursts of color [which] call
forth oohs and ahs on all pages," Wildsmith has also created
the graphics for the motion picture of the same name.

*BIOGRAPHICAL/CRITICAL SOURCES: New York Her-
ald Tribune Books,* May 12, 1963; *Publishers Weekly,* August 16, 1976; *Children's Literature Review,* Volume II,
Gale, 1976.*

*   *   *

WILKIE, Kenneth 1942-

PERSONAL: Born May 26, 1942, in Dundee, Scotland; son
of George Wilson and Betty (Bruce) Wilkie. *Education:* Attended St. Martin's College of Art, 1962-64, and University
of London; London College of Journalism, diploma, 1966.
Home: Brouwersgracht 158, Amsterdam, Netherlands. *Office:* P.O. Box 696, Amsterdam, Netherlands.

CAREER: Bank clerk in Dundee, Scotland, 1959-61; publisher's assistant in London, England, 1961; pianist in London, England, 1962-65; *Enfield Weekly Herald,* London,
England, reporter, 1966-67; *Glasgow Herald,* Glasgow,
Scotland, feature writer, 1967-69; *Holland Herald,* Amsterdam, began as writer and sub-editor, became editor. *Member:* International Press Club, National Union of Journalists.

WRITINGS: The Van Gogh Assignment, Paddington, 1978.
Contributor to *Sunday Times.*

SIDELIGHTS: Wilkie writes: "I speak French, Dutch, and
Latin, without which I could not have followed my inquiries
into the life of Van Gogh. I have also had first-hand knowledge of life with mental patients (my mother). In the course
of my work in the last seven years I have traveled to Japan,
Hong Kong, Australia, the Philippines, Indonesia, Thailand, Singapore, Tunisia, Tanzania, France, Kenya, Belgium, Denmark, Germany, Brazil, Surinam, Curacao, Aru-
ba, the United States, and Canada."

BIOGRAPHICAL/CRITICAL SOURCES: Guardian, November 9, 1970; *Sun Monthly,* Number XI, 1972; *Sunday
Times,* March 19, 1978.

*   *   *

WILLIAMS, Maureen 1951-

PERSONAL: Born August 12, 1951, in Kent, England;
daughter of Herbert William and Eva (a secretary; maiden
name Foster) Eves; married Guy Williams (a media resources officer), September 4, 1971; children: Thomas Sean.
Education: Attended Folkestone School of Art, England,
1968-71. *Home and office:* 51 Lansdowne Rd., Purley, Surrey, England.

CAREER: Illustrator; part-time teacher. Held various full-
and part-time office positions, 1971-73.

WRITINGS: (Self-illustrated) *Bd-Dd,* Macmillan, 1975;
(self-illustrated) *On Safari,* Macmillan, 1975. Also author of
The Blue Book, published by Macmillan.

Illustrator: *Storytime From Playschool,* Piccolo, 1974;
Southgate St. James, *The Ghost of Beestley Zoo,* Macmillan,
1974; Geranne Leonard, *The Mandarin's Daughter,* Abelard, 1975; Terry Wilson, *Beginner's Spanish: An Introduction to Conversational Spanish,* Hodder & Stoughton, 1975;
Diana Webster, *Pilbeam's Circus,* Macmillan, 1975; *Child's
Talk,* Heinemann, 1977.*

*   *   *

WILLIAMSON, Jeffrey G(ale) 1935-

PERSONAL: Born November 26, 1935, in New Haven,
Conn.; married in 1958; children: two. *Education:* Wesleyan
University, Middletown, Conn., B.A., 1957; Stanford Uni-
versity, M.A., 1959, Ph.D., 1961. *Office:* Department of
Economics, University of Wisconsin, Madison, Wis. 53706.

CAREER: Vanderbilt University, Nashville, Tenn., assistant professor of economics, 1961-63; University of Wisconsin—Madison, assistant professor, 1963-64, associate professor, 1964-68, professor of economics, 1968—, member of
executive committee of Center in Economic Development
and International Economics at Social Systems Research
Institute, 1968-74, director, 1969-71. Visiting professor at
University of the Philippines, 1967-68, Harvard University,
1972, and Stanford University, 1976-77. Participant in and
administrator of seminars and workshops. Member of policy
board of Economics Institute (Boulder, Colo.), 1969-72;
consultant to International Bank for Reconstruction and
Development, Agency for International Development, and
U.S. Department of State. *Member:* American Economic
Association, Economic History Association. *Awards, honors:* Cole Prize from Economic History Association, 1971,
for article, "Writing History Backwards: Meiji, Japan Revisited."

*WRITINGS: American Growth and the Balance of Pay-
ments, 1820-1913: A Study of the Long Swing,* University of

North Carolina Press, 1964; (contributor) S. Cohen and F. Hill, editors, *American Economic History: Essays in Interpretation*, Lippincott, 1966; (contributor) A. R. Hall, editor, *The Export of Capital from Britain, 1870-1914*, Methuen, 1968; (contributor) L. Needleman, editor, *Regional Analysis: Selected Readings*, Penguin, 1968; (contributor) *Economic Theory and Practice in the Asian Setting: Macroeconomics*, Wiley Eastern, 1968.

(Contributor) S. Engerman and R. W. Fogel, editors, *The Reinterpretation of American Economic History*, Harper, 1971; (with A. Kelley and R. J. Cheetham) *Dualistic Economic Development: Theory and History*, University of Chicago Press, 1972; (with Kelley) *Lessons from Japanese Development: An Analytical Economic History*, University of Chicago Press, 1974; *Late Nineteenth-Century American Development: A General Equilibrium History*, Cambridge University Press, 1974; (contributor) P. David and M. Reder, editors, *Nations and Households in Economic Growth*, Academic Press, 1974; (contributor) D. C. Klingaman and R. K. Vedder, editors, *Essays in Nineteenth-Century Economic History*, Ohio University Press, 1975; (contributor) L. Schnore, editor, *The New Urban History*, Princeton University Press, 1975; (contributor) P. Uselding, editor, *Research in Economic History*, Volume I, Johnson Associates, 1976; (contributor) Manning Nash, editor, *Essays on Economic Development and Cultural Change*, University of Chicago Press, 1977.

Also contributor to *Exports and National Economic Growth*, edited by R. Caves, J. Price, and D. North, Princeton University Press; *A National Policy Toward Regional Change: Alternatives to Confrontation; Distribution, Poverty, and Development; Modelling the Distribution and Inter-Generational Transmission of Wealth*.

General editor of "Social Science and the Modern Historian: An International Monograph Series," Johnson Associates, 1975—. Contributor of about sixty articles and reviews to economic journals in the United States and abroad. Member of editorial board of *Explorations in Economic History*, 1965-69, 1973-74, 1977-80, co-editor, 1969-73, associate editor, 1974-77; member of editorial board of *Economic Development and Cultural Change*, 1969—; associate editor of *Review of Economics and Statistics*, 1972—.

WORK IN PROGRESS: A *Macroeconomic History of American Inequality*, with a companion volume on the British experience, with P. Lindert; *Accumulation and the State: Macromodelling Japanese Growth Since the Late Meiji*, with L. DeBever; editing *Essays in General Equilibrium History;* continuing research on economic growth, accumulation, and distribution.

*   *   *

WILLIS, Jerry W.   1943-

PERSONAL: Born January 27, 1943, in Tuscumbia, Ala.; son of Elbert Carter (a steamfitter) and Lavice (a psychiatric aide; maiden name, McAlpin) Willis; children: Amy Elizabeth. *Education:* Union University, B.A., 1966; University of Alabama, M.A., 1967, Ph.D., 1970. *Politics:* Democrat. *Religion:* Unitarian-Universalist. *Home address:* R.R. 2, Box 69-AA, Lubbock, Tex. 79415. *Office:* College of Education, Texas Tech University, Lubbock, Tex. 79409.

CAREER: Worked as Project director of Alabama Department of Mental Health, 1970-72; University of Guelph, Guelph, Ontario, assistant professor of psychology, 1972-74; University of Western Ontario, London, assistant professor of psychology, 1974-76; University of British Colum-

bia, Vancouver, assistant professor of psychology, 1976-78; Texas Tech University, Lubbock, member of faculty, 1978—. *Member:* American Psychological Association, Royal Society of Arts (fellow).

WRITINGS: (With Jeane Crowder and Joan Willis) *Guiding the Psychological and Educational Growth of Children*, C. C Thomas, 1976; (with Donna Giles) *Great Experiments in Behavior Modification*, Harper, 1976. Also author of *Peanut Butter and Jelly Guide to Computers*, with Deborrah Smithy and Brian Hyndman, Dilithium Press.

SIDELIGHTS: Willis writes: "I am addicted to learning and change. I live on a few acres outside Lubbock and am into solar energy, underground houses, homemade adobe bricks, and personal computers. I feel there must be someone who builds a bridge between the basic research literature and the consuming public. Through my books I try to be that person."

*   *   *

WILLIS, Meredith Sue   1946-

PERSONAL: Born May 31, 1946, in Clarksburg, W.Va.; daughter of Glenn Ernest (a school principal) and Lucille (a teacher; maiden name, Meredith) Willis. *Education:* Attended Bucknell University, 1964-66; Barnard College, B.A., 1969; Columbia University, M.F.A., 1972. *Politics:* "Deeply involved in radical student politics in the late sixties." *Religion:* "Raised a Baptist." *Home:* 236 Clinton St., Brooklyn, N.Y. 11201. *Agent:* Wendy Weil, Julian Bach Literary Agency, Inc., 3 East 48th St., New York, N.Y. 10017.

CAREER: Volunteers in Service to America (VISTA), Washinton, D.C., volunteer worker for Southeastern Tidewater Opportunity Project in Norfolk, Va., 1966-67; Goddard-Riverside Community Center, New York City, group worker with senior citizens, 1967-68; Bellevue Hospital, New York City, recreation therapist, 1969-70; Cuando Community Center, New York City, teacher of remedial reading and writing, 1970-71; Teachers & Writers Collaborative, New York City, consultant in creative writing, 1971—. Has given readings in New York and New England. *Member:* Feminist Writers Guild, Phi Beta Kappa. *Awards, honors:* Won *Mademoiselle*'s college fiction contest, 1969, with story, "The Babysitter"; fellowship from Mary Roberts Rinehart Foundation, 1976; Bernard de Voto Fellowship in Fiction from Bread Loaf Writers' Conference, 1978; National Endowment for the Arts fellowship, 1978-79.

WRITINGS: A *Space Apart* (novel), Scribner, 1979.

Work represented in anthologies, including *Mademoiselle Prize Stories*, M. Evans, 1975. Contributor to *Whole Word Catalogue #2*. Contributor of more than twenty-five stories and articles to education journals and literary magazines, including *Little Magazine*, *Commentary*, *Epoch*, and *Minnesota Review*.

WORK IN PROGRESS: Another novel.

SIDELIGHTS: Willis writes: "I have done a lot of odd jobs in my life and I value these very highly. I have worked with wheelchair patients, been a disc jockey for a college radio station, and given workshops for teachers and students of all ages in video tape and acting as well as creative writing. I participated passionately in many demonstrations and sit-ins, I work in a recycling center, and write painstaking letters in Spanish to dictators and other unsavory characters for Amnesty International. I like seeing everything—teaching, childhood, books I've read, jobs I've had, come together in fiction."

WILMER, Valerie (Sybil) 1941-

PERSONAL: Born December 7, 1941, in Harrogate, England; daughter of Eustace (a civil servant) and Kathleen Sybil (Rogers) Wilmer. *Education:* Attended Polytechnic of Central London, 1959-60. *Politics:* "Socialist feminism." *Home:* 10 Balham Park Mansions, Balham Park Rd., London S.W.12, England.

CAREER: Writer and photojournalist. Worked as a darkroom technician. Photographs shown in traveling exhibitions, including "Keep Music Live" and "Young British Photographers." Has held her own exhibition at Victoria and Albert Museum in London, 1973, which subsequently went on tour. Participant in collective women's shows at Half Moon Gallery, 1974 and 1975. *Member:* National Union of Journalists. *Awards, honors:* Grants from Arts Council of Great Britain, 1974 and 1976, to photograph black women in Mississippi.

WRITINGS: (And photographer) *Jazz People* (interviews), Allison & Busby, 1970, Bobbs-Merrill, 1971; (and photographer) *The Face of Black Music*, De Capo Press, 1976; *As Serious as Your Life*, Allison & Busby/Quartet Books, 1977. Contributor to periodicals, including *Melody Maker, Spare Rib, Time Out, Swing Journal, Jazz Magazine, Coda, Jazz Forum, Jazz Journal, Black Music, Jazz Monthly, Crescendo, Jazz News, Jazz Beat, Jazz & Blues, Into Jazz, Blues Unlimited, Tropic, Flamingo, Drum,* and *Soul Illustrated.* British correspondent for *Downbeat,* 1967-74.

Photographer: Charles Fox, *The Jazz Scene*, Paul Hamlyn, 1972; Brian Case and Stan Britt, *The Illustrated Encyclopaedia of Jazz*, Salamander Books, 1978; Kitty Grime, *Jazz at Ronnie Scott's*, R. Hale, 1979; Dave Laing, *There Was Only the Pit*, Quartet Books, 1979. Contributor of photographs to periodicals, including *London Times, Observer, Time Out, Creative Camera,* and *New Musical Express.* Photographs featured in films, including "Jazz Is Our Religion," 1972, and "Born to Swing," 1972.

WORK IN PROGRESS: Research with percussionist Andrew Cyrille "into the work of those black American drummers who have influenced music over three decades"; continuation of photography project on black women in Mississippi.

SIDELIGHTS: Wilmer told *CA:* "I work equally as a journalist and photographer. I dislike being classified as either 'writer' or 'photographer' for this reason. Were I to accept such qualification, it would detract from part of the whole. I do not believe in the notion of 'hobbies'—everything I do is important to me and is pursued with the same degree of dedication."

Wilmer has managed to apply her skills as a writer and photographer to her interest in African-American music. "Basically, most writers don't have any idea of what being a musician is about," she told an interviewer. "They're just pundits, they don't understand what they're talking about beyond the superficiality of it.

"When I had to make my own living out of doing something which was a craft, writing and photography, and became mature enough to put things in perspective, then I understood what the musicians had been telling me." Wilmer also revealed that "the difference between the photographer who knows and the one who doesn't is the feeling [for the subject]."

As jazz music originates from black culture, much of Wilmer's work has revolved around studying that culture. In her book *As Serious as Your Life*, Wilmer constantly refers to jazz as black music. In anticipation of critics who would accuse her of racism, Wilmer stated that "my attitude isn't a racist one. I don't belive that if it's black it must be good. That's rubbish. I just believe that you should put things in their historical context. This music is the creation of African-American people . . . I don't see that there's any harm in describing it as black music or African-American music. I think if people do object to that, then it's for their own racist reasons. . . ."

Wilmer has also defended her choice of including feminist politics in *As Serious as Your Life*. "Well, what I've written certainly doesn't offer any devastating analysis," she admitted, "but if it might make some people think about it then it will have been worth including." Wilmer revealed that much of the substance in her section on feminism came from personal experience: "Once you've had that experience [feminist consciousness-raising], then you never look back."

BIOGRAPHICAL/CRITICAL SOURCES: New Musical Express, May 7, 1977; *Time Out,* November 11-17, 1977; *London Morning Star,* January 10, 1978.

* * *

WILSON, Ian (William) 1941-

PERSONAL: Born March 30, 1941, in London, England; son of William Thomas (a clerk) and Doris (a school secretary; maiden name, Bentall) Wilson; married Judith Mary Dyett (a psychologist), December 9, 1967; children: Adrian Peter, Noel Christopher. *Education:* Magdalen College, Oxford, B.A., 1963, M.A., 1977. *Religion:* Roman Catholic. *Home and Office:* 18-A Flax Bourton Rd., Failand, Bristol BS8 3UW, England.

CAREER: Bristol United Press Ltd. (newspaper publishers), Bristol, England, publicity and promotions manager, 1969-79; full-time writer, 1979—. *Awards, honors:* Gold Award from Miami Film Festival, 1978, for "The Silent Witness"; British Academy Robert Flaherty Award for best feature documentary of the year, 1978, for "The Silent Witness."

WRITINGS: The Shroud of Turin, Doubleday, 1978 (published in England as *The Turin Shroud*, Gollancz, 1978).

Co-author of screenplay, "The Silent Witness" (based on *The Turin Shroud*), released by Screenpro Films, 1978. Contributor to magazines and newspapers, including *Sunday Times.*

WORK IN PROGRESS: Mind Out of Time, a study of experiences of "seeing" into the past with and without hypnosis, publication by Victor Gollancz expected in 1980.

SIDELIGHTS: Ian Wilson told *CA:* "A compulsion to investigate the unexplained has perhaps been the chief motivating factor in my writing career. This began as early as 1955 when I first became aware of the Turin shroud and found myself, as an agnostic, quite unable to dismiss the cloth's image as the work of any forger. In 1973 I was able to examine the shroud at a rare private showing, and began serious work on a book, but found myself unable to interest British publishers in what seemed to them such an obscure subject. Then in 1976, after a *Catholic Herald* article on the shroud appeared, I was contacted by Doubleday and *The Shroud of Turin* was born. The film *Silent Witness* followed, and today the book has already been translated into French and Japanese, with further foreign language editions in progress.

"In 1979 I decided to commence a full-time writing career, with a view to researching in depth the phenomenon of apparent past-life recall. As I am now a Roman Catholic, the phenomenon raises precisely the same quarrel in my mind as originally raised by the shroud. It is impossible to tell at this stage what the eventual verdict will be, but after *Mind out of Time* I have promised myself to choose a more frivolous subject.

AVOCATIONAL INTERESTS: Art history, foreign travel, painting, photography.

* * *

WILSON, Kenneth L. 1897(?)-1979

OBITUARY NOTICE: Born c. 1897; died February 1, 1979, in Evanston, Ill. Athletic coach and administrator. A 1920 Olympic participant, "Tug" Wilson was the athletic director at Drake University and then at Northwestern University until 1945. In that year he became commissioner of the Big Ten athletic conference, a position he held until his retirement in 1961. Wilson also served several terms as president of the United States Olympic Committee and belonged to the President's Council on Youth Fitness. He co-authored a history of the athletic conference, *The Big Ten,* in 1967. Obituaries and other sources: *New York Times,* February 3, 1979.

* * *

WILSON, Michael 1914-1978

PERSONAL: Born July 1, 1914, in McAlester, Okla.; died April 9, 1978, in Beverly Hills, Calif.; married wife, Zelma (an architect); children: Rebecca, Roseanna. *Education:* University of California, A.B., 1936. *Politics:* Communist.

CAREER: Screenwriter. *Military service:* U.S. Marine Corps. *Awards, honors:* Academy Award for best screenplay from Academy of Motion Picture Arts and Sciences and best screenplay award from Writers Guild, both 1951, both for "A Place in the Sun"; nominations for Academy Award and Writers Guild award, both 1952, both for "Five Fingers"; award from Writers Guild, 1956, for "Friendly Persuasion"; Best Dramatic Screenplay Award from British Writers Guild, 1962, for "Lawrence of Arabia."

WRITINGS—Screenplays: (With Frederick Kohner and Paul Trivers) "The Men in Her Life" (adapted from the novel by Lady Eleanor Smith, *Ballerina*), Columbia, 1941; "Border Patrol," United Artists, 1942; "Colt Comrades," United Artists, 1944; (with Norman Houston and Mortimer Grant) "Bar 20," United Artists, 1944; (contributor) Frances Goodrich, Albert Hackett, and Frank Capra, "It's a Wonderful Life" (adapted from the short story by Philip Van Doren Stern, *The Greatest Gift*), RKO, 1946.

(With Harry Brown) "A Place in the Sun" (adapted from the novel by Theodore Dresier, *An American Tragedy*), Paramount, 1951; "Five Fingers" (adapted from the non-fiction book by L. C. Moyzisch, *Operation Cicero*), Twentieth Century-Fox, 1952; "Friendly Persuasion" (adapted from the novel by Jessamyn West), Allied Artist, 1956; "The Bridge on the River Kwai" (adapted from the novel by Pierre Boulle) Columbia, 1957; (with Robert Bolt) "Lawrence of Arabia" (adapted from the book by T. E. Lawrence, *Seven Pillars of Wisdom*), Columbia, 1962; (with Martin Biberman) *Salt of the Earth* (released independently, 1954), Beacon Press, 1965; (with Dalton Trumbo) "The Sandpiper," Metro-Goldwyn-Mayer (MGM), 1965; (with Rod Serling) "Planet of the Apes" (adapted from the novel by Boulle), Twentieth Century-Fox, 1968; (with Sy Bartlett) "Che!," Twentieth Century-Fox, 1969.

SIDELIGHTS: Wilson was among those screenwriters working in the film industry who were victims of the anti-communist paranoia of the early 1950's. Prior to his banishment from Hollywood, Wilson had achieved recognition for his work on "A Place in the Sun." Acknowledged as one of the finer screenwriters at the time, Wilson soon found himself in trouble for his refusal to respond to intimations that he was a communist. Shortly after, he was blacklisted.

Despite his exile from Hollywood, Wilson continued to impress people in filmmaking with work he'd completed before the blacklisting. Prominent among those works was "Friendly Persuasion," a film about conscientious objectors during the Civil War. Wilson was nominated for an Academy Award for his screenplay but the Academy, anticipating his nomination, resolved that only those who'd cleared themselves of association with the Communist Party could actually win an award.

Wilson finally left the United States for France where he lived for eight years. While in France, he was again persecuted by film moguls who deprived him of screen credit for "The Bridge on the River Kwai"; they opted to give credit to Pierre Boulle, on whose novel the film was adapted from.

In the 1960's, Wilson returned to Hollywood where he once again worked as a screenwriter. He retired in 1969.

OBITUARIES: New York Times, April 10, 1978; *Washington Post,* April 11, 1978; *Newsweek,* April 24, 1978.*

* * *

WOLF, Christa 1929-

PERSONAL: Born March 18, 1929, in Landsberg an der Warthe, Germany (now Gorzow, Poland); married Gerhard Wolf; children: Annette, Katrin. *Education:* Attended University of Jena and University of Leipzig, 1949-53. *Address:* c/o Aufbau Verlag, Postfach 1217, Franzoesische Strasse 32, DDR-108 Berlin, East Germany.

CAREER: Novelist, essayist, and writer of short stories. Former editor of *Neue Deutsche Literatur* (periodical) and reader for book publishers; also worked in a factory manufacturing railroad freight cars, 1959-62. *Member:* P.E.N. German Academy of Arts. *Awards, honors:* Heinrich Mann Prize, German Academy, 1963; National Prize of German Democratic Republic, 1964; Fontane Prize, 1972; Bremen Literature Prize, 1978.

WRITINGS: (Editor with husband, Gerhard Wolf) *Wir, unsere Zeit* (title means "We in Our Time"), Aufbau Verlag, 1959; (editor) *In diesen Jahren: Deutsche Erzaehler der Gegenwart* (title means "In These Years: Contemporary German Short Story Writers"), P. Reclam, 1957; (editor) *Proben junger Erzahler: Ausgewaehlte deutsche Prosa* (title means "A Sampler of Work by Young Short Story Writers: Selected German Prose"), P. Reclam, 1959; *Moskauer Novelle* (title means "Moscow Stories"), Mitteldeutscher Verlag, 1961; *Der geteilte Himmel* (novel), Mitteldeutscher Verlag, 1963, translation by Joan Becker published as *Divided Heaven: A Novel of Germany Today,* Seven-Seas Press, 1965; *Nachdenken ueber Christa T.* (novel), Mitteldeutscher Verlag, 1968, translation by Christopher Middleton published as *The Quest for Christa T.,* Farrar, Straus, 1971; *Lesen und Schreiben,* (essays; title means "Reading and Writing"), Aufbau Verlag, 1972, translation published as *The Reader and the Writer,* International Publishing Co., 1978; (with G. Wolf) *Till Eulenspiegel,* Aufbau Verlag, 1973; *Unter den Linden: Drei unwahrscheinliche Geschichten* (title means "Under the Linden Tree: Three Improbable Stories"), Luchterhand, 1974; *Kindheitsmuster* (title means "Patterns of Childhood"), Aufbau Verlag, 1976.

WORK IN PROGRESS: A story, *Kein Ort. Nirgends* (title means "No Place. Nowhere").

SIDELIGHTS: Unlike her earlier novel, *Divided Heaven,* Christa Wolf's *The Quest for Christa T.* has caused much controversy in her homeland of East Germany. It was publicly attacked at the Sixth East German Writers Congress which condemned it "as a pessimistic attempt to replace Marx with Freud." In fact, prior to its release "East German censors postponed its publication for two years and it finally appeared in a limited edition of 4,000 copies" with booksellers being given special orders to sell it only to "well-known customers professionally involved in literary matters." *The Quest for Christa T.* has since been removed and is no longer on sale in East Germany.

But why should this book cause such criticism for the author who previously received the German Democratic Republic's National Prize for *Divided Heaven* and who also was chosen as an alternate member in the party's Central Committee (a position which she later left due to "a conflict over literary freedom")? Praised by Western critics, *The Quest for Christa T.* was described by a *New York Times Book Review* critic as a "beautifully written, imaginative novel [that] has nothing explicitly to do with politics." *New Leader* noted that *The Quest for Christa T.* "succeeds in creating that fictional rarity, a character who is ordinary and engaging, complex and credible, and well worth knowing."

Perhaps it is the attitude of the character Christa T. that was responsible for the uproar in East Germany. Through the use of Christa T.'s papers and letters, she is revealed to be an ordinary woman who graduates from a university, teaches school, marries and bears children, and who dies at the age of thirty-five of leukemia. Unlike the heroine in Wolf's earlier novel who finally decides to continue living in East Germany rather than live with her lover in the West, Christa "is unable to reconcile herself to East Germany's noisy parades, pompous speeches and mass meetings with flags and songs, and she is particularly affected by the general air of servility, the subservience to official precepts. . . . She is convinced . . . that one has the right to question, to doubt, to investigate and to lead a unique and independent life listening to one's inner voice and making personal decisions." In addition, this novel has been criticized specifically because the character is ordinary "when East German literature is under strict orders to produce what has been described as 'Socialist folk heroes.'" Finally, the character's preoccupation with death towards the end of the novel has been denounced by Communist critics as being "antisocial."

Nevertheless in *The Quest for Christa T.*, Wolf, according to a *New Leader* critic, "displays a gentle respect for selfhood and for spiritual values. In one short scene the virtues are contrasted with the materialism and frivolity of Christa's friends in West Berlin. The episode illustrates how philosophical differences among individuals are more profound and divisive than any inherent differences between sociopolitical systems. . . ." A *Times Literary Supplement* critic called it "a remarkable novel, not merely because it deviates from the prescribed ideological pattern, a fact which has earned it an inflated reputation in the West and a difficult passage in the East, but because it respects the delicacy of individual personality despite threatening restraints."

Wolf's most recent work, *Kindheitsmuster,* which she considers to be her most important and extensive literary contribution, is autobiographical, recalling her life under the growing influence of Hitler in Nazi Germany and her family's experiences during the Second World War. She begins *Kindheitsmuster* by stating: "What is past is not dead. It is not even past. We separate ourselves from it and pretend to be strangers." It is in this manner that Wolf's recent work differs from the norm of East German literature because, unlike their counterpart, the East Germans "have maintained that the establishment of a socialist state created an entirely new order untainted by complicity in Nazi atrocities. . . . To suggest that the citizens of the new Republic might have been scarred so deeply by life under Hitler that not even a profession of faith in Marxism could completely eradicate its effect would be quite unthinkable."

Wolf does more than just suggest. She retraces her life under the rule of the fuehrer: at the age of five his very name brings a lump in her throat, her father joins the Party, she progresses through various Nazi youth organizations, in school she learns of racial purity and begins to fear the alien race—the Jews, and finally, she states that no objections are made "not even at the euthanasia programme, that costs the family their simple-minded aunt Jette."

In 1971, Christa Wolf and her husband, daughter, and brother made a trip to her birthplace, now a town in Poland. It is in this narrative, according to Peter Graves of the *Times Literary Supplement,* that the book's greatest strengths are revealed. The mother must now confront her daughter with the truth of what happened and how it could have happened. Graves called *Kindheitsmuster* "a courageous book that breaks taboos . . . it is infused with an integrity and a deep moral concern that raise it far above the narrow and self-conscious partisanship of much GDR literature. It speaks equally to East and West Germany—itself a daring accomplishment for an East German author—but also, with its atmospheric depiction of a fateful era and its patent and compelling truthfulness, to wider audiences beyond."

BIOGRAPHICAL/CRITICAL SOURCES: Brian Keith-Smith, editor, *Essays on Contemporary German Literature,* Oswald Wolff, 1966; *Nation,* February 13, 1967; *New York Times,* June 3, 1969; *Times Literary Supplement,* July 24, 1969, August 13, 1971, April 7, 1978; *New York Times Book Review,* October 19, 1969, January 31, 1971; H. M. Waidson, *The Modern German Novel,* Oxford University Press, 1971; *Saturday Review,* May 8, 1971; *New Leader,* May 31, 1971; *New York Review of Books,* September 2, 1971; *Books Abroad,* winter, 1975, spring, 1975; Alexander Stephan, *Christa Wolf,* Edition Text und Kritik, 1976.

*   *   *

WOLOSZYNOWSKI, Julian 1898-1978

OBITUARY NOTICE: Born in 1898 in Poland; died in March, 1978, in Warsaw, Poland. Polish writer best known for his biography of the poet, *Slowacki,* and his historical novel, *Rok 1863.* Woloszynowski also wrote verse and theatre criticism. Obituaries and other sources: *The Penguin Companion to European Literature,* McGraw, 1969; *World Literature Today,* spring, 1979.

*   *   *

WOOD, Barbara 1947-

PERSONAL: Born January 30, 1947, in England; came to United States; daughter of Alfons (a painter) and Ruth (Pemberton) Lewandowski; married George Wood (a surgical technician), June 25, 1966. *Education:* Attended University of California, Santa Barbara, 1964-66. *Home:* 852 21st St., #C, Santa Monica, Calif. 90403. *Agent:* Harvey Klinger, 250 West 57th St., New York, N.Y. 10019.

CAREER: Writer. Santa Monica Hospital, Santa Monica, Calif., surgical technician, 1973-77; writer, 1977—.

WRITINGS: The Magdalene Scrolls, Doubleday, 1978; *Hounds and Jackals,* Doubleday, 1978; *Curse This House,* Dell, 1978; *Yesterday's Child,* Doubleday, 1979; (with Gareth Wootton) *Night Trains,* Morrow, 1979.

AVOCATIONAL INTERESTS: Travel, foreign languages, ancient history.

* * *

WORTHEN, Blaine Richard 1936-

PERSONAL: Born October 10, 1936, in Murray, Utah; son of Donovan H. (a construction superintendent) and Grace (a secretary; maiden name, Middleton) Worthen; married Barbara Allen (a writer), January 16, 1959; children: Jeffrey, Lynette, Bradley. *Education:* University of Utah, B.S. (with high honors), 1960, M.S., 1965; Ohio State University, Ph.D., 1968. *Religion:* Church of Jesus Christ of Latter-day Saints (Mormons). *Home:* 175 Quarter Circle Dr., R.F.D., Logan, Utah 84321. *Office:* Department of Psychology, Utah State University, Logan, Utah 84321.

CAREER: Elementary school teacher in Sandy, Utah, 1960-62; University of Utah, Salt Lake City, instructor at campus school, 1962-64, part-time instructor in education, 1964-65; Ohio State University, Columbus, associate director of Evaluation Center, 1967-69, assistant professor of educational psychology, 1968-69; University of Colorado, Boulder, assistant professor, 1969-71, associate professor of educational psychology, 1971-73, co-director of Laboratory of Educational Research, 1969-73; Northwest Regional Educational Laboratory, Portland, Ore., director of Research and Evaluation Services, 1973-75, and Division of Research, Evaluation, and Instructional Technology, 1975-78; Utah State University, Logan, professor of psychology and head of department, 1978—. Guest lecturer at Canberra College of Advanced Education, 1977; lecturer at College of Southern Utah, summer, 1964; participant in academic symposia and conferences; organizer of training and development workshops. Member of executive committee of Centers for Educational Development and Research Evaluators, 1974-75; member of National Evaluation Network, 1975—; director of technical assistance in evaluation training for Hawaii Department of Education, 1976-77.

MEMBER: American Psychological Association, National Council of Measurement in Education, American Educational Research Association (head of task force on research training, 1970-71; member of publications committee, 1977—), National Society of Professors of Educational Research, National Working Group on Evaluation. *Awards, honors:* Named distinguished scholar by Australian Association of Research in Education, 1977; grants from Phi Delta Kappa, 1968-70, U.S. Office of Education, 1969-70, 1970, 1970-71, 1971-72, 1972-73, 1973, 1976-77, Ohio Department of Education, 1972, University of British Columbia, 1974-75, Alaska Department of Education, 1974-75, Hawaii Department of Education, 1976-77, and National Institute of Education, 1977-78.

WRITINGS: (Editor with D. L. Clark, and contributor) *Preparing Research Personnel for Education,* Phi Delta Kappa, 1967; (with J. R. Sanders) *Educational Evaluation: Theory and Practice,* Charles A. Jones Publishing, 1973; (with M. D. Hock) *A Simulation Approach to Training Evaluation Personnel: Instructor's Manual,* Charles A. Jones Publishing, 1973; (with A. L. Roaden) *The Research Assistantship: Recommendations for Colleges and Universities,* Phi Delta Kappa, 1975.

Contributor: J. M. Scandura, editor, *Research in Mathematics Education,* National Council of Teachers of Mathematics, 1967; R. E. Ripple, editor, *Readings in Learning and Human Abilities,* Harper, 1971; G. J. Mouly, editor, *Readings in Educational Psychology,* Holt, 1971; W. G. Hack and other editors, *Educational Administration,* Allyn & Bacon, 1971; H. D. Schalock, editor, *Conceptual Frameworks for Viewing Educational Research, Development, Diffusion, and Evaluation,* Oregon State System of Higher Education, 1972.

Author of training materials and multi-media kits. Contributor of about twenty-five articles and reviews to education journals. Guest editor of *Theory Into Practice,* June, 1967; advisory editor of *Journal of Educational Measurement,* 1969-73.

WORK IN PROGRESS: Research on methods for evaluating publicly supported programs.

SIDELIGHTS: Worthen commented: "The writings listed above reflect my efforts to improve the theory and practice of evaluation and research in the fields of education and psychology. These two fields collectively touch most persons in our society, and it is satisfying to provide assistance in these areas. It is my belief that the greatest advances in education and psychology will come through careful research to generate new knowledge and through systematic evaluation of the worth and effectiveness of all programs, products, and processes in these fields. It is my hope that my writing has been of some help in this effort."

AVOCATIONAL INTERESTS: Lapidary, photography, art, travel (including New Zealand, Micronesia, and Polynesia).

* * *

WRIGHT, Richard B(ruce) 1937-

PERSONAL: Born March 4, 1937, in Midland, Ontario, Canada; son of Laverne and Laura Willette (Thomas) Wright; married Phyllis M. Cotton (a library technician), September 2, 1966; children: Christopher, Andrew. *Education:* Ryerson Polytechnic Institute, graduate, 1959; Trent University, B.A., 1972. *Politics:* Conservative. *Religion:* Anglican. *Home:* 21 Ridley Rd., St. Catharines, Ontario, Canada L2S 2H5. *Agent:* Georges Borchardt, Inc., 136 East 57th St., New York, N.Y. 10022. *Office:* Department of English, Ridley College, St. Catharines, Ontario, Canada.

CAREER: CFOR-Radio, copywriter, 1959-60; Macmillan Publishing Co., Inc., Toronto, Ontario, editor and sales manager, 1960-68; Ridley College, St. Catharines, Ontario, teacher of English and head of department, 1975—. *Awards, honors:* Book award from City of Toronto, 1974; Canada Council junior fellow, 1971-72, senior fellow, 1973-74; Ontario Arts Council fellow, 1975-76.

WRITINGS: Andrew Tolliver (juvenile), Macmillan, 1965; *The Weekend Man,* Macmillan, 1971; *Farthing's Fortunes,* Macmillan, 1971; *In the Middle of a Life,* Macmillan, 1973.

WORK IN PROGRESS: Another novel.

* * *

WURLITZER, Rudolph 1938(?)-

HOME: 234 East 23rd St., New York, N.Y. 10010.

CAREER: Writer. Worked as actor in motion picture "Pat Garrett and Billy the Kid," 1973.

WRITINGS—Novels: Nog, Random House, 1969, published as *The Octopus,* Weidenfeld & Nicolson, 1969; *Flats,* Dutton, 1970; *Quake,* Dutton, 1972.

Screenplays: (With Will Corry) *Two-Lane Blacktop* (released by Universal, 1971), Award Books, 1971; (with Lorenzo Mans and Jim McBride) "Glen and Randa," UMC Pictures, 1971; "Pat Garrett and Billy the Kid," Metro-Goldwyn-Mayer, 1973.

SIDELIGHTS: Wurlitzer's first novel, *Nog,* was described by Richard M. Elman as "a marvy new experimental novel—it can be said, I think, that it is beyond interpretation. Its intention is to be boring and it succeeds mightily." Many critics have had difficulty discerning an actual plot in *Nog.* Howard Junker confessed: "The plot line is cloudy.... An 'I' who is on a beach, tracks a girl in a supermarket, falls in with zonked-out renegades, is deposited in the wilderness, walks into a mini-apocalypse, takes (is taken on) flight. A voyage by sea, one ocean to the next. At last, by cab, then plane to New York."

Geoffrey Wolff seemed confused about the novel. "I can tell you two things about *Nog* and its author," he wrote. "The title is the name of a drug-user whom the unnamed narrator might have met once and from whom he might have bought a plastic octopus that seems to figure rather crucially in the tale. And Mr. Wurlitzer likes the word 'ding,' for he repeats it fifty times in a single paragraph." Wolff conceeded that "I should read *Nog* again, but nothing could make me agree to do that."

Richard Poirier viewed Wurlitzer's obscure and abstract writing style differently. He wrote: "Wurlitzer's writing, if only in its incessant ruptures of tone, alerts the reader to the weirdness, the disguised anguish, the ridiculous comic presumption about spatial presence lurking in the ordinary language by which we try to locate ourselves. His books are a reminder that we live in a hallucination of space; that, like it or not, each of us is forever on a trip; and that by the time our language catches up with us the trip is over or we are off on quite a different one." Lore Segal's summation was close to Poirier's. He advised readers, "Read it as a 'how to' book: how to write the life of a character in a novel when you are minus assumptions about life and about novels." Segal had praise for the book though. "I liked this book so much I read it anxiously in case it should disappointment me," he wrote. "Wurlitzer's writing is full of crazy, beautiful invention."

Not all critics were impressed with *Nog.* While acknowledging that the novel did contain "some brilliant passages," Sara Blackburn also wrote that "only the most devoted reader will be able to struggle through the anesthetic quality of the rest to get from one reward to another." Similarly, Elman mused, "One wonders who would care to make such an effort after confronting Wurlitzer through his naked prose." He described Wurlitzer as "a kind of fop of despair, but not so despairing that he wouldn't like to see his sham of a 'Nog' elevate him to the pantheon of pedants of the new novel."

With the publication of his second novel, *Flats,* some critics were already finding Wurlitzer passe. John Leonard wrote, "The old cultural forms are comatose ... reality is a bad trip ... fragments express our existential disrelation, and shards are our shared experience ... *ad nauseum* and beat vigorously." The novel itself is set near a swamp. The area is inhabited by survivors of a dead culture and they each bear the name of an American city. A reviewer in *Virginia Quarterly Review* wrote, "Mr. Wurlitzer's brief book can be only designated a novel by courtesy, for all commonly accepted criteria are conspicuously absent. His work has every affectation of profundity." Leonard claimed that "unless Mr.

Wurlitzer is putting down the drug scene, which is unlikely, this is last year's sports pages. Spatial presence? Language as a pawn shop for hot metaphors? The problematic as a lifestyle? The phenomenologists have already been there." Ronald De Feo simply observed, "The greatest virtue of Rudolph Wurlitzer's second novel, *Flats,* is that it is five pages shorter than his first novel, *Nog.*"

Flats inspired many critics to compare Wurlitzer's works with Samuel Beckett's, often as a means of pointing out flaws in the former. Leonard proclaimed that *Flats* "might just as well be called 'Linoleum' or 'Malone Dies with Friends from an Overdose of Epistemology.'" In pursuing "why a Beckett succeeds and a Wurlitzer does not," De Feo discovered, "Behind Beckett's prose ... we sense a profoundly dedicated, intelligent artist. Behind Wurlitzer's work—thin, incoherent, tedious—we sense only a dabbler." Michael Wood was less harsh in his comparison of Wurlitzer with Beckett. "Like Beckett," noted Wood, "Wurlitzer is often darkly funny about his images of despair—'I don't like the way things are going,' the narrator says when a turtle arbitrarily appears in the text—and my only real quarrel with his book is with its tendency at times to explain too much."

In defense of both *Nog* and *Flats,* Douglass Bolling argued: "*Nog* and *Flats* are worthy experiments and possess the form and finesse that will win them increasing acceptance.... The best experimental fiction of recent years has revealed few limitations beyond which genuinely creative writers cannot take us. Wurlitzer shares with many of them an interest in probing beneath the layers of cultural conditioning and compromise to expose the truth of man's solitary being."

Morris Dickstein noted Beckett's influence in *Quake,* Wurlitzer's third novel. Calling Wurlitzer's writings "heavily indebted to Beckett," Dickstein continued, "Wurlitzer never makes clear whether the catatonic types who people his world are sad cases, the expectable debris of a culture without meaning or satisfaction or modest heroes." He added that *Quake* was Wurlitzer's "most realistic and conventional novel, his first with genuine narrative thrust." However, Dickstein was not pleased with the overall effect of the novel. He related, "Whether Wurlitzer's more fervent admirers will find it as unpleasant as I do I have no way of knowing."

Edward Butscher wrote, "As a sociological fable, *Quake* is clever and chillingly apt." His complaint was that *Quake* "weakens its own firm, if far too narrow, *raison d'etre,* through its adolescent obsession with sexual quirks." Butscher also declared that "the sex here is too often arbitrary, external, the result of the author's personal hang-up rather than a legitimate causal or thematic factor."

BIOGRAPHICAL/CRITICAL SOURCES: New York Times Book Review, February 16, 1969, September 20, 1970, October 22, 1972; *Washington Post,* February 24, 1969; *Nation,* February 24, 1969; *Newsweek,* March 17, 1969; *New Republic,* March 29, 1969; *Village Voice,* May 1, 1969; *Virginia Quarterly Review,* spring, 1969, winter, 1971; *Observer,* January 25, 1970; *London Magazine,* May, 1970; *New York Times,* September 17, 1970; *New York Review of Books,* March 11, 1971; *New Leader,* December 28, 1971; Richard Poirier, *The Performing Self,* Oxford University Press, 1971; *Critique: Studies in Modern Fiction,* Volume XIV, number 3, 1973; *Carleton Miscellany,* fall/winter, 1973-74; *Contemporary Literary Criticism,* Gale, Volume 2, 1974, Volume 4, 1975; Morris Dickstein, *Gates of Eden: American Culture in the Sixties,* Basic Books, 1977.*

WYNNE, Nancy Blue   1931-

PERSONAL: Born March 9, 1931, in Tulsa, Okla.; daughter of Clarence H. (an architect) and Helen (Oglesby) Blue; married: Charles A. Wynne (a fuel consultant), August 1, 1950; children: David Blue, Charles Alan. *Education:* University of Oklahoma, B.A., 1952. *Politics:* Democrat. *Religion:* Protestant. *Home:* 495 West Fremont Dr., Littleton, Colo. 80120.

CAREER: Worked as teacher in public and private schools in Oklahoma and Texas, 1952-58, 1968-70; associated with Waldenbooks, 1978; Denver University, Denver, Colo., instructor in mystery fiction, 1977—. *Member:* Mystery Writers of America.

WRITINGS: An Agatha Christie Chronology, Ace Books, 1976.

WORK IN PROGRESS: The Deadly Distaff: The Importance of Women Writers in Mystery Fiction.

SIDELIGHTS: Wynne told *CA:* ''My only book was really an outgrowth of my teaching and lecturing on the subject [of Agatha Christie].''

Y

YAFFE, Barbara 1953-

PERSONAL: Born March 4, 1953, in Montreal, Quebec, Canada; duaghter of Allan (in sales) and Anne (a typist) Yaffe. *Education:* Attended McGill University, 1971-74; University of Toronto, B.A., 1974; Carleton University, B.J., 1975. *Religion:* Jewish. *Home:* 50 Rosehill Ave., Apt. 1107, Toronto, Ontario, Canada M4T 1G6. *Office: Toronto Globe and Mail,* 444 Front St. W., Toronto, Ontario, Canada M5V 259.

CAREER/WRITINGS: Montreal Gazette, Montreal, Quebec, reporter, 1975-76; *Toronto Globe and Mail,* Toronto, Ontario, reporter, 1976—. *Member:* Canadian Centre for Investigative Journalism. *Awards, honors:* Shared in Roland Michener Award to *Toronto Globe and Mail,* from governor-general of Canada, 1978, for a series of articles.

WORK IN PROGRESS: Research on Canadian provincial politics and on national health and social welfare issues.

SIDELIGHTS: Yaffe's work as an investigative journalist has included such diverse activities as undercover observation of politicians' lifestyles, posing as a pregnant teenager seeking an abortion, surveying conditions at a maximum-security prison for women, researching shock therapy used on some of Ontario's most retarded children, and assessing Canadian investments in Florida.

She writes: "I choose not to join clubs or associations which would, I feel, encumber me with affiliations and special interests which could affect my work as a reporter.

"I love to write, to be creative, and to challenge or test the mettle of existing conditions and institutions. I am driven by an appreciation of the supreme importance of the individual in society and his freedom and rights. I believe an individual has strong obligations to his society and, in return, society must serve him well and respect his uniqueness, be flexible enough to accommodate him. Hence, my interest in researching social services and the way the state treats those of its members in special need.

"I despise war because war forgets altogether about individual human beings. Life is more precious to me because I am keenly aware of death.

"On a personal note: I believe women are born with a few strikes against them. It's still a man's world. We lack the role models, most of us lack the guts, and we lack the biological freedom of our male counterparts."

AVOCATIONAL INTERESTS: Travel.

YODER, Don 1921-

PERSONAL: Born August 27, 1921, in Altoona, Pa.; son of Jacob H. (a mechanical engineer) and Ora M. (Cronister) Yoder. *Education:* Franklin and Marshall College, B.A., 1942; University of Chicago, Ph.D., 1947. *Religion:* Society of Friends (Quakers). *Home address:* P.O. Box 304, Devon, Pa. 19333. *Office:* University of Pennsylvania, Logan Hall, Box 13, Philadelphia, Pa. 19174.

CAREER: Union Theological Seminary, New York, N.Y., instructor, 1946-48; Muhlenberg College, Allentown, Pa., instructor, 1948-49; Franklin and Marshall College, Lancaster, Pa., assistant professor, 1949-54; University of Pennsylvania, Philadelphia, 1956—, began as associate professor of religious thought, became professor of folklife studies and adjunct professor of religious studies, chairman of graduate program in folklore and folklife, 1966-70. Member of board of trustees of Library of Congress's American Folklife Center, 1976-78. Participant in conferences and symposia; consultant to Smithsonian Institution.

MEMBER: American Folklore Society, Schweizerische Gesellschaft fuer Volkskunde, Deutsche Gesellschaft fuer Volkskunde, Historical Society of Pennsylvania, Genealogical Society of Pennsylvania, Phi Beta Kappa. *Awards, honors:* Grants from American Philosophical Society and National Carl Schurz Association, fellow of Winterthur Museum, 1977-78.

WRITINGS: (With Albert F. Buffington and Walter E. Boyer) *Songs Along the Mahantongo,* Pennsylvania Dutch Folklore Society, 1951, revised edition, Folklore Associates, 1964; *Pennsylvania Spirituals,* Pennsylvania Folklife Society, 1961; (contributor) Fife and Glassie, editors, *Forms Upon the Frontier,* Utah State University Press, 1969; (contributor) Richard M. Dorson, editor, *Folklore and Folklife: An Introduction,* University of Chicago Press, 1972; (editor) *Symposium on Folk Religion,* University of California Press, 1974; (editor) *American Folklife,* University of Texas Press, 1976.

Contributor to folklore, history, and religious studies journals in the United States and Europe. Co-founder and co-editor of *Pennsylvania Dutchman,* 1948-58; co-editor of *Pennsylvania Folklife,* 1958-61, editor, 1961-78; member of editorial board of *Pennsylvania Genealogical Magazine,* 1970—, and *Winterthur Portfolio,* 1978—.

WORK IN PROGRESS: Translating *Haeuser und Land-*

schaften der Schweiz, publication by University of Tennessee Press; *Occult Pennsylvania,* a documentary study of witchcraft and folk healing; translating two German travel books on early America; research on Quaker culture in the Delaware Valley, Pennsylvania German history and ethnography, and linguistic history of Pennsylvania Germans.

* * *

YORKE, Henry Vincent   1905-1974
(Henry Green)

PERSONAL: Born October 29, 1905, near Tewkesbury, Gloucestershire, England; died in 1974; married Mary Adelaide Biddulph, 1929; children: one son. *Education:* Attended Eton College and Oxford University. *Residence:* London, England.

CAREER: Writer. Began as laborer and became managing director of H. Ponifex & Sons (a food engineering firm), in Birmingham and London, England. *Military service:* Served in British National Fire Service, 1939-43.

WRITINGS—All under pseudonym Henry Green; all novels, except as indicated: *Blindness,* Dutton, 1926, reprinted, Viking, 1978; *Living,* Dent, 1929 (also see below); *Party Going,* Hogarth, 1939, Viking, 1951 (also see below); *Pack My Bag* (autobiography), Hogarth, 1940; *Caught,* Hogarth, 1943, Viking, 1950; *Loving,* Hogarth, 1945, Viking, 1949 (also see below); *Back,* Hogarth, 1946, Viking, 1950; *Concluding,* Hogarth, 1948, Viking, 1951; *Nothing,* Viking, 1950; *Doting,* Viking, 1952; *Loving, Living, and Party Going* (collection of three novels), Penguin, 1978.

SIDELIGHTS: John Updike recently declared Henry Green to be "one of the most piquant and original English writers not only of his generation but of the century." W. H. Auden once called him "the best English novelist alive." "*Loving* by the late Henry Green is one of the best novels I have ever read," Anatole Broyard announced in a recent review. Green has received accolades from Evelyn Waugh, Christopher Isherwood, and Eudora Welty as well. But until the recent reprinting of several of his novels, Green had been a neglected writer in the United States.

Green himself aided in his relegation to obscurity. He kept his lives as the author, Henry Green, and as the wealthy industrialist, Henry Vincent Yorke, scrupulously separate. Although he had writer friends, he avoided involvement in literary circles. He refused to be photographed, except from the back, in an effort to obscure his identity. "I found my happiness in life," he once said, "not through earning my living or through gardening or fishing but through writing. And I employ it as a kind of solitary self-control which has now, to my considerable embarrassment, made me an object of interest outside my own country."

In an often-quoted declaration of artistic purpose, Green wrote: "Prose is not to be read aloud but to oneself at night, and it is not quick as poetry, but rather a gathering web of insinuations which go further than names shared can ever go. Prose should be a long intimacy between strangers with no direct appeal to what both may have known. It should slowly appeal to feelings unexpressed, it should in the end draw tears out of the stone."

Updike has glorified Green as "a saint of the mundane." Anatole Broyard commented: "Common men and women have never been shown to be so uncommon as they are in Mr. Green's novels. He may have had the finest ear for demotic speech of any novelist in English. And this may be because he was hard of hearing. Instead of parroting his

characters, as some writers do, he imagines what they would say if they were true to themselves. That's what I find so wonderful about his books: Although most of his characters are ordinary people, they are true to their ordinariness, and this amounts to a condition of grace."

Green elucidated his preoccupation with the trivial. He remarked: "The true life has nothing to do with sudden death and great tragedy, and as such, as a writer, I do not consider that the field of the novel is concerned with major (international) issues. Rightly or wrongly, having arrived at this decision—I particularly emphasize this, as I do not criticize any novelist's work which is not on my own lines—I consider that the novel should be concerned with the everyday mishaps of ordinary life."

Although his subjects are common, his means of depicting them are not. Green once stated that his novels were "an advanced attempt to break up the old-fashioned type of novel." Dialogue is the cudgel Green used to accomplish this. Many critics have cited Green's gift for language. Robert S. Ryf explained why he found Green's dialogue to be so exemplary. He wrote: "[Green] has already indicated his view that art is not representational: communication, it then follows, is not a direct, one-to-one affair, nor is dialogue representational either. His own dialogue does not represent exactly the way people talk; it is oblique, and for a very good reason. 'For if you want to create life the one way not to set about it is explanation.' Life itself does not explain itself; it is oblique in its impact on us. That is why, Green tells us, the time has come for a change from traditional narrative techniques to an increased emphasis on oblique dialogue, which must 'mean different things to different readers at one and the same time.'"

Green's facility with dialogue is illustrated in an examination of his second and third novels. While they are concerned with completely different social milieus, the speech of characters in each novel is both true and illuminating. *Living,* Green's second novel, concerns the lives of lower-class factory workers, whom Green was able to observe when he was a laborer. The novel was praised for its careful and affectionate characterizations. Green used the somewhat peculiar device of eliminating articles, "in an attempt to forge a prose as 'taut and spare' as the milieu he was writing about," Christopher Porterfield explained. While some critics accused him of mannerism, Porterfield found that the technique "has a surprising force, giving the characters a simple, massive dignity." He continued: "The density of the novel is formidable. It achieves an epic tone without epic proportions." Evelyn Waugh simply called the novel "a triumph."

Green moved to his own upper-class society for his third novel, *Party Going.* Although the characters are the social opposites of the characters in the previous novel, Green again successfully captured their idiosyncratic speech. With the conversation in *Party Going,* P. H. Newby remarked, Green "gets close to the very nerve of life which animates the half-dozen or so principal characters who are waiting to set off on holiday together." But Green's gift for dialogue is more than simply mimetic, as Eudora Welty explained. She commented that Green's talent is for "turning what people say into the fantasy of what they are telling each other, at the same time calling up out of their own mouths their vital spirit."

Blindness, Green's first novel, was unusual because it was begun when he was seventeen and a student at Eton (where he was a member of the aesthete-decadent crowd led by Harold Acton and Brian Howard). He completed the novel while at Oxford, but by the time it was published when he was twenty-one, Green had left the university to work as a laborer at the family manufacturing plant. "More virtuoso performance than novel," Michael Dirda wrote, "*Blindness* remains beguiling for its prefiguration of the major themes and techniques of Green's mature fiction: the exact rightness of the conversation of both landed gentry and servants, the machinations of people at cross-purposes, symbolism in nature and names, the young and old locked together in death-grip relations, and much humor and sadness." Similarly, Updike commented, "*Blindness,* an astoundingly sophisticated and compassionate work for an undergraduate to have produced, is yet less cunning than the later books, and bares some preoccupations that his fully developed, highly oblique art was to conceal."

BIOGRAPHICAL/CRITICAL SOURCES—Books: Henry Green, *Pack My Bag,* Hogarth, 1940; P. H. Newby, *The Novel 1945-1950,* Longmans, 1951; Harvey Breit, *The Writer Observed,* Redman, 1957; John Russell, *Henry Green: Nine Novels and an Unpacked Bag,* Rutgers University Press, 1960; Kingsley A. Weatherhead, *A Reading of Henry Green,* University of Washington Press, 1961; Paul West, *The Modern Novel,* Hutchinson, 1963; Walter Allen, *The Modern Novel: In Britain and the United States,* Dutton, 1964; Robert S. Ryf, *Henry Green,* Columbia University Press, 1967; Anthony Burgess, *The Novel Now: A Guide to Contemporary Fiction,* Norton, 1967; Frederick R. Karl, *A Reader's Guide to the Contemporary English Novel,* Farrar, Straus, 1972; *Contemporary Literary Criticism,* Volume 2, Gale, 1974.

Articles: *Partisan Review,* May, 1949; *Time,* October 10, 1949; *Newsweek,* March 27, 1950; *New York Herald Tribune Book Review,* November 8, 1950; *Times Literary Supplement,* August 26, 1977, February 10, 1978, June 23, 1978; *Spectator,* August 27, 1977; *Observer,* August 28, 1977, December 18, 1977; *New Statesman,* September 23, 1977, June 9, 1978; *New York Review of Books,* May 18, 1978; *Chronicle of Higher Education,* November 13, 1978; *New York Times,* December 2, 1978; *New York Times Book Review,* December 10, 1978; *New Yorker,* January 1, 1979; *Harper's,* February, 1979. Obituaries: *AB Bookman's Weekly,* April 15, 1974.*

*　　*　　*

YOUNG, Marjorie W(illis)

PERSONAL: Born in Mansfield, Ohio; daughter of John Edgar and Mary Adelle (Reiter) Willis; married James Russell Young (a publisher), October 2, 1934; children: Willis Patterson. *Education:* Attended Cornell University, 1924, Art Students League and Cooper Union, both 1925-27, New York University, 1925, 1944, Columbia University, 1925-26, 1943, Sorbonne, University of Paris, 1928-30, and Japanese Language School, Tokyo, 1934-35. *Politics:* Democrat. *Religion:* Episcopal. *Home:* 2003 Laurel Dr., Anderson, S.C. 29621. *Office:* Safety Journal International, P.O. Box 4189, Anderson, S.C. 29622.

CAREER: International News Service, Tokyo, Japan, author of Far East column, 1938-41; *Saturday Pictorial Review,* New York City, feature writer, 1941-45; David McKay Co., Inc. (publisher), New York City, promotion director, 1945-48; *Anderson Independent Tribune,* Anderson, S.C., feature writer and travel editor, 1949—. Lecturer for National Concert & Artists Corp., 1942-43; moderator of "Holiday Decorating" on WAIM-TV, 1953, "Safety Program," 1953-77, and "How to Cut and Sew," 1954-77; travel editor for WAIM-Radio, 1953-77. Member of research department for "Believe It Or Not," 1946-48; assistant technical director for "Behind the Rising Sun," a film released by Radio-Keith-Orpheum, 1943. Member of board of directors of Capitol City Communications, Inc. Director of Chinese War Orphans Relief, 1941-45.

MEMBER: Veterans of Safety International (president, 1978-79), Society of American Travel Writers, American Women in Radio and Television, Garden Writers Association, American Society of Safety Engineers (affiliate; head of South Carolina chapter), National Press Photographers Association, Writers Association of America, National Recreation Association, American Horticulture Council, Far East Society, Overseas Press Club of America, Daughters of the American Revolution, Caroliniana Society, South Carolina Recreation Society (vice-president, 1954—), Anderson County Historical Society (president, 1978-80), Washington Press Club, Cornell Women's Club. *Awards, honors:* Public relations award from American Society of Safety Engineers.

WRITINGS: Decorating for Joyful Occasions, Laurel Publishers, 1952; *It's Time for Christmas Decorations,* Palmetto Publishing, 1957; (editor) *Textile Leaders of the South,* J. R. Young, 1963; *Japanese-American Cook Book: Kindaiteki katei seiyo ryori ho* (bilingual edition), Droke, 1972; *South Carolina's Women Patriots,* R. Bryan, 1978.

Feature writer for King Features Syndicate in Tokyo, 1939; feature editor and author of a column in *Wilmington Sunday Star,* 1946-48; feature writer and travel editor of *Anderson Daily Mail,* 1949-73; editor of "What's What," a monthly feature in *Veterans of Safety.* Editor of *Safety Journal International,* 1953—; editor of *Fodor's Tour Guide of South Carolina,* 1966-68, and *Fodor's Tour Guide of Georgia,* 1966-67; editor of *South Carolina Newsletter* of American Society of Safety Engineers; associate editor of *New South,* 1966-73; travel editor of *Quote,* 1977-78.

AVOCATIONAL INTERESTS: World travel.

Z

ZACHARIAS, Lela Ann 1944-
(Lee Zacharias)

PERSONAL: Born December 1, 1944, in Chicago, Ill.; daughter of Joseph Ryan (an oil worker) and Dorothine (a cafeteria manager; maiden name, Hurley) Ives; married Richard Kirk Zacharias, October 29, 1966 (divorced, 1976). *Education:* Indiana University, A.B., 1966; Hollins College, M.A., 1973; University of Arkansas, M.F.A., 1975. *Residence:* Greensboro, N.C. *Agent:* Rhoda A. Weyr, William Morris Agency, 1350 Avenue of the Americas, New York, N.Y. 10019. *Office:* Department of English, University of North Carolina, Greensboro, N.C. 27412.

CAREER: Indiana University, Bloomington, assistant director of publications at Research Center of Language Sciences, 1967-70; University of North Carolina, Greensboro, assistant professor of English, 1975—, coordinator of writing program, 1977—. Has taught photography to children. *Member:* Poets and Writers, Associated Writing Programs. *Awards, honors:* Writing and photography awards from Virginia Commonwealth University, University of Arkansas, and Virginia Museum.

WRITINGS—Under name Lee Zacharias: *Helping Muriel Make It Through the Night* (short stories), Louisiana State University Press, 1976. Contributor to academic journals, literary journals, and popular magazines, including *Redbook, New Writers,* and *New England Review.* Editor of *Greensboro Review,* 1977—.

WORK IN PROGRESS: Lessons, a novel, publication expected in 1980.

SIDELIGHTS: Zacharias writes: "Although my work is often autobiographical in atmosphere, it is never autobiographical in event, and very rarely in character. I remain interested in photography, but it plays almost no role in my writing. I find fiction a far more flexible compromise with reality."

*   *   *

ZACHER, Mark W. 1938-

PERSONAL: Born March 4, 1938, in Boston, Mass.; married; children: two. *Education:* Yale University, B.A., 1961; Columbia University, M.A., 1963, Ph.D., 1966. *Home:* 1721 West 68th Ave., Vancouver, British Columbia, Canada V6P 2V9. *Office:* Institute of International Relations, University of British Columbia, Vancouver, British Columbia, Canada V6T 1W5.

CAREER: University of British Columbia, Vancouver, assistant professor, 1965-70, associate professor of political science, 1970—, director of Institute of International Relations, 1971—.

WRITINGS: Dag Hammarskjold's United Nations, Columbia University Press, 1970; (editor with R. Stephen Milne) *Stability and Conflict in Southeast Asia,* Doubleday, 1974; (editor with Barbara Johnson) *Canadian Foreign Policy and the Law of the Sea,* University of British Columbia Press, 1977; *International Conflicts and Collective Security,* Praeger, 1979; (with Michael McGonigle) *Pollution, Politics, and International Law,* University of California Press, 1979.

WORK IN PROGRESS: "A book on the political foundations of international institutions."

*   *   *

ZARETSKY, Eli 1940-

PERSONAL: Born February 29, 1940, in Brooklyn, N.Y.; son of David (a hairdresser) and Pauline (Silverman) Zaretsky; divorced; children: Natasha. *Education:* University of Michigan, B.A., 1960; Brooklyn College of the City University of New York, M.A., 1963; University of Maryland, Ph.D., 1978. *Home:* 504 Clayton St., San Francisco, Calif. 94117. *Office:* Institute for the Study of the Family and the State, Institute for Policy Sciences, Duke University, Durham, N.C. 27706.

CAREER: Wells College, Aurora, N.Y., instructor in history, 1967-69; *Socialist Review,* Oakland, Calif., managing editor, 1969-76; San Francisco State University, San Francisco, Calif., instructor in history, 1978; Duke University, Durham, N.C., fellow of Institute for the Study of the Family and the State, Institute for Policy Sciences, 1978—. Instructor at the Pentagon, summer, 1967, Andrews Air Force Base, summer, 1968, and University of California, Berkeley, 1973-74; lecturer at various colleges and universities. Committee for Research on Women fellow.

WRITINGS: Capitalism, the Family, and Personal Life, Harper, 1976. Contributor of more than fifteen articles and translations to magazines, including *Insurgent Sociologist, New Left Review,* and *Journal of Psychohistory.* Associate editor of *Psychohistory Review.*

WORK IN PROGRESS: A revised edition of *Capitalism, the Family, and Personal Life;* a history of theories of the family; a book on the state and the family.

* * *

ZEROF, Herbert G. 1934-

PERSONAL: Born August 18, 1934, in New York, N.Y.; son of Albert (in furniture business) and Mary Jane (Allen) Zerof; married Aletta McDonald (an office manager), July 5, 1959; children: Linda Marie, Cheryl Anne. *Education:* Attended University of Miami, 1951-52; Stetson University, A.B., 1955; Southeastern Seminary, B.D., Th.M., 1959; further graduate study at Florida State University, 1959-60; University of Pennsylvania, Ed.D., 1968. *Home:* 3126 Ferncliff Rd., Charlotte, N.C. 28211. *Office:* Marriage and Family Institute, 4401 Colwick Rd., Charlotte, N.C. 28211.

CAREER: University of Pennsylvania, Philadelphia, instructor in psychiatry, 1965-68; Hahnemann School of Medicine, Philadelphia, senior instructor in psychiatry, 1968-70; University of North Carolina, Charlotte, associate professor of guidance and counseling, 1971-73; associated with Marriage and Family Institute, Charlotte. Director of student counseling at Swarthmore College, 1964-70. Visiting lecturer in Australia and New Zealand, 1973. Consultant to U.S. Navy and National Institute of Mental Health. *Member:* American Psychological Association, American Orthopsychiatric Association (fellow), American Association of Marriage and Family Therapists, North Carolina Association of Marriage and Family Therapists. *Awards, honors:* Robert L. Dickinson Writing Award from American Association of Marriage and Family Therapists, 1964.

WRITINGS: Relationship: The Medium of Help, U.S. Navy, 1968; *Finding Intimacy: The Art of Happiness in Living Together,* Random House, 1978. Contributor to medical journals.

WORK IN PROGRESS: Studying popular psychology, especially as it relates to marriage and the family.

SIDELIGHTS: Zerof comments: "I am concerned with the breakdown of family life in the United States, and with what can be done practically and realistically to improve the quality of life in this regard." *Avocational interests:* Biology.

* * *

ZIMBARDO, Philip G(eorge) 1933-

PERSONAL: Born March 23, 1933, in New York, N.Y.; son of George and Margaret (Bisicchia) Zimbardo; married Rose Abdelnour, 1958 (divorced, 1969); married Christina Maslach (a professor), August 10, 1972; children: Adam, Zara. *Education:* Brooklyn College (now of the City University of New York), A.B. (summa cum laude), 1954; Yale University, M.S., 1955, Ph.D., 1959. *Politics:* Liberal Democrat. *Religion:* Roman Catholic. *Home:* 25 Montclair Ter., San Francisco, Calif. 94109. *Office:* Department of Psychology, Stanford University, Stanford, Calif. 94305.

CAREER: Yale University, New Haven, Conn., assistant professor of psychology, 1959-60; New York University, New York City, assistant professor of psychology, 1960-67; Columbia University, New York City, associate professor of psychology, 1968; Stanford University, Stanford, Calif., professor of psychology, 1968—. *Member:* American Psychological Association, American Association for the Advancement of Science, Phi Beta Kappa. *Awards, honors:* Distinguished teacher award from American Psychological Foundation, 1975; distinguished research award from California State Psychological Association, 1978.

WRITINGS: Psychology and Life, Scott, Foresman, 1971, 10th edition, 1979; (with Ebbe Ebbesen and wife, Christina Maslach) *Influencing Attitudes and Changing Behavior,* Addison-Wesley, 1969, 2nd edition, 1977; *Cognitive Control of Motivation,* Scott, Foresman, 1969; (with Robert Abelson) *Canvassing for Peace: A Manual for Volunteers,* Society for the Psychological Study of Social Issues, 1970; *Psychology and Life,* Scott, Foresman, 1971, 10th edition, 1979; (with Ebbe Ebbesen and wife, Christina Maslach) *Shyness: What It Is, What to Do About It,* Addison-Wesley, 1977; (with Shirley Radl) *Shyness Workbook,* A & W Press, 1979; (with Shirley Radl) *Shy Child,* McGraw, 1980.

Contributor: (With Craig Haney) J. Tapp and F. Levine, editors, *Law, Justice, and the Individual in Society,* Holt, 1972; M. Deutsch and H. Hornstein, editors, *Applying Social Psychology,* L. Erlbaum Association, 1975. Also contributor to psychology journals.

WORK IN PROGRESS: The Stanford Prison Experiment, nonfiction based on his own 1971 research "which analyzes the psychology of evil and the subtle controls on human feelings"; *The Rational Basis of Madness,* on "how normal people go crazy, a new theory on research that helps us understand the process by which pathology of thought, feeling, and action arises."

SIDELIGHTS: Zimbardo writes: "All my work has as its original purpose improving the human condition by illuminating ways we can go or have gone wrong. I try to show the power of situations to overwhelm people. It is important in my research and writing that I am of the people, learn from them, and give back to them all that I believe may help improve the human condition."

BIOGRAPHICAL/CRITICAL SOURCES: Human Behavior, April, 1976; *New West,* May 9, 1977; *People,* June 27, 1977.

* * *

ZIMMER, Anne Y(oung) 1920-

PERSONAL: Born December 19, 1920, in Detroit, Mich.; daughter of Arthur Frederick (an electrical work foreman) and Jessie (Clements) Young; married D. Robert Stewart, October 3, 1942 (died July 26, 1944); married Arnold E. Zimmer (a systems analyst), April 7, 1951; children: (first marriage) Robert Arthur; (second marriage) Kathleen Anne (deceased). *Education:* Wayne State University, B.S., 1962, M.A., 1964, Ph.D., 1966. *Politics:* Independent. *Religion:* Protestant. *Home:* 813 Anita Ave., Grosse Pointe Woods, Mich. 48236. *Office:* Department of History, Wayne State University, Detroit, Mich. 48202.

CAREER: Standard Accident Insurance Co. (now Reliance of Philadelphia), Detroit, Mich., in personnel, 1944-46, bond underwriter, 1946-51; worked in hospital administration and as medical secretary in Detroit, 1954-59; Wayne State University, Detroit, instructor, 1966-67, assistant professor and administrator of graduate programs, 1967-77, associate professor of history, 1977—. *Member:* American Historical Association, Organization of American Historians, Institute of Early American History and Culture, American Association of University Women, Smithsonian Institution, Southern Historical Association (member of nominating committee, 1978-80), Pi Lambda Theta, Zonta Club of Detroit (president, 1978-79).

WRITINGS: Jonathan Boucher: Loyalist in Exile, Wayne State University Press, 1978. Contributor to encyclopedias and history journals.

WORK IN PROGRESS: Women in American Life and Thought; a biography of Loyalist printer Hugh Gaine; journal articles.

SIDELIGHTS: Zimmer writes: "The idea for a biography of Jonathan Boucher began in England with the chance finding of a series of letters over a thirty-year period which were written by Boucher to a close friend in Britain. The letters were exceptionally candid, expressing opinions on a variety of subjects including economics, religion, politics, social life and personal affairs. They revealed an intelligent, ambitious, romantic dynamo of energy, whose career was as adventurous as that found in good fiction. The letters, however, contradicted in large measure Boucher's established reputation as a consistent High Tory of the American Revolution. I saw a challenge in amending some two hundred years of scholarship by setting straight the record of his politics as they developed in America and in England."

* * *

ZINBERG, Norman E(arl) 1921-

PERSONAL: Born November 30, 1921, in Harrisburg, Pa.; son of Louis and Esther (Wilner) Zinberg; married Dorothy Shore (a sociologist), April 4, 1956; children: Sarah, Anne. *Education:* University of Maryland, A.B., 1942, M.D., 1947; Boston Psychoanalytic Society and Institute, graduated, 1957. *Home and office:* 11 Scott St., Cambridge, Mass. 02138.

CAREER: Sinai Hospital, Baltimore, Md., intern, 1947-48; Spring Grove Hospital, Catonsville, Md., resident in psychiatry, 1948-51; Harvard University, Cambridge, Mass., assistant in psychiatry, 1951-54, instructor, 1954-63, clinical associate, 1963-64, assistant clinical professor, 1964-74, associate clinical professor of psychiatry, 1974—; in private practice of psychiatry and psychoanalysis, 1954—; Beth Israel Hospital, Boston, Mass., assistant director of psychiatric service, 1955-67; Boston Psychoanalytic Institute, Boston, faculty member, 1962—; Tufts University, Medford, Mass., scholar-in-residence, 1969-71; Clark University, Worcester, Mass., professor of education, 1971-72; Children's Hospital Medical Center, Boston, senior associate in psychiatry, 1972—; Washington Center for Addictions, Boston, chief psychiatrist, 1972; Cambridge Hospital, Cambridge, staff psychiatrist, 1973—. Fulbright-Hays senior lecturer at London School of Economics and Political Science, London, 1968-69. Coordinator of Task Panel on Psychoactive Drug Use/Misuse, of the President's Commission on Mental Health, 1977-78; member of National Advisory Council on Drug Abuse, of Alcohol, Drug Abuse, and Mental Health Administration, 1978-81; senior consultant to Drug Abuse Council, Inc.

MEMBER: American Psychiatric Association (fellow), American Psychoanalytic Association, Massachusetts Association for Mental Health (member of board of directors and chairman, both 1970—). *Awards, honors:* Guggenheim Fellowship, 1968-69; grant from Walter F. Meyer Foundation, 1968-69; Field Foundation fellowship, 1969-71.

WRITINGS: (Editor with Irving Kaufman) *The Normal Psychology of the Aging Process,* International Universities Press, 1963, revised edition (with Kaufman and R. J. Kahana), 1978; (editor) *Psychiatry and Medical Practice in a General Hospital,* International Universities Press, 1964; (with J. A. Robertson) *Drugs and the Public,* Simon & Schuster, 1972; (with G. M. Edinburg and Wendy Kelman) *Clinical Interviewing and Counseling: Principles and Techniques,* Appleton, 1974; (with H. N. Boris and Marylynn

Boris) *Teaching Social Change: A Group Approach,* Johns Hopkins Press, 1976; (editor) *Alternate States of Consciousness,* Free Press, 1977; (with Margaret Bean) *Psychoanalysis and the Treatment of Alcoholism,* Free Press, 1980; *Control: Social and Psychological Concomitants in Intoxicant Use,* Free Press, 1980. Author of "Forum/Drugs" and "Forum/Alcohol," columns in *Boston Globe.* Contributor of more than a hundred articles to professional journals and popular magazines.

WORK IN PROGRESS: Research on conceptual issues in substance use and habitual behavior.

SIDELIGHTS: Zinberg writes: "At this time my chief interest, in addition to my specific research on how people control the use of intoxicants, is to work out what is necessary for nonmedical degree people, in particular mental health workers who have no specific professional backgrounds, to know (and not know) in order to turn the work they do into effective therapeutic encounters. Essentially, this entails conceptualizing dynamic theory so that it applies to all levels of client/therapist interaction and not simply to a specific therapeutic situation."

* * *

ZONKER, Patricia

PERSONAL: Born in Huntington Park, Calif.; daughter of Alfred (a merchant) and Mildred (a secretary and bookkeeper; maiden name, Niquette) Mathewson; married Thomas Zonker (a president of a butane equipment distributorship), October 14, 1950; children: Laurie Zonker Pevytoe, Jenny Zonker Ashcroft, Daniel, Gregory. *Education:* Attended Los Angeles City College. *Home:* 11532 Samoline Ave., Downey, Calif. 90241.

CAREER: Secretary, 1947-48; Aladdin Employment Agency, South Gate, Calif., co-owner, 1948-55; writer, 1966—. *Member:* International P.E.N., California Writers Guild, Writers Workshop (West), Writers Club of Whittier.

WRITINGS: Murdercycles (nonfiction), Nelson-Hall, 1979. Contributor of articles and stories to newspapers and popular magazines, including *'Teen, Good Housekeeping, Christian Home, St. Anthony Messenger, National Jewish Monthly,* and *Lady's Circle.*

WORK IN PROGRESS: A novel.

SIDELIGHTS: Patricia Zonker writes: "A hitch in a hospital orthopedic ward from a yachting accident made me write *Murdercycles.* Hobbling around the halls on crutches, I became aware the place was overflowing with motorcycle accident patients. Doctors were hacking off legs as casually as chopping wood. This, and the fact that several friends have sons physically and mentally disabled from motorcycle accidents, made my writer's blood boil.

"I hit the research trail, with personal attendance at motorbike training schools, interviews with doctors, nurses, and patients (some as young as fifteen years old). Motorcycle parks and police departments were visited. Other motorcycle issues fell into place, such as use of public land, the noise factor, the mass media, motorcycle toys, and more.

"The book was born. Welcome or not, these machines are coming at us from all sides, invading every home. There is no escaping. It is an epidemic. Why all the fuss about *Jaws*? There are only about fifty shark attacks annually in the entire world. The public was hungry for a book blasting motorcycles. *Murdercycles* will *save lives.*"

AVOCATIONAL INTERESTS: Travel, especially in Ireland, Greece, Yugoslavia, Italy, Austria, Mexico.

ZUMWALT, Elmo Russell, Jr. 1920-

PERSONAL: Born November 29, 1920, in San Francisco, Calif.; son of Elmo Russell (a physician) and Frances (a physician; maiden name, Frank) Zumwalt; married Mouza Coutelais-du-Roche, October, 1945; children: Elmo Russell III, James Gregory, Ann F., Mouza C. *Education:* Received degree (cum laude) from U.S. Naval Academy, 1942; attended Naval War College, 1953, and National War College, 1962. *Politics:* Democrat. *Religion:* Protestant. *Residence:* Arlington, Va. *Office:* 1500 Wilson Blvd., Suite 1700, Arlington, Va. 22207.

CAREER: U.S. Navy, 1942-74; commissioned ensign, 1942, assigned to U.S.S. *Phelps;* served as lieutenant of U.S.S. *Saufley* and U.S.S. *Zellars,* 1944-48; became commander, 1955; served as commanding officer of U.S.S. *Arnold J. Isbell,* 1955-57, and U.S.S. *Dewey,* 1959-61; became rear admiral, 1965; served as commander of U.S.S. *Flotilla Seven,* 1965-66; director of systems analysis division, Office of the Chief of Naval Operations, 1966-68; commander of U.S. Naval Forces and chief of naval advisory group, Vietnam, 1968-70; chief of naval operations, 1970-74; retired as admiral, 1974. Visiting professor at Vanderbilt University, 1974-75; guest lecturer at Stanford University, 1974, University of Pennsylvania, 1974-75, University of Michigan, and Whittier College. President of Americans for Energy Independence, Inc., 1975. Member of board of directors of Phelps-Stokes Fund, Esmark, Inc., Organization Resources Counselors, Inc., American Health Foundation, American Building Maintenance Industries, Presidential Classroom for Young Americans, and SOGen International Fund, Inc. Consultant to System Planning Corporation.

AWARDS, HONORS: Recipient of more than forty national and international citations and decorations for military service, including the Legion of Merit, China Service Medal, National Defense Service Medal, Order of Military Merit (Korea), Order of the Rising Sun (Japan), National Order of Vietnam Medal, United Nations Service Medal, Great Star of Military Merit of Chile, Grand Cross of the Division of King George I (Greece), and Grand Cross of St. Olav (Norway). L.L.D., Villanova University, University of North Carolina; D.Hum. Litt., United States International University; Dr. Public Service, Central Michigan University.

WRITINGS: On Watch, Quadrangele, 1976. Contributor of articles to the *New York Times, Washington Star, Daily Progress,* and *American Legion Magazine.*

SIDELIGHTS: Elmo Zumwalt, Jr. was the youngest four-star admiral in U.S. naval history. *Avocational interests:* Jogging, tennis.

*   *   *

ZWEIG, Paul 1935-

PERSONAL: Born July 14, 1935, in New York, N.Y.; son of Samuel H. and Celia (Berkin) Zweig; married Michele Katz (a painter), September, 1963 (marriage ended); married Francine Harris, March 31, 1968. *Education:* Columbia University, B.A., 1956, M.A., 1958; University of Paris, Ph.D., 1964. *Politics:* "Anarchist, I suppose." *Religion:* Jewish. *Home:* 610 West 110th St., Apt. 2-A, New York, N.Y. 10025. *Office:* Department of English, Queens College of the City University of New York, 65-30 Kissena Blvd., Flushing, N.Y. 11367.

CAREER: Writer. Columbia University, New York, N.Y., assistant professor, 1966-68; currently associated with Queens College of the City University of New York, Flushing, N.Y. Has taught and written in France. *Military service:* U.S. Army Reserve, 1960-66.

WRITINGS: (Translator from the French) Aloysius Bertrand, *From Gaspard of the Night,* Minard (Paris), 1964; (translator from the French) Antonin Artaud, *Black Poet,* Minard, 1966; *Lautreamont ou les violences du Narcisse,* Minard, 1967, translation published as *Lautreamont: The Violent Narcissus,* Kennikat, 1972; (editor) *Yuan Goll: Selected Poems,* Kayak, 1968; *The Heresy of Self-Love: A Study of Subversive Individualism,* Basic Books, 1968; *Against Emptiness* (poems), Harper, 1971; *Images & Footsteps* (poem), Plain Wrapper Press, 1971; *The Dark Side of the Earth,* Harper, 1974; *The Adventurer,* Basic Books, 1974; *Three Journeys: An Automythology,* Basic Books, 1976; *Muktananda: Selected Essays,* Harper, 1977.

Contributor of poems and essays to periodicals, including *New Yorker, Poetry, Nation,* and *Harper's.*

SIDELIGHTS: As a poet, Paul Zweig has provoked mixed reactions from his critics. For example, when his first book of poems, *Against Emptiness,* appeared, James Naiden described Zweig's use of imagery and metaphor as "accomplished and sure" and Zweig himself as "a poet whose talents are quite diverse, despite (in this case) a continually shifting focus." Similarly, Bill Zavatsky criticized Zweig's "hazy symbolist vocabulary and stilted phraseology," but added this praise: "By working against the grain of language, the kind of verse to which he seems to aspire has broken new verbal paths."

Zweig's emphasis on death was noted by reviewers of his second collection of poetry, *The Dark Side of the Earth.* Poet David Ignatow wrote, "The feeling I always come up with about Zweig's work is of a most paradoxical luxuriousness in the treatment of death, and it always leads to the realization that this is a poet affirming his pleasure in living, even at its most extreme, which is the act of dying." However, other critics did not interpret Zweig's emphasis on death as affirmative. Disapproving of Zweig's "fascination with death," Judith Moffet nevertheless saw fit to "give Paul Zweig high marks for word masonry and let it go at that."

Zweig's critical prose has been more consistently appreciated. Mary Ellman considered *The Heresy of Self-Love* to be "lucid without simplification, and temperate without condescension." *The Adventurer* was also highly lauded by John Gardner: "Zweig writes with splendid originality and insight, such a set of analyses as we haven't seen in years." The autobiographical *Three Journeys* was applauded, too. Christopher Lasch thought the book "painfully authentic," and Francine Du Plessix Gray, noting the swift alternations between the "mordantly witty" and the "nebulously contemplative," finally praised the "seduction and power" as well as the "translucent prose" of Zweig's book.

BIOGRAPHICAL/CRITICAL SOURCES: Nation, March 31, 1969; *New York Times Book Review,* December 26, 1971, December 22, 1974, May 2, 1976; *Poetry,* May, 1972, December, 1975; *New York Review of Books,* September 30, 1976; Paul Zweig, *Three Journeys: An Automythology,* Basic Books, 1976.*

CONTEMPORARY AUTHORS

CUMULATIVE INDEX VOLUMES 1-88

This index includes references to all entries in the series listed below.
References in the index are identified as follows:

Volume number only—*Contemporary Authors* Original Volumes
R after number—*Contemporary Authors* Revised Volumes
CAP before number—*Contemporary Authors—Permanent Series*
CLC before number—*Contemporary Literary Criticism*, Volumes 1-11
SATA before number—*Something About the Author*, Volumes 1-16
AITN before number—*Authors in the News*, Volumes 1-2

Copyright © 1980 by Gale Research Company